THE SEVENTEENTH MENTAL MEASUREMENTS YEARBOOK

EARLIER PUBLICATIONS IN THIS SERIES

BUROS CENTER DIRECTOR AND EDITOR
KURT F. GEISINGER

DIRECTOR AND EDITOR, EMERITA
BARBARA S. PLAKE

ASSOCIATE DIRECTOR AND EDITOR
ROBERT SPIES

EDITOR
JANET F. CARLSON

MANAGING EDITOR
LINDA L. MURPHY

ASSISTANT EDITOR
GARY L. ANDERSON

CLERICAL ASSISTANTS

CHRISTA HAKE	ROSEMARY SIECK
CARINA McCORMICK	CAROL SUTTON

RESEARCH ASSISTANTS

JEFFREY BABL	ALEJANDRO MORALES
STACEY DeSCHANE	ERIN RHOADS
M. KELLY HAACK	ANJA RÖMHILD
TABETHAH MACK	MICHELLE SIMPSON

INSTITUTE SECRETARY
RASMA STRAUTKALNS

THE SEVENTEENTH MENTAL MEASUREMENTS YEARBOOK

KURT F. GEISINGER, ROBERT A. SPIES,

JANET F. CARLSON, and BARBARA S. PLAKE

Editors

LINDA L. MURPHY
Managing Editor

The Buros Institute of Mental Measurements
The University of Nebraska-Lincoln
Lincoln, Nebraska

2007
Distributed by The University of Nebraska Press

LC 39-3422
ISBN 910674-60-4

Manufactured in the United States of America.

The paper used in this publication meets the minimum requirements of American National Standard for Information Sciences—Permanence of Paper for Printed Library Materials, ANSI Z39.48-1984.

Note to Users

TABLE OF CONTENTS

INTRODUCTION

The Seventeenth Mental Measurements Year-book (*17th MMY*), like all yearbooks in this series, is designed to serve as a guide to the complex task of test evaluation, selection, and use. Oscar K. Buros (1905-1978) began its production over 70 years ago. His primary goal was to provide users with access to critical information and independent reviews for a wide variety of testing products. With this publication, he also sought to provide the testing community with professional evaluations that would improve both the science and practice of testing.

As current editors of the MMY, we remain committed to continuing this long-standing history of independent test review. The increasing complexity of tests and questions of appropriate test use are often discussed in the professional literature, but no other forum consistently has provided users with specific information on which to base their vital selection decisions. We recognize both its importance to users and the debt we owe contributors to the MMY series.

THE SEVENTEENTH MENTAL MEASUREMENTS YEARBOOK

The *17th MMY* contains reviews of tests that are new or significantly revised since the publication of the 16th MMY in 2005. Reviews, descriptions, and references associated with many older tests can be located in other Buros publications: previous *MMY*s and *Tests in Print VII*. Criteria for inclusion in this edition of the *MMY* remain that a test be (a) new or substantively revised since it was last reviewed in the MMY series, (b) commercially available from its publishers, (c) available in the English language, and (d) published with adequate developmental and technical documentation.

Content. The contents of the *17th MMY* include: (a) a bibliography of 209 commercially

available tests, new or revised, published as separates for use with English-speaking individuals; (b) 376 critical test reviews from specialists selected by the editors on the basis of their expertise in measurement and, often, the content of the test being reviewed; (c) a test title index with appropriate cross-references; (d) a classified subject index; (e) a publishers directory and index, including publisher addresses and other contact information with test listings by publisher; (f) a name index including the names of authors of all tests, reviews, or references included in this *MMY*; (g) an index of acronyms for easy reference when only a test acronym is known; and (h) a score index to identify for users test scores of potential interest.

Appendix. Three separate listings appear in the *17th MMY* for users requiring additional information when a specific test cannot be otherwise located in the Mental Measurements Yearbook series. Beginning with the *14th MMY* (2001), a test qualifying for review must provide an adequate developmental history and sufficient evidence describing the instrument's technical properties. Not all tests submitted for evaluation meet these two criteria for review in the *MMY* series. A listing of tests received (but not reviewed) is included to make users aware of the availability of these tests, albeit without supporting documentation or reviews. The Appendix also provides a list of tests that meet review criteria but were received too late for review in this volume. These tests (plus additional tests received in the following months) will be reviewed in *The Eighteenth Mental Measurements Yearbook*. Test reviews that are completed prior to publication of the *17th MMY* are available electronically for a small fee on our web-based service Test Reviews Online (www.unl.edu/buros). A third list in the Appendix includes titles of tests requested from publishers but not yet received as of this volume's publication. This listing includes tests for which the publishers decline to provide review copies as well as tests from publishers who routinely make their instruments available for review but who have failed at this point to provide a new or revised test for evaluation.

Organization. The current *MMY* series is organized like an encyclopedia, with tests being ordered alphabetically by title. If the title of a test is known, the reader can locate the test immediately without having to consult the Index of Titles.

The page headings reflect the encyclopedic organization. The page heading of the left-hand page cites the number and title of the first test listed on that page, and the page heading of the right-hand page cites the number and title of the last test listed on that page. All numbers presented in the various indexes are test numbers, not page numbers. Page numbers are important only for the Table of Contents and are located at the bottom of each page.

TESTS AND REVIEWS

The *17th MMY* contains descriptive information on 209 tests as well as test reviews by 258 different authors. Statistics on the number and percentage of tests in each of 18 major classifications are contained in Table 1.

TABLE 1
TESTS BY MAJOR CLASSIFICATIONS

Classification	Number	Percentage
Vocations	43	20.6
Personality	24	11.5
Neuropsychological	19	9.1
Developmental	17	8.1
Intelligence and General Aptitude	16	7.7
Miscellaneous	16	7.7
Behavior Assessment	14	6.7
Reading	13	6.2
English and Language	12	5.7
Education	10	4.8
Speech and Hearing	9	4.3
Achievement	7	3.3
Sensory Motor	6	2.9
Mathematics	3	1.4
Fine Arts	0	0.0
Foreign Languages	0	0.0
Science	0	0.0
Social Studies	0	0.0
Total	209	100.0

TABLE 2
NEW AND REVISED OR SUPPLEMENTED TESTS BY MAJOR CLASSIFICATION

Classification	Number of Tests	Percentage New	Percentage Revised
Achievement	7	42.9	57.1
Behavior Assessment	14	50.0	50.0
Developmental	17	29.4	50.6
Education	10	60.0	40.0
English and Language	12	58.3	41.7
Fine Arts	0	0.0	0.0
Foreign Languages	0	0.0	0.0
Intelligence and General Aptitude	16	62.5	37.5
Mathematics	3	33.3	66.7
Miscellaneous	16	81.3	18.7
Neuropsychological	19	89.5	10.5
Personality	24	66.7	33.3
Reading	13	61.5	38.5
Science	0	0.0	0.0
Sensory Motor	6	66.7	33.3
Social Studies	0	0.0	0.0
Speech and Hearing	9	55.6	44.4
Vocations	43	81.4	18.6
Total	209	65.6	34.4

The percentage of new and revised or supplemented tests according to major classifications is contained in Table 2. Overall, 137 of the tests included in the *17th MMY* are new and have not been listed in a previous *MMY* although some descriptions may have been included in *Tests in Print VII* (*TIP VII*; 2006). The Index of Titles may be consulted to determine if a test is new or revised.

Test Selection. A new policy for selecting tests for review became effective with the *14th MMY* (2001). This new policy for selecting tests for review requires at least minimal information be available regarding test development. The requirement that tests have such minimal information does not assure the quality of the test; it simply provides reviewers with a minimum basis for critically evaluating the quality of the test. We select our reviewers carefully and let them and well-informed readers decide for themselves about the essential features needed to assure the appropriate use of a test. Some new or revised tests are not included because they were received too late to undergo the review process and still permit timely publication, or because some reviewers did not meet their commitment to review the test. A list of these tests is included in the Appendix and every effort will be made to have them reviewed for *The Eighteenth Mental Measurements Yearbook*, and included before then through our web-based service Test Reviews Online (TROL).

There are some new or revised tests for which there will be no reviews although these tests are described in *Tests in Print VII*. The absence of reviews occurred for a variety of reasons including: We could not identify qualified reviewers, the test materials were incomplete so reviews were not possible, the tests were sufficiently obscure that reviews were deemed unnecessary, the publisher advised us the test is now out-of-print before reviews were completed, or the test did not meet our criterion for documentation. Descriptions of all these tests still in print were published in *TIP VII* and are included in the Test Reviews Online database.

Reviewer Selection. The selection of reviewers was done with great care. The objective was to secure measurement and subject specialists who would be independent and represent a variety of different viewpoints. It was also important to find individuals who would write critical reviews competently, judiciously, fairly, and in a timely manner. Reviewers were identified by means of extensive searches of the professional literature, attendance at professional meetings, and recommendations from leaders in various professional fields. Perusal of reviews in this volume also will reveal that reviewers work in and represent a cross-section of the places in which testing is taught and tests are used: universities, public schools, businesses, and community agencies. These reviewers represent an outstanding array of professional talent, and their contributions are obviously of primary importance in making this *Yearbook* a valuable resource. A list of the individuals reviewing in this volume is included at the beginning of the Index section.

Active, evaluative reading is the key to the most effective use of the professional expertise offered in each of the reviews. Just as one would evaluate a test, readers should evaluate critically the reviewer's comments about the test. The reviewers selected are competent professionals in their respective fields, but it is inevitable that their reviews also reflect their individual perspectives.

The *Mental Measurements Yearbook* series was developed to stimulate critical thinking and assist in the selection of the best available test for a given purpose, not to promote the passive acceptance of reviewer judgment.

INDEXES

As mentioned above, the *17th MMY* includes six indexes invaluable as aids to effective use: (a) Index of Titles, (b) Index of Acronyms, (c) Classified Subject Index, (d) Publishers Directory and Index, (e) Index of Names, and (f) Score Index. Additional comment on these indexes is presented below.

Index of Titles. Because the organization of the *17th MMY* is encyclopedic in nature, with the tests ordered alphabetically by title throughout the volume, the test title index does not have to be consulted to find a test if the title is known. However, the title index has some features that make it useful beyond its function as a complete title listing. First, it includes cross-reference information useful for tests with superseded or alternative titles or tests commonly (and sometimes inaccurately) known by multiple titles. Second, it identifies tests that are new or revised. Third, it may cue the user to other tests with similar titles that may be useful. Titles for the 50 tests not reviewed because of insufficient technical documentation are included in the Index of Titles. It is important to keep in mind that the numbers in this index, like those for all *MMY* indexes, are test numbers and not page numbers.

Because no *MMY* includes reviews of all tests currently in print, a particular test of interest may not be reviewed in this volume. To learn if a commercially published test has been reviewed in this or an earlier volume of the *MMY*, users may access the Buros page on the World Wide Web (www.unl.edu/buros). A search of Test Reviews Online (TROL) will indicate if a test has been reviewed and also will indicate the yearbook in which the review can be found. TROL also provides electronic access to reviews provided in recent *MMY*s (most current reviews only) and test reviews that have been finalized since the publication of the most recent *MMY*. Therefore, TROL provides ready access, for a small fee, to the majority of tests that have been reviewed in *The Mental Measurements Yearbook* series. As an alternative,

Tests in Print VII provides a cross-reference to reviews of still-in-print tests in the *MMY* series.

Index of Acronyms. Some tests seem to be better known by their acronyms than by their full titles. The Index of Acronyms can help in these instances; it refers the reader to the full title of the test and to the relevant descriptive information and reviews.

Classified Subject Index. The Classified Subject Index classifies all tests listed in the *17th MMY* into 14 of 18 major categories: Achievement, Behavior Assessment, Developmental, Education, English and Language, Fine Arts, Foreign Languages, Intelligence and General Aptitude, Mathematics, Miscellaneous, Neuropsychological, Personality, Reading, Science, Sensory-Motor, Social Studies, Speech and Hearing, and Vocations. (No tests in the Fine Arts, Foreign Languages, Science, and Social Studies categories are reviewed in the *17th MMY*.) Each test entry in this index includes test title, population for which the test is intended, and test number. The Classified Subject Index is of great help to readers who seek a listing of tests in given subject areas. This index represents a starting point for readers who know their area of interest but do not know how to further focus that interest in order to identify the best test(s) for their particular purposes.

Publishers Directory and Index. The Publishers Directory and Index includes the names and addresses of the publishers of all tests included in the *17th MMY* plus a listing of test numbers for each individual publisher. Also included are the telephone and FAX numbers, email, and Web addresses for those publishers who responded to our request for this information. This index can be particularly useful in obtaining addresses for specimen sets or catalogs after the test reviews have been read and evaluated. It also can be useful when a reader knows the publisher of a certain test but is uncertain about the test title, or when a reader is interested in the range of tests published by a given publisher.

Index of Names. The Index of Names provides a comprehensive list of names, indicating authorship of a test, test review, or reviewer's reference.

Score Index. The Score Index is a listing of the scored parts of all tests reviewed in the *17th MMY*. Test titles are sometimes misleading or ambiguous, and test content may be difficult to define with precision. In contrast, test scores often represent operational definitions of the variables the test author is trying to measure, and as such they can define test purpose and content more adequately than other descriptive information. A search for a particular test is most often a search for a test that measures some specific variable(s). Test scores and their associated labels can often be the best definitions of the variable(s) of interest. The Score Index is a detailed subject index based on the most critical operational features of any test—the scores and their associated labels.

HOW TO USE THIS YEARBOOK

A reference work like *The Seventeenth Mental Measurements Yearbook* can be of far greater benefit to a reader if some time is taken to become familiar with what it has to offer and how it might be used most effectively to obtain the information wanted.

Step 1: Read the Introduction to the *17th MMY* in its entirety.

Step 2: Become familiar with the six indexes and particularly with the instructions preceding each index listing.

Step 3: Use the book by looking up needed information. This step is simple if one keeps the following procedures in mind:

1. Go directly to the test entry using the alphabetical page headings if you know the title of the test.

2. Consult the Index of Titles for possible variants of the title or consult the appropriate subject area of the Classified Subject Index for other possible leads or for similar or related tests in the same area, if you do not know, cannot find, or are unsure of the title of a test. (Other uses for both of these indexes were described above.)

3. Consult the Index of Names if you know the author of a test but not the title or publisher. Look up the author's titles until you find the test you want.

4. Consult the Publishers Directory and Index if you know the test publisher but not the title or author. Look up the publisher's titles until you find the test you want.

5. Consult the Score Index and locate the test or tests that include the score variable of interest if you are looking for a test that yields a particular kind of test score.

6. If after following the above steps you are not able to find a review of the test you want, consult the Appendix for a list of tests that are not reviewed. Reasons tests are not reviewed include (a) they did not meet our selection criteria, (b) the reviews were not completed in time for publication in this volume, or (c) the publisher failed to respond in a timely manner to our request for testing materials. You also can consult *TIP VII* or visit the Buros web page (www.unl.edu/buros) and use the Test Reviews Online service (TROL) to identify the *MMY* that contains the description and any available reviews for a test of interest.

7. Once you have found the test or tests you are seeking, read the descriptive entries for these tests carefully so that you can take advantage of the information provided. A description of the information in these test entries is presented later in this section.

8. Read the test reviews carefully and analytically, as suggested above. The information and evaluations contained in these reviews are meant to assist test consumers in making well-informed decisions about the choice and applications of tests.

9. Once you have read the descriptive information and test reviews, you may want to contact the publisher to order a specimen set for a particular test so that you can examine it firsthand. The Publishers Directory and Index provide the address information needed to obtain specimen sets or catalogs.

Making Effective Use of the Test Entries. The test entries include extensive information. For each test, descriptive information is presented in the following order:

a) TITLE. Test titles are printed in boldface type. Secondary or series titles are set off from main titles by a colon.

b) PURPOSE. For each test there is a brief, clear statement describing the purpose of the test. Often these statements are quotations from the test manual.

c) POPULATION. This describes the groups for which the test is intended. The grade, chronological age, semester range, or employment category is usually given. For example, "Grades 1.5–2.5, 2–3, 4–12, 13–17" means that there are four test booklets: a booklet for the middle of

first grade through the middle of the second grade, a booklet for the beginning of the second grade through the end of third grade, a booklet for Grades 4 through 12 inclusive, and a booklet for undergraduate and graduate students in colleges and universities.

d) PUBLICATION DATE. The inclusive range of publication dates for the various forms, accessories, and editions of a test is reported.

e) ACRONYM. When a test is often referred to by an acronym, the acronym is given in the test entry.

f) SCORES. The number of part scores is presented along with their titles or descriptions of what they are intended to represent or measure.

g) ADMINISTRATION. Individual or group administration is indicated. A test is considered a group test unless it may be administered only individually.

h) FORMS, PARTS, AND LEVELS. All available forms, parts, and levels are listed.

i) MANUAL. Notation is made if no manual is available. All other manual information is included under Price Data.

j) RESTRICTED DISTRIBUTION. This is noted only for tests that are made available to a special market by the publisher. Educational and psychological restrictions are not noted (unless a special training course is required for use).

k) PRICE DATA. Price information is reported for test packages (usually 20 to 35 tests), answer sheets, all other accessories, and specimen sets. The statement "$17.50 per 35 tests" means that all accessories are included unless otherwise indicated by the reporting of separate prices for accessories. The statement also means 35 tests of one level, one edition, or one part unless stated otherwise. Because test prices can change very quickly, the year that the listed test prices were obtained is also given. Foreign currency is assigned the appropriate symbol. When prices are given in foreign dollars, a qualifying symbol is added (e.g., A$16.50 refers to 16 dollars and 50 cents in Australian currency). Along with cost, the publication date and number of pages on which print occurs is reported for manuals and technical reports (e.g., 1999, 102 pages). All types of machine-scorable answer sheets available for use with a specific test are reported in the descriptive entry. Scoring and reporting services provided by publishers are reported along with information on costs. In a few cases, special computerized scoring and interpretation services are noted at the end of the price information.

l) FOREIGN LANGUAGE AND OTHER SPECIAL EDITIONS. This section concerns foreign language editions published by the same publisher who sells the English-language edition. It also indicates special editions (e.g., Braille, large type) available from the same or a different publisher.

m) TIME. The number of minutes of actual working time allowed examinees and the approximate length of time needed for administering a test are reported whenever obtainable. The latter figure is always enclosed in parentheses. Thus, "50(60) minutes" indicates that the examinees are allowed 50 minutes of working time and that a total of 60 minutes is needed to administer the test. A time of "40–50 minutes" indicates an untimed test that takes approximately 45 minutes to administer, or—in a few instances—a test so timed that working time and administration time are very difficult to disentangle. When the time necessary to administer a test is not reported or suggested in the test materials but has been obtained from a catalog or through correspondence with the test publisher or author, the time is enclosed in brackets.

n) COMMENTS. Some entries contain special notations, such as: "for research use only"; "revision of the ABC Test"; "tests administered monthly at centers throughout the United States"; "subtests available as separates"; and "verbal creativity." A statement such as "verbal creativity" is intended to further describe what the test claims to measure. Some of the test entries include factual statements that imply criticism of the test, such as "1999 test identical with test copyrighted 1980."

o) AUTHOR. For most tests, all authors are reported. In the case of tests that appear in a new form each year, only authors of the most recent forms are listed. Names are reported exactly as printed on test booklets. Names of editors generally are not reported.

p) PUBLISHER. The name of the publisher or distributor is reported for each test. Foreign publishers are identified by listing the country in brackets immediately following the name of the publisher. The Publishers Directory and Index must be consulted for a publisher's address and other contact information.

q) FOREIGN ADAPTATIONS. Revisions and adaptations of tests for foreign use are listed in a separate paragraph following the original edition.

r) SUBLISTINGS. Levels, editions, subtests, or parts of a test available in separate booklets are sometimes presented as sublistings with titles set in small capitals. Sub-sublistings are indented and titles are set in italic type.

s) CROSS REFERENCES. For tests that have been listed previously in a Buros Institute of Mental Measurements publication, a test entry includes—if relevant—a final item containing cross references to the reviews, excerpts, and references for that test in those volumes. In the cross references, "T7:467" refers to test 467 in *Tests in Print VII*, "14:121" refers to test 121 in *The Fourteenth Mental Measurements Yearbook*, "8:1023" refers to test 1023 in *The Eighth Mental Measurements Yearbook*, "T3:144" refers to test 144 in *Tests in Print III*, "7:637" refers to test 637 in *The Seventh Mental Measurements Yearbook*, "P:262" refers to test 262 in *Personality Tests and Reviews*, "2:1427" refers to test 1427 in *The 1940 Yearbook*, and "1:1110" refers to test 1110 in *The 1938 Yearbook*. In the case of batteries and programs, the paragraph also includes cross references—from the battery to the separately listed subtests and vice versa—to entries in this volume and to entries and reviews in earlier Yearbooks. Test numbers not preceded by a colon refer to tests in this Yearbook; for example, "see 45" refers to test 45 in this Yearbook.

RIGHTS AND RESPONSIBILITIES OF TEST TAKERS

In order to more fully publicize the efforts of the Test Taker Rights and Responsibilities Working Group of the Joint Committee on Testing Practices, we are printing this document in the final section of *The Seventeenth Mental Measurements Yearbook*. It is common for both test takers and test publishers to be unfamiliar with this publication. We believe that by bringing additional attention to this document, all appropriate groups will gain increased awareness of these general guidelines.

ACKNOWLEDGMENTS

The publication of *The Seventeenth Mental Measurements Yearbook* has required the concerted effort and the contributions of many individuals without whom this edition would not have been possible. The editors gratefully acknowledge the talent, expertise, and dedication of all individuals who have assisted in the publication process.

Although Barbara S. Plake is a co-editor of this edition of the *MMY*, her primary participation ended with her retirement as Director of the Buros Institute of Mental Measurements in May 2006. Throughout the nearly 30 years that the Buros Institute has been in Nebraska, it has enjoyed able leadership, first of James V. Mitchell and, until very recently, of Dr. Plake. Her term as Director of the Buros Institute began with *The Tenth Mental Measurements Yearbook* and continued through the beginning of this 17th edition. Although she continues to be extremely active serving in the field, she is missed at the Buros Institute and throughout the University of Nebraska. The other three editors continue to admire and look to her for wisdom. An expert in standard setting, it is perhaps not surprising that she set high standards herself, standards that the new leadership of the Buros Institute are committed to keep. We hope that readers and reviewers alike will consider this as a seamless transition.

Linda Murphy, Managing Editor, has long been an essential individual in the publication of each new edition of the *MMY* series. Her attention to detail, good humor, and steadfast commitment to the production of this series makes our job as editors far more agreeable than would otherwise be possible. Her wise counsel and historical insights keep us alert to the many errors that might occur if not for her thoughtful presence and diligence. Nor would the publication of this volume be possible without the substantive efforts of our Assistant Editor, Gary Anderson, who balances his ongoing support as webmaster for the Buros Institute's website with his good-natured communications to all of our reviewers. Rasma Strautkalns, Institute Secretary, and Rosemary Sieck, Clerical Assistant, also must be recognized for their important contributions to the success of our efforts. In addition, we would like to cite other members of the Buros Center for Testing, our parent organization, for their support and encouragement during the publication of this edition of the *MMY*. Former editor James C. Impara, as well as Chad W. Buckendahl, Susan L. Davis, Theresa Glanz, and Janice Nelsen have all made generous contributions to discussions of our current and future directions. We appreciate the efforts of all permanent staff, each of whom contributes more than their share to the development and production of products from the Buros Institute of Mental Measurements. We also enjoy the respect, collegiality, and support of the organizations within which the Buros Institute exists. In particular we thank Ralph De Ayala, department chair, and Marjorie Kostelnik, college dean, for their encouragement and backing.

This volume would not exist without the substantial efforts of test reviewers. Based on the recommendations of our National Advisory Council, the Buros Institute began recognizing reviewers of long-standing with the publication of *The Sixteenth Mental Measurements Yearbook* series. Individuals submitting reviews to six or more publications, beginning in 1985 with *The Ninth Mental Measurements Yearbook*, were designated as "Distinguished Reviewers" for their enduring contribution to the field of testing and measurement. A listing of these reviewers is referenced on page 922 of this edition. Reviewers who became eligible with the publication of *The Seventeenth Mental Measurements Yearbook* are listed on page 921. We are very grateful to the many reviewers (and especially to those Distinguished Reviewers recognized in this edition) who have prepared test reviews for the Buros Institute of Mental Measurements. Their willingness to take time from busy professional schedules and to share their expertise in the form of thoughtful test reviews is very much appreciated. The *Mental Measurements Yearbook* series would not exist were it not for their efforts.

The work of many graduate and undergraduate students helps make possible the quality of this volume. Their efforts have included writing test descriptions, fact checking reviews, verifying test references, proofreading, and innumerable other tasks. We thank Graduate Research Students Jeffrey Babl, Stacey DeSchane, M. Kelly Haack, Tabethah Mack, Alejandro Morales, Erin Rhoads, Anja Römhild, and Michelle Simpson for their assistance. We also wish to thank Christa

Hake, Carina McCormick, and Carol Sutton, who contributed primarily in the area of word processing and proofreading, even in the face of our sometimes atrocious handwriting.

Appreciation is also extended to the members of our National Advisory Council for their willingness to assist in the operation of the Buros Institute of Mental Measurements and for their thought-provoking suggestions for improving the *MMY* series and other publications of the Institute. During the period in which this volume was prepared, the National Advisory Council has included Gregory Cizek, Lawrence Rudner, Milton Hakel, Terry Gutkin, Angee Baker, and Neal Schmitt.

The Buros Institute of Mental Measurements is part of the Department of Educational Psychology of the University of Nebraska-Lincoln. We have benefited from the many departmental colleagues who have contributed to this work. We are also grateful for the contribution of the University of Nebraska Press, which provides expert consultation and serves as distributor of the *MMY* series.

SUMMARY

The Mental Measurements Yearbook series is an essential resource for both individuals and organizations seeking information critical to the evaluation, selection, and use of specific testing instruments. This current edition contains 376 test reviews of 209 different tests.

Test reviews from recent *MMY* editions are now available electronically through EBSCO Publishing or Ovid Technologies at many university, medical, and research libraries. Test reviews also are available over the internet directly from the Buros Institute (www.unl.edu/buros) through our Test Reviews Online ecommerce website.

For almost 70 years the *MMY* series has been published to support the interests of knowledgeable professionals and an informed public. By providing candid reviews of testing products, this publication also has served test publishers who wish to improve their tests by submitting their products to this independent review process. Given the critical importance of testing, we hope test authors and publishers will carefully consider the comments made by these reviewers and continue to refine and perfect their assessment products.

Kurt F. Geisinger
Robert A. Spies
Janet F. Carlson
Barbara S. Plake
July 2007

Tests and Reviews

[1]

Abbreviated Torrance Test for Adults.
Purpose: To assess creative thinking ability.
Population: Adult.
Publication Date: 2002.
Acronym: ATTA.
Scores, 23: Norm-Referenced Measures (Fluency, Originality, Elaboration, Flexibility, Total Scaled Score), Criterion-Referenced Creativity Indicators (Richness and Colorfulness of Imagery, Emotions/Feelings, Future Orientation, Humor: Conceptual Incongruity, Provocative Questions, Verbal Responses Total, Openness: Resistance to Premature Closure, Unusual Visualization/Different Perspective, Movement and/or Sound, Richness and/or Colorfulness of Imagery, Abstractness of Titles, Articulateness in Telling Story, Combination/Synthesis of Two or More Figures, Internal Visual Perspective, Expressions of Feelings and Emotions, Fantasy, Figural Responses Total), Creativity Index.
Administration: Group.
Price Data, 2005: $15.45 per nonreturnable sample set including manual (39 pages) and 1 booklet; $27.55 per starter set including 10 booklets and manual; $16.75 per 10 booklets; $12.75 per manual.
Time: 15 minutes.
Comments: Based on 1980 Demonstration Form of the Torrance Tests; may be self-administered; norm- and criterion-referenced.
Authors: Kathy Goff and E. Paul Torrance.
Publisher: Scholastic Testing Service, Inc.

Review of the Abbreviated Torrance Test for Adults by JAMES A. ATHANASOU, Faculty of Education, University of Technology, Sydney, Australia:

DESCRIPTION. The Abbreviated Torrance Test for Adults (ATTA) is a projective assessment of creative thinking abilities. It has a substantial pedigree of theory and application and is in-tended—as the title implies—to be a shortened adult version of the Torrance Tests of Creative Thinking. The target population for the test is adults, and the ultimate purpose of this test of figural and verbal creative thinking aptitudes is to provide an indicator of real-life creative achievement.

The administration of the ATTA is straightforward, and clear instructions are provided for users. The total testing time for the three separate tasks is 9 minutes. The test yields results for four norm-referenced abilities: Fluency, Originality, Elaboration and Flexibility. It also provides criterion-referenced creativity indicators for (a) verbal responses (Richness and Colorfulness of Imagery; Emotions/Feelings; Future Orientation; Humor—Conceptual Incongruity; Provocative Questions), and (b) figural responses (Openness—Resistance to Premature Closure; Unusual Visualisation—Different Perspective; Movement and/or Sound; Richness and/or Colourfulness of Imagery; Abstractness of Titles; Context: Environment for Object, Articulateness in Story telling; Internal Visual Perspective; Expressions of Feelings and Emotions; Combination/Synthesis of Two or More Figures; and Fantasy).

Each of the four raw scores for Fluency, Originality, Elaboration, and Flexibility is converted to a normalized scales score (broadly equivalent to a stanine). Each of the 15 criterion-referenced indicators is scored on a 3-point scale of 0, 1, or 2. The sum of these indicators is added to the scaled scores to yield a *Creativity Index*, which is then norm-referenced and a standards-based interpretation is provided. The results are summarized as a Creativity Index with a mean of 69.4 ($SD = 10.9$) and which ranges from minimal levels with scores of 1–50 to substantial level with scores of 85 or more.

The guidelines for scoring are detailed and helpful, but the scoring requires a great deal of familiarity and practice because it is not entirely objective in its grading. For instance, originality of the verbal responses is the ability to produce ideas that are not common. This is relatively straightforward to assess because any responses that are not listed as common responses are given 1 point each. Criterion-referenced scoring for richness and colorfulness of imagery is on the basis of the variety, vividness, and strength of imagery. A rating of single plus (+) is given for any indicator appearing once and a rating of double plus (++) is given for any indicator appearing more than once (manual, p. 7). This requires a degree of judgment and expertise in decision making. An indication of the expertise required is that 17 out of the 38 pages in the manual are devoted to scoring.

DEVELOPMENT. The ATTA was created from the Demonstration Form of the Torrance Tests that were published in 1980. The development of the three items is not described specifically other than to state that the ATTA originated from the Torrance Tests and the shorter demonstration form. The ATTA is described as "essentially an alternate form of the TTCT" (manual, p. 1). It is not possible to discern from the manual the results of any pilot testing or to comment on the selection of items.

The user is directed to a reference list for details of the original test development and the assumptions underlying the construct of creative thinking. For all intents and purposes, however, the creativity that is assessed is essentially a simple, linear, and mathematical function of figural and verbal responses (across the norm-referenced and criterion-referenced creativity indicators).

TECHNICAL. There is minimal information about the norm sample. The norm sample is described as 141 of the original 249 adults who completed the Brief Demonstrator of the Torrance Tests of Creative Thinking. This group comprised adults aged 19 to 89 years and "represented retirees, college students, business owners etc." (manual, p. 30). To these 141 were added 34 persons who completed that ATTA in 2000. Thus the norms are based on an unspecified geographic, occupational, educational, and social cohort of 175 persons. It is impossible to state to what extent

this sample matches any intended testing population and it is not clear to what extent the norms are appropriate for different gender or ethnic culture groups.

The evidence for score consistency is based first on the Kuder-Richardson 21 formula applied to the composite score. The Creativity Index has a KR-21 value of .69 and a corresponding standard error of measurement of 8.23. Kuder-Richardson 21 coefficients were calculated for fluency, originality, elaboration, and flexibility and range from .38 to .84. Interrater reliabilities are greater than .95 but the devil is in the detail; actually the interrater reliabilities were derived from the predecessor test and it is stated that "interrater reliability studies are ongoing" (manual, p. 34). Finally, the manual described how a score of 18 is higher than a score of 17 (p. 28) but these scores may actually overlap (16.5 to 19.4 versus 15.5 to 18.4) and does not heed its own advice to users on a reasonable allowance of two standard errors of measurement.

The interpretation and potential uses of the test results really hinge upon the validity of scores from the Torrance Tests of Creative Thinking; reference is also made in the manual to a Quality of Life study as support for the validity of the results. No specific studies examining the validity of the ATTA are reported. It seems likely that on the basis of the evidence available the test adequately samples fluency, originality, elaboration, and flexibility but further information should be presented, especially with regard to the differential validity across gender, racial, ethnic, and culture groups.

COMMENTARY. The overall strength of the test lies in the content and its origins from the earlier work of Torrance. It provides a brief and usable assessment that is standardized. It is not subject to faking but special training is required to score the ATTA.

SUMMARY. The ATTA may be useful as a qualitative assessment of divergent thinking or creative potential with adults. It presents three novel tasks and may find wider application beyond the assessment of creative thinking. It is not yet supported by substantial psychometric evidence of the validity and reliability of the results and users are best referred to the original Torrance Tests of Creative Thinking (T7:2662) for a more substantial assessment of individuals where high-stakes personal, educational, or vocational decisions are involved.

Review of the Abbreviated Torrance Test for Adults By ALAN C. BUGBEE, JR., Director of Psychometrics, American Society for Clinical Pathology, Chicago, IL:

DESCRIPTION. The Abbreviated Torrance Test for Adults (ATTA) is designed to be a measure of creative thinking ability in people over 18 years old. According to the manual, it is a form of the Torrance Tests of Creative Thinking (T7:2662). The ATTA is a short test consisting of three tasks. Each task is performed by the test taker in no more than 3 minutes. Including the instructions to the test taker, which are read by the test administrator, this test could probably be administered in no more than 15 minutes. The manual also mentions that the ATTA could be self-administered, although no directions for doing this are provided. At the beginning of the test, the test takers are told that they are being tested on how good they are at thinking creatively and solving problems. All questions are answered in the testing booklet.

There are three activities that constitute the entire test. Test takers are asked to describe and complete a set of novel tasks. These tasks require writing and drawing to different stimuli and scenarios.

The test is scored using a worksheet in the back of each test booklet. The ATTA uses two sets of scores, Norm-Referenced Measures and Criterion-Referenced Creativity Indicators. The Norm-Referenced Measures are based on Fluency and Originality for the first task. The second task or activity scores are also based on Fluency and Originality, plus Elaboration. The third task has these three plus Flexibility. The scoring for these categories is done by assigning points to the responses. How points are assigned comes from a lengthy section of the manual (pp. 5-6, 8-14). Although the methods used for this scoring require some judgment and attention to detail, no special training seems to be required to score it. The raw score for each of the categories is based on the frequency of responses that are assigned a point, following the manual's instructions. For example, Fluency, for the first activity, "is a simple count of the pertinent responses, scored by first reading each response and making a judgment as to whether the response is in fact relevant to the situation" (manual, p. 6). After raw scores are calculated for each category, these scores are converted to scaled scores, based on a table on the last page of each test booklet. These derived scores are then summed together to create a total scaled score for Norm-Referenced measures.

In addition, there are 15 Criterion-Referenced Creativity Indicators. The scores for these areas are also based on the three tasks performed: 5 for Activity #1 and 10 for Activities #2 and #3. The 5 indicators for Activity #1 are: Richness and Colorfulness; Emotions/Feelings; Future Orientation; Humor: Conceptual Incongruity; and Provocative Questions. The 10 indicators for Activity #2 and Activity #3 are: Openness: Resistance to Premature Closure; Unusual Visualizations/Different Perspective; Movement and/or Sound; Richness and/or Colorfulness of Imagery; Abstractness of Titles; Articulateness in Telling Story; Combination/Synthesis of Two or More Figures; Internal Visual Perspective; Expressions of Feelings and Emotions; and Fantasy. These indicators are scored by counting the frequency of each occurrence, as defined in the manual, and assigning them relative values, as indicated by a single plus sign (+) or a double plus sign (++). Each indicator is then given a numeric score of 0 for a blank rating, 1 for a single plus sign rating, and 2 for a double plus sign rating. It is noted that not all of the indicators may be present in each of the activities. A total score for Criterion-Referenced Creativity Indicators is calculated by summing the raw scores for these 15 areas and the 5 indicators for Activity #1. The Criterion-Referenced Creativity Indicators for Activities #2 and #3 scores may range from 0 (all blanks) to 30 (all 2 points in all 15 areas).

After all of the scores are calculated and summed for the Norm-Referenced Measures and the Criterion-Referenced Creativity Indicators, the total scores for these two groups are summed together to form the Creativity Index. According to the manual, this is a composite score of all of the subscores. This composite score is converted to a 7-point scale, called the Creativity Level, using a table at the end of the test booklet. According to the manual, "The creativity index...perhaps provides the best single overall indicator of creative ability for the individual being tested" (p. 29).

DEVELOPMENT. As mentioned above, the Abbreviated Torrance Test for Adults (ATTA) is a short form of the Torrance Tests of Creative Thinking (TTCT); "(the ATTA) is essentially an alternate form of the TTCT, though in an abbreviated context combining both Verbal and Figural activities" (p. 1). According to the manual, since it was developed, the TTCT has become a standard for assessing creative thinking. However, the TTCT takes 1 hour and 15 minutes to administer—45 minutes for the Verbal section and 30 minutes for the Figural section. Apparently, this made Torrance believe that a shorter version for adult administration was necessary. This led to the Demonstration Form of the Torrance Tests (D-TTCT) in 1980. According to the manual, the D-TTCT was successful. This led to the development of the ATTA.

The ATTA was first developed as a Brief Demonstrator of the Torrance Tests of Creative Thinking (BD-TTCT) in 2000. The BD-TTCT was converted to the ATTA in 2002. This conversion consisted of reducing the number of creative indicators from 19 to 15 and the expansion of the scoring directions. The normative data used for the BD-TTCT (n = 249 adults, ages 19 to 89) were rescored with the new directions. From the original 249 subjects, 141 records were available for rescoring. These records were added to 34 records from subjects who were tested in 2000. This led to a total of 175 records that were rescored using the new guideline. These became the norms for the ATTA and the source for the technical information presented in the manual.

TECHNICAL. The Torrance Tests of Creative Thinking (TTCT) has existed since 1966 and has been researched extensively. Perhaps within that research there is evidence that there was a need for a shorter form, leading to the ATTA. Perhaps there is also a demonstration that this form of the TTCT does the same as the complete test. Several studies are cited that apparently demonstrate these points (Torrance, Wu, & Ando, 1980; Torrance & Goff, 2000 [This is cited (p. 30), but not referenced, in the manual; it may be referring to Torrance (2000), which is referenced]), but the evidence is not presented in the manual. If there are other materials available as part of the test package beyond the test manual and the test booklet that would demonstrate that the ATTA is a form of the TTCT, they were not provided.

This lack of a comprehensive summary of the evidence of the validity of the results from this test is not in keeping with the *Standards for Educational and Psychological Testing* (American Educational Research Association, American Psychological Association, National Council on Measurement in Education, 1999, especially Standards 1.1, 1.6, 1.8, 1.14, 1.16, 1.17, 1.20, 1.21). Because the ATTA says that it is an alternate form of the TTCT, the least that it should do is provide evidence of its relationship with the TTCT. No such evidence is provided, at least in the test manual, other than citations of some studies. Brief information is provided about the development of the Creativity Index, the composite score, and the distribution of scores.

Reliability. The reliability estimates of the composite raw scores (Total Ability and Total Ability + Indicators) and of the separate ability scores (Fluency, Originality, Elaboration, Flexibility) are reported in the manual. All of the reliabilities range from .38 (Originality) to .90 (Total Abilities + Indicators).

The manual also mentions coefficients of interrater reliability that range from .95 to .99. However, these reliabilities were not calculated for this form of the examination, but for the BD-TTCT. The manual also reports that interrater reliability studies "are ongoing as different scores become involved" (p. 34). It is hoped that this information is included in future editions of the ATTA.

There is no report on reliability or standard error of measurement for the 15 creativity indicators. This is not in keeping with the criteria for reliability (AERA et al., 1999, Standards 2.1, 2.2, 2.9, 2.10, 2.17). Because the test results are affected by the number of responses—as well as their quality—for each activity, this information should be provided to test takers (AERA et al., 1999, Standard 2.8).

As mentioned previously, the ATTA is an alternate form of the Torrance Tests of Creative Thinking (TTCT). However, there is a lack of information about how this form or its predecessors (D-TTCT and BD-TTCT) is related to the TTCT. No equating or relational information is provided. It also lacks information about self-administration, although the manual specifically mentions this as a method.

COMMENTARY. The ATTA seems to be written under the assumption that potential users already know all about the TTCT. The manual is more concerned with providing the user with scoring guidelines than with providing evidence that the ATTA is indeed an alternate form of the TTCT. The manual provides a great deal of information about the scoring process. Twenty-one of the manual's 37 pages (57%) deal specifically with scoring. Whether this provides sufficient information and guidelines for scoring is hard to say.

It is quite possible, and indeed probable, that the ATTA is a valid and reliable quick measure of the creative thinking ability of an adult. Unfortunately, the evidence that it is this sort of instrument is not presented in its test manual or its test booklet. It is hoped that the authors of this test will provide the evidence necessary for it to be accepted as a short version of the Torrance Tests of Creative Thinking.

SUMMARY. The Abbreviated Torrance Test for Adults (ATTA) is a short measure of creative thinking. It is intended to be an alternate form of the widely used Torrance Tests of Creative Thinking (TTCT), specifically for adults (19 years or older). Unfortunately, the ATTA does not present the necessary information to demonstrate that it is either a valid and reliable instrument to assess the creative thinking ability of adults or that it is a viable alternate form of the TTCT. It is unclear whether the necessary work in demonstrating the ATTA as a useful instrument has been done and is not presented in the manual or if it still needs to be done. It is hoped that this necessary information will be explicitly provided in the next version of this test.

REVIEWER'S REFERENCES

American Educational Research Association, American Psychological Association, & National Council on Measurement in Education. (1999). *Standards for educational and psychological testing*. Washington, DC: American Educational Research Association.

Torrance, E. P. (2000). *Research review for the Torrance Tests Of Creative Thinking: Figural and Verbal Forms A and B*. Bensenville, IL: Scholastic Testing Service, Inc.

Torrance, E. P., Wu, T. H., & Ando, T. (1980). *Preliminary norms—technical manual: Demonstrator Torrance Tests of Creative Thinking*. Athens, GA: Georgia Studies of Creative Behavior.

[2]
Abuse Disability Questionnaire.

Purpose: "Designed to assess both the extent of exposure to partner abuse, as well as its associated consequences."

Population: Women ages 18 years and older.

Publication Date: 2005.

Acronym: ADQ.

Scores, 8: Relationship Disability, Psychological Dysfunction, Substance Abuse, Anxiety, Life Restriction, Health Status Issues, Inadequate Life Control, Concern with Physical Harm.

Administration: Individual or group.

Price Data, 2006: $70 per complete kit including 50 questionnaires/profile forms and manual (27 pages); $45 per 50 questionnaires/profile forms; $30 per manual.

Time: (5-15) minutes.

Comments: Includes a self-report questionnaire/profile form and an information/diagnostics form to be completed via an interview.

Author: John R. McNamara.

Publisher: Stoelting Co.

Review of the Abuse Disability Questionnaire by SHERI BAUMAN, Associate Professor, Department of Educational Psychology, University of Arizona, Tucson, AZ:

DESCRIPTION. The Abuse Disability Questionnaire (ADQ) is a self-report paper-and-pencil screening instrument designed to assess quickly the level of an adult woman's impairment in several domains that are associated with abuse in an intimate-partnered relationship. The brief questionnaire, which the author states can be completed independently by anyone who has completed elementary school, consists of three parts. In the first part, respondents rate the amount of exposure to physical, psychological/emotional, and sexual abuse on a 5-point scale ranging from 0 (*none*) to 4 (*excessive*). The circled numbers are summed to derive an Abuse Exposure total score, which is compared to the means and standard deviations of a shelter sample and a well-functioning community sample provided on the cover page of the questionnaire. The next section, designed to assess degree of impairment, is composed of 30 statements to which the respondent indicates her level of agreement on a 5-point Likert scale from *Strongly Agree* to *Strongly Disagree*. The sum of the responses on the 30 Likert-scale items is the Impairment Level, which is rated from low to severe using score ranges provided on the cover page. Using a matrix provided on the form, eight subscale scores are also derived from these items. They are: Relationship Disability, Life Restriction, Psychological Dysfunction, Health Status Issues, Substance Abuse, Inadequate Life Control, Anxiety, and Concern with Physical Harm. Scores on the subscales are interpreted by comparing them to the means of a sample of women in a shelter; intervention should be considered when the client's score is equal to or above that of the shelter sample. The final section is a Supplemental and Diagnostics Form to be administered in a clinical interview. There are no guidelines for use of the Supplemental Information and Diagnostics Form.

No special qualifications are required to administer the questionnaire, and time needed to complete the form is estimated to be less than 10 minutes. Scoring is straightforward and is likely to require only a few minutes. The questionnaire is available only in English.

DEVELOPMENT. The ADQ was copyrighted in 1999; the manual bears a 2005 copyright. The author takes a "disability perspective" (manual, p. 4) on intimate partner violence, which focuses on the negative self- and worldview that is the consequence of the stress of abuse. The author suggests that when a person's strategies for coping are overwhelmed, as is the case in victims of partner abuse, the person becomes disabled by the negative way she comes to evaluate herself and the world. The conceptual grounding is in a view of psychopathology as a functional impairment or disability (Bergner, 1997).

The manual presents a concise case for the prevalence and harmful psychological consequences of intimate-partner abuse, but is less effective at demonstrating a rationale for the disability view of psychopathology. Although the implication is that information about psychological disabilities is clinically useful, it is not clear how this information has an advantage over traditional diagnostic information. Many women who have been victims of intimate partner violence will qualify for a diagnosis of posttraumatic stress disorder and/or depression. For both of these diagnoses, assessment instruments with established reliability and validity are available, and efficacious treatment approaches for these disorders have been identified via randomized clinical trials.

Much of the argument in favor of a disability perspective is presented in McNamara and Brooker (2000); it is unfortunate that it was omitted from this brief manual. In that article, the authors observe that traditional assessments focus on trauma-related symptoms, whereas the ADQ assesses the altered way in which the client views herself and the world. They argue that such information is important in generating epidemiological information; understanding different patterns of disability that may exist in those whose abuse has been primarily physical, psychological, or sexual;

and in providing clinically useful profiles of disability to guide treatment.

The questionnaire was developed by generating statements about disabilities resulting from partner abuse based on clinical experience and a review of relevant literature. Women's shelter counselors provided input on items and clinically relevant impairments, and the pool of items was reduced to the current 30 items. The manual does not indicate the number of items in the original pool; the information provided implies that those counselors who reviewed the items were all from a single women's shelter. There is no indication that the questionnaire was piloted and revised based on performance of a pilot version.

The manual justifies the omission of male victims from the development of this questionnaire by the ratio of female-to-male victims and the increased rate of injuries in female victims. No mention is made of women who are abused by other women in same-sex relationships. No scales are available to determine whether the client might be exaggerating or minimizing impairment other than observing whether a particular response set (answering all items with the same response level) is evident and noting whether there are obvious discrepancies between the elevations in the Abuse Exposure and Impairment Level sections.

TECHNICAL. Normative data are provided only for the original sample on which the instrument was developed. Means and standard deviations are provided, and scores above the mean for the shelter group are considered worthy of attention.

The principal components analysis (PCA) that was used to develop the subscales raises some questions that are not answered in the manual or in the article cited above. The sample size of 132 may not be adequate for a PCA on a 30-item questionnaire. The manual provides indications of a much larger number of ADQ samples; it is not clear why confirmatory factor analysis was not conducted. Various rules of thumb exist, but a minimum sample size of 150 is often suggested (with five cases for each variable being a widely used guideline). Other experts recommend 20 subjects per factor, and as eight factors were extracted, this sample size does not appear adequate for the analysis. Further, no data regarding the factorability of the correlation matrix are given; values for Bartlett's test of sphericity and/or Kaiser-Meyer-

Olkin values are commonly reported. The author does not identify the criteria used for determining the number of factors to retain, and the small proportion of variance accounted for by several other factors renders that information particularly important. One factor (or subscale) has only 2 items, whereas a minimum of 3 items per factor is often recommended. The author acknowledges in the article, but not in the manual, that two of the factors (Anxiety and Concern with Physical Harm) are "not straightforward" (McNamara & Brooker, 2000, p. 176). The fact that these two factors had low internal consistency is not surprising considering their small size in terms of items.

Reliability data are reported in the manual based on two different shelter samples. Internal consistency (alpha) values for the total Impairment scores are very good (.88 and .93). Coefficient alphas for four of the subscales are above .70 in both samples, but the values are below that level, usually considered a minimum, for the other four subscales. The Anxiety and Concern with Physical Harm scales have particularly low coefficients (.37 and .48 for the former, and .52 in both samples for the latter). Temporal stability values over a 12-day period were calculated based on a very small sample (16–20) and with the exception of the Substance Abuse subscale, were adequate. Given that the sample was in treatment, it is expected that some changes would be evident over time.

Although validity data are reported, all studies were conducted by the author and use the same data reported in development and reliability studies. Correlations are reported between the Total Impairment and Abuse Exposure scores in two samples, a negative correlation was found with self-esteem, and positive correlation with depression. Although all correlation coefficients were statistically significant, they are in the low to moderate range, with the exception of a correlation with psychiatric symptomatology, which is a high positive correlation. The reported concurrent validity is based on the correlation between the impairment scores and scores on the Center for Social Research Abuse Index (a measure of exposure). This analysis is based on a sample of only 29 women, although this number was provided in the article and omitted from the manual. The manual reports evidence for divergent validity in the differential scores of shelter samples, community Mental Health patrions, and community samples of well-functioning women. There is a need for independent researchers to undertake validity studies on this instrument.

COMMENTARY. Assessment of victims of intimate-partner violence is hampered by relatively few available instruments specifically designed for this population. The most widely used measures conceptualize intimate-partner abuse as a trauma, and identify trauma-related profiles and diagnoses. The ADQ approaches screening of adult female victims of intimate-partner violence from a slightly different perspective than other assessments that identify symptoms of psychiatric disorders. The value of this perspective has yet to be established.

The questionnaire can be completed in less than 10 minutes even by clients with limited education. Scoring and interpretation is straightforward, and requires no special training for administration. Thus, results are quickly available to clinicians who can then use them for treatment planning.

There are some concerns about the format of the questionnaire. On the first page, which includes space for the client's name and date, the scores for Abuse Exposure and Impairment Level used in interpreting the results are clearly presented. Because this questionnaire is not designed as a self-assessment (compared to a self-report), the effect of having these data available is unknown. In addition, all of the 30 impairment items are negatively worded and face valid. Most questionnaires will vary the direction of items to avoid response sets. Given that the questionnaire is described as a screening measure, which suggests it would be given to some individuals who will not be positive for partner abuse, a more balanced wording of items might be preferable.

The factor analysis, which is the basis for the subscale structure, is not adequately described. Coupled with the low values for subscale internal consistency, concerns with the analysis suggest that perhaps further development and additional analyses might have been useful prior to publication.

The utility of the instrument over existing ones has not been clearly demonstrated. The Impact of Events Scale (Horowitz, Wilner, & Alvarez, 1979) is well established for both research and clinical uses. The Trauma Symptom Inventory

(Briere, 1995; T7:2678) has 10 clinical scales including one called Impaired Self-Reference that would seem to tap a similar construct as does the ADQ, and also contains critical items and validity scales. Both of these scales have established validity with diverse groups; information about the shelter samples indicates only that the sample was 67% Caucasian.

SUMMARY. The ADQ is a brief pencil-and-paper screening questionnaire for women who have experienced intimate-partner violence. The results identify the extent that the client has adopted a negative evaluation of self and life, presumably as a result of the abuse. Although easy to administer and score, there are questions about the psychometric attributes that suggest caution in interpreting some subscales. The manual could be expanded by inclusion of much of the material in the journal article that describes the development of the same questionnaire. For clinicians who are interested in a quick assessment of overall exposure and impairment, improving the manual would be useful. Caution is urged in making clinical decisions based on the results; further research is needed to establish the overall value of this measure.

REVIEWER'S REFERENCES

Bergner, R. M. (1997). What is psychopathology? And so what? *Clinical Psychology: Science and Practice, 4,* 235-248.

Briere, J. (1995). *Trauma Symptom Inventory: Professional manual.* Lutz, FL: Psychological Assessment Resources.

Horowitz, M., Wilner, N., & Alvarez, W. (1979). Impact of Events Scale: A measure of subjective stress. *Psychosomatic Medicine, 41,* 209-218.

McNamara, J. R., & Brooker, D. J. (2000). The Abuse Disability Questionnaire: A new scale for assessing the consequences of partner abuse. *Journal of Interpersonal Violence, 15,* 170-183.

Review of the Abuse Disability Questionnaire by CARL J. SHEPERIS, Assistant Professor of Counselor Education, Mississippi State University, and TIFFANY D. CHANDLER, Doctoral Candidate, Mississippi State University, Starkville, MS:

DESCRIPTION. The Abuse Disability Questionnaire (ADQ) is a self-report screener designed to assess the extent of exposure to partner abuse, as well as the impact of that abuse on psychological functioning. The instrument is designed for use with adult women 18 years of age or older. Use of this instrument with younger age groups such as high school and middle school was mentioned but there are no normative data for these populations. According to the author of the manual, the ADQ has only been administered to women because "they experience the most extreme consequences from partner abuse and suffer disproportionately from it" (manual, p. 5).

The ADQ typically takes 10 minutes or less to complete and requires only an elementary school education. Individuals needing special assistance to complete the ADQ may take longer. Though it can be administered in a group setting, individual administration is preferred. Items are rated on a Likert scale using *strongly agree* (SA), *agree* (A), *neither agree nor disagree* (N), *disagree* (D), and *strongly disagree* (SD).

The ADQ contains 30 items within eight subscales (i.e., Relationship Disability, Life Restriction, Psychological Dysfunction, Health Status Issues, Substance Abuse, Inadequate Life Control, Anxiety, and Concern with Physical Harm). Scores on these scales reflect the level of impact (i.e., disability) on the psychological functioning of the respondent. There are no *formal* validity scales to determine the influence of personal bias with regard to the self-report. Decisions regarding the severity of an individual's Abuse Disability should be based only on the Total Abuse Exposure (AE) Score indicating the individual is experiencing *problematic* levels of abuse. The AE Score is calculated by adding the circled responses to the client's perception of the amounts of Psychological/Emotional Abuse, Physical Abuse, and Sexual Abuse she has experienced. The Impairment Level (IL) Score is used to determine level of disability and is calculated by adding the scores in each column at the bottom of the page. Totals from the first page of the survey are added to totals on the second page. Grand totals are then compared to means and standard deviations of impairment ratings in the shelter sample and well-functioning community sample, both of which are described briefly below. Scores are entered on the front page of the ADQ (i.e., profile form).

DEVELOPMENT. The ADQ was developed in consideration of clinical concerns that arise when working with victims of partner abuse. The ADQ was developed from a theoretical basis by conducting a review of the literature pertinent to abuse. Through the review, the author concluded that substance use, mental and physical health, relationship issues, and safety concerns and life control issues were central themes and generated a questionnaire with statements reflective of the above areas. Counselors at a women's shelter were used to evaluate content validity of the items by indicating which of the areas would most likely require treatment. Evaluation of these answers served as the basis for the development of this brief, 30-item instrument.

The ADQ is accompanied by a 27-page manual, complete with five chapters discussing the development, administration, scoring, interpretation, psychometric properties, case studies, and research of the instrument. Although there is a section of the manual dedicated to test development, little information is presented about the actual process. Test users should note that the ADQ is not a comprehensive assessment but does allow "staff in domestic violence shelters and other human service agencies to quickly screen for the degree of impairment associated with abuse, so appropriate interventions or referrals can be made" (manual, p. 2).

TECHNICAL. As part of the normative process, 939 women (18 and over) completed the ADQ. Normative data samples were obtained from six different groups including domestic violence shelter residents, Chamber of Commerce women, women at an outpatient mental health clinic, women prisoners, and women at outpatient health clinics. With the exception of women from Chamber of Commerce, the mean ages for the samples of women were in their 30s.

The manual author reports internal consistency and test-retest stability for the ADQ. McNamara and Brooker (2000) and McNamara and Fields (2001) reported reasonably high internal consistency reliability coefficients in two different shelter samples. The first sample resulted in internal consistency reliability for the IL score of .88 with subscale reliabilities ranging from .37 to .90. The second sample resulted in internal consistency reliability of .93 for the IL score with the subscale reliabilities ranging from .48 to .90. In their analysis of the ADQ, McNamara and Brooker reported test-retest reliabilities by subscales (across an average period of 12 days): Relationship Disability = .95, Life Restriction = .77, Psychological Dysfunction = .55, Health Status Issues = .88, Substance Abuse = .36, Inadequate Life Control = .74, Anxiety = .73, and Concern with Physical Harm = .75. Reliability estimates for some of the subscales are rather low. As a result, the manual author cautions decisions based on individual subscale scores.

The author of the manual reported several types of validity for the ADQ including construct, concurrent, and divergent validity as demonstrated by independent research studies. Item content was developed through evaluations with counselors as well as guidance from empirical literature and the expertise of psychologists who have significant clinical experience with victims of abuse. According to the manual, there is a strong relationship between partner abuse and, consequently, lowered self-esteem in the victim. McNamara and Brooker (2000) demonstrated concurrent validity between the IL score and the Center for Social Research Abuse Index ($r = .41$, $p < .05$). Divergent validity was demonstrated through different base rates of abuse in multiple samples of women. Domestic violence shelter samples reportedly had higher exposure to abuse and higher impairment than women seeking services at a community mental health center who reported moderate rates, still higher than women in the Chamber of Commerce reporting the lowest rates. The ADQ has shown sensitivity in detecting rates of abuse and impairment in community versus shelter samples.

COMMENTARY. Strengths of the ADQ include (a) quick and easy administration and scoring, (b) a user-friendly manual that is well organized and employs numerous case studies for further clarification and detailed tables to convey technical information, (c) a summary and profile form attached to the questionnaire that aids in interpretation and explanation of results, (d) a supplemental and diagnostics form to provide a fuller picture of the client's situation [back page of ADQ], (e) an adequate standardization sample, and (f) good reliability of the IL score. Weaknesses include (a) reliance on subjectivity as this measure employs self-report, (b) reliability of the individual subscales, and (c) clarity of validity of this measure.

SUMMARY. The ADQ appears to be an adequate screening measure to detect abuse and impairment resulting from abuse in women over 18 years of age. Use for younger populations has not been substantiated by normative data. The ADQ was also not designed for use with men. The instrument provides scores across eight subscales as well as a global Abuse Exposure score and an Impairment Level score. The instrument does not provide validity scales that assess for the influence of beliefs and feelings or personal bias. Although rating scales and questionnaires are often used by professionals because of their efficiency, the ADQ should be utilized as an initial step or component in which high scores result in a more thorough assessment battery. Finally, further investigation with populations and instruments other than those used by the author of the ADQ will continue to provide valuable information about the psychometric properties and clinical utility of the instrument.

REVIEWERS' REFERENCES

McNamara, J. R., & Brooker, D. J. (2000). The Abuse Disability Questionnaire: A new scale for assessing the consequences of partner abuse. *Journal of Interpersonal Violence, 15*, 170-183.

McNamara, J. R., & Fields, S. (2001). The Abuse Disability Questionnaire: Internal consistency and validity considerations in two samples. *Journal of Family Violence, 15*, 37-45.

[3]

Academic Intervention Monitoring System.

Purpose: Guidebook and intervention planning questionnaires "designed to provide teachers and other school-based professionals with the resources they need for developing, monitoring, and evaluating classroom-based, empirically supported interventions for academic difficulties."

Population: Grades K–12.

Publication Date: 2001.

Acronym: AIMS.

Scores: Not scored.

Administration: Individual.

Forms, 3: Student, Parent, Teacher.

Price Data, 2004: $133 per complete kit including manual (147 pages), 25 each of Student, Parent, and Teacher forms; $19 per 25 Student forms; $19 per 25 Parent forms; $36 per 25 Teacher forms; $95 per manual.

Time: (10–15) minutes.

Comments: Developed in conjunction with the Academic Competence Evaluation Scales (16:1); student and parent forms available in Spanish.

Authors: Stephen N. Elliott, James C. DiPerna, with Edward Shapiro.

Publisher: The Psychological Corporation, A Harcourt Assessment Company.

Review of the Academic Intervention Monitoring System by KATHLEEN M. JOHNSON, Psychologist, Lincoln Public Schools, Lincoln, NE:

DESCRIPTION. The Academic Intervention Monitoring System (AIMS) is an intervention framework with four main objectives, according to the authors. The system is a descriptive, solution-focused process with intervention forms to be completed by teachers, parents, and older students. The first objective of the AIMS, according to Elliott, DiPerna, and Shapiro, is to provide a review of the factors for teachers and intervention teams to consider in planning how to address academic difficulties. Secondly, the AIMS framework gives guidance about optimal impact points for academic and behavior interventions. The third objective is to provide information on numerous empirically supported academic and behavioral interventions for the users of the AIMS. Finally, the authors provide a review of various methods for monitoring and evaluating the effectiveness of interventions. The AIMS includes the Guidebook, the Teacher Intervention Form, the Parent Intervention Form (English and Spanish Editions), and the Student Intervention Form (for Grades 6–12). The AIMS was developed in conjunction with the Academic Competence Evaluation Scales (ACES; DiPerna & Elliott, 2000; 16:1) and it is recommended by the authors that the ACES and the AIMS be used together. A brief description of the ACES is included in the guidebook. The ACES is an assessment tool for measuring academic competence, which includes teacher and student scales for rating academic skills and academic enablers ("behaviors that interact with instruction to enable the learning and productive use of academic skills," guidebook, p. 5). The ACES reportedly provides efficient and reliable data to facilitate the identification of the specific concerns for a student and help guide intervention. Specifically, the authors state, "The ACES and AIMS together represent an integrated approach to the assessment of a student's academic competence, the planning of specific classroom-based interventions to address academic difficulties, and the monitoring and evaluation of the effectiveness of the interventions" (guidebook, p. 7).

The AIMS materials are designed to help address the academic concerns displayed by students in kindergarten through 12th grade. The AIMS is to be used by educational professionals and intervention teams in the context of a problem-solving model (using a five-step process: identify concerns, analyze concerns, plan intervention, implement intervention, evaluate intervention). The 163-page guidebook documents the need for an efficient and systematic process for applying empirically based interventions to address the academic and related concerns of students, preferably before the concerns result in educational failure. A review of the ACES process for identifying target behaviors and a discussion of the importance of carefully defining target behaviors is included in the guidebook. The authors endorse the use of the stimulus-organism-response-consequence (SORC) model (Kanfer & Goldstein, 1986) as the optimal means of analyzing behaviors and for identifying potential impact points for intervention (e.g., intervening on antecedent events, on the student's cognitive mediation, on the student's response, or on the consequences given). Various monitoring and evaluation methods (specifically, the use of pretest/posttest changes on the ACES, goal attainment scales, direct observations, and curriculum-based measurements) are reviewed in the guidebook as options for documenting academic and behavioral changes.

The research base underlying the development of the AIMS intervention forms (questionnaires) is summarized in the guidebook. The forms are intended to provide information to the problem-solving team about the key factors in the instructional and home environments and to aid in the selection of appropriate intervention strategies. The instructions for completing the intervention forms are printed on each form, and each form is estimated to take about 15 minutes to complete. The parent and student forms can be completed as part of a semistructured interview with a member of the intervention team, as an alternative to having them complete the forms independently. The items included on the intervention forms are used to help pinpoint the strategies/interventions that are perceived by the teacher, parent, and/or student as helpful and feasible to implement, as a basis for planning the educational intervention. For example, the respondent is asked to rate how helpful a strategy would be (response choices: no, somewhat or moderately, very much) and how possible/feasible it would be (response choices: no, yes, yes with help/training). A sample item on the teacher form is as follows: "Include the student in identifying rewards and consequences for specific behaviors." The assumption by the authors is that the strategies that are rated as very helpful and feasible to implement should be considered first by the intervention team as part of the plan to address the identified concerns.

The AIMS guidebook contains detailed information on numerous empirically supported intervention strategies to aid the AIMS user in designing plans to help students improve their academic enablers and their academic skills. For example, general strategies (such as antecedent control, behavioral rehearsal, positive reinforcement, reductive strategies, etc.) and specific strategies (such as peer tutoring, school-home notes, SQ3R, mnemonic memory techniques, etc.) are outlined for assisting students to improve study skills, interpersonal skills, task engagement, and student motivation. Likewise, general strategies (such as modeling, activating prior knowledge, coaching, etc.) and specific strategies (such as folding-in, previewing, self-management spelling, visual cueing, etc.) for addressing academic skill deficits are described in detail. The authors provide strategy examples for improving reading, language arts, math, and critical thinking skills and a quick reference chart to assist the AIMS user in choosing the appropriate strategies for intervention plans.

Two detailed case studies are also presented in the guidebook to show how the AIMS (and the ACES) can facilitate the application of specific interventions to address specific educational concerns. For each case the entire process is described within the context of the five-step team problem-solving process, beginning with the assessment of the concerns and proceeding with the development of the intervention plan and the ongoing monitoring/evaluation of the intervention plan.

DEVELOPMENT. The development of the AIMS Intervention Forms is described in the guidebook. Initially, the authors used research on effective teaching and learning (Elliott, Kratochwill, Littlefield-Cook, & Travers, 2000) and research on the impact of family/home factors on academic competence (Christenson, Rounds, & Gorney, 1992) to identify a variety of intervention strategies to include in pilot versions of the forms. Items for the teacher and parent forms were written first and the items for the student form were generated to supplement the teacher and parent forms. Previous work by Elliott (1988) on the Prereferral Behavior Inventory also influenced the item development, according to the authors. No other information on the development of the specific items is provided in the guidebook. Approximately 20 teachers, 20 parents, and 20 students reviewed the initial items and provided written feedback. Based on the feedback from these reviewers, the items were revised prior to the collection of the standardization data.

According to the authors the "initial feedback was positive with minor suggestions for rewording a few items" (guidebook, p. 22).

The final, standardization version of the AIMS Teacher Intervention Form had 50 items representing the 11 key characteristics of effective instructional environments: (a) expectations for student learning, (b) standards for classroom behavior, (c) classroom routines, (d) instructional orientation, (e) instructional delivery, (f) instructional grouping, (g) progress monitoring, (h) review and reteaching, (i) learning time, (j) teacher-student interactions, and (k) incentive and rewards. Each factor was described by 3 to 6 items. On the Parent Intervention Form, 40 items were used to represent five key factors: (a) parent expectations for learning and achievement, (b) behavior management, (c) parent-child relationship, (d) home-school communication, and (e) support for learning. On the final version of the Student Intervention Form, 48 items were used to cover seven key areas: (a) expectations for learning and achievement, (b) rewards and consequences, (c) self-monitoring and evaluation, (d) learning resources, (e) homework and assignments, (f) maximizing learning during instruction, and (g) time management and organization. Finally, the respective AIMS intervention forms were completed by a sample of teachers, parents, and students for standardization purposes.

TECHNICAL. The AIMS standardization sample consisted of 101 teachers, 130 parents, and 116 students. The authors provide descriptive data for the sample. Of the 101 teachers who participated by completing the AIMS intervention form, 87% were females and most of them were from the Northeastern (23%), Southern (36%), and Western (22%) regions of the U.S. The teachers had varying years of teaching experience and nearly half had a master's degree level of education. Of the 130 parents who participated, 51% were females and the parents were from all areas of the country (Northeast 15%, North Central 23%, South 37%, and West 25%). A wide range of educational backgrounds was represented in the parent sample. The student sample of 116 was 52% female and the students came from various parts of the U.S., similar in percentages to the geographical regions of the parent sample. No data are presented in the guidebook as to the average age of the students or

how they were selected as part of the standardization sample.

The authors cite content validity support based upon item-percentage data for two identified criteria (helpfulness and feasibility) for each item on the intervention forms. Overall, the data showed that most (84%) of the teacher respondents rated every item on the Teacher Intervention Form as being helpful (either moderately or very much) and being feasible to implement (either independently or with help/training). Most of the parent respondents rated every item on the intervention forms as being helpful (89% responded with either somewhat or very much) and being feasible to implement (84% responded with either independently or with help/training). The difference in the wording for the helpfulness criterion between the teacher and parent forms should be kept in mind when examining these data (i.e., teacher choices for the items: no, moderately helpful, and very much helpful vs. the parent choices for the items: no, somewhat helpful, and very much helpful). At least 80% of the student respondents rated 47 of the 48 items as being helpful (either somewhat or very much) and over 80% rated every item as being feasible to implement (either independently or with help/training). The authors conclude that most teachers, parents, and students in the sample group perceived the research-based interventions (as represented by the items on the forms) as both helpful in promoting educational success and feasible to implement. Additional data from actual AIMS application cases (e.g., the extent to which the AIMS components are actually applied, user satisfaction feedback) would lend further support for this assumption.

COMMENTARY. The Academic Interventions Monitoring System (AIMS) is a descriptive, solution-focused system for efficiently examining the many factors involved in designing educational interventions for students that are both research-based and able to be implemented with students. The AIMS guidebook includes a wealth of information on numerous empirically supported intervention strategies, as well as methods for monitoring the integrity and effectiveness of the interventions. The information is very thorough and includes both general and specific intervention suggestions to address concerns about both academic skills and academic enablers (for example, study skills, on-task behavior, and motivations). The AIMS framework, as described by the authors, is consistent with best practices in terms of problem-solving and behavior analysis methods. The authors recommend the use of the AIMS companion materials (ACES; DiPerna & Elliott, 2000) as an efficient method of identifying the target behaviors for the interventions and for evaluating progress; however, other methods of selecting target behaviors and measuring progress would also work well with the AIMS. The AIMS intervention forms (questionnaires) consist of items that describe elements of effective instruction and learning (e.g., the importance of having classroom and study routines or reteaching concepts to reach mastery levels). The intervention forms provide a structured means of gathering input from teachers, parents, and older students in terms of perceived intervention helpfulness and intervention feasibility. Having this information organized and ready to share at the problem-solving team meeting is a major advantage because it may help keep the process solution-focused and time-efficient. The validity of the AIMS intervention forms is based upon research on effective instruction and learning (in both school and home environments) and item percentage data. No other analysis of the concepts or items included in the intervention forms is presented. The case examples described in the guidebook provide the reader with excellent details about the overall application of the AIMS, as well as the use and interpretation of the Teacher Intervention Form. There is, however, no reference to data from the Parent and Student Intervention Forms for the sample cases. Despite this omission, the authors make a strong case for gathering information from multiple sources as a means of making the intervention process more collaborative and subsequently more effective.

SUMMARY. The AIMS is a descriptive, solution-focused intervention framework for use with K–12 students. It provides a structured means (intervention questionnaires) of gathering input from teachers, parents, and older students (Grades 6–12) about the perceived helpfulness and feasibility of various empirically supported educational interventions. It also provides a thorough, organized, and systematized procedure for pairing identified concerns with the relevant and empirically based interventions. The AIMS guidebook also includes descriptions of methods for monitoring

and evaluating the impact of educational interventions. Problem-solving teams (i.e., teachers, school psychologists, consultants, and administrators) will find these materials useful and relatively easy to use to address the educational needs of individual students. In the AIMS guidebook, the authors discuss the importance of various factors relevant to educational problem solving and provide a guiding framework. Some of the factors reviewed in the guidebook include: using data-gathering tools to maximize the time efficiency of the problem-solving process, using data from multiple sources to enhance collaboration while designing interventions, using interventions perceived as helpful and feasible to optimize intervention implementation, and monitoring and evaluating the effectiveness of educational interventions for individual students.

REVIEWER'S REFERENCES
Christenson, S. L., Rounds, T., & Gorney, D. (1992). Family factors and student achievement: An avenue to increase students' success. *School Psychology Quarterly, 7*, 178-206.
DiPerna, J. C., & Elliott, S. N. (2000). Academic Competence Evaluation Scales. San Antonio, TX: The Psychological Corporation.
Elliott, S. N. (1988). Acceptability of behavioral treatments in educational settings. In J. C. Witt, S. N. Elliott, & F. M. Gresham (Eds.), *Handbook of behavior therapy in education* (pp. 121-150). New York: Plenum Press.
Elliott, S. N., Kratochwill, T. R., Littlefield-Cook, J. L., & Travers, J. F. (2000). *Educational psychology: Effective teaching, effective learning.* Boston: McGraw-Hill.
Kanfer, F. H., & Goldstein, A. P. (Eds.). (1986). *Helping people change: A textbook of methods* (3rd ed.). New York: Pergamon.

Review of the Academic Intervention Monitoring System by JEFFREY SMITH, Professor, The University of Otago, Dunedin, New Zealand:

DESCRIPTION. The Academic Intervention Monitoring System (AIMS) "is a guidebook designed to provide teachers and other school-based professionals with the resources they need for developing, monitoring, and evaluating classroom-based, empirically supported interventions for academic difficulties" (guidebook, p. 1). The AIMS utilizes three intervention planning forms (one each for teachers, students, and parents) that are described extensively in the guidebook. The AIMS program also uses the Academic Competence Evaluation Scales (ACES) that are discussed in the guidebook, but readers are referred elsewhere for an extensive presentation of those forms (DiPerna & Elliott, 2000; 16:1). The question that arises for the reviewer is: What is being reviewed here—the AIMS intervention forms or the program for academic intervention and monitoring that is described in the guidebook?

Actually, this is a welcome problem. A real strength of the AIMS program, and therefore the

AIMS intervention forms, is that they are part of an instructional outlook and process. They do not stand apart from the theoretical base in which they are applied. The authors are fundamentally saying, "Here is a model of how to work with children who have learning difficulties and here is a set of instruments developed to work within that model." Thus, AIMS is a system of instruction that utilizes the AIMS intervention forms as an integral part of instruction, fundamentally as the assessment component that informs decision making. This review focuses primarily on the quality of these three intervention forms as they exist within the overall model. It is not the primary purpose here to comment on the quality of the model, although some consideration of the model is necessary to frame the review.

All three intervention forms have the same structure. A series of statements are presented categorized under general headings. Individuals (teacher, student, or parent) respond in two fashions: First, they mark whether they think the concept being presented will help the student; second, they mark whether they think the concept is possible to accomplish. For example, under the Student Intervention Form, one statement is: "Find out what my teacher expects from me before I begin an assignment." The response options for, "Will this help me?" are: "No," "Somewhat," and "Very Much." The response options for "Can I do it?" are: "No," "Yes," and "Yes, with help."

The Teacher Intervention Form contains 50 statements organized under 11 headings. An example statement under the heading of Progress Monitoring is: "Provide timely feedback that is clear and understandable." The teacher responses are very similar to the pattern described above. The Parent Intervention Form contains 40 statements categorized under 5 headings. An example statement under the heading of Behavior Management is: "Plan with my child what he or she will receive for good behavior." The Parent Intervention Form is also available in Spanish. The Student Intervention Form contains 48 statements categorized under 7 headings.

The AIMS intervention forms are a component of an overall approach to working with children who are experiencing academic difficulties. The purpose of the AIMS is to provide classroom-based interventions for children in order to address needs without a formal referral for special education services. The intervention strategy is described as a cognitive-behavioral approach; it includes specific instructions on how to approach interventions, how to develop strategies, and how to monitor student progress. Educators familiar with behaviorally oriented approaches to special education intervention will find this approach to be situated within such approaches. The authors are careful to document the research base that guides their ideas for intervention. They drew widely from the effective practice literature in a variety of domains to put their program together. In looking at several case studies presented in the manual, it appears that the AIMS forms primarily serve as a review of possible strategies that might be employed to help the child. They are a type of checklist of suggestions to teachers, parents, and children of activities that are known to be helpful in learning.

DEVELOPMENT. The AIMS intervention forms were developed in three phases. The first phase involved using the research literature base to develop the initial pool of items for each of the three AIMS measures. The approach here appears to have been quite thorough. This system was clearly developed by researchers familiar with the literature and with classrooms. These pools were then tested with a group of roughly 60 teachers, parents, and students to check for readability, clarity, etc. Minor modifications were made based on this review. The final forms were then tested on groups of parents, teachers, and students, and are described below in the section discussing content validity.

TECHNICAL. Reliability is a difficult issue for a form of this nature. There is no notion of an internal consistency reliability coefficient such as coefficient alpha or a split-half coefficient that would be appropriate here. The items on the forms are to be used individually, and not summed into a total score. A reliability measure of stability over time would be possible, but not without problems. There would have to be at least 80 for each form (two each for each item, one for helpfulness, and one for feasibility). Even with these difficulties, it would have been useful to see if respondents hold some level of consistency over a short time interval.

Content validity is often hard to separate cleanly from development issues. In addition to the development work described above, the forms were administered to samples of teachers, parents, and students, with *n*s of 101, 130, and 116, respectively. Responses from these samples serve as baseline data for comparison purposes in the program. The authors note that almost all of the strategies presented in the forms are strongly endorsed as being at least potentially helpful to students and possible to implement. The only concern here is whether the list is exhaustive; it is clear that the current items are endorsed by individuals who should have a good idea of what will be helpful and possible. But this does not rule out the possibility that there are other effective strategies that have not been included. Overall, content validation evidence appears to be solid for the AIMS, especially given the difficulty of collecting such data from teachers and parents of students with learning difficulties, as well as from the students themselves. The responses from these samples also serve as a kind of standardization sample, although the use of the forms would not really call for reference to any kinds of norms.

The AIMS is part of an ambitious approach to help children who are experiencing learning difficulties in classrooms. It would be difficult to parcel out the AIMS survey component of this package to see if it were living up to traditional validity concerns. However, it would not be difficult to gather data on whether the approach as a whole seems to be effective in helping children, and to see how the AIMS forms function within that approach. The validity concerns are not the traditional ones, but they are not impossible to address in a reasonable fashion. Unfortunately, no data are presented as to the overall efficacy of the program, or the utility of the AIMS forms within it. The authors discuss the benefits of avoiding referral for students, which reflects on the consequential validity of the program, but do not present data on the degree to which the AIMS can be effective in reducing referrals. The lack of validity evidence beyond content validity is a singular failing in an otherwise impressive package.

COMMENTARY. The AIMS package is a serious attempt to implement a cognitive-behavioral approach to working with children with learning difficulties. This approach may be too prescriptive and too heavily behavioral for some educators. There are charts and rewards, and a host of other terms and approaches that are funda-

mentally behavioral in nature. However, the combination of the scholarly approach the authors take to the issue, combined with very practical and detailed recommendations, is impressive. Because the forms being reviewed here are intended more as vehicles to engender discussion and action than to provide scores on traits, traditional concerns of reliability and norming are not central to the discussion. However, the idea of validity does need to be addressed. Validity here would mean that the forms lead to identification of areas of intervention that can be acted upon to lead to increased learning. Research that demonstrates that this results from the use of the forms, and the program in general, is currently lacking and needs to be addressed.

SUMMARY. The AIMS forms, and the approach to prereferral intervention of which they are a component, appear to be a carefully researched, well-thought-out package for helping children with learning difficulties. The only shortcoming, and it is a substantial one, is that there simply is no concrete evidence of the efficacy of the approach, and therefore of the validity of the forms. It is not possible to recommend the use of the AIMS without that evidence, but it certainly seems to be a program with promise that a school district might want to explore on a pilot basis and draw its own conclusions.

REVIEWER'S REFERENCE

DiPerna, J. C., & Elliott, S. N. (2000). *Academic Competence Evaluation Scales*. San Antonio, TX: The Psychological Corporation.

[4]

Achievement Motivation Inventory.

Purpose: Designed to evaluate "all major aspects of job-related achievement motivation."

Population: Adults.

Publication Date: 2004.

Acronym: AMI.

Scores: 17 scales: Compensatory Effort, Competitiveness, Confidence in Success, Dominance, Eagerness to Learn, Engagement, Fearlessness, Flexibility, Flow, Goal Setting, Independence, Internality, Persistence, Preference for Difficult Tasks, Pride in Productivity, Self-Control, Status Orientation.

Administration: Individual or group.

Price Data, 2006: $188 per complete kit including manual (60 pages), questionnaire, 20 score sheets, 20 score profiles, and case; $18 per questionnaire; $68 per 20 response sheets; $12 per 20 score profiles; $98 per manual.

Time: Administration time not reported.

Authors: Heinz Schuler, George C. Thornton III, Andreas Frintrup, Rose Mueller-Hanson.
Publisher: Hogrefe & Huber Publishers.

Review of the Achievement Motivation Inventory by JEFFREY A. JENKINS, Associate Professor, Roger Williams University, Bristol, RI:

DESCRIPTION. The Achievement Motivation Inventory (AMI) is an instrument intended for identifying and measuring various aspects of achievement motivation as a personality construct.

Achievement motivation is conceived by the authors as multidimensional, allowing users to examine particular aspects of achievement motivation depending on the purpose of the assessment. These purposes may include, for example, personnel selection, decision making in the work setting, athletic performance, and sports psychology. Some applications in educational settings may also be appropriate.

The AMI consists of 170 items measuring 17 dimensions of achievement motivation. The items are presented in Likert format on a scale from 1 (*does not apply at all*) to 7 (*applies fully to me*). Ten items are used to measure each of these dimensions, which are reported as subscales. The dimensions and some example items are: Compensatory Effort ("When faced with an important task, I would rather prepare myself too thoroughly than not enough"), Competitiveness ("The wish to be better than others is a major incentive for me"), Confidence in Success ("Even when faced with a difficult task, I am always confident"), Dominance ("I like to decide what others should do"), Eagerness to Learn ("I spend considerable time learning new things"), Engagement ("I don't feel comfortable when I have nothing to do"), Fearlessness ("I have not undertaken some activities for fear of not being successful"), Flexibility ("My everyday life is full of things that interest me"), Flow ("I often lose myself in what I'm doing"), Goal Setting ("The future is too uncertain to make long-term plans"), Independence ("I like being solely responsible for what I do"), Internality ("Most of what happens in life depends more on others than on oneself"), Persistence ("When I am doing my work, there is hardly anything that can disturb me"), Preference for Difficult Tasks ("Difficult problems appeal more to me than simple ones"), Pride in Productivity ("I like to think about all the things I have accomplished"), Self-Control ("Even when I do not have any real desire to work, I can still force myself to concentrate"), and Status Orientation ("I want to be admired for my achievements").

Subscale scores on these dimensions are produced using a preprinted carbon response sheet, and consist of the simple summation of item values within each subscale. Reverse scoring is necessary for some items (as may be seen by some of the previous examples), but this adjustment is automatically made on the publisher-provided response sheet. Scores may then be plotted on a score profile form, which shows the relations among the dimensions for a respondent. The profile may also be compared to percentile scores for a norm group ($N = 2,178$) from the U.S. and Germany. U.S. norms are also reported separately for males and females.

DEVELOPMENT. The AMI broadly approaches the measurement of achievement motivation as a multifaceted construct related to generally accepted dimensions of personality. Thus, rather than considering achievement motivation solely as a unified concept that may be represented as a single global index, the authors conceptualize achievement motivation as multidimensional, composed of a set of interrelated aspects of personality reflected in the subscale dimensions measured.

The AMI is based on a German instrument, the Leistungsmotivationsinventar (LMI), which was translated from German to English, adjusting for language discrepancies in item meaning and interpretation, to create the AMI. The LMI was originally developed for both psychological research and practical applications in "all areas of life where achievement motivation and its consequences can be observed" (manual, p. 5). Initially, a set of 728 items were developed, from which smaller sets of items in each dimension were selected and, following a series of pilot testing with groups of students and working adults, the final version of 170 items was produced.

TECHNICAL. The AMI manual is a well-organized and helpful booklet that discusses the development, use, and technical characteristics of the AMI. It also provides appendices with the actual test items organized into subscales, explanations of the subscales, norm tables, sample profiles, and tables reporting results of reliability and validity studies. The discussion of reliability and validity, though brief, should be understandable for most users; numerous references are also given for those wishing to learn more about research using the AMI.

Both internal consistency and test-retest reliability estimates are provided in the manual. Generally, reliability of the AMI is sufficiently high. Reported internal consistency (coefficient alpha) estimates for the subscales based on the total norm sample of 2,178 individuals ranged from .66 (Independence) to .83 (Confidence in Success and Preference for Difficult Tasks). Given the various dimensions of achievement motivation measured by the AMI using only 10 items each, these estimates are relatively high. As would be expected for a 170-item instrument, total score reliability is very high (.96), although the total measure of achievement motivation appears to be of lesser importance for most purposes. For only 3 of the 17 subscales (Goal Setting, Independence, and Internality) were internal consistency estimates less than .70 (.69, .66, and .68, respectively), and the publisher explains that these facets of achievement motivation are somewhat more heterogeneous in nature and therefore less likely to be highly interrelated. Also, test-retest estimates for these subscales appear to be adequate (.84, .81, and .79, respectively), as are test-retest reliabilities for the other 14 subscales, which range from .71 to .89. Test-retest estimates were based on a 2-week interval using a sample of 48 participants. Characteristics of either the participants or their method of selection was not reported. Nonetheless, for research purposes, the reliability of the AMI is satisfactory. For other applications, reliability for most subscales should be sufficient, although caution should be used for individual decision making.

As is appropriate, the manual provides various sources of evidence of validity for the AMI. Content validity is addressed in terms of the instrument development process and is supported by a brief review of the literature relating to achievement motivation, the theoretical basis for the facets measured, and the process of item selection and refinement.

Construct validity is also examined. Evidence of the factor structure of the AMI is reported as interrelationships among the subscales, rather than interrelationships among items that support the AMI's measurement of the 17 subscales. Although this is unfortunate (because

evidence to support the reporting of 17 separate scores is necessary), the results do indicate the existence of three "higher order" factors, labeled Self-Assurance, Ambition, and Self-Control. These factor labels are used on the Score Profile form, with the subscales defining the factor organized within each. The reported factor-analytic results (both exploratory and confirmatory) also provide indirect evidence for the measurement of the 17 subscales, inasmuch as the results show the interrelationships among the subscales and their organization as three more general constructs.

Evidence of criterion-related validity is also presented. Specifically, the results of a study examining the relationship between AMI subscales and two aspects of social desirability measured by the Balanced Inventory of Desirable Responding (BIDR), termed Self-Deception and Impression Management are summarized. Although not definitive, the pattern of correlations between these instruments provides some support for the distinct measurement of some of the AMI subscales. In addition, the relationship between AMI subscales and individual personality characteristics measured by the Revised NEO Personality Inventory (NEO-PI-R) is reported. These results also lend some support for the convergent and discriminant validity of the AMI subscales, as well as the three "higher order" factors measured.

Taken together, the evidence presented, though not compelling, suggests a fairly high degree of validity for the AMI. Generally, the results of these studies demonstrate that the AMI can be used with some confidence for measuring aspects of achievement motivation, within the scope and limitations of its intended purposes.

COMMENTARY. The AMI is a beneficial addition to the measurement of achievement motivation. By approaching the measurement of achievement motivation as a multidimensional construct, the publisher has expanded the usefulness of the instrument to a variety of applications—work, school, sports, and research—where aspects of personality are relevant and important. Strengths of the AMI include scores reported on the numerous dimensions of achievement motivation measured, the availability of both U.S. and German norms, and the clearly organized profile reporting and interpretation. Potential weaknesses include the questionable reliability and validity of some of the subscales (such as Goal Setting and

Flow). Also noteworthy is the absence of scores for the three general factors measured (Self-Assurance, Ambition, Self-Control), and the failure of the publisher to explain why these are not calculated or reported, despite the organization of the profile report in terms of these three factors. Scores on these factors would likely be useful in a variety of practical and research situations.

SUMMARY. Those interested in the measurement of achievement motivation will find much to like about the AMI. For an instrument of its type, and given the potential difficulties in identifying and measuring separable aspects of personality related to behavior, the AMI has much to recommend it. It benefits from relatively strong technical characteristics, and clearly presented score report profiles. It also is easy to administer and score, and may be used in individual and group settings. Although some caution is in order when using the instrument in work or school settings for individual decision making, the AMI can be recommended for research purposes.

Review of the Achievement Motivation Inventory by ELEANOR E. SANFORD-MOORE, Vice-President of Research and Development, MetaMetrics, Inc., Durham, NC:

The Achievement Motivation Inventory (AMI) was developed by Schuler, Thorton, Frintrup, and Mueller-Hanson. The original assessment (Leistungsmotivationsinventar; LMI), was developed in German to meet the new conceptualizations of achievement motivation within a single test. The Achievement Motivation Inventory was developed for use in personnel selection, personnel development, professional counseling in regard to job decisions, and sports psychology. The AMI is based on a trait-oriented concept of achievement motivation, and, as such, can be used by researchers, counselors, or personnel specialists by "choosing the facets of achievement most relevant to alternative applications" (manual, p. 1). The 17 facets of achievement motivation are grouped into three themes—self-assurance, ambition, and self-control—for interpretation.

ADMINISTRATION. The Achievement Motivation Inventory can be administered to individuals or groups in a paper-and-pencil format. The AMI consists of 170 statements employing a 7-point Likert rating scale (1—*Does not apply at all*

to 7—*Applies fully to me*). Statements are worded both in positive and negative directions. Items for each of the dimensions of achievement motivation are distributed throughout the inventory, thus any evidence of fatigue is consistent across all dimensions and interest is maintained.

Scales are presented in rows on the answer sheet for ease in hand scoring. A computer-scoring program is under development. Raw scores are calculated for each scale by summing the responses (1–7) and are then converted to percentiles. The norming population consisted of 2,178 German and United States students and working adults. Results of the Achievement Motivation Inventory are reported on a profile that provides insight into the individual's motivational pattern across the three themes.

DEVELOPMENT. The Achievement Motivation Inventory employs a "very broad diagnostic procedure that covers all dimensions that are considered by one or more theorists to be a part of achievement motivation" (manual, p. 1). Initially, 728 statements were developed and grouped into 38 preliminary dimensions. Each item was reviewed by independent evaluators for clarity and applicability to a wide range of examinees. The revised pool consisted of 445 items grouped into 24 dimensions of achievement motivation.

An initial feasibility study was conducted to determine the comprehensibility of the items. A sample of 20 individuals participated in the study. From this study, 187 items were deleted and the remaining 258 items were grouped into 19 dimensions. The final pilot study was conducted with 256 individuals and resulted in the removal of 88 items. The final 170 items were grouped into 17 dimensions or scales (Fearlessness, Flexibility, Independence, Preference for Difficult Tasks, Confidence in Success, Dominance, Goal Setting, Eagerness to Learn, Competitiveness, Compensatory Effort, Engagement, Pride in Productivity, Status Orientation, Flow, Internality, Persistence, and Self-Control). When the decision was made to develop the test in English, the items were translated from German into English and then back-translated to German to ensure that the meaning of the items had been maintained.

Using factor analysis, the 170 items were grouped into three clusters—Self-Assurance, Ambition, and Self-Control. Using three samples of examinees (German, $N = 1,433$; Israeli, $N = $

688; and U.S., N = 745), similar factor structures were produced with similar factor loadings and intercorrelations.

RELIABILITY. The internal consistency estimates (coefficient alpha) for 14 of the 17 scales were above .70 (.66 to .83) and for the total score was .96 (N = 2,178). The test-retest reliability estimates over 2 weeks for 14 of the 17 scales were in the .80s (.71 to .89) and for the total score was .94 (N = 48). The standard error of measurement is 4 points.

VALIDITY. Content validity was built into the Achievement Motivation Inventory from a research base of theories to develop a comprehensive list of facets of achievement motivation. The AMI exhibits low to moderate correlations between the scales with a median of .35 (-.14 to .60).

Criterion-related validity was examined by correlating individual demographic characteristics (age, gender, and ethnicity) with results from the AMI. Few differences between groups were evidenced and were small.

The construct validity of the Achievement Motivation Inventory has been investigated through correlations between AMI scores and scores on other assessments. The first area of construct validity investigations examined the correlation between the AMI and the Self-Deception and Impression Management scales of the Balanced Inventory of Desirable Responding (N = 201). The results indicate which scales of the AMI are more susceptible to the intentional forms of social desirability (8 AMI scales with correlations significant at the .01 level) and the less conscious forms of social desirability (13 AMI scales with correlations significant at the .01 level).

The second area of construct validity investigations examined the social validity of the AMI as a reasonable questionnaire for an organization to use in making selection decisions. A seven-item questionnaire that examined the instrument's acceptability, reasonableness, level of stress to complete, and usefulness of results by an organization was administered to 653 U.S. students and working adults and the results were positive (agreements with the statements ranged from 82% to 93%).

The third area of construct validity investigations examined how biographical antecedents correlated with AMI scores. From a sample of 84

U.S. students, results showed the following moderate correlations with the AMI scales: early academic achievement (r = .21 to .36; median = .33), positive academic attitude (r = .22 to .35; median = .24), popularity (r = .26 to .43; median = .29), and early rewards/successes (r = .22 to .42; median = .28). The correlation between the AMI Total Score and grade point average was .22 for 201 U.S. college students.

The fourth area of construct validity investigations examined how personality characteristics correlated with AMI scores. A sample of 201 colleges students were administered the AMI and the NEO-PI-R (Costa & McCrae, 1992), which assesses Conscientiousness, Neuroticism, Agreeableness, Extraversion, and Openness to Experience. Moderately high correlations were observed between NEO-PI-R scores and AMI scales that were expected to measure similar constructs (e.g., Conscientiousness and AMI/Self-Control, r = .72; and Eagerness to Learn and AMI/Openness to Experience, r = .41) and between NEO-PI-R scores and AMI scales that measured opposite aspects of a construct (e.g., Neuroticism and AMI/Fearlessness, r = -.56; and Competitiveness and AMI/Agreeableness, r = -.40).

SUMMARY. The Achievement Motivation Inventory is an easy-to-use and interpret instrument to examine achievement motivation. The AMI is a well-researched and well-developed instrument for examining achievement motivation in personnel selection, personnel development, professional counseling in regard to job decisions, and sports psychology situations. Validity and reliability information is provided that supports the uses of the test. Reliability results are acceptable at the total score level for use with individual examinees, but no information is provided at the cluster/theme level. Some individual scales have reliability estimates lower than desirable when making individual decisions.

The AMI manual provides good interpretative information and examples of profiles for individual examinees and for groups of examinees used in the norming population. The manual further states that each researcher needs to consider how the instrument is relevant to his or her research goals before interpreting and using the results.

REVIEWER'S REFERENCE

Costa, P. T., & McCrae, R. R. (1992). *The Revised NEO Personality Inventory (NEO-PI-R) and NEO Five-Factor Inventory (NEO-FFI) professional manual.* Odessa, FL: Psychological Assessment Resources.

[5]
Air Conditioning Specialist (Form SWA-C).

Purpose: For selecting candidates with knowledge of air conditioning.

Population: Applicants and incumbents for jobs requiring air conditioning knowledge and skills.

Publication Dates: 1992–2002.

Scores, 7: Print Reading/Electrical/and Test Equipment, Controls, Welding/Piping and Plumbing, Mechanical Maintenance and Machines & Equipment, Heating & Ventilation and Combustion, Air Conditioning and Refrigeration, Total.

Administration: Group.

Price Data, 2007: $20 per consumable self-scoring test booklet (minimum order of 20); $24.95 per manual (2002, 16 pages).

Time: (60) minutes (untimed).

Author: Roland T. Ramsay.

Publisher: Ramsay Corporation.

Review of the Air Conditioning Specialist (Form SWA-C) by JAMES A. PENNY, Senior Psychometrician, CASTLE Worldwide, Morrisville, NC:

DESCRIPTION. The Air Conditioning Specialist examination was originally created in 1992. A shorter version, Form SWA-C, was developed in February 2002 and is a 60-item pencil-and-paper test using 4-point multiple-choice items. An online form, SWA-E, created in October 2002, is used for electronic administration. The only reported difference between the two 2002 forms is the adjustment of the size of a graphic used with one item so that the graphic may be viewed appropriately on a computer screen.

The test is intended to assess knowledge and skill in the area of air conditioning. The target audience of the examination is journey-level air conditioning technicians.

The instructions, equipment, and conditions for test administration are straightforward, and should be easily accomplished with very little difficulty. Nonclinical staff can administer, score, and interpret the SWA-C. Examiners should have taken or should be familiar with the examination. The examiner instructions indicate there is no time limit on the examination administration, but the instructions also indicate that the exam should not require more than 2 hours to complete.

Answers are recorded on a separate answer sheet, and those sheets are scored by hand. The scoring instructions indicate that the score on the exam is the number of correct answers. Items left unanswered are scored as incorrect. No penalty for guessing is incorporated in the scoring formula.

DEVELOPMENT. The documentation in the manual for administration & scoring indicated that a job analysis was performed to determine the appropriate content for the SWA-C. The documentation did not indicate the date of that job analysis. However, the SWA was published in January 1992, suggesting that the initial job analysis occurred earlier than 1992. No indication of a job analysis revision was provided in the documentation for when the Shortened version, the SWA-C was developed in February 2002 or when the online version, the SWA-E, was developed in October 2002 by reducing the size of one item to make the graphic render appropriately on a computer screen.

The job analysis study described in the manual for administration & scoring indicated that the applicable title of the job was Heating and Air Conditioner Installer Servicer [*sic*], which is defined in the *Dictionary of Occupational Titles* from the U.S. Department of Labor. The corresponding O*NET title is Heating and Air Conditioner Mechanics. The manual for administration & scoring presents both definitions in detail.

In addition to a descriptive job title, the job analysis study produced a three-level hierarchy of knowledge and skill areas to form a content outline. There were 12 major areas, each with two to eight secondary levels. Although the list was titled to include skills, most elements of the content outline appeared to represent knowledge. Only a few elements appeared to reference a skill, and even those were nuclear in their description of the skill. One element did look out of place, that being the inclusion of psychometrics under heating and ventilating.

A group of 10 content experts ranked the elements of the content outline by importance, and those rankings were then used to determine the content sampling plan of the examination. The documentation did not indicate how "importance" (manual for administration & scoring, p. 5) was defined in this portion of the job analysis study. The elements of the knowledge and skill areas were reorganized and re-aggregated to form the content sampling plan. No description of the manner in which the examination items were developed is presented in the manual for administration & scoring.

TECHNICAL. The reliability of the SWA-C was reported as internal consistency using KR-20. Using a sample of 97 test takers from two companies during an undocumented period, the value of KR-20 was found to be .88. The *SEM* in that sample was 3.3. These values are not unreasonable for an examination of this type and length. However, the manual for administration & scoring referred to the reliability as "excellent," and that description seems excessive and perhaps motivated by marketing purposes. The mean score and standard deviation in the studied sample were 35.48 and 9.64, respectively.

No evidence to suggest similar functioning of the SWA-E was provided. However, it seems unlikely that changing the size of the one graphic on one item to accommodate computerized delivery would influence the internal consistency of the examination substantially in either direction.

Using data that were gathered from air conditioning specialists through February 2002, the authors computed the classical item indices for both item difficulty and discrimination. Item difficulty was not defined in the manual for administration & scoring, but the values provided were indicative of the percent of test takers answering the item correctly.

Item discrimination was computed as the point-biserial correlation between item score and test section score. Test sections were not defined in the documentation, but a reasonable inference of the section definitions was the re-aggregation of the knowledge and skill areas produced for the examination content sampling plan.

The values of item difficulty appeared generally reasonable for an examination of this type. However, the difficulty of six items was below .30, suggesting the items were too difficult for the intended purpose with the studied sample. Only one item appeared too easy (i.e., difficulty greater than .90) in the sample.

The values of item discrimination were also generally reasonable for an examination of this type. However, two items did exhibit values of discrimination above .60. Such high values can often be an artifact of candidate sampling variability more than extremely good item discrimination.

The manual for administration & scoring presented documentation of four types of validity for the SWA-C. Content validity was posited directly on the pre-1992 job analysis. As such, the content validity of the SWA-C was adequately established. The question that remains unanswered concerns the continued content validity of the examination. No evidence of job analysis revisions that accommodate technological advances over the past 15 years was presented.

No direct evidence of criterion-related validity was presented in the manual for administration & scoring. However, the authors cited the work of Hunter and Hunter (1984) to support the inference that content validity usually promotes criterion-related validity. Consumers who plan to make use of this examination for employee selection would be well advised to study that inference carefully before exposing companies to the legal actions that can result when that inference is not valid for the given company and situation.

The manual for administration & scoring made a brief case for the construct validity of the SWA-C using the results of the job analysis. No empirical evidence of construct validity was presented, and the authors indicated that no such studies had been conducted. Those consumers considering the use of this examination for employee selection should assume that no direct evidence of the construct validity of the SWA-C exists, at least until data to the contrary are presented.

The manual for administration & scoring presented normative (i.e., raw score with percentile rank) data for the SWA-C using 97 test takers from two sources, a Southwestern communications company and a Midwest manufacturing plant. It is unclear that these 97 test takers represent a sufficient sample to support the use of the presented norms in employee selection.

COMMENTARY. The focus of the examination is quite clear, that being the assessment of the knowledge and skill necessary to function as a competent journey—level air conditioning technician. The content underpinning of the examination was well defined for use circa 1992. That this content underpinning is sufficient for use in 2007 remains undetermined.

Persons considering the use of this examination for employee selection are cautioned that the practice of journey air conditioning specialists has likely changed since 1992. A close examination of examination content and content sampling to determine that the examination is sufficiently up-to-date for the intended use is warranted.

No evidence was presented to demonstrate the current content validity of the examination given the technological advances of the past 15 years, and although it is certain that resistors, capacitors, and thermocouples still function much as they have for several decades, it is the advances in computer controls, the more sophisticated use of electronics, and the revised safety protocols that should compel the test authors to reexamine and document the propriety of this examination for use with current journey-level air conditioning technicians.

Furthermore, the use of validity generalization (VG) to infer the criterion-related validity of this examination for employee selection is, at best, just that, an inference. Taking VG to its logical conclusion, a driver's license examination might be sufficient and cheaper. Those consumers considering this examination for use with employees should require empirical evidence to support this inference.

No passing standard study was presented for use with this examination, and the presentation of norms, if based on 97 test takers from two environments, suggested that the passing standard is left to the consumer using this examination either for selection or for training. It seems reasonable to think that a single passing standard could be established, even across industries, by an overarching organization. However, such an organization might not exist, and no such overarching passing standard appeared to exist. To this end, those who plan to use this examination, whether for employee selection or development, should consider carefully how a passing standard could be established and defended for use in their particular context.

[6]
Amsterdam Short-Term Memory Test.

Purpose: Designed to be used in "neuropsychological evaluation of persons who claim to have memory and/or concentration problems, but in whom these problems are not clinically obvious, while the possibility exists that they are exaggerating or simulating their problems."
Population: Individuals who claim to have memory and/or concentration problems, but do not have clinical symptoms.
Publication Dates: 1999–2005.
Acronym: ASTM.
Scores: Total score only.
Administration: Individual.

Price Data, 2006: EURO350 per complete kit including manual (2005, 75 pages), computer program for administration, and 100 record forms; EURO49.50 per manual; EURO29.95 per 100 record forms.
Foreign Language Editions: Manual and record forms are also available in German and Dutch.
Time: (10–30) minutes.
Comments: Test is administered via computer; computer program is available on a CD.
Authors: Ben Schmand and Jaap Lindeboom with collaboration of Thomas Merten and Scott R. Millis.
Publisher: PITS: Psychologische Instrumenten Tests en Services [The Netherlands].

Review of the Amsterdam Short-Term Memory Test by DANIEL C. MILLER, Professor, Texas Woman's University, Denton, TX:

DESCRIPTION. The Amsterdam Short-Term Memory Test (ASTM) was designed to assess short-term memory and concentration in adults who appear to have deficits in these areas and who may be exaggerating or simulating their complaints. Therefore, the test attempts to measure a negative response bias or insufficient effort that would contribute to poor performance. The test authors suggest that the ASTM would be useful in forensic neuropsychology and in clinical practice when a clinician needs to differentiate actual memory dysfunction from cognitive complaints due to somatization or other psychiatric states. The test authors state specifically that the ASTM is not intended for use with adult patients with Alzheimer's disease, Korsakoff's psychosis, or traumatic brain injury who are still in a state of posttraumatic amnesia. The test was originally developed in Dutch, with English and German versions added later.

The ASTM materials consist of a computer program for test administration and a record form for recording patients' responses. Although the test has a computer program to standardize stimulus presentation, it is not intended to be self-administered. The system requirements for the computer program include: (a) personal computer with 12 MB of hard disk space and a 486 or higher processor, (b) Windows 98(SE) or higher (not Linux or Macintosh), (c) VGA or higher resolution video adaptor, and (d) a Microsoft mouse or compatible pointing device. Microsoft Powerpoint Viewer is necessary for item presentation, which can be installed from the Program CD. Installation of the ASTM requires an activation code.

There are 30 trials on the ASTM. Each trial is administered in the same fashion. The patient is shown a list of five stimulus words on the computer screen for 8 seconds. Next, the patient is shown a simple arithmetic problem and asked to verbally state the answer. The arithmetic problem is meant to be a distracter. The patient is then shown five response words on the computer screen, three of which appeared on the original list of words. The patient is asked to identify the three words that appeared on the original list of words prior to the arithmetic problem distracter. The total test takes approximately 10–15 minutes to administer. Malingerers and other underperformers may take much longer to finish the test. The ASTM may be discontinued if the patient makes six or more errors after the first 15 items or performs quickly with no more than two errors. One point is assigned to each of the correctly identified words for a total of 3 points per item. The total possible raw score for the test is 90 points (30 items X 3 points each). Total raw scores falling within the 85–90 range are considered normal. Scores falling below 85 are suspicious and may reflect performance that is below actual level of competence or may be indicative of insufficient effort. Scores less than or equal to 48 are very likely indicative of malingering.

DEVELOPMENT. The stimulus materials were chosen from a normative study of semantic category dominance words (Battig & Montague, 1969). Battig and Montague listed words generated by 442 individuals in response to specific categories (e.g., "precious stones" elicited "diamond" as the first response from 435 of the 442 individuals). Words with high response frequencies were used in order to be comparable across languages.

TECHNICAL.

Standardization. The ASTM was standardized on 17 groups of patients and normal controls for a total sample of 1,503. The clinical sample consisted of patients with neurological conditions (e.g., Parkinson's disease, brain tumors), patients with memory complaints, legal cases that involved whiplash or chronic toxic encephalopathy, and patients with chronic fatigue syndrome. Normal participants of all ages typically perform almost perfectly on the ASTM, whereas malingerers achieve much lower overall test scores.

Reliability. The reliability of the ASTM appears to be satisfactory. Internal consistency measures in several patient samples revealed alpha coefficients of .87 (Schagen, Schmand, de Sterke, & Lindeboom, 1997) and .91 for the total standardization sample database (test manual). Test-retest reliability after 1 to 3 days in a sample of neurologically mixed patients (e.g., traumatic brain injury, cerebrovascular diseases, inflammatory diseases) was .84. Using a cutoff score of 84 to classify insufficient effort yields a specificity index of 89% and a sensitivity index of 91%.

Validity. The ASTM was cross-validated with several other measures of symptom validity including the recognition score of the Rey's Auditory Verbal Learning Test (1964), the Dot Counting Test (Lezak, 1995), the Distraction Test (Baker, Hanley, Jackson, Kimmance, & Slade, 1993), Test of Memory Malingering (Tombaugh, 1996), the Portland Digit Recognition Test (Binder, 1993), and the Word Memory Test (Green, 2003). The ASTM appeared to be more sensitive to biased responding than all of the tests listed above except for the Word Memory Test, which was equally sensitive. The ASTM has been cross-validated in three languages: Dutch, English, and German.

COMMENTARY. The ASTM was designed to assess short-term memory and concentration in adults who claim to have deficits in these areas but for whom the possibility exists that they may be exaggerating or simulating complaints. Therefore, the test attempts to measure a negative response bias or insufficient effort that would contribute to poor performance. The test is well standardized although further demographic data regarding the standardization samples (such as the mean age, gender composition, geographic representation, socioeconomic background, and so forth) would strengthen the test. The psychometric properties of the test (reliability and validity) are solid. The test appears to be a good addition to adult neuropsychology, forensic neuropsychology, and adult clinical neuropsychology for differential diagnosis of malingering and biased responding.

SUMMARY. The ASTM is a solid psychometric instrument designed to measure malingering and biased responding in adults. The ASTM has been cross-validated in Dutch, English, and German, which increases its cross-cultural utility. As a diagnostic tool for assessing malingering in adults, it has several advantages to other similar tests. The test does not use the familiar two-word forced-choice recognition format, but rather requires the patient to choose three of the five target words. This format reduces the "50–50" chance factor and therefore improves the validity of the test. The ASTM also uses high incidence words for targets and low incidence words for the foils, which increases the likelihood of patients putting forth good effort. The administration manual is easy to read and provides concise information about the technical properties of the test and clear administration directions.

REVIEWER'S REFERENCES

Baker, G. A., Hanley, J. R., Jackson, H. F., Kimmance, S., & Slade, P. (1993). Detecting the faking of amnesia: Performance differences between simulators and patients with memory impairment. *Journal of Clinical and Experimental Neuropsychology, 15,* 668-684.

Battig, W. F., & Montague, W. E. (1969). Category norms for verbal items in 56 categories: A replication and extension of the Connecticut category norms. *Journal of Experimental Psychology Monograph, 80,* 1-46.

Binder, L. M. (1993). Assessment of malingering after mild head trauma with the Portland Digit Recognition Test. *Journal of Clinical and Experimental Neuropsychology, 15,* 170-182.

Green, P. (2003). *The Word Memory Test for Windows: User's manual and program.* Edmonton, Canada: Green's Publishing.

Lezak, M. D. (1995). *Neuropsychological assessment* (3rd ed.). New York: Oxford University Press.

Rey, A. (1964). L'examen clinque em psychologie. Paris: Presses Universitaires de France.

Schagen, S., Schmand, B., de Sterke, S., & Lindeboom, J. (1997). Amsterdam Short-Term Memory Test: A new procedure for the detection of feigned memory deficits. *Journal of Clinical and Experimental Neuropsychology, 19,* 43-51.

Tombaugh, T. N. (1996). Test of Memory Malingering (TOMM). North Tonawanda, NY: Multi-Health Systems.

[7]

Anger Disorders Scale.

Purpose: "Designed to help practitioners identify clinically dysfunctional anger."

Population: Ages 18 and over.

Publication Date: 2004.

Administration: Individual or group.

Forms, 2: Anger Disorders Scale; Anger Disorders Scale: Short.

Price Data, 2006: $135 per ADS complete kit including technical manual (2004, 184 pages), 10 reusable item booklets, and 25 each ADS and ADS:S QuikScore forms; $64 per technical manual; $42 per 25 ADS QuikScore forms; $40 per 25 ADS:S QuikScore forms; $23 per 10 reusable item booklets.

Authors: Raymond DiGiuseppe and Raymond Chip Tafrate.

Publisher: Multi-Health Systems, Inc.

   a) ANGER DISORDERS SCALE.

   Acronym: ADS.

   Scores, 22: Reactivity/Expression (Scope of Anger Provocations, Physiological Arousal, Duration of Anger Problems, Rumination, Impulsivity, Coercion, Verbal Expression, Total), Anger-In (Hurt/Social Rejection, Episode Length, Suspiciousness, Resentment, Tension Reduction, Brooding, Total), Vengeance (Revenge, Physical Aggression, Relational Aggression, Passive Aggression, Indirect Aggression, Total), Total.

   Time: (20) minutes.

   b) ANGER DISORDERS SCALE: SHORT.

   Acronym: ADS:S.

   Scores, 4: Reactivity/Expression, Anger-In, Vengeance, Total.

   Time: (5–10) minutes.

Review of the Anger Disorders Scale by LAURA L. B. BARNES, Associate Professor of Research, Evaluation, Measurement, and Statistics, Oklahoma State University, Tulsa, OK:

DESCRIPTION. The Anger Disorders Scale (ADS) is a 74-item paper-pencil or computer-administered scale designed to "assess and identify aspects of anger that may lead to dysfunction and impairment in clinical populations" (technical manual, p. 1). The ADS comprises 18 subscales clustered into five domains (provocations, arousal, cognitions, motives, and behaviors), plus a positive impression index. Scores are obtained for each of the 18 scales, three higher order factors (Reactivity/Expression, Anger-In, and Vengeance) plus a total score. There is also a short form, the ADS:S containing 18 items, one from each subscale. Scores obtainable for the short form correspond to the three higher order factors from the long form plus a total score.

The ADS was developed for the purpose of assessing dysfunctional anger to help practitioners devise individualized treatment plans. The authors also intended for the subscales to "assess relevant criteria needed for potential anger disorder diagnoses to be considered in future versions of the Diagnostic and Statistical Manual" (technical manual, p. 1).

The ADS scales are intended for individuals 18 years of age and up who are already believed to have anger problems such as aggression, domestic violence, sexual assaults, substance abuse, and marital problems, and/or who have been referred for a forensic evaluation or for employment concerns. The short form is recommended for screening or as part of an intake assessment battery or psychosocial assessment.

Individuals completing the long form are presented with an item booklet containing 74 item stems with a five-option response format and a separate response sheet. Response formats primarily tend to measure frequency (e.g., *never or rarely to almost every day*), though some measure duration (e.g., *a week or less* to *a year or more*) or scope (*almost nothing* to *almost everything*). The 18-item short form items are included in the same booklet as the short form response sheet. The Dale-Chall procedure indicated the scales have a fifth grade reading level. The authors suggest the ADS should take about 20 minutes to complete and 5-10 minutes to complete the short form. Detailed administration instructions are provided in the manual.

The QuikScore Form is arranged to facilitate scoring and developing norm-referenced score profiles for males or females by age group. The top sheet of the QuikScore Form is the response sheet, which is perforated for easy top-half tear-away once the respondent is finished. This reveals a tear-away scoring form with instructions and beneath that are profile sheets for converting raw scores to percentiles separately for males and females by age group. Appendices in the technical manual include both percentiles and *T*-scores that are linearly derived, thus preserving the positively skewed distribution of raw scores.

DEVELOPMENT. The authors write that the scales mainly focus on characteristics that represent anger as a form of pathology because these characteristics are important to developing anger interventions. They provide an extensive review of current measures and note their limitations—both general measures such as the MMPI-2, Symptom Checklist-90-Revised, 16PF, and MCMI-III; and anger specific measures such as the Novaco Anger Scale, Spielberger STAXI-2, Buss-Durkey Hostility Inventory, and Siegel's Multidimensional Anger Inventory. These and other scales were considered to be limited in their theoretical formulation, their lack of utility for treatment planning, or lack of empirical support for their scale structure. The authors note that the ADS is unique in that, as well as measuring the four domains proposed by Novaco (1994), the ADS includes an additional domain of Motives. Thus, the five domains for which ADS items were to be developed were as follows: provocations, which represent the eliciting stimuli; cognitions, representing how stimuli are interpreted; arousal, which includes intensity, duration, and physical aspects of anger; motives, which includes the use of emotions to cope with stressful events; and behaviors that emerge to cope with stress.

Several versions of the ADS were developed and tested. The first version of the ADS contained only seven subscales. As research was conducted with various groups, additional subscales were developed to better assess the differences in anger experience of these groups. Items were required to load on a single factor, to discriminate between clinical and nonclinical groups, and to have correlations of at least .6 with other items on the same subscale or with other anger measures. Items not meeting these criteria were reworded or discarded. Items in the current version of the ADS have factor loadings of .3 or greater on their respective factors. The ADS:S (short form) was developed by selecting the single best item from each ADS subscale based on the above criteria.

TECHNICAL EVALUATION. The normative sample was composed of "normal" individuals who were not clinical referrals or indicating pathology at the time of testing. The total sample consisted of 1,429 individuals with complete data who were recruited from among college students in New York, Connecticut, and southern Indiana (21%), and through various places of employment in metropolitan New York. Further, 674 individuals were recruited through two internet sites. This sample was 64% Caucasian, 13% African American, and 12% Hispanic, with a mean age of 33. The final standardization sample used all 578 males and a random sample of 619 females from the total sample in order for the gender representation to be more balanced (48% male). The final standardization sample was 1,197.

Norms are presented for the final standardization sample of 1,197 and separately for males (*n* = 578) and females (*n* = 851, the total female normative group) in each of three age groups (18-29, 30-49, and 50 plus). The sample sizes are generally adequate for the two younger gender/age groups, though rather small for the over-50 group (78 for men, 103 for women). There were significant, though generally small, gender differences for several of the subscale and higher order factor scores, though no differences on the total score. Men scored significantly higher on Physical Aggression, Coercion, Revenge, and Indirect Aggression subscales; whereas women scored higher on Rumination, Episode Length, Scope of Anger Provocations, Hurt/Social Rejection, Resentment, and Suspiciousness subscales. The authors note the patterns of these subscale differences and the lack of total score differences on the ADS support the multidimensional structure of the ADS. On the short form, women scored higher on the higher order factor scores of Reactivity/Expression and Anger-In; whereas, men scored significantly higher on Vengeance. Women scored significantly higher than men on the total score of the ADS:S. Separate age norms are presented because of a sharp increase in total anger scores during the early 60s. Though separate ethnic norms were not developed because differences were small (generally within one score point), the authors recommend that cultural differences be taken into account in interpretation.

A separate clinical sample consisted of 1,015 individuals. These included aggressive drivers who completed the survey over the internet, psychotherapy general outpatients, mental health clients with anger problems, court referrals to a court intervention program, male and female medium security inmates, and incarcerated sex offenders. The authors report no score differences between those who completed the survey by internet and those who completed the paper/pencil version.

Reliability. Stratified alpha (often used when test data are multidimensional) was used to estimate the internal consistency of the scores in the standardization sample. Coefficients for the ADS total score for all normative groups and the clinical sample are .97 and above. For the ADS higher order factor scores, coefficients range from .90 to .96 for all groups except Women Over 50 where alpha = .85. ADS subscale alphas ranged from .70 to .88 in the overall sample (mean alpha = .81); from .71 to .90 in the clinical sample (mean alpha = .82); and have a mean alpha for women of .80 and for men of .82 in the age/gender groups. For the ADS:S total score alphas range from .83 to .88; for all but one subscale ADS:S score alphas are in the range of .55 to .84, with one subscale alpha at .41 (median alpha = .73). Two-week test-retest coefficients for ADS and ADS:S total and subscale scores from 65 college students range from .75 to .92. The manual reports standard errors of measurement based on coefficient alpha, and standard errors for prediction based on test-retest coefficients.

Validity. The standardization sample was randomly split into a derivation sample (*n* = 595) for exploratory factor analyses (EFA) and a replication sample (*n* = 605) for confirmatory factor analyses (CFA). Principal axis EFAs with oblique rotation and CFAs conducted separately on items within each of the 5 theoretical domains tended to support the subscale structure of the ADS. Support for the Relational Aggression subscale was rather weak in that these items did not load on one scale but were split across Physical Aggression and Passive Aggression. The authors acknowledge the exploratory nature of this construct and decided to retain this subscale.

The authors originally hypothesized four higher order factors based on Spielberger's theory of anger-in and anger-out. A four-factor EFA extraction failed to converge so the authors adopted a three-factor solution after oblique rotation as the basis for the higher-order factor scores. The three factors were Anger-In (primarily loaded by Hurt/Social Rejection, Suspiciousness, and Brooding); Vengeance (primarily loaded by Relational Aggression and Indirect Aggression); and Reactivity/Expression (primarily loaded by Physiological Arousal, Rumination, Impulsivity, and Verbal Expression). All subscales were assigned to the higher order factor on which they had the highest loading though only 11 of the 18 loaded significantly on a single factor and 6 had significant loadings on two factors. CFA fit indices for this correlated three-factor solution revealed a marginally acceptable fit. The three higher order factor scores were then submitted to a principal factor analysis (PFA) and a single factor emerged accounting for about 79% of the variance, providing support for a Total score.

Results of EFA of the 18 ADS:S items generally supported the three-factor structure of the long form. It was considered desirable for the two forms to share the same scoring structure so any differences in the empirical factor structure were resolved by assigning ADS:S items to the same factor scales as they were assigned on the long form. An EFA of the three factor scores on the short form supported a one-factor solution thus supporting the interpretation of a Total score.

Four hundred forty-three individuals from the standardization sample also completed Spielberger's STAXI. The correlation between the Anger-In and Anger-Out subscales of the STAXI on the sample was .38; whereas the correlation between the higher order factors of Anger-In and Reactivity-Expression on the ADS was .62; and between ADS Anger-In and Vengeance was .51.

The authors suggest these results may be due to the ADS measuring a broader range of anger reactions than the STAXI. Based on this and additional research with the ADS, the authors hypothesize that Anger-In and Anger-Out, rather than being independent dimensions of anger, are strongly related among individuals with dysfunctional anger.

Evidence for validity of the ADS and ADS:S scores for clinical and research purposes is presented via a number of studies examining the relationship of ADS scores to scores from other instruments. Correlations of ADS scales with scales from other anger measures (e.g., Spielberger State-Trait Anger Inventory, STAXI; Aggression Questionnaire, AQ) were consistent with the theoretical structure of the ADS; patterns of correlations with MCMI-III clinical syndromes scales are consistent with the ADS measurement of anger as psychopathology. However, the authors note that the correlations, though significant, are small, which they interpret to indicate that the DSM-IV "poorly represents anger in the present representation of psychopathology" (technical manual, p. 90). Other research examined the validity of the Positive Impression Index, which was found to correlate as expected with other impression management indices and to differ among clinical groups as expected.

COMMENTARY AND SUMMARY. The authors present a compelling case for the development of the ADS both in terms of its theoretical justification and the unique niche filled by this instrument as a clinically useful multidimensional measure of pathological anger. The long form scales possess good psychometric characteristics; reliability is generally adequate for the short form, though a bit low for the Anger-In subscale (range = .55 to .68 across age groups) and alpha = .41 for Vengeance Among Women Over 50. The authors have assembled an impressive collection of evidence to support the use of these scales for their intended purpose. The factor structure is generally well-supported though the higher order factor scores may be influenced by some subscales with relatively low loadings. Additional reported research regarding the equivalence of scores derived from the long and short forms would be welcome. The technical manual is well-written and contains substantial guidance regarding clinical interpretation. The authors have written an informative literature covering theories and measures of anger as well as a section on next steps in research with the ADS. These instruments should be very useful to clinicians and researchers alike.

REVIEWER'S REFERENCE

Novaco, R. (1994). Anger as a risk factor for violence among the mentally disturbed. In J. Monahan & H. J. Steadman (Eds.), *Violence and mental disorders.* Chicago: University of Chicago Press.

Review of the Anger Disorders Scale by MATTHEW E. LAMBERT, Assistant Clinical Professor of Neuropsychiatry, Texas Tech University Health Sciences Center, Lubbock, TX:

DESCRIPTION. The Anger Disorders Scale (ADS) was designed "to assess and identify aspects of anger that may lead to dysfunction and impairment in clinical populations and to help practitioners devise individualized treatment plans" (technical manual, p.1). It is available in two forms: the 74-item Anger Disorders Scale, which produces 22 scores (18 subscale scores, 3 factor scores, and a total score); and the 18-item Anger Disorders Scale: Short (ADS:S), which produces 4 scores. The ADS also produces a Positive Impressions Index, which assesses aberrant response styles. All items are responded to on 5-point Likert scales and the entire instrument is hand-scored using tear-apart QuikScore forms. Scores from the ADS/ADS:S are then plotted as raw scores on the profile form according to age and sex. Raw scores can then be converted to percentiles. Percentiles of 75 or greater indicate anger pathology. *T*-scores for age and gender are provided in the appendices. *T*-scores at 61 or greater are viewed as clinically significant scale elevations.

The ADS/ADS:S is intended for use with adults age 18 years and older; with three age ranges used for plotting scores: 18- to 29-year-olds, 30- to 49-year-olds, and those 50 years of age and older. The full-length ADS requires approximately 20 minutes to complete whereas the ADS:S requires 5 to 10 minutes to complete. A 172-page test manual accompanies the test and extensively discusses all aspects of ADS/ADS:S development and validation.

DEVELOPMENT. The ADS was developed to provide a clinically meaningful assessment of anger that was not available prior to its development. Although previous theories of anger had focused on anger as a trait, those instruments reportedly did not allow for the clinical assessment of anger necessary for development of remediation plans. This required anger to be considered a multidimensional phenomena involving both anger-in and anger-out, with differences in how various aspects of anger are displayed. Ultimately, the ADS was based on a five domain model of anger: (a) Provocations Domain, which addresses anger triggers; (b) Arousal Domain, involving the physiological arousal of anger along with intensity and duration; (c) Cognitions Domain, including aspects of appraisal and attitude impacting anger; (d) Motives Domain, reflecting the rationale for anger ranging from it being helpful, selfish, or emphasizing revenge; and (e) Behaviors Domain, ultimately anger expression or restraint. Each of these domains reflects a number of constructs ranging from only two for the Provocations Domain (i.e., Scope of Anger Provocations and Hurt/Social Rejection) to six for the Behaviors Domain (i.e., Brooding, Verbal Expression, Physical Aggression, Relational Aggression, Passive Aggression, and Indirect Aggression). A total of 18 constructs formed the foundation for the five anger domains. These then provide the basis for the 18 ADS subscales.

Items were written to assess each of the 18 constructs and administered to normal and clinical populations. Any item that correlated less than .6 with other items from the subscale or with other anger measures, and that could not discriminate clinical and normal groups was either discarded or reworded. Additional items were added to subscales with inadequate reliability and items that loaded on more than one subscale were rewritten to reflect the meaning of just that subscale. Each subscale ultimately was made up of between three and six items. The ADS:S was constructed by drawing one exemplary item from each of the 18 subscales.

TECHNICAL. The psychometric properties of the ADS and ADS:S were determined from eight sample populations that included: normals (normative sample), aggressive drivers, psychotherapy outpatients, individuals seeking mental health treatment for anger problems, court intervention referrals, correctional institution inmates, incarcerated sex offenders, and individuals seeking anger treatment at a Canadian medical school. The normative sample was recruited from a variety of collegiate and governmental and nongovernmental entities, as well as from two internet sites. A total of 1,429 individuals comprised the norma-

tive sample with gender, age, and ethnicity differences being accounted. It is noted, however, that over 50% of the normative sample resided in New York State with 47 other states and the Canadian province of Ontario contributing less than 3% each to the normative sample.

ADS factor analytic studies were conducted by dividing the standardization sample into two equivalent derivation and replication samples. Both exploratory and confirmatory factor analyses were conducted for the items from the 18 subscales. Oblimin rotations accurately reflected the hypothesized ADS subscales and better goodness of fit was noted for the Provocations, Arousal, Cognitions, and Motives domains than for the Behaviors domain. Further factor analyses supported the creation of the higher order factor scores: Anger-In, Vengeance, and Reactivity/Expression along with an overall ADS Total score. Similarly, ADS:S factor analyses with oblimin rotations produced a higher order ADS:S total factor and three second order factors of Anger-In, Vengeance, and Reactivity/Expression.

Internal consistency for the overall standardization sample, age and gender subgroups, and clinical sample was assessed using a Stratified Alpha and found to be .97 to .98 for the ADS Total and .91 to .96 for the higher order factor scores. Cronbach's alpha for the 18 ADS subscales ranged from .60 to .97. As well, Cronbach's alphas for the ADS:S and its higher order factors ranged from .62 to .86. Two-week test-retest correlations for all ADS scores ranged from .79 to .92 whereas test-retest correlations for the ADS:S scores ranged from .83 to .92.

Validity studies were undertaken by comparing the ADS and ADS:S subscales and major factors to various widely used anger instruments. The ADS/ADS:S total scores correlated highly with the Spielberger Trait Anger Expression Inventory-2 (STAXI-2) Trait Anger subscale, $r = .73$ and .70, respectively. As well, a factor analysis based on 400 participants from the standardization sample and 100 prison inmates compared the ADS and STAXI-2 subscales to assess concurrent validity. A five-factor solution was determined, which reflected considerable overlap between the two instruments. Yet, the ADS was also noted to add significant information from the Provocations, Cognitions, and Motives domains that the STAXI-2 did not include.

Similarly, the ADS was compared to the Aggression Questionnaire (AQ) with correlations for the ADS total and factors scores and the ADS subscale scores. This was conducted with a portion of the normative sample as well as individuals from the anger disorders clinic. Correlations between the ADS and the five AQ scores for the normative sample ranged from .11 to .62 and all but seven of the correlations reached a .01 significance level, indicating good concurrent validity. For the anger disorders clinic group the correlations ranged from .09 to .86, although a smaller number of those correlations reached the .01 significance level. This suggested both concurrent and discriminant validity for a clinical population. A factor analysis of the ADS and AQ subscales, however, suggested that the two instruments measure different aspects of anger.

Also, to address concurrent validity, the ADS was compared to the Millon Clinical Multiaxial Inventory-III (MCMI-III) to assess the interaction of ADS concepts with DSM-IV-TR diagnostic signs. Correlations were again calculated between the ADS/ADS:S scores and the MCMI-III Clinical Syndrome and Personality Disorders scales. Again, moderate correlations were noted between the various scales reflecting consistent concurrent validity to the MCMI-III.

Finally, differences between the various sample populations were determined for the ADS/ADS:S total, factor, and subscale scores. Angry outpatients scored highest from among the sample groups, with other groups who had designated anger problems scoring higher than those who had fewer anger problems. This suggested that the ADS/ADS:S possess adequate levels of discriminant validity.

COMMENTARY. The ADS and ADS:S were developed to provide a clinical assessment of anger to be used in treatment planning. As such, it provides a broad assessment of anger that should allow for individualized patient treatment plans in which the focus is the elements of anger that are problematic. This is in contrast to other anger assessment instruments that are less broad and more focused on anger as a trait versus a topic for clinical intervention. Although the broad nature of the ADS is a strength, the number of subscale scores produced may make it somewhat unwieldy as there may be too many permutations to try to account for in a clinical intervention.

Although the number of scores produced by the ADS may make it unwieldy, the true strength of the ADS/ADS:S lies in its psychometric underpinnings. Good reliability and concurrent validity data exist for all ADS/ADS:S scales. The only ADS/ADS:S psychometric weakness may be the normative sample's somewhat restricted demographic range. It is unknown whether the ADS/ADS:S reflects a regional bias as the bulk of the sample was drawn from New York state.

With the good reliability and concurrent validity data present, however, there still is a need for further predictive validity data. This is particularly so because the ADS/ADS:S is designed for use in treatment planning. Being able to predict responsiveness to anger treatment would be an important component for treatment planning.

SUMMARY. The ADS/ADS:S provides a positive step in measuring clinically significant aspects of anger for treatment planning. It is an easily administered, psychometrically sound instrument that can be used in treatment planning and possibly treatment outcome assessment. The large number of scores produced may be somewhat unwieldy and there is yet to be good predictive validity for it. With these minor limitations the ADS/ADS:S meets all expectations as an anger assessment instrument.

[8]

Applicant Risk Profiler.

Purpose: "Designed to assist companies in determining which applicants are a potential risk or threat to their supervisors, coworkers and/or themselves."

Population: Job applicants.

Publication Date: 2001.

Acronym: ARP.

Scores, 5: Deception, Integrity, Illegal Drug Use, Workplace Policy Compliance, Workplace Aggression.

Administration: Individual.

Price Data, 2005: $99.99 per starter kit including manual (44 pages), 5 tests, and 1 test log; $34.99 per manual; $13.29 per paper-and-pencil version test (sold in quantities of 10; quantity discounts available); $13.29 per on-line test.

Time: (30) minutes.

Comments: Online and paper-and-pencil administration available; online version includes interpretive reports and follow-up interview questions.

Author: J. M. Llobet.

Publisher: G. Neil.

Review of the Applicant Risk Profiler by RICHARD E. HARDING, Director of Research, Kenexa Technology, Inc., Lincoln, NE:

DESCRIPTION. The Applicant Risk Profiler (ARP) is a tool that was intended to provide employers the means to measure the potential risk or threat of the applicant to people in the workplace. There are four workplace behaviors measured by 65 scaled statements. These behaviors are: Integrity (this involved the likelihood of stealing and/or inappropriate behaviors); Illegal Drug Use (the potential that an applicant comes to work under the influence of illegal drugs); Workplace Policy Compliance (the likelihood that an applicant will disregard the company's policies and procedures); and Workplace Aggression (this measures the potential for an applicant to be overly aggressive at work). The scaled statements use a 5-point scale from *Strongly Disagree* to *Strongly Agree* with the midpoint being labeled as *Neutral*. Each of the scales is composed of 15 statements. There is an additional scale consisting of 5 statements. This scale is called the Deception scale score, which provides information on the test-taker's attempt to fake the results in order to present him/herself in a more favorable or positive manner.

Test-takers are instructed to take the test by considering each statement and how it applies to them in their everyday work. There is no time limit for completion. The test-taker booklet is well designed with very clear instructions. Given the number of statements, it does appear that this will take most test-takers about 15 to 20 minutes to complete, depending on reading and comprehension abilities.

The scoring key is provided within the test booklet. After completion, a perforated seal is broken and the responses for each statement are on a carbonless scoring key. The statements that go into each scale are easily identified with the weighting for each response given. The statements in each scale are then summed and the scale scores used in interpretation.

The manual indicates that the ARP in its present form of 60 items has been reduced recently (no date given) from 80 items and the 5-item Deception scale added. A table is also included at the scale level that shows each revised scale and its correlation to the earlier version. These correlations range from .85 to .98 based on sample sizes from 153 to 206. Conclusions drawn by the author suggest that the new ARP, although reduced by 25%, still measures the same constructs as the older, larger version.

The manual covers many aspects of testing and how it applies to the test user and the ARP. The author indicates that a test of this nature can be useful in the candidate selection process but, quite appropriately, should not be used as the sole source of information with which to make a decision. The manual points out, in many sections, the test users' responsibility to monitor their selection processes for adverse impact, establish their own "cut scores," do a job analysis, keep relevant records, consult an attorney, and consult with an I/O psychologist or psychometrician on questions of validity and reliability. These recommendations are very much in keeping with both the letter and spirit of Section II, Chapter 11, pages 111–118 of the *Standards for Educational and Psychological Testing,* (American Educational Research Association, American Psychological Association, & National Council on Measurement in Education, 1999). Other areas of caution are also noted with respect to the Uniform Guidelines on Employee Selection Procedures, Title VII, The Americans with Disabilities Act.

In summary, many parts of the manual are very useful and offer excellent ideas and points for the test user to consider. Other areas are quite limited and disappointing, especially in the validity and adverse impact sections.

DEVELOPMENT. Very little information regarding how the ARP was developed can be found in the manual. Other than mention that the tool was formerly referred to as the Applicant Risk Detector and was recently (no date given) revised and reduced to its present form, no developmental information is presented. This is a glaring omission in the manual, especially for an integrity test that brings risk to employers using it for selection purposes.

TECHNICAL. Interpretation of each of the four scales is provided using a raw score. For example, a raw score of 50–75 on the Integrity scale shows that 85% of the participants, in a validity study presented in the manual, engaged in self-reported stealing or deception at least once in the last year at work. Similar statistics are available for the Illegal Drug Use scale, the Workplace Policy Compliance scale, and the Workplace Aggression scale. Each scale has score ranges associated with Low Risk, Low/Moderate Risk, Moderate Risk, and High Risk based on a validity study. Each scale also has norms based on samples ranging in size from 156 to 210 participants. The manual also suggests users develop their own norms by administering the ARP to their current employees.

There are several (five) concurrent validity studies presented in the manual. Four of the five validity studies are criterion related whereas the final one is a construct validation study. The criteria used in these studies range from self-report scales around integrity, illegal drug use, policy compliance, and workplace aggression to supervisor ratings. Sample sizes range from 56 to 199 for the criterion-related studies and up to 206 for the construct study.

The validity coefficients are generally acceptable. For example, on a sample of 100 entry level through management employees enrolled in a college class, a correlation of .42 ($p < .001$) was found between the Integrity scale on the ARP and self-reported times the participant had stolen from their employer in the past year. Furthermore, on a sample of 80, a correlation of .35 ($p < .001$) was noted between the Illegal Drug Use scale on the ARP and the self-reported number of times the participant showed up to work in the past 6 months intoxicated from illegal drug use. Although these validity coefficients may seem impressive at first glance, no data on the base rate of these behaviors is presented. Of the 100, how many had actually stolen; of the 80, how many did show up intoxicated? These kinds of data would have made the validity coefficients much more interpretable and may or may not have allowed the test user to gain higher confidence in the ARP. In only one instance can data of this sort be found and that is because there were no instances of physical fights between a participant and customer so no validity coefficient could be calculated.

In the study where overall job performance is used as the criterion, a validity coefficient of -.24 ($p < .079$, $n = 56$) is noted. This is somewhat lower than the mean validity of .41 reported by Ones, Viswesvaran, and Schmidt (1993) in their meta-analytic study. This involved more than 650 validity coefficients and how well integrity tests predict job performance. The meta-analytic study does allow a test user to place more confidence in integrity tests than any single small sample study allows such as those presented in the manual.

The reliability coefficients for the scales range from .70 to .88. Each scale is composed of 15 items. The reliability measure used was one of internal consistency.

Additional analyses are presented around the adverse impact of the ARP. Comparisons were shown between samples of African Americans, Hispanics, and Whites on each of the four scales. There are 9 to 25 African Americans, 97 to 115 Hispanics, and 28 to 52 Whites, depending on the scale. Apparently, multiple and independent t-tests were used to demonstrate no difference between groups on each scale. No mention is made of the potential for inflators of Type I error rate. Using this technique, only one difference was noted and that was between Whites and Hispanics on the Integrity scale. Hispanics scored lower (desirable) on the scale. Given this methodology and the relatively small sample sizes, the recommendation in the manual that test users monitor the selection process carefully for evidence of adverse impact is one that should be heartily endorsed if using the ARP.

COMMENTARY. The use of an integrity test is a decision that should never be taken lightly by an employer. When in the hiring process it is to be administered, how it is interpreted, what weight it is given in the final decision, and confidentiality of results are all issues that should be determined prior to implementing. These are all mentioned in the manual as issues to consider.

However, the manual is not detailed enough in some areas to help make a truly informed decision on using the ARP. It is difficult to understand how the ARP was developed and revised. Few descriptions of any of the samples used in the validity studies are provided. Some of the analytic methodologies seem questionable (i.e., the use of multiple independent t-tests, as well as the description of one validity coefficient as "approaching significance"). The validity evidence presented seems acceptable but is still difficult to judge given the lack of detail in the sample statistics.

SUMMARY. Users of integrity tests can feel some confidence given the meta analysis by Ones, Viswesvaran, and Schmidt (1993). The ARP fits into this category of tests. Before adopting the ARP, employers should ask the test publisher many questions about the validity studies and any new work with the ARP. It is very possible that the ARP could be a very effective device in helping to select employees but the test manual makes it difficult to have a high degree of confidence in using the ARP at this time.

REVIEWER'S REFERENCES

Ones, D. S., Viswesvaran, C., & Schmidt, F. L. (1993). Comprehensive meta-analysis of integrity test validities: Findings and implications for personnel selection and theories of job performance [monograph]. *Journal of Applied Psychology, 78,* 679-703.

American Educational Research Association, American Psychological Association, & National Council on Measurement in Education. (1999). *Standards for educational and psychological testing.* Washington, DC: American Educational Research Association.

Review of the Applicant Risk Profiler by WIL-LIAM I. SAUSER, JR., Associate Dean and Professor, Business and Engineering Outreach, Auburn University, Auburn, AL:

DESCRIPTION. In a 1998 review of research on integrity testing, Ones and Viswesvaran noted that evidence continues to mount that integrity tests are valid predictors of employee theft and a host of other counterproductive behaviors at work. They claimed, based on their research, that: (a) U. S. businesses lose in excess of $40 billion in cash and merchandise to employee theft per year, (b) as many as 5,000 companies may use pre-employment screening tests, assessing about 5,000,000 applicants yearly, and (c) there are 45 commercial integrity tests available in the United States (p. 244). Clearly, integrity testing is a lucrative market for test publishers; reviews of several of these tests are found in the *Mental Measurements Yearbook* series indexed under such scores as "integrity" and "theft."

The Applicant Risk Profiler (ARP) is a recently revised (2001) version of an earlier test, the Applicant Risk Detector. It is an attractive and potentially useful product in the integrity testing market and should be considered by those searching for an easily administered and scored screening device for prospective employees. The test consists of 65 short statements (e.g., "All employees bend the rules now and then") with which the examinee is asked to indicate, on a 5-point scale, level of agreement ("strongly agree," "agree," "neutral," "disagree," "strongly disagree"). Fifteen items are used to measure each of four key issues of concern to most employers: Integrity (the potential for theft or deception), Illegal Drug Use, Workplace Policy Compliance, and Workplace Aggression. Five of the items comprise a Deception scale intended to reveal the extent to which an examinee

may be "faking" his or her answers in an effort to present a favorable appearance.

The directions for testing are clear, concise, and comprehensive, and the manual provides suggestions for dealing with any questions that might occur prior to test administration. This reviewer was pleased to see recommendations in the manual for making appropriate accommodations for those with various disabilities. This is just one example of the test publisher's helpful guidance throughout the manual for compliance with federal and state law respecting employment testing. The paper version of the ARP can be administered in group or individual settings. The test is not timed; most examinees who are literate in English can easily complete the instrument within 20 to 30 minutes. Potential users of the ARP are specifically warned to "consult with an attorney before subjecting any test-taker to an adverse employment decision on the basis of English language deficiencies" (administrator's manual, p. 8).

The instrument is cleverly designed so that, by tearing off the cover sheets, the scoring template is revealed. Scoring consists of simple tabulations; reversed-item scoring is already built into the scoring system. The manual indicates that a computer-administered version of the ARP is also available, but that version was not supplied to this reviewer. The manual provides excellent guidance in how to interpret each of the five scores.

DEVELOPMENT. The manual does not provide much detail on how the items were generated and analyzed, but it does note that "the questions that make up the ARP were developed from an extensive review of the psychological literature focusing on what variables and personality characteristics lead to theft in the workplace, illegal drug use, rules and policy noncompliance and aggressive tendencies" (administrator's manual, p. 6). The test publishers take pains to indicate that the ARP is not a "clinically-based" personality assessment instrument, but was instead designed "specifically with the employment environment in mind" (administrator's manual, p. 6). The items appear to possess considerable face validity.

TECHNICAL. The manual describes a series of five studies undertaken to establish and further investigate the psychometric properties of the ARP. Participants in these studies were various groups of employed college students and employees of a specific marketing company with "a wide range of jobs" (administrator's manual, p. 32). These validation samples ranged around 100 each, not the thousands of participants that would be desirable for a test of this nature. Interpretive tables found throughout the manual display results of these various studies in terms of the probability of employee malfeasance associated with each range of scores. For example, 85% of test-takers in one study scoring 50–75 on the Integrity scale admitted engaging in stealing or deceptive behavior at least once during the past year (p. 11).

Internal consistency reliability coefficients for the four substantive scales of the ARP range from .70 (Integrity) to .88 (Illegal Drug Use); these values are acceptable but not as high as desired. Correlations of ARP scores with those of the earlier version (the Applicant Risk Detector) range from .85 (Workplace Aggression) to .98 (Illegal Drug Use), indicating that the two versions are virtually identical and are closely parallel. Throughout the manual, validity coefficients are presented between ARP dimension scores and a variety of self-reported behavioral criteria; these coefficients are typically statistically significant at the .05 to .001 level of probability. Such values suggest that the scores may be useful measures of the constructs they are designed to represent. "Overall" concurrent validity coefficients reported in the manual for the four substantive scales are .51 for Integrity, .59 for Illegal Drug Use, .45 for Workplace Policy Compliance, and .33 for Workplace Aggression. Percentile scores are supplied alongside the raw scores for each of the four substantive scales.

Although some would perceive the evidence presented above supporting the psychometric quality of the ARP as relatively impressive, three weaknesses of the validation work done to date must be considered. First, as mentioned above, the sample sizes used in the studies are small (though they did apparently provide enough statistical power to detect significant relationships among the variables). Second, all of the studies are "concurrent" in nature; no predictive studies are reported in the manual. Third, most of the studies are based on self-reported criteria; only two studies (#3 and #4 in the manual) use criteria collected from supervisors, and the validity coefficients in these two studies are rather modest (ranging from -.22 to -.24). This reviewer encourages the publisher to continue collecting validity information about the ARP and to

include more evidence in future editions of the manual.

COMMENTARY. Business losses due to employee malfeasance are staggering; the test publisher suggests they can range to "$120 billion in financial losses each year" (administrator's manual, p. 5). Given the significance of this problem, it makes sense for employers to search for and use employee screening devices that can help them "weed out" potential problem employees. The ARP appears to be a promising device for this purpose, and the publisher is encouraged to continue collecting research evidence regarding the usefulness of the instrument for this practical purpose. Employee screening can be a tricky process from a legal perspective, and this reviewer again commends the publisher for pointing out to potential users of the ARP how to conduct a proper job analysis, examine adverse impact, identify task linkages, and collect company- and job-specific validity evidence before proceeding to use the ARP in an employee selection program.

The fine manual for this inventory deserves special mention. A major strength of this instrument's manual is that it focuses considerable attention on important issues relating to the legal use of tests in the employment setting. Several pages of the manual are devoted to a primer on assessment, legal issues in testing, adverse impact, job relatedness, the *Uniform Guidelines on Employee Selection Procedures*, recordkeeping requirements, and state and local laws. Throughout the manual potential users of the ARP are encouraged to seek the advice of testing experts and employment law specialists and to follow appropriate procedures for job analysis, task linkage, local validation, and production of company-specific norms and cutoff scores. Potential users are specifically warned in the manual that "assessment results should always be interpreted along with other information gathered through your selection process, to ensure that you get a complete picture of the job candidate or employee" (administrator's manual, p. 4). The manual also provides suggestions on how to discuss ARP results with job applicants and how to ask follow-up questions during the interview process to reveal "insights into the applicant's unique style or tendencies" in interpreting various items within the instrument (p. 22).

SUMMARY. The Applicant Risk Profiler is an attractive, face valid instrument that is easy to administer and score. It results in four substantive dimension scores of considerable interest to potential employers: Integrity, Illegal Drug Use, Workplace Policy Compliance, and Workplace Aggression, as well as a Deception score used to detect incidence of "faking good." Evidence of the ARP's psychometric quality is promising to date, and the publisher is encouraged to continue validation research with the instrument (using larger samples and criteria other than self-reported behavior) and to report the results of these studies in future editions of the manual. Following the caveats and very helpful advice provided by the test publisher, employers could find the instrument useful as a component of an employee selection strategy.

REVIEWER'S REFERENCE

Ones, D. S., & Viswesvaran, C. (1998). Integrity testing in organizations. In R. W. Griffin, A. O'Leary-Kelly, & J. Collins (Eds.), *Dysfunctional behavior in organizations* (pp. 243-246). Greenwich, CT: JAI Press.

[9]

Assessment of Classroom Communication and Study Skills.

Purpose: Designed to "provide classroom teachers and specialists with a tool that efficiently comments on the quality of a student's school language skills."

Population: Grades 5—12.

Publication Dates: 1998—2000.

Acronym: ACCSS.

Scores, 2: Total Score, Vocabulary Score.

Administration: Group or individual.

Forms, 3: ACCSS—Long Form, ACCSS—Short Form, ACCSS—esl.

Price Data, 2006: $40 per test and manual (1998, 211 pages).

Time: (40—60) minutes.

Comments: Criterion-referenced measure; includes an audio cassette containing the administration scenario; revised and expanded edition of the Classroom Communication Screening Procedure.

Author: Charlann S. Simon.

Publisher: Thinking Publications.

Review of Assessment of Classroom Communication and Study Skills by THOMAS EMERSON HANCOCK, Everett School District, Everett, WA:

DESCRIPTION. The Assessment of Classroom Communication and Study Skills (ACCSS) was designed to identify the deficient language and learning skills of those students who are likely to experience difficulties coping with classroom demands. Those skills are assessed in four sections: (a) comprehending a text passage; (b) following oral and written directions; (c) using reasoning, writing, and metalinguistic skills; and (d) matching definitions to vocabulary. The students targeted are (a) early adolescents (Grades 5 to 8); (b) adolescents (Grades 5 to 12) who have learning disabilities; and (c) high school ESL students.

The ACCSS can be administered to class groups (preferred) using a script or to individual students using an audio cassette. There are detailed instructions provided for test administration, scoring, and interpreting results; however, it is suggested that norms be established locally. In addition, the background and rationale for the test as a whole and for every item are both thoroughly described and grounded in relevant research literature.

Students' responses on the ACCSS can be used to identify those who might not succeed in the regular classroom setting without focused help. That focus is designed to come as the interventionist uses the Descriptive Summary where student responses can be grouped according to the following categories and subcategories: (a) Cognition and Comprehension (oral directions, written directions, concepts in text/directions, analysis/evaluation, and integration/inference); (b) Language Analysis and Expression (vocabulary definition, metalinguistic skills, word/symbol response, sentence composition and/or unscrambling words); and (c) Study Skills and Habits (working memory, task persistence and accuracy, and test-taking behavior). Some follow-up instructional suggestions are also provided.

There are three formats to the basic instrument: a long form, which requires about 60 minutes for administration; a short form requiring about 45 minutes; and an ESL form. There is also an observational checklist with thorough directions. Materials and summary forms are provided in reproducible forms.

DEVELOPMENT. A rich foundation for the ACCSS is provided in explicit statements and logic drawn from current educational philosophy and research. Upon this foundation and out of a concern for the success of early adolescents in school, the ACCSS was developed. The author had found that existing instruments were not adequate to assess communication and study skill tasks in early adolescents as they transition to middle school.

It is stated that the instrument is built upon the following philosophy for success in school: (a) Instruction reflects an understanding of the relationship between language and thought; (b) the gaps between school and nonschool language must be identified; (c) reading instruction must reflect a synthesis of phonic and whole language orientations; (d) metalinguistic skills must be evaluated; (e) valid assessment of school tasks must use realistic school tasks; (f) assessment of literacy-related skills comes by observing students' linguistic, metalinguistic, and reasoning abilities; and (g) assessment of classroom skills must occur in the classroom.

The author also explains in detail how the items in the ACCSS are drawn from specific tasks that the research literature has identified as predictors of classroom success: (a) integrating segments of information for inferences or summary, (b) using working memory to process and act on details, (c) applying metalinguistic skills in reading and writing, (d) meaningfully using vocabulary, and (e) persisting and monitoring accuracy.

There are detailed explanations and data showing how words were chosen for the vocabulary portion of the instrument. It appears that the items selected for the other parts of the test were simply based on the good logic of the author. That is, other than a few anecdotal references, there is no evidence for any refining of the items, pilot testing, or evaluations of appropriateness.

TECHNICAL. The ACCSS was tested in metropolitan Phoenix and a graduate student analyzed the data from 500 respondents. It appears that the main concern was determining item difficulties for that sample. Various statistics are somewhat haphazardly reported, including: item difficulty values, means for Grade 5 and 6 respondents, and the labels for six factors from a factor analysis. The difficulty values show a respectable range. However, it is not clear how these difficulty levels might apply to some other sample, as there are few demographic details reported. The factors from the factor analysis appear to have some overlap with the author's grouping of items, though there is no further discussion of this analysis and its results and no statistics from the factor analysis are reported.

There is some validity evidence, but with few methodological details. It was reported that students in this Phoenix sample had lower scores when English was not their first language. Also, when the Iowa Basic Skills reading scores were below the 40th percentile, students in the fourth quartile were clearly discriminated from the other students. However, there were no statistical details provided. The author concluded that the ACCSS was effective in finding the at-risk population who needed immediate support upon their arrival at the middle school.

No reliability data are reported.

There seems to be some evidence of what some call consequential validity. It is reported that many school district administrators use the instrument because they like "authentic assessment" and find the results of the ACCSS more helpful than those from traditional standardized tests. The ACCSS author wrote (C. Simon, personal communication, January 4, 2007) that one district consultant using the instrument reported that "teachers know from the beginning of the year which literacy and study skills need the most attention" and thus are helped to incorporate instruction on how to learn. In addition, it is reported that speech-language pathologists (SLPs) using the instrument obtain easier access to classrooms because the teachers see that the SLPs are concerned about communication/learning behaviors that are directly related to classroom success. However, all of this consequential evidence is anecdotal.

The author states that school systems report that the ACCSS scores correlate with standardized reading scores, but no details are provided. This reviewer requested and was provided some of that data. All the students ($n = 263$), Grades 5–8, at a low-income school with a "high proportion" of ELL students were administered the ACCSS. The percent correct scores from the ACCSS were correlated with recent, scaled normal-curve equivalents (NCEs) from a standardized test, AIMS: reading, .70; language, .64; math, .56. Thus, there is evidence here for aspects of construct validity. In addition, this reviewer administered the short form of the ACCSS instrument to 12 spring-term fifth graders. These same students were also rated independently by their teacher (and blind to the ACCSS scores) on a scale of 1 to 10 for "need to be monitored and assisted within the classroom context." A correlation of .90 was found—good evidence for predictive validity.

COMMENTARY AND SUMMARY. The Assessment of Classroom Communication and Study Skills is the result of an attempt to fill a gap in our educational system. That is, children transitioning from elementary to middle school, and also ESL students, often do not have the communication and study skills needed to succeed in classroom situations. For example, some lack the ability to follow directions and persist with a task, or do not appropriately use metalinguistic skills, or have a poor understanding of vocabulary. These children may not qualify for special programs but nonetheless are in need of special help with student skills.

The items or tasks in the ACCSS attempt to measure these and other skills or abilities that research has shown to be important for success in school. Though there are occasional typographical errors, the test administration directions, scoring helps, and other support materials are thorough and appropriate. The ACCSS can easily be administered to an entire classroom. In addition, support materials provide the structure for arranging instruction targeted to the identified needs of at-risk students.

The ACCSS has strong content and construct validity, in that the instrument as a whole, the methods for administration, and each item are logically grounded with firm support in the research literature. However, the meaningful application of statistical analysis and scientific methods for validation of the instrument are lacking. It is hard to assess the data reported from the one ACCSS-related research study that is reported, as the methods and results are inadequately described. There are no other results provided from research studies testing the ACCSS. It appears that the instrument was created to address a local school district need, that the local administration changed, and that the author has not been motivated to continue to refine her instrument.

It is recommended that the author heed her own statements that more can be accomplished through collaboration and that "research can help us to analyze patterns in data we have collected for purposes of refinement and/or revision of original hypotheses" (manual, p. 179). This reviewer, in his own investigations, did find content and predictive validity. However, there is much more that might be done. For example, the instrument might become more powerful if the categories for group-

ing responses in the Descriptive Summary were more precisely conformed to the six factors identified in the factor analysis. If the ACCSS were tested further with a few diverse samples, then differential validity could be assessed across gender, racial, and culture groups and the instrument could be improved accordingly. With an appropriate collaborator, the ACCSS could be easily and validly evaluated for reliability, concurrent validity, predictive validity, and its impact and those results could be communicated according to current paradigms for reporting research, so that users might have more confidence. It seems likely that the instrument would be validated and probable that its items could be made even more effective. Such analyses and appropriate reporting would make the ACCSS more appealing for potential users and perhaps many more at-risk children could be helped.

Review of the Assessment of Classroom Communication and Study Skills by S. KATHLEEN KRACH, Assistant Professor, University of Nevada Las Vegas, Las Vegas, NV:

DESCRIPTION. The author states, "The *primary purpose* of ACCSS is to *systematically survey* the integrity of classroom communication (i.e., school language) and study skills" (manual, p. 15). Specifically, the Assessment of Classroom Communication and Study Skills (ACCSS) was designed to assess a child's understanding of classroom directions, ability to pay attention to details, capability to understand and use information presented in writing, and awareness needed to self-monitor understanding of academic information. The measure is divided into four sections: Answering Questions on a Text Passage, Following Directions, Language Detective, and Vocabulary/Definition Matching.

The ACCSS is available in a long form, a short form, and a form for speakers of English as a second language (ESL). All items on each form are administered to every student. The long form consists of the four sections described above with 26 mini-assignments. Instructions for each item can either be read to the student(s) by the examiner, or individual students can listen to instructions from an audiotape. The short form is divided into the same four sections described above; however, only 15 mini-assignments are administered. In the short form, items can only be read aloud from the manual. The ESL form contains 17 mini-assignments; however, these are not the same mini-assignments administered in the short form. These mini-assignments were selected based on common tasks performed in the average English-as-a-Second-Language (ESL) classroom. In any of the three forms, students answer the responses to each item on an answer sheet, which can either be copied from the manual or be bought through the publisher. Scores are then transferred onto the Quantitative Summary Chart to analyze percentage correct for the entire test and for the individual mini-assignments. Also, the Descriptive Summary Chart is provided to document performance across types of tasks (e.g., oral, written, memory) based on subjective descriptions such as "adequate," "marginal," and "weak."

In addition to the ACCSS itself, the manual provides three examples of additional observational procedures, sample IEP objectives linked to the information from the ACCSS, additional items to assess and help develop study skills and classroom communication, and research from the test developer.

Although the ACCSS is a curriculum-referenced measure, the test author states that local norms can and should be gathered for the instrument. The author describes that the best procedure for interpreting raw scores is to transform them into percent correct scores, which are then compared to peer performance. According to the manual, if children's scores fall lower than half a standard deviation below the mean of their peers, then these scores should be considered nonpassing.

DEVELOPMENT. The ACCSS is an adaptation of an earlier screening test called the Classroom Communication Screening Procedure: A Test of School Language Proficiency. Items for the ACCSS were designed to match research concerning classroom communication and study skills. To this end, the researched rationale for each type of item on the ACCSS is provided in the manual. No specific origin for items was provided except for the items in the Vocabulary/Definition Matching section. The 10 vocabulary items were selected from a pool of 41 words obtained from the 1981 World Book Dictionary's Grade 3 through Grade 5 wordlists.

Information on item difficulty was analyzed using data based on 500 Grade 5 and Grade 6 students, and was reported in terms of the average number of students who answered that specific item correctly. Data reported ranged from items that most children answered correctly (.94 or 94%) to items that most children did not answer correctly (.18 or 18%). However, none of these data on item difficulty appeared to be used in determining item selection.

TECHNICAL. The ACCSS manual did not specifically report any reliability or validity data. In fact, the words "validity" and "reliability" were not included in the manual anywhere that the reviewer could locate; however, topics related to validity were described. Content validity appeared to be addressed throughout the majority of the manual. Items included were based on extensive research into what types of items provide the best information about classroom communication and study skills. Based on an informal observation of the items and the research presented, the item types appear to match what the test is intended to measure. Concurrent validity appears to be reflected in an evaluation of test performance on the ACCSS as compared to the Iowa Test of Basic Skills (ITBS). Results indicated that students who performed lower on the ACCSS (below 70% accuracy) also performed lower on the ITBS (below the 40th percentile).

COMMENTARY. The ACCSS appears to be an adequate informal measure of classroom communication and study skills. Although item selection was described in some detail and validity was referred to obliquely, the psychometric data presented were not sufficient to make conclusions about actual item suitability and score reliability. Therefore, this measure may be used as a screener for general problems and an aid in providing guidance toward treatment planning, but it should not be used alone to make any educational, linguistic, or psychological diagnostic decisions. The author stated this limitation specifically when she wrote that the ACCSS "is *not* to determine who should be referred to special education. Rather, the results indicate who needs to be monitored and assisted within the classroom context" (manual, pp. 15-16).

The main strength of this instrument appears to be that it is a direct evaluation of children's study and classroom communication skills. Other measures on the market, such as the Learning and Study Strategies Inventory (LASSI; Weinstein, Schulte, & Palmer, 2002; 105) and the School

Motivation and Learning Strategies Inventory (SMALSI; Stroud & Reynolds, 2006), although psychometrically better supported, are simple questionnaires and do not directly assess these skills. Thus, a combination of instruments such as the ACCSS for direct assessment and the LASSI or SMALSI for indirect assessment may provide the most accurate and psychometrically sound description of a child's study and classroom communication skills.

A second strength for the ACCSS is its ease of use. Entire classrooms of students can be evaluated simultaneously and data collected by assessment staff with very little need for additional training. Given the need for local norms and/or local estimates of means and standard deviations to interpret the scores produced by the ACCSS, this simplicity is extremely important.

SUMMARY. The ACCSS is an adequate school- or classroom-wide screener of study and classroom communication skills. Given the paucity of psychometric information available on the measure, it should only be used for gross estimates of skills. The ACCSS is best used in combination with other, more psychometrically sound measures, teacher reports, and classroom observations when making any diagnostic decisions.

REVIEWER'S REFERENCES

Stroud, K. C., & Reynolds, C. R. (2006). School Motivation and Learning Strategies Inventory. Los Angeles: Western Psychological Services.
Weinstein, C. E., Schulte, A. C., & Palmer, D. R. (2002). Learning and Study Strategies Inventory (LASSI). Clearwater, FL: H&H Publishing Company.

[10]

Attention Deficit Disorders Evaluation Scale—Third Edition.

Purpose: Designed "to provide a measure of the ADHD characteristics of inattention and hyperactivity-impulsivity in the DSM-IV."

Population: Ages 4–18.

Publication Dates: 1989–2004.

Acronym: ADDES-3.

Scores, 3: Inattentive, Hyperactive-Impulsive, Total Score.

Administration: Individual.

Forms, 2: School Version, Home Version.

Price Data, 2006: $232 per complete kit including 50 Pre-Referral Attention Deficit checklists, 50 Intervention Strategies Documentation forms, School Version technical manual (2004, 48 pages, 50 School Version rating forms, Home Version technical manual (2004, 48 pages), 50 Home Version rating forms, 50 ADDES-3/DSM-IV forms, Attention Deficit Disorders Intervention manual, and the Parent's Guide to Attention Deficit Disorders; $15 per technical manual (specify School or Home Version); $30 per Attention Deficit Disorders Intervention manual; $35 per 50 rating forms (specify School or Home Version); $30 per 50 Intervention Strategies Documentation forms; $30 per 50 Pre-Referral Attention Deficit checklists; $22 per 50 ADDES-3/DSM-IV forms; $20 per Parent's Guide to Attention Deficit Disorders; $35 per Quick Score computerized Windows program (specify English or Spanish); $35 per 50 Spanish rating forms (specify School or Home Version).

Foreign Language Edition: Spanish edition available.

Time: (20) minutes.

Comments: Scale is rated by parent/caregiver or an educator.

Authors: Stephen B. McCarney and Tamara J. Arthaud.

Publisher: Hawthorne Educational Services, Inc.

Cross References: For reviews by Hugh W. Glenn and Beverly M. Klecker of the second edtion, see 14:27; for reviews by Deborah Collins and Stephen Olejnik of the original edition, see 12:38 (1 reference).

Review of the Attention Deficit Disorders Evaluation Scale—Third Edition by TIMOTHY J. MAKATURA, Consulting Psychologist, Allegheny Children's Initiative, Pittsburgh, PA:

The Attention Deficit Disorders Evaluation Scale—Third Edition (ADDES-3) is the latest version of an instrument that has been developed by Stephen B. McCarney to provide a comprehensive method to assess for symptoms of Attention Deficit Hyperactivity Disorder (ADHD). The ADDES-3 consists of a 46-item Home Version (HV), a 60-item School Version (SV), Parent's Guide to Attention Deficit Disorders, and The Attention Deficit Disorders Intervention Manual. The HV and SV provide an environment-specific and systematic measure of the symptoms of ADHD that are identified in the *Diagnostic and Statistical Manual, Fourth Edition* (DSM-IV) for students ages 4 through 18 years. The HV and SV specifically accommodate the criterion that the ADHD behaviors "must be present in at least two settings." The ADDES-3 was designed specifically to provide an objective and comprehensive assessment of critical behaviors involved in the diagnosis of ADHD as well as provide resources to suggest goals, objectives, and behavior interventions to address these behaviors.

It is interesting to note that the author does not comment on the specific differences between the ADDES-3 and the previous version of this instrument. The manual is confusing on this point because the discussion on development of the instrument refers exclusively to the ADDES-2 versions and there is no comment on updates or item changes on the rating form. It does seem that the rating forms for the HV and SV are unchanged from the previous version; however, a different standardization population was used to determine the statistical properties of the scale.

DESCRIPTION. Two rating scales comprise the ADDES-3, a 46-item scale for the Home Version (HV) and a 60-item scale for the School Version (SV). Items on each form are grouped into two subscales, one with descriptive statements of inattention and the other with descriptive statements of hyperactivity. Each statement is given one of six ratings indicating frequency of occurrence, not developmentally appropriate, or not observed. There are identical items on the two rating forms as well as similar items that are specific to each environment.

The ADDES-3 provides normative information for the Home Version (HV) and the School Version (SV). Normative information for the HV was gathered from 2,848 children, aged 4.0 to 18 years, from 21 states. Normative information for the SV was gathered from 3,903 students from 26 states. Both normative samples were proportionally matched to the national population in terms of gender, race, residence, geographic area, and parent's occupation. Due to significant age and gender differences found on both scales, 13 standardization groups were developed for the HV and 15 standardization groups were developed for the SV.

TECHNICAL. For the Home Version (HV) of the ADDES-3, test-retest reliability was determined by rating 156 randomly selected children who were part of the standardization sample following a 30-day interval. The total score reliability coefficient was .86 and subscale coefficients for Inattentive and Hyperactive-Impulsive were .86 and .82, respectively. Interrater reliability is based on the rating of 68 children by pairs of parents or caregivers. These coefficients ranged from .87 for the Inattentive subscale to .85 for the Hyperactive-Impulsive subscale. Overall interrater reliability was .89. Measures of internal consistency for the Inattentive and Hyperactive-Impulsive subscales resulted in alpha coefficients of .96.

For the School Version (SV) of the ADDES-3, test-retest reliability was determined by rating 855 randomly selected students who were part of the standardization sample following a 30-day interval. The total score reliability coefficient was .91 and subscale coefficients for Inattentive and Hyperactive-Impulsive were .92 and .88, respectively. Interrater reliability was based on the rating of 455 students by pairs of educators with equal knowledge of the student. These coefficients ranged from .78 for the Inattentive subscale to .84 for the Hyperactive-Impulsive subscale. Overall interrater reliability was .85. Measures of internal consistency for the Inattentive and Hyperactive-Impulsive subscales were .98 and .99, respectively.

Evidence for construct validity is based on convergent lines of reasoning involving correlations, factor analysis, and comparison studies. The correlations between items and total score exceeded .54 on the HV and .57 on the SV. On both the HV and SV, all individual items correlated with their respective subscales at levels greater than .65. Factor analytic procedures for the Inattentive and Hyperactive-Impulsive subscales resulted in factor loadings that closely correspond to the factors structure of the ADDES-3. However, certain items had significant loadings on more than one factor. The author reports that content validity for the HV and SV was initially established through "extensive review, field testing and statistical analysis .... The ADDES-3 SV, HV was enhanced with the meticulous review by the diagnosticians and educators" (p. 16). For the HV, concurrent validity was established by correlating the subscales of the HV with the ADD-H Comprehensive Teacher's Rating Scale—Second Edition Parent Form (ACTeRS) and eight subscales of the Conners' Parent Rating Scale—Revised: Short Form (CPRS-R:S). Correlations between the HV and these two instruments ranged from .76 to .93. For the SV, concurrent validity was established by correlating the subscales of the SV with the ADD-H Comprehensive Teacher's Rating Scale—Second Edition (ACTeRS) and eight subscales of the Conners' Teacher Rating Scale—Revised: Long Form (CTRS-R:L). Correlations between the SV and these two instruments ranged from .68 to .92.

SUMMARY. The ADDES-3 is the latest version of an instrument that has been developed to provide a comprehensive method to assess for symptoms of ADHD. This current version has reasonably good psychometric properties that are based on a large normative population. The scale is relatively easy to administer and score, and provides varied formats to consider the scores in relation to one another. Generally, this scale meets the stated purpose to provide a comprehensive method to assess for symptoms of ADHD.

Overall, there are no doubts regarding the utility of this scale but there is some question regarding the need for this recent revision as the previous version seemed to utilize the same rating scales and have adequate psychometric properties. In reviewing the entire ADDES-3, significant differences between the current and previous versions of this scale are not apparent. Although this scale continues to be useful, it remains a mystery what advantage the new scale provides over the old.

Review of the Attention Deficit Disorders Scale—Third Edition by JAMIE G. WOOD, Associate Professor of Psychology, Pittsburg State University, Pittsburg, KS:

DESCRIPTION. The Attention Deficit Disorders Evaluation Scale—Third Edition (ADDES-3) has both a Home Version (ADDES-3HV) and a School Version (ADDES-3SV). The ADDES-3HV is a rating scale containing 46 items and two subscales (Inattentive, Hyperactive-Impulsive). The ADDES-3SV contains 60 items divided into the same two subscales. The forms are designed to be completed by teachers or other school personnel who know the student well and parents or other caregivers, respectively. The scales are appropriate for children ages 4 to 18. Raters are asked to rate each item on a 0 to 5 scale. The rating values for both the Home and School Versions are 0 = *Not Developmentally Appropriate for Age*, 1 = *Not Observed*, 2 = *One to Several Times per Month*, 3 = *One to Several Times per Week*, 4 = *One to Several Times per Day*, and 5 = *One to Several Times per Hour*. Once raw scores are totaled for each of the subscales and total score they can be converted to standard scores and percentile ranks. The manual also provides standard error of measurement values for the subscale and total scores.

DEVELOPMENT. The ADDES-3 is the latest version (copyright, 2004) of an instrument that has been under development since the mid-1990s (ADDES-2; McCarney, 1995). Ironically,

the latest version is not really a new version other than the fact that new norms have been developed. The technical manuals for both the ADDES-3SV and the ADDES-3HV provide detailed information on processes used to select items for inclusion in the ADDES-2. Materials also provided by the publisher for this review included the Attention Deficit Disorders Intervention Manual—Second Edition (McCarney, 1994) and the Parent's Guide to Attention Deficit Disorders—Second Edition (McCarney & Bauer, 1995). Apparently, third editions of these materials are not yet available. Both the ADDES-3SV and the ADDES-3HV were standardized on a variety of age groups of both genders from several states representing every region of the United States. Other demographic characteristics include race, residence (metropolitan or nonmetropolitan), geographic area, mother's occupation, and father's occupation. The developers attempted to align the demographics of their sample with data from the 2000 U.S. Census. The developers report that the standardization sample included both youth with and without ADHD. The number of students in each category was not specified.

TECHNICAL. The technical manuals for each version of the ADDES-3 note that factor analytic evaluations establish the two distinct subscales of each instrument. Tables are provided noting the factor loadings for each item. These tables confirm the rationale for including different items into the different subscales although most items load at least marginally into both subscales. This is not surprising, of course, given that "a student demonstrating problems in one area of attention-deficit/hyperactivity disorder is likely to have problems in the other area, also" (ADDES-HV manual, p. 13). The subscales on each version are highly correlated (values range from .93 to .95) with the total score.

The reliability of the ADDES-3 is reported through methods of test-retest, interrater, and internal consistency. The developers tested sizeable samples on both version of the ADDES-3 for test-retest reliability. These youth were reevaluated 30 days after the first rating. Test-retest reliability was very strong ranging from .82 to .86 for the subscales and total scale on the Home Version and from .88 to .92 on the School Version. Evidence for interrater reliability is strong for both the Home and School Versions. The analyses were conducted by asking pairs of educators or parent/caregivers to rate single students. Coefficients for the School Version range from .78 to .85 for the subscales and total score and from .85 to .89 for the Home Version. The developers claim that the pairs of individuals who participated in this activity knew the student equally well although this criterion is not further defined. Internal consistency reliability data are strong for both versions of the ADDES-3. Coefficients reported for both subscales and total score for each version are all above .95. Overall, ample evidence is available to support the ADDES-3 scales' reliability. Despite these findings, it should be noted that the standard deviation for the total raw score is significantly higher for the School Version than for the Home Version (55.87 versus 34.07). Both educators' and parents'/caregivers' mean ratings per item were fairly low (HV = 1.81 and SV = 1.87). Thus their mean ratings per item were between *Not Observed,* and *One to Several Times per Month.* This finding seems to suggest that the students rated in the standardization sample demonstrated mild symptoms in general. Because data on the numbers of students with ADHD and without ADHD are not provided, one has to wonder if the majority of the sample consisted of students without ADHD. Equally crucial and lacking is information on the number of students with ADHD who were actively receiving treatment (e.g., medications or other interventions) for ADHD. Obviously, this is an important factor in the level of symptoms in ADHD students.

Both versions of the scale offer support of content, construct, and concurrent validity. Content validity for each of the instruments was established by the involvement of educational and diagnostic professionals who evaluated an initially large pool of items. This large number was reduced to the final number of items after the aforementioned experts agreed upon items that offered the "most educationally relevant indicators of behavior typically demonstrated by students with ADHD" (p. 16). Construct validity is strongly supported through factor analysis, subscale interrelationships, and item validity. The developers demonstrate concurrent validity by comparing scores on the ADDES-3HV with two subscale scores on the ADD-H Comprehensive Teacher's Rating Scale-Second Edition Parent Form (ACTeRS; Ullmann, Sleator, & Sprague, 2000), and with eight subscale scores on the Conners' Parent Rating Scale: Short Form (CPRS-R:S; Conners, 2001). The ADDES-3HV subscales of Hyperactive-Impulsive and Inattentive were moderately correlated with similar scales on the ACTeRS (Ullmann et al., 2000), *r*s = .76 to .78. The ADDES-3HV subscales were more highly correlated with the Cognitive Problems/Inattention and Hyperactivity subscales CPRS-R:S (Conners, 2001), *r*s = .83 to .93. It is interesting that the results of the comparisons with the other six subscales are not reported. One has to wonder what the other scales were and why the correlation was attempted in the first place. The above concurrent validity relationships were investigated with only 27 students. The ADDES-3SV has documented concurrent validity as well. Correlations with the ADD-H Comprehensive Teachers Rating Scale-Second Edition (ACTeRS) (Ullmann et al., 2000) ranged from .78 to .80, depending on the subscale. Similarly, correlations with eight of the subscales of the Conners' Teacher Rating Scale—Revised: Long Form (CTRS-R:L; Conners, 2001) were completed. Results of each of these comparisons are reported and indicate strong concurrent validity, *r*s = .82 or higher, with the appropriately matched subscales. These concurrent validity relationships were explored with 79 students. The School Version manual cites a study comparing 78 students from the norm group with 78 students with ADHD who "were receiving program services from school districts participating in the standardization activity" (p. 17). The description of this study provided in the manual seems to imply that the 78 students without ADHD were not otherwise a part of the standardization sample. The Home Version provides no data indicating any discriminant validity studies.

COMMENTARY. Significant concerns regarding the ADDES-3 scales exist. The concerns evolve not so much from reported data, which are supportive of use, but from data that are missing and crucial in the decision to use a rating scale in the assessment of ADHD. The developers of the ADDES-3 scales deserve to be commended on the production of scales that offer a comprehensive number of questions about symptoms of ADHD. Further, the scales have strengths in test-retest reliability, interrater reliability, and internal consistency reliability. Data are also sufficient for content validity, construct validity, and concurrent validity. Three significant problems exist with the

ADDES-3 scales. First, a lack of information on the number of students with ADHD in the standardization samples is particularly troublesome. Given the low means of ratings supplied on both scales, a hypothesis that asserts that few students with ADHD were included in the norm groups seems to be a reasonable possibility. Other instruments such as the ADHD Rating Scale-IV (Home and School Versions; DuPaul, Power, Anastopoulos, & Reid, 1998) have sizeable populations of students with ADHD included in their norm groups.

The second concern involves the valuable psychometric property of discriminant validity. In other words, does the instrument provide distinct scores when used to rate students with ADHD and those without ADHD. Support for this imperative property is limited at best. One study utilizing 78 students who apparently were not included in the norm group makes the use of the School Version tenuous at best.

The final concern involves the scoring criteria for each individual item. When a behavior is "not observed" it is to be rated as a 1. Such a system could result in a slightly elevated total placing the child into the ADHD range on either of the subscales and/or the total score. Why "not observed" and "not developmentally appropriate for age" cannot each receive the value of 0 is puzzling.

With the availability of the aforementioned ADHD-IV Rating Scale and other psychometrically sound measures such as the Behavior Assessment System for Children—Second Edition (BASC-2; Reynolds & Kamphaus, 2004), the Connors' Rating Scales—Revised (Conners, 2001), and others, the field of ADHD assessment is not limited to choosing less than psychometrically strong instruments.

SUMMARY. The ADDES-3 contains both Home and School Versions that have been renormed since the instrument was published as the ADDES-2 in 1994. Apparently only updated norms differentiate the latest version from the previous. The developers deserve credit for conducting studies to establish certain types of reliability and validity. The scales lack sufficient evidence of the important property of discriminant validity. One small comparison study of students with ADHD and those without ADHD is offered in the School Version. The study seems to have

utilized students with ADHD who were not in the norm group. Neither scale provides figures on the number of ADHD students included in the respective norm groups. Mean ratings for items on the Home Version were 1.81 and 1.87 for the School Version, possibly indicating that the norm sample contained few students with ADHD or those with very mild symptomology. With a variety of other more reliable and valid instruments available for the assessment of ADHD, neither the Home nor School current version of the ADDES is recommended at this time.

REVIEWER'S REFERENCES

Conners, C. K. (2001). Conners' Rating Scales—Revised. North Tonawanda, NY: Multi-Health Systems.
DuPaul, G. J., Power, T. J., Anastopoulos, A. D., & Reid, R. (1998). *ADHD Rating Scale-IV: Checklists, norms, and clinical interpretation.* New York: Guilford Press.
McCarney, S. B. (1995). The Attention Deficit Evaluation Scale (2nd ed.). Columbia, MO: Hawthorne Educational Services, Inc.
McCarney, S. B., & Bauer, A. M. (1995). *Parent's guide to attention deficit disorders* (2nd ed.). Columbia, MO: Hawthorne Educational Services, Inc.
Reynolds, C., & Kamphaus, R. (2004). Behavior Assessment System for Children (2nd ed.). Circle Pines, MN: American Guidance Service.
Ullmann, R. K., Sleator, E. K., & Sprague, R. L. (2000). *ACTeRS teacher, parent, and self-report forms manual* (2nd ed.). Champaign, IL: MetriTech, Inc.

[11]

The Autobiographical Memory Interview.

Purpose: "Provides an assessment of a subject's personal remote (retrograde) memory."
Population: Ages 18–80.
Publication Date: 1990.
Acronym: AMI.
Scores, 8: Personal Semantic (Childhood, Young Adult, Recent, Total), Autobiographical Incidents (Childhood, Young Adult, Recent, Total).
Administration: Individual.
Price Data, 2006: £84 per complete kit including manual (24 pages) and 25 scoring sheets; £104 per 50 scoring sheets.
Time: Untimed.
Comments: Semistructured interview format.
Authors: Michael Kopelman, Barbara Wilson, and Alan Baddeley.
Publisher: Harcourt Assessment [England].

Review of The Autobiographical Memory Interview by CAROLYN M. CALLAHAN, Commonwealth Professor of Education, University of Virginia, Charlottesville, VA:

DESCRIPTION. The Autobiographical Memory Interview (AMI) is a 52-item semistructured interview protocol to be used with hospitalized or institutionalized patients from the age of 18 onward who are experiencing memory loss as a result of injury or illness. The instrument measures personal remote or retrograde memory (loss of memory about facts or incidents that occurred prior to the trauma). It purports to help in understanding the nature of memory deficits exhibited, to allow for more adequate advice and counseling, and to provide guidance for therapy with those patients. In addition, the authors suggest the AMI may be used in research to investigate disassociation of retrograde and anterograde amnesia.

The items on the AMI are divided into three sections (Childhood, Young Adult, Recent Life). Each section includes questions requiring patients to recall facts from their personal lives during each of the three given time periods (Personal Semantic) and items requiring descriptions of specific incidents associated with that same time period (Autobiographical Incidents). Directions are given for scoring items according to correctness and specificity of the response yielding 8 scores (1 for each time period within Personal Semantic and Autobiographical Incidents, a total score for each category). Each score (out of a possible 21 on each scale) can be translated into a category of "acceptable" (within one standard deviation of the mean of scores of 34 healthy controls), "borderline" (one to two standard deviations below the mean), "probably abnormal" (more than two standard deviations below the mean), or "definitely abnormal" (no one in the sample scored below this point). The manual does not provide specific guidelines or restrictions regarding the qualifications for administration, scoring, or interpretation of the instrument. No estimate is given for the time necessary to administer the AMI.

DEVELOPMENT. No information is provided about the development of the scale (choice of items), selection of the individuals used to establish norms, or demographic characteristics of the norm group.

TECHNICAL. The items on this scale differ from those on other remote memory scales in calling for personal memories rather than knowledge of public events or familiar faces, thus reducing the potential for items to become dated. Directions for scoring the scales on the form are definitive for the Personal Semantic scale. The scoring of the autobiographical items is more open-ended with the instruction to award 3 points for "episodic memory, specific in time and place; two points for specific personal memory, in which time and place are not recalled, or for a less

specific event for which time and place are recalled; one point for a vague personal memory" (manual, p. 7). No points are given for no response or for responses that relate to semantic memory. Notably, the prompts included on the protocol do not probe time or place as would be expected given the scoring protocol, but rather probe people who might have been involved in the incident. The appendix includes examples of scoring. Scoring of items is dependent on the provision of "correct" information, which may or may not be verifiable by the examiner. The authors report that verification by relatives of the personal semantic responses given by 16 Korsakoff and 16 Alzheimer patients indicates that patients are accurate in about 90% of responses provided and conclude, "While it is clear some inaccuracy and confabulation occurs, the amount is small when compared to the deficit between patients and controls" (manual, p. 21). Talking to relatives or friends, checking for consistency in responses, and consulting the patient's records or conferring with hospital staff are suggested as means of verification.

The items reflect a British cultural bias and a generational bias. In some cases, alternate American options are provided, but in others they are not. For example, one item asks respondents to recall "Qualifications obtained after leaving school." And some items require unusual recall for full credit (e.g., the first and last name of an elementary school teacher or the date of birth of a relative's or close friend's child if one has not had children of one's own). Finally, the recent life section seems to include items that are post-trauma and reflect anterograde memory.

The categorizations of the scores into levels of normalcy in memory are based on only 34 "healthy subjects." No demographic data are available for the norm population nor for patients who have been otherwise documented as falling into the designated categories. No correlations were found between age and scores on the AMI, and thus, the same norms are used for all age groups. The AMI's purpose is to discriminate between healthy individuals and those with a range of clinical disorders ("organic amnesic syndrome, ...dementing disorders, ...and possibly various psychiatric disorders," manual, p. 5). The authors claim that the AMI has proved useful in differentiating amnesiacs from normal persons; however, the manual does not provide guidance in interpretation of scores beyond the chart for normalcy and does not provide interpretations of profiles that reflect differences across the varied life span periods or categories of memory.

The manual reports that three raters scored responses with correlations between pairs of testers ranging from .83 to .86. No information on the characteristics or qualifications of those raters is provided. An assertion is made by the authors that if the data are to be used for research purposes, it would be preferable to use a second rater–a troubling note because it presumes a need for "greater precision" (manual, p. 7) in research that runs counter to advice regarding decisions about patients. No stability estimates are provided.

The validity data include one study in which the scores of control subjects differed from those of patients (from a range of etiologies) on both the total Personal Semantic scale and the Autobiographical scale. In a second study, there were no significant correlations between the AMI and other measures of remote memory (the correlation between Personal Semantic Memory and Autobiographical Incident was .379) in a control group. Small, but significant correlations were found between the Personal Semantic scale and four other assessments of remote memory (coefficients ranged from .31 to .42) in a patient population, but only one small significant correlation ($r = .27$) of the Autobiographical incidents with other measures of remote memory was found. When the samples were combined, there were significant correlations between all assessments ($r = .28$ to $r = .93$). In addition, graphic information is provided to illustrate the expected decrease in scores on both the Personal Semantic and Autobiographical scores of Korsakoff patients.

COMMENTARY. The value of the AMI as a measure of remote personal memory is limited first by the lack of clear guidelines for use of the data provided and by the lack of systematic and comprehensive validity data that support the stated purposes of the instrument. Insufficient evidence supporting the underlying construct of memory to support the use of two distinct categories of memory assessed by the scales, the independence or meaningfulness of the life-span categories, and the lack of diagnostic guidance for interpretation of the scales make constructive use of the scales problematic.

SUMMARY. The AMI's interview protocols are easily administered and appear to be non-threatening. The interrater reliability is adequate; however, stability has not been documented sufficiently. Insufficient validity evidence supporting the use of the instrument for understanding the nature of memory deficits exhibited or for providing guidance in counseling or therapy for patients combined with questionable rationale for the creation of rating categories and interpretation of the scores seriously limits the usefulness of the instrument as a diagnostic tool.

Review of The Autobiographical Memory Interview by MICHAEL FURLONG, Professor and Chair, and DIANE TANIGAWA, Doctoral Candidate, Department of Counseling, Clinical, and School Psychology, University of California, Santa Barbara, CA:

DESCRIPTION. The Autobiographical Memory Interview (AMI) is a semistructured interview to assess retrograde memory for individuals ages 18 and older with conditions (e.g., Alzheimer's, Korsakoff syndrome) that impair memory related to the events and issues in a person's life. Respondents are asked to recall facts and events from three time periods of their personal life (childhood, early adult, and recent). Personal Semantic scores (total and three time-period subscale scores) are obtained for recollections of personal facts (e.g., address), and Autobiographical Incident scores (total and three time-period subscale scales) are obtained for the recollection of personal events (e.g., an incident that occurred during secondary school). Directions for administering and scoring the AMI include specific instructions for the administration and scoring of the Autobiographical Incidents Schedule section. Administration only requires the use of the examiner manual and the scoring sheet, which summarizes information to be solicited from the respondent. Scoring examples for the Autobiographical Incident Schedule section are provided in an appendix. Scores are interpreted as falling in one of four clinical ranges: Acceptable, Borderline, Probably Abnormal, and Definitely Abnormal.

DEVELOPMENT. The procedures used to develop the AMI are not thoroughly described in the brief manual, which reports that the AMI was created to address some of the limitations of other measures of retrograde memory. The objective was to obtain information in a simple and straightforward manner and to reduce test bias by having respondents recall personal recollections rather than information from a particular culture and time period, as is done with some other memory measures. The AMI's structure (assessment of Personal Semantic Memory and Autobiographical Memory across the three life periods) was fashioned to determine the degree to which respondents are able to generate memories from each phase of life and to permit comparisons between the AMI and other tests of semantic memory. The developers of the AMI highlight that assessing autobiographical memory aids in understanding the nature of the memory deficit as well as in providing suggestions for appropriate intervention.

TECHNICAL.

Norming. Criteria for all four clinical ranges (Acceptable, Borderline, Probably Abnormal, and Definitely Abnormal) were determined by examining the performance of 34 healthy controls. Scores fall in one of the four categories based on whether they are within ±1 *SD* of the mean, between -1 and -2 *SD* below the mean, -2 *SD* below the mean, and below any of the scores obtained from the healthy controls, respectively.

Interrater reliability. The AMI reports interrater reliability coefficients between .83 and .86. These estimates were derived by comparing scores provided by three judges who reviewed written descriptions of memories recalled. In addition, interjudge agreement is only one form of reliability that is needed; no information about the stability of ratings is provided.

Validity. The authors report more detailed information about the AMI's validity. Although based on small clinical samples, significant differences were found between amnesic patients and healthy controls in both total Personal Semantic score and total Autobiographical Incidents score. Recent research (e.g., Irish et al., 2006; Meeter, Eijsackers, & Mulder, 2006) found significant differences between amnesic patients and healthy controls on the AMI as well. No significant correlations were found between the AMI and other remote memory tests with normal individuals. However, significant correlations were found between the AMI and other remote memory tests involving amnesic patients and the total group

(combination of amnesic patients and normal individuals). Among amnesic patients, significant intercorrelations between the AMI and the other tests ranged from .22 to .42. Among the total group, significant intercorrelations between the AMI and the other tests ranged from .28 to .68.

The pattern of temporal gradients on the AMI for normal controls and amnesic patients was similar to the pattern of temporal gradients for normal controls and amnesic patients using another remote memory test. The developers only report on the accuracy of amnesic patients' responses to personal semantic items. Correlations between respondents' original scores and scores corrected after consulting with relatives were all greater than .87. Meeter et al. (2006) report a correlation of .93 between amnesic patients' original scores and scores obtained after consultation with spouses.

COMMENTARY.

Strengths. The AMI appears to be an adequate measure of autobiographical memory, and current literature supports its use as a tool in differentiating amnesic clients from normal controls. The AMI may be considered more cultural-free and time-free than other tests of remote memory because it requires respondents to recollect personal information rather than public knowledge from specific time periods. Clinicians and researchers will appreciate the structure of the AMI because it provides total scores and scores across three phases of life in Personal Semantic Memory and Autobiographical Memory. In addition, clinicians and researchers may find the AMI relatively easy to administer and score. Recently, AMI applications have been extended by researchers to include other clinical conditions that affect personal memory recall (e.g., depression and schizophrenia).

Weaknesses. Although the AMI is intended for those as young as 18 years of age, young adults may not have enough life experiences to answer items in the "early adulthood" section and answers to questions from the "recent" section may describe events that actually occurred during the young adults' "childhood" or "early adulthood." Future studies on the norming of the AMI should include a larger sample size because the current norms are based on only 34 healthy controls. Furthermore, the appropriateness of the norms for gender and ethnicity/culture was not discussed, and there is no evidence supporting the validity of the interpretation of scores. Although the interrater reliability for the AMI as a whole is reported, the interrater reliability for each subscale (Personal Semantic Schedule and Autobiographical Incidents Schedule) is not reported. Considering that the scoring procedure for the Autobiographical Incidents section employs qualitative standards, it is important for professionals and researchers to know the interrater reliability of this subscale. The statistical significance of the comparison between the pattern of temporal gradients produced by amnesic clients and normal controls on the AMI and another remote memory test is not reported. The developers of the AMI assert that the similarity of the patterns lends support to the validity of the AMI. Future studies investigating the pattern of temporal gradients with normal controls and amnesic patients on the AMI and other remote memory tests need to confirm this initial finding.

SUMMARY. The AMI provides an adequate measure of autobiographical memory. The AMI assesses Personal Semantic Memory (recollection of personal facts) and Autobiographical Memory (recollection of personal events) across three life periods: childhood, early adulthood, and recent. There are some technical weaknesses in the AMI, therefore, interpretations of scores and patterns of temporal gradients need to be made with caution. Nonetheless, the AMI is being used in various research studies and the manual would be greatly enhanced by updating it to include these recent developments. Despite these limitations, clinicians should find the knowledge gained from the AMI useful in understanding and intervening with their patients, and researchers should find it a valuable measure in assessing remote memory with various populations.

REVIEWERS' REFERENCES

Irish, M., Cunningham, C. J., Walsh, J. B., Coakley, D., Lawlor, B. A., Robertson, I. H., & Coen, R. F. (2006). Investigating the enhancing effect of music on autobiographical memory in mild Alzheimer's disease. *Dementia and Geriatric Cognitive Disorders, 22*, 108-120.
Meeter, M., Eijsackers, E. V., & Mulder, J. L. (2006). Retrograde amnesia for autobiographical memories and public events in mild and moderate Alzheimer's disease. *Journal of Clinical and Experimental Neuropsychology, 28*, 914-927.

[12]

The Balloons Test.

Purpose: "Designed to detect visual inattention following brain injury."
Population: Adults.
Publication Date: 1998.

Scores, 4: Total A, Total B, Generalized Inattention Index, Lateralized Inattention Index.
Administration: Individual.
Price Data, 2006: £130 per complete kit including manual, test cards, and 20 scoring sheets; £39.50 per 40 scoring sheets.
Time: [5–10] minutes.
Authors: Jennifer A. Edgeworth, Ian H. Robertson, and Thomas M. McMillan.
Publisher: Harcourt Assessment [England].

Review of The Balloons Test by MARY (RINA) M. CHITTOORAN, Associate Professor and Chair, Department of Educational Studies, Saint Louis University, St. Louis, MO:

DESCRIPTION. The Balloons Test is a simple screener that may be used to identify visual inattention in adults subsequent to brain injury. It also permits examiners to distinguish between problems related to attention and those stemming from visual field deficits. The test is designed to be used by clinicians; training needs for administration, scoring, and interpretation are minimal. There is no time limit specified, although most subjects in pilot studies completed the task in under 3 minutes.

Test materials, which are stored in a large, yellow plastic case, include a paperback 10-page manual, two tear-off pads of Stimulus Sheets A and B (each 11 1/2 inches by 16 1/2 inches), a laminated stimulus sheet for each subtest, and two plastic scoring templates, one each for Subtests A and B. Each stimulus sheet includes black line drawings of stylized balloons interspersed among circles. The back of Stimulus Sheet B includes an area to record subject performance in English as well as in 10 other European languages.

Pages 9 and 10 of the manual include brief instructions for administration, scoring, and interpretation. Test Takers are first administered Subtest A, which includes 22 target balloons and 180 distractors. After being given a brief sample, they are asked to cross off all the balloons they see in a 3-minute period, switching to a different color pen halfway through the task. Task demands for Subtest B, which includes 22 target circles and 180 distractors, are similar except that the participant crosses off circles, instead of balloons. Test takers are not permitted to move the stimulus sheet during either subtest.

Both quantitative and qualitative assessments of performance are available on the Balloons Test.

Three types of scores are obtained by simply counting the number of targets cancelled for each subtest; Total A is the number of targets cancelled on Subtest A, Total B is the number of targets cancelled on Subtest B, and Laterality B relates to the number of circles cancelled on the left of Subtest B expressed as a percentage of the total number of circles cancelled. The test also offers two indices of inattention. The Generalized Inattention Index is characterized by a Total B score less than 17; if the Total A score is greater than the Total B score, it is unlikely that the omissions are due only to visual field deficits. The Lateralized Inattention Index is a measure of unilateral deficits in visual attention and is characterized by a Total B score less than 17 and a Laterality B score less than 45%. Behavioral observations of performance can help identify left or right hemispheric lesions because affected patients exhibit distinct search patterns on visual perceptual tasks.

DEVELOPMENT. The Balloons Test is based on the work of Treisman and colleagues (Treisman & Gelade, 1980; Treisman & Gormican, 1988) in the area of perceptual "popout." The identification of certain types of targets (e.g., a small number of balloons that are interspersed among circles) is less difficult than the identification of a small number of target circles that are interspersed among balloons. Therefore, Subtest A is intended to serve as a control in that attentional demands during "serial search" are minimized. Subtest B, on the other hand, with its more complex task demands, serves as a measure of visual neglect. Differences in subtest performance are designed to help the examiner identify problems in visual attention as well as in peripheral vision.

TECHNICAL. Seventy-two patients with right cerebrovascular damage subsequent to stroke participated in the standardization and were assigned to either a visual neglect group (n = 39) or nonvisual neglect group (n = 33) based on their performance on another test of visual neglect, the Star Cancellation subtest of the Behavioural Inattention Test (BIT). Both groups of patients were then compared with a group of nonimpaired individuals (n = 55) whose performance on Subtest B provided normative data. Patients with brain damage were considered to have problems with visual attention and visual field detection if their score was lower than the lowest score of any control

subject on Subtest B (that is, lower than 17 or lower than 45% on Laterality B).

Both groups of patients as well as the control group were administered the Balloons Test; results of multivariate analyses of variance and post-hoc analyses revealed significant differences between the visual neglect and nonvisual neglect groups as well as between the patient and control groups.

Test-retest reliability was examined by administering Subtest B to 29 subjects on two occasions, with a mean retest interval of 7.7 days. Correlations of .64 and .71, respectively, were obtained for the Generalized Inattention Index and the Lateralized Inattention Index. Further, there was 83% agreement between the number of visual neglect cases identified across the two test administrations.

Concurrent validity of the Balloons Test as a measure of visual neglect was studied by examining the relationship (r = .78) between scores on the BIT's Star Cancellation subtest and the Balloons' Subtest B. Criterion-related validity was studied by examining the relationship between scores on the Balloons Test and caregiver ratings on the Catherine Berego Scale, which is a measure of functional difficulties associated with neglect; this yielded a correlation coefficient of .67.

COMMENTARY. The Balloons Test is founded in the research on visual-spatial attention and may be useful as a bedside screener for patients following brain injury. Administration, scoring, and interpretation are a simple matter and, indeed, the unusual nature of the tasks might be appealing to some test takers. The laminated stimulus sheets may be useful to examiners who are permitted by the publisher to photocopy them instead of having to order additional stimulus sheets from the publishing company. Finally, the inclusion of scoring sections in 10 languages is a rather nice addition to the test.

Despite its positive features, however, the Balloons Test has some rather undesirable features that outweigh its advantages. First, its theoretical foundations appear tenuous, given the research on which it is based. There is little published research about the link between visual inattention and the popout phenomenon; it is possible, therefore, that additional studies in this area could significantly limit the usefulness of the test. Efforts at test development, at least as described in the test manual, appear to be minimal. The standardization sample is limited, as it includes only 55 normal subjects, and there is no mention of subjects with visual-perceptual deficits, their race/ethnicity, or other demographic data. Further, normative data are scant, and there are no data on patients with left hemisphere damage. There has been some effort to establish reliability and validity but results are based on very small samples and obtained correlations are moderate.

The manual is flimsy and, because of its brevity, lacks important information. The stimulus sheets are large and rather unwieldy and do not lend themselves either to convenient storage or portability. Further, if the test is to be administered at a patient's bedside, as suggested, the size of the stimulus sheets and the thinness of the paper could pose further problems.

The instructions for Subtest A and B both have grammatical errors (e.g., referring to the subject, the manual states, "When the subject indicates they [sic] have understood...."). This kind of error appears several times in the instructions for both subtests. Also, the instructions on Subtest A state, "If the subject incorrectly reports they have completed the task before the end of the time limit" as opposed to, on Subtest B, "If the subjects report they have completed the task." Is one incorrect but the other one not? This is not entirely clear. The words "swap pens" in the instructions for administration may not be understood by everyone. Further, there is no guidance as to how examiners might interpret the search patterns of examinees. Although the ability to record in other languages is useful, it is unclear why this is included. One would assume that there would also be corresponding instructions in each of those 10 languages but there are not. What about evaluations of people who do not speak English?

The plastic scoring template for Subtest A, which is designed to be placed over the stimulus sheet so that the red balloons line up with the balloons on the stimulus sheet, do not line up exactly; neither does the template for Subtest B. It is not entirely clear (unless the examiner places the templates over the stimulus sheet, or refers back to the manual), which template belongs with which stimulus sheet. The manual ends rather abruptly after a brief discussion of scoring and interpretation. One nice addition might have been a section

on implications of results or interventions for subjects with particular test profiles.

SUMMARY. The Balloons Test appears to be one of the few published measures of its kind and, because it is rather easy to use, may serve a useful purpose as an initial assessment of visual inattention and neglect. It also may be useful if it is supplemented by other standardized measures of visual perception and if interpretations of results are made by experienced clinicians. On the other hand, the Balloons Test has a number of less than positive features that cannot be ignored and that preclude a positive recommendation.

REVIEWER'S REFERENCES

Treisman, A., & Gelade, G. (1980). A feature-integration theory of attention. *Cognitive Psychology, 12,* 97–136.
Treisman, A., & Gormican, S. (1988). Feature analysis in early vision: Evidence of search asymmetrics. *Psychological Review, 95,* 15–48.

Review of The Balloons Test by D. ASHLEY COHEN, Clinical Neuropsychologist, Forensic Psychologist, CogniMetrix (private practice), San Jose, CA:

DESCRIPTION. The Balloons Test is an individually administered screening measure for adults, designed to assist neuropsychologists and other clinicians in determining whether and to what extent a patient is experiencing visual inattention, or what is often termed "neglect" (e.g., left neglect from a right-sided cerebrovascular accident). The test also allows uncoupling of visual field defects that may be present in some of these persons, from any attentional problems they may be having. The Balloons Test can be used as a screening test or as a stand-alone brief measure, or it may be incorporated into a larger neuropsychological test battery.

This measure was first published in 1998 by the Thames Valley Test Company, Limited of Suffolk, England. It was sold initially in the United Kingdom and Europe, becoming more widely available in the United States when it began being offered through The Psychological Corporation, which is now owned by Harcourt Assessment.

The second author of The Balloons Test, Ian Robertson, is first author of the book, *Spatial Neglect: A Clinical Handbook for Diagnosis and Treatment* (Robertson & Halligan, 1999). Dr. Robertson is an internationally known expert in visual-spatial neglect and visuospatial disorders. He frequently emphasizes the importance of this area of knowledge by noting that unilateral neglect is both the most common and the most disruptive symptom occurring subsequent to right-sided cerebrovascular accident (CVA); yet it remains poorly understood, is often overlooked in clinical assessments, and very often has deleterious effects upon the patient's rehabilitation and recovery.

The test authors' preferred use of The Balloons Test is as a screening tool to determine if more in-depth testing for visual-spatial neglect is warranted. In the latter case the test developers recommend the Behavioural Inattention Test (BIT; Wilson, Cockburn, & Halligan, 1987). The BIT is a larger, more comprehensive assessment instrument, composed of six so-called "conventional" subtests (such as Figure Copying, Line Bisecting, and Letter Cancellation), along with nine "behavioral" subtests. The latter are similar to neuropsychological tests that are referred to as having "ecological validity," and draw on skills such as navigating a map, sorting coins, setting the time on a clock, and reading a magazine article, among others.

The Balloons Test kit contains a manual, Subtest A and B test forms (a scoring and summary form is printed on the back of the B sheet), two scoring keys, and two laminated master sheets.

Each of the two subtests uses a single sheet of A3 size paper, with an identical distribution of objects on each. In Subtest A, there are 10 target "balloons" (a circle with a line extending from the lower portion) interspersed among 90 plain circles, on both right and left sides of the large page. There are 22 balloon targets to be cancelled, among 202 total stimuli. Two of the balloons are in the midline of the paper and are used to demonstrate the task to the examinee. The patient's task is to locate and draw a line through each balloon within a 3-minute time period.

In Subtest B, there are 10 target circles scattered among 90 balloons, on either side of the midline. Here the patient is asked to ignore the balloon and instead to cancel out as many of the circles as can be found within a 3-minute time period. On both subtests, if the examinee reports that he or she is finished before time has expired, the person is instructed to continue searching until the examiner calls time. Also on both A and B, if some targets still remain at the end of 90 seconds, the examinee is handed a different colored pencil and told to continue searching.

Administration time is approximately 5 to 10 minutes. Scoring consists of counting the number of targets cancelled for both A and B subtests. The number of targets cancelled on the left side only of Sheet B derives a Laterality B index, a percentage of left side targets located, compared to the total number of cancelled targets.

Three scores may then be calculated: Total A, Total B, and Laterality B index. Interpretation is as follows:

1. Generalized Inattention Index. Patients with a Total B score of less than 17 have generalized visual inattention.

2. If Total A is higher than Total B, it is highly unlikely that omissions are attributable to peripheral visual (field) defects.

3. Lateralized Inattention Index. Patients with a Total B score of less than 17 and a Laterality B score of less than 45% have a left unilateral visual attention deficit. Examiners are also asked to record on which side of the page the patient begins to search for targets and whether the search is systematic or haphazard.

DEVELOPMENT. Unlike several currently available psychological measures, The Balloon Test was not developed merely from an apparently good idea formulated by the test authors. It is based upon a phenomenon long known in cognitive psychological research literature, called "perceptual pop-out." Detection of certain stimuli embedded within others that are sufficiently different (e.g., searching for 5 yellow rectangles scattered among a field of 50 black rectangles), involves parallel processing, such that the target is relatively easy to discern, no matter how many distractors are present; the yellow rectangles appear to "pop out" from their background. The time to find pop-out type targets is not extended as the number of distractors is increased. The above condition applies to Subtest A, making it the control trial.

By contrast, Subtest B requires serial searching, with the targets much more difficult to detect among their distractors (e.g., locating a few light gray pentagons among many light gray hexagons). Patients with neglect syndromes evidence much greater pathology when confronted with a task such as that in Subtest B. There are many studies in cognitive psychology demonstrating that serial search performance is far more impaired than parallel processing in persons with unilateral neglect.

Validation studies of The Balloons Test indicate that the test is particularly useful in a hard-to-diagnose group, that of partially recovered hemi-inattention patients who have learned to try to compensate for their difficulty by reminding themselves to scan the left side of a paper in front of them. They often believe they have overcome their problem, despite continued difficulty in daily life activities because of neglect. They still show as impaired on The Balloons Test if they continue to experience some level of visual neglect.

It should also be noted that The Balloons Test enables the examiner to rule out simple visual field defects as the cause of omissions on the patient's left side. Subtests A and B are similar, visually; when more errors are made on Subtest B than on A, this demonstrates that the problem may be neglect, not a primary visual field defect. The test authors believe that enforcing a time limit on examinees is important because it reduces the likelihood of false positives, which are often caused by persons who prematurely stop working on a test because of feeling discouraged, fatigued, or some other factor unrelated to spatial inattention.

TECHNICAL.

Standardization. There was a fairly small normative population used in test standardization, comprising 72 right hand dominant individuals with a recent right-sided CVA (confirmed by CT scan), and 55 persons (outpatient rheumatology patients) with no brain injury. The entire normative sample was drawn from the United Kingdom.

Gender ratio was essentially equal, with 52.7% males; neither were there significant differences between the experimental and control groups in terms of age, or time since CVA. Ethnicity was not specified. Standardization subjects were largely older adults (mean = 66.9 years). The precise age ranges of subjects in each group were not specified.

Reliability. Only one type of reliability was calculated, test-retest reliability. Over an interval of approximately 1 week, correlations were reasonably strong for both primary indices—.64 and .71 for the Generalized Inattention Index and Lateralized Inattention Index, respectively. The percentage of individuals with visual neglect who were correctly identified across the first and second test administration was 83%.

Validity. Construct validity was established with the finding of a strong correlation (.78) between The Balloons Test results and a cancellation task from the BIT. The authors further compared performance on The Balloons Test with findings from a published questionnaire assessing ratings of functional neglect made by intimates of the patient. The resultant correlation coefficient was .67.

The authors also made an effort to link the results of their test with real world performance and patient problems, an attempt to demonstrate ecological validity. They acknowledge that the Behavioural Inattention Test is a more robust resource for measuring this factor.

COMMENTARY. The test authors assert that The Balloons Test is superior to other screening tests for visuospatial neglect, and this reviewer concurs. Their unique incorporation of time limits helps factor out mere lack of sustained general attention, as well as minimizing any possible interference from motivational or emotional matters. The test was designed to reduce false positives. The Balloons Test yields a clear pattern of scores when a patient has unilateral inattention.

The task itself is not objectionable for test takers; it is not confrontational, nor overly personal in nature. No distinct social or cultural understandings are required. The entire test is so brief the examinee will not show a drop off in performance because of motor or mental fatigue. Neither will the examiner become exhausted with intricate scoring, or calculating of complex indices. Scoring is straightforward and simple, and the rules for deriving indices are clear.

There are very detailed, sequential administration instructions, giving both wording of the test instructions to the examinee, and explanations for the examiner. There are also several helpful suggestions addressing how to manage misunderstandings or forgetfulness on the part of the patient. The scoring overlay sheets fit the test forms amazingly well, requiring only minor adjustments to match them with the test sheets below.

Although the authors caution that administering the test at bedside is not ideal, instructions for giving the test in this setting are supplied, which is a nice nod to reality in many settings in which neuropsychologists work. Similarly, although the examiner is urged to purchase more testing sheets when the kit is emptied, the manual contains detailed instructions for photocopying more sheets for oneself, if desired, and two useful laminated templates are included for this purpose.

There was a clear description of the authors' criteria for how they formed their experimental groups, and statistics showed that all three groups were well separated. For example, the status of the CVA patients was independently determined through use of brain imaging, thus excluding a large source of messy variance that surrounds erroneous self-report, possible inaccurate recollection by the patient, and faulty assessment by family members. Other potential confounds were eliminated when it was found that factors such as age and gender did not yield significant differences.

The few negatives coming to the attention of this reviewer were relatively trivial. The "A" and "B" cards were not marked, and this was confusing when first examining the test. The total number of standardization subjects was low, particularly as they are divided into three groups. The fact that all the control group subjects were outpatient individuals with a particular condition (some form of rheumatic disease) may be a difficulty. This reviewer would have liked to see a control group of inpatients as well as outpatient controls and patients with one or two other disease types.

SUMMARY. In the opinion of this reviewer, The Balloons Test is a solid, fairly simple, but genuinely useful short test for visuospatial inattention. It is based upon theory and findings from cognitive psychology and from perceptual processing research. Several possible confounds were eliminated (age, gender, time since CVA, the presence of ordinary visual inattention, or visual field defects), making test results all the more credible. Variations in patient motivation are also controlled to some extent by the use of timed subtests, in which the patient cannot stop too early nor work indefinitely. The instructions are readily understood by patients, even those with impaired intellectual abilities, and examinees do not find the test unpleasant. Neither is The Balloons Test a major administration chore for the examiner, not in time, techniques of administration, nor in scoring and interpretation. Clear cutoff scores are provided for determining the presence or absence of inattention, and if so present, whether it is generalized or lateralized inattention. The Balloons Test should be a welcome addition to a neuropsychologist's armamentarium.

REVIEWER'S REFERENCES

Robertson, I. H., & Halligan, P. W. (1999). *Spatial neglect: A clinical handbook for diagnosis and treatment.* East Sussex, U.K: Psychology Press.
Wilson, B., Cockburn, J., & Halligan, P. W. (1987). *Behavioural Inattention Test.* Bury St. Edmunds, UK: Thames Valley Test Company.

[13]
Basic Achievement Skills Inventory.

Purpose: Designed "to measure reading, written language, and math skills among children and adults."
Population: Grades 3 & 4, 5 & 6, 7 & 8, 9–12, and ages 8 to 80.
Publication Date: 2004.
Acronym: BASI.
Administration: Individual or group.
Tests, 2: Comprehensive, Survey.
Price Data, 2007: $115 per Comprehensive starter kit including manual (382 pages), 1 test booklet for each level (Levels 1–4, Forms A and B), and 12 hand-scored answer sheets (3 for each level); $185 per Mail-in Scoring Service Comprehensive starter kit with Student Summary Report, includes same materials as hand-scored starter kit but with scannable answer sheets; $160 per Q Local Comprehensive starter kit with Student Summary Report, includes same materials as hand-scored starter kit but with scannable answer sheets and 12 Q Local administrations, which require separate purchase of Q Local Software of $89 (desktop version) or $250 (network version) annual license fee; $55 per Survey starter kit including manual (146 pages), 1 test booklet (Math and Verbal), and 3 hand-scored answer sheets; $65 per Q Local Survey starter kit with Summary Report, includes same materials as hand-scored starter kit but with scannable answer sheets, and 12 Q Local administrations, which require separate purchase of Q Local Software; quantity discounts available for the reports.
Comments: Form A is for August–December testing; Form B is for January–July testing.
Author: Achilles N. Bardos.
Publisher: Pearson.

a) BASI COMPREHENSIVE.
Population: Grades 3 & 4, 5 & 6, 7 & 8, 9–12.
Scores, 9: Reading (Vocabulary, Reading Comprehension, Total), Written Language (Spelling, Language Mechanics, Total), Math (Math Comprehension, Math Application, Total).
Subtests, 6: Vocabulary, Spelling, Language Mechanics, Reading Comprehension, Math Computation, Math Application.
Levels, 4: Grades 3 & 4, Grades 5 & 6, Grades 7 & 8, Grades 9–12.
Forms, 2: A, B at each level.
Time: 115 minutes.
b) BASI SURVEY.
Population: Ages 8 to 80.
Scores, 7: Verbal Skills (Vocabulary, Language Mechanics, Reading Comprehension, Total), Math Skills (Math Computation, Math Application, Total).
Subtests, 2: Verbal Skills, Math Skills.

Price Data: $36.05 per 10 test booklets (Math and Verbal).

Time: 50 minutes.

Comments: Brief version of the Comprehensive Test.

Review of the Basic Achievement Skills Inventory by ELIZABETH KELLEY RHOADES, Associate Professor of Psychology at West Texas A&M University, Canyon, TX:

DESCRIPTION. The Basic Achievement Skills Inventory (BASI) is a norm-referenced, group-administered achievement test series. There is a Comprehensive version and a briefer Survey version. The Comprehensive version consists of six subtests (Vocabulary, Spelling, Language Mechanics, Reading Comprehension, Math Computation, and Math Calculation) in four levels (Level 1 for Grades 3–4, Level 2 for Grades 5–6, Level 3 for Grades 7–8, and Level 4 for Grades 9–12). Based on these six subtests, three composite scores are obtained (Written Language, Reading, and Math). The six subtests take 115 minutes to complete. The test uses the familiar multiple-choice format common to many group-administered achievement tests.

The test author describes a number of recommended uses for the Comprehensive version of the test, some of which are: Diagnosing learning disabilities in reading, written expression, and math; evaluating students for gifted programs; placing college students; practicing for or predicting performance on a high-stakes test; efficiently completing triennial evaluations for students with an IEP or 504 plan; and identifying a child's or adult's academic strengths and weaknesses.

The Survey version has two subtests, a general Verbal Skills, which includes Vocabulary, Language Mechanics, and Reading Comprehension items, and a general Math Skills with questions on Math Calculation and Math Application. Each of these Survey tests takes 25 minutes to administer.

Norms for the Comprehensive version are included for individuals in Grades 3 through 12. Each level has a Form A with fall norms and Form B with spring norms. Norms for the Survey version are for ages 8 to 80 years.

DEVELOPMENT. Development of the BASI began with the construction of a test blueprint that was compared to a database of local, state, and national educational standards. This blueprint led to the creation of achievement area standards for each Comprehensive subtest at each level. These matrices are included in the test manual. The initial item pool included 2,665 items authored by teachers in the appropriate content areas. Items were further reviewed by content experts and pilot tested. Final item selection was based on item analyses statistics.

TECHNICAL. The test standardization occurred during the 2002–2003 academic year and was matched to the 2000 U.S. Census using a sample stratified based upon gender, race/ethnicity, parental education, and geographic region. The standardization included 2,439 children in Grades 3 through 12 for Form A and 2,130 children for Form B. The results of each individual in the standardization sample were weighted to ensure a closer match to the U.S. Census.

The test author chose to examine the measure's reliability through measures of internal consistency, test-retest performance, and alternate-forms reliability. Measures of internal consistency were calculated for each subtest at each level for both forms of the Comprehensive test. Alpha coefficients ranged from a low of .69 to a high of .96 for individual subtest scores. Composite score coefficients were naturally higher, ranging from .83 to .98. Test-retest data were provided only for Levels 1, 2, and 3. After a 2-week interval, test-retest stability coefficients ranged from .54 to .89 for individual subtests and .70 to .92 for the composite scores. Alternate-forms reliability was examined for Levels 1, 2, and 3 by having a small sample of students take the Form B test during the week after having taken the Form A test. Alternate-forms reliability coefficients ranged from .57 to .80 for the individual subtests and .67 to .87 for the composite scores.

Validity studies compared the BASI with other group-administered achievement tests. Level 1, 2, and 3 results were compared to the Iowa Test of Basic Skills (ITBS) for a sample of 184 students. Correlation coefficients ranged from a low of .14 to a high of .60 across subtests. Correlations were not necessarily strong when comparing subtests purporting to measure the same concepts although they were generally higher for the higher grade ranges. For example, at Level 1 the Math Computation subtests on the two measures had a correlation of only .34 although this value was considerably higher, .59, for Level 3. Level 4

BASI results were compared to the Iowa Tests of Educational Development (ITED) with resulting correlation coefficients of .34 to .80 across subtests with fairly strong results across subtests that attempted to measure similar fields. For example, Vocabulary subtests on the two measures correlated .80. BASI Level 4 Form A results were compared to the Tests of Adult Basic Education (TABE) for a sample of 40 high school students. Individual subtest correlations ranged from .17 to .72, not uniformly particularly strong correlations between subtests measuring similar constructs. For example, the two Reading Comprehension subtests correlated only .49. The two Math composite scores correlated only .54. Another study compared BASI Level 4 Form B and TABE results on a sample of 161 high school students. Results were similar to the study on Form A. Reading Comprehension subtests across the two measures correlated at only .37, and Math composite scores correlated at only .45.

A study of BASI Comprehensive Test results were compared to BASI Survey test results for a sample of 1,500 students. Correlations between Comprehensive and Survey scores in the same skill areas were not strong overall, ranging from .30 in Math Application for Level 1 Form B to .65 in Vocabulary for Level 4 Form A. Modest correlations were found with the WIAT-II, again with surprisingly low correlations across similar content. For example, the Reading Comprehension subtests correlated only .45 and the Math composite scores only .57. Similar results were found with comparisons to the Woodcock-Johnson Psychoeducational Battery III. Reading Vocabulary subtests correlated only at .44 and Math Calculation at .60. No examination of predictive validity was provided.

COMMENTARY. The BASI Comprehensive version is a group-administered achievement test with norms for Grades 3 through 12. As such, the Comprehensive version appears to have relatively good testing materials, a useful and informative manual, and some adequate psychometric characteristics. It could prove useful for making group analyses of school performance in the tested domains and broad judgments about educational achievement. The Survey version is not recommended.

However, the BASI is not recommended for use in several of the areas that are recommended in the manual. First, although the test manual reports that the BASI may be used as an individually administered test, there is neither data nor standardization for this approach and it is therefore not recommended. The test does not have sufficient psychometric strength to be used for individual assessment of learning disabilities or giftedness. The subtests lack sufficiently low items (floors) to provide valid assessment of disability, and there are insufficient high or challenging items (ceilings) to assess academic giftedness, particularly in older students.

Although the test materials say that the test may be used with adults and for college placement decisions, this use is also not recommended. The Comprehensive version of this test lacks standardization and norms for an adult population. There is no evidence of appropriate use for individuals beyond Grade 12.

SUMMARY. The BASI is a group-administered test that broadly measures academic achievement in Grades 3 through 12. The Comprehensive version appears adequate for making broad, group-based analyses of academic performance of children at these grade levels. It is not recommended for making individual or high-stakes decisions or use with adults.

Review of the Basic Achievement Skills Inventory by MICHAEL S. TREVISAN, Professor, Educational Psychology, Washington State University, Pullman, WA:

DESCRIPTION. The Basic Achievement Skills Inventory (BASI) is a standardized, norm-referenced achievement test that assesses Reading, Written Language, and Mathematics. The test has four levels spanning Grades 3–12. Each level has two forms. Form A was normed in the fall and Form B was normed in the spring. All tests are composed of multiple-choice items.

There are two versions of the test: Comprehensive and Survey. The Comprehensive version has six subtests across academic subjects and takes slightly less than 2 hours to administer. The Survey version has two tests, each requiring 25 minutes to administer. For both versions, the subtests can be administered in any order.

The developers recommend use of the BASI for student placement, program evaluation, and assessment of educational achievement. Both versions have norms for students in Grades 3–12.

The Survey test also has adult norms. One of the key advantages offered by the developers is the ease with which the BASI can be used. In addition to relatively short administration requirements, each version of the BASI can be administered individually or in a group. There is a variety of scoring options that include scoring by hand or by computer. Percentile ranks, grade and age equivalents, and standard scores are available for each version of the BASI. To enhance interpretation, confidence interval estimates are also provided. In addition, the authors offer the BASI for those desiring criterion-referenced information. In this case, tests may be administered in an untimed manner. Percentage correct scores are recommended for interpretation.

DEVELOPMENT. The BASI is a relatively new test battery, having been first published in 2004. The norms were obtained during the 2002–2003 school year, and initial development and item writing started in the spring of 2001. Curriculum experts, educators, and item writers were employed in the test development. Items were piloted during 2001 and 2002.

The content of the BASI subtests was based on curriculum standards obtained from the Model Curriculum and Assessment Database (MCAD). According to the manual for the BASI Comprehensive Test, the standards "are an amalgamation of the 'best-of-the-best' local, state, and national U.S. educational standards" (p. 3). MCAD was also used in the development of the BASI Survey test. Content descriptions are well presented and articulated in the manual for each version.

TECHNICAL. A stratified random sampling approach was used to obtain the norming sample, incorporating important demographic variables with the intent of matching the U.S. 2000 Census. The norming window is quite wide, with Form A being normed in Fall 2002 and Form B in Spring 2003. No start or end dates were identified.

The developers provide a variety of reliability data including internal consistency, test-retest, and alternative forms for the BASI Comprehensive test. The internal consistency measures using coefficient alpha, show generally high consistency across forms, grades, and subtests. Most reliability estimates are above .80.

To gauge the stability of scores over time, test-retest reliability estimates were computed by correlating a first and second testing for the same group of students, with 2 weeks between testings. These estimates were obtained for Form A only and Levels 1–3 only. No explanation for this approach was provided. Although based on relatively small samples, test-retest reliability estimates were fairly strong, with most above .70. These results suggest scores on the BASI are fairly stable over time.

With regard to equivalence, the developers correlated scores on Form A with Form B for the same group of students for Levels 1–3. Most estimates were modest to fairly high.

Two types of validity evidence were provided: content and construct validity. For content validity, a test blueprint was used and conventional item writing standards employed. Not mentioned nor built into the test blueprint are the kinds of thinking skills assessed by the items. Subtests for the Comprehensive version of the test in Mathematics, for example, are referred to as Computation and Application, respectively. Likewise, Spelling, Vocabulary, Language Mechanics, and Reading Comprehension are labels applied to subtests in Reading and Written Language.

For construct validity, intercorrelations between subtests of the BASI Comprehensive Levels 1–3, and selected commercially available group- and individually administered tests were obtained. The group-administered tests include the Iowa Tests of Basic Skills, Iowa Tests of Educational Development, and the Tests of Adult Basic Education. The individually administered tests include the Wechsler Individual Achievement Test II and the Woodcock-Johnson Psychoeducational Battery III. Correlations range from low to high. The preponderance of evidence suggests a relationship between the BASI and the achievement tests listed. In some cases, the sample sizes of students used to correlate the BASI with another test were small, likely producing unstable correlations and, therefore, somewhat uncertain validity data.

The developers also presented data from special education and bilingual education students, suggesting the appropriate use of the BASI with these students. No other discussion or presentation of validity data was provided. The authors cite and briefly discuss the *Standards for Educational and Psychological Testing* (AERA, APA, & NCME, 1999), implying that the *Standards* were considered in the test development process.

COMMENTARY. The developers provided test manuals that were professionally done and indicate that much of the development of the BASI followed test industry standards. It is clear that the test was built with great care and professionalism. The developers offer the BASI for wide use and it is in such use, however, where problems occur for the following reasons. First, the norming for each form used a testing window across several months. For Form A, students tested in the same grade in December, for example, presumably have acquired more of the content than students in August of the same year, although this is the testing window recommended by the developers. The same logic can be applied from January to July, the testing window for Form B. Thus, the accuracy of the norms is in question. Second, Level 4 reflects Grades 9–12. That is, when using the BASI, any high school student would take the same level or form. Creating BASI test Level 4 in this way stretches the content domain so thin that it is likely unreasonable to make judgments about student achievement at any one grade level. Third, the development of the BASI was based on curriculum standards and is reflected in test specifications or blueprints in the manual. What are disregarded in the specifications are the thinking skills involved in any one content domain or subtest. Thus, it is not possible to determine student achievement based on higher order thinking skills specific to a particular content domain, skills that presumably most states now expect, given recent state and national education reform policies. This lack decreases the usefulness of the test for assessment of student achievement in particular, a specific use articulated in the manual. Fourth, the developers offer the BASI for criterion-referenced purposes. The practice of offering a norm-referenced test for criterion-referenced purposes is not uncommon with nationally standardized achievement tests. However, given the wide norming window for each form, the fact that all high school grades take the same test level, and that there is no differentiation of relevant thinking skills, the use of the BASI for criterion-referenced purposes cannot be recommended for high school students. There are simply not enough differentiated items within level to make good judgments about student achievement. Caution is recommended for use at earlier grades.

With regard to validity evidence, the developers used logical strategies for constructing these achievement tests, strategies with substantive relevance and historical precedence (i.e., content validity and intercorrelations with other tests). The developers argue that validity is an ongoing process with test development. This reviewer agrees and as such, suggests taking the validity argument a step further and developing a validity framework as recommended by validity theorists (e.g., Shepard, 1993). This framework could include the results from tested hypotheses. Although no simple undertaking, a positive outcome would be that users would have better information to judge appropriate use, and developers would have more solid data with which to market the test.

SUMMARY. The BASI is professionally developed and forms the basis for a potentially useful achievement test. The test, however, is offered for much too wide a use given its current state. This reviewer can recommend, with caution, Levels 1–3 for norm-referenced use (given the wide and unspecified norming window). This reviewer also recommends the criterion-referenced use, again with caution and reasoned judgment, also for Levels 1–3 (given the lack of detail concerning thinking skills at the item level). At this time, use of Level 4 for Grades 9–12 is not recommended.

REVIEWER'S REFERENCES

American Educational Research Association, American Psychological Association, & National Council on Measurement in Education. (1999). *Standards for educational and psychological testing*. Washington, DC: American Educational Research Association.

Shepard, L. A. (1993). Evaluating test validity. In L. Darling-Hammond & J. A. Banks (Eds.), *Review of research in education* (pp. 405-450). Washington, DC: American Educational Research Association.

[14]

Batería III Woodcock-Muñoz.

Purpose: Designed to "measure intellectual abilities and academic achievement" in Spanish-speaking individuals.

Population: Ages 2–90+.

Publication Dates: 1982–2007.

Acronym: Batería III.

Administration: Individual.

Price Data, 2007: $1,283 per complete Batería III with 2 carrying cases including Cognitive Standard and Extended test books, examiner's manual (2005, 158 pages), examiner's training workbook, audio recording, 25 test records and subject response booklets, 5 BIA test records, scoring guides, Achievement Standard and Extended test books, examiner's manual (2005, 180 pages), examiner's training workbook, audio recording,

25 test records and subject response booklets, WJ III NU Compuscore® and Profiles Program, and scoring guides; $799 per Batería III Cognitive Battery with carrying case including Cognitive Standard and Extended test books, examiner's manual, examiner's training workbook, audio recording, 25 test records and subject response booklets, 5 BIA test records, WJ III NU Compuscore and Profiles Program, and scoring guides; $374 per Diagnostic Supplement including test book, examiner's manual (2005, 151 pages), 25 test records, audio recording, WJ III NU Compuscore and Profile Program, and scoring guides; $597 per Batería III Achievement Battery with carrying case including Achievement Standard and Extended test books, examiner's manual, examiner's training workbook, audio recording, 25 test records and subject response booklets, WJ III NU Compuscore and Profiles Program, and scoring guides.

Foreign Language Editions: All of the materials are in Spanish including the examiner's manuals and the technical manual.

Time: (5–10) minutes per test.

Comments: The Batería III Woodcock-Muñoz is the parallel Spanish adaption/translation of the Woodcock-Johnson III (15:281).

Authors: Ana F. Muñoz-Sandoval, Richard W. Woodcock, Kevin S. McGrew, and Nancy Mather (test); Fredrick A. Schrank, Kevin S. McGrew, Mary L. Ruef, Criselda G. Alvarado, Ana F. Muñoz-Sandoval, and Richard W. Woodcock (manual).

Publisher: Riverside Publishing.

a) PRUEBAS DE HABILIDADES COGNITIVAS (Tests of Cognitive Abilities).

Acronym: Batería III COG.

Scores: 20 tests: Standard Battery (Comprensión Verbal, Aprendizaje Visual-Auditivo, Relaciones Espaciales, Integración de Sonidos, Formación de Conceptos, Pareo Visual, Inversión de Números, Palabras Incompletas, Memoria de Trabajo Auditiva, Memoria Diferida—Aprendizaje Visual-Auditivo), Extended Battery (Información General, Fluidez de Recuperación, Reconocimiento de Dibujos, Atención Auditiva, Análisis-Síntesis, Rapidez en la Decisión, Memoria Para Palabras, Rapidez en la Idenificación de Dibujos, Planeamiento, Cancelación de Pares).

1) *Suplemento Diagnóstico (Diagnostic Supplement).*

Acronym: Batería III SD.

Scores: 11 tests: Memoria Para Nombres, Integración Visual, Configuración de Sonidos—Vocalizada, Series Numéricas, Números Matrices, Tachar, Memoria Para Frases, Rotación de Bloques, Configuración de Sonidos—Musical, Memoria Diferida—Memoria Para Nombes, Comprensión Verbal Bilingüe—Español/Inglés.

b) PRUEBAS DE APROVECHAMIENTO (Tests of Achievement).

Acronym: Batería III APROV.

Scores: 22 tests: Standard Battery (Identificación de Letras y Palabras, Fluidez en la Lectura, Rememoración de Cuentos, Comprensión de Indicaciones, Cálculo, Fluidez en Matemáticas, Ortografiá, Fluidez en la Escritura, Comprensión de Textos, Problemas Aplicados, Muestras de Redacción, Memoria Diferida—Rememoración de Cuentos), Extended Battery (Análisis de Palabras, Vocabulario Sobre Dibujos, Comprensión Oral, Corrección de Textos, Vocabulario de Lectura, Conceptos Cuantitativos, Conocimientos Academicos, Análisis de Sonidos, Discernimiento de Sonidos, Puntuación y Mayúsculas.

Cross References: For reviews by Robert B. Frary and Maria Prendes Lintel of a previous edition, see 13:27; for reviews by Jack A. Cummings and by Steven W. Lee and Elaine Flory Stefany of the Woodcock-Johnson Psycho-Educational Battery—Revised, see 12:415 (36 references); see also T4:2973 (90 references) and T3:2639 (3 references); for reviews by Jack A. Cummings and Alan S. Kaufman of an earlier edition of the Woodcock-Johnson Psycho-Educational Battery, see 9:1387 (6 references).

Review of the Batería III Woodcock-Muñoz by BETH DOLL, Professor of Educational Psychology, and COURTNEY LeCLAIR, Doctoral Student in Educational Psychology, University of Nebraska-Lincoln, Lincoln, NE:

DESCRIPTION. The Batería III Woodcock-Muñoz (Batería III) is the Spanish-language version of the Woodcock-Johnson III (WJ III; Woodcock, McGrew, & Mather, 2001; 15:281) and is composed of the Pruebas de Habilidades Cognitivas (Batería III COG; parallel to the WJ III Tests of Cognitive Abilities) and the Pruebas de Aprovechamiento (Batería III APROV; parallel to the WJ III Tests of Achievement). It is designed to provide a comprehensive, norm-referenced, individual assessment of general cognitive ability and academic knowledge for individuals who speak Spanish. All tests of the Batería III have either been translated or adapted from the WJ III, and the four Batería III manuals are direct translations of the English WJ III manuals: the Tests of Cognitive Abilities examiner's manual, the WJ III Diagnostic Supplement examiner's manual, the WJ III Tests of Achievement examiner's manual, and the WJ III technical manual. For further information regarding characteristics of the WJ III, and the theory underlying its development, the reader may consult reviews of the WJ III by Cizek (2003) and Sandoval (2003), and reviews of the WJ III Diagnostic Supplement to the Tests of Cognitive Abilities by Sares (2005) and Thompson (2005).

Like the WJ III, The Batería III kits include both the Standard and Extended Batteries. Tests within each battery may be selectively administered based on assessment needs. In total, the Batería III COG contains 20 tests; the Standard Battery of the Batería III COG consists of 10 tests (e.g., Relaciones Espaciales, Pareo Visual, Palabras Incompletas, Comprensión Verbal), and the Extended Battery includes 10 additional tests (e.g., Atención Auditiva, Rapidez en la Decisión, Planeamiento). A diagnostic supplement to the Batería III COG, the Suplemento Diagnóstico para las Pruebas de Habilidades Cognitivas (Batería III SD), is also available as an extension to the Batería COG to provide an additional 11 tests. The Batería III APROV consists of 22 total tests. The standard battery of the Batería III APROV includes 12 tests (e.g., Fluidez en la Lectura, Cálculo, Ortografía) and a Handwriting Evaluation scale. The extended battery includes 10 additional tests (e.g., Comprensión Oral, Análisis de Sonidos, and Vocabulario Sobre Dibujos). The Batería III record form includes a Spanish translation of the Language Exposure and Use Questionnaire to assess the individual's prior exposure to and current use of primary and secondary languages.

The total Batería III can be administered to Spanish-speaking individuals aged 5 to 90+ years; portions can be administered to individuals as young as 2 years old. Each test takes an average of 5–10 minutes to administer. Administration of the Batería III follows the WJ III guidelines, although Batería III examiners must be fluent in Spanish. Results can be hand-scored, or scores can be computed using the Batería III Compuscore and Profiles program that is included with the kit. Like the WJ III, the Batería III yields raw scores, standard scores, grade and age equivalents, percentile ranks, W scores, Relative Proficiency Index (RPI), Instructional Zones, Cognitive Academic Language Proficiency (CALP levels), and discrepancy scores for tests and clusters of the Cognitive and Achievement batteries. Scores can be used to examine two types of discrepancies: discrepancies between individuals' cognitive ability and their academic achievement (ability-achievement), and discrepancies in achievement in different academic skills (intra-achievement). If both the WJ III and the Batería III have been administered, a Comparative Language Index (CLI) can be derived to compare an individual's scores for the oral language, broad reading, and written language clusters as an index of his or her relative proficiency in the two languages.

DEVELOPMENT. The Batería III was developed from the WJ III and from earlier editions of the Batería including the Batería Woodcock Psico-Educativa en Español (Woodcock, 1982) and the Batería Woodcock-Muñoz—Revisada (Woodcock & Muñoz-Sandoval, 1996). Like the WJ III, the Batería III is based on the Cattell-Horn-Carroll (CHC) model of cognitive abilities, a theory that merged Horn and Cattell's development of the Gf-Gc theory of fluid and crystallized intelligence with Carroll's theory of hierarchical cognitive ability (Carroll, 1997). Most items and instructions for the Batería III are direct translations from the WJ III; for these items, stimuli were exactly the same, and directions were simply translated into Spanish. Examples of tests that were directly translated included the visual-spatial thinking, quantitative ability, fluid reasoning, and processing speed subtests. When the shift in language would alter the nature or difficulty of a task, subtests were adapted from the WJ III. In these instances, items were changed, but the general measurement concept remained the same. Examples of subtests that required adaptation included the comprehension-knowledge, auditory, long-term retrieval, short-term memory, oral language, reading, and writing tests.

Many translated and adapted items on the Batería III had been used in the two previous versions of the Batería. The original Batería translation was developed by professional translators who were native speakers of Spanish, and the first revision was developed in consultation with Spanish linguists and a Spanish translation expert. This tradition continued with the Batería III, for which the author of the test consulted closely with two professional translators who were native speakers of Spanish. Subsequently, critical feedback on the translation and item adaptation was secured from Batería III standardization examiners who were native speakers from diverse Spanish-speaking countries. Still, despite the careful attention that was given to the item translation, it is not clear what procedures were used to verify the translation. Neither is there evidence that the translation was systematically verified across the many dialects of Spanish that are spoken in the United States. Examiners who use the Batería III should be aware that linguistic terms and conventions can vary substantially depending upon a family's country of origin and language history, and some errors on test items could be due to confusing language. Finally, even though items were translated into Spanish, the cultural knowledge underlying a few items reflects history specific to the United States and similar culture including items asking about cultural icons and holidays in the United States and about Euro-American fairy tales.

The Batería III was not actually standardized as a measure in its own right. Instead, the scale was administered to a small nonsystematic sample of 1,413 participants, the majority of whom were from the United States, Mexico, and Costa Rica. Participants from the United States were drawn from nine states; one third of the U.S. participants were residents of Texas and 42% had been born in Mexico. These results were used to "calibrate" the scale, that is, to equate it statistically to the English-language WJ III. First, items on both the WJ III and the Batería III were scaled according to their item difficulty using Rasch-model technology. Calibration statistics were then examined for equivalent items, and Batería III item difficulties were statistically adjusted to the scale of the WJ III. Using these comparisons, each test in the Batería III was scaled or equated to their empirical difficulty in the WJ III. An advantage of this calibration procedure is that the Batería III scores and WJ III scores can be directly compared. However, important disadvantages are that the small calibration sample was not sufficient to provide extensive information about the psychometric properties of the Batería III subtests in their own right; and the standardized scores that are provided for Spanish-speaking individuals who complete the Batería III use the standardization sample of the WJ III as a comparison group. Such a comparison may provide a very appropriate answer to questions about individuals' performance relative to their English-speaking counterparts in U.S. communities and schools, but the scores cannot be defended as fair or appropriate comparisons to other Spanish-speaking children with similar sociodevelopmental histories.

Another controversial issue raised by standardized tests administered in Spanish is that of examiner qualifications. Appropriate use of the Batería III requires both a thorough facility with the Spanish language and advanced professional training in standardized assessment. Because Spanish-speaking assessment professionals may not always be readily available, the manual for the Batería III recommends that ancillary Spanish-speaking examiners could be trained in the administration of the test, as long as an assessment professional retained responsibility for interpreting and presenting the results. Consequently, in the *Folleto de instrucciones para la capacitación del examinador* (Wendling & Mather, 2005), the Batería III provides materials for training fluent speakers of Spanish in each test's exact administration and scoring procedures, and explaining the importance of standardized examination procedures. This compromise position, although pragmatic, does not meet the professional standard that would be expected of examiners of English-speaking children. For this reason, the use of ancillary examiners is not widely accepted and has been criticized as de facto discrimination against Spanish-speaking children.

At first glance, the four test manuals released with the Batería III are impressive. However, these manuals are direct translations of the equivalent WJ III manuals and do not provide any specific information about the development or technical properties of the Batería III. Moreover, additional interpretive procedures incorporated in the Batería III, such as the Language Exposure and Use Questionnaire and the Comparative Language Index (CLI), are not described in the examiner's manuals. Some of this information is available in the Assessment Service Bulletin No. 1 (Schrank et al., 2005). Information about the reliability and validity of the Batería III, independent of that provided for the WJ-III, was not found in any other manual or published source.

SUMMARY. The development of a Spanish version of any cognitive or achievement measure is a technically sophisticated task. It is understandable that, like other test developers, the authors of the Batería III struggled to identify a nationally representative sample of Spanish-speaking individuals, to verify a Spanish translation of items that was satisfactory for all regional or national dialects of Spanish, and to develop items that were largely independent of U.S.-specific culture and history. Other shortcomings of the Batería III are more difficult to justify. Current standards for tests and measures demand that the authors routinely disseminate technical information about the scale's development and psychometric properties with the release of the scale. Current standards for cross-linguistic research have established various procedures as essential to verify translations of critical information such as test items. Still other practices endorsed by the Batería III have not yet been resolved by the professional assessment community. In particular, the use of ancillary examiners and the utility of scores comparing Batería III performance to WJ-III norms continues to be controversial. In some respects, the Batería III represents the best available Spanish-language measure of cognition and achievement. In other respects, users of the Batería III would need to interpret results very carefully and relative to each individual's educational history and country of origin.

REVIEWERS' REFERENCES

Carroll, J. B. (1997). The three-stratum theory of cognitive abilities. In D. P. Flanagan, J. L, Genshaft, & P. L. Harrison (Eds.), *Contemporary intellectual assessment: Theories, tests and issues* (pp. 122-130). New York: Guilford Press.

Cizek, G. J. (2003). [Review of the Woodcock-Johnson III]. In B. S. Plake, J. C. Impara, & R. A. Spies (Eds.), *The fifteenth mental measurements yearbook* (pp. 1020-1024). Lincoln, NE: Buros Institute of Mental Measurements.

Sandoval, J. (2003). [Review of the Woodcock-Johnson III]. In B. S. Plake, J. C. Impara, & R. A. Spies (Eds.), *The fifteenth mental measurements yearbook* (pp. 1024-1028). Lincoln, NE: Buros Institute of Mental Measurements.

Sares, T. (2005). [Review of the Woodcock-Johnson III Diagnostic Supplement to the Tests of Cognitive Ability]. In R. A. Spies & B. S. Plake (Eds.), *The sixteenth mental measurements yearbook* (pp. 1151-1153). Lincoln, NE: Buros Institute of Mental Measurements.

Schrank, F. A., McGrew, K. S., Ruef, M. L., Alvarado, C. G., Muñoz-Sandoval, A. F., & Woodcock, R. W. (2005). *Overview and technical supplement* (Batería III Woodcock-Muñoz Assessment Service Bulletin No. 1). Itasca, IL: Riverside Publishing.

Thompson, D. L. (2005). [Review of the Woodcock-Johnson III Diagnostic Supplement to the Tests of Cognitive Ability]. In R. A. Spies & B. S. Plake (Eds.), *The sixteenth mental measurements yearbook* (pp. 1153-1155). Lincoln, NE: Buros Institute of Mental Measurements.

Wendling, B. J., & Mather, N. (2005). *Folleto de instrucciones para la capacitación del examinador* (Batería III Woodcock-Muñoz). Itasca, IL: Riverside Publishing.

Woodcock, R. W. (1982). Batería Woodcock Psico-Educativa en Espanol. Itasca, IL: Riverside Publishing.

Woodcock, R. W., McGrew, K. S., & Mather, N. (2001). Woodcock-Johnson III. Itasca, IL: Riverside Publishing.

Woodcock, R. W., & Muñoz-Sandoval, A. F. (1996). Batería Woodcock-Muñoz. Itasca, IL: Riverside Publishing.

Review of the Batería III Woodcock-Muñoz by ARTURO OLIVAREZ, JR., Associate Professor of Educational Psychology, and ALLISON BORODA, Graduate Research Assistant in Educational Psychology, Texas Tech University, Lubbock, TX:

DESCRIPTION. The Batería III Woodcock-Muñoz contains two co-normed instruments: *Pruebas de habilidades cognitivas* (COG and SD) and *Pruebas de aprovechamiento* (APROV). Their primary purpose is to provide a comprehensive system for measuring general intellectual ability, specific cognitive abilities, scholastic aptitude, oral language, and academic achievement. The Batería III COG: *Pruebas de habilidades cognitivas*, intended to measure cognitive abilities, is composed of 31 tests measuring general intelligence, general and specific cognitive ability, and executive functioning. The names of some of these tests within the Batería III COG/SD scale include Comprension Verbal, Formacion de Conceptos, Atencion Auditiva, Planeamiento, and Series Numericas. There are two versions of the battery: (a) the Standard Battery (Tests 1–10 for COG; Tests 1–12 for APROV) and (b) an Extended Battery (Tests 11–20 for COG and Tests 13–22 for APROV). Additional supplemental diagnostic tests (Tests 21–31 for Batería III COG/SD) are included for diagnostic purposes, with special utility in evaluating young children and bilingual individuals. Pruebas de aprovechamiento (APROV), intended as a measure of achievement, includes 22 tests ranging from oral language, reading and writing skills, and phonological awareness to mathematic and academic knowledge bases. Some of the test names within the Batería III APROV include Identificación de Letras y Palabras, Fluidez en la Lectura, Cálculo, Análisis de Palabras, Comprensión Oral, Conceptos Cuantitativos, and so on.

The Batería III is a direct Spanish translation and adaptation of the Woodcock-Johnson III (WJ III; 15:281), which is meant to underscore the application and implementation of the Cattell-Horn-Carroll model of cognitive ability (CHC). An overview of CHC application and implications underlying construction of the Batería III are readily available and clearly outlined in their Overview and Technical Supplement (Schrank, McGrew, Ruef, Alvarado, Muñoz-Sandoval, & Woodcock, 2005). The COG and APROV portions of the Batería III (technical manual, 2005) are described as appropriate for individuals between the ages of 5 and 95; however, a few of the tests even may be used for children at 24 months of age.

Administration and scoring. For all three of the instruments, Batería III COG, Batería III APROV, and Batería III COG supplement diagnostics (SD), an examiner must be proficient in the Spanish language. There are three direct translations from the WJ III examiner's manuals presenting a detailed description of the qualifications, necessary abilities, and experiences the examiner must possess in order to administer any of the individual tests or clusters appropriately. Similar qualifications are emphasized for those examiners who may be administering the Batería III instruments (Mather & Woodcock, 2005a, 2005b). Additionally, the Batería III includes new examiners' training workbooks with extensive instructions for the appropriate administration and interpretation of test scores with heavy emphasis on close adherence to guidelines adopted by AERA, APA, and NCME (1999). These manuals emphatically declare that the battery examiners need to possess both Spanish and English language skills in order to administer and interpret appropriately and correctly the performance of their examinees. The three instruments may be administered to a single individual or specific test clusters from each of the instruments may be chosen by the test administrator based on the specific evaluative or diagnostic need of a particular examinee.

The materials for all the Batería III instruments include folding, easel-type binders for easy and efficient presentation of individual test items, the administrators' response recording sheets, CD audios for some tests within the Batería III requiring standard sounding of words and phrases in Spanish, and the scoring system WJ III NU Compuscore and Profiles Program. The battery also includes correct-answer scoring templates for each of the instruments to obtain raw scores. These materials are of professional grade quality and the software has received all the benefits inherited from the multiple improvements conducted with the WJ III's Compuscore and Profiles Program counterpart software. In its present version, administering and scoring the Batería III is relatively easy. The Batería III is computer scored, which saves scoring effort and time. Directions for administration and scoring are clearly stated on the first page of each instrument, with additional guidelines for scoring found in the examiners' manuals.

DEVELOPMENT. As stated earlier, the Batería III is based on close translation and interpretation of the WJ III. Because the WJ III is modeled after CHC theory, the Batería III is also meant to underline CHC's nine factors of cognitive ability. The authors state that the Batería III is meant to be used with "monolingual Spanish-speaking individuals" (overview and technical supplement, p. 10). It is the third version of the Bateria, originally known as the Batería Woodcock psico-educativa en español. Original and updated test items follow the plan set by Woodcock and Muñoz-Sandoval and are meant to transfer across worldwide Spanish-speaking communities. In most cases, items are direct translations of the WJ III, although some tests were adapted when the concepts were identical but items needed to be changed. Additionally, this newest version of the Batería provides two new interpretive features about appropriate assessment of language proficiency. First, the Batería uses an oral language proficiency level based on predicted performance in instructional situations using the cognitive-academic language proficiency (CALP) measure (Cummins, 1984; Woodcock & Muñoz-Sandoval, 1993). The second interpretive feature was the Comparative Language Index (CLI), which allows direct comparisons of Spanish and English language proficiencies within a single index (overview and technical supplement, 2005, p. 11).

The sample used to calibrate initial items on the Batería III consisted of 1,413 primary Spanish-speaking individuals from around the world, including individuals within the U.S. Of those individuals, 279 came from nine states in the United States: Arizona (15 cases), California (27 cases), Colorado (27 cases), Florida (7 cases), Georgia (7 cases), New Mexico (41 cases), New York (28 cases), Oregon (35 cases), and Texas (92 cases). Selection criteria included: (a) being a primary Spanish-speaker, and (b) having (for U.S. participants) dominance of Spanish over English. The initial Batería III data were calibrated with WJ III norms using Rasch-modeling and the comparability and equating standards from the *Standards for Educational and Psychological Testing* (AERA, APA, & NCME, 1999).

TECHNICAL.

Standardization. The Batería III inherits most of the psychometric properties found in the WJ III (Woodcock, McGrew, & Mather, 2001) normalization sample ($n = 8,818$) and examiners are encouraged to make use of age and grade equivalent tables for those tests that possess equivalent items and clusters for the appropriate score interpretations. A rather complete technical manual provides descriptive statistics results stratified across age. Reliability and standard errors of measurement for W scores and for Standard scores are provided for each test across age groups ranging from age 2 to 80+. The technical manual also provides detailed statistical test information for the individual tests and the different clusters within the cognitive and achievement measures. Additionally, the technical manual provides a large amount of evidence for content, factorial, internal structure, relational to other similar measures, and confirmatory validity. However, for purposes of determining the specific psychometric properties related uniquely to the Batería III's individual test scores and cluster scores, one needs to refer to the technical manual's detailed explanations for use of a calibration sample of Spanish-speaking individuals (Schrank, et al., 2005). The Batería III calibration sample data were equated to the WJ III norms (see reviews in *The Fifteenth Mental Yearbook* by Gregory Cizek [2003] and Jonathan Sandoval [2003]). Rasch-model technology facilitated this scaling task by equating the test data for each Batería III to that of the WJ III. The technical supplement provides a detailed account of the additional steps taken by the test developers in their calibration process leading to the final version of the Batería III (overview and technical supplement, 2005, p. 16).

Reliability. Although not directly stated in the technical supplement, it appears that the method for computing the internal consistency of the Batería III tests for the calibration sample data was the split-half method and the Rasch analysis procedures for the speeded adapted and translated tests. Reliability of the Batería III COG and APROV appears to be good with reliability coefficients for the COG subtests ranging from .80 (Palabras Incompletas) to .93 (Comprensión Verbal) and reliabilities for the APROV subtests ranging from .77 (Rememoracion de Cuentos) to .98 (Comprensión de Indicaciones and Discernimiento de Sonidos). Reliability coefficients for the cluster scores also indicate adequate reliability. Within the COG clusters, reliability coefficients range from .94–.95 for Habilidad Verbal-Escala Extendida, .86–.91 for Procesamiento Auditivo, .86–91 for Perception Fonemica, and .88–.90 for Alcance de la Memoria Auditiva. Within the APROV clusters, internal consistency reliability coefficients are .99 for Amplia Lectura and APROV Total, .97 for Destrezas Académicas, .96 for Aplicaciones Academicas and Comprensión de Lectura, and .90 for Expresión Escrita. The remaining clusters (Destrezas Básicas en Lectura, Lenguaje Oral-Estándar, Lenguaje Oral-Extendida, Comprensión Auditiva, Expresión Oral, Razonamiento en Matemáticas, Amplio Lenguaje Escrito, Destrezas Basicas en Escritura, Conocimientos Académicos, and Conocimiento de Fonemas y Grafemas) have internal consistency reliability coefficients ranging from .78–.98. The lowest median reliability coefficient found within the COG component of the Batería III was .80 for both Palabras Incompletas and Memoria de Trabajo Auditiva tests, whereas the Comprensión Verbal reported the highest internal consistency coefficient of .93. Similar reliability indices are reported for the COG clusters (a low of .88 and a high of .94). No median reliability was provided for the APROV clusters; however, the technical supplement provides reliability values for three broad age groups ranging from 6 to 29 years of age for 16 different test clusters for this component of the Batería III. The lowest reliability coefficient (.78) was found for the Lenguaje Oral-Estándar and the highest reliability value (.99) was observed for the Amplia Lectura cluster for all age groups. Overall, the internal consistency values for the Batería III yielded more than adequate internal consistency reliabilities for each of the test and cluster measures.

Validity. As observed above, the Batería III inherits some of the strong pieces of evidence for its content, internal structure, and construct validity from the WJ III battery of tests. The technical supplement sheds very little light in terms of the whole process of building evidence for the tests' content with only a brief mention as to how the internal structure of the Batería III tests intercorrelate. No actual subtest intercorrelations and factor-analytical results for the tests or clusters were available for any of the adapted and translated tests. However, a brief presentation of the results obtained in determining proposed organizational structure of these tests in support of the CHC theory was presented. The results of the confirmatory factor analyses suggest that the CHC model of cognitive abilities indeed underlies the Batería III (construct validity). Factor loadings indicate that there is a relatively good fit between the Batería III and the nine components of the CHC model. Using the calibration data, the pattern and relative magnitude of the factor loadings and model fit statistics resulted in moderate to high factor loadings and an overall good model fit (GFIs greater than .95). Furthermore, these results suggest that the Batería III is a good fit to the theory across the selected age groups. The proposed model appears to have adequate invariance qualities across the age groups. Although this information is promising and useful and corroborates the test developers' model, the Overview and Technical Supplement booklet does not include evidence of any other kind of validity evidence, such as criterion-related or construct validity. It is the opinion of these reviewers that such information should be provided in order to help administrators evaluate an examinee's COG and APROV scores on the Batería III. Assuming validity from results in Englsih with the WJ III is not certain.

COMMENTARY. Overall, the Batería III provides a measurement tool unmatched by any other standardized test in the market. Its close alignment with the WJ-III battery results in an excellent array of desirable psychometric properties making it an easy selection for those test users interested in assessing ability/achievement performance for Spanish-speaking populations. The Batería III is supported by the solid evidence of its construct validity provided through analyses using the Spanish calibration sample data. Although a larger sample would have been more desirable, the results provide more than adequate psychometric results obtained in their calibration sample. Although there are many strong features of the Batería III, the battery contains some potential features that may hinder administration and score interpretation due to the magnitude of tasks and constructs that are measured. Another potential difficulty with the Batería III is the fact that the calibration sample does not account for differences in language exposure and dialect within different regions of the United States, in that the subsamples are too small for comparison. In addition, although the authors state that the Batería III is intended primarily for monolingual Spanish-speakers, the authors do not fully resolve the issue of other language exposure. They explain that they used criteria "to verify that the Spanish-language development of individual subjects had been maintained and was not arrested due to the introduc-

tion of a second language" (p. 15), thus excluding any influences of other-language exposure that might elevate students' performance or mask ability. Finally, focusing on the Batería III COG Supplemental Diagnostic Test #31 (a, b, c, and d) intended for bilingual populations, the nature of some of the test items may lead to an overrepresentation of students in special education programs due to the level of difficulty for some of the test items. Item analyses specific to one particular section of the battery may help indicate the level of familiarity that individuals have with certain items.

SUMMARY. The Batería III Woodcock-Muñoz is a revised and updated comprehensive set of tests that assess both cognitive abilities and achievement levels of Spanish-speaking examinees ages 2–90+ years. The tests are parallel Spanish versions of the WJ III and are updated revisions of the Batería-R. The Batería III instruments may be used for measurement of general intellectual ability, specific cognitive abilities, oral language, and academic achievement. The battery also provides a language-reduced general intellectual score to measure the intellectual ability of bilingual individuals, a broad cognitive ability-low verbal score, and a comparative language index to determine language dominance, CALP score (Cummins, 1984). The assessment tool attempts to provide several options for brief, as well as comprehensive, assessment of an individual's cognitive and/or academic performance in Spanish based on the CHC theory. The Batería III uses cluster scores to interpret examinees' performance and also offers a Brief Summary report that is available in both English and Spanish. In summary, the Batería III is an instrument that can be used to assess important aspects of an individual's cognitive processes and achievement accurately. Although the purchaser of the instrument receives much valuable information, one must seriously weigh the benefits with the cost inherent in acquiring this assessment tool.

REVIEWERS' REFERENCES

American Educational Research Association, American Psychological Association, & National Council on Measurement in Education. (1999). *Standards for educational and psychological testing*. Washington, DC: American Educational Research Association.

Cizek, G. J. (2003). [Review of the Woodcock-Johnson III]. In B. S. Plake, J. C. Impara, & R. A. Spies (Eds.), *The fifteenth mental measurements yearbook* (pp. 1020–1024). Lincoln, NE: Buros Institute of Mental Measurements.

Cummins, J. (1984). *Bilingualism and special education: Issues in assessment and pedagogy*. Austin, TX: PRO-ED.

Mather, N., & Woodcock, R. J. (2005a). *Woodcock-Johnson III. Pruebas de habilidades cognitivas: Manual del examinador*. Itasca, IL: Riverside.

Mather, N., & Woodcock, R. J. (2005b). *Woodcock-Johnson III. Pruebas de aprovechamiento: Manual del examinador*. Itasca, IL: Riverside.

Sandoval, J. (2003). [Review of the Woodcock-Johnson III]. In B. S. Plake, J. C. Impara, & R. A. Spies (Eds.), *The fifteenth mental measurements yearbook* (pp. 1024-1028). Lincoln, NE: Buros Institute of Mental Measurements.

Schrank, F. A., McGrew, K. S., Ruef, M. L., Alvarado, C. G., Muñoz-Sandoval, & Woodcock, R. W. (2005). *Batería III Woodcock-Muñoz—Assessment service bulletin number 1: Overview and technical supplement.* Itasca, IL: Riverside Publishing.

Woodcock, R. W., McGrew, K. S., & Mather, N. (2001). Woodcock-Johnson III. Itasca, IL: Riverside Publishing.

Woodcock, R. W., & Muñoz-Sandoval, A. F. (1993). *Woodcock-Muñoz Language Survey: Comprehensive manual.* Itasca, IL: Riverside Publishing.

[15]

Battelle Developmental Inventory™, 2nd Edition.

Purpose: "Screening, diagnosis, and evaluation of early development."

Population: Birth to 7 years, 11 months.

Publication Dates: 1984–2005.

Acronym: BDI-2™.

Administration: Individual.

Forms, 2: Full Assessment, Screening Test.

Foreign Language Editions: Test items available in Spanish translation/adaptation for use by bilingual examiner or with a Spanish monolingual examiner.

Comments: Screening Test available as separate; hand-scoring, web-based, or stand-alone computer scoring (current version is called Data Manager) and Palm-powered electric data collection capability with Electronic Record Forms (ERF) available for full assessment and Screening Test in English and Spanish.

Author: Jean Newborg.

Publisher: Riverside Publishing.

a) FULL ASSESSMENT.

Purpose: Assess and identify "strengths and opportunities for learning of typically developing infants, preschoolers, kindergarteners, and early primary school students, as well as those who are advanced," and "children who have a disability or delay in any area of development."

Scores, 19: Self-Care, Personal Responsibility, Adaptive Total, Adult Interaction, Peer Interaction, Self-Concept and Social Role, Personal-Social Total, Receptive Communication, Expressive Communication, Communication Total, Gross Motor, Fine Motor, Perceptual Motor, Motor Total, Attention and Memory, Reasoning and Academic Skills, Perception and Concepts, Cognitive Total, Total.

Domains, 5: Adaptive, Personal-Social, Communication, Motor, Cognitive.

Administration Methods, 3: Structured Procedure, Observation Procedure, Interview Procedure.

Price Data, 2007: $444.50 per complete kit including 5 test item books, examiner's manual (2005, 256 pages), stimulus book, set of presentation cards, 15 scoring booklets, 15 workbooks, the Screening Test item book with 30 Screening Test booklets, set of screening visuals, and carrying case; $489 per manipulatives kit; $902.25 per complete kit with manipulatives; $70.25 per examiner's manual; $43.75 per 15 scoring booklets; $43.75 per 15 workbooks; $238.25 per Data Manager (new program released in 2007) software kit (PC); $238.25 per Data Manager software kit (Web) single; $59.25 per Palm Application Kit.

Time: (60–90) minutes.

b) SCREENING TEST.

Purpose: Provides "method for determining in which areas of development, if any, a comprehensive assessment is needed for a given child."

Scores, 6: Adaptive, Personal-Social, Communication, Motor, Cognitive, Total.

Price Data: $299 per Screener Kit including Screening Test Item Book with 30 Screening Test booklets, set of Screening visuals, examiner's manual, Quick Reference Guide, manipulatives needed to administer the Screening Test, and a canvas carrying case; $178.25 per Screener Kit including the Screening Test item book with 30 Screening Test booklets, and set of screening visuals (must purchase BDI-2 examiner's manual separately); $70.25 per examiner's manual; $51.50 per 30 Screening Test booklets.

Time: (10-30) minutes.

Cross References: See T5:265 (15 references) and T4:263 (4 references); for reviews by Judy Oehler-Stinnett and Kathleen D. Paget of an earlier edition, see 10:25 (1 reference); for information about the Screening Test, see T5:266 (4 references) and T4:264 (1 reference); for reviews by David W. Barnett and by Joan Ershler and Stephen N. Elliott of an earlier edition of the Screening Test, see 11:30.

Review of the Battelle Developmental Inventory, 2nd Edition by MICHELLE ATHANASIOU, Professor of School Psychology, University of Northern Colorado, Greeley, CO:

DESCRIPTION. The Battelle Developmental Inventory, 2nd Edition (BDI-2) is an individually administered test of development for children from birth through 7 years, 11 months of age. It is designed to measure developmental strengths of children with and without disabilities, to screen children considered to be at risk for developmental delays, to assist with the development of individualized family service plans and individualized education plans, and to monitor short- and long-term progress. The BDI-2 measures development in five domains, each contributing equally to the Total score, and each made up of several subdomains. The Adaptive (ADP) domain includes Self-Care (35 items) and Personal Responsibility (25 items) subdomains. The Personal-Social (P-S) domain includes Adult Interaction (30 items), Peer Interaction (25 items), and Self-Concept and Social Role (45 items) subdomains. The subdomains included in the Communication (COM) domain are Receptive Communication (40 items) and Expressive Communication (45 items). The Motor (MOT) domain consists of three subdomains: Gross Motor (45 items), Fine Motor (30 items), and Perceptual Motor (25 items). Finally, the Cognitive (COG) domain includes Attention and Memory (30 items), Reasoning and Academic Skills (35 items), and Perception and Concepts (40 items) subdomains. The items corresponding to various subdomains are administered based on the child's age, so not all subdomains are measured for all children. For example, Self-Care items are only administered to children 5 years, 11 months and younger. A screening test consisting of 100 of the total test's 450 items is also included (20 items from each domain). Scores for each of the domains are available using the screening test, but subdomains are not included. BDI-2 Complete provides a Total score, domain, and subdomain scores. Scores may include developmental quotients, percentile ranks, NCEs, *T*-scores, and *Z*-scores, and age equivalents at subdomains only.

The BDI-2 consists of an examiner's manual, separate test item books for each domain and the screening test, screening and full battery record forms, a student workbook (used for select Fine Motor, Perceptual Motor, and Reasoning and Academic Skills items at the upper ages), screening and full battery stimulus books, presentation cards, and a plastic puzzle/strip sheet. Manipulative kits are available but are not included with the complete BDI-2 kit. Consumers can choose to purchase a complete set of manipulatives or a specialized set, containing only those items that are unique to the BDI-2 and/or would be difficult to purchase separately. Also available separately are a web-based computer-scoring service and stand-alone computer scoring software, as well as a PDA administration module. A Spanish version of the BDI-2 is also available.

Administration times for the full battery are 1 hour for children under 2 years and over 5 years, and 90 minutes for children between 2 and 5 years. Screening test times are between 10 and 30 minutes, depending on the age of the child. The test item books include a standard set of information and instructions for each item, making administration relatively clear. The BDI-2 includes three administration procedures for items: structured test, observation, and interview. Instructions for each item are found in the test item books and describe which of the procedures are acceptable for that item. The flexibility in administration format is very useful, especially for items that cannot be assessed easily in a test setting (e.g., helping with simple household tasks or imitating the play activities of other children), and for instances when young children refuse to complete test items. The flexibility does, however, make establishing basals and ceilings more challenging, as it means items might be administered out of order (i.e., items using the same administration procedure are likely to be administered together). An additional useful feature of the BDI-2 is the description of test accommodations that can be used when testing children with various impairments or disabilities. The norm tables are easy to use, and each of the subdomains and domains demonstrates adequate floors, ceilings, and item gradients.

DEVELOPMENT. The BDI-2 is based on the concept of developmental milestones, with items written to reflect behaviorally based indications of such. Item content is consistent with that of commercially available early childhood curricula. As a result, a strong assessment-intervention link is created, whereby intervention ideas for specific BDI-2 items can be found in various curricula.

The BDI-2 is a comprehensive revision of the earlier version of the instrument (BDI; Newborg, Stock, Wnek, Guidubaldi, & Svinicki, 1984). Improvements over the BDI include new artwork, updated item content, and clearer administration instructions. Additionally, the BDI-2 reduced the number of subdomains from 22 to 13, resulting in more items per subdomain. Scoring criteria, although improved, remain somewhat ambiguous for certain items. The procedures used to develop the final BDI-2 item set are nicely detailed in the examiner's manual.

TECHNICAL. The BDI-2 was standardized on a sample of 2,500 children in more than 30 states. The sample was stratified on the bases of age, sex, race/ethnicity, geographic region, and socioeconomic level. The sample very closely matches 2001 U.S. Census data, but children with disabilities were not included. Because the instrument is designed in part to measure the developmental skills of children with disabilities, such children should have been included in the norm sample at a rate reflective of national demographics.

Median internal consistency estimates for each age level and subdomain meet accepted standards for diagnostic purposes (Salvia & Ysseldyke, 2001), although certain subdomains at certain ages are problematic. For example, indices for the Attention and Memory subdomain drop below .8 after age 3 1/2, and the ADP and MOT domains are insufficiently reliable above age 6. Total test scores and screening test scores are adequately reliable. Test-retest reliability estimates are based on a sample of 252 children at 2 and 4 years of age over a 2- to 25-day retest interval. Problems are noted with stability for the Attention and Memory subdomain, as well as the COM and COG domains. Additional stability studies using the entire age range of the test would be helpful. Interscorer agreement was calculated only on 17 items that require examiners' interpretation, such as the Fine Motor and Perceptual Motor items in the student workbook. These items appear to be reliable, but indices for all items would be helpful, given the relatively ambiguous scoring criteria for some object scoring items.

Evidence for content validity consists of judgments of professionals regarding coverage of important constructs, as well as empirical item analysis procedures including item-total correlations, age trends, and model-data-fit statistics. Items deemed unsatisfactory based on these procedures were deleted.

Criterion-related evidence for validity was investigated by correlating BDI-2 scores with those of other measures of development, as well as measures of other constructs (e.g., phonological processing, intelligence, and academic achievement). Patterns of correlations generally support the BDI-2 constructs, but some of the samples were relatively small. Additional criterion-related evidence for validity is needed. Construct validity evidence is provided in the forms of factor analyses, age differentiation, and patterns of intercorrelations. These indices support the BDI-2 as a measure of development.

COMMENTARY. The BDI-2 is a solid measure of development for young children. It has several useful characteristics that differentiate it from other tests of its kind. First, flexibility in administration procedures has the potential to provide a better estimate of children's highest skills, especially for younger children. Second, the items' correspondence with early childhood curricula makes the instrument much more useful for program planning and outcome monitoring. Nevertheless, the BDI-2 is wanting in some regards. Most notably, very little evidence for test fairness is provided in the manual. Aside from differential item functioning analyses based on race and expert judgment regarding potentially biased items, no attention is paid to empirical determinants of test fairness. Also, despite the reduction in subdomains with the second edition of the instrument, the BDI may be attempting to cover too much ground to provide useful information about all subdomains.

SUMMARY. The BDI-2 is a comprehensive, relatively user-friendly, and overall technically adequate measure of early childhood development. It represents a significant improvement over its predecessor. This revision renders the instrument highly competitive with other instruments of its kind. It is hoped that evidence of test fairness will be forthcoming.

REVIEWER'S REFERENCES

Newborg, J., Stock, J. R., Wnek, L., Guidubaldi, J., & Svinicki, J. (1984). *Battelle Developmental Inventory examiner's manual.* Allen, TX: DLM Teaching Resources.
Salvia, J., & Ysseldyke, J. E. (2001). *Assessment* (8th ed.). Boston: Houghton Mifflin.

Review of the Battelle Developmental Inventory, 2nd Edition by LAUREN R. BARTON, Early Childhood Researcher, and DONNA SPIKER, Program Manager, Early Childhood Program, Center for Education and Human Services, SRI International, Menlo Park, CA:

DESCRIPTION. The Battelle Developmental Inventory, 2nd Edition (BDI-2; see http://www.riverpub.com/products/) is a standardized developmental assessment battery for children from birth through 7 years, 11 months. It is an updated and improved version of the Battelle Developmental Inventory that was originally published in 1984. The BDI-2 is intended to assess developmental strengths and opportunities for learning in young children with disabilities, those "at risk" in any developmental area, or those who are developing typically. Developers ambitiously identify that it can be used for team assessment, to guide development of intervention and educational plans, to monitor a child's short- or long-term progress, or to evaluate child outcomes in programs serving young children. Examples of appropriate BDI-2 examiners include early childhood teachers, infant interventionists, special educators, psychologists, health professionals, and various other therapists or specialists. The manual provides clear directions as well as case examples to support effective administration, scoring, and interpretation.

BDI-2 procedures include individually administered items in a structured test format, and a combination of interviewing parents and observing the child in natural settings for items that are not easily assessed with structured procedures.

The manual provides administration instructions and the scoring rubric for each item using different appropriate procedures (structured task administration, observation, and interview). The manual suggests that "When there is a choice of administration procedures, structured is most preferred and the Interview is least preferred, because the examiner can observe and document the response of the child directly, rather than depend on the observation, interpretation, and reporting skills of another person" (p. 48). The observation procedure is only recommended if "the examiner has extended contact with a child to observe him or her in a natural setting at great length. A good rule of thumb is to use the Observation procedures when the examiner has, on average, at least 1 hour of contact per day with the child for at least 2 weeks. *If only limited contact with a child can be arranged, it is best to use the Interview procedure instead*" (p. 29; emphasis in original).

Items are grouped into five domains (Adaptive, Personal-Social, Communication, Motor, and Cognitive) and 13 subdomains (Self-Care, Personal Responsibility, Adult Interaction, Peer Interaction, Self-Concept and Social Role, Receptive Communication, Expressive Communication, Gross Motor, Fine Motor, Perceptual Motor, Attention and Memory, Reasoning and Academic Skill, and Perception and Concepts). The Adaptive and Personal-Social domains are assessed primarily through parent interview, whereas the other domains require the most direct assessment time. The full BDI-2 battery is available either in English or Spanish translation. It includes 450 test items, with subsets selected using basal and ceiling

rules. The full BDI-2 reportedly averages 60–90 minutes to administer; that is, 60 minutes for children under 2 or over 5, and 90 minutes for children 2–5 years. When needed, testing may occur over several days, preferably within a 2-week period.

CD-ROM, PDA, and Web-based scoring software are available in addition to hand-scoring approaches. Item scoring on a 3-point continuum (0, 1, 2) is recorded either on paper or electronic record forms developed for the PDA. Raw scores are computed for each subdomain and converted into age equivalents, scaled scores (with a mean of 10, range 1–19, standard deviation of 3), and corresponding percentile ranks for scaled scores based on age level. Sums of scaled subdomain scores generate scaled scores and percentile ranks for each domain or for overall BDI-2 composite performance. Scores from the five domains and overall performance can be converted into developmental quotient (DQ) scores with a mean of 100 and a standard deviation of 15. Percentile ranks and confidence intervals are provided for each DQ. Information is provided for further conversion of scores to z-scores, T-scores, and normal curve equivalents. Subdomain scaled scores and DQ composite scores can be plotted and displayed graphically to see the variation across scores. Additional reports, including reports on individuals, classes, or larger groups of children in a program for one or across multiple test administrations and with different kinds of scores (z-, T-, standard scores, percentile ranks, and NCEs), are available with use of the computerized scoring option. Special reports, including conservative narrative versions, designed for Head Start monitoring, the Screening Test, and for IEP/IFSP development are available.

In addition to the full assessment, a separate screening test, the Battelle Developmental Inventory, 2nd Edition, Screening Test, was developed to identify children in the broad population who should receive the full assessment due to their potential risk for developmental delays. The screening test consists of 100 items, or two items at each of 10 age levels for the five domains. For children under 3 years and over 5 years of age, screening administration requires 10–15 minutes. For 3–5-year-old children, 20–30 minutes is needed for screening. Raw scores are calculated for each domain and compared to cutoff scores provided for -1.0, -1.5, and -2.0 standard deviations.

DEVELOPMENT. The BDI-2 is an updated revision to the original BDI published in 1984 and originally reviewed in *The Tenth Mental Measurements Yearbook* (Oehler-Stinnett, 1989; Paget, 1989). The BDI was initially developed in response to a need for a uniform measure of children's progress in achieving milestones that also could serve as a tool to evaluate programs serving children with disabilities. Differences highlighted between the BDI and BDI-2 include: an expanded normative sample and norm tables with smaller age ranges; updated test items and reduction from 22 to 13 subdomains; fewer subtrials on most items; more specific guidance in directions, interview questions, and scoring procedures; more colorful and child-friendly materials; computer software for scoring; availability of electronic and paper record forms; a Spanish translation/adaptation; revised basal and ceiling rules; and use of scaled, standard, and percentile scores for interpretation. All of these features are improvements over the original BDI.

A great deal of effort went into this revision in terms of redesigning the items and materials and conducting a standardization study. Items in the initial BDI were selected by evaluating more than 4,000 items in existing instruments with expert review, followed by analysis of the psychometric characteristics of items in sample data to select the final subset. The developers of the BDI-2 reviewed research literature that used the BDI, examined critiques published on the BDI's technical qualities, surveyed users of the BDI about experiences with the instrument, and observed the use of the BDI screening test. Updated items to address identified concerns, plus approximately 150 new items, were reviewed against criteria for inclusion, classified into domains and subdomains by experts, and field tested with small groups for face validity, ease of administration, and relevance to the subdomain concept. Then the developers studied a new tryout edition with approximately 700 of the most promising items. Two groups of approximately 425 children each were administered half of the tryout assessment (either two or three domains each). Sample composition for the tryout is not provided. Analyses included item difficulty across age groups, item gradients, reliability, factor analyses, differential item function-

ing, and analysis of test fairness across gender and ethnic groups. Developers also considered examiner feedback regarding the items and children's reactions to items and materials, to refine the final standardization edition of the test.

The standardization study was undertaken with 2,500 children given 492 items to inform the selection of 450 items in the final BDI-2 composition. Using appropriate statistical techniques, items were checked for high item discrimination, appropriate difficulty for the targeted age range, differentiation of responses from high- and low-ability examinees, proper progression, and score values across ages, and they met at least 80% agreement threshold between the way examiners scored items and the approach of trained quality assurance investigators using the score sheets. Analyses suggested that conceptual development and perceptual discrimination should be, and therefore were merged into one subdomain under the cognitive domain. Minor wording enhancements to some instructions and items were provided based on examiner feedback.

The 100-item BDI-2 Screening Test is a subset of the 450 BDI-2 items that represented critical developmental milestones, usually included items from across the subdomains, had item-total score correlations of .70 or higher, had item difficulty values of approximately .75, and had generally good predictive qualities (sensitivity and specificity from .75–.91 for different groups of children with diagnosed disabilities).

TECHNICAL.

Standardization. The BDI-2 was standardized, with appropriate quality control measures described, using a nationally representative sample of 2,500 children from birth to 7 years, 11 months in 3- or 6-month intervals. The sample was stratified by child age, sex, race/ethnicity, geographic region of residence, and socioeconomic level as indicated by mother's educational attainment. The standardization sample focused on milestones achieved by typically developing children. Those who had been referred for services, were receiving support services during more than 50% of the day, or were documented with a disability were excluded from the standardization sample. Standardization protocols did not permit significant accommodations or adaptations to the standardized test administration. Percentages of child, family, and community characteristics in the sample closely matched percentages reported from the United States 2000 Census information. However, the low percentage of Asian children (2.9%) in the standardization sample may make interpretations questionable for this group. Although 18.9% of the standardization sample identified themselves as Hispanic, the standardization assessments were conducted only in English. Therefore, this group may represent a more highly acculturated group of Hispanic or Latino children than in the general population. The developers state that although a Spanish translation of the BDI-2 has been made available, normative information applies only when direct assessment items are presented in English; they suggest presenting items first in English to children with limited English proficiency and retesting missed items in Spanish as needed. However, this approach to test administration seems problematic given the short attention spans of young children, individual differences in responses and effort following failure, and potential score differences resulting from practice effects. Although this concern may be viewed as a problem with the BDI-2, it is one that applies to almost all other early childhood assessment tools as well.

Data from the standardization sample and related simulations were analyzed to consider the appropriateness of basal and ceiling rules and starting points. Age equivalents representing the median raw score for all children at an age level were computed, plotted, and smoothed. Means and standard deviations were tabulated for each subdomain and plotted in two graphs by age group and the trend curves were fitted by polynomial regression to provide smoothed means and standard deviations. Linear scale transformations and analyses involving linear interpolation and extrapolation of adjacent age-group values were calculated to create the final set of subdomain scaled scores and associated percentile ranks. Sums of scaled scores were computed for each domain and, for the child's overall performance, smoothed using a compound binomial procedure that maintained a mean of 100 and a standard deviation of 15.

Reliability. The manual provides detailed information showing that the BDI-2 has good reliability. Internal consistency was assessed in the standardization sample using the split-half method, corrected by the Spearman-Brown formula. Averaged across ages, reliabilities on subdomains varied from .85–.95, and reliabilities on domains ranged from .90–.96, and were fairly consistent across ages. The relatively weak areas included the Perception and Concepts subdomain for infants 6–23 months (.70, .58, and .76 over the three age groups), Fine Motor subdomain for the 60–71-months group (range .75–.76), and Adaptive domain from the 12–17-months group (.79). The overall BDI-2 test score reliability was .99, and for the screening test score it was .91.

Standard errors of measurement (*SEM*) are provided for subdomains, domains, and total scores based on data in the standardization study. Generally, they are less than 1/3 of a standard deviation, with higher *SEM*s in the same subdomains and domains where weaker reliability was noted.

Test-retest stability was examined using 126 2-year-old and 126 4-year-old children in racial/ethnic categories similar to U.S. Census breakdowns, with 2–25 days after the initial assessment (median = 8 days, 80% within 2 weeks). Overall DQ stability was high (.93 for 2-year-olds, .94 for 4-year-olds). No further test-retest information is available for other ages. This seems especially important for children younger than 2 years of age whose performance is more variable and when language plays less of a role in the assessment. Reliability coefficients were stronger for domains than subdomains for both 2-year-olds (.77–.90 subdomains, .87–.90 domains) and 4-year-olds (.74–.91 subdomains, .87–.92 for domains), with Attention and Memory showing the weakest subdomain stability in both groups. The authors recommend test administrations in normal use be conducted at least 6 months apart.

During preliminary field testing, potential items were examined for equivalence in scores across direct assessment, observation, and interview approaches. Seven percent of the items were flagged for further inspection by developers and these did not show a consistent method bias, supporting equivalence of methods. However, the manual does not report how many of these items were included in the final set of 450 items.

According to the manual, "the vast majority" (p. 115) of examiners made no omissions or errors in scoring during the standardization study quality control checks. The developers attribute this finding to objective scoring parameters in the instructions that do not require the examiner's interpretation. No information is provided about interscorer agreement from two examiners present at the same assessment. However, trained examiners independently scored at least 120 responses to each of 17 items (1/3 each with 0, 1, and 2 scores) from the Fine Motor and Perceptual Motor subdomains expected to have the greatest potential for scoring interpretation problems and found 94–97% agreement across examiners. No information was provided about either test-retest stability or interobserver agreement on the BDI-2 Screening Tool items specifically.

Validity. The manual provides detailed information indicating that the BDI-2 generally has good validity. Content validity is supported by drawing heavily on content representing milestones from the previous BDI, supplementing additional items based on more recent developmental literature, and having potential items examined by expert review panels to consider their consistency in measuring the well-established childhood domains. Hundreds of professional examiners who conducted assessments on children also rated every item in the tryout and standardization editions for relevance, concerns, and fairness. Item analyses were conducted using classical and item response theory methods. Items with poor discrimination in Rasch-fit statistics, high differential item functioning analysis (using gender and racial/ethnic groups), bias reviewer concerns, or a lack of contribution to the domain structure were dropped from successive versions.

Criterion-related validity is described through convergent validity with many widely used instruments assessing progress toward developmental milestones. Instruments include the original BDI, the Bayley Scales of Infant Development, 2nd Edition (BSID-II), the Denver Developmental Screening Test-II (DDST-II), the Preschool Language Scales (PLS-4), the Vineland Social-Emotional Early Childhood Scales (Vineland SEEC), the Comprehensive Test of Phonological Processing (CTOPP), the Wechsler Preschool and Primary Scale of Intelligence—Third Edition (WPPSI-III), and the Woodcock-Johnson III Test of Achievement (WJ III ACH). Information presented in the manual provides preliminary evidence of relationships between expected components of these tests commonly used in the field and relevant domains or the total BDI-2 score. Correlations are generally in the .60–.75 range. Correlations between subscales or domains where

one would not expect correspondence tend to be in the .30–.50 range. Samples are generally small (ranging between 30 to 191 and spanning a large age range) and include a racially and ethnically diverse population, resulting in subgroups that generally are too small to ensure that there are not consistent trends in bias or poor measurement relationships.

A series of studies compared mean BDI-2 differences and effect size differences between various groups of children with identified disabilities or at risk for developing them to an equal number of matched children from the standardization sample who had more typical developmental patterns. These groups included children with autism ($n = 44$, ages 2 to 7), cognitive delays ($n = 42$, ages 2 to 7), developmental delays ($n = 58$, ages 2 months to 6 years), motor delays ($n = 40$, ages 2 months to 6 years, 7 months), premature births ($n = 45$, ages 1 month to 4 years), and speech/language delays ($n = 72$, ages 1 to 7 years). Several of the above samples include no Asian-Americans. In each case, the results yielded large effect sizes indicating that the group of children with the identified risk condition, delay, or disability scored lower than their matched peers on each of the domains of the BDI-2 and in the overall score. In each study, the domain expected to be the most impaired showed the greatest effect size for differences. However, in most cases BDI-2 scores were more than one standard deviation below the mean in all domains. Sample information provided was not detailed enough to identify if lower scores should have been expected in primarily one domain or to show this pattern of scores. Sensitivity in detecting those with the expected condition at the one standard deviation below the mean level with the BDI-2 ranged from .75–.91 across these studies. Sensitivity was below .80 for the developmental delay, motor delay, and speech/language delay groups, representing the three samples with more heterogeneous populations. Specificity to avoid falsely identifying a child who is developing typically ranged from .75–.91, with the motor delay and speech/language delay groups having lowest specificity (at or below .80).

Using the BDI screening items to identify children performing at or below one standard deviation below same age peers yielded sensitivity of .72–.93 and specificity of .79–.88. Sensitivity and specificity were lowest for children in the speech/language group. The broad sample of children with developmental delays also had sensitivity of .72, but yielded higher specificity (.86) than for the speech/language group. The BDI-2 was sensitive in detecting children with cognitive delays, but it had a lower level of specificity (.81) than most of the other samples.

These studies concerning specific populations of children at risk for or with established delays or conditions employ samples that span large age ranges and children of diverse ethnicities. They are not sufficient to determine potential problems with using the BDI-2 on specific age, gender, ethnic, or socioeconomic subgroups of children at risk for or with diagnosed delays or conditions. Overall, these studies provide preliminary evidence that the BDI-2 provides lower scores for children who are at risk for or have delays or diagnosed conditions compared to those with more typical developmental patterns. Like many other early childhood assessment tools, the standardization sample for the BDI-2 does not include adequately large subgroups of children with specific disabilities at different ages to generalize to those groups.

BDI-2 scores do show expected increases in raw scores across ages and growth, with steeper age-graded increases in the first 3 years than later. The manual includes a table of intercorrelations among domains and subdomains and includes factor analysis results that support the convergence of the domain/subdomain structure and the presence of related, but divergent, properties with other domains and subdomains based on the standardization study.

COMMENTARY. The BDI-2 presents a strong set of preliminary evidence supporting its use in assessing developmental skills among children who are developing typically (i.e., those similar to the normative sample). Some evidence suggests that the BDI-2 reflects lower scores in some populations at risk or with diagnosed conditions or delays. Those studies did not include children with sensory impairments. No normative information is provided for those populations studied. Likewise no normative information or reliability/validity information is provided for the Spanish-translation version. This lack of information yields uncertainty about the measurement properties and effectiveness of the BDI-2 in these groups. Although far too commonly overlooked, the estab-lished best practice recommendation in assessment is to use assessments only on populations for which they have been normed. In this case, this drawback is particularly important for those considering use with Spanish-speaking populations or for children with disabilities or delays.

Overall, the revision of the BDI-2 represents a thoughtful development and validation effort to address some shortcomings in the original BDI. Efforts to enhance guidance for use of interview and observation to supplement the direct, structured assessment approach and to update the instructions and materials are appreciated. Administration time and recommended intervals for administration remain key considerations, especially when a comprehensive assessment in all developmental domains is necessary. However, this concern is not unique to the BDI-2. Use of the screening tool may help determine need for the full administration, but it still requires significant time, especially for preschool-aged children. Moreover, if a child has potential speech or language concerns, additional assessment is recommended.

The BDI-2 retains the established approach of identifying developmental status by assessing achievement of predictive developmental skills or milestones as categorized in common sequences and split into domains. Consistent with many other commonly used assessment tools, the BDI-2 was not derived from a specific theoretical approach, it is not based on an integrated curriculum, and it does not focus item selection around functional performance of skills. Thus, the BDI-2 may not be the most useful assessment approach for informing individualized interventions and educational plans and for capturing short-term progress toward identified goals. Although BDI-2 content largely reflects common developmental milestones, no validity evidence is provided to support the tool's usefulness in guiding intervention and educational plans, monitoring individual child change (no longitudinal change studies/data presented), or for evaluating outcomes in programs serving young children (or intervention effectiveness studies). Further validation of the effectiveness of the BDI-2 for these purposes would be a contribution to the field.

SUMMARY. This revised and updated BDI-2 is an improvement over the original BDI. The detailed and well-written manual provides in-depth information about how the revision was done, guidelines for administration and use in program planning, and the standardization process and reliability and validity data. Users may still find this tool to be time-consuming to administer. Caution is advised in using the tool with Spanish-speaking and other non-English-speaking children, but this concern is a nearly universal issue for users of early childhood assessment instruments. Similarly, although the instrument can generally help distinguish which children have disabilities or delays, it has not been standardized on children with special needs. These issues related to non-English speakers and children with disabilities apply to almost all early childhood assessment instruments as well. The flexibility of administration of the BDI-2 (direct assessment, interview of parents or familiar caregivers, observation) is a strength of this instrument that could serve to mitigate against these problems. The measure allows knowledgeable users to take full advantage of its flexibility.

REVIEWERS' REFERENCES

Oehler-Stinnett, J. (1989). [Review of the Battelle Developmental Inventory]. In J. C. Conoley & J. J. Kramer (Eds.), *The tenth mental measurements yearbook* (pp. 66–70). Lincoln, NE: Buros Institute of Mental Measurements.

Paget, K. D. (1989). [Review of the Battelle Developmental Inventory]. In J. C. Conoley & J. J. Kramer (Eds.), *The tenth mental measurements yearbook* (pp. 70–72). Lincoln, NE: Buros Institute of Mental Measurements.

[16]

Battery for Health Improvement 2.

Purpose: A psychomedical assessment designed "to provide relevant information and treatment recommendations to professionals who treat injured patients in a variety of settings."

Population: Ages 18–65, individuals who are being treated for a physical injury.

Publication Dates: 1996–2003.

Acronym: BHI 2.

Scores: 18 scales: Validity (Self-Disclosure, Defensiveness), Physical Symptoms (Somatic Complaints, Pain Complaints, Functional Complaints, Muscular Bracing), Affective Scales (Depression, Anxiety, Hostility), Character Scales (Borderline, Symptom Dependency, Chronic Maladjustment, Substance Abuse, Perseverance), Psychosocial Scales (Family Dysfunction, Survivor of Violence, Doctor Dissatisfaction, Job Dissatisfaction).

Administration: Group or individual.

Price Data, 2007: $104 per Q Local scoring starter kit with enhanced interpretive reports including manual (2003, 291 pages), 1 soft-cover test booklet, and answer sheets; $94 per Q Local scoring starter kit with basic interpretive reports; $71 per Q Local scoring starter kit with profile reports; $114 per mail-in starter kit with enhanced interpretive reports including manual, 1 soft-cover test booklet, and answer sheets; $102 per mail-in starter kit with basic interpretive reports; $80 per mail-in starter kit with profile reports; $89 per Desktop Version Q Local Software (requires annual license fee); $250 per Network Version Q Local Software (requires annual license); $47 per manual; $10.25 per 5 test booklets; $21.50 per 25 answer sheets; $51.50 per compact disc; quantity discounts available for the reports.

Foreign Language Editions: Spanish forms available.

Time: (30–45) minutes.

Comments: Computer administration and audio CD; mail-in scoring, Q Local software, fax-scoring.

Authors: Daniel Bruns and John Mark Disorbio.

Publisher: Pearson.

Cross References: For reviews by Gregory J. Boyle and Ephrem Fernandez of an earlier edition, see 14:36.

Review of the Battery for Health Improvement 2 by MICHAEL G. KAVAN, Associate Dean for Student Affairs and Associate Professor of Family Medicine, Creighton University School of Medicine, Omaha, NE:

DESCRIPTION. The Battery for Health Improvement 2 (BHI 2) is a 217-item self-report instrument designed for the psychological assessment of medical patients. Specifically, its purpose is to provide information and treatment recommendations to professionals who treat injured patients in settings that include general medicine, physical medicine and rehabilitation, and vocational rehabilitation programs.

The BHI 2 includes 18 scales organized into five domains including Validity (Self-Disclosure, Defensiveness), Physical Symptom (Somatic Complaints, Pain Complaints, Functional Complaints, Muscular Bracing), Affective (Depression, Anxiety, Hostility), Character (Borderline, Symptom Dependency, Chronic Maladjustment, Substance Abuse, Perseverance), and Psychosocial (Family Dysfunction, Survivor of Violence, Doctor Dissatisfaction, Job Dissatisfaction) scales. In addition, the BHI 2 contains 40 content areas that fall under the four latter-mentioned domains as well as under a Critical Item Content Area domain.

The BHI 2 was designed to be administered to patients between the ages of 18 and 65 years who are being evaluated or treated for an injury. The BHI 2 has English and Spanish versions in paper-and-pencil, computer-administered, and audio CD formats. The BHI 2 should be administered in a supervised setting and patients should have at least a sixth-grade reading level. The answer sheet requests general demographic information as well as date of injury and legal status of the case. The test administrator also designates a Pain Diagnostic Category based on the patient's primary complaint, which is used for providing diagnostic probabilities within the Enhanced Interpretive Report. Patients then complete four parts of the test including items related to the patient's pain experience over the past month, general physical symptoms over the past month, level of agreement/disagreement with a host of MMPI-2-type statements, and level of agreement/disagreement on issues related to job satisfaction. Standard administration time is estimated to be between 30 and 45 minutes.

Scoring options include mail-in scoring, on-site computer scoring using NCS Pearson software, and fax-in scoring. Users may obtain a profile report, an interpretive report, or an enhanced interpretive report from the publisher. The basic profile report includes raw scores and *T*-scores for both patient and community samples for the 18 major scales. Validity and critical item information are also included along with comparisons of the patient to other "patients" on the 40 content areas. Interpretive and enhanced reports provide more in-depth interpretations, summaries, and treatment recommendations.

Although the authors promote the BHI 2 in assessment and treatment planning throughout the manual, they do note that interpretations of BHI 2 results "should be considered in conjunction with other clinical [and medical] findings" (manual, p. 75) in order to determine the relationship between psychological factors and physical complaints. The authors stress that the BHI 2 is not intended for making diagnoses, but to be one source for making clinical hypotheses.

DEVELOPMENT. The origin of the BHI 2 dates to 1985 with the development of several prototype versions. In total, an item pool of over 1,000 items was developed and then subdivided into 80 content areas based on the authors' clinical experience and patient input. From this item pool, the authors developed a 600-item research version (BHI R). The BHI R and a variety of other psychological measures were then administered to patients and community participants. Patients were being treated in a variety of medical settings such as physical therapy, chronic pain, vocational rehabilitation, and work-hardening programs for either a physical injury or pain due to an injury.

BHI items were initially assigned to scales based on the consensus of the authors and expert judges. Criteria included: how well items were judged to represent each content area; how well items differentiated patients from community subjects; and item-to-scale, item-to-criterion, and scale-to-criterion correlations. The Somatic Complaints and Pain Complaints scales were developed based on the selection of representative items for each area. The same general method was used for the Anxiety scale; however, its items also had to correlate higher with its own scale versus the other Affective scales. Finally, the Validity Index items were selected due to their rare endorsement. This resulted in a 202-item instrument that included a validity index, 14 scales, 10 critical items, items addressing a history of physical or sexual abuse, and research items.

The BHI has since been revised utilizing essentially this same method. The BHI 2 now has 217 items and includes two new scales (Survivor of Violence and Functional Complaints), two new validity measures (Defensiveness and Self-Disclosure), and revisions of 6 of the 14 original scales. Content areas were developed for purposes of making "finer discriminations of a patient's symptomatology" (manual, p. 6) by having a 12-member panel of physical rehabilitation and chronic pain psychologists assign items to content definitions. As a result of this process and subsequent item reassignment, the BHI 2 currently has 40 content area scales.

TECHNICAL. The BHI 2 was designed for patients with at least a sixth-grade reading level; however, no Flesch-Kincaid method or Bermuth formula data are provided within the manual. The authors state that a unique feature of the BHI 2 is that each scale is double normed so that it produces both a patient *T* score and a community *T* score. The patient *T* score may be compared to a national sample of patients in rehabilitation, whereas the community *T* score allows comparison to a national sample of people in the community. Means and standard deviations are provided for the patient (*n* ranging from 517 to 527) and community (*n* ranging from 716 to 725) samples; sample sizes were somewhat smaller for the Job

Dissatisfaction scale. In addition, means and standard deviations are provided for reference groups asked to fake-bad or fake-good, and demographic data are provided for these and six additional pain-specific subgroups. Limited normative data are provided within the manual for these groups.

Internal consistencies (alpha coefficients) for all 18 BHI 2 scales were computed for the patient, community, and combined samples. For the patient sample, alphas ranged from .74 (Chronic Maladjustment) to .96 (Self-Disclosure), whereas those for the community sample ranged from .73 (Substance Abuse) to .97 (Self-Disclosure). Alphas for the combined sample ranged from .75 (Substance Abuse) to .97 (Self-Disclosure). Test-retest reliability for each of the 18 BHI 2 scales was computed for patients (n ranging from 58 to 86) in a physical rehabilitation setting. Average time between test administrations was 6.7 days (range was 5–10 days). Correlations ranged from .88 (Hostility, Borderline, Symptom Dependency, and Doctor Dissatisfaction) to .97 (Somatic Complaints and Job Dissatisfaction).

Internal consistencies were also computed for the 40 BHI 2 content areas for all three groups. Alpha coefficients ranged from .25 (Entitlement) to .83 (Cognitive Dysfunction and Aggressiveness) in the patient sample, .31 (Compensation Focus) to .83 (Severe Depression and Helplessness and Cynical Beliefs) in the community sample, and .41 (Rx Abuse Risk and Entitlement) to .83 (Severe Depression and Helplessness) in the combined sample. Test-retest correlations for the content areas ranged from .76 (Interpersonal Dynamics) to .97 (Company Dissatisfaction). These calculations were made on samples ranging from 59 to 87 patients with a test-retest interval range of 5 to 10 days.

In order to establish criterion-related validity, the BHI 2 was administered concurrently with the Minnesota Satisfaction Questionnaire—Short Form, the McGill Pain Questionnaire, the Scored Pain Drawing scales, and scales from the Brief Battery for Health Improvement 2, the MMPI-2, and the Millon Clinical Multiaxial Inventory-III. Data provided within the manual suggest respectable concurrent validity for most scales; however, relatively weak support was provided for the Symptom Dependency, Survivor of Violence, and Doctor Dissatisfaction scales due mainly to the concurrent measures selected to support their validity.

Also, the Pain Range Calculation showed only nominal correlations with the Scored Pain Drawing and the McGill Pain Questionnaire.

Interscale correlations were also computed for the patient, community, and combined samples and most are in the expected direction. Intercorrelations among the various content areas are also provided within the manual and most seem appropriate. Factor analysis of the 40 content areas revealed seven factors including demanding dependency, aggressiveness, somatic concerns, helpless depression, job dissatisfaction, addictive tendencies, and worries and ineffectiveness. Two scales (i.e., Self-Efficacy and Proactive Optimism) failed to meet the authors' criterion for the final factor configurations. The seven factors accounted for 67.4% of the variance. No data are provided within the manual supporting the ability of the BHI 2 to predict patient outcome in physical rehabilitation, vocational rehabilitation, and general medicine settings.

COMMENTARY. The stated purpose of the BHI 2 is to "provide relevant information and treatment recommendations to professionals who treat injured patients in a variety of settings, including physical rehabilitation, vocational rehabilitation, and general medicine" (manual, p. 2) sites. The authors state that the BHI 2 was designed to address the APA's Guidelines for Test User Qualifications (Turner, DeMers, Fox, & Reed, 2001), which include classification, description, intervention planning, tracking, and prediction.

So, how does the BHI 2 fare? The BHI 2 is an instrument with strong internal consistency and test-retest reliability. However, several scales fall short in their coverage of relevant symptomatology. For example, the 14-item Depression Scale covers, at best, four of the nine symptoms of Major Depressive Episode based on DSM-IV-TR criteria (American Psychiatric Association, 2000). Correlations with a variety of other measures show reasonable concurrent validity; although one questions the use or non-use of certain collateral measures to support concurrent validity. Overall, although the BHI 2 should not be used independently to diagnosis a patient's condition, it effectively describes a patient's symptomatology and allows for a comparison with patient and community samples.

The BHI 2 also assists clinicians in treatment planning by providing information on relevant risk factors and treatment issues that may be addressed early on and throughout the treatment process. Progress may also be tracked by comparing patient profiles over time. Where the BHI 2 falls short is in the area of predictive validity. No data are presented within the manual regarding its ability to predict rehabilitative progress or outcome, surgical outcome, pain management, or program outcome. Although the test publisher's website provides a link to articles on presurgical psychological screening (Devlin, Ranavaya, Clements, Scott, & Boukhemis, 2003) and psychological factors associated with whiplash (Richter et al., 2004), these manuscripts include no data supporting the BHI 2.

Although the authors are praised for the development of both patient and community samples, limited additional data are available regarding specific problems and treatment settings. As such, comparisons are somewhat difficult.

SUMMARY. The authors are commended for developing an instrument that specifically addresses the psychological assessment needs of patients in medical or rehabilitation settings. The BHI 2 is an improvement over the original. Its multitude of scales and content areas provide rich fodder for promoting the understanding and treatment of patients in these settings. The key concern remains a lack of predictive validity data and, thus, the authors should direct their future efforts toward responding to this issue. Until then, the BHI 2 should be used, as the authors suggest, as only one source of information within the context of other patient factors and information.

REVIEWER'S REFERENCES

American Psychiatric Association. (2000). *Diagnostic and statistical manual of mental disorders* (4th ed., text revision). Washington, DC: Author.
Devlin, K. J., Ranavaya, M. I., Clements, C., Scott, J., & Boukhemis, R. (2003). Presurgical psychological screening in spinal cord stimulator implants: A review. *Disability Medicine, 3,* 43–48.
Richter, M., Ferrari, R., Otte, D., Juensebeck, H-W., Blauth, M., & Krettek, C. (2004). Correlation of clinical findings, collision parameters, and psychological factors in the outcome of whiplash associated disorders. *Journal of Neurology, Neurosurgery, and Psychiatry, 75,* 758–764.
Turner, S. M., DeMers, S. T., Fox, H. R., & Reed, G. (2001). APA's guidelines for test user qualifications: An executive summary. *American Psychologist, 56,* 1099–1113.

Review of the Battery for Health Improvement 2 by ROMEO VITELLI, Private Practice, Hamilton, Ontario, Canada:

DESCRIPTION. The Battery for Health Improvement 2 (BHI 2) is the latest version of the self-report inventory first developed in 1996 as a measure of psychosocial recovery in rehabilitation settings. The 217-item test is designed to provide rehabilitation professionals with a comprehensive profile measuring various aspects of patient functioning and therapeutic change. The BHI 2 profile consists of 18 scales including two measures of validity (Self-Disclosure and Defensiveness), four physical symptom scales (Somatic Complaints, Pain Complaints, Functional Complaints, and Muscular Bracing), three affective scales (Depression, Anxiety, and Hostility), five Character scales (Borderline, Symptom Dependency, Chronic Maladjustment, Substance Abuse, and Perseverance), and four Psychosocial scales (Family Dysfunction, Survivor of Violence, Doctor Dissatisfaction, and Job Dissatisfaction). The test also contains 31 critical items designed to assess a wide range of risk factors to supplement the test scales. Comprehensive normative data based on census-matched community and patient populations are provided. Time for administration is 35 to 45 minutes and requires test-takers to have a minimum sixth-grade reading level. An audio version of the BHI 2 is also available for patients with reading difficulties. Available formats include pencil and paper, CD-based, or direct computer administration.

The BHI 2 can be administered and scored by nonclinical staff although the test manual recommends interpretation be limited to experienced professionals familiar with accepted standards of test usage. The test manual includes guidelines and case studies that promote consistent interpretation of test results. The test authors give specific cautions concerning the use of the BHI 2 as the sole criterion for clinical decision making and recommend its use as part of an integrative assessment process including clinical interviews, collateral sources of information, and additional psychometric assessment. Clinical judgment is also recommended when using the BHI 2 with patients who do not fall within the 18–65 age range on which the test was normed.

Computer-generated interpretative reports are available in three formats ranging from a simple profile form to an enhanced interpretive form. Test scoring options include mail-in scoring, fax-based scoring, and use of Q-Local software. The BHI 2 can also be used in conjunction with the shorter Brief Battery for Health Improvement 2 (BBHI 2; 17:30).

DEVELOPMENT. The development history of the BHI dates back to 1985 with the initial development of a 600-item research version (BHI R). Successive versions of the BHI instruments were standardized on community-based and patient subjects across 30 U.S. states to provide a stratified nationwide sampling. The patient subjects were recruited from a wide variety of medical settings including vocational rehabilitation, chronic pain, and physical therapy clinics. Community sample data were obtained from a large sample of census-matched subjects from 16 U.S. states. Additional reference groups were obtained to provide BHI 2 reference norms for specific injury populations as well as fake-bad and fake-good conditions

The BHI 2 represents a substantial expansion of the BHI with the inclusion of two new clinical scales (Survivor of Violence and Functional Complaints) and two new validity measures (Defensiveness and Self-Disclosure) as well as revisions of six of the original BHI scales. Content analysis of BHI 2 items using a 12-member panel of expert judges yielded 40 content areas and a mean interjudge agreement level of 91%. The test manual outlines the development and validation of the BHI family of tests and their use in numerous research studies that are cited in the bibliography.

TECHNICAL. Information on the normative samples and the standardization process is provided in the BHI 2 user's manual. Reliability data for the BHI 2 are provided with alpha reliability coefficients falling in the .73–.97 range for the different normative samples. Test-retest reliability coefficients fall into the .88–.97 range for a physical rehabilitation patient sample showing reasonable stability over a 7-day test period. Information about interscale correlations for community-based and patient samples is also provided.

Criterion-referenced validation of the BHI 2 scales uses the MMPI-2 (Butcher, Dahlstrom, Graham, Tellegen, & Kaemmer, 1989) and the MCMI-III (Millon, Davis, & Millon, 1997) as the principal criterion validity measures. Additional criterion measures include the McGill Pain Questionnaire (Melzack, 1975) and the MMPI-2 Hypochondriasis (HS) Scale to validate the BHI 2 Pain Complaints Scale. The manual outlines a series of correlation findings using data from the patient samples.

Analysis of variance studies of the BHI 2 validity scales showed significant differentiation between the fake-good, fake-bad, community, and patient samples. Correlation analyses also showed

that BHI 2 physical symptom, affective, character, and psychosocial scales strongly correlated with the MMPI-2 and MCMI-III analogues.

Factor analysis of the 40 BHI 2 content areas yielded a seven-factor model accounting for 67.4% of total variance. The obtained factors include Demanding Dependency, Aggressiveness, Somatic Concerns, Helpless Depression, Addictive Tendencies, Job Dissatisfaction, and Worries. The manual describes the obtained factor model and content loadings.

Overall, the validation process meets the psychometric standards for test validation as specified in the Standards for Educational and Psychological Testing (AERA, APA, & NCME, 1999).

COMMENTARY. The BHI 2 is the culmination of over 18 years of research into developing a flexible measure of patient pain, disability, and psychosocial impediments to patient recovery. It was designed for ease of administration and scoring that can be used and reused to address the treatment and care needs of clients in different clinical settings. The reliability and validity research of the BHI 2 demonstrates that it is one of the best instruments available for assessing the broad range of treatment needs in clinical populations.

The test authors acknowledge the need for predictive validation research on the BHI 2 and discussed the ongoing collection of normative data in clinical and community-based populations. Although the BHI 2 validity scales have been found to be useful in discriminating fake-good and fake-bad test subjects, further research is needed to assess the vulnerability of the BHI 2 scales to factitious disorders, random responding, and malingering. Further research is also needed to evaluate the validity of many of the newer BHI 2 scales (i.e., Substance Abuse, Survivor of Violence, and Doctor Dissatisfaction). Other potential avenues for development include research into the role of cultural influences in patient functioning, and further examination of the role of sociodemographic factors in patient recovery. The BHI 2 can be viewed as a valuable addition to the clinical tools that treatment professionals can draw upon for treatment and research.

SUMMARY. The BHI 2 is a 217-item test designed to provide rehabilitation professionals with a comprehensive profile measuring various aspects of patient functioning and therapeutic change. It is part of a family of related instruments that promote flexible measurement of physical symptomatology, affective functioning, psychosocial functioning, and personality. Test formats include pencil and paper, CD-based, and direct computer administration. Guidelines and case studies are provided to enhance consistent interpretation of test results. The test manual outlines the development and validation of the BHI 2 as well as comprehensive community-based and patient population norms.

REVIEWER'S REFERENCES

American Educational Research Association, American Psychological Association, & National Council on Measurement in Education. (1999). *Standards for educational and psychological testing.* Washington, DC: American Educational Research Association.

Butcher, J. N., Dahlstrom, W. G., Graham, J. R., Tellegen, A., & Kaemmer, B. (1989). *MMPI-2 (Minnesota Multiphasic Personality Inventory-2) manual for administration and scoring.* Minneapolis: University of Minnesota Press.

Melzack, R. (1975). The McGill Pain Questionnaire: Major properties and scoring methods. *Pain, 1,* 277–299.

Millon, T., Davis, R., & Millon, C. (1997). *MCMI-III (Millon Clinical Multiaxial Inventory-III) manual* (2nd ed.). Minneapolis: NCS Pearson.

[17]
Bayley Scales of Infant and Toddler Development–Third Edition.

Purpose: Designed to "assess the developmental functioning of infants and young children."
Population: Ages 1-42 months.
Publication Dates: 1969-2006.
Acronym: Bayley-III.
Scores, 19: Cognitive, Language (Receptive Communication, Expressive Communication, Total), Motor (Fine Motor, Gross Motor, Total), Social-Emotional, Adaptive Behavior (Communication, Community Use, Functional Pre-Academics, Home Living, Health and Safety, Leisure, Self-Care, Self-Direction, Social, Motor, Total).
Administration: Individual.
Price Data, 2006: $895 per complete kit including administration manual (2006, 266 pages), technical manual (2006, 163 pages), 25 Cognitive, Language, and Motor record forms, stimulus booklet, picture book, manipulative set, 25 Social-Emotional/Adaptive Behavior Questionnaires, 25 Caregiver Report forms, rolling case, and PDA Administrative Assistant; $98 per 25 Cognitive, Language, and Motor record forms; $75 per 25 Social-Emotional/Adaptive Behavior Questionnaires; $225 per stimulus booklet; $15 per picture book; $150 per administration manual; $150 per technical manual.
Time: (30-60) minutes.
Comments: Hand scored or scored with use of a PDA.
Authors: Nancy Bayley.
Publisher: The Psychological Corporation, A Harcourt Assessment Company.

Cross References: See T5:270 (48 references); for reviews by Carl J. Dunst and Mark H. Fugate of a previous edition, see 13:29 (130 references); see also T4:266 (58 references); for reviews by Michael J. Roszkowski and Jane A. Rysberg of an earlier edition, see 10:26 (80 references); see also 9:126 (42 references) and T3:270 (101 references); for a review by Fred Damarin, see 8:206 (28 references); see also T2:484 (11 references); for reviews by Roberta R. Collard and Raymond H. Holden, see 7:402 (20 references).

Review of the Bayley Scales of Infant and Toddler Development—Third Edition by RENÉE M. TOBIN, Assistant Professor of Psychology, and KATHRYN E. HOFF, Associate Professor of Psychology, Illinois State University, Normal, IL:

DESCRIPTION. The Bayley Scales of Infant and Toddler Development—Third Edition (Bayley-III) consists of five scales designed for use with young children aged 1 month to 42 months. The Bayley-III assesses young children's developmental functioning across five domains: Cognitive, Language (Receptive and Expressive), Motor (Fine and Gross), Social-Emotional, and Adaptive (Conceptual, Social, and Practical) Behavior. Its stated purposes are to identify children with developmental delay(s) and to provide data for intervention planning. The Bayley-III builds on previous versions of the test by using multiple methods of assessment. That is, children complete tasks to provide data about their Cognitive, Language, and Motor Development and primary caregivers provide questionnaire data about children's Social-Emotional and Adaptive Functioning. A more focused measure of test observations has also been incorporated into the Bayley-III with the express goal of better informing intervention planning. Testing time for children ages 1 month to 12 months is estimated at 50 minutes; testing time for older children (13 to 42 months) is expected to take 90 minutes.

DEVELOPMENT. This edition of the Bayley has maintained the objectives and general assessment approach of its predecessors. For instance, the authors kept an eclectic theoretical approach to the test without focusing on any one theory over another. Rather, the test developer focused on relevant research in child development. The Bayley-III also has maintained or improved on the psychometric properties of previous editions. Accordingly, the author updated the norms based on the 2000 U.S. Census. To maintain its high standards, it also includes updated stimulus materials, revised instructions for item administration, and improved caregiver involvement.

Those familiar with the Bayley Scales of Infant Development, Second Edition (BSID-II) will notice some improvements to this version. First, the author opted to incorporate established measures of social-emotional and adaptive functioning into the Bayley-III. More specifically, she replaced the Behavior Rating Scale with an adapted version of the Greenspan Social-Emotional Growth Chart: A Screening Questionnaire for Infants and Young Children. She also incorporated the Parent/Primary Caregiver form of the Adaptive Behavior Assessment System—Second Edition (ABAS-II; Harrison & Oakland, 2003) into the Bayley-III, allowing for more comprehensive coverage of these areas of functioning that map onto current special education law and the AAMR (1992) guidelines. Further, the Bayley-III provides norms at 10-day intervals of infants between the ages of 16 days and 5 months 15 days to allow for more precise measurement during this period of rapid development.

Another major improvement is the increased clinical utility of the instrument because of the new inclusion of growth scores. That is, the Bayley-III provides charts on which to graph a child's development in each area over time. This provision has direct implications for intervention planning and progress monitoring. Additionally, the manual was reorganized, and the instructions were revised for clarity and to reduce demands on abilities outside the domain being assessed (e.g., reduced motor demands for cognitive items, reduced language demands for motor items). The test materials were also improved by a more play-based focus and by extending the ceilings and floors for the subtests, allowing for better measurement at the extremes (i.e., high and low performers). The author also wisely split the text relevant to the test into two manuals: administrative and technical.

TECHNICAL. In general, the psychometric properties of the Bayley-III far exceed the guidelines recommended by the American Educational Research Association, American Psychological Association, and National Council on Measurement in Education (1999). The author provides impressive data about the reliability and validity of this instrument. For example, separate studies

were conducted to examine the Bayley-III in relation to the BSID-II, WPPSI-III, PLS-4, PDMS-2, and the ABAS—II Parent/Primary Caregiver Form. She also provides detailed data regarding the use of the Bayley-III with special populations including children with Down syndrome, pervasive developmental disorders, cerebral palsy, specific language impairment, at-risk for developmental delay, asphyxiation at birth, prenatal alcohol exposure, small for gestational age, and born premature or with low birth weight. Overall, the research conducted during the development of the Bayley-III was exemplary.

The normative sample for the Cognitive, Language, and Motor Scales of the Bayley-III consists of 1,700 children between the ages of 16 days and 43 months 15 days. The normative sample was stratified by race/ethnicity, age, sex, parent educational level, and geographic location. Participants in the normative sample were recruited through identification by examiners, health clinics, child development centers, university research centers, speech therapy clinics, hospitals, places of worship, and other children's organizations. The manual does not state how many participants were found with each recruiting method. Participants were excluded from the normative sample if they were receiving Early Childhood Intervention (ECI) services; were diagnosed with attention-deficit/hyperactivity disorder, chromosomal abnormality, congenital infections, disorder secondary to prenatal exposure to toxic substances (e.g., fetal alcohol syndrome), disorders reflecting disturbance of the development of the nervous system, genetic or congenital disorder, or mental retardation; inborn errors of metabolism; intraventricular hemorrhage; respiratory disorder; severe attachment disorder; severe sensory impairment; low birth weight; prematurity; and currently admitted to a hospital, mental, or psychiatric facility. Special group studies examining the groups listed were later conducted and a proportion (about 10%) of these participants were later included in the normative group.

The norms for the Social-Emotional Scale were obtained from 456 children (.5 months to 42 months) who were included in the normative sample of the Greenspan Social-Emotional Growth Chart (Greenspan, 2004); similarly, the norms for the Adaptive Behavior Scale were obtained from

1,350 children (birth to 5 years 11 months) in the ABAS-II normative sample.

The overall reliability coefficients (coefficient alpha for individual scales), as calculated with Fisher's z transformation, ranged from .86 (Fine Motor) to .91 (Cognitive, Expressive Communication, and Gross Motor). The reliabilities of the Social-Emotional and Adaptive Behavior Scales were similarly strong (.83 to .94; .79 to .98, respectively). Taken together, these results suggest strong internal consistency for the measurement of functioning within these five domains.

A separate study was conducted examining the test-retest reliability of the Cognitive, Language, and Motor Scales of the Bayley-III with a sample of 197 children falling within four representative age groups in the standardization sample. Results indicate a strong consistency in responding over time (with a mean retest interval of 6 days). Discrepancies, when they occurred, were attributed to maturation and/or practice effects. Similarly, the test-retest reliability (mean interval of 12 days), as measured by product-moment correlation coefficients for 207 children, for the Adaptive Behavior Scales was strong. No data were provided for the test-retest reliability of the Social-Emotional Scale.

Confirmatory factor analyses suggest that a three-factor structure fits best with separate factors emerging for Cognitive, Language (with two subtests), and Motor (with two subtests) factors. Intercorrelations among these three factors were not provided.

COMMENTARY. The Bayley-III manuals are well written and clear. The test materials are simple, durable, and well designed. The test is relatively easy to learn, administer, and score, particularly with the assistance of the new computer and/or PDA scoring. The test maker also provides a helpful video in which many of the subtests are demonstrated and administrative suggestions are provided. Like its predecessor, it is not a light test kit; however, the test maker has improved its portability significantly by providing a bag with wheels much like a small carry-on suitcase. Initially packing the case requires considerable visual-spatial ability to get the many stimulus materials, manuals, and protocols in the compact space. In addition to the stimulus materials provided in the test kit, the examiner will need to supply facial tissue, five

small coins, food pellets (e.g., Cheerios), blank 3 x 5 cards, safety scissors, a stopwatch, sheets of blank white paper, and a standard set of stairs.

The Bayley-III is laudable for adding components that increase its clinical utility for intervention planning. In particular, the growth charts and the adaptive behavior scale increase its usefulness. It is clear that the test was updated to allow for progress monitoring and to address the target areas identified by the AAMR. With its extended floors and ceilings, the Bayley-III is better able to assess infants and toddlers who are low or high functioning. In addition, the Bayley-III has been extensively researched during its development as demonstrated by its large representative standardization sample, its reliability, and its convergent and discriminant validity. Although it is unlikely that this instrument will be particularly useful in developing behavioral goals, future research will determine how effective these changes are in assisting with intervention planning.

SUMMARY. The Bayley Scales of Infant and Toddler Development—Third Edition (Bayley-III) is an individually administered assessment targeting the current developmental functioning of infants and toddlers aged 1 to 42 months. It includes five scales assessing the areas of Cognitive, Language, Motor, Social-Emotional, and Adaptive Functioning. The engaging stimulus materials, improved task instructions, and simplified administrative directions allow for a comprehensive assessment of these five areas. The Bayley-III includes several new additions to previous versions of the instrument. For example, it provides growth scores, extended ceilings and floors for subtests, improved clarity of instructions, and a reorganization of the manual (broken into administration and technical). The psychometric properties of the Bayley-III are solid with evidence of strong reliability, convergent and discriminant validity, and research with special populations. These results also highlighted the natural variability of children in this age range, thus, caution in interpretation is recommended. It is unclear how well it will address its second goal, to assist in intervention planning, but it appears to be an improvement over its predecessors. Additional research and use will dictate conclusions about its clinical utility. In general, this instrument is strongly recommended.

REVIEWERS' REFERENCES

American Educational Research Association, American Psychological Association, & National Council on Measurement in Education. (1999). *Standards for educational and psychological testing.* Washington, DC: American Educational Research Association.

Greenspan, S. I. (2004). Greenspan Social-Emotional Growth Chart: A Screening Questionnaire for Infants and Young Children. San Antonio, TX: Harcourt Assessment, Inc.

Harrison, P. L., & Oakland, T. (2003). Adaptive Behavior Assessment System—Second Edition. San Antonio, TX: The Psychological Corporation.

Review of the Bayley Scales of Infant and Toddler Development—Third Edition by JOHN J. VENN, Professor of Special Education, University of North Florida, Jacksonville, FL:

DESCRIPTION. The Bayley Scales of Infant and Toddler Development—Third Edition (Bayley-III) is a comprehensive battery consisting of five scales for evaluating deficits in Cognitive development, Language, Motor proficiency, Social-Emotional development, and Adaptive Behavior. The Language scale includes Receptive and Expressive subtests, and the Motor scale has Fine and Gross Motor subtests. Designed for use with infants and toddlers from 1 to 42 months of age, administration time for the Bayley-III is from 50 to 90 minutes depending on the age of the child. The purpose of the Bayley–III is to measure strengths and weaknesses and to identify current levels of performance in the major developmental domains. The Bayley-III uses a parent-oriented approach, in which the parent/caregiver actively participates in specific parts of the administration. This involvement enables assessment of infants and toddlers in a play-like situation with someone they know and trust.

Appropriately trained, experienced practitioners, including early intervention, early childhood, and child development specialists, school psychologists, and assessment specialists can give, score, and interpret the Bayley-III. The evaluator administers the items in the Cognitive, Language, and Motor domains directly to the child. In contrast, assessment of Social-Emotional and Adaptive skills is conducted by having a parent or primary caregiver respond to a questionnaire. Assessment with the Bayley-III also includes having the evaluator and the parent complete a behavior observation inventory to gauge the child's behavior during the evaluation and to measure the child's behavior at home.

Bayley-III scores include scaled scores, composite scores, and percentile ranks for all five scales. Confidence intervals are available for the scores from the five scales. Growth scores and developmental age scores are available for the Cognitive, Language, and Motor scales. The growth scores are used to create a chart of progress over time for each subtest. The growth scores range from 200 to 800 with a mean of 500 and a standard deviation of 100.

DEVELOPMENT. The original Bayley Scales of Infant Development, published in 1969, were created using several different infant developmental scales and a wide range of research on infants and toddlers. The second edition, published in 1993, included updated normative data, an expanded age range, improved content coverage, upgraded stimulus materials, and revised psychometric properties. The Bayley-III development process was based on extensive review of the literature and critical reviews as well as input from experts, practitioners, and examiners. New features of the third edition include updating the normative data, developing five scales to meet new guidelines for early childhood assessment, strengthening the psychometric qualities, improving the clinical utility, simplifying the administration procedures, updating administration of individual items, and updating the stimulus materials. These improvements were accomplished while maintaining the basic qualities of the scales.

TECHNICAL. The Bayley-III development process began with several experimental editions that helped finalize the test framework. After creating the framework, the developers completed a pilot study, conducted a national tryout with more than 1,900 children, carried out the standardization study, and assembled and evaluated the test. The standardization included a national sample of 1,700 children representative of infants and toddlers between ages 16 days to 43 months 15 days and samples of children from various special groups. A stratified sampling plan ensured inclusion of representative proportions of infants and toddlers for the variables of parent education, race/ethnicity, and geographic region. The sample included approximately equal numbers of boys and girls for each age group. The manual provides detailed information about the standardization sample including the quality control steps taken to collect the best possible standardization data.

The developers established the reliability of the Bayley-III based on several studies including investigations of internal consistency, test-retest stability studies, and an examination of the interrater reliability of the Adaptive Behavior scale. The manual reports high internal consistency reliability coefficients for the subtests and composites (an average range of .86 to .93). The Social-Emotional scale displayed moderately high coefficients (an average range of .83 and .90). The reliability coefficients for the Adaptive Behavior scale were also moderately high (an average range of .79 to .92) for the skill areas and domains by age group. The test-retest results yielded lower coefficients, which is not unusual when assessing infants and toddlers. The corrected subtest and composite stability coefficients for ages 2–4 months were the lowest (a range of .67 to .80). The coefficients were higher for children in the older age groups. For ages 9–13 months the coefficients ranged from .77 to .86; for ages 19 to 26 months they ranged from .71 to .88; and for ages 33–42 months they ranged from .83 to .94. The interrater reliability coefficient of the general adaptive composite score (GAC) was .82. The coefficients for the three adaptive domains averaged .79, and the average for the skill areas was .73.

The Bayley-III manual provides comprehensive validity information including detailed descriptions of the content, concurrent, and construct validity of the instrument. The content validity information includes descriptions of the comprehensive literature searches and expert reviews conducted to ensure appropriate test items and test construction. The manual explains that the Social-Emotional and Adaptive Behavior scales were derived from existing scales that had prior research to support validity. The Social-Emotional scale was adapted from the Greenspan Social-Emotional Growth Chart: A Screening Questionnaire for Infants and Young Children. The Adaptive Behavior scale is a questionnaire with items and skill areas from the parent/primary caregiver form of the Adaptive Behavior Assessment System—Second Edition (ABAS-II-P). The concurrent validity of the Bayley—III was established by examining the scale's relation to other instruments including the Bayley Scales of Infant Development, Second Edition (BSID-II), the Wechsler Preschool and Primary Scale of Intelligence—Third Edition (WPPSI-III), the Preschool Language Scale—Fourth Edition (PLS-4), the Peabody Developmental Motor Scales, Second Edition (PDMS-2), and the Adaptive Behavioral Assessment System—Second Edition, Parent/Primary Caregiver Form (ABAS-II-P). In addition to these studies comparing Bayley-III scores with scores from these tests, further evidence to support the validity of the Bayley-III as a comprehensive diagnostic assessment tool was provided through several special group studies. The special groups in the studies included children with Down syndrome, pervasive developmental disorders, cerebral palsy, language impairment, at risk for developmental delay, asphyxiation at birth, prenatal alcohol exposure, small for gestational age, and premature or low birth weight. The special group studies also included a review of the validity of the Adaptive Behavior scale with children from other special groups. Evidence to support the construct validity of the instrument included a factor analysis of the subtests. This study used the overall sample of 1,700 children. The results supported a three-factor model and confirmed that the instrument measures motor, language, and cognitive development.

COMMENTARY. Benefits of the Bayley-III include the addition of language and adaptive behavior subtests, which enable more comprehensive evaluation, clearer directions, improved materials, the ability to use subtests by themselves as standalone measures, and the availability of a separate and complete parent report. The Bayley-III also displays excellent overall technical characteristics. However, the Bayley-III takes longer to administer than the previous version, and it still has all of the issues associated with infant and toddler assessment. These include questionable predictive validity, the importance of child and parent comfort with the assessment environment to insure accurate results, and the inherent variability of the day-to-day behavior of infants and toddlers. Despite these limitations, the Bayley-III is an excellent tool for use in a number of situations. Hundreds of researchers have used the Scales as a dependent measure in a variety of investigations with very young children, and a number of researchers have investigated the technical qualities of the earlier versions of the test. The Bayley-III will certainly continue to be used in these ways. The Bayley-III is also useful as a tool for conducting comprehensive evaluations, for use in early intervention team assessment, and as an instrument for documenting progress over time.

SUMMARY. The well-designed and carefully constructed Bayley Scales of Infant and Toddler Development, Third Edition is an individually administered measure of the developmental performance of young children from 1 to 42 months of age. The Bayley-III has an impressive and expanding research base, and this latest revision includes attractive new features. The Bayley-III should be strongly considered as the instrument of choice for assessing infants and toddlers. Users should keep in mind the limitations associated with infant and toddler assessment and use appropriate caution when interpreting Bayley-III results.

[18]

Bayley Scales of Infant and Toddler Development—Third Edition, Screening Test.

Purpose: Designed to "briefly assess the cognitive, language, and motor functioning of infants and young children."
Population: Ages 1-42 months.
Publication Date: 2006.
Acronym: Bayley-III Screening Test.
Scores, 5: Cognitive, Receptive Communication, Expressive Communication, Fine Motor, Gross Motor.
Administration: Individual.
Price Data, 2006: $225 per screening test kit including screening test manual (138 pages), 25 screening record forms, screening stimulus book, picture book, and screening manipulative set; $35 per 25 screening record forms; $100 per stimulus booklet; $15 per picture book; $50 per manual.
Time: (15-30) minutes.
Author: Nancy Bayley.
Publisher: The Psychological Corporation, A Harcourt Assessment Company.

Review of Bayley Scales of Infant and Toddler Development—Third Edition, Screening Test by R. ANTHONY DOGGETT, Assistant Professor of Educational Psychology, and KRISTIN N. JOHNSON-GROS, Assistant Professor of Educational Psychology, Mississippi State University, Starkville, MS:

DESCRIPTION AND DEVELOPMENT. The Bayley Scales of Infant and Toddler Development—Third Edition, Screening Test (Bayley-III Screening Test) is an individually administered screening instrument designed to assess the cognitive, language, and motor abilities of infants and toddlers ranging in age from 1 month to 42 months. The Bayley-III Screening Test includes a subset of items from subtests included in the Bayley Scales of Infant and Toddler Develop-

ment—Third Edition (Bayley-III; Bayley, 2006; 17). According to the test author, the primary purposes of the screening instrument "are to determine quickly whether a child is progressing according to normal expectations and to determine if further, more comprehensive evaluation is needed" (manual, p. 1).

The Bayley-III Screening Test includes five subtests. The Cognitive subtest contains 33 items that assess attention, problem solving, concept formation, novelty preference and habituation, exploration and manipulation, play, object relatedness, and other forms of cognitive development. The Receptive Communication subtest includes 24 items that evaluate auditory acuity (e.g., responding to voices, discrimination sound, localizing sound), vocabulary development (e.g., identification of referenced objects and pictures), and morphological development (e.g., pronouns) in addition to items that assess social referencing and verbal comprehension. The Expressive Communication subtest includes 24 items that assess preverbal communication, vocabulary development (e.g., naming objects and pictures), and morphosyntactic development (e.g., two-word utterances, plurals, verb tense). The Fine Motor subtest contains 27 items that assess visual tracking, reaching, object manipulation, and functional hand skills. The Gross Motor subtest includes 28 items that assess movement of limbs and torso including static positioning (e.g., sitting, standing), dynamic movement (e.g., locomotion and coordination), balance, and motor planning. The subtests may be administered in any order; however, the authors noted that the Receptive Communication subtest must be administered before the Expressive Communication subtest because some items are similar in content across both subtests and exposure to the Expressive Communication subtest may spoil some of the child's responses on the Receptive Communication subtest.

The Bayley-III Screening Test takes approximately 15–20 minutes to administer to children 12 months and younger and approximately 30 minutes to administer to children 13 months and older. The authors noted that no more than three adults should be in the testing area when the screener is administered with the ideal arrangement being the examiner, the child, and one parent or primary caregiver in the room. The authors further encouraged examiners to avoid having other siblings or children in the room to avoid unnecessary distractions that could lead to unusable results. The instrument can be administered, scored, and interpreted by psychologists, early childhood specialists, and other professionals who have obtained training and applied experience in assessment. Although trained technicians or paraprofessionals may be allowed to administer and score the Bayley-III Screening Test, only professionals who have received standardized training in educational or psychological assessment should interpret the results of the instrument.

The Bayley-III Screening Test should be used to "identify young children's degree of risk for developmental delay and to assist the practitioner in determining whether further evaluation is necessary" (manual, p. 2). As such, a cut score may be obtained for each administered subtest in order to determine if the child demonstrates competence in age-appropriate tasks, shows evidence of emerging age-appropriate skills, or demonstrates performance that is suggestive of being at-risk for potential developmental delay. As such, the instrument is not designed to identify specific strengths or weaknesses in the areas assessed, identify degree of impairment, or provide a diagnosis of developmental delay. When such information is needed or diagnosis is warranted, more comprehensive instruments, such as the full Bayley-III Scales should be used.

The Bayley-III Screening Test is accompanied by a 138-page, well-written manual, complete with four chapters discussing the content and structure, development, administration, scoring, interpretation, reliability, validity, and standardization of the instrument. The authors provided thorough discussions about the theoretical and empirical basis for the inclusion of items, development of the subtests, and normative and validation procedures. The stimulus book and manipulatives are housed in a small soft black case that is much easier to manage than the cases provided with previous versions of the Bayley Scales.

TECHNICAL.

Norming-standardization procedures. The standardization sample for the Bayley-III Screening Test included 1,675 children from the larger sample of 1,700 children included in the Bayley-III Scales. Children in the sample ranged from 1 month through 42 months of age. The children were divided into nine distinct age groups where the number of children in each age group ranged from 300 in the 1–3-month age group to 115 in the 31–36-month age group. The sample consisted of approximately equal numbers of female and male children across the nine age groups. Data gathered in October 2000 by the U.S. Bureau of the Census provided the basis for stratification along the variables of parent education level, race/ethnicity, and geographic region. Impressive standardization procedures were followed including extensive literature reviews, expert consultation, and pilot studies designed to evaluate the structure of the instrument, item content, basal and ceiling rules, and bias related to gender and ethnicity.

Reliability. The manual reports internal consistency, test-retest reliability, and interscorer agreement. Internal consistency estimates were obtained using the split-half method corrected by the Spearman-Brown formula. Overall, the average reliability coefficients of the Bayley-III Screening Test ranged from .82 on the Fine Motor subtest to .88 on the Receptive and Expressive Communication subtests. The reliability coefficients by subtest by age band ranged from .73 for the 1–3-month age group on the Fine Motor subtest to .96 for the 31–36-month age group on the Receptive Communication subtest. The internal consistency for the instrument was also assessed on a sample of 622 children from nine specific groups including children diagnosed with Down syndrome, Cerebral Palsy, and Pervasive Developmental Disorder, as well as children having prenatal alcohol exposure, premature or low birth weight, asphyxiation at birth, language impairment, at-risk for developmental delay, and being small for gestational age. This evaluation was conducted to estimate the generalizability of the instrument and revealed that all of the subtest reliability coefficients across all of the identified groups were similar, and in some cases, higher than those reported for the normative sample.

Test-retest reliability of the instrument was assessed in a separate study of 203 children across four age groups ranging from 2 months to 42 months who were tested twice. The interval between the two administrations ranged from 2 to 30 days with a mean retest interval of 7 days. Test-retest stability was estimated using the Pearson product-moment correlation coefficient for subtests and the stability for the overall sample was calculated by averaging the coefficients across the four age groups using the Fisher's z transformation. Results from this investigation revealed that stability coefficients ranged from .80 to .83.

Interscorer agreement was assessed on the entire Bayley-III standardization sample of 1,700 children by comparing the item scores assigned by two independent scorers and then calculating the percent of agreement for each subtest across each age group. Additionally, anchor protocols developed by the research team were used to assess scoring drift. Interscorer reliabilities were high, ranging from .98 to 1.00 across all five scales and all age groups.

Validity. Several sources of validity evidence for the Bayley-III Screening Test were obtained including data related to test content, response processes, relationships to other variables, and studies with special populations. In order to ensure that the instrument appropriately tapped a broad range of domains including cognitive processing, receptive and expressive language, and motor skills, extensive literature reviews, expert reviews, and thorough evaluation of items from the BSID-II were conducted. The test developers and an advisory panel evaluated the response processes of the screener by investigating if the tasks (a) focused on the intended skill, (b) only relied on required skills that were age-appropriate for the item, (c) minimized confounding processes, and (d) focused on child-friendly and child-familiar themes. Although a screening instrument is not intended to yield results with the same accuracy of an in-depth assessment, the results obtained from the screener should be in concordance with the results of the in-depth assessment. As such, the classification accuracy of the Bayley-III Screening Test was compared to that of the Bayley-III Scales. This analysis was accomplished by converting the raw scores obtained on the instruments to age-corrected z-scores and then applying a linear transformation to the z-scores in order to establish a common unit of measurement between the scores of the two instruments. Overall results revealed that the classification accuracy of the Bayley-III Screening Test was moderate to high in this reviewer's opinion.

A number of special group studies were conducted concurrently with the standardization study in order to evaluate the clinical utility of the instrument. Results of these studies revealed that the subtest mean scores were significantly lower than the corresponding mean scores of the matched control group on all subtests for children identified with Down syndrome, Pervasive Developmental Disorder, and Cerebral Palsy. Differences were also obtained, on specific subtests, between the matched control group and children diagnosed with specific language impairment, at-risk for developmental delay, asphyxiation at birth, prenatal alcohol exposure, or being identified as small for gestational age, although effect sizes were generally smaller. No significant differences were observed between the matched control group and children who were born prematurely or with low birth weight on the Bayley-III Screening Test, suggesting that children in this group are "indistinguishable on average from children born at or near term" (manual, p. 104). Other studies designed to calculate the sensitivity, specificity, positive predictive power, and negative predictive power of the screener were conducted with four groups (e.g., Down syndrome, Pervasive Developmental Disorder, Specific Language Impairment, and Cerebral Palsy). Overall, the results from these studies revealed that the instrument has sufficient diagnostic accuracy with these populations. Detailed information on the validity of the instrument is included in the manual for the interested reader.

COMMENTARY. The Bayley-III Screening Test has several important strengths. These include (a) easy administration and scoring, (b) a user-friendly manual that is well-organized and employs graphics to convey technical information and artwork to assist in administration of items, (c) summary and profile forms that aid in interpretation and explanation of results, (d) thorough and impressive standardization procedures, (e) overall good reliability and validity evidence, (f) a sound theoretical basis, and (g) inclusion of additional subtests not present on previous editions of the Bayley Scales. Despite these strengths, the authors strongly caution test users and professionals that the instrument is only a screener and should never be used for purposes of diagnosis or identification of strengths and weaknesses.

SUMMARY. The overall goal of the Bayley-III Screening Test is "to identify children with possible developmental disorders who should be referred for complete diagnostic evaluation" (manual, p. 90). The screener contains five subtests that are designed to assess cognitive functioning, receptive and expressive language, and fine and gross motor skills of children ranging in age from 1 month to 42 months. Although efficient for use as a screener of potential developmental problems, the instrument will be best utilized as a component of a thorough assessment battery for individuals suspected of experiencing delays or meeting criteria for a disorder. Finally, further investigation with populations and instruments other than those used by the authors will continue to provide valuable information about the psychometric properties and clinical utility of the instrument.

REVIEWERS' REFERENCE

Bayley, N. (2006). Bayley Scales of Infant and Toddler Development-Third Edition. San Antonio, TX: Harcourt Assessment, Inc.

Review of the Bayley Scales of Infant and Toddler Development—Third Edition, Screening Test by THERESA GRAHAM, Adjunct Faculty, University of Nebraska-Lincoln, Lincoln, NE:

DESCRIPTION. The Bayley Scales of Infant and Toddler Development—Third Edition, Screening Test (herein referred to as Bayley-III Screening Test) is a norm-referenced test that provides a quick assessment of the cognitive, language, and motor function of infants and young children between the ages of 1 month and 42 months. It is intended to determine whether development in the above areas is proceeding according to normal expectations or whether more evaluation is needed. Using cut scores, the Bayley-III Screening Test can "identify young children's degree of risk for developmental delay" (manual, p. 2).

The Bayley-III Screening Test consists of five subtests: Cognitive, Receptive Communication, Expressive Communication, Fine Motor, and Gross Motor. The Cognitive subtest assesses aspects of cognitive development such as attention, novelty preference and habituation, and problem solving. The Receptive Communication subtest assesses vocabulary development, social referencing, and sound discrimination. The Expressive Communication subtest assesses preverbal communication in infants and vocabulary development in toddler-aged children. The Fine Motor subtest assesses skills such as motor planning, motor speed, and visual tracking. Finally, the Gross Motor subtest assesses the movement of the limbs and

torso. The items included in these subtests are a subset of the items included in the Bayley Scales of Infant and Toddler Development—Third Edition (Bayley III; 17). Item administration and scoring are the same across the two instruments. However, the names of some of the items and the materials used have been changed.

The Bayley-III Screening Test is designed to be administered individually and should be administered by a trained childhood professional. As the test relies on multiple materials and because the target population is vulnerable, it is critical that the administrator be very familiar with the test materials, test protocol, and early childhood assessment. The Bayley-III Screening Test manual provides an excellent description of the general testing guidelines in terms of standard procedures, testing environment, establishing rapport, and test materials. Because the test is intended for use with very young children, the authors suggest having a caregiver present during the administration to aid in obtaining a child's typical performance.

The Bayley-III Screening Test manual also outlines the general administration guidelines in terms of administration time, reversal and discontinue rules, and positions. It is estimated that for children ages 12 months and younger the administration time for complete administration of the five subtests ranges between 15 and 20 minutes. For children older than 13 months, administration time is approximately 30 minutes. It is recommended that all subtests be given during a single administration. However, the subtest order is not strictly prescribed. The only required testing order is that the Receptive Communication subtest be administered before the Expressive Communication subtest.

Information regarding completing the Screening Test record form is provided in the Bayley-III Screening Test manual. Calculating age and starting point are described in the manual and are recorded on the record form. Adjustments are made for prematurity. The test manual also provides a detailed description of the protocol for each item, the materials used, and the scoring criteria used. The record form provides a brief description of each item, including the name of the task, the materials used, and the scoring criteria. A "1" is circled for items correctly demonstrated, and a "0" is circled for items incorrectly demonstrated. Space is provided for comments that the test administrator may want to record regarding the child's performance. In both the manual and the record form, five icons are printed along the side bar of the page to help tab the different subtests: a puzzle piece, a building block, a rattle, a teddy bear, and a ball. At first glance, it would seem that each subtest would be tied to a different icon. However, that is not the case. The cognitive subtest is indicated by the puzzle piece. The Receptive Communication and Expressive Communication subtests are indicated by the building block. The Fine Motor and the Gross Motor subtests are indicated by the rattle. The teddy bear icon and ball icon, although printed on every page, are never utilized. Similarly, the authors note that the subtests are differentiated by different colors on the record form. However, only three colors are used. The same color is used for the Receptive Communication and Expressive Communication subtests and for the Fine Motor and Gross Motor subtests. There may be some internal confusion as to whether the test consists of three subtests or five subtests.

Performance on the subtests is evaluated by calculating the raw scores and then converting them to cut scores by specific age groupings. Raw scores are based on the total number of items on which the child has received full credit. Items that precede the starting point are credited to the child and are included in the raw score. Ceiling is established and testing for each subtest is stopped when the child has received a score of "0" for four consecutive items. Raw scores are noted on the record form. Appendix A, located in the testing manual, provides a conversion table to transform the raw scores to cut scores for each subtest for different age groupings. Three risk categories include: At Risk, Emerging, and Competent. Children whose scores fall in the "competent" range are considered to be at low risk for developmental delay. Children whose scores fall in the "emerging" range may be at some risk and may require more comprehensive evaluation. Children who are designated as "at risk" are considered to be at high risk for developmental delay and most likely will require further evaluation. Because the primary purpose of the Bayley-III Screening Test is to identify children who may need further evaluation, the authors note that the scoring is somewhat biased to avoid cases in which children score in a low risk category (competent) but are later identified with a developmental delay.

DEVELOPMENT. Because the items used on the Bayley-III Screening Test were selected from the Bayley-III, the authors provide a brief description of the development of the Bayley-III. Test development of the larger instrument included a conceptual development phase, a pilot phase, a national tryout, standardization, and final evaluation. Items for the Bayley-III were derived from a literature search and guidance from experts. The items for the Bayley-III Screening Tests were generally selected to cover the main components of the Bayley-III, all age groups, and "have the highest discrimination of the standardization sample at the 25th percentile" (manual, p. 84). It is estimated that between 31% and 50% of the items from the Bayley-III were included for the Bayley-III Screening Test subtests. Although the authors include information regarding a pilot test analysis that was used to evaluate items for the Bayley-III, no specific pilot test results for the Bayley-III Screening Test were described.

TECHNICAL.

Standardization. The sample used to standardize the Bayley-III Screening Test was a subset of the sample used to standardize the Bayley-III. The standardization sample for the Bayley-III Screening Test included 1,675 children divided into nine age groups, ranging in age from 1 month to 42 months. The sample represents the U.S. population in terms of gender, race/ethnicity, region, and parental education. To be included in the sample, children needed to meet specific criteria. Generally, the authors were trying to compose a sample of typically developing children. Therefore, children who were born with significant medical complications, or were currently diagnosed or receiving treatment for a developmental difficulty were excluded from the sample. (However, approximately 10% of the sample was composed of children with developmental needs.) Tables are provided in the manual that compare the standardization sample with U.S. Census information in terms of race/ethnicity, geographic region, and parent education level. In addition to the standardization sample, children with special developmental needs were recruited. A total of 622 children with various special needs (e.g., Asphyxia, Cerebral Palsy, Down Syndrome) were administered the Bayley-III Screening Test. The results of these separate studies were used to address the validity of the instrument.

Cut scores to determine the risk categories were calculated based upon the distribution for each age group and each subtest. The "At Risk" category represents 2 standard deviations from the mean or the 2nd percentile (i.e., 2% of the sample scored at or below the cut score). The "Emerging" category represents .67 standard deviations from the mean or the 25th percentile (i.e., 25% of the sample scored at or below the cut score).

Reliability. Reliability was assessed in terms of internal consistency and test-retest reliability. Internal consistency was determined using the split-half method. Reliability coefficients are presented for the nine age groups and each subtest. Coefficients ranged from .73 to .96, indicating adequate internal consistency. In addition, satisfactory internal consistency was met with the mixed special groups. Although some age groups were combined because of sample size, reliability coefficients ranged from .87 to .97.

Test-retest stability was assessed with a group of 203 children who were given the test twice. The sample was obtained from the standardization sample from four age groups: 2–4 months, 9–13 months, 19–26 months, and 33–42 months. The retest occurred anywhere between 2 and 30 days with the average retest time being 1 week. The test-retest reliability coefficients ranged from .80 to .83.

Validity. Evidence of validity of the Bayley-III Screening Test was assessed in four ways: test content, response processes, relationship to other variables, and special studies. The authors contend that content validity was addressed by conducting an extensive review of the literature concerning the developmental domains assessed in the Bayley-III Screening Test and by soliciting expert reviews. Unfortunately, the authors did not cite any of the specific literature examined.

Concurrent validity was evaluated in two ways. First, the relationship of performance of the Bayley-III Screening Test and the Bayley-III was examined. The authors wanted to confirm that the three category assignments (At Risk, Emerging, and Proficient) corresponded to the scaled scores on the Bayley-III. To do this, the authors used the sample from the Bayley-III Screening Test standardization. Indeed, the results indicate that no children who were classified as Proficient on the Bayley-III Screening Test received a scaled score of 1–4 on the Bayley-III on any of the subtests. Similarly, no children who were classified as At Risk on the Bayley-III Screening Test received a scaled score of 8–19 on the Bayley-III on any of the subtests. At the extremes, then, no children would have been sent for further evaluation who did not warrant it, and more importantly, no children who needed to be sent for further evaluation were assessed as proficient. Thus, the percent of children correctly identified according to the Bayley-III Screening Test was high.

The Bayley-III Screening Test was also evaluated in terms of its clinical utility. That is, does the screening test serve to identify children correctly from special population groups for more in-depth evaluation? The authors present a number of studies to examine that question. However, they appropriately caution the reader that the studies are flawed in terms of sample recruitment (the samples were not randomly obtained), sample size (the sample sizes in the studies tend to be small), and sample ages (not all ages for which the Bayley-III Screening Test is intended were fully examined). Nine studies are discussed that included children with Asphyxia, Cerebral Palsy, At Risk for Developmental Delay, Down Syndrome, Fetal Alcohol Syndrome/Effects, Language Impairment, Prematurity, Pervasive Developmental Disorder, and Small for Gestational Age. In addition, the authors present data that address the sensitivity, specificity, and negative and positive predictive power of the Bayley-III Screening Test for some of these special groups. For children with Down Syndrome, Pervasive Developmental Disorder, Specific Language Impairment, and Cerebral Palsy, the Bayley-III Screening test has a very low false negative rate. The percent of children misdiagnosed was very low, ranging from 2 to 8%.

COMMENTARY. The Bayley-III Screening Test is intended to provide a quick tool to evaluate children from 1 month to 42 months to determine whether further evaluation might be indicated. Indeed, the screening test can be completed in less than 30 minutes. Moreover, the studies done to evaluate the sensitivity and specificity of the instrument suggest that the instrument does a good job in accurately identifying children who need further evaluation. However, it is difficult to provide a complete endorsement of the Screening

Test because some of the technical information is either missing or incomplete. As noted earlier, the standardization sample for the Bayley-III Screening Test was a subset of the sample used to standardize the Bayley-III. It is unclear whether both tests were given or in what order. More information regarding the standardization study would be helpful. Similarly, the list of the references used to develop the items is necessary. In terms of the validity of the instrument, results of the Bayley-III Screening Test are only compared to results of the Bayley-III. Validity would have been more strongly supported if the Screening Test had been compared with other developmental measures, such as the Battelle Developmental Inventory, Second Edition, which also has a full version and a shorter screening instrument.

SUMMARY. In general, the Bayley-III Screening test provides a good overall measure of cognitive, language, and motor functioning of young children. The positive reports of clinical utility make it a helpful tool. It is a good first step in identifying children who may need further evaluation. It will be important in future validation studies to include other measures of early childhood development.

[19]
Becker Work Adjustment Profile: 2.

Purpose: Designed to "assess work habits, attitudes, and skills of people with special needs" and to assess level of supports needed.
Population: Individuals ages 13 and over, who are mentally retarded, physically disabled, emotionally disturbed, learning disabled, and/or economically disadvantaged.
Publication Dates: 1989–2005.
Acronym: BWAP:2.
Scores, 5: Work Habits/Attitudes, Interpersonal Relationships, Cognitive Skills, Work Performance Skills, Broad Work Adjustment.
Administration: Individual.
Price Data, 2007: $70.75 per value kit including 25 test booklets and manual (2005, 76 pages); $33.75 per 25 test booklets; $40 per manual; $41 per starter set including 2 test booklets and manual; quantity discounts available.
Time: (10–20) minutes.
Comments: Ratings by teachers, counselors, or other vocational professionals; 5 levels of work supports are also assessed.
Author: Ralph L. Becker.
Publisher: Elbern Publications.

Cross References: See T5:275 (1 reference); for reviews by Brian Bolton and Elliot L. Gory of an earlier form, see 11:33.

Review of the Becker Work Adjustment Profile: 2 by JAMES T. AUSTIN, Senior Research Specialist, and STEPHANIE D. TISCHENDORF, Senior Program Associate, Center on Education and Training for Employment, College of Education and Human Ecology, The Ohio State University, Columbus, OH:

DESCRIPTION. The Becker Work Adjustment Profile: 2 (BWAP:2) is an instrument completed by a rater-observer that measures vocational competency in special needs populations in competitive or sheltered work situations. It can best be described as a restandardization of the 1989 Work Adjustment Profile (as the items have not changed). The 1989 first edition was a revision of a rating scale developed as a part of a 1965 Federal grant. In particular, individuals from categories of mental retardation, learning disabled, physically disabled, emotionally disturbed, and economically disadvantaged were included in the restandardization sample.

The BWAP:2 questionnaire booklet is laid out as follows. Page 1 provides a section for documenting background information about the examinee and the evaluator (name, sex, date, grade, date of birth, age in years/months, IQ, school/facility, primary disability, secondary disability, name of evaluator, title of evaluator). Instructions to the rater-observer are provided at the bottom of the first page. Pages 2 through 12 present 63 ratings distributed across domains named Work Habits/Attitudes (HA) with 10 items, Interpersonal Relations (IR) with 12 items, Cognitive Skills (CO) with 19 items, and Work Performance Skills (WP) with 22 items. For each item, anchor statements range from 0 to 4 (from the lowest level to the highest level of vocational competence). A rater or evaluator completes the BWAP:2, adds the number of points, and enters the totals at the end of each domain. Page 13 of the BWAP:2 contains an Individual Profile Form in sections including (a) background information (duplicated from p. 1), (b) score summary featuring entries for the raw score, *T*-score, Percentile, Work Placement, and Work Support needs together with specific Norm Used and Broad Work Adjustment (BWA), and (c) Vocational Competency Profile with *T*-scores and a set of work/

training placements. Page 14, titled Interpretation of Results supports a narrative interpretation.

An extensive user's manual is provided with the tool. In this manual, the developer begins by defining relevant constructs. First, the author defines four major methods of client work evaluation: work samples, job analysis, standardized tests, and situational assessment. The BWAP:2 is placed in the category of situational assessment (which features associated advantages and disadvantages, for example knowledge of and opportunity to observe rated individuals). Second, the nature of vocational competence as being closely related to work adjustment is discussed. In addition, vocational competence is considered to be typical rather than maximal performance. The entire profile is discussed in the manual, the questionnaire booklet is briefly described including the Level B requirement for rater competence, and research topics are offered as examples of BWAP:2 usage.

The user's manual presents the basics of administration, scoring, and use while providing technical evidence on reliability and validity. The instrument should be completed by a rater who has, according to the user's manual and questionnaire booklet, "closely observed the daily work behavior of the client and has knowledge of the individual's work adjustment" (questionnaire booklet, p. 1). The estimated time to complete the instrument is 15 minutes, probably not including the interpretation of results. A Work Habits/Attitudes figure in the user's manual is useful, and it is clear how interventions might be structured from the items (that is, eating habits at work could be a target for a hypothetical individual). Material concerning completion of the individual profile form and the interpretation of raw and normative scores is presented. A sample Individual Profile Form is helpful in that it provides quantitative and qualitative information, in addition to a visual representation of a sample profile. Normative procedures are also presented as discussed below.

DEVELOPMENT. Extensive information is available regarding the restandardization of the BWAP:2 between 2002-2005. The approach is norm-referenced and employs classical test theory. The user's manual provides reliability and validity support for use of the BWAP:2. Because the profile items are unchanged, this review focuses upon the technical section below.

TECHNICAL. We reviewed the questionnaire booklet and a 69-page user's manual authored by the developer (Becker, 2005). The questionnaire booklet was described above. The user's manual contains six chapters, references, and two appendices (Appendix A provides Normative Tables and Placements/Supports Guidelines; Appendix B provides three case studies). No other technical documents were provided for review by the publisher. We considered, in addition, the reviews of the first edition of the BWAP by Bolton (1992) and by Gory (1992) to identify and verify changes suggested for the BWAP:2.

Standardization. The developer provided extensive information regarding the restandardization of the revised Work Adjustment Profile. The user's manual categorizes the standardization sample by diagnostic category and gender and presents numbers, means, and standard deviations for chronological age and IQ, and IQ range. No information is given about the method of IQ assessment, which makes it hard to evaluate the procedure. The sample was geographically diverse as shown. Sites in 20 states were included in the norm sample, with random samples drawn by the administrator of each site. A breakdown of the standardization sample into four levels of mental retardation: mild, moderate, severe, and profound is also presented. The normative data are found in Appendix A, collapsed across age levels, with T-scores, raw scores for each of the domains, Broad Work Adjustment, and percentiles.

Reliability. The user's manual provides reliability information. The author presents different estimates of reliability for the BWAP:2 derived from subsamples based on diagnostic category (Ns ranging from 76 to 105). The reliability estimates are presented and discussed and include internal consistency (coefficient alpha) for domain (.80 to .93) and for BWA total score (.87 to .91), retest estimates over a 2-week interval (range .82 to .96 across domains), standard errors of measurement (.91 to 5.84), and interrater reliability estimated by pairs of raters for a sample of 117 adults in three sheltered workshops (range .82 to .89 across domains, .87 for Broad Work Adjustment). These numbers represent both multiple estimates of reliability and normally acceptable values. The importance of taking into consideration the standard error of measurement and using measures other than the BWAP:2 scores in making decisions regarding vocational competence is discussed separately. The standard error of measurement for the BWAP:2 is summarized as a matrix (domain X category) with three levels of confidence (95, 90, 68). This section of the manual also includes a brief example of interpreting an individual's scores using the standard error of measurement.

Validity. The user's manual also provides validity information, which is decomposed into the traditional evidence categories of content, criterion, and construct. This tripartite view is itself a relic of pre-1999 *Standards* interpretations, as the testing standards now emphasize the primacy of construct validity. Evidence of content validity is asserted in two ways: (a) rationales for the four domains and (b) statistical item analysis. The former rationale is based on research conducted in the mid-1960s and may require revisiting at some point in time to incorporate recent advances (Schaylock, Baker, & Croser, 2002). The scale analysis ($N = 1,194$ from the standardization sample) is a combination of test item analysis (depending heavily on the point biserial correlations) and exploratory principal factors analysis (using common variance as the starting point). The item analysis resulted in median point biserial coefficients that seem large relative to commonly reported values in technical reports (.67, .61, .79, .65 for the domains and .70 for BWA). The factor analysis resulted in a four-factor solution accounting for nearly identical proportions of variance compared to the first edition scale (same items, different standardization sample). A confirmatory approach to factor analysis provides a stronger test of the items as assigned to the domain structure, and could facilitate a comparison between a general factor model (Broad Work Adjustment only) and a four-factor solution, or a hierarchical solution with first-level factors and a second level BWA factor. This analysis was not performed, however.

Criterion related validity is discussed, although aspects of the description seem primarily to portray convergent validity, indicating separate instruments that measure the same characteristics or traits are highly correlated. Criterion-based validity typically is regarded as how well an instrument predicts success in some external outcome. The author describes correlation of the BWAP:2 scores with the AAMR Adaptive Behavior Scale, which also, in part, measures vocational competence. These data are used to address the recommendation by Bolton (1992) not to use the placements provided with the first edition. Development of supports, to the credit of the developer, is also discussed in light of Bolton's (1992) critique that the work placement levels and work supports should be disregarded because of a lack of supporting evidence. The use of overlap statistics and cross-validation samples helps in this regard. Follow-ups on placements and supports would add evidential strength. Finally, construct validity is addressed explicitly in the user's manual. The treatment consists of a definition and proposal of six testable hypotheses. Additional issues would include consequential validity associated with use of the instrument, as well as categories of evidence identified by Messick (1995).

COMMENTARY. This restandardization is based on an instrument that was revised and reviewed in *The Eleventh Mental Measurements Yearbook* by Bolton (1992) and by Gory (1992). Some issues requiring clarification that would be helpful to address in future documentation and revision of the BWAP:2 are:

1. The economically disadvantaged subgroup is a curious category to include with various mentally and psychologically disabled groups. A more detailed rationale for the inclusion of this particular group, including supportive information would be beneficial (e.g., the "generational poverty" stream of research and intervention; Payne, 1998, 1999). Further, the learning-disabled group is a wide-ranging category and additional detail would be helpful.

2. The largest emphasis is provided on mental retardation, and the theoretical model, although never clearly stated, may be dated when compared with recent approaches to concepts such as learning disability (Flanagan, Ortiz, Alfonso, & Mascolo, 2001).

3. Modern test theory might be helpful in analyzing data and conceptualizing the constructs, and confirmatory factor analysis might be employed productively in evaluating the construct validity of the four domains and the BWA composite score.

4. Comparing systematically ordered levels of "opportunity to observe" or familiarity across rater-observers might establish the validity of ob-

servational data. It is important that the familiarity of vocational competence is standardized across all raters.

5. Another consideration would be to increase the length of the retest period to more than 2 weeks and to compare the results to the results of the 2-week retest period. A combination of longer retest period and high obtained values would strengthen the reliability evidence.

6. It would be interesting to have the results of the standardization sample ($N = 4,019$) further broken down by age (instead of mean age by disadvantage), ethnicity, and sex. It would also be beneficial to have the data provided that would include any statistically significant differences in regard to age, ethnicity, and sex.

SUMMARY. The shifts in practice and policy occurring within the field of mental retardation (cf. Schaylock, Baker, & Croser, 2002) mean that reliable, valid, and unbiased client evaluation is crucial for a range of purposes. These purposes range from individual intervention planning to program evaluation and from basic research to policy evaluation. The BWAP:2 was restandardized to improve the rating of vocational competency by observers of individuals from five special populations. Four domains and a total composite score (Broad Work Adjustment) are used in developing a profile and work placement that can be related to work support needs. The BWAP:2 instrument is easily administered and scored by raters with ample opportunity to observe the focal individual. The evidence provided concerning the revision and standardization may well support the use of scores from the instrument in appropriate situations. Consider that a large sample of 4,019 was used to develop the norms, although it is unbalanced in favor of mental retardation diagnosis (1621/4019 = 40%). Several improvements have been made to this instrument, including a revised version of the score summary (IPF), expanded normative tables, updated normative standardization data, example case studies, and attention to previous *MMY* reviewer suggestions. Any issues that remain do not preclude a recommendation to use the BWAP:2 but rather suggest continuing to develop its knowledge base.

REVIEWERS' REFERENCES

Bolton, B. (1992). [Review of the Becker Work Adjustment Profile.] In J. J. Kramer & J. C. Conoley (Eds.), *The eleventh mental measurements yearbook* (pp. 83–84). Lincoln, NE: Buros Institute of Mental Measurements.

Flanagan, D. P. Ortiz, S. O., Alfonso, V. C., & Mascolo, J. T. (2001). *Achievement test desk reference (ATDR): Comprehensive assessment and learning disability.* Boston: Allyn & Bacon.

Gory, E. L. (1992). [Review of the Becker Work Adjustment Profile.] In J. J. Kramer & J. C. Conoley (Eds.), *The eleventh mental measurements yearbook* (pp. 84–86). Lincoln, NE: Buros Institute of Mental Measurements.

Messick, S. (1995). Validity of psychological assessment. *American Psychologist, 50,* 741–749.

Payne, R. K. (1998). *A framework for understanding poverty.* Highlands, TX: RFT Publishing Company.

Payne, R. K. (1999). *Bridges out of poverty: Strategies for professionals and communities.* Highlands, TX: RFT Publishing Company.

Schaylock, R. L., Baker, P. C., & Croser, M. D. (Eds.). (2002). *Embarking on a new century: Mental retardation at the end of the 20th century.* Washington, DC: American Association on Mental Retardation.

Review of the Becker Work Adjustment Profile: 2 by PAM LINDSEY, Associate Professor, Curriculum and Instruction, Tarleton State University, Stephenville, TX:

DESCRIPTION. The Becker Work Adjustment Profile: 2 (BWAP:2) is a revision of the 1989 version of this instrument and is designed to assess an individual's vocational competence. Like its predecessor, the BWAP:2 uses an observer rating scale format to assess the work habits, attitudes, and skills of an individual with disabilities.

The questionnaire booklet contains 63 items organized in four domains or factors and provides a Broad Work Adjustment (BWA) profile. The domains are Work Habits/Attitudes, Interpersonal Relations, Cognitive Skills, and Work Performance Skills. Vocational personnel familiar with the daily demands of the work environment and the individual being assessed complete the questionnaire.

The instrument uses a rating scale format from 0–4 for each item in specific domains. The rating of zero represents a negative rating with 4 representing a positive rating. Raw scores for each domain are translated into T scores and percentile ranks by disability category, and an overall Broad Work Adjustment score is also provided. Sample case studies are also provided with examples of profile scoring and interpretation.

DEVELOPMENT. The BWAP:2 was developed based on the construct of vocational competence, which is purported to be a central component of rehabilitation for people with disabilities. Vocational competence is defined as qualitative statements about the work functioning of persons with a variety of disabilities or economic disadvantages (user's manual, p. 2).

Many of the items from the BWAP were retained for the new edition. Additional domains and items were developed due to the changes in knowledge about the work behaviors and vocational assessment in general for people with disabilities. The 63 items were analyzed using an item analysis procedure. Results showed adequate support for the validity of the items.

TECHNICAL. The BWAP:2 was normed on a population of 4,019 individuals with various disabilities throughout the United States, Canada, and Puerto Rico. Standardization data are presented by individual disability characteristics, gender, and region.

Construct and criterion-related validity data were reported as adequate. Criterion-related validity was investigated by comparing the BWAP:2 scores of 167 individuals with mental retardation with their scores on the AAMR Adaptive Behavior Scale, which measures vocational adjustment as well as adaptive behavior. The analysis yielded evidence of adequate validity.

Internal consistency, test-retest, and interrater reliability studies were conducted. Internal consistency measures indicate adequate reliability across domains and total battery for diverse groups of individuals. Test-retest results using intervals of 2 weeks suggested BWAP:2 scores were stable over this period of time. Interrater reliability data showed coefficients ranging from a low of .82 for the Work Habits/Attitudes Scale to a high of .84 on the Work Performance Skills and .87 for the total test. Overall, technical data appear to support adequate reliability and validity.

COMMENTARY. Like other observational instruments, the BWAP:2 has the inherent "bias" of the observer's personal perceptions and prejudices. The instrument has merit to help professionals assess the vocational competence of persons with disabilities on the job, assist them in developing appropriate rehabilitation plans, and target areas for intervention. It has adequate technical soundness and provides standardized scores that may be compared with other measures such as adaptive behavior or cognitive abilities.

SUMMARY. The BWAP:2 is an easy-to-use instrument that provides useful information about the work and personal habits of people with disabilities. It should be considered as part of an overall assessment process to help professionals target areas of strength and weakness for on-the-job training and

support for their clients. It is not meant to be a comprehensive assessment of an individual's ability to work or be successful on the job.

[20]

The Beery-Buktenica Developmental Test of Visual-Motor Integration, 5th Edition.

Purpose: "Designed to assess the extent to which individuals can integrate their visual and motor abilities (eye-hand coordination)."

Publication Dates: 1967–2004.

Acronym: BEERY VMI.

Scores, 3: Beery VMI, Visual Perception [optional], Motor Coordination [optional].

Administration: Group or individual.

Forms, 2: Full, Short.

Price Data, 2007: $110 per starter kit including manual (2004, 210 pages), 10 Full forms, 10 Short forms, 10 Visual Perception forms, and 10 Motor Coordination forms; $55 per manual; $90 per 25 Full forms; $67 per 25 Short forms; $14.95 per 25 Visual Perception forms; $14.95 per 25 Motor Coordination forms (bulk discounts available for forms); $140 per Teaching Materials starter kit including My Book of Shapes, My Book of Letters and Numbers, Developmental Teaching Activities, Developmental Wall Chart, and 25 Stepping Stones Parent Checklists; $36.25 per My Book of Shapes; $36.25 per My Book of Letters and Numbers; $47 per Developmental Teaching Activities; $26 per Stepping Stones Parent Checklist; $20.75 per Developmental Wall Chart for Visual-Motor Integration.

Comments: The subtests must be given in the appropriate sequence.

Authors: Keith E. Beery and Natasha A. Beery.

Publisher: Pearson.

   a) BEERY VMI.
     1) *Full Form.*
      Population: Ages 2–100.
      Time: (10–15) minutes.
     2) *Short Form.*
      Population: Ages 2–7.
      Time: (5–15) minutes.
   b) VISUAL PERCEPTION [OPTIONAL].
     Population: Ages 2–100.
     Time: (3–7) minutes.
   c) MOTOR COORDINATION [OPTIONAL].
     Population: Ages 2–100.
     Time: (3–7) minutes.

Cross References: For a review by Jan Visser of an earlier version, see 14:119; see also T5:815 (52 references); for reviews by Darrell L. Sabers and James E. Ysseldyke of the Third Revision, see 12:111 (25 references); see also T4:768 (42 references), 9:329 (15 references), and T3:701 (57 references; for reviews by Donald

A. Leton and James A. Rice of an earlier edition, see 8:870 (24 references); see also T2:1875 (6 references); for a review by Brad S. Chissom of an earlier edition, see 7:867 (5 references).

Review of The Beery-Buktenica Developmental Test of Visual-Motor Integration, 5ᵗʰ Edition by THERESA GRAHAM, Adjunct Faculty, University of Nebraska-Lincoln, Lincoln, NE:

DESCRIPTION. The Beery-Buktenica Developmental Test of Visual-Motor Integration, 5ᵗʰ Edition (herein referred to as the Beery VMI) is a norm-referenced test used to assess "the extent to which individuals can integrate their visual and motor abilities (eye-hand coordination)" (administration, scoring, and teaching manual, p. 1). The Beery VMI is intended to provide an early screening for children ages 2 to 18. Research suggests that the ability to copy geometric forms is correlated with academic achievement and reading readiness. The authors purport that using the Beery VMI allows for early identification of children who have not integrated fully their motor and visual abilities and provides specific guidance in intervention. The current edition of the Beery VMI includes 2 forms: the Full Form and the Short Form. The Full Form consists of 30 items and can be used with children ages 2 to 18 years and adults to age 100. The Short Form includes 21 items and is used with children ages 2 through 7 years. Two additional standardized tests are provided: the Beery VMI Visual Perception test and the Beery VMI Motor Coordination test. These tests use the same geometric forms as the Beery VMI and are intended to provide information regarding visual and motor performance separately. The fifth edition extends the scope by including standardizing information for 2-year-olds. In addition, the authors identified 600 "Stepping Stones" or milestones that may serve as precursors for visual-motor integration for birth through age 6. The Stepping Stones have been listed in both the Parent Checklist and in the VMI instrument as a reference guide. Developmental Teaching Activities based on the Stepping Stones were also developed for this edition. Finally, the fifth edition provides updated standardization information.

The Beery VMI allows for either individual or group administration (although it is recommended that preschool children be tested individually). The assessment takes about 10 to 15 minutes. Although administration of the supplemental standardized tests is not necessary, the authors stress that if they are used, the Beery VMI should be administered first, followed by the Visual Perception test and then the Motor Coordination test. The Short Form and Full Form differ in that the Short Form only includes the first 15 geometric shapes included on the Full Form. Additional information on test administration and the protocol are described in the administration, scoring, and teaching manual. Both suggested prompts and directions on what not to do in administering the test are provided to help ensure uniformity in test administration. Children indicate their answers by drawing or copying the shape on the answer form.

The recording and scoring sheet are included in the Beery VMI test booklet. Copied or traced forms receive either "1" for a correct or "0" (no-score) for items not copied or traced correctly. Specific guidelines regarding scoring are outlined in the administration, scoring, and teaching manual. Pictorial examples as well as specific scoring criteria are provided for each geometric form. Although testing may continue beyond a child's ability level, scoring is stopped after three consecutive forms have received a "no score." The raw score consists of the total number of correct forms until the ceiling. The child's raw score is converted to the standard score using the conversion charts provided. Finally, the standard score is used to calculate the percentile score for the child's specific age range. Tables for each of these scores are provided in the administration manual and the Beery VMI test booklet.

Separate test booklets for the Visual Perception and the Motor Coordination tests are provided. Information regarding test administration and scoring are detailed in the administration manual. Raw scores are noted on the specific supplemental test, but then can be transferred to the Beery VMI test booklet in the summary section to obtain standard scores, scaled scores, and percentiles.

In addition to the assessment tools included in the VMI Fifth Edition, four materials are provided that are meant to enhance the teaching of visual-motor integration. The Beery VMI Stepping Stones Parent Checklist includes about 200 of the "Stepping Stones" milestones that a parent can observe and note on a check list. The Beery

VMI Developmental Teaching Activities contains about 250 activities geared to help children from birth to age 6 develop skills to facilitate visual-motor development. The Beery VMI My Book of Shapes provides 100 activities that may assist later "teaching of letter and numeral shapes" (administration, scoring, and teaching manual, p. 118). The Beery VMI My Book of Letters and Numbers extends upon the earlier activities and provides 100 additional exercises providing more practice with numerals and upper- and lower-case letters.

DEVELOPMENT AND STANDARDIZATION. The original Beery VMI was developed in the early 1960s. Since that time, the Beery VMI has been normed five times with over 11,000 children. In all of the norming studies that have been conducted, no changes in the mean raw scores for children ages 3 through 18 have been noted. Moreover, the authors report that although the scoring system changed between the third and fourth edition, the two norms correlated .99. Given the similarity, the authors cite many earlier studies that have been conducted to evaluate the validity and reliability of the Beery VMI.

The administration manual provides information about the development and publication of the original test in 1967, which consisted of 27 items. All of the items are geometric forms (i.e., no numerals or alphabetic figures are used to reduce bias). The current version includes three additional, new items for each of the tests to extend the range through age 2 years. These items were developed on the basis of a literature search (although no references are cited). The three items include Imitated Marking, Spontaneous Marking, and Contained Marking. Although the authors state that a pilot test was done with a pool of items with 1- to 3-year-olds, specific information regarding the pilot test (e.g., other piloted items, mean age of each group) was not provided.

TECHNICAL. The current norming study was conducted with 2,512 children from across the United States, including 23 child-care, preschool, public, and private schools with children ranging from 1 year through 18 years of age. Information regarding age, ethnicity, urban versus nonurban residence, and parental information is provided. Unfortunately, mean ages for each age group are not provided. This is important given that the standard scores are presented in 3-month intervals.

Reliability. Much of the information regarding reliability and validity of the Beery VMI is based on earlier norming studies. The authors state that because there has been high consistency in the earlier Beery VMI editions, they would present the data from earlier studies. For example, Rasch-Wright results are provided for data based on administration of the 1995 fourth edition and therefore did not include the three items developed for the 2-year-olds. Similarly, internal consistency results were reported on a study using the third edition. Although the results of both of these reliability analyses are well within an accepted range, it is difficult to determine the reliability of the items developed specifically for the 2-year-old children.

Time sampling and interscorer reliability were assessed using the fifth edition. Time sampling was assessed with a group of 115 children between the ages of 5 and 11. With a retest average time of 10 days, the retest raw score coefficients were .89 for the Beery VMI, .85 for Visual Perception, and .86 for Motor Coordination.

Interscorer reliability was evaluated with two professionals independently scoring 100 randomly selected testings from the norming group. The interscorer reliabilities were .92 for the Beery VMI, .98 for Visual Perception, and .93 for the Motor Coordination. The authors do not give any information regarding what age groups were randomly selected. Given that the administration and scoring of the three items developed for the 2-year-old groups are scored during the administration of the test, it is not clear how independent scorers would be able to evaluate the responses accurately.

Finally, the authors present a table of overall reliability indicating three major error sources: interscorer, content sampling, and time sampling. The averages range from .85 to .98. These data should be somewhat cautiously interpreted for the 2-year-old sample given the different versions used to assess these measures of reliability.

Validity. Content validity, concurrent validity, construct validity, predictive validity, and bias are each addressed in the administration manual. In terms of content validity, the authors relied upon the Rasch-Wright measure that was used in norming the fourth edition and that was discussed in the reliability section above. Again, the fourth version did not include the three items added to the fifth version. Similarly the evidence provided for adequate concurrent validity was based on a study using the fourth edition. In that study, results of the Beery VMI were correlated with parts of the Developmental Test of Visual Perception (DTVP-2) and the Wide Range Assessment of Visual-Motor Abilities (WRAVMA) Drawing Subtest. Although the correlations ranged from .52 to .75, there were no comparisons with tests using younger children. Nor could those comparisons be made with the measures chosen. The DTVP-2 is intended for ages 4 and above, and the WRAVMA is used with children ages 3 and above.

Seven hypotheses were generated to assess construct validity. Hypotheses such as whether the Berry VMI is developmental, the extent to which the Beery VMI is related to its supplemental tests, the relationship between the Beery VMI and nonverbal aspects of intelligence and academic achievement, and performance on the Beery VMI of populations with disabling conditions were addressed. Using test results from the fifth edition, the authors demonstrated that indeed the raw scores increased with age. In addition, performance on the Beery VMI was significantly related to performance on the supplemental tests for each age group. Interestingly, the correlation differs significantly from one age to another. For example, the correlation between the Beery VMI and the Visual Perception test for the 12-year-olds is only .08. However, for the 2-year-olds it is .57. The authors provided no explanation of this finding. With respect to the other hypotheses, the authors cite data using earlier versions, which support the hypotheses generated (e.g., performance on the Beery VMI is related to nonverbal intelligence and achievement).

In terms of predictive validity, most of the research cited addressed the issue of reading readiness. The Beery VMI helps to predict reading difficulties at school entry. Other studies looked at school achievement and retention. However, the authors point out that these predictive correlations seem to decline as children get older.

BEERY VMI TEACHING TOOLS. In addition to the Beery VMI and supplemental tests, the authors developed four sets of materials to facilitate the teaching of visual-motor integration from birth through age 6. The "Stepping Stones" were created on the basis of a literature search for

"'milestones' in gross motor, fine motor, visual, and visual-motor development" (administration, scoring, and teaching manual, p. 93). Initially, thousands of milestones were generated. This list was reduced to 600 by applying a set of criteria based on how many sources cited the milestone and whether the milestone related to an age norm. The 600 Stepping Stones are organized into four categories: gross motor development, fine motor development, visual development, and visual-motor development. In addition, specific age (in months) is provided next to the behavior. The Beery VMI Stepping Stones Parent Checklist lists about 200 of the 600 stepping stones. This list is intended for parents to mark development over time. In this context, the stepping stones are organized into 6-month intervals. It is not clear what criteria were used to select the subset included in the parent checklist. Also, given that the authors emphasize that age-equivalent scores should be interpreted cautiously, it was surprising that they placed specific age (in years and months) for specific visual-motor milestones (e.g., 1 yr 5 month, Begins to run). Most developmental literature would designate a milestone as that which occurs within a specific range of time.

The Beery VMI Developmental Teaching Activities, the Beery VMI My Book of Shapes, and the Beery VMI My Book of Letters and Numbers are workbooks that the authors developed with a team of early childhood teachers and resource specialists. Face validity was assessed with a group of 100 teachers and specialists who evaluated the materials. Ninety-eight teachers and resource specialists gave the materials a top rating.

COMMENTARY AND SUMMARY. The Beery VMI, 5ᵗʰ Edition was intended to expand the earlier version by standardizing the instrument to include 2-year-old children. In addition, the authors wanted to introduce the 600 Stepping Stones and to provide materials intended to teach visual-motor integration. Given the issues raised in the reliability and validity sections, it seems that the authors only met part of their goal. In terms of the Stepping Stones and teaching materials, the authors provide useful and practical information, suggestions, and activities for facilitating the visual-motor development of children under the age of 6. The workbooks are easy to use and would be helpful to parents and educators. Although the authors state that these materials have sufficient face validity, there is no other technical information provided. The authors contend that future studies will be needed to ascertain the impact of these interventions on children's visual-motor development.

In terms of the extension of the Beery VMI to include 2-year-olds, it is not clear whether this version adequately measures visual-motor integration in 2-year-olds because much of the reliability and validity data were based on studies using earlier versions of the Beery VMI. More information on how the three new items were generated, and a study assessing the reliability and validity of the instrument with 2-year-olds would have been important to include. Moreover, the authors never provide a solid rationale for why it was necessary to extend the standardization to 2-year-old children. Results of this instrument with 2-year-olds must be cautiously interpreted. Yet, given these limitations, The Beery VMI, 5th Edition is still a useful tool for assessing visual-motor development in preschool and school-age children and providing specific materials for enhancing that development.

Review of The Beery-Buktenica Developmental Test of Visual-Motor Integration, 5th Edition by THOMAS McKNIGHT, Psychologist, Private Practice, Spokane, WA, and TIFFANY CHANDLER, Doctoral Student, School Psychology Program, Mississippi State University, Starkville, MS:

DESCRIPTION. According to the authors, this newest edition of the VMI and its two supplemental subtests "provide the most valid and economical visual-motor screening battery available for preschool to adult ages" (administration, scoring, and teaching manual, p. 14). The authors note that an examination with the VMI is often followed with an assessment of visual-perception and motor abilities, using either informal clinical evaluation (detailed in the manual) or The Beery-Buktenica Developmental Test of Visual-Motor Integration, 5th Edition (Beery VMI) new and standardized Visual Perception and Motor Coordination supplemental tests. There is a clear recommendation to use the supplemental tests to get additional clinical information, even if performance on the VMI is adequate, and there is a specific notation that tests must be administered in the order they were normed: VMI, Visual Perception, and Motor Coordination. Raw scores are converted to age-equivalent scores, for those institutions that "still require them" (administration, scoring, and teaching manual, p. 91) and there is the often unheeded notation that age scores "should be used with caution" (p. 91). Raw scores are also converted to standard scores, T scores, scaled scores, and percentile rank.

The VMI Full Form consists of 30 items and can be used individually or with groups, within 15 minutes. The Short Form (21 items) is typically used individually, with children ages 2 through 7, and requires about 10 minutes. Each of the supplemental tests, used with ages 2 through 100, reportedly takes about 5 minutes to complete.

The current edition of this long-used instrument includes the administration-technical manual, short and full formats of the test, and supplemental tests. In addition, teaching material (shapes and letters/numbers) workbooks, details of age-appropriate Developmental Teaching Activities (for youngsters through 6 years, 11 months), and a Parent Checklist to aid parents' tracking the child's development are included.

DEVELOPMENT. The original edition of the VMI was published in 1967 and quickly embraced by clinics and schools needing information about the visual-perceptual and motor development of children. Geometric forms, rather than letters or numbers, were selected, to minimize the impact of culture and/or education. In 1964, the VMI was normed on 1,030 children from Illinois. The next edition was cross-validated with a sample of 2,060 California children in 1981, and the 1989 study included a national sample of 2,734 children. The 1995 sampling used 2,614 children, representing five major geographical areas of the United States. Although the VMI has been normed in some other countries, such values are not provided in the manual. The 5th edition (including supplemental tests) was normed (January 2003) on 2,512 children, across four major regions of the United States. The authors note that norms, "over time and place have been consistent, particularly at the preschool and elementary grade level for which it was designed" (administration, scoring, and teaching manual, p. 96).

TECHNICAL ASPECTS. The 2003 normative sample, the basis for the current edition of the VMI, reflects the 2000 U.S. Census, relative to gender, ethnicity, urban versus nonmetropolitan, region, and parent education. Children used in the normative study were spread evenly across ages 2–17, with fewer children selected for ages 1 and 18.

Coefficient alpha reliability varies from mid .70s to high .80s, with mean alpha of .82 for VMI and Motor Coordination, and .81 for Visual Perception. Overall test-retest reliability, reported in the manual, is in the mid-to-high .80s, a slight improvement over the 4th edition. Historically, interrater reliability for earlier editions has varied, depending on level of training and familiarity with the material, but the manual for the current edition reports overall mean interrater reliabilities of .92, .91, and .90 for the VMI, Visual Perception, and Motor Coordination, respectively.

Concurrent validity is rather modest: .52 with 122 students tested with the Wide Range Assessment of Visual Motor Abilities (Drawing test), .63 with the Comprehensive Tests of Basic Skills, .80 with chronological age, and .66 with the Wechsler Intelligence Scale for Children—Revised (WISC-R). Mean correlations between the Bender-Gestalt and earlier editions of the VMI range from .29 to .93 (median .56). Although the manual references a number of studies related to predictive validity, few findings are reported and only one of the referenced studies is less than 5 years old; the rest are 10–20+ years old. Validity research with the supplemental tests is not reported and there is no information about the effectiveness of the Developmental Teaching Material.

COMMENTARY. The current revision of the VMI clearly focused on the "stepping stones" of developmental progress, from birth to age 6, so parents can track a child's growth and development. The age range of the VMI was extended downward to age 2, clearly appropriate for this end. Administration and scoring procedures are clear. Reliability is somewhat improved over earlier editions. Validity remains a question. Although the manual noted the VMI was particularly able to identify high-risk boys in kindergarten who subsequently had reading difficulty and referenced a number of other studies related to predictive validity, statistical information is all but absent.

SUMMARY. The Beery-Buktenica Developmental Test of Visual-Motor Integration, 5th Edition is the somewhat expanded version of earlier editions. Reliability is somewhat improved but recent information about predictive validity is seriously limited. There is no information about the effectiveness of the supplemental teaching material. The VMI has long held a place in clinics and schools that deal with children and this usage is expected to continue. More information about predictive validity, with false negatives and false positives, and research to evaluate the effectiveness of the Developmental Teaching Material are needed. The VMI continues to be a valuable screening instrument of children's visual-motor skills.

[21]
Behavior Assessment System for Children [Second Edition].

Purpose: Designed "to facilitate the differential diagnosis and educational classification of a variety of emotional and behavioral disorders of children and to aid in the design of treatment plans."

Population: Ages 2–25.

Publication Dates: 1992–2004.

Acronym: BASC-2.

Administration: Individual.

Forms, 11: Teacher Rating Scales–Preschool, Teacher Rating Scales–Child, Teacher Rating Scales–Adolescent, Parent Rating Scales–Preschool, Parent Rating Scales–Child, Parent Rating Scales–Adolescent, Self-Report of Personality—Child, Self-Report of Personality—Adolescent, Self-Report of Personality—College, Structured Developmental History, Student Observation System.

Price Data, 2007: $120 per examination set including manual (2004, 606 pages), and 1 sample each of the hand-scored forms for all levels of the Teacher Rating Scales, Parent Rating Scales, and Self-Report of Personality, Parent Feedback Report, the Structured Developmental History, and the Student Observation System; $249.99 per ASSIST software for Windows and Macintosh (nonscannable version); $589.99 per ASSIST software for Windows and Macintosh (scanning version); $85.75 per manual; $125 per BASC-2 Training Video (DVD or VHS); additional price data available on publisher's website (www.pearsonassessments.com).

Foreign Language Editions: Spanish edition available for the Parent Rating Scales, the Self-Report of Personality, and the Structured Developmental History.

Comments: Also available are Parent Feedback Reports for the Teacher Rating Scales, Parent Rating Scales, and Self-Report of Personality forms; computer programs (BASC-2 ASSIST and BASC-2 ASSIST Plus, which includes optional content scales) to score and report results are also available; computer version of the student Observation System (BASC-2 Portable Observation Program) is available for use with Windows (Win 98 SE, 4.0 NT, 2000, ME, XP), Macintosh (OS 9.2, 10.x), Palm (OS 3.x, 4.x, 5.x), and Pocket PC (2000, 2002); audiorecordings are available for administration of the Parent Rating Scales and Self-Report of Personality forms.

Authors: Cecil R. Reynolds and Randy W. Kamphaus.

Publisher: Pearson.

a) TEACHER RATING SCALES.

Price Data: $32.25 per 25 hand-scored forms; $26.75 per 25 computer-scored forms; $42.75 per 25 scannable forms; $26.75 per 25 Parent Feedback Reports.

Time: (10–15) minutes.

1) *Teacher Rating Scales—Preschool.*

Population: Ages 2–5.

Scores, 19: Externalizing Problems (Aggression, Hyperactivity), Internalizing Problems (Anxiety, Depression, Somatization), Adaptive Skills (Adaptability, Social Skills, Functional Communication), Behavioral Symptoms Index, Attention Problems, Atypicality, Withdrawal, Content Scales (Anger Control, Bullying, Developmental Social Disorders, Emotional Self-Control, Executive Functioning, Negative Emotionality, Resiliency).

2) *Teacher Rating Scales—Child.*

Population: Ages 6–11.

Scores, 23: Externalizing Problems (Aggression, Hyperactivity, Conduct Problems), Internalizing Problems (Anxiety, Depression, Somatization), School Problems (Attention Problems, Learning Problems), Adaptive Skills (Adaptability, Social Skills, Leadership, Study Skills, Functional Communication), Behavioral Symptoms Index, Atypicality, Withdrawal, Content Scales (Anger Control, Bullying, Developmental Social Disorders, Emotional Self-Control, Executive Functioning, Negative Emotionality, Resiliency).

3) *Teacher Rating Scales—Adolescent.*

Population: Ages 12–21.

Scores, 23: Externalizing Problems (Aggression, Hyperactivity, Conduct Problems), Internalizing Problems (Anxiety, Depression, Somatization), School Problems (Attention Problems, Learning Problems), Adaptive Skills (Adaptability, Social Skills, Leadership, Study Skills, Functional Communication), Behavioral Symptoms Index, Atypicality, Withdrawal, Control Scales (Anger Control, Bullying, Developmental Social Disorders, Emotional Self-Control, Executive Functioning, Negative Emotionality, Resiliency).

b) PARENT RATING SCALES.

Price Data: $32.25 per 25 hand-scored forms; $26.75 per 25 computer-scored forms; $42.75 per 25 scannable forms; $26.75 per 25 Parent Feedback Reports.

Time: (10–20) minutes.

1) *Parent Rating Scales—Preschool.*

Population: Ages 2–5.

Scores, 20: Externalizing Problems (Aggression, Hyperactivity), Internalizing Problems (Anxiety, Depression, Somatization), Adaptive Skills (Adaptability, Social Skills, Activities of Daily Living, Functional Communication), Behavioral Symptoms Index, Attention Problems, Atypicality, Withdrawal, Control Scales (Anger Control, Bullying, Developmental Social Disorders, Emotional Self-Control, Executive Functioning, Negative Emotionality, Resiliency).

2) *Parent Rating Scales—Child.*

Population: Ages 6–11.

Scores, 22: Externalizing Problems (Aggression, Hyperactivity, Conduct Problems), Internalizing Problems (Anxiety, Depression, Somatization), Adaptive Skills (Adaptability, Social Skills, Leadership, Activities of Daily Living, Functional Communication), Behavioral Symptoms Index, Attention Problems, Atypicality, Withdrawal, Control Scales (Anger Control, Bullying, Developmental Social Disorders, Emotional Self-Control, Executive Functioning, Negative Emotionality, Resiliency).

3) *Parent Rating Scales—Adolescent.*

Population: Ages 12–21.

Scores, 22: Externalizing Problems (Aggression, Hyperactivity, Conduct Problems), Internalizing Problems (Anxiety, Depression, Somatization), Adaptive Skills (Adaptability, Social Skills, Leadership, Activities of Daily Living, Functional Communication), Behavioral Symptoms Index, Attention Problems, Atypicality, Withdrawal, Control Scales (Anger Control, Bullying, Developmental Social Disorders, Emotional Self-Control, Executive Functioning, Negative Emotionality, Resiliency).

c) SELF-REPORT OF PERSONALITY.

Price Data: $32.25 per 25 hand-scored forms; $26.75 per 25 computer-scored forms; $42.75 per 25 scannable forms; $26.75 per 25 Parent Feedback Reports.

Time: (20–30) minutes.

1) *Self-Report of Personality—Interview.*

Population: Ages 6–7.

Scores, 8: Anxiety, Attitude to School, Attitude to Teachers, Atypicality, Depression, Interpersonal Relations, Social Stress, Emotional Symptoms Index.

2) *Self-Report of Personality—Child.*
Population: Ages 8–11.
Scores, 20: School Problems (Attitude to School, Attitude to Teachers), Internalizing Problems (Atypicality, Locus of Control, Social Stress, Anxiety, Depression, Sense of Inadequacy), Inattention/Hyperactivity (Attention Problems, Hyperactivity), Emotional Symptoms Index (Social Stress, Anxiety, Depression, Sense of Inadequacy, Self-Esteem, Self-Reliance), Personal Adjustment (Relations with Parents, Interpersonal Relations, Self-Esteem, Self-Reliance).

3) *Self-Report of Personality—Adolescent.*
Population: Ages 12–21.
Scores, 26: School Problems (Attitude to School, Attitude to Teachers, Sensation Seeking), Internalizing Problems (Atypicality, Locus of Control, Social Stress, Anxiety, Depression, Sense of Inadequacy, Somatization), Inattention/Hyperactivity (Attention Problems, Hyperactivity), Emotional Symptoms Index (Social Stress, Anxiety, Depression, Sense of Inadequacy, Self-Esteem, Self-Reliance), Personal Adjustment (Relations with Parents, Interpersonal Relations, Self-Esteem, Self-Reliance), Content Scales (Anger Control, Ego Strength, Mania, Test Anxiety).

4) *Self-Report of Personality—College.*
Population: Ages 18–25.
Scores, 23: Internalizing Problems (Atypicality, Locus of Control, Social Stress, Anxiety, Depression, Sense of Inadequacy, Somatization), Inattention/Hyperactivity (Attention Problems, Hyperactivity), Emotional Symptoms Index (Social Stress, Anxiety, Depression, Sense of Inadequacy, Self-Esteem, Self-Reliance), Personal Adjustment (Relations with Parents, Interpersonal Relations, Self-Esteem, Self-Reliance), Content Scales (Anger Control, Ego Strength, Mania, Test Anxiety).

d) STRUCTURED DEVELOPMENTAL HISTORY.
Price Data: $41.75 per 25 history forms.
e) STUDENT OBSERVATION SYSTEM.
Price Data: $35.25 per 25 observation forms.
Time: (15) minutes.
Cross References: for reviews by James Clyde DiPerna and by Robert Spies and Christina Finley Jones of an earlier version, see 14:40; see also T5:280 (6 references); for reviews by Jonathon Sandoval and by Joseph C. Witt and Kevin M. Jones of an earlier edition, see 13:34 (6 references).

Review of the Behavior Assessment System for Children [Second Edition] by STEPHANIE STEIN,

Professor and Chair of Psychology, Central Washington University, Ellensburg, WA:

DESCRIPTION. The Behavior Assessment System for Children [Second Edition] (BASC-2) is a 2004 revision of the original BASC, published in 1992. The BASC-2 claims to be a multimethod, multidimensional system, intended to assess observable behavior and self-perception ratings of individuals, ages 2–25. It provides a triangulated view of a child's behavioral functioning by considering ratings and observations by others (teachers and parents), self-ratings, and background information. The primary purpose of the BASC-2 is to assist in the educational classification of emotional and behavioral disorders in children as well as facilitate the design of treatment plans. Other uses addressed in the manual include assisting with clinical diagnoses using DSM-IV-TR, IEP planning, manifestation determination (determine whether a student's misbehavior is a direct result of their disability), assessment of students with vision or hearing impairments, program evaluation, forensic evaluation, and research. However, little or no evidence is provided to show that the BASC-2 has been specifically designed and validated for all of these uses.

The BASC-2 contains the same five components as the BASC: a Teacher Rating Scale (TRS), a Parent Rating Scale (PRS), a student Self-Report of Personality (SRP), a Structured Developmental History (SDH), and a Student Observation System (SOS) for use with observed classroom behavior. Three separate levels of rating forms are available for the TRS and PRS (Preschool, Child, and Adolescent) and the SRP (Child, Adolescent, and College). The BASC-2 focuses on both positive and adaptive behaviors as well as negative and maladaptive behaviors.

The manual describes several changes in the BASC-2, compared to the original BASC. The changes outlined in the manual include improved reliability and the addition of scales in Functional Communication (TRS and PRS), Activities of Daily Living (PRS), Adaptability (TRS-A and PRS-A), and Attention Problems and Hyperactivity (SRP). All of this was accomplished, apparently, without lengthening any of the rating forms. The BASC-2 also provides new "content scales" intended as an option for interpreting the primary scales. Other changes in the BASC-2 include item changes and item development, the development of a College-Level SRP, provision of more detailed clinical norms, improved software, and minor improvements in the SDH.

The items on the BASC-2 TRS, PRS, and part of the SRP are presented on a 4-point response scale. The BASC-2 provides *T*-scores and percentile ranks on the two rating scales (TRS and PRS) and the self-report measure (SRP). Scores are based on national norms and can be separated by age grouping, gender, or clinical status. These three instruments provide both overall composite scores and individual scale scores. In addition, each rating scale includes validity checks to guard against untruthful or biased responding, misunderstandings or carelessness by the raters, and other potential threats to validity. The instruments can be scored either by hand or computer. The manual provides solid and clear guidelines regarding administration and scoring of the rating scales. It includes an interpretive guide for each scale and composite, provides score classifications based on *T*-scores, identifies High or Low scale scores (comparing the score to the composite mean, adjusted for multiple comparisons) and provides parent feedback reports where the TRS, PRS, or SRP composite scores can be graphed.

DEVELOPMENT. The BASC-2 and its predecessor, the BASC, were developed through a careful examination of the theoretical literature, review of other prominent behavior rating scales and self-report instruments, and extensive clinical consultation and feedback. Teachers, students, and experts were involved in the initial item generation for the BASC, and all items were piloted and passed through a series of reviews by experts as well as statistical reviews prior to their inclusion in the BASC. Confirmatory factor analysis was used to analyze items and resulted in the construction of the scales and the composites. One of the main goals of the authors was to include both positive and adaptive behaviors as well as problematic or maladaptive behaviors.

In the BASC-2, the authors have strived to provide more consistent content across the two external rating scales (TRS and PRS) and have shortened the length of the TRS, presumably to make it more manageable for busy teachers to complete. After a study on the use of an alternative response format for the SRP to improve reliability and improve measurement at the extremes, the SRP was redesigned to include a 4-point response scale (*Never/Sometimes/Often/Almost Always*) in addition to the True/False response format used in the original BASC SRP. Overall, the items and scales of the BASC and the BASC-2 appear to be the result of a careful and thorough development process.

TECHNICAL. The manual for the BASC-2 provides considerable, detailed information about the technical characteristics of the TRS, PRS, and SRP. On the other hand, no technical information is provided on the SDH or SOS.

Standardization. The updated norms for the BASC-2 were collected between 2002 and 2004. Over 13,000 cases were included for ages 2–18 in the general norm sample. The general norms closely reflect U.S. population estimates for race and ethnicity and, for the most part, are well represented for gender and mother's education level with the exception at the youngest age level (2 to 3 years) where the sample is approximately half of the U.S. population estimates. Although the general norms are fairly well-matched to the U.S. population by geographic region, an examination of the testing locations reveals that, especially in the West, the samples tended to be tightly clustered in relatively few areas, leaving some geographic expanses largely or completely unsampled. The College Level norms (SRP-COL) included 706 students (ages 18–25) from a variety of postsecondary institutions. Other than the sample including more females than males, there is little information about the demographic characteristics of this limited norm sample.

The clinical norms were drawn from 1,779 children, ages 4–18, who were identified by parents as having a clinical diagnosis or classification. Classification categories included Learning Disability, Speech-Language Impairment, Mental Retardation/Developmental Disability, Emotional/Behavioral Disturbance, Hearing Impairment, Attention Deficit/Hyperactivity Disorder, Pervasive Developmental Disorders, and Other. Clinical norms were also created for high school students aged 19–21, most of whom were enrolled in special education classes. Other than age, gender, and number of cases per form, no additional data are provided on this group. The clinical samples were not matched demographically like the general norm group and included more males than females at every age level.

Reliability. The BASC-2 manual includes detailed internal consistency and test-retest reliability estimates for the TRS, PRS, and SRP and interrater reliability on the TRS and PRS. Internal consistency coefficients are generally high for all three measures. The TRS composite scores for the general norm group yield the most consistently high alpha coefficients, with most falling in the low to mid .90s. Coefficients for the PRS composites are strong as well. The SRP composites yield mostly alpha coefficients in the mid-to-high .80s. The clinical norms have reliability coefficients that are almost equivalent or just slightly lower. Other relatively lower alpha coefficients (still mid .80s, however) are on the School Problems composite for the TRS (clinical norms); the Externalizing Problems for Preschoolers on the PRS; and the School Problems, Inattention/Hyperactivity, and Personal Adjustment composites of the SRP. The Externalizing Problems (except for PRS Preschoolers), Adaptive Skills, and Behavioral Symptom Index on the TRS and PRS all yield coefficients above .90 with the exception of the Behavioral Symptoms Index for PRS in the College clinical sample. As expected, the individual scale scores of the TRS, PRS, and SRP tend to be lower than the composite scores. This is especially noted in the Activities of Daily Living scale on the PRS (.65 to .78) and the Somatization (.61 to .74) and Self-Reliance (.68 to .74) scales of the SRP. Because a minimum alpha coefficient of .90 is recommended for making decisions about individuals (Salvia & Ysseldyke, 2004), the composite scales should be the preferred scores on the BASC-2 for decision-making purposes.

The test-retest reliabilities were based on a median time span of about 6 weeks for the TRS and PRS and approximately half that time for the SRP. Adjusted reliabilities for composites on the TRS ranged from a low of .81 for Internalizing Problems in adolescence to a high of .93 for BSI for children. They ranged from a low of .64 for Anxiety scales in the adolescent age group to a high of .90 on several scales. On the PRS, the mother was usually the rater. The composite adjusted reliabilities ranged from a low of .78 (Child—Internalizing) to a high of .92 (Child—BSI). The reliability coefficients ranged from low of .65 for the Somatization scale in the Child age group to a high of .88 for Conduct Problems in the Adolescent age group. On the SRP, the composite scales

yielded test-retest reliabilities mostly in the upper .70s to lower .80s (somewhat higher for the College level). On the individual scales, the reliability coefficients ranged from a low of .61 for the Self-Reliance scale in the Adolescent age group to a high of .99 for Alcohol Abuse in the College age group. For the most part, composite scales yielded higher test-retest reliabilities than the individual scales on all three measures. Within the age groups, the Child age group yielded the highest median reliability on the TRS (.86) and the PRS (.84), whereas the College group yielded the highest median reliability (.84) on the SRP.

As one would expect, interrater reliabilities on the TRS and PRS are lower than both internal consistency and test-retest reliability values. This is especially true for the TRS, where the median adjusted reliabilities range from a low of .53 for the Adolescent age group to a high of .65 for the preschool group. Some low reliability estimates (.19) occurred on the TRS individual scales of Somatization and Withdrawal at the Adolescent level. On the PRS, the median adjusted interrater reliability estimates ranged from a low of .69 at the Child level to a high of .77 at the Adolescent level. No individual scale reliability estimates for the PRS fell below the mid .50s.

Validity. The evidence for validity of the BASC-2 provided in the manual includes scale intercorrelations (divergent and convergent); factor analyses (covariance structure analysis and principal axis analysis); concurrent validity; and TRS, PRS, and SRP profiles of various clinical groups. For the most part, the scale intercorrelations reveal expected relationships between the scales on each measure. A few scales that seem to be less related to the others include Somatization on the TRS and PRS, Anxiety on the PRS, and Sensation Seeking on the SRP.

The bulk of the validity data described in the manual involves correlational studies between the three measures on the BASC-2 and other well-known teacher, parent, and self-report measures. The TRS and Achenbach System of Empirically Based Assessment (ASEBA) correlate highly on similar constructs, especially in externalizing problems (range of .75 to .85). Internalizing problems correlations were lower overall (ranging from .64 to .80). With the Conners' Teacher Rating Scale—Revised and the TRS, higher correlations were found in the child age group than the adolescent sample. Most scales of similar constructs on these two measures were moderately to highly correlated except for low correlations between the anxiety scales (.26 to .35), apparently due to significantly different content on these scales of the TRS and the Conners. Correlations between the TRS on the BASC-2 and the original BASC resulted in very high correlations, as expected, with the lowest being .83 (Atypicality scale).

As with the TRS, the concurrent validity correlations between the PRS and the ASEBA are high on similar constructs, especially in externalizing problems (ranging from .73 to .84). Likewise, internalizing problem correlations were lower overall (ranging from .65 to .75). Similarly, correlations between the Conners' Parent Rating Scale—Revised and the PRS were higher in the child sample than the Adolescent sample, with moderate to high correlations most scales of similar constructs except for the Anxiety scales (.35 to .41). Correlations between the PRS and the Behavior Rating Inventory of Executive Functioning (BRIEF) Parent form were also moderate to high. Finally, the very high correlations between the PRS on the BASC-2 and the BASC mirror the pattern on the TRS, with the lowest correlations occurring on the Atypicality scale (.73) in the child sample.

Concurrent validity studies with the SRP show moderate to strong correlations with both the ASEBA Youth Self-Report and the Conners-Wells' Adolescent Self-Report Scale. Comparisons between the SRP and the Children's Depression Inventory indicate that the SRP correlates much better on depression scales at the Adolescent level (.69) than the Child level (.29). Correlations between the SRP and the Revised Children's Manifest Anxiety Scale (RCMAS) are moderate in both the Child and Adolescent samples. The College level sample of the SRP was compared on both the Brief Symptom Inventory and the Beck Depression Inventory-II and resulted in moderate correlations. Also at the College level, the SRP and MMPI-2 correlated moderately to high on anxiety scales; moderately in depression, self-esteem, parent/family, and alcohol abuse scales; and low to moderate in somatization scales. Finally, the correlations between the BASC-2 and the BASC on the SRP were low (median of .51 for Children and .68 for Adolescents). Though the change in the response format on the SRP could

account for somewhat lower correlations, the authors hypothesize that the low N may be the cause of the lower than expected correlations in the Child sample.

Evidence in support of the construct validity of the BASC-2 is provided through the clinical scale and composite score profiles on the TRS, PRS, and SRP for the Child and Adolescent age groups. The resulting profile patterns are mostly consistent between the age groups and generally reflect behavioral strengths and weaknesses that one would expect within the clinical groups. In each case, the most divergent age group profiles occur in the sample diagnosed with mood disorders (bipolar or depression). The authors advise caution when interpreting these profiles due to the relatively low N.

COMMENTARY. The impressive psychometric properties of the TRS, PRS, and, to a lesser degree, the SRP are probably the greatest strengths of the BASC-2. The authors go to exhaustive lengths to describe the reliability and validity data on these instruments. In addition, the standardization and national norms (both general and clinical) and the development of the instruments are well documented and should be considered relative strengths. For the most part, the lengthy manual is very thorough, with detailed chapters on the use and interpretation of each component of the BASC-2. Extensive norm tables are available. Other more specific strengths include the use of validity scales and the careful blending of both positive and negative items within the instruments.

Two obvious weaknesses of the BASC-2 are the largely ignored SDH and SOS. It is true that any good assessment of a child's functioning should include a developmental history and some sort of direct observation of the child's behavior in an educational setting. What is unclear is whether these two instruments are the best choice for the job because no psychometric information is provided on these components of the BASC-2. Though a visual scan of the SDH reveals a fairly broad range of developmental questions, the medical section seems unnecessarily lengthy and detailed, whereas the behavioral and educational sections appear to be overly brief. The SOS is even more problematic, mostly because it is framed as an actual assessment instrument rather than just a source of potentially useful background information (as with the SDH). The SOS relies on 3-second time-sampling within 30-second intervals. Though this may provide a relatively easy form of observation, it does not necessarily provide an accurate measure of behavior. A 3-second snippet is likely to miss a number of low frequency but potentially serious behaviors. Other weaknesses of the SOS include an overly vague scale on the behavior key and checklist, a predetermined list of behaviors with no operational definitions, limited options for including individually identified target behaviors, no utilization of a peer reference, and minimal attempts to systematically integrate the observation of environmental factors. The BASC-2 would probably be a more useful system of measures if it eliminated the SOS altogether and instead included a detailed chapter in the manual on how to conduct a meaningful and useful behavioral observation, tailored to the relevant, operationally defined target behaviors for the child and incorporating a systematic and integrated observation of antecedents and consequences.

Another criticism of the BASC-2 is an echo of concerns stated in the initial reviews of the BASC: There is no clear way to integrate the information from all of the different components of the system, especially for the hand-scored instruments. The inclusion of a summary recording form would be helpful towards addressing this issue. Finally, the manual states "When all BASC-2 components have been collected along with a clinical interview and a review of school and clinical records and histories, the professional will have the information needed for a thorough, comprehensive evaluation of behavior, personality, and context" (p. 7). That is a strong claim. The BASC-2 is good, but probably not *that* good. It also tells the practitioner next to nothing about treatment implications.

SUMMARY. The BASC was considered an exemplary instrument in its original form so one could argue that the BASC-2 is simply making a good thing better. In some ways, that is probably true. The components that count (the rating scales and self-report measure) have strong psychometric properties. However, despite its claim of providing multimethod and multidimensional assessment, the BASC-2 is still just one piece (albeit a hefty piece) of the diagnostic picture. In the limited scope of measuring external and self-report ratings of behavior, the BASC-2 does what it does well.

Any valid attempt at diagnosis, though, should include multiple *other* measures as well. One of these measures should be a defensible method of directly observing the child's behavior and functioning in the relevant environment, something that is not provided by the BASC-2.

REVIEWER'S REFERENCE
Salvia, J., & Ysseldyke, J. E. (2004). *Assessment* (9th ed.). Boston: Houghton Mifflin.

Review of the Behavior Assessment System for Children [Second Edition] by T. STEUART WATSON, Chair and Professor, and KATHERINE WICKSTROM, Assistant Professor, Department of Educational Psychology, Miami University, Oxford, OH:

DESCRIPTION. The Behavior Assessment System for Children [Second Edition] (BASC-2) is a multimethod, multidimensional system used to assess emotional and behavioral difficulties in persons aged 2 through 25 years. The following five components may be used individually or in combination with one another: Teacher Rating Scales (TRS), Parent Rating Scales (PRS), Self-Report of Personality (SRP), Structured Developmental History (SDH), and Student Observation System (SOS). The primary purposes of the BASC-2 are: clinical diagnosis, educational classification, manifestation determination, assessment of children with sensory impairments, program evaluation, forensic evaluation, and research.

The TRS can be completed by someone who has knowledge of the child in the educational context, such as teachers, teacher aides, or preschool caregivers and includes questions regarding both adaptive and problem behaviors that occur in the school setting. The PRS is completed by a parent, guardian, foster parent or other custodial caregiver with regard to a child's adaptive and problem behaviors in the home and community settings. Both the TRS and the PRS target three age levels (Preschool, 2–5 years; Child, 6–11 years; and Adolescent, 12–21 years) with separate forms and number of items for each (e.g., TRS-P includes 100 items, PRS-A includes 150 items). Each scale is completed by an informant using a four-choice response format, ranging from *Never* to *Almost Always*. The TRS and PRS assess broad domains or Composites [Adaptive Skills, Externalizing Problems, Internalizing Problems, and School Problems (TRS only)], as well as primary scales for all age levels. Differences in the scales occur between levels due to developmental age changes as well as various behaviors that are more likely to be observed in one setting versus the other. The Behavioral Symptoms Index (BSI) is a broad composite score for the TRS and PRS and is designed to assess the overall level of problem behavior. New to the BASC-2, the TRS and PRS include content scales that are intended to supplement the clinical interpretation of other BASC-2 scales. The seven optional content scales are more specific or syndrome-oriented and include items that are part of the primary scales as well as items not part of any primary scale; examples include Anger Control, Bullying, and Resiliency. The TRS and PRS may be interpreted in terms of General and Clinical norm groups and include validity scales in order to detect a negative informant response set (F index), identify invalid forms (Response Pattern Index), and identify inconsistencies in responding (Consistency Index).

The SRP is a self-report inventory used to assess the emotions and self-perceptions of children or young adults. Some of the items are completed using a True or False response, and others use the four-choice response format. The SRP is written at approximately the third grade level and includes three levels: Child (ages 8–11), Adolescent (ages 12–21), and College form for young adults attending postsecondary school (ages 18–25). The age levels overlap in scales, structure, and item content, with Child and Adolescent having identical composites (Inattention/Hyperactivity, Internalizing, Personal Adjustment, School Problems, and the Emotional Symptoms Index). Similar to the BSI on the TRS and PRS, the Emotional Symptoms Index (ESI) is an overall composite score. However, unlike the BSI, the ESI includes problem (negative) and adaptive (positive) scales. The SRP also includes the optional content scales and may be interpreted with reference to General and Clinical norms. The validity scales (F index, Response Pattern Index, Consistency Index) are integrated, as well as an additional index (the V index) to distinguish invalid responses due to poor understanding or comprehension, failure to follow directions, or inappropriate contact with reality.

In addition to the rating and self-report scales, the BASC-2 includes a developmental history form and an observation form. The Structured Developmental History (SDH) may be used by a clinician as an interview with a parent or guardian or completed by a parent/guardian in the home, school, or clinic. The SDH gathers information on the child and family regarding development, social, and medical histories. The Student Observation System (SOS) may be used in order to gather direct behavioral information on the child in the classroom setting on both adaptive behaviors (e.g., teacher-student interaction) and problem behaviors (e.g., inappropriate vocalization). An electronic version of the SOS, the BASC-2 Portable Observation Program (BASC-2 POP), may be purchased separately and used on a laptop computer or Personal Digital Assistant (PDA).

Users of the BASC-2 should have received formal academic training and supervised clinical experience in the administration, scoring, and interpretation of behavior rating and personality scales. A comprehensive manual provides instructions for administering, scoring, and interpretation of the TRS, PRS, and SRP, as well as guidance in using the SDH and SOS. The manual also includes all norm tables, the development of the BASC-2, and technical characteristics. The TRS, PRS, and SRP are all rating scales in which data may be entered in one of three formats: hand scored, computer entry, and scannable. The BASC-2 ASSIST and BASC-2 ASSIST Plus computer scoring programs may be used with computer entry forms to score and report TRS, PRS, and SRP results. The Plus software includes additional features to report content scales and tie into the DSM-IV-TR diagnostic criteria. There are three summary reports for parents, called the Parent Feedback Report, to summarize TRS, PRS, and/ or SRP scores. Spanish editions are available for the PRS, SRP, and the SDH.

DEVELOPMENT. The BASC-2 is a revision of the Behavior Assessment for Children (BASC; Reynolds & Kamphaus, 1992). Key features of the BASC-2 include improved reliabilities and additional scales without lengthening the forms, updated standardization sample, greater content overlap across levels and between the TRS and PRS, the newly devised content scales, the mixed response-format of the SRP, extended age ranges, more detailed clinical norms, newly developed computer scoring software, and additions to the SDH.

The TRS, PRS, and SRP of the BASC-2 are highly similar to the original BASC. Initial constructs for the BASC were developed based on a comprehensive review of existing behavior and self-report rating scales, as well as consultations with clinicians. In addition, teachers and students were involved in the item-generation process. Extensive pilot, tryout, and standardization testing, along with statistical item analysis of both traditional and innovative (confirmatory factor analysis) techniques resulted in final scales for the original BASC.

Item development for the BASC-2 TRS and PRS focused on increasing the consistency of content across age levels of each form. For example, items that were absent from a particular form but were viewed as appropriate for a certain developmental level (or setting) were added to the standardization edition for reevaluation using the new sample. New test items were also written for all scales, with special consideration to scales with lower reliabilities. Additionally, new scales were created for the standardization forms to broaden content domains.

Development for the SRP items on the BASC-2 addressed the forced-choice response format of True and False, low reliabilities, and restricted normative distributions on the original BASC. An extensive study to evaluate alternative response formats regarding technical adequacies of the scales (e.g., test/retest reliability, internal-consistency reliability) resulted in the use of both a 4-point response scale as well as a True/False scale on the BASC-2 SRP. In addition, a new version (SRP-COL) for use with college-aged students (18 through 25) was developed based on the SRP-A.

Final item selection and scale definition were based on the standardization sample and were submitted to extensive statistical analyses. Covariance Structure Analysis (CSA; confirmatory factor analysis) was the primary means for item analysis and scale development.

TECHNICAL DATA. As with the original BASC, the BASC-2 rating scales were nationally standardized to reflect the general (nonclinical) population of children as well as the clinical population of children. The General norm samples (TRS, n = 4,650; PRS, n = 4,800; SRP, n = 3,400) were matched to target U.S. population estimates from the 2001 Current Population Survey for socioeconomic status, race/ethnicity, geographic region, and special education classification. Chil-

dren identified by their parents as being diagnosed or classified as having behavioral, emotional, or physical problems comprised the Clinical norm sample. There was considerable overlap across the TRS, PRS, and SRP forms, as well as between the General norm samples.

For each scale (TRS, PRS, and SRP), several indices of reliability were presented. Across all age levels, internal consistency of the composites (.80s to .90s) and scales (.60s to .90s) for both the General and Clinical norm samples were satisfactory. Lower reliabilities were evident in scales on the SRP.

For each rating scale at every level, a sample of children was rated twice by the same teacher or parent/caregiver- or self-respondent using an 8- to 70-day interval between ratings. Overall, moderate to high retest correlations were obtained. Test-retest reliabilities for the TRS Composites ranged from the middle .80s to the low .90s, with the exception of Internalizing Problems at the adolescent level (.78). The PRS test-retest reliabilities for the Composites were generally in the low .80s to the low .90s. For the SRP, test-retest reliabilities ranged from the middle .70s to the low .90s.

In order to evaluate the agreement of ratings between two different raters (e.g., teachers, parents/caregivers) at similar time periods, interrater reliability studies were conducted with samples at each age level of the TRS and the PRS. For the TRS, acceptable interrater reliabilities were obtained with median reliability estimates of .65, .56, and .53 for the Preschool, Child, and Adolescent levels, respectively. For the PRS, median interrater reliabilities were also adequate at .74, .69, and .77 for the Preschool, Child, and Adolescent levels, respectively.

Construct validity of the TRS and PRS was stronger for the Externalizing Problems composites with all scales loading on this composite having high loadings across all levels. The Internalizing Problems factor was primarily defined by only three factors for each scale (Depression, Atypicality, and Withdrawal for TRS; Anxiety, Depression, and Atypicality for PRS).

When comparing the BASC-2 TRS and PRS rating scales to other behavior measures, such as the Achenbach System of Empirically Based Assessment (ASEBA; Achenbach & Rescorla, 2001) and the Conners' Teacher/Parent Rating Scales (CTRS-R, CPRS-R; Conners, 1997), moderate to high correlations between scales that measure similar constructs were obtained. Higher correlations were obtained in the child samples than in the adolescent samples. For the SRP, correlations on composite scores with similar scales on the Achenbach Youth Self-Report (Achenbach & Rescorla, 2001) and the Conners-Wells' Adolescent Self-Report Scale (CASS; Conners, 1997) were satisfactory.

MANUAL AND FORMS. The manual is quite comprehensive and cumbersome (590 pages in length) and is replete with tables and figures that contain psychometric data that assist in the interpretation of scores. It also contains the administration and scoring guidelines for each of the scales. In its current state, the manual is not very user-friendly and would likely prove to be daunting even to many experienced assessors. Given the length of the existing manual, it would seem to make sense, for ease and practicality of use, to divide the manual into a technical manual and a users' manual (with administration, scoring, and interpretation guidelines). All of the forms (i.e., protocols) appear to be easily completed and are straightforward. Most clinicians, however, will probably condense the Structured Developmental History due to its length, depending upon the nature of the referral and the type of assessment data needed.

COMMENTARY. As with the original BASC, the BASC-2 has several strengths over similar existing measures, including its extensive and rigorous standardization, Spanish language versions, strong psychometric properties, and inclusion of both problematic and adaptive behaviors. There are, however, several limitations of the BASC-2 worthy of comment. First, the correlations between the TRS-C and PRS-C Composites (*md* = .48) and scales (*mn* = .38) are modest at best. Second, the Parent Feedback Reports are an added feature, but may not be very practical in that they may overwhelm some parents due to the inclusion of a great deal of information on the forms in a somewhat technical manner. Third, as with any other "one-point-in-time" measure, information is lacking as to the reliability and validity of the diagnostic and classification decisions made with such measures. Ongoing, repeated measurement of a child's behavior along with his or her response to an intervention is vital to classification (Individuals with Disabilities Education Improvement Act, 2004).

Finally, the value of the BASC-2 in aiding in the design of treatment plans is questionable. An essential component to treatment plans is *ongoing* evaluation of the treatment. Although the developers recommend its use for evaluation at both the individual and program levels, the repeated and frequent use of the TRS, PRS, and/or SRP to monitor an individual intervention is not likely to provide sufficient sensitivity to measure changes associated with a specific intervention. In addition, frequent use of such rating scales would be labor intensive on the part of the respondents, and the scores would be highly suspect due to the effects of repeated assessment.

SUMMARY. The BASC-2 is a well-developed multimethod, multidimensional system for assessing the behavioral and emotional concerns in children and young adults. The inclusion of teacher-, parent-, and self-perceptions along with gathering developmental history and direct behavioral observations pulls together needed information for the primary purpose of clinical diagnosis and classification. However, as with other one-point-in-time measures, the reliability and validity regarding the *decisions* clinicians make when using such measures should be examined. Future investigations should focus on the clinical importance and relevance of using the BASC-2 in the diagnosis and classification of children and young adults.

With respect to the seven stated purposes of the BASC-2, perhaps it is most useful for *aiding* in making clinical or educational diagnoses/classifications, program evaluation, and research. Manifestation determination, with or without data from the BASC-2, is a risky proposition at best. Data collected as part of the BASC-2 assessment do not seem to be very helpful in determining whether or not a particular behavior is due to a person's identified disability or some other phenomena. In addition, it has not been established that the BASC-2 is more effective than other similar measures for assessing children with sensory impairments. The BASC-2 has sufficient psychometric properties and indices of dissimulated responding that potentially make it useful for some types of forensic evaluations.

REVIEWERS' REFERENCES

Achenbach, T. M., & Rescorla, L. A. (2001). *Manual for the ASEBA school-age forms and profiles.* Burlington, VT: University of Vermont, Research Center for Children, Youth, and Families.

Conners, C. K. (1997). Conners' Rating Scales—Revised. North Tonawanda, NY: Multi-Health Systems.

Individuals with Disabilities Education Improvement Act, 20 U.S.C. 1400. (2004).

[22]
Behavior Evaluation Scale—Third Edition.

Purpose: Designed "to contribute to the early identification and service delivery for students with serious emotional disturbance or behavior disorders."

Population: Ages 4–19.

Publication Dates: 1990–2005.

Acronym: BES-3:L, BES-3:S.

Scores, 6: Learning Problems, Interpersonal Difficulties, Inappropriate Behavior, Unhappiness/Depression, Physical Symptoms/Fears, Total Score.

Administration: Individual.

Forms, 4: Long—School Version; Long—Home Version; Short—School Version, Short—Home Version.

Price Data, 2006: LONG VERSION: $208.50 per complete kit including Long—School Version technical manual (2005, 77 pages), 50 Long—School Version rating forms, Long—Home Version technical manual (2005, 75 pages), 50 Long—Home Version rating forms, 50 Intervention Strategies Documentation forms, 50 Long—Pre-Referral checklists, Long—Intervention manual, and one Parent's Guide; $20 per Long—technical manual (specify School or Home Version); $30 per Long—Intervention manual; $35 per 50 Long—rating forms (specify School or Home Version); $35 per 50 Long—Home Version Spanish rating forms; $30 per 50 Intervention Strategies Documentation forms; $30 per 50 Long—Pre-Referral checklists; $8.50 per the Parent's Guide; $35 per Long—Quick Score computerized Windows program; SHORT VERSION: $206.50 per complete kit including Short—School Version technical manual (2005, 83 pages), 50 Short—School Version rating forms, Short—Home Version technical manual (2005, 77 pages), 50 Short—Home Version rating forms, 50 Intervention Strategies Documentation forms, 50 Long—Pre-Referral checklists, Short—Intervention manual, and one Parent's Guide; $20 per Short—technical manual (specify School or Home Version); $28 per Short—Intervention manual; $35 per 50 Short—rating forms (specify School or Home Version); $35 per 50 Short—Home Version Spanish rating forms; $30 per 50 Intervention Strategies Documentation forms; $30 per 50 Short—Pre-Referral checklists; $8.50 per Parent's Guide; $35 per Short—Quick Score computerized Windows program.

Foreign Language Editions: Long—Home and Short—Home Version Spanish rating forms available.

Time: (20) minutes.

Comments: Includes 4 forms: Long—School Version, Long—Home Version, Short—School Version, Short—Home Version; scale is completed by parent/caregiver or an educator.

Authors: Stephen B. McCarney and Tamara J. Arthaud.

Publisher: Hawthorne Educational Services, Inc.

Cross References: See T5:284 (1 reference); for reviews by Bert A. Goldman and D. Joe Olmi of a previous edition, see 12:47; for reviews by J. Jeffrey Grill, Lester Mann, and Leonard Kenowitz of an earlier edition, see 9:128.

Review of the Behavior Evaluation Scale— Third Edition by MATTHEW K. BURNS, Associate Professor of Educational Psychology, University of Minnesota, Minneapolis, MN:

DESCRIPTION. The third edition of the Behavior Evaluation Scale Long Form (BES—3:L) is the latest version of one of the most widely used behavioral rating scales in K–12 schools. Like its predecessor, the current edition includes a Home Version with 73 items as well as the School Rating Scale with 76 items. The two forms are parallel in format in that behaviors described in the items for both are rated on a 7-point (1 to 7) Likert scale ranging from *not personally observed* (1) to *continuously throughout the day* (7). Moreover, the items are grouped into five subscales based on the federal special education eligibility criteria for emotional and behavior disorder. The two scales also come with a companion intervention manual and a parent's guide to suggest solutions for problems in both home and school settings.

The two scales of the BES—3:L are designed to rate the behavior of children ages 4 to 19 years in order to identify children with behavioral disorders in the schools. The authors also suggest the data could be used for measuring behavioral change over time, identifying areas in need of behavioral intervention, and identifying subsequent goals and objectives for individual students. Raw data are converted to age-, grade-, and gender-specific subscale standard scores, which are then converted to a quotient that measures overall behavior problems. Percentile ranks and standard errors of measurement are provided for both types of scores.

Administration of the two scales requires approximately 20 minutes each and can be completed by anyone familiar with the student's behavior. Specific criteria for "familiar" are provided and are probably quite helpful in selecting raters. Moreover, the items are fairly straightforward, and the rating system is perhaps as objective as a rating scale can be with understandable descriptions of each Likert point. Thus, both scales seem easily administered with simple scoring procedures.

DEVELOPMENT. The scales of the BES—3:L were developed to be consistent with commonly used criteria for serious behavioral disorders while following guidelines for psychometrically sound behavior rating scales. Items were initially developed for the original version of the scale (School–1983 Version and Home–1994 Version) through research literature reviews and input from professionals across the country. The number and content of the items remained the same between the current and the second edition scales. However, the items of the third edition were subjected to relatively extensive empirical analysis, including factor analyses and item correlations with the subscale and total scores. Although the items were highly correlated with subscale and total scores, the factor analyses were less convincing. Both the Home and School Versions had items that generally loaded most strongly on the appropriate factor, but many items demonstrated significant factor loading on as many as four other factors. Although the items were extensively tested, the manual did not mention specifically whether items were revised as a result.

TECHNICAL.

Standardization. The Home Version of the BES—3:L was normed on 4,643 children. The School Version was normed on 5,124 children. Both samples adequately matched the 2000 United States Census data, with an acceptable slight overrepresentation of males in the School Version. The School Version provides norm tables for 16 gender-specific age groupings and 26 gender-specific grade groups (Pre-K–K to 12th grade). The Home Version contains norm tables for 14 gender-specific age groupings and the same 26 gender-specific grade groups as the School Version. All of the normative groupings contained at least 100 participants in each group, with the exception of 4-year-old females in the Home Version and 14-year-old females in the School Version, both of which exceeded 90. Thus, the norms seem adequate for the intended ages and grades, and probably for most ethnic groups. Although the

standardization sample included children with behavioral difficulties, precise numbers were not provided. If children with behavioral difficulties were underrepresented, there is a possibility that the norms may overestimate behavioral difficulties.

Reliability. Data regarding test-retest and interrater reliability coefficients are provided for both scales. The technical manuals report reliability coefficients that exceed .78 for all subtests, except the test-retest reliability estimate for the Unhappiness/Depression subtest of the Home Version, which was .65. In addition, internal consistency reliability estimates were reported for both versions, by subtest and total scores. Alpha coefficients were in the upper .80s or .90s, consistently. All coefficients for the Total scores were at least .90, across the various forms of reliability that were addressed. However, reliability estimates should be provided for the various age/grade groups, rather than for the sample in its entirety. Of the 15 reliability estimates provided for the Home Version scale 10 were at or above .85. Three of these coefficients exceeded .90. For the School Version, 14 of the subtest reliability estimates exceeded .85, 9 of which exceeded .90. Of note, the test-retest reliability study for the Home Version was based on only 24 participants. The test-retest interval used was 30 days.

Validity. Content validity was supported with expert judgment. Factor analyses conducted during test development were used to support construct validity. These approaches seem somewhat limited, but probably acceptable. However, how items were revised as a result of these processes should be stated explicitly.

Concurrent validity data were obtained by correlating scores from the BES—3:L Home and School Versions with other behavior rating scales. The resulting coefficients were moderate to high, ranging from .62 to .95, for the subtests. Correlations for the Total scores ranged from .78 to .94. These data offer good support for concurrent validity of the BES—3:L.

The test manuals suggest that criterion-related validity could be established with group differentiation data. In other words, if a significant difference in scores between students with and without behavior disorders is found, the data could be judged to have sufficient criterion-related validity. BES—3:L scores were compared between the standardization samples and 96 children in the

Home Version and 154 for the School Version. This is a curious approach to "criterion-related validity," but could be useful data if more information was provided. The results found mean subtest scores of either 4 or 5 for the children with behavior disorders, whereas the standardization sample resulted in a mean standard score of 10. Given that the groups were not matched on important demographic variables, these results are difficult to interpret.

COMMENTARY. The Home and School Versions of the BES—3:L offer many important strengths including being based on school-based criteria defined in special education mandates, ease of administration and scoring, and the ability to derive age-, grade-, and gender-specific standard scores. Moreover, the use of ratings to provide information about behavior in the home is an important component of any ecologically valid assessment model.

The test authors offer a modicum of support for the reliability and validity of the BES—3:L that suggest the scale is appropriately used for screening purposes. However, this test does not seem to make a unique contribution to the field. Purportedly BES—3:L data are useful for measuring behavioral change over time, identifying areas in need of behavioral intervention, and identifying subsequent goals and objectives for individual students in addition to the early identification of behavioral disorders. However, no data were presented to support the other purported uses. Thus, the tests should probably be used only for screening, but the Behavior Disorders Identification Scale—Second Edition (BDIS:2; McCarney & Arthaud, 2000; 16:26) already exists, was developed from the same criteria, was written by the same authors, and published by the same publishers. It is unclear how the BES—3:L is different from the BDIS:2.

The title of the BES—3:L scales is somewhat misleading. The data from the Home and School Versions provide information about school-based behavioral disorders, not about behavior in general. All of the items in the two scales are ratings of clinically significant behavior (i.e., symptoms), with no ratings of any prosocial or adaptive skills. The test manuals state that the data also measure the "ability to be successful in the residential (Home version)/educational (School version) environment as compared to the standard-

ization population" (p. 28), but this is not the case. There is more to successful behavior in the school and/or home, and to being mentally healthy than a lack of abnormal behavior (U.S. Department of Health and Human Services, 1999). The BES—3:L only measures the existence or lack of pathology, which in and of itself is not sufficient for mental health at any age. For an ecologically sensitive measure of behavior that includes both clinical symptoms and prosocial behavior, readers should examine the Behavior Assessment System for Children–Second Edition (Reynolds & Kamphaus, 2004; 17:21).

SUMMARY. The BES—3:L provides data from raters familiar with a child in the home/residential setting and the school that could be used for an initial screening of behavior disorders. The scale was developed from school-based criteria for behavioral disorders and exhibits sufficient psychometric properties for screening purposes. However, it is similar to the BDIS:2 and does not provide information about adaptive or prosocial behavior. Thus, the data are limited in their use until they are further researched.

REVIEWER'S REFERENCES

McCarney, S. B., & Arthaud, T. J. (2000). Behavior Disorders Identification Scale (2nd ed.). Columbia, MO: Hawthorne Educational Services.
Reynolds, C. R., & Kamphaus, R. W. (2004). Behavior Assessment System for Children (2nd ed.). Circle Pines, MN: AGS.
U.S. Department of Health and Human Services. (1999). *Mental health: A report of the surgeon general.* Rockville, MD: U.S. Department of Health and Human Services, Substance Abuse and Mental Health Services Administration, Center for Mental Health Services, National Institutes of Health, National Institute of Mental Health.

Review of the Behavior Evaluation Scale— Third Edition by MARK E. SWERDLIK, Professor of Psychology, and W. JOEL SCHNEIDER, Assistant Professor of Psychology, Illinois State University, Normal, IL:

DESCRIPTION. The BES-3 consists of four components including the Behavior Evaluation Scale—Third Edition: Long School Version (BES-3:L-SV), the Behavior Evaluation Scale—Third Edition: Long Home Version (BES-3:L-HV), BES:L Intervention Manual, and the Parent's Guide: Solutions to Today's Most Common Behavior Problems in the Home. The BES was first developed as a school rating scale in 1983, expanded (from 52 to 76 items), and restandardized in 1994 as the BES-2. The BES-3:L-SV rating scale represents a restandardization of the BES-2 with new normative tables based on a national standardization sample. The BES-3:L-HV represents a restandardization of the Behavior Evaluation Scale—Second Edition Home Version (BES:2-HV).

The purpose of the BES-3, both the SV and HV, is to facilitate the early identification and program planning for students with emotional disturbance or behavior disorders. In addition, an updated version of the companion book, the intervention manual, was developed for use in the development of a student's Individual Educational Plan (IEP) including goals, objectives, and interventions. The parent guide was first published in 1990 and is not keyed directly to the HV as the intervention manual is to the SV.

The BES-3, both SV and HV, is appropriate for use with children and adolescents as young as age 4 through age 19. The scales are also designed to identify areas of need for use in program planning and for progress monitoring or the measurement of behavior change over time as a result of programming. The SV has both a long form consisting of 76 items and a short form with 54 items. The HV provides a measure of a child/youth's behavior in the home/residential environment with a long form consisting of 73 items and a short form of 52 items.

The SV includes a rating form to be completed by educational personnel (e.g., teachers, paraprofessionals) who work with the student in instructional settings and who have had "extended observational opportunities." For the HV, similar criteria for parents or caregivers (e.g., parents, guardians, group home counselor, babysitter) exist for those who rate behaviors in the residential/home setting. Ratings are to be completed independently based on observations of the "typical performance" of the student in the educational or home/residential setting.

Rating options for both rating scales include "not personally observed," "is developmentally advanced for age group," "less than once a month," "approximately once a month," "approximately once a week," "more than once a week," "daily at various times," or "continuously throughout the day." Respondents are instructed to rate "conservatively" (i.e., using the highest quantifier that accurately describes the student's behavior).

Although the SV and HV scales are untimed, the authors suggest that they can be completed within approximately 20 minutes but no data are provided to support this estimate. Directions are clearly printed on each of the rating forms. Scoring is simple and consists of summing the ratings for each item to compute raw scores for each of the five subscales and the sum of the Standard Scores derives the Quotient. Tables (for each rating scale) provide corresponding scaled scores ($M = 10$, $SD = 3$) for the subscale scores and index scores ($M = 100$, $SD = 15$) for the composite Quotient.

The intervention manual is organized by items corresponding to the SV and is designed for school personnel who use this scale. Items are organized sequentially and each has a list of possible IEP Goals and Objectives followed by a variable number of interventions with a brief description of each. The parent's guide is organized into "102 most common behavior problems" that occur in the home setting (e.g., Does Not Complete Chores, Makes Rude Comments) followed by a variable number of "solutions." The parent's guide is designed to be a resource for parent-training groups and parent problem-solving sessions with therapists and counselors.

The technical manuals for the SV and HV are comprehensive and generally clearly written. The intervention manual, parent's guide, and the SV and HV rating forms/profile sheets are attractively produced and clearly written. The rating form/profile sheet is combined into one form and includes space for the child's demographic information, each of the items are printed, space for the respondent to provide their individual item ratings, a section for a summary of scores, and a printed graph to pictorially display all subscale scores and the Quotient.

The authors do not provide information related to the professional training or positions of potential test users other than "diagnosticians." The authors indicate that the SV and HV cannot be used as the sole data sources for determining diagnoses for emotional disturbance/behavior disorder but rather should be a part of a more comprehensive evaluation.

DEVELOPMENT. The BES-3 is based upon an ecological model that includes both a school and a home/residential version. This allows for observations of the child in both the school and home settings, which is consistent with state guidelines requiring home-based observations as part of a comprehensive evaluation.

The theoretical construct upon which the SV and HV are based is the educational definition of serious emotional disturbance that is included in past and current reauthorizations of the Individuals with Disabilities Education Act (2004). This definition has its roots in Bower's (1959) definition and represents the most commonly used state definition of this disability category. The authors also conducted a review of the research that confirmed the basic characteristics included in Bower's definition but give no details on this review. These characteristics include learning problems, interpersonal problems, inappropriate behavior or feelings under normal circumstances, unhappiness or depression, and physical symptoms or fears, which also comprise the five subscales of the SV and HV rating scales. In addition to the behaviors being judged as to their occurrence by students with serious emotional disturbance, the frequency, intensity, and context of the behavior also must be considered in identification.

The authors provide no information on how the goals, objectives, and particular interventions were selected for inclusion in the intervention manual for each of the SV items. A one-page introduction provides some very general behavioral principles related to analyzing problem behaviors and choosing interventions. Users are instructed to use "professional judgment" in choosing specific interventions. Student characteristics including age, gender, grade level, local community standards, and disability (if one exists) also should be considered. The intervention manual is suggested for use by a team of professionals including either a general or special education teacher. The authors claim the interventions have been found useful in either general or special education classroom environments.

The authors of the parent's guide also provide no specific information on how the particular 102 most common behavior problems were selected other than they were chosen by "surveying parents." Further, there is no specific information presented on the selection criteria for the various "solutions" provided for each of the behavior problems other than only the "most logical and common sense approaches" that "are the ones that work best with children" were included and those that had "the greatest likelihood of success that can be easily shared by counselors, social workers, child psychologists, pediatricians, etc., with parents individually" (parent's guide, p. 5). The authors also note that parents in the home can practice the strategies chosen for inclusion in the parent's guide without the aid of a therapist or counselor.

TECHNICAL. The SV standardization sample includes 5,124 students ages 4 through 19 residing in 29 states, enrolled in classes for students with behavior disorders and in general education classrooms. The SV sample includes 2,770 males and 2,354 females. Standardization generally approximates the demographics from the 2000 U.S. Census. The specific percentage of students in the standardization sample who were enrolled in general education as compared to those identified as having a behavior disorder was not specified.

SV age norms are based on a range of 174 students at age 4 to 579 boys at ages 5–7 and a minimum of 92 girls at age 14 to 682 at ages 4–7. Age divisions differed for boys and girls, and there was no theoretical rationale provided for these age divisions other than it was based on an analysis of the standardization data. Grade placement groups range from Pre-Kindergarten–Kindergarten though Grade 12 and are more evenly distributed.

The HV standardization sample includes 4,643 identified behaviorally disordered and general education students, ages 4 through 19 years from 29 states and the District of Columbia. Although drawn from the same number of states as the SV standardization sample, the HV standardization sample was drawn from different states. Standardization generally approximates the demographics from the 2000 U.S. Census. The specific percentage of students in the standardizations sample who were enrolled in general education as compared to those identified as having a behavior disorder also was not specified for the HV.

HV age norms are based on over 100 individuals although some age ranges were collapsed and include a range of 188 at ages 17–19 to 508 boys at ages 12–14 and a minimum of 96 girls at age 4 to 561 at ages 10-12. Age divisions differed for boys and girls and there was no theoretical rationale provided for these age divisions other than it was based on an analysis of the standardization data. Age distributions and divisions are different for the HV and SV ratings scales. As for the SV, grade placement groups range from Pre-Kindergarten–Kindergarten through Grade 12. Standard scores, quotient, and percentiles are provided by gender, age, and grade placement for both the SV and HV ratings scales.

Strong internal consistency reliability was reported for both the SV (.98) and the HV (.98) Total scores and above .88 for each of the five SV subscales with only Physical Symptoms/Fears below .90 (.88) and above .87 for all five HV subscales with Learning Problems (.89), Unhappiness/Depression (.87), and Physical Symptoms/Fears (.88) below .90. This lower internal consistency reliability can be attributed in part to smaller numbers of items comprising each of the HV subscales with an internal consistency reliability coefficient below .90 for several HV subscales (e.g., the Unhappiness/Depression SV scale has 17 items whereas the HV subscale has 7 items).

Test-retest reliability appears very strong for the SV scale (total score .93 with subscales all at or above .84), for a randomly selected sample of 185 students evaluated 30 days apart. Similarly strong, albeit somewhat lower (total score .90 with subscales all at or above .65 and none above .88), test-retest reliability coefficients were found for the HV. There exists a need to use a variety of samples of different ages to establish more completely the test-retest reliability of the SV and HV.

Interrater reliability studies of the SV and HV were conducted. The SV study included 160 students selected from the standardization sample and 68 children from the HV standardization sample. Interrater reliability for the SV was unusually high with .95 for the total score and a range of .88–.91 for the five subscales and also high for the HV with .93 for the total score and a range of .80–.93 for the five subscales. Standard errors of measurement, with confidence intervals, are provided for all subscales and Quotients by gender and age.

Related to content validity of both SV and HV items, behavioral descriptors of students with behavior disorders they had observed were compiled by the authors, teachers of children with behavior disorders, diagnosticians, and other school personnel. The items, representing educationally relevant indicators of behavior disorders, were then reviewed by a panel of special education teachers and related service personnel who were instructed to eliminate any that did not represent the behaviors of students with behavior disorders, clarify any items, and add items that would improve the evaluation of a student with a suspected behavior disorder. A similar procedure was used for the development of the HV.

Construct-identification validity evidence for both the SV and HV included principal components analysis with varimax rotation of the interitem correlations for the entire instrument, a principal components analysis of the logically defined subscale, an item analysis of each logically defined subscale, and an internal consistency reliability analysis of each logically defined subscale. Results of the exploratory factor analyses for both the SV and HV indicated a large first factor accounting for 41% of the SV variance and 40% of the HV variance.

For both the SV and HV scales, there were a significant number of items that loaded on more than one factor. Item analysis of each logically defined subscale indicated that most of the items within each subscale loaded primarily on that factor but others were retained even with less than expected factor loadings due to theoretical considerations. Some SV subscales (e.g., Unhappiness/Depression) loaded almost evenly on two factors. The correlations between the SV subscales and the total score ranged from .59 to .95 indicating that those students exhibiting behavior problems in one area tend to have them in other areas and are not so related as to measure identical constructs. For the HV scale, four primary factors emerged, whereas the fifth factor contained only a very weak loading for all but four items. Substantial item validity, based on item to subscale/total score correlations for both the SV and HV, was demonstrated.

Decisions were made as to items being retained on a particular subscale based upon if the item discriminated in a positive direction, had item to subscale/total scores in a positive direction, and had acceptable content validity. However, with a strong general factor, almost any item will load positively on any subscale.

Discriminative validity included group differentiation (differentiating students with and without behavior disorders) and was based on a sample of 250 male and female students ages 4 through 19. Standard score means for the identified group ranged from 4 to 5 and were compared to the standard score of 10 representing the mean subscale standards scores for the standardization sample. However, groups were not matched according to important demographic variables. Further, no comparisons were made for mean age and gender differences.

No other criterion-related validity evidence was presented such as relationships of the subscale scores with other valid measures of these characteristics (e.g., interpersonal problems) nor for other purposes suggested by the authors. For example, no validity data were presented for BES-3 uses such as the sensitivity of the scale for the purposes of progress monitoring or how the ratings lead to the development of more effective IEPs.

Concurrent validity studies included comparing the SV with the BES-2 SV. In one such study, 93 students from age levels 4 through 19 were randomly selected for a concurrent validity study, and correlations for the total score and all five subscales were above .90 except for Unhappiness/Depression (.87) and Physical Symptoms/Fears (.67). Concurrent validity of the SV and the Devereaux Behavior Rating Scale—School Form for the four subscales that overlap (Interpersonal Difficulties, Inappropriate Behavior, Unhappiness/Depression, and Physical Symptoms/Fear) ranged from .62 (Physical Symptoms/Fears) to .82 (Inappropriate Behavior). A concurrent validity study comparing the SV with the Behavior Rating Profile: Second Edition reported a .88 correlation for the Total scores from both scales.

Similar concurrent validity studies were conducted with the HV using 67 children/youths between the ages of 4 and 19, who were randomly selected from the HV standardization sample for a study comparing the HV and the BDIS-2 HV. All coefficients fell at or above .85 indicating a strong association with the Total score correlating .92. Sixty-nine participants were also selected from the HV standardization sample and were administered the Behavior Rating Profile—Second Edition (BRP-2) yielding a correlation coefficient of .78. A similar criterion-related validity identification of groups study was conducted with the HV using 96 male and female students ages 4 though 19 years, identified as having a behavior disorder. As was true for the SV, standard score means differed significantly between the identified group and nonidentified students from the standardization sample.

Related to the interventions/solutions provided in the intervention manual and parent's guide, there was no review provided of evidence-based interventions that were included in the list. Further, there are no treatment validity data presented that demonstrate use of results from the SV or HV rating scales and selection of interventions

from one or both of these manuals leads to more positive outcomes of children and adolescents.

COMMENTARY. Strengths of the BES-3 include assessing behaviors in both the school and home/residential settings. The intervention manual can be used to develop goals, objectives, and choose intervention strategies for IEPs. The parent's guide provides solutions to common behavior problems in the home or residential setting. Administration time of approximately 20 minutes is efficient and scoring is simple. Use of the SV and HV allows for multiple independent ratings, which increases objectivity. A large and generally representative standardization sample characterizes both the SV and HV. Strong internal consistency reliability evidence is presented. However, test-retest and interrater reliability data are presented only across the entire age range and not for each age or grade level.

No validity data are presented that relate to the correlation with more direct measures of behavior (e.g., frequency counts of aggressive behavior), teacher ratings of overall classroom behavior, or peer sociometric ratings. Further no correlations with self-report measures are presented, which are particularly critical for internalizing disorders, or validity data related to the BES-3 sensitivity as a measure of progress monitoring. Related to the theoretical model upon which the BES-3 is based, some argue that the conceptualization of school-based emotional problems by Bower and incorporated into federal and state special education law provides a weak conceptual and empirical base on which to design rating scale items and upon which to base item and scale construction (Floyd & Bose, 2003). However, the BES-3 authors argue that this represents the criteria upon which special education eligibility for serious emotional disturbance is based. Yet, this definition may not be as useful for treatment selection and progress monitoring—two other major purposes of the SV and HV scales.

For a large number of items, more than one factor is measured. Factor analytic evidence does not support the interpretation of the subscales as distinct constructs. This weakens the validity of interpretations based on these subscales and ultimately will lead to less valid treatment decisions. It is reasonable that, for practical purposes, the BES-3 includes subscales related to Bower's categories. However, the authors also should include subscales that fit the factor structure of the items better. Informal inspection of the factor analyses suggests that the structure of the BES-3 is not that different from other instruments that measure similar content domains (e.g., CBCL, BASC-II). Although short forms are referred to in the SV and HV manuals, no technical data are presented about the short forms—how the particular items were chosen, reliability, or validity evidence.

Having an intervention booklet linked to the BES-3 is a feature that could potentially set it apart from similar behavior rating scales. Unfortunately, the BES-3 manuals do not present an analysis of the problem or linking of the interventions to more comprehensive assessment data. Interventions appear atheoretical and it is unclear if interventions are evidence based. Only one-page instructions are provided. Further, no effectiveness data are presented related to the use of the interventions in general or special education settings. The interventions are not described with enough detail to insure implementation integrity. It can be hoped that clinicians using the BES-3 will implement better interventions because of the easy availability of an intervention booklet, but no evidence has been presented to support that hope. Without a treatment outcome study proving the superiority of the BES-3, it is hard to recommend it over more established measures.

SUMMARY. The BES-3 consists of two rating scales to assess behavior and two manuals that describe interventions to implement in both school and home/residential settings. Based on the reliability and validity data presented, the BES-3 represents a reliable and valid global measure of behavior problems, which can be used for the purposes of screening or as part of a multimethod, multisource, and multisetting assessment. Interventions based on only a BES-3 subscale or item score must be implemented with caution and the sensitivity of the SV and HV scales to behavior change for their use in progress monitoring is unclear.

REVIEWERS' REFERENCES

Bower, E. M. (1959). The emotionally handicapped child and the school. *Exceptional Children, 26,* 6-11.
Floyd, R. G., & Bose, J. E. (2003). Behavior ratings scales for assessment of emotional disturbance: A critical review of measurement characteristics. *Journal of Psychoeducational Assessment, 21,* 43-78.

[23]

Behavior Rating Inventory of Executive Function—Adult Version.

Purpose: Designed to capture "views of an adults own executive functions, or self-regulation, in his or her everyday environment."

Population: Ages 18–90.
Publication Dates: 1996–2005.
Acronym: BRIEF-A.
Scores, 12: 9 subscales: Inhibit, Shift, Emotional Control, Self-Monitor, Initiate, Working Memory, Plan/Organize, Task Monitor, Organization of Materials; 3 composite scores: Behavioral Regulation Index, Metacognition Index, Global Executive Composite.
Administration: Individual.
Price Data, 2007: $189 per introductory kit including professional manual (2005, 147 pages), 25 self-report forms, 25 informant report forms, 25 self-report scoring summary/profile forms, and 25 informant report scoring summary/profile forms; $55 per professional manual; $45 per 25 self-report forms; $45 per 25 informant report forms; $30 per 25 self-report scoring summary/profile forms; $30 per 25 informant report scoring summary/profile forms.
Time: (15) minutes.
Comments: It is preferable to administer the informant report form to a knowledgeable informant such as a spouse, adult child, caregiver, or other person who has frequent face-to-face interaction with the individual completing the self-report form.
Authors: Robert M. Roth, Peter K. Isquith, and Gerard A. Gioia.
Publisher: Psychological Assessment Resources, Inc.

Review of the Behavior Rating Inventory of Executive Function-Adult Version by GARY J. DEAN, Professor and Chairperson, Department of Adult and Community Education, Indiana University of Pennsylvania, and SANDRA F. DEAN, Instructor, Pennsylvania Highlands Community College, Indiana, PA:

DESCRIPTION. The Behavior Rating Inventory of Executive Function—Adult Version (BRIEF-A) is a self-report and informant-report measure of adults' self-regulation in their everyday environment. It is intended to be administered to adults between the ages of 18 and 90 who have a wide "variety of developmental disorders and systemic, neurological, and psychiatric illnesses such as attention disorders, learning disabilities, autism spectrum disorders, traumatic brain injury, multiple sclerosis, depression, and schizophrenia" (professional manual, p. 1). The BRIEF-A has nine clinical scales to measure executive functions and three validity scales. According to the manual, the executive functions are Inhibit (the extent to which people can control their own impulses and stop their behavior at the appropriate time), Shift (employing flexibility to solve problems or moving from one situation to another), Emotional Control (modulating their emotional responses), Self-Monitor (awareness of behavior in social context), Initiate (initiating activities and generating ideas), Working Memory (maintaining and manipulating information to complete a task), Plan/Organize (anticipating future events and planning for them), Task Monitor (assessing performance in accomplishing a task), and Organization of Materials (keeping workspace and living areas clean and orderly). In addition, the three validity scales address Negativity (the extent to which responses show an unusually negative manner possibly indicating depression), Infrequency (the extent to which the respondent answers selected items in an unusual or infrequent direction), and Inconsistency (the extent to which the respondent answers similar items inconsistently).

The inventory consists of two versions, each containing 75 items: a Self-Report Form and an Informant-Report Form. For each item, respondents indicate whether the behavior described occurred "never," "sometimes," or "often," in the past month. Upon completion of the inventory, responses are transferred to a removable portion of the inventory to generate the scores for the nine clinical and three validity scales. The scale scores are further summarized and interpreted on the Self-Report Scoring Summary or Informant-Report Scoring Summary. The scoring summaries include the raw score, T-score, percentile, and 90% confidence interval for each of the nine clinical scales. The negativity scale is scored by counting the number of times the respondent responded "often" to 10 selected items on the inventory. The Infrequency score is based on responses to 5 items on the inventory. Certain responses to these items occur infrequently and indicate unusual behavior. The Inconsistency score is obtained by comparing 20 paired items on the inventory and then subtracting the numerical value of the response to 1 item from the response to the other. The difference scores are then totaled.

In addition, scores for two indexes, the Behavioral Regulation Index (BRI) and the Metacognition Index (MI), and the Global Executive Composite (GEC) are computed. The BRI measures an adult's ability to maintain regulatory control over behavior and emotional responses. The Inhibit, Shift, Emotional Control, and Self-Monitor scales contribute to this index. The MI index measures an individual's ability to

systematically solve problems and is composed of the Initiate, Working Memory, Plan/Organize, Task Monitor, and Organization of Materials scales. The GEC is a summary measure that reflects all of the clinical scales of the BRIEF-A.

Interpretation of scores is facilitated by tables showing T-scores and equivalent percentile ranks for the nine clinical scales as well as the BRI, MI, and GEC. These tables report norms for the following age groups: 18 to 29 years, 30 to 39 years, 40 to 49 years, 50 to 59 years, 60 to 69 years, 70 to 79 years, and 80 to 90 years.

DEVELOPMENT. The BRIEF-A was developed from the BRIEF (for children), the BRIEF-P (for preschool children), and the BRIEF-SR (self-report for adolescents). Items for the BRIEF-A were developed from several sources. The existing BRIEF instruments served as a starting point for the item pool. This pool was augmented by items developed from case files from the authors and other professionals. This pool of items was broadened to include additional items consistent with the nine executive functions. Finally, other inventories were reviewed to identify possible gaps in coverage, for which additional items were needed. The resulting pool of 160 items was reduced to 146 items that were subjected to try-out studies.

Using a sample of 313 adults for the Self-Report form and 289 for the Informant-Report form, the authors examined the statistical properties of individual items, calculated the correlation of each individual item score with the total score for each scale, and conducted a principal factor analysis with orthogonal rotation to clarify scale structure resulting in 75 items for each form. Care was taken to develop norm samples for both forms (Self-Report form n = 1,050 and the Informant-Report form n = 1,200) that represent the adult population of the U.S. according to age, gender, race, education, and geographic region.

TECHNICAL INFORMATION. The authors established reliability for the BRIEF-A in three ways: internal consistency, test-retest stability, and interrater agreement. Internal consistency estimates were based on coefficient alpha. Correlations are reported for two groups per form. For the Self-Report form, coefficients ranged from .73 to .90 for the norm sample (n = 1,050) and .80 to .94 for a mixed sample of clinical patients and healthy adults (n = 233). Correlation coefficients for the indexes (BRI and MI) and GEC ranged from .93 to .96 for the norm sample and .96 to .98 for the mixed sample. For the Informant-Report form, coefficients ranged from .80 to .93 for the norm sample (n = 1,200) and .85 to .95 for a mixed sample (n = 196). For the indexes (BRI and MI) and the GEC, the coefficients ranged from .95 to .98 for the norm sample and .96 to .98 for the mixed sample.

Test-retest correlations were computed for a variety of samples with an approximate 4-week interval in testing. For the Self-Report form, a small sample (n = 50) was used that resulted in a range of correlation coefficients from .82 to .93. The BRI, MI, and GEC coefficients for the Self-Report form ranged from .93 to .94. For the Informant-Report form (sample size = 44), the coefficients ranged from .91 to .94, whereas the BRI, MI, and GEC coefficients were all .96. In addition, absolute mean T-score differences between the first and second testing were computed for both forms. For the Self-Report form, the mean differences ranged from a low of 1.88 (for Inhibit) to a high of 3.26 (for Initiate). The BRI, MI, and GEC mean differences ranged from 2.12 to 2.28. For the Informant-Report form, the T-score mean differences ranged from 1.32 (Emotional Control) to 2.18 (Self-Monitor), whereas the BRI, MI, and GEC mean differences ranged from 1.43 to 1.61.

Finally, in an attempt to establish reliability between the Self-Report and Informant-Report forms, the authors conducted an interrater study with a mixed clinical and healthy adult sample (n = 180). The resulting correlation coefficients ranged from .44 (for Shift) to .68 (for Emotional Control).

Evidence of validity is presented in four ways: item content, convergent and discriminant validity through comparison of the BRIEF-A with other instruments, internal structure of the BRIEF-A, and profiles of BRIEF-A scale scores for various clinical groups. In addition to the development of items described earlier, the authors asked 10 professionals familiar with the concept of executive function to rate each item as to whether it belonged in its assigned scale. Their agreement, averaged within each scale, ranged from a low of 35% (Self-Monitor) to a high of 98% (Emotional Control).

Evidence of convergent and discriminant validity was obtained by comparing the BRIEF-A with seven other instruments. Sample sizes for these validity studies ranged from 9 to 69. The instruments used for comparison were the Frontal Systems Behavior Scale (FrSBe), the Dysexecutive Questionnaire (DEX), the Cognitive Failures Questionnaire (CFQ), the Clinical Assessment of Depression (CAD), the Beck Depression Inventory II (BDI-II), the Geriatric Depression Scale (GDS), and the State-Trait Anxiety Inventory (STAI). Statistically significant (p < .05) correlations were reported for the FrSBe Executive Dysfunction scale and six of the nine clinical scales of the BRIEF-A Self-Report form and two of the clinical scales of the BRIEF-A Informant-Report form. Comparison of the FrSBe Disinhibition scale with the BRIEF-A yielded statistically significant results for four scales of the Self-Report form and six scales for the Informant-Report form.

Correlations with the DEX, which measures executive functions, ranged from .38 to .80 for the Self-Report form and from .54 to .88 for the Informant-Report form with all but one correlation statistically significant at p < .01 (the exception was significant at p < .05).

Correlations between the BRIEF-A clinical scales and the CFQ, which measures lapses in executive function, ranged from .34 to .81 for the comparison between the self-report forms of the two instruments. Comparison between the two informant-report forms of the two instruments resulted in correlations ranging from .52 to .86. All but one of the correlations were statistically significant at p < .05 or better.

Studies comparing the BRIEF-A to measures of depression were carried out with the CAD, BDI-II, the GDS, and STAI. For the CAD scales of Depressed Mood, Anxiety/Worry, and Diminished Interest, coefficients ranged from .03 to .62. Correlations were slightly higher for the CAD's Cognitive and Physical Fatigue scale, ranging from .33 to .65. Correlations with the BDI-II, GDS, and STAI were more substantial. Correlations with the BDI-II ranged from .29 to .55 (all statistically significant at p < .05). Correlations with the GDS ranged from .31 to .54 (all statistically significant at p < .05 or better). Finally, correlations with the Trait Anxiety scale of the STAI ranged from .38 to .54 (all statistically significant at p < .01).

To establish the validity of the internal structure of the BRIEF-A, the authors conducted principal factor analyses (two factors) with both norm samples. For the Self-Report form ($n = 1,050$), the factor correlation was .783 (which accounted for 73% of the variance). For the Informant-Report form ($n = 1,200$), the factor correlation was .799 (81% of the variance).

Finally, the authors conducted a series of studies with people diagnosed with various conditions (ADHD, Alzheimer's, MS, traumatic brain injury, and epilepsy). Two groups of ADHD adults, those receiving medication ($n = 16$) and those who were not ($n = 27$), were compared to a group of healthy adults ($n = 42$). MANOVAs revealed that there were statistically significant differences ($p < .05$) between the two ADHD groups and the control group for all nine clinical scales and the BRI, MI, and GEC scales. Another study compared normal adults ($n = 26$) to adults with Alzheimer's ($n = 7$), mild cognitive impairment ($n = 23$), and normal adults with memory loss ($n = 26$). The resulting MANOVAs indicated that there were statistically significant differences for eight of the nine clinical scales (excluding Inhibit) and the BRI, MI, and GEC. A study comparing individuals with MS ($n = 14$) to a matched sample of healthy adults ($n = 14$) showed statistically significant differences for T scores ($p < .05$) for eight of the nine clinical scales (excluding Organization of Materials) and both indexes and the GEC. A study comparing a sample of people with MS ($n = 8$) to a matched sample of healthy adults ($n = 8$) had mixed results. There were statistically significant differences ($p < .05$) for four of the nine clinical scales (Shift, Initiate, Working Memory, and Task Monitor) as well as for the BRI, MI, and GEC. Similarly, there were mixed results when samples of people with traumatic brain injury ($n = 23$ for the Self-Report form and $n = 11$ for the Informant-Report form) were compared to matched samples of healthy adults. A final study with a sample of people with epilepsy ($n = 10$) was compared to a healthy adult sample ($n = 10$) with results showing statistically significant differences ($p < .05$) for seven of the nine clinical scales (excluding Inhibit and Shift) and the BRI, MI, and GEC.

COMMENTARY. Evaluating standardized instruments such as the BRIEF-A can be based on three broad questions: Are the underlying constructs supportable, to what extent does the instrument adequately measure the constructs, and how useful is the instrument to clients and professionals? These questions will be used to guide the commentary on the BRIEF-A.

There is some debate in the literature regarding the constructs of executive function. According to Royall et al. (2002), there are two main themes in the literature: "ECF [executive control function] is associated with higher cognitive functions such as insight and judgment, which are mostly dependent on the frontal lobes" and "ECF is made visible only by the disorganized operation of nonexecutive functions" (p. 379). The latter appears to be the position taken by the authors of the BRIEF-A. Given that there is still debate regarding the meaning of executive function, it is important for practitioners to be well grounded in its underlying theory. Although the authors state that practitioners need to have graduate education in psychology or a related area to interpret the BRIEF-A, it would appear that in-depth knowledge of executive function is required to effectively understand and use the BRIEF-A in practice.

The adequacy of the BRIEF-A to measure executive dysfunction is supported in a number of ways. Although, in general, the test development procedures employed by the authors are exemplary, there are some points about which practitioners should be aware. The samples used to develop the norms are more than adequate, correcting the problems of sample size and geographic distribution noted by Fitzpatrick (2003) for the BRIEF. The process of item selection and refinement was built upon the earlier BRIEF inventories. Benton and Benton (2005) and Martinez-Pons (2005) noted that expert ratings for item assignment to scales in the BRIEF-SR were not made clear. This issue has been addressed in the BRIEF-A, albeit with mixed results. The authors note that a panel of 10 experts reviewed each item to determine its appropriateness for the scale in which it was included. Expert ratings of items varied from 0% to 100% agreement indicating that there were some items for which the experts did not agree with the author's placement in that scale. This was particularly apparent in the Self-Monitor scale.

The extensive tests for reliability through internal consistency, test-retest, and interrater reliability studies demonstrate that there is substantial reliability for the BRIEF-A. The authors went to extensive lengths to establish the validity of the BRIEF-A. Comparisons of the BRIEF-A with other instruments to establish convergent and discriminant validity were, in general, supportive although most were based on small samples. The studies with various diagnostic groups of adults, however, had mixed results. There were inconsistent results with studies of people with multiple sclerosis, traumatic brain injury, and epilepsy indicating the BRIEF-A may not be as useful with these groups. In addition, the sample sizes in many of these studies were quite small indicating that the findings might not be generalizable.

With regard to the usefulness of the BRIEF-A in the field, it is clear that the BRIEF-A can make a positive contribution to practitioners. The BRIEF-A is easy to administer although scoring and interpretation may be challenging for some practitioners. Practitioners will find the case studies provided in the manual especially useful for learning to interpret and use the BRIEF-A with clients. The manual itself is thorough, well organized, and provides the information necessary to administer, score and interpret the BRIEF-A. More information could be supplied regarding the theoretical basis of executive function. In addition, the careful selection of the norm samples to match the demographics of the U.S. makes the instrument especially useful for practitioners. An important question raised by Martinez-Pons (2005) in regards to the BRIEF-SR is the extent to which children and adolescents can adequately self-report regarding their executive functions. The same question might be raised concerning adults who have diminished capacities. The use of the Informant-Report form, therefore, becomes important in practice.

SUMMARY. The BRIEF-A is a carefully developed instrument built on the success of previous instruments and the authors' extensive experience. It is thoroughly researched and the development of the instrument followed exacting procedures. Practitioners should find the BRIEF-A useful for assessing executive dysfunctions in their clients. Professionals in a variety of agencies serving a variety of clients will find the BRIEF-A useful. It should yield data that will help both the agencies and clients better understand their diagnoses and make realistic treatment plans for coping with diminished executive function.

REVIEWERS' REFERENCES

Benton, S. L., & Benton, S. (2005). [Review of the Behavior Rating Inventory of Executive Function—Self-Report Version.] In R. A. Spies & B. S. Plake (Eds.), *The sixteenth mental measurements yearbook* (pp. 119–121). Lincoln, NE: Buros Institute of Mental Measurements.

Fitzpatrick, C. (2003). [Review of the Behavioral Inventory of Executive Function.] In B. S. Plake, J. C. Impara, & R. A. Spies (Eds.), *The fifteenth mental measurements yearbook* (pp. 113–115). Lincoln, NE: Buros Institute of Mental Measurements.

Martinez-Pons, M. (2005). [Review of the Behavioral Inventory of Executive Function—Self Report.] In R. A. Spies & B. S. Plake (Eds.), *The sixteenth mental measurements yearbook* (pp. 121–123). Lincoln, NE: Buros Institute of Mental Measurements.

Royall, D. R., Lauterbach, E. C., Cummings, J. L., Reeve, A., Rummans, T. A., Kaufer, D. I., LaFrance, W. C., Jr., & Coffey, C. E. (2002, November). Executive control function: A review of its promise and challenges for clinical research: A report from the committee on research of the American Neuropsychiatric Association. *The Journal of Neuropsychiatry and Clinical Neurosciences, 14*, 377-405.

Review of the Behavior Rating Inventory of Executive Function–Adult Version by KATHY E. GREEN, Professor of Education, University of Denver, Denver, CO:

DESCRIPTION. The Behavior Rating Inventory of Executive Function–Adult Version (BRIEF-A) is a self-report assessment of executive function in the daily environment. Executive or higher order cognitive functions serve to direct and organize behavior, emotional response, and cognition. Disorders affecting the frontal lobe of the brain can result in executive dysfunction. Disorders can result from brain trauma, degenerative or other diseases, or substance abuse, among other causes. The BRIEF-A is a screening tool for executive dysfunction.

The 75-item measure is intended for use with adults ages 18 through 90 with a fifth grade or higher reading level. The response options are *never, sometimes,* and *often.* The BRIEF-A can be administered by persons without formal training but interpretation of results requires graduate training in psychology, psychiatry, neurology, or a related field. Nine scale scores (Inhibit, Shift, Emotional Control, Self-Monitor, Initiate, Working Memory, Plan/Organize, Task Monitor, and Organization of Materials) are provided plus two index scores (Behavioral Regulation and Metacognition), one composite score (Global Executive Composite), and three validity scores (Negativity, Infrequency, and Inconsistency). There is also an informant version to be completed by an individual familiar with the respondent, such as a spouse, parent, or child. The BRIEF-A takes approximately 15 minutes to complete. A scoring sheet attached to the BRIEF-A as a carbonless copy makes summing responses to generate the nine subscale scores easy. These nine scores are then transferred to a separate scoring summary sheet on which raw scores for Inhibit, Shift, Emotional Control, and Self-Monitor are added to calculate the Behavioral Regulation Index. Raw scores for Initiate, Working Memory, Plan/Organize, Task Monitor, and Organization of Materials are added to form the Metacognition Index. The sum of the two index raw scores forms the Global Executive Composite. Raw scores are converted to T-scores, percentiles, and 90% confidence intervals by referring to age-appropriate norms in the professional manual. T-scores exceeding 65 are called clinically significant. The professional manual contains six case illustrations or profiles to aid in score interpretation. Validity scores are computed by circling and counting specified responses to marked items. Cutoff scores for each validity scale identify the most extreme 1% of respondents and may indicate compromised validity of the assessment.

DEVELOPMENT. The BRIEF-A is one of a series of measures of executive functioning designed for different populations (e.g., BRIEF for school-aged children, Gioia, Isquith, Guy, & Kenworthy, 2000, 17:23; BRIEF-SR adolescent self-report, Guy, Isquith, & Gioia, 2004, 16:28). BRIEF development was informed by models of executive function, research regarding the neurodevelopment of the frontal regions of the brain, neuropsychological tests, and clinical assessment of executive dysfunction and as such has an extensive, if not uniformly agreed upon, theoretical basis. BRIEF-A items were modeled upon BRIEF items and revised to reflect adult behaviors. Additional general items plus items taken from clinical interviews of adults were added. An item pool of 160 items was reduced to 146 items by eliminating redundant or unclear items, and cut to 78 items via principal factor- and item-analyses with 3 poorly fitting items later discarded. Respondent and informant samples of 313 and 289 were enlisted to try out the initial measure. Parallel analyses were conducted for informant data with generally parallel results.

TECHNICAL. The 140-page BRIEF-A professional manual contains well-written chapters on development and standardization, reliability and validity, and score interpretation. Standardization was conducted on a sample of 1,050 adults in the United States selected to approximate the demographic distribution of the U.S. population from the Current Population Survey, March 2002. Subgroup analysis resulted in minimal score differences by gender, socioeconomic status, race/ethnicity, and educational level, but more substantial differences by age. Separate T-score norms were constructed for age groups.

BRIEF-A reliability was assessed via internal consistency, stability, and interrater (self- and informant) estimates. Internal consistency reliability estimates were generally high, ranging from .73 to .90 for the clinical scales based on self-report and from .80 to .93 for informants in the norming sample; index and composite score alphas exceeded .93 for both samples. A second sample of mixed clinical and healthy adults (233 respondents and 196 informants) yielded higher coefficient alphas (all $\geq$ .80). Test-retest data were collected for a small subsample of the norming samples (n = 50 for self-report and n = 44 for informants). Scale stability coefficients over approximately 4 weeks were .82 to .93 for respondents and .91 to .94 for informants; index and composite stability coefficients were .93 to .96 for the two groups. Correlations between self- and informant-report were moderate (.44 to .63) for all scales, indices, and the composite. Aside from the norming sample, sample selection (e.g., subsampling) was not well described.

Validity evidence came from evaluation of content, convergent, and discriminant relationships with other measures, structure, and differences between groups with diagnoses suggesting executive dysfunction. Content review was conducted by an expert panel of 10 neuropsychologists/psychologists. Reviewers addressed allocating items to scales, with agreement ranging from 35% (self-monitor) to 98% (emotional control). BRIEF-A scores were correlated with scores on the Frontal Systems Behavior Scale (Grace & Malloy, 2002), the Dysexecutive Questionnaire (Wilson, Alderman, Burgess, Emslie, & Evans, 1996), the Cognitive Failures Questionnaire (Broadbent, Cooper, Fitzgerald, & Parkes, 1982), the Clinical Assessment of Depression (Bracken & Howell, 2004), the Beck Depression Inventory II (Beck, Steer, & Brown, 1996), the Geriatric Depression Scale (GDS; Yesavage et al., 1983), and the State-Trait Anxiety Inventory (STAI; Spielberger, Gorsuch, & Lushene, 1970). Sample sizes ranged from 9 to 69 in 10 studies and comprised groups of adults with mixed or no diagnosis, or informants related to those adults. Moderate to high correlations were found for most scales, with lower correlations with the GDS and the STAI.

BRIEF-A internal structure was evaluated separately for self- and informant-report data using principal factor analysis with oblique rotation. Two factor solutions accounted for 73%, 81%, 76%, and 78% of the variance in samples of, respectively, 1,050 respondents, 1,200 informants, 233 mixed clinical/healthy adult respondents, and 196 informants of the mixed clinical/healthy adult sample. Two-factor structures also emerged when the normative samples were split into two age groups (ages 18–49 and 50–89). Tables present only the highest factor loadings, so it was not possible to determine scale crossloadings.

Thirteen separate samples of individuals with or informants for individuals with and without executive dysfunction diagnoses were assessed. Diagnoses were ADHD, Alzheimer's, cognitive impairment, multiple sclerosis, traumatic brain injury, epilepsy, controls with health complaints, and five healthy control groups. Group sample sizes ranged from 7 to 42. Control participants were matched to diagnosed adults on age, gender, and ethnicity. Mean differences between controls and adults diagnosed with ADHD were statistically significant at $p < .001$ for all scales, indices, and the composite, with large effect sizes. Differences and effect sizes were less pronounced for individuals diagnosed with Alzheimer's, mild cognitive impairment, and multiple sclerosis, though still statistically significant across groups. Significant differences for the traumatic brain injury sample were found for some scales; differences for individuals diagnosed with epilepsy were significant for all scores except Inhibit and Shift. In most though not all comparisons, effect sizes were large (Eta Squared > .15).

COMMENTARY. The BRIEF-A is grounded in the literature and also in clinical practice. It fills a gap in assessment of executive function problems in that it reflects everyday settings. Strengths of the BRIEF-A include a sound development process, simple administration and scoring, a user-friendly manual, score interpretation aids, a standardization sample reflective of the U.S. population, good reliability, and support for validity through varied types of evidence. Weaknesses include lack of confirmation of the measure's structure. Confirmatory factoring techniques, rather than exploratory, would be preferable. Also, it appears that analysis was at the scale not the item level so empirical item grouping by scale has not been confirmed. As the factor structure of the BRIEF-A differs from the structure of the BRIEF, an explanation of why structures differ would be interesting. Reliability coefficients by age group would be informative as would reliability coefficients for the samples of individuals with executive function diagnoses. Further validity studies with known groups would be useful, including prediction of job functioning, use of the BRIEF-A with differently lesioned patients, relationships to performance-based executive function measures, and classification/misclassification rates by scale, index, and composite scores. A further consideration is the inventory's reliance on reading, which limits its use.

SUMMARY. The BRIEF-A is a well-constructed, soundly based, easy-to-use inventory of executive functioning in everyday life. It adds an ecologically sensitive assessment to be used, as the authors recommend, in conjunction with other sources of information "to facilitate focused treatment and educational planning for adults with executive function difficulties" (professional manual, p. 5). Continued research regarding the factor structure and predictive and convergent validity will contribute to understanding results, indicate validity of scale scores versus indices, and focus its use.

REVIEWER'S REFERENCES

Beck, A. T., Steer, R. A., & Brown, G. K. (1996). Beck Depression Inventory-II (BDI-II). San Antonio, TX: The Psychological Corporation.

Bracken, B. A., & Howell, K. (2004). Clinical Assessment of Depression. Lutz, FL: Psychological Assessment Resources, Inc.

Broadbent, D. E., Cooper, P. F., Fitzgerald, P., & Parkes, K. R. (1982). The Cognitive Failures Questionnaire (CFQ) and its correlates. *British Journal of Clinical Psychology, 21*, 1-16.

Gioia, G. A., Isquith, P. K., Guy, S. C., & Kenworthy, L. (2000). Behavior Rating Inventory of Executive Function. Odessa, FL: Psychological Assessment Resources.

Grace, J., & Malloy, P. F. (2002). Frontal Systems Behavior Scale (FrSBe). Lutz, FL: Psychological Assessment Resources, Inc.

Guy, S. C., Isquith, P. K., & Gioia, G. A. (2004). Behavior Rating Inventory of Executive Function—Self-Report Version. Lutz, FL: Psychological Assessment Resources, Inc.

Spielberger, C. D., Gorsuch, R. L., & Lushene, R. E. (1970). State-Trait Anxiety Inventory (STAI Form C1). Palo Alto, CA: Consulting Psychologists Press.

Wilson, B. A., Alderman, N., Burgess, P., Emslie, H., & Evans, J. J. (1996). Behavioural Assessment of the Dysexecutive Syndrome. Bury St. Edmunds, Suffolk, England: The Thames Valley Test Company.

Yesavage, J. A., Brink, T. L., Rose, T. L., Lun, O., Huang, V., Adez, M., et al. (1983). Development and validation of a geriatric depression screening scale: A preliminary report. *Journal of Psychiatric Research, 17*, 37-49.

[24]

Behavioural Assessment of the Dysexecutive Syndrome in Children.

Purpose: Tests the executive functioning of children and adolescents.

Population: Children and adolescents ages 7 to 16.

Publication Date: 2003.

Acronym: BADS-C.

Scores, 8: Playing Cards Test, Water Test, Key Search Test, Zoo Map Test 1, Zoo Map Test 2, Six Parts Test, Dysexecutive Questionnaire for Children, Total Score.

Administration: Individual.

Price Data, 2007: £382 per complete kit including manual (41 pages), 25 scoring sheets, stimulus cards, three-dimensional plastic materials, timer, 25 Dysexecutive Questionnaire for Children (DEX-C), independent rater questionnaires, beads, nuts, bolts, and washers; £19.39 per 25 record sheets; £15.86 per 25 DEX-C questionnaires.

Time: (35–45) minutes.

Comments: Adaptation of Behavioural Assessment of the Dysexecutive Syndrome (T7:302); examinee IQ-score must be available to determine scaled score and percentile rank.

Authors: Hazel Emslie, F. Colin Wilson, Vivian Burden, Ian Nimmo-Smith, and Barbara A. Wilson.

Publisher: Harcourt Assessment [England].

Review of the Behavioural Assessment of the Dysexecutive Syndrome for Children (BADS-C) by LORRAINE CLEETON, Faculty Mentor in the Ph.D. Program in Education, Walden University, Minneapolis, MN:

DESCRIPTION. The Behavioural Assessment of the Dysexecutive Syndrome for Children (BADS-C) is described as an ecologically valid and reliable test of executive functioning in children with standardized "child-friendly" administration, standardized scoring procedures, and comprehensive norms. The test authors maintain that a brain injury occurring in adulthood has an effect on separate skills of executive functioning and the primary impairment to individuals is in initiating these skills, self-monitoring, and using performance information to adjust their behavior. The test authors noted a paucity in the literature of studies on executive abilities in children and adolescents and found that executive functioning possibly did not emerge until adolescence. Because most standard psychometric tests for children are not sensitive to executive functioning, the test authors started using parts of the Behavioral Assessment of the Dysexecutive Syndrome (BADS) to assess adolescents and younger children. The test authors do not specify which parts of the BADS were used.

DEVELOPMENT. The BADS-C is based on the BADS (Behavioural Assessment of the Dysexecutive Syndrome; Wilson, Alderman, Bargess, Emslie, & Evans, 1996). The BADS was designed to be used by occupational and speech therapists as well as psychologists. Essentially, this test for adults assesses frontal lobe damage and comprises the characteristics: inflexibility, perseveration, novel problem solving, impulsivity, planning, and the ability to utilize feedback and moderate one's behavior as necessary. Collectively, these characteristics make up the dysexecutive syndrome.

The BADS test battery includes different situations that use tasks analogous to those used in everyday life involving executive functioning (a "set of behavioral competencies which include the ability to plan, sequence behaviors, sustain attention, resist interference, utilize feedback, co-ordinate simultaneous activity, change set, and generally deal with novel situations associated with frontal lobe damage," manual, p. 5).

The norming process for the BADS-C is comprehensively described by the test authors, and the individuals chosen were taken from a wide-ranging representative sample even though the total number of participants was small. It was based on a total of "265 children comprising approximately equal numbers of individuals balanced for gender across each of eight bands" (manual, p. 9) recruited from a wide range of schools (urban, rural, industrial/high–tech, social/private housing) and drawn from across the socioeconomic spectrum. The children were given the Wechsler Objective Reading Dimensions Test to obtain eligibility and establish IQ. Students whose scores fell two or more standard deviations below the mean were dropped from the sample. A total of 114 children with a variety of developmental and neurological disorders, independently diagnosed by hospital consultants, were tested on the BADS-C battery and a range of other neuropsychological tests. "The teachers and/or parents of all children were asked to complete two questionnaires, the Dysexecutive Questionnaire for Children (DEX-C) and the Strengths and Difficulties Questionnaire (SDQ)" (manual, p. 10).

"Children who were referred for assessment because of learning and/or behavior difficulties differed significantly from the controls in all tasks except the Zoo Map Test 2" (manual, p. 24). In contrast, children with dyslexia performed similarly to controls in all tests. Neither of these findings were explained further. However, the authors did give some explanation of why children with ADHD (attention deficit hyperactivity disorder) scored better on the Water Test but did not describe why they had difficulty with the Six Part Test and Key Search Test and lesser difficulty with the Playing Cards Test. According to the test authors, children with ADHD performed marginally better than controls on the Water Test in which it was thought that their frequent changes of strategy helped them in finding a solution.

DESCRIPTION OF TESTS. The test authors explain how the BADS tests were either modified or dropped based on their appropriateness for children to evolve into the BADS-C. The BADS-C comprises six subtests and one questionnaire. They are the Playing Cards Test (evaluates a child's ability to alter a pre-existing response pattern); the Water Test (requires a plan of action to solve a problem); the Key Search Test ("examines a child's ability to plan an efficient, systematic, implementable plan of action, monitor their own performance, and take into account factors which are not explicitly stated," manual, p. 7); Zoo Map Tests 1 and 2 (the former is an "open-ended task where little structure is provided so the planning abilities of the child are rigorously tested" (manual, p. 8) and the latter is a "low demand, rule-governed task" in which the instructions state "Your job is to draw a line to show where you would walk to visit the animals and places pictured below" (manual, p. 8); the Six Part Test (test of planning, task scheduling and performance monitoring); and the Dysexecutive Questionnaire for Children (DEX-C), a 20-item questionnaire derived from the Dysexecutive Questionnaire that is part of the BADS.

The DEX-C questionnaire "has been constructed to reflect the range of problems usually associated with the Dysexecutive Syndrome.... the questions probe four main areas of possible difficulty: emotional/personality, motivational, behavioural, and cognitive" (manual, p. 9). Examples of items include statements such as "Acts without thinking, doing the first thing that comes to mind" (manual, p. 9) The scoring and individual characteristics of the Dysexecutive Syndrome range from 1, abstract thinking problems, to 20, unconcern for social rules. It might have been helpful for practitioners if the authors had

included some questionnaire results obtained from children with various disabilities.

The scoring of each subtest of the BADS-C is briefly discussed. The authors point out that "conversion tables have been created so that the raw score for each of the component tests can be converted to a scaled score, which is adjusted for the child's age and estimated IQ" (manual, p. 14). Complete scored examples are included for each test on pages 16–22. These are very helpful to the practitioner.

TECHNICAL DATA. Test-retest reliability was addressed using 25 controls aged 8–14 years and drawn from all ability bands. Participants performed "slightly better on the tests on the second occasion than they did on the first" (manual, p. 22), although differences were statistically significant only for the Playing Cards Test and Six Part Test. "There is a fairly high correlation between the scaled scores achieved on the first and second occasions on the Key Search Test (as it was in the adult BADS), and moderate correlations in the other … tests with the lowest being in the Playing Cards Test and Zoo Map Test" (manual, p. 22).

According to the test authors, similar findings occurred in the adult version of this test (the BADS) even when a longer interval was employed. It may be unreasonable to expect high test-retest reliability coefficients for test of executive functions because the tasks are not novel when presented for the second time. Also, the authors state that improvement in test scores "might also reflect normal developmental changes in children" (manual, p. 23).

Interrater reliability. Across the 6 tests 14 items are scored and interrater reliability is very high, ranging between .53 and 1.00 with complete agreement on 6 out of 14 measures. The exception was the perseveration measure in the Water Test (.53). This errant finding was not explained.

Internal consistency. This method of estimating reliability could have been used to prune weak items. It was not addressed in the test manual.

The main purpose of the BADS-C was to produce an ecologically valid test of executive functioning that would predict the presence and severity of executive problems in everyday life. Information about difficulties encountered by children was collected using the DEX-C and Goodman's Strengths and Difficulties Questionnaire (SDQ), "which yields measures of total difficulties as well as emotional symptoms, conduct problems, hyperactivity, and peer problems.... There were significant negative correlations between BADS-C total and DEX-C total scores and all measures on the SDQ: the higher the difficulties score on the DEX-C or SDQ the lower the BADS-C score" (manual, p. 34). According to the test authors, "a satisfactory performance on the BADS-C test is indicative of low ratings of the presence and severity of problems as perceived by parents or teachers whereas poor scores on the BADS-C are associated with increased reporting on the part of teachers or parents of the presence of difficulties and higher ratings of their severity" (manual, p. 34).

Significant correlations between the DEX-C and all the subtests except the Water Test are used by the BADS-C authors to claim construct validity. The test authors also report further correlations between measures associated with the dysexecutive syndrome and some of the different subtests of the BADS-C. For example, word fluency, sometimes considered to be a measure of frontal lobe function, correlates only with the Playing Cards Test, and memory correlates only with Zoo Map Test 2 and the BADS-C total score. Further discussion of these correlations and their associations with the test battery would have been useful to the practitioner.

SUMMARY. According to the authors, "the BADS-C has been standardized and normed for children and adolescents between the ages of 8 and 16.... It has been designed to predict everyday problems arising from the Dysexecutive Syndrome (DES)" (manual, p. 37). It was based on the adult BADS, which involves tasks of the supervisory system with which children with DES have most difficulty.

The test authors claim the BADS-C is a "sensitive, reliable, ecologically valid tool for assessing executive impairment that has child friendly administration, a standard scoring system and comprehensive norms" (manual, p. 37). They also assert that this test will assist in early, reliable identification of deficits in executive functioning in children to try to prevent or ameliorate secondary social and learning deficits that tend to emerge over time. Additional test-retest reliability studies are needed to support this assertion.

The BADS-C allows for a wide range of practitioners to administer the test including clinical and educational psychologists, neuropsychologists, child psychiatrists, pediatricians, research assistants and health professionals working with children with impairments as compared to the BADS (occupational and speech therapists, as well as psychologists). The modification procedure involved in creating the BADS-C from the BADS is not well defined with enough supporting evidence. The length of each test is not adequately described. More research is needed to establish the relationship between test scores and different disabilities.

REVIEWER'S REFERENCE

Wilson, B.A., Alderman, N., Burgess, P., Emslie, H., & Evans, J. (1996). Behavioural Assessment of the Dysexecutive Syndrome. Suffolk, England: Thames Valley Test Company.

Review of the Behavioural Assessment of the Dysexecutive Syndrome for Children by RAMA K. MISHRA, Department of Psychiatry, Medicine Hat Regional Hospital, Medicine Hat, Alberta, Canada:

DESCRIPTION. The Behavioural Assessment of the Dysexecutive Syndrome for Children (BADS-C) is a test of "impaired executive functioning and self-regulation" (manual, p. 5) for 8- to 16-year-old children and adolescents. The identification of these deficits would be useful in the neuropsychological assessment of Pervasive Developmental Disorder, Traumatic Brain Injury, Attention Deficit Disorder, and other conditions in which frontal and prefrontal lobe dysfunction is suspected. This test is claimed to be "ecologically valid and reliable" and "child-friendly" (manual, p. 5).

The test authors have defined executive functioning as "behavioral competencies which include the ability to plan, sequence behaviors, sustain attention, resist interference, utilize feedback, co-ordinate simultaneous activity, change set, and generally deal with novel situations" (manual, p. 5). Baddeley's (1986) concept of "dysexecutive syndrome" has been used to identify these deficits.

In traditional tests of cognitive functioning the test taker usually has a single problem to solve. The trials are initiated by the clinician and criteria for success are specified. However, the opportunity for prioritization of tasks, organization, and planning of activities over a relatively longer period of time are rarely assessed. The

BADS-C is designed to capture these aspects of executive functioning that are important in everyday activities.

The BADS-C battery has six tests, namely the Playing Cards Test, Water Test, Key Search Test, Zoo Map Test 1 and 2, and Six Part Test. In addition to the child's level of performance on these tasks, a 20-item questionnaire is completed by the teacher and parents to identify emotional/personality, motivational, behavioral, and cognitive problems associated with the dysexecutive syndrome. The subtests and total scores are converted to scaled scores and percentiles based on age (provided in intervals of 12 months) and estimated IQ bands (e.g., 70 to 89, 90 to 110, and above 110). The BADS-C total age-scaled score can be converted to an overall Scaled Score (Mean = 100, SD = 15) and an Overall Classification from six categories (e.g., impaired, borderline, low average, average, high average, and superior). The estimated administration time is between 35 and 45 minutes.

DEVELOPMENT. The BADS-C was developed as a downward extension of the adult version of the Behavioural Assessment of the Dysexecutive Syndrome (BADS; Wilson, Alderman, Burgess, Emslie, & Evans, 1996; T7:302). In a pilot study, the BADS was administered to children. Certain items and subtests were identified as inappropriate or difficult for children. Therefore, these sections of the adult version (BADS) were dropped and replaced with age-appropriate items for children. It was reported that clinical observations, unavailability of tests for children in this area, and uniqueness of item formats (e.g., reflective of everyday activities) guided the development process.

Detailed information regarding test development is lacking. The description of operational definitions, process of test and item selections, and steps of the norming process are very brief or absent from the test manual.

TECHNICAL. The standardization of the BADS-C used 265 eight-to sixteen-year-olds with approximately equal numbers of boys and girls in each of eight age groups. Six children were dropped from the sample due to very low IQ Scores based on the Basic Reading Test from the Wechsler Objective Reading Dimensions Test (WORD). Additionally, the clinical groups consisted of 114 children with a variety of developmental and neurological disorders. The diagnosis of these conditions was done independently by hospital consultants in England.

Reliability evidence for the BADS-C is reported in the manual. Interrater reliability was determined by asking two examiners to record all relevant responses independently for 25 children between the ages of 8 and 14 years. "Absolute agreement" (r = 1.0) was obtained for 6 of the 14 items of the six tests. Seven items demonstratd very high correlations and ranged from .91 to .99. The only exception was the perseveration measure on the Water Test, which—at .53—was considered a moderate correlation.

Test-retest reliability estimates were developed by readministering the test to a sample of 25 children in 3 to 4 weeks after the first assessment. The correlation coefficient was found to be high for Key Search Test (r = .81) and moderate for Zoo Map Test 1 (r = .59) and Six Parts Test (r = .44). The correlations were low for Zoo Map Test 2 (r = .29) and Playing Cards Test (r = -.24). The test authors argue that test-retest correlations are expected to be low as the test is familiar when it is given for the second time. Thus, they expected that the scores would improve when it is readministered. Accordingly, they found that the scores were significantly higher for the Playing Cards Test and Six Part Test (p < .05 in both). On the Water Test, test-retest correlations or group difference were not calculated as the participants obtained maximum score (reached ceiling) when the test was administered for the second time. Overall, test-retest reliability indices are quite mixed.

Some basic reliability estimates such as internal consistency of the various tests were not reported. It is suspected that, due to the small number of items, internal consistency estimates would be quite low.

Validity evidence for the BADS-C was determined in a number of ways. First of all, the authors demonstrated that the control group and the clinical groups were found to be significantly different on Playing Cards Test, Zoo Map Test 2, Six Parts Test (all p < .001), Key Search Test (p < .05), and Water Test (p < .05). The Zoo Map Test 1 was nearly significant (p = .06). The test authors also reported that children with learning and/or behavioral difficulties were found to be significantly different from control subjects on all but the

Zoo Map Test 2. A group of children with congenital adrenal hyperplasia (CAH; $n = 10$), diabetic hypoglycemia ($n = 13$), and traumatic brain injury ($n = 23$), also were found to be lower than the control subjects on the Zoo Map Test 1, Zoo Map Test 2, and the Total score. Additionally, DEX-C Ratings for children with learning and/or behavioral problems were significantly higher in terms of number and severity of executive problems compared to the controls. However, children with hypoglycemia and CAH were rated similar to the controls.

The relationship of performance on the BADS-C and ratings of executive problems were reported to demonstrate that this test is ecologically valid. The ratings of executive functioning were the DEX-C and the Strengths and Difficulties Questionnaire (SDQ; Goodman, 1999). The correlation matrix (p. 35) showed significant negative correlations between the BADS-C total and DEX-C total scores and all total scores on the SDQ, namely, the Emotional Symptoms, Conduct Problems, Hyperactivity, and Peer Problems. However, the magnitudes of relationships were found to be quite low (e.g., -.18 to -.26).

Correlations of BADS-C with other cognitive tasks also were presented. The Word fluency (as measured by COWAT) demonstrated a significant relationship with the Playing Cards Test ($r = -.35$). Memory category (measured by RBMT & RBMT-C) demonstrated a significant relationship with Zoo Map Test 2 ($r = -.41$) and the BADS-C Total score ($r = -.38$). On the attention domain, assessed by the Test of Everyday Attention for Children (TEA-ch), Inhibition demonstrated a significant relationship with the BADS-C total score ($r = .34$), the Water Test ($r = .22$), and the Zoo Map Test 1 ($r = .26$). Visual Selective Attention demonstrated a significant relationship with Zoo Map Test 2 ($r = .24$). Sustained and Divided Attention measures were not found to be related to any of the BADS-C tests.

These results provide some evidence in support of convergent and discriminant validity, as well as concurrent validity. However, further studies are needed to establish the construct validity of this instrument. More importantly, it would be useful to identify the sensitivity and specificity of the test in identifying children who are diagnosed with impaired executive functioning based on empirical evidence (e.g., clinical diagnosis, and/or

determined by other established tests such as Delis Kaplan Executive Function System).

COMMENTARY. The BADS-C has been a welcome addition to the handful of tests available to assess executive functioning, particularly in children. The combination of a battery of six cognitive tasks and a parent/teacher rating scale provides a comprehensive assessment of deficits in executive functioning. The tasks are quite engaging for children. This test is also unique in the sense that it helps the examiner to assess the child's ability to prioritize, allocate time judiciously, and demonstrate flexibility in his or her response. These skills are expected from an individual in everyday activities. Thus, this test is likely one of the very few ecologically valid tests available today.

On the down side, additional studies are needed to establish reliability and validity of this test battery. Due to the small range of scores on the subtests, and small sample size in each age group, a lot of the subtests were found to have reached ceiling very quickly. For example, on the Key Search Test, a score of 13 for a 15-year-old is equivalent to an age-scaled score of 9. But a score of 14 has an age-scaled score of 16 (see p. 33). The maximum possible score for this task is 14.

SUMMARY. The BADS-C is a novel test of executive functioning with many features that are attractive for clinicians. The authors have tried to incorporate the main themes of executive functioning from a problem-solving point of view that reflect everyday behavior rather than performance on specific tasks. However, the basis of the selection of the subtests and items is not explained adequately. The small number of items in the subtests and small sample size are one of the major problems of this test for converting raw scores to scaled scores. The reliability and validity information of this battery is quite limited at this time as well. Clinicians and researchers looking for a psychometrically more robust test may want to consider the Delis–Kaplan Executive Function System (Delis, Kaplan, & Kramer, 2001; 15:74). Nevertheless, the BADS-C is expected to be used by clinicians and researchers, particularly in rehabilitation settings, where assessment and monitoring of real life decision-making skills are very important.

REVIEWER'S REFERENCES

Baddeley, A. D. (1986). *Working memory*. Oxford: Clarendon Press.
Delis, D. C., Kaplan, E., & Kramer, J. H. (2001). Delis-Kaplan Executive Function System. San Antonio, TX: Harcourt Assessment.

Goodman, R. (1999). The extended version of the Strengths and Difficulties Questionnaire as a guide to child psychiatric caseness and consequent burden. *Journal of Child Psychology and Psychiatry*, 40, 791-799.

Wilson, B. A., Alderman, N., Burgess, P., Emslie, H., & Evans, J. (1996). *Behavioural Assessment of the Dysexecutive Syndrome*. Suffolk, England: Thames Valley Test Company.

[25]
Behavioural Inattention Test.

Purpose: Developed to measure unilateral visual neglect.

Population: Ages 19–83.

Publication Date: 1987.

Acronym: BIT.

Scores, 17: Conventional Subtest Scores (Line Crossing, Letter Cancellation, Star Cancellation, Figure and Shape Copying, Line Bisection, Representational Drawing, Total), Behavioural Subtests (Picture Scanning, Telephone Dialling, Menu Reading, Article Reading, Telling and Setting the Time, Coin Sorting, Address and Sentence Copying, Map Navigation, Card Sorting, Total).

Administration: Individual.

Price Data, 2006: £229.50 per complete kit including manual, various stimuli, test, playing cards, and clock face; £60.50 per 50 scoring sheets.

Time: (40) minutes.

Authors: Barbara Wilson, Janet Cockburn, and Peter Halligan.

Publisher: Harcourt Assessment [England].

Review of the Behavioural Inattention Test by WILLIAM R. HORSTMAN, Forensic Neuropsychologist, Private Practice, San Francisco, CA:

DESCRIPTION. Slightly larger in both length and width than the Wechsler Adult Intelligence Scale-Third Edition (WAIS-III) brief-case, the Behavioural Inattention Test (BIT) is packaged in a flimsy 2-inch deep plastic black file folder with Velcro closing. There is no handle; the black file folder broke after 1 week. Clearly intended for a British population, the folder has a bold red strip with white printing announcing "Behavioural inattention test."

The "test" is in actuality a composition of some proprietary and nonproprietary conventional and behavioral subtests. The six conventional subtests have been used for decades either alone or in combination to screen for unilateral visual neglect. Instructions state that all stimuli must be placed directly in front of the subject's mid-line plane. Familiar to most neuropsychologists, they include Line Crossing, Letter Cancellation, Star Cancellation, Figure and Shape Copying, Line Bisection, and Representational Drawing, which

yield both an individual test score and total score. In addition, there are nine behavioral subtests: Picture Scanning, Telephone Dialling, Menu Reading, Article Reading, Telling and Setting the Time (clock face), Coin Sorting, Address and Sentence Copying, Map Navigation, and Card Sorting (deck of standard playing cards).

DEVELOPMENT. As promoted by the publisher, the BIT is described as "an objective behavioral test of everyday skills relevant to visual neglect, aimed at increasing the understanding of specific difficulties patients experience" (BIT product information, www.harcourtassessment.com). There are two parallel versions, each comprising six "conventional" subtests and nine behavioral subtests. Short and easy to understand and interpret, the BIT is applicable to a wide range of environmental settings. "The BIT has been validated against conventional tests of neglect and therapists' reports." "The BIT has excellent interrater, test-retest, and alternate form reliability" (Overview-Product-Behavioral Inattention Test, www.harcourtassessment.com). Actually, the parallel Versions A and B are only for the nine behavioral subtests.

If only the above statements were factually correct, given that the manual and 15 subtests were developed and subsequently normed against one sample, involving only one study. Participants were recruited from the Rivermead Rehabilitation Centre in Oxford, England, over an 18-month period (average length of recruitment status post-cerebral vascular accident [CVA] equaled 2 months; no *SD* given). On page 6 of the manual, of the 125 patients, all had "a presumed unilateral cerebral lesion." Thirty patients were excluded "because of bilateral motor weakness, apraxia, severe visual impairment, general cognitive deterioration, or severe language comprehension deficits. Those with milder language difficulties were, however, included in the study" (p. 6). Another 15 patients were excluded as they evidenced other aetiologies rather than cerebrovascular (no explanation given). Finally, from the resulting patient group, the authors present the following nonsequitorial reason as to baseline assessment of visual neglect: "Information from the complete neurological examination of each patient on admission was taken into account when assessing them neuropsychologically" (p. 6). There was no statistical or systematic explanation as to what was "taken into account."

The remaining sample was subsequently skewed by incomplete data. More specifically, left CVAs dropped 19% from 26 to 21 patients; right CVAs dropped 4% from 54 to 52. Therefore, the total N for stroke patients was 73. The control sample of 50 volunteers was equally bewildering in selection. They were recruited from numerous sources which, according to the manual, included hospital employees, volunteers from community-based groups, and members of the Oxford University subject panel. Apparently, none were subjected to neurological screening. No mention is made that any brain imaging or neurophysiological testing was ever employed to substantiate stroke lateralization in participants or to rule out loss of organic integrity in the controls.

TECHNICAL. It is only a single study upon which reliability, validity, norms and cutoff scores of the BIT are based, and the sample for analysis was relatively small (80). Contrary to the manual's assertion, the control group was in no way matched to the patient group. For example, the controls were significantly more likely to be female ($p <$ .0001 by Fisher's exact test) and had significantly higher IQ scores ($p =$ .0003 by t-test).

Reliability. Interrater reliability is .99 based on 13 participants. The authors give a p-value of .001, which just says the reliability is not zero.

Parallel form reliability was established by having 10 people take both Version A and Version B. The correlation was .91. Again, a confidence interval would be appropriate. Nothing is said about the time interval between the two tests.

Test-retest reliability was based on 10 participants completing the test 15 days apart. Again, $r =$ .99. There is no mention of how these participants were selected.

Presumably, all these reliabilities were done on patients. The distribution of scores for the controls is so tight that their reliabilities would likely be poor.

Nothing is said about internal consistency. Because the authors added up the scores for the conventional subtests, they should provide alpha coefficients to show that these subtests are all working in the same general direction. Finally, there is no evidence of *SEM*, a fundamental requisite for any neuropsychological test.

Validity. In order to establish validity of the BIT as a measure of visual neglect, the test developers correlated the raw score sum of the behav-

ioral subtests with the raw score sum of the conventional tests, which produced $r =$ .92 ($p <$ .001). The authors do not seem to appreciate that validity is the degree to which the BIT can be used to establish visual neglect. Validity in and of itself is not an inherent property of a test, but rather the syndrome the test is designed to identify, in this case unilateral visual neglect. Hence, the BIT is composed by scores on the conventional and behavioral subtests. Thus, simple correlation between the two does not establish any sort of validity.

The next validity correlation was between the behavioral scores and a therapist assessment, which yielded $r =$ .67. If there were multiple patients per therapist, then this correlation would not be valid because the data pairs would not be independent. Again, confidence intervals are necessary to establish a lower boundary for the correlation.

In the result section, the authors present the actual maximum score, mean score, standard deviation, and range of scores on each of the conventional and behavioral subtests for only the control group. Why do we not see the corresponding statistics for the patient group? That is, how would construct validity be assessed?

Finally, this reviewer found a relevant research paper by Teea Brunila, Maarit J. Jalas, Arja B. Lindell, Olli Tenovuo, and Heikki Hämäläinen, titled *The Two Part Picture in Detection of Visuospatial Neglect* (2003). Psychometrics are excellent, as is the theoretical foundation and review of the literature. The resulting two-part picture test is clearly superior in both sensitivity and specificity to the BIT.

Scoring. The manual states, "A subject was considered to have visual neglect if his/her aggregate score on the six conventional subtests fell below that of any control subject" (p. 9). This is not correct. The aggregate cutoff of 129 was construed by summing the lower range minus 1 for each of the subtests. It is unlikely one control participant had all the lower range values. The lowest total for the controls could be considerably above 129.

Neglect. If the finding of neglect is strongly associated with right hemispheric strokes (two-thirds of patients with right hemispheric strokes have some degree of unilateral spatial neglect, hence the base rate of neglect approach 66%), then the BIT conclusion of neglect (cutoff score for total of conventional subtests = 129) should show good discrimination between the two subgroups of patients (laterality of lesion).

To measure the discrimination of the conclusion of neglect with respect to laterality of lesion one can compute the sensitivity and specificity of this test. The sensitivity is the proportion of right hemispheric lesions categorized as neglect, and the specificity is the proportion of left hemispheric lesions categorized as nonneglect. According to Table 4, page 9 of the BIT manual, the sensitivity is then 26/54 = .48 and the specificity is 22/26 = .85. The sensitivity of .48 is not very impressive, particularly given the high base rate of neglect in a right hemisphere CVA. The specificity is adequate; however, the question remains how useful is a test that produces such a high rate of false negatives (28/54) = .52.

The above results are based on the conventional subtests only. Later in the manual (page 9), the authors suggest a patient scoring above 129 but falling at or below the cutoff scores for an individual subtest should then be assessed with the behavioral subtests. They provide cutoff scores for those subtests (total = 67), so presumably the overall rule is:

If conventional score ≤ 129, declare neglect.

If conventional score > 129, but one or more subtests ≤ their individual cutoff score, then administer the behavioral subtests. If the total subtest scores ≤ 67, declare neglect, if ≥ 68 declare nonneglect.

If conventional scores > 129 and no subtests are ≤ their specific cutoff score, declare nonneglect.

These formulas required several hours to determine. Indeed, if these are the rules the authors mean to suggest, why not use them in the analysis of the current sample or apply them to another acute CVA group for cross validation?

SUMMARY. In conclusion, the BIT and its corresponding manual have not been updated since the original publication in 1987. The norms and corresponding test stimuli reflect their British development and, as such, render the behavioral subtests difficult to comprehend for the average American stroke patient.

Given the above factors, specifically the nonupdated BIT and corresponding 20-year-old manual, *caveat emptor*, as the following Ethical Principles are relevant to this review:

9.05 Test Construction. Psychologists, who develop tests and other assessment techniques, use appropriate psychometric procedures, and current scientific or professional knowledge for test design, standardization, validation, reduction or elimination of bias, and recommendations for use.

9.08 Obsolete Tests and Outdated Test Results.

(a) Psychologists do not base their assessment or intervention decisions or recommendations on data or test results that are outdated for the current purpose. (American Psychological Association, 2002, p. 1072)

The errors in test construction, reliability, and validity are so numerous that they are beyond the scope of this review. It is suggested that prospective users refer to the *Standards for Educational and Psychological Testing* (AERA, APA, & NCME, 1999) for further consideration.

On a positive note, either the conventional or behavioral subtests of the BIT have been used in well over 100 studies since 1987 (Medline, September 2006). In addition, they are commented upon at length by Lezak, Howieson, Loring, Hannay, and Fischer (2004) and by Strauss, Sherman, and Spreen (2006). In light of these findings, some of the subtests and, in a few instances, the entire BIT, proved empirically useful in the assessment of visual neglect.

REVIEWER'S REFERENCES

American Educational Research Association, American Psychological Association, & National Council on Measurement in Education. (1999). *Standards for educational and psychological testing.* Washington, DC: American Educational Research Association.

American Psychological Association. (2002). *Ethical principles of psychologists and code of conduct. American Psychologist, 57,* 1060–1073.

Brunila, T., Jalas, M. J., Lindell, A. B., Tenovuo, O., & Hämäläinen, H. (2003). The two part picture in detection of visuospatial neglect. *The Clinical Neuropsychologist, 17*(1), 45-53.

Lezak, M. D., Howieson, D. B., Loring, D. W., Hannay, H. J., & Fischer, J. S. (2004). *Neuropsychological assessment* (4th ed.). New York: Oxford University Press.

Strauss, E., Sherman, E. M. S., & Spreen, O. (2006). *A compendium of neuropsychological tests: administration, norms, and commentary* (3rd ed.). New York: Oxford University Press.

Review of the Behavioural Inattention Test by ROBERT M. THORNDIKE, *Professor of Psychology, Western Washington University, Bellingham, WA:*

DESCRIPTION. The Behavioural Inattention Test (BIT) is a 15-subtest instrument developed in the United Kingdom "for measuring unilateral visual neglect (UVN). UVN refers to the heterogeneous and often transitory phenomenon commonly associated with right hemisphere strokes" (manual, p. 4). UVN is not further defined in the manual for the test except to note that patients suffering from the condition are unaware of material in the contralateral visual field.

The 15 subtests are divided into a set of six "conventional" tests requiring various forms of psychomotor behavior (Line Crossing, Letter Cancellation, Star Cancellation, Figure and Shape Copying, Line Bisection, and Representational Drawing) and nine "behavioural" subtests (Picture Scanning, Telephone Dialling [*sic*], Menu Reading, Article Reading, Telling Time, Coin Sorting, Address and Sentence Copying, Map Navigation, and Card Sorting), which seem to differ from the conventional subtests only in relying more on objects found in the examinee's normal environment. No particular rationale is offered for the division into these two sets. Scores are calculated for each of the 15 subtests and for the conventional and behavioural areas, but no total score is obtained. In light of the lack of any practical or theoretical justification for the division of the subtests into two areas, the absence of a total score seems questionable.

DEVELOPMENT. The description, and perhaps the facts, of the development of the BIT are completely inadequate. All we are told is that "Tasks in the *Behavioural inattention test* [*sic*] were selected by psychologists and occupational therapists who were familiar with the everyday problems encountered by patients with UVN. The practical selection of these items was determined by their testability and relevance to daily life" (manual, p. 4). There is no indication in the manual that anything other than clinical judgment guided the selection of items for the final form of the test, or that the items were given any sort of tryout prior to final standardization. Given the psychomotor nature of many of the items, it is doubtful that tryouts would have revealed anything useful about individual items, but there is also no evidence presented that particular subtest scores differentiate between individuals with UVN and those without it.

The manual makes no mention of speed of performance or time limits, so we must assume examinees work at their own pace for as long as they wish. Testing time is estimated to be 40 minutes, but it could easily be much more or much less depending on the personality characteristics of the examinee, and this could affect scores. For example, an impulsive examinee could easily fall into the UVN category due to impatience rather than presence of the condition.

In general, the test materials are reasonably well constructed and durable. Users are advised that they have permission to duplicate certain test materials that would be consumed in the process of testing. However, certain materials needed for testing are not provided. For example, behavioral Subtest 2, Telephone Dialling, requires a disconnected telephone and Subtest 6, Coin Sorting, requires 18 coins (in English currency) that are not provided. Occasionally the printing of materials is a little sloppy.

TECHNICAL. This instrument is intended to lead to a binary decision: UVN present or not. For this reason, norms in the ordinary sense are not needed, but a sound justification for the recommended cutting score is essential. The cutting scores were developed by comparing 80 patients who had been diagnosed as experiencing a stroke with 50 nonstroke control participants of similar age and cognitive ability. Of the 80 patients, 54 had experienced a right-side event and 26 had experienced a left-side event. A potential confound in these data is that 65% of the patients were men, whereas only 28% of the controls were men. The authors do not address this issue.

As one would expect for untimed psychomotor tasks, control participants achieved almost perfect scores on all subtests, the most notable exceptions being Letter Cancellation and Picture Scanning. Cutting scores for the "conventional" subtests were set at 1 point below the lowest score earned by any control participant. The cutting score for the sum of conventional subtest scores was set 1 point below the lowest total score earned by any control participant, which was 129 out of a possible 146. (Similar cut scores are provided for the "behavioural" tests, but these tests are not used in making the original diagnosis.) Using the cutting score of 129, 30 of the 80 patients were diagnosed with UVN. Of these 30, 26 had experienced a right-side stroke, leaving 28 right-side stroke victims either unaffected by UVN or missed by the testing and 4 left-side stroke victims either misdiagnosed or presenting a rare occurrence of the syndrome. Because the authors do not discuss the prevalence of the syndrome among right-side stroke victims, we have no way to assess whether the 48% rate is reasonable or not. We are also not told how many patients missed the cutting score by 1 or 2 points.

Evidence of reliability is offered for interrater agreement based on 13 participants whose performance was simultaneously scored by two raters. The authors report a correlation of .99, but we have no idea what the range of scores was, which makes this coefficient largely uninterpretable. To establish temporal stability of scores, 10 participants were retested over a 15-day average interval. Again, the correlation was .99, and again we have no report on the range of scores.

Alternative sets of stimuli (Form B) are provided for several of the subtests. Ten participants were given both forms. Scores on the two forms correlated .91, but again, without information on the range of scores, this coefficient is uninformative. In summary, the evidence offered by the authors concerning the reliability of scores on the BIT is woefully inadequate by contemporary standards.

Two types of validity evidence are offered for the BIT. First, the correlation between scores on the "conventional" tests and the "behavioural" tests for all 80 patients was found to be .92. This indicates that the two types of materials are measuring the same thing, whatever it is, but this is more an issue of reliability than of validity. Second, BIT scores were correlated with "responses to a short questionnaire completed by the relevant therapist at the time of the assessment" (manual, p. 8). The correlation was .67. Inasmuch as we do not know what these "responses" were, this coefficient is uninformative. In summary, no useful evidence concerning the validity of the BIT for its stated purpose is provided in the manual other than the claim of professional judgment.

COMMENTARY. The manual for the Behavioural Inattention Test is 19 pages long, with many pages given over to white space or very brief and inadequate directions for test administration. The best and most adequate aspect of the supporting materials for this instrument is the layout of the response profile, which is well-organized and easy to use. As stated earlier, the test materials seem well-made, but some of the items are dated (a reading passage about contemporary events in the U.S.S.R.) or inappropriate for an environment other than Great Britain (British coins). In the Picture Scanning subtest one picture is of a plate of food. The examinee is to identify the items. I could not tell what the items to be identified as cheese and potatoes were. In other pictures it was hard to determine what the "major items" (manual, p. 13) were. The Telephone Dialling task involved 5-, 6-, and 7-digit numbers. Presenting the first two as telephone numbers might be confusing to an American examinee. Overall, the instructions for administration and scoring lacked necessary detail.

SUMMARY. Given the support materials presented, I have no idea, other than from the appearance of the test tasks, whether this test yields scores that are appropriate for their stated purpose. An experienced clinician might examine the test tasks and decide, based on personal clinical experience, that the test would yield useful information, but nothing produced by the authors or publisher supports the use of this instrument. Although most of the tasks are culture-neutral, some are clearly inappropriate for other than British examinees. The test materials, including the manual, appear not to have been evaluated or updated in 20 years. Based on the material available to me, I cannot recommend that anyone use this test. I am surprised and disappointed that The Psychological Corporation/Harcourt Assessment would put their name on this instrument.

[26]

Benchmark of Organizational Emotional Intelligence.

Purpose: "Designed to measure the level of emotional intelligence in an organization as a whole and across departments, teams, or divisions."

Population: Ages 18 and over.

Publication Date: 2005.

Acronym: BOEI.

Scores, 24: 7 scale scores (Job Happiness, Compensation, Work/Life Stress Management, Organizational Cohesiveness, Supervisory Leadership, Diversity and Anger Management, Organizational Responsiveness), 14 subscale scores (Pay, Benefits, Stability, Stress Management, Work/Life Balance, Coworker Relationships, Teamwork, Diversity Climate, Gender/Racial Acceptance, Anger Management, Training and Innovation, Optimism and Integrity, Courage and Adaptability, Top Management Leadership), 2 validity scale scores (Positive Impression, Negative Impression), Total Score.

Administration: Group or individual.

Price Data, 2007: $330 per Online Organizational Report kit including technical manual (176 pages) and

1 Organizational Report; $300 per Online Organizational Report; $50 per technical manual; $50 per Online Group Report comparing up to 5 groups; $13 per Online Individual Report; $35 per 10 item booklets; $20 per 25 faxable response sheets.

Time: (30) minutes.

Comments: Test can be administered over the internet.

Authors: Steven J. Stein and Multi-Health Systems Staff.

Publisher: Multi-Health Systems, Inc.

Review of the Benchmark of Organizational Emotional Intelligence by MALINDA HENDRICKS GREEN, Professor, College of Education, University of Central Oklahoma, Edmond, OK:

DESCRIPTION. The Benchmark of Organizational Emotional Intelligence (BOEI) is a 143-item instrument, administered either paper-and-pencil or online, "designed to measure the level of emotional intelligence (EI) in an organization as a whole and across departments, teams, or divisions" (technical manual, p. 1). All 143 items are Likert scales with five options and a "Not Applicable" (NA) option allowing that item to be skipped if it did not apply to the respondent. The BOEI allows the inclusion of up to 10 anchored custom items and/or 2 open-ended custom items to both administration options of the BOEI. Responses are combined for a total of 24 scores including: a Total BOEI score, 7 scale scores, 14 subscale scores, and 2 validity scale scores. The 7 scale scores are: Job Happiness, Compensation, Work/Life Stress Management, Organizational Cohesiveness, Supervisory Leadership, Diversity and Anger Management, and Organizational Responsiveness. The 14 subscale scores are: Pay, Benefits, Stability, Stress Management, Work/Life Balance, Coworker Relationships, Team Work, Diversity Climate, Gender/Racial Acceptance, Anger Management, Training and Innovation, Optimism and Integrity, Courage and Adaptability, and Top Management Leadership.

The BOEI can be administered by individuals without formal training in psychometrics or organizational development. According to the test authors, a "thorough reading and understanding of the procedures" (p. 4) in the technical manual would be sufficient. However, interpretation of results is reserved for individuals qualified such as human resource professionals, organizational development specialists, organizational psychologists, or other professionals who are trained in the principles of testing and psychometrics. The BOEI's intended use is with working adults over the age of 18 years. The reading level reported in the manual is at the North American ninth-grade level based upon the Dale-Chall formula. Regardless of the administration method (paper-and-pencil or online) most individuals need between 30 to 45 minutes to complete the instrument. The online version tends to require a bit less time. No time limits are imposed, but the instrument should be completed "during one sitting, without interruption, and at a steady pace" (technical manual, p. 9).

The BOEI provides results that can be customized. Possible reports include one for the entire organization, one for each individual, and "custom groups," which would be determined before the administration of the BOEI. Suggested custom groups include by location, work unit, type of employment, or job classification. The scoring of the surveys includes the number of employees surveyed and the number of invalid protocols. An invalid protocol is defined in the manual as those "with *more than* the allowable number of missing items" (technical manual, p. 25). For example, on the Total BOEI with 143 items, the individual must respond to at least 127 or the survey is deemed invalid and the results are excluded from the reports. Each scale and subscale has a minimum number of valid responses required for the scale score to be calculated. The response option of "Not Applicable" is treated as a missing response. The obtained (raw) scores of the individuals are converted to standard scores with a mean of 100 and standard deviation of 15. This transformation facilitates comparisons among the individuals, the groups, and the organization, and to normative standards.

DEVELOPMENT. The BOEI was developed to assess several factors based upon the belief that emotional and motivation aspects of employees at work are related to their job performance. The BOEI is predicated upon the notion that the individual's emotional intelligence is an important part of that person's ability to contribute in a meaningful manner to an organization's success. The manual provides a historical review of literature of the progression of organizational surveys in general and emotional intelligence in particular with the idea of an individual's organizational emotional intelligence. Beginning by conceptualizing a general theory of what constitutes organizational emotional intelligence, items were generated to measure possible factors that could rationally be drawn from the principal concept. Literature is reviewed in the manual highlighting each of the 7 scales and 14 subscales present in the current version of the BOEI.

The manual provides extensive information on the development, statistical analysis, theoretical basis, and relationships among these elements. Normative data are reported as being collected in 2002 and the copyright for the BOEI is 2005. The manual provides an in-depth discussion as to organizational emotional intelligence and how the BOEI attempts to assess it. The theoretical anchors of the instrument and its scales along with the subscales are presented in logical and historical context.

TECHNICAL. The BOEI reports data collection for two different versions; the first contained 160 items and the second 203 items. Items were removed and added between the two along with modifications of the wording mainly in terms of third person pronouns, positive to negative or vice versa, and change of the meaning of the statement. The present version arranges the scale items dispersed throughout the questionnaire. Items with mean scores for the 155 items in common to both versions were compared using independent samples t-tests. The second set of data included 811 individuals and was examined for validity scales of missing responses, which resulted in analysis based upon 759 individuals. Criteria were established for the analysis, which removed 18 items. A factor analysis was run on the 185 items. A principal components analysis was used with a varimax rotation examining all possible solutions. An eight-factor solution resulted in the removal of 9 items that failed to load on any factor. The factor analysis was run again on the remaining 160 items. A chi-square difference test compared the new seven-factor model to the previous eight-factor model yielding an improvement ($X^2 = 126.279$, $df = 14$, $p < .01$). Each factor was further analyzed for the subscale structure, which removed several more items. A confirmatory factor analysis was run for each factor, scale, and subscale. The fit was best with multiple scales. Normative data were collected in 2002 on 811 individuals at 17 sites (data from 759 of these individuals were used because 52 had too many

missing responses and were removed from the data set); 7 sites used the paper-pencil version ($n = 248$) and 10 sites used the web version ($n = 511$).

Reliability is reported as test-retest stability through t-test comparisons on each scale and subscale with no significant difference found on any. Internal consistency reliability coefficients were calculated for scales and subscales. Cronbach alpha values ranged from .69 to .96. Standard errors of measurement for individual scales are provided along with means and standard deviations in the manual.

Validity was first checked by administering the BOEI with another existing tool used for organizational assessment, the Campbell Organizational Survey. For comparison, the scores on each instrument were ranked on a 7-point scale. A table is provided with the rankings on the seven comparable scales. To test its ability to assess social and emotional functioning with an organization, the BOEI was co-adinistered with established social and emotional competency instruments in two separate organizations: the Emotional Quotient Inventory (EQ-i) short version and the EQ-i (long version) and the Mayer-Salovey-Caruso Emotional Intelligence Test. Correlational results ranged from $r = .27$ to $r = .69$, indicating some construct validity.

COMMENTARY. The BOEI appears to be a remarkably well-developed instrument. The theoretical constructs are presented and supported with a thorough review of literature. The item development was thoughtful and well documented. The technical analysis to establish the underlying factors is perhaps the most significant quality of this instrument. The manual is detailed in describing the factor-analytic processes, reliability analyses, and evidence of theoretical as well as empirical validity.

The authors of the BOEI are to be commended for the comprehensive theoretical discussion of the constructs of emotional intelligence and organizational emotional intelligence. The logic provided as to the factors that comprise the 7 scales, 14 subscales, and 2 validity scales is not only clear and solid, but also as extensive as this reviewer has seen. Further, acknowledgement is deserved for the detailed manual, which included the above-described information as well as chapters on BOEI reports available, interpretation of the results of any assessments, and several appendices on pre-administration information, sample instruction, scale compositions, sample reports, a scoring organizer; and a flowchart of setup, administration, and scoring processes.

This reviewer finds little if anything missing from the BOEI and would recommend a review of the instrument and supplements for anyone developing quality assessment tools. Special compliments are extended for the avoidance of extremely technical language as much as possible and clear explanations when it is required. The samples of reports and interpretations should prove particularly helpful to lay-persons wanting to utilize the BOEI.

SUMMARY. The developers of the BOEI have accomplished what they intended: an instrument that assesses organizational emotional intelligence from multiple perspectives, provides a comprehensive view of an organization's level of functioning, and provides useful feedback from numerous participants. The manual describes all aspects of the development, theory, refinement, normative data, and applications of results for the BOEI remarkably well. Any organization interested in measuring aspects of organizational emotional intelligence of its employees in such key performance factors as job happiness, compensation, work/life stress management, organization cohesiveness, supervisor leadership, diversity/anger management, or organizational responsiveness would do well to give the BOEI careful consideration. The added features of on-line administration, customized items, and reports make this an attractive option. The developers include an encouragement to provide feedback on the BOEI including suggestions and research findings.

Review of the Benchmark of Organizational Emotional Intelligence by MICHAEL J. ZICKAR, Associate Professor of Psychology, Bowling Green State University, Bowling Green, OH:

DESCRIPTION. The Benchmark of Organizational Emotional Intelligence (BOEI) is a 143-item test that measures components thought to be related to organizational emotional intelligence (OEI). The test manual describes OEI as "an organization's ability to successfully and efficiently cope with change and accomplish its goals while being responsible and sensitive to its employees, customers, suppliers, networks, and society" (p. 2). There are seven scales (Job Happiness,

Compensation, Work/Life Stress Management, Organizational Cohesiveness, Supervisory Leadership, Diversity and Anger Management, and Organizational Responsiveness), along with 14 subscales, and two validity scales (Positive Impression and Negative Impression). The items use a 5-point Likert format.

The BOEI was designed to assess different areas of organizational effectiveness; the test developers claim that the inventory can be used by leaders to assess aspects and units of the organization that need attention. They also claim that the test can be used to help team-building activities and to monitor organizational change by administering the instrument longitudinally. The test is designed to be completed by working adults who are over the age of 18. The test requires a ninth-grade reading level.

The test manual recommends that the test be administered and supervised by a person who has received training in tests and measurement. The test can be administered electronically over the Internet or using a paper-and-pencil-based test booklet, which is then scored by the test developer. The test manual states that most respondents complete the BOEI in 30 to 45 minutes. The test manual includes a detailed protocol for administering the test, obtaining respondent buy-in, and presenting feedback. Score reports can be generated for the individual, group, and organization level.

DEVELOPMENT. The development of the test was based on the definition of organizational emotional intelligence presented earlier. The dimensions of the BOEI were chosen based on their impact on employee motivation and organizational performance. The BOEI was developed iteratively with an initial version that consisted of 160 items and then a second version was developed that eliminated 5 items and added 48 additional items, along with changing format and wording of remaining items. Item analysis was conducted on a sample of 759 respondents to the second version of the BOEI. Items were retained that had reasonable variability, low missing data, item-total correlations greater than .30, high factor loadings (greater than .35), and little redundancy with other items. Based on those initial criteria, 18 items were chosen for deletion. After that, a series of principal components analyses were conducted that resulted in elimination of additional items along with identification of seven substantive factors (the two validity scales, Positive and Negative Impression, were not included in these factor analyses). Finally, confirmatory factor analyses were run for each of the seven dimensions, showing that the unidimensional structure of each dimension was adequate. It should be noted that these confirmatory analyses were not run together, preventing the analysis of items that had errors correlated with items from other factors.

TECHNICAL. The sample used for scale construction was also used for normative information. The data were collected in 2002 from 17 sites that ranged from 14 to 175 employees. Seven of the sites used the paper-and-pencil version whereas 10 used the online version. The norm sample was roughly equal in gender, with a mean age of 37.9 years. Organizations were located in Canada, the United States, Australia, Hungary, the United Kingdom, and Bahrain. The industries were diverse including consulting, construction management, software design, health services, and educational institutions. There was no description of the ethnicity breakdown of the normative sample.

Two types of reliability information are presented in the test manual. Internal consistency was analyzed using coefficient alpha for each of the subscales (there are no reports on scale composite reliability). Alpha estimates ranged from .69 to .96. Two of the subscales (Stability and Stress Management) have internal consistency below .70, four have internal consistency in the .70s, nine in the .80s, and three (Supervisory Leadership, Optimism and Integrity, and Organizational Courage and Adaptability) have internal consistencies in the .90s. It should be noted that these internal consistencies are based on the individual level of analysis. Given some of the low levels of internal consistency, caution should be used when interpreting subscale information at the individual level.

Stability information was evaluated using a single organization that had employees complete the survey at two time periods, separated by a month ($n = 19$ for the first time and $n = 22$ for the second time). It was assumed that there were no major changes in the organization and so means should be similar across the two times. Given concern for confidentiality, the stability of the organization mean was compared across the two time periods with no significant differences ob-

served for any of the scales. It should be noted that power to detect any differences would have been low given the small sample of employees. It should also be noted that the stability information is relevant only to an organizational level analysis; inferences about individual level of stability cannot be made based on the data presented in the manual.

Validity was assessed by correlating the BOEI with other instruments thought to measure similar constructs. The Campbell Organizational Survey (COS; Campbell & Hyne, 1995) was administered to a mid-sized company along with the BOEI. The seven BOEI scales were matched to relevant scales on the COS and each scale's ranking was compared. In this company, for example, Job Happiness was ranked highest on the BOEI whereas it was ranked second highest on the COS. The Spearman correlation of BOEI rankings with COS rankings was .79. This evidence provides modest evidence that there was convergence across the two instruments but given that the results are limited to a single organization, these results should be taken merely as suggestive of convergent validity.

Additional validity evidence is provided by correlating the BOEI with two other measures of individual-level emotional intelligence, the short version Emotional Quotient Inventory (EQI; Bar-On, 1997) and the Mayer-Salovey-Caruso Emotional Intelligence Test (Mayer, Salovey, & Caruso, 2002). Two organizations were used for these analyses ($n = 57$ and $n = 30$). Some expected relationships were found; for example, the BOEI Coworker Relationships scale was positively correlated with Emotional Intelligence (measured by the EQI) at the individual level. Some of the findings with the MSCEIT were counterintuitive, such as negative correlations with Emotion Management and many of the BOEI scales. As of now, the validity evidence for the MSCEIT is merely suggestive.

Gender differences and occupational-level differences were also examined. Significant differences were found across gender for five scales. Men scored significantly higher than women on stability and negative impressions whereas women scored higher than men on diversity climate, gender/racial acceptance, and top management leadership. With respect to occupational differences, the normative sample was broken into the categories of upper management, middle management, and staff. Significant differences were found on a majority of dimensions, with the general finding that upper management viewed the organization more favorably than middle management, which was generally more favorable than staff. Both the findings related to gender differences and occupational level differences suggest that these findings should be taken into consideration when evaluating different areas within an organization.

COMMENTARY. The BOEI provides an impressive range of organizational dimensions that could be useful in assessing an organization's strengths and weaknesses. The notion that this test measures emotional intelligence at the organizational level is tenuous at best. Although there are correlations between some of the scales of the BOEI with individual level measures of emotional intelligence, some correlations are in unexpected directions. Also, the definition of organizational emotional intelligence used by the test developers seems so broad as to include dimensions that would be irrelevant to emotional intelligence. This reviewer would recommend that the test developers collect additional validity data with measures of emotional intelligence to understand the relationship of the BOEI measure to the individual level construct better. In addition, correlations of the BOEI measures with traditional measures of organizational assessment, such as job satisfaction and job stress, should be examined. Finally, validity data should be collected that show that using the BOEI can help improve organizational effectiveness and team-building as advertised.

Other issues that should be addressed are whether the validity scales are useful and how they should be used when interpreting data along with issues of aggregation and levels of analysis. The instrument is touted as a measure that can be used at the individual, departmental, and organizational level. There are complex issues related to data aggregation that should be worked out. For example, does it make sense to present a department-level mean if the individuals have large amounts of variability within that unit?

SUMMARY. The BOEI provides a detailed measure of 16 dimensions that are hypothesized to be related to organizational effectiveness. The dimensions, for the most part, are similar to others that have been used by organizational psychologists for assessing organizations. Although the BOEI measures a vast array of important con-

structs important to organizations, it is unclear whether it is appropriate to call this a measure of organizational emotional intelligence.

REVIEWER'S REFERENCES
Bar-On, R. (1997). *Bar-On Emotional Quotient Inventory technical manual.* Toronto, ON: Multi-Health Systems.
Campbell, D. P., & Hyne, S. A. (1995*). Campbell Organizational Survey manual.* Minneapolis, MN: National Computer Systems.
Mayer, J. D., Salovey, P., & Caruso, D. R. (2002). *Test manual for the Mayer, Salovey, Caruso Emotional Intelligence Test.* Toronto, ON: Multi-Health Systems.

[27]
BEST Plus: Oral English Proficiency Test.

Purpose: Designed "to assess the oral language proficiency of adult" nonnative speakers of English "who need to use English to function in day-to-day life in the United States."
Population: Adults.
Publication Dates: 2003–2005.
Acronym: BEST Plus.
Scores: 3 subscales: Listening Comprehension, Language Complexity, Communication, Total.
Administration: Individual.
Levels, 3: 1 (low proficiency), 2 (middle proficiency), 3 (high proficiency); measures Student Performance Levels (SPLs) 0–10.
Versions, 2: Computer-adaptive version, print-based version.
Forms, 3: A, B, C (all for print-based version).
Price Data, 2007: $30 per 20 print-based test administrations; $15 per picture cue book; $20 per replacement test administrator guide; $30 per test administrator guide (included in price of training); $10 per replacement BEST Plus Test CD; $5 per replacement practice CD; $25 per technical report; $1.50 per administration for 20–280 computer administrations; $1.25 per 300–380 computer administrations; $1 per 400 and more computer administrations.
Time: (5–15) minutes.
Comments: An adaptation of the Basic English Skills Test (T7:256); computer administrations must be ordered in multiples of 20 or 50; BEST Plus Administrator Training, administered only by certified BEST Plus trainers, is required for all individuals wishing to administer the BEST Plus.
Authors: The Best Plus Development Team.
Publisher: Center for Applied Linguistics.

Review of the BEST Plus: Oral English Proficiency Test by S. KATHLEEN KRACH, Assistant Professor, University of Nevada Las Vegas, Las Vegas, NV:

DESCRIPTION. The publishers describe the purpose of the BEST Plus as measuring "oral language proficiency of adult English language learners" (test administration guide, p. 1). Specifically, this test measures aspects of informal, day-to-day language (e.g., oral, conversational language that is unrehearsed) instead of formalized language (e.g., analogies, reading passages, single-word identification).

The BEST Plus can be administered either using a computer or via one of three paper versions (Form A, Form B, or Form C). The computer version adapts the test administration sequence based upon a student's performance on previous items. For the paper version, locator items are administered prior to test items to determine which levels of the test to administer. Once that is determined, all items in that level are administered.

Items derive from common domains used in teaching adult English Language Learners, including Personal (e.g., housing, health), Occupational (e.g., getting a job and on the job), and Public (e.g., civics, education). Both the computerized version and the paper version require the test administrator to administer the test items, judge the items based on three criteria (Listening Comprehension, Language Complexity, and Communication), and enter the score (either into the software program or onto the paper form; scores on the paper form must be entered into the score management software to reach the final scale score).

The BEST Plus is administered individually to adult English language learners by a trained test administrator. The measure provides two types of scores: one, norm referenced and the other, criterion referenced. The criterion-referenced score is called a Student Performance Level (SPL) score, and falls along a continuum with SPL 0 being the lowest and SPL 10 being the highest.

DEVELOPMENT. The BEST Plus, an adaptation of the oral interview portion of the Basic English Skills Test (BEST), was developed in two cycles. The first cycle resulted in a prototype of the BEST Plus. Only approximately 25% of the items are common to both the prototype and the final version of the BEST Plus.

Items developed for the prototype were designed to measure topics within the three global domains (Personal, Occupational, and Public) across three levels of difficulty (low, intermediate, and high level oral language proficiency). Field-testing of the prototype was conducted using data from more than 700 students. Results from the field testing indicated that the items were valid and reliable; however, the low-level language items did not provide sufficient information to be useful.

Thus, during the second cycle, item writers reevaluated how the items were constructed to ensure that test takers at all language levels could be evaluated. Final test items were reviewed and piloted until only items the publishers felt were the best indicators of oral language proficiency across three aspects of oral language (Listening Comprehension, Language Complexity, and Communication) were included. Item field tests were then conducted across 25 programs using data from 2,400 students to calibrate the difficulty level of each item using a Rasch measurement technique. Although the technical report devotes several pages to explain how the test items were developed, only descriptions of item suitability were noted. No numerical or statistical data were presented in the technical report to justify item suitability in the revision process.

TECHNICAL. The normative sample for the BEST Plus included more than 2,000 adult English Language Learners ranging from under 20 years old to over 55 years old. The sample contains scores from students born in approximately 100 different countries and speaking more than 80 different languages. Students in the sample received English language instruction ranging from less than 1 month to more than 24 months. Only minimal data were reported on how participants were selected.

Reliability studies were performed using measures of interrater reliability, test-retest reliability, parallel-form reliability, and precision of measurement. Raters were placed into two groups, ranging from low amounts of training using the instrument (2 hours) to very experienced using the instrument. Interrater reliability scores for all three domains fell at or above .90 across both groups. Examinees were given two administrations (one with Group A administrators and one for Group B administrators). The total scores for both administrations correlated at .89. Parallel-form reliability data were generated from administration of the print forms. The mean parallel-form reliability coefficient was .91. Finally, Rasch estimates used to determine the precision of the measurement produced a value of .97, a statistic the authors state should be interpreted in a manner similar to other reliability values.

The developers address content, construct, and concurrent validity in the technical report. Content validity was addressed during the item development stage using trained item-content creators, and by having second language-acquisition specialists observe testing sessions and rate English language proficiency skills independently from the test administrators.

Construct validity was assessed by comparing scores on the BEST Plus with the placement level of the students in the English language class (using the assumption that students with better language skills should be in higher classes). The average correlation between class level and BEST Plus score was .72.

Comparing scores on the BEST Plus with other measures of English language proficiency assessed concurrent validity (BEST, TABE, and CASAS). The correlation between examinee performance on the BEST Plus and the BEST Literacy Skills test was .62, and correlations ranged from .75 to .89 when comparing the BEST Plus to the BEST oral interview. The Tests of Adult Basic Education (TABE) was also correlated with the BEST Plus, producing a correlation coefficient of .65. Correlations on the Comprehensive Adult Student Assessment System (CASAS) tests of Listening Skills (.76) and Reading Skills (.67) were similar to the other tests compared. Overall, concurrent validity values were only moderate. Given the nature of the tasks on the BEST Plus (with its emphasis on oral daily interaction skills) versus the tasks on the CASAS (which measures reading and writing skills) and the TABE (which measures reading, writing, and math skills), the moderate correlations evaluating concurrent validity should not be unexpected.

COMMENTARY. The BEST Plus appears to be a good measure of oral English-language proficiency for adults. The psychometrics are sound enough to interpret results with some degree of score accuracy.

The main strength of this test is that it uses everyday situations to evaluate oral language proficiency. Therefore, if one wishes to know how well a person can speak on a day-to-day basis, this seems to be a good instrument. However, the test's focus on everyday language is also a weakness, as there may be some concern that only Basic Intercommunication Skills (BICS) are evaluated and not Cognitive Academic Language Proficiency

(CALP). Thus, the test administrator should be wary of assuming that a high score on this measure indicates a student's capability for high levels of academic work. For more information about BICS and CALP, see Cummins (1984).

A second strength of this measure is its very short administration time. However, because it is so short, it is not designed to assess several areas of English-language literacy (e.g., reading, writing). Thus, again the administrator is limited to interpreting the results in terms only of listening and speaking skills.

The biggest problems with the test have to do with usability. It appears that, once a person is set up with the software program and has been sufficiently trained in its use, test administration runs smoothly. However, the reviewer had to call the customer help line three separate times to get the software to work. Also, it should be noted that the software program itself does not actually score the items. Test items are scored by the examiner based upon a rubric and are then entered manually into the software program by the examiner.

This scoring rubric is somewhat subjective on the surface, but with the required 6-hour training the rubric may become more objectively administered. One would think that for assessment specialists who are well-trained in administering tests, it should be possible to pick up the materials and immediately be able to administer the instrument. However, even for the most experienced assessment staff, formal training specifically for the BEST Plus is needed to accurately score and interpret these results.

SUMMARY. The BEST Plus can be a good measure of oral English language proficiency for adults. However, in order for the test to produce accurate scores, formal training on the scoring criteria for this instrument must be completed. In addition, the test should only be used to assess listening and speaking language at a basic intercommunication level, but not to assume higher levels of academic language proficiency or proficiency in reading or writing. As long as the BEST Plus is used only for its appropriate purpose by trained assessment personnel, it should be considered a useful addition to the classroom of any teacher of adult English language learners.

REVIEWER'S REFERENCE

Cummins, J. (1984). *Bilingualism and special education: Issues in assessment and pedagogy.* San Diego: College-Hill.

Review of the BEST Plus: Oral English Proficiency Test by ANNITA WARD, Associate Professor, Salem International University, Bridgeport, WV:

DESCRIPTION. The BEST Plus: Oral English Proficiency Test is an adaptation by the Center for Applied Linguistics (CAL) of the Basic English Skills Test (BEST) oral interview. Its purpose is to test the oral language proficiency of adults who are nonnative speakers of English. The test administrator guide suggests that results of assessment can be used to make placement decisions, to assess student progress, to evaluate language programs, and to provide diagnostic feedback on students' oral English proficiency. There are two versions of the BEST Plus, the computer-adaptive version on CD-ROM and the print-based version (with three parallel forms: A, B, and C). Both versions are individually administered scripted interviews covering a variety of themes that have been identified as meaningful to adult English language learners. Each test administration should begin with a warm-up session so that students will feel comfortable in the testing situation. The test administration guide offers direction to administrators on how to do a warm-up for examinees. The actual test questions are scored for three aspects: *listening,* where the response is evaluated in terms of how well the examinee understands a question; *language complexity,* where the response is evaluated for organization and elaboration; and *communication,* where the response is evaluated for communication of meaning. The Listening Comprehension section of the scoring rubric consists of a 3-point range (0–2); the Language Complexity section represents a 5-point range (0–4), and the Communication section 4 points (0–3). Computer software places raw scores within appropriate Student Performance Levels (SPLs). Students' scale scores will fall within a particular range of scores and each range corresponds to 1 of 11 SPLs. (SPLs are numbered 0–10.) The test manual has a description for each of the SPLs. SPL Level 0 is described in the test manual as "no ability whatsoever." The SPLs are partitioned into three distinct instructional levels. SPLs 0–4 fall within the beginning level, 4–7 within the intermediate level, and 7–10 within the advanced level. For a computer score report, however, three raw scores must be entered into the computer program to reach an accurate SPL.

When the computer-adaptive version of the test is given, the administrator reads to an examinee a question printed on a computer screen, scores the examinee's response using the BEST Plus Scoring Rubric, and enters the score into the computer. The computer displays the next question for the examiner to read. The computer chooses the next question based on the score that was just entered by the examiner.

Both versions of the test are administered face-to-face. The test administrator, who must have completed 6 hours of training prior to giving either version of the test, gives an individual locator test to determine which level (1, 2, or 3) to administer to the test-taker. Once the level is determined, the administrator reads all questions at that level one at a time to an examinee. The test administrator scores each response immediately after it is offered, using the BEST Plus Scoring Rubric. Both responses from the computer-adaptive test and the print-based version are scored with the same rubric.

The specialized training for test administrators includes giving and scoring practice tests. Test administrators also must have an excellent command of English as well as experience interacting with speakers of English as a second language. Those who administer the test via computer must have basic computer skills such as the ability to use a mouse, save information to the hard disk, and load a CD, as well as those skills required by the print-based version.

On average the test takes about 15 minutes to administer, but if an examinee's English is particularly limited, the test administration may take less than half that time. There are three forms of the print-based version of the test.

DEVELOPMENT. The BEST Plus is an adaptation of the oral interview section of BEST (Center for Applied Linguistics, 1984). It was developed as a response to the need for an oral language assessment that could be quickly administered and could be used for both a pretest and a posttest. A 10-member nationally representative team of professionals worked with CAL staff to complete a prototype in June 2000. The Office of Vocational and Adult Education (OVAE) funded the development of the prototype and operational versions of BEST Plus, through a contract with CAL.

The first cycle of test development began in the fall of 2000 and ran for 1 year. Three types of items were developed. Type 1 questions were designed to elicit low level responses and were usually based on a photograph; Type 2 questions were designed to draw intermediate level responses; Type 3 questions were designed to assess higher level language skills (well-developed vocabulary, complex sentence structures, etc.). In 2001 a small scale field test was performed involving seven programs and 15 administrators. This study focused on how to use the computerized administration and to apply the scoring rubric. Data from 738 student performances were available for analysis. According to the BEST Plus technical report, the items performed well, as those designed to be most challenging were most challenging to test-takers and those designed to be less challenging were indeed not as challenging as other test items. Of the 156 items used in the small scale field test, 114 were chosen for use in a small scale reliability test done in November 2001. According to the technical report, this study of the computer-adaptive version of the test gave reliable results when administered by different test administrators to the same students.

In January 2002, a second cycle of test development was initiated. The CAL staff wanted to develop test items that would be more engaging for examinees. Seven question types were developed for each thematic folder of the test ranging in difficulty from easy to advanced: Photo Description, Entry Question, Yes/No questions, Choice Questions, Personal Expansion, General Expansion, and Elaboration. A full scale field test was conducted in 2002. More than 40 administrators gave the test to 2,400 students. Every test item was administered to at least 100 students. Field testing data were used to calibrate difficulty of items in the final version of the test. The adaptive test was calibrated using the software Facets, which is an application of the many faceted Rasch measurement model.

TECHNICAL. The BEST Plus development project studied the reliability of the computer-adaptive version of the test. In November 2002, an interrater reliability study was done using two groups of scorers of computer-adaptive responses. Each group consisted of a test administrator, an experienced scorer, and a novice scorer who had about 2 hours' training. These scorers considered responses of 32 students. Interrater reliability between the two groups of scorers on each subsec-

tion (Listening Comprehension, Language Complexity, Communication) was quite high, ranging from a correlation coefficient of .96 to .99 for the first group (Group A) to correlations of .90 to .98 for the second group (Group B).

To establish test-retest reliability the same 32 students were administered the BEST Plus by two separate test administrators. The computer-adaptive test was given at all administrations. The correlation between the two final scores from the two administrators was .89.

The BEST Plus paper-scripted test has three forms: A, B, and C. In a study to establish parallel-form reliability, 48 adult ESL students were divided into three groups of 16 each and members of each group were given two different forms of the test; 16 took Form A and Form B; 16 took Form A and Form C; 16 took Form B and Form C. The correlation between the two scores of the examinees who took Form A and Form B was .93; for those who took Form A and Form C the correlation was .96; for those who took Form A and Form B the correlation was .85. The average correlation was .91. The technical manual reports that students who scored high on one form of the test also scored high on another form and those who scored low on one form scored low on another form.

Validity. Various studies were performed to establish test validity. Twenty-four English language programs reported on the placement level for 1,866 adult students. A correlational study was done between BEST Plus scores and placement levels. Correlations ranged from .35 to .87 with an average correlation across all programs of .72.

The BEST Oral Interview and BEST Plus were given to the same 304 students who were enrolled in five different language programs. A correlation of .75 was found between the scores derived from the administration of these two assessments. CASAS Listening scores were obtained for 101 students who were enrolled in four different ESL programs. These students were also administered the BEST Plus. Correlation between the two sets of scores was .76. The correlation between BEST Plus scores and Test of Adult Basic Education (TABE) scores was .62.

COMMENTARY. The BEST Plus can be administered as a paper-scripted test or as a computer-adaptive test. CAL offers no evidence that the two versions of the test will yield the same score when administered to the same examinee under the same testing conditions. Interrater reliability studies, which were reported in the technical report, focused on the administration of the computer-adaptive test. A parallel-forms reliability study reported correlations between forms of the paper-scripted test.

The same rubric is used to score the computer-adaptive test and the three forms of the paper-scripted test, but it is likely that examinees may view having questions read to them from a computer screen differently from having questions read to them from a paper script. They may respond to questions about pictures shown on a computer screen differently than they do to questions about pictures on a piece of paper. It is certainly true that a computer-adaptive test in which the computer chooses the next question is not the same test as a paper-scripted test in which the questions are read from a paper in a predetermined order.

Another shortcoming of this assessment is the manner in which it is scored. Each response is scored immediately by the test administrator who refers to the rubric and then enters the score into the computer. There are two problems for such a scoring plan. First, it is likely to be distracting to test-takers to have their scores entered as they are taking the test. As use of a second language by people who are not proficient requires the user to concentrate, such a distraction may affect examinees' scores on the test. Second, particularly when assessing advanced levels of proficiency, the scorer may need to hear a response twice in order to use the rubric most effectively. If responses are scored immediately, the scorer may not be able to apply the rubric accurately in assessing those responses. Tape-recording responses and scoring from tapes may be more time-consuming, but such a procedure is likely to yield a more accurate score and for examinees whose scores determine their exit from or progression through programs, this approach may be a fairer method of scoring an assessment.

Scripts for questions for the assessment are provided and the testing manual cautions test administrators to read the questions exactly as they are scripted, to repeat questions only once, and not to rephrase or explain questions. For Entry Item 1 the script states "I like living in my neighborhood. What about you?" "What about you?" is used as a follow-up question to a number of statements in the paper scripts. But, this is not really how a question is normally asked in English for the statements that are offered in the scripts. For the example cited, in everyday conversations the follow-up question is likely to be "do you like living in yours?" The second-language speaker when confronted with "What about you?" as an entry question may not clearly understand its meaning and perhaps may even believe the examiner is asking if the examinee wants to live in the examiner's neighborhood. As the purpose of the test is to assess an examinee's ability to understand and produce oral English, it may be questionable to make that assessment based on language that is not readily used or perhaps even always understood by primary speakers of English.

As explained in the description above, scale scores for the BEST Plus are placed in bands that correspond to Student Performance Levels (SPLs). Each SPL is briefly described in the test administrator guide in an effort to help teachers and program administrators understand the skills possessed by students whose scores fall within each SPL. However, the examinee's general language levels are as much described in terms of what the native speaker can do when interacting with the second language speaker as they are in terms of what the second language speaker can do. This approach is a useless and stereotypical way to describe an examinee's skills and may lead to a misunderstanding of what language skills the test taker actually has. Although the communicative aspect of language is crucial, it does not constitute general language ability. Yet in this test, it is nearly all that is used to describe such ability in the descriptors provided for general language ability. These descriptions are useless for teachers and program administrators as they are too vague for anyone to give real meaning to them. For example, for SPL 9 the manual offers the following as the description of general language ability: "Can participate fluently and accurately in practical, social, and work situations. A native English speaker not used to dealing with limited English speakers can communicate easily with a person at this level" (test administrator guide, p. 17). Such a generalization is meaningless and perhaps misleading for several reasons. First, what does "dealing with" mean? We need some clarification for this phrase before we can put meaning to the description. Second, the ability to communicate "easily" with people who are speaking our primary language as a second language is determined by many factors, such as accent, attitude of both parties, etc.; none of these factors are addressed in the testing manual's descriptor.

The descriptor for SPL Level 10, general language ability, is perhaps most confusing and stereotypical. It says "ability equal to that of a native speaker of the same socioeconomic level" (test administrator guide, p. 17). This descriptor suggests that linguistic proficiency must be described by determining a person's socioeconomic level. The descriptor is meaningless because although it is used to describe general linguistic proficiency at SPF 10, the highest performance level, it says nothing about the actual skills of a person at this level and apparently such skills vary from person to person if, in fact, socioeconomic level is indicative of linguistic proficiency.

SUMMARY. The BEST Plus is an easily administered assessment for making general determinations about students' oral language proficiency. However, the scoring technique of scoring responses immediately and in the presence of the examinee makes it likely that testing results will not be precise or accurate as scorers will not have time to consider the rubric carefully and examinees may be negatively affected by having scoring done in their presence.

CAL has not established the reliability between scores on the computer-adaptive version of the test and the paper-scripted version. Therefore, users of the results of testing must be careful when comparing results on the two different versions of the test.

The BEST Plus should not be used alone in making determinations about students' placement in programs or for evaluation of programs although the testing manual suggests such uses for the test. The scoring procedures for this test make it likely that results are not precise and accurate and, therefore, they should not be the sole basis for such important decisions.

[28]
The Birkman Method.

Purpose: "Developed as a self-report questionnaire eliciting responses about perception of self, perception of social context and perception of occupational opportunities."
Population: Ages 25–65.

Publication Dates: 1992–2001.
Scores, 33: Esteem Usual, Esteem Need, Acceptance Usual, Acceptance Need, Structure Usual, Structure Need, Authority Usual, Authority Need, Advantage Usual, Advantage Need, Activity Usual, Activity Need, Challenge Usual, Challenge Need, Empathy Usual, Empathy Need, Change Usual, Change Need, Freedom Usual, Freedom Need, Thought Usual, Thought Need, Persuasive Interest, Social Service Interest, Scientific Interest, Mechanical Interest, Outoor Interest, Numerical Interest, Clerical Interest, Artistic Interest, Literacy Interest, Musical Interest, Stress Behaviors.
Administration: Group.
Price Data: Available from publisher.
Time: [45] minutes.
Comments: Publisher advises that 2006 edition is available for ages 15 and up. However, these new materials were not made available for review.
Author: Roger W. Birkman.
Publisher: Birkman International, Inc.

Review of the Birkman Method by DAVID F. CIAMPI, Adjunct Professor, International Homeland Security Defense Coalition and Homeland Security Project, Region 6, MA:

DESCRIPTION. The Birkman Method is a 298-item, self-report questionnaire designed to elicit responses about perception of self, perception of social context, and perception of occupational opportunities in normally functioning male and female adults from 25 to 65 years of age. Versions of this assessment instrument are available in English, Spanish, French (Canadian), Dutch, and Mandarin languages. It is administered in paper-and-pencil form in conjunction with a three-part survey booklet or by desktop computer-based administration. Directions for administering the questionnaire to examinees are provided. Test takers who complete the questionnaire are asked to provide their name, address, the name of their employer, previous job titles, highest attained level of education, as well as optional information, such as gender, age, and ethnicity in the front inside cover of the survey booklet. The data are then entered into a confidential computerized file to facilitate computer scoring and final report preparation. The computer-generated advanced report provides narrative and graphic summaries of the test results.

All items are of the selection type and consist of 250 true or false items and 48 two-choice item sets. The 48 two-choice item sets require first choice and second choice responses. This assessment instrument has four major scales with corresponding components that "measure constructs relevant to the particular grouping of scales" (Reliability and Validity manual, 2001, p. 4). The following major scales are listed with their associated components shown in parentheses: Usual Behavior (11), Stress Behavior (11), Underlying Needs (11), and Interests (10). The first two parts of the survey instrument measure three major scale types: "Usual Behavior" that refers to a test taker's effective and interactive style with relationships and tasks; "Underlying Needs" that assess the requirements in a relationship or situation in order for the test taker to feel good; and, "Stress Behavior" that describes a test taker's ineffective style when engaging in relationships or tasks. The third and last part of the survey instrument measures "Interests" that refer to preferences for job titles. It is unclear from reviewing the Instructions for Administering The Birkman Method Questionnaire, the Birkman Reliability and Validity Manual, and the Questionnaire Survey Booklet, whether a nonclinical staff member can administer the instrument. The average time required for test administration is not specified in the manual. The online version indicates 30 minutes are needed to complete the test. The instructions to prospective test takers are clear and concise.

DEVELOPMENT. The Birkman Method is the result of research and investigation that has its beginnings in the 1940s when its developer became interested in the relationship between visual, interpersonal impact misperceptions and pilot performance while serving as a pilot instructor for the United States Air Force. Hence, the Birkman Method was constructed to measure perceptual characteristics related to individual's perceptions of self, perceptions of social context, and perceptions of occupational opportunities. According to the author, this instrument is not based on a particular theory of personality structure nor designed to be used as a statistical map of personality characteristics. The questionnaire was developed to measure individual characteristics that affect one's perceptions, behaviors, and motivations.

Documents furnished by the developer (The Birkman Method Reliability and Validity manual, The Birkman Survey Instrument, and the Birkman Advanced Report) provide substantive and extensive information regarding test development and normative data that has been compiled in the United States (N = 107,539), Canada (N = 8,707), Australia (N = 8,745), England (N = 970), Ireland (N = 252), Mexico (N = 4,916), Puerto Rico (N = 232), South America: Ecuador, Colombia, and Venezuela (N = 3,525), the Netherlands (N = 4,189), and China (N = 804). A restandardization of the scales and reevaluation of the item structure of this instrument was undertaken by the author in 2000 with the objective of increasing internal consistency of the existing constructs. According to the developer, the content structure has remained relatively unchanged with the exception of subtle and minor rewording of a few items in order to coincide with changes in language usage.

TECHNICAL. The developer addressed issues of reliability by relying on alpha coefficients, split-half reliability estimates with Spearman Brown correction for scale length, and test-retest reliability estimates of the scales. Internal consistency was computed using both coefficient alpha and split-half reliability estimates. The alpha coefficients for the revised (2000 Scaling) Usual Behavior Scale ranged from .48 for the Freedom component to .80 for the Empathy component. The split-half estimates ranged from .54 for the Freedom component to .80 for both the Esteem and Acceptance components. Alpha coefficients for the Needs Scale ranged from .60 for both the Change and Authority components to .85 for the Challenge component. The split-half estimates ranged from .57 for the Authority component to .82 for the Advantage component. Internal consistency coefficients for the Interest Scale ranged from .74 for the Scientific component to .91 for the Numerical component. The split-half estimates for the Interest Scale ranged from .79 for the Scientific component to .91 for the Numerical component.

Test-retest reliability of the Usual and Needs Scales using Pearson product-moment coefficients were also computed by the author in three different samples. In the immediate sample (Sample 1), the Pearson coefficients for the Usual Scale ranged from .69 for the Activity component to .87 for the Advantage component. The Pearson coefficients for the Needs Scale ranged from .76 for both the Freedom and Authority components to .94 for the Acceptance component. In the 2-weeks sample (Sample 2), the Pearson coefficients for the Usual Scale ranged from .52 for the Activity component to .84 for both the Esteem and the Empathy components. The Pearson coefficients for the Needs Scale ranged from .48 for the Activity component to .85 for the Acceptance component. The Interest scales had test-retest Pearson coefficients ranging from .58 for the Numerical component to .84 for the Clerical component. In the 15-months sample (Sample 3), Pearson coefficients for the Usual Scale ranged from .21 for the Acceptance component to .62 for the Change component. The Pearson coefficients for the Needs Scale ranged from .40 for the Acceptance component to .69 for the Advantage component. The Interest Scale had Pearson coefficients that ranged from .65 for the Persuasive scale to .81 for the Artistic, Musical, and Scientific components. The author noted that, "the 15-month study utilized college freshmen and found lower levels of reliability for the behavioral constructs but reasonably high reliability for the Interest scales" (Reliability and Validity manual, 2001, p. 8). It was observed that lower reliability estimates for college-aged students were consistent with the findings of other instruments. Longer term test-retest studies are currently being conducted, according to the author.

Numerous data are presented to support the validity of the Birkman Method. For example, validity was assessed in a study of 91,672 individuals who completed the survey instrument between 1993 and 1999. The Birkman Method was also subjected to rotated component factoring using the Direct Oblimin procedure to five factors for both the Usual and Need Scales components. Other validity data reported include comparisons of the Birkman self-report scales with three scales of the MMPI (i.e., Ego Strength, Depressiveness, and Psychopathic Deviancy) and the Eysenck and Eysenck Personaility Inventory (EPI). Validity coefficients for the Birkman Method and the MMPI were .36 for the Psychopathic Deviancy scale, .45 for the Depressiveness scale, and -.80 for the Ego Strength scale. Correlational data were also provided for the Birkman scales and the EPI. The author rationalized that, "The correlations of Extraversion and Neuroticism from the EPI and the Birkman self-report scales are useful in understanding how The Birkman Method relates to these important personality constructs" (Reliability and Validity manual, 2001, p. 16). There is a moderate to high correlation between the Birkman

scales and the EPI's Extraversion scale with a coefficient of .73 and the EPI's Neuroticism scale with a coefficient of .86.

COMMENTARY. The Birkman Method appears to have reasonably adequate reliability and validity. A thorough review of the comparative data for various translation and linguistic versions of the Birkman Method have also been made based on the data provided. This reviewer concurs with the author that caution should be exercised when interpreting the results. The author expounds on the intercultural utility of the Birkman Method by stating that "we should always acknowledge that approach to interpersonal and business issues do differ between some cultures and may influence results of instruments such as The Birkman Method" (Reliability and Validity manual, 2001, p. 84).

SUMMARY. The Birkman Method provides a unique view of an individual's perceptions of self, perception of social context, and perception of occupational opportunities. This instrument has adequate psychometric properties; however, caution should be exercised when interpreting results in an intercultural context. The questionnaire items are well constructed and written in a clear, concise manner. The Reliability and Validity Manual also contains a great deal of technical data based on the collection of questionnaire data from 1993 to 2000. The author cautions readers to be cognizant of the problematic challenges associated with attempting to draw conclusions about gender differences and the Birkman Method, as well as discouraging individuals from drawing conclusions about behavioral or expectation differences between men and women.

Review of the Birkman Method by GYPSY M. DENZINE, Associate Dean and Professor of Educational Psychology, Northern Arizona University, Flagstaff, AZ:

DESCRIPTION. Roger W. Birkman, Ph.D., began developing his assessment tool in the 1940s when he served as a pilot instructor for the U.S. Air Force. In response to his observation of students who demonstrated both visual and interpersonal misperceptions of impact in pilot situations, he sought to measure human characteristics he believed influenced the perceptions, behaviors, and motivation among normally functioning adults. The scale provides scores for the following four primary structures that allow for the description of individual differences: Usual Behavior, Underlying Needs, Stress Behavior, and occupational preferences that represent Interests. Behavioral descriptors are obtained from reviewing scores on the Usual and Stress subscales. Descriptions of one's motivations are obtained from Needs and Interests subscale scores. The measure was initially titled "Test of Social Comprehension," which reflects Birkman's intent to combine respondents' perception of self and perception of social context. The Interest subscale was added later in the test development and is considered to be relevant to the other three subscales. Interest scores are presented separately and can be interpreted independently, whereas scores on the Usual, Need, and Stress scales are intimately connected and should be considered and interpreted together as a set of related constructs.

The Usual Behavior subscales assess an individual's effectiveness in dealing with relationships and tasks when the person feels good about himself or herself and the situation. Thus, Usual Behavior measures "socially correct" (Reliability and Validity manual, p. 2) behaviors as social correctness is understood by the respondent. By design, this scale is related to social desirability, and it describes a person's behavioral style rather than level of effectiveness in dealing with relationships and tasks.

The Underlying Needs scales represent individuals' expectations regarding how relationships and situations should function regardless of perceived social correctness. Needs items measure how people would like or need others to treat them and what types of behaviors the person wants to be required to express. The Need scale assesses how people want to be treated by others rather than the "socially correct" behaviors people believe they must demonstrate early in relationships or in formal contact situations. The underlying assumption behind this scale is that most people know what is acceptable behavior in a relationship or task but may prefer a different style of behavior over extended periods of time.

Items underlying the Interest scales are combined to form the following 10 Interest scales: Persuasive, Social Service, Scientific, Mechanical, Outdoor, Numerical, Clerical, Artistic, Literary, and Musical. The Reliability and Validity Manual provides a brief description of the Interest Scales,

and users are referred to Birkman International's "Coaching Guide" for a more in-depth treatment of the scales.

Birkman does not claim he relied on any specific theories in developing his method. Rather, the Birkman Method was based on matching interview-based descriptions of people by others with their own answers to the questionnaire. Scale development was derived from emerging commonly recurring themes in the interview-based matching procedures rather than a statistical approach to test theories of personality structure, characteristics, or development. The authors of the Reliability and Validity Manual claim the Birkman method is unique in that it assesses individual differences in both personality and interest structure, whereas most instruments measure either personality or interest. The Reliability and Validity Manual was last updated in 2001. For the most recent information about the instrument, interested persons should access the Birkman Method web site (http://www.birkman.com/), which contains a wealth of information about the test and its potential uses. Information about test costs and certification training consultants is presented on the web site.

Administration. The Birkman assessment package includes access to the online questionnaire, a 40–50-page report, and a 60–90-minute one-on-one consultation either in person or by phone with a Certified Birkman Consultant. Administration time is approximately 45 minutes. Items are clear and straightforward.

The first scale presented in the booklet is titled "How Do You See Most People?" and contains 125 True/False items. The second scale is titled "How Do You See Yourself" and is also composed of 125 True/False items.

Using The Birkman Method requires a Birkman Certified Consultant. According to the Birkman Method website there are currently over 2,000 Certified Consultants in over 25 countries worldwide. The Certification Training program appears to be targeted towards performance consultants, organizational psychologists, and human resources personnel. One benefit of having a person within the organization trained as a Consultant is that the individual will receive a database that contains all of the data for the people he or she had complete the questionnaire. This database is housed within the Birkman's secure systems, and additional data can be added upon request. Certified Consultants are required to complete 20 hours of professional development every 3 years to insure that they remain current with the latest Birkman Method approaches and resources.

Scoring and interpretation. The test is a self-report scale with scoring and interpretation provided by Birkman International, Inc. Test-takers who complete the on-line version (referred to as "BirkmanDirect") receive via email a unique link (or a unique password) to access the Birkman 298-item questionnaire. Completed over the internet, the questionnaire is available in multiple languages. Results for the online version are available immediately upon questionnaire completion. Respondents can create and print over 40 PDF format reports, which can be printed or saved to a disk for future use. Reports are generated based on an organization or an individual's needs and can be sent electronically to qualified users directly. Non-electronic versions of the test must be mailed to Birkman International, Inc. for scoring and processing.

The sample "Advanced" report I received to review contained 39 pages of interpretation. All interpretative documents were professional looking, well-organized and labeled, and clear to understand. Results included 12 pages of individualized brief narrative descriptions of the sample respondent's strengths and needs, as well as some possible stress reactions. Scores were not intended to be interpreted in a normative manner, and the manual does not contain norms for any groups of individuals.

Strengths and needs are measured by respondents' self-reported behaviors and motivations. Each Strength and Need page of the sample report contained an outline of one's Usual Behavior (i.e., Strength), which was worded in a positive manner. Following the Usual Behavior summary was an overview of the person's Basic Needs, which was meant to help the person understand that his or her capability to be maximally productive was contingent on having certain basic needs met. In the last section of the Strengths and Needs page was the Stress Behavior description, which listed some potential behaviors in situations in which the Basic Need was not met. Neither the strengths or coping with stress reactions were described in detail but the terms in the sample report were fairly self-explanatory and should be

familiar to most readers (e.g., energetic, restless tension, driven, feelings of inadequacy). The Strengths and Needs pages were intended to provide nonjudgmental style descriptions and did not contain information on numerical scores. The Advanced report also contained a Needs graph, which illustrates the respondent's Usual Behavior, Basic Needs, and Potential Stress behaviors in 11 domains. The bar graph mapped the actual component scores in areas such as: Demands of Work, Dealing with Change, and Personal Independence.

The second section of the Advanced report covered the career and interest dimensions of the Birkman Method. This section began with a Career Narrative description, which displayed the respondent's similarity to different job strengths and projects.

It is not clear exactly how the subscale scores are derived. One is left to assume simple means are computed for the various subscales and no weighting of items is employed.

DEVELOPMENT. The Birkman Method has been used for more than 50 years, and nearly two million people have completed the scales. As of 2001, the Birkman Method was available in the following languages: English, Dutch, French (Canadian), Mandarin, and Spanish.

Although it is clearly stated in the Reliability and Validity Manual that the Birkman Method was not created based on factor analytic results, a considerable amount of attention is given to comparison of the Birkman Method to other widely used psychological scales.

Between 1993 and 1999, 91,672 individuals completed the Birkman questionnaire by paper or direct computer administration and scores were interpreted using the scale revisions from the Year 2000. These scale scores were subjected to a principal component analysis using the Direct Oblimin rotation method, which resulted in the interpretation of five factors. The factor structure resulting from this analysis was used to compare Birkman scores to the structure underlying the Big Five. Unfortunately, the authors of the Reliability and Validity Manual do not provide any references or cite any empirical work related to the Big Five. The authors of the Reliability and Validity Manual note the Birkman Method differs from the Big Five theory of personality in that it deals with more specific behaviors and motivations compared to the Big Five structure. The validity section of the Birkman Reliability and Validity Manual provides a conceptual mapping of the Big Five factors. For example, the first Usual Behavior factor is compared to the Birkman Activity Scale and opposed to the Empathy and Thought scales. Items comprising this factor relate to level of energy, desire to work fast, feeling bitter or sad, and ability to handle emotions when upset. This factor is believed to be conceptually aligned with the Big Five factor labeled Negative Emotionality (also, referred to as the Neuroticism scale by some researchers). To the trained professional familiar with the Big Five factors of personality, the comparison between the Big Five structure and the Birkman Method appears to have some face validity; however, empirical validity would be much more credible and convincing. Similarly, the scores on the Birkman Method scales are compared to Cattell's 16PF© Factors. Unfortunately, no references or other information about Cattell's theory and/or the 16PF© scale are presented in the Birkman manual. The Birkman manual does provide an empirical comparison of its scale scores and 16PF© scores. Based on data collected from a sample of 318 college students, a principal components analysis with a Varimax rotation was conducted on respondents' 16PF© and Birkman Self scale scores. Overall, there is some conceptual coherence to the results obtained from this combined principal components analysis. For example, the first factor is composed of items from the 16PF© factors of Anxiety and Neuroticism and items from the Birkman scale scores of Emotionality and Neuroticism. Caution needs to be used in evaluating the results presented in the Birkman manual on the comparison to 16PF© because scores from the Birkman Method were from the original scales rather than the revised scales.

As criterion data accumulated, Birkman periodically added criterion-referenced scales. In 2000, however, Birkman embarked on extensive examination of the basic scales and the item structure of each scale. The purpose of the 2000 revisions was to increase internal consistency of the four measured constructs rather than to remove or add new constructs. Most revisions occurred at the item level, and Birkman shifted items, deleted items, and added some new items. One substantial revision involved the Challenge scale, which was originally computed through a ratio of more basic scales. After re-examining the Challenge scale in 2000, Birkman revised this scale so that scores are derived from direct items underlying the Challenge construct.

TECHNICAL. Evidence for the validity of the Birkman Method resides in the results of numerous factor analytic investigations, which are summarized in the Reliability and Validity Manual. Overall, the manual contains important information about the samples utilized for establishing reliability and validity of the constructs.

The Reliability and Validity Manual provides a thorough discussion of the appropriateness of this scale for different gender or ethnic/culture groups and empirical data are presented in tables for various demographic groupings (e.g., age, gender, ethnicity, and English-speaking cultures). In addition, a table is presented in the manual comparing the scale means for various language translations (i.e., English, Dutch, Mandarin, and Spanish).

Internal consistency reliability for the four subscales of the Birkman Method has been well established by numerous studies and is presented in the Reliability and Validity Manual. Based on a sample of 91,762 persons who completed the test between 1993 and 1999, the researchers report alpha coefficients for the component scales ranging from .48 (Usual-Freedom subscale) to .85 (Need-Challenge subscale). Alpha coefficients for the 10 Interest scales ranged from .74 (Scientific subscale) to .90 (Mechanical subscale and Clerical subscale). Internal consistency reliabilities are reported separately for the original scales and the 2000 test version. Overall, there were considerable improvements in internal consistency for the 2000 revised version of the Birkman Method compared to the original instrument. It is noted, however, that five of the Usual component scales had alpha coefficients below .70 (Authority, Advantage, Change, Freedom, and Thought). Three of the Need subscales had alpha coefficients below .70 (Authority, Change, and Thought).

The Reliability and Validity Manual contains information on three studies in which test-retest reliabilities were computed. In a sample of 42 male prisoners, immediate test-retest coefficients ranged from .69 (Usual-Activity subscale) to .91 (Need-Empathy subscale). In another study, test-retest reliabilities (2-week time interval) for a sample of 132 individuals aged 9–11 who were tested in school resulted in coefficients ranging from .48 (Need-Activity subscale) to .85 (Need-Acceptance subscale). One concern about this sample is that the manual states the Birkman Method was designed for older individuals (25 years or older), yet, reliability coefficients are reported for a sample involving youth as young as 9 years of age. In a third study, results from a 15-month time interval test-retest study are reported. Fifty 17–18-year-old college students completed the Birkman scales with test-retest coefficients ranging from .21 (Usual-Acceptance subscale) to .69 (Need-Advantage subscale). For this sample, test-retest coefficients for the Interest scales ranged from .65 (Persuasive) to .81 (Scientific, Artistic, and Musical subscales). Again, it is noted the college sample was younger than the recommended minimum age.

COMMENTARY. According to the authors of the Reliability and Validity Manual, "scale development was not driven by a particular theory of personality structure (or personality development) and was not intended to establish a statistical map (factor structure) of personality characteristics" (p. 1). Although the developers of the method are most interested in practical uses of the Birkman Method, it seems the neglect of theory and construct development is a missed research opportunity, especially in light of the large data warehouse existing on Birkman Method scores.

The Reliability and Validity Manual provides definitions for the scales and key terms; however, there is a need for more operational definitions related to the constructs. For example, the Underlying Needs scale is based on the assumption that most people know what is acceptable behavior in a relationship or task but may prefer a different style of behavior over extended periods of time. What is lacking is a prediction or evidence of what constitutes an "extended period of time." The potential user does not know if extended time is meant to refer to weeks, months, years, or decades.

In a few cases, the Reliability and Validity Manual provides incomplete information about some issues related to test development. For example, although the authors provide good details about the samples and methodologies employed in gathering the criterion-referenced scales for the career family validities, the treatment of the Interview Guide scales is vague and somewhat confusing.

The Birkman Method is purported to have a wide range of applications related to measuring nonclinical human behavior and occupational strengths. For example, the test developer claims the Birkman Method is appropriate for the following uses: organizational team building, career guidance, conflict management, stress management, mergers and acquisitions, workplace diversity, crisis management, retirement planning, marital counseling, leadership development, executive coaching, and more. This wide range of applications raises questions due to the lack of evidence of predictive validity. Moreover, the use of the Birkman Method for career counseling and/or marital counseling raises serious questions because Consultants are not required to have a background or training in the helping professions. The web site and manual do not explicitly state only trained and qualified professionals should use the Birkman Method for personal counseling purposes.

My literature search did not reveal any published articles on the psychometric properties of the Birkman Method in professional journals. With the exception of two journal articles, the search did not reveal any studies using this scale. The journal articles discussed the benefits of using the Birkman Method for an organization; however, no empirical evidence supporting the psychometric properties of the Birkman Method was presented. An internet search, however, revealed this scale is widely used in business and industry training, and numerous newspaper articles surfaced in which the practical uses of the Birkman Method for an organization were described. It is a concern that the Birkman Method has garnered no support from the professional literature such as studies that provide evidence of convergent, divergent, or criterion-related validity.

SUMMARY. The Birkman Method is a straightforward measure of one's perception of self, social context, and occupational opportunities. The reports produced are interesting and presented in a clear manner free of jargon and evaluative judgments. The Reliability and Validity Manual provides some evidence related to psychometric properties. Given the research to date on item and scale development, the Birkman Method can be recommended for use with nonclinical populations aged 25 and above. In addition to the benefits for individual and group interpretation, one of the primary strengths of the Birkman

Method is that researchers who choose this method enter a very large data base and have the potential to conduct cumulative research on a variety of constructs including furthering the investigation of the psychometric properties of the Birkman Method.

Overall, the technical manual accompanying the Birkman Method does not meet the standards outlined by professional organizations (APA, AERA, & NCME, 1999) in education and psychology to recommend its use in personal counseling and some career development settings. In conclusion, it seems one of the primary strengths of the Birkman Method is that it allows for the examination of one's strengths, which may be capitalized upon through greater self-awareness and social awareness. There is a need for further research on the psychometric properties of the Birkman Method, which would ideally be conducted by independent researchers who are not connected to Birkman International, Inc.

REVIEWER'S REFERENCE

American Educational Research Association, American Psychological Association, & National Council on Measurement in Education. (1999). *Standards for educational and psychological testing.* Washington, DC: American Educational Research Association.

[29]

The Boston Diagnostic Aphasia Examination—Third Edition.

Purpose: Designed to help "identify and distinguish among disorders of language function and neurologically recognized aphasic syndromes."
Population: Individuals with aphasia.
Publication Dates: 1972–2001.
Acronym: BDAE.
Scores, 59: Conversational and Expository Speech (Simple Social Responses, Free Conversation, Picture Description [Discourse Analysis—Segmentation into Utterances], Severity Rating and Profile of Speech Characteristics), Auditory Comprehension (Word Comprehension [Basic Word Discrimination, Supplemental Test], Commands and Complex Ideational Material Test), Oral Expression (Oral Agility [Nonverbal Agility and Verbal Agility], Automatized Sequences, Recitation, Melody, and Rhythm [Recitation, Melody and Rhythm], Repetition [Single Word Repetition and Repetition of Sentences], Naming [Responsive Naming, Boston Naming Test—Visual Confrontation Naming, Screening for Naming of Special Categories]), Reading (Basic Symbol Recognition [Matching Across Cases and Scripts and Number Matching], Word Identification [Picture-Word Match], Phonics [Homophone Matching], Derivational and Inflectional Morphology

[Free Grammatical Morphemes], Oral Reading [Basic Oral Word Reading and Oral Reading of Special Word Lists (Mixed Morphological Types and Semantic Paralexia-Prone Words)], Oral Reading of Sentences with Comprehension, Reading Comprehension—Sentences and Paragraphs), Writing (Mechanics of Writing, Basic Encoding Skills [Primer Word Vocabulary, Regular Phonics and Common Irregular Forms], Written Picture Naming and Narrative Writing) and Apraxia Assessment (Natural Gestures, Conventional Gestures, Use of Pretend Objects without an Action Goal, Use of Pretend Objects with an Action Goal and Bucco-Facial Respiratory Movements).
Administration: Individual.
Forms, 3: Short, Standard, Extended.
Price Data, 2005: $190 per complete kit including manual (2001, 136 pages), 147 long form stimulus cards picture book, 25 long form record booklets, 27 short form stimulus cards picture book, 25 short form record booklets, Boston Naming Test stimulus cards picture book, 25 Boston Naming Test record booklets, and videotape; $71 per manual; $33 per videotape; $52 per Boston Naming Test kit including Boston Naming Test stimulus cards picture book and 25 Boston Naming Test record booklets; $15 per 25 Boston Naming Test record booklets; $40 per Boston Naming Test stimulus cards picture book.
Time: (35–45) minutes.
Comments: Previously listed as The Assessment of Aphasia and Related Disorders, and that is the title of the manual.
Authors: Harold Goodglass with the collaboration of Edith Kaplan and Barbara Barresi.
Publisher: PRO-ED.

a) SHORT FORM.
Purpose: Designed "to provide a comprehensive, but brief sampling of the performances necessary for an informed quantitative assessment" of individuals with aphasia.
Price Data: $42 per short form kit including 27 short form stimulus cards picture book and 25 short form record booklets; $15 per 25 short form record booklets; $30 per short form stimulus cards picture book.
Time: (30–45) minutes.
Comments: The short form consists of shortened or omitted sections that are included in the standard form.
b) EXTENDED FORM.
Purpose: Designed to be a "more probing evaluation of particular language functions within each area of testing."
Scores, 18: Aesop's Fables, Word Comprehension in Categories, Syntactic Processing (Touching A with B, Reversible Possessives, Embedded Sentences), Repetition of Nonsense

Words, Naming in Categories, Advanced Phonic Analysis – Pseudo-homophone Matching, Bound Grammatical Morphemes, Derivational Morphemes, Uncommon Irregularities, Nonsense Words, Oral Spelling, and Cognitive/Grammatical Influences (Part of Speech Effects: Dictated Words, Subtest 2: "Dictated Functor Loaded Sentences").

Price Data: $148 per long form kit including manual, 147 long form stimulus cards picture book, and 25 long form record booklets; $20 per 25 long form record booklets; $61 per long form stimulus cards picture book.

Time: Administration time not reported.

Comments: All scores included in the standard form are also included in the extended form.

c) BOSTON NAMING TEST, SECOND EDITION.

Population: Ages 55–59.

Scores: Total score only.

Time: Administration time not reported.

Authors: Edith Kaplan, Harold Goodglass, and Sandra Weintraub.

Cross References: See T5:199 (18 references) and T4:207 (105 references); for reviews by Rita Sloan Berndt and Malcolm R. McNeil of an earlier edition, see 10:15 (3 references); see also 9:86 (2 references) and T3:308 (28 references); for reviews by Daniel R. Boone and Manfred J. Meier of an earlier edition, see 8:955 (1 reference).

Review of the Boston Diagnostic Aphasia Examination—Third Edition by SHAWN K. ACHESON, Associate Professor of Neuropsychology, Department of Psychology, Western Carolina University, Cullowhee, NC:

DESCRIPTION. The Boston Diagnostic Aphasia Examination (BDAE) was designed more than 40 years ago. The initial purpose of the BDAE, to assess a variety of aphasic disorders in terms of diagnosis, breadth and nature of linguistic deficit, and as a guide to treatment, remains central to the current revision of this well-established and highly respected instrument. The BDAE is intended for use by psychologists and speech pathologists with those adults who have acquired language deficits. It is an individually administered test that yields percentile scores based on a sample of aphasic individuals.

The BDAE assesses five linguistic domains including conversational speech, auditory comprehension, oral expression, reading, and writing. There is also a supplemental component designed to assess a number of nonlanguage processes including constructional apraxia, finger agnosia, acalculia, and right-left confusion.

DEVELOPMENT. The third edition of the BDAE is a much expanded version of the original BDAE. Unlike the 1983 version, there are now a number of extended subtest features that can be used to provide more information about the client's deficit. The Standard Form remains similar to previous versions of the test and there is now a Short Form. This Short Form includes a selection of the subtests found in the Standard Form. Moreover, each of these selected subtests has fewer items than are found in the corresponding Standard Form subtest. The authors of the BDAE have also introduced a number of clusters that represent the amalgamation of several subtests each. These clusters include Auditory Comprehension, Oral Expression, Reading, and Writing. The BDAE now also includes an omnibus measure of language function referred to as the Language Competence Index. Unlike the Severity Rating Scale (an essentially ordinal scale), this new composite score was intended to provide an interval scale measure of language ability that might be more effectively used in the course of research.

Unfortunately, there is little information provided in support of these new features. To start, there is no description of the process by which the extended testing items were created, evaluated, or selected. Similarly, this reviewer could find no explanation or rationale to explain why certain subtests and subtest items were selected for the Short Form whereas others were excluded. The test authors report subtest intercorrelations for each of the new clusters but no information concerning factor-analytic confirmation of these clusters. There is also no discussion of the process by which subtests were chosen for the Language Competence Index (LCI). Moreover, the calculation of the LCI involves the summation and averaging of several subtest percentiles. Percentile scores are effectively ordinal scale scores and as such they are not amenable to basic addition, subtraction, multiplication, or division.

TECHNICAL. The BDAE is an instrument based on the assumption that many aphasic symptoms are not normally distributed in the population. In most cases, the types of language errors and deficits seen in aphasics are not seen in those with normal language. Given this, technical psychometric characteristics of the BDAE are not what we might expect to find in measures of abilities that are normally distributed (e.g., the Wechsler Adult Intelligence Scale—Third Edition [WAIS-III]).

The standardization sample is based on data collected from 1999 that included 85 aphasic and 15 healthy elderly participants. These data were supplied by field examiners (licensed speech pathologists) from across the country. The size of this normative sample is considerably smaller than that of the 1983 normative sample. There is also no demographic information (age, sex, ethnicity, education, or diagnosis) provided for either the aphasic or the normal sample.

Generally, internal consistency reliability for standard and extended testing subtests ranged from a low of .71 to a high of .98. One extended testing subtest had a reliability coefficient of .54, and one standard subtest had a coefficient of .64. No reliability information was provided for the shortened subtests found on the short form, the clusters, or the LCI. Validity was not discussed at all in the Statistical Background chapter of the manual. Given the overlap between the present version and the 1983 version of the BDAE for the standard subtests, one might assume that the weight of the history of this measure stands in its favor. However, new research needs to be done to support the validity of the Short Form and its modified subtests, the new clusters, and the LCI.

COMMENTARY. The heart of the BDAE remains essentially unchanged and as such retains much of its fundamental value as a measure of language dysfunction. However, in its attempt to keep pace with changes in our understanding of aphasia and language function it falls short in the development of a new Short Form, cluster scores, and the omnibus composite measure of language competence. Much work remains to be done on these newer components before they should be widely used in a clinical setting. At the very least they should be used with great caution and only in conjunction with other more psychometrically sound measures. The purpose of these new components is certainly worth the effort, but they need additional psychometric qualification.

The materials themselves are also worth some comment. The stimulus books are well constructed and the layout of the record forms makes administration and scoring easy. However, the manual itself was poorly prepared and edited. It lacks both necessary and relevant content (e.g., reliabilities for cluster scores) and contains many typographic errors, especially within the tables. There is a long and rich literature that supports the validity of the BDAE, none of which is found in the current edition of the manual.

This reviewer wishes to comment on the qualitative and subjective nature of the BDAE. This instrument requires a thorough understanding of language and aphasia. It might be best to think of the BDAE as a structured framework through which clinicians can observe the nature and extent of their clients' linguistic deficits. This type of measurement comes in sharp contrast to some more current measures that present as an essential litmus test for the presence or absence of some neurocognitive disorder. Such measures are often used in an algorithmic fashion for the purpose of diagnosis and prognosis whereas measures such as the BDAE provide important and valuable information relevant to understanding the underlying neurocognitive process.

SUMMARY. The history of psychological assessment is replete with flash-in-the-pan tests and measures. The BDAE is one of those rare instruments that appear to have gotten it right early on and remained useful and effective for more than 4 decades. There is no doubt that this version of the BDAE will survive and even improve with time. Practitioners will find the current BDAE as useful as before, and if used cautiously, may provide insights and understanding of clients' language impairments that previous versions could not.

Review of The Boston Diagnostic Aphasia Examination—Third Edition by ANTHONY T. DUGBARTEY, Visiting Assistant Professor, Department of Psychology, University of Victoria, Victoria, British Columbia, and Forensic Psychologist, Forensic Psychiatric Services Commission, Victoria, British Columbia, Canada:

DESCRIPTION. The Boston Diagnostic Aphasia Examination (BDAE) was first published in 1972 (Goodglass & Kaplan, 1972) as a means of assessing the verbal communication and language functioning deficits that occur following brain injury. A second edition of the manual was published in 1983, and a survey of professional neuropsychologists showed that this battery received the most frequent use from among a list of other extant aphasia test batteries (Butler, Retzlaff, & Vanderploeg, 1991). The third edition of the Boston Diagnostic Aphasia Examination (BDAE-3) is designed to assist in the differential diagnosis of aphasic syndromes, assess change in symptoms over time, and aid in the rehabilitation of neurolinguistic impairments. The BDAE-3 is substantially different from its predecessor, both in format and scope of language processes measured. In many respects, the changes reflect two major realities. First, advances in neurolinguistic research culminated in the development of an Extended version to incorporate empirically based methods for appraising additional aspects of language function. Second, the economics of health service delivery has imposed a premium on time-limited assessments, which consequently led to the development of a Short Form.

The BDAE-3 is divided into five functional sections. The first, Conversational and Expository Speech, incorporates four subtests that serve the dual function of establishing rapport and evaluating speech output. The Auditory Comprehension section, also comprising four subtests, assesses a broad variety of receptive language skills. The Oral Expression section includes subtests that assess automatized speech, repetition, confrontation naming, and melodic and rhythmic aspects of speech. The Reading section is made up of subtests that assess a broad variety of domains ranging from basic symbol recognition to oral reading. The fifth section assesses a variety of writing skills. An additional section is also devoted to the assessment of apraxia, a condition that frequently co-occurs with aphasia. A second edition of the Boston Naming Test (BNT-2) has now been incorporated in the BDAE-3, and includes a new, multiple-choice version.

The BDAE-3 was designed to be administered to individuals ranging in age from 16 years through adulthood. The authors, however, include norms for children (ages 5 to 12 years) on the BNT-2. Administration of the entire BDAE-3 takes approximately 90 to 110 minutes, and the Short Form takes 40 minutes to 1 hour to administer. The administration rules are fairly straightforward, but scoring, especially of the Rating Scale Profile of Speech Characteristics, requires extensive training and experience in aphasiology and the process approach to neuropsychological assessments. Examiners are encouraged to tape record the examinee's responses to certain subtests, particularly from the Conversational and Expository Speech section, in order to enhance scoring accuracy. Of note, the BDAE-3 test kit comes with a nicely presented instructional video to help facilitate learning of the administration and scoring guidelines.

DEVELOPMENT. The BDAE was originally modeled after late 19th century classical neurological traditions in clinicopathological conceptualization of aphasia syndromes. With the current edition, an attempt has been made to incorporate modern cognitive neuroscience descriptions of language functions and aphasia. The primary goal of the developers of this test battery, in spite of any changes, has remained clinical utility and measurement of performances that are diagnostically distinctive for aphasia. The Extended Testing format was incorporated with the stated objective of achieving comprehensiveness in assessing all major aspects of neurolinguistic performance.

Work on the development of the BDAE-3 departed from the previous editions, which relied upon an accumulation, over several years, of protocols from successively admitted aphasic inpatients at the Boston Veterans Administration Medical Center. The current edition utilized field examiners from multiple sites who sampled patients concurrently from a variety of settings, including inpatient and outpatient medical facilities, and from private practice clinics. For this reason, the normative data for the BDAE-3 have a more even distribution on the Aphasia Severity Rating Scale than its predecessors. The field examiners were all certified speech pathologists. No pilot studies or data regarding test tryout analyses are reported. Although there is no indication that traditional psychometric principles of item analyses were followed in the development of this test battery, the choice of items was based upon expert selection. In fact, the authors encourage examiners to use the BDAE-3 as a framework for sampling language performance, and as a springboard for further exploration of linguistic skills. Although not explicitly stated, ceiling scores are expected to be attained, at least on the language tests of the BDAE-3, among normal individuals.

TECHNICAL. Information describing the norming process is presented in very simple terms. The normative data for the BDAE-3 were derived from a standardization sample of only 15 normal elderly individuals and 85 aphasic patients. Not all 85 of the patients were administered the entire battery, and the authors offer no clear justification for this strategy. A percentile conversion table is presented for subtests on which items are identical for the BDAE-3 and its predecessor. Summary statistics (i.e., means, standard deviations, and ranges) of performance on the 15 normal controls are outlined in the BDAE-3 manual. The authors note that with one exception where one individual from the normal control group failed 7 of the 12 items on the syntax comprehension subtest, all normal controls reached full criterion on the BDAE-3 items.

Internal consistency reliability estimates using the Kuder-Richardson method were modest for the BDAE-3 as a whole, but generally high (above .85) for the majority of the Oral Expression, Auditory Comprehension, and Writing subtests. Internal consistency statistics are not presented for the Language Competence Index (LCI), and this omission represents a fairly major concern, especially because the LCI made its debut in the BDAE-3. The authors did not present stability (test-retest reliability) coefficients, with the sound explanation that fluctuations in language performance occurs to a greater degree among aphasics than most other neurological patient populations. Although this may be true of aphasic patients in the acute and immediate post-acute stages, there is little justification for not performing empirically based stability statistics on patients whose recovery has stabilized. Consequently, the authors' assurance, however, that "Once recovery has stabilized… most aphasic patients will repeat their earlier performance fairly closely on retest" (manual, p. 16) requires empirical corroboration.

The Short Form of the BDAE-3 compares quite favorably with the Standard Form, with correlations ranging from .90 to .99 for most subtests except the Word Discrimination (.77), Matching Numbers (.76), Complex Ideational Material (.87), Picture-Word Matching (.86), Naming (.84), and Irregular Phonics (.88) subtests. Interrater reliability coefficients are not provided in the BDAE-3 manual.

Limited validity information for the BDAE-3 is available in the examiner's manual. Only partial correlation matrices for the BDAE-3, with coefficients .60 or greater, are displayed in the manual. No external validity data are presented for the BDAE-3. For now, applicability of this battery must be limited to monolingual native English-speaking North American populations. Ecological validity data, including empirical support for applying the BDAE-3 to return-to-work assessments for which its predecessor was occasionally applied (see Rabin, Barr, & Burton, 2005), are lacking.

COMMENTARY AND SUMMARY. The BDAE-3 has several strong features. First, it provides an omnibus assemblage of tests and procedures for assessing a myriad of language functions following brain injury. Second, the introduction of a Short Form, as well as some modest inclusion of information-processing concepts in current neurolinguistic research reflects current trends in research and professional practice. Third, inclusion of the Boston Naming Test in the current edition of the BDAE is a welcome addition. Also, the BDAE-3 examiner manual, coupled with the illustrative video, presents a wealth of information about the major aphasic syndromes and illustrative patient performances. Some weaknesses include the still lengthy administration time of the Short Form. Second, as has been suggested by Strauss, Sherman, and Spreen (2006), knowledge of the process approach to neuropsychological examinations is a necessary prerequisite for interpretation of the BDAE-3. The limited reliability and validity information, as well as inadequate description of the standardization sample, are major shortcomings of the BDAE-3, as is the rather small number of individuals comprising the clinical and normal standardization samples. Third, rather disappointing is the missed opportunity of the BDAE-3 authors in giving some attention to the application of the BDAE-3 to such degenerative disorders as Primary Progressive Aphasia (Mesulam, 1982; Weintraub, Rubin, & Mesulam, 1990) and Frontotemporal dementia.

In sum, despite the weaknesses of the BDAE-3, it would remain an indispensable test battery whenever a detailed assessment of aphasia is warranted. Although further empirical validation support is needed, the BDAE-3 is a welcome revision over its predecessor and an excellent addition to the armamentarium of the aphasiologist.

REVIEWER'S REFERENCES

Butler, M., Retzlaff, P., & Vanderploeg, R. (1991). Neuropsychological test usage. *Professional Psychology: Research and Practice, 22*, 510-512.

Goodglass, H., & Kaplan, E. (1972). Boston Diagnostic Aphasia Examination (BDAE). Philadelphia: Lea & Febiger.

Mesulam, M. M. (1982). Slowly progressive aphasia without generalized dementia. *Annals of Neurology, 11,* 592-598.

Rabin, L. A., Barr, W. B., & Burton, L. A. (2005). Assessment practices of clinical neuropsychologists in the United States and Canada: A survey of INS, NAN, and APA Division 40 members. *Archives of Clinical Neuropsychology, 20,* 33-65.

Strauss, E., Sherman, E. M. S., & Spreen, O. (2006). *A compendium of neuropsychological tests: Administration, norms, and commentary.* New York: Oxford University Press.

Weintraub, S., Rubin, N. P., & Mesulam, M. M. (1990). Primary progressive aphasia. Longitudinal course, neuropsychological profile, and language features. *Archives of Neurology, 47,* 1329-1335.

[30]

Brief Battery for Health Improvement 2.

Purpose: Designed for "assessing medical patients who may be experiencing problems with pain, functioning, somatization, depression, anxiety, or other factors relevant to rehabilitation and recovery."

Population: 18–65 years.

Publication Date: 2002.

Acronym: BBHI 2.

Scores, 6: Validity Scale (Defensiveness), Physical Symptom Scales (Somatic Complaints, Pain Complaints, Functional Complaints), Affective Symptom Scales (Depression, Anxiety).

Administration: Individual.

Parts, 4: Part I (Pain Complaints scale), Part II (Somatic Complaints scale), Part III (Functional Complaints scale), Part IV (Depression, Anxiety, and Defensiveness scales).

Price Data, 2007: $140 per starter kit with Standard or Extended Reports including manual (151 pages) and 10 fax-in answer sheets and scoring; $110 per starter kit with Standard or Extended Reports including manual, 10 answer sheets, and 10 Q Local administrations; $36.50 per manual; $51.50 per compact disk administration; $26.50 per 25 fax-in answer sheets; $13.50 per fax-in service of 1 fax-in answer sheet; $9.50 per 5–9 Patient Assessment Device Reports; $89 per Q Local Software Desktop version (annual license fee); $26.50 per 25 Q Local answer sheets; $9.50 per 5–9 Q Local Standard or Extended Reports; No Charge for Q Local Progress Reports; $12.50 per 5–9 mail-in answer sheets and Standard or Extended Reports; quantity discounts available for reports.

Foreign Language Edition: Spanish materials available.

Time: (7–10) minutes.

Comments: Shorter version of the Battery for Health Improvement 2 (BHI 2; 17:16); mail-in and fax-in scoring available from publisher along with on-site computer (Q Local software) and hand-held electronic device (Patient Assessment Device) scoring; three automated reports available (Standard Report, Extended Report, Progress Report).

Authors: John Mark Disorbio and Daniel Bruns.

Publisher: Pearson.

Review of the Brief Battery for Health Improvement 2 by THEODORE L. HAYES, Principal Selection Research Scientist, The Gallup Organization, Washington, DC:

DESCRIPTION. The technical manual for the Brief Battery for Health Improvement 2 (BBHI 2) states that "The BBHI2 test was developed to serve as a tool for assessing medical patients who may be experiencing problems with pain, functioning, somatization, depression, anxiety, or other factors relevant to rehabilitation and recovery" (p. 1). The inventory is meant to provide clinicians and patients a perspective on the respondent's degree of pain, perceived functioning, and specific well-being. The BBHI 2 is composed of 63 patient self-presentation items. It can be administered to patients between the ages of 18 and 65 with at least a sixth grade English-language reading competence who are undergoing treatment for a physical injury. Optionally, the BBHI 2 can be administered on multiple occasions, and a Progress Report will plot changes in scores over time. The authors claim that BBHI 2 completion time should be less than 10 minutes. Completed response sheets are supposed to be sent to the publisher for scoring; on-site electronic scoring is optional. Three types of reports are available: a standard report with scale means, pain indicators, and a clinical summary (plus various optional reporting details); a report option that extends the summary report with more in-depth clinical insights plus diagnostic probabilities; and a progress report chart for multiple administrations. Report output includes scale scores in raw score, *T*-score, and percentile formats; the percentile scores are shown for patient "community" samples.

DEVELOPMENT. In addition to its thoughtful content and construct coverage, a unique strength of the BBHI 2 is its integration of pain conceptualization and measurement into the assessment report. The BBHI 2 is the latest iteration of a previous assessment published by the same publisher and authors. These assessments purport to evaluate different facets of recovery diagnostics in order to integrate pain perceptions and "state" (as opposed to "trait") levels of defensiveness, physical symptoms, and psychological reactions (anxiety, depression) into the clinician's report and treatment evaluation. Presumably a clinician would chart BBHI 2 assessment results to evaluate the patient's progress both in terms of pain reduction and psychological readjustment. No rehabilitation model is presumed or suggested, which means that the BBHI 2 measurements should be valuable to the various members of a rehabilitation team. The BBHI 2's authors have gone to great lengths to assess the instrument in both patient and nonpatient samples, in the process using a cross-validation design. Finally, it seems likely that further refinements and linkages to other measures may be unveiled in future editions.

TECHNICAL. The validity of use of the BBHI 2 results arises primarily through the authors' clinical experience and their review of the theoretical and practice-based issues in medical psychology and rehabilitation. Pain assessment is integral in the BBHI 2, and it seems appropriate for the purposes of the inventory. The other constructs—Depression, Anxiety, Somatic Complaints, Defensiveness (response validity), and specific items—all are clearly presented, have a strong research base rationale summarized in the manual, and are measured efficiently. The interpretive guide offered in the manual is vivid and realistic. In all, the construct and content-based evidence for the BBHI 2 are strong.

Empirical validation is not a strength of BBHI 2. The entire criterion-oriented validity evidence of the BBHI 2 might fairly be described as incomplete. On the plus side, the first case made for criterion validity in the BBHI 2 manual is based on differentiating patient respondents from "community" (nonpatient) respondents. (Other groups of respondents, such as the "fake good" and "fake bad" conditions, are presented as needed.) This is a laudable keying criterion for validation, and the resulting average standardized mean difference (.62) is encouraging.

The authors attempt to demonstrate that the racial, gender, and age compositions of the patient and community databases are comparable to the U.S. Census distributions of those categories. Further allusion is made to sampling respondents in the "four geographic regions of the United States" (manual, p. 19). However, these comparisons serve to undermine the well-intentioned appeal to demographic representation. The samples are clearly unbalanced in all categories relative to U.S. Census values. The end result is that there are no "normative database values" as claimed, though a reasonable description might be "comparison database values." The authors then use several cross-validation analyses to derive scales and expected score distributions. These again are well-intentioned and certainly better than no attempt, but the rationale for two cross-validations is missing, and the sample splitting strategy varies inexplicably from cross-validation to cross-validation.

The best evidence for the validity of the BBHI 2 would be indication of change after clinical intervention, or correlation with independent/non-self-report indicators. Changes in scores are not presented as criteria, nor are correlations with external ratings (e.g., clinical ratings of impairment) or other indicators such as duration of treatment, time to return to work, etc.

Based on the case studies provided in the manual, the BBHI 2 can be administered at least monthly to track change. The manual does not indicate how much change should be expected. The authors should provide standard errors of measurement to help guide clinical judgment. The only test-retest reliability information is presented for 87 individuals over 5–10 days, and not surprisingly, the stability of the instrument is quite high. Unfortunately, the manual text and table labels conflict with each other such that it is not clear whether the tabled values are internal reliability or stability estimates. The scale-level internal reliability estimates vary between .72 and .86, with no reported average overall score internal reliability. The average scale intercorrelation is around .58. One cannot rule out the possibility that there is one predominant dimension in the instrument.

COMMENTARY. The BBHI 2 is on many levels an evolutionary leap forward for the psychological assessment of patient functioning. The BBHI 2 seems well-grounded in the current nomological network of constructs and content germane to the subject matter at hand. Thus, this inventory's rationale is at least as compelling as the coordinate material in the R-SOPAC (Hayes, 2005), which was itself preferable to previous measures. The development process seems carefully executed and reasonable. As with the R-SOPAC, there are no external criterion-oriented validity data for the BBHI 2, its reliability evidence is weak, and its incremental conceptual utility remains untested. Practitioners using the R-SOPAC may wish to consider the BBHI 2; however, the R-SOPAC has fewer items and (allegedly) lower reading demands, and it too has much conceptual utility.

SUMMARY. The BBHI 2 provides measurements of perceived pain and psychological distress. These measurements have strong conceptual validity and internal reliability. Until further studies are reported, the BBHI 2 in its current form may be better used as an indicator of the patient's overall emotional well-being at the time of the clinician visit rather than an ongoing indicator of rehabilitation progress. The instrument may be useful to professionals who wish to employ a standardized intake interview, or possibly to corporate health survey sponsors who wish to create localized databases of patient functioning. Further claims as to its diagnostic or predictive value are currently unwarranted, though future research may substantiate them. Relative to other standardized assessments, though, the BBHI 2 has much to recommend it.

REVIEWER'S REFERENCE

Hayes, T. L. (2005). [Review of the Rehabilitation Survey of Problems and Coping.] In R. A. Spies & B. S. Plake (Eds.), *The sixteenth mental measurements yearbook* (pp. 877-879). Lincoln, NE: Buros Institute of Mental Measurements.

Review of the Brief Battery for Health Improvement 2 by WES SIME, Professor, Emeritus, University of Nebraska–Lincoln, Lincoln, NE:

DESCRIPTION AND PURPOSE. The Brief Battery for Health Improvement 2 (BBHI 2) is designed to be used with medical patients who may be in physical pain and/or rehabilitation with other somatic dysfunctions. It is particularly relevant where there is a need to assess the patient's personal (individual) symptomatic experience before, during, and after various medical interventions. It is a 63-item test (multiple choice) that can be administered by one of four different scoring methods aimed at identifying factors that interfere with recovery from a physical rehabilitation and/or pain management case. The BBHI 2 can be filled out in paper-pencil format to be mailed or faxed in to Pearson Assessments or there is also a computer-scored version with Pearson Assessments software in addition to a hand-held stand-alone electronic device for instantaneous scoring. The computer-generated scoring protocol is based upon six scales, 21 pain variables, and 17 critical items and uses two norm groups (patient and community) and eight other reference groups (chronic pain, head injury, neck injury, back injury, upper extremity injury, lower extremity injury, fake good, and fake bad) to produce an automated printed report. The computer narrative yields a detailed report with a wide variety of interpretative summaries and reports. The test requires a sixth grade reading level, and there is a CD presenting the questions as might be needed where literacy is an issue.

The test authors assert that the BBHI 2 provides a unique assessment in a population of medical patients where the presence of clinical signs and symptoms may violate assumptions made by other psychological instruments resulting in a tendency to overpathologize the patient's psychological condition (Bruns & Disorbio, 2005). They state that the American Academy of Pain Management advocates accurate assessment of pain, functional status, mood state, actual cost of medical treatment, misuse of medications, and cost of case settlement (where damages are reimbursable) for which the BBHI 2 appears appropriate. Further, the instrument is designed to help caregivers understand patient problems objectively as to how they feel physically (e.g., type of pain) and emotionally (e.g., frustration or anger).

Regarding the assessment of pain complaints (Part I), there are 10 items ranging from headache, abdominal pain, and feet pain wherein an 11-point Likert-type scale is provided. Four additional items address highest and lowest level of pain together with current pain and the highest level the patient could tolerate and still work, thus getting on with life. Part II assesses somatic complaints on a 4-point Likert scale on 11 items such as being irritable, having difficulty sleeping, and having difficulty concentrating.

Part III addresses functionality complaints on a 4-point scale including 17 items relating to sleep disorder, perceived disability, and ability to work. The last section, Part IV, has 21 items related to mood and affect. These include factors that reveal degree of anxiety and depression related to these medical conditions.

Presence of sleep problems, post-traumatic stress disorder, and psychosis are screened for indication of need to assess in greater detail. The BBHI 2 is used routinely to screen for classification of a particular physical medical disorder as well as for tracking progress and predicting the ultimate outcome of a therapeutic regime.

The authors argue the presence of a "psychological fallacy" that exists when symptoms such as change in sleep habits and appetite are used to diagnose depression. Most other psychological tests fail to control for the influence of medical signs and symptoms whenever there is a conjoint diagnosis of psychological condition along with a medical disorder (Disorbio, Bruns, & Barolat, 2006).

There are 17 "critical items" covering 15 areas of concern. These are used to elicit red flags, such as substance abuse, that can be an obvious concern in this population where pain symptoms often prompt patients to self-medicate with alcohol or recreational drugs. A second area tapped by these critical areas is family dysfunction that may exacerbate symptom manifestation. A third area is dissatisfaction with physician or other medical care provider. This is important to assess periodically as patients who tend to withhold complaints are less likely to make progress in therapy.

DEVELOPMENT. The BBHI 2 is the shortened version of the Battery for Health Improvement 2 (BHI 2; 17:16) and was developed concurrently with it. The BHI 2 was derived from two previous instruments that originated with a 600-item research version (BHI-R) in 1985 followed by the Battery for Health Improvement (BHI) in 1996. Data were collected on over 2,400 community and patient subjects representing 36 states and four geographical regions of the U.S.A. intending to differentiate patient from community (normal) subjects. For the BHI 2 in 2003, a 12-member panel of experts (all experienced in pain and rehabilitation) was convened to validate the appropriate categorical placement of test items into the appropriate content area.

Ultimately there were 250 developmental patient samples and 527 normative patient samples who did not exhibit physical rehabilitative or pain symptoms among their medical complaints.

In addition, patient data were contrasted with 250 individuals who were tested and categorized as the developmental community sample along with 725 normative community sample participants, none of whom had any primary symptoms of pain that required physical rehabilitation.

A Defensiveness scale is used to assess tendency to either minimize or magnify symptoms or problems to determine fake-good and fake-bad indicators. Questions such as "My life should not be this hard" versus "My life is much better than it used to be" were used in a study with 50 fake-good and 50 fake-bad patients combined with

patient populations to elicit the Defensiveness scale. The authors were conscientious in developing the final instrument from 1993 to 2004 before initiating the research documenting the utility, validity, and reliability for a wide variety of clinical populations ranging from chronic musculoskeletal pain (Bruns & Disorbio, 2000a; Davis, 1999) to those with violent behavior (Bruns & Disorbio, 2000b) or intent to sue the caregiver (Fishbain, Bruns, Disorbio, & Lewis, in press).

Probable users of the BBHI 2 include physicians, occupational and physical therapists, as well as health psychologists working in pain management with bad outcomes, including violence (Bruns, Disorbio, & Hanks, in press) or with patients suffering from chronic illnesses such as non-cancer-related chronic pain (Bruns, Disorbio, Bennett, et al., 2005).

TECHNICAL. The test manual provides information on psychometrics, including internal consistency and test-retest stability. For internal consistency, alpha coefficients ranged from .69 to .87 for patients, .72 to .86 for the community sample, and .72 to .86 for the combined groups. Test-retest reliability estimates ranged from .88 to .96. As expected, scale intercorrelations were moderately high. Affective scales for anxiety and depression were .56 to .64, whereas the intercorrelations for the physical symptoms ranged from .43 to .66.

Validity was assessed by correlating the scales of the BBHI 2 with the MMPI 2 (Minnesota Multiphasic Personality Inventory-2) and the Millon Clinical Multiaxial Inventory-III (MCMI-III) for affective measures and with both the McGill Pain Questionnaire and the Scored Pain Drawing for physical symptoms. Somatic complaints and pain measures were correlated with the MMPI-2 and McGill; coefficients ranged from .59 to .73 on measures including Hypochondriasis, Hysteria, Anxiety, Depression, and Psychasthenia. For functional complaints and affective scales the correlations were .53 to .91.

A unique feature of the BBHI 2 is that it is double normed against both community (normal) and patient populations. It is intended to be helpful in the measurement of pain as well as readiness to return to work and current state of depression. The automated reports include a profile with a horizontal bi-directional deviation bar chart. The Defensiveness scale shows significance for both high and low values. Actual values throughout the results include black diamond for patients and white diamond for community. If one diamond or both are outside of the normed range, the test authors suggest that it is likely a very severe concern.

Defensiveness is determined by a combination of the diffuse physical symptom scales, problems with personal disclosure, and potential for functional weakness. Affective measures include feeling helpless, despondent, and anxious. Validity measures are obtained using the Defensiveness data.

COMMENTARY. Reports provided for the BBHI 2 are automated in three different formats. The first is a standard report that could be used in discussion with the patient. The extended report is essentially the same, but includes more precise data that can be used for insurance and workers' compensation documentation as needed. The last of the three report formats is for noting progress over time with a series of simple line graphs that report the changes that have occurred from one time period to the next in therapy.

The instrument has potential to measure alexithymia, an important psychological dimension where the patient simply has no words to explain feelings or does not recognize the disillusioned state.

The value of the BBHI 2 in chronic medical conditions that are associated with severe pain is quite good. It uses relatively few descriptive words (on average eight words per item), which is about 80% fewer words per item than for the average BDI-II item. This makes the BBHI 2 administration go relatively fast, an advantage when it is used for quick assessment of progress at various stages of the therapeutic intervention.

One limitation of the BBHI 2 test manual (but not the instrument) is that it was published in 2002 at a time when there were very few documented publications supporting the utility and therapeutic benefits of the instrument. However, in reviewing the literature it is clear that there are now a substantial number of publications supporting the use of this instrument to aid in both the diagnosis and the prognosis for showing therapeutic benefits of various treatment interventions such as spinal cord stimulator implants (Devlin, Ranavaya, Clements, Scott, & Boukhemis, 2003).

Another concern, of lesser importance perhaps, is the name of the test. The authors apparently sought to de-pathologize the instrument by leaving out reference to pain and instead highlighting health improvement. The title Health Improvement instead of Pain and Frustration (for example) may make it more conducive for the patient to cooperate with testing, but it does not describe the test content as one might expect.

One big advantage of this instrument relates to the fact that in most psychological testing, medical patients often produce elevated scores on measures of somatization because patients obviously report more medical symptoms. The BBHI 2 scale addresses symptoms of somatization, and/or physical symptoms of depression, with data stratified across disorders (i.e., cardiac, neurological, orthopedic, GI, pulmonary). Thus a high score on select somatic complaints would not be identified inappropriately as somatization. The intent is to be sure that medically ill patients are not wrongly categorized as somatizers. However, patients can still be identified with the stratification process to aid in diagnosis of a particular medical disorder and in directing patients toward appropriate treatment.

SUMMARY. The authors of this instrument have produced a concise measure of several important variables in the lives of patients with chronic disabling pain conditions (Bruns, in press). They have included important psychological dimensions of anxiety and depression that will magnify or minimize actual symptoms for most patients. In addition, they have addressed the issues of fake-good or fake-bad variance that might be related to pending litigation and/or family manipulation issues. Now that research documentation has accumulated supporting many of the important validation measures for this instrument, there is little question about the potential for the BBHI 2 to serve both psychologists and physicians in the physical medicine and rehabilitation fields.

REVIEWER'S REFERENCES

Bruns, D. (in press). Chronic pain. In F. T. L. Leong (Ed.), *Encyclopedia of counseling*. Thousand Oaks, CA: Sage.

Bruns, D., & Disorbio, J. M. (2000a, August). *Functional rehabilitation of employees with chronic musculoskeletal pain: A comparison of two BHI measures of faking*. Paper presented at the National Convention of the American Psychological Association, Washington, DC.

Bruns, D., & Disorbio, J. M. (2000b). Hostility and violent ideation: Physical rehabilitation patient and community samples. *Pain Medicine, 1*(2), 131-139.

Bruns, D., & Disorbio, J. M. (2005). Chronic pain and the natural history of biopsychosocial disorders: The BHI 2 approach to classification and assessment. *Practical Pain Management, 5*(7), 52-61.

Bruns, D., Disorbio, J. M., Bennett, D., Simon, S., Shoemaker, S., & Portenoy, R. K. (2005). Degree of pain intolerance and adverse outcomes in chronic non-cancer pain patients. *The Journal of Pain*, (3 Supplement), s74.

Bruns, D., Disorbio, J. M. & Hanks, R. H. (in press). Chronic pain and violent ideation: Testing a model of patient violence. *Pain Medicine.*

Davis, F. N. (1999). Functional rehabilitation of employees with chronic musculoskeletal pain. *The Case Manager, 10*(3), 55-59.

Devlin, K. J., Ranavaya, M. I., Clements, C., Scott, J., & Boukhemis, R. (2003). Pre-surgical psychological screening in spinal cord stimulator implants. *Disability Medicine, 3*(2), 43-48.

Disorbio, J. M., Bruns, D., & Barolat, G. (2006). Assessment and treatment of chronic pain: A physician's guide to a biopsychosocial approach. *Practical Pain Management, 6*(2), 11-27.

Fishbain, D., Bruns, D., Disorbio, J. M., & Lewis J. (in press). What variables are associated with a wish to sue a physician? *Archives of Physical Medicine.*

[31]

BRIGANCE® Diagnostic Inventory of Early Development-II.

Purpose: Designed to "determine readiness for school; track developmental progress; provide a range of scores needed for documenting eligibility for special education service; enable a comparison of children's skills within and across developmental domains in order to view strengths and weaknesses; determine entry points for instruction; and assist with program evaluation."

Population: Developmental ages birth to age 7.

Publication Dates: 1978–2004.

Acronym: IED-II.

Scores, 24: Fine Motor (Drawing/Visual Motor, Writing, Total), Gross Motor (Nonlocomotor, Locomotor, Total), Total Motor, Receptive Language (Nouns and Early Listening, Actions, Total), Expressive Language (Isolated Skills, Contextual Skills, Total), Total Language, Academic/Cognitive (Quantitative/General, Prereading/Reading, Total), Daily Living (Self-Help, Prevocational, Total), Social-Emotional (Play Skills and Behaviors, Engagement and Initiative, Total), Total Adaptive Behavior.

Administration: Individual.

Price Data, 2005: $185 per complete inventory including standardization and validation manual (2004, 248 pages); $35 per 10 record books; $159 per inventory only; $40 per standardization and validation manual; $329 per 100 record books; $14 per class record book; $65 per testing accessories kit; $35 per 10 standardized record books; $329 per 100 standardized record books; $99.95 per scoring software with standardization and validation manual; $59.95 per Goals and Objective Writer software on CD-ROM; customized price information for web-based Screens Data Management System available from publisher.

Time: (20–35) minutes.

Comments: Criterion-referenced and norm-referenced; previous edition entitled Revised BRIGANCE® Diagnostic Inventory of Early Development (12:326).

Authors: Albert H. Brigance (test) and Frances Page Glascoe (standardization and validation manual).

Publisher: Curriculum Associates, Inc.

Cross References: For reviews by C. Dale Carpenter and Douglas A. Penfield of the previous edition, see 12:326; see also T4:2256 (3 references); for reviews by Stephen J. Bagnato and Elliot L. Gory of an earlier edition, see 9:164.

Review of the BRIGANCE® Diagnostic Inventory of Early Development-II by ANDREW S. DAVIS, Assistant Professor, Department of Educational Psychology, Ball State University, and W. HOLMES FINCH, Assistant Professor, Department of Educational Psychology, Ball State University, Muncie, IN:

DESCRIPTION. The assessment of infants and toddlers is a difficult task due to test-taking skills such as attention, receptive language, and executive functioning that are usually necessary for psychological and neuropsychological tests. The BRIGANCE Diagnostic Inventory of Early Development-II (IED-II) is a revision of the widely used BRIGANCE Diagnostic Inventory of Early Development—Revised (IED-R; Brigance, 1991) and shows great promise for assessing children from birth to 7 years old. The IED-R was a criterion-referenced assessment, and the IED-II represents an improvement upon the earlier version by providing a standardized and norm-referenced element. The IED-II still maintains the criterion-referenced component, and the norm-referenced section should be seen as an addition and not a replacement. The IED-II has several uses, including as an assessment tool, a guide for instruction, and a record-keeping system. It also contains a wealth of information about child development. The IED-II would also be a valuable addition to a school system, especially for children who are too young to undergo traditional standardized intelligence tests, but still need to be tested for placement into special education.

Both the criterion-referenced and norm-referenced components of the IED are administered via a combination of parent and teacher interviews, observations, or from an examinee-examiner interaction. The complete IED-II system includes an optional class record book, a developmental record book, and a standardized assessments record book. A box of toys and common household items is available from the test publishers, or can be provided by the examiner or examinee. The optional class record book is designed to be used by classroom teachers to identify children with similar instructional objectives who can be taught together. The developmental record book is what will likely be most familiar to traditional users of the IED-R and includes a system of identifying areas of developmental delay and obtaining instructional objectives. There is also a comprehensive skill sequence, which is useful for assessing children with suspected developmental delays and obtaining more detailed information about developmental skills. The class record book and the developmental record book are used for assessing 11 broad developmental domains: Preambulatory Motor Skills and Behaviors, Gross Motor Skills and Behaviors, Fine Motor Skills and Behaviors, Self-Help Skills, Speech and Language Skills, General Knowledge and Comprehension, Social and Emotional Development, Readiness, Basic Reading Skills, Manuscript Writing, and Basic Math. The standardized and norm-referenced aspect of the IED-II assesses five broad domains: Motor, Language, Academic/Cognitive, Daily Living, and Social-Emotional. These five skills are used to create an Adaptive Behavior composite. Both the criterion-referenced and norm-referenced elements of the IED-II contain several subdomains. The standardized component of the IED-II yields derived quotient scores, confidence intervals, percentiles, age equivalents, and instructional ranges. Although teachers and other educators should be able to use the developmental record book, use of the standardized and norm-referenced test would require training in psychological assessment in order to understand the statistics for test interpretation well.

DEVELOPMENT. Although many of the items of the criterion-referenced and standardized elements of the IED-II are the same, the development of the tests should be considered separately. The development of the criterion-referenced component of the IED-II is not well explained in the test manual. It seems as if extensive research was conducted to develop the developmental skills that are assessed by this test, and each domain provides a list of references that were used to develop the skill sequence that is assessed. However, there is little information regarding the logistics of the test development (i.e., pilot study, item analysis). It is also unclear how many items are new or were retained from the IED-R. The information regarding the standardized and norm-referenced component of the IED-II is contained in the IED-II standardization and validation manual. The standardized part of the IED-II likely will be more valuable to school and other psychologists who need norm-referenced scores for differential diagnosis or educational placement, and "the IED-

II meets state and federal assessment requirements and can be used as the educational and adaptive behavior portion of a battery that identifies children with learning disabilities, mental retardation, language impairment, or other exceptionalities" (standardization and validation manual, p. 1). The IED-II standardization and validation manual does an excellent job of describing the relevant aspects of child development that comprised the development of the IED-II, including discussions on developmental malleability, social mediation, and risk of disabilities. Akin to other sections of the manuals for the IED-II, readers will find that the standardization and validation manual by Glascoe would be a welcome addition to a course on child development and/or psychological assessment. The norm-referenced component of the IED-II was standardized under multiple settings with psychologists, teachers, and healthcare professionals, and the normative data provided in the manual are quite extensive. A panel consisting of child development experts reviewed the IED-II to select items appropriate for the validation study. The validation study was conducted on a sample that was roughly representative of the United States with regard to demographic information. The subtests were reviewed for reliability, and all were retained for inclusion.

TECHNICAL. Because part of the IED-II is criterion-referenced, there is not information regarding normative data for that aspect of the measure. This part of the IED-II seems to have been carefully constructed based upon the author's extensive review of the literature and in consultation with child development experts. There is no reliability information presented for the criterion-referenced component of the IED-II, but reliability information is presented based upon data gathered for a standardization study in 1991. However, as mentioned above, the lack of information regarding the similarities between the two measures limits the amount of generalizability from the IED-R to the IED-II. However, the internal consistency reliability statistics for the study were quite adequate. Because much of the IED-II is based on observation of skills, it would be helpful to have interrater reliability coefficients presented for all subtests. The manual does provide useful definitions of key psychometric terms for readers who have not been introduced to them before or who would welcome a reminder.

The standardization data for the norm-referenced component of the IED-II were collected on a sample of 1,171 children ranging in age from birth to 7 years old. The sample is somewhat representative of the United States population in regard to the ethnic background, parents' level of education, parents' marital status, and family income, though a disproportionate percent of the participants were recruited from health care settings. Data were collected from 24 states and territories with participants being about evenly split between males and females. Unfortunately, information is not provided regarding the neurological or psychiatric status of the normative sample, including no base rates of occurrence for any identifiable disorders. A large number of normative tables, stratified by ages, are available to provide normative data for domains and subdomains. More scores are available for older children to account for a wider range of measurable abilities. Quotient scores with a mean of 100 and a standard deviation of 15 can be calculated, along with percentile ranks, age-equivalent scores, instructional range, and confidence levels. There are no studies with clinical groups reported in the manual.

Glascoe reported reliability studies in the standardization and validation manual. Both Coefficient alpha and Guttman Lambda coefficients are reported providing information regarding the internal consistency for the five domains, subdomains, and the Total Adaptive Behavior scale. The values of alpha range from a low of .34 to a high of 1.00, with the majority being greater than .80. The Guttman coefficients were used as an alternative to alpha due to the latter's tendency to underestimate actual reliability. The Guttman values range from about .86 to .99. The test-retest reliability was explored with 36 children from birth to 12 months (test was administered twice within 1 week), and the author also reports the results from a study in 1991 that had 1,156 students (interval between test and retest was not provided). Coefficients for these two studies ranged from .68 to 1.00. Glascoe indicated that the new test items for the IED-II were "concentrated" between the ages of birth and 1 year, which accounts for the limited analysis with the new measure. However, as before, this study raises the question of the similarities of the test items between the IED-II standardization sample developed in 2003 and the one reported in the manual

from 1991. Readers may wonder if this version of the IED-II was used in 1991 (for all items except the 0- to 12-months study).

Interrater reliability, in the form of percent agreement, is reported from a 1988 study (Brulle & Ivarie, 1988, as cited in the IED-II standardizaiton and validation manual) in which two experienced teachers assessed 20 children with 17 of 22 subtests, obtaining percentages above .60. Glascoe reported that interrater reliability was assessed for the 2003 standardization sample "by having a second examiner retest thirty-six children with the IED-II. Children were retested within one week" (standardization and validation manual, p. 98). Results are provided that combine these two interrater reliability studies, with percentages ranging from .82 to .98. However, the second component of this study deviates from the traditional approach of interrater reliability in which two individuals simultaneously observe the same individual. It would have been preferable if the authors had addressed the issue of interrater reliability using Generalizability Theory and/or Kappa, both of which have been shown to be superior to simple rater agreement (Shouki, 2004).

The validity of the norm-referenced component of the IED-II was assessed in a number of ways, including measures of content, construct, concurrent, and discriminant validity. The content validity of the IED-II was established by extensive reviews of the literature and with help from child development experts. There is also a study that shows that the raw scores increase as children of increasing ages are tested (which should happen for a test that assesses the progression of developmental skills). Although the manual refers to this analysis as a content validity study, it can more correctly be thought of as evidence of construct validity, in that theory would suggest that as children age their scores on a developmental measure would increase.

The construct validity was determined by examining intercorrelations among all of the IED-II subtests and through factor analysis. The correlations among the subtests were generally adequate, though the results consist primarily of a very large table with very little explanatory text. Although the authors discuss in general terms the generally high correlation values among the subtests designed for very young children, they do not describe which subtests these might be. Given that the correlations presented in the table range from below .2 to nearly 1.0, it would have been helpful had they described more fully how these values support the construct validity. Nonetheless, the values do tend to be high, which arguably supports the construct validity of the instrument. The underlying factor structure was examined using a factor analysis with varimax rotation, which yielded a three-structure solution accounting for 84% of the total variance. Glascoe indicated the three factors were: Understanding and Expressing, Movement and Social Activity, and Academic/Preacademic. Although some of the factor compositions seem to fit with these labels intuitively, others do not. For example, Quantitative/General load highly on Understanding and Expressing, but not Academic/Preacademic, and the same pattern is found for the Nouns and Early Listening domain. In addition, some of the domains appear to be strongly associated with multiple factors, including Writing, Actions, Prereading/Reading, Prevocational and Self-Help, which calls into question the integrity of the factor structure posited by the authors. This problem is not addressed in the manual. It would be beneficial for future research to attempt to validate the structure identified in this study using confirmatory factor analysis.

The concurrent validity was assessed with a sample of 484 children who were part of the standardization sample. The children were administered comprehensive measures of cognitive, achievement, language, motor, social-emotional, and adaptive behavior skills. Glascoe reported that the concurrent validity studies used widely acknowledged and respected measures for their respective domains and listed and explained each in the standardization and validation manual. The correlations are reported between the IED-II and "Other Diagnostic Measures," but it is unclear how the variables were formed for the other measures; they seem to be combined from several measures. For example, the results are presented with correlations between IED-II domains and the variable "Academic/Cognitive," but the author describes five measures of cognitive and achievement functioning that seem to have been used. There is also no indication of how many children of what age took each test, or what the correlations were with individual tests. Although the reported correlations are mostly significant, the above concerns limit the interpretability of these results.

Discriminant validity was assessed in four different analyses, where children were categorized based on separate criteria. One of the studies compared children who were born prematurely with those who were not, whereas the second study compared those identified as having psychosocial risk with those who were not at psychosocial risk. The third analysis compared those with and without known developmental disabilities, and the fourth compared those with and without "highly advanced development." For each of these small studies, discriminant analysis was used to differentiate between the groups using the subtests of the IED-II. The results of the analyses showed that in all four cases, the groups of children were significantly different on at least some of the IED-II subtests. Results are provided so that the reader can ascertain which of these scales provided the greatest differentiation between the groups under consideration. The authors do not describe the samples that were used in these discriminant analyses, so it is not possible to ascertain how generalizable the results are to practice. Neither the sample sizes nor the methodology used to classify individuals into the groups are discussed at all, nor are any demographics of the samples reported. Further discriminant validity evidence is provided in the form of a series of analyses of covariance comparing scores for children by ethnicity, parental education, and participation in programs for the poor such as Medicaid and free/reduced lunch. These results demonstrate that although there were no differences by ethnicity, children whose parents did not complete high school had lower mean scores than those whose parents did, and those who received government assistance had lower mean scores than those who did not. Finally, the authors present prior discriminant validity studies for a subset of scores on the IED-II that also appeared on the BRIGANCE Screens. They report significant differences on these screening instruments between children with learning disabilities and those without, as well as between children enrolled in special education and those not. In summary, the discriminant validity of the IED-II appears promising for a variety of groups. However, the lack of information about the nature of the sample(s) limits the degree to which the interested practitioner can generalize these results.

COMMENTARY. The IED-II is a valuable addition to the limited number of tests that can be used to assess infants and toddlers. The addition of the norm-referenced component to the IED-II renders this measure an important addition to a child psychologist's staple of tests. The measure is extremely well constructed, the materials are easy to use and administer, and a wealth of information regarding child development is contained within the test manuals. The multiple recording techniques make this battery a very flexible tool that could be used by a myriad of professionals, including teachers, school psychologists, and neuropsychologists. Teachers will find the class record book to be a useful tool for grouping young children together for instructional purposes. The IED-II would be an excellent choice for a school district that assesses a large number of children prior to starting preschool, especially because instructional objectives are readily identified. Indeed, the ease with which interventions could be designed based upon the criterion-referenced and norm-referenced scores should be considered a major strength of the IED-II.

The addition of the norm-referenced component now allows the IED-II to be used for identification of deficits with a normative approach. The norm-referenced standardization sample is of sufficient size (1,171 children) and is drawn from a sample that is approximately equivalent to the demographics of the United States. The large number of normative tables, stratified by age, allows examiners to make ipsative and normative comparisons using derived quotient scores, percentiles, age-equivalent scores, and instructional ranges. The previous version of the IED-II, the IED-R, is a well-studied and validated instrument, and the test manuals report several studies that were conducted with this previous instrument. The standardization and validation information for the norm-referenced component is contained in a separate test manual, and extensive reliability and validity studies were conducted. However, the limited amount of information that is reported for some of these studies is quite frustrating. For example, demographic data for the participants in the studies is not sufficiently reported and the procedures seem to be inadequately explained. For example, there is no indication of neurological or psychiatric status in the standardization sample, nor is there any explanation of any perinatal complications that could have affected this sample. In addition, there is a lack of

information regarding any demographic information (aside from the total number of subjects) who participated in the concurrent validity study, which is a problem because different numbers of children seem to have taken a wide variety of tests. Similarly, there is no information about the samples used in the discriminant groups validity studies. This lack of reported information is a significant oversight because it limits the interpretability of the author's quality psychometric findings. It is hoped that future research will appear in the literature that rectifies this omission, because this is practically the only blemish on an otherwise excellently presented test.

SUMMARY. The IED-II should be considered an important addition to any mental health professional that must assess infants, toddlers, and young children's developmental levels. This type of assessment is often necessary to identify children at risk, to help with differential diagnosis, and to create instructional objectives for these children. A major strength of the IED-II is the versatility of the battery. The IED-II could easily fit into the philosophy and practice of a developmental preschool program or a pediatric hospital because such a wide range of developmental skills are assessed, and parts of the battery do not require advanced training in psychological assessment. The IED-II is easy to learn how to administer, and it can be given in an interview format if direct observation is not feasible. The addition of a norm-referenced component rectifies one of the few limitations of earlier measures of the IED-II. Although extensive standardization and validation seem to have been conducted, at times the manual does not provide sufficient information for readers to ascertain the limitations of the psychometric information. It is hoped that the test authors or independent research will rectify this problem, because the IED-II is an extremely promising instrument.

REVIEWERS' REFERENCES

Brigance, A. H. (1991). *Revised Brigance Diagnostic Inventory of Early Development.* North Billerica, MA: Curriculum Associates, Inc.
Brulle, A. R., & Ivarie, J. (1988). Teacher checklists: A reliability analysis. *Special Services in the Schools, 5,* 67-75.
Shouki, M. M. (2004). *Measures of interobserver agreement.* Boca Raton, FL: Chapman & Hall, CRC.

Review of the BRIGANCE® Diagnostic Inventory of Early Development-II by LAUREN R. BARTON, Early Childhood Researcher, and DONNA SPIKER, Program Manager, Early Childhood Pro-

gram, Center for Education and Human Services, SRI International, Menlo Park, CA:

DESCRIPTION. The BRIGANCE® Diagnostic Inventory of Early Development-II (IED-II) is a developmental assessment battery with both criterion-referenced and standardized, norm-referenced options for children from birth through developmental age 6 years, 11 months. It is the updated version of the original BRIGANCE Diagnostic Inventory of Early Development (IED), published in 1978, and revised in 1991 (IED-R) (see previous reviews noted in test description above). The IED-II is intended to determine the developmental or performance level of an infant or child under 7 years of age. Developers suggest that it can be used for diagnostic purposes, and for classroom assessment, progress monitoring and identification of instructional objectives, and program evaluation. It also can serve as an instructional guide and resource, as a recordkeeping tracking system, and as a tool for developing and communicating an individualized education program (IEP).

Most of the IED-II is administered via direct assessment, although interviews with family members, teacher observations, group administrations, and informal appraisals of the child's performance in school are also cited as appropriate methods for many of the items. (Eleven out of 46 assessment areas on the standardized IED-II version can be administered using teacher/parent report rather than direct administration. Guidance is given about appropriate questions to elicit this information.) Administration procedures were designed to be simple and may be administered by early childhood professionals, or in criterion-referenced usage, by paraprofessionals under supervision. Individuals are encouraged to consider individual differences and to avoid rigid adherence to assessment procedures for informal, criterion-referenced testing, although using this approach does not derive valid normative scores (available only from the standardized assessment).

The criterion-referenced IED-II can be used to estimate skill development and mastery in individual children and to track changes even at short intervals (e.g., every 6–8 weeks). Skills are scored as fully mastered or not. Item numbers of mastered skills are circled, and initials are written to indicate use of parent report, observation, or direct assessment. No cumulative scores or scoring mechanisms are associated with a specific area or cluster of skills during criterion-referenced use. However, the manual suggests that users could compare the percent of skills mastered within a given area at two or more times to yield percent improvement during that period. The manual also suggests that one could examine the percent of skills mastered relative to the average number of skills mastered by other children that age (based on average raw scores for age in the norm charts) rather than based on the total number of skills in the area. Conducting this comparison requires use of the same items and directions as in the standardized approach, limiting its usefulness to users as a criterion-referenced measure.

The same developmental record book is used on multiple occasions to track progress by changing pen colors for scoring. A class record book can be used to summarize a group of children's skills and objectives for planning purposes. The developmental record book contains items ordered in typical milestone sequences that are in sufficient detail for most children. Additional comprehensive skill sequences may be used in situations where it is useful to have more intermediate skills in sequences to describe incremental progress over time. Supplemental skill sequences also are included; this category includes activities that may be a useful part of the curriculum and appropriate for informal observation and curricular planning, but they are not essential areas for assessment (e.g., puzzles, use of clay). However, neither the comprehensive skills nor the supplemental skill sequences are integrated into the content of the developmental record book, which makes recording these skills more unwieldy. Specialized materials beyond those found in most early childhood settings are not required; a testing accessories kit with 13 items is available for purchase.

The IED-II contains numerous items organized into one structure for criterion-referenced use, and a smaller subset of these, organized into a different structure, for standardized administration. For criterion-referenced use, items are grouped into 10 areas (preambulatory motor skills, gross motor, fine motor, self-help skills, speech and language skills, general knowledge and comprehension, social and emotional development, readiness, basic reading skills, and basic math) and further subdivided by content into 88 very specific skill clusters. Given the extensive array of content on the IED-II, users are not expected to assess all areas comprehensively in a single session; instead, they are encouraged to use professional judgment to select the most relevant skill areas for assessment and to consider the appropriate length for each child's assessment.

Standardized IED-II assessment. A subset of items in the IED-II may be administered as a standardized assessment to yield scores for a diagnostic purpose or to compare a child's performance to same-age peers. The items for the standardized assessment are identified with a special symbol in the instruction manual. Performance is recorded in a separate record book using the same item level recording approach (circles and underlines), with additional summative scoring sheets and information about suggested entry points, basal levels, and ceiling levels. Item and page numbers are cross-referenced between materials to support ease of administration. The standardized IED-II subset includes items grouped into five domains (Motor, Language, Academic/Cognitive, Daily Living, and Social-Emotional). Motor and Language domains each are divided into two subdomains (Fine Motor, Gross Motor; Receptive Language, Expressive Language). The domains are divided into 14 composite areas that are derived from 46 specific assessment areas that vary in applicability by the child's age. This structure is not identical to the structure in the criterion-referenced approach. Notably, no composite, subdomain, or domain scores are produced related to social-emotional development for children above 3 years, 8 months of age. For children 5 years, 8 months and older, the IED-II primarily provides information on Language and Academic/Cognitive Skills.

The guidelines for standardized administration of the IED-II differ in some substantive ways from criterion-referenced use. When the guidelines are followed during the assessment, the IED-II generates standardized scores at the domain, subdomain, and composite levels and a total adaptive behavior score. The total adaptive behavior score uses the median score across domains assessed to reflect overall skill levels. (At least four or more domains must be assessed to compute a total adaptive behavior score.) The manual encourages flexible administration procedures for criterion-referenced use, but strict adherence to administration directions is required to generate valid normed scores from the standardized assessment. The standardized assessment does not have alternative item sets like the comprehensive or supplemental skill sequences. Examiners follow one defined set of items that is often given in its entirety, but they also have the option of administering only certain subdomains or composites of skills that are most relevant to the child's needs. Components of the assessment may be administered in any order and/or spread out over "a few days" (p. 35) if needed. The manual reports that the whole standardized version of the IED-II can be administered in 20–55 minutes, depending on child age. (Twenty minutes of direct administration time is expected for infants, and 50–55 minutes is expected for most 4–5-year-olds.) Like many other assessments, the IED-II provides age-recommended entry points and requires examiners to follow basal and ceiling rules. The number of correct and incorrect responses needed to reach a basal or a ceiling varies across composite sections. Although the manual includes a table to organize these requirements and notes about specific rules are embedded in the standardized assessment record book, this variation has the potential to contribute to administration error by many examiners.

The IED-II assigns points for mastery of specific skills that can be summed and converted into normative data with confidence intervals, including developmental quotients (mean = 100, standard deviation = 15), percentiles, age equivalents, and instructional ranges. A developmental profile also is provided to plot quotients on a grid and to assess and discuss the child's strengths and weaknesses. Scores from multiple assessment periods may be plotted on the same graph to convey the trajectory of changes over time. The process for score conversion is well described in the manual, but the Academic/Cognitive domain uses a different process than other domains and may be a source of potential confusion for some users. Computer software to facilitate scoring and writing goals and objectives is available on CD-ROM. A customized web-based data management system and screens also are available from the publisher.

DEVELOPMENT. The IED-II is the latest revision of the BRIGANCE Diagnostic Inventory of Early Development (IED), initially published in 1978 and later revised (IED-R) in 1991. The IED was designed as a criterion-referenced instrument. The IED-R included a number of changes to content based on the sequences of development identified in the more recent literature, the inclusion of a Social-Emotional domain, the availability of an optional testing accessories kit, and the introduction of the comprehensive and supplemental skill sequences at the end of some sections. These changes are retained in the IED-II.

The major change in the IED-II is that content was designed and validated so that the assessment also could be used as a norm-referenced instrument when such information is needed. Prior to the standardization of the IED-II, the developers reviewed recent literature on child development for information about the content, sequence, and age ranges for skills. This process was conducted in a similar manner to that used for previous versions of the IED. As a result, some new items were added (primarily in the birth to 1-year-old age group, although information was not provided in the manual) and care was taken to ensure that item sequences were placed appropriately and were predictive of developmental outcomes and school success. A panel of child development professionals identified assessment content to include in the standardization study that was likely to be important in normal child development. The panel also reviewed standardization directions for clarity and replicability. No information is provided about item analyses or decision making about item removal to determine the final IED-II content.

Items were translated into Spanish, although no information on the process used to validate the translation of the instrument is provided. This Spanish version was administered to 8.6% of participants in the standardization study; however, a Spanish translation of the instrument is not publicly available for purchase and no information is available on analysis of differential performance between children administered the English and Spanish versions.

TECHNICAL. No reliability or validity information is provided for criterion-referenced usage. Unless otherwise noted, the sections below refer to use of the standardized IED-II.

Standardization. Initial standardization data were collected with the IED-R from 1,156 children who were 13 months to 6 years old. Detailed information on this sample is not provided. The IED-II is based on a standardization undertaken in 2003 with efforts to use a nationally represen-

tative sample of 1,171 children from all four U.S. Census regions. The overall sample characteristics are fairly similar to 2003 projected U.S. Census statistics for race/ethnicity, parental education, and free/reduced lunch program participation, with a somewhat more highly educated and urban/suburban-residing population than the U.S. population. However, detailed information about the sample size and characteristics, using the age intervals upon which norms were generated, is not provided in the manual. The standardization sample derives norms from a relatively small number of children, especially in the youngest and oldest age groups. In addition, 18 percent of the sample was recruited from Child Find or special education sources, but no further information is provided about the kinds of risk factors, delays, or disabilities this group had, any adaptations permitted in the assessment process for them, and the distribution of this group of children across ages. Like many other assessment tools, it is difficult to be confident that the IED-II norms are representative for children of all racial and ethnic backgrounds or all kinds of delays or disabilities at each age interval. In this case, it is a concern because norms were based on a diverse and relatively small number of children in each age grouping; special caution should be used with Asian and Native American populations where participation was especially limited and with those assessed in Spanish. (About 8.9% of the sample was assessed with a Spanish translation, but no analyses are reported about any potential differences between use of the two versions.) Despite all of these issues, the IED-II data show the expected pattern of ascending median scores across increasing age groupings, providing some support for the effectiveness of the sample to represent the expected set of skills.

Reliability. The standardization manual describes a number of actions that were taken to investigate the reliability of the standardized IED-II. However, the manual provides little description of the actual data for independent review and often combines data from the IED-II and the IED-R for analysis. For instance, they report that "all subtests behaved with reasonable reliability and none were removed from the pool of standardized subtests" (p. 91). A table describing the internal consistency of the assessment areas/subtests included in both the IED-R and the IED-II shows data from the 1991 sample assessed with the IED-R rather than the nationally representative sample given the IED-II. (Although the assessment area/subtest may have been in both versions, it is not clear if some modifications to those assessment areas still occurred, such as an addition of or revisions to items.) It does not include information on children 1 year of age and under or span the entire upper age limit. Although use of IED-II standardization data would be significantly more informative, the data shown suggest that the IED-R generally had strong alpha coefficients (> .80), especially when collapsed across ages and within assessment areas. The lowest alpha coefficients were found for children over 5 years old. In this group, over 36% (16/44) of the coefficient alphas were below .70, and 68% (30/44) of the alphas reported were below .80. The nonlocomotor composite had the weakest internal consistency, showing coefficient alphas from .61–.76 for each age grouping (.86 total, collapsed across ages). In the 2003 restandardization, Guttman Lambda coefficients were computed for composites, subdomains, and domains collapsed across child ages. These coefficients were greater than .85, and only one (Drawing/Visual Motor) was less than .90.

Test-retest reliability was high, with data for a sample of 36 infants spanning ages 0–12 months for whom the test was administered twice within 1 week (coefficients > .93 in all areas, except Daily Living [.88] and Social-Emotional [.83]). The manual provides test-retest reliability information at the subdomain level from the 1991 standardization study with 1,156 children (test-retest interval was not provided). To the extent that these findings remain applicable, test-retest reliability was good; Fine Motor (.83 total, .77–.93 within various ages) was the only subdomain with a coefficient less than .90 when collapsed across ages. In the test-retest data, children 61 months and older demonstrated the lowest level of reliability.

Interrater reliability was examined by retesting the same children with different raters within a week (although this procedure is usually used for test-retest reliability). Observed agreement between two raters was considered for 36 children 0–12 months old on the IED-II. These data were coupled with similar data on the IED-R for children at older ages and yielded good percentage agreements from .80–.98 across domains.

Validity. The manual presents several types of validity data. Content validity was assessed in three ways. A panel of experts reviewed the appropriateness of item content. Criterion-referenced item content and sequences, a subset of which forms the standardized IED-II, were derived by relying on existing and recent literature. Finally, evidence of content validity was gleaned from the broad use of the earlier criterion-referenced forms of the assessment tool by practitioners with feedback about its usefulness in ongoing monitoring and planning curricular objectives.

Although the manual describes that the IED-II "correlates highly with criterion measures of academics and intelligence, and of language, social, and motor skills" (p. 3), specific information about the correlations of relevant domains or scores with some in other individual assessments or even with performance on the IED and IED-R versions are not provided. The data contained in the manual (p. 108) do not allow the reader to know the ages of children tested and which specific tests were used in a table of correlations to support claims about construct validity, although correlations with these domains ranged from .51 (Social) to .88 (Academic/Cognitive).

It is clear that further demonstration of construct validity is needed. A factor analysis did not replicate the expected five-domain structure of the standardized IED-II. Rather, it generated a three-factor model (factors labeled: understanding and expressing, movement and social activity, academic/preacademic). Further, not enough information is provided in the manual to interpret the factor analysis results and age groupings on which they were based.

Discriminant validity was assessed by dividing children in the standardization sample into four groups based on the presence or absence of: (a) a birth history of prematurity, (b) psychosocial risk, (c) known developmental disabilities, or (d) known highly advanced development; group performance on various subdomains of the IED-II was compared using discriminant function analysis. The results presented are difficult to interpret without more information about the samples including the types of children's disabilities, degree of prematurity, or specific psychosocial risk conditions. As expected, significant differences in scores on the standardized IED-II were found between each of these groups; however, information to interpret the direction of these differences is not provided. Key data on the sensitivity or specificity of group predictions based on scores from the IED-II also are not reported. Further information is needed to support diagnostic use of the IED-II.

Other validity data are presented showing variability in scores for different groups in the expected directions (e.g., children in different ethnic groups, with parents with different educational attainment levels; different household income levels). The manual also reports data showing that children's performance did not differ significantly between those recruited from general medical settings (pediatric offices, public health clinics) and those from educational settings (day care, preschool, Head Start). However, children from both medical and educational settings displayed significantly higher scores than children recruited from Child Find and special education settings, supporting usefulness in distinctions between these populations.

The manual also offers validity information about the IED-II based on data from the BRIGANCE Screens (i.e., based on some overlapping items). This information is difficult to assess because details and data from the other research were not provided in the IED-II manual.

COMMENTARY. The IED-II builds on a long history of development and use as a criterion-referenced assessment. The IED-II retains the established approach of informing about developmental progress over time by periodically assessing achievement of predictive developmental skills or milestones, categorized by common sequences and domains. Consistent with other commonly used assessment tools, the IED-II was not derived from a specific theoretical approach and has not focused item selection around functional performance of skills. Although the IED-II is not based on a fully integrated curriculum, skills within a curriculum were carefully considered to try to provide content so that the curriculum-referenced IED-II could inform and guide curricular objectives. Care was taken to develop and refine item content and create sequences of items that were consistent with the developmental literature and also were comprehensive enough to be useful for intervention and curricular planning. Thus, the IED-II will likely continue in its tradition of usefulness for this practice.

The manual and supporting materials are well-written to help individuals from a wide range of backgrounds administer and use the IED-II to support their ongoing work with children. The manual includes a case example of a developmental evaluation and practical suggestions for effective assessment, for example. More clearly outlining changes in item content from the IED-R to the IED-II and describing the reasons for these changes would have been helpful for users of the previous version. Existing item content is well organized and provides details about questions to ask, direct administration procedures, and/or focal skills being assessed. However, because the content is too extensive to administer in a comprehensive manner, the examiner must determine the areas to assess with each child. Thoughtful preparation also is needed to organize materials including copying any needed comprehensive or supplemental skill sequences, copying stimulus materials for administration in situations where sitting across the table from the child is not optimal, to flag relevant items or sections for administration, and to insure familiarity with cross-referenced page numbers and needed materials, especially for administration in home settings.

The primary change in the revision to the IED-II was to standardize and validate the use of item content embedded within the criterion-referenced assessment for use as a standardized, norm-referenced assessment to permit greater flexibility in use. This change will be helpful for programs currently using the assessment tool for criterion-reference use, but who require a standardized format as well for diagnostic or reporting purposes. Although both the criterion- and norm-referenced IED-II assessment share one manual (norm-referenced items are an identified subset of criterion-referenced items), they function effectively as two separate assessment tools with separate scoring books (standardized items are not flagged in the developmental record book). Users who wish to supplement a norm-referenced assessment with additional content from the criterion-referenced assessment will likely need to use multiple scoring books despite the integrated manual. The two approaches also have quite different guidelines about the stringency of administration. Users need to understand clearly distinctions between the two approaches and not inappropriately apply normative information to the criterion-referenced IED-II; at present, there are no supporting psychometric data for use of the

IED-II in a criterion-referenced approach. Likewise, despite the comprehensiveness of the criterion-referenced IED-II, users of the standardized IED-II need to know that it does not provide scores in all areas at all ages. The standardized IED-II has a notable emphasis on language and cognitive skills after 5 years, 8 months. It lacks Social-Emotional scores for children older than 3 years, 8 months, but for younger children, it does contain a set of items about social-emotional skills that have strong face validity, making for an efficient assessment of this domain.

The standardization and validation manual provides some preliminary support for the reliability and validity of the IED-II in a nationally representative sample. However, the manual lacks sufficient detail in some instances to evaluate the technical merits of the standardized IED-II. Further, the manual presents information that combines data collected with the IED-R in with data collected with the IED-II. The standardization sample mirrors the U.S. population in many ways, including in racial/ethnic diversity and indicators of income. However, it appears that the children in this sample have more highly educated parents than is representative of the U.S. population, a factor that clearly relates to children's performance on developmental assessments. The large sample size is subdivided between many norming age groups resulting in relatively small groups of children, especially in those 5 years of age and older. As a result, data presented repeatedly show the greatest weakness for this oldest age group. Given the relatively small numbers on which norms were based and the lack of careful assessment of norms for specific groups, results should be interpreted with caution for racially/ethnically diverse groups, children over 5 years, children whose parents have more limited educational attainment, Spanish-speaking families, and children with disabilities or other special needs. Further research using this assessment tool with larger numbers of children in these populations would be a contribution to the field. These challenges and concerns are common to many existing assessments for young children and further support the importance of relying on information from multiple sources for effective assessment of young children.

Despite these concerns, the norms produced show the expected pattern of increasing scores with age and showed significant differences between groups of children in areas that prior studies have established to have different developmental trajectories. Initial reliability and validity information that combine the IED-R and IED-II seem promising, but the appropriateness of combining these data is questionable. Further analyses with the 2003 standardization sample data are needed. These should include analyzing data in smaller age groups, providing further attention to construct validity, and analyzing sensitivity and specificity information when the IED-II is used for diagnostic purposes. Additional studies to establish the other psychometric characteristics of both the criterion-referenced and the standardized IED-II, including reliability, validity, sensitivity to monitoring individual child change longitudinally, and usefulness in evaluating outcomes in programs, will be a service to the field. Many individuals who are already committed to using the IED-II as a criterion-referenced tool should find use of the standardized approach a useful extension to further inform understanding about a child's development.

SUMMARY. The IED-II retains many of the features of the criterion-referenced tool that users have appreciated for many years. The IED-II now offers two distinct assessment tools, including the flexibility of a standardized assessment tool that follows a format similar to that of the criterion-referenced one. However, the standardized tool needs additional psychometric validation data than are presented in the manual. Users of this tool are advised to use multiple sources of information until further psychometric information is available.

[32]

BRIGANCE® Early Preschool Screen-II.

Purpose: Criterion-referenced and norm-referenced screen designed to identify "those who may have developmental problems such as language impairments, learning disabilities, or cognitive delays"; also used to "identify children who may have academic talent or intellectual giftedness."

Population: Ages 2-0 to 2-11.
Publication Dates: 1990–2005.
Administration: Individual.
Price Data, 2005: $110 per manual (2005, 108 pages) with building blocks; $58 per technical report (2005, 262 pages); $38 per 30 data sheets; $48 per 10 class folders; $25 per Spanish directions booklet; $117.95 per Screens Scoring Software CD with technical report;

customized price information for web-based Screens Data Management System available from publisher.
Foreign Language Edition: Spanish directions available.
Time: (15) minutes.
Comments: Can be used to identify a child's strengths and weaknesses to determine what kinds of additional evaluations are needed; includes prompts for behavioral observations, and supplemental rating scales for parents and teachers; Screens Scoring Software provides percentile ranks, standard scores, and age equivalent scores; web-based Screens Data Management System reports individual and program-wide progress including growth indicators, cutoff scores, and other standardized scores.
Author: Albert H. Brigance (test) and Frances Page Glascoe (technical manual).
Publisher: Curriculum Associates, Inc.

a) TWO-YEAR-OLD CHILD.

Scores, 9: Identifies Body Parts, Gross-Motor Skills, Picture Vocabulary, Identifies People in Picture by Naming, Knows Use of Objects, Visual Motor Skills, Verbal Fluency, Builds Tower with Blocks, Total.

Subtests, 5: Visual/Fine/and Graphomotor, Gross Motor, Receptive Language, Expressive Vocabulary, Articulation/Verbal/Fluency/Syntax.

b) TWO-AND-A-HALF-YEAR-OLD CHILD.

Scores, 12: Personal Data Response, Identifies Body Parts, Gross-Motor Skills, Knows Use of Objects, Repeats Sentences, Visual Motor Skills, Quantitative Concepts, Builds Tower with Blocks, Matches Colors, Picture Vocabulary, Plural s and –ing, Total.

Subtests, 8: Visual/Fine/and Graphomotor, Gross Motor, Receptive Language, Expressive Vocabulary, Articulation/Verbal/Fluency/Syntax, Quantitative Concepts, Personal Information, Prereading/Reading Skills.

Cross References: For reviews by William M. Bart and Joseph M. Ryan of an earlier edition, see 11:49.

Review of the BRIGANCE® Early Preschool Screen-II by MICHELLE ATHANASIOU, Professor of School Psychology, University of Northern Colorado, Greeley, CO:

DESCRIPTION. The BRIGANCE® Early Preschool Screen-II is an individually administered screening instrument for identifying children ages 2 years, 0 months to 2 years, 11 months who might have developmental problems or academic talent/intellectual giftedness, and therefore would benefit from further testing. Additionally, the author purports that the screens are useful for identifying strengths and weaknesses, helping

teachers create instructional goals, and for measuring progress over time.

The BRIGANCE Early Preschool Screen-II includes separate forms for children 2 years, 0 months to 2 years, 5 months and 2 years, 6 months to 2 years, 11 months. Both forms measure motor and communication skills. The 2 1/2-year-old form also measures academic/preacademic skills. In addition to these forms, several optional forms are available, including supplemental assessments that elicit higher level skills than those found on the screen, a screening observations form (screens for various sensory, physical, and emotional problems), teacher and parent rating forms, and a background information form. Self-help and Social-Emotional scales and a Reading Readiness Scale are also optional; however, little information about them beyond norm tables is presented in the manual. The BRIGANCE Early Preschool Screen-II comes with a technical report manual, forms in triplicate for 2- and 2 1/2-year-olds, a class summary record (for teachers to track screening results for a whole class), test administration book, Spanish instructions, colored wooden blocks, and scoring software.

According to the manual, the BRIGANCE Early Preschool Screen-II can be administered and scored in approximately 15 minutes. Materials needed to administer the instrument are the test administration book, the data sheet for the child's age level, unlined 8.5" X 11" sheets of paper, a crayon, and wooden blocks. Directions for administration are clearly presented in the test administration book, along with time requirements, scoring criteria, and suggestions for skills/characteristics to observe while the child completes the item. The record forms also include information about the items, so that examiners familiar with them would not need to rely heavily on the test administration book while directly interacting with young children. In addition to recording credited items, examiners can choose to test the limits by assessing emerging skills. Total scores earned are compared to cutoff scores demarking suspected developmental delay and possible advanced development in 3-month increments. Separate cutoff scores are provided for children at risk because of psychosocial disadvantage. Scores can be converted to quotients, age equivalents, and percentiles for purposes of program evaluation and assessment of progress. The record forms also include space to record observations (e.g., handedness, hearing, vision), summary information when children are screened within a group, and recommendations. Procedures for conducting error analysis are also outlined in the manual, but users should be cautioned that such analysis is based on very small numbers of items. Finally, significant attention is paid in the manual to the measurement of performance on the Screens over time for the purposes of evaluating student progress, evaluating program effectiveness, and planning instruction.

DEVELOPMENT. Little information about the development of the BRIGANCE Early Preschool Screen-II is provided in the manual. The items were taken from the BRIGANCE Diagnostic Inventory of Early Development (IED). According to the manual, a group of professionals selected items from the IED, and these items were field tested in 35 schools spread across 13 states. The IED was a criterion-referenced measure of language, motor, cognitive, self-help, academic, and readiness skills. The instrument was revised in 2003 to include standardization data for norm-referenced scoring. The test author states that every decade instruments need revising due to changes in curricula and information to which children are exposed–such change is reportedly the rationale for the revision. However, no information about how the content was revised is provided in the manual. It appears that the content is identical. Content appears appropriate for the constructs measured, but little or no information is provided about *why* the specific items/skills were chosen.

TECHNICAL.

Standardization. As stated, the BRIGANCE Early Preschool Screen-II is a revision/restandardization of the 1979 version of the BRIGANCE Screens, which was composed of items from the BRIGANCE Diagnostic Inventory of Early Development (IED). In 2005 new data on the screens were collected. These data were combined with existing data from the IED-II (normed in 2003), the Comprehensive Inventory of Basic Skills-R (CIBS-R; normed in 1998), data from the original BRIGANCE Screens, and restandardization data collected in 1995 from four cities. According to the author, this collection of information ensured that the standardization sample in total accurately represented the U.S. population. A preferred method would have been

to include a sufficiently large and representative number of children in the BRIGANCE Screens-II 2005 standardization sample. A significant issue with the 2005 restandardization sample is that only 75 and 71 children, respectively, were included at 2 years and 2 1/2 years of age. More detailed information about the sample is not available. Morever, information about gender, race and ethnic background, and parent education level is not broken down by age.

Reliability. Internal consistency of the BRIGANCE Early Preschool Screen-II is .98 and .97 for the 2- and 2 1/2-year forms, respectively, based on Guttman scalability coefficients (*N* not provided). Stability of the Early Preschool Screen-II is not directly measured. Rather, results of the IED, IED-II, and CIBS-R for 1,197 children were used. Specifically, the items from those three instruments that are used on the Early Preschool Screen-II were pulled, and reliability estimates were calculated (i.e., .84 and .91 for 2- and 2 1/2-year-olds, respectively). The test-retest interval is not specified. Interrater agreement was measured similarly. Results for interrater agreement are aggregated for all children 2 years old and higher, so specific estimates for the Early Preschool Screen-II are also not available.

Validity. As evidence of content validity, the author of the technical manual states that the content of the BRIGANCE Screens was selected based on the test author's extensive readings of developmental and readiness literature. Furthermore, she cites literature touting the merits of the BRIGANCE Screens. The literature cited predates the BRIGANCE Early Preschool Screen-II. Factor-analytic results are presented as evidence of construct validity; however, these analyses appear to have been conducted on the original version of the BRIGANCE Screens (i.e., they do not include more recent data). Concurrent validity data presented in the manual are equally problematic. Information comparing IED-II and CIBS-R items found on the Early Preschool Screens-II with various measures (not specifically named) is presented as evidence that the most recent editions of the four BRIGANCE Screens-II (i.e., Infant and Toddler Screen, 15:41; Preschool Screen-II, 17:34; K & 1 Screen, 17:33; and Early Preschool Screen-II) are valid. Without more specific information, it is difficult to interpret these indices. Correlations between Screens-II factor scores and those of the IED-II and CIBS-R are provided, but are not sufficiently useful for evaluating the validity of the Screens-II. Accuracy of the Screens-II for correctly identifying those with delay and academic talent/giftedness was measured using two samples of children in 2001 and 2005. Accuracy is above 70%, leading the author of the technical manual to conclude that the Screens-II are highly accurate.

COMMENTARY. The BRIGANCE Early Preschool Screen-II is brief and focuses on skills pertinent to early childhood development. It is relatively user-friendly, is amenable to group screening, and it can readily be used for program planning and evaluation of outcomes. On the surface, it appears to be an appropriate choice for a developmental screener. Nevertheless, there are several problems with the instrument. First, the standardization sample includes several smaller groups of children aggregated to provide a representative sample. These samples include children tested 10 years prior to the current edition of the instrument, many of whom were actually tested with the complete IED or CIBS-R batteries (with relevant items subsequently used in analyses). Pulling items from a comprehensive battery is not equal to actually administering the screener as it is intended. Second, evidence of test-retest and interrater reliability also comes from IED and CIBS-R data, making it difficult to determine the reliability of the Screens-II. Third, evidence for validity presented in the manual is weak, using either earlier versions of the Screens, IED and CIBS-R data, or not providing sufficient information for interpreting correlations between the Screens and measures of other constructs. Finally, there are problems with the norm tables. Specifically, the cutoff scores used to determine children who are in need of further testing for developmental delay are high in some cases. For example, for children 2 years, 6 months to 2 years, 9 months, the cutoff score corresponds to a quotient of 111 ($X = 100$; $SD = 15$). There are also floor and ceiling problems with domain scores (i.e., language, motor, and academic) at some ages. The author states that the quotients should be used only for progress monitoring and program evaluation, but they are problematic nonetheless.

SUMMARY. The BRIGANCE Early Preschool Screen-II is a brief screener of development in the areas of language, motor, and (for 2 1/2-year-olds) academic skills. It has several features to recommend it, including clear administration and scoring instructions, some data (although not carefully specified) to support their accuracy for identifying children with delay and/or giftedness, optional forms for more in-depth assessment, and some utility for progress monitoring and instructional planning. However, the instrument is poorly standardized, has little reliability and validity evidence, and has problems with norm tables. Furthermore, it is not clearly stated in the manual how the instrument was revised, as well as how items were specifically selected for inclusion. These problems negate the positive features and leave the instrument seriously lacking as a developmental screener.

Review of the BRIGANCE® Early Preschool Screen II by GENE SCHWARTING, Associate Professor, Education Department, Fontbonne University, St. Louis, MO:

DESCRIPTION. The purpose of the BRIGANCE® Early Preschool Screen-II is to quickly identify those children between their second and third birthdays who are experiencing developmental delays or advanced development. The two versions of this norm- and criterion-referenced, standardized instrument are for the 2-year-old child (ages 2 years, 0 months to 2 years, 5 months), and the 2 1/2-year-old child (ages 2 years, 6 months to 2 years, 11 months). The former measure consists of 8 subtests in two domains (communication and motor) and the latter of 11 subtests in three domains (communication, motor, and pre-academic), with both having a total of 100 points. Areas addressed include receptive and expressive vocabulary, language, fine- and gross-motor, quantitative, color identification, and visual-motor skills. Supplemental assessment items, as well as self-help and social-emotional scales, are also provided.

This test is designed to be used by teachers, paraprofessionals, physical or occupational therapists, nurses, physicians, or other individuals who have been trained to conduct such assessments. Screening time is estimated at 15 to 20 minutes, and it is recommended that this instrument should be administered by one examiner rather than a team due to the need to establish a relationship with the child. Also, the impact of vision or hearing deficits on assessment results are noted, with the resultant need to determine if concerns exist in these areas. The test kit includes a thorough, easily used assessment manual, three-part NCR score sheets, a set of colored blocks, a technical manual, a directions book in Spanish, and class summary records. The administrator needs to provide paper, crayons or primary pencils, and a timing device.

Scoring is straightforward, as the examiner circles the correct responses on the answer sheet, multiplies by a point value for that item, and sums the scores obtained. Directions are simple, although some items do not indicate acceptable answers, raising concerns as to interrater reliability.

It is emphasized by the author that the major function of the BRIGANCE Early Preschool Screen-II is to identify those children in need of further assessment, and that the instrument should not be used to make decisions as to program eligibility. Cutoff scores are provided based on 3-month age intervals, with the recommendation made that children who score below these points receive further evaluation. It is also suggested that assessment sites consider developing their own cutoffs based upon community norms. Performance across levels of the various Brigance Screens is provided through tables of growth indicators in the manual.

DEVELOPMENT. The BRIGANCE Early Preschool Screen-II is one component of a comprehensive assessment system covering the age span from birth through 7 1/2 years, dating back to the publication of the Diagnostic Inventory of Early Development in 1978. The first of the screening instruments, the BRIGANCE K & 1 Screen, dates to 1982, whereas the initial version of the Early Preschool Screen was published in 1990.

The BRIGANCE Early Preschool Screen-II (along with the Preschool Screen-II and the K & 1 Screen-II) was revised in 2005. Adjustments were made in some test items to increase the level of difficulty and hence the scale ceiling, so as to reflect changes in the development of children, as well as updating of standardization and norms.

TECHNICAL. In 2005 a partial renorming of the Early Preschool Screen-II was conducted, involving 75 children at age 2 and 71 children at age 2 1/2; it is reported that normative data from four of the earlier BRIGANCE scales encompassing the years 1995–2003 were "folded in" with the

new data. Information from 2005 indicates an uneven distribution geographically, with the West being significantly underrepresented. Data as to gender, race, and parent education are presented for the entire 2005 group, but not isolated for the Early Preschool Screen-II. Reliability information from 2005 finds internal consistency (Guttman Lamda coefficient) to be .98 for 2-year-olds, and .97 for 2 1/2-year-olds; internal consistency of the self-help and social-emotional scales ranges from .88 to .93.

Test-retest reliability information includes data from previous standardizations, and is reported at .84 for age 2 and .91 for age 2 1/2 (administration interval not reported but indicated as a "short interval of time," technical report, p. 115). Specific content validity is not reported; rather, comments are made noting the history of the scales as a whole and the wide usage of the instrument. Construct validity evidence for 2005 involving factor analysis indicated for the 2-year-olds that two factors corresponding to the domains were obtained, with the 8 tasks showing significant loadings ranging from .55 to .92; for the 2 1/2-year-olds three factors were found to correspond to the three domains with the 11 tasks having significant loadings ranging from .45 to .91. Finally, concurrent validity for 2005 was documented by significant comparing the Early Preschool Screen-II to the Inventory of Early Development-II and the Comprehensive Inventory of Basic Skills—Revised. These correlations ranged from .66 to .97 dependent on domain, with language being highest. Finally, as a screening instrument, the issues of sensitivity (the ability to correctly identify possible concerns) as well as specificity (the ability to correctly identify those without concerns) must be addressed. A study using small samples (22 two-year-olds and 28 two-and-one-half-year-olds) found sensitivity to be .80 and 1.00, respectively; specificity was .94 and .73, respectively for the two age groups.

COMMENTARY. The Early Preschool Screen-II is part of a sequence of instruments that have a long history in the field of assessment of young children. It is simple to administer, provides supplemental assessment items and scales, has a user-friendly manual, and includes developmentally appropriate items. The directions in Spanish are a plus. Limited directions are provided for scoring of some items, so examiners will need to coordinate what responses they will accept as correct. The utility of the validity and reliability evidence is questionable due to the minimal renorming done in 2005 and the incorporation of previous normative data with the new information. As with many screening instruments, the cutoff scores are significantly impacted by age; for example, a child 2 years, 2 months, and 29 days of age would have a cutoff score of 47 whereas the next day it would be 61. Therefore, examiners are urged to be cautious regarding the use of the cutoffs.

SUMMARY. Those who need to perform screening of young children will find the BRIGANCE Early Preschool Screen-II an improvement over its predecessor, and will note that along with the other BRIGANCE instruments it is well worth consideration. As with any early childhood assessment tool, the results obtained will not only reflect the skills of the child but also the opportunities and stimulation provided in the home. Therefore, examiners must use the information carefully so as to avoid cultural or economical bias.

[33]
BRIGANCE® K & 1 Screen-II.

Purpose: Criterion-referenced and norm-referenced screen designed to "identify quickly and accurately those who may have developmental problems such as language impairments, learning disabilities, or cognitive delays"; also used to "identify children who may have academic talent or intellectual giftedness."

Population: Grades K, 1.

Publication Dates: 1982-2005.

Administration: Individual.

Price Data, 2005: $110 per manual with building blocks; $58 per technical report; $38 per 30 data sheets; $48 per 10 class folders; $25 per Spanish directions booklet; $117.95 per Screens Scoring Software CD with technical report; customized price information for web-based Screens Data Management System available from publisher.

Foreign Language Edition: Spanish directions available.

Time: (15) minutes.

Comments: Can be used to identify a child's strengths and weaknesses in order to determine what kinds of additional evaluations are needed; includes prompts for behavioral observations, and supplemental rating scales for parents and teachers; Screens Scoring Software provides percentile ranks, standard scores, and age equivalent scores; web-based Screens Data Management System reports individual and program-wide progress including growth indicators, cutoff scores.

Authors: Albert H. Brigance (test) and Frances Page Glascoe (technical report).

Publisher: Curriculum Associates, Inc.

a) KINDERGARTEN.

Scores, 14: Personal Data Response, Identifies Body Parts, Gross-Motor Skills, Color Recognition, Visual Motor Skills, Draws a Person (Body Image), Prints Personal Data, Rote Counting, Numeral Comprehension, Number Readiness, Reads Uppercase Letters, Alternate-Reads Lowercase Letters, Syntax and Fluency, Total.

b) FIRST GRADE.

Scores, 13: Personal Data Response, Recites Alphabet, Visual Discrimination-Lowercase Letters and Words, Reads Lowercase Letters, Auditory Discrimination, Phonemic Awareness and Decoding, Listening Vocabulary Comprehension, Word Recognition, Draws a Person (Body Image), Prints Personal Data, Computation, Numerals in Sequence, Total.

Cross References: For reviews by Ronald A. Berk and T. Steuart Watson of the previous edition, see 12:53 (1 reference); see also T4:331 (3 references); for reviews by Ann E. Boehm and Dan Wright of an earlier edition, see 9:166.

Review of the BRIGANCE® K & 1 Screen-II by KORESSA KUTSICK MALCOLM, School Psychologist, Augusta County Public Schools, and Adjunct Faculty Member, Mary Baldwin College, Staunton, VA:

DESCRIPTION. The BRIGANCE® K & 1 Screen-II is part of a recently revised series of developmental assessment systems designed to screen young children for potential developmental delays or for giftedness. The K & 1 Screen-II is appropriate for use with children in the kindergarten/first grade age span. Information regarding a child's skill development in the areas of language, cognition, and motor functioning can be obtained. There are also supplemental scales provided to obtain information regarding the social, self-help, and reading readiness skills of children in the 5 years to 5 years, 11 months range. The K & 1 Screen-II was designed to be a criterion- and a norm-referenced test. English and Spanish versions are available.

The K & 1 Screen-II is divided into two forms for kindergarten or first grade students. The screening is composed of several basic skill assessment activities that reflect common developmental milestones and achievements for children in these grades. There are 12 basic assessments or subtests in the kindergarten level screening and 13 in the first grade level screening test. The tasks involved in these basic assessments include items such as identifying body parts, balancing activities, color recognition, rote counting, letter and/or word identification, expressive language, number recognition, drawing, and matching. The assessment tasks can be presented to children in a standardized fashion, so that normative information about the child's performance can be obtained. These tasks can also be presented in less structured formats in order to obtain criterion-referenced data used to monitor a child's developmental growth. The supplemental rating scales provided to screen a student's social-emotional functioning, self-help skills, and reading readiness skills are administered through parent/caregiver or teacher responses to provided rating scales. Interview data can also be used to complete these scales in cases where a parent's reading skills are limited.

The BRIGANCE K & 1 Screen-II is an individually administered screening test. The screening tasks can also be presented as part of a station-based screening process with various professionals and nonprofessionals administering the evaluation tasks. This station-based approach is useful when large numbers of children must be screened. The administration process is straightforward with clear and simple directions provided for each task. It takes about 15 minutes to complete the screening assessment. Most of the materials needed to administer the screening items are presented in a flip-style booklet format. A one-page data sheet, with attached NCR copies that can be distributed to parents or other professionals, is provided to record student performance on each item. A few materials, such as paper and child-sized crayons or pencils, need to be provided by examiners. Group data collection folders are provided for those wanting to keep a list of student scores. Teacher and parent rating scales for the social/emotional, self-help, and reading readiness scales are presented in the back of the administration manual and can be copied and used as needed. Several other reproducible materials are presented in the technical manual. These include a registration and background information form that can be used to gather personal data for each child being screened and handouts to provide parents with ideas for building particular skill areas for their child.

Scoring the K & 1 Screen-II is a fairly simple process. Correct items for each of the basic assessments are tabulated, recorded on the right side of the data sheet, and weighted by assigned point values. The total score can then be compared to cutoff scores, presented in the technical manual, to determine which children might be at risk for delays, or who might be showing indicators of advanced development. Scores can also be converted to normative information either through comparisons of scores to tables presented in the technical manual, or this information can be obtained by use of a computer-assisted scoring program. Scoring can also be accomplished through an online process. Curriculum Associates offers to provide online users with an aggregate data collection system for maintaining information that might be used for system-wide program evaluations or other projects and studies. Yielded scores include raw scores, percentile ranks, age equivalents, and quotients. Standard error of measurement and standard deviations are also provided. The mean of the quotient is 100 with a standard deviation of 15.

DEVELOPMENT. The BRIGANCE K & 1 Screen-II is part of a series of four screening instruments (including The BRIGANCE Infant & Toddler Screen [15:41], the Early Preschool Screen-II [17:32], and the Preschool Screen-II [17:34]) that have evolved from the BRIGANCE Diagnostic Inventory of Early Development. The K & 1 Screen-II utilizes items that reflect curricular demands of kindergarten and first grade. The original version of the BRIGANCE K & 1 Screen was a criterion-referenced instrument that was revised in 1995 to be a standardized norm-referenced test as well as a criterion-referenced test. Users of the original version had reported a need for standard scores from the BRIGANCE Screen so that test results could be used in child placement or programming decisions. This prompted the inclusion of normative information for the 1995 edition.

Changes in the 2005 edition from previous editions focused on updating the standardization information of the test. New norms were developed. Some changes in items were made better to reflect current curriculum trends in kindergarten and first grades. For example, more items were added to include early literacy skills. A Spanish version of the test was also prepared.

Developers of the BRIGANCE K & 1 Screen-II noted that data for the 2005 standardization process were obtained from subject assessment information generated for the new version, as well as from selected information from the normative and standardization processes of other recently revised BRIGANCE tests (the inventory of Early Development-II in 2003; the Comprehensive Inventory of Basic Skills—Revised in 1998; and the BRIGANCE Screens in 1995). The actual process utilized here was somewhat vague. It was difficult to discern exactly how much of the data came from new subjects and how much was a compilation of data from the other tests. Data from 1,366 children's item and test performances were utilized to establish normative information for the K & 1 Screen-II. The descriptive information of these children was reported to be reflective of U.S. population demographics related to geographical region, gender, and parental education level, although it was noted that no children from major metropolitan areas of the nation were included.

The authors of the BRIGANCE K & 1 Screen-II noted that during the standardization process of the test when a child's or parent's primary language was Spanish the Spanish versions of the test or rating scales were given. No specific data regarding comparisons of scores obtained on these instruments with the English versions were provided.

TECHNICAL ASPECTS. Minimal reliability information regarding the 2005 version of the K & 1 Screen was provided in either the administration or the technical manual. Most of the presented data summarized research in this area on previous editions of the K & 1 Screen or on the Infant and Toddler Screen. The authors note that Guttman Scalability coefficients for the K & 1 Screen-II ranged from .90 for the kindergarten screen and .99 for the First Grade screen. The process of obtaining this data was not clearly defined in the technical manual. Some test-retest reliability and interrater reliability data were provided; however, again the procedures utilized to obtain this information were not clearly stated.

Validity information presented for the K & 1 Screen-II is generally based on review of predecessor tests. Face and content validity were suggested from reviews of previous versions of the BRIGANCE Screens and discussions of the match of test item content to early childhood curriculum. Evidence offered for construct validity noted factor analytic studies that identified a three-factor structure of language, motor, and academics. Analysis of the provided data, however, indicated some interesting results that suggested the factor structure was not as clean as might be desired (i.e., multiple high loadings on more than one structure). For example, the Personal Data item was found to have a significant relationship with both the academic and motor factors, yet there is no motor task involved with the item. Concurrent validity was based on comparing the K & 1 Screen to the Inventory of Early Development-II. Positive moderate to moderately high correlations were obtained; however, this was not surprising because the author maintained the K & 1 Screen-II was derived, at least in part, from these tests. Discriminant validity was purported to be demonstrated by references made to how well the K & 1 Screen-II can identify children with learning or developmental issues, or with advanced functioning such as giftedness. Results indicated there were strong positive correlations between children's scores on the language and academic domains and their developmental status.

COMMENTARY. The BRIGANCE K & 1 Screen-II holds good promise for being a useful screening instrument for use by early childhood professionals. The format and structure of the test does represent the long-term history and experiences of the developers in the field of early childhood assessment and education. The screening process is easy to follow, and the assessment tasks are related to basic skills required of children in the kindergarten and first-grade years. The flow of item presentation is child-friendly. The short administration time and ease of presenting the assessment tasks to children would be positive features for examiners.

The theoretical basis of the test is appropriate. Positive features here include awareness by the test's authors that development is a continuous process. This philosophy is obviously built into the structure of the BRIGANCE K & 1 Screen-II. Use of the range of the various BRIGANCE Screens could enable examiners to monitor and chart a child's development from birth through their first years in school.

The multiple scoring procedures and data management options offered are positive features of the K & 1 Screen-II. Examiners might find use of the online data collection system to be of value to monitor the effectiveness of interventions provided to different categories of children.

Another positive feature of the K & 1 Screen-II is the extensive descriptions and case studies provided by the authors to exemplify how results of the screens can be used in a decision tree format to identify students who are at risk for, or who may have, developmental difficulties. It is also a positive feature that the K & 1 Screen-II includes identification processes to determine potentially gifted children.

Weaknesses of the K & 1 Screen-II still lie in the amount of statistical data available to support claims that the test results are highly reliable and valid. The technical report spends a great deal of time summarizing previous versions of the test, as well as general descriptors of the types of reliability and validity information that can be generated for a test, but falls short on providing specifics for the K & 1 Screen-II. Additional research in the area would be appropriate and encouraged.

It would also be helpful for the developers to delineate better the exact process of standardization followed for the K & 1 Screen. For example, it would be necessary to highlight exactly what information was used from existing data on previous tests and what data were gathered from new studies/processes specific to the 2005 version. If subsequent revisions of the K & 1 Screen are undertaken, it would be wise to base standardization information on new data gathered only. A minor addition the K & 1 Screen-II that would be helpful to examiners would be to provide a space on the student data sheet where scores can be recorded.

SUMMARY. The BRIGANCE K & 1 Screen-II is a quick and easily administered screening system that covers basic functioning of children in kindergarten and first grade. The instrument holds promise; however, additional work on the psychometric properties of the test would strengthen its value for early childhood professionals.

Review of the BRIGANCE® K & 1 Screen-II by THERESA VOLPE-JOHNSTONE, Clinical and School Psychologist, Pleasanton, CA:

DESCRIPTION. The BRIGANCE® K & 1 Screen-II is a norm-referenced evaluation allowing individual and group comparisons. Items are criterion-referenced in that they sample a well-defined set of skills. This tool comprises two parts of a comprehensive screening system for children from birth to 7 years, 6 months of age. The Brigance K & 1 Screen-II includes protocols for Basic Assessments for screening children within the age ranges of 5 years, 0 months to 5 years, 11 months for the kindergarten screener and from age 6 years, 0 months to 7 years, 6 months for the first-grade screener. Each screen takes up to 20 minutes to administer and score. Basic assessments include preacademic/academic, communication, and motor domains with the goals of identifying children who may have language, learning, or global developmental problems, to identify children who may have academic talent, to provide teachers with individualized information for curricular planning, and to assist professionals in monitoring aspects of a child's progress over time. The BRIGANCE K & 1 Screen-II can be used for eligibility in remedial programs or to identify children who need assistance for other reasons. Entry using the basic assessment test book begins with Item 1 on both screens. Discontinuance is clearly identified for each item in the test book (generally after three incorrect responses); there is no ceiling. Performance is scored on a separate data sheet, which clearly identifies the page number in the administration BRIGANCE Screen test book with which the skill corresponds along with scoring point values. Scores in subtests are weighted, totals are compared to cutoffs established for age groups, and raw scores are converted to standard scores, percentiles, quotients, age equivalents (not recommended), percentages of delay, and deviation scores. Scoring software is available as is online scoring for administrators/teachers to track progress or view performance across classrooms. A Spanish-language direction booklet is available and there is a section in the manual for adapting the tasks for children with exceptionalities. It can be administered by teachers, paraprofessionals (after supervision and training), special educators, psychologists, physicians, occupational and physical therapists, speech-language pathologists, and early childhood teachers. Optional supporting information is available through ratings by a parent or teacher and is included in the Basic Assessment screen book.

DEVELOPMENT. The BRIGANCE K & 1 Screen-II was based on an understanding of the developmental nature of child growth influenced by environmental and innate factors. The manual describes the malleability of development through parental influences and quality early intervention or prevention programs as well as the children's own temperaments and personalities and how they interact with the adults in their lives. In addition, child development is moderated by age-related manifestations as certain skills do not become visible until particular ages. When skills are developing, they are inconsistent and can be targeted for instructional planning based on the results of the BRIGANCE K & 1 Screen-II. The restandardization of the BRIGANCE screens in 2005 used 1,366 children who were stratified on the basis of ethnicity, geographic location, and an estimate of socioeconomic status. As part of that restandardization, the K & 1 Screen-II involved 591 of those children. The BRIGANCE K & 1 Screen-II contains 24 brief subarea items, 12 for the kindergarten level and 12 for the first-grade level. Items were selected if, after review by a large group of teachers, diagnosticians, and curriculum supervisions across the United States, 90% of them agreed on the degree of correspondence between items and curriculum objectives. After these items were selected, field testing in 35 different schools/districts and 13 states was conducted using an experimental version of the screen and item selection was finalized, item content was clarified, and directions for administration and scoring were refined.

TECHNICAL. In restandardizing the BRIGANCE K & 1 Screen-II, data were drawn from 2005 standardization and validation studies; 2003, 1998, and 1995 norming data; and the online scoring service. As mentioned above, the sample was stratified across geographic location, parents' level of education (as a proxy for SES), and ethnicity. Separate norms were not developed to adjust for socioeconomic and cultural differences as the authors rationalized that an overcorrection for these "factors may lead to underidentification of children in need of special assistance" (manual, p. 99) and that they will continue to compete and be held to the same standards of performance as other children in the classroom. The manual provides item-by-item means, standard deviations, and standard errors of measurement for the BRIGANCE K & 1 Screen-II and for its supplemental scales. Reliability measures included those for internal consistency, test-retest reliability, stability, and, interrater and intra-examiner reliability. For internal consistency, defining the construct of developmental and readiness skills, Guttman Lambda coefficients were found to be .90 and .99 for the total kindergarten and first-grade child screens, respectively. Test-retest reliability was assessed as part of validation studies using this measure, the Inventory of Early Development (IED), and the Comprehensive Inventory of Basic Skills—Revised (CIBS-R), which all contained tasks found on the BRIGANCE K & 1 Screen-II. Results yielded concordance rates of .84 and .90 for total kindergarten and first-grade child screens, respectively. Interrater agreement was less well described in the manual, but for a small sample (n = 52) of kindergarten students, 96% agreement was found across two examiners. There were no data on the first-grade screen.

Content validity has been built into the measure not only through the authors' extensive work with developmental and readiness skills but also with collaboration of professionals in the field, curricular content being reflective of the skills addressed, and the similarity of the BRIGANCE screens to other measures tapping into the items assessed. Factor analysis revealed a three-factor solution for the BRIGANCE K & 1 Screen-II, which captured 74% of the variance. Factors included Language, Motor, and Academic/Preacademic domains with minimal overlap, which suggests measurement of unique dimensions have been made. Correlations of the BRIGANCE K & 1 Screen-II with the IED-II and CIBS-R ranged from .67 to .80 for the Kindergarten Total screen and from .68 to .83 for the First-Grade Total screen. Factor scores all demonstrated adequate-to-strong correlations on the criterion measures as did the supplemental measures. As a result, concurrent validity was easily demonstrated. Discriminant validity was established by categorizing children into two groups from their assessment results on the CIBS-R or IED-II, typically developing/gifted or delayed. Average performance in the two groups was calculated. The BRIGANCE K & 1 Screen-II discriminated between those who were average or advanced (p < .01) and those who were developmentally delayed (p < .005). As a screening tool, it was important for the BRIGANCE K & 1

Screen-II to identify accurately children with true problems (i.e., sensitivity) and those without true difficulties (i.e., specificity) by using optimal cut-off scores. For screening measures, the author cited values of 70% or better to be appropriate. When analyses were conducted to determine cut-off scores, correct identifications of delayed children were .91 for the Kindergarten screen and .84 for the First-Grade screen. Excellent sensitivity was also found for identifying gifted/talented children (.81 for the Kindergarten screen and .80 for the First-Grade screen). The results of the reliability and validity studies demonstrated to this reviewer that the BRIGANCE K & 1 Screen-II are highly reliable tools. They sample readiness skills considered to be important, measure dimensions of developmental and readiness skills, correlate with more comprehensive measures, discriminate between patterns of performance in children, and identify children with and without developmental problems.

COMMENTARY. This edition of the BRIGANCE K & 1 Screen-II has many advantages. Using the screens with children at risk for academic difficulty may provide the test user with a wealth of information useful in identifying risk factors, making referral decisions, improving instruction for the child, and evaluating student progress by using growth indicators. It guides the assessor to specific items in the broader BRIGANCE Inventories that are prerequisite to the ones on the screener that are not emerging or mastered. The manual offers suggestions on building skills that can be shared with parents. The BRIGANCE K & 1 Screen-II offers standardized scoring and although age-equivalent scores can be attained, they are always to be used with extreme caution and are not recommended by the author or this reviewer. The screening tests can be administered in Spanish via the Spanish direction booklet available. In addition, adaptations for children with exceptionalities are suggested. The BRIGANCE K & 1 Screen-II includes quick measures that are easy to administer and score, and it can be used as a repeated measure. The screening stimuli plates are laminated and uncomplicated. Supplemental assessments are included in the Basic Assessments book and the data sheets are straightforward. Validity and reliability studies are strong.

SUMMARY. The BRIGANCE K & 1 Screen-II appears to be an excellent screening tool for kindergarten and first-grade children as it offers much information in a short period of time. It is easy to administer and score. Results of the screenings can be considered reliable and valid for appropriate purposes. An evaluator can feel confident that recommendations they make based upon an assessment using this tool for further developmental assessment or advanced assessment would likely be good referrals. The additional information provided for parental resources and supplemental assessments are helpful. This reviewer considers the BRIGANCE K & 1 Screen-II a welcome and recommended tool.

[34]

BRIGANCE® Preschool Screen-II.

Purpose: Identifies children who may have "developmental problems such as language impairments, learning disabilities, or cognitive delays" or "academic talent or intellectual giftedness."

Population: Ages 3–4.

Publication Dates: 1985–2005.

Administration: Individual.

Price Data, 2005: $110 per manual (2005, 104 pages); $38 per 30 data sheets; $48 per 10 class folders; $58 per technical report (2005, 262 pages); $25 per Spanish directions booklet; $117.95 per Screens Scoring Software CD with technical report; customized price information for web-based Screens Data Management System available from publisher.

Foreign Language Edition: Spanish directions available.

Time: (10–15) minutes.

Comments: Criterion-referenced and norm-referenced.

Authors: Albert H. Brigance (test) and Frances Page Glascoe (technical report).

Publisher: Curriculum Associates, Inc.

a) AGE 3.

Scores: 11 skills: Personal Data Response, Color Recognition, Picture Vocabulary, Knows Use of Objects, Visual Motor Skills, Gross Motor Skills, Number Concepts, Builds Tower with Blocks, Identifies Body Parts, Repeats Sentences, Prepositions and Irregular Plural Nouns.

b) AGE 4.

Scores: 11 skills: Personal Data Response, Color Recognition, Picture Vocabulary, Visual Discrimination—Forms and Uppercase Letters, Visual Motor Skills, Gross Motor Skills, Rote Counting, Identifies Body Parts, Follows Verbal Direction, Number Concepts, Syntax and Fluency.

Cross References: For reviews by Edith S. Heil and Timothy L. Turco of an earlier edition, see 10:36.

Review of the BRIGANCE® Preschool Screen-II by SHAWN POWELL, Director, Wyoming National Guard Youth ChalleNGe Program, Guernsey, WY and Graduate Lecturer, University of Northern Colorado, Greeley, CO:

DESCRIPTION. The BRIGANCE® Preschool Screen-II is one of the BRIGANCE Screens, an assessment screening system used to assess children from birth to age 7 years, 6 months. It is designed to screen children, ages 3 and 4 to determine if they need additional testing or special programming. It includes childhood development assessments across Motor, Communications, and Academic/Preacademic domains. It has eight subtests: Visual, Fine, and Graphomotor; Gross Motor; Receptive Language; Expressive Vocabulary; Articulation, Verbal Fluency, and Syntax; Quantitative Concepts; Personal Information; and Prereading and Reading Skills. When children perform above or below given cutoff scores it is recommended they should be referred for additional testing.

Formal training in assessment is not required to administer, score or interpret the BRIGANCE Preschool Screen-II. However, it is recommended evaluators using this test have knowledge of, and experience with, children in the developmental age group(s) being evaluated. Directions to administer the test in Spanish are available.

The BRIGANCE Preschool Screen-II is described as both a criterion-referenced and a norm-referenced test. It is a criterion-referenced test as it contains skills children at given ages should be able to demonstrate competently, such as 3-year-old children reciting their names. Specific cutoff scores for identifying children who should be referred for additional testing due to developmental delays or to measure gifted/talented potential are provided. It is also described as a norm-referenced test as it yields quotient scores, percentiles, and age-equivalent scores.

The BRIGANCE Preschool Screen-II has 11 assessment areas and routinely takes 15 minutes to administer. The total number of test items administered depends upon the child's performance. The directions provide clear guidance on discontinuing rules. The stimulus picture book contains colorful pictures and shapes. In addition to the data sheet used to record a child's performance on specific test items, the BRIGANCE Preschool Screen-II has observation, teacher rating, and parent rating forms that can be used to obtain a well-rounded assessment of a child from various data sources.

The BRIGANCE Preschool Screen-II manual provides numerous examples to assist examiners in learning how to administer, score and interpret the test. The test publisher also provides free web-based training to increase an evaluator's competency. Administration instructions are concise, and the data sheets contain clear directions for administering each test item.

DEVELOPMENT. The BRIGANCE Screening system was developed to assist in identifying children who may exhibit developmental difficulties, screening children who may be gifted or talented, planning instruction, and monitoring a child's progress over time. With these goals in mind, the BRIGANCE Preschool Screen-II was revised in 2005. The technical manual for the BRIGANCE Screens lists six factors related to child development and the assessment of child development. The first factor is malleable, described as the extent to which the environment either promotes or hinders a child's developmental progress. The second factor is the interaction of nature and nurture in a child's development. The third factor is age-related manifestations, described as the manner in which various behaviors and skills become apparent as a child matures. The fourth factor is the risk of a child having a disability. The technical manual cites research indicating 20% to 25% of all preschool children will need either prevention services, further evaluations, or special programming. The fifth factor recommends that school readiness measures need to weigh factors directly correlated with school performance (i.e., language abilities) more heavily than other developmental domains (i.e., gross-motor skills). The final factor suggests children display and master new skills in an inconsistent manner depending on their familiarity with their setting and the directions used to convey performance requests.

TECHNICAL.

Standardization. When the BRIGANCE Preschool Screen-II was revised in 2005 the new normative group contained 95 three-year-olds and 86 four-year-olds. The standardization group for all the BRIGANCE Screens ranged in age from birth to 6 years plus, and consisted of 1,366 children. This standardization group was divided into four geographical areas: south, west, north, and central and included 24 states.

The 2005 normative sample was stratified for gender, racial and ethnic background, and parents' level of education. The normative sample's racial composition was reported as African American (14%), Asian/other (7%), Caucasian (65%), and Hispanic (14%). The normative group for all of the BRIGANCE Screens revised in 2005 had 690 females and 676 males ranging form birth to 6 years plus. On the BRIGANCE Preschool Screen-II females outperformed males.

Reliability. Estimates of the internal consistency of the BRIGANCE Preschool Screen-II were obtained by use of Guttman's Lambda coefficients. The internal consistency estimate for both the 3-year-old and 4-year-old age groups was .99. The BRIGANCE Preschool Screen-II's standard errors of measurement were 1.29 for the 3-year-old group and 1.26 for the 4-year-old group.

Test-retest reliability estimates for the study conducted in 1991 are provided as evidence of the current version of the BRIGANCE Preschool Screen-II. No newer studies of the test-retest reliability are proved in the technical manual.

Interrater reliability is discussed in the technical manual for the BRIGANCE Preschool Screen-II. Studies showing interrater agreement for this specific test are not provided. The technical manual presents evidence of interrator reliability, ranging from .80 to .96, across the three domains measured by all the BRIGANCE Screens.

Validity. The validity of the BRIGANCE Preschool Screen-II is provided in the form of content validity, construct validity, concurrent validity, and discriminate validity. The test's content validity is provided by research studies conducted in 1984, 1985, and 1986. The technical manual also references that concept developmental scores should increase with age and suggests the test has good content validity as the median test scores of the new normative groups increase with age.

A factor analysis is used to begin to indicate the BRIGANCE Preschool Screen-II's construct validity. The analysis generally supports a three-factor model that corresponds to the three domains the test reportedly measures. The 3-year-old version has five assessment tasks loaded on the language domain, three assessment tasks loaded on the motor domain, and three assessment tasks loaded on the academic/preacademic domain. The 4-year-old version has four assessment tasks loaded on the language domain, two assessment tasks loaded on the motor domain, and five assessment tasks loaded on the academic/preacademic domain.

In providing evidence of the BRIGANCE Preschool Screen-II's concurrent validity, correlations with criterion measures ranging form .87 to .93 are presented. Discriminant validity is displayed in the form of correlations of the test's ability to identify children as either delayed or gifted and talented accurately. Presented data suggest the ability of the BRIGANCE Preschool Screen-II to discriminate between these two groups is best accounted for by its measurement of academic and language domains as opposed to the motor domain.

COMMENTARY. The BRIGANCE Preschool Screen-II is easy to administer, interpret, and score. It is most appropriately used as a criterion-based screening test of child development. It has the ability to predict if a child needs additional evaluations to determine if special programming is warranted. The concurrent and discriminate validity studies support this use of this test.

The BRIGANCE Preschool Screen-II's standardization is significantly limited, which raises serious concerns about its use and description as a norm-referenced test. For example, the sample sizes used in revising the BRIGANCE Preschool Screen-II are quite small. The 3-year-old group's normative sample included 95 children, and the 4-year-old normative group included 86 children. These small sample sizes do not allow accurate comparisons to a national normative group. Additionally, if the BRIGANCE Preschool Screen-II is to be utilized as a norm-referenced test the development of gender-based norms should be undertaken as females outscored males in the presented tasks.

Studies on the test-retest reliability of the current version of the BRIGANCE Preschool Screen-II need to be conducted. The technical manual does not contain evidence of current studies having been performed to obtain an estimate of the stability of the test's scores over time. Additionally, there is limited evidence of the test's interrater reliability.

Another area for additional study is comparing the current version of the Brigance Preschool Screen-II to recent editions of other cognitive measures. The technical manual does not contain evidence of the relationship of this to other measures of childhood development. This also reduces the test's usefulness as a norm-referenced test.

SUMMARY. The BRIGANCE Preschool Screen-II is a revised version of an assessment measure that enjoys widespread use as a screening measure for childhood development. It is based on sound development theory and is useful in identifying children who need further evaluation or special programming to be successful. Concerns with its psychometric properties reduce its ability to be described or used as a norm-referenced test. The major contribution of the BRIGANCE Preschool Screen-II to the field of childhood assessment is as a criterion-referenced screening assessment of child development and school readiness.

Review of the BRIGANCE® Preschool Screen-II by JOHN J. VACCA, Assistant Professor of Individual and Family Studies, University of Delaware, Newark, DE:

DESCRIPTION. The BRIGANCE® Preschool Screen-II is an individually administered, criterion-referenced/norm-referenced test that is designed for children ages 3 to 4 years. The primary purpose is to identify children who may have developmental problems such as language impairments, learning disabilities, cognitive delays, or have academic talent or intellectual giftedness. Major domains of development are addressed, and the results can be used by school systems and other related agencies that comply with the regulations set forth by Part B of the Individuals with Disabilities Education Act (IDEA). Part B of IDEA provides special education and related services for identified individuals from age 3 to 21 with disabilities in public-funded school programs or state-approved private schools.

The approximate total testing time of the Preschool Screen-II is 15 minutes. The author of the technical manual states that the results from the Preschool Screen-II can be linked to items on the BRIGANCE Inventory of Early Development-II (IED-II) in order to provide information for future assessments and the development of educational programs. Further, as with any developmental screening measure, the primary purpose of the Preschool Screen-II is to identify those children in the community who may benefit from more in-depth evaluation of their development due to concerns about the possibility of developmental delay or a specific disability.

The present Preschool Screen-II now includes items tapping literacy and phonemic awareness, which is reflective of increasing emphases seen across the nation on school readiness in early childhood and initiatives such as the Early Reading First where information is needed to help those children who are at-risk for school-related difficulties. This revised edition also includes standard quotients, age equivalents, and percentile ranks across each of the developmental domains.

Included with the Preschool Screen-II are rating forms for teachers, examiners, and parents. There is also a Spanish version of the Preschool Screen-II. The examiner is provided with a data sheet that lists the subtests, items, and scoring criteria. There is a maximum of 24 items per subtest. Some subtests, however, may have fewer items depending on the age of the child being screened. Materials include illustrations in the test book and a set of colored blocks. Other materials such as crayons and paper may be helpful to have alongside, especially when establishing rapport with the child.

With administration, the manual provides clear instructions for both individual and group administrations of the Preschool Screen-II. These include guidelines for setting up the testing situation, testing with parents or caregivers present, establishing rapport (especially with very young children), and positioning of test materials. In terms of scoring, correct responses are circled on the data sheet. All correct responses are totaled and then weighted to produce an overall score (maximum = 100). Total scores are then compared to cutoff scores respective of the child's chronological age. The cutoff scores reflect probable delay, normal, or probable gifted. Traditional hand scoring can be completed, or the examiner can use the scoring software program provided with the purchase of the kit. Online options are also available through Curriculum Associates, Inc. to enter data from the Preschool Screen-II and track the progress of individual children. The author notes that it takes 1 to 2 minutes to score. Case examples are also provided to assist the examiner further in accurate scoring and interpretation. The author is to be commended for also including a section in the technical manual on explaining screening results to parents as well as sections on working with children in at-risk categories. Finally, the author includes elaborate tables that align the Preschool

Screen-II with the BRIGANCE Kindergarten and First Grade Screen as well as the BRIGANCE Inventory of Early Development-II (IED-II). A third table is provided that aligns the Preschool Screen-II with the IED-II and the Head Start Outcomes Framework Mandated Assessments.

DEVELOPMENT. Much of the work that went into the redesign and updated standardization of the Preschool Screen-II came from the original works of Albert Brigance in the development of the IED (1979). Data from two studies (one conducted in 1995 and another in 2005) were collapsed to reflect the current norming sample. Demographics were based on the 2005 U.S. Census. Data stratified accordingly across geographic region, gender, age, ethnicity, and at-risk groups.

TECHNICAL.

Reliability. Measures of internal consistency were calculated using Guttman Lambda coefficients. Standard Errors of Measurement were also determined. Review of the values indicates strong reliability at the .99 levels and corresponding narrow *SEM*s of 1.29 and 1.26. Similar values were reported for the supplemental scales as well. With test-retest reliability (administration interval indicated as "short intervals of time," technical report, p. 115), moderate to strong values were reported for 3- and 4-year-olds (.53 to .99). Finally, estimates of interrater reliability were determined to be strong as well with coefficients ranging from .80 to .96.

Validity. The author reports that all of the BRIGANCE screens have substantial content validity evidence. Factor analyses provide ample support for construct validity and the developmental domains being assessed. Concurrent validity as a result is also highly supported. The author cautions that considering the recency of publication of the Preschool Screen-II, more data are needed for the documentation of predictive validity. Finally, with any screening measure, estimates of discriminant validity are important to establish to avoid the occurrences of false positives and/or false negatives. The factors of Language and Academic demonstrated the highest predictive power with coefficients ranging from .70 to .91.

COMMENTS AND SUMMARY. The redesign and development of the BRIGANCE Preschool Screen-II represents a significant contribution to the early childhood field. Given the national focus on school readiness and overall accountability, educators and professionals alike are requesting increasing amounts of guidance on how to identify those children who may be in need of support for their development either now or in the future when they are in school. Use of the BPS-II provides one approach to use when collecting information on children that can be used to qualify referrals for more in-depth assessments. The inclusion of the Head Start Framework and how the Preschool Screen-II compares with the outcomes identified in the framework is very timely and will benefit many educators in the field who need a system for monitoring child progress. The technical manual author's educational and professional preparation in the field of psychometrics and with children is clearly illustrated in the care she took in the design of the standardization studies and in the inclusion of the supplemental forms for parents and teachers. The instructions for administration are clear and the scoring rubric is simple to follow, and therefore use of the Preschool Screen-II is compatible in either one-to-one or group screening sessions. Overall, it is impressive to see an early childhood screening measure with such strong psychometric support and content that is consistent with national priorities.

[35]

Burns/Roe Informal Reading Inventory: Preprimer to Twelfth Grade, Sixth Edition.

Purpose: Provides information about the reading skills, abilities, and needs of individual students in order to plan an appropriate program of reading intervention.

Population: Beginning readers–Grade 12.

Publication Dates: 1985–2002.

Acronym: IRI.

Scores, 2: Word Recognition, Comprehension.

Administration: Individual.

Levels, 14: Preprimer, Primer, First Reader, Second Grade, Third Grade, Fourth Grade, Fifth Grade, Sixth Grade, Seventh Grade, Eighth Grade, Ninth Grade, Tenth Grade, Eleventh Grade, Twelfth Grade.

Price Data, 2005: $55.56 per Informal Reading Inventory manual including reproducible teacher pages.

Time: (40–50 minutes).

Authors: Betty D. Roe and Paul C. Burns.

Publisher: Houghton Mifflin Company.

Cross References: For reviews by Felice J. Green and Timothy Shanahan of the Fifth Edition, see 14:56; see also T5:357 (1 reference) and T4:343; for reviews by Carolyn Colvin Murphy and Roger H. Bruning and by Edward S. Shapiro of an earlier edition, see 10:37.

Review of the Burns/Roe Informal Reading Inventory: Preprimer to Twelfth Grade, Sixth Edition by JOYCE MEIKAMP, Professor of Special Education, and CAROLYN H. SUPPA, Professor of Counseling, Marshall University Graduate College, South Charleston, WV:

DESCRIPTION. The Burns/Roe Informal Reading Inventory: Preprimer to Twelfth Grade, Sixth Edition (IRI) assesses multiple aspects of a student's reading skills in an authentic format. Individually administered, the IRI is designed to match readers to text via identification of reading levels and a student's related strengths and weaknesses. Use of the IRI is not constrained by formal directions, time limits, or restricted procedures. Directions for administration and interpretation of the inventory are straightforward, although organization of the material in the manual could be better.

The inventory itself consists of two sets of graded word lists and four forms of reading passages from preprimer through 12th grade. Text is primarily narrative and both fiction and nonfiction. Essentially the graded word lists function as placement tools to assist the examiner in deciding where to begin administering the reading passages. Based upon the results from orally reading the word lists, the student reads graded passages that gradually increase in difficulty. These passages are then used to assess the student's oral and silent reading and listening comprehension.

As the student reads, the examiner observes and records strengths and weaknesses and asks questions probing for understanding and knowledge. The bulk of the IRI's diagnostic information comes from reading the passages. Each time the student finishes reading a passage, the examiner asks 8 to 10 comprehension questions. The types of questions asked include main idea, detail, inference, sequence, cause-and-effect, and vocabulary. Thus, emphasis is placed on learning about the reading skills, abilities, and needs of the student.

Although the classroom teacher working most closely with the student typically administers the IRI, the manual suggests it can be administered by a reading teacher or other trained professional. The authors also suggest instructors of developmental or diagnostic and corrective reading courses may find it useful as a training tool with preservice teachers. Finally, it is reported the inventory is particularly useful as a tool in planning instruction for students experiencing reading difficulties.

The authors propose both quantitative and qualitative information can be gleaned from the instrument. Grade equivalent scores as well as a student's independent, instructional, frustration, and listening comprehension levels are generated from the inventory. The percentage of word recognition accuracy and percentage of correct answers to comprehension questions are used for determining a student's various reading levels. Qualitative analysis can be utilized to determine individual strengths and weaknesses in word recognition, reading rate, oral reading, reading comprehension, and listening comprehension. Numerous forms are available to assist with the qualitative analysis.

DEVELOPMENT. Although the IRI is long on history, it is short on providing specific data related to its development. The IRI authors describe the construction of the graded word lists, reading passages, and comprehension questions; however, specifics as to the population on which it was developed and field tested are not provided. Other than noting the instrument was field tested on pupils in the representative grade ranges, specific details on the population itself are nonexistent. No mention is made of the population's size, sex, ethnicity, or location. Thus, the generalizability of any findings from the instrument must be questioned.

Although the IRI has at least a 20-year history, the authors provide sparse technical details of its development. For example, much of the development and field testing of the IRI comprehension questions appears to have been done with little more than classes of graduate students in reading education courses. In describing the development of the instrument, the authors frequently make statements, yet provide little supporting data. No mention is made about how the various comprehension questions were categorized. Moreover, they leave the reader to wonder what the rationale was behind their choices. For example, the authors indicate the graded word lists were randomly selected from vocabulary lists of two basal reading series; the reading passages were selected from three different basal reading series and leveled by the Spache Readability Formula and the Fry Readability Formula. Why were these particular reading series selected as the basis for the reading passages? Other than readability, exactly what were the criteria for their inclusion in the inventory?

Reportedly the second edition updated the passages to be representative of minority groups. No mention is made as to how many or what minority groups were given consideration. Generalizability is called into question. Passages and questions were revised for the third edition so as to be timely and of high interest. Operational definitions for timely and high interest are not provided. Apparently in field testing the passages the authors did little more than ask students if they liked the stories. What children and how many were asked?

Except for the addition of an appendix listing leveled books and their authors, the current edition of the IRI remains unchanged from the previous edition. Each of the levels has as many as 21 and as few as 6 books listed. The authors indicate they could be used for recreation or instruction and are at the appropriate reading level. Other than reading level, specific criteria or a further explanation for their inclusion is not provided. The relative utility of such a resource has to be questioned given more extensive lists are readily available from other sources such as the internet.

TECHNICAL. Although the IRI was first developed over 20 years ago, the current edition still does not address technical adequacy. To date the IRI authors have not reported nor discussed any type of reliability evidence. Not even interrater reliability, one of the most basic of all types of reliabilities, has been addressed. Because passage selection is not prescribed and examiners can administer any of the passages at a given reading level, alternate forms reliability of the IRI is an important consideration (Spector, 2005). Yet it is not addressed in the manual. Although the authors suggest the IRI is useful for instructional planning with students in resource rooms and reading clinics, caution should be exercised when using this instrument to make such high stakes decisions as determining eligibility for receiving services for reading difficulties.

COMMENTARY. Despite the fact IRIs are time-honored assessment tools in education, one has to ask if the time has not come to address technical adequacy. Although the IRI may be regarded as a harmless tool because it is not a standardized test, any instrument has the potential for harm if its results are misleading or utilized inappropriately. Recently, developers of some IRIs have begun addressing the technical adequacy of their instruments. In a study of nine manuals from recently revised IRIs including the Burns/Roe IRI, Spector (2005) found four had reported reliability evidence. Using Burns/Roe IRI results to determine whether or not a student requires intervention for reading difficulties is a high stakes decision. Although reliability alone does not define technical adequacy, without it an instrument has limited usage.

SUMMARY. Much of the inherent attraction of the Burns/Roe IRI is its relevance and close resemblance to the reading process. However, the current edition of the Burns/Roe IRI is sorely in need of even the most basic attention to technical adequacy. Caution should be exercised in utilizing results for high stakes decisions that impact the lives of students.

REVIEWERS' REFERENCE

Spector, J. E. (2005). How reliable are informal reading inventories? *Psychology in the Schools, 42*, 593–603.

Review of Burns/Roe Informal Reading Inventory: Preprimer to Twelfth Grade, Sixth Edition by RAYNE A. SPERLING, Associate Professor of Educational Psychology, and CRYSTAL M. RAMSAY, Doctoral Student, Pennsylvania State University, University Park, PA:

DESCRIPTION. The Burns/Roe Informal Reading Inventory (IRI), as with other available informal reading inventories (e.g., Shanker & Ekwall, 2000; Stieglitz, 2002), is designed for use as a diagnostic assessment to determine a student's reading level. Teachers, clinicians, special educators, reading specialists, school psychologists, and other practitioners and researchers commonly use informal reading inventories to diagnose students' reading levels. The information gained from administration of an IRI is used to plan instruction as well as to determine appropriate reading materials for individual learners. The Burns/Roe Informal Reading Inventory includes word lists, listening comprehension tests, and independent reading comprehension assessments. The new edition also includes a list of leveled trade books that can be used in classroom instruction. For convenience, all of the test materials are provided within the manual.

The Burns/Roe Informal Reading Inventory provides assessment materials to evaluate preprimer through 12th grade readers. Readers are assigned grade level equivalents corresponding to texts appropriate for each student's independent level, instructional level, and frustration level. The IRI also provides a listening comprehension assessment. The amount of time taken to administer the IRI varies as an administrator may elect not to give all of the assessments to a given learner. In addition to assessing K–12 learners, informal reading inventories are often used in assessment of at-risk college learners. Some research and the manual also suggest that the Informal Reading Inventories can also serve as an instructional tool in reading methods classes for preservice teachers (e.g., manual, p. vii; Traynelis-Yurek & Strong, 2000).

DEVELOPMENT. The Informal Reading Inventory (IRI) is in the sixth edition and has a long history. Previous editions have been reviewed in earlier *Mental Measurements Yearbooks* (see Green, 2001; Murphy & Bruning, 1989; Shanahan, 2001; Shapiro, 1989). The assessment has changed little since the first edition published more than 20 years ago, and concerns from the previous reviews remain unaddressed. For example, Murphy and Bruning (1989), Shanahan (2001), and Shapiro (1989) noted concerns with the lack of psychometric properties available for the assessment, and Green (2001) noted concerns that pronunciation guides were not provided for international names in the passages. No new passages have been added since the revisions made to the third edition of the assessment. The fourth and fifth editions focused on revisions that expanded and clarified directions (manual, p. 226). As noted, the new edition includes graded reading lists. These reading lists are recommended for assigning texts to learners. The word lists in the assessment were developed from two prominent basal reading series (manual, p. 225). It seems that these word lists have remained constant for all six editions of the IRI. The reading passages rely on grade equivalents established by the Spache readability formula (Spache, 1953) and the Fry Readability graph (Fry, 1977). The Spache formula is best used to assess primary grade texts and therefore may be of limited value for the range of texts used in the assessment (e.g., Wright, 2006). In contrast, the Fry graph remains a commonly used technique to assess readability (Sperling, 2006).

TECHNICAL. As noted in previous reviews (e.g., Murphy and Bruning, 1989; Shanahan, 2001; Shapiro, 1989), a serious limitation of the Burns/ Roe Informal Reading Inventory is the lack of any evidence of its psychometric properties. The IRI does not include standardization information as is available for a limited number of other informal reading inventories (e.g., Johnston, 1982). Although the Informal Reading Inventory is not designed as a normative assessment, the lack of psychometric information regarding the instrument remains problematic. The manual contains a flow chart to guide administration as well as scoring aids for each passage and suggests that administrators practice. These may also serve to increase consistency of administration. During the assessment, each reader's answers and errors can be recorded on a scoring sheet. Although initially cumbersome, with practiced administrators, the scoring sheets likely serve to increase the reliability of the scores from the assessments. There are opportunities to address other measures of reliability, but these are not reported. For example, students could be administered more than one passage per grade level, and an alternate form reliability estimate could be reported. Similarly, consistency within the answers to comprehension questions could also be reported. Further, test/ retest reliability could also be assessed. Of course, practice would inflate such an estimate if the administrations were too close in time and history, and maturation will play a role if the time frame is too large. Nonetheless, formal reliability estimates would enhance the assessment.

The comprehension questions are designated by category (e.g., main idea, details, inference, vocabulary, structure related questions). These categories reflect current beliefs about assessing comprehension and are supported by research literature. These comprehension questions, coupled with the word lists, suggest content validity of the assessment. Data from the administration of the component assessments (word lists, listening comprehension, and reading comprehension) can be triangulated, which should increase confidence in the obtained scores. Again, no psychometric properties are provided for the assessments.

COMMENTARY. As noted, most informal reading inventories are not standardized and few have psychometric data to support the technical properties (e.g., evidence of reliability and validity). The Burns/Roe Informal Reading Inventory is no exception and might best be used only with other information when making decisions regarding the reading level of individual learners. There are numerous informal reading inventories available, and most practitioners can use the Informal Reading Inventory with some practice. The manual suggests potential for broad use of the assessment. The amount of time to individually administer the full assessment, however, suggests more limited application is likely in practice.

Practitioners can use data from the administration of the IRI to assist them in developing instructional programs for individual learners. The data collected through administration of the inventory can provide recommendations regarding what level of instructional materials learners may be able to comprehend independently or with support. Limitations noted in previous reviews remain drawbacks in the current edition. Although previous reviews noted that the reading passages in the assessment included some diversity (Green, 2001), this is considered one weakness of the instrument. Most passages have a "traditional" feel. One benefit of the IRI is the wide range of learners targeted by the assessment. This breadth is also a limitation of the assessment. For example, the assessment lacks subword skills as are often found in other informal reading inventories, and the words for the older learners will be of limited diagnostic value. The largest benefit of the IRI is the compact and accessible nature of the assessments.

SUMMARY. Although with practice one can become facile in administration and recording, initially administration is cumbersome. Experienced educators and specialists often can readily obtain similar information about their readers through other measures and may not elect to widely use the inventory. Assessments such as the IRI, however, are often helpful in individual cases with learners who demonstrate mixed skill sets or inconsistent reading comprehension. In conclusion, the Burns/Roe Informal Reading Inventory can be of assistance to researchers and practitioners as an individually administered diagnostic reading assessment.

REVIEWERS' REFERENCES

Fry, E. (1977). Fry's readability graph: Clarifications, validity, and extension to level 17. *Journal of Reading Behavior, 21*(3), 242–252.

Green, F. J. (2001). [Review of the Burns/Roe Informal Reading Inventory: Preprimer to Twelfth Grade, Fifth Edition.] In B. S. Plake & J. C. Impara (Eds.), *The fourteenth mental measurements yearbook* (pp. 195–196). Lincoln, NE: Buros Institute of Mental Measurements.

Johnston, M. C. (1982). Johnston Informal Reading Inventory. Tucson, AZ: Educational Publications.

Murphy, C. C., & Bruning, R. H. (1989). [Review of the Burns/Roe Informal Reading Inventory: Preprimer to Twelfth Grade, Second Edition.] In J. C. Conoley

& J. J. Kramer (Eds.), *The tenth mental measurements yearbook* (p. 116). Lincoln, NE: Buros Institute of Mental Measurements.

Shanahan, T. (2001). [Review of the Burns/Roe Informal Reading Inventory: Preprimer to Twelfth Grade, Fifth Edition.] In B. S. Plake & J. C. Impara (Eds.), *The fourteenth mental measurements yearbook* (pp. 196–198). Lincoln, NE: Buros Institute of Mental Measurements.

Shanker, J. L., & Ekwall, E. (2000). Ekwall/Shanker Reading Inventory (ESRI), 4th Edition. Boston, MA: Allyn & Bacon.

Shapiro, E. S. (1989). [Review of the Burns/Roe Informal Reading Inventory: Preprimer to Twelfth Grade, Second Edition.] In J. C. Conoley & J. J. Kramer (Eds.), *The tenth mental measurements yearbook* (pp. 117–118). Lincoln, NE: Buros Institute of Mental Measurements.

Spache, G. (1953). A new readability formula for primary grade reading materials. *Elementary School Journal, 55*, 410–413.

Sperling, R. A. (2006). Assessing reading materials for students who are learning disabled. *Intervention in School and Clinic, 41*(3), 138–143.

Stieglitz, E. L. (2002). Stieglitz Informal Reading Inventory (SIRI). Assessing Reading Behaviors from Emergent to Advanced Levels, 3rd edition, Boston, MA: Allyn & Bacon.

Traynelis-Yurek, E., & Strong, M. W. (2000). Preservice teachers' ability to determine miscues and comprehension response errors of elementary students. *Journal of Reading Education, 26*(1), 15–22.

Wright, J. (2006). OKAPI! On-line manual. Retrieved March 5, 2006 from www.interventioncentral.org

[36]

Cambridge Prospective Memory Test.

Purpose: Designed to "assess prospective memory" (remembering to do previously planned actions).

Population: Ages 16 and over.

Publication Date: 2005.

Acronym: CAMPROMPT.

Score: Total score only.

Administration: Individual.

Forms, 2: Parallel Forms A and B.

Price Data, 2006: £171.50 per complete kit including manual, 25 record forms, quiz question cards, puzzle cards, message card, clock, and two timers; £36.50 per 25 record forms.

Time: 20(25) minutes.

Authors: Barbara A. Wilson, Hazel Emslie, Jennifer Foley, Agnes Shiel, Peter Watson, Kari Hawkins, Yvonne Groot, and Jonathan J. Evans.

Publisher: Harcourt Assessment [England].

Review of the Cambridge Prospective Memory Test by MARK A. ALBANESE, Professor of Population Health Sciences, University of Wisconsin School of Medicine and Public Health, Madison, WI:

DESCRIPTION. The Cambridge Prospective Memory Test (CAMPROMPT) is designed to aid clinical psychologists, neuropsychologists, geriatricians, occupational therapists, speech and language therapists, and other health professionals working with people who have prospective memory impairments. "Prospective memory is defined as the ability to remember to do previously planned actions" (manual, p. 1) and, to paraphrase some of the qualifying additional elements, executing them at the designated time or within certain time limits. Examples of prospective memory tasks include remembering to take medication on time or to keep an appointment with one's physician. Prospective memory function has five phases: formation and encoding of intention and action, the retention interval, the performance interval (where success depends on the person recognizing the retrieval context, associating it with a particular intention, and recalling the task conditions), the initiation and execution of the intended action, and the evaluation of the outcome. Prospective memory functions have been classified in various ways, but for the use in this instrument, they are divided into time-based tasks that must be carried out at a particular moment in time, or within a certain time interval or when a particular event occurs. The CAMPROMPT assesses both time-based and event-based types of tasks, a feature that distinguishes it from other types of memory tests. The CAMPROMPT was built upon experience working with the Cambridge Behavioural Prospective Memory Test. The CAMPROMPT reduced the number of tasks of the two types from four each to three each, reduced testing time from 40 minutes to 25 minutes, standardized the lag time across tasks before prompting occurred, and developed a scoring system that incorporated timing of the action and the action itself. There are six prospective memory tasks that the examinee carries out in a 25-minute period while they work on a number of "background" distractor pencil-and-paper tasks (e.g., general knowledge quiz, word-finder puzzle). Examinees can use any strategy they wish as a memory aid in conducting the tasks (e.g., writing them down on paper provided). Of the three time-based tasks, two are cued by a countdown kitchen timer and the third is cued by a clock. Both the timer and clock are on the table in front of the examinee. The three event-based tasks are cued by: (a) encountering a specific distractor task, (b) a verbal prompt from the examiner, and (c) a beeper going off followed by a prompt from the examiner. What the examiner does and says is carefully scripted. Different sets of distractor tasks are provided. There are two forms of the exam to enable sequential testing without specific task remembering affecting scores. Each of the six tasks is scored up to 6 points. Coding is done at the time of the exam into alphabetic codes from A–H to minimize feedback to the examinee. The exact coding scheme is supposed to be described in the manual, but it appears to have been left out. However, the coding awards 6 points for

doing the task as requested at the time appointed, 4 points if there is a single prompt, 2 points if two prompts are needed, 1 point and 0 points if performance requires more prompting or if the examinee completely fails to do the task.

DEVELOPMENT. The CAMPROMPT assesses the ability of a test taker to implement time-based and event-based tasks while being preoccupied by light mental diversions. It is an outgrowth of preliminary work using the Cambridge Behavioural Prospective Memory Test. It was developed by shortening (from 45 minutes to 20–25 minutes) and addressing some of the administrative weaknesses of the earlier exam. Two parallel forms of the test were created. Validity and reliability estimates were obtained from a study involving 237 participants the test authors refer to as controls who were recruited from a wide variety of sources. The exclusion criteria used in selection were a history of head injury resulting in loss of consciousness, other neurological or psychiatric condition, or learning disability. Control participants ranged in age from 16–92 and were approximately equally represented by gender. A group of 72 participants with clinical findings of traumatic brain injury (TBI) or cerebrovascular accidents (CVA) were tested as well.

TECHNICAL.

Scoring. The CAMPROMPT reports a single overall score that can range from 0–36 and is derived from summing scores from each of the six tasks. Task scores each range up to 6 points and are created by awarding the 6 points for task completion and then taking away points depending upon the number and nature of prompts that were needed before the task was completed.

Standardization. The CAMPROMPT has not been standardized in the sense of administering it to a representative sample of some specific population. The manual reports results for 72 participants with traumatic brain injury (TBI; $N = 35$) and various neurological problems ($N = 37$). It also reports results from a control group of 237 participants presumed to be representative of the general population. However, selection of members of the control group did not follow what might be considered an approach that would yield a nationally representative probability sample. However, it probably is about as close as one might come for such a "hands-on" diagnostic instrument. The characteristics of the control sample are described in sufficient detail that one can make relatively informed decisions about whether the results might apply to a given population of individuals. Norms are reported by six categories of CAMPROMPT performance (impaired, borderline, poor, average, above average, very good) for three IQ ranges (<90, 90–110, >110) and four age ranges (16–35, 36–50, 51–65, >65). The six descriptive categories for the CAMPROMPT were derived from various performance levels by the control participants (impaired: < = 5th percentile, borderline: 5–10th percentile, poor: 10–25th percentile, average: 25–75th percentile, above average: 75–95th percentile, very good: > 95th percentile). No justification is provided for the placement of the six descriptive labels to the particular percentiles.

Reliability. Interrater reliability was estimated from 22 control patients with a second examiner present at the time of the assessment. The correlation between the two examiners' scores was .998. Test-retest reliability was estimated from 10 control participants who completed Form A and then 7–10 days later completed Form B and another 10 who completed the two forms in reverse order with the same time lag. This study found a correlation of .64 (Kendall's Tau-b). The instrument did show a practice effect with scores rising by an average of 3.8 points from the first to the second testing, *p* < .001 via Wilcoxon test. Parallel-form reliability was assessed using 23 participants, 12 of whom completed form A and then a week later did Form B and 11 of whom took the forms in reverse order. The correlations between the two forms were not reported, but there was no significant difference in mean scores on the two forms administered at a given time. Neither internal consistency reliability nor correlations between the time- and event-based subscores are reported, a curious omission.

Validity. Data for the clinical participants are reported on the correlation of the CAMPROMPT score and subscores with an assortment of concurrent measures. The correlation of CAMPROMPT total score with the Rivermead Behavioural Memory Test was .38. Of the subscores, the event-based subscore correlated .47 (*p* < .01), whereas the time-based subscore correlated .21 (*p* > .05), showing a differential functioning of the two scores. Correlations of the CAMPROMPT with a battery of other scores found correlations ranging between .20–.50 (absolute value). A timed map search test produced a higher correlation with the time-based CAMPROMPT score than with the event-based score. Conversely, the opposite pattern was found for a measure of "Executive Processing" from the Behavioural Assessment of the Dysexecutive Syndrome test and Speed and Capacity of Language Processing test, with correlations of .50 (*p* < .01) for the first and -.46 (*p* < .05) for the latter. The correlations with the time-based score ranged from .04 to .26 (*p* > .05).

COMMENTARY. The CAMPROMPT provides an extremely well-written and detailed set of guidelines for administration and to a lesser extent for scoring. The theoretical justification is clear and strong and the authors are credible, with at least three peer-reviewed publications to their credit in the domain. The instrument itself is very clever and has substantial "face" validity. The distracting tasks are engaging and likely to keep the examinee distracted while the memory tasks play out. Having two forms is very helpful, particularly in light of a documented practice effect. That there is a practice effect is not terribly surprising. The ability to use any memory aid desired is likely to lead examinees to selecting better strategies in a second time through the test. Also, the tasks that examinees are asked to perform while in the midst of the exam might have caught them somewhat by surprise the first time, but would be expected in a second taking. The norms provided are one of the strengths of the instrument, particularly the criteria for determining impairment. The estimates of reliability that are provided are at least satisfactory; however, it is perplexing that internal consistency reliability is not reported. The differential functioning of the time- and event-based scores causes one to wonder to what extent they are homogenous. Internal consistency estimates (separate and combined) would help to indicate the extent to which they are. Related to this omission is the lack of construct validity data that would be provided by a factor analysis. With the large body of control group data, it would be very helpful to report to what extent the total score represented a single factor.

Although the strengths of the CAMPROMPT are the scoring and norms for criteria for impairment, they are also the main weaknesses because the details of how they were both determined are not provided. Although the scoring method has a certain intuitive appeal, more details of the logic behind it and how it was developed would be helpful. More importantly, it appears that impairment is defined as being in the lowest 5% of the control group (specificity = .95). However, it would be very helpful to indicate why that point was chosen and what percent of the clinical group would fall into that score range (sensitivity).

SUMMARY. The CAMPROMPT is designed to aid clinical psychologists, neuropsychologists, geriatricians, occupational therapists, speech and language therapists, and other health professionals working with people who have prospective memory impairments. What separates this exam from other assessments of memory is that it focuses on prospective memory, the ability to do future tasks that are stimulated by the passage of time or anticipated events. These are the types of memory impairments that are the most frustrating for caregivers and can have the greatest implications for health care lapses. The use of distractor tasks to keep the examinee occupied as the time passes or events unfold is clever and effective. Having two forms is a plus for many applications. The examination is relatively short, taking approximately 25 minutes. Data from 237 control participants with no known neurological assault or deficit are used to produce reliability estimates and norms for performance and 72 patients with diagnosed neurological problems provide evidence for the clinical sensitivity/validity of the instrument. The interrater (.998) and test-retest (.64) reliabilities and validity estimates (.20–.50) provided are adequate to good. But many are based upon small subsets (< 30) of the larger database, and it is often unclear if it is the control participants or the clinical participants who are assessed. The lack of construct validity via factor analysis and internal consistency estimates coupled with the differential correlations of the time-based and event-based scores with various criteria raises questions about the homogeneity of the scores produced. Although the CAMPROMPT has the potential to be useful for identification of memory-impaired patients, those wishing to use it as a diagnostic tool should clarify whether the reliability and validity data are relevant for their patient/client population. Further, if the CAMPROMPT is to be used in making decisions about whether a

patient should be allowed to live independently, much care should be exercised in its use. For this purpose, administration should be by a clinician who weighs the results as part of the larger constellation of information used in assessing a patient's ability to live independently.

Review of the Cambridge Prospective Memory Test by LINDA E. BRODY, Johns Hopkins University, Center for Talented Youth, Baltimore, MD:

DESCRIPTION. Prospective memory is the ability to remember to carry out actions that were previously planned such as remembering to take scheduled medication. Because failure to remember such a task can have serious consequences, assessment of prospective memory in an individual whose memory appears to be declining can be especially useful for caretakers and clinicians. The Cambridge Prospective Memory Test (CAMPROMPT) was developed to provide a standardized assessment of an individual's prospective memory to aid in diagnosis and guide intervention decisions.

The CAMPROMPT consists of six prospective memory tasks that the examinee must carry out during a 20–25-minute session while he or she is also working on a number of "background" distractor tasks. The distractor tasks are puzzles and knowledge quizzes of various kinds that are provided as part of the test battery. These range in difficulty from very easy to very difficult, and the examiner is instructed to choose ones that are appropriate for the examinee's cognitive level in order to engage interest but not cause frustration.

While the examinee is working on the puzzles, he or she is also being asked to follow through on specific tasks, three of them cued by time and three by events. Of the time-based tasks, two use a kitchen timer and the third a clock (these items are included with the test materials). There is an interval of time between when the request is made and when the response should occur, with the response cued by either the timer or the clock. The event-based tasks are cued by either a verbal prompt from the examiner, the beeper going off followed by a prompt from examiner, or a specific question.

As the examinee completes each task, or fails to do so appropriately, the examiner is instructed to respond to his or her actions. When the response is appropriate and on time, the examiner says "Good. Thank you." Additional prompts or words of encouragement are given when the response is not accurate. The examinee can use any aids, including writing a reminder on a piece of paper.

There are two parallel versions of this test, Forms A and B. The instructions for administering and scoring the CAMPROMPT are exceptionally clear and easy to follow. Training examiners to administer this test should not be difficult.

DEVELOPMENT. For the purpose of developing this assessment, the authors decided to operationally define prospective memory as "failure to remember to do things at the right time, or within a certain interval or when a particular event occurs" (manual, p. 3). They also chose to make the test items analogous to everyday life behavior following on the example of such tests as the Rivermead Behavioural Memory Test (RBMT), the Behavioural Assessment of the Dysexecutive Syndrome (BADS), the Behavioural Assessment of the Dysexecutive Sysndrom for Children (BADS-C), and The Test of Everyday Attention (TEA). In particular, the CAMPROMPT was influenced by concepts and items found in an earlier test, the Cambridge Behavioural Prospective Memory Test (CBPMT). Because that test of prospective memory discriminated between clinical examinees and controls, it was thought that it could be the basis for developing a standardized test of prospective memory.

After conducting pilot testing of the CBPMT, however, it was decided that certain changes were needed in the development and construction of the CAMPROMPT. These included: (a) ensuring that the time intervals between being asked to do the task and responding appropriately at the right moment are balanced across cueing conditions, (b) having a set pattern of responses to examinees' actions or lack of actions, and (c) having a sensitive scoring system that takes into account both the timing of the action and the action itself.

A somewhat longer version of the CAMPROMPT was initially developed, but pilot studies of the test revealed that it could be shortened without loss of sensitivity. Thus, the final test includes only the three event-based and three time-based tasks and can be administered in 20–25 minutes.

TECHNICAL.

Standardization and norms. The norms are based on the results obtained by 214 control subjects who participated in the standardization study. The researchers began by recruiting 237 control subjects; validation studies were also conducted on a group of clinical patients.

One hundred of the participants in the control group were chosen because their age, gender, and ability levels were already known from other sources (e.g., many had volunteered for other research studies). The remaining participants in the control group were recruited individually from various settings such as farms, prisons, and clubs. Those with any history of head trauma, neurological or psychiatric conditions, or learning disabilities were excluded. An attempt was made to assure representation by gender, general ability, and socioeconomic status, as well as representation across the four age bands that were assessed, ages 16 to above 66.

The 214 control participants who became the normative sample were all administered Version A of the CAMPROMPT as their first test. The other 23 control participants were given Version B as their first test to assess test-retest reliability, and these individuals were not included in the norm group. All of the controls were administered the National Adult Reading Test (NART) as an estimate of IQ. Although this measure may be possibly considered a fairly rough estimate of IQ, especially because even gifted individuals can exhibit reading disorders, and reading levels are influenced by education, the NART has been used by others for this purpose.

The ages of the 214 participants from whom the norms were derived ranged from 16 to 92 years, with a mean of 42.2 years. Their IQ scores, based on the NART, ranged from 69 to 131 with a mean of 105.5.

In an analysis of the performance of these participants, there were no gender effects, but there were significant effects for age. A gradual decline in memory with aging was observed in the results of this test. When the participants were separated into four bands by age groups, there were no significant differences between adjacent age groups but differences emerged between nonadjacent groups. Differences in memory were also found to relate to estimated IQ scores with the higher IQ participants outperforming lower ones on the memory assessment.

Following this research, norms were developed based on the performance of the control group. The differences that were found in this group as a result of age and ability are reflected in the norm table in the manual. Clinicians can compare the performance of a patient to the norm group based on three levels of general mental ability (above average, average, and below average) within each of four age groups (16–35, 36–50, 51–65, and 66+ years). In comparison with typical performance on this assessment, a patient's prospective memory can be classified as impaired, borderline, poor, average, above average, or very good, a classification that reflects the 5th, 10th, 25th, 75th, and 95th percentile scores for the norm group.

Although the authors worked to use a standardization sample representative of the general population in many ways, ethnicity is not mentioned, so one might assume that the sample was not ethnically diverse. Also, because age and ability turned out to be factors in performance, the numbers in each cell (one of three IQ bands and one of four age bands) is smaller than one might like to see. Additional research with larger numbers would be advisable.

Reliability. To evaluate consistency of scoring the CAMPROMPT, 22 of the participants from the control group, representing all of the ability and age groups in the sample population, were tested with a second tester present. Both examiners recorded all responses and scored the test. The correlation of scores from the two examiners was .998, which is extremely high. It suggests that the directions for scoring the test are reliable and that scoring should be consistent regardless of who administers the test.

Test-retest reliability was also assessed. Ten control participants who had taken Version A and 10 who took Version B were tested 7–10 days later on the same version of the test that they had taken to see if the results were stable on retesting within a short period of time. There was a small practice effect (a mean increase of 3.8) for 11 of the participants, but the correlation between performances was .64. The authors concluded that the test can be administered a second time within a period of weeks. However, the number of individuals who participated in this assessment was rather small. It would also be useful to evaluate stability over a longer period of time and also to minimize the practice effect.

Finally, parallel-form reliability was assessed utilizing 23 control participants, 12 of whom took Version A, followed a week later by Version B, while 11 took Version B, followed a week later by Version A. No significant differences in performance were found for either group between versions. Once again, however, the size of the sample was rather small for drawing conclusions.

Validity. In order to compare the performance of the control subjects to a clinical group, the CAMPROMPT was also administered to 76 patients with a variety of neurological disorders including brain injury and degenerative conditions such as multiple sclerosis. These individuals were recruited primarily from hospital or rehabilitation settings. Three participants later withdrew and one died, leaving 72 in the final group. Their ages ranged from 18–83, with a mean of 45.2, and IQ (based on the NART) ranged from 62–128 with a mean of 104.10, reasonably similar to the control group. The gender balance in the group was also reasonable. Though this group was smaller in size, these statistics compare reasonably well with those of the control group.

The clinical participants performed significantly less well than the control group on all aspects of the CAMPROMPT. Their time-based, event-based, and total scores were lower. One factor in this difference was explicit note-taking, which was less common in this group; patients who made few or poor notes had much lower scores whereas patients who made good notes performed as well as those in the control group who also made good notes. The effects of age and IQ, and especially of the patients' neurological and memory problems, are not clear in the results reported for the clinical group, however.

The clinical participants were also tested on a number of cognitive measures to determine the extent to which the results correlated with their performance on the CAMPROMPT. Because prospective memory tasks have a retrospective component, the relationship between the CAMPROMPT and the Rivermead Behavioural Memory Test (RBMT) was investigated. Significant correlations were found between scores on the RBMT and the total and event-based items, but not on the time-based CAMPROMPT tasks, leading the authors to conclude that the CAMPROMPT includes retrospective memory measures but the additional time-based tasks provide a more comprehensive test of prospective memory.

The 1-minute Map Search test from the Test of Everyday Attention correlated significantly with the total, event-based, and timed-based CAMPROMPT scores, and the 2-minute Map Search with the total and timed scores confirming, claim the authors, the role attention plays in assessing prospective memory on the CAMPROMPT. The Modified Six Elements Test from the Behavioural Assessment of the Dysexecutive Syndrome (BADS) Test, a measure of executive processing, correlated with the total score and the event-based tasks on the CAMPROMPT but not the time-based. And the Speed of Comprehension Test from the Speed and Capacity of Language Processing (SCOLP) Test, a measure of verbal information processing, correlated only with the event-based tasks, confirming that this factor plays only a minor role in prospective tasks, in the opinion of the test authors.

Although this line of research is interesting and informative, it seems as though similar data should be collected on nonclinical patients before drawing conclusions. Because these clinical patients, as a group, performed rather poorly on the CAMPROMPT compared to the norm group, this reviewer believes that high scorers from the norm group should have been included in any study of the test's validity.

Most important to the question of validity on this test is the need to assess the relationship between CAMPROMPT performance and the individual's ability to remember tasks in the real world. Does this test predict or correlate with the clinical indices that are being investigated? Specifically, among the clinical patients, are those who are having the greatest difficulties in remembering to do things in their daily lives, within this group, also the ones who score lowest on this test? And what about the relatively low scorers in the norm group; are they having difficulty in their daily lives? Presumably this concern is being left up to the clinician to determine but the question is crucial to accepting the validity of the CAMPROMPT for its stated purpose.

COMMENTARY. Our lives are full of important things we plan to do in the future and then must remember to do when the time comes. Whether it's taking medication on time, paying bills, or keeping appointments, systematically forgetting to follow through on such events can cause serious problems. Thus, identifying the cause and degree of difficulty with prospective memory in individuals whose memory appears to be failing has important implications for diagnosis and treatment. Because clinical judgment can be subjective, a standardized instrument to complement clinical judgment can be extremely useful.

The CAMPROMPT is the first standardized test designed to assess prospective memory. Its authors have worked hard to conduct a standardization study and to provide evidence of the reliability and validity of the test. They have developed norms based on a carefully chosen national sample of participants after comparing their performance on the CAMPROMPT with clinical participants. The statistics they present with regard to reliability and validity are reasonably satisfactory.

I would like to see more research done, however, before supporting the widespread use of this test. Because of the influence of age and IQ on scores, the fairly large sample tested actually breaks down into fairly small cells by age and IQ. Replication of the study on more people is recommended, particularly with a more ethnically diverse sample.

Perhaps even more important, however, is the need for predictive validity studies. The authors need to relate the test results to the real world behavior of individuals, because that is actually the purpose of the assessment. Undoubtedly that was the intent in comparing clinical to control participants, but we have little understanding of the exact nature of the problems experienced by the clinical patients, and there were high and low scorers in both the standardization and clinical samples. We need assurance that there is a high correlation between scores and real-world memory issues.

It is certainly hypothetically possible that some individuals might perform well on the CAMPROMPT because it tests short-term memory but they have difficulty remembering to do things over a longer period of time, whereas others might do poorly on the test because the tasks have little meaning to them but they do remember the important things in their own lives. The authors need to provide evidence that this is not the case, that those individuals who struggle with memory every day are the same ones who consistently perform poorly on the CAMPROMPT, whereas the high scorers function well in their everyday lives. Basically, we need a better understanding of how scores on the CAMPROMPT predict real world behavior.

SUMMARY. The CAMPROMPT is the only standardized assessment of its kind to aid clinicians in diagnosing prospective memory problems in their patients. Being able to compare a patient's results to a national sample of tested individuals is certainly a useful tool to supplement clinical judgment, particularly because age and IQ have been taken into consideration. However, the brevity of the instrument and lack of data related to predictive validity suggests it should be used cautiously until the research base is stronger. If the results of this assessment agree with a judgment that has already been made, that may be comforting to the clinician, but if it contradicts clinical judgment more work is needed before the CAMPROMPT should be used for diagnosis.

[37]

Career Directions Inventory [Second Edition].

Purpose: "Designed to identify areas of greater or lesser interest from among a wide variety of occupations."

Population: Adolescents and adults ages 15 years or older.

Publication Dates: 1986–2003.

Acronym: CDI.

Scores, 49: 15 Basic Interest Scales (Administration, Art, Clerical, Food Service, Industrial Art, Health Service, Outdoors, Personal Service, Sales, Science, Teaching/Social Service, Writing, Assertive, Persuasive, Systematic); 7 General Occupational Themes (Realistic/Practical, Enterprising, Artistic/Communicative, Social/Helping, Investigative/Logical, Conventional, Serving); 27 Job Clusters (Computer and Mathematical Science, Science and Engineering, Electronic Technology, Medical and Health Care, Health Record Technology, Social Science, Banking and Accounting, Funeral Services, Architectural Technology/Drafting and Design, Word Processing and Administrative Assistant, Public and Protective Services, Art, Social Services, Sales, Administration, Performing Arts, Communication Arts, Food Services, Education, Hospitality and Travel Services, Law Enforcement, Agriculture and Animal Science, Personal Care, Renewable Resource Technology, Marketing and Merchandising, Skilled Trades, Library Science).

Administration: Group.

Price Data, 2006: $25 per examination kit including manual on CD and question and answer document for the mail-in extended report; $15 per manual on CD; $85–$95 per 10 mail-in extended reports; $105 per SigmaSoft CDI for Windows Software including complete installation package and 10 coupons; $8 per online password.

Time: (30) minutes.

Comments: Test may be administered through mail-in scoring, SigmaSoft for Windows Software, or via the internet at www.sigmatesting.com.

Author: Douglas N. Jackson.

Publisher: Sigma Assessment Systems, Inc.

Cross References: For reviews by Darrell L. Sabers and Fredrick A. Schrank of an earlier edition, see 9:44.

Review of the Career Directions Inventory [Second Edition] by BERT A. GOLDMAN, Professor, University of North Carolina at Greensboro, Greensboro, NC:

DESCRIPTION. The Career Directions Inventory (CDI) [Second Edition] developed by Douglas Jackson contains 100 items in triad format requiring the respondent to select within each triad the most and least liked activities. Administration can be accomplished with a paper-and-pencil, mail-in scoring version or by a computer-administered and scored version using a SigmaSoft for Windows software package or over the internet at www.sigmatesting.com. Administration requires 30 to 50 minutes for the majority of respondents with the average respondent completing the CDI in 25 to 35 minutes. A vast array of detailed printed information provides respondents with profiles on 15 basic interest scales, 7 general occupational themes, 27 job clusters, and 100 different educational fields. Respondents also receive administrative indices that show how much confidence can be placed in the results, and finally, respondents receive suggestions to help them explore their career options. Profile results are given in percentages for females, males, and combined, but the actual profile is prepared for the respondent's gender. Given the CDI's approximate sixth grade vocabulary level, its simplistic and relatively brief administration, along with items describing familiar activities, this instrument is appropriate for the general population as well as with junior high school level students who are at least 15 years of age. The CDI is intended for use in educational and career counseling and decision-making. Jackson further suggests that the instrument lends itself to research in vocational interest, job satisfaction, and personnel classification.

DEVELOPMENT. According to the manual, the present CDI is the second edition of the instrument for which the first edition appeared in 1986. The author modeled the instrument after his Jackson Vocational Interest Survey (JVIS; 15:129) with entirely different items and serving a broader target population by being appropriate, not only for those planning post-secondary education, but for those high school graduates or nongraduates planning direct entry into the work force. Jackson clearly lists each step that was taken in constructing the instrument over several years with a detailed step-by-step flow chart. Then he describes in detail how he accomplished each step. Jackson's construction process included the following steps: developing a statement of objectives; making decisions regarding domain and scale definitions; writing and editing items; conducting an initial item analysis identifying the basis for item triads, evaluating different populations, and conducting additional item analyses and revision; conducting administration to standardized groups; developing verification keys and a reliability index; selecting final normative groups; and developing the psychometric bases for profiles reflecting General Occupational Themes, Similarity to Job Clusters, and Similarity to Educational Specialty Groups. Discussion of the test construction process appears to be focused on the First Edition of the test.

TECHNICAL. The manual provides norms for the 15 basic interest scales. One table provides a comparison between "old" and "new" norms broken down by male, female, and total for each of these 15 scales. No dates are given for when these data were collected. Also the table indicates that the new norm data comprise 1,250 males and 1,250 females, for a total of 2,500. However, a second norm table for the 15 basic interest scales provides a breakdown by gender for each of six age groups and gives the number in each age group, but these numbers total 1,169 for males, not 1,250, and only 1,151 for females, not 1,250. Thus, the grand total is not 2,500 persons, but 2,320 [Editor's Note: The publisher has corrected this in the manual as of June 2006]. Also the manual indicates that the norm population represents a wide geographic area, but no information

is given to describe the area other than to indicate that the population came from the United States and Canada.

Test-retest reliability over an average of 4 weeks was based on data collected from 34 male and 36 female high school students. No information is given to indicate how, from where, or why this type of student was selected. A table presents reliability coefficients for each of the Basic Interest Scales, General Occupational themes, Administrative Indices, and Occupational Clusters containing coefficients ranging from .67 to .96, with most in the .80s. The same table also contains alpha coefficients without administrative indices, but these were developed from the old norm data of 1,000 subjects with no explanation given for using the original norms from which to collect these alpha coefficients. The alpha coefficients ranged from .62 to .92 with most in the .80s.

Validity information was presented in two tables and 20 figures. The two tables provide comparison cumulative percentiles for each of three cluster groups with those of people in general. In each case, as expected, the cluster groups scored higher than people in general. The data for the people in general were from the old norms and no information is given as to how or when the cluster group data were collected. The 20 figures provide graphic examples revealing that 20 different target groups scored substantially higher than people in general. However, in these examples, too, the people in general were from the old norms and there was no indication of how or when the target groups were selected.

Correlations between the 15 Basic Interest Scales were computed, and the majority of these correlations were in the .30s or less indicating a reasonable degree of independence between scales. Higher correlations are expected in a few cases where one would expect some relationship between scales to exist, such as between Persuasive and Administrative (.62). However, by the same token, one would therefore expect Persuasive to correlate highly with Sales, but the correlation was fairly low at .37. The manual contains no mention of this low relationship. The correlations between the 15 Basic Interest scales, too, are based on the old norm data.

COMMENTARY. The Career Directions Inventory enables a broad range of the general population, as young as 15 years, to identify within 30 to 50 minutes, levels of interest in a variety of both blue collar and professional careers. Administration is relatively easy through a paper-and-pencil, machine-scored version or through a computer-administered and scored version using a software package or on the internet. Regardless of the administrative method employed, a vast array of material is generated for the respondent to absorb. Although respondents may find their way through a self-interpretation of the results, given the variety of scales about which much information is printed, as well as the need to consider such characteristics as achievements, aptitudes, personality, values, etc., most respondents will surely need the assistance of a professional career counselor. The identification of interests and disinterests, which can be determined by the CDI, does provide valuable supplemental information for career decision-making.

New norms are given for six age groups broken down by male, female, and total, but the Ns in the table presenting these data do not agree with the Ns described in the manual narrative, nor are dates given for when the data were collected. Also the geographic area from which the norm population was drawn and how it was selected are not given.

Internal consistency reliability coefficients and validity evidence based upon comparisons between specialty groups and people in general, although acceptable, were developed from old norm data. With the exception of new norms from which little technical data are compiled, the addition of four new job clusters, and the division of one job cluster into two, the second edition of the CDI with its accompanying manual appears to be identical to the first edition, which was published in 1986.

SUMMARY. The Career Directions Inventory provides a supplement to the career counselor's arsenal of data-producing instruments for use with clients as young as 15 years of age. The professional counselor relatively easily accomplishes administration, scoring, and interpretation, but not so for the client without professional assistance. Reliability and validity data are acceptable; however, the author should provide more timely information, and although a newer set of norms is provided, a more thorough description of the norm population should be given.

Review of the Career Directions Inventory [Second Edition] by CLEBORNE D. MADDUX, Foundation Professor of Counseling and Educational Psychology, University of Nevada—Reno, Reno, NV:

DESCRIPTION. The Career Directions Inventory (CDI) [Second Edition] is a computer-scored, individual or group-administered, career interest inventory designed to identify occupations of greater or lesser interest across a wide variety of careers or occupations. It is for use with adults and can also be used with children as young as those in junior high school, although the manual cautions that vocational interests are not stable in individuals under the age of 15 years.

The inventory consists of 100 items, each made up of three statements describing different job-related activities or tasks. The forced-choice format requires the respondent to indicate which of the three statements is most liked, and which is least liked. The third statement in each triad is left blank. Average reading level of the test is said to be approximately sixth grade, and steps were taken to identify and eliminate words that were difficult to read or to understand.

An extensive report is computer-generated for each respondent. This report "identifies interest patterns by providing a variety of profiles and scores relating to basic interest scales, general occupational themes, similarity to educational and occupational clusters, similarity to criterion groups, and indices relating to the validity of respondents' answers" (manual, p. 9).

The second edition of the inventory incorporates several changes. New norms were determined based on a sample of 2,500 participants from the U.S. and Canada, half male and half female. The job clusters have been changed by dividing the Food and Hospitality cluster from the original edition into the Food Services cluster and the Hospitality and Travel Services cluster. New clusters were added for Social Science, Library and Information Science, Funeral Service, and Computer and Mathematical Sciences. In addition, the World Wide Web administration option was added.

Unlike some other career interest inventories, the CDI is not intended solely for those who intend to pursue a university education followed by a professional career. The CDI can be used with such individuals, but is also intended for use by those planning to enter specialized training for blue collar jobs, and for those who intend to enter the world of work immediately after high school. The focus on technical or skilled careers and the simplified language is what differentiates the CDI from the Jackson Vocational Interest Survey (15:129), which was developed by the same author.

The manual, which must be printed from the CD containing the test software, suggests that the inventory is for use in education and career counseling as well as for use in research on vocational interests, job satisfaction, and personnel classification. The manual emphasizes that the inventory is for use in predicting a person's long-term satisfaction with an educational program of study or work but is not appropriate as a predictor of future job performance nor for use as a measure of aptitude. Interests are considered predictive of long-term job satisfaction because they play a critical role in determining job enjoyment, and thus they contribute to a person's willingness to remain in a given career path over a long period of time.

The inventory must be scored by computer but can be administered in any of three ways: (a) by filling out a machine-scorable, question/answer booklet, (b) through use of the SigmaSoft CDI for Windows software (supplied on CD), or (c) on the World Wide Web at http://www.livecareer.com. (The manual lists an obsolete URL with an automatic forward to the valid site.) The inventory cannot be scored by hand regardless of mode of administration. If the machine-scorable booklet is used, it must be mailed to an address in Michigan or to one in Canada. The manual asserts that reports will be mailed back within 24 to 48 hours of receipt. If the computer software or the World Wide Web is used for administration, the instrument is computer scored and the lengthy report is generated on the spot.

Reports are impressively detailed and consist of different forms for respondent and counselor. According to the manual, these are available in U.S., Canadian English, and French versions. (However, the manual contains no information about whether or not there are Canadian English or French versions of the inventory itself.) The report consists of profiles and bar graphs showing interest scaled scores on the 15 basic interest scales, the seven general occupational themes, the 27 job clusters, and 100 different educational fields.

Each profile presents percentile ranks for each measure with the respondent's performance compared to males, females, and males and females combined. A bar graph plots percentile rank with those in the same gender as the respondent making up the comparison group. The report suggests that scores less than 30 indicate low interest or dislike, whereas scores greater than 70 indicate high interest. In addition, a section on administrative indices provides a measure of consistency of results, and a section entitled "Where to go from here?" provides suggestions for further career exploration.

DEVELOPMENT. The CDI was conceived and developed by Douglas N. Jackson, who also developed the Jackson Vocational Interest Survey (JVIS; 15:129). The CDI is theoretically similar but is intended to be more useful for nonprofessional careers and to be easier to read and understand the items.

TECHNICAL.

Normative data. The first edition of the CDI was normed with 1,000 respondents who were a subsample of the 12,846 respondents (6,113 males and 6,733 females) from 138 educational specialty groups who were in the initial validation sample. No information is available in the manual concerning how these original 12,846 respondents were selected or how the norm sample of 1,000 was selected. The new norms for the second edition were based on a sample of 2,500 respondents (1,250 males and 1,250 females) from the U.S. and Canada. Again, no information is provided about these respondents or how they were selected. The new norms are reported for six age groups: 15 years or less, 16 to 17 years, 18 to 19 years, 20 to 30 years, 31 to 40 years, and 41 years or greater.

Reliability. Reliability data for the CDI consist of a table in the manual reporting over 120 test-retest coefficients and alpha coefficients. The test-retest coefficients were calculated on a small sample: 70 senior high school students, 34 males and 36 females, who were given the original CDI on two occasions that were an average of 4 weeks apart. These range from the high .60s to the mid-.90s, with most in the .70s or .80s. The alpha coefficients were calculated on the scores from the 1,000 individuals in the original normative sample, and range from the low .60s to the .90s, with most in the mid- to high .80s.

Validity. Validity is addressed in a nontraditional way. The manual expresses this as follows: "The validities of the CDI scales were appraised by comparing the distributions of scores on different educational specialty groups and cluster scales obtained by individuals in particular relevant specialty groups with those obtained by the 1000 people forming the normative groups, designated as 'people in general'" (p. 98). The comparisons are made visually by plotting the two distributions on a single graph and inspecting the graph for degree of separation.

COMMENTARY. The CDI is a promising instrument but has shortcomings. Reliability is acceptable, but validity data are incomplete. One problem is with use of the term "people in general," who actually appear to be students in a variety of educational programs. A problem in the original edition that has not been corrected in this edition is that data on the performance of student groups rather than actual groups of workers in various jobs or occupations are used when comparing a respondent's performance to the performance of those in a given occupational title. There is no way to determine whether or not these "educational specialty groups" are representative of groups actually working in the occupational titles identified in the CDI. Because of these problems, the instrument must be considered one in which validity has not been satisfactorily established.

SUMMARY. The CDI is quick and easy to administer, and produces extensive and high-quality reports—one for the respondent and one for the counselor. It can be administered in paper-and-pencil format, on a personal computer, or on the World Wide Web. The instrument is intuitively appealing and interesting to respondents, and the report is understandable to most of them, although some respondents may need a short explanation concerning the meaning of percentile ranks and how to interpret the bar graphs that are featured on almost every page. The manual contains clear and well-written instructions and a script for administration, although the CDI is one of a growing list of assessment instruments in which no hard copy of the manual is provided and a copy must be printed from the CD. This is unfortunate, because lack of a paper copy is almost sure to encourage some users to forego a close examination of the manual, which is over 116 pages in length and will be time-consuming to

print in its entirety. The manual does a good job of cautioning that the inventory is a measure of career interest and possible future job satisfaction but should not be interpreted as predictive of future job performance or aptitude.

Procedures used for item selection and refinement were meticulous and thorough. The instrument has acceptable test-retest reliability and internal consistency. However, as with the first edition, there are problems with validity. What is needed is more convincing evidence that performance on the CDI is predictive of job satisfaction among workers in given careers rather than simply among students preparing to enter those careers. This problem was understandable in a new instrument. However, it is somewhat disappointing that validity concerns have not been satisfied in the second edition, especially because the instrument is a highly promising one. This problem aside, career counselors will find the instrument to be useful in working with clients who are not college bound and who are seeking a more thorough understanding of their own vocational interests.

[38]

Checking Individual Progress in Phonics.

Purpose: Designed to "assess pupils' progress in phonics, identify their learning strategies and improve their skills."

Population: Ages 6 to 7.

Publication Date: 2001.

Acronym: ChIPPs.

Scores: Total words read correctly.

Administration: Individual.

Forms: 2 parallel forms: Version 1 and Version 2.

Price Data: Price data for complete set including teacher's manual (106 pages), test materials, and reproducible Individual, Class, and Pupil record sheets available from publisher.

Time: Administration time not reported.

Authors: Sue Palmer and Rea Reason.

Publisher: NFER-Nelson Publishing Co., Ltd. [England]

Review of Checking Individual Progress in Phonics by JORGE E. GONZALEZ, Assistant Professor, Department of Educational Psychology, and REBEKAH HAYNES, Research Graduate Assistant, Texas A&M University, College Station, TX:

DESCRIPTION. Checking Individual Progress in Phonics (ChIPPs) is an individually administered measure of phonics skill, specifically the ability to read words with sound/letter correspondence of increasing difficulty. ChIPPs target populations include primary school students ages 5 to 7 learning phonics or older learners with special needs. Recommended uses of the ChIPPs include pretesting prior to teaching, progress monitoring, developing individual plans, and planning differentiated instruction for whole group or individual students. The ChIPPs consists of two parallel versions, each with seven sets of words (10 words per card) in three broad bands: (a) Set 1 includes simple consonant-vowel-consonant (CVC) words; (b) Sets 2, 3, and 4 include consonant digraphs and blends at the beginning and ends of words; and (c) Sets 5, 6, and 7 include vowel digraphs, usually in the middle of a word. Included in the seven sets are five "real" and five "non-words." The nonwords are meant to evaluate a child's phonics skill without providing the child recognizable cues. The ChIPPs is an untimed measure.

Administration instructions are described briefly. The test begins with five demonstration nonword training items. The student is then instructed to start with the first word and continue reading as many words as she or he can. The examiner begins with the word sets and discontinues when the examinee has read four or fewer words correctly in a set. Using individual record sheets, the examiner marks errors, "passes," and correctly read words. The total score is the number of words read correctly. Scores can then be compared to six categories of fluency ranging from Category 1 ("The child struggles with set 1 and has not started to develop fluency," manual, p. 13) to Category 6 ("The child reads all sets of words with ease and fluency," manual, p. 13). Individual scores can be transferred to a class record sheet to get a quick assessment of class achievement patterns. Five broad performance levels of phonics proficiency can be used to describe whole class performance. The broad levels of proficiency are described in detail in the manual, but range from Group 1 ("There are children who struggle with CVC words in set 1," teacher's manual, p. 14) to Group 5 ("There are some children who zoom through all seven sets of ChIPPS so easily and effortlessly that one wonders whether phonics is really a skill to be built up by practice," teacher's manual, p. 15). Group performance can subsequently be mapped onto differentiated approaches

to instruction. Subsequently, Version 2 of the ChIPPs can be used to monitor individual and class-wide progress on the differentiated instruction. The ChIPPs manual also provides seven banks of words and nonwords from which teachers can create customized word lists with targeted phonic elements. The manual includes recommendations for weekly planning and record keeping with a section on selecting activities (e.g., Sound Bingo, Rhymes and Chimes) to accelerate phonics development. Both the word banks and recommended activities appear to be mapped onto an instructional framework titled "The National Literacy Strategy Progression in Phonics," a United Kingdom Department of Education and Employment curricular initiative.

DEVELOPMENT. Detailed information on ChIPPs item development is limited. Word sets were apparently informed by the "English National Literacy Strategy"—a curricular initiative of the United Kingdom's Department of Education and Employment. Virtually no information is provided on the psychometric properties of the instrument either. The use of a bar graph depicting a positively skewed slope of correct words by "set" as evidence for progressive difficulty is one example of the problematic approach taken to establish confidence in the instrument. A more useful concept would have been employment of some kind of intrinsic item difficulty assessment, defined in terms of the item's content, context, or characteristics and the task demands set by the items. Instead, the authors report studies demonstrating the word sets become increasingly difficult as they move from Set 1 to Set 7 for monolingual and bilingual students. A third study following students for 2 years demonstrated scores on each word set increased from Year 1 to Year 2. These studies are the only evidence of meaningful test construction provided in the manual. The second version of the ChIPPs was developed with feedback from the teachers involved in the first study.

TECHNICAL. The ChIPPs assessment is a nonstandardized instrument. The authors report that norm-referencing was not needed for the ChIPPs because it is intended as a method of instructional planning for teachers. The authors do, however, describe five heuristic performance "ability" groups. These groups are based on trials of the ChIPPs, but specific information about the trials, such as the location and number of children assessed, is unknown. No reliability data, in the conventional psychometric sense, were provided. The only analyses done involved a comparison of 200 (100 Year 1 and 100 Year 2 students) students' performance on Version 1 with their performance on Version 2 of the ChIPPs (one test immediately after the other in counter-balanced design). No statistical difference between the versions was found. It is unknown why the authors did not conduct conventional reliability analyses such as alternate-form reliability or split-half analysis to estimate the consistency of the scores. For validity, the authors provide some evidence of content validity by demonstrating that word sets get progressively more difficult. This evidence lacks, however, detail on the appropriateness of the items and the completeness of the content other than how it aligns to the "English National Literacy Strategy." There is also no evidence of the relationship between the measure and other measures that assess phonics, nor is there evidence of convergent or discriminant power. Without this important information it is difficult to know whether knowledge of a student's score on the ChIPPs is an accurate estimate of future performance on some defined criterion. No studies validating the test for its intended uses are included, making it difficult to determine whether the test is "valid" for its intended purpose.

COMMENTARY. The ChIPPs purports to measure phonics performance for 5-to-7-year-olds learning phonics and older children with special needs. The instructions and attached stimulus cards are teacher friendly. The attached stimulus cards are attractive and can be seen easily by an individual examinee. There are, however, threats to the internal and external validity of this measure that limit its potential value. First, the ChIPPs provides little or no information on the theoretical or conceptual underpinnings of the importance of phonics and its relation to reading. To understand phonics, the user needs to know how phonics is different from phonemic awareness, how it relates to phonological awareness, and the broader phonological processing construct. Little or no attempt is made by the authors to explain "why" phonics is important in beginning reading. The authors could have easily referenced the works reported in the National Reading Panel (National Institute of Child Health and Human Develop-

ment, 2000) and from the seminal works in *Preventing Reading Difficulties in Young Children* (Snow, Burns, & Griffin, 1998) as theoretical justification for the instrument's intended purpose. Second, the limited psychometric information on the development of the ChIPPs casts doubt on its usefulness. Researchers, teachers, and other professionals alike should be wary of scores derived from this measure. When scores are used, they should be interpreted with caution, especially when generalizing beyond the development sample. Third, the authors state that the test is derived from and maps onto the *English National Literacy Strategy* phonics teaching curriculum, which "has provided the basis for ChIPPs" (teacher's manual, p. 8). The test appears to have been developed to assess U.K. 5–7-year-old's phonics performance and progress for those exposed to U.K.'s *English National Literacy Strategy* curriculum. How this maps onto current trends in other countries (e.g., *Reading First* in the United States) is unknown.

SUMMARY. The ChIPPs may prove to be useful to teachers who simply want a progress-monitoring tool for their students' skills in phonics. The test does provide teacher-friendly features that make it useful for planning differentiated phonics instruction. The authors should be commended for developing a user-friendly, curriculum-based assessment of phonics. Conversely, the ChIPPs falls short on its intended purposes. Insufficient reliability and validity evidence exists to place confidence on the scores derived from this measure. Readers seeking a phonics test should consult more well-researched instruments such as the subtests relevant to phonics on the Brigance Diagnostic Comprehensive Inventory of Basic Skills (CIBS-R; Brigance, 1998).

REVIEWERS' REFERENCES
Brigance, A. H. (1998). Brigance Diagnostic Comprehensive Inventory of Basic Skills, Revised. North Billerica, MA: Curriculum Associates, Inc.
National Institute of Child Health and Human Development. (2000). *Report of the National Reading Panel. Teaching children to read: An evidence-based assessment of the scientific research literature on reading and its implications for reading instruction: Reports of the subgroups* [NIH Publication No. 00-4754]. Washington, DC: U.S. Government Printing Office.
Snow, C. E., Burns, S. M., & Griffin, P. (Eds.). (1998). *Preventing reading difficulties in young children.* Washington, DC: National Academy Press.

Review of Checking Individual Progress in Phonics by WILLIAM K. WILKINSON, Consulting Educational Psychologist, Boleybeg, Barna, County Galway, Republic of Ireland:

DESCRIPTION. Checking Individual Progress in Phonics, herein referred to by its acronym (ChIPPs), is intended for use by teachers, most likely reading support teachers. All of the information and word lists are contained in a single manual. The remaining description is based entirely on the information in this document.

From the information presented in the first section of the manual, it appears that the ChIPPs is a measure of one element of a multicomponent literacy strategy used in the U.K. Specifically, within the "word level" component there are targets for phonics and this, it seems, is where the ChIPPs fits in. The age group for ChIPPs is 5 to 6 years, although the authors contend the word lists also may be relevant for older children. The authors note that the ChIPPs is curriculum based, but they suggest it can also provide diagnostic information for identifying specific phonics strengths and weaknesses. It is clear that the ChIPPs is not a norm-referenced instrument.

The ChIPPs consists of two versions of seven word sets, each set containing five words and five nonwords. The sets are progressively more difficult, measuring a hierarchy of phonics skills. For example, Set 1 begins with simple CVC (consonant-vowel-consonant) words, with the middle sets including consonant digraphs/blends, and the latter sets containing vowel digraphs. The word sets are presented to the child from the manual. In addition, the manual contains material to be photocopied, such as a sheet to record the child's responses to each word in each set, a progress sheet for entire class use, and materials for the child (e.g., "My Target Words").

The second section of the manual provides verbatim test administration instructions to the teacher who will be conducting assessments. This section also covers general administration issues such as discontinue rules, scoring, and keeping record sheets.

Section 3 of the manual provides information on how to analyze children's phonics skills using ChIPPs outcomes. Topics covered include where to start teaching, how to proceed, and how to individualize teaching given various rates of progress. This section is cross referenced with Section 5—word banks. There are seven word banks, with the first four relating directly to the seven word sets. For example, Word Bank 1 relates to Word Set 1; both are CVC words. The word banks break word patterns into further phonic categories.

The fourth section of the manual outlines remedial teaching activities, such as sound bingo, making up silly sentences, word chains, etc. Each teaching activity includes a subsection related to the purpose of the activity, materials needed, and instructional procedure.

"Technical Information" is provided in the manual, including data regarding the level of difficulty of the word sets, performance difference based on age for each set, and the equivalence of the two different "forms."

DEVELOPMENT. The ChIPPs is a curriculum-based procedure. The authors seek to measure one component of word analysis, which is phonics. There is an emphasis on progress, and, in this regard, the word sets come in two separate versions. This availability enables the teacher to cross-check one particular word pattern before and after a period of instruction. Further, the teacher can then move a student to increasingly difficult phonics skills, teach, and retest to determine progress.

As a curriculum-based procedure, the need for a carefully selected norm sample is less relevant. Therefore, the only reference to "samples" is a brief description of the children used to determine whether the word sets do indeed increase in difficulty and whether the forms are, in fact, parallel.

The authors could provide more information about the "population" of words and nonwords that comprise the word sets. For example, a reference to the materials used to sample word sets would be useful. The U.K. National Literacy Strategy is alluded to, so a possible link between this policy, or some other reference to a population of words is required, especially in the case of a curriculum-based procedure.

TECHNICAL. Technical data cover three basic questions, as follows. The first question is: Are the sets of words in fact progressively more difficult? A bar chart reflecting mean raw score performance for a sample of children shows a clear stepwise decrement in performance for sets. Thus, the sets are more difficult on average.

A second question is: Do older children perform better than younger children across the word sets? Again, mean raw score performance is higher for slightly older children compared to younger children across word banks. Thus, there is a degree of "differential population validity."

Finally, are the two versions of the test parallel? Again, the bar chart reflecting mean raw score performance is not statistically different, so the user can be confident that the forms provided are equivalent, although this proof is far less than would be necessary to demonstrate that they are equivalent forms, much less that scores from each correlate highly with each other.

It would be interesting to validate the ChIPPs through the test-teach-test method. This type of validity would be especially pertinent because the test purportedly measures progress. Even the presentation of several case studies using raw score performance, pre- and postinstruction, would speak to the validity of the test.

COMMENTARY. If the potential user is a reading support teacher who wishes to teach an array of phonic skills, the ChIPPs would appear useful. The inclusion of instructional strategies, the clear delineation of subsets of phonics skills, and the test-retest philosophy, are amenable to individual educational planning.

The ChIPPs is not a norm-referenced test. Reading support teachers may find it useful as one component of a multifaceted assessment approach.

SUMMARY. The ChIPPs is a curriculum-based procedure that covers various elements of phonics development. The intended age group for the ChIPPs is 5 to 6 years, roughly the period when beginning reading instruction begins. A hierarchy of phonics skills is measured by word sets, seven in total, each set containing 10 words (5 nonwords and 5 real words). There is a detailed analysis of performance and how to teach given different outcomes. The technical information shows that the two versions of the test are parallel and that the sets do indeed increase in difficulty. The ChIPPs would seem a useful barometer of teaching and child progress and, in this regard, it is suggested that future data be provided about the reliability and instructional validity of the test.

[39]
ChemTest (Form AC).

Purpose: For selecting candidates with basic chemical knowledge.

Population: Applicants and incumbents for jobs requiring knowledge of chemical principles.

Publication Dates: 2001–2002.

Scores, 9: Physical Knowledge, Acids/Bases & Salts, Compounds, Elements, Miscellaneous, Chemical Knowledge, Mechanical Principles, Gases & Fluids, Total.

Administration: Group.

Price Data, 2007: $21 per consumable self-scoring test booklet (minimum order of 20); $24.95 per manual (2002, 13 pages).

Time: (60) minutes (untimed).

Comments: Self-scoring instrument.

Author: Roland T. Ramsay.

Publisher: Ramsay Corporation.

Review of the ChemTest (Form AC) by JOHN TIVENDELL, Professor of Psychology, Université de Moncton, Moncton, New Brunswick, Canada:

DESCRIPTION. The Ramsay Corporation Job Skills ChemTest is part of a series of multiple-choice basic job skills tests that are put out by Roland Ramsay's company. There are many organizations that have jobs that involve manipulating chemical products, including printing shops and paint manufacturers, and they could indeed use a tool to assess pertinent skills and knowledge. This RCJS ChemTest (Form AC) is a self-scoring 43-item, four-option, multiple-choice test of some basic knowledge of physics and chemistry, to be used as part of a selection process for operating technicians in a chemical field. There are seven district content areas: first so-called Physical Knowledge (i.e., 6 items about such things as the role of electrical fuses and the different boiling points of household liquids); next 6 items about the chemical differences between Acids, Bases and Salts; a third called Compounds has 6 items mostly about recognizing chemical formulae; the fourth section called Elements includes 6 items, half of these about simple properties of metals and half on recognizing the chemical symbol for these; the sixth section has only 4 items about so-called Chemical Knowledge such as evaporation and measuring heat and weight; the seventh and largest section has 8 often diagram-related items measuring basic knowledge of Mechanical Principles such as in welding, and about torque and fulcrums. The final section has 4 items about knowledge in handling household Gases and Fluids. The fifth section has 3 items about measurement and is labeled Miscellaneous. The test is available in Spanish, too, which is certainly useful in many regions of the U.S.A. and elsewhere.

The 9-page test booklet is professional in appearance and not overly academically formatted. There is a clear and simple instruction page with two example items, and the back page acts as the multicolumned answer sheet. There are 7 pages of descending widths corresponding to these columns that present the multiple-choice questions. There is also a simple, straightforward, if very sparse, 13-page manual. Although 4 of its pages give the directions for administration and scoring, the manual introduces the test by simply citing the 1991 Dictionary of Occupational Titles' definition of a Chemical Operator III. There is little attempt at promoting its potential usefulness. Finally, the manual goes on to relate the development of the test and presents the limited information available as to its psychometric properties.

DEVELOPMENT. According to the manual, in 1996 the author and a colleague developed a 60-item paper-and-pencil pilot version of the test. Ten chemical-plant-based job experts later reduced these to 43 items, which then made up a computer-delivered version called Form A that was administered to 169 male and female job applicants. Their answers on the 43-item Form A test are the basis for the manual's KR-20 internal consistency reliability coefficient (.86), the item analysis table in the manual reporting on item difficulty, and the percentile ranks table also in the manual that forms the normative data reported by the authors of the test. However, in the introduction to the item analysis table, the author reports that 18 of these 43 items have since been modified by Ph.D level trainers at a chemical company in the mid-Atlantic area. This new and final version, Form AC, at best may have been used only once in one recent validity study (Scott, 2001).

TECHNICAL. Note that this test uses a multiple-choice format and does not measure a single job skill or job skills' factor but rather a combination of knowledge and skills in different areas, and it appears similar to a typical high-school level exam. Perhaps because of the appearance, the test authors employed KR-20 approach, a variation of coefficient alpha used for dichotomous data (Charter, 2003), albeit a standard for estimating reliability for a single administration of a single form test. However, given the heterogeneous nature of the items on the test, a high alpha reliability may not be possible despite the fact that the reliability coefficients for better tests are said to fall between .80 and .85 (Patock, 2004). Because the items on this test are multiple-choice items, an analysis of the patterns and rules of candidates' response errors might provide useful information.

Finally, the author has reported (Ramsay, 2002) that the second study was carried out to validate the test on a sample of 151 incumbent chemical operators. In the manual there are three correlation coefficients, presumably Pearson coefficients, of .20, .21, and .25 for the prediction of three unnamed job performance rating criteria used in this study. Unfortunately, we have no further information about the nature and form of these criteria, nor are there any scatterplots of their distribution. Surprisingly there are no specific data reported in the manual for this Form AC of the test, although it is probable that the unpublished content validity study, which was carried out by another management consultancy firm (see Scott, 2001), used the new form. The manual only states that the difference between Form A and Form AC is that the latter no longer contains the original 17 extra items and that 18 of the remaining computer-delivered Form A items have since been changed slightly to reflect simplification and readability. Changing the nature and the number of test items could affect the reliability and validity data, but changing the response format from a computer delivered to a paper and pencil type could also affect the results.

SUMMARY. There is certainly a need for specific job skills tests, such as this ChemTest, given the number of jobs that may require such competencies and the cost of putting the wrong candidate in the wrong job. The test booklet itself is clear and simple to use, albeit requiring high-school-level linguistic skills. The manual only deals with a few basic notions in chemistry and actually contains more questions on physics and measurement, but such knowledge is probably what is needed in most journey-level jobs. However, the manual is especially sparse, and users need to know more about the reliability and validity of this test, specifically of the Form AC. If possible, it should be tested on larger samples. The author acknowledges this latter point in his manual and asks readers to share any available normative data. Finally, it is also possible that biographical information about a candidate's performance, such as his or her results on a simple high school exam, could suffice for most organizations' purposes.

REVIEWER'S REFERENCES

Charter, R. A. (2003, July). A breakdown of reliability coefficients by test type and reliability method, and the clinical implications of low reliability. *Journal of General Psychology*. Retrieved February 7, 2007, from http://www.findarticles.com/p/articles/mi_m2405/is_3_130/ai_107124690/print

Patock, J. (2004). *A guide to interpreting the item analysis report*. University Testing Service, Arizona State University. Retrieved February 7, 2007, from http://www.asu.edu/uts/InterpIAS.pdf

Ramsay, T. (2002, July). *Tests you may want to use*. [member contribution to quarterly news publication of the Society for Industrial and Organizational Psychology, Inc.] Retrieved February 7, 2007, from http://www.siop.org/TIP/backissues/TIPJuly02/pdf/401_002.pdf

Scott, B. (2001). *Refinery operators validation study* [in-house study]. Pittsburg, PA: Development Dimensions International.

[40]

Child and Adolescent Risk Evaluation: A Measure of the Risk for Violent Behavior.

Purpose: Designed to screen "for violence risk and protective factors in childhood and adolescence."

Population: Ages 2–19.

Publication Date: 2003.

Acronym: CARE.

Scores, 3: Risk, Resiliency, Total.

Administration: Individual.

Price Data, 2005: $75 per complete kit including manual (37 pages), 25 assessment forms, and 25 case management planning forms; $19.95 per manual; $29.95 per 25 assessment forms; $29.95 per 25 case management planning forms.

Time: Administration time not reported.

Comments: Assessment includes record review and interviews with subject, family, and caregivers.

Author: Kathryn Seifert.

Publisher: Research Press.

Review of the Child and Adolescent Risk Evaluation: A Measure of the Risk for Violent Behavior by CHRISTOPHER A. SINK, Professor and Chair, School Counseling and Psychology, Seattle Pacific University, and BEVERLY J. WILSON, Associate Professor, Graduate Psychology, Seattle Pacific University, Seattle, WA:

DESCRIPTION. The Child and Adolescent Risk Evaluation: A Measure of the Risk for Violent Behavior (CARE) manual overviews the theoretical, research, and technical background and potential uses of the CARE Assessment Form (originally called the Child and Adolescent Risk for Violence [CARV]; Seifert, Phillips, & Parker, 2001), a measure designed to screen for violence risk and protective factors in children and youth. The precise age range for which CARE results are valid is not enumerated in the test manual or in other relevant publications (e.g., on the publisher's [Research Press, 2006]) or Seifert's [2005] web site). According to the author, knowing an examinee's total CARE score (a) enhances the test administrator's understanding of the child or youth at risk for violent behavior; (b) indicates the number of risk and protective factors present in the child's or adolescent's life; and (c) assists with planning appropriate treatment. The instrument also can be deployed in at-risk prevention and intervention studies.

In terms of the CARE assessment process, the manual outlines the following steps. The examiner should (a) review case history notes on the child or youth at risk for violent behavior; (b) conduct an interview with the examinee; (c) complete the CARE Assessment Form; and (d) develop, if warranted, an appropriate treatment plan using the Case Management Planning Form.

Directions for scoring the CARE are relatively clear and easy to follow. Three types of scores are calculated: (a) Risk score (raw scores for Risk Factors Items 1–41 are summed), (b) Resiliency score (raw scores for Protective Factors Items 42–49 are summed), and (c) total CARE score (difference between Risk score and Resiliency score). Although the Protective Factors dimension has no subsections, the Risk Factors component is composed of items representing four subdomains: Youth Characteristics (Items 1–24), Peers (Items 25–28), School and Education (Items 29–33), and Family Characteristics (Items 34–41). The range of possible raw scores ascribed to a particular item relates to the dimension or subdomain in which the item is listed. For instance, each Risk Factors item is assigned a 0, 1, 2, or 3. If an examinee had assaulted an authority figure (Youth Characteristics, Item 4), the item would be assigned a score of "3"; whereas, should the child or youth commit a sexual assault or other violation of another (Youth Characteristics, Item 3), the examinee is given a score of "1." For the eight items in the Protective Factors dimension used to generate the examinee's CARE Resiliency score, responses are awarded a -1 or -2. There are no derived or standardized scores. Even though Seifert indicates that the scoring procedure is based on research, in our view, the method appears idiosyncratic.

Other major considerations need to be weighed before administering the CARE. First, the examiner needs to have access to relevant information from the child's or youth's case history. Second, in addition to the 15 to 30 minutes required to complete and hand score the rating scale (an optional CARE tabulation software package is available), the examiner also needs to have adequate time to conduct the personal interview and review a client's file. Third, a total score cannot be tabulated if more than 33% of items cannot be rated. Fourth, although there is no explicit information in the manual about the qualifications required to fill out and interpret the CARE, we believe the examiner must have at least a psychology-related graduate education (e.g., mental health, clinical psychology) before doing so.

Interpretation of the severity of behavior problems is based on comparing the Total CARE Score to those youth with mild, moderate, and severe behavior problems who were previously tested on the instrument. In the manual, five cutoff points are provided, each one representing a higher severity level of youth behavior problems and a concomitant level of intervention intensity. In other words, as the examinee's total score increases, the intensity level of structure and treatment needed for this client also escalates. No threshold levels or intervention suggestions are provided for pre-adolescent children. Interpretation of scores for youth with sexual offenses or psychiatric disorders, without other behavioral acting out, may be problematic because assessments of these adolescents may produce low CARE ratings.

DEVELOPMENT. The CARE manual neglects to review the scale development process adequately. It does, however, point out that the background work on the measure commenced in 1996, with early data collection conducted at seven sites primarily within Atlantic and Midwestern states. Without providing details, the CARE Assessment Form was administered to "children and adolescents with mild to severe behavior problems and a history of violence" (manual, p. 16). With a 5-year data set, the author refined the items and codified the scoring procedures. It is unclear from reading the manual whether extensive pilot studies and item analyses were conducted on the scale during the test development phase. Moreover, the CARE's theoretical underpinnings and the empirical research supporting its various domains are only broadly reviewed in the manual and elsewhere (e.g., Seifert, 2003, 2005; Seifert et al., 2001). Further discussion of these issues would be helpful.

TECHNICAL. According to the manual, the technical sample used to examine the CARE's psychometric properties was composed of 463 individuals. Of this number, 414 were children and youth (ages 2–19) drawn principally from nonspecified mid-Atlantic ($n = 359$, 86.5%) states. Data were disaggregated into two age groups: ages 2–12 ($n = 139$, 34%) and 13–19 ($n = 275$, 66%). The convenience sample was composed of youth in (a) outpatient treatment facilities ($n = 295$, 71%), (b) residential settings ($n = 89$, 21%), (c) prisons and charged as adults for the violent crimes ($n = 17$, 4%), and (d) other juveniles ($n = 2$, .5%). Matching in part the ethnic breakdown in the U.S. population with serious emotional difficulties, the ethnicities of juveniles assessed by the CARE were: European American or white ($n = 232$, 56%), African American ($n = 139$, 34%), Hispanic ($n = 16$, 4%), Asian ($n = 5$, 1%), and other ($n = 22$, 5%). Males represented approximately 73% of the sample. The participants' individual histories were summarized as follows: 43% ($n = 181$) had no assault history and 56% ($n = 231$) had some assault on their record. Of the latter group, most had a history of problems including family violence as well as some type of mental disorder and learning difficulty. It should be noted that in the same year the CARE manual was published, Seifert (2003) reported somewhat different numbers and background data when describing the CARE technical sample. Subsequently, Seifert (2005), in an unpublished manuscript, indicated that the technical sample had increased to 825 individuals, ages 2–19.

Item statistics and item-total score correlations were reported in the manual. The means and SDs for Items 2 through 49 were similar across all but one item (Item 1). Item-total score correlations were largely in an acceptable range ($rs = .25$–$.65$). Somewhat disconcerting, however, 12 items (24.4%) yielded Pearson rs below .30, including 6 items (12.2%) with item-total score rs less than .21. Given these 12 questions appear to be contributing little variance to the overall score, we question why they were retained in the final version of the CARE.

Reliability evidence for the CARE is reviewed in the manual as internal consistency coefficients and stability estimates (Pearson rs). The magnitude of the alphas reported for the full scale was adequate for a measure such as this one ($r = .83$). The split-half reliability analysis (unequal length Spearman-Brown) yielded a coefficient of

.72. Alpha coefficients calculated on both halves of the items were .81 and .61, respectively. More recently, Seifert (2005) reported a full-scale alpha of .85 and split-half reliabilities ranging from .54 to .85 ($N = 825$). The test-retest stability coefficient was estimated from a very small convenience sample ($N = 25$ juveniles) following a time gap varying from 5 to 45 days after the initial testing. All data were collected before the start of therapy or in the initial assessment period of therapy producing a Pearson r of .99 (unbiased $r = .83$). Given the subjective nature of the CARE items and clinic skill needed to appraise the at-risk behavior of children and youth, the manual inexplicably does not report interrater reliability estimates.

Seifert (2003, 2005, and in the test manual) provided some evidence for the CARE's validity. For instance, the moderate alpha coefficient and the trend of increasing CARE scores across the severity of participants' behavior problems show some support for the measure's construct validity. However, the manual did not provide any confirmatory evidence of the CARE's underlying dimensionality (e.g., factorial validity studies).

Support for the CARE's predictive validity and construct validity was summarized in the manual. Data from a subsample of 112 individuals were used to determine if the CARE's total score was a good predictor of future violence and assault. Six months after the initial assessments, therapists working with the youth were asked to submit a sample of case files of individuals who had and had not committed assaults. The total CARE score was a relatively useful indicator of future behavioral problems ($r = .65$, $p < .001$). However, neither standard errors of measurement nor estimate are reported. Construct validity was assessed by examining the mean total CARE scores of psychiatric ($M = 22.17$, $SD = 13.83$, $n = 320$) and nonpsychiatric ($M = 17.15$, $SD = 13.88$, $n = 91$) clients. A significant main effect for group was reported; the clients with mental disorders had significantly higher mean CARE scores than the nondisordered sample.

Remarkably, outside of the item analyses conducted, evidence for the measure's content validity was not fully discussed, and there was no way to determine whether risk evaluation experts scrutinized the CARE items. Examples provided for several items are vague and ill-defined. In summary, unlike the evidence for the measure's reliability, the empirical documentation marshaled in support of the instrument's content validity and construct validity was less than passable for these types of screening inventories.

COMMENTARY. The CARE's value to appraise respondents' perceptions of the level of behavioral problems in children and adolescents consistently, as well as what interventions may be useful to adolescents at risk, is relatively well documented in the manual. Extreme caution must be exercised, however, when using individual item scores to determine potential behavior problems and plan relevant interventions.

Because the CARE seems to have little or no research support from school-based studies and the technical sample appears to be largely composed of adolescents drawn from clinical milieus, the CARE's value as a school-based screening device for at-risk students is questionable. We suggest, therefore, that the CARE Assessment Form be utilized as a screening device only with adolescents in clinical and mental health milieus. It should be noted as well, we could not find any published studies using the CARE except those by Siefert.

Evaluators must keep in mind the following caveats when assessing adolescents with the CARE. First, additional research needs to be collected with much larger samples gathered from a variety of settings around the country to corroborate the soundness of its psychometric properties. Mental health and school-based validity evidence for the rating scale falls short of accepted professional testing standards for attitudinal-like screening measures. Second, the terminology used on the CARE Assessment Form and the Case Management Planning Form requires substantial graduate-level training in a psychology-related discipline. Test administration and score interpretation (as well as intervention planning) should be, therefore, left to competent professionals (e.g., mental health counselors, clinical psychologists, and clinical social workers). Third, although Seifert indicates in the test manual that the CARE is an efficient screening device, if evaluators actually follow the steps outlined in the manual, the time needed to complete the assessment could be as long as 2 to 3 hours. Finally, to enhance the CARE's utility, sample real-world case studies should be provided in the manual. These need to walk the examiner through the administration process and its steps coherently, as well as provide information on how to effectively interpret and use the Case Management Planning Form.

SUMMARY. The Child and Adolescent Risk Evaluation is in part user-friendly and reliable and, if used with significant caution, a serviceable clinical instrument to estimate risk levels for adolescents for behavior problems as well as their risk and protective factors. Although, the CARE may be a helpful assessment tool for well-trained mental health clinicians, we do not recommend that the instrument be used by individuals without graduate-level training in psychology. Further, given the lack of research on the utility of the CARE with younger children in nonclinical settings, it is recommended that it not be used with children under 13 years of age and in school settings. Before fully endorsing the CARE as an efficient and effective screening tool, from our perspective, the measure requires: (a) further refinements to the manual and to the test items, (b) additional psychometric analyses with a much larger and more representative sample of children and youth at risk, and (c) stronger evidence of its interscorer reliability as well as its validity (e.g., content, construct).

REVIEWERS' REFERENCES

Research Press. (2006). *CARE Kit Child and Adolescent Risk Evaluation: A Measure of the Risk for Violent Behavior.* Retrieved March 17, 2006, from http://www.researchpress.com/product/item/5205/

Seifert, K. (2003). Childhood trauma: Its relationship to behavioral and psychiatric disorders. *The Forensic Examiner, 12*(9-10), 27-33.

Seifert, K. (2005). *Development of the youth version of the CARE.* Retrieved March 17, 2006, from http://articles.careforusall.com/CARE.html

Seifert, K., Phillips, S., & Parker, S. (2001). Child and adolescent risk for violence (CARV): A tool to assess juvenile risk. *The Journal of Psychiatry and Law, 29*, 329-346.

Review of the Child and Adolescent Risk Evaluation: A Measure of the Risk for Violent Behavior by JAMIE G. WOOD, Associate Professor of Psychology, Pittsburg State University, Pittsburg, KS:

DESCRIPTION. The Child and Adolescent Risk Evaluation: A Measure of the Risk of Violent Behavior (CARE) is an instrument that screens children and adolescents for their risk of violence. This form contains 49 questions in five different areas: Youth Characteristics, Peers, School and Education, Family Characteristics and Environmental Factors, and Protective Factors (Resiliency). An individual's risk for violence is judged on a combination of the number of risk factors combined with his or her resiliency factors. Completion of the CARE Assessment Form pro-

vides three scores: the Risk Score, the Resiliency Score, and the Total CARE Score. A Case Management Planning Form for the CARE is also provided. Based on the total CARE score as well as scores from individual items, the Case Management Planning Form provides suggestions for specific interventions. The CARE manual provides scoring directions, technical data, and samples of completed CARE and Case Management Planning Forms. During the process of completing this review, the reviewer received information on additional technical studies conducted on the CARE. The date(s) on which these studies were completed is not provided nor is any reason given for the lack of inclusion of this research in the published manual.

DEVELOPMENT. This discussion of the development of the CARE is based on information from the CARE manual as well as the aforementioned studies. Work on the development of the CARE reportedly began in 1996. Data were collected over a 5-year period. Along the way, items were refined and scoring rules for the items were developed to produce the final CARE Assessment Form. Data were collected on youth in outpatient treatment programs (treatment for what not specified), residential settings, and from those charged as adults and imprisoned for violent crimes. According to the manual, the sample consisted of 414 individuals, ages 2 to 19, which the author refers to as "juveniles." The sample contained primarily males from the Midwestern and mid-Atlantic regions of the United States. Ethnically, the group was composed of primarily Caucasian and African American youth although a few Hispanic-American and Asian-American youth were included. It should be noted that the sample group, in the case of this instrument, were youth who were rated by examiners. Although the manual implies that there was more than one examiner, the exact number is not provided. The examiners divided the individuals in the sample group into six categories based on severity of behavior problems. These groups ranged from no behavior problems to severe behavior problems with Level 2 assaults. The examiners who were asked to rate the children and adolescents were familiar with each of their case histories.

In the additional studies sent to the reviewer, a sample of 924 youth is reported, within the aforementioned age range. Gender and ethnic percentages are similar to those in the sample contained in the manual. These studies also report on the development of four CARE Subscales: Chronic Violence, Sexual Behavior Problems, Attachment Problems, and Psychiatric Problems. Although the information describes how to calculate the subscale scores, the "CARE Subscale packet" used to record the scores and provide suggested interventions was not provided to the reviewer.

TECHNICAL. The manual reports that the reliability coefficient for the full scale score (assumed by the reviewer to be Total CARE Score) was .83. The reliability technique used for this analysis is not reported. Split-half reliability analysis was also performed, and a coefficient of .56 was reported. Further reliability studies mention that the alpha for Part 1 was .81 whereas the alpha for Part 2 was .61. Although not described clearly in the manual, the reviewer assumed that the author is referring to the Total Risk Score and the Total Resiliency Score as Parts 1 and 2, respectively. A test-retest reliability investigation was conducted utilizing a convenience sample of 25 individuals from the original sample. The test-retest period ranged from 5 to 45 days, and a coefficient of .99 was reported. It is assumed that the same examiner rated the individuals on both the first and second dates. No information is provided on interrater reliability.

The items on the CARE Assessment Form were evaluated for their correlation with the Total CARE Score. The manual describes all items as "highly correlated" with the Total CARE Score despite the fact that many of the items appear minimally correlated. For example, Item 2b (Two or three assaults) has a coefficient of .069 and Item 49 (Treatment for 6 months or more) has a coefficient of .089. The highest coefficient for a single item is .792 for Item 1 (Severity of behavior problems). Correlation coefficients for all other items range from .143 to .646. Not surprisingly, the resiliency (Protective Factors) items are negatively correlated to the Total CARE Score.

Several analyses are cited as evidence for the validity of the CARE. The first such investigation assessed the relationship between the aforementioned severity of problem behavior (six different levels) and the Total CARE Score. The manual does not mention a correlation coefficient for this analysis but reports that the findings were statistically significant. Likewise, a multivariate analysis, which controlled for age factors, also found a statistically significant relationship between severity of problem behavior and the Total Care Score. Surprisingly, the author reports that this second finding offers evidence of validity of the instrument for adults although there is no previous mention of any adults in the sample. Two studies attempting to establish predictive validity are also mentioned in the manual. First, the relationship between scores on the CARE (specific score not specified) and future violent behavior was conducted with a convenience sample of 112 youth. Each of these individual's files were reviewed 6 months after the completion of the CARE. The resulting correlation coefficient was .646. Secondly, there was a subsequent investigation of the association between CARE Score and whether the individual was in a community or a secure placement. The resulting correlation coefficient was .344. Finally, the manual cites evidence of divergent validity by attempting to correlate CARE Scores with number of psychiatric disorders. Although cited as statistically significant, the coefficient is reported as .149.

Several studies were conducted to investigate the validity of the various CARE subscales. Most of the investigations focused on attempts to correlate a subscale score with likelihood of engaging in a specific behavior (e.g., the Chronic Subscale Total Score and three or more unprovoked assaults, or the Sexual Behavior Problems Subscale and a history of sexually inappropriate behaviors). What professionals rated the youth in these subscales and examined their charts for the behaviors is not provided.

COMMENTARY. The author of the CARE deserves a great deal of credit for attempting to develop an instrument capable of making predictions about violent behavior. The type of research necessary to gather the necessary psychometric values can be quite time-consuming. Perhaps one of the more important aspects of such investigations is establishing operational definitions of what a history of sexually inappropriate behaviors means. Such tasks are not easily accomplished and the author deserves credit for attempting to establish some precision to predicting violent and other related behaviors.

In reviewing the CARE and its supplemental materials, one quickly notices a variety of flaws in many areas, most of which center around concerns with ambiguity in defining behaviors or traits. Many of the items contain descriptors that leave an examiner wondering how to score them. For example, Item 3 is titled "sexual assault or violence of another." In the descriptors for this item, an adolescent earns the same score if they have raped or molested another as they do if they have made an obscene phone call. Item 42 allows the examiner to find the results of an adolescent's IQ test or "estimate from what is known." Equally ambiguous is the way in which the total CARE score corresponds to arbitrarily defined ranges of necessary intervention.

The various samples associated with original and subsequent analyses appear to be samples of convenience. Very little information is provided on how the samples were selected or the characteristics of the individuals in the various analyses. Without knowing the representativeness of the sample, using the instrument with a specific group seems tenuous at best.

The manual does not provide any details on who the examiners were in most of the studies. If the examiners were not independent raters, the correlations between various scores and actual behaviors are less meaningful. If the examiners who scored the child or adolescent are also their caseworkers responsible for charting the youth's behaviors, strong correlations would be anything but surprising. In general, the questions concerning methodology of the attempts to establish validity and reliability makes one question the data provided.

CONCLUSIONS. The CARE is a measure of the risk for violent behavior. The total CARE score should lead to recommended interventions when used with the Case Management Planning Form. In addition to the psychometric investigations reported in the manual, other studies have been conducted by the author and were considered by this reviewer. The attempt to establish a useful predictive tool in this important area is a noble effort by the author. However, the lack of precision in many data-collecting procedures is troubling. Far too many questions exist about how samples were obtained, what their demographics were, why the ambiguous descriptors for items were used, and who the examiners were. The CARE seems at face value to ask important and reasonable questions useful for predicting vio-

lence. With revision of vague items, higher quality investigations of psychometric properties, and the use of multiple raters, the CARE could become a valuable instrument in this important field. However, at this time, it merely represents some valuable questions that may be important for planning intervention for youth at possible risk of committing violent behaviors. Assigning scores to the questions or interpreting the scores to be specifically predictive is not recommended at this time.

[41]

Children's Depression Inventory [2003 Update].

Purpose: "Evaluates the presence and severity of depressive symptoms in children."

Population: Ages 7–17.

Publication Dates: 1977–2003.

Administration: Individual.

Price Data, 2007: $193 per complete user's package including technical manual (2003, 170 pages), 25 CDI QuikScore forms, 25 CDI:S Quikscore forms, 25 CDI:P QuikScore forms, and 25 CDI:T QuikScore forms; $70 per specimen set including technical manual, 3 each of CDI Quikscore forms, CDI:S Quikscore forms, CDI:P Quikscore forms, and CDI:T Quikscore forms; $62 per technical manual; $43 per 25 CDI Quikscore forms; $41 per 25 CDI:S QuikScore forms; $39 per 25 CDI:P or CDI:T QuikScore forms; $90 per CDI V.5 Software kit including technical manual, CDI V.5 Getting Started Guide, and 25 Profile Report uses.

Foreign Language Editions: Translation of the CDI available in Afrikaans, Arabic, Bulgarian, Cantonese, Czech, Dutch, French (European), French (Canadian), German, Hebrew, Italian, Japanese, Lithuanian, Malay, Norwegian, Polish, Portugese (South American), Russian, Spanish (European), Spanish (South American), Swedish, Turkish, and Ukranian.

Comments: New edition adds parent and teacher report forms; paper-and-pencil or computer formats available.

Author: Maria Kovacs.

Publisher: Multi-Health Systems, Inc.

a) CHILDREN'S DEPRESSION INVENTORY.

Acronym: CDI.

Scores, 6: Negative Mood, Interpersonal Problems, Ineffectiveness, Anhedonia, Negative Self Esteem, Total.

Time: (15) minutes.

b) CHILDREN'S DEPRESSION INVENTORY: SHORT VERSION.

Acronym: CDI:S.

Scores: Total score only.

Time: (5) minutes.

c) CHILDREN'S DEPRESSION INVENTORY: PARENT VERSION.
Acronym: CDI:P.
Scores, 3: Emotional Problems, Functional Problems, Total.
Time: (10) minutes.
d) CHILDREN'S DEPRESSION INVENTORY: TEACHER VERSION.
Acronym: CDI:T.
Scores, 3: Same as *c* above.
Time: (10) minutes.
Cross References: See T5:472 (235 references) and T4:450 (71 references); for reviews by Michael G. Kavan and Howard M. Knoff of an earlier edition, see 11:66 (63 references).

Review of the Children's Depression Inventory [2003 Update] by JANET F. CARLSON, Professor, Department of General Academics, Texas A&M University at Galveston, Galveston, TX:

DESCRIPTION. The Children's Depression Inventory (CDI) [2003 Update] is an extension of the original CDI, first published in 1992. The CDI provides a direct assessment of the presence and severity of depressive symptomatology in children between the ages of 7 and 17, inclusive. It is a brief, paper-and-pencil self-report measure that may be administered in groups or individually. Respondents indicate which of three options best describes his or her mood, belief, action, or degree of enjoyment, in the context of everyday living. The CDI may be used to screen for symptoms of depression, to identify individuals in need of more comprehensive assessment, to assess treatment response, and for research purposes. The CDI is not intended as a diagnostic instrument.

Hand scoring is completed using the two-sided carbonless answer form supplied. The CDI provides a Total score and factor scores on five domains of depression. Total raw scores range from 0 to 54, with higher scores associated with greater levels of depressive symptomatology. All responses contribute to one of the five subscales as well as to the Total scale. Subscale scores range from 0 to 12, 8, 8, 16, and 10 for Negative Mood, Interpersonal Problems, Ineffectiveness, Anhedonia, and Negative Self-Esteem, respectively. Raw scores may be converted to *T*-scores by plotting raw scores on the Profile form that is part of the QuikScore response sheet. A series of tables presented in the test manual allow the conversion of raw scores to percentile equivalents for Total and subscale scores of the original (CDI), Parent

(CDI:P), and Teacher (CDI:T) forms, and for the total score of the Short version (CDI:S). Several clinical case illustrations provide guidance for scoring and interpretation.

Materials sent by the publisher included the 158-page test manual and several copies of each type of record form (CDI, CDI:S, CDI:P, and CDI:T). The test manual indicates that software may be purchased to permit responses to be made by keyboard entry.

DEVELOPMENT. The original CDI was based on the Beck Depression Inventory (BDI; Beck, 1967). For the most part, 21 items from the original BDI were extracted with some semantic modifications for age-appropriate language and content. Five items were added to address peer and school functioning. Item tryouts were conducted using clinical and nonclinical samples. Based on the tryouts, one item was added that addressed self-blame. The resultant 27-item scale was administered to a clinical sample (*n* = 39), a known nonclinical sample (*n* = 20), and a public school sample (*n* = 127). Several changes in the scale were indicated, following data analyses. Further refinements occurred following a second pilot test. Factor analyses were conducted and a five-factor solution was selected, despite underwhelming statistical indicators. All factors correlate significantly with one another at the *p* < .001 level.

The 10-item Short version of the CDI was developed from the original, using a backward stepwise internal consistency reliability analysis. This method maximizes internal consistency of the scale. The 17-item CDI-Parent and the 12-item CDI-Teacher versions also were developed from the original CDI, with appropriate adjustments to language to facilitate third party reporting and with an eye toward maximizing validity. Exploratory factor analyses were conducted. A two-factor solution emerged as optimal for both Parent and Teacher versions, using data from clinical and nonclinical samples. Nearly all scales and subscales correlate significantly with one another at the *p* < .05 level.

TECHNICAL. Information presented in the introduction to the test manual under the heading "Applicable Populations" (p. 5) states that norms were based on samples of Canadian, American, and Australian children. No further information about the relative proportions of the groups is provided here or in the chapter on "Normative Data" (pp. 45–49).

The original CDI was normed on 1,266 students from public schools in Florida, using data collected between 1979 and 1984. Gender distribution is reported as 592 boys and 674 girls. Other sample characteristics are not known with certainty. The test author used school district demographic data to estimate that 77% of the sample was White and 23% non-White. About 20% of the children comprising the sample were believed to be from single-parent households.

The Parent and Teacher versions of the CDI were developed later, with normative data collected from 1997 to 2003. The clinical sample included 167 Parent evaluations and 114 Teacher evaluations of children with various psychiatric conditions. The nonclinical sample included 1,187 Parent and 631 Teacher evaluations. Tabulated information for age and gender subgroups is presented in the test manual.

Results from 16 research studies are presented in the test manual to address test-retest reliability for the CDI. Coefficients vary widely. The test author offers a standard disclaimer about test-retest reliabilities of inventories such as the CDI, noting that the scale "measures a state rather than a trait" and suggests, "the retest interval for assessing reliability should be short (2 to 4 weeks)" (p. 60). Yet two studies that each used an interval of 1 week account for both the lowest (.38) and the highest (.87) coefficients reported. Generally, test-retest reliability coefficients fall in the mid .70s for retest intervals up to 4 weeks. Item-total score correlations (corrected) ranged from .22 to .58, with a median value of .41.

Internal consistency reliability estimates are reported for the normative sample on the original CDI (.86) and the CDI:S (.80). Estimates for the five CDI factors ranged from .59 to .68. Internal consistency of the Parent and Teacher versions are reported for clinical and nonclinical samples. Across samples, alpha coefficients were in the high .80s for the Total scores. Factor scores (Emotional Problems and Functional Problems) were nominally lower for the Teacher scale (.79 to .86) and the Emotional Problems factor on the Parent scale (.82 and .85). The Functional Problems factor on the Parent scale demonstrated alpha coefficients of .76 and .68 for clinical and nonclinical samples, respectively. The test manual also presents summary data from several research studies concerning reliability of the CDI.

A large number of findings reported by other researchers and cited or annotated in the CDI test manual establish much of the basis for validity of the CDI. Considering the wealth of research that has been conducted using the CDI, this seems a reasonable and parsimonious approach. Validation evidence for the CDI addresses a variety of types of validity and cites numerous studies published over the last 25 years or so in which results obtained with the CDI were compared with those obtained with other inventories and checklists. The test author presents this information in a series of tables, under the heading of construct validity. Test users can locate annotated bibliographic information for many of the cited works in Appendix A of the test manual. The appendix information summarizes the research and presents, briefly, the findings (e.g., correlation coefficients obtained). For example, one annotated reference (Nieminen & Matson, 1989) compared assessment of depressive symptoms using the CDI, Reynolds Adolescent Depression Scale (RADS), and corresponding subscales of the Behavior Problem Checklist (BPC), and the Walker Problem Behavior Identification Checklist. Participants were school children ($n = 76$; 63 boys, 13 girls) between 11 and 18 years of age, with severe behavior problems. Significant correlation coefficients ($p < .001$) were obtained for the RADS (.56), the BPC (.43), and the Walker (.36). Research studies cited in the test manual but not annotated in Appendix A are listed in Appendix B together with more complete reference information, so users can identify and locate the article on their own.

The test author offers appropriate caveats to potential users, concerning the use of the CDI in clinical settings. For example, the test author cautions that the CDI is not a diagnostic instrument and recommends it for use as a screening tool. To support this use, the test author cites 23 research studies in which the CDI has been found to be effective in differentiating between depressed and nondepressed children.

COMMENTARY. Representativeness of the sample on which norms were developed is difficult to assess, as demographic data are incomplete. Likewise, it is impossible to ascertain the extent to which the norming process was appropriate.

The CDI readily allows multirater assessment, which probably works in favor of accurate recognition of children in need of further evaluation. However, the items comprising each version of the inventory are transparent and, therefore, easily faked or manipulated by respondents inclined to do so. In those cases where test takers might be motivated to deceive (e.g., juvenile justice scenarios, custody hearings), the respondent easily could respond in a manner consistent with achieving his or her aims. The test author suggests repeated administration of the CDI over intervals as short as 2 weeks to assess treatment progress. The nature of the items and the brevity of the inventory make this application unreasonable, as respondents who recall their previous responses may strive to answer in the same way or in accordance with demand characteristics (i.e., if one is receiving treatment for depression, one should report fewer depressive symptoms as treatment proceeds).

Although the CDI is available in more than 20 languages, the validity of using the CDI in cross-cultural applications has not been established, as diagnostic classifications and symptoms vary from culture to culture. Test takers easily understand the CDI. It is presented in a rather familiar format that most respondents will complete properly. Although the math is simple, scoring and plotting results by hand involves several steps that may allow for clerical mishaps in transcription. The test author states that interpretation must remain the purview of qualified clinicians, although administration and scoring may be accomplished by paraprofessionals or technicians with proper training.

The CDI provides a preliminary indication of depressive symptoms and indicates who may need more comprehensive evaluation. With the growth in attention given to the detection and treatment of depression in children, it is not surprising that the CDI has been rather widely used. As a screening measure and in research, it is likely to continue to enjoy considerable use. The five domains comprising the subscales are closely related to the dimensions recognized as the hallmarks of depression in the most widely used diagnostic and classification systems. As described in the test manual, the reading level required to complete the CDI has not been identified unequivocally.

SUMMARY. The CDI uses a pencil-and-paper, self-report format to screen for depressive symptomatology in children. Its subscale scores align well with current perspectives on the major domains that comprise depression. It is reasonably priced, brief, and easy to administer, using individual or group administration procedures. Supportive documentation provided in the test manual is quite thorough in its coverage. On balance, the CDI is a reasonable choice for test users who wish to screen children, individually or in groups, for the presence of depressive symptoms.

REVIEWER'S REFERENCES

Beck, A. T. (1967). *Depression: Clinical, experimental, and theoretical aspects.* New York: Harper & Row.
Nieminen, G. S., & Matson, J. L. (1989). Depressive problems in conduct-disordered adolescents. *Journal of School Psychology, 27*, 175–188.

Review of the Children's Depression Inventory [2003 Update] by STEPHEN J. FREEMAN, Professor and Chair, Department of Counseling, Texas A&M University-Commerce, Commerce, TX:

DESCRIPTION. The Children's Depression Inventory (CDI) [2003 Update] is a self-report inventory purported to evaluate the presence and severity of depressive symptoms in children 7-17 years of age. The manual states the CDI may be administered individually or in a group setting. The CDI [2003 Update] is composed of the original 27-item CDI, a 10-item short version (CDI:S), and a new 17-item CDI Parent (CDI:P) and a 12-item CDI Teacher (CDI:T). The CDI and the CDI:S ask children to respond to items by identifying which of three choices (absence of symptoms, mild symptoms, or definite symptoms) best fits their feelings and ideas over the past 2 weeks. Items on the CDI:P and CDI:T versions were taken from the original CDI and rephrased. Parents and teachers are asked to select one response (*not at all, some of the time, often,* or *much or most of the time*) that best describes their observations on the child over the past 2 weeks. The CDI yields a Total score and scores on five subscales: Negative Mood, Interpersonal Problems, Ineffectiveness, Anhedonia, and Negative Self-Esteem. The CDI:S yields a Total score only. The CDI:P and CDI:T both yield two subscales (Emotional Problems and Functional Problems) in addition to a Total score. For evaluation and interpretation scores are converted to T scores.

The CDI self-report requires approximately 15 minutes or less to complete whereas the CDI:S (which was developed as a quick screening measure of depressive symptoms) takes approximately 5–10 minutes. The CDI:P and CDI:T can also be completed in under 10 minutes. Scoring and profile plotting can be accomplished in approximately 5–10 minutes. The entire procedure can be completed in 30 minutes. A software version is available. Computer administration times are comparable to those obtained with paper forms; however, score and profiles are completed in minutes.

DEVELOPMENT. Modeled after the Beck Depression Inventory (T7:275), the original CDI was initially developed in 1977 and published in 1992. The aim of the self-report instrument was to measure depression in children and adolescents between the ages of 8 and 15 years. However, in the mid-1990s, responding to the identified importance of multirater assessment, the CDI Parent and CDI Teacher were developed as an effective method of supplementing the CDI self-report. The four inventories (CDI, CDI:S, CDI:P, and CDI:T) comprise the CDI [2003 Update].

TECHNICAL. The norming sample for the CDI and CDI:S consisted of 1,266 Florida public school students in Grades 2 through 8, collected from 1979 to 1984. The sample included 592 boys ages 7 to 15 and 674 girls ages 7 to 16. Data on the children's ethnicity are unavailable.

Normative data for the CDI:P and CDI:T versions were gathered from 1997 to 2003 and included clinical and nonclinical samples. Data were gathered on children and adolescents in Grades 1 to 13 ranging in age from 7 to 17. The nonclinical sample consisted 1,187 parent and 631 teacher evaluations. The clinical sample consisted of 167 parent and 114 teacher evaluations of children with varied clinical diagnoses. The manual reports that only a subset of these were specifically diagnosed with a depressive disorder. The ethnicity of the nonclinical population was 83.4% Caucasian, 4% African American, 3.8% Hispanic, and 2.8% Asian. The clinical population was 77.9% Caucasian, 2.9% African American, 3.9% Hispanic, and 4.4% Asian.

The manual reports three estimates of reliability for the CDI: internal consistency, test-retest, and standard error of measurement. Internal consistency as measured using coefficient alpha was reported as .86 with a diagnostically heterogeneous psychiatric sample of 75 children, .71 with a pediatric medical outpatient group of 61, and .87 with a large sample (n = 860) of Toronto school

children. Internal consistency for the CDI:P and CDI:T was calculated using coefficient alpha. Reliabilities for the nonclinical sample ranged from .68 to .88 and for the clinical sample ranged from .76 to .89. The manual states that the CDI measures a state rather than a trait and therefore test-retest intervals should be short (2–4 weeks). Test-retest reliability coefficients for intervals of 1 to 4 weeks ranged from .38 to .87. However, for longer intervals of 6 weeks, these values ranged from .54 to .67; for intervals of 6 months, these values were .54; and for 1 year the values were .41 to .69. No test-retest data were provided for the CDI:P and CDI:T. Standard error of measurement was provided for total scores and ranged from 2.6 to 2.8 and for subscales ranged from .6 to 1.6.

The manual discusses various types of validity and contains numerous tables but provides little interpretable data to support the validity of the uses of the instrument. Some evidence supporting concurrent validity is presented in forms of reports that boys' and girls' self-rated depression correlated (boys .67; girls .72) with lowered self-esteem as measured by the Coopersmith Inventory and that the Piers-Harris Children's Self-Concept Scale and the CDI correlated .66.

COMMENTARY. The value of the CDI [2003 Update] seems compromised on several levels. First, the normative data for the CDI and the CDI:S were gathered from 1979 to 1984. The data for the CDI:P and the CDI:T were gathered from 1997 to 2003. Data on the normative samples' demographic, socioeconomic, and cultural/ethnic variables are also lacking.

Secondly, although internal consistency reliability is good, test stability and whether the CDI is measuring a state or a trait variable needs to be further defined and clarified. Data supporting interscorer reliability on the CDI:P and CDI:T are also needed.

Third, evidence supporting the validity of use of the CDI [2003 Update] is indeed far from adequate. Although the manual talked about validity, little convincing data were provided.

Finally, studies are needed of the cultural test bias with the CDI scores by ethnic group and by gender. No instrument can be recommended for use with ethnic minorities without such supporting studies.

SUMMARY. The author has developed a much needed instrument that is easy to administer and score. However, despite the popularity of the instrument the value of the CDI [2003 Update] is questionable. Significant criticism can be made regarding the normative sample indicating that it is time to renorm using a national sample. The CDI [2003 Update] does warrant further research in order to continue its development, and to document its validity as a clinical diagnostic tool. The potential usefulness of the CDI [2003 Update] will be contingent on the outcome of this research. Until such supportive work is forthcoming, clinical use is not recommended.

[42]

Children's PTSD Inventory: A Structured Interview for Diagnosing Posttraumatic Stress Disorder.

Purpose: "Designed for the identification and assessment of posttraumatic stress disorder in children and adolescents."
Population: Ages 6–18.
Publication Date: 2004.
Scores, 7: Exposure, Situational Reactivity, Reexperiencing, Avoidance and Numbing, Increased Arousal, Significant Distress, Total.
Administration: Individual.
Price Data, 2007: $141 per complete kit including manual (52 pages) and 25 inventory forms; $52 per 25 inventory forms; $66 per manual.
Time: (5–20) minutes.
Comments: Inventory forms also available in Spanish and Canadian French; five overall diagnostic categories (PTSD Negative, Acute PTSD, Chronic PTSD, Delayed Onset PTSD, or No Diagnosis) provided.
Author: Philip A. Saigh.
Publisher: The Psychological Corporation, A Harcourt Assessment Company.

Review of the Children's PTSD Inventory: A Structured Interview for Diagnosing Posttraumatic Stress Disorder by ROBERT CHRISTOPHER, Professional, Clinical and Forensic Assessments, LLC, Sparks, NV:

DESCRIPTION. The Children's PTSD Inventory is designed as a structured interview, intended for assessment of posttraumatic stress disorder in children and adolescents between 6 and 18 years of age. The Inventory consists of an answer sheet, a scoring sheet, and the manual. The item set consists of five sections of questions that closely follow the DSM-IV-TR diagnostic criteria for PTSD: Exposure and Situational Reactivity,

Reexperiencing, Avoidance and Numbing, Increased Arousal, and Significant Distress or Impairment. The questionnaire component can be completed in approximately 15–20 minutes with children who exhibit PTSD symptomatology, and less than 5 minutes with children with a history of stress exposure who do not manifest PTSD symptoms.

DEVELOPMENT. Many of the Children's PTSD Inventory's test items have subsets, and multiple endorsements within a subset are recorded as a single numerical score. Negative responses to certain items signal an examiner to discontinue further inquiry, whereas affirmative responses warrant continuation of assessment. Most of the items are supplemented with additional inquiries about the specific time frame of the symptom's onset and duration. Total score on the Inventory yields four diagnostic options: PTSD Negative, Acute PTSD, Chronic PTSD, or Delayed Onset PTSD.

Normative samples for the Children's PTSD Inventory consisted of two groups of stress-exposed and stress-unexposed youths. Sample 1 included 150 youths—109 with a history of stress-exposure, and 41 without. A range of stressors were included, specifically sexual assaults, physical attacks, stabbings/shootings, attempted abduction, World Trade Center Attack, dog attacks, motor vehicle/bicycle accidents, hand injuries, smoke inhalation, witnessing traumatic events, and sequelae of someone's suicide. This sample consisted of 56% males and 44% females with an age range from 7.1 to 18.7 years (60.7% Hispanic, 19.3% African American, 13.3% Caucasian, 6% Asian, and .7% other), and the second sample consisted of 54.8% males and 45.2% females, with a mean age of 12.5 years and a range of 6.3 to 17.9 years (48.7% Hispanic, 29.3% Caucasian, 17.1% African American, and 4.9% Asian).

TECHNICAL. Internal consistency estimates for the Children's PTSD Inventory were in the moderate to high range (.58 to .89) within individual clusters. Coefficient alpha for Overall Diagnosis was .95. Interrater reliability of diagnoses derived from two separate administrations of the Inventory (n = 150) indicated that 39 participants were identified to have the PTSD diagnoses, 106 were identified as PTSD negative, and no rating was given for 2 participants. Disagreement among raters occurred for only 3 cases or 2%. The manual reports 88.3% correspondence with DSM-IV diagnostic criteria. Additional instruments used to demonstrate criterion-related validity included the Diagnostic Interview for Children and Adolescents—Revised PTSD Module, Structured Clinical Interview for DSM PTSD Module, and clinical interviews. Moderate to high levels of sensitivity (.84–.92) and specificity (.93–98) were obtained, with positive predictive power (PPP = .93–.95) and negative predictive power (NPP = .95–.99), and diagnostic efficacy ranging from .93 to .95.

To test construct validity a comparison was made between a number of items endorsed on the Inventory and total and subscale standard scores of the Revised Children's Manifest Anxiety Scale (RCMAS), Children's Depression Inventory (CDI), Junior Eysenck Personality Inventory (JEPI), and Child Behavior Checklist (CBCL). "The total number of symptoms endorsed on the Children's PTSD Inventory was significantly associated with continuous psychological variables from RCMAS and CDI" (manual, p. 37). The correlation between the Children's PTSD Inventory and the JEPI is provided as supporting evidence for discriminant validity. The association between the Inventory and the CBCL Internalizing scales is used to illustrate convergent validity, whereas a lack of significant correlations between CBCL Externalizing scores and the Children's PTSD Inventory provided additional evidence of discriminant validity.

COMMENTARY. The Children's PTSD Inventory is designed to follow the format of a structured interview for diagnosing Posttraumatic Stress Disorder in children and adolescents. It guides an examiner along a narrow path of the DSM PTSD diagnostic criteria, which is essentially developed for assessment of adult patients. Shortcomings of diagnostic approaches to classifying children have been documented (Evans, 1991; Scotti, Morris, McNeil, & Hawkins, 1996). Applying a uniform diagnostic standard to children, adolescents, and adults may lead inexperienced clinicians to overlook symptom overlaps and symptom variations caused by age, etiology, and environmental contingencies. Diagnostic frameworks applied to children historically come from those developed for adults. Although diagnostic criteria have been significantly revised to make them more relevant to the younger population of trauma patients, antecedents, symptom spectrum, and sequence of traumatic experiences may differ with this population in many respects from adult versions (Tierney, 2000).

The Children's PTSD Inventory is intended for examinees between the ages of 6–18. This age range may contain a number of developmental stages, each with specific characteristics and complexities that may not be identical across the entire age range. Thus, a likelihood exists that scores would not meet empirical thresholds and could result in diagnoses that are inappropriate for similar symptoms at different developmental stages. Although structured interviews are perhaps the closest approximation to what some clinicians consider to be a "gold standard" of assessment (Angold & Costello, 2000), other researchers agree that the current diagnostic system may not be appropriate for children (Carrion, Weems, Ray, & Reiss, 2002) and that further developmental modifications are needed for certain symptom clusters.

The normative samples used in standardization of the Children's PTSD Inventory appear to be demographically unbalanced, bringing into question diagnostic sensitivity and specificity of the instrument regarding a number of trauma diagnostic variations reported in the literature for demographic features such as age, gender, race, ethnicity, culture, and so forth (Brown, 2004; Bryant-Davis, 2005; Fitzpatrick, Piko, Wright, & LaGory, 2005; Flores, Cicchetti, & Rogosch, 2005; Gollwitzer, Eid, & Jürgensen, 2005; Horowitz, McKay, & Marshall, 2005; Koss, et al., 1996; Kubiak, 2005; Marshall, & Orlando, 2002; McKay, Lynn, & Bannon, 2005; Ng-Mak, Salzinger, Feldman, & Stueve, 2004; Pole, Best, Metzler, & Marmar, 2005; Pottinger, 2005; Ruef, Litz, & Schlenger, 2000; Voisin, 2005; Weisman et al., 2005).

When selecting normative samples for the Children's PTSD Inventory, differences in the prevalence rates of PTSD diagnoses among children exposed to a single trauma (Type I) as compared to chronic long-term trauma (Type II) were not taken into consideration. However, after Hurricane Hugo in 1989, Shannon, Lonigan, Finch, and Taylor (1994) conducted a study with a large population of school-age children. Their findings indicated that only 5.42% of the children and adolescents involved in the disaster developed posttraumatic disturbances. On the other hand,

McLeer, Deblinger, Henry, and Orvaschel (1992) found that approximately 44% of sexually abused children met the full criteria for PTSD.

SUMMARY. Given the developmental complexities of children and adolescents, conflicting issues with the conceptual framework of PTSD (Yehuda & McFarlane, 1995), as well as known concerns about the applicability of current psychiatric diagnostic systems to youth (Beutler & Malik, 2002; Carrion et al., 2002; Evans, 1991; Scotti et al., 1996; Tierney, 2000; and others), the author's statement that this instrument may be administered by an examiner with an undergraduate degree in psychology or equivalent, after only 2 hours of laboratory training, should be taken with some reservation. However, the Children's PTSD Inventory can be a practical assessment instrument if used by skillful, knowledgeable, and experienced clinicians who are particularly cognizant of numerous diagnostic limitations inherent with demographically varied population samples, and particularly children and adolescents.

REVIEWER'S REFERENCES

Angold, A., & Costello, J. E. (2000). The child and adolescent psychiatric assessment (CAPA). *Journal of the American Academy of Child & Adolescent Psychiatry, 39,* 39–48.

Brown, L. S. (2004). Feminist paradigms of trauma treatment. *Psychotherapy: Theory, Research, Practice, Training, 41,* 464-471.

Bryant-Davis, T. (2005). Coping strategies of African American adult survivors of childhood violence. *Professional Psychology: Research and Practice, 36,* 409-414.

Buetler, L. E., & Malik, M. L. (2002). *Rethinking the DSM, A psychological perspective.* Washington, DC: American Psychological Association.

Carrion, V. G., Weems, C. F., Ray, R., & Reiss, A. L. (2002). Toward an empirical definition of pediatric PTSD: The phenomenology of PTSD symptoms in youth. *Journal of the American Academy of Child and Adolescent Psychiatry, 41,* 166–173.

Evans, I. M. (1991). Testing and diagnosis: A review and evaluation. In L. H. Meyer, C. A. Peck, & L. Brown (Eds.), *Critical issues in the lives of people with severe disabilities* (pp. 25-44). Baltimore: Paul H. Brooks.

Fitzpatrick, K. M., Piko, B. F., Wright, D. R., & LaGory, M. (2005). Depressive symptomatology, Exposure to violence, and the role of social capital among African American adolescents. *American Journal of Orthopsychiatry, 75,* 262-274.

Flores, E., Cicchetti, D., & Rogosch, F. A. (2005). Predictors of resilience in maltreated and nonmaltreated Latino children. *Developmental Psychology, 41,* 338-351.

Gollwitzer, M., Eid, M., & Jürgensen, R. (2005). Response styles in the assessment of anger expression. *Psychological Assessment, 17,* 56-69.

Horowitz, K., McKay, M., & Marshall, R. (2005). Community violence and urban families: Experiences, effects, and directions for intervention. *American Journal of Orthopsychiatry, 75,* 356-368.

Koss, M. P., Figueredo, A. J., Bell, I., Tharan, M. et al. (1996). Traumatic memory characteristics: A cross-validated mediational model of response to rape among employed women. *Journal of Abnormal Psychology, 105,* 421-432.

Kubiak, S. P. (2005). Trauma and cumulative adversity in women of a disadvantaged social location. *American Journal of Orthopsychiatry, 75,* 451-465.

Marshall, G. N., & Orlando, M. (2002). Acculturation and peritraumatic dissociation in young adult Latino survivors of community violence. *Journal of Abnormal Psychology, 111,* 166-174.

McKay, M. M., Lynn, C. J., & Bannon, W. M. (2005). Understanding inner city child mental health need and trauma exposure: Implications for preparing urban service providers. *American Journal of Orthopsychiatry, 75,* 201-210.

McLeer, S. V., Deblinger, E. B., Henry, D., & Orvaschel, H. (1992). Sexually abused children at high risk for post-traumatic stress disorder. *Journal of the American Academy of Child and Adolescent Psychiatry, 31,* 875-879.

Ng-Mak, D. S., Salzinger, S., Feldman, R. S., & Stueve, C. A. (2004). Pathologic adaptation to community violence among inner-city youth. *American Journal of Orthopsychiatry, 74,* 196-208.

Pole, N., Best, S. R., Metzler, T., & Marmar, C. R. (2005). Why are Hispanics at greater risk for PTSD? *Cultural Diversity & Ethnic Minority Psychology, 11,* 144-161.

Pottinger, A. M. (2005). Children's experience of loss by parental migration in inner-city Jamaica. *American Journal of Orthopsychiatry, 75*(4), 485-496.

Ruef, A. M., Litz, B. T., & Schlenger, W. E. (2000). Hispanic ethnicity and risk for combat-related posttraumatic stress disorder. *Cultural Diversity & Ethnic Minority Psychology, 6,* 235-251.

Scotti, J. R., Morris, T. L., McNeil, C. B., & Hawkins, R. P. (1996). DSM-IV and disorders of childhood and adolescence: Can structural criteria be functional? *Journal of Consulting and Clinical Psychology, 64,* 1177-1191.

Shannon, M. P., Lonigan, C. J., Finch, A. J., & Taylor, C. M. (1994). Children exposed to disaster: I. Epidemiology of post-traumatic symptoms and symptom profiles. *Journal of the American Academy of Child & Adolescent Psychiatry, 33,* 80-93.

Tierney, J. A. (2000). Post Traumatic Stress Disorder in children: Controversies and unresolved issues. *Journal of Child and Adolescent Psychiatric Nursing,* October 1.

Voisin, D. R. (2005). The relationship between violence exposure and HIV sexual risk behavior: Does gender matter? *American Journal of Orthopsychiatry, 75,* 497-506.

Weisman, A., Feldman, G., Gruman, C., Rosenberg, R., Chamorro, R., & Belozersky, I. (2005). Improving mental health services for Latino and Asian immigrant elders. *Professional Psychology: Research and Practice, 36,* 642-648.

Yehuda, R., & McFarlane, A. C. (1995). Conflict between current knowledge about posttraumatic stress disorder and its original conceptual basis. *American Journal of Psychiatry, 152,* 1705–1713.

Review of the Children's PTSD Inventory: A Structured Interview for Diagnosing Posttraumatic Stress Disorder by BETH DOLL, Professor of Educational Psychology, and ALLISON OSBORN, Doctoral Student, University of Nebraska-Lincoln, Lincoln, NE:

DESCRIPTION. The Children's PTSD Inventory is a structured clinical interview designed to identify posttraumatic stress disorder (PTSD) in children and adolescents, ages 6–18. Its five sections correspond to the five DSM-IV-TR (American Psychiatric Association, 2000) symptoms clusters for PTSD: The child has experienced a traumatic event (Exposure and Situational Reactivity); is troubled by intrusive memories of the event (Reexperiencing); avoids experiences associated with the event and undergoes diminished interest or emotional detachment in the aftermath (Avoidance and Numbing); has difficulty sleeping and concentrating (Increased Arousal); and these symptoms have been pronounced and persistent (Significant Distress or Impairment). The inventory is a structured clinical interview that should be administered only by a licensed psychologist or a bachelor's level examiner working under a psychologist's supervision. Use of the inventory is intended to promote the early identification and treatment of children with PTSD which, in turn, can significantly improve the children's social and academic outcomes.

The Children's PTSD Inventory is a sophisticated interview composed of a series of open and closed questions. Appropriate administration requires that the examiner have a thorough knowledge of the onset and progression of PTSD because, once each question is asked as written, the examiner must follow-up with appropriate probes and inquiries to more fully describe the child's experience. Only examiners familiar with the assessment and treatment of PTSD will know how to respond to children's answers. Completion of the interview usually requires 15–20 minutes, but can take much less time for some children because the interview is discontinued at any point if the child's answers rule out a diagnosis of PTSD.

In the first section of the inventory, the children are asked to recount their traumatic experience. The examiner records their description verbatim and then asks additional probing questions to define the nature of that event. If the child does not report a traumatic experience, the interview is discontinued. The next three sections of the inventory include "yes" or "no" questions about specific symptoms of PTSD, and the examiner asks about symptom duration whenever a child responds "yes" to a symptom. To continue the interview, the child must report at least one symptom lasting 1 month or longer. The final section of the interview assesses the degree of distress that the child is experiencing.

The complexity of the Children's PTSD Inventory is heightened by shifts from one section to the next in scoring rules and the number and kinds of symptoms. Despite this complexity, the manual's administration and scoring instructions span only seven pages and provide insufficient detail for the typical examiner. Instead, instructions and the script for examiners are incorporated into the inventory form, but the form is complex and sometimes difficult to follow. Examiners who plan to administer the inventory will need to review the instructions carefully prior to beginning.

DEVELOPMENT. The Children's PTSD Inventory was developed from the diagnostic criteria for PTSD in the DSM-IV-TR. Inventory items were written in language that could be easily understood by children. Then, to assess the phrasing and improve clarity, the test items were read aloud to 8-year-old children and their comments and level of understanding were noted. Next, one co-chair and two members from the DSM-IV/PTSD advisory group reviewed the scale and verified that it corresponded with the diagnostic criteria for PTSD in the DSM-IV (agreement = 90%). Additional reviews were conducted by several practicing psychologists who provided feedback on the agreement of inventory questions with DSM-IV-TR diagnostic criteria.

TECHNICAL. The reliability of the Children's PTSD Inventory has been described in two recent, peer-reviewed publications based on overlapping samples: 150 youth (109 of whom were stress-exposed) who had been seen at a large urban hospital or a private clinic in the Northeastern United States, and an additional 11 youth also seen at a private clinic. The manual essentially restates information from these two publications. Results are quite promising. The internal consistency reliability of the overall diagnosis based on the inventory was very strong (alpha = .95), and four of the five inventory sections showed adequate internal consistency with alphas equal to or greater than .70. The exception was the alpha for Situational Reactivity (.58). Interrater reliability was similarly high with 98% agreement for the overall diagnosis across two independent examiners. Test-retest reliability was examined using a subset of 42 participants and showed 98% agreement across a 2-week interval. These levels of reliability are adequate to support the scale's use in applied settings, if they are confirmed in subsequent research.

In the same two studies, the validity of the Children's PTSD Inventory was strongly supported by its high agreement and correlation with parallel measures of the symptoms of PTSD: the Diagnostic Interview for Children and Adolescents—Revised, PTSD module (Reich, Leacock, & Shanfeld, 1994) and the Structured Clinical Interview for the DSM—IV, PTSD module (First, Gibbon, Williams, & Spitzer, 1996); and moderate correlations with closely related measures: the Revised Children's Manifest Anxiety Scale (r = .73; Reynolds & Richmond, 1985), the Children's Depression Inventory (r = .61; Kovacs, 1992), the Junior Eysenck Personality Inventory Neuroticism (r = .57; Eysenck, 1965), and the Child Behavior Checklist (r = .47 for the total scale, and .54 for the Internalizing subscale; Achenbach, 1991). To be convincing, these results will need to be replicated in additional, nationally representative samples.

COMMENTARY AND SUMMARY. The Children's PTSD Inventory is a complex diagnostic interview that requires thorough knowledge of PTSD to administer. Minimal instructions in the manual, and a very complex inventory form, require that examiners review the inventory carefully before beginning its administration. The inventory's reliability and validity are promising, but are predicated on only two publications by the author and his research group. Early indications are that the Children's PTSD Inventory will be a very strong diagnostic tool. If these results are confirmed by additional research, the scale could be appropriate for use in clinical settings.

REVIEWERS' REFERENCES

Achenbach, T. M. (1991). *Manual for the Child Behavior Checklist and Revised Child Behavior Profile*. Burlington, VT: University of Vermont, Department of Psychiatry.

American Psychiatric Association. (2000). *Diagnostic and statistical manual of mental disorders* (DSM-IV-TR). Washington, DC: Author.

Eysenck, S. B. (1965). Junior Eysenck Personality Inventory. San Diego, CA: Educational and Industrial Testing Service and Human Services.

First, M., Gibbon, M., Williams, J. B., & Spitzer, R. L. (1996). *Structured Clinical Interview for the DSM-IV* (SCID). Biometrics Research Department, New York State Psychiatric Institute.

Kovacs, M. (1992). The Children's Depression Inventory. North Tonawanda, NY: Multi-Health Systems.

Reich, W., Leacock, N., & Shanfeld, C. (1994). Diagnostic Interview of Children and Adolescents—Revised (DICA-R). St. Louis, MO: Washington University.

Reynolds, C. R., & Richmond, B. O. (1985). *Revised Children's Manifest Anxiety Scale: Manual*. Los Angeles, CA: Western Psychological Services.

[43]
Children's Speech Intelligibility Measure.

Purpose: "Designed to provide clinicians with an objective measure of single-word intelligibility of children ages 3.0 to 10.11 whose speech is considered unintelligible."

Population: Ages 3.0–10.11.

Publication Date: 1999.

Acronym: CSIM.

Scores: Total score only.

Administration: Individual.

Price Data, 2004: $94 per complete kit including manual (140 pages), 15 record forms, and microphone switch; $15 per 15 record forms; $50 per manual.

Time: (10-20) minutes.

Authors: Kim Wilcox and Sherrill Morris.

Publisher: The Psychological Corporation, A Harcourt Assessment Company.

Review of the Children's Speech Intelligibility Measure by CONNIE T. ENGLAND, Associate Professor/Department Chair, Graduate Counseling and Guidance, Lincoln Memorial University, Knoxville, TN:

DESCRIPTION. The Children's Speech Intelligibility Measure (CSIM) is an individually administered measure of single-word intelligibility of children ages 3 years, 0 months to 10 years, 11 months. It is intended to be an objective measure of a child's intelligibility and purports to control for (a) listener familiarity with the subject, (b) context clueing associated with connected speech, (c) eliciting procedures, and (d) content of materials.

To address issues related to listener familiarity, all judges are expected to be unfamiliar with the child's particular speech patterns. The authors have chosen a multiple-choice presentation of phonetically balanced words from which the judge is to select the target word most similar to the speaker's production. The authors support this method of assessment arguing that contextual cues are lessened and do not provide the supportive cues of a continuous speech sample. Elicitation of the single word speech sample is accomplished through oral presentation of the stimulus word by the examinee followed by the audiotaping of only the examinee's response. The measure relies on 600 carefully selected target words organized into 50 sets of 12 phonetically similar words. The words in each group serve as phonetically similar foils for the target word. The words also serve as alternate forms. The authors state that having a large cadre of stimulus lists reduces the likelihood of "practice effects" typically associated with frequent retesting of children.

Although speech-language pathologists will be the typical examiner, the manual states that other individuals with experience and training in giving tests may also administer the CSIM. Examiners for the CSIM must also be experienced in working with preschool- and elementary-school-aged children. The examiner is also responsible for soliciting the help of a person unfamiliar with the examinee's specific speech patterns to act as judge in completing the scoring.

The CSIM consists of a manual, record form, a stimulus list, and a hand-switch box with a 1/8-inch connector plug. (The hand-switch box is used to mute the administrator's presentation of the target word and record the child's repetitions, with the tape running continuously.) Additional equipment required for administration, but not provided in the test kit, are a microphone with a 1/8-inch adapter, a tape recorder equipped with a jack for an outside microphone, and a blank audiocassette tape. After completing the identifying information on the record form, the examiner selects a stimulus list. (The manual notes that a grid is provided at the bottom of each list so that the examiner can keep a record of how often a specific list is used.)

To administer the CSIM the examiner models the target word and the examinee responds by repeating the word. Only the examinee's responses are taped, thus preventing the judge from hearing the stimulus word. The manual states that to accomplish this form of taping it is necessary for the examiner to release the record button on the hand-switch box, thus stopping the recording each time the examiner says the stimulus word. Beginning with the first stimulus word and then with every fifth word the examiner records on tape the number of the item (examinee does not respond). This procedure is used to assist the judge keep place on the record form. After the examinee's 50 words have been recorded this recording is given to the judge for scoring. Each correct item gets 1 point, incorrect items get zero. To calculate the percent intelligibility the total raw score is multiplied by 2. The manual also provides *SEM*s for percentages at the 90% confidence level.

DEVELOPMENT. The CSIM is an adaptation of Yorkston and Beukelman's 1984 Assessment of Dysarthric Speech. Yorkston and Beukelman modeled their studies with dysarthric clients on Haagen's original studies of multiple-choice intelligibility measures. Yorkston and Beukelman created a master pool of 50 sets of 12 similar-sounding words, which when combined into a four-option format gave the highest score of intelligibility. The authors of the CSIM adopted the Yorkston and Beukelman master pool of similar-sounding words for their stimulus sets.

During the development of the CSIM the authors responded to two concerns raised. One concern was that the list of words needed to be unfamiliar to young children and not impact their performance on the test. The authors addressed this issue by evaluating the words and finding that the list of words was relatively equal in its unfamiliarity to most young children. The other concern was that the lists of stimulus words needed not only to be phonetically similar but also had to sample each vowel phoneme adequately and appear only once on the word list. These concerns were addressed by revising Yorkston and Beukelman's word lists, thus the final list contains 165 word changes from the original 600 words. Furthermore, during pilot testing an additional 17 words were replaced because examination of judges' responses indicated that the words were not being chosen as incorrect responses as frequently as the other words on the list.

The standardization sample for the CSIM consisted of 152 children, ages 3 years to 10 years, 11 months. Each child selected for the study had to be English-language dominant and exhibit unintelligible speech as identified by a speech pathologist. Seventy-nine speech-language pathologists administered the standardization version of the CSIM. Each speech-language pathologist was required to recruit a judge to complete the scoring phase.

Demographic characteristics of the sample are reported by gender, ethnicity, and geographic regions of the United States and by age. Of the 152 children, 90 were male, 107 were Caucasians, and 61 were from the south. The sample was separated into three age groups. There were 54 children in the 3 years to 4 years, 11 months age group; 57 children in the 5 years to 6 years, 11 months age group; and 41 children in the 7 years to 10 years, 11 months age group.

TECHNICAL. Each child in the standardization sample completed four tests. Each test was administered by a speech-language pathologist and scored by a judge. Results of testing and scoring were sent to The Psychological Corporation, the publisher of the test, where additional judging of the cassette tapes was conducted.

Test-retest reliability, using the same form, was conducted with three forms of the test. The time interval between the first and second administration was not less than 1 week and not more than 2 weeks. Overall, the results of the test-retest study indicate moderate to strong correlations (e.g., .79–.91) for all groups with the exception of the 3-year to 4-year, 11 month age group. The authors suggest that "it is plausible that the significant variability among this particular age group is due to factors other than variability in the test form" (manual, p. 22). For example, they suggest that actual changes in the child's intelligibility may have resulted from interventions to the child's speech. Results of the alternate form reliability study revealed a pattern consistent as test-retest (same form), with the lowest correlations occurring in the youngest age group.

Interrater reliability was accomplished by having one judge from the same geographic location as the child score the tape and the other judge an employee of The Psychological Corporation. Presumably this arrangement allowed for a judge who was not only unfamiliar with the child's speech (as was a requirement for all judges) but was also unfamiliar with regional dialectal features the child may be using. The results indicate a strong correlation between these two groups $r = .8$. Once again lower correlations for interrater reliability occurred with the youngest age group. A somewhat unexpected finding for ages 3 years to 4 years, 11 months was that interrater agreement was actually higher than intrarater agreement for this group. To account for these results, the manual suggests that because of the small number of judges used for this study, a "practice effect," or "judge familiarity" factor may have impacted the results. The manual also suggests that in clinical practice this effect would most likely be minimized.

Content validity data for the CSIM (i.e., evidence that the items of the instrument are an appropriate measure of the construct) are based on Yorkston and Beukelman (1980) studies with dysarthric clients. Modeled on Haagen's original studies on multiple-choice intelligibility measures, Yorkston and Beukelman created a master pool of 50 sets of 12 similar-sounding words. Yorkston and Beukelman found that the four-option format gave the highest score of intelligibility. With only a few minor adjustments the authors of the CSIM adopted the Yorkston and Beukelman master pool of similar sounding words.

The authors posit that their underlying theory of intelligibility is that it can be measured as a single coherent construct. To that end measuring a one-dimensional construct should reveal high internal consistency coefficients. The authors refer to reliability alpha internal consistency coefficients averaging between .79 and .90 across age levels to support their supposition.

The authors state that no comparable single word intelligibility assessments are currently available so they had to rely on other speech intelligibility measures for correlational validation. Correlation validity evidence comprised two separate studies. One study compared the speech intelligibility scores from the CSIM with participants' performances on the Goldman-Fristoe Test of Articulation. The authors report a moderate negative correlation (-.55 to -.65) between these two measures (i.e., as articulation errors increase intelligibility decreases), and conclude based on these results that the CSIM shows adequate concurrent validity.

In another study, speech-language pathologists and clinicians were asked to provide intelligibility estimates for children's connected speech. The manual states that by doing this they were able to determine the level of agreement between trained and untrained listeners when judging intelligibility, and were able to investigate the relationship between intelligibility based on single word utterances versus intelligibility based on connected speech. This study resulted in a moderate level of agreement between the trained listeners' and average listeners' estimation of intelligibility. The authors conclude that because, as the manual states, the CSIM was designed to measure an average listener's understanding of a child's speech intelligibility, the level of agreement between listeners gives additional evidence of the CSIM's correlational validity.

COMMENTARY AND SUMMARY. The CSIM was designed to provide clinicians with an objective measure of single-word intelligibility of children ages 3 years to 10 years, 11 months whose speech is considered unintelligible. The manual states that the use of a single-word intelligibility format contrasts sharply with the current use of more subjective measures of intelligibility. The authors support their single word utterance measure of intelligibility by suggesting that commonly used connected speech samples lack control over speech content, rarely result in identical pre/post test situations, and require lengthy speech samples that must be transcribed by a trained professional.

Unfortunately, the CSIM provides only sparse data to support claims of adequate reliability and validity. The manual fails to provide sufficient empirical documentation, other than the phonetic similarity of words, for selecting a list of similar-sounding words once intended for use with dysarthric clients. The authors' argument that most of the words in the sets are unfamiliar to young children fails to justify adequately the selection of these specific words for the assessment. Additional research is needed to determine the validity and efficacy of this selection of phonetically matched word sets.

Furthermore, the soliciting of independent judges as part of the evaluation process seems both cumbersome and unrealistic. As noted in the manual, field testers both supported and criticized the use of independent judges. Although independent judges were able to provide an objective opinion of the child's speech, finding such a person is too time-consuming and may ultimately end in the overuse of some judges, thus eradicating the basic premise of the assessment (i.e., to have objective data provided by judges unfamiliar with the child's speech patterns).

A final note regards the mechanics of the assessment. The taping device suggested in the manual requires three separate pieces of machinery (e.g., external microphone, hand-switch box [provided in test kit] and a tape recorder with a 1/8-inch plug). Newer technology makes the proposed machine set-up seem impractical and outdated. One suggestion is the use of a hand-held microcassette with an external microphone. It is highly portable, allows for fast review of recordings, easily goes from recording mode to "pause" mode allowing for the taping of only the examinee's responses, and presents fewer potential problems for the examiner and judge. Because technology advances are fast-paced and seemingly never-ending even this device may benefit from updating.

REVIEWER'S REFERENCE

Yorkston, K., & Beukelman, D. R. (1980). A clinician-judged technique for quantifying dysarthric speech based on single-word intelligibility. *Journal of Communication Disorders, 13,* 15–31.

Review of the Children's Speech Intelligibility Measure by GABRIELLE STUTMAN, Private Practice, Westchester and Manhattan, NY:

DESCRIPTION. The Children's Speech Intelligibility Measure (CSIM) is an objective measure of single-word intelligibility for ages 3 years to 10 years, 11 months. It utilizes a standardized presentation method and controls for list-learning effects, listener familiarity, and contextual cues. The test administrator may choose any of 200 lists of 50 words. The large number of lists permits frequent retesting without list-learning effects. The child is asked to repeat each of the 50 words into a tape recorder. A muting device is included in the test kit so that only the child's responses are recorded; the examiner must purchase a tape recorder with an external microphone jack. The examiner must also find an independent judge, unfamiliar with the child, to score the tape recording using a multiple-choice format. The judge chooses each word they hear from a list of 12 similar-sounding alternatives on the record form, a process that requires about 10 minutes. A tape library can be maintained to aid discussion of a child's progress and document improvement.

The manual gives detailed instructions for setting up the muting apparatus, administering, and scoring the 50-word list. A "Percent Intelligibility" score is obtained by doubling the number correct. Raw scores, estimated true scores, and confidence intervals (90%) have been developed for age groups of 3 years to 4 years, 11 months; 5 years to 6 years, 11 months; and 7 years to 10 years, 11 months, and are listed in an appendix.

DEVELOPMENT. The CSIM is an adaptation of the Assessment of Intelligibility of Dysarthric Speech (Yorkston & Beukelman, 1984; T7:207), which was designed for assessing adults. The Yorkston and Beukelman word list was compared to a list of word frequencies in children's speech (ages 4 years, 6 months to 5 years), to determine that each of the 600 words on the list was equally unfamiliar to young children. The list was revised to assure an adequate sample of each vowel phoneme represented, and that the words within each of the 12-item comparison lists were phonetically similar. The age range of the list was expanded during standardization to include children up to 10 years, 11 months of age. However, some words appear to be at a higher level of vocabulary than others, which creates an iatrogenic difficulty for younger children.

A pilot testing of 15 native English-speaking preschool children refined the recording procedures, instructions, and phonetic similarities of the 12-word comparison lists. A tryout testing of 19 preschool children confirmed the practicality of the testing process, and provided an initial assessment of the validity (high correlation with the Goldman-Fristoe Test of Articulation and teacher ratings) and reliability (test-retest and item analysis) of the instrument.

TECHNICAL. The test was standardized on a sample of 152 English dominant children, with unintelligible speech but adequate hearing, ages 3 years to 10 years and 11 months, from April to July of 1998. It was administered by 79 speech-language pathologists who recruited their own judges to complete the scoring phase of the test. The sample was standardized by gender, ethnicity, geographic region, and age. However, there is no comparison of the sample with population statistics. Each child completed two test sessions consisting of one test with a unique word list and one test with a repeated word list in each session, for a total of four tests. The sessions were given 1 to 2 weeks apart.

With regard to reliability, the test-retest, alternate form, interrater, and intrarater reliability measures were lower for the 3 years to 4 years and 11 months group, compared with the 5 years to 10 years and 11 months age groups. The most deficient rating was for the alternate form (age 3 years to 4 years and 11 months; $r = .64$). This weakness supports the authors' suggestion to take an average across several tests for enhanced reliability and validity. All reliability ratings were moderate to strong for the older two groups ($r = .80-.91$). Internal consistency (coefficient alpha = .79–.93) is acceptable for all tests and age groups.

Validity measures are reasonably good. The content validity of a multiple-choice format, using 12 different but phonetically similar comparison words on each administration, appears to minimize intelligibility ratings thus minimizing any ceiling effect. The authors' unidimensional theory of intelligibility is made possible by their use of single words to control for linguistic context, and of a naïve judge to control for familiarity. The result is the relatively high coefficients of internal consistency cited above. Correlational validity was assessed in two ways. First, a comparison of the CSIM with the Goldman-Fristoe Test of Articulation was made. This yielded correlations of moderate magnitude in the predicted direction ($r = -.55$ to $-.65$), where negative correlations were expected. Second, the intelligibility of the children's speech was rated by the children's speech-language pathologist or clinician, and compared with those of untrained individuals. This yielded only low to moderate levels of agreement ($r = .38-.52$). The authors' interpretation of this result is its usefulness in increasing people's understanding of a child's "improvement," despite little perceived change in intelligibility. I tend to agree that it is the naïve listener who must understand the child, if that child is to succeed in social and academic contexts. No examination of differential reliability or validity of this test was made across gender, racial, ethnic, or cultural groups. With the caveat that one needs to compensate for the higher variability of children in the youngest age group, the CSIM provides a good diagnostic measure of childhood dysarthria and of change in intelligibility over time.

SUMMARY. The CSIM, a diagnostic and evaluative tool for quickly measuring single word intelligibility, serves its stated purpose well. It puts less pressure on the child, compared to the Goldman-Fristoe, because only repetition of a heard word is required. However, the evaluator should be aware that information is lost when a speech sample does not include the child's ability to connect the sounds of multiword phrases. The manual provides a thorough description of administration procedures, 200 alternate forms, age-normed confidence intervals, a brief summary of test development, and generally acceptable technical data. However, reliability of scores in the youngest group should be enhanced by averaging more than one testing. Its primary weakness is that the administrator needs to find a tape recorder that will mesh well with the muting device and an independent rater to score the responses. However, children's motivation is enhanced because they enjoy pressing the buttons and hearing their own voice on the tape recorder. The ability to maintain a record that provides an objective rating of single word intelligibility, while minimizing practice effects, and relatively rapid administration (20-25 minutes) are also strong points.

REVIEWER'S REFERENCE

Yorkston, K., & Beukelman, D. R. (1989). Assessment of Intelligibility of Dysarthric Speech. Austin, TX: PRO-Ed.

[44]

Clerical Skills Test.

Purpose: "Designed to assist companies in identifying individuals who have strong reading, mathematical and analytical skills."

Population: Current and prospective employees.

Publication Dates: 1999–2001.

Acronym: CST.

Scores, 7: Writing, Analyzing, Proofreading, Filing, Math, Checking, Total.

Administration: Group.

Price Data, 2005: $79.99 per starter kit including administrator's manual (2001, 28 pages), 5 tests, and 1 test log; $29.99 per administrator's manual; $9.25 per test (online or paper-and-pencil version; paper-and-pencil version sold in quantities of 10).

Time: 21(26) minutes.

Comments: Paper-and-pencil and online versions available.

Author: J. M. Llobet.

Publisher: G. Neil.

Review of the Clerical Skills Test by ELEANOR E. SANFORD-MOORE, Vice-President of Research and Development, MetaMetrics, Inc., Durham, NC:

The Clerical Skills Test (CST) was developed by J. M. Llobet and is part of the G. Neil HR Assessments Series. The test was designed to measure an individual's reading, mathematical, and analytical skills necessary to complete the basic skills required of most clerical positions. The manual states that the test can be used to select applicants or to test current employees for training needs. When used as a selection tool, the manual recommends that the test results should be used in conjunction with other tools.

The test consists of six subtests: Writing Skills, Analyzing Skills, Proofreading Skills, Filing Skills, Math Skills, and Checking Skills. These subtests measure an individual's ability to read instructions, write and analyze reports, file, and handle basic computations. There are both print and electronic versions of the instrument.

ADMINISTRATION. The Clerical Skills Test can be administered in both a print mode and an electronic mode. Each subtest is timed and the total test takes less than 30 minutes to administer. Each subtest can be considered a speed test because the examinee is asked to complete as many items as possible in the defined administration time.

The Writing Skills subtest is scored by the administrator using judgment based on the level of the job in which the applicant is interested. The items on four of the remaining five subtests—Analyzing Skills, Filing Skills, Math Skills, and Checking Skills—are scored right-wrong, and raw scores are used for each of the subtest scores. The score for the Proofreading subtest is calculated by subtracting the number of errors marked that are not errors from the number of correctly identified errors. The Total Score for the Clerical Skills Test is the sum of the five subtest scores (Writing Skills is excluded).

Norms for each subtest (excluding Writing Skills) and the total test are provided. The norming population consists of 113 employees employed in various positions (e.g., secretary, file clerk, accounting clerk, shipping and receiving clerk, marketing coordinator) in 12 organizations. The manual cautions that this normative information should be used to guide the development of local norms based on current employees.

DEVELOPMENT. No information is presented concerning the development of the instrument.

RELIABILITY. No information is presented concerning the reliability of the instrument. That interrater reliability has not been checked is especially concerning for the Writing Skills subtest as judgment is used in its scoring.

VALIDITY. The validity information presented in the manual consists of two studies conducted to assess the construct validity of the instrument. The first study consisted of 113 employees who were administered the Clerical Skills Test and for whom job performance data were collected. The job performance data consisted of Likert ratings of the five scored tasks on the Clerical Skills Test—perceptual accuracy, analyzing skills, proofreading skills, math skills, and filing skills—and overall job performance. Although the correlations between the ratings and the scores on the subtests were low ($r = .18$ to $.30$), most were significant at the .05 level. Correlations between the Clerical Skills Test subscores and the rating of overall job performance were low and generally not significant at the .05 level ($r = .17$ to $.24$).

The second validity study involved 47 of the employees from the first study. Each of the 47 employees was also administered the Personnel Ability Test (a measure of overall intelligence). Scores on the Clerical Skills Test subtests and the overall score on the Personnel Ability Test were moderately correlated ($r = .47$ to $.67$). The correlation between the Total Score on the Clerical Skills Test and the overall score on the Personnel Ability Test was .72 (significant at the .001 level).

SUMMARY. The Clerical Skills Test is easy to administer and score. The manual does not provide information in relation to the development and reliability of the instrument, and the validity information is not adequate for making individual decisions. If decisions are to be made based upon the results from the test, adequate reliability and validity need to be ensured. The manual does stress that the interpretation of the test results should be done locally, be job-specific, and not be based on national norms. Each test user should conduct job analyses and validation studies to determine the usefulness and appropriateness of the results for his or her specific situation.

The manual provides considerable information related to guidelines associated with personnel selection testing: Title VII of the Civil Rights Act of 1964, the Americans with Disabilities Act, and various other topics. In addition, the manual describes steps to follow for proper administration, adverse impact monitoring, and interpretation of results when instruments are used for employee selection.

[45]
Clinical Assessment of Articulation and Phonology.

Purpose: Designed to "assess English articulation and phonology in preschool and school aged children."
Population: Ages 3 to 9 years.
Publication Date: 2002.
Acronym: CAAP.
Administration: Individual.
Price Data, 2006: $219 per complete kit including examiner's manual (2002, 136 pages), 50 Articulation Inventory forms, 30 Phonological Checklists forms, stimulus easel, 5 Clinical Assessment of Articulation and Phonology Pals, and Clinical Assessment of Articulation and Phonology Stickers; $29.99 per 50 Articulation Inventory forms; $29.95 per 30 Phonological Checklists forms; $45 for examiner's manual.
Comments: This is a norm-referenced instrument.
Authors: Wayne A. Secord and JoAnn S. Donohue.
Publisher: Super Duper Publications.
    a) ARTICULATION INVENTORY.
    Scores, 2: Consonant Inventory Score, School Age Sentence Score.
    Time: (15–20) minutes.
    b) PHONOLOGICAL PROCESS CHECKLISTS I AND II.
    Scores, 10: Final Consonant Deletion, Cluster Reduction, Syllable Reduction, Gliding, Vocalization, Fronting, Deaffrication, Stopping, Prevocalic Voicing, Postvocalic Devoicing.
    Time: (20) minutes.

Review of the Clinical Assessment of Articulation and Phonology by STEVEN LONG, Speech Pathology and Audiology, Marquette University, Milwaukee, WI:

DESCRIPTION. The Clinical Assessment of Articulation and Phonology (CAAP) is a norm-referenced test of Standard American English consonant articulation. The test has two parts, Consonant Inventory and School Age Sentences, that assess consonant production in single word and connected speech, respectively. The Consonant Inventory subtest can be administered to individuals 2.5 to 9 years of age and yields standard scores

for both phoneme errors and phonological process occurrences in single-word naming. The School Age Sentences subtest is suitable for individuals 5 to 9 years of age and has norms for errors occurring in repeated sentences. Administration time for both subtests together is 15–20 minutes.

Test responses are recorded on two forms, an Articulation Inventory and a Phonological Process Checklist. Scoring on the Inventory form differs for the two subtests. Responses from the Consonant Inventory subtest are recorded either as correct or by type of error (omission, substitution, distortion). Responses from the School Age Sentences subtest are simply scored as right or wrong. The Phonological Process Checklist also offers two forms of scoring. Checklist I uses the response data from the Articulation Inventory, analyzing it for phonological process occurrence. Checklist II requires the child to again name the test stimulus pictures in a different order. Process occurrence is then judged on-line for each word as it is spoken. Whichever checklist is used, additional time is required beyond the estimated 15–20 minutes. If all sections of the CAAP are administered, then three raw scores are calculated: Consonant Inventory, School Age Sentences, and either Phonological Process Checklist I or II.

DEVELOPMENT. The CAAP belongs to a large group of tests that assess children's speech sound production skills. In design, the CAAP is intended to be time efficient, to sample consonant singletons and clusters across mono- and multisyllabic words representatively, and to provide a comparison of speech accuracy on single-word and connected speech tasks. The CAAP offers the option of introducing the test through a "story" involving five puppet characters. Although these puppets are prominently featured on all the test forms and stimuli, the rationale for using them is meager and they seem included mostly for marketing purposes. To simplify administration, the Consonant Inventory subtest only tests consonant production in initial and final position and samples two targets (singleton or cluster) in all elicited words. The lack of medial consonant sampling is justified by the claim that such consonants behave similarly to initial and final consonants, according to their position within a syllable. This view is not shared by others in the field (e.g., Grunwell, 1987; Hodson, 2004), who point to children's sound changes, such as glottal substitution, that are more prominent word-medially. Vowels are not sampled in the CAAP.

TECHNICAL. The CAAP was standardized on a total sample of 1,707 American and Canadian children. The sample generally mirrors the demographic characteristics of the United States (2000 U.S. Census data) with respect to region, gender, race, maternal education, and home language. Information about the initial pilot study, field testing, and standardization testing is included in the manual. The dialectal status of the children tested (e.g., Standard American English, African American English, English-Spanish bilingual) is not reported. Furthermore, the demographic data are not cross-tabulated, so that the dialectal composition of the sample cannot be inferred from race and socioeconomic data. More importantly, the norms themselves are not tabulated by race, dialect, or gender, making it impossible to compare a speaker to his or her linguistic or gender peers.

The standardization data for the CAAP was collected by 220 American and Canadian speech pathologists. No requirements for participation in the standardization study are cited. Hence, it is unclear whether examiners were actually required to demonstrate proficiency in judging the accuracy of children's speech. Without this information, one cannot judge the level of training needed to administer the CAAP accurately and reliably.

Test-retest reliability was measured on the raw scores from 32 children. Comparing total raw scores, the correlation was .975. Comparing just the School Age Sentences raw score from children 5 to 9 years, the correlation was .865. Interexaminer reliability was computed on just four examiners. Analyses of variance performed on their scores from 56 protocols showed a reliability coefficient of .99. This figure represents the reliability of the average of four examiners, not the reliability of a single rater. The examiners who participated in the reliability studies are not identified and therefore cannot be evaluated for how well they represent the typical CAAP user. Furthermore, the reliability estimates are only for presence of error, not type of error. Thus, any interpretation of test results that relies on information from phonetic transcription (e.g., the ratio of omissions to substitutions and distortions) rather than correct/incorrect judgments cannot be assumed as reliable. Finally, the authors of the CAAP do not report

the severity of the samples compared for reliability purposes. As the data from the standardization sample indicate, the average number of errors produced on the test falls dramatically, to less than nine, after age 4. The reliability of perceptual judgments is greatly inflated when the sample(s) to be judged contain mostly normal behaviors (Kearns & Simmons, 1988).

COMMENTARY. There are now a large number of standardized articulation tests available to clinicians that, for the most part, cannot be differentiated by the volume or diversity of their standardization data. The value of one test over another therefore rests largely in (a) design features that render a particular test faster or simpler to use, or (b) analytical features that provide clarity in interpretation or offer insights into a child's speech behavior that are not available from other instruments. The CAAP fits into the mix of other articulation tests as one that is adequately but perhaps not impressively standardized and that offers no particular advantages in design or analysis.

As a norm-referenced test, the CAAP compares unfavorably on several points to other available tests. Sentence error norms are only provided for ages 5 years 0 months to 8 years 11 months, so the test cannot be used to compare errors in single word and connected speech with preschool children. The CAAP provides conversion of raw scores to standard scores, age equivalent scores, and percentile ranks. However, the first two of these are best avoided in clinical practice because the normative data regarding the test were not normally distributed and articulation skill does not develop linearly through childhood and adolescence. The CAAP standardization sample was not analyzed for gender differences, despite the fact that years of normative research have indicated more rapid speech normalization in girls during the preschool years (e.g., Smit, Hand, Freilinger, Bernthal, & Bird, 1990). Moreover, the test remains biased against speakers of nonstandard or regional dialects because no allowance is made in scoring for pronunciations that are acceptable dialectal variations.

Within each section of the CAAP are weaknesses in design that detract from its accuracy and informativeness. In the multisyllabic words section of the Consonant Inventory, deleted syllables are recorded but only count as errors if they occur on the initial or final syllables of the word. However, in 7/9 of the words, the weak (unstressed) syllable(s) are neither the first nor last. In the majority of instances, then, syllable deletion occurring in these multisyllabic words would not be reflected in the child's error score. The summary tables of the Consonant Inventory form tally information about consonant singletons only. Thus, there is no convenient way to interpret a child's performance with consonant clusters or multisyllabic words, apart from his raw score in those categories. Ages of mastery are not reported for consonant clusters and one cannot easily compare a child's production of consonant singletons to those clusters in which the same phonemes occur (e.g., /r/ versus /br/, /tr/, /gr/).

In the School Age Sentences subtest, only the number of errors is counted. There is no analysis comparing types of errors or phonemes produced in error between word and sentence samples. The sentence production task thus potentially confounds phonological and morphosyntactic errors. The examiner's manual does not acknowledge this lack and provides no guidance on how to score sentences where words or bound morphemes are omitted (e.g., if a child repeats the word "paints" as "paint"). The Critical Difference Calculation purports to evaluate the statistical significance of any difference between a child's score on the Consonant Inventory and School Age Sentence subtests. A cutoff value is given for each of the four school-age intervals. No explanation is provided in the manual of how these cutoff values were calculated from the standardization data.

The use of two Checklists (I and II) to evaluate phonological process occurrence seems possibly unnecessary. Phonological Checklist II, if administered, adds to the total administration time, with no gain in assessment information because the child merely names the same set of pictures a second time. The child must also be engaged in the naming task longer, which should be avoided when a child's attention span is short. At the very least, the scoring form should have provided a convenient way to evaluate the child's consistency of production of the same target words. The rationale for Phonological Checklist II, which involves an online judgment of process occurrence, is that it saves time over Checklist I, which involves transferring information from one part of the scoring form to another. No evidence is pro-

vided by the authors that this greater efficiency is real, and intuition suggests to this reviewer that it is not. Because of a printing delay, standard scores for the Phonological Process Checklists are contained in a supplemental examiner's manual, which also explains how to score the Checklists. The supplemental manual does not explain the interpretation of the Phonological Process norms. The user is referred back to the primary manual, which says little on the subject. Of particular importance is the fact that the manuals provide no guidance on how to interpret together the two standard scores that the test yields, one from the Articulation Inventory, the other from the Phonological Process Checklists.

SUMMARY. In most aspects, the CAAP is a traditional test of speech sound production in children and, as such, it is a reasonably well-designed and standardized instrument. However, the developers have attempted to introduce some innovative features that they believed would create greater motivation in test-takers and save time for examiners. Unfortunately, this reviewer believes that these features do not improve the test. Fortunately, examiners can avoid them (i.e., they can ignore the introductory "story" of the test and can use Checklist I rather than II). If this type of administration is done, then one is left with a norm-referenced instrument that can be used to document the existence of an articulation impairment and qualify the examinee for clinical services. The CAAP does not offer very many or very good options for analyzing children's error patterns, which is needed for treatment planning, especially with individuals who demonstrate severe articulation disorders. Other tests, such as the Hodson Assessment of Phonological Patterns—Third Edition (HAPP-3; Hodson, 2004;17:87), or other methods of manual or computerized phonological analysis must be employed for this purpose.

REVIEWER'S REFERENCES

Grunwell, P. (1987). *Clinical phonology.* Second edition. Baltimore, MD: Williams & Wilkins.

Hodson, B. (2004). Hodson Assessment of Phonological Patterns—Third Edition. Austin, TX: Pro-Ed.

Kearns, K. P. & Simmons, N. N. (1988). Interobserver reliability and perceptual ratings: More than meets the ear. *Journal of Speech and Hearing Research, 31,* 131-136.

Smit, A. B., Hand, L., Freilinger, J., Bernthal, J., & Bird, A. (1990). The Iowa articulation norms project and its Nebraska replication. *Journal of Speech and Hearing Disorders, 55,* 779-799.

Review of the Clinical Assessment of Articulation and Phonology by ROGER L. TOWNE, Associate Professor, Department of Communication Sci-

ences and Disorders, Worcester State College, Worcester, MA:

DESCRIPTION. The Clinical Assessment of Articulation and Phonology (CAAP) is a norm-referenced test of English articulation and phonology appropriate for preschool and school-aged children. According to the authors, the CAAP was developed to provide a quick way of assessing articulation in young children, to measure overall articulation competency, to compare word- and sentence-level articulation ability in school-aged children, and to estimate the occurrence of common phonological processes in children's speech. It is designed to be administered by speech-language pathologists or others who have specific training in the assessment and treatment of articulation and phonological disorders.

The test includes an examiner's manual, a stimulus easel, separate scoring forms for the Articulation Inventory and Phonological Process Checklists, five foam character "dolls" called CAAP Pals, and CAAP Pal stickers. The Articulation Inventory tests for production of 24 consonants and one vowel using 44 words. Consonants are tested in the prevocalic position, the postvocalic position, or within clusters at three levels of difficulty; singleton consonants in mostly single syllable words; consonant clusters in single syllable words; and multisyllabic words. A total of 97 test items make up the articulation inventory. For children 5 years of age and older the articulation inventory also includes a School Age Sentence section in which articulation accuracy in sentences is measured by the number of words correctly articulated. There are eight sentences of varying lengths incorporating a total of 73 words.

The Phonological Process Checklists (I and II) each assess "the occurrence of ten (10) phonological processes commonly observed in normal acquisition and in the speech patterns of children with delayed phonological development" (examiner's manual, p. 1). These 10 phonological processes are described with examples in the examiner's manual. The two separate checklists allow for assessing phonological processes either from the child's responses obtained from the consonant inventory (Checklist I) or from the Phonological Probe Section in the Stimulus Easel (Checklist II) depending on the responses of the child.

Administration of the CAAP is simple and straightforward and follows the general protocol

of other tests of articulation and phonological processes. That is, children are presented visual and/or verbal stimuli designed to elicit the production of a particular word containing targeted phonemes or phonological processes. Based on these productions, decisions are made as to whether a sound was produced correctly or incorrectly, the nature of an incorrectly produced sound, and the presence or absence of 1 of the 10 phonological processes. The visual stimuli used in the CAAP and contained in the stimulus easel consist of large colored drawings of common objects that should be easily recognized by most children.

Administration begins with the Articulation Inventory followed by the School Age Sentence section for those children 5 years of age or older. The Phonological Probes section would then be administered if using the Phonological Checklist II, otherwise the Phonological Checklist I can be completed later using the responses already obtained from the Articulation Inventory.

Scoring the Articulation Inventory is facilitated by the color-coded record form. Each verbal response is first analyzed relative to the target phoneme or phonemes and recorded as either produced correctly, deleted from the word, distorted, or substituted with a different phoneme. If substituted, the substituted phoneme is also recorded. The number of phoneme errors made are then added up and separately recorded for consonant singletons, clusters, and multisyllabic words. These three are further summed to provide the Consonant Inventory Score. Similarly, the number of phoneme errors made on the School Age Sentences is also calculated and recorded as the School Age Sentence Score. For both the Consonant Inventory and School Age Sentences total scores are converted to standard scores, 90% confidence intervals, percentile ranks, and age equivalent scores. In addition, a Critical Difference Calculation between the child's performance on the Consonant Inventory and the School Age Sentences can also be calculated, and patterns of errors relative to phoneme manner of production and syllable position can also be made.

Scoring either of the two Phonological Process Checklists involves analyzing the child's verbal productions for the presence or absence of the 10 phonological processes on a separate scoring form. Each phonological process is analyzed separately and the total number of occurrences for each process is calculated. A percent occurrence is then calculated by dividing the number of occurrences of each process by the number of opportunities for that process to have occurred. Percentage "calculators" in the form of easy-to-use tables are provided on the scoring sheet. The total number of occurring processes from either checklist becomes the Phonological Process Score that can then be converted to a standard score, 90% confidence interval, percentile rank, and age equivalent.

DEVELOPMENT. As previously noted, the CAAP was developed to provide a quick means of assessing the articulation skills and phonological process occurrence in young children. The CAAP was developed in three stages over an 18-month period. First, a pilot study was conducted on a small number of children ($N = 32$) to determine if the initial picture stimuli and directions were appropriate and effective. Next, the test was field tested on 135 children grouped into those with no history of articulation impairments and those with diagnosed disorders of articulation and phonology. In addition to differentiating performances between these two groups, the field test resulted in further refining the picture and verbal stimuli and the administrative process in preparation for national standardization.

TECHNICAL. Standardization of the CAAP involved 1,707 apparently normal children in terms of language development between the ages of 2 years 6 months and 8 years 11 months: 1,619 children from 35 states representing all geographic areas of the country and 88 children from four Canadian provinces. The examiner's manual presents several tables that compare the standardization sample distribution to U.S. population distribution for age, region, gender, socioeconomic status, and primary language spoken at home. Examination of these data suggests that the standardization sample distribution does generally represent the U.S. population on these variables. Technical aspects of the CAAP are further discussed following 10 criteria for evaluating norm-referenced standardized tests established by McCauley and Swisher (1984).

According to the authors, face validity was established during test construction and preliminary testing. Examination of the content of the test "illustrates the breadth of assessment and the degree to which the CAAP does indeed give the appearance of evaluating articulation in a compre-hensive manner" (examiner's manual, p. 81). Concurrent validity (a.k.a., criterion-related validity) was established by comparing CAAP performance of 49 children with identified articulation and phonological problems to their concurrent performance on the Bankson-Bernthal Test of Phonology (Bankson & Bernthal, 1990). This comparison included raw (word) and standard (word) scores for articulation performance as well as five selected phonological processes. Pearson product-moment correlations for these comparisons ranged between .62 and .88, whereas Spearman rho correlations ranged between .56 and .84; all correlations were significant beyond $p < .01$. Based on these analyses, the authors conclude that "both tests are examining the same underlying processes" (examiner's manual, p. 81). Discriminant predictive validity was established by examining how well the CAAP "predicted" that the 49 children indeed had articulation and/or phonological problems. According to the authors "approximately 84% of the sample earned a standard score of one standard deviation or less below average" (examiner's manual, p. 82) with most also exhibiting 40% or more occurrence of one or more phonological processes.

Two types of reliability were established and reported: test-retest reliability and interexaminer reliability. Test-retest reliability was established by administering the CAAP twice to 32 children within a 7- to 45-day period. Test-retest correlation for raw scores on the Consonant Inventory was .98 and on the School Age Sentences was .87 suggesting strong test-retest reliability. Interexaminer reliability was based on a comparison of results obtained by four trained examiners who each administered the CAAP to a group of 26 younger preschool children and a group of 27 school-aged children. Using an analysis of variance approach, the reliability coefficient in the preschool group was .99 and the reliability coefficient in the school-age group was also .99. Based on these data, interexaminer reliability for trained examiners is very high.

COMMENTARY. The CAAP joins a relatively large group of published articulation and/or phonology assessment tools (e.g., 20 listed under speech and hearing at the Buros Institute of Mental Measurements website: www.unl.edu/buros/bimm/html/index17.html as of June 2006). As such, speech-language pathologists have a wide selection from which to choose. Choice generally depends on the test's appropriateness for the age of the targeted population, the ability of the test to elicit targeted verbal responses consistently, ease of recording and analyzing responses, and the degree to which the test provides information to help with interpreting the results. To these criteria the CAAP would seem to be an attractive choice for some; its format seems most appropriate for the 2 years 6 months to 8 years 11 months age-targeted population; its visual stimuli are large, colorful, and interesting; its recording forms are well-organized, color-coded, and informative; and its norm referencing could be a considerable help in interpreting test performance. In addition, the test's ability to compare single word articulation to articulation within sentences, and its ability to assess both articulation and the occurrence of phonological processes makes the CAAP relatively unique.

However, like other tests of articulation and/ or phonology, the CAAP collects only a limited structured sample of a child's speech performance. Therefore, clinical decisions regarding a child's articulation and phonological competency should be based on more than a single test and include samples of the child's speech in a variety of settings. For this reason, tests such as the CAAP do serve as the foundation of these assessments and provide extremely variable information. Therefore, it is incumbent upon clinicians to select tests that will provide a valid and reliable measure of a child's articulation and/or phonological status. The CAAP would seem to serve that purpose rather well.

SUMMARY. The CAAP is a newly developed norm-referenced test of young children's articulation and phonology. Among such tests it is somewhat unique in that it targets a relatively narrow age group (3 to 9 years) and provides for an assessment of both articulation skills and phonological development as measured by the presence of phonological processes. It uses a format similar to other articulation tests presenting carefully selected pictorial and/or verbal stimuli to elicit specific verbal responses, which presumably are an accurate representative sample of a child's speech. Although the CAAP has some attractive features, it does not represent a new format for sampling articulation and phonology, nor does it preclude the need for additional testing and sampling of a child's speech in order to make accurate clinical decisions. In this

regard the CAAP joins several other valid and reliable measures of articulation and/or phonology from which clinicians can choose.

REVIEWER'S REFERENCES

Bankson, N., & Bernthal, J. (1990). Bankson-Bernthal Test of Phonology. Chicago: Applied Symbolix.
McCauley, R. J., & Swisher, L. (1984). Psychometric review of language and articulation tests for preschool children. *Journal of Speech and Hearing Disorders, 49,* 34-42.

[46]

Clinical Assessment of Attention Deficit—Adult.

Purpose: Designed to provide a "comprehensive assessment of attention deficit with and without hyperactivity (ADD/ADHD)" in adults.

Population: Ages 19—79.

Publication Dates: 1994—2005.

Acronym: CAT-A.

Scores, 17: Clinical Index, Childhood Memories Clinical Index (Inattention, Impulsivity, Hyperactivity), Childhood Memories Context Clusters (Personal, Academic/Occupational, Social), Childhood Memories Locus Clusters (Internal, External), Current Symptoms Clinical Index (Inattention, Impulsivity, Hyperactivity), Current Symptoms Context Clusters (Personal, Academic/Occupational, Social), Current Symptoms Locus Clusters (Internal, External).

Administration: Group or individual.

Price Data, 2007: $152 per introductory kit including professional manual (2005, 239 pages), 25 rating forms, and 25 score summary/profile forms; $65 per professional manual; $68 per 25 rating forms; $26 per 25 score summary/profile forms; $185 per unlimited use scoring software CD (CAT-SP).

Time: (20—25) minutes.

Comments: Can be computer scored; a child and adolescent form (CAT-C; 17:47) is also available and shares the same professional manual.

Authors: Bruce A. Bracken and Barbara S. Boatwright.

Publisher: Psychological Assessment Resources, Inc.

Review of the Clinical Assessment of Attention Deficit–Adult by RAMA K. MISHRA, Department of Psychiatry, Medicine Hat Regional Hospital, Medicine Hat, Alberta, Canada:

DESCRIPTION. The Clinical Assessment of Attention Deficit-Adult (CAT-A) is a self-report measure with 54 items on Part I for Childhood Memories and 54 items on Part II for Current Symptoms. Each item has four response choices, namely Strongly Disagree, Disagree, Agree, and Strongly Agree. The test protocols can be scored manually by the autoscore forms or by an unlimited-use software program.

Both parts of the scale provide scores on three clinical scales (Inattention, Impulsivity, and Hyperactivity), three context clusters (Personal, Academic/Occupational, and Social), and two locus clusters (Internal and External). Additionally, this test provides three validity indices, namely Negative Impression, Infrequency, and Positive Impression. The context clusters are designed to indicate the contexts in which the target symptoms are most problematic. The locus clusters are expected to indicate whether the symptoms are experienced as sensations (Internal) or as behaviors (External).

The scores on the scales and clusters are converted to standard scores, percentiles, confidence intervals, qualitative classification, and graphical profile displays for all clinical scales, context clusters, and locus clusters. In addition, the validity scales indicate whether the range of scores in each index is typical, atypical, or very atypical. The overall Clinical Index is calculated from all three clinical scales from both parts of the test. Qualitative ranges such as "normal range," "mild clinical risk," "significant clinical risk," and "very significant clinical risk" are provided for the overall Clinical Index.

DEVELOPMENT. This instrument has been developed to identify adult forms of Attention Deficit/Hyperactivity Disorder (ADHD), which is conceptualized as a lifelong condition beginning in early childhood. The Clinical Assessment of Attention (CAT) includes two separate instruments, one for children and adolescents and the other for adults. Both forms are similar in structure and format. The main difference is that the adult form tries to identify both childhood and current symptoms, and the child form focuses solely on current symptoms. In addition, the children's version has three forms, the self-report form, parent report form, and teacher report form. The adult version has only the self-report form. The test manual contains information for both Clinical Assessment of Attention-Adult and Child versions. The forms are, however, separate for children and adults. The scoring software can be purchased separately or with the instrument.

TECHNICAL. The technical information for the instrument is documented in the professional manual. The items for the instrument were based on a review of the literature, item content from existing instruments, DSM-IV diagnostic criteria,

and input from clinicians and researchers in the field. The original instrument consisted of 144 items, 108 of which were retained in the final version. The Clinical Assessment of Attention for Adults was standardized on a sample of 800 adults between the ages of 19 and 79 years. Normative data were collected from 13 states in the United States. Except for some ethnic samples, the standardization sample matched the population parameter of the 2001 U.S. Census Bureau.

Reliability and validity information are presented in separate chapters in the professional manual. Two main types of reliability coefficients are reported. Internal consistency estimates ranged from .68 to .96, with an average and median internal consistency coefficient of .85. Test-retest reliability for a 3-week interval ranged from .78 to .88 with an average and median coefficient of .83. The difference in ratings for this interval was reported to be generally less than one T-score for all 19 scales.

Extensive validity information for this instrument appears in the validity chapter of the professional manual. First of all, the CAT-A is reported to demonstrate strong content validity. The item selection process was quite exhaustive and included review of journal articles, textbooks, reference books, DSM-IV, and existing ADD/ADHD rating scales. The items were chosen deliberately to represent the three core clinical symptoms, three life contexts, and two loci. All three clinical scales on Part I (Childhood Memories) and Part II (Current Symptoms) were independent of each other with no overlapping items and consisted of 18 items each. Table D20 in Appendix D (pp. 190–191) provides a list of how items are assigned to each of the three domains (clinical scale, context cluster, and locus cluster).

Internal structure-related validity was demonstrated by intercorrelations of the scales and exploratory factor analysis. As expected, moderate correlations were reported among the three clinical scales (.36 to .76). Moderate to high correlations also were reported between the clinical scales and the clusters for Childhood Memories (.75 to .88) and Current Symptoms (.64 to .84). The factor analyses indicated three factor solutions with appreciable factor loadings (.49 to 1.03) for Inattention, Hyperactivity, and Impulsivity parcels with the first factor for Inattention, second for Hyperactivity, and third for Impulsivity scales.

However, it was not indicated if they conducted any factor analysis on the items to see if, in fact, they represented the three clinical scales. As well, factor loadings were quite good for the locus clusters (.70 to .83) with the first factor for internal locus and second factor for external locus. However, the factor loadings of the context clusters were somewhat mixed (.36 to .92). For example, the first factor included both social and personal context parcels. Additionally, the second factor consisted of the academic and occupational context scales for childhood memories but not for current symptoms (see p. 99 of the test manual). The third factor consisted of only one of the personal context parcels on both Part I and Part II.

Criterion-related validity for this instrument was documented by concurrent administration of other available tests such as the Conners' Adult ADHD Rating Scales (CAARS), Brown ADD Scales (B-ADD), and Clinical Assessment of Depression (CAD). CAT-A clinical scales were found to have a moderate to high correlation with the CAARS scales (.52 to .79). As expected, the correlations were slightly lower for the Childhood Memory clinical scales than for the Current Symptoms clinical scales. These correlation coefficients were also found to be similar for a mixed clinical sample and a separate normal control sample. The CAT-A was found to have low to moderate correlations with the Brown ADD scales. The reasons for the low correlations were attributed to the fact that there were no comparable scales on the two instruments. However, the Brown scale produced higher T-scores compared to the CAT-A. The rationale for providing relationship with a depression scale was that both tests measure "negative affect" that stem from different disabilities. Therefore, the relationship should be moderately positive. As expected, CAT-A was found to have a correlation of .42 with CAD.

Additional validity studies were carried out with several clinical samples. These studies demonstrated that the ADD/ADHD sample earned a mean score of about 1.5 standard deviations above the normative mean on both parts of this instrument. The Mixed Clinical group had a mean score of one standard deviation above the normative mean, and the Learning Disability sample had a mean score of about .75 standard deviations above the normative mean.

COMMENTARY. The CAT-A is obviously expected to provide several important pieces of clinical information that are not available from any other commercially available scales or tests of attention for adults. The item content is quite exhaustive with 108 items and captures a broad range of symptoms relevant to this disorder. All three nonoverlapping clinical scales assess Inattention, Hyperactivity, and Impulsivity. Of more importance, the contexts (e.g., personal, social, and academic/ occupational) in which these symptoms manifest are assessed. The additional domain of locus focuses on whether the symptoms are experienced internally as sensations, or are acted upon as behaviors. The most unique feature of this instrument is the inclusion of three validity scales. Because self-ratings can be easily distorted, it would be useful to identify if the responses are disproportionately influenced by a certain response style (e.g., negative, positive, or infrequent) so that they can be addressed more appropriately.

Missing from the technical information is a good study of sensitivity and specificity. It is hoped that independent studies will be published in the future to identify the rate of false positives and false negatives in identifying individuals with ADHD from the CAT-A scores.

Because this instrument provides a number of new features compared to the currently available instruments, this instrument should be very popular. Time will tell if these additional features are clinically useful or not. It is suspected that the context cluster scales would be somewhat difficult to complete and interpret, particularly due to the inadequate differentiation in the normative sample. When the publisher introduces the "observer rating" version of this instrument in the future, it would provide a comprehensive assessment of attention for adults. The authors have tried their best to stay close to the conceptualization of ADHD defined by DSM-IV. It will be important to stay abreast of developments in this area, however, such as evidence that supports emerging subtypes of ADHD (see Barkley, 2006) and other models of conceptualizations (Doucette, 2002). Finally, all assessments for ADHD should include a diagnostic interview (structured or semistructured), corroborating history, self-report and observer-report, laboratory tests of attention (e.g., Integrated Visual and Auditory Continuous Performance Test, Visual Search and Attention Test, Stroop Color-Word Identification Test, Test of Everyday Attention, etc.), and screening for affective disorders (e.g., Beck Depression Inventory, Beck Anxiety Inventory, Personality Assessment Inventory) for differential diagnosis.

SUMMARY. The Clinical Assessment of Attention Deficit for Adults is expected to fill a great gap in the assessment of attentional difficulties. It has many features that are not available in other tests in the field. This instrument has quite impressive reliability and validity and would be appreciated by both clinicians and researchers in the field. However, clinicians would probably appreciate a parallel observer-rating form to be completed by a family member or another person known to the patient. It is hoped that an observer rating scale would be available in the near future. Experienced clinicians should continue to use additional sources of information for appropriate differential diagnosis, particularly to rule out bipolar and other affective disorders.

REVIEWER'S REFERENCES

Barkley, R. A. (2006). *Optimizing ADHD treatment: Subtypes and comorbidity.* Paper presented at the Southern Alberta Children's Hospital, Calgary, Canada, on April 25, 2006.

Doucette, A. (2002). Child and adolescent diagnosis: The need for a model-based approach. In L. E. Beutler & M. L. Malik (Eds.), *Rethinking the DSM: A psychological perspective* (pp. 201-220). Washington, DC: American Psychological Association.

Review of the Clinical Assessment of Attention Deficit-Adult by SEAN REILLEY, Assistant Professor of Psychology, Morehead State University, Morehead, KY:

DESCRIPTION. The Clinical Assessment of Attention Deficit-Adult (CAT-A) is a self-report rating form for adults (aged 19-79) that provides information concerning current symptoms of Attention Deficit/Hyperactivity Disorder (ADHD) as well as childhood recollections of behavior. The CAT-A contains a total of 108 items that are evenly distributed across Childhood Memories (Part I—54 items) and Current Symptoms (Part II—54 items) domains. The CAT-A has more items than most other comparable adult ADHD rating scales but can be easily completed in as little as 20 to 25 minutes in an individual or group setting. Respondents endorse how well each statement is descriptive of their behavior by circling one of four response options ranging from strongly agree to strongly disagree. Raw responses are automatically transferred to a scoring sheet via an underlying carbon form. Clinicians and appropriately trained staff can easily tabulate subscale and cluster scores from the scoring sheet. The CAT-A professional manual facilitates conversion

of these scores to gender- and age-adjusted t-scores, percentiles, and 90th percentile confidence intervals. Alternatively, a computer-scoring program can be purchased for scoring and interpretive assistance. Central to DSM-IV-TR diagnostic considerations for ADHD, both Part I (Childhood Memories) and Part II (Current Symptoms) yield three clinical ADHD subscales (Inattention, Impulsivity, and Hyperactivity), and a Clinical ADHD Risk Index. An overall CAT-A Clinical Index can be calculated using the Clinical Risk Indices from Part I and Part II. A strength of the CAT-A is its ability to provide additional, detailed information concerning the breadth, locus, and severity of attention problems. For such purposes, cluster scores are calculated that measure the impact of clinical symptoms within three contexts (Personal, Academic/Occupational, and Social) as well as the locus of experienced symptoms (Internal or External). Clinical risk classifications ranging from "normal" to a "very significant clinical risk" can be calculated and graphed for each of these subscales. Three validity scores are calculated to assess infrequent responding and positive and negative response distortion using items drawn from the entire instrument (Parts I and II). Severity classifications can be made for these scores ranging from "typical" to "very atypical."

DEVELOPMENT. The CAT-A uses a logical ADHD model that relies heavily on current clinical knowledge about ADHD from published sources and symptom criteria found in the DSM-IV. An overriding goal of the development of the CAT-A was to provide the clinician with a multidimensional, norm-referenced assessment of ADHD behavior across the lifespan. A variety of CAT-A items were initially written to accomplish this goal. A 144-item version of the CAT-A was field tested with a sample of 108 students (84% female). Estimates of temporal stability were acceptable (range .74 to .84), although the test-retest window is not reported in the professional manual. Internal consistency for clinical and context indices for both Parts I and II ranged from marginal to excellent (coefficient alphas ranged from .61 to .95). Based on these analyses, one item on the academic/occupational cluster was replaced prior to validation work.

A validation study was conducted with a sample of 370 adults that included community and higher education adults (aged 17-53; gender distribution unreported) from the Carolinas, classified into one of four groups. The ADHD group was formed using scores on two other indices of attention deficit. The remaining three groups were based on self-reports. Across all four groups, 36% to 58% of diagnoses were independently verified. The selectively reported CAT-A discriminant classification rates (reported range .66 to .85) for specific clinical scales and clusters appear appropriate. However, the stepwise discriminant classification technique employed capitalizes on chance associations, and, thus, cross validation on a new sample is commonly recommended. Internal consistency for clinical and context indices for both Parts I and II of the validation version of the CAT-A were slightly improved (coefficient alphas ranged from .75 to .97). No test-retest reliability data were reported in the manual for the validation study.

TECHNICAL. A standardization sample of 800 adults (aged 19-79) was recruited from 13 states via solicitation letters to community members and mental health professionals and academicians. This sample compared fairly well with the 2001 United States Census Bureau data reported in the CAT-A manual. Minor disparities include standardization respondents being somewhat more educated than census individuals, undersampling of Hispanic/Latino Americans, geographical oversampling in Midwestern and Northeastern regions, and undersampling in the Western region. A broader and more representative standardization sample would enhance the generalizability of the CAT-A for diverse populations including rural, multi-ethnic, and geriatric adults, as well as those with lower education and/or socioeconomic status.

Readability analyses were conducted for CAT-A items using the Flesch-Kincaid method. Unfortunately, detailed item-level statistics are not provided to substantiate the overall fourth grade reading level that is suggested in the manual. Basic internal consistency and temporal stability estimates are similar to those reported for previous CAT-A versions and were used to guide final item selection. The range of item total correlations for Child Memories (Part I item total correlations range from .12 to .74) and Current Symptoms (Part II item total correlations range from .09 to .67) suggests the CAT-A could benefit from some additional item revisions or deletions. However,

no items were deleted, revised, or added at this stage of development. High temporal stability estimates were obtained (correlations ranging from .77 to .87), but were drawn from a small portion of the standardization sample ($n = 83$) over an average period of approximately 3 weeks (range 8 to 63 days).

To evaluate content validity, exploratory factor analyses are reported for the CAT-A clinical and cluster scores using data from the standardization sample. Pseudorandom parcels of clinical and cluster scores were selected using items from each respective clinical and cluster domain. This process of factoring scores versus items is known to differentially affect the resulting latent variable factor model. In the case of the CAT-A, high intercorrelations between clinical and cluster scores for both Childhood Memories (Part I—correlations ranging from .59 to .91) and Current Symptoms (Part II—correlations ranging from .36 to .89) are noted, which could lead to model misfit. As such, more advanced modeling procedures such as structural equation modeling are suggested with the entire CAT-A item pool to clarify its underlying latent variable structure.

Concurrent validity of the CAT-A is based on a sample of adults ($n = 116$), including individuals with an attention deficit disorder ($n = 41$), learning disorders without ADHD ($n = 30$), those with ADHD comorbid with a learning disorder ($n = 45$), or individuals without any of these conditions ($n = 30$). The obtained correlations between scores on the CAT-A and the Conners' Adult ADHD Rating Scale—Self Report—Screening version (CAARS-S:SV) are moderate to high for childhood memories and current symptoms. Lower correlations emerged between the CAT-A and the Brown Attention-Deficit Disorder Scales, which, unlike the CAT-A and the CAARS-S:SV employs a theoretical model different than some aspects of the DSM-IV conception of ADHD. Finally, some partial divergent validity is provided by 590 adults from the standardization sample who completed CAT-A and the Clinical Assessment of Depression (CAD). Childhood Memories subscales of the CAT-A yielded low to moderate correlations with the CAD measure, whereas the CAT-A Current Symptoms subscales yielded moderate relationships.

COMMENTARY. The CAT-A appears to be a potentially valuable, multidimensional, ADHD rating scale for adults. Most, but not all symptom criteria for ADHD are addressed by the CAT-A using exact diagnostic nomenclature found in the DSM-IV-TR. Several issues need to be addressed in order to firmly anchor the psychometrics and enhance the utility of the CAT-A. First, no childhood age or uniform time frame is associated with Childhood Memories (Part I) or Current Symptoms (Part II), despite diagnostic requirements for both in the DSM-IV-TR. External validation work is needed to gauge the accuracy of the scoring systems and cut scores for validity scales. Application of advanced structural equation modeling would help clarify or solidify the CAT-A factor structure. Finally, additional clinical validation studies are needed that employ standardized, semistructured interview techniques and collateral reports.

SUMMARY. The developers, to their credit, have produced a potentially valuable multidimensional, adult rating scale for childhood and current ADHD symptoms. In order for this instrument to become a gold standard, careful, continued validation work will be required to establish the CAT-A factor structure, to enhance its reliability, and to clarify and improve its validity scales and positive and negative predictive power. As a whole, this inventory is recommended for clinical purposes with an eye to its current DSM-oriented limitations for diagnostic decision making.

[47]
Clinical Assessment of Attention Deficit—Child.

Purpose: Designed to provide a "comprehensive assessment of attention deficit with and without hyperactivity (ADD/ADHD)" in children and adolescents.
Population: 8–18 years.
Publication Dates: 1994–2005.
Acronym: CAT-C.
Scores, 12: Clinical (Inattention, Impulsivity, Hyperactivity), Clinical Index, Context (Personal, Academic/Occupational, Social), Locus (Internal, External), Validity (Negative Impression, Infrequency, Positive Impression).
Administration: Individual.
Parts, 3: Self-Report, Parent Report, Teacher Report.
Price Data, 2007: $265 per introductory kit including professional manual, 25 Self-Rating Forms, 25 Parent Rating Forms, 25 Teacher Rating Forms, 25 Self-Rating Score Summary/Profile Forms, 25 Parent

Score Summary/Profile Forms, and 25 Teacher Score Summary/Profile Forms; $65 per professional manual; $52 per 25 Self-Rating forms; $52 per 25 Parent Rating Forms; $52 per 25 Teacher Rating Forms; $22 per 25 Parent Score Summary/Profile Forms; $22 per 25 Self-Rating Score Summary/Profile Forms; $22 per 25 Teacher Score Summary/Profile Forms; $185 per unlimited use CAT-C SP scoring software CD.
Time: (10–20) minutes.
Comments: An adult form (CAT-A; 17:46) is also available and shares the same professional manual.
Authors: Bruce A. Bracken and Barbara S. Boatwright.
Publisher: Psychological Assessment Resources, Inc.

Review of the Clinical Assessment of Attention Deficit–Child by GEORGE J. DEMAKIS, Associate Professor of Psychology, University of North Carolina at Charlotte, Charlotte, NC:

DESCRIPTION. The Clinical Assessment of Attention Deficit—Child (CAT-C) is a 42-item rating scale designed to assist in the diagnosis of Attention Deficit/Hyperactivity Disorder (ADHD) in children and adolescents from ages 8 to 18. The test consists of three Clinical scales (Inattention, Impulsivity, and Hyperactivity) that assess the key behavioral symptoms of ADHD, three Context clusters (Personal, Academic/Occupational, and Social Domains) that assess these symptoms in multiple settings, as well as two Locus clusters (Internal and External) that assess the individual's experience of symptoms. An overall Clinical Index can be obtained by adding all the Clinical scales. There are also three validity scales: Negative Impression assesses the degree to which responses are in an unusually negative or impaired manner; Infrequency measures the extent to which responses are in an extreme manner compared to the standardization sample; Positive Impression assesses the degree to which responses are in an unusually positive manner. Scales and clusters are assessed separately via parallel self, parent, and teacher ratings. For example, an item that loads on the Hyperactivity Clinical scale for self-rating is "I do not like to sit still and read," whereas for parent and teacher rating the question is "Does not like to sit still and read." All test items are scored on a 4-point basis with responses ranging from *Strongly Disagree* to *Strongly Agree*.

To collect self, parent, and teacher ratings, there are three separate rating forms. Each rating form has an answer sheet with the questions (top part of form) and a scoring sheet (bottom part of form). After the respondent completes the top rating form, the examiner can remove it to score the test easily. On each scoring sheet, circled responses for each item are transferred to the relevant column in the areas listed above. Column scores are then totaled to obtain the raw scores for each measure. These scores are then transferred to a separate score summary sheet where they are converted to T scores (with 90% confidence interval), percentiles, as well as a qualitative classification (Normal Range, Mild Clinical Risk, Significant Clinical Risk, and Very Significant Clinical Risk). Raw scores for each validity scale are also transferred to this sheet and are classified as Typical, Atypical, or Very Atypical. If desired, a visual profile can be plotted using T-score. An adult form of the test also is available (Clinical Assessment of Attention Deficit-Adult [CAT-A]) and is presented in the same manual as the child version reviewed here.

DEVELOPMENT. Initial scale development included a review of relevant literature, review of item content of existing instruments, examination of current diagnostic criteria based on the DSM-IV, and suggestions from colleagues. An initial CAT-C 54-item scale was developed from a downward extension of the CAT-A. Parallel measures of parent and teacher ratings were developed as well, though these are not included on the CAT-A. Initial research on this scale in a small group of elementary-aged children demonstrated attractive psychometric properties and, based on these promising data, the final instrument was subsequently normed. Items with poor item-total reliability were deleted from the initial 54 to obtain the final 42 items.

TECHNICAL. The three forms of the CAT-C were normed on 800 children and adolescents, 800 matched parents, and 550 teachers of these children. The standardization sample is fairly representative of the U.S. population, though Hispanic participants were undersampled (e.g., in self and parent ratings for 8- to 11-year-olds, Hispanics represent 17.7% of the U.S. population, but are only 5% of the standardization sample) and the Western U.S. geographic region was oversampled (for 12- to 18-year olds in the U.S. population the rate is 23.4%, whereas the standardization sample had 37.4% from this region). Despite such differences, age, gender, race, parental education level, and geographic region accounted for less than 1%

of the variance in scale or cluster scores for self, parent, or teacher rating. Moreover, scores from the standardization sample for self, parent, and teacher ratings are fairly consistent with predictions based on the normal distribution, indicating that scores are normally distributed. For instance, the following percentage of scores for parent rating on the Clinical Index were obtained in each of the following T-score areas in the standardization sample with the predicted percentages in parentheses: Normal Range $T \leq 59$ = 82.8% (81.59%), Mild Risk T of 60 to 69 = 15.0% (15.33%), Significant Clinical Risk T of 70 to 79 = 2.1% (2.69%), and Very Significant Clinical Risk $T \geq 80$ = .1 % (.9%).

The test manual presents data on internal, test-retest, and interrater (e.g., teacher and parent ratings of the same child) reliability. Internal reliabilities, as assessed via coefficient alpha reliabilities, are uniformly high, typically above .90, on Scale and Cluster measures for self, parent, and teacher ratings. Across the two normative age groups, 8 to 11 years and 12 to 18 years, as well as across gender and race, internal reliabilities were very similar. Stability across time, as assessed via test-retest correlations, of self and parent ratings are high, typically above .80, when assessed over a short intertest interval. The stability of teacher ratings, however, was somewhat lower, but still above .7. Not surprisingly, interrater reliabilities were much lower, typically in the .4 to .5 range (e.g., the overall Clinical Index correlation between teachers and parents was .47). Rather than suggesting poor reliability, this reflects the fact that these individuals see the rated child in different situations and for different periods of times—data that might be clinically meaningful.

The test manual presents various types of validity data including content and criterion (concurrent) validity, as well as findings from intercorrelations (not reviewed here), factor analyses, and performances of clinical samples. A series of exploratory factor analyses was performed on each scale with the relevant items or, according to the test manual, "parcels" of items. Findings were broadly consistent with the test's design. For instance, on the self-rating scale, items on the clinical scale tapping Hyperactivity, Inattention, and Impulsivity loaded on three separate factors, whereas for the parent rating scale items on the Context cluster tapping Academic/Occupational,

Personal, and Social loaded on three separate factors. Overall, factor analyses of self, parent, and teacher ratings consistently accounted for approximately 90% of the variance with either three-factor solutions for Clinical scale and Context cluster or two-factor solutions for Locus cluster. Concurrent validity was assessed via correlation of the CAT-C with various other well-known measures of ADD such as the Conners' Adolescent Self-Report, Parent, and Teacher Rating Scales; the Attention-Deficit/Hyperactivity Disorder Test; and the Clinical Assessment of Depression. The CAT-C was moderately correlated with a variety of other attentional rating measures in expected fashion. For instance, the CAT-C self-rating was more highly related to the Conners' Adolescent Self-Report Scale (rs = .56 to .76) than to the Clinical Assessment of Depression (rs = .40 to .55). Finally, clinical samples composed of children and adolescents with ADD/ADHD, learning disorders, or a mixed clinical sample were evaluated on the CAT-C. The pattern of scores is broadly supportive of this measure's validity, as the participants with attention deficits consistently scored higher than the learning disordered participants on self, parent, and teacher ratings. For instance, the parent rating of the Clinical Index score for ADD/ADHD participants was 65.13, but only 56.46 for learning disordered participants. Not surprisingly, when all the clinical participants were combined, they were less likely to score in the Normal Range and more likely than the standardization sample to score in the Clinical Risk Range.

COMMENTARY. The test manual is clearly written and provides compelling data for use of this measure with children and adolescents. The standardization sample is appropriately diverse and without evidence of age, gender, racial, geographic region, or parental educational bias. Various types of reliability (internal and test-retest) and validity (factor analytic and criterion-related) are addressed and evidence supporting them provides a strong psychometric basis for use of this measure. Data on clinical samples support validity claims, as participants with ADD/ADHD scored higher than other groups, but additional information (besides demographics) would have been helpful here. For instance, how and from where were these participants obtained? What were the inclusion/exclusion criteria for each clinical group? How many participants were diagnosed with various subtypes of either ADHD or learning disorder, respectively? What types of participants were in the mixed clinical group? Given that there is currently no published research on this instrument, such information would be helpful for initial clinical use of this instrument.

In addition to the above psychometric issues, the actual test items are developmentally appropriate and easy to understand, and the test appears easy to use and administer. A particularly attractive feature of this test is that validity measures are included, including positive and negative impression management, as well as infrequent item endorsement. Given the increasing knowledge and emphasis of these issues in clinical practice, this is a welcome feature.

SUMMARY. The CAT-C is a rating scale of ADD symptoms in children and adolescents measured via self, parent, and teacher rating. From each of these sources, the following scales/clusters are obtained: Clinical scale (Inattention, Impulsivity, and Hyperactivity); Context cluster (Personal, Academic/Occupational, and Social); Locus cluster (Internal and External). Validity measures of Negative Impression, Positive Impression, and Infrequency are also obtained. Overall, the test appears easy to administer and score and data in the test manual clearly outline a standardization sample that is fairly representative of the U.S. population. The test also has strong psychometric properties. Although additional information about the presented clinical samples would have been useful in the test manual, as is, this test appears to be a promising rating form for use in the diagnosis of ADHD in children and adolescents.

Review of the Clinical Assessment of Attention Deficit—Child by ROSEMARY FLANAGAN, Associate Professor/Director, Masters Program in School Psychology, Adelphi University, Garden City, NY:

DESCRIPTION. The Clinical Assessment of Attention Deficit—Child (CAT-C) is a screening instrument for children ages 8-18 that includes the behavior and criteria for Attention-Deficit/Hyperactivity Disorder (ADHD). The kit contains separate Parent, Teacher, and Child (self-rating) forms, Profile Forms, and a test manual. The test items were based on the diagnostic criteria specified in the *Diagnostic and Statistical Manual* of *Mental Disorders, Fourth Edition* (DSM-IV; American Psychiatric Association, 1994), and should be useful for clinical, educational, and research applications.

Clinical and educational applications include aiding the diagnosis of ADHD, treatment planning, and monitoring. The CAT-C identifies the contexts in which behaviors are most likely to be problematic by assessing clinical symptoms across multiple contexts. Moreover, because the scales are operationalized similarly across age levels, functioning can be tracked. Potential research applications are facilitated by a uniform operational definition.

The CAT-C includes Clinical Scales (Inattention, Impulsivity, and Hyperactivity) and Context (Personal, Academic/Occupational, Social) and Locus (Internal, External) Clusters. Validity scales assess faking good (Positive Impression), malingering (Negative Impression), or responding in an infrequent manner. An overall rating, called the Clinical Index, is available. It is useful as a gross screening device because it is an aggregate of the Scales and Clusters, the latter of which provide information more useful to practitioners. The Clinical Index may be useful to researchers.

The CAT-C forms are printed on carbonized paper, which when separated, reveal the scoring rubric. The first page includes directions to the respondent. The second and third pages include a place for demographic information and the 42 test questions. Items are identical across respondents and are presented using a 4-point scale, with 1 = *strongly disagree* and 4 = *strongly agree*. The scoring rubric contains columns organizing responses according to their respective scales; to the right are columns for the validity scales. The profile forms are separate and organize data according to clusters. The reverse side of the form contains a graph for a visual display of functioning. The forms are user-friendly for respondents and evaluators. Data are reported as T-scores (Mean = 50, SD = 10).

DEVELOPMENT. Development of the CAT-C was preceded by reviewing child development literature, other scales, and DSM-IV diagnostic criteria. Pilot studies used an initial pool of 52 items, later reduced to 42 items. Children with diagnoses of ADHD, children without psychiatric diagnoses, their parents, and their teachers completed the CAT-C pilot scale and the Attention Deficit Disorders Evaluation Scale (McCarney,

1989) in order to establish interrater reliability and concurrent validity. Validation of the pilot scale was conducted using a discriminant function; classification accuracy for teachers was 83%, for mothers, 88%.

The standardization sample was 800 children aged 8-18; 800 parents of these individuals and 550 teachers also participated. Stratification variables included: parent education level, gender, race/ethnicity, geographic region, and age. Census tract data were approximated, although Hispanics were undersampled, and Caucasians were slightly oversampled. The Midwest was slightly oversampled, the Northeast and South were undersampled. There were some statistically significant differences in responses provided by 8–11-year-olds and 12–18-year-olds; two age groups were used for developing norms. Despite unevenness in sampling, the distribution of T-scores across the normal and clinical ranges approximates normality.

TECHNICAL. Bracken's (1987) guidelines for technical adequacy were used as a benchmark. Coefficient alpha was reported for the total sample for the Clinical Index and across the Clinical Scales and the Context and Locus Clusters for all forms/raters. Coefficient alphas are acceptable, ranging from .92–.97 for the Clinical Index; for the Clinical Scales, values ranged from .90–.94 for teachers, .85–.91 for parents, and .77–.85 for children. The components of the scales and clusters follow a similar pattern, with coefficient alpha for the Context Cluster ranging from .89–.91, .85–.89, and .75–.84, for the teachers, parents, and children, respectively. For the Locus cluster, coefficient alpha was .94 for all teacher scales, .91 for all parent scales, and .86–.87 for child scales. Further examination of the data indicates that for two cohorts (ages 8–11, 12–18) across gender, coefficient alpha was remarkably stable for all forms/raters. Coefficient alpha was not as strong for African American children aged 8-11 as compared to other groups for some isolated scale and cluster components.

The stability of the CAT-C falls short of the desired value of at least .90. The corrected reliabilities for the Clinical Index are .82, .83, and .73 for the child, parent, and teacher forms, respectively. This may be attributable to sample size ($N = 38$–41), the interval (17–20 days), or possibly to the raters themselves, as well as variability in perceived symptoms. Interrater reliability seems weak, as the reported values across forms/raters ranges from .41–.49. Data are also reported in terms of the mean differences in T-scores; these values are consistently less than one T-score point, minimizing this possible concern.

Validity data are empirical and theoretical. Three clinical samples were used: ADD/ADHD ($N = 23$, $N = 24$, $N = 21$), Learning Disorder, and Mixed Clinical. Specific information about settings from which these samples were obtained, and details about the disorders, such as severity, is not provided. Information is reported on mean age, gender, parental education, and race/ethnicity; educational level was unknown for 4.3% of the parents (13% had an 11th grade education or less; the remainder had more education). There were no African American children in the ADD/ADHD group and 33.3% of the Learning Disorder group was Hispanic. The mean T-score data indicate close agreement between children in the ADD/ADHD group and their parents, as the Clinical Indices were 57.22 and 65.13, respectively. Teachers rated this same group less favorably, with the mean T-score being 58.04. Less agreement across raters is noted for the Learning Disorders group, with mean Clinical Indices of 50.33, 56.46, and 53.42, for children, parents, and teachers, respectively. The Mixed Clinical group had mean Clinical Indices most similar to the ADD/ADHD group, raising concerns about the ability of the scales to rule out problems comorbid with ADHD. Structure of the CAT-C was explored by principal components analyses. All scales within each form are moderately to highly correlated with one another for the entire standardization sample. Using odd-even item versions of the scales, data support a three-factor structure for the Clinical Scales and Context Cluster, and a two-factor structure for the Locus Cluster for the Child and Parent forms. The factor structure is less clean for the Clinical Scales and the Context Clusters for the Teacher form, although the data generally support the same factor structure as the Child and Parent forms. Factor loadings are provided in the test manual.

Concurrent validity was demonstrated by group separation. Combinations of normal and clinical groups (to increase sample size) were used across raters/forms, making comparisons complex. Correlations of the CAT-C scales and cluster components with the subscales of the Conners, Ratings Scales (Conners, 1997) ranged from .47–.76; 20% were below .50, and 10% were .70 or above. Correlations with the Attention Deficit/Hyperactivity Disorder Test (Gilliam, 1995) show a similar pattern, with correlations ranging from .19–.85; 15% were below .50, and 33% were .70 or above. The relationships are stronger for the teacher versions than the parent versions. Other validity data include correlations in the expected directions with scales of the Clinical Assessment of Behavior (CAB; Bracken & Keith, 2004). Across the forms, correlations between the CAT-C and the CAB were positive for the CAB clinical scales and negative for the CAB adaptive scales. Scores for ADHD sample were similar to the mixed clinical group on both measures.

COMMENTARY. The CAT-C is an addition to the test libraries of clinical and school psychologists. Among its advantages are its user-friendliness, relatively brief length, identical forms for all respondents, adequate psychometric properties, and scales that assess the context of behavior. Limitations include its minimal practical utility of the Clinical Index for practitioners and sampling weaknesses. Utility of the scales for those assessing African American populations is uncertain; practitioners are urged to exercise caution because the standardization sample was not sufficiently representative, and internal consistency is weak. This problem is not unique to this measure. The rationale for using principal components analysis rather than specifying a model and validating it by using structural equation modeling was not provided. Preliminary validity data are encouraging. More research is needed to determine the suitability of this measure for practice.

SUMMARY. The CAT-C is a multiple rater form that was developed for the school-age population. It is distinguished by being briefer than its competitors, using the exact same questions across forms, and by providing information by context. The standardization procedures are appropriate and the technical properties are adequate; the standardization sample is small. Additional validity data are needed to determine the suitability for clinical practice. Its likely use is as a screening device, or as a standardized source of contextual information that questionnaires typically do not provide. Researchers may find the instrument useful.

REVIEWER'S REFERENCES

American Psychiatric Association. (1994). *Diagnostic and statistical manual of mental disorders* (4th ed.). Washington, DC: Author.

Bracken, B. A. (1987). Limitations of preschool instruments and standards for minimal levels of technical adequacy. *Journal of Psychoeducational Assessment, 5*, 313-326.

Bracken, B. A., & Keith, T. Z. (2004). *Clinical Assessment of Behavior professional manual.* Lutz, FL: Psychological Assessment Resources.

Conners, K. (1997). Conners' Rating Scales-Revised. North Tonawanda, NY: Multi Health Systems.

Gilliam, J. E. (1995). Attention Deficit/Hyperactivity Disorder Test. Austin, TX: ProEd.

McCarney, S. B. (1989). Attention Deficit Disorders Evaluation Scale (ADDES): School and Home Versions. Columbia, MO: Hawthorne Educational Services.

[48]

Clinical Assessment of Depression.

Purpose: "Developed to aid in the clinical assessment and diagnosis of depression."

Population: Ages 8 to 79.

Publication Dates: 1994–2004.

Acronym: CAD.

Scores, 14: Symptom Scale Scores (Depressed Mood, Anxiety/Worry, Diminished Interest, Cognitive and Physical Fatigue, Total), Validity Scale Scores (Inconsistency, Negative Impression, Infrequency), Critical Item Cluster Scores (Hopelessness, Self-Devaluation, Sleep/Fatigue, Failure, Worry, Nervous).

Administration: Group.

Price Data, 2007: $130 per introductory kit including professional manual (2004, 96 pages), 25 rating forms, and 25 score summary/profile forms; $185 per scoring program (CD-ROM) including unlimited scoring and reports.

Time: 10 minutes.

Authors: Bruce A. Bracken and Karen Howell.

Publisher: Psychological Assessment Resources, Inc.

Review of the Clinical Assessment of Depression by MICHAEL G. KAVAN, Associate Dean for Student Affairs and Associate Professor of Family Medicine, Creighton University School of Medicine, Omaha, NE:

DESCRIPTION. The Clinical Assessment of Depression (CAD) is a 50-item self-report instrument designed to assist with the assessment of depression in children, adolescents, and adults, ages 8 to 79 years. Whereas the CAD is meant to be general enough to assess depressive symptomatology across the lifespan, it is also purported to address the unique characteristics associated with depression in children/adolescents and adults. The test authors developed this instrument so that it would be more technically sound, comprehensive, and useful than currently available scales for depression. The CAD is also meant to assist in intervention planning and the monitoring of treatment progress.

The CAD includes a Total Scale score that reflects an overall level of depressive symptomatology and four symptom-based scales including Depressed Mood, Anxiety/Worry, Diminished Interest, and Cognitive and Physical Fatigue. In addition, the CAD contains Inconsistency, Negative Impression, and Infrequency validity scales. The test authors also suggest that users examine six critical item clusters that provide additional information on Hopelessness, Self-Devaluation, Sleep/Fatigue, Failure, Worry, and Nervousness.

Based on a Flesch-Kincaid reading level analysis, the CAD is written at a third-grade reading level. No alternative language versions of the CAD are available. Administration of the CAD may be accomplished by persons with little training; however, they should be supervised by a qualified professional. Test materials include the CAD Rating Form, which includes answer and scoring sheets, and the Score Summary/Profile Form sheet. Clients are asked to circle *Strongly Disagree, Disagree, Agree,* or *Strongly Agree* to items based on "how you have been feeling *lately*" (professional manual, p. 10). The CAD may be completed in approximately 10 minutes.

Scoring of the CAD may be accomplished by hand or hand-entered for computer scoring. Hand scoring entails separating the answer sheet from the scoring sheet and then transferring the circled score items to the appropriate scale boxes. These scale scores are then tabulated and transferred to the Score Summary sheet where they are converted to T scores, percentiles, and 90% confidence intervals based on tables within the manual. The Inconsistency score also must be tabulated on the Score Summary sheet. The Negative Impression and Infrequency scores are simply transferred from the Scoring Sheet to the Score Summary sheet. Finally, T scores are transferred to the Profile Form and plotted. Scoring program software is available from the publisher and provides basically the same information for the user.

In regard to interpretation, the test authors recommend that properly licensed or certified personnel follow a five-step process that includes consideration of the CAD Total Scale score, the symptom scales, individual items, follow-up clinical interview data, and other related information. They go on to say that the Total Scale score is the "best overall measure of the client's general affectivity" (professional manual, p. 17). However, they suggest that test users consider closely the validity scales, symptom scales, and critical item clusters when interpreting the total score.

DEVELOPMENT. The test authors developed items for the CAD following a review of the literature and existing instruments, an assessment of current diagnostic criteria, and consultation with colleagues. Various versions were developed and piloted, and eventually a 75-item instrument showed moderate-to-high correlations with the Multiscore Depression Inventory, the Beck Depression Inventory, and the Children's Depression Inventory. Analyses of variance demonstrated a significant main effect for age and gender, but no main effects for race/ethnicity. There were small effect sizes for the difference between the child and adolescent groups and between the child and adult groups; however, differences across ages were not deemed of developmental importance. Slightly larger effect sizes were seen for gender. Additional content and factor analyses resulted in the current 50-item version with its total scale and four symptom scales labeled Depressed Mood (23 items), Anxiety/Worry (11 items), Diminished Interest (6 items), and Cognitive and Physical Fatigue (10 items).

TECHNICAL. The standardization sample included 1,900 children, adolescents, and adults between the ages of 8 and 79 years in 22 states. Samples are fairly similar to the U.S. population in most respects; however, the CAD normative sample is skewed toward being better educated and from the Midwest. T-scores and percentiles are provided for the CAD total scores and for the four subscales by four normative age groups (i.e., 8–11 years, 12–17 years, 18–25 years, and 26–79 years).

Internal consistencies (coefficient alpha) and standard errors of measurement for the CAD Total Scale and symptoms scales were computed by age, gender, and race/ethnicity for the total sample (n = 1,900). By age group, coefficient alphas for the CAD Total Scale ranged from .96 (8–11 and 18–25 years) to .97 (12–17 and 26–79 years). Alpha coefficients for the four symptom scales range from .78 (Diminished Interest scale for the 8–11 age group) to .96 (Depressed Mood scale for both the 12–17 and 18–25 age groups). By gender and race/ethnicity, alpha coefficients were nearly identical for the CAD Total Scale scores; however, mild variations in alphas existed on several symptom scale scores.

For the clinical sample (n = 378), alpha coefficients for the CAD Total Scale scores ranged from .97 (8–18 years) to .98 (19–79 years and total clinical sample). Coefficients for the symptom scales ranged from .85 (Diminished Interest for the 8–18 age group) to .97 (Depressed Mood for the ages 19–79 and total clinical sample groups). The clinical sample was composed of mainly Caucasian females who apparently have major depression (n = 48), dysthymia (n = 33), and a mixed clinical presentation (n = 108). No information is provided within the manual on factors such as how participants were classified, inpatient versus outpatient status, and so forth.

Corrected test-retest reliabilities for the CAD Total scale and symptom scales were computed for child/adolescent (n = 40) and adult (n = 59) samples over a mean time interval of 17.53 days (range of 7 to 36 days) for the former and 13.27 days (range of 1 to 51 days) for the latter. Coefficients for the CAD Total Scale ranged from .81 (child/adolescent) to .87 (adult). Corrected coefficients for the symptom scales ranged from .64 for Diminished Interest (child/adolescent) to .89 for Anxiety/Worry (adult).

In terms of content validity, the test authors state that this is ensured by the CAD's inclusion of items representing symptoms associated with depression within the literature and those noted within diagnostic criteria such as the DSM-IV. In support of criterion-related validity, a 75-item version of the CAD was shown to correlate .74 with the Multiscore Depression Inventory and .68 with the Beck Depression Inventory in a sample of adults, and .80 with the Children's Depression Inventory in a sample of children/adolescents.

The 50-item CAD was administered to nonclinical control (n = 67) and combined clinical (n = 189) samples. The nonclinical youth sample is skewed toward being older adolescents (mean age = 17.5 years), and the nonclinical adult sample is skewed toward being younger adults (mean age = 24.7 years). Both groups are composed of mainly Caucasians (93.3% and 97.3%, respectively). Within the combined clinical sample, the mean age of the youth group is 13.1 years and the mean age for the adult group is 37.1 years. Whereas the race/ethnicity breakdown for the youth group is appropriate, over 94% of the adult combined clinical sample is Caucasian and none are African American. In addition, the child/adolescent nonclinical and adult combined clinical groups are predominantly female.

Correlations between the CAD Total Scale score and the Beck Depression Inventory-II (BDI-II) were .71 (child/adolescent), .87 (adult), and .86 (overall) in the combined clinical group and .67 (child/adolescent), .70 (adult), and .69 (overall) in the nonclinical group. Correlations between the CAD Total Scale score and the Reynolds Adolescent Depression Scale (RADS) were .64 (child/adolescent), .90 (adult), and .83 (overall) in the combined clinical group and .82 (child/adolescent), .83 (adult), and .85 (overall) in the nonclinical group. CAD symptom scale correlations with the BDI-II ranged from .42 (Anxiety/Worry) in nonclinical adults to .85 (Depressed Mood) for adults in the combined clinical group. Correlations with the RADS ranged from .49 (Diminished Interest and Cognitive and Physical Fatigue) in the child/adolescent combined clinical sample to .87 (Depressed Mood) in the adult combined clinical sample.

A University of Western Kentucky study with 122 mainly Caucasian adolescents found the CAD and its symptom scales correlating from .64 (Diminished Interest) to .75 (Depressed Mood) with the BDI-II and from .71 (Cognitive and Physical Fatigue) to .86 (Depressed Mood) with the RADS. Total scale correlations were .77 with the BDI-II and .88 with the RADS.

Evidence for the validity of the CAD based on its internal structure is provided within the test manual. Item-with-total scale correlations ranged from .41 to .74. Intercorrelations among the symptom scales ranged from .68 to .82 in a sample of 700 8–17-year-olds and from .68 to .81 in a sample of 1,200 18–79-year-olds. Intercorrelations among the symptom scales for the total standardization sample ($n = 1,900$) ranged from .68 to .81. A confirmatory factor analysis was performed, and results favor a four-factor model including Depressed Mood, Anxiety/Worry, Diminished Interest, and Cognitive and Physical Fatigue. No information is provided within the manual supporting the use of the critical item clusters, particularly the claim that their content is "especially sensitive to individuals who may be at risk for harming themselves" (p. 7). Neither is there evidence to support the test authors' contention that the CAD may be useful in planning interventions or for monitoring treatment progress.

COMMENTARY. The CAD was developed in order to provide "a more technically sound, comprehensive, and useful scale" (professional manual, p. 5) for assessing depression in children, adolescents, and adults. It is also meant to be useful in planning interventions and monitoring treatment progress. The test authors' overall goal was to publish an instrument that is an improvement over existing scales.

So, how does the CAD measure up? First, in terms of its technical soundness, the CAD is an instrument with strong Total Scale internal consistency and relatively strong symptom scale internal consistency. Test-retest reliability is slightly less than desirable; however, given the variable nature of the affective states being measured it is not problematic. The CAD demonstrates reasonable internal consistency and correlates well with other measures of depression including the BDI-II and the RADS. One concern lies in the normative samples and their skewness toward better-educated, Caucasian females and the general lack of descriptive information regarding the clinical samples. Despite this, the CAD appears to meet the test authors' objective of developing an empirically supported instrument that is appropriate for measuring depression across age groups.

In terms of comprehensiveness, the CAD includes 50 items designed to be sensitive to depressive symptomatology. However, the CAD items only completely cover four (i.e., depressed mood, diminished interests/pleasure, fatigue/loss of energy, and concentration difficulties/indecision), partially cover three (i.e., sleep issues, feelings of worthlessness/guilt, and psychomotor retardation [not agitation]), and fail to cover two (i.e., changes in weight/appetite and thoughts of death or suicide) of the nine DSM-IV-TR (APA, 2000) criteria for major depressive episode. Other instruments (e.g., BDI-II, Zung Self-Rating Depression Scales) do as well or better in this respect. Also, an accurate diagnosis of depression is made difficult because the CAD asks respondents to rate how they have been feeling "lately" versus over the same 2-week period as required by the DSM-IV-TR criteria.

In terms of its usefulness, most would likely agree that the CAD is an easily administered and scored instrument for depression. Its true utility lies in its ability to assess depression across the life span and in its validity scales that may assist the clinician to determine various response sets.

Finally, with regard to the CAD being useful in planning interventions and monitoring treatment progress, the jury is still out. Although, intuitively, one suspects that scores from the various scales on the CAD would be helpful in planning interventions and monitoring progress, no data are provided within the test manual to support these assertions. Additional studies must be conducted in these areas.

SUMMARY. The CAD is a self-report instrument designed to assess depression in children, adolescents, and adults. The test authors should be given credit for developing a technically sound instrument that may assess depression across the ages. The incorporation of validity scales may also be useful for clinicians. CAD problems include limited descriptions of the normative clinical samples, which makes interpretation difficult, and the lack of data within the test manual regarding the use of the CAD in planning interventions or monitoring treatment. Instruments that are more comprehensive in their DSM-IV-TR coverage and possess a wealth of data associated with their use include the original BDI, the Zung Self-Rating Depression Scale, and the Reynolds Adolescent Depression Scale—2nd Edition. Although more age restricted, these scales may be deemed more appropriate for clinical use until additional studies are conducted on the CAD.

REVIEWER'S REFERENCE

American Psychiatric Association. (2000). *Diagnostic and statistical manual of mental disorders* (4th ed., TR). Washington, DC: Author.

Review of the Clinical Assessment of Depression by JODY L. KULSTAD, Adjunct Professor, Seton Hall University, South Orange, NJ:

The Clinical Assessment of Depression Scale (CAD) is a relatively brief, comprehensive, psychometrically sound measure of depression in individuals from childhood to late adulthood. Closely linked to DSM-IV-TR criteria, the 50-item CAD provides a diagnostically driven assessment of major, minor, and subclinical depressive episodes. The primary purpose of the CAD is for clinical use, allowing clinicians the ability to not only diagnose, but also to monitor symptoms and severity across the individual's lifespan. In addition, the CAD can be used in epidemiological or outcome research studies to measure depression longitudinally or cross-sectionally.

The CAD is a pencil-and-paper self-report measure of depression. Test materials include the 88-page professional manual, The CAD Rating Form (a carbonless rating form that includes the answer sheet on top and the scoring sheet underneath), and the CAD Profile Form/Score Summary. The CAD is intended for individuals from age 8 to 79. Each of the 50 items addresses diagnostic criteria or clinical manifestations of depression across the lifespan. Content includes age-sensitive symptoms (e.g., irritability in childhood) as well as hallmark criteria (e.g., anhedonia) for depression. Items are written in first person, with response options including *strongly disagree, disagree, agree,* and *strongly agree.*

The CAD provides a total score assessing overall level of depression as well as four symptom scales: Depressed Mood (23 items), Anxiety/Worry (11 items), Diminished Interest (6 items), and Cognitive and Physical Fatigue (10 items). The CAD also provides validity scales as well as six critical item clusters measuring Hopelessness, Self-Devaluation, Sleep/Fatigue, Failure, Worry, and Nervous.

ADMINISTRATION, SCORING, AND INTERPRETATION.

Administration. The CAD takes approximately 10 minutes to complete and can be administered by individuals with training in administering and scoring self-report measures. Although specialized professional training is not necessary, administration and scoring should be done under the supervision of a qualified professional. The measure can be administered in individual or group settings, but the location needs to be as private as possible and free from distraction. The test manual recommends rapport be established prior to administering the CAD, as this may motivate the individual to respond in a more open and accurate manner. Individuals respond to the 50 items regarding how they have been feeling lately. Respondents should be strongly encouraged to carefully read and answer all items, selecting only one response per item. If the respondent changes his or her mind about a response, he or she must mark an "*x*" over the incorrect response and circle the intended response. Responses should not be erased, as this will appear as a smear on the scoring sheet. Though the instrument is written at an overall third-grade reading level, examiners should be cautious about assuming reading ability and should monitor the administration. For some, the examiner may need to administer the assessment orally.

Also, because the CAD is available only in English, use with individuals who are non-English-speaking or speak English as a second language should be undertaken only with great caution, and the examiner should ensure comprehension of the items prior to scoring and interpretation.

Scoring. After the respondent has completed the CAD, the examiner should review the form for missing responses or multiple responses to one item. The CAD can be hand scored easily or can be computer scored using the CAD Scoring Program, available from the publisher.

When hand scoring, remove the perforated edge to separate the answer sheet from the scoring sheet. The individual's responses and information will show on the scoring sheet, with boxes to the left for the four symptom scales and to the right for the validity scales. To calculate the total raw scores and raw symptom scale scores, follow these steps. First, transfer the individual's circled response value to the box to the left of the item. When all items are recorded in the appropriate box, sum the boxes and record the subtotal in the box provided at the bottom of the column. Then, transfer the column totals for Items 1–25 (left-hand page) to the corresponding boxes provided at the bottom of the columns on the right-hand page. Sum the two subtotal boxes at the bottom of the column to arrive at a Total CAD raw score and a total raw score for each of the four symptom scales. Then, transfer all five raw scores to the Score Summary Sheet. Raw scores may be converted to *T* scores using the age-based Raw Score Conversion tables provided in the appendices of the professional manual. In addition to *T* scores, percentiles and 90% confidence intervals are recorded.

To score the validity scales, there are three steps to follow. Step 1 entails recording a "1" in the Negative Impressions (NI) and Infrequent Response (IF) boxes, where available, to the right of the respondent's circled score, for each item marked a "4." For example, if the respondent indicated a 4 on Item 1, then the person scoring the form would record a 1 in both the NI and IF boxes, because both boxes are shown. However, if the respondent indicated a 4 on Item 2, a "1" would be recorded in the NI box only, because that is the only box shown. As with calculating the total and scale scores, the next step is to tabulate the total NI and IF scores from the left-hand page and record the score in the box provided on the

right-hand page. Step 3, then, is to calculate a total score for the NI and IF scales and then transfer that total score to the Score Summary form.

The third validity scale, the Inconsistency scale (IN), is tabulated differently than the previous scores. Only 10 pairs of items (20 items total) are used to tabulate the IN score, so careful attention must be paid when transferring the scores from the scoring sheet to the Score Summary form. First, on the scoring sheet, in some of the boxes to the left of the respondent's circled number, there is an "I" in the right side of the box. These are the items used for the IN scale. For each box that shows an "I," one records the value in that box on the Score Summary form. When all 20 values have been recorded on the form, one then subtracts the lower value from the higher value and records the difference in the "total" column. Then, sum each total value for an overall inconsistency score.

Interpretation. Although the CAD can be administered and scored by nonprofessionals, the professional manual cites professional training and clinical experience as necessary for interpreting the CAD. Interpretation follows a five-step protocol.

First, omitted items or multiply marked items can invalidate an individual's CAD. As such, the reason for their occurrence needs to be discussed with the respondent. The clinician/researcher needs to determine whether this impacts the overall validity of the responses. Regardless of the reason, if more than 10% of any scale's items are omitted or mismarked, the scale is invalid. The only exception is Diminished Interest, which requires responses for all items in order to be valid. Then, the validity scales are reviewed. Using the Score Summary form, the clinician compares the IN, NI, and IF scores to the classification table at the bottom of the form. Classifications of Atypical or Very Atypical raise a red flag and need further exploration. High IN scores may suggest unreliable or careless responding. High NI scores may suggest a highly negative response set that requires close review to determine specific areas of concern. High IF scores could indicate a fake good or fake bad profile.

Once validity is established, the CAD Total Score (TS) is examined. With the exception of the validity scales, all scores are reported as *T* scores with scores of 60 or above suggesting clinical relevance. *T* scores between 60 and 69 reflect Mild Clinical Risk (MCR), between 70 and 79 reflect

Significant Clinical Risk (SCR), and scores 80 or above reflect Very Significant Clinical Risk (VSCR). Thus, Total Scores (TS) above 60 reflect varying levels of depression. Though scores falling below 60 on the TS reflect "No Risk" (NR), scale scores and critical item clusters may evidence specific problem areas needing intervention so evaluation of the individual's protocol should continue beyond the TS assessment.

Symptom Scales are interpreted in a similar way, along the same classification parameters. Elevations in each of the areas result in a classic presentation of a depressed individual: depressed, anxious, unmotivated and disinterested, and fatigued. Elevations on all four would tend to reflect high CAD Total Scores, but it is important to remember that each individual may manifest depression differently and so each scale needs to be carefully examined for symptom pattern.

The fourth component of the interpretation is the critical item clusters. The goal of exploring these six clusters is twofold: to determine if there are any symptom endorsements that require immediate attention, and to glean information useful for planning therapy. Because there are no cutoffs to use in interpreting the clusters, the clinician should review the individual's responses to each item to determine specific areas of client concern.

Finally, the clinician should review each item in the CAD to ensure that no clinically significant information needs to be explored further or acted on. The manual recommends following up the administration, scoring, and interpretation with a clinical interview to provide further information, and then to consider the results of the CAD and the interview in light of any other data obtained.

DEVELOPMENT. The CAD was developed to fill a void in the assessment of depression. According to the professional manual, the CAD was designed to address the psychometric and content-related shortcomings of existing measures. A major benefit was the development of a single form for use with children to older adults. Content was developed based on review of the professional literature, existing measures, consideration of age-related depressive symptoms, and the DSM-IV-TR diagnostic criteria. This process generated a pilot version consisting of 175 items across 16 domains, that demonstrated a full scale coefficient alpha of .99. The scale was subsequently reduced

to 130, then 80, then 75 items and was administered to a wide range of respondents, including children and adolescents, all resulting in total scale coefficient alphas of .96 and higher. Following further factor and content analyses, the CAD was reduced to the current 50 items. No information on these analyses was included in the test manual.

TECHNICAL. The CAD was standardized on a sample of 1,900 individuals age 8 to 79 obtained from a range of settings (e.g., schools, clinicians, community organizations). The sample was a close match to the 2001 U.S. Census, with only educational level higher than that of the Census values. Results from ANCOVA analyses evidenced no effect of demographic variables on variance in CAD scales. Despite only minor mean differences between age groupings, derived scores were developed with associated T scores, percentiles, and 90% confidence intervals.

Reliability. The CAD evidences reliability through internal consistency, standard error of measurement, and test-retest reliability. Coefficient alphas for the CAD Total Scores across age groups were .96 and higher, and were .97 for both genders. Symptom scale reliabilities ranged from .78 (Diminished Interest, 8–11-year-old age group) to .96 (Depressed Mood, 18–25-year-old age group), with all but one above .80. Lowest values were found for the 8–11-year-old sample. Standard error of measurement for the CAD Total Score and Symptom Scales is between 2 and 5 T score points, which indicates that a person's obtained score is likely to be very similar to his or her true score. The CAD stability reliabilities, obtained from all age groups (interval ranging from 7 to 36 days for the child/adolescent group and 1 and 51 days for the adult sample), was .84 overall and ranged from .74 to .84 (uncorrected) and .81 to .87 (corrected), with higher stability values for the adult sample. It is important to note, even though the values dip below the desired .90 criterion, the mean score differences were one T score point or less in all cases.

Validity. The CAD evidences validity via content, criterion, and construct validity. All information comes from the CAD professional manual. Content validity is evidenced through scale development. The test authors based item content on professional literature, accepted diagnostic criteria, and other widely used scales that assess depression. Criterion validity is evidenced through moderate to high correlations with other widely used instruments as assessed on the various versions of the CAD during the scale development process. More recent comparisons (Bowers, 2004; Tinsley, 2004) also showed high correlations with existing instruments (i.e., Beck Depression Inventory-II [BDI-II] and Reynolds Adolescent Depression Scale [RADS]). Concurrent validity for the final version was obtained by comparing clinical and nonclinical samples across age ranges, where clinical samples scored significantly higher than the mean and most age groups in the nonclinical sample scored below the normative mean. Construct validity is shown through both internal structure and confirmatory factor analysis (CFA). High coefficient alpha values suggest that the items are measuring a similar construct. This is supported by moderate to strong scale intercorrelations and moderate item-with-total scale correlations. CFA results show the CAD to be a multidimensional scale assessing one overall construct, Depression, and four secondary constructs (Depressed Mood, Anxiety/Worry, Diminished Interest, and Cognitive/Physical Fatigue).

COMMENTARY. Depression is one of the leading psychiatric illnesses across the lifespan. It is only in more recent times that we as a society have begun to fully appreciate the extent to which this disorder affects the young and the old. As a result, our assessment of depression has been more limited. Although there are some very good scales available, such as the Beck Depression Inventory (T7:275), Children's Depression Inventory (17:41), and Hamilton Rating Scale for Depression (T7:2161), to name a few, all have limitations. Most are age specific and some are theoretically driven, paying less attention to the multidimensional nature of depression. This is where the CAD shows its greatest strength. The CAD offers a single form, which can be used with children up to older adults, and addresses basic symptom presentation needed for diagnosis but also aspects of depression that may be more unique to the developmental level or specific situation of the individual. The CAD's applicability across the lifespan is a real benefit; however, this asset must be viewed with some caution, as the manifestation of the depression varies so greatly across developmental levels. This is seen in the reliability and validity studies, which show that values tended to be lower in the younger groups. Even though they

were somewhat lower, the values were still good and suggest that the CAD is a psychometrically sound instrument for use with individuals from age 8 to 79. Although the CAD appears to offer a very attractive alternative to other depression measures, it is unclear why it is not being seen more in the professional literature. A literature search for studies using the CAD yielded no results. However, this could be more related to the relative newness of the CAD than any statement of its value in research or clinical settings. That being said, this review is limited by the fact that all information was obtained from the professional manual and the publisher's website.

SUMMARY. The CAD offers clinicians a brief, psychometrically sound, comprehensive method for assessing depression in clients. Its multilayered content and interpretation possibilities, combined with its ease of use, make the CAD a good option for the busy clinical professional as well as researchers.

REVIEWER'S REFERENCES

Bowers, S. L. (2004). *Concurrent validity of the Clinical Assessment of Depression with the Beck Depression Inventory—Second Edition.* Master's Thesis, Western Kentucky University, Bowling Green.

Tinsley, B. W. (2004). *Concurrent validity of the Clinical Assessment of Depression with the Reynolds Adolescent Depression Scale.* Master's Thesis, Western Kentucky University, Bowling Green.

[49]

Clinical Evaluation of Language Fundamentals Preschool—Second Edition.

Purpose: Designed as a "clinical tool for identifying, diagnosing, and performing follow-up evaluations of language deficits."

Population: Ages 3–6.

Publication Dates: 1992–2004.

Acronym: CELF Preschool-2.

Scores, 16: 11 subtests (Sentence Structure, Word Structure, Expressive Vocabulary, Concepts and Following Directions, Recalling Sentences, Basic Concepts, Word Classes, Recalling Sentences in Context, Phonological Awareness, Pre-Literacy Rating Scale, Descriptive Pragmatics Profile); 5 Composites (Core Language, Receptive Language, Expressive Language, Language Content, Language Structure).

Administration: Individual.

Price Data, 2007: $329 per complete kit; $89 per examiner's manual (2004, 220 pages); $219 per Stimulus Book #1; $52 per Stimulus Book #2; $62 per 25 record forms.

Time: (15–20) minutes.

Comments: A downward extension of the Clinical Evaluation of Language Fundamentals—Fourth Edition (16:53).

Authors: Elisabeth H. Wiig, Wayne A. Secord, and Eleanor Semel.
Publisher: The Psychological Corporation, A Harcourt Assessment Company.
Cross References: See T5:539 (2 references); for reviews by Janet A. Norris and Nora M. Thompson of an earlier edition, see 13:67 (2 references).

Review of the Clinical Evaluation of Language Fundamentals Preschool—Second Edition by RICK EIGENBROOD, Assistant Dean for Graduate Studies and Assessment, Seattle Pacific University, Seattle, WA:

DESCRIPTION. The Clinical Evaluation of Language Fundamentals Preschool—Second Edition (CELF Preschool—2) is a norm-referenced test intended for use with children ages 3 years, 0 months through 6 years. It is a downward extension of the Clinical Evaluation of Language Fundamentals—Fourth Edition (CELF-4; Semel, Wiig, & Secord, 2003; 16:53). The test is individually administered with a relatively short administration time for the Core Language composite score (15–20 minutes), plus varying additional time for remaining subtests depending on which additional optional subtests are selected. According to the manual, major revisions for the current edition reflect new norms based on a national and representative standardization sample (2003) and include increased evidence for reliability and validity, easier and quicker administration, an expanded test floor to increase diagnostic value for ages 3–4, an expanded ceiling for ages 5–6, an increase in the testing efficiency by including administration directions in the stimulus book, and an expansion of the original CELF-Preschool to assess early literacy fundamentals and communication in context (pragmatics) and add composite scores to evaluate content (semantics) and structure (morphosyntax).

Materials included in the test kit include the examiner's manual, two stimulus books, record forms (protocol), a Pre-Literacy Rating scale, a Descriptive Pragmatics Profile, and a Concepts and Following Directions stimulus sheet. Directions for administering and scoring each of the subtests are clearly presented in the manual with additional directions provided in the stimulus book for ease of administration. Subtests for the test include Sentence Structure, Word Structure, Expressive Vocabulary, Concepts and Following Directions, Recalling Sentences, Basic Concepts, Word Classes, Recalling Sentences in Context, Phonological Awareness, a Pre-Literacy Rating Scale, and a Descriptive Pragmatics Profile.

The manual recommends that testing begin with the three subtests that make up the Core Language composite score in the order that they appear on the record form (protocol)—Sentence Structure, Word Structure, and Expressive Vocabulary. Other subtests may then be administered in any order as needed but alternating between receptive and expressive subtests.

According to the CELF Preschool-2 manual, the test is a "clinical tool for identifying, diagnosing, and performing follow-up evaluations of language deficits in children 3-6 years" (p. 1). Results may be used to identify a child's current language and communication skills and strengths, which can then be used to make recommendations for intervention and accommodation.

The test manual specifies that the test should be administered only by those who have training and experience in administering and scoring standardized tests. Additionally, test administrators should have experience with the testing of young children from similar cultural and linguistic backgrounds and comparable clinical histories. The person giving the test should be familiar with the test and practice administration of the test before administering it for clinical purposes. The directions in the manual reflect standardized and typical requirements for the administration of standardized tests. The manual states that it is important to accept dialectical variations during the testing process. Additionally, instructions are explained for special situations that may require modifications. If the modifications do not change the standardized procedures, stimuli, or scoring, the norms may still be used. However, if changes are substantial (e.g. additional repetitions of the stimuli) then only raw scores should be reported.

Scores reported for the CELF Preschool-2 include scaled scores ($M = 10$, $SD = 3$) and percentile ranks for Sentence Structure, Word Structure, Expressive Vocabulary, Concepts and Following Directions, Recalling Sentences, Basic Concepts (ages 3–4), Word Classes–Receptive (ages 4–6), Word Classes—Expressive (ages 4–6), and Word Classes—Total (ages 4–6). All scaled scores and percentiles are reported with confidence intervals. A standard composite Core Language score ($M = 100$, $SD = 15$) is reported for all ages (3–6), and additional composite standard scores can be calculated by using various combinations of the subtests' scaled scores–Receptive Language (ages 3–4 and 5–6), Expressive Language (ages 3–6), Language Content (ages 3–4 and 5–6), and Language Structure (ages 3–6).

In addition to the scaled and standard scores, criterion-referenced scores (meets or does not meet) can be reported for two of the subtests–Phonological Awareness (ages 4–6) and Basic Concepts (ages 5–6) and for two checklists–the Pre-Literacy Rating Scale and Descriptive Pragmatics Profile. Finally, raw scores on the Recalling Sentences in Context subtest are converted to percentile ranks only.

The test record form also provides the ability to complete an item analysis for each of the scaled subtests. The manual provides thorough and psychometrically sound discussion for interpreting the results.

DEVELOPMENT. The development of the CELF Preschool-2 was based largely on professionally accepted test development standards (see e.g., Gall, Gall, & Borg, 2002). Steps in the development of the test included feedback from those who had previously used the first edition (CELF-Preschool), feedback from a panel of experts on child language development, a review of current literature, an initial tryout study, and a national standardization of the instrument. The initial CELF-Preschool was reviewed by a panel, and based on that feedback changes were introduced to the CELF Preschool-2. A pilot study was then carried out with a sample of 40 children (23 females and 17 males) to evaluate the new subtests and two CELF-Preschool tests that had been substantially revised. The composition of the sample should be considered adequate for a pilot study of the new and revised subtests. Based on analysis of the pilot sample, additional changes were made (e.g., the addition of items and the selection of a new story for the test).

The next step in the test development was a "tryout research" of the CELF Preschool-2 with 487 children, ages 3 years, 0 months to 6 years, 11 months. An additional 230 children who had previously been identified as having language disorders were also included in a clinical study. The sample demographics for both the tryout sample and the clinical study were well described in terms of gender, ethnicity, geographical region, and parent education. The manual states that statistical analyses including item difficulty, item discrimination, subtest construct, and reliability were performed. Unfortunately, the statistical data were not reported in the manual, though the authors state that additional changes were made to the test (e.g., the Word Class subtests were dropped for the 3-year-olds).

The final version of the CELF Preschool-2 was standardized on a sample of 800 children with 100 children in each of the eight 6-month age groups. The manual provides evidence that the standardization sample was representative of the U.S. population in terms of gender, racial, and ethnic background; geographic region; and primary-caregiver education. In addition, the sample included appropriate representation of students with special needs (i.e., children receiving services for special education).

The theoretical grounding for the CELF Preschool-2 is well discussed in the manual and the theory behind each of the subtests is addressed individually. However, the use of citations to research to substantiate the theoretical basis is stronger for some of the subtests than others. For example, there are no substantiating references for Concepts and Following Directions, Word Class, Recalling Sentences, and only two of the instrument's authors are cited for Sentence Structure (Wiig & Semel, 1984).

TECHNICAL. The CELF Preschool-2 manual reports three types of evidence for reliability–test-retest, internal consistency, and interrater reliability. Reported test-retest corrected correlations for subtests by age ranged from a high of .94 for Expressive Vocabulary (ages 5 years to 5 years, 11 months) to a low of .75 for Sentence Structure (ages 6 years to 6 years, 11 months), and correlations across all ages range from a high of .90 for Expressive Vocabulary and Recalling Sentences to a low of .78 for Sentence Structure. A number of the correlations do not meet the recommended test-retest reliability correlations expected of a diagnostic assessment (.90), and some of the correlations fall below the recommended correlations for a screening instrument (.80) (Salvia & Ysseldyke, 2003). The time between the two testings was 2–24 days.

The manual also reports evidence for internal consistency by reporting both coefficient alpha and split-half reliability corrected correlation coefficients for both the standardization sample and the clinical sample. Average alpha coefficients across all ages for the standardization sample ranged from a high of .95 for the Pre-Literacy Rating Scale and the Descriptive Pragmatics Profile to a low of .77 for Basic Concepts. A review of the coefficient alpha reliability coefficients for the various age categories indicated that some were unacceptably low (e.g., Basic Concepts, .59 for ages 5 years to 5 years, 6 months and .61 for ages 5 years, 6 months to 5 years, 11 months). The reported split-half reliability coefficients indicated a similar pattern for internal consistency. Average internal consistency evidence was strong for the clinical groups with both overall test average alpha coefficient and split-half reliability coefficients at .90 or higher for most of the subtests. The test manual provides acceptable evidence for interater reliability.

Evidence to support the validity of the CELF Preschool-2 is extensive. First, the authors discussed the instrument's content validity in terms of how the various subtests and composite scores are linked to scientifically based research literature. All items, as well as the test structure were reviewed by a panel of experts, and where indicated modifications were made to the test. The manual also describes the use of response analysis (response process) during the test development. In brief, the evidence for the CELF Preschool-2's content validity is adequate.

Construct validity for the CELF Preschool-2 is summarized in terms of two areas–a study of intercorrelations and factor analyses. According to the test manual, moderate to high subtest intercorrelations indicate that the subtests and composite scores appear to tap various elements of the same construct.

The appropriateness for the CELF-Preschool model, or its construct validity, was also examined through the use of confirmatory factor analyses on the subtest scores for ages 3 to 4 and 5 to 6. Though the results presented in the manual were limited and somewhat confusing, the data presented do suggest adequate support for the construct validity of the test. In short, the evidence provided in the manual to establish the CELF Preschool-2's construct validity is adequate.

Evidence for the CELF Preschool-2's criterion-related validity is limited. Even though concurrent validity data between the test and the original CELF-Preschool, the CELF-4, and the Preschool Language Scale-4 (PLS-4; Zimmerman, Steiner, & Pond, 2002) were reported at the moderate to high levels, the authors omitted essential background information suggested by Salvia and Ysseldyke (2003). For instance, the criterion measure (PLS-4) was not well described and the rationale for its selection was not made explicit.

COMMENTARY. The CELF Preschool-2 appears to be a useful test for the assessment of young children's language development. Description of the test's development is strong and reflects best professional practice in test construction. Though the evidence for criterion-related validity is not adequately established, content and construct validity appear strong. However, reliability data presented in the manual indicate lower than acceptable reliability for some of the subtests at certain age groups. Clinicians should use caution when interpreting the results for individual children where reliability coefficients fall below accepted standards (Salvia & Ysseldyke, 2003).

SUMMARY. The CELF Preschool-2 is a norm-referenced assessment of early language development that can be efficiently used for screening and diagnostic purposes. The instrument can be administered and scored in a relatively efficient manner. However, the CELF Preschool-2 should be used with some caution when used as a diagnostic tool because of lower than acceptable reliability for some of the subtests and age groups.

REVIEWER'S REFERENCES
Gall, J. P., Gall, M. D., & Borg, W. R. (2002). *Educational research: An introduction* (7th ed.) Boston: Allyn and Bacon.
Salvia, J., & Ysseldyke, J. E. (2003). *Assessment: In special and inclusive education* (9th ed.). Boston: Houghton Mifflin.
Semel, E. M., Wiig, E. H., & Secord, W. A. (2003). Clinical Evaluation of Language Fundamentals—Fourth Edition. San Antonio, TX: The Psychological Corporation.
Wiig, E. H., & Semel, E. M. (1984). Language Assessment and Intervention for the Learning Disabled (2nd ed.). Columbus, OH: Charles E. Merrill.
Zimmerman, I. L., Steiner, V. G., & Pond, R. E. (2002). Preschool Language Scale-Fourth Edition. San Antonio, TX: The Psychological Corporation.

Review of the Clinical Evaluation of Language Fundamentals Preschool—Second Edition by GENE SCHWARTING, *Associate Professor, Education/Special Education, Fontbonne University, St. Louis, MO:*

DESCRIPTION. The Clinical Evaluation of Language Fundamentals Preschool—Second Edition (CELF Preschool-2) is a standardized, norm-referenced assessment tool for measuring the language development of children ages 3–6 years. It is to be administered individually, and is intended to be used by speech/language pathologists, school psychologists, special educators, and educational diagnosticians. The CELF Preschool-2 is a four-level, flexible assessment system to determine if a language disorder exists, the nature of the disorder, to measure early classroom and literacy fundamentals, and to evaluate language and communication in context. The test includes a core language score, incorporating measurement of Sentence Structure, Word Structure, and Expressive Vocabulary with an estimated administration time of 15–20 minutes. In addition to this core component, other subtests include Concepts and Following Directions, Recalling Sentences, Basic Concepts, Word Classes, Recalling Sentences in Context, Phonological Awareness, Pre-Literacy Rating Scale, and a Descriptive Pragmatics Profile, which if administered results in additional assessment time.

The CELF Preschool-2 consists of an examiner's manual, two easel-type stimulus books, record forms, checklists, and a stimulus sheet. Administration and specific scoring directions are found in the stimulus books, and the general directions and norms tables are found in the examiner's manual.

Each subtest begins with Item 1, so basals are not needed. The ceiling rules vary from one subtest to another, as do the point values of correct responses. The subtest raw scores are converted to subtest scaled scores with a mean of 10 and a standard deviation of 3. These are combined to obtain standard scores, percentiles, and confidence intervals for Core Language, Receptive Language, Expressive Language, Language Content, and Language Structure. Age equivalents may be obtained as well.

It is recommended that the three subtests of the language core be administered in sequence to determine if a language impairment exists. Then, other subtests may be administered in any order based upon clinical judgment, language concerns, and the original referral question.

DEVELOPMENT. The CELF Preschool-2 is a revision of the original 1992 CELF-Preschool, as well as a downward extension of the 2003 Clinical Evaluation of Language Fundamentals—Fourth Edition (CELF-4), from which its format was derived and some of whose items it shares. Nevertheless, the CELF Preschool-2 was developed with the goals of strengthening the validity and reliability, expanding the floor for younger children and the ceiling for older ones, improving usability, and expanding the areas assessed. Pilot studies were conducted in 2002, followed by a large tryout study and the actual standardization in 2003. The normative group included 100 children in each of eight age groups at 6-month intervals. Using the 2000 U.S. Census, this sample of 800 children was stratified based closely on age, sex, ethnicity, geographic region, and the primary caregivers' education level. Children with a diagnosed disability were included, as well as those from bilingual homes as long as the primary language of all participants was English.

TECHNICAL. Test-retest reliability was determined on 120 children from the norm group with the times between testing ranging from 2–24 days. When ages were combined, reliabilities of the subtests were all above .80 except for sentence structure at .77. However, the reliabilities of composite scores were all greater than .90 and consistent across age groups. Internal consistency of the subtests, using coefficient alpha, varies from .80 for Sentence Structure to .97 for the Pre-Literacy Rating Scale. For composites, all measures exceed .90 with Core Language being .92. The standard error of measurement for subtests ranges from .55 for the Pre-Literacy Rating Scale to 1.4 for Basic Concepts, and for composites varies from 3.75 for the Expressive Language Index to 4.37 for the Receptive Language Index.

The authors indicate that content validity is strong, and they note that test items were reviewed by experts in the field, response processes were studied, factor analysis was conducted, and the intercorrelation of subtests found the existence of highly intercorrelated relationships (.50–.93). Because language is a focus throughout the subtests, and because the various composites incorporate different combinations of the same subtests, high intercorrelations are to be expected. Concurrent validity is measured by examining the relationship of the CELF Preschool-2 with the CELF-P and the CELF-4. Because these instruments have designs and items in common, the strong relationships of the composite scores (.75 to .88 with the CELF-P, and .69 to .84 with the CELF-4) are not a surprise. When compared to the Preschool Language Scale—Fourth Edition, the relationships found are .73 for Receptive Language, .76 for Expressive Language, and .73 for Total Language.

COMMENTARY. The CELF Preschool-2 is easy to use, contains items that are developmentally appropriate, and seems to be an improvement over its predecessor. Reliability and validity, although adequate, could be stronger—particularly for the subtests. Sensitivity (the ability of the test to identify a language disorder correctly) is .85; whereas specificity (the ability to identify nondisordered students correctly) is .82. Therefore, this error rate suggests that the CELF Preschool-2 not be used as the sole diagnostic tool.

SUMMARY. Overall, the CELF Preschool-2 is a sound, well-developed instrument that exists as a part of a diagnostic system. It provides a variety of information about a child if the entire instrument is administered. Alternatively, the core language components can be used to measure abilities in this area alone. As with many instruments for this age level, it is recommended that a second instrument also be administered for determination of disabilities.

[50]

College Survival and Success Scale.

Purpose: Designed to "identify the concerns college students are experiencing or the concerns that prospective college students can anticipate."

Population: Individuals interested in attending college, or agencies that work with individuals interested in attending college.

Publication Date: 2006.

Acronym: CSSS.

Scores, 5: Commitment to Education, Self-/Resource-Management Skills, Interpersonal/Social Skills, Academic Success Skills, Career Planning Skills.

Administration: Individual or group.

Price Data, 2006: $37.95 per complete kit including 25 test booklets and 1 administrator's guide (8 pages).

Time: (15–25) minutes.

Author: John Liptak.

Publisher: JIST Publishing, Inc.

Review of the College Survival and Success Scale by HEIDI M. CARTY, Associate Director, Student Research & Information, University of California, San Diego, San Diego, CA:

DESCRIPTION. The College Survival and Success Scale (CSSS) was designed as a tool to measure a person's knowledge and attitude about the skills needed for college survival and success. In identifying one's strengths and weaknesses, the CSSS provides student advisors and career counselors with information on areas in which a student or potential student needs counseling or assistance in developing effective skills for college survival and success. The CSSS contains 60 statements representing five major scales, including commitment to education, self- and resource-management skills, interpersonal and social skills, academic success skills, and career planning skills. For each question one responds selecting from a 4-point scale, meaning "a lot like me" to "not like me." The CSSS is easy to administer, score, and interpret. Responses to statements are made using a pen or pencil. Total and scale scores are calculated by simply summing the response value for each section. The CSSS takes approximately 20 minutes to complete.

Materials provided by the author include a test booklet and an administrator's guide. The test booklet includes a five-step process for completing the scale, calculating, interpreting, and profiling scores, and developing a plan for success. Included in the administrator's guide are sections describing the theoretical framework underlying the process, directions and guidelines for administering the scale, how to calculate and interpret scores, an illustrative case, development of the scale, and a brief description of the psychometric properties.

DEVELOPMENT. The CSSS was published in 2006. According to the author, the research underlying the development of the CSSS is based on a thorough review of the literature regarding college success, transition to college, and college preparation. The author also mentions using a variety of academic and professional sources to identify the five content areas that represent college success skills (p. 5). A list or description of these "sources" was not provided in the materials. Missing from the scale are statements or questions regarding academic ability. As scores on standardized tests and high school grades are highly correlated with college success (i.e., retention and graduation rates), including two or three questions regarding one's academic abilities seems important, if only to add to the collection of information for counseling purposes.

Although the scale was developed from a sample comparing scores from both males and females, the sample size was small ($N = 156$) and presumably was not randomly selected. A description of the sampling methodology was not provided. Therefore, the results from the sample may not be generalizable to the entire population of current or potential college-bound students. In addition, it is not clear whether respondent racial or ethnic background or socioeconomic status was taken into account when developing the scale. It would have been useful for the author to look at patterns among various socioeconomic classes and racial and ethnic background with regard to item responses, particularly considering the number of questions regarding knowledge of student aid and financial services available.

TECHNICAL. There is no information regarding the standardization of the CSSS. As mentioned, the scale was developed using a relatively small sample. No normative data are provided for racial and ethnic minorities or by socioeconomic status.

The author provided evidence in support of reliability by measuring the internal consistency and stability of the scales. Measures of internal consistency (split-half) and stability (test-retest) are generally high for each scale of the instrument ranging from .88 to .94.

The CSSS does not meet the minimum accepted psychometric standards for substantiating validity evidence established in the *Standards for Educational and Psychological Testing* (AERA, APA, & NCME, 1999). For each scale, the author provides interscale correlations and the mean and standard deviations from one small sample (N = 156). Although it is important to provide these statistics, they do not provide evidence of validity. It would be useful for the author of the manual to provide evidence of construct, content, and criterion-related validity. It would be useful to replicate the study on a new, larger, randomly selected sample and compare results. It would also be useful to correlate the results from the CSSS to other tests and variables with which a relationship would be expected. Further, it would also prove useful to examine differences with respect to race and ethnicity and socioeconomic status.

Finally, other unanswered validity issues include the relationship of the scale scores to college grade-point averages, to scholastic ability, and to improvement in study skills and college success rates. How effective is the five-step process and what are the long-term effects as a result of participating in this process? Do students or potential students who participate in this process become successful in college and ultimately graduate? Are they retained at a higher rate than nonparticipants? Do they graduate at higher rates than nonparticipants? Do they obtain financial aid and learn money management at a higher rate than nonparticipants? Are they more successful in selecting a career than those students who do not participate? Long-term effects as a result of participating in the CSSS five-step process need to be addressed.

COMMENTARY. Although the theoretical framework underlying the CSSS—based on college success, the transition to college, and college preparation—appears well grounded, the psychometric properties providing evidence for the validity of the study are absent. At best the scale appears to serve the advisors of students and career counselors as a simple resource or checklist for determining the nonacademic (with the exception of study skills) areas of weakness that may hinder a student on the road to college success.

As the CSSS was developed using a relatively small, nonrandom sample, the section for interpreting scores should be used with caution as they may not be generalizable to the general population. In addition, as stated above, validity studies need to be conducted. These studies need to employ a larger, randomly selected sample and take into account possible differences by race and ethnicity as well as socioeconomic status.

Finally, the short-term and long-term effects of participating in the program compared to nonparticipants need to be addressed. How successful is the program and what are the long-term effects?

SUMMARY. Overall, the CSSS may serve as an easily administered checklist in identifying the areas in which students could benefit most from educational intervention if psychometric evidence regarding the criterion-related validity and construct validity are not required. Validity studies need to be conducted using a large broad-based, randomly selected group of college-bound or current college students, so the results may be generalized to the general population of current and potential college students. Norms for racial and ethnic groups should be established, and the short-term and long-term effects of the program should be determined.

REVIEWER'S REFERENCE

American Educational Research Association, American Psychological Association, & National Council on Measurement in Education. (1999). *Standards for educational and psychological testing.* Washington, DC: American Educational Research Association.

[51]
Combined Basic Skills (Form LCS-C & Form B-C).

Purpose: To evaluate literacy and cognitive skills.
Population: Applicants and incumbents for jobs requiring literacy and cognitive skills.
Publication Dates: 1998–2003.
Scores, 4: Reading, Arithmetic, Inspection and Measurement, Process Monitoring & Problem Solving.
Administration: Group.
Price Data, 2006: $15 per consumable self-scoring test booklet (minimum order of 20); $24.95 per manual (2003, 30 pages).
Foreign Language Editions: Available in Spanish.
Time: (48) minutes.
Comments: Self-scoring instrument; two alternate equivalent forms.
Author: Roland T. Ramsay.
Publisher: Ramsay Corporation.

Review of the Combined Basic Skills (Form LCS-C & Form B-C) by CHER N. EDWARDS, Assistant Professor, School Counseling and Psychology, Seattle Pacific University, and SCOTT F. BEERS, Assistant Professor, Curriculum and Instruction, Seattle Pacific University, Seattle, WA:

DESCRIPTION. The Ramsay Corporation Job Skills Test, Combined Basic Skills (Form LCS-C & Form B-C), is a multiple-choice, 52-item timed test administered by paper-and-pencil. The test is designed to assess arithmetic, inspection, measurement, process monitoring, and problem solving skills as well as evaluate the reading and comprehension levels of production, maintenance, and operating workers. For each skill area a score is generated, which can be used to identify strengths and weaknesses among applicants within a group. Scores may then be combined to provide an overall measure of a test-taker's basic skills. The manual for administration and scoring indicates that data are being collected for norming purposes, which will enable administrators in the future to interpret an applicant's score as a percentile rank.

Administrator qualifications are not indicated. Instructions and user-friendly scripts for administration and testing conditions are provided. Adding to the ease of use, test booklets are self-scoring, thus allowing for results within 5 minutes. Scores are generated for each skill area assessed, which may be combined for an overall

score. No recommendations or calculations of the raw score are provided, although a percentile score can be determined based upon preliminary norming data. Administrators are expected to use these scores to make more informed personnel decisions.

DEVELOPMENT. The Ramsay Corporation Job Skills Combined Basic Skills Test (Form LCS) was developed in 1997, based upon four longer "predecessor" tests upon which the current test is based. Feedback from initial administrations of these tests indicated that they were too long, leading the Ramsay Corporation to develop abbreviated versions. Form LCS-C, the self-scoring format, was developed in 1998, and Form B-C (a "parallel equivalent" or alternate form) was developed in 2002. The manual for administration and scoring provides limited information about the development of the original test and the modifications that led to the current forms. The manual indicates that two industrial psychologists selected representative items from the longer predecessor tests to create the shorter version, in the hopes of maintaining the "content integrity" and reliability of the larger tests. No theoretical selection criteria for the items are provided, and empirical data supporting the claims of preserved content integrity are lacking.

Although no theoretical rationale for the skill areas is provided, three of the four sections of the test appear to assess distinct skill areas that may apply to diverse jobs (Reading, Arithmetic, and Inspection and Measurement). The fourth section (Process Monitoring and Problem Solving), however, seems to measure a wide array of skills and background knowledge that only loosely fit the category.

TECHNICAL. The norming process for the test is currently incomplete. The manual provides preliminary norming data by including tables of cumulative percents for each of the four skill areas assessed, although these tables are based upon only two administrations of Form LCS-C in 1998 (*N* = 473). Further, these two administrations of the test provide substantially different results, leading to notable differences in the reported norms for the test. For example, a raw score of 13 (out of 16) among the applicants in one group tested would result in a cumulative percent of 72.2, whereas the same score among applicants in another tested group would result in a cumulative percent of 53.8. Until additional norming *data* are collected and calculated, the relevancy of these reported norms is questionable.

The Reading section items on both test forms (16 items, Forms LCS-C and B-C) call for literal-level information, akin to following directions or finding specific information in a given text. Several of the questions may not be text-dependent, so that test-takers with experience in production work may be able to answer questions correctly without accurately reading the passages. Because test-takers may already know answers about production/operation topics, scores on the Reading portion of the test may be inflated. In one administration of Form LCS-C to 437 applicants at a manufacturing plant (1998), the mean score was 12.34 (out of a possible 16), suggesting a possible ceiling effect (SEM = 1.45).

The Arithmetic section (14 items) includes basic computation skills such as addition, subtraction, multiplication, and division, and calculating percentages, along with interpreting tables and graphs. The Inspection and Measurement section (10 items) includes estimating lengths of objects (with rulers graphically represented), reading gauges, and matching lengthy identification numbers from among a list of similar numbers. The Process Monitoring and Problem Solving section (12 items) seemingly draws upon a wider range of skills, from basic knowledge of engine/machine function to solving word puzzles and reading flow charts.

Internal consistency reliability coefficients for each of the skills areas are reported twice, based upon two administrations of the test. In the first of these administrations (437 applicants at a manufacturing plant), reliability coefficients (KR_{20}) range from .71 (Inspection and Measurement) to .80 (Reading). For achievement tests these reliability coefficients are at best marginal; achievement tests generally are expected to report coefficients above .80. In the second administration (36 applicants at a metals plant), the reliability coefficients are higher, ranging from .90 (Arithmetic) to .92 (Inspection and Measurement). The differences between the two administrations of the test, both of which used Form LCS-C, are surprising and not explained. Generally larger samples provide more stable results, but in this case, the smaller sample yielded higher internal consistency coefficients. We speculate that the populations appeared to have different skill levels; the larger group scored higher in every skill area with means 1–2 points higher, raising the possibility of ceiling and restricted range effects. The disparity in reliability coefficients between the two administrations and the marginal reliability coefficients from the larger sample serve to undermine the manual's assertion of "excellent reliability" (manual for administration & scoring, p. 14). No test-retest reliability is reported.

Evidence to support the validity of the test is inconsistent. Several concurrent validity scores demonstrating correlations between tested skill areas and employee performance ratings are provided but without sufficient detail. For example, the test reports that the Reading portion correlates with overall job performance (r = .49) and other performance-related "various criteria" (not named, correlation coefficients ranging from .21 to .35). These low-to-moderate correlations, however, are based upon Reading Form A, which is the longer "predecessor" form (40 items) upon which the shorter forms (LCS-C and B-C, 16 items) are based. No content validity analyses are reported for the Reading portion of the current shorter forms, although they are said to be of similar content.

In another validation study, which was not referenced, the combined Basic Skills score was significantly correlated (r = .29) with supervisor performance ratings. As with the Reading test, validation data appear to rely upon previous forms of the test instead of the current forms (LCS-C and B-C). Low to low-moderate correlations with job performance ratings are reported for Arithmetic (r = .21, Form CO), Inspection and Measurement (correlation coefficients from .16 to .35, Form LCI-C), and Process Monitoring/Problem Solving (correlation coefficients from .21 to .31, form unknown).

The developer asserts that each construct measured is "attained by the procedures of development" (manual for administration & scoring, p. 19), although evidence of this process is lacking. These procedures are not explained to our satisfaction.

COMMENTARY. The value of this test as a measure of job skills seems to depend upon the type of job one may be offering. In a somewhat circular argument, the developers assert that the test is useful if the job requires the use of the skills that the test measures. Although this logic may be obvious, it also demonstrates the serious limitations of the test. High among these limitations are reliability concerns. When two target populations of applicants produce substantially different mean scores and reliability coefficients, it is difficult to assume that the test itself is a reliable measure. Second, the test manual includes norming data based upon these two sets of scores, resulting in two different "norms." Until more extensive norming data are provided, interpretation of scores from the Combined Basic Skills is left to the judgment of the administrators.

Demographic information gathered on the examinees whose scores were utilized for norming data was not provided. Instructions for test administration indicates that any significant behavior should be noted. One example provided was regarding English Language Learner status, which suggests that the test is appropriate for individuals for whom English is a second language (instructions recommend administering the test and indicating a comment that the test taker is a nonnative English speaker). Despite the inclusion of this group, no information is provided regarding norming for nonnative English speakers. Ethnicity and gender were also not included although it may be that neither impacted test score results.

SUMMARY. If reliability and validity are further documented then the Ramsay Corporation Combined Basic Skills may be a useful tool to assess basic skills of identified importance for production, maintenance, and operating workers. This instrument is brief and efficient and requires no administration or scoring expertise. Limitations include significant reliability issues as well as a lack of extensive norming data needed for valid interpretation of test scores. The test manual suggests the instrument is appropriate for bilingual or multilingual populations although there are no data to support this indication.

[52]
Comprehensive Testing Program 4.

Purpose: "Designed to provide instructionally useful information about student performance in key areas of the school curriculum: listening, reading, vocabulary, writing, and mathematics"; beginning with the spring of Grade 3, includes verbal and quantitative reasoning tests to measure higher order thinking skills.
Population: Grades 1–2, 2–3, 3–4, 4–5, 5–6, 6–7, 7–8, 8–9, 9–10, 10–11.
Publication Dates: 1974–2004.
Acronym: CTP 4.

Administration: Group.
Levels, 10: 1–10.
Price Data: Available from publisher.
Time: (300) minutes for total battery.
Comments: Machine scoring by the publisher; provides "Independent," "Suburban Public," and "National" norms; hand-scoring keys and norms booklets are also available from the publisher; partial battery is an option; allows for nonstandard administration.
Author: Educational Records Bureau.
Publisher: Educational Records Bureau.

a) LEVEL 1.
Population: Grade 1 spring or Grade 2 fall.
Scores, 4: Auditory Comprehension, Reading Comprehension, Word Analysis, Mathematics Achievement.
b) LEVEL 2.
Population: Grade 2 spring or Grade 3 fall.
Scores, 5: Same as for Level 1 plus Writing Mechanics.
c) LEVEL 3.
Population: Grade 3 spring or Grade 4 fall.
Scores, 7: Verbal Reasoning, Auditory Comprehension, Reading Comprehension, Writing Mechanics, Writing Concepts and Skills, Mathematics Achievement, Quantitative Reasoning.
d) LEVEL 4.
Population: Grade 4 spring or Grade 5 fall.
Scores, 7: Verbal Reasoning, Vocabulary, Reading Comprehension, Writing Mechanics, Writing Concepts and Skills, Mathematics Achievement, Quantitative Reasoning.
e) LEVEL 5.
Population: Grade 5 spring or Grade 6 fall.
Scores, 7: Same as for Level 4.
f) LEVEL 6.
Population: Grade 6 spring or Grade 7 fall.
Scores, 7: Same as for Levels 4 and 5..
g) LEVEL 7.
Population: Grade 7 spring or Grade 8 fall.
Scores, 7: Same as for Levels 4, 5, and 6.
h) LEVEL 8.
Population: Grade 8 spring or Grade 9 fall.
Scores, 8: Same as for Levels 4, 5, and 6, plus Algebra 1.
i) LEVEL 9.
Population: Grade 9 spring or Grade 10 fall.
Scores, 8: Same as for Level 8.
j) LEVEL 10.
Population: Grade 10 spring or Grade 11 fall.
Scores, 7: Same as for Levels 8 and 9 except for omission of Algebra 1.
Cross References: For reviews by Steven J. Osterlind and Darrell L. Sabers of an earlier edition, see 13:83; for a review by Kathleen Barrows Chesterfield of an earlier edition, see 9:397.

Review of the Comprehensive Testing Program 4 by KORESSA KUTSICK MALCOLM, School Psychologist, Augusta County Public Schools, Fishersville, VA, and Adjunct Faculty Member, Mary Baldwin College, Staunton, VA:

DESCRIPTION. The Comprehensive Testing Program 4 (CTP 4) is a standardized group assessment instrument designed to measure the academic skills and abilities of students who are attending high-achieving schools. The CTP 4 is composed of a battery of tests designed to provide instructionally relevant data for children in Grades 1 through 11. Student skills in the areas of listening, reading, vocabulary, writing, and mathematics are assessed.

The CTP 4 was designed for two major purposes. One goal of the CTP 4 was to provide information about individual student performances that would enable educators to pinpoint the skill strengths and weaknesses of very successful students. These students were defined as those who would obtain top scores on group achievement tests used by most public schools in the nation. The other major goal of the CTP 4 was to provide data that would enable administrators, teachers, and others to review curricular strengths and weaknesses of their educational programs in high-performance schools.

The CTP 4 is composed of both achievement and reasoning tests. Comparisons of scores in these areas can be made to determine if students' skills are at levels consistent with their potential for learning.

There are two major formats of the subtests of the CTP 4. One is a standard multiple-choice styled test. The other is what the test's developers refer to as "constructed-response" tests. The tests are provided for the areas of reading comprehension and mathematics. In the reading comprehension constructed-response items, students are asked to integrate information from several reading passages and to answer presented questions in their own words. In the mathematics constructed-response items, students must show their work to reflect the problem-solving processes they used to solve the presented problem.

Administration of the CTP 4 can take up to 6 hours total time, depending on the age of the student and whether or not the entire battery of tests for a grade level is administered. Fall and spring norms are available.

Computer scoring of the multiple-choice items is provided for the CTP 4. Younger children can mark their responses in a scannable test booklet. The Educational Testing Service scores the constructed-response items on-line. Student responses are scored by trained reviewers under a supervised process.

DEVELOPMENT. The Comprehensive Testing Program was developed under the direction of the Educational Records Bureau (ERB), which was founded in 1927. One of the missions of the ERB was to address concerns that assessment programs designed for public schools did not always differentiate the skills and abilities of high-achieving students. This was felt to be especially true for students who attended high performance and high expectation schools, such as those found in private schools, suburban public schools, and other independent school programs. Over the course of their history, ERB contracted with Educational Testing Service to develop a standardized ability and achievement test that would provide detailed academic assessment data for top-performing students.

The CTP 4 technical report, content standards manual, and administrator and teacher manuals provide detailed explanations regarding the developmental history of this test. Thorough discussions of the conceptualization of the test, review of user needs for the assessment instrument, the development of the test's table of specifications, item development, and test scaling procedures are provided. Extensive information regarding the design of the structure and format of the CTP 4 was gathered through focus groups, user reviews, and expert opinions.

Verbal reasoning and language arts test items were developed to reflect standards established by the 1996 National Council of Teachers of English/International Reading Association in the Standards for English Language Arts. The verbal tests of the CTP 4 include Verbal Reasoning, Vocabulary, Auditory Comprehension, Reading Comprehension, Word Analysis, Writing Mechanics, and Writing Concepts and Skills. Math items were noted to be reflective of the 2000 National Council of Teachers of Mathematics' "Principles and Standards for School Mathematics." The mathematics tests of the CTP 4 include Mathematics Achievement, Quantitative Reasoning, and Algebra 1.

TECHNICAL. Each of the achievement subtests of the CTP 4 was standardized on 800 to 1,500 students selected from school systems across the country. Student participants were stratified by school type, geographical census division, type of locale (urban, rural, etc.), minority status of the school, and school enrollment size. Students attending private schools (including those from the Bureau of Indian Affairs and the Department of Defense) and public schools were included in the standardization sample. Specific information regarding the ratio of minority students included in the study and a breakdown of gender status for students in this sample was not provided. Data were collected in the spring of 2002. The national norming study did not include any testing in the fall. The statistical information provided for students who might be tested in the fall of a year were based on estimates of growth reported by the test developers for students from one spring to the next.

Minimal reliability information is available for the CTP 4. The authors present tables that summarize intercorrelations between the CTP 4 subtests. These tend to be moderate to moderately high. No information was provided for specific types of reliability other than for internal consistency. Correlations here were high in the .72 to .94 range. No summary or discussion of these data was presented in the manual. The standard error of measurement of the CTP 4 was low across all subtests. Item to total correlations were moderate, which would be expected for an achievement test.

COMMENTARY. Schools have utilized the Comprehensive Testing Program across the U.S. for over 30 years. The CTP 4, the most recent in the series, has several positive features. The test developers spent a great deal of time surveying the needs of consumers of their testing program and attempted to design an achievement test that would meet these needs. The content sampling and item development processes of the CTP 4 were extensive. The types of information provided for each student evaluated by the CTP 4 would help teachers and administrators plan for skill and instructional refinement. The aggregate data would also be useful to those developing curricula and monitoring instructional program needs.

For a standardized, group-administered test, the CTP 4 provides several positive features for students. For example, younger students can mark their responses in a scannable record booklet. This minimizes transfer mistakes that can be made when young students are unfamiliar with score sheets. The inclusion of timed as well as untimed items, reasoning and skill tests, and content response questions would provide for a wide range of assessment of student achievement, thinking, and reasoning. Rather detailed information can be obtained for each student assessed. The processes of item and score analysis built into the CTP 4 would provide valuable information regarding the skills of each student and group of students assessed.

The materials provided for teachers and administrators (i.e., the handbook) contain useful information regarding the interpretation of test scores. Test administrators can select which types of score reports they would like to receive. This option of score report would help administrators make the most of the presented data. It is also a positive feature that the developers of the CTP 4 offer information and training to help teachers and administrators understand the information they receive from the CTP 4 and then to present test data to parents, school boards, etc.

The major weaknesses of the CTP 4 involve the limited statistical information provided regarding the reliability and validity for uses of the test. Additional research to build the support for claims that the scores are both reliable and valid for the intended purposes would be in order. The authors seemed to have much of this data (such as test-retest information and interrater comparisons) but did not include it in clear presentations that could be used by consumers.

SUMMARY. The Comprehensive Testing Program was reported to be a widely used test for more than 30 years. The current revision, the CTP 4, was designed to meet the assessment needs of students in Grades 1 through 11 who are attending high performance educational programs. The CTP 4 is a well-designed test of its nature. The test has many positive features for consumers of group tests. The test's developers are encouraged to provide additional statistical information regarding the technical quality of the CTP 4 to make it a strong contender in the testing market. This information would also be necessary to demonstrate that the CTP 4 actually does differentiate skills for top students.

Review of the Comprehensive Testing Program 4 by WILLIAM D. SCHAFER, Affiliated Professor

(Emeritus) of Measurement, Statistics, and Evaluation, University of Maryland, College Park, MD:
DESCRIPTION.

Purpose and Nature. The Comprehensive Testing Program 4 (CTP 4) consists of two series of tests designed to assess verbal and mathematics achievement in grade levels from 1st to 11th. The content standards of the verbal tests are taken from the 1996 statement of recommended standards from the National Council of Teachers of English and the International Reading Association. The mathematics content standards are taken from the 2000 recommendations of the National Council of Teachers of Mathematics. The technical manual has a copyright date of 2004, but the tests have evolved from earlier editions of the testing program.

There are 10 levels of multiple-choice items in each series with optional constructed-response items. The assessments were developed by Educational Testing Service (ETS) under contract with Educational Records Bureau (ERB), a nonprofit organization that offers several series of assessments designed to be used in independent and suburban public schools. A 180-page Content Standard Manual with a 2002 copyright date describes the domain of each CTP 4 test and gives sample items. The manual has a chart identifying the target grades for each level of the test and the subtests, including subtopics, and numbers of items for each.

Two handbooks, one for administrators and one for teachers, describe the score reports each receives. Both have a 2002 copyright date. The administrator handbook discusses ways to communicate the test information to various audiences, school boards, parents, and teachers. The teacher handbook discusses ways the data can be used instructionally and draws heavily on interviews with teachers.

The reports include a student report that gives points earned versus points possible overall and for subtests that vary in length down to as few as 7 points, and for each score a percentile rank and a stanine is given for three norm groups: national, suburban public schools, and independent schools. A graph displays, overall and for each subtest, a selected norm group percent correct versus the student's percent correct. A second item analysis report groups the multiple-choice items into content subdomains and gives for each

item the keyed answer, and the percent correct in the school and for school-selected norm groups. This report also gives the item-level responses of each student. A companion item analysis report gives parallel information for constructed-response items. Other reports are available for administrators and teachers as well as for parents.

DEVELOPMENT.

Norms. Norm groups for the CTP 4 represent its target users, which are high-achieving independent schools and public schools. Data are gathered each year from those schools that used the test, beginning in the fall of 2002 and the spring of 2003. The initial year's data are reported in the technical manual. However, percentile ranks are to be reported based on the three most recent years of data for suburban public and independent schools.

National norms are also reported. Testing occurred in spring 2002. The national norm group was selected using a multistage, systematic selection procedure separately for the four consecutive pairs of grades, 3rd through 10th, within school types, regions, locale, minority status, and enrollment. Schools (or substitutes) were selected and then classes were selected within schools. Locally, teachers were shown contiguous tests, at and below their students' grade levels, and asked to select the one most appropriate to administer. In all, 417 schools were selected; the number of tests administered varied by grade. Not all subtests were given at any one grade; no one grade received all subtests and no subtest was given at all grades.

Proportions of examinees at each cell in a two-way table, grade level by scale score, were estimated for each reported subtest scale using a log-linear model. A score's national percentiles for a grade level for the spring norms were found by estimating the score's cumulative percentage at the grade level. Fall norms were interpolated by estimating for grade levels midway between the spring grade levels.

The technical manual gives selected raw-score distribution characteristics for each subtest separately for the suburban and independent school samples. These are highest score possible, sample size, mean, median, standard deviation, chance score, percent of examinees below chance, and skewness.

Scales. The assessments report scale scores, percentile ranks, stanines, and raw scores. The scale score scale was established to be consistent with that used in the earlier version of the tests (CTP III) using common-item equating. The scale is continuous across test (and therefore grade) levels for each content area, and users are encouraged to compare scores across adjacent levels.

Standardized differences between standardized performance on various subject-matter achievement versus reasoning tests are evaluated for (in)consistency. For primary grades (Test Levels 1 and 2), subtest scores are evaluated in terms of achievement levels: developing, meets expectations, and exceeds expectations, as determined by standard-setting panels of teachers, although the frame of reference they were using is unclear.

TECHNICAL COMMENTARY.

Reliability evidence. Reliability and standard errors are based on classical test theory. Only unconditional standard errors of measurement are presented. The reliability coefficients for the subtests are all .76 and above for the suburban school sample and .72 and above for the independent school sample. The large majority of the coefficients are well above these lower limits, and most are large enough to support subtest score interpretations at the individual student level.

Validity evidence. The Content Standards manual is the primary evidence source for validity. For each test level, the subdomains are described in terms much like those in the councils their standards were drawn from and sample test questions are provided. Schools are encouraged to evaluate the match between their local content coverage and that of the tests.

Although the manual uses the language of the councils' recommendations and has sample items, which gives more clarity than is commonly found in nationally marketed testing programs, it is still not always clear from the specifications whether certain specific content is or is not within the domain from which test items could be sampled. Constructions such as "various types of ..., including ..." leave open the possibility that types beyond the list could appear in the test items. A set of domain specifications that allows consistent judgments among all groups of education professionals about whether any content element is or is not within the scope of the tests' intended domains would be helpful to users who want to evaluate the alignment of their curriculum objectives with the CTP 4, as recommended in the CTP 4 materials.

The assessments come in only one form per level. Repeated use over time is best restricted to situations where there are no stakes for students, teachers, or schools. Otherwise, exposure of item content to students or to teachers, who might strive to ensure that their instruction covered those objectives actually on the test, could compromise the ability to generalize from student performance to the domains of the assessments.

Intercorrelations among the subtests appear to show less differentiation than is desirable. Particularly at the lower levels, the correlations between the verbal and quantitative subtests are not very different from correlations among the verbal subtests. It is not clear from these intercorrelations that interpretations solely based on comparisons among the subtest scores for individual students are justified. The justification for the consistency (standardized difference) score report seems better for the quantitative domain.

Tables of typical speededness statistics are given for suburban and independent school samples. The data show that the large majority of examinees reach the last items; apparently the time limits are adequate for those tests that are timed.

The technical manual does not specify how scale scores were originally developed. This is an important omission because the manual claims that scale scores from adjacent levels of the test are comparable, which justifies allowing teachers to select the test level to administer to their students in developing norms. Differences between test levels along such dimensions as content coverage and overall test difficulty may be problematic in generating comparable scale scores. An evaluation of the success of the links among the levels of the tests through the common scales running from 1st through 11th grades would be helpful.

Utility. Directions for administration are straightforward and appear easy to use. The test materials are attractively designed.

There is little direction given for nonstandard administrations for students with disabilities. Teachers are provided only three examples in a paragraph and given a phone number to call for questions.

COMMENTARY AND SUMMARY. The CTP 4 tests are designed to be used with high-achieving students and appear to cover reasonably demanding material. Their content standards are appropriately drawn from those recommended by the most respected national disciplinary associations of teachers, among others. The tests are well designed and seem straightforward to use (with the possible exception of nonstandard administrations). Score reports are clear and materials available to teachers and administrators should enhance the value of the assessments to users. Looking to the future, some further technical work seems needed.

Although reliability evidence appears adequate, conditional standard errors of measurement are not provided. It would be helpful to have conditional standard errors reported by test level. Migration from classical to item-response-theory-based psychometric models could facilitate that work.

More support is needed around three aspects of validity. First, the assumptions underlying the development and use of continuous scales across the test levels should be specified and evaluated. Second, the degree of differentiation among the subtests should be studied. It is not clear that the data support separate reporting of all subtest scores. Third, definitive domain specifications that elaborate the rules for item content inclusion would be helpful, particularly for applications in multiple settings where curricula can differ significantly.

[53]
Contextual Test of Articulation.

Purpose: "Designed to ... identify phonetic contexts that facilitate correct production of phonemes incorrectly produced by children ... who display speech sound production disorders."

Population: Ages 4–9.

Publication Date: 2000.

Acronym: CTA.

Scores: 6 subtests: Consonant Singleton /s/, Consonant Singleton /l/, Consonant Singleton /k/, Consonant Singleton /r/, Semivowel, Consonant Clusters.

Administration: Individual.

Price Data, 2006: $129 per complete kit including manual (46 pages), easel-style spiral, and 195 full-color picture plates.

Time: (15–25) minutes per subtest.

Comments: This test should be administered "after a child's phonemes production errors have been identified."

Authors: Dawn Aase, Charity Hovre, Karleen Krause, Sarah Schelfhout, Jennifer Smith, and Linda J. Carpenter.

Publisher: Thinking Publications.

Review of the Contextual Test of Articulation by JEFFERY P. BRADEN, Professor of Psychology, North Carolina State University, and SANDYE M. OUZTS, Graduate Student in Psychology, North Carolina State University, Raleigh, NC:

DESCRIPTION. The Contextual Test of Articulation (CTA) is designed to help speech-language pathologists identify phonetic contexts that facilitate a child's correct articulation of phonemes. The intended population is children aged 4 years and older with speech sound production disorders. The CTA is intended to be given as a follow-up test to a formal diagnostic test of articulation or phonological processes (i.e., after the child's phoneme production errors have been identified). Test results are intended to help examiners create practice materials and identify specific targets for phonologically based interventions. The test was designed to address limitations of other contextual articulation tests (i.e., A Deep Test of Articulation and the Secord Contextual Articulation Tests; S-CAT) by including pictorial (rather than textual) items to assess phonemes in spontaneous speech in response to multiple phonetic contexts. Phonetic contexts are defined as the phonemes that precede or follow the target phoneme and can be simple (single consonants) or compound (consonant clusters).

The spiral bound test easel includes a test manual, reproducible response forms, information related to phonemes assessed by the CTA, information about consonant and vowel production assessment, International Phonetic Alphabet symbols, and 186 color images that depict a variety of objects and concepts. The images are designed to elicit a specific word that contains certain phonemes in the initial or final position. Each item includes three prompts if the child does not immediately name the object (i.e., provide the target word). The first prompt provides an incomplete sentence (i.e., cloze item) with the target word missing. The second prompt poses a question with the target word as the answer. The third prompt elicits an imitative response (i.e., the examiner provides the word to the child, and asks the child to repeat it). Any or all three prompts may be used, and the clinician is encouraged to modify the prompts to elicit a spontaneous response as needed. Items are designed to assess 4 consonants, 1 semivowel, and 15 consonant blend phonemes that are among the most commonly misarticulated sounds in English. The easel is designed to allow the child to see images on one side, and provides examiner directions and prompts on the other side.

Examiners record the number of phonemes the child produces correctly in each consonant/ semivowel/consonant blend. Standardized scores are not provided. In the summary chart at the bottom of each score form, a check is placed in the box(es) that represent phonetic contexts for which the child scored at a level of 100% accuracy. The information from these charts may be transferred to a summary form showing the child's performance across all areas assessed. Typically, examiners only administer items relevant to the child's identified articulation errors (typically identified by another test).

DEVELOPMENT. Stimulus words were chosen that were appropriate for testing with children, aged 4 years and above, that included frequently occurring sound combinations, and that could be depicted in pictures. Stimulus materials and scoring forms were field-tested multiple times and were revised according to feedback. Preliminary testing included administration of the test to 43 children aged 3 to 5 years at early childhood daycare and education facilities in two Wisconsin communities. Stimulus materials and record forms were also revised based on feedback from four undergraduate clinicians from a university communication disorders clinic. Materials were revised on the basis of this information, although neither the revision process nor outcomes are described. Speech language pathologists provided feedback about the appropriateness of test materials for use with children from linguistically and culturally diverse backgrounds (n = 13). Two groups of children from university and school settings also participated in field testing, although the number and characteristics of these samples are not described.

The test booklet includes six sets of items and is color-coded accordingly. The first four sets of items include 132 images to assess the singleton consonants /s/, /l/, /k/, and /r/ (in that order); the next set includes 9 images to assess the semivowel; and the last set includes 45 images to assess the 15 consonant blends. All of the consonant blends and semivowel/consonant combinations are tested in prevocalic (initial) and postvocalic (final) positions. All of the singleton consonants except /r/ are tested in prevocalic and postvocalic positions;

the singleton consonant /r/ is tested only in the prevocalic position.

In addition to prevocalic and postvocalic categories, items are further categorized to facilitate the identification of facilitative contexts. Consonant singleton items are categorized according to the vowel sound in the phonetic context. The semivowel/consonant combination items include words that require nasal/glide, fricative/affricate, and plosive manner of production. Consonant clusters are categorized into different types of clusters. The prevocalic cluster items include /s/ + nasal, /s/ + liquid, /s/ + stop, stop + liquid clusters, and the postvocalic clusters include only nasal + stop clusters.

TECHNICAL. The CTA does not provide standardized scores; therefore, no standardization process was included in its development. Neither reliability nor validity is discussed in the manual, nor was a rationale for selecting the four targeted consonant singletons (and omitting the other six most common and most commonly misarticulated) provided. Furthermore, although abutting connections (i.e., spaces between syllables) are identified as relevant for phoneme production, no rationale is given for why the test excludes them.

EVALUATION. *The Code of Fair Testing Practices in Education* (Joint Committee on Testing Practices, 2004) outlines standards that test developers should meet when offering a test for use. Because the American Speech-Language-Hearing Association (ASHA) is a member of the Joint Committee, and because the CTA is intended to be used by ASHA members (i.e., speech-language pathologists) in educational contexts, the standards in the Code should apply to the CTA. Unfortunately, the CTA materials correspond to few of those standards. Given that the CTA manual does not reference those (or any other) standards, it seems likely that the test developers were not aware of the Code (or other test standards), and therefore failed to address many relevant standards in the development of the CTA. It would appear that only one of the nine standards for test developers (Standard #4: Provide guidance on the levels of skills, knowledge, and training necessary for appropriate review, selection, and administration of tests) was adequately addressed in the CTA manual.

The most important standards not addressed are a description of test strengths and limitations

(Standard #1), descriptions of how the content and skills to be tested were selected and how the CTA was developed (Standard #2), information about test characteristics (Standard #3), evidence that the technical quality, including reliability and validity, of the test meets its intended purposes (Standard #4), and evidence on the performance of test takers of diverse subgroups, including significant efforts to obtain sample sizes that are adequate for subgroup analyses (Standard #9). Most telling is that the CTA omits even the most basic information expected of a test (viz., evidence of reliability and validity). Two forms of reliability evidence appear to be most important: interrater agreement (i.e., would two or more raters observing the same child score the child's responses in the same way?), and test-retest stability (i.e., would a child produce the same performance across two or more test sessions?). Other measures of internal consistency (e.g., to what degree do items intended to measure the same skill agree with each other, and with other items?) would also be useful in helping test users judge the precision of test outcomes, and the degree to which fluctuations in test performance are due to error versus genuine changes in speech articulation abilities.

Because there is no evidence of reliability, there can be no basis for inferring that test results have meaning (i.e., validity) for their stated purposes. The CTA test developers omitted discussion of a number of important issues in the test materials, in addition to test content (which was not systematically reviewed for bias), evidence of response processes (e.g., that children's production of phonemes is due to their articulation difficulties and not the nature of information demanded), internal structure (e.g., the degree to which portions of the test converge and diverge in expected directions), relationships to other variables (e.g., other tests of articulation, independent observations of speech in other contexts), and test consequences (e.g., use of the test in fact guides treatments and produces gains in speech production, see AERA, APA, NCME, 1999, which is also recognized by the Joint Committee for test development).

These omissions in the development of the CTA are, unfortunately, not unique. Reviews of other tests of children's speech articulation (e.g., the Children's Articulation Test; Kenney, 1995; Turton, 1995) often note the complete lack of even rudimentary evidence supporting test reliability and validity. Apparently, many professionals who are interested in developing tests of articulation are unaware of the standards that should govern test development. This deficiency is unfortunately ironic and lamentable, because these developers produce tests that fail to meet the standards demanded of test users in the *Code of Fair Testing Practices in Education*, meaning developers produce tests that professionals are advised by their own professional organizations not to use. Furthermore, a search of Social Sciences Citation Index found no subsequent (i.e., postpublication) research on the CTA that would provide such evidence, although one study (Cascella, 2006) also noted the CTA failed to meet even minimal standards for use with individuals who have intellectual disabilities.

SUMMARY. The CTA is a test of English speech articulation that promises to evaluate children's abilities to articulate target phonemes within phonemic contexts. However, the complete lack of evidence to support the reliability and validity of the CTA render it unusable for clinical practice. Until such evidence is available, either from the test developer or from postpublication research, clinicians should follow the standards in the Code and avoid using the CTA.

REVIEWERS' REFERENCES

American Educational Research Association, American Psychological Association, & National Council of Measurement in Education. (1999). *Standards for educational and psychological testing.* Washington, DC: American Educational Research Association.

Cascella, P. W. (2006). Standardised speech-language tests and students with intellectual disability: A review of normative data. *Journal of Intellectual & Developmental Disability, 31*(2), 120-124.

Joint Committee on Testing Practices. (2004). *Code of fair testing practices in education.* Washington, DC: Author. Retrieved February 13, 2007, from http://www.apa.org/science/FinalCode.pdf

Kenney, K. W. (1995). [Review of the Children's Articulation Test.] In J. C. Conoley & J. C. Impara (Eds.), *The twelfth mental measurements yearbook* (pp. 183–184). Lincoln, NE: Buros Institute of Mental Measurements.

Turton, L. J. (1995). [Review of the Children's Articulation Test.] In J. C. Conoley & J. C. Impara (Eds.), *The twelfth mental measurements yearbook* (p. 184). Lincoln, NE: Buros Institute of Mental Measurements.

Review of the Contextual Test of Articulation by REBECCA J. McCAULEY, Professor of Communication Sciences, University of Vermont, Burlington, VT:

DESCRIPTION. This individually administered test is intended to aid qualified speech-language pathologists in selecting treatment stimuli for children with speech sound disorders affecting one or more of the following sounds or sound sequences: /s/, /l/, /k/, consonantal /r/, vocalic /r/, and/or the 15 consonant clusters. Each of the six subtests is designed to help identify one or more facilitating phonetic contexts for the target sound or cluster. Facilitating phonetic contexts represent those that appear to be associated with better productions and could be used to promote early success in treatment of the affected sound.

Test stimuli consist of colored picture plates and accompanying verbal prompts that are used to elicit spontaneous or delayed imitative productions. Each subtest may be given alone and requires about 20 minutes to administer and score. Scoring consists of determining the percentage of correct responses in different phonetic contexts, with 100% correct performance described as demonstration of a facilitating context.

DEVELOPMENT. This test was developed by a group of undergraduate students and a faculty member from the University of Wisconsin-Eau Claire based on the concept of facilitative contexts, which was defined by McDonald (1964a) and incorporated in an assessment tool called the Deep Test of Articulation (McDonald, 1964b). Numerous textbooks in the field of speech-language pathology have endorsed this strategy for the identification of treatment targets, although it has received relatively little empirical study.

Stimulus words were selected to address sounds that occur frequently in English within a variety of phonetic contexts (pre- and postvocalic singletons as well as pre- and postvocalic consonant clusters). Words were also selected based on expectations that they could be found in the vocabulary of children 4 years of age and older and could be represented by a picture. Words containing singleton consonants were chosen to sample up to seven frequently occurring vowels. Three prompts were created for each stimulus word and were described as being field tested. Although participants and goals for two sets of field tests were described, no details were provided about how field test data were used to reach decisions to retain, discard, or modify test items.

TECHNICAL. No reliability or validity data were provided.

COMMENTARY. Positive aspects of this measure include its use of colorful, easily recognizable pictures and its systematic inclusion of consonantal and vocalic contexts for many of the sounds that are likely to be present in the productions of children with speech sound disorders. Its very significant weaknesses, however, are related to its minimal development as a standardized test. Dis-

cussion of empirical data concerning reliability and validity were absent from the test manual, and claims concerning the validity of content coverage and relevance were implied rather than made explicitly.

SUMMARY. The test presents a resource for clinicians who are looking for stimuli to incorporate in informal probes used to aid initial decisions concerning treatment targets. An additional use for these stimuli that was not mentioned by the test authors would be as untreated, or "control," probe items that could be used to track generalization in treatment (Bain & Dollaghan, 1991). If used with an understanding of its considerable limitations, the CTA may well prove a somewhat worthwhile addition to the materials used in the treatment of children with speech sound disorders who are quite young. Alternatively, clinicians may want to examine the Secord Contextual Articulation Tests (Secord & Shine, 1997), a measure that includes pre- and posttest probe forms and a story-telling task designed to assess productions in connected speech. It also provides probes for a larger number of speech sounds than the CTA Although it shares the psychometric weaknesses of the CTA, it nonetheless appears to offer standard probes that can used more flexibly in informal assessments.

REVIEWER'S REFERENCES

Bain, B., & Dollaghan, C. (1991). The notion of clinically significant change. *Language, Speech, and Hearing Services in Schools, 22,* 264-270.
McDonald, E. T. (1964a). *Articulation testing and treatment: A sensory-motor approach.* Pittsburgh, PA: Stanwix House.
McDonald, E. T. (1964b). A Deep Test of Articulation. Pittsburgh, PA: Stanwix House.
Secord, W., & Shine, R.E. (1997). Secord Contextual Articulation Tests. Sedona, AZ: Red Rocks Educational Publications.

[54]

Dean-Woodcock Neuropsychological Battery.

Purpose: Designed to provide a "comprehensive assessment of sensory-motor functioning."
Population: Ages 4-0 and over.
Publication Date: 2003.
Acronym: DWNB.
Administration: Individual.
Price Data, 2007: $309.50 per complete kit including manual (269 pages), stimulus book, 25 test records, 25 interview forms, 25 emotional status forms, and a plastic storage box containing a comb, scissors, key, candle, nail, paper clip, pen, ball, plastic fork, plastic spoon, stylus, eye occluder, and three blindfolds; $49.25 per 25 test records; $40.50 per 25 interview forms; $58.75 per 25 emotional status forms.

Comments: Examiner's manual provides verbal instructions in Spanish and English.
Authors: Raymond S. Dean and Richard W. Woodcock.
Publisher: Riverside Publishing.

a) DEAN-WOODCOCK SENSORY-MOTOR BATTERY.
Acronym: DWSMB.
Scores, 21: Sensory (Near Point Visual Acuity, Visual Confrontation, Naming Pictures of Objects, Auditory Acuity), Tactile (Palm Writing, Object Identification, Finger Identification, Simultaneous Localization, Total), Motor (Lateral Preference, Gait and Station, Romberg, Construction, Coordination, Mime Movements, Left-Right Movements, Finger Tapping, Expressive Speech, Grip Strength, Total), Impairment Index.
Time: (30–45) minutes.

b) DEAN-WOODCOCK STRUCTURED NEUROPSYCHOLOGICAL INTERVIEW.
Scores: Not scored.
Time: (30) minutes.
Comments: Structured interview can be administered to the subject, a parent, or "other informant who knows the subject well."

c) DEAN-WOODCOCK EMOTIONAL STATUS EXAMINATION.
Scores: Not scored.
Time: (30) minutes.
Comments: May be administered to subject or to an informant.

Review of the Dean-Woodcock Neuropsychological Battery by RIK CARL D'AMATO, M. Lucile Harrison Professor of Excellence, School of Applied Psychology and Counselor Education, College of Education and Behavioral Sciences, University of Northern Colorado, and JUSTIN M. WALKER, Doctoral Student in School Psychology, School of Applied Psychology and Counselor Education, University of Northern Colorado, Greeley, CO:

DESCRIPTION. The Dean-Woodcock Neuropsychological Battery (DWNB) is one component of the Dean-Woodcock Neuropsychological Assessment System (DWNAS). The DWNAS is one of the most comprehensive and psychometrically sound measures available in the field today. This battery includes the Dean-Woodcock Neuropsychological Battery (DWNB), the Woodcock-Johnson III Tests of Cognitive Abilities (WJ-III-COG; Woodcock, McGrew, & Mather, 2001a; 15:281), and the Woodcock-Johnson Tests of Achievement (WJ-III-ACH; Woodcock, McGrew, & Mather, 2001b; 15:281). The

DWNAS provides a comprehensive outlook of an individual's neuropsychological, emotional, cognitive, and academic functioning.

The DWNB consists of the Dean-Woodcock Sensory Motor Battery, a Structured Neuropsychological Interview, and an Emotional Status Examination. Despite the complexity of most neuropsychological measures, few materials are needed to administer this measure. A stimulus book and the examiner's manual are used by the examiner and most of the necessary materials come in a small box the size of a paperback book. However, some important items (i.e., finger tapper, hand dynometer) are not included in this kit.

The first component of the DWNB is the Dean-Woodcock Sensory Motor Battery (DWSMB), which is the most comprehensive part of this instrument. Ten of the 18 DWSMB subtests measure motor functioning and the remaining 8 subtests measure sensory functions such as visual, auditory, and tactile perception. A set of interview materials provide the examiner with additional information, such as the client's motivation, attention, emotional problems, and medical disorders that may contribute to their performance on certain measures. The final component, an Emotional Status Examination, is used to explore signs and symptoms of psychiatric disorders. This protocol contains two parts: the examination conducted with the client and a section on clinical observations and impressions that is completed by the examiner. Further, the Emotional Status Exam is translated into Spanish and a section of the manual is dedicated to using the DWNB with Spanish-speaking clients. This noteworthy translation is a positive addition to any neuropsychological battery.

The DWSMB can be administered in approximately 30 to 45 minutes. Similarly, the Structured Neuropsychological Interview and the Emotional Status Examination each take about 30 minutes and can be administered at any time during the evaluation. Although the DWSMB is relatively easy to administer and score, only individuals well trained in psychological testing should administer the measure. The manual details that interpretation should be left only to those who are specially trained in neuropsychology.

DEVELOPMENT. The DWSMB is a measure that has been derived mostly from traditional qualitative neurological tests. Tests of sensory and motor ability were selected from measures with a history of clinical utility. Each subtest relies on a small number of items because most mature, normal individuals taking the tests will obtain near perfect scores on the measures. The subtests are primarily concerned with measuring the bottom end of ability, which will help identify age differences and assist the examiner in making inferences about specific functions.

Practitioners subscribing to the Dean-Woodcock Cognitive Neuropsychological Model (Brinkman, Decker, & Dean, 2005) may find the attributes of the DWNB especially appealing. By integrating assessment of cognitive abilities with sensorimotor functions, a broad interpretation of an individual's neuropsychological functioning can be made. Integrated within the Cattell-Horn-Carroll (CHC) and information processing theories, a variety of cognitive and noncognitive factors contribute to the cognitive and motor performance of a client. Application of this model is useful in test interpretation and assists in recommending interventions to a client (Brinkman et al., 2005).

TECHNICAL. Although many of the tests used in the DWSMB may seem familiar to behavioral neurologists and neuropsychologists, a particular strength of the DWSMB is that these adapted measures have now been standardized with respect to administration and scoring. A sample of 1,011 individuals ranging in age from 2 to 95 was closely matched to variables in the 2000 U.S. Census Bureau data. The stratification variables included sex, race, Hispanic status, age, and handedness. Geographic region was not mentioned by the authors as a consideration in the sampling. The sample consisted of 233 young children (ages 2–10), 265 adolescents and young adults (ages 11–24), and 513 adults (ages 25–95). Further weighting of participants was used to obtain a distribution that was exactly proportionate to the U.S. Census.

Reliability for the DWSMB was estimated using several methods including interrater agreement and the split-half method. Interrater agreement—the correlation of scores for the same client when rated by different examiners—was established in a separate study (Woodward, Ridenour, Dean, & Woodcock, 2002). Seven of the tests most susceptible to scoring error were investigated. The examiner's manual reports correlations

that ranged from .45—1.00 (median of .85). These findings suggest adequate to excellent rater agreement for most of the tests included in the DWSMB. Internal consistency of individual subtests was calculated by the split-half method using odd and even items on each subtest. Most coefficients were .90 or better, although about 15% of them fell below .70. The manual does not state if a formula was used to correct scores.

Reliability and validity data are lacking for the interview and Emotional Status Exam. A summary score is not used in interpretation. However, qualitative information is presented in the manual and may have some utility when used in clinical training. Preliminary evidence of content-related and construct-related validity is presented in the DWSMB examiner's manual. Due to the relatively recent release of the DWNB, few validation studies exist. Future research needs to establish the reliability and validity of this measure with various types of clients. As with any complex measure, validity is reliant on the quality of the administration and interpretation of the DWSMB.

Many of the tests used in the DWSMB have a significant clinical history of use in neuropsychology. Although some changes were necessary for standardization purposes, these measures appear to retain content validity in assessing clients.

The DWSMB has been examined from the perspective of a two-factor (sensory and motor) and a three-factor solution (sensory functions, cortical motor functions, and subcorticol motor functions), which proved more supportive (Hill, Lewis, Dean, & Woodcock, 2001). Further research is necessary in testing factor solutions and their relationship to intelligence and achievement. Overall, there is some established reliability and validity evidence for the DWSMB. Research suggests a relationship between sensory and motor constructs as well as a relation to cognitive ability.

COMMENTARY. One particular advantage of the DWNB over other batteries is that it was designed for use by a wide range of practitioners. This further increases its utility in a variety of settings, including schools. Also, the fact that the DWSMB includes standardized tests reduces the ambiguity of certain neuropsychological measures of the past. Given the wide number of measures available today and the history of use regarding such measures, a particular advantage of the DWNB is the presence of current norms. The ease of administration and scoring further support the usefulness of the DWNB with various types of clients. Another particular advantage of the DWNB is the inclusion of a glossary of neuropsychological terms, which is quite helpful and is rarely included as a part of other measures.

Given the underlying theoretical construct that drives the DWNB, it seems appropriate to include the entire DWNAS battery in one's assessment. Cognitive, academic achievement, motor, and sensory information as well as emotional status and relevant background information can all be achieved with one comprehensive assessment system.

SUMMARY. The field of clinical neuropsychology has suffered for decades because of a lack of psychometric sophistication regarding the development and norming (including reliability and validity) of neuropsychological tests. Some of this lack of sophistication grew out of the use of procedures first used in medicine and later adapted for neuropsychology. After evaluating the field, Reynolds, Lowe, and Saenz (1999, p. 549) argued for major change, noting, "In God we trust, all others must have data." At the same time, the field has begun to embrace scientifically driven evidence-based practices. Clinical neuropsychology, like psychology in general, has been in need of a firm psychometric foundation. This is especially true given the use of neuropsychological data in forensic practice. Consequently, the DWSMB should be hailed as a major accomplishment in our field. This newly standardized measure offers norms for individuals from a variety of ages on most major motor and sensory tasks. This represents a major achievement in our field because the Dean-Woodcock Sensory and Motor tests along with the larger Woodcock-Johnson Achievement and Woodcock-Johnson Cognitive batteries offer the potential for establishing clinical neuropsychology as a specialty area that is as psychometrically sound as clinical and school psychology. The use of "standardized" measures for evidence-based practice in the field of clinical neuropsychology is long overdue.

REVIEWERS' REFERENCES

Brinkman, J., Jr., Decker, C. L., & Dean, R. S. (2005). Assessing and understanding brain function through neuropsychologically based ability tests. In R. C. D'Amato, E. Fletcher-Janzen, & C. R. Reynolds (Eds.), *Handbook of school neuropsychology* (pp. 303–326). Hoboken, NJ: Wiley.

Hill, S. K., Lewis, M. N., Dean, R. S., & Woodcock, R. W. (2001). Constructs underlying measures of sensory-motor functions. *Archives of Clinical Neuropsychology, 15*, 631–641.

Reynolds, C. R., Lowe, P. A., & Saenz, A. L. (1999). The problem of bias in psychological assessment. In C. R. Reynolds & T. B. Gutkin (Eds.), *The handbook of school psychology* (3rd ed.) (pp. 549-596). New York: Wiley.

Woodcock, R. W, McGrew, K. S., & Mather, N. (2001a). Woodcock-Johnson III Tests of Cognitive Ability. Itasca, IL: Riverside.

Woodcock, R. W., McGrew, K. S., & Mather, N. (2001b). Woodcock-Johnson III Tests of Achievement. Itasca, IL: Riverside.

Woodward, H. R., Ridenour, T., Dean, R. S., & Woodcock, R. W. (2002). Generalizability of sensory and motor tests. *International Journal of Neuroscience, 112,* 115-137.

Review of the Dean-Woodcock Neuropsychological Battery by W. JOEL SCHNEIDER, Assistant Professor of Psychology, Illinois State University, Normal, IL:

DESCRIPTION. The Dean-Woodcock Neuropsychological Battery (DWNB) is a set of three integrated measures designed for neuropsychological assessment: the Dean-Woodcock Sensory-Motor Battery (DWSMB), the Dean-Woodcock Structured Neuropsychological Interview, and the Dean-Woodcock Emotional Status Examination.

Experienced neuropsychologists are already familiar with most of the tests on the DWSMB because it consists mostly of classic neuropsychological assessment screening procedures that previously had been used informally without the benefit of norms from a nationally representative standardization sample. The sensory tests measure visual acuity, visual field defects, auditory acuity, picture naming, and tactile discrimination. The motor tests measure lateral preference, gait and station, balance, visual construction, coordination, miming ability, fine motor control, expressive speech, and grip strength. Performance on each test can be classified as within normal limits and above, mildly impaired, moderately impaired, or severely impaired. The DWSMB can be administered to examinees ages 4 to 90+. Administration time typically is less than 1 hour.

The Emotional Status Examination is a mental status interview/checklist similar to many other mental status examinations. It covers mood symptoms, anxiety symptoms, cognitive functions, psychotic symptoms, somatic symptoms, executive functions, attention and vigilance, behavior control, asocial behavior, and personality. After completing the initial interview and examination, the clinician rates the examinee's orientation, attention, comprehension, speech, consciousness, grooming, appearance, mood, affect, and psychotic symptoms, among other things. The Structured Neuropsychological Interview covers biographic information, chief complaints, medical history, history of mental health evaluations and treatments, personal and social history, psychiatric and neurologic family history, and developmental history. No composite scores or normed indices are associated with the Emotional Status Examination or the Structured Neuropsychological Interview. Both are to be used qualitatively and informally to guide interpretations of other test data.

DEVELOPMENT. Each test from the DWSMB has a long history of use in the screening of sensory and motor deficits. Each test was designed to be brief and easy to administer to both children and adults by a wide variety of clinicians with differing levels of training. Neurologically intact adults generally obtain perfect scores on most tests because the DWSMB is designed to measure sensory and motor deficits instead of strengths.

TECHNICAL.

Standardization. The standardization sample for the DWSMB included 1,011 participants with an age range of 2 to 95. Norms are included for ages 4 to 80 because there were too few participants outside that range to create reliable norms. All participants were screened to be free of psychiatric symptoms, diagnoses, or history of psychiatric treatment. Participants also had to be free of any known neurological disorders, orthopedic conditions, serious medical defects, learning disabilities, serious head injuries, or sensory impairments (with the exception of corrective lenses). Other than those exclusions, the standardization sample was selected to be broadly representative of the U.S. population. A weighting algorithm corrected for demographic variables (sex, race, Hispanic ethnicity, age, and handedness) in the standardization sample that differed from the 2000 U.S. Census data.

Reliability. An interscorer reliability study for the DWSMB tests with two doctoral students scoring the same protocols and videotaped administrations established that nearly all tests requiring rater judgment could be scored reliably by different raters.

Most of the subtests of the DWSMB have excellent internal consistency (coefficients > .90) at most age ranges. However, 32% of the 72 internal consistency statistics presented for each test (18 tests at four different age ranges) were below .80. Ten of these were below .70. Somewhat lower internal consistency is to be expected given that the tests are intended as screening instruments to help decide if more reliable tests are warranted. Mime Movements appeared particularly inconsistent (coefficients ranged from .29 to .57) probably because it only has five very easy items. Such low internal consistency typically indicates that a test is too unreliable to use for diagnostic purposes. However, the DWSMB was developed from an Item Response Theory perspective in which reliability is viewed not as a property of a test as a whole but instead as a joint function of the test and the examinee's ability. That is, reliability of a test differs for examinees of differing levels of ability. For most of the DWSMB subtests, the abilities of examinees in the average range or higher are measured with less precision than the abilities of examinees with low scores. One of the great features of the DWSMB manual is that it lists the standard errors of measurement associated with each raw and W-score, allowing the clinician to estimate how likely the examinee is to be truly low in any particular area. Thus, a subtest with low internal consistency (such as Mime Movements) can still be useful for examinees who score so low that their abilities fall into the range in which they are estimated with sufficient precision that diagnostic impressions can be formed.

Validity. Most of the validity evidence relevant to the DWSMB is indirect because each of the tests in the battery has been investigated extensively by researchers. The manual alerts test users to relevant reviews of the history and validity of each test.

Direct validity research with the DWSMB has only recently begun to be collected. Factor analyses of the DWSMB suggest a three-factor solution in which the visual, auditory, and tactile perception tests form a general sensory factor, the complex motor tasks form a cortical motor function factor, and the Romberg and the Gait and Station tests form a subcortical motor function factor. In a study of 250 adults with neurological impairment and 250 adults without impairment, the DWSMB was able to correctly classify 87% of the sample (Volpe, David, & Dean, 2006).

COMMENTARY. The Dean-Woodcock Neuropsychological Battery is a welcome addition to the neuropsychologist's tool box. It has provided, for the first time, nationally representative norms for many of the sensory and motor function screening tests that neuropsychologists have been using informally for decades. The manual is clearly written and practical in orientation. The tests are easy to administer and their interpretation is relatively straightforward, although the amount of information that can be gleaned from the test will vary considerably depending on the sophistication and knowledge of the clinician.

The use of W-scores instead of standard scores will seem strange at first. But the advantages of using W-scores to evaluate functional impairment instead of age-corrected relative ability metrics soon becomes apparent (e.g., an 80-year-old with "average" auditory acuity may still need hearing aids).

The manual presents an ambitiously comprehensive model of assessment that integrates sensory and motor assessment with the cognitive and academic tests of the Woodcock-Johnson-III and also provides tools to assess emotional status and developmental/neuropsychological history. At this time, this integration is based more on theoretical and logical grounds than empirical findings. Although there is a chapter in the manual that asserts that the integrative interpretation of these domains of functioning can be facilitated with these tests, the chapter does not provide much practical help beyond a few vague suggestions. The intercorrelations between the DWSMB and the symptoms measured by the Dean-Woodcock Emotional Status Examination are not presented and the relations between the DWSMB and the subtests of the Woodcock-Johnson-III are not published in the manual. Thus, clinicians will continue to have to base their integrative interpretations on educated guesses. When such information becomes available, the Dean-Woodcock Neuropsychological Battery may well become indispensable to practicing neuropsychologists.

One weakness of the DWSMB is that the tests appear to have been chosen based on their ease of administration and their demonstrated utility rather than a well-validated taxonomy of sensory and motor functioning. This is not a fault of the test developers as there is no taxonomy of sensory and motor functioning with the same clout as Gf-Gc theory has among intelligence researchers. Perhaps the DWSMB will facilitate further research to make such a theoretical advance possible. In the meantime, the Dean-Woodcock Neuropsychological Battery is a commendable tool that represents a practical advance forward for the field of neuropsychological assessment.

SUMMARY. The Dean-Woodcock Neuropsychological Battery is a collection of measures that provide neuropsychologists the ability to screen for motor and sensory deficits and to briefly assess emotional and psychological symptoms relevant to neuropsychological concerns. Because most of the tests are already used informally by many neuropsychologists, the primary benefit of using the battery is that it provides reliable norms for a wide range of ages (4 to 90+). The tests are reasonably reliable and a wealth of data supports their utility in assessment. Overall, the Dean-Woodcock Neuropsychological Battery is an excellent product that will be very helpful for practicing neuropsychologists.

REVIEWER'S REFERENCE

Volpe, A., Davis, A., & Dean, R. (2006). Predicting global and specific neurological impairment with sensory-motor functioning. *Archives of Clinical Neuropsychology, 21,* 203-210.

[55]

Detroit Tests of Learning Aptitude—Primary, Third Edition.

Purpose: "Measures general aptitude."
Population: Ages 3–9.
Publication Dates: 1986–2005.
Acronym: DTLA-P:3.
Scores, 7: Verbal-Enhanced, Verbal-Reduced, Attention-Enhanced, Attention-Reduced, Motor-Enhanced, Motor-Reduced, General Ability.
Administration: Individual.
Price Data, 2006: $200 per complete kit including examiner's manual (2005, 128 pages), picture book, 25 examiner record booklets, and 25 response forms; $62 per picture book; $37 per 25 response forms; $50 per 25 examiner record booklets; $60 per manual.
Time: (15–45) minutes.
Comments: Adaptation of the Detroit Tests of Learning Aptitude—Second Edition.
Authors: Donald D. Hammill and Brian R. Bryant.
Publisher: PRO-ED.
Cross References: See T5:799 (2 references); for reviews by Terry A. Ackerman and Robert T. Williams of an earlier edition, see 12:106 (1 reference); for reviews by Cathy F. Telzrow and Stanley F. Vasa of an earlier edition, see 10:84 (1 reference).

Review of the Detroit Tests of Learning Aptitude—Primary, Third Edition by BETHANY A. BRUNSMAN, Assessment/Evaluation Specialist, Lincoln Public Schools, Lincoln, NE:

DESCRIPTION. The Detroit Tests of Learning Aptitude—Primary, Third Edition (DTLA-P:3) was designed as a relatively quick and easy measure of general aptitude for children ages 3 to 9. Specifically, the examiner's manual lists the following four purposes: "(a) to help qualify children for special needs programs; (b) to identify aptitude in children where it might not be obvious; (c) to make predictions about future performance; and (d) to serve as a research tool in studies investigating aptitude, intelligence, and cognitive behavior" (p. 6). The authors suggest that this instrument be used in conjunction with prior educational history, home situation, and interests to make decisions about children.

The DTLA-P:3 is individually administered and takes 15–45 minutes, depending on the age and ability level of the child. It consists of 100 identification and production items that are scored either correct or incorrect based on an answer key and sample responses. The examiner reads all of the directions to the child. The child responds to both verbal directions and verbal directions with visual stimuli in an easel format. What items a child completes depends on the age of the child and the correctness of the child's responses. The items are ordered based on difficulty. The examiner establishes a "basal" below which all items are scored correct and a "ceiling" above which all items are scored incorrect. The child does not respond to items before the basal or after the ceiling.

Scores include "General Ability," which is a standard score based on all of the 100 items available, and subscale scores for Verbal-Enhanced, Verbal-Reduced, Attention-Enhanced, Attention-Reduced, Motor-Enhanced, and Motor-Reduced. Standard scores in General Ability and in the subscales have a mean of 100 and a standard deviation of 15. The subtests are not mutually exclusive; they are based on overlapping sets of items. As a result, only scores within a domain (e.g., Attention) may be compared with one another. The examiner calculates the raw scores by hand by summing correct answers and converts the raw scores to standard scores, percentile ranks, and age equivalents using the tables provided in the manual. The examiner record booklet is set up to aid in the calculation of General Ability and the subscale scores.

The manual recommends that examiners have formal training in assessment, including a basic understanding of test statistics, test administration and scoring, interpretation of test scores,

and knowledge of the mental ability literature. Additionally, examiners need to read through the instructions and scoring criteria carefully and practice administering the assessment. The tasks and directions are varied, some of the items include a visual stimulus and others do not, and many of the items are subjectively scored. Examiners need to take special care to develop rapport with the child and to attend to whether the assessment needs to be administered in more than one session because of the dwindling attention of the child.

DEVELOPMENT. The DTLA-P:3 is an update to the DTLA-P and the DTLA-P:2, which were published in 1986 and 1991, respectively. According to the examiner's manual, the changes include: the addition of color to the item drawings (the items are the same otherwise), a new norm sample, and additional evidence of lack of bias.

The manual contains a brief summary of some of the conceptualization of aptitude and intelligence and the relationships between aptitude and achievement in the literature with references provided. The authors view aptitude as both heavily influenced by previous learning and predictive of future learning.

The authors cite consistency with theoretical frameworks proposed by Horn and Cattell (1966) and Das (1972) as content-related evidence of validity. The items for the DTLA-P were originally selected based on a range of difficulty values from .15 to .85 and discrimination values above .30. Mean item difficulties and discriminations are provided for each of the subscales of the DTLA-P:3, but item difficulty indices for individual items are not provided. Given the way the basal and ceiling are determined, it is important that the items be ordered in terms of difficulty. Evidence that the items continued to function similarly for the DTLA-P:3 norm group, particularly given that items needed to be reordered for the DTLA-P:2 based on item statistics collected for that norm group, would have provided additional validation for DTLA-P:3 norms.

TECHNICAL. The norm group consists of a sample of 901 children from four states in different geographic regions and an additional 110 children from other states. The total norm group of 1,011 is smaller and less geographically diverse than the norm groups for the DTLA-P or DTLA-P:2. No rationale is provided for the reduction in sample size. Data provided in the manual suggest that the DTLA-P:3 norm group is relatively representative of the United States population as measured by the 2000 U.S. Census in terms of gender, geographic area, family income, and educational attainment of parents. The proportions of "White," "Hispanic," and "Black" participants also fairly closely mirror those in the population. The sample slightly underrepresents children of "Other" ethnicities and those with disabilities. Children ages 3 through 9 were included in the norm group. The subgroup participation in some of the age groups is small (as low as 3 children in the 3-year-old "Other" and "Hispanic" ethnicity groups).

Data on the internal consistency of the scores of children at each age in the norm group and standard errors of measurement (*SEM*s) based on these estimates of reliability are provided in the manual. The coefficient alpha internal consistency reliability coefficients for the subscales ranged from .82 to 92 and for General Ability from .92 to .95. The *SEM*s ranged from 3 to 6 points for the subscales and General Ability. Coefficient alphas calculated for the scales for the different gender and ethnic groups were relatively similar to those for the whole population. Additionally, the authors report that a sample of student responses were double scored by two PRO-ED research staff and the correlations between the original scores and the staff scores were .99 for all subscales; this is a strong indication of interrater reliability. This evidence of reliability of scores for the norm group is acceptable, assuming that the children who participate in the assessment are well-represented by the norm group.

A Differential Item Functioning (DIF) analysis based on gender and two ethnicity groups ("Black" and "Hispanic") using the data for the norm group revealed only one item with a moderate effect size. Because the norm group contained only small numbers of children at some ages and not all of the children answered all of the items, this statistical technique for detecting item bias may have been insufficient. Perhaps a better approach would be to combine the statistical identification of potential bias with a judgmental process in which people who represent different groups are trained to identify bias and review all of the items. A judgmental process would also provide information about other groups of examinees represented in very small numbers or not easily identified in the norm sample (e.g., certain ethnicities, low income).

The manual cites studies conducted using the DTLA-P and DTLA-P:2 as evidence of the validity of the DTLA-P:3. This reviewer disagrees, however, with the authors' statement, "Because the three editions have almost identical items, one may assume that the findings of studies that used the first two editions are applicable to the DTLA-P:3 as well" (examiner's manual, p. 53). To make that assumption, one would also have to assume that the scores function the same way for all three norm groups.

As construct-related evidence of validity of score interpretations, the authors present data to support several predicted relationships between DTLA-P:3 scores and other variables (age, ethnicity, and cognitive disabilities) for children in the norm group. As predicted, older children had higher mean scores than younger children, children of several ethnicities had mean scores in the average range, and children with cognitive disabilities scored lower on average than other children in the norm group. Exploratory and confimatory factor analysis results support the use of the overall and subscale scores. The results of a second confirmatory factor analysis were consistent with a theoretical model the authors described as the Cattell-Horn-Carroll theory of cognitive abilities.

COMMENTARY. The brief discussion about Aptitude, Intelligence, and Achievement in the manual nicely summarizes some of the thinking on the relationships between these concepts. The authors present several theoretical models for aptitude along with references for further reading. The directions for administering and scoring the assessment are thorough and clear. The authors provide a clear rationale for many of their development and validation decisions and for their recommendations for administration and scoring of the DTLA-P:3 and the interpretation of results.

The smaller size of the norm sample of the DTLA-P:3 compared to the previous versions of the DTLA-P and the lack of validity studies based directly on DTLA-P:3 norms are somewhat troublesome, as is the fact that children with disabilities are slightly underrepresented compared to the census population. Given that one of the purposes of the DTLA-P:3 is to identify children for special needs programs, evidence to support its use with students with disabilities is important. Additional studies of the relationships between the DTLA-P:3 and other related measures and with other groups of children are needed. A judgmental process for reviewing items for bias would also strengthen the evidence of technical quality of the assessment.

Caution should be used in interpreting the DTLA-P:3 results of children who are not native English speakers and children of various cultures who are not well represented in the norm sample. Children whose primary or first language is not English are not addressed at all in the norm sample or the validity studies. And the number of children in some ethnic groups in the norm sample at some ages, although representative of the numbers in the general population, are nonetheless very small.

The authors point out that a number of the average item difficulties approach .9 for the subscales for children ages 7 to 9 (depending on the specific subscale). The ceiling effect that results from these relatively easy items for these age groups limits the utility of the DTLA-P:3 for identifying older children for gifted programs.

SUMMARY. The DTLA-P:3 was designed as a measure of aptitude. The authors provide adequate evidence related to the reliability of scores for the norm group and subgroups within that group and that the measure is consistent with several conceptual frameworks of aptitude. Some construct-related evidence of validity is available based on analyses of scores of the norm sample and other variables, but additional evidence should be collected to document the interpretations of scores recommended by the authors. Particular caution should be used in interpreting scores for children from certain linguistic and cultural groups.

REVIEWER'S REFERENCES
Horn, J. L., & Cattell, R. B. (1966). Refinement and test of the theory of fluid and crystallized intelligence. *Journal of Educational Psychology, 57*, 253-270.

Das, J. P. (1972). Patterns of cognitive ability in nonretarded and retarded children. *American Journal of Mental Deficiency, 77*, 6-12.

Review of the Detroit Tests of Learning Aptitude—Primary, Third Edition by SHAWN POWELL, Director, Wyoming National Guard Youth ChalleNGe Program, Guernsey, WY, and Graduate Lecturer, University of Northern Colorado, Greeley, CO:

DESCRIPTION. The Detroit Tests of Learning Aptitude—Primary, Third Edition (DTLA-P:3) is designed to assess aptitude in children ages 3 to 9. This test reportedly measures aptitude across three domains: Verbal, Attention, and Motor. It provides seven scores including a General Ability score and six subtest scores: Verbal-Enhanced, Verbal-Reduced, Attention-Enhanced, Attention-Reduced, Motor-Enhanced, and Motor-Reduced. Formal training in assessment is required to administer and interpret the DTLA-P:3.

The DTLA-P:3 has 100 items and takes 15 to 45 minutes to administer. The number of test items administered depends upon a child's age and ability. The test authors identify six age-based starting points and provide clear guidance on basal and ceiling rules. The stimulus picture book contains both color and black-and-white pictures.

The DTLA-P:3 manual provides numerous examples to assist examiners in learning how to administer and score the test. Directions for administering the test are explicitly clear, and the record booklet contains concise instructions for the test items. Verbal directions read aloud during test administration are printed in blue.

DEVELOPMENT. The authors of the DTLA-P:3 define aptitude as "the ability a person must have in order to achieve some purpose" (examiner's manual, p. 1). The test is purported to involve 16 different mental abilities: articulation, matching of semantic concepts, reproducing of designs, repeating digits, drawing a person, letter sequencing, following verbal directions in the performance of manual dexterity tasks, sequencing pictures, following oral directions, identifying incomplete pictures, object identification, repeating verbal sentences, visual abstract reasoning, visual discrimination skills, knowledge of antonyms, and repeating word lists. These 16 abilities are grouped into Verbal, Attention, or Motor domains. Each domain has two subtests that reportedly assess the following abilities: Verbal-Enhanced assesses word knowledge and usage; Verbal-Reduced assesses items not involving language; Attention-Enhanced assesses concentration and short-term memory; Attention-Reduced assesses long-term memory; Motor-Enhanced assesses visual-motor skills and manual dexterity; and Motor-Reduced assesses relatively motor-free items. A child's overall or general aptitude is taken from the total number of test items correctly answered.

TECHNICAL.

Standardization. The DTLA-P:3 normative sample included 1,011 children from 15 states and was collected from 2001 to 2003. Of these 1,011 children, 901 came from four testing centers located in Pennsylvania, Wisconsin, Texas, and Colorado. Each of the remaining 110 children in the normative sample were tested in 1 of the other 11 states involved in the standardization of the DTLA-P:3. The normative sample's racial composition was reported as Black (13%), White (79%), and Other (8%). The sample had 494 females (49%) and 517 males (51%) spread across seven age groups from 3 years to 9 years old.

Reliability. The authors of the DTLA-P:3 provide four indices of the test's reliability. The DTLA-P:3's internal consistency was obtained by use of coefficient alpha. Internal consistency estimates for the DTLA-P:3 range from .82 to .92 across the six subtests and age group categories of the normative sample. The General Ability internal consistency estimates range from .92 to .95 across the seven age categories. The DTLA-P:3's standard errors of measurement range from 4 to 6 points across the six subtests and normative sample's age categories. The General Ability standard error of measurement estimates are 3 to 4 points across the seven age categories.

Test-retest reliability estimates are provided in the results of three studies conducted in Texas involving 1-week intervals between testing sessions. The results of these studies indicate the DTLA-P:3 stability estimates range from .68 to .89.

The last measure of reliability provided by the test authors is interscorer agreement. In obtaining the interscorer agreement, two staff members of the test's publishing company independently scored 50 randomly selected protocols from the normative sample. The resulting interscorer agreement was .99.

Validity. The DTLA-P:3's validity is provided in the from of content validity, item analysis, criterion/predictive validity, and factor analysis. The authors provide comparisons of the DTLA-P:3 to well-known assessment taxonomies and theories. The median percentages of item difficulty for the six subtests range from .22 to .97 across seven age groups and from .23 to .94 for the General Ability score across seven age groups.

To show the DTLA-P:3's criterion/predictive validity, the results of 14 studies published from 1986 to 1994 that compared earlier editions of the test to other assessment measures are provided. In explaining this approach the authors suggest all versions of the DTLA have similar test items. Studies showing comparisons of the current version of the DTLA-P:3 to other assessment instruments are not provided.

The DTLA-P:3's exploratory factor analysis suggests the test measures one factor. This exploratory factor analysis resulted in a multiple-factor model; however, the first factor had an Eigenvalue of 124.94. A subsequent confirmatory factor analysis resulted in item parcel factor loadings between the domain subtests of .98 for the Verbal domain, .99 for the Attention domain, and .99 for the Motor domain. The test manual does not contain a complete correlation matrix between all the subtests and the general ability score. However, the test authors provide three intercorrelation statistics between the domain subtests that range from .81 to .87.

COMMENTARY. The DTLA-P:3 is easy to administer and score. Each test item contributes to the General Ability score and three subtest scores. For example, test items requiring the repetition of verbal word lists contribute to the General Ability score and to the Verbal-Enhanced, Attention-Enhanced, and Motor-Reduced subtest scores. The test authors suggest subtest comparisons should only be made between subtests within a given domain (i.e., Verbal-Enhanced score compared to Verbal-Reduced score) as each test item loads on three different subtests. This stated limitation is problematic as it is difficult to determine exactly what is being measured by a given test item. It is obvious that the repetition of words requires verbal ability, attention, and motor responses. However, having each test item contribute to three different subtests raises questions regarding the ability to differentiate test items into given domains. The validity studies for the test also prompt questions regarding the independence of the subtest scores.

The range of scores on the DTLA-P:3 is concerning. For children 5 years and no months to children 6 years and 5 months old the DTLA-P:3 General Ability, or total standard score, ranges from less than 55 to more than 140. The ranges of available standard scores for children on either side of these ages are significantly smaller. A child who is 3 years and no months old may receive a General Ability score ranging from 69 to more than 140. A child who is 9 years, 6 months old may receive a General Ability score ranging from less than 55 to 120. As the range of standard scores children can obtain varies significantly depending on their age, the DTLA-P:3 may not be useful for some diagnostic situations (e.g., identifying students with specific learning disabilities and differentiating various levels of mental retardation).

The test authors suggest the standardization sample was reflective of the 2000 U.S. Census. However, only 110 children in the normative sample were tested outside of four testing centers. Additionally, the authors did not provide racial data regarding their normative sample beyond three categories (i.e., Black, White, and Other). The 2000 U.S. Census Bureau's data contain 16 different categories for racial identity (U.S. Census Bureau, 2001).

The test authors suggest the current edition of the DTLA has similar items to those of earlier editions of the test. In reporting on the validity of the instrument they provide the results of earlier studies conducted before the current version of the test was revised and subsequently published in 2005. This is a questionable procedure. Comparing the current version of the test to recent editions of other cognitive measures would have reduced the degree of uncertainty regarding the DTLA-P:3's true validity.

SUMMARY. The revised version of the DTLA-P:3 is an updated version of a test that has existed for 20 years. It is easy to score and administer. The normative sample was smaller than other measures used to assess children's abilities (e.g., WISC-IV, CAS) and came from 15 states. A larger normative sample taken from a wider geographical area may have improved the overall psychometric properties for the test. As each test item contributes to three subtest scores, it is difficult to determine if different aptitudes are truly being assessed. It appears the best contribution to childhood evaluation the DTLA-P:3 provides is an overall estimate of a child's aptitude obtained by assessing specific developmental tasks. The authors are to be commended for revising this useful assessment instrument and are encouraged to continue to explore its psychometric properties.

REVIEWER'S REFERENCE

U.S. Census Bureau. (2001). *Profile of general demographic characteristics: 2000 geographic area: United States.* Retrieved April 16, 2006, from http://censtats.census.gov/data/US/01000.pdf

[56]

The Devine Inventory [Revised].

Purpose: Designed as a comprehensive measure of work-related behaviors to assist in employee selection and promotion decisions.

Population: Employees and prospective employees.
Publication Dates: 1989–2005.
Acronym: DI.
Scores, 29: Self-Responsibility, Role Clarity, Approaches Problems Realistically, Openness to Change And Experience, Growth And Development/Learning, Response to Crisis, Trust in Self, Trust in Others, Dominance/Leadership, Negotiating, Decisiveness, Thinking, Detail Mindedness, Structure, Follow-Through, Diligence/Work Ethic, Goal Orientation, Response to Change, Mobility, Energy, Quiescence, Assertiveness, Authority Relationships/Loyalty, Following Rules and Procedures, Recognition, Sociability/Gregariousness, Belonging, Intimacy, Influence Through Trust.
Administration: Individual.
Price Data: Available from publisher.
Foreign Language Editions: Spanish, French, and German editions available.
Time: Administration time not reported.
Comments: Administered and scored via the internet.
Author: Donald W. Devine.
Publisher: The Devine Group, Inc.
Cross References: For reviews by Phillip Benson and William L. Deaton of an earlier edition, see 12:113.

Review of the Devine Inventory [Revised] by THEODORE L. HAYES, *Principal Selection Research Scientist, The Gallup Organization, Washington, DC:*

DESCRIPTION. The Devine Inventory is a 184-item self-presentation inventory that purports to measure 29 work-related construct dimensions. The constructs were developed based on critical incident interviews in a variety of work settings. Construct dimensions are meant to have narrow bandwidth; they can be mapped into 33 broader behavioral dimensions. Dimension scores can be used at the individual level for selection or employee development, or in hybrid applications at the group level such as team building and talent mapping. Items are presented via access to the publisher's website. A paper/pencil version is available. The publisher claims that the Devine Inventory is written at an eighth grade reading comprehension level. Apparently a Spanish language version is available, but it is not further described or alluded to in the manual. Of the 184 items, 29 are presented using a 10-point Likert-type scale and 155 are presented with a keyed response option (along the lines of "I like making decisions") and a single seemingly equally valid alternative (along the lines of "I like working with people") keyed to another dimension. The manual inadvertently alludes to the fact that the inventory's 155 item pairings result in ipsative measurement, though there is no further discussion of the effect this methodology has on results. The forced-choice approach was adopted "in an effort to reduce the 'social desirability' response bias that plagues most behavioral instruments" (technical manual, p. 3); no further attention is paid to social desirability in the manual. Completion time seems to be about 30 minutes for the entire inventory. However, the publisher refers to "tailored" inventory versions (with fewer items) that could be completed in about 10-15 minutes.

DEVELOPMENT. The manual states that the Devine Inventory was developed in the early 1970s based on critical incident interviews with managers and executives regarding important behavioral characteristics of successful employees. These characteristics were sorted through expert judgment into distinct categories. The Devine Inventory was designed "to be comprehensive and to measure 29 constructs considered important in the workplace of today and the workplace of the future" (technical manual, p. 6). The Inventory purports to measure behaviors, "which are defined as a person's predisposition to act" (technical manual, p. 5). The manual further states that "Our goal in developing the Devine Inventory was to make available a comprehensive test of behaviors that are truly work related and to avoid the psychological orientation and jargon associated with many behavioral tests" (technical manual, p. 6). The critical incident approach seems to have been used to great effect in the inventory, as the face validity of the items and behavioral definitions is quite high. Also, the authors stress that the inventory is not meant to be a stand-alone test but rather a part of a selection/development process, which seems reasonable given the inventory's developmental history.

TECHNICAL. The information presented in the Devine Inventory manual is based on a 2004 revision with some research occurring in 2005. In terms of standardization, there is no information presented as to the basis for revising the Inventory, no information on sample characteristics, etc. The manual states that items were written (presumably by content-matter experts) based on original inventory items, dimensions, and concepts, and then tested on a "representative sample" (p. 24) of respondents. No reference or percentile values are presented in the manual. There is an overall descriptive statistics table with the number of items, means, standard deviations, score ranges, and coefficient alphas for each dimension; it is not clear how large this sample is or how it was derived.

Reliability evidence for the inventory is mixed. The authors inexplicably picked .60 as a level of adequate internal reliability, which is low. Only 11 of 29 dimensions have internal reliability at or above the .60 level. The manual contains a lengthy footnote near the data table claiming that the inventory's low reliability is a function of scale ipsativity, extreme polar responding, and using the KR-20 formula rather than coefficient alpha (although the two are conceptually identical). Regardless, the dimension-level internal consistencies as presented are unusually low.

Test-retest stability estimates are provided along with standard errors of measurement. Data are based on 42 individuals retaking the inventory after about 3 months. The median stability estimate is .68 (mean, about .66). This is good information to have, yet the variance of the measures may vary across applications—that is, people taking the inventory for selection may differ from those taking it for development or strictly for research. Differences in variability will drive differences in standard errors. Because the inventory is intended to be used for any of several applications, it would be better to report standard errors (along with other dimension analytics) for each of those separate applications.

Validation evidence for the inventory must be considered incomplete. How much personal change (or score change) might be expected using the Devine Inventory for coaching, development, etc.? Coaching and development is a featured use of the inventory. This is not to say that the inventory is deficient in this function, and certainly there are other assessments where the same information is lacking (e.g., Hayes, 2001). In any event, it is lacking here.

The manual states that the median interdimension correlation, based on 217 respondents, is .11 (mean, about .13; the authors insist on converting negative correlations to positive values before averaging them, and without this function the mean interdimension correlation would be .02). Nearly 26% of the interdimension correlations are -.10 or lower. They would appear almost independent.

The authors put a great deal of effort into attempting to establish the convergent and divergent validity of the Devine Inventory relative to the Hogan Personality Inventory (HPI) and the NEO Personality Inventory-Revised (NEO-PI-R). Using a sample of 70 respondents who took both the NEO and Devine, and 76 who took the HPI and Devine, the authors make a reasonable attempt to assess whether the Devine dimensions correlate as hypothesized with the "Big Five" personality scales. They claim most differences between average hypothesized Devine/Big Five scale correlations and average nonhypothesized Devine/Big Five scale correlations as "evidence" of construct validity. However, because they do not utilize confidence intervals for hypothesized and nonhypothesized averaged correlations (e.g., Hunter and Schmidt, 1990, p. 112ff; Meng, Rosenthal, & Rubin, 1992) the authors make more out of marginal differences than would be warranted.

Nine concurrent validation studies are presented in the manual. In five of these nine studies, the authors "validate" the Inventory by showing that members of a specific job group (e.g., senior managers) have higher average scores than other groups, such as entry-level managers or respondents in general. But organizational level does not indicate performance within role and so this is not a highly valid criterion for empirical validation. In the studies where an external criterion is presented, there are no studies where more than 11 Devine Inventory dimensions are significantly correlated with the criterion, and a large subset of these significant correlations have negative values yet are counted as validity evidence. The manual does not explain why a lower score is desirable or explicable from a selection perspective other than it is significantly correlated with performance. And should an organization consider developing the skills of those with lower scores when the lower score is actually significantly related to performance?

Finally, the authors present evidence regarding demographic group differences. The authors claim that the Devine Inventory is "ADA-compatible," and although the Devine certainly is not a medical examination, some of its behavioral dimensions ("Mobility," "Emotional Composure," "Vitality") seem to be clumsily named, at least regarding people with disabilities. There seem to be no pervasive age, gender, or racial/ethnic group differences as presented in the manual. However, given the Inventory's history, the number of data points per group seems low. It also must be noted that the authors try to explain away some significant male-female score differences as "not surprising," and although the authors are certainly entitled to believe this, it is odd at least to see gender stereotypes used to explain empirical test score differences in this manner.

COMMENTARY. The company's website claims that "over 1,500 leading organizations across the U.S." (www.ecassoc.com/devine.html as of October 2006) used the previous version of the Inventory in 2004, and in another place on its website the organization claims it is willing to "leverage" its historical database to customize profiles. Given all that, it would not be unfair or burdensome to expect more and better information would be available on the Devine Inventory than is presented in the manual. Use of the NEO and HPI tests as criteria for construct validation all but explicitly concedes that the Devine Inventory is a personality test.

SUMMARY. The Devine Inventory has a long history of use. Its content seems reasonable and conceptually there is a strong rationale for the Inventory. The Devine Inventory could be said to have strong consulting utility—its concepts are business related and consultants who have used the Inventory over time are probably familiar with its scope and intent. The empirical analyses presented in the manual leave much to be desired. It is unclear whether this dearth is due to the inventory's 2004 revision, the inventory itself, poor editing choices, or some combination of factors. Future editions of the Devine Inventory and manual may clarify these issues.

REVIEWER'S REFERENCES

Hayes, T. L. (2001). [Review of the Prospector: Discovering the Ability to Learn and Lead.] In B. S. Plake & J. C. Impara (Eds.), *The fourteenth mental measurements yearbook* (pp. 962-964). Lincoln, NE: Buros Institute of Mental Measurements.
Hunter, J. E., & Schmidt, F. L. (1990). *Methods of meta-analysis: Correcting error and bias in research findings.* Newbury Park, CA: Sage.
Meng, X.-L., Rosenthal, R., & Rubin, D. B. (1992). Comparing correlated correlation coefficients. *Psychological Bulletin, 111*(11), 172-175.

Review of the Devine Inventory [Revised] by PAUL M. MUCHINSKY, Joseph M. Bryan Distinguished Professor of Business, The University of North Carolina at Greensboro, Greensboro, NC:

DESCRIPTION. The Devine Inventory (DI) is a comprehensive personality assessment designed to assist in selection and promotion decisions. It is intended for applicants and employees in a wide range of jobs. The DI yields scores on 29 personality constructs: Self-Responsibility, Role Clarity, Approaches Problems Realistically, Openness to Change and Experience, Growth and Developmental/Learning, Response to Crisis, Trust in Self, Trust in Others, Dominance/Leadership, Negotiating, Decisiveness, Thinking, Detail Mindedness, Structure, Follow-Through, Diligence/Work Ethic, Goal Orientation, Response to Change, Mobility, Energy, Quiescence, Assertiveness, Authority Relationships/Loyalty, Following Rules and Procedures, Recognition, Sociability/Gregariousness, Belonging, Intimacy, and Influence Through Trust. The test is administered and scored via the internet, and is available in a Spanish edition. Neither administrative time nor cost information is presented by the publisher. An earlier version of the DI was reviewed by Phillip Benson and William Deaton (see 12:113).

DEVELOPMENT. The DI evolved from dissertation research conducted in the early 1960s. Over subsequent years the DI has been revised, and additional psychometric assessments were conducted. The current version of the DI consists of 184 items. In the first set of items (1–56), the candidate is to indicate which of two items is most descriptive of his or her attitudes, opinions, and behavior (e.g., "I like new challenges" vs. "I like learning new things"). Items 57–85 consist of statements (e.g., "I like working as part of a team") to which the candidate is to respond on a 10-point scale ranging form *least descriptive to most descriptive*. Items 86–184 use the same format as the first set of items. The manual reports that the items were equated for social desirability. Using the critical incident technique based on job analytic interviews, 33 job behaviors (ranging from aggressiveness to vitality) were identified as being critical to successful performance in a wide range of jobs. In some fashion not explained in the manual, a score for each of the 33 behaviors is derived from a composite of several of the 29 personality constructs. For example, the manual describes one behavior ("task completion") is derived from combining the scores of the measured personality constructs of "follow-through," "work hard," and "structure." The scoring weights used to derive the prediction of each of the 33 behaviors are described as being proprietary.

TECHNICAL. The authors of the technical manual are to be complimented for the thoroughness of the description of how the DI was developed and validated. The psychometric information includes a discussion of item content, internal consistency and test-retest reliability, convergence and divergence of personality scales score from the DI with both the NEO-Personality Inventory-Revised (NEO-PI-R; Costa & McCrae, 1992) and Hogan Personality Inventory (HPI; Hogan & Hogan, 1995), the results from criterion-related validity studies, and the results from adverse impact studies on age, gender, and race. However, although the authors conducted a thorough psychometric analysis of the DI, they seem impervious to the meaning and interpretation of some of the results of their own analyses. Many such examples abound. The internal consistency reliability estimates (alpha coefficients) of the 29 personality constructs ranged from .40 to .74. The median alpha was .55. The authors concluded, "Overall, the majority of alpha coefficients were at acceptable levels" (technical manual, p. 27). Even if one were to consider these alpha coefficients are truncated because most of the scale items are presented in a binary format, these results do not inspire confidence in the homogeneity of the items comprising each construct. A group of 42 individuals took the DI twice in a time period separated by 3 months. The test-retest reliability coefficients of the 29 constructs ranged from .35 to .84, with a median of .68. If one's personality is deemed to be a stable attribute (at least over 3 months), the magnitude of these test-retest reliability coefficients is also not impressive. The results from the reliability analyses aside, the results from the criterion-related validity studies are more troublesome. To the authors' credit, they conducted and explained the results of nine such studies. The nature of the criterion was either job level or evaluated performance within a job. Samples included real estate agents, car salespeople, and sales call center agents; out of the 29 personality constructs assessed, 15, 7, and 12 scales of the DI predicted job performance, respectively. The criterion of "successful prediction" was the alpha level of statistical significance. The authors also combined the significant individual scale scores into a composite, and reported a level of combined predictability of the aggregated scale scores. Two aspects of these validational data are of concern.

First, there was not a high degree of generalizability across the numbers of constructs that predicted job success from one study to another, nor in their identity. Second, most of the individual validational studies were based on fairly large sample sizes (ranging between 63–545). The sample sizes were large enough for the authors to have cross-validated their findings. I suspect there could be considerable shrinkage, especially involving those analyses where the individual statistically significant constructs were preselected to create the composite index. Finally, the results of the adverse impact (fairness) studies reveals that members of one group (e.g., racial majority group members) would score significantly higher on some constructs than another group (e.g., racial minority group members). This phenomenon would also occur in reverse—the racial minorities would score higher than racial majorities on some other constructs. Thus, in its totality, the DI does not exhibit adverse impact. The problem with this interpretation is that in reality only certain constructs (not all 29) are predictive of job performance, thus the degree of adverse impact against some group is a function of which constructs are being considered in making personnel decisions.

COMMENTARY. My biggest concern with the DI as a selection or developmental aid pertains to how the test results are to be used in making personnel decisions. According to the manual, the hiring organization is to be highly familiar with the knowledge, skills, and behaviors needed for job success based upon a job analysis and knowledge/experience requirements. Then the candidate takes the DI, and the results reveal the scores on each of the 29 constructs. "This process reviews the degree of strength in critical constructs related to on-the-job success… This step will give the hiring managers insights into a person's strengths and weaknesses" (technical manual, pp. 10-11). Not so fast. The authors' own validational research reveals that different constructs predicted job success across different jobs. Furthermore, many logical or plausible relationships between constructs and job performance did not manifest themselves in the authors' own research. For example, in the study of sales and call center agents, the measured constructs of negotiating, approaches problems realistically, self-responsibility, follow-through, energy, assertiveness, following rules and procedures, and influence through trust all failed to predict job performance. In the absence of a local validational study, the hiring organization would be making personnel selection decisions based on construct scores that could have absolutely no relationship to performance in the job in question. All of the constructs are labeled with positive terms (e.g., "energy"), yet the assessed energy construct may not be related to job performance. What candidate with a very low score on "energy" would be deemed acceptable by any rational hiring manager? Because all 29 of the constructs reflect desirable, positive attributes, a candidate's low score on one or more of these constructs could well be construed as a legitimate (albeit unsubstantiated) basis for rejection.

SUMMARY. There is no mention of recommended cut scores in the manual; one might presume none are provided in the scoring. The link between the 29 constructs and the 33 behaviors, from an operational standpoint, is most confusing. In reading the manual, it appears the test results are reported in construct scores, not behavior scores. If behavior scores are also included, the hiring organization would now be presented with 62 scores per candidate (33 behavior plus 29 scale scores). In the final analysis, the actual use of the test results would seemingly fall to the "folk wisdom" of the hiring organization as to whether someone with high Trust in Self is preferable to someone with high Trust in Others, for example. In addition to relying on statistical significance levels to determine the practical significance of the scores, the authors also play fast-and-loose with the relationship between n and p. In the section on adverse impact examining differences in test scores of various groups, the statistical significance of the difference between scores is dismissed because, "Due to the large sample size, the t statistics are prone to show significance" (technical manual, p. 115). Yet this same caveat is not offered to explain the statistical significance of the validity findings. In conclusion, the DI was developed using professionally acceptable standards of test development. However, undeterred by the results of their own analyses, the authors have produced an enticing array of 29 (or possibly 62) test scores that offer a hiring organization an invitation to justify making plausible false positive and false negative hiring decisions. Candidates can be selected for scoring high on some constructs, or rejected for scoring low on others, neither of which may be related to job performance to any meaningful degree.

REVIEWER'S REFERENCES
Costa, P. T., & McCrae, R. R. (1992). The NEO-Personality Inventory—Revised (NEO-PI-R). Lutz, FL: Psychological Assessment Resources.
Hogan, R., & Hogan, J. (1995). Hogan Personality Inventory (HPI). Tulsa, OK: Hogan Assessment Systems.

[57]

Diagnostic Evaluation of Language Variation—Norm Referenced.

Purpose: Designed "to be used by clinicians to identify speech and language disorders (or delays) in children."

Population: Ages 4-0 to 9-11.

Publication Date: 2005.

Acronym: DELV-Norm Referenced.

Scores, 5: Total Language Composite, Syntax, Pragmatics, Semantics, Phonology.

Administration: Individual.

Price Data, 2006: $145 per complete test kit including examiner's manual (209 pages), picture manual, and 25 record forms; $85 per examiner's manual; $85 per stimulus book; $59 per 25 record forms.

Time: (45) minutes.

Comments: Appropriate for use with children for whom English is their first and primary language.

Authors: Harry N. Seymour, Thomas W. Roeper, and Jill de Villiers.

Publisher: The Psychological Corporation, A Harcourt Assessment Company.

Review of the Diagnostic Evaluation of Language Variation—Norm Referenced by DONNA KELLY, Associate Professor, and THOMAS GUYETTE, Professor and Chair, Department of Audiology and Speech Pathology, University of Arkansas at Little Rock and University of Arkansas for Medical Sciences, Little Rock, AR:

DESCRIPTION. The Diagnostic Evaluation of Language Variation—Norm Referenced edition (DELV—Norm Referenced) is a formal diagnostic instrument given by speech-language pathologists and other professionals with training in test administration. Its purpose is to assess the status of four language domains (i.e., Phonological, Syntactic, Semantic, and Pragmatic) in children ages 4 years, 0 months through 9 years, 11 months. A unique aspect of the DELV—Norm Referenced is that it targets areas of language development that are common to both Mainstream American English (MAE) variations and African American English (AAE) variations. Additionally, the test content and pictorial stimuli were carefully selected for young children from diverse ethnic and cultural backgrounds.

Administration time is estimated at 45 minutes, and the derivation of standard scores and interpretation of the four test domains is estimated at 15 minutes. The instructions are relatively straightforward and include specifics such as how to administer the trial items and when to repeat test items; thorough instructions for recording and scoring the test items are provided. Another unique aspect of the DELV—Norm Referenced is that it includes both Adjusted and Unadjusted derived scores. Prior to test administration, the clinician determines which type to utilize based on parental education level (PEL); the Unadjusted Scores have NOT been adjusted for the PEL whereas the Adjusted Scores have been so adjusted. Clinicians have four PEL levels to choose from, PEL1 = 11 or less years of school; PEL2 = high school degree/GED; PEL3 = 1 to 3 years of college or technical school; PEL4 = bachelor's degree or higher. As noted by the authors, there is empirical evidence in the literature, which demonstrates that the educational level of a child's primary caretaker has a significant impact on the rate of language acquisition.

The Phonology domain is derived differently from the other domains; for this area a percentile band is used to guide the clinician's interpretation of the child's abilities. Raw scores from the three primary language domains (i.e., Syntax, Pragmatics, and Semantic) may be used to derive the following scores: Scaled Scores, Critical Value for Confidence Intervals, Scaled Score Confidence Intervals, Percentile Ranks, Percentile Rank Confidence Intervals, and Test-Age Equivalents. The DELV—Norm Referenced also provides a Total Language Composite Score from the three primary domains, and allows for the derivation of age-equivalent scores. Clinicians may also elect to chart a child's strengths and weaknesses across the four domains.

DEVELOPMENT. The DELV—Norm Referenced began as a contract awarded by the National Institute on Deafness and Communication Disorders (NIDCD) of the National Institutes of Health (NIH) to the test authors in 1994. The original grant goals were expanded by an NIH contract in 1998, which allowed for the construction of a culturally fair and unbiased language assessment tool for both MAE and AAE children. Another unique aspect of the DELV—Norm Referenced is that it draws on both linguistic (e.g., movement rules) and language processing (e.g., fast mapping) constructs, which have been supported in the literature. A contrastive/noncontrastive assessment model posited by the first author of the test (Seymour & Seymour, 1977) was also used to guide the item content.

Each of the four domains contains subdomains that are grounded in theoretical frameworks and empirical research findings. For example, the Syntax domain contains four subdomains: *Movement Rules*, which examine a child's knowledge of how words and/or parts of sentences can move to different locations within a sentence (e.g., placement of question words); *Variables*, which examine a child's ability to reference the appropriate item or set of items posited by a wh-question; *Passive Sentence Constructions*, which tap a child's knowledge of three different aspects of passive sentence comprehension; and *Articles*, which target comprehension and appropriate use of "a" and "the." The Pragmatic domain includes four subdomains: *Speech Acts*, which explores a child's understanding of communicative intentions (e.g., naming, requesting); *Narrative Development*, which examines the child's development of the properties of coherence and cohesion; *Theory of Mind*, which examines a child's awareness of the mental states of other people; and *Question Asking*, which taps a child's ability to request missing information. The Semantic domain contains three subdomains: *Lexical Organization*, which taps a child's understanding of hierarchical word categories; *Quantification*, which examines comprehension of terms commonly used in mathematical word problems (e.g., every, all, some); and *Fast Mapping*, which taps the ability of a child to infer meaning from a new word after hearing it used in context. Finally, the Phonological domain contains two subdomains; one distinguishes between phonological differences and disorders using *Contrastive/NonContrastive Elements*, which may be produced differently by MAE and AAE speakers and *Consonant Clusters* such as *stove* and *scratch*, which are not produced differently by MAE and AAE speakers.

The DELV—Norm Referenced was piloted in both public and private schools in Connecticut and Massachusetts on over 500 MAE and AAE speakers between 4 and 6 years of age. Following modifications, a total of 247 items were compiled into a tryout version; this version contained only those items that demonstrated minimal differences between MAE and AAE speakers. The tryout version sampled four groups of children: (a) typically developing MAE speakers, (b) typically developing AAE speakers, (c) MAE speakers who had been previously diagnosed with a language disorder (or delay), and (d) AAE speakers who had been previously diagnosed with a language disorder (or delay). Finally, a small sample of children who spoke an alternative variety of English (e.g., Appalachian, Cajun, Southern) was also collected. Results from the items tryout were used to select the final version of the DELV—Norm Referenced; these items were found to (a) elicit consistently the intended response from the typically developing children, (b) yield essentially similar findings between the MAE and AAE speakers, and (c) differentiate clearly between the typically developing children and the children with a previous diagnosis of a language disorder (or delay).

TECHNICAL. Normative information is based on 900 children; there were 100 children in each of the following age groups: 4 years to 4 years, 5 months; 4 years, 6 months to 4 years, 11 months; 5 years to 5 years, 11 months; 5 years, 6 months to 5 years, 11 months; 6 years to 6 years, 5 months; 6 years, 6 months to 6 years, 11 months; 7 years to 7 years, 11 months; 8 years to 8 years, 11 months; and 9 years to 9 years, 11 months. Eighty-one percent of the children spoke MAE, and 8% spoke AAE. Participant characteristics such as gender, race/ethnicity, region of U.S., and parent years of education are readily available; these tables may be used to establish whether or not the DELV—Norm Referenced is an appropriate instrument for a particular child.

The manual provides one chapter devoted to the reliability of the test and one chapter that provides evidence of its validity. For example, test-retest reliability was examined over an interval of 6 to 28 days with a sample size of 239 children across all of the age ranges tapped by the DELV—Norm Referenced. Correlation coefficients for the four domains range from .71 to .96 with small *SEM*s; total test coefficients ranged from .87 to .94. Internal consistency was also evaluated and yielded coefficient alpha reliability coefficients for the Total Language Score between .81 and .92, with individual domain coefficients ranging between .59 and .95. The authors also examined evidence of reliability for the children who had a previous diagnosis of language disorder (or delay), and found that this instrument is reliable for measuring language skills in both "clinical" and "non-clinical" samples. In general, reliability levels declined with the oldest groups of children; the authors stated that this trend was expected given likely ceiling effects for the typically developing children. Additional reliability information is available in the manual.

Several areas of test validity were examined for the DELV—Norm Referenced (e.g., test content, internal structure, and diagnostic accuracy). Evidence of validity for this measure appears to be adequate, particularly when contrasted with other formal language measures that tap the same constructs. The diagnostic accuracy of the DELV—Norm Referenced appears to be particularly strong. The manual reports strong levels of sensitivity and adequate specificity when the cut score is 1 *SD* below the mean.

COMMENTARY. The authors of the DELV—Norm Referenced have exceeded typical standards of test construction and standardization in their quest to create a nonbiased language assessment for use with MAE and AAE speakers. Although few, if any, measures contain a requisite sample of all the participant characteristics of interest, the DELV—Norm Referenced has made great strides in the development of a valid language assessment for middle- and low-SES AAE speakers. The test content was based on input from several theoretical frameworks and appears to be empirically grounded. Pilot and tryout editions of the test were utilized to select those items most likely to differentiate validly between language differences and language disorders (or delays) for MAE and AAE speakers. Adequate levels of reliability and validity are reported, and the DELV—Norm Referenced appears to exceed reliability and validity values reported by the vast majority of child language assessment measures. Good sensitivity and adequate specificity are documented. The authors are to be commended for developing a language measure that can be validly utilized with AAE speakers.

SUMMARY. The DELV—Norm Referenced is a valid and reliable measure of four aspects of language (i.e., Syntax, Pragmatics, Semantics, and Phonology) for children ranging in age from 4 years, 0 months to 9 years, 11 months.

The DELV—Norm Referenced is the only child language measure that clearly differentiates children with language differences and disorders (or delays) in both MAE and AAE speakers. Another valuable attribute of the DELV-Norm Referenced is that test score interpretation includes parental education level, an essential factor when assessing children across socioeconomic levels.

REVIEWERS' REFERENCE

Seymour, H. N., & Seymour, C. M. (1977). A therapeutic model for communicative disorders among Black English speaking children. *Journal of Speech and Hearing Disorders, 42*, 247–256.

Review of the Diagnostic Evaluation of Language Variation–Norm Referenced by AIMÉE LANGLOIS, Professor, Department of Child Development, Humboldt State University, Arcata, CA:

DESCRIPTION. The Diagnostic Evaluation of Language Variation—Norm Referenced (DELV—Norm Referenced) test is designed to identify children who have "speech and language disorders (or delays) ... regardless of the variety of English the child speaks" (manual, p. 1). The authors state that the test assesses language constructs that are both essential to the acquisition of linguistic competence and common to all dialects of English. To that effect, the test can be administered to children between the ages of 4 and 10 who speak either Mainstream American English (MAE) or one of its variations. According to the authors, clinicians who use the test can thus be sure that test results reflect a child's true language competence and may use these results as a base for remediation.

The DELV—Norm Referenced assesses Syntax, Pragmatics, Semantics, and Phonology. The assessment of these language components, except that of Phonology, is further divided into three subdomains for Syntax and Pragmatics, and four for Semantics. The test includes an examiner's manual and a stimulus book, as well as a 24-page record form to complete for each child. Detailed instructions for administering and scoring the test are provided in the examiner's manual and on the record form. The authors strongly caution potential test users to read the examiner's manual before administering the test. They emphasize that examiners "must" (p. 9) become familiar with the materials, follow the scripted procedures exactly, practice administering the test, and ensure that the test environment be comfortable.

They also provide detailed instructions for administration, recording, and scoring. In addition, the manual includes a valuable interpretation section that includes case studies. However, during testing the examiner must consult both the manual and the record form simultaneously in order to administer the test according to the specified instructions and enter an appropriate score. This complex procedure can become unwieldy given that the examiner must also handle the stimulus book (set between the child and clinician who must sit side by side) and point to pictures while maintaining rapport with and encouraging the child. However, the authors' suggestions for such encouragement, in the form of praise and statements such as "you're doing a good job" contradict best practice for providing feedback (Kohn, 2001) and should be modified according to suggestions provided by Kohn.

The 24-page record form includes a cover page on which the examiner enters scores and identifies for each language domain the tested child's strengths and weaknesses as well as his or her profile based on the scores. To that effect, the examiner must follow instructions provided in the examiner's manual. Although the explanations for converting raw scores into scaled scores and percentile ranks are easy to follow, those for determining confidence intervals and determining strengths and weaknesses are not, which can jeopardize the accuracy of interpretation.

The last page of the record form is devoted to an item analysis of the child's errors whereas the remainder of the record form includes, for each test item, specific instructions, a space in which to enter the child's response, and the numbers 0, 1, and 2, one of which the examiner must circle to reflect the child's response level. The examiner then adds the circled numbers to determine a child's raw score for each domain. At first glance, the test appears easy to administer given the specificity of the instructions. However, two factors negatively affect ease of administration. One, related to the logistics of handling the materials, is discussed above; the other compounds this first and relates to the amount of information on the score form, which is overwhelming; it includes scripts that users must read, instructions test administrators must follow, common children's responses, and lines for writing additional information.

DEVELOPMENT. The authors offer a sound rationale for the development of the DELV—Norm Referenced test and its use. They point to the frequent misdiagnosis of language disorders in children whose language is simply different from MAE. They convincingly argue that, because of such misdiagnoses, minority children are overrepresented in special education programs. The DELV—Norm Referenced test was therefore developed to obviate this problem, especially for African American children.

The authors provide information regarding subdomain and item development. They also describe pilot studies and a tryout research in terms of objectives, sites, subjects, results, and review. The selection of the final set of items therefore represents results of thorough research.

TECHNICAL.

Standardization. The DELV—Norm Referenced test was standardized, following the pilot and tryout studies, on 900 (100 in each of nine age groups) children who represented "as closely as possible, the 2002 U.S. Census Current Population Survey of children ages 4-9 years" (manual, p. 109). The representativeness of the norm sample is supported in the examiner's manual with six tables that favorably compare the demographics of the children in the standardization sample with those of the U.S. population in terms of gender, age, region, race/ethnicity, and parent education level. Given that age is the determinant factor for assigning scaled and percentile scores, the number of children in each age group (100) is deemed adequate for test standardization (AERA, APA, & NCME, 1999). According to McCauley and Swisher (1984), subgroups of at least 100 individuals ensure that norms are stable, which appears to be the case in this instance.

Reliability. The authors provide evidence that they assessed the test-retest, coefficient alpha, split-half, and interexaminer reliability of the test. Coefficients range from adequate (.70) to excellent (.90) for each reliability type and each language domain. Of particular concern, however, are the small to medium score gains in the test-retest data, which the authors attribute to practice effects. If, as the authors assume, a child benefits "from having heard and completed the items once before" (manual, p. 120), that child's performance on a first administration of the test may not reflect his or her true abilities. The availability of confidence intervals and standard errors of measurement help mitigate this problem. Clinicians should therefore be sure to consider these data when interpreting results and making recommendations for treatment.

Validity. The authors attended to the following types of validity: content, response process, internal structure, evidence based on relationship to other variables, and evidence based on clinical studies. The authors' detailed rationale for the selection of the test's subdomains attests to its content validity. Results of pilot studies and a tryout phase further support content validity for each item. The changes made to the items that yielded unintended responses during the pilot studies ensure that the test measures intended skill and thus has high response process validity. Positive correlations of domains and composite scores demonstrate the internal structure of the test. Moderate correlations with Part II of the DELV—Screening Test, on one hand, and four subtests of the CELF-4, on the other, show the test's relationship to other variables. Moderate correlations might lead one to question the test's concurrent validity. However, given the purpose of the test, the rationale that supports it, and the constructs that it assesses, there are no instruments at this time with which to establish its concurrent validity. Therefore, in light of the high content validity of the test, this omission might not be an issue.

Finally, the authors provide evidence of validity based on clinical studies. Although two tables show differences in scores between typically developing children and those diagnosed with language or articulation disorders, the discussion in this section is particularly confusing and thus of limited value.

Qualifications of examiner. The manual specifies that "speech-language pathologists, psychologists, early childhood specialists, educational diagnosticians, and other professionals who have experience in training and assessment" (p. 6) as well as with the International Phonetic Alphabet can administer, score, and interpret the DELV-Norm Referenced test. Its high interexaminer reliability established with individuals with such training supports the fact that individuals who use the test should have the above qualifications.

COMMENTARY. The DELV—Norm Referenced test, as a means to identify children who have language disorders regardless of the variety of English they speak, meets a special need. The authors emphasize this point eloquently throughout the manual. In addition, the test was standardized on a large sample of children representative of the U.S. population, a complex task to say the least. It appears that the strengths of the test lie in its potential to facilitate the identification of non-MAE children who have language disorders, and in its content validity and high interexaminer reliability. In addition, clinicians can use children's responses on the test to determine how their use of English compares to that used for instruction at their school, as a departure point for selecting additional assessment procedures, as an explanation for their performance on such an assessment, and as a guide to determine treatment goals when warranted.

However, several concerns about test administration, reliability, validity, and unclear passages in the examiner's manual weaken the usefulness of the test in terms of the accuracy of scores obtained and their interpretation.

SUMMARY. The DELV—Norm Referenced test addresses the problem of misdiagnosing children who speak a variation of English as having language disorders. The authors eloquently explain their purpose and the rationale that together support the development of the test with a review of the literature. They attended to many of the psychometric criteria that help establish the value of this instrument. As such, the test is to be recommended though clinicians must heed the advice of the authors of the test to become thoroughly familiar with the test before using it and exercise caution in interpreting results.

REVIEWER'S REFERENCES

American Educational Research Association, American Psychological Association, & National Council on Measurement in Education. (1999). *Standards for educational and psychological testing.* Washington, DC: American Educational Research Association.
Kohn, A. (2001). Five reasons to stop saying "Good Job." *Young Children, 56*(5), 24-30.
McCauley, R. J., & Swisher, L. (1984). Psychometric review of language and articulation tests for preschool children. *Journal of Speech and Hearing Disorders, 49,* 34-42.

[58]

Doors and People.

Purpose: Designed to "provide comparable measures of visual and verbal memory" and "test both recall and recognition."

Population: Ages 16–80.

Publication Date: 1994.

Scores, 14: Verbal Recall (People), Visual Recognition (Doors), Visual Recall (Shapes), Verbal Recognition (Names), Overall, Combined Visual Memory, Combined Verbal Memory, Combined Recall, Combined Recognition, Forgetting (Verbal), Forgetting

(Visual), Overall Forgetting, Visual-Verbal Discrepancies, Recall-Recognition Discrepancies.
Administration: Individual.
Price Data, 2006: £251 per complete kit including manual (20 pages), 25 scoring sheets, and 3 stimulus books; £39.50 per 50 scoring sheets.
Time: [35–40] minutes.
Authors: Alan Baddeley, Hazel Emslie, and Ian Nimmo-Smith.
Publisher: Harcourt Assessment [England].

Review of Doors and People by WILLIAM K. WILKINSON, Consulting Educational Psychologist, Boleybeg, Barna, County Galway, Republic of Ireland:

DESCRIPTION. The full title of this test is "Doors and People: A Test of Visual and Verbal Recall and Recognition." As the name implies, there are four separate quadrants measured: Visual Recall, Visual Recognition, Verbal Recall, and Verbal Recognition. In addition, there are two "forgetting" scores. Although the authors never explicitly define their target population, they repeatedly use the word "patients" and "brain damage." Because normative data are provided for ages 16 to 80+ we take it that the test is intended for use with adults who suffer some form of classifiable brain injury. With this target group in mind, specific uses of the test are given as (a) assessing the degree to which brain injury impacts learning and memory and (b) assessing the degree to which the patient might benefit from therapy.

Test materials include a technical manual, scoring sheets, a bound book called the "Doors Test," a smaller bound booklet with the label "Names Test," and one more booklet called the "People Test and Shapes Test." In administrative order, the purpose of the People Test is to measure Verbal Recall and requires the examinee to scan a total of four stimulus cards, each with a pictured person and his name/profession typed below the picture (e.g., "Dawn Smith—Teacher"). The score for this test is the correct recall of first name, second name, and correct pairing of the two when given the profession as a prompt. A maximum of three trials is allowed to achieve complete recall. Later, after completing the second test in the battery, a delayed measure of Verbal Recall is obtained by asking the examinee to recollect the names.

The Doors Test is a Visual Recognition test where one is asked to recognize a series of 12 doors of different types (e.g., garage, front, church, shed). Each of the 12 target pictures is presented briefly followed by the 12 recognition items (correct door and three distractors). The test is repeated with a second set of 12 more doors where target and distractor are intentionally more difficult.

Visual Recall is the purview of the Shapes test. The stimuli are four line drawings of crosses. The examinee views each shape for 5 seconds, then draws it. Scoring is based on the quality of the reproduction, where each shape has three scoring criteria, yielding a total maximum raw score of 12. As with the People Test, the Shapes Test is re-administered after an interference test, which is described next.

The last domain, Verbal Recognition, is the focus of the Names Test. Logically related to the Doors Test, the patient views 12 target names in succession and then selects targets from nontargets. There are two sets of names, one all female, the other all male.

Each test yields a raw score, which is converted to a "scaled score" and a corresponding percentile. All trial scores for each subtest, total subtest scores, score conversation, and so forth are made on the scoring sheet for the examinee. A handy feature of the scoring sheet is that it includes administrative instructions for each subtest. The cover of the scoring sheet is where all of the score conversations are made. In addition to the four Visual/Verbal and Recall/Recognition scores, the user can compare disparity in performance in domain pairings, such as Visual versus Verbal and Recall versus Recognition. Finally, Visual and Verbal Forgetting scores are also obtained, as well as an Overall Forgetting score.

DEVELOPMENT. The test authors ask the question, "Why another test of memory," and go on to name several reasons for doing so. Concerning just the question of development, a case is made for the dichotomy between "visual" and "verbal." Test materials are face valid in regard to the four processes of Visual, Verbal, Recall, and Recognition. However, the actual importance of the separate areas is reduced by the ensuing data, which show that an overwhelming degree of variation in test performance is due to a "general memory factor." They add that a much smaller amount of variance is accounted for by the visual/verbal distinction. To their credit, the test developers recognize that the most valid score from the battery of tests is the overall memory score (the sum of each domain score). However, this admission would, to some degree, negate the importance of the visual/verbal split.

The authors do appear to have overcome some of the limitations in the format of previous tests. For example, the use of doors would seem to reduce access to "specialized memory" systems such as the kind possibly used in face recognition tests.

Another claim for a new memory test is the need for more representative norms. In this regard, the authors used a stratified sample of 238 individuals with strata based on census data. The individuals were grouped into five age categories: 16–31, 32–47, 48–64, 65–79, and 80+ years. It would be helpful if more information was included in the manual about the sample, such as how recruitment took place, location of participants, and other relevant tests used. The authors mention that members of the sample were administered other tests (e.g., adult reading test), but the reasons for, and results of, these tests are not included in the discussion. This information is particularly relevant if the test consumer is trying to assess the authors' comment that the norms are somehow more representative compared to other memory tests.

The scoring of the test is very clear and straightforward. The user may have to make some subjective decisions in the scoring of the Shapes Test (e.g., exactly how off center does the square need to be from the intersecting lines). Otherwise, the scoring is clear, as is the scoring sheet.

It is obvious from the normative tables that the standard score is a subtest conversion: mean of 10, standard deviation of 3. One of the authors' original points is that a new memory test should avoid floor and ceiling effects. Although some of the separate scores do result in adequate raw score distributions, others are more suspect. The major problem is the Shapes Test (Visual Recall), especially for the two youngest age strata. For these age groups, a perfect Shapes raw score results in a scaled score of 12. Further, the loss of one raw score point results in a scaled score of 11, and a further 1 point lower, we arrive at the scaled score mean of 10. The impact of this problem is to undercut the overall score and the resultant aggregative visual memory score for the youngest age groups on which the test is designed. This test

may need to be modified for this particular age group in the future. Alternatively, other concerns might relate to the scoring of this test or some atypical attribute of the 16- to 47-year-old normative samples as it relates to this measure.

The authors include percentile norms corresponding to raw score performance. Because not all raw score outcomes correspond to a "decile," the potential user will have to arrive at approximations of exact percentile scores through interpolation.

Finally, it was disappointing that the authors did not address some of the points they make in justifying the development of a new memory test in the ensuing manual coverage. Take, for example, the notion that the test is "unstressful" to a range of subjects. Is this actually the case?

TECHNICAL. Given the ease of scoring of most subtests and the clear score outcomes in the domains measured, one would expect a plethora of reliability and validity data in the manual. Thus, the comment "relevant studies will be reported elsewhere" (manual, p. 7) was perplexing. The only data in the manual indicate that performance, across all four subtests, declined with age. It is hoped that in a supplement the authors will summarize the relevant reliability and validity data to date.

COMMENTARY. The Doors and People measure may prove to be a valuable asset in the future. The materials used are original and seem to address some of the shortcomings of other memory tests. The scoring sheet is well presented and thorough. Some of the reservations noted here could be addressed by simply providing additional information in the technical manual (e.g., normative sample, technical data). Some of the issues raised may require revision in some tests for some age groups (e.g., Shapes Test for youngest age groups).

SUMMARY. The Doors and People Test purports to measure four cognitive processes— Visual Recall, Visual Recognition, Verbal Recall, Verbal Recognition—of particular relevance for the brain-injured population. It also includes two forgetting measures. Technical data—reliability and validity—regarding all six of these areas needs to be documented before the consumer can be confident that this test does what the authors claim it does.

[59]
Draw-A-Person Intellectual Ability Test for Children, Adolescents, and Adults.

Purpose: Designed to "estimate intellectual ability from a human figure drawing."

Population: Ages 4-0 to 89-11.

Publication Date: 2004.

Acronym: DAP: IQ.

Score: DAP IQ.

Administration: Individual or group.

Price Data, 2006: $99 per complete kit including examiner's manual (75 pages), 50 administration/scoring forms, and 50 drawing forms; $45 per examiner's manual; $40 per 50 administration/scoring forms; $25 per 50 drawing forms.

Time: (8—15) minutes.

Authors: Cecil R. Reynolds and Julia A. Hickman.

Publisher: PRO-ED.

Review of the Draw-A-Person Intellectual Ability Test for Children, Adolescents, and Adults by ROBERT W. HILTONSMITH, Professor of Psychology, Radford University, Radford, VA:

DESCRIPTION. The Draw-A-Person Intellectual Ability Test for Children, Adolescents, and Adults (DAP: IQ) is a human figure drawing (HFD) test for which the stated purpose is to "improve the pervasive practice of evaluating human figure drawings as a measure of cognitive ability" (examiner's manual, p. v). It provides what the developers believe is an objective scoring system for deriving an estimate of intellectual ability from a drawing of a human figure that was obtained through a standardized administration procedure. In doing so, the DAP: IQ "provides an estimate of cognitive development that is at least an estimate of the lower bound of the person's ability and does so with a task and scoring criteria that have less cultural specificity than most intelligence tests, verbal or nonverbal" (examiner's manual, p. vi).

The DAP: IQ is normed for ages 4 years and 0 months through 89 years and 11 months, thus distinguishing it from prior draw-a-person tests that typically provide norms only for children. Test materials are minimal and include the examiner's manual, the administration/scoring form, the drawing form (where the examinee draws his or her sketch), and two sharpened pencils with erasers. The administration instructions simply ask the examinee to draw the best picture possible of him- or herself, adding that the requested sketch should be a frontal view of the examinee's entire body. The test may be administered to either individuals or groups, using essentially similar directions. The test takes approximately 8 to 15 minutes to administer, though the manual suggests that most individuals complete the requested drawing in 5 minutes or less. The drawing is then scored by assigning varying numbers of points for 23 scoring elements (some elements receive a maximum of 1 point, whereas others can receive 2, 3, and, in the case of the mouth, 4 points). The raw score is the total number of points awarded for all 23 scoring criteria. Raw scores are then transformed into standard scores with a mean of 100 and a standard deviation of 15. Using a continuous norming procedure, the developers determined the optimal breakdown of age grouping for the normative tables. These tables include half-year intervals for ages 4 through 8, 1-year intervals through age 16, and then multiple-year intervals through age 89. Percentile ranks are included, as well as *T*-scores, *z*-scores, and stanines.

DEVELOPMENT. The DAP: IQ was developed with several purposes in mind. First, all intelligence tests, including human figure drawing tests, have normative data that become outdated and less useful over time. HFD tests have had extensive norming data collected since at least the 1920s, but no norming studies have been done since the late 1980s. Second, prior HFD norming studies have been restricted to children and adolescents and have not been applicable to adult populations. Third, prior HFD scoring systems, according to the test developers, "have tended to infuse the derived score with motor skill" (examiner's manual, p. 2), though the developers offer no evidence to support this contention. The DAP: IQ was therefore developed to provide a rapid and easy-to-use scoring system for HFDs that includes up-to-date normative data on adults as well as children and adolescents, and that emphasizes the "conceptual quality of the examinee's performance" (examiner's manual, p. 2).

TECHNICAL. The examiner's manual provides detailed information about the procedures used to norm the DAP: IQ. This information includes the methods employed to select the sample, the demographic characteristics of the sample, and the derivation of the various normative scores noted earlier. The DAP: IQ was initially normed on a sample of 3,290 individuals residing in 46 states. This sample was pared to 2,295 individuals in order to make the sample "a near-perfect match to the U.S. Bureau of the Census demographic characteristics" (examiner's manual, p. 13). Each of the four major geographic regions of the United States was represented in the selection of the norming sites. The sites themselves were selected by two methods that are described in considerable detail in the examiner's manual, along with data that generally support the test developer's claim regarding how closely the DAP: IQ sample matches all relevant demographic characteristics of the U.S. population in 2001.

It is somewhat less clear how the 23 scoring elements used to assess the obtained HFDs (the "items" on the DAP: IQ) were derived. At one point in the examiner's manual, the developers note that the DAP: IQ scoring elements are "certainly reminiscent of [prior] systems and were generated on the basis of our knowledge of the literature" (p. 25). These prior scoring systems include familiar ones by Florence Goodenough and Dale Harris, Elizabeth Koppitz, and Jack Naglieri. A few sentences later, however, the developers note that "we generated the DAP: IQ scoring elements initially without formal reference to any other scoring criteria" (examiner's manual, p. 25). Regardless of their genesis, the scoring elements were reviewed by experts to make sure they were plausible, clear, and objective.

The examiner's manual provides separate chapters on the reliability and the validity of the DAP: IQ, with the chapter on validity being especially thorough. In terms of reliability, the test developers present data on the status of DAP: IQ scores relative to three sources of error variance: content sampling (internal consistency reliability), time sampling, and interscorer differences. For content sampling, the median internal consistency reliability across all ages using coefficient alpha is .82, with the lowest being .74. Time sampling reliability estimates were derived using the test-retest method with a small sample of 45 individuals who were tested and retested after a 1-week period. The resulting test-retest coefficient was .84. Finally, interscorer differences were investigated through two studies involving a total of 179 DAP: IQ drawings. Interscorer reliability estimates of .91 and .95 were obtained for the two studies. The test developers conclude, appropriately, that "the overall reliability of the DAP: IQ

standard scores is quite good" (examiner's manual, p. 22).

The chapter on validity focuses on presenting evidence that supports the interpretation of the DAP: IQ as "a component of general ability that is more closely aligned with nonverbal or fluid aspects of ability than with abilities in the verbal domain" (examiner's manual, p. 23). Toward this end, the developers present theory-based, logic-based, and empirically based evidence related to the interpretation of performance on the DAP: IQ. A detailed discussion of this evidence is beyond the scope of this brief review. Perhaps of most interest is the evidence presented by the developers relating DAP: IQ scores to measures of intellectual ability and academic achievement. The relationship of DAP: IQ scores to measures of intellectual ability was assessed in two studies, one using 1,233 children and relating their DAP: IQ scores to scores on the Detroit Tests of Learning Aptitude—Primary: Second Edition (DTLA-P:2) and the second using 211 children whose scores on the DAP: IQ were correlated with their scores on the Wechsler Intelligence Scale for Children-III (WISC-III). Correlations generally were from .40 to .60, with higher correlations with the nonverbal sections of both intellectual ability tests. Although the developers acknowledge that prior research has shown that scores from HFDs tend to underestimate intellectual ability, this finding was not shown for either the DTLA-P:2 or the WISC-III. In terms of academic achievement, DAP: IQ scores for children referred to a clinic for learning disabilities were correlated with scores on the Woodcock-Johnson–Revised Tests of Achievement (WJ-R) and the Wechsler Individual Achievement Test (WIAT). The correlations were significant but only moderate in magnitude, with the highest correlations being between DAP: IQ scores and Woodcock—Johnson math achievement and the WIAT spelling test.

COMMENTARY AND SUMMARY. The DAP: IQ has a number of distinct advantages for those examiners wishing to employ human figure drawings in their assessment regimen. The norms are representative of the U.S. population and are presently up-to-date. A variety of derived scores are available, including the familiar mean of 100 and standard deviation of 15. Furthermore, the DAP: IQ is appropriate for use with adults as well as with children and adolescents. The main challenge for many examiners may be to determine just how to use scores from the DAP: IQ in the overall context of the assessment results for an examinee, particularly with the current availability of brief measures of intellectual ability such as the Kaufman Brief Intelligence Test—2nd Edition (KBIT-2) and the Reynolds Intellectual Screening Test (RIST), which take only a little more time to administer and score than the DAP: IQ and yield, in this reviewer's opinion, much richer and direct data about the examinee's intellectual functioning.

Review of the Draw-A-Person Intellectual Ability Test for Children, Adolescents, and Adults by JONATHAN SANDOVAL, Professor of Education, University of the Pacific, Stockton, CA:

DESCRIPTION. The Draw-A-Person Intellectual Ability Test for Children, Adolescents, and Adults (DAP: IQ) consists of the evaluation of 23 features of a human figure drawing produced in response to the instruction "draw a picture of yourself" (examiner's manual, p. 5). Examinees are asked to draw a full figure from a frontal view. Each of the drawing features (e.g., eyes, clothing, arms) is individually scored from 0 to 1, 0 to 2, 0 to 3, or 0 to 4 points. A maximum score of 49 points is possible. Raw scores may be converted into a single standard score, an IQ with a mean of 100 and standard deviation of 15, a T-score, a z-score, or a stanine. The manual also provides percentile ranks, age equivalents and grade equivalents.

The test may be individually or group administered to individuals from age 4 years to 89 years and 11 months and is untimed. The time to administer and score the test is from 8 to 15 minutes. Administration requires a pencil with eraser and drawing form. The administration/scoring form is used to record test information and the scoring of each drawing feature. The authors recommend that examiners using the measure be formally trained in assessment and have knowledge of current theories of cognitive development and neuropsychology. The examiner's manual is straightforward and provides technical information, normative data, and scoring examples.

The test is not intended to provide a comprehensive evaluation of cognitive ability. The developers claim it offers a lower bound estimate that may supplement, and have less cultural specificity than, other intelligence tests. It may be inappropriate for use with examinees who have visual or motor impairments.

DEVELOPMENT. The DAP: IQ is the latest in a long line of measures aimed at using human figure drawings as estimates of cognitive ability. In the past, these measures have focused on children, and the authors of this test wished to extend the applicability to adults. Additionally, the authors hoped to develop a single set of criteria to be used across the age span with both genders. Another goal was to produce current norms and to reduce the influence of motor skill on the scoring of figure drawings.

TECHNICAL. Norms for the test were based on 2,295 individuals matched to U.S. Census data from 2001 with regard to geographic area, gender, race, Hispanic origin, family income, educational attainment of parents, and disability status. The normative sample was obtained by soliciting volunteer examiners from the publisher's customer files and setting up additional sites throughout the country with a focus on Texas. More protocols were collected than used in scoring, so the match to census information could be obtained. Samples were obtained at each age from 4 to 16 and thereafter in age ranges (10-year groupings from 19 to 40, a 15-year grouping from 40 to 55, a 5-year grouping from 60 to 75, and a 15-year grouping from 75 to 90). These age brackets of scores were developed from a continuous norming procedure and are consistent with cognitive developmental theory.

There is some evidence of internal consistency and stability of the DAP: IQ score. The coefficient alpha estimates for the age groupings varied from .74 at age 4 to .87 at age 30–39, with a mean and median value of .82. The standard errors of measurement vary between 4 and 5 points. Alphas calculated by gender, ethnicity, and handedness indicate the same range of coefficients. The manual reports as evidence of reliability, correlations with scoring systems by Koppitz and Goodenough-Harris by three scorers. These correlations are .85, .86, and .86. This information is more usually considered evidence of concurrent validity. Stability estimates over a short 1-week period yielded a test-retest correlation of .84 (n = 45). Interscorer reliability was estimated at .95 for protocols selected from across the sample, and at .91 for the more difficult-to-score age group of 6 to 11. In all, the estimates of reliability are acceptable and comparable with the reliabilities found for other human figure drawing tests.

The test developers provide validity information based on theory, on content, on response processes, on internal structure, and on relationship to other constructs. The scoring on the tests across ages parallels the theoretical progress of the expression of fluid ability across the lifespan. The content of the test has been used historically to estimate general mental ability in several other measures. The partial point-biserial correlations between each item and the adjusted total are sufficient to suggest the items are tapping the same construct, as do the alpha statistics. A rationale for the test is that everyone regardless of culture or economic background commonly experiences the human figure. The content is also less influenced by education and the task is simple.

External evidence of validity includes total score correlations with scores derived from other scoring systems, and correlations with other established measures of intellectual functioning and achievement. Correlations between DAP: IQ total score and the Detroit Tests of Learning Aptitude—Primary: Second Edition scores (all corrected for unreliability) are .60 for Nonverbal, .42 for Verbal, and .54 for General Mental Ability. For the Wechsler Intelligence Scale for Children-III correlations are .33 with Verbal, .49 with Performance, and .46 with Full Scale. The DAP: IQ correlates .39 with Woodcock Johnson—Revised (WJ-R) Broad reading, and .36 with Wechsler Individual Achievement Test (WIAT) Reading. Correlations with Math are .46 with WJ-R Broad math and .43 with WIAT Math. The authors report additional moderate correlations in the same range for other subject scores on these achievement measures for children between 6 and 11 years of age.

Both convergent and divergent validity data are reported. The DAP: IQ has moderate correlations (around .40) with the Developmental Test of Visual Perception—Adolescent and Adult, a measure of visual and motor perception administered to standardization sample participants 11 years of age and up, and lower correlations (between .36 and .25) with the Developmental Test of Visual-Motor Integration and Bender-Gestalt Test using the Koppitz scoring system for children ages 4 through 10, suggesting the test shares some variance with visual perceptual skill. The low correlation of .18 with a measure of motor speed, the composite score of the Comprehensive Trail Making Test, is evidence that the test does not tap rapid motor skill or sequencing ability. Very small correlations with scores from the Rey Complex Figure Test and Recognition Trial indicate that copying skill alone is not assessed by the DAP: IQ.

The examiner's manual also presents data on subgroup performance. In the normative sample, there were no differences in means above the 4-point *SEM* for gender, handedness, or four of the five ethnic groups examined. However, the African American mean was 6 points below average. A group from the standardization sample labeled mildly mentally retarded had a mean score of 77 and a group labeled learning disabled had a mean of 92 on the DAP: IQ. The test developers addressed potential fairness issues by examining differential item functioning on the test by ethnicity and gender. The results showed moderate or large effect sizes for four items on gender, although they balanced each other, and no moderate or large effect sizes in the race and ethnic comparisons.

COMMENTARY. Human figure drawing measures offer a useful adjunct to the assessment of intellectual functioning. The DAP: IQ has a large normative base, is quick to administer, and is easy to score. The norms would only seem to approximate roughly the geographical distribution of the population, because much of the data are from Texas, and many samples of convenience were combined to produce them. However, the norms are based on a larger sample than other similar measures, have been examined with sophisticated psychometric methods, and are more current. Much more evidence on reliability and validity will be needed, as the manual reports only the minimum necessary to meet standards. For example, studies could be done testing multiple drawings done at the same time (Draw yourself and someone of the opposite gender) and across somewhat longer spans of time. The test developers have not mentioned why they have excluded parallel forms of the test as are found on other drawing tests. Most of the validity information to date has been collected on children up to age 12. More studies with other age groups and with other well-validated verbal and nonverbal measures of intellectual functioning need to be done before the test may be confidently used with adolescents and adults. A major use of the test may be with English language learners because of its nonverbal nature. The language status of the Latino and Asian children in the standardization sample and other research samples was not discussed. Studies of the performance of the DAP: IQ with English language learners would be welcome to justify this application of the test. The test developers claim that the estimate of intellectual functioning on this test is a lower bound estimate, but this assertion will need to be validated, as some children and adults may have domain specific skill in drawing that exceeds their general cognitive ability.

SUMMARY. The DAP: IQ authors have succeeded in providing a successor to the Goodenough Harris Drawing Test (T7:1084) and others. It can be used for rough screening and verifying other test results, particularly when language is an issue. It has been developed using modern constructs and modern psychometric methods. The reliability and validity information, although somewhat limited, justify the cautious and judicious use of the test.

[60]

Dutch Eating Behaviour Questionnaire.

Purpose: Assesses "the structure of an individual's eating behaviour."

Population: Ages 9 to adult.

Publication Date: 2002.

Acronym: DEBQ.

Scores, 3: Emotional Eating, External Eating, Restrained Eating.

Administration: Individual.

Price Data, 2006: £87 per complete kit including manual (24 pages), questionnaire, and 25 scoring sheets; £47 per 50 questionnaires and scoring sheets.

Foreign Language Editions: German, French, Swedish, Portugese, Chinese, Greek, and Korean editions available.

Time: (10) minutes.

Author: Tatjana van Strien.

Publisher: Harcourt Assessment [England].

Review of the Dutch Eating Behaviour Questionnaire by ROBERT CHRISTOPHER, Professional, Clinical, and Forensic Assessments, LLC, Sparks, NV:

DESCRIPTION. The Dutch Eating Behaviour Questionnaire (DEBQ) is an instrument that consists of 33 items scored on a 5-point Likert scale. The DEBQ can be given in both individual and group settings with the total administration time of approximately 10 minutes. On one side of the scoring sheet demographic data are collected including name, sex, and age, along with data pertaining to body weight, height, weight history, and patterns of breaking eating restraints. On the other side of the answer sheet, raw scores are obtained by totaling answers to 33 test items with response choices "Never," "Rarely," "Sometimes," "Often," and "Very often."

Items are categorized into five scales and the scoring transparency categorizes scales membership for each item. The five scales are: Emotional Eating (13 items), Emotional Eating—diffuse emotions (4 items), Emotional Eating—clearly labeled emotions (9 items), External Eating (10 items), and Restrained Eating (10 items). A score for each scale is obtained by dividing the raw scale score by a total number of items endorsed on that scale. Classification of each scale score is derived by comparing it to the tables for each scale developed from scores compiled from normative samples. Classifications are: Very High, High, Above Mean, At the Mean, Below the Mean, Low, and Very Low. Classification is dependent upon the category of the normative sample to which the respondent belongs. Categories of normative samples include: female obese patients, female readers of a Dutch magazine "Margriet," sportswomen, female dancers, high school boys, nonpatient obese females, restricting anorexia nervosa patients, bulimic anorexia nervosa patients, patients with bulimia nervosa, and patients with binge eating disorder.

DEVELOPMENT. The theoretical foundation of the Dutch Eating Behaviour Questionnaire (DEBQ) is derived from three psychological frameworks of eating disorder: the psychosomatic theory, the externality theory, and the restraint theory. The psychosomatic theory postulates that for some individuals emotional arousal such as anger, fear, anxiety, or stress will result either in loss of appetite, decreased eating, and weight loss, or an excessive intake of food. This behavior is labeled emotional eating and is generally caused by a lack of somatosensory awareness. Individuals characterized by this theoretical framework do not successfully identify the source and nature of their affective discomfort and are most likely to manifest either excessive or diminished eating habits. Specific therapeutic recommendations discussed in the manual focus on development of insight into psychological correlates of their eating behaviors such as identification of impulses, feelings, and needs, rather than directly on weight loss or gain.

The second component of the DEBQ's theoretical framework emphasizes external environmental determinants as primary causes of disturbances in eating behavior such as heightened sensitivity to sight, smell, and other food-related cues. Treatment focus with this type of individual would be on modification of eating behaviors, such as eating at the same time and place, eating slowly, taking small bites, and avoiding places with tempting cue exposure.

The third theoretical component emphasizes the restraint or attempt to preserve body-weight ratio. Potential disturbances in the ratio may evoke physiological defenses such as an arousal of sensation of hunger. Disinhibition of self-control over body-weight ratio results in disturbances in eating habits. Treatment focus would be on relearning sensations of hunger and satiety and developing an acceptable degree of comfort with one's weight.

The DEBQ's initial item pool of 100 items was chosen from several other instruments, based on the items' relatedness to the theoretical framework of the DEBQ. Instruments from which items were initially derived included: The Eating Patterns Questionnaire (EPQ; Wollersheim, 1970), the Fragenbogen für Latente Adipositas (FLA; Pudel, Metzdorff, & Oetting, 1975), and the Eating Behavior Inventory (EBI; O'Neil et al., 1979). Items were translated into Dutch and initially administered to 120 subjects including overweight as well as normal weight male and female subjects. All items were rated on a Likert scale with response options of 1 = *never*, 2 = *seldom*, 3 = *sometimes*, 4 = *often*, and 5 = *very often*.

TECHNICAL. The manual reports significant correlations between emotional and external eating behaviors with emotional disturbances such as anxiety, depression, phobias, suicidal behaviors and ideation, sexual contacts, and intimate interpersonal relationships. Correlations with psychopathology included those with alexithymia, represented by uncertainty in accurate identification of visceral sensations related to hunger and satiety. Correlations with change in body mass, according to the manual, were reliable indicators of prediction of weight gain in men. Correlations between

DEBQ restraint scores and intake of fat and sugar were negative; significant positive correlations were found between restraint and magnitude of deviation from energy requirements.

COMMENTARY. One shortcoming of the DEBQ is that all normative samples utilized in the development were native to the Netherlands without cross-cultural considerations. This approach may assume that the findings relevant to the original normative sample would be valid for eating behaviors with other populations. Therefore, more detailed analyses of culture- and race-specific variations in eating behaviors need to be incorporated in this instrument's norms.

SUMMARY. The Dutch Eating Behaviour Questionnaire may have practical applications within the domains of behavioral health. One of its strengths is that it specifically addresses therapeutic interventions as related to each domain of the DEBQ: Emotional Eating, External Eating, and Restrained Eating. The manual points out that one of many possible reasons that various weight reduction programs have only temporary effects may be due to an absence of proper fit between treatment specificity and demographic variations among individuals, each requiring specific approaches to treatment in order to achieve more permanent results.

REVIEWER'S REFERENCES
O'Neil, P. H., Currey, H. S., Hirsch, A. A., Malcolm, R. J., Sexauer, J. D., Riddle, F. E., & Taylor, C. I. (1979). Development and validation of the Eating Behavior Inventory. *Journal of Behavioural Assessment, 1*, 123–132.
Pudel, V., Metzdorff, M., & Oetting, M. (1975). Zur Persönlichkeit Adipöser in psychologischen Tests unter Berücksichtigung latent Fettsüchtiger. *Zeitschrift für Psychosomatische Medizin und Psychoanalyse, 21*, 345–362.
Wollersheim, J. P. (1970). Effectiveness of group therapy based upon learning principles in the treatment of overweight women. *Journal of Abnormal Psychology, 78*, 462–474.

[61]

Dyslexia Early Screening Test [Second Edition].

Purpose: "Designed to pick out children who are 'at risk' of reading failure early enough to allow them to be given extra support at school."

Population: 4 years, 6 months to 6 years, 5 months.

Publication Dates: 1996–2004.

Acronym: DEST-2.

Scores, 13: Tests of Attainment (Digit Naming, Letter Naming), Diagnostic Tests (Rapid Naming, Bead Threading, Phonological Discrimination, Postural Stability, Rhyme/First Letter, Forwards Digit Span, Sound Order, Shape Copying, Corsi Frog, Vocabulary), At Risk Quotient.

Administration: Individual.

Price Data, 2006: £125 per complete kit including examiner's manual (2004, 106 pages), envelope 1 (containing 7 subtest cards and sample permission letter), envelope 2 (containing score keys), Forward Digit Span tape, Sound Order tape, Corsi Frog, beads, cord, blindfold, balance tester, scoring software with manual, and 50 score sheets in a carrying case; £83 per upgrade kit including examiner's manual, envelope 1 (containing 7 subtest cards and sample permission letter), envelope 2 (containing score keys), Corsi Frog, scoring software with manual, and 50 score sheets in carrying case; £24.50 per manual; £38.50 per 50 score sheets.
Time: (30) minutes.
Authors: Rod I. Nicolson and Angela J. Fawcett.
Publisher: Harcourt Assessment [England].
Cross References: For reviews by Kathleen M. Johnson and William K. Wilkinson of the earlier edition, see 15:88.

Review of The Dyslexia Early Screening Test [Second Edition] by LORRAINE CLEETON, Faculty Mentor in the Ph.D. Program in Education, Walden University, Minneapolis, MN:

DESCRIPTION. The Dyslexia Early Screening Test, [Second Edition] has evolved from the Dyslexia Early Screening Test (DEST) first published in 1996. The authors advise early identification of possible slow learners and potential dyslexic children around ages 5 or 6 but do not describe the distinction of identifying the slow learner as opposed to the potential dyslexic child. They also do not cite the specific research to support the early age identification.

The Dyslexia Early Screening Test (DEST) was specifically designed to detect children who were "at risk" of reading failure at the 2-year age group between ages 4 years, 6 months and 6 years, 5 months. The DEST and DEST-2 can be used by teachers, special needs coordinators, or school nurses instead of educational psychologists. In the U.K. the DEST has had an effect on the early identification of dyslexia as acknowledged in the Code of Practice for Special Educational Needs (Department for Education and Skills, 2001).

The DEST-2 enables the teacher to know whether a further full assessment by school or educational psychologists is necessary; it provides a profile of strengths and weaknesses that can be the starting point for charting the child's development and initiating additional in-school support. The DEST-2, as compared to the DEST, enabled the test authors to evaluate the strengths and weaknesses of the DEST. They found that

the DEST seemed to be very effective in early identification, especially in introducing the category of "mild risk." Also, an area omitted from the DEST, was a test of visual skills as noted by the teachers involved in the original study. The authors have added a test of visual skills for the second edition, taken from the companion test, the PREST (Fawcett, Nicholson, & Lee, 2001), and normed for the older age group. Also, included is a test of receptive vocabulary modified from the British Picture Vocabulary Scales (BPVS). The norming process is not described for either test. Administration time of either the DEST or DEST-2 is approximately 30 minutes.

DEVELOPMENT. The DEST originally consisted of 10 subtests (2 tests of attainment, "Digit Naming" and "Letter Naming," and 8 diagnostic tests related to phonological processing [e.g., Sequencing Sounds], motor skills [e.g., Threading Beads, Postural Stability], and Memory Ability [e.g., Sound Order]). The two new tests known as Test 11–Corsi Frog and Test 12–Vocabulary are explained in terms of content and administration in the manual. The former is a test of spatial memory using a card and a plastic toy frog in which the tester demonstrates the frog jumping from water to a specific lily pad and back to start. The child is supposed to copy the demonstration of the presenter. Scoring of the Corsi Frog is 1 mark for each correct jump, and a mark is given only if the full sequence (e.g., 5,3,7) is correct (maximum 14).

The Vocabulary test is designed to be administered on a group basis or one-on-one administration. Children aged 6+ should be able to complete this task in a class, but younger children aged 4 and 5 or children with special needs might need a small-group setting. The authors state that receptive vocabulary skills might indicate the need for remediation and give teachers additional help in the development of an Individual Education Plan (IEP). This test is designed to measure receptive vocabulary in a multiple-choice format. Some questions included reasoning ability. The scoring of the Vocabulary test is 1 mark for each correct answer.

For the DEST-2, the intercorrelations for the Corsi Frog and Vocabulary tests were taken from a small sample of 30 children. The composition of this group is not described.

TECHNICAL DATA.

The construct validity of the DST (Dyslexia Screening Test) in diagnosing dyslexia in older children is used to compare the construct validity of the DEST-2, inasmuch as they both follow a very similar format. The DST has been well validated (a panel of 17 previously diagnosed dyslexic children and 20 control children were tested with it and all except 2 were correctly classified). The construct validity of the DST therefore provides further convergent evidence as to the construct validity of the DEST-2 because both tests measure the same set of skills including phonological and cerebellar skills. The test authors assume that the DEST-2 has similar construct validity as the DST.

The reliability of the DEST was assessed by one administration of the test on separate occasions about a week apart to groups of children aged 5 years, 5 months to 6 years, 5 months. In total, 26 children participated and all tests showed a significant test-retest correlation at least at the .001 probability level. The Corsi Frog and Vocabulary tests show a significant test-retest correlation at least at the .01 probability level based on the participation of 21 children but their ages are not given. The test authors state, without evidence or support, that reliability might have been increased if the samples included larger numbers and more age groups. Also, in line with the WISC–III U.K., it is advised not to give the DEST-2 twice within a 6-month period.

The interrater reliability of the DEST-2 was not included as the authors stated that most of the subtests were fully objective and there was little or no chance of possible differences in interpretation between different testers. Because there were two new tests introduced subsequent to the publication of the DEST, interrater reliability should have been included.

The DEST–2 case study provided in the manual gives a completed response sheet of all the tests and an interpretation of the scores and profile and possible remedial action. Administration of the DEST or DEST-2 is approximately 30 minutes each. DEST-2 computer software allows the tester to enter the scores and generate the At Risk Quotient (ARQ) report and profile for each child tested. In terms of the interpretation of the profile, the authors have modified the ARQ in line with the findings of their validation studies (some teachers had concerns regarding the DEST that the ARQ might be used to support an all-or-none approach to dyslexia, in which a child with an

ARQ of 1.0 is investigated further and a child with an ARQ of .9 is not). The DEST-2 includes a classification of "mild risk" with an ARQ of .6–.8, a modification of strong risk to .9, in line with the author's validation study, which is described in the manual.

The authors highlighted the significance of individual subtests in line with recent research findings and provided some information on the use of the DEST-2 with other learning disabilities. Their findings were that dyslexic children will normally score poorly on phonological skill, motor skill/balance, and rapid naming compared to children with general learning difficulties scoring normally on balance, but showing speed deficits. These data were derived from the authors' blind study in a unit for children with special educational needs, which included both children with low IQ and those only with dyslexia. The authors did not indicate the number of children in the study with and without dyslexia.

The 65-page manual of the DEST, which included the detailed administration and scoring instruction of each instrument, has been extended to 106 pages for the DEST-2. The latter includes a case study that provides a detailed examination of a student's scores and explanations and possible remediation. This material is very helpful to the special educator.

SUMMARY. The DEST was based on the fact that few studies assessed performance of dyslexic children and normal children matched for IQ and age on this range of tasks. The authors assessed the relative impairments on a whole range of tasks and established that it was possible to provide a simple index that was sufficient to dissociate the dyslexic from the nondyslexic child. This index was derived by combining indications of difficulties in phonological skill, balance, and speed of processing. This finding provided the basis of the DEST. In the DEST-2, the authors incorporated the established literature on visual difficulties and have included a test of visuospatial memory, designed to tap this aspect of dyslexic impairment. The authors consider that all aspects of the dyslexic deficit have been covered with this addition. In adding the test of receptive vocabulary and spatial memory the authors do not go into the research supporting these additions. Also, the authors state that using the DEST-2 provides information that may be used to distinguish between dyslexia and other learning disabilities but such diagnoses are not definitive and give the special educator little confidence in using the DEST-2 to make the distinction.

REVIEWER'S REFERENCES

Department for Education and Skills. (2001). *Special Educational Needs Code of Practice* (DFES Publication No. 581).
Fawcett, A., Nicholson, R., & Lee, R. (2001). Pre-School Screening Test. London: Harcourt Assessment.

Review of the Dyslexia Early Screening Test [Second Edition] by KATHARINE SNYDER, Associate Professor of Psychology, Methodist College, Fayetteville, NC:

DESCRIPTION. The Dyslexia Early Screening Test [Second Edition] (DEST-2) is a quick measure, composed of 12 subtests, for educators to identify children (4 years, 6 months to 6 years, 5 months of age) reportedly in danger of developing reading difficulties and in need of professional evaluation. Subtests include the following: Rapid Naming (speed of picture identification), Bead Threading, Phonological Discrimination (determining whether word pairs, such as pat and bat, are the same or different), Postural Stability (subjective ratings of the effect of small lower back pushes, using an included device, ranging from "rock solid" to "marked loss of balance"), Rhyme/First Letter Identification, Forwards Digit Span, Digit Naming, Letter Naming, Sound Order, Shape Copying, Corsi Frog (spatial memory), and Vocabulary.

At-risk categories for each subtest are as follows: "- -" for percentile 1–10, "-" for percentile 11–25, "O" for percentile 26–75, "+" for percentile 76–90, and "++" for percentiles above 90. An overall At-Risk Quotient (ARQ) is derived by multiplying the number of subtests receiving "- -" scores by two, then adding the number achieving "-" scores, and finally dividing by the total number of subtests administered. Authors recommend audiology and optometric testing. An ARQ of .9 or greater is considered "strong risk," whereas an ARQ of .6–.8 is considered "mild risk."

DEVELOPMENT. New to the second edition are the Corsi Frog and Vocabulary subtests as well as the "mild risk" category. Subtests are chosen primarily by their relationship to other measures (e.g., Nathlie Badian battery) and educational policy within the United Kingdom. Minimal discussion about the relationship of the measure to the concept of dyslexia is provided. Authors mention that the DEST-2 should not serve a diagnos-

tic function, yet references to dyslexia classification are numerous. Many items within the 12 subtests are adaptations of other measures, yet little discussion is offered as to why some items were selected but not others. The Corsi Frog subtest is reportedly added to assess visual perceptual skills, but seems more adequately a measure of spatial memory. A Vocabulary subtest was added as a "test of attainment," yet evaluators should be aware that this and several other subtests reach ceilings quickly, particularly for the upper age intervals.

TECHNICAL: STANDARDIZATION. Because norms accrue from a sample limited in size and representativeness, generalization of some items is unclear. For instance, a picture of a two-story bus is a test item that children in some countries may have never seen. Over 1,400 children from schools in Sheffield, England and Wales constituted the normative sample. No description of representativeness in terms of gender, race, socioeconomic status, parental education, or early educational experience is provided.

TECHNICAL: RELIABILITY. Reliability assessments are based on limited test-retest and interrater methods. The DEST-2 was given twice, with approximately 1 week between, to 26 children (no demographic characteristics are provided). Coefficients were .87 for Digit and Letter Naming; over .80 for Shape Copying, Postural Stability, and Rhyme/First Letter; .70 or above for Bead Threading and Rapid Naming; and .60 or above for Digit Span, Sound Order, and Phonological Discrimination. Test-retest coefficients were also calculated for 21 children (no further description is provided) receiving the new subtests, Corsi Frog (.548) and Vocabulary (.596). Test-retest information for ARQ scores is not provided. Videotapes of 14 children undergoing Postural Stability testing were shown to two "experienced testers" (.98 correlation) and one "inexperienced tester" (.94 correlation). Further assessment of interrater agreement would be useful, especially on the Shape Copying subtest. Intercorrelation data among the subtests are provided, but no interpretation is given to these values. The following intercorrelations were above the .60 level: Phonological Discrimination correlated with Digit Naming (.627), Sound Order (.619), and age (.684); Rhyming correlated with Digit Naming (.602) and Letter Naming (.687); Digit Naming correlated with Letter Naming

(.711), Sound Order (.643), and age (.657); and Sound Order correlated with age (.645). Reliability problems could result from the small number of items in each subtest. Salvia and Ysseldyke (2007) stress the importance of higher reliability standards for measures used extensively in educational decisions.

TECHNICAL: VALIDITY. For tests aimed at identifying children at risk of developing reading difficulties, predictive validity is most imperative. Ninety-seven children in Sheffield were given the DEST (M = 5.4 years) and retested (M = 7.9 years) with the Wechsler Oral Reading Dimensions (WORD). No further sample details are provided. Twenty children exhibited a 1-year WORD discrepancy, 15 of which had ARQs of 1.0 or higher (DEST standard) and 18 of which had ARQs of .9 or higher (DEST-2 standard). A phonetics and word building intervention study was undertaken with 62 children (no demographic characteristics are provided). Exact means and standard deviations are not provided. A graph with large variance bars and relatively small visually derived mean differences (e.g., approximately 89 at pretest and 93 at posttest for the reading training group) is given. Statistical and practical (e.g., Cohen's *d*) significance values are not discussed. Postintervention, children were assigned to problem reader (less than 6 months improvement), intermediate (no operational definition), or recovered reader (no reading age deficit) groups. Letter Names, Rhyme, Postural Stability, Rapid Naming, and Beads are reported to have the best prediction rates for problem and recovered readers. Of the 16 problem readers, 7 had DEST scores of .9 or worse.

Another intervention was carried out with 432 children in 11 schools. Of these, 90 were classified as at-risk and another 90 children were selected as controls (no further description is provided). Authors report that the DEST and the Wide Range Achievement Test 3 (WRAT 3) were successful predictors of at-risk (32nd reading percentile) and control (75th reading percentile) group membership in Year 1, Terms 1 through 3. Of the children labeled as at-risk on the DEST, 18% were reportedly above the 75th percentile on the WRAT 3 at Term 3. Nonbeneficiaries (children who do not benefit from early literacy intervention using phonologically based strategies) scored significantly lower than beneficiaries (those

who do benefit) on Phonological Discrimination (p = .01) and Postural Stability (p = .01).

Information on construct validity is very limited. A paragraph beginning with the sentence, "This is not the place to describe current theoretical views of dyslexia" (manual, p. 72) proceeds to describe how subtest selection is loosely related to three theories, one emphasizing phonological deficits, another auditory processing speed, and the third "automatising skills." Authors report that the DEST has much in common with Nathlie Badian's battery, but convergent and divergent validity data are not discussed. The Dyslexia Screening Test (DST) for older children is reportedly a companion test to the DEST-2. Authors state the following: "The construct validity of the DST therefore provides further convergent evidence as to the construct validity of the DEST-2, since both tests measure the same set of skills" (manual, p. 73).

COMMENTARY. Data collection is limited and more research is required to establish a clearer association to the concept of dyslexia. As previously noted, norms accrue from a limited sample and no information on representativeness is provided. Technically, the DEST-2 is poor in reliability and validity support. It would be particularly useful to have reliability information on the ARQ categories. It is unclear whether the addition of the mild risk category in the DEST-2 contributes to predictive validity. A chief obstacle is that this age group displays a great deal of variability on evaluations of this type, making prediction difficult, especially in brief inventories. Gauging potential difficulties early and intervening is a commendable purpose, which underlies the need for more preschool measures. However, the risk of remedial educational services being contingent upon labeling is that this may set up expectations that hamper subsequent accomplishments (Salvia & Ysseldyke, 2007). Authors state that the DEST-2 cannot be used for diagnostic purposes, yet references to dyslexia identification are frequently made.

Other features of the DEST-2 should be noted. As mentioned, some subtests reach ceilings rapidly for the upper age groups, leaving little range for variation. Little justification is provided for rhyming and first letter identification tasks constituting one score rather than two. Copying is subjectively rated (no length or angle specifications), and example scores are not given for one of the figures (the diamond). Administration instructions are highlighted in the manual, but it might be useful to have some directions and scoring guidelines on the profile form, perhaps as a second page, because record keeping is a proposed role of the DEST-2. For example, score categories on Postural Stability would be useful for those viewing the record without the manual (authors give permission to copy completed original record forms for parents, teachers, referrals, etc.). Although advocated that nonreply to the parental permission form be interpreted as parental consent, evaluators should be wary of even the most remote possibility of finding a "marked loss of balance" (manual, p. 16).

SUMMARY. The DEST-2 is a quick screening measure purporting to identify children at-risk of reading difficulties for early intervention and referral for formal testing. The measure is adequate for use by teachers to justify professional assessment. However, in agreement with prior reviews of the DEST (Johnson, 2003; Wilkinson, 2003), the DEST-2 does not offer much more than an experienced teacher could gain for documentation through informal and classroom means.

REVIEWER'S REFERENCES

Johnson, K. M. (2003). [Review of the Dyslexia Early Screening Test.] In B. S. Plake, J. C. Impara, & R. A. Spies (Eds.), *The fifteenth mental measurements yearbook* (pp. 338-340). Lincoln, NE: Buros Institute of Mental Measurements.
Salvia, J., & Ysseldyke, J. E. (2007). *Assessment in special and inclusive education* (10th ed.). Boston: Houghton Mifflin.
Wilkinson, W. K. (2003). [Review of the Dyslexia Early Screening Test.] In B. S. Plake, J. C. Impara, & R. A. Spies (Eds.), *The fifteenth mental measurements yearbook* (pp. 340-342). Lincoln, NE: Buros Institute of Mental Measurements.

[62]

Early Literacy Skills Assessment.

Purpose: "Designed to provide preschool programs and teachers with an authentic and meaningful way to assess young children's early literacy skills."
Population: Ages 3–5 years.
Publication Dates: 2005–2007.
Acronym: ELSA.
Scores: 12 scores in 4 areas: Comprehension (Prediction, Retelling, Connection to Real Life), Phonological Awareness (Rhyming, Segmentation, Phonemic Awareness), Alphabetic Principle (Sense of Word, Alphabet Letter Recognition, Letter-Sound Correspondence), Concepts About Print (Orientation, Story Beginning, Direction of Text).
Administration: Individual.
Price Data, 2006: $149.95 per complete kit including 2 copies of *Violet's Adventure* or *Dante Grows Up*, user guide (48 pages), 60 score sheets, 60 Child Summary forms, 12 Class Summary forms, and 60 Family Report forms; $199.95 per Spanish version complete kit including 2 copies of *La Aventura de Violeta* or *El Combio en Dante*, user guide, 60 score sheets, 60 Child Summary forms, 12 Class Summary forms, and 60 Family Report forms; $39.95 per *Violet's Adventure* or *La Aventura de Violeta*; $39.95 per *Dante Grows Up* or *El Cambio en Dante*; $84.95 per DVD Scoring the ELSA: Establishing Reliability.
Foreign Language Edition: Spanish edition (2006) available.
Time: (15–20) minutes; (20–25) minutes for Spanish edition.
Author: Andrea DeBruin-Parecki.
Publisher: High/Scope Educational Research Foundation.

Review of the Early Literacy Skills Assessment by RICK EIGENBROOD, Assistant Dean for Graduate Studies and Assessment, Seattle Pacific University, Seattle, WA:

DESCRIPTION. The Early Literacy Skills Assessment (ELSA) is a criterion-referenced test for use with children ages 3 years, 0 months through 5 years, 11 months. The test is relatively short (15–20 minutes) and is designed to assess early literacy skills believed to be associated with later reading achievement. The manual states that it is designed to be an authentic assessment.

Testing is done individually by reading with the child one of two children's books during which the person administering the test asks the student questions, which are embedded in the text as part of the story. The content areas tested are Comprehension—Prediction (4 items), Retelling (2 items), Connection to Life (2 items), Phonological Awareness—Rhyming (2 items), Segmentation (1 item), Phonemic Awareness (1 item), Alphabetic Principle—Uppercase Letter Recognition (1 item), Lowercase Letter Recognition (1 item), Letter Sounds (1 item), Sense of Word (1 item), Concepts about Print—Book Orientation (1 item), Story Start (1 item), Direction of Text (left to right and top to bottom; 1 item each), Front and Back Covers (1 item each), and Title (1 item).

Raw scores are used to determine a single developmental level for three skill areas (Comprehension, Phonological Awareness, Concepts about Print) as Early Emergent-Exploration (Level 1), Emergent–Awareness (Level 2), or Competent Emergent–Application (Level 3). In the case of Alphabetic Principle the four items have multiple parts, and each of the four items is used to determine a development level for each subarea, plus an overall developmental level.

According to the ELSA manual, the test is primarily to be used to assess the early literacy skills of young children (ages 3–5). Results may be used to plan instruction for all young children, but especially those using the "Growing Readers Early Literacy Curriculum" (High/Scope Educational Research Foundation, 2005). In addition, scoring and summary sheets allow practitioners to create a class summary that can be used for program evaluation in addition to individual growth assessment. Test items are individually administered while reading one of two children's books with the child—*Violet's Adventure* or *Dante Grows Up*. Both books are also available in Spanish. While reading one of the books with the child, test items are individually administered by asking the child to respond verbally or perform a task (e.g., "show me the front cover of the book"). Instructions for item administration and scoring appear clearly explained.

The test manual does not identify any specific qualification about which professionals should administer the test except that the tester should be familiar with the story and the way the questions fit into the narrative of the story. It is suggested that the test should be administered by the child's teacher or other adult familiar to the child. Instructions for administering the test are clearly presented in the manual, and scripted questions are provided in the storybook. Although the manual states that the tester should not "give hints or prompts other than the ones provided as part of the assessment" (p. 4), the tester has somewhat more flexibility in administering the test than is typical for most traditional standardized tests by allowing some rephrasing of the questions, nor are there any time limits for responses.

DEVELOPMENT. To determine the ELSA's psychometric properties, a pilot study was conducted with a convenience sample of 630 children (ages 3–5) in 31 classrooms in Florida (10 classrooms), Maine (9 classrooms), and Michigan (21 classrooms). There was no discussion of item selection. Demographic data for the pilot study indicated a disproportionately high number of students with special needs (23.7%). The manual also states that there were statistically significant differences in special needs, ages, and previous preschool experiences across the three states used in the pilot study. For example, 40% of

the children in Florida were identified as having special needs.

Regarding the theoretical grounding for the test, the manual discusses only in a limited manner the relationship of the four content areas assessed to those that have been identified as crucial skills for early literacy. Although the manual refers to early literacy principles in the federal No Child Left Behind Act (U.S. Department of Education, 2002), the National Reading Panel (2000), and the National Early Literacy Panel (Strickland & Shanahan, 2004), there is virtually no description of how the four areas assessed by the ELSA correspond to the above noted principles. The theoretical and practical utility of the instrument is based on the assumption that the skills assessed by the ELSA are important for later academic success.

TECHNICAL. General information about the norming process was inadequate, and limited to a brief description of the convenience sample of 31 classrooms in Florida, Maine, and Michigan. There was no discussion of how the sample was selected. The ELSA manual presents demographic information for the 630 children used as the standardization sample. The sample was comparable to that of the U.S. population for gender and race/ethnicity. The ELSA manual states that there were statistically significant differences across the three states for age and the percentage of students with special needs. Descriptive data such as score means and variance are not reported in the manual.

ELSA subscale internal consistency coefficients were computed by administering the test to all subjects in the pilot sample during the fall and the spring (both samples between 500–600 test takers). Alpha coefficients ranged from .57 for Phonological Awareness in the fall to .83 for Comprehension in the spring. However, the manual states that if the Phonological Awareness area was examined at the subscale item level, the corresponding reliability coefficients were much higher (.85 and .88). The reliability coefficients were higher for each of the subscales for the spring administration for each of the four areas with large differences for Comprehension (.69–.83) and Phonological Awareness (.57–.67). Such large differences between the fall and spring should raise concern about the stability of the instrument, especially because no other data are reported to support the stability of the test. If the ELSA is to be used primarily as a screening tool for the purpose of instructional planning as the authors recommend, then the derived reliability coefficients are generally acceptable (Salvia & Ysseldyke, 2004).

Evidence to support the validity of the ELSA is sparse. First, the authors vaguely discuss the instrument's content validity in terms of how the four areas assessed are linked to scientifically based research literature. Unfortunately, no specific analysis of this research base is presented beyond that discussed previously in this review's theoretical basis. There was no discussion in the manual of how the items were selected or whether the items were submitted for external expert analysis. In brief, the evidence for the ELSA's content validity is limited.

The manual also fails to establish the ELSA's criterion-related validity. Even though concurrent validity between the ELSA and the Get Ready to Read! Screening Tool (GRR; Whitehurst & Lonigan, 2001) was reported at the moderate to high level for three of the four scales (there was not a significant correlation with the comprehension scale), the authors omitted essential background information discussed in Salvia and Ysseldyke (2004). For instance, the criterion measure (GRR) was not well described and the rationale for its selection was not made explicit. Additionally, concurrent validity was only provided for one of the two story books used to assess children (*Violet's Adventure*), and the manual states that it was not possible to report any concurrent validity for Comprehension because no acceptable criterion measures are available. The manual does not provide a thorough accounting of the statistical analyses used or a description of the sample examined.

Evidence of construct validity is primarily based on a factor analysis of the ELSA items (Varimax solution) using data from the spring administration of the pilot group. There is strong evidence that items that make up Comprehension, Phonological Awareness, and Alphabetic Principle areas are well matched to the appropriate constructs. However, the items in the Concepts about Print scale appear to represent two distinct factors, as acknowledged by the authors of the ELSA, who state that changes have been made to the instrument and that future research will likely indicate only four distinct factors. In addition to the factor analysis, the authors also report that

there were statistically significant differences in children's early literacy abilities, as measured by the ELSA, for age and disability status (typical vs. special needs), and that these differences should be considered evidence for the soundness of the underlying construct. In addition to factor analysis data provided in the manual, the authors do present additional factor analysis data in a supplemental technical manual. The confirmatory factor analysis data presented in this technical manual do support the construct validity of the ELSA model.

COMMENTARY. The usefulness of ELSA scores to estimate accurately early literacy skills must be downgraded for several reasons. First, the process of item selection is not discussed. Second, the measure's underlying construct(s) and its subcomponents (i.e., ELSA model) were not established in the research documented in the test manual nor by a solid corpus of previous empirical studies. Third, there were multiple areas of the test manual that were unclear, especially the more technical elements of the standardization process and the ELSA's psychometric properties.

SUMMARY. The ELSA is considered a criterion-referenced authentic assessment that can be efficiently used for instructional planning, especially when linked with the "Growing Readers Early Literacy Curriculum" (High/Scope Educational Research Foundation, 2005). The instrument can be administered and scored in a relatively efficient manner. However, the ELSA falls short of accepted professional and technical testing standards and cannot be recommended for use as a diagnostic tool, though it may be useful as a screening instrument.

REVIEWER'S REFERENCES
High/Scope Educational Research Foundation. (2005). *Growing readers early literacy curriculum.* Ypsilanti, MI: High/Scope Press.
National Reading Panel. (2000). *Teaching children to read: An evidence-based assessment of the scientific research literature on reading and its implications for reading instruction* (NIH Pub. No. 00-4754). Washington, DC: U.S. Department of Health and Human Services.
Salvia, J., & Ysseldyke, J. A. (2004). *Assessment: In special and inclusive education* (9th ed.). Boston, MA: Houghton Mifflin.
Strickland, D., & Shanahan, T. (2004). Laying the groundwork for literacy. *Educational Leadership, 61*(6), 74-77.
U.S. Department of Education. *No Child Left Behind Act of 2001.* Public Law (PL) 107–110 115 stat 1425 (08 January, 2002).
Whitehurst, G. J., & Lonigan, C. (2001). *Get ready to read! An early literacy manual: Screening tool, activities, and resources.* Washington, DC: National Center for Learning Disabilities.

[63]
Early Reading Success Indicator.

Purpose: "To identify children at risk for developing reading difficulties."
Population: Ages 5–10.

Publication Date: 2004.

Acronym: ERSI.

Scores: RAN-Letters, Phonological Processing, Speeded Naming, Word Reading, Pseudoword Decoding.

Administration: Individual.

Price Data, 2007: $69 per complete kit including manual (89 pages), stimulus book, 25 record forms, Pseudoword Decoding Card, and Word Reading Card; $30 for 25 record forms.

Time: (20–25) minutes.

Comments: A brief battery of cognitive tests composed of subtests selected from various products from this publisher: Process Assessment of the Learner: Test Battery for Reading and Writing (16:199), NEPSY: A Developmental Neuropsychological Assessment (T6:1696), and Wechsler Individual Achievement Test—Second Edition (15:275).

Authors: PsychCorp.

Publisher: The Psychological Corporation, A Harcourt Assessment Company.

Review of the Early Reading Success Indicator by JENNIFER N. MAHDAVI, Assistant Professor of Special Education, Sonoma State University, Rohnert Park, CA:

DESCRIPTION. The Early Reading Success Indicator (ERSI) is a standardized, norm-referenced measure designed to identify children who are at risk of developing reading difficulties. The manual clearly states that the ERSI is not meant to be used to diagnose a reading disorder, but that it can be one factor in a multidisciplinary assessment to determine whether reading skills are developing appropriately. Administration and interpretation of the test should be undertaken only by an individual with graduate-level training in psychological testing.

This test, for use with children in kindergarten through Grade 5 (ages 5 to 10), consists of five subtests: Rapid Automatic Naming-Letters, Phonological Processing, Speeded Naming, Word Reading, and Pseudoword Decoding. The subtests were drawn from three assessments published by Harcourt Assessment, Inc. The Process Assessment of the Learner: Test Battery for Reading and Writing (PAL-RW) was the source of RAN-Letters. Both Phonological Processing and Speeded Naming were pulled from the NEPSY: A Developmental Neuropsychological Assessment. The Wechsler Individual Achievement Test-Second Edition (WIAT-II) was the source of the final two subtests. Raw scores on each of these tests

were converted to age-based scaled scores with a mean of 10 and standard deviation of 3. Scoring the ERSI involves finding the age-based subtest scaled scores that correspond to raw scores using normative tables in the manual.

Test administration is described in the manual and stimulus book and more briefly within the protocol. An estimated length of the test period is not offered, but it does not appear to be a time-consuming measure. Because the subtests were drawn from three different published measures, the administration procedures differ slightly for each. Some have age- or grade-related starting points, others are simply timed. Discontinue rules are either 5 or 7 consecutive scores of 0, depending on a given subtest. Raw scores are recorded, but the manual does not make it clear that items that were not administered because they were below the starting point also should be counted as correct. Professionals administering the ERSI must read all the administration directions very carefully.

DEVELOPMENT. As mentioned above, the ERSI was developed by bringing together subtests from three previously available standardized assessments. As such, the method for developing items on each subtest is not described in this test manual, nor was the ERSI extensively pilot-tested.

The five subtests were selected to comprise the ERSI because they were, according to the manual, easy to administer and score, had the data necessary to convert the scores to a common scaled score metric, covered the age span desired, and were sensitive to reading difficulties. Also, all subtests were from larger tests offered by the same publisher.

A chapter of the manual offers an overview of reading research to support the ERSI construct. Brief statements related to the factors that lead to reading difficulties were made and sources cited. The factors were: genetic, sociodemographic, environmental, and personal. In addition, cognitive skills associated with reading difficulties were identified, including phonemic awareness and phonological processing, rapid automatic naming, working memory, and Verbal IQ, and were reviewed as were predictors of reading ability. The research review, although brief, connects reading success clearly to the ERSI and its subtests.

TECHNICAL.

Standardization. Because the ERSI is culled from three different assessments, there is not one norm sample that was used in standardizing the measure. The standardization of each of the three assessments, the PAL-RW, NEPSY, and WIAT-II, is described very briefly. For each assessment, the stratification of the norming sample by age, gender, ethnicity, and parent education level is described and appears to match U.S. Census data. Information about socioeconomic status and region is not included. However, special attention is paid to the proportion of the samples that had been identified as having reading difficulty or disorders. The standardization and norming of the ERSI appears to be appropriate for its intended population.

Reliability. Reliability coefficients, established in the standardization of the original measures, are provided for each subtest and each age range for the ERSI. The reliability coefficients are quite high, from .97–.99 on the WIAT-II subtests of Word Reading and Pseudoword decoding across the represented ages (5–10 years). The NEPSY Speeded Naming subtest had the lowest reliability scores, based on the generalizability coefficient, and ranged from a low of .62 for 9- and 10-year-olds, to a high of .86 for 7- and 8-year-olds. The NEPSY Phonological processing reliability coefficients ranged from .87–.93. The PAL-RW RAN-Letters reliability coefficients, using test-retest correlations, where the time interval was not provided, were uniformly .92. Although the Speeded Naming subtest appears to have moderate reliability, the ERSI as a whole would seem to be a reliable way of measuring components relevant to early reading ability.

Validity. The validity of the ERSI is well reported in the test manual. The stated purposes of the validation studies to evaluate the sensitivity of the ERSI to reading difficulties were: to differentiate children with or without reading difficulties, to correlate the ERSI subtests with the WIAT's measures of reading decoding and reading comprehension, and to identify children performing at different percentile ranks on the WIAT's measures of reading decoding and reading comprehension.

The RAN-Letters assessment had statistically significant, moderate correlations with WIAT-II Word Reading ($r = .40$) and Reading Comprehension ($r = .52$) subtests. Children with scaled scores of 7 or below typically also had standard scores of less than 90 on the WIAT tests.

The NEPSY tests of Phonological Processing and Speeded Naming were also validated against the WIAT reading subtests. Speeded Naming and WIAT Basic Reading were not significantly correlated, but other correlations were moderate and significant. As with RAN-Letters, if children scored below a scaled score of 7 on Speeded Naming or Phonological Processing, they were likely to also have received standard scores below 90 on the WIAT subtests.

Overall, the predictive and discriminant validity of the ERSI appear to be within appropriate limits. Each subtest is sensitive to reading difficulties. The manual also offers a section to help inform clinical decisions about whether a child needs reading intervention. This section discusses in depth how scaled scores on different subtests might be combined to select cutoff scores and identify children who are at-risk for reading failure.

COMMENTARY. The Early Reading Success Indicator is a theoretically sound and well-developed compilation of tests of early reading skills. It assesses prereading abilities of rapid naming and phonological awareness as well as the alphabetic principle. The connections between the ERSI and other well-known, well-developed tests are clear and consistent. The assessment is not lengthy and scoring procedures are simple. That the manual includes extensive information about how to identify children who might need additional intervention to develop reading skills is a strength. The ERSI is up-to-date and addresses new theories, research, and developments in the federal special education law, Individuals with Disabilities Education Act (IDEA), regarding how learning and reading disabilities will be diagnosed.

Because the five subtests have been selected from three different previously published assessments, the administration directions and rules for discontinuation vary across subtests. These differences may be confusing to people who use the ERSI rarely or who have not studied the manual carefully.

As a relatively brief measure of skills necessary for early reading ability that can easily be used with common assessments, such as the WIAT II and the Wechsler Intelligence Scales for Children-Fourth Edition, the ERSI provides valuable information to a multidisciplinary assessment team who is working to identify and remediate weakness in reading. The ERSI can also serve as a beneficial measure in research studies about reading.

SUMMARY. The Early Reading Success Indicator is a useful addition to the collection of standardized, norm-referenced assessments of reading ability. It is an indicator of what weaknesses a child might exhibit in different early reading skills. It may not be the most specific indicator of what precise weaknesses a child has, but it can help educational professionals decide what skills to probe more deeply for the purpose of establishing an intervention plan.

Review of the Early Reading Success Indicator by DIANE J. SAWYER, Murfree Professor of Dyslexic Studies, Middle Tennessee State University, Murfreesboro, TN:

DESCRIPTION. The Early Reading Success Indicator (ERSI) is a brief battery of tests, in five categories, intended to assess the likelihood that students, ages 5–10, are at-risk of experiencing difficulty in reading acquisition. The publisher indicates that the battery of tests should be considered a screening tool or indicator of increased risk rather than a tool to diagnose a reading difficulty.

The test is composed of subtests or tasks intended to assess components of word reading efficiency and reading difficulty. These include RAN-Letters–two sets of stimuli for naming letters and letter pairs; Phonological Processing—(a) recognition of a spoken segment of a word represented by a picture and (b) phoneme deletion and phoneme replacement in spoken words; Speeded Naming-rate and accuracy in naming sequences of shapes in different sizes and colors; Word Reading—naming printed letters and words; and Pseudoword Decoding—reading printed nonwords. Pseudoword Decoding is administered only to ages 8–10. All other tasks may be administered to ages 5–10.

Scoring and interpretation. Total raw scores for each subtest are converted to scaled scores using tables provided in the manual. Criteria for interpretation are provided on the inside cover of the record form for ages 5–7 and 8–10. "The criteria used by the ERSI for identifying children at risk for reading difficulties are scores from the Word Reading (for ages 5–10) and Reading Comprehension (for ages 8–10) subtests of the Wechsler Individual Achievement Test–Second Edition (WIAT-II, The Psychological Corporation, 2002)" (scoring and interpretation manual, p. 3). Information is also provided to augment the diagnostic potential of the ERSI by integrating interpretation of ERSI scores with subtest and full scale scores on the Wechsler Intelligence Scale for Children-Fourth Edition (WISC-IV).

DEVELOPMENT. The publisher states that the ERSI is designed for students in Grades K–5 (ages 5–10). The cognitive tests included in the battery were chosen because research has shown they relate to reading and measure skills known to be relevant to early reading skills.

The ERSI subtests were taken from other tests previously published by Harcourt Assessment, Inc.: Process Assessment of the Learner: Test Battery for Reading and Writing (2001); NEPSY: A Developmental Neuropsychological Assessment (1998); the Wechsler Individual Achievement Test, Second Edition (2002). The publisher provides brief descriptions of the original test batteries, their norming samples, and any adjustments made to the original scores for use in the ERSI.

TECHNICAL. The publisher offers fairly detailed descriptions of the validity studies for each ERSI subtest as these studies were performed with the original test battery from which each was drawn. The samples referenced were relatively small (i.e., 83 children ages 5–10 with a reading disability in one study of the RAN-Letters subtest, 83 controls and 2 children with a reading disability in a second study; 36 and 38 individuals included in studies of Phonological Processing and Speeded Naming respectively). No independent assessment of reliability for the ERSI battery is reported. Inferences (estimates) of being at-risk are based upon conversions of raw scores to scaled scores. Scaled scores are the result of corrections for age formulas applied to the scores originally developed for the source or parent test.

Users of the ERSI are encouraged to establish a criterion or cutoff score that best fits the individual school situation. The rationale offered is that school resources (limited or not) and socioeconomic status of the student body (high or low) could influence the degree of being at-risk a school chooses to address. To accommodate these differences in identification goals, the publisher provides tables of criterion standard score equivalents for each subtest and the relative likelihood (percent of cases identified) of a reading impairment in word reading or reading comprehension at the 5th, 9th, 16th, and 25th percentiles. For example, a cutoff standard score of 7 or less on the RAN-Letters subtest could be expected to identify 67% of students at the 5th percentile but only 57% of students at the 25th percentile on Word Reading performance.

COMMENTARY. All claims for the utility of the battery as a screening tool for the early identification of students at-risk of reading difficulty rest on two principal elements: (a) the body of research that supports the significance of the tasks comprising this battery, to success in word reading and, subsequently, to reading comprehension; (b) the concurrent validity of each subtest as assessed when the test batteries from which they were drawn were being developed. No specific studies of the validity or reliability of the battery of tests newly configured into the ERSI are reported. Estimates of degree of being at-risk are based on the "standardization sample and L.D. cases" for the RAN-Letters (scoring and interpretation manual, p. 60) or on "combined standardization and reading disorder sample" for Phonological Processing and Speeded Naming subtests or both combined (scoring and interpretation manual, pp. 61–63). As noted earlier, the validity samples specifically associated with the subtests in the ERSI appear to have been quite small and could not support a claim of representing students in the 5–10-year age range nationally.

SUMMARY. The ERSI is a battery of tests intended to help schools screen for students in Grades K–5 who may be at-risk for reading difficulty. The tasks are well documented in research for their relevance to beginning reading and the early stages of skilled reading. However, the tasks are imported from three different previously published tests normed on three different norming samples in different years. The reported sample sizes specifically related to the three early predictor tasks–RAN-Letters, Phonological Processes, and Speeded Naming—are small and cannot reasonably be described as representative of the population. This concern significantly compromises the validity of the estimates of the percent of those who may be at-risk when specific cutoff scores (standard scores from the previously published tests now corrected for age) are considered.

The principal value of the ERSI perhaps stems from the explicit alignment of phonological processes and speed of letter naming on one hand with subsequent achievement in word reading on

the other. Further, the inclusion of a speeded naming task provides an entré for consideration of rapid retrieval of familiar information from long-term memory, early on, as a possible contributor to reading difficulties that is independent of skills specifically related to word reading.

The ERSI offers a research-based supportive framework for understanding some of the important elements that support reading acquisition. Identification of those who might be at-risk of low achievement, in the opinion of this reviewer, is not well supported due to the absence of an independent assessment of the reliability and validity of the ERSI. Such a study should involve a large national sample of students, ages 5–10, representing the demographics typical of U.S. schools currently.

[64]

Eating Disorder Inventory-3.

Purpose: Designed to "provide a standardized clinical evaluation of symptomology associated with eating disorders."

Publication Dates: 1984–2004.

Acronym: EDI-3.

Administration: Group.

Price Data, 2007: $246 per introductory kit including professional manual (2004, 223 pages), referral form manual (2004, 36 pages), 25 item booklets, 25 answer sheets, 25 percentile/T-score profile forms, 25 symptom checklists, and 25 referral forms; $260 per CD-ROM based scoring program.

Author: David M. Garner.

Publisher: Psychological Assessment Resources, Inc.

a) EATING DISORDER INVENTORY-3.

Population: Females ages 13 to 53 years.

Scores, 21: 6 composite scores (Eating Disorder Risk Composite, Ineffectiveness Composite, Interpersonal Problems Composite, Affective Problems Composite, Overcontrol Composite, General Psychological Maladjustment Composite), 12 primary scores (Drive for Thinness, Bulimia, Body Dissatisfaction, Low Self-Esteem, Personal Alienation, Interpersonal Insecurity, Interpersonal Alienation, Interoceptive Deficits, Emotional Dysregulation, Perfectionism, Asceticism, Maturity Fears), 3 response style indicators (Inconsistency, Infrequency, Negative Impression).

Time: (20) minutes.

Comments: Full battery.

b) EATING DISORDER INVENTORY-3 REFERRAL FORM.

Population: Adolescents and adults ages 13 and older.

Acronym: EDI-3 RF.
Scores, 4: Drive for Thinness, Bulimia, Body Dissatisfaction, BMI.
Time: (10) minutes.
Comments: Abbreviated referral form of Eating Disorder Inventory-3 "used to identify individuals who are at risk for eating disorders."
c) EATING DISORDER INVENTORY-3 SYMPTOM CHECKLIST.
Population: Adolescents and adults.
Acronym: EDI-3 SC.
Scores: Frequency ratings.
Time: (10) minutes.
Comments: Symptom checklist used as an aid in the diagnosis of eating disorders.
Cross References: See T5:893 (54 references); for reviews by Phillip Ash and Steven Schinke of an earlier edition, see 12:130 (38 references); see also T4:847 (38 references); for a review by Cabrini S. Swassing of an earlier edition, see 10:100 (16 references).

Review of the Eating Disorder Inventory-3 by JEFFREY A. ATLAS, Clinical Psychologist, SCO Family of Services, Queens, NY:

DESCRIPTION. The Eating Disorder Inventory-3 (EDI-3) is the latest edition of an instrument developed through 20 years of research in national and international populations of eating-disordered individuals. The manual is encyclopedic in scope, providing adequate instructional information on the EDI-3, textbook-like introductions to topics in the field, and digressions into such areas as cross-cultural comparisons, which may whet the appetite of researchers. The EDI-3 presents itself as both an evaluative measure and an ongoing research program.

The EDI-3 inventories information relevant to the phenomenology, severity, and clinical course of eating disorders in females ages 13–53 years. In combination with interview evaluation, and, where appropriate, medical examination, the EDI-3 may increase confidence in accurate assessment of eating disorders following the nosologies of the DSM-IV-TR and the ICD-10 definitions of Anorexia Nervosa, Bulimia Nervosa, and Eating Disorders Not Otherwise Specified (NOS). It does not address the newer, but important category of Binge Eating Disorder, describing obese individuals with little dietary restraint who do not purge.

A tripartite, potentially stepwise organization of the scale broadens its clinical utility. The Referral Form (RF), with separate manual, provides a weight algorithm and an abbreviated self-report measure (pitched at a sixth-grade reading level) as a separable vehicle for referral for more in-depth assessment. Height and weight values are indexed to a Body Mass Index, which provides critical threshold values for thinness. A 25-item questionnaire is drawn from the full instrument, with critical items keyed to the EDI Drive for Thinness (DT) and Bulimia (B) scales, which research has shown to demonstrate good temporal stability. A modified Likert-type scale yields severity ratings for items such as "If I gain a pound, I worry that I will keep gaining" or "I stuff myself with food."

Part B of the questionnaire canvases the frequency of behavioral weight-control measures such as binge-eating and laxative use. Referral can be based on positive cutoff scores on the 25-item scale, behavior questionnaire, or BMI Index. Advantages of the RF are the brevity and flexibility of administration (group or individual), and plausibility of confidential directing of information from at-risk groups (e.g., aspiring ballet dancers, wrestlers), while permitting the provision of test materials to be handled by on-line staff or entry-level mental health professionals. The RF is a carbonized questionnaire that is easily scorable directly by a teacher, coach, or counselor or via referral to another source for purposes of confidentiality. An example of such use would be in helping an athlete whose drive to maintain a weight designation leads to health-threatening starvation.

A brief Symptom Checklist (SC), written at the sixth-grade level and designed to be administered under the guidance of a healthcare professional, provides for direct canvassing of symptoms keyed to DSM-IV-TR diagnosable eating disorders (e.g., percentage of time aimed at controlling weight, average number of vomiting episodes). By itself or in combination with the RF, the SC may be used as an additional screening device alerting the worker to usefulness or feasibility of administration of the full EDI-3 scale. Failure to meet critical thresholds would indicate nonclinical eating patterns, or, not uncommonly, denial of problems by self-report, which would preclude or postpone use of the EDI-3 until such time as the participant can be engaged in truthful discussion.

DEVELOPMENT. The DT and B are foundational scales of the EDI that anchor the 12 primary subscales of the EDI-3. The other 10 subscales, presented as a continuum of "themes" in eating-disordered populations, are Body Dissatisfaction, Low Self-Esteem, Personal Alienation, Interpersonal Insecurity, Interpersonal Alienation, Interoceptive Deficits, Emotional Dysregulation, Perfectionism, Asceticism, and Maturity Fears. Scale items based on these constructs were generated by experienced clinicians, operationalized and subject to empirical adequacy in terms of goodness-of-fit and stability with clinical populations. The recruitment of normative samples from the United States, Canada, Europe, and Australia is consistent with prevalence of these eating disorders in Westernized industrial societies. Females and young adults, the predominant clinical demographic of eating disorders, form the principal study samples.

The EDI-3 item booklet, written at an overall fourth-grade reading level, takes about 20 minutes to complete. The sorting of items into exemplars of different scales reflects reasonable face validity and empirical grounding. The "Interoceptive Deficits" scale is the authors' description for items comprising affective fears of confusion, such as, "I don't know what's going on inside me." Testing of items on the successive three versions of the scale was aimed at maximizing homogeneity of individual scales (comparing item-total scale correlations with the target scale), which feature item-total scale correlations of about .40 or greater for eating-disorder samples.

TECHNICAL.

Reliability. The EDI-3 was assessed for reliability on the normative samples of U.S. Adult Clinical (N = 983), International Adult Clinical (N = 662), and U.S. Adolescent Clinical (N = 335) populations. A composite T-score comprising the scales' Drive for Thinness, Bulimia, and Body Dissatisfaction produced alpha coefficients ranging from .90 to .97 across the three normative groups and diagnostic categories of Anorexia Nervosa-Restricting, Anorexia Nervosa-Bulimic/Purging, Bulimia Nervosa, and Eating Disorder NOS. The remaining subscales demonstrated somewhat lower, but acceptable, alpha coefficients, with medians of .84, .74, and .85 for the respective normative samples. By this accounting the EDI-3 shows good internal consistency of item scales.

Test-retest stability of scores was assessed through a sample of 34 females who had undergone earlier treatment for eating disorders, ranging in age from 15–55 with an average age of 25.2. The test-retest interval ranged from 1 to 7 days with an average of 2.6. Correlation coefficients ranging from .86 (for Asceticism) to .98 (for Interpersonal Alienation) suggested excellent stability of subscale and composite scores, albeit on a very restricted study sample.

Validity. Confirmatory factor analysis of the EDI-3 on the U.S. Adult and Adolescent Clinical samples yielded meaningful scale groupings of Ineffectiveness, Interpersonal Problems, Affective Problems, and Overcontrol Composites. The fact that the factorial analysis failed to meet acceptable levels related to mean square errors of approximation leads the test author to conclude that "the primary consideration in constructing the EDI-3 scales was clinical relevance" (professional manual, p. 137).

Other sources of validity may be examined. A nonclinical sample of 543 females administered the EDI-3 and Rosenberg Self-Esteem Scale yielded an inverse correlation of .82 between the Low Self-Esteem subscale of the EDI-3 and the Rosenberg, supporting convergent validity. The manual provides "descriptive data" on moderate-size samples of U.S. and international male and female adults, as well as international male and female adolescents. Although statistical tests are not provided, the author notes higher female raw scores on the Body Dissatisfaction and Drive for Thinness scales, but otherwise relatively small differences between females and males without eating disorders. The gender contrasts are consistent with the impact of Western social norms. However, the absence of T-score comparisons makes the issue of differential validity difficult to evaluate.

COMMENTARY. Despite the voluminous work and care that appeared to go into the development of the EDI-3, it is ultimately disappointing. The instrument appears "front-loaded" in the sense that its preliminary screening components may be more efficient and valid than the full scale. Empirically, the Drive for Thinness and Bulimia measures, as well as the Body Mass Index and canvassing of symptoms, converge with other research and clinical knowledge in presenting reasonable measures for further assessment. As the extended EDI-3 shows questionable factor structure and discriminant subscale utility, with the author's own dictate that it does not substitute for a structured clinical interview, the question comes up as to whether the added diagnostic contributions of the EDI-3 warrant the time and expense. Given some of the theoretical and empirical lacunae of this instrument, one might conclude otherwise, as the state of evidence-based studies in the field combined with advances in diagnostically focused interview techniques may make the EDI-3 unnecessary.

SUMMARY. The EDI-3 reflects the development of an ambitious research, assessment, and intervention program in the field of eating disorders. The full instrument may have been surpassed in its usefulness by advances in the field itself, but the EDI-3 screening components, particularly the RF, would seem useful in settings such as high school and college counseling clinics where rapid assessment and referral of clients at risk for eating disorders is of critical importance.

Review of the Eating Disorder Inventory-3 by ASHRAF KAGEE, Professor of Psychology, Stellenbosch University, Matiland, South Africa:

DESCRIPTION. The Eating Disorder Inventory-3 is the third edition of a widely used 91-item self-report paper-and-pencil test used to measure psychological traits that are relevant to persons with eating disorders. The purpose of this instrument is to test the continuum model of anorexia nervosa (Nylander, 1971), to assess risk factors associated with this condition, to measure outcome, and to predict response to treatment. The instrument has been largely designed for use in clinical settings but has been consistently researched over several decades. It is easily administered and scored, and yields 12 nonoverlapping scale scores and 6 composite scores that may be used to create clinically meaningful profiles, which in turn may be linked to treatment plans, specific interventions, and treatment monitoring. It is important to note that the EDI-3 is not designed to arrive at a diagnosis of an eating disorder. Instead the emphasis is placed on the measurement of psychological traits relevant to the development and maintenance of such disorders.

Test takers are provided with the EDI-3 item booklet, and an answer sheet. The first page of the item booklet contains questions about demographic information and physical characteristics. The remaining 91 items address psychological constructs associated with eating disorders. The answer sheet is used by the test-taker to record item responses. The scoring sheet and the score summary sheet are used by the examiner to calculate validity scale scores, scale raw scores, T scores, and percentiles. Test takers are asked to respond to items on a 6-point Likert-type scale containing the response options *Always, Usually, Often, Sometimes, Rarely,* and *Never.* The test materials are presented in an attractive box set that facilitates ease of use for both the test taker and test administrator.

DEVELOPMENT. The materials furnished by the developers provide useful information concerning how the instrument was developed. The EDI-3 was formulated using an approach to construct validation emphasizing both the rational and empirical methods of scale development. Constructs were chosen based on a review of the major theories in the clinical literature, and scales were identified by clinicians experienced in the area of eating disorders in order to operationally define these constructs. The scales and composites included in the final version of the EDI-3 were based on empirical adequacy as well as scale stability.

The rationale behind the development of the EDI was to test the continuum model of anorexia nervosa, which states that this disorder is the final stage of a continuous process beginning with voluntary dieting and progressing to more stringent forms of dieting accompanied by progressive loss of insight. The difference between mild or subthreshold symptoms is thus conceptualized as quantitative rather than qualitative. This matter of whether the severity of eating disorders is chiefly qualitative or quantitative in nature has not been settled in the literature in this area. However, the implications are that it is important to recognize the heterogeneity of cases in terms of symptom severity, to identify meaningful psychological typologies that may lead to better clinical decision-making, and to conduct research on these psychological constructs that could yield information regarding etiology, prognosis, prediction of relapse, and biological and cultural factors.

TECHNICAL. The standardization process of the EDI-3 is described in great detail. The Eating Disorder Risk Composite Scale reliability estimates range from .90 to .97 (median = .94) across four diagnostic groups and three normative groups. For the three Eating Disorder Risk scales, all reliability estimates were generally in the high .80s and low .90s across all the groups that formed part of the assessment. The median reliability coefficients for the psychological scales were .84, .74, and .85 for the American Adult Clinical, International Adult Clinical, and American Adolescent samples, respectively. The test-retest stability coefficients (retest interval of 1 to 7 days) were .98 and .97 for the Eating Disorder Risk Composite and General Psychological Maladjustment Composite scales, whereas the Eating Disorder Risk and Psychological scales had median coefficients of .95 and .93, respectively.

In terms of construct validity in addition to other measures, the various subscales of the EDI-3 were correlated with corresponding subscales of the Eating Attitudes Test (EAT-26), the Bulimia Test Revised (BULIT-R), and the Rosenberg Self-Esteem Scale. Scale correlations ranged from low (-.13) to very high (.83).

The underlying relationships of the items were examined by means of exploratory factor analysis. The analysis showed that a three-factor model for the American Adult Clinical and sample accounted for 63.0% of the total variance, whereas the models for the International Adult Clinical and American Adolescent samples accounted for 60.8% and 65.6% of the variance, respectively.

COMMENTARY. The EDI-3 appears to be a thorough assessment tool for use in a clinical context. It has been extensively researched and has undergone three revisions over the past several decades. The major advantage conferred by the EDI-3 over other similar measures is that it is more likely than those to lead to refinements in clinical decision making due to the psychological typologies provided by the subscales.

From the data provided in the test manual, it is apparent that this instrument has been subjected to considerable empirical research. However, additional and more robust studies that assess divergent and convergent validity are necessary to examine its construct validity in a more rigorous fashion.

The item booklet and item answer sheet are easy to read for most people. On the whole, the instrument is easy to administer and score. The norms provided in the appendix of the manual were obtained from American and international samples (Australia, Canada, Italy, and the Netherlands), indicating that efforts have been made to generate evidence of cross-cultural validity for the instrument. At this point in the research trajectory

of this instrument it may be appropriate to test its utility and relevance in developing countries, such as those in South America, Africa, and Asia. If this instrument is to gain usage in these parts of the world, additional culture-specific norms will need to be developed.

SUMMARY. The developers have made considerable efforts to refine the newest version of the EDI. The strength of this instrument lies in its thorough treatment of the psychological correlates of eating disorders. Despite a reasonable amount of research on this instrument, further studies correlating the instrument with other measures of similar constructs may need to be pursued. Of particular interest is the cross-cultural applicability of the EDI-3. Although studies in countries other than the United States have been undertaken, it would also be of benefit to determine the extent to which the measure may be applicable in developing countries.

REVIEWER'S REFERENCE

Mylander, I. (1971). The feeling of being fat and dieting in a school population: An epidemiologic interview investigation. *ACTA Socio-Medica Scandinavica, 3,* 17–26.

[65]
Electrical Aptitude Test (Form EA-R-C).

Purpose: For evaluating electrical aptitude skills.
Population: Applicants for jobs that require the ability to learn electrical skills.
Publication Dates: 2003–2004.
Scores: Total score only for 6 areas: Mathematics, Electrical Concepts, Electrical Schematics, Process Flow, Signal Flow, Electrical Sequences.
Administration: Group.
Price Data, 2007: $21 per consumable self-scoring test booklet (minimum order of 20); $24.95 per manual (2004, 10 pages).
Time: (18) minutes.
Comments: Self-scoring instrument.
Author: Roland T. Ramsay.
Publisher: Ramsay Corporation.

Review of the Electrical Aptitude Test (Form EA-R-C) by MARTIN W. ANDERSON, Director of Administration, Connecticut Department of Administrative Services, Hartford, CT, and Adjunct Professor, University of New Haven, West Haven, CT:

DESCRIPTION. The Electrical Aptitude Test (Form EA-R-C) is a 36-item multiple-choice test that is administered using a paper-and-pencil test form. The test can be administered individually or to a group under a time limit that should be monitored by stop watch or accurate timer. There is a 10-page Manual for Administration and Scoring (copyright 2004). There are no special qualifications for administrators of the test. The manual includes verbatim instructions to be read to anyone taking the test. The test and manual are published by Roland T. Ramsay, Ph.D., of the Ramsay Corporation of Pittsburgh, PA. Testing forms can be used only once. Scoring the test requires counting the number of correct marks that have been left behind on an "NCR" sheet of paper. This sheet of paper is exposed by the test administrator after the examinee completes the test by pulling a perforated tab from the edge of the score sheet to expose the self-scoring grid. There are line drawings, printed test items, and multiple-choice answers in the test booklet.

DEVELOPMENT. The manual contains few details about the test development other than it was developed by the Ramsay Corporation in April of 2002; it was developed to enable a quick evaluation of electrical aptitude; and it was written by two Industrial/Organizational psychologists to cover six content areas said to be Mathematics, Electrical Concepts, Electrical Schematics, Process Flow, Signal Flow, and Electrical Sequences. Each area is represented by six items with the areas selected "from a review of recent books, tests and training materials" (manual, p. 1) that were not described. Furthermore, electrical aptitude is not operationally defined and the test is also said to measure electrical aptitude skills or knowledge with the same content. There is no specific information provided describing test takers for whom the test is appropriate for administration. The manual and supplemental abstract state that the test is for "Applicants for jobs that require the ability to learn electrical skills" (manual, p. 8).

TECHNICAL. Most data presented are based on the same group of 113 "male and female trainees and job experts" (manual, p. 9). There are no breakdowns for age, gender, or other characteristics of these persons. Data presented are based on what is assumed to be a version of the test with the identical content as the Form EA-R-C but are referenced as coming from Form REA-R. There is an 18-minute time limit for administering the test with no explanation of how the time limit was set. The manual reports one KR_{20} internal consistency reliability coefficient of .80 along with the mean, standard deviation, and SEM of scores, which the author concludes indicates "adequate reliability" (manual, p. 6). Difficulty and point-biserial coefficients are published for each item, but there is no discussion on whether these data were used in any way to improve items or decide which items would be included for administration. The manual states that content-related validity is "assured when the behaviors required on the test are also required on the job" (manual, p. 8). Neither of these issues is explicated. A criterion-related validity coefficient of .47 is reported between the Electrical Aptitude Test and a 15-item test of electrical job knowledge (that was not described) for 97 male and female postsecondary technical school students and job experts. They also reported a correlation of .41 with GPA although it was not explained where the GPA data were obtained and what can be inferred from that relationship. No construct validity evidence is reported. The author states that the construct measured by the test is the ability to learn and perform jobs involving electricity. Percentile ranks are reported for raw scores although how scores should or should not be used is given no explanation and the size and representativeness of the norm sample might be questioned. Furthermore, there is simply no explanation of how scores relate to electrical aptitude measured or evaluated by any other means (e.g., convergent validity).

COMMENTARY. There are only the sketchiest data reported for the Electrical Aptitude Test as a measure intended to evaluate electrical aptitude skills (the stated purpose of the test), and the data are not necessarily helpful in supporting the use of the test. It is unknown what these skills are that are being tested, and the six "areas" of the test are listed as "knowledge areas." The item analysis statistics show that a number of improvements could have been made to the test items but were not. A review of the items and the processes needed to answer them correctly suggests that there are far fewer areas being measured than the six that are listed. Clearly, data need to be collected to demonstrate better what, if any, value this test has in assessing electrical aptitude. Publishing a plea at the end of the manual for "normative data, test results, or validation information" (manual, p. 9) that might be used to update the manual is not sufficient. At best, the author should label this test as a research instrument.

SUMMARY. The Electrical Aptitude Test (Form EA-R-C) is a timed paper-and-pencil test stated to have the purpose of evaluating electrical aptitude skills. The test comes with consumable self-scoring forms and a 10-page manual. Reliability and validity statistics are presented but are of questionable value and do not represent the necessary work needed to assess reliability or validity. Norms are based on 113 persons who are not described in the manual in any detail. The most fundamental information about how test scores should be used is not made available to the user.

[66]
Emotional Competence Inventory.

Purpose: "Designed to assess emotional intelligence (the ability to recognize and manage emotions [yours and other])."

Population: Coaches, executive coaches, mid to senior level managers.

Publication Dates: 1999–2002.

Acronym: ECI.

Scores: 4 clusters, 18 competencies: Self-Awareness (Emotional Self-Awareness, Accurate Self-Assessment, Self-Confidence); Self-Management (Emotional Self-Control, Transparency, Adaptability, Achievement Orientation, Initiative, Optimism); Social Awareness (Empathy, Organizational Awareness, Service Orientation); Relationship Management (Developing Others, Inspirational Leadership, Influence, Change Catalyst, Conflict Management, Teamwork & Collaboration).

Administration: Group or individual.

Price Data, 2005: $3,000 Accreditation (2-day program); $1,800 Accreditation (one-day master class); once accredited internet assessments are $150 per participant (this includes unlimited raters); online development tool available for $75 annual subscription.

Time: (50–60) minutes.

Comments: Accreditation required; multirater assessment to be administered by accredited consultants only; accreditation programs run approximately every second month; the publisher advises that newer versions of this instrument are now available including the ESCI introduced in 2007 but the reviewer did not have access to these materials.

Authors: Daniel Goleman, Richard Boyatzis, and the Hay Group.

Publisher: Hay Group.

Review of the Emotional Competence Inventory by T. STEUART WATSON, Professor and Chair, Department of Educational Psychology, Mi-ami University, Oxford, OH, and TONYA S. WATSON, Assistant Professor, Department of Family Studies and Social Work, Miami University, Oxford, OH:

DESCRIPTION. The Emotional Competence Inventory (ECI) is a 110-item instrument for which the purpose is to assess emotional competency, which is defined as the ability to recognize and manage one's own emotions and the emotions of others and the ability to motivate oneself. The four clusters of "competencies" or skills measured by the ECI are (a) Self-Awareness, (b) Self-Management, (c) Social Awareness, and (d) Social Skills. Each cluster is composed of an additional three to eight specific competencies that are considered to make up the more general competency. For instance, the Self-Awareness cluster includes emotional awareness, accurate self-assessment, and self-confidence. In all, 20 competencies are assessed on the ECI.

DEVELOPMENT. The theoretical foundation of the ECI is based on the work of Daniel Goleman and Richard Boyatzis. Items were derived from the emotional competencies identified by Goleman and from the Generic Dictionary of Competencies and Self-Assessment Questionnaire. One need not agree with the theoretical construct of emotional intelligence to find some aspects of this instrument useful. The test authors provide a very cursory treatment regarding the development of the ECI, which at times is confusing because they discuss the ECI 2.0 at the end of the test manual. It would make more sense for the reader if all test development information were in one place in the manual, so that the processes for selecting the items and iteration of the instrument are readily apparent.

TECHNICAL. The manual reports a number of reliability and validity studies with diverse geographic and ethnic populations. Most of these studies are limited in some significant manner, which leaves questions regarding the strength of the instrument's psychometric properties. Internal consistency, based on a large sample of both third-party ratings ($n = 3,931$) and self-ratings ($n = 4,001$), is judged to be adequate with alpha coefficients ranging from .60 to .96. As expected, alpha coefficients for self-ratings were consistently lower than those for ratings completed by others. The only test-retest evidence presented is from a sample of 20 Brazilian executives with a 7-month assessment interval. Stability coefficients ranged widely—from .05 to .82 for self-ratings on the 20 competencies and from .19 to .92 for others-ratings. Given the small sample size, the lack of supporting empirical data, and the length of time between assessments, there is little evidence that the test is stable over time. Evidence of content validity is offered by a study cited by the test authors that examined self- and others-ratings on each competency using 427 individuals who were categorized as scoring either high or low on Accurate Self-Assessment. Those who scored low on the Accurate Self-Assessment competency showed a significantly larger gap between self-ratings and ratings by others compared to respondents who scored high on Accurate Self-Assessment. This finding lends support to the claim of content validity for the specific competencies studied, but not for the overall inventory.

The manual presents the results of six studies in which ECI competencies were correlated with scores from the Myers-Briggs, a Type A/B personality measure, the NEO-PI, the Managerial Style Inventory, and the Organizational Climate Survey. Overall, the results from these studies showed low to moderate correlations with each of the measures. Curiously, the authors did not report data from one of the studies. Correlations between competencies and Managerial Styles were unimpressive. Overall, the construct validity of the ECI, based on the limited number of studies, the restricted samples, and the size of the correlation coefficients, is suspect. The same limitations apply to the discriminant validity data.

Perhaps the most important type of validity for an instrument like the ECI is criterion validity. Six studies are reported, but none have particularly impressive results. For instance, correlations between scores on the ECI and two measures of performance indicators for 92 U.K. principals were low and mostly nonsignificant. Of the two correlations that reached significance, the coefficients were .20 and .18, hardly meaningful from a practical perspective. As another example, a study using 40 Turkish financiers between the ages of 31 and 36 yielded significant correlation coefficients (ranging from .24 to .53) between the ECI clusters and various indices of job and life success (salary, subjective job, and personal success).

The ECI materials include a 29-page Feedback report, which details the results of one's completed and scored ECI. A great deal of information is contained in this report, much of which may be confusing to the person reading the report. Numerous graphs and charts are included, but they do little to clarify the meaning of scores on many of the scales. The rating booklet is easy to understand and well organized. However, the response choices are a bit confusing in that there are four choices (slightly, somewhat, very, N/A) for each item but there is a range of one to three ovals for each choice. It is not entirely clear which oval the rater is supposed to use or if it matters which oval is filled.

COMMENTARY. The test manual, although fairly comprehensive, is not well organized. It begins with a very brief summary of the development of the ECI but does not include more general information about the construct of emotional intelligence, which would be helpful to readers who may not be familiar with the theoretical foundation of this concept. The next two sections, Reliability and Validity, inexplicably precede the section on Descriptive Statistics. The section on Emotional Intelligence Training and Development is out of place and seems unrelated to the evaluation of the instrument itself. Given the normative data and validity studies presented, the ECI is probably best used for assessing the emotional "skills" of individuals within business settings. The ECI is certainly a heuristic device that may serve to add to the variance accounted for in managerial success and related outcomes.

SUMMARY. The ECI may be a reliable instrument. Currently, little empirical evidence has been offered to support this property. Validity, too, is questionable, given the many limiting factors of the studies reported in the test manual. These criticisms were acknowledged by the authors and were purportedly addressed by a revision of the ECI (i.e., the ECI 2.0). The inventory certainly shows promise, but much more work needs to be completed to establish its psychometric properties as well as its applicability to a wider range of job professions.

[67]
English Placement Test, Revised.
Purpose: Designed to "quickly place English language students into homogenous ability levels."
Population: English language learners.
Publication Dates: 1972–1993.

Acronym: EPT.

Scores: Total score only.

Subtests, 4: Listening Comprehension, Grammar, Vocabulary, Reading.

Administration: Individual or group.

Forms, 3: A, B, C.

Price Data: Price data for examiner's manual (1993, 8 pages), cassette or CD containing Forms A, B, and C of Listening Comprehension, test booklets for Forms A, B, and C, and answer sheets available from publisher.

Time: (75) minutes.

Authors: Testing and Certification Division, English Language Institute, University of Michigan.

Publisher: English Language Institute, University of Michigan.

Cross References: See T4:908 (3 references); for a review by John L. D. Clark of an earlier form, see 8:102.

Review of the English Placement Test [Revised] by JAMES DEAN BROWN, Professor of Second Language Studies, University of Hawaii at Manoa, Honolulu, HI:

DESCRIPTION. The English Placement Test (EPT) is a multiple-choice paper-and-pencil test available in three forms (A, B, & C) of 100 items each. The EPT was designed to measure four skills: Listening Comprehension (Items 1–20), Grammar (Items 21–50), Vocabulary (Items 51–80), and Reading (Items 81–100). The 20 three-option multiple-choice Listening Comprehension items are of two types: either the examinees hear a question and select the appropriate response from among the options, or they hear a statement and select the option that best matches or summarizes that statement. These two formats are intermixed in one subtest, which might be a source of confusion for some examinees. Each of the 30 four-option multiple-choice Grammar items presents a short conversation between two people. A blank appears in the second person's response. The examinee must select the word or phrase that correctly completes that response. The 30 four-option multiple-choice Vocabulary items each present a sentence with a blank. The examinees must choose the word that correctly fits the blank. The 20 Reading items require the examinees to read a sentence and then answer a four-option multiple-choice question about its meaning. The examinees are not required to read anything longer than a sentence in this "reading" subtest.

The EPT is designed for administration, scoring, and interpretation by the staff of a university intensive ESL program. During the test administration, the examiner reads all of the directions and then can use a cassette tape to play the Listening Comprehension subtest. If that cassette tape is not available, scripts are provided for the three different Listening Comprehension subtest forms.

The EPT includes three 13-page test booklets, examiner's manual, a cassette tape with all three Listening Comprehension subtest forms on it, answer sheets, and a scoring template.

Each of the test booklets (Forms A, B, & C) starts with a one-paragraph introduction to the test. Then directions and two example items are provided for the Listening Comprehension subtest. The next page contains all 20 Listening Comprehension items. That is followed on page 3 by directions for the Grammar, Vocabulary, and Reading Comprehension subtests along with one example item for each subtest type. The remaining 10 pages are taken up by the 80 Grammar, Vocabulary, and Reading items. The item types shift from one subtest to another within these 80 items with no heading or visible break to delineate the subtests, which might cause confusion for some examinees. In addition, the relatively short 50 minutes allowed to finish the 80 items would probably make this a speeded test rather than a power test for many examinees, some of whom might not finish (especially the Reading section) for lack of time. However, high proficiency university students should have time to correctly answer all of the items on the EPT if they know the answers.

The short eight-page examiner's manual is made up of six parts: Descriptive Information and Administration Procedures; Scripts; Scoring Keys; Establishing Cut Points; Equating Scores from Different Test Forms; and Reliability Estimates. The Descriptive Information and Administration Procedures part gives a brief overview of the development of the EPT, describes the content of the various subtests, and very briefly lists the test administration procedures. The three Scripts, one for each form, provide exactly the words that are given on the cassette tapes, each including directions and example items for the Listening Comprehension subtest and the questions or statements on the tape for each of the 20 listening questions. Scoring keys are also provided for all 100 items on all three forms. The very short discussion in the Establishing Cut Points section includes four lines of text and a table. In the Equating Scores from Different Test Forms section, a table is given that shows the equivalencies for raw scores on Forms A, B, and C. The Reliability Estimates section shows descriptive statistics and reliability estimates.

DEVELOPMENT. The EPT was developed for group administration to university ESL students like those in the Intensive English Program at the University of Michigan and was used in that program from 1972 until the program was phased out in 1987. At some unspecified point (probably 1993), the EPT was revised. Hence, it carries the copyright dates 1972, 1978, and 1993. No other information is provided in the examiner's manual about how the EPT was developed.

TECHNICAL. The text of the Establishing Cut Points section of the examiner's manual begins by explaining that there are "no pre-established cut scores" (p. 6) for the EPT. It then goes on to give the cut scores previously used in the Intensive English Program at the University of Michigan for six levels: beginner (0–29), beginner high (30–47), intermediate low (48–60), intermediate (61–74), advanced low (75–84), and advanced (85–100). The Reliability Estimates section provides descriptive statistics for different small samples of examinees (ranging in size from *n* = 29 to *n* = 58) for 1977 administrations of the three forms along with unspecified internal consistency estimates (ranging from .89 to .96) and parallel forms reliability estimates (ranging from .89 to .95).

A number of technical issues pose problems for using the EPT. First, no mention is made of the possibility of using the standard error of measurement in cut-point decisions. Second, it is not clear which of the three sets of raw scores (for Forms A, B, or C) should be used as the basis for those decisions, even though the raw scores are clearly not exactly the same in the equating table. Third, no information is given about how the three forms were equated. Fourth, no explanation is provided for how the raw score equivalencies were determined. Fifth, no discussion of validity is provided, much less any discussion of the interpretation, use, social consequences, or values implication issues related to validity.

COMMENTARY. Aside from the five technical problems mentioned in the previous section, a number of other potential problems exist in the design of the EPT. First, no attempt is made to make use of separate scores for Listening Comprehension, Grammar, Vocabulary, and Reading Comprehension skill areas, or to show how they could be interpreted in equivalent ways for the three forms. Second, all of the items on this test are multiple-choice, which might be appropriate in traditional grammar-translation or audio-lingual ESL classes, but would make little sense in EFL/ESL programs that offer more recently developed communicative or task-based teaching. Third, no mention is made of potential problems for validity and fairness that might arise from reading the script instead of using the cassette tape. Nor is there any discussion of similar problems that might arise if low quality audio equipment is used to play the cassette tapes. Fourth, the vocabulary items were taken from the most common 2,500 words in the Thorndike and Lorge (1944, 1959) word list. This word list is quite outdated by now, and other much more recent word lists are available.

SUMMARY. For those who have university-level ESL students and need a quick, traditional placement test in three forms with subtests for grammar, vocabulary, listening, and reading comprehension as measured by discrete-point multiple-choice items, the EPT may serve their purposes. However, the lack of information about ways to use the standard error of measurement in decision making, how the forms were equated, how score equivalencies were determined, and what the scores mean in terms of validity all pose real and important limitations on the technical quality of the EPT. In addition, because no information is given about how to use the separate scores for Listening, Grammar, Vocabulary, and Reading or how to interpret those separate scores as equivalent across the three forms, the test scores may be of limited use. Finally, other problems, like the fact that all of the items are multiple-choice, that unfairness issues might arise from reading the script aloud or using low quality audio equipment, and that the vocabulary items were taken from an outdated wordlist, amount to serious validity and fairness concerns. All in all, I would only use the EPT for placement of university ESL students for very specific purposes after myself piloting, equating, and validating the three forms for those purposes.

REVIEWER'S REFERENCE

Thorndike, E. L., & Lorge, I. (1944, 1959). *The teacher's word book of 30,000 words.* New York: Teachers College, Columbia University.

[68]
Entrepreneurial Style & Success Indicator [Revised].

Purpose: Designed to help individuals identify their preferred entrepreneurial style and its related strengths and weaknesses, as well as comparing their background to the background of other successful entrepreneurs.
Population: Adults.
Publication Dates: 1988–2006.
Acronym: ESSI.
Scores, 4: Behavioral/Action, Cognitive/Analysis, Interpersonal/Harmony, Affective/Expression, plus 28 Entrepreneurial Success Factors.
Administration: Individual or group.
Price Data, 2006: $19.95 per test booklet (2006, 32 pages); $14.95 per Indicator In-Depth Interpretations booklet (2006, 48 pages); $34.95 per code for online version; $69.95 per Professional's Guide (2006, 62 pages); $38 per Trainer Guidelines (1996, 18 pages); $159.95 per Power Point CD & Binder 126 slides; $23.95 per participant workbook entitled Discovering Your Pathway to Entrepreneurial Success (2006, 64 pages).
Time: [120–180] minutes for Basic; [360–720] minutes for Advanced.
Comments: Test can be self-administered and self-scored.
Authors: Ken Keis, Terry D. Anderson, and Howard Shenson.
Publisher: Consulting Resource Group International, Inc.
Cross References: For a review by Stephen F. Davis of an earlier edition, see 13:120.

Review of the Entrepreneurial Style and Success Indicator by FREDERICK T. L. LEONG, Professor of Psychology, Michigan State University, East Lansing, MI:

DESCRIPTION. The Entrepreneurial Style and Success Indicator (ESSI) was designed by the authors to be an integrated learning and communication instrument regarding both entrepreneurial style and entrepreneurial success factors. It consists of three parts: (a) revised version of the "Personal Style Indicator" (b) revised form of the "Foundations of Entrepreneurial Assessment" developed by Shenson, and (c) an interpretative summary based on the integration of the entrepreneurial tendencies and success factors.

Essentially, the ESSI is based on a combination of the Personal Style Indicator developed by Terry Anderson and the Foundations of Entrepreneurial Assessment developed by Howard Shenson. With a reading level set at 10th grade, the ESSI was designed to be a self-administered, self-scored, and self-interpreted learning and communication tool. Throughout the professional's guide to the ESSI, the authors maintain that it is not a psychological test in the usual psychometric tradition.

The professional's guide also discusses the Job Style Indicator (JSI; 17:99) but it is somewhat ambiguous as to the relationship between the JSI and the ESSI. It seems that the JSI is also based on the Personal Style Theory that underlies the Personal Style Indicator, which comprises the first part of the ESSI. The JSI is based on a four-part classification of orientations to work consisting of (a) Behavioral Action, (b) Cognitive Analysis, (c) Interpersonal Harmony, and (d) Affective Expression. These four patterns in turn can be combined in various ways to provide a 21-fold profile, which is described in the In-Depth Interpretation of each of these patterns. For example, a pure Behavioral Action type (B) would be classified as Directing whereas a pure Cognitive Analysis type (C) would be Rational. Combining two patterns, an individual who is B + C would be classified as Self-Reliant. On the other hand, a C + B individual is classified as Calculating.

The authors proposed that the ESSI would be useful for individuals and groups interested in entrepreneurial potential. Consultants, coaches, and counselors can also use the ESSI to help others understand their business and career plans, and managers can use it to identify entrepreneurial strengths in their employees. Researchers could also use the ESSI to evaluate entrepreneurial style and its relationship to productivity and morale among workers.

The authors of the ESSI have maintained that it was designed as a "communication and learning tool" (manual, p. 1) and not a psychological test. They carefully remind users that the ESSI should not be used to predict entrepreneurial behaviors. Yet, there are mixed messages contained within the professional's guide. Despite numerous disclaimers that the ESSI is not a psychometric measure or test, the authors go on to provide correlation coefficients between actual entrepreneurial success and scores on the Foundations of Entrepreneurial Assessment (Part 2 of the ESSI). Interestingly, as indicated above, they cite that one of the applications of the ESSI is for "researchers interested in assessing entrepreneurial style and its relationship to management or other job responsibilities" (professional's guide, p. 3). Furthermore, they issue a call for continuous development and research of the ESSI by making the following statement: "Although this instrument was not designed to be a psychological test, questions of reliability and validity nonetheless apply. CRG invites qualified researchers to pursue further investigations" (professional's guide, p. 8). This approach seems to be a strange shift of responsibility to future researchers because the normative pattern has been for the developer of a psychological test to conduct the research to establish basic psychometric properties of their test before "going public."

TECHNICAL AND COMMENTARY. It appears quite common for certain corporations and consultants to develop a variety of learning tools or group exercises and then avoid the work on evaluating the psychometric properties of their assessment instruments by claiming that they were not designed as psychological tests. This reviewer has previously taken the position in his review of the Teamness Index (Leong, 1992) that an instrument that provides scores and profiles is an assessment device and therefore should be subject to all the standards pertaining to tests outlined in the *Standards for Educational and Psychological Testing* (AERA, APA, & NCME, 1999). This reviewer also believes that this requirement applies to the ESSI as well. As such, the ESSI is quite inadequate because scant or no reliability or validity data have been collected to justify its use in any settings.

Furthermore, because the ESSI is based in part on the Personal Style Theory as represented in the Personal Style Indicator (PSI; 17:144) and the Job Style Indicator (JSI; 17:99), a critique from Schmitt (1998) in his review of the JSI is also relevant here. Schmitt points out that because the JSI is based on a theory of personality or personal styles, evidence should be presented on the validity of this theory (aside from the test) in accounting for human behaviors. Yet, no such evidence has been presented other than a description of the personality styles. Instead, the authors assume that

if a personal style is described it must be true or valid. Without scientific evidence for the personality theory on which the JSI and the ESSI are based, one cannot really recommend the use of this test or "learning tool."

SUMMARY. The Entrepreneurial Style and Success Indicator (ESSI) was designed to aid individuals, groups, counselors, consultants, and researchers in identifying entrepreneurial style and potential. However, the ESSI is lacking any supporting research on its reliability and validity as a psychological test. The authors have insisted that the ESSI was not designed as a psychological test, but this reviewer strongly disagrees with that disclaimer and has reviewed it as a psychological test. Furthermore, as pointed out by Schmitt, there has been an absence of any scientific evidence supporting the validity of the personality theory that underlies both the ESSI and the JSI. Although both the test and the personality theory underlying it are intuitively appealing, use of the ESSI in any applied settings is not warranted given the lack of basic psychometric data as well as lack of scientific evidence for the underlying personality theory.

REVIEWER'S REFERENCES

American Educational Research Association, American Psychological Association, & National Council on Measurement in Education. (1999). *Standards for educational and psychological testing*. Washington, DC: American Educational Research Association.
Leong, F. T. L. (1992). [Review of the Teamness Index.] In J. J. Kramer & J. C. Conoley (Eds.), *The eleventh mental measurements yearbook* (pp. 921-923). Lincoln, NE: Buros Institute of Mental Measurements.
Schmitt, N. (1998). [Review of the Job Style Indicator.] In J. C. Impara & B. S. Plake (Eds.), *The thirteenth mental measurements yearbook* (pp. 561-564). Lincoln, NE: Buros Institute of Mental Measurements.

Review of the Entrepreneurial Style and Success Indicator by MYRA N. WOMBLE, Associate Professor of Workforce Education, University of Georgia, Athens, GA:

DESCRIPTION. The Entrepreneurial Style and Success Indicator (ESSI) is a self-administered, self-scored, and self-interpreted three-section instrument. It is designed to stimulate self-exploration and self-discovery. The first section, including the response sheet, is designed to assess entrepreneurial style and explain how it is related to success in different business situations. The second section assesses how well attitudes and previous experiences may already be providing suitable foundations for entrepreneurial achievement. The third section shows how to increase potential for success as an entrepreneur and provides suggestions for emphasizing personal strengths and overcoming weaknesses. The ESSI was designed with a dual entrepreneurial focus of examining style and success factors. The reading level is 10th grade. It is not recommended to administer the ESSI to those under 16 years of age without direct supervision and explanation from an adult.

A separate In-depth Interpretations manual with guidelines is available and provides further insight into business and entrepreneurial tendencies characterized by individuals' style behaviors. Persons using the ESSI also have access to a 55-page professional's guide. Other support materials available when using the ESSI include (a) ESSI Trainer's Guidelines, (b) CRG Models, (c) Discovering Your Pathway to Entrepreneurial Success Workbook, (d) ESSI PowerPoint Deluxe, (e) Job Style Indicator, (f) Train-the-Trainer DVD, and (g) Train-the-Trainer Program.

DEVELOPMENT. The first part of the ESSI is a revised version of the Personal Style Indicator (PSI; 17:144). The second section derives from Shenson's (1975) original work on the Foundations of Entrepreneurship Assessment (FEA). Shenson used interviews with entrepreneurs and reviews of literature on entrepreneurship to identify specific experiences and attitudes he believed were associated with a tendency toward, and success in, entrepreneurial activities. These identified experiences and attitudes served as the model for development of standards that were field tested, then modified. An inventory designed to encourage individuals to evaluate their entrepreneurial potential by comparing their own attitudes and experiences to those of successful entrepreneurs resulted. Shenson used informal interviews and data collected from over 1,000 entrepreneurs to arrive at 21 factors in his original Foundations of Entrepreneurship Assessment. He later expanded the instrument, including seven additional factors, based on patterns seen from field research involving over 4,000 persons who described themselves and were described by others as entrepreneurial. This second edition of the assessment, with 28 factors, was edited to comprise the second section of the ESSI with 21 patterns.

The third section of the ESSI is a brief interpretation of style tendencies and success factor considerations, presumably summarized from a more detailed interpretation provided in a separate booklet entitled ESSI: In-depth Interpretations.

Users are encouraged to select and read a maximum of three in-depth interpretations found in this booklet. The in-depth interpretations were written jointly by the authors based on their experiences, observations, and research. It is assumed that the interpretation summaries are the style interpretations for the behavioral, cognitive, interpersonal, and affective quadrants, which "were based on Anderson's Personal Style Theory (PST) and the results of Shenson's research using the assessment" (p. 6).

TECHNICAL. This section is divided into three categories: standardization, reliability, and validity, and addresses findings from validation procedures used for the three sections of the ESSI.

Standardization. The first section of the instrument is an ipsative measure producing four interrelated scales. The developers suggest that this type of measure prevents this section of the ESSI from being used as a normative measure. Psychometric concerns and issues do arise when using ipsative measures, especially those with a small number of scales. Such measures are not easy to norm because results would only produce an internal measure of a respondent's entrepreneurial self-assessment.

The intended population of users of the ESSI is broadly identified as clients, students, and employees. However, information about the demographic composition of the norm samples used in developing Sections 2 and 3 of the ESSI is limited. For example, the second section of the ESSI results from Shenson's field research over a 6-year period, which included over 4,000 persons from various professions and industries who self-identified or were considered by others as entrepreneurial. Similarly, the third section of the ESSI, written by the authors, includes style tendencies and success factor considerations written as an interpretive summary and based on the experiences, observations, and research of the authors over the past decade. The authors collected observations and feedback from individuals in more than 300 small groups who described themselves as having a mix of two specific entrepreneurial styles. Gender norms or ethnic and cultural norms are not identified in either section.

Reliability. No estimates of reliability are provided for the ESSI, possibly because the ESSI does not claim to be a psychometric-type instrument. Even so, any standardized procedure for measuring behavioral and/or psychological attributes is usually thought to have psychometric qualities, and to serve as a test designed to measure psychological variables. A possible problem with no evidence of reliability, however, is that an instrument cannot be valid if it is not reliable. The ESSI professional's guide offers this statement, "By not claiming to be a psychometric test, by sharing the results in an interactive environment with respondents, and by drawing upon an integrated perspective of personality and entrepreneurial research, the ESSI avoids some of the traditional pitfalls associated with self-report approaches to assessment" (p. 7). This assumption is also offered, "The ESSI assumes that people do not often have a clear sense of who they are as individuals and why they tend to behave the way they do in different circumstances in daily life. The ESSI is fundamentally interested in assisting people to improve this ability; it provides a tool for helping people develop greater self-awareness and self-control over their lives. Paradoxically, they do this by embracing the essential subjectivity of the process as the key to improving the objectivity of the results" (p. 7). The ESSI professional's guide also provides information about the instrument's limitations, specifically in terms of scoring on the first section, an ipsative measure. Also, issues of reliability and validity are acknowledged and independent research and further study is encouraged.

Validity. Information about establishing validity for the first section of the ESSI was not provided, but may be available in the PSI professional's guide. However, in terms of validity for the second section of the ESSI, primarily the FEA, a strong positive correlation between total score and actual entrepreneurial success was found, as measured by business results obtained in self-reported annual corporate incomes, self-perceptions of entrepreneurial success, and the perceptions of others regarding entrepreneurial success: success self-reported: $r = .87$; success other reported: $r = .79$; and success independent measure: $r = .81$. These correlation coefficients seem remarkably high. Validity of the original and revised versions of the FEA was determined based on administration of the instrument to more than 4,000 individuals who identified themselves as entrepreneurs and who had been successful entrepreneurs to some degree. Over 3,000 such individuals were administered the revised version to

examine validity. Users are cautioned that less than 8% of successful entrepreneurs did not score high on all three of these measures and less than 3% of unsuccessful entrepreneurs did score high. Therefore, those administering the ESSI are cautioned to share this information during training or consulting sessions and avoid creating the impression that failure to score high means a person will be a failure as an entrepreneur. Content validity for the third section of the ESSI, the interpretations, was established through using "college and university students and professionals in the fields of business, psychology, counseling and business coaching" (p. 6) as well as through the experiences, observations, and research of the developers.

COMMENTARY. Because the groups used in developing much of the ESSI are not thoroughly described, it is possible that many of the characteristics the ESSI attributes to entrepreneurs do not accurately reflect those of all entrepreneurs or business owners. Information about age, race, gender, and ethnicity are not given in describing the norm sample, which means the ESSI could be culturally, sexually, or otherwise biased, thereby affecting interpretation of results. In the ESSI's professional's guide, the authors offer a caution: "a minority (less than 8%) of successful entrepreneurs did not score high on all three of the above measures on the Foundations of Entrepreneurship Assessment and a few (less than 3%) unsuccessful entrepreneurs who did score high" (p. 6). The guide suggests that this fact should be stressed when administering the ESSI and a concerted effort made not to give clients the impression that failure to score high means he or she cannot become a successful entrepreneur. Further, Shenson's results "reveal differences in item-by-item responses on the part of test subjects, but show a high degree of correlation on both self-reported and externally measured success in entrepreneurial ventures for the inventory as a whole" (p. 6).

There are a number of measures available in books and on the Internet that purport to determine a person's entrepreneurial traits, style, or attitudes. The difficulty lies in selecting an appropriate measure that is (a) relatively easy to administer, score and interpret; (b) norm-based, including comparative normative information; and (c) appropriately tested to validate effectiveness. Each of these factors is addressed below. The ESSI is designed to be self-administered, self-scored, and self-interpreted. However, with regard to the first difficulty, self-administering and self-scoring appear relatively simple, but the materials needed for self-interpretation could be overwhelming (many support materials are needed when presenting this assessment) to individuals or administrators and prevent them from making accurate interpretations. The second difficulty as it relates to the ESSI is due to limited normative information. In the second and third sections of the ESSI, users cannot be sure that the information provided is representative because details related to appropriate reference populations are not available. The ESSI is also subject to the third difficulty, validation, in that its first section is an ipsative measure, and its second and third sections were developed using data from groups that may not represent the norm well and may exclude groups such as women, older persons, or persons of various racial and ethnic groups.

SUMMARY. Materials provided for review of the ESSI include the Entrepreneurial Style and Success Indicator, which includes three sections, the ESSI professional's guide, and the In-depth Interpretations. Each of these documents contains an abundance of useful information, especially the guide for administrators. The In-depth Interpretations is likely to be the most difficult for self-interpretation. The first part is an ipsative measure, and the authors note why they believe it cannot be used as a normative measure. However, this limitation may be more due to design than necessity. Therefore, because the publisher will support any studies that continue to improve the design or application of the ESSI, the authors and/or others may consider developing and testing an alternative version of the first section. It may be possible to develop the ipsative measure in a more normative form, thereby avoiding issues of reliability, construct validity, and equivalence in measuring characteristics of entrepreneurs, but meeting requirements of independence in statistical analyses. There are a few possible alternatives to use rather than the ESSI for individuals, counselors, coaches, and other professionals including the Strong Interest Inventory Interpretive Report, the Strong/MBTI Career Report, and the Myers-Briggs Type Indicator.

REVIEWER'S REFERENCE

Shenson, H. L. (1975). Foundations of Entrepreneurship Assessment. Woodland Hills, CA, Unpublished assessment instrument.

[69]

ERB Writing Assessment Program [Revised].

Purpose: "Designed to assess six domains of writing proficiency."
Population: Grades 3–4, 5–6, 7–8, 9–10, 11–12.
Publication Dates: 1989–2004.
Acronym: ERB WrAP.
Scores: 6 writing traits: Overall Development, Organization, Support, Sentence Structure, Word Choice, Mechanics.
Administration: Group.
Price Data, 2006: $7.75 per student for test materials (minimum order of $50 per level) plus shipping; $35 per data disk (ASCII file); $7 per additional set of anchor papers; $8 per perusal set (per level) including technical manual (2004, 45 pages), writing booklet, rubric, anchor papers, and report of individual student results; $10 per technical manual.
Comments: Writing samples scored by Measurement Incorporated.
Author: Educational Records Bureau.
Publisher: Educational Records Bureau.
a) ELEMENTARY LEVEL.
Purpose: To assess a student's narrative writing.
Population: Grades 3 and 4.
Time: Two [40–60] minute sessions.
b) INTERMEDIATE LEVEL.
Purpose: To assess a student's descriptive writing.
Population: Grades 5 and 6.
Time: Two [40–50] minute sessions.
c) MIDDLE SCHOOL LEVEL.
Purpose: To assess a student's expository writing.
Population: Grades 7 and 8.
Time: Two [40–50] minute sessions.
d) SECONDARY LEVEL.
Purpose: To assess a student's persuasive writing.
Population: Grades 9 and 10.
Time: Two [40–50] minute sessions.
e) COLLEGE PREP LEVEL.
Purpose: To assess a student's critical thinking.
Population: Grades 11 and 12.
Time: Two [40–50] minute sessions.
Cross References: For reviews by G. Michael Poteat and Wayne H. Slater of an earlier edition, see 13:122.

Review of the ERB Writing Assessment Program [Revised] by THOMAS P. HOGAN, Professor of Psychology, University of Scranton, Scranton, PA:

DESCRIPTION. The ERB Writing Assessment Program [Revised] (ERB WrAP) is presented as a direct measure of student writing ability for students in Grades 3–12. There are five levels: Elementary for Grades 3–4, Intermediate for 5–6, Middle for 7–8, Secondary for 9–10, and College Preparatory for 11–12. The "mode of discourse" (technical manual, p. 3) varies by level: Narrative, Descriptive, Expository, Persuasive, and Critical Thinking, respectively. These levels differ slightly from the first edition of the WrAP, reviewed in a previous *Mental Measurements Yearbook* (13:122; see cross references above).

Materials for the assessment consist of an 8-page Directions for Administering covering all levels; a 1-page Directions for First Draft, varying somewhat by level to accommodate the differences in modes; a 4-page folder of scoring rubrics, the same for all levels; sets of anchor papers for each level; a 4-page final draft booklet, the same for all levels, and including bubble-in identification information on the front cover; and a 40-page technical manual.

Scoring of the written products is completed by Measurement Incorporated in Durham, NC. The WrAP features analytic scoring on what the publisher refers to as six writing traits: Overall Development, Organization, Support, Sentence Structure, Word Choice, and Mechanics. Each score is on a 6-point scale from 1 (low) to 6 (high). As is typical for scoring of writing, two independent ratings are made, with discrepancies beyond 1 scale point being referred to a third reader. The different analytic scores are all obtained at once, rather than through separate ratings. According to the technical manual, use of the analytic scores is supposed to measure writing process rather than just the end product. The WrAP materials specifically eschew use of the more customary holistic score. Scores returned to users include, for each of the six writing traits, raw scores (average of the two ratings) plus within-grade percentile ranks and stanines. A total score (sum of the ratings on the six writing traits) is also provided, along with a scaled score for this total.

The WrAP's actual writing task is rather unusual in that it proceeds in two separate phases and on separate days. First, students prepare a draft. The teacher supplies ordinary paper for this purpose. Students are given a set of directions containing several "prewriting suggestions" and "editing suggestions," and teachers read these to the students. Students have approximately 50 minutes (see comment later on this point) to work on a draft. Then, the following day, students complete a final draft in the test booklet, again having about 50 minutes. This latter document is the product that is scored. Nothing is done with the draft. Final drafts may be done in word-processed form, but teachers are asked to disable spelling and grammar functions. Teachers are supposed to ensure that students have ready access to dictionaries and thesauruses for both writing periods. The actual writing prompts presented to students change each year.

Ordinarily, the publisher of a test is irrelevant for purposes of evaluating the instrument. In this case, there is some relevance. The publisher, Educational Records Bureau (ERB), exists primarily to serve independent and high-end suburban schools. It has a long and distinguished record of doing so. The WrAP is obviously aimed at this audience.

DEVELOPMENT. The WrAP technical manual provides minimal information about development of the test. Regarding the use of six writing traits, the manual references a project with teachers in one school system, working with staff of the Northwest Regional Educational Laboratory (NWREL) and asserts that this work has been widely accepted. Oddly, the manual lists seven traits arising from this project but does not reconcile the difference between these seven and the six used by the WrAP. [Editor's Note: The test publisher informed the Buros Institute of Mental Measurements late in the process, after these reviews had been written, that there were some mistakes in the technical manual for the WrAP. They advised that they were in the process of correcting and reprinting the manual. A correct listing of the writing traits assessed on the WrAP would have included "Voice" and "Word Choice," and not "Voice Choice."] Regarding the five modes of discourse, changing with each level of the test, the manual simply states that the levels are consistent with those recognized by the National Council of Teachers of English; it claims, without support, that the changes by level correspond to the typical order of instruction. Regarding specific prompts, the manual reports that 16 prompts were selected from 24 that were field tested in 2001–2002. Criteria for selection of the final prompts are not clear.

TECHNICAL INFORMATION. Regarding validity, the technical manual devotes most attention to factor analysis of the six scores, interchangeably referred to as traits or domains. The analytic procedure was principal components with oblique (oblimin) rotation. The results usually yielded two factors, labeled form and content, with the two oblique factors themselves intercorrelated approximately .80; the two factors coalesce into a single factor at the higher grades. Incredibly, the manual claims that these results support the six-score structure of the test. Clearly, they do not. One could quibble as to whether there is just one dimension or possibly two highly correlated dimensions here (most experts, I think, would opt for one), but there certainly are not six. In apparent reference to content validity, the manual simply states that the modes of discourse are valid if those modes are the ones addressed by a school in particular grades. Such a tautology is not very helpful. Although mentioned under scaling rather than under validity, the manual notes that scores tend to increase from grade to grade within a level and from fall to spring within grade: a sort of Binet-like argument for validity. However, as the manual notes, there are some untidy reversals in the expected patterns. Finally, the manual claims that, by having six writing traits and by requiring an initial draft, the assessment is addressing process rather than end product. Clearly, that is not the case. What is scored and reported is based on a finished product and one that is essentially unidimensional. The writing process is not analyzed.

Regarding reliability, the manual reports generalizability analyses with students, domains, and readers (raters) as components. Given that domains are not distinct, as just noted, these analyses reduce to simple interrater agreement reliabilities. They are high, generally above .90. This is what would be expected from an organization like Measurement Incorporated, which has vast experience in scoring writing materials. However, the manual makes no mention of variance due to topics or occasions, which are the principal sources of unreliability for writing assessments— and they are typically found to be very substantial (see, for example, the summary of relevant research by Hayes, Hatch, & Silk, 2000; and the analyses by Koretz, Stecher, Klein, & McCaffrey, 1994). It is misleading to imply that overall reliability is high when treating only interrater reliability (domain reliability being largely irrelevant here).

Regarding norms, the manual reports a scaling project to allow for conversion of raw scores (average of two ratings) into a scaled score cutting across all levels. This transformation is apparently done only for the total score, based on the sum of the six domain scores. Further, selected percentiles are presented separately for independent school and suburban school students. No information is provided about the nature of either the independent or suburban groups. The actual norms are updated each year based on a rolling 3-year combination of users. Perhaps information about the nature of the norm groups is given in separate publications along with annual updates in the norms. However, the technical manual should at least provide information about the original groups.

The first edition of the WrAP was justifiably criticized for total absence of a technical manual (Poteat, 1998; Slater, 1998). This second edition has a technical manual, but it is clearly deficient both in what it omits and in what it includes but with inappropriate inferences.

COMMENTARY. On the positive side, the WrAP uses a reasonable set of prompts, although restricted to only one mode of discourse per level. The scoring rubrics and sample anchor papers are also commendable. Certainly the scoring contractor (Measurement Incorporated) can supply high interrater reliability. However, in addition to the technical deficiencies noted earlier, the WrAP has some troublesome administrative features. Of greatest concern is the 2-day administration format. Students start a draft on Day 1 and then complete the final draft on Day 2. Almost certainly, there is unwelcome variance due to discussing the topic with parents, caregivers, peers, and perhaps even teachers between days. The directions for timing present another opportunity for unwanted variance. According to the Directions for Administering (for upper levels, p. 2), "students will have up to 50 minutes to work on their writing samples, including directions from the proctor." Almost certainly, teachers (if they follow the directions) will differ in how long they take to give directions and answer questions, resulting in varying amounts of time actually devoted to writing. One also wonders about how uniformly diligent teachers can be in disabling (and keeping disabled) the spelling and grammar functions when students use the word processing option. These potential problems are not addressed in the WrAP materials.

SUMMARY. The WrAP has very substantial administrative and technical problems. In this reviewer's opinion, it is not recommended for use. Schools interested in a standardized assessment of writing skill would be better served with the writing assessments available with most of the widely used standardized achievement batteries. Typically, the writing assessments accompanying these batteries offer a choice of different modes of discourse for prompts at all grade levels and a choice of either holistic or analytic scoring. If a school does use the WrAP, school personnel should be made aware that they are not measuring six relatively independent traits, that the reliability of the measure is substantially less than what is portrayed by the manual, that there may well be irrelevant sources of variance attributable to the 2-day administration, and that the norms must be carefully explained.

REVIEWER'S REFERENCES

Hayes, J. R., Hatch, J. A., & Silk, C. M. (2000). Does holistic assessment predict writing performance? *Written Communication, 17*, 3-26.
Koretz, D., Stecher, B., Klein, S., & McCaffrey, D. (1994). The Vermont portfolio assessment program: Findings and implications. *Educational Measurement: Issues and Practice, 13(3)*, 5-16.
Poteat, G. M. (1998). [Review of the ERB Writing Assessments]. In J. C. Impara & B. S. Plake (Eds.), *The thirteenth mental measurements yearbook* (pp. 426–427). Lincoln, NE: Buros Institute of Mental Measurements.
Slater, W. H. (1998). [Review of the ERB Writing Assessment]. In J. C. Impara & B. S. Plake (Eds.), *The thirteenth mental measurements yearbook* (pp. 427–428). Lincoln, NE: Buros Institute of Mental Measurements.

Review of the ERB Writing Assessment Program [Revised] by BRUCE G. ROGERS, Professor Emeritus of Educational Psychology, University of Northern Iowa, Cedar Falls, IA:

DESCRIPTION. The Educational Records Bureau (ERB) Writing Assessment Program [Revised] was developed to directly measure the writing ability of students as they progress through school. The current edition, developed in 2002 to reflect the refinement of the original six domain (factor) model, has been expanded to five levels, with two grades per level, encompassing Grades 3 through 12. A technical manual was developed for this edition, which should be carefully analyzed by any potential customer prior to a decision to purchase. The authors have developed, for each of the five levels, a booklet containing 20 Anchor papers for the single question prepared for that level. Following each Anchor paper, the six domains are assigned a score, followed by one sentence (sometimes two) of explanation for the score that was assigned. The Anchor booklets were assembled to show teachers and administrators how the student responses will be graded by "scorers [who] have been certified as having passed an intensive training and qualifying program" (technical manual, p. 1).

The students, at each level, are given a printed prompt (or question) of one or two sentences and instructions to write a rough draft during the next 40 to 50 minutes, which constitutes the first period. In the second period, either the same day or the next day, the students receive their rough draft with instructions to prepare a final draft. A three-page writing booklet is provided for the final draft, which is mailed to the publisher to be scored.

The five levels, called "modes," are given the names Narrative, Descriptive, Expository, Persuasive, and Critical Thinking, in that sequence. Writing experts will recognize this as a widely used sequence. Each writing sample is scored by two trained readers, independently, on each of the six domains (also called writing traits), labeled: Overall Development, Organization, Support, Sentence Structure, Word Choice, and Mechanics. Again, experts in writing assessment will recognize these as having a long, established use in professional evaluation.

DEVELOPMENT. The authors trace the history of the program for over 20 years, beginning in public schools in the state of Oregon. Teachers and other educators began the evolution of their six-trait model, to assess the writing of elementary students, as was being done in several other states across the nation. They also evolved the grade-level structure, which eventually resulted in five levels, each assessed with a distinct mode of discourse (previously identified in this review). These efforts led to the development and tryout of items in 2001, the administration of the new test in 2002, and the subsequent preparation of the manual.

TECHNICAL. The test was standardized using the fall 2002 test administration data, but no description of the standardization sample is given. Only the total scores, not the domain scores, are reported in the manual.

The total scores are converted into percentiles for ease of interpretation by the student and other users. The manual shows an excerpt from the conversion table, for the raw scores associated with the percentile values of 10, 25, 50, 75, and 90. Because each mode includes two grade levels, it would be expected that the higher grade in the pair would have a higher raw score for a given percentile. In the actual reported data, there were a few exceptions, which might be the result of the effects of sampling variability or rater inconsistency.

Raw scores were also converted to scale scores via a logistic function, but the authors did not provide their rationale, a deficiency that could be addressed in future printings. The resulting scale scores were fitted in a plot to show continuous growth across grade levels. The shapes of the curves reflect the logistic transformation, which gives an ogive-type shape; however, the authors did not give an interpretation of the shapes in terms of expected learning curves. Although the authors state that the scaling "has yielded an easily interpretable set of values" (technical manual, p. 12), some readers of the manual may not find it so "easy" and might appreciate further explanation.

For evidence of test reliability, it is always desirable to seek, if possible, some alternate-form data, but the authors have not yet chosen to do that. They might consider the advantage of doing so in the future. They did analyze their existing data for internal consistency, using generalizability analysis, and claimed that they used a "different approach" (technical manual, p. 17) from correlation-based techniques, but generalizability theory is often conceptualized as a "generalization" of simple correlation. The manual displays 10 analyses, all of which have values of G and Phi greater than .90. The variance component values for the Students were satisfactory, for the Domains were small (near .02), and for the Readers were very small. Indeed, the Reader values were so small as to raise some concern. Of the 10 values, 8 had four zeros after the decimal. Although the Readers were well trained, their judgments still involved subjectivity, so one might expect some chance variation. When variability is below chance expectation, researchers will often investigate further for an explanation. The data show that, in over 10% of the cases, there was a 1-point difference between the scores of the two readers, thus suggesting some variability in this source.

With respect to validity, the authors mention establishing content validity through input from teachers, but do not provide supporting detail to constitute evidence. Criterion-related validity is not mentioned, but it might be worthwhile to gather data from an established instrument, such as the Stanford Writing Assessment Program, Third Edition (Harcourt Brace Educational Measurements, 1996), to examine the relationship. For construct validity, the authors reported a factor analysis with a nonorthogonal rotation procedure and reported two factors correlated at .72–.82. They said that these two factors, which they labeled Content and Form, could form a "reasonable underlying structure" (technical manual, p. 13) for the data. Although those data are pertinent, it might be desirable to have further evidence that the factor loadings were reflective of the hypothesized constructs. As the authors state, validity is a judgment of the degree to which "empirical evidence and theoretical rationales" (technical manual, p. 2) support the inferences. More of that evidence and reasoning would enhance the validity of this test.

COMMENTARY. Both reviewers (Poteat, 1998; Slater, 1998) of the earlier edition pointed out what they perceived to be areas in need of improvement and made constructive suggestions. The test authors apparently chose not to give serious attention to those suggestions, which, in the opinion of this reviewer, was an unfortunate choice. This reviewer suggests that the authors might carefully analyze those suggestions. The modes postulated for this test seem attractive, but the authors do not give any theoretical justification for them. Can it be assumed that successive levels are inclusive? That would seem reasonable so that the students could display their skills as their writing ability increases in complexity. It would be useful if the authors could address that in their subsequent revisions of the manual. Likewise, the domains seem reasonable, so readers might appreciate a theoretical rationale by the authors.

The authors claim that analytical scoring is preferable to holistic scoring because it "isolates teachable skills" (technical manual, p. 4). However, the technical manual does not show a six-variable intercorrelation table that could show evidence pertaining to the distinctiveness of the domains. Further, because the same rater generated all six scores, both rater-effect and halo-effect could be confounded with the skill. Finally, the six domain scores are added to obtain a total score. The authors might consider scoring a set of papers with holistic scoring and then correlating those scores with the total scores. That could lead to a discussion of how the analytic scores could be used in feedback to the student, which is not presently in the manual.

One concern that this reviewer has with the validity data is that some of the sample prompts appear to be deficient in how we want students to think. For example, a student taking the test is presented with a prompt that describes a current controversy. The student is asked to write an essay presenting his or her position on this issue. Educated people can see both pros and cons on this issue, so the student needs to be aware of both of those views prior to forming a position. Asking the student to write a position statement prior to showing a clear understanding of both the pros and cons appears to me to be in inverse order and thus may interfere with the ability of the educated student to clearly write what they know. I suggest that the authors consider this philosophical position, because Persuasion is a common topic in writing classes.

A second concern of this reviewer is with reliability. Only one writing sample is generated in the two periods. Have the authors analyzed the data obtained in only one writing session to examine the adequacy of that sample in terms of reliability? For many years, researchers have reported that reliability is enhanced with more than one writing sample. The authors might consider collecting a separate writing sample in each session, even though each sample may be shorter.

CONCLUSION. The ERB Writing Assessment Program [Revised] shows evidence of being constructed on professionally accepted Domains and Modes. It is scored in a professional manner, based on stated criteria. However, it has limitations, as pointed out in this review and in the two reviews of the previous edition. This reviewer thinks that research indicates that reliable and valid results can be obtained in a much shorter testing time. Given its limitations, potential users might also consider an established instrument such as the Stanford Writing Assessment Program (Harcourt Brace Educational Measurement, 1996; T7:2417). For students with adequate keyboard skills, one of the newer computer-based scoring programs, such the Criterion Online Writing Evaluation (see www.ETS.org), might be considered. However, if substantial changes are made by ERB, a revision of this instrument may prove feasible for use in schools to complement the teacher's assessment of pupil writing skills.

REVIEWER'S REFERENCES

Harcourt Brace Educational Measurement. (1996). Stanford Writing Assessment Program, Third Edition. San Antonio, TX: Harcourt Assessment, Inc.

Poteat, G. M. (1998). [Review of the ERB Writing Assessment]. In J. C. Impara & B. S. Plake (Eds.), *The thirteenth mental measurements yearbook* (pp. 426–427). Lincoln, NE: Buros Institute of Mental Measurements.

Slater, W. H. (1998). [Review of the ERB Writing Assessment]. In J. C. Impara & B. S. Plake (Eds.), *The thirteenth mental measurements yearbook* (pp. 427–429). Lincoln, NE: Buros Institute of Mental Measurements.

[70]

Facial Expressions of Emotion-Stimuli and Tests.

Purpose: Designed to "assess recognition of facial expressions of emotion."

Population: Adults.

Publication Date: 2002.

Acronym: FEEST.

Administration: Individual.

Price Data, 2006: £384 per CD-ROM including tests and manual.

Time: Untimed.

Comments: Computer administered; requires Pentium PC running Windows 98, 64 Mb RAM and CD-ROM drive; also runs on Apple Macintosh System 7.5 through 9; 2 tests: Ekman 60 Faces, Emotion Hexagon.

Authors: Andrew Young, David Perrett, Andrew Calder, Reiner Sprengelmeyer, and Paul Ekman.

Publisher: Harcourt Assessment [England].

a) EKMAN 60 FACES.

Scores, 7: Anger, Disgust, Fear, Happiness, Sadness, Surprise, Total.

b) EMOTION HEXAGON.

Scores, 7: Same as *a* above.

Comments: Uses computer-morphed expressions to manipulate test difficulty.

Review of the Facial Expression of Emotion—Stimuli and Tests by ALBERT M. BUGAJ, Professor of Psychology, University of Wisconsin-Marinette, Marinette, WI:

DESCRIPTION. The Facial Expressions of Emotion—Stimuli and Tests (FEEST) CD contains the Ekman 60 Faces Test (ESFT), the Emotion Hexagon Test (EHT), 1,000 images of facial expressions (FEEST Stimuli), a software utility to copy the images to a computer, and test and software manuals. The manual (overview, pp. 10–11) states various purposes of the FEEST: (a) examination of deficits in facial expression recognition; (b) using FEEST stimuli to create supplementary tests for specific purposes (e.g., whether a person can match different emotional representations); (c) examination via neural imaging of responses of the brain to different emotions; and (d) experiments studying phenomena such as priming effects.

Neither the ESFT nor the EHT are timed. The manual does not indicate the qualifications necessary to administer or interpret the tests' results. Brief, easily understood instructions for both tests appear on the computer screen. The ESFT consists of pictures of 10 individuals depicting six basic emotions (Anger, Disgust, Fear, Happiness, Sadness, Surprise). The program presents each picture one at a time in random order for 5 seconds. The test-taker then has an unlimited time to identify the emotion represented by clicking on the proper label on the computer screen using the mouse, or by pressing a corresponding key on the keyboard. Making a choice activates the next picture. Six practice trials precede the test. The total score for the ESFT is 60 points, 10 points for each emotion.

For the EHT, photographs of one person (male) from the EFST stimulus set were "morphed" to create stimuli of graded difficulty (e.g., manipulating "disgust" to gradually look more and more like "anger"). The EHT presents stimuli one at a time for 5 seconds. As in the ESFT the test-taker must decide which of six emotions the picture represents. The test begins with a 30-image practice session, followed by five test blocks of 30 trials each. The program allows a rest period between each block. The total possible score for the test is 120 correct, 20 for each emotion.

The program saves EHT and EFST scores in an Excel-compatible format and EFST scores in a graphical representation as well. The software records the file name of each photo and the participant's response. For the EHT, this allows the individual analyzing the results to determine whether errors made are of the same type as normal perceivers, and whether the errors tend to be for expressions not easily recognized, or for particular facial muscle movements.

DEVELOPMENT. Ten models (6 female, 4 male) from the Ekman and Friesen (1976) Pictures of Facial Affect form the basis of the FEEST stimuli. None of the models appear to be of minority ethnic background. Each model displays a neutral pose, plus six basic emotions that form the stimuli for the EFST. In the FEEST stimuli these are "morphed" through computer manipulation. "Emotion megamixes are continua showing transitions between one expression and another"

(manual, overview, p. 7). "Caricatures" exaggerate differences between emotions making them easier to recognize. "Anti-caricatures" are less intense and harder to recognize. "Morphed and caricatured continua" are continua of single faces ranging from a neutral pose to an intensely expressed emotion.

To obtain comparison data for the EFST, tests of 227 individuals (ages 20 to 70) were performed. Analysis of variance assessed the effects of age, gender, and intelligence (as measured via the NART-R when scores were not available from other sources). This revealed a borderline effect for age for the total score. Based on the results of subsequent analyses of variance, the manual provides comparison data for the total score and each emotion for the total group, as well as subdivided into three age groups.

Comparison data for the EHT were developed by testing 125 individuals, aged 20 to 75, with intelligence test scores of 90 or above (estimated using the NART-R when scores were not available from existing records). Analyses of variance indicated no differences due to age, gender or intelligence for the total score. A significant interaction between age and emotion did occur. The manual thus presents comparison data for the total score and each emotion for the total group, as well as subdivided into three age groups. Cutoff scores defining the border between normal-range and impaired performance for each age group for both tests were determined at the nearest integer score to a z value of 1.65 (p = .05) using the standard deviation of the entire group to estimate the degree of variability of recognition of each emotion.

TECHNICAL. Split-half reliabilities for the ESFT total score and all emotions except Fear and Happiness were in the .60 to .66 range, that for Fear was .53, and that for Happiness was .21. All reliabilities except that for Happiness were significant at the .001 level. The split-half reliability for "happiness" was insignificant for both the ESFT and EHT as scores were at ceiling. For the remaining emotions on the EHT, significant split-half reliabilities (all at the .001 level) ranged from a low of .33 for "surprise" to a high of .92 for the total score. There was no examination of test-retest reliability so it is impossible to ascertain whether scores are stable over time.

As one examination of the EFST's validity, the percentage correct rate of participants in the normative sample aged 20 to 30 years (n = 105) was found to be correlated with data provided by American college students who participated in a recognition test performed by Ekman and Friesen in 1976 (r = .081, df = 58, p < .001). EHT and EFST scores were also converted to a percentage correct rate for all participants in the normative samples. Total scores for the two tests were found to be significantly correlated (r = .68, df = 65, p < .001). Scores for each emotion except Happiness (where scores were at ceiling) were also significantly correlated, ranging from an r of .27 (df = 65, p < .05) for Disgust, to .54 (df = 65, p < .001) for Sadness.

The manual refers to several published case studies as well as group studies. Both types of studies utilized earlier variants of the tests (e.g., presentations of actual, rather than computer-generated, pictures, and verbal responses). The case studies involve individuals with various types of neurological damage (e.g., to the amygdala) and with obsessive-compulsive disorder (OCD). In most cases of neurological damage the individuals scored below cutoff on the ESFT for recognition of Fear, with more individuals below cutoff on the EHT. Similar results occurred for recognition of Disgust by individuals with OCD. Although providing the ages of the individual cases, the manual includes no information concerning gender or minority status of the individuals examined.

The manual does not discuss group studies, requiring the reader to locate them. Results of one study (Springelmeyer et al., 1996) indicated Huntington's patients (n = 13) had greater difficulty recognizing all emotions but happiness, compared to healthy adults (n = 17). Huntington's patients also had significantly lower scores than the control group on the Benton Test of Facial Recognition (BTFR), for which scores were within the normal range. Springelmeyer et al. (1997) found that individuals with OCD (n = 12), and individuals with Tourette's Syndrome accompanied by OCD (n = 5) scored significantly lower on recognition of disgust than 18 control individuals.

COMMENTARY. If the purpose of the EFST and EHT is for use in neural imaging studies and as stimuli in social psychological experiments, the tests could prove to be powerful research tools. If they are meant to be diagnostic tools, then their usefulness must be questioned. No examination of the test-retest reliability of either test has occurred. Likewise, there has been no effort to establish their concurrent validity through comparison with already established tests of neurological impairment. Although some research used the BTFR, these studies did not utilize the present forms of the EHT and EFST. The results of group and case study research, although suggesting the utility of the EHT and EFST as diagnostic tools, have been too few in number to make solid conclusions concerning criterion-related validity of the tests.

Based on the results of the analysis of variance of the normative data the manual assumes that "recognition of some emotions (especially fear) declines across age" (Section 1, p. 8). This assumption ignores the possible occurrence of cohort effects on the data (see Schaie, 1965, 1996), as well as the complex nature of changes in reaction time in adulthood (see Cerella, 1990; Salthouse, 1996). This is a rich area for future research, and does not negate the need to divide the tests' norms by age.

Additional investigations should examine adequate samples of individuals with specific neurological impairments to determine the adequacy of the cutoff scores and patterns of responses specific to particular disorders. The test-retest reliability and criterion-related validity of the EHT and EFST must be examined. Another area for further investigation is the relationship of age to responsiveness to emotional stimuli.

SUMMARY. The FEEST can be recommended as a research tool for social psychologists studying the perception of emotions and the effects of emotional stimuli. Until further research demonstrates its utility as a diagnostic tool it should be used in the field of neurological psychology only on an experimental basis in conjunction with more established instruments. The psychometric properties of the FEEST tests of emotional recognition are relatively unexamined.

REVIEWER'S REFERENCES

Cerella, J. (1990). Aging and information-processing rate. In J. E. Birren & K. W. Schaie (Eds.), *Handbook of the psychology of aging* (3rd ed., pp. 201–221). San Diego, CA: Academic Press.

Ekman, P., & Friesen, W. V. (1976). *Pictures of facial affect*. Palo Alto, CA: Consulting Psychologists Press.

Salthouse, T. A. (1996). The processing-speed theory of adult age differences in cognition. *Psychological Review, 103*, 403–428.

Schaie, K. W. (1965). A general model for the study of developmental change. *Psychological Bulletin, 64*, 92–107.

Schaie, K. W. (1996). *Intellectual development in adulthood: The Seattle Longitudinal Study*. New York: Cambridge University Press.

Springelmeyer, R., Young, A. W., Calder, A. J., Karnat, A., Lange, H. W., Hömberg, V., Perrett, D. I., & Rowland, D. (1996). Loss of disgust: Perception of faces and emotions in Huntington's disease. *Brain, 119*, 1647–1665.

Springelmeyer, R., Young, Q. W., Pundt, I., Springelmeyer, A., Calder, A. J., Berrios, G., Winkel, R., Vollmoeller, W., Kuhn, W., Sartory, G., & Przunte K. H. (1997). Disgust implicated in obsessive-compulsive disorder. *Proceedings of the Royal Society: Biological Sciences, B264*, 1767–1773.

Review of the Facial Expressions of Emotion—Stimuli and Tests by DENICE WARD HOOD, Associate Professor of Educational Psychology, Northern Arizona University, Flagstaff, AZ:

DESCRIPTION. The Facial Expressions of Emotion—Stimuli and Tests (FEEST) is designed to test recognition of affect (as indicators of emotion) from facial expression. The FEEST consists of three computer-administered sections. "All of the images used in the FEEST are derived from pictures of facial expressions in the Ekman and Friesen (1976) series of Pictures of Facial Affect" (manual, overview, p. 2). The Ekman 60 Faces Test uses 60 facial expressions of basic emotions (Anger, Disgust, Fear, Happiness, Sadness, and Surprise) in addition to neutral facial expressions. The Emotion Hexagon Test consists of 5 sets of 30 computer-morphed images from the Ekman and Friesen series to test recognition of basic emotions with stimuli of graded difficulty (manual, overview, p. 6). The examples provided in the Emotion Hexagon Test are more ambiguous than those included in the Ekman 60 Faces Test. The hexagonal representation refers to the emotions that tend to be confused most frequently with each other. The FEEST stimuli contains approximately 1,000 unmodified, facial expressions and computer-manipulated images of faces (prototyped expressions) from the Ekman and Friesen series. Morphed and caricatured versions of the computer-manipulated images allow the creation of novel tests and experiments. The FEEST stimuli can be utilized to create tests with emotions expressed in varying levels of intensity.

The FEEST, designed for adults, was created to assess the recognition of facial expressions of emotion. The FEEST is provided on a CD-ROM, which can be used in both a PC and a Macintosh computer. The examinee can use the mouse or keyboard to select the emotion they think describes the facial expression provided on the screen. The tests are untimed; however, each of the facial expressions, appearing in random order, is on the screen for 5 seconds. There is not a time limit for the examinee's response. The Ekman 60 Faces Test yields a maximum score of 60 for all six emotions; 10 for each basic emotion. The Emotion Hexagon Test generates a maximum score of 120; 20 for each of the six emotions. The CD also contains practice blocks which are not scored. The software scores the test and saves the summary to a file.

DEVELOPMENT. The pictures used in the FEEST (copyright, 2002) originated from Ekman's cross-cultural studies conducted 40+ years ago to determine the emotion shown in a series of photographs. Six basic emotions were found to be achieved when subjects moved their facial based muscles into particular patterns. The Pictures of Facial Affect (POFA) was developed on the authors' assumptions that particular muscle movements signified each emotion. The Psychology Manual provided by the developer described the origin of the FEEST pictures. Original judgments were made by U.S.-born college students. The Facial Action Coding System (FACS) was subsequently created as selection criteria for emotional expression. The FACS is a "measurement technique for scoring any observed facial behavior, in still photographs, film or video" (manual, section 6, p. 4). The original series of photographs was shown to individuals in "literate and preliterate cultures" (p. 2). The reader is directed to Ekman (1999) for a complete review of these studies.

TECHNICAL. The Psychology Manual describes the sample used to establish the performance norms. These norms were based on an opportunity sample of 227 individuals aged 20–70 (Ekman 60 Faces Test) and 125 aged 20–75 (Emotion Hexagon Test). The National Adult Reading Test (NART-R) was used to estimate intelligence when IQ scores were unknown. Average scores by sex, age, and IQ range were provided but no further demographic information (e.g., race, ethnicity, frequency by group) was given. This is cause for concern regarding the norm-setting process given the weaknesses inherent in the sampling procedure and the paucity of descriptive detail for the sample. The process for establishing the cutoff scores is described but not justified. Additional validity studies for the Ekman 60 Faces are referred to (manual, section 1, p. 2) but the results of these were not included in the documentation. The split-half reliability method was employed for both the Ekman 60 Faces Test and the Emotion Hexagon Test using data from 50 and 40 participants respectively. The values for split-half reliabilities were .92 for the total and above .33 for each of the emotions with the exception of Happiness because the two sets of scores were at ceiling. Comparison data on the correlation ($r = .81$) of recognition rates between the Ekman and Friesen (1976) data (which utilized college students as the sample) and the FEEST data (age group range 20–30) was offered as further evidence of reliability. The only information provided on these two samples was the approximate age range. Information on the extent to which the FEEST correlates with any other measures is not provided. No additional validity evidence is offered: The authors assert that "the validity of the items used in the Ekman 60 Faces test does not need to be established here, since the Ekman and Friesen (1976) series has been the most extensively used set of stimuli in research on recognition of facial expressions" (manual, section 1, p. 10). The authors cited several studies where some variation of the Ekman 60 Faces test was used in addition to two studies where the test was used with Möbius syndrome and frontal variant frontotemporal dementia.

COMMENTARY. The authors acknowledge that "testing of facial expression recognition is notoriously tricky" (manual, overview, p. 5). Facial expressions, the words used to describe them, and the meaning associated with those words may vary slightly from culture to culture and context to context. Concomitantly, without adequate information on the representativeness of the sample it is unclear if the inferences drawn from the scores are valid for various groups that range in age, gender, ethnicity, race, and social class. For example, the Psychology Manual does not address the rationale for the pictures appearing to be exclusively of Anglo men and women. The test is relatively easy to use requiring only a minimum of computer skills to navigate. The Emotion Hexagon test was long, but it contains scheduled breaks to help relieve fatigue. Because this test contained the morphed images of only one face from the Ekman and Friesen (1976) series, it became a bit tedious to take. The order of the emotion selection buttons was randomized to help reduce response perseveration.

SUMMARY. The FEEST CD-ROM is a self-contained set of facial expression emotion recognition tests that can be self-administered and computer-scored (numerically and graphically). Age, sex, and IQ differences were considered in the norming process but neither race nor ethnicity were discussed for either the sample description or the faces used in the database. The results yield detailed information on emotion recognition in addition to areas of specific deficiency in response.

This may be of particular utility in clinical applications and contexts. Potential users may wish to review the literature, which may address questions regarding validity and reliability issues.

REVIEWER'S REFERENCES
Ekman, P., & Friesen, W. V. (1976). *Pictures of facial affect*. Palo Alto, CA: Consulting Psychologists Press.
Ekman, P. (1999). Facial expressions. In T. Dalgleish & M. Power (Eds.), *The handbook of cognition and emotion* (pp. 301–320). Sussex, U.K.: John Wiley and Sons, Ltd.

[71]

Fast Track.

Purpose: Designed as a "simple screening tool to identify those who have literacy needs below Level 1 and/or numeracy needs below Entry Level of the Basic Skills Standards."

Population: Adults.

Publication Date: 2000.

Scores: Total score only.

Administration: Individual.

Forms, 3: Fast Track 20 Questions, Fast Track Assessment—Written, Fast Track Assessment—Oral.

Price Data, 2000: £15 per complete kit including manual (24 pages), 50 Fast Track 20 Question, 50 Fast Track Assessment—Written, and 50 Fast Track Assessment—Oral; £9 per manual; £3 per 50 Fast Track 20 Questions; £3 per 50 Fast Track Assessment—Written; £3 per 50 Fast Track Assessment—Oral.

Time: (5–15) minutes.

Comments: This test can be completed as part of a 1:1 interview.

Authors: The Basic Skills Agency.

Publisher: The Basic Skills Agency [England].

Review of the Fast Track by PAM RAMSDEN, Senior Lecturer, University of Bolton, Bolton, Lancashire, England:

DESCRIPTION. The Fast Track assessment is designed to identify basic skills deficiencies for front line advisers, outreach personnel, and occupational development workers in contact with young people and adults. Fast Track is written in British terminology with the use of British monetary denominations (British pound) for numeracy and is therefore only appropriate to individuals and agencies familiar with both. The instrument consists of two basic forms. The first is a series of 20 basic informational type questions and the second is a reading task with an additional 6 questions. The informational 20-questions form is designed to assess basic reading and numerical ability and consists of questions such as, "How often do you read a newspaper?" and "How often do you write letters/notes/anything?" The second form is task oriented where the person taking the test is asked to read an advertisement about a job description and then answer 6 questions relating specifically to the statement.

The Fast Track assessment can be administered either verbally or in written form. The complete instrument measures two basic abilities: (a) basic communication skills such as reading and understanding a short feature in a newspaper, the ability to use reference materials such as a dictionary, ability to deal with forms and write formal letters, reports, or notes; (b) basic numeracy skills such as using money, checking change, comparing the price of goods, understanding and using simple tables, graphs, and bar charts.

The instructions for the Fast Track assessment are clear and well detailed, and participants are required to provide answers in either short answer form, yes/no, or a 4-point Likert-type scaling. The directions are standardized for ease of administration. The 20-question portion of the instrument requires approximately 5 minutes to complete, and the written/task portion takes approximately 10 minutes for an overall total of 15–30 minutes for both sections depending upon reading ability. The handbook provides clear scoring and an easy-to-read result guide that directs the scorer/administrator to refer the participant for further assessment dependent upon the individual's score.

DEVELOPMENT. The Fast Track assessment material was piloted in 23 different organizations from career services to college outreach programs. The various centers were asked to assess up to six individuals with one version of the material and were then asked to use Version 2 of the agency's initial assessment test "to provide a baseline for the reliability and scoring of the new materials. A total of 177 assessments were distributed and 141 returned" (user guide, p. 18). Percentages were reported for score correlation with initial assessments of between 77% and 81%. Additionally, centers were invited to make a qualitative evaluation of the material. Results were provided in three different categories: acceptability to clients (95%-yes), ease of administration (100%-yes), and easy to mark (90%-yes).

TECHNICAL. Outside of the summary results reported in basic percentages, no other technical information was available. There appear to

be no formalized norms, or research conducted on the reliability or validity of this instrument. The instrument relies entirely on face validity and has no further information concerning current measurement standards.

COMMENTARY. The Fast Track assessment appears to be a basic instrument of British design created to identify deficiencies in communication skills and numeracy particularly related to work type settings. Its strengths are in its ability to assess work-related skills quickly in adult populations, and it is best used in occupational screening organizations for which functions are to assist in job placement. The manual provides no reliability or validity information as well as no information on gender, age, and ethnic differences. Scoring is easy and straightforward as well as standardized administration information.

SUMMARY. The Fast Track assessment is a primary instrument for estimating deficiencies in basic skills in communication and numeracy mainly related to occupational functioning. It is written and designed in the U.K. and therefore uses British English terminology as well as U.K. currency for its numeracy functions. It is rather limited as there is no reliability or validity information as well as no information on norms in terms of gender, age, and ethnic differences. Its usefulness will be limited to basic screening and the identification of individuals who lack basic skills in reading and writing enabling support organizations to rectify these deficiencies.

[72]

Feedback Edition of the Strength Deployment Inventory.

Purpose: Designed to elicit feedback to describe how a person uses his/her personal strengths in relationships.

Population: Adults.

Publication Dates: 1973–1996.

Acronym: SDI/PVI.

Scores, 20: 7 Motivational Values (Altruistic-Nurturing, Assertive-Directing, Analytic-Autonomizing, Flexible-Cohering, Assertive-Nurturing, Judicious-Competing, Cautious-Supporting), plus 13 scores reflecting Progression through Conflict.

Administration: Individual or group.

Price Data, 2001: $4.50 per test booklet; $30 per manual (1996, 146 pages).

Time: (20–40) minutes.

Comments: Uses self-ratings and ratings of a significant other person; manual is entitled Relationship Awareness Theory Manual of Administration and Interpretation (9th Ed.).
Author: Elias H. Porter.
Publisher: Personal Strengths Publishing.

Review of the Feedback Edition of the Strength Deployment Inventory by RICHARD E. HARDING, Director of Research, Kenexa Technology, Inc., Lincoln, NE:

DESCRIPTION. The Strength Deployment Inventory (SDI) was designed to provide information on the motivation of an individual and an understanding about how a person responds to conflict. The SDI is a learning tool that includes training on interpretation. As such, the SDI is not intended to be used as an employee selection instrument. The author feels that an individual could answer in a way that would produce results that an employer may want but would not be an accurate depiction of the person.

The author of the SDI, Elias H. Porter, Ph.D., based it on his Relationship Awareness Theory. The basic premise of the theory is that relationships grow as individuals seek gratification from others. The theory views motives as the basis for behavior and gives understanding in why people do what they do. Within the theory are seven clusters called the Motivational Values System, four of which are primary and three are a blending of the primaries. These are in effect when "all is going well" for the person. The seven clusters are: Altruistic—Nurturing, Assertive—Directing, Analytic—Autonomizing, Flexible—Cohering, Assertive—Nurturing, Judicious—Competing, and Cautious—Supporting.

Conflict resolution is also part of the theory and is measured in the SDI. Conflict is defined as occurring "when a person is faced with a situation that threatens their sense of self-worth or value" (Manual of Administration and Interpretation, p. 23). Much of the interpretation centers on conflict style as it relates to motivation.

The SDI is composed of 10 sentence stems with three possible completion responses, with the respondent being directed to weight the three response possibilities. The first 10 are answered on the basis of situations at home, school, work, or with friends where "things are going well and you feel good about yourself." The next 10 are where "things are going wrong and you are in conflict

with others." The respondent is directed to use 10 total points for each question and assign point values, that always sum to 10, across the three possible completion responses. The point values are then summed into six columns, which become the basis for analysis. Respondents then plot their column scores on a triangular grid, which is then interpreted according to the Manual of Administration and Interpretation.

There are so many interpretive nuances in the manual that training seems like a necessity for use of the SDI. Training is offered by the publishers for this purpose. The manual also provides some other teaching methods and exercises to use in working with people on the SDI.

The directions to complete the SDI and chart the scores on the interpretive triangle are clear and relatively easy to follow. The triangle is color coded in blue, green, and red for interpretive purposes. These colors are referred to throughout the manual. The triangle is also well labeled and descriptive of the motivational values and conflict resolution types.

DEVELOPMENT. The history of the development of the SDI is covered in 11 pages in the manual. It is an edited paper by the late Dr. Porter on his evaluation and discovery of the Relationship Awareness Theory. This is a well-written and descriptive treatise on how he came to the realization of the theory through his work in the late 1930s to his death in 1987. No data are presented but rather a conceptual development linking or distancing the theory to work by Fromm, Cattell, Skinner, Tolman, Erikson, and Horney. Conceptual arguments are presented as to where the theory is congruent to and incongruent to these works.

TECHNICAL. There is a chapter in the manual that provides evidence on reliability and validity. A test-retest reliability study is reported on 100 individuals. No description of the sample is provided nor is the study dated. The time between administrations was 6 days to 2 weeks. For the Altruistic-Nurturing scale, the reliability coefficient was .78, for Assertive—Directing it was .78, and for Analytic—Autonomizing it was .76. Item level data were also analyzed where item discriminations are listed in how well an item discriminates between high and low scores on the respective scales. These data look acceptable in terms of item significance. No other data are presented on reliability although anecdotal evidence of an experiential nature yields a conclusion that "a high degree of consistency is found no matter how long the intervening length of time between test and retest" (manual, p. 68).

The validity of the results is considered to be relatively unimportant due to the intended use of the tool for educational and self-awareness purposes rather than as a personnel selection test. Yet, the results of a validity study conducted in 1988-89 are included. The sample of 564 respondents is described according to gender, racial/ethnic background, income, and education. The study was more of a construct validation study than a criterion-related study. Internal consistency was re-examined and was supportive of the previous study of 100. Factor analysis was completed and indicated that the factor loadings were appropriate at the item level. No traditional tables associated with factor analysis were presented except for the factor loadings. There are statements that the SDI has been analyzed in a similar fashion for Spanish, Dutch, German, French, and Japanese versions. No data are included in the manual for these versions, but the conclusions are that it is appropriate for use internationally.

COMMENTARY. Because the SDI is not to be used as a personnel selection instrument, the authors did not see the need to include lengthy and detailed psychometric properties of the tool. Users are expected to take on face value the quality of the SDI, with little statistical evidence. Even if the use is intended for educational and self-awareness reasons, one still would like assurances that the tool has acceptable properties of validity and reliability. The expectations of the salient statistics surrounding these issues were not met in the manual.

Another concern centers on the use of the SDI without a training workshop. The manual is very detailed but still would present problems to an untrained user with all of the analytical nuances presented for appropriate interpretation. This reviewer could not find any information in the manual on who can administer the SDI, who can interpret the SDI, or the training, licensures or certificates necessary. The web site for the publisher (www.prersonalstrengths.com) does indicate that the facilitator for the SDI must be qualified.

SUMMARY. The goal of this review was not to evaluate the theory upon which the SDI was built but rather to provide readers with an understanding of the properties of the tool. The research evidence one would expect to support use of the instrument was not present. Yet with the stated purpose of the SDI around self-awareness in relationships, motivations, and conflict resolution the tool is acceptable. It does seem like it would provide an excellent framework for discussion between a counselor and client with regard to relationships and conflict. And it is to the publisher's credit that they indicate very clearly the SDI is not intended for personnel selection.

[73]

Feedback Portrait of Personal Strengths.

Purpose: Designed to elicit feedback to describe how a person uses his/her personal strengths in relationships.
Population: Adults.
Publication Date: 1997.
Scores, 3: Profile, Top Strengths, Least Deployed Strengths.
Administration: Individual or group.
Price Data, 2001: $5.50 per test booklet; $100 per manual.
Time: (20–40) minutes.
Author: Personal Strengths Publishing.
Publisher: Personal Strengths Publishing.

Review of the Feedback Portrait of Personal Strengths by FREDERIC MEDWAY, Professor of Psychology, University of South Carolina, Columbia, SC:

DESCRIPTION. The Feedback Portrait of Personal Strengths (referred to as Portrait in this review) is designed as a tool or exercise "to produce feedback that describes how a person uses their personal strengths in relationships" (test response form). The user is asked to sort 28 traits or characteristics (personal strengths) described on peel-apart stickers into piles that are most like and least like himself or herself using a diamond-shaped response grid. The grid assigns each personal strength a numerical value between 1 (least like person) and 9 (most like person). Scores are summed to yield values on four personality dimensions: Altruistic-Nurturing, Assertive-Directing, Analytic-Autonomizing, and Flexible-Cohering. The sort is then compared with one provided by a feedback provider (e.g., another with whom the person has a close or conflicted relationship). In most cases a feedback recipient would choose from whom they would like to receive feedback. The tool provides a chart that allows one to compare one's own personal strength views with those provided by another person both in terms of each personal strength and in terms of the four broad dimensions of personality. Personal strengths with values three or more points apart as rated by feedback recipient and feedback provider are used to generate discussion. The publisher claims that the Portrait's directions are easy to understand and that it is easy for individuals to rank order specific strengths. The Portrait is described as a vehicle for communicating compliments to others and as a learning tool for the feedback recipient and feedback provider. It is one of several feedback tools developed by Personal Strengths Publishing. The measure is to be used in counseling and consultation settings and was designed to lead to action plans to improve personal relationships.

DEVELOPMENT. The Feedback Portrait of Personal Strengths and related educational tools are based on Relationship Awareness Theory developed by Elias H. Porter, Ph.D. The publishing company produces a manual of interpretation and administration that describes the theory and provides information about some of the feedback tools. This manual does not specifically address the development of the Portrait or its characteristics.

Relationship Awareness Theory is a motivational theory of interpersonal relationships founded on the premise that individuals engage in purposeful behavior to obtain positive affirmation. It is based on the idea that individuals seek positive connections with others and that this drive begins in infancy. The theory also distinguishes between behavior exhibited when individuals are free to pursue interpersonal gratifications and behavior exhibited under conditions of conflict or opposition. The theory further notes that individuals exhibit personal strengths when interpersonal interactions are mutually gratifying. They exhibit a personal weakness (defined as overdoing a personal strength) when interpersonal interactions are not mutually productive and potentially destructive. A final aspect of the theory is the use of clear concepts and terms that can serve as a basis for self-discovery and understanding others. One such concept is Valued Relating Style—a predisposition to relate to others in a certain way that leads to rewards and personal empowerment. The

theory also describes seven clusters of ways of relating to others called Motivational Value Systems. The Portrait and other feedback measures from this company such as the Strength Deployment Inventory (SDI; T7:2436) help individuals identify their preference for 28 personal strengths (characteristic ways of responding) grouped into four primary motivational value systems: Altruistic-Nurturing, Assertive-Directing, Analytic-Autonomizing, and Flexible-Cohering.

TECHNICAL. The feedback recipient and feedback provider complete the tool independently and then discuss the results. Although group administration can be used, individual administration would appear preferable. The Portrait is described as an education tool and as such has not been subjected to basic test development standards. As noted, the manual does not contain technical information on the Portrait, but it does describe limited reliability and validity information on other assessment tools of the company (e.g., SDI). These other tools are similar in nature to the Portrait and data on them *may* be applicable to the Portrait as well. For example, SDI development was based on the assumption that individuals would be equally distributed across the first three value systems. Test-retest reliability ranges from $r = .76$ to .78 over a time period ranging from 6 days to 2 weeks; significant score changes over time are not considered likely. SDI items do appear to distinguish between high scorers and low scorers. The scale also yields profiles that would be expected from individuals in certain occupations (e.g., nurses were found to be highly altruistic and business majors found to be highly assertive). A large ($n = 564$) 1988 SDI validation study also demonstrated scale internal consistency and clear factor structure.

COMMENTARY. The Portrait is an educational tool designed to generate self-awareness of relationship styles. As such it appears to have high face validity, is easy to complete, and is easily scored. The 28 personal strengths are fairly easy to understand, at least by individuals with college educations. Although not designed as a test per se, the manual for its administration and interpretation does not provide any information on scale development and characteristics. This is a limitation in that such information is provided on related feedback measures, even if the quality of these studies may be questionable. The user of the tool does so without knowing if the tool is equally applicable across gender, ethnicity, educational level, etc. The scoring guidelines hold that score differences between feedback recipient and feedback provider exceeding three points are worthy of discussion and represent substantive disagreement in self and other perception. There is no justification provided for this recommendation, nor any discussion of what discrepancies exceeding three points may reveal. The manual does not present any illustrative cases to demonstrate the value of the scale or its limitations.

SUMMARY. The Feedback Portrait of Personal Strengths appears to be an interesting and engaging vehicle both for self-exploration and for obtaining feedback. It has been developed primarily as a springboard for discussion rather than a psychological test per se. It is felt that the exercise itself will generate self-learning by giving someone the chance to get systematic interpersonal feedback from another. Unfortunately, there is little information available to judge the merits of the tool. Because of this limitation, potential users may require supervision or instruction from an experienced user or may have to try out the Portrait a few times. This practice would seem especially valuable when used in interpersonal settings in which the feedback recipient and provider may have relationship issues or in which the interpersonal climate is not harmonious. The tool is presented as having the power to build positive relationships. However, in the hands of a novice or inexperienced user, individuals could come to doubt the validity of their own self-perceptions or become defensive or anxious when the feedback from others does not match their own self-views. Dealing with potential problems resulting from feedback discrepancies or the conversations that follow would seem to require considerable clinical training.

Review of the Feedback Portrait of Personal Strengths by JAMES A. PENNY, Senior Psychometrician, CASTLE Worldwide, Morrisville, NC:

DESCRIPTION. The Feedback Portrait of Personal Strengths is a diagnostic tool used to provide insight into the possible causes of harmony or conflict in the relationship between two people. No particular training is required to use this assessment, though some familiarity with relationship awareness theory would be helpful to frame the follow-up discussions the assessment intended to motivate.

In the instructions, one of the two people called the feedback provider; the other person called the feedback recipient. (Caution is urged this point because the designations, *provider* an *recipient*, are apparent misnomers. The reason f this caution appears later in this review.)

The feedback recipient uses a Q-sort arrange 28 squares each representing a streng (e.g., persevering, tolerant, self-confident, moest) onto a diamond shape where the top of tl diamond contains the strength most like the fee back recipient. The strength placed at the botto of the diamond is the strength that is least like tl feedback recipient.

There are nine horizontal lines from tl bottom to the top of the diamond on which tl strengths are arranged. From top to bottom, tl nine lines accommodate 1, 2, 3, 5, 6, 5, 3, 2, ar 1 strength(s). When the Q-sort is finished, tl feedback recipient records the line number on tl comparison chart. The line numbers correspor to the number of points to be given to eac strength. The strength at the top of the diamor receives nine points, whereas the strength at tl bottom of the diamond receives one point.

The feedback provider also performs the C sort to arrange the strengths in a pattern that be describes the feedback provider, not the provide impression of the recipient. (To this end, tl designations of *provider* and *recipient* are inappr priate to the context. Hence, the caution regardir the apparent misnomer.) When the Q-sort finished, the feedback provider also transcribes tl points for each of the strengths to the comparisc chart. If the feedback recipient and the feedbac provider differ by three or more on the poin assigned to a given strength, that strength is flagge by marking an oval.

The 28 strengths are arranged on a compar son chart in four columns. The columns are la beled (a) Altruistic-Nurturing, (b) Assertive-D recting, (c) Analytic-Autonomizing, and (c Flexible-Cohering. These columns are colo. coded. The seven strength scores from the recip ent and the provider in each of the four colum are added to create composite scores for the recip ent and the provider.

Suggested follow-up points of discussic include (a) the strengths flagged for being three c more points different in score, (b) the strengths appearing on the top three lines of the diamond for the provider and the recipient, (c) the strengths appearing on the bottom three lines of the diamond for the provider and the recipient, and (d) do the observed differences reflect different interpretations of the words used to describe the strength, or do those differences arise from perceptions of behaviors.

DEVELOPMENT. Personal Strengths Publishing of Carlsbad, California provided documentation of the development of the Feedback Portrait of Personal Strengths in the form of the book, *Relationship Awareness Theory: Manual of Administration and Interpretation*, published in 1996. However, explicit reference to the Feedback Portrait of Personal Strengths was not discernible in the manual. Instead, the manual focused on the development of relationship awareness theory along with several related inventories. The Feedback Portrait of Personal Strengths appeared to be a component of one of these inventories, the Strength Deployment Inventory (SDI; T7:2436) to be specific, and the Feedback Portrait of Personal Strengths is sold on the Personal Strengths Publishing web site (http://www.personalstrengths.com/main.html) as a component of the SDI, Premier Edition. (The Feedback Portrait of Personal Strengths assesses four of the seven motivational value systems assessed by the SDI.)

The SDI (and the Feedback Portrait of Personal Strengths) were developed using the framework of Relationship Awareness Theory as described in the manual and as posited on four major premises. These premises are (a) behavior traits arise from the purposeful search for gratification ameliorated by considerations of the appropriate actions necessary to achieve the gratifications; (b) behavior is predictable in the absence of conflict, but variable in the presence of conflict; (c) a weakness is a strength that is overused; and (d) the better the concepts of a personality theory describe how a person experiences the self, the better those concepts promote and support self-discovery.

It appears that no attempt was made to relate these premises to the factors of the Big 5 or the Myers-Briggs personality assessments, though much of the description of the motivational value systems identified using the SDI was distinctly reminiscent of the feedback reports of the more commonly used personality inventories.

The seven motivation value systems identified by the SDI are (a) Altruistic-Nurturing, (b) Assertive-Directing, (c) Analytic-Autonomizing, (d) Flexible-Cohering, (e) Assertive-Nurturing, (f) Judicious-Competing, and (g) Cautious-Supporting. Four of these systems are assessed by the Feedback Portrait of Personal Strengths, as mentioned earlier. No documentation was presented in the manual of the manner in which the strengths used to underlie these motivation value systems were identified and validated.

TECHNICAL. Technical information regarding the reliability and validity of the Feedback Portrait of Personal Strengths was not provided in the manual. Some information regarding the technical characteristics of the Strength Deployment Inventory was provided. Given that the Feedback Portrait of Personal Strengths represents a subset of the SDI, we were left to infer the technical aspects of the Feedback Portrait of Personal Strengths from those of the SDI.

The reliability of the SDI, from which we might infer the reliability of the Feedback Portrait of Personal Strengths, was provided in the form of test-retest reliability and "Parsonian" (*sic*) correlation coefficients. Retestings ranged from 6 days to 2 weeks after initial testing. These coefficients range from .76 to .78, though were presented for only three of the seven scales. Estimates of test-retest reliability for the remaining four scales were not presented. Other estimates of reliability (e.g., coefficient alpha, generalizability theory) were not reported. Although the test-retest evidence of reliability was encouraging, sufficient evidence to infer the test-retest reliability of the Feedback Portrait of Personal Strengths was not presented.

The validity of the SDI was presented in two forms from two studies. One study involved 100 people; the other study involved 564 people. The first example of the validity of the SDI takes the form of item discrimination. The title of both tables was "Validity as Internal Consistency of the Scales," which is generally more related to reliability then validity.

However, in both studies, the discrimination of the items was presented as the level of statistical significance achieved in a chi-square analysis to contrast high and low scorers on a given scale. The chi-square statistic is dependent on sample size, and even in the presence of a small effect, a sufficiently large sample generally will produce statistical significance. The validity evidence presented was not sufficient to infer any form of validity for the Feedback Portrait of Personal Strengths.

The second form of validity was presented as "Validity as Congruence with External Reality." In this set of studies, the authors gave the SDI to persons from different professions (e.g., nurses, social workers, engineers). The report indicated that the performance of the participants on the SDI was generally as predicted by what would be expected from those workers (e.g., nurses should display Altruistic-Nurturing behavior). In addition, anecdotal evidence was presented indicating that some workers whose strengths were incongruent with their profession subsequently changed to jobs that were more congruent with their inventory scores, achieving, then, greater personal satisfaction with their work. However, no empirical evidence was presented to support the extent of these findings and claims.

COMMENTARY. As a mechanism to promote fruitful discussion between two people working together, the Feedback Portrait of Personal Strengths might do its job. Similarly, as a tool to promote self-understanding as well as the understanding of others, the Feedback Portrait of Personal Strengths might provide some degree of new insight. However, the same and much more can be said of a great many other inventories designed for personal and professional development.

What is lacking with the Feedback Portrait of Personal Strengths is any substantive theoretical underpinning and empirical analyses to support the claims made by the author. Other well-studied inventories that dissect personal and professional strengths and weaknesses while providing feedback for development are readily available from other sources (e.g., The Center for Creative Leadership, CPP, Discovery Learning, Kaplan, Lominger Ltd.), and these sources provide a wealth of technical documentation to support the claims made of the inventories.

Persons contemplating the use of the Feedback Portrait of Personal Strengths to support personal or professional development should cast their vision wide to determine if other sources might provide assessments with greater evidence of technical quality.

[74]
Five Factor Wellness Inventory.

Purpose: Designed to "assess characters of wellness as a basis for helping individuals make choices for healthier living."

Population: Elementary, high school, and adults.

Publication Date: 2005.

Acronym: 5F-Wel.

Scores, 28: Wellness (Creative Self [Thinking, Emotions, Control, Positive Humor, Work], Coping Self [Realistic Beliefs, Stress Management, Self-Worth, Leisure], Social Self [Friendship, Love], Essential Self [Spirituality, Self-Care, Gender Identity, Cultural Identity], Physical Self [Exercise, Nutrition]), Local Context, Institutional Context, Global Context, Chronometrical Context, Life Satisfaction Index.

Administration: Group or individual.

Levels, 3: Elementary, Teen, Adults.

Price Data, 2005: $40 per manual (71 pages); $10 per adult web-based administration; $160 per 20 reports of one verion; bulk pricing is available.

Foreign Language Editions: Hebrew, Korean, Turkish.

Time: (10–20) minutes.

Comments: Users can administer the factor scales only or all scales; can be self-administered; web-based administration and reporting including a development guide.

Authors: Jane E. Myers and Thomas J. Sweeney.

Publisher: Mind Garden, Inc.

Review of the Five Factor Wellness Inventory by GERALD E. DeMAURO, Managing Educational Assessment Scientist, American Institutes for Research, Voorheesville, NY:

DESCRIPTION. The Five Factor Wellness Inventory yields 17 third-order factor scores, five second-order factor scores, and one overall wellness score. Five contextual scores with theoretical meaning are also provided. Three forms of the instrument are available, having maximum reading levels at third, sixth, and ninth grades and composed of 77, 80, and 73 items, respectively. The theoretical model is based on the Wellness Evaluation of Lifestyle (Myers, Sweeney, & Witmer 1996; 2004) and on the Wheel of Wellness model (Witmer, Sweeney, & Myers, 1998), which delineates components of overall wellness, their theoretical interrelationships, and associated life tasks.

DEVELOPMENT. The adult version of the Five Factor Wellness Inventory (5F-Wel-A) was developed from the Wellness Evaluation of Lifestyles (WEL; Hattie, Myers, & Sweeney, 2004;

Myers et al., 1996; 2004), through structural equation modeling. The theoretical model of wellness is of an integral approach to well-being.

Twenty-nine items were eliminated from an original pool of 132 because they had poor psychometric properties. Maximum-likelihood exploratory factor analysis decomposed 103 of these items to 17 factors related to the original Wheel of Wellness model (Hattie et al., 2004).

A structural model specified a restricted factor pattern permitting each item to load on 1 specified scale of the 17. The scales, in turn, were restricted to load on one of five second-order factors. The loadings on the 17 scales ranged from .35 to .91, and the loadings of the five second-order factors onto a single global factor ranged from .51 to .98. A maximum-likelihood restricted factor analysis that specified the five factors demonstrated that 2 of the 17 scales did not load above .30 on any of the five superordinate factors. The highest loading for Work was .26 on the Creative superordinate factor, whereas the highest loading for Realistic Beliefs was .25 on the Coping superordinate factor.

TECHNICAL.

Reliability. Alpha coefficients for the five second-order factors ranged from .90 to .94. The coefficient for Total Wellness was .94. Among the five third-order scales, alpha coefficients ranged from .79 to .88 for the five scales composing Creative Self, .58 to .91 for the four scales composing the Coping Self, .92 to .95 for the two scales composing the Social Self, .85 to .92 for the four scales composing the Essential Self, and .87 to .89 for the two scales composing the Physical Self. Context measures—Local, Institutional, Global, and Chronometrical—yielded alpha coefficients of .74, .73, .66, and .79, respectively. These data are based on a sample of 3,343. The coefficients are respectable given that the numbers of items comprising the 17 scales never exceeds six. Because the examinees are at least 18 years old, the data appear to be based on the 5F-Wel-A (ninth grade reading level) form.

Validity. Three items measuring global self-perceptions of happiness, health, and life satisfaction were field-tested as validity checks to the Inventory. Only Life Satisfaction, which had the largest correlation (.38) with Total wellness, was retained. A multivariate predictive study assessing the incremental contribution of global self-assessments within ethnic groups might contribute greater clarity to the wellness construct.

Several sources of convergent validity evidence are reported. Psychological well-being was correlated to major life tasks of the theoretical model of wellness (Hermon, 1995). Body shame and wellness were negatively related among undergraduate women, whereas the appearance control beliefs variable (Sinclair & Myers, 2003) was positively related to wellness. The healthy love styles variable was positively related to the life tasks delineated in the Wheel of Wellness (Shurts & Myers, 2004), and job satisfaction and mattering (both Connolly, 2000) were positively related to the life tasks of wellness delineated in the Wheel model.

The authors report large scoring differences among various population groups. Clearly, an analysis of Differential Item Functioning, more typically used in ability and achievement testing, would benefit the user and inventory development. The tables presented in the technical manual evidence large differences in dispersions across population groups and scales, even after linear transformation. For example, among Caucasian examinees, the standard deviation for Realistic Beliefs is 12.14, whereas the standard deviation for Love is 19.75. Among African American examinees, the standard deviation for Realistic Beliefs is 12.86, whereas the standard deviation for Love is 26.01, more than double that for Realistic Beliefs. Differences of this magnitude might have some theoretical significance in terms of the prevalence of the trait, or alternatively, they may reflect sampling issues in the samples studied.

Administration. The scales are each self-administered, with an average time of 10 to 20 minutes. The Inventory may be administered individually or in groups. Large-type versions are available.

Scoring and score profiles. Each statement on the Inventory is scored on a 4-point Likert-type scale ranging from *strongly agree* (4) to *strongly disagree* (1). A linear transformation is performed to yield the raw score: The total number of points is divided by the number of items that comprise the scale and then multiplied by 25. Thus, the scores ranged from 25 to 100.

Although the rationale for the transformation is to put the scales on a common metric, the differences in dispersion among the scales make it difficult to compare performance across the wellness factors. Standardizing the scores would enable such comparisons. Nevertheless, conversion of transformed raw scores to the norm-referenced scores provided does achieve much of the same advantages. This analytic procedure raises the question of the need for raw score linear transformations at all.

COMMENTARY. The Five Factor Wellness Inventory has strong ties to a theoretical model in its development. Validity rests heavily on global self-perceptions of wellness. These may suffer from the same biases that influence the choice of responses to the Inventory. Validity could be strengthened by relating Inventory scores to nonobtrusive or behavioral indices of wellness. This would increase the sensitivity of the instrument to more objective measures of wellness to supplement its current sensitivity to self-perceptions of wellness. Finally, although all scores are interpreted in normative terms, and advice is provided for evaluating the scores, there do not appear to be any score values that could be interpreted as values that call for intervention. The Inventory might take advantage of standard-setting techniques that could serve to help examinees interpret scoring anomalies in their profiles.

SUMMARY. The Five Factor Wellness Inventory is a measure of the self-perception of global wellness, as it is expressed in 17 scales, five second-order factors or scales, one global measure, and four context scores. Careful development and research support the model. Some suggestions are made for further development.

REVIEWER'S REFERENCES

Connolly, K. (2000). *The relationship among wellness, mattering, and job satisfaction.* Unpublished doctoral dissertation, University of North Carolina at Greensboro, Greensboro, NC.

Hattie, J., Myers, J. E., & Sweeney, T. J. (2004). A factor structure of wellness: Theory, assessment, analysis, and practice. *Journal of Counseling and Development, 82,* 354-364.

Hermon, D. (1995). *Adherence to a wellness model and perceptions of psychological well-being.* Unpublished doctoral dissertation, Ohio University, Athens, OH.

Myers, J. E., & Sweeney, T. J. (1999). The Five Factor Wellness Inventory. Greensboro, NC: Authors.

Myers, J. E., Sweeney, T. J., & Witmer, J. M. (1996; 2004). The Wellness Evaluation of Lifestyle. Redwood City, CA: Mind Garden, Inc.

Shurts, M., & Myers, J. E. (2004). Measuring positive emotionality: A review of instruments assessing love. *Measurement and Evaluation in Counseling and Development, 34,* 238-254.

Sinclair, S. L., & Myers, J. E. (2004). Weighty issues: Objectified body consciousness and wellness in heterosexual Caucasian college women. *Journal of College Counseling, 7,* 151-160.

Witmer, J. M., & Sweeney, T. J., & Myers, J. E. (1998). The Wheel of Wellness. Greensboro, NC: Authors.

Review of the Five Factor Wellness Inventory by SUSAN LONBORG, Professor of Psychology, Central Washington University, Ellensburg, WA:

DESCRIPTION. According to the publisher's website, the Five Factor Wellness Inventory (5F-Wel) is a self-report questionnaire "designed to assess characteristics of wellness as a basis for helping individuals make choices for healthier living" (Mind Garden, n. d.). Three versions of the 5F-Wel are available: Adult (5F-Wel-A), Teen (5F-Wel-T), and Elementary (5F-Wel-E). The 5F-Wel-A is the result of a structural equation modeling analysis of data for a previous version of the instrument, the Wellness Evaluation of Lifestyle (WEL; Myers, Sweeney, & Witmer, 1996; 2004). The Adult version of the 5F-Wel is designed for teens and adults with a ninth grade reading level or below; whereas the Teen version is intended for adolescents (i.e., middle school students) with a sixth grade reading level or below. The 5F-Wel-E is purportedly designed to measure wellness in elementary-school-aged children with a maximum third grade reading level.

The 5F-Wel Inventory manual lists 91 self-statement items for the 5F-Wel-A, 97 items for the 5F-Wel-T, and 94 items for the 5F-Wel-E. The Adult form of the 5F-Wel contains 73 items on the Total Wellness scale, 21 items on the Creative Self scale, 19 items on the Coping Self scale, 8 items on the Social Self scale, 15 items on the Essential Self scale, and 10 items on the Physical Self scale. In addition, there are 5 items assigned to Local Context, 4 items for Institutional Context, 3 items for Global Context, and 4 items for Chronometrical Context. The Adult form also contains a Validity Index (that is only 1 item) and 7 demographic questions. The manual indicates that the Teen version of the inventory (i.e., 5F-Wel-T) contains 80 items on the Total Wellness scale, which are further distributed among the second-order subscales as follows: Creative Self ($n = 23$), Coping Self ($n = 19$), Social Self ($n = 11$), Essential Self ($n = 18$), and Physical Self ($n = 9$). Like the Adult version of the inventory, the 5F-Wel-T also contains Local Context ($n = 5$), Institutional Context ($n = 4$), Global Context ($n = 3$), and Chronometrical Context ($n = 4$) items as well as the Validity Index (again, only a single item) and a single demographic question concerning the respondent's primary cultural background. The Elementary version of the instrument (i.e., 5F-Wel-E) assigns 77 items to the Total Wellness scale. Like the Adult and Teen versions, the 5F-Wel-E contains a 22-item Creative Self scale, an

18-item Coping Self scale, an 11-item Social Self scale, a 17-item Essential Self scale, and a 9-item Physical Self scale. The 5F-Wel-E also has the same number of items assigned to the Local Context Institutional Context, Global Context, Chronometrical Context, and Validity Index scales as the Adult and Teen versions of the instrument. Finally, elementary students are also asked to respond to a single demographic question (i.e., "What is the primary cultural background with which you most closely identify"); however, it is interesting to note that this item has a Flesch-Kinkaid reading level of Grade 9.7.

It is, however, important to mention a discrepancy between the number of items described in Table 2 of the manual and copies of each instrument printed on pages 49–62 of the manual. An inspection of the 5F-Wel-A indicates 91 scale items, plus an additional 7 demographic items. In contrast, in the Table 2 list of scales and the Validity Index, the number of items totals 90. [Editor's Note: The publisher advises that there is an error on Table 2. The Self-Care scale has 4 items, not 3, bringing the total to 91.]

According to the manual, "the 5F-Wel-A and T are designed for self-administration" and "the instruments may be administered individually or in groups" (p. 17). However, according to both the publisher's website and customer service representative, the three versions of the 5F-Wel are only available for Web administration and scoring. Furthermore, the manual suggests that "for group administrations, the instructions may be read aloud" (p. 17). Although the instrument itself is apparently only available for Web administrations, an accompanying printed workbook may be purchased individually or in bulk from the publisher.

The average time required to complete each of the three versions is reportedly between 10 and 20 minutes, although more time may be required if the 16 context items are also included in the administration. For each item on the 5F-Wel, respondents are instructed to answer in a way that is "true for you most or all of the time." Respondents are further encouraged to consider how they most often see themselves, feel, or behave. After reading each of the item statements, respondents are asked to endorse one of the following four answers: "strongly agree," "agree," "disagree," or "strongly disagree."

The current revision of the original WEL is apparently designed for Web administration and scoring only. However, the manual also provides a description of scoring procedures. Each item response is converted from a qualitative response (i.e., "Strongly Agree") to a numerical score ranging from 4 ("Strongly Agree") to 1 ("Strongly Disagree"). Item responses are then summed for each subscale. With the exception of five items on the Realistic Beliefs subscale and "one of the items on the Safety scale" (manual, p. 18) that are to be reverse-scored, all items are worded positively. It should be noted that the 5F-Wel makes no mention of a "Safety scale" though the instructions for reverse-scoring an item on this scale are nonetheless included in the current 5F-Wel manual. [Editor's Note: The publisher advises that the "safety" scale measures local context, but this is not well explained in the manual.] The manual indicates that a scale should not be scored unless a minimum of three items on the scale are endorsed.

The authors suggest that in order to ensure a common metric for scales, each scale score must be converted to one that ranges from 25 to 100. Each converted score is obtained by dividing the mean score for the scale by the number of items and then multiplying by 25. According to the manual, the obtained linear transformations aid in interpreting scores; these percentages are construed to represent a percent of total wellness. As noted in an earlier critique of the original WEL, the use of percentages to interpret scale scores is problematic, given that these scores do not represent true ratio scales (Farmer, 2005).

The manual indicates that "5F-Wel items can be keyed into web forms to get profiles and scored data if the administration is by paper rather than the web" (p. 18). Although the publisher states that paper administration is no longer available, the web-based administration apparently yields both scoring and a profile report. Individual scores are provided for the 17 third-order factors (i.e., scales), the 5 second-order factors, the Total Wellness scale, the four context scales, and the one-item Life Satisfaction measure. It is also suggested that "a group profile may be prepared to provide comparative data (local norms) for specific subgroups of individuals that may complete the instrument" (manual, p. 18).

According to the manual, the 5F-Wel may be used in counseling to assess clients in identifying major wellness areas for further exploration and intervention. For the purposes of screening clients, the authors recommend initial inspection of the profile for second-order factor scores and the Total Wellness factor. Once target areas for intervention are identified, an analysis of third-order factor scores may be beneficial. The manual also provides a detailed presentation of the authors' four-phase model for wellness assessment and intervention (Myers, Sweeney, & Witmer, 2000) and a sample client profile. In addition, according to the authors, *The Wellness and Habit Change Workbook* is a recommended resource for clients and is available from the publisher. It should be noted, however, that no data are presented to support claims about the efficacy of either the four-phase model or the wellness workbook.

DEVELOPMENT. The 5F-Wel-Adult is a revision of the previous version of the WEL. Although the original WEL was based on the authors' lifespan model of wellness as represented by the "Wheel of Wellness," the current 5F-Wel is based on a new formulation called the "The Indivisible Self: An Evidence-Based Model of Wellness" (Myers & Sweeney, 2004). Both the Wheel and Indivisible Self models are primarily based on the Adlerian concept of holism; however, the latter conceptualization of wellness (i.e., the IS-WEL) represents the results of a structural equation modeling analysis of a large database of scores from the original WEL. According to the manual, this unifying definition of wellness represents "a way of life oriented toward optimal health and well-being in which body, mind, and spirit are integrated in a purposeful manner with the goal of living life more fully" (p. 3).

In describing the development of the 5F-Wel-A, the authors apparently relied on both exploratory and confirmatory factor-analytic procedures. Initially, 29 of the original 132 WEL items were eliminated, apparently due to "poor psychometric properties" (manual, p. 3). According to the manual, the authors specified, in this exploratory analysis, "17 clear factors based on the original theoretical, circumplex Wheel of Wellness model" (p. 3). Based on the results of this maximum-likelihood factor analysis, the authors purportedly re-examined the structure of wellness, yet claimed that the data provided support for the original 17 scales, or components, of the Wheel of Wellness. Next, the authors apparently specified a restricted load pattern in which the questionnaire

items were allowed only to load on their identified third-order factors; in turn, these factors (or scales) loaded on five second-order factors and one higher order factor (i.e., Total Wellness). The authors report that factor names were assigned by studying the items and scales contained in these five second-order factors: the Creative Self, Coping Self, Social Self, Essential Self, and Physical Self. Each of these five factors are purported to represent the "Indivisible Self" proposed in the current conceptual model of wellness.

In addition to the higher order, second-order, and third-order factors, the 5F-Wel also includes items intended to measure "contextual variables." The authors suggest that one's Indivisible Self maintains a reciprocal relationship with the surrounding world; consequently, four levels of context are reportedly assessed by the current instrument. These are identified as local (e.g., families, communities), institutional (e.g., education, religion), global (e.g., politics, the environment), and chronometrical (i.e., change over time) contexts. According to the manual, "these contexts emerged from extensive literature reviews and were not part of earlier empirical studies" (p. 9).

Surprisingly, the inventory manual does not describe the specific procedures used to identify items for the 5F-Wel-T. Although the authors report that recent research with the 5F-Wel-T is "promising" and the manual does provide teenage norms, no additional information about item development is readily available. The 5F-Wel-E is apparently based on a pilot test conducted with 10 elementary school students. Prior to this pilot test, the 5F-Wel-E was developed by "examining each of the items of the 5F-Wel-A and 5F-Wel-T and trying to lower the reading level to no higher than 3.0 while maintaining the intent of the original item" (manual, p. 28). In addition, professionals with expertise in working with children were consulted about "possible dynamics of wellness" in children that might differ from those in teenagers and adults. Following these discussions, "a number of items" were apparently added to the original 5F-Wel scales, though the specific nature of these additions is not explicitly described in the manual.

Although the manual suggests that the 5F-Wel-A (Adult version) is designed for adolescents and adults with at least a ninth grade reading level, there is no mention in the manual of the procedure used to develop or verify this requirement.

There is also no evidence supporting the claim that the 5F-Wel-T is intended for adolescents with at least a sixth grade reading level. Although the 5F-Wel-E presumably requires only a third grade reading level, the manual notes that test instructions are written at a fifth grade level. Although this level of reading ability required apparently assumes that elementary students would require an adult test proctor, it is unclear how such an administration would occur in light of the fact that the instrument is currently available only through a web-based administration.

A number of issues related to the development of the three versions of the 5F-Wel remain to be addressed. First, the procedures for scoring the inventory items are unclear. Unfortunately, the items described in the manual do not clearly correspond to items in the factor model. More specifically, the item numbers represented in the Five-Factor Structural Model in the manual (p. 4) appear to be different from those in the 5F-Wel Adult version of the instrument. Second, although the 5F-Wel published in 2005 is apparently based on a 5-factor wellness model, the authors also published a new 4-phase model in the same year. The relation between the 5F-Wel and the 4-phase model is not addressed in the manual.

TECHNICAL. It is somewhat difficult to evaluate the psychometric properties of the current versions of the 5F-Wel given that estimates of the reliability and validity of the instrument are apparently based on either the original WEL data or nonrepresentative convenience samples. For example, the authors report alpha coefficients for the five second-order factors based on a sample of 3,043 individuals who completed the original WEL; "however, only the 73 items that comprise the 5F-Wel were examined in [this] reliability analysis" (manual, p. 14). This procedure assumes, of course, that individuals will respond similarly to the 73 items of the 5F-Wel in both a 73-item administration and the longer 132-item WEL administration, despite the fact that this assumption should instead be treated as an empirical question. Similarly confusing is the fact that the manual also reports on the reliability analysis for a new database that presumably makes use of scores on the newer 5F-Wel. According to the manual, alpha coefficients for this new sample of "2,093 persons" are presented in the manual (p. 14). Unfortunately, an inspection of that analysis indicates that the alpha coefficients of internal consistency were apparently based on a sample of 3,343 individuals using a version of the instrument that provides five, rather than four, response options. [Editor's Note: The publisher advises that the number 2,093 on p. 14 was a typographical error and that the correct sample size is 3,343.] More specifically, these estimates of internal consistency rely on an instrument that includes "Undecided" or "Neutral" as an additional response option. Nonetheless, the alpha coefficients reported in the manual suggest reasonable internal consistency for the higher order Total Wellness factor (.98) and for the five second-order factors (.89 to .96). Alpha coefficients become much more variable when examining the internal consistency of the third-order factors and are considerably lower (.66 to .79) for the contextual variables. No test-retest reliability data are reported for the three versions of the 5F-Wel, although estimates of 2-week test-retest reliability for the original WEL in a sample of 99 undergraduate students "exceeded .68, with most above .80" (Hattie, Myers, & Sweeney, 2004, p. 356).

One section of the 5F-Wel manual describes the demographic characteristics "of the 3,343 persons who comprise the norm group for the 5F-Wel-A" (p. 19). Again, it should be noted that this norm group apparently completed the original WEL instrument. According to the authors, there are a number of "deviations from a nationally representative sample" (e.g., underrepresentation of males, overrepresentation of African Americans, high proportion of individuals with graduate degrees); consequently, users are "strongly encouraged to develop and use local norms for score interpretation" (manual, p. 19).

Similarly, questions may be raised about the representativeness of the normative sample for the 5F-Wel-T. The normative sample included 1,142 participants recruited for a number of doctoral dissertation studies supervised by the authors. Given that these dissertations were completed prior to the development of the 5F-Wel, participants presumably responded to items on the original WEL. The majority of respondents in the teenage normative sample were between the ages of 14 and 18. Given concerns about the overrepresentation of some ethnic groups (e.g., Caribbean Americans) in this norm group, users might also consider the development of local norms for this version of the 5F-Wel.

It is important to note that there are no published normative data for the 5F-Wel-E, the elementary version of this instrument. The authors indicate, however, that it is currently available for "large scale testing and research" (manual, p. 28).

The test manual describes a relatively large number of studies that reportedly provide support for the validity of the 5F-Wel as a measure of wellness. Unfortunately, this superficial discussion of validity data, coupled with the fact that many of the studies cited actually used a previous version of the instrument—the WEL—makes a careful assessment of the psychometric properties of the current instrument rather difficult. With the exception of one unidentified report of data from a single study correlating the 5F-Wel Total Wellness score with unidentified measures of happiness (r = .30), health (r = 30), and life satisfaction (r = .38), no specific correlations are provided as evidence of support for the concurrent or predictive validity of the current instrument. Some might also argue that happiness and life satisfaction represent different constructs and, as such, would not provide the best evidence for the validity of the 5F-Wel. Furthermore, although the 5F-Wel manual was published in 2005, the authors fail to mention an earlier published report suggesting that a four-factor, rather than five-factor, solution provides the best fit for the data (Myers, Luecht, & Sweeney, 2004).

COMMENTARY. Though the work of the authors and their research colleagues represents an ambitious effort to define and measure the construct of wellness, the 5F-Wel and its test manual continue to suffer from a number of the shortcomings associated with the previous version of this instrument, the WEL. First, questions remain about the specific number of items actually associated with the 5F-Wel-A. Second, the extent to which items represent the definitions of the higher order and second-order factors and scales described in the manual is unclear. For example, when describing the procedures for scoring the 5F-Wel, the manual refers to a "Safety" scale; yet there is no other mention of this scale nor the items intended to measure such a dimension. Furthermore, many of the 5F-Wel items appear to measure perceived satisfaction rather than wellness behaviors per se. For example, "I am satisfied with

the quality and quantity of foods in my diet" seems to measure one's satisfaction with food choices, rather than an objective assessment of the extent to which one's dietary habits represent a commitment to good health. This problem is compounded further when a closer examination of the items indicates that some measure beliefs, whereas others inquire about specific behaviors per se. For example, one item on the Physical Exercise scale requires individuals to respond to the statement, "I think I am an active person," yet another states, "I do some form of stretching activity at least three times per week" (manual, p. 51). The confounding of attitudes and behaviors is particularly troubling in light of the extant literature suggesting that attitudes are often poor predictors of health-related behavior.

As stated previously, serious questions remain about the psychometric properties of the three versions of the 5F-Wel. Most notable is the absence of any empirical evidence for the reliability or validity of the 5F-Wel-E, an instrument formulated on the basis of informal discussions with professionals and a pilot study with 10 elementary school children. Perhaps even more troubling is the incomplete discussion of the instruments' validity, particularly when many of the studies cited were actually conducted with the original WEL rather than the 5F-Wel.

In light of the aforementioned problems, caution should be exercised in the use of the 5F-Wel for wellness assessment, intervention, and counseling. Perhaps an important agenda for future research is the empirical investigation of the authors' proposed four-phase counseling model as well as attention to the psychometric issues related to the instrument noted above.

Finally, it should be noted that the 5F-Wel manual suffers from a number of editorial problems. The reference list is apparently incomplete, given that a number of studies cited in the manual are not included in this list. Inconsistencies in reports of the number of items associated with each of the three versions of the 5F-Wel should also be resolved. Finally, care should be taken to ensure that clearer distinctions are made between those studies using the original WEL and those reporting the results of psychometric research with the 5F-Wel.

SUMMARY. Although wellness remains an important topic for research and clinical practice, the current versions of the 5F-Wel are hampered by a number of unresolved problems. Most notable are: (a) inconsistencies in reports of the number of items included in the measure; (b) obvious discrepancies between specific item content and descriptions of factors and scales contained in the manual; (c) questions about the extent to which the instrument measures wellness-related beliefs versus behaviors; (d) inadequate data regarding the psychometric properties of the 5F-Wel in contrast to the original WEL; (e) challenges associated with the interpretation of factor and scale scores, particularly with respect to the issue of using percentages to describe respondents' degree of wellness; and (f) the lack of evidence for the efficacy or effectiveness of the four-phase model of wellness assessment and intervention proposed by the authors. As stated previously, caution should be exercised when using this measure for counseling purposes and further research is necessary to establish the reliability, validity, and representative norms for the three versions of this instrument before it is used in the manner for which it has been envisioned.

REVIEWER'S REFERENCES

Farmer, R. F. (2005). [Review of the Wellness Evaluation of Lifestyle (2004 Update).] In R. A. Spies & B. S. Plake (Eds.), *The sixteenth mental measurements yearbook* (pp. 1127-1130). Lincoln, NE: Buros Institute of Mental Measurements.
Hattie, J. A., Myers, J. E., & Sweeney, T. J. (2004). A factor structure of wellness: Theory, assessment, analysis, and practice. *Journal of Counseling and Development, 82,* 354-364.
Mind Garden, Inc. (n. d.). Five Factor Wellness Inventory. Retrieved February 7, 2007 from http://www.mindgarden.com/products/5fwels.htm
Myers, J. E., Luecht, R. M., & Sweeney, T. J. (2004). The factor structure of wellness: Reexamining theoretical and empirical models underlying the Wellness Evaluation of Lifestyle (WEL) and the Five-Factor Wel. *Measurement and Evaluation in Counseling and Development, 36,* 194-208.
Myers, J. E., Sweeney, T. J., & Witmer, J. M. (2000). The Wheel of Wellness counseling for wellness: A holistic model for treatment planning. *Journal of Counseling and Development, 78,* 251-266.
Myers, J. E., & Sweeney, T. J. (2004). The Indivisible Self: An evidence-based model of wellness. *Journal of Individual Psychology, 60,* 234-244.
Myers, J. E., Sweeney, T. J., & Witmer, M. (1996; 2004). *Wellness Evaluation of Lifestyle manual.* Menlo Park, CA: Mind Garden, Inc.

[75]

Full Range Test of Visual Motor Integration.

Purpose: Designed to assess the ability of individuals to "accurately relate visual stimuli to motor responses" and "to assist in differentiating normal from pathological aging."
Population: Ages 5–74.
Publication Dates: 1996–2006.
Acronym: FRTVMI.
Scores: Total score only.
Administration: Group or individual.
Price Data, 2006: $169 per complete kit including examiner's manual (2006, 102 pages), 25 profile/examiner record forms for ages 5–10, 25 profile/examiner record forms for ages 11–74, and scoring transparency; $51 per examiner's manual; $59 per 25 profile/examiner record forms for ages 5–10; $59 per 25 profile/examiner record forms for ages 11–74; $6 per scoring transparency.
Time: (15–30) minutes.
Comments: Extensive revision and redevelopment of the Test of Visual-Motor Integration.
Authors: Donald D. Hammill, Nils A. Pearson, Judith K. Voress, and Cecil R. Reynolds.
Publisher: PRO-ED.
Cross References: For a review by Deborah Erickon of the Test of Visual-Motor Integration, see 14:395; see also T5:2722 (1 reference).

Review of the Full Range Test of Visual Motor Integration by RIK CARL D'AMATO, M. Lucile Harrison Professor of Excellence, School of Applied Psychology and Counselor Education, College of Education and Behavioral Sciences, University of Northern Colorado, and JAMIE E. VANNICE, Doctoral student in School Psychology, School of Applied Psychology and Counselor Education, University of Northern Colorado, Greeley, CO:

DESCRIPTION. The Full Range Test of Visual Motor Integration (FRTVMI) is designed to assess the ability to reproduce visual stimuli using motor responses for children, adults, and the elderly. The test is easy to administer allowing the examiner to assess, document, and identify individuals with potential visual-motor difficulties. This test was expanded in order to differentiate potential neuropsychological and psychological conditions in the elderly. Accordingly, the words "full range" indicate an expanded age range that is now available when administering the test.

The FRTVMI test consists of 18 geometric shapes and figures administered to the examinee from a seven-page booklet with six figures in boxes on each page. The geometric designs are to be replicated by the examinee directly beneath the figure provided. Several variables impact the length of the test including the examinee's age, ability to accurately reproduce figures, and the individual's speed of copying task. Administration of the test should take approximately 10 to 30 minutes.

DEVELOPMENT. The administration and scoring section of the examiner's manual is clearly written and easy to follow. Instructions for administering the test are provided for individuals as well as for groups. Helpful suggestions are also provided in an effort to assist the examiner in conducting an individual and group administration. One of the challenges of this test is the ability of the examiner to score an examinee's drawings accurately. The scoring section of the examiner's manual provides four examples for each 0-, 1-, 2-, and 3-point response for every test item. In addition, there is a detailed description of the requested shapes as well as a description of item gestalts and criteria for scoring at each point level. Moreover, the test breaks down the scoring for 5–10-year-olds and 11–74-year-olds and includes a transparency in order to help the examiner efficiently determine criteria met for specific point responses.

TECHNICAL. The interpretation section of the test manual provides a detailed explanation of the types of scores the test yields as well as a thoughtful discussion concerning the limitations or reservations regarding the raw scores and age equivalents. The FRTVMI was standardized using Roid's continuous norming procedure (Roid, 1989). The authors indicate that normative data were collected from 3,153 individuals residing in 22 states over an 8-year period. The authors specify the demographic characteristics of the normative sample including geographic area, gender, ethnicity, family income, exceptionality status, and age, demonstrating that the sample was representative of the United States.

Test reliability or the ability to yield accurate results across time is thoroughly examined and explained in the manual. Cautions concerning reliability are clearly explained including evidence of reliability from three sources, covering content sampling, time sampling, and interscorer differences. The content sampling method was reported using coefficient alpha for computing item correlations with a mean of .85 for 5- to 10-year-olds and .90 for 11- to 74-year-olds (Salkind, 2006). The test was also evaluated for reliability for seven subgroups within the normative sample and it was found that the scores were equally reliable for all the subgroups investigated. Analyses also indicated little or no bias relative to the subgroups. A test-retest model was used to evaluate consistency of the FRTVMI over time. This procedure indicated a 1-week stability correlation coefficient of .85 for 5- to 10-year-olds and .85 for 11- to 74-year-olds. The interscorer reliability was assessed with two scorers each completing 30 protocols for

5- to 10-year-olds, which yielded a coefficient of .92. Additionally, the scorers completed 30 protocols for 11- to 74-year-olds yielding a coefficient of .96. The scores for the FRTVMI appear to be reliable.

The validity section demonstrated the accuracy of measuring what the test is intended to measure. The FRTVMI manual examined three types of validity: content-description validity, criterion-prediction validity, and construct-identification validity. The authors provided little support for their rationale in selecting particular items. Although the authors were clear about which model they utilized to design the FRTVMI, no rationale regarding the choice of this particular model was provided.

An item analysis was performed using the entire normative sample with all median item discrimination indexes exceeding .35 and item difficulties ranging from .34 to .63. Dichotomous scoring was utilized to determine that differential item functioning (DIF) was assessed using a logistic regression procedure. Although comparisons were made between pairs of demographic groups, only five comparisons were statistically significant, but further investigation indicated negligible effect sizes. The authors concluded that all test items were fair across groups within the normative sample.

The concurrent validity of the FRTVMI was assessed by correlating it with similar measures. Initially, the FRTVMI was correlated with the Developmental Test of Visual Motor Integration for 5- to 10-year-olds. This analysis yielded a coefficient of .85 indicating high equivalency between measures. The FRTVMI was also correlated with the Developmental Test of Visual Perception—Adolescent and Adult (DTVP-A) addressing criterion-prediction validity for 11- to 74-year-olds. This analysis yielded a coefficient of .93 for the Copying subtest and .63 for the Visual-Motor Integration Index. The Visual-Motor Integration Index had a slightly lower coefficient because the DTVP-A includes scores from other subtests, which measured more than figure reproduction in isolation. These reported correlations supported the validity of the FRTVMI for both 5- to 10-year-olds and 11- to 74-year-olds.

COMMENTARY. The value of the FRTVMI appears to be very specific to one skill set. This brief measure would be assistive in providing screening to persons over a large age range to identify any visual-motor integration issues. This measure can now be used to investigate markers across a wide range of ages and abilities. This measure does not provide the examiner with subtests to discriminate between visual impairments and motor impairments, therefore requiring professionals to seek out a separate measure to identify the specificity of the issue. The addition of quick subtests would further enhance the value and usefulness of the FRTVMI.

SUMMARY. The FRTVMI is a brief measure that can help professionals assess the various components that comprise visual-motor integration abilities. The FRTVMI appears to be a useful instrument and appears to be both valid and reliable when used appropriately. Another desirable attribute of this measure is its ability to evaluate a single skill area. One test can now be used to evaluate individuals or groups of individuals from a wide variety of age ranges. This test could be useful in multiple disciplines including educational, clinical, and research applications because it is focused, fast, and efficient.

REVIEWERS' REFERENCES

Roid. G. H. (1989). *Programs to fit skewed distributions and generate percentile norms for skewed or kurtotic distributions: Continuous norming with the first four moments* (Tech. Rep. No. 89-02). Salem, OR: Assessment Research.
Salkind, N. J. (2006). *Tests and measurement for people who (think they) hate tests and measurement.* Thousand Oaks, CA: Sage.

Review of the Full Range Test of Visual Motor Integration by KATHARINE SNYDER, Associate Professor of Psychology, Methodist College, Fayetteville, NC:

DESCRIPTION. The Full Range Test of Visual Motor Integration (FRTVMI) evaluates the ability to associate motor responses with visual stimuli through copying figures. Reportedly, the FRTVMI can assess visual-motor deficits, identify individuals for referral, document progress, assist research, and differentiate neuropsychological symptoms. Assessing visual-motor skills within the context of copying is utilized in planning rehabilitation programs for brain-injured adults, particularly those with constructional dyspraxias. Many educational aptitude and readiness tests also include perceptual-motor items, assuming these abilities are necessary for academics and basic skills (Salvia & Ysseldyke, 2007).

Administered individually or in groups (10–15 minutes), participants receive either the 5–10-year-old booklet or the 11–74-year-old booklet. Each contains 18 figures whereby participants copy figures within a box below. Without time limitations, examinees complete items until a ceiling is reached (three consecutive items scoring zero). Final scores consist of raw totals, age equivalents, percentiles, standard scores, and qualitative descriptors. Items score a "three" if line segments are straight (within 1/16 inch), lines that should be of the same length are (within 1/16 inch), curvatures have a smooth arc, segments do not go beyond or fail to meet intersections (within 1/16 inch), and angles are within 2 degrees. If any of the above criteria are not met, additional lines are added, overstrikes are used, or lines extend beyond/touch the box, a score of two is given. One point is awarded for the general idea, otherwise zero points are given. Authors note that visual or motor impairment, cerebral insult, intellectual difficulties, or individual factors (e.g., attention, fatigue, motivation) can lower performance. Limitations inherent in the use of age equivalents are also discussed. It is recommended that examiners be formally trained and knowledgeable of the Standards of the American Educational Research Association, American Psychological Association, and the National Council on Measurement in Education (1999). Credentials required depend on testing rationale (e.g., neuropsychologist, school psychologist).

DEVELOPMENT. The FRTVMI is an extension of the original Test of Visual Motor Integration (TVMI) to older individuals (ages 5–74). The relationship between copying and perceptual-motor integration is clear. However, there is minimal discussion as to the adequacy of utilizing copying as the sole measure of visual-motor integration. Furthermore, no information is given as to why particular items were selected. More discussion about the choice of such a large age interval for Form 2 (11–74 years) would be useful.

TECHNICAL: STANDARDIZATION. Authors report that data from a normative sample of 3,153 individuals were collected. Reportedly, this sample was representative of the 2001 U.S. Census with regard to geographic region, gender, ethnicity, family income, exceptionality status (Learning Disorder, Articulation Disorder, Emotional Disturbance, ADD/ADHD, other disability), and age.

TECHNICAL: RELIABILITY. Because visual-motor integration is believed to be a stable construct, FRTVMI scores should be reliable. To establish test-retest reliability, two samples received the test twice within a week or less. Sample description is limited. A first sample consisted of twenty-seven 5–10-year-olds in New York and Texas, and a second sample consisted of thirty-one 20–57-year-olds in Texas. Test-retest coefficients for both were .85. To establish interrater reliability, two PRO-ED employees scored 30 tests from each version. Coefficients were .92 for the 5–10-year-old forms and .96 for the 11–74-year-old forms. Given the small samples tested, reliability is good.

TECHNICAL: VALIDITY. Content validity assessments were undertaken to ascertain the representativeness of items in measurement of the visual-motor integration construct. Because the alpha coefficients all exceeded .80 and 42% were higher than .90, the FRTVMI exhibits internal consistency reliability. Additional item analysis was undertaken to ascertain that items had a sufficient range of difficulty. The proportions of participants passing (scores of 2 or 3) or failing an item ranged between .34 to .63.

Differential Item Functioning Analysis (DIF) uses regression to identify differences between item performance across groups. DIF analysis compared two regression models, one with ability (subtest scores) as the sole predictor and another using both ability and group (male/female, African American/Non-African American, Hispanic American/Non-Hispanic American) as predictors. Of all item comparisons, only five reached significance at the .001 level. These five comparisons were not discussed, but authors report that none reached Cohen's standards of practical significance.

Predictive validity assessments were also undertaken to ascertain that the FRTVMI is effective in forecasting the abilities of test takers to carry out particular tasks. In Study 1, 20 individuals (ages 5–10) completed both the FRTVMI and the Developmental Test of Visual Motor Integration. A correlation coefficient of .85 was found, but descriptions of the "neurological impairments" (examiner's manual, p. 4) of this small sample are needed before conclusions about concurrent validity can be drawn. In Study 2, all individuals 11 years of age or older from the normative sample completed both the FRTVMI and the Developmental Test

of Visual Perception for Adolescents and Adults (DTVP-A). A correlation of .93 was found between the FRTVMI and the DTVP-A Copying Subtest, which is strong.

Because copying is the only measure of visual-motor integration, the FRTVMI is limited with regard to construct validity. Admirably, authors attempt to establish construct validity by assessing how well the construct visual-motor integration, conceptualized as copying, promotes the generation of testable hypotheses. First, it was hypothesized that visual-motor integration correlated with age. For participants receiving the 5–10-year-old form, age and raw score means correlated at .55. For participants receiving the 11–74-year-old form, the correlation was .04. Authors report that raw score means increase until 29 years, then decline. This finding is reportedly consistent with declines in the Rey Complex Figure scores after 25. More details about when the inverse relationship between age and FRTVMI scores becomes practically significant would be helpful. Second, it was hypothesized that FRTVMI standard score means would vary as a function of group. Unlike gifted individuals ($M = 102$), learning disabled ($M = 86$) and cerebrovascular accident ($M = 70$) cases scored in the below-average range. More details on the statistical and practical significance of this finding would be helpful. Third, it was hypothesized that FRTVMI scores would be related to copying-based assessments of intelligence. Both the FRTVMI and the Draw-a-Person tests were administered to all individuals in the normative sample who were 11 years of age or older. A modest correlation of .39 was discovered. Finally, it was hypothesized that there would be a relationship between FRTVMI standard scores and performance on the Rey Complex Figure Test (RCFT). Thirty adults (20–57 years old) were given both measures. A modest correlation of .44 was found between the FRTVMI and RCFT immediate recall, whereas a correlation of .49 was found between the FRTVMI and RCPT delayed recall.

COMMENTARY. Assessment of perceptual-motor skills in general is problematic. It is difficult to conceptualize and therefore not easy to measure, yet many educators believe that it underlies reading skills (Salvia & Ysseldyke, 2007). When construct definitions of perceptual-motor integration are limited, the danger of circular reasoning must be considered (e.g., if all learning-disabled individuals have perceptual-motor deficits and a particular student exhibits a deficit, this student is therefore learning disabled). To the credit of the authors, it is stressed that improvements in hand-eye coordination do not relate to better academic performance, but rather that remediation will help with other aspects (e.g., running, catching, throwing, tracing, copying, penmanship). Additionally, the authors emphasize the importance of assessing visual and motor skills independently before making FRTVMI conclusions, which is a crucial control factor.

Other features of the FRTVMI could be expanded upon. Many of the figures in the FRTVMI overlap those found in other assessments. Discussion as to why particular figures were chosen would be helpful. Salvia and Ysseldyke (2001) commented that additional cross-tabs within the standardization sample of the TVMI would be useful (e.g., where are the lower SES subjects from?). The FRTVMI could still expand on this. It may also be useful to have a subscale score and comparative norms for the three-dimensional items. Many measures of copying are currently available, but the advantage of the FRTVMI is that it can be administered in group settings and scored rapidly with the transparency template. It may be useful to test group versus individual administration as a predictive variable. Future research may also consider the development of immediate and delayed recall and/or recognition components.

SUMMARY. The FRTVMI is a well-done measure of visual-motor integration, within the context of copying, for children and adults. This reviewer believes it will be useful in many contexts. To the credit of developers, the measure can be administered, scored, and evaluated in a fairly rapid manner with a reasonable cost. When administered in conjunction with tests of visual perception and motor integrity, the FRTVMI can be a valuable tool.

REVIEWER'S REFERENCES

American Educational Research Association, American Psychological Association, & National Council on Measurement in Education. (1999). *Standards for educational and psychological testing*. Washington, DC: American Educational Research Association.
Salvia, J., & Ysseldyke, J. E. (2001). *Assessment* (8th ed.). Boston: Houghton Mifflin.
Salvia, J., & Ysseldyke, J. E. (2007). *Assessment in special and inclusive education* (10th ed.). Boston: Houghton Mifflin.

[76]

Functional Assessment of Academic Behavior.

Purpose: Designed as an ecological approach to "evaluate learners in context and address needed instructional, home, and home-school supports for learning."
Population: Grades PreK-12.
Publication Dates: 1987-2002.
Acronym: FAAB.
Scores, 23: 12 classroom components: Instructional Math, Instructional Expectations, Classroom Environment, Instructional Presentation, Cognitive Emphasis, Motivational Strategies, Relevant Practice, Informed Feedback, Academic Engaged Time, Adaptive Instruction, Progress Evaluation, Student Understanding; 5 home components: Home Expectations and Attributions, Discipline Orientation, Home-affective Environment, Parent Participation, Structure for Learning; 6 home-school relationship components: Shared Standards and Expectations, Consistent Structure, Cross-setting Opportunity to Learn, Mutual Support, Positive/Trusting Relationships, Modeling.
Administration: Individual.
Forms, 11: 5 required forms: Instructional Environment Checklist, Instructional Environment Checklist: Annotated Version, Instructional Needs Checklist, Parental Experience With Their Children's Learning and Schoolwork, Intervention Documentation Record; 6 supplemental forms: Observation Record, Student Interview Record, Teacher Interview Record, Parent Interview Record, Supplemental Teacher Interview Questions, Supplemental Student Interview Questions.
Price Data, 2006: $61.95 per Functional Assessment of Academic Behavior book (2002, 105 pages).
Time: Administration time not reported.
Comments: Replaces The Instructional Environment System-III (T6:1223).
Authors: James Ysseldyke and Sandra L. Christenson.
Publisher: Sopris West.
Cross References: See T5:1275 (1 reference); for reviews by Michael J. Furlong and Jennifer A. Rosenblatt and by Jerry Tindal of The Instructional Environment System-II, see 13:150; for reviews by Kenneth W. Howell and by William T. McKee and Joseph C. Witt of an earlier form, see 10:149.

Review of the Functional Assessment of Academic Behavior by JONATHAN SANDOVAL, Professor of Education, University of the Pacific, Stockton, CA:

DESCRIPTION. The Functional Assessment of Academic Behavior (FAAB) consists of a manual subtitled Creating Successful Learning Environments, with a series of checklists, questionnaires, and rating scales contained in the appendices. The manual outlines the authors' approach to using the findings from research to improve academic outcomes for individual students. It catalogues the environmental conditions that enhance a student's academic success and development in school based on his or her review; it outlines nine steps to structure an intervention planning process for referred students; and it provides examples of interventions that may be used to enhance school and home instructional supports for learning. To facilitate the planning process, five required forms and six supplemental forms have been provided that may be reproduced by the user. The five key forms are the Instructional Environment Checklist (23 items), the Instructional Environment Checklist: Annotated Version (128 items plus summaries), the Instructional Needs Checklist (98 items), the Parental Experience with Their Child's Learning and Schoolwork (42 items), and the Intervention Documentation Record (form with six headings). Supplemental forms, taken from a previous version of the manual by the authors, are the Observation Record, the Student Interview Record, the Teacher Interview Record, the Parent Interview Record, the Supplemental Teacher Interview Questionnaire, and the Supplemental Student Interview Questionnaire.

These forms are not tests, for the items are not compiled, and there are no normative or other psychometric data available. The checklists and other forms instead are intended to be used by educational professionals in assessing the presence or absence of environmental conditions related to reasons why a child may not be making sufficient academic progress in school. The professionals, using the information gleaned from the forms, should be better able to plan interventions for learners in concert with educational professionals working directly with the students.

The items on the form are derived from three areas the authors deem important for academic success: Classroom Instructional Support for Learning, Home Support for Learning, and Home-School Support for Learning. Within Instructional Support are 12 components (e.g., Instructional Match, Motivational Strategies), within Home Support are 5 components (e.g., Home Expectations and Attributions, Parent Participation), and within Home-School Support are 6 Components (Shared Standards and Expectations,

Positive Trusting Relationships). These components make up the content of or underlie the various forms.

DEVELOPMENT. The FAAB is the successor to The Instructional Environment System-II (TIES-II). The supplemental forms come from that work. Since the TIES-II was published, the authors have continued to review the literature, have done work of their own, and have responded to the current movement encouraging empirically based intervention and practice. Christenson's work on the home school connection (Christenson & Sheridan, 2001) has influenced this revision and resulted in the inclusion of the new area of Home-School Support with its six components. The theoretical and empirical literature supporting the content of the FAAB has been substantially updated in this version of the manual.

TECHNICAL. The manual presents no traditional technical data. There are references to research literature that supports the content of the scales. However, there are no reports of the reliability or validity of the decision making or interventions based on the use of the FAAB.

COMMENTARY. The concepts underlying this systematic look at improving educational outlooks for children seem sound and are well justified. The materials are attractively packaged and the manual is very readable. Allowing the reader to copy the forms makes it economical and convenient to use. The manual's review of possible interventions by instructional component provides useful reminders of good educational practice.

Some of the forms are labeled "required" and some as "supplemental." A rationale for these labels has not been provided and of the five required forms, two differ only in the amount of detail. Are both required?

Other readers of the educational research might come up with a different taxonomy of alterable variables or additional areas of instructional support. It is not clear that the FAAB contains an exhaustive list. For example, there is no mention of peers or peer influences and group dynamics included in the system. Another aspect missing in the FAAB is an acknowledgement of the role of culture or language competence in supporting learning. Also, it is not clear at what age these supports or interventions are most relevant, although based on the wording of the items, the focus would seem to be roughly Grade 3–6.

Certain aspects of the FAAB may be less useful in secondary settings. Clearly the developmental level of students should be taken into account in evaluating responses to the items and planning instruction. Developmental considerations seem absent from the discussion.

The manual is vague about the qualifications necessary to use the FAAB effectively. The items may be understood very differently depending on the user's education and training, theoretical orientation, and experience. In most school settings, the information from the forms would be used by interdisciplinary teams to plan interventions for children who are having difficulty learning. The manual does not indicate how this problem solving might take place other than outlining a nine-step process, and the FAAB has not been evaluated as a consultation process. A similar approach to developing interventions to address academic problems, Instructional Consultation (Rosenfield & Gravois, 1996), has been more thoroughly implemented and evaluated.

SUMMARY. The FAAB offers educational professionals a set of informal data collection devices for examining a student's academic functioning and considering modifications. The focus of the assessment forms is on areas that have been validated as important for supporting academic learning. The system may be a help to those seeking to devise empirically based interventions. The FAAB is not a traditional assessment device. There is no guarantee that it will be used effectively in schools, because it depends heavily on the skill of the users to reach its goal of improving academic supports. That said, it provides a road map for creative, research-based thought about good instructional settings.

REVIEWER'S REFERENCES

Christenson, S. L., & Sheridan, S. L. (2001). *Schools and families: Creating essential connections for learning.* New York: Guilford Press.
Rosenfield, S. A., & Gravois, T. A. (1996). *Instructional consultation teams: Collaborating for change.* New York: Guilford.

Review of the Functional Assessment of Academic Behavior by SANDRA WARD, Professor of Education, The College of William & Mary, Williamsburg, VA:

DESCRIPTION. The Functional Assessment of Academic Behavior (FAAB) is a system, including checklists, interviews, and observations, that is designed to identify the presence or absence of environmental conditions that enhance a student's academic success and progress in school.

Specifically, the authors assert that the purposes of the FAAB are to "(a) gather information relevant to a referral concern for an individual student, (b) assess the instructional needs for the student, (c) assess supportive learning conditions, and (d) assist educators in designing feasible instructional interventions" (manual, p. 2). The FAAB is intended for use in Grades PreK through 12 in any classroom setting. The FAAB is designed to obtain information about a student's learning environments from multiple informants, including teachers, parents, and the student.

The FAAB includes five required forms: (a) The Instructional Environment Checklist, (b) The Instructional Environment Checklist: Annotated Version, (c) The Instructional Needs Checklist, (d) Parental Experience with Their Child's Learning and Schoolwork, and (e) The Intervention Documentation Form. Six additional forms are provided to inform educators about methods and types of data collection. All forms are reproducible, and users are encouraged to employ the forms that are relevant for the student of concern.

The FAAB Instructional Environment Checklist includes 23 components associated with positive academic performance. These variables are divided into three categories: (a) instructional support for learning (12 components), (b) home support for learning (5 components), and (c) home-school support for learning (6 components). The authors define each of the variables in the manual. Based on the data collected through various methods, the user of the FAAB marks the components for each variable on the checklist that applies to the student of concern. The annotated version of this checklist provides specific examples for each component in the three categories. This information will prove helpful for a less experienced user of the instrument.

The authors recommend nine steps in the use of the FAAB. This process matches the procedures of major consultation models. First, the referral concern should be identified. In Step 2, the Instructional Needs Checklist and Parental Experience with Their Child's Learning and Schoolwork form are used to understand the student's instructional needs according to the teacher and parents, respectively. The Instructional Needs Checklist is completed by teachers who check off items if they apply to the student of concern. The Parental Experience with Their

Child's Learning and Schoolwork form includes a section for the parent to identify concerns from a list. Parents also respond Yes or No to a series of statements regarding their observations of the child.

During the third step, the user of the FAAB collects data on the student's instructional environment. The authors do not prescribe data collection methods; however, they recommend that users of the FAAB employ at least two methods of data collection. These methods may include observation, interviews and rating scales, record review, and test results. The FAAB includes an Observation Record in the appendices. Additionally, the authors provide a Student Interview Record, a Parent Interview Record, and a Teacher Interview Record. The authors provide clear directions for the data collection methods, including common errors associated with each technique.

In Step 4, the user of the FAAB prioritizes and plans interventions to meet the student's instructional needs. At this stage the Instructional Environment Checklist should be used to identify the top three components that need to be changed for the student to demonstrate greater academic success. A plan is developed to meet these needs. The user employs the Instructional Environment Checklist's Home Support for Learning and Home-School Support for Learning components in Step 5 to identify ways to enhance student learning outside of school hours. In Step 6, the intervention is implemented, and in Step 7, the intervention's effectiveness is evaluated. If necessary, the user proceeds to Step 8, which includes revising the intervention plan. The final step is to document the intervention and report the results. The Intervention Documentation Record is designed to help in this process.

DEVELOPMENT. The FAAB is intended to replace the Instructional Environment System-II (TIES-II). The authors provide a strong rationale for the use of the FAAB and its potential impact on a student's academic performance. The FAAB maintains a focus on identifying and coordinating instructional, home, and home-school supports for a referred student. The emphasis on functional assessment stresses the importance of antecedents in the student's learning environment that lead to positive consequences for learning. The FAAB adds an essential piece to the assessment of academic behavior by examining evidence-based factors that predict greater academic

success. The authors cite numerous research studies to support the learning components of the FAAB, but specific information about the development of the instrument is not provided.

TECHNICAL. The FAAB is not a standardized instrument, so information on norms is immaterial. The authors do not provide any information on the reliability of the FAAB. It would have been particularly helpful if the authors offered estimates of interrater reliability for the Instructional Environment Checklist, the Instructional Needs Checklist, and the Observation Checklist. The inclusion of these data would inform the instrument's users of the consistency of results between and across the scales. Additionally, such data also would indicate the stability of the constructs being observed.

The FAAB has strong face validity. The items on the checklists appear reasonably related to the construct being measured, and the authors provide a logical explanation for the inclusion of specific components. Support for the instrument's content validity is inferred from the research that is cited by the authors to support the inclusion of the support for learning components. The test's content validity would be strengthened if the authors reported the specific details of the instrument's development, including a blueprint, rationale for particular emphases on content areas, and any expert reviews. Without this information, the test user must rely on the authors' interpretations of the cited studies.

The FAAB manual does not include any data to support empirical validity. Although the authors claim that the results of the FAAB can be linked to intervention, they do not provide any evidence on predictive validity. Specifically, the test user does not know whether the use of the FAAB and recommended interventions resulted in any changes in a student's outcome.

COMMENTARY. The FAAB is a potentially useful system to evaluate the ecological variables of a student's learning environment that may enhance or inhibit a student's academic progress. The authors provide a strong rationale for the impact of environmental variables on students' learning outcomes, which is supported by numerous research studies. The manual does not include any information about the instrument's reliability. The instrument does possess strong face validity. Although the authors claim that the FAAB adds a structure for examining evidence-based factors that predict greater academic success, they provide no evidence of empirical validity to support this statement. The components of the FAAB and the interventions that are recommended by the authors appear to be logical and research-based. However, the authors need to provide evidence that demonstrates that the use of the FAAB and the subsequent implementation of interventions actually results in students' academic success and progress in school.

SUMMARY. The FAAB is a comprehensive system that can be used in Grades PreK through 12 to evaluate the presence or absence of environmental conditions that enhance a student's academic success. The manual is clearly structured, and the authors are commended for their detailed descriptions of the components of positive academic performance. However, the instrument may be difficult for novice users to implement due to the complexity of the construct. The annotated version of the Instructional Environment Scale will assist these users, but they will need to practice applying this system to be efficient in the process. Chapter 3 in the manual provides examples of interventions that users of the FAAB will find extremely helpful. The FAAB can be a valuable component to a comprehensive assessment of a student. Its emphasis on the learning environment highlights an important variable with regard to a student's academic success that should be considered when making instructional decisions. The FAAB provides a systematic framework for examining the home and school environments. It appears to offer a planned method to approach academic difficulties from an ecological perspective, but the authors do not clearly connect the use of the FAAB with effective outcomes.

[77]

Gifted and Talented Evaluation Scales.

Purpose: Designed to "identify persons who are gifted and talented."
Population: Ages 5–18.
Publication Date: 1996.
Acronym: GATES.
Scores, 5: Intellectual Ability, Academic Skills, Creativity, Leadership, Artistic Talent.
Administration: Individual.
Price Data, 2006: $110 per complete kit including examiner's manual (50 pages) and 50 summary/response forms; $65 per examiner's manual; $50 per 50 summary/response forms.
Time: (5–10) minutes.
Comments: This test is to be completed by a teacher, parent, or guardian of the individual being assessed.
Authors: James E. Gilliam, Betsy O. Carpenter, and Janis R. Christensen.
Publisher: PRO-ED.

Review of the Gifted and Talented Evaluation Scales by LINDA E. BRODY, Johns Hopkins University, Center for Talented Youth, Baltimore, MD:

DESCRIPTION. The Gifted and Talented Evaluation Scales (GATES) is a behavioral checklist intended to assist in the identification of gifted and talented students ages 5–18. Designed to be completed easily by parents, teachers, and others who have had sustained contact with the student being evaluated, the GATES assesses performance in five areas derived from the federal definition of giftedness: Intellectual Ability, Academic Skills, Creativity, Leadership, and Artistic Talent. Each of these areas is measured by 10 items that compose a scale.

The rater is instructed to compare the student to average students of the same age by completing a 9-point Likert scale for each item, with the points falling into three broad bands: "Below Average" (1–3 points), "Average" (4–6 points), and "Above Average" (7–9 points). A raw score is computed for each of the five scales, which can be converted into standard scores (with a mean of 100 and standard deviation of 15) and percentile ranks (based on a comparison norm group of identified gifted and talented students). The results are depicted graphically on a form provided by the publisher to demonstrate the student's profile across the five talent areas.

The GATES is not intended to be the sole assessment tool for identifying gifted students, an important caution because the brevity of the instrument and the subjectivity of raters would be of concern if it were to be used to eliminate candidates from consideration for gifted programming without evaluating other factors. The authors support the use of numerous data sources including standardized tests, behavioral observations, parent interviews, and other indices of high ability and achievement.

DEVELOPMENT. In addition to wanting to reflect the categories of giftedness depicted in the federal definition, the authors were influenced in the development of this test by the work of Barbara Clark, Joseph Renzulli, and others who have described the characteristics of gifted students. After reviewing these sources, the authors generated a pool of 25 items per scale for a total pool of 125 items. These items were then reviewed by teachers of the gifted, university professors, and testing experts, and edited based on the feedback received. Existing rating scales were examined to determine if the GATES items failed to measure any important traits or skills.

The items were submitted to point-biserial correlation analysis to determine how well the items on each subtest discriminated between the high and low scorers on that subtest. A confirmatory item analysis was done on the strongest 60 items with 500 subjects from the normative sample. To reduce the size of the test, two items were removed from each scale and the shorter test was also analyzed. The published scales resulted from this process.

TECHNICAL.

Standardization. The GATES was normed on 1,083 individuals who resided in 32 states and Canada and had been identified as gifted and talented (G/T). To solicit this sample, 5,000 teachers were randomly selected from a purchased mailing list and asked to help in norming the GATES on the gifted students they taught. Sixty-eight teachers participated, 34 of whom were G/T teachers, 26 were general teachers who also taught G/T students, and 8 were special education teachers who primarily taught students with disabilities. Additional G/T teachers were added to enhance the geographic representation of the sample. In all, ratings were done on 1,787 students. Students who had not been identified as gifted and talented were omitted from the normative sample, but they were included in the validation studies.

Thus, all of the students in the norm group had been identified by their schools as gifted and talented, though the criteria used were not specified. Because schools vary in their methods for identifying gifted students, the assumption that this norm group might represent some consistent standard for defining giftedness could be faulty. Also, because students are being compared to average students in this assessment, it might have been better to use a national comparison group consisting of students of all ability levels for the normative sample, ensuring that the higher scores are achieved by the gifted students within that group, rather than restrict the sample to gifted students.

The authors hope that the GATES may be useful for identifying gifted students across cultural, gender, and age groups, and representation of these various groups was evident in the normative sample. However, it is difficult to evaluate, based on the data presented in the manual, whether the test serves subgroups of gifted students equally well or whether the GATES can identify underrepresented gifted students who would not otherwise be identified. In particular, because the rating scales are not necessarily being completed by individuals familiar with the specific characteristics of underachieving gifted students, the GATES may not be helpful in identifying twice—exceptional students as well as underachieving gifted students from disadvantaged backgrounds.

Reliability. Internal consistency reliability was assessed using coefficient alpha. Coefficients were computed for the scales using 400 of the students from the gifted norm sample and 210 average students, separately by gender. All coefficients were above .90, suggesting that the items within each scale are homogeneous and reliable. An analysis by type of rater (parents, G/T teachers, etc.) found that internal consistency was maintained within these groups. However, this analysis appears to have been done with different raters evaluating different children; it would have been helpful to determine the reliability when different raters evaluate the same children.

Two test-retest reliability studies were also conducted to assess the stability of the GATES. In both studies, the correlation coefficients were lower for the gifted students than for average students or for those with handicaps, which the authors attribute to restriction of range in the gifted group. Sample sizes were small, with only 17 gifted students participating in each of the two studies. Though combining students from both studies resulted in higher coefficients, it would have been wise to pursue this further with a larger sample of gifted students. The standard error of measurement on the GATES was determined to be 3 points, which is reasonably acceptable for a measure of this kind, though it is important that educators be aware of this if any cutoff scores are utilized for admission to programs.

Validity. The authors assert that content validity for the GATES is supported by their literature review on what constitutes giftedness and the internal consistency of the scales. To evaluate criterion-related validity, the correlation of the GATES with each of three other behavioral rating scales commonly used to identify gifted students (the Renzulli-Hartman Scales, the Williams Scale, and the Comprehensive Scales of Student Abilities) was computed and resulted in moderate to strong correlations. Sample sizes in these studies were small, however.

To assess construct validity, the correlations among the scales were computed and found to be strong. The authors suggest that these findings validate the idea that the GATES is true to its mission to identify gifted individuals, but it may also suggest that the scales lack the independence needed to identify students gifted in one domain but not others. Other evidence that the test does what it is supposed to do is that it was found to discriminate between average students and those identified as gifted; however, these results may have been biased because the rating scales were completed in the pilot studies, for the most part, by teachers who were already aware of who had been identified as gifted.

What is lacking is any assessment of the predictive validity of the test. When identifying students as gifted, we should be looking for students who are ready to excel in more advanced work. There is no evidence that these scales have been successfully used for this purpose. In addition, no studies have been presented that specifically measure the validity of this instrument for identifying traditionally underrepresented gifted students.

COMMENTARY. The GATES attempts to provide a standardized alternative to nonstandardized nomination forms and checklists used to identify students for gifted and talented programs. In spite of the efforts that went into establishing a normative comparison group and evaluating the test's reliability and validity, more work is needed to demonstrate the value of this tool.

The validity of the GATES depends heavily on the fact that the students in the norm group were accurately identified as gifted, yet little information is provided to evaluate the appropriateness of that identification. Assuming the students in the norm group were accurately identified based on other measures, it is not clear what value-added role the GATES plays in an identification that still includes all of those measures.

Most importantly, studies of the predictive validity of the GATES are needed. Does it accurately predict high achievement among the students who score high on this assessment? And are students who receive low ratings less likely to be high achievers in the future? In addition, more information is needed about the usefulness of the GATES for identifying students who belong to specific subgroups of gifted children, including students who differ by age, ethnicity, cultural background, and specific talent areas.

SUMMARY. A lack of consensus in the gifted community about how to define giftedness has led to a lack of consistency in the methods used to identify and serve gifted learners. Thus, we might welcome a new tool for identification that addresses these concerns. To their credit, the authors of the GATES have gone to considerable effort to establish a defensible rationale and methodology for these scales. In spite of these efforts, the validity for all of its purposes and the value-added role of the GATES remain unclear. Perhaps more research can provide a stronger justification for using this product.

Review of the Gifted and Talented Evaluation Scales by CAROLYN M. CALLAHAN, Commonwealth Professor of Education, University of Virginia, Charlottesville, VA:

DESCRIPTION. The Gifted and Talented Evaluation Scales: A Norm-Referenced Procedure for Identifying Gifted and Talented Students (GATES) is a set of five rating scales to be completed by teachers, teacher assistants, parents, or other persons "knowledgeable about the student being rated" (examiner's manual, p. 11). Each scale is composed of 10 items, each rated on a 9-point Likert scale. The items for each scale (Intellectual Ability, Academic Skills, Creativity, Leadership, and Artistic Talent) are printed on a "Summary/Response Form" and are completed under the supervision of the examiner by a rater who needs only be familiar with how the items are completed, how the data will be used, and the student who will be rated. Raters indicate their "impression" of students in comparison to "average students of the same age" (examiner's manual, p. 12) on the characteristic by circling a number on the form provided. The examiner sums the ratings for each scale on the front of the form and uses conversion tables to determine standard scores (mean of 100 and standard deviation of 15) and percentile scores, entering those on a profile and determining the probability of giftedness (ranging from *Very Unlikely* to *Extremely Probable*) from a chart provided on the form. The authors also claim that the GATES may be used as a diagnostic instrument and may be used to "document progress as a consequence of special intervention programs, and...to measure changes in behavior in research projects" (p. 8).

The authors recommend that an "examiner" responsible for administering the GATES be a member of the identification and placement committee responsible for screening gifted and talented students. No particular professional qualifications or training other than familiarization with the underlying tenets of the test, the test manual, and an understanding of norm-referenced assessment are called for in examiner qualifications.

DEVELOPMENT. The items for the GATES scales were generated by reviewing literature on the characteristics of students who are gifted and talented. Reviews of those items by teachers, university professors, and test construction experts were used by the authors to "edit" items. No criteria are specified for selection of the item reviewers, nor are the criteria that were given to raters delineated. Other rating scales were consulted to identify gaps in the coverage for each scale. Point-biserial correlations were calculated on each item. A confirmatory factor analysis using 500 cases from the normative sample was used to reduce the initial pool of 125 items to 60 items (12 per scale), and then two items were deleted from each scale. No detail is provided on the criteria used in deleting those items.

The norming of the GATES was carried out by seeking volunteer teachers selected from a mailing list of teachers to rate students in their classrooms. Of the 1,787 students rated by 68 teachers returning forms, 1,083 were identified as gifted and talented. Only the students identified as gifted and talented were used in the norming sample; however, a heterogeneous group was used in the confirmatory factor analysis and point-biserial correlational analysis.

TECHNICAL. Directions for completing the scales on the form are vague and require broad interpretations by the rater. Examples for completing the scale are incomplete, and thus, are not helpful in clarifying the ways in which one would distinguish among the nine possible ratings. Although the manual gives a more specific example, it does not specify that this example should be read to or otherwise presented to the rater. It is also not clear which directions (those on the form or those in the manual) were provided to those completing the ratings in the norming sample.

Norming data that serve as the basis for cutoffs for the various score levels on the GATES are vague. The authors report that the "test" was normed on a nationally representative sample of 1,083 students in 32 states and Canada who were identified as gifted and talented in their respective school districts. However, information on the definition of giftedness used in those schools, the basis for giftedness identification in the schools, or the success of students in gifted and talented programs are not provided. Further, given that the scales range across academic, intellectual, artistic, and leadership constructs, it may be inappropriate that the same sample would be used for setting of norms on all the scales. The authors report that there was very little difference in ratings across age but do not present supporting data.

Point-biserial correlations of the items with total scale scores are presented as both reliability and validity evidence, but the data appear to have been calculated based on the completion of the full complement of 125 items. No evidence is presented on the reliability when only the 50-item instrument is completed. Internal consistency estimates (coefficient alphas) were calculated according to teacher gender and role. The results are very high and yield standard errors of measurement ranging from 2.1 to 4.5 when separated by type of rater. Stability estimates based on a small sample of 17 students identified as gifted and talented, 30 average students, and 14 students with mild handicaps by undergraduate college students in an education course over a 1-week period yielded stability estimates ranging from .42 (Intellectual Ability) to .68 (Leadership and Artistic Talent). In a second study, 20 graduate students rated students they taught (17 gifted students, 33 average students, 14 students with mild handicaps). The coefficients ranged from .70 (Intellectual Ability) to .87 (Creativity and Leadership) for the gifted and talented students. The similar numbers of students in each sample rated and the setting suggest the same students were rated in both estimates of reliability, but no interrater reliability is presented. The degree to which the raters were aware of the designation of students as gifted and talented or handicapped (a potential bias in the rating) is not noted.

The scales are not based on clearly defined constructs. Though noting that there is no commonly accepted definition for giftedness, these scales fail to identify the parameters of the definitions of giftedness underlying the GATES or the defining parameters of the categories of giftedness they have chosen to use as the basis for the GATES scales. Further, they do not provide a rationale for or evidence of the effectiveness of using the scales in identifying students who will benefit from the many curricular, instructional, or programmatic options that are suggested for meeting the educational needs of gifted students.

Evidence in support of the validity of the scales on the GATES is limited. Although the authors claim that the scales on the GATES are "independent scales" and that a confirmatory factor analysis documented that "most" items strongly correlated with their respective scales, no factor-analytic data are provided to confirm those findings or to document that the items did not also load on multiple scales. Claims that point-biserial correlations provide powerful and sophisticated evidence of construct validity may not be warranted. An examination of the items calls their independence into question. Many items on the Intellectual Ability scale overlap considerably with items on the Academic Skills scale. The scales are also extremely redundant internally, failing to tap a range of behaviors. In several cases, constructs rather than behaviors make up the items (e.g., creativity itself is an item on the Creativity scale).

Content validity is based on the expert review described above and presentation of item discrimination data documenting that there is internal consistency of scales. Criterion-related validity is based on correlating the GATES scales with other frequently used instruments. The first study, comparing the GATES and the Renzulli-Hartman Scales (Renzulli, Smith, White, Callahan, & Hartman, 1976) found all correlations significant, thus failing to provide the convergent and discriminant validity one would expect. For example, the correlation of the two Creativity subscales was lower than the correlation between the Creativity scale (GATES) and the Learning subscale of the Renzulli-Hartman. Correlations

with the Williams Scale Creativity Assessment Packet (Williams, 1980) are not discussed in terms of concurrent, convergent, or discriminant validity and do not add to an understanding of the validity of the GATES. The correlations between scales of the Comprehensive Scales of Student Abilities (Hammill & Hresko, 1994) and the GATES scales on a small sample are insufficient in conception or discussion to support validity. For example, the authors note correlations in expected directions, but fail to discuss significant correlations between Handwriting and Leadership or Social Behavior and Artistic Talent.

The discussion of discrimination between diagnostic groups is weakened by the lack of evidence as to whether raters were already aware of the diagnostic categories prior to rating the students, hence calling into question the objectivity of ratings. If teachers were already aware that the students were labeled gifted, they might be more likely to rate the students higher on the scales. No evidence is provided for diagnostic validity of the scales.

The manual suggests that parents or others familiar with the student can be raters; however, the norming process and limited psychometric analysis were all completed using teacher raters only. The ability of parents to rate their own children relative to other students of the same age presumes a wide range of parental experience with children of the same age.

COMMENTARY. The value of the GATES as a measure of "giftedness" or even the individual constructs identified on the five scales is limited first by the lack of a clear definition of the meaning of those constructs for purposes of interpretation. The authors' attempt to create a universal definition of gifted and talented as a basis for a single instrument limits its usefulness. Second, data presented on the independence of the scales and their content and construct validity are insufficient to warrant great confidence in their use.

The manual makes claims that standard scores can also be "added, subtracted, and otherwise manipulated statistically" (p. 18) which may lead to the incorrect assumption that adding together scores on the scales will yield a meaningful index of a unitary concept of giftedness.

The interpretations of the profile scores are suspect. The authors claim that "low scores are indicative of persons with little or no exceptional abilities" (examiner's manual, p. 15). In fact, they are indicative only of someone's *perceptions* of the student. Further, if *all* the students in the sample were gifted and talented, low standard scores simply place the child at the low end of the range of gifted and talented students, not necessarily in a category unlikely to be gifted. No rationales are provided for the categories used or for the cutoff scores used to create the category beyond an explanation that "Approximately 50% of the subjects who are gifted and talented scored in this range [between 90 and 110]. Standard scores above 110 are highly indicative of students who are gifted and talented" (examiner's manual, p.19).

SUMMARY. The GATES appears to be an instrument that can be easily administered and scored and that is internally consistent. Neither stability nor interrater reliability has been sufficiently documented. Insufficient validity evidence combined with questionable rationale for the creation of rating categories and interpretation of the scores limit the usefulness of the scores and unsatisfactory interpretation and documentation of probabilities that a student is gifted invites incorrect judgments about student potential.

REVIEWER'S REFERENCES

Hammill, D. D., & Hresko, W. P. (1994). Comprehensive Scales of Student Abilities. Austin, TX: PRO-ED.
Renzulli, J. S., Smith, L. H., White, A. J., Callahan, C. M., & Hartman, R. K. (1976). Scales for Rating the Behavioral Characteristics of Superior Students. Mansfield Center, CT: Creative Learning Press.
Williams, F. (1980). Creativity Assessment Packet. Austin, TX: PRO-ED.

[78]
Gilliam Autism Rating Scale—Second Edition.

Purpose: Designed to help professionals "identify children with autism from children with other severe behavioral problems."

Population: Ages 3–22.

Publication Dates: 1995–2006.

Acronym: GARS-2.

Scores: 3 subscales: Stereotyped Behaviors, Communication, Social Interaction, plus Autism Index.

Administration: Individual.

Price Data, 2006: $131 per complete kit including examiner's manual (2006, 85 pages), 50 summary/response booklets, and instructional objectives manual (2006, 26 pages); $60 per examiner's manual; $45 per 50 summary/response booklets; $28 per instructional objectives manual.

Time: (5–10) minutes.

Comments: Appropriate raters include parents, teachers, or other caregivers who have had regular, sustained contact with the individual for at least 2 weeks.

Author: James E. Gilliam.

Publisher: PRO-ED.

Cross References: For reviews by Donald P. Oswald and Steven Welsh of an earlier form, see 13:130.

Review of the Gilliam Autism Rating Scale, Second Edition by DOREEN WARD FAIRBANK, Professor of Psychology, Meredith College, Raleigh, NC:

DESCRIPTION. The Gilliam Autism Rating Scale—Second Edition (GARS-2) is the second edition of a scale originally published in 1995. The author developed the instrument for clinicians and educators as a screening/diagnostic instrument to assist in the identification of individuals with autism and for educational planning and research. According to the manual, there were several reasons for this revision that were based on test reviews, published articles, individuals' queries, and observations. The major changes were to revise the Developmental Disturbances subscale into a parent interview format, clarify several items, renorm and update the demographic characteristics of the normative sample based on 2000 U.S. Census data, change the Autism Quotient to the Autism Index, add a separate chapter on discrete target behaviors for each test item, and add a separate booklet, Instructional Objectives for Children Who Have Autism.

The Gilliam Autism Rating Scale—Second Edition was designed to provide an instrument for distinguishing individuals aged 3 through 22 years with autism from others who have severe behavioral problems. The information provided from this test should help the assessor to interpret an individual's present level of functioning and how best to develop a program for educational or therapeutic interventions. There are 42 clearly stated items that are divided into three subscales (Stereotyped Behaviors, Communication, and Social Interaction) that describe specific, observable, and measurable behaviors. The three subscales were based on two definitions of autism, one from the Autism Society of America and the other from the diagnostic criteria for autistic disorder published in the DSM-IV-TR (American Psychiatric Association, 2000). Each subscale contains 14 items and is scored on the frequency of occurrence from 0 (*never observed*) to 3 (*frequently observed*). The GARS-2 also includes a parent interview with 25 yes/no questions divided into a "Delays in" and

"Abnormal Functioning in" format. The "Delays in" section evaluates social interaction and language used in social communication, and the "Abnormal Functioning in" examines social interaction, language used in social communication, and symbolic or imaginative play. An additional section, "Key Questions," includes 11 questions that assist the examiner in reaching a diagnostic conclusion. The last section of the Summary/Response booklet provides space for interpretation and recommendations. The GARS-2 is completed using several techniques including interviewing the parents, a rater's response to the direct observation of the child, and the examiner completing the Key Questions and Interpretation and Recommendations sections. The manual states that the rater needs to be someone who knows the individual well, such as a classroom teacher, parent, or other caregiver. The examiner should be a school psychologist, an educational diagnostician, an autism specialist, a speech-language pathologist, or a similarly trained professional who knows how to interpret test information and use it to diagnose autism.

The Gilliam Autism Rating Scale—Second Edition consists of an examiner's manual, Instructional Objectives for Children Who Have Autism, and a Summary/Response booklet. The Summary/Response booklet is divided into 9 sections that are intended to assess, summarize, and make diagnostic inferences. The sections are: Section I Identifying Information, Section II Score Summary, Section III Interpretation Guide, Section IV Profile of Scores, Section V Individual Item Responses (the three subscales), Section VI Parent Interview, Section VII Key Questions, Section VIII Interpretation and Recommendations, and Section IX Characteristics, which contains a summary of characteristics of the instrument that an examiner might want to have immediately available. The rater/examiner does not need any additional material or supplies to complete this instrument. The Instructional Objectives for Children Who Have Autism is a new addition to this revision. Sample instructional objectives for behavioral problems are given for each item from the GARS-2 and are designed to help in writing Individualized Education Programs and behavior management plans. These goals and objections also can serve as a guide for program development.

DEVELOPMENT. The Gilliam Autism Rating Scale—Second Edition is the latest revision. The original test was published in 1995 based on two definitions of autism, one from the Autism Society of America and the other from the diagnostic criteria for autistic disorder published in the DSM-IV. The manual gives a brief history of autism, prevalence and definitions of autism, characteristics and associated features of autism, differential diagnosis, and diagnostic issues relating to autism. It gives detailed information and instructions on the administering, scoring, and interpretation of this instrument. There are several sections in the manual on normative information, reliability, and validity of the GARS-2. The manual also includes a chapter on "Application of GARS-2 Items for Applied Behavior Analysis." This chapter provides a detailed list of behavioral descriptors for each test item so that the behaviors can be used in applied behavior analysis studies.

TECHNICAL. The Gilliam Autism Rating Scale—Second Edition was researched and standardized with a nationwide sample of 1,107 individuals diagnosed with autism between the ages of 3 and 22. Additional data were collected on a similar aged population with disabilities other than autism and from a control group of individuals without disabilities. The nonautism groups were used in the validity studies but not in establishing the norms for this instrument. Ethnicity, gender, geographic regions, and age of individuals comprising the norming sample are discussed in the user's manual. The manual illustrates how this sample is representative of the U.S. 2000 Census data. Subscales are all norm-referenced. The normative scores are given in the manual for subscale standard scores, percentile ranks, and Autism Index.

Internal consistency reliability, as assessed by coefficient alpha was calculated using data from the normative sample. The coefficients of internal reliability were .84 for the Stereotyped Behavior subscale, .86 for Communication, .88 for Social Interaction, and .94 for the total test. Over a 1-week interval, test-retest reliability estimates ranged from .64 for Communication to .82 for Social Interaction, .83 for Stereotyped Behaviors, and .84 for the Autism Index.

The manual provides substantial evidence for content validity (using a variety of techniques including item discrimination coefficients ranging from .35 to .64), criterion-related validity, and construct-identification validity. The GARS-2 is an instrument that can discriminate persons with autism from other individuals with severe behavioral disorders based on the validity studies discussed in the manual.

COMMENTARY. The Gilliam Autism Rating Scale—Second Edition is a well-standardized, reliable, and valid instrument to screen/diagnose individuals with autism from 3 to 22 years of age. The rater can complete the instrument in about 10 minutes, and as long as the rater is well familiar with the individual being assessed, additional training is not necessary. One limitation involves the subscale on Communication. The instructions inform the rater that if the individual is unable to communicate using oral language or signs, then try to encourage them. If there is still no communication after 2 weeks of effort, omit the Communication subscale. The GARS-2 can still be scored without this subscale. The test should include some type of evaluation of alternative communication systems or the individual's attempt to communication, as this is valuable information for programming.

SUMMARY. The Gilliam Autism Rating Scale—Second Edition is a screening instrument intended for use with individuals with autism, ages 3–22 years. The instrument is completed through parent interview, observation of the child, and direct administration of test items to the child. The test is self-contained, and the raters do not need to gather materials before administering the test. The manual contains excellent information regarding standardization, reliability, and validity. The instrument can be used as a reliable diagnostic tool, as well as an instrument for monitoring behavior and education/communication progress. The instrument along with the Instruction Objectives booklet provides a systematic method to collect and organize information across areas of social, educational, and language development and to enhance program development for individuals with autism.

REVIEWER'S REFERENCE

American Psychiatric Association. (2000). *Diagnostic and statistical manual of mental disorders* (4th ed., text rev.). Washington, DC: The Author.

Review of the Gilliam Autism Rating Scale— Second Edition by ADRIENNE GARRO, Assistant Professor of Psychology, Kean University, Union, NJ:

DESCRIPTION. The Gilliam Autism Rating Scale—Second Edition (GARS-2) is a 42-item, norm-referenced instrument developed to assist in the identification of individuals with autism ages 3—22. Although the GARS-2 is described as a screening test, its purposes, as stated in the examiner's manual, extend to diagnosis, intervention planning, and progress monitoring. According to the manual, the GARS-2 can be completed by a teacher, parent, or other caregiver who has knowledge of and regular contact with the individual being evaluated. The estimated time of administration is 5 to 10 minutes. The main section of the GARS-2 is divided into three subscales—Stereotyped Behaviors, Communication, and Social Interaction—which are based upon the Autism Society of America's definition of autism and diagnostic criteria from the DSM-IV (American Psychiatric Association, 2000). The items on these subscales are answered using a frequency scale from 0–3 (0 = *Never Observed*, 3 = *Frequently Observed*). These rating categories are further specified in the manual and the response booklet. Each subscale generates a standard score (mean = 10, SD = 3) with a corresponding percentile rank. The subscale standard scores are then summed to produce an Autism Index (mean = 100, SD = 15). Higher standard scores and Autism Indices are indicative of more problematic behavior. Scoring also includes a Probability of Autism classification (*Very Likely, Possibly, Unlikely*). Unfortunately, these categories are somewhat vague and have minimal empirical evidence to back them.

In addition to the main subscales, the GARS-2 includes sections for score summarization and interpretation, a parent interview, key questions to assist in diagnosis, and a booklet of instructional objectives to help develop interventions. According to the manual, the GARS-2 should be administered by professionals who have training and experience in working with individuals with autism such as school psychologists, educational diagnosticians, and autism specialists.

DEVELOPMENT. The GARS-2 is the second edition of an instrument that was first published in 1995. According to the test manual, the second edition reflects several positive changes such as: (a) updated, more clearly described norms; (b) rewriting of some items and the scoring guidelines to improve clarity; and (c) a section that provides specific item definitions and examples for applied behavior analysis and research projects. The process of item development for the GARS-2 is not thoroughly described. Although the names of the subscales correspond to the main DSM-IV criteria for Autistic Disorder, the items do not correspond absolutely to the behavioral characteristics listed under these criteria or to the traits listed on the website of the Autism Society of America. The author notes that item development was based upon several general principles about people with autism (e.g., "they perceive and respond to sensory and cognitive input in unique ways," examiner's manual, p. 46). To the author's credit, information regarding item discrimination is provided to help support content validity of the GARS-2.

TECHNICAL. The normative sample for the GARS-2 consisted of 1,107 individuals between the ages of 3 and 22 residing in the United States who had been diagnosed with autism. Almost 73% of the sample were students or other individuals who were rated by teachers, diagnosticians, and other personnel from school districts and treatment centers specializing in autism and other disabilities; and 27% were individuals whose parents submitted internet data through the Asperger Syndrome Information and Support website. Although the manual emphasizes the importance of differential diagnosis between autism and other disorders, the normative sample may have included individuals with a variety of pervasive developmental disorders (PDDs). Based upon comparisons to 2001 U.S. Census data, the sample roughly approximated national characteristics with respect to geographic region and race, though the manual delineates only three racial categories (White, Black, and Other). The percentage of Hispanics is specified, but it is unclear if this term refers to ethnicity or language spoken. The sample was appropriately divided with respect to gender (81% male, 19% female), given that autism disproportionately affects males. When it comes to age, the sample is unevenly distributed with 54% of the individuals falling in the range from 3–8 years, 25% in the range from 9–12 years, and the remainder in the range from 13–22 years.

With respect to reliability, the GARS-2 shows good internal consistency for the three subscales and the total scale with coefficient alphas ranging from .84–.94. The test manual reports one study for test-retest reliability. The results indicated good stability over a one-week interval for the subscales and the Autism Index, but should be regarded with caution due to the small sample size (n = 37) used.

The developer of the GARS-2 provides some basic information supporting its validity, but additional studies are clearly warranted. The instrument's content was guided by basic principles regarding autism, but there is little theoretical and empirical information to support the development and selection of specific items. In addition, evidence supporting the instrument's factor structure is limited to the discrimination indices previously described. As evidence of construct validity, the manual notes that the three subscales are strongly intercorrelated with each other. Although these intercorrelations indicate that GARS-2 items measure the intended underlying construct, they offer little support for the separation of some items into distinct subscales. As further evidence of construct validity, the developer describes several hypotheses that were tested. The first of these (GARS-2 scores will not be highly correlated with chronological age) is questionable because it does not specifically examine the characteristics of autism as defined by the instrument. The remaining hypotheses are more meaningful, and, in general, the results provide preliminary support for the validity of the Autism Index as a broad diagnostic indicator. For example, in one study, this index did successfully discriminate among different diagnostic groups and a nondisabled group. With respect to criterion-related validity, scores from the GARS-2 and the Autism Behavior Checklist were compared. Results indicated significant correlations between the total scores of the two instruments and between subscales that were hypothesized to be related to each other, but there were also significant correlations between other subscales. In another study, prediction analyses yielded significant results that seem to support the Autism Index as an identifier of autism.

COMMENTARY. The value of the GARS-2 depends upon its intended purpose and the user's need for a specific diagnostic tool. The overall content is clearly linked to characteristics of people with PDDs but does not follow a theoretical framework specific to autism. It would be beneficial to describe more fully the rationale for item development and input from expert clinicians and researchers as part of content validation. One clear drawback regarding the development of norms is that the process used did not control for inconsistencies and inaccuracies in the diagnostic process. More specifically, although it was specified that sample participants should have been diagnosed with autism, there is no information about the specific diagnostic criteria that were actually used. Although the norms are not based upon age, the underrepresentation of older children and young adults suggests that users need to exercise caution when using the instrument with individuals from these age groups.

Further research with samples beyond the norm group is warranted to strengthen evidence that supports validity and reliability. One shortcoming is the absence of research related to interrater reliability, which is important because users may include multiple raters in the assessment process. Although it is realistic to expect some interrater differences due to environmental fluctuations in individual functioning, the nature of autism implies some consistency in characteristics across settings and situations. Therefore, the main value of the GARS-2 is its utility as a screening instrument to help identify individuals who may fit the criteria for autism or another PDD. To this end, the Autism Index is the most valuable and reliable score provided by the instrument. As previously noted, the Probability of Autism classification lacks a strong empirical basis and is subject to misinterpretation; therefore, it should be avoided by all except the most experienced diagnosticians. Although there is some evidence of item discrimination, users will find that several items from different subscales overlap with one another. Review of item wording suggests that a number of items could be grouped under more than one subscale. The majority of the individual items appear to correspond with the subscale they represent, though the significances of individual item correlations were not reported. On a positive note, the manual provides comprehensive information, including several cautions for interpretation of results. If this information is followed carefully, the GARS-2 provides useful information as part of a comprehensive assessment for PDDs.

SUMMARY. The GARS-2 has a number of distinct features that contribute to its utility in assessing autism and other PDDs. These include its ease of administration, use of specific frequency ratings, flexibility to accommodate different raters, and applicability to a wider age range. The content of the instrument covers a number of behavioral characteristics that clearly apply to in-

dividuals with PDDs. Despite these strengths, the GARS-2 demonstrates several shortcomings: (a) the subscales require better differentiation, (b) many items are not necessarily specific to autism, and (c) some aspects of norming require expanded clarification. In addition, although the developer provides preliminary support for the psychometric properties of the GARS-2, a more solid research base is needed, especially with respect to interrater reliability and construct and criterion-related validity. Due to these factors, the GARS-2 is most effective as a screening tool for PDDs in general, but not autism specifically.

REVIEWER'S REFERENCES
American Psychiatric Association. (2000). *Diagnostic and statistical manual of mental disorders:* (4th ed., text rev.). Washington, DC: Author.
Autism Society of America. (n.d.). *Learn the signs.* Retrieved September 25, 2006 from http://www.autism-society.org/site/PageServer?pagename=whatisautism#Signs

[79]
Graded Nonword Reading Test.

Purpose: Designed to "identify reading difficulties associated with impaired phonological skills."
Population: Ages 5–11.
Publication Date: 1996.
Acronym: GNWRT.
Scores: Total score only.
Administration: Individual.
Price Data, 2006: £84 per complete kit including manual (32 pages), 100 scoring sheets, and stimulus book; £26.50 per 100 scoring sheets.
Time: (5) minutes.
Authors: Margaret J. Snowling, Susan E. Stothard, and Janet McLean.
Publisher: Harcourt Assessment [England].

Review of the Graded Nonword Reading Test by KAREN MACKLER, School Psychologist, Lawrence Public Schools, Lawrence, NY:

DESCRIPTION. The Graded Nonword Reading Test assesses a school-aged child's ability to read novel letter strings, or nonsense words. The authors state that this measure is useful for the identification of children with impaired phonological skills, common in children who struggle with reading.

The measure consists of 20 nonsense words, ordered by difficulty. There are 10 one-syllable items, followed by 10 two-syllable items. Prior to the formal administration of the stimuli, the child is presented with five practice items, all following a one-syllable, CVC (consonant-vowel-consonant) pattern. Each nonword is presented individually, nd the participant is asked to read the word loud. If the child cannot be successful on the practice pretest, administration is abandoned. Entire administration requires approximately 5 minutes. Normative data were collected for children ages 5 years to 11 years of age, but the authors state that the measure is also suitable for older children and adults with suspected reading difficulties.

Students taking the test are informed that they are to read "silly nonsense words" (manual, p. 1) that were made up by the examiner. The student is asked to read each nonword and is told if his or her response is correct. If the response is incorrect, or if the student fails to respond, he or she is asked to sound out each of the letters and then to blend them together, such as: "w," "u," "t," "wut." If the child still is having difficulty, the examiner is to demonstrate the technique. This type of assistance is only to be given on the initial practice items, with corrective feedback given as needed. During the actual test administration, praise and encouragement are to be given without letting the child know if each individual response is correct or incorrect. Every child is given the practice items, and the test is discontinued after six consecutive incorrect responses. The response is credited with 1 point per item up to a maximum score of 20 on the test. The correct phonetic responses are provided to the examiner on the scoring sheet. Consonant pronunciations are to be scored strictly, whereas examiners are asked to use their discretion when scoring the pronunciation of vowels, due to regional accents that might come into play. Appropriate sequencing of the sounds is to be strictly adhered to, as many students who experience difficulty with reading transpose the sequence of letter sounds, omit letter sounds, or insert letter sounds, all of which result in no credit earned.

The thin manual has a section dedicated to interpreting the results, which acknowledges that because the test is not timed, the resulting score may be an overestimate of decoding skills. The interpreter is also told to use resulting scores in conjunction with chronological age or reading age. The score obtained on this measure is reported as a centile equivalent. The 50 centile is considered normal for age, whereas scores falling below the 10 centile are considered to be within an impaired range. An examiner may also use a reading age

obtained from the British Abilities Scales, although this would not be feasible in the United States. In addition, a reading age equivalent score may be computed based on the number of nonwords correctly read by an individual student.

DEVELOPMENT. This measure was developed by the authors while conducting studies on developmental dyslexia. Results indicated that children with dyslexia have difficulty in reading nonwords. Based on the history of reading acquisition, the authors contend that a graded nonword reading list is a useful component of an assessment of a child's written language skills, and a direct measure of decoding. The authors do not provide any detailed information about the initial studies conducted in the development of this current measure, but appear to compile information based upon the theory of reading acquisition, rather than on actual empirical data. The authors do state that although the measure is age-normed and can stand on its own as an assessment tool, the primary value of the test is the diagnostic information it provides.

TECHNICAL. Standardization of the Graded Nonword Reading Test was conducted on a large sample of 653 children between the years of 1990–1993. Standardization was conducted in three regions of England. It is unclear how the children might differ based upon their residence, as there is no mention of type of location, such as rural or suburban. The standardization sample was not equalized for age, so although 142 children were 8 years of age, only 54 were 11. The British Abilities Scale Word Reading Test, which requires single-word reading, was also administered to each child in the sample. No technical data were provided for the British Abilities Scale Word Reading Test. In addition, no information regarding gender differences, if any, was given.

Internal reliability data were obtained by completing an item analysis on protocols obtained from 246 participants from one primary school. The measure was administered without any discontinuation rule in effect. Coefficient alpha was .96, suggesting strong indication that the test items were measuring the same attribute.

A group of approximately 90 children ages 6, 8, and 10 years were given the test on two separate occasions, separated by approximately 1 week. There were approximately 30 children of each age group. Correlations were .90 or higher, indicating adequate test-retest reliability over this short period of time. Practice effects were measured by computing the mean number of nonwords read correctly during each session. The mean number was very similar for the two sessions, suggesting minimal learning or practice effects.

Concurrent validity was assessed by comparison of scores on this measure with those obtained on the British Abilities Scales Word Reading Test of single-word reading (BAS). The correlation coefficients that resulted were in the .60s. Predictive validity was assessed by administering the test to 12 children selected from a school for children with dyslexia. These scores were compared to those of 12 children with typical reading skills, matched for chronological age, and 12 reading-age-matched controls. The children with dyslexia obtained significantly lower scores on the Graded Nonword Reading Test than the chronologically matched controls. The group with dyslexia also read significantly fewer nonwords than the reading-age controls, suggesting that the measure can discriminate between children with reading difficulties and those with typical reading abilities.

COMMENTARY. This measure provides a quick assessment of phonetic decoding skills. It is packaged nicely and is quite easy to administer. It is not a comprehensive measure and should not be used as a stand-alone assessment of reading ability. However, students should find the format appealing, almost game-like, as they try to figure out the pronunciation of the nonsense words. Much qualitative information is derived from the administration of this measure in terms of strategies used to decode novel words, and what kind of errors the student tends to make. For example, the evaluator can count the frequency of errors involving each vowel sound. Based on the information gained, remediation strategies might be developed. A difficulty with this test could be in using it in the United States with norms from Great Britain. The administrator needs to be aware that scores are based on British norms, and centile scores are provided, which is not how scores are typically reported in the United States. As such, it is difficult to integrate this tool with others used in a typical U.S. assessment, where percentile ranks and standard scores may be generated. There appears to be merit in the authors' belief that this measure is a suitable measure of phonetic decoding, justifying the resulting reading-age equivalent score. They readily acknowledge that this score does not give information about other skills such as reading comprehension and word recognition (sight words). Overall, however, this instrument may be a nice addition to a reading assessment, especially as an ice breaker to get the student involved in a nonthreatening activity that does not seem to be reading at all.

SUMMARY. The Graded Nonword Reading Test provides a quick measure of phonetic decoding skills, as measured by reading nonsense words. The test was developed as part of several studies assessing readers with dyslexia, and might be helpful as part of a comprehensive assessment to determine areas of reading difficulty. It has acceptable reliability and validity. It was normed in Great Britain, which might make it difficult to integrate scores with the results of testings using measures more commonly used in other countries, such as the United States. The test should not be used as a sole determinant of reading difficulty. The test may provide useful qualitative data regarding phonetic strategies and an error analysis, which might be helpful in generating remedial plans.

Review of the Graded Nonword Reading Test by JEFFREY SMITH, Professor, The University of Otago, Dunedin, New Zealand:

DESCRIPTION. The Graded Nonword Reading Test is a set of 20 items of letter strings that are not English words, but approximate them in terms of appearance and pronunciation. For example, "kib" and "chamgalp" are two of the items on the test. It is intended as a measure of decoding ability. Children are presented with the words one at a time and asked to pronounce them. Items are ordered from least difficult to most difficult. Acceptable pronunciations are presented in the manual provided with the test. Items are scored as right/wrong, and a total score is calculated as the sum of the correct responses. The test can be discontinued when a student gets 6 items in a row wrong. Norms are provided based on a modest sample of students from England. The test is designed to be used with children aged 6 to 11 years, or with individuals with reading difficulties. The test takes roughly 5 minutes to administer and does not require special training or certification.

DEVELOPMENT. The Graded Nonword Reading Test appears to have been developed in the late 1980s. The publication date for the test is 1996. The authors present a brief description of the theory behind looking at children's ability to pronounce nonwords in order to learn about their reading abilities and difficulties. Given the publication date, the theoretical work is somewhat dated. Also, the authors do not engage the great reading debate over whole language approaches to literacy development versus phonics-based approaches. The authors also do not discuss how the specific list of words used in the test was created or chosen, or whether they conducted pilot tests to determine how well the items were working. All of the items conform to standard pronunciation rules and are of the consonant-vowel-consonant variety for the easier nonwords, working up to consonant-consonant-vowel-consonant-consonant-vowel-consonant (e.g., "sloskon") for the most difficult nonwords. No double vowel nonwords and no nonwords with long vowel sounds are used.

TECHNICAL INFORMATION. The technical information provided for the test is fairly brief. Internal consistency reliability (coefficient alpha) was estimated at .96 for a sample of 246 children in a single primary school. The ages of the children in this sample were not presented. Test-retest reliability was estimated at between .90 and .95 for three small samples (ns = 26, 30, 31) of 6-, 8-, and 10-year-old students. Testing occurred over a 1-week time interval. Thus, even though the age range of the students in the internal consistency measure would clearly affect the estimate, even though the ns are quite small in the test-retest reliability estimates, and the time interval between testing is short, reliability does not seem to be an issue.

Validity information is scant, but some does exist. The authors found that for a sample of 646 British school children (ages 5–11), the correlation between the Graded Nonword Reading Test and the British Abilities Scales Word Reading Test (reading single words) was .78. When age was covaried out of the results, the correlation was .63. Additionally, the authors compared performance on the test for a group of students with dyslexia, a group of chronologically age-matched students, and a group of reading age-matched students (n = 12 for each group). The students with dyslexia performed less well than either the chronologically age-matched sample or the reading-age matched sample.

Norming information based on the sample of roughly 650 British school children described above is provided. Also included are a series of individual sample responses with brief interpretations. Although one might question the representativeness of the sample, particularly for use with students outside England, the norming tables are well-presented and easy to use.

COMMENTARY. The Graded Nonword Reading Test has rather modest aspirations, but it does appear to be adequate for the task at hand. The reliability and validity information provided clearly supports the use of the test, but there is not a whole lot of such information. The question that arises with regard to the use of the test is whether it does what it is purported to do: provide a good measure of decoding ability. It would be useful to see how well the measure relates to other approaches to assessing decoding ability (e.g., letter sound—picture association). Also, it would be good to see how well the measure compares to teacher assessments of reading difficulties.

One of the issues the authors do not discuss has to do with the relationship between the instruction children have had in decoding words and how well they perform on the test. In some reading programs, there is little or no instruction on decoding, and in others there is a heavy emphasis. A child who does not perform well on this measure coming out of a strong whole language instructional program would probably be very different from a child with the same performance coming out of a strong phonics-based program.

Another concern with the measure has to do with the nature of the words selected. Children at ages 8 and above are encountering many words that have more complex architecture than the ones on the test. There are no words that end in vowels on the test, nor any double vowel words, nor any that use nonintuitive pronunciations (such as "gh" making an "f" sound, or "ea" making a long "a" sound). It seems that decoding stops at a fairly rudimentary level on this test.

Finally, there is not much guidance in the manual about what to do about children who do not do as well as expected on the test. There are some sample cases that look at performance of children on the test in combination with other measures, but not much in the way of advice on what to do next in given circumstances.

SUMMARY. The Graded Nonword Reading Test appears to provide a solid assessment of decoding ability at a basic level. Reliability and validity data are not extensive, but the data available support the use of the test. The test is quick and easy to administer. It could be used by classroom teachers or reading specialists. As a measure of early decoding ability, it is probably quite adequate for the job.

[80]

Gray Diagnostic Reading Tests—Second Edition.

Purpose: Designed as "a comprehensive measure of reading skills ... to determine strengths and weaknesses, document progress in reading programs, [and] help diagnose specific reading problems."

Population: Ages 6-0 to 13-11.

Publication Dates: 1991–2004.

Acronym: GDRT-2.

Scores, 10: Decoding (Letter/Word Recognition, Phonetic Analysis, Total), Comprehension (Reading Vocabulary, Meaningful Reading, Total), General Reading, Listening Vocabulary, Rapid Naming, Phonological Awareness.

Administration: Individual.

Forms, 2: A, B.

Price Data, 2006: $250 per complete kit including examiner's manual (2004, 113 pages), Adventures in Fancyland Storybook, Student Book Form A, Student Book Form B, 25 record Forms A, 25 record Forms B, and storage box; $73 per examiner's manual; $50 per Student Book Form A; $50 per Student Book Form B; $5 per Adventures in Fancyland Storybook; $47 per 25 record Forms A; $47 per 25 record Forms B.

Time: (45-60) minutes.

Comments: Norm–referenced; revision of the Gray Oral Reading Tests-Diagnostic.

Authors: Brian R. Bryant, J. Lee Wiederholt, and Diane Pedrotty Bryant.

Publisher: PRO-ED.

Cross References: See T5: 1130 (2 references); for reviews by William R. Merz, Sr. and Steven A. Stahl of the original edition, see 11:149 (1 reference).

Review of the Gray Diagnostic Reading Tests— Second Edition by HOWARD MARGOLIS, Reading and Special Education Consultant, Voorhees, NJ, and ANTONIA D'ONOFRIO, Professor of Education, Center for Education, School of Human Service Professions, Widener University, Chester, PA:

DESCRIPTION. The Gray Diagnostic Reading Tests—Second Edition (GDRT-2) is an individually administered battery of norm-referenced reading and related tests. The battery, designed for children ages 6 years, 0 months to 13 years, 11 months, has two forms, Form A and Form B.

The GDRT-2 contains four core subtests and three supplemental subtests. The four core subtests are Letter/Word Recognition, Phonetic Analysis, Reading Vocabulary, and Meaningful Reading; the three supplemental subtests are Listening Vocabulary, Rapid Naming, and Phonological Awareness. According to the examiner's manual (manual), the core subtests directly "measure different aspects of reading" (p. 2), whereas the supplemental subtests measure factors that represent "only a correlative relationship to reading" (p. 4). Because the core subtests are theoretically related to one another, their scores can be combined into composite ability scores (composites) for Decoding, Comprehension, and General Reading. In contrast, because the supplemental subtests are theoretically unrelated to one another and do not directly assess the reading process, their scores cannot be combined.

The manual claims that the GDRT-2 is "well suited" for identifying the skills that "require remediation or further study" (p. 4). Two of its specific purposes are to determine a child's weaknesses and strengths in reading, and to document progress in reading. Progress can be documented by comparing children's performances on Forms A and B. Qualifications for administering and interpreting the GDRT-2 include "some form of training in reading assessment" (manual, p. 7), basic knowledge of test administration and interpretation, and an understanding of the legal requirements governing assessment.

TECHNICAL. The GDRT-2 was standardized by combining two samples. One sample, consisting of 1,018 students, was drawn from four major geographical regions in 17 U.S. states in the Northeast, Midwest, South, and West. The other was drawn from previous purchasers of the publisher's reading tests; they were invited to contribute between 5 and 20 students to the investigation. These procedures yielded a standardization sample of 1,414 students, ages 6 through 13.

The manual reports that this sample reflects the distributions of race, ethnicity, gender, disability, family income, and parents' educational levels in the sampled regions. Although the manual states that the percentages of school children correspond "closely" to U.S. Census figures, the lack of correspondence in some Census categories may limit the usefulness of the test for some school children. The percentage of children from families with incomes under $24,999 was 8% lower than the national percentage; the percentage of children with disabilities exceeds the national figures by 7%; younger children from the South were overrepresented in the standardization sample; males outnumbered females by 10% or more in the 6-, 12-, and 13-year intervals; and females outnumbered males by 10% or more in the 7- and 8-year-old intervals.

Internal consistency for Forms A and B was evaluated for the core subtests, supplemental subtests, and composites using coefficient alpha. Of the 80 possible coefficients for each form (for eight age intervals across seven subtests and three composites), coefficients for all composites reached a standard of .85, as did most correlations for the subtests. For Form A, four coefficients did not; they fell between .83 and .84; similarly, for Form B, five fell between .81 and .84. Of the nine coefficients that fell below the .85 standard, five were for the Reading Vocabulary Subtest. Coefficients were uniformly high (alpha = .85 or higher) when differentiated by sex, race, ethnicity, and classification (Gifted and Talented, Learning Disabled, and Attention Deficit Hyperactivity Disorder).

Alternate forms reliability was tested in both immediate and delayed formats. In the immediate format, GDRT-2 Forms A and B were administered in the same testing session, with half the children first given Form A and half Form B; for the other half, the sequence was reversed. In the delayed administration, only 40 children (5–11 years) were tested. Unfortunately, the manual failed to report the time interval between administrations.

To show that two forms of a test are equivalent, the correlations between forms must be close to 1.0 (Anastasi & Urbina, 1997). For the immediate administration of alternate forms, reliability varied considerably across core and supplemental subtests ($r = .74$ to .99). When different age groups were examined, the Listening Vocabulary and Reading Vocabulary subtests yielded the majority of lower coefficients ($r = .74$, age 11, and $r = .75$, age 11, respectively). For each age group, the coefficients for the Decoding and General

Reading composites exceeded .90. In contrast, for ages 11 and 12, the coefficients for the Comprehension composite were .84 and .86, respectively.

To assess children's progress, the GDRT-2 manual suggests that examiners compare children's performance on Forms A and B. This suggestion makes the delayed administration of alternate forms a particularly important form of reliability as it "estimate[s] test error that relates to both content sampling and time sampling" (manual, p. 49). Unfortunately, coefficients for the delayed administration of alternate forms suggested that for many subtests and composites the GDRT-2 did not maintain temporal stability. The coefficients measuring alternate forms reliability fell below .90 for all but one composite and two subtests: General Reading composite (.92), Reading Vocabulary subtest (.92), and Rapid Naming subtest (.91). Possibly, the sample's small size ($n = 40$) led to low coefficients.

Other information indicates that some subtests were insufficiently stable over time. Test stability is essential because it demonstrates that, absent intervening conditions and change, test scores are unlikely to fluctuate randomly, and that errors of measurement are low enough to warrant fairly stable assessments of individual ability over time (Anastasi, 1982). Ideally, when making important decisions about individual children, "the minimum standard should be .90" (Salvia, Ysseldyke, & Bolt, 2007, p. 141). For five of the seven GDRT-2 subtests, the test-retest reliability coefficients with the same form of the test fell below .90: Letter/Word Recognition ($r = .89$), Phonological Awareness ($r = .89$), Meaningful Reading ($r = .84$), Listening Vocabulary ($r = .82$), and Phonetic Analysis ($r = .82$). Two of these, however, were close to .90. The relatively lower correlations for the Meaningful Reading, Listening Vocabulary, and Phonetic Analysis subtests suggest that examiners should be cautious in interpreting scores from these subtests, especially if they will be used in making decisions about individual children. On the positive side, the reliability coefficients for all three composites ranged from .90 to .94.

Because the GDRT-2 is offered as a diagnostic test, it must differentiate readers unequivocally. To this end, the manual reports an average item discrimination index for core subtests, supplemental subtests, and composites, for relevant age groups. The distribution of discrimination coefficients indicated that the subtests and composites were appropriately difficult for given levels of reading ability. Conditional logistic regression was used to evaluate whether items favored some groups of readers over others. Only 2% of 2,472 comparisons could be attributed to systematic bias, indicating that nearly all items assessed ability only.

One way to assess a test's validity is to determine the degree to which it, or its subtests, correlates with independent measures of the same or similar construct(s). The correlations between the GDRT-2 and measures of related abilities were moderate and acceptable. The manual briefly describes several validity studies. In one study of 28 children in rural Georgia, four reading tests and three reading clusters of the Woodcock-Johnson Psycho-Educational Battery—Revised were positively correlated with the four core subtests and the three composites of the GDRT-2, Forms A and B. The correlations, however, varied widely, from .58 to .94. In another study of 61 children in Texas, the Fluency and Comprehension subtests of the Gray Oral Reading Test-4, as well as its Oral Reading Quotient, correlated significantly with the GDRT-2's Letter/Word Recognition, Phonetic Analysis, and Meaningful Reading subtests and its Decoding, Comprehension, and General Reading Composites (rs ranged from .51 to .74). In studies like these, moderate correlations are not undesirable, as a case can be made that tests should not measure exactly the same reading constructs, and that perfect correspondence between measures of reading ability would indicate that the tests were redundant. Of course, the question always remains, how valid are the tests against which the newer test is compared? In this case, the answers are debatable.

To begin to assess construct validity, the authors measured the degree to which the GDRT-2 corresponded to its theoretical underpinnings. They posited that (a) reading ability would improve with age, (b) subtests would be internally consistent, (c) subtests would correlate with cognitive ability, and (d) the distribution of reading ability, as measured by the GDRT-2, would reflect reading differences in the general population. Much of the validity data supported their predictions. Raw scores on most subtests were positively correlated with chronological age. The internal consistency of the composites and many subtests

was sufficient. Intercorrelations among composites and core subtests were both positive and significant. Moderate-to-high correlations were found between Wechsler Intelligence Scale for Children, Third Edition (WISC–III) tests of verbal and nonverbal intelligence and GDRT-2 subtests. As theorized, group means were significantly lower for children with Attention Deficit Hyperactivity Disorders or Learning Disabilities than for the sample as a whole; conversely, group means for children classified as gifted and talented were higher, particularly on core subtests and composites.

COMMENTARY. The manual is well written. It contains some important admonitions for those making assessments. For example, it says, "Too often examiners forget the dictum that 'tests don't diagnose, people do' and base their diagnoses exclusively on test results, a hazardous enterprise at best. Test results are merely observations, not diagnoses. They specify a performance level at a given time under a particular situation, but they do not tell the examiner why a person performs as he or she did" (p. 34). The manual points out that even highly reliable tests "still possess considerable error" (p. 34).

Despite being well written and offering some helpful insights about test interpretation, the manual often presents minimal information about critical aspects of administrating and interpreting the GDRT-2. Compared to a test manual like that of the Qualitative Reading Inventory-4 (QRI-4; Leslie & Caldwell, 2006), it presents minimal information about the rationale for the inclusion of its subtests and procedures. Examiners are forced to depend almost totally on their background knowledge of reading, which may be insufficient for properly interpreting test findings. Consider, for example, one of the core subtests, Meaningful Reading. Level B of this subtest, the level for children who understand the conventions of print (e.g., children who can show the examiner a specific part of a booklet), uses a modified cloze procedure that requires children to supply missing words in short passages (e.g., John was happy. He just hit the baseball with a b____). Other than a few brief statements indicating that this subtest measures a basic component of comprehension, the reader is given little information about cloze. Its limitations are ignored. Many examiners with insufficient knowledge of reading might not know that cloze has limited utility for measuring comprehension, even if it is paired with reading vocabulary, as the GDRT-2 does to attain the Composite Ability Score for Comprehension. For example, Carlisle and Rice (2005) noted that (a) cloze and multiple-choice questions are only moderately correlated, (b) "cloze tests are not ideal ... to assess understanding and recall of ideas and information in natural passages" (p. 535), and (c) no task is best for measuring reading comprehension. Similarly, Tierney and Readence (2004) noted that "very little research supports the use of Cloze as a procedure for testing ... comprehension" (p. 517).

Like the manual, the testing materials also have some major drawbacks. The children's test book is printed on paper stock that is unlikely to last for many administrations. Of even more concern are some of the test layouts. Level B of the Reading Vocabulary subtest may prove visually overwhelming for many children; it has 33 items arranged in six columns, totaling 198 numbers and words. For each item, children must point to two words that are opposites, from an array of five words across five columns. Similarly, the pages of the Meaningful Reading and Listening Vocabulary subtests are crammed with information. Busy, crammed pages like these can adversely affect children who are highly anxious about being tested, and who have low self-efficacy for the task—often the kind of struggling reader to whom the GDRT-2 would be administered. With children who respond quickly, examiners may have difficulty scoring the Word Opposites part of the Reading Vocabulary subtest, as children may quickly point to two different words that examiners cannot quickly discern on the busy page. Finally, the graphics in the test book are poor; they are outmoded line drawings. It is a shame that the paper, the layout, and the pictures are of such poor quality.

The GDRT-2 has two strengths that can help busy examiners. First, learning to administer it is easy, as is administration and scoring. Second, it can be used to assess quickly critically important areas of reading. Paradoxically, this last strength is also one of its major weaknesses. Because none of the reading passages on the Meaningful Reading subtest are as long or as involved as passages children must typically read in Grades 3 and above, and because the diversity of items on several of its subtests is very limited (e.g., Reading Vocabulary, Phonological Awareness), the GDRT-2 lacks the depth and breadth needed to assess children's reading difficulties fully. It lacks the variety of tasks that are needed by examiners to make a more detailed analysis of a child's reading and related abilities. Nor can it identify children's instructional and independent reading levels. It can, however, serve as an initial component of a reading assessment by identifying areas in need of a more intensive, more fine-grained assessment.

Here too, it has some weaknesses. For example, a child might score within the average range on the Meaningful Reading subtest, but have great difficulty comprehending longer, expository passages found in textbooks or informal reading inventories, such as the QRI-4 (Leslie & Caldwell, 2006) or The Stieglitz Informal Reading Inventory (2002). A child might do well recognizing pictures on the Listening Vocabulary subtest, but have difficulty understanding abstract words that are hard to illustrate, and are thus not found on tests like the GDRT-2. Nevertheless, if used by an examiner who has discussed the child's reading abilities with the child's teachers, and who plans to supplement the GDRT-2 with other assessments, the GDRT-2 may function fairly well as an initial test battery that helps inform assessment efforts.

SUMMARY. To its credit, the GDRT-2 reflects its theoretical underpinnings. For example, it differentiates between different groups of readers and is moderately correlated with other tests of reading. For the composites and many subtests, internal consistency is good. However, several reliability concerns are evident. Correlations between Form A and Form B are equivocal in demonstrating stable assessments over time. Similarly, some subtests are insufficiently stable over time, signaling a need for cautious interpretations.

As a diagnostic battery, the GDRT-2 has numerous limitations. Nevertheless, it may prove valuable in providing a quick overview of a child's reading abilities. Such an overview, though not definitive, can help inform further assessment. In no case, however, should examiners use the GDRT-2 alone to place children in reading materials or to determine the nature of a remedial reading program. Other assessments are needed. The manual states that the test "provides clues as to what skills require remediation or further study" (p. 4). Examiners should emphasize the words *clues* and *further study*. These words suggest that the Gray is not definitive—it can provide a few small pieces of a large jigsaw puzzle, but leaves too many holes. As such, the word *Diagnostic* in the test's name exaggerates its potential.

REVIEWERS' REFERENCES

Anastasi, A. (1982). *Psychological testing* (5th ed.). Boston: Macmillan Publishing Co.

Anastasi, A., & Urbina, S. (1997). *Psychological testing* (7th ed.). Upper Saddle River, NJ: Prentice-Hall, Inc.

Carlisle, J. F., & Rice, M. S. (2004). Assessment of reading comprehension. In C. A. Stone, E. R. Silliman, B. J. Ehren, & K. Apel (Eds.), *Handbook of language and literacy: Development and disorders* (pp. 521–540). New York: Guilford.

Leslie, L., & Caldwell, J. (2006). Qualitative Reading Inventory–4. Boston: Allyn & Bacon.

Salvia, J., Ysseldyke, J. E., & Bolt, S. (2007). *Assessment in special and inclusive education* (10th ed.). Boston: Houghton-Mifflin Company.

Stieglitz, E. L. (2002). The Stieglitz Informal Reading Inventory: Assessing Reading Behaviors from Emergent to Advanced Levels (3rd ed.). Boston: Allyn & Bacon.

Tierney, R. J., & Readence, J. E. (2005). *Reading strategies and practices: A compendium* (6th ed.). Boston: Allyn & Bacon.

Review of the Gray Diagnostic Reading Tests—Second Edition by LISA F. SMITH, Senior Research Fellow, University of Otago—Educational Assessment Research Unit, Dunedin, New Zealand:

DESCRIPTION. The Gray Diagnostic Reading Tests—Second Edition (GDRT-2) is a revised edition of the Gray Oral Reading Tests—Diagnostic (Bryant & Wiederholt, 1991) that may be used independently or in conjunction with the Gray Oral Reading Tests—Fourth Edition (GORT-4; Wiederholt & Bryant, 2001) and/or the Gray Silent Reading Tests (Wiederholt & Blalock, 2000). The GDRT-2 is designed to measure oral reading ability from 6 years, 0 months through 13 years, 11 months. Two parallel forms comprise four core subtests (Letter/Word Identification, Phonetic Analysis, Reading Vocabulary, and Meaningful Reading), and three supplemental subtests (Listening Vocabulary, Rapid Naming, and Phonological Awareness). Scaled scores from the core subtests may be combined into a Decoding composite, made up of Letter/Word Recognition and Phonetic Analysis; a Comprehension composite, made up of Reading Vocabulary and Meaningful Reading; and, a General Reading composite, made up of all four core subtests. The authors state that the GDRT-2 may be used to determine strengths and weaknesses in reading skills, document progress in reading programs, help diagnose specific reading problems, and serve as a research tool.

The GDRT-2 is administered individually. Examiner qualifications, entry points, basals, ceilings, and general guidelines are explained clearly in the examiner's manual, with varied examples, clarifications for scoring, and appropriate cautions to interpret only within what is being measured on any given subtest. A sample cover page from the examiner's record booklet is also provided with the scoring completed. Six scores are obtained: raw scores, standard (scaled) scores for the subtests, composite ability scores, percentile ranks, age equivalents, and grade equivalents. Only the Rapid Naming subtest is timed, with a maximum of 2 minutes allowed. Appendices contain easy-to-use tables for the conversion of raw scores to scaled scores, percentile ranks, age equivalents, and grade equivalents. Additional tables permit the conversion of scaled scores to composite ability scores and percentile ranks.

The composite ability scores have a mean of 100 and a standard deviation of 15. Although the authors argue that the mean of 100 and standard deviation of 15 were selected because they are familiar to examiners who use other popular tests of intelligence and aptitude, there are both philosophical and empirical problems with that position. In addition, there is no substantiation in the section describing the composite scores for some of the authors' speculations, such as, students with high General Reading composite scores are likely to have been read to at home, or students with high Comprehension composite scores are likely to read for pleasure. Information about conducting discrepancy analyses is also provided.

TECHNICAL.

Standardization. Normative data were collected during 1999–2002. The norming sample included *n* = 1,018 students from 17 states. Large areas of the United States are not represented, including much of the southeast and the majority of the states in the mountain and western regions. The sample appears to be representative of nationwide statistics as reported in U.S. Census information (U.S. Bureau of the Census, 2000) with regard to gender, race, ethnicity, family income, educational level of parents, disability status, and age. An additional convenience sample (*n* = 396) solicited from the PRO-ED customer database was tested and included as part of the normative sample.

Reliability. Evidence of reliability is provided using coefficient alpha, alternate forms (immediate and delayed), test-retest, and interrater scoring. For coefficient alpha, results for various age groups range from .81 to .98; however, a large number of the coefficients seem unusually high. Similar results were obtained for selected demographic subgroups, with coefficients almost exclusively greater than .90. For alternate forms (immediate administration), coefficients by age groups are good, ranging from .74 to .98. It is not stated whether the administration of forms was counterbalanced. For alternate forms (delayed administration), 40 children ranging in age from 5 through 11 years were tested in a counterbalanced design with 2 weeks between administrations. Other than a descriptive summary of age and ethnicity, no information is given on these examinees. Coefficients for different scales range from .72 to .92, but these are difficult to evaluate given the absence of information about the sample. Test-retest coefficients computed using a formula from Anastasi and Urbina (1997) are satisfactory, ranging from .82 to .97. Evidence of interrater reliability for two scorers using a random sample of 30 protocols was high, with coefficients ranging from .95 to .99. Given the clear scoring instructions, this excellent finding is not unexpected.

Validity. The authors provide evidence of content-related validity by relating each subtest to established tests in use. A differential item functioning analysis for gender, African American versus non-African American, Hispanic American versus non-Hispanic American, and European American versus non-European American comparisons yielded significant results at the .001 level for fewer than 50 items out of almost 2,500 comparisons.

Limited evidence of criterion-related validity was provided, based on three studies. The first compared 28 students from rural Georgia, who took the GDRT-2 and selected tests from the Woodcock-Johnson Psycho-Educational Battery—Revised (WJ-R; Woodcock & Johnson, 1989). Uncorrected correlations ranged from .45 with the GDRT-2 Letter/Word Recognition subtest and the WJ-R Passage Comprehension test, to .74 with the GDRT-2 Comprehension composite and the WJ-R Broad Reading test. Participants in the second study were 61 students in Austin, Texas who took the GDRT-2 and selected tests from the GORT-4. Uncorrected correlations ranged from .44 with the GDRT-2 Letter/Word Recognition subtest and the GORT-4 Comprehension subtest,

to .71 with the GDRT-2 Letter/Word Recognition subtest and the GORT-4 Fluency subtest. Participants in the third study were 29 students in Austin, Texas who took the GDRT-2 and selected subtests from both the WJ-R and the Comprehensive Test of Phonological Processing (CTOPP; Wagner, Torgesen, & Rashotte, 1999). Uncorrected correlations were .39 for Rapid Naming with the CTOPP Rapid Naming subtest, .55 for Phonological Awareness with the CTOPP Elision subtest, and .65 for Listening Vocabulary with the WJ-R Picture Vocabulary subtest. The authors provide correlations corrected for unreliability for these studies, but these would be inappropriate as the underlying validity question pertains to how closely the measures are related, not the constructs they represent.

For evidence of construct validity, the authors examine performance on the GDRT-2 in terms of age, intercorrelations of the subtests and total test score, measures of aptitude/intelligence, and known groups for reading ability. Mean raw scores increase with age; however, standard deviations within age groups tend to be large. The intercorrelations among the core subtests are significant. The authors state that, "The lower correlations for Listening Vocabulary, Rapid Naming, and Phonological Awareness subtests are a function of the fact that these subtests do not measure reading; they measure abilities that are only related to reading" (examiner's manual, p. 68). With regard to intelligence, scores on the GDRT-2 for 39 students from rural Georgia were correlated with scores on the Wechsler Intelligence Scale for Children-Third Edition (Wechsler, 1991) and the Broad Cognitive Ability, Standard Scale from the WJ-R (Woodcock & Johnson, 1989). Uncorrected correlations were mostly small to moderate; corrected correlations were understandably better. Scale scores based on the normative sample provide evidence for construct validity for the subgroups.

COMMENTARY/SUMMARY. The GRDT-2 can be a useful tool as part of a comprehensive testing program to assess reading skills and help diagnose specific reading problems. Additional research is needed to establish criterion-related validity and construct validity. However, for the most part, the GRDT-2 lives up to its stated purposes.

REVIEWER'S REFERENCES

Anastasi, A., & Urbina, S. (1997). *Psychological testing* (7ᵗʰ Ed.). Upper Saddle River, NJ: Prentice-Hall.

Bryant, B. R., & Wiederholt, J. L. (1991). *Gray Oral Reading Tests—Diagnostic.* Austin, TX: PRO-ED.

U.S. Bureau of the Census. (2000). *The statistical abstract of the United States: 2000* (120ᵗʰ ed.). Washington, DC: Author.

Wagner, R. K., Torgesen, J. K., & Rashotte, C. A. (1999). Comprehensive Test of Phonological Processing. Austin, TX: PRO-ED.

Wechsler, D. (1991). Wechsler Intelligence Scale for Children—Third Edition. San Antonio, TX: Psychological Corporation.

Wiederholt, J. L., & Blalock, G. (2000). Gray Silent Reading Tests. Austin, TX: PRO-ED.

Wiederholt, J. L., & Bryant, B. R. (2001) Gray Oral Reading Tests—Fourth Edition. Austin, TX: PRO-ED.

Woodcock, R. W., & Johnson, M. B. (1989–1990). Woodcock-Johnson Psycho-Educational Battery—Revised. Allen, TX: DLM.

[81]

Greenspan Social-Emotional Growth Chart.

Purpose: Designed to help determine a child's social-emotional development and growth.

Population: Birth to 3.5 years.

Publication Date: 2004.

Scores, 3: Total Growth Chart Score, Sensory Processing Score, Highest Stage Mastered.

Administration: Individual.

Price Data, 2006: $99 per complete kit including manual, 25 caregiver reports, and 25 questionnaires; $80 per manual; $25 per 25 caregiver reports; $35 per 25 questionnaires.

Time: (5–15) minutes.

Comments: It is recommended that the questionnaire be administered at each developmental stage.

Author: Stanley I. Greenspan.

Publisher: The Psychological Corporation, A Harcourt Assessment Company.

Review of the Greenspan Social-Emotional Growth Chart by CAROL M. McGREGOR, Content Development Specialist, The Learning House, Louisville, KY:

DESCRIPTION. The Greenspan Social-Emotional Growth Chart was developed to screen for functional emotional milestones through the interview process with parents and caregivers. The framework for this norm-referenced assessment tool is to provide a progression of developing emotional capacities from birth through 42 months of age. The purpose of this screening device is to provide early identification of social-emotional delays or deficits when interventions can be more effective.

The Greenspan Social-Emotional Growth Chart is in the form of a 35-item questionnaire to be completed, in approximately 10 minutes, by parents or individuals who have primary or major

responsibility for the child. The questionnaire is divided into eight age groups and includes six areas of functional emotional milestones: Growing Self-Regulation and Interest in the World, Engaging in Relationships, Using Emotions in an Interactive Purposeful Manner, Using Interactive Emotional Signals to Communicate and Solve Problems, Using Symbols to Convey Intentions or Feelings and Express More Than Basic Needs, and Creating Logical Bridges Between Emotions and Ideas. The final score indicates three categories: Full Mastery, Emerging Mastery, and Possible Challenges.

Although administration of this instrument requires professional supervision, it can be administered by clinicians or educators (including paraprofessionals) who work with children and families and are familiar with developmental testing considerations.

Also included in the materials for this screening assessment is a Caregiver Report. Along with results of the summary of screening results, activities are listed that are said to encourage social-emotional development. The author asks that with this report, the test user should not disclose or copy the questionnaire items, which would compromise the security and validity of the instrument.

The user qualifications, copyright restrictions, and guidelines are consistent with the *Standards for Educational and Psychological Testing* (American Educational Research Association, American Psychological Association, & National Council on Measurement in Education, 1999).

DEVELOPMENT. In designing this assessment, Greenspan has examined some of the functional emotional developmental capacities that are necessary for healthy development but are missing in some children: joint attention, social reciprocity, functional language, selected early motor capacities, motor planning, and sequencing abilities. He also considered the Child Neurology Society of the American Academy of Neurology, which describes disorders that indicate developmental delays—no babbling by 12 months; no gesturing, pointing, waving "bye-bye" by 12 months; no single words by 16 months; no two-word spontaneous phrases by 24 months; and any loss of language or social skills at any age—as universal indicators of a need for intervention. He was also concerned with the interaction of sensory processing with functional emotional development.

Greenspan states that his premise or theoretical base is formulated from a variety of traditional models such as psychoanalytic, psychodynamic, and cognitive developmental models through modern theorists including Tomkins, Izard, Ekman, LeDoux, Schacter, Ainsworth, Bruner, Brazelton, and others.

This model is described as a Functional Emotional Developmental Approach. In this model, Dr. Greenspan depicts emotions as the "orchestra leader" (manual, p. 18) for critical mental capacities and for providing the basis of levels of consciousness and social group functioning. His belief is that through interactions with caregivers, emotions begin to enable a child to gain the ability to use signals, order social functions, and become an "architect of cognitive, language, social, and reflective reasoning capacities" (manual, p. 18).

From these considerations were developed the Developmental Structuralist Theory and the Developmental, Individual-Difference, Relationship-Based model (DIR). In relationship to this theory, the Functional Emotional Developmental Approach is used to provide a means of evaluating how various aspects of development, including cognitive, language, sensory, and motor functioning, work together when organized by the emotional processes. This method of evaluating a child from the functional emotional approach provides a means of learning those emotional capacities that are operational and those that are deficit or missing. Determining these strengths and weaknesses during a child's early life can provide ample time to provide needed supports that might either remediate or correct the problem areas.

TECHNICAL. The sample for this screening device was 456 children in the United States, ages 15 days to 42 months, collected in 2003. The sample was chosen to represent the U.S. population of children ages birth to 4 years in the 2000 U.S. Census survey, stratified according to race/ethnicity, region, and parent or guardian educational level. Gender was generally equal at all age levels and geographic representation was proportionate to the population of the sample group. The manual states that examiners were selected based on their familiarity with assessment procedures as well as instructions on use of the test and recording information.

Responses are on a scale with five levels of behavior frequency from "All of the time" down to "None of the time." There is also a category of "Can't tell" but directions state that examiners are to attempt to ascertain some level of competence rather than using "Can't tell."

Reliability is based on internal consistency measures using alpha coefficients. These ranged between .83 and .94 for the Total Growth Chart Score, with higher scores gained at higher age levels. The Sensory Processing coefficients were between .76 and .91, based on eight items within the scale.

It appears that construct validity was the considered method of determining validity and that items were considered valid when the majority of children mastered the item. There was no discussion of concurrent or predictive validity.

In a clinical study, children with a variety of developmental delays were matched with the control group from the standardization study and found to have less developed social and emotional skills than the control group. A bias study was also done which, using the Mantel-Haenszel bias analysis, indicated that items on the test were not biased on gender or racial characteristics. Appendices in the manual include a scoring index along with a variety of guidelines for encouraging social and emotional growth.

COMMENTARY. Dr. Greenspan's years of experience and work with young children, especially those with autism, define him as an expert in the area of social and emotional growth. This screening test appears to meet the criteria for the purposes for which it was designed. Wording in the test items is clear and should be easily understood by parents or caregivers for more valid responses. The coloring on the page of test items appears somewhat dark on every other item. It is possible this shading could cause anyone with limited vision or limited light to misread the statement and provide an invalid response. As with many screening tests, test items are limited at each age (2 items for each age below 14 months), necessarily limiting a variety of behaviors to be considered.

This screening test relies heavily on language-based items, particularly at the upper level. Some other developmental tests, such as The Brief Infant-Toddler Social and Emotional Assessment (BITSEA; 17:95), seem to look more specifically at some other problems of early childhood such as self-regulation and attachment issues. One real advantage the Greenspan screener has over most other good developmental tests on the market is that it screens from 15 days after birth whereas most others begin somewhere around 12 months. The Bayley Scales of Infant and Toddler Development—Third Edition (Bayley-III; 17:17) has adapted the Greenspan Social-Emotional Growth Chart to use as its new social-emotional subtest.

SUMMARY. The Greenspan Social-Emotional Growth Chart is a 35-item, norm-referenced, developmental screening tool designed to assess maturing emotional functioning in children from 15 days to 42 months of age. It can be completed by anyone with basic psychometric skills with information gained from parents or caregivers. Sampling was carefully done in relation to generally used parameters. Validity and reliability are adequate. Pretend play is included at all upper stages, but there is a heavy dependence on language for determining emotional status. The manual includes appendices with suggestions and games to offer parents to encourage emotional development.

REVIEWER'S REFERENCE

American Educational Research Association, American Psychological Association, & National Council on Measurement in Education. (1999). *Standards for educational and psychological testing.* Washington, DC: American Educational Research Association.

Review of the Greenspan Social-Emotional Growth Chart by GRETCHEN OWENS, Professor of Child Study, St. Joseph's College, Patchogue, NY:

DESCRIPTION. The Greenspan Social-Emotional Growth Chart is a brief screening measure designed to determine the level of social and emotional development of infants and young children under the age of 3 1/2. It is also suggested for use as a screening measure to detect potential social and emotional problems. It can be completed in less than 10 minutes by a parent or other caregiver who has extended interactions with the child on a daily basis.

The Questionnaire booklet has a total of 35 items. Twenty-seven of them are designed to indicate whether children have acquired particular skills that allow them to express their needs, deal with feelings, and communicate with others (caregivers and peers). Eight additional ones are related to sensory processing. Because there are stopping points for each of the eight age groups, the parent completes between 11 and 35 items. For each item, the caregiver indicates the frequency with which the child exhibits that behavior. Later, a clinician calculates a total score, with 0–5 points awarded for each item based on the frequency reported by the caregiver (0 points for *Can't tell,* 1 point for *None of the time,* 2 points for *Some of the time,* 3 points for *Half of the time,* 4 points for *Most of the time,* and 5 points for *All of the time*). The raw score is then converted to a rating of Full Mastery, Emerging Mastery, or Possible Challenges. A Sensory Processing Score is derived and converted in the same way, based upon the caregiver's responses to the first eight items.

Finally, the clinician looks back to find the highest section of the test (each section indicating a particular stage of development) for which the caregiver checked *Most of the time* or *All of the time* for every item. The Highest Stage Mastered is recorded and plotted on a Social-Emotional Growth Chart that allows comparison of a theoretical normal growth curve with the child's current level. The author suggests that the Questionnaire be re-administered at each stage of development in order to plot the child's actual growth curve over time. The kit also comes with a Caregiver Report that indicates the child's level of mastery (Full, Emerging, or Possible Challenges), his or her position on the Social-Emotional Growth Chart, and six examples of activities to encourage social-emotional growth, along with references to two of Greenspan's books.

DEVELOPMENT. Unlike some of the other social-emotional instruments that are available in the field of early intervention, this one is built upon a strong theoretical base, the fundamental tenets of which are presented in the test manual. Stanley Greenspan is a prolific and respected child psychologist who has published extensively in the area of social-emotional development. His theoretical formulations, both the earlier Developmental, Individual-Difference, Relationship-Based model (DIR) and the later Functional Emotional Developmental Approach, have led to plans for comprehensive assessment (Greenspan, DeGangi, & Wieder, 2001) and intervention programs to help children develop critical functional skills in this domain (Greenspan, 1992; Greenspan & Wieder, 1998). Because a Sensory Processing Score is included in the Greenspan Social-Emotional Growth Chart, the manual also includes a brief description of some ways in which inadequate sensory processing can affect emotional responses.

In the manual, Greenspan states that he selected the questionnaire items based on his 30 years of clinical work and research. (The manual contains no description of the specific method used to choose this particular set of 35 items, nor any indication whether there was a larger pool from which they were selected.) Rather than simply providing a checklist of specific social and emotional skills, his aim was to identify "larger emotional patterns that define healthy emotional functioning and provide purpose to many mental processes" (manual, p. 1). The underlying structure of the Growth Chart is his stage theory of emotional development, with the various stages indicated by the child's ongoing acquisition of what he calls "functional emotional milestones" (manual, p. 1). The age groupings in the Growth Chart seem to be based on typical ages for achievement of these milestones, and therefore are of varying ranges (0–3 months, 4–5 months, 6–9 months, 10–14 months, 15–18 months, 19–24 months, 25–30 months, and 31–42 months).

In the manual, Greenspan reports that the Growth Chart was developed as part of the "prestandardization data collection efforts of the Bayley Scales of Infant and Toddler Development—Third Edition" (manual, p. 29). The technical manual for the Bayley-III (Bayley, 2006; 17:17) confirms that the newly added Social-Emotional subtest is based on Greenspan's Social-Emotional Growth Chart. It is not stated in the Growth Chart manual exactly how much overlap there is between the two, but perusal of the Bayley-III subtest shows that all items in the two measures are the same.

After qualified examiners had been recruited, protocols had been collected, and appropriate quality control measures had been carried out, psychometric studies were conducted. Cut points for the Growth Chart Index were selected to represent roughly the 2nd and 25th percentiles at each age, and these were used to set up the table for converting raw scores to levels of mastery (Possible Difficulty, Emerging Mastery, or Full Mastery).

TECHNICAL.

Standardization. During the spring of 2003, the measure was individually administered to 456 children ranging in age from 15 days to 42 months. The number of participants in each age grouping varied, with 50–56 children in seven of the groups and 89 in the 0- to 3-month category. The children were selected (presumably from the larger Bayley-III standardization sample), using a stratified random sampling plan, to approximate the 2000 U.S. Census data. The sample as a whole matches the U.S. population quite well in terms of sex, parent education levels, race/ethnicity, and geographic region. The only sample disparity that appears to be potentially problematic is that at the 6- to 9-month level, males are overrepresented, whereas at the 19- to 24-month level, females are. No information is given about performance differences by gender, but other research suggests that even at young ages, girls demonstrate greater social competence (Fagot, 1994; LaFreniere & Dumas, 1996), so having a disproportionate number of girls in the sample may adversely affect boys' scores.

Exclusion criteria are listed in the manual, and include non-English speakers, children with sensory disabilities, and those with developmental risk factors based on SES or parent education factors. There is no indication that any of the children in the standardization sample had been diagnosed with developmental problems, which presents a dilemma common to many of the childhood measures that were developed earlier, but which has been corrected in most recent revisions. Assessment standardization samples should include children of all levels of ability and skill. The omission of low-functioning children from a norm group makes it hard to interpret a low score, which shows only that a given child is at the low end of the group of *normally developing* children.

Greenspan also recruited an additional clinical sample of 130 children with diagnosed delays in the cognitive, language, motor, or adaptive domains (including an unspecified number with autism and mild or moderate mental retardation) for a validity study, but they were not included in the standardization process, and separate norms are not provided for this group (which would be a helpful inclusion for future editions). No demographic information is given about the clinical sample.

Reliability. The manual presents evidence of internal consistency, with alpha coefficients ranging from .83–.94 for the Total Growth Chart Score, and .76 to .91 for the Sensory Processing Score, with three age groups (4–5 months, 6–9 months, and 15–18 months) falling below .80 on the Sensory Processing scale. No other evidence of reliability, including interrater agreement or test-retest reliability, is provided. In fact, the author makes the assertion (manual, p. 34) that due to inevitable changes in the individual and/or the testing situation, test-retest studies must of necessity fail to match the theoretical definition of reliability. Nevertheless, other social-emotional measures have reported acceptable to excellent test-retest reliability data after periods of 1–4 weeks, and similar analysis of the Growth Chart's reliability is needed.

Validity. In regard to validity, the author asserts that "analyses indicate that the items are age-appropriate and match the age range in which these behaviors are typically mastered" (manual, p. 35). The only analysis that is reported in this context is that items were considered appropriate for a particular age group if the average score for that item was at least 4.0 in the standardization sample. Rather than indicating that the "vast majority of children showed mastery of that item," as asserted in the manual (p. 35), this finding could signify that as few as half of them exhibited the behavior "most of the time" or "all of the time."

Two bias studies were conducted to test the differential validity of the measure across racial/ethnic and gender lines. Although an unspecified set of items statistically favored particular gender or racial/ethnic groups, the author asserts without further elaboration that "examination of the data and content indicates the instrument is not biased on gender or racial/ethnic characteristics" (manual, p. 36).

The other validity evidence reported in the manual derives from comparison with the clinical group. From the clinical sample (N = 130), 68 children aged 4–42 months were matched with a control group from the standardization sample according to demographic characteristics. Questionnaire scores of the clinical group were significantly lower than those of the control group, but only the means and standard deviations for each group as a whole are reported, so it is impossible to tell whether their lower scores would in fact place the children from the clinical group at the "Possible Challenges" level. The various tables in the Bayley-III manual listing mean subtest scores for specific clinical subgroups do include their mean scores on the Social-Emotional subtest (the same set of items as are on the Greenspan Social-Emotional Growth Chart), but the user should not have to go to a different test to get needed

technical information. No percentages are provided to indicate the measure's specificity or sensitivity, so it is unclear to what extent it over- or underidentifies children who warrant further evaluation. Lack of this crucial evidence makes it impossible to determine how valid the Growth Chart is in meeting its intended purpose as a screening measure.

Best practice recommendations in the field of early intervention encourage family involvement in the assessment process as well as doing assessments in the child's natural environment. A caregiver checklist such as this one meets both conditions. However, it is important to demonstrate the validity of caregiver ratings. Such a check could be done by correlating Growth Chart scores with scores on other measures that have been demonstrated to be valid, as well as by conducting studies in which parent ratings are compared to those given by another rater who knows the child well. With these missing from the Growth Chart manual, one is left with no clear indication of the extent to which this caregiver-completed measure presents an accurate depiction of the child's skills. Confounding the issue further, Greenspan suggests in one part of the manual that respondents could also be preschool instructors or childcare providers (p. 5), but there is no indication of the degree to which their scores correspond to those of parents.

COMMENTARY. Though P.L. 99-457 includes social-emotional ability as one of the five domains that must be assessed as part of a comprehensive evaluation, there are major challenges to doing so. Wide variations in the ways in which cultures and families socialize children, along with marked individual differences in children's personalities and ways of relating, compounded even further by the normative developmental challenges that arise at particular ages, make it far from easy to identify accurately which children need further evaluation. Greenspan has chosen to approach this potentially daunting task by creating a theory-based measure that looks for behavioral indicators that the infant or young child has or has not reached particular social-emotional milestones.

As would be expected in light of Dr. Greenspan's long and distinguished record of work in developmental psychology, there are praiseworthy aspects to this measure. The items chosen do go beyond isolated social skills and easily observable emotions to look at several more complex aspects of emotional functioning, including emotional signaling, expression of wishes and feelings, and pretend play. Obtaining input from parents or other primary caregivers about typical behaviors is invaluable in assessing social-emotional skills, and the rating scale they are asked to complete provides clear descriptors based on frequency (e.g., *half of the time*). The activity ideas suggested for parent use also could be helpful for professionals who are setting up an intervention program.

However, there are problems with the current product. In several ways, the manual seems conflicted regarding its purpose and its audience. On the one hand, the sections on theoretical underpinnings are clearly written for professionals (though they are heavy going even for the average clinician who is not already well versed in Greenspan's theory). On the other hand, the interventions that are found in the manual and the Caregiver Report are written for parents. Though designed for caregiver implementation, these suggestions are not consistently presented in parent-friendly language ("Note your baby's sensory processing skills," manual, p. 49) and for the most part are neither clear nor specific enough to be particularly helpful. (Typical suggestions: "Challenge the child to do things to you" or "Help the child build up to a continuous flow of circles of communication," manual, p. 50.)

Another problem that sometimes arises seems to be an unintended result of Greenspan's conceptualization of emotional capacities as the integrating force ("orchestra leader" [manual, p. 18], as he puts it) of the other domains of development. The implied presumption is that children's skill levels in the various domains will parallel one another. This supposition becomes problematic with children who exhibit language delays. In the Social-Emotional Growth Chart, Stages 4b, 5a, and 5b have one item each—and Stage 6 has four items—that cannot be credited unless the child uses words rather than gestures or other actions as the medium of social communication (e.g., "Does your child tell you what he or she wants with one or a few words?"). This confounding of different domains of development can lead to conflicting results within the measure. One 24-month-old child with whom this examiner tried out the Growth Chart, who was being evaluated for early intervention services primarily because of language

delay, scored at the Full Mastery level on the Questionnaire (and also scored fine on two independent social measures), but his Highest Stage Mastered placed him at the 10- to 14-month level on the Growth Chart, a year behind where he should be. For a variety of good reasons, most education agencies are moving away from allowing use of age equivalents for eligibility decisions, but in states that still allow services based on a 1-year delay or a 33% delay, this anomaly in the Greenspan measure could lead to confusing results at best and inappropriate decisions about eligibility at worst.

A couple of procedural clarifications are needed in the manual. First, the examiner is not told whether to drop extra days or to round up in calculating chronological age; the only example provided in the manual has less than 15 days. Second, the section on plotting social-emotional growth could be clearer. Though the protocol itself incidentally mentions how one determines which is the "highest milestone mastered by the child," the step-by-step instructions in the manual should include the information as well.

Though the Greenspan Social-Emotional Growth Chart is billed as a "norm-referenced screening" measure (manual, p. 2), its three-category approach will not be enough for early interventionists who are required to report standard scores. Those who need standard scores could go to the Social-Emotional subtest of the Bayley-III, which is identical to the Greenspan Social-Emotional Growth Chart. (However, this Bayley subtest, like the Growth Chart from which it came, provides insufficient evidence of validity or reliability to warrant a wholehearted recommendation at this time.)

In the meantime, the Growth Chart could be used for the other purpose the developer suggests: monitoring social and emotional growth. One could imagine it being used as a relatively inexpensive measure to be filled out during routine visits to clinics or doctors' offices. Health care providers often have little time to conduct developmental appraisals of babies' and young children's motor and language skills, let alone of their social development (and children's social behavior in such an unfamiliar setting is not necessarily an accurate indicator of their capabilities anyway). As parents complete the Growth Chart, the items on it could inform them about normal social-emotional development and give them ideas for activities they can be doing with their child to enhance his or her social skills. In addition, the Growth Chart could be used productively in research with high-risk populations.

SUMMARY. The Greenspan Social-Emotional Growth Chart, the screening version of the Social-Emotional subtest of the Bayley Scales of Infant and Toddler Development—Third Edition, is built upon a comprehensive theoretical foundation. It meets some but not all of the criteria for appropriate screening instruments for young children: The instrument is brief, inexpensive, and reasonably easy to score. However, these features do not obviate the need to address psychometric considerations carefully. Screening measures are not held to as high reliability standards as diagnostic instruments are, but developers of screening tests do need to demonstrate that their measures are valid ways of determining which children need further evaluation. The manual for the Growth Chart does not provide sufficiently convincing evidence that this is the case. More complete data are needed regarding validity and reliability, as well as test sensitivity and specificity, before this instrument can be viewed as an appropriate screening measure.

For informal uses that are confined to the determination of approximate social-emotional developmental levels, it can be recommended. However, for formal screening purposes, a more convincing case needs to be made that it indicates accurately whether further assessment is needed.

REVIEWER'S REFERENCES

Bayley, N. (2006). *Bayley Scales of Infant and Toddler Development* (3rd ed.). San Antonio, TX: Harcourt.

Fagot, B. I. (1994). Peer relations and the development of competence in boys and girls. In C. Leaper (Ed.), *Childhood gender segregation: Causes and consequences* (pp. 53-65). San Francisco: Jossey-Bass.

Greenspan, S. I. (1992). *Infancy and early childhood: The practice of clinical assessment and intervention with emotional and developmental challenges.* Madison, CT: International Universities Press.

Greenspan, S. I., DiGangi, G. A., & Wieder, S. (2001). *The Functional Emotional Assessment Scale (FEAS) for infancy and early childhood: Clinical and research applications.* Bethesda, MD: Interdisciplinary Council on Developmental and Learning Disorders.

Greenspan, S. I., & Wieder, S. (1998). *The child with special needs: Encouraging intellectual and emotional growth.* Cambridge, MA: Perseus Publishing.

LaFreniere, P. J., & Dumas, J. E. (1996). Social competence and behavior evaluation in children ages 3 to 6 years: The short form (SCBE-30). *Psychological Assessment, 8,* 369-377.

[82]

Group Environment Scale, Third Edition.

Purpose: Designed to "measure the actual, preferred, and expected, social environments of task-oriented, social, psychotherapy, and self-help groups."

Population: Group members and leaders; clinicians, consultants, and program evaluators.

Publication Dates: 1974–2002.

Acronym: GES.

Scores, 10: Cohesion, Leader Support, Expressiveness, Independence, Task Orientation, Self-Discovery, Anger and Aggression, Order and Organization, Leader Control, Innovation.

Administration: Group.

Forms, 3: Real (R), Ideal (I), Expectations (E).

Price Data, 2007: $40 per sampler set including manual (2002, 64 pages), 3 forms, answer sheet, scoring key, and blank profile; $120 per duplication set including permissions statement allowing buyer to reproduce up to 150 copies of the survey for one year from date of purchase; other reproduction prices available from publisher.

Time: Administration time not reported.

Comments: A component of the Social Climate Scales.

Author: Rudolf H. Moos.

Publisher: Mind Garden, Inc.

Cross References: See T5:1141 (5 references) and T4:1095 (5 references); for a review by Arthur M. Nezu of an earlier edition, see 10:132 (6 references); for reviews by Michael J. Curtis and Robert J. Illback, see 9:435 (4 references); for reviews by David P. Campbell and Robyn M. Dawes, see 8:573; see also T3:1015 (1 reference); for a review of the Social Climate Scales, see 8:681.

Review of the Group Environment Scale, Third Edition by LAURA L. B. BARNES, Associate Professor of Research, Evaluation, Measurement, and Statistics, Oklahoma State University, Tulsa, OK:

DESCRIPTION. The Group Environment Scale, Third Edition (GES) is one of the 10 Social Climate Scales developed by Moos and his colleagues. There are three forms of the GES developed to measure individuals' perceptions of the actual (Form R—Real), ideal (Form I), and expected (Form E) social environments of groups they are in or may consider joining. Items are identical across the scales except for a change in verb tense (e.g., "The group is …" on Form R becomes "The group will be…" on Forms I and E). Items on the GES form 10 subscales of 9 items each and are true/false statements describing the group. The subscales are intended to measure three dimensions of group environments: Relationship (Cohesion, Leader Support, Expressiveness), Personal Growth (Independence, Task Orientation, Self-Discovery, Anger and Aggression), and System Maintenance and Change (Order and Organization, Leader Control, Innovation). The instrument itself has not changed since the 1981 edition, though the manual has been revised. The authors report that the third edition of the manual includes updated norms, an expanded literature review, and more information on clinical, consulting, and program evaluation uses of the GES. The authors intended for the GES to be used with a wide variety of groups ranging from social/recreational groups (e.g., book clubs), task-oriented (e.g., peace action groups), self-help/support groups (e.g., Alcoholics Anonymous), and psychotherapy groups (e.g., groups for chronic mentally ill patients).

The "Real" form of the test is reported to be useful for clinicians, consultants, and program evaluators to evaluate group climates, track changes in groups, understand individuals' perceptions of groups they are in (e.g., therapy groups), or identify a group's impact on individual members. The manual reports that GES scores are useful in research into the antecedents of group climate, comparisons of groups, and the relationship between group climate and outcomes on both the aggregate and individual level. The authors clearly intend for Form R to be used both as a measure of individual perception and as a descriptive measure of actual group characteristics. The "Ideal" form was designed for purposes of examining preferred group environment; the "Expectations" form might be useful for helping members adjust to a group environment by examining the discrepancy between what they expect and what they experience in a group environment.

Administration and scoring is relatively straightforward. Items on the test and answer sheet are arranged to facilitate hand-scoring of subscales. However, for information on administration options, reading level, form selection, or setting policies regarding anonymity and use of GES results, users are referred to a different manual, *The Social Climate Scales: A User's Guide* (p. 4).

The true/false answers to items are converted to raw scores by summing up the number of answers matching keyed responses on each subscale. Raw scores are converted to standard scores via a set of tables in the appendices. Separate tables in the appendix are given for converting individual scores to standard scores and for converting group means to standard scores. The same scoring key is provided for all three forms though standard scores are provided only for Form R.

DEVELOPMENT. Neither the constructs being measured nor the underlying theory are well-described in the third edition of the manual. The authors, throughout the manual, state that the instrument is designed to measure characteristics of the social climate or social environment. These terms are used somewhat interchangeably but are never defined in the manual. The authors present a conceptual framework of stress and coping theory intended to guide a review of the relevant research. This model fits group experiences into a larger context and suggests uses for the instrument but does not provide insight into the working theory of social climate that informed the development of the instrument.

The author wanted an instrument of between 80 and 100 items so, with 10 dimensions to cover, a target was set of 9 to 10 items per dimension. Of the original 200 or so items, those selected for the final form reportedly met the following criteria: (a) endorsement rates (true or false) of between 20% and 80%, (b) items correlated more highly with their own subscale than any other, (c) approximately half the items on each subscale keyed in the "true" direction, (d) subscales had low to moderate interscale correlations, and (e) "each subscale should discriminate significantly among groups" (manual, p. 16). It was not clear what specific groups the authors refer to in establishing this last criterion. The item selection criteria reported in the manual was for Form R. There is no mention of the item selection criteria applied to the other two forms.

The items appear to be logically organized into three dimensions with three or four subscales each, though the manual provides no theoretical basis for these dimensions or subscales. These are the same three dimensions that underlie all 10 of the Social Climate Scales. Factor-analytic studies for the GES are only vaguely reported; thus, there is very little to go on with respect to item/construct relationships.

TECHNICAL. The manual reports that some raw data for the GES norms for the first and second editions of the manual were lost in the aftermath of the 1989 earthquake. Therefore, the updated norms were based on adding new data to the original subscale means and standard deviations. For Form R, the new norms are based on a total of 305 groups (of which approximately half are apparently new data) and 2,436 individuals.

Thirty-three percent of the groups included in the sample are task-oriented, 20% are social-recreational, 18% are psychotherapy/supervision, and 29% are self-help/mutual support. Group level norms were based on old and new data but it is likely that the individual norms are based on a subset of the groups due to the loss of some individual level data. The manual does not elaborate on this factor, nor do the authors provide any demographic information for the individuals in the sample. For Form I, individual level subscale means and standard deviations based on 684 cases are provided. Normative data are absent for Form E.

The manual provides evidence of substantial and predictable subscale differences among the four group types on Form R. Nevertheless, there is a single set of group norms for interpreting scores from groups as diverse as psychotherapy groups and book clubs. Likewise, a single set of individual norms is available. It is difficult to imagine how such undifferentiated norms can be useful. The authors provide subscale group-level means and standard deviations for the four types of groups so savvy users can construct their own standard scores for group-level data though the number of groups (i.e., the sample size) would be quite small. Not even this group-type information is provided for interpreting individual level scores.

Internal consistency reliabilities of subscale scores for Form R were computed on a sample of 246 group members and leaders representing 30 groups. Coefficients ranged from .62 (Independence) to .86 (Cohesion) with a median alpha of .76. One-month test-retest coefficients were computed on a sample of 63 members and leaders from groups of an unknown number or type. Scale correlations ranged from .65 (Independence) to .87 (Anger and Aggression) with a median correlation of .76. Because the reliabilities were computed on individual scores, not group means, these coefficients apply to the stability of individual-level scores, not group means. A profile-stability coefficient of sorts was computed for 10 staff teams by computing a subscale mean for each group at four points in time. For each team, a correlation was computed between adjacent points in time with the observations for each correlation being the 10 GES subscale scores. Averaged over the 10 teams, the mean correlation was .92 over 4 months, .91 at 8 months, .84 at 12 months, and .78 at 24 months. These results appear to suggest fairly good stability of GES profiles for groups.

The author asserts that the focus of GES interpretations may be at either the group or individual member level. However, the evidence to support these multilevel inferences is woefully inadequate. No studies are reported that attempt to distinguish individual from group effects. This is a very serious shortcoming for an instrument purporting to measure both group climate and individual perception. Confusion over these two constructs is evident when the author interprets the results of correlations computed on individuals ($n = 246$ individuals representing 30 groups) to reflect group phenomena. "More cohesive groups tend to be high on leader support and expressiveness; ...as expected, task-oriented groups tend to be well-organized..." (manual, p. 18). To represent group-level constructs, at least these correlations should be based on group means, with some indication of within-group agreement, though 30 groups is a rather small sample. Further, the extent to which group-level scores measure actual characteristics of the groups rather than just an aggregate of individual perceptions needs to be demonstrated. The author's claim that, "Overall, actual characteristics of a group are the major determinants of members' perceptions of the group" (manual, p. 22) is supported only by passing reference to minimal relationship between individuals' perceptions of group environments and their demographic or personality characteristics. The confusion over units of analysis in the Social Climate Scales was noted by a reviewer as far back as *The Eighth Mental Measurements Yearbook* (1978).

In general, though the manual summarizes a large number of studies that have utilized the GES, just what it measures at the group or individual level is debatable. The author reports that factor-analytic studies conducted on the GES have identified from three to eight factors depending on the type of group studied, conceptual considerations, and methodology. For example, three factors were reported in a study of students and leaders in freshmen seminars; four different factors were identified in a study of student teachers in mental health consultation groups. Two other studies on unspecified populations resulted in five and eight factors.

COMMENTS AND SUMMARY. A potential strength of the GES is its relationship to the other Social Climate Scales in the series—all the scales are based in the same set of dimensions.

However, there is little evidence in the present manual to suggest how well the GES measures these dimensions or whether the construct of social climate is comparable across the different types of environments measured in the series (e.g., family, school, work). Certainly, the sketchy factor-analytic evidence presented for the GES suggests that across group types the constructs vary considerably, thus presumed construct equivalence is highly questionable. As noted by previous reviewers (in the 9th and 10th MMYs, see cross references above), the lack of any systematic approach to validation of the GES continues to be a very serious limitation. Another serious threat to valid use of these scores is the lack of attention to differences in individual-level and group-level use of the instrument. The author interprets individual-level correlations as representing group effects. No consideration is given to computing within-group agreement when aggregating data and some sample sizes for computing group means are as small as 5 (p. 7). Further, as pointed out by the reviewer in the 10th MMY, there is still a lack of meaningful norms. Though additional normative data have been collected and means and standard deviations are reported for four different group types, the only table for converting raw scores to standard scores lumps all four group types into a single table. Further, the lack of sample description is still a huge problem. There is no sound basis for utilizing standard scores based on the norms provided in the manual. Essentially, the problems that were noted by reviewers as far back as the 8th MMY continue to be serious problems—little effort seems to have gone into addressing the previous reviewers' concerns. I cannot recommend the use of this instrument at this time.

Review of the Group Environment Scale, Third Edition by MALINDA HENDRICKS GREEN, Professor, College of Education, University of Central Oklahoma, Edmond, OK:

DESCRIPTION. The Group Environment Scale, Third Edition (GES) is 1 of 10 Social Climate Scales available from Rudolf Moos, the author, and his colleagues at the Center for Health Care Evaluation at Stanford. The GES has 10 subscales for which the purpose is to measure the actual, preferred, and expected social environments of task-oriented, social, psychotherapy, and self-help groups. These 10 subscales are intended

to measure three dimensions: relationship, personal growth, and system maintenance/change. The Relationship Dimension is divided into three categories: Cohesion, Leader Support, and Expressiveness. The Personal Growth Dimension includes four: Independence, Task Orientation, Self-Discovery, and Anger/Aggression. The System Maintenance and Change Dimensions reports three: Innovation, Leader Control, and Order/Organization. The GES has three parallel forms, each with 90 items responded to as true or false. The Form R (Real) tries to assess members' and leaders' perceptions of the current group. Form I (Ideal) considers the members' and leaders' conceptions of ideal group settings, groups they prefer including goals and value orientations. Form E (Expectations) examines prospective members' or leaders' expectations about group settings or beliefs about a task-oriented or social group they are about to enter. There are new normative data and new information on the clinical, consulting, and program evaluation uses of the GES.

DEVELOPMENT. The GES was developed by first conducting structured interviews and using information from observation as well as adapting some items from the other Social Climate Scales. Initially, 211 items (Form A) were composed under the formulation of three sets of social climate dimensions. Form A was administered to 30 groups including task-oriented, social/recreation, and psychotherapy or self-help. Data were analyzed to determine and to remove redundant items. Normative data for Form R were obtained for an overall sample of 305 groups: 101 task-oriented groups, 62 social-recreational groups, 54 psychotherapy-supervision groups, and 88 self-help groups. Normative data for Form I included 684 individuals from 59 groups. Means were reported for the groups, and standard deviations were reported for groups and individuals.

TECHNICAL. Results from several applications of the GES were investigated through factor analysis. The manual reports a 1986 study that identified three factors, a 1982 study that found eight factors, and a different 1986 study that found four. The authors of the GES do not report any factor analysis studies conducted by themselves to examine the validity of the dimensions or the subscales.

Reliability is considered through internal consistency measures (coefficient alpha), test-retest correlations, and profile stability through correlations. Alpha coefficients range from .62 to .86, whereas the test-retest correlation coefficients range from .65 to .87. The profile stability was reported on assessments after 4 months ($r = .92$), 8 months ($r = .91$), 12 months ($r = .84$), and 24 months ($r = .78$). These would all suggest moderate reliability values for the instrument.

Validity evidence reported includes discussions of face and content validity. Support for content validity was based upon the formulating of definitions of specific constructs, preparing items based on theoretical definitions, and selecting items consistent with dimension concepts. Construct validity evidence was presented through a discussion of the literature on groups and the factors that influence them. Additional evidence was reported from research applications of the GES regarding its capacity to discriminate among groups, to identify the determinants of group climate, and to examine the interaction among the group climate and the group's as well as member's outcomes.

COMMENTARY. In response to the concerns raised in the review of the second edition of the GES, the manual does present additional applications of the GES in research through case studies of groups as well as individuals. However, all the concerns raised in that review (*10th MMY*) regarding the data have yet to be addressed. Norms continue to be reported by subscale from data collapsed across a wide range of groups for both members and leaders. Also, the concern of combining the data from groups of differing structure has not been adequately resolved. Therefore, users of this instrument may find the GES scores and the accompanying norms to be misleading. The second concern raised in the earlier reviews regarding the validity has been at least acknowledged in this edition. There is an expanded review of literature supporting the conceptual framework on which the GES is based. Unfortunately, no efforts by the authors of systemic efforts to cross validate the results from the GES are reported.

SUMMARY. The intent of the GES is worthwhile, and the efforts to consider the theoretical work in the development of the items is laudable. The reliability information for the GES is acceptable. Also, the inclusion of additional research applications of the GES is a step in the direction of validity verification. The use of the GES to assess the areas of cohesion, leader support, and

the other subscales would continue to require the interpretations and/or inferences to be applied cautiously. The GES is a promising instrument and with continued improvements should prove highly useful in the assessment of clinical, self-help, and/or psychotherapy/mutual support groups.

[83]

Group Mathematics Assessment and Diagnostic Evaluation.

Purpose: A group-administered diagnostic mathematics test that measures individual skills in key areas, including concepts, operations, computation, and applications.

Population: Grades K–12.

Publication Date: 2004.

Acronym: G·MADE.

Administration: Group.

Forms: 2 parallel forms, A or B, for each of 9 levels.

Price Data, 2007: $110.99–$184.99 per Form A classroom sets (specify Level) including teacher's manual (102 pages), hand-scoring templates, answer sheets, and 30 student booklets; $201.99—$303.99 per Forms A & B classroom sets (specify Level); $31.99 per norms supplement (specify age-based or grade-based out-of-level); $34.99 per technical manual (122 pages); $349.99 per Scoring and Reporting Software v. 2.1 PC and Mac Version; $2,295.99 per Scoring and Reporting Software Single PC Scanning Version 2.1; $114.99 per Resource Library (specify Level).

Time: (60–90) minutes per level.

Author: Kathleen T. Williams.

Publisher: Pearson.

   a) LEVEL R.

   Population: Ages 5-0 to 7-11.

   Scores, 3: Concepts and Communication, Process and Applications, Total.

   b) LEVEL 1.

   Population: Ages 6-0 to 8-11.

   Scores, 4: Same as *a* above plus Operations and Computation.

   c) LEVEL 2.

   Population: Ages 6-0 to 9-11.

   Scores, 4: Same as *b* above.

   d) LEVEL 3.

   Population: Ages 7-0 to 10-11.

   Scores, 4: Same as *b*.

   e) LEVEL 4.

   Population: Ages 8-0 to 12-11.

   Scores, 4: Same as *b*.

   f) LEVEL 5.

   Population: Ages 9-0 to 18-0 and above.

   Scores, 4: Same as *b*.

g) LEVEL 6.
Population: Ages 10-0 to 18-0 and above.
Scores, 4: Same as *b*.
h) LEVEL M.
Population: Ages 11-0 to 18-0 and above.
Scores, 4: Same as *b*.
i) LEVEL H.
Population: Ages 12-0 to 18-0 and above.
Scores, 4: Same as *b*.

Review of the Group Mathematics Assessment and Diagnostic Evaluation by JOSEPH C. CIECHALSKI, Professor, East Carolina University, Greenville, NC:

DESCRIPTION. The Group Mathematics Assessment and Diagnostic Evaluation (G•MADE) is a norm-referenced, standards-based assessment of mathematics skills. The G•MADE includes nine test levels, each having two forms (A&B). Eight of the nine G•MADE test levels contain three subtests: Concepts and Communication, Operations and Computation, and Process and Application. The lowest level, Level R, does not include the Operations and Computation subtest.

The Concepts and Communication subtest measures the words and language of mathematics. All 28 items in this subtest are multiple-choice items that present a symbol, word, or short phrase followed by four choices that may be pictures, symbols, or numbers. The Process and Applications subtest measures the student's ability to apply the appropriate operations and computation to solve a word problem. Each multiple-choice item consists of a short passage of one or more sentences followed by four choices. The choices may be numbers, pictures, or symbols. Levels R-4 in this subtest contains 28 items, and Levels 5, 6, M, and H contain 30 items. The Operations and Computation subtest contains 24 items that consist of an incomplete math equation followed by four possible answers or solutions. This subtest is not included in Level R because Kindergarten students have not been instructed in how to reason with the basic mathematical operations.

The Directions for Administering the G•MADE are included in the teacher's manual and are very easy to read and follow. Depending on the level of the test, a student's responses may be recorded in the test booklet or on a separate answer sheet. Although the G•MADE is not a timed test, it takes about 60–90 minutes to administer. The use of calculators is not permitted.

Scoring the test is very simple. For example, Level R is scored using an answer key whereas the remaining eight levels may be scored either by hand or by using the G•MADE Scoring and Reporting Software. Scores may be reported in a number of ways. For example, scores may be reported as standard scores, percentile, normal curve equivalents, stanines, etc.

DEVELOPMENT. The G•MADE was developed as a diagnostic instrument to determine what mathematical skills students have and what skills they need to be taught. Work on the G•MADE began in 2000 with a yearlong research study of state standards, curriculum benchmarks, the scope and sequence plans of commonly used math textbooks, and a review of the best practices for the teaching and learning of math concepts and skills. The technical manual contains the components of this research study.

The foundation of the G•MADE is based on the National Council of Teachers of Mathematics (NCTM) Standards, which include five content standards (Numbers and Operations, Algebra, Geometry, Measurement, and Data Analysis and Probability) and five process standards (Problem-Solving, Reasoning and Proof, Communication, Connection, and Representation). The technical manual contains a summary of these standards as represented by the G•MADE subtests. In addition, surveys collected at national meetings and surveys mailed to over 800 math educators were also examined. Based on these results, the test blueprints for the three subtests were developed and test items were written.

In early 2002, the G•MADE was tried out nationally at 52 sites with nearly 11,000 students in Grades K–12 sampled. All testing was completed in a group or classroom setting with the directions read either by a teacher or administrator familiar to the students. Race and ethnicity were also represented in this sample, and the respective proportions and their representativeness are provided in the technical manual.

Based on the results of this national tryout, the data were analyzed in four stages. Stage 1 consisted of three phases that analyzed the items based on (a) difficulty and discrimination, (b) the goodness-of-fit of each item to the Rasch model, and (c) an analysis of each item's distracters. Stage 2 analyzed items for bias. In stage 3, the questionnaires included in the tryout administrations were analyzed. Stage 4 involved the development of parallel forms.

The resulting version of the G•MADE included nine test levels each with two parallel forms (A & B). The technical manual lists the subtests by level and the number of subtest items for each form. The G•MADE was ready for the development of the fall 2002 and spring 2003 national norms.

TECHNICAL. A total of 26,099 students were tested at 143 sites nationwide in the fall 2002 and spring 2003 and comprise the norming sample. The four major geographic areas of the United States (Northeast, North Central, South, and West), an equal number of males and females, a balance of race and ethnicity, and students receiving special education services were represented in this norming sample.

Internal reliability coefficients were computed for each grade level using the split-half method and then adjusted for test length using the Spearman-Brown formula. The median total test reliability coefficients were reported as .92 (Form A) and .93 (Form B) in the fall and .93 (Form A) and .94 (Form B) in the spring. Split-half reliability coefficients were also computed for 13 age groups by level and form. The median reliability coefficients of the total test scores for the groups were .93 (Form A) and .94 (Form B) with a range of .91 to .98. Alternate-form reliability coefficients ranged from .84 to .96. Test-retest reliability coefficients ranged from .78 to .91 for Grades K–4 (median = .86) and .90 and greater for Grades 5–12 (median = .93). The standard error of measurement (*SEM*) ranged from a low of 2.8 to a high of 4.5.

Content validity was addressed by considering how well the three subtests assess the various skill areas of math. The test blueprint was based on collected documents and materials and summarized in a document. The foundation of the content validity was based on the *Principles and Standards for School Mathematics* published by the NCTM in 2000. The technical manual presents the NCTM content standards with the G•MADE subtest tasks, and the content covered by each of the three subtests are included in the same manual. Concurrent validity was based on correlating the G•MADE with the Iowa Tests of Basic Skills, the TerraNova, the Iowa Tests of Educational Development, and one standardized state test. All concurrent validity coefficients were high. In addition, the KeyMath-R was administered to 30

students with coefficients above .80. Predictive validity studies based on how well the G•MADE predicted performance on the math subtests of a group standardized achievement test (ITBS) were high. Construct validity was examined using evidence of a standards-and-curriculum-driven test structure, of consistency of growth across G•MADE levels and grade enrollment, of the performance of students identified as having learning disabilities, and of both convergent and divergent validity. The latter is supported in part in the *Standards for Educational and Psychological Testing* (AERA, APA, & NCMR, 1999), "Relationships between test scores and other measures intended to assess similar constructs provide convergent evidence, whereas relationships between test scores and measures purportedly of different constructs provide discriminate evidence" (p. 14).

COMMENTARY. The G•MADE is a well-developed math diagnostic instrument. The technical manual is especially noteworthy. It contains numerous tables that help to clarify, among other things, the development of norms, the various validity and reliability studies, and an Appendix (B) that contains a comprehensive listing of item objectives for all levels of the G•MADE that math teachers will find very useful in developing math examples. To permit diagnostic analyses, Part 4 of the teacher's manual includes several test profiles and information on how to complete diagnostic analyses of each G•MADE subtest for both individual students and classes.

SUMMARY. Overall, the G•MADE has been constructed upon sound mathematical standards and has undergone extensive research in its development and standardization. Several validity and reliability studies were conducted, and high validity and reliability coefficients were reported. Therefore, I recommend the G•MADE as a very useful math diagnostic instrument.

REVIEWER'S REFERENCE

American Educational Research Association, American Psychological Association, & National Council on Measurement in Education. (1999). *Standards for educational and psychological testing*. Washington, DC: American Educational Research Association.

Review of the Group Mathematics Assessment and Diagnostic Evaluation by KEVIN D. CREHAN, Professor of Educational Psychology, University of Nevada, Las Vegas, Las Vegas, NV:

DESCRIPTION. The Group Mathematics Assessment and Diagnostic Evaluation (G•MADE) is designed as a diagnostic mathematics skills inventory for students in kindergarten through high school. The G•MADE has nine levels, labeled R, 1, 2, 3, 4, 5, 6, M, and H, with two forms, A and B, at each level. Sources for determining the contents of the test levels included: the National Council of Teachers of Mathematics (NCTM, 2000), Principles and Standards for School Mathematics; selected state curricula; popular textbook series; and research on best practice for teaching and learning mathematics. All level tests, except Level R, have three subtests labeled: Concepts and Communications (28 items), Operations and Computation (24 items), and Process and Applications (28 or 30 items). The R level omits the Operations and Computation subtest. All items use the multiple-choice format. Scoring keys, norm conversion tables, and templates for individual and class summaries are provided. Additional templates are provided for analysis by subtest and item-objective summary by subtest. Raw score conversions are provided for standard scores (mean = 100, standard deviation = 15), percentile ranks, normal curve equivalents, stanines, and grade equivalents. Additionally, a scaled score named the growth scale value (GSV) is provided for total score. This score is purported to allow tracking growth in mathematics knowledge over time using different G•MADE levels and forms.

Administration of the G•MADE is group or individual with a recommendation that small group or individual administration be used for kindergarten and first graders. The test is not timed, but takes 60 to 90 minutes. Breaks or multiple sessions are suggested as permissible. Accommodations are suggested for students with reading or language difficulties, visual or hearing impairments, and students requiring individual testing. It is recommended that younger students, through Grade 3, mark their answers in the test booklet or, if testing is individually performed, have their answers recorded by the test administrator. Older students, Grade 4 and above, can use the answer sheet provided. Answer sheets can be hand scored using a template or machine scored using available scoring and reporting software.

Suggested uses of results include student placement and instructional planning at classroom and individual levels, measuring growth in mathematics achievement, and research applications.

DEVELOPMENT. Test specifications or blueprints were developed based of the author's integration of content suggested by the National Council of Teachers of Mathematics (2000), Principles and Standards for School Mathematics; selected state curricula; popular textbook series; and research on best practice for teaching and learning mathematics. Three separate tables of specifications over the nine test levels were developed for (a) Concepts and Communication, (b) Operations and Computation, and (c) Process and Applications.

The Concepts and Communication table lists content in algebra, comparison, geometry, measurement, money, numeration, quantity, sequence, statistics, and time. Cell entries are the number of items for each content area over the nine test levels. The number of items varies from zero to as many as 16 for Level M numeration.

The Operations and Computation table lists the operations of addition, subtraction, multiplication, division, and multiple operations with representation subcategories of whole numbers, fractions, decimals, percents, exponents, signed numbers, square roots, and algebra. When crossed with the nine test levels, this table has 810 cells. The number of items in each cell indicates content coverage. As might be expected, most cells are blank. All items use whole numbers up through Level 3, and there is a gradual increase over levels in items using the other types of representation.

The Process and Applications table has the headings: algebra, comparison, geometry, measurement, money, numeration, quantity, sequence, statistics, and time. Each heading has subheadings of one-step, multiple-step, and process (except time, which omits process). Again, the cell entries are the number of items for each heading over the nine levels of the test.

This reviewer found no indication as to the origin of test items. That is, item development and selection are not discussed in the technical manual. The degree of fit between the actual items and content specifications is uncertain because no information on this match is provided. Because no independent verification of item to test specification (content validation) is available, the prospective test user must make this judgment.

TECHNICAL. A national tryout administration of the item pool was conducted with over 10,000 students. The sample is described as having an equal representation of males and females and an overrepresentation of African American and Hispanic students as compared to White students. There is no rationale given for the overrepresentation of African American and Hispanic students. Items were screened using classical item difficulty and discrimination indices and calibrated using a one-parameter Rasch analysis. Items were screened for bias using both quantitative and qualitative methods. Parallel forms for each level were developed following tryout screening.

A national standardization sample of 26,099 students from kindergarten through Grade 12 was tested during the fall of 2002 and spring of 2003. Reports are provided showing the sample to national percentage by ethnicity, geographic region, type of community, and percent free lunch.

Raw scores were converted to normalized standard scores (mean = 100, standard deviation = 15) for fall and spring samples for the three subscale and total scores. Standard scores were converted to percentile ranks, normal curve equivalents, and stanines. Total raw score to grade equivalents and growth scale values were also determined. All conversions are tabled in the teacher's manual accompanying each level test.

Split-half reliability evidence is provided on both forms for the three subscale scores and total score of all nine level tests for both fall and spring administrations using estimates based on the standardization sample data. Most median subscale coefficients are in the high .8 range for the operations and computations subscale and in the low .8 range for the other two subscales. Total score split-half estimates are all in the .9 range. Split-half reliabilities are also reported by age range with 1-year increments and test level for both forms on total scores. These median estimates are also in the .93–.94 range for both forms. Parallel-forms reliability estimates for total score are in the mid .8 to mid .9 range when corrected for restriction of range. Selected levels test-retest reliabilities over short periods (most less than 1 month) for total score ranged from .78 to .94, with a median of .915, when corrected for restriction of range.

The discussion of content validity evidence points to the tables of specifications developed for the test levels and suggests that potential users judge the degree of content validity for their situation. Concurrent criterion-related evidence presents correlations between G•MADE level subtest and total test scores and comparable scales of the Iowa Test of Basic Skills (ITBS), the TerraNova, Second Edition (CTBS), the Iowa Test of Educational Development (ITED), the TAKS, and the KeyMath-R. Subscale-to-subscale correlations are difficult to summarize due to the similarities and differences in subscale labels. Fourteen total mathematics score correlations ranged from .74 to .90 with a median of .84. In addition to concurrent correlations, some predictive correlations are reported for the ITBS, ITED, TerraNova, and TAKS.

COMMENTARY. The G•MADE appears to be the product of a well thought out test development process. Care was taken to develop tables of specifications that are representative of current views on the mathematics curriculum from the NCTM professional organization, textbook publishers, and state curricula. Detailed content specifications are provided by a thorough listing of objectives for each subscale for each test level. Tryout and standardization methods seem to be generally sound, and reliability and some of the validity evidence is good. There are, however, a few concerns deserving mention:

Although the tables of specifications and the listing of objectives are very detailed, the origin of test items and the process of matching items to the content dimensions are not mentioned in the technical manual. Then again, given the detail and descriptive nature of the objectives, the author may have assumed the correspondence was obvious.

The standardization sample is underrepresentative of Hispanic students by about 6% and overrepresentative of White students by 5% in comparison to the national statistics. The standardization sample also substantially overrepresents urban students and underrepresents poorer students.

A less than compelling argument for evidence of construct validity is given using the comparison of the mathematics to mathematics score (convergent) correlations with mathematics to reading and language score (divergent) correlations. Although the mathematics to mathematics score correlations are mostly higher than the reading/language to mathematics score correlations, there are exceptions and the differences are smaller than would be expected to support evidence of divergence.

The multiple-choice items with numeric options consistently ignore the item-writing guideline concerning the ordering of numeric options.

The overall appearance of the tests is unimpressive.

SUMMARY. The detail of the content specifications and the listing of specific objectives provide potential users with excellent information to allow a comparison of the test's contents to the scope and sequence of the local curriculum. It is recommended that the adoption decision be informed by the results of this local content validation. The results of this local content validation will establish the value of the test and its accompanying resources for local instructional decisions.

[84]

Gudjonsson Suggestibility Scales.

Purpose: "Developed in order to measure objectively the vulnerability or proneness of people 'to suggestive influence and/or' to give erroneous accounts when interviewed," particularly in forensic contents.
Population: Ages 6 and over.
Publication Date: 1997.
Scores, 7: Immediate Recall, Delayed Recall, Yield 1, Yield 2, Shift, Total Suggestibility, Confabulation.
Administration: Individual.
Forms: 2 parallel forms: GSS1, GSS2.
Price Data: Available from publisher.
Time: Administration time not reported.
Author: Gisli H. Gudjonsson.
Publisher: Taylor & Francis [England].

Review of the Gudjonsson Suggestibility Scales by MARC JANOSON, President, Forensic Psychology PC, New York, NY, and BRUCE FRUMKIN, Director, Forensic and Clinical Psychology Associates, South Miami, FL:

DESCRIPTION. The Gudjonsson Suggestibility Scales (GSS) is presented as a memory test. A short narrative paragraph containing 40 facts is read to the person being tested with that person being asked to try to remember everything he or she can about the story. He or she is then asked to state everything that can be remembered about the story. Unless the person being tested has very poor recall initially, after a 50-minute delay, he or she is again asked to recall what they can about the story.

After the recall portion(s) of the test, the test taker is asked 20 standardized questions about the story, 15 of which have been specifically designed as subtly leading (i.e., they lead the subject toward an inaccurate reporting of what they believe they remember about the story). The extent to which a test taker *yields* to the 15 leading questions comprises the Yield 1 score of the GSS. All participants are clearly and firmly told, "You have made a number of errors. It is therefore necessary to go through the questions once more, and this time try to be more accurate" (manual, p. 11). The examiner is then able to assess how much the person "yields" to the 15 questions after being pressured, the scoring of which leads to the Yield 2 score. The extent to which a test taker *shifts* from the original response, right or wrong, to a different response after pressure, comprises the Shift score. The Yield 1 (0 to 15) and Shift (0 to 20) are combined for a Total Suggestibility score. These scores can be compared to various normative groups on a number of dimensions including age, legal status, and intellectual ability.

The GSS comprises two parallel forms, the GSS 1 and the GSS 2. They are identical in structure except for the narrative paragraph and the questions asked about the paragraph.

DEVELOPMENT. Gisli Gudjonsson developed the GSS in order to measure, subtly yet objectively, the construct of *interrogative suggestibility*. *Interrogative suggestibility* is the extent to which an individual comes to accept messages or information communicated during formal questioning, essentially coming to believe the information presented as true. As measured by the Yield and Shift scores, information is obtained about the degree to which an individual yields to leading or misleading questions and gives in to negative feedback or pressure.

In addition to use for research, the GSS was developed for clinical use, such as assessing the psychological vulnerability of a defendant or witness to yielding to leading questions and to shifting from one response, right or wrong, to a different response, under pressure. This use has applications in providing data to the court regarding an individual's susceptibility to providing false information during police questioning, which is highly relevant when the trier of fact is assessing the validity of a confession or witness statements. The measure also has applications when a court is determining the voluntariness of a confession or *Miranda* rights waiver.

TECHNICAL. The scoring of the Yield and Shift scales is highly nondiscretionary and generally clear cut. Interscorer reliability for the suggestibility scales (Yield 1, Yield 2, Shift, Total GSS Score) ranges from .949 to .992 for the GSS 1 and .989 to .996 for the GSS 2 (Richardson & Smith, 1993).

In light of the nature of the GSS, where individuals are likely to remember some of the narrative paragraph over time, test-retest reliability scores have not been obtained for the individual scales. Instead, temporal consistency scores have been obtained, comparing the GSS 1 with the GSS 2 for a variety of populations over different time frames. All the correlations for suggestibility were highly significant. Using a forensic population retested the same day, the correlation was .92 for the Total GSS score and ranged from .80 to .90 on the individual scales (Yield 1, Yield 2, and Shift). Another forensic group retested from one day to 18 months later had a correlation for Total GSS score of .83 and .74 to .78 on the individual scales.

Grisso (1986) reviewed the early validation studies on the GSS 1 and concluded "Construct validation research with the GSS has placed the forensic examiner in a good position to use the GSS scores when considering questions of an examinee's decreased resistance to suggestion or subtle pressure in interrogations by law enforcement officials" (p. 147). Since that initial review, additional research has been done. Suggestibility has been shown to correlate with a number of cognitive variables. Gudjonsson (2003, p. 360-412) summarized the relevant research. There is a negative relationship of suggestibility scores to intelligence and memory. Poor assertiveness, evaluative anxiety, state anxiety, and avoidance coping strategies correlated with suggestibility. Research has also shown that although adolescents do not "yield" to leading questions any more than adults, they are more likely to have higher Shift scores (i.e., change a response when provided with pressure or negative feedback). Sleep deprivation is also correlated with suggestibility. Mental illness per se does not correlate with suggestibility. Significantly, research has shown that false confessors have higher GSS scores than forensic patients and those who have maintained their innocence.

COMMENTARY. The GSS was developed using normative data from Great Britain and Iceland. Yet this test is quite appropriate for use with populations from the United States. The reader should be reminded that London, like many big cities in the United States, is a multicultural city. There is perhaps no reason to believe that those detainees residing in London would score as a group much differently than comparable populations in any multiculturally diverse American cities although American norms would be quite useful. Moreover, there were few differences in performance between those residing in Iceland and those in Great Britain. Relatively little research has been performed on cross-cultural factors and the GSS. Although Gudjonsson, Rutter, and Clare (1995) found that Afro-Caribbean police detainees scored significantly higher on all GSS 2 scores compared to their Caucasian counterparts, such factors as intelligence, memory, and anxiety produce more of an effect in suggestibility scores than ethnicity. Even without data normed on an American population, the GSS provides excellent behavioral data relating to how an individual responds when given leading questions and pressured with negative feedback. Certainly norms from American subjects would enhance the perceived applicability of this test in the United States.

The GSS can be used in a variety of forensic, clinical contexts. Although it might be argued that the test is only relevant in situations in which a defendant has potentially produced a *coerced-internalized false confession* (has faulty memory for events surrounding an offense but is led to believe by police through leading questions and/or pressure that in fact he or she committed the crime), the GSS has far more applicability when episodic or autobiographical memory is an issue during police questioning. The GSS measures behavioral responses to leading questions and negative feedback, the same processes that occur in many interrogations. Although the GSS does not provide a direct measure of *compliance* (which does not require personal acceptance of the information provided or request made), research has shown a correlation between GSS scores and that construct as measured by the Gudjonsson Compliance Scale (GCS; Gudjonsson, 2003). The correlations for Yield 1, Shift, and Total GSS score were .40, .53, and .54, respectively.

When testing is performed in a forensic context, the clinician must address issues of response distortion or malingering. The GSS is particularly resistant to exaggeration or feigning of interrogative suggestibility. First, test takers believe they are being given a memory test. Also, a study by Baxter and Bain (2002) demonstrated that even when individuals were informed that the test measures suggestibility and were told to feign suggestibility on the test, only the Yield 1 score was susceptible to faking.

SUMMARY. Gudjonsson has successfully produced objective tests (GSS 1 and GSS 2) to help assess interrogative suggestibility and related constructs in the context of police questioning of suspects and witnesses. The GSS enables comparison of a person's suggestibility to normative groups and provides behavioral samples relevant to those behaviors a defendant may have exhibited when confronted with leading questioning or negative feedback during a *Miranda* waiver or confession (see Frumkin, in press). The GSS should not be used to assess whether a *Miranda* waiver or confession was voluntary or whether a confession was false.

The reviewers note that the GSS has limitations. Its normative data are based upon populations in Great Britain and Iceland. Its simplicity invites misuse whereby clinicians put undue weight on individual scores without viewing the data as one piece of what needs to be a comprehensive assessment to address issues pertinent to *Miranda* waiver and confessions. It is also not meant to provide data suggesting whether or not a confession is true of false. Someone may have high GSS scores, be highly suggestive, and be susceptible to influence, yet still have committed the offense for which he or she confessed. Nevertheless, psychologists now have a unique, objective, standardized test to help in their assessment in confession-related forensic cases.

REVIEWERS' REFERENCES

Baxter, J., & Bain, S. (2002). Faking interrogative suggestibility: The truth machine. *Legal and Criminological Psychology, 7*, 219–225.
Frumkin, I. B. (in press). Psychological evaluations in *Miranda* waiver and confession cases. In R. Denny & R. Sullivan (Eds.), *Clinical neuropsychology in the criminal forensic context.* New York: Guilford Publications.
Grisso, T. (1986). *Evaluating competencies: Forensic assessments and instruments.* New York: Plenum Press.
Gudjonsson, G. (2003). *The psychology of interrogations and confessions: A handbook.* West Sussex, England: John Wiley & Sons.
Gudjonsson, G., Rutter, S., & Clare, I. (1995). The relationship between suggestibility and anxiety among suspects detained at police stations. *Psychological Medicine, 25,* 875–878.
Richardson, G., & Smith, P. (1993). The inter-rater reliability of the Gudjonsson Suggestibility Scales. *Personality & Individual Differences, 14,* 251–253.

Review of the Gudjonsson Suggestibility Scales Report by ROMEO VITELLI, Private Practice, Hamilton, Ontario, Canada:

DESCRIPTION. The Gudjonsson Suggestibility Scale (GSS1) and its parallel form (GSS2) were designed to provide professionals with a concise and self-contained test of interrogative suggestibility and verbal recall for use in research, forensic, and clinical applications. Although originally developed for use in forensic contexts, the GSS scales may be valuable tools in any interview setting. Interrogative suggestibility is defined in the GSS manual with a quote from an earlier article as: "the extent to which, within a closed social interaction, people come to accept messages communicated during formal questioning" (Gudjonsson & Clark, 1986, p. 84). Research using early measures of the GSS (Gudjonsson, 1984) has identified two critical components of suggestibility: Yield (tendency to give in to leading questions) and Shift (tendency to shift responses due to interpersonal pressure), and the GSS1 and GSS2 have been designed to measure both components. In addition to interrogative suggestibility measures, the GSS1 and GSS2 provide objective measures of response distortions and fabrications (the two components associated with confabulation), as well as measures of immediate and delayed verbal recall. To complement the information provided by the GSS1 and GSS2, the Gudjonsson Compliance Scale (GCS), a 20-item, self-report measure of compliance using a true/false format is also provided.

The GSS1 and GSS2 are designed to be presented to the test taker as a test of verbal recall. In each version of the GSS, a brief story is presented. It may be either read by the examiner or presented using the audiotape provided with the test package. Immediate and delayed (usually after 50 minutes) recall is measured verbatim, and 20 questions relating to the story are given. Following negative feedback, the 20 questions are re-administered to score for Yield and Shift measures. The test manual provides comprehensive instructions for scoring suggestibility, recall, and confabulation measures. The GCS can be administered either using the printed test sheet or read to the subject if literacy problems prevent standard administration. Scoring the GCS is done using the provided scoring key. The test author gives specific cautions concerning the use of the GCS for individuals whose IQ falls below 70 or who might have difficulty understanding the test items.

For the purpose of interpretation, normative data are provided for adult, adolescent, and forensic populations. GSS norms are also provided for use with persons suffering from intellectual disabilities. The test author specifically notes that the GSS1, GSS2, and GCS represent only one component in a comprehensive forensic assessment and cannot be used exclusively to make conclusions about witness validity.

DEVELOPMENT. Although the formats of the GSS1 and GSS2 are identical with respect to administration and scoring criteria, the nature of the narrative paragraphs and corresponding interrogative questions differ in specific content with the GSS1 story having a forensic context (a robbery) whereas the GSS2 story has a nonforensic content (a couple saving a boy from an accident). The GSS2 was developed to provide a nonforensic narrative to complement the forensic objectives of the GSS1.

The GCS was originally developed using 28 true/false items selected to measure compliance in an interrogation setting. The original 28 GCS items were administered to a sample of 164 subjects and factor-analyzed to identify 20 items with a high loading on the compliance factor (the manual presents the loadings for the final 20 GCS items). The GCS is presented in two forms: Form D as the standard administration and Form E for use as part of the interview process.

TECHNICAL. Information on the normative samples and the standardization process is provided in the GSS user's manual. Normative data were collected using samples from a variety of different clinical populations from various studies over the years. Information on the sample demographics for the normative and clinical samples are given, and statistics are provided for adults, juvenile offenders, forensic populations, and intellectually disabled offenders. Separate norms for male and female respondents are not provided. Percentile rankings are provided for most of the norms. Analyses of the role of age, forensic status, and clinical diagnosis in test responding are also described.

Interscorer reliability analyses for the GSS1 and GSS2 are provided with coefficients falling in the .95–.99 range for measures of verbal recall and suggestibility with slightly lower results for measures of confabulation (.72–.80 range). Due to the format of the scales, test-retest reliability coefficients are not provided for the GSS1 and GSS2 although "temporal consistency" involving correlations of scores for respondents who had completed both the GSS1 and GSS2 are provided. All correlations are highly significant with correlations for Shift being consistently lower for Yield 1 than Yield 2. Coefficient alpha reliabilities appear to be slightly higher for the GSS2 than the GSS1. Test-retest reliability data for the GCS are provided for a sample of hospitalized forensic patients over a 1- to 3-month time interval (.88 between the two time periods). Standard error of measurement scores for each of the GSS subscales are provided, determined by the relationship between the GSS1 and GSS2 scores when both scales are administered. Given the parallel nature of the GSS measures, the length of time between administrations of both tests has been found to impact on the variability of the scores with longer intervals between test sessions being more appropriate in forensic contexts.

The test manual provides a series of validation studies although the test author also refers readers to the author's comprehensive review of validation studies of the GSS1 and GSS2 (Gudjonsson, 1992).

Factor-analytic studies of the Yield and Shift items of both tests have found strong correspondence to the two-factor model on which the tests were based. Changes in scoring procedures have yielded stronger item loadings and have been incorporated into the current test and norms. Factor analysis of the GCS items has yielded a three-factor model reflecting avoidance of confrontation, eagerness to please, and general compliance.

Suggestibility as measured by the GSS has been linked to a number of cognitive variables in the hypothesized direction for adults, children, and adolescents. The effects of avoidant coping strategies, anxiety, and poor assertiveness have also been found to correlate significantly with Yield and Shift suggestibility scores. Other factors such as sleep deprivation, intellectual disabilities, mental illness, and the role that they play in susceptibility to leading questions are also discussed.

Research assessing the predictive validity of the GSS1 and GSS2 has identified a strong negative correlation between measures of Shift and Yield and interrogative experience. GSS1 suggestibility measures have also been found to relate to level of accuracy in police interviews. Despite the problematic nature of research into "false confessions," research using the GSS1 has identified a linear relationship differentiating "false confessors," "resisters" (respondents denying their involvement in crimes of which they were accused), and forensic patients. False confessors were also found to score more highly on the GCS than other prisoners in a prison sample.

Although confabulation measures were found to be less reliable than suggestibility measures, validation studies have suggested that personality factors may play a greater role than psychiatric diagnosis. Overall, the studies cited and the validation process meets the psychometric standards for test validation as specified in the *Standards for Educational and Psychological Testing* (AERA, APA, & NCME, 1999).

COMMENTARY. The increasing use of psychological testimony to investigate issues of suggestibility in obtaining confessions has resulted in the Gudjonsson scales being used in research and forensic settings in countries around the world as well as becoming the focus of an impressive body of research into interrogative suggestibility and compliance.

There continues to be a need for the collection of normative data in the U.S. and in other countries to counterbalance the predominantly U.K.-based norms compiled to date. As well, further research is required to validate the confabulation measures and to investigate the role of cultural influences in interrogative suggestibility and the applicability of the GSS1 and GSS2 with pre-adolescent populations. Another line of investigation should focus on the vulnerability of the Gudjonsson scales to the effects of malingering given its increasing usage in criminal cases and the possibility of "coaching" designed to provide the appearance of suggestibility.

Despite these concerns, the Gudjonsson scales are well-designed and well-validated and can be viewed as a valuable addition to the clinical tools that forensic psychologists can draw upon.

SUMMARY. The GSS1, GSS2, and GCS are well-developed instruments based on extensive research into suggestibility, compliance, and confabulation. They are designed to provide professionals with concise measures of interrogative suggestibility, verbal recall, and compliance for use in research, forensic, and clinical applications. The parallel format provides needed flexibility to accommodate client needs and to address forensic and nonforensic applications across clinical populations. Guidelines and scoring examples are pro-

vided to enable consistent interpretation of test results. The test manual outlines the development and validation of the GSS1, GSS2, and GCS and their use to identify potential problems in witness testimony based on numerous research studies that are cited in the bibliography.

REVIEWER'S REFERENCES

American Educational Research Association, American Psychological Association, & National Council on Measurement in Education. (1999*). Standards for educational and psychological testing*. Washington, DC: American Educational Research Association.
Gudjonsson, G. H. (1984). A new scale of interrogative suggestibility. *Personality and Individual Differences, 5*(3), 303-314.
Gudjonsson, G. H. (1992). *The psychology of interrogations, confessions, and testimony*. Chichester, England: John Wiley & Sons.
Gudjonsson, G. H., & Clark, N. K. (1986). Suggestibility in police interrogation: A social psychological model. *Social Behaviour, 1*, 83-104.

[85]

The Hayling and Brixton Tests.

Purpose: Designed to assess executive functions.
Population: Ages 18–80.
Publication Date: 1997.
Administration: Individual.
Price Data, 2006: £136 per complete kit including manual (20 pages), stimulus book, and 25 scoring sheets; £39.50 per 50 scoring sheets.
Authors: Paul W. Burgess and Tim Shallice.
Publisher: Harcourt Assessment [England].

a) HAYLING TEST.
Scores, 4: Response Latency, Error Score, Time Taken to Respond, Total.
Time: [5] minutes.
Comments: Administered verbally; requires no reading or writing.
b) BRIXTON TEST.
Score: Total score only.
Time: [5–10] minutes.

Review of The Hayling and Brixton Tests by KATHLEEN D. ALLEN, Assistant Professor of Education, St. Martin's University, Lacey, WA:

DESCRIPTION. The Hayling and Brixton assessment is composed of two tests created to assess neuropatients with suspected frontal lobe damage. Although neuroimaging can successfully determine the location of brain lesion or injury, the Hayling and Brixton Tests are designed to ascertain how damage to this particular part of the brain could affect a patient's everyday functioning. The frontal lobes are considered the brain's central executive processing system. Therefore, damage to the frontal lobes is often referred to as *dysexecutive syndrome*. The four prevalent factors affecting everyday functioning for patients with dysexecutive syndrome assessed in the Hayling and Brixton Tests are response time, suppression of automatic response, pattern detection, and the ability to monitor changes appropriately.

The Hayling Sentence Completion Test is a measure of response time and suppression of automatic responses that consists of two sections of answer completion. Each section consists of 15 questions that are scored with a stopwatch for response time. Raw scores in each section are converted to scaled scores and totaled to create an overall scaled score ranging from 1 (*impaired*) to 10 (*very superior*).

In the first section, the patient's response is timed to determine how many seconds it takes to supply the missing word that completes a sentence in a connected and meaningful manner. For example, when the examiner gives the partial sentence "When you go to bed, turn off the _____" the patient's answer is recorded, along with the response time in whole second intervals. For scoring purposes, the response times for all 15 questions are added together to create a raw score. A provided table is used to convert the raw score into a 1–7 scaled score.

For the second section of the Hayling Tests, the patient is told to complete the sentence in a totally unconnected manner, such as "She called the husband at his ...elephant." For this task, the patient must suppress an automatic response connected to the phrase ("work"). Answers are scored according to three criteria: unconnected ("elephant"), connected ("office"), or somewhat connected ("telephone booth"). The number of errors ("connected" and "somewhat connected" answers) are totaled separately, and then added together to be converted to a scaled score. Response times for this section are totaled as per Section 1, but the scaled scores are calibrated differently.

The Brixton Spatial Anticipation Test assesses rule detection and the ability to monitor changes appropriately. Each page has 10 numbered circles in two rows of 5. One circle on each page is colored blue according to a pattern (i.e., the blue circle's position could be 1,2,1,2 on four consecutive pages). The pattern of the positioning of the blue circles changes about nine times during the test. Participants are asked to anticipate which of the 10 circles will be blue on the next page and point to the correct numbered circle. The number of errors are totaled and converted into one scaled score.

DEVELOPMENT.

Theoretical framework. The Hayling and Brixton Tests were designed according to the neuropsychological theory of impairments associated with frontal lobe damage. This theory originates from years of brain imaging and cognitive task studies. The authors used the results of these studies to find the predominant impairments associated with everyday functioning. Sentence completion and spatial anticipation tasks were then developed to assess these impairments.

Task development. The Hayling Sentence Completion Test was adapted from sentence completion norms by Bloom and Fischler (1980). These norms were used to select 30 sentence completion items that had a high rate of accuracy for participants producing the correct response. The second section of the test was designed to measure suppression of automatic response. This is similar in concept to the Stroop Test (1935), an older cognitive test also designed to measure automatic suppression. In the Stroop Test, one of the three tasks is giving the participants color words printed in a different ink color (the *word* blue printed in the *color* red) and asking them to suppress the reading of the words and identify the ink color instead.

The Brixton Spatial Anticipation Test is a pattern detection and monitoring test. Participants base their responses on determination of a preset pattern. This concept is also measured in the well-known Wisconsin Card Sorting Test (Heaton, Chelune, Talley, Kay, & Curtiss, 1993; T7:2787), as well as the Color Trails (Mitrushina, Boone, & D'Elia, 1999; 15:56) assessment, but the Brixton Test was designed to be quicker to administer and score.

TECHNICAL.

Standardization. The norm sample selected for scaling production was a control group of 121 brain-healthy volunteers between the ages of 18 and 75. For comparison purposes, 71 and 73 control group members were used for the Hayling and Brixton Tests, respectively. Control group members were matched based on age, WAIS (Wechsler Adult Intelligence Scale) score, and NART (National Adult Reading Test) WAIS FSIQ equivalent. Nonnative English speakers and individuals with a <85 IQ were not included in the sample. The three dysexecutive syndrome groups were all neurological patients with lesions categorized from a CT scan as in the frontal lobes only (bifrontal), elsewhere in the cortex (posterior), or both (anterior).

The standardization results are indicative of the test theory construct that the factors of response time, suppression factors, pattern detection, and monitoring are connected to frontal lobe functioning. Group effects were measured with an ANOVA, and highly significant differences were found between the neurological lesion and control groups for all four factors. Post hoc comparisons of specific groups indicated significance between the participants with (anterior and bifrontal groups) and the participants without (posterior and control groups) frontal lobe damage. However, comparison between the two groups of participants without frontal lobe involvement (posterior and control) did not achieve significance.

Reliability. The split half reliability study with 118 Hayling control group participants generated reliability coefficients of .35 (H1 time), .83 (H2 time), and .41 (errors). The 47 anterior group participants produced split-half reliability coefficients of .93, .80, and .72 for H1 time, H2 time, and errors, respectively. Although the anterior group coefficients were good, the split-half reliability study of the control group participants yielded less than adequate coefficients for H1 time and errors. The test-retest reliabilities for the Hayling were .62 (H1 time), .78 (H2 time), and .52 (automatic suppression errors). The reliability coefficient for the overall Hayling score was .76. Test-retest reliability was fair for response time and overall measurements but inadequate for the error scoring. Moderate reliability results were achieved with the Brixton (split-half .62, test-retest .71).

Validity. The test manual cites more than 50 studies as evidence of construct validity. These studies include assessment of frontal lobe functioning during neuroimaging and task performance as well as behavioral evaluations of a patient's daily life. This research also demonstrates the Hayling and Brixton's *ecological* validity, as the factors assessed in the tests are the most prevalent factors in difficulties experienced by patients with dysexecutive syndrome during everyday living. Concurrent validity is evident in the comparison studies between the Hayling and Brixton and similar well-known cognitive tests (Stroop, Wisconsin Card Sorting, and Color Trails) that measure the same factors.

Correlational data (*N* = 116) are provided in the test manual that support the relationships between the Hayling and Brixton Tests, age, gender, and general intelligence (IQ). These data indicate significant correlations of age (for all tasks) and IQ (for the Brixton, H1 time, Hayling errors, and overall score). The test manual also provides cutoff scores for each task weighted for the effects of aging and premorbid intellectual function (*N* = 121).

COMMENTARY. The most impressive strength of the Hayling and Brixton is its origin in cognitive theory with evidence provided for construct validity. The focus on ecological validity is another advantage of this assessment. Because the test authors focused the test only on the most important factors of everyday functioning, it can be efficiently administered and utilized by clinicians. The manual includes many statistical analyses to demonstrate reliability and validity. Some changes to the standardization sample size, scale score measures, and the testing instructions and materials would strengthen the power of those analyses for research and application purposes.

The standardization sample size of 121 and the sten scoring scale seem inadequate for the evaluation of an assessment with the complexity inherent in brain functioning. According to Crawford and Henry (2005), a standardization study is in publication with a larger norm sample (*N* = 222) and using *T* scores instead of sten scores for the Brixton Test. Even more large sample size research studies are needed to create norms across diverse groups for the Hayling and Brixton scores. For example, Bielak, Mansueti, Strauss, and Dixon (2006) have evaluated 457 non-brain-injured adults from the ages of 53–90 to provide normative data on Hayling-Brixton scores for the effects of aging, education level, and gender.

Because the factor of error administration and scoring is inherent in both Hayling reliability tests, perhaps the test manual directions on response classification could be improved. Bielak, et al. (2006) suggest that the authors create a list of novel or hard-to-classify responses for interrater reliability and include them in the manual. An interrater reliability rating would be an asset to the data provided in the manual, and the difference in responses across cultures or geographic location, even within the parameter of those who are native English speakers, should be addressed.

In the Hayling Section 1 directions, the test manual does not provide correct answers. It is also unclear how to score incorrect answers for this section, except that a time maximum of 60 seconds is recorded for each correct answer. Therefore, the implication is that an incorrect answer is scored as a 60-second response time, and even one incorrect answer could affect the participant's scale score.

SUMMARY. In a recently published article, one of the test authors suggests that neurological assessments move beyond proof of construct and into practical application (Burgess, Alderman, & Forbes, 2006). This seems like a reasonable goal, and well worth pursuing. Although earlier cognitive assessments, such as the Stroop and Wisconsin Card Sorting Task, added to the construct of prevalent factors in frontal lobe functioning, the Hayling and Brixton is an important attempt to provide an assessment of those factors that can be evaluated for patient benefit. The next step is investigating how to use the information generated by the Hayling and Brixton Tests to design and monitor an individualized rehabilitation plan for a patient's success in everyday functioning.

REVIEWER'S REFERENCES

Bielak, A. A., Mansueti, L., Strauss, E., & Dixon, R. A. (2006). Performance on the Hayling and Brixton tests in older adults: Norms and correlates. *Archives of Clinical Neuropsychology, 21*, 141-149.

Bloom, P. A., & Fischler, I. (1980). Completion norms for 329 sentence contexts. *Memory and Cognition, 8*, 631-642.

Burgess, P. W., Alderman, N., & Forbes, C. (2006). The case for the development and use of "ecologically valid" measures of executive function in experimental and clinical neuropsychology. *Journal of the International Neuropsychological Society, 12*(2), 194-209.

Crawford, J. R., & Henry, J. D. (2005). Assessment of executive dysfunction. In P. W. Halligan & D. T. Wade (Eds.), *Effectiveness of rehabilitation for cognitive deficits* (pp. 233-245). New York: Oxford University Press.

Heaton, R. K., Chelune, G. J., Talley, J. L., Kay, G. G., & Curtiss, G. (1993). *Wisconsin Card Sorting Test manual: Revised and expanded*. Odessa, FL: Psychological Assessment Resources.

Mitrushina, M. N., Boone, K. B., & D'Elia, L. (1999). *Handbook of normative data for neuropsychological assessment*. New York: Oxford University Press.

Stroop, J. R. (1935). Studies of interference in serial verbal reactions. *Journal of Experimental Psychology, 18*, 643–662.

Review of The Hayling and Brixton Tests by EUGENE P. SHEEHAN, Dean, College of Education and Behavioral Sciences, University of Northern Colorado, Greeley, CO:

DESCRIPTION. As the name suggests, the Hayling and Brixton Tests are actually two tests. They are designed to assess functions that are known to be impaired when there is damage to the frontal lobes. Basic task initiation speed, performance on a response suppression task, and the detection and following of rules are functions that have been shown to exist in dysexecutive patients. The Hayling Test measures task initiation speed and performance on a response suppression task, whereas the detection and following of rules are functions measured by the Brixton Test. Both tests are short and can be administered in a brief period of time. Scoring is straightforward and is accomplished on an easy-to-use scoring sheet.

Specifically, the Hayling Test is a sentence completion test composed of two sections, each of which consists of 15 sentences missing the last word. In the first section the participant completes the sentence as quickly as possible, using a word that makes sense. For example, "The old house will be torn ...down" (manual, p. 4). In the second section, the participant is requested to complete the sentence with a word that is unconnected to the sentence in any way. The manual provides the example: "The captain wanted to stay with the sinking ... lightbulb" (manual, p. 4).

Using a stopwatch, the examiner measures response latencies (time from when the examiner ceases speaking to when the participant begins a reply) in both Sections 1 and 2. A coding scheme is provided for the response suppression task. Participants can make two types of errors in this task: inappropriate responses and last word completions. Interpretation of the coding scheme is straightforward. The response latencies and the scores are entered on a scoring sheet. Instructions for the conversion of the scores into an overall scaled score provided on the scoring sheet are easy to follow.

The manual refers to the Brixton Test as a concept attainment task. The test consists of a 56-page stimulus book, with each page containing a set of 10 circles in two rows of 5. One of the circles on each page is filled in. As the examiner moves from page to page the participant's task is to predict which circle will be filled in on the next page. Clinical research has shown that the cognitive tasks involved in this test are affected by damage to the frontal lobes.

DEVELOPMENT. The Hayling and Brixton Tests derive their theoretical underpinnings from work that has identified certain intellectual and cognitive tasks that are affected by damage or lesion to the frontal lobes. The manual contains a brief summary of the literature in this area, describing several tasks that are impacted by frontal lobe damage. The implicit rationale in the selection of the three tasks (initiation speed, performance on a response suppression task, and detection and following of rules) is that they are functions known to be commonly impaired.

The Hayling Test is based on comparisons between a group of 91 lesion patients referred for "routine neuropsychological assessment" (manual, p. 5). One interesting caveat about the lesion group is that they were above average on premorbid intelligence, a peculiarity of patients referred to the particular hospital from which they were drawn. The standardization process for the Brixton Test is similar to that of the Hayling Test: a lesion group compared with a control group.

TECHNICAL. The manual is rather short with respect to background psychometric data. For the Hayling Test, the test manual provides a comparison between lesion and control group scores, split-half reliability, and test-retest reliability. The results of the comparisons between the lesion and control groups are significant and in the expected direction: Those with frontal lobe damage perform at a poorer level than do control group members or participants with other nonfrontal lobe lesions. Thus, despite the small sample sizes, there is evidence for discriminant validity of this instrument. Although the control group split-half reliabilities are low (.35 to .83), those for the impaired group are both more consistent and higher (.72 to .93). The difference is attributed to the lack of variability in the control group's performance. Test-retest reliabilities for the Hayling range from .52 to .78, which the test authors deem adequate for this type of test.

Results of the psychometric analyses of the Brixton Test (comparison between lesion and control, split-half reliability, and test-retest reliability) are generally comparable to those of the Hayling Test.

Correlational analyses between scores on the Hayling and Brixton Tests reveal statistically significant relationships between all the Hayling and Brixton measures. Additionally, age and IQ were related to performance on the tests. When age and IQ are partialled out, the correlation between the Hayling overall score and the Brixton Test becomes nonstatistically significant suggesting that the relationship between the tests is indicative of shared age and IQ. The authors therefore suggest that the Hayling and Brixton Tests "probably measure different cognitive processes or resources" (manual, p. 13).

COMMENTARY. The main value of the Hayling and Brixton Tests lies in their potential to provide a preliminary screening of patients presenting with dysexecutive syndrome. Using these tests, a therapist or doctor could quickly assess a patient with symptoms of frontal lobe impairment. Data from the tests could then be used in conjunction with other information about the patient to make a decision about future testing.

SUMMARY. The Hayling and Brixton Tests are designed to assess the dysexecutive syndrome that can accompany damage to the frontal lobes. The tests measure cognitive processes shown to be affected by frontal lobe lesions: basic task initiation speed, performance on a response suppression task, and the detection and following of rules. Both tests are remarkably quick and easy to administer and score. Supporting psychometric data indicate adequate split-half and test-retest reliabilities and the ability of the tests to discriminate between patients with frontal lobe damage and control groups.

[86]

Hines Functional Dysphagia Scale.

Purpose: A quick scale for measuring swallowing behavior "to distill the results of a videofluoroscopic swallow study."

Population: Ages 20–86.

Publication Date: 2005.

Acronym: HFDS.

Scores, 6: Food, Liquid, Aspiration, Efficiency, Compensations, Total Score.

Administration: Individual.

Price Data: Not available.

Time: (3–5) minutes.

Comment: The publisher advised in April 2007 that this test is now out of print.

Authors: Barry M. Klor, Mary J. Bacon, Barbara S. Cook, and Franklin J. Milianti.

Publisher: PRO-ED.

Review of the Hines Functional Dysphagia Scale by REBECCA McCAULEY, Professor of Communication Sciences, and MOIRA DALY, Lecturer of Communication Sciences, University of Vermont, Burlington, VT:

DESCRIPTION. The purpose of the Hines Functional Dysphagia Scale (HFDS) is to assist speech-language pathologists in the description of and tracking of changes in swallowing over time based on one or more videofluoroscopic swallow studies (VFSSs).

The HFDS consists of five items rated following a VFSS using a 3 point scale (0, 1, 2), where lower scores indicate greater severity of dysphagia. The five items address the following five aspects of swallowing: (a) level of restriction on food intake (NPO [nothing by mouth], restricted consistency, all allowed), (b) level of restriction on liquid intake (NPO, restricted consistency, all allowed), (c) presence of aspiration (yes, some with clearing cough, none), (d) efficiency of swallow (poor, decreased, good), and (e) effects of compensations, such as head positioning (unable/no benefit, some compensations required, none required). The sum of scores on the five items results in a total dysphagia severity rating, with a higher numerical score (maximum possible = 10) indicating a more functional swallow. Optional fields are also provided to capture additional parameters of patient performance. These include Prognosis for Improvement, Immediate Improvement with Compensations, and whether intervention was provided since any previous VFSS. Each form can be used to track performance across multiple VFSSs (up to 5). In addition, space is provided to allow the clinician to follow the American Speech-Language-Hearing Association National Outcomes Measurement System (NOMS).

"Qualified examiners include clinicians who have training in the interpretation of VFSS data" (examiner's manual, p. 7), as well as in dysphagia assessment and treatment. Estimated time required to complete a HFDS scoring sheet following a VFSS is 3 to 5 minutes.

DEVELOPMENT. The total severity score is considered criterion-referenced by the test developers. The procedure was developed by speech-language pathology staff members of the Hines Veterans' Affairs (VA) Hospital in Hines, Illinois. Its development was internally funded and appeared to have occurred within limitations associated with a clinical setting.

TECHNICAL.

Standardization. The authors describe a standardization sample of 1,000 individuals seen consecutively at the Hines VA Hospital for VFSS over a 3 1/2-year period. Eleven etiological categories were represented among the sample patients, with cerebrovascular accident (*n* = 218) and head and neck cancer (*n* = 164) the most frequent. Patients ranged in age from 20 to 86, with a mean of 64.7 years. Only seven women were included in the sample. The 3 point rating scale used for each of the five test items was based on the clinical

judgment of the speech-language pathology staff, whose experience and training were not described.

Reliability. Four types of reliability were examined—internal consistency, intrarater reliability, interrater reliability, and test-retest reliability. High and statistically significant evidence of internal consistency was found for the entire test using the coefficient alpha method. Very high Spearman rank-order correlation coefficients (range = .94 to .97) were reported for intrarater reliability using three clinicians who rated 20 VFSSs across sessions that were scheduled within 2 weeks of each other based on clinical exigencies. Similarly, very high interrater reliability coefficients (range = .91 to .95) were obtained using four raters who reviewed the same VSSs for 30 patients. The training and credentials of the raters were not provided. Test-retest reliability was examined for 65 patients who were referred for clinical reasons for two VFSSs within a 2-week period (Mean = 6.85 days between assessments). Although a high Spearman rank-order correlation coefficient was obtained for the two sets of scores (rho = .89), that time interval may be problematic given that recovery from dysphagia can occur within 2 weeks of acute stroke (Ramsey, Smithard, & Kalra, 2003). In addition, when differences between scores across administrations were examined, 30 of the 65 patients displayed no change in total score, 29 exhibited a change of plus or minus 1, and 6 exhibited a change of plus or minus 2.

Validity. The standardization sample was described both in terms of total scores on the HFDS and on a separate 7-point dysphagia severity score that had been in use at the hospital since 1985. The test manual described the development of the measure and offered high positive correlations between each of the five test items and the overall score on the HFDS as well as moderate, positive correlations among the test items as content evidence of validity. Criterion-related validity evidence consisted of correlations between the total HFDS score and the dysphagia score as well as the total HFDS score and the ASHA NOMs scores for 300 of the 1,000 participants from the standardization sample. Neither of these measures has received sufficient study to serve as a reasonable criterion. The authors provided a factor analysis based on the entire standardization sample to support the construct validity of the five items comprising the test, as each appeared to represent a separate factor.

COMMENTARY. This scale formalizes observations made in relation to the VFSS, which is often considered the gold standard for the evaluation of dysphagia (Ramsey et al., 2003). However, the bases on which the ratings are to be made are very poorly described. For example, a rating of 1 on Efficiency is said to correspond to "swallowing is slow (rule of thumb: 2 times the normal duration of swallowing)" (examinee's manual, p. 11); however, no indication of what constitutes "normal" is given. Measures of oral and pharyngeal transit times can be quantified to provide a more objective means of describing decreased efficiency. The reliability evidence offered in support of the HFDS is problematic because insufficient information was provided concerning the raters and kinds of patients studied, and because the relationship of etiologies and course of swallowing performance (e.g., recovery, decline) was not considered in the design and description of the reliability studies. There is also no accounting for etiology (either anatomical or physiological) regarding the nature of the dysphagia resulting in any aspiration and/or decreased efficiency that may be documented on the HFDS. Thus, there is no rationale provided for chosen compensations. The purpose of the VFSS is to provide more objective data regarding a patient's swallowing than a mere checklist. Therefore, the information provided by the HFDS really cannot be used to direct treatment and/or account for any change that may be noted upon subsequent administrations of the tool. This tool fails to capture the nature of the dysphagia, and thus the reason for any recovery of function. One may expect very different swallowing recovery rates in a CVA patient versus a head-and-neck cancer patient experiencing the acute effects of radiation therapy. Further, the vague basis on which items were rated suggests that reliability data obtained by individuals not directly involved in the test's development may be far less impressive than the data described in the current test manual. Initial validity evidence related to content and construct identification showed some promise. However, evidence that use of the HFDS results in better outcomes for patients than outcomes achieved with current practice patterns is sorely needed.

SUMMARY. Typically, clinicians view the videographic materials created during the VFSS, apply their clinical expertise to reach several decisions regarding the status and management of observed swallowing deficits, and document those decisions within the clinical record. Although the HFDS seemed to be designed to improve consistency and utility of information obtained from VFSSs, further development is needed before it can be recommended for use in either description or on-going assessment. In the interim, the Penetration-Aspiration Scale (Rosenbek, Robbins, Roecker, Coyle, & Woods, 1996), which provides a much greater description of one component of the swallow, appears to present a superior alternative for use in the interpretation of VFSSs.

REVIEWERS' REFERENCES
Ramsey, D. J. C., Smithard, D. G., & Kalra, L. (2003). Early assessments of dysphagia and aspiration risk in acute stroke patients. *Stroke, 34*, 1252-1257.
Rosenbek, J. C., Robbins, J., Roecker, E. G., Coyle, J. L., & Woods, J. L. (1996). A penetration-aspiration scale. *Dysphagia, 11*, 93-98.

Review of the Hines Functional Dysphagia Scale by ROGER L. TOWNE, Associate Professor, Department of Communication Sciences and Disorders, Worcester State College, Worcester, MA:

DESCRIPTION. The Hines Functional Dysphagia Scale (HFDS) is a rating scale designed to summarize the results of a videofluroscopic swallowing study (VFSS) performed during dysphagia evaluation. It was designed by the speech-language pathology staff at the Hines Veterans Affairs Hospital in Hines, Illinois and is an extension of a 7-point dysphagia severity rating scale used at that facility for many years. The HFDS was developed to provide a more complete multidimensional picture of a patient's swallowing problem while maintaining minimum administration time.

The HFDS uses a 3-point forced-choice scoring system to assess a patient in five parameters of swallowing: ability to eat food, ability to drink liquid, aspiration status, efficiency of eating and drinking, and response to compensatory swallowing techniques. In addition, the scale provides for an assessment of a patient's prognosis for improvement and whether they demonstrate immediate improvement with compensation. The HFDS is designed to assess the results of a single VFSS or multiple VFSS studies whereby a patient's change over time can easily be charted and evaluated.

The HFDS consists of a single-sheet recording form divided into four sections. Section 1 contains patient identifying information, which includes name, date of birth, gender, and diagnosis. Section 2 is the record of scores obtained on the five parameters of swallowing assessed. Each parameter receives a score of 0, 1, or 2 where 0 represents a significant, nonfunctional deficit in that parameter, 1 represents a parameter that is functional but with limitations due to dysphagia, and 2 represents a functional parameter at the patient's baseline. Scores received in each of the five parameters are then added together to calculate the HFDS Total Score, which can range from 0 to 10. The HFDS is then converted to one of a seven-level HFDS Severity Rating ranging from severe (total score = 0–2) to normal (total score = 10). Section 3 is a summary of the data obtained for the patient. It includes the HFDS Total Score, the HFDS Severity Rating, optional scores from any additional severity ratings, and the rating from the National Outcomes Measurement System (NOMS), as well as notations relative to the patient's prognosis for improvement, any immediate improvement with compensations, and any intervention provided since the latest VFSS. Section 4 consists of the HFDS Severity Ratings used to convert the HFDS Total Score.

Administration of the HFDS is simple and straightforward and according to the authors should take approximately 3–5 minutes. Following a review of the patient's VFSS findings the clinician completes Section 2 of the HFDS assigning a score to each of the five parameters of swallowing, and then calculates the HFDS Total Score. The examiner's manual contains guidelines and criteria for scoring each of the five parameters. Section 3 is then completed summarizing the data from the HFDS as well as any other administered severity ratings. Based on these results the clinician then completes the section relative to prognosis, compensation, and intervention. Although uncomplicated to complete, the authors note that the HFDS should only be administered by "clinicians who have training in the interpretation of VFSS data and dysphagia assessment and treatment" (examiner's manual, p. 7).

DEVELOPMENT. As noted, the HFDS was developed as a multidimensional extension of a 7-point dysphasia severity rating scale used for many years. Selection of the five parameters of swallowing assessed in the HFDS was based on the staff's experience and "thought to tap the factors of greatest importance to swallowing therapists" (examiner's manual, p. 3). The 3-point forced-choice scoring system was selected to assign a patient's performance in each parameter to one of three functional categories: within normal limits, compromised performance, or precludes oral intake. Following a 1 month trial period the staff evaluated the scale and their ability to make consistent judgments in scoring by viewing and independently scoring samples of VFSS tapes. They reported "excellent agreement among clinicians" (examiner's manual, p. 3). At that time a decision was also made to include the other additional notations relative to Prognosis for Improvement, Immediate Improvement with Compensations, and intervention. The HFDS was then standardized.

TECHNICAL. The HFDS was standardized over a 3 1/2-year period on 1,000 consecutive patients referred to the Hines VA Hospital for a VFSS. As all referred patients were included in the standardization data they represented a broad age range (20 to 86 years), a variety of etiologies, and a greatly disproportionate distribution of gender (993 males and 7 women). The HFDS is a criterion-referenced test in that the HFDS Total Score can be interpreted to reflect specific levels of performance. This scale was made to be criterion-referenced by comparing each patient's HFDS Total Score to their assigned severity level on the internal Hines 7-point severity rating scale. As noted, this scale had been used for many years and was based on "descriptions of behavioral features of dysphagia that discriminate severity" (examiner's manual, p. 16). Through this comparison specific HFDS Total Scores could be assigned to one of the seven levels of severity described by the other severity rating scale.

Reliability of the HFDS was established in four areas: internal consistency, intrarater reliability, interrater reliability, and test-retest reliability. Internal consistency, the degree to which the HFDS items correlated with one another, was measured using the coefficient alpha method yielding an alpha of .84 suggesting a strong internal consistency. Intrarater reliability was established by having three clinicians view and judge 20 VFSS recordings twice with 2 weeks between each viewing. Spearman rank-order correlation coefficients between the two viewings ranged from .94 to .97, suggesting high intrarater reliability. Interrater reliability was established by having four clinicians view and score 30 VFSS recordings, which were then correlated using a Spearman rank-order correlation coefficient. Interrater correlations ranged from .91 to .95 indicating good agreement between the four judges. Finally test-retest reliability was established using the data from 65 patients who received a second follow-up VFSS within 2 weeks of their first evaluation. A Spearman rank-order correlation coefficient between the patients' first and follow-up HFDS was .89 (p <.001), and a Wilcoxon signed ranks test between the two administrations resulted in a nonsignificant statistical difference. Together these two measures suggest good test-retest reliability.

Validity of the HFDS was established in three areas: content validity, criterion-related validity, and construct validity. According to the authors, content validity (establishing that the HFDS covers a representative sampling of swallowing behaviors) had to be built into the scale at the time it was developed. It is their position that the five parameters of swallowing selected for inclusion in the HFDS are consistent with current knowledge about dysphagia. In addition, Spearman rank-order part-whole correlations computed between these five parameters indicated that "all five HFDS parameters contributed positively to the test score and, therefore, support content validity of the HFDS" (examiner's manual, p. 19). Concurrent criterion-related validity, the degree to which performance on the HFDS predicts a patient's performance on another similar (criterion) measure, was established by comparing patients' performances on the HFDS to their performances on the Hines 7-point severity scale administered at the same time. Spearman rank-order correlation between the two measures was r = -.94 (p < .001) indicating a strong correlational relationship between the two measures. Additionally, a Spearman rank-order correlation was also calculated between the performances of 300 patients on the HFDS and their rating on the NOMS completed at the same time, resulting in a correlation of .91 (p < .001) and again supporting the HFDS as a valid measure of dysphagia. Finally, construct validity, the degree to which the HFDS reflects theoretical models of dysphagia, was based on how well each individual parameter of the scale measured the underlying behaviors associated with dysphagia. Construct validity was established by a factor analysis of a large data set in which only one specific factor emerged for each of the five proposed factors. Thus each factor appears to represent a unique yet similar attribute related to dysphagia. Based on the data presented by the authors, the HFDS appears to be a reliable and valid measure of dysphagia as represented by performance on the swallowing parameters assessed.

COMMENTARY. As the authors note in the examiner's manual, there have been many instruments developed for the assessment of dysphagia—many of them checklists or scales. The HFDS joins this group of relatively short and easy-to-administer instruments designed to measure swallowing behavior and changes in performance over time. A unique aspect of the HFDS is its purpose in providing summative data relative to the results of a videofluroscopic swallowing study, whereas other scales usually assess swallowing behaviors via questionnaires and patient self-report, or those directly observed by a clinician at "bedside." It must be noted, however, that the HFDS, like other scales or checklists, only collects reports of the signs and symptoms of dysphagia without reference to their underlying physiological and/or anatomic etiology. Therefore, although the HFDS may be a helpful tool in summarizing the symptoms of dysphagia observed during a VFSS, it cannot substitute for a comprehensive report that discusses these observed symptoms with respect to the underlying dysfunctions of anatomy or physiology that are responsible for them. As dysphagia therapy and compensatory swallowing strategies are designed to alter and modify the physiologic processes involved in swallowing, such a detailed description of these processes forms the necessary basis from which dysphagia management decisions are made. Such decisions cannot be made solely on the information contained in the HFDS or other scales or checklists of swallowing behavior.

SUMMARY. There are several available scales and checklists that provide a means of summarizing various aspects of dysphagia symptoms and behaviors. The HFDS provides a means of specifically summarizing those behaviors observed during administration of a VFSS and to track changes in those behaviors in individuals who have multiple VFSS procedures. To that extent some clinicians may find the HFDS a useful tool. However, management of dysphagia requires much more detailed information regarding the underlying etiologies for these observed behaviors. Therefore, the HFDS should be regarded as a supplemental evaluation summary and not a substitute for a necessary detailed report regarding the dysphagic behaviors observed during a VFSS and their underlying anatomic and/or physiologic etiology.

[87]
Hodson Assessment of Phonological Patterns—Third Edition.

Purpose: Designed to "assess and analyze phonological deviations of children with highly unintelligible speech."
Population: Ages 3 to 8.
Publication Dates: 1986-2004.
Acronym: HAPP-3.
Scores, 14: Word/Syllable Structures Omissions (Syllables, Consonant Sequences/Clusters, Prevocalic Singletons, Intervocalic Singletons, Postvocalic Singletons, Total), Consonant Category Deficiencies (Liquids, Nasals, Glides, Stridents, Velars, Anterior Nonstridents, Total), Total Occurrences of Major Phonological Deviations.
Administration: Individual.
Levels, 3: Comprehensive, Preschool Screening, Multisyllabic Word Screening.
Price Data, 2004: $189 per complete kit including examiner's manual (2004, 64 pages), 25 Comprehensive Phonological Evaluation Record Forms, 25 Major Phonological Deviations Analysis Forms, 25 Substitutions and Other Strategies Analysis Forms, 50 Preschool Phonological Screening Record Forms, 50 Multisyllabic Word Screening Record Forms, 1 Multisyllabic Word Screening Picture Sheet, 30-piece object kit, and 13 picture cards; $71 per examiner's manual.
Time: (15–20) minutes.
Comments: 3 levels: Comprehensive Phonological Evaluation, Preschool Phonological Screening, Multisyllabic Word Screening; norm referenced and "criterion referenced"; formerly called The Assessment of Phonological Processes.
Author: Barbara Williams Hodson.
Publisher: PRO-ED.
Cross References: See T5:214 (19 references); for reviews of an earlier version by Allen O. Diefendorf, Michael K. Wynne, and Kathy Kessler and by Kathryn W. Kenney, see 12:36; see also T4:220 (4 references); for a review by Sheldon L. Stick, see 9:91 (1 reference).

Review of the Hodson Assessment of Phonological Patterns—Third Edition by DAVID P. HURFORD, Director of the Center for the Assessment and Remediation of Reading Difficulties and Professor Psychology and Counseling, Pittsburg State University, Pittsburg, KS:

DESCRIPTION. The Hodson Assessment of Phonological Patterns—Third Edition (HAPP-3) is an assessment instrument created to assess and examine the phonological patterns of children with highly unintelligible speech between the ages of 3 years and 7 years and 11 months. The HAPP-3 is composed of two screening instruments (the Preschool Phonological Screening and the Multisyllabic Word Screening) that are to be used to determine if a more detailed assessment of phonological deviations is needed, plus a comprehensive assessment of phonological deviations (the Comprehensive Phonological Evaluation). To administer either of the screening instruments, or the Comprehensive Phonological Evaluation, requires knowledge in phonetics, phonology, diagnostic evaluation, speech pathology, and very good phonetic transcription abilities.

The HAPP-3 has six intended uses: (a) screening to determine if a comprehensive evaluation is necessary, (b) to identify children with disordered phonological systems, (c) to analyze children's phonological deviations, (d) to determine a rating of severity for the children who have phonological deviations, (e) to identify potential optimal target patterns for training purposes, and (f) to document progress following intervention. Only one version of the HAPP-3 is available, which is not the optimal situation when performing multiple assessments as is the case when documenting progress or engaging in research that requires multiple assessments. As will be seen below, the HAPP-3 is a psychometrically sound test to accomplish these intentions.

The HAPP-3 is composed of two screening instruments, the Preschool Phonological Screening (PPS) and the Multisyllabic Word Screening (MWS), and a comprehensive evaluation aptly named the Comprehensive Phonological Evaluation (CPE) that can be used if either of the two screening instruments indicate that it is necessary or if prior arrangements have been made.

The PPS instrument assesses consonant category deficiencies and omissions among preschool children including children as young as 2 years of age. The PPS can typically be administered in less than 2 or 3 minutes and consists of 12 three-dimensional objects that can readily be recognized and named by preschoolers.

The MWS instrument assesses four types of phonological deviations that are common among children older than 8 years of age who have grave difficulty pronouncing complex multisyllabic words. The MWS can also be typically administered in less than 2 or 3 minutes and consists of 12 stimulus pictures arranged equidistantly on a laminated 22 cm x 28 cm card. The stimulus pictures were selected because they represented multisyllable words for which the structure was complex and easily recognizable by elementary students.

The CPE is used when either the PPS or MWS indicate that a more detailed and comprehensive assessment is necessary. Forty-eight three-dimensional objects and three parts of the body (i.e., thumb, nose, and mouth) are used to elicit the 50 stimulus words that comprise the CPE. The stimulus words provide ample opportunities to assess the phonologic deviations of children with highly unintelligible speech, which is the purpose of the HAPP-3.

It is required that the administrations of each of the PPS, MWS, and CPE be recorded on an audio device. During the administration of the CPE, the Transcriptions of Stimulus Words form is completed as the student names the objects.

The child's utterances from the Transcriptions of Stimulus Words form are then analyzed with the Major Phonological Deviations Analysis form. This form is used to assess the student's speech-sound deviations. The child's utterances from the Transcriptions of Stimulus Words form are also assessed with the Substitutions and Other Strategies Analysis form.

From the above-mentioned forms, the Major Phonological Deviations-Occurrences and Percentages form is completed. This form summarizes the child's phonological deviations into Word/Syllable Structure Omissions, Consonant Category Deficiencies, and Total Occurrences of Major Phonological Deviations (TOMPD). The substitutions and other strategies that were produced are also listed by type and number of occurrences. The consonants that the student spontaneously produced, omitted, or substituted are inventoried along with the vowels that the child was able to produce. Finally, the consonant, consonant sequences, and vowels that were not spontaneously produced are listed in terms of stimulability.

The major scores derived from the CPE are the TOMPD, the Consonant Category Deficiencies Sum, and the Ability Score and its percentile.

But it also provides a wealth of descriptive information as a function of transcribing the student's performance onto the various forms described above.

DEVELOPMENT. The HAPP-3 was standardized with a norming group of 886 children from 22 states and the District of Columbia in which 97% of the sample had no disability, 2% had phonological impairments, and 1% had "other" disabilities. The normative sample was weighted, which resulted in a sample that was very similar to the demographic characteristics of the population of the United States.

TECHNICAL. Reliability was assessed using internal consistency, test-retest, and interscorer indices. Internal consistency was assessed by computing coefficient alphas for the 50 stimulus words for the age levels 3, 4, 5, 6, and 7 years. Coefficient alphas ranged from .95 (for 6-year-olds) to .97 (for 3- and 7-year-olds) with an average of .96. Coefficient alpha was also calculated for 11 of the patterns of phonological deviations from the Major Phonological Deviations Analysis form for a sample of 30 children who experienced phonological deviations. Coefficient alphas for these 11 deviation categories ranged from .87 (Prevocalic/Intervocalic Singletons) to .99 (Postvocalic Singletons) with an average of .96 for Word/Syllable Structures and .95 for Consonant Category Deficiencies.

Test-retest reliability was assessed with a group of 59 children ranging in age from 3 through 7 years and a test-retest interval of 2 weeks. Although the group was diverse in terms of geographical region and race, there was no information regarding the children's phonological abilities. The resulting coefficient of reliability was .99; however, a separate sample that included only children with phonological deviations or some indication of the percentage of children with phonological deviations who comprised the sample was necessary to adequately address test-retest reliability.

Interrater reliability was assessed by examining the results of two individuals who independently scored 30 completed Major Phonological Deviations Analysis forms. Although this method assesses the likelihood of arriving at similar results when the protocols have been completed by individuals trained to administer the HAPP-3, it does not directly assess interrater reliability. To adequately assess this type of reliability requires that two individuals independently administer the HAPP-3 to the same children, transcribe the utterances of the children, and then score the protocols. Although the authors report in the manual that the interrater reliability was .98, this is an incomplete evaluation of interrater reliability.

Validity was assessed with content validity (including item rationale, conventional item analysis, and differential item functioning analysis), criterion-related validity, and construct validity. With regard to content validity, the HAPP-3 was originally created and subsequently modified as a function of past and current theory (e.g., Distinctive Feature Theory, Chomsky & Halle, 1968; Natural Phonology, Stampe, 1969; Nonlinear Phonology, Bernhardt & Stoel-Gammon, 1994).

The median item discrimination values ranged from .47 (4-year-olds) to .68 (7-year-olds). The item discrimination and item difficulty scores fall within values that support the technical quality of scores from the HAPP-3.

To examine the possibility of item bias in the HAPP-3, items were subjected to Differential Item Functioning (DIF) analysis to assess for potential gender and ethnic bias. The particular type of DIF analysis that was utilized examined two logistic regression solutions. The first examined Ability scores alone to predict item performance. The second solution used Ability scores and group membership to predict item performance. If the second solution provides a better solution than the first, it would indicate that group membership was important in predicting item performance, thus suggesting that the items were biased toward particular groups. The groups that were examined included males versus females, African Americans versus non-African Americans, and Hispanic-Americans versus non-Hispanic-Americans. One-hundred and fifty DIF comparisons were carried out, of which only 11 were determined to be significant; only 3 were of moderate effect size. The HAPP-3 does not appear to be biased with regard to gender or ethnicity. In addition, administrators are instructed to refer to the child's linguistic community when making decisions regarding appropriate pronunciations of the various stimulus words, thus reducing bias further.

Finally, construct validity was assessed utilizing age and group differentiation. Phonological production abilities should improve with age. As a result, phonological production errors should decrease with age. Data provided in the manual indicated that the raw score means for the normative data decreased with age, thus supporting validity. The correlation coefficient reported was .41. Group differentiation, like age differentiation, can be used to support validity. A test of language development should be able to differentiate between groups of young children who are known to have phonological impairment and those who do not have phonological impairment. Although data reported in the manual indicated that individuals who had phonological processing impairment ($n = 21$) had a mean Ability Score ($M = 75$) lower than the normative sample ($n = 886$, $M = 97$), there were no statistical procedures to indicate the significance of this difference. In addition, there were no differences between males and females, or between Caucasians, African Americans, Hispanic-Americans, and others. Again, there were no statistical procedures performed to substantiate the lack of difference between these groups' means.

Construct validity is also typically examined by comparing the results of a particular test with others that are purported to measure the same construct. This type of assessment of construct validity was not performed. Item validity was assessed instead in which a coefficient is produced by correlating each item with the total score on the test, which was obviously quite similar to the conventional item analysis reported above.

In conclusion, the case for validity was established. Age differentiation data indicated that phonological deficiencies decreased with age, which provides validity evidence given that phonological production errors are purported to decrease with age. The case for group differentiation also supported validity in that children with phonological impairments had lower mean Ability scores than the mean of the normative sample.

The PPS record form and the MWS record form are quite similar and provide sections for identifying information (e.g., child's name, gender, grade, and age [date of examination, date of birth, chronological age], parent/caregiver, school/agency, and examiner's name); record of phonological deviations (e.g., transcriptions, consonant omissions, consonant category deficiencies, metathesis migration, assimilations, and other deviations); and a short section for the summary of the performance. In this section, there are several questions to be answered by the examiner. If two or more of the questions are answered "yes" the child is referred for the Comprehensive Phonological Evaluation.

The stimulus materials for the two screening instruments and the CPE are appropriate for the age of the child to be assessed. The examiner's manual is very well written and provides specific and useful information regarding the administration of the HAPP-3. In addition, the manual has very good chapters regarding developing intervention priorities and developing phonological interventions.

SUMMARY. The HAPP-3 is an assessment instrument that can be used to screen the phonological production ability of children aged 3 years to 7 years, 11 months of age, and to carefully assess the phonological deviations of children who have unintelligible speech. The HAPP-3 has only one form. Therefore, with no alternative form, it is limited for research studies that assess phonological deviations more than one time of measurement. Research designs typically require that alternative forms of a test be used at different times of testing to reduce the likelihood of time of measurement or practice effects. The most recent edition of the HAPP-3 provides a reliable and valid measure of the phonological deviations of children aged 3 years to 7 years, 11 months who have unintelligible speech.

REVIEWER'S REFERENCES

Bernhardt, B., & Stoel-Gammon, C. (1994). Nonlinear phonology: Introduction and clinical application. *Journal of Speech and Hearing Research, 37,* 123-143.
Chomsky, N., & Halle, M. (1968). *The sound pattern of English.* New York: Harper & Row.
Stampe, D. (1969). The acquisition of phonetic representation. *Papers from the fifth regional meeting of the Chicago Linguistic Society* (pp. 443-454). Chicago: Chicago Linguistic Society.

Review of the Hodson Assessment of Phonological Patterns—Third Edition by VINCENT J. SAMAR, Associate Professor, Department of Research, National Technical Institute for the Deaf, Rochester, NY:

GENERAL DESCRIPTION. The Hodson Assessment of Phonological Patterns—Third Edition (HAPP-3) is a norm-referenced and criterion-referenced test that assesses and analyzes phonological deviations in children with highly unintelligible speech. The test is also designed to provide a treatment direction for these children and to provide posttreatment data that can be used to document evidence-based practice. The HAPP-3 is capable of identifying broad patterns of phonological deviations, including (a) Word/Syllable Structure deviations (e.g., omissions of syllables, consonants in sequences/clusters, and singleton consonants), (b) Consonant Category Deficiencies deviations (e.g., omissions and specific substitutions of consonants), and (c) Substitutions and Other Strategies that children use to compensate for speech sounds with which they have difficulty (e.g., assimilations). The test includes a Preschool Phonological Screening component for children ages 2 and up, a Multisyllabic Word Screening component for children older than age 8, and a longer Comprehensive Phonological Evaluation component for detailed analysis of phonological deviations in children ages 3–8.

The HAPP-3 is a revision and extension of the earlier Assessment of Phonological Processes—Revised (APP-R; Hodson, 1986). The HAPP-3 is a substantial improvement due to updating the target words to generalize better internationally across English language communities; improving the usability of forms; adding three-dimensional objects to the kit to elicit utterances; and, most importantly, adding norms, reliability data, and evidence of validity.

The HAPP-3 kit is provided with an examiner's manual, 50 Preschool Phonological Screening record forms, 50 Multisyllabic Word Screening record forms, 25 Comprehensive Phonological Evaluation record forms, 25 Major Phonological Deviations Analysis forms, 25 Substitutions and Other Strategies Analysis forms, 1 Multisyllabic Word Screening picture sheet, a 30-piece kit of common, easily recognized objects, and 13 picture cards.

Test administration. The HAPP-3 is administered individually to children. The Preschool Phonological Screening and Multisyllable Word Screening, each of which contains 12 target items and requires only about 2–3 minutes to administer, can be used to screen large numbers of children quickly. For the Preschool Phonological Screening, the examiner uses 11 three-dimensional objects (and a pointing reference to the examiner's own nose) to elicit speech from the child. For the Multisyllable Word Screening, the examiner uses 12 pictures to elicit speech from the child. Children who do not pass the screening tests can be administered the Comprehensive Phonological Evaluation for in-depth follow-up evaluation (20 minutes administration time). For the Comprehensive Phonological Evaluation, the examiner uses a combination of three-dimensional objects (e.g., a toy boat, a package of gum) and pictures (e.g., a cloud) to elicit production of 50 specific stimulus words.

Manual, forms, and materials. The HAPP-3 manual provides a brief overview of the design and usage of the HAPP-3; information about the qualifications of examiners; the criteria for selecting children to be tested and administration of the HAPP-3 components; extensive directions for analyzing phonological deviations, transcribing stimulus words, and completing the HAPP-3 forms; a discussion of how to determine and interpret HAPP-3 severity levels and how to prioritize the selection of target phonemes for intervention; a description of the Cycles Phonological Remediation Approach, the phonological remediation program originally developed by the author; an appendix that describes the HAPP-3 normative sample, its reliability, and its validity; and an appendix that provides a table for converting HAPP-3 consonant category deficiencies raw scores to an ability score (a standardized score) and to percentile ranks for different ages.

The forms are logically organized and easy to use. Each prescreening form is clearly laid out for recording and classifying specific phonological deviations for 12 target stimuli. A convenient checklist summarizing performance appears at the bottom of the screening forms and permits a rapid decision whether to administer the longer Comprehensive Phonological Evaluation. For the Comprehensive Phonological Evaluation, the evaluator transcribes the child's speech deviations during naming, using a convenient, one-page transcription form organized in a grid structure. These transcriptions are later transferred to the Major Phonological Deviations Analysis form for error classification, organized in columns according to Word/Syllable Structures and Consonant Category Deficiencies, and subdivided into error pattern categories within these broad classifications. An additional Substitutions and Other Strategies Analysis form provides a checklist grid to classify 28 specific substitutions, distortions, additions, and position changes in a word. Finally, the Comprehensive Phonological Evaluation record form is used to summarize the specific occurrences of major phonological deviations and of substitutions

and other strategies, to compute percentages of major phonological deviations, and to record the child's normative ability score and percentile rank for the Consonant Category Deficiencies Sum by reference to the tabled norms in the manual.

The HAPP-3 stimulus materials are generally easily identified. Most pictures do not contain any text (i.e., the object they represent can be identified by the child without reading). However, occasionally a picture contains text labels (e.g., "aluminum foil") that are required to disambiguate the stimulus target represented by the drawing. These items may be more difficult for a child to recognize and therefore to name verbally if the child has a reading disability in addition to an intelligibility problem. Therefore, it is important that the evaluator be aware that a child's production target and production speed on such items may be affected by a reading problem.

Adequacy of the normative sample, reliability, and validity. The HAPP-3 is based on a normative sample drawn from 22 states and the District of Columbia. The demographic characteristics of the sample compare favorably with the socioeconomic and ethnicity demographics of the 2001 U.S. Census. However, the demographic characteristics given in the manual list only "white," "black," and "other" under the category of race. It is unclear from the demographic characteristics given in the manual to what the designation "other" refers. Therefore, it is unclear whether the demographic sample contained a representative percentage of either Hispanics or Asian/Pacific Islanders, a numerically substantial segment of the U.S. population.

Reliability statistics indicate generally high overall reliability. Content sampling reliability, as indicated by coefficient alpha, for the whole normative sample was very high on average and at each age from 3 to 7 years (above .95). The manual does not address the acceptability of the content sampling reliability of the HAPP-3 for different genders and ethnicity groups because it does not provide separate coefficients alpha for these groups, a concern that should be corrected in a subsequent revision. Coefficient alpha for 11 separate patterns of major phonological deviations, obtained from a small sample of 30 specifically phonologically impaired children, were generally high as well (from .87 to .99). Time sampling reliability, using test-retest correlations, obtained from a small sample of 59 children over a period of about 2 weeks, was .99. Finally, interscorer reliability correlation coefficients between two scorers, for 30 children drawn randomly from the normative sample, ranged from .89 to .99 across 11 categories of major phonological deviation patterns.

The content-description validity of the HAPP-3 is sound and well grounded in phonological theory. However, the empirical validity studies presented in the manual, although a good beginning, are limited in scope. Conventional item analysis suggests acceptable item validity, and differential item functioning analysis suggests that less than 1% of the items on the test are potentially biased for gender or for race/ethnicity (limited to comparisons of African American versus non-African American groups and Hispanic-American versus non-Hispanic-American groups). Differential item functioning analyses should be studied with respect to other racial/ethnic American groups (e.g., Asian/Pacific Islander).

Construct validity is suggested by the results of a study that shows diminishing normative raw score values as a function of increasing age, as expected from the fact that phonological skills are developmental in nature. Construct validity is also suggested by a study that shows that different gender and ethnicity groups from the normative sample had equivalent high normative raw score values on average, whereas a group of independently sampled children with phonological impairment had numerically depressed normative raw score values on average compared with the other groups. (The statistics defining this result were not presented in the manual.)

Curiously, the results of a concurrent validity study conducted by the HAPP-3 test developer were not included in the section of the manual on validity, but rather appear in connection with a discussion on determining HAPP-3 severity levels. The study showed that the HAPP-3 Total Occurrences of Major Phonological Deviations (TOMPD) score, which sums phonological deviations with consonant category deficiencies, correlated -.98 with an independently developed measure of the severity of phonological deviations (the Percentages of Consonants Correct-Revised metric). This result appears to provide substantial empirical support for the criterion-related validity of the TOMPD metric provided by the HAPP-3.

Further studies, involving larger samples of children and extended to additional racial/ethnic

groups, are needed to quantify and verify the validity of the HAPP-3 and its sensitivity to types and severity of phonological deviations.

SUMMARY. The HAPP-3 is a carefully designed screening tool and comprehensive evaluation instrument for the identification and assessment of phonological deviation in children. The HAPP-3 is a significant improvement over its predecessor (the APP-R) both by virtue of design and of the inclusion of a serious initial demonstration of its reliability and validity. The HAPP-3 is particularly valuable because of its ability to provide significant evidence-based input to the clinical determination of intervention priorities and to the evaluation of the success of intervention.

[88]
Index of Teaching Stress.

Purpose: Designed to "assess the effects of a specific student's behavior on a teacher's stress level and self-perception."

Population: Teachers from preschool to 12th grade.

Publication Dates: 2003–2004.

Acronym: ITS.

Scores, 12: Total Stress Score, Attention-Deficit/Hyperactivity Disorder, Student Characteristics (Emotional Lability/Low Adaptability, Anxiety/Withdrawal, Low Ability/Learning Disability, Aggressive/Conduct Disorder, Total); Teacher Characteristics (Sense of Competence/Need for Support, Loss of Satisfaction From Teaching, Disruption of the Teaching Process, Frustration Working With Parents, Total).

Administration: Group.

Price Data, 2007: $134 per introductory kit including manual (2004, 89 pages), 25 reusable item booklets, 25 answer sheets, and 25 profile forms.

Time: (20–25) minutes.

Authors: Richard R. Abidin, Ross W. Greene, and Timothy R. Konold.

Publisher: Psychological Assessment Resources, Inc.

Review of the Index of Teaching Stress by MILDRED MURRAY-WARD, Dean, College of Education, California State University, Stanislaus, Turlock, CA:

DESCRIPTION. The Index of Teaching Stress (ITS) is a unique instrument that measures teacher stress in relation to interactions with students. Unlike other instruments that measure teacher stress by focusing on global measures of job satisfaction, the ITS focuses on specific student behaviors and teachers' specific feelings of self-efficacy as a teacher in the student-teacher relationship.

The primary purpose of the ITS is to measure teacher stress experienced through interactions with a specific student. The authors state that the ITS allows assessment of students and provides data for consultation with teachers to maximize teacher effectiveness with a specific child. Indeed, the last section of the manual contains suggestions for clinical and research applications. The manual also provides profiles or case studies presenting score profiles and interpretations of results. In addition, the authors claim that through this assessment process teacher stress may be reduced, teacher objectivity could be increased, and teacher student relationships could be enhanced.

The target group for whom the instrument is intended is composed of teachers in preschool to 12th grade in regular or special education classroom settings.

The instrument is composed of 90 statements, organized through careful development and analysis into three scales. The first is the Attention-Deficit/Hyperactivity Disorder Domain composed of 16 items. Second is the Student Characteristics Domain (31 items), including the following scales: Emotional Lability/Low Adaptability, Anxiety/Withdrawal, Low Ability/Learning Disability, and Aggressiveness/Conduct Disorder. Third, the Teacher Characteristics Domain is composed of 43 items, including the following scales: Sense of Competence/Need for Support, Loss of Satisfaction From Teaching, Disruption of the Teaching Process, and Frustration Working With Parents.

Respondents use two different 5-point response scales. For Part A, respondents choose from: 1—*Never Stressful* to 5—*Very Often Stressful*. For Part B, respondents use: 1—*Never Distressing* to 5—*Very Distressing*.

DEVELOPMENT. The ITS was developed based on a model of Teaching Stress initially designed in 1989 in response to the need for a teacher stress instrument comparable to the Parenting Stress Index (Abidin, 1983, 1995). The model uses six understandings of human behavior:

(a) recognition that temperament plays a major dispositional role in exhibited behavior; (b) attachment style and interpersonal relationships are both motivational sources and moderators of disposition; (c) cultural and social skills are factors that influence the expression and interpretation of behavior; (d) behavior is learned, shaped, and

influenced by behavioral factors ranging from cues to reinforcements; (e) human behavioral and emotional responses are both produced and moderated by perceptions and cognitions; and (f) behavior is embedded in social and physical contexts that influence behavioral expression, cognitions, and emotions. (professional manual, p. 2).

The ITS was created from a strong theoretical foundation clearly explained in the professional manual. The items were created through examination of the impact of students on teacher behavior and teachers' attitude toward self. The authors claim that the instrument is unique in that it focuses on students and their relationship to teacher stress and not other occupational factors that may contribute to teacher stress levels.

The authors created the 90-item instrument by first conducting focus groups with teachers who reported student characteristics, thoughts about themselves, and school contexts. A total of 108 items were generated from the information obtained from the focus groups. The 108 items were reduced to 90 and factor analyzed into two scales. The authors clearly described this process and their rationale for technical decisions, including the reasoning behind establishing a separate ADHD scale.

TECHNICAL.

Standardization. Technical qualities of the ITS are clearly discussed in the manual. The final instrument was normed on a sample of 814 teachers who rated randomly selected students. The teachers ranged from 1 to 41 (mean of 14.0) years of experience, with the majority in regular classrooms (16.4% in special education classrooms). The students ranged from ages 5 to 18 years (mean of 10.9). The teachers and students were matched to the most recent U.S. Census and included teachers from Georgia, Massachusetts, New York, Texas, and Virginia. Student characteristics were matched to 1995 NCES data on student populations.

The 674 teachers who rated students with specifically identified behavior problems had a mean of 13.7 years of experience, with 17.3% in special education classrooms. The rated students were from 5 to 18 (mean 10.2) years of age. It was not clear whether there was any overlap in the group of teachers who rated randomly selected students and those with specific behavior problems. Again, the group selected was matched to 1995 NCES data.

Normative scores include percentiles and *T*-scores. The authors also looked at possible grade-level effects on ratings and found no significant differences in ratings of students from three different grade levels.

The authors recommend choosing the Randomly Selected Student Sample norms when determining teachers' scores relative to other teachers, child study, and in case consultation and other clinical situations. The authors recommend using both sets of norms to illustrate findings such as comparing teacher scores with those teachers who also teach behavior problem students, and in gauging the relative severity of the classroom situation.

Reliability. Both internal consistency and test-retest reliability of the ITS were examined. Internal consistency reliability alpha coefficients exceeded .90 for the ITS domains and Total score for the Behavior Problem Student and Randomly Selected Student samples. Test-retest reliability was estimated with 42 white teachers' ratings of the same Behavior Problem Students using a 1-month interval. Reliabilities ranged from .30 to .70 for the domains, .57 for Student Characteristics, .70 for Teacher Characteristics, and .65 for Total Stress. The reliability studies provide evidence that the instrument is internally consistent and moderately sensitive to "episodic" student behavior.

Validity. In the area of validity, the authors established the content validity of the items through the use of teacher focus groups and using the responses to generate ITS items. The authors also explored discriminant and concurrent validity. The discriminant validity studies revealed that the scores were not related to general stress of teachers. In addition, the scores are sensitive to intervention and positively related to teacher ratings of likelihood of the student being referred for services. Concurrent validity studies indicated that scores on the ITS are positively related to the students' social skills, and negatively related to the quality of the teacher-student relationship. Interestingly, female teachers were more stressed with male students and male teachers were more stressed with female students.

COMMENTARY. The ITS is a unique and interesting instrument that may help in assessing teacher-student relationships. It serves a vital need in examining student-related stress in teachers that could impact classroom interactions and resulting learning environments. The instrument has several strengths. First, it possesses a strong theoretical foundation and research base. Second, the technical qualities and processes of development appear excellent. Of particular note are the studies establishing content validity and the procedures used to develop the scales. The authors were also careful to examine cutscore ranges that could trigger intervention.

Although the instrument does possess excellent qualities, there are some weaknesses and notes of caution. First, although the authors clearly discuss the application of the Randomly Selected Student Sample, they do not provide as clear directions on use of the Behavior Problem Student Sample. In addition, the authors provide some interesting case studies using profiles of teachers and specific students. Although these are interesting examples, the profiles include interpretation of scores and accompanying actions not validated in previous studies. Because these cases are not based on empirical studies, the reader is cautioned not to overinterpret the scale scores.

SUMMARY. The ITS is a high quality instrument designed to examine teacher stress levels. The instrument is an important addition to the field because teacher stress can impact the quality of the learning environment and, therefore, the learning potential for students. The authors' careful attention to instrument development make it an excellent tool in forming an understanding of student-teacher interaction as information used in part to generate student interventions. As with any instrument, this reviewer recommends the use of multiple data sources. Therefore, when using the ITS, additional data on classroom environment should be collected and considered in making such determinations.

REVIEWER'S REFERENCES

Abidin, R. R. (1983). Parenting Stress Index. Charlottesville, VA: Pediatric Psychology Press.
Abidin, R. R. (1995). *Parenting Stress Index: Professional manual* (3rd ed.). Odessa, FL: Psychological Assessment Resources.

[89]

Infant/Toddler Environment Rating Scale—Revised Edition.

Purpose: Designed to assess programs for children from birth to 30 months of age in group care settings.
Population: Infant/toddler day care centers.
Publication Dates: 1990–2006.
Acronym: ITERS-R.

Scores, 8: Space and Furnishings, Personal Care Routines, Listening and Talking, Activities, Interaction, Program Structure, Parents and Staff, Total.
Administration: Individual.
Price Data, 2006: $14.95 per rating scale (2006, 79 pages) including administration and scoring instructions and score sheet and profile that may be photocopied.
Time: (180) minutes to observe and rate.
Authors: Thelma Harms, Debby Cryer, and Richard M. Clifford.
Publisher: Teachers College Press.
Cross References: See T5:1264 (6 references); for reviews by Norman A. Constantine and Annette M. Iverson of an earlier edition, see 12:188.

Review of the Infant/Toddler Environment Rating Scale—Revised Edition by KAREN CAREY, Professor of Psychology, California State University, Fresno, CA:

DESCRIPTION. The Infant/Toddler Environment Rating Scale—Revised Edition (ITERS-R) considered in this review is not a revision, per se, but according to the authors is an updated edition. The ITERS, a criterion-referenced test, was first available in 1990 and updated in 2004 as the ITERS-R. The scale is designed to assess child care programs for children from birth to 30 months. The scale can be used by a classroom teacher or outside observer and a video training package is available from Teacher's College Press. A training sequence led by experienced trainers is recommended, and users should conduct at least two practice observations with experienced trainers. Three hours are recommended for observation, and an additional 20–30 minutes are required for questions of the teacher or other staff members. The spiral-bound booklet contains the items and a scoring sheet. The scale consists of 39 items (with 467 indicators) that are categorized into seven subscales: Space and Furnishings, Personal Care Routines, Listening and Talking, Activities, Interaction, Program Structure, and Parents and Staff. Indicators are examples provided on each item. According to the authors, items were selected based on research from health, development, and education; best practices; and real world constraints of providing child care to very young children; however, the specifics of how items were generated and selected is not described in the brief eight-page "Introduction to the ITERS-R." Each subscale contains from 3 to 10 items. Items are rated on a 7-point scale from 1 (inadequate), 3 (minimal), 5 (good), and 7 (excellent). One of the changes on the revised edition includes indicators under each level of quality (e.g., 1, 3, 5, or 7) numbered so that they can be a given score of "Yes," "No," or "Not applicable (NA)."

DEVELOPMENT. The revision was based on research of child care environments, a content comparison of the ITERS with other instruments, research with the ITERS by the co-authors, and feedback from users of the scale provided through a questionnaire. Changes on the revised edition included elimination of scoring exceptions on the ITERS; expanded Notes for Clarification; additional indicators and examples; new items added for some subscales; combining items on some subscales to eliminate redundancy; the use of gradual scaling on some subscales to better reflect varying levels of health practices, and changes to the materials (each item is printed on a separate page, and sample questions are now included for indicators that may be difficult to observe). Specific information about these changes and updates is not included in the manual.

TECHNICAL. To establish reliability of the ITERS-R a two-phase study of interrater reliability was completed, including a pilot and a "more formal" study. Ten trained observers in groups of two to three participated in the study using a revised version of the scale and conducted 12 observations in nine centers. Data obtained from this study resulted in modifications to the scale, although information in the manual does not describe what specific modifications were made. The formal study included six trained observers who conducted 45 paired observations lasting 3 hours followed by a 20–30-minute teacher interview. Centers included in the study were selected based on North Carolina award rankings for quality. A center meeting basic requirements received a star of 1 point whereas centers with very high standards received a 5-star ranking. Of the centers selected for inclusion in the study, 15 had a 1–2-star ranking, 15 had a 3-star ranking, and 15 had a 4–5-star ranking. For the paired observations, 15 children were under 12 months of age, 15 were between 12 and 24 months, and 15 children were between 18–30 months of age. Interrater reliabilities ranged from .79 to .97 for indicator reliability, from .64 to .98 for item reliability, and .92 for intraclass correlations. Internal consistency for the subscales using coefficient alpha ranged from .47 to .80, .92 for the overall scale, and .92 for child-related items. Information related to concurrent and predictive validity of the revised scale was not provided in the manual. According to the authors, "Since the concurrent and predictive validity of the original ITERS is well established and the current revision maintains the basic properties of the original instrument, the studies of the ITERS-R have focused on the degree to which the revised version maintains the ability of trained observers to use the scale" (manual, p. 2).

COMMENTARY. The ITERS-R appears to be an interesting tool for assessing the ecology of a child care environment and may provide some useful information; however, without knowledge of the ITERS or information provided through training, the technical adequacy of the instrument is unknown as provided in the current manual. The authors do note that further studies are needed to establish content and construct validity, as well as test-retest reliability of the ITERS-R. Information related to best practices in conducting observations, how to interpret the scale, and recommendations for changing child care environments is also not provided in the manual.

SUMMARY. The ITERS-R has the potential to be a useful tool to assess the child care environments of young children. However, the manual needs substantial revision as it does not meet the *Standards for Educational and Psychological Testing* (AERA, APA, & NCME, 1999). The technical adequacy of the scale needs to be thoroughly researched before it is used by practitioners wanting to determine the quality of child care settings.

REVIEWER'S REFERENCE

American Educational Research Association, American Psychological Association, & National Council on Measurement in Education. (1999). *Standards for educational and psychological testing*. Washington, DC: American Educational Research Association.

Review of the Infant/Toddler Environment Rating Scale—Revised Edition by JOSEPH C. KUSH, Associate Professor, Duquesne University, Pittsburgh, PA:

DESCRIPTION. The original version of the Infant/Toddler Environment Rating Scale (ITERS) was reviewed in the 12th edition of *The Mental Measurements Yearbook*. The ITERS-R does not directly measure the behaviors of young children; rather it was created as a rating scale for day care and preschool settings and was adapted from the original Early Childhood Environment Rating Scale (ECERS; Harms & Clifford, 1980). The

criterion-referenced instrument consists of 39 items, organized into seven subscales, and is intended to assess programs for children from birth to 30 months of age. The authors indicate that the instrument was designed to be used by preschool teachers and day care staff, or by agency administrators, to assist with program planning and evaluation. Additionally the authors recommend that the ITERS-R can be used for research purposes.

In the Introduction to the ITERS-R, the authors write, "The Infant/Toddler Environment Rating Scale-Revised Edition (ITERS-R) is a thorough revision of the original Infant/Toddler Environment Rating Scale (ITERS, 1990)" (manual, p. 1). Changes between the ITERS and the ITERS-R, identified in the manual include: (a) Indicators under each level of quality in some items were numbered so that they could be given a score of "Yes," "No," or "Not Applicable." (b) Negative indicators were removed from one item. In the minimal, good, and excellent levels only indicators of positive attributes are listed. This change eliminates the one exception to the scoring rule in the original ITERS. (c) Several subscales and indicators were slightly revised (e.g., "Cultural awareness" was renamed: "Promoting acceptance of diversity"; "Caregiver-child interaction" was renamed: "Staff-child interaction"). (d) Several items in the Space and Furnishings subscale were combined to remove redundancies, and two items were dropped in Personal Care Routines. (e) The scaling of several items in Personal Care Routines was made more gradual to better reflect varying levels of health practices in real life situations. (f) New items were added to several subscales.

Following the revision of the scale, the ITERS-R then underwent a minor update. In the preface to the updated edition, the authors write, "This updated edition of the ITERS-R is not a revision. It contains all of the ITERS-Revised Edition with all items and indicators intact" (manual, p. v). Specifically, the ITERS-R now includes Additional Notes (previously available via the website), a new expanded scoresheet, and an improved spiral binder.

The seven subscales of the ITERS-R have been slightly renamed and include: Space and Furnishings, Personal Care Routines, Listening and Talking, Activities, Interaction, Program Structure, and Parents and Staff. As indicated by the authors, the goal of the scale is to "assess provision in the environment for the protection of children's health and safety, appropriate stimulation through language and activities, and warm, supportive interaction" (manual, p. 1). Guidelines for the completion of the ITERS-R are improved from the previous version, and scoring criteria are also more thoroughly detailed.

The authors indicate that individuals who are familiar with the day care facility will require approximately 2 hours to observe the setting and complete the instrument. Individuals who are outside observers and are not a member of the teaching staff should set aside a minimum of an additional 3 hours for a comprehensive and valid rating. Additional suggestions for administration alert the observer that some questions are only able to be observed at specific times of the day or only after sufficient observation time has elapsed. Observers are encouraged to allocate approximately 20–30 minutes for asking questions of the teacher regarding indicators that could not be directly observed. Finally, observers are cautioned to situate themselves in an observational location that does not disrupt the class, not talk to or interrupt the staff or children, and to maintain a pleasant but neutral facial expression.

The 10-page ITERS-R score sheet allows users to record ratings for indicators, items, subscale and total scores, and provides an area to record comments. Indicator examples have been added to the scale to make items more precise and culturally sensitive. The accompanying profile sheet allows users to present this information graphically in order to compare areas of strength and weakness visually. The score sheet includes opportunities to record both indicator and item scores. Indicator scores are Y (Yes), N (No), and NA (not applicable). Additionally, item quality scores rank observations from 1 (Inadequate) through 7 (Excellent). Because subscales are based on varying numbers of items, the instruction manual now instructs users that in order to compare subscales accurately, these subscale scores must be divided by the number of items in the subscale. Because the ITERS-R is criterion-referenced, no norms are provided.

RELIABILITY. Reliability values reported in the user's manual were based on 90 observations with two paired observations in 45 group settings. This represents an increase from the 60 observations (30 paired observations) obtained during the development of the original ITERS. All centers were located in central North Carolina. The user's manual reports an overall coefficient alpha of .93 for the ITERS-R Full Scale (Items 1–39). Subscale alphas range from .47 (Space and Furnishing) to .80 (Interaction). Many of the subscale internal consistency reliabilities are actually unacceptably low (e.g., Personal Care Routines .56; Parents and Staff .68) despite the author's claim that, "Cronbach's alphas of .6 and higher are generally considered acceptable levels of internal consistency" (manual, p. 4). The authors do recognize this limitation to some degree by acknowledging, "caution should be taken in using the Space and Furnishing and Personal Care Routines subscales" (manual, p. 4). Possible explanations for these low levels of internal consistency reliability as well as any attempt to improve these levels since the time of the publication of the original ITERS are glaringly absent. Also unfortunately absent is the reporting of any standard errors of measurement values.

Regarding indicator reliability, the total level of agreement across all indicator scores is reported to be 91.65%. Only one item was reported to have an indicator agreement level of less than 80% (Item 11, Safety practices), whereas staff professional needs (Item 35) produced an agreement level of 97.36%. For the Full Scale, an intraclass correlation of .92 is reported.

Individual item reliabilities are reported both by percentage of rater agreement and by Cohen's Kappa statistic. Using a criterion of agreement between raters such that rater scores were within 1 point of each other on the 7-point scale, an overall agreement level across the full 39 items was obtained in 85% of the cases. Again using this criterion, paired-observer agreement ranged from 64% (Room arrangement, Item 4) to 98% (Evaluation of staff, Item 38). Similarly a Cohen's Kappa value of .58 was reported for the full 39-item scale. Individual items ranged from .14 to .92. Several items were identified by the authors as possessing unacceptable Kappa values (Diapering/toileting .14; Safety practices .20), and the authors subsequently made unspecified "minor changes to improve the reliability of the item without changing its basic content" (manual, p. 3) although no follow-up statistics are reported. Finally, no test-retest reliability coefficients are reported in the user's manual. As mentioned previously, although several of the low reliability coefficients are pointed out in the manual, the implications of these results are not fully explained nor are suggestions for improving reliability coefficients (e.g., improved scoring rubrics).

VALIDITY. No evidence of any type of validity is reported in the user's manual. Potential users are merely provided with the author's statement, "Since the concurrent and predictive validity of the original ITERS is well established and the current revision maintains the basic properties of the original instrument, the studies of the ITERS-R have focused on the degree to which the revised version maintains the ability of trained observers to use the scale reliably" (manual, p. 2). Quite simply, the omission of empirical data supporting the validity of the scale is grossly unacceptable.

In the previous MMY reviews of the ITERS (Constantine, 1995; Iverson, 1995), it was reported that content-related validity was established by an item-by-item comparison of the ITERS with seven other infant/toddler program assessment instruments and with eight sets of program standards. Content-related evidence of validity was also based on the ratings that five experts subjectively assigned to each ITERS item. Criterion-related validity was supported by a single study that compared experts' sorting of 12 classrooms into high and low quality groups, producing an overall agreement rate of 83%. Again, this study is not reported in the manual of the current ITERS-R.

Finally, despite concerns expressed previously by both MMY reviewers, the current ITERS-R continues to provide no evidence of any type to support the construct validity of the scale. Correlations among the subscales are not provided, and there is no reported factor-analytic research. As a result, it remains unknown whether the theorized subscales do in fact provide distinct and discreet information, separate from what is yielded from the Full Scale score.

SUMMARY. The ITERS-R continues to provide a criterion-referenced checklist of criteria that can be used to evaluate day care and preschool environments. Although the overall scale may have some value for program planning, the lack of solid reliability evidence makes its use for program evaluation or research purposes entirely unacceptable. Previous reviews expressed reservations about the clinical utility of the scale and the revised version fails to address many of these concerns. Internal consistency is adequate for the overall scale but subscale reliabilities vary substantially. There are, additionally,

some unanswered questions about the construct validity of the scale, and it remains unclear exactly how many subscales are being adequately measured by the ITERS-R. It is also unclear how sensitive these subscales are to accurately measuring changes in program quality as a result of training or programmatic structural changes. Finally, although the authors claim that numerous validity studies have been conducted to support the ability of the scale to discriminate among quality of environments and the relationship of quality to child development outcomes, neither these validity statistics nor their citations are reported in the users manual.

REVIEWER'S REFERENCES

Constantine, N. A. (1995). [Review of the Infant/Toddler Environment Rating Scale]. In J. C. Conoley & J. C. Impara (Eds.), *The twelfth mental measurements yearbook* (pp. 483–485). Lincoln, NE: Buros Institute of Mental Measurements.

Harme, T. & Clifford, R. M. (1980). Early Childhood Environment Rating Scale. New York: Teachers College Press.

Iverson, A. M. (1995). [Review of the Infant/Toddler Environment Rating Scale]. In J. C. Conoley & J. C. Impara (Eds.), *The twelfth mental measurements yearbook* (pp. 485–486). Lincoln, NE: Buros Institute of Mental Measurements.

[90]

InstrumenTest (Form AIT-C).

Purpose: For selecting instrument technicians.
Population: Applicants and incumbents for jobs requiring technical knowledge and skills of instrumentation.
Publication Dates: 2001–2005.
Scores, 8: Mathematics & Basic AC/DC Theory, Analog & Digital Electronics and Power Supplies, Schematics & Electrical Print Reading, Process Control, Test Instruments, Mechanical and Hand & Power Tools, Computers & PLC, Total.
Administration: Group.
Price Data, 2007: $21 per consumable self-scoring test booklet (minimum order of 20); $24.95 per manual (2005, 15 pages).
Time: (60) minutes (untimed).
Comments: Self-scoring instrument.
Author: Roland T. Ramsay.
Publisher: Ramsay Corporation.

Review of the InstrumenTest (Form AIT-C) by SUZANNE YOUNG, Associate Professor of Educational Research, University of Wyoming, Laramie, WY:

DESCRIPTION. The InstrumenTest (Form AIT-C), published by the Ramsay Corporation, was developed to test the skills and knowledge of applicant and incumbent instrument technicians. According to the manual, this form is a shortened version of the RCJS Instrumentation Technician Test. The test is available only in paper form.

According to the test manual, this 60-item test is not timed. Examiners are told that the test-takers should not need more than an hour to complete the test. However, the manual asks the examiner, in preparation for the testing, to bring a stopwatch or other timer. Also, the manual states that specified time limits must be observed. In a review of an earlier version of this test, the Instrument Technician published in 1990, a reviewer (Bugbee, 1998) noted the same discrepancy.

The test administration instructions are very detailed and surprising in some ways. The author scripts the precise administration instructions and also explains the tone and attitude the examiner should exhibit. The examiner is told to "unobtrusively ... check the work of each examinee" (manual, p. 5) during the test to be sure directions are being followed. Although this reviewer agrees that the administration of tests is important and should be consistent, asking examiners to take a look at each examinee's work seems somewhat improper to this reviewer. In addition, the examiner is told to watch the examinees carefully and to make note of "any significant behavior" (manual, p. 5). Test examiners may or may not be well prepared to observe or recognize such behavior; they may need some additional training to develop skills so they understand what is in the normal range.

The test is a self-scoring test booklet. Each section of the test receives its own total score, and section totals are summed for an overall score. The manual does not provide any interpretation of section scores or the total score. It appears that the examinees do not do the scoring but that is not specifically stated.

DEVELOPMENT. According to the manual, the InstrumenTest is a shortened version of the Instrumentation Technician Test (two versions) published in 1993. Although the author states that job analyses were conducted during the development stages of the test, the details of the job analysis are lacking. The manual includes a table showing 10 general knowledge and skills areas and says that these correspond with the actual job skills and body of knowledge. Evidence to support that claim is not provided.

The author explains how the items for the shortened version were chosen; 60 items were selected proportionally from seven categories using item difficulty indices and point-biserial correlations. Of the 60 items, 23 items have difficulty indices greater than .75, indicating they were difficult questions. The remaining item difficulties are between .25 and .75; they were neither difficult nor easy for the development sample. Clearly this test was designed to be quite challenging. The point-biserial correlations are all positive, ranging from .31 to .68, showing that the items correlate appropriately with the overall test score. In one of the reviews of an earlier version (the Instrument Technician test, published in 1990), the reviewer (Bugbee, 1998) commented that some items had negative point-biserial correlations; test-takers who missed these items generally scored well on the test. The author eliminated these poorly functioning items in the development of the current version.

TECHNICAL. The validation sample was described in the manual as instrument technician applicants, but no further details of their characteristics were provided. The manual includes a table showing the cumulative percents of the applicants' raw scores. According to the table, the quartiles for the 140 applicants were raw scores of approximately 35 (first quartile), 42 (second quartile), and 48 (third quartile) out of 60 possible points. Thus only 25% of the sample had raw scores of 48 or greater. The mean score for the sample was 40.62 with a standard deviation of 8.84.

The author provided the reliability and standard error of measurement for the validation sample. The reliability was reported to be .87, but the author does not specify the type of reliability, making it difficult to evaluate. The standard error of measurement was identified as 3.19, indicating a relatively wide interval for interpreting an individual's score. For example, at a 95% confidence level, the true score for an individual with a test score of 45 would be between approximately 39 and 51 (between 65% and 85% correct).

The manual includes a discussion of content, criterion, and construct validity. The primary evidence is content validity, based on the correspondence between test items and the job itself. According to the *Standards for Educational and Psychological Testing* (AERA, APA, & NCME, 1999), the primary basis for validity when tests are used to make employment decisions should be job analysis. However, the manual does not provide a discussion of the job analysis in any detail, other than to say that job analysis studies were conducted during the development of the original test. Evidence for the test is based on content-related validity; the logic apparently is that if the evidence for content validity is strong, test scores would likely predict job performance. The author suggests that construct validity is evidenced by the development of the test; however, the development is based on content validity.

COMMENTARY. The InstrumenTest is attractive because it uses the best items from a longer version of the same test. The reliability for the test is strong but the validity is questionable. The author should provide more detail about the job analysis originally conducted, considering that the development and validity of the InstrumenTest are based almost entirely on the original test. The entire argument for validity is circular and unconvincing: Job analysis, which is not described, is the basis for content validity, content validity is the basis for criterion validity, and the test is useful in measuring the construct of knowledge and skill in instrumentation because of the content.

Given that the test is to be used for applicants as well as those who are currently on the job, a study using instrument technicians would be useful. In addition, the author should provide a more detailed description of the sample.

Based on an earlier version of this test that was reviewed in *The Thirteenth Mental Measurements Yearbook*, the Instrument Technician Test (13:151), the author made significant revisions: larger validation sample, instructions for administering the test, and selection of items that function more efficiently. However, the test reviewers for the earlier version noted many of the same issues: validity evidence, type of reliability, description of the validation sample, the issue of whether or not the test is timed, and the origin of the items themselves. The development of the original test was weak, and little has changed in the current version.

SUMMARY. It is difficult to recommend the use of this test, considering the weaknesses that continue to be apparent. The author could have easily addressed many of the issues that were raised in the reviews of the earlier version but apparently did not do so. For example, it would be a simple matter to state the type of reliability. It is possible that the test items accurately measure the knowledge and skills for an instrument technician, but the test comes up short in too many critical areas, especially those relating to the documentation of its validity.

REVIEWER'S REFERENCES

American Educational Research Association, American Psychological Association, & National Council on Measurement in Education. (1999). *Standards for educational and psychological testing*. Washington, DC: American Educational Research Association.

Bugbee, A. C., Jr. (1998). [Review of the Instrument Technician.] In J. C. Impara & B. S. Plake (Eds.), *The thirteenth mental measurements yearbook* (pp. 515–517). Lincoln, NE: Buros Institute of Mental Measurements.

[91]
Interpersonal Intelligence Inventory.

Purpose: Intended "to identify the teamwork skills individuals demonstrate" in cooperative learning situations.

Population: Grade 6–adult.
Publication Date: 2002.
Acronym: III.
Scores, 5: Attends to Teamwork, Seeks and Shares Information, Communicates with Teammates, Thinks Critically and Creatively, Gets Along with Team.
Administration: Group.
Price Data, 2007: $38 per starter kit including manual of administration and interpretation (46 pages), 10 definitions of team skills booklet, 1 pad of 10 Team Skills Profile forms, and 1 pad of 20 Teamwork Skills forms; $21 per additional manual of administration and interpretation; $23 per additional package of 10 booklets, 1 pad each of Team Skills Profile forms, Team Scoring forms, and Teamwork Skills forms; $24 per sample set (nonreturnable) including 1 manual, 1 booklet, 1 Team Skills Profile form, 1 Team Scoring form, and 1 Teamwork Skills form.
Time: Varies.
Comments: Test can be administered in middle school, high school, college, and universities.
Authors: Paris S. Strom and Robert D. Strom.
Publisher: Scholastic Testing Service, Inc.

Review of the Interpersonal Intelligence Inventory by BRUCE BISKIN, Director of Learning Assessment, Thomas Edison State College, Trenton, NJ:

DESCRIPTION. The Interpersonal Intelligence Inventory (III) was designed as a tool to aid in the assessment of team-building skills. The authors' focus in the manual is on using the III to help team members understand and assess their team-building skills and to help teachers/trainers evaluate the effectiveness of team-building training. The essential information collected and organized by the III comprises peer- and self-endorsements of 25 statements representing five high-level teamwork domains: (a) Attending to Teamwork, (b) Seeking and Sharing Information, (c) Communicating with Teammates, (d) Thinking Critically and Creatively, and (e) Getting Along in a Team. The III is intended to be used for both formative and summative assessment of teamwork skills, and the manual describes how to use the III as part of a 5-week team-building program. The authors maintain that the III is appropriate for teams with members aged 10 through adult.

Participants in team building groups endorse whether each statement applies to themselves and to each other member of the group. Endorsement rates for statements of others in the group are aggregated and percentages reported for both the formative assessment and the summative assessment on the Team Scoring form. These are recorded on the Team Skills Profile form for each participant in the group. Changes in both peer and self-endorsements between the formative and summative assessment are noted on the profile. Though the manual indicates scan forms can be used for collecting participant ratings, preprinted scan forms are not included in the testing materials. The Team Scoring forms that come from the publisher are designed for groups comprising up to six members, which the authors believe to be the optimal group size.

The authors suggest that the III profiles can add value to student portfolios in assessing individual and class performance and for selecting interventions, aiding in teacher development and evaluation, increasing parental involvement in schooling, and evaluating and improving school programming.

DEVELOPMENT. The III is based on Collaboration-Integration Theory (CIT), the authors' model of learning and instruction. The theory, in turn, is built on conceptions of interpersonal intelligence (e.g., Gardner, 2000) and cooperative learning. The manual carefully builds up to the development of the instrument from the theory and its precursors. It also provides a good introduction to the rationale for the III and includes pertinent references for the user who needs further grounding in the theory. The authors are less detailed about describing the links between the model and the creation of the 25 statements that presumably represent the domain of interpersonal intelligence and/or CIT. Though they note that the 25 items were drawn from relevant professional literature, it is unclear whether the 5 items per content cluster are adequate to represent each domain, or whether the inclusion of 5 items per domain is simply a convenience of inventory construction.

The authors have chosen to cluster items in each domain together on the III. For example, the first five items all represent skills that constitute the larger domain of "Attends to Teamwork."

Though the manual states that the III was field tested "extensively with community college and university populations before determining its suitability for adolescents" (manual of administration and interpretation, p. 12), it provides no specific description about the development work with postsecondary students. The authors do provide a reference to such work (Strom & Strom, 2002); however, it would have been useful to provide a summary of this work in the manual.

TECHNICAL. Despite the intent of using the III with a range of high school and college students to assess the effectiveness of training in teamwork skills and cooperative learning, the data presented in the manual are limited to about 300 high school students, almost equally divided between boys and girls. No further subgroup breakdown of the data is available. Because sex differences in self-endorsement of a substantial number of skill statements were found between boys and girls—and the differences were even more pronounced in the peer ratings—subgroup data based on ethnicity and culture also would have been desirable. Data for college students would also have been useful for evaluating the III's imputed appropriateness for that group.

Norms. The authors never refer to the data they provide as "norms," nor should the data be construed as such. Indeed, the sample on which the manual's data are based was not intended to be representative. If users develop local norms, inferences about III ratings for *individuals* based on normative data should be made cautiously—if at all—because of the dependency of individual ratings on the groups to which the individuals belong.

Administration. Each member of a team rates every other member—including themselves—on each of the 25 statements. The peer ratings must then be tallied across team members. If the III is being used as suggested by the authors, it must be administered twice during a training program. Particularly among high school students, there is a risk of "drift" in the consistency of a participant's ratings of the first team member to her or his ratings of the last. After the second set of ratings, profile sheets are completed for each team member and include both self-ratings, peer ratings, and changes in each. Particularly if the III is hand scored and profile sheets are manually generated, there is a high risk of clerical error. In that case, depending on the skill of the scorer, it may be wise to have an independent check of the scoring and recording.

Reliability. The manual does not identify the fundamental level of analysis for evaluating the III. Though skill items are clustered into groups of five, ostensibly representing higher order domains, data are presented primarily at the item (skill) level. Evidence for reliability of scores, however, is presented at the level of the internal consistency (coefficient alpha) for the *entire 25-item instrument*. Based on item-construct correspondence, this reviewer expected the authors to provide separate reliability estimates for each cluster of skills, and an interpretation of the magnitude of the reliability estimates in terms of their consistency with, and representativeness of, the underlying model. In addition, rater reliability and agreement estimates of peer ratings are both pertinent in evaluating the consistency of evaluations across peers, at the levels of both individual statements and skill domains. Finally, correlations between ratings taken at two appropriate points in time (e.g., 2 to 4 weeks apart) with no intervening teambuilding training would provide an estimate of stability of the III, and could serve as a benchmark for evaluating effects of training.

Validity. The authors present scant validity evidence in the manual. Evidence to support the validity of inferences from III scores is limited to the statement, "(a)ll faculty participants in the field test reported that the cooperative learning skills necessary for performance at the high school level are included and well defined" by the III (manual of administration and interpretation, p. 12). I would like to have seen a more detailed description of how the responses were solicited from teachers. With no further description, this statement provides very weak support for the III's content adequacy. The authors do provide agreement percentages between self- and peer-reports as support for validity, noting that agreement was 90% or more for 23 of the 25 statements. However, most of the statements had high endorsement percentages, which result in a high base rate for agreement and confound agreement with positive response style.

This reviewer would have liked the scale authors to have included the results of some type of covariance analysis—such as a factor analysis or structural equation model analysis—to determine whether the structure of III responses—peer, self, and differences between the two types—corresponds to predictions based on the CIT model. Even a simple set of item discrimination analyses by domain could have been useful for evaluating the consistency of the III with the model. The high school data included in the manual would seem to be appropriate for conducting these types of analyses.

COMMENTARY. From a psychometric perspective, the support for the III as a measure of "interpersonal intelligence" is very weak, given the type of reliability estimates and dearth of validity evidence included in the manual. The authors fail to make a convincing argument that the 25 statements adequately represent the five domains of teambuilding skills, which is operationally linked to "interpersonal intelligence" by the III. The authors' conclusions in the manual for the adequacy of reliability and their explanation for unavoidable limitations on collecting evidence for validity of score interpretation (pp. 12-13) simply do not hold up to scrutiny.

Because of the lack of support for the reliability of III scores and the validity of inferences made from those scores, the clearest value of the III is as a tool for teaching teambuilding skills in high school. The manual contains a detailed description of a five-session training module, including how to use the III for both formative and summative assessment. Unless further study supports scores from the III as an adequate operational definition of interpersonal intelligence and the CIT model, the apparent value of the III as a teaching/training tool outstrips its value for summative assessment.

SUMMARY. The developers of the III have taken a significant step in creating a tool that may facilitate teaching and assessing teambuilding skills. More work remains to be done to evaluate how much promise it holds for generating scores about teambuilding skills and interpersonal intelligence that are useful for the various purposes suggested by the authors. If used in training high school students to learn cooperatively, manual scoring and profiling can be burdensome and the results prone to clerical error. Scoring time and errors could be minimized by using optical scan sheets to collect ratings and to generate profiles directly by computer. Until further research is conducted to support the inferences the authors would like to make from III scores, the III's primary value will be as a tool to facilitate teaching teamwork skills.

REVIEWER'S REFERENCES

Gardner, H. (2000). *Intelligence reframed: Multiple intelligences for the 21st century.* New York: Basic Books.
Strom, P. S., & Strom, R. D. (2002). Overcoming limitations of cooperative learning among community college students. *Community College Journal of Research and Practice, 26*(4).

Review of the Interpersonal Intelligence Inventory by ARTHUR S. ELLEN, School Psychologist, New York City Department of Education, New York, NY:

DESCRIPTION. The Interpersonal Intelligence Inventory (III) is an informal assessment used to collect feedback from students engaged in cooperative group learning. Students endorse 25 teamwork skill statements (items) about others in their group (peer) and themselves (self). Skill statements are evenly divided into five categories: Attends to Teamwork, Seeks and Shares Information, Communicates with Teammates, Thinks Critically and Creatively, and Gets Along in the Team. The skill statements include the observable, "This peer arrives on time for team meetings" in the Attends to Teamwork category and the more inferential, "This peer keeps trying even when the task becomes hard" in the Gets Along in the Team category. Each skill is individually interpreted, so no part or total score is derived. Individual skill statements are intended to promote student understanding of group work and to let teachers evaluate group functioning.

Junior-high school to university-level teachers form groups of four to six students who work together for at least 10 weeks. Teachers administer the III twice: first about midterm (formative) and second at about semester's end (summative). Prior to the formative assessment, teachers follow a carefully scripted yet flexible sequence of five exercises to promote group cohesion, to teach students the authors' approach to cooperative group learning, and to facilitate accurate use of the III. For example, in one exercise students study and discuss the Definitions of Teamwork Skills, a five-page booklet providing illustrative statements for each skill. Another exercise has groups discuss sources of rating bias such as favoritism and leniency.

After these group exercises, students privately complete the formative assessment, using two 8.5-inch by 11-inch forms: the Team Scoring form and the Teamwork Skills form. The Team Scoring form has six columns, and each column is to be labeled with the name of one peer. The sixth and last column is reserved for self. In each column below a student's name are the numbers from 1 to 25; each number represents 1 of the 25 skill statements. The second form, the Teamwork Skills form, lists the text of the 25 skill statements. Once the two forms are aligned, a student reads the skill statement on the Teamwork Skills form and then circles its corresponding number on the Team Scoring form. The number corresponding to a specific skill is circled (endorsed), either for peer or self, *only* if a skill has been demonstrated in the group.

The Team Skills Profile form summarizes a student's group performance. This form lists the 25 teamwork statements and provides a series of columns to record student responses. For each group in a class, a teacher transfers a student's item endorsements from the Team Scoring form to a tally column on that student's Team Skill Profile form. These tallies are converted to percentage endorsements and recorded in another column. Percentages are interpreted based upon a mastery rule: 100% means students should continue to demonstrate the skill already mastered; 0% means students should focus on acquiring the skill; and any percentage value between those two indicates students require growth. When peer- and self-endorsements are compared, students consider consistencies or discrepancies between how they see themselves and how others in their groups see them. After at least 5 weeks of group work, this process repeats itself, resulting in the summative evaluation. The Team Skills Profile form includes columns for both formative and summative student results and a column to indicate either positive or negative change. The manual provides a scored profile and instructions, which facilitate scoring and interpreting the III.

DEVELOPMENT. The III reflects the authors' educational philosophy and instructional method for cooperative group learning. Their philosophy, Collaboration-Integration Theory, in part, emphasizes students practicing clearly defined, assigned group roles and learning by receiving anonymous group feedback. Their method, Cooperative Learning Exercises and Roles, has students try various, flexibly defined roles such as summarizer, discussant, organizer, and evaluator. The III is used to hold students accountable to group roles, thereby increasing skill acquisition and reducing social loafing. These roles are practiced during at least a 10-week schedule of group work. The manual does not detail exactly how this schedule and its accompanying exercises integrate into a semester course.

The manual indicates that teamwork skill statements for the III were collected from the available literature on group process, yet sources were not cited nor was the method of item selection indicated. In deciding upon an item format, the authors argue that it would be too difficult for students to use a Likert rating scale. Instead, they rely on having students endorse a skill only when a student has demonstrated it.

TECHNICAL. The authors report previously developing and refining the III with community college and university students. However, the sample used for reporting analyses comes from 10 classes in different subject areas in a single high school, albeit one that emphasized peer-assisted instruction (Strom, Strom, & Moore, 1999). These 10 classes resulted in a sample of 303 students and 1,136 peer reports. Percentages of self- and peer-item endorsements for this sample are reported in the manual's appendix. For example, the highest percentage of self-endorsement, 94%, was for the skill statement, "This peer does a fair share of the work expected of everyone." And the lowest percentage of peer-endorsement, 33%, was for the statement, "This peer brings reading materials for the group to examine."

To obtain an estimate of the III's reliability, the 25 items were considered as a single test, even though the inventory is not used as such. This resulted in a coefficient alpha of .79 for self-scores and .87 for peer-scores.

The authors argue for content validity when they anecdotally report that faculty in the current sample thought the III statements adequately covered cooperative learning skills. Face validity was based upon a post-test question, which found teachers and students largely agreeing that the ratings were truthful. Because the authors claim they could not locate a similar instrument to provide a basis for concurrent validity, they used agreement between peer- and self-ratings to infer concurrent validity. Although high levels of agreement were reached, this finding may be explained by students wanting to give each other good ratings or to be liked, not by truthfulness in reporting.

To some extent the limited psychometric analyses for the III results from the authors' intent to provide an easily scored, classroom inventory. Their approach requires little in the way of score conversions other than item percentages. Because the authors have striven to create an inventory for such a wide range of students and courses, norms may not be appropriate. Still, even if only briefly, the authors have attempted to provide descriptive data, reliability estimates, and evidence of content, face, and concurrent validity.

COMMENTARY. Peer nominations are a dependable method to inquire how individuals are perceived by group members. In fact, nominations have proved reliable and valid in a number of research and applied settings (Anastasi, 1982). The III employs a nomination technique akin to the Peer Nomination Inventory method (Wiggins, 1973). This technique has students decide whether or not their classmates exhibit specific traits. The III, however, has not retained many of the strengths of the Peer Nomination Inventory. These include the rigorous clinical and conceptual derivation of item content, rationally formulated subtests, class-size ratings, and psychometrically verified scale structure. In contrast, the III implements a peer-nomination process with counts and percentages at the item level. This process is done at the cost of having multiple paper forms and extensive teacher hand scoring, which can be labor intensive. Therefore, computer implementation of a general peer rating process is advantageous (Freeman & McKenzie, 2002).

Teachers should carefully examine the use of the III and its interpretation. Although the manual reports a Flesch-Kincaid grade level of 6.85, suggesting starting III use at about seventh grade, students may need to be older and have developed the metacognitive skills to reflect upon group processes. Additionally, the manual only provides empirical support for the III's use with a limited group of high school students. The authors partially acknowledge these limits, indicating that teachers may select particular items for use depending upon course purpose and student grade level. In regard to interpretation, small group size (four to six group members), use of individual items, several possible rating biases, and the intricacies of small group processes may result in unreliable or misleading feedback. Hence, teachers need to consider how groups are functioning and be sensitive to how students might respond to negative peer feedback.

SUMMARY. The III is a clever paper-and-pencil adaptation of the peer nomination inventory technique for use in educational settings where sustained cooperative group projects are integrated into classroom instruction. The III provides item-by-item feedback to individuals from the endorsements of group members and their own self-ratings. III instructions are clear and detailed; scoring is somewhat cumbersome. Because the authors have spelled out what they require for team participation, the III results are readily understood by students and useful to teachers. The authors believe that an obstacle to successful implementation of cooperative group learning is the lack of effective group feedback. Because the III does provide such feedback, it merits consideration by teachers who include cooperative group learning in their courses.

REVIEWER'S REFERENCES

Anastasi, A. (1982). *Psychological testing* (5th ed.). New York: Macmillan.
Freeman, M., & McKenzie, J. (2002). SPARK, a confidential web-based template for self and peer assessment of student teamwork: Benefits of evaluating across different subjects. *British Journal of Educational Technology, 33,* 551-569.
Strom, P. S., Strom, R. D., & Moore, E. G. (1999). Peer and self-evaluation of teamwork skills. *Journal of Adolescence, 22,* 539-553.
Wiggins, J. S. (1973). *Personality and prediction: Principles of personality assessment.* Reading, MA: Addison-Wesley.

[92]

Iowa Algebra Aptitude Test™, Fifth Edition.

Purpose: Designed to "help teachers and counselors make the most informed decisions possible regarding the initial placement of students in the secondary mathematics curriculum."

Population: Grades 7—8.

Publication Dates: 1931—2006.

Acronym: IAAT™.

Scores, 5: Pre-Algebraic Number Skills and Concepts, Interpreting Mathematical Information, Representing Relationships, Using Symbols, Total.

Administration: Group or individual.

Forms, 2: A, B.

Price Data, 2006: $31 per manual Forms A and B; $78 per 25 test booklets (Form A or B); $8 per Directions for Administration booklet (Forms A and B); $35 per 25 self-scoring answer sheets (Forms A and B); $98 per 100 Mark Reflex answer sheets (Forms A and B);

$33 per 25 Report to Families booklets (Forms A and B); $1,250 per Licensed Norms (Forms A and B).

Time: 40 minutes for the battery (i.e., 10 minutes for each of four subtests) plus approximately 10 minutes for distribution and collection of materials.

Comments: "Designed to be used in conjunction with other indicators of student progress, such as grades and teacher evaluations."

Authors: Harold L. Schoen and Timothy N. Ansley.

Publisher: Riverside Publishing.

Cross References: For reviews by John W. Fleenor and Judith A. Monsaas of an earlier edition, see 12:195; see also T2:681 (7 references); for reviews by W. L. Bashaw and Cyril J. Hoyt, and an excerpted review by Russell A. Chadbourn of an earlier edition, see 7:505 (8 references); for reviews by Harold Gulliken and Emma Spaney of an earlier edition, see 4:393; for a review by David Segel, see 3:327 (2 references); for reviews by Richard M. Drake and M. W. Richardson, see 2:144 (1 reference).

Review of the Iowa Algebra Aptitude Test, Fifth Edition by DAVID MORSE, Professor, Counseling, Educational Psychology and Special Education, Mississippi State University, Mississippi State, MS:

DESCRIPTION. The Iowa Algebra Aptitude Test, Fifth Edition (IAAT) comprises 60 four-option, multiple-choice items, arranged in four subtests of 15 items each, targeted for pre-algebra students in Grades 7 and 8. The test is administered in paper-and-pencil format in about 50 minutes. Two alternate forms (A and B) are available in reusable booklets. According to the Manual for Test Use, Interpretation, and Technical Support, the principal purpose of the IAAT is to "help teachers and counselors make the most informed decisions possible regarding the initial placement of students in the secondary mathematics curriculum" (p. 1). The authors also state that the IAAT may be used to communicate student readiness for algebra to parents, to evaluate instructional programs, and the subtest scores can be used to "provide diagnostic information" (p. 5).

Administration of the IAAT requires no special training, and tests may be scored locally, by hand via "self-scoring" answer sheets, or by machine using machine-scorable answer sheets. Directions for administration are straightforward and should present no special difficulty for school staff or faculty. Use of calculators is allowed, according to the technical manual, but no mention is made in the administration manual of whether calculators may be used. The technical manual does not address whether the normative (standardization) sample was or was not permitted to use calculators or whether different norms might be needed depending on the local choice to use or not use calculators. Each of the four subtests is timed (10 minutes). The test was not intended to be sharply speeded, though the reported completion rates show that fewer than 75% of the normative sample completed the first part, under 90% completed Parts 2 and 3, and more than 90% completed Part 4 in the allotted time. No mention is made in either the technical or administration manual of whether large print or other versions of the IAAT are available for examinees with visual impairments or whether versions in languages other than English are available. There is no discussion of what sort(s) of accommodations to the testing conditions (e.g., additional time for students identified as learning disabled) may be permitted without endangering the integrity of the norms.

Normative scores are available as percentile ranks (for both subtests and the total, or composite score), standard scores (M = 150, SD = 15), stanines, and normal curve equivalents (the last three for composite scores only). Given that the principal purpose of the IAAT is to determine whether students are ready for placement in an algebra course, one might expect some sort of qualitative classification of performance level based on No Child Left Behind type levels, such as "Basic," "Proficient," and "Advanced." However, authors recommend that the IAAT score is but one component of the decision-making process, and should be given less weight than the recommendations of the student's teacher. Because local standards may vary, it is up to the school staff to determine the score threshold(s) on the IAAT that would represent a sufficient level of readiness for algebra.

DEVELOPMENT. The IAAT is the newest version (2006 copyright) of a test that first appeared in 1931. Revisions were published in 1942, 1967, and 1993. Normative data were collected in February–May of 2005. The content of the most recent (2000) Principles and Standards for School Mathematics of the National Council of Teachers of Mathematics formed the basis for the fifth edition of the IAAT. In addition, the authors consulted current algebra and pre-algebra texts and other resources. Item development and tryout

took place from 2001–2003. Once the final set of items was prepared, item sensitivity reviews were conducted by members of a diverse panel, looking for instances of concerns about the items based on perception of fairness, culture, geographic region, gender, and urban-rural.

Each item is identified in two ways: by subtest and by skill within the subtest area. Part (or subtest) 1, Pre-Algebraic Number Skills and Concepts, includes two broad skills: Using numerical expressions (5 items) and Solving problems (simple and complex, 10 items total). Part 2, Interpreting Mathematical Information, covers Graphs (8 items) and Novel mathematical formulations (both comprehension and application of symbols, 7 items total). Part 3, Representing Relationships, measures two skills, Inferring functional relationships (7 items) and Expressions with variables (8 items). Part 4, Using Symbols, covers Solving algebraic expressions (7 items), Applying symbolic representation (3 items), and Identifying relationships among variables in a formula (5 items).

Nontest materials available from the publisher include the norms-technical manual (Manual for Test Use, Interpretation, and Technical Support), an administration manual (Directions for Administration), and a parent guide (Report to Families).

TECHNICAL. Overall, the standardization sample, comprising 6,346 students from Grades 7 and 8 in 38 schools in 24 states, was relatively close to matching the stated population percents, typically within 7%, except for the Great Lakes/Plains region, which was overrepresented in the sample by more than 14%. Other stratification variables included district enrollment and socioeconomic status, to which the sample was also generally well matched. Ethnic minority subgroups were underrepresented a bit, but weights were used to adjust for all stratification variables.

The technical manual offers a traditional presentation of information: item p-values, biserial correlations of item-total test score, subtest intercorrelations, internal consistency reliability estimates (subtest and total), estimates of reliability of difference scores for subtests, and what appear to be classical theory standard errors of measurement for both raw scores and by decade for the standard scores, which range from 100–200. As biserial correlations were used as the measure of item discrimination, these will tend to be biased upward over a point-biserial or corrected item-total biserial correlation. In addition, statistical checks for differential item functioning (DIF), using the Mantel-Haenszel method, were conducted for male-female, White-African American and White-Hispanic comparisons. Only one item from all 120 (60 each on the two forms) was flagged for statistical DIF (showing female-male difference), but the item was apparently retained.

No information on alternate-forms reliability or test-retest reliability is offered. This deficiency was also noted by reviewers of the previous edition of the IAAT (Fleenor, 1995; Monsaas, 1995). There is no evidence that any part of the standardization sample took both forms of the IAAT, so that the equivalence or equating of the two forms is entirely presumptive of equal populations having taken the two forms. Of the available equating designs, that is among the weakest methodologically.

The internal consistency reliability estimates from the total (composite) scores are good enough for making judgments about individual examinees (.90 or better), according to guidelines such as those given by Cronbach (1990). The same cannot be said about individual subtest scores, of which four (of eight—that is, two forms each with four subtests) of the estimates are below .75. Form B reliabilities are uniformly lower by subtest than Form A reliabilities. However, even these subtest reliability estimates would be high enough to warrant use of subtest scores when summarizing the ability of groups of examinees. The estimated reliabilities of difference scores among subtests are low enough to give pause to anyone wishing to interpret profiles of student scores; these are as low as .30.

Authors of the technical manual show evidence of having consulted the 1999 Standards (AERA, APA, & NCME, 1999), but the evidence presented concerning validity is sorely lacking in this version of the technical manual. There is a brief discussion about items having been judged for content congruence to the subtest skills but without much detail as to how this process took place, or the degree of congruence in rater judgment that items were required to meet. Also, there is no criterion-related validity information presented. A study done in 1991 on the fourth edition of the IAAT is discussed, but because the fifth edition is different, those results should not be considered as suitable evidence. The authors do say that a validation study is underway and will appear in a later version of the technical manual. There is no discussion of evidence that the IAAT taps a construct of algebra readiness and not a more general mathematics proficiency.

COMMENTARY. The IAAT offers a competently developed measure of prowess on a blend of algebra and pre-algebra skills coupled with recent normative data. As such, it would appear to be a potentially viable option for schools where staff believed that placement decisions for pre-algebra students could be strengthened by inclusion of a relevant, objective test. The test is easily and relatively quickly administered, easily scored, and the layout of items within the subtests is generally very good. Form B does have several items for which the options appear in two columns (subtest) rather than a single column (subtest), however. There is a colorful illustration or picture appearing on most pages of the test, making the pages and items more visually appealing. Each subtest has at least one "sample exercise," so students have some sense of what is to come, though the answer is always given and shown on the sample answer grid.

In light of the stated purpose of the IAAT, it is disappointing that appropriate validity information is yet to be collected and presented. Even the old (1991) study cited by the authors, which used the previous edition of the IAAT, was not the most prescient of the studies available. Pinkham and Ansley (1996) presented data on the fourth edition of the IAAT, which showed that scores on the IAAT correlated with grades in mathematics (both overall and disaggregated for algebra, pre-algebra, and general mathematics classes) less well than did the total mathematics score on the Iowa Tests of Basic Skills. Further, in predicting student grades in their current algebra course, scores from the earlier edition of the IAAT added only about 1% explained variation to what could be accounted for by the previous grade in a mathematics course, which by itself explained about 53% of the variation. Since the passage of the No Child Left Behind legislation, states and schools annually appraise the mathematics proficiency of their pre-algebra students, typically in a way that permits normative comparisons. Thus, many schools may currently be using a mathematics achievement test from which the scores would serve the stated purpose of the IAAT as well or perhaps even better than the IAAT itself. So the potential utility of the IAAT is something that the school or district staff should consider carefully, when the validity information for the IAAT becomes available. This was noted by Hoyt (1972, p. 901) in a review of the third edition of the IAAT, wherein he cited authors of that version suggested that the IAAT might be considered a "luxury" if a school had in place an appropriate achievement test battery, and that the potential virtue of the IAAT may lie in its face validity.

There are a few other concerns about the IAAT materials, mostly minor. First, the authors claim in the technical manual that Forms A and B of the IAAT are parallel forms. They are not parallel (cf., Lord & Novick, 1968, pp. 47–50); they are alternate forms. Second, the sample student profile given in the Report to Families document, used to communicate results to parents or guardians, suggests that the difference between the 83rd and 87th percentile is a meaningful one when interpreting subtest scores for a student, disregarding the error of measurement associated with each score. That is potentially misleading. The example is also potentially confusing to the reader because the 87th percentile subtest score came from a lower percent correct than did the 83rd percentile subtest score. Third, the only normative data come from the spring of the school year, presumably from students in the second semester of year-long courses in mathematics. For schools using block scheduling, this time frame might not be optimal. Fourth, the technical manual lists mean item discrimination values that do not agree with the means of individual item discrimination values given later in the manual, either by simple average or Fisher-z transformation. Averages of individual item-total biserial correlations are uniformly lower than those reported. Finally, on most of the subtests, there are substantial correlations between item difficulty (p-values) and discrimination (item-total biserial correlation) values; these are as high as .71 (Form B, Part 4) and with one exception are generally in the .40s or higher. Ideally, item difficulty and item discrimination should generally be independent of one another. The trend for the IAAT is that easier items are more discriminating and more challenging items are not lending as much to the discrimination power or overall internal consistency reliability of the test, at least for the standardization sample. For Part 2 on Form A, the correspondence of item difficulty and discrimination is admirably low (-.09). For Form B, however, the correlation for Part 2 was strong (.62). That discrepancy suggests some potential differences between the forms. However, the correlations for the other three parts are fairly consistent across forms.

SUMMARY. The IAAT may have merit as an additional bit of information in helping to place students in algebra or a pre-algebra course. It is simple to administer, can be scored locally by hand or by machine, and may be used for small or large groups of examinees (with appropriate proctoring assistance). Potential users should first examine the instrument to judge whether the skill set measured is consistent with their vision of what students need in order to succeed in an algebra course. However, those interested in this instrument are advised to wait until such time as validity evidence is presented to show that this version of the IAAT differentiates between students who are and students who are not capable of passing algebra. Once that information becomes available, the salient question would then be whether the use of the IAAT facilitates better decision making, when combined with the student's past performance and teacher judgment, than would the results from a mathematics achievement test that may already be in place.

REVIEWER'S REFERENCES
American Educational Research Association, American Psychological Association, & National Council on Measurement in Education. (1999). *Standards for educational and psychological testing.* Washington, DC: American Educational Research Association.
Cronbach, L. J. (1990). *Essentials of psychological testing* (5th ed.). New York: Harper Collins Publishing.
Fleenor, J. W. (1995). [Review of the Iowa Algebra Aptitude Test-Fourth Edition]. In J. C. Conoley & J. C. Impara (Eds.), *The twelfth mental measurements yearbook* (pp. 504-506). Lincoln, NE: The Buros Institute of Mental Measurements.
Hoyt, C. J. (1972). [Review of the Iowa Algebra Aptitude Tests-Third Edition]. In O. K. Buros (Ed.), *The seventh mental measurements yearbook* (pp. 900-901). Highland Park, NJ: Gryphon Press.
Lord, F. M., & Novick, M. R. (1968). *Statistical theories of mental test scores.* Reading, MA: Addison-Wesley.
Monsaas, J. A. (1995). [Review of the Iowa Algebra Aptitude Test-Fourth Edition]. In J. C. Conoley & J. C. Impara (Eds.), *The twelfth mental measurements yearbook* (pp. 506-507). Lincoln, NE: The Buros Institute of Mental Measurements.
National Council of Teachers of Mathematics. (2000). *Principles and standards for school mathematics.* Reston, VA: Author.
Pinkham, A. K., & Ansley, T. M. (1996, April). *Predicting achievement in secondary mathematics courses.* Paper presented at the annual meeting of the American Educational Research Association, New York. (Educational Resources Information Services Document ED 402 341)

Review of the Iowa Algebra Aptitude Test by BRUCE G. ROGERS, *Professor Emeritus, University of Northern Iowa, Cedar Falls, IA:*

DESCRIPTION. The Iowa Algebra Aptitude Test (IAAT) is a 60-item multiple-choice test, comprising four subtests of equal length. Because the computations are one-digit arithmetic, a student will probably do the problems faster without a calculator, therefore, calculators are not recommended, but are also not prohibited. The four subtests are called Parts. Pre-Algebraic Number Skills requires considerable understanding of concepts. The numbers may be 2 and 3, but the student must decide whether to add, divide, etc., and sometimes, how to estimate the value of a fraction. Interpreting Mathematical Information requires the student to read instructions, to follow them carefully, and to learn new material. A formula is written in words and the student is asked to use it with numbers. Representing Relationships requires the student to look at two sets of numbers and reason out a formula that will pair them. Using Symbols draws upon recent cognitive research to require the student to see the relationship among symbols. When given an algebraic equation, the student must reason out how changes in the independent variables will affect the dependent variable.

The classroom teacher can administer the test in a typical 50-minute class period. The answer sheets can be hand-scored or machine-scored using available software. The test was specifically designed for the purpose of helping teachers, counselors, administrators, parents, and students, working together, to assist in accurately determining whether the student should be placed in pre-algebra or is ready for Algebra I. Teachers can also use the data to help in their evaluation of their teaching strategies to help improve their instruction. The authors emphasize that the test results are to be used only in combination with other professional information, including teacher recommendations, standardized test batteries, and local screening tests. The test was developed to assist in that process of placement decisions.

DEVELOPMENT. The IAAT is the fifth edition of a test for which development began in 1931. Each edition has been an attempt to reflect the curriculum of the era. This 2006 copyrighted version was adapted to reflect the content of the 2000 NCTM Standards. Supporting materials provided to this reviewer included a Report to Families (4 pages), Directions for Administration (10 pages), and a Manual for Technical Support (26 pages). Overall, these materials reflect careful writing for clear interpretation by the intended users. It appears that the authors have attempted to benefit from feedback from teachers and previous test reviews; therefore, it is from that perspective that this review is written as a constructive critique for both potential users and the authors.

TECHNICAL. The normative information provides a reasonably clear explanation of the national standardization procedure. A total of 24 states are listed with 38 school districts. Over 6,000 students participated. There are some limitations in the sampling. For example, for the state of California, only one school was chosen, which appears to be a private school. Thus, in that very large state, not even one public-school student exists in the sample. There is, perhaps, room for improvement in sampling stratification in the opinion of this reviewer. However, the authors do present evidence to demonstrate that, overall, the standardization sample can be construed to be reflective of the national population by size of geographic region (four regions), size of district enrollment, socioeconomic status, and ethnic representation.

Readers might ask why there are only spring norms, when batteries usually list both fall and spring norms. It appears to this reviewer that decisions for algebra placement are made in the spring, therefore, those are the only appropriate norms. Readers might also wonder, because these norms were developed from students in Grades 7 and 8 who could enroll in algebra the next academic year, if the data could be used for students in Grade 6 or in a community college. If the user follows the instructions in the manual, it appears to this reviewer that these norms would be useful in making decisions for students in those groups.

Data are presented, in the manual, for item difficulty. Let me make a comment about that term. The "difficulty index" is actually an "easiness index," and the authors might help readers by pointing out that the term "difficulty" continues to be used because of traditional use. Likewise, many readers, if they have not had instruction in measurement theory, may misinterpret the term "discrimination index." Do these authors not know that we should not discriminate against females, minorities, etc.? Yes, of course they do, and therefore, it might be useful if they clearly explain, when they first introduce that term, how it is properly used in psychometric literature. Also, in the paragraph on item difficulty, the terms P_{90} and

P_{10} (in Table 9, under Difficulty) are not defined. It would be useful to define terms when they are first used. They are later defined in the paragraph for item discrimination. In Table 10 in the manual, it is stated that "n = number of response options." Although that is technically correct, it may be confusing, because almost every reader knows that "n" is commonly used for the number of subjects in the sample. Choosing a different letter might be helpful to the reader. Harold Gullikson (1950) suggested the letter "f" (p. 371) and Lord and Novick (1968) suggested the letter "A" (p. 304).

The authors write, "the typical student will succeed on only a little more than half of the test items" (manual, p. 10). From this statement, we can infer that, on the "typical item," only a "little more than half" of the students will succeed. Let us reason on this: If half of the students "know" the correct answer, then half the students do not "know" the correct answer, but one-fourth of the latter will be expected to choose the correct answer if their guessing is correct at the chance level. Thus, we would expect about 62% of all students to get the item correct. However, Table 9 shows that the obtained difficulty values were less than that, on the average. Are we to infer that, in actuality, these items are, on the average, harder than "medium" difficulty? This inference would also suggest that the total scores on 60 items would be approximately 37, but Table 8 in the manual shows mean values of 32 and 29, for Forms A and B. Test administrators might consider this in interpreting raw scores, and the authors might consider this in their test planning and construction.

The data show that these items have very desirable discrimination values. All the items have values greater than .30, and over 90% of the items have values greater than .40. This level of item discrimination results in high values of internal consistency, even greater than KR20 = .90. Very few students, less than 2%, "hit the ceiling" (perfect score) on any subtest, and relatively few, approximately 7%, "hit the floor" (chance-level score) on any subtest. The test is able to give a meaningful score for almost all students.

There is evidence of a certain amount of speededness in the test because over 10% of the students are expected not to finish all of the items in each subtest. However, these same students may experience difficulty in an algebra class be-

cause the tests in those classes also require the students to complete the tests within a set time. These limitations of the test probably do not change the decisions about placement decisions, because cutpoints are typically near the center of the distribution.

Evidence to support the validity of the tests is presented in two areas. In terms of content validity, the authors stated that they examined algebra and pre-algebra texts, along with other relevant literature. They wrote that "a rigorous development plan" was followed; however, they did not show any development plan in the manual. If it was a written plan, many readers might like to see it. The authors wrote that "content experts" (i.e., "mathematics educators") "scrutinized" (manual, p. 13) the items; however, those individuals did not get their names listed in the manual. Because the authors stated that they planned to issue a revised manual, it might be useful to consider adding those names. Another group of experts were asked to look at the items for "fairness" or "bias." Those experts did get their names and positions listed, so readers can judge their qualifications. In addition, a statistical analysis was conducted for DIF (Differential Item Functioning). This analysis is a positive feature and the results are presented.

The evidence for criterion-related validity consists of correlations with test grades in an algebra class. The correlations are about .50 or above. The authors might also consider correlating the test scores with the results of a standardized algebra test given at the end of the algebra course. They might also look at grades and standardized test scores for those students who were placed in the pre-algebra course. The authors stated that a multiple regression analysis was run to examine the extent to which the IAAT added to the prediction of algebra grades from standardized test battery scores. They said that they obtained positive results, but they did not provide any details on what they did. Perhaps they will consider including these results in their revised manual.

Evidence for reliability consists of KR20 data. The subtests show values above .70 and the composite score above .90. Because reliability is a property of the data and not the test, per se, readers can be reasonably confident that their data will show high values also. The authors might explore the possibility of running an alternate-form reliability analysis if they can motivate students to participate. That motivation is a possibility, because the students may actually enjoy these test items and might want to see if they can improve their score. Standard errors are also shown in a table in the manual. Unfortunately, the authors did not mention confidence bands. I suggest that, in their revised manual, they tell how to construct a confidence band and then explain how we could be 2/3 confident that, if John took the alternate form, his second score would be within the confidence band around the first score.

The norms tables show how to convert raw composite scores to standard scores (mean = 150, sd = 15), percentiles, stanines, and normal curve equivalents (NCE). Percentiles are also shown for each of the four subtests. A section on interpretation of scores emphasizes proper uses and limitations of scores.

COMMENTARY. The IAAT can be a valuable tool for predicting algebra success when appropriately used. The table of specifications is properly constructed and shows emphasis on important algebraic concepts. Evidences for reliability and validity are sparse, so readers should look forward to a revised manual to judge the extent to which these concerns have been addressed.

There is a potential danger in using this test. Because the test reflects the "new math" and the 2000 NCTM Standards, it may not be appropriate to use it in a class that has not been exposed to that curriculum. Students need to have been taught to these standards from the perspective of instructional validity. The authors might want to emphasize this possible limitation further in their manual. Teachers should avoid this test if they have not chosen to teach their students the skills and concepts covered in the standards and, hence, this test.

In my opinion, teachers should look carefully at this test, understanding that it reflects the NCTM standards to ensure that it matches their curriculum. The authors should continue their work to gather reliability and validity data for the test, and they should consider preparing revised forms to reflect improvement in the items.

SUMMARY. The Iowa Algebra Aptitude Test (IAAT) is a credit to the authors and can be of benefit to students and teachers when it is properly used. It can be administered, scored, and interpreted in a manner that will prove enjoyable and valuable to students. To do so will require that the students be properly taught the concepts, particularly those concepts that emphasize comprehension of basic understandings, including the recent cognitive research on correcting misconceptions that can hinder the progress of the student.

The quality of this test is such that it may be viewed, in the future, as the criterion toward which other mathematics tests will be compared. The criticisms raised by this reviewer should be interpreted in a constructive manner because they were written to inspire both users and the authors to continue to look for ways to improve its applications. The authors must not be complacent, for they have much to do in fulfilling their promise to produce a revised manual with further technical supporting data. Teachers must not be complacent about their teaching, for this test requires them to teach their students at a higher level of understanding than has previously been expected of teachers and students. Toward that goal, this test can be recommended to every dedicated math teacher who is preparing students for the world of algebra.

REVIEWER'S REFERENCES

Gullikson, H. (1950). *Theory of mental tests*. New York: Wiley.
Lord, F. M., & Novick, M. R. (1968). *Statistical theories of mental test scores*. Reading, MA: Addison-Wesley.

[93]

Iowa Tests of Basic Skills®, Forms A and B.

Purpose: Designed to measure skills and achievement in fundamental content areas of school curricula's vocabulary, word analysis, reading comprehension, language arts, mathematics, social studies, science, and sources of information.

Population: Grades K–9.

Publication Dates: 1955–2003.

Acronym: ITBS®.

Administration: Group.

Levels, 10: 5–14.

Forms, 2: A and B; 3 batteries: Complete (Levels 5–14), Core (Levels 7–14 only), and Survey (Levels 7–14 only).

Price Data: Available from publisher.

Comments: Provides scores for both norm-referenced and criterion-referenced interpretations.

Authors: H. D. Hoover, S. B. Dunbar, D. A. Frisbie, K. R. Oberley, V. L. Ordman, R. J. Naylor, G. B. Bray, J. C. Lewis, and A. L. Qualls.

Publisher: Riverside Publishing.

a) LEVEL 5.
Population: Grades K.1–1.5.
Scores, 8: Vocabulary, Word Analysis, Reading Words, Listening, Language, Mathematics, Reading Profile Total, Core Total.
Time: Untimed, approximately 120–145 minutes.
b) LEVEL 6.
Population: Grades K.7–1.9.
Scores, 10: Same as *a* above, with the addition of Reading Comprehension and Reading Total.
Time: Untimed, approximately 163 minutes.
c) LEVELS 7 and 8.
Population: Grades 1.7–3.2.
Scores, 18: Vocabulary, Word Analysis, Reading Comprehension, Reading Total, Listening, Spelling, Language, Math Concepts, Math Problems, Math Computation, Math Total, Core Total, Social Studies, Science, Sources of Information, Composite, Reading Profile Total, Survey Battery Total.
Time: Untimed, approximately 260–284 minutes for Core Battery; approximately 344–374 minutes for Complete Battery; approximately 114–136 minutes for Survey Battery.
d) LEVELS 9–14.
Population: Grades 3.0–9.9.
Scores, 21–23: Vocabulary, Reading Comprehension, Reading Total, Spelling, Capitalization, Punctuation, Usage and Expression, Language Total, Math Concepts and Estimation, Math Problem Solving and Data Interpretation, Math Computation, Math Total, Core Total, Social Studies, Science, Maps and Diagrams, Reference Materials, Sources of Information Total, Word Analysis (Level 9 only), Listening (Level 9 only), Composite, Reading Profile Total (Level 9 only), Survey Battery Total.
Time: 250–360 minutes for Core Battery; 362–515 minutes for Complete Battery; 101–142 minutes for Survey Battery.
Cross References: See T5:1318 (24 references); for reviews by Susan M. Brookhart and Lawrence H. Cross of Forms K, L and M, see 13:159 (110 references); see also T4:1280 (33) references; for reviews by Suzanne Lane and Nambury S. Raju of Form J, see 11:184 (24 references); for reviews by Robert L. Linn and Victor L. Willson of Forms G and H, see 10:155 (45 references); for reviews by Peter W. Airasian and Anthony J. Nitko of Forms 7 and 8, see 9:533 (29 references); see also T3:1192 (97 references); for reviews by Larry A. Harris and Fred Pyrczak of Forms 5-6, see 8:19 (58 references); see T2:19 (87 references) and 6:13 (17 references); for reviews by Virgil E. Herrick, G.A.V. Morgan, and H. H. Remmers, and an excerpted review by Laurence Siegel of Forms 1-2, see 5:16. For reviews of the modern mathematics supplement, see 7:481 (2 reviews).

Review of the Iowa Tests of Basic Skills, Forms A and B by GEORGE ENGELHARD, JR., Professor of Educational Measurement and Policy, Emory University, Atlanta, GA:

DESCRIPTION. The Iowa Tests of Basic Skills, Forms A and B (ITBS), is a group-administered, norm-referenced battery of achievement tests for students in kindergarten through eighth grade (ages 5 to 14). The tests are ordered by levels ranging from Levels 5 to 14. The levels correspond to target ages and grade levels based on academic achievement. For example, Level 5 is targeted for students with a chronological age of 5 in the first month of kindergarten (K.1) to the fifth month of first grade (1.5), whereas Level 12 is targeted for 12-year-olds in sixth grade (6.0 to 6.9).

The ITBS is available in various combinations of tests within three batteries (Complete, Core, and Survey) with the number of items and content areas varying across levels and batteries. Helpful tables are presented to aid the potential user in the selection of the appropriate test battery. The total number of items in the Complete battery varies from 146 items for Level 5 to 515 items for Level 14. The Core and Survey Batteries have fewer items. Content areas tested vary by level, and the following scores are available for the Complete Battery: Level 5 (Vocabulary, Word Analysis, Listening, Language, Mathematics, Reading Words, Reading Profile Total, and Core Total), Level 6 (same as Level 5 with addition of Reading Comprehension and Reading Total), Levels 7 and 8 (Vocabulary, Word Analysis, Reading Comprehension, Reading Total, Listening, Spelling, Language, Math Concepts, Math Problems, Math Computation, Math Total, Core Total, Social Studies, Science, Sources of Information, Composite, Reading Profile Total, Survey Battery Total), and Levels 9 to 14 (Vocabulary, Reading Comprehension, Reading Total, Spelling, Capitalization, Punctuation, Usage and Expression, Language Total, Math Concepts and Estimation, Math Problem Solving and Data Interpretation, Math Computation, Math Total, Core Total, Social Studies, Science, Maps and Diagrams, Reference Materials, Sources of Information Total, Word Analysis [Level 9 only], Listening [Level 9 only], Composite, Reading Profile Total [Level 9 only], and Survey Battery Total). Raw scores, percent-correct scores, two developmental scores (grade equivalents and developmental standard scores), and three status scores (percentile ranks, stanines, and normal curve equivalents) are available for most content areas. Item-by-item normative data are also provided. Extensive documentation and manuals are available that provide very detailed directions for administration and interpretation of scores. These manuals are targeted for various audiences including parents, teachers, counselors, and school administrators.

According to the authors, the ITBS has been designed to "measure growth in fundamental areas of school achievement: vocabulary, reading comprehension, language, mathematics, social studies, science, and sources of information" (Guide to Research and Development, 2003, p. 1). More specifically, there are three main purposes: (a) to obtain information that can support instructional decisions made by teachers in the classroom, (b) to provide information to students and their parents for monitoring the student's growth from grade to grade, and (c) to examine yearly progress of grade groups as they pass through the school's curriculum.

DEVELOPMENT. The ITBS includes a range of 6 to 15 tests designed to measure achievement across content areas for students in kindergarten through eighth grade. The ITBS was first published in 1955, but its roots go back over 70 years to the Iowa Every-Pupil Tests of Basic Skills. The Iowa Tests have a long history of development grounded in a strong program of research in educational measurement by scholars at the University of Iowa. In looking over the research supporting the ITBS, the authors of these reports and publications represent many of the top measurement specialists in the 20th century.

The development of the tests was guided by the major purpose of the ITBS, which is to measure growth in the fundamental areas of school achievement. The selection of content for the ITBS was guided by a consideration of (a) typical course coverage across the country, (b) current textbooks and teaching methods, and (c) recommendations of national curriculum groups. Extensive documentation is provided regarding the content of each of the tests, and helpful manuals are provided to aid practitioners and potential users regarding the content measured within each subject area and level. The ITBS has an outstanding

set of manuals written for teachers, counselors, test administrators, and parents. As with all aspects of the ITBS, the authors provide a detailed description of the steps and rationale for the major decisions made during the development of the ITBS.

TECHNICAL. The authors of the ITBS provide a Guide to Research and Development Manual (GRD manual) that includes clear and detailed descriptions of all aspects of test development. Throughout the development process, the authors of the ITBS were guided by the *Standards for Educational and Psychological Testing* (AERA, APA, & NCME, 1999). As a result, the ITBS and supporting technical material are of very high technical quality.

The national standardization of the ITBS was based on the 2000 spring and fall administration of the tests to a carefully selected random sample. This norming sample was designed to represent the national population of school children in grades K to 8 as closely as possible with careful weighting of the scores to ensure proportional representation of various subgroups (public/private schools, geographic regions, SES categories, district and diocese size, grade level, and race/ethnicity). The total unweighted sample for spring 2000 was approximately 170,000 students, and approximately 76,000 for the fall 2000 normative sample. Item, student, and school level normative data are provided. The GRD Manual provides a list by state of the districts and schools that participated in the national standardization of the ITBS. The ITBS has been restandardized with new norms approximately every 7 years, and therefore new norms may be available soon. [Editor's note: The publisher advised the Buros Institute in June 2007 that during the 2004-05 school year, a representative subsample of districts from the original standardization participated in a renorming of the ITBS.] The process used to select and weight the normative data used in the national standardization provides a textbook-perfect example of how to create nationally representative norms.

The authors provide several types of scores, and careful descriptions of how to interpret these scores. As with other aspects of the ITBS, a great deal of time and effort went into teaching potential users about correct interpretations and pointing out inappropriate interpretations. Three general frameworks for providing meaningful scores are available with the ITBS. These three scoring frameworks are (a) raw scores and percent-correct scores, (b) developmental scores (grade equivalents and developmental standard scores), and (c) status scores (percentile ranks, stanines, and normal curve equivalents). In support of these scoring frameworks, the authors conducted a variety of scaling, norming, and equating activities. Within the Iowa Testing Program, scaling is defined as the development of "longitudinal score scales for measuring growth in achievement" (GRD manual, p. 51) (developmental standard scores and grade equivalents); norming is defined as the estimation of national performance and long-term trends in achievement including evidence of strengths and weaknesses for individuals and groups (percentile ranks, stanines, and normal curve equivalents); and equating is defined as methods for obtaining comparable scores on equivalent forms.

First, raw scores and percent-correct scores are available for most tests and subtests. In the interpretive guides for teachers, counselors, and administrators, the authors indicate that these scores have little meaning in themselves, and that they are usually converted to other types of scores. The second framework is based on two developmental scoring systems: developmental standard scores and grade equivalents. It is important to point out that the developmental grade equivalent scores are a monotonic derivation of the developmental standard scores. The authors suggest that the developmental scales should be used to estimate student development or year-to-year growth, and caution that they are ill-suited for identifying student standing within a group or diagnosing areas of relative strength and weakness in educational achievement. It cannot be stressed enough that the grade-equivalent scoring framework used in the ITBS is not the same as the grade equivalents described in most measurement textbooks (Linn & Miller, 2005). Grade-equivalent scoring systems have always had great potential for misinterpretation, and the hybrid developmental grade equivalents reported with the ITBS may be even more likely to confuse some users. Renaming the scoring systems as developmental grade equivalents with the label "DGE" may lessen the potential confusion. By definition, the developmental grade equivalents provide a scoring system where the "average student 'grows' one unit on the scale each year" (GRD manual, p. 54). Users must be cautious about how this "average" or typical stu-

dent is defined. The final scoring framework provided for the ITBS is status scores (percentile ranks, stanines, and normal curve equivalent scores). These status scores are recommended for use in describing the relative strengths and weaknesses in various content areas based on a comparison to student achievement in these areas for the normative sample. Overall, the methods used for creating the developmental scores are not defined in sufficient detail in the GRD Manual. For example, so-called Hieronymus Scaling was used to create the Developmental Standard Scores in conjunction with a "growth model ... consistent with the patterns of growth over the history of the Iowa Tests and with the experience of educators in measuring student growth and development" (GRD manual, p. 54). A detailed description of what happens in this black box should be included in the GRD Manual, and would aid the potential users in understanding and evaluating the quality of the developmental scoring system.

The equating of Forms A and B for the Complete Battery was done with a comparable-groups design (Petersen, Kolen, & Hoover, 1989) using an equipercentile method based on raw score distributions from samples of students in the fall 2000 standardization sample. According to the authors, Forms A and B are equivalent to previous ITBS Forms K, L, and M in most respects. Before 1992, grade equivalent scores were defined by the Hieronymus Method, whereas other scales were defined using Thurstone's Method. Beginning with Forms K, L, and M, both developmental standard scores and developmental grade-equivalent scores were derived with the Hieronymus Method. Therefore, developmental standard scores and grade equivalents are comparable across Forms K, L, M, A, and B, but they are not directly comparable for earlier forms.

Extensive evidence regarding the reliability of the ITBS scores is provided in the GRD Manual. This evidence is presented in terms of a variety of reliability coefficients, and also in terms of conditional standard errors of measurement. As would be expected for a norm-referenced (NR) test battery that emphasizes student separation and ranking, the internal consistency coefficients based on Kuder-Richardson Formula 20 (KR20) are quite high. Internal consistency and equivalent forms reliabilities are in the expected range with most reliability coefficients ranging from the middle

.80s to low .90s. Subtest reliabilities tend to be lower. Reliability coefficients for shorter tests and for younger students also tend to be lower on average. These reliability coefficients are likely among the best found for any achievement test battery. In addition to KR20, the GRD manual also presents information regarding other sources of error variance in the ITBS scores. Estimates of equivalent-forms reliability and test-retest reliabilities are provided. These estimates of score stability and consistency are comparable to those obtained for other NR-test batteries. Conditional standard errors of measurement (*SEM*) are reported by score levels. The conditional standard errors of measurement are calculated with a fairly complex model. Additional advice should be provided for users regarding why the conditional *SEM*s increase and decrease over the range of the score scales. The evidence reported regarding the reliability of the ITBS scores is more than sufficient to support its recommended uses.

The authors provide a nice description of the concept of validity that highlights validity evidence as a function of the purposes and proposed uses of the ITBS, that reflects the perspective that obtaining evidence of validity is an ongoing process, and that stresses the important roles that judgments play in the validation process. Content validity is of major importance for achievement test batteries, and the authors recommend that potential users conduct item-by-item inspections of the test. This suggestion is sound advice. The underlying philosophy is that "evaluating an elementary school achievement test is much like evaluating other instructional materials" (GRD manual, p. 25), and that "the guiding principle for the development of the Iowa Tests is that materials presented to students be of sufficient quality to make the time spent testing instructionally useful" (GRD manual, p. 26). In support of this philosophical position, extensive material is provided regarding the content of the various subject tests at each level.

In addition to content-related evidence, statistical data are also provided including summaries of conventional item analyses (item *p*-values and discrimination indices), and reliability coefficients. Item fairness reviews and statistical analyses of differential item functioning were conducted for various subgroups of students. Because the validity process is an ongoing set of activities, the Iowa

Testing Program has maintained a continuous program of research on the ITBS. As with other aspects of the development of the ITBS, the authors have been very thoughtful and cautious in describing the validity evidence. More than enough information is provided for potential users to determine whether or not the ITBS will be useful in making decisions and recommendations about their students. In the interpretive guides for teachers, counselors, and school administrators, detailed descriptions are provided regarding appropriate and inappropriate uses of the ITBS scores. As the authors rightly point out, the final decisions regarding test selection and appropriate use of test scores comes down to judgments by potential users based on both available statistical data and a careful consideration of the content of the tests.

COMMENTARY. What can be said about an achievement test battery with such a long and distinguished history? Reading previous test reviews of earlier forms of the ITBS provides a snapshot of how measurement issues and concerns regarding standardized achievement tests have evolved over the 20th century. These earlier test reviews suggest that the ITBS and the overall Iowa Testing Programs continue to be responsive to current measurement policy and psychometric concerns. There is a clear historical record that the Iowa Testing Programs have maintained a high level of quality and a strong commitment to a goal to "provide information that can be used to improve instruction and learning" (GRD manual, p. 1).

The ITBS is a well-developed instrument that should be considered for use by practitioners who require a comprehensive achievement test battery. The GRD Manual provides very detailed descriptions regarding the appropriate uses of the ITBS, cautions about the limitations, and sufficient detail regarding the psychometric quality of the ITBS. The GRD Manual does not assume that the reader is an expert in psychometrics, and provides enough detail to teach the potential user about a variety of measurement issues.

It is important to stress that the ITBS was developed based on a norm-referenced (NR) theoretical perspective. This has important implications for all aspects of the test development process ranging from item selection to the framework provided for reporting meaningful and useful score interpretations. For example, an NR-perspective on item selection is guided by evaluations of item quality based on difficulty (items that are too easy or too hard might be flagged for deletion), and item-discrimination indices. The best and most discriminating items from an NR-perspective are answered correctly by about 50% of the students. The sine qua non of NR-measurement is the ranking and separation of students on an underlying achievement continuum. This perspective can be contrasted with a criterion-referenced (CR) perspective that focuses on content with the meaning of the scores derived primarily from a comparison of scores to a performance standard or criterion (cut) score. CR scores are obtained in most statewide assessment systems, and CR scores are used to inform many of the policy decisions embedded in the federal No Child Left Behind Act of 2001. The point here is not to revisit the NR versus CR debates, but to remind the potential user that the ITBS is grounded within an NR-theoretical perspective, and that this theoretical perspective has implications for test use and score interpretation. Of course, sound educational decisions can and should be informed by both NR and CR perspectives.

Previous test reviews of the ITBS criticized aspects of the norm-referenced scores. However, parents and other stakeholders continue to want information regarding how the performance of their students and schools compares to other students in the nation. The ITBS does an excellent job in performing this function. It is also important to point out that there may eventually be disillusionment with the current incarnation of criterion-referenced tests that have changed from their original purposes. For example, many stakeholders are just beginning to comprehend that CR tests that vary by state with performance standards that vary by state cannot be used to compare the educational achievement of students across states. The concept of a performance standard has also evolved over time, so that current cut scores are an amalgam of both criterion-referenced and norm-referenced judgments about achievement levels. In the fluctuating world of educational assessment, the ITBS may provide a less ambiguous view of changes in educational achievement over time in the United States than other assessment systems.

SUMMARY. In summary, the ITBS is as good as it gets for users requiring a comprehensive, norm-referenced achievement test battery for elementary school students (Grades K to 8). The

ITBS is one of the oldest and most venerable standardized, norm-referenced achievement test batteries in existence today. Many parents and other stakeholders continue to want norm-referenced scores in addition to criterion-referenced information about student achievement, and the ITBS provides extensive normative information that fulfills this need. The information supplied through the administration of the ITBS, and the appropriate use of the accompanying scores and user manuals, provides a useful framework for improving educational practices.

REVIEWER'S REFERENCES

American Educational Research Association, American Psychological Association, & National Council on Measurement in Education. (1999). *Standards for educational and psychological testing.* Washington, DC: American Educational Research Association.
Linn, R. L., & Miller, M. D. (2005). *Measurement and assessment in teaching* (9th ed.). Upper Saddle River, NJ: Prentice-Hall, Inc.
Petersen, N. S., Kolen, M. J., & Hoover, H. D. (1989). Scaling, norming, and equating. In R. L. Linn (Ed.), *Educational measurement* (3rd ed., pp. 221–262). Washington, DC: American Council on Education.

Review of the Iowa Tests of Basic Skills, Forms A and B by SUZANNE LANE, Professor of Research Methodology, University of Pittsburgh, Pittsburgh, PA:

DESCRIPTION. The Iowa Tests of Basic Skills, Forms A and B is the latest version of a widely used achievement test battery consisting of multiple-choice items with 10 overlapping levels, Level 5 to Level 14. The ITBS is suited for children ranging from kindergarten to Grade 8. Educational achievement is assessed in 6 to 15 different subject areas depending on the level and battery. [Editor's note: Riverside has now published Form B of Levels 5 and 6, as well as Level 5 books with optional Reading tests for both Forms A and B.] As indicated by the authors, the main purpose of the ITBS is to provide information that can be used to inform instruction and improve student learning.

A Complete Battery is provided for Levels 5 and 6 with achievement tests in Vocabulary, Word Analysis, Listening, Language, Mathematics and Reading. For Levels 7 and 8 there is a Core Battery with tests in Vocabulary, Word Analysis, Reading, Listening, Spelling, Language, Math Concepts, Math Problems, and Math Computation; a Complete Battery that includes the 9 tests in the Core Battery and tests in Social Studies, Science and Sources of Information; and a Survey Battery that consists of 3 shorter 30-minute tests in Reading, Language and Mathematics. For Levels 9 through 14, Forms A and B are available for a Complete Battery and a Survey Battery at each Level. There are 13 achievement tests in the Complete Battery and 2 additional tests (Word Analysis and Listening) at Level 9 only. The 11 Core Battery tests are included in the Complete Battery. The Survey Battery includes 3 shorter 30-minute tests in Reading, Language, and Mathematics. There is also a machine-scorable Form A Complete, Core, and Survey Battery for Level 9.

For Level 5, the administration time for the Complete Battery is 2 hours and 25 minutes, and for the Level 6, it is 2 hours and 43 minutes. For Levels 7 and 8, the administration time for the Survey Battery is 1 hour and 25 minutes, for the Core Battery it is 3 hours and 5 minutes, and for the Complete Battery it is about 4 hours and 25 minutes. For Levels 9 through 14, the test administration time is 1 hour and 30 minutes for the Survey Battery, 3 hours and 31 minutes for the Core Battery, and 5 hours and 26 minutes for the Complete Battery.

The tests assess a range of skills and processes in each subject area. As an example of items that assess higher level thinking skills, mathematical problem-solving items may involve multiple steps for solving the problem, require identification of extraneous or insufficient information, or require students to select an appropriate solution method.

As with past forms of the ITBS, there is a wide range of written documentation that supports test users in administering the test and interpreting the test scores including Directions for Administration, Message to Parents, Report to Students and Parents, Content Classifications with Item Norms, Test Coordinator Guide, Norms and Score Conversions, and the ITBS Guide to Research and Development. In addition, the Interpretive Guide for School Administrators and the Interpretive Guides for Teachers and Counselors provide valuable information on how to use the results for enhancing instruction and student learning. Practice tests and practice test directions are also available at various levels. The practice tests for Levels 5 and 6 are especially important given that children in primary grades may not be accustomed to sitting for a standardized test.

The two Interpretive Guides for Teachers and Counselors, Levels 5–9 and Levels 9–14, are comprehensive, and begin with a discussion on the appropriate uses of the ITBS including using the

results to support instructional decision making, report individual progress to parents and students, and evaluate the progress of groups of students. The Interpretive Guides also discuss inappropriate uses of the test results. The authors provide in-depth information on the content of the tests at each level and how the test was developed. The sections on how to interpret score reports and use the ITBS for both norm-referenced and criterion-referenced interpretations are especially well-written. In particular, the section describing common misunderstandings in interpreting grade equivalents is very clear. The authors indicate that due to scale development techniques that are unique to the ITBS, certain interpretations that are typically inappropriate for grade equivalents are possible for interpreting ITBS grade equivalents. If teachers and administrators use grade equivalents, this discussion on their interpretation is most informative.

Numerous score reports that describe results for individuals as well as groups (i.e., class, school, district) are available to teachers for instructional planning and are displayed in the Interpretive Guides. As an example, the Class Item Analysis Report provides scores useful for both norm-referenced and criterion-referenced interpretations. This report indicates the percentage of students who respond correctly for content/skill areas within a subject area for the class, building, system, and nation, allowing teachers to determine the strengths and weaknesses of their students relative to the school, district, and the nation.

In addition to providing examples of reports, the Interpretive Guides also provide general guidelines on how to use the test results for instructional planning. In this section, particular score reports are presented and informative discussions follow on how to interpret the scores and use the information for instructional decision making. There are also reminders that many factors affect the test scores of a student and a group such as cultural characteristics, student commitment, and mobility of students.

The Interpretive Guide for School Administrators also describes the purpose of the ITBS, how the ITBS was developed, the content of each test, and how to interpret scores and score reports. Of particular interest to school administrators are sections on selecting scoring service reports and using the test results for administrative services. The latter section provides examples of reports that are useful in evaluating and monitoring system-level performance. As an example, the System Performance Profile provides criterion- and norm-referenced information on the performance level of the system within subject areas. This information is useful for identifying strengths and weaknesses of the system's curriculum at a particular grade level.

Student norms and school average norms are provided in the Norms and Score Conversions document. For student norms, tables are provided for raw score to standard score conversions; and standard score to grade equivalent, percentile rank, and normal curve equivalent conversions. For school norms, tables are provided for standard score to percentile rank conversions.

DEVELOPMENT. The development of the ITBS, Forms A and B is documented in several publications including the Guide to Research and Development, Interpretive Guide for School Administrators, and Interpretive Guide for Teachers and Counselors. These documents indicate that new forms of the ITBS are developed based on a thorough examination of local, state, and national curriculum guidelines, and when possible, reflect shifts in curriculum and instructional practice. Content and fairness reviews are also conducted.

The Guide to Research and Development describes how the emphasis of the curriculum in particular subject areas in this country has changed over time, and how the ITBS has adapted over time to reflect these curriculum changes. Forms A and B differ from the previous forms in a number of ways. There is more of a focus on categorizing items by core skills rather than fewer specific skill categories. This change reflects the national attempt to identify a smaller number of core ideas on which to focus within subject areas at a particular grade. The Reading Comprehension test at Levels 9 through 14 is administered in two separately timed sections as opposed to a single, timed administration. A preliminary administration and analysis of the Reading Comprehension test indicated better completion rates and item statistics with two rather than one timed administration. In the mathematics tests at Levels 9 through 14 there are a number of changes reflected in Forms A and B. There is an increased emphasis on probability and statistics, and the estimation section was shortened by approximately 50%. Problem-solving and data interpretation are integrated, and problem

contexts, tables, and graphs are based on real data and are connected to other curriculum areas. The testing time and number of items for the Computation test was reduced by approximately 25%.

The ITBS measures a range of thinking skills, and many of its items measure inferential and analytical skills, problem solving and reasoning. The items for Levels 9 through 14 are classified on the basis of content and process requirements. Further, the authors classified each item in terms of the critical thinking demands required for successful performance. A continuum is presented with critical thinking at one end and remembering at the other end, with low-level application in the middle. An example the authors provide of critical thinking is inferring an author's viewpoint after reading several passages. The authors also attempt to integrate subject areas. As an example the reading passages from previously published material used for Levels 9 through 14 represent a wide variety of material that students are exposed to in and out of school including narrative, informational, and poetry, as well as topics in social studies and science.

The procedures used to try out items for the ITBS are notable. As part of the Iowa Testing Program, over 350 school systems are administered the tryout items in a 20-minute testing period. Close to 200,000 students in kindergarten through Grade 8 participated in the preliminary tryout of items for Forms A and B. Because student performance in Iowa differs from the national performance, item difficulties are adjusted to account for the difference. In addition to examining biserial correlations, items that have increasing percents correct (item easiness) in successive grades are looked upon favorably because they are sensitive to students' developmental progression. After examining the data from the preliminary item tryout, a national item tryout was conducted for Forms A and B in the fall of 1998 and the spring and fall of 1999. Approximately 11,000 students per grade in kindergarten through Grade 8 were tested, and 10,370 items were included in the national item tryouts. Given that the total number of items for the Complete Battery ranged from 146 to 515 depending on the Level, there were ample items from which to choose to create Forms A and B. Final item selection was based on the content coverage and the discrimination, difficulty, and differential item functioning analyses.

The mean, standard deviation, and standard errors of measurement are provided for the Fall and Spring for each of the tests at each Level in the Norms and Score Conversions document. Difficulty levels of each of the tests at each Level are also provided in the document.

TECHNICAL. The Guide to Research and Development and the Norms and Score Conversions documents provide a rich supply of data to evaluate the technical quality of the ITBS.

Standardization. The standardization of Forms A and B of the ITBS was done in conjunction with the standardization of the Iowa Test of Educational Development (ITED) and the Cognitive Abilities Test (CogAT) in the spring and fall of 2000. [Editor's note: Forms A and B were subsequently renormed during the 2004-05 school year. The reviewer had access to Form A only while preparing this review.] Both individual student norms and school norms are provided in Norms and Score Conversions. In addition to providing both fall and spring norms based on the standardization testing dates, interpolated norms are available for all quarter months outside of these dates.

To obtain a national probability sample that was representative of students across the nation, a stratified sampling procedure was used with geographic region, district enrollment, and socioeconomic status of the school district serving as the stratifying variables. In addition to the public school sample, a Catholic school sample and a private (non-Catholic) school sample were also obtained. The demographics for the standardization samples are compared to the population percentages in the Digest of Education 2000.

In the spring of 2000, students took the appropriate levels of the ITBS Complete Battery, Form A and the CogAT, Form 6. The spring norming group consisted of 170,000 students in kindergarten through Grade 8. As expected, the obtained samples in the spring were not representative of the population for some stratification categories so the sample percentages were weighted to reflect the population percentages better. The sample characteristics are presented in both the Guide to Research and Development and Norms and Score Conversions. To a small extent, the obtained sample overrepresented the Great Lakes and the Plains, and underrepresented New England, the Mideast, and the Farwest. There was also a small underrepresentation for Hispanics or Latinos.

In the fall of 2000, a more complex design was used. Students in Grades 2 through 8 participated in two units of testing with the order being counterbalanced. Each student took one of the ITBS Forms for the Complete Battery and the other Form for the Survey Battery. The fall 2000 standardization served several purposes: (a) to obtain fall norms, (b) to equate Form A and Form B of the Complete Battery and the Survey Batteries of Forms A and B to the Complete Batteries, and (c) and to obtain national item statistics for the Complete Battery, Form B and Survey Battery, Forms A and B. The fall norm group consisted of 76,000 students, with a subset of the schools drawn from the spring standardization sample. Unfortunately, the sample characteristics for the fall are not provided in either the Guide to Research and Development or Norms and Score Conversions. School districts that want to administer the test in the fall are not provided with information to determine the extent to which the fall norm group is representative of the population. For both the spring and fall standardizations, information should be presented on the percentage of schools that declined participation for those schools that were contacted as a first choice, second choice, and third choice.

Validity. Curricular relevancy should be the driving force for schools in deciding which standardized achievement test to adopt. Thus, schools should carefully determine whether the content assessed by the ITBS is reflective of their curriculum in kindergarten through Grade 8. The Interpretive Guide for School Administrators and the two Interpretive Guides for Teachers and Counselors provide rich information regarding the number of items measuring each content/process skill assessed by the tests within each subject area. This enumeration will prove valuable to administrators and educators who are evaluating the ITBS for adoption in their school system.

Content validity evidence is of paramount concern for achievement tests like the ITBS, and the process used for the development of the test specifications, individual items, and test forms provides rich validity evidence for the interpretation of the test scores. To provide validity evidence supporting the content of the ITBS, the authors indicate that it was developed to correspond with common goals of instruction across schools in the nation and the content and process specifications for the ITBS have been continuously revised. As discussed in the Development Section of this review, the process used to design the ITBS, including curriculum reviews, preliminary and national item tryouts, fairness reviews, and form design within and across levels, adhere well to national standards for test design (AERA, APA, & NCME, 1999).

To provide internal structure evidence, correlation matrices are presented showing the relationships among subtests and composite scores within each level of the ITBS. As expected, the correlations are moderate to high, and also as expected, correlations across subject areas are slightly lower than correlations within subject areas.

In addition to sensitivity reviews by content and fairness committees, standard errors of measurement for subgroups, overall gender differences, and differential item functioning (DIF) were examined. Tables provide the standard errors of measurement for boys, girls, Blacks, and Hispanics. The standard errors are similar across subgroups. A table provides the male-female effect sizes for average achievement for Form A indicating that girls score higher than boys in Reading Comprehension, Language, Computation, and Reference Skills, and these gender differences increase with level. In an attempt to explain these differences, the variability of the distributions for boys and girls was examined as well as the effect sizes computed at the 10th, 50th, and 90th percentiles. The results are provided for Grades 4 and 8 and indicate that boys tend to be more variable than girls, and for some subject areas such as Mathematics Problems and Data Interpretations, boys tend to outperform girls at the upper end of the distribution but girls tend to outperform boys at the lower end of the distribution. Tables in the manual also show that Whites tend to outperform Blacks and Hispanics. These differences in performance, however, are consistent with differences reported by NAEP. Data also are provided that indicate a narrowing of the gap between Whites and Blacks over time, also consistent with NAEP's findings. The narrowing of the gap is most likely due to changes related to opportunities to learn rather than any major changes in tests.

Reliability. Internal consistency estimates of reliability and equivalent-forms reliability were obtained. Using the Kuder-Richardson Formula 20, the majority of the internal consistency estimates for the subtests are in the .80s and .90s across Forms A and B, and most of the estimates for the reading totals, math totals, core totals, and composites are in the .90s. As expected, the lowest estimates are for primary grade levels. As an example, for Form A of the Complete Battery, the internal consistency estimates for Level 5 which is appropriate for kindergarten children, range from .699 to .882, whereas the internal consistency estimates for Level 14 range from .837 to .984.

Equivalent-forms reliability was obtained for Forms K and A from the spring 2000 equating of those forms, and for Forms A and B from the fall 2000 standardization sample. Most of the correlations for subtests between Forms K and A are in the high .70s and .80s. The correlations between Forms A and B for the Reading, Language, Math, and Core Totals were obtained from Levels 9 through 14 and they ranged from .811 to .942. The slightly lower equivalent-forms reliabilities as compared to the internal consistency estimates is to be expected given that more sources of error are reflected in the equivalent-forms reliabilities.

Stability coefficients were also obtained using the data from the 2000 national standardization. These were based on a sample of students who had taken Form A in the spring of 2000 and were then administered the next level of Form A or Form B in the fall of 2000. Correlations were obtained based on the developmental standards scores from these two administrations. Most of the coefficients were in the .70s and .80s.

Conditional standard errors of measurement are also reported for various score levels for the subscores and composite scores. The reporting of conditional standard errors of measurement is attractive given that measurement accuracy varies across a particular score scale.

COMMENTARY. The ITBS has a long history of use in schools as one of the most well-developed commercial standardized achievement tests, and the ITBS, Forms A and B continue the tradition. The authors are to be commended for their efforts in developing items that require students to integrate information across subject areas and to use complex thinking and reasoning skills. Careful attention was given to the design of the test specifications and items for the ITBS, Forms A and B. There is ample information provided about the content of the test to help potential test users determine its match to their curriculum.

The documents accompanying the ITBS that provide information on its development, purpose, and score interpretation are excellent. The Interpretive Guides have a strong instructional focus that enables teachers and administrators to evaluate individual student-, class, school-, and system-level achievement, including strengths and weaknesses. Information is provided for both criterion-referenced and norm-referenced interpretations. Clear examples are provided that illustrate the correct interpretation of different types of individual and group level scores as well as how to interpret score reports and how to use the information for instructional decision making.

The internal consistency estimates for subtest scores from most of the levels are moderate to high and allow for relatively reliable score interpretations at the subtest level. Item development and tryout procedures were extensive. The spring 2000 standardization sample was well-documented, but more information is needed on the characteristics of the fall 2000 standardization sample.

SUMMARY. The ITBS is a well-designed achievement test that reflects great care in the design of the instrument and the accumulation of evidence to support the validity of the score interpretations. Documents describing the design of the ITBS make it relatively easy for a prospective user to evaluate the alignment between the content of the test and the school curriculum. Reliabilities for the composite and subtest scores are very respectable. The accompanying documents that facilitate test administration and score interpretation and use are impressive. The ITBS should be given serious consideration for users who want to assess student achievement for grades K-12.

REVIEWER'S REFERENCE

American Educational Research Association, American Psychological Association, & National Council on Measurement in Education. (1999). *Standards for educational and psychological testing.* Washington, DC: American Educational Research Association.

[94]

IPT Early Literacy Test.

Purpose: Designed to "assess the skill development of English learners in kindergarten and first grade relative to their becoming proficient English language readers and writers."

Population: Grades K–1.

Publication Dates: 2000–2004.

Administration: Group.

Price Data: Available from publisher.

Comments: Measures students' developmental stages of reading and writing and helps educators develop instructional programs tailored to meet students' specific needs.

Authors: Beverly Amori and Enrique F. Dalton.

Publisher: Ballard & Tighe Publishers.

a) READING.

Scores, 9: Visual Recognition, Letter Recognition, Phonemic—Initial Sounds, Phonics—Initial Blends and Digraphs, Reading Vocabulary, Reading for Life Skills, Reading for Understanding Sentences, Reading for Understanding Stories, Total Reading.

Time: (10–30) minutes.

b) WRITING.

Scores, 5: Copy Letters, Write Name and Copy the Sentence, Descriptive or Narrative Writing, Spelling, Total Writing.

Time: (30–45) minutes.

Review of the IPT Early Literacy Test by MERITH COSDEN, Professor of Counseling, Clinical and School Psychology, University of California, Santa Barbara, Santa Barbara, CA:

DESCRIPTION. The IPT Early Literacy Test is one of a series of tests published by the authors on reading and writing proficiency. Their earlier instruments were written for students in 2nd through 12th grades, whereas this one was designed for students in kindergarten and 1st grade. The test has eight Reading and four Writing subtests. The Reading subtests assess Visual Recognition, Letter Recognition, Phonemic Awareness-Initial Sounds, Phonics-Initial Blends and Digraphs, Reading Vocabulary, Reading for Life Skills, Reading for Understanding Sentences, and Reading for Understanding Stories. First graders take each subtest, and kindergarteners take all but the Phonics and Reading for Understanding Stories subtests. The Writing test has four subtests: Copy Letters, Write Name and Copy the Sentence, Descriptive or Narrative Writing, and Spelling. First graders take each subtest, and children in kindergarten take all but the Spelling subtest.

The test can be administered to students in small groups. There are well-delineated standardization procedures for administering and scoring the test. Standardization for administration describes how the environment and the student should be prepared for the test and how much help should be given by the examiner. For example, the examiner is advised to have an assistant to help supervise, and to refer to the test as "work to be done," instead of a test, in order to reduce anxiety. Instructions for each subtest are provided in detail. Initial instructions can be given in the child's primary language, but once the test begins, test items need to be presented in English. Beyond assuring that the child is using the answer forms correctly, no assistance should be given. Although there is no time limit for the test, approximate times for each subtest are provided.

Although most of the subtests have objective criteria for scoring, the Descriptive or Narrative Writing subtest requires comparison of student responses to sample protocols, which are provided. An answer key for objective items, and sample protocols, are provided in the examiner's manual, as are tables that allow comparison of the student's scores to norms obtained for students at that grade level. Tables with standard scores, percentile ranks, and normal curve equivalents are available, as is a table associating the child's score with a stage of development in Reading (i.e., Pre-Reader, Beginning Reader, or Early Reader) and Writing (i.e., Pre-Writer, Beginning Writer, or Early Writer).

DEVELOPMENT. There were a number of stages to the test development. Prior to creating the test, the authors reviewed current research on the development and assessment of early literacy, early reading programs, and expectations for reading and writing for kindergarteners and first graders. The authors created a test committee, composed of practitioners experienced in teaching or assessing early literacy, and the test authors, whose charge it was to conceptualize the areas to be covered by the test. Their first task was the development of a shared definition of reading. Given the diversity of opinions in the field on how early literacy should be defined, the authors' definition, which guided development of the test, and their interpretation of test scores, is provided below:

> Reading is an active, cognitive process of gaining meaning from printed, graphic and written symbols, resulting in communication between the writer and the reader. Meaning is in the mind of the reader and depends upon his or her cultural and linguistic background; on his or her prior knowledge and experience; on the content and text form presented; on his or her skills in language processing; and on his or her purpose, interest, and motivation for reading. (technical manual, p. 3)

The committee then operationally defined three developmental stages of reading and writing for this age group: Pre-Reading and Writing, Early Reading and Writing, and Beginning Reading and Writing. The eight Reading subtests and four Writing subtests listed above were developed to measure the skills viewed as distinctive and seminal to each of these stages. The authors used three approaches for measuring literacy: Some of the subtests are discrete point tests, measuring specific reading and writing skills; some are integrative tests, assessing more than one domain at a time in a holistic manner; and some are pragmatic, focusing on aspects of literacy that require higher order thinking. Item development within each subtest also went through a comprehensive review process, with a larger number of items developed and discussed and modified on the basis of pilot testing.

The instrument that emerged after pilot testing was field tested in 2000 on 560 kindergarten and first-grade students across nine, largely southwestern states. The norms are based on this sample. Although the sample is ethnically diverse, with 58% Hispanic, 17% Native American, 17% Caucasian, and 8% from other ethnic groups, the authors appear to have used convenience sampling, relying on cooperating schools and students, rather than a stratified, random sampling plan.

TECHNICAL. Reliability data are provided primarily for the Reading subtests. The coefficient alpha is .89 for their kindergarten sample, and .90 for their first graders, which suggests strong internal consistency for this measure. The standard error of measurement for each grade level also suggests that the child's true score will fall within a few points of his or her tested score. However, there are no corresponding analyses for the Writing subtest. Interrater reliability was calculated for both Reading and Writing domains. These analyses were conducted on a diverse sample of 154 students collected across three states. Correlations of test scores over a 2-week period, with tests conducted and scored by two different assessors, was significant for both Reading and Writing tests, but lower for the Writing test (.48 for kindergarten; .76 for first grade) than for the Reading test (.87 for kindergarten and .85 for first grade).

The content validity for the test is evident in the match of items to the major tasks the authors describe for early literacy. Construct validity is noted in two ways for the Reading test. Intercorrelations among the Reading subtests are moderate (between .3 and .5), and significant, suggesting that they measure related domains. In addition, scores are higher in each domain for each grade level, as would be anticipated. Although not explained, the same analyses were not conducted on the Writing subtests.

Criterion-related validity was determined by correlating test scores with teacher ratings of students' academic abilities. Although the teacher rating scale was not provided, aside from the nonsignificant correlation with first graders' Visual Recognition, all other correlations were moderate and significant, ranging from .24 to .51 (Visual Recognition correlation was .20). Teachers were also asked to classify their students as Pre-Readers, Beginning Readers, or Early Readers, and Pre-Writers, Beginning Writers, and Early Writers, based on descriptors of these constructs provided by the test authors. The average test score for children categorized in this manner was in the anticipated direction, although mean test score differences between teacher-designated Early Reading and Early Writing, and Beginning Reading and Beginning Writing groups was small. Finally, the authors developed their cutoff scores for Pre-, Beginning, and Early Reading and Writing groups based on the test scores associated with teacher designations of students as English language learners. No subsequent analyses are cited, however, to determine the validity of these designations relative to classroom performance.

COMMENTARY. Although there is not a consensus regarding a definition of early literacy, the authors provide a well-considered definition that overlaps with many others in the field. The IPT Early Literacy Test was systematically constructed based on review of research and classroom needs, expert opinion, and pilot testing. However, the psychometric properties of the test are not uniformly strong. For example, criterion-related validity is based on correlations with teacher ratings of student abilities, and, although most of the correlations with Reading subtests are significant, some are low (.24), and similar analyses were not available on the Writing subtests. In addition, the normative data appear to be based on a convenience sample, and may not represent the skills and needs of students across the country. Stan-

dardized scores, percentiles, and normal curve equivalents are provided, but their usefulness is restricted by the sample used to generate them and limited study of their relationship to school performance. The authors caution against labeling students as Non-, Limited, or Competent English Readers; however, the value of their own student groupings of Pre-, Beginning, and Early Readers and Writers is not evident. It is the specific subtest scores that appear most useful in determining the types of experiences the child needs to improve his or her reading and writing skills.

SUMMARY. Although no assessment can measure all aspects of reading and writing ability, the IPT Early Literacy Test provides a thoughtful assessment of students' skills congruent with the test authors' definition of literacy. The test was carefully developed, with items tested and revised prior to the final version. Although the normative sample is not nationally representative, and the value of the global classification of students as Pre-, Early, and Beginning Readers and Writers unproven, the utility of the test lies in its ability to provide an assessment of students' reading and writing in a manner that will allow teachers to provide students with the experiences they need to improve their skills.

Review of the IPT Early Literacy Test by PATTI L. HARRISON, Professor of School Psychology, The University of Alabama, Tuscaloosa, AL:

DESCRIPTION. The IPT Early Literacy Test is described as an assessment for English language learners in kindergarten and first grade relative to skills in becoming proficient English readers and writers. A caution in the examiner's manual notes that the assessment is not designed for administration to non-English speakers. Furthermore, the examiner's manual emphasizes that inferences regarding a student being non-, limited, or competent as a reader or writer should not be made using the results of the test. Instead, the assessment purports to provide information relative to stages of reading and writing development (pre-, beginning, or early) that will assist in making curricular and instructional decisions.

Administration occurs in small groups and is conducted by a teacher or other trained staff member. The Reading test consists of eight subtests: Visual Recognition, Letter Recognition, Phonemic Awareness, Initial Sounds, Phonics, Reading

Vocabulary, Reading for Life Skills, Reading for Understanding Sentences, and Reading for Understanding Stories. The Writing test consists of four subtests: Copy Letters, Write Name and Copy the Sentence, Descriptive or Narrative Writing, and Spelling.

The examiner's manual contains detailed procedures for testing, instructions to be read to children by examiners, and a helpful summary of rules for testing. An answer key is provided for simple scoring of items for the Reading test. Scoring of the Writing test is more complex. The manual suggests that the scorer should not know the examinees being rated, which may be impractical in many classrooms. The examiner's manual includes extensive instructions, samples, and rubrics for scoring Writing items. Before conducting scoring for examinees, pairs of scorers must learn procedures by independently rating samples in the manual.

The correct Reading items across all subtests are summed to yield a total score for a student. Examiners may then use a table in the Reading test booklet to determine a student's overall English stage (pre-, beginning, or early reader) compared to criterion scores for fall kindergarten, spring kindergarten, or first grade. In the Writing test booklet, student scores on each subtest of the Writing test are used to identify a pre-, beginning, or early writer of English stage compared to criterion scores for fall kindergarten, spring kindergarten, or first grade. An indication of a student's overall English writing stage is determined as pre-writer (all subtests scored as pre-writer), beginning writer (any combination of subtest stages except those for the pre-writer or early writer), or early writer stage (all subtests scored as early writer). Stages are described as useful for placement and identification. Examiners may use optional diagnostic profiles to graph students' subtest scores in comparison to means obtained by the norm sample; these charts are described as useful for grouping students for instruction.

In addition, using tables in the examiner's manual, examiners may determine norm-referenced scores for total Reading and Writing, including standard scores (mean of 350 and standard deviation of 50 for kindergarten children and mean of 500 and standard deviation of 50 for first-grade students), percentile ranks, and normal curve equivalents (NCEs). NCEs are described as useful

for accountability and tracking progress. An IPT 2004 Addendum includes additional NCEs for Reading and Writing and provides options of deriving a comprehension score and overall proficiency score using the IPT Early Literacy Test and IPT-I Oral test.

The test manuals include only general information about interpreting test scores and provide little information directed toward outcomes and uses of the IPT Early Literacy Test. The stated purposes of placement, identification, grouping, accountability, and tracking progress are not described in detail, and there is little information about how to use the test for these purposes.

DEVELOPMENT. The examiner and technical manuals for the IPT Early Literacy Test include a general description of the development of the items and subtests of the Reading test and Writing test. Test authors and a committee of experts conducted reviews of research in early literacy and identified key competencies and objectives. Test authors wrote a large pool of items to reflect objectives, and committee members selected the items that best met the objectives. Items were reviewed, including review for cultural bias and representation of ethnicity and gender. Questionable items were administered to students and analyzed. A pilot test was conducted in which teachers critiqued content and test procedures.

In an IPT 2004 Addendum, the relationship between the test and No Child Left Behind requirements is described. The publisher offers to create alignments between the test and state standards.

TECHNICAL. The norm and field test studies included data collection with relatively small samples of kindergarten students (N = 317) and first-grade students (N = 243) in Spring 2000 and kindergarten students (N = 411) in Fall 2000. School districts in nine states in Spring 2000 and five states in Fall 2000 participated; although all regions of the country were represented, the majority of the norm samples were in the western states. The norm samples do not reflect U.S. Census data, and no other source of information was provided to judge the population for which the norm sample is representative. The majority of children in the samples were reported to be Hispanic, and additional race and ethnic groups were also included. A total of 55% in Spring 2000 and 82% in Fall 2000 were designated by their school districts as fluent English speakers or English-only speakers, although the assessment is described as one for English language learners. Fewer students were non- or limited-English speakers. Although the examiner's manual includes a caution that the test is not designed for administration to non-English speakers, a number of non-English speakers were included in the norm samples. Additional demographics described for the samples include primary language and country of origin, but important demographics used in typical test normings, such as socioeconomic status or community and school size, are not reported.

Data reported in the technical manual result in many concerns about the test's normative scores. Tables of item characteristics report that large percentages of children in the norm samples obtained perfect item scores, and means of subtest scores and total scores are also high, especially for the spring norm samples. The test authors suggest that, based on item data, the test is not appropriate for English-only students at the high end of the achievement range; this suggestion is in stark contrast to the norm samples, in which the majority of students were fluent in English or were English-only speakers. The authors also describe a tendency for school districts to select their best classes for field tests, casting further doubt on the appropriateness of the norm samples for comparison purposes. The characteristics of the norm samples and resulting high item, subtest, and total scores for the normative samples raise serious concerns about normative scores providing relevant information regarding the population for which the test was designed: *English language learners.*

A number of additional concerns about the normative scores were identified. The total scores for the Reading test and Writing test are based on the sum of raw scores for the subtest; because some subtests have more items than others, these subtests have higher weight in the total scores. The test authors note that it was decided not to weigh any of the subtests differently, but the unequal weights resulting from 10-item subtests having greater weights than 5- or 6-item subtests impacts the total score. Although the examiner's manual includes optional diagnostic profiles to plot children's subtest scores in comparison to average normative sample scores, there are no instructions for interpreting scores that are 1, 2, 3, etc. points below the mean. The high subtest

mean scores for the normative samples may result in subtest scores below the mean for most English language learners in the intended population for use of the instrument.

The examiner's manual includes tables for converting raw scores to standard scores, percentile ranks, and NCEs. The rationale for setting different standard score means of 350 for kindergarten children and 500 for first-grade children was not explained and is a source of potential confusion for examiners. In addition, standard scores may not be normalized. A percentile rank of 50 is associated with the mean standard score in a normal distribution. However, on the Reading test of the IPT Early Literacy Test, a percentile rank of 40 is associated with a standard score of 501 (in a distribution with a mean of 500) for first graders.

Two sources of NCEs are provided in the manuals. NCEs are included in an examiner's manual table that contains standard scores and percentile ranks. Additional tables of NCEs are provided in an IPT 2004 Addendum in both the examiner and technical manuals. However, the NCEs in the two tables are not consistent. For example, a raw score of 50 for first graders on the Reading test has an NCE of 38 in the first table and an NCE of 44 in the second table. The reason for this discrepancy in the NCE tables is not clear and is potentially confusing to examiners.

The technical manual includes cross-tabulation tables of the percentages of children classified with the IPT Early Literacy Test as pre-, beginning, and early readers or writers and classified by teachers as non-, limited, fluent, or English-only speakers. Although correlations between these two classification systems are reported as quite low (.06 to .39), the authors describe the cross-tabulation tables as the basis for establishment of cutoff scores in tables that identify a student in the pre-, beginning, or early English reader and writer stages. It is not clear how the cross-tabulation tables were used to identify cutoff scores, and the manual does not provide an adequate rationale for scores to define pre-, beginning, or early English reader and writer stages.

Internal consistency coefficients are reported for the Reading test and range from .23 to .84 for subtests and .88 to .90 for Total Reading; the low coefficients for subtests may relate to the small number of items found in some subtests. A reliability study involved administration of the Reading test and Writing test to a sample of 107 kindergarten students and 47 first-grade students and re-administration 2 weeks later by another examiner. Although labeled as an "inter-rater reliability" study, the study actually combines both interrater and test-retest reliability; thus, the source of error variance is unknown and may be due to raters, time, practice effects, etc. Correlation coefficients for the Reading test were .87 for kindergarten and .85 for first grade, and for the Writing test were .48 for kindergarten and .76 for first grade; no coefficients for subtests are provided. Standard errors of measurement are not reported for the reliability studies.

Several types of validity are described. The test authors support content validity based on sampling of test items to match specific objectives, as determination by experts during test development. Construct validity is described with intercorrelations between subtests and reporting of mean raw scores for students in kindergarten and first grade who were designated as non-, limited, fluent, or English-only speakers. Criterion-related validity data consist of correlations between teacher opinion of academic ability and Reading subtest scores, and the generally low correlations range from .11 to .51. The procedure for obtaining "teacher opinion" is not described. In addition, criterion-related data report average IPT Early Literacy Test Reading and Writing scores for groups of students ranked as pre-, beginning, and early readers and writers by teachers; Reading and Writing scores were different for the three groups.

All reliability and validity studies were apparently conducted with students in the norm samples. Thus, no reliability and validity studies focus specifically on the population of English language learners for whom the test is intended. COMMENTARY AND SUMMARY. The IPT Early Literacy Test contains well-designed administration procedures. The process for development of items appears to be extensive. However, there are many concerns about this instrument. The subtests have small numbers of items. The nature of the population represented by the norm samples is not apparent, but the majority of students were Hispanic and lived in western states. The samples have large numbers of students who were fluent or English-only speakers, in contrast to the test's intended use with English language learners. The norm samples obtained generally high scores on the test, and resulting normative data may not provide an appropriate comparison. There are a number of questions and inconsistencies about criterion scores for the pre-, beginning, and early Reading and Writing developmental stages and other norm-referenced scores. Reliability studies are limited, and a number of coefficients are low. Validity data also are limited. There are no reliability or validity studies that support the use of the test with the intended population of English language learners. Overall, the technical data do not support using the IPT Early Literacy Test for the stated purposes of placement, identification, grouping, accountability, and tracking progress relative to skills in becoming proficient readers and writers in the English language.

[95]

ITSEA/BITSEA: Infant-Toddler and Brief Infant-Toddler Social and Emotional Assessment.

Purpose: Designed to identify children "who may have social-emotional and behavioral problems and/or delays, or deficits in social-emotional competence."

Population: Ages 12-0 to 35-1 months.

Publication Date: 2006.

Administration: Individual.

Parts: 2 assessments: Brief Infant Toddler Social Emotional Assessment, Infant Toddler Social Emotional Assessment.

Forms, 2: Parent, Childcare Provider.

Price Data, 2006: $275 per ITSEA/BITSEA comprehensive kit including ITSEA/BITSEA Scoring Assistant software, ITSEA manual, BITSEA manual, 10 ITSEA Parent Forms, 10 ITSEA Childcare Provider Forms 25 BITSEA Parent Forms, and 25 BITSEA Childcare Provider Forms.

Foreign Language Editions: Parent and Childcare Provider Forms available in Spanish.

Comments: These tests are to be completed by a parent/guardian and a childcare provider; the parent form may be completed as an interview.

Publisher: The Psychological Corporation, A Harcourt Assessment Company.

a) BRIEF INFANT TODDLER SOCIAL EMOTIONAL ASSESSMENT.

Acronym: BITSEA.

Scores, 2: Problem Total, Competence Total.

Price Data: $99 per complete kit including BITSEA manual (2006, 62 pages), 25 BITSEA Parent Forms, and 25 BITSEA Childcare Pro-

vider Forms; $50 per BITSEA manual; $35 per 25 BITSEA Parent Forms; $35 per 25 BITSEA Childcare Provider Forms.
Time: (5–10) minutes.
Authors: Margaret J. Briggs-Gowan and Alice S. Carter.
b) INFANT TODDLER SOCIAL EMOTIONAL ASSESSMENT.
Acronym: ITSEA.
Scores, 20: Externalizing (Activity/Impulsivity, Aggression/Defiance, Peer Aggression), Internalizing (Depression/Withdrawal, General Anxiety, Separation Distress, Inhibition to Novelty), Dysregulation (Sleep, Negative Emotionality, Eating, Sensory Sensitivity), Competence (Compliance, Attention, Imitation/Play, Mastery Motivation, Empathy, Prosocial Peer Relations), Maladaptive Item Cluster, Social Relatedness Cluster, Atypical Item Cluster.
Price Data: $150 per complete kit including ITSEA manual (2006, 180 pages), 10 BITSEA Parent Forms, and 10 ITSEA Childcare Provider Forms; $25 per ITSEA manual; $25 per 10 ITSEA Parent Forms; $25 per 10 ITSEA Childcare Provider Forms; $75 per ITSEA Scoring Assistant.
Time: (20–30) minutes.
Authors: Alice S. Carter and Margaret J. Briggs-Gowan.

Review of the ITSEA/BITSEA: Infant-Toddler and Brief Infant-Toddler Social and Emotional Assessment by ABIGAIL BAXTER, Associate Professor, Department of Leadership and Teacher Education, University of South Alabama, Mobile, AL:

DESCRIPTION. The Infant-Toddler Social and Emotional Assessment (ITSEA) assesses social-emotional development in 1- to 3-year-olds. The Brief Infant-Toddler Social and Emotional Assessment (BITSEA) is a social-emotional development screening test. Both measures sample two types of problem behaviors: (a) typical behaviors that are excessive or insufficient in frequency or intensity and (b) behaviors that are never developmentally appropriate. Social-emotional competencies are also assessed. Both have Parent (PF) and supplemental Childcare Provider forms (CPF) and can be self-administered or used for interviews. Both were written at the fourth to sixth-grade reading levels.

The ITSEA should be administered by professionals with training and experience administering and interpreting standardized tests who have also had supervised developmental and mental health training with young children and par-

ents. BITSEA administrators should understand screening tests and the need for follow-up with further assessment, or be supervised by someone with these qualifications.

The ITSEA-PF has 170 items forming three problem domains (externalizing, internalizing, dysregulation) and one competence domain with three to six subscales per domain. Maladaptive, Social Relatedness, and Atypical Item Clusters are also scored. Items are rated with a 3-point scale: 0 = *not true/rarely*, 1 = *somewhat true/sometimes*, 2 = *very true/always*. "N" (no opportunity) can be scored on certain items. Inclusion of reverse-scored items helps to prevent response sets. There are maximum numbers of missing responses allowed on each subscale. The measure can be computer- or hand-scored; hand scoring is complex but the manual's directions are clear. Subscale average raw scores are summed and averaged (by number of questions answered) and converted to domain *T*-scores and percentile ranks divided by age bands (12–17 months, 18–23 months, 24–29 months, and 30 months–35 months, 30 days) and gender. Problem domain *T*-scores of 65 or more are "of concern" and Competence domain scores of 35 or less are also "of concern" and suggest a developmental deficit or delay. Subscale and item cluster percentile ranks of 10 or below are interpreted as "of concern." These scores are not diagnostic, however, and should be interpreted in light of a more comprehensive evaluation.

The CPF includes the PF and seven items specific to child care. It has no norms but is scored like the PF. Parents' and childcare providers' ratings are compared to understand the child better.

The BITSEA PF and CPF contain the same 42 items and result in separate Problem and Competence Total scores. Total scores with percentile rankings greater than the 25th percentile for Problem scales and 15th for the Competence scale indicate possible problems. When such thresholds are triggered, further assessment is suggested.

DEVELOPMENT. The ITSEA was developed as a parent report of social-emotional development based upon the developmental psychology and psychopathology literatures. The authors decided, a priori, to assess social-emotional and behavior problems as well as social-emotional competencies. Literature and clinical reviews led to the development of 200 items assessing the three problem domains, their constructs, social-emotional competencies, and rare but clinically significant problem behaviors across the proposed age range. These items were reviewed by 12 national experts in social-emotional development and psychopathology and the number of items was expanded. These items were pilot-tested with a clinical sample and changed for readability (sixth grade level) and formatting ease. The final version of the ITSEA was field-tested with a nonclinical sample and fine-tuned with a cohort sample.

An expert panel identified ITSEA items that should be included on the BITSEA screener. ITSEA subscale items with the highest loading were added. Finally, several ITSEA fear and emotion questions were combined into one fear and one emotion question on the BITSEA.

TECHNICAL. The standardization sample for both tools is 600 children from 42 states: 150 in each age band, equally divided between boys and girls. Age bands are stratified by ethnicity, parent education, and region as in the 2002 Census.

The ITSEA has test-retest, interrater, and internal consistency reliability. Internal consistency coefficient alphas and standard errors of measurement (SEM) are available for all ages and both genders. There is internal consistency within domains and subscales. Test-retest reliability (average 6 days) was assessed with 84 families. The test-retest correlations are .76–.91 for the domains; subscale correlations are comparable (.75–.92). For the total sample, only the Externalizing and Dysregulation domain scores and three subscale scores meet the .90 or greater criteria for making individual decisions (Salvia & Ysseldyke, 2004). However, the authors state very clearly that the ITSEA is not a diagnostic tool and it should be part of a comprehensive assessment. This caution, in conjunction with the lability of performance when testing infants and toddlers, may make these reliabilities understandable. Interrater reliability was assessed by having both parents of 94 children rate their child separately and comparing scores with Intraclass Correlation Coefficients (ICC). ICCs greater than .75 were deemed excellent, and .60–.74 were good. All domain ICCs were between .72 and .79. Two subscale ICCs (Depression/Withdrawal and Mastery Motivation) and two of the Item Cluster (Atypical Item Cluster and Social Relatedness) ICCs were below .60 for the entire sample. There was only a small average difference between the two parents' ratings.

BITSEA test-retest reliability coefficients were based on the same 84 families as used with the ITSEA. The Pearson correlations for the Problem Total scores were all in the .90 range for the total sample and boys and girls separately. Competence Total scores' correlations were in the low .80s for these groups. These numbers meet/exceed the minimal standard for screening tools. Evidence of score stability across a year is reported. The SEMs were larger for Problem Total scores (1.64–1.89) than for Competence Total Scores (1.15–1.34). There is evidence of interrater reliability from 94 families with two parents completing the BITSEA.

The ITSEA has many types of validity. Content validity may be inferred from the literature and expert reviews. Confirmatory factor analysis indicated that the subscales are coherent and reflective of their domains. The patterns of domain and subscale correlations also provide validity evidence. Divergent and convergent validity studies comparing scores from the ITSEA and the Child Behavior Checklist 1.5–5, Ages and Stages: Social-Emotional, Adaptive Behavior Assessment System II, and the Bayley Scales of Infant and Toddler Development III reveal a pattern of measures of similar constructs being positively correlated and measures of dissimilar constructs being negatively correlated. Finally, when children from special groups were compared to control children on the ITSEA, it was sensitive to differences between the groups in ways that point to sensitivity and specificity of the ITSEA.

Validity of the BITSEA is based upon correlations with ITSEA scores and relationships with other measures as described above. Likewise, BITSEA scores differentiated special populations from the norm group. The BITSEA also provides a sensitivity-specificity analysis, a crucial criterion for a screening instrument. Sensitivity refers to the correct identification of clinical cases and specificity refers to correct identification of normalcy. A sensitivity-specificity analysis with a sample of children with autism indicated that the Competence scores (using the 15th percentile cut scores) have excellent specificity and sensitivity in detecting children with autism. The BITSEA identified 100% of the children with autism by their Competence scores, and misidentified 9.1% of the control children as having autism. With Problem scores, 97% of the normal children were classified as normal (using the 25th percentile cut scores) but only 63.6% of the children with autism were identified.

COMMENTARY. The ITSEA and BITSEA assess a very important component of development that is often overlooked: social-emotional development. This developmental domain is rather important because of the impact it has upon the child's life. The ability to detect social-emotional and behavior problems as well as competencies in young children will help professionals intervene earlier. The foci on problem behaviors and competencies will allow interventionists to address inappropriate behaviors while trying to facilitate the development of acceptable behaviors.

The ITSEA and BITSEA are unique in that they can be easily completed by both parents and childcare providers. Using information from these two raters, clinicians can look for contextual effects on children's behavior. Often these dual perspectives are missing in the assessment of young children's social skills.

The internal consistency, interrater, and test-retest reliabilities of the ITSEA and BITSEA are acceptable. The test-retest reliability for the ITSEA, however, is low. Further information is needed. For the ITSEA to have some clinical utility, test-retest reliabilities of stable characteristics must meet accepted minimal levels.

Validity evidence for the ITSEA and BITSEA is extensive. Evidence of construct, convergent, and divergent validity is available and indicates that both tools measure multiple components of social-emotional and behavioral problems as well as social-emotional competencies in young children. In addition, with a sample of children with Autism Spectrum Disorder, the BITSEA Competence scores reflected both sensitivity and specificity.

SUMMARY. The ITSEA and BITSEA assess important dimensions of infants' and toddlers' social-emotional development. Unlike other tools that include social-emotional development as one of the domains assessed, on the ITSEA and BITSEA it is the only domain assessed. As a result, a better picture of the child's strengths and needs in this domain emerges. If problems are detected they can be pinpointed and addressed. The use of multiple informants, flexible administration methods, and computer scoring are also benefits of using the ITSEA and/or BITSEA.

REVIEWER'S REFERENCE

Salvia, J., & Ysseldyke, J. E. (2004). *Assessment: In special and inclusive education* (9th ed.). Boston: Houghton Mifflin.

Review of the ITSEA/BITSEA: Infant-Toddler and Brief Infant-Toddler Social and Emotional Assessment by TIMOTHY R. KONOLD, Associate Professor of Research, Statistics, and Evaluation, University of Virginia, Charlottesville, VA:

DESCRIPTION. The Infant-Toddler Social and Emotional Assessment (ITSEA) is a self-report measure designed for use with young children 12 to approximately 35–36 months of age. The ITSEA measures four domains related to social-emotional and behavioral problems (i.e., Externalizing, Internalizing, Dysregulation, and Competence) with three or more subtests for each. In addition, item clusters defined as Maladaptive, Social Relatedness, and Atypical are also available.

Respondents rate the behavioral statements listed on the protocol using a 3-point scale ranging from *not true/rarely* to *very true/often*. The accompanying examiner's manual provides clearly articulated instructions for completing the protocols.

Several hypothetical case studies are also provided in the examiner's manual that are useful in illustrating various interpretative frameworks offered on the ITSEA. Separate versions of the ITSEA are available for parents and childcare providers.

The Brief Infant-Toddler Social and Emotional Assessment (BITSEA) is also available and can serve as an initial screening tool or for use when examiners are faced with time limitations. The BITSEA is appropriate for use with the same age group as the ITSEA. It covers less comprehensively the same four domains as the ITSEA and includes the Atypical Behaviors Item Cluster. As with the ITSEA, both parent and childcare provider forms are available. Items located on the BITSEA were derived from the more comprehensive ITSEA measure.

DEVELOPMENT. The motivation to develop the ITSEA emerged from a lack of measurement tools focusing on social-emotional behavioral problems and competencies in very young children. Construction of the ITSEA was guided by existing literature, the author's earlier work in this area, and a review of previously published instruments designed for use with older children. An initial pool of 200 items was constructed to tap the aforementioned domains. Items were scrutinized to ensure fit with both of the areas intended to be measured with the ITSEA and the age group for which it was designed. Nationally recognized developmental psychologists with expertise in the fields of social-emotional development and psychopathology in early childhood were called upon to provide item reviews. Revised items were pilot tested with clinic-referred children and further revised for readability and ease of use. Two additional field tests were conducted in order to examine the psychometric properties of the instrument and provide additional modifications to items to ensure adequate content coverage, respectively.

TECHNICAL. The standardization sample for the ITSEA is composed of N = 600 children between the ages of 12 to 35 months, 30 days who were selected from 42 states. Age bands of approximately 6-month intervals are composed of 150 children each (N = 75 boys). Children within each interval are stratified in accordance with 2002 U.S. Census data by ethnicity, parent education level, and region. Norms are provided in 6-month age bands and are available separately for boys and girls in standardized T-scores. Base rates are also available to facilitate score interpretations.

Reliability. Several investigations into the reliability of scores are presented in the form of internal-consistency, test-retest, and interrater agreement for the parent form. Internal-consistency (alpha) estimates for the ITSEA are provided separately for girls and boys within each of four age bands. In addition, overall estimates for boys and girls are provided. All overall estimates for boys and girls at the domain level are well within acceptable limits (e.g., > .80), whereas the majority of subscale estimates across these groups are somewhat lower. Estimates are not provided for item clusters.

A test-retest reliability study (N = 84) is reported for the parent form across an average testing interval of approximately 6 days. Estimates are provided for the total sample and separately for boys and girls across domain, subscale, and item cluster scores. Coefficients generally range from .76 to .92 for the total sample, with the exception of the Social Relatedness cluster, which yielded a value of .64. Interrater agreement estimates between parent pairs (N = 94) are very favorable for an informant-based assessment of children within this developmental age range. Standard errors of measurement are provided for domain and subscales

to facilitate score interpretations. These estimates are provided separately for boys and girls within each of the four age bands.

Validity. It is widely recognized that validity refers to the accumulation of evidence to support the interpretation of test scores in the context of their purpose. The ITSEA examiner's manual reports several validity studies for the parent form, the majority of which can be characterized as related to internal structure and convergent/discriminate validity. Internal structure is largely explored in the examiner's manual through zero-order correlations among the various scales contained within the ITSEA. The pattern of relationships presented is largely consistent with expectations and suggests that few of the scales are so highly correlated as to render them redundant, with the majority of correlations within the low to moderate range. A more complete investigation of the internal structure of the scales emerges through factor analysis. Users are provided a very brief summary of findings previously published in peer-reviewed journals that support the internal structure of the ITSEA through confirmatory factor analysis that incorporated cross-validation.

Scores on the parent version of the ITSEA were examined in relation to four external child rating instruments. These studies, which ranged in size from N = 37 to N = 112, are presented to support the construct validity of the ITSEA parent form scores. Results from these investigations were generally favorable in demonstrating good convergent and discriminate validity for the parent form.

The final set of reported studies examined mean ITSEA parent form score differences between clinical samples (developmentally delayed, language delayed, premature, autistic, and mental health) versus control samples matched from the standardization sample on age, sex, ethnicity, and parental education level. Results generally demonstrated statistically significant score differences between the clinical and control groups, suggesting that the ITSEA parent form is useful in discriminating between these groups. This finding was perhaps most apparent for comparisons directed between the autistic disorder group and matched controls, and least apparent for comparisons between premature birth and matched controls.

COMMENTARY/SUMMARY. The primary value of this assessment tool lies in its comprehensive coverage for a young population of infants and toddlers. The ITSEA measures a large number of social-emotional problems and competencies, and provides several layers of interpretation through its subscales, domains, and cluster scores that should be useful for developing a profile of children's behavior problems and competencies. The BITSEA represents a shorter version of the ITSEA that can be used when administrators are faced with time constraints or when the goal is to determine whether a more complete assessment of children's behavior problems and competencies is needed. This screening measure was derived from the ITSEA and was scrutinized in many of the same ways as the ITSEA in terms of its psychometric characteristics.

Demonstrating the extent to which scores are free from error (reliable) and that the scores are appropriate for their intended use (valid) is an ongoing process. The examiner's manuals accompanying the ITSEA and BITSEA address many important psychometric issues relating to the interpretation of scores and appropriateness of score use with this young population of children. These studies provide a good foundation for understanding the parent versions in terms of the consistency of scores they produce, their relationship with other measures of child behaviors, and their ability to discriminate between clinical and nonclinical samples. In balance, however, it is important to note that in addition to the parent form, the ITSEA and the BITSEA both provide a childcare form. Very little is mentioned about the childcare form in the examiner's manuals, particularly in terms of empirical support for the reliability and validity of its scores. The lack of empirical research presented on the usefulness of these scores limits the confidence users will have with this form of the instrument.

[96]

IVA+Plus [Integrated Visual and Auditory Continuous Performance Test].

Purpose: "Designed primarily to help in the diagnosis and quantification of the symptoms of Attention-Deficit/Hyperactivity Disorders (ADHD)."
Population: Ages 6 to adult.
Publication Dates: 1993–2007.
Acronym: IVA+Plus CPT.
Scores, 28: Auditory Response Control Quotient, Prudence Auditory, Consistency Auditory, Stamina Auditory, Visual Response Control Quotient, Prudence Visual, Consistency Visual, Stamina Visual, Full Scale Response Control Quotient, Auditory Attention Quotient, Vigilance Auditory, Focus Auditory, Speed Auditory, Visual Attention Quotient, Vigilance Visual, Focus Visual, Speed Visual, Full Scale Attention Quotient, Fine Motor Regulation Quotient (Hyperactivity), Balance, Readiness Auditory, Readiness Visual, Comprehension Auditory, Comprehension Visual, Persistence Auditory, Persistence Visual, Sensory/Motor Auditory, Sensory/Motor Visual.
Administration: Individual.
Price Data, 2007: Option 1: $495 per starter kit with Investigator including CD-ROM, interpretation, administration and technical support manuals (included on CD), and 10 testing administrations (licensed for use at one computer); $149 per 10 additional test administrations for starter kit preferred customer ($269 per 25); Option 2: $899 per registration kit with Investigator including CD-ROM, interpretation, administration, and technical support manuals (included on CD), and 10 testing administrations; $139 per 25 additional test administrations for registration kit preferred customer; Option 3: $1,895 per unlimited use kit with Investigator including CD-ROM, interpretation, administration, and technical support manuals (included on CD), and unlimited testing administrations at one computer station; $99 per preferred customer plan; Investigator included with test (unlimited use); $10 per demonstration CD; $249 per Interpretive Report Writer; $99 per technical support package.
Foreign Language Editions: Option available to allow the test stimuli to be spoken in a foreign language (Arabic, Danish, Dutch, French, German, Greek, Hebrew, Hindi, Indonesian, Italian, Japanese, Mandarin, Pashto, Polish, Portuguese, Russian, Spanish, Swahili, Swedish, and Taiwanese Dialect) for an additional charge of $269.
Time: (13) minutes.
Comments: Computer administered; requires IBM computer with a Pentium 166 or higher processor, Windows 2000, ME, XP, or Vista, Internet Explorer 6.0 or higher, and speakers; optional analyses (Investigator and Special Analyses) and report writers (Standard Report, ADHD Report, Special Analyses Report) may be added to software; the Preferred Customer Plan provides software or normative updates, free technical support for one year, and discounts on the cost of additional testing administrations and Add-Ons.
Authors: Joseph A. Sandford and Ann Turner.
Publisher: BrainTrain.
Cross References: For reviews by Harrison Kane and Susan C. Whiston and by Martin J. Wiese of an earlier edition, see 14:180.

Review of the IVA+Plus [Integrated Visual and Auditory Continuous Performance Test] by CLEBORNE D. MADDUX, Foundation Professor of Counseling and Educational Psychology, University of Nevada, Reno, Reno, NV:

DESCRIPTION. The IVA+Plus [Integrated Visual and Auditory Continuous Performance Test] is a computer-administered and computer-scored, individual, continuous performance test (CPT) for use with individuals from ages 6 to adult. The test requires a total of 20 minutes for administration and is designed to assess two major factors: *response control* and *attention*, measured in both visual and auditory modes. Its purpose is "to be useful in following the diagnostic criteria provided in the DSM-IV by providing data to help differentiate between the four sub-types of Attention-Deficit/Hyperactivity Disorder-ADHD..." (interpretation manual, p. 6). The manual goes on to suggest that the test can also be useful in evaluating attention and self-control problems in individuals with a variety of other medical and psychological problems, and can also be useful in assessing the effects of medication or other therapies.

The test is different from many other continuous performance tests in that the items involve both visual and auditory modes. The test program requires a USB mouse, sound card, speakers, Internet Explorer 6.0 or later, and a screen resolution set to 1024 X 768. The test is made up of 500 trials, each requiring 1.5 seconds, in which respondents click the mouse button of a computer each time the screen displays a "1" or the computer-synthesized voice speaks the word "one," and refrains from pressing the mouse button each time the screen displays a "2" or the computer-synthesized voice speaks the word "two." The computer keeps track of reaction times in milliseconds and other data related to responses to the auditory and visual stimuli such as errors of commission (said to indicate *impulsivity*) and errors of omission (said to measure *inattention*).

The test is made up of four stages: (a) the warm-up period, (b) the practice period, (c) the main test, and (d) the cool-down period. The main test, from which the scores are derived, takes approximately 13 minutes.

The IVA+Plus yields six global composite quotient scores (mean of 100, standard deviation of 15), which includes a full scale response control quotient, auditory response control quotient, visual response control quotient, full scale attention quotient, auditory attention quotient, and visual attention quotient. The profile also lists 22 subscales divided into four groups: response control, attention, attribute, and symptomatic. Each of these latter four groups are further divided to make the 22 scales, all but one with both an auditory and a visual quotient. The response control group is made up of auditory and visual prudence, consistency, and stamina; the attention group is made up of auditory and visual vigilance, focus, and speed; the attribute group is made up of balance and auditory and visual readiness; and the symptomatic group is made up of auditory and visual comprehension, persistence, and sensory/motor scales. There is also a fine motor regulation scale and two additional scales for use with the interpretive flowchart for ADHD: the sustained auditory attention quotient and the sustained visual attention quotient. According to the manual, the 22 subscales "provide data to help clarify the nature of problems with inhibition, consistency of response, stamina, inattention, variability of attention, and overall speed of discriminatory reaction time" (interpretation manual, p. 8).

The way the quotients are organized is complex, and descriptions in the manual are somewhat difficult to follow, partly because there is no complete sample report printed on consecutive pages in the manual (there is a complete sample report on the website), and also because there are two manuals (the administration manual and the interpretation manual) and numerous other technical or informational documents, all of which must be printed out from separate files on the CD or accessed on the Website. Then too, neither manual contains a concise statement of the differences between the original IVA and the current IVA+Plus. For the IVA+Plus, it appears that the normative sample has been increased to 1,700 and the name of one of the four groups into which the 22 scaled scores are organized has been changed from "validity" to "symptomatic." A phone call to the publisher revealed the additional information that The Investigator, a supplementary computer routine, is included free in the IVA+Plus, but was not free in the IVA. The Investigator is designed to permit analyses of results test by test, quintile by quintile, or response by response. The IVA+Plus also offers two different types of narrative reports, each of which can be produced in three different styles as well as a special analyses report that focuses on mental concentration, performance under high and low demand conditions, and the possibility of malingering.

DEVELOPMENT. The IVA+Plus is based on a number of concepts and theories related to the nature of ADHD, especially those of Barkley (1993), who posits ADHD to be caused by a deficit in response inhibition. The IVA+Plus consequently is said to be designed to maximize errors of response inhibition. The manual includes several pages devoted to research studies conducted by others that have been used in the design of the IVA+Plus.

TECHNICAL.

Normative data. The normative group of the IVA+Plus was expanded to 1,700 in December of 1999. The manual contains only a general description of the normative group and states that "Normative data were collected from individuals not known to have past neurological disorders, not on medication (except birth control and nasal sprays), not currently active in psychotherapy or counseling, not known to have learning and/or attentional problems and not known to demonstrate hyperactivity" (interpretation manual, p. 25). The website contains more descriptive information, but is still incomplete. There is no mention of characteristics of the sample such as ethnicity, social class, or other demographics other than the fact that individuals were located in Texas, California, Michigan, and Florida; that they are grouped across 21 age levels; and that approximately equal numbers of males and females were in each of these levels. Numbers at each age level are adequate, and summary statistics from the normative group can be downloaded from the CD.

Reliability. The only reliability information presented is one test-retest study of the 22 raw scale scores and the six composite quotient scales carried out with 70 individuals 5 to 70 years of age, tested 1 to 4 weeks apart. This appears to be the test-retest study carried out with the IVA when it was first developed. There is no information available on how these individuals were selected, and no detailed demographics are presented. The manual states only that 60% were female and 40% were male; they were volunteers; and none had identified physical, psychological, attention, self-control, or learning problems. For the six composite quotient scores, test-retest correlations ranged from .37 to .75, with all but two of these below .70. For the 22 scale scores, test-retest correlations range from .02 to .88, with 15 of these below .70.

Validity. Evidence of validity is limited to what appears to be the original validity study that investigated the discriminative and concurrent validity of the IVA. This was a study involving 26 children who had been diagnosed as having ADHD and 31 children with no history of such a diagnosis. The children were between 7 and 12 years of age, and the IVA correctly identified 92% of the ADHD children and 90% of the non-ADHD children. Concurrent validity was studied by comparing the percentage correctly and incorrectly identified by the IVA and by four other continuous performance tests and rating scales. These ranged between 90% and 100%. Of the five instruments, the percent of false negatives was lowest for the IVA (7.7%).

COMMENTARY. The IVA+Plus is quick and easy to administer, and its greatest strength is its assessment of both auditory and visual processes in a single instrument. However, reliability and validity data are not sufficient. Test-retest reliability is low for some of the quotients and has been studied only in a group of 70 individuals ages 5 to 70. Concurrent and predictive validity evidence for the overall test is quite good, at least for the small group studied (26 with ADHD and 31 without ADHD). However, as pointed out in an earlier review of the IVA (Kane, 14:180), the instrument has not been shown to be valid for distinguishing between non-ADHD subjects and subjects with the four subtypes of ADHD. Until this is provided, the claim in the manual that the instrument will help differentiate among the four subtypes of ADHD must be regarded as unsubstantiated.

SUMMARY. The IVA+Plus is a continuous performance test (CPT) that is quick and easy to administer. It assesses attention in both auditory and visual modes. Scoring is entirely by computer and the profile that is produced is complete and easy to understand. Information about the IVA+Plus should be consolidated in a smaller number of files on the CD. The manuals and supplementary files contain sufficient information concerning the characteristics of the scores and their interpretation.

The instrument is promising, but the normative sample, though sufficiently large, is insufficiently described. Reliability and validity data are incomplete. Future reliability and validity studies should make use of larger samples across the entire age range for which the instrument is normed, and evidence produced to validate the instrument for distinguishing among subtypes of ADHD. Information derived from use of the instrument should be regarded as merely suggestive, and any assessment of ADHD should make use of multiple data sources and types.

REVIEWER'S REFERENCE
Barkley, R. A. (1993). A new theory of ADHD. *The ADHD Report 1*(5), 1-4.

Review of the IVA+Plus [Integrated Visual and Auditory Continuous Performance Test] by WES SIME, Professor, Emeritus, University of Nebraska-Lincoln, Lincoln, NE:

DESCRIPTION. The IVA+Plus is a computerized assessment tool used to assess specific dimensions of Attention-Deficit/Hyperactivity Disorder (ADHD) and other motor learning-performance functions. Based upon criteria outlined in the DSM-IV, the authors assert that the IVA+Plus helps the clinician diagnose and differentiate between the four subtypes of ADHD: (a) Predominantly Inattentive Type (formerly called ADD), (b) Predominantly Hyperactive-Impulsive Type, (c) ADHD Combined Type, and (d) ADHD Not Otherwise Specified. This test also may be useful as part of a neuropsychological test battery (Tinius, 2003). It is commonly used to measure treatment effectiveness for behavioral as well as pharmacological treatments. It is a relatively brief (13 minutes) testing process that involves 500 trials of either seeing or hearing the numbers "1" or "2" in a pseudorandom pattern, requiring the shifting of sets between visual and auditory modalities. The respondent's continuous performance task is to click the mouse button when the number "1" appears and to forego (withhold) responses whenever the number "2" appears on the screen or is heard through the earphones.

The performance assessment begins with the examiner documenting the client profile with very minimal demographic information most notably age and gender, which are the primary factors that influence the interpretation of results. Scores are automatically computed, graphed, and converted to a text explaining the results. The assumption for conduct of testing includes the fact that the user has an understanding of motor learning, developmental stages of children, signal detection theory, and statistical inference before engaging in the testing process. During some segments of the test, the 1s are more common

than the 2s, creating a response set that "invites" errors of commission (clicking erroneously when a 2 appears), or impulsivity. During alternating segments of the test the 1s occur rarely, which "invites" more errors of omission (failing to click when a 1 appears), or inattention, because the subject must remain vigilant while he or she waits for a 1 to occur. The authors provide an extended narrative in the interpretive report, but in practical application the narrative is not easily understood and requires significant editing to be included in a clinical report. Training in how to interpret the results would be recommended in order to use the test most effectively.

All scores are presented both as raw scores and as quotient scores. The quotient scores have a mean of 100 and a standard deviation of 15 and are divided into four categories: (a) Attention, (b) Response Control, (c) Attribute, and (d) Symptomatic. The primary diagnostic scales are the Response Control Quotient (RCQ) and Attention Quotient (AQ). The RCQ is based on separate Auditory and Visual Response Control Quotients derived from both visual and auditory analysis of Prudence, Consistency, and Stamina scales. Prudence is a measure of impulsivity and response inhibition as determined by recording errors of commission. Consistency is a measure of the reliability and variability of response times and reflects the ability to stay on task. Stamina is determined by comparing the difference in reaction times (of only the correct responses made) during the first 200 trials versus the last 200 trials and serves as a measure of ability to sustain attention and effort over time.

By contrast, the AQ is derived by examining separate Auditory and Visual Attention Quotients based on measures of visual and auditory Vigilance, Focus, and Speed. Vigilance is a measure of inattention (errors of omission), whereas "Focus reflects the total variability of mental processing speed for all correct responses" (interpretation manual, p. 9). On the other hand, Speed is determined by recording the average reaction time for all correct responses throughout the test and is purported to help identify attentional problems related to slow discriminatory mental processing.

Another feature of this instrument is the Fine Motor Regulation scale that provides an assessment of "off-task" behaviors with the mouse, such as multiple clicks, spontaneous clicks during instruction periods, anticipatory clicks, and holding the mouse button down. The authors suggest that "the Fine Motor Regulation score quantifies fidgetiness and restlessness associated with small motor hyperactivity" (interpretation manual, p. 10). In addition they claim learning style can be determined by calculating Attribute scores in two dimensions: (a) Balance, wherein the client may process information more quickly visually or aurally, or is equally quick in either modality and (b) Readiness, wherein the client may process information more quickly when the demand is quicker or when it is slower. The Readiness scale may provide a subtle measure of inattention when the client just "can't quite keep up" with the demand.

Finally, the IVA+Plus has symptomatic scales for measures of Comprehension, Persistence, and Sensory/Motor deficiency. Comprehension identifies random responding, which would lead to faulty interpretation of other IVA+Plus scale scores. The authors suggest that Comprehension is the single most sensitive subscale in discriminating ADHD, whereas Persistence is a measure of motivation as the client is asked to do "one more thing" at a time when fatigue may be setting in. By contrast, the Sensory/Motor scales may rule out possible neurological, psychological, or learning problems as evidenced by particularly slow reaction time.

DEVELOPMENT. The IVA+Plus is a relatively quick measure of both auditory and visual inattention and impulsivity as well as learning style that yields objective data supportive of other self-report and behavioral observations (Solanto, Etefia, & Marks, 2004). The results are presented in the same format as the IQ scoring system familiar to most clinicians. Further, the results of the test address both emotional and neurological problems, in addition to cognitive deficiencies. Results are available immediately via the computerized scoring system and can be stored and transferred to data files for research purposes.

In comparing this instrument to another similar tool, the Conners' Continuous Performance Test II (CPT-II; 15:66), there are many similarities. The format and the length of the test are comparable. However, the CPT-II uses letters for the correct target stimuli and a Bold "X" for the noncorrect target. In addition, the CPT-II offers either space bar or the mouse for client responses. It would appear that the IVA+Plus provides more clinically relevant information in that the CPT-II addresses only attention, vigilance, impulsivity, and "erraticness" through the measures of reaction time, commissions, and omissions. Furthermore, the response mode is visual only for the CPT-II, whereas the IVA+Plus offers an integrated visual and auditory assessment.

The authors also market a software and hardware training package under the heading of Captains Log that addresses learning deficiencies in children and young adults.

TECHNICAL. Normative data include a sample of 1,700 individuals divided by gender, and grouped by age as follows: 6, 7, 8, 9, 10, 11, 12, 13, 14, 15, 16, 17–18, 19–21, 22–24, 25–29, 30–34, 35–39, 40–44, 45–54, 55–65, and 66–96 years of age. The normative database included a broad representation of ethnicity (not documented) and was collected regionally in Virginia, Texas, Michigan, California, and Florida excluding clinical patients with any history of learning disability, hyperactivity, or attention problems. Approximately equal numbers of males and females were included in each age/sex group.

Insufficient evidence is offered with regard to reliability and validity. For each psychometric property, results from a single study are presented using 70 individuals to assess test-retest reliability (over a 1- to 4-week interval) and 57 individuals to assess validity. Reliability estimates varied widely (.02 to .88) across composite quotients and scale scores. Validity coefficients proved somewhat more credible, as the IVA+Plus correctly identified the vast majority of ADHD and non-ADHD children (92% and 90%, respectively) and compared well with other instruments designed to discriminate these same groups.

COMMENTARY. Research documentation on the clinical relevance of the test is well established for not only ADHD but also autism (Corbett & Constantine, 2006). It may be particularly useful where there is potential for either malingering (Quinn, 2003) or faking the symptoms of ADHD because the results are much more objective than self-reports or behavioral observations (Solanto et al., 2004). In complex cases where cognitive function and a history of brain injury are in question, the objective nature of this test is useful in neuropsychological testing (Tinius, 2003). It should be noted that the most definitive measure of attention is accomplished with the TOVA (Test of

Variables of Attention, TOVA; T6:2566), which has a longer history and more common usage, but takes 2–3 times longer to be completed.

SUMMARY. The authors of this instrument have produced a concise measure of both auditory and visual indicators of attentional deficit (ADHD) in varying types. For the most part, psychometric soundness of the IVA+Plus has yet to be demonstrated. This instrument has some advantage over two other similar measures (TOVA and CPT-II) in expediency and comprehensiveness. Outcome measures of Prudence, Consistency, Stamina, Vigilance, Focus Speed, Balance, Readiness, Comprehension, Persistence, and Sensory/Motor Deficiency provide highly specific and relevant information on the various dimensions of ADHD. The instrument is easy to administer and provides results rapidly. Although the interpretive report is long and somewhat unwieldy for most clinical applications, the information provided is very useful in diagnosing ADHD as well as in determining progress in therapy. There is little question about the advantages of using the IVA+Plus to serve both psychologists and educators in helping those with this disorder to overcome the difficult behavioral and learning deficits.

REVIEWER'S REFERENCES

Corbett, B. A., & Constantine, L. J. (2006). Autism and attention deficit hyperactivity disorder: Assessing attention and response control with the integrated visual and auditory continuous performance test. *Child Neuropsychology, 12*, 335-348.
Quinn, C. A. (2003). Detection of malingering in assessment of adult ADHD. *Archives of Clinical Neuropsychology, 18*, 379-395.
Tinius, T. P. (2003). The Integrated Visual and Auditory Continuous Performance Test as a neuropsychological measure. *Archives of Clinical Neuropsychology, 18*, 439-454.
Solanto, M. V., Etefia, K., & Marks, D. J. (2004). The utility of self-report measures and the continuous performance test in the diagnosis of ADHD in adults. *CNS Spectrum, 9*, 649-659.

[97]

James Madison Test of Critical Thinking.

Purpose: "Designed to evaluate the in-depth critical thinking ability of middle school students through adults."

Population: Grades 7–12+.

Publication Date: 2004.

Scores: Total score only.

Acronym: JMTCT.

Administration: Individual or group.

Forms, 2: A, B.

Price Data, 2006: $64.99 per 50-use CD (specify form); $103.99 per 50-use CD including both forms; quantity discounts available; $9.99 per test online administration.

Time: 50 minutes.

Comments: Can be administered online, over a network, or on a stand-alone computer (Windows or Macintosh); both forms can be used as a pretest or posttest; formerly known as the Comprehensive Test of Critical Thinking.

Authors: Don Fawkes, Bill O'Meara, and Dan Flage.

Publisher: The Critical Thinking Co.

Review of the James Madison Test of Critical Thinking by JERRELL C. CASSADY, Associate Professor of Psychology, Department of Educational Psychology, Ball State University, Muncie, IN:

DESCRIPTION. According to the authors, the James Madison Test of Critical Thinking (JMTCT) is the most comprehensive pencil-and-paper measure of critical thinking that can be accomplished in the time frame permitted (50 minutes). The JMTCT provides assessment of some 47 unique critical thinking skills in a 55-item, multiple-choice format. The manual provides support addressing the claim that the JMTCT covers all the primary skills covered in the leading critical thinking assessment alternatives (e.g., California Critical Thinking Skills Test, Cornell Critical Thinking Tests, Watson-Glaser Critical Thinking Appraisal). There are two forms for the JMTCT, both delivered and scored by a computer interface that can be managed on a local computer or through a network server. This aspect of the JMTCT is the true mark of distinction relative to the standard critical thinking assessments that are widely used.

Review of all 47 proposed skills addressed would be overly laborious. However, the scale can be broken into 14 main areas of critical thinking that are addressed: Distinguish between paragraphs that are arguments and those that are not; identify main conclusions of arguments; analyze sufficient and necessary conditions; analyze the structure of arguments based on experimental results in science; judge strengths and weaknesses of additional evidence supporting inductive arguments; draw conclusions from Aristotelian and other forms of deductive arguments; draw direct conclusions from given statements; judge logical equivalence of two statements; judge arguments that are fallacious or ambiguous; judge if hypothetical claims and additional information support an argument leading to a definite conclusion; supply missing assumptions or premises that guarantee stated conclusions are true; assess relevance of claims to other claims, questions, descriptions, etc.; judge whether conditional claims have been satisfied by the provided information to draw correct conclusions; identify the claim that will best support a target argument; and discern whether pairs of claims are consistent, contrary, contradictory, or paradoxical.

The computer interface system allows individual and group summaries based on the 14 parts of the JMTCT as well as performance estimates on each of the 47 skills proposed to be assessed. The performance summaries are currently provided as raw scores and percent correct. It is also possible to generate comparison printouts between different test takers, again using raw and percentage correct scores. No standardization information is provided in the version reviewed.

DEVELOPMENT. The manual outlines the history of the development of the JMTCT, essentially the collaborative endeavor of three faculty members at James Madison University (Bill O'Meara, Dan Flage, and Don Fawkes). The work was reportedly inspired by an interest in developing a new test of critical thinking that took on more tasks than the traditional measures as well as attempted to overcome the perceived barriers of existing measures: lengthy items, excessive use of jargon, and low clarity in the intended purposes of the assessment.

After the initial creation of the JMTCT, the authors undertook a revision effort at the prompting of the president of the Critical Thinking Company, a business that provides online critical thinking measures across the lifespan, with particular focus on elite institutions. The purpose for the revision was apparently to make the original university-oriented items accessible for testing for children as young as seventh grade. Support for the supposition that the revised version meets that developmental period is provided through a series of scores on a variety of readability calculations, which ranged from the Flesch Grade Level of 3.9 to the FORCAST Grade Level of 9.4 (an additional 6 calculations all put the test within the seventh grade range of readability).

Finally, the manual outlines a sampling done with 830 incoming students to James Madison University (443 Form A, 387 Form B). The results of that testing sample provides some score averages and indications that the internal consistency estimates were acceptable, but not strong (.58 and .65). These low levels of internal consistency were attributed to the variety of tasks encompassed by the JMTCT.

Overall, there is little explicit information documenting the development of this scale. For example,

there is no indication that there were any scale analyses leading to the creation of subfactors and no demonstration of the impetus for item generation.

TECHNICAL. The technical manual provides insufficient evidence to declare confidently that the scale is reliable or valid. The manual is embedded in the CD-ROM that comes with the test server software and provides only one measure of reliability (noted above) for what is reported as a pilot sample (collected in 2004). There is no evidence provided for validating the scale. That is, there are no comparisons to existing measures of critical thinking to demonstrate construct validity; nor is there any indication of correlations with meaningful constructs related to critical thinking.

The administration of the test can be done either through a local server or via the Internet. There is an advertised price of $9.99 per test when conducted online (with various discounts for bulk testing), but the CD-ROM-based server testing application costs are generally less, if many individuals are tested. The technical support for the software is excellent; requests for information or support on installing the software to run the JMTCT were promptly met and expertly managed.

The scoring is automatized and can be exported through a variety of output options. The score report provides simple raw score values for each of the 47 skills, 14 sections, and an overall value for the scale as a whole. The scores are also presented as percentage correct, but no standard scores are available at this time. Furthermore, all analyses are provided without attention to age of the subject. There is an option to list a set of scores together, identifying performance on the 14 parts of the test, again making simple raw score or percentage correct comparisons.

COMMENTARY. The JMTCT may indeed be the test of the future for critical thinking assessment. The items are similar to existing measures, with the caveat of providing a multitude of additional critical thinking tasks for assessment. Several of the items provide realistic analysis of research, science, or logic that can tap into applied critical thinking skills. The online or computer-based testing process was simple and allowed the testing administrator to set up individual, class, or multiclass testing situations. The automated printouts are ideal for speedy response to data.

However, there are several issues to be resolved with the version of the test made available for review. From an instrumentation and measurement perspective, it is disconcerting that most critical thinking skills are assessed with only one item. Furthermore, providing a 50-minute timed test of critical thinking with the same items for individuals ranging in age from seventh grade through adulthood raises the concern that most seventh grade students will not reach the latter portions of the test. Although many of the items meet the goal of providing clear instruction without undue jargon, there were still many items that were unnecessarily abstract and ambiguous—likely to be confusing to the younger populations in particular.

The scoring for the JMTCT is a critical barrier to utility in any avenue other than research studies investigating change over time at this point. That is, until there are standard scores available with disaggregation based on age, gender, culture, and other relevant factors, there can be no comparative statements made for the general population. As it stands, researchers could use the two forms as pre- and posttests to measure the impact of a program on critical thinking, or perhaps correlate critical thinking with other dependent measures. However, this usage would be poorly advised at this point, as there exists no evidence to support the scale as a valid measure of critical thinking.

SUMMARY. The JMTCT has potential to be a meaningful addition to the field. However, the current status of the scale is one of incompletion. Although the computer-based testing and reporting process was efficient and effective, there is little use in the scores that are generated to this point. To meet the needs of a test of critical thinking for diagnostic, comparative, or evaluative purposes, the JMTCT will need to have a greater degree of explanation for the development of the scale, provide standardized performance information, detail age-related differences, and provide extensive psychometric evidence to demonstrate that the measurement of 47 skills with 55 items is not prone to excessive measurement error.

Review of the James Madison Test of Critical Thinking by SUZANNE YOUNG, Associate Professor of Educational Research, University of Wyoming, Laramie, WY:

DESCRIPTION. The James Madison Test of Critical Thinking (JMTCT) was developed to measure the degree to which respondents exhibit skills used in typical everyday life to think critically. Critical thinking, according to the authors, is made up of more than 250 skills; the JMTCT tests 14 of these skills (including 38 subskills). The rationale for developing this test was that the authors wanted to develop a test that had less jargon and tested more critical thinking skills than comparable tests. There are two forms of the test available, and it was developed for test-takers who are in the seventh grade and beyond.

The test itself includes 55 objective items and respondents are expected to complete the test in 50 minutes. The test items are written at a seventh-grade reading level; sentence structure is simplistic and vocabulary is relatively jargon-free. Items are presented in a multiple-choice format, and each set of items is preceded by a brief introduction. The test is only available electronically: on CD, over a network, or online. Test takers receive a total score when the test is completed.

The authors do not provide information about the test administration in the test manual. Also, they do not offer an explanation for interpreting test scores.

DEVELOPMENT. In the test manual, the authors describe their test development conducted using students at James Madison University. The initial administration was used to revise items so that scores would yield similar standard deviations for Form A and Form B. The authors do not explain how the original items were developed, but it is clear that items were based on skills that relate to critical thinking. The authors also mention that the test was piloted with other small groups of students during development; although they do not report those statistics, they suggest that the results from the pilots were similar to the later versions of the test.

TECHNICAL. The test was validated using freshmen at James Madison University. Form A was administered to 443 students and Form B was given to 387 students. The authors report the means and standard deviations for the students' scores on the two forms ($M = 28.6$ and $SD = 5.15$ for Form A; $M = 28.4$ and $SD = 5.59$ for Form B). However, they do not describe the sample except to say they were incoming freshmen.

Reliability was found using coefficient alpha (internal consistency). Coefficient alpha was reported for both forms of the test, using the same two samples described above. Reliability was reported to be .58 for Form A and .65 for Form B. The authors note that reliability coefficients are typically low for tests of critical thinking; certainly internal consistency estimates would be expected to be low for a set of items that are written to assess a number of different skills. The authors do not provide the standard error of measurement, although they are easily calculated with the statistics provided (3.34 for Form A and 3.31 for Form B).

Validity of the tests was not addressed except that the authors suggest the test items were developed to address identified critical thinking skills. According to the authors, critical thinking is made up of more than 250 separate skills. Although the JMTCT does not test all 250 skills, according to the test authors it does cover the same skills as other popular tests plus 24 additional skills. They include a table that shows the correspondence between skills and items; if these are indeed the skills that define critical thinking, this is solid evidence for content validity.

COMMENTARY. The most compelling feature of the James Madison Test of Critical Thinking is that it assesses critical thinking skills more thoroughly than its popular competitors (Cornell Critical Thinking Tests measures seven skills, California Critical Thinking Skills Test covers five general skills, Watson-Glaser Critical Thinking Appraisal assesses five skills). The JMTCT is also designed so that it is readable at the seventh-grade level. Although these are both strengths of the test, they are also weaknesses.

Although the authors describe the test as usable for seventh-grade students and older, their validation sample was limited to college freshmen. As noted, they provide evidence of content validity in the design of the test but they do not provide other evidence of validity. Because critical thinking is likely used primarily in educational settings, one would expect to see evidence of construct and criterion-related validity. Can critical thinking skills be taught? If so, how do critical thinking skills relate to achievement? The authors could certainly have collected more data from their 830 freshmen to support the validity of this test. Also, the internal consistency coefficients of the two forms are weak, very likely due to the fact that the test is assessing so many different critical thinking skills. A more appropriate reliability estimate would have

been alternate-forms reliability and could have been done by giving both forms of the test to all 830 freshmen. Although the authors note that the difficulty of developing a new test is the scarcity of psychometric data, they could easily have designed their validation study to provide more evidence of validity and reliability. In addition, writing a test so that it is readable at a seventh-grade level is very different from developing a test that is appropriate for seventh graders (or others). Their development sample was college students; based on this sample, it is a stretch to suggest the test is appropriate to be used with 12-year-olds, graduate students, and other adults in nonacademic settings.

SUMMARY. Considering the weaknesses of the psychometric information, it is difficult to recommend the use of the JMTCT. It does have the potential to be more useful that its competitors but based on the low reliability, lack of validity evidence, and the fact that the validation sample was college freshmen, the test developers need to do more to convince potential users of its usefulness. Other tests of critical thinking are recommended for more narrow populations, report higher reliability estimates, and some offer stronger evidence of validity. Until the authors can produce more compelling evidence, this reviewer suggests that potential users choose the Watson-Glaser Critical Thinking Appraisal (T7:2742).

[98]
Job Search Knowledge Scale.

Purpose: Designed to "measure a person's knowledge about finding a job."
Population: Job seekers.
Publication Date: 2005.
Acronyms: JSKS.
Scores, 5: Identifying Job Leads, Direct Application to Employers, Resumes/Cover Letters, Employment Interviews, Following Up.
Administration: Individual or group.
Price Data, 2006: $34.95 per complete kit including 25 test booklets and administrator's guide (8 pages).
Time: (15–25) minutes.
Comments: This test can be self-administered and self-scored.
Author: John Liptak.
Publisher: JIST Publishing, Inc.

Review of the Job Search Knowledge Scale by GARY J. DEAN, Professor and Chairperson, Department of Adult and Community Education, Indiana University of Pennsylvania, Indiana, PA:

DESCRIPTION. The Job Search Knowledge Scale (JSKS) is designed to measure a person's knowledge about searching for employment. It is intended to be administered to people seeking employment to determine in what areas they have sufficient job search knowledge and in what areas they need to strengthen their job search knowledge. The inventory consists of 60 true-false items that are arranged into five scales with 12 items per scale: Scale 1—identifying job leads, Scale 2—submitting direct applications to employers, Scale 3—writing resumes and cover letters, Scale 4—conducting employment interviews, and Scale 5—following up after the interview. It can be administered to an individual or group and can be self-administered and self-scored.

The instrument folds out from 8.5" x 11" to 22" x 17" and includes the 60 true-false items and scoring and interpretation guides. The format is easy to follow and colorful and attractive. Taking the inventory is expedited by clearly marked steps on the instrument: (a) take the inventory, (b) total the scores, (c) understand the results, (d) review the answers, and (e) develop a job search action plan.

The JSKS is scored based on the number of true-false items to which the job seeker correctly responds on each scale. The true–false responses are labeled A or B or C or D. To score each scale, the respondent totals the number of B and C responses (regardless of whether they were true or false) and records that number in a box next to the items. These scores (correct responses) for each scale range from 0 to 12. The score for each scale is then recorded in a grid, which allows for comparison of the five scale scores. Interpretation is provided in two ways. First, score ranges are interpreted. These are 9 to 12 = a "great deal of knowledge about the job search topic," 4 to 8 = job search knowledge "similar to that of other people," and 0 to 3 = "little knowledge about the job search topic." The second form of interpretation is that each item on the inventory is explained in a narrative that describes the correct responses and the reasons why those responses are correct.

DEVELOPMENT. The five scales on the JSKS were identified through reviewing a variety of job search books and workbooks. The item pool was developed based on a review of literature related to employment counseling and job search training. In addition, the author consulted with individuals providing counseling services in government funded training programs, rehabilitation counseling programs, and private outplacement and career counseling businesses. The resulting item pool was reviewed in terms of the five scales to determine their appropriateness and to eliminate duplicate and unrelated items. The author also stated that he used language that is consistent with current job search literature and that all references to ethnicity, race, and sex in the items were removed. Samples of adults from a variety of places, including prisons, government funded programs, and career counseling programs, completed drafts of the instrument, and alpha coefficients and interscale correlations were computed to identify the final pool of 60 items.

TECHNICAL INFORMATION. Reliability was established through the use of alpha coefficients and test-retest correlations. The alpha coefficients were computed based on a sample of 155 adults from a combination of private and community agencies and are as follows: Scale 1 = .75, Scale 2 = .82, Scale 3 = .90, Scale 4 = .84, and Scale 5 = .91. The test-retest correlation coefficients were from a subsample of the previous sample (n = 100) with a 1-month interval and are as follows: Scale 1 = .82, Scale 2 = .79, Scale 3 = .87, Scale 4 = .85, and Scale 5 = .90.

Validity was established through interscale correlations and, according to the manual, mean scores for men and women on the five scales. The interscale correlation coefficients ranged from .19 (between Scales 3 and 5) to .47 (between Scales 4 and 1). The mean scores and standard deviations for each scale are reported for a total sample of 135 and for subsamples of men (n = 65) and women (n = 70). The mean scores for all (n = 135) range from 7.88 (interviews) to 8.20 (direct application to employers). The mean scores for men indicated that their strongest area is interviews (mean = 8.53) and their weakest area is identifying job leads (mean = 7.76). For women, the strongest area is direct application to employers (mean = 8.20) and their weakest area is interviews (mean = 7.79).

COMMENTARY. The author established five guidelines for the JSKS. To provide commentary on the instrument each of the guidelines will be examined in turn.

1. "The instrument should measure a wide range of job search skills" (administrator's guide, p. 5). The JSKS appears to have a good representation of items for the five scales. In addition, the

five scales do represent the commonly accepted major areas of job search knowledge and skill needed to be successful in the job market. The scale and instrument development and selection process appear to have been well thought out and carried out with attention to appropriate instrument development procedures. On the other hand, only a few references are provided; no in-depth information is provided about the "thorough review of the literature" (administrator's guide, p. 5) that the author stated he conducted. Also, the items appear to represent a white-collar job bias with many of the items representing tasks peculiar to searching for white-collar jobs.

2. "The instrument should utilize a user-friendly format" (administrator's guide, p. 5). The true-false format does, in fact, lend itself to ease of completion by the user. However, sophisticated users (in terms of general worldly experience and/or test taking savvy) will be able to pick the correct answer for many items even if they do not know the correct response. This susceptibility to testwiseness generally will have the result of inflating their job search knowledge score in one or more of the scales.

3. "The instrument should be easy to administer, score, and interpret" (administrator's guide, p. 5). In this area the author succeeded admirably. The overall layout of the instrument and the easy-to-follow five-step format allows the instrument to be completed by an individual with little or no guidance. Furthermore, the administrator's guide contains clear directions for administering, scoring, and interpreting the JSKS.

4 and 5. "The instrument should apply to both men and women and the instrument should contain items which are applicable to people of all ages" (administrator's guide, p. 5). In this area there are some limitations to assessing how well the author met his guidelines because of the lack of information in the administrator's guide. Although the author does indicate that one of the samples consisted of both men and women, there is surprisingly little detail offered about the samples used in the development and reliability and validity studies. For example, there is no description of the samples used to generate the final pool of 60 items other than indicating that they came from a variety of areas. Also, there was no detail provided on the statistical procedures used to arrive at the final pool of 60 items. Finally, the samples re-

ported in the reliability and validity studies give us no information about the make-up of those samples in terms of age, race, geographic area, or previous employment experience. The absence of this information is disturbing because it would appear to make a great deal of difference in understanding the generalizability and applicability of the norm groups. Also, how the means for men and women relate to validity is not clear.

SUMMARY. The JSKS appears to meet several of the guidelines established by the author. The instrument appears to be useful for measuring the job search knowledge of job seekers and could be a useful tool to both job seekers and counselors assisting them. The major problem is in the lack of information in the administrator's guide. In summary, although the reliability studies appear to be adequate to demonstrate the usefulness of the JSKS, the validity studies are weak. The administrator's guide contains too little information about the norm groups to be able to make a good judgment as to whom the JSKS is applicable.

Review of the Job Search Knowledge Scale by KEITH HATTRUP, *Associate Professor of Psychology, San Diego State University, San Diego, CA:*

DESCRIPTION. The Job Search Knowledge Scale (JSKS) is a paper-and-pencil measure of an individual's knowledge of how to find, apply for, interview, and negotiate for positions of employment. As stated in the administrator's guide, the goals of the measure are to provide diagnostic information for job seekers about the most effective ways of finding employment. The measure is especially designed for use in the context of career guidance programs, including school- and college-based programs, employment counseling programs, rehabilitation counseling programs, and similar agencies. The author presents a very good explanation of the need for the measure in the administrator's guide. The measure provides an assessment of the instructional needs of the job seeker that can assist career counseling staff, and provides self-assessment information that may increase the job seeker's motivation and ability to acquire new knowledge relevant to the job search process.

DEVELOPMENT. The JSKS includes five scales that each contain 12 items; all 60 of the resulting items are answered with a True/False response format. The five scales included in the measure are: Identifying Job Leads, Direct Application to Employers, Resumes and Cover Letters, Employment Interviews, and Following Up. These scales are designed to measure the factors, or dimensions, that are represented in a thorough job search effort, based on the author's review of the literature. According to the administrator's guide, the appropriateness of the five dimensions was confirmed by three independent "job search experts" who all agreed that the five dimensions are important in finding and securing employment. Thus, the measure was developed rationally, and little empirical evidence of either the comprehensiveness or conceptual structure of the item domain was provided.

TECHNICAL. The measure can be administered to individuals or groups, requires about a ninth-grade reading level, and takes about 20 minutes to complete. Very clear instructions are provided for examinees and administrators, and the measure itself appears easy to understand and simple to complete. Scoring is done by the user, following simple instructions in the manual. A separate score is calculated for each scale by summing the 12 items in each scale using codes that identify correct answers for each item. Instructions to examinees and administrators indicate that scores between 4 and 8 represent a level of knowledge that is "similar to that of other people" (administrator's guide, p. 4), whereas higher or lower scores represent more or less knowledge than average, respectively. However, normative data provided in the administrator's guide show that means for the five scales ranged from 7.88 to 8.20 in a sample of 135 adult males and females, with standard deviations between 1.04 and 1.72. This finding implies that scores between about 7 and 9 represent average performance on each scale, whereas the range presented by the author probably represents somewhat lower than average performance.

The normative data, provided separately for both males and females and for the groups combined, were based on responses of 65 adult male and 70 adult female participants. Internal consistency reliability estimates are based on a sample of 155 adults who were clients of agencies or services dedicated to helping individuals who were having difficulty finding employment. Of the sample of 155, about 100 participants were tested a second time after a 1-month delay to derive test-retest reliability estimates. Correlations among the five scales are derived from a sample of 105 adults. The degree of overlap between the sample that provided normative data and the sample that was used in calculating interscale correlations is not indicated in the administrator's guide. Participants' ages ranged from 18–65. Information is not presented about participants' ethnicities, education levels, or job experience; thus, the generalizability of the results presented in the administrator's guide is difficult to ascertain.

Internal consistency reliability estimates ranged from .75 to .91 across the five scales. Test-retest reliabilities varied between .79 and .90. The Resumes and Cover Letters and Following Up scales showed the highest reliabilities in both analyses. Standard errors of measurement (SEMs) are not provided in the manual, but would assist in the interpretation of differences among scores.

Evidence of validity of the measure is limited to observed correlations among the five scales, which varied from .19 to .47. After correcting the correlations for attenuation due to measurement error (based on internal consistency estimates), these values vary between .21 and .59. The author suggests that male-female differences in scale scores (which are in fact very small) provide additional construct validity evidence, without explaining how or why.

COMMENTARY. Much more evidence of the test's reliability and validity must be presented before a clear understanding of the measure is possible. Exploratory or confirmatory factor analyses would significantly bolster the conceptual model underlying the measure.

SUMMARY. The Job Search Knowledge Scale is a newer measure designed to fill a need for an assessment of job search knowledge within the context of career or job search counseling. If its use is limited to the stated purposes of providing an approximate assessment of training needs and self-knowledge, where psychometric considerations are secondary to overall counseling goals, then the JSKS is likely to prove useful. However, its use for making classification decisions, making differential assignments to training conditions, or other purposes that require stronger inferences about the meaning of specific score differences must be avoided until more thorough and supportive empirical evidence of reliability and validity is obtained.

[99]
Job Style Indicator [Revised].

Purpose: Designed to help understand "the work behavioral style and task requirements" of a job and to provide "a job compatibility rating when used with the following CRG style assessments: personal, Sales, Instructional, Entrepreneurial, and Quick."

Population: Adults.

Publication Dates: 1988–2006.

Acronym: JSI.

Scores, 4: Behavioral/Action, Cognitive/Analysis, Interpersonal/Harmony, Affective/Expression.

Administration: Individual or group.

Price Data, 2006: $7.95 per test booklet; 47.95 per access code online version; $69.95 per professional's guide (2006, 64 pages).

Time: [30–60] minutes.

Comments: Self-administered and self-scored; may be used in conjunction with Personal Style Indicator (17:144), Sales Style Indicator (17:251), Quick Style Indicator (17:249), Entrepreneurial Style and Success Indicator (17:68), and the Instructional Style Indicator (17:232).

Authors: Ken Keis, Terry D. Anderson, and Everett T. Robinson.

Publisher: Consulting Resource Group International, Inc.

Cross References: For reviews by Neal Schmitt and David M. Williamson of an earlier edition, see 13:164.

Review of the Job Style Indicator [Revised] by M. DAVID MILLER, Professor, College of Education, University of Florida, Gainesville, FL:

DESCRIPTION. The Job Style Indicator [Revised] (JSI) is a tool used to understand the style expectations of a job or work position. That is, job style is the features that are required by a job if the job is to be performed well. The JSI has two primary functions described in the manual. First, the JSI is used to define a position from a hiring or development perspective to the company. Second, the JSI provides a job description that employers can compare with potential employee assessments for making employment decisions.

In some ways, the Job Style Indicator is not a measurement of a person as much as it is a description of a job. The JSI is used to describe a job along four dimensions: Behavioral, Cognitive, Interpersonal, and Affective. The instrument is completed by a manager, a management team, or individuals currently holding a given position to describe the job—not a person in the job but the requirements of the job in the ideal. Once the job description is completed with the Job Style Indicator, the Personal Style Indicator (also reviewed in this *Yearbook*; 17:144) is administered to determine a potential employee's match to the job profile as specified by the JSI. The JSI provides a target profile, whereas the Personal Style Indicator is used for employee selection; therefore, the latter bears the onus of providing validity and reliability evidence for its use in employee selection.

The Job Style Indicator is composed of 16 items. Each item is a set of four descriptions of job-related behaviors or tasks (e.g., goal-oriented, structured, considerate, outgoing). For each item, the manager, management team, or individuals holding the job would rank-order how accurately each job description describes the job requirements (4 = most accurate to 1 = least accurate). Each set of four descriptions represents the four dimensions of Behavioral, Cognitive, Interpersonal, and Affective. Scores on the dimensions are defined by the sum of the rankings on the 16 items for the appropriate descriptors. Thus, a job with higher cognitive requirements would result in a higher score on that dimension and a lower score on other dimensions. Scores on the four dimensions provide the company with a Job Style Profile.

DEVELOPMENT. The Job Style Indicator was developed based on evidence that the foundation of any successful business is hiring the right person for the right job. The instrument assumes there are four primary dimensions for understanding general job style: Behavioral, Cognitive, Interpersonal, and Affective. The Behavioral dimension is defined as a job that requires action and being willing to change things. The Cognitive dimension is defined as a job that requires analysis and handling of data. The Interpersonal dimension is defined as a job that requires harmony and relating to people. Finally, the Affective dimension is defined as a job that requires expression and exploring ideas. For each dimension, the manual describes the general orientation, the typical strengths, and the common difficulties of individuals with those characteristics. The instrument was developed with job characteristic descriptors to match the above definitions.

TECHNICAL. No technical information (e.g., reliability and validity) is provided for the Job Style Indicator. Given the use of the instrument to provide a method whereby a company can come to agreement on a job style profile and its use as a target for employment decisions, the lack of formal reliability and validity evidence may be appropriate. Again, this evidence should be closely examined for the instrument used to assess the potential employee match to the job style description (e.g., the Personal Style Indicator; 17:144).

However, additional information is provided to understand better the job style ratings and the roles and responsibilities of the job. After completing the ratings, the users of the JSI are given a checklist for the job to describe the position better. For each dimension, a checklist of job strengths and difficulties is provided. Job strengths are characteristics/abilities that are important to the job whereas difficulties are traits that need to be minimized for the job. It is noted that a high score on a dimension should have more strengths checked and fewer difficulties. In contrast, a lower score on a dimension should have fewer strengths checked and more difficulties. This checklist provides specific behaviors for the specific job that can be used in employee selection. Interrater reliability would have been useful.

COMMENTARY/SUMMARY. The Job Style Indicator provides a qualitative description of the work behavioral style and task requirements of a job. The JSI does not provide psychometric evidence because it is not an instrument to measure a potential employee's fit for a job. The psychometric information rests rather with its companion measure, the Personal Style Indicator, or other measures of the potential employee. The strength of the JSI is in forcing a company to consider the job style pattern explicitly and the specific behaviors for a specific job that should be considered prior to making employment decisions. Thus, the JSI helps a company organize perceptions of the requirements for a job.

[100]

Job Survival and Success Scale.

Purpose: Designed to "identify a person's attitudes and knowledge about keeping a job and getting ahead in the workplace."
Population: Job seekers.
Publication Date: 2005.
Acronym: JSSS.
Scores, 5: Dependability, Responsibility, Human Relations, Ethical Behavior, Getting Ahead.
Administration: Individual or group.

Price Data, 2006: $37.95 per complete kit including 25 test booklets and administrator's guide (8 pages).
Time: (15—25) minutes.
Comments: This test can be self-administered and self-scored.
Author: John Liptak.
Publisher: JIST Publishing, Inc.

Review of the Job Survival and Success Scale by JAMES T. AUSTIN, *Senior Research Specialist, and* STEPHANIE D. TISCHENDORF, *Senior Program Associate, Center on Education and Training for Employment, College of Education and Human Ecology, The Ohio State University, Columbus, OH:*

DESCRIPTION. The Job Survival and Success Scale (JSSS) is a tool that claims to identify job seeker attitudes and knowledge regarding job retention and success skills. The layout of the JSSS is colorful and divided into sections relating to five constructs that span attitudes, skills, and knowledge. The construct-scale names or skill sets are Dependability, Responsibility, Human Relations, Ethical Behavior, and Getting Ahead. For each skill set, 12 statements are provided. The respondent, usually a job seeker or incumbent, responds to 4-point Likert scales and sums the number of points received for each section. For each section a raw score ranging from 12 to 48 is given that is categorized as Low, Average, and High. Scores that fall within 12–23 points correspond to a Low rating, 24–36 points correspond to an Average rating, and 37–48 points correspond to a High rating. A chart is provided for plotting scores in order to illustrate a person's profile. Fairly general recommendations are given for improvement by section if scores fall within the Low or Average categories. The results and suggested interpretations of scores indicate areas for which job seekers may wish to improve to retain or advance in a job. Administration and scoring of the JSSS was intended to be completed individually, but it may also be done in a group setting. Results are available immediately because respondents score themselves.

DEVELOPMENT. Some information is available regarding the development of the JSSS within a framework of "soft skills," emotional intelligence, and confluence counseling. The author states that he used a literature review and "academic and professional sources" to develop the five subscales. A conference presentation by the developer available on the Internet provides important additional details about the conceptual background (Liptak, 2005). An article developing the construct of employability by Fugate, Kinicki, and Ashforth (2004) and an edited treatment of workforce readiness (O'Neil, 1997) are recommended additions.

It appears that the JSSS was pilot tested, but too little information was provided for evaluation. An indeterminate number of items were developed and piloted, and the number of pilot participants was not disclosed. The developer claimed that the JSSS contains language consistent with that used in current employment programs, but he did not explain how this was substantiated. Items were reviewed and revised with regard to bias in sex, race, culture, and ethnicity. It is asserted that basic reliability and validity statistics were collected, including coefficient alpha and interscale correlations, but the author did not provide this information describing the pilot study. Item statistics and respondent feedback aided in the process to determine which items were dropped, resulting in the current 60-item JSSS. Items were then reviewed and revised with regard to bias in sex and race to create the final form.

TECHNICAL. The short administrator's guide provides information regarding the reliability, validity, and standardization of the JSSS. No other technical documents were provided by the publisher for review.

Standardization. The developer provided little information regarding the standardization process. The only information given regarding the pilot sample was that persons in different age brackets were selected from high schools, colleges, universities, employment agencies, and training programs. The scant information provided regarding the final sample was that it consisted of successfully employed persons in businesses and organizations. The author did not report how long they had been employed in their business or organization, how long they had held their current position, or whether they had been promoted within the company (as an index of job success). These factors would have been helpful in determining whether the reported results reflected job retention and success. Summary information regarding sex, ethnicity, race, or cultural background was not given for the pilot or the final sample. The developer did not indicate from which area in the country the pilot sample was obtained, and only

provided the general region for the final sample as the Southeastern coast. The developer did not state whether the JSSS is intended for local or national use. It is impossible to deduce whether the sample is representative of others who might consider utilizing the JSSS. Finally, the total sample size of 110 is small for making any kind of confident generalizations even if the population were specified.

Reliability. The author provided internal and retest estimates of reliability for each subscale of the JSSS in its final form. Alpha coefficients for internal consistency ranged from .87–.92 (n = 110). The test-retest correlations for stability estimates ranged from .79–.89 (n = 75), with the retest interval of 2 months. Although these methods appear to be appropriate estimates of reliability and the obtained levels are adequate, the low number of participants used for calculating each estimate is a possible concern.

Validity. The author did not address the potential uses of the JSSS and also did not provide much to support use of the instrument. One form of validity evidence that is claimed is interscale correlations between the five subscales. Values for the five subscales ranged from .20–.39 (n = 65). The author claimed that because the values are low, the subscales were independent of each other. However, these correlations do not provide convincing evidence. Furthermore, the author incorrectly identified the highest correlation (.39) to be between the measures of Dependability and Human Relations. Based on the summary table provided, the highest correlation (.39) was between the measures of Responsibility and Human Relations. The low number of participants used for these validity calculations also may contribute a lack of confidence in the sample statistics.

The only other evidence provided to substantiate the validity of the JSSS was means and standard deviations presented in three tables: high school students (ages 16–18; n = 98), college students (ages 17–23; n = 52), and adults (ages 20–67; n = 51). It is unclear whether the purpose was to show that older adults would score higher on the subscales than younger adults as a form of validity evidence. The summary tables provided descriptive statistics, but in and of themselves did not form validity evidence for this instrument. There was also no analysis performed to indicate whether bias was an issue for sex, race, culture, or ethnicity. Furthermore, the low number of respondents may not permit such analysis.

COMMENTARY. The current utility of the JSSS to a potential job seeker or job incumbent is unknown. A conceptual framework is provided, but the process by which the items were developed is not detailed. The author also did not provide details regarding the demographics of the samples, nor was the intended population indicated. Details of how items were aligned to the five domains were similarly not provided. Psychometric evidence was lacking, especially for validity. Norms are neither provided nor mentioned, but a confusing term "reliability and validity norms" is mentioned (administrator's guide, p. 5). Therefore, most of these data should be weighted cautiously because the samples were small and may not be representative. Another issue to consider is whether participants would present themselves in a positive manner. However, the JSSS is easy to read, administer, score, and interpret, and the layout is simple. With more information concerning development and psychometric evidence to support score interpretations, the JSSS could be a useful tool in determining job retention and success. At the present time we cannot determine that it is not useful.

SUMMARY. The JSSS was designed to measure a job seeker's attitudes and knowledge regarding job retention and success. For areas that participants score in ranges that correspond to Low or Average ratings, recommendations are provided for improvement in those areas. The instrument is self-administered and scored, and the results and interpretations are concise and clear. However, although reliability evidence may be adequate, the psychometric evidence does not support this instrument. Validity evidence in the form of content, criterion, internal/external structure, and consequences of usage is required before this instrument can be recommended. More specific information must be provided on test assembly, norm sample compilations and standardization techniques, and sample representativeness. A larger sample size would also be helpful in supporting interpretations and making generalizations. It would also be useful to have participants who were exposed to this instrument evaluate the usefulness of the JSSS in their job retention and success, either prospectively or retrospectively.

REVIEWERS' REFERENCES
Fugate, M., Kinicki, A. J., & Ashforth, B. E. (2004). Employability: A psycho-social construct, its dimensions, and applications. *Journal of Vocational Behavior, 65,* 14–38.
Liptak, J. J. (2005, July). *Helping students succeed in college: Identifying, exploring, and enhancing emotional intelligence skills.* Presented at the 18th International Conference on the First-Year Experience, University of Southampton, England.
O'Neil, H. F., Jr. (Ed.). (1997). *Workforce readiness: Competencies and assessment.* Mahwah, NJ: Erlbaum.

Review of the Job Survival and Success Scale by STEPHEN B. JOHNSON, *Psychometrician, CASTLE Worldwide, Morrisville, NC:*

DESCRIPTION. The Job Survival and Success Scale (JSSS) is intended for quick assessment of workplace soft-skills for clients ages 16+, as part of a protocol for events such as job-placement screening or on-the-job counseling. A related scale by the same author, The College Survival and Success Scale (17:50), is also available.

The JSSS is an untimed 60-item test administered in a paper-pencil format. All items are 4-point Likert type anchored by *A Lot Like Me* to *Not Like Me.* There are no qualifications required for test administration, and it can be self-administered. The JSSS takes an average of 20 minutes to complete.

The JSSS is designed to assess five dimensions of an individual's "attitude and knowledge about keeping a job and getting ahead in the workplace" (administrator's guide, p. 3): Dependability, Responsibility, Human Relations, Ethical Relations, and Getting Ahead. Each of the five dimensions is measured by 12 items.

Respondents answer a general prompt "On the job, I would/I do …," which then describes an attitude or behavior such as "Simply quit if I did not like my job."

The JSSS is scored by hand on the consumable test form provided. A total score for each of the five dimensions is calculated and charted on a score profile section on the consumable form. Each dimension has a score range of 12 to 48. The scores are categorized into three bands. For each dimension, a score of 12 to 23 is Low, 24 to 36 is Average, and 37 to 48 is High.

The form presents a series of suggestions for success in each dimension. The respondent checks those they are already doing, concurrently identifying strategies they could be implementing to improve employment success.

The separate administrator's guide details the intent and theory behind the JSSS and outlines the test development process and basic measurement statistics. It also provides means and standard deviations for the five dimensions for three groups of test takers: college students (ages 17–23), high school students (ages 16–18), and successfully employed adults (ages 20–67). As of this review, the JSSS costs US$37.95 for a pack of 25 forms.

DEVELOPMENT. The JSSS's theory of action is based on two concepts. The first is Goleman's (1995) of Emotional Intelligence, which holds that there are learnable skills, competencies, and abilities (e.g., goal achievement) that are key to successfully functioning in society. Second, data indicate that employers are seeking not only "hard" job-specific skills and knowledge, but also soft skills such as interpersonal skills.

From this foundation, the author suggests that employee success is the intersection of social competence skills (skills related to interactions between individuals), personal competence skills (e.g., personal strengths and weaknesses and self-esteem), and job search skills (traditional career management skills). The author proposes that the role of the career counselor is to help clients develop the emotional intelligence skills needed to succeed in the workplace using a Confluence Counseling model that integrates personal and career counseling strategies.

The author established five guidelines in developing the instrument:

1. Assess a wide range of job survival and success skills.
2. Be user friendly.
3. Be easy to administer, score, and interpret.
4. Apply to a variety of populations.
5. Apply to a range of ages.

The five dimensions of job success were developed through a literature review conducted by the author. From this a pool of items was developed. A draft form of the JSSS was administered to youth and adult populations at high schools, colleges, universities, and employment and training programs.

Following this pilot study, item statistics (coefficient alpha and interscale correlations) were generated and a pool of 60 items chosen to represent the five dimensions. These 60 items were then reviewed for content, clarity, style, and potential gender or race bias.

TECHNICAL. The test-retest reliability of the instrument was obtained from a sample of 75 individuals with a 2-month interval in test administration. Individual dimension test-retest correlations range from .79 (Human Relations) to .89 (Getting Ahead). Alpha coefficients were also obtained from a sample of 110 "successfully employed people" (administrator's guide, p. 6) from the southeastern coast of the United States. This sample provided internal consistency coefficients for each dimension ranging from .87 (Human Relations) to .92 (Responsibility).

The presented validity evidence consists of concurrent validity, defined as interscale correlations for the five dimensions, and construct validity, defined as differences in the means of the five dimensions for three population groups: high school students ($N = 98$), college students ($N = 52$), and adults ($N = 51$). Interscale correlations range from .20 (Getting Ahead vs. Human Relations) to .39 (Human Relations vs. Responsibility). Differences between the means for the three populations range from .06 (College vs. High School Dependability) to 3.44 (High School vs. Adult Responsibility), and standard deviations range from 5.14 to 8.93, with most around 7. Information about how the cut scores for each band of the five dimensions were developed is not provided.

COMMENTARY. Researchers who study the transition from school to work are well aware of the difficulties many individuals, even those with years of experience in the workplace, have in providing evidence they have the appropriate soft skills necessary. It is not always the most technically proficient person who best fits. The JSSS certainly provides a tool for helping individuals think about their behaviors in the workplace, and for counselors, and perhaps even employers, to review an individual's soft skills. That the JSSS also arises from a plausible theory of action is certainly a big plus in its favor.

The data presented by the author for the JSSS provides some initial validity evidence but is not persuasive in linking career and job skills, personal and social competencies, to employment success. This gap reduces the overall credibility of the instrument.

Developing an instrument's credibility does not happen overnight. Credibility for the JSSS could be enhanced. As an initial step, I would have liked more details about the item development phase, for example, how many items were initially developed, who developed and reviewed the items, who reviewed the entire instrument, and what does it mean that a "careful examination" was conducted to eliminate any possible race or gender bias? (For example, Was it statistical? Content-focused? Who conducted it?) The last point is especially important as the author claims that the instrument is valid for a variety of audiences but provides no evidence of an analysis by sex, race, or class. I also would have liked to see a map that linked the five JSSS scales to the Confluence Counseling model (is Getting Ahead a social or personal competence?).

Statistically based validity evidence for the instrument also needs to be developed. A review of the three datasets provided indicated that there were no significant differences between the groups in the mean responses for each dimension. This suggests that data for the three groups could be collapsed enabling a confirmatory factor analysis. Furthermore, the author's theory of action does not imply that there would be group differences as a result of age-only job experience.

The largest credibility gap is the JSSS's relationship to actual employment success. The author makes the somewhat tenuous claim that the 110 "successfully employed" (administrator's guide, p. 6) adults provide some measure of validation. However, the definition of successful is not presented (e.g., what was the average length of employment, across what industries or functions?).

This definitional gap results in a divergent validity problem. A naïve reader may expect that college and high school students would score significantly lower than successfully employed adults on the assumption that they are less experienced, and therefore potentially less successful in the workplace. Indeed, this chain of reasoning appears to underlie the author's presentation of minor differences in dimension means. However, as previously noted, data contained in the tables show no statistical differences in the scale means between adults and students. From this finding, the naïve reader would have to conclude that the JSSS cannot distinguish between successfully employed and inexperienced individuals. However, approximately 40% of U.S. college students work, with over 30% working more than 20 hours per week (e.g., Fox, Connolly, & Snyder, 2005), which suggests that many youth are experienced and successful in the workplace, and therefore may not be different from the successful adult population.

A stronger validation argument could be made by assessing the difference between long-term employed individuals (e.g., more than 12 months) with short- and/or long-term unemployed individuals, with age as a covariant. Credibility would also be enhanced by assessing the predictive validity of the instrument by working with a job retraining program and/or school counseling service to undertake research as to the link between the JSSS and later employment. It would also be improved with evidence that respondents who scored in each of the three bands differed in their employment success.

SUMMARY. In the opinion of this reviewer, the JSSS is a tool that provides enough initial evidence to be usable by counselors to assess areas of soft skills. The gaps in information about test development, lack of construct, predictive and divergent validity data, and the non-existent definition of successfully employed, undermine the credibility of the instrument to assess the theory of action. Over time I would hope for a more complete analysis of the instrument, perhaps through users pooling their data with the author, and validation of the link between the five dimensions, the competencies, and employment success.

REVIEWER'S REFERENCES
Fox, M. A., Connolly, B. A., & Snyder, T. D. (2005). *Youth Indicators 2005: Trends in the well-being of American Youth*. National Center for Education Statistics (NCES 2005–050), U.S. Department of Education, National Center for Education Statistics. Washington, DC: U.S. Government Printing Office.
Goleman, D. (1995). *Emotional intelligence*. New York: Bantam Books.

[101]

Joseph Picture Self-Concept Scale.

Purpose: Designed to measure "self-concept in children" and "identify children whose negative self-appraisals signal that they are at risk for academic and behavioral difficulties."

Publication Date: 2004.

Scores: Total Self-Concept Score.

Administration: Individual.

Parts, 4: Light-Skin Boys, Dark-Skin Boys, Light-Skin Girls, Dark-Skin Girls.

Price Data, 2006: $198 for complete kit for younger children including 2 stimulus booklets, 20 AutoScore forms, and manual (86 pages); $121 for complete kit for older children including 2 stimulus booklets, 20 AutoScore forms, and manual; $44 per manual; $40 per 20 AutoScore forms (specify Form Y [younger] or Form O [older]); $64 for choice of stimulus booklets; $28.50 for either Form O light-skin or Form O dark-skin version stimulus booklet.

Time: (5–10) minutes.

Comments: Both forms of this test allow participants to "respond using pictures rather than words."
Author: Jack Joseph.
Publisher: Western Psychological Services.
  a) FORM Y—YOUNG CHILD INTERVIEW.
  Population: Ages 3-0 to 7-11 years.
  b) FORM O—OLDER CHILD INTERVIEW.
  Population: Ages 7-0 to 13-11 years.

Review of Joseph Picture Self-Concept Scale by EUGENE V. AIDMAN, Senior Research Scientist, Defense Science and Technology Organisation & Senior Lecturer, University of Adelaide, Adelaide, Australia:

DESCRIPTION. According to the test developer, the Joseph Picture Self-Concept Scale (The Joseph) is intended for the assessment of self-concept in children aged 3 to 13. The Joseph is an updated and expanded version of the Joseph Preschool and Primary Self-Concept Screening Test (Joseph, 1978). As the original Joseph, the new Joseph is a structured interview instrument, with pictorial assistance both for item presentation by the examiner and for test-taker response. Each item is illustrated by a pair of contrasting line drawings depicting situations related to self-evaluation, such as a child being scolded or comforted by the parent, praised or disciplined by the teacher. The examiner first establishes whether the test taker can properly distinguish between the two pictures and then asks which of the two situations happens more often to the test taker. A 3-point response format is utilized—the child can choose either of the two pictures or indicate that he or she is not sure. The number of uncertain responses is asserted to have diagnostic value. There are 21 items in the Young Children Interview (Form Y) and 30 items in the Older Children Interview (Form O).

DEVELOPMENT. Compared to the earlier Joseph, the new Joseph extends the test-taker age range to include older children and preadolescents. The Older Child Form (Form O) was developed to cater to the latter group. Pictures in both Form O and Form Y items portray either boys or girls, each of whom can be either light-skinned or dark-skinned—making four different versions for each form. The standardization sample included 934 children aged 3–13, with 379 for the Young Child and 555 for the Older Child forms. The examination of the normality of the test score distribution is missing but a brief inspection of

descriptive statistics and score conversion tables suggests that the distribution is negatively skewed. Mean scores approach the maximum possible scores especially for the Young Child group (e.g., the mean for Form Y is within one standard deviation of the highest score). Quite appropriately then, the test utilizes raw score conversion to normalized T-scores—but without articulating the rationale for doing so.

TECHNICAL. The reliability of the Joseph's total score was evaluated on the standardization sample (n = 934) and a clinical sample (n = 260). Internal consistency estimates reported in the manual are slightly higher for the clinical sample (.77 and .78, for Form Y and Form O, respectively), with the standardization sample returning .77 for Form O and .67 for Form Y. The latter estimate causes some concern over the simultaneous reliability of Form Y. An inspection of individual item reliabilities adds to this concern, with several item-total correlations below .20 and some as low as .06.

Temporal stability of the Joseph is well documented. Test-retest reliability of the total score ranged from .95 and .87 for a 1-week interval (with n = 92 and n = 115) to .69 for a 7-month interval, between .58 and .80 for a 12-month interval, .65 for a 2-year interval, and .43 for a 3-year interval. The test author suggests that the longer interval correlations are more indicative of construct stability than test-retest reliability. It does not, however, compare temporal stability of the Joseph with that of established self-concept measures.

Evidence of the Joseph's validity, as presented in the test manual, is rather limited and poorly organized. Correlations between the total Joseph score and the corresponding Joseph Preschool and Primary Self-Concept Screening Test score range from .80 for the Older Child Form to .92 for the Younger Child Form, indicating good correspondence between the two versions of the test. These data, however, are more accurately interpreted as evidencing parallel form reliability, rather than validity, of the Joseph tests. Convergent validity is evidenced by predictable correlations of the total Joseph score with teacher ratings of self-esteem, social skills, and problem behaviors for the Younger Child Form and, in addition, with a range of self-concept questionnaire measures for the Older Child Form. The latter include a .85 correlation with the total score of the Piers-Harris (Piers, 1984) Children's Self-Concept Scale and .69 with Bracken's (1992) Multidimensional Self-Concept Scale. The same table in the test manual lists a correlation of -.78 with Kovacs' (1982) Children's Depression Inventory (CDI) as further evidence of convergent validity. An inspection of individual items confirms the presence of several items with depression-related contents (e.g., happy vs. sad, smiling vs. crying) and no direct self-concept reference. Items like these tend to reduce discriminant validity as they add to the method artefact in comparing theoretically related constructs.

Criterion validity evidence derives from the known-group validation strategy. The data show a predictable decline in the Joseph total score among children referred for treatment of emotional/behavioral disorders, but not for specific learning or other disabilities. Associations of the Joseph total score with teacher-rated academic achievement are somewhat mixed: significantly positive in the Older Child Form but unrelated in the Younger Child Form. Some evidence of predictive validity was found using a sample of 170 preschoolers of whom 36 scored below 41 T-score points; 4 years later 75% of this low-scoring group was characterized by poor academic and behavioral outcomes, to the point of requiring at least 1 year of special education services. Another important aspect of discriminant validity is social desirability contamination. Correlations between the Joseph Form O total score and the test's four-item Response Distortion Index (RDI) are statistically significant and range from .17 (p < .001) for the standardization sample (n = 555) to .40 (p < .001) for the clinic-referred sample (n = 201). The test manual does not address reliability of the RDI, but item-total correlations indicate that its internal consistency is probably similar to that of the Joseph total score. Given an acceptable reliability of RDI, the Joseph total score is quite likely to be contaminated by social desirability—and to a greater extent in the clinic-referred population. This contamination is of some concern, but its level is similar to that of the majority of self-concept questionnaire measures. Overall, evidence of the Joseph's validity is either incomplete (see below) or not compelling.

COMMENT. The test has provisions for the calculation of three theoretically meaningful subscale scores—(a) Significance (self-perceptions of how one is valued by significant others), (b) Competence (self-appraisals of mastery in various domains), and (c) General Evaluative Contentment. These scales are consistent with the distinction in the current literature between self-liking and self-competence—the subdimensions of global self-esteem that are discernable both conceptually and in measurement (Aidman, 1998; Tafarodi & Swann, 1995; Tafarodi & Vu, 1998). The Joseph also contains four items contributing to a Response Distortion Index, which is claimed to measure socially desirable responding. Unfortunately, the test developer does not provide any evaluation of reliability and validity for the Joseph subscales—their psychometric properties remain unknown. The only psychometric evaluation presented is for the total self-concept score, which makes the Joseph a single-score instrument, effectively measuring global self-esteem.

A proportion of items on both Joseph forms use what the manual terms "neutral-contrast" picture pairs—where the pictures have no contents to illustrate the examiner's verbalizations and serve only as their visual anchors. These picture pairs present children with different neutral attributes (e.g., hair style, clothing) that are asserted to be sufficient for differentiation. This assertion remains to be proven—at least to this reviewer the "neutral-contrast" picture pairs do not seem particularly contrasting. Relative position (i.e., right vs. left page) is likely to be a stronger differentiator. The overall rationale for the "neutral-contrast" items is not clear. The rationale for the dark-skinned versions of test booklets is not clear either. The only change from the light-skinned versions is some grey shading to open skin areas, with the essentially Caucasian features of all the line drawings remaining unaltered.

Finally, the power of visual stimulus material seems to be underutilized in the Joseph. The pictures are intended to serve as simple, unambiguous, and straightforward illustrations to the examiner's verbalizations, as well as placeholders for the test taker's responses. As such, they are unlikely to add much value to the verbal protocol. It seems that a pair of plain colored cards—a pink and a blue one, for example—would be nearly as effective as the Joseph's line drawings, especially for the "neutral-contrast" items. Visual stimulus material has been used in self-concept measurement—both in photographs (Liggett, 1959) and line drawings form (Aidman, 1999)—and it has shown the potential to tap into less articulated, more implicit aspects of self-concept. Notably, the pictorial items in these methods are used to contribute directly to the measurement rather than being a dispensable service to the verbal protocol.

SUMMARY. The Joseph is an interesting instrument, with an original item and item response format supporting a structured interview to assess the young test taker's self-views. The test's conceptual foundation, reflected in its item contents, is eclectic—if not confused, with items ranging from competence self-appraisals through expected evaluations by significant others to general self-acceptance. These potentially promising subdimensions remain undeveloped. Although the reliability of the Joseph is acceptable, evidence of its validity, as currently documented, is limited. Some item contents are questionable. The Joseph may be worth considering as a novel interview protocol but not as a standard clinical instrument—at least until more validation data become available.

REVIEWER'S REFERENCES

Aidman, E. V. (1999). Measuring individual differences in implicit self-concept: Initial validation of the Self-Apperception Test. *Personality and Individual Differences, 27*(2), 211-228.

Aidman, E. V. (1998). Analysing global dimensions of self-esteem: Factorial structure and reliability of Self-liking/Self-Competence Scale. *Personality and Individual Differences, 24*(5), 735-737.

Bracken, B. A. (1992). *Multidimensional Self-Concept Scale: Manual.* Austin, TX: Pro-Ed.

Kovacs, M. (1982). *Children's Depression Inventory: Manual.* Toronto, Ontario: Multi-Health Systems.

Liggett, J. (1959). The paired use of projective stimuli. *British Journal of Psychology, 50,* 269-275.

Piers, E. V. (1984). *Piers-Harris Children's Self-Concept Scale: Revised manual.* Los Angeles: Western Psychological Services.

Tafarodi, R. W., & Swann, W. B. (1995). Self-liking and self-competence as dimensionality of global self-esteem: Initial validation of a measure. *Journal of Personality Assessment, 65,* 322-342.

Tafarodi, R. W., & Vu, C. (1997). Two-dimensional self-esteem and reactions to success and failure. *Personality and Social Psychology Bulletin, 23,* 626-635.

Review of the Joseph Picture Self-Concept Scale by CARLEN HENINGTON, Associate Professor of School Psychology, Mississippi State University, Mississippi State, MS:

DESCRIPTION. The Joseph Picture Self-Concept Scale (the Joseph) is designed as a measurement of self-concept, defined as "beliefs and attitudes about one's own behavior, abilities, and personal characteristics" (manual, p. 3), for ages 3-0 to 13-11 years. A revision of the Joseph Preschool and Primary Self-Concept Screening Test (Joseph, 1979), the Joseph is purported to enhance the original measure through: (a) revised items and stimulus materials, (b) expansion to older

children, and (c) updated norms. The Joseph is administered as an interview using one of two forms: Form Y for young children (3-0 to 7-11 years) and Form O for older children (7-0 to 13-11 years). A short version (e.g., 10 items) of Form Y is also briefly presented. The stimulus booklets contain a set of gender-specific pictures, available in a Light-Skin Version (for light-complexioned children) and Dark-Skin Version (for dark-complexioned children), to be used as reference picture pairs for Form Y (picture pairs for each item) and Form O (picture-pairs for the first 3 items and the same pair for subsequent items).

Administration time is 5 to 10 minutes for most children. The two forms use similar instructions and procedures in that the administrator presents a set of pictures and corresponding questions related to an aspect of self-concept. For Form Y, administration begins with the Identity Reference Drawing (IRD) in which the child is directed to draw his or her face on an outline line drawing of a human figure. This drawing is used as a reference for the questions and, potentially, as clinical information during interpretation. The administration of each item involves a three-step presentation of the picture-pair: (a) presentation step; (b) distinguish step (used to determine an understanding of the difference between the pair of pictures) and selection ("Now which one is most like you?"); and (c) confirm step. For older children, the distinguish step is modified. The child's response to the question "which one is most like you?" is recorded in the appropriate box. Two alternative scenarios to the expected response should be monitored during administration: (a) a response of younger children that indicates confusion about the picture meaning (mark box labeled "C") and (b) an ambivalent response (i.e., no clear choice of the two response options) provided by a child of any age (mark box labeled "?").

Scoring is straightforward and facilitated by automatic transfer into a numeric response on the scoring worksheet located on the inside of the protocol. Dependent upon the form used, a response could be awarded one of four scores: (a) a negative self-concept response (0 points), (b) a positive self-concept response (2 points), (c) an ambivalent response (1 point), and (d) a confusion response, Form Y only (related to response validity with no impact on the total score). The points are totaled by the administrator and entered as a Raw

Total Score (range = 0 to 42 and 0 to 52, for Forms Y and O, respectively). A conversion table is used to obtain a normalized T-score. The number of confusion and ambivalent boxes are also recorded. For older children, Form O also yields a measure of response validity (e.g., defensiveness or socially desirable response patterns) with the Response Distortion Index (RDI) composed of four items.

The Total Self-Concept Score is the focus of both forms; however, several additional scores may be useful in interpretation. These include the three theoretical self-concept dimension scores: Significance (SIG)—items related to interpersonal functioning and relational issues, Competence (COM)—items reflective of skill and mastery in daily activities, and General Evaluative Contentment (GEC)—items related to overall satisfaction with perceived functioning. Specific functional domains represented within the content of each question (e.g., school functioning, authority relations, family relations) may also be useful in interpretation. Furthermore, the ambivalent response (1-point), confusion response, and the IRD are useful as clinical indicators. The author presents several interpretive tables for each form: (a) identification criteria for six categories of self-concept classification with corresponding T-score ranges and comparisons to the standardization and clinical samples; (b) an interpretation rubric with information on item content, theoretical dimension, functional domain, self-perception associated with a negative response, and differentiation between the clinical and nonclinical sample; (c) brief interpretive descriptions for each self-concept classification; and (d) suggestions for item content analysis to assist in treatment design. The author also provides case studies for each form to illustrate the usefulness in the clinical setting.

DEVELOPMENT. This instrument is based on the "view that self-concept forms the core of a person's social and emotional development," and that self-appraisal and sense of self-worth interact with "emotional growth, interpersonal functioning, and academic and vocational achievement" (manual, p. 55) and are mediated by two contemporary constructs (emotional intelligence and emotional resilience). Although he cites a number of supporting references, the author does not offer a specific underlying theoretical foundation. Six theoretical assumptions are foundations for the Joseph:

(a) conscious self-perceptions are based on functioning and experience, (b) self-report is reliable, (c) young children's self-perceptions are measurable, (d) early intervention can address behavioral and academic problems, (e) self-concept is composed of both global and specific hierarchical dimensions relative to global self-evaluation, and (f) self-perceptions are developmental with complexity related to maturation.

In the revision of the Joseph, the goal was to expand the instrument for use with older children and to provide updated norms. To revise the Joseph, 17 items were developed; six of these items "appeared to represent self-concept issues that were developmentally appropriate for young children" (manual, p. 58) and were combined with the original 15 items (some reworded) to comprise the 21 items for the new Form Y. The IRD was retained. The picture-pairs were modified from black line drawings to the current illustrations with versions for light- and dark-complexioned children. The 21 items were piloted and subjected to item analysis examining inter-item and item-total correlations and internal consistency. Finally, the five classification categories were expanded to six categories. Form O was developed using the same pool of 32 items developed for Form Y with some wording changes to reflect age-appropriate situations (e.g., a reprimand versus spanking for misbehavior). It is uncertain how the items were selected or rejected for inclusion in the instrument, and no information is provided on how each item was determined to relate to the three theoretical dimensions (SIG, COM, GEC).

TECHNICAL. Standardization was based on a sample of 934 children and preadolescents (3 to 13 years; $n = 379$ for Form Y, $n = 555$ for Form O). Demographic data indicate ethnicity and gender numbers reflective of the 2000 U.S. Census, fewer were from the lowest SES category, and participants were predominately from the northeast (61%).

Normalized T-scores and percentiles are provided for children ages 3 to 5 years and 6 to 7 years (Form Y), and across all ages (Form O). No rationale was provided for the use of 7 years of age as the differentiation between the two forms, nor for the combination of all ages within Form O, but the two sets of norms for Form Y were based on the two groups' raw scores differing by more than 5 points (considered to be large) for 16 of the

21 items (76%). No score differences were noted for gender or ethnicity (possible effects for language in a Spanish-speaking sample were noted) and descriptive statistics for a clinic-referred sample (*n* = 59 and 201, Forms Y and O, respectively) were also provided.

Alpha coefficients were used to estimate internal consistency (Form Y = .67 and .77, Form O = .77 and .78, for the standardization and clinical samples, respectively), and a 1-week test-retest reliability was high (Form Y Total Score = .95, Form O Total Score = .97, and Form O RDI = .83).

Content validity of the three major dimensions of self-concept was established for the original Joseph, and revised items were designed to reflect these same dimensions. Convergent validity studies showed high correlations between the new and original Joseph (.92 and .80 for Forms Y and O, respectively) and for teacher ratings on the Behavioral Academic Self-Esteem Rating Scale (Coopersmith, 1981; .60 and .73 for Forms Y and O, respectively), the Piers-Harris Children's Self-Concept Scale (Piers, 1984; .85, Form O), and the Multidimensional Self-Concept Scale (Bracken, 1992; .69, Form O). Divergent validity was supported with negative correlations with rating on the Social Skills Rating System—Problem Behaviors (Gresham & Elliott, 1990; -.52 and -.24, for Forms Y and O, respectively).

To support the use of the RDI as a measure of response validation, correlation coefficients between the four RDI items and Total Score ranged from .04 to .21 for the standardization sample (with two significant items at the .05 level) and coefficients ranging from .11 to .39 for the clinic-referred sample (with three of the four items significant) and patterns consistent with the standardization sample.

COMMENTARY. The Joseph appears to be useful as a brief measure of self-concept for children, ages 3 years to 13 years, 11 months. Although the author provides cautionary statements about the use of the Joseph as a single diagnostic indicator, he provides several case studies in which that advice is not followed. Perhaps the greatest concern is the use of the IRD to inform intervention design. This is beyond the scope of the Joseph. The Joseph is an instrument suited to evaluate the effects of an intervention (either behavioral or academic) upon a child's self-concept within a clinical or research venue.

The author is to be commended for his efforts to provide an instrument suitable for use with very young children; however, he neglects to provide a strong theoretical foundation to support the use of the additional items in the new version of the Joseph and in the expansion of the instrument to older children. An additional strength is the addition of the RDI as a measure of response bias. It is believed that the value of this instrument is likely to outweigh the concerns established in this review.

SUMMARY. The Joseph is a reliable and valid instrument—easy to administer, score, and interpret as a measure of self-concept in children (3 to 13 years)—with adequately established norms. It yields a Total Score (*T*-score) and offers three dimensional scores (i.e., interpersonal functioning, skill and mastery in daily activities, overall satisfaction with perceived functioning) to assist in determining appropriate intervention targets and/or effects. Although similar to the Pictorial Scale of Perceived Competence and Social Acceptance for Young Children (Harter & Pike, 1984), the Joseph offers several relative strengths: use with very young children and those with low cognitive functioning, and an estimation of the validity of a child's response to the overall instrument. An additional strength is its strong convergent and divergent validity with well-researched instruments (e.g., Piers-Harris Self-Concept Scale, Social Skills Rating Scale).

REVIEWER'S REFERENCES

Bracken, B. A. (1992). *Multidimensional Self-Concept Scale: Manual.* Austin, TX: Pro-Ed.
Coopersmith, S. (1981). *Behavioral Academic Self-Esteem Rating Scale: Manual.* Palo Alto, CA: Consulting Psychologists Press.
Gresham, F. M., & Elliott, S. N. (1990). *Social Skills Rating System: Manual.* Circle Pines, MN: American Guidance Service.
Harter, S., & Pike, R. (1984). The pictorial scale of perceived competence and social acceptance for young children. *Child Development, 55,* 1969-1982.
Joseph, J. (1979). *Joseph Preschool and Primary Self-Concept Screening Test: Manual.* Wood Dale, IL: Stoelting.
Piers, E. V. (1984). *Piers-Harris Children's Self-Concept Scale: Revised manual.* Los Angeles: Western Psychological Services.

[102]
Kaufman Brief Intelligence Test, Second Edition.

Purpose: Intended as a brief measure of verbal and nonverbal intelligence.
Population: Ages 4–90.
Publication Dates: 1990–2004.
Acronym: KBIT-2.
Scores, 3: Verbal, Nonverbal, IQ Composite.
Subtests, 3: Verbal Knowledge, Riddles, Matrices.
Administration: Individual.

Price Data, 2005: $199.99 per complete kit including easel, manual (2004, 147 pages), 25 individual test record forms, and carry bag; $39.99 per 25 individual test records; $59.99 per scoring and administration manual.

Time: (15–30) minutes.

Comments: Examiners are encouraged to teach individuals, using teaching items, how to solve the kinds of items included in subtests.

Authors: Alan S. Kaufman and Nadeen L. Kaufman.

Publisher: Pearson.

Cross References: See T5:1380 (21 references); for reviews by M. David Miller and John W. Young of an earlier version, see 12:205 (9 references); see also T4:1344 (4 references).

Review of the Kaufman Brief Intelligence Test, Second Edition by RONALD A. MADLE, Licensed Psychologist, Miflinburg, PA, and Adjunct Associate Professor of School Psychology, The Pennsylvania State University, University Park, PA:

DESCRIPTION. The Kaufman Brief Intelligence Test, Second Edition (KBIT-2) is a brief intelligence test for individuals from 4 to 90 years of age. It is designed for traditional brief assessment purposes such as screening, conducting periodic cognitive reevaluations, and assessing cognitive functioning when it is a secondary consideration. Interestingly, in light of recent changes in IDEA, the manual recommended it to estimate cognitive functioning of children referred for specific learning disabilities evaluations when comprehensive intellectual measures are not included in the assessment battery.

The KBIT-2 includes a full-color stimulus book, manual, and test forms. Administration, which can be done by trained technicians or paraprofessionals as well as qualified professionals, takes about 15 to 30 minutes. A properly qualified professional, however, should always interpret the results.

The KBIT-2 yields Verbal and Nonverbal subscales in addition to an IQ Composite. The Verbal scale is composed of two combined subtests that assess receptive vocabulary and general information (Verbal Knowledge) as well as comprehension, reasoning, and vocabulary knowledge (Riddles). The Nonverbal scale uses a Matrices subtest to tap the ability to complete visual analogies and understand relationships. Clear administration instructions and scoring criteria are provided in a well-designed easel, with some questions in the test booklet. All responses involve either pointing or one-word answers with binary scoring. Little querying is required. Basals for all subtests involve passing the first three items at an age-based entry point, with a procedure to drop back a starting point until they are passed. Failing four consecutive items constitutes a ceiling. In addition, two subtests include teaching items when early errors are made.

The manual presents acceptable administration variations for using the Verbal or Nonverbal scales separately in special situations such as deafness, limited English proficiency, or severe visual impairments. Additionally, the Verbal subtests can have directions given and responses accepted in languages other than English, although items are always presented in English. In fact, Spanish instructions and response options are included.

The trifold 8.5 by 11-inch record form has all identifying and summary information on the front page, with items on the remaining five sides. Spaces are provided for standard scores, 90% confidence intervals, percentile ranks, descriptive categories, and age-equivalents. All standard scores have a mean of 100 and standard deviation of 15, with the average range being defined as scores between 85 and 115. Subsequent descriptors are at 15-point intervals.

DEVELOPMENT. The KBIT-2 development goals were to retain the K-BIT's strong features, to correct any problems, and to obtain up-to-date norms. Based on a survey of many K-BIT users, a major goal was to replace the K-BIT's Definitions subtest; this involved reading clues after age 7. There was concern that reading proficiency might taint the intellectual estimates. The final revision process resulted in updated norms, use of full-color stimuli, a completely new Verbal scale, an updated Matrices subtest, and use of the same tasks across the entire life span.

The KBIT-2 was developed in conjunction with the Kaufman Assessment Battery for Children, Second Edition (KABC-II; 16:123) and drew on a number of similar constructs. Although all three subtests are used on the KABC-II, there is no item overlap. The interpretive framework for both scales is based on the Cattell-Horn-Carroll (CHC) theory of intelligence, with the Verbal scale as Crystallized Ability and the Nonverbal scale as an amalgam of Fluid Reasoning and Visual Processing. The Nonverbal scale also can be viewed through the lens of Luria's model as representing simultaneous processing and planning ability.

TECHNICAL.

Standardization. The KBIT-2 standardization sample of 2,120 individuals was stratified on race/ethnicity, geographic region, and educational level using the *March 2001 Current Population Survey.* A close match was obtained except for region, where the South was overrepresented (44.2% versus 36.0%) and the Northeast was undersampled (11.4% versus 19.8%). Equal gender representation was used rather than approximating the increasing proportion of females in later adulthood. Non-English speakers, institutionalized individuals, and those with significant physical, perceptual, or psychological impairments were excluded, although special education and gifted/talented students were included at school age.

The 23 normative age groups varied in size, with the largest (*n* = 125) at ages 5 through 10. Four-year-olds and the 11- to 15-year age groups used 100 participants each, whereas the 16- and 17–18-year age groups had 75 participants. Beyond age 18 the age spans were larger and had 50 to 100 participants per group. Examination of the norm tables show the KBIT-2 has floors of at least -3.20 standard deviations and ceilings of 3.33 standard deviations or better. The items gradients (Bracken & Walker, 1997) involve a respectable minimum of 4.86 items per standard deviation.

Reliability. The KBIT-2's IQ Composite internal consistency coefficient of .93 across ages (.89 to .96) is quite good, with reliabilities increasing with age. The Verbal (.91) and Nonverbal (.88) coefficients are somewhat lower but within acceptable ranges, although the Nonverbal scale coefficients are only .78 at ages 4 and 5.

IQ Composite test-retest stability was .90 over mean intervals of 22.5 to 30.8 days, with a mean performance increase of 4 points. The Verbal (*r* = .91) and Nonverbal (*r* = .83) scales each showed similar increases on retesting. Coefficients at different ages were adequate (.83 or higher) except for the Nonverbal scale for the 4- through 12-year age groups (.76).

Validity. Several types of construct validity evidence are present. These involve demonstrating no meaningful differences across gender as well as showing increases in raw scores across age groups.

In older examinees, the expected lifespan declin in performance (Baltes, Staudinger Lindenberger, 1999) were noted. Matrices, as measure of fluid ability, peaked during early adu hood and then began a slow decline, whereas t Crystallized-Verbal scales increased or remain stable until old age.

Special group studies revealed mean sco of groups that involve intelligence as a key part their definition had expected results (intellectua gifted = 115.0; mentally retarded = 61.1), as d other groups with likely intellectual deficits (tra matic brain injury = 73.4; dementia = 74.1). Grou that typically show average or slightly decreas cognitive scores did so on the KBIT-2 as well learning disability (88.0), speech and langua impaired (85.3), and attention-deficit/hyperacti ity disorder (90.5).

Concurrent validity evidence included da on the relationship with several other measures intelligence. KBIT-2 scores were lower than t K-BIT by about 2 points, which is consistent wi expected declines due to the Flynn Effect (Flyn 1987). Adjusted correlations for the IQ Compo ite were substantial, ranging from .80 to .8 except for correlations of only .47 for the Nonve bal scale in 4- to 7-year-old children. Compa sons showed Full Scale and Performance IC about 4.5 points and 7 points higher on t Wechsler Abbreviated Scale of Intelligenc (WASI) than on the corresponding KBIT-2 scale even though the correlations were strong.

Correlational studies were reported with se eral comprehensive Wechsler scales. The Fu Scale-IQ Composite correlations with the WISC III and WISC-IV were .76 and .77, respectivel The WAIS-III correlation was .89. Mean Fu Scale IQs, however, ranged from 1.3 points low (WISC-IV) to 5 to 7 points higher (WAIS-II than the KBIT-2 IQ Composite.

Finally, the KBIT-2's relationship with tw achievement measures showed typical IQ-achieve ment correlations for the KTEA-II (about .6 and WRAT3 (about .50).

COMMENTARY AND SUMMARY. Ove all, the KBIT-2 appears to be a well-designe screening test that was built on the solid found tion of the original version. It is easily admini tered and scored across a wide age range. Th primary criticism of the K-BIT—possible con tamination with reading ability—has been co rected in the revision. For a brief test the KBIT-2 has very respectable floors, ceilings, and item gradients. The KBIT-2's psychometric characteristics are strong, with the possible exception of the Nonverbal scale for preschool and primary age children. The Nonverbal scale requires some interpretive caution at these ages.

Although the KBIT-2 correlated highly with various Wechsler scales, data suggest lower mean IQs, with a KBIT-2 gifted sample mean of only 115, compared to the more commonly found means in the low to middle 120s for gifted groups in validation studies. Although this is based on a limited sample and should be further researched, this would be a factor to consider when the KBIT-2 is used for gifted screening programs.

In addition, the ability to give instructions and accept answers in languages other than English, while a positive feature, can be a double-edged sword because non-English speakers were excluded from the normative sample. This reduces the likelihood of obtaining artificially low IQs with English language learners, but still makes the meaning of the scores unclear to some extent.

REVIEWER'S REFERENCES

Baltes, P. B., Staudinger, U. M., & Lindenberger, U. (1999). Lifespan psychology: Theory and application to intellectual functioning. *Annual Review of Psychology, 50*, 471–507.

Bracken, B. A., & Walker, K. C. (1997). The utility of intelligence tests for preschool children. In D. P. Flanagan, J. L. Genshaft, & P. L. Harrison (Eds.), *Contemporary intellectual assessment: Theories, tests, and issues* (pp. 474–592). New York: Guilford.

Flynn, J. R. (1987). Massive IQ gains in 14 nations: What IQ tests really measure. *Psychological Bulletin, 101*, 171–191.

Review of the Kaufman Brief Intelligence Test, Second Edition by STEVEN R. SHAW, Assistant Professor of Educational and Counselling Psychology, McGill University, Montréal, Québec, Canada:

DESCRIPTION. The Kaufman Brief Intelligence Test, Second Edition (KBIT-2) is a short, individually administered test of intelligence for children and adults. The KBIT-2 is an update and renorming of the popular Kaufman Brief Intelligence Test (Kaufman & Kaufman, 1990). In addition to updating the normative sample, several changes have been made. An additional Verbal subtest, Riddles, has been added. Additional items have been added to expand the floor and ceiling of all subtests. And full color plates have been added to the subtests.

The KBIT-2 manual suggests several uses and purposes. Among these are screening to identify high-risk children, screening cognitive ability in the gifted and talented selection process, assisting in adolescent and adult job placement decisions, estimating intelligence as part of a personality evaluation, reassessing the intellectual status of a child or adult who has already had a full cognitive evaluation, and measuring cognitive ability for research purposes.

The KBIT-2 provides three scores: Verbal, Nonverbal, and IQ Composite. The Verbal score is composed of Verbal Knowledge and Riddles subtests. Verbal Knowledge involves the examiner requesting the examinee to point to a word or phrase (e.g., "Point to … winter"). The examinee then simply points to one of six presented pictures on the stimulus easel that best represents the word or phrase. This is a familiar format for many examiners, much like the Peabody Picture Vocabulary Test (T7:1866). Riddles is a new subtest for the KBIT-2. Riddles involves a simple question with two or three variables (e.g., "What has whiskers, is a common household pet, and meows?"). All responses require a one-word oral or signed response. The manual states that responses on Riddles must be exact or nearly exact matches to the correct responses provided on the test protocol. The Matrices subtest, the sole marker for the Nonverbal score, is similar to matrices tasks on a variety of tests such as the Wechsler Intelligence Scale for Children—Fourth Edition (16:262), Raven's Progressive Matrices (T7:2122), and the Reynolds Intellectual Assessment Scales (16:213). Like the Verbal Knowledge subtest, Matrices requires only a pointing response to select from six presented options.

The KBIT-2 is intended for examinees aged 4 through 90 years of age. The KBIT-2 requires between 15 and 30 minutes to administer. Adults, high ability children, and examinees with the reflective style of test taking may take longer. It is also worth noting that none of the three subtests on the KBIT-2 are timed.

The KBIT-2 is reported to be easy to administer and may be administered by technicians or paraprofessionals, if those individuals have received appropriate training in standardized testing by appropriately qualified professionals. The protocol and easel format stimulus book are well designed and nearly self-explanatory. Basal and discontinue rules are simple and consistent across the three subtests. The only potential complex component of administering the KBIT-2 is the "teaching items." When examinees fail to understand the task, further explanation of the task and instructions is permitted. These items are labeled as teaching items in the protocol. The purpose of teaching items is to ensure that the examinee completely understands the task. Teaching items are not intended for coaching or giving problem-solving strategies to the examinee. The distinction between explaining directions and coaching the examinee can be subtle to inexperienced examiners.

Although administration of the KBIT-2 is extremely simple, analysis and interpretation of test scores require some level of psychometric sophistication and clinical experience. The KBIT-2 manual discusses interpretation of test scores from the vantage point of the Cattell-Horn-Carroll (CHC) theory of intelligence, and interpretation of KBIT-2 scores based on Luria's neuropsychological theory of simultaneous and successive processing. Such sophisticated interpretations of test scores are not likely to be appropriate for technicians and paraprofessionals who may be administering this test.

DEVELOPMENT. The KBIT-2 was developed in conjunction with the Kaufman Assessment Battery for Children, Second Edition (KABC-II; 16:123). Verbal Knowledge and Riddles are parallel forms of subtests that also appear on the KABC-II. Matrices is based on the original KBIT. Approximately half the items on the KBIT-2 Matrices subtest also appeared on the original KBIT Matrices. A large-scale try-out administration of potential Matrices items was conducted with 463 examinees aged 4 through 18 years. The Rasch procedure was used to identify items that may indicate bias. Based on this study and one additional tryout study, several items were dropped due to bias. Items were also selected based on development of adequate subtest reliability, appropriately low floor, appropriately high ceiling, and correlations with other subtests.

TECHNICAL.

Standardization. The KBIT-2 was normed on a sample of children, adolescents, and adults aged 4 through 90 who speak English, are not institutionalized, and did not have physical, perceptual or psychological impairments that may affect cognitive functioning. Data were collected on 2,120 examinees in 34 states and the District of Columbia. The normative sample is a fairly good match to the 2001 U.S. Census data on educa-

tional status (for adults), mothers' educational lev (for children and adolescents), geographic regio and race and ethnicity. The only minor deviatio from an otherwise excellent match with Censu data is that the normative sample overrepre sented the Southern and Northeastern regio of the United States. In addition, validatio studies were conducted on several special popu lations. These populations include persons wit learning disabilities, persons with speech an language disorders, persons with attention defic hyperactivity disorder, persons with mental reta dation, persons identified as gifted or talente individuals with traumatic brain injury, and ind viduals with dementia.

Reliability. The KBIT-2 manual reports tes retest reliability and internal consistency reliabili estimates. Internal consistency reliabilities calcu lated by age range from .86 to .96 on the Verb score. Internal consistency reliabilities range fro .78 to .93 on the Nonverbal score. IQ Composit internal consistency reliabilities range from .89 t .96. Test-retest reliabilities are based on two ad ministrations of the KBIT-2 to 271 examinee aged 4 through 89. The interval between tes sessions ranges from 6 to 56 days with the mea interval of about 28 days. Test-retest reliabilitie range from .76 (Nonverbal score for ages 4-12) t .93 (Verbal score for ages 13-21). From first test ing to second testing the mean gain in scores fo IQ Composite was 4 standard score points.

Validity. Validity data consist primarily of series of concurrent validity studies with well established tests of cognitive ability and academi achievement. Data are reported for studies wit the Wechsler Abbreviated Scale of Intelligenc (WASI), Wechsler Intelligence Scale for Chil dren: Third Edition and Fourth Edition, Wechsle Adult Intelligence Scale: Third Edition, Wid Range Achievement Test: Third Edition, and th Kaufman Test of Educational Achievement: Sec ond Edition. Correlation coefficients are consis tently in the moderate to high range and provid strong evidence of construct validity. Likewise, th validation studies using special populations indi cate differences from the norm sample in expecte directions. For example, scores for the gifted spe cial population are significantly higher than that o the mean of the norm sample. And scores from the mental retardation sample are significantl lower than the mean of the norm sample. Ther are no confirmatory factor analytic studies supporting the CHC or neuropsychological interpretation of the KBIT-2.

COMMENTARY. The KBIT-2 is a well-designed brief measure of general cognitive ability. The manual is comprehensive, clear, and useful. The KBIT-2 compares favorably to other brief measures of intelligence such as the Wechsler Abbreviated Scale of Intelligence (WASI; T7:2745; The Psychological Corporation, 1999) and Reynolds Intellectual Screening Test (16:213; Reynolds & Kamphaus, 2003) on features of brevity, psychometric characteristics, theoretical soundness, ease of administration and interpretation, and attractiveness of materials. The KBIT-2 represents another well-conceived and professionally executed assessment instrument by Alan and Nadeen Kaufman and published by American Guidance Service [Editor's Note: AGS tests are now published by Pearson].

SUMMARY. The KBIT-2 is an update and renorming of the original Kaufman Brief Intelligence Test. The changes and updates are fairly minor, yet represent an improvement over the previous edition. The developmental and technical aspects of the KBIT-2 meet high standards of psychological and educational assessment development.

REVIEWER'S REFERENCES

Kaufman, A. S., & Kaufman, N. L. (1990). Kaufman Brief Intelligence Test. Circle Pines, MN: American Guidance Service.
Reynolds, C. R., & Kamphaus, R. W. (2003). Reynolds Intellectual Screening Test. Lutz, FL: Psychological Assessment Resources.
The Psychological Corporation. (1999). WASI: Wechsler Abbreviated Scale of Intelligence. San Antonio, TX: Author.

[103]

Language Processing Test 3: Elementary.

Purpose: Designed to identify "students' language processing strengths and weaknesses in a hierarchical framework."
Population: Ages 5-0 to 11-11.
Publication Dates: 1985—2005.
Acronym: LPT 3.
Scores, 8: Labeling, Stating Functions, Associations, Categorization, Similarities, Differences, Multiple Meanings, Attributes.
Administration: Individual.
Price Data: Available from publisher.
Time: (30) minutes.
Authors: Gail J. Richard and Mary Anne Hanner.
Publisher: LinguiSystems, Inc.
Cross References: See T5:1424 (5 references); for reviews by Thomas W. Guyette and Lyn Haber of an earlier edition, see 10:169.

Review of the Language Processing Test 3: Elementary by NATALIE RATHVON, Assistant Clinical Professor, The George Washington University, Washington, DC, and Private Practice Psychologist and School Consultant, Bethesda, MD:

DESCRIPTION. The Language Processing Test 3: Elementary (LPT 3) is an individually administered, norm-referenced instrument designed to identify language deficits and guide remediation for children between the ages of 5 years and 11 years, 11 months. The authors assert that the test is based on Luria's model of brain functioning (Luria, 1970, 1982) and was developed because they believed that existing language tests were misidentifying or underidentifying many students with language deficits. Materials include a spiral-bound, tabbed examiner's manual and 20 student response booklets, packed in a box.

The LPT 3 consists of two pretests and six subtests, all with 12 items, arranged in a presumed hierarchy of language skills from simple to complex. The two pretests—Labeling (naming common objects) and Stating Functions (naming the function of the same common objects)—are intended as introductory activities and are not scored, but no rationale is presented for including two 12-item pretests rather than a small set of practice items specific to each subtest. Moreover, Labeling requires examinees to name pictured objects, an activity that differs from the task requirement of the subtests, which involve only auditory stimuli. The six subtests consist of Associations (naming an object associated with the same stimulus nouns used in the pretests), Categorization (naming at least 3 items in a specific category), Similarities (stating how two objects are the same), Differences (stating how similar objects are different), Multiple Meanings (providing definitions for a stimulus word [a homonym] used in three sentences), and Attributes (providing attributes of nouns).

Administration. With the exception of Multiple Meanings, which is not administered to 5-year-olds, all subtests are administered to every examinee. There are no basals and ceilings. The manual states that the LPT 3 can be administered in approximately 35 minutes, but the publisher's catalog indicates 45 minutes, which is closer to this reviewer's experience.

Scoring. Scoring is dichotomous for all items on the first four subtests, which increases scorer consistency but reduces the sensitivity of subtests such as Similarities and Differences to individual differences in expressive language. For Multiple Meanings, the examinee must provide at least two of three definitions for each stimulus word to receive credit. Scores on Attributes items range from 0 to 8, depending on how many different attributes the examinee identifies. According to the authors, scoring standards were established through an extensive review of the responses for each participant in the norm group and additional in-depth analyses.

Raw subtest scores can be converted to standard scores ($M = 100$, $SD = 15$), percentiles, and age equivalents. A total test score can be derived, but interpretation is entirely at the subtest level. Norms are in 1-year increments for the entire age range. Although 1-year intervals are adequate for children ages 8 and up, norm-group intervals should be no more than 6 months for children 7 and younger, whose language skills are developing rapidly (Rathvon, 2004).

DEVELOPMENT. This is the third edition of the LPT (1985, 1995). The authors claim that the LPT 3 is based on Luria's model of brain organization, but they provide no specific information as to how subtest organization, format, and content reflect Luria's model or any other model of brain organization. A pilot version of the LPT 3 with 120 items was administered to an unspecified number of children ages 5 through 11 in Illinois and Iowa. Criteria for retaining items were an increasing percentage of examinees passing at successive age levels and significant discrimination between high and low scorers at each age level. The year of the pilot study is not provided, and there is no discussion of the item review, modification, and deletion process. The authors state that they have made minor revisions in this edition to "make the test more user-friendly" (examiner's manual, p. 7) but make no mention of reviewers' concerns regarding the theoretical basis and technical adequacy of an earlier version (Guyette, 1989; Haber, 1989). Unfortunately, there have been many concerns regarding this test and these have not been substantively addressed in this edition, as discussed in the technical section below.

TECHNICAL ADEQUACY.

Standardization. Standardization was conducted from March 2005 to July 2005 on 1,313 students ages 5 years to 11 years, 11 months from 49 states and the District of Columbia (excluding Delaware), using certified speech-language pathologists as examiners. According to the authors, an attempt was made to ensure minority representation to match U.S. 2000 Census figures. Characteristics are reported by gender, race, and income (high, middle, low) for the seven age groups but no information is provided regarding the number or percentage of examinees tested by state or geographic region or regarding other important demographic characteristics, such as disability status, residence, or parental educational level. The authors state that examinees with "language-learning disorders" (examiner's manual, p. 64) were included in the sample but fail to indicate the number or percentage of examinees with language impairments in terms of the total sample, age levels, or demographic groups. Evaluating representativeness even for the three stratification variables is difficult because information is not presented uniformly in the standardization table in the manual—gender and income are reported in terms of number but not percentage, whereas race is reported in terms of percentage but not number. Moreover, the standardization table does not include the relevant Census figures for comparative purposes, so that potential users must consult other resources to assess sample representativeness. In fact, a review of U.S. 2000 Census data for school-aged children reveals that although gender and race proportions in the LPT 3's normative group are a close match to national figures, examinees from low-income families (defined in the LPT 3 manual as families with incomes of $20,000 or less) are overrepresented and constitute nearly third (32%) of the norm group. The inclusion of such a disproportionately large number of examinees from low socioeconomic (SES) backgrounds is likely to depress the means, given the well-documented relationship between SES status and language development (Hart & Risley, 1992). Age group sizes range from 178 for age 9 to 195 for age 7, which is adequate for 1-year intervals. As stated above, however, 1-year intervals are too broad for tests intended for children under 8 years of age.

Reliability. KR-20 reliability coefficients reported by age for all subtests except Attributes range from .43 to .79, with average values generally in the .60s, well below the acceptable level of .80 for a screening measure, much less the accept able level for a diagnostic measure (.90), as this instrument purports to be. Internal consistency estimates should also be reported by age and subtest for key demographic variables, such as gender, race/ethnicity, and disability status. Stability coefficients for small samples of 14 to 21 examinees (test-retest intervals unspecified) at each of the seven age intervals vary widely by subtest and age level (rs = .13 to .93), with more than two-thirds of the values falling below the minimum criterion of .80. Test-retest reliabilities for total test scores are somewhat higher (rs = .69 to .92), but six of the seven values fall below the .90 criterion for instruments designed for diagnosis and individual programming. Moreover, examiners cannot adequately evaluate the extent of practice effects because mean scores are not reported.

Interscorer reliability was evaluated by having seven speech-language pathologists independently score 21 completed protocols randomly selected from the normative sample. Although the authors state that each pathologist scored all of the items in each record, they go on to say that the items scored were those "in the expressive domain for which individual judgment as to correctness of response is a factor in scoring" (examiner's manual, p. 68), leaving open to question which items were considered to require individual judgment or how many items each pathologist scored. Another problem is that percent agreement is presented for the total number of comparisons across the 21 protocols (31,320) rather than by subtest, and even these estimates range from 85% to 89%. Moreover, because these values are based on completed protocols, they provide no information about examiner variance for tasks involving prompts, such as Differences and Attributes, or scorer variance for subtests involving extended verbal production, such as Multiple Meanings and Attributes.

Validity. Evidence of validity based on test content is very limited. According to the authors, the subtests were selected following an extensive review of the literature and available tests, but no details about the review are provided, and no studies or measures are cited in support of subtest organization, format, content, or item types. Of the 27 citations in the reference list, 17 date from the 1980s or earlier, none refer to specific tests, and the only 2 directly cited in the text of the manual refer to Luria's work, making it unclear to what extent these sources contributed to test de-

velopment. Nor is there any evidence that advisory panels, curriculum experts, or other external reviewers participated in the development, piloting, and validation process for this or earlier editions.

The manual reports biserial correlations between item and subtest scores (excluding Multiple Meanings for age 5 and Attributes), but because mean values are reported by item rather than by subtest across age groups, it is very difficult for potential users to evaluate the discriminating power of the various subtests for their own student populations. Half of the Categorization items fall below the acceptable level of .30 for the 11-year-old group, indicating that those items have little power to differentiate among individual examinees at this age level. *P*–values for each item are reported by age for three of the four racial groups (Caucasian, African American, and Hispanic), but analyses are based on subgroups randomly sampled from the normative sample rather than the entire norm group. Values for many Categorization items exceed the criterion level of .85 across all three groups, even at age 5, indicating that the items are too easy to provide an accurate assessment of individual performance. Item difficulty indices should be calculated with the entire standardization sample, and median values reported for each subtest by age.

To evaluate possible gender bias, *t*-tests were conducted to compare mean raw scores for males and females for each subtest and total test by age. Differences for total test were not significant at any age level, whereas there were three instances of significant subtest differences, all in favor of females and all less than 2 points. Analyses of racial performance differences are based on the same matched subgroups in the item difficulty studies rather than on the entire normative sample. Although only 5% of the comparisons were significant for race, subtest means are not presented for the subgroups, so that examiners cannot determine the degree to which the differences are clinically meaningful. A series of ANOVAs analyzing differences among nine racial/SES groups (e.g., middle-SES Hispanics) randomly sampled from the norm group indicated significant effects for 19% of the analyses, with effects occurring primarily at ages 10 and 11. Neither raw score nor standard score means for the groups are presented on a sample-wide basis, and the Attributes subtest was omitted from all of the analyses. Moreover, there is no evidence that flagged items were examined to determine the characteristics contributing to their greater difficulty for a particular subgroup. Similarly, although judgmental procedures are insufficient to detect differential item functioning (DIF), there is no indication that sensitivity reviews with representatives of various demographic groups were conducted to minimize the potential for gender, racial, ethnic, or cultural bias. Such reviews might have discovered that male gender pronouns are used to refer to a single individual throughout the manual.

No concurrent validity evidence is presented to document the LPT 3's relationship to other standardized tests of language, vocabulary, reading, cognitive ability, or other relevant domains, nor to contextually relevant measures of performance, such as teacher ratings or classroom grades. Predictive validity evidence is also lacking. LPT 3 subtests demonstrate increases in raw score means across age groups, indicating that the abilities being measured are developmental in nature, in support of construct validity, although no correlations with age are presented. Intersubtest correlations reported for the entire normative group and by age interval are generally low to moderate. Most item-subtest correlations are significant, but evaluating subtest homogeneity is difficult because item values are averaged across the seven age groups rather than by subtest. No evidence is presented in support of the presumed hierarchical organization of the subtests. In fact, contrary to that claim, Categorization mean raw scores are higher than Associations mean raw scores in the normative sample across all seven age groups, mean raw scores for Similarities and Differences differ by less than half a point across all age levels, and Multiple Meanings mean raw scores approach or exceed Associations mean raw scores beginning at age 8.

Diagnostic utility was evaluated by contrasting mean raw scores of examinees randomly selected from the norm group with matched samples of students identified as language disordered (total of 28 to 42 examinees at each age interval). It is not clear whether all of the students with language disorders in these analyses (total $n = 115$) were included in the standardization sample or whether they represent a subgroup. Total test raw score means significantly discriminated between groups at all seven age intervals. Subtest differences between groups were significant for 30 of 41 comparisons, although Associations demonstrated significant differences only for the age 5 group. Because the analyses are based on raw scores rather than standard scores, however, examiners cannot readily determine whether the observed differences are clinically meaningful. When this reviewer used the norms tables to convert the reported raw mean scores to standard scores, total test mean standard scores for the language-disordered groups fell 13 to 28 standard score points lower than those for normal controls. For the age 6 sample, however, mean standard scores for both groups were within the average range (mean standard score = 93 vs. 106, respectively). Subtest standard score differences between normal controls and disability groups ranged from 5 to 34 points, with scores for both groups falling within the average range for more than 20% of the comparisons (9 of 41). Evidence of group differentiation should be based on comparisons between normal controls and several disability groups, such as students with articulation disorders, language delay, language impairment, learning disabilities, and mental retardation, rather between normally achieving students and a single disability group. No evidence that the LPT 3 can identify individual children with language impairment (i.e., sensitivity or specificity indices) is presented.

COMMENTARY. The LPT 3 may appeal to practitioners because of its low cost and ease of administration, but usability cannot compensate for lack of psychometric soundness, and the LPT 3 has numerous technical shortcomings that are likely to result in overidentification or misidentification of students with language impairment.

Administration procedures for the Attributes subtest are problematic and are likely to compromise both reliability and validity. For the demonstration item (*horse*), the examinee is given the directions: "Pretend I don't know what a horse is. Tell me about a horse; anything you can think of" (examiner's manual, p. 38). To earn full credit, the examinee must provide eight attributes per noun: function, parts, color, accessory/necessity, size/shape, category, composition, and location/origin. If the examinee does not provide all eight attributes spontaneously for the demonstration item, the examiner delivers category-specific prompts (e.g., "What color can a horse be?"), but the only prompts permitted on test items are "Tell me about…" and "Are you finished?" Are examinees expected to derive the task requirements by memorizing the categories of their unprompted responses as well as the categories of the examiner's questions? The authors justify the lack of prompting on the basis that "inability to expand on a response is a diagnostic indicator for language processing problems" (examiner's manual, p. 60), but the lack of querying, coupled with the vague scoring guidelines, increases construct-irrelevant variance rather than diagnostic validity. The manual also contains a discrepancy between the directions and the list of acceptable responses. For example, "A watermelon is black" (examiner's manual, p. 38) is given as an example of inappropriate use of color, whereas later in the manual, black is listed as an acceptable response in the color category for this question.

The rationale and criteria for scoring decisions are sketchy, making the LPT 3 highly vulnerable to interscorer variance. A few examples of the numerous scoring problems are provided below.

> Associations—Item 1: "What goes with shoe?" *Sock* is correct; *shoelace* is not. Item 6: "What goes with soap?" *Holder* is correct; *container* is not. Item 7: "What goes with milk?" *Glass* is correct; *carton* is not. *Cow*, which was listed as incorrect in an earlier version, is not listed as acceptable or unacceptable in this edition.
>
> Categorization—Item 4: "Things that take you places." *Car*, *boat*, and *horse* are correct, but *trailer*, *camper*, *skateboard*, and *inline skates* are among the incorrect answers.
>
> Multiple Meanings—Item 1: *rose*. For the sentence "The sun rose over the mountains," acceptable definitions are given in the present rather than past tense (*ascend, come up, rise, move up, go up/high*). Although this may be an editorial oversight, it should be corrected, especially in view of accumulating evidence that tense may serve as a clinical marker of specific language impairment (Rice & Wexler, 1996; Rice, Wexler, & Hershberger, 1999). Item 5: *cut*. One of the three stimulus sentences involves a slang expression ("Cut it out").

The norm group for the LPT 3 is of questionable representativeness and includes a disproportionately large number of examinees from low-income families. This may have lowered the means.

Despite their assertion that the LPT 3 can be used to diagnose specific language deficits and plan remediation, the authors provide remarkably little assistance to users in interpreting test performance or linking assessment results to intervention. They suggest that normally performing students would display stronger language skills on the early subtests and then deteriorate markedly at a given level (i.e., subtest), whereas students with language impairments would deteriorate earlier than expected and might also demonstrate uneven performance across subtests. At one point, the authors recommend beginning remediation at the Associations level if a student scores one standard deviation below the mean on Categorization, but it is by no means clear that they intend this criterion to serve as a cutoff score, leaving examiners with no specific criteria for determining the presence or severity of a language impairment. Moreover, no empirical evidence is provided to support the use of a cut score of one standard deviation below the mean to identify language impairment at either the total test or subtest level. In fact, because of the floor effects noted below, 6-year-olds cannot obtain standard scores lower than 89 on Multiple Meanings. No case examples are presented to illustrate the scoring and interpretative process or to demonstrate how to use the results to design remediation. Similarly, although an intervention kit by the authors is listed in the references, the manual contains no information on treatment strategies, curricular programs, or best practices for addressing the identified deficits.

Despite the appropriate cautions about age equivalents included in the manual, the front page of the record booklet displays an age equivalency profile along with a standard score profile, and in the scores section, age equivalents are listed first, before percentile ranks and standard scores. No cautions are provided regarding the use of the LPT 3 with students from diverse linguistic or cultural backgrounds or the importance of considering multiple sources of data in diagnosis and treatment planning, such as performance-based assessments, teacher interviews, and classroom observations, in addition to standardized tests. Also absent is any information to assist examiners in explaining the results to parents or classroom teachers.

Given the limited number of items per subtest, it is not surprising that floors for several subtests are inadequate at the younger age levels. Floors for Similarities, Differences, and Attributes are inadequate below age 7, and floors for Multiple Meanings are inadequate below age 8. Total test floors are inadequate for ages 5 and 6. Although ceiling effects are less critical than floor effects for a test intended to identify language deficits, several subtests also demonstrate ceiling effects, with effects for Categorization beginning at the 5-year-old level. Because of the restricted score ranges, item gradient violations, defined as fewer than 10 items between the subtest mean and floor (Rathvon, 2004), are pervasive across all subtests and all age groups, reducing the sensitivity of the test to small differences in performance.

Many subtests have unacceptably low levels of internal consistency, and test-retest and scorer consistency cannot be adequately evaluated. Inadequate norm group intervals, floor effects, and item gradient violations further reduce the LPT 3's ability to identify low-performing children and to distinguish small differences in performance among children. Evidence documenting what the LPT 3 is actually measuring is also limited. The authors do not provide an in-depth discussion of the LPT 3's theoretical basis and how its subtests map onto Luria's model or any other model, and the LPT 3 has not been correlated with any other criterion measure. Notably absent from the manual is any discussion of the contribution of current research in language disorders or assessment, as well as evidence that external reviewers participated in the development and validation of this edition. There is some evidence that the LPT 3 discriminates between children with language disorders and normally developing children, although more than 20% of the mean subtest standard scores for the clinical groups fell within the average range, limiting its ability to identify language impairment. Moreover, the primary evidence required to support the use of a test designed to identify language impairment does not consist of mean differences between normally developing students and clinical groups, but evidence of sensitivity and specificity (Spaulding, Plante, & Farinella, 2006), which is lacking here.

SUMMARY. In view of the numerous psychometric problems noted above, the LPT 3 cannot be recommended for screening, diagnosis, progress monitoring, or intervention planning purposes. Alternatives include the Test of Lan-

guage Development–Primary, Third Edition (Newcomer & Hammill, 1997; T7:2598) for children ages 4 through 8 and the Test of Language Development—Intermediate, Third Edition (Hammill, & Newcomer, 1997; T7:2597) for children ages 8 through 12. Both of these instruments have much more adequate theoretical and empirical documentation and include measures of phonology, morphology, and syntax, as well as semantics. For practitioners assessing children from birth through age 6, the Preschool Language Scale, Fourth Edition (Zimmerman, Steiner, & Pond, 2002; 16:198) is a technically sound instrument that provides sensitivity and specificity indices in addition to other validity evidence.

REVIEWER'S REFERENCES
Guyette, T. W. (1989). [Review of the Language Processing Test.] In J. C. Conoley & J. J. Kramer (Eds.), *The tenth mental measurements yearbook* (pp. 432-434). Lincoln, NE: Buros Institute of Mental Measurements.
Haber, L. (1989). [Review of the Language Processing Test.] In J. C. Conoley & J. J. Kramer (Eds.), *The tenth mental measurements yearbook* (pp. 434-435). Lincoln, NE: Buros Institute of Mental Measurements.
Hammill, D. D., & Newcomer, P. L. (1997). Test of Language Development—Intermediate, Third Edition. Austin, TX: PRO-ED.
Hart, B., & Risley, T. R. (1992). American parenting of language-learning children: Persisting differences in family-child interactions observed in natural home environments. *Developmental Psychology, 28*, 1096-1105.
Luria, A. R. (1970, March). The functional organization of the brain. *Scientific American, 222*, 66–78.
Luria, A. R. (1982). *Language and cognition*. New York: John Wiley & Sons.
Newcomer, P. L., & Hammill, D. D. (1997). Test of Language Development–Primary: Third Edition. Austin, TX: PRO-ED.
Rathvon, N. (2004). *Early reading assessment: A handbook for practitioners*. New York: Guilford Press.
Rice, M. L., & Wexler, K. (1996). Toward tense as a clinical marker of specific language impairment in English speaking children. *Journal of Speech and Hearing Research, 39*, 1239-1257.
Rice, M. L., Wexler, K., & Hershberger, S. (1999). Tense over time: The longitudinal course of tense acquisition in children with specific language impairment. *Journal of Speech, Language, and Hearing Research, 41*, 1412-1431.
Spaulding, J., Plante, E., & Farinella, K. A. (2006). Eligibility criteria for language impairment: Is the low end of normal always appropriate? *Language, Speech, and Hearing Services in Schools, 37*, 61-72.
Zimmerman, I. L., Steiner, V. G., & Pond, R. E. (2002). Preschool Language Scale, Fourth Edition. San Antonio, TX: Harcourt Assessment.

[104]
Leadership Spectrum Profile.

Purpose: To identify leadership business priorities in a given situation, develop business acumen, improve team effectiveness, enhance strategic thinking, and to reflect that leadership requirements change by context or circumstance.

Population: Individuals in leadership positions.

Publication Dates: 1998–2000.

Acronym: LSP.

Scores: 6 choices: Inventor (new products/services), Catalyst (market growth), Developer (reduce risk and improve accountabilities), Performer (increase efficiency, quality, and resource utilization), Protector (build culture and develop talent), and Challenger (position for the future, check assumptions and trends).

Administration: Group.

Price Data, 2005: $24.95 per manual/test booklet (2000, 31 pages), volume discounts available; $45 per Priority Balancing Handbook (110 pages); price information for online version is available from publisher.
Foreign Language Edition: Japanese language version is available.
Time: (12–18) minutes.
Comments: Results reflect the business priorities that are currently driving the leader; online version is available at www.leadershipspectrum.com.
Author: Mary Lippitt.
Publisher: Enterprise Management Ltd.

Review of the Leadership Spectrum Profile by JANET F. CARLSON, Professor, Department of General Academics, Texas A&M University at Galveston, Galveston, TX:

DESCRIPTION. The Leadership Spectrum Profile (LSP) identifies leadership priorities, or principles and values used by leaders to make decisions and communicate with others in an organization. It is a brief, paper-and-pencil, self-report measure that may be completed individually, in groups, or online. A respondent indicates which of six options best captures his or her action, emphasis, or priority in given business situations. Respondents also indicate their second choice in response to each of 14 situations. A Team Composite report may be generated for groups whose organizations purchase this online option.

Self-scoring is easily completed using the multiple-carbon-copy answer form supplied. The LSP provides scores on six leadership preferences associated with an individual's priorities in the context of the workplace: Inventor, Catalyst, Developer, Performer, Protector, and Challenger. Leadership profile scores may range from 0 to 28, but extreme scores are unlikely. One or more "primary profiles" typically emerge; the test manual does not address how to interpret scores when all or most of the profiles are clustered tightly. Interpretation is simply a matter of noting one's highest score and the associated description of that profile, while considering the life cycle of the particular organization in which one functions. The test manual also provides some ideas and exercises (in the form of open-ended questions) to contextualize results and help test takers clarify decision-making criteria, improve communication, and enhance their influence within the organization.

Materials sent by the publisher included the 31-page manual/test booklet, an order form, a profile response sheet, and five photocopied pages (pp. 66-70) from a book, manual, or technical report, containing sketchy information on test development, validity, reliability, respondent demographics, and norms. Hereafter, the photocopied pages are referred to as "test materials" to distinguish them from the "test manual." This reviewer also consulted and used information on the LSP web site to complete the review.

DEVELOPMENT. The LSP was developed using 192 items, written to measure six leadership profiles. The final version of the LSP consists of 84 items (14 per concept), matched for social desirability. Test materials offer vague descriptions of test development procedures, noting that a "series of analyses" were used "to identify a subset of items which optimally measured these six concepts" (test materials, p. 66). Other information states that seven experts conducted a Q-sort to identify items that functioned poorly. Who were considered "experts," and "experts" in what, is not specified. The test materials sent also mention that a factor analysis was performed for each of the six leadership profiles, and that coefficient alpha values were used to determine whether an item should be retained or deleted. Insufficient detail was provided in the test materials to evaluate whether the procedures employed in the Q-sort, factor analyses, or alpha determinations were appropriately implemented and applied.

TECHNICAL. The test materials refer to norms that are updated and posted regularly on a corresponding web site. These norms appear to consist of descriptive statistics that derive from self-reporting by test takers who opt to submit their data for inclusion in the database. Means and standard deviations, as well as medians, are presented for each profile, grouped in a series of four tables by gender, job title, job function, and type of industry, respectively. Standard demographic information about ethnicity, age, race, educational level, and so on, is not provided in the test manual or online.

In general, means and medians appear to be similar. Another discernible pattern across all four tables relates to standard deviations, which tend to be quite large. An example provided in the test materials concerning use of the norms (p. 70) suggests that a female inventor's score of 10 "falls far above 50% of other female inventors." Given the size of the standard deviation, however, the example (score of 10) actually falls within one standard deviation (3.68) of the mean (6.66), according to data posted online on March 21, 2006. Individual scores that fall within one standard deviation of the mean seldom warrant attention. More often, such scores are considered to be within normal limits.

Internal consistency reliability received brief mention in the test materials provided to this reviewer. Details are sketchy, but the author claims a reliability estimate of .91. No other forms of reliability are addressed in the test materials provided by the publisher.

The test materials suggest that the LSP demonstrates face validity, because an unspecified number of individuals who completed the instrument "said they agreed with the results" (test materials, p. 67). No other forms of validity evidence are addressed in the test materials provided by the publisher.

COMMENTARY. Representativeness of the sample on which descriptive statistics are based and presented online cannot be assessed, as demographic data are not provided, either online or in the test manual. Only the entire sample size is provided online. As of this writing, the number exceeds 5,000. The number of respondents per category (gender, job title, job function, type of industry) is not provided. It is impossible to ascertain the extent to which the norming process was appropriate and to understand how or if various demographic features should be used in interpreting scores.

The test manual is not written at a sufficiently high level of sophistication to satisfy individuals with even a modicum of measurement expertise. The LSP test manual contains superficial descriptions of technical features, making the review process—by this reviewer or prospective users—difficult and incomplete. It makes only passing mention of procedures employed during test development and assessment of psychometric properties. Consequently, prospective users will not have enough information to make an informed decision about the suitability of the LSP for their intended purposes. With a brief, self-report measure such as the LSP, establishing consistency over time via test-retest reliability would be accomplished easily, yet apparently no such process has been undertaken. Evidence presented in support of validity is similarly weak. For example, instead

of addressing content validity by considering whether the domain content had been adequately sampled, the test developers merely decided that 14 sets of six items was adequate in length because "time limitations and individuals getting tired were "particularly important [considerations] in a business environment" (test materials, p. 68). The only type of validity mentioned is face validity. Face validity is recognized widely as the weakest form of validity, with some measurement experts suggesting that it is too weak to be considered a psychometric concept at all.

As far as the interpretive statements contained in the LSP manual, Barnum effects loom large. Descriptions attached to the six leadership profiles contain many statements that would be widely applicable to many people, rather than to a single leadership profile. For example, many would agree that the following statement applies to them: "Concerned that blindspots or narrow perspectives may limit opportunities, the [individual] seeks diverse ideas and people to prepare the enterprise for the future" (manual, p. 12). Thus, it is not surprising that participants in the reliability sample study agreed that the LSP provided "descriptions [that] captured their priorities and contributions" (test materials, p. 67).

The LSP itself is easily understood by test takers and is presented in a format that facilitates proper completion. Prospective users would be well advised to contact the publisher directly for answers to specific questions that are not addressed, or are addressed incompletely, in the materials one receives.

SUMMARY. The LSP uses a pencil-and-paper, self-report format to identify leadership priorities under a number of business situations. It is brief and easily administered using individual or group administration procedures or online. Documentation provided in the LSP manual is lacking in many ways, but especially insofar as information needed to assess its technical adequacy.

Review of the Leadership Spectrum Profile by L. CAROLYN PEARSON, Professor of Educational Foundations, and SHARON ANN RICHARDSON, Assistant Professor of Educational Leadership, University of Arkansas at Little Rock, Little Rock, AR:

DESCRIPTION. The Leadership Spectrum Profile is a 14-item paper-and-pencil or online instrument used to identify current leadership pri orities, or the perspectives and actions a person values as a leader in their enterprise. All of the multiple-choice items have six response possibilities that generate scores for six scales: Inventor, Catalyst, Developer, Performer, Protector, and Challenger. The directions for taking the instrument in paper-and-pencil format are clear, and a separate answer sheet allows for easy scoring of the items by totaling the labels that correspond to each of the six scales within two sections. Although not indicated in the instructions, it is estimated that time for administration is about 15 minutes. The instrument is also available in a Japanese-language version. There are two sections on the response sheet in which the user first indicates the response that most represents the action that would be taken (Most Like You) and then the response that represents the action that is next likely to be taken (Next Most Like You). The primary profile is determined by the highest score on the six scales and indicates the type of actions a person would take in meeting their enterprise's goals and making decisions. Once the primary profile is determined the user is referred back to the manual for interpretation. The manual includes five sections with corresponding exercises that address understanding the primary profile, understanding the organizational life cycle, developing leadership effectiveness, understanding how to influence others, and understanding team composite profiles. Although the author provides these exercises, there is no scoring process and it is up to the user to interpret the results.

DEVELOPMENT. Materials furnished by the developer (including the manual, instrument construction, and demographic information) provide some insight regarding initial development. Seven experts were briefed on the theoretical framework and were given a detailed description for each of the six constructs that the scales were based on and then participated in refining an initial pool of 192 items (grouped into 32-item sets) down to a pool of 132 items (grouped in 22-item sets) by using a Q-sort method in which five or more had to agree on the scale classification of an item for each of the six sets. The test author wrote that the experts were also asked to rate the social desirability of each item on a 5-point Likert-type scale, but gave no information as to how items were evaluated using this rating process. Factor analysis was then performed separately for

each of the six scales, and correlations between the individual items and the factor were used to determine which were to be retained on the final version of the instrument, which resulted in 84 items (14 sets of 6). According to the authors, items that had extreme means and standard deviations were eliminated, and the coefficient alpha internal consistency reliability was also determined, but again no information was provided as to which items were retained using this information. The test author states that the final version of the instrument comprises 14 items, each with six choices. However, the development information states that there are 84 items (i.e., each choice for the 14 items is actually considered an individual item, which does yield a total of 84).

TECHNICAL. Information describing the norming process is very vague, and what is provided by the developer makes reference to demographic data collected from 5,003 respondents and includes the six scale means, standard deviations, and medians by gender, title (supervisor/team leader, manager, executive, other), job function (engineering/technical, finance/accounting, manufacturing/operations, sales/marketing, administrative/human resources, other), and industry (business, nonprofit/association, public sector/government), but no analyses regarding demograhic subgroups are presented with the exception of gender, for which no differences were found. One might assume that the developer is continuing to collect data in order to develop norms and conduct future research because users are requested to return a database page included with the response and scoring pages. The 14 items are presented with six choices that represent each of the six scales and focus on perspectives and behaviors that leaders demonstrate in their enterprise. The six choices do appear to be linked to the stems of the 14 items and are worded neutrally because there are no right or wrong answers.

Internal consistency reliability was determined during instrument development for item selection but no coefficients are provided. Reliability of the final version was "assessed by the consistency of priority classification—the level of consistency between all pairs of items" (handbook, p. 68), and the contingency coefficient was used to quantify the classification. The Spearman-Brown prophecy formula was used to determine the average value of 91 calculated contingency coefficients for a reliability coefficient of .91, but no justification was provided as to why this method was used. Other reliability estimates to support the consistency of the scores for this instrument are lacking.

Evidence to support the validity of the scores is very limited. Again only the initial factor analysis used for scale construction is mentioned, and there are no efforts to establish concurrent validity of the scores with other existing leadership inventories or predictive validity of the scores in the particular job setting included in the demographic information. The developer refers to both reliability and validity in terms of the coefficient already discussed ($r = .91$) and does not differentiate the two concepts, but merely refers to the face validity of the instrument.

COMMENTARY. The Leadership Spectrum Profile, as a measure of identifying leadership priorities, has some limitations. First, the author has not provided a solid conceptual framework from which the items, and the constructs they purport to measure, were derived, although the author does make mention of it. The items seem to demonstrate content validity; however, there is no indication of how they were derived from the research on leadership. Second, the author needs to make clear that the answer choices to the 14 items correspond to the six scales; therefore, there are 84 items rather than 14, an issue that could easily confuse some users. Next, the author should conduct analyses using the job titles/functions mentioned to determine any potential biases that could exist when attempting to generalize the scores to the groups that are represented. Also, other than the initial development information, empirical evidence to support the reliability and validity of the scores is lacking, and in the future the author should clearly delineate the two concepts.

SUMMARY. The author has produced a leadership profile that can be administered, scored, and interpreted rather easily. An attempt was made to delineate clearly the 6 constructs that are being measured, but the information presented was from the initial validation process. Ongoing validation efforts are lacking and such insufficient evidence brings into question whether the instrument can produce reliable and valid scores for any of its constructs. Readers seeking an alternative test will find several that measure leadership behaviors/skills or style (e.g., Leadership Practices Inventory [T7:1412], Styles of Leadership Surve [T7:2473], Leader Behavior Analysis I [T7:1403]), although they do not measure leader ship priorities per se.

[105]

Learning and Study Strategies Inventory Second Edition.

Purpose: Designed to assess "students' awarenes about and use of learning and study strategies related t skill, will and self-regulation components of strateg learning."

Population: Grades 9 and over.

Publication Dates: 1987-2002.

Acronym: LASSI.

Scores, 10: Anxiety Scale, Attitude Scale, Concen tration Scale, Information Processing Scale, Motiva tion Scale, Self-Testing Scale, Selecting Main Idea Scale, Study Aids Scale, Time Management Scale, Tes Strategies Scale.

Administration: Individual or group.

Foreign Language Edition: Spanish Version avai able for college students.

Time: (15-20) minutes.

Comments: This test can be self-administered an self-scored; can be computer administered and score

Authors: Claire E. Weinstein, Ann C. Schulte, an David R. Palmer.

Publisher: H&H Publishing Company, Inc.

   a) COLLEGE VERSION.

   Population: College students.

   Price Data: $3.25 per complete kit includin test booklet and user's manual (2002, 28 pages)

   b) HIGH SCHOOL VERSION.

   Population: Grades 9-12.

   Price Data: $2.75 per complete kit includin test booklet and user's manual (2002, 28 pages)

   c) SPANISH VERSION.

   Population: College students.

   Price Data: $3 per complete kit including te booklet and user's manual (2002, 28 pages).

Cross References: See T5:1455 (13 reference and T4:1417 (1 reference); for reviews by Martha V Blackwell and Steven C. Hayes of an earlier edition, s 11:198 (3 references).

Review of the Learning and Study Strategi Inventory, Second Edition by HEIDI M. CART Associate Director, Student Research & Informatio University of California, San Diego, San Diego, C

DESCRIPTION. The Learning and Stud Strategies Inventory, Second Edition (LASSI) is revised edition of the LASSI first published i 1987. The LASSI is designed to serve as a diag nostic tool to help identify a student's study patterns and learning skills for which they could benefit from educational interventions.

The LASSI 2nd Edition consists of 80 questions, yielding 10 scales (8 questions per scale) including: Anxiety, Attitude, Concentration, Information Processing, Motivation, Selecting Main Ideas, Self-Testing, Study Aids, Test Strategies, and Time Management. The LASSI 2nd Edition is administered via pen or pencil and is self-scoring. An on-line version is also available with automated scoring; an Excel file of raw data is available upon request.

The materials provided by the developers include a self-scoring survey and user's manual. Included in the user's guide are sections describing uses of the LASSI, its administration and scoring, the individual LASSI scales, the development of the first edition of the LASSI, development of the LASSI 2nd Edition, field testing and norming sample data, summaries of the item statistics for each LASSI 2nd Edition scale, individual scale statistics, interscale correlations, and LASSI 2nd Edition scale norms.

DEVELOPMENT. One criticism about the LASSI was the redundancy of items within and between scales (Blackwell, 1992). The authors appear to have addressed this issue in creating a new instrument over a 5-year period. The authors mention pilot testing the items on a large (*n* = 2,400) sample of students, employing "a team of developmental educators, educational psychologists, and educational psychometricians" (user's manual, p. 17) to examine the pool of items, utilizing student feedback and field tests. The authors used "77 items from the LASSI 1st Edition, 29 items from the pilot test version and 60 new items written for the field test" (user's manual, p. 17). As a result of field testing, 86 items were eliminated resulting in a final instrument of 80 items. No rationale was provided for why items were eliminated. The authors mention updating the LASSI 2nd Edition to remove dated items and wording and improve the psychometric properties of the instrument.

TECHNICAL. With the LASSI 2nd Edition the authors attempted to improve the psychometric properties of the instrument. The authors provided evidence of internal consistency reliability by providing coefficient alphas for each scale; these alphas range from .73 to .89.

As discussed in prior reviews by Blackwell (1992) and Hayes (1992), the lack of empirical evidence for external validity of the first edition of the LASSI is of concern. The developers did not respond to this concern and have not presented the psychometric properties for substantiating the validity of the scales. Therefore, the LASSI 2nd Edition continues not to meet the minimum accepted psychometric standards for substantiating validity evidence established in the *Standards for Educational and Psychological Testing* (AERA, APA, & NCME, 1999).

Other validity issues that need to be addressed are the short-term and long-term effects of utilizing the information produced by the LASSI 2nd Edition. What are the short-term and long-term effects of using the instrument to identify areas of weakness with regard to one's study and learning skills? Do the students who utilize the instrument ultimately benefit from the information and receive the necessary educational intervention as identified by the instrument? What is the relationship of the scale scores to improved scholastic ability, college GPA, and college success rates?

With the LASSI 2nd Edition, the developers created national norm data based on a more broad-based sample compared to the first edition of the LASSI. According to the authors, their "sample was drawn from twelve different institutions representing different geographical regions as well as university, community college, state college and technical institutions" (user's manual, p. 16). The authors include sample size statistics by type of institution (e.g., university, community college), gender, ethnicity, age, and GPA; however, norm statistics by these subject characteristics are not provided, rather just overall norm statistics. It would be useful to have norm data by gender, ethnicity, age, type of institution, and one's GPA.

COMMENTARY. Although the theoretical framework underlying the LASSI 2nd Edition, based on interviews with professionals in both developmental education and educational psychology, and a review of relevant research, related textbooks, and other learning assistance materials appears well grounded, the psychometric properties providing evidence for the validity of the instrument are absent. The usefulness of this instrument is in the face-validity of the questions and the ease of both administration (on-line and paper-and-pencil versions) and interpretation.

SUMMARY. Overall, if psychometric evidence regarding the construct and criterion-related validity are not required, the LASSI 2nd Edition may serve as an easily administered instrument that is intended to identify whether a student has the attitudes and learning skills that may be needed to ultimately graduate from college. The LASSI 2nd Edition is available on-line with automated scoring to enhance the ease in administering the instrument. Validity studies need to be documented and the short-term and long-term effects of the program need to be determined.

REVIEWER'S REFERENCES

American Educational Research Association, American Psychological Association, and National Council on Measurement in Education. (1999). *Standards for educational and psychological testing.* Washington, DC: American Educational Research Association.
Blackwell, M. W. (1992). [Review of the Learning and Study Strategies Inventory.] In. J. J. Kramer & J. C. Conoley (Eds.), *The eleventh mental measurements yearbook* (pp. 449-450). Lincoln, NE: Buros Institute of Mental Measurements.
Hayes, S. C. (1992). [Review of the Learning and Study Strategies Inventory.] In. J. J. Kramer & J. C. Conoley (Eds.), *The eleventh mental measurements yearbook* (p. 450). Lincoln, NE: Buros Institute of Mental Measurements.

Review of the Learning and Study Strategies Inventory, Second Edition by CLAUDIA R. WRIGHT, Professor Emerita, California State University, Long Beach, Long Beach, CA:

DESCRIPTION. The Learning and Study Strategies Inventory, Second Edition (LASSI, 2nd Edition) is an 80-item, 10-scale (with 8 items per scale), self-report assessment that can be administered individually or in groups using a self-scoring, paper-and-pencil form or an online, web-based version that is scored automatically. The authors offer the LASSI, 2nd Edition as a measure for obtaining presumably reliable and valid scores for screening, diagnosing, planning, evaluating, and advising college-level and post-secondary students about their awareness levels of cognitive, affective, and control components considered to support study practices and to enhance learning. To assess various strategies for acquiring knowledge, 3 of the 10 scales make up the Skill Component: Information Processing (INP; learning new information), Selecting Main Ideas (SMI), and Testing Strategies (TST). To measure affective aspects that can impact learning, 3 scales form the Will Component: Anxiety (ANX; school-related), Attitudes (ATT; achievement-related), and Motivation (MOT; self-discipline and effort). And, to assess management and control strategies, 4 scales

support the Self-Regulation Component: Concentration (CON), Self-Testing (SFT), Study Aids (STA), and Time Management (TMT). The inventory employs a 5-point Likert-type formatted scale with response options ranging from (a) *Not at all typical of me* to (e) *Very much typical of me.*

DEVELOPMENT. The authors sought to improve item content and the psychometric properties of the LASSI scales by incorporating new content consistent with research in metacognition and development (particularly self-regulation) and in higher education and instructional psychology (particularly changes in instruction and related practices). The concept of "strategic learning" is offered without documentation as the underlying framework for the LASSI's three components of Skill, Will, and Self-Regulation. This argument is used to explain conceptual overlap found among the components and among items of different scales.

Building on the original 77-item, 10-scale version of the LASSI, additional items were constructed and subjected to content validation procedures. This item pool was piloted with a sample of 2,400 entering freshmen who attended a southwestern university during 1998 and 1999; SAT, GPA, and high school rank data were also collected. Subsequent item analyses, input from content experts, and student feedback produced a 166-item inventory that was later field tested. The results of the field test guided the construction of the final 80-item version of the inventory and the collection of normative data.

TECHNICAL.

Standardization. Norms were based on data collected from the responses of 1,092 students enrolled in 1 of 12 U.S. institutions (3 universities, 3 state colleges, 5 community colleges, and 1 technical school) representing different geographical regions. Respondents were classified as White, 65%; African American, 14%; Hispanic, 14%; Asian or Pacific Islander, 1%; or Other, 6%. Females made up 65% of the sample and males, 35%–a relationship that holds across ethnic groups (with the exception of the small Asian cohort, with 56% female and 44% male). About 65% of the sample was 19 years old or younger, consistent with expected ages of entering freshman out of high school and 35% were 20 or older. Approximately 36% of White students earned GPAs less than 3.0 contrasted with 72% of African American, 45% of Hispanic, 44% of Asian, and 51% of Other students.

A table for "national norms" provides an easy reference for identifying percentile scores that correspond to scale scores for each of the 10 scales. Although ethnicity, gender, and age data were available, there are no norms for gender or age and insufficient data precluded norms by ethnicity or institution.

Scoring. Clear instructions are provided for manual self-scoring. However, because of the complexity of the scoring template, test administrators might assess the general skill level and arithmetic proficiency of the examinees to determine what supervision, if any, might be required during the scoring phase. A handy chart is provided that lays out percentiles and corresponding scale scores and allows for an examinee to plot each score. Demarcations for the 50th and 75th percentiles facilitate interpretation of scores so that a scale score at or above the 75th percentile is explained as identifying an area of relative strength; a score at or below the 50th percentile suggests relative weakness and lack of development in the skill area; and a score falling between these two positions indicates a need for improvement. Students are referred to learning resources in their college for additional information.

The range of possible scores for each scale is from 8 to 40. Although 50% of the items are reverse scored, the pattern is not random across scales. For example, all 8 items for the Anxiety Scale are reverse scored, so that a respondent who declares that each corresponding statement is *Not at all typical of me* would earn a score of 40; whereas, none of the items for Information Processing or Self Testing scales are reverse scored so that a response of *Very much typical of me* for each statement of the respective scales would produce a score of 40. An issue of possible response bias is not addressed.

Reliability. A series of tables displays the item statistics separately for each of the 10 scales including item-total correlations. Acceptable coefficient alphas ranged from .73 to .89 (*mdn* = .84) and reflect modest improvement over the original LASSI scales. Although scales were ordered alphabetically, alpha coefficients for scales are ordered here by components: Skill Component, INF = .84, SMI = .89, TST = .80; Will Component, ANX = .87, ATT = .77, MOT = .84; and Self-

Regulation Component, CON = .86, SFT = .84, STA = .73, TMT = .85. No other reliability estimate is provided.

Validity. Standard content validation procedures were employed and appear sound. "User validity" was offered as evidence, which was based on the "high degree of usefulness" (user's manual, p. 16) feedback expressed by test administrators. Unfortunately, important criterion-related validity evidence is lacking even though the authors indicate that (a) data collected over the years included SAT, GRE, GPA, and high school rank variables; and (b) LASSI scores had been validated against performance measures. In addition, important construct-related validity evidence is lacking even though, reportedly, LASSI scores had been compared to other tests with subscales measuring similar factors. None of the tests or measures for any validation effort were specifically identified and no statistics were reported.

COMMENTARY. It appears that the LASSI, 2nd Edition has been used most extensively in classroom settings where students have access to structured, informed feedback and resources. How students might fare using the inventory on their own has not been addressed.

The sample upon which the normative data are based lacks sufficient representation from Asian, African American, and Hispanic student groups. It is quite possible that patterns of responses to the LASSI items are "ethnic" free, but this circumstance has yet to be verified. As the publisher boasts broad usage of the LASSI in post-secondary and higher education settings, oversampling from these groups would seem warranted. Further, the authors refer to one of the uses of the LASSI, 2nd Edition as focusing on those "thoughts, behaviors, attitudes, motivation, and beliefs that ...can be altered" (user's manual, p. 4). As shown in the technical manual tables, the students from underrepresented groups appeared to have the largest number of underperformers as measured by GPA; evidence that interventions designed to address "diagnosed" weaknesses on the LASSI have led to "altered" behaviors and subsequent increases in academic performance for such students would be very useful.

Because one function of LASSI scores is to provide "diagnostic" information for students, it appears that only scores related to the 10 scales have been considered relevant for analysis. That

said, hearsay claims of the value of this instrument for diagnostic and prescriptive purposes would be stronger if the authors provided additional empirical evidence. Test administrators would benefit from publication of relevant psychometric statistics and related analyses to support criterion-related validity such as correlations between the 10 LASSI scales and achievement-related variables. Support for construct validity could be obtained by obtaining correlates of the LASSI scales with selected self-regulation measures and academic attitude scales. Factor-derived scales could enhance the efficacy of the LASSI approach.

Some editing of materials is needed for consistency and accuracy. Among the demographic tables printed in the technical manual, at least one table heading is mislabeled and overlapping ranges for GPA occur throughout.

SUMMARY. Support for use of the LASSI, 2nd Edition comes from the face validity of items. Its utility as a tool for the purposes intended (screening, diagnosing, planning, evaluating, and advising students about their awareness levels of learning and practice skills) relies solely on anecdotal evidence. The lack of sound psychometric support for the construction of the scales limits the usefulness of the instrument for research and ultimately for its application in student advisement settings.

[106]
Learning Styles Inventory, Version III.

Purpose: Designed to identify "student preferences for particular instructional techniques."
Population: Elementary and middle school students.
Publication Dates: 1978–2002.
Acronym: LSI-III.
Scores, 9: Direct Instruction, Instruction through Technology, Simulations, Projects, Independent Study, Peer Teaching, Drill and Recitation (Elementary school only), Discussion (Middle school only), Teaching Games (Middle school only).
Administration: Group.
Forms, 3: Elementary school, Middle school, Teacher.
Price Data, 2004: $17.95 per technical and administration manual (2002, 95 pages); $29.95 per class set including 30 student instruments, 1 teacher instrument, and 1 classroom summary sheet.
Time: (15) minutes.
Authors: Joseph S. Renzulli, Mary G. Rizza, and Linda R. Smith.
Publisher: Creative Learning Press, Inc.

Cross References: See T5:1474 (2 references) and T4:1435 (1 reference); for a review by Benson P. Low of a previous edition, see 9:608.

Review of Learning Styles Inventory, Version III, by THEODORE COLADARCI, Professor of Educational Psychology, University of Maine, Orono, ME:

DESCRIPTION. The Learning Styles Inventory, Version III (LSI-III) "is designed to measure student preferences for nine instructional strategies commonly found in elementary and middle school classrooms" (technical and administration manual, p. 1). The LSI-III takes 15 minutes to complete, is self-scoring, and has forms for elementary (Grades 2–5) and middle-levels (Grades 6–8). Equipped with a 5-point rating scale (0 = *really dislike*, 1 = *dislike*, 2 = *not sure*, 3 = *like*, 4 = *really like*), students communicate their preferences for Direct Instruction, Instruction through Technology, Simulations, Projects, Independent Study, Peer Teaching, Drill and Recitation (elementary form only), Discussion (middle-level form only), and Teaching Games (middle-level form only). Sample items are "Listen to your teacher explain new information" (Direct Instruction), "Use a computer program to solve a problem" (Instruction through Technology), "Interview adults about careers you are interested in pursuing" (Simulation), "Study on your own to learn new information" (Independent Study), "Prepare a written report with a committee" (Projects), "Have a friend help you learn difficult material" (Peer Teaching), "Be quizzed by your teacher to see if you understand a story you read" (Drill and Recitation), "Have a discussion on a topic suggested by the teacher" (Discussion), and "Practice vocabulary words by playing a word game" (Teaching Games). Through a scoring process described below, students ultimately receive for each instructional strategy a "converted score" that putatively corresponds to one of five preference levels: *very low* (converted scores of 1–2), *low* (3–4), *average* (5–6), *high* (7–8), and *very high* (9–10). Teachers are encouraged to use these converted scores "to help create a more responsive learning environment" (technical and administration manual, p. v) by matching instructional practices to students' preferences "whenever appropriate" (technical and administration manual, p. 4).

DEVELOPMENT. This latest version of the LSI is "the result of a lengthy process that began with a review of the items found on the original instrument" (technical and administration manual, p. 11). Curiously, the rationale and development of the original instrument—which provides the basis for LSI-III—are left to the imagination of the potential user. In any case, the review involved feedback from classroom teachers, experts in gifted education (for an undisclosed reason), university professors, and graduate students. Together, the collection of reviews resulted in 85 items that were then factor analyzed. The factor analyses, conducted on a research sample of 2,260 elementary and middle-level students from 14 states, produced the 56-item elementary LSI-III (seven factors) and the 62-item middle-level LSI-III (eight factors).

TECHNICAL. The LSI-III technical manual provides information on scoring, reliability, and validity, each of which raises troubling questions about the integrity of this instrument. Regarding scoring, a student's converted score (or preference level) for a particular instructional strategy has a decidedly norm-referenced flavor, because the authors use T-scores, based on research-sample data, to translate raw scores to converted scores. The composition of the research sample, therefore, is of legitimate concern to potential users, for it is the likes and dislikes of these students that provide the normative context within which users ultimately interpret their students' preferences levels. What we find is not encouraging. For example, the research sample is predominantly Caucasian (elementary, 88%; middle level, 96%), and, further, a disproportionate number of students in the sample are gifted—inexplicably more so at the elementary level (41%) than at the middle level (17%). About 62% of the middle-level sample is from the suburbs, compared to 40% for the elementary sample; for urban areas, the figures are 17% and 1%, respectively. Further, there are many more fourth and fifth graders than third graders in the elementary research sample (even fewer second graders), and half of the students in the middle-level research sample are sixth graders. In short, although the authors announce that "there are no norms" for the LSI-III (technical and administration manual, p. 3), the scoring process nevertheless raises questions about the representativeness of the research sample and, therefore, the appropriateness of the LSI-III for various segments of the population. This problem

easily could have been avoided by using a reporting scheme that relies directly on the raw scores, the interpretation of which would be guided by the language of the rating scale (0 = *really dislike*, 1 = *dislike*, 2 = *not sure*, 3 = *like*, 4 = *really like*).

The authors report coefficient alpha for each LSI-III subscale. These internal consistency reliability coefficients range from .74 (Peer Teaching) to .85 (Direct Instruction) for the elementary form and .76 (Discussion) to .89 (Direct Instruction) for the middle-level form. The corresponding standard errors of measurement, which are not provided but can be calculated from available information, result in marked uncertainty regarding a student's converted score and, therefore, about the reported preference level itself. Consider the direct instruction subscale (elementary), where $SD = 6.1$ and coefficient alpha = .86. The raw-score standard error of measurement is thus 2.36. If we apply this value to a raw score of 18, we see that the 95% confidence band extends from 13.3 to 22.7. Although a raw score of 18 corresponds to a converted score of 5 (an "average" preference level), the lower and upper limits of this confidence band correspond to converted scores of 4 ("low") and 7 ("high"), respectively. Such imprecision is unacceptable. Unfortunately, it is not unique to this particular subscale of the LSI-III.

As for validity, the authors' argument is thin. As noted above, no information is provided regarding the rationale and development of the original instrument. For starters, why *these* instructional strategies? And how is the LSI-III superior to competing instruments? Turning to statistical evidence, the authors' factor analyses show that LSI-III items cluster generally as intended, although there are several curious exceptions where an instructional strategy surfaces for one grade span but not the other. For example, there is no Teaching Games factor at the elementary level, even though such games arguably are relevant to these students as well. In their post hoc explanation of this discrepancy, the authors invoke the middle-level student's "maturity and metacognitive understanding" (technical and administration manual, p. 29). Nevertheless, it is difficult to understand why items about spelling bees, flash cards, board games, and the like fail to find a statistical home in the elementary-level factor analyses (but succeed to do so at the middle level).

Further, the authors' interpretation of factors sometimes is questionable. Regarding the Projects factor, for instance, an examination of item language suggests that this factor is more about a preference for collaboration than for project-based work. And consider the Drill and Recitation factor, which includes "Work on assignments that have questions that you can correct on your own," "Fill in the missing word to complete a sentence on an assignment," and several other items that bear little unique relation to this method of instruction as I understand it. In short, when the LSI-III reports a high preference level for a student (the aforementioned problem of imprecision notwithstanding), the teacher does not necessarily know what it is that the student prefers.

A final comment on validity: The authors provide scant evidence in support of adapting instruction to a student's learning style. Validity evidence in this regard boils down to the results of a few unpublished studies and two published studies of questionable relevance. (The research participants were airmen in one and university students in the other.)

In the learning styles literature, it seems that the strongest claims about the underlying research base tend to come from those in the instrument-development business, whereas decidedly less positive conclusions tend to be reached by individuals having no vested interest in this enterprise. Even though three decades old, the conclusion reached by Cronbach and Snow (1977) in their seminal *Aptitudes and Instructional Methods* is just as appropriate today. After considering the extant research, they concluded that "[t]hese studies cast doubts upon the appropriateness of assigning students to their preferred instructional method. . . . All in all, . . . the evidence discourages the romantic view that self-selection of the instructional diet pays off" (p. 478). A similar conclusion was reached by Doyle and Rutherford (1984, p. 22): "Advocates of matching models often claim that their methods increase student achievement . . . .. The weight of the evidence does not, however, support such claims" (p. 22). Further, the LSI-III authors do not acknowledge an important caveat to the matching argument, which is that students also are well served by striving to accommodate the various instructional strategies and modes of presentation they face in school—and will continue to face in the postschool world. It is in this spirit, I believe, that Sternberg and Williams (2002, p. 143) encourage teachers to develop flexibility in the student by providing "some instruction that fits students' learning styles but other instruction that *challenges them to adjust the way they learn*" (also see Good & Stipek, 1983, p. 34; italics added). It's about functioning in a world that does not always cater to our preferences. In any case, absent a strong empirical basis for matching instruction to student preference—which the LSI-III authors encourage potential users to do—it is not clear why one would adopt the LSI-III.

SUMMARY. The LSI-III scoring process raises troubling questions about the adequacy of the research sample, reliability coefficients point to considerable imprecision in the preference levels, and validity evidence is weak. In his review of an earlier edition of the LSI-III, Low (1985) opened by stating that the instrument "does not appear to be a useful measure of learning styles" (p. 841). Unfortunately, the intervening decades do not permit a more positive conclusion for the LSI-III.

REVIEWER'S REFERENCES

Cronbach, L. J., & Snow, R. E. (1977). *Aptitudes and instructional methods.* New York: Irvington.
Doyle, W., & Rutherford, B. (1984). Classroom research on matching learning and teaching styles. *Research Into Practice, 23,* 20-25.
Good, T. L., & Stipek, D. J. (1983). Individual differences in the classroom: A psychological perspective. In G. D. Fenstermacher (Ed.), *Individual differences and the common curriculum* (pp. 9-43). Eighty-second yearbook of the National Society for the Study of Education, Part 1. Chicago: University of Chicago Press.
Low, B. P. (1985). [Review of Learning Styles Inventory.] In J. V. Mitchell, Jr. (Ed.), *The ninth mental measurements yearbook* (p. 841). Lincoln, NE: Buros Institute of Mental Measurements.
Sternberg, R. J., & Williams, W. M. (2002). *Educational psychology.* Boston: Allyn & Bacon.

Review of the Learning Styles Inventory, Version III by JENNIFER N. MAHDAVI, Assistant Professor of Special Education, Sonoma State University, Rohnert Park, CA:

DESCRIPTION. The Learning Styles Inventory, Version III (LSI-III), is a questionnaire that classroom teachers may use to examine their students' preferences about activities for learning. Nine learning styles are identified within the measure. The manual contains sections detailing inventory administration and scoring as well as information about how teachers interpret scores and alter teaching to match learning styles. Teachers are advised to help students understand their own learning styles. The second half of the manual contains technical information about the development, reliability, and validity of the LSI-III. An appendix offers the theoretical basis for the measure.

The LSI-III comes in versions for elementary school and middle school students. The inventory is designed for group or individual administration and takes approximately 15 minutes to complete. Also included in the LSI-III is an instrument that the teacher can use to assess whether his or her teaching matches the learning preferences of the students in the class.

The elementary school level inventory consists of 56 statements broken out into seven learning styles: Direct Instruction, Instruction through Technology, Simulations, Projects, Independent Study, Peer Teaching, and Drill and Recitation. The middle school inventory consists of 62 items, with the same categories as above, except for Drill and Recitation. Two additional categories for the middle school survey are Discussion and Teaching games.

Students are to indicate whether each statement is something they would like to do in school. They circle a numerical rating of 4 for *really like* down to 0 for *really dislike* in response to each statement. The rating of 2 corresponds to *not sure*. At the end of the survey, students self-score their survey by adding up their scores in each area and circling the appropriate range of scores in the Section Totals box on the back of the survey.

Section Total raw scores relate to "converted scores," which are also given in the box on the back of the survey. The converted scores were created by transforming the raw data into T-scores and then converting into a scale with a range of 1—10, a mean of 5, and standard deviation of 2. A converted score of 9—10 indicates a very high preference level for a learning style, whereas a 1—2 indicates very low preference.

DEVELOPMENT. The manual offers an extensive review of the research literature describing the importance of understanding the different ways that students best learn and of gearing instruction to match their preferences. The authors of the LSI-III base their inventory on the theory that meeting the learning preferences of students will improve the quality of the education they receive, that is, the quality of their learning.

The LSI-III is the result of revising and updating the previous version. The authors obtained feedback from teachers who suggested that some items were not relevant to typical classroom instruction and that the use of technology should be included as a preference in the measure. Professors, graduate students, and classroom teachers who were experienced in the field of gifted instruction reviewed all old and new items and the proposed factor structure. The grammar of the items was changed to a more active voice with simpler sentence structures. Items with negative connotations were dropped and the influence of technology was recognized in new items, such as "Search sources in the library or on the Internet" (technical and administration manual, p. 12). Items relating to enrichment activities and grouping were added. The experimental inventory had 85 items.

A total of 2,260 students (1,157 in elementary school and 1,103 in middle school) from 14 states participated in the development of the measure. Each group (elementary and middle school) in the sample was stratified by grade, ethnicity, gender, and placement and divided in two. The experimental inventory was administered to the participants of the first group and an exploratory factor analysis was conducted. This analysis yielded seven factors for elementary school children and eight for middle school. Items were retained if they loaded at least .40 on a factor without cross-loading on others. Items were also removed for redundancy, resulting in a 61-item scale for elementary school and 68 items for middle school. The manual describes each removed item and provides factor loadings for each remaining item. Confirmatory factor analysis was done using survey results from the second half of the sample and supported the results of the exploratory analysis.

The data from the sample were used to obtain means and standard deviations that were converted into *t*-scores for each subscale. These *t*-scores were, in turn, converted into a scale more easily interpreted by novices and described above.

TECHNICAL.

Sample. The students who participated in the development of the instrument were well described. The sample included children in Grades 2–8, divided approximately in half, with one group being the second through fifth graders in the elementary school level, and the other half being fifth through eighth graders in the middle school level. The stratification by grade was not equal; second graders made up approximately 10% of the elementary group whereas sixth graders comprised nearly half of the middle school group.

Gender was evenly divided. Caucasian students predominated in the samples, making up 95% of the middle school group and approximately 87% of the elementary. This sample is not representative of the larger population, nor is the classification of the setting, with urban students making up only 1% of the middle school group and approximately 16% of the elementary. The middle school sample was predominately suburban, whereas just under half of the elementary group was suburban. The 14 states from which the sample was drawn were not distributed across the country.

Students in gifted education placements predominated in the elementary group, comprising about 40% of the sample. This proportion is clearly not reflective of the population for which this instrument is intended, in which approximately 2% are considered eligible for gifted education. Similarly unbalanced representation is found among the students who qualify for special education programs—about 1% of the elementary school group and less than that in the middle school group. Special education typically comprises 10% of a school population.

Reliability. Coefficient alpha reliability coefficients were computed for each of the factors on each of the versions of the inventory. The range of coefficient alphas for the elementary instrument ranged from .74 to .85 and on the middle school instrument from .76 to .89. These coefficients are within acceptable limits for an instrument of this type.

Validity. The content validity of the LSI-III is more than adequately described in the manual. Not only do the developers extensively discuss the process of selecting and justifying items in collaboration with experts in the education field, they provide an appendix in the manual that overviews learning styles literature and orients the reader to their theoretical perspective.

To address construct validity, the instrument was also validated through the use of factor analysis. The process of factor analyzing the data is well described in the manual and factor loadings for each item are presented.

No information is presented about differences in answers to the questions by any stratification variable. Such information may not be necessary as the instrument is designed to inform the teacher about student preferences for learning on an individual level. However, the significant underrepresentation of children of color and children with disabilities and the overrepresentation of children considered gifted is a concern. Also, sampling across settings (urban, rural, suburban) and states was uneven. That the LSI-III reflects the learning preferences of all children from all backgrounds equally well is not established.

COMMENTARY. The LSI-III is easy to administer and easy to score. The manual is well written and easy to understand so that any classroom teacher could quickly implement the inventory and utilize its results. The theoretical underpinnings of the measure are very well described. Additionally, there is attention paid to engaging students in understanding their own learning preferences and understanding what conditions they require to help them learn efficiently.

The only area of concern is the sample upon which the factor analysis and construct validity measures were based. This mostly Caucasian, disproportionally academically gifted, mostly suburban or rural sample does not reflect accurately the population of American school children. Teachers using this measure with groups not well represented in the initial sample may want to interpret the results with some caution.

SUMMARY. The Learning Styles Inventory, Version III not only helps teachers and students discover learning preferences, but the manual also offers clear descriptions of the different learning styles and implications for adapting teaching to meet the needs of each style. A section of the manual contains information and tools to help teachers develop a "Total Talent Portfolio" for each student that can be used to inform decisions about how to provide the best enrichment activities for him or her. This teacher-friendly assessment can be easily and effectively used to improve classroom instruction for students with diverse learning preferences.

[107]

The Level of Service Inventory—Revised [2003 Norms Update].

Purpose: Designed as a "quantitative survey of attributes of offenders and their situations relevant to level of service decisions."
Population: Ages 16 and over.
Publication Dates: 1995–2003.
Acronym: LSI-R.

Scores: Total score only.
Administration: Individual.
Price Data, 2007: $204 per LSI-R U.S. Norms complete kit including manual (2001, 63 pages), LSI-R U.S. Norms Supplement (2003, 16 pages), 25 interview guides, 25 QuikScore forms, and 25 U.S. ColorPlot profile forms; $74 per LSI-R manual, LSI-R Norms Supplement, and 1 U.S. ColorPlot profile form; $124 per 25 each of interview guides, QuikScore forms, and ColorPlot profiles; $81 per 25 interview guides; $50 per 25 QuikScore forms; $25 per 25 U.S. Norms ColorPlot profile forms; $97 per specimen set including LSI-R manual, LSI-R U.S. Norms Supplement, 3 interview guides, 3 QuikScore forms, and 3 U.S. ColorPlot profile forms.
Foreign Language Editions: LSI-R is available in Spanish but the U.S. ColorPlot profile forms are not.
Time: (30–45) minutes.
Comments: Windows computerized version available on CD or 3.5-inch disk; French-Canadian and Spanish forms, interview guides, and ColorPlot profiles available.
Authors: Don A. Andrews and James L. Bonta.
Publisher: Multi-Health Systems, Inc.
Cross References: For reviews by Solomon M. Fulero and Romeo Vitelli of an earlier edition, see 14:212.

Review of The Level of Service Inventory— Revised [2003 Norms Update] by DAVID F. CIAMPI, Adjunct Professor, Homeland Security University Projects, Region 6, MA:

DESCRIPTION. The Level of Service Inventory—Revised (LSI-R) is a norm-revised, 54-item quantitative assessment instrument relevant in both male and female offender treatment planning and for assessing levels of freedom and supervision by identifying minor and major risk factors as a basis for comprehensive risk/needs assessment. It is administered and scored in the paper-and-pencil form in conjunction with the LSI-R Interview Guide, QuikScore form, and ColorPlot Profile form. An online or QuikEntry assessment is also available to facilitate computer administration and scoring. The computer-generated scoring protocol, which runs on a Microsoft Windows platform, produces fast and reliable onsite test results and report generation within several minutes.

All items are of the selection type and predominantly consist of either "Yes or No" responses or a 4-point Likert scale with a rating range from 0 to 3 (*A very unsatisfactory situation* to *A satisfactory situation*). Changeable and dynamic offender attributes and situations relevant to level of service decisions are generated for each of the following subcomponents with number of items in parentheses: Criminal History (10), Education/Employment (10), Financial (2), Family/Marital (4), Accommodation (3), Leisure/Recreation (2), Companions (5), Alcohol/Drug Problems (9), Emotional/Personal (5), and Attitudes/Orientation (4).

According to the Level of Service—Revised manual, the subcomponents are "indicators of major risk factors identified by both theory and research" (p. 1). The LSI-R QuikScore form is utilized and requires an "X" to be placed over each item based on the client's response, or the number of the item should be circled when the answer is unknown. The LSI-R total score is the sum of the Xs in columns A and B of the QuikScore form. The Profile Form converts raw scores to percentiles based on normative group data. The authors state that, "the score and the subcomponent score will suggest a client's level and area of risk/needs, guide level and area of service decisions" (manual, p. 5).

The developers also point out that the responsible staff person who administers, scores, and interprets the LSI-R should have an understanding of the basic principles of psychological testing and interpretation, as well as realize the limitations associated with screening and testing procedures. The authors claim that the users of this assessment instrument should be familiar with the testing standards and ethics as promulgated by the American Educational Research Association, the American Psychological Association, and the National Council on Measurement in Education (1999).

DEVELOPMENT. The LSI–R is based on the social learning theory of criminal behavior, research in criminal conduct, and risk (Andrews & Bonta, 1994). This instrument was initially developed and tested with Canadian offenders. Although the test itself remains unchanged, the current normative data consist of 23,721 male and female inmates, as well as community offenders from five geographic regions in the United States. It should be noted that the original normative data were limited to 2,370 Canadian inmates (956 males and 1,414 females, respectively). Thus, the revised normative data represents a substantial improvement in this instrument's utility for assessing levels of risk among American offenders. Documents furnished by the developers (including the Level of Service—Revised Manual, U.S. Norms Manual Supplement, LSI-R Interview Guide, QuikScore form, and ColorPlot Profile form) provide substantive information regarding initial test development, as well as the revised normative data on United States inmates and community offenders.

TECHNICAL. Andrews and Bonta obtained psychometric information using samples of 23,721 United States inmates and community offenders in their current U.S. Norms Manual Supplement (2003). Internal consistency reliability and standard error of measurement using coefficient alpha, as well as total LSI-R scores, were presented in the 2003 updated norms manual based on several published investigations (Andrews & Bonta, 2003; Lowenkamp & Latessa, 2002a, 2002b; Flores, Lowenkamp & Latessa, 2003). As would be expected, the internal consistency reliability of the total score was higher than those associated with the subcomponent scores in three of the following four studies that provided internal consistency reliability coefficients: .87 (range = .27 to .85, Andrews & Bonta, 2003); .86 (range = .51 to .78, Lowenkamp & Latessa, 2002b); and .86 (range = .43 to .80, Lowenkamp & Latessa, 2002a). The internal consistency reliability total score and range of subcomponent scores in the fourth study were: .84 (range = .31 to .98, Flores, Lowenkamp, & Latessa, 2003). Internal consistency values for the Financial subcomponent were fairly low, falling below .50 in all four studies. The developers of the LSI-R noted that the reliability coefficient tends to be affected by the number of items in each subcomponent and that a fairly low coefficient alpha for the Financial subcomponent may be due to the fact that there are only two items in this particular subcomponent. This finding is nevertheless somewhat puzzling because the Leisure/Recreation subcomponent that also has two items is presented with internal consistency values that are above .50 for all four studies. The developers also obtained standard error of measurement values for overall, as well as male and female total LSI-R scores. Overall, this inventory does appear to have adequate reliability, stability, and consistency.

The developers also describe several investigations that examined the predictive and concurrent validity of the LSI-R. A moderate to strong relationship between LSI-R and recidivism was found (Andrews & Bonta, 2003; Lowenkamp, Holsinger, & Latessa, 2001; Lowenkamp & Latessa, 2002a, 2002b; Lowenkamp & Latessa, 2002a, 2002b; Washington State Institute for Public Policy, 2002, 2003). The studies cited appear to meet acceptable standards for substantiating validity of this particular inventory instrument.

SUMMARY. The LSI-R appears to be a well-developed instrument for assessing American offenders' dynamic and changeable risks/needs as a means to reduce risk. The developers, to their credit, have produced an instrument that can be administered, scored, and interpreted in a relatively cost-effective and efficient manner. They have provided supplemental normative data that improve the utility of assessing inmate and community offender populations in Canada, as well as the United States. The developers have considered thorny questions such as the effects of age and race on LSI-R scores. As the developers mentioned, the LSI-R should not be used as the sole assessment instrument for ascertaining the level of service required for an inmate or community offender. It is also contraindicative to utilize this instrument to identify mitigating and aggravating factors relevant to criminal sanctioning.

REVIEWER'S REFERENCES

American Educational Research Association, American Psychological Association, & National Council on Measurement in Education. (1999). *Standards for educational and psychological testing.* Washington, DC: American Educational Research Association.
Andrews, D. A., & Bonta, J. (1994). *The psychology of criminal conduct (3rd ed.).* Cincinnati, OH: Anderson.
Andrews, D. A., & Bonta, J. (2001). The Level of Service Inventory—Revised (LSI-R). Toronto, Ontario, Canada: Multi-Health Systems, Inc.
Andrews, D. A., & Bonta, J. (2003). Level of Service Inventory—Revised: U.S. norms manual supplement. Toronto, Ontario, Canada: Multi-Health Systems, Inc.
Flores, A. W., Lowenkamp, C. T., & Latessa, E. J. (2003). *A profile of offenders in a central state using the LSI-R.* Unpublished manuscript, University of Cincinnati, OH.
Lowenkamp, C. T., Holsinger, A. M., & Latessa, E. J. (2001). Risk/need assessment, offender classification, and the role of childhood abuse. *Criminal Justice and Behavior, 28,* 543–563.
Lowenkamp, C. T., & Latessa, E. J. (2002a). *A profile of offenders in a northern state using the LSI-R.* Unpublished manuscript, University of Cincinnati, OH.
Lowenkamp, C. T., & Latessa, E. J. (2002b). *Norming and validating the LSI-R: Northwestern state sample.* Unpublished manuscript, University of Cincinnati, OH.
Washington State Institute for Public Policy. (2002). *Washington's Offender Accountability Act: An evaluation of the department of corrections' risk management identification system.* Olympia, WA: Author.
Washington State Institute for Public Policy. (2003). *Washington's Offender Accountability Act: Update and progress on the act's evaluation.* Olympia, WA: Author.

Review of The Level of Service Inventory-Revised [2003 Norms Update] by ANDREW A. COX, Professor, Counseling and Psychology, Troy University, Phenix City, AL:

DESCRIPTION. The Level of Service Inventory—Revised (LSI-R) is a 54-item test. Test items are answered in a YES or NO format or a 0 to 3 rating. The test is administered through an interview format with specific questions and collateral information used to compile data. Items cover criminal history, education and employment, financial, family and marital information, accommodation, leisure and recreation, companions, alcohol and drug problems, emotional and personal, and attitudes and orientation.

The test instrument is designed to compile criminal justice offender risk and needs information. It is designed to bring together in a systematic manner risk and needs information that is thought to be important in planning offender treatment and determining the level of required offender supervision. Test content is based upon the recidivism literature, and views of probation personnel. A social learning perspective of criminal behavior underlies the theoretical construct of the instrument.

This review describes The Level of Service Inventory—[2003 Norms Update] (Revised U.S. Norms Manual Supplement). The original inventory was developed in 1995. Fulero (2001) and Vitelli (2001) evaluated the content, uses, and technical characteristics of the original revised edition of the inventory. The initial inventory was taken from a population of Canadian inmates. The inventory used in the U.S. norms edition does not differ in item content from the original Level of Service Inventory-Revised. Accordingly, the Level of Service Inventory—Revised U.S. norms edition adds to the psychometric properties of the original instrument.

DEVELOPMENT. Normative data for the U.S. norms edition consists of 23,721 male and female offenders. Both inmates and community offenders are included within this sample. Seven corrections departments from the United States provided 19,481 inmates from the Northeastern, Midwestern, Northwestern, Northern, and Southern regions of the United States. The community offender sample consisted of 4,240 individuals from Midwestern, Southern, and Northeastern states.

Male and female inmate and community offender samples were of predominantly Caucasian and African American ethnic background. Small samples of Hispanic, Asian, Native American, and American Indian individuals were included within the sample. Male inmates ranged in age from 17 to 90 years of age, and the male community offender sample ranged from age 17 to 81 years. The female inmate sample was age 16 to 67 years, and the female community offenders were 18 to 60 years of age. The dates and manner in which the normative sample was selected are not described. It is not indicated if sampling conformed to offender frequencies reported for the United States correctional population.

Materials for The Level of Service Inventory—Revised include an Interview Guide to assist the test examiner in eliciting information required to provide item ratings or YES/NO answers to inventory items using a semistructured interview process. This guide also includes probes that the interviewer can use to elicit more detailed information. A "multiscore or QuikScore" score sheet is also provided to facilitate ratings and recording of YES/NO responses with an attached scoring profile. The U.S. norms edition also provides a "ColorPlot" profile form with separate forms for males and females. This profile allows plotting of obtained total raw scores, with cumulative frequencies for inmates and community offenders. This profile promotes interpretation of the offender's raw score relative to high risk and needs or low risk and needs. The "ColorPlot" profile used in the U.S. norms supplement does not promote the specificity of interpretation as provided by the original profile. The latter profile allows differentiation of risks and needs into high, medium, moderate, low/moderate, or low risk/needs. Fulero (2001) indicated that interpretation materials available for the earlier revised edition allow interpretation of specific scale subcategories with associated percentiles. The U.S. norms supplement materials do not allow for this preciseness in interpretation. Fulero (2001) further stated that the earlier revised edition had cutoff scores relative to risk/needs categories for test takers other than female offenders. Such cutoff scores are not reported for the U.S. norms supplement.

TECHNICAL. The Level of Service Inventory—Revised user's manual describes instrument reliability and validity data for the instrument. The reader is referred to Fulero (2001) and Vitelli (2001) for analysis of this data. Fulero (2001) suggested that the Level of Service Inventory—Revised possesses adequate psychometric properties.

The Level of Service Inventory—Revised U.S. Norms Manual Supplement reports internal consistency and standard error of measurement (*SEM*) data in support of the instrument's reliability. Internal consistency alpha coefficients gathered from three U.S. studies range from .27 to .98 with the average coefficient being .66 for subcomponents. The average total-score internal consistency related coefficient was .87. These data suggest that adequate reliability exists for the Level of Service Inventory relative to the U.S. sample in terms of internal consistency. Using the standard error of measurement (*SEM*), test users can calculate confidence intervals for both the subcomponent and total scores for greater ease of use and interpretation.

Validity data are reported in the U.S. Norms Manual Supplement. For the U.S. sample, relationships were found between LSI-R scores and criminal history. The authors conclude that the measure is a "promising tool" (manual supplement, p. 8) for estimating recidivism with several United States predictive validation studies that correlate with offender recidivism and reincarceration described in the manual. Moderate correlations for male and female offender scores and various outcome variables are also described. Data are reported in the manual regarding gender, ethnic, and age factors used in support of the instrument's generalizability to United States offender populations.

COMMENTARY. The test developers have done an excellent job relative to numbers and geographical location represented by the U.S. norms sample. However, the test developers need to provide more detail describing the U.S. norms. As noted, information regarding sample selection methodology and how the sample represents frequencies found within the U.S. correctional population would be useful. Supplemental normative samples would also be recommended to identify further unique considerations that may be present with various minority populations that make up the U.S. correctional population.

The Level of Service Inventory—Revised user's manual indicates that the measure is not a substitute for clinical judgment and should be used with other collateral measures of risk and correctional needs. This recommendation should be strongly considered by instrument users within their respective settings. The LSI-R appears to have utility as a means to quantify clinical judgment, interview data, and case review and other collateral material by correctional personnel.

Though some validation work has taken place in the development of this instrument, more work is needed. The instrument uses a social learning perspective in understanding and interpreting criminal behavior. More construct validation work would be recommended to further quantify the usefulness of this construct in clinical interpretation of the measure.

More research is also needed in specifying the validity of scale subcomponents. Such validation work currently focuses upon criminal history.

The "ColorPlot" profile used with the U.S. norms supplement does not promote the specificity of interpretation as found in the earlier Canadian norms interpretative materials. It is recommended that the test developers make this "ColorPlot" more useful and specific for use by United States corrections workers. In addition earlier "ColorPlot" editions allow interpretation of cutoff and subcategory scores according to Fulero (2001). This type of interpretation is not possible with U.S. norms data.

More research using the LSI-R with U.S. correctional populations would be recommended. Such research would further solidify and outline parameters of the instrument's use with U.S. inmate populations and settings. An informal literature review conducted by this reviewer indicates that much of the current research reported with this instrument continues to be with Canadian correctional populations (Kroner & Mills, 2001; Simourd, 1998, 2004).

SUMMARY. As reported by Fulero (2001) and Vitelli (2001), the original Level of Service Inventory—Revised is a useful assessment in correctional settings. Further improvement and utility of the instrument is promoted through the development of U.S. norms. This enhancement is a development in the right direction in further advancing the use of this instrument with U.S. correctional populations and settings.

The Level of Service Inventory–Revised has merit for use in correctional environments in the United States. As noted by the test authors and by Vitelli (2001), the instrument should not be used alone but to supplement other interview, records review, clinical insight, or psychometrically derived data that may be available to correctional workers. The uses described for this measure within the manual and by Vitelli (2001) appear to be valid. Accordingly, the LSI-R could be a useful tool for corrections work.

REVIEWER'S REFERENCES

Fulero, S. M. (2001). [Review of the Level of Service Inventory–Revised.] In B. S. Plake & J. C. Impara (Eds.), *The fourteenth mental measurements yearbook* (pp. 692–693). Lincoln, NE: Buros Institute of Mental Measurements.

Kroner, D. G., & Mills, J. F. (2001). The accuracy of five risk appraisal instruments in predicting institutional misconduct and new convictions. *Criminal Justice and Behavior, 28*, 471–489.

Simourd, D. J. (1998). Reliability and validity of the Level of Service Inventory—Revised among federally incarcerated sex offenders. *Journal of Interpersonal Violence, 13*, 261–274.

Simourd, D. J. (2004). Use of dynamic risk/need assessment instruments among long-term incarcerated offenders. *Criminal Justice and Behavior, 31*, 306–323.

Vitelli, R. (2001). [Review of the Level of Service Inventory—Revised.] In B. S. Plake & J. C. Impara (Eds.), *The fourteenth mental measurements yearbook* (pp. 693–695). Lincoln, NE: Buros Institute of Mental Measurements.

[108]

Level of Service/Case Management Inventory: An Offender Assessment System.

Purpose: Designed to help "determine an offender's risk/needs level so that an appropriate level of service can be provided."

Population: Offenders ages 16 and over.

Publication Date: 2004.

Acronym: LS/CMI.

Scores: 8 Risk/Need factors: Criminal History, Education/Employment, Family/Marital, Leisure/Recreation, Companions, Alcohol/Drug Problem, Procriminal Attitude/Orientation, Antisocial Pattern.

Administration: Individual.

Price Data, 2007: $255 per complete kit including user's manual (228 pages), scoring guide, and 25 each of interview guides, offender history forms, Quikscore forms, ColorPlot profiles, and case management protocols; $162 per reorder kit including 25 each of interview guides, offender history forms, Quikscore forms, ColorPlot profile forms, and case management protocols; $75 per user's manual; $81 per 25 interview guides; $16 per 25 offender history forms; $49 per 25 QuikScore forms; $22 per 25 ColorPlot profile forms; $243 per software kit.

Time: (20–30) minutes.

Comments: Computer version available.

Authors: D. A. Andrews, James L. Bonta, and J. Stephen Wormith.

Publisher: Multi-Health Systems, Inc.

Review of the Level of Service/Case Management Inventory: An Offender Assessment System by SHERI BAUMAN, Associate Professor, Department of Educational Psychology, University of Arizona, Tucson, AZ:

DESCRIPTION. The Level of Service/Case Management Inventory: An Offender Assessment System (LS/CMI) is based on the Level of Service Inventory—Revised (LSI-R; Andrews & Bonta, 1995). It was produced to reflect the increased information and data about offender risk assessment that have accumulated since the publication of the previous version. The LS/CMI is one of a group of related inventories designed to assist those in "management and treatment planning … in justice, forensic, correctional, prevention, and related agencies" (user's manual, p. 1). The system is designed for use with male and female offenders age 16 and over; there is an adolescent version for younger offenders. The system includes a QuikScore form, an offender history form, a Case Management protocol, a ColorPlot profile for male and female offenders, an interview guide, a scoring guide, and a user's manual. An errata sheet (dated January 2006) is included that lists several postpublication changes to the user's manual, scoring guide, and interview guide. There are 11 sections in the LS/CMI (scored "yes" or "no" by the assessor), with space for supplementary information. The assessor gathers the necessary information from file records and a client interview.

Section 1 (General Risk/Need Factors) is almost entirely derived from the LSI-R, and contains 43 items reflecting the "big eight" factors that researchers have found to be most salient in risk assessment: Criminal History, Education/Employment, Family/Marital, Leisure/Recreation, Companions, Alcohol/Drug Problems, Pro-criminal Attitude/Orientation, and Antisocial Pattern. The QuikScore form provides cutoff scores to determine level of risk (five categories from *Very Low* to *Very High*) for each of the eight factors and for the total of Section 1. There is also space to indicate the presence of strengths in each of the eight areas. Section 2 examines Specific Risk/Need Factors, including Personal Problems with Criminogenic Potential and History of Perpetration (sexual assaults, nonsexual physical assaults and other violence, and other forms of antisocial behavior). Section 3 covers Prison Experience—Institutional Factors to be used with incarcerated offenders only, addressing the History of Incarceration, Past and Present Incarceration, and Barriers to Release. Section 4 focuses on Other Client Issues (Social, Health, and Mental Health), and Section 5 includes Special Responsivity Considerations such as cultural, intelligence, anxiety, etc. In Section 6, the professional determines a score-based risk/need level. This is based directly from the total score in Section 1; then based on Sections 2 through 5 consideration can be made on whether to use the clinical override. There is also an option for an administrative/policy override, and a final risk/need level determination. Section 7 provides a graphic profile of the offenders' risk/needs in the eight areas mentioned above, whereas Section 8 is the area where program/placement decisions are indicated. The separate Case Management protocol utilizes the information from previous sections to create the management plan, including goals, interventions, and time frames. If Special Responsivity Considerations were listed earlier in the document, the assessor recommends approaches to address the issue. A progress record is included in this part of the protocol, as is a discharge summary.

DEVELOPMENT. This system is based on a personality and social learning theoretical perspective. The authors consulted both users and researchers in creating the current edition. The system reflects the eight risk factors that have been identified through empirical research and the increased risk of recidivism that is associated with these factors. For those aspects of the risk factors that are *dynamic* (changeable, in contrast to *static* factors that are not), an increase in services has reduced rates of recidivism in high risk cases. A previous reviewer (Fulero, 2001) of its immediate predecessor, the LSI-R, expressed concern that the normative data for that version were based entirely on samples from Ontario (Canada). The LS/CMI includes normative data from 60,156 male and female offenders in nine U.S. jurisdictions. Separate norms are provided for each legal and demographic group to enable the user to compare the offender's score with those of a comparable group.

Several computer-scoring programs are available for this system. Smart-Link allows up to four users to enter the information to be automatically scored. A database stores these results. The software developer kit that allows data from this assessment to be integrated with other databases is also available for large organizations with many users.

TECHNICAL. Internal consistency reliability data for the total score for North American (U.S. and Canadian combined) samples ranged from .89 to .94 for all groups (incarcerated and community, male and female). The subsection coefficients were somewhat lower, as would be expected given the smaller number of items. The manual includes numerous tables of internal consistency data for the various subgroups. The authors state that interrater and test-retest reliabilities are less important for this assessment due to the dynamic nature of the factors being rated. However, the authors do report the test-retest reliability coefficients for a small (N = 18) sample of offenders who were re-tested (usually in another setting by another assessor) in an average of 26 days. Coefficients varied considerably, from .88 for Section 1 Total score and .91 for Criminal History, to .16 for Procriminal Attitude and Orientation.

Considerable validity data are also provided in the user's manual. In general, there was a consistent relationship between risk level and recidivism, such that the higher the risk rating, the greater the percentage who recidivate (within 1 year). Much of the research reported in the manual involves the LSI-R (Andrews & Bonta, 1995), from which most of Section 1 on the LS/CMI is directly taken. The results of two prospective risk assessment studies are also reported. In one study with 454 adult male inmates and 176 adult male community-based offenders, the LS/CMI total score correlated with recidivism at $r = .39$. The relationship was stronger for general recidivism than for violent recidivism. Variation was observed in various subgroups, and these data are also provided. In these studies, conviction on a new offense was the outcome variable, and offenders were tracked for an average of 2 1/2 years. Another reviewer of the LSI-R had reservations because the instrument was not sensitive to sex-offender specific risk factors (Vitelli, 2001). For this version, validity data were similar for sex offenders and nonsexual offenders. Assessors of sex offenders might nevertheless prefer to utilize sex-offender-specific assessment tools with that population in addition to the LS/CMI.

Validity studies were conducted with U.S. samples using the LSI-R, and strong associations between total scores and recidivism rates were reported for both males and females. As predicted, re-incarceration rates were significantly different among the risk categories (low, medium, and high risk groups). It is important to note that an analysis of U.S. data by ethnic groups, with at least 1,000 cases of each group (African American, Hispanic, Asian, Native American, and Caucasian) found no significant differences on scores for different groups, or for males and females. These results suggest the system can be used with members of these groups without concern for bias.

COMMENTARY. This assessment system is impressive on several grounds. First, the extensive empirical research that has been conducted on this and previous versions of the system is unusual in its size and scope. Second, the revision was made based on both empirical data and consultation with users, researchers, and with regard for theory. The resulting changes are clearly useful for the user and will allow for continued empirical research. Finally, the user's manual is thorough, well-organized, and clearly written. The scoring guide contains administration instructions that are clear and detailed. The assessor using this system will be confident using such a well-designed system that is so comprehensive. The only disappointment is that interrater reliability studies have not yet been conducted for this version.

SUMMARY. The LS/CMI is a revision of the LSI-R (Andrews & Bonta, 1995) that incorporated both input from users, researchers, and trainers and considerable empirical data in developing the current version. This assessment system is one of several integrated tools that have been developed by the first author. This version consists of eight sections using a yes/no format that are completed by an assessor from data collected from files and an interview (using a provided protocol). Results provide an overall level of risk that is used in preparing a Case Management plan that can be used for both planning and tracking progress to discharge. Excellent psychometric properties provide sound support for the use of this system.

REVIEWER'S REFERENCES

Andrews, D. A., & Bonta, J. (1995). *Level of Service Inventory—Revised: User's manual.* Toronto, Canada: Multi-Health Systems.

Fulero, S. M. (2001). [Review of the Level of Service Inventory—Revised.] In B. S. Plake & J. C. Impara (Eds.), *The fourteenth mental measurements yearbook* (pp. 692–693). Lincoln, NE: Buros Institute of Mental Measurements.

Vitelli, R. (2001). [Review of the Level of Service Inventory—Revised.] In B. S. Plake & J. C. Impara (Eds.), *The fourteenth mental measurements yearbook* (pp. 693–694). Lincoln, NE: Buros Institute of Mental Measurements.

Review of the Level of Service/Case Management Inventory: An Offender Assessment System by GEOFFREY L. THORPE, *Professor of Psychology, University of Maine, Orono, ME:*

DESCRIPTION. The Level of Service/Case Management Inventory (LS/CMI™): An Offender Assessment System was designed to help professionals working with male and female offenders 16 years of age and older in correctional and similar facilities, and specifically to serve as (a) a comprehensive measure of risk and need factors and (b) a broad-ranging case management tool. The package of materials received from the test publisher consists of a more than 212-page user's manual and copies of: a 43-item QuikScore form; an Offender History form; a Case Management protocol; separate ColorPlot profiles for male and for female offenders; interview guides for Sections 1 through 5; and an errata sheet with corrigenda and addenda.

The LS/CMI comprises 11 sections: (1) General Risk/Need Factors; (2) Specific Risk/Need Factors; (3) Prison Experience—Institutional Factors; (4) Other Client Issues (Social, Health, and Mental Health); (5) Special Responsivity Considerations; (6) Risk/Need Summary and Override; (7) Risk/Need Profile; (8) Program/Placement Decision; (9) Case Management Plan; (10) Progress Record; and (11) Discharge Summary.

Section 1, General Risk/Need Factors, is the most important component. It includes the "big eight" factors identified by the test developers as among the best-validated predictors of recidivism on the basis of contemporary research findings and evaluative literature reviews: Criminal History (8 test items), Education/Employment (9 items), Family/Marital (4 items), Leisure/Recreation (2 items), Companions (4 items), Alcohol/Drug Problem (8 items), Procriminal Attitude/Orientation (4 items), and Antisocial Pattern (4 items). For each factor, quantitative guidelines allow test users to designate respondents' risk/need levels as *Very Low, Low, Medium, High,* and *Very High,* with latitude for assessor discretion in including extraneous sources of information in making these designations. The total score from all 43 items is also interpretable in itself. Because of their potential as protective factors and to improve predictive accuracy, respondents' strengths may be noted, but these are not scored quantitatively.

Section 2, Specific Risk/Need Factors, includes questions about relevant personal problems and respondents' criminal history, and Section 3,

Prison Experience—Institutional Factors, contains items identified by correctional staff as having prognostic significance. The remaining sections allow test users to record supplementary information needed for treatment, service, and discharge planning, including a running log of offenders' progress in reaching case management objectives (Section 10, Progress Record).

The LS/CMI is intended for use by physicians, mental health professionals, probation and parole officers, institutional case management personnel, and paraprofessionals. Appropriate test-user qualifications are necessary unless the test administrator is supervised by a professional with psychometric expertise and credentials. The instrument is administered and scored in paper-and-pencil format in conjunction with the LS/CMI interview guide. The QuikScore™ form includes everything needed for test scoring.

DEVELOPMENT. The LS/CMI (Andrews, Bonta, & Wormith) is the latest addition to the Level of Service Inventory (LSI) series that includes three prior contributions (1995, 1998, and 2002) by Andrews and his colleagues. Cited as a "true fourth generation risk assessment tool" (user's manual, p. 107) because of its inclusion of dynamic risk assessment tied to case management recommendations, the LS/CMI is grounded in a comprehensive model of risk/need assessment that encompasses the four key areas of general risk/needs, specific risk/needs, responsivity, and strengths. The test authors justify the inclusion of general and specific responsivity factors (such as assessing offenders' suitability for specialized cognitive-behavioral intervention programs) in their broad-ranging protocol by stressing the "criminogenic need principle," and note that "targeting the dynamic aspects of the major risk factors has been found to decrease recidivism rates" (user's manual, p. 1). However, although actuarial research has established the fundamental importance of assessing certain static risk factors in predicting offender recidivism (e.g., Quinsey, Harris, Rice, & Cormier, 1998), the inclusion of dynamic risk factors has not improved predictive accuracy in recent studies (e.g., Philipse, Koeter, van der Staak, & van den Brink, 2006).

TECHNICAL. The development samples used to create the LS/CMI norms consisted of adult and youth offenders, institutionalized or in the community, in Ontario, Canada ($n = 97,791$) and nine jurisdictions in the United States ($n = 60,156$). Thus the total sample size approached 158,000. Test items were drawn from pilot work with archival data, and validation and recidivism studies were conducted with various subsets of offenders, including male inmates and institutionalized and community-based female offenders. The user's manual provides norms and descriptive statistics for a variety of specific offender groups, chiefly from the 43 items of Section 1, and includes at least 16 tables and six figures. Frequency distributions of risk levels, based on the prescribed cutoff scores in the user's manual, are provided in a series of 6 tables.

Information on the reliability of the LS/CMI is presented in the manual, encompassing internal consistency, test-retest reliability, and standard error of measurement (*SEM*). Values for coefficient alpha for Section 1 ranged from .89 to .94 for the authors' entire North American sample, and reports by other groups working with the instrument gave similar results. Other components of the instrument produced more variable results. Test-retest reliability coefficients were presented for a small sample of 18 offenders retested after 26 days by another investigator, giving $r = .88$ for Section 1 and a range of values for the subcomponents. Because the instrument measures dynamic as well as static factors, the authors argue, test-retest reliability estimates are confounded by true changes in offenders. Consistent with that argument, the highest value recorded ($r = .91$) was for Criminal History, presumably static within the time-frame of the study, and the lowest ($r = .16$) was for Procriminal Attitude/Orientation, a dynamic factor that could be expected to show favorable change after successful interventions. Information on parallel-forms reliability (very high) and on its standard error of measurement is also provided.

Information on predictive validity is presented in several tables of correlation matrices. For example, in nearly 1,500 probationers and inmates, Section 1 scores correlated moderately ($r = .44$) with any recidivism within 1 year of release. Similar results were found in a prospective, longitudinal study of 630 male offenders who were followed for 2 to 3 years. The authors note that assessing recidivism rates within the five risk levels identified by the LS/CMI revealed a "consistent and steady increase" on all measures (user's manual, p. 144). Attesting to the instrument's concurrent validity, strong correlations were observed between the LS/CMI and two other inventories purportedly measuring the same construct.

COMMENTARY. Since 1995 the LS/CMI and its predecessor have been administered to a very large sample of probationers and inmates in Canada, the United States, the United Kingdom, and Singapore. Descriptive statistics are provided for practically all imaginable subsets of respondents—males and females, probationers and inmates, adults and juveniles, in federal versus other jurisdictions, by country, and so forth. The resulting tables of normative data provide a wealth of information, potentially the basis for many possible applications. Test users are free, of course, to set their own cutoff scores higher or lower in adjusting the balance of selectivity and specificity for their own contexts and purposes.

The authors acknowledge their commitment to appropriate ethical and professional standards, advising test users that significant decisions should not be based on the results of a single test, however solid its psychometric basis. They not only urge test users to bring their own judgment and expertise to bear on the interpretation of test results with individuals, but also make specific provision for professional overrides of test scores when circumstances so dictate. There is the danger here that, by straying too far from the objective test results, a user might sacrifice the established validity of actuarially based assessment in succumbing to the beguiling (yet unsubstantiated) allures of clinical wisdom and insight. However, the authors' data indicate that the professional override capability is rarely used in practice.

Such a huge data set as the LS/CMI developers have accumulated has allowed them to answer with authority almost all of the questions typically posed by users of classical test theory methodology. There is an opportunity here for the authors or others to take advantage also of modern test theory methodology (Embretson & Reise, 2000), for example, by examining each of the 43 items of Section 1 for their levels of "difficulty" and discrimination vis-à-vis the hypothesized latent trait of risk of recidivism. In this context, risk could be assessed by offenders' total scores on Section 1 or by actual recidivism rates in longitudinal studies of test respondents. Among other things, such methods have the potential for identifying and scaling the most important predictors of recidivism.

SUMMARY. The LS/CMI is a set of paper-and-pencil rating forms to be used in criminal justice settings to classify offenders' risk of recidivism and need for particular services. The 43-item Section 1 involves assessing the most important predictors that have been identified by actuarial research, an investigative strategy that has produced compelling results that have informed current practice in this area. The test developers have provided a user's manual of over 200 pages with extensive documentation of the test's psychometric properties and tabulations of the data from almost 158,000 offenders in North America, together with some information from European and Asian respondents. The authors have established five categories of risk based on ranges of test scores, but users are encouraged to bring their professional discretion to bear when interpreting test results with individual offenders. Sophisticated test users can make use of the huge data set summarized in the many tables and figures of the manual to adjust cutoff scores as appropriate to their own settings and referral questions. Together with its predecessor, the LSI, the LS/CMI has generated an expanding research literature and is widely used by mental health and criminal justice professionals in the correctional arena.

REVIEWER'S REFERENCES

Embretson, S. E., & Reise, S. P. (2000). *Item response theory for psychologists.* Mahwah, NJ: Lawrence Erlbaum.
Philipse, M. W. G., Koeter, M. W. J., van der Staak, C. P. F., & van den Brink, W. (2006). Static and dynamic patient characteristics as predictors of criminal recidivism: A prospective study in a Dutch forensic psychiatric sample. *Law and Human Behavior, 30,* 309–327.
Quinsey, V. L., Harris, G. T., Rice, M. E., & Cormier, C. A. (1998). *Violent offenders: Appraising and managing risk.* Washington, DC: American Psychological Association.

[109]

Life Attitude Schedule: A Risk Assessment for Suicidal and Life-Threatening Behaviors.

Purpose: Designed to "measure the cognitive, affective, and action-oriented components of suicide proneness."

Population: Ages 15–20.

Publication Date: 2004.

Administration: Individual or group.

Forms, 2: Life Attitudes Schedule, Life Attitudes Schedule: Short.

Price Data, 2007: $118 per complete kit including technical manual (70 pages), 10 item booklets, and 25

QuikScore forms each for LAS and LAS:S; $49 per technical manual; $25 per 10 item booklets (reusable); $39 per 25 LAS QuikScore forms; $33 per 25 LAS:S Quikscore forms.

Authors: Peter M. Lewinsohn, Jennifer Langhinrichsen-Rohling, Paul Rohde, and Richard A. Langford.

Publisher: Multi-Health Systems, Inc.

a) LIFE ATTITUDES SCHEDULE.

Acronym: LAS.

Scores, 12: Composite Scores (Physical, Psychological), Content Scales (Health-Related, Death-Related, Injury-Related, Self-Related), Modality Type Scales (Actions, Thoughts, Feelings), Valence Scales (Negative, Positive), Total.

Time: (30) minutes.

b) LIFE ATTITUDES SCHEDULE: SHORT.

Acronym: LAS:S.

Scores, 3: Physical, Psychological, Total.

Time: (10) minutes.

Review of the Life Attitudes Schedule: A Risk Assessment for Suicidal and Life-Threatening Behaviors by THOMAS P. HOGAN, Professor of Psychology, University of Scranton, Scranton, PA:

DESCRIPTION. The Life Attitudes Schedule: A Risk Assessment for Suicidal and Life-Threatening Behavior consists of a regular or long form (LAS) and a short form (LAS:S). According to the technical manual (p. 1), "The LAS was created to identify adolescents and young adults who are at increased risk of suicidal and/or life-threatening behavior." The target behavior is not simply suicide but, more broadly, life-risking behavior and even the absence of life-enhancing behaviors. The test authors note that they hope the schedule will be useful to both clinicians and researchers.

The long form (LAS) contains 96 items in a four-page booklet. Each item is a brief declarative statement, for example, "I love dangerous activities" and "Getting enough sleep at night is important to me," all reportedly at a fourth-grade reading level. Responses use a True/False format (True = agree or describes me, False = disagree or does not describe me). Answers are recorded on a separate carbonized form. On this form, the client records answers on the top page; the second page contains a scoring grid, where answer marks are summed for the simple scores; the third page has space for score calculations, that is, combining simple scores into various composites; and the last four pages are score profiles, separately by gender and age.

Items are categorized in a 4 x 3 x 2 matrix with four items in each of the resulting 24 cells. There are four content areas: Death-Related, Health-Related, Injury-Related, Self-Related; three modalities: Actions, Thoughts, Feelings; and two valences: Negative, Positive. Thus, one item might be Death-Related/Actions/Negative; another might be Self-Related/Thoughts/Positive. Each Content area (4), Modality (3), and Valence (2) yields a score, for a total of 9 scores. Based on the 4 x 3 x 2 matrix, Content scores have 24 items each; Modality scores, 32 items each; and Valence scores, 48 items each. Then, there are 3 additional scores: Physical, the sum of Health-Related and Injury-Related Content scores; Psychological, the sum of Death-Related and Self-Related Content scores; and Total, the sum of all scores. Thus, LAS yields 12 scores in all. It is a nice conceptual scheme. However, that is a lot of scores for 96 items.

In addition, seven items are identified as "critical items" (direct endorsements of life-threatening actions or feelings). These items, if endorsed in an undesirable direction, require special attention regardless of any of the formal scores.

The short form (LAS:S) contains a subset of 24 items from the regular or long form. Both items and responses appear on a single sheet atop a carbonized form, with the second sheet allowing for determination of scores based on the responses, followed by a profile sheet on which scores are entered. Profiles again are completed separately by gender and age. LAS:S yields three scores: the Physical score and Psychological score, each based on 12 items, plus the Total score, the sum of the two subscores. These scores correspond conceptually to the comparably named scores in the long form, although based on fewer items. The LAS:S also contains 1 of the 7 critical items.

The LAS has an 80-page, eight-chapter technical manual covering both long and short forms. Chapter 1 gives a description of the problem (suicide and life-threatening behaviors) and its prevalence, plus a brief description and key features of the LAS. The chapter contains a commendable discussion of user qualifications and potential misuses—more than the often perfunctory statement on these matters. Chapter 2 outlines the instrument's conceptual framework, essentially an expanded statement of how the authors are thinking about this topic and how they plan to attack it. Chapter 3 presents procedures for administration and scoring, including very nice examples of completed scoring forms. Chapter 4 offers suggested steps for interpretation, including helpful descriptions of five clients in terms of their backgrounds and LAS score profiles. No cases are presented for the short form. Chapter 5 reviews pilot-testing procedures. Chapter 6 describes normative samples. Chapter 7 presents reliability and validity data. The very brief (one-page) Chapter 8 suggests directions for future research (and the need for an adult form of the schedule).

DEVELOPMENT. As noted above, Chapter 2 describes the conceptual background for the LAS. Chapter 5, labeled "Development of the LAS," describes pilot testing and selection of final items. From a practical viewpoint, LAS items are an outgrowth of the authors' work on an interview-based assessment. Using this and supplementing it with other sources, originally over 600 items were created, according to the manual. These were winnowed through author review and, finally, by pilot-testing in four samples. Procedures for item selection seem reasonable, although samples are purely convenience samples, without much description.

TECHNICAL INFORMATION.

Norms. For both the long and short forms, the LAS manual presents norms by gender and age (for each age 15–20). All norms are in *T*-score form. The norm groups are clearly of the ad hoc, convenience type, a common feature for instruments of this type. The manual emphasizes total numbers of cases (LAS, 1,229; LAS:S, 2,071), but the actual norm groups (by gender and age) have some groups as low as 55 for LAS, with median of 88; and as low as 38 for LAS:S. The total groups are described by age and race, but there is no information about such potentially important characteristics as socioeconomic level, intellectual ability, or educational achievement, or (for the college students) major field of study. In addition, the manual does not address the comparability of norms for the long and short forms. Clearly, the practitioner will need some experience with the norms to get a feel for them. As they stand, they cannot be taken as representative of any clearly defined population.

Reliability. The LAS technical manual provides internal consistency reliabilities (alpha coefficients) separately by age and gender for all 12

LAS scores and the three LAS:S scores. The manual states (p. 45) that the "internal consistencies were uniformly high." That is simply not true. Some alpha coefficients are in the .50s and .60s, with many in the .70s. The total scores do have high reliability estimates, and *some* of the subscore reliabilities are quite respectable. But many do not reach a level of reliability needed for ordinary, practical work. The database for the test-retest reliabilities is sketchily described; and data are not presented separately by gender and age, or even for all scores. More importantly, what data are presented show that some scores (including the total scores) have good stability, whereas others do not. The manual's claim (p. 45) of "very good temporal stability" is not warranted.

Validity. The manual reports correlations of LAS with corresponding scores in the Life Attitudes Interview Schedule (LAIS). The LAIS is an unpublished instrument (the authors overlapping with LAS), thus making it difficult to know exactly what is being assessed. Correlations between the LAS and the LAIS are presented for the four Content scores, three Modality scores, and the Total score. The correlations are relatively high (median = .76), but more information is needed about the criterion measures. Correlations are also reported between the Content, Modality, and Total LAS scores and three Suicidal Behavior indicators on the LAIS. Correlations are in the expected direction and mostly significant, especially with "lifetime history of suicide attempt" (technical manual, p. 49).

The manual devotes the majority of space under validity to confirmatory factor analysis (CFA) of each form. For the long form, there is some evidence to support the matrix-based organization of scores. It would have been helpful to present the original correlation matrix for the scores to allow for alternative views of the structure. For the short form, the manual concludes that the analysis supports the two-part structure (Physical and Psychological); however, the correlation of .82 between the scores suggests the short form may be tapping a single underlying dimension.

Regarding the extensive presentation of CFA, there is a disconnect between the bases for norms and reliability reports, on the one hand, and for the factor analytic work, on the other hand. The manual emphasizes the need for norms separately by gender and age; this emphasis carries over to most of the reports of reliability. However, for the factor analytic work, all cases are combined. If, in fact, it is important to separate by gender and age, then combining these groups means that much unwanted variance has been included in the factor analytic results. It becomes difficult to distinguish between variance due to underlying dimensions versus that due to gender or age differences.

COMMENTARY. The LAS provides a meaningful conceptual framework for assessing its target area: suicide and life-threatening behavior, with such behavior broadly defined to include actions, thoughts, and feelings, both positive and negative. The long and short forms have the usual trade-off between breadth and administrative convenience: 12 scores and 30 minutes administration time versus 3 scores and 10 minutes time. The short form is comparable in many ways to the currently popular measures of suicidal ideation. The long form provides a much richer array of information than currently popular forms.

The LAS presents a reasonable array of technical information, especially for a new entry in the field, although there are certainly weaknesses in the array. Adequate internal consistency data are given but more caution is needed in their interpretation. Additional test-retest data are needed. Similarly, a more frank discussion of limitations in the normative data is warranted. Several types of validity data are presented, with some favorable results. Clearly, more validity studies are needed. Contrasted group studies (suicide attempters versus nonattempters and similar contrasts) would be particularly welcome.

Calculation of LAS scores, using the carbonized form, is not a trivial task. The manual (p. 10) notes that "scoring of the LAS takes under 15 minutes." That is actually quite a bit of time for a 96-item, true-false inventory. It would be a simple matter to construct a computer program to develop all the scores and profiles automatically (and with less chance of error) just by keying in the 96 T-F responses; the publisher should do so.

SUMMARY. The LAS is a promising instrument for assessment of suicide and life-threatening behavior. Both the long and the short forms can be recommended for clinical work, with some cautions. Total scores on both are quite reliable and supported by some reasonable validity evidence. However, subscores on both forms require considerable caution in interpretation. Normative comparisons also require caution. The long form has excellent potential for contributing to research in this area.

Review of the Life Attitudes Schedule: A Risk Assessment for Suicidal and Life-Threatening Behaviors by JANET SMITH, Associate Professor, Department of Psychology and Counseling, Pittsburg State University, Pittsburg, KS:

DESCRIPTION. The Life Attitudes Schedule (LAS) is a 96-item self-report pencil-and-paper measure designed to identify increased risk of suicide and life-threatening behavior in adolescents and young adults ages 15 to 20. The questionnaire takes approximately 30 minutes to complete and can be hand-scored in under 15 minutes. There is also a 24-item short version of the Life Attitudes Schedule (LAS:S) designed to be used as a brief screening instrument, for example to monitor progress in treatment or for use with clients with limited concentration abilities. Raw scores are converted into T-scores by plotting them on a profile form. Minimum qualifications are required for test administration and scoring, but interpretation needs to be completed by a licensed or certified professional meeting b-level qualification standards.

The LAS yields 12 scores, including a Total score, 2 Composite scores, 4 Content scores, 3 Modality Type scores, and 2 Valence scores. The Total score is an overall indicator of suicide proneness, incorporating the extent of suicidal and suicide-related behaviors as well as presence or absence of life-promoting behaviors. The instrument encompasses three modalities: Actions, defined as behaviors engaged in by the individual; Thoughts, encompassing ideas, beliefs, opinions, and plans; and Feelings, involving affective and emotional state. In addition, four content areas are assessed: the Death-Related scale is closest to most traditional measures of suicidality and is composed of suicide and death-related items as well as views of life and longevity; the Health-Related scale addresses illness and lack of self-care along with health and wellness; the Injury-Related scale addresses potential for injury and risk-taking, along with safety-related behavior; and the Self-Related scale addresses self-worth and self-image. The Death-Related and Self-Related Content scores are summed to produce the Psychological Composite score. This score is considered a measure of probability of suicidal ideation, with high scores indicating a combination of death-associated behaviors along with low self-worth, depression, and hopelessness. The Health-Related and Injury-Related Content scores are summed to produce the Physical Composite score. This score is conceptualized as being indicative of the extent to which individuals are engaging in a broad range of behaviors associated with increased probability of injury or death, regardless of presence or absence of expressed suicidal intent. The Valence scales are composed of the Negative scale, addressing extent of life-threatening thoughts, behaviors, and feelings across the content areas and the Positive scale indicating extent of presence or absence of life-promoting thoughts, behaviors, and feelings. Finally, a select set of questions are identified as indicators of imminent suicide risk.

DEVELOPMENT. The theoretical construct underlying the LAS is suicide proneness, which the authors define as an individual's propensity to engage in suicidal behaviors. The construct of suicide proneness is treated as a bipolar continuum, with negative, self-destructive behaviors at one end of the continuum and positive, life-extending behaviors at the other extreme. The instrument addresses both ends of this continuum, assessing life-enhancing thoughts, feelings, and behaviors as well as the more traditional life-threatening aspect of suicidality. Incorporation of the four content areas was based on a review of the literature in the area of suicide proneness. The authors developed an item pool of 600 items based on previous suicide assessment devices as well as from daily self-monitoring records completed by high school volunteers. Items from this initial pool were scrutinized by the test authors, then pilot data were collected from four separate samples, including adolescents and college students. For the final version of the LAS, the test authors selected items with low correlations with social desirability, age, and gender along with high correlations with the Total LAS score. In addition, final items were selected only if they were endorsed by a minimum of 5% and maximum of 95% of the sample. The LAS:S was constructed by selecting 1 item from each of the 24 cells resulting from combining Content scales (4), Modality Types scales (3), and Valence scales (2). Items were selected on the basis of highest correlation with

the LAS Total score in combination with low association with gender.

TECHNICAL. Gender and age-specific norms are provided. The normative sample for the LAS is composed of 1,229 high school and college undergraduate students from the Midwest. There is an overrepresentation of individuals in the 18- and 19-year-old age groups along with a higher percentage of females. The test manual also provides information on racial distribution, with the majority of individuals being Caucasian. Although the racial distribution is somewhat representative of the U.S. population, the sample has a very small actual number of males and females for some racial groups. The LAS:S normative sample consists of 2,071 high school and college students, predominantly from the South. The majority of individuals are also predominantly Caucasian and not evenly distributed in terms of age and gender, with an underrepresentation of 19- and 20-year-olds.

Internal consistency of all subscales was moderately high, with coefficient alphas for individual ages and gender ranging from .50 to .95, with most being in the .7 or .8 range. Total score for each age group showed high internal consistency, with alpha coefficients mostly above .90. Test scores showed moderate stability over time, with test-retest reliability coefficients for subscales ranging from .71 to .90 over a 1-month interval. Test-retest reliability for the Total score, again with a 1-month test interval, was .85. Stability of scores on the LAS:S subscales was somewhat lower, with test-retest scores over a 1-month test interval ranging from .67 to .80, but stability of the LAS:S Total score was comparable to that of the LAS Total score, with a test-retest reliability coefficient of .84. The test manual did not provide any information regarding size or characteristics of the sample used to establish test-retest reliability, other than to note that participants were a subsample of the development sample. Test-retest data were not provided for the Valence scales or Composite scores. Standard errors of measurement are provided for LAS subscale T-scores by age and gender, and range from 2.24 to 7.07, with most values in the 3 to 6 range. Standard error of measurement for the Total score ranges from 2.24 to 3.32, dependent on age and gender.

The test manual describes several studies that provide evidence of validity for the LAS.

Scores on the LAS were compared to the Life Attitudes Interview Schedule (LAIS; Lewinsohn, Langhinrichsen-Rohling, & Langford, 1989) in a sample of 757 high school students. Correlations were significant between scores on the LAS and corresponding scales on the LAIS. However, correlations with noncorresponding scales were also high, raising questions about the degree of specificity of scale scores. It also should be noted that the LAIS is an unpublished scale. For the same sample, LAS scores were shown to be correlated with criterion measures identified by the LAIS, including history of accidental injury (for Total score, $r = .27$, $p < .01$), history of intentional injury (for Total score, $r = .29$, $p < .01$), and most significantly, lifetime history of suicide attempt (for Total score, $r = .45$, $p < .001$). Confirmatory factor analyses using the developmental samples supported underlying structure of the LAS, specifically in terms of the Modality, Content, and Valence scales. Factor analysis also supported the existence of a second-order factor, consistent with use of a Total score to measure a more general construct of suicide proneness. Positive and Negative constructs showed a strong inverse correlation, supporting the notion of a bipolar continuum. Results of factor analyses were consistent across different groups in terms of gender and social desirability. The only exception to expected correlations and factor loadings noted in the test manual is that Death-Related Actions did not load significantly on the Actions construct. The authors attribute this finding to the low frequency of many of the behaviors assessed in this category. In addition, there were high intercorrelations between the Modality Type scales and, to a lesser extent, high intercorrelations between the Content scales, raising questions about the independent contribution of each of these scales. Evidence of validity using the full normative sample was a little more mixed. Although support was provided for the Content and Modality scales, direct evidence for the Positive and Negative scores was not found and could only be inferred. In addition, lack of adequate fit was found for Content scores loading onto the Total score, which resulted in the creation of the two additional Physical and Psychological scales. These two scales were found to be highly correlated, which was seen as evidence supporting use of a Total score.

Validity of the LAS:S was established by showing significant correlations for the LAS:S Total score and individual scales with established depression and hopelessness scales. In a sample of 32 adolescents, LAS:S Total score was used to identify participants with lifetime suicidal ideation, with a sensitivity of .80, specificity of .77, and positive predictive value (PPV) of .62. In summary, the authors note that the LAS:S correctly classified 78.1% of the adolescents. The authors further noted that the full LAS showed the same level of accuracy. In a further study of 1,742 high school students, the LAS:S was correlated with suicidality and depression, a wide range of problem behaviors, personality factors, as well as family and peer factors. The LAS:S was also found to be associated with past suicide attempt.

COMMENTARY. The manual is comprehensive, very well organized, and easy to follow. In addition, the test itself is well-designed, and easy to administer and score, requiring only a fourth grade reading level for completion. The greatest strength of the test is the scope of the assessment of suicide proneness, extending beyond the traditional focus of depression and hopelessness, and incorporating a life-enhancing aspect or positive valence score. A significant weakness is that normative data are not representative of the U.S. population and do not include adolescents who did not remain in high school or young adults outside of a college student population. Reliability of both the LAS and LAS:S is high. Validity of the scales appears mostly adequate, although there is considerable intercorrelation between scales, calling into question the utility of specific individual scales, and some validity evidence is based on correlations with an unpublished scale. It should be noted that no evidence of predictive validity is reported in the manual, which underscores the test authors' caution that the instrument is not designed as an instrument to be used in the prediction of suicide. Although the test authors caution about possibility for response bias, the instrument does not include any scales to assess an individual's approach to the test.

SUMMARY. The LAS differs from most existing measures of suicide proneness in that the scope of the instrument extends beyond traditional components of hopelessness and depression and attempts to assess absence of positive life-promoting behaviors in addition to engagement in a broad range of negative behaviors. The test authors caution, however, that the instrument does not claim to be predictive of suicide. However, both the LAS and LAS:S can provide invaluable information regarding overall suicide proneness, suggesting further areas to be evaluated and targeted in treatment. Depending on purpose of the assessment, the LAS:S may be just as useful as the full LAS. It would be desirable for future editions of the instrument to include norms more representative of the U.S. population as well as provide further evidence of validity, particularly for individual subscales. But, overall, the LAS is a welcome addition in the area of assessment of suicide proneness.

REVIEWER'S REFERENCE

Lewinsohn, P. M., Langhinrichsen-Rohling, J., & Langford, R. A. (1989). The Life Attitudes Interview Schedule. Unpublished manuscript.

[110]

Lindamood Auditory Conceptualization Test—Third Edition.

Purpose: Designed to measure "the ability to (a) discriminate one speech sound or phoneme from another and (b) segment a spoken word into its constituent phonemic units."

Population: Ages 5-0 through 18-11.

Publication Dates: 1971–2004.

Acronym: LAC-3.

Scores, 6: Isolated Phoneme Patterns, Tracking Phonemes, Counting Syllables, Tracking Syllables, Tracking Syllables and Phonemes, Total.

Administration: Individual.

Price Data: Available from publisher.

Time: (20–30) minutes.

Comments: "Criterion referenced"; requires no reading by examinees.

Authors: Patricia C. Lindamood and Phyllis Lindamood.

Publisher: PRO-ED.

Cross References: See T5:1503 (16 references) and T4:1465 (2 references); for reviews by Nicholas G. Bountress and James R. Cox of a previous edition, see 9:623 (1 reference).

Review of the Lindamood Auditory Conceptualization Test—Third Edition by VINCENT J. SAMAR, Department of Research, National Technical Institute for the Deaf, Rochester, NY:

GENERAL DESCRIPTION. The Lindamood Auditory Conceptualization Test (LAC-3) is a norm-referenced test that assesses an individual's ability to perceive and conceptualize speech sounds in isolation and within and across syllables. Auditory conceptualization refers to essentially the same construct as the more widely known reading precursor skill known as phonemic awareness or (sometimes interchangeably) phonological awareness. The primary value of the LAC-3 is its ability to contribute to diagnosis of reading disability in individual children, longitudinal educational evaluation of literacy development in individual children, and research on the developmental foundations of reading ability and disability.

The LAC-3 is intended to assess one primary component of literacy development, namely phonemic awareness/auditory conceptualization (decoding skill). As the manual emphasizes, literacy development, or the reading "gestalt," is also dependent on visual image processing (sight word recognition) and language knowledge (oral vocabulary and the ability to use context). The LAC-3 provides focused assessment of only the phonemic awareness/auditory conceptualization component of literacy development, and, as such, is intended to be used diagnostically within the context of a more comprehensive evaluation of total reading ability.

DEVELOPMENT. The LAC-3 is a revision and extension of the earlier LAC-R (Lindamood & Lindamood, 1979). The LAC-3 provides norms for a broader range of ages (5.0 years through 18.11 years) and extends the variety and complexity of phonemes and syllables tested. The LAC-3 is based on a normative sample that is intended to be representative of U.S. socioeconomic and ethnicity demographics as of the 2001 U.S. Census. The reliability and validity of the LAC-3 are now grounded more firmly in new studies, and quantitative evidence is provided for a general freedom from item bias with respect to gender and ethnicity.

The LAC-3 kit is supplied with a comprehensive manual, 25 examiner record booklets, 24 colored plastic blocks to visually represent phonemes, six colored felt squares to visually represent syllables, and an examiner presentations audio CD that demonstrates the presentation of instructions and helps the examiner standardize pronunciation of the targeted phonemes, syllables, and phonological contrasts used in the LAC-3.

Test administration. The LAC-3 is administered to individual children. On each item trial, a child listens to the examiner produce a sequence of individual phonemes or syllables. The child then uses colored blocks to represent the target phoneme sequence and/or colored felt patches to represent the target syllable sequence. A unique and valuable feature of this approach is its ability to allow the child to demonstrate simultaneous awareness of both the syllable sequence and the syllable-internal phoneme structure of a target utterance by laying the colored blocks (representing phonemes) on top of the appropriate felt patches (representing the syllables that contain the phonemes).

The LAC-3 begins with a short precheck task that requires manipulation of the color sequence of the blocks in response to the examiner's verbal instructions. The precheck is intended to establish that the child is able to follow directions and to understand the basic concepts of sameness and difference. Subsequently, the examiner administers five categories of spoken items, and the child uses the colored blocks and felt squares to model each spoken item. The five categories are: (a) Isolating Phoneme Patterns, which requires the child to model sequences of phonemes spoken in isolation; (b) Tracking Phonemes, which requires the child to model sequences of phonemes spoken as blended single syllables and to track phoneme additions and substitutions to the internal syllable structure; (c) Counting Syllables, which requires the child to model the number of syllables spoken in a multisyllable utterance and to represent the auditory distinctions among its syllables; (d) Tracking Syllables, which requires the child to model sequences of syllabic additions and substitutions within multisyllable utterances; and (e) Tracking Syllables and Phonemes, which requires the child to model sequences of phonemic and syllabic additions and substitutions within multisyllable utterances.

The LAC-3 manual provides a clear description of the rationale for the LAC-3 and its assessment domain within the whole reading process, information about the qualifications of examiners and the eligibility of the children tested, administrative and scoring procedures, interpretation, description of the normative sample, reliability, validity, controlling test bias, and diagnostic and remedial issues and recommendations. The examiner form is easy to use. The audio CD demonstrating the instructions and

pronunciation of the targeted items is a boon t new LAC-3 test administrators.

TECHNICAL. Based on a comparison c the LAC-3 normative sample with the U.S. 200 Census Bureau data the manual claims that th LAC-3 sample is representative of the nation as whole. However, the demographic characteristic given in the manual list only "white," "black," an "other" under the category of race. It is unclea from the demographic characteristics given in th manual to what the designation "other" refers.

Reliability statistics indicate generally hig overall reliability, as well as high reliability fo different ages, genders, certain race and ethnicit groups, and children with learning disabilities With respect to race and ethnicity, reliability sta tistics are reported for White, Black, and His panic-origin children only. No reliability data ar reported for the substantial American subpopu lation of Asian/Pacific Islander children, which in a representative sample of 1,003 children should have been sampled in sufficient number to compute reliability statistics. The lack o reliability statistics for this subgroup is an omis sion that should be corrected in future revisions o the LAC-3.

Evidence presented in the manual indicate that the LAC-3 has acceptable overall validity ir terms of its content validity, criterion-related va lidity, and construct validity. The LAC-3 doe appear to measure necessary precursor skills re lated to developmental patterns of reading and spelling, and to reading and spelling disability. In addition, differential item functioning analysis indicated that the LAC-3 is robust against gender, racial, and ethnic bias, at least for those racial and ethnic groups tested. Again, the lack of validity work that specifically targets Asian/Pacific Islander children is an omission that should be corrected in future revisions of the LAC-3.

To the credit of the LAC-3 authors, the manual includes a separate chapter that addresses the issue of test bias for targeted demographic groups, and how to control it. As the authors point out, a test is biased if it differentiates between members of various groups (e.g., ethnic groups) on bases other than the characteristics being measured. They further acknowledge that the standard remedies for test bias are to include targeted demographic groups in the normative sample, obtain specific reliability and validity statistics for targeted groups, and examine group behavior on each item as a basis for unbiased item selection. The LAC-3 normative sample and its reliability and validity studies have been designed to satisfy these conditions to a reasonable first approximation for at least some ethnic groups.

COMMENTARY. Against this background of otherwise cautious test development and recommendations, it was disconcerting to see the manual claim that "the LAC-3 is appropriate for use with individuals ages 5-0 through 18-11, including those ... who are deaf or hearing impaired" (p. 9). There is probably no group of American children, not already included in the existing LAC-3 norms, to whom it is less likely that those norms would fortuitously generalize than deaf and hard-of-hearing children. There is certainly evidence that phonological coding and phonological awareness are associated with reading ability in some subgroups of deaf children (Harris & Beech, 1998). However, the development of these skills follows a very different timecourse than for hearing children, and both the development of these skills and their predictive relationship to reading acquisition depend on several additional population-specific factors, including speech intelligibility level, type and amount of language exposure, degree of residual hearing, and so on. Obviously, performance on any auditory-based test can be seriously compromised by hearing loss itself, independent of phonetic awareness/auditory conceptualization. The deaf and hard-of-hearing population is so heterogeneous in its educational, linguistic, and audiometric characteristics that it is not even clear at this point that a useful set of norms could be developed for the majority of that population on the LAC-3. Certainly, the LAC-3 might turn out to be useable with certain subgroups of deaf children, such as cochlear implant users, once appropriate validation studies are done that target those subgroups. However, the validation of the LAC-3 for the deaf and hard-of-hearing population in general may present serious roadblocks, especially in dealing with the problem of separating the effects of auditory discrimination from auditory conceptualization. Therefore, it is clearly inappropriate at this stage for the authors of the LAC-3 to suggest that phonemic awareness/auditory conceptualization can be successfully measured in any deaf or hard-of-hearing children by the LAC-

3, and by implication, that the existing LAC-3 norms can be used for their educational assessment or diagnosis. Doing so without sound normative and validation work, and without clear guidelines for ensuring the testing eligibility of individual deaf and hard-of-hearing children, places these children at risk for serious misassessment and educational misplacement. The claim that the LAC-3 is appropriate for use with deaf and hard-of-hearing children should be removed from the manual.

SUMMARY. The LAC-3 is a well-designed, reasonably well-validated instrument, and its use for assessment and diagnosis of hearing children at risk for reading failure is well motivated. The LAC-3 should not be used for the assessment of phonemic awareness/auditory conceptualization or for diagnosis of reading disabilities in deaf and hard-of-hearing children until such time as the difficult task of norming and validating this instrument on that population or on any of its subgroups is satisfactorily completed.

REVIEWER'S REFERENCES

Harris, M., & Beech, J. R. (1998). Implicit phonological awareness and early reading development in prelingually deaf children. *Journal of Deaf Studies and Deaf Education, 3,* 205-214.
Lindamood, C. H., & Lindamood, P. C. (1979). The LAC Test: Lindamood Auditory Conceptualization Test. Austin, TX: PRO-ED.

Review of the Lindamood Auditory Conceptualization Test—Third Edition by DOLORES KLUPPEL VETTER, Professor Emerita, University of Wisconsin–Madison, Madison, WI:

DESCRIPTION. The Lindamood Auditory Conceptualization Test—Third Edition (LAC-3) was designed to assess phoneme awareness/auditory conceptualization. The test taker is asked to represent the sound sequence(s) heard by manipulating colored blocks or felt squares to mark the detection of phonemes, patterns of phonemes within syllables, syllables in pseudowords, and patterns in syllables within pseudowords.

The LAC-3 is appropriate for youth, ages 5-0 to 18-11 years, including those who have hearing impairments, or have educable developmental delays, articulation disorders, or are non-English-speaking. The participants' performances on five categories (i.e., subtests) relevant to proficient auditory conceptualization are assessed through the use of small colored blocks and/or colored felt squares. A colored block represents a phoneme and a colored felt square represents a syllable. The participant assigns the colored objects to phonemes/syllables and sequences them from left to right. The LAC-3 typically is completed in 20–30 minutes.

Examiners must have intact phoneme awareness, be competent in the administration of educational or psychological tests, and be knowledgeable of the procedures for administering and scoring the LAC-3. They are encouraged to practice the stimuli and to compare their productions with the demonstrations on the LAC-3 audio CD included with the test.

After a "precheck" during which there is a determination of the participant's competence to demonstrate the concepts of same-different, left-right, first-last, and number concept to four, the examiner instructs and provides models prior to initiating each category. There are varying numbers of items in the categories, but the discontinuation rule is the same: five errors, not necessarily consecutive. Responses are recorded as the color(s) and pattern of the block(s) or felt(s) chosen.

Tables are provided to permit the conversion of raw scores into standard scores (mean = 100, $SD = 15$), percentile ranks, and age and grade equivalents. There are four purposes stipulated for the LAC-3: (a) identification of problems in phoneme awareness/auditory conceptualization; (b) quantification of the problem(s) identified; (c) tracking progress in auditory conceptualization as a function of treatment; and (d) research where auditory conceptualization is being investigated. The authors caution that the LAC-3 should never be used in isolation as a diagnostic tool, but rather that other data and observations should be incorporated in forming a diagnosis.

DEVELOPMENT. The LAC-3 is the second version of the Lindamood Auditory Conceptualization Test. The LAC was originally developed to evaluate an individual's basic abilities to detect specific characteristics (e.g., the identity, number, and sequence of phonemes) in spoken sounds because of the importance of these skills to reading, spelling, and writing. Participants were asked to make same-different distinctions as well as contrasts incorporating the number and order of speech sounds; these distinctions were indicated through the manipulation of colored blocks. There were two alternate forms of the instrument and subsequently a Spanish translation was added.

Although the initial normative sample of participants was relatively small and from a single school district, it was argued that its demographic characteristics and sampling techniques made "exemplary" in its research design. Participants from a second school district were tested for the purpose of establishing test-retest reliability. The validity criterion employed was reading level.

The LAC-R evaluated additional participants and extended the age/grade range of the normative sample. This publication also added validity studies conducted at first and third grades as well as at college level. Statistical information was expanded in this revision and an item analysis was included. Several reviewers wrote praising the novel manner in which the Lindamood Auditory Conceptualization Test–Revised Edition and its predecessor assessed the subjects' competencies in phoneme awareness/auditory conceptualization. However, they also indicated that there should be additional studies of reliability and validity. To their credit, the test authors responded to the recommendations as well as to comments and suggestions from educators and speech/language clinicians who used the instrument; they also had their own ideas about how the instrument should be modified. The result is the Lindamood Auditory Conceptualization Test—Third Edition.

The LAC-3 provides more specific information about the normative sample (i.e., socioeconomic factors, gener, ethnicity), increased normative data (i.e., standard scores, percentile ranks, age, and grade equivalents for persons between the ages of 5 years and 18 years, 11 months), increased information about individual items (i.e., conventional item analysis and differential item functioning), reliability coefficients for subgroups of the normative sample (e.g., African American, Hispanic, gender), and additional validity studies. New items were added to the original categories and three new categories were added; the result is that the difficulty level of the instrument has been expanded. The new categories assess the individual's ability to count and track multisyllables and their ability to track syllables and phonemes in multisyllable pseudowords.

TECHNICAL.

Standardization. A sample of 1,003 individuals was chosen from eight states (e.g., California, Florida, Illinois, Maryland, Nebraska, New Hampshire, New Jersey, and Pennsylvania) and tested during the years 1998 through 2002. The authors compared characteristics of their sample (i.e., geographic area, age, gender, ethnicity, family income, education of the parents, and disability status) with those reported for the school population in the United States in the Statistical Abstract of the United States (2001) and concluded that their sample is representative of the population from which it was drawn.

Raw scores were transformed into standardized scores with a mean of 100 and a standard deviation of 15. The manual contains a table with descriptive ratings and percentages that are associated with a range of standard scores (e.g., the description for a score of 121–130 is "superior" and the percentage included in that range of scores is 6.87%). In addition, it provides a thorough discussion of the type of interpretation the examiner might provide for a range of certain, and perhaps more usual, standard scores. The manual does not, however, provide a reason for the intervals chosen for interpretation (i.e., greater than 110, 90–110, 80–89, and below 80). Given that many statistical interpretations use the standard deviation as a typical interval about a score, it is somewhat surprising that the authors did not choose to use it (i.e., 15). Examiners should be aware of this difference and remind themselves of it when using recommendations from the manual for writing reports.

Tables are presented for three other types of scores: percentile ranks, age, and grade equivalents. The authors caution users to be aware of the many concerns expressed in the literature about the use of these types of scores and present appropriate references to the original sources of these criticisms. Finally, they discuss factors that they believe should be taken into account in the interpretive process.

Reliability. Coefficient alphas and their associated standard errors of measurement are presented for 14 age intervals and for selected subgroups (i.e., gender, ethnicity, and disability status). They range from .91–.95 for the various ages and .95–.97 for the selected subgroups. Test-retest reliability coefficients calculated separately for participants in elementary ($N = 33$), middle ($N = 20$), high school ($N = 27$), and for all ages ($N = 80$) were either .96 or .97.

Validity. For content validity, the categories and items in categories were chosen using empirical evidence and a theoretical model. Original selection was based upon extensive data from a teaching program (i.e., ADD: Auditory Discrimination in Depth, 1969 and its revision in 1975); later a model employing psycholinguistic rationale was developed. After the normative data were collected, conventional item analysis and differential item functioning were calculated; they provided additional statistical information applicable to the manual's discussion of item difficulty and item bias.

Concurrent validity was established by evaluating the relationship between the LAC-3 and several other instruments measuring phonological awareness (i.e., the Elision and Blending words subtests and Phonological Awareness composite portions of the Comprehensive Test of Phonological Processing, the Alphabet/Word Knowledge subtest from the Diagnostic Achievement Battery—Third Edition, and the Test of Phonological Awareness Skills) on three independent groups of participants (sample sizes were from 94 to 123). A second study correlated corrected scores on the LAC-R (items were removed that are also in the LAC-3) with the LAC-3; the resulting correlation was .88. This result might be interpreted as more of an internal consistency measure than one of concurrent validity, but it is still of note.

The rationale for construct validity is dependent upon basic constructs attributed to the LAC-3, that is, phoneme awareness/auditory conceptualization should show developmental progression in individuals, and because phoneme awareness/auditory conceptualization underlies phonics and is associated with written language, it should be correlated with tests of reading and spelling. The authors also argue that as a result of these propositions, the LAC-3 should also provide scores that discriminate between good and poor readers and spellers, and that there should be significant correlations between item performance and total scores. Evidence in the manual indicates that there is support for these basic premises: There is an increase in mean raw scores in the early years (up to age 11 years) with the rate slowing through age 18 years and the LAC-3 identifies poor readers versus good readers of the Wide Range Achievement Test—Third Edition (WRAT-3).

COMMENTARY. The LAC-3 is a relatively brief, but seemingly thorough, test of phoneme awareness/auditory conceptualization appropriate for use for a wide range of youth. Because of its unique methodology it may be used with persons who have hearing and/or articulation impairments, educable developmental disabilities, as well as for non-English-speaking individuals (e.g., a Spanish translation is included in the test package).

Efforts to assure that the examiner is proficient in administering the category items are supported through specific instructions in the manual as well as through the use of an audio CD. All of the information needed for administering the LAC-3 is conveniently contained in the examiner record booklet. Score interpretation is discussed extensively in the manual, and prototypical statements that may be used in providing feedback regarding results are also included.

There are no apparent flaws in the LAC-3 if the stipulated definition of phoneme awareness/auditory conceptualization is accepted. The authors appropriately caution the interpretation of some of the available scores (e.g., age and grade equivalent scores) in the text, but they present the conversion tables as though they have the same status as standard scores. Finally, because of small sample sizes, additional evidence for reliability and validity would be desirable.

SUMMARY. The LAC-3 is an instrument useful in assessing phoneme awareness/auditory conceptualization in individuals 5 years to 18 years, 11 months. Because of its unique presentation and response requirements, it can be used with those who are hearing impaired, have educable developmental delays, have articulation disorders, or are non-English-speaking. The instrument is useful for identification and quantification of phoneme awareness/auditory conceptualization problems, for tracking progress in treatment, and for research purposes.

[111]

Location Learning Test.

Purpose: To measure visuo-spatial learning and recall.
Population: Elderly adults.
Publication Date: 2000.
Acronym: LLT.
Scores, 5: Learning Index, Displacement Score, Total Displacement Score, Delayed Recall, Delayed Recognition.
Administration: Individual.
Forms, 2: A, B.

Price Data, 2006: £113.50 per complete kit including manual (15 pages), 25 scoring sheets, test grids, practice grids, and picture cards; £35.50 per 50 scoring sheets.
Time: (25) minutes.
Authors: Romola S. Bucks, Jonathan R. Willison, and Lucie M. T. Byrne.
Publisher: Harcourt Assessment [England].

Review of the Location Learning Test by ANITA M. HUBLEY, Associate Professor of Measurement, Evaluation, and Research Methodology, University of British Columbia, Vancouver, British Columbia, Canada:

DESCRIPTION. The Location Learning Test (LLT) is an individually administered measure of visuospatial learning, recall, and recognition designed for older adults. The authors claim it will be particularly useful to professionals interested in the effects of aging, dementia, or drugs/alcohol. There are two forms of the test. Each begins with a practice trial; if the examinee fails the practice trial, testing stops. Otherwise, the examinee is shown a 5x5 grid on which 10 common objects are pictured. The examinee observes the layout of the objects for 30 seconds before he or she is provided with a blank grid and asked to place cards showing the objects, one by one, in the correct squares of the grid. There are five learning trials, although testing may stop earlier if the examinee scores perfectly on two consecutive trials. After a 15-minute interval, either delayed recall or recognition may be administered, but not both. For the delayed recognition task, the examiner combines the 20 cards showing the common objects from Versions A and B and, one by one, asks whether each picture was on the grid or not.

The administration instructions are clear and easy to follow. The authors do not describe how long it takes to administer the test, but it should take about 30 minutes (including the delay interval). Recording performance and computing displacement scores (i.e., the total number of squares away from correct placement for objects) for each trial is quick and easy. Four key scores are computed. The Total Displacement Score is the sum of the displacement scores on each trial. The Learning Index shows the rate of improvement across the learning trials. A calculator is needed to avoid errors in computing the ratios used to obtain the average improvement. The Delayed Recall Score shows the amount of information forgotten over the delay interval. Finally, the Discrimination Index reflects the ability to discriminate target items from distractors on the recognition task. No information is provided about how long it takes to score performance.

DEVELOPMENT. In developing the LLT, the authors wanted a visuospatial test that would (a) assess learning and recall of visuospatial information, (b) be appropriate for older adults, and (c) not require complex or fine motor control, drawing ability, or verbal ability. The authors trace the origins of the LLT to "some informal work" (manual, p. 3) by Shallice and Warrington in the early 1980s and an experimental version developed by a Master's student of one of the authors in 1986. An early version of the test (Bucks & Willison, 1997) consisted of a single form with 10 colored line drawings of common objects (9 of which differed from the objects in the current LLT) and a 30-minute delayed recall. A recognition trial was administered after the first learning trial. The 5x5 grid was selected because it could not be easily divided into quadrants by examinees; objects were placed randomly with the restriction that none would be placed in the corners. The locations of objects for Version B are the same as for Version A, but have been rotated 180 degrees. Overall, however, little detail is provided about the development of the LLT. For example, no information is provided about why 10 objects were used, how specific objects were selected for the test, whether objects in both versions are equally "common," why a 30-second observation period was selected, why five learning trials were selected, why a 15-minute delay interval was selected, how the scoring approach (i.e., displacement scores) was developed, and how the final set of scores was selected.

TECHNICAL. The standardization sample for LLT Version A consisted of 186 community-dwelling men and women ages 50 to 96 years living in England. The majority of the sample was from the Bristol area (n = 128). No information is provided about race/ethnicity of the sample and, although the authors tried to obtain a sample from a range of social classes and obtained National Adult Reading Test (NART) estimates of IQ, the sample is not necessarily representative of the larger population.

Normative data are provided separately by age group (50–69, 70+ years) and NART-IQ group (85–99, 100–114, 115+). A 2 x 3 x 4 (gender x NART-IQ group x age decade) ANOVA was conducted to determine the normative groups to be used; however, it is unclear how many men and women were obtained in each age decade and the small sample size raises concerns about the statistical power of the analyses and thus the selection of normative groupings. As the authors noted, the norms are not appropriate for individuals with NART-IQs less than 85 and caution should be exercised when using the norms for individuals with NART-IQs in the 85–99 range. Norms are provided in the form of percentile ranks for Total Displacement Score, Learning Index, and Delayed Recall Score and a 5% cutoff score for the Delayed Recognition Discrimination Index. Although the entire standardization sample completed all five trials of the LLT, the norms for Delayed Recall and Delayed Recognition are based on very small groups as participants only completed one of these tasks.

Meaningful estimates of reliability for memory tests are often difficult to obtain due to features such as item interdependence within and between trials and practice or recall effects. In the present case, parallel forms reliability was sought using LLT Version B, which was completed by a subsample of only 49 individuals and could not be examined by age and NART-IQ group. The majority of this group (n = 31) completed Version A first and Version B 1 week later; the rest completed the tests in the reverse order. The two versions correlated .71 for the Total Displacement Score and .49 for the Learning Index. The correlation of the two versions at delay was not reported.

Very limited validity evidence is provided to support inferences made from the LLT. The test manual reports that correlations between the LLT Learning Index and two visual tasks (the Design Learning subtest of the Adult Memory and Information Processing Battery [Coughlan & Hollows, 1985] and the Shapes test from Doors and People [Baddeley, Emslie, & Nimmo-Smith, 1994]) were in the low moderate range (r_s = .49 and .44, respectively) but were higher than the correlation (r_s = .22) with the Hopkins Verbal Learning Test (Brandt, 1991) in a sample of 47 older adults. Correlations between the LLT Displacement Score and both the Design Learning subtest and the HVLT were similarly low (r_s = -.24 and -.29) whereas the correlation with the Shapes test was slightly higher (r_s = -.37). This is fairly weak evidence. Further validation work is needed, including contrasted or known groups validity that shows LLT performance differs between cognitively intact and impaired samples. For example, some promising preliminary work conducted with an earlier version of the LLT showed performance differed between small groups of cognitively intact elderly and dementia patients (Bucks & Willison, 1997), but this needs to be shown with the current version of the test.

COMMENTARY. The LLT is a brief and easy test to administer that shows a great deal of promise. Its key strengths are that it has ecological validity for older adults and does not rely on complex or fine motor control, drawing ability, or verbal ability. Scoring is not too difficult but does require a calculator. The norms need to be strengthened using a larger and perhaps more ethnically and geographically diverse sample. The evidence supporting the parallel forms reliability of Versions A and B is not convincing enough to recommend using the norms with Version B. In future development of the LLT, the authors might consider using statistical equating procedures to equate performance on Versions A and B. Most critically, however, validity evidence is extremely limited. It is surprising that a test that the authors describe as "particularly useful to … those concerned with the effects of dementia and ageing, as well as the effects of drugs and stressors such as alcohol, benzodiazepines and cholinesterases" (manual, p. 4) is presented without any validity evidence to back up these claims. Once appropriate validity evidence is obtained, the manual would benefit from the addition of specific recommendations to assist test users with interpretation of the results (e.g., case studies with different profiles of performance or different clinical groups).

SUMMARY. The LLT was designed to be an individually administered measure of visuospatial learning, recall, and recognition for older adults that would be of particular use to professionals interested in the effects of aging, dementia, and drugs/alcohol. The test meets its goal of assessing visuospatial learning, recall, and recognition in an ecologically valid manner and stands out from the majority of visuospatial tests in that it does not rely on complex motor control or drawing ability. Unfortunately, very little validity evidence is pro-

vided to support the inferences to be made from the LLT and the lack of known groups validity evidence, in particular, means the LLT cannot be recommended for clinical use at this time.

REVIEWER'S REFERENCES

Baddeley, A., Emslie, H., & Nimmo-Smith, I. (1994). Doors and People: A Test of Visual and Verbal Recall and Recognition. Bury St. Edmunds, England: Thames Valley Test Company.
Brandt, J. (1991). The Hopkins Verbal Learning Test: Development of a new memory test with six equivalent forms. *The Clinical Neuropsychologist, 5*, 125–142
Bucks, R. S., & Willison, J. R. (1997). Development and validation of the Location Learning Test (LLT): A test of visuo-spatial learning designed for use with older adults and in dementia. *The Clinical Neuropsychologist, 11*, 273–286.
Coughlan, A. K., & Hollows, S. E. (1985). The Adult Memory and Information Processing Battery (AMIPB). Leeds: AK Coughlan, St. James's University Hospital.

Review of the Location Learning Test by CLAUDIA R. WRIGHT, Professor Emerita, California State University, Long Beach, Long Beach, CA:

DESCRIPTION. The Location Learning Test (LLT) is a timed, nonverbal test designed to assess one's ability to recall spatial arrangements of everyday objects and to demonstrate learning over time. A two-fold purpose is (a) to distinguish healthy older adults from those who have difficulty with learning or retaining new spatial information, who exhibit episodic memory problems, or who are at risk for dementia; and (b) to help support the work of clinical psychologists, occupational therapists, speech and language therapists, and other professionals and researchers concerned with the effects of aging, dementia, drugs, and/or other stressors on recall. Step-by-step instructions are provided for placement of materials and examinee prompts during one practice, five testing, and one delayed-recall or recognition trials. Detailed examples are presented to facilitate calculation and interpretation of five scores generated from an examinee's responses. The Displacement Score is the sum of errors in a single trial determined by the number of grids between misplaced objects and their corresponding targets (the higher the score the poorer the recall). The Total Displacement Score is the sum of displacement scores over five trials. The Learning Index provides an estimate of the rate of improvement and is the arithmetic average of four ratios derived from the Displacement Score for each trial (Trial 1—Trial 2)/Trial 1, (Trial 2—Trial 3)/Trial 2, and so on, and ranges from 0 ("no learning") to 1 ("perfect learning"). The Delayed Recall Score assesses the amount of information lost after a 15-minute delay between the Displacement Score for the fifth trial and that for the delayed recall session

Finally, the Discrimination Index is the difference between the number of correctly remembered objects and the number of misidentified objects. The authors caution test examiners to interpret LLT scores with consideration of the context of an examinee's personal and clinical histories and performance on other assessments.

DEVELOPMENT. Although a number of assessments can be used to differentiate between healthy older adults and those with dementia on abilities to learn over time and to accurately recall information, many have relied on skills that require verbal recall or an ability to reproduce patterns by drawing or manipulating objects. Research with the original form of the LLT (Bucks & Willison, 1997) reportedly distinguished between adults diagnosed with dementia and those without as well as between those diagnosed with dementia who demonstrated learning over trials from those who did not. The newly revised version of the LLT was designed with skill limitations in mind and employs only pictures of common objects that older adults frequently misplace. LLT materials include a technical manual, two sets of laminated stimulus (picture) cards, two 2x2 laminated grids (approximately 6"x7"), one stimulus grid with two objects pictured on it for practice and one blank for testing, and three 5x5 laminated grids (approximately 15"x16", two of these each contain 10 pictures of everyday objects [e.g., glasses, scissors, watch, comb] randomly distributed across the grids, and one is blank for testing).

TECHNICAL.

Norms. Normative data were based on responses from a sample of 186 adults aged 50 to 96 living in communities in or near Bristol, England: 128 (69%), Bristol; 37 (20%), Wirral; 10 (5%), Manchester; 6 (3%), Wales; and 5 (3%), South East. Across social classes, 38 (20%) were classified as I (Professional); 78 (42%), II (mid-level professionals and managers); 35 (19%), IIIN (skilled non-manual); 21 (11%) IIIM (skilled manual); 13 (7%) IV (partly skilled); and 1 (.5%) V (unskilled). In addition, an estimate of intelligence for classification purposes was obtained from scores on the National Adult Reading Test (NART-IQ; 12:252), which purportedly measures "premorbid intelligence levels" in adults thought to be experiencing deteriorating cognitive functions. The NART-IQ is a verbal test composed of 50 words of increasing difficulty with irregular pronunciations. LLT examinees were classified into one of three NART-IQ groups with scores ranging from 85–99 (low-to-average, -1 $SD < M$), 100–114 (average-to-high, $M \leq \pm 1$ SD), and 115 or higher (high, > +1 SD). Statistically significant ANOVA comparisons and corresponding post-hoc analyses identified two age groups (50-69 years and 70+ years) and three NART-IQ groups (85–99, 100–114, 115+) for which norms were generated. Three tables constructed for the three LLT scores of Total Displacement, Learning Index, and Delayed Recall, display norms for each of six groups (2 age x 3 IQ ranges) corresponding means, minimum and maximum scores, and percentiles. A fourth table displays Discrimination Index cutoff scores for each of the six groups.

Reliability. An estimate of parallel-forms reliability ($r = .71$, $p < .001$) was obtained from a subsample of 49 respondents who agreed to take a second form of the LLT 1 week later; 63% received Version A first and Version B, 1 week later; 37% received Version B first. Adequate statistical comparisons were conducted to support the conclusion that the subsample and total sample were comparable with respect to gender and social class proportions. Although a comparison of means on the NART-IQ for the two groups revealed that the mean for the subsample (118.5, $SD = 8.5$) was significantly higher than that for the total sample (114.4, $SD = 10.5$; $t[232] = -2.5$, $p < .05$), it was concluded that the correlates were sufficiently low between NART-IQ scores and each of the four LLT measures (absolute values of r ranged from .01 to .23, $mdn = .21$) to assuage concern the scores on the parallel form would be compromised. Further, mean Total Displacement Scores were subjected to a repeated-measures ANOVA revealing no statistically significant differences between the two versions and no order effect.

Validity. To assess concurrent validity, LLT scores were correlated with several measures using a subsample of 47 participants. Scores on the Design Learning (DL) subtest of the Adult Memory and Information Processing Battery (AMIPB; Coughlan & Hollows, 1985), based on the placement accuracy of a design's form that an examinee reproduces on a grid, yielded Spearman's rank correlations of -.23 (n.s.) with LLT's Total Displacement Score and .49 with the Learning Index ($p < .01$). The Shapes Test (Baddeley, Emslie, & Nimmo-Smith, 1994) involves the reproduction of an increasingly complex design, assessing learning across trials; Shapes Test Total scores correlated -.37 (p < .05) with the Total Displacement Score and .44 (p < .01) with the Learning Index. Scores on the Hopkins Verbal Learning Test (HVLT; Brandt, 1991), derived from three trials where one attempts to learn a list of 12 words, correlated -.29 with the Total Displacement Score and .22 with the Learning Index (all p > .05). Intercorrelations among the scores of these three measures yielded a single statistically significant coefficient between the Shapes Test Total and the DL Total (r_{sp} = .47, p < .01), suggesting low-moderate overlap between the two sets of scores; coefficients between HVLT scores and Shapes and DL scores were not statistically significant (r_{sp} = .28 and .16, respectively). A fourth measure included as a correlate with each of the four LLT scores but not specifically identified as part of the validation process was the Mini-Mental State Examination (MMSE; 15:166), which provides a total score that is used to estimate severity of cognitive impairment. MMSE scores range from 0 to 30 (category ranges are *normal*, 27–30; *mild impairment* 21–26; *moderate* 11–20; and *severe* 0–10). For the total sample (N = 186), the mean for the MMSE was 27.5 (SD = 1.8) with a range of 20–30. Scores on the MMSE for the subsample fell into the mild to normal ranges. Low-to-moderate Pearson product-moment correlations were obtained between MMSE scores and the LLT's Total Displacement Score (r = -.36, p < .001), Learning Index (r = .33, p <.001), Discrimination Index (r = .24, p < .05), and Delayed Recall (r =.08, p > .05). The correlation between MMSE scores and NART-IQ scores was .38 (p < .001).

COMMENTARY. It appears the normative data were obtained from a sample of relatively healthy older adults living in communities in southwest England; 62% (N = 186) were classified in the top two social classes (professional and mid-level professionals); 30% had IQ scores of 100–114 and 60%, 115 or higher. Although it is said efforts were made to obtain a representative sample, no comparative statistics are provided to support this assertion.

It is not known how closely characteristics of social-class ranks in England compare to those socioeconomic strata in the United States or other countries. Further, no ethnic comparisons on LLT scores have been made. Additional research may help clarify the utility of the LLT in more diverse settings and in countries other than Great Britain. Although data were collected that included estimates of cognitive impairment, no explanation was given for the variable's exclusion from the analyses. Also, missing from the technical manual are descriptions and rationales for tests selected for classification and validation purposes.

SUMMARY. For professionals working with aging clients suffering from or at risk for dementia, the LLT offers a face-valid, nonverbal measure to assess visuospatial learning over time and delayed recall. An advantage of the LLT over similar measures is that the testing format requires no verbal recall or fine motor movements, both of which can help to minimize test-related anxiety in older adults. Modest concurrent validity support for test scores has been demonstrated for a small subsample of examinees.

REVIEWER'S REFERENCES

Baddeley, A., Emslie, H., & Nimmo-Smith, I. (1994). Doors and People: A Test of Visual and Verbal Recall and Recognition. Bury St. Edmunds, England: Thames Valley Test Co.
Brandt, J. (1991) The Hopkins Verbal Learning Test: Development of a new memory test with six equivalent forms. *The Clinical Neuropsychologist, 5,* 125–142.
Bucks, R. S., & Willison, J. R. (1997). Development and validation of the Location Learning Test (LLT): A test of visuo-spatial learning designed for use with older adults and in dementia. *The Clinical Neuropsychologist, 11,* 273–286.
Coughlan, A. K., & Hollows, S. E. (1985). The Adult Memory and Information Processing Battery (AMIPB). Leeds: AK Coughlan, St. James's University Hospital.

[112]

Maintenance Electrician A Test (Form BTA-C).

Purpose: For selecting manufacturing or processing maintenance candidates.

Population: Applicants and incumbents for jobs requiring electrical knowledge and skills at the highest level.

Publication Dates: 2000–2005.

Scores, 8: Motors, Digital Electronics and Analog Electronics, Schematics & Print Reading and Control Circuits, Power Supplies/Power Distribution and Construction & Installation, AC/DC Theory and Electrical Maintenance & Troubleshooting, Test Instruments and Computers & PLC, Mechanical Maintenance, Total.

Administration: Group.

Price Data, 2007: $21 per consumable self-scoring test booklet (minimum order of 20); $24.95 per manual (2000, 17 pages).

Time: (60) minutes.

Comments: Self-scoring instrument.

Author: Roland T. Ramsay.

Publisher: Ramsay Corporation.

Review of the Maintenance Electrician-A Test (Form BTA-C) by KEVIN R. KELLY, Head, Department of Educational Studies, Purdue University, West Lafayette, IN:

DESCRIPTION. The Maintenance Electrician-A Test (Form BTA-C) is designed for selecting personnel with advanced knowledge of electrician job activities. It is focused above entry-level electrical knowledge and skill. This self-scorable test consists of 60 multiple-choice items and yields a single overall score of advanced electrician knowledge and skill.

DEVELOPMENT. The authors of the test began by defining the domain of advanced electrician knowledge. They analyzed the *Dictionary of Occupational Titles* job descriptions for maintenance electrician (829.261-018) and industrial maintenance repairer (899.261-014), which yielded 14 knowledge and skill areas. The authors then developed a bank of items to reflect each knowledge/skill area; they did not specify the number of items in the test bank. The authors next identified 10 maintenance supervisors as "job experts"; the method used to determine their expert status was not specified. These job experts were given three tasks. First, they ranked the importance of the 14 knowledge/skill areas in the position of advanced electrician. Second, they weighted the percentage of each knowledge/skill area in the typical performance of an advanced maintenance electrician. Finally, the experts assigned items from the test bank to 1 of 7 knowledge/skill areas: Motors; Digital and Analog Electronics; Schematics & Print Reading and Control Circuits; Power Supplies, Power Distribution, and Construction & Installation; Basic AC/DC Theory and Electrical Maintenance & Troubleshooting; Test Instruments and Computers & PLC; and Mechanical Maintenance. The authors did not describe how or why they reduced the number of knowledge/skill areas from 14 to 7.

A total of 50 individuals were administered the potential test items; the authors did not specify the number of potential items. The authors calculated point-biserial correlations between individual items and the total test score. The Maintenance Electrician-A (Form BTA) consists of the 60 items with the best point-biserial discrimination indices. The authors did not specify why they chose their final total of 60 items. The Form BTA was developed in 1993. A revised Maintenance

Electrician-A (Form BTA-C) was developed in 2000. The Form BTA-C appears to be a more difficult test than the Form BTA. For example, a raw score of 40 was at the 70th percentile for the Form BTA but at the 99th percentile for the Form BTA-C.

TECHNICAL.

Reliability. The Form BTA-C was administered to 49 job applicants at an automotive plant. The KR-20 internal consistency reliability coefficient was .75. This coefficient was lower than the KR-20 coefficient of .87 found for the original Form BTA for a group of job applicants and employees at a metal finishing plant. The authors did not address the lower internal consistency coefficient that resulted for the revised Form BTA-C. No temporal stability data were reported. No data were reported regarding the equivalence of Forms BTA and BTA-C.

Validity. The authors appear to have done a good job of establishing the content validity of the Form BTA-C. Advanced electrician knowledge and skill content were derived from DOT job descriptions. Job experts determined the composition of the discrete knowledge/skill areas in the position of an advanced maintenance electrician. The authors did not report any evidence of criterion-related validity for the original Form BTA or the revised Form BTA-C.

COMMENTARY. The Form BTA-C appears to cover the domain of advanced electrical knowledge adequately. The authors carefully analyzed and described the content domain and used expert judges to weight coverage of the domain. This test is also easy to administer and score. There are, however, four limitations to this test. First, the authors did not fully describe their test construction procedures. There are a number of unanswered questions about the procedures used to develop and select test items. Second, there was a complete lack of information about the rationale and procedures for developing the revised Form BTA-C. One can presume that there was a need to update test content because of advances in the field of electronics. However, there is no way to determine whether or not the authors were successful in accomplishing their goals for test revision because those goals were not specified. It was somewhat troubling to see that the revised Form BTA-C had lower internal consistency than the original Form BTA. Third, the validity data were quite limited. This reviewer was expecting to see data relating test scores to independent ratings of work knowledge and performance. Because the BTA-C is a test of advanced electrical knowledge, data should have been provided comparing the test performance of advanced electricians with that of either entry- or second-level electricians. In fact, neither the original Form BTA nor the revised Form BTA-C was administered to a homogeneous group of entry-level or advanced maintenance electricians. There is no convincing criterion-related evidence that this test measures advanced electrical knowledge, that it can be used to select candidates with advanced knowledge, or that it predicts quality of performance in jobs requiring advanced electrical knowledge. Finally, the authors provided no normative data. There is no way to tell which score represents baseline knowledge/skill for advanced maintenance electricians.

SUMMARY. The Maintenance Electrician-A Test (Form BTA-C) is a test of electrician knowledge and skill with satisfactory internal consistency. This test reflects the requisite job activities of electrician maintenance workers and industrial maintenance repairers. Although designed as a test of advanced electrician knowledge, it is not clear that the Form BTA-C can be used for the purpose of selecting advanced electricians or distinguishing entry-level from advanced electricians.

[113]
Maintenance Electrician B Test (Form BTB-C).

Purpose: For selecting manufacturing or processing maintenance candidates.
Population: Applicants and incumbents for jobs requiring electrical knowledge and skills.
Publication Dates: 2000–2005.
Scores, 8: Motors, Digital Electronics and Analog Electronics, Schematics & Print Reading and Control Circuits, Power Supplies/Power Distribution and Construction & Installation, AC/DC Theory and Electrical Maintenance, Test Instruments and Computers & PLC, Mechanical Maintenance and Hand & Power Tools, Total.
Administration: Group.
Price Data, 2007: $20 per consumable self-scoring test booklet (minimum order of 20); $24.95 per manual (2000, 16 pages).
Time: (60) minutes (untimed).
Comments: Self-scoring instrument.

Author: Roland T. Ramsay.
Publisher: Ramsay Corporation.

Review of the Maintenance Electrician B Test (Form BTB-C) by JAY R. STEWART, Director and Associate Professor Rehabilitation Counseling Program, Division of Intervention Services, Bowling Green State University, Bowling Green, OH:

DESCRIPTION. The Maintenance Electrician B Test (Form BTB-C) is a 60-item achievement test. All items are multiple-choice with four options. The instrument was designed for selecting workers for jobs requiring electrical knowledge and skills. The knowledge and skill areas are: Motors (5 items), Digital Electronics (3), Analog Electronics (5), Schematics & Print Reading (5), Control Circuits (6), Power Supplies (2), Power Distribution (3), Construction & Installation (4), AC/DC Theory (6), Electrical Maintenance (8), Test Instruments (4), Computers & PLC (4), Mechanical Maintenance (3), and Hand & Power Tools (2).

The manual contains test administration and scoring instructions. The test is designed to be untimed—although it usually takes no more than an hour to complete—and should be administered in a room with tables and chairs. Pencils, test booklets, and a four-function calculator are required for taking the test. The number of persons taking the test at one time is limited to 20 for each test monitor. According to the manual, the test monitors must stay in the room at all times to ensure that test takers have adequate reading comprehension levels (sixth grade), are physically able to take the test, and are not disturbed during testing.

Test scoring is a simple process. To the examinee it appears that the bottom page of the test booklet is the answer sheet, but hidden from examinee's view, below the answer sheet, is the self-scoring grid. The examinee marks the answer boxes on the answer sheet, which is carbon copied onto the self-scoring grid. If examinees wish to change answers, they circle the first answer and check another box. The self-scoring grid, when uncovered, indicates if each answer is correct and the test scorer adds all correct answers to arrive at a total test score.

DEVELOPMENT. The BTB-C development began about 15 years ago. At that time, 10 maintenance supervisors were given a list of maintenance electrician knowledge and skill areas, which they independently ranked on importance. The supervisors then estimated the percent of test items needed for each knowledge and skill area. The needed number of items was then calculated. Supervisors then selected test items from the Ramsay Corporation's test bank. The items were chosen for both content and difficulty. They also chose an item concerning job safety for each test section. The Maintenance Electrician-B Test was made up from these items and administered to 81 persons, electrical maintenance applicants and employees in processing plants and in the metals industry. Sixty items were chosen from the original test items based on item point-biserial discrimination indexes and item difficulty, keeping proportions of content areas the same. These 60 items now comprise the BTB-C test.

TECHNICAL.

Standardization. There is no reported norm sample; therefore, there is, at present, no ability to statistically compare individual scores on this test to scores of a population of maintenance electricians or job applicants for maintenance electrician positions (Kline, 2000). Obviously, there is also no ability to compare scores to special populations based on gender, race, age, or disability status.

Reliability. Reliability was determined through the KR20 (.87) and Standard Error of Measurement (3.43), indicating excellent reliability. However, there are no reports of test-retest reliability measures and stability of performance may be important.

Validity. Content validity would seem to be adequate, based on the use of maintenance supervisors to establish appropriate content areas and test items. There appears to be no independent research on the content by other job expert raters. Additionally, rapidly evolving industrial and electrical technology might invalidate some of the content areas. Criterion validity has not been reported. Research correlating test scores to subsequent job performance has yet to be conducted. Test scores have not been compared to parallel or even approximately similar tools of processes that measure successful maintenance electricians' skill and knowledge levels. The requisite skills and knowledge needed to be a competent worker certainly compose a complex construct. The construct has not been formally researched, but one might see indicators of potential construct

validity through having used job experts in constructing the test.

COMMENTARY. Identifying and hiring competent skilled workers is essential for the economic survival of the United States. Additionally, good maintenance electricians can maintain expensive equipment and poor maintenance hires could cause severe injury to production workers by improperly working on production equipment. This test has made a good effort at simulating a work sample with a paper-and-pencil test. An actual work sample would be more valid as a test (Truxillo, Donahue, & Kuang, 2004). The BTB-C does seem to approach the value of a work sample because electrical problems often demand diagram reading, formula application, and mathematic calculations. To this end, test items have the feel of grappling with a real electrical problem needing diagnostic and problem-solving skills, which leads to practical solutions.

The BTB-C can provide a vital service if appropriately researched and applied. Unfortunately, possibly due to the fact that assessment is limited to a relatively small population of electrical maintenance workers, exploration into reliability and validity issues has not been adequately conducted. However, this test does appear useful in identifying, in a broad manner, skill and knowledge levels of maintenance electricians both overall and in specific task areas. Additionally, a norm group study could provide comparison and cutoff scores.

SUMMARY. Because employers are subject to EEOC action if they use hiring instruments that discriminate against gender, race, and disability groups, it is wise to use only selection instruments that have been assessed for potential bias (Aiken, 2003). The BTB-C does have the advantage of being faithful to measuring the essential job functions of maintenance electrician positions, but does need research on how the test assesses protected groups. Using this test with other hiring and assessing processes may aid in reducing selection bias. Developing standardized scores would expand the test use. At present, employers would have to individually set cutoff scores and identify their own priorities for skill areas. This test appears to be a candidate for further research and refinement, possibly ultimately making it a quality industrial assessment tool.

REVIEWER'S REFERENCES

Aiken, L. R. (2003). *Psychological testing and assessment* (11th ed.). Boston: Allyn & Bacon.

Kline, P. (2000). *Handbook of psychological testing* (2nd ed.). London: Routledge.

Truxillo, D. M., Donahue, L. M., & Kuang, D. (2004). Work samples, performance tests, and competency testing. In J. C. Thomas & M. Hersen (Eds.), *Comprehensive handbook of psychological assessment: Vol. 4. Industrial and organization assessment overview* (pp. 345-370). Hoboken, NJ: John Wiley and Sons, Inc.

[114]

MAINTEST (Form NL-1R, Form B, & Form C).

Purpose: Measures practical mechanical and electrical knowledge.

Population: Applicants and incumbents for jobs requiring practical mechanical and electrical knowledge and skills.

Publication Dates: 1991–2005.

Scores, 22: Hydraulics, Pneumatics, Welding, Power Transmission, Lubrication, Pumps, Piping, Rigging, Mechanical Maintenance, Shop Machines and Tools & Equipment, Combustion, Motors, Digital Electronics, Schematics & Print Reading, Control Circuits, Power Supplies, Basic AC & DC Theory, Power Distribution, Test Instruments, Computers & PLC, Electrical Maintenance, Total.

Administration: Group.

Price Data, 2007: $60 per consumable test booklet; no charge for manual (2005, 28 pages).

Time: (150) minutes (untimed).

Comments: Tests scored by publisher; Forms B and C are alternate forms of Form NL-1R.

Author: Roland T. Ramsay.

Publisher: Ramsay Corporation.

Cross References: For reviews by Nambury S. Raju and William J. Waldron of an earlier edition, see 13:189.

Review of the MAINTEST (Form NL-IR, Form B, & Form C) by MICHAEL J. ZICKAR, Associate Professor of Psychology, Bowling Green State University, Bowling Green, OH:

DESCRIPTION. The MAINTEST is a 153-item test, administered via paper-and-pencil, designed to assess applicants and incumbents for maintenance jobs that require mechanical and electrical skills and knowledge. The test assesses 21 different content areas. The content areas range from Hydraulics, Lubrication, Digital Electronics, Control Circuits, to Electrical Maintenance. All items have a four-option multiple-choice format. Most of the items are knowledge-based though some of the items require interpretation and analysis of diagrams. Scores are reported for each of the 21 content areas as well as an overall score. There are

currently four forms of the MAINTEST: Form NL-1, Form NL-1R, Form B, and Form C.

The test manual provides explicit instructions for test administrators, including physical descriptions of the room arrangement, demeanor for the administrator, and verbal scripts to be read to applicants. Respondents use an NCS answer sheet provided by the Ramsay Corporation and scoring is conducted by the developer. Individual scoring sheets can be provided, which present raw scores as well as percentile scores based on both local and national norms. Although the test manual does not mention this possibility, according to the publisher's website, it now appears that the MAINTEST can be administered on-line. There is no time limit set for the test, though the test manual claims that respondents should be done within 2.5 hours.

DEVELOPMENT. The MAINTEST Form NL-1 was first developed in 1991 by the Ramsay Corporation. Forms B and C were developed in 1996 and 1999, respectively. In 2004, Form NL-1 was revised with 18 items being modified or revised. The manual for administration and scoring, provided by the developer, mentions that the test was developed based on job analyses of the jobs Maintenance Mechanic and Electrician, Maintenance, as defined by the *Dictionary of Occupational Titles* (United States Department of Labor, 1991) or the general O*NET (United States Department of Labor, 2002) job title Industry Machinery Mechanic. There is no description of the method of job analysis used.

The test manual describes that the items on the MAINTEST Form NL-1 were selected by the Vice President of Maintenance of a Fortune 500 uniform rental company. The manual does not describe how items were generated for Forms B and C, though the manual provides tables that convert scores from Forms NL-1, B, and C so that test-takers can be compared across those forms. At present, there are not enough data to provide conversion tables that include Form NL-1R. It is unclear what method was used for creating the conversion tables, though this reviewer suspects that the method was based on equipercentile equating. If so, the sample sizes seem small to ensure accuracy in the equating.

TECHNICAL. Normative data are provided for Forms NL-1 and Form B. The manual describes that the Form NL-1 norm percentiles were based on 5,699 employees "in maintenance jobs in a variety of industries" (p. 23), whereas the norm percentiles for Form B were from a national sample of maintenance employees and applicants. The manual does not specify how these normative samples were collected, whether they were sampled randomly from the population of maintenance workers or were based on a convenience sample of companies that have worked with the Ramsay Corporation. There is no information provided about the gender or ethnicity of the normative samples.

The manual provides extensive information on the reliability of Form NL-1 and Form B. For each item in both forms, item difficulty (percentage getting the item correct) and point-biserial discrimination indexes are presented. In addition, reliability coefficients and corresponding standard errors of measurement are presented for seven different samples, ranging in size from 54 to 5,699. The types of reliability coefficients are not specified, though one might assume that they refer to internal consistency measures such as KR20. The range of reliabilities is from .88 to .94, indicating that in general the test has high reliability. There is no mention of test-retest reliability in the document.

The test manual states that there is both content-related validity as well as criterion-related validity. The manual states that the test has content validity because the test measures knowledge identified by job analyses. There is no information presented about the methodology used in the job analysis, though detailed descriptions of each of the test's 21 content areas are provided in the manual.

Two studies are reported that are related to criterion-related validity. In a Uniform Rental company ($n = 201$), test scores were significantly correlated with job performance ratings of know-how, technical knowledge, supervisory skills, problem solving, and interpersonal skills. In a sample of 95 employed maintenance workers, the researchers found that using tests would have resulted in a workforce of 22% poor employees, whereas without the test, 33% of workers were rated as poor. Although there was little information provided about the samples and methodology in these two studies, they both suggested that the test had significant criterion-related validity when administered to incumbent samples.

COMMENTARY. The MAINTEST appears to be a well-developed test that is designed to assess the skills of applicants and incumbents for maintenance worker positions. The test relies heavily on a content-validation approach; there are listings of the content bases that underlie each of the 21 content areas. In the opinion of this reviewer, all potential users should compare these test specifications to a detailed job analysis conducted for the specific organization that uses the test. This task is especially important given that there is little information provided in the manual regarding the initial job analysis that was used to develop this test. Criterion-related validity evidence is positive, although the details of the study methodology are minimal.

Although Form NL-1R appears to be an improvement over the previous version, there are no normative data for this version nor is there any method for converting scores from that version to other versions. According to the manual, the developer is committed to collecting the necessary data to equate scores on this new version with the other forms.

SUMMARY. This test is designed for improving hiring and personnel decisions related to the job of maintenance worker. Tests designed for this specific job are important, and this test should be given serious consideration for those hiring into this specific position. Given that the test is supposed to be designed on the foundation of content validity, it is recommended that potential test users conduct a detailed job analysis and compare the results of their job analysis with the content of this test.

REVIEWER'S REFERENCES

United States Department of Labor. (1991). *Dictionary of occupational titles* (4th ed., rev.). Washington, DC: U.S. Government Printing Office.
United States Department of Labor. (2002). *The O*NET dictionary of occupational titles*. Indianapolis, IN: JIST Works, Inc.

[115]

Management and Organizational Skills Test.

Purpose: Measures "an individual's knowledge and understanding of how relatively complex organizations function as well as knowledge of the competencies and skills required for success in management and executive positions."

Population: Job applicants.
Publication Date: 2004.
Acronym: MOST.
Scores: Total score only.

Administration: Group.
Price Data, 2005: $29.95 per manual (10 pages); $50 per 10 test booklets.
Time: (45–60) minutes.
Comments: Web-based test version is self-administering.
Authors: E. P. Prien and Leonard D. Goodstein.
Publisher: HRD Press, Inc.

Review of the Management and Organizational Skills Test by PAUL M. MUCHINSKY, Joseph M. Bryan Distinguished Professor of Business, University of North Carolina, Greensboro, NC:

DESCRIPTION. The Management and Organizational Skills Test (MOST) measures an "individual's knowledge and understanding of how relatively complex organizations function, as well as knowledge of the competencies and skills required for success in management and executive positions. The purpose of this instrument is to differentiate between those individuals who possess this knowledge and understanding of general organizational and management principles and those who do not" (technical and administrative manual, p. 1). It is proposed that the MOST be used both for pre-employment screening, and as a diagnostic measure to be used in career planning.

The "MOST consists of 165 multiple-choice items that present a representative array of organizational and business scenarios" (technical and administrative manual, p. 1). Next presented are 12 case-oriented practical business situations. The number of items devoted to each situation ranges from 4 to 18. In total, 109 items comprise the first section. The second section consists of 10 terms or concepts used in business. The candidate must select whether the concept concerns what kind of business the company is conducting, or how the business operates. The final section consists of 45 multiple-choice items with four alternatives. The items most typically assess the definitions of business terms or how to handle situational problems.

The MOST is available in both paper-and-pencil and web-based versions. There is no time limit, but the manual indicates it typically takes 45–60 minutes to complete the test. There is a manual scoring system for the paper-and-pencil version of the test. The candidate's responses are recorded on a separate answer sheet, and the time needed to score each test is estimated at 30 seconds.

DEVELOPMENT. This test was developed out of the authors' repeated experiences in working with managers. They concluded some managers did not understand the obstacles to achieving organizational goals and objectives, based on a lack of knowledge about what was required. It was thus concluded an assessment was needed to measure knowledge of management practices, including an overall systems approach to understanding organizations and their effectiveness. The authors examined the research-based literature on organizational effectiveness and the determinants of that effectiveness, particularly in terms of level of business knowledge and other differences among individuals. Next the authors wrote descriptions of work and organization settings representing different levels and areas of business. Over several preliminary versions of the MOST, the items were developed, edited, and revised, ultimately producing the current 165-item version of the test. The author determined that the MOST requires a level of reading comprehension associated with 2 years of college.

TECHNICAL. Reliability and validity evidence to support use of the MOST is sparse. Based on an unspecified sample size, the internal consistency reliability (coefficient alpha) of the test is .85. Validity evidence is limited to two studies. In an assessment of criterion-related validity, 243 individuals serving in various supervisory and management positions were administered the test. Scores on the test were correlated with 10 validity indices of rated job performance. Three of the 10 validity coefficients were statistically significant ($p < .05$): coaching and developing ($r = .16$); planning, organizing and, scheduling ($r = .15$); and problem solving ($r = .18$).

The second validity study was to correlate scores on the MOST with scores on a second test developed by the authors that measures planning, organizing, and scheduling. The reported validity coefficient was $r = .33$ ($p < .01$).

The final item of technical information is a percentile table based on the one sample of 243 managers who were administered the test. The median score on the test was 109, the standard deviation was 10.56, and the range of scores was from 79 to 127. The above-noted research findings constitute the sum total of technical information available on the MOST. The Technical and

Administrative Manual, which presents this technical information, is only 7 pages in length.

COMMENTARY. Similar to the authors, it has been my experience in working with business people that some individuals have high business acumen, whereas some others seem to have very little. As such, I can readily see how the idea for this test came to be. However, I believe it is easier to differentiate individuals with little or no business sense from those with moderate business acumen, than to differentiate individuals with high business acumen from those with middling talent. There are "right and wrong answers" to questions that can differentiate business talent at the lower end of the distribution, but evidence of high business acumen involves something far different (and more complex psychologically) than knowing right answers from wrong. Herein lies the fundamental question behind the development of this test: Do business problems and situations inextricably have right and wrong answers? My answer would be "no," as what is right and what is wrong can depend upon a myriad of conditional and contextual factors that cannot be woven into any test format in an efficient manner. To illustrate my point, we need not go any farther than a sample question posed at the start of the test. A problem situation is posed to the examinee, and four responses are asked about it. The examinee is supposed to respond as to whether each of the four responses would contribute to, or detract from, the effectiveness of the organization. Here is the sample question as presented in the test (p. 2):

> You have recently been promoted to a supervisory position with a group of six subordinates. Two of them are casual acquaintances, three are older than you, and two are new employees. During the first month in your new position would it be desirable for you to...
>
> 1. Talk to each person individually to get a sense of their skills and ask about any problems they may be having that you should address.
>
> 2. Have a group meeting your first day on the job to "lay down the law" because you have heard rumors that the previous supervisor was too casual.
>
> 3. Talk privately with your two acquaintances about the work habits of the others.

> 4. Observe the work and skills of all your subordinates as you get to know them and their strengths and weaknesses.

The authors provide the "correct answers" to these four responses regarding whether each would contribute to, or detract from, organizational effectiveness. Not surprisingly, #2 is indicated as a detracting response. Equally obvious, #1 and #4 are both indicated as contributing responses. However, the "correct answer" of #3 was surprising (and somewhat disturbing) to me—it is listed as a contributing response. I can readily envision that if the entire work group learned that two of their peers "had the ear" of the new supervisor, yet they were nothing more than casual acquaintances (as described in the stem of the question), concerns could be raised that the new supervisor already had identified his "favorites," resulting in what has been referred to as "in group" and "out group" members. The perceived formation of cliques within an organization setting can hardly be described as "contributing to" organizational effectiveness. Conversely, if total confidence and discretion could be assured among the new supervisor and the two acquaintances, such a response might well contribute to organizational effectiveness. In short, the "right answer" to Response #3 is most likely "it depends." Aside from definitional questions, one could reasonably pose challenges to the supposed "right answer" to many of the items in this test. Nowhere in the manual does it state how the right answers to the questions were determined. Furthermore, recent research on international business practices (House, Hanges, Javidan, Dorman, & Gupta, 2004) reveals that cultural differences strongly influence what is regarded as acceptable or appropriate behavior. For example, in some cultures a supervisor would never deign to ask subordinates for their opinions. Such a practice is founded on Western values of participative decision making and low status differential concepts that are far from universal. It is the *lack* of "right answers" to many business situations that makes highly skilled business leaders rare individuals, and thus are people truly vital to the organization's effectiveness.

Although my overwhelming concern is how the right answers to this knowledge test were derived, I would be remiss if I did not call the reader's attention to a major flaw in the construction of the test. The final seven questions of the test (#159 to #165) are direct repeats of the preceding questions (#152 to #158). Although some lengthy tests include two presentations of the same question to serve as a consistency check, this pattern of obviously repeated questions is a major compositional error in the test.

SUMMARY. I think the MOST holds promise as a developmental aid to assist individuals in understanding the rudiments of business. Its usage should be limited to the lower end of talent in the business world. Given the paltry validity evidence, it should not be used for making personnel selection decisions. Paradoxically, the major value of the test might be antithetical to the precepts underlying its creation. Although some problems and situations in business do have patently right and wrong answers, many do not. It might be instructive for supervisors and managers to consider conditional and contextual factors (of the type I described previously) as a way to stimulate thinking about the complexities of business situations. Such an understanding might be the most useful contribution of this test in enhancing organizational effectiveness, the stated purpose of the test.

REVIEWER'S REFERENCE

House, R. J., Hanges, P. J., Javidan, M., Dorman, P. W., & Gupta, V. (Eds.). (2004). *Culture, leadership, and organizations: The GLOBE study of 62 societies.* Thousand Oaks, CA: Sage.

Review of the Management and Organizational Skills Test by CAROLYN L. PEARSON, Professor of Educational Foundations, University of Arkansas at Little Rock, Little Rock, AR, and IBRAHIM DUYAR, Assistant Professor of Educational Administration, University of Arkansas at Little Rock, Little Rock, AR:

DESCRIPTION. The Management and Organizational Skills Test (MOST) is a 165-item, paper-and-pencil and online instrument used to measure individual knowledge and understanding of how relatively complex organizations function, and knowledge of the competencies and skills required to be successful in management and executive positions. As the developers also state, the MOST is designed to measure individual differences for use in pre-employment screening, as a diagnostic measure to be used in career planning and development, and in assessing the overall knowledge and skill levels of organizations. All of the items are multiple-choice questions that generate a total score from three sections that contain different item types. The first section contains two item types that focus on organizational effectiveness/success; the first type is composed of 25 simple statements that describe a condition, situation, or action; the second type consists of 12 situations followed by a series of possible actions (total of 84 items), and both types require the user to determine whether the statement or action "contributes to" or "detracts from" organizational effectiveness/success. The second section, which is much shorter than the others, contains 10 items that are various actions that represent long-range strategic planning issues that require the user to determine "what kind" of business the company will engage in or "how" the business will be conducted. The third section actually contains 45 items with four multiple-choice responses that inquire into general knowledge about appropriate managerial behavior and organizational functioning and require the user to determine the "correct" or "best" answer and do not require industry-specific experience or education in any particular area of business. The directions for taking the instrument are clear, and a separate answer sheet, which is arranged according to the three sections, allows for easy scoring of the items by totaling the correct answers in the designated boxes for a total raw score. As indicated in the manual, the estimated time for administration is 45–60 minutes. Once the total score is obtained the user is referred back to the manual to convert the raw score to a percentile.

DEVELOPMENT. Materials furnished by the developer (including the manual, test booklets, and answer sheets) provide some insight regarding the initial development of the instrument. The authors state that development of the MOST was guided by the revised *Standards for Educational and Psychological Testing* (AERA, APA, & NCME, 1999) and the revised *Principles for the Validation and Use of Personnel Selection Procedures* (Society for Industrial and Organizational Psychology, Inc., 2003) yet are unclear about how the individual items were derived from any theoretical framework. Reference is made to the conduct of an extensive literature review on organizational effectiveness, and drafting descriptions of work and organizational settings representing different areas and levels of business that stemmed from critical incident episodes that were gathered from conducting organizational analysis and evaluation studies and conversations with managers and supervisors. From this process, 18 sections were derived and items were pretested on a small sample of individuals to determine item clarity, followed by a sample of personnel from a large corporation as part of a management assessment, and then to a sample of business school students who lacked prior experience so that criterion groups of experienced and inexperienced respondents were obtained. No information regarding the previous samples was provided even though the final version reports data collected from 243 respondents. Whether the instrument measures what it purports to measure remains to be determined by the user. The authors further state that conventional item analysis was performed by demonstrating significant differences in group membership (experienced versus inexperienced) and detecting significant correlations between the scores of the MOST and the scores from measures of general mental ability, critical thinking, and mathematical reasoning, but no indices are reported. The instrument was refined to reduce the level of reading comprehension needed and was next administered to a small sample of college students majoring in business administration and was incorporated in an individual assessment battery for a corporation for positions that ranged from entry-level supervisor to higher level management positions, but no data were reported from this refinement. The present version of the MOST was administered to a convenience sample of industrial managers that contained equal numbers of men and women with a representative group of African Americans, concurrently with a performance appraisal developed using "behaviorally anchored rating scales (BARS)" (technical and administrative manual, p. 3) similar to the MOST items, yet the authors report no data from this study nor the rationale behind using the anchored rating scales, although it may be assumed this was an attempt to establish concurrent validity of the instrument's scores.

TECHNICAL. There is no information regarding any norming process for the MOST in the manual. Although data were gathered on both gender and race, no analyses were reported regarding potential biases, and one may assume that the authors are still engaged in the development process. The 165 items are presented with choices that do represent each of the types of answers that are possible and appear to cover a wide range of conditions, situations, actions, long-range planning issues, and general knowledge as stated.

Internal consistency reliability from the initial versions of the instrument yielded alpha coefficients that ranged from .70 to .90, and for the current version, .85. Other reliability measures to support the consistency of the scores for the MOST are lacking.

Evidence to support the validity of the scores, similar to reliability, is for the most part lacking for the initial versions. The authors reference the initial attempt at determining the construct validity of the scores with the criterion-group analysis of experienced versus inexperienced, and also mention that similar results were obtained with later versions by different degrees of educational attainment. There was also mention of detecting significant correlations between the scores of the MOST and the scores from measures of general mental ability, critical thinking, and mathematical reasoning, but no indices are reported from any of these analyses. For the current version, the MOST was administered to 243 individuals in various supervisory or management positions in a large industrial organization, along with other measures, in which scores on the MOST demonstrated small but significant correlations with ratings from the BARS (Coaching and Developing, $r = .16$; Planning, Organizing and Scheduling, $r = .15$; and Problem Solving, $r = .18$). The scores from the MOST also demonstrated a significant and moderate correlation with scores from the Planning, Organizing, and Scheduling Test (POST, $r = .33$).

COMMENTARY. The MOST, as a measure of knowledge and understanding of organizational functioning, and knowledge of the competencies and skills required to be successful in management and executive positions, has several limitations. First, the authors have not provided a solid conceptual framework from which the items, and any underlying constructs they purport to measure, were derived, although the authors did make mention of an extensive literature review during the development process. The items seem to demonstrate content validity; however, there is no indication of how they were derived from the research on organizational effectiveness. Second, the authors should make it clear if the differing item types corresponding to the three sections represent individual scales, and if so, there are concerns over a lack of construct articulation and differentiation among the scales. Next, the authors should conduct analyses using the various groups and organizational types mentioned to determine any potential biases that could exist when attempting to generalize the scores to the groups that are represented. Also, rather than the initial development information, empirical evidence to support the reliability and validity of the scores is lacking and the authors should conduct further research regarding the technical aspects of the instrument.

SUMMARY. The authors have provided an organizational and management knowledge and skills instrument that can be administered, scored, and interpreted rather easily. An attempt was made to use a variety of items, but most of the information presented was from the initial validation process, and it is still unclear as to what the instrument actually measures because there is no demonstrated linkage between the items and the literature from which they were derived. Also, in addition to the question of what the items actually measure, ongoing validation efforts are lacking and such insufficient evidence brings into question whether the MOST can produce reliable and valid scores for its intended purpose. Although there are few alternatives for measuring organizational knowledge and understanding per se, readers seeking an alternative instrument will find several that measure management competencies and skills including the Kirkpatrick Management and Supervisory Skills Series (T7:1369); the General Management In-Basket (T7:1066), also designed to be independent of any particular job classification; Management & Leadership Systems (T7:1493); and to a lesser degree two instruments that measure managerial strengths and weaknesses, the Management Development Questionnaire (T7:1497) and the Management Effectiveness Profile System (T7:1498).

REVIEWERS' REFERENCES

American Educational Research Association, American Psychological Association, & National Council on Measurement in Education. (1999). *Standards for educational and psychological testing.* Washington, DC: American Educational Research Association.

Society for Industrial and Organizational Psychology, Inc. (2003). *Principles for the validation and use of personal selection procedures.* Bowling Green, OH: The author.

[116]

Mechanical Aptitude Test (Form MAT-AR2-C).

Purpose: For evaluating mechanical aptitude.

Population: Applicants for jobs that require the ability to learn mechanical skills.
Publication Dates: 2002–2004.
Scores: Total score only covering 4 areas: Household Objects, Work-Production and Maintenance, School-Science and Physics, Hand and Power Tools.
Administration: Group.
Price Data, 2007: $21 per consumable self-scoring test booklet (minimum order of 20); $24.95 per manual (2004, 12 pages).
Time: (20) minutes.
Comments: Self-scoring instrument.
Author: Roland T. Ramsay.
Publisher: Ramsay Corporation.

Review of the Mechanical Aptitude Test (Form MAT-AR2-C) by M. DAVID MILLER, Professor of Educational Psychology, University of Florida, Gainesville, FL:

DESCRIPTION. The Mechanical Aptitude Test (Form MAT-AR2-C) was developed in May 2004 as an updated version of the MAT. This updated version allows self-scoring. The MAT measures the ability to learn and perform production and maintenance job activities. The new version of the test uses stimuli from daily home and work life. The MAT manual reports four reasons for the updated version. First, the test is an updated measure of mechanical aptitude in its content. Second, the MAT provides a short and user-friendly measure of mechanical aptitudes that can be self-scored. Third, the MAT is free of references to city/rural or gender-based content. Fourth, the test is developed to be more appropriate to the context of the 21st century. In the administration directions, the MAT is described as being used for employee selection.

DEVELOPMENT. The MAT is a 36-item test written by Industrial/Organizational psychologists based on their review of other tests and books. The 36 items cover four areas of mechanical aptitude: Household Objects (11 items), Work Production and Maintenance (9 items), School Science and Physics (6 items), and Hand and Power Tools (10 items). Item analyses are based on the 30 items that were on the earlier version of the MAT. Item level data are not reported for the current version of the test. For the 30 items, item difficulties range from .33 to .94 with a median of .68. Item discriminations (point-biserial correlations) range from .12 to .45 with a median of .36.

TECHNICAL. Technical information is provided for the MAT. However, it is not always clear what form of the test was used in the validity studies. Data are provided on reliability, validity, and norms.

Reliability coefficients (KR20) and standard errors of measurement are reported from three studies. The three studies represent three populations: post-secondary technical school students, applicants for food production jobs, and a mixed pool of applicants, students, and others. The internal consistency reliability coefficients range from .65 to .72. The range of reliability coefficients is directly related to differences in sampling. That is, lower reliabilities are associated with more restricted ranges in sampling (i.e., lower standard deviations). The standard errors of measurement also vary as a function of the sampling and are approximately 2.50 units on the 36-item test.

Validity evidence is reported using the more traditional content-related, criterion-related, and construct rather than the current emphases in the *Standards for Educational and Psychological Testing* (AERA, APA, & NCME, 1999). Content-related validity is reported as the care taken to measure competencies required on the job in the test development process. No additional content studies using outside experts were conducted after the test was initially developed. Criterion-related validation data are reported from two studies. For two samples of postsecondary technical school students, the MAT was positively correlated with a test of mechanical job knowledge (.48) and GPA (.40). For a sample of hourly workers at a food industry plant, the MAT was positively correlated with supervisor ratings on their ability to troubleshoot equipment (.21) and their ability to enter and receive information using the computer (.32). Finally, construct validity was established by examining correlations between the MAT and another measure of mechanical aptitude. The MAT had high positive correlations with the Wiesen Test of Mechanical Aptitude (.72).

Normative data are provided for each form of the MAT. The sample sizes for the norms range from $N = 109$ (Form 1) to $N = 994$ (Form MAT-AR2). The normative data show the conversion from raw scores to percentile rank.

COMMENTARY. The reliability of the MAT is adequate but not high. This finding suggests that the use of the MAT is limited for high-stakes decisions (e.g., employment). Although the manual reports that the test was developed as "a series of exercises to be used in employee selection" (p. 5), the reliability data suggest that other information should be used in addition to the MAT. That is, the reliability data suggest that the MAT could be useful in helping to make employment decisions but only as part of a larger portfolio of information on the candidate. Clearly, these test scores alone are not sufficient for making high stakes decisions about individuals.

Validity is not a property of the test but instead is based on particular uses and interpretations of the test scores. The manual suggests that the test can be used for employee selection. However, validity evidence should be produced locally for this type of use until enough evidence is established to conduct a validity generalization study.

The test has been shown to be correlated with other measures of mechanical knowledge and ability, which may provide evidence of the construct being measured (i.e., mechanical aptitude). These data provide good evidence for interpreting scores but are not adequate for using the scores for employee selection. Evidence on employee selection is based on a single study of hourly workers at a food industry plant in the Midwest. Although the evidence in that study is convincing, it is also limited to a single occupation within one plant in the Midwest. When considering using the MAT for employee selection, additional validation would be required for the local use of the test with a clear specification of the jobs and the criteria for job success. At a minimum, the company should review the content of the test for relevance to their particular job and correlations should be established between job performance and the MAT.

The norms for the MAT are based on samples that are similarly limited. Presumably, random sampling techniques were not used. The manual also does not provide a description of the populations or the samples on which the norms are based. Based on the data described for the reliability and validity studies, it appears that the norms may be based on samples limited by a single job description in a single context (e.g., school or plant).

SUMMARY. Employee selection is a high-stakes use of a test that requires sound psychometric evidence that the test is useful for that purpose. The Mechanical Aptitude Test (Form MAT-

AR2-C) has gathered psychometric evidence to show that it measures the construct well, although this evidence is limited in scope. Moreover, moderate reliability suggests that other information should also be used in making decisions about employment. In addition, the evidence for predicting job performance is limited to a single study. The study is limited by occurring in a single plant with a single job type. Thus, the MAT is promising as a measure for predicting job performance, but additional studies are still needed for usage in employee selection except in those narrow contexts within which it has been used.

REVIEWER'S REFERENCE

American Educational Research Association, American Psychological Association, & National Council on Measurement in Education. (1999). *Standards for educational and psychological testing.* Washington, DC: AERA.

[117]

Mechanical Maintenance Trainee (Form UKM-1C).

Purpose: Selecting mechanical maintenance trainees.
Population: Applicants with mechanical training and experience necessary for entry into a training program.
Publication Dates: 1998–2005.
Scores, 13: Hydraulics, Pneumatics, Print Reading, Welding, Power Transmission, Lubrication, Pumps, Piping, Rigging, Maintenance, Shop Machines, Tools/Material & Equipment, Total.
Administration: Group.
Price Data, 2007: $21 per consumable self-scoring test booklet (minimum order of 20); $24.95 per manual (1999, 18 pages).
Time: (60) minutes (untimed).
Comments: Self-scoring instrument.
Author: Roland T. Ramsay.
Publisher: Ramsay Corporation.

Review of the Mechanical Maintenance Trainee Test (Form UKM-1C) by KEVIN J. McCARTHY, Staff Psychologist, State of Louisiana, Department of Health and Hospitals, ELMHS Facility, Jackson, LA:

DESCRIPTION. The Mechanical Maintenance Trainee Test (Form UKM-1C) is an instrument designed to assess the mechanical aptitude of trainees, specifically testing knowledge and skills. It consists of 60 multiple-choice questions administered under supervision as a paper-and-pencil examination. There are two items that serve as practice exercises to familiarize the candidate with the test format. There is no time limit for completing the task, but examinees are told that "you should not need more than an hour" (manual, p 9). The test booklet contains illustrations in each section to assist the candidate in understanding the knowledge and skills being evaluated. The 60 item test is divided into 12 test sections. The items included under all test sections were "independently ranked by eight job experts (maintenance supervisors)" (manual, p. 4).

The test sections include: Hydraulics (6 items); Pneumatics (5); Print Reading (5); Welding (4); Power Transmission (6); Lubrication (5) Pumps (3); Piping (3); Rigging (3); Maintenance (9); Shop Machines (4); and Tools, Materials and Equipment (7). The test items are referenced to drawings, prints, and diagrams, which are essential to making the correct answer selections. Answers are recorded on a separate self-scoring answer sheet within the test booklet. Including the answer page, the test booklet is 11 pages.

The Mechanical Maintenance Trainee Test appears to be a rationally derived instrument in which the items evaluate the candidate's understanding of the basic concepts of maintenance work skills. Items were chosen for meaningfulness and relationship to necessary skills and job knowledge. The test utilizes problem-solving strategies as an essential mechanism for determining the strengths and weaknesses of individual applicants. The test publisher noted that a "job analysis" was conducted in the development of this test (manual, p. 1). The instrument is an adequate measure of the candidate's ability to function in a work environment. The test appears to be organized in a logical format. The authors have included several caveats that direct the administrator's attention to possible problem situations that could influence the test outcome. These include the following examples: "examinee did not have bifocal glasses examinee felt ill and nauseous; examinee was educated in another country and is somewhat slow in reading English; examinee had less than six years of education and reads with difficulty" (manual, p 7). The examiner's instructions have been documented in a helpful manner.

DEVELOPMENT. The Mechanical Maintenance Trainee Test (Form UKM-1C) is published by Ramsay Corporation. It is noted in the manual that "the job of trainee differs from apprentice.... An apprenticeship usually requires from 3 to 4 years and begins from a very basic level. The trainee usually begins at a higher level and requires up to 2 years of training" (manual, p. 1). The original test items were selected from the Ramsay Corporation's item bank by a group of job experts. The test was then administered to 1,079 individuals. At that point in its developmental stage, two Industrial/Organizational psychologists selected the best 60 items according to point-biserial discrimination indexes and item difficulty.

The test manual does not contain a viable breakdown of the group membership from the item selection study (N = 1,079) in terms of descriptive statistics or referent data, which might be helpful in determining the usefulness of this instrument in specific applications. The data provided for review contain no reference to the diversity of the group membership, or its unique characteristics. The manual does include (Table 4, p. 12) an analysis of item difficulty and point-biserial discrimination indexes for all test items.

TECHNICAL. The reliability coefficient and standard error of measurement were reported in table format. The reliability coefficient (.87) is acceptable and the standard error of measurement (3.48) is reasonable. The author's efforts should be focused upon expansion of the reliability data to enhance the utility of this instrument. Little is known about the referent group; therefore, the resulting test data have limited usefulness. In terms of validity data, there were few useful data offered to support the contentions of the test author. Content-related validity was based upon a summary statement containing no supporting data. No criterion-related validity studies were completed on this instrument. Rather, the author chose to address this gap in psychometric analysis by offering the hypothesis that "it would be predictive of job performance" (manual, p. 13). Construct validity was also addressed using a summary statement containing no supporting data. Normative data were addressed in a similarly insufficient manner. The author did provide a table of cumulative percents for Form UKM-1C (manual, pp. 15–16). Altogether, the author's identification of psychometric properties for this test is deficient and in need of revision or significant supplemental data analysis.

COMMENTARY. The format of the test booklet lends itself to clarity, enhancing the ability of test takers to conceptualize and understand the knowledge being evaluated. The author captured the essence of the basic skills and knowledge necessary to perform mechanical maintenance jobs. It appears to be a useful measure based upon a review of the target job-related concepts. The primary problem with the instrument is the limited data available to support its psychometric properties. This limitation should be addressed to ensure the future adaptation of this instrument in appropriate settings.

SUMMARY. The conceptual framework utilized in developing the Mechanical Maintenance Trainee Test (Form UKM–1C) appears to be sound. The instrument itself is illustrated and self-contained in a self-scoring format. Upon inspection, it seems to be an adequate measure of basic mechanical maintenance concepts. The test focuses upon the requisite knowledge of necessary skills and abilities to transition to this type of work environment successfully. Its value will be substantially improved through pertinent research studies and the development of data that will further clarify its psychometric properties.

[118]
Mechanical Technician A.

Purpose: For selecting mid-journey level maintenance technicians for jobs in the metals or manufacturing industry.

Population: Applicants and incumbents for jobs requiring mechanical maintenance knowledge and skills at the highest level.

Publication Dates: 2003–2005.

Scores, 6: Hydraulics & Pneumatics, Print Reading, Power Transmission & Lubrication, Pumps & Piping, Mechanical Maintenance Principles, Total.

Administration: Group.

Forms, 2: MTA-XC, MTA-YC.

Price Data, 2007: $21 per consumable self-scoring test booklet (minimum order of 20); $24.95 per manual (2005, 18 pages).

Time: (60) minutes (unitmed).

Comments: Self-scoring instrument; Form MTA-YC is an alternate equivalent of Form MTA-XC.

Author: Roland T. Ramsay.

Publisher: Ramsay Corporation.

Review of the Mechanical Technician A by MICHAEL D. BIDERMAN, Professor of Psychology, and BART L. WEATHINGTON, Assistant Professor of Psychology, University of Tennessee at Chattanooga, Chattanooga, TN:

DESCRIPTION. The Ramsay Corporation Job Skills (RCJS) Mechanical Technician *A* is a 60-item multiple-choice test developed to measure the highest level of knowledge and skills required for maintenance technicians. Intended specifically for jobs requiring maintenance knowledge and skills, representative job titles based on the *Dictionary of Occupational Titles* (U.S. Department of Labor, 1991) definitions are Maintenance Repairer, Industrial, Maintenance Mechanic, and Millwright.

Two forms of the test are available. Form MTA-YC uses a separate answer sheet and is scored with an overlay key. Form MTA-XC is in a self-scoring format. Both formats assess nine basic knowledge areas: Hydraulics, Pneumatics, Print Reading, Power Transmission, Lubrication, Pumps, Piping, Mechanical Maintenance Principles, and Safety. For scoring purposes, however, an overall score is calculated based on total number of items answered correctly.

DEVELOPMENT. Originally developed as part of a series of 80-item measures for C, B, and A Mechanical Technicians in 1995, the forms of the test reviewed here are shortened and consist of 60 items. Form MTA-YC was created in 2003 and the self-scoring version (Form MTA-XC) was created in 2005. Both forms were designed to be equivalent and cover the same knowledge areas.

For the original test development, 18 job experts (maintenance supervisors) were given a list of knowledge and skill areas thought to be necessary for the position of Maintenance Technician A. No information is provided in the test manual about how these knowledge and skill areas were identified. Each supervisor independently ranked the importance of each area and estimated the percent of time spent in each. Specific results are not provided in the test manual. The Ramsay Corporation's database was then used to identify and to assess each category. No information is provided on the initial development of these items.

The process by which the 80-item versions of the test were reduced to 60 items is vague. The test manual states that two industrial psychologists picked the 60 items according to both item point-biserial discrimination indices and item difficulty. The items were selected in the same proportions that were represented in the original 80-item tests.

TECHNICAL.
Standardization. Standardization was base on two small samples—one sample of 27 mainte nance applicants and one sample of 38 mechanic maintenance applicants both assessed in 200: The first sample was given Form MTA-XC an the other sample was given Form MTA-YC. table in the manual gives percentile ranks for eac sample. All respondents achieved scores of 24 c higher on Form MTA-XC and 27 or higher o Form MTA-YC. Mean score for the 27 respon dents given Form MTA-XC was 39.63 with SD 6.43. Mean of those given Form MTA-YC wa 41.79 with SD = 5.68. No measure or test c equivalence of the two forms was presented.

Reliability. Reliability estimates are based o the above-mentioned small samples. For the firs sample (N = 27) the KR_{20} estimate was .76. Fo the second sample (N = 38) the KR_{20} estimat was .73. These values are somewhat lower tha the .85 recommended as the "absolute minimur in most selection situations" by Gatewood an Field (2001, p. 145). Estimated standard error of measurement were 3.15 and 2.95 for Sample 1 and 2, respectively. No test-retest reliabilit estimates are available nor are correlations be tween the two forms.

Validity. No criterion-related validity dat are presented although the manual mentions tha similar tests developed by the test manufacture have shown significant correlations with supervi sory ratings of job performance. The manual cite another manual for administration and scoring c a test called MecTest in this regard. The manua argues that the content validity is the appropriat model for such a test, saying that the test is paper-and-pencil form of a work sample. No othe formal evidence for content validity is presented No formal studies of construct validity are re ported by the manual. The manual states that th construct of knowledge and skill in maintenance i represented by knowledge areas listed in a table c the knowledge areas sampled by the MTA-X(and MTA-YC. This table contains a list of th areas Hydraulics, Pneumatics, Print Reading Power Transmission, Lubrication, Pumps, Piping Mechanical Maintenance Principles, and Safety.

COMMENTARY. The test represents a sub stantial first step in the measurement of knowl edge and skills of mechanical technicians. Th lack of criterion-related validity is clearly an argu ment against its use. The lack of construct validity information is also a problem. For example, users of the test might wish to know whether test scores correlate with general cognitive ability to assess the extent to which use of the test might create adverse impact. It is unclear how well the items in the test will stand the test of time. Many of the items referenced what appear to be specific mechanical devices or processes. It would be desirable to have some indication of the generality of these references and of the likelihood of their being important for future users of the test.

SUMMARY. Examination of the items of the MTA-XC test clearly suggests to a psychologist not trained in mechanics that the items have high content validity. The MTA-XC test booklet is quite legible and it appears that self- or administrator scoring of an individual booklet would be easy. The time to take the test should be no more than 60 minutes. Reading level appears to be no higher than would be expected of a mechanical technician, although the test items contain many technical terms and phrases (e.g., "Vickers balanced piston-type relief valve," "micrometer," "reciprocating compressor," "false brineling") that only such a technician would be expected to understand. If one accepts the argument presented in the manual that content validity is the appropriate model for such a test, then the content of the test items appears to support that model. The lack of criterion-related validity data, in spite of the fact that the most recent Form MTA-YC has been available since 2003 is discouraging, however. Because the test is designed for use in selection and promotion and because criterion-related validity is of primary importance in such applications, users of the test should make every effort to obtain such criterion-related validity data.

REVIEWERS' REFERENCES

Gatewood, R. D., & Field, H. S. (2001). *Human resource selection* (5th ed.). New York: Harcourt.
U.S. Department of Labor. (1991). *Dictionary of occupational titles* (4th ed., rev.). Washington, DC: U.S. Government Printing Office.

Review of the Mechanical Technician A by MARY L. GARNER, Associate Professor of Mathematics, Kennesaw State University, Kennesaw, GA:

DESCRIPTION. The Mechanical Technician A test is a paper-and-pencil test that has 60 multiple-choice items. The test is designed to assess the skills of a job applicant who is applying for a position as an advanced journey-level maintenance mechanic. There are two forms of the test:

MTA-YC, which is in a standard booklet form; and MTA-XC, which is in the form of a self-scoring test booklet. Each form has 18 items addressing Hydraulics and Pneumatics, 5 addressing Print Reading, 15 addressing Power Transmission and Lubrication, 11 addressing Pumps and Piping, and 11 addressing Mechanical Maintenance Principles. The manual for administration and scoring provides a script for test administration and simple directions for scoring. Test-takers have an unlimited amount of time for the test, but administrators are instructed to record the amount of time taken by each examinee.

DEVELOPMENT. Skills necessary for an advanced journey-level maintenance mechanic were ranked in order of importance by 18 maintenance supervisors. No information is provided about how these maintenance supervisors were selected, nor specifically what skills were ranked. Interrater agreement is reported as .90. The maintenance supervisors then picked 80 items for each form of the test from the Ramsay Corporation's database, for a total of 80 items in eight categories of Hydraulics, Pneumatics, Print Reading, Power Transmission, Lubrication, Pumps, Piping, and Mechanical Maintenance Principles. Two industrial psychologists then selected 60 of the 80 items, reportedly according to item difficulty and item point-biserial correlation coefficients as indices of discrimination.

TECHNICAL. Data were provided from two samples of job applicants—Form MTA-XC was administered to a sample of 27 and Form MTA-YC was administered to a sample of 38. Both samples consisted of applicants for mechanical maintenance jobs at a "large metals manufacturer" (manual, p. 10). No further information on the samples is provided. Under "Normative Data," raw scores on each of the tests are converted to percentiles, but essentially no information regarding the sample population is provided. Raw scores on the tests ranged from 24 to 52 with a mean of 39.63 (*s.d.* 6.43) on the MTA-XC and 27 to 51 with a mean of 41.79 (*s.d.* 5.68) on the MTA-YC. Item difficulties ranged from .15 to .96 on the MTA-XC and .05 to 1.00 on the MTA-YC. Point-biserial discrimination indices are also provided. The KR-20 reliability coefficient was .76 for the MTA-XC and .73 for the MTA-YC.

No evidence of validity is provided, except the statement that the skills tested are required for the job. No information is provided as to how to interpret the results of the test or what level of achievement on the test is adequate for effectively accomplishing the tasks of a maintenance mechanic.

COMMENTARY. The test has a very specific, well-defined content domain and much face validity. There is, however, little evidence presented of the reliability and validity of the test including the equivalence of the two forms. There is no evidence presented of the test's ability to predict on-the-job success, the main purpose of the test. The items on the test were originally part of the corporation's database, but no background data on the items were provided. The only analysis of the two tests is a summary of the data collected on a sample of 27 job applicants for one test form, and 38 job applicants for the other test form. There is not much that can be concluded from such a small sample with unknown characteristics.

Great detail is included in the instructions for administration, including recording the time an examinee takes to complete the test. No information is provided, however, about how the test should be used or how the timing of the test should influence its use.

SUMMARY. The Mechanical Technician A is a pencil-and-paper, 60-item multiple-choice test with two forms. It was designed to assess job applicants' skills associated with an advanced journey-level maintenance mechanic. Administration and scoring are straightforward. The reliability and validity of the test are not addressed.

[119]
Mechanical Technician B.

Purpose: For selecting mid-journey level maintenance technicians for jobs in the metals or manufacturing industry.
Population: Applicants and incumbents for jobs requiring mechanical maintenance knowledge and skills.
Publication Dates: 2003–2005.
Scores, 8: Hydraulics & Pneumatics, Print Reading, Burning/Fabricating/Welding & Rigging, Power Transmission & Lubrication, Pumps & Piping, Mechanical Maintenance Principles, Shop Equipment & Tools, Total.
Administration: Group.
Forms, 2: MTB-XC, MTB-YC.
Price Data, 2007: $21 per consumable self-scoring test booklet (minimum order of 20); $24.95 per manual (2005, 18 pages).

Time: (60) minutes (untimed).
Comments: Self-scoring instrument; Form MTB-YC is an alternate equivalent of Form MTB-XC.
Author: Roland T. Ramsay.
Publisher: Ramsay Corporation.

Review of Mechanical Technician B by GREGORY J. CIZEK, Professor of Educational Measurement and Evaluation, University of North Carolina Chapel Hill, Chapel Hill, NC:

DESCRIPTION. The Mechanical Technician B (MTB) examination is the second of three-test series covering beginning, intermediate and advanced levels, respectively, of mechanical knowledge and skill relevant to U.S. Department of Labor occupations Industrial Maintenance Repairer, Maintenance Mechanic, and Millwright. The precise purpose of the test is somewhat ambiguous. In some locations in the test manual it is stated that the test is an "achievement test" (manual, p. 14) and is "intended for use with applicants and incumbents for jobs where maintenance and skill are necessary parts of job activities" (p. 1). However, in another location it is stated that the test is "to be used in employee selection" (p. 8). As can be seen, the distinction is important as regards the appropriate sources of validity evidence and warranted interpretations of examinee test performance.

Available test materials include two forms of the MTB that are intended to be "alternate-equivalent" versions. Both forms consist of 60 four-option, multiple-choice items. The forms differ in some technical ways (as is described in a subsequent section of this review) but also in form design. One of the forms (Form MTB-YC) is designed as a reusable test booklet intended to be hand-scored using an overlay key. The other form (Form MTB-XC) is consumable and intended to be easily scored by the test taker, although it does not seem likely that a potential employer would want a presumably high-stakes selection instrument to be scored by the test takers themselves.

Both forms of the MTB are well formatted, clear, and fairly easy to use, although there are several aspects that could be improved. For example, the practice items for one form are printed on the outside of the test booklet cover so that examinees do not see the actual test items until told to begin working. On the other form, the practice items are printed on the left-facing page with the actual items easily visible to examinees on the right-hand page. An instruction to "Go on to the next page" is printed on one of the pages of Form MTB-YC, but not on others. And, in the same form, one of the items printed in the test booklet apparently needed to be replaced; a sticker with a new item printed on it has been pasted into the test booklet. The method for choosing an answer requires examinees to place an X in a box for each item; however, examinees are instructed not to erase any answers, but to indicate a changed response by circling the original response and placing an X by the intended choice. Such directions are odd indeed and are likely very novel to examinees and a potential source of response recording mistakes or scoring error. It is not clear what an examinee would do if he or she wished to change back to a circled response, and it is unclear why the test requires number 2 pencils (presumably with erasers attached) when erasures are not permitted and the answer documents are not intended for optical scanning. The test administration manual indicates that a "stopwatch or accurate timer" is a required item for administering the test, although examinees are told, according to the script provided, that "there is no time limit" (manual, p. 9). Finally, the instructions for the test require examinees to record, in addition to name, date, and other customary information, their social security numbers. Although the requirement that social security number be recorded is likely for identification purposes, it is also likely that some examinees might justifiably balk at disclosing that information in an era of rampant identity theft and when other equally accurate methods would suffice for this purpose.

The directions for test administration are succinct and exemplary on many counts. For example, the manual directs test administrators to ensure, in advance of testing, that the testing conditions are comfortable, secure, and conducive to accurate measurement. Cautions are provided regarding distractions; possession by examinees of devices that could send, receive, or store test information; and positive identification of test takers. The manual provides specific instructions that test administrators, prior to the test, "should have taken the tests, should be familiar with the procedures for administering each test, and should be familiar with the test items" (manual, p. 7) and

should "strive to put examinees at ease so that they may do their best work" (p. 6). During the first minutes of the test, administrators are directed to "rapidly, but unobtrusively and quietly, check the work of each examinee to see that directions are being carried out and there are no misunderstandings of the procedures to be followed" (p. 7). For the remainder of the testing period, test administrators are instructed to "make notes regarding any significant characteristics and behavior which might indicate that the test results may not represent accurate measurements of ability" (p. 7). In summary, it is apparent that the test developers had as a clear goal the fair and accurate measurement of the intended content.

DEVELOPMENT. The MTB forms reviewed here were developed in 2003 and are actually shortened forms of an 80-item test, called Maintenance Technician B, developed in 1995. The longer version covers 11 content areas. Those 11 areas were reduced to 7 areas in the shortened forms with varying numbers of items. The categories (with numbers of items shown in parentheses) include: Hydraulics & Pneumatics (13); Print Reading (4); Burning, Fabricating, Welding, & Rigging (10); Power Transmission & Lubrication (12); Pumps & Piping (8); Mechanical Maintenance Principles (10); and Shop Equipment & Tools (3). The reduction from 11 to 7 content areas was accomplished by combining categories. For example, two previously separate categories of Pumps and Piping were merged to form the single area, Pumps & Piping. Scoring of the MTB forms yields subscores in each of the 7 content areas and a total score. However, no apparent use is made of the subscores, and all technical information provided with the MTB forms pertains to the total (raw) score.

Development of the shorter MTB-XC and MTB-YC forms drew heavily from the longer version. The technical manual for the shorter forms describes their development largely in terms of the procedures used to create the longer version. The manual indicates that 18 maintenance supervisors ranked the importance of each entry on a list of knowledge and skill areas provided to them on a "Maintenance Activity List" and that rater agreement was .90. In addition, the raters provided estimates of the percentage of time that maintenance technicians spend in each of the 7 content areas. Finally, the same panel then chose items from an extant item pool to create the original 80-item form.

Unfortunately, much information necessary to evaluate the development of the MTB forms is not provided. For example, it is not stated how the maintenance activity list was obtained, how many entries appeared on the list, what qualifications or other characteristics the raters possessed, how the rankings were done, how the agreement coefficient was calculated, or how the importance and frequency ratings were combined to derive test specifications. The most serious omission is the fact that no information on item development is provided. A potential test user does not know the qualifications of the item developers; what, if any, guidelines were used to create the items; what, if any, procedures were employed to ensure item validity, clarity, readability, absence of bias, and accuracy of item stems, graphics, and answer keys; and what, if any, procedures were used for field-testing the items.

From the 80-item form, the two shortened forms appear to have been created by deleting poorly performing items from the longer version. According to the manual, this task was performed by two industrial psychologists who selected 60 items for the shortened forms in proportion to the content category percentages in the longer version and by using "criteria of item point biserial indexes and item difficulty" (manual, p. 5). The selected items comprised 7 content areas representing a reconfiguration of the 11 content areas in the longer version. No other information on the development of the forms is provided. In addition to addressing the omissions listed previously, it would seem necessary for the manual to provide information such as the qualifications of the industrial psychologists who performed the test construction task, the discrimination and difficulty targets they used as criteria, and what empirical work, if any, was performed to support the content category reconfiguration.

TECHNICAL. Extremely limited technical information is provided in the manual accompanying the MTB-XC and MTB-YC. The manual has sections labeled Reliability, Item Analysis, Validity Data, and Normative Data.

Information on the reliability of MTB scores is limited to KR_{20} reliability estimates and associated standard errors of measurement (*SEMs*) obtained in two samples (n = 30 and 26, respectively)

of "Applicants for maintenance jobs at a larg[e] metals manufacturer" (manual, p. 10). The re[-] ported values of KR_{20} for the two forms are .79 an[d] .69, with *SEMs* of 3.13 and 3.10, respectivel[y.] Although reliabilities of this magnitude are mo[d]est to good for a test of this length, the samp[le] sizes are too small to be confident in the stabili[ty] of the reliability estimates and the groups o[n] which the estimates are based were more homog[-]enous—all of them were applicants—than would b[e] desirable given that the MTB claims utility f[or] both applicants and job incumbents. In additio[n,] the standard deviations of the test scores for th[e] two groups (S_x = 6.84 and 5.57, respectively[)] suggest that the groups were also dissimilar i[n] unknown ways. No information about the group[s] beyond the sample sizes, means, and standar[d] deviations is provided. Finally, the suggestion i[n] the manual that "These reliabilities are expected t[o] improve when larger samples are tested" (p. 10) [is] misleading, as the magnitude of the reliabilit[y] estimate has little to do with the sample size. T[o] the extent that a future sample of whatever siz[e] has similar characteristics to the (unknown) char[-]acteristics of the sample used to obtain the curren[t] reliability estimates, the future reliability estimate[s] would likely be similar to the current ones. Only t[o] the extent that a future sample is *dissimilar* to th[e] research sample (for example, by being more het[-]erogeneous) would one expect the reliability esti[-]mate to increase.

Several recommendations come to mind [if] additional information on reliability can be incor[-]porated in a revision of the technical manua[l.] Considerably more detail on the characteristics o[f] the research samples is necessary. Information o[n] the stability of scores (via a test-retest coefficien[t) would be desirable. Evidence, rather than merel[y] claims of form equivalence, should be presented b[y] including an alternate-forms reliability coefficien[t.]

In the section labeled "Item Analysis," [a] table of item difficulty indices (*p*-values) and dis[-]crimination indices (point-biserial correlations) i[s] provided, which shows these values for the 6[0] items on each form. In general, these values seer[m] appropriate for a test of this type. For example, th[e] point-biserial indices, with few exceptions, ar[e] positive and exceed .20. On the surface, this resu[lt] might appear to be the product of high-qualit[y] item development and refinement. However, [a] note describing the calculation of the discrimina[-] tion indices reveals that the item-total correlations were calculated using the subarea scores as the criterion variable. Because the MTB has some very small subareas (comprising as few as 3 items), it is likely that the item-total correlations are spuriously high due to the fact that the item score itself is included in–and often contributes a large proportion to–the criterion score. For the future, it is recommended either that a corrected item-total correlation be used or that the total test score (i.e., not the subarea score) be used as the criterion variable, or both.

Concerning the validity of score interpretations, empirical evidence is essentially nonexistent and the theoretical rationales provided are weak. The validity section is divided according to the outdated three-part view of validity with no apparent recognition of the unitary view of validity or the guidelines comprising the *Standards for Educational and Psychological Testing* (AERA, APA, & NCME, 1999) or the more recent *Principles for the Validation and Use of Personnel Selection Procedures* (Society for Industrial and Organizational Psychology, 2003).

Information on content validity–claimed elsewhere in the manual to be the primary source of validity evidence–consists of merely two sentences. The first sentence (in its entirety) claims that "The content-related validity of the test is assured when the behaviors required on the test are also required on the job" and the second sentence (in its entirety) asserts that the MTB test "is a paper-and-pencil form of a work sample" (manual, p. 14). Although there is some logical support for validity that accrues from the sampling of essential job behaviors, no job analysis data are provided and no evidence of alignment between job demands and item content is presented.

For an instrument used for selection decisions, criterion-related validity evidence would seem to be paramount. The single paragraph on criterion-related validity indicates that "the test has not been part of a criterion-related validation study" (manual, p. 14). The manual states only the hypothesis that test scores should be "predictive of job performance measures in jobs requiring knowledge of maintenance" (p. 14) and the claim that "Similar knowledge and skills tests developed [by the test publisher] have shown significant correlations with supervisory ratings of job performance" (p. 14). The single paragraph on construct validity

evidence similarly reveals that "No formal studies of construct validity have been conducted, but construct validity may be enhanced by the procedures of [test] development" (p. 14). Although this assertion has merit, it does not add support to the validity argument (Kane, 2006) that needs to be made to support the use of scores on the MTB forms, particularly because the test development procedures used are (as described previously) so poorly documented.

Two sentences and a single table comprise the information on standardization. The norms were developed based on the same two samples used for calculating the reliability estimates described previously in this review, and the same concerns are in order regarding the very small and unrepresentative samples, the instability of the results–in this case, the norms–and the need for much greater information on the participants and procedures used. Separate norms are reported for each of the two samples, and the percentile ranks associated with the same raw score differ. The same raw score is often associated with dramatically different percentile ranks; for example, the percentile ranks associated with a raw score of 50 are 83.3 on one form of the MTB and 98.1 on another. Further, because of the small, restricted-range samples, norms are essentially only available for raw scores between 25 and 50. Perhaps most troubling is that no cut scores or predictive validity are available and prospective users are not provided with any information that would assist them in using the data.

SUMMARY AND OVERALL EVALUATION. The Mechanical Technician B test purports to be useful as an achievement measure for employee selection with new or incumbent workers in mechanical repair and maintenance positions. Although the materials supporting the use of the test have a modest veneer suggesting appropriateness for that purpose, there is little in the way of any empirical evidence that the test can be used for the intended purpose. Overall, the test development procedures used appear to have modest face validity, but specific information on the development of the MTB is seriously inadequate in the opinion of this reviewer.

The strengths of the test include its clarity, ease of use, and attention to detail in administration directions. However, these strengths are far outweighed by weaknesses in test development procedures and documentation, skimpy reliability data, absence of evidence for validity of scores, unstable and nonrepresentative norms, and lack of any apparent grounding in professionally accepted standards for test development and analysis. Potential users of the test are not provided even the barest of information on the ways in which test results might be used properly, and the best advice is probably that the test should not be used for any selection or classification decisions until far more work is done to bolster its psychometric properties.

REVIEWER'S REFERENCES

American Educational Research Association, American Psychological Association, & National Council on Measurement in Education [AERA/APA/NCME]. (1999). *Standards for educational and psychological testing.* Washington, DC: American Educational Research Association.

Kane, M. T. (2006). Validation. In R. L. Brennan (ed.), *Educational measurement* (4th ed.; pp. 17-64). New York: American Council on Education/Praeger.

Society for Industrial and Organizational Psychology. (2003). *Principles for the validation and use of personnel selection procedures.* Bowling Green, OH: Author.

[120]

Mechanical Technician C.

Purpose: For selecting entry-journey level maintenance technicians for jobs in the metals or manufacturing industry.

Population: Applicants and incumbents for jobs requiring mechanical maintenance knowledge and skills.

Publication Dates: 2003–2005.

Scores, 8: Hydraulics & Pneumatics, Print Reading, Burning/Fabricating/Welding & Rigging, Power Transmission & Lubrication, Pumps & Piping, Mechanical Maintenance Principles, Shop Equipment & Tools, Total.

Administration: Group.

Forms, 2: MTC-YC, MTC-XC.

Price Data, 2007: $21 per consumable self-scoring test booklet (minimum order of 20); $24.95 per manual (2005, 18 pages).

Time: (60) minutes (untimed).

Comments: Self-scoring instrument; Form MTC-YC is an alternate equivalent of Form MTC-XC.

Author: Roland T. Ramsay.

Publisher: Ramsay Corporation.

Review of the Mechanical Technician C by RUSSELL W. SMITH, Senior Psychometrician, Alpine Testing Solutions, Henderson, NY:

DESCRIPTION. The Mechanical Technician C (MTC) is a 60-item, selected-response test administered by paper-and-pencil. There are two alternate forms, one of which is self-scoring. It is a starting-level examination intended to measure knowledge and skill for maintenance jobs. The specific job titles are Maintenance Repairer, In-

dustrial; Maintenance Mechanic, and Millwright. The examination has seven content areas: Hydraulics and Pneumatics; Print Reading; Burning, Fabrication, Welding, and Rigging; Power Transmission and Lubrication; Pumps and Piping; Mechanical Maintenance Principles; and Shop Equipment and Tools.

DEVELOPMENT. The current version of the examination was developed in 2003 as a shortened version of the original. The original version of the exam, developed in 1995, was the starting-level test of three tests in a hierarchical series. The original test consisted of a series of 80-item forms. The current version of the exam has two alternate 60-item forms that are said to be equivalent.

The manual for administration & scoring for the self-scored form of the examination describes a job analysis in which 18 maintenance supervisors rated the importance and the amount of time spent in knowledge and skill areas for the position of Maintenance Technician C. The same subject matter experts then selected the 80 questions in 11 different categories for each form from a database of items.

A subset of 60 items was selected based on the statistical properties of the items to meet the same content specifications proportionately for the current version. The item statistics on which the decisions were made are included in the manual. The self-scoring version, Form MTC-XC, was based on an analysis of 63 candidates. The other version, Form MTC-YC, was based on an analysis of 42 candidates. The samples were described as "mechanical maintenance applicants" (manual for administration & scoring, p. 11).

Some of the 11 original categories were combined, resulting in the seven previously listed content areas in the current version. No mention is made in the manual of reevaluating the job analysis for the current version. No mention is made of reference materials, reading lists, or resources.

TECHNICAL. The norming sample described in the manual is based on samples of 63 and 42 candidates on which the item selection decisions were made for the current forms. A table of percentile ranks for each form based on these samples is provided in the manual. No description is provided regarding the make-up of the sample used for item selection and norming, nor is evidence provided that the sample is representative of the target population.

The internal test score reliability, reported as KR-20, is .75 and .71 for the self-scoring and proctored forms, respectively. These values are described by the manual as "very good" and "good" (p. 10), respectively. The manual also states that "these reliabilities are expected to improve when larger samples are tested" (manual for administration & scoring, p. 10). No validity studies have been conducted for this exam.

COMMENTARY. The strengths of the examination include the convenience of the self-scoring form and the ease of use of the test. The weaknesses include the lack of empirical validity evidence, the lack of evidence of sample representation, and the relatively small sample size on which the norms and item statistics are based. The sample size and possible lack of representation call the reliability estimates into question. Caution should be taken when considering the item statistics, percentile ranks, and reliability indices.

SUMMARY. The Mechanical Technician C examination is designed to measure skills and knowledge necessary for beginning journey-level maintenance mechanics. It appears to have reasonable face validity and is easy to administer and score. Potential users should review the content categories and the items carefully to see if they are appropriate for the user's intended purpose. The lack of empirical validity evidence should raise serious caution for the interpretation of test scores. The norming sample is not sufficient for making normative interpretations.

[121]
Mechanical Understanding Test.

Purpose: Designed to assess how well people understand "the basic principles of physics and mechanics that determine success in handling and manipulating objects and machines."
Population: Adults.
Publication Date: 2004.
Acronym: MUT.
Scores: Total score only.
Administration: Group.
Price Data: Available from publisher.
Time: (30–40) minutes.
Authors: Erich P. Prien, Leonard D. Goodstein, and Kristin O. Prien.
Publisher: HRD Press, Inc.

Review of the Mechanical Understanding Test by PHILLIP L. ACKERMAN, Professor of Psychology, Georgia Institute of Technology, Atlanta, GA:

DESCRIPTION. The Mechanical Understanding Test (MUT) is a 65-item test, administered with paper and pencil in either individualized or group settings. Instructions for the test have no explicit timing recommendation (although the manual indicates about an hour is needed for the full administration), but appear to take a couple of minutes. The test is speeded, with a time limit of 30 minutes for completing the items. There are several varieties of items that range from traditional mechanical principles (e.g., center of mass, gravity) to abstract spatial visualization (selecting shapes that differ from other shapes) to a set of 10 map planning items (based on the Kit of Factor-Referenced Cognitive Tests; Ekstrom, French, Harmon, & Derman, 1976). The answers are selected from 3–4 multiple-choice options. The test is hand-scored, with a carbonless copy second sheet that indicates the correct answers. Only one score is derived, the total number of correct answers (so participants are not penalized for guessing). Raw scores can be converted to a percentile score, based on a single table, based on a heterogeneous set of opportunistic work and college student samples and two samples of machine operators and mechanics. The publisher notes that the test was "originally titled the Work Skills Test" but that the title did not adequately describe the "content and purpose" (technical and administrative manual, p. 3), and therefore changed the title to the Mechanical Understanding Test. The publisher represents the test as a "gender-unbiased measure of mechanical comprehension, i.e., there are no differences between the average scores of men and women" (www.hrdpress.com, downloaded January 2, 2006).

DEVELOPMENT. The Mechanical Understanding Test "was designed to assess how well people understand the principles underlying how things work in the physical world" (technical and administrative manual, p. 1). The test was developed by observing workers in the context of the *Dictionary of Occupational Titles*. Sixteen core "physical principles" were identified by the authors, including concepts that are typically included in other mechanical principles and mechanical knowledge tests (e.g., force, mass, and gravity, motion in one or two directions), but also constructs that are traditionally considered separate from the underlying construct of mechanical knowledge (e.g., perceptual speed and spatial visualization). In addition, 10 items, based on the Spatial Scanning Marker Test of Cognition, were added to the test that represent a "cognitive/planning" construct (not included in the list of 16 core physical principles identified by the authors). The test manual does not indicate how the items on the test are aligned with the final developed test (and the only item analysis presented is a list of items associated with six factors from a factor analysis of the items). The six factors identified included the Cognitive/Planning factor identified with the 10 map planning items, followed by factors of Spatial Visualization, Materials/Force/Heat/Volume, Motion/Electricity/Hydraulics, Mass/Friction/Gravity, and Center Gravity/Energy.

TECHNICAL.

Norms. Means and standard deviations are provided for a sample of "212 individuals" by gender, though there are no indications of what the nature of the sample is, other than gender. The normative sample of 1,012 individuals is a mixture of occupational and college student groups, with no separate indicators of means and standard deviations by group. No recommendations are provided regarding the population of individuals to whom these norms should be relevant or useful.

Reliability/validity. The only reliability information provided by the publisher is a reported Cronbach's alpha of .81, with an unidentified sample size and type. The publisher reports this as "indicates a quite high degree of stability" (technical and administrative manual, p. 5), but there are no indications of test-retest reliability. Because the alpha coefficient confounds item homogeneity and stability (e.g., see Ackerman & Humphreys, 1990), it is impossible to ascertain how stable the test scores are from one occasion to the next. Construct validity evidence is reported for small samples (from $N = 51$ to 85) via correlations with the Bennett Mechanical Comprehension Test (Bennett, 1994), a well-established test of mechanical knowledge, and the Trouble Shooting Test, about which no information is presented. Correlations with the Bennett test are adequate, though they are lower for mechanics than they are for college students. Concurrent criterion-related validity information is presented for two small

groups of mechanics and operators (the validity correlations were .28 and .24, respectively). The manual indicates that these validity coefficients are "sufficient to make a significant contribution to the prediction of success in jobs requiring mechanical comprehension" (technical and administrative manual, p. 6). Additional criterion-related validity evidence is reported for overall college grade point average and a college student sample. The correlation of $r = .57$ is represented as "strong support for the predictive value of the MUT, especially for the ten items tapping cognitive/planning skills—successful intelligence—in tasks requiring an aptitude for learning" (technical and administrative manual, pp. 6–7). However, given that the test is described as a measure of mechanical understanding, such a correlation appears to suggest that the test does not show discriminant validity (in that the correlations with college GPA are nearly as high as the correlations with the Bennett Test). Instead, this indicator suggests that the MUT is more of a test of intelligence than it is of mechanical understanding (e.g., see Anastasi, 1976; Murphy & Davidshofer, 2001; Nunnally, 1959).

An additional aspect of the test is noted in the manual as "gender bias" though it actually refers only to the differences between men and women in terms of average scores on the test. The manual reports that the test is not gender biased because the means for men and women are quite close (with women having a small advantage). However, the test manual fails to take account of any developments in the assessment of gender bias (e.g., differential item functioning, different validity regressions; see AERA/APA/NCME, 1999). There is also a discussion of adverse impact concepts in the manual, but no mean, reliability, or validity data were presented for different racial and ethnic groups.

COMMENTARY. The sparse presentation of information about the test (e.g., item analyses, reliability, validity) in the manual, along with the apparent heterogeneity of underlying constructs that entered into the construction of the test (mixing mechanical principles with cognitive/planning items), make it difficult to understand exactly what constructs the test is assessing. The limited criterion-related validity data suggest that the test is perhaps a better representation of general intellectual abilities than it is a measure of mechanical understanding. Coupling the low predictive validity of the test for performance of workers in jobs that appear to require mechanical understanding with the lack of gender differences that appear in most mechanical principles or mechanical knowledge tests (e.g., see Bennett, 1994), and the higher reported correlation with college grades, suggests that the test may not perform well for the intended purposes or populations, in comparison to existing tests of mechanical principles or mechanical knowledge. Furthermore, the absence of separate norms for samples from the intended use population make it difficult to determine whether an individual test taker is qualified for selection purposes. The lack of substantial supporting reliability/validity/norming data for the purposes of selection suggest that the test does not compete well for application purposes, in comparison to existing tests of mechanical abilities.

SUMMARY. Retitling the test from "Work Skills" to "Mechanical Understanding" does not appear to have made the test better matched to the underlying constructs. Ultimately, the test appears to be an amalgamation of different constructs that are not well integrated or representative of the construct of mechanical understanding, at least in the context of extant theory and empirical research and application (e.g., see Carroll, 1993, pp. 525-526 for a discussion and review of "factors of mechanical and technical knowledge").

REVIEWER'S REFERENCES

Ackerman, P. L., & Humphreys, L. G. (1990). Individual differences in industrial and organizational psychology. In M. D. Dunnette & L. M. Hough (Eds.), *Handbook of industrial and organizational psychology* (Vol. 1, pp. 223–282). Palo Alto, CA: Consulting Psychologists Press.
American Educational Research Association, American Psychological Association, & National Council on Measurement in Education. (1999). *Standards for educational and psychological testing.* Washington, DC: Author.
Anastasi, A. (1976). *Psychological testing* (4th ed.). New York: MacMillan.
Bennett, G. K. (1994). *Bennett Mechanical Comprehension Test (2nd ed.) manual.* San Antonio, TX: Psychological Corporation.
Carroll, J. B. (1993). *Human cognitive abilities: A survey of factor-analytic studies.* New York: Cambridge University Press.
Ekstrom, R. B., French, J. W., Harmon, H. H., & Derman, D. (1976). *Manual for Kit of Factor-Referenced Cognitive Tests.* Princeton, NJ: Educational Testing Service.
Murphy, K. R., & Davidshofer, C. O. (2001). *Psychological testing: Principles and applications* (5th ed.). Upper Saddle River, NJ: Prentice-Hall.
Nunnally, J. C., Jr. (1959). *Tests and measurements: Assessment and prediction.* New York: McGraw-Hill.

Review of the Mechanical Understanding Test by MICHAEL B. BUNCH, Senior Vice President, Measurement Incorporated, Durham, NC:

DESCRIPTION.

General. The Mechanical Understanding Test (MUT), developed by Erich P. Prien, Leonard D. Goodstein, and Kristin O. Prien, consists of a test booklet, answer document, and a technical and administrative manual. It is the successor to the Work Skills Test (WST), marketed by the same publisher, and renamed the MUT in 2004. The test is composed of 65 multiple-choice items. The answer document is a two-part carbonless form with the key printed on the second sheet. The manual combines administration instructions with all technical information about the test.

The test. The 65 items in the test have either three or four response options. The first 55 items measure a variety of concepts, based on 16 core physical principles: Motion in a straight line; Motion in two directions; Force, mass, and gravity; Center of gravity; Circular motion; Properties of materials; Heat; Gas; Electricity; Sound; Hydraulics; Number facility; Perceptual speed; and Spatial visualization. If this seems like only 14 principles, it might be helpful to count force, mass, and gravity as 3 principles, rather than one. The final 10 items measure what the authors call Cognitive/Planning.

The answer document. The answer document is a two-part carbonless form on which examinees place Xs in boxes to indicate their answers. These responses are transferred to the scoring key directly beneath. Correct answers appear as Xs in white boxes, whereas incorrect answers appear as black boxes.

The manual. The 16-page manual provides an introduction to the test, some technical information, and two pages of administration directions, followed by norms and the answer key.

COMMENTARY. The distribution of items across the 14 or 16 core principles is extremely uneven, and some of the items are difficult to match to any of the principles. At least one appears to be miskeyed. The design of the answer document is flawed in that only two sides are sealed; the top and bottom are unsealed, revealing the correct answers below.

The manual is brief, general, and not very useful. The authors play fast and loose with statistical significance tests. For example, when some items yield performance differences between men and women, they note that the differences are significant but small. Later, they tout significant correlations between MUT scores and scores on other tests as evidence of a high degree of validity, without noting that the correlations are modest and at best indicate less than 50% shared variance and at worst only 5% or 6% shared variance. In other instances, analyses and results (e.g., factor analyses, norms) are not sufficiently documented to permit independent conclusions.

SUMMARY. I cannot recommend this test. Anyone interested in a test of mechanical understanding would be better served by investigating the Bennett Mechanical Comprehension Test (reviewed in *The Sixteenth Mental Measurements Yearbook*; 16:31) or the Revised Minnesota Paper Form Board Test, 2nd Edition (reviewed in *The Thirteenth Mental Measurements Yearbook;* 13:316).

[122]
Merrill-Palmer—Revised Scales of Development.

Purpose: Designed to assess cognitive, social-emotional, self-help, and fine and gross motor development in infants and children.
Population: Ages 0-1 to 6-6 years.
Publication Dates: 1926–2004.
Acronym: M-P-R.
Administration: Individual.
Price Data, 2006: $925 per complete kit including manual (2004, 267 pages), infant stimuli book, easel book, Fido book, choke-safe toys and manipulatives, 20 Cognitive Battery record forms, 20 Social Emotional Development Parent Scales, 20 Social Emotional Temperament Style Parent Forms, 20 Gross Motor record forms, 20 Self-Help/Adaptive Development Scale Parent Forms, 20 Expressive Language Evaluator Forms, 20 Expressive Language Parent Forms, 20 Summary Reports/Growth Score Profiles, 20 Copying Response Sheets A, and 20 Copying Response Sheets B; $55 per manual; $30 per 20 Cognitive Battery record forms; $10 per 20 Social Emotional Development Parent Scales; $20 per 20 Spanish Social Emotional Development Parent Scales; $10 per 20 Social Emotional Temperament Style Parent Forms; $20 per 20 Spanish Social Emotional Temperament Style Parent Forms; $20 per 20 Gross Motor Record Forms; $10 per 20 Self-Help/Adaptive Development Scale Parent Forms; $20 per 20 Spanish Self-Help Parent Report Forms; $10 per 20 Expressive Language Evaluator Forms; $10 per 20 Expressive Language Parent Forms; $20 per 20 Summary Reports/Growth Score Profiles; $2.50 per 20 Copying Response Sheets A; $2.50 per 20 Copying Response Sheets B.
Foreign Language Editions: Spanish editions of parent reports available.
Time: (40–50) minutes.
Comments: Portions of this test are to be completed by a parent/guardian; previous edition entitled Merrill-Palmer Scale of Mental Tests.

Authors: Gale H. Roid and Jackie L. Sampers.
Publisher: Stoelting Co.
a) EXPRESSIVE LANGUAGE—EXAMINER FORM.
1) *Element of Attire, Body Parts, Verbs.*
Population: Ages 1-1 years and older.
2) *Adverbs, Adjectives, Prepositions, Pronouns.*
Population: Ages 1-6 years and older.
b) EXPRESSIVE LANGUAGE—PARENT REPORT.
Scores: 2 scales, 4 subscales: 0–12 months, 13 months and older (Word Combination, Word Meanings/Semantics, Gestural, Expressive Verbal).
c) SELF-HELP/ADAPTIVE—PARENT.
Forms, 5: 0–11 months, 12–23 months, 24–35 months, 36–37 months, 48–78 months.
d) GROSS MOTOR—EXAMINER.
Scores: 7 scales, 23 subscales: 0–12 months (Lifts Head, Supported Sitting, Reaching, Rolls, Balance Responses, Independent Sitting, Stomach Creep, Hand/Knee Creep), 13–24 months (Pull to Standing, Cruises Furniture, Independent Walking), 25–36 months (Child Squats to Pick Up Toy, Climbing Into Chair, Stairs, Special Walking), 37–48 months (Running, Jumping #1), 49–78 months (Throwing/Catching, Kicking, Dynamic Walking, Static Balance, Jumping #2, Hopping Movements), Quality of Movement, Tone.
e) SOCIAL-EMOTIONAL DEVELOPMENTAL—PARENT.
Forms, 5: Same as *c* above.
f) SOCIAL-EMOTIONAL TEMPERAMENT—PARENT.
Forms, 2: 0–17 months, 18–78 months.
g) COGNITIVE BATTERY—EXAMINER.
Scores, 6: Cognitive, Memory, Fine Motor, Speed, Receptive Language, Visual Motor; 8 scales, 49 subscales: 1–5 months (Warm-up, Visual Regard, Small Rattle Play, Visual Preference), 6–12 months (Spin Toy, Large Rattle Play, Dangle Toy, Push-Spin Toy, Object Permanence), 13–23 months (Novel Problem, Blocks, Chips in the Box, Round Peg Board (A), Body Parts, Pop Out, Simple Puzzle, Square Peg Board (B), Fido Book), 24–35 months (Ring Stack, Color Matching, Identifies Emotions, Picture Details, Goodnight Baby, Bead Stringing, Two Puzzles, Find It, Goes Together, Square Pegs, Same), 36–47 months (Fingers, Questions, Where Do They Go?, Word Pictures, See It?, Shapes Puzzle), 48–59 months (Puzzle Fun, Big/Small, Touch Picture, Draw It, Hidden Picture, Different Pictures), 60–78 months (Find 'em, High/Low, Count 'em, Fun with Cards, Touch 'em, What's Next?, Different Pictures, Let's Draw It).

1) *Testing Behaviors—Examiner.*

Scores: 4 scales, 6 subscales: 1–5 months (Emotionality), 6–11 months (Attention), 12–17 months (Fearful/Cautious), 18–78 months (Organized/Cooperative, Active/Eager, Angry/Oppositional).

b) SUMMARY REPORT—EXAMINER.

1) *Developmental Index.*

Scores, 7: Developmental Index, Cognitive, Fine Motor, Receptive Language, Memory (ages 1–4 years and older), Speed (ages 1–4 years and older), Visual Motor.

2) *Gross Motor.*

Score: Gross Motor.

3) *Language.*

Scores, 2: Overall Expressive Language, Overall Language.

4) *Social-Emotional.*

Score: Social-Emotional.

5) *Self-Help.*

Score: Self-Help/Adaptive.

Cross References: See T5:1653 (29 references) and T4:1614 (19 references); for a review by Jack A. Naglieri of an earlier edition, see 9:697 (4 references).

Review of the Merrill-Palmer-Revised Scales of Development by SANDRA LOEW, Associate Professor, University of North Alabama, Florence, AL:

DESCRIPTION. The Merrill-Palmer-Revised Scales of Development (M-P-R) is designed to assess the cognitive, social, emotional, and fine and gross motor development of infants and children. It includes four parent reports and two examiner reports. Parents or caregivers are asked to answer questions in the areas of Expressive Language, Social-Emotional Development, Social-Emotional Temperament, and Self-Help/Adaptive. The examiner reports are in the areas of Expressive Language, Cognitive Battery, and Gross Motor Skills.

There is a summary report form where the examiner gathers and tabulates the scores from the preceding forms and plots a Growth Score Profile, which indicates performance delays in the various areas. The kit includes all of the reporting forms, a manual, and a large laminated poster that shows pictures and captions explaining fine motor, gross motor, visual, and visual motor skills at various ages. The kit includes manipulatives, toys, and puzzles that come in a backpack with wheels, which makes it easy to transport the equipment. The manipulatives are contained in heavy duty plastic containers, which should hold up to wear and tear. The backpack is of high quality, and it includes name-brand toys and everything an examiner would need to complete the test, including batteries for the stop watch.

DEVELOPMENT. This test was developed to provide sensitivity in scoring. Therefore, it employs smaller increments of improvement in infant's and children's development than most tests of infant and child development. It is an expansion of the Merrill-Palmer Scales of Development using more recent research to update the assessment.

The authors of the test researched, planned, pilot tested, field tested, normed, and did statistical analyses over a 6-year period in the development of the M-P-R. One of the goals was to allow for testing of infants and to recognize smaller increments of growth in children with developmental delays.

The Cognitive Battery is based on the Cattell-Horn-Carroll Model and the exploratory play model. There is limited information in the manual concerning the exploratory play model, and it is unclear how that model contributed to the development of the test. It seems that the abilities measured by the Merrill-Palmer-Revised Scales of Development such as Visual Spatial and Visual Memory are only a small portion of the overall Cattell-Horn-Carroll Model, and large portions of that theory did not appear to drive the construction of the test.

TECHNICAL. The 2000 U.S. Census was used as the benchmark to develop a stratified sample for the normative studies for this test. Children from the ages of 1 month to 6 years, 6 months were selected. The sample includes the same proportions concerning race, ethnicity, geographic region, and socioeconomic status as the population in the U.S. according to the 2000 Census. Community size was also considered as a variable.

The developers were careful to consider special populations, and the final version of the test has recommendations for adapted-testing methods. The test also has been created to be fair to children with exceptionalities such as language, hearing, visual, or orthopedic impairment, and those children for whom English is not their first language. There is also a Spanish language version of the parent report forms available.

Internal consistency estimates range from .70 to .98, and this reviewer considers them quite good. Internal consistency suggests that the items in the assessment are highly interrelated.

Test-retest reliability coefficients ranged from .84 to .90 (3-week retest interval), but these estimates excluded the assessment for Expressive Language. The Standard Error of Measurement for the Cognitive Battery Scales had a range of 2.12 to 8.26, with the higher variations being in Memory and Speed. The lowest variations were for the 0–12-month age group.

A factor analysis was done on the examiner rating of test session behavior to document that items loaded on the proper scales or factors. Subsequently, factor internal consistency coefficients ranged from .71 to .94, which would indicate that the test session behavior forms are fairly consistent.

The content validity of this test appears to be high. The developers did extensive research and pilot and field testing before publishing this test, and it contributed to the creation of a test that clearly evaluates the developmental progress of infants and children.

The M-P-R Cognitive Scale has a correlation coefficient of .92 with the Bayley Scales, which suggests strong criterion-related validity. The only concern is that a small sample size was used in the validation study, and there are no indications of how that sample was derived or how the small size or demographic features might have impacted the correlation coefficients.

Other assessment instruments, such as the Leiter International Performance Scale—Revised, were used to test for criterion-related validity. All showed correlations that would suggest good criterion-related validity.

COMMENTARY. The M-P-R is a useful tool to assess developmental delays and ascertain improvements that are being made during treatment and intervention. The research that was cited is sound; however, it is unclear why only some of the theoretical constructs were used in the development of the test. It would be useful for the test user to find more information in the test manual that explains the reasons for the omission of some of the theoretical constructs.

The reliability estimates are strong, and the interrater reliability estimates, which may be the most difficult challenge in this type of test, are also strong. The test seems to have good construct and criterion-related validity that suggests it is testing what it was developed to test, and it is in line with other tests that also assess development of infants and children. Extensive testing on various populations contributed to the overall quality of the assessment making it a good tool to use with children with exceptionalities.

The parent reports may be challenging for some parents whose first language is not English or who have a low reading level. Although the Spanish-language version of the parent reports is a commendable addition to the test, it does not solve the problem for parents with poor reading skills or other language barriers. Parental input is essential in the evaluation of infants, but four separate forms for parents to fill out may seem daunting for some.

SUMMARY. The Merrill-Palmer-Revised Scales of Development is a strong assessment system that clearly evaluates the development of infants and children. The cost is over $900, which is not excessive for these types of tests, and the quality of the testing equipment is well worth the cost. The high quality toys and manipulatives will withstand years of use and cleaning, which makes the M-P-R a sound investment. This test kit can be useful in assessing the development of infants and children, and their growth during and following intervention.

Review of the Merrill-Palmer-Revised Scales of Development by LORAINE J. SPENCINER, Professor, and DOLORES J. APPL, Associate Professor, College of Education, Health, and Rehabilitation, University of Maine at Farmington, Farmington, ME:

DESCRIPTION. The Merrill-Palmer-Revised Scales of Development (M-P-R) is a norm-referenced assessment developed for the purpose of determining eligibility for early intervention and/or special education services under the Individuals with Disabilities Education Act (IDEA). Designed for children between the ages of 1 month and 6 years, 6 months, the instrument measures the cognitive, language, motor, self-help, and social-emotional domains. This broad coverage of the developmental domains is consistent with the eligibility term, *developmental delay,* which is used with young children from birth to age 3. In addition, states may elect to use the term to determine eligibility of young children through age 9, according to the discretion of the state and local education agency [20 USC Sec 602 (3)B].

The Merrill-Palmer-Revised Scales of Development consists of four discrete assessment batteries and includes both examiner forms and, for some domains, parent reports. The Cognitive Battery measures general cognitive, receptive language, and fine motor areas. It also provides supplemental scores for memory, speed of cognition, and visual motor ability. The Gross Motor Scale consists of general gross motor development, unusual movements, and atypical movement patterns. There are four Social-Emotional scales including Examiner Observation Form/Test-Session Behavior, the Social-Emotional Developmental Scale-Parent Report, the Social-Emotional Temperament Scale-Parent Report, and the Social-Emotional Problem Indicators. The Expressive Language Scale includes both examiner and parent report. The Self-Help/Adaptive Scale consists of the parent report. For each of the batteries, directions for the examiner are available in both English and Spanish. Three of the parent reports (Social-Emotional Developmental Scale, Temperament Scale, and the Self-Help/Adaptive Scale) are available in Spanish but not the Expressive Language Scale, which only measures English usage.

Test administration begins with the Cognitive Battery and proceeds to the Gross Motor Development Battery. Other batteries are administered according to examiner discretion. According to the examiner's manual, the Cognitive Battery takes between 30–40 minutes. Raw scores may be transformed into standard scores, percentiles, age equivalents, and growth scores. These derived scores are recorded on the Summary Report and may be plotted to indicate patterns of strengths and weaknesses. Additional analysis may be completed by using Rasch growth scores.

DEVELOPMENT. In the development of this revision of the original Merrill-Palmer Scales of Development, the authors sought to update cognitive assessment by examining models of cognitive abilities. The examiner's manual contains a brief description of the theoretical basis of the Merrill-Palmer-Revised Scales of Development, including an explanation of the Cattell-Horn-Carroll model for the structure of cognitive abilities. This model provides the foundation for the Cognitive Battery. In addition, the M-P-R includes updated test materials and the inclusion of

additional assessment domains. Some of the expressive language test items from the original Merrill-Palmer were eliminated due to the high level of English required. Other test items were dropped if they included materials too small for infants and toddlers to use safely.

TECHNICAL. According to the examiner's manual, the M-P-R was developed over 6 years and included a pilot test, a national field test of the Tryout Edition, and national norming of the Standardization Edition. From the Tryout Edition, some tasks and items were eliminated based on level of complexity, technical flaws, or for ethnic or gender issues.

For the Spanish language version, a "nationally-recognized expert" (manual, p. 119) in test translation developed the initial set of examiner prompts using a procedure that would produce the same meaning, rather than a literal translation. This work was later reviewed by psychologists and educators and a national panel of school psychologists and education diagnosticians representing different regional variations in Spanish usage.

The M-P-R was standardized on over 1,068 children, ages 1 month to 6 years, 6 months. This sample was stratified by gender, ethnicity, parental educational level, and geographical region, according to 2000 U.S. Census percentages.

The examiner's manual reports several types of reliability including classical approaches to reliability estimation and item-response theory. Internal consistency for the Cognitive Battery scales (cognitive, receptive language, fine motor, and visual motor) and all of the Gross Motor Battery scales are high (exceeding .90). Within the Cognitive Battery, reliability coefficients for memory and speed are lower (.70 to mid .80s), indicating that items in these scales are not as homogenous as the other scales. The manual reports reliability coefficients on a small test-retest reliability study (involving 41 children ages 3–70 months who took the test twice with about 3 weeks between testings) involving the Cognitive Battery. However, additional studies must be completed for the examiner to have assurance that this battery and the others comprising this instrument are reliable. Test-information curves provide visual representation of the measurement of error and the accuracy at different growth scores. These indicate that there is adequate discrimination across age levels. However, information for very young children is less reliable than for older children.

The examiner's manual presents evidence of both traditional validity (content-related, criterion-related, and construct-related validity) and evidence of consequential validity. Data from a small sample of children whose scores on the M-P-R were correlated with the Bayley Scales of Infant Development, Second Edition indicated a high correlation (.92) between the Mental Scale and the overall cognitive composite score as well as fine motor, receptive language, expressive language, and memory scores. Additional studies must be completed to provide assurance that the M-P-R is a valid instrument.

COMMENTARY. Available in either English or Spanish, this instrument is based on a theoretical perspective of respected infant experts including the early work of Uzgiris and Hunt. The instrument includes adaptations for children with limited expressive language and some items have "teaching" components (e.g., items on the Cognitive Scale: simple puzzle, color matching, and picture details). On the other hand, some test materials may be hazardous. For example, chips used with 13 month olds are too large to be a choking risk, but could get lodged in the child's mouth.

The assessment allows information to be interpreted by selecting from several different derived scores. Derived scores are helpful in determining eligibility for early intervention and/or early childhood special education services. This assessment also allows the use of growth scores, designed using item-response theory. Growth scores allow members of the early childhood team to examine small changes in growth. Additionally, "Since the child's overall ability, and task performance ability, are placed along an interval scale, it is possible to determine what kinds of tasks are too hard, too easy, or 'just about at the right difficulty level' for the child on each domain of cognition sampled by the task in the M-P-R" (manual, p. 81). Thus, this information would be helpful in planning and monitoring progress once early intervention or special education services have begun.

The examiner's manual includes a well-written section concerning test accommodations under *Accommodations and Adaptations in Test Administration*, with suggestions for specific accommodations when a child has a severe disability. The information would be very helpful to the examiner facing such a situation.

Some sections in the manual include extensive information regarding assessment procedures for working with very young children. These sections, such as *Timing, Pacing, and Stop Rules* and *Establishing Rapport*, need to be edited carefully to reflect best practices when working with infants and toddlers. Many factors are relevant when gathering information about very young children. For example, how is the child's inability to do the task versus motivation to do the task versus using items in a novel way taken into consideration?

The examiner must have a solid foundation in child development as well as knowledge and skills in working with infants, toddlers, and preschoolers. For example, being responsive to children's cues is especially important for an examiner working with young children who naturally have limited attention spans. Additionally, very young children often experience anxiety during interactions with an unfamiliar adult whereas preschoolers may lack motivation to use materials in ways directed by an adult. Thus, knowledge and training in working with young children should be a requirement under *User Qualifications* in the examiner's manual.

SUMMARY. The Merrill-Palmer-Revised Scales of Development (M-P-R) is a norm-referenced assessment developed for the purpose of determining eligibility for early intervention and/or special education services under IDEA. The instrument assesses typical developmental domains for children of ages 1 month through 6 years, 6 months. The M-P-R should be used only by examiners with a solid foundation in child development as well as knowledge and skills in working with infants, toddlers, and preschoolers. Additional research studies will provide assurance that this instrument is both reliable and valid.

REVIEWERS' REFERENCE

Individuals with Disabilities Education Improvement Act of 2004, (20 USC).

[123]

MIDAS: The Multiple Intelligences Development Assessment Scales [Revised].

Purpose: "Designed to provide an objective measure of the multiple intelligences."
Publication Dates: 1994–2005.
Acronym: MIDAS.

Administration: Group or individual.

Price Data, 2006: $250 per Professional kit including MIDAS Questionnaire (select 2 age groups—reproducible), 50 MIDAS Profiles (pre-paid bulk scoring), The MIDAS: A Professional Manual (2005, 136 pages), and 1 interpretive workbook (reproducible); $350 per Classroom kit including MIDAS Questionnaire (select 1 age group—reproducible), 100 MIDAS Profiles (bulk pre-paid mail-in scoring included), The MIDAS Teacher's Handbook, Common Miracles in Your School, Select 1 of the two (2) reproducible workbooks above, 1 hour technical support, and discount bulk scoring rate; $900 per Guidance kit including MIDAS Questionnaires for Teens and Adults (reproducible), 200 MIDAS Profiles (pre-paid bulk scoring), The MIDAS: Professional Manual, The Challenge! Guide to Career Development, Student High Impact Project (SHIP) reproducible, and 1 hour technical support; $2,500 per School kit including MIDAS Questionnaires for 2 age groups—reproducible, bulk scoring for 1,000 profiles, web administration and scoring available using the Online MIDAS System (OMS), The MIDAS: A Professional Manual, Common Miracles in Your School (bulk pricing available), Student High Impact Project (SHIP) (reproducible), Teacher's Handbook for MI in the Classroom (bulk pricing available), Stepping Stones: A Teacher's Workbook (reproducible), Stepping Stones: Student Workbook for MI (reproducible), The Challenge! Guide to Career Success (reproducible), 2 hours on-site training (plus travel expenses), and 3 hours of telephone (free), Discounted Bulk Scoring Rate; $500 per Staff Development kit including MIDAS Questionnaire for adults (reproducible), 100 MIDAS Profiles (pre-paid bulk scoring), Teacher's Handbook: Multiple Intelligences in the Classroom, Common Miracles in Your School, Stepping Stones Workbook for Teachers (reproducible), 1 hour of technical support, Staff Development Packet (reproducible)—forthcoming, inquire; $40 per MIDAS preview package including 3 profiles, 1 book, interpretative packet, and Teacher's Handbook for MI in the Classroom; $45 per Teacher's Profile Package including Teacher's Handbook for MI in the Classroom, Common Miracles in Your School, and 1 MIDAS Adult Profile; $150 per The Basic Research kit, 100 MIDAS profiles, Professional Manual or Teacher's Handbook, Brief Interpretative Packet, data imported into database (either SPSS or Excel database—upon request), and 1 workbook (upon request); $300 per 100 MIDAS Profiles (with kit purchase); $400 per 100 MIDAS Profiles (without kit purchase); $100 per MIDAS Database; $7 per MIDAS Personal Profile (with purchase of book or package); $15 per MIDAS profile (bulk discounts available); $20 per Teacher's Handbook: Multiple Intelligences in the Classroom; $40 per The MIDAS: A Professional Manual.

Foreign Language Editions: Research editions available in Singaporean, Spanish, Chinese, Danish, Malaysian, Korean, German, Romanian, Venezuelan, Persian, Arabic, Turkish, and French.

Time: (20–35) minutes via self-completion; (60-90) minutes via structured interview.

Comments: This test can be administered via self-completion or as a structured interview; can be completed by an individual who is close to the subject.

Author: C. Branton Shearer.

Publishers: Multiple Intelligences Research and Consulting, Inc.

a) MIDAS.

Population: Ages 20 and up.

Scores: 11 scales and 26 subscales: Basic Scales: Musical (Appreciation, Vocal Ability, Instrumental Skill, Composing), Kinesthetic (Athletics, Dexterity), Logical-Mathematical (Strategy Games, Everyday Skills with Math, Everyday Problem Solving, School Math), Spatial (Spatial Awareness, Artistic Design, Working with Objects), Linguistic (Rhetorical Skill, Expressive Sensitivity, Written/Academic Ability), Interpersonal (Social Sensitivity, Social Persuasion, Interpersonal Work), Intrapersonal (Personal Knowledge/Efficacy, Self/Other Efficacy, Calculations, Spatial Problem-Solving), Naturalist (Animal Care, Plant Care, Science), Intellectual Style Scales: Leadership (Social Adeptness, Communication Skill, Managerial Skill), Innovation (Musical, Kinesthetic, Logical-Mathematical, Spatial, Linguistic, Interpersonal, Intrapersonal), General Logic (Logical-Mathematical, Spatial, Interpersonal, Intrapersonal).

b) TEEN-MIDAS.

Population: Ages 14–18.

Scores: Same as *a* above.

c) MIDAS-KIDS: ALL ABOUT ME.

Population: Ages 9–14.

Scores: 10 scales and 24 subscales: Basic Scales: Musical (Musicality, Vocal, Appreciation, Instrument), Kinesthetic (Physical Ability, Dance, Working with Hands), Logical-Mathematical (Problem Solving, Calculations), Spatial (Artistic, Constructions, Imagery), Linguistic (Linguistic Sensitivity, Writing, Reading), Interpersonal (Leadership, Understanding People, Getting Along with Others), Intrapersonal (Self Knowledge, Managing Feelings, Effective Relationships, Goal Achievement), Naturalist (Animal Care, Earth Science), Intellectual Style Scales: Technical, Innovative.

d) MIDAS-KIDS: MY YOUNG CHILD.

Population: Ages 6-9.

Scores: Same as *c* above.

Cross References: For reviews by Abbot Packard and Michael S. Trevisan of an earlier version, see 14:234.

Review of the MIDAS: The Multiple Intelligences Developmental Assessment Scales [Revised] by ROBERT W. HILTONSMITH, *Professor of Psychology, Radford University, Radford, VA:*

DESCRIPTION. Since Howard Gardner published his theory of multiple intelligences over 20 years ago in *Frames of Mind* (Gardner, 1983), several efforts have been made to develop methods and instruments to assess the original seven "intelligences" (referred to by Gardner as "biopsychological potentials" or as "constructs"). These include Linguistic, Logical-Mathematical, Spatial, Kinesthetic, Musical, Interpersonal, and Intrapersonal intelligences. "The Multiple Intelligences Developmental Assessment Scales (MIDAS) are designed to provide an objective measure of the multiple intelligences as reported by the person or by a knowledgeable informant" (manual, p. 3), although it should be noted that later in the manual (p. 65) the author states that "the MIDAS is not an objective test of intelligence because the findings are compiled from the perceptions of the person or a knowledgeable observer." Results from the MIDAS provide a "reasonable estimate" (manual, p. 3) of the person's "intellectual disposition" in each of the intelligences, as well as 24 or more kinds of skills associated with each intelligence. (The eighth intelligence is called "Naturalist" and was added later in the development of the MIDAS.) In addition, the MIDAS includes "several intellectual style scales" that "estimate the person's proclivity for Innovation, General Logic and Leadership" (manual, p. 3).

There are four general forms of the MIDAS for different age groups. The MIDAS for adults is a 119-item self (or other) report. Teens from 14–18 years of age respond to a slightly modified version of the adult form. There are also two 80-item versions of the "MIDAS-KIDS." The first, "All About Me," is self-completed for children aged 9–14, whereas "My Young Child" is completed by parents of children ages 6 to 9 years. The questionnaires may be group administered via self-completion or individually as a structured interview. Individuals who are unable to read at a fifth-grade level should have the test administered through a structured interview. Administration time is approximately 20–35 minutes for the individual and group administration formats, and approximately one hour to one and a half hours for the structured interview. The questions ask about activities of everyday life that require cognitive ability, involvement, and judgment, such as "Can you sing in tune?" or "Are you good at playing checkers or chess?" The items are written in three basic forms. Some inquire about the frequency or duration of time that the person participates in a particular activity, whereas others focus on either the person's skills in the activity or their enthusiasm for the activity. Each item uses a 5-point Likert scale, with response anchors tailored to the specific content of the question. A "does not apply" or "I don't know" option is provided for every item so the respondent is not forced to guess or answer beyond his or her actual level of knowledge.

The manual notes that "A MIDAS computerized scoring program is necessary to score and interpret the assessment" (p. 23). Two options exist for obtaining computerized scoring: (a) using the Online MIDAS System (OMS) web administration, or (b) mailing in completed forms to the publisher using the scannable answer sheet and an accompanying transmittal form. The computerized scoring program provides the MIDAS user with a multipage printout that typically includes: (a) an introduction and overview of the MIDAS assessment, (b) scores for the eight main scales, and (c) scores for the 24–29 subscales for each of the eight main scales. In addition, an interpretative packet is supplied, which varies according to the needs of the user. Typically, the packet includes information about the MIDAS and its scales and subscales, study strategies for each intelligence, recommendations (or strategies) for choosing a college major based on the subject's MIDAS profile, and a list of activities and occupations associated with each intelligence.

DEVELOPMENT. The MIDAS was developed in 1987 as a structured interview instrument to assess the multiple intelligences for adolescents and adults undergoing cognitive rehabilitation (Way & Shearer, 1990). It was later adapted as a self-report measure that can be completed by adolescents and adults. The goal in developing the MIDAS was to provide information "to increase the person's self understanding and appreciation for his [sic] intellectual profile in order to increase personal satisfaction and achievement" (manual, p. 39). Additionally, the manual notes that "The MIDAS Profile serves as the beginning of a dialogue that will lead to the creation of a narrative description of the person's intellectual and creative life" (p. 4). The test developer claims that using the profile can provide useful learning strategies for adolescents and adults, claiming that the highest score in the profile reflects the subject's "best developed abilities and will facilitate new learning" (manual, p. 32). High profile scores are also said to be helpful to individuals who are trying to decide on a college major.

The manual contains detailed information about the four-stage plan for developing the MIDAS. Briefly, Phase 1 was devoted to the development and testing of items that focused on "critical incidents or behaviors" in a person's life that were consistent with Gardner's multiple intelligences theory. Factor analyses supplied guidance and support for the placement of items on the seven scales that correspond to the original seven multiple intelligences. In Phase 2, additional items were added, and field testing and expert reviews of items were completed. In Phase 3, interrater reliability studies were conducted and subscales were created for the main scales. Finally, in Phase 4, the eighth intelligence scale ("Naturalist") was added and pilot tested. The manual includes similar information for the development of the MIDAS-KIDS.

TECHNICAL. The test developer has made a concerted effort to test the reliability and validity of the MIDAS against standards used to evaluate objective tests, while cautioning the user that "The MIDAS is not an objective test of intelligence because the findings are compiled from the perceptions of the person or a knowledgeable observer" (manual, p. 65). These studies are clearly presented in a separate chapter in the manual devoted to psychometric properties of the MIDAS.

Five studies examined the internal consistency of the items within each of the original seven MIDAS scales (the "Naturalist" scale is considered separately in the same chapter). The overall alpha coefficients range from .78 for Kinesthetic to .89 for Musical and Linguistic, with an overall mean of .86. Temporal stability was examined through three studies to see if respondents changed their ratings during a second completion of the

questionnaire. The results indicated adequate stability in all three studies, with reliabilities in the range of .76 to about .92. Interrater reliability was assessed in two studies. Results from the largest of these using 212 people showed a pairwise agreement rate for individual items of 75–85%. Cultural bias was also investigated in a study with 119 college students and strong support was found for the notion that the MIDAS is not culturally biased.

The validity of the MIDAS has been examined in six studies that are described in the manual. These studies provide evidence about content validity, construct validity, concurrent validity, predictive validity, and contrasted criterion groups. As noted earlier in this review, factor analyses provide support for the seven hypothetical constructs of intelligence, and studies of discriminant and convergent validity provided evidence that the MIDAS "obtains a 'reasonable estimate' of a person's multiple intelligence profile" (manual, p. 72). Concurrent validity was demonstrated by correlations in the mid- to upper- .50 level between the MIDAS scales and selected, matched, and standardized aptitude, cognitive, and achievement tests. A study of predictive validity indicated that college students' self-ratings on the MIDAS are in "reasonably close agreement with measurements provided by expert raters" (manual, p. 78). Finally, evidence is provided that the "magnitude of the mean MIDAS scores, as well as their patterns, are logically consistent with what would be expected of college students thought to be either high or low in specified skills" (manual, p. 79). For example, college musicians averaged a high score of 72% on the Musical scale of the MIDAS.

COMMENTARY AND SUMMARY. The MIDAS is offered as a screening instrument for providing data about a person's multiple intelligences as described by Gardner (1983). Like many assessment tools, the MIDAS should be administered and interpreted within a conceptual framework. In the case of the MIDAS, this framework contains a number of assumptions that are not without controversy. For instance, users must conceptualize the eight major constructs on the MIDAS as relating in some meaningful way to human intelligence, and not as indicators of perceived interest preference, talent, or aptitude. Additionally, for the MIDAS results to be useful in providing insight into personally effective study skills, the user must believe in the effectiveness of aptitude-treatment interactions, for which the evidence is, at best, equivocal (Reschly & Ysseldyke, 2002). With these caveats aside, it would appear that the MIDAS is a useful tool for, as the test developer intended, beginning a dialogue that can help inform both personal and career decisions.

REVIEWER'S REFERENCES

Gardner, H. (1983/1993). *Frames of mind: The theory of multiple intelligences.* New York: Basic Books.

Reschly, D. J., & Ysseldyke, J. E. (2002). Paradigm shift: The past is not the future. In A. Thomas & J. Grimes (Eds.), *Best practices in school psychology: IV* (pp. 3-20). Bethesda, MD: National Association of School Psychologists.

Way, D., & Shearer, B. (1990, October). *Phase 1: Development of the Hillside assessment of pre-trauma intelligences.* Paper presented at the annual meeting of the Midwest Educational Research Association, Chicago, IL.

Review of the MIDAS: The Multiple Intelligences Developmental Assessment Scales [Revised] by W. JOEL SCHNEIDER, Assistant Professor of Psychology, Illinois State University, Normal, IL:

DESCRIPTION. The MIDAS: Multiple Intelligences Developmental Assessment Scales [Revised] is an instrument intended to assess aspects of Gardner's (1983/1993, 1999) Theory of Multiple Intelligences for adults (MIDAS-adult), adolescents (TEEN-MIDAS; for ages 14–18), and children (MIDAS-KIDS; for ages 6–14). All versions can be completed by the person being assessed (if older than 8) or by a knowledgeable informant. All versions can be used as traditional questionnaires, but an interview format is preferred in order to gain more accurate information and more qualitative information that would not surface in a questionnaire. The MIDAS can also be taken using a computer program.

The MIDAS is not so much a "test" as it is a method that provokes dialogue between the clinician and client about the client's intellectual strengths. When the MIDAS yields information that is inconsistent with the client's understanding of his or her (i.e., one's own or one's child's) strengths, the client is encouraged to talk about the results with the clinician and, if necessary, to rearrange the results to fit the client's understanding.

The MIDAS takes less than an hour to complete (20–35 minutes is typical) and can be scored using the Online MIDAS System for web administration or by a mail-in bulk scoring service. Information necessary for hand scoring is not included in the professional manual and thus, hand scoring is not possible.

The MIDAS-adult has 119 items. The TEEN-MIDAS has these same 119 items but some are slightly modified to be relevant to adolescents. The MIDAS-KIDS has an 93-item questionnaire for children called "All About Me" and an 93-item questionnaire for parents and other informants called "My Young Child."

The questions ask about a person's abilities, preferences, habits, experiences, accomplishments, and training in a wide variety of domains. Sometimes the answer stems only allow the person to evaluate themselves positively (e.g., *Fair, Pretty Good, Good, Very Good,* or *Excellent*). Most of the questions have answer stems that allow people to evaluate themselves negatively but only slightly so (e.g., "Not really," "Not very good," or "Less than average"). There are never any answer choices that allow a person to state that an activity or ability is an extreme problem or weakness. Thus, low scores are achieved by a failure to acknowledge excellence in a domain.

Items are grouped into several types of scales and subscales. The main scales measure eight of Gardner's intelligences, including Musical (subscales: Vocal Ability, Instrumental Skill, Composing and Active Listener/Appreciation), Kinesthetic (subscales: Athletics and Physical Dexterity), Logical-Mathematical (subscales: School Math, Everyday Skill with Math, Everyday Problem Solving, and Strategy Games), Spatial (subscales: Spatial Awareness, Working with Objects, and Artistic Design), Linguistic (subscales: Expressive Sensitivity, Rhetorical Skill, and Written-Academic Ability), Interpersonal (subscales: Social Sensitivity, Social Persuasion, and Interpersonal Work), Intrapersonal (subscales: Personal Knowledge/Efficacy, Self/Other Effectiveness, Calculations, and Spatial Problem Solving), and Naturalist (subscales: Animal Care, Plant Care, and Science). The intellectual style scales use items from all of the different main scales to measure different ways the eight intelligences are expressed. The intellectual style scales include Leadership (subscales: Social Adeptness, Communication Skill, and Managerial Skill), Innovation, General Logic, and Technical Skill. The scores are presented as "percentages" but it is not at all clear how they are calculated as the details necessary for hand scoring the MIDAS are not presented in the manual. The "percentages" are grouped according to the following general categories: Very High (80–100), High (60–79), Moderate(40–59), Low (20–39), and Very Low (0–19).

The computerized score report profile includes information about each of the scales and guidelines as to how to interpret the MIDAS. Clients are encouraged to reflect on which scores they think are too high, too low, surprising, or puzzling. Clients are also encouraged to reflect on what the results have helped them learn about themselves.

The score report includes lists of careers and college majors that are linked to each of the multiple intelligences and a guide to use each of the intelligences to study effectively. Clients are encouraged to think of the results as tentative and changeable rather than as fixed abilities. Examiners using the MIDAS do not label evaluees without their participation and consent.

DEVELOPMENT. The professional manual covers the development of the MIDAS-adult in great detail. The initial items were developed by a team of psychologists who are knowledgeable about the Theory of Multiple Intelligences. These items were revised several times based on feedback from different samples of participants. Factor analyses and item analyses were also used to eliminate items, identify items in need of revision, and identify domains that needed additional coverage. Additional questions were revised to make sure that the items did not exceed a sixth-grade reading level. Several experts (including Howard Gardner) reviewed the items for readability, cultural bias, and fit to the Theory of Multiple Intelligences. The TEEN-MIDAS and the MIDAS-KIDS were developed along similar lines.

TECHNICAL. Evaluating the psychometric properties of the MIDAS is complicated because the MIDAS does not purport to be a traditional psychometric instrument for which standardized norms and checks on reliability and validity are of paramount importance. For the same reason that music critics do not fault soul singers for not having operatic-quality voices (or opera singers for not singing soulfully), it is difficult to fault the MIDAS for failing to demonstrate the same kinds of psychometric properties and validity data as traditional assessment instruments. In contrast to other instruments, the MIDAS does not claim to measure any "ability" that people "have" in an objective sense. In this sense, the MIDAS is beyond reproach because it claims no (objective) virtues. It is a true post-modern assessment tool. Even so, the psychometric properties of the instrument do hold up reasonably well when evaluated by standard criteria. Thus, enthusiasts can have it both ways: They can cheer when findings support the MIDAS and when they do not, enthusiasts can say, "Aw shucks! This nomothetic finding just isn't relevant to an idiographic measure like the MIDAS."

Standardization. Although the database of MIDAS scores now includes tens of thousands of test administrations from people of all ages, there has never been an attempt to collect a nationally representative standardization sample. Because the MIDAS measures intelligence in an ipsative and idiographic fashion, representative norms are at best irrelevant and possibly misleading. Nevertheless, means and standard deviations of scores from different criterion groups (e.g., physics majors, Mensa members, and high school students) are available.

Reliability. Reliability data have been collected from many samples of participants in various studies designed to assess qualities of the MIDAS. All scales are reasonably internally consistent (coefficient alpha ranges from .78 to .89) and stable (1-week test-retest reliability ranges from .76 to .92). Interrater reliability data are reported in an idiosyncratic fashion. Self-report data for 212 adults were compared with ratings from two knowledgeable informants for each participant. The manual lumps self-informant correlations with informant-informant correlations and does not distinguish between the two types of comparisons. Furthermore, instead of reporting intraclass correlations, as should be done with interval-level data from indistinguishable dyads, informants were arbitrarily designated as "Primary" and "Secondary" and scores were then chopped up into 5 categories (Very High, High, Moderate, Low, and Very Low). Exact agreement rates and agreement rates plus or minus one category were calculated. Exact agreement ranged between 35% to 49%. Agreement between raters (plus or minus one category) ranged from 71% to 88%. No rationale was given for this deviation from standard practices for reporting interrater reliability.

Validity. A series of the manuscripts available at www.miresearch.org supplements the manual's review of studies that have attempted to demonstrate the validity and utility of the MIDAS. As of the writing of this review, none of these manuscripts have undergone peer review. Five dissertations using the MIDAS were also found on PsycInfo. Despite the manual's warning that the MIDAS does not measure intelligence as if it were a trait that a person can "possess" in an objective sense, the dissertations, unpublished manuscripts, and even the professional manual itself often lapse into language that reifies MIDAS scores into entities in ways that seem very "thing-like." Perhaps this wording is an unavoidable consequence of psychological researchers' underdeveloped vocabulary for issues involved in idiographic, ipsative, and narrative assessment procedures such as the MIDAS.

The validity data presented include anecdotes from parents, teachers, counselors, research participants, and clients who were satisfied with the MIDAS and who claimed to have learned things that they might not have otherwise learned using standard psychoeducational assessment procedures. Given the theoretical orientation of the author, it would seem that a rigorous and systematic qualitative study of these anecdotes would provide the best validity data for the MIDAS. Unfortunately, there is no indication that these anecdotes were collected or presented in a systematic fashion.

In addition to the anecdotal data, the professional manual and the unpublished manuscripts document a large number of traditional quantitative validity studies. The nature of these studies is surprisingly similar to that of studies used to validate the original IQ tests almost a century ago. For example, many of the studies show that teacher ratings of student competencies correlate in theoretically expected ways with MIDAS scores. In addition, criterion groups expected to have competence in specific domains tend to have MIDAS profiles with peaks and valleys that one would expect (e.g., engineers rate themselves lower on Interpersonal abilities but higher on Logical-Mathematical abilities. Professional dance instructors rate themselves high on everything but rate themselves particularly high on Kinesthetic and Musical abilities). The MIDAS scales (i.e., Linguistic and Logical/Mathematical intelligences) expected to correlate with traditional IQ tests do, in fact, correlate robustly with IQ (r = .48 to .54). It should be noted that a few unexpected correlations with IQ were also evident (e.g., .32 with Musical, .54 with Intrapersonal). Interpersonal intelligence

correlated with Performance IQ (r = .28) but not with Verbal IQ.

Factor-analytic data on large samples (N > 10,000) generally support the theoretical factor structure of the MIDAS. However, a very large general factor caused by a robust positive manifold (i.e., all scales are strongly and positively intercorrelated) is very clearly evident in the data and goes unremarked in any discussion in any of the papers. Thus, it is noted here that in each of the factor analyses, the first factor dwarfs all others. A large first factor in rating scale data usually indicates that some process causes many people to tend to rate themselves as similar in all abilities (high, average, or low across domains). Although no such interpretation is offered by the manual, the matter is referred to indirectly when the validity of profiles that are both flat and low was questioned. It was suggested that people with such profiles are depressed or have low intrapersonal abilities. It is not stated directly but it appears that the assumption is that no one who can evaluate themselves with accurate insight should have uniformly low scores. Some of the other manuscripts demonstrate that the MIDAS scales correlate with theoretically predicted scales derived from Sternberg's (1985) Triarchic Theory of Intelligence and Goleman's (1995) Emotional Intelligence Theory.

COMMENTARY. The MIDAS professional manual and supplementary research documents are well-written and mostly well-conceived presentations of a kind of approach to assessment that is vastly different from traditional psychoeducational approaches to intelligence. The validity data are persuasive that the MIDAS does a good job of operationally defining Gardner's Multiple Intelligences Theory. Indeed, Gardner himself congratulates the author in the Foreword of the manual (although he appears to have reservations about measurement of any kind of intelligence and worries that instruments such as the MIDAS might be used by some people to come to conclusions such as "Johnny is linguistic" or worse, "Sally is not spatial").

If the MIDAS were purported to measure abilities with accuracy and abilities are things that exist independent of raters' perspectives, then the weight of unanswered questions and legitimate criticisms of the instrument might crush any hope of it earning respect or acceptance among hard-nosed researchers. However, the theoretical ratio-nale for the MIDAS ducks most forms of vulner-ability to empirical falsification. Reasonably well-controlled outcome studies comparing the outcomes of clients given the MIDAS with clients given standard assessments might go a long way to persuade reasonable skeptics. For now, its *raison d'être* appears to be that it is a good way to bolster the confidence and self-esteem of those being assessed and that it helps clinicians and parents focus on the strengths rather than the weaknesses of those being assessed. In this goal, it probably succeeds in helping people sidestep the implicit question of IQ tests, "How smart are you?" and instead focus on Gardner's famous reversal of that question, "How are you smart?"

Other than the opportunity costs associated with the time it takes to administer the MIDAS, it probably would not hurt anyone if clinicians used the MIDAS regularly. However, clinicians, parents, teachers, and those being evaluated will probably find it very difficult to refrain from talk-ing about multiple intelligences as if they were reified "things" (as Gardner fears that they will). If they do, the MIDAS becomes just another test that measures an eclectic mix of personality, interests, motivation, and cognitive and emo-tional abilities but does so with a lot of error, especially for people with a poor capacity to evaluate themselves (or their children). Unfor-tunately, people with a poor capacity to rate themselves are typically the people in most need of help. Instead, users should hold fast to the stated purpose of the MIDAS: to promote mu-tual, wide-ranging, and exploratory dialogue be-tween clinician and client about the evaluee's in-tellectual strengths. If clinicians can facilitate this process, the MIDAS is likely to improve greatly the quality of assessments and, ultimately, of in-terventions based on those assessments.

SUMMARY. The MIDAS is a questionnaire that measures aspects of Gardner's Theory of Multiple Intelligences. The overall thrust of the growing, but unpublished research literature sup-porting the use of the MIDAS, is that the data it provides are not random, the scores are reasonably reliable, the scales correlate reasonably well with measures that they should, and that many people like the test and find it helpful. Its primary pur-pose is to facilitate discussion of evaluees' cogni-tive strengths and to help clinicians design more

helpful interventions. It has yet to be established that it accomplishes any of its goals better than existing measures (e.g., and in particular, a well-constructed IQ test).

REVIEWER'S REFERENCES

Gardner, H. (1983/1993). *Multiple intelligences: The theory in practice.* New York: Basic Books.
Gardner, H. (1999). *The disciplined mind: What all students should understand.* New York: Simon & Schuster.
Goleman, D. (1995). *Emotional intelligence.* New York: Bantam Books.
Sternberg, R. J. (1985). *Beyond IQ: The triarchic theory of human intelligence.* New York: Cambridge University Press.

[124]
The Middlesex Elderly Assessment of Men-tal State.

Purpose: "Developed as a screening test to detect gross impairment of specific cognitive skills in the elderly."

Population: Adults.

Publication Date: 1989.

Acronym: MEAMS.

Scores, 12: Orientation, Name Learning, Naming, Comprehension, Remembering Pictures, Arithmetic, Spatial Construction, Fragmented Letter Perception, Unusual Views, Usual Views, Verbal Fluency, Motor Perseveration.

Administration: Individual.

Forms, 2: Version A, Version B.

Price Data, 2006: £131 per complete kit including manual, 25 scoring sheets, and 2 stimulus books; £33.50 per 50 scoring sheets.

Time: [10] minutes.

Author: Evelyn Golding.

Publisher: Harcourt Assessment [England].

Review of The Middlesex Elderly Assessment of Mental State by STEPHEN J. FREEMAN, Professor and Chair, Department of Counseling, Texas A&M University—Commerce, Commerce, TX:

DESCRIPTION. The Middlesex Elderly Assessment of Mental State (MEAMS) was de-veloped as a screening test to detect gross impair-ment of specific cognitive skills and differentiate between functional illnesses and organically based cognitive impairment in the elderly ages 65 to 93. The MEAMS is individually administered and takes approximately 10 minutes. There are two versions of the MEAMS, Versions A and B. Each version contains 12 subtests: Orientation, Name Learning, Naming, Comprehension, Remember-ing Pictures, Arithmetic, Spatial Construction, Fragmented Letter Perception, Unusual Views, Usual Views, Verbal Fluency, and Motor Perseveration.

The Orientation subtest assesses orientation to time, place, and person by asking the test taker her or his name, age, date of birth, current location, and the current date. The Name Learning subtest assesses memory by displaying a photograph of a named person and asking the test taker to remember the photograph and name later in the test. The Naming subtest is a test of impaired naming ability (anomia). The Comprehension subtest assesses the comprehension of spoken language by requiring the test taker to name three items from their verbal descriptions. The Remembering Pictures subtest assesses recognition memory by presenting 10 line drawings of common objects and later asking the test taker to recognize them from a set of 20. The Arithmetic subtest requires test takers to perform two simple addition and one simple subtraction problem. Inability to perform these tasks is purported to be sensitive to dementia. The Spatial Construction subtest assesses perceptual motor ability by asking the test taker to reproduce paper-and-pencil designs. The Fragmented Letter Perception subtest assesses the test taker's ability to perceive an item when it is represented in fragmented and incomplete form. The Unusual Views subtest assesses test takers' perceptual ability by presenting pictures of objects photographed at unusual angles and asking them to identify the object. The test taker is required to identify objects this time photographed from a usual view point and purports to differentiate problems of perception from sensory deficit or anomia. The Usual Views subtest is administered if the test taker fails any items of the previous subtest; otherwise it is discretionary. The Verbal Fluency subtest assesses the ability to produce spontaneous speech fluently and requires the test taker to name as many animals as possible in 2 minutes. The Motor Perseveration subtest assesses executive function by instructing the test taker to reproduce a tapping sequence adding or eliminating a single tap as requested.

Each subtest of the MEAMS is scored either pass (1) or fail (0) with the highest score (12) equaling the total number of subtests, including both the Unusual and Usual Views subtests. The MEAMS is a cognitive screening instrument and not meant to diagnosis; therefore, scores are suggestive only. Scores between 10 and 12 are suggested as normal, 8 to 9 are suggested as being borderline and should be scrutinized, and scores of 7 or below should be referred for further investigative assessment.

DEVELOPMENT. The current MEAMS test evolved from an earlier more extensive range of tests developed at the Middlesex Hospital. To enhance the test's assessment of memory two additional subtests were added from the then recently developed Rivermead Behavioural Memory Test.

TECHNICAL. Technical information on the MEAMS is reported based on 10 subtests. The Name Learning and Remembering Pictures subtests comprised the Rivermead Behavioural Memory Test which was added to the current MEAMS. Technical information on these subtests was not contained in the manual.

The norming sample for the MEAMS consisted of 120 elderly patients, 28 males and 92 females ages 65-93, who attended the Latimer House Day Hospital, the Middlesex Hospital, London for a first assessment.

The manual reports two estimates of reliability for the MEAMS interrater reliability and parallel forms reliability. Parallel forms reliability was established by having 28 patients take both versions of the MEAMS. The correlation between the two forms was reported as .91.

The manual presents information on four diagnostic groups (Alzheimer's disease, multi-infarct dementia, depression without dementia 1, and depression without dementia 2). The two groups of patients diagnosed with dementia (Alzheimer's and stroke) performed substantially worse on all 10 subtests than did the group of patients diagnosed with depression without dementia. Comparisons (t-test) between the dementia and nondementia groups revealed significant differences on all subtest performance with the exception of the stroke and depression group on the Usual Views subtest.

COMMENTARY. Significant criticism can be made regarding the sample size and the lack of demographic information on the normative sample. A larger sample and better balance between males and females is needed. The current sample included an age range of 29 years, which does little for sensitivity. Groups consisting of at least 50 participants with age intervals of 5 years would be more consistent with the goal of sensitivity to older adults.

Parallel forms reliability was provided for the whole test and viewed as adequate. Lacking were coefficients for each of the subtests. Similarly, the MEAMS was shown in one study to differentiate between patients with dementia and those with depression; however, greater sensitivity needs to be clearly demonstrated with various age groups. Conspicuously absent were other forms of validity (e.g., concurrent, predictive).

SUMMARY. The MEAMS appears to be a collection of item types similar to those suggested by Strub and Black (2000) in their classic book, *The Mental Status Examination in Neurology*. Though a screening and not a diagnostic instrument, the MEAMS appears to differentiate patients with dementia from those with depression; however, given the problems with the norming sample and the lack of technical information demonstrating acceptable levels of reliability and validity for the intended uses, no serious support for the use of the MEAMS can be made. The lack of clear technical strength and meaningful difference (greater sensitivity) preclude its ability to accomplish its mission. Until such supportive work is forthcoming, use of the MEAMS is not recommended.

REVIEWER'S REFERENCE

Strub, R. L., & Black, F. W. (2000). *The mental status examination in neurology* (4th ed.). Philadelphia: F. A. Davis Company.

Review of The Middlesex Elderly Assessment of Mental State by MATTHEW E. LAMBERT, Assistant Clinical Professor of Neuropsychiatry, Texas Tech University Health Sciences Center, Lubbock, TX:

DESCRIPTION. The Middlesex Elderly Assessment of Mental State (MEAMS), originally published in 1989, is a screening examination to assess basic functioning of elderly adults ages 65 to 93 years across 12 cognitive tasks: Orientation, Name Learning, Naming, Comprehension, Remembering Pictures, Arithmetic, Spatial Construction, Fragmented Letter Perception, Unusual Views, Usual Views, Verbal Fluency, and Motor Perseveration. The MEAMS subtests are included in a standing flip-chart arranged such that instructions are on the page facing the administrator and test stimuli face the examinee. Instructions are read to the examinee with responses recorded on a scoring form. Most subtest items have explicitly correct answers. Yet, some judgment is required for scoring the Spatial Construction items in relation to comparison drawings.

Passing scores for the subtests range from 100% accuracy to some percentage thereof. The total number of subtests passed is then used to determine whether the examinee falls in a normal (i.e., score of 10 or above), borderline (score of 8 or 9), or further evaluation (score of 7 or below) group. Although the test manual suggests that all examinees scoring below 7 should be referred for "full neuropsychological/psychological assessment of cognitive functioning" (p. 11) those falling in the borderline range should also be given further scrutiny to determine if further evaluation is necessary.

Completion of the MEAMS requires approximately 10 minutes and consists of two alternate forms to allow for sequential administrations. A 14-page manual describes the 12 cognitive areas assessed, validity and reliability data, and interpretation of scores.

DEVELOPMENT. There is a dearth of information included in the test manual regarding any underlying assumptions to the MEAMS's development. The MEAMS items were selected from a larger and extensive set of tests developed at the Middlesex Hospital, but no discussion was provided of the rationale for selecting those items for the current instrument. It is also noted that the two memory subtests were drawn from the "Rivermead Behavioral Memory Test." These subtests were added because the 10 original MEAMS subtests were not satisfactory in their assessment of memory function. A review of several subtests (e.g., Orientation, Naming, Arithmetic, Spatial Construction), however, reflects their commonality to many mental status type examinations. Yet, other subtests (e.g., Fragmented Letter Perception, Unusual Views, Usual Views) are less obvious as to why they were included in this particular mental status examination. There is also no rationale as to why the specific number of items was selected for each subtest. Furthermore, there is no indication about why the MEAMS was necessary as compared to other mental status examinations.

TECHNICAL. Statistical validation of the individual MEAMS items is not presented in the test manual, except for the memory items. Reliability and validity issues for the nonmemory items were addressed when developing the original instruments and not reviewed. As such, there is not an independent assessment of most MEAMS items in the current configuration. MEAMS validation focused on its utility in assessing cognitive functioning.

The MEAMS's psychometric properties were assessed with 120 patients undergoing treatment at a day hospital that was attached to the Middlesex Hospital. Each new patient was administered the MEAMS as part of the admission process, along with additional psychological and medical evaluations. Each patient then received a diagnosis from a psychiatrist who was unaware of MEAMS scores. The first 40 Alzheimer's disease, first 40 multi-infarct dementia, and first 20 depressed but not demented patients admitted to the day hospital were included in the validation study. An additional 20 depressed but not demented patients, for whom MEAMS scores were known prior to diagnosis, were also included to give equal numbers to each group. Across all groups the patients were predominantly female with extreme skewing of gender for all but the multi-infarct dementia group.

Interrater reliability for 22 patients produced a Pearson Product Moment correlation of .98 for the number of subtests failed. Yet, it is uncertain from which patient group those 22 patients were drawn. Similarly, both versions of the MEAMS were administered to 28 patients, with uncertainty over patient characteristics, producing a Pearson Product Moment correlation of .91 for the number of subtests failed.

MEAMS validation focused on whether the two dementia groups differed from the combined group of depressed patients or from each other, for each of the 10 nonmemory subtests. Student t-tests were conducted comparing the multi-infarct dementia versus depressed groups, Alzheimer's disease versus depressed groups, and the multi-infarct dementia versus Alzheimer's disease groups. Twenty-five of the 30 tests showed significant differences with 4 of the nonsignificant tests being for the multi-infarct dementia versus Alzheimer's disease comparisons. As such, it was noted that both dementia groups performed poorer than the depressed group and that the Alzheimer's group performed poorer than the multi-infarct dementia group. The reason for this latter difference did not draw any specific interpretations.

A separate validation of the MEAMS memory items was first drawn from the Rivermead Behavioral Memory Test data. This involved comparing performances for Alzheimer's Disease patients to elderly depressed patients or age-matched normal controls. Following demonstration that the memory items were sensitive to the impairments of Alzheimer's Disease, the items were then administered to a group of stroke patients who demonstrated the MEAMS items to be related to overall performance on the larger memory test. Based on these studies, a Pass-Failure score was set for the memory items and those items were then included as two of the MEAMS's 12 subtests.

Based on the validation data and experience with the MEAMS, it appears the authors set cut scores to characterize performances. Unfortunately, there is no documentation as to the statistical or clinical basis for setting those cut scores. There also is no rationale for distinguishing those who pass 8 or 9 subtests from those who pass no more than 7 subtests as each group is recommended to have further assessment. As such it would seem that a single screening score would be more appropriate.

COMMENTARY. It has now been over 15 years since the MEAMS was first published and the manual presents only the original psychometric data. Moreover, the psychometric data are inadequate for determining how the MEAMS was developed and validated. Interrater reliability is based on Pearson Product Moment correlations for the number of failed subtests rather than using more typical interrater reliability approaches (e.g., Kappa). Although the number of subtests failed may be appropriate for interrater reliability of the single-items subtests, it is not adequate for those items requiring subjective judgment or having numerous items. Similarly, the absolute number of subtests failed was used to determine parallel-form reliability. Assessing the duplicity of each subtest would have been more appropriate as individual subtest performance differences could occur and still produce the same number of subtests failed.

The MEAMS's validation is also problematic as too much reliance was made on the validity bases for the original instruments. As such, there is no construct validity assessment as it relates to the 12 areas of cognitive functioning assessed or to the concept of impairment for which screening scores seem to have been set.

Although discriminant validity may exist for the MEAMS in distinguishing demented patients from depressed or normal elderly patients based on the results presented, the validity analysis is marred by two common and errors: small and restricted sample and too many statistical tests conducted without adequate error control. The sample size is small for use in test development and restricted to patients at one facility. And, based on the manual's documentation, all diagnoses were made by a single psychiatrist with no assessment of diagnostic accuracy. The validity analysis also included over 30 tests of difference. These problems raise questions about generalization and the potential that some results were erroneous.

Given that the MEAMS was developed over 15 years ago, a revision of the manual is needed that provides expanded psychometric data acquired over the intervening years.

SUMMARY. The basis for the MEAMS is laudable in that is was developed as a screening tool to assess several areas of basic cognitive functioning in elderly patients. Its actual use, however, may be to screen patients who warrant further evaluation of cognitive function as it seems to have little utility in discriminating across various cognitive domains. Unfortunately, the MEAMS also has a very weak psychometric foundation. Issues of reliability and validity have not been fully addressed. There also is limited generalization from the setting in which it was developed to other settings. As such, this instrument would only appear applicable to settings that have similar characteristics to where it was developed. Finally, it also is unknown what the MEAMS offers beyond other instruments also commercially available.

[125]

Millon Index of Personality Styles Revised.

Purpose: "Designed to measure personality styles of normally functioning adults."
Population: 18 years and older.
Publication Dates: 1994–2004.
Acronym: MIPS Revised.
Scores, 28: 6 Motivating Styles (Pleasure-Enhancing, Pain-Avoiding, Actively Modifying, Passively Accommodating, Self-Indulging, Other-Nurturing), 8 Thinking Styles (Externally Focused, Internally Focused, Realistic/Sensing, Imaginative/Intuiting, Thought-Guided, Feeling-Guided, Conservation-Seeking, Innovation-Seeking), 10 Behaving Styles (Asocial/Withdrawing, Gregarious/Outgoing, Anxious/Hesitat-

ing, Confident/Asserting, Unconventional/Dissenting, Dutiful/Conforming, Submissive/Yielding, Dominant/Controlling, Dissatisfied/Complaining, Cooperative/Agreeing), 3 Validity Indices (Positive Impression, Negative Impression, Consistency), Clinical Index.
Administration: Group or individual.
Forms: 1 form with 2 reporting options: Interpretive, Profile.
Price Data, 2007: $46 per manual (2004, 176 pages); $21 per 10 test booklets; $21 per 25 answer sheets; $41.50 per 50 hand-scoring answer sheets; $89 per Q Local desktop software; $250 per Q Local network software; quantity discounts available.
Time: (25–30) minutes.
Comments: Paper-and-pencil or computer administration available.
Author: Theodore Millon.
Publisher: Pearson.
  a) Q LOCAL SCORING AND REPORTING SOFTWARE.
  Price Data: $88 per Q Local starter kit with interpretive reports including manual, 3 answer sheets, 1 test booklet, and 3 Q Local administrations (does not include Q Local software); $17.25 per Q Local interpretive report administration; $9 per Q Local profile reports administration.
  b) MAIL-IN SCORING SERVICE.
  Price Data: $95 per mail-in starter kit with profile reports including manual, 3 answer sheets, and 1 test booklet; $20.25 per mail-in interpretive report scoring and answer sheet; $12 per mail-in profile report scoring and answer sheet.
  c) HAND-SCORING MATERIALS.
  Price Data: $169 per hand-scoring starter kit including manual, 10 test booklets, 50 answer sheets, and answer keys.
Cross References: See T5:1688 (1 reference); for reviews by James P. Choca and Peter Zachar of an earlier version, see 13:202.

Review of the Millon Index of Personality Styles Revised by S. ALVIN LEUNG, Professor, Department of Educational Psychology, The Chinese University of Hong Kong, Hong Kong, China:

DESCRIPTION. The Millon Index of Personality Styles Revised (MIPS Revised) is a measure of general personality of normal-functioning adults ages 18 or older with an eighth-grade reading skill. The instrument was theoretically grounded in an evolutionary perspective, presuming that "normal personality" has adaptive and survival functions. Personality is manifested in one's styles of perceiving, feeling, thinking, and acting. Under this evolutionary tenet, the themes and nature of the MIPS Revised scales were derived from concepts of classic personality theories including those of Freud, Jung, Sullivan, and Leary.

The MIPS Revised can be administered to adults with diverse concerns, in helping contexts such as employee development programs, career guidance, and screening for marital compatibility. The MIPS Revised has a total of 180 test items, including 12 pairs of bipolar content scales (165 items) and three validity indicators, which are Negative Impression (NI) (10 items embedded within the 165 items), Consistency scale (5 items), and Positive Impression (PI) (10 items). All the items are presented in true-false format. There are three groups of content scales, which are Motivating Styles, Thinking Styles, and Behaving Styles. The Motivating Styles cluster has three pairs of scales, which are Pleasure-Enhancing and Pain-Avoiding, Actively Modifying and Passively Accommodating, and Self-Indulging and Other-Nurturing. The Thinking Styles cluster has four pairs of scales, which are Externally Focused and Internally Focused, Realistic/Sensing and Imaginative/Intuiting, Thought-Guided and Feeling-Guided, and Conversation-Seeking and Innovation-Seeking. The Behavior Styles cluster has five pairs of scales, which are Asocial/Withdrawing and Gregarious/Outgoing, Anxious/Hesitating and Confident/Asserting, Unconventional/Dissenting and Dutiful/Conforming, Submissive/Yielding and Dominant/Controlling, and Dissatisfied/Complaining and Cooperative/Agreeing.

The MIPS Revised can be administered online or through an on-site automated computer version in which individualized profiles and reports are generated. There are also two paper-and-pencil formats. Answer sheets are either hand-scored (using scoring templates from the publisher) or sent to the publisher for scoring and report generation. The interpretive report provides users with a cover page, test scores and profiles, and an interpretive summary. Most test takers could complete the test in about 20 to 30 minutes.

DEVELOPMENT. The MIPS Revised test items were developed through a systematic process. First, prototypical items consistent with the theoretical content of scales were written and expert psychologists with no prior knowledge of item affiliation sorted them into scales. Items that were correctly sorted were selected. Additional items were developed for the validity indicators, including a Positive Impression (PI) scale, Consistency scale, and Negative Impression (NI) scale. This process resulted in a 300-item test booklet, which was then administered to college and adult standardization samples.

Based on data from the adult standardization sample, partial correlation was used to examine the relationship between each individual item and scale scores. Prototypical items with a high partial correlation with the target scale were each given a weight of 3 points. When a prototypical item for a target scale was also empirically found to relate to another theoretically consonant scale, a weight of 2 points or 1 point was assigned, depending on the strength of association. Meanwhile, items with low partial correlations and weak substantive relations to the target constructs were dropped. This process resulted in a 165-item inventory, and due to the use of a multiple keying system a maximum of 627 raw score points could be generated.

Prevalence scores (PS) were used rather than standard scores such as T-scores. The range of PS was 0 to 100, with a PS score of 50 as the reference point separating individuals who possess the trait and those who do not. Prevalence scores of 50 or above on each MIPS Revised content scale corresponds with the prevalence of individuals in the general population who possess the measured trait. The higher the score is above 50, the more a person possesses the measured trait, and vice versa. In addition, the frequency and intensity with which an individual might exhibit a particular trait is also a function of his or her position in the polar opposite scale. A scaling procedure involving the use of actuarially estimated prevalence rates in the general population was used to transform raw scores to PS, a procedure not clearly described in the test manual. Separate gender norms are available based on the assumption that the prevalence rates of personality traits in men and women are not the same.

TECHNICAL. The adult normative sample consisted of 500 females and 500 males from eight cities in each of four regions in the U.S. that were matched to the population by race/ethnicity (African American, Hispanic, White, and Other), age, education level, and employment status. The college normative sample consisted of 1,600 students (800 females and 800 males) from 14 colleges and universities whose demographic backgrounds were equivalent to the general college student population. Despite apparent attention to demographic characteristics of the standardization sample, no information as to whether differences in test scores emerged within any of the demographic groups is offered in the test manual. Possible ethnic group differences in test scores and implications for score interpretation are important issues to address in assessment, including personality assessment.

Among the general adult sample, the median internal consistency reliability coefficients (alpha) of the 24 content scales for females and males were .76 and .78, respectively, and the range was .67 to .84 for females and .67 to .85 for males. The median split-half reliability coefficient was .80 for both gender groups (range for females was .72 to .87, range for males was .72 to .88). The test-retest reliability of the scales was examined with a sample of 50 adults (20 to 82 days), and the median correlation coefficient was .85 (range was .73 to .91).

Similarly, the median internal consistency reliability coefficients of the scales among female and male college students were .78 and .76, respectively, and the range was .69 to .88 for females and .69 to .87 for males. The median split-half reliability coefficient was .80 for both females (range was .72 to .89) and males (range was .74 to .87). The test-retest reliability of test scores (21 to 23 days) was assessed with a sample of 110 college students, and the median correlation coefficient was .84 (range was .78 to .90). Overall, the reliabilities of the MIPS scales appear adequate and consistent with what is expected for a comprehensive personality assessment instrument.

Patterns of convergence and divergence among the MIPS Revised scales were used as evidence of internal validity. As predicted, inverse correlations were found between pairs of opposing scales, as well as between scales that were theoretically dissonant. Conversely, positive correlation was observed between scales that were theoretically consonant. The potential impact of using an "overlapping keying" approach was assessed through counting only prototypical items in scale scoring, and the resultant patterns of correlations among the scales were similar to those when all items were counted. Overall, with the exception of the opposing pairs of scales in which negative correlations were expected, it is not clear from the

conceptual framework of the MIPS Revised which pairs of scales were expected to be "consonant" and "dissonant," and in the absence of specific "a priori" theoretical proposition it is difficult to interpret the observed patterns of correlation.

The patterns of correlation between the MIPS Revised scales and a number of established personality inventories were used as evidence of external validity. For example, high correlations ($N = 100$, $r > .70$) were found between the MIPS Revised Thinking-Styles scales and the corresponding scales in the Myers-Briggs Type Indicator (MBTI). Similarly, selected MIPS scales were found to correlate with corresponding scales and/or factors of established personality measures such as the 16PF Questionnaire, the California Psychological Inventory, the NEO Personality Inventory, and the Minnesota Multiphasic Personality Inventory-2 (MMPI-2).

In order to establish the validity of the PI and NI scales, participants were asked to either answer the items honestly or to present themselves positively or negatively through their responses. The findings were used to establish cutoffs to identify profiles that might be questionable in terms of validity due to distorted response styles.

Research findings were reported to show the validity and diverse applications of the MIPS Revised scales. A study with military recruits ($N = 297$) showed that those who were judged to be fit for military service had higher PS values on positively toned scales, and lower PS values on negatively toned scales, than those who were judged to be unfit for military service. A composite Clinical Index was constructed by aggregating PS values of a number of scales based on their conceptual meanings. A high degree of agreement was found between the value of the Index (using T score ≥ 35 as a cutoff) and the judgment of clinical psychologists regarding the fitness of recruits for military service. The findings from this study were used as a basis for the interpretation of the Clinical Index in the interpretive report, in which a T-score of 35 or lower suggested that someone might be "experiencing psychological distress and who may benefit from a separate, more comprehensive, psychological evaluation" (manual, p. 75).

In another study, composite indexes on Adherence to Work Ethics, Thoroughness and Attentiveness to Details, Sensitivity to the Interest of Others, and Emotional Stability were constructed. The various composite indexes were found to be predictive of police officer trainees' (*N* = 47) field training performance ratings and performance on simulated field situations. Other studies on the use of the MIPS Revised for career development issues also were reported, including studies on personality styles of career undecided college students (*N* = 100), the association between leadership ratings and personality styles among mid-level managers (*N* = 51), and the relationship between personality styles and absenteeism and disciplinary actions of hourly municipal employees (*N* = 41).

COMMENTARY. A major limitation of the MIPS Revised is related to its theoretical clarity and specificity. The theoretical structure of the instrument appears broad but loose, encompassing concepts from key psychoanalytically oriented theorists such as Freud, Jung, and Leary, tied together under an evolutionary umbrella. A higher degree of conceptual specificity is needed in at least three areas. First, it is not clear how positions in the 24 scales denote different degrees of normal or dysfunctional adaptation. More specific guidelines on *score interpretation* in relation to personality functioning should be developed to aid in the interpretive process. Second, in addition to pairs of bipolar personality styles, the test manual put forth other examples of theoretically consonant and dissonant scales, especially in the section in which internal validity is discussed. It appears that what constitutes consonance and dissonance internally within the instrument remains fluid and unclear. Third, the test authors state "no score can be interpreted independent of its relative and configural position with other scale scores" (manual, p. 7), yet there is a lack of conceptual specificity and guidelines on how different groups of scales, including scales within the same domain, could be understood and interpreted in aggregate. Enriching conceptual clarity in the above three areas will greatly enhance the power and utility of the MIPS Revised scales.

A number of indexes have been developed, including the Clinical Index and indexes related to personality assessment of police officers. Because these indexes were initially conceived theoretically based on the additive meanings of scales and items, their validity should be further examined empirically to establish construct validity, especially given that the studies reported so far were based on samples limited in size and demographic diversity. More central than others is the construct validity of the Clinical Index because it is reported in the Interpretive Profile. More research studies are needed to strengthen its conceptual underpinnings and empirical foundation.

Additional studies should be carried out to examine the validity of the NI and PI scales. The items and the cutoff points of these two scales were chosen based on laboratory studies requesting participants to present themselves positively or negatively. There is no information on whether the scales could correctly identify distorted profiles in actual assessment settings, and the impact of distortion on different MIPS Revised scales is unknown. Generating more empirical findings on the NI and PI scales would strengthen the utility of these validity indicators.

There is no information on how the automated interpretive report is generated and how it is structured to provide valid, constructive, and easy-to-understand feedback to clients. Meanwhile, there should be more specific guidelines on how counseling professionals should approach the task of test interpretation with and without the aid of the report.

SUMMARY. The MIPS Revised is a carefully constructed instrument measuring an array of normal personality dimensions. The personality dimensions were conceptually grounded in the diverse psychological literature on personality. There was evidence showing that the MIPS Revised was a reliable instrument. A number of carefully planned research studies showed evidence of convergent, divergent, and construct validity. At this point, this instrument could be used in counseling or other applied settings to facilitate self-understanding and awareness so as to strengthen an individual's adaptive functioning. However, given the limitations of conceptual clarity and construct validity, the MIPS Revised should be used with caution in situations in which formal clinical assessment or personnel selection are involved.

Review of the Millon Index of Personality Styles Revised by DAVID J. PITTENGER, Associate Provost for Academic Administration, The University of Tennessee at Chattanooga, Chattanooga, TN:

DESCRIPTION. The Millon Index of Personality Styles Revised (MIPS Revised) is a refinement of the previously published version of this inventory. The revised version contains 180 items as does the previous edition. Moreover, test developers renamed the scales to facilitate a ready description of the personality traits the instrument purportedly measures. For the most part, the inventory follows the structure and purpose of the original version of the inventory, which is to provide a broad and readily understood measure of personality as defined by Millon.

As with other popular measures of personality, the MIPS Revised assesses personality by reporting the individual's relative position on a bipolar scale. Unlike the Myers-Briggs Type Indicator (MBTI; T7:1710), which produces an absolute categorization of personality type, the MIPS Revised produces weighted scores for each personality dimension. This procedure affords the opportunity to determine the extent to which individual scores deviate from population norms. Therefore, the MIPS Revised is comparable in structure to the NEO Personality Inventory (NEO-PI; T7:1729) as an omnibus measure of personality.

Although the test may be used in a variety of clinical settings, it appears to be well suited for use in nonclinical settings where issues of personality disorder are not of particular concern. Indeed, the labels for the personality trait dimensions tend to be value neutral and lend themselves to teambuilding exercises. Given the high correlation between the subscales of the two instruments, one may use the MIPS Revised as an alternative to the MBTI or the NEO-PI.

The MIPS Revised assesses 12 underlying bipolar personality traits that represent three main personality styles. The revised names for these styles are Motivating, Thinking, and Behaving. The Motivating trait purports to measure the individual's propensity to manipulate the surrounding environment and react to reinforcement. The subscales include the bipolar traits Pleasure-Enhancing—Pain-Avoiding, Actively Modifying—Passively Accommodating, and Self-Indulging—Other-Nurturing. The Thinking Styles assess how the individual prefers to process information and includes the dimensions Externally Focused—Internally Focused, Realistic/Sensing—Imaginative/Intuiting, Thought-Guided—Feeling-Guided, and Conservation-Seeking—Innovation-Seeking. The Behaving Styles consist of a cluster of five traits related to the individual's interpersonal style and method of interacting with others. The subscales

are Unconventional/Dissenting—Dutiful/Conforming, Submissive/Yielding—Dominant/Controlling, Dissatisfied/Complaining—Cooperative/Agreeing, Asocial/Withdrawing—Gregarious/Outgoing, and Anxious/Hesitating—Confident/Asserting.

These personality dimensions represent Millon's theory of personality, which is described in the second chapter of the manual. Briefly, this theory of personality borrows from older theories of personality (e.g., Freud and Jung) as well as more contemporary theories (e.g., the Big Five). Although this chapter provides a lengthy description of the evolution of Millon's theory it does not provide a critical analysis of the potential superiority of this theory to other perspectives of personality. Indeed, there is little analysis of the theory as a more effective characterization of personality than other perspectives.

The test consists of a reusable test pamphlet and a separate machine-readable answer sheet. Users of the test also may hand score the answer sheet or purchase a software package for the computer administration and scoring of the responses. Each item is a declarative statement about the individual (e.g., "I am very confident") to which the individual responds true or false. According to the test manual, the test can be completed by individuals with an eighth grade reading level and within 30 minutes.

DEVELOPMENT. The authors of the test manual take pains to make clear that the construction of the inventory was theoretically rather than empirically driven. Consequently, items were first written because they were thought to represent a specific bipolar trait. Those items that were consistently judged to be consistent with the trait were retained for subsequent analysis.

Most of the subsequent development of the inventory follows common practice among measures of personality. Specifically, preliminary versions of the scale were administered to a broad range of Americans who matched population norms regarding age, education, race, geographic area, and sex. Resultant data were used to establish normative values for scale interpretation. The manual provides adequate detail for the collection of the normative data as well as an exegesis of item construction processes.

TECHNICAL. Scoring the individual bipolar traits produces a "prevalence score," which can range from 0 to 100, the extremes of the scale, with 50 representing the midpoint of each scale. According to the test manual, prevalence scores of 29 and 69 represent the respective medians of the subpopulations of individuals classified on either pole of the bipolar trait. Although the prevalence scores present information related to the magnitude of the personality trait, the score is not as readily interpreted as a percentile or standardized score. The consequence of this scoring procedure may require that those who administer the inventory will need to spend considerable time explaining the proper meaning of the score.

The evidence of reliability includes measures of coefficient alpha, split-half reliability, and test-retest reliability. All reliability measures represent relatively high measures of consistency.

The evidence of validity is less encouraging. Several factors lead to this guarded assessment. First, there is considerable intercorrelation among the scales. Second, there is a relatively strong correlation between the MIPS Revised scales and scales for other popular measures of personality including the CPI, MBTI, and NEO-PI. Finally, the available data have not been subjected to the types of statistical analyses, such as a confirmatory factor analysis, that would confirm the primacy of the latent traits implied in the theory. Each of these concerns is more fully elaborated in the following paragraphs.

The intercorrelation observed among the traits may reflect the fact that many of the items are used as indices for more than one trait. This practice raises important questions about the theoretical independence of the underlying traits as well as the degree to which each trait scale assesses unique variance. In brief, the level of intercorrelation suggests the need for fewer traits and therefore a more parsimonious explanation of personality. Although the test authors may wish to preserve the theoretical structure of personality, there comes a time when the data suggest that the theory may imagine more than what can be measured.

This assessment is confirmed when considering the correlations between scales of various personality measures. One would expect clear evidence of convergent validity among the multiple measures of personality as these instruments measure traits commonly included in omnibus measures of personality. To the extent that the MIPS Revised purports to be a unique measure of personality one would expect to find evidence of discriminant validity where the instrument captured variance among individuals not assessed by other instruments.

Finally, the most important verification of the MIPS Revised's theoretical structure is missing from the data analysis. The manual makes no reference to any attempts to verify the validity of the instrument using commonly available confirmatory factor analytic tools. Such an analysis would allow one to confirm that the unique scoring of the MIPS is a statistically superior model to potential alternatives. Unfortunately, the author of the test manual places greater emphasis on preserving the theory rather than allowing the data to shape and refine theory.

SUMMARY. The MIPS Revised provides a serviceable measure of personality that may be readily used with nonclinical populations. The structure and labeling of individual bipolar traits can be presented easily in a nonthreatening manner to members of diverse populations. As such, the instrument may be seen as an alternative to the NEO-PI or the MBTI. Indeed, the instrument appears to correlate well with those instruments. Although this attribute may make the instrument appealing as an alternative personality inventory, there is not compelling evidence that the MIPS Revised offers a unique measure of personality traits not captured by those instruments.

[126]
Millon Pre-Adolescent Clinical Inventory.

Purpose: To "identify, predict, and understand a broad range of psychological disorders that are common in 9–12 year olds seen in clinical settings."

Population: Ages 9–12.

Publication Date: 2005.

Acronym: M-PACI.

Scores: 16 scales: Emerging Personality Patterns (Confident, Outgoing, Conforming, Submissive, Inhibited, Unruly, Unstable), Current Clinical Signs (Anxiety/Fears, Attention Deficits, Obsessions/Compulsions, Conduct Disorder, Disruptive Behaviors, Depressive Moods, Reality Distortions), Response Validity Indicators (Invalidity, Response Negativity).

Administration: Individual or group.

Price Data, 2005: $215 per hand-scoring starter kit including manual (115 pages), 50 answer sheets, 50 profile forms, and answer keys; $86 per mail-in scoring starter kit including manual and 3 answer sheets; $81 per Q local starter kit with interpretive reports including manual, 3 answer sheets, and 3 Q local administrations; $89 per Q local software for desktop version; $250 per Q local software for network version; $38 per manual; quantity discounts available.

Time: (15–20) minutes.

Comments: Hand-scored, mail-scored, or computer-based administration, scoring, and interpretation available.

Authors: Theodore Millon, Robert Tringone, Carrie Millon, and Seth Grossman.

Publisher: Pearson.

Review of the Millon Pre-Adolescent Clinical Inventory by JEFFREY A. ATLAS, Clinical Psychologist, SCO Family of Services, Queens, NY:

DESCRIPTION. Psychologists brought up on Theodore Millon's integrative-evolutionary approach to personality, as students and teachers of his tests, may welcome his latest instrument with interest.

The Millon Pre-Adolescent Clinical Inventory (M-PACI) has as its purpose to "identify, predict, and understand a broad range of psychological issues that are common in 9–12-year-olds seen in clinical settings" (manual, p. 3). As with other, particularly new, psychological instruments, the inventory appears most successful in its first aim of identification. "Prediction," presumably of clinical course, would presuppose longitudinal research and accrual of data pertaining to the instrument. Evaluation of the "understanding" of disorders provided by the M-PACI necessitates examination of its 16 scales and their relationship to interpretive reports.

The administration of the scale is fairly straightforward and user-friendly, assuming examiners' psychology licensure or graduate degree with tests and measurements experience. The combined answer and score sheets are cleverly designed to permit examinee completion of the 97-item True-False questionnaire, with the administrator having the option of hand-scoring the measure using a series of plastic templates.

The measure yields 16 percentile scales subsuming seven emerging personality patterns (Confident, Outgoing, Conforming, Submissive, Inhibited, Unruly, Unstable) and seven clinical signs (Anxiety/Fears, Attention Deficits, Obsessions/Compulsions, Conduct Problems, Disruptive Behaviors, Depressive Moods, Reality Distortions). The items are pitched at a third grade reading level and flow easily, tapping aspects of a Westernized-pre-adolescent's universe of everyday experiences (e.g., "I have many talents ... My teacher has to remind me to pay attention ... My parents tell me that I have mood swings"). In addition, there are two validity scales, a Resonse Negativity one, which may tap unusually high or low self-portrayals, and an Invalidity scale. In the latter, the authors reject earlier endeavors to nest false response sets in mutually exclusive or distorting responses and simply pose four widely spaced iterative items to the examinee asking if they are lying (e.g., "I'm not answering this test in an honest way," and "Many of my answers to these questions are a lie"). These items fairly jump out of the page and seem to lack face validity inasmuch as a respondent admitting deception would be unlikely to have the motivation to complete the entire scale. The authors report that only 1% of the development sample endorsed each of these items, but as this could variously reflect poor comprehension, limited English, attention problems, or lying, the Invalidity Scale is virtually uninterpretable and in this reviewer's opinion is of questionable usefulness to the measure.

DEVELOPMENT. Six of the seven emerging personality pattern scales derive from Millon's configuration of personality traits as encompassing active or passive polarities in individuals demonstrating independent or dependent orientations. In this matrix, for example, Submissive personalities emerge at the intersection of passive and dependent orientations, Confident from passive and independent orientations, whereas self-other ambivalence in a passive individual issues in a Conforming personality style. The Unstable personality designation describes more serious personality issues.

The seven Clinical Signs scales are seen as "extensions of underlying personality" vulnerabilities or as "potentially biologically driven conditions" (manual, p. 10). Following Millon's biosocial learning model, there is a natural unfolding or continuity between certain personality patterns and clinical signs, such as Inhibited Personality and Depressive Mood.

In developing the M-PACI, the authors wrote items for the postulated personality dimensions and signs in assembling a research inventory, and then had this administered to 9- to 12-year-olds in a variety of clinical settings. Independent ratings of these individuals by their clinicians provided a basis for correlational analysis and final inventory development.

Inspection of the research sample demographics table suggests reasonable aproximation to U.S. Census data. African American individuals are somewhat underrepresented at 7.7%. Males are overrepresented at 68.7% but this is consistent with child guidance referrals. It should be noted that about half of the subject pool is drawn from private practice settings, as opposed to a bit over a third in public settings such as residences, clinics, and schools. Over half of the 292 research subjects were seen five or more times by participating clinicians. Six research protocols were set aside as invalid, leaving a final pool of 286.

Clinicans were asked to rate particiants on the scales based on first- and second-most prominent patterns and signs. Unruly personality pattern and Disruptive clinical signs figured high in prominence, whereas Reality Distortions were quite low, as one would expect from a representative clinical pre-adolescent sample. Subject item-endorsements in a provisional scale were correlated with clinician ratings to yield a final set of prototype and subsidiary items for each scale.

The "base rate" for each scale were converted into percentiles to maintain the relative differences in prevalence rates between scales. For example, almost a fifth of subjects had a base rate of zero on the Reality Distortions scale. The lack of normalization of the distribution of traits and signs is not unusual in inventories as opposed to tests, inasmuch as it is not prudent to assume that loss of reality orientation, for example, follows a bell-curve population distribution presumed to characterize intelligence. The lack of standardized scores such as T-scores does, however, put a greater interpretive burden on the examiner and report-writer. The authors eschewed establishing prevalence-based diagnostic cutoffs due to their belief in the malleability of pre-adolescent personality.

Combined (single) norms for boys and girls similarly preserved real differences in base rate scores. The result that boys scored higher on Unruly, Attention Deficits, and Disruptive Behaviors, and girls scored higher in Conforming, Inhibited, Anxiety/Fears, and Depressive Moods is consistent with prevalence rates commonly seen and may be viewed as informally contributing to construct validity. The authors encourage looking at the scatter plot or profile of percentile scores versus elevation in understanding individual pre-adolescents from an idiographic, or intraindividual perspective. In a sense, the M-PACI presumes what it purportedly sets out to measure. Rather than offering guideposts in diagnosing disturbance, the inventory is restricted to "troubled" populations and offered as a map in assessing the personality typology of individual pre-adolescents. Mental health professionals hoping to "understand" the degree or tye of psychopathology shown by their clients might be frustrated by this scale on the basis of its presuppositions.

TECHNICAL. Accepting that the "standardization" sample of the M-PACI is actually a select group drawn from the universe of pre-adolescence, one may proceed to evaluate relevant reliability and validity data.

Reliability. Coefficient alpha reliability values for the 14 scales are presented in the manual. The alpha coefficients are moderately high, ranging from .63 for Obsessions/Compulsions to .84 for Unruly. The results suggest satisfactory internal consistency of scales considering the overlap in scales measuring different dimensions of personality.

One would wish the authors had presented some data, if only preliminary, on test-retest reliability of scores from the M-PACI before it was published. Even allowing for some fluidity in personality presentation over time within the pre-adolescent years, some indication of stability in scores would make the descriptive project of this instrument more compelling.

Factor analysis of the scale intercorrelations yielded two factors most contributive to variance, labeled Externalizing and Internalizing. The Externalizing factor had high loadings for the Unruly, Conduct Problems, and Disruptive Behaviors scales whereas the Internalizing factor featured high loadings of the Submissive, Inhibited, and Depressive Moods scales. A three-factor loading separated out the Confident and Outgoing scales, which may be seen as indices of positive environmental adjustment. Overall, the factor structure is consistent with the logic of the scales of the M-PACI and serves to support the construct validity of the instrument.

Validity. Convergent validity coefficients of the final M-PACI with clinician ratings were mild to moderate, all statistically significant (at least $p <$

.05, two-tailed). This would suggest that the instrument is successful in discriminating those participants with the personality dimensions under examination.

Correlation of the M-PACI base rate scores with the raw scores of administered Children's Depression Inventories yielded a coefficient of .65. The Revised Children's Manifest Anxiety Scale Total Anxiety Scale registered a .75 correlation with the M-PACI Obsessions/Compulsions scale. These high ratings support concurrent validity of the M-PACI.

Demographic comparisons of M-PACI scores show few significant differences between mean scores. Younger (9–10-year-old) children scored higher than older (11–12-year-old) children on the Submissive scale. White participants scored higher than nonwhite on the Outgoing scale. The convergent validity score (comparing M-PACI and clinicians' scores) was .42 for white participants and -.07 for nonwhite. Although these results raise some concerns, perhaps relating to a slight underrepresentation of African Americans in the research sample, overall the results of differential demographic analyses are very good.

COMMENTARY. A preliminary caution by the test's authors is that "because the M-PACI inventory was normed using children who had already been identified as troubled, it should not be used to screen general populations of children for psychological problems" (manual, p. 3). Although psychometrically sound, the dictum to not generalize outside of a "troubled" population raises numerous theoretical and practical issues. As Millon views pre-adolescent disturbances as inchoate and not necessarily predictive of adult disorders, the discontinuity implied between clinical and nonclinical populations is discordant with a premise of the underlying personality typology (stability of traits), as well as limiting the usefulness of the measure. If a mental health professional limits the use of the M-PACI to already-identified "troubled" populations, and the great majority of school-referred cases of pre-adolescents involve some variety of unruly behavior, the extra diagnostic yield of a 20-minute instrument (with matching hand-scoring time) must be carefully evaluated.

The test authors provide some useful guidelines for interpretation of the M-PACI. Inspecting the percentile elevations of the Submissive,

Inhibited, Unruly, and Unstable personality scales may cue the clinician into emerging problem areas. Very high scores on the Reality Distortions scale may signal the presence of a psychotic disorder. In some instances, a notably high score on one of the emerging personality patterns, coupled with another high score, may indicate early evidence of personality or character styles (e.g., Submissive-Inhibited). Coupling of certain clinical signs scales (e.g., elevated Attention Deficits and Disruptive Behaviors) may suggest the presence of Attention-Deficit/Hyperactivity Disorder, Combined Type.

Integrating and contrasting select scale combinations leads the authors to apparent attempts at limited predictions of behavior. The manual thus details a contrast between two Submissive 12-year-olds, one Submissive-Inhibited-Depressive, the other Submissive-Outgoing-Depressive. Although both girls may be Submissive and Depressive, one might anticipate the Inhibited girl to "be more susceptible to severe and potentially protracted depressive episodes marked by a dysphoric mood, a withdrawn stance, fatigue and weakness, pessimistic thoughts, and negative self-esteem" (manual, p. 68). In contrast, the response of Submissive-Outgoing personalities "is to attempt to ward off the depressive feelings by engaging others and soliciting attention and support" (manual, p. 68).

The algorithms of prominent scale combinations appear to underlie the computer-generated "ideal-typical" interpretive reports provided in the appendix of the manual. As these reports draw from particular but unspecified items, some of the statements have an oracular quality (e.g., an 11-year-old boy "can be a challenge to manage, but trust and respect can temper this tendency," manual, p. 90). In addition, from the snapshot of items there are vague intimations of causality: "His assertive and bullying behavior contributes to an impulsive and quixotic emotionality" (manual, p. 91).

The lack of transparency between groups of predictors and inventory items makes it difficult for other professionals to evaluate the validity of such computer-generated reports. In more traditional projective personality testing one may at least preface inferences with citations of, for example, Rorschach movement and color responsivity and particular content. In the M-PACI sample reports, the participant appears reified or dislocated, in a literal sense in Sample Report #2, which is left blank after a standard introductory section (manual, p. 98).

Mental health professionals who trust and value the ease of computer-driven reports may find these reservations quibbling and take advantage of this scoring method. In the present reviewer's opinion, the limitations of the M-PACI's test development sample and the absence of cutoff scores restricts the usefulness of this measure. One may imagine a niche in which it finds some utility in instances of pre-adolescents in initial stages of assessment who demonstrate poor verbal productivity regarding the nature of their problems.

SUMMARY. The M-PACI is a novel new instrument that extends Millon's personality typology into pre-adolescence. The decision to limit its development to a clinical sample instead of establishing population norms restricts its utility. With one or two exceptions the test is attractively packaged. Clinicians working with less verbal troubled youth might find this instrument of value in identifying problem areas and foci for treatment.

Review of the Millon Pre-Adolescent Clinical Inventory by STEVEN I. PFEIFFER, Professor and Director of Clinical Training, PhD Program in Combined Counseling and School Psychology, Florida State University, Tallahassee, FL:

DESCRIPTION. The Millon Pre-Adolescent Clinical Inventory (M-PACI) is a multidimensional self-report inventory for use with 9- to 12-year-olds. It is designed for a pre-adolescent clinical population as a downward extension of the Millon Adolescent Clinical Inventory (Millon, 1993; T7:1636). The test consists of 97 True/False items that can be administered by paper-and-pencil or computer and takes approximately 20 minutes to complete. The inventory has 14 profile scores grouped into two clusters: Emerging Personality Patterns and Current Clinical Signs.

Scores are reported as base rate (BR) scores that reflect the relative prevalence of the characteristics that they purportedly measure. The inventory can be scored by computer or by hand. Computer scoring provides two options: a profile report with scores only or a more detailed, interpretive report that includes scores and automated interpretive text.

The wording (third grade reading level) and number of items (fewer than 100) were selected to make the M-PACI interesting and user-friendly for a pre-adolescent clinical population. The M-PACI is based on comprehensive theory of personality (Millon, 1990) and, as mentioned above, shares a common theoretical foundation with the Millon Adolescent Clinical Inventory (Millon, 1993). The test is designed for use in clinical settings as well as for use in the schools by students referred for behavioral and/or emotional problems.

The M-PACI consists of seven scales that measure "emerging personality patterns": Submissive, Outgoing, Confident, Unruly, Conforming, Inhibited, and Unstable. The inventory also consists of seven scales that measure "current clinical signs": Anxiety/Fears, Attention Deficits, Obsessions/Compulsions, Conduct Problems, Disruptive Behaviors, Depressive Moods, and Reality Distortions. There are two validity scales: Invalidity (4 items; 2 or more endorsed items suggest an *invalid* test) and Response Negativity (high scores suggest *faking bad* and low scores suggest *faking good*).

The inventory was normed using pre-adolescents identified with psychological difficulties; as such, it is not appropriate for use as a general screening test. The test is designed for use by credentialed and qualified mental health professionals.

DEVELOPMENT. The development of the M-PACI was guided by the same theoretical model underlying Millon's other multiaxial clinical inventories. Millon's theory of personality postulates three primary polarities: self-other, active-passive, and pleasure-pain. Eighteen initial constructs were identified (seven personality patterns variables, seven clinical signs variables, and four expressed concerns variables), and then items were generated to reflect these constructs. A research version was constructed and administered in 53 sites to a sample of 286 nine- to twelve-year olds being seen in clinical settings. The research version consisted of 135 items.

All 286 participants in the total research sample completed the M-PACI; a "cross-validation" subsample of 100 individuals was "pulled" from the total research sample for subsequent comparison analysis. It is unclear why the authors did not recruit an independent cross-validation sample. Clinicians at the 53 sites independently completed a Clinician's Research Form for each person in the sample. Statistical analysis evaluated degree of item overlap among scales—some overlap among scales was desired to allow a set number of constructs with fewer total items.

Seven "emerging personality patterns" scales and the seven "current clinical signs" scales were retained in the final M-PACI version, whereas the four "expressed concerns" scales were eliminated. Between five and eight "prototype" items were selected for each of the 14 retained scales, based on endorsement frequencies. Additional "subsidiary" items were added to the 14 scales to supplement the prototype items and increase the total number of items in the inventory. Final item "pruning" and adjustments were made to optimize internal consistency, correlations with clinician ratings, and conceptual mapping to the scales.

Standardized scores are reported as base rate (BR) scores. BR scores are a departure from the typical approach for determining standardized scores with which most practitioners are familiar (i.e., each scale has a similar mean [e.g., $T = 50$], standard deviation [$SD = 10$], and overall score distribution). BR scores are scaled to reflect the relative prevalence of syndromes measured by the inventory. For example, the base rates for conduct problems and obsessions/compulsions are different in the clinical population; the M-PACI scores for these two scales reflect these differing base rates.

The BR scores were refined through a series of iterations, in each successive round comparing the percentage of participants who scored highest and second highest on each scale with the clinician rating frequency targets. The goal was to obtain a match between the participant BR score percentages and the clinician rating percentages for the scale set as a whole. BR scores are monotonic transformations of the raw scores. The method used is consistent with an intraindividual (idiographic) approach to clinical test interpretation, focusing on the configuration, rather than on the absolute elevation, of scale scores. The M-PACI adopts a combined-gender norm group that "ensures that true differences between pre-adolescent girls and boys in the characteristics measured by the M-PACI inventory are preserved in the conversion of raw to standardized scores" (manual, p. 26).

TECHNICAL. The manual does not provide information on the geographic representation of the sample. The list of institutions, clinics and private practitioners in the Acknowledgements (manual, p. ix), however, suggests that the normative sample represents a wide range of communities across the U.S. The normative sample consists of individuals already identified as troubled. However, the manual does not provide independent clinical information on the normative sample to afford users an opportunity to evaluate the representativeness and generalizability of the M-PACI clinical sample.

M-PACI scales consist of relatively few items (7 to 12 items each). Coefficient alpha reliability values range from .63 to .84, with an average of .707 for the seven scales measuring Emerging Personality Patterns, and .728 for the seven scales measuring Current Clinical Signs. The manual considers these moderate internal consistency values "acceptable." Many test experts would suggest a more circumspect and conservative interpretation for any scale with a coefficient alpha below .80. Data are not provided on test-retest reliability.

The intercorrelations among BR scores on the 14 scales provide fairly consistent conceptual support for the scales. For example, the intercorrelations among the unruly emerging personality pattern scale and the disruptive behaviors and conduct problems current clinical signs scales are, as expected, the three highest in the matrix (.77-.86). Principal factor analysis with varimax rotation of the scales suggested either a two- or three-factor solution; the two-factor solution was more interpretable (externalizing-internalizing) and consistent with most models of developmental psychopathology. The normative sample ($n = 286$) was too small to conduct an item-level factor analysis, which is unfortunate because the coefficient alphas for the scales are only adequate.

Validation evidence for the M-PACI was derived from two sets of studies. The first validation study correlated M-PACI scores on the scales with clinician ratings of the same constructs. These "validation" data are the same data that were used in initial test construction efforts. The second set of validation studies correlated M-PACI scores with scores from three self-report instruments administered to a subsample of the standardization group.

The majority of correlations between the M-PACI profile scale scores and clinician ratings suggest moderately strong convergent validity. The average convergent validity coefficient for the seven emerging personality patterns scales was .40, and the average convergent validity coefficient for the seven current clinical signs scales was .36.

Correlations with the three self-report instruments (Behavior Assessment System for Children: Self Report of Personality, BASC; Children's Depression Inventory, CDI; Revised Children's Manifest Anxiety Scale, RCMAS) provide additional support for convergent validity. Most correlations between the M-PACI scales and the BASC (sample = 104), CDI (sample = 61), and RCMAS (sample = 51) were significant and in the expected direction. However, correlations were not very high. Support for the validity of the M-PACI would have been strengthened immeasurably with at least one study that correlated parent or teacher ratings with the self-ratings on the M-PACI.

The manual acknowledges some unanticipated and inexplicable findings. For example, the clinical participants who completed both the BASC and M-PACI self-report inventories obtained mean scores on the BASC in the normal, nonclinical range (T ranges from 47.7–50.7).

A study explored the validity of the response negativity (RN) scale—an effort to test the sensitivity of the RN scale to deliberate faking. When instructed to pretend to be either "someone who is really unhappy and has lots of problems" or "someone who is really happy and has no problems," 75% of the fourth, fifth, and sixth graders were able to create M-PACI fake-good and fake-bad ratings.

COMMENTARY. The M-PACI is a multidimensional self-report inventory designed for pre-adolescent clients presenting with behavioral or emotional problems. The test builds upon the significant work of Theodore Millon. The M-PACI goes beyond existing multidimensional self-report inventories by including scales that purport to measure emerging personality patterns. Interpretation includes configuration or pattern analysis. This is both the most exciting and innovative aspect of the M-PACI and the most controversial and empirically unsubstantiated aspect of the test. There is no evidence that the personality scales or that the interpretation of scale configurations/patterns provide any additional information to

better understand, more precisely conceptualize, or more effectively treat a pre-adolescent.

The normative sample consists of a clinical group. Independent clinical data were not collected on the sample; it is impossible to know whether the sample is representative of other children seen in clinical practice. It is a concern that a subsample of the clinical standardization group obtained scores in the normal range on the BASC. Further compromising the generalizability of the test is the underrepresentation of minority group children in the standardization sample (80.6% were White, only 7.7% were African American, and only 7.7% were Hispanic/Latino), and the overrepresentation of males (almost 70%). It is puzzling why more care was not taken to ensure that the standardization sample was representative of *both* the U.S. population and of pre-adolescents seeking mental health services.

There is logic in the choice of using base rate scores, which are sensitive to the different prevalence rates across clinical syndromes (i.e., scales). However, most practitioners will not welcome the departure from standardized score transformations in which each scale has the same mean, standard deviation, and overall score distribution. Many practitioners would prefer having both a normal and clinical standardization sample with which to compare their scores.

SUMMARY. The M-PACI is an ambitious self-report inventory that attempts to go beyond providing information on clusters of clinical symptoms to provide more profound psychological information on a child's personality. The M-PACI professes to conceptually link emerging personality patterns with clinical symptoms to provide important clinical information that helps the practitioner better understand and more effectively treat pre-adolescent clients. These are laudable but as yet unsubstantiated goals.

The Behavior Assessment System for Children (BASC; 17:21; Reynolds & Kamphaus, 1998) is arguably the most widely used self-report clinical inventory. The BASC is easy-to-use and interpret and includes both a normative and clinical standardization group. There is *no* evidence that the M-PACI is any more diagnostically useful than the BASC; furthermore, the theoretical model underlying the M-PACI may be a stumbling block for potential users unfamiliar with Millon's work or unsure of how personality relates to the choice of empirically validated treatment interventions.

The M-PACI promises the user a comprehensive and in-depth look at a referred child's clinical problems and personality patterns. Considerable research is warranted before we can be assured that the promise of the M-PACI is realized.

REVIEWER'S REFERENCES

Millon, T. (1990). *Toward a new personology.* New York: Wiley.
Millon, T. (1993). *Millon Adolescent Clinical Inventory manual.* Minneapolis, MN: NCS Pearson, Inc.
Reynolds, C. R., & Kamphaus, R. W. (1998). *Behavior Assessment System for Children manual.* Circle Pines, MN: American Guidance Service, Inc.

[127]
Multi-Craft Aptitude Test.

Purpose: To evaluate mechanical and electrical aptitude.
Population: Applicants for jobs that require the ability to learn mechanical and electrical skills.
Publication Dates: 2004–2005.
Scores: Total score only covering 9 areas: General Science, Power Tools, Hand Tools, Household Items, Electrical Concepts, Electrical Schematic Maze, Process Flow, Signal Flow, Electrical Sequences.
Administration: Group.
Price Data, 2007: $21 per consumable self-scoring test booklet (minimum order of 20); $24.95 per manual (2005, 12 pages).
Time: (20) minutes.
Author: Roland T. Ramsay.
Publisher: Ramsay Corporation.

Review of the Multi-Craft Aptitude Test by KEVIN J. McCARTHY, Staff Psychologist, State of Louisiana, Department of Health and Hospitals, ELMHS Facility, Jackson, LA:

DESCRIPTION. The Multi-Craft Aptitude Test (Form A) is an instrument designed to assess the mechanical and electrical aptitude of potential employees or trainees. It consists of 40 multiple-choice questions administered under supervision as a paper-and-pencil examination. The first 4 items serve only as practice exercises. The candidate is given 20 minutes to complete both the mechanical and electrical sections of the test. The test booklet is well illustrated to enhance the applicant's ability to understand the concepts being examined. Items 5 through 25 each contain three options from which to choose a correct response. Items 26 through 40 vary from six responses on Items 26 and 27, to four response choices on each of the remaining questions. The later items address the candidate's understanding of reading Electrical Schematic Mazes, Process Flow, Signal Flow, and Electrical Sequences. All test items from 26 through 40 are based upon clearly plotted diagrams that are integral to making the appropriate answer selections. Answers are recorded on a separate answer sheet.

The Multi-Craft Aptitude Test appears to be a rationally derived instrument for which the items reflect an awareness of the basic concepts of work-related skills. Items were chosen for meaningfulness and to evaluate the applicant's ability to understand basic mechanical and electrical concepts, while utilizing problem solving strategies. The author has noted that he has "used objects and elements from daily home and work life in this test" (manual for administration & scoring, p. 1) to determine an individual's "ability to learn and perform mechanical and electrical production and maintenance job activities" (manual for administration & scoring, p. 1). Though simplistic in design, the instrument is an adequate measure of the candidate's potential adaptability in the work or training environment. Its value is further enhanced by the organization of test items in a concise format. The author has included several caveats that direct the administrator's attention to possible problem situations that could influence the test outcome. These include the following examples: "examinee did not have bifocal glasses; examinee felt ill and nauseous; examinee was educated in another country and is somewhat slow in reading English; examinee had less than six years of education and reads with difficulty" (manual for administration & scoring, p. 4).

The two knowledge areas being evaluated are further subdivided into specific aspects of understanding. Mechanical capacities include: General Science, Power Tools, Hand Tools, and Household Items. Electrical capacities include: Electrical Concepts, Electrical Schematic Maze, Process Flow, Signal Flow, and Electrical Sequences. The author has also documented important considerations to be observed in terms of test-taking conditions. Instructions to the test examiner are written in a clear and comprehensive manner. The conceptual framework in which this test was developed is addressed by the test publisher, noting that it was "developed to address the following requirements: (1) The need for an updated measure of multicraft aptitude; (2) The need for a short and user-friendly measure of multicraft aptitude; (3) The creation of a measure without reference to city/rural or gender-based content; (4) The development of a measure appropriate to the context of 21st century life" (manual for administration & scoring, p. 1).

DEVELOPMENT. The authors of the test items, who are both Industrial/Organizational psychologists, identified the nine areas of aptitude following a review of training materials, recent relevant literature, and tests. Item analysis was based upon data from a total of 88 male and female job applicants, students from a technical school, and job experts. The test manual does not contain any further breakdown of this group, or referent data that might be helpful in determining the usefulness of this instrument in specific applications.

The data provided for review contain no reference to the diversity of the group membership, or its unique characteristics. The manual does include (Table 3, p. 8) an analysis of item difficulty and point-biserial discrimination indexes for all test items. Comments on methodology were summarized in the statement, "Data were analyzed using a statistics program" (manual for administration & scoring, p. 8).

TECHNICAL. The reliability coefficient, descriptive statistics, and standard error of measurement were reported in brief format. Although the (KR20) reliability coefficient (.76) is adequate and the standard error of measurement (2.17) is acceptable, further effort should be focused upon expansion of the reliability data to increase the utility of this instrument.

Because little is known about the referent group, the descriptive statistics offered in the manual have limited usefulness. In terms of validity data, few useful data were offered to support the author's contentions. Content-related validity was based upon a summary statement containing no supporting data. Criterion-related validity was derived from assessment of "67 male and female post-secondary technical school students" (manual for administration & scoring, p. 9). The reference specifically noted that "their scores were found to be significantly correlated, $r = .40$, $p < .01$, with scores on a test of multicraft knowledge" (manual for administration & scoring, p. 9). The author further posited that "for the same group ($N = 66$) ... scores on the

RCJS Multi-Craft Aptitude Test were found to be significantly correlated, $r = .38$, $p < .01$, with grade point average (GPA)" (manual for administration & scoring, p. 9). The final form of validity offered was construct validity, identified as "the ability to learn and perform production and maintenance jobs" (manual for administration & scoring, p. 9). The test booklet indicates that "Portions of RCJS Multi-Craft Aptitude Test have been found to correlate highly with Wiesen Test of Mechanical Aptitude (WTMA). Scores on the WTMA have been found to correlate highly, r ($N = 161$) = .80, $p < .01$, with scores on the Bennett Test of Mechanical Aptitude ... Where mechanical and electrical aptitude is required, the test is useful" (manual for administration & scoring, p. 9). There was no identification of the relevant portions of the RCJS Multi-Craft Aptitude Test to which the author had previously referred. Normative data were offered only in the form of a table of percentile rankings ($N = 88$). Altogether, the author's identification of psychometric properties for this test is deficient and in need of revision or significant supplemental data analysis.

COMMENTARY. The format of the test booklet lends itself to clarity, enhancing the ability of test takers to conceptualize and understand the knowledge being evaluated. The authors captured the essence of the basic skills and abilities necessary to learn and perform mechanical and electrical production and maintenance jobs. It appears to be a sound measure based on a review of the target concepts. The primary problem with the instrument is the limited data regarding psychometric properties that can be used to identify suitable applicants. This limitation can and should be addressed to ensure the future adaptation of this instrument in appropriate settings.

SUMMARY. The conceptual framework utilized in developing the Multi-Craft Aptitude Test appears to be sound. The product itself is well illustrated and seems to be an adequate measure of basic mechanical and electrical concepts. The test focuses upon the requisite knowledge of necessary skills and abilities to adjust to this type of work environment or training activity successfully. Its value would be substantially improved through research studies and the development of data that would further clarify its psychometric properties.

[128]

Multi-CrafTest.

Purpose: For selecting maintenance employees.
Population: Applicants and incumbents for jobs requiring electrical knowledge and skills.
Publication Dates: 2000–2002.
Scores, 8: Hydraulics & Pneumatics, Welding & Rigging, Power Transmission/Lubrication/Mechanical Maintenance & Shop Machines/Tools and Equipment, Pumps/Piping & Combustion, Motors/Control Circuits & Schematics and Print Reading, Digital Electronics/Power Supplies/Computers & PLC and Test Instruments, Basic AC & DC Theory/Power Distribution and Electrical Maintenance, Total.
Administration: Group.
Forms, 2: MC-C, B.
Price Data, 2007: $21 per consumable self-scoring test booklet (minimum order of 20); $24.95 per manual (2002, 19 pages).
Time: (60) minutes.
Comments: Self-scoring instrument; Form B is an alternate equivalent of Form MC-C.
Author: Roland T. Ramsay.
Publisher: Ramsay Corporation.

Review of the Multi-CrafTest by VICKI S. PACKMAN, Senior Assessment Analyst, Salt River Project, Phoenix, AZ:

DESCRIPTION. The Multi-CrafTest consists of a 60-item, multiple-choice, paper-and-pencil test that measures the practical mechanical and electrical knowledge and skills required for maintenance workers. The test has seven scales: Hydraulics & Pneumatics; Welding & Rigging; Power Transmission, Lubrication, Mechanical Maintenance, & Shop Machines, Tools and Equipment; Pumps, Piping & Combustion; Motors, Control Circuits, & Schematics and Print Reading; Digital Electronics, Power Supplies, Computers & PLC, and Test Instruments; and Basic AC & DC Theory, Power Distribution and Electrical Maintenance. The Multi-CrafTest is scored by hand. Test administrators count the number of correct responses on the pressure-sensitive grid on the last page of the test booklet.

The Multi-Craft test has two forms: MC-C and B. The two forms contain the same scales and the same amount of items in each scale, but the test items on each form are different. Only form MC-C is discussed in the manual. Form B is mentioned in the description of the test supplied by the publisher to Buros as an alternative equivalent of Form MC-C, and it was also included in the reviewer's packet. It is interesting that the publisher does not mention Form B because on initial review, Form B has more face validity as it appears more up-to-date in appearance. Form MC-C was copyrighted in 2000 but appears rather outdated in appearance and scoring. The test booklet is printed in blue, and each page becomes less wide to accommodate the increasing width of the pressure-sensitive answer sheet on the last page of the test booklet. Form B appears more modern with black print and a General Purpose Pearson NCS answer sheet and can be scored manually or by a scanner. Form B comes with a plastic overlay key with the correct answers punched out.

DEVELOPMENT. The Manual For Administration & Scoring is 19 generously spaced pages in length and contains a minimal amount of documentation regarding the development and validation of this assessment. This reviewer asked the publisher if they had any additional documentation regarding the development and validation of the Multi-CrafTest and received a half-page document entitled "Test Analysis Report, Summary of Test Statistics." Some of the statistics on this document are in the manual and some are not. It appears that not all of the research conducted is documented in the manual.

The Multi-CrafTest (Form MC-C) was developed in 2001 from the MainTest, which was developed in either 1991 (pp. 6 and 11) or 1997 (p. 2). The manual states on page 6 that: "Multi-CrafTest – Form MC-C (1/01) is a shortened version (60 items) of RCJS MainTest – Form NL-1, a 153-item test developed in 1991. Two Industrial Organizational Psychologists selected 60 items (proportionally) from the 153 items on the MainTest-Form NL-1 based on their difficulties and point Biserial correlations." This is about the extent of the information presented regarding how the Multi-CrafTest was developed.

TECHNICAL. The manual contains administration procedures that are general in nature and are clearly written for those with little or no experience in test administration. Some of the instruction has a harsh tone. For example, the manual states that "The examiner should be as objective as possible in all statements or answers to questions, avoiding any remark, tone or mannerism which might be construed as sarcastic or antagonistic" (p. 8).

The manual also contains specific directions for administering the Multi-CrafTest. Some of the instruction is confusing. Examinees are told there is no time limit but they should not need more than 1 hour. Examiners are then instructed on page 10 to "Mark the time they [the examinees] took on their test papers above their names." No information is provided as to why the time is collected or how it should be utilized.

The manual implies that the Multi-CrafTest is content valid because it "samples" the body of knowledge presented in Table 1 on page 15 of the manual. The table lists 21 knowledge areas with each knowledge area having between 3 and 10 categories with a total of 128 categories. The manual gives no information as to the specific knowledge areas and categories the test samples. The test may sample all 21 knowledge areas, but it is impossible for a 60-item test to sample all of the 128 categories. No rationale is presented as to why the publisher would list categories that are not actually measured by the test.

The manual also mentions a criterion-related validity study that was conducted on the MainTest in 1991. The sample is described merely as 201 maintenance employees at a Fortune 500 Uniform Rental Company. There are no data presented regarding the race, sex, age, job classification, or tenure of the individuals comprising this sample. The documentation regarding this study is vague. The manual states that "Job performance ratings were obtained for 95 to 97 persons in the areas of Know-how, Technical Knowledge, Supervisory Skills, Problem Solving, Interpersonal Skills and Total of the preceding criteria" (p. 15). There is no additional information to substantiate why a range was used to describe the number of performance ratings obtained, how the knowledge areas were defined, or what kind of a scale was used to collect the ratings. The 1991 data were re-evaluated with the Multi-CrafTest at a later date. Significant correlations were obtained between the Multi-CrafTest scores and the performance areas of Technical Knowledge, Supervisory Skills, and Problem Solving with Total Performance. The value of these correlations is overshadowed by the lack of documentation regarding how they were obtained.

The manual presents the means, standard deviations, reliability coefficients, and standard errors of measurement for the samples of both the MainTest and Multi-CrafTest tests. The reliability statistics are impressive (KR-20s of .93 and .86) but the documentation regarding how they were obtained is again weak. The MainTest had a sample of 201 "Employees in maintenance jobs in a processing plant" (manual, p. 11). The Multi-CrafTest sample included the 201 employees utilized in the MainTest study plus an additional 364 from a "National sample of maintenance employees/applicants in maintenance jobs" (p. 11). Again, no data are presented regarding the race, sex, age, job classification, or tenure of the individuals comprising these two samples.

The manual also reports the KR-20 internal consistency reliability coefficients and standard errors of measurement for the seven subtests in the Multi-CrafTest for an N of 565. The numbers range from .39–.66 and could be considered moderate, but there is no documentation regarding how they were obtained. The paragraph describing these data is confusing. The manual states that "The data ... below show the reliability and subtest information for a sample of 565 applicants and employed maintenance workers on the Multi-CrafTest-Form MC-C. These data indicate sufficient reliability for use in counseling individuals on developmental curricula" (p. 12). The second sentence seems out of context, and this reviewer is totally mystified as to what it means and why it is in the manual.

The manual lists the item difficulty and point-biserial discrimination for each of the 60 items based on a sample of 565. The "point-biserial correlations [were] computed on item versus test section rather than item versus total test" (p. 14). The numbers are good and indicate that the test items are related to the test section in which they appear.

COMMENTARY. The value of the Multi-CrafTest for selecting maintenance workers is questionable. The manual does not present sufficient documentation regarding how the test was developed or validated to really evaluate the psychometrics behind this test.

The MainTest is mentioned so frequently in the manual that the reviewer wonders why they do not change the title of the manual to include both tests.

There is very little information in the manual to assist test users in interpreting the test scores of examinees. The Mean, Standard Deviation, and

Standard Error of Measurement are presented for both the MainTest and Multi-CrafTest, and raw scores and percentiles are also presented. These portrayals are the only data in the manual that pertain to scores. This reviewer questions how users can make good decisions regarding test scores with such limited information.

SUMMARY. The Multi-CrafTest has some serious deficiencies that need to be corrected. This reviewer recommends a thorough upgrading of the manual by someone trained in psychometrics so that information is presented regarding how to interpret test scores, a break down of test scores by occupation and tenure, and that the validation samples and the research conducted be described in much more detail. It is also recommended that the publisher update Form MC-C to model the appearance of Form B and to discuss Form B in the manual regarding how it was developed and how it correlates to the MainTest and Form MC-C.

[129]

Multidimensional Perfectionism Scale.

Purpose: Designed to assess "different aspects of perfectionism."
Population: Ages 18 and over.
Publication Date: 2004.
Acronym: MPS.
Scores: 3 subscales: Self-Oriented Perfectionism, Other-Oriented Perfectionism, Socially Prescribed Perfectionism.
Administration: Individual or group.
Price Data, 2007: $89 per complete kit including manual (100 pages) and 25 QuikScore forms; $61 per manual; $44 per 25 QuikScore forms; $63 per Profile Report Kit-Web including manual and 3 profile reports; $113 per software kit including manual, Getting Started Guide, and 25 interpretive reports.
Time: (15) minutes.
Comments: Self-report inventory.
Authors: Paul L. Hewitt and Gordon L. Flett.
Publisher: Multi-Health Systems, Inc.

Review of the Multidimensional Perfectionism Scale by COLLIE CONOLEY, Professor of Counseling, Clinical, and School Psychology, University of California, Santa Barbara, Santa Barbara, CA:

The Multidimensional Perfectionism Scale (MPS) is a 45-item self-report measure of a three-dimensional model of trait perfectionism developed by the test authors (Hewitt & Flett, 1991a).

The three dimensions of perfectionism are Self-Oriented Perfectionism (requiring self-perfection), Other-Oriented Perfectionism (requiring others to be perfect), and Socially Prescribed Perfectionism (believing that others require themselves to be perfect). The scores of the three dimensions are not to be combined. The MPS can be used for research or clinical purposes.

The MPS has separate norms for men and women who are 18 years of age or older from community and clinical populations. The reading level was judged at the fourth-grade level. The assessment takes less than 15 minutes to complete. The scoring and norm transformation graphs are contained within the questionnaire packet. After the questionnaire packet is completed front and back by the subject, the administrator tears open the packet to total the responses that have been transferred onto the scoring sheet. The totals are transcribed onto the included profile sheet that allows discerning the *T*-scores.

Hewitt and Flett's (1991a) model of perfectionism views perfectionism as comprising trait dimensions, self-presentational dimensions, and cognitive features. The MPS has been used in many studies examining the relationship of perfectionism with other psychological variables.

DEVELOPMENT. The development of the Multidimensional Perfectionism Scale (MPS) was based upon the theoretical model of Hewitt and Flett (1991a). The manual reflects the attention to detail that a measure of perfectionism demands. Four students generated 162 initial items. Each item was written to tap one of the three theorized constructs. The items were edited and culled to 122 items. The 104 female and 52 male York University students of unknown ethnicity responded to the items and the Marlowe-Crowne Social Desirability scale. Items were retained if: (a) the mean of the item was between 2.5 and 5.5 on a 1 to 7 scale, (b) the item-to-total correlation with the appropriate dimension was larger than .40, (c) the item-to-total correlation with the other dimensions was smaller than .25, and (d) the item-to-total correlation with social desirability measure was smaller than .25. This yielded three subscales of 15 items each.

TECHNICAL. Exploratory factorial studies supported the validity of the three subscales of the MPS. Using samples of 1,106 university students and 263 psychiatric inpatients, a principal components analysis was performed on each sample separately (Hewitt & Flett, 1991b). The items received loadings as anticipated with the exception of two in the first analysis and then seven items in the next. The scree test supported three significant factors in both analyses.

Concurrent validity was demonstrated in 10 studies where the MPS was correlated with two other perfectionism assessments, Frost's Multidimensional Perfectionism Scale (Frost, Marten, Lahart, & Rosenblate, 1990) and the Revised Almost Perfect Scale (Slaney, Rice, Mobley, Trippi, & Ashby, 2001). With 2,049 participants including college students, depressed patients, and seventh grade gifted students the studies produced moderately high correlations in the expected comparisons.

Convergent and discriminant validity was provided by describing the results of seven studies. The correlations were fairly impressive using the NEO-PI-R subscales. For example, Angry-Hostility was correlated with Other as expected but not with Self. Depression was correlated with Social as expected but not with Other. Unfortunately, Depression was not correlated with Self either. Conscientiousness was highly correlated with Self but not with Other and was negatively correlated with Social.

The test manual presents six samples that compared the MPS with measures of psychopathology. The correlations were higher with patient populations. The test authors explained that for the Self subscale to correlate with depression the patient must have a failure experience, which is more likely in the clinical population.

The test manual reviews the literature indicating that subscales of the MPS correlated with depression, suicide, relationship difficulties, and procrastination fitting with theoretical predictions. For example, both Self-Oriented and Socially Prescribed Perfectionism scales were correlated with depression in college students (e.g., Flett, Hewitt, Blankstein, & O'Brien, 1991; Hewitt & Flett, 1991b, Joiner & Schmidt, 1995; Saddler & Sacks, 1993). Self-oriented and socially prescribed perfectionism were correlated with suicide in adult psychiatric patients (Hewitt, Flett, & Weber, 1994).

Response bias was addressed by reporting three studies examining the correlation between the MPS and Marlowe-Crowne Social Desirability Scale and one study correlating the MPS with the Lie scale of the Eysenck Personality Questionnaire. The MPS Self subscale did not correlate with social desirability, and none of the MPS subscales correlated with the Lie scale. However, college students' MPS Social ($r = -.39$) and Other ($r = -.25$) subscales were negatively correlated with social desirability. There was no correlation for college students in a second sample nor a psychiatric sample. The demographic data that perhaps could have helped account for the contradictory results were not presented. The three subscales intercorrelated between $r = .20$ and $.60$ depending upon the population sampled.

The community nonclinical normative sample was 1,350 women and 814 men from college and community settings including Canada and the U.S. The mean age was about 24 years with an approximate standard deviation of 10 years. The ethnicity of three quarters of the sample was unknown. Of the 533 whose ethnicity was reported, 36% were European American; 33%, African American; 15%, Hispanic; 12%, Asian; and 3%, Native American.

The clinical sample ($N = 1,476$) was older than the nonclinical sample with a mean age of about 37 years and standard deviation of 11 years. The diagnostic categories were primarily represented by major depression (27%), schizophrenia (20%), alcohol/drug problems (14%), and personality disorders (11%). No ethnicity data for the sample were included.

The test manual includes a table of raw subscale score means and standard deviations for specific populations. The samples are from studies that include some specific diagnostic categories and assorted other sample criteria.

A 3-month test-retest reliability study (Hewitt & Flett, 1991b) of 34 university students produced correlations of .88 for Self, .85 for Other, and .75 for Social. Eight studies were presented to represent the sample's internal consistency coefficients. Self-Oriented perfectionism varied from .84 to .90, Other-Oriented perfectionism from .74 to .83, and Socially Prescribed perfectionism from .80 to .87.

COMMENTARY. The purpose of the instrument was to measure the constructs of the test authors' perfectionism model. There is good support for the validity of the MPS. The authors include a wealth of information in the

MPS manual. The user will find the manual informative regarding their model of perfectionism, how to use the MPS results, their steps in developing the instrument, and many validation studies.

The major omission was not addressing ethnic differences. No attempt was made to address ethnicity other than stating that in one nonclinical sample statistically significant differences were found among ethnic groups. The test authors deemed the difference not practically significant in terms of size. The origin of the sample was not revealed. It is probable that the sample was a college sample. The test authors did not entertain the possibility that under stress ethnic groups might react differently (i.e., in a clinical sample). Neither did they acknowledge that the ethnic sample was small. The test authors did provide separate norms for females and males as well as clinical and nonclinical populations. A concern in the normative community sample was a possible overreliance upon college students.

The amount of information in the test manual demonstrates that the test authors are more than somewhat interested in perfectionism. The reader will find a wealth of information to inform the user for clinical and research perspectives.

The test authors present the construct of perfectionism as traits. There was no report of the MPS showing sensitivity to change. The user may wish to investigate the measure closely if one's purpose is to track change of perfectionism in therapy.

SUMMARY. The Multidimensional Perfectionism Scale (MPS) appears to well represent Hewitt and Flett's model of perfectionism. The MPS is made up of three scales that have good reliability and validity across many populations. Construct validity was supported by exploratory factor analyses, correlations with other measures, internal consistency measures, as well as convergent and discriminant predictions. Missing was confirmatory factor analysis. Finally, the applicability for use with ethnic groups other than European Americans from Canada and the U.S. is unknown.

REVIEWER'S REFERENCES

Flett, G. L., Hewitt, P. L., Blankenstein, K. R., & O'Brien, S. (1991). Perfectionism and learned resourcefulness in depression and self-esteem. *Personality and Individual Differences, 12,* 61–68.

Frost, R. O., Marten, P., Lahart, C., & Rosenblate, R. (1990). The dimensions of perfectionism. *Cognitive Therapy and Research, 14,* 449–468.

Hewitt, P. L., & Flett, G. L. (1991a). Dimensions of perfectionism in unipolar depression. *Journal of Abnormal Psychology, 100,* 98–101.

Hewitt, P. L., & Flett, G. L. (1991b). Perfectionism in the self and social contexts: Conceptualization, assessment, and association with psychopathology. *Journal of Personality and Social Psychology, 60,* 456–470.

Hewitt, P. L., Flett, G. L., & Weber, C. (1994). Dimensions of perfectionism and suicide ideation. *Cognitive Therapy and Research, 18,* 439–460.

Joiner, T. E., & Schmidt, N. B. (1995). Dimensions of perfectionism, life stress, and depressed and anxious symptoms: Prospective support for diathesis-stress but not specific vulnerability among male undergraduates. *Journal of Social & Clinical Psychology, 14,* 165–183.

Saddler, C. D., & Sacks, L. A. (1993). Multidimensional perfectionism and academic procrastination: Relationships with depression in university students. *Psychological Reports, 73,* 863–871.

Slaney, R. B., Rice, K. G., Mobley, M., Trippi, J., & Ashby, J. S. (2001). The Revised Almost Perfect Scale. *Measurement and Evaluation in Counseling and Development, 34,* 130–145.

[130]

Multifactor Leadership Questionnaire, Third Edition.

Purpose: Measures a broad range of leadership types; identifies the characteristics of a transformational leader and helps individuals discover how they measure up in their own eyes and in the eyes of those with whom they work.

Population: Researchers, consultants, leaders, supervisors, colleagues, peers, direct reports.

Publication Dates: 1985–2004.

Acronym: MLQ.

Scores, 12: Transformational Leadership (Idealized Attributes, Idealized Behaviors, Inspirational Motivational, Intellectual Stimulation, Individualized Consideration), Transactional Leadership (Contingent Reward, Management-by-Exception: Active), Passive-Avoidant Behaviors (Management-by-Exception: Passive, Laissez-Faire), Extra Effort, Effectiveness, and Satisfaction with the Leadership.

Administration: Group.

Forms, 3: Leader 5X-Short, Rater 5X-Short, Actual-Ought.

Price Data: Available from publisher (www.mindgarden.com).

Foreign Language Editions: Translations and reports available in English, German, Italian, Swedish, Spanish, Turkish, and Portuguese; MLQ translations only: French, Norwegian, Hebrew, Arabic, Chinese, Thai, Korean, and others.

Time: (15) minutes.

Comments: Both paper form-based and Web-based forms are available; scoring and reporting provided by publisher (including both multirater and an Actual vs Ought Feedback Report); previous edition listed as Multifactor Leadership Questionnaire for Research, Second Edition.

Authors: Bruce J. Avolio and Bernard M. Bass.

Publisher: Mind Garden, Inc.

Cross References: For a review by David J. Pittenger of an earlier edition, see 14:248; see also T5:1736 (5 references); for reviews by Frederick Bessai and Jean Powell Kirnan and Brooke Snyder of an earlier edition, see 12:247 (5 references); see also T4:1684 (5 references).

Review of the Multifactor Leadership Questionnaire, Third Edition by JOHN W. FLEENOR, Director of Knowledge Management, Center for Creative Leadership, Greensboro, NC:

DESCRIPTION. According to its authors, the Multifactor Leadership Questionnaire (MLQ) measures individual leadership styles ranging from passive leaders, to transactional leaders (who give contingent rewards to followers), to transformational leaders (who transform their followers into becoming leaders themselves). The purpose of the MLQ is to reveal significant factors that differentiate between effective and ineffective leaders at all levels of an organization. The instrument can be used to identify characteristics of transformational leadership and to enable leaders to compare their self-assessments of their leadership styles with the assessments of their co-workers.

The current version of the MLQ (Form 5X-Short; 45 items) includes rating forms for self and co-workers, as well as scoring instructions and a technical manual. The short form (MLQ 5X-Short) provides measures of 12 "full-range" leadership styles.

A web-based version of the MLQ is available, or the rating forms can be mailed or faxed into a scoring service. A comprehensive development report detailing the results of the assessment is provided to the leaders. Parallel instruments are available for three organizational levels (individual, team, and organization); however, only the individual-level measure is discussed in this review.

DEVELOPMENT. The theoretical foundation of the MLQ is based on the seminal work of Bass (1985), who suggested that transformational leadership accounts for unique variance in ratings of performance beyond that accounted for by transactional leadership. According to Bass (1985, 1998), transformational leaders are more likely to emerge in times of change, growth, and crisis.

Since 1985, the MLQ has undergone a number of significant revisions. Based on a series of confirmatory factor analyses, the six-factor model proposed by Bass was expanded to the current nine-factor model that Avolio and Bass (1991) term the "full-range" of leadership styles, although the six-factor solution was also appropriate.

On the most recent revision of the MLQ (Form 5X; 2004), the items were pooled from a number of sources. Items from the previous version of the MLQ (Form 5R) provided the base for the item pool of the current version. The authors also developed new items based on current findings on the distinguishing characteristics of transformational leaders. The revised item pool was then reviewed by six leadership experts who made recommendations on modifying and/or eliminating items based on a conceptual model of the full-range of leadership (Avolio & Bass, 1991). The resulting 63 items comprise the long form of the MLQ. Additionally, the authors developed a short form of the instrument containing 45 items.

TECHNICAL. The MLQ manual (2004) has been expanded to provide updated summaries of research conducted with the MLQ. Updated chapters are included on the development, theory, and use of the instrument, as well as new coverage of topics such as gender differences and diversity. Norms are presented for self and co-worker ratings based on a total sample of more than 27,000 individuals.

In the manual, a number of validity studies conducted on the MLQ are discussed, including the relationship of the instrument with the five-factor model of personality. In a 2003 study, Antonakis, Avolio, and Sivasubramaniam examined the validity of the measurement model and the factor structure of Form 5X of the MLQ. They hypothesized that assessments of leadership are often affected by the context in which leadership is being evaluated. Using large samples of raters who assessed same-gender leaders, Antonakis et al. found support for the nine-factor leadership model proposed by Avolio and Bass (1991). Mean differences were found between the male and female samples on four of the leadership factors. The findings suggested that the same constructs were validly measured in both the male and female groups.

In a second study, Antonakis et al. (2003) tested the nine-factor model and found it was stable within homogenous contexts. These contextual factors included environmental risk, leader-follower gender, and leader hierarchical level.

COMMENTARY. Bernard Bass is one of the leadership field's foremost thinkers, particularly in the area of transformational leadership. With the assistance of Bruce Avolio, a distinguished leadership researcher in his own right, Bass has done an excellent job of operationalizing his theory in an assessment instrument. Judging from reviews of earlier versions of the MLQ (e.g., Pittenger, 2001), this revision represents a significant improvement over earlier versions. In the manual, Avolio and Bass admit that the current version was developed in response to criticisms of the earlier versions.

The manual contains in-depth discussions of the theory and the leadership model underlying the MLQ; however, it is poorly organized, making it difficult to locate specific information in the manual. For example, there do not appear to be any reliability data for the MLQ reported in the manual, although one might reasonably presume that such studies have been conducted.

Overall, a number of studies have shown that the MLQ is a valid measure of leadership style. Such studies have been conducted in an array of settings including banks, community agencies, oil companies, the military, and state-run industries (see Hoffman, 2002).

One of the strengths of the MLQ is the feedback report that is provided to the leaders (ratees) in the assessment process. The feedback report contains detailed summaries of the assessment data, including feedback that indicates how the leader can be more effective. A separate report and form allows a leader to compare how they "actually" are versus how they "ought" to be.

SUMMARY. According to the authors, scores on the MLQ have been found to predict individual and group performance in organizations and to explain between 45% and 60% of the variance in organizational performance. For example, transformational leadership has been found to predict higher levels of product innovation in R&D teams. The authors assert that the MLQ can be used to identify transformational leaders who are able to create greater alignment around an organization's strategic vision and mission. Transformational leaders also are able to create greater unit cohesion, commitment, and safer work environments, which, in turn, can lower turnover. Additionally, transformational leadership has been associated with increases in sales, market share, earnings, and return on investment.

Although the claims of its authors may be slightly overstated, the MLQ does appear to be valid across a number of cultures and types of organizations. The instrument is easily administered (requiring 15 minutes to complete), extensively researched and validated, and has become known as the benchmark measure of transformational leadership. It is recommended for the measurement of transformational leadership styles in all appropriate settings.

REVIEWER'S REFERENCES

Antonakis, J., Avolio, B., & Sivasubramaniam, N. (2003). Context and leadership: An examination of the nine-factor full-range leadership theory using the Multifactor Leadership Questionnaire. *Leadership Quarterly, 14,* 261–295.

Avolio, B., & Bass, B. (1991). *The full-range of leadership development.* Binghamton, NY: Center for Leadership Studies.

Bass, B. (1998). *Transformational leadership: Individual, military and educational impact.* Mahwah, NJ: Erlbaum.

Bass, B. M. (1985). *Leadership and performance beyond expectations.* New York: Free Press.

Hoffman, E. (2002). *Psychological testing at work.* New York: McGraw Hill.

Pittenger, D. J. (2001). [Review of the Multifactor Leadership Questionnaire for Research]. In B. S. Plake & J. C. Impara (Eds.), *The fourteenth mental measurements yearbook* (pp. 806–808). Lincoln, NE: Buros Institute of Mental Measurements.

Review of the Multifactor Leadership Questionnaire by EUGENE P. SHEEHAN, Dean, College of Education and Behavioral Sciences, University of Northern Colorado, Greeley, CO:

DESCRIPTION. The Multifactor Leadership Questionnaire (MLQ) is a learning and development tool aimed at assisting leaders at all levels in identifying their strengths and weaknesses, especially in relation to the transformational theory of leadership. The instrument uses the 360-degree feedback approach, with as many as 24 raters providing leaders with feedback on their performance. Feedback from the MLQ is a computer-generated report that summarizes the frequency with which leaders engage in a series of leader-relevant behaviors. Leaders can also evaluate their self-perceptions against the observations of their associates. The authors state that the MLQ can be used in selection, transfer, promotion, and for field and laboratory research.

Specifically, the MLQ purports to measure four major components of leadership: transformational, transactional, and nontransactional leadership, and outcomes of leadership. These four components provide 12 scores grouped as follows: Transformational (Idealized Attributes, Idealized Behaviors, Inspirational Motivation, Intellectual Stimulation and Individualized Consideration); Transactional (Contingent Reward, Management-by-Exception: Active, Management-by-Exception: Passive); Nontransactional (Laissez-Faire); and Outcomes Of Leadership (Extra Effort, Effectiveness, and Satisfaction with the Leadership). The short form (5X-short) contains 45 items and is designed for organizational research purposes and for the development of individual leader reports. Individuals completing the MLQ evaluate how frequently (0 = *Not at all;* 1 = *Once in a while;* 2 = *Sometimes;* 3 = *Fairly often;* and 4 = *Frequently, if not always*) they have observed a leader engage in leadership-related behaviors.

DEVELOPMENT. The MLQ derives its theoretical underpinnings from the literature on transformational, transactional, and passive/avoidant leadership styles. As the authors point out in the manual, much of the research in the area of leadership has focused on dimensions such as democratic/autocratic, relationship/task focus, or initiation/consideration behavior. The need to facilitate and nurture positive organizational change has resulted in the focus on the transformational leadership. The assumption is that the transformational leader is better positioned to foster the change needed in modern organizations. Transformational leaders are in a position to shift from the traditional focus on quantity to a focus on quality and speed.

The manual contains an in-depth analysis and summary of the transactional and transformational leadership styles. The authors point to the inherent problems in the transactional style and how this style does not result in significant long-term organizational change. Through a focus on enhancing associate self-efficacy, transformational leadership concentrates on motivating associates to be more productive than they originally thought possible. The manual builds a strong case for transformational leadership, including providing a summary of each of several dimensions of transformational leadership: idealized influence, inspirational influence, intellectual stimulation, individualized consideration, and cascading effect. It is important to note that the authors point out that transformational leaders know how to work to change their environment so that the environment will be more conductive to a transformational leader. The transformational leadership style has been shown in many studies in an array of organizations to enhance organizational effectiveness.

TECHNICAL. The manual provides a great deal of helpful information regarding the psychometric properties of the instrument. Appropriate psychometric steps were taken in the development of the MLQ. External validity for the effects of transformational leadership on associates and or-

ganizational effectiveness is strong. Studies in a variety of different organizations and in both the U.S. and abroad have demonstrated several positive outcomes for transformational leadership. Demonstrating its strong empirical base, "the latest version of the MLQ, form 5X, has been used in almost 300 research programs, doctoral dissertations, and master's theses" (manual, p. 35).

The authors explain in great detail how they selected items and assured the construct validity of the MLQ. The items selected for the instrument are clear and are obviously focused on leadership behaviors. All the items deal with issues that would be readily observable to associates as they reflect upon their leader's performance. A series of factor analyses resulted in a six-factor model, with adequate reliabilities for all scales, although other models, such as a nine-factor one, were also appropriate.

Additional validity evidence is provided through a summary of correlations between the MLQ and a variety of personality tests. These correlations are in the predicted direction and lend credence to the psychometric soundness of the instrument.

COMMENTARY. The main value of the MLQ is its potential for use in management and leadership training. Its use of the 360-feedback approach in the analysis of a leader's style is very effective. The results produced by this instrument can be easily incorporated into a management-training program. They certainly would cause managers to reflect upon their performance. Working with a change agent, the report produced by the MLQ could serve as a strong catalyst for change.

The developers have paid considerable attention to the theoretical underpinnings of this instrument. The basis in transformational leadership is clear. Further, they provide considerable data that summarize the psychometric properties of the instrument. Construct and external validities are well documented and scale reliabilities are adequate.

SUMMARY. The MLQ is designed to assess leadership styles in the context of transformational leadership framework. The questionnaire can be easily and efficiently administered and scored. The resulting feedback report should provoke leaders to assess their style of interacting with and motivating their followers. The instrument could be a strong addition to a management or leadership-training program. Particularly useful is the 360-feedback nature of the report. The psychometric properties of the instrument described by the developers reveal the MLQ to be based on sound theory and to have strong construct and external validity.

[131]
Naturalistic Action Test.

Purpose: Designed to "assess errors of action in the performance of routine activities of daily living."
Population: Adults.
Publication Dates: 2002–2003.
Acronym: NAT.
Scores, 8: Accomplishment Score, Error Score, Naturalized Attention Test (NAT) Score for Task 1: Toast and Coffee, NAT Score for Task 2: Present, NAT Score for Task 3: Lunchbox and Schoolbag, Total NAT Score, Comprehensive Error Score, Lateralized Attention Score.
Administration: Individual.
Price Data, 2006: £319.50 per complete kit including manual (22 pages), 25 scoring sheets, work space template, 2 master score sheets, bell, doll, plastic lunchbox, flask, paper bags, and cardboard boxes; £41.50 per 50 scoring sheets.
Time: (30–40) minutes.
Comments: Adaptation of Multi-Level Action Test.
Authors: Myrna F. Schwartz, Laurel J. Buxbaum, Mary Ferraro, Tracy Veramonti, and Mary Segal.
Publisher: Harcourt Assessment [England].
[Editor's Note: The publisher advised in December 2006 that this test is now out of print.]

Review of the Naturalistic Action Test by MARK A. ALBANESE, Professor of Population Health Sciences, University of Wisconsin School of Medicine and Public Health, Madison, WI:

DESCRIPTION. The Naturalistic Action Test (NAT) is designed, primarily, as a diagnostic instrument to assist neuropsychologists, occupational therapists, and other rehabilitation clinicians who work with adult neurological populations (individuals with stroke, traumatic brain injury-TBI, and progressive dementia, including patients with hemiparesis, weakness, and range of motion limitations and some patients with aphasia). Compared to the various indices of Activities of Daily Living that rely on reports of care-givers and penalize physical limitations, this is a highly standardized performance-based measure of whether the patient can accomplish, with limited assistance, three ordinary tasks: prepare buttered toast and coffee, wrap a gift, and pack a boxed lunch and school bag. There are two diagnostic scores that are combined into a single overall score that can range between 0-18 (maximum of 6 points for each task). The two diagnostic scores are: task accomplishment (percent of steps in task sequence accomplished) and error scores (specific missteps made along the way to accomplish the task-operationally coded in two levels: ≤ 1 error and >1 error). If the session is videotaped, additional scoring can be done for specific types of errors and for spatial attention biases associated with unilateral lesions.

DEVELOPMENT. The NAT is an outgrowth of a decade of work completed at the Moss Rehabilitation Research Institute in Philadelphia. It was developed by shortening and greatly simplifying the scoring procedures of a research instrument called the Multi-Level Action Test (MLAT). The NAT derived validity and reliability estimates from a study involving 45 right-hemisphere (RCVA) and 30 left-hemisphere (LCVA) stroke patients, 25 traumatic brain injury (TBI) patients, and 28 age-matched controls (CVA = 20, TBI = 8). A follow-up study, conducted 6 months post-discharge with 48 of these patients, was used to determine if the test predicted functional abilities after discharge.

TECHNICAL.

Scoring. The NAT reports a single overall score that can range from 0–18 and is derived from summing scores from each of the three tasks. Task scores range up to 6 points and are created by combining a percent of task steps accomplished assessment with an assessment of errors committed during completion of the task. The assignment of NAT points is based upon the percent of task steps being in a certain range and whether the assessment of errors is less than or equal to or greater than 1. A lower error score puts the score into the higher of two categories that correspond to a given range in percentage of task steps accomplished. For example, on the first task, a percentage of task steps accomplished in the range of 75–99 would yield a point score of 3 or 4, with the higher score given if no more than 1 error is made.

Standardization. The NAT has not been standardized in the sense of administering it to a probability sample of some specific population. The manual reports results for 100 cerebrovascular accident (CVA) patients, and 25 traumatic brain injury (TBI) patients and 28 age-matched nonneurological controls (CVA = 20, TBI = 8). The results are reported by the percentage of patients who score in each three NAT score ranges: 0–6, 7–12, and 12–18. Separate percentages are reported for patients with CVA and TBI and in three different age ranges: less than 36 years, 36 to 60, and over 60 years.

Reliability. Interrater reliability was estimated from 20 patients rated by "a relatively inexperienced clinician" compared to an experienced coder's scoring from videotape (manual, p.11). Weighted kappa estimates of chance corrected percentage agreement ranged from .95–1.0 for the accomplishment score and from .70–1.0 for the error coding. Internal consistency derived from the patient sample was .75 and increased to .79 when the controls were added.

Validity. Data are reported on concurrent criterion, construct, and predictive validity. The evidence for the concurrent criterion-related validity of the NAT is based upon the relationship of the NAT score to those from the Functional Independence Measure (FIM), a criterion assessing disability. The NAT correlated .50 with both the physical and cognition subscales of the FIM.

Construct validity of the NAT was assessed by correlating it with a battery of attention tests. The NAT correlated -.68 with a measure of processing speed/arousal and .61 with a measure of visuospatial attention. The authors state that these results suggest that diminished arousal/resource capacity as well as visuospatial impairments are factors that contribute to error vulnerability. The NAT also correlated significantly with measures of working memory (only a p value is provided, that being $p < .001$).

Predictive validity was assessed by correlating NAT scores with those from the Instrumental Activities of Daily Living (IADL), "a widely used measure of functional independence in home and community" (manual, p. 12). A correlation of .58 was found between the NAT and a follow-up IADL score. A multiple regression showed that the success of NAT in predicting IADL was "independent of its correlation with FIM, age or the various attention measures" (manual, p. 12). Finally, the correlation between the NAT and IADL administered at the same time was .64.

COMMENTARY. The NAT is a very impressive set of materials and provides an extremely well-written and detailed set of guidelines for administration and scoring. The theoretical justification is clear and strong, and the authors are credible, with years of experience and at least nine peer-reviewed publications to their credit in the domain. The instrument itself has substantial "face" validity with the three tasks comprising the test being straightforward and undeniably reasonable in the expectation that someone who could not do them would be impaired in their ability to function. The attention to detail is especially impressive with specifications even given to the dimensions and shape of the work station used to assess patients. The manual indicates that a workstation is available from Smith and Nephew that conforms to the dimensions of the NAT. The estimates of reliability and various forms of validity are impressive. The interrater reliability estimates reported are especially impressive given that they employ the relatively conservative kappa chance corrected agreement statistic.

The main problems with the NAT pertain to the sparse description of how the sample of 100 patients and 28 controls was obtained, how the scoring algorithm was developed and the paucity of normative data provided. The test manual does not describe subject recruitment (including eligibility criteria), the time frame over which the data were collected, nor how the investigators were involved in the data collection process as raters, care givers, data analysts, and so on. These are significant omissions because the credibility of the instrument is based upon its ability to distinguish among patients and controls in this study and correlations with an assortment of other instruments administered to these 128 individuals.

The scoring algorithm is rather unusual in that it translates performance originally obtained as a percentage of expected steps to be taken and the errors made while taking the steps into a 6 point scale. There is no theoretical or empirical justification for such a reductionist approach. Although the approach has a certain amount of intuitive logic, it would be extremely helpful to provide data to show that the scoring method does not "waste" information contained in the original percentages and error counts.

The reporting of normative data is also limited. Data reported in the manual in table form include the percentage of the subjects who scored between 0-6, 7-12, and 13-18. In the text, the means and standard deviations (in parenthesis) for the overall score for each type of subject were reported to be: TBI = 12.6 (5.8), RCVA = 10.3 (4.9), LCVA = 10.3 (6.0), controls = 17.3 (1.2). For the individual tasks, means and standard deviations (presented parenthetically) are reported to be 4.55 (2.04), 3.35 (2.42), and 2.95 (2.23), respectively, for the patient sample and means for the control group were from 5.57-5.86, near the ceiling of 6.0. In an unpublished study described in the Auxiliary scoring systems, the authors used 2 *SD* below the control mean (~15 if the control *SD* is used) to classify subjects as impaired or nonimpaired. This is the only information on how to use the scores for assessing patient performance. If these data are to serve as norms, or at least to provide clinical guidelines for their use, it would be extremely helpful to report sensitivity and specificity for the NAT scores. It is not clear if the NAT can distinguish between TBI, RCVA, and LCVA, although the two CVA scores are substantially below those of the TBI patients. One way to present this information would be in the form of receiver-operator curves (ROCs). Such a format would allow users to set thresholds on the NAT for clinical applications. In the present form, it is hard to know what constitutes a NAT score of concern.

Space may be an issue for this test. A U-shaped work station occupying a minimum 4'x6' footprint is needed with a 36"x18" space directly in front of the patient and an 18"x48" space on either side. The table system is available for purchase from Smith and Nephew Rehabilitation Division. However, unless the demand for using the NAT is great, dedicating space for its use may be prohibitive. There is also the added cost of creating or purchasing the workstation that must be considered.

Maintaining skilled NAT administrators may be an issue. The manual is confusing on this front. At one point it says that the NAT procedures are "reliably mastered with approximately eight hours of supervised experience" (manual, p.4, Column 1). However, on the same page in the second column it says "Formal training is unnecessary; all the information needed to achieve reliable scoring is present in this instruction manual." If all that is needed for administrator training is contained in the manual, there is little guidance regarding how to assess whether an administrator is sufficiently well-trained to reliably administer the NAT. If, however, training requires supervised experience, it is not clear where that experience can or should be obtained. It also may represent an upfront cost that will need to be considered in adopting the NAT. If the NAT is not used on a constant basis, there may be issues pertaining to maintenance of administration skills that need to be considered.

SUMMARY. The NAT is designed, primarily, as a diagnostic instrument to assist neuropsychologists, occupational therapists, and other rehabilitation clinicians who work with adult neurological populations. Compared to other indices of Activities of Daily Living that rely on third-party reports and penalize physical limitations, this is a highly standardized performance-based measure of whether the patient can accomplish, with limited assistance, three ordinary tasks. Interrater reliability coefficients ranged from .70-1.00 and internal consistency estimates ranged from .70-.75. Concurrent criterion, construct, and predictive validity estimates ranged between .50-.68. Thus, for a relatively short assessment containing three tasks and usually taking less than 45 minutes to complete, its psychometric properties meet most accepted standards. The main concern about this instrument is the lack of information about how participants were selected for the norming group, scoring methods, and determination of cut scores. In addition, the NAT requires upfront cost for administrator training and workstation purchase as well as ongoing commitment to dedicating space for a large workstation and maintenance of administrator skills. Although the NAT has the potential to be useful for identification of impaired patients, those wishing to use it as a diagnostic tool should refer to the research underlying its development to determine if the patient population used in its development would be representative of those they serve. Further, if the NAT is to be used in making decisions about whether a patient should be allowed to live independently, much care should be exercised in its use. For this purpose, administration should be by a clinician who weighs the results as part of the larger constellation of information used in assessing a patient's ability to live independently.

Review of the Naturalistic Action Test by JAMES W. PINKNEY, Professor of Counselor and Adult Education, East Carolina University, Greenville, NC:

DESCRIPTION. The Naturalistic Action Test (NAT) consists of three tasks intended to assess "learned, sequential, object-oriented behavior" (manual, p.4). This is the test authors' definition of naturalistic action that occurs in meeting the everyday goals of independent living. The target population is people who have suffered brain damage through trauma, stroke, or progressive dementia, but the manual suggests the NAT is appropriate for anyone with deficits in cognitive functioning. The three tasks (making a breakfast of coffee and toast, wrapping a present as a gift, and packing a lunch and backpack for a child's day at school) are arranged for increasing difficulty and complexity. The NAT is completed by most examinees in 30-45 minutes.

Each task is scored by the examiner for accomplishing steps to complete the task and errors committed during the process of completing each task. The observations generate an accomplishment score and an error score that are then combined into a NAT score. The tasks are also scored to generate a Lateralized Attention Score (LAS).

The LAS is based on how many objects the examinee touches in a standardized layout of the items needed for each task. For a right hemisphere stroke the proportion of objects touched on the right side of the layout is subtracted from the left side proportion. This is reversed for left hemisphere strokes. The manual suggests the LAS be determined from a videotape of the administration of the NAT because the examiner's attention is taken up by recording accomplishments and errors while the NAT is conducted. The manual includes pictures of how materials for each task must be laid out and suggests that both the administration and scoring are straightforward and require minimal training.

DEVELOPMENT. The NAT was derived from the Multi-Level Action Test (MLAT) with the intent of shortening the assessment task and simplifying the scoring procedures. Scoring the NAT is a matter of checking off accomplished steps of each task and checking off errors as they occur. One advantage the manual claims is that administration and scoring of the NAT can be reliably mastered with 8 hours of supervised experience. The manual clearly spells out how to set up the NAT materials, what kinds of assistance can be given, and the timing of when to offer assistance.

A major purpose of the NAT's development was to provide rehabilitation clinicians with a tool that would aid in measuring the impairment of naturalistic action, set treatment goals, and help patients understand the nature and extent of their adjustment to diminished functioning. The manual also suggests the NAT may have utility for researchers in establishing baselines, matching levels of functional disability, and as an outcome measure in treatment studies. These latter possibilities seem premature given the short life and limited use of the NAT to date.

TECHNICAL. The NAT was standardized on two small groups of 25 traumatic brain-injured (TBI) patients and 75 who suffered strokes (CVA). The NAT scores for these groups were then compared to a control group of 28 participants who completed the NAT. Further breakdown of these groups was based on age—over and under 35 years of age for the TBI group, and over and under 60 years of age for the CVA group. The test manual presents no rationale for selecting either age. Information on gender and education levels is provided as well.

The test manual notes that the NAT items are ordered for increasing difficulty but presents no information about task selection or how difficulty was determined. Low scores on Task 1 (making breakfast) and Task 2 (wrapping a present) are noted to be very predictive of a low score on Item 3 (fixing a school lunch and filling a book bag with school supplies). Thus, low scores on the first two tasks are considered to comprise sufficient evidence of impairment.

There is limited information presented on the reliability of the NAT, concerning interrater scoring, test-retest, and internal consistency. The reliability of the scoring apparently rests on one report. An inexperienced clinician scored 20 patients during testing, and an experienced coder then scored the patients from a videotape of the NAT being taken. Based on this, the manual reports a weighted kappa coefficient for the accomplishment score of .98 and a median percent agreement of 98% for the presence or absence of errors. A test-retest administration of the NAT produced a correlation coefficient of .66. For the standardization sample, an internal consistency estimate by coefficient alpha was .75.

It should be pointed out that these relatively high values may be an artifact of the scoring system used. The scoring sheets used are devised so all scoring is a matter of checking off a correct step (accomplishment) or a mistake that is made (error). No judgment is involved except to decide if something did or did not occur.

The validity of the NAT is briefly reviewed in the test manual. The correlation of the NAT with a criterion for disability measurement based on clinician ratings was .50. The manual also reports consistent correlations with a measure of processing speed (r = -.68) and a measure of visuospatial attention (r = .61). In addition, the range of scores and score separation between the treatment groups and the control group are used to support the validity of the NAT. The lowest score in the control group was 14 with 71% of the controls scoring a perfect 18. The patients' scores ranged from 0–18 and about two-thirds of the patients scored below the control group's range.

COMMENTARY. The NAT is presented as a standardized assessment of impairment in individuals who have had a stroke, traumatic brain injury, or progressive dementia. It suggests that a simplified scoring system reduces training time and increases consistency for research purposes. No information or reasoning is given on how the three tasks of the NAT (making breakfast, wrapping a present, and packing a school lunch/book bag) were determined as the content of the NAT or best suited to assess impairment.

As small as this sample of behavior is for assessing impaired ability to perform naturalistic actions, the manual strongly suggests that the difficulty gradient of the NAT means the third task need not be attempted if poor scores are obtained on the first two tasks. Potential users would want to think carefully if the three (or two) tasks of the NAT are a reasonable sample of behavior for their particular group of patients and their particular organization's role.

Another issue for users would be the cost of the NAT. For over $300 the basic kit contains a template for setting up tables, a plastic drawer, a plastic lunch box, two flat boxes with wrapping paper, a plastic thermos, a small doll, scoring sheets, and a door bell/chime. Everything else for the NAT's administration (food items and utensils) is provided by the user.

SUMMARY. The NAT was designed to be a quick (30–45 minutes) assessment of impairment of the ability to perform naturalistic actions involving everyday activities. Its best points are the simplified scoring sheets to standardize the assessment and the clear instructions on how to administer it for consistent results. Potential users would want to consider carefully the cost of the NAT and how applicable the three tasks are for a specific population of patients. If speed and ease of training are not important issues, the Multi-Level Action Test (Buxbaum, Schwartz, & Montgomery, 1998), which was used for the development of the shorter NAT, could be considered.

REVIEWER'S REFERENCE

Buxbaum, L. J., Schwartz, M. F., & Montgomery, M. W. (1998). IDEA Ideational apraxia and naturalistic action. *Cognitive Neuropsychology, 15,* 617-643.

[132]
Nelson-Denny Reading Test CD-ROM Version 1.2.

Purpose: "To provide a trustworthy assessment of student ability in three areas of academic achievement: vocabulary, reading comprehension, and reading rate."

Population: Grades 9–16 and adults.

Publication Dates: 1929–2000.

Scores, 4: Vocabulary, Comprehension, Total, Reading Rate.

Administration: Group.

Forms, 2: G and H.

Price Data, 2007: $22.05 per Manual for Scoring and Interpretation; $7.30 per administration for 25 to 499 test administrations; quantity discounts available for administrations.

Time: 35(56) minutes.

Comments: Requires Windows 95, 98, NT, or 2000; creates reports including the Individual Narrative, Individual Longitudinal, Group Longitudinal, Group Longitudinal Summary, List of Student Scores, and the Group Summary; a computerized alternative identical in content to paper-pencil Forms G and H and considered by the publisher to be parallel forms.

Authors: James I. Brown, Vivian Vick Fishco, and Gerald S. Hanna.

Publisher: Riverside Publishing.

Cross References: See T5:1767 (9 references); for reviews by Mildred Murray-Ward and Douglas K. Smith of Forms G and H, see 13:206 (52 references); see also T4:1715 (30 references); for reviews by Robert J. Tierney and James E. Ysseldyke of Forms E and F, see 9:745 (12 references); see also T3:1568 (38 references); for reviews by Robert A. Forsyth and Alton L.

Raynor of Forms C and D, see 8:735 (31 references); see also T2:1572 (46 references); for reviews by David B. Orr and Agatha Townsend and an excerpted review by John O. Crites of Forms A and B, see 6:800 (13 references); for a review by Ivan A. Booker, see 4:544 (17 references); for a review by Hans C. Gordon, see 2:1557.

Review of the Nelson-Denny Reading Test, CD-ROM Version 1.2 by ALICE CORKILL, Associate Professor, Department of Educational Psychology, University of Nevada-Las Vegas, Las Vegas, NV:

DESCRIPTION AND DEVELOPMENT. The Nelson-Denny Reading Test, CD-ROM Version 1.2 is a computerized version of Forms G and H of the paper-and-pencil Nelson-Denny Reading Test (T7:1727). Both the interpretive guide and the technical manual clearly indicate that the CD-ROM version is identical to Forms G and H of the paper-and-pencil test. As a result, the following review does not include information related to the creation of the instrument. In addition, the manuals indicate that the Suggested Uses for the Test are based on the paper-and-pencil versions of Forms G and H. Therefore, information related to these topics are in a prior edition of the *Mental Measurements Yearbook* (Murray-Ward, 1998; Smith, 1998). The following review focuses exclusively on issues related to the computerized version.

The user's guide provides instructions for installing the test in the relatively typical "computer-eze" that many people find difficult to interpret. The ease with which the CD-ROM version may be installed will vary with the technical expertise of the user. Three settings had to be changed in my computer configuration in order to install and run the test. These were changes that I was unable to complete without assistance. The configuration changes made other programs look different than they had previously, which was problematic. This implementation may be a phenomenon related only to the operating system from which I was working (Windows XP). Once the test was installed, however, it was fairly easy to navigate from login through to the main screen.

The main screen offers the user nine option buttons: (a) Help, (b) About, (c) Order Wizard, (d) Test Session Wizard, (e) Manual Scoring Wizard, (f) Management, (g) Reports, (h) Logoff, and (i) Exit. The function of each button with the exception of "Logoff" and "Exit" will be described in turn. Clicking on the "Help" button opens a typical help window with a variety of help topics that may be accessed via a brief description or a search initiated by the user. The provided descriptions are clear and easy to understand. Clicking on the "About" button opens a window that provides basic test information (publisher, title, author, and so forth) and acknowledgements. Clicking on the "Order Wizard" button opens a window that assists the user in purchasing additional Nelson-Denny CD-ROM administrations or processing the activation code. The minimum number of administrations for purchase is 25. Twenty-five to 499 administrations cost roughly $7 per administration. The cost is reduced to roughly $6.50 per administration for 500–999 administrations and to approximately $6 per administration for more than 1,000 administrations. The test may be purchased by supplying a credit card or purchase order number. This process appears to be straightforward.

Clicking on the "Test Session Wizard" opens a window that begins the test administration session. A variety of test session information must be entered before the test may be started including: an examinee ID number, examinee name, selection of Form G or H, selection of the appropriate norms (high school, 2-year college, 4-year college), and selection of the appropriate grade level (9 through 14). This window will also allow an existing database of test takers to be searched by either ID number or last name. Either search format will enable the user to find previous test scores, including information about the type of test (computerized or manual), test date, and test form. Test taker information that is required is indicated by red type. Optional information is indicated by black type. Users should be sure that the examinee is ready to begin the test before clicking on the "Start Test" button. Once the test has begun, it is difficult to exit from the program.

The test screen contains a text box on the left side. A "Back" button, "Next" button, "Start" button, and two colored bars are located on the lower right portion of the screen. The two colored bars are provided to help the examinee track his or her progress on the test. The upper bar indicates page number (e.g., "page 5 of 6") or item number (e.g., "item 18 of 80"). The lower bar shows a blank horizontal window that becomes progressively filled with blue as the examinee proceeds. A timer is located in the extreme lower right corner of the screen. Examinees may confuse the "blue bar" with the amount of time left for completing the test because it is located immediately above the timer and because it fills with blue from left to right as the examinee moves through the test.

The six instruction pages explain how to use the computerized features of the test and give examinees an opportunity to click on the buttons and so forth until they feel comfortable. The examinee is given three practice items for the Vocabulary test. The examinee is allowed to move backwards and forwards through the test and may leave items blank and return to them at the end of the test, time permitting. In order to select a response, the examinee only needs to move the cursor over the chosen box. The box color changes when the cursor is over it. One click of the mouse selects the answer. The examinee must click on the "Next" button to proceed. When the examinee feels comfortable with the mouse, the buttons, and so forth, she or he may start the Vocabulary test. The timer starts a second-by-second countdown from 15:00 minutes. In the actual test, as opposed to the practice items, the questions advance automatically as soon as an examinee has selected a response. As indicated previously, the examinee may skip items on the test and return to them should time permit. Unfortunately, in order to return to a skipped item, the examinee must click the "back" button through every item between wherever she or he is in the test to the skipped item. If the examinee completes the test before time has run out, she or he is reminded that she or he may return to items to change answers. The examinee is not reminded of whether she or he left items unanswered. If the examinee is finished, she or he is required to click a button to so indicate. If time expires before the examinee completes the test, a window appears that so indicates and the examinee is automatically moved on to the next portion of the exam.

Once the examinee has completed the Vocabulary test she or he is immediately moved to the Comprehension test instructions. Both the Reading Rate and Comprehension portions are explained. There are no practice items. When the examinee clicks the "Start" button, a text box appears on the left side of the screen and the timer starts a second-by-second countdown from 60 seconds. This 60 seconds is for the Reading Rate portion of the test. The reading selection for the Reading Rate portion of the exam is longer than will fit in the text box. Therefore, most examinees will need to use the scroll bar during the Reading Rate portion of the exam. This necessity may affect Reading Rate scores. In addition, the second-by-second countdown in the extreme lower right corner of the screen may be unnerving for some examinees. Nevertheless, once the 60 seconds has elapsed, the examinee is prompted to click on the last word he or she read. Clearly examinees are not obligated to select the last word they actually read and they may select a word further along in the passage. In this version of the test, the timer stops while the examinee selects the last word read. In the paper-and-pencil versions, the timer continues while the examinee records information about his or her Reading Rate. Regardless, once the Reading Rate information has been recorded, a text box appears on the upper right side of the screen within which examinees will see a multiple-choice question to go along with the text that is still available in the text box on the left side of the screen, and the timer begins a second-by-second countdown from 19:00 minutes. Examinees may respond to the question at any point during the test. The questions advance automatically as soon as an examinee has selected a response. As in the Vocabulary test, the examinee need only position the cursor over the box within which she or he finds her or his answer choice and click. When the cursor is over a response, the box changes color. Examinees may skip items and return to them later, time permitting. As with the Vocabulary test, an examinee must back up over all items between the current item and a skipped item in order to provide a response. Once all questions for a passage have been answered, the next passage appears in the left screen text box with a question in the right screen text box. This process continues until all items have been answered or time elapses. Most passages fit completely within the text box on the left. Therefore, the entire passage is available for inspection while the examinee selects a response. As with the Vocabulary test, if the examinee completes the test before time has run out, she or he is reminded that she or he may return to unanswered items. The examinee is not reminded of whether she or he left items unanswered. If the examinee is finished, she or he is required to click a button to so indicate. If time expires before the examinee completes the test, a window appears and indicates that time is up and the exam is over.

Immediately upon conclusion of the test, an "Individual Narrative Report" for the examinee appears on the screen. This report includes a graphic that depicts the examinee's Vocabulary, Reading Rate, and Comprehension percentile ranks. The examinee is also provided with a report in a small box that includes standard scores, grade equivalent scores, stanines, and percentile ranks for Vocabulary, Comprehension, Total, and Reading Rate. A description of what each score represents is also included. After closing the "Individual Narrative Report" window, the test administrator must indicate whether the test was successfully administered. If so, the scores are recorded and the administration is counted against the number purchased. At this point, the Individual Narrative Report may be printed for the examinee. If the test administrator determines that the test administration was not successful, the test administrator must provide a reason. An unsuccessful administration is not counted against the number purchased, and the Individual Narrative Report is not available for printing.

Clicking on the "Manual Scoring Wizard" button begins an easy three-screen process of entering paper-and-pencil Nelson-Denny test scores (Forms G and H only) into the CD-ROM database, a useful feature for users who wish to store data from previously administered paper-and-pencil tests. Clicking on the "Management" button opens a window that displays nine option buttons: (a) Groups, (b) Database, (c) Assign Groups, (d) Export to Riverside, (e) Users, (f) System Configuration, (g) Test Sessions, (h) Help, and (i) Main Screen. Each button (with the exception of the "Help" and "Main Menu" buttons) provides the user with features designed to help him or her organize test information.

Clicking on the "Reports" button takes the user to a screen where six reports may be accessed/created: (a) Individual Narrative Report, (b) Individual Longitudinal Report (Pre-test/Post-test Growth), (c) List Report, (d) Group Summary Report, (e) Longitudinal Report (Pre-test/Post-test Growth), and (f) Longitudinal Summary Report (Pre-test/Post-test Growth). The Individual Narrative report was described in a previous sec-

tion of this review. The List Report provides individual test scores in a format different from the Individual Narrative Report. The examinee's raw scores, standard scores, grade equivalent scores, normal curve equivalent scores, stanines, and percentile ranks are displayed for Vocabulary, Comprehension, Reading Total, and Reading Rate in a chart. Percentile ranks for the four scores are displayed in a bar chart format. The chart is clear and easy to understand. The Group Summary Report provides both the chart feature (as described for a List Report) and the graphic described for the Individual Narrative Report. The scores on this report are averages based on the examinees included in the group. Groups may be assigned by the user through the "Management" and "Assign Groups" options.

I was unable to view an Individual Longitudinal Report, a Longitudinal Report, or a Longitudinal Summary Report. These reports are based on pre- and posttest data for individuals or groups of test takers. Despite my best efforts, I was unable to find reference to how to set up a test as a pre- or posttest in the manuals. There were no references to pre/post test in "Help."

On many of the screens a user would be accessing while working with this test, an "Okay" button is included. Sometimes the "Okay" button appears to have a function. For example, while working in the "Report" section of the test, clicking the "Okay" button will cause a report to be generated and displayed on the screen. Sometimes the "Okay" button appears to have no function and clicking it results in no discernable activity. Many screens also include a "Cancel" button. Clicking this button prompts the user to exit the program. This aspect was especially bothersome while working in the test session wizard. As mentioned previously, it is extremely difficult to back up or exit from the "Test Session Wizard" once it has been activated. A user must either complete the test and designate it an unsuccessful administration or quit the program via some other method (e.g., Windows Task Manager).

It is not possible to acquire a printout of an examinee's responses to the test items. On the Comprehension portion of the test, half of the items are labeled "literal" and half are labeled "interpretive." A list of which items are on each form of the test is provided in the technical manual. Because actual examinee responses are unavailable, a test administrator's option to consider differential performance on literal and interpretive items is not possible.

TECHNICAL. The Nelson-Denny Reading Test CD-ROM version was standardized on high school, 2-year, and 4-year college students. Reports in the technical manual suggest totals of nearly 2,000 high school students, 1,000 two-year college students, and 1,500 four-year college students participated. Actual numbers provided in the technical manual are: 1,548 high school students, 948 two-year college students, and 1,310 four-year college students. These values are based on the sample sizes reported for Vocabulary, Comprehension, and Total. Separate sample size values are listed for Reading Rate. The samples were drawn from 17 public and parochial high schools (how many of each type is not reported), 27 two-year colleges, and 23 four-year colleges. The sample represents three geographic regions: (a) East/Mideast/Southeast (roughly 38% of the total standardization sample including institutions from AL, AR, DE, GA, KY, LA, MS, NH, NJ, NY, NC, PA, TN, and VA); (b) Great Lakes/Plains (roughly 47% of the total standardization sample including institutions from IL, IN, KS, MN, MO, NE, OH, OK, and WI); and (c) West/Far West (roughly 15% of the total standardization sample including institutions from AK, AZ, HI, OR, and TX). As with the paper-and-pencil versions of Forms G and H, middle-America is overrepresented and the West/Far West is underrepresented. As in previous versions of the test, enrollment was considered as a selection criteria. Unlike previous versions of the test, including the paper-and-pencil versions of Forms G and H, no attempt to address ethnicity or SES is included with respect to the standardization sample for the CD-ROM version.

Reliability (KR20) estimates are reported for both Forms G and H for Grades 9 and 10, Grades 11 and 12, Grades 13 and 14 at a 2-year college, and Grades 13 and 14 at a 4-year college. For the Vocabulary portion of the test, reliability estimates range from .92 to .94. For the Comprehension portion of the test, reliability estimates range from .85 to .91. For the Total test score (Vocabulary plus 2 times the Reading Comprehension score), reliability estimates range from .94 to .95.

Alternate-forms reliability estimates were also provided. For the alternate Forms CD-ROM Form G and paper-and-pencil Form H, reliability estimates (based on approximately 90 participants) for Vocabulary = .92, Comprehension = .76, Total = .90, and Reading Rate = .54. For the alternate Forms CD-ROM Form H and paper-and-pencil Form G, reliability estimates (based on approximately 116 participants) for Vocabulary = .87, for Comprehension = .68, for Total = .85, and for Reading Rate = .67.

The technical manual includes a report of a test equating study between Forms G and H in the CD-ROM version and Forms G and H in the paper-and-pencil version. A one-paragraph description of the test equating study and a table are provided. The explanation and the table do not provide adequate information for interpreting the equivalence of the CD-ROM and paper-and-pencil versions of Forms G and H.

No validity information is provided in the manuals that accompany the CD-ROM version of the test. An evaluation of the validity of Forms G and H (paper-and-pencil version) may be found in a previous edition of the *Mental Measurements Yearbook* (Murray-Ward, 1998; Smith, 1998).

SUMMARY. The most appropriate use for the test is for screening. Researchers in need of a quick and relatively reliable measure of reading comprehension may find the test useful. Sufficient time has passed since the norming of the paper-and-pencil versions of Forms G and H (published in 1993) to have resulted in additional studies of the test. None, however, are reported in the manuals available with the CD-ROM version. The same information related to use of the test from the paper-and-pencil versions is reported instead.

From an examinee's perspective, the Nelson-Denny Reading Test CD-ROM is likely easy to use. From a test administrator's perspective, the CD-ROM version may be problematic until she or he acquires sufficient knowledge of the program features. This version incorporates some useful tracking and data management features. The ability to receive scores immediately and print out easy-to-understand score reports is an attractive feature of the CD-ROM version.

REVIEWER'S REFERENCES

Murray-Ward, M. (1998). [Review of the Nelson-Denny Reading Test, Forms G and H]. In J. C. Impara & B. S. Plake (Eds.), *The thirteenth mental measurements yearbook* (pp. 683-685). Lincoln, NE: Buros Institute of Mental Measurements.

Smith, D. K. (1998). [Review of the Nelson-Denny Reading Test, Forms G and H]. In J. C. Impara & B. S. Plake (Eds.), *The thirteenth mental measurements yearbook* (pp. 685-686). Lincoln, NE: Buros Institute of Mental Measurements.

Review of the Nelson-Denny Reading Test, CD-ROM Version 1.2 by DARRELL L. SABERS, Professor of Educational Psychology, and AMY M. OLSON, Doctoral Student, University of Arizona, Tucson, AZ:

DESCRIPTION. The Nelson-Denny Reading Test, CD-ROM Version 1.2 (Forms G & H) is the latest version of the Nelson-Denny Reading Test first published in 1929. The test is targeted towards students in Grades 9–14. The CD-ROM offers an alternative to the paper-and-pencil administration of Forms G and H published in 1993. With items identical to Forms G and H of the paper-and-pencil test, the computerized version assesses student achievement in three areas: Vocabulary, Comprehension, and Reading Rate.

The Vocabulary subtest has 80 multiple-choice items to be completed in 15 minutes. The Comprehension subtest includes seven reading passages and 38 multiple-choice items. Reading Rate is assessed during the first minute of the 20-minute Comprehension subtest. Forms G and H of the paper-and-pencil test include directions for an extended-time administration in which the test can be given in two sessions (Vocabulary in 24 minutes and Comprehension in 32 minutes).

The software immediately scores tests and produces student and group score reports. Users can also manually score tests by entering raw score information from administration of the paper-and-pencil test. For manual test scoring, additional norms are available for Grades 15–16, law enforcement academies, and extended-time administration. The user is unable to evaluate these norms directly as they are not included in the manual for the CD-ROM version of the test. These norms are derived from research on the 1993 paper-and-pencil test and are included in the Manual for Scoring and Interpretation for the paper-and-pencil version of the test.

DEVELOPMENT. The CD-ROM version of Forms G and H is an exact presentation of those two forms; thus users of the CD-ROM test may wish to purchase the paper-and-pencil test and accompanying technical report (1993) for more complete development information. Murray-Ward (1998) and Smith (1998) already reviewed the test's development, and the strengths and short-comings described in those reviews remain in the CD-ROM version.

Because the test is administered via computer, one cannot review items in great detail. The overall impression of Vocabulary items is that they are generally well constructed, requiring students to match difficult words to easier synonyms. Interpretative Comprehension items are passage dependent for the most part but, at least in some cases, literal items can be answered correctly through matching phrases. This strategy is particularly true in biographical passages that ask students to answer what happened when the student was a certain age or during a historical event. For all items, it would be helpful if the authors had included difficulty indices and evidence of relevance.

TECHNICAL. The CD-ROM Forms G and H were standardized between September 1999 and January 2000; the technical manual (p. 5) describes the match between the sample and the nation with regard to region and enrollment size of high schools, 2-year colleges, and 4-year colleges. As noted in the Murray-Ward (1998) and Smith (1998) reviews of the paper-and-pencil test, those norms tend to overrepresent the Midwest (now the Great Lakes/Plains) region and small schools. The norms for the CD-ROM version have those same flaws, including only 10.4% of high school students in the West/Far West region where 32% of the population should have been represented in 1990 (and more in 2000). The large school districts' target was 45.4%, but only 19% of the students came from those districts. The college and university samples are also nonrepresentative, appearing to be more a collection of scores from users than a national sampling. It appears that the university sample may also be biased in favor of remedial classes, given that high school students were more likely to complete the test than university students (technical manual, Table 7, p. 9). There is no way these norms should be considered "national" norms. The CD-ROM manuals do not include the ethnic and SES norm data that were available with the paper-and-pencil test.

The authors assume that the CD-ROM version is equivalent to the paper-and-pencil Forms G and H, an assumption not fully supported by the alternate-forms reliability estimates obtained in the equating study. For example, the Mantel-Haenszel approach to differential item functioning (DIF) was used in preparing the paper-and-pencil test, but the authors assume the same items were "potentially biased" in the standardization sample for the CD-ROM test 6 years later and no further analyses were conducted (technical manual, p. 4).

The authors caution against interpreting raw scores, and especially warn against the temptation to use the Reading Rate score as a traditional measure of words per minute. Raw scores on the Comprehension subtest are doubled before obtaining derived scores, and the Total test score includes the doubled Comprehension score as well. The authors note this doubling is made because the standard deviation for the shorter Comprehension test is half the size of the standard deviation for the Vocabulary test. However, users must be cautious to use the doubled Comprehension score when entering the tables provided in the technical manual. The computer-scoring package automatically doubles the Comprehension score when calculating and reporting the Total score.

Derived scores include percentile ranks, stanines, NCEs, developmental standard scores (also called scale scores), and grade equivalents. The authors admit that basing the grade equivalents on pooled nonequivalent samples of all grades does not account for attrition and results in larger estimates of growth. They caution readers against relying on the grade equivalents, but one might wonder why grade equivalents are even included. The purported "equal-interval" properties of the developmental standard or scale scores are also suspect given that the standardization populations are not national samples.

The sample score profiles provided in the interpretation manual use the suspect grade equivalents along with standard scores and percentile ranks. The text included in score reports is not customized for individual respondents, and although the general interpretation and tips may assist a first-time test-taker, the lack of specificity renders individual longitudinal reports relatively unhelpful. Problems exist with the group reports as well; the use of individual norms to evaluate group averages results in an underestimation of high-performing groups and overestimation of low-performing groups.

Interitem reliability estimates are provided by KR-20 reliability coefficients, but the authors note that these are not appropriate to use with the speeded test. KR-20 estimates are provided for the Total Score (Vocabulary + 2*Comprehension), but there is no explanation of how the KR-20 coefficients were computed for such a composite. Additional reliability estimates are provided from the equating study between the CD-ROM version and the paper-and-pencil version of Forms G and H. The authors refer to these estimates as alternate-forms reliability, but the coefficients also reflect the variance attributed to differences between the CD-ROM and paper-and-pencil versions. All students received both forms within a 3-week interval. These alternate form/comparable-administration coefficients range from .54–.92, with Vocabulary and Total score demonstrating higher reliability estimates than Reading Rate and Comprehension. Given that the test is primarily used for making decisions about individuals, many of these coefficients are lower than would be desired.

The authors suggest that the test can be used for the same predictive and screening purposes as the paper-and-pencil version. However, empirical validity evidence for these uses is restricted to citing studies using previous forms of the Nelson-Denny Reading Test. The authors also indicate the test may provide diagnostic information. A "rule of thumb" (technical manual, p. 16) for interpreting subtest score differences in percentile ranks is provided, and this use of score-level standard errors is appreciated. However, no mention is made of how these standard errors were calculated. The authors further suggest that users may interpret "word power" (technical manual, p. 15) by comparing Vocabulary and Comprehension scores and may use Reading Rate as an indicator. Unfortunately, no evidence supporting these interpretations is provided.

No information is provided to establish whether this test is representative and relevant for current high school and college students, and past reviewers (Murray-Ward, 1998; Smith 1998) indicate that this may be a weakness in the paper-and-pencil versions as well. Comprehension items are classified as "largely interpretive" or "primarily literal," but the authors do not provide a description of the process used to classify items. The user cannot evaluate responses item-by-item when the test is computer administered; so item classification does not help in interpreting test performance. Comprehension items are further categorized by subject, but the authors caution against using categorization when interpreting scores due to intercorrelations (not provided) between items. Moreover, upon examining the item categories, it appears that the social sciences content was drawn from college sources whereas the humanities and science content was mostly drawn from high school sources.

COMMENTARY. Previous reviewers (Murray-Ward, 1998; Smith, 1998) have found validity information to be lacking or to be based on previous versions of the test, and this dearth continues to be a problem with the CD-ROM. Intersubtest correlations available for earlier pencil-and-paper Forms C and D have not been provided for later forms. Correlations between the subtests would assist a reviewer or user in understanding the construct being measured.

To the authors' credit, the chance-level score issue discussed in the reviews of Forms C and D by Forsyth (1978) and Raygor (1978) has been resolved with the increase to 15 minutes and reduction to 80 items in the Vocabulary subtest. The authors should be commended for addressing the difference between 2-year and 4-year colleges and universities. But this test is a disappointment given the number of years and the extensive reviews available for assistance.

SUMMARY. The Nelson-Denny provides assessments of student performance on three generally accepted reading measures. Users interested in assessing students transitioning from high school to college may find the test especially useful if local norms are developed and used for interpreting student performance. The CD-ROM version is simple to administer and scoring is automatic, which may contribute to the continued popularity of the Nelson-Denny Reading Test.

REVIEWERS' REFERENCES

Forsyth, R. A. (1978). [Review of the Nelson-Denny Reading Test, Forms C and D]. In O. K. Buros (Ed.), *The eighth mental measurements yearbook* (pp. 1207-1209). Highland Park, NJ: The Gryphon Press.

Murray-Ward, M. (1998). [Review of the Nelson-Denny Reading Test, Forms G and H]. In J. C. Impara & B. S. Plake (Eds.), *The thirteenth mental measurements yearbook* (pp. 683-685). Lincoln, NE: Buros Institute of Mental Measurements.

Raygor, A. L. (1978). [Review of the Nelson-Denny Reading Test, Forms C and D]. In O. K. Buros (Ed.), *The eighth mental measurements yearbook* (pp. 1209-1211). Highland Park, NJ: The Gryphon Press.

Smith, D. K. (1998). [Review of the Nelson-Denny Reading Test, Forms G and H]. In J. C. Impara & B. S. Plake (Eds.), *The thirteenth mental measurements yearbook* (pp. 685-686). Lincoln, NE: Buros Institute of Mental Measurements.

[133]

Nonverbal Personality Questionnaire and Five-Factor Nonverbal Personality Questionnaire.

Purpose: Designed to "measure normal personality characteristics" with the use of pictures instead of words.
Population: Ages 18 and over.
Publication Date: 2004.
Administration: Group or individual.
Price Data, 2005: $20 per manual (72 pages).
Comments: Tests can be administered together and use the same manual; can be used in research, counseling, and business settings.
Authors: Sampo V. Paunonen, Douglas N. Jackson, and Michael C. Ashton (manual).
Publisher: Sigma Assessment Systems, Inc.

a) NONVERBAL PERSONALITY QUESTIONNAIRE.
Acronym: NPQ.
Scores, 17: Achievement, Affiliation, Aggression, Autonomy, Dominance, Endurance, Exhibition, Thrill-Seeking, Impulsivity, Nurturance, Order, Play, Sentience, Social Recognition, Succorance, Understanding, Deviation.
Price Data: $40 per handscorable examination kit including manual, picture booklet, 5 answer sheets, and 5 profile sheets; $50 per 10 picture booklets; $62.50 per 25 answer sheets; $40 per 25 profile sheets.
Time: (20–35) minutes.
Authors: Sampo V. Paunonen and Douglas N. Jackson.

b) FIVE-FACTOR NONVERBAL PERSONALITY QUESTIONNAIRE.
Acronym: FF-NPQ.
Scores, 5: Extraversion, Agreeableness, Conscientiousness, Neuroticism, Openness to Experience.
Price Data: $40 per examination kit including manual, picture booklet, 5 answer sheets, and 5 profile sheets; $50 per 10 picture booklets; $50 per 25 answer sheets; $32 per 25 profile sheets.
Time: (10–15) minutes.
Authors: Sampo Paunonen, Douglas N. Jackson, and Michael C. Ashton.

Review of the Nonverbal Personality Questionnaire and Five-Factor Nonverbal Personality Questionnaire by ASHRAF KAGEE, Professor of Psychology, Stellenbosch University, South Africa:

DESCRIPTION. The Nonverbal Personality Questionnaire (NPQ) and Five-Factor Nonverbal Personality Questionnaire (FF-NPQ) are two paper-and-pencil questionnaires that were constructed to measure personality characteristics in adults. The two questionnaires are presented in tandem in the test manual but measure separate sets of constructs. The NPQ is a 136-item form designated to measure 16 different personality traits, which are: Achievement, Affiliation, Aggression, Autonomy, Dominance, Endurance, Exhibition, Thrill Seeking, Impulsivity, Nurturance, Order, Play, Sentience, Social Recognition, Succorance, and Understanding. The FF-NPQ is a shorter 60-item questionnaire designed to measure five broad factors of personality, the so-called Big Five, namely, Extraversion, Agreeableness, Conscientiousness, Neuroticism, and Openness to Experience. The unique feature of these two instruments is that the items consist of illustrations rather than verbal statements. Respondents are asked to choose their answers to each nonverbal item from a range of alternatives or response options. As the instruments are structured, little training in scoring the test results is required.

The nonverbal items of the NPQ consist of line drawings showing a main person engaging in personality-relevant behaviors. The primary advantage of both instruments is that they may be used with people who have difficulty with the language of the assessment. Thus they are among clients who have problems with illiteracy, dyslexia, age, or attention deficit disorder, or have difficulty with English. In this sense, the measures may be of use in multicultural contexts, especially as they require no translation into other languages. Indeed, in some multicultural situations where there is an absence of adequate translation facilities, the use of these measures may be indicated so that differences in assessment results due to poor or inadequate translation of verbal items may be minimized. Importantly, the authors of the instruments are careful not to make the claim that they are culture-free. Indeed, it is accepted that they may be mainly relevant to Western, educated, middle-class respondents.

DEVELOPMENT. The materials furnished by the developers provide useful information concerning how the instruments were developed. The nonverbal items of the NPQ and FF-NPQ were originally created to address a debate in the personality literature regarding the meaning of trait and behavior ratings, rather than for the purposes of personality assessment. The chief aim of the test developers was to address the Semantic Similarity Hypothesis, which states that both self-ratings and observer ratings of personality reflect consistencies in the language of personality. Thus, people tend to ascribe personality characteristics to themselves and others without any necessary knowledge of the person's behavior. Instead, they have certain assumptions about what personality characteristics tend to occur together in the language of personality. The authors argue that this link between descriptions of personality is not necessarily based on real personality traits but instead on shared elements of meaning between words describing personality traits. The NPQ and FF-NPQ attempt to circumvent the problem of shared elements of meaning accounting for personality ratings by eliminating verbal behavior information in personality judgment tasks. Thus, the assumption of the scales is that a set of behavioral acts could be considered exemplars of common personality traits to be used in describing an individual. Rather than using words, the scale uses visual depictions. The developers commissioned an artist to draw cartoon-like pictures of a person performing specific behaviors in specific situations. Respondents are asked to consider the behavior depicted in each illustration and then rate the probability that they would engage in the behavior on a 7-point Likert scale.

TECHNICAL.

NPQ: Information about the standardization process is described in detail for both instruments. Large samples were recruited in the standardization process of the NPQ (468 men, 794 women, and a combined sample of 1,267). The data sets were obtained in Canada, Finland, Germany, Poland, Norway, the Netherlands, England, Russia, Israel, and Hong Kong. The cross-cultural data were aggregated in order to provide a large group of respondents for the calculation of norms. The psychometric properties for the NPQ appear to be adequate and reliability coefficients cluster around .70. The developers describe in detail the procedures involved in arriving at the final form of the NPQ in that items that displayed poor item reliability and other scale properties were deleted. They also present a flowchart showing how decisions were made to include and exclude items. Five meta-factors were extracted from the scales of the pooled data, accounting for 83.8% of the scales' variance, and closely resembled the Big Five personality dimensions. The data obtained from the factor analysis are consistent with the claim that the structure of personality has some generality across cultures and that the structure tends to resemble the Five-Factor Model.

FF-NPQ: The FF-NPQ is similar to the NPQ in appearance. The norms for this measure were developed using the scale scores of a sample of Canadian university students, which consisted of a total of 319 male and female respondents. These norms make it possible to compare the scores of individuals by sex. The procedures for test development are described in detail. The items were taken from the item pool offered by the NPQ by calculating correlations between the items and the NEO-FFI developed by Costa and McCrae (1992). In an attempt to advance an argument for the cross-cultural validity of the NPQ, the data were collected from samples in Canada, England, Finland, Germany, Norway, Poland, and Russia. The results showed that the NPQ scales had similar means and standard deviations to those of the original Canadian sample, indicating cross-cultural applicability of the instrument.

COMMENTARY. The NPQ and FF-NPQ are useful instruments for consideration in contexts in which there are concerns regarding clients' linguistic ability or literacy. From a psychometric perspective the instruments appear to be robust and well-validated. However, it is important to recognize the cultural limitations of the measure despite efforts to bridge cultural differences. The pictures to be presented to respondents are very primitive from an artistic point of view. In following revisions of the scale the developers may consider more sophisticated artwork for inclusion. Some of the items are also difficult to interpret, which is likely to create confusion among respondents and poor item reliability. It seems that further work on this instrument may be warranted.

SUMMARY. The developers have made a robust effort to develop a pair of instruments to measure personality that precludes items that rely on respondents' verbal skills. The strengths of these tests lie in their application among populations for whom verbal language and literacy are compromised. However, the cross-cultural applicability of the NPQ and FF-NPQ is likely to be somewhat limited.

REVIEWER'S REFERENCE

Costa, P. T., Jr., & McCrae, R. R (1992). *Revised NEO Personality Inventory (NA-PI-E) and NEO Five-Factor Inventory (NEO-FFI): Professional manual.* Odessa, FL: Psychological Assessment Resources, Inc.

Review of the Nonverbal Personality Questionnaire and Five-Factor Nonverbal Personality Questionnaire by SEAN REILLEY, Assistant Professor of Psychology, Morehead State University, Morehead, KY:

DESCRIPTION. The Nonverbal Personality Questionnaire (NPQ) consists of 136 nonverbal items that measure 16 adult personality characteristics highlighted in Murray's (1938) system of needs. The NPQ also yields a validity score (Deviation) in an effort to detect random responding. The NPQ appears to be appropriate for administration on an individual or group basis, and requires 20 to 25 minutes for completion. Adults (aged 18 years and older) are given a picture booklet containing 17 pages of NPQ items. An initial sample item is provided with directions indicating that participants should provide a numerical rating of their likelihood for engaging in the type of behavior shown. Using on a 7-point Likert scale ranging from *extremely unlikely* to *extremely likely*, respondents rate their probable level of engagement for each item on the NPQ answer sheet. Scores for each of 16 personality scales and 1 validity scale are derived by summing across predetermined rows of items on the answer sheet. Using the professional manual, total NPQ raw scores are converted to gender-specific percentiles and graphed on a gender-specific profile sheet. The order of the 16 raw scores on the answer sheet are arranged under five broad personality dimensions represented in the literature as the Big Five Personality Factors: Extraversion, Agreeableness, Conscientiousness, Neuroticism (labeled as Social Dependency on the NPQ), and Openness to Experience. As such, the NPQ provides information concerning 16 lower level personality traits and five broad personality dimensions common in contemporary literature.

If only a nonverbal assessment of the Big Five Personality Factors is desired, a 60-item Five-Factor NPQ (FF-NPQ) can be completed. The FF-NPQ uses a large subset of the NPQ items for each FF-NPQ scale with the exception of the Neuroticism scale. Respondents complete the FF-NPQ in approximately 10 minutes using an eight-page FF-NPQ picture booklet, a FF-NPQ answer sheet, and ratings procedures similar to those of the NPQ. Reverse scoring for selected FF-NPQ items is completed prior to summing down predetermined columns on the answer sheet to calculate raw scores. Percentiles are then obtained from the professional manual and graphed on the gender-specific FF-NPQ profile sheet. Unlike the NPQ, scores of a greater magnitude for each FF-NPQ scale uniformly correspond with higher percentiles on the profile sheet.

DEVELOPMENT. Two hundred and two line drawings were professionally commissioned to depict a genderless person engaging in behaviors thought to represent 17 of the personality traits described in Murray's (1938) system of needs. These traits were the same as those measured verbally on Jackson's Personality Research Form (PRF, Form E). These initial NPQ items were piloted with the PRF in two small groups of undergraduate students from North America and one small group from Finland. Internal consistency was found to be fair for the overall sample (average coefficient alpha = .71). Item analyses were conducted using a sequential ranking procedure that compared item-parent scale and item-nonparent scale, parent scale-validity scale, and determined whether the correlation between NPQ and like PRF scales was acceptable. It is unclear from the manual which item-nonparent scales were chosen and if formal statistical tests were performed to evaluate magnitude differences between correlations. Similarly, the magnitude of the correlation needed for acceptable status is unclear when like NPQ and PRF scales were compared. Based on these procedures, however, one personality scale, Abasement, was dropped from the final version of the NPQ and the remaining 16 personality scales and the validity scale were reduced to eight items each.

The FF-NPQ was developed to address the need for a brief, nonverbal assessment of the Big Five Personality Factors. Rather than create a new instrument, 60 existing NPQ items were piloted along with the NEO-FFI in a small sample (n = 304) of North American university students. Correlations greater than .30 with the NEO-FFI were used to retain like scales for the FF-NPQ. Using this procedure, three FF-NPQ scales were dropped. Re-pooling of the remaining items resulted in retention of a total of 56 items. Scale reliabilities were re-calculated using the same sample, which would likely lead to a biased estimate of reliability. Thirteen new Neuroticism items were created due to lower reliability and were administered to a small sample (n = 178) of North American university students. Ultimately, 12 items were retained, 3 per Neuroticism facet scale, using factor analytic techniques that are not well detailed in the manual.

TECHNICAL. Ten small, international samples drawn from 10 countries were combined for a total NPQ standardization sample of 1,267 adults (794 females, 468 males, 5 unidentified). Because of gender differences on various subscales, separate conversion tables were developed to transform raw scores to percentiles.

Internal consistency estimates (alphas ranging from .60 to .84) are generally minimally acceptable to good for each personality scale for the combined normative sample. Attempts to validate the factor structure of the current NPQ version are reported using meta-factor-analytic techniques. This approach allows the researcher to examine the overall factor structure using pooled aggregate correlation matrices drawn from the 10 international samples. Ultimately, a five-factor personality model had fairly acceptable convergence using all 16 personality subscale scores as loadings with the exception of the Dominance and Understanding scales. The two Neuroticism loadings suggests Neuroticism as measured on the NPQ reflects social dependency in contrast to negative affect commonly seen in other instruments. NPQ responses from a small Korean sample (n = 221) were recently fit to a five-factor model with mixed results. The authors attributed the results to different rotations used in the sets of factor analyses. Alternative explanations should also be investigated to account for model misfit given sample size and factoring choices. Test-retest reliability data are currently lacking for the NPQ. Estimates of convergent validity are provided for a portion of the standardization sample that completed both the NPQ and PRF. Moderate convergence was observed between the NPQ and PRF (M correlation = .46). Modest self-collateral correlations were noted for one North American sample for both the NPQ (r = .21) and the PRF (r = .24). These values are significantly below those afforded by the NEO-PI-R (r = .43), another widely used instrument to assess the Five Factor Personality Model. As noted by the test authors, however, the degree of acquaintanceship varied widely within dyads, which may account in part for the lower coefficients that were observed for the NPQ and the PRF.

The normative sample for the FF-NPQ is small (*n* = 319) and serves at best as a preliminary normative sample. Internal consistency estimates (alphas ranging .77 to .85) are generally fairly acceptable to good for each of the five FF-NPQ subscales. Similarly, two follow-up replications with smaller North American samples yielded internal consistency estimates of a similar range and magnitude. Archival cross cultural data (*n* = 701) for the FF-NPQ are provided, but for an earlier version of the FF-NPQ.

COMMENTARY. The NPQ and FF-NPQ are potentially valuable nonverbal, personality instruments for use with international, nonclinical populations. In order to improve utility, reliability evidence is needed to anchor factor structures and to provide temporal stability estimates. A larger and more representative sample is needed for the FF-NPQ. At present, the current standardization sample for the FF-NPQ is best viewed as preliminary and needs to be expanded in the future if this scale is to be used. Further, the positive and negative predictive power of the NPQ and FF-NPQ in relation to other personality instruments needs to be established, and inquiries into the conversion metrics for percentiles needs to be explored further.

The attempt to provide an international standardization sample is a strength of the NPQ. As a non-verbal instrument, no minimum reading level is suggested; however, the respondent would need to understand the directions and scaling procedures involved. As such, future work to determine the applicability of the NPQ for lower functioning levels is needed.

The process of factoring personality scores versus items is known to differentially affect the resulting latent variable factor model. In the case of the NPQ, the underlying factor structure might be clarified if advanced modeling using individual items was employed.

SUMMARY. The developers, to their credit, have produced two potentially valuable nonverbal personality instruments, the NPQ and the FF-NPQ, for international, nonclinical populations. Further validation work involving factor structure and evidence supporting temporal stability is needed for both instruments. A larger

and more representative standardization sample is desirable, especially for the FF-NPQ.

REVIEWER'S REFERENCE

Murray, H. A. (1938). *Explorations in personality*. New York: Oxford House.

[134]

Novaco Anger Scale and Provocation Inventory.

Purpose: "Designed to assess anger as a problem of psychological functioning and physical health and to assess therapeutic change."

Population: Ages 9–84 years.

Publication Date: 2003.

Acronym: NAS-PI.

Scores: INC Index.

Administration: Individual or group.

Price Data, 2007: $92 per complete kit including 25 AutoScore test forms and manual (64 pages); $53 per manual; $43.50 per 25 AutoScore test forms (bulk discounts available); Computerized Components: $152.50 per 25-use Computer Scoring CD for Windows; $16.50 per 100 PC answer sheets.

Comments: Can be administered as a whole or as two separate parts.

Author: Raymond W. Novaco.

Publisher: Western Psychological Services.

a) THE NOVACO ANGER SCALE.

Purpose: Designed to assess "how an individual experiences anger."

Scores: Cognitive, Arousal, Behavior, NAS Total, Anger Regulation.

Time: (10–20) minutes.

b) THE PROVOCATION INVENTORY.

Purpose: Designed to identify "the kinds of situations that lead to anger."

Scores: PI Total.

Time: (5–15) minutes.

Review of the Novaco Anger Scale and Provocation Inventory by ALBERT BUGAJ, Professor of Psychology, University of Wisconsin-Marinette, Marinette, WI:

DESCRIPTION. The Novaco Anger Scale and Provocation Inventory (NAS-PI), designed for individual assessment, outcome evaluation, and research purposes, consists of the 60-item Novaco Anger Scale (NAS) and the 25-item Provocation Inventory (PI). The NAS, which focuses on an individual's experience of anger, results in an overall scale score, and scores on Cognitive, Arousal, Behavioral, and Anger Regulation subscales. High NAS scores may indicate a need for clinical intervention, although they also may show an effort by the test-taker to "look tough."

The Provocation Inventory (PI), intended to assess the types of situations that lead to anger in five content areas such as "disrespectful treatment," results in an overall scale score. Results of the PI can elicit discussions of settings that provoke strong anger in a client; discussion of items leading to low scores can result in an understanding of how the client utilizes effective coping skills.

A trained technician can administer the NAS-PI in individual or group settings, although only individuals with clinical training in psychological testing should interpret the results. A paper-and-pencil test, NAS-PI responses are hand-scored, although the test manual indicates a computerized version is available. A formula developed by Barrett (2001), provided in the test manual, allows the values of missing responses to be estimated when three or fewer items are left incomplete. The test manual also includes a method for checking for inconsistent response patterns.

DEVELOPMENT. A theory of anger devised by Novaco (1977) formed the basis of the preliminary set of 101 items for the NAS-PI. A sample of 171 undergraduate students responded to these items. Results of this test administration and interviews with 45 hospitalized patients led to the creation of a revised instrument containing 88 items. Two additional waves of testing produced the final instrument.

TECHNICAL. The standardization sample of the NAS-PI consisted of 1,546 individuals (ages 9 to 84) from nonclinical settings. The manual indicates slight underrepresentation in the sample of males, individuals of minority ethnic backgrounds, and those with lower levels of education. Statistical examination of the scores (Cohen's d) indicated that although scores of men and women were comparable, scores of younger test-takers (ages 9 to 18) and adults (19 and older) differed significantly; the manual thus provides separate norms for the two age groups.

The manual notes that African Americans' scores were higher than the average of the standardization sample on some scales, a result also found in other research (cited in the test manual) with African American and Hispanic samples. Individuals with lower educational levels also acquired scores departing from the average. The test

manual suggests further research is necessary to uncover why these groups depart from the norm.

The NAS and PI exhibit high levels of internal consistency. Alpha coefficient for the NAS total score for the standardization sample was .94. Alpha values ranged from .76 for the Anger Regulation subscale to a high of .89 for the Behavior subscale. Coefficient alpha for PI total score was .95, and ranged from .73 to .84 for its subscales.

Median test-retest reliability over a 2-week period for a group of 27 individuals from the standardization sample was .78, ranging from .47 on the cognitive subscale to .82 on the PI total score. The test author acknowledges the small size of the sample. Higher test-retest reliabilities resulted from studies (utilizing larger sample sizes) of hospitalized inpatients in California and Scotland, and Canadian prison inmates.

The test manual cites several studies that examined the concurrent validity of the NAS-PI using samples from clinical and correctional populations. For example, in a study involving 141 male and female psychiatric patients in California, the NAS total score was strongly correlated to the total score on the Buss-Durkee Hostility Inventory (r = .82); the Caprara Scales of Irritability (r = .78) and Rumination (r = .69), the Cook-Medley Hostility scale (r = .68), and the STAXI Trait Anger Scale (r = .84). With regard to the PI, the test author concludes that although the PI total score is closely related to other measures of anger, specific content areas of the PI "seem to have some selective relationships with other measures" that are difficult to interpret (manual, p. 38), and calls for further research into this area.

More problematic, therapist ratings of severity of past and current offenses committed by a sample (n = 59) of juvenile delinquents in a residential treatment facility were for the most part unrelated to NAS-PI scores. However, the "Rated Anger Level" of 39 paroled sex offenders was related to NAS total scores (r = .42) and the Behavior subscale (r = .51). The Behavior subscale was also related to the therapists' ratings of the parolees' offensive history (r = .45), appropriateness for participation in anger management groups (r = .33), and parolees' current offense severity (r = .29).

A number of intercorrelations within the NAS and PI subscales proved to be moderate to high in the standardization sample, with those between subscales of the NAS and PI generally lower than those within the two scales. Factor analysis of the NAS resulted in three factors each consisting of items from at least two subscales. Factor analysis of the PI resulted in five factors. Another factor analysis (n = 1,101 civil commitment patients) utilized a different set of Cognitive items, and did not include Regulation items.

In one study of predictive validity, NAS (r = .46) and PI (r = .43) total scores and several subscales were found to be predictive of STAXI State Anger. In a retrospective analysis, the NAS total was predictive of hospitalized patients' number of convictions for violent crimes. In a study of 1,100 discharged patients, the NAS was predictive of violence during the first 20 weeks after discharge and at 1 year.

Although several other studies are supportive of the NAS, homicidal patients in the standardization sample obtained higher Irritability scores than the "normal" standardization subsample, but reported higher Anger Regulation. Juvenile delinquents in the group reported poorer Anger Regulation, but problematically, less Anger Provocation. A number of groups (Homicide Perpetrators in Psychiatric Treatment, Incarcerated Sex Offenders, and Juvenile Delinquents in Residential Care) reported higher scores on the Crowne-Marlowe Social Desirability Scale than did other groups. Three studies reported in the test manual examined the NAS-PI as a measure of anger treatment outcomes with positive results.

COMMENTARY. Numerous studies (only some of which are referred to in this review) attest to the concurrent validity, as well as the test-retest reliability, of the NAS-PI. However, as the test author intimates, the test is not without problems. One must question the suitability of the NAS-PI for use with minority populations, as data indicate African Americans and Hispanics score differently than the normative population. The same may be said for individuals with lower levels of education.

Although the test author states that most people with a fourth-grade reading ability can read the test, there is no indication of an empirical examination of the readability of the items. One may thus question the use of the NAS-PI with younger or less educated populations. One must also wonder if lower levels of education or reading ability do not lead to the lower scores of younger populations.

On the basis of the factor analysis reported in the test manual, the question arises as to whether the subscale structure of the test is correct. One would expect items related to particular subscales to load on the same factor. This was not the case in the reported factor analysis where items from two and sometimes three subscales loaded on the same factor. Although this outcome does not detract from the potential worth of the overall scale scores, further examination of the subscale structure of the test is suggested.

The most problematic issue concerning the NAS-PI is the issue of social desirability. The test manual concludes with a suggestion that the test administrator obtain an estimate of response bias (for example, through use of the Crowne-Marlowe Social Desirability Scale) when using the NAS-PI in forensic settings. The manual also states that very high scores might indicate an effort to "look bad" (p. 13) or "look tough" (p. 15). If this is the case, it may be questioned why the test authors did not devise scales measuring social desirability and the need to "look tough" during the inception of the scales.

None of this is to say the NAS-PI is not a useful test. A good deal of research has gone into determining the psychometric properties of the test, with regard to its validity and reliability. A sound and elaborate theory, which should be used to further refine the test's factor structure, forms the basis of the NAS-PI.

SUMMARY. Used with proper caution, the NAS-PI should prove useful in assessing anger in clinical and forensic populations. The test possesses adequate reliability, and concurrent and predictive validity. Caution must be taken, however, when the test is used with minority, younger, or less educated populations. Test users also must be wary of social desirability effects and efforts by the test-taker to "look tough."

REVIEWER'S REFERENCES

Barrett, P. (2001). *Prorating error in test scores*. Retrieved on August 11, 2006, from http://www.liv.ac.uk~pbarrett/statistics_corner.htm
Novaco, R. W. (1977). Stress inoculation: A cognitive therapy for anger and its application to a case of depression. *Journal of Consulting and Clinical Psychology, 45*, 600–608.

Review of the Novaco Anger Scale and Provocation Inventory by GEOFFREY L. THORPE, Professor of Psychology, University of Maine, Orono, ME:

DESCRIPTION. The Novaco Anger Scale and Provocation Inventory (NAS-PI) is a two-part self-report test consisting of 85 items. The NAS component assesses how an individual experiences anger, with questions like: "If someone bothers me, I react first and think later." Respondents rate each of the 60 items of the NAS on a 3-point scale (1 = *Never true*, 2 = *Sometimes true*, 3 = *Always true*), producing four subscale scores (Cognitive, Arousal, Behavior, and Anger Regulation) and a total score. The PI component describes situations that may lead to anger, such as: "Being accused of something that you didn't do." Respondents rate each of the 25 items of the PI on a 4-point scale to indicate how angry the situation described would make them feel (1 = *Not at all angry*, 2 = *A little angry*, 3 = *Fairly angry*, 4 = *Very angry*), producing a single total score.

The NAS-PI was designed "to assess anger as a problem of psychological functioning and physical health and to assess therapeutic change" (manual, p. 1). The test author cites a broad range of stress-related health problems and mental disorders in which anger is prominent, and argues that the assessment of anger disposition and its modification is an important task for many healthcare professionals.

The materials received from the test publisher consist of a 64-page manual and a package of NAS-PI profile sheets and AutoScore forms. The profile sheets, printed separately for Adolescent (age range 9–18) and Adult (ages 19 and over) respondents, present *T*-scores and percentiles corresponding with the various subscale and total score ranges.

DEVELOPMENT. The NAS-PI components were developed separately. NAS items are clinically oriented and reflect the guiding theoretical orientation that anger comprises elements of cognition, arousal, and behavior, "linked by feedback and regulation mechanisms and embedded in an environmental context" (manual, p. 21). Items in the Cognitive domain represent the dimensions of justification, suspiciousness, rumination, and hostile attitude; in the Arousal domain, intensity, duration, somatic tension, and irritability; and in the Behavioral domain, impulsive reaction, verbal aggression, physical confrontation, and indirect expression.

PI items were selected to assess the intensity of anger elicited by a variety of provocative situations in five content areas. These areas are: disre-spectful treatment, unfairness, frustration, annoying traits of others, and irritations.

An initial set of 101 test items for the NAS-PI was pilot-tested with 171 undergraduate students, who also completed a battery of tests that included other anger inventories. The set of items was reduced to the 88 with the best psychometric properties that also represented the most realistic match with the experiences of state hospital patients with severe anger problems. The revised instrument was administered to 142 psychiatric inpatients, a subset of whom provided test-retest reliability data. Further refinements followed, and the final form of the NAS-PI was re-assessed with similar samples of inpatients. A set of 16 item pairs was identified to serve as a rough index of consistent responding, the criterion being that each pair selected showed a minimal intercorrelation of .40 or greater (these correlations range from .42 to .66).

TECHNICAL. The standardization sample consisted of 1,546 respondents, ranging in age from 9 to 84, from public schools, college classrooms, senior centers, religious organizations, and other community settings. In addition to a table of raw score means and standard deviations for the subscales and total scores in the entire standardization sample, the test author (Novaco) provides tabulations of the sample's demographic characteristics (gender, age, ethnic background, socioeconomic status, and geographic region), indicating a fairly close match with data from the U.S. Census of 2000. Novaco presents *T*-scores for males and females, for racial/ethnic subgroups, for nine age ranges, and for five educational levels in the normative group. He argues that the use of *T*-scores makes effect sizes immediately apparent, so that *T* = 56 in one subgroup in comparison with *T* = 50 in another reveals a large effect size of .6 in standard deviation units. On that criterion, the observed statistically significant difference between males and females on the NAS behavior subscale (the only scale to produce a significant sex difference) is not clinically meaningful, as the corresponding effect size is only .31.

The internal consistency (alpha) estimates for the standardization sample were very high for the total scores: .94 for the NAS and .95 for the PI. Alpha coefficients for the NAS subscales ranged from .76 to .89. Similar results were obtained for juveniles and adults, and for psychiatric inpatients in California and Scotland. Test-retest reliability estimates in a subsample of the standardization sample were .76 for the NAS and .82 for the PI. These estimates were drawn from a very small subset of 27 respondents who were tested 2 weeks apart. More compelling are the test-retest correlations of .84 (NAS) and .86 (PI) in 126 California state hospital inpatients with a 2-week intertest interval.

The construct validity of the NAS was assessed by obtaining its correlations with the Buss-Durkee Hostility Inventory, the STAXI Trait Anger Scale, and two other anger scales, producing coefficients ranging from .69 to .84 in a sample of 141 inpatients. Data from inpatients in a high security forensic unit in Scotland showed a similar range of intercorrelations of the NAS-PI with other anger measures, but much lower correlations with the Beck Depression Inventory, attesting to the NAS-PI's discriminant validity.

A study with 110 male inpatients in a forensic facility for the developmentally disabled compared NAS-PI scores with, among other measures, a ward behavior rating scale, yielding low correlations (e.g., .28 for the NAS total score and .34 for the NAS cognitive subscale). However, it seems likely that these correlation coefficients could have been limited by a truncated range of scores produced by the respondents in that setting.

The NAS-PI correlates modestly with STAXI state anger scores obtained 2 months later, indicating a level of predictive validity for Novaco's instrument. The manual provides detailed information on factor analytic studies of the NAS-PI and on its sensitivity to anger treatment outcome.

The test-retest reliability, parallel-form reliability, concurrent validity, and discriminant validity of the NAS were found to be satisfactory in 204 male offenders in Canada (Mills, Kroner, & Forth, 1998). This study and many like it exemplify the substantial professional literature that has developed in recent years from Novaco's research on the assessment of anger.

COMMENTARY. The NAS-PI is a two-part self-report inventory of anger and its components that was designed for practicality and ease of use by respondents and examiners. The items were written at a fourth-grade reading level, and the test takes about 25 minutes to complete. Hand-scoring is straightforward and convenient. The test was developed and standardized with commu-

nity, clinical, and forensic samples, and is offered as an assessment instrument for research, individual assessment, and outcome measurement. The NAS-PI was originally standardized with about 1,500 respondents who were broadly representative of the U.S. population. Many further studies have provided normative data from clinical and forensic populations in diverse geographic regions. The test manual's extensive tabulation of norms and detailed appraisal of the NAS-PI's psychometric properties confirm that the instrument is psychometrically sound and that its author has reached his intended goals.

Readers familiar with Novaco's early work will recall the original Novaco Anger Scale from the 1970s that consisted of 80 anger provocation items similar to those in the current PI. The early scale was used in research by Novaco and others and was not commercially available. The development of the new NAS to reflect cognitive, emotional, behavioral, and self-regulatory dimensions of anger drawn from theory was a constructive move that has helped to advance the field. Retaining a list of potentially anger-arousing situations in the PI allows clinicians and researchers to continue to use assessment methodology similar to that of Novaco's original research on anger control.

SUMMARY. The NAS-PI can be recommended as a convenient self-report assessment of anger and its principal dimensions to be used in community, clinical, and forensic settings, both as a snapshot index of current anger levels and as a barometer of progress and change. The instrument is extensively norm referenced and has satisfactory psychometric properties of internal consistency, test-retest reliability, and concurrent and predictive validity. Despite the strong internal consistency of the scales, the interitem correlations and factor-analytic work described in the manual appear to indicate that the NAS-PI scale items are not interchangeable and make different contributions to assessing the measured constructs. It would be interesting to see future researchers use the methodology of modern test theory to ascertain specific test items that are most informative in distinguishing respondents with varying levels of anger, and to aid in scaling items for the level of anger they typically represent.

REVIEWER'S REFERENCE

Mills, J. F., Kroner, D. G., & Forth, A. E. (1998). Novaco Anger Scale: Reliability and validity within an adult criminal sample. *Assessment, 5,* 237–248.

The OAD Survey.

Purpose: "Measures seven work-related personality traits and seven perceptions of how an individual believes he/she must behave in his/her job."
Population: Employees.
Publication Dates: 1990–2002.
Acronym: OAD.
Scores, 7: Autonomy, Extroversion, Patience, Detail, Versatility Level, Emotional Control, Creativity.
Administration: Individual and group.
Restricted Distribution: Completion of a 3-day seminar is required for participants to administer and use the survey within their organization.
Price Data: Available from publisher.
Foreign Language Editions: Available in 10 languages.
Time: Not timed.
Comments: Web-based scoring process is available.
Author: Michael J. Gray.
Publisher: Organization Analysis and Design LLC.

Review of the OAD Survey by ARTHUR S. ELLEN, School Psychologist, New York City Department of Education, New York, NY:

DESCRIPTION. The OAD Survey (Organization Analysis and Design) is a 110-item adjective checklist—called a word list survey by the publishers—for use in personnel selection (job analysis and selection) and management (organizational analysis and staff development). The checklist is available as part of a consulting relationship with the management firm Organization Analysis and Design. Test use requires test administrators to complete a 3-day training to learn how to interpret the OAD and integrate the results into their organization. Test takers check only those adjectives that describe themselves. They complete the identical checklist under two conditions: first, to describe yourself (traits) and second, to describe how you must behave in your current or most recent job (perceived job behaviors). The selected adjectives are summed into seven scales: Assertive/Autonomy (A; bold, self-confident, and independent); Extroversion (E; outgoing, friendly, and talkative); Patience (P; deliberate, calm, and efficient); Detail Orientation (D; exacting, conscientious, and cautious); Versatility Level (VL; the sum of A, E, P, D); Emotional Control (EC; composed, restrained, and steady); and Creativity (CR; inventive, original, and innovative). The VL scale has been hypothesized to measure flexibility and resiliency in the face of stress and organizational change. The seven OAD scales have from 13 to 22 adjectives, apparently without item overlap. The Survey includes several experimental adjectives.

OAD interpretation proceeds as follows. First, all scales, except VL, are converted to decile scores. Then, the A, E, P, and D scales are averaged, and each of these four scales is compared to the average decile. This intraindividual or ipsative interpretation produces a series of profile types. The Perfectionist type, for example, results when A and E are below and P and D are above a person's average. This kind of person is considered low-key, solid, and steady and one who works in a way that is deliberate, patient, exacting, and always tries to be correct. Second, the VL raw score is reported, and for purposes of interpretation, it is placed into one of five descriptive categories relative to the average of the normative group (very high, high/above average, average, low/below average, and very low). Higher VL levels mean a person can more easily modify his or her behavior, needs more diverse kinds of stimulation, and is more resilient when experiencing stress. It is important to note that either exceptionally low or high VL scores are used to flag protocols suspected of distortion, reflecting either over- or underendorsement of adjectives. Finally, the EC and CR scales are interpreted relative to the normative sample. Higher EC deciles indicate a person who is more controlled, unflappable, and may be viewed as emotionally detached, whereas lower EC deciles indicate someone who is more guided by emotions and may act impulsively. CR scores below the third decile indicate concrete thinking whereas higher deciles point to abstract, creative thinking.

Although a paper checklist and stand-alone software are mentioned, the OAD is available, either in English or French, on the publisher's easy-to-use web site, which includes a database for administered tests and automated report production. A five-part report includes two graphs, one for traits and the other for perceived job behaviors, and four narrative sections, which include a summary and descriptions of traits, perceived job behaviors, and preferred work environments (which deal with motivating needs as based on the trait scales). The report alerts the user when there is a concern about a distortion, which requires contacting an OAD consultant. In regard to impression management or enhancement, the publishers take the position that an individual clever enough to provide a specific profile may fool an interviewer too.

DEVELOPMENT AND TECHNICAL. The initial OAD 250-item adjective pool was conceptually based upon the five-factor personality model (Costa & McCrae, 1992), the 16 Personality Factor Questionnaire (16PF; Cattell, Eber, & Tatsuoka, 1970), and the author's work experience (Gray, 2001). Through repeated item and factor analysis and consideration of the number of adjectives in each domain, the 250 items were reduced to the current 110 adjectives. Little information in support of content validity was provided, and the analyses for the initial scale development were unavailable.

Norms are based upon 234 U.S. participants split evenly by gender. No further descriptive information for these norms was reported. Additionally, it is unclear if these norms apply to both the trait and perceived job behavior sections and how form equivalence between paper-and-pencil administration, computer delivered administration, and translated forms (English-French) has been evaluated. Two applications of these norms prove worrisome. First, the OAD report employs an 11-point scale (0 to 10). However, it is unclear if the extremes of this scale are the zero and 99th percentile ranks. Second, decile scores are treated as if they formed an equal-interval scale, not an ordinal scale. Such scale issues may mislead interpretation when the A, E, D, and P scales are averaged for an ipsative reference and when decile scores are shown at equal intervals in the graphs in the report.

Internal consistency reliability estimates based upon the U.S. normative sample and a large U.K. data set yielded adequate indices in the high .70s or .80s for all scales, except the shorter 13-item P scale. Absent, however, were any reports for the intercorrelation among the seven scales, for the VL scale's internal reliability, or for the short-term stability of any scale.

Validity for the OAD has been explored through factor analysis and several concurrent validity studies. Using the normative data, a six-factor solution emerged: The first factor consists of the A and CR scales, Factors 2 through 5 related to the remaining four scales (EC, D, E, and P, respectively), and there was an unlabeled sixth factor. For those items that did not clearly load on a single factor, it was not possible to fully understand this analysis because the items were not given their adjective labels.

Studies with the OAD trait section and personality measures provide limited support for the meaning of the seven scales. Four scales (A, E, D, and EC) positively correlated better than .40 with clearly similar scales of either the NEO-Five Factor Inventory (Costa & McCrae, 1992) or 16PF (i.e., A with 16PF Dominance, E with NEO-FFI Extraversion, D with the NEO-FFI Conscientiousness, and EC with the 16PF Controlled). Less clear were the correlations of P with the NEO-FFI Agreeableness (.36), CR with the 16PF Openness to Change (.46), and CR with the NEO-FFI Openness to Experience (.25). A validity study with the Adjective Checklist (Gough & Heilbrun, 1983) merits consideration because the ACL employs the identical method and has scales that might provide convergent (Dominance, Orderliness, and Self-Control) and divergent (Nurturance and Succorance) validity.

Though hypothesized to reflect resiliency, the meaning of the VL scale may be elusive. There were only small correlations between the VL scale and two similar scales of the Pressure Management Indicator (Williams & Cooper, 1998—Contentment (.28) and Resilience (.29). However, possibly useful correlations between the VL scale and the NEO-FFI Neuroticism and 16PF Perfectionism were not reported. Ultimately, because the meaning of the VL scale will vary depending upon the different contributions of the A, E, D, and P scales, multidimensionality will interfere with convergent validity.

Evidence supporting the job relatedness of the OAD comes from three exploratory studies with sales associates and retail and restaurant managers. These studies found that the A, E, D, and EC scales all showed some promise for possible future use in job selection. The value of these studies, however, would be enhanced with better subject description, operational definitions of outcome measures, and reports of effect magnitude not just significance levels.

COMMENTARY. Adjective checklists achieve their versatility because they are easy and quick to administer, nonthreatening, interesting, can generate little participant resistance, and have high face validity. Yet there are challenges to the valid use of the method such as response biases, intentional distortion, under- and overreporting, and the distorting impact of social desirability (Craig, 2005). Empirically, the influence of social desirability upon the OAD has not been considered, but given the use of the OAD in a selection setting, slanting of responses is a substantial issue. In fact, many of the adjectives on the OAD appear to have a positive connotation; this orientation may act to induce social desirability.

Changing adjective checklist instructions is an aspect of the method's flexibility and a challenge to the test construct. Masterson (1975) pointed out that changing experimental conditions not only changes the scale reliability, but it also influences which items belong on the checklist. On the OAD, therefore, it seems unlikely that a person would check such adjectives as indifferent, moody, or nervous when describing how one must behave in their current job, though the same adjectives might be relevant for self-description. Moreover, differences in scale reliabilities for the traits and perceived job behavior sections were not considered.

The OAD publishers caution that these scales should be interpreted as either higher or lower on a particular trait, yet some users might interpret scales as being bipolar. For example, people with lower E scores are considered introverted. There is, however, no evidence that the scales exhibit such bipolarity. There are few adjectives that reflect introversion (e.g., shy, reserved, 2nd introspective). Additionally, there is no indication of bipolarity from the OAD factor analysis, which would show positive and negative item loadings on a scale's factor.

Though the use of personality variables in the prediction of work performance had fallen into disfavor, recent improvements in methodology have led to a resurgence of research and interest (Hogan, Hogan, & Roberts, 1996). Improvements include better definition of work-related personality measures, use of more reliable work outcome measures, and establishing a strong logical link between a personality measure and work performance. When the OAD scales were correlated with composite, thus more reliable, measures of work performance, results seemed promising. Consequently, applying these improved methods to establish personality-perfor-

mance linkages might prove efficacious in establishing additional validity for OAD scales and score profiles.

SUMMARY. Organization Analysis and Design LLC developed an adjective checklist for the complex and challenging area of personnel selection and management. Despite strengths in applying and interpreting the OAD, a number of crucial psychometric aspects of the OAD are reported either with insufficient detail or need to be more extensively evaluated. These include the rational and empirical development of scales; the adequacy of the score metric and norms; the meaning of the VL scale; and the validity of scales, score profiles, and the computer-based report narratives. Certainly, the versatility of the adjective-checklist method, despite its limits, merits serious consideration for use in personnel work. Unfortunately, the current conceptual and psychometric shortcomings of the OAD do not recommend this kind of use at this time.

REVIEWER'S REFERENCES

Cattell, R. B., Eber, H. W., & Tatsuoka, M. M. (1970). *Handbook for the Sixteen Personality Factor Questionnaire (16PF)*. Champaign, IL: Institute for Personality and Ability Testing, Inc.

Costa, P. T., Jr., & McCrae, R. R. (1992). *Revised NEO Personality Inventory (NEO-PI-R) and NEO-Five Factor Inventory (NEO-FFI) professional manual*. Odessa, FL: Psychological Assessment Resources.

Craig, R. J. (2005). Assessing personality and mood with the adjective check list methodology: A review. *International Journal of Testing, 5*, 177-196.

Gray, M. J. (2001). The OAD Survey—Taxonomy of general traits. Retrieved July 26, 2006, from Organization Analysis and Design Web site: http://www.oad2.com/OADTaxonomy.pdf.

Gough, H. G. & Heilbrun, A. B. (1983). *The Adjective Checklist manual*. Palo Alto, CA: Consulting Psychologists Press.

Hogan, R., Hogan, J., & Roberts, B. W. (1996). Personality measurement and employment decisions: Questions and answers. *American Psychologist, 51*, 469-477.

Masterson, S. (1975). The adjective checklist technique: A review and critique. In P. McReynolds (Ed.), *Advances in psychological assessment* (Vol. 3, pp. 275-312). San Francisco: Jossey-Bass.

Williams, S., & Cooper, C. L. (1998) Measuring occupational stress: Development of the pressure management indicator. *Journal of Occupational Psychology, 3*, 306-321.

Review of the OAD Survey by JEFFREY A. JENKINS, Associate Professor, Roger Williams University, Bristol, RI:

DESCRIPTION. The OAD (Organization Analysis and Design) Survey seeks to measure aspects of personality relevant to the workplace as well as employees' perceptions of their current jobs in terms of these personality characteristics. It is a central part of a "management development process" through which business people and organizational leaders can diagnose the way in which the organization functions, plan by examining business goals and systems for human resource development, and provide information about the "temperaments" of the individuals within the organization in order to learn ways to maximize individual and group effectiveness. As a part of this process, the OAD is not intended as a stand-alone measurement tool, but to be used in conjunction with the program of consulting services offered by the publisher.

Specifically, the OAD assesses individuals using six personality "trait clusters," and these same six characteristics form the basis for individuals' perceptions of their jobs. The traits include Autonomy, Extroversion, Patience, Detail, Emotional Control, and Creativity. An additional trait, identified as Versatility Level, is a linear combination of scores on the first four traits. These traits are used to produce a profile of the individual that may be useful for a variety of human resource management decisions in the workplace.

As a self-report measure, the instrument consists of a word list of 110 descriptors from which respondents choose to describe themselves or their job. It may be administered in a paper-and-pencil format or online, where immediate scoring and feedback is available. Completion is untimed and consists of two sections. The first section presents respondents with the list of 110 adjectives; in a box next to each descriptor, respondents place a check mark if they would use the word to describe themselves, and a question mark if they are uncertain about the meaning of the word. The list includes, for example, such descriptors as Self-assured, Efficient, Individualistic, Demanding, Popular, Impulsive, and Respectful. The second section contains the same word list presented in the same order, but respondents are asked to select those that "describe how you must behave in your current job." The survey instrument is therefore easy to administer and complete and, although untimed, should not take more than 10 minutes for a typical respondent to complete.

Both sections of the OAD are scored by summing the selected items for each of the traits, which become subscales by converting the raw scores to percentiles based on a national norm distribution of 234 participants. The first four subscale scores (Autonomy, Extroversion, Patience, and Detail Orientation) are graphed as a profile, allowing users to make comparisons among the subscales. Versatility Level is calculated by summing the raw scores of the first four subscales and converting to a mean decile score, which is shown on the profile to allow comparison of the four traits to their mean value. Deciles for Emotional Control and Creativity are shown separately on the profile graph. All scoring is accomplished through the publisher's website, and narrative explanatory summaries of both the individual respondent's traits and perceived job behaviors are provided. Interpretation of scores and profiles is explained in detail in written documentation available through the publisher's seminars or consulting services.

DEVELOPMENT. The OAD was developed and initial validation studies were performed from 1987 to 1990. Although the OAD seeks to measure work-related characteristics of individuals and their perceptions of work, and does not attempt the general assessment of personality, it relies on well-known approaches to personality assessment, including Cattell's theoretical work in the development of the 16PF (Cattell, Eber, & Tatsuoka, 1970) and McRae and Costa's (1987) research on the five-factor personality model.

The publisher's website (www.oadllc.com) provides considerable information about the instrument and other services, including short articles relating to the OAD and a more detailed technical manual, entitled "The OAD Survey—Taxonomy of General Traits" (referred to here as the "manual"). Although the OAD Survey can only be obtained if used in conjunction with an OAD seminar or other consulting services of the publisher, this method of distribution and use appears appropriate given the settings and purposes for which the instrument was designed.

TECHNICAL. The manual provides information regarding subscale scoring, reliability, and validity. This information is particularly helpful and necessary given the self-report nature of the instrument and the use of one-word descriptors to represent the complexity of the personality traits measured.

Reliability of the OAD Survey appears to be satisfactory. Reported internal consistency estimates based on a sample of 234 U.S. participants ranged from .77 (Patience) to .88 (Creativity), and for a larger U.K. sample (2,842) ranged from .69 (Patience) to .84 (Assertiveness). The selection process for these samples is not reported, but given the otherwise thorough work of the publisher in disclosing technical information, there is no reason to believe these samples are not representative.

The developers of the OAD Survey provide a variety of information and study results relating to validity. In addition to an explanation of the theoretical basis for the traits measured and the process of item selection, the construct validity of the instrument is discussed. The factor structure of the OAD Survey generally supports the reporting of the subscales measuring four of the six intended personality traits. The publisher notes that the Autonomy and Creativity subscales are not independent and may be measuring a single construct. Although the manual reports factor loadings for items within each subscale, it does not give the actual word items from the survey instrument to which the factor loadings correspond. This deficiency makes it difficult to examine the factor-analytic results in any detail, which is problematic given the possibility of interrelationships between single-word items that may be synonyms. Nonetheless, the publisher should be commended for presenting factor-analytic results at all, particularly given other evidence of validity that was also presented. The manual also summarizes a study of the relationship between the OAD Survey subscales and those of the 16PF (Form C, 1978). The reported correlation coefficients offer evidence of convergent validity by significant relationships between the OAD subscales and corresponding 16PF traits, and evidence of discriminant validity by the lack of significant relationships among dissimilar traits.

In addition, evidence of criterion-related validity is presented by reporting the results of three studies that examined the relationship between the OAD Survey and different predictive criteria. The criteria were performance measures for three different groups: fashion sales associates, retail store managers, and restaurant management staff. Generally, the results of these studies demonstrate that the OAD Survey has a reasonable degree of predictive validity for its intended purposes.

COMMENTARY. The OAD Survey has much to commend it. Grounded in personality theory, it is an instrument that is designed for assessing aspects of work-related personality for targeted populations and purposes, and appears to do that well. Although it apparently may only be obtained and used in conjunction with other services provided by the publisher, the training provided for using and interpreting results from the instrument is likely necessary and beneficial.

Strengths of the OAD include its adaptation of personality concepts to business settings, the resulting usefulness for workplace applications, and the ease of administration. Weaknesses include the limited sample on which percentile scores are based and the potentially tenuous relationship between individual subscale scores and the same individuals' perceptions of job requirements.

SUMMARY. Attendees of an OAD seminar will undoubtedly find the OAD Survey to be an interesting approach to understanding workers and potential hires, as well as being useful in workplace decision making. The OAD Survey benefits from relatively strong technical characteristics and clearly presented score report profiles. Although the instrument should certainly not be used as the sole basis for any decisions regarding employee or potential employee work assignments, when used in combination with other relevant information it may assist organizations in their operations.

REVIEWER'S REFERENCES

Cattell, R. B., Eber, H. W., & Tatsouka, M. M. (1970). The 16 Personality Factor Questionnaire. Champaign, IL: IPAT.
McRae, R. R., & Costa, P. T., Jr. (1987). Validation of the five-factor model of personality across instruments and observers. *Journal of Personality and Social Psychology, 52*, 81–90.

[136]

OQ-10.2 [A Brief Screening & Outcome Questionnaire].

Purpose: "Designed as a brief screening instrument … intended to alert the physician to the possibility that the patient was experiencing enough psychological distress to consider follow-up with other specific diagnostic tests or interviews."

Population: Ages 17–80 years.

Publication Dates: 1998–2000.

Acronym: OQ-10.2.

Scores: Total score only.

Administration: Individual or group.

Restricted Distribution: Requires licensure from American Professional Credentialing Services LLC.

Price Data, 2006: Licensing cost available from publisher; $25 per administration and scoring manual (1998, 10 pages); $25 per test.

Foreign Language Editions: English, Spanish, and French editions available.

Time: (1–5) minutes.

Authors: Michael J. Lambert, Arthur M. Finch, John Okishi, Gary M. Burlingame (manual only), Celeste McKelvey (manual only), and Curtis W. Reisinger.

Publisher: OQ Measures LLC.

Review of the OQ-10.2 [A Brief Screening & Outcome Questionnaire] by JODY L. KULSTAD,

Adjunct Professor, Seton Hall University, South Orange, NJ:

DESCRIPTION. The OQ-10.2 is a 10-item brief screening tool used to identify individuals needing referral for a more complete psychological evaluation. For medical practitioners, the OQ-10.2 can serve as a "psychological vital sign" (administration & screening manual, p. 1) to be used to screen their patients for emotional distress, which may require further assessment and/or treatment. The OQ-10.2 is particularly useful in settings where routine screening is undertaken, but complete evaluation is typically precluded (e.g., family and general practice settings). The OQ-10.2 may also be used to evaluate well-being of large groups and monitor the behavioral health of health-related organization consumers (e.g., HMOs, community health centers).

The OQ-10.2 is intended for individuals aged 17 to 80 (the standardization sample age range). The OQ-10.2 is available in several languages, including English, Spanish, and French, though the manual is available only in English. Administration and scoring are clear and easily completed, allowing a range of persons to administer the measure. However, to use the assessment one needs to obtain a use license from OQ Measures, LLC. Licenses range in price from $30 for a student to $7,000 for single states (multistate, national, and international prices are available from the developer); with the exception of the student license, all are lifetime licenses. All licenses come with one manual and one reproducible form. Manuals can be ordered for an additional fee.

Administration and scoring. The OQ-10.2 is brief and unobtrusive, making it easy to integrate into the office visit, particularly as part of the intake forms. Although there is no time limit, most will complete the measure in about 2 minutes. Respondents need only the paper measure and a writing instrument. Neither the manual nor test developer's website (www.oqmeasures.com) address administration modifications for those who cannot read the assessment form. In the medical setting, the manual recommends not sharing with the patient what the results will be used for, but rather to inform them that the doctor is interested in how they have been feeling. They should be told to read each item carefully before responding and to mark the category that best reflects how they are feeling, with values ranging from 0–4.

Scoring is done by hand, using simple addition. The total score is obtained by summing the number located below each box the respondent checked. The first five items are reverse scored with values ranging from 4 to 0. Total scores range from 0 to 40. No guidance for interpretation is provided in the manual, and different studies used to evaluate the psychometrics of the OQ-10.2 suggest different cutoff values.

DEVELOPMENT. The OQ-10.2 was developed from the OQ-45.2, a measure used to track patient progress in treatment. Although the parent measure is also a general measure of psychological well-being and distress, the developers felt an even briefer, more unobtrusive measure was needed. The developers submitted the 45 OQ-45.2 items to a discriminant function analysis (DFA). The 10 items selected were the items that best discriminated between patients with known psychiatric disorders and nonpatient community members. Using DFA and a cutoff score of 19, the OQ was shown to identify 75.7% of the patient sample correctly as well as 83.7% of the nonpatient sample. Sample specifics are not included, but the manual points the reader to an alternate source for the information. Also, the manual does not detail the development of the OQ-45.2 and provides no resources from which to glean this information.

Items selected for inclusion measure both the subjective experience of the person as well as his or her overall quality of functioning. Items tap general symptoms and are not intended to be symptomatic of any one particular psychiatric disorder. Although the manual does not note subscales, researchers (Seelert, Hill, Rigdon, & Schwenzfeier, 1999) have identified a two-factor structure suggesting the measure is composed of items addressing psychological well-being and psychological distress.

TECHNICAL. Information describing the norming process is not included in the manual.

Standardization sample. The source of the standardization data is not identified. Raw scores are reported for "various samples" (manual, p. 3) so it is unclear if this information was obtained from a variety of studies or a more formal standardization process. The samples reported included "community normals," college students, medical patients being seen by a general practitioner, and persons seen at an Employee Assistance Program, outpatient mental health facility, inpatient setting, and community mental health center. No information is available on demographics of the sample or total numbers used for standardization. The data that are reported suggest no overall or item level differences were present based on sex or age. Also, no statistical differences in overall scores were found based on ethnoracial classifications for Caucasian, African American, or Hispanic respondents (numbers for other ethnic groups were too small to draw conclusions). However, item-level differences were found between African Americans and Caucasians on items relating to loneliness (African Americans scored higher) and feeling loved and wanted and feeling one's relationships are complete (Caucasians scored higher). It is noted in the manual that ethnicity-based information was obtained from the EAP sample, so these findings can really only be extrapolated to other working individuals and their spouses.

Reliability. Internal consistency and temporal stability reliabilities were computed. Internal consistency estimates for a community sample were .82 and higher, with some values as high as .92 for an EAP sample. In a separate study of medical patients (Seelert et al., 1999), scores on the OQ-10.2 yielded a coefficient alpha of .88. All estimates indicate good internal consistency suggesting the items are measuring the general construct. The manual reports test-retest values for the OQ-10.2 based on a 3-week interval of .62, in the average range.

Validity. The OQ-10.2 evidences good concurrent, criterion, content, and construct validity. Seelert et al. (1999) compared the OQ-10.2 to the Duke Health Profile subscales, finding good concurrent validity with correlations ranging from .23 to .77, with low correlations on scales not expected to correlate (e.g., Pain, Perceived Health) and high correlations on those expected to correlate (e.g., Mental Health, .77; and Anxiety-Depression, .72). Using a cutoff score of 12 on the OQ-10.2 and a cutoff score of 30 on the Anxiety-Depression subscale of the Duke, the OQ-10.2 evidenced good specificity and sensitivity, suggesting good criterion validity. Other studies provide additional evidence of validity with scores on the OQ-10.2 correlating to higher prescription use (Anderson, Rigdon, Hill, & Smooth, 1996; Schwenzfeier, Rigdon, Hill, Anderson, & Seelert, 2002) and more time spent in the medical clinic (Rigdon, Hill, Anderson, & Li, 1996 as cited in the administration and scoring manual). In addi-

tion to concurrent validity using the Duke Health Profile as a comparison, the OQ-10.2 shows concurrent validity with the Symptom Checklist-90-R (.75), the Beck Depression Inventory (.58), the Inventory for Interpersonal Problems (.68), and the Social Adjustment Rating Scale (.71), suggesting that the OQ-10.2 is a similar, though not exact, measure of psychological distress. Previously reported internal consistency estimates suggest good content validity. Finally, as noted previously, Seelert et al.'s (1999) factor-analytic study confirms the two-dimensional nature of the OQ-10.2 with the two-factor structure replicated by Schwenzfeier, Rigdon, Hill, Anderson, and Seelert (2002).

INTERPRETATION. Psychological issues affect the health and welfare of all individuals. Today's health care environment needs to find a way to determine whether and to what extent a person's concerns are psychologically related, particularly because many health insurance companies' health maintenance organization plans still require primary care physician referral for behavioral health assessment and intervention. Primary care settings have neither the time nor the expertise to provide complete psychological evaluations. As such, screening measures should be in place. Due to the time demands, moreover, measures must be brief, but they also must be reliable and valid. There are measures that fill this void, such as the Brief Patient Health Questionnaire, the Duke Health Profile, and the Brief Symptom Inventory. The benefit of the OQ-10.2 is its brevity in comparison as well as more of a focus on a general sense of well-being. The OQ-10.2 appears to be a good option as a valid and reliable screener. That being said, the greatest weakness of the OQ-10.2 is its manual. Development and normative information are not fully addressed. And perhaps the most important weakness is that there is no stated guide for interpreting the total score for the OQ-10.2. Developers need to have clear guidelines for when a referral is needed. Overall, benefits of the OQ-10.2 recommend it as a brief screening tool for use in primary care settings. Because no data were presented to assess its use as a measure of community wellness, caution should still be used when using the OQ-10.2 for this purpose.

REVIEWER'S REFERENCES

Anderson, N. S., III, Rigdon, M. A., Hill, R. D., & Smooth, C. (1996). Psychological vital signs assessing patient distress. *IHC Psych Resources Update, 7,* 1–3.

Rigdon, M., Hill, R. D., Anderson, N., & Li, L. (1996, May). *The utilization of a "Psychological Vital Sign" as a preventive intervention to improve primary care services in community-based family practice.* Paper presented at the Rocky Mountain Psychological Association, Park City, UT.

Seelert, K. R., Hill, R. D., Rigdon, M. A., & Schwenzfeier, E. (1999). Measuring patient distress in primary care. *Family Medicine, 31,* 483–487.

Schwenzfeier, E. M., Rigdon, M. A., Hill, R. D., Anderson, N. S., III, & Seelert, K. R. (2002). Psychological well-being as a predictor of physician medication prescribing practices in primary care. *Professional Psychology: Research & Practice, 33,* 478–482.

Review of the OQ-10.2 [A Brief Screening & Outcome Questionnaire] by MICHAEL J. SCHEEL, Associate Professor, Department of Educational Psychology, University of Nebraska-Lincoln, Lincoln, NE:

DESCRIPTION. The OQ-10.2 is a brief screening instrument to be used in the offices of primary care physicians. Its intended purpose is to alert physicians to possibilities of high levels of psychological distress that accompany physical complaints of patients. Patients are to be recommended for further assessment when scores fall above an established cutoff score. The authors view the OQ-10.2 as a tool to assess the link between psychological and physical illness. In addition, the authors recommend the OQ-10.2's use for research to monitor outcomes of behavioral health of consumer groups broadly due to changes in managed care benefit policies.

Instructions to respondents direct them to look back over the previous week to provide the best description of the respondent's "current situation." The measure consists of 10 items, each accompanied by a 5-point anchored Likert-type scale ranging from 4 to 0. Although the OQ-10.2 is purportedly a measure of a univariate construct, the scale is written in two parts. The first part consists of 5 items that evidently represent psychological health ("I am a happy person") with a corresponding scale in descending order starting with "4" (i.e., "Never"). The second part consists of 5 items worded as psychologically unhealthy ("I feel fearful"), starts with "0" (i.e., "Never"), and is listed in ascending order. Higher scores indicate psychological distress with a range of 0 to 40.

TEST DEVELOPMENT. The OQ-10.2 is based on the well-known and longer Outcome Questionnaire 45.2 (OQ-45; 16:176). The authors considered the OQ-45 to be too long for its intended purpose as a screening instrument in a physician's office. The measure was constructed to be brief and not to offend patients through the use of items that could be considered to be "too personal" or "too odd" (manual, p. 2), because

patients will have come for medical treatment, not psychological treatment.

The 10 items of the OQ-10.2 were taken exactly from the OQ-45, and were selected on their ability to discriminate between nonpatient community members ($N = 104$) and patients ($N = 511$) diagnosed with DSM, Axis I disorders. In a discriminate analysis of these groups, the OQ-10.2 correctly classified 75.7% of the patient group and 83.7% of the nonpatient group when a cutoff score between the two designations was set at 19. This data set was obtained by Lambert et al. (1996) from the normative sample of the OQ-45.

TECHNICAL. Administration is intended to be conducted by any medical office worker with the purpose of the questionnaire not revealed to the respondent. The approximate amount of time to complete the instrument is 2 minutes. Scoring is straightforward by adding the 10 item scores together. Due to the change from descending to ascending order between the first five items and the last five, the scorer is warned to look under each square to check for the corresponding number so that errors in scoring can be avoided. Mean scores for "normals" and "college students" are 10.2 and 9.8, respectively, whereas patient scores average between 14.7 (Employee Assistance Program clients) and 23.2 (inpatient psychiatric) as reported in the OQ-10.2 administration and scoring manual.

No significant differences were detected between males and females in the normative sample. Similarly, normative data do not suggest variation due to age. The authors considered the effect of race by comparing Caucasian, Hispanic, and African American respondents, finding no significant differences among the three groups for the total scale score. However, African Americans were found to score significantly higher for Item 9, "I feel lonely." Caucasians scored higher on Items 4 ("I feel loved and wanted") and 5 ("I feel my love relationships are full and complete"). Hispanics did not vary significantly from the other two groups on any of the items.

Internal consistency alpha coefficients of the OQ-10.2 were found to be lower than its parent instrument, the OQ-45, but acceptable at .82 for a community sample and .92 for an EAP group. Test-retest reliability over a 3-week period was calculated and yielded a Pearson r of .62. The OQ-45 substantially outperforms the shorter OQ-10.2 both in internal consistency and test-retest reliability. However, this is to be expected due to the brief nature of the OQ-10.2.

Seelert (1997) compared the OQ-10.2 with the Duke Anxiety-Depression subscale. The two possess similar purposes of using a brief instrument to identify patients with significant levels of psychological distress. The Pearson r was found to be .72. Seelert also discovered an optimal cutoff score of 12. Using this cutoff, 48.6% of patients were recommended for further screening. In a study by Anderson, Rigdon, Hill, and Smooth (1996), 39% of all patients scored in the moderate to high range on the OQ-10.2, and this group took almost twice as many medications in comparison to the low distress score patients. Further construct validity evidence is provided by Rigdon, Hill, Anderson, and Li (1996) through research findings that indicated high distress score patients (higher than 15) required significantly more case management time than lower scorers. The OQ-10.2 also compares favorably to other screening instruments such as the Symptom Checklist-90-R (r = .75), the Beck Depression Inventory (r = .58), the Inventory for Interpersonal Problems (r = .68), and the Social Adjustment Rating Scale (r = .71). Results from factor analysis with varimax rotation yielded two factors named Psychological Wellness accounting for 49.9% of the variance and Psychological Distress accounting for 13.3% of the variance (Seelert, 1997). The two factors correspond to the first five items and the second five items, respectively.

COMMENTARY. The OQ-10.2 is intended as a brief screening instrument. The instrument seems quite adequate for this purpose. The authors have designed it to be taken in a waiting room of a physician's office in only 2 minutes. The utility of the instrument is excellent. Additionally, discriminant analyses demonstrated its ability to select most clients involved in mental health treatment, and to also mostly select "normals" not involved in any kind of psychological treatment. The measure also possesses a moderately high correlation with other symptom checklist instruments. Score interpretation can be guided by the cutoff scores that have been established through research.

The instrument possesses a number of strengths. However, the worry is that the instrument may be used inappropriately due to the ease of administration. Results may be overgeneralized to cases needing much more specific assessment before giving a diagnosis or planning treatment. It is hoped that physicians will be trained to use the OQ-10.2 appropriately as a screening instrument, not as a final and complete assessment of psychological distress.

Therefore, the OQ-10.2 should not be the sole means of evaluation for mental disorders or psychological symptoms because of its brief nature and broad focus. Some patients may deny psychological symptoms assessed through the instrument, and the OQ-10.2 does not possess a means by which detection of socially desirable or psychologically healthy response sets can be achieved. The instrument might benefit from one or two items that could test the validity of responses similar to L scale items of the MMPI-2. A recommendation to accompany this instrument should also be the necessity for further assessment when scores from the OQ-10.2 indicate psychological distress. An interview conducted by the physician or a nurse may suffice to catch those patients with psychological symptoms not detected through the OQ-10.2. Furthermore, because the OQ-10.2 does not possess items that could be judged by respondents as too odd or too personal, the OQ-10.2 is insufficient for diagnosis or treatment planning.

SUMMARY. The purpose of the OQ-10.2 is to screen broadly for psychological aspects of a patients' complaints during visits to primary care physicians' offices. The instrument was developed from its parent instrument, the OQ-45.2, and its items are drawn directly from the longer instrument. The OQ-10.2 appears to screen successfully for most psychological aspects of physical complaints of patients visiting their primary care physician. Less is known about its ability as an outcome measure on which to base judgments of the effects of managed care benefits decisions, as the authors of the OQ-10.2 suggest. The instrument demonstrates strong reliability for its purposes. Construct and concurrent validity evidence is also strong. Cutoff scores have been established to base judgments about further recommendations for assessment of psychological distress. The instrument is exceptionally easy to administer, and due to this ease, caution is advised to not use the OQ-10.2 for purposes beyond its purpose as a brief screening device. Ill-trained users may be tempted, due to the ease with which the OQ-10.2 can be administered, to use the instrument inappropriately for outcome research or as a diagnostic tool. Nonetheless, the OQ-10.2 possesses sufficient evidence of its utility as a screening instrument.

REVIEWER'S REFERENCES

Anderson, N., Rigdon, M., Hill, R. D., & Smooth, C. (1996). *Psychological vital signs assessing patient distress. IHC Psych Resources Update, 7,* 1-3.

Lambert, M. J., Hansen, N. B., Umphress, V., Lumen, K., Okiishi, J., Burlingame, G. M., Huefner, J. C., & Reisinger, C. W. (1996). *Administration and scoring manual for the OQ-45.2.* Stevenson, MD: American Professional Credentialing Services.

Rigdon, M., Hill, R. D., Anderson, N., & Li, L. (1996). *The utilization of a "Psychological Vital Sign" as a preventive intervention to improve primary care services in community-based family practice.* Paper presented at the Rocky Mountain Psychological Association, Park City, UT.

Seelert, K. R. (1997). *Validation of a brief measure of distress in a primary care setting.* Masters Thesis, University of Utah, Department of Educational Psychology.

[137]

OQ-30.1 [Outcome Questionnaire for Adults].

Purpose: Designed to "measure patient progress following psychological and medical interventions."

Population: Ages 17–80 years.

Publication Dates: 2001–2003.

Acronym: OQ 30.1.

Scores: Total score only.

Administration: Individual or group.

Restricted Distribution: Requires licensure from American Professional Credentialing Services LLC.

Price Data, 2006: Licensing cost available from publisher; $25 per administration and scoring manual (2003, 18 pages); $25 per test.

Foreign Language Editions: English, Spanish, and French editions available.

Time: (2–15) minutes.

Comments: Test can be administered orally.

Authors: Michael J. Lambert, Derek R. Hatfield, David A. Vermeersch (manual only), Gary M. Burlingame, Curtis W. Resinger, and G. S. (Jeb) Brown (manual only).

Publisher: OQ Measures LLC.

Review of the OQ-30.1 [Outcome Questionnaire for Adults] by COLLIE CONOLEY, Professor of Counseling, Clinical, and School Psychology, University of California, Santa Barbara, Santa Barbara, CA:

DESCRIPTION. The OQ-30.1 (A Brief Outcome & Tracking Questionnaire for Adults) is designed to measure an individual's psychological functioning over multiple administrations, indicating the progress of treatment. The OQ-30.1 is a 30-item paper-and-pencil test that is self-administered and hand scored. The OQ-30.1 consists of 30 items empirically selected from its forbearer, the OQ-45.2. The test is estimated to take 4 minutes for the typical user. Each item is a simple declarative sentence that is evaluated using five categories from "*never*" to "*almost always occurring.*" The OQ-30.1 is intended to measure the degree of a person's functional disturbance and

also to track the degree of disturbance over time via repeated administrations. The measure is not for diagnostic purposes. The OQ-30.1 provides a single score and 4 critical items that signal potential problems with suicide or substance abuse. A high score reflects an admission of symptoms of distress (i.e., anxiety, depression, somatic problems, and stress) and interpersonal difficulties (i.e., work and social problems). The manual provides rudimentary normative information and a computed reliable change index. The user age range is listed from 17 to 80 years old. The cost is a one-time charge based on the status of the user and the number of users in the organization.

The OQ-30.1 is the 30-item adult measure as contrasted with the OQ measures that have different numbers of items (i.e., 10 and 45) and those that are designed for younger populations. The OQ-30.1 does not have multiple scales as the OQ-45.2 (16:176) does (e.g., symptom distress, interpersonal functioning, and social role).

DEVELOPMENT. The purpose of the OQ-30.1 development was to provide a brief measure of functioning that could be administered repeatedly for the purpose of demonstrating improvement in functioning during psychological or medical interventions. The items of the OQ-30.1 were selected from the larger OQ-45.2. The original selection of items for the OQ-45 was not included in the manual.

However, the criteria of selecting the OQ-30.1 items from the OQ-45 was the: (a) size of the item's sensitivity to change in pre- and posttreatment administrations (Vermeersch, Lambert, & Burlingame, 2000); (b) item's identifying commonly occurring problems across a wide spectrum of disorders; (c) item's relevance to many types of people; and (d) item's describing the characteristics affecting a person's social life. The strengths of the item selection process were the size of the Vermeersch et al. (2000) study's sample and the variety of psychological problems the sample included. The sample included 1,460 people from four mental health settings (i.e., a university counseling center, a university training clinic, private practitioners, and a managed care facility), which should have spanned multiple diagnostic categories and levels of functioning. However, the selection process for the items' sensitivity or "socially relevant characteristics" was not explicated. Also, European Americans represented around 92% of the sample.

TECHNICAL. The reliability for the OQ-30.1 reported in the manual used several studies addressing internal consistency as well as test-retest reliability. The first reliability study used 157 college students with a mean age of 23 years. The sample was 66% female and 94% Caucasian. The internal consistency coefficient alpha was .93, and the test-retest reliability coefficient was .84 (tested weekly over a ten-week period). A second study using 289 employee assistance clients with undisclosed demographics had a coefficient alpha of .93.

A third reliability study used 56 undergraduate students with unknown demographics who took the OQ-30.1 once a week or once biweekly for 10 weeks. This study was performed to examine the stability of the scores as well as the effects of repeated testing. Correlating the scores from Week 1 with Week 2 through Week 10 yielded correlation coefficients varying from .66 to .86. The slightly diminishing size of the correlation coefficient over time was interpreted by the authors as meaning that the OQ-30.1 is fairly stable over time and appropriate for tracking progress through the course of therapy. The authors assert that the size of correlation would be larger over time if the repeated administration influenced the scores. This assertion is addressed in the Commentary section of this review.

Validity. Validity was based upon a number of studies that used the OQ-30 and OQ-45.2. When the OQ-45.2 was used, it appears that the statistics are based on only the OQ-30.1 items. Concurrent validity was established by correlating the OQ-30.1, the Symptom Checklist-90-R, the Beck Depression Inventory, the Inventory of Interpersonal Problems, and the Social Adjustment Scale. The correlations of the OQ-30.1 with the other scales ranged from .593 to .698. This research was interpreted as supporting the OQ-30.1 having moderately high concurrent validity with a variety of measures. The manual did not describe the sample used for the validity study, but the sample was probably the 56 undergraduate students used in the previously described reliability study.

Data supported the sensitivity of the OQ-30.1 to the presence of psychopathology and its sensitivity to change across psychotherapy sessions. Data from the Vermeersch et al. (2000) study consisting of 1,176 patients compared to 284 controls seemed to be the basis for this study. Although the original study examined the OQ-45.2, the items of the OQ-30.1 were used in this study. The OQ-30.1 was able to differentiate the clinical versus the community subjects in a *t*-test at the .001 level. There is no information about the effect size of the difference. The second study compared the clinical group's pretreatment OQ-30.1 mean score to the posttreatment mean score. A *t*-test yielded significance beyond the .0001 level indicating that the OQ-30.1 scores were different after psychotherapy. Again, no effect size was given.

Normative data. The authors provided normative data based upon 905 volunteers who were not receiving psychological services and 8,410 who were receiving outpatient services. The nonpatient subjects were primarily undergraduate students (Utah, Idaho, and Ohio) and around 208 community members (Utah). The clinical sample consisted of a university counseling center, an employee assistance program, and an outpatient clinic in a university setting. The clinical sample probably had a good cross section of diagnostic types; however, there were no data to support this.

The normative sample seems to have a geographic bias of the Utah, Idaho, and Ohio area. The nonpatient volunteers seem to be heavily influenced by college students. The authors state that there was no difference between the subgroups nor between males and females. Adults between the ages of 17 and 80 are reported to exist in the sample as a whole, and age did not correlate with the OQ-30.1 score. The distribution of ages in the sample was not given.

Means and standard deviations for the normative groups of community volunteers and mixed outpatient samples were reported as was a cutoff score of 44 for separating the two samples based on the formula from Jacobson and Truax (1991). The authors also use the normative data to calculate a Reliable Change Index of 10 units. A Reliable Change Index represents the change in an individual score that is considered clinically significant (Jacobson & Truax, 1991).

COMMENTARY. The OQ-30.1 is a very brief assessment of general dysfunction that appears to have good reliability, validity, and sensitivity to change. The brevity and ability to use the measure weekly to plot change are the OQ-30.1's strongest attributes. The norm data are beneficial in working with a Caucasian or European American clinical population. The four critical items provide the user a rudimentary alert that signals a need for further investigation into suicide and substance abuse problems.

The major concern is the lack of information regarding the demographics of the norm groups and the vague criteria for selecting the items from the OQ-45.2. The manual glossed over demographic issues, electing to present a singular set of norms. The OQ-30.1 may well represent all demographic groups with one set of norms but the manual was unconvincing. There were no data to support the stance.

The PacifiCare Behavioral Health Inc. company was listed as the repository of thousands of data sets of the OQ-30.1. Regrettably, the vast amount of information was not available to inform the manual about key demographic or population issues.

Perhaps the most significant omission was ethnicity. The manual stated that there were no differences found between ethnic groups. However, there was no statement of which ethnic groups were examined.

Of some concern was the logic for substantiating the validity of using the OQ-30.1 on a weekly basis. The slightly diminishing size of the correlation coefficient between Time 1 and later administrations was interpreted by the authors as meaning that the OQ-30.1 is appropriate for tracking progress through the course of therapy. The authors assert that the size of correlation would be larger over time if the repeated administration influenced the scores. This reviewer believes that logic dictates that the latter administrations may correlate more highly with each other but not necessarily to Time 1 if the instrument is losing validity. These data were not presented. Additionally, it would have been helpful to compare the internal consistency scores of Week 1 with Week 10 to see if the internal consistency changed to any great extent.

REVIEWER'S REFERENCES

Jacobson, N. S., & Truax, P. (1991). Clinical significance: A statistical approach to defining meaningful change in psychotherapy research. *Journal of Consulting and Clinical Psychology, 59,* 12-19.

Vermeersch, D. A., Lambert, M. J., & Burlingame, G. M. (2000). Outcome Questionnaire: Item sensitivity to change. *Journal of Personality Assessment, 74,* 242-261.

Review of the OQ-30.1 [Outcome Questionnaire for Adults] by PAM RAMSDEN, Senior Lecturer, University of Bolton, Bolton, Lancashire, England:

DESCRIPTION. The OQ-30.1 [Outcome Questionnaire for Adults] is designed to be utilized as a measure of patient progress during and after psychological/medical interventions. The instrument consists of 30 items on a 5-point Likert scale that queries patients concerning their current state of functioning and emotional status. The OQ-30.1 takes approximately 10–15 minutes to complete depending upon the participant's reading ability and current functioning state. The manual does indicate that under normal circumstances individuals can easily complete the instrument in approximately 4 minutes. The OQ-30.1 does include provisions so that it can be verbally administered if necessary.

The OQ-30.1 is self-administering and requires no instructions beyond those printed on the protocol. The instrument does not require a high level of professional training but does appear to be subject to possible influences based upon administrator "attitude"; the manual indicates that negative attitudes by clinicians and other administrators of the instrument can severely impair its validity. Specificity of the types of "negative attitudes" was not clarified, and it was uncertain whether the attitude was directed at the patient while completing the test or the test itself. The only specific reference was that test administrators should encourage subjects to be "honest and conscientious" (manual, p. 1) while filling out the instrument.

Patient progress on the OQ-30.1 is measured along three dimensions: subjective discomfort (intrapsychic functioning), interpersonal relationships, and social role performance. The instrument contains no subscales that incorporate these three dimensions and provides a single score that acts as a global measure of these factors.

The best use of this instrument is to measure patient progress, and the instrument is specifically designed for repeated administration during the course of treatment and at termination. The test designers state that the true value of the OQ-30.1 is to track change over time and the instrument's design can ascertain if patients are improving, not changing, or getting worse. The manual further suggests that one administration prior to each treatment session is ideal; however, they comprehend the burdensome element and suggest that administering it on the first, second, third, fifth, and every fifth session thereafter would capture the clinical changes in a meaningful way. The OQ-30.1 was not designed to be used for patient diagnoses, and its sole purpose is to monitor change in patient progress over a short duration of time.

The OQ-30.1 was intended to be a therapeutic tool that was of low cost, sensitive to change over short periods of time, and had the ability "to monitor common symptoms across a wide range of adult mental disorders and syndromes including stress related illness and v. codes" (manual, p. 1).

Scoring is straightforward and involves simple addition of the 30 items. Each item is scored on a 5-point scale (range 0–4). Four items are reverse scored. Scores range from 0–120 with the higher score indicating the higher levels of distress that is being acknowledged. There are two additional scoring criteria: the Significant Change Index and the Reliable Change Index. For the clinically significant change index, a cutoff score of 44 was calculated between the community sample and several of the clinical samples. Patients scoring 43 and less are in the functional range whereas those with a score of 44 or higher are functioning more like patients than normals. The specific formulas devised for these calculations are provided in the manual. The Reliable Change Index (RCI) is used to determine if the change exhibited by an individual in treatment is clinically significant. The RCI value was computed using reliability estimates from the community samples. A change of 10 is utilized for this value, and an individual's score must change by at least 10 points in either direction to be considered a clinically significant change.

DEVELOPMENT. The OQ-30.1 is an abbreviated version of the OQ-45.2 (16:176). Both outcome measures were designed to be used in behavioral and medical health care to measure patient progress, during and after intervention. Neither instrument was designed to be used for patient diagnoses. The OQ-30.1 is an abbreviated version and contains only one scale, whereas the OQ-45.2 contained three subscales. The 30 items were chosen from the original instrument based on their individual sensitivity to change. The item selection was based on three criteria: (a) Items were chosen that were commonly occurring problems in a wide range of disorders, (b) items were chosen to tap symptoms that occur across patients regardless of problems, and (c) items were selected that affected the quality of life in an individual. In addition, the entire set selected needed to be administered in a brief time period.

TECHNICAL. The norms were collected from undergraduate and community samples across three states: Utah, Idaho, and Ohio. The partici-pants included 796 students and 208 community members from Utah. Data were collected from clinical samples from a large private western university counseling center, an Ohio-based community mental health center, and an employee assistance program. No specific information was provided on gender, age, or ethnic differences but where the data were available researchers indicate that there were no apparent differences that existed between any of the subgroups. Normative values were computed on the nonpatient community volunteers (n = 905) and mixed outpatient samples (n = 8,410).

Reliability was assessed using a sample of 157 students. Internal consistency was also calculated on a subset of 298 patients from the employee assistance program. Both were high and were a respectable .93. The test-retest reliability correlation coefficient was .84 but was conducted only on the student population (tested weekly for a 10-week period). Additionally a test-retest value of .796 was found on a separate student sample (n = 53) after a 3-week interval. Correlation coefficients between test administration over a 10-week period ranged from .82 at Week 1 to .66 at Week 10. The data do appear to indicate that the OQ-30.1 is fairly stable over time and is consistent with the goal of tracking patient progress during the course of treatment. Concurrent validity was conducted on frequently used clinical scales: the Symptom Checklist-90-R (Derogatis, 1977), Beck Depression Inventory (Beck, Ward, Mendelson, Mock, & Erbaugh, 1961); Inventory of interpersonal Problems (Horowitz, Rosenberg, Baer, Ureno, & Villasenor, 1988) and Social Adjustment Scale (Weissman & Bothwell, 1976). The OQ-30.1 had moderately high concurrent validity with all measures indicating that it provides a broad index of mental health functioning.

One more element of construct validity was the OQ-30.1's response to treatment over time and the element of sensitivity to change, which was assessed by comparing 1,176 patients to 284 controls who were not in treatment. The results indicated that the patients had significantly more movement in scores than the controls, as well as improvement in their scores following each incident of treatment. Additional results on psychopathology also indicated that the instrument was capable of discriminating between clinical and nonclinical groups.

COMMENTARY. Research has been conducted on the clinical usefulness of the OQ-30.1 specifically in terms of establishing benchmarks in outcomes in treatment. Preliminary research has indicated that the OQ-30.1 could possibly be a reliable way of establishing a measure for these outcomes provided that comparisons are made in similar populations (i.e., diagnoses and severity of symptoms). In certain populations the utility of the instrument is clear. However, the simplistic design may be its downfall as it is subject to false positives or negatives as well as the positive or negative attitudes of the administrator. There are no validity scales so individuals could easily indicate more or less distress than is actually present. Additionally, there is little information on gender, age, and ethnic differences and the norming populations were inadequately described. The test authors simply stated that contrasts between ethnic groups were limited to people in similar school or work settings. The manual does state that the instrument has been administered to adults between the ages of 17 and 80 but no supporting data have been provided concerning the upper age limits.

SUMMARY. The OQ-30.1 is an outcome questionnaire designed to chart a patient's progress during the course of a therapeutic intervention. One of the goals of this instrument was to address the limitations in other current outcome measures, and it does adequately achieve that goal. It has good reliability and some validity and appears to be able to measure accurately a subject's change over time as well as discriminate psychopathology in clinical populations. The instrument provides an index of mental health and correlates with a variety of clinician scales that are currently used in clinical practice to assess a variety of mental health issues such as anxiety, depression, quality of life social adjustment, and interpersonal functioning. The major limitation of this instrument is its lack of information concerning gender, age, and ethnic differences.

REVIEWER'S REFERENCES

Beck, A. T., Ward, C. H., Mendelson, M., Mock, J., & Erbaugh, J. (1961). An inventory for measuring depression. *Archives for General Psychology, 4,* 53-63.

Derogatis, L. R. (1977). *The SCL-90 manual: Scoring, administration and procedures for the SCL-90.* Baltimore: Johns Hopkins University School of Medicine, Clinical Psychometrics Unit.

Horowitz, L. M., Rosenberg, S. E., Baer, B. A., Ureno, G., & Villasenor, V. S. (1988). Inventory of interpersonal problems: Psychometric properties and clinical applications. *Journal of Consulting and Clinical Psychology, 56,* 885-892.

Wiessman, M. M., & Bothwell, S. (1976). Assessment of social adjustment by patient self-report. *Archives of General Psychiatry, 33,* 1111-1115.

Orleans-Hanna Algebra Prognosis Test, Third Edition.

Purpose: Designed to "determine algebra readiness" and as a predictor of student success in first-year algebra.

Population: Grades 7–11.

Publication Dates: 1928–1998.

Scores: Total score only.

Administration: Group.

Price Data, 2005: $85 per 25 test booklets and manual (1998, 55 pages); $35 per 25 hand-scorable answer documents including class record; $21 per key to use with hand-scorable answer documents; $30 per 25 student report forms; $35 per 25 machine-scorable answer documents.

Time: 35(40) minutes.

Author: Gerald S. Hanna.

Publisher: The Psychological Corporation, A Harcourt Assessment Company.

Cross References: See T4:1910 (3 references); for reviews by Dietmar Küchemann and Charles Secolsky of an earlier edition, see 9:912 (1 reference); see also T2:688 (11 references); for reviews by W. L. Bashaw and Cyril J. Hoyt of an earlier edition, see 7:510 (3 references); for reviews by Harold Gulliksen and Emma Spany, see 4:396 (1 reference); for a review by S. S. Wilks, see 2:1444 (4 references).

Review of the Orleans-Hanna Algebra Prognosis Test, Third Edition by JOSEPH C. CIECHALSKI, Professor, East Carolina University, Greenville, NC:

DESCRIPTION. The Orleans-Hanna Algebra Prognosis Test is designed to predict student success in first-year algebra. The test booklet consists of five algebra lessons, each followed by six multiple-choice items. A review test consisting of 20 multiple-choice items based on middle school math concepts is also included.

Directions for administering the test are clearly written. All directions read to the students are highlighted in color. Students are required to place their answers on a separate answer sheet. In addition to the normal demographic data, students must include their most recent report card grades in math, science, English, and social studies on the answer sheet. The test has a 35-minute time limit.

The Algebra Prognosis Test may be scored using the stencil key or it may be machine scored. Specific directions for hand scoring the test and for preparing the answer sheet for machine scoring are concise and easy to understand. The hand scoring stencil is not only used to determine the raw scores but is also used to assign point values for each subject grade reported by the student. The maximum possible raw score points is 48. Each of the 50 multiple-choice items on the test is worth 1 point. Thus, the highest possible total score is 98.

The total raw score points are converted to percentile ranks using one of the four conversion tables found in the test manual. There are two separate conversion tables for seventh- and eighth-grade students who have completed seventh- and eighth-grade math as well as two tables for seventh- and eighth-grade students who have completed first-year algebra.

DEVELOPMENT. The first edition of the Orleans-Hanna Algebra Prognosis Test was published in 1928. It was updated in 1950, revised in 1968, and again in 1982. Three major domains (aptitude, achievement, and affective) were identified and included in this third edition.

The questionnaire section and the work-sample approach used in previous editions were retained. This approach was designed to measure how well students learn algebra from the five brief learning lessons. A section designed to assess middle school math skills as well as review items based on the five learning lessons was included in this edition.

Over 200 test items were developed and edited. The resulting 198 items were divided into four experimental forms: two forms that approximated the format and length of the final test and two forms used to try out additional items for inclusion for the review middle school math test. Each form was administered to over 300 students. Based on the results, the current version of the test was developed.

Sixteen questionnaire items were included in the norming version of the test. Multiple regression analyses were performed to determine which combination of items would yield the most power for predicting success in algebra. Of the original 16 questionnaire items, only 4 questionnaire items contributed significantly and were included in the test. These surviving items were the four most recent self-reported report card grades in math, science, social studies, and English. Thus, the final version includes four questionnaire items based on report card grades; five teaching lessons each followed by 6 multiple-choice items; and 20 multiple-choice items based on the middle school math curriculum and the five teaching lessons in algebra.

TECHNICAL. The norming sample was selected to represent the nation's seventh and eighth graders who have not enrolled in first-year algebra. A stratified, random, multistage, cluster sample design was used to sample the national population of school districts. The sample included four sections of the country, three strata of socioeconomic status, and three categories of urbanicity (urban, suburban, and rural) resulting in an interaction of 36 cells (4 regions, 3 strata, and 3 urbanicity). The sample included 159 districts in 39 states.

Evidence of content-related validity is reported by having the test users evaluate whether the work sample section is suitable, whether the content of the achievement-testing section is consistent with the local curriculum, and whether the balance between the above is appropriate. These areas could be successfully presented by developing a table of specification or test blue print.

Predictive validity evidence is provided in two tables. One presents the predictive validity evidence coefficients for both seventh and eighth graders who have earned a grade in algebra as .60 with the corrected validity coefficients reported as .63 and .67 for seventh and eighth graders, respectively. The second table presents the predictive validity coefficients for seventh and eighth graders who took an end-of-year algebra achievement test as .80 and .68 for seventh and eighth graders, respectively corrected as .83 for seventh graders and .76 for eighth graders. In addition, expectancy tables were developed for the above and are reported in two tables in the manual.

Evidence for construct-related validity is described by the author by indicating that the Orleans-Hanna Algebra Prognosis Test scores are not influenced or contaminated by things the test is not supposed to measure. By using multiple-regression predictions, the author presents evidence that the test attains greater predictive qualities by considering the test along with past grades in predicting academic success in algebra. Finally, the author compares the validity of predictions made by the test with other less specialized measures like the Otis-Lennon School Abilities Test and the predictive validity of the students' most recent report card grades in math.

Test-retest reliability coefficients were reported as .95 for the total test and .94 for the items alone over a 2-week period. Using the KR-20 formula, the internal consistency coefficient was .95 for the seventh-grade sample and .94 for the eighth-grade sample. Correlations for the old (1982) and the current edition of the test were found for each of the four subject areas, the questionnaire items, the test items, and total score. The resulting reliability coefficients ranged from .88 to .92. In addition, item discrimination indices for the tests are reported in the manual. The median biserial correlations for the seventh- and eighth-grade students were .68 and .65, respectively.

COMMENTARY. The Orleans-Hanna Algebra Prognosis Test has a long and distinguished history. It was first published in 1928 and has undergone several revisions since that time. New items were written, field tested, edited, and incorporated into the current edition of the test. In 1985, the test was reviewed by Küchemann and Secolsky. What changes have been made since their reviews?

In Küchemann's (1985) review, he stated, "At a minimum, it would have been useful to know the predictive validity of the test items and grades separately" (p. 1105). Two tables in the current test manual address this issue. Both Küchemann (1985) and Secolsky (1985) along with this reviewer find the two expectancy tables very useful devices to help individuals predict algebra success.

The 1985 version of this test reported the test results in both percentile ranks and stanines. The current edition reports the scores in percentile ranks only. Stanines are easier to interpret than percentile ranks, and I believe that they should be made available in future revisions of the test.

A concern that I have involves the content validity. Küchemann (1985) states, "The most disappointing aspect of the manual is the lack of detailed discussion of the actual content" (p. 1105). A table of specifications would be able to resolve this concern. In addition, norming data for males, females, and minorities should be considered for inclusion in future revisions.

SUMMARY. Overall, I find the Orleans-Hanna Algebra Prognosis Test, Third Edition to be a useful predictor of algebra success. The author is to be commended for eliminating some of the weaknesses of the previous version. Although more evidence of content validity is needed, the validity and reliability evidence is sound. The test manual is easy to read and understand. Therefore, I recommend this test to anyone in need of an algebra prognosis test.

REVIEWER'S REFERENCES

Küchemann, D. (1985). [Review of the Orleans-Hanna Algebra Prognosis Test.] In J. V. Mitchell, Jr. (Ed.), *The ninth mental measurement yearbook* (p. 1105). Lincoln, NE: Buros Institute of Mental Measurements.
Secolsky, C. (1985). [Review of the Orleans-Hanna Algebra Prognosis Test.] In J. V. Mitchell, Jr. (Ed.), *The ninth mental measurements yearbook* (pp. 1105–1106). Lincoln, NE: Buros Institute of Mental Measurements.

Review of the Orleans-Hanna Algebra Prognosis Test, Third Edition by KEVIN D. CREHAN, Professor of Educational Psychology, University of Nevada, Las Vegas, NV:

DESCRIPTION. The original version of this test, the Orleans Algebra Prognosis Test, was published in 1928. This test was subsequently revised in 1950, 1968, and 1982. The author of the present (1998) revision was reportedly motivated to incorporate the current NCTM Curriculum and Evaluation Standards for School Mathematics, strengthen the contribution of the questionnaire items to the total score, and go beyond the work-sample approach used in earlier editions.

The test is organized into five "lesson" segments with each lesson followed by 6 multiple-choice items covering the concepts introduced in the lessons. A 20-item review follows the five lesson segments for a total test length of 50 multiple-choice items. The five lessons introduce exponents, letters to represent unknown numbers, order of operations, function notation, and factorials to determine permutations. The 20-item review section covers "topics from middle-school mathematics" (manual, p. 35) and a review of the concepts introduced in the five lessons presented earlier in the test. Also included as part of the test score are responses to 4 questionnaire items that ask examinees to self-report their grades in mathematics, science, English, and social studies. Each of the four self-reported grades is "scored" on a 13-point scale from F = 0 to A+ = 12. The maximum total for reported grades would be 48 in the case of an examinee reporting four A pluses. Number correct on the 50 test items is added to the reported grade "score" to obtain a total score with the maximum being 98. Because the reported standard deviations for the test scores and grade "scores" are similar, 10.05 and 10.9 respectively, the two variables are given close to an equal weighting in the composite.

An expectancy table is provided that relates 16 test score categories to final algebra grade. Four raw score-to-percentile-rank conversions are provided for norm samples of (a) seventh graders who completed seventh-grade mathematics, (b) seventh graders who completed seventh-grade mathematics and first-year algebra the following year, (c) eighth graders who completed eighth-grade mathematics and, (d) eighth graders who completed eighth-grade mathematics and first-year algebra the following year.

DEVELOPMENT. The revised test content is reportedly guided by the coverage in current algebra texts, trends reported in the literature, content specialists, and the National Council of Teachers of Mathematics 1989 publication *Curriculum and Evaluation Standards for School Mathematics*. Factors assessed for possible inclusion in the tests were aptitude, achievement, and affective traits. Aptitude is measured by performance on items that follow lessons designed to teach the concepts. Achievement is measured by items tapping mathematics knowledge and essential skills requisite to learning algebra. The affective traits, measured by a questionnaire, included interest, motivation, self-efficacy, study habits, affect for mathematics, and effort. Additionally, students were asked to report previous grades as described above.

Selection of the 50 items for inclusion in the final test form was based on results of pilot testing of a pool of 198 items on a sample of over 300 middle school students distributed among 13 school districts in three states. The affective measures were dropped from the final version of the test following regression analyses that failed to show a significant contribution of these items to prediction of algebra grades. The only questionnaire items retained were the self-reported grades.

TECHNICAL. The norm sample included 9,195 seventh graders and 6,743 eighth graders closely representative of United States geographic region, socioeconomic status, population density, ethnicity, and school control. Internal consistency reliability was quite high at .95 for the seventh-grade sample and .94 for the eighth-grade sample. Item analyses showed a good range of item difficulties from around .30 to around .80 with median proportions correct of .58 for seventh graders and

.63 for eighth graders. The median biserial correlations were .68 and .65 for seventh-and eighth-grade samples, respectively.

The manual appropriately cautions potential users of the test to make local decisions on the appropriateness of using the test to guide placement decisions regarding algebra courses. The manual also appropriately suggests that potential users evaluate the test content against local curriculum content.

Evidence of predictive validity includes correlation of prognosis test scores with algebra grades attained by the subgroups of seventh ($n = 2,260$) and eighth graders ($n = 1,845$) who took algebra in the year following the norm data collection. The correlation was .60 for both subgroups. Also reported is the correlation between prognosis test scores and a specially developed end-of-course algebra achievement test. These correlations were .80 for the seventh grade subgroup and .68 for the eighth-grade subgroup. Additional evidence is reported that shows the prognosis test had higher correlations than the OLSAT with both the algebra grades and the end-of-course algebra test.

COMMENTARY. The manual for the Orleans-Hanna Algebra Prognosis Test presents evidence of effort and expertise in the development and norming of the measure. The lesson and test format of the first 30 items and review nature of the remaining 20 items seems appropriate for a summary assessment of aptitudes and achievements predictive of success in an algebra course. There is, however, a question regarding the use of self-reported grades as half of the composite used as the reported score for this measure. The manual reports that "self-reported grades were better at predicting the (algebra) grade criterion" (p. 34) than the score on the 50 items, although surprisingly, the manual does not report this higher correlation. It would seem that, because regression analysis was used to decide which questionnaire items to retain, regression analysis would also be used to determine the relative contributions of test scores and self-reported grades in predicting algebra course grades. Especially of interest is the incremental increase in prediction of the algebra grade attained by adding the prognosis test scores to self-reported grades in the regression analysis. It is important for potential users to know the unique contribution to prediction of the prognosis test scores alone.

Potential users of this test most likely have a student's actual grades. Therefore, they do not need the self-reported grades supplied by the examinee. Obviously, the actual grades are more accurate than self-reported grades. It would be a simple task to translate the actual letter grades to numbers using the F = 0 to A+ = 12 conversion and combine this value with a student's score on the 50 items. It could well be that this more accurate composite score would be a better predictor than the composite that relies on self-reported grades.

SUMMARY. The Orleans-Hanna Algebra Prognosis Test appears to be a well-developed measure of a student's ability to learn some basic algebra concepts during testing. It also provides a summary measure of core concepts taught in pre-algebra mathematics courses. The test manual suggests that test scores are to be used to counsel students on whether and when to take algebra. However, the unique usefulness of scores on the test, by itself, as a predictor of algebra course grade is in question. The manual fails to report how much the score on the test adds to the prediction of algebra course grade over a student's previous achievement. The manual reports that previous achievement is a better predictor of algebra grade. A counselor might be advised to use a student's previous achievement and teacher recommendations to offer advice on mathematics course selection and save the time and expense of testing. The manual suggests that other uses of test scores are to plan instruction and decide on levels of instruction. Sufficient evidence is not supplied to comment on the appropriateness of these suggested interpretations.

[139]
Overeating Questionnaire.

Purpose: Designed to measure "key habits, thoughts, and attitudes related to obesity."
Population: Ages 9–98 years.
Publication Date: 2004.
Acronym: OQ.
Scores, 12: 2 Validity scores (Inconsistent Responding, Defensiveness), 6 Eating-Related Habits and Attitudes scores (Overeating, Undereating, Craving, Expectations About Eating, Rationalizations, Motivation to Lose Weight), 4 general Health Habits and Psychosocial Functioning scores (Health Habits, Body Image, Social Isolation, Affective Disturbance).
Administration: Group or individual.

Price Data, 2007: $93.50 per complete kit including 25 AutoScore answer sheets and manual (51 pages); $42.50 per 25 AutoScore answer sheets (bulk discounts available); $55 per manual; Computerized components: $307.50 per 25-use computer disk for Windows; $16.50 per 100 PC answer sheets.
Time: 20 minutes.
Comments: Written for individuals with a fourth-grade reading level and higher.
Authors: William E. O'Donnell and W. L. Warren.
Publisher: Western Psychological Services.

Review of the Overeating Questionnaire by JAMES P. DONNELLY, Assistant Professor, Department of Counseling, School & Educational Psychology, University at Buffalo, Amherst, NY:

DESCRIPTION. The Overeating Questionnaire (OQ) is an 80-item self-report measure of attitudes and behaviors related to obesity. In the test manual, the authors indicated that the OQ was developed to meet a growing need for a comprehensive measure useful in the treatment of obesity, especially in individualized treatment planning. They also noted that the wide age range covered by the norms for the measure meets the increasing need for assessment of children and adolescents in weight-loss programs. Users are advised that the test is not intended to be used in diagnosis of eating disorders such as anorexia or more general mental health issues like depression.

The measure includes two validity scales (Inconsistent Responding and Defensiveness) as well as 10 clinically oriented scales. The six clinical scales specifically related to eating include: Overeating, Undereating, Craving, Expectations about Eating, Rationalizations, and Motivation to Lose Weight. The remaining four clinical scales address more general health-related issues thought to be central to weight loss treatment, including Health Habits, Body Image, Social Isolation, and Affective Disturbance. The measure also includes 14 items related to patient identity, demographics, weight, and general health behavior.

The OQ can be completed via paper form or computer, and can be administered by a technician. Interpretation of results, which include raw scores, normalized T scores, percentiles, and a graphic profile plot, should be done by a professional with competence in psychometrics sufficient to be able to read and understand the test manual. Time for test completion is said to average about 20 minutes and requires a fourth-grade reading level. The paper or "autoscore" version is printed on a cleverly designed form that integrates all items, scoring instructions and worksheet, and a scoring page (or "profile sheet") that includes raw score, percentile, and T score equivalents. Hand scoring on the worksheet is facilitated by a combination of arrows, boxes, and shading, which makes the computation of raw scale scores relatively quick and easy. The profiling of scores facilitates efficient visual identification of relative strengths and vulnerabilities, but is not intended for classification of subtypes of test takers. The computer version of the test was not available for this review; however, the manual provides a description and a sample report.

DEVELOPMENT. The development process appears to have generally followed accepted scale development practices (e.g., DeVellis, 2003), though some irregularities in the manual report cause concern. Item development and evaluation included two sequences of literature review, data collection, and item and scale analysis. No specific theory was cited. Following an initial literature review, 140 items thought to be related to overeating and responsiveness to weight loss interventions were written. Constructs represented in this item set included attitudes toward weight, food, eating, and self-image. Items reflecting defensiveness and general psychosocial functioning were also included. The initial item set was studied in a sample of convenience in a university medical school setting (no other description of the participants or their number is given). Based on examination of correlations, 129 items were retained, supplemented by an additional 59 new items generated from feedback from the pilot sample and additional literature review. The second item set was evaluated based on responses of 140 nursing students. The manual notes that the scale structure based on the new data was generally similar to the original set with two minor exceptions, yet no specifics on how scale structure was studied are given. For final inclusion, an item had to correlate at least .30 with its intended scale, and had to show discrimination of at least .10 greater correlation with its own versus any other scale. In addition, final decisions were made with regard to item readability and content uniqueness, resulting in the final 80-item set.

As noted, there are two validity scales, Inconsistent Responding Index (INC) and Defensiveness (DEF). The INC scale includes 15 pairs of items with correlations of .5 or greater in the standardization sample. The scale is scored by counting all of the item pairs in which the response differed by at least 2 scale points. The test authors computed the average INC score for 200 randomly generated scores to provide an interpretive guide vis-à-vis the probability that an INC score reflects random responding. For example, an INC score of 5 is associated with a 71% likelihood that the scale was completed randomly. The Defensiveness scale includes seven items representing idealized self-evaluations (e.g., "I am always happy"). Relatively less information is provided on this scale, except that T scores above 60 are said to suggest caution in interpretation and reassurance for anyone completing the scale in the context of treatment.

TECHNICAL.

Standardization. The standardization sample of 1,788 was recruited nationally from schools and community settings. A table of breakdowns by gender, age, race/ethnicity, education, and region are provided with national proportions for each variable for comparison, with the exception of age (perhaps because the categories used for the test were not comparable to U.S. Census records, though no explanation is given). Overall, as the test authors noted, the sample resembles national data with some underrepresentation of males and some minority groups. The sample data were then transformed to normalized T scores, which were the basis for both the examination of subgroup differences and for the clinical scoring procedures.

The analysis of subgroups involved inspection of means with interpretation of differences guided by a general statement regarding effect sizes (.1–.3 = small, .3–.5 = moderate, greater than .5 = large). The use of effect sizes as an interpretive guide is laudable, but more specific reference to the meaningfulness of these numbers in the context of obesity research and treatment would be a significant improvement. For example, some of the subscales may represent attitudes and behaviors that are more difficult to change in treatment than others; some scales may be more stable following treatment than others; and some may be more highly correlated with other treatment outcomes such as Body Mass Index, any of which would significantly affect interpretation. We can hope that future research provides such data. Nevertheless, the tables indicate that most of the subgroup mean differences are less than the 3 *T*-score points the authors suggest is the upper limit of a small effect. The differences beyond this level are noted in text, and further research is acknowledged as important in these instances. The overall conclusion that the subgroup differences are minimal simplifies the matter of scoring and interpretation because the *T*-score norms essentially become a "one size fits all" scoring protocol, a trade of simplicity for specificity that may be welcomed in the clinical setting on purely practical grounds, but cannot be said to reflect strong evidence-based assessment at this point in time.

Reliability. Reliability data for the OQ are presented in terms of internal consistency for the standardization sample, and 1-week test-retest reliability for a separate group. The coefficient alpha estimates for the 10 clinical scales and the Defensiveness scale show evidence of strong internal consistency, with a range of .79 to .88 across the subscales for the full sample. Interestingly, the test authors separately examined internal consistency for the 68 children aged 9 or 10 in the sample. For this group, one scale (Health Habits) dipped below .70 (to .66), but otherwise the reliability estimates remained reasonably strong (range = .72–.88). In the same table, the authors also provided corrected median item-total correlations for the items in each scale, along with ranges for these estimates. Again, the evidence points toward desirable internal consistency. The 1-week test-retest data are also strong if we merely examine the range of the estimates (.64–.94), but is much more limited when taking into account the small number in this sample (*n* = 24), the fact that no information is given about the sample, and the absence of any theoretical or other comment on why this interval was chosen or whether the constructs measured by the scales *should* be stable over this interval.

Validity. The manual reports evidence of construct validity that reflects internal and external validity characteristics of the scales. The internal validity report includes tables of scale intercorrelations as well as the results of a principal components analysis on the standardization sample. The external validity data include correlations with a number of other scales and variables chosen to reflect plausible relationships that would provide convergent and divergent validity evidence.

The table of intercorrelations and the accompanying interpretive text are consistent with previously described internal structure of the measure. The principal components analysis was conducted separately for seven scales measuring vulnerabilities (e.g., Overeating) and the remaining three measuring strengths (e.g., Motivation to Lose Weight). The table reporting this analysis includes only the component loadings. No other information on important details of the analysis that should typically be reported is given (e.g., rotation, extraction criteria, eigenvalues) (Henson & Roberts, 2006). The authors noted that the loadings are generally consistent with indicated scales, though, for example, two clearly distinct but adjoining components are combined in a single scale.

Additional construct validity data are presented in the form of correlational studies further examining the relationship of OQ scales to person characteristics such as BMI in the standardization sample, and a small sample (*N* = 50) study of OQ correlations with five previously established self-report measures of related constructs (e.g., eating, self-concept, stress). In addition, a study of Piers-Harris Self-Concept and OQ scores for 268 of the "youngsters" from the standardization sample was mentioned (no other information is given on this subsample). The authors' conclusion that the overall pattern is consistent with expectations given the nature of the OQ scale constructs is quite global but not unreasonable.

COMMENTARY. Strengths of the OQ include the efficiency of a single instrument for virtually anyone who might be seen in treatment, ease of administration and scoring, attention to response style, inclusion of specific eating and more general health behaviors, a reasonably large standardization sample of children and adults, internal consistency reliability, face validity, and some evidence of construct validity. The question of to what extent the standardization sample resembles the likely clinical population is not directly addressed. A case could be made that the sample is, in fact, a good comparison one because a large proportion of the U.S. population is overweight and at some point may seek professional assistance. The use of effect sizes in interpretation is commendable, but should eventually be more specifically associated with clinical data in the intended population in future versions of the scale. In addition, some details of the measure development process are missing from the manual (e.g., minimal reporting of the pilot samples, few details of the principal-components analysis).

SUMMARY. The OQ is a relatively new measure attempting to address a major health issue with a comprehensive and efficient set of scales intended for use in individualized treatment of overeating. The test manual sets a relatively circumscribed goal of aiding in individual treatment planning, but that process must be undertaken without the benefit of any predictive data. The OQ ambitiously attempts to provide a single measure for children through older adults with a single set of norms. In providing a user-friendly format and some good psychometric evidence, it is potentially useful in the expressed goal of aiding in treatment planning. Further research is needed to enhance the clinician's ability to confidently employ the measure, especially in understanding the relationship of scores and profile patterns to treatment process and outcome.

REVIEWER'S REFERENCES

DeVellis, R. F. (2003). *Scale development*. Thousand Oaks, CA: Sage.
Henson, R. K., & Roberts, J. K. (2006). Use of exploratory factor analysis in published research: Some common errors and some comment on improved practice. *Educational and Psychological Measurement*, 66, 393-416.

Review of the Overeating Questionnaire by SANDRA D. HAYNES, *Dean, School of Professional Studies, Metropolitan State College of Denver, Denver, CO:*

DESCRIPTION. The Overeating Questionnaire is an 80-item self-report questionnaire designed to measure key habits, thoughts, and attitudes related to obesity in order to establish individualized weight loss programs. Such an instrument is rare as tests of eating behavior are typically geared toward anorexia nervosa and bulimia nervosa. The paper-and-pencil version of the questionnaire can be administered individually or in a group and takes approximately 20 minutes to complete. The administration time for the PC version is similar but, as suggested, administration is accomplished using computer keyboard and mouse. After completing identifying information including age, gender, education, and race/ethnicity, examinees are asked to answer questions in Part I regarding height, historical weight and eating patterns, use of alcohol and drugs, health problems, and perceptions of weight in self and others. Part II consists of a list of 80 statements that the examinee is asked to rate with regard to agreement on a 5-point scale: *Not at all* (0), *A little*

bit (1), *Moderately* (2), *Quite a lot* (3), and *Extremely* (4). Care should be taken to ensure that clients respond to all statements on the questionnaire. If an item has been left blank and an answer cannot be obtained from the client, the median score for that item is used in scoring. No written instructions are given to the client regarding the correction of responses made in error. The sample scoring sheet shows errors being crossed out. Verbal instruction should be given.

Scoring is manual using the paper-and-pencil AutoScore™ form or computerized using the PC version. Using the AutoScore™ form, responses are automatically transferred to an easy score worksheet. Raw scores for each question are transferred to a box under the appropriate scale heading. Numbers from columns representing each of 11 scales are then summed and transferred to the profile sheet. The profile sheet contains corresponding normalized T-scores and percentiles, and provides a graphic representation of results. Scores greater than or equal to $60T$ are considered high; greater than or equal to $70T$ are very high. Scores less than or equal to $40T$ are considered low. A 12th score, the Inconsistent Responding Index (INC), is calculated by finding the differences between 15 INC similar item pairs.

Remarkably little attention is paid to the computerized scoring in the text of the manual. (It is described in an appendix.) Using this method, the client uses a computer to complete the questionnaire. Scoring is quicker and multiple tests can be scored at the same time. An interpretive report is automatically produced. Even so, care should be taken to ensure accuracy of the report.

As mentioned, 12 scores are generated from the questionnaire. Of the 12 scores, 2 are validity scores. These are Inconsistent Responding (INC) and Defensiveness (DEF). Using INC, an inconsistency is noted if the difference between the paired items is greater than or equal to 2. There is no absolute cutoff score for a high INC score. An INC of 5 or more indicates a 71% probability of random or careless responding. Clients should be queried about their distractibility during test taking. The results of the INC score should be discussed in the interpretative report. The DEF score corresponding to items is indicative of an idealized self. If the DEF score is elevated, accuracy of responding to the questionnaire as a whole is questionable.

Of the 10 remaining scores, 6 of the scores are classified under the category Eating-Related Habits and Attitudes. This cluster of scores identifies positive and negative habits and attitudes that enhance or interfere with maintenance of healthy body weight. These scores are: Overeating (OVER), Undereating (UNDER), Craving (CRAV), Expectations About Eating (EXP), Rationalizations (RAT), and Motivation to Lose Weight (MOT). The 4 remaining scales are classified as General Health Habits and Psychosocial Functioning. These scores are: Health Habits (HEAL), Body Image (BODY), Social Isolation (SOCIS), and Affective Disturbance (AFF). This cluster of scores identifies positive and negative aspects of the environment that enhance or interfere with the maintenance of healthy body weight. Taken together, these scores are designed to help the clinician and client develop an effective, personalized weight reduction plan.

DEVELOPMENT. The OQ was formulated after extensive literature review, creation of an initial item pool of 140 items, and modification of the item pools and scales in two pilot tests. The initial items were related to attitudes toward weight, food and eating, self-image, and defensive response. Related questions were placed into different scales as they were identified in the pilot testing process. The 80-item questionnaire was derived from an intercorrelation evaluation of "fit" within the scales and from feedback from respondents. The INC score was incorporated after the final 80 questions were decided upon by correlation of item pairs. Pairs with a correlation of .50 or higher in the standardization sample were included in the sample. Readability was taken into consideration and the reading level for the final form is fourth grade.

TECHNICAL.

Standardization. A standardization sample of 1,788 individuals ranging in age from 9 to 98 from public, nonclinical settings (such as public schools) was used to standardize the OQ. Males, persons of color, and those with less education were somewhat underrepresented. Nonetheless, the authors examined differences among gender, ethnicity, age, education, and region of the United States. Standard scores held relatively true for these demographic variables. The authors are well aware of the need to continue their research in the area of differences among individuals from various demographic backgrounds.

Reliability. Estimates of internal consistency (coefficient alpha), item-to-scale correlations, and test-retest reliability were examined. All measures of reliability indicate that the OQ is a reliable measure. Specific values are generally acceptable to high with an internal consistency median value of .82 (.77 for respondents aged 9–10), item to scale correlations median value of .55, and test-retest correlation median value of .88. The first two estimates of reliability were conducted using the entire standardization sample. Test-retest reliability used a subgroup of 24 individuals aged 27–64 with a 1-week interval between testing. Further investigation of test-retest reliability is warranted given the small sample size and short retest interval.

Validity. Construct and discriminate validity measures were used to assess the validity of the OQ. Construct validity was evaluated in three ways: interscale correlations, a factor analysis showing the relationships among responses given to test items, and correlations between a scale and other measures of a similar characteristic. The first two measures showed strong evidence that the OQ scales measure unique although sometimes related constructs. The third measure indicated good correlation with other measures of similar characteristics and good negative correlation with other measures of opposite characteristics.

Discriminate validity was assessed in two ways. First, three subgroups from the standardization sample who indicated in one of three ways they were overweight were compared to the overall sample. As expected, individual scores from these groups differed significantly from those without weight problems on most scales. However, females scored differently on more scales than did males. Such a finding underscores the need for further research into gender and other demographic differences in scoring. Second, the standardization sample was compared to a group of individuals who were in treatment for mood disorders. All of these individuals were overweight. All but three scores were above average for this group as compared to the standardization group.

COMMENTARY. The major strength of the OQ is its measurement of the key habits, thoughts, and attitudes related to obesity in order to establish individualized weight loss programs. Thus, not only does the questionnaire focus on an important, yet often neglected area of eating disorders—obesity—it appears that it may be a useful instrument in the development of personalized weight loss programs. The efficacy of the latter claim needs further research, however. Administration and scoring are straightforward and the ability to administer the OQ to individuals or to a group is a plus.

The manual is well organized and is easy to read. Psychometric concepts are explained prior to giving the specific measures of the OQ and were well evaluated. More supporting interpretive comments would make the test more useful in clinical situations.

SUMMARY. The OQ appears to be a well-researched measure of factors that influence obesity. More research is needed in the efficacy of the instrument in establishing effective treatment protocols.

[140]

Paced Auditory Serial Attention Test.

Purpose: "To evaluate the capacity for sustained attention and rate of information processing."
Population: Ages 9–69.
Publication Date: 1998.
Acronym: PASAT.
Scores, 16: Response Type Summary, Total Correct Responses, Total Incorrect Responses, Total No-Responses, Total Correct Strings, Longest Correct String, Suppression Failures, Suppression Failure Index, Reaction Time Summary (Average [mean] Correct Responses, Average [mean] Incorrect Responses, Average [mean] Suppression Failures, Average [mean] Total Responses, Median Correct Responses, Median Incorrect Responses, Median Suppression Failures, Median Total Responses).
Administration: Individual.
Price Data: Not available.
Time: Administration time not reported.
Comments: Test is a software package and can be administered as standard, revised, abbreviated, children's, or customized version; the publisher advised in May 2007 that this test is now out of print.
Author: The Psychological Corporation.
Publisher: The Psychological Corporation, A Harcourt Assessment Company.

Review of the Paced Auditory Serial Attention Test by RUSSELL N. CARNEY, Professor of Psychology, Missouri State University, Springfield, MO:

DESCRIPTION. The Paced Auditory Serial Attention Test (PASAT) is a proprietary, computer-administered version of the Paced Auditory Serial Addition Test developed three decades ago

in New Zealand by Dorothy Gronwall and her associates (e.g., Gronwall, 1977; Gronwall & Wrightson, 1974). The general PASAT task requires examinees to "add pairs of numbers that are presented serially [aurally], while suppressing successive additions of numbers" (user's guide, p. 1). The current PASAT is presented via computer and was developed by John Cegalis and Walter Birdsall. It consists of Standard (60 frames), Revised (50 frames), Abbreviated (29 frames), and Children's (60 frames) versions. (A frame contains a pair of sequential numbers added to yield a sum.) The children's version is referred to as the CHIPASAT. This computerized version of the PASAT comes on four 3.5-inch disks and is designed for IBM-based PCs. Further system requirements are listed in the publisher's catalog. The computerized version utilizes seven computer screens that are titled as follows: Logon, Subject Data, Observation Setup, DSM Classification, Observations, Select Test, Instructions, Score a Test, Score Responses, and Summarize Data Screens.

To briefly illustrate the test administration, consider the 60-frame (Standard) version. The Standard version presents a pseudorandom set of 61 single-digit numbers (i.e., 1–9) aurally via computer at fixed intervals, and asks the examinee to add successive pairs, saying each sum aloud. That is, the first and second numbers are added, then the second and third numbers are added, and so forth through the 61 numbers presented. Four passes are made through this set of 61. The first pass is at a rate of 2.4 seconds per item, and is followed by passes at 2.0, 1.6, and 1.2 seconds per item. Other versions vary in terms of number of digits and timing. Also, although the sums on adult tests are no greater than 18, the sums on the children's version cannot be more than 10. Examinee performance is recorded in a database on the computer. One can also enter written comments.

The computerized version of the PASAT makes an audio recording of the responses that can then be manually checked against the correct answers presented on the computer screen. Reaction time is also recorded. From these data, 15 scores can be derived. Seven of these deal with Response Type (e.g., Total Correct Responses) and 8 deal with Reaction Time. These results are then portrayed both numerically and graphically on the screen titled Summarize Data. "The graph presents correct, incorrect, suppression failure, and no responses, with corresponding response times. The number of correct strings (2 or more consecutively correct responses) and the longest string are presented" (user's guide, p. 15).

The user's guide states that the PASAT is a "popular test of attention in neuropsychological and psychopathology research" (p. 1) and can be used by researchers and clinicians to get at such things as sustained attention, working memory, and information processing. The guide reports that this instrument is effective in discriminating between head-injured populations and normal populations, and is also useful in measuring recovery from mild head injury. In addition, PsychCorp's website (2006) suggests that the test gets at mental calculating abilities and the "ability to serially track numbers presented orally." The website goes on to say that the test is useful for measuring attention deficits in individuals with ADHD or who are blind.

DEVELOPMENT. Minimal information is provided in the user's guide regarding test development. The auditory-tape-based Paced Auditory Serial Addition Test was developed by Gronwall and her colleagues in New Zealand in the 1970s. Gronwall's goal was to distinguish individuals who had sustained a head injury from those who had not. Her version was an auditory modification of Sampson's (1956) PASAT. The children's version of the PASAT (i.e., the CHIPASAT) was developed by Dyche and Johnson in 1991.

TECHNICAL. The manual states that the use of norms is complicated by the fact that different response measures have been used over the years. That is, "differing sets of normative data have been derived from differing research paradigms" (p. 23). For example, Gronwall used 60 frames, whereas Levin used 50 frames, and so forth. Normative data are provided in the user's guide based on three studies, each published in 1991. Table 3 (n = 90) provides means and standard deviations (SDs) for 60 frames at the four presentation rates for three age groups (16–29, 30–49, 50–69). Table 4 (n = 519, IQs = 90–109) provides means and SDs for 50 frames at the four presentation rates for three age groups (25–39, 40–54, and >54). Finally, Table 5 (n = 70) provides just the means for 60 pairs (for sums <10) for the four presentation rates for six age groups (9–10, 10–11, 11–12, 12–13, 13–14, and 14–15 years).

Very little reliability information is provided in the user's guide for the adult portions of the PASAT. The guide mentions that Gronwall (1977) published evidence that practice effects on the PASAT were minimal. Also, Egan (1988) reported split-half reliability as .96. Of greater interest here would be estimates of test-retest reliability. However, such information is not provided for adults in the user's guide. The guide does provide test-retest reliability estimates for children. A study is cited that found test-retest reliabilities for the CHIPASAT ranging from .77 to .90, with the interval ranging from 18–35 days (mean = 25 days).

Although the term validity is not listed in the user's guide index, the guide does cite research results with adults and with children that provide evidence for validity. For example, several early research studies by Gronwall, Wrightson, and others demonstrated that brain-injured individuals do worse on the PASAT than do normal individuals. This research suggests that the test is valid for the purpose of identifying head injury and in measuring recovery. Further, the PASAT (which, again, is purported to get at attention and speed of information processing), correlates with the various performance subtests of the Wechsler IQ test—subtests that tap nonverbal abilities involving processing speed. The correlation of the PASAT with nonverbal intelligence was .71. Further, researchers have found that the PASAT loads most highly on the widely recognized third factor of the WAIS-R (i.e., working memory). Such findings represent convergent validity evidence for the PASAT. Further studies found correlations with Raven's Standard Progressive Matrices (r = .63) and Cattell's Culture-Fair Intelligence Test (r = .62). Raven's test is believed to be a relatively pure measure of general intelligence (i.e., g), and Cattell's test is designed to measure fluid intelligence (i.e., g_f). Also, researchers have described age effects for the PASAT. As expected, older individuals (60–75 years) had poorer performance than younger (18–50 years).

COMMENTARY. My review of the PASAT is based primarily on a careful review of the user's guide—and on actually taking the briefer, 29-frame version on a computer. Given the three-decade history of clinical practice and research with this instrument, one would expect to find thorough documentation of the test's reliability—at least in the audiotape format. However, the user's guide provides only minimal information in this regard. No test-retest reliability coefficients were provided for the adult version of the PASAT—although data were reported for children. The reliability data for the CHIPASAT seemed reasonable.

Validity evidence was reported under headings such as "Initial Research with Adults" and "Additional Research with Adults," rather than appearing in a "Validity" section per se. These sections provided support for some of the uses described in the user's guide. In general, the user's guide could be improved by providing more complete sections on the topics of reliability and validity. Indeed, the term "validity" does not appear in the guide's appendix. Given the test's lengthy history in different forms, I believe that additional reliability and validity information is out there—it just needs to be located and summarized in the guide. And, given the current version's ease of administration and scoring, new reliability and validity data based on the computerized version could be obtained and reported.

The computerized version of this test has a number of advantages over the prior audiotape version. These include such things as ease of administration, a reliable presentation rate (versus audiotapes, which can stretch), exact measurement of reaction time, computer storage of the data, and a nice summary of the results. In taking the 29-frame version, I offer the following observations. Installation via the four disks was straightforward, and the computer screens were fairly easy to negotiate. In taking the 29-frame version, I certainly found that it tapped concentration and the ability to do rapid mental calculations. Although I tried to say each sum quickly, some of my utterances were cut off on the computer's audio recording, making scoring those particular items difficult. It seems I was not stating the answer into the microphone quickly enough. The PASAT task in general may be a frustrating (and, perhaps, aversive) one for individuals who have more serious head injuries than those in the mild category. Finally, the user's guide cautions that storing audio/sound files from test administrations takes up a good deal of memory.

Two clinical examples are provided in the guide that illustrate how the PASAT can discriminate between head-injured and normal performance. However, citing the 1985 *Standards for Educational and Psychological Testing*, the guide rightly notes that the examiner needs the proper training to interpret this test (see Standard 11.3 in the *Standards*, AERA, APA, & NCME, 1999). Further, the user's guide provides the caveat that the PASAT should not be used in isolation to make a diagnosis (Standard 11.20 in the *Standards*, 1999).

SUMMARY. The Paced Auditory Serial Attention Test (PASAT) is a proprietary, computer-administered version of the classic Paced Auditory Serial Addition Test developed in the 1970s. After reviewing this test, and given its long history and wide use in clinical practice and research, I believe the PASAT is a useful tool for the clinician or researcher interested in measuring basic processes such as rate of information processing and sustained attention. Although limited reliability and validity data are provided in the manual, I suspect that the test would be helpful for the purpose of identifying those suffering mild head injury and measuring their subsequent recovery. More broadly, it may be useful in working with those who may have attention deficits.

REVIEWER'S REFERENCES

American Educational Research Association, American Psychological Association, & National Council on Measurement in Education. (1999). *Standards for educational and psychological testing.* Washington, DC: American Educational Research Association.
Egan, V. (1988). PASAT: Observed correlations with IQ. *Personality and Individual Differences, 9,* 179–180.
Gronwall, D. (1977). Paced auditory serial-addition task: A measure of recovery from concussion. *Perceptual and Motor Skills, 44,* 367–373.
Gronwall, D. M., & Wrightson, P. (1974, September 14). Delayed recovery of intellectual function after minor head injury. *Lancet,* 605–609.
Sampson, H. (1956). Pacing and performance on a serial addition task. *Canadian Journal of Psychology, 10,* 219–225.

Review of the Paced Auditory Serial Attention Test by ELIZABETH KELLEY RHOADES, Associate Professor of Psychology, West Texas A&M University, Canyon, TX:

DESCRIPTION. The Paced Auditory Serial Attention Test (PASAT) is a software package designed to "evaluate the capacity for sustained attention and rate of information processing" (user's guide, p. 1) for individuals aged 9 to 69. The examinee must listen to a series of numbers and add them while suppressing or ignoring the numbers heard previously. The test is designed to help identify those with deficits related to head injury and to gauge their recovery.

The test includes the necessary computer disks and a user's manual. A desktop or laptop computer is required for test administration, which involves a prerecorded set of instructions and a series of single digits presented aurally. The examiner must manually score each item by selecting the examinee's response. Results are stored and analyzed using a standardized database format.

The examiner determines the rate of the test (presentation of stimuli from 4.0 to 1.2 seconds) and the number of items (60, 50, or 29) for both the adult and children's versions. The computerized analysis of responses includes response accuracy, reaction time, frequency of correct and incorrect items, frequency of suppression failure, frequency of failure to respond, and tables of all data.

DEVELOPMENT. The test is an adaptation of Gronwall's 1974 Paced Serial Addition Test, which was itself an auditory adaptation of a test originally designed by Sampson in 1956. Although Gronwall's original test was designed to identify individuals with brain damage, the current measure purports to be useful for assessing attention in a variety of clinical populations as well as measuring recovery from head injury.

The original PASAT was based on Gronwall's theory that the test measures information processing capacity and sustained attention. Later work by Gronwall and Wrightson (1981) further proposed that the PASAT measures complex information processing under time pressure. Numerous studies have shown that Gronwall's earlier test can illustrate the cognitive deficits associated with brain injury (Gronwall & Wrightson, 1981). Dyche and Johnson (1991a, 1992b) developed a children's version of the measure. The original PASAT appears sensitive to the initial deficits and quick initial recovery period of head injury (Cripe, 1987).

TECHNICAL. The user's guide contains virtually no information about the development, standardization, reliability, or validity of the current instrument. There are some limited data on the original PASAT, but its relation to the newer test is unknown. For example, Egan (1988) reported that Gronwall's version of the PASAT had a split-half reliability coefficient of .96. No data could be found for the current version.

COMMENTARY. The Paced Auditory Serial Attention Test is an outgrowth of Gronwall's original PASAT. Although there is some limited information available on the development and psychometric properties of the original test, little is known about this adaptation. The user's guide provides very limited information and contains several errors such as missing and incorrect citations. Although the guide provides the "bare bones" necessary to administer and score the test, it is not easily understandable and lacks even the most basic background information. The PASAT may be useful for research purposes and appears to offer some improvements to the original PASAT. However, the current measure requires further study and establishment of its psychometric properties before it can be recommended for clinical use.

SUMMARY. The Paced Auditory Serial Attention Test is a revised version of Gronwall's PASAT, which uses computerized administration of the serial addition task. It gives the examiner options about the pace of the test, the number of items, and whether to use the adult or children's version of the measure. Little information is provided in the test materials concerning the psychometric properties of the test.

REVIEWER'S REFERENCES

Cripe, L. I. (1987). The neuropsychological assessment and management of closed head injury: General guidelines. *Cognitive Rehabilitation*, 18–22.

Dyche, G. M., & Johnson, D. A. (1991a). Development and evaluation of the CHIPASAT, an attention test for children: II. Test-retest reliability and practice effects for a normal sample. *Perceptual and Motor Skills, 72*, 563–572.

Dyche, G. M., & Johnson, D. A. (1991b). Information processing rates derived from the CHIPASAT. *Perceptual and Motor Skills, 73*, 720–722.

Egan, V. (1988). PASAT: Observed correlations with IQ. *Personality and Individual Differences, 9*, 179–180.

Gronwall, D., & Wrightson, P. (1981). Memory and information processing capacity after closed head injury. *Journal of Neurology, Neurosurgery, and Psychiatry, 44*, 889–895.

[141]

Parents' Observations of Infants and Toddlers.

Purpose: "Designed to identify young children with potential problems who may be in need of further diagnostic assessment."

Population: Ages 2–36 months.

Publication Date: 2006.

Acronym: POINT.

Scores, 4: Being Healthy & Early Moving Skills, Thinking/Talking & Early Learning Skills, Feelings/Learning About Others & Everyday Skills, Total.

Administration: Individual.

Levels, 6: Level 1 (2–6 months), Level 2 (6–9 months), Level 3 (9–12 months), Level 4 (12–18 months), Level 5 (18–24 months), Level 6 (24–36 months).

Price Data, 2007: $200 per complete basic kit including manual (2006, 112 pages), 12 record forms for each level in choice of Spanish or English, 1 set of record forms in the other language, 1 set of transparent scoring masks for each level, 1 set duplication masters of POINT Parent Conference Plan form, and the POINT Report Card in English and Spanish; $230 per complete bilingual kit including manual, 12 record forms for each level in both English and Spanish, 1 set of transparent scoring masks for each level, 1 set of duplication masters of the POINT Parent Conference Plan form and POINT Report Card in English and Spanish; $30 per POINT Portfolio; $35 per 12 record forms for each level in English or Spanish; $15 per 24 record forms for one level; $30 per 6 sets of transparent scoring masks; $10 per set of 3 Conference Plan and Report Card duplication masters.

Foreign Language Editions: Spanish version available; standardized in Spanish and English.

Time: (15–20) minutes.

Comments: Test to be completed by one or two parents/guardians and/or one or two caregivers.

Authors: Carol D. Mardell and Dorothea S. Goldenberg.

Publisher: Master Publishing, Inc.

Review of the Parents' Observations of Infants and Toddlers by JEAN N. CLARK, Associate Professor of Educational Psychology, University of South Alabama, Mobile, AL:

DESCRIPTION. The Parents' Observations of Infants and Toddlers (POINT) is a 128-item reporting tool for parents and primary caregivers of children ages 2–36 months. It is targeted to chart normal developmental milestones and to screen for current or potential problems in cognitive, physical, social-emotional, language, or school readiness development.

The instrument is administered at six levels on Forms 1–6: 2–6 months, 6–9 months, 9–12 months, 12–18 months, 18–24 months, and 24–36 months. The first section of the form requests demographic information about the child and responder. In the second section, parents and caregivers are asked 30–75 questions, to which they respond by marking a 3-point annotated scale, with choices being *Yes/Almost Always, Sometimes,* and *No/Almost Never/Not Yet.* Most items are repeated at two or more age levels. The items assess development in three areas: (a) Being Healthy and Early Moving Skills; (b) Thinking, Talking, and Early Learning Skills; and (c) Feelings, Learning about Others, and Everyday Skills.

The third section of the instrument contains four open-ended questions. The manual suggests these should be used, along with scores on the three variables, by the screening coordinator in follow-up conferences with the parents. The instrument is available in English and Spanish, and may be completed by parents or caregivers; or questions may be asked orally by a screening coordinator who records the responses. The assessment kit also contains an overlay "mask" for scoring, a POINT report card for noting scores and interpretation, and a Parent/Caregiver Conference Plan form.

DEVELOPMENT. The POINT is a new instrument, developed over 6 years (1999–2005) according to principles proposed by the National Education Goals Panel, which sets standards for such programs as Headstart. The manual contains a thorough review of literature and rationale for the variables assessed.

The instrument contained 218 items, which were screened by a panel of experts for clarity and cultural fairness (the authors call this a prevalidation stage), revised, sent to 17 reviewers in six countries, and then given a third review by a panel of eight experts. The third panel was asked to categorize items into eight discrete categories, but a preset 80% consensus was not reached. Specific analyses of these reviews were not presented in the manual. The panel was then asked to categorize the items according to five developmental areas used in the Individuals With Disabilities Education Act (IDEA). The manual reports that "consensus was easily reached" (p. 64), which resulted in the three variables in the current form. However, again neither methodology nor analyses were offered to describe this consensus.

Once the instrument was revised, a field study was conducted. The sample consisted of 213 English-speaking parents and caregivers, and 60 Spanish-speaking parents and caregivers. Data collection from eight U.S. states and Mexico was reported. A Generalizability or G-coefficient was used, described as an interrater coefficient "conceptually equivalent to the theoretically expected Cronbach Alpha" (manual, p. 66). The manual reports that 35% of the forms were completed by 4 respondents, and the other 65% were completed by 2 or 3 respondents. However, there is a reported G-coefficient of .9829 "using either a parent or a caregiver" (manual, p. 66). This index suggests that some forms were indeed completed by only 1 person. Other reported coefficients include .9872 using 1 parent and 1 caregiver, and .9895 using 2 parents and 2 caregivers.

Means for children already classified as special needs children were significantly lower (Mean = 403.32, *S.D.*= 76.70) than for regular children (Mean = 432.42, *S.D.* = 84.25), supporting the use of this instrument as a stage-one screening tool.

The manual states that significant differences were not found for gender, language (Spanish vs. English), or forms used. Again, specific supporting data analyses for these statements were not furnished.

TECHNICAL.

Sample. The sample used for standardization and normalization consisted of ratings for 1,142 children, drawn from 29 sites in 23 states. Site coordinators were recruited, who in turn recruited parents and caregivers to complete the forms. Although the field study had three age-level forms, the standardization process included the six forms as described above. No explanation for this change was offered. Because the authors used the standardization sample as the norming sample, the authors attempted to match population parameters to the 2000 U.S. Census by gender, nationality, family structure, and geographic location.

Reliability. An alpha coefficient was used to report "summative classical reliability" (manual, p. 68) for each of the three assessment categories: Being Healthy and Early Moving Skills; Thinking, Talking, and Early Learning Skills; and Feelings, Learning About Others, and Everyday Skills. Scores ranged from .62 to .85 on the 2–6-month form, .67 to .90 on the 6–9-month form, .62 to .88 on the 9–12-month form, .73 to .84 on the 12–18-month form, .74 to .93 on the 18–24 month form, and .67 to .94 on the 24–36-month form.

Interrater reliabilities of .63 to .83 were reported using Pearson correlation coefficients. Dyad ratings were reported on 96 children who were rated by four adults: two parents and two center-based caregivers. Dyads consisted of parent-parent, primary parent-caregiver, secondary parent-caregiver, and caregiver-caregiver. These results were based on the field study data, and no analogous analyses were reported for the standardization sample. Generalizability theory analyses also were used to evaluate interrater reliability. The G-coefficients ranged from .70 to .89.

Estimated cutoff scores for regular versus problematic scores were established using Phi (lambda) scores, which were all at or above the .99 level. Although the results are encouraging, the application of this relatively new theoretical model has not been used before in assessing an instrument such as the POINT; therefore, any positive support for reliability may be tenuous. On the other hand, this application may provide ancillary documentation of analysis via the generalization theory.

With the standardization sample, item discrimination among variables within each level showed moderate discrimination power of items. Gender and cultural analyses were reported, but they were the results from the field study sample only.

Validity. For content validity, the authors referred to the process used in the field study. No additional content review was reported for the standardization sample. To investigate instrument discrimination between regular and special needs children, means and standard deviations were compared, as in the field study. Even though the standardization sample was much larger than the field study sample, the number of special needs children was smaller; significant differences were found only in the three older groups. To assess "process-based evidence" (manual, p. 77) the authors attempted to determine whether the parents perceived the item as the item was intended. The assessment consisted of audio-tapes of adults who rated 61 children, and the responders were asked to process out loud as they scored the forms. The tapes were transcribed and submitted to qualitative analysis. Twelve items were subsequently revised or discarded.

COMMENTARY. The three categories that comprise the POINT contain critically different areas of development. The study began with eight categories, then five, then three. The reduction was based on a lack of agreement by experts about categorizing items. However, such a drastic reduction has blurred vitally needed specificity in determining developmental areas of "regular" versus "need" in interpretation. The moderate item discrimination power underlines this conclusion. A suggestion is to review these categories, attempting to define specific development in a larger and more discrete set of variables.

Validation support for the standardization sample was either retrospection to the field study, or described in general terms in the manual with no analytical support. Reliability was addressed by means of four methods, showing an overall consistency among items, raters, and developmental sequence.

In reporting data analyses, tables were found in the manual, its appendices, and an accompanying set of looseleaf printouts from the companion website. This dispersed representation of analysis, results, and interpretation is disturbing, and the authors refer the reader to the companion website, citing "saving trees" as partial rationale. A suggestion is to collect all data analyses and results under one umbrella, using statistical reports to substantiate claims now made only in expository form.

SUMMARY. The POINT forms are clear and straightforward, and it is reasonable to expect responders to complete them in the allocated 15–20 minutes, at 2–6-month intervals during the child's development. The process of completing a report and planning a parent conference is facilitated by the accompanying forms and the instructions in the test manual.

The manual is a strong teaching tool. The review of literature is thorough, and summaries are clear, easy to understand, and useful. In the technical sections, the tables are preceded by specific and informative descriptions of rationale and application.

The sample is large enough for the number of items and variables. The analyses are thorough, vigorous, and well-planned. However, a clear one-third of the results are described but not corroborated with actual data. In addition, the analyses from the field study and the standardization process are mixed, so that a careful scrutiny and distinction are necessary burdens of the reader.

The instrument can be useful, and the form itself is user-friendly. With more attention to rigorous analytical reporting and a review of variable content, the tool could become a standard for multicultural and multidisciplinary use.

Review of the Parents' Observations of Infants and Toddlers by LORAINE J. SPENCINER, Professor of Special Education, University of Maine at Farmington, Farmington, ME:

DESCRIPTION. The Parents' Observations of Infants and Toddlers (POINT) is a developmental screening instrument for children ages 2 months through 36 months of age. The POINT materials include a manual, six color-coded forms that coincide with specific age levels, scoring templates, and a reproducible planning form for the parent conference and "report card."

The manual uses the term "screening coordinator" rather than "examiner" who administers, scores, and interprets the assessment. The qualifications of this individual, in part, include knowledge of and experience with administrative procedures, experience with infants and toddlers and parents from diverse linguistic and cultural backgrounds, skills in establishing rapport with adults, and competence in administering, scoring, and interpreting the POINT.

The age-level color-coded screening form, which may be completed by the parent or caregiver, consists of three parts. In Part I: Personal/Medical Facts, questions focus on the family and the child's health history. The manual points out that this section is included because the research indicates a relationship between these factors and developmental problems.

Part II: Current Growth consists of a series of questions appropriate to a child's age level. According to the manual, the instrument "includes an empirically-based developmental sequence of behaviors in motoric, cognitive, communicative, adaptive, and social-emotional areas" (p. 2). Items in these areas are reported under one of three subscales: (a) Being Healthy and Early Moving Skills; (b) Thinking, Talking and Early Learning Skills; and (c) Feelings, Learning about Others and Everyday Skills. The parent(s) and/or the primary caregiver complete the form by reading each question and checking one of three responses: *yes/almost always, sometimes,* or *no/almost never/not yet.* The form is available in English or Spanish. According to the manual, questions are written at a third-grade reading level to accommodate adults with first languages other than English or Spanish. The questions may be read to the respondent, if necessary. The screening coordinator uses a scoring template to score responses to Part II.

In Part III: Overall Growth the parent or caregiver responds to open-ended questions about the child's development. Questions are worded to provide the respondent an opportunity to indicate both strengths and concerns about the child's development.

In calculating POINT scores, raw scores are converted to standard scores with a mean of 100 and a standard deviation of 15. The POINT uses three cutoff criteria: -1.0 standard deviation, -1.3 standard deviations, or -1.5 standard deviations. On the scoring form, these are reported in cutoff percentiles: 15th, 10th, and 7th, respectively. Scoring tables in the manual allow the screening coordinator to use the cutoff percentile to identify the child's score as "possible problem" or "OK."

The Parent/Caregiver Conference Plan form provides a format for discussing screening results and developing a follow-up plan with the parent or caregiver. The manual includes a description of how to synthesize information and how to use the Checkpoint Discussion and Talking Point Discussion during the conference. According to the manual, Checkpoints include items that are criterion-referenced as well as norm-referenced and provide a "double check on functional developmental milestones" (p. 36). The Checkpoints are indicated on the scoring template to assist the screening coordinator in identifying important areas to discuss, based on the child's score. Similarly, the service coordinator identifies Talking Points, which indicate difficulties that the child may be having.

The Report Card form provides a format for documenting each of the child's screenings. With parent consent, this form may be sent to the child's doctor or an agency working with the family.

DEVELOPMENT. During the development of this screening instrument, test items first were assessed by a prevalidation panel of experts to review on relevance, representativeness, cultural fairness, and appropriate wording. Next, the items were reviewed by individuals in the U.S., Mexico, Argentina, Israel, Sweden, and Taiwan to assess on the previous dimensions as well as from a cultural viewpoint. These studies resulted in some items being deleted due to cultural bias and rewording, according to the manual.

Additionally, a content validation panel, consisting of experts representing different disciplines, reviewed the test items. When panel members did not reach a minimum of 80% agreement, the test item was eliminated, resulting in the elimination of additional test items. For interested reviewers, all names of individuals who served on these prevalidation and content validation panels are listed in the manual's appendix.

The manual also describes the link between theory, research findings, and items within each of the three subscales. References to the literature are generally within the last 10 years.

TECHNICAL. According to the manual, the POINT was standardized in 2002–2003 on a total of 1,142 children. There were 947 English-speaking parents or caregivers and 195 individuals who indicated Spanish as the primary language spoken at home. This latter group completed the Spanish version. The sample approximated the U.S. 2000 Census data according to gender, race/ethnicity, family structure, and geographic location. Norms were developed for each 2 month interval from 2-months through 36 months of age.

The manual reports both classical and contemporary reliability information. Internal consistency, estimated through the coefficient alpha, is generally high (most subtests falling in the .70 to .80 range). The manual includes a thorough discussion of the difficulties with interrater reliability when an instrument relies on caregivers' reports. The POINT recommends that providers with the *primary* care-giving responsibility complete the report.

Each of the age-level forms were evaluated for classification reliability. Using Phi Lambda, coefficient method (generalizability theory, Brennan, 2001), the manual reports high values of cutoff scores for all age groups. Based on this information, it appears that the POINT may be used with a high degree of confidence in identifying children who should be referred for further assessment.

Rasch analyses were used to supplement the classical item analysis and to determine if the selected test items were placed in the appropriate age level forms. Inconsistencies were examined and final item placement was based on the following: Rasch difficulty parameters, child development theory, and known facts.

The manual reports contemporary validity measures based on the Testing Standards (American Educational Research Association, American Psychological Association, & National Council on Measurement in Education, 1999). Content validation included prevalidation and validation panels of experts who reviewed test items on a number of dimensions. Evidence based on response-based process is reported in the manual as the results of an independent study and subsequent discarding or further modifying of items.

Evidence based on relations with other variables included analyses of the scores of premature infants and children with special needs. Due to inadequate numbers of children with special needs in the younger age categories, statistical tests were not performed; in the three older age categories, children who were developing typically scored about one standard deviation above the group of children with special needs.

COMMENTARY. The POINT is a well-constructed screening measure that provides a parent or primary caregiver's perspective on the development of the child. The response form is available in English or Spanish. During the development of this instrument, the authors paid careful attention to cultural fairness and relevance of test items. Certainly, careful attention to these areas is critical for instruments entering the market today.

The POINT is designed to be used by a "screening coordinator," an individual with skills in working with infants and toddlers and families and competence in using and interpreting the POINT. Unquestionably, knowledge and skills in working with very young children and their families are necessary for individuals who conduct screenings of this age group and the manual clearly outlines these skills. The provision of a scoring template minimizes the potential for scoring errors. The manual also includes helpful examples of how to calculate subscores and the total score. These are well-written and welcome additions for someone learning how to use this instrument and/or who may not have had formal coursework in tests and measurements. Of particular note is a chapter in the manual entitled "Interpreting POINT Results with Parents and Caregivers." This chapter provides the screening coordinator with valuable information and suggestions for organizing screening information and for sharing with parents.

However, the discussion of standard scores and percentiles for determining cutoffs could be confusing for the individual who has a minimal background in assessment. The manual simply offers, "Prior to screening any children, the screening coordinator should first select one of three common cut-off criteria used in early childhood assessment to identify problematic children" (p. 31). Usually screening cutoffs are determined by the agency or the local team of professionals. In a high-stakes decision, such as selecting a screening cutoff, it is both inappropriate and potentially harmful for an individual with minimal formal training to make this decision.

The POINT terminology in each of the three subscales (Being Healthy and Early Moving Skills; Thinking, Talking and Early Learning Skills; and Feelings, Learning About Others and Everyday Skills) provides an indication that this screening is family-friendly. These subscales remain the same throughout each of the six age levels. Because children are usually screened and rescreened several times during the early childhood years, the consistency of these categories across age levels will assist in comparing an individual child's scores.

In contrast with the fitting terms discussed above, the manual fails to use appropriate terminology when referring to children with disabilities. Since 1997, when the Individuals with Disabilities Education Act first mandated the use of people-first language, the child is mentioned first, then the disability. In a future edition, the authors should correct the manual by inserting this more appropriate language.

SUMMARY. The Parents' Observations of Infants and Toddlers (POINT) is a well-constructed developmental screening instrument for children ages 2 months through 36 months of age. The parent or primary caregiver completes the form based on knowledge and observation of the child. Forms are available in either English or Spanish. The manual reports information regarding the standardization sample, reliability, and validity measures. The POINT appears to be technically adequate and may be used with assurance for the purpose of screening very young children and to identify those children who may have a disability and should be referred for further assessment.

REVIEWER'S REFERENCES

American Educational Research Association, American Psychological Association, & National Council on Measurement in Education. (1999). *Standards for educational and psychological testing.* Washington, DC: American Educational Research Association.
Brennan, R. (2001). *Generalizability theory.* New York: Springer-Verlag.

[142]

PDD Behavior Inventory.

Purpose: Designed to assist in the assessment of children who have been diagnosed with a pervasive developmental disorder.

Population: Ages 1-6 to 12-5.

Publication Dates: 1999—2005.

Acronym: PDDBI.

Scores, 51: 29 Approach/Withdrawal Problems scores: Approach/Withdrawal Problems Composite, Receptive/Ritualistic/Pragmatic Problems Composite, Sensory/Perceptual Repetitive Approach Behaviors (Visual Behaviors, Non-Food Taste Behaviors, Touch Behaviors, Proprioceptive/Kinesthetic Behaviors, Receptive Manipulative Behaviors), Ritualism/Resistance to Change (Resistance to Change in the Environment, Resistance to Change in Schedules/Routines, Rituals), Social Pragmatic Problems (Problems with Social Approach, Social Awareness Problems, Inappropriate Reactions to the Approaches of Others), Semantic/Pragmatic Problems (Aberrant Vocal Quality When Speaking, Problems with Understanding Words, Verbal Pragmatic Deficits), Arousal Regulation Problems (Kinesthetic Behaviors, Reduced Responsiveness, Sleep Regulation Problem [extended form only]), Specific Fears (Sadness When Away From Caregiver/Other Significant Figure/or in New Situation, Anxious When Away From Caregiver/Other Significant Figure/or in

New Situation, Auditory Withdrawal Behaviors, Fears and Anxieties, Social Withdrawal Behaviors [extended form only]), Aggressiveness (Self-Directed Aggressive Behaviors, Incongruous Negative Affect, Problems When Caregiver or Other Significant Figure Returns From Work/an Outing/or Vacation, Aggressiveness Toward Others, Overall Temperament Problems [extended form only]), 22 Receptive/Expressive Social Communication Abilities scores: Receptive/Expressive Social Communication Abilities Composite, Expressive Social Communication Abilities Composite, Social Approach Behaviors (Visual Social Approach Behaviors, Positive Affect Behaviors, Gestural Approach Behaviors, Responsiveness to Social Inhibition Cues, Social Play Behaviors, Imaginative Play Behaviors, Empathy Behaviors, Social Interaction Behaviors [parent/caregiver form only], Social Imitative Behaviors), Expressive Language (Vowel Production, Consonant Production at the Beginning/Middle/and End of Words, Diphthong Production, Expressive Language Competence, Verbal Affective Tone, Pragmatic Conversational Skills), Learning/Memory/Receptive Language (General Memory Skills, Receptive Language Competence [extended form only]), Autism Composite, SOCPP-SOCAPP Discrepancy Score, SEMPP-EXPRESS Discrepancy Score.

Administration: Individual or group.

Forms, 4: Parent/Guardian or Teacher, Standard or Extended.

Price Data, 2007: $230 per complete kit including professional manual (2005, 545 pages), 25 Parent Rating forms, 25 Teacher Rating forms, 25 Parent Score Summary sheets, 25 Teacher Score Summary sheets, and 50 Profile forms; $75 per professional manual; $60 per 25 Parent Rating forms; $60 per 25 Teacher Rating forms; $15 per 25 Parent Score Summary sheets; $15 per 25 Teacher Score Summary sheets; $25 per 50 Profile forms; $225 per unlimited use PDDBI Scoring Program Software CD.

Time: (30—45) minutes for Extended forms; (20—30) minutes to Standard forms.

Comments: Ratings from both parents and multiple teachers/school personnel is desirable.

Authors: Ira L. Cohen and Vicki Sudhalter.

Publisher: Psychological Assessment Resources, Inc.

Review of the PDD Behavior Inventory by KAREN CAREY, Professor of Psychology, California State University, Fresno, CA:

DESCRIPTION. The PDD Behavior Inventory (PDDBI) is designed for the assessment of children from ages 1 year, 6 months to 12 years, 5 months, who have been diagnosed with any of the Pervasive Developmental Disorders described in the DSM-IV. The primary application of the PDDBI is to assess children with Autism, but it can be used to assess children with Asperger's Disorder, Rett's Disorder, and Childhood Integrative Disorder. The PDDBI consists of a Parent Rating form (188 items), a Teacher Rating form (180 items), a Parent Score summary sheet, a Teacher Score summary sheet, and a Profile form. Extended and Standard forms are available for both the Parent and Teacher ratings (one form is used for parents and teachers, but fewer items are required for the Standard form). The Extended form takes 30–45 minutes to administer, and the Standard form takes 20 to 30 minutes to administer. The authors recommend that the Extended form be administered if areas of behavior other than those associated with autism (e.g., fears or aggression) are of concern.

Formal training is not required to administer the PPDBI; however, only individuals with graduate training in clinical, school, or counseling psychology, or developmental/behavioral pediatrics should interpret the inventory, as a complete understanding of the DSM-IV is needed for interpretation. Informants should know the child well, and should have had contact with the child either in the school or home setting for a minimum of 4 weeks. Those with the most recent and frequent contact should be asked to complete the forms. Scoring can be completed by hand or by using the PDDBI Scoring Program, which yields a score report. Cluster raw scores are first calculated, followed by calculations of each domain resulting in a composite score. Composites include Repetitive, Ritualistic, and Pragmatic Problems; Approach/Withdrawal Problems; Expressive Social Communication Abilities; and Repetitive/Expressive Social Communication Abilities. Scores are then transferred to the appropriate summary sheet. T scores are obtained from the normative tables contained in the manual and include an Autism Composite, as well as Discrepancy scores (i.e., calculation of differences between specific clusters). Scores can then be transferred to the profiling graph sheet, and T scores can be plotted. Shading on the profile indicates an average range for children with Autism (T scores between 40 and 60). Domain scores are divided into two sections, Approach/Withdrawal and Receptive-Expressive Social Communication. The authors stress that for the Approach/Withdrawal Problems domain, higher T scores indicate increasing levels of severity; for the Receptive-Expressive Social Communication Abilities domain, higher T scores suggest increasing levels of competency. The manual provides extensive information about the interpretation of the PDDBI including 10 domains for each rating form, five composite scores, and three discrepancy scores.

DEVELOPMENT. The manual provides excellent information about the development and standardization of the PDDBI. The rationale for inclusion and definitions of clusters, domains, composites, and discrepancies are extensive and provide the examiner excellent information for interpreting the scale. The domains selected for inclusion were based on their relevance to the diagnosis of Autism and their relevance to other behaviors frequently associated with Autism. Items selected were based on the authors' observations of working with children with PDD, the social communication literature, the autism literature, and children's language usage. Domains were developed independently in order to allow researchers to assess behaviors that may change over short periods of time.

The PDDBI was developed over a period of 9 years. Pilot testing of the initial version contained 306 items in seven domains. Field tests were conducted in New York and California, and results of principal components and internal consistency analyses resulted in several modifications of the instrument, including adding and combining domains.

TECHNICAL. The inventory was normed on 369 parents and 277 teachers of children from 1 year, 6 months to 12 years, 5 months with PDD and nine age groups resulted from the analyses. Approximately 75% of the children rated by parents and teachers were male, and 86% of all cases were rated as having Autism. Diagnoses were confirmed in the majority of cases by the Autism Diagnostic Interview—Review (ADI-R) and the Autism Diagnostic Observation Schedule (ADOS). The parents were predominantly Caucasian, with African Americans, Hispanics, Others, and Unknowns included in the sample, although proportions were not specified for parents, teachers, or children.

Internal consistency reliability was moderate to high for all domains and composite scores on both the Extended and Standard forms (alpha coefficients from .80s to .90s) except for four domains. The alpha coefficients for the Social Pragmatics Problems domain in the youngest age group was .60 and .41 for both Parent and Teacher scales, respectively, and .73 for the Semantic/Pragmatic Problems domain on the Parent scale. On the Teacher scale for the Ritualisms/Resistance to Change domain, an alpha coefficient of .55 was obtained. Stability was assessed using 28 cases, comparing parent ratings approximately 12 months (range 92 to 910 days) following the initial assessment. Correlations for the Extended and Standard forms domain and composite scores ranged from .38 to .91. Interrater reliability estimates were based on 237 children where both the parent and teacher completed the Standard and Extended forms, or where two teachers completed the Extended and Standard forms ($N = 20$). Interrater reliabilities for the Parent and Teacher forms double corrected for restriction of range were between .24 and .82. For the Teacher-to-Teacher forms, interrater reliability correlations double corrected for restriction of range were between .32 and .92. Verbally mediated domains yielded the highest interrater reliabilities.

The content validity of the PDDBI of each form indicated overall differential validity of the domains and composites. Construct validity was examined through principal components analysis to confirm the Approach/Withdrawal Problems and the Receptive/Expressive Social Communication Abilities structure of the PDDBI. Criterion-related validity was examined by comparing the PDDBI forms to the Childhood Autism Rating Scale (CARS), the Nisonger Child Behavior Rating Form (CBRF), the Vineland Adaptive Behavior Scales, and the Griffiths Mental Development Scales with correlations ranging from very low (.00) to high (.84). Clinical validity, "the extent to which the domain and composite scores are informative regarding diagnosis, clinical classifications of adaptive functioning level, and comorbidity issues" (professional manual, p. 73) were examined. Statistical comparisons between The Autism Diagnostic Interview—Revised (ADI-R), the Autism Diagnostic Observation Schedule—Generic (ADOS-G), the Vineland Adaptive Behavior Scales, and Seizure Disorder history and the PDDBI indicated that the PDDBI scores are strongly predictive of functioning on these scales.

COMMENTARY. With the increase of children diagnosed with autism over the last 10 to 15 years, instruments with good technical adequacy are needed to insure not only appropriate diagnoses, but more importantly, whether children are responding to the interventions developed and implemented. Many of the instruments currently available to assist clinicians in diagnosing autism are qualitative in nature, do not provide age-standardized scoring, and do not yield standard scores. Others assess only problem behaviors. The PDDBI can be used with both teachers and parents, and the comparisons can be useful in determining differences in child behavior from home to day care/school settings. Test-retest reliability of instruments generally is done over a period of weeks. The fact that the authors conducted follow-up studies with some children from 3 months to almost 3 years (average = 1 year) provides a start for clinicians wanting to determine the effectiveness of interventions developed for children with PDD.

SUMMARY. The PDDBI appears to be a good instrument for diagnosing and developing interventions for children with autism, and for assessing response to intervention. Few instruments have demonstrated acceptable levels of test-retest reliability over a 1-year interval, and although the sample size for this study was small (*N* = 28), the authors are commended for doing so. The authors provide an extensive manual with complete tables, research, and case studies to document the technical adequacy of the inventory, meeting the requirements of the *Standards for Educational and Psychological Testing* (AERA, APA, & NCME, 1999). The standardization sample size is small and more information is needed related to the demographics of the sample, including the children and teachers. Further research is needed with the inventory to demonstrate usefulness.

REVIEWER'S REFERENCE

American Educational Research Association, American Psychological Association, & National Council on Measurement in Education. (1999). *Standards for educational and psychological testing.* Washington, DC: American Educational Research Association.

Review of the PDD Behavior Inventory by KATHRYN E. HOFF, *Associate Professor, and* RENÉE M. TOBIN, *Assistant Professor, Psychology Department, Illinois State University, Normal, IL:*

DESCRIPTION. The PDD Behavior Inventory (PDDBI) is an individual rating scale designed to assist in the assessment and treatment of children from the age of 1 year, 6 months to 12 years, 5 months who have been diagnosed with a pervasive developmental disorder (PDD) as de-

fined by the DSM-IV (American Psychiatric Association, 1994). The PDDBI was developed to (a) provide age-standardized scores for parent and teacher ratings, (b) measure adaptive and problem behaviors pertinent to autism, (c) assess generality of change using both parent and teacher inventories, (d) evaluate change over time and responsiveness to intervention, and (e) be useful across a variety of settings (e.g., research applications and clinical or educational settings).

The test kit contains Parent and Teacher Rating forms, Parent and Teacher Score summary sheets, a PDDBI Profile form, and a professional manual. The manual is well organized, easy to understand, and information regarding administration and scoring is straightforward. The authors provide a brief overview of autism and PDD, such as co-morbidity, prevalence, diagnostic history, and assessment. The Standard form takes between 20 to 30 minutes to complete, and the Extended form takes approximately 30 to 45 minutes to complete.

The Parent and Teacher rating forms include a standard set of items (Parent = PDDBI-P and Teacher = PDDBI-T, consisting of 124 items each) to assess behaviors specifically associated with autism and an optional extended set of items (Parent = PDDBI-PX, with 188 items; Teacher = PDDBI-TX, with 180 items) to assess other relevant behaviors that may be of concern (e.g., specific fears or aggression). The PDDBI Standard rating form consists of items in six domains for both the Parent and the Teacher versions, and the Extended Rating Form consists of 10 domains (6 maladaptive and 4 adaptive). Domain scores are divided into two sections: (a) Approach/Withdrawal Problems and (b) Receptive-Expressive Social Communication Abilities. Additionally, domain scores are grouped into five composite scores: (a) Repetitive, Ritualistic, and Pragmatic Problems Composite; (b) Approach/Withdrawal Problems Composite (Extended Form only); (c) Expressive Social Communication Abilities Composite; (d) Receptive/Expressive Social Communication Abilities Composite (Extended Form only); and (e) Autism Composite.

Items are rated on a 4-point Likert-type scale reflecting frequency (*does not show behavior* = 0 and *usually/typically shows behavior* = 3). To the right of the response options, there is a question mark column (indicating "Don't understand") for the respondent to circle if they do not understand or have questions. Scoring is accomplished by first summing items within each cluster to obtain cluster scores then calculating a domain raw score by summing the corresponding cluster scores. Raw cluster scores are converted to a percentile range (low, moderate, high, and very high), and raw domain/composite scores are converted to norm-referenced scores (*T*-scores and percentiles).

DEVELOPMENT. The development of the PDDBI was guided by professional theory and practice in autism assessment. According to the authors, the PDDBI was created due to limitations of existing autism assessment instruments (e.g., lack of age-standardized scoring, measuring response to intervention, and assessing adaptive behavior). Items on the PDDBI were derived from the research literature and the authors' clinical experiences. However, the manual contains limited information about the development of items, why certain items were included, criteria for item selection, or the relevancy of items to other indicators.

TECHNICAL.

Standardization. The normative sample is based on ratings from 369 parents and 277 teachers of children from 1 year, 6 months to 12 years, 5 months of age. The sample was approximately 75% male and there was a wide distribution across different ages. For specific age categories, participant numbers ranged considerably from 17 to 44 for Teacher ratings and from 31 to 54 for Parent ratings. The sample is limited in terms of racial/ethnic diversity, with approximately 68% Caucasian, 3% African American, 3% Hispanic American, 6% Other, and 19% unknown. The geographical representativeness of the sample was not specified. Children in the normative sample included approximately 86.35% diagnosed with autism (between 63–70% of cases confirmed with the ADI-R and/or ADOS-G), 11.5% PDD-NOS, and 2.3% Other.

Reliability. Test-retest reliabilities for the parent form were collected over several intervals for a sample of 28 children during a 12-month period; however, specific information regarding the demographics of children in the subsample is lacking. Thus, the representativeness of the sample cannot be determined. Correlation coefficients on the parent form ranged from .38 to .91. Test-retest reliability was in the acceptable to good range (.77–.93) for the Approach/Withdrawal

Problems Composite, Social Approach Behaviors, Expressive Language, Expressive Social Communication Abilities Composite, and Receptive/Expressive Social Communication Composite. All other scales were in the poor to moderate range (.38–.68), including the Autism Composite (.65). Test-retest data for the Teacher form were collected from a sample of 17 teachers rating students in an early intervention program over a 2-week interval and ranged from .60 to .99. Ratings of these same youth were also collected after 6 months, and stability coefficients ranged from .58 to .99.

Internal consistency reliability coefficients collapsed across age groups were acceptable for all domains and composite scores (range = .80–.98 for parent and .81–.98 for teacher). Alpha coefficients by age indicate low reliability for some domains at specific ages. Interrater reliability evidence was based on Parent and Teacher ratings of the same child (*N* = 237) or ratings from two teachers on the same child (*N* = 20). Similar to results obtained from other cross-informant rating scales, a low to moderate degree of convergence was obtained for most categories between Parent and Teacher ratings (range = .23–.82) and higher convergence among two teacher raters (range = .40–.99). In general, higher interrater reliability coefficients were obtained for verbally mediated domains.

Validity. The authors assessed developmental validity of domain and composite scores using one-way analyses of variance with age as the independent variable. Results indicated a significant change in raw score means for most domain and composite scores; however, it is important to note that these data were generated from the cross-sectional sample rather than a longitudinal one. Criterion validity was assessed by comparing PDDBI parent and teacher ratings with other well-established measures (Childhood Autism Rating Scale, the Nisonger Child Behavior Scales, Autism Diagnostic Interview—Revised, the Autism Diagnostic Observation Schedule—Generic, the Vineland Adaptive Behavior Scales, and the Griffiths Mental Development Scales). Correlations between the PDDBI and other established instruments were generally in the low to moderate range, with the exception of adaptive scales of the PDDBI, which were moderately to highly correlated with sections of the Vineland Adaptive Behavior Scales and Griffiths Mental Development Scales. Although the authors state the Childhood

Autism Rating Scale was used as a validity check for the Autism Composite score, there were low to moderate correlations (.48 Parent and .32 for Teacher).

COMMENTARY. The PDDBI has several strengths. The authors investigated a population that warrants further attention, and the instrument incorporated information on maladaptive and adaptive behaviors. This instrument would nonetheless benefit from continued research with a larger normative group. The manual is clear and easy to use. The instructions for administration and scoring are straightforward and the authors provide many examples. Criterion validity was assessed comparing the PDDBI with a variety of other hallmark autism assessment instruments. Further, the reliability data were satisfactory for some subscales and age groups, but caution should be used with several age ranges and scales.

There are a number of limitations of the PDDBI. Foremost is a limited standardization sample. The standardization sample is of particular concern due to the small number of participants that make up some of the age groups. For example, some specific age categories included as few as 17 individuals, which is a concern for assessing such a heterogeneous sample as children with autism. Additionally, data were not provided about the functioning of youth within the standardization sample (low, medium, high, and very high functioning), despite these categories being used with the scale. Further, almost 98% of the standardization sample consisted of children with autism or PDD-NOS. Information about how the sample relates to the normal population is lacking. In addition, because of the low numbers of students diagnosed with a pervasive developmental disorder other than autism (e.g., Rett's Disorder or Asperger's Disorder), it is questionable whether this scale can be used with the full range of autism spectrum disorders.

One of the main objectives of the PDDBI was to create a measure to assess change over time and responsiveness to intervention for children diagnosed with a pervasive developmental disorder. Although this would clearly be a contribution to the diagnostic treatment planning literature, the authors provided no evidence supporting the use of the PDDBI for intervention planning or monitoring. A second main objective of the PDDBI was to assist in the assessment of children with a possible pervasive developmental disorder. However, validity data supporting the use of the PDDBI as a diagnostic tool are limited. The standardization sample consisted solely of youth diagnosed with a pervasive developmental disorder (i.e., typical children and children with mental retardation were not included in the sample), and no data were provided on the discriminant validity or sensitivity/specificity of the PDDBI. Evidence offered in support of clinical validity is insufficient to document that the PDDBI accurately differentiates between low-functioning, typical, or high-functioning individuals with autism. Thus, its value for diagnosis, making educational decisions, facilitating interventions, and assessing response to intervention is limited.

SUMMARY. The PDD Behavior Inventory (PDDBI) is a rating scale completed by parents and teachers and is designed to assist in the assessment and treatment of a child with a pervasive developmental disorder. The PDDBI is easy to administer, score, and interpret, and the manual provides detailed information for the examiner. However, validity evidence is limited and the purported uses of this test are not fully substantiated. The standardization sample is also limited. The psychometric properties of the PDDBI do not support its use for decision-making or treatment-monitoring purposes. Currently, this scale is recommended for research purposes but cannot be recommended for clinical use until further testing and analysis have been completed.

REVIEWERS' REFERENCE

American Psychiatric Association. (1994). *Diagnostic and statistical manual of mental disorders* (4th ed.). Washington, DC: Author.

[143]
Performance Series.

Purpose: A computer-adaptive assessment of student performance and progress, modified to measure the different academic objectives of individual state standards.

Population: Grades 2–10.

Publication Dates: 2002–2006.

Scores, 21: Reading (Vocabulary, Fiction, Nonfiction, Long Passages, Total), Mathematics (Number & Operations, Algebra, Geometry, Measurement, Data Analysis & Probability, Total), Language Arts (Capitalization, Parts of Speech, Punctuation, Sentence Structure, Total), Science (Ecology, Science Processes, Living Things, Total), Total.

Administration: Group.

Price Data, 2006: $12–$15 per student annual subscription cost.
Time: (60) minutes per subject area.
Comments: Web-administered, computer-adaptive instrument for Windows or Macintosh platforms; bookmarking allows students to take assessments over more than one test period.
Author: Scantron Corporation.
Publisher: Scantron Corporation.

Review of the Performance Series by CARLEN HENINGTON, Associate Professor of School Psychology, Mississippi State University, Mississippi State, MS:

DESCRIPTION. The Performance Series Computer Adaptive Internet Assessment for Schools (the Performance Series) is an untimed internet-delivered computer-adaptive test (CAT) designed to provide schools with diagnostic assessment data regarding students' (Grades 2–10) levels of academic competence and progress on curriculum and classroom instruction. The author indicates that the system works with national, state, and district standards and relies on Item Response Theory to determine specific test items administered to an individual student in Reading (Grades 2–10), Mathematics (Grades 2–9 nationally and Grades 2–12 in some states), Science (Grades 2–8), and Language Arts (Grades 2–8). A fixed form is also available. Units of performance covered include: (a) Reading—Vocabulary, Fiction, Nonfiction, and Long Passage; (b) Mathematics—Algebra, Geometry, Measurement, Data Analysis & Probability, and Number & Operations (problem solving and computational skills); (c) Science—Living Things, Ecology, and Science Processes; and (d) Language Arts—Capitalization, Parts of Speech, Punctuation, and Sentence Structure. As a criterion-referenced test, the Performance Series provides a variety of scores for individual and group comparison for curriculum placement, progress tracking, and prediction of performance on high stakes tests. These scores include: scaled scores (range 1300–3700), gain score (gain from one testing session to the next), standard item pool score (probability of answering each item within the item pool correctly), reading rate, and a Lexile measure (a developmental reading scale to assist in selection of text with a 75% comprehension rate). The scale score and the state curriculum alignment guide (for Math, Science, and Language Arts) can be used to identify skills

aligned with state standards. Additionally, student reading profile reports (e.g., reading rate, skill level) and the student math profile offer information on specific areas of strengths and weaknesses.

The Performance Series, designed to take 1 hour per subject area (approximately 50 questions per student), may be used three times a year to monitor progress. Longer administration time may be required for those with skill levels significantly different from grade peers. The authors suggest two 1-hour class periods be held for the set-up and testing for each subject area. Specific test questions are not published; and, due to the adaptive nature of Performance Series, no two students are expected to have the same sequence of questions.

The Performance Series can be used to show annual yearly progress (AYP), as well as to provide projected scores of individuals and groups on statewide tests. Available reports include: student, testing status, class, grade or district level, and gains/history profiles and Suggested Learning Objectives (SLO) reports. Each report can be sorted by a variety of demographics and can be stored long-term with "rollover" from year to year. Two days of mandatory training (pretest site set-up training and posttest data interpretation training) are provided either online or onsite.

DEVELOPMENT. The current version (Performance Series 4.0) was released by the Scantron Corporation in July 2006. Testing materials, extensive support materials, and all reports are located online within the program with well-written manuals available for administrators and users. The Performance Series is constructed to align with national, state, and district standards and relies upon Item Response Theory to adapt to individual ability. Although no data are provided about correlations with measures of performance on standards, the authors indicate that alignment can be accomplished for any purpose through the use of the Curriculum Alignment Guide (displaying the standards next to the corresponding learning objectives for Math, Language Arts, and Science). No alignment guide is available for Reading due to the consistency of learning objective (i.e., comprehension). To this end, the authors have developed an extensive list of skills and learning objectives commonly taught across the U.S. The technical manual provides an extensive list of skills (70 pages) for the four content areas to which items are compared on aspects such as critical skill needed, grade appropriateness, and comparison to grade-level objectives.

A team of developers engaged in a number of activities to develop items initially: (a) grade level of Reading passages was determined based on a number of reading indices (e.g., Flesch, Fry Graph); (b) Mathematics, Language Arts, and Science were examined for grade-level and contextual appropriateness; and (c) depth of knowledge was rated based on two taxonomies (Bloom's Taxonomy [1956] and one developed by Robert Marzano [2001]). For most items, knowledge depth was reported at Levels 1 through 3, of the five levels. Then, a group of independent editors (e.g., teachers, university professors) reviewed item content for age appropriateness, interest level, bias (e.g., gender, active versus passive voice, ethnicity/cultural diversity), sentence structure, vocabulary, clarity, and grammar/spelling. Once items passed this phase, they were examined statistically: (a) item analysis (pilot test) to determine initial p-values and distractor functioning; (b) review (field test) to obtain refined p-value and point biserial for each item; and (c) calibration (fixed, computer-administered forms) to determine item difficulty parameters. The calibration stage was conducted in Mathematics and Reading with a minimum of 200 students per grade. Criteria p-values were set between .30 and .75, with a minimum point biserial of .30. Recalibration was conducted in 2002 using an iterative approach with a Pearson correlation coefficient of greater than .9996 for both Mathematics and Reading. A principal component analysis on the standardized residual was conducted on 20,000 students to assure unidimensionality (items measure the same construct) in all four content areas. Finally, Differential Item Functioning (Plake, 1995) was used to determine differences in performance by subpopulations of examinees (i.e., gender, ethnicity; reported squared correlation estimates exceeded .997 for all four subjects). To replenish items, an item embedding process is used with a reported average of 5,000 new items introduced yearly for the four subject areas. These are examined on four occasions with statistical examinations conducted at each stage (e.g., item difficulty, point biserial correlations). Overexposed items are retired out of the tests.

TECHNICAL. Fall and spring norms were developed for Grades 2 through 8 and high school based on gender, ethnicity (five larger ethnic groups roughly representative of census numbers), and geographic area (central, northeastern, western, southeastern) in Mathematics and Reading only. Tables are provided to assist teachers in understanding the standard scores, which vary depending upon the content area and grade level of the student. Additional tables provide interquartile scaled scores for each grade and high school for each content area, fall and spring. Observed gain ranges for each grade are also presented so that comparisons of a given child or population can be made to the norm sample to determine appropriate expectations. Grade level equivalent and national percentile conversion tables are also available.

The authors indicate the use of the standard error of measurement (*SEM*) as "the only meaningful way to express an instrument's reliability/precisions" (technical manual, p. 35) in CAT. The criteria were set at less than .30 logits for each examinee ("roughly equivalent to a conventional reliability coefficient of 0.91," technical manual, p. 35). For all grades this standard was achieved in Mathematics (Total *SEM* Mean = .27, with a mean of 58.5 items administered to 136,914 participants); Language Arts (Total *SEM* Mean = .30, with a mean of 49.5 items administered to 54,945 participants); and Science (Total *SEM* Mean = .28, with a mean of 53.6 items administered to 30,994 participants). In Reading, where individuals needed to read entire passages to respond to associated items, there was greater variability (Total *SEM* Mean = .33, with a mean of 46.4 items administered to 137,164 participants).

Content validity was examined through item and sampling validity. Each item went through a series of examinations to determine content appropriateness (e.g., skill alignment, bias, item content, and quality). To have sampling validity, items must span the content area to be tested. By the very nature of CAT, content areas can be divided in subunits or "testlets during test administration" (technical manual, p. 40); as such, students are not restricted in the item range they are given in any content area. The correlation of scores between the component testlets was examined for each content area: (a) Mathematics—range from .463 to .876 (61% above .65); (b) Reading—range from .748 to .967 (70% above .82); (c) Language Arts—range from .678 to .915 (70% above .72); and (d) Science—range from .778 to .937 (67% above .81). Correlations with high stakes tests (e.g.,

ITBS, SAT9) were also computed for Mathematics and Reading, with correlations generally in the mid to high .70 range.

COMMENTARY. The Performance Series appears to be useful as a brief measure of achievement in the four content areas (Mathematics, Reading, Science, Language Arts) for children in Grades 2 through high school. This test's strength is that it is a computer-adaptive test and may be administered individually or to a group of students. The nature of the reports may prove helpful to teachers and administrators to determine beginning and growth levels of students. It is important to note that there are a number of computer adaptive tests on the market; however, a web-based search indicated the Performance Series is the one most frequently cited. Other tests such as the DIBELS (Dynamic Indicators of Basic Early Literacy Skills, Sixth Edition, 16:73) are not adaptive, test across four subject areas, and are not so extensively aligned with various standards. Although this test is appropriate for broad screening of individuals to make predictions about which students are likely to be successful on high stakes tests or will need intervention, it is not a curriculum-based assessment instrument appropriate for monitoring short-term gains required in the Response to Intervention or similar intervention monitoring models.

The authors are to be commended for their efforts to align with standards to assist teachers in determining mastery of a set of skills. The link of these skills to standards, thereby leading to development of a set of learning objectives, is an additional strength. The Performance Series is a tool that many teachers and administrators will find beneficial as they are held increasingly accountable for their students' performance on high stakes tests.

SUMMARY. The Performance Series appears to be a reliable and valid instrument—easy to administer, score, and interpret as a measure of academic competence in four subject areas (Mathematics, Reading, Language Arts, and Science) for children in Grades 2 through high school. It yields standard scores that can be used to compare students in a wide variety of reports. The Performance Series offers several strengths: alignment with a large number of standards, ability to provide a number of very useful reports in real time for immediate curriculum decisions, ease of administration, adaptation to students' functioning

to provide close assessment of skill achievement, and the provision of suggested learning objectives.

REVIEWER'S REFERENCES

Bloom, B. S. (Ed.). (1956). *Taxonomy of educational objectives: The classification of educational goals: Handbook I, cognitive domain.* New York: D. McKay.

Marzano, R. J. (2001). *Designing a new taxonomy of educational objectives.* Thousand Oaks, CA: Corwin Press.

Plake, B. S. (1995). Differential item functioning in licensure tests. In J. C. Impara (Ed.), *Licensure testing: Purposes, procedures, and practices* (pp. 205-218). Lincoln, NE: Buros Institute of Mental Measurements.

Review of the Performance Series by DAVID MORSE, Professor, Counseling, Educational Psychology and Special Education, Mississippi State University, Mississippi State, MS:

DESCRIPTION. The Performance Series is a computer-adaptive, online (web-based) testing and integrated reporting package covering four traditional discipline areas: Reading (Grades 2–10), Mathematics (2–9), Language Arts (2–8), and Science (2–8). Each subject area covers three to five major units and comprises a pool of four-option, multiple-choice items that have been targeted by grade level and by Rasch-calibrated difficulty. In addition, the Performance Series offers a wide range of reports that users may request any time, in the form of dynamic-content web pages, that give the most current information about a student, class, subgroup, school, or district possible. Portrayed as principally criterion-referenced measures, the Performance Series subject area tests do offer normative information, though at present just for the Reading and Mathematics subtests. One of the key points about the Performance Series is the Curriculum Alignment Guide (which does not cover Reading), which the publisher asserts allows for tying items to individual state curriculum frameworks, so that schools or districts trying to measure and report on student attainment on state (or local) benchmarks will be able to do so with ease.

Administration of a test for a subject area takes approximately 1 hour. Test sessions are not timed, however. The technical manual suggests that with set-up, preparation, log-on, and initial explanation to an examinee, one should plan for up to 2 hours for a test session. There are no special skills required for administration, though the publisher indicates that test administrators must attend and complete a mandatory 2 days of training. It is not clear whether this training is solely for system administrators or for all teachers and administrators who might have occasion to interact with the package. Because the examinee's responses are scored by the testing package, no special skills are needed to obtain the results of the test, which are available immediately (on-line) or any time thereafter. Permissible testing accommodations are not well explained, though time is not an issue. Other accommodations, such as a reader, and their possible impact on the integrity of the norms are not discussed. On the Mathematics test, use of a calculator is a local choice. The technical manual does not indicate whether the normative sample did or did not use calculators, or what effect, if any, this option might have on the pertinence of the normative results.

The Performance Series is not purchased and held by the user; one leases access to the system each year, with a charge based on the number of students in the school or district. However, the package incorporates the testing, scoring, and reporting, with no apparent limits on how often one might choose to test or call for reports at a variety of levels. Because it is all web-based, the costs to the user beyond the annual contract fee would be mostly for printing of reports. Of course, one would need access to a web-enabled computer for each student who was to be tested.

Scores are available in a variety of scales, though the publisher's chosen scale that cuts across all grade levels and subject areas is from 1300–3700, representing a linear transformation of Rasch-type logits (log units) (e.g., scaled score = 200(logit) + 2500). Additionally, normative percentiles and grade level equivalents are offered, though the technical manual warns against relying on the GLE scores. Lexile scores can be obtained for Reading, though this is an optional reporting feature. An ersatz domain score estimate is available, expressed as the percent of items in a subject area pool that an examinee (with a specific estimated scaled score) would be expected to answer correctly, and is termed the item pool score or standards item pool score. There is no automatic link of student performance to No Child Left Behind (NCLB) qualitative classifications (e.g., Minimal, Basic, Proficient, Advanced). Because these vary by state, it would be up to the individual school or district to decide what scaled scores, or what item pool score, for a given grade and given subject area, suitably represented the threshold separating any two of those NCLB classifications.

DEVELOPMENT. The Performance Series is a new package; all of the items currently in the pools were said to have been developed from scratch, not adapted or taken off-the-shelf from other measures or item pools. Additionally, the item pools are promised to change over time, with new items added each year and old items eventually retired, so as to avoid overexposure of items. As a step in test development, items were submitted to "bias editing," in which review for gender bias (e.g., main characters and presence of active or passive voice in reading passages), and socioeconomic and ethnic or cultural diversity was undertaken. Identification of misrepresentation by gender or racial/ethnic identity resulted in the item (or passage) being revised by the development team.

Initial item pilot testing began in 2000 (for Reading and Mathematics), with subsequent field tests in 2001 and 2002. For Language Arts and Science, the pilot testing began in 2002, with field tests concluding in 2003. Normative data were collected, for the Reading and Mathematics areas, from fall 2002 and spring 2003. Norms are available for Grades 2–8, and for high school, which groups Grades 9–12 together. Norms are not yet available for Language Arts and Science.

Each item is tied to a discipline area (e.g., Reading), unit (e.g., Fiction), target grade level, and calibrated difficulty. Skills within units were generated from a compendium of state curriculum standards, published text series, and reports of selected professional organizations (e.g., National Council of Teachers of Mathematics). This survey, referred to as Scantron's Curriculum Designer project, of the skills sets that appear to be common across the country is what allows a Performance Series user to obtain reports of attainment tied to specific standards.

Nontest materials available from the publisher include the norms-technical manual (Performance Series Technical Manual), a user-manual (Performance Series User's Guide: Administrator's Version), and an executive summary (Above and Beyond: Applying Adaptive Technology to Diagnose Student Performance and Progress). No mention is made of materials to send to parents, either to assist in preparing students for testing or in interpreting the results of testing, nor of materials for teachers, though these may be available.

TECHNICAL. For the normative sample, participating schools and districts were sampled by region from the U.S.A. The representation by the four regions was a bit off from the target percentages for two regions. By gender and ethnicity, the normative sample did meet the target goals of relative percentage representation.

The technical manual indicates that initial item trials involved inspection of classical item statistics (e.g., *p*-values, distractor functioning, point-biserial correlations), with calibration samples (using fixed, computer-administered forms having 8–10 anchor items per form) including at least 200 students per grade level in each content area (this is specified for Mathematics and Reading, but not explicitly stated for Language Arts and Science). Other analyses performed include checks for dimensionality, and differential item functioning (DIF). Gender and ethnicity were used for DIF analysis, which resulted in as many as 12% of items being dropped from a subject area. A further check was performed for differential test functioning, which appears to have been the examination of correlations of item calibration estimates across different groups.

No information on test-retest reliability is offered in the technical manual. As each test is potentially unique, a near zero-interval test-retest reliability estimate would serve as the proxy for alternate-forms reliability. In the absence of this information, one cannot be sure of the stability of an estimated performance level over time. The technical manual describes the option for having student gains reported across two administrations, with an estimated standard error (the report can be for individuals or groups). However, these would apply to long-term intervals and even with this approach, no data are given on how stable scores tend to be, whether over the short- or the long-term. The issue of reliability of gain scores (always lower than that of either score from which the gain is calculated, unless one has perfectly reliable scores) is not directly addressed.

Internal consistency reliability estimates for total scores tend to be very good, due to the stopping rule of having an estimated standard error of measurement (*SEM*) of less than .3 logits. A *SEM* of .3 implies an estimated total score reliability of about .91, which is high enough for making decisions about individuals (Cronbach, 1990). However, no information is given about estimated reliability of unit scores, such as Geometry (Mathematics), Sentence Structure (Language Arts), Vocabulary (Reading), or Ecology (Science), or for scores tied to a specific state standard. Given the Rasch difficulty information, however, such estimates could be generated and reported for each student on each testing occasion. It would be helpful for potential users, however, to have an inkling of the dependability of such scores prior to adopting the package. From spring 2004 data, the typical test length differs by subject area, averaging about 46 items for Reading, 49–50 items for Language Arts, 53–54 items for Science, and 58–59 items for Mathematics.

Validity information provided in the test materials addresses several aspects of validity. These include content validity judgments, made by panels of content area experts for individual items (including the item bias review). However, the technical manual does not state what sort of consensus was necessary for an item to be retained, modified, or discarded. Sampling validity, an issue mostly for assuring that an adaptive testing framework covers the relevant units, is handled by treating the units (e.g., capitalization) as a mandatory "testlet" to be included in any administration. The technical manual does report inter-testlet correlations, but it is not at all clear how these assure item and sampling validity so much as they indicate that student performance is moderately to highly correlated across testlets/units. Criterion-related validity comes in the form of samples of schools or districts in which students took both the Performance Series and another standardized achievement test. For Mathematics, the total score correlations of the Performance Series and other achievement tests tended to average in the .70s, as was the case for Reading. No such evidence is yet included for Language Arts or Science. For decision-makers who are considering replacing an achievement test battery with the Performance Series, the absence of such information makes the decision substantially more challenging. The APA/AERA/NCME Joint Standards (1999) outline the importance of criterion-related validity as part of the relevant evidence for the suitability of a measure (pp. 13–15).

COMMENTARY. Using the Performance Series is fairly straightforward. Once a student has logged in correctly, the actual mechanics of taking a test are simple. Likewise, for a teacher or administrator, navigating the numerous reporting options is fairly easy to accomplish. The user's manual outlines many of the actions in a screen-by-screen manner.

The stopping criteria for a test (essential in an adaptive testing framework) are: (a) maximum number of items administered (though these limits are not stated); (b) length of time (again, not stated); or (c) *SEM* estimated at .3 or less. When items are selected for an examinee, his or her previous exposure to items is also taken into account, so as to minimize the number of times that a student might encounter the very same item from the pool. The starting point for a sixth grade student would typically be a few items near the fifth grade level; system administrators can adjust the desired starting point up or down from the default for individual students (e.g., for ESL learners). Within a test, the units are said to always be administered in the same sequence (e.g., Vocabulary, Long Passage, Fiction, and Nonfiction for Reading). Within a test, students would not be exposed to items more than three grade levels from their listed grade, unless this was modified by the user.

However, as this reviewer sampled some of the tests, attempting to emulate the performance of very proficient and very inept students, it is apparent that the item pools at the extremes of the performance continuum are fairly shallow. For example, in emulating a student with very low Science mastery, the test ended up asking a series of questions about the five senses. If a student does not know what an eye is for, it is not likely that he or she would fare any better on the ear or nose, yet that may be the only set of very low difficulty items available. Such an occurrence may be less likely over time, if the publisher's promise to add thousands of items each year to the pools is realized. The numbers of items put through the pilot testing in 2003 for Science and Language Arts were 383 and 419, respectively, to cover Grades 2–9 (though this may have been a misprint in the technical manual; 2–8 is given elsewhere). For seven grades (assuming 2–8), that is only about 55–60 items per grade on average. If the test length is close to 55 items, on average, for Science, there is obviously a serious need to increase the number of items in the pool.

There are some instances throughout the Performance Series materials in which the documentation disagrees. For example, in the frequently asked questions section, the grades covered by the Reading test are said to be from 2–10. Yet, the description of how reading vocabulary is assessed indicates that, for first grade and below, the task is to match a word to a picture; for grades 2–10, the task is to choose the synonym for a word; whereas for Grades 11–12, the task is to identify the meaning of a word in context.

Elements that are not measured anywhere in the Performance Series include Spelling and Composition (Language Arts) and Health Issues and Evolution (Science). The units that are measured include: Vocabulary, Fiction, Nonfiction, and Long Passages (Reading); Number & Operations, Algebra, Geometry, Measurement, and Data Analysis & Probability (Mathematics); Capitalization, Parts of Speech, Punctuation, and Sentence Structure (Language Arts); and Living Things, Ecology, and Science Process Skills (Science).

Long-term adopters of the Performance Series can apparently access prior years' data, which suggests that longitudinal studies can be undertaken. It is not clear what would happen to a school or district's historical data if they decided to use the Performance Series for a while, stop their annual lease for a year or two, then re-adopt. One would expect such instances to be rare, however.

One logistics concern that might arise in a school setting is that of how to handle group testing. Aside from the need for as many internet-capable computers as one has students to be tested at a given moment, how to best handle the situation wherein some students finish their tests long before (or after) their peers might prove to be a bit of a challenge, although not entirely different from paper-and-pencil testing.

One final concern about the Performance Series package is its strict reliance on multiple-choice questions as the mode for eliciting information about student attainment. Many states are adopting hybrid assessment systems, involving elaborated responses with scoring rubrics to aid in the understanding of reasoning, organization, and other skills considered to be critical for academic success. Those who embrace more "authentic" assessment methods will find this package to be lacking. In fairness, that is not a criticism unique to the Performance Series package.

SUMMARY. The Performance Series is perhaps best characterized as a work in progress. For the areas of Reading and Mathematics, normative data for fall and spring and criterion-related validity data are currently available. For Language Arts and Science, however, such information is currently lacking. The initial item pools are not necessarily as thick as they might be in the future. Using the package is fairly simple; it provides a rich variety of reports that can be obtained in real time. Once students are acclimated to the format and taking a test on-line, subsequent administrations should go more easily. The system can track and report on students, classes, teachers, schools, or larger groups; results can be disaggregated by subgroups, and changes over time can be indicated.

Choosing a system like the Performance Series is a bit different from selecting fixed-forms measures of achievement. In this package, one does not have to count test forms, store tests, bundle up answer sheets, and ship them off for scoring; a test can be given virtually any time, and the results are then available. Potential users should consider whether the information furnished about the package is sufficient to assure them that their needs for appropriate, dependable, and valid assessment and reporting will be met. Because setting up the initial data base takes some time and effort, the adoption decision is most likely for more years than just 1 or 2.

REVIEWER'S REFERENCES

American Educational Research Association, American Psychological Association, & National Council on Measurement in Education. (1999). *Standards for educational and psychological testing*. Washington, DC: American Educational Research Association.
Cronbach, L. J. (1990). *Essentials of psychological testing* (5th ed.). New York: Harper Collins Publishing.

[144]

Personal Style Indicator [Revised].

Purpose: Designed to increase mutual understanding, acceptance, and communication among people and to increase self-awareness.
Population: Ages 15 years—adults.
Publication Dates: 1988–2006.
Acronym: PSI.
Scores, 4: Behavioral/Action, Cognitive/Analysis, Interpersonal/Harmony, Affective/Expression.
Administration: Individual or group.
Price Data, 2006: $13.95 per test booklet (2006, 20 pages); $14.95 per In-Depth Interpretations booklet (2006, 28 pages); $69.95 per Professional's Guide (2006, 64 pages); $35 per Trainer's Guidelines (1996, 70 pages); $159.95 per PSI PowerPoint CD and binder (116 slides); $23.95 per participant workbook Building Relationships With Style (2006, 68 pages); $22.95 per Why Aren't You More Like Me? Book second edition (1994, 226 pages); $109.95 per CRG Models Master Handout binder and CD for PSI-color PDFs (2006, 26 pages).

Foreign Language Editions: Available online in English, French, and German, and in print in English, French, Japanese, Dutch, and Spanish; the In-Depth interpretations booklet is available in English, Japanese, Dutch, Spanish, and French.
Time: [90] minutes; [180–720] minutes advanced.
Comments: Self-administered and self-scored.
Authors: Ken Keis, Terry D. Anderson, and Everett T. Robinson.
Publisher: Consulting Resource Group International, Inc.
Cross References: For reviews by James T. Austin and Kusum Singh of an earlier edition, see 13:228.

Review of the Personal Style Indicator [Revised] by GYPSY M. DENZINE, Associate Dean and Professor of Educational Psychology, Northern Arizona University, Flagstaff, AZ:

DESCRIPTION. The developers of the Personal Style Indicator [Revised] (PSI) state the purpose of the PSI "is to help people understand themselves better—both their uniqueness as individuals and their similarities to other people" (PSI/JSI professional's guide, 2005, p. 5). According to the authors, the PSI is intended to foster self-exploration in regard to how an individual perceives, approaches, and interacts with his or her environments, which form the basis of one's personal style. The authors state one of the major intended goals of the PSI is to help individuals begin to appreciate the influence of personal style on their daily behaviors.

The PSI scales were designed to measure "personal styles" rather than "personality types" because the authors intended to move away from a fixed view of personality. Instead, they prefer "to refer to each person's natural—and perhaps largely biologically determined—predisposition to act or behave in certain ways" (professional's guide, p. 2). The identified list of over 50 different uses of the PSI includes the following suggested uses: career planning, customer service, dating compatibility, life coaching, sales, stress management, working with teenagers, wellness programs, and more. According to the authors, it is appropriate to use the PSI as a communication tool during personal, marriage, and family counseling sessions.

Personal style is described in terms of four dimensions: (a) Behavioral—energy to behave or take action, (b) Cognitive—to think about or analyze, (c) Interpersonal—to be concerned with harmony toward others, and (d) Affective—to be expressive in an intuitive, creative manner. The model is grounded in the assumption that people have a limited amount of energy, which can be distributed among the four dimensions of personal style. Thus, if an individual is very strong in one personal dimension then he or she will have less intense personal style levels in the other three dimensions. The intensity of one's four personal style dimensions is believed to be influenced by the development factors of (a) brain side preference (left/right), (b) reticular activating system (more or less sensitive), and (c) arousal level (more or less aroused by the environment). In addition to providing feedback about one's interpersonal style at the four different levels, profile reports provide specific action steps for understanding relations in the work place and team dynamics.

The authors state the PSI was developed using the theoretical assumptions underlying the work of Marston (1927), Jung (1928), Lewin (1936), Horney (1942), and Fromm (1964). The authors also note the influence of Merrill and Reid's (1981) work on "interpersonal style," which contains the concept of "social-style versatility." This work was used to form Anderson's idea of "style-shifting" in the development of the PSI. Style-shifting is a topic covered in the *PSI In-Depth Interpretations* guide, and test takers are encouraged to develop greater personal and social awareness to improve their interpersonal relationships and on-the-job performance. According to the authors, one of the major features of the PSI is that it is designed to measure a person's strengths and assist the individual in understanding, developing, and expressing his or her personal style strengths. It is further posited that one's strengths can be capitalized upon through greater self-awareness, practice, self-control, and social awareness. A final conceptual tenet underlying the PSI discussed in this review is the assumption that an individual's weaknesses are intensified in times of stress or when their style conflicts with other people.

Although not explicitly stated in the technical manual, this scale appears to be a tool most appropriate for nonclinical adult populations. The authors note the PSI is appropriate for individuals 14 or 15 years of age and older and respondents should be able to read at the ninth- to tenth-grade level.

Administration. The PSI is available in both print and online formats. The test is a self-report rating scale, which was developed to be self-administered, self-scored, and self-interpreted. The PSI can be administered to individuals or in a group format. Individuals obtain their scores by completing the Personal Style Indicator® response sheet, which contains 64 descriptor words presented in 16 rows (4 words per row). Respondents are instructed to rank-order each set of 4 words with the highest ranking score of 4 representing words best descriptive of how they see themselves most of the time, with most people, in most situations. For example, the following words comprise one of the sets in which the individual is required to complete a within-set ranked order: self-reliant, disciplined, dependable, and expressive. A ranked score of 1 represents words least descriptive of them. After completing all 16 sets of 4 words, individuals are instructed to total the numbers they placed beside each word within four columns. The four columns are labeled on the response sheet as Artistic, Technical, Productive, and Supportive. The four column scores are then added together to total a score of 160. If the respondent does not obtain a total score of 160 for the sum of the four columns, they are instructed to go back to the response sheet and check their rankings and/or column sum totals for accuracy. Scoring of the PSI may involve a second step for individuals. If an individual scores between 35 to 39, he or she is instructed to calculate a Secondary Pattern, which means the individual has a tendency to operate out of his or her primary dimension. The authors note in the manual that most people have a Secondary Pattern meaning they have inherent style-flex or versatility. Although not specified in the test manual, completion time appears to be about 30 minutes.

PSI scores can be cross-validated by obtaining PSI scores from others who indicate their perceptions of the respondent. PSI self-ratings and other-ratings are compared to provide cross-validation information. The authors note PSI scores are not derived by complicated tests that need to be administered by highly specialized individuals under structured, standardized conditions.

Scoring and interpretation. The PSI is an ipsative measure that results in test takers receiving four scale scores that are interrelated. Due to the ipsative nature of the scale scores, the PSI should not be used as a normative measure and the test authors explicitly state that scores should not be used to compare individuals. Nor are scores intended to be used for making hiring decisions in an employment setting. The authors note the forced-choice item format and resulting ipsative scale scores present problems for researchers who are traditionally used to seeing results from correlations and factor analyses. They cite Johnson, Wood, and Blinkhorn's (1988) work on the difficulties related to establishing adequate reliability and validity measures for ipsative tests. They also caution users about using standard statistics with PSI scores due to their ipsative nature.

PSI scores are easy to compute and are available immediately without technical assistance. All information needed to interpret scores is contained in an accompanying booklet. Respondents are encouraged to purchase the Personal Style Indicator In-Depth Interpretation booklet, which is a 47-page resource providing 2 pages of detailed text about each of the 21 style patterns. This booklet is purported to contain narrative information related to one's: Strengths, Common Difficulties, Reactions to Stress, Team Compatibility, Leadership Implications, and suggestions for increasing one's Effectiveness.

DEVELOPMENT. The development of the PSI began in 1979 when Dr. Terry Anderson desired to create a tool for helping students in his classes begin to self-explore characteristics of their behavior. The PSI went through several revisions during the development period between 1979 and 1986. The most recent version of the PSI was published in 2005. According to the test manual, the development of the PSI "was often intuitive and eclectic rather than a series of precise stages" (professional's guide, p. 19).

The manual contains an overview of the major theories used to develop the scale; however, the theoretical integration is conceptual rather than empirical. According to the authors, more than four personal style dimensions were initially considered for the PSI. In the end, the test developers decided to utilize the four-quadrant model because it aligned better with the theoretical perspectives underlying the personal style construct and because the four-quadrant model was consistent with Anderson and Robinson's observations of how humans behave. Another reason for keeping the four-quadrant model was because it fit better into a 2 x 3 matrix, which is needed to evaluate personal style similarities and differences. The test manual

does not contain any empirical justification for interpreting a four-quadrant model of personal style.

Item development occurred over a 2-year period in which the test developers used "informal and subjective procedures of item analysis" (professional's guide, p. 30) to field test the rank-ordering of words. The initial instrument was developed based on Anderson's assessment of several hundred participants in college classes, counseling sessions, and consultations in private practice. No empirical evidence is reported comparing the psychometric properties of the PSI for the various groups used in the test development stage. Early in the development process the PSI was revised to produce a final version after the scale was administered to colleagues and acquaintances of the researchers. The manual does not contain detailed demographic information about the samples used for item and scale development. Ongoing field testing also occurred for the development of the PSI In-Depth Interpretations based on feedback from college students and participants in public and private seminars. Some changes in the readability of the PSI were made after feedback was obtained from a lifeskills coach who used the instrument with federal prison inmates to gain self-awareness and improve communication skills. In 1987, Anderson made some significant changes to the PSI in order to incorporate the concept of "style-shifting," which resulted in the inclusion of an *application* focus in the scale interpretation process. Much of the evidence cited in support of the validity of the PSI was obtained from college students' self-reported confidence ratings of the PSI results and In-Depth Interpretations. In 1988, 455 college students used a 5-point semantic differentiated scale to rate the accuracy of the sentences contained in the In-Depth Interpretations. The majority of the participants in this activity rated their PSI interpretation as "highly accurate" with four respondents rating their interpretation as "inaccurate" (21 students responded they were "not sure" about the overall accuracy of their PSI interpretation). It is noted this research was obtained from an earlier version of the PSI and In-Depth Interpretations booklet. This type of field-testing is not reported in the test manual for the more recent version of the PSI (fourth edition) and the PSI-In-Depth Interpretations (fifth edition), which were revised by Keis in 2004.

The technical manual lacks specific information regarding who can administer and interpret PSI scores, which conflicts with the *Standards for Educational and Psychological Testing* (AERA, APA, & NCME, 1999). The manual offers information on numerous training resources for sale (e.g., PSI Trainer's Guidelines and Train-the-Trainer DVD). It appears anyone can obtain the 3-day Train-the-Trainer program via the 10-disc DVD set as no specific educational background or previous training is required to obtain the program.

TECHNICAL. Overall, the manual lacks important information about the samples utilized for item and scale development. Also missing is an in-depth discussion of the appropriateness of this scale for different gender or ethnic/culture groups.

The authors claim "Although these instruments [PSI and JSI] were not designed to be psychometric tests, questions of reliability and validity nonetheless apply" (professional's guide, p. 38). Reliability data are provided in internal consistency form ($N = 20–25$; correlation coefficients of greater than .85) on each of the four scales. The authors state the need for independent research to conduct larger investigations with heterogeneous populations. No reliability data are provided in test-retest form.

Issues of validity were discussed in general terms in the manual. Information regarding other researchers' conceptual and empirical support of the personal style model or PSI scale was not included.

Although the authors claim the PSI is intended to help individuals appreciate the influence of personal style on their daily behaviors, no studies providing evidence of predictive validity are reported. Nor is any empirical evidence provided for the hypothesis that an individual who is able to understand, develop, and express his or her personal style has good or improved interpersonal relations or on-the-job success. The authors state that an individual's basic style forms the foundation of interpersonal, communication, parenting, counseling, decision-making, learning, management, preferred job, and leadership styles and much more. How people see themselves (self-perception) is presumed to influence the way people act. Yet, the manual does not contain any results from research investigating the claims previously mentioned. Evidence of predictive or construct validity is noticeably absent. Further, there is no evidence of concurrent validity tests with other measures of interpersonal behavior, communication style, and personality. In addition, my review of the professional literature did not reveal studies providing evidence supporting the convergent, divergent, or criterion-related validity of the PSI.

COMMENTARY. Perhaps the greatest strength of this test is the ease of the administration and the availability of immediate results. The reports are user-friendly and provide for some interesting self-reflection. Although I found some aspects of my own profile to be interesting and have some practice evidence of face and content validity, the limitations of the technical manual and lack of attention paid to item and test development cannot be ignored.

The potential user of the PSI should be aware of the conceptual and empirical limitations of this scale. There is minimal evidence that the theoretical model of interpersonal behavior is supported by the use of this test. Moreover, to the trained psychologist, the PSI will raise a concern as the authors claim that it is "a powerful communication and learning tool that will help you discover your client's individual personality and how it 'fits' into the world around him or her" (professional's guide, p. i). Yet, the test manual is void of theoretical and empirical references connecting the PSI to personality psychology.

Of concern is the fact that no empirical investigations are cited on the relations between personality measures and PSI profiles. Overall, the technical manual provides incomplete and superficial treatment of important test development information. Moreover, no published articles on the psychometric properties of the PSI could be found in any professional journals. Nor did a literature search reveal any empirical studies using this scale. However, an internet search reveals this scale is widely used in business and industry training.

The manual does not explicitly state only trained and qualified professionals should use the PSI for counseling purposes. Also of concern, the authors note the PSI can be used with adolescents and individuals above the age of 14 years. Noticeably missing in this discussion is the necessity to obtain parent/legal guardian approval when assessing individuals under the age of 18.

SUMMARY. Although the PSI is easy to administer and score, and the reports are interesting and easy to interpret, there are several elements missing in the demonstration of a psycho-metrically sound measure of personal style. Given these limitations, there is a need for more sophisticated and ongoing research on the PSI before its use can be recommended.

REVIEWER'S REFERENCES

American Educational Research Association, American Psychological Association, & National Council on Measurement in Education. (1999). *Standards for educational and psychological testing.* Washington, DC: American Educational Research Association.

Fromm, E. (1964). *The heart of man, its genius for good and evil.* New York: Harper and Row.

Horney, K. (1942). *Self analysis.* New York: Norton.

Johnson, C., Wood, R., & Blinkhorn, S. (1988). Spuriouser and Spuriouser: The use of ipsative personality tests. *Journal of Occupational Psychology, 61,* 153-162.

Jung, C. (1928). *Contributions to analytic psychology.* New York: Harcourt, Brace and Company.

Lewin, K. (1936). *Principles of topological psychology.* New York: McGraw-Hill.

Marston, W. (1927). Motor consciousness as a basis for emotion. *Journal of Abnormal and Social Psychology, 22,* 140-150.

Merrill, D., & Reid, R. (1981). *Personal styles and effective performance.* Radnor, PA: Chilton Book Company.

[145]

Personal Styles Inventory [PSI-120] [1999 Revision].

Purpose: Provides a comprehensive assessment of nonpathological personality characteristics.

Population: Adults.

Publication Dates: 1990–2005.

Acronym: PSI-120.

Scores, 24: Styles of Expressing Emotions (Sympathetic, Enthusiastic, Expansive, Confronting, Self-Willed, Reserved, Modest, Patient), Styles of Doing Things (Agreeing, Sociable, Excitement-Seeking, Venturing, Restless, Self-Directed, Self-Motivated, Organizing), Styles of Thinking (Traditional, Dedicated, Imaginative, Inquiring, Individualistic, Analytical, Practical, Focused).

Administration: Group or individual.

Price Data: Available from publisher.

Time: (20–30) minutes.

Comments: Computerized interpretation reports are available online.

Authors: Joseph T. Kunce, Corrine S. Cope, and Russel M. Newton.

Publisher: Educational & Psychological Consultants, Inc.

Cross References: See T5:1954 (1 reference); for reviews by Paul A. Arbisi and Mary Henning-Stout of an earlier edition, see 13:229 (2 references); see also T4:1993 (4 references).

Review of the Personal Styles Inventory [PSI-120] [1999 Revision] by FREDERIC MEDWAY, Professor of Psychology, University of South Carolina, Columbia, SC:

DESCRIPTION. The Personal Styles Inventory [PSI-120] is a self-report personality inventory that measures three major aspects of personality: emotions, action, and thinking. The test is appropriate for ages 16 and older. The PSI-120 asks respondents to rate themselves in terms of 120 common, easily recognizable, everyday behaviors rather than behaviors that describe abnormal or pathological states. Thus, the measure does not indicate degree of maladjustment but rather assesses the probabilities that individuals will exhibit certain traits and behavioral styles. The PSI-120 was derived from the Personal Styles Model of Personality (Kunce & Cope, 1987) and is intended for a wide variety of clinical and nonclinical uses including fostering self-awareness, exploring career and vocational issues, studying in-depth personality styles, examining social and interpersonal behaviors, facilitating adaptation and coping with stress, and diagnosing behaviors that may be relevant in counseling and organizational consultation contexts.

A 92-page (not including appendices) test manual describes the rationale of the PSI-120, defines key terms and concepts, and explains administration procedures, the scale's technical characteristics, score interpretation, and the research evidence supporting the measure. It also contains examples of the different types of reports that can be derived from the PSI-120. The test can only be scored using a computer disk program or by establishing an internet account with the publisher.

The PSI-120 booklet contains two parts and asks respondents to answer in ways describing their general behavior in different situations. The first part consists of 96 items answered on a 3-point scale (*like me, not certain, unlike me*). The second part contains 24 items answered on a 5-point scale from *definitely like me* to *definitely unlike me*. The PSI-120 can be administered in individual or group setting and takes about 25 minutes to complete.

The PSI-120 provides information on 8 global personal styles or traits as manifested across emotion, action, and thinking, thus producing 24 specific personal styles. These are considered the core domains of personality and are arranged in a circular (circumplex) format to reflect the complexity of the styles and relationships among them. They include Supporting, Preserving; Encouraging, Facilitating; Promoting, Inspiring; Creating, Designing; Improvising, Inquiring; Evaluating, Investigating; Applying, Constructing; and Systematizing, Arranging. These 8 styles are ordered on two dimensions that demonstrate how the trait is manifested: external/internal orientation (similar to introversion-extroversion) and stability/change orientation. Styles adjacent to one another in the circular format are similar (e.g., encouraging and promoting both reflect an external orientation) whereas dissimilar styles appear on the opposite side of the circle (e.g., systematizing reflects stability whereas improvising reflects change). The global personality styles produce scores indicating whether the style is a basic behavior ("natural for the person") or a learned (acquired or desired) behavior. Scores for basic (or inner-self-aspects) and learned behaviors (or outer-self-aspects) can be considered to determine if a particular style of reacting is pervasive, is occasional or infrequent, or depends on particular situations. It is argued that differences between basic and learned responding may signify stress for the individual.

The PSI-120 user can choose from several varieties of scoring presentations based upon the goal of assessment and the amount of detail desired. For example, a summary report provides brief interpretations written in everyday language useful for sharing directly with the client. Alternatively, one can obtain detailed reports that include data on response sets, means and standard deviations for the eight traits and 24 styles, percentages of items endorsed, correlations among items, linear graphs, and color-coded octagonal maps including one map for the eight personality traits and three maps for the eight elements that make up styles of emotion, action, and thinking.

DEVELOPMENT. The original development of the PSI-120 began in the 1980s and was based on the authors' desire to create a personality inventory based on nonpathological tendencies and behaviors. A decision was made to organize the eight personality styles into a circular or circumplex arrangement that orders the styles along the stability/change and the external/internal orientations. Personality characteristics were intentionally divided into the three domains or styles of emotion, action, and thinking. Finally, the test authors developed the scale to be able to distinguish between enduring and situational personality tendencies, thus reflecting a state-trait personality distinction. The test manual describes how this organizational approach is consistent with other models of personality. Once the circumplex

model of personality was developed, the test authors wrote items that represented each style and its place in the circumplex model rather than using factor analytic procedures. Items were subsequently rewritten or discarded based upon how each correlated with its intended scale. Over several years different versions of the measure were developed and modified leading up to the newest version that contains 120 items with revised names describing the styles and traits.

TECHNICAL. The test manual presents mean scores, internal consistency reliability data, and test-retest reliability for various samples. However, in most cases sample sizes are not large (ranging from 23 to 238 respondents) and research samples include psychology undergraduates, students seen at a campus health clinic, and "gifted" high school students. The test development samples are not described in detail but *do not* appear representative of the U.S. population. This is particularly problematic because of the wide-ranging purported uses of the scale for adults faced with both clinical and everyday concerns. Another potential problem is that these restricted development samples were used to create procedures to detect invalid protocols. The authors report that random responding occurs in only 7% of cases; however, this percentage may not be accurate when the PSI-120 is administered to individuals who are less educated, of lower SES, or older than the research sample participants.

Measures of internal consistency are generally respectable for the eight traits (range of .71 to .85). However, these estimates are not always high for the personal styles (range of .35 to .81); internal consistency coefficients are lowest for styles of thinking. Test-retest correlations range from .68 to .86 over periods of 4 months or less. Profiles show few gender differences; profiles do show differences for various occupations and degree of mental health impairment. However, it is not clear what group differences would be theoretically expected. Validity evidence is presented showing that the PSI-120 traits correlate with behaviors on other personality measures such as the 16PF, Jesness, and Minnesota Multiphasic Personality Inventory (MMPI). There are no data showing PSI-120 relationships with standard vocational and interest inventories. The manual reviews several studies relating PSI-120 scores to various outcomes such as problem behaviors, learning styles, behavior disorders, alcohol dependence, and job roles. Although these relationships between PSI-120 profiles and outcomes often appear to make some sense when interpreted after the fact, there is little use of the PSI-120 to test a priori notions.

COMMENTARY. The PSI-120 is a measure that appears to have held up well over time, and it has been used in several research studies. To the authors' credit it has been continually improved and is built on a comprehensive model of personality. The test is easy to administer, computer scored, and can be used in individual or group administrations. The manual presents several cases to aid in test interpretation.

Despite these strengths the PSI-120 appears to have several limitations. One primary limitation is the lack of any representative, normative sample. This is especially problematic given that the inventory was designed to measure personality in normal individuals and designed to illuminate a large number of situations in which personality understanding would appear critical. A second limitation is that users would need considerably more understanding of this model of personality than is presented in the test manual (about 6 pages) in order to interpret the data effectively. Thus, users may be forced to rely too heavily on conclusions from computerized test reports because they lack key understandings about the personality model. The model refers to the distinction between basic personality and learned personality, and defines the former as "innate" or "natural" for a person. However, the existence of innate personality traits is arguable; rather, the test authors should have focused on generalizable and situational tendencies and avoided the suggestion that some traits are fixed at birth. The test manual also is not clear on what changes in the inventory were made in the last revision except revising the names of some of the traits and styles. Finally, potential users should wonder why there is little recent research using the PSI-120. Since 1996 only one empirical study on the PSI-120 appeared in a list of research articles provided by the publishing company, leading one to wonder if more recently devised measures are more advantageous.

SUMMARY. The PSI-120 would appear to be a useful measure of general personality traits and styles in the hands of users who have more than passing familiarity with general personality theory and this specific approach. It can provide useful interpretations of personality that can potentially lead to useful counseling and consultation interventions. It is not recommended for use as a sole measure when important life decisions must be made. Additional normative data and recent research are needed, particularly studies that compare the advantages of the PSI-120 with other personality inventories with similar objectives.

REVIEWER'S REFERENCE

Kunce, J. T., & Cope, C. S. (1987). Personal styles analysis. In N. C. Gysbers & E. J. Moore (Eds.), *Career counseling: Skills and techniques for practitioners* (pp. 100–130). Englewood Cliffs, NJ: Prentice Hall.

Review of the Personal Styles Inventory [PSI-120] [1999 Revision] by JANET SMITH, Associate Professor, Department of Psychology and Counseling, Pittsburg State University, Pittsburg, KS:

DESCRIPTION. The Personal Styles Inventory (PSI-120) is a 120-item self-report measure of personality, specifically in terms of an individual's personal styles of emotions, actions, and thinking. The questionnaire takes approximately 25 minutes to complete and is designed for individuals ages 16 and older. According to the manual, younger persons can take the PSI-120, provided that they have the requisite academic capability. The completed questionnaire must be computer-scored, either using a disk on a local machine or through an internet account with the publisher. The PSI-120 cannot be hand-scored due to complexity of statistical procedures used in scoring. The computerized scoring program generates an option of eight different types of reports, which can be selected depending on the setting, personal preferences, and intended use of the instrument. For example, reports with numerical data, graphic representation, and/or interpretive narrative are available. The purpose of the PSI-120 is to increase self-awareness of personality, social interactions, stress, coping strategies, potential for change, and preference for job activities. Emphasis is placed on recognition of positive aspects. According to the manual, the test is appropriate for use in individual, couples, or group counseling, as well as career counseling, team building, and management consulting.

The PSI-120 assesses 24 specific personal styles, eight global personality traits, and two underlying dimensions. The instrument is designed for use in both clinical and nonclinical settings, but the scale descriptors are deliberately nonpathological in nature. The specific personal styles are categorized into three major areas: emotion, action, and thinking. Examples of styles of emotion include: Sympathetic, Reassuring; Confronting, Spirited; and Patient, Unassuming. Examples of styles of action include: Sociable, Affiliating; Venturing, Daring; and Organizing, Cautious. Examples of styles of thinking include Imaginative, Abstract; Practical, Realistic; and Focused, Systematic. The personality attributes are arranged in a circumplex model to capture the complexity of the model as well as highlight similarities and differences among the styles. Each personal style is measured twice, with one score representing learned behavior ("outer self") and the other indicative of an underlying basic tendencies ("inner self"). Combinations of these two scores identify how each style is exhibited: pervasive, basic, learned, or occasional. The manual describes learned behavior as indicative of one's "outer self," which is readily recognized by others. In contrast, basic behavior represents ones "inner self," which may be less obvious to observers. In addition to the external/internal dimension there is a second stability/change dimension. These dimensions underlie state versus trait aspects of each personal style. Validity of each protocol is established by ensuring that there is a sufficient degree of correlation between basic and learned style scores, as well as mean response set scores (how frequently an individual endorses items as "like me") and their standard deviations being within established acceptable ranges.

DEVELOPMENT. The PSI-120 is based on an underlying model of personality developed by Kunce and Cope (1987). Specifically, the model views personality in terms of three domains: emotions, actions, and thoughts. In addition, the personality traits are arranged in a circular format on the basis of two bipolar and orthogonal dimensions. The external/internal dimension of personality is represented along the vertical axis, and stability/change is indicated along the horizontal axis. This generates a circular model with eight sectors, each representative of a personal style. Adjacent sectors represent personality styles most similar in nature, and opposite sectors are most dissimilar in nature. The instrument was developed by initially writing items that addressed each of the personality styles, taking into account internal/external, stability/change, and the three domains of emotion, action, and thinking. Items focus on everyday behaviors and are written in neutral or nonpathological terms. Items from the initial pool were retained only if they correlated highly with their identified target scale. The PSI-120 has been developed over a period of several years. Earlier versions of the scale, the Personal Styles Inventory, contained a greater number of items, and the most recent version, the PSI-120 was published in 1990. For this version, each scale has "its own 4 separate items plus 2 of the most similar items 'borrowed' from each of its adjacent scales" (manual, p. a-9). The manual was revised in 2005 and includes changes in scale names to better represent the underlying concepts, with focus still on nonpathological terminology.

TECHNICAL. The revised manual provides no comprehensive normative data. However, scores are intended to be interpreted in an ipsative manner, with any individual's raw scores statistically adjusted to produce an average score of 50. Mean scores are provided for small separate samples of male (n = 58) and female (n = 58) college students, as well as gifted male (n = 15) and gifted female (n = 29) high school students. No standard deviations are given and no data are provided for age, race, or other demographic variables. In terms of reliability, data are provided for both internal consistency and stability of scores. Coefficient alphas for the 24 specific personal styles show considerable variability and range from .35 to .85 in two samples of students, with a median value of .68. The eight personality traits show more respectable internal stability, with coefficient alphas ranging from .71 to .85 in the same student populations. Test-retest data are based on a sample of 31 university students seeking outpatient treatment for depression and anxiety, tested at admission and 4 months later, with a median value of .76 for the basic aspect of the 24 personal styles and .68 for the learned aspect of the same personal styles. For the same sample, median test-retest reliability of the eight personality traits was .83 for basic behaviors and .68 for learned behaviors. The test manual presents evidence for the validity of the circumplex model, with adjacent traits showing significant positive correlation coefficients in the range of .50 to .75, and opposite scales showing significant negative coefficients of -.75 to -.95. Considerable information on implications of test scores is presented in the manual, but there is meager evidence of validity to support these uses of test scores. The manual lists significant correlations between scores on the PSI-120 and several major personality instruments, including the 16PF, Myers-Briggs Type Indicator (MBII), Jesness Inventory, and Minnesota Multiphasic Personality Inventory (MMPI). However, actual values of the coefficients are not provided, nor is there any description of the participant sample. In addition, the test manual makes general statements about PSI-120 scores and several areas, including self-reported problem behaviors, learning styles, behavior disorders, career implications, alcohol abuse/dependence, and counseling implications. However, the statements in each category are rather sweeping and no actual data are provided, substantially limiting the studies' contributions to establishing validity.

COMMENTARY. The manual is well-organized and easy to follow. Numerous examples of client data are provided, along with implications of scores in a number of different settings, such as counseling, career, and management consultation. However, psychometric data to support such use of test scores are severely lacking. Conceptually, the overall model is sound and the circumplex aspect of the model has empirical support. But there are minimal data to support interpretation of the various scales. Although interpretation is intended to be ipsative in nature, lack of adequate normative data severely restricts complete score interpretation, especially as no information is given in terms of impact of demographics—such as age, gender, and race—on test scores. In terms of internal consistency, reliability of the eight personality trait scales appears adequate, but several of the specific personal style scales show problems. Test-retest data are less than adequate as they are based on such a limited clinical sample, where change would naturally be expected. Although many potentially valuable interpretations and uses of test scores are posited in the manual, additional research is needed to adequately establish validity. Ideally, additional research should include a broader range of participants, with clearly identified demographic characteristics, as a great deal of the research findings presented in the test manual are based on university students.

SUMMARY. In summary, the PSI-120 is an appealing instrument because of its broad scope, covering emotion, action, and thinking across a wide range of different aspects of personality. In addition, the emphasis on everyday, nonpathological test items and scale descriptors allows for focus on adaptive behaviors and enables a clinician or counselor to address problematic behaviors in a nonthreatening, constructive manner. With additional research, the instrument could potentially make a valuable contribution to the field of personality assessment. However, despite the conceptual appeal of the instrument, there are serious psychometric limitations that make it difficult to recommend use of the PSI-120 at this time.

REVIEWER'S REFERENCE

Kunce, J. T., & Cope, C. S. (1987). Personal styles analysis. In N. C. Gysbers & E. J. Moore (Eds.), *Career counseling: Skills and techniques for practitioners* (pp. 100-130). Englewood Cliffs, NJ: Prentice Hall.

[146]

Personnel Assessment Form.

Purpose: To measure mental ability and intelligence for employee selection and placement planning.
Population: Ages 16 and older.
Publication Dates: 2004–2006.
Acronym: PAF.
Scores, 2: Verbal Subtest Score, Quantitative Subtest Score.
Subtests, 2: Verbal Subtest, Quantitative Subtest.
Administration: Group.
Forms, 2: A, C.
Price Data, 2007: $18 per manual (2006, 28 pages); $20 per report, volume discounts available.
Time: 14(20) minutes.
Comments: The PAF is available through fax-in scoring and online administration at www.sigmatesting.com.
Author: Douglas N. Jackson.
Publisher: Sigma Assessment Systems, Inc.

Review of the Personnel Assessment Form by JEAN P. KIRNAN, *Professor of Psychology, The College of New Jersey, Ewing, NJ:*

[Editor's Note: Subsequent to the writing of these reviews and during the test publisher's fact-confirmation of these reviews, the test publisher advised that the test manual had been revised (2006). In reacting to some comments in the reviews, they shared the new test manual with the Buros staff. There was not time to share the new manual with the original reviewers, whose comments were accurate at the time they were written, based on the (2004) test materials they had been provided. Therefore, the editors made some updates in the test description but the reviews have not been changed to reflect the new manual. Potential users should know that the new manual now provides guidance in terms of which form should be used dependent upon the test taker's educational level, briefly addresses the use of calculators, and has reformatted and better labeled figures that were previously difficult to understand. The publisher also improved the answer sheet.]

DESCRIPTION. The Personnel Assessment Form (PAF) is a test of general mental ability (GMA) intended for use in employee selection or career counseling. Designed for individuals 16 years of age or older, the test purports to capture many aspects of GMA including reasoning, planning, problem solving, abstract thought, comprehending complex ideas, and the ability to learn from experience.

Inspired by the Multidimensional Aptitude Battery-II (MAB-II; T7:1688), the PAF provides a quick and convenient alternative to the measurement of GMA. The PAF eliminates most of the subscores of the MAB-II, providing only verbal and quantitative scores. Each subtest takes about 10 minutes to administer, including directions, for a total of approximately 20 minutes compared to the nearly 2 hours of testing required by the MAB-II (Jackson, 1998). Two forms of the PAF are available: Form A is more difficult and purportedly "more accurate at a higher range" (manual, p. 2); whereas Form C is "more accurate at the lower range of scores" (manual, p. 2). However, this description is insufficient for the test user. An employer would benefit from guidance as to the job types or educational levels appropriate for each form. The website does offer some guidance of this type, but this information should be in the manual.

Both the 36-item Verbal subtest and the 21-item Quantitative subtest utilize a five-option, multiple-choice format. Verbal items are mainly vocabulary or general knowledge with a mix of sentence completion, synonym, antonym, and analogy. Math items are short word problems representing a mix of ratios, rates, and percents. Items have a face validity that most pre-employment tests lack. Responses are recorded on a separate answer sheet that is then faxed to a scoring service, and a score report is returned via fax within a few minutes. The reverse side of the answer sheet provides a sample item with instructions for recording responses. However, the example is inappropriate as it is a personality item and the response format requires that one choose two responses ("one most like me" and "one least like me") as opposed to the single response option and GMA items that actually appear on the PAF.

The PAF manual provides clear administrator's instructions in the form of a script, thus ensuring uniform procedures. However, other aspects of the manual are unclear. No mention is made of the use of calculators, data are selectively presented from cited scholarly articles, and figures are poorly formatted lacking axis labels or with double printing of axes (Hunter & Hunter, 1984; Schmidt & Hunter, 1998). Finally, one-third of the PAF manual is dedicated to detailing the benefits of mental abilities tests in general with no discussion of their shortcomings such as adverse impact against protected groups. Research in cognitive skills testing consistently reports mean differences with ethnic minority groups scoring a full standard deviation below nonminorities (Kaplan & Saccuzzo, 2001; Outtz, 2002). The manual leaves the naïve reader with an unrealistically favorable impression of general mental abilities tests.

The manual is also deficient in terms of score reporting and score interpretation. Although the manual states that two scores are provided, Verbal and Quantitative, no sample score report or interpretation of scores appears. The website, however, does have a sample score report with Verbal, Quantitative, and total scores. Although raw scores and percentiles are presented and are reportedly based on a sample of job candidates, this information is insufficient for test users. Information on how to interpret test results for selection decisions or career counseling should be added.

DEVELOPMENT. No information is provided on the construction of the PAF items. Form A was equated with the MAB-II. [Editor's Note: The 2006 manual eliminates all reference to the link with the MAB-II, but it is discussed several times in the 2004 manual.] The MAB-II was normed on a group of 1,600 individuals who were reported as roughly representative of the U.S. population in terms of gender, ethnicity, and geographic region. The normative group consisted equally of employees in managerial, professional, or specialty jobs and technical, sales, service, and labor occupations (Thompson, 2003). A group of 363 individuals took both the PAF and relevant subtests of the MAB-II (Comprehension, Arithmetic, and Similarities). However, the demographics of this group were not reported, except that their ages ranged from 25 to 34 years. An algorithm was developed to equate the three PAF scores (Verbal, Quantitative, and Total) with

MAB-II scores, although the process described is not entirely clear. Thus, MAB-II norms could then be used to interpret the PAF score. Form C was normed on a group of 245 blue-collar workers for whom neither demographics nor industry were reported.

Lack of information regarding the normative groups makes scores difficult to interpret. Because Form A and Form C are intended for individuals with different educational levels [Form A is for college graduates] (Jackson, 2004), the educational level of these normative groups should have been reported and should have consisted of college educated for Form A and nondegreed for Form C. It would be useful to report gender, ethnicity, industry, and length of time on job so that the norms could be properly interpreted. Competing instruments, such as the Wonderlic, provide separate norms for educational levels, and minimum scores are reported for over 140 job positions (Wonderlic, 1999).

TECHNICAL. Only one reliability study is reported in the manual, and there is no indication as to which form was analyzed. The sample used in the reliability study is referred to as a group of 88 managers from a food service organization. However, there is no information as to the gender or ethnic composition of this group. Internal consistency measures yielded good coefficients (alpha) of .89 for Verbal, .87 for Quantitative, and .94 for Total score. The publisher claims that these are likely underestimates of the true reliability because of restriction of range and that the application of appropriate formulas would produce a higher estimate. The publisher should either apply those formulas and report the results or they should conduct the reliability study with a larger, more heterogeneous sample.

The validity of the PAF was demonstrated by correlating PAF scores with other acceptable measures of general intelligence and also with job performance. Form A reports a correlation of .80 with the MAB-II using what appears to be the same sample of 363 individuals cited above in PAF development. It seems no surprise that these two measures would correlate because the algorithm used to derive PAF scores utilizes scores on the MAB-II. At a minimum, a new sample of respondents should have been used to demonstrate this validity. Form C was correlated .85 with the Wonderlic using a sample of 245 individuals for whom no demographic information was provided.

In terms of job performance, data were reported only for Form C in a study of 88 first-line supervisors in the food service industry. Employees were rated on job aspects such as Public Relations, Administration, Communication, Management, Policy Following, and Routine Job Tasks. A Cohen set correlation, which takes into account all significant canonical variates, was $r^2 = .26$. Individual criterion measures were much smaller and only a few are reported, such as .35 between Verbal score and Communication. For the Quantitative score, correlations of .20 and .25 were reported with Administration and Communication, respectively. It is unclear why only select individual correlations were reported.

No information is reported on the fairness of the PAF. As stated earlier, GMA tests are known to routinely demonstrate large and consistent score differences of approximately one standard deviation deficit for racial and ethnic minority groups. The authors should conduct studies of separate gender and ethnic groups and report on score differences as well as prediction.

COMMENTARY. At first glance, the PAF appears to be a viable option when choosing a test of GMA. The layout and face validity of the instrument are excellent, which is a problem with other measures of GMA. However, the psychometric properties of the instrument have not been well documented and the studies that are presented are lacking. The manual provides selective information and contains numerous editorial errors. The publisher failed to provide sufficient information regarding the composition of samples used to determine norms or to demonstrate reliability or validity. Finally, at a cost of $17 per answer sheet (Jackson, 2005), the PAF is prohibitive when other instruments cost less than half and provide superior normative data (e.g., the Wonderlic costs $7.50 for orders under 100 and $3 for orders of 100 or more; Wonderlic, Inc., personal communication, February, 21, 2006).

SUMMARY. The PAF could be a viable alternative to existing measures of GMA. However, the paucity of research, lack of normative information, high cost, and lack of information as to the instrument's fairness, lead this reviewer to recommend not using the instrument until more information is available.

[The reviewer would like to thank Brian Kirby for his assistance on this critique. His insights and perspectives contributed significantly to the review.]

REVIEWER'S REFERENCES

Hunter, J. E., & Hunter, R. F. (1984). Validity and utility of alternate predictors of job performance. *Psychological Bulletin, 96,* 72-98.

Jackson, D. N. (1998). Multidimensional Aptitude Battery-II. Sigma Assessment Systems. Retrieved February 7, 2006, from http://www.sigmaassessmentsystems.com/assessments/mab.asp

Jackson, D. N. (2004). Personnel Assessment Form. Sigma Assessment Systems. Retrieved February 1, 2006, from http://www.sigmaassessmentsystems.com/assessments/paf.asp

Jackson, D. N. (2005). PAF prices. Sigma Assessment Systems. Retrieved February 3, 2006, from http://www.sigmaassessmentsystems.com/prices/paf.asp

Kaplan, R. M., & Saccuzzo, D. P. (2001). *Psychological testing.* Wadsorth: Belmont, CA.

Outtz, J. L. (2002). The role of cognitive ability tests in employment selection. *Human Performance, 15,* 161-171.

Schmidt, F. L., & Hunter, J. E. (1998). The validity and utility of selection methods in personnel psychology: Practical and theoretical implications of 85 years of research findings. *Psychological Bulletin, 124,* 262-274.

Thompson, D. L. (1998). [Review of the Multidimensional Aptitude Battery-II.] In B. S. Plake, J. C. Impara, & R. A. Spies (Eds.), *The fifteenth mental measurements yearbook* (pp. 603-607). Lincoln, NE: Buros Institute of Mental Measurements.

Wonderlic Personnel Test & Scholastic Level Exam user's manual. (1999). Libertyville, IL: Wonderlic Inc.

Review of the Personnel Assessment Form by JAMES W. PINKNEY, *Professor of Counselor and Adult Education, East Carolina University, Greenville, NC:*

DESCRIPTION. The Personnel Assessment Form (PAF) is a multiple-choice inventory of 57 items for assessing general mental ability (GMA) as an estimate of intelligence. There are two components: a 36-item Verbal subtest and a 21-item Quantitative subtest. These components form an estimate of GMA with the Verbal items looking at words, concepts, and diverse topics and the Quantitative items looking at numerical problems to estimate problem solving and abstract reasoning skills.

All items of the PAF are taken from the Multidimensional Aptitude Battery-II (MAB-II; T7:1688), and the publisher apparently assumes that the psychometric properties of the MAB-II are preserved in this considerably shortened version. No explanation of this assumption is given in the manual, even though longer assessments are generally found to be more reliable. [Editor's Note: All reference to the link the MAB-II is eliminated in the 2006 manual.]

There are two versions of the PAF, and both are to be attempted by the employee or applicant in less than 15 minutes (7 minutes per subtest). The two versions differ in the difficulty of the items. Form A is more difficult and presumed to be more discriminatory at the higher range of mental ability (intelligence) whereas Form C is presumed to be more useful at the lower range of mental ability. Both versions are intended for use with normal, functional individuals, and use of the PAF is discouraged for people with psychopathology or borderline cognitive abilities.

The PAF is taken with a fax-ready answer sheet that is scored by the publisher. The promotional advertising mentions a turnaround time of 30 minutes for a report to be received by the user. No other scoring option is offered, and the cost is $17 per report. Volume discounts are mentioned that would lower this cost to $11 per report for more than 2,500 reports.

DEVELOPMENT. The manual for the PAF takes a rather unusual approach to presenting the development of the instrument. Instead of the developmental history of the PAF, the manual focuses on the predictive validity of cognitive ability. Essentially, the potential user is presented the argument that any job will be performed better by candidates and employees with higher levels of mental ability. Because the intent of the PAF is to provide a rapid assessment of mental ability, it should be a useful component in both hiring and promotion decisions.

There is no information presented in the manual on how items were selected from the longer MAB-II, how the level of difficulty was determined, or what determined the length of the two subtests. On inspection, the Verbal subtest consists of vocabulary items and analogies. The Quantitative subtest consists of arithmetic operations and a few algebra problems. Potential users are left with the assertion that the PAF is a reliable measure of GMA with the advantage of being faster than most tests of intelligence because of the reduced number of subtests. Again, no information is provided about which MAB-II subtests were dropped, why the two subtests of the PAF were selected, or the reasoning behind this process.

TECHNICAL. The two forms of the PAF were standardized using two different groups. Form A (for higher levels of GMA) used a sample of 363 participants drawn from the norming process of the MAB-II. An equating algorithm was created to link the PAF raw score to the MAB. This generated MAB percentiles for the PAF scores. The participants were drawn from the age group of 25–34-year olds. The manual states that this age group is characteristic of job applicants, but no information is given on how the participants were drawn.

Form C (for lower levels of GMA) was standardized on a group of 245 participants described only as "blue-collar employees." The manual reports that the distribution of the scores obtained from this group approximated the general population. No information is given about any other aspects for either of the two groups used in the standardization process.

Information on the PAF's reliability is sketchy. The manual reports one published study that used 88 food service managers and reported coefficient alpha reliability values of .89 for the PAF Verbal score, .87 for the PAF Quantitative score, and .94 for the total PAF score. The only other information about the PAF's reliability is that the above sample of 88 managers had scores in the top half of GMA range. An attenuation of range in scores tends to lower reliability estimates slightly.

The manual presents little information to support the validity of the PAF for its two primary uses: personnel selection and promotion decisions. The promotional literature suggests its primary use is career counseling, but there is no mention of this in the manual. The author appeals to a meta-analysis of numerous validity studies as adequate support for this argument and, by extension, for the "validity" of the PAF.

No information is provided on item selection other than the comment that it is intended to be a short version of the MAB-II. The potential user is left with the manual's assertion that the PAF is a measure of GMA that takes less time to administer than most tests of intelligence. It should be noted that GMA, intelligence, is a very broad construct with numerous facets that can be very different from each other. The information about what the two subtests attempt to assess is very brief and provides no details on how the items were selected, designed, or tested. This omission is especially troubling because two versions of the PAF are available with one for the higher levels of GMA and the other for the lower levels of GMA.

The manual reports that the two standardization groups also took another assessment of GMA and that the correlations support the PAF as a measure of GMA. The Form A group of 363 participants also took three parts of the MAB-II (Comprehension, Arithmetic, and Similarities) and found a correlation of .80 between the two measures.

The Form C group of 245 participants took the Wonderlic Personnel Test, which generated a correlation of .85 with the PAF. The only other information about validity provided by the PAF manual is a brief table illustrating how a second predictor can supplement the predictive validity of GMA assessments.

COMMENTARY. The PAF is a recent effort and as such has had little time to develop a background of research, either supporting it or not supporting it as an assessment of GMA. The manual attempts to promote the PAF on logical arguments and on the extensive efforts that went into producing its forerunner, the MAB-II. The use of the PAF for personnel selection and promotion is presented as a shortened version of an already proven assessment. Potential users would need to think carefully about several assumptions involved in the construction of the PAF.

The assumption that any job will be done better by a smarter worker is an overgeneralization. Not every job requires high levels of creativity, intelligence, and quickness. Overqualified workers can easily create problems as well as results. A faster assessment has a cost, and speed may not be an issue in many personnel situations, either for hiring or for promotion. Whether a 15-minute estimate of GMA is cost effective would be a relevant and reasonable question that potential users should think about.

The assumption is also made that because the MAB-II has good psychometric properties, the PAF inherits those properties. This logic is suspect in the sense that the PAF is much shorter than the MAB-II. Shorter assessments tend to be less reliable and more narrow in focus. For example, the Verbal subtest is based solely on vocabulary items and a few analogies.

SUMMARY. The PAF is intended to provide a quick estimate of general mental ability. Potential users would want to consider seriously whether or not speed is an issue in many hiring and promotion decisions, two uses the manual suggests. If speed is not an issue, the original MAB-II, reviewed by Thompson (2003) and Widaman (2003) would be a better choice. Cost would be an issue for many users. The PAF should not be used for career counseling.

REVIEWER'S REFERENCES

Thompson, D. L. (2003). [Review of the Multidimensional Aptitude Battery-II]. In B. S. Plake, J. C. Impara, & R. A. Spies (Eds.), *The fifteenth mental measurements yearbook* (pp. 603-605). Lincoln, NE: Buros Institute of Mental Measurements.

Widaman, K. F. (2003). [Review of the Multidimensional Aptitude Battery-II]. In B. S. Plake, J. C. Impara, & R. A. Spies (Eds.), *The fifteenth mental measurements yearbook* (pp. 605-607). Lincoln, NE: Buros Institute of Mental Measurements.

[147]

Personnel Tests for Industry—Oral Directions Test [Second Edition].

Purpose: A test of general ability designed to "assess an individual's ability to follow directions presented orally" and as a selection tool "to predict performance in a variety of vocational and technical training settings."
Population: Adolescents and adults.
Publication Dates: 1974–1995.
Acronym: PTI-ODT.
Scores: Total score only.
Administration: Individual or group.
Forms, 2: S, T.
Price Data, 2007: $200 per complete set including recording, manual (1995, 67 pages), script, key, 100 answer documents, directions for administering, and cassette tape Form S or T; $50 per examination kit including scripts and answer documents for both forms and manual.
Time:(15) minutes.
Comments: Tape-recorded administration; one of three subtests of Personnel Tests for Industry (T7:1938).
Author: Charles R. Langmuir.
Publisher: Harcourt Assessment, Inc.
Cross References: For information for Personnel Tests for Industry, see T5:1974 (1 reference), T4:2008 (5 references), T3:1808 (3 references), T2:433 (5 references), and 7:373 (3 references); for a review by Erwin K. Taylor, see 5:366; see also 4:309 (1 reference); for reviews by Charles D. Flory, Irving Lorge, and William W. Turnbull of the Oral Directions Test, see 3:245.

Review of the Personnel Tests for Industry—Oral Directions Test [Second Edition] by CAROLINE M. ADKINS, Professor Emeritus, School of Education, Hunter College, City University of New York, New York, NY:

DESCRIPTION. The Personnel Test for Industry—Oral Directions Test (PTI-ODT) is a 15-minute test of "general mental ability" that was designed to be used as part of an employment selection process. Two equivalent forms of the test are available, Forms S and T, with each composed of 16 items. Directions and questions on both forms of the test are administered from prerecorded cassette tapes. Items in the questions move from simple "draw a circle inside the first square and then make an x in the second square" to more complicated and complex items. Some items include 10 different sequences for listening and responding.

Paper-and-pencil answer sheets are provided for responses that require marking an x, letters, or numbers in different squares, circles, and triangles. A scoring key accompanies each form and is used to hand score the test. Raw scores are converted to percentile rankings, expressed in terms of the percent of people in a variety of norm groups scoring above or below a given raw score.

The manual for the PTI-ODT includes information about the first 1974 version of the test along with information collected from 19 new norm groups in the early 1990s. According to the authors, the PTI-ODT was designed to "predict success in certain production, maintenance and service jobs…that require the comprehension of oral directions" and "to determine whether a trainee can benefit from specific vocational training" or "remediation" (manual, p. 11). The authors also suggest that the PTI-ODT can be used with people who have a limited education because it only requires printing either alphabet letters or simple numbers. It can also be used, the test authors say, to determine how well people with non-English backgrounds can comprehend verbal English.

DEVELOPMENT. The PTI-ODT was developed "specifically for use in industry" (manual, p. 8). The manual describes a sequence of pilot tests conducted from 1946–1974 to explore item clarity, reliability, validity, ease of administration, and relevance of norms. These studies resulted in shorter versions of the PTI-ODT and the eventual development of the two equivalent forms, S and T. It is not clear from the manual why these were developed. One can assume they were for equivalent-form reliability studies or retesting but such explanations are not described in the manual. Other than identifying the test as an ability test (rather than an achievement test), a test of general mental ability, and a test of ability to follow oral directions, no mention is made in the manual of any concepts, theories, or behavioral domain samples that were used to develop items for the PTI-ODT. The absence of this dimension of the test relates negatively to the test's validity.

TECHNICAL. Studies done in the early 1990s focused primarily on developing new sets of norms. They included 7,797 adults in 13 different occupational groups (e.g., "entry-level production applicants at a Midwestern paper mill, applicants for semi-skilled jobs at a county government" [manual, p.20] and six rehabilitation training groups). In the new norm tables, data for males and females and different ethnic groups are combined. Users of the test are advised to "look for a group that is similar to the individual or group being tested" (manual, p. 19). The manual also advises developing local norms whenever possible to reflect local job demands and labor market conditions.

The standardization norm samples are of sufficient size and essential for converting raw scores into percentile ranks and for interpreting the meaning of scores for applicants to specific positions. It is difficult to determine exactly what type and level of occupation the PTI-ODT is best suited. The norm groups are generally described as "technician applicants," "maintenance applicants," or "vocational rehabilitation clients" (manual, p. 21). Norms that specify educational level, skilled or unskilled occupations, type of occupation, or different enterprises would be helpful to the user who needs to ascertain the usefulness of this measure for different groups of interest.

Reliability studies for the PTI-ODT are primarily for the 1974 version of the test. Internal consistency reliability was examined by calculating standard errors of measurement and split-half reliability coefficients for six different groups. The coefficients are acceptable ranging from .73 to .86. Test-retest reliability analyses were done with five different groups. Given the fact that examinees were retested immediately following completion of the first form one cannot have much confidence in the measure's stability over time. Because the PTI-ODT manual describes the test as having "characteristics of both a *speeded* [examinees have a very limited time, 5 to 10 seconds, to respond to varying items] and a *power* test [composed of easy and difficult items]" (manual, p. 11), it would be helpful to know the extent to which differences in test scores are attributed to speed and how much to power and how much they both affect scoring reliability.

The test manual clearly lays out the validity issues and analyses that were conducted to address them. Emphasis is placed on criterion-related validity and the relationship of PTI-ODT scores to job performance ratings and construct validity, correlating scores on the PTI-ODT with achievement and intelligence test scores. Strangely missing is a description of how content valid the PDI-ODT is with the manual suggesting that "those

interested in content validity should demonstrate that the jobs in question require the oral comprehension abilities measured by the PDI-ODT" (manual, p. 31). This is a central problem with respect to the test's validity. Because we have no information about from where the measure's items are derived, we can have little confidence that the domain of items is a representative sample of tasks, behavior, and knowledge necessary to perform specific jobs.

With respect to criterion-related validity, the PTI-ODT studies are better. Data are presented from 22 studies that examine the relationship between test scores and either job performance ratings or grades in training courses. For the most part, the correlations vary a great deal ranging from good (.52) to quite doubtful (.04). (A couple are even negative.) The user needs to examine this table very carefully to determine whether or not the correlations are appropriate for the jobs for which they are interested in selecting applicants. One example of sample differences relates to the correlation between scores and job performance for a sample of white males versus a sample of minority males. These correlations are, on five indices, .21 to .43 for white males and .01 to .18 for minority males.

Construct validity studies are extensive and generally correlate scores on the PTI-ODT with scores on the Fundamental Achievement Series, Stanford Achievement Tests, Wide Range Achievement, and Wechsler Adult Intelligence Scale. These studies are relevant in the sense that the authors claim the PTI-ODT is a measure of "general mental ability" (p. 37). The average correlations of combined samples for these analyses range from .47 to .78, suggesting moderate to substantial overlapping constructs with these measures. These validity studies add evidence to the claim that it is measuring some part of intelligence.

COMMENTARY. The concept of who can take directions and who cannot is basically a good one and becomes critical in some occupations (e.g., fireman, nurse, platoon leader). It is difficult to see, however, what the relationship is between items in the PTI-ODT and the ability to understand and follow verbal directions. The items' complexity, sequencing, use of numbers, circles, squares, diagrams, and directions require much more than the ability to listen to and follow directions. They require a special type of cognitive processing, perceptual speed, motor coordination, and memory function involving sequencing and positioning of numbers. In some instances the items were so complex that it was very difficult to follow the directions even after reading them several times. At the very least the items reflect a measure of intelligence as defined in some theories. The authors describe it as a test of general mental ability without defining what general mental ability they are testing.

Various norm groups in the PTI-ODT include employees in entry-level positions. It is difficult to see how the PTI-ODT would not adversely affect applicants with limited educational backgrounds who have a lack of familiarity with academic type tasks or who may have limited English-language proficiency. More valid tests of ability to follow oral directions would need to include situationally relevant directions, more emphasis on verbal rather than numerical concepts, attention to sequence and following, interaction clarification, and judgment. Questions can also be raised about the predictive value of any such tests. Perhaps the focus should be on the training of employees to follow directions in their own occupational areas rather than excluding potential employees with spurious selection procedures.

SUMMARY. The PTI-OTD may have been attractive in a prior time when employers were looking for a quick (15-minute) measure that could be orally administered and hand scored. There is still probably a need for measures with these characteristics, but the PTI-OTD has such fairness and validity issues in the areas of its relevance to job performance and ability to follow oral directions that it cannot be recommended as a selection measure.

Review of the Personnel Tests for Industry—Oral Directions Test [Second Edition] by BRUCE BISKIN, Director of Learning Assessment, Thomas Edison State College, Trenton, NJ:

DESCRIPTION. The test manual [Second Edition] for the Personnel Tests for Industry—Oral Directions Test (PTI-ODT) notes that it was designed as a "wide range test of general mental ability" (p. 7) that would be "simple and practical for use in testing adolescent and adult groups" (p. 7). Its intended uses include employment selection, research, counseling, training, and vocational rehabilitation. The manual indicates

that the PTI-ODT is targeted at differentiating among individuals who do not have extensive education and so is not appropriate for use with highly educated individuals. The limits of education for which the test is appropriate, however, are not clearly spelled out.

The PTI-ODT manual, in its second edition, is a good example of a classic technical manual for a published test. It contains an overview, followed by a short section on "general mental ability." A fairly detailed description of the construction and uses of the PTI-ODT ensues. The manual also includes clear and specific instructions for the test administration and scoring, and an extensive set of psychometric information, including multiple norms and reliability estimates. It also includes evidence to support the validity of the scores.

The PTI-ODT is available in two forms (S and T). The test forms are contained on a separate prerecorded audiocassette tape. Each form comprises 16 items, though some items require multiple responses. The two forms, though intended to be completely parallel, have a slightly different structure: Form S elicits 39 scorable responses and Form T elicits 36. Each scorable response is weighted equally, and there is no penalty for an incorrect response. Responses are manually recorded by the examinee on a printed answer sheet. Machine scoring is not available. The examination kit did not include cassette tapes (though it did include transcripts of the tapes), nor did it contain the answer keys.

DEVELOPMENT. The development of the PTI-ODT, as described in the manual, apparently began in the mid-1940s, with the first version—a longer form than either of the current forms—published in 1946. Form S was published in 1954, followed by Form T in 1974. No further versions have been published in over 30 years, though additional normative data, included in the manual, were collected in 1993 and 1994. Though the PTI-ODT is purported to be a measure of general mental ability, the manual contains no substantive discussion of the construct, nor does it contain specific references that would link the development of the PTI-ODT with the construct. The psychometric development of the test—that is, the procedural and statistical methods used to refine the development through a series of iterative studies—is described in detail and reflects a high degree of attention to psychometric practices of the time.

TECHNICAL.

Norms. The manual presents an extensive set of norms from 1994 for samples with a variety of job titles and for several vocational rehabilitation samples. The manual includes the older norms from 1954 and 1971 for research purposes only. It also takes great care to inform the user about the limitations of *all* the published norms, appropriately recommending that the user make high-stakes decisions—like employee selection—using locally developed norms.

Administration. The PTI-ODT is not designed to be self-administering. Administration begins with preparatory instructions by the test administrator—after which the cassette is started and the administrator provides no further instruction until the test is completed. Because each form has different items—and therefore different oral directions—multiple forms can be used simultaneously only if the two audio feeds are segregated. This can be done using separate rooms or a dedicated audio lab/testing room that allows each test taker's audio feed to be isolated from the others. However, no specific instruction or guidance is provided in the manual for administering the PTI-ODT to multiple test takers using headphones. Because the use of headphones could affect scores, the construction of local norms using this method of administration would be even more important than the manual states.

Scoring. The manual (p. 18) describes the scoring process for each item on Forms S and T. Each scorable response is weighted equally, and there is no penalty for an incorrect response. Several items have multiple responses and require the scorer to make a series of evaluations to determine the score value of a response. As a result, scoring can be complex and prone to errors. Scoring should always be checked, ideally by a second person.

Reliability. Extensive reliability information is provided in the manual. The alternate-form reliability estimate reported in the manual for Forms S and T was .79, based on a combined sample of 350 individuals who took both forms in counterbalanced order. Ten Spearman-Brown-corrected split-half reliability estimates, reprinted from the 1974 manual, ranged from .73 to .86, with a median of .81. Eight of the 10 estimates were based on four independent groups, each of which

took both Forms S and T. The difference between the reliability estimates for the two forms in those four groups was .03 or less, suggesting scores from the two forms are approximately equally reliable. In addition, 5 independent test-retest reliability estimates (also first reported in the 1974 manual) ranged from .79 to .93, with a median of .82.

All these estimates, when taken together, support the use of the PTI-ODT in research where data are aggregated, and in making low-to-moderate stakes decisions where the reliability estimates in the .80 to .90 range may be sufficient for such uses. However, users should be cautious about using scores from the PTI-ODT for making high-stakes decisions, such as employment selection. Of course, if the PTI-ODT scores are used to supplement other information, reliability estimates in this range may be sufficient for help in making high-stakes decisions. The *incremental* reliability of the decision when the PTI-ODT scores are added to the decision process should be of primary concern. The manual notes that base rates should be considered in evaluating the utility of PTI-ODT scores in decision making. Although this advice is good, the manual could have included other factors, such as selection ratio and tolerance for false positives and false negatives, as well as individual and joint reliability of various information sources that contribute to the decision. The bottom line is that users should understand the impact of *how* they use PTI-ODT scores in making high-stakes decisions.

Validity. The presentation of *validity* in the manual is more consistent with the conceptualization of validity prevalent in 1974—the date of the previous revision—than in 1995, the last time the PTI-ODT manual was revised. In particular, the manual refers to different, discrete *types* of validity, rather than to different *sources of evidence* of validity, which is a more modern conception. The older conception attributes validity to the test, whereas the modern conception attributes validity to the inferences and decisions made for a specific purpose based on test *scores.* As a result, the manual presents discussions of three types of validity—content, criterion-related, and construct—in separate sections with no attempt to unify the evidence.

The section on content validity presents no content-related evidence to support the validity of the PTI-ODT for any particular purpose. This reviewer would have liked to see a rationale for the item structure chosen, particularly given the complex scoring.

Evidence of criterion-related validity consists of a tabular summary of 22 samples, originally included in the 1974 version of the manual, comprising correlations of PTI-ODT scores with a variety of job-related criteria. Likewise, the section presenting evidence of construct validity consists of a table summarizing 34 samples in which PTI-ODT scores were correlated with scores from tests of mostly general mental ability and mechanical ability. (Note: some of the "construct validity" correlations appear to be based on the same samples reported under "criterion-related validity.") The manual provides minimal interpretation of the criterion-related and construct evidence for validity, assuming—and relying on—a moderate amount of statistical/psychometric sophistication on the part of the user.

The correlational evidence included under "criterion-related validity" is variable from sample to sample, possibly reflecting variability and idiosyncrasies in the quality and reliability of local criterion measures. These factors, when combined with relatively small samples of participants—ranging from less than 25 participants to 136 (median = 52)—may explain why most of the correlations failed to reach statistical significance. Even without using statistical significance to evaluate the various correlations, there is no intuitively obvious pattern in the correlations with various criterion measures that would support a consistent argument for the validity of PTI-ODT scores in making selection decisions. I suspect those wanting to evaluate the PTI-ODT for making high-stakes employee selection decisions, unless they are highly trained or very experienced with the PTI-ODT, would have difficulty applying the construct validity evidence for their local purposes.

The construct-related evidence was reasonably consistent across studies. A summary statement suggesting that "the relationships with measures of numerical, verbal, and clerical ability are substantial, while correlations of the PTI-ODT with measures of mechanical ability tend to be moderate" (manual, p. 37) is as definitive as the manual gets for interpreting evidence to support the validity of PTI-ODT scores. No evidence for the validity of the PTI-ODT as a measure of understanding oral instructions is included in the manual except as that construct might be part of general mental ability.

COMMENTARY. The last major revision of the PTI-ODT was done over 50 years ago, though new norms were published in 1974 and 1995. The manual consistently cautions users to collect local norms. All too often, technical manuals read like they were edited by a marketing department, but the PTI-ODT manual appears to be well-balanced. The extensive criterion-related evidence for validity was spotty. Given the more consistent construct-related evidence for validity, as opposed to the criterion-related evidence, one wonders more about the quality of the *criterion measures* used in the reported studies than the efficacy of the PTI-ODT itself. Still, the paucity of criterion-related evidence is a concern, given the longevity of the PTI-ODT. After 50+ years, one would have expected a more solid track record in criterion-related validity evidence.

Test administration materials have not changed to adapt to modern technology. Cassette tapes and players are becoming obsolete and no longer represent an optimal way to record, store, or deliver high-quality audio. Indeed, some potential users may not have cassette players with high-quality reproduction. The publisher should consider the value of redesigning the test materials to include CD and other digital media that can be played on high-quality sound systems or computers. In addition, advice—preferably research-based—on the use of headphones with a single machine or in a networked environment (such as a testing center or language lab) should be included in the manual.

The publisher might also consider adapting the PTI-ODT so that examinees can record answers on a computer or other device that can automate scoring. If feasible, automated scoring could improve accuracy and turnaround of scores.

Changes in administration format and equipment could make current norms obsolete, so major changes should be made only after studies show that the changes have no negative impact on the interpretation of scores, or after studies show that use of current norms has no substantive impact on decisions or inferences based on those norms.

SUMMARY. The PTI-ODT is described primarily as a short measure of general mental ability for use in employee selection, counseling, and vocational rehabilitation. It is beginning to show its age by not adapting to changes in test administration, response-recording, and scoring technologies. Criterion-related validity evidence for employment selection is surprisingly variable, though construct-related validity evidence is more consistent.

[148]

Pervasive Developmental Disorder in Mental Retardation Scale [Second Revised Edition].

Purpose: "A simple classification and screening instrument designed for the identification of Pervasive Developmental Disorders in persons with mental retardation/intellectual disability."
Population: Ages 2—80.
Publication Dates: 1990—2006.
Acronym: PDD-MRS.
Scores: Total score only.
Administration: Individual.
Price Data, 2006: EURO123,40 (U.S. $148.08) per starter set including manual (2006, 53 pages) and 75 record forms; EURO49,50 (U.S. $59.40) per manual; EURO73,90 (U.S. $88.68) per 75 record forms.
Foreign Language Editions: First published in Dutch; English, German, and Italian versions are available.
Time: (10—20) minutes.
Comments: Norms of the scale are based on data of 1,230 children, adolescents, and adults in the profound, severe, moderate, and mild ranges of mental retardation.
Authors: D. W. Kraijer.
Publisher: PITS: Psychologische Instrumenten Tests en Services [The Netherlands].

Review of the Pervasive Developmental Disorder in Mental Retardation Scale [Second Revised Edition] by TAWNYA MEADOWS, Assistant Professor of Psychology, University of Nebraska Medical Center, Omaha, NE:

DESCRIPTION. The Pervasive Developmental Disorder in Mental Retardation Scale [Second Revised Edition] (PDD-MRS) is an instrument designed to screen and classify Pervasive Developmental Disorders (PDD) in individuals, ages 2 to 80, with mental retardation. Twelve items are scored based upon behaviors exhibited over the past 2- to 6-month period. Information is obtained though interview, observation, and record review. There are 12 individual items, some having more than one stem. Each stem is scored individually with some being weighted more than others.

The 12 items comprise four categories: social interaction with adults, social interaction with peers, language and speech, and other behavior. Raw scores for the 12 items are added together into a total score, with each item being weighted from 1 to 3. The maximum total score is 19. The total score is used to classify individuals as having No Pervasive Developmental Disorder (N), Presence of a Pervasive Developmental Disorder Doubtful (D), and Pervasive Developmental Disorder (PDD).

Administration may be conducted by anyone with familiarity of autism and autism-related disorders, as well as mental retardation. It is highly recommended that the administrator be emotionally detached from the individual being assessed to reduce subjectivity and increase accuracy. Finally, the test administrator must be able to make observations, interview relevant individuals, and review patient records. However, interpretation is recommended to be done by either a psychologist or psychiatrist.

DEVELOPMENT. The PDD-MRS is the most recent version (copyright, 2006) of the instrument that has been in various development stages since the late 1980s. Three reasons for the development of the revised PDD-MRS are provided in the manual. First, the PDD-MRS may be used with children and adults, as other instruments at that time were designed to measure or screen PDD in children only. Second, most instruments during the late 1980s were designed to measure strictly autistic disorder and not PDD in general. Third, the PDD-MRS was designed to be used with individuals with mental retardation, whereas previous instruments were not designed specifically for this population. The author purports that previous instruments not designed for the mental retardation population were often leading to either diagnostic overshadowing or diagnostic underrepresentation.

The manual provides extensive information regarding rationale for the development of another autism scale and requirements of the instrument the test developer wanted to meet. Many requirements are congruent with Practice Parameters for the Diagnosis and Evaluation of Autism (Filipek et al., 1999). Items were derived from behavioral descriptions of autistic children with mental retardation from field experts and diagnostic criteria. However, one significant criticism of the instrument is that items are strongly based upon diagnostic criteria of the DSM III-R. Thirty-seven preliminary items were derived from these two sources and were narrowed down by the results from a series of pilot studies. The remaining items were reworded for clarity and ease of interpretation and then subjected to statistical analysis via coefficient kappa and discriminability between PDD and non-PDD individuals.

TECHNICAL. The normative sample consists of 1,230 individuals from 2 to 80 years of age, including 71 children who were 2 years old. Individuals in the normative sample came from 5 of the 12 provinces of the Netherlands and all had a measured level of mental retardation. Individuals from the norm sample resided in institutions, group homes, or lived at home but were involved in day-care centers or special treatment clinics. In addition, the manual did not include information either as to the recruitment process nor did it include information either regarding socioeconomic class or ethnicity of participants.

Internal consistency reliability was computed for those in the norm group with functional speech and those without functional speech. The resulting alpha coefficients were .86 and .81, respectively. In addition, interrater reliability was calculated by comparing ratings of 99 participants made by medical and psychological experts and yielded a Pearson correlation coefficient of .83. Interrater reliability was also calculated by comparing ratings of two psychology experts for groups, sizes 76 and 42, and was found to be .85 and .89, respectively. Finally, test-retest reliability was calculated from a group of 97 participants with ratings provided by psychological and medical experts, with Pearson correlation coefficients of .81 and .86, respectively. Although the manual did provide reliability coefficients and a brief description as to calculation methodology, the author did not provide reference to empirical studies making these claims.

Several methods of calculating validity were discussed in the manual. The author provided citations to several of his studies over the years that supported his position that the PDD-MRS satisfactorily discriminates between groups. Sensitivity and specificity values were reported to be satisfactory to good. Data based on specific subgroups were also reported. Lower sensitivity was found for participants diagnosed with borderline intelligence or who were early-life blind. In addi-

tion, the participant group who had severe blindness exhibited a high misclassification rate. A high misclassification rate was also found for participants diagnosed with Fragile X. Validity was also enhanced by factor analysis via varimax rotation with Kaiser normalization yielding satisfactory results. Discriminative validity was calculated by comparing PDD-MRS scores to scores on three scales related to gross motor skills, maladaptive behavior, and social functioning. Gross motor skills, self-help skills, and aggressive maladaptive behaviors were not found to be affected by the presence of a PDD. Meanwhile, verbal and mixed maladaptive behavior and communication, persistence, and social skills subscales were impacted by the presence of a PDD diagnosis. Therefore, concurrent and discriminative validity of the scale appear satisfactory.

COMMENTARY. The PDD-MRS does appear to fulfill sufficiently its role as an autism screening instrument for individuals with mental retardation. The test was developed with clear goals in mind, and it appears the author successfully achieved this aim. There are several positive attributes of the instrument such as its ease of administration, short administration time, and its recommendation that information should be obtained from multiple sources. The manual is clear in providing information regarding administration procedures that could be quickly mastered by the administrator. Added to the ease of administration are very clear and thorough directions provided to assist in the scoring of each item. For example, numerous behavior examples were provided with operational definitions of many terms. It is also beneficial that the test developer included a few key developmental milestones and typical age of achievement to assist in qualitatively rating the patient on daily living skills, motor skills, and social interaction skills. Furthermore, a sample completed and scored instrument is provided in the manual. However, the PDD-MRS focuses so closely on current symptomology on a narrow range of behaviors that information obtained is limited in its ability to assist in treatment planning. It should be noted that the test developer recognizes this limitation and makes it clear that the instrument is not intended to be used in isolation for diagnosis. In addition, as stated earlier, it would be beneficial and critical that future revisions of this instrument take into consideration DSM-IV-TR diagnostic criteria. As mentioned previously, validity and reliability data for the PDD-MRS are satisfactory for individuals in the mental retardation range but not so for those in the borderline range. It will be helpful when the normative sample extends beyond the Netherlands as well.

SUMMARY. The PDD-MRS is a promising and useful instrument for screening PDD among individuals with mental retardation. According to a review by Berney (2007), the PDD-MRS deserves more recognition and attention. This instrument appears to be the only instrument on the market that was specifically designed for this particular population. Other PDD instruments are restricted in use with children and adolescents, whereas the PDD-MRS may be used with adults, as well as children and adolescents. An additional advantage to this measure is its quick administration time with little specialized training required. As an added bonus, administration of this screener is not dependent upon cooperation of the patient. Nonetheless, the PDD-MRS does not appear to be adequate for use in individuals with borderline or higher intelligence and its items are based on old diagnostic criteria.

REVIEWER'S REFERENCES

Berney, T. (2007). Pervasive developmental disorder in mental retardation scale (PDD-MRS). *Journal of Intellectual Disability Research, 51*, 250-251.
Filipek, P. A., Accardo, P. J., Baranek, G. T., Cook, E. H., Dawson, G., Gordon, B. et al. (1999). The screening and diagnosis of autistic spectrum disorders. *Journal of Autism and Developmental Disorders, 29*, 439-484.

[149]
Pervasive Developmental Disorders Screening Test, Second Edition.

Purpose: Designed as "a clinical screening tool for autism (autistic disorder)/AD and other pervasive developmental disorders, such as pervasive developmental disorder, not otherwise specified (PDD-NOS) and Asperger's Disorder."
Population: Ages 12 to 48 months.
Publication Date: 2004.
Acronym: PDDST-II.
Scores: Total score only.
Administration: Individual.
Forms, 3: Stage 1—Primary Care Screener, Stage 2—Developmental Clinic Screener, Stage 3—Autism Clinic Severity Screener.
Price Data, 2007: $125 per complete kit including manual (42 pages) and record forms; $30 per 25 Stage 1 record forms; $30 per 25 Stage 2 record forms; $30 per 25 Stage 3 record forms.
Time: (10–20) minutes.
Comments: Parent-report screening measure.

Author: Bryna Siegel.
Publisher: Harcourt Assessment, Inc.

Review of the Pervasive Developmental Disorders Screening Test, Second Edition by MARY (RINA) M. CHITTOORAN, Associate Professor and Chair, Department of Educational Studies, Saint Louis University, St. Louis, MO:

DESCRIPTION. The Pervasive Developmental Disorders Screening Test, Second Edition (PDDST-II) is used to screen for Autism Spectrum Disorders (including autism; other pervasive developmental disorders; pervasive development not otherwise specified; and Asperger's Syndrome) in children between the ages of 12 and 48 months of age. It is a revision of the old Pervasive Developmental Disorder Screening Test that has been available for clinic use for the past decade or so. The PDDST-II includes three response forms that are designed to be completed by parents or a person familiar with the child and then interpreted by clinicians. Stage 1, the Primary Care Screener (PCS), can be used in primary care settings for children, 12–18 months. Stage 2, the Developmental Clinic Screener (DCS), can be used in clinics where children are being screened for possible developmental delays. Finally, Stage 3, the Autism Clinic Severity Screener (ACSS), can be used in clinics that are conducting a complete diagnostic assessment on children with Autism Spectrum Disorders. The manual also includes 41 supplemental items that provide additional information about children's behaviors. The major purposes of the PDDST-II are (a) to screen for possible Autism Spectrum Disorders (ASD) in the first 4 years of life and (b) to help differentiate between ASDs and other neurodevelopmental disorders in young children.

Because the PDDST-II is intended to be completed by parents and interpreted by nonspecialist clinicians, training requirements for administration, scoring, and interpretation are minimal. Each rating form is a single page, printed back and front, and is in a different color that corresponds with the various stages. Ratings can be completed in about 15 minutes by parents or a "person familiar with the child's behavior" (manual, p. 2). Raters respond to 22 items on the PCS, 14 items on the DCS, and 12 items on the ACSS. Each item is in the form of a question such as, "Did your baby ever seem bored or uninterested in conversation going on around him/her?" or "Did you think, at times, that your toddler didn't care if you were there or not?" with the rater responding, "Yes, Usually True" or "No, Usually Not True." The manual suggests that both parents complete ratings, either together or independently. It also suggests that clinicians can use the questions in an interview format for parents who speak English as a Second Language, are not literate, or who are themselves developmentally delayed. If a parent is not available, a day care provider may complete the ratings. Finally, if there is any question about the validity or reliability of parent ratings, it is recommended that an additional rater be used. The item glossary provides further information about each test item, including Qualities (information about severity that may indicate risk), Threshold (points above and below which behaviors may be of concern), and Probes (specific questions aimed at eliciting more information). If an item has been left blank, the clinician is encouraged to help the rater provide a response. The clinician who interprets the form can do so in 5 minutes or less by referring to the cut score printed on the bottom of the form. A cut score can indicate a positive screen (raw score equal to or greater than the cut score) or a negative one (raw score less than the cut score). The manual provides suggestions for further action in the event of positive or negative screens.

DEVELOPMENT. Research into the development of the PDDST-II first began in 1986, in an effort to develop an effective measure for the early screening of autism. Initial data were gathered on children who were being seen in clinic settings to confirm or rule out Autism Spectrum Disorders. Items for each screening stage were arranged in developmental fashion, that is, those items that related to behaviors most likely to be noticed early were placed first. Effort was given to distinguishing between behaviors that are unique to autism and those that could characterize other neurodevelopmental disorders. Test development continued through 2002 with subsequent item analyses resulting in the addition, deletion, or refinement of particular test questions.

TECHNICAL. The standardization sample included 943 children (714 males, 229 females), from 19 months to over 4 years old, and who had one of the following conditions: Autistic Disorder, PDD-NOS/Asperger's, Language Disorder,

Mental Retardation only, Very Low Birth Weight, and other neuropsychiatric condition.

Cut scores, which were determined "based on research results and clinical judgement" (manual, p. 14), were related to sensitivity (which refers to the probability that a child with a condition will test positive for it) and specificity (which refers to the probability that a child without a particular condition will test negative for it). For Stage 1, the cut score was determined to be 5 (sensitivity = .92; specificity = .91); for Stage 2, the cut score was determined to be 5 (sensitivity = .73; specificity = .49); and finally, for Stage 3, the cut score was determined to be 8 (sensitivity = .58; specificity = .60). An appendix to the manual also includes detailed information about the sensitivity and specificity of each item at Stages 1 through 3 and is offered as a way to determine which items best discriminated between groups.

COMMENTARY. The PDDST-II is grounded in the growing body of research on Autism Spectrum Disorders and could be a useful addition to the arsenal of tools available to assess such disorders. It is the result of several decades of research and appears to be based on developmentally appropriate practices. The test is appealing, primarily because of its simplicity and its relatively low cost. Items on the PDDST-II are generally easy to read and interpret, and the addition of the item glossary is particularly nice. The author is to be commended for emphasizing the screening nature of the test instead of making unfounded claims about its utility. There appears to have been some attention paid to test validity with regard to item sensitivity and specificity.

Despite these positive features, the following issues are of some concern. The standardization sample does not seem to reflect the general population; it might have been nice to compare the clinic sample with children in nonclinic settings (surprisingly, descriptions of the earlier version of the PDDST-II do mention control populations). There is no discussion of the parents who must have served as raters during the development of the test; if they were indeed volunteers, that would be problematic. There is no mention of internal consistency, interrater reliability, or test-retest reliability; these are particularly important omissions given the nature of this rating form. Furthermore, the manual does not discuss concurrent validity nor does it include any information about predictive validity, which would seem to be particularly important for a measure that is to be used for screening purposes. Discussions of divergent and convergent validity could have been enhanced by pointing out for readers which items across the three scales best discriminated between groups.

The PDDST-II could be improved by the addition of a greater number of items on each form, particularly on the response forms at Stages 2 and 3. Items on the response form could be leading because they are all worded positively; that is, a parent, particularly one who is worried about his or her child's functioning, may respond positively—and possibly incorrectly—to certain items. For example, which parent, reading an item such as, "Did your child play with some toys in ways that aren't the main way such toys are meant to be used?" would not answer "Yes"?

Although the manual states that items can be read to raters with limited English proficiency, it does not address the historic difficulty of obtaining oral ratings, particularly from those who speak minimal English. More descriptive anchors could have been provided for words such as "Usually" and "Not Usually" as these terms are open to interpretation. Ratings are based on children's behaviors during a particular age range (e.g., birth to 6 months) and may, therefore, be dependent on the accuracy of a parent's memory of behaviors that occurred a long time ago. Responses to these items may be misleading, resulting in false positives as well as false negatives; such inaccuracies may be obviated by repeating ratings on several occasions and by supplementing them, if possible, with independent behavioral observations in both home and school settings. Finally, there is no longitudinal research cited that could support the predictive validity of ratings; it is possible, therefore, that further studies in the area could significantly influence the utility of the PDDST-II.

SUMMARY. The PDDST-II is the result of years of ongoing research into the early assessment of Autism Spectrum Disorders and, given the growing interest in this area, is a welcome addition. It requires minimal training and time for administration and interpretation; however, documentation of its technical merits, particularly with regard to reliability and validity, are questionable. The PDDST-II is not intended to be used by itself for eligibility decisions in special education, and caution is suggested when dealing with parent

ratings of behavioral concerns in their children. On the other hand, it is recommended as a quick screening measure of behaviors that may indicate the need for further assessment to confirm or rule out Autism Spectrum Disorders. It may also be useful when ratings are completed by more than one individual, when it is used in conjunction with other measures of Autism and independent behavioral observations, and when it is included as part of a comprehensive assessment battery.

Review of the Pervasive Developmental Disorders Screening Test, Second Edition by THERESA VOLPE-JOHNSTONE, ACFE, Clinical and School Psychologist, Pleasanton Unified School District, Pleasanton, CA:

DESCRIPTION. The Pervasive Developmental Disorders Screening Test, Second Edition (PDDST-II) is composed of three brief screening tools developed for administration in three clinical settings referred to as "stages" where a child might regularly be seen for developmental concerns. They all use parents/caregivers as respondents using a yes/no format where they must try to recall the child's behavior during a specified age range. Stage 1 is recommended for primary care settings such as pediatrician visits and is composed of 22 yes/no questions, 9 of which ask about the age range of 12—18 months and 13 of which ask about the age range of 18—24 months. Stage 2 is recommended for administration for children who may be entering developmental services such as Child Find, Early Start, special education, or departments of developmental services. Stage 2 is composed of 14 yes/no questions, 1 that asks about the age range of birth—6 months, 1 that asks about the age range of 6–12 months, 5 of which ask about the age range of 12–18 months, and 7 of which ask about the age range of 18–24 months. Stage 3 is recommended to aid in the differentiation of autism from other pervasive developmental disorders and can offer a suggestion of the severity of the autism disorder. Stage 3 is composed of 12 yes/no questions, 1 that asks about the age range of birth–6 months, none of which ask about the age range of 6–12 months, 3 of which ask about the age range of 12–18 months, 4 of which ask about the age range of 18–24 months, 2 of which ask about the age range of 24–30 months, and 2 of which ask about the age range of 30–36 months. The PDDST-II also provides 41 supplemental items describing behaviors that could be symptomatic of an Autism Spectrum Disorder (ASD) or other non-ASD.

All stages yield a Total score determined by the sum of "yes" responses. This sum is compared to a "cut" score. A Total score equal to or greater than the cut score is considered to be a positive rating for that respective screening measure. A score below the cut is considered a negative rating. Stage 1 positive screenings suggest a referral for further diagnostic testing, Stage 2 positive screenings suggest to the assessing clinic to conduct further evaluation, and Stage 3 positive screenings should prompt the assessment for differentiation of ASDs. In addition, each age band has designated supplemental items that would reflect atypical development at that developmental time and could be referred to for more detailed information from the respondent using the manual. The manual also has descriptions of each item in each stage composed of Qualities, Thresholds, and Probes, which aid in the interview or follow-up process or can be used to refresh a parent's memory.

DEVELOPMENT. Development of the PDDST-II was purported to begin with 1986 research from the earlier edition, the PDDST, with data analysis and inclusion of data since 1994. The four primary considerations for the development of this second tool was to have available early and efficient screening measures, to determine the absence of expected and presence of atypical patterns of behavior, to offer measures that can be used across a variety of early child health care settings, and to have observationally detectable items for reliable parent report. There was no information on item development for any stage, but the children used in the study had received "extensive multi-method diagnostic assessments that resulted in diagnoses made by a clinician" (manual, p. 5) involved in developing DSM-III-R and DSM-IV criteria for Pervasive Developmental Disorders. There is no information on the readability level of each item although if English is a second language or if the responder has a low literacy level or is developmentally disabled, a guided interview can, and should, be conducted. Items clustered by age range appear to have been determined by what would be markers of ASDs of a child at that developmental age. Markers under age 12 months were used with caution as descriptive behaviors in the first year of

life may not be unique to ASDs but become more definitive into the second and third year.

TECHNICAL. The total standardization sample size was 943 children ages 19 months to 8 years who were assessed and diagnosed between 1985 and 2002 at an autism clinic. Specific location, demographic data, and ethnic background were not indicated. Five diagnostic groups, Autistic Disorder, PDD-NOS/Asperger's, Language Disorder, other neuropsychiatric disorder, and mental retardation (only) made up 687 of the cases. The remaining 256 were very low birth weight (VLBW) children and were used as the "negative" or "specificity" group for the Stage 1 screener as their development was atypical but not ASD. Cut scores were determined by sensitivity and specificity, that is, the probability that a child who has ASD will test positive and the probability that someone who does not have an ASD will test negative, respectively. Based on research results and clinical judgment, a cut score was recommended for each stage rating scale. Stage 1 compared the At-Risk for ASD ($n = 681$) to the VLBW ($n = 256$). Stage 2 compared ASD ($n = 490$) to ASD-referred children for which ASD was subsequently ruled out ($n = 194$). Stage 3 compared Autistic Disorder ($n = 355$) to PDD-NOS/Asperger's Disorder ($n = 99$). As a result of these comparisons, cut scores were determined where results would yield the greatest probability of true positives and true negatives. From the data presented, it would appear that the PDDST-II has adequate ability to discriminate on the Stage 1 measure, has moderate ability to discriminate on the Stage 2 measure, and mild ability to discriminate on the Stage 3 measure. Reliability studies and construct validity studies were not conducted.

COMMENTARY. The PDDST-II Stage 1 screener appeared to be the strongest of this three-stage screener. Its benefit lies in it being a quick measure and easily available to primary care physician offices where ASDs are typically overlooked to the detriment of early intervention. It does not require extensive training, and the scoring system is straightforward enough to generate a referral for further consideration of ASD to appropriate professionals if necessary. The Stage 1 screener would also be a beneficial tool for speech pathologists as they are often a first resource for children with ASD due to the usual language delay that prompts that visit. The probes provided in the item glossary for each stage are positive aspects of this tool as they can assist in eliciting responses to each item. The supplemental items are informational and can be supportive evidence when presenting parents with the diagnosis of ASD relative to their child. The Stage 2 screener does not appear useful for clinical consideration due to its moderate sensitivity (.73) and low specificity (.49). However, for the setting in which this screener is to be used, it may have some utility if it generates further evaluation by a person qualified to continue evaluation for a clinical diagnosis. For example, if it is used by occupational therapists, an appropriate referral can be made. The objective of the Stage 3 screener, presented as "to differentiate autism from other pervasive developmental disorders" (manual, p. 3), is unnecessary in this reviewer's perspective because by the time differential diagnosis is required, the child is within the throes of a full assessment by a clinical team, which should diagnose differentially. Although the author indicated that this screener provides an estimate of the severity that is empirically based, the screener simply suggests a course of action to "assess whether the child is more likely to have autistic disorder, PDD-NOS, or Asperger's Disorder" (manual, p. 12), which requires differential diagnosis not possible through the PDDST-II. Weaknesses of the measure include that the author did not provide technical standardization data including demographic information or explain why it was not included; did not describe how items for the scales were developed; did not examine correlations with other measures of ASDs; and did not consider interrater reliability measures, particularly from preschool settings because 63% of the sample population were over the age of 32 months with 54% of them over 3 years of age. A potential confound is that parent/caregivers are asked to recall the child's behavior retrospectively, which may prove challenging. Using the probes can alleviate some of this method. Not knowing the reading level necessary to understand the statements on each screener can be a potential problem. The term "cut" score may be novel to some and may be better understood using the term "cut-off" score, and a Stage 3 screener does not seem necessary given the setting for which it would be used.

SUMMARY. The PDDST-II is composed of three brief questionnaire scales called Stage 1, 2, and 3, which should prompt different referral actions if positive "cut" scores are reached after finding the Total score.

Parent/caregivers are respondents using a yes/no format. Each stage is recommended for different types of settings a child might be in. Supplemental items, which can be consistent with ASDs, are also provided in the manual. It is quick and easy to administer and score, and the Stage 1 screener may have the most utility for early intervention. The weaknesses outlined above should be considered before using this tool in a clinical setting.

[150]
Position Classification Inventory.

Purpose: Designed "as an inventory for classifying positions and occupations" to assess the demands, rewards, and opportunities of work environments.
Population: Adults.
Publication Date: 1991.
Acronym: PCI.
Scores, 6: Realistic, Investigative, Artistic, Social, Enterprising, Conventional.
Administration: Individual or group.
Price Data, 2007: $90 per introductory kit including manual, 25 reusable item booklets, and 25 answer sheets/profile forms; $27 per manual; $35 per 25 reusable item booklets; $34 per 25 answer sheets/profile forms.
Time: (10) minutes.
Authors: Gary D. Gottfredson and John L. Holland.
Publisher: Psychological Assessment Resources, Inc.

Review of the Position Classification Inventory by KEITH HATTRUP, Associate Professor of Psychology, San Diego State University, San Diego, CA:

DESCRIPTION. The Position Classification Inventory (PCI) is a paper-and-pencil measure designed to assess the demands, rewards, and opportunities of work environments. Its purpose is to classify work environments (e.g., jobs, occupations, work settings) according to Holland's well-known typology of persons and situations. Thus, the measure provides scores on six dimensions, labeled Realistic, Investigative, Artistic, Social, Enterprising, and Conventional, that are included in Holland's hexagonal model that summarizes the similarities and differences among the dimensions (the RIASEC model). Whereas Holland's Self-Directed Search (SDS; T7:2289) and Vocational Preference Inventories (VPI; T7:2728) are designed to measure dimensions of persons according to the RIASEC model, the PCI is designed to provide commensurate measurement of environments. As such, the PCI represents one of a large number of approaches for measuring characteristics of jobs and work environments. Such measures may be particularly useful when analyzing jobs to determine the importance of specific tasks or behaviors, and the rewards and opportunities provided by jobs and work environments.

The PCI is unique, however, in providing a measure of environments that produces scores that are parallel with those used to represent persons in Holland's model. In this sense, the PCI, particularly when used in conjunction with the SDS or VPI, operationalizes one of a large number of models of person-environment (PE) fit. PE fit, of course, is seen by many as an essential element of individual adjustment, success, and well-being. The goals of the PCI, therefore, are to (a) contribute to an understanding of the demands, rewards, and opportunities of work environments; (b) provide information relevant to occupational choice and vocational counseling; (c) assess sources of disagreement within work settings about jobs and their requirements; and (d) contribute to an understanding of sources of various individual and organizational outcomes, such as satisfaction, commitment, or turnover, that relate to person-environment fit.

The PCI includes 84 items that are answered with a 3-point scale, anchored *Often*, *Sometimes*, and *Seldom/Never*. There are 13 items in each of the 6 scales, and six experimental items that are not scored. Separate test booklet and answer sheets are used, and the measure can be completed in about 10 minutes. Instructions for completing and scoring the measure are very easy to follow, and the measure does not appear to require a high level of reading ability. Scale scores are calculated by simply adding the number of keyed responses in each scale. A 3-point "Holland Code" is created by identifying the three scales with the highest scores; the scales with the lowest scores are effectively ignored. The use of a 3-point code for interpreting PCI responses provides some minor practical advantage in terms of increasing the simplicity of the approach. However, at the same time, it ignores potentially important information, as it may be just as useful to understand what an environment supports, requires, or encourages as it is to understand what it does not support or what it discourages. A differentiation

index can also be calculated for each respondent, which measures the relative difference among the highest and lowest scale scores. The manual provides very good theoretical background, clear instructions, many practical examples, detailed technical information, a complete reference list, and even a short knowledge test for users of the PCI. The authors demonstrate appropriate restraint in their discussion of the instrument, noting that the measure lacks perfect reliability and should be used in conjunction with other information about positions and respondents.

DEVELOPMENT. The PCI evolved out of an active program of research by the authors to operationalize and test various aspects of the RIASEC model. Earlier attempts to operationalize the environment in Holland's PE fit model relied on very gross classifications of positions based on the profile of interests of incumbents, the judgment of observers, or job task information. The PCI, thus, represents an important advance by providing a method to assess work environments directly using a set of items derived from the RIASEC theory. Items were written using a rational approach designed to operationalize the theory. Scale reliability and item analyses were then performed to refine the measure by deleting items and adding new ones. In all, data from 2,172 participants were used to evaluate the original and revised set of items, representing a wide range of occupations. Broad sampling of occupations is, of course, necessary given that the goal of the PCI is to measure work environments.

TECHNICAL. Scale means, standard deviations, and percentile ranks are provided for supervisors and incumbents and for males and females. Percentile ranks are also provided for the differentiation index. These overall norms collapse across a wide range of occupations and positions. The manual also provides means, SDs, and Holland Codes for 37 specific occupations, using samples ranging between 8 and 33 individual respondents.

Internal consistency reliabilities were calculated separately for supervisors, male incumbents, female incumbents, and a mixed sample. Across all groups, coefficient alphas ranged from .70 to .94 for the six scales. Alphas were lowest for the Conventional scale (.70 to .75), whereas they were higher for the Realistic (.80 to .91) and Artistic (.78 to .94) scales. Test-retest reliabilities are not provided but would be a valuable addition. Of course, one of the potential applications of the PCI would be to evaluate change in work environments over time, which is surely to be expected in many occupations. Correlations between PCI scores for incumbents and supervisors who evaluated the same positions are provided, and range from .25 for the Conventional scale, which had the lowest alphas, to .60 for the Realistic and Artistic, which had consistently higher internal consistency. These correlations might be considered relevant to interrater reliability; however, given that one goal of the PCI is to measure the relationships between work environment perceptions of organizational members, these correlations might also be indicative of meaningful similarities and differences in the ways in which different organizational members conceptualize and react to job settings. Standard errors of measurement are provided for the six scales for both supervisors and incumbents.

Several analyses reported in the manual are relevant to the construct validity of the PCI. First, correlations among the six scales are presented for both incumbents and supervisors, and range from -.15 to .54. The highest of these correlations was between the Social and Enterprising scores obtained from incumbents. After correcting this value for attenuation due to unreliability (using coefficient alphas of .82 and .78, respectively), the correlation reaches .68, implying that up to about 46% of the reliable variance is shared between these factors. Although this high value suggests these two scales may be somewhat less unique than desired, none of the other correlations exceeded .48. Moreover, the authors note that correlations partially followed the expected pattern, with higher correlations observed among hexagonally adjacent scales (including the Conventional and Enterprising scales) than among scales that are more distant from each other on the hexagon. However, many of the correlations failed to follow the hypothesized pattern. For example, although the Enterprising scale failed to correlate as expected with the adjacent Conventional scale in the sample of supervisors ($r = -.04$), the Enterprising scale correlated higher than expected with several of the scales among both supervisors and incumbents. As has been observed with measures of Holland's personality types, results generally fail to support the circumplex hypothesis implied by the RIASEC theory (Tinsley, 2000).

A second analysis examines the agreement in the classification of positions based on scores obtained from the PCI and the classification of the same positions in the *Dictionary of Holland Occupational Codes* (DHOC; Gottfredson & Holland, 1989). Agreement in the first letter of 3-point Holland Codes between the methods occurred between 49% to 60% of the time, depending on the sample and version of the PCI used to classify the positions. Disagreements in the first-letter coding of positions occurred somewhat more frequently for classifications that were adjacent on the hexagonal model. Overall, the evidence of consistency in the classification of positions according to the RIASEC model using two very different methodological approaches provides good support for the construct validity of the PCI.

Analyses of scale intercorrelations, correlations among supervisors and incumbents, and agreement in classifications between the PCI and DHOC are provided after collapsing data across individual positions to the level of broad occupations. As expected, correlations among PCI ratings provided by independent sources increase after aggregating larger numbers of individual respondents. Agreement in the first-letter classification of occupations according to the PCI and DHOC ranged from 72% to 89%, depending on the number of inventories combined when aggregating responses to the occupation level.

SUMMARY AND COMMENTARY. The PCI is a measure of work environments that may have a number of applications in research, and in the practical contexts of job/organization analysis and vocational counseling. It follows from Holland's highly influential theory of person-environment fit and provides a direct operationalization of elements of the theory. Although empirical evidence has generally failed to support the circumplex hypotheses implied by the hexagonal RIASEC theory, good evidence of the agreement of the PCI with independent classifications of positions and occupations is provided in the manual. More generally, despite its influence on the field, many of the hypotheses that follow from the RIASEC model have not been well-supported empirically, due to a variety of reasons (Furnham, 2001; Tinsley, 2000). The PCI may provide unique information about work settings, and it may contribute to an understanding of the fit between individuals and their work situations.

However, researchers and practitioners are strongly encouraged to supplement their investigation of persons and environments with measures that derive from other theoretical perspectives, such as the Five-Factor Model of (FFM) personality, the Theory of Work Adjustment (Dawis & Lofquist, 1984), models of job demands and worker abilities, and recent models of the dimensionality of work behavior and job performance.

REVIEWER'S REFERENCES

Dawis, R. V., & Lofquist, L. H. (1984). *A psychological theory of work adjustment.* Minneapolis: University of Minnesota Press.

Furnham, A. (2001). Vocational preference and P-O fit: Reflections on Holland's theory of vocational choice. *Applied Psychology: An International Review, 50,* 5-29.

Gottfredson, G. D., & Holland, J. L. (1989). *Dictionary of Holland occupational codes* (2nd ed.). Odessa, FL: Psychological Assessment Resources.

Tinsley, H. E. A. (2000). The congruence myth: An analysis of the efficacy of the person-environment fit model. *Journal of Vocational Behavior, 56,* 147-179.

[151]

Pragmatic Language Skills Inventory.

Purpose: Designed to help identify children "who have pragmatic language disabilities."

Population: Ages 5–12.

Publication Date: 2006.

Acronym: PLSI.

Scores: 3 subscales: Classroom Interaction, Social Interaction, Personal Interaction; and Pragmatic Language Index.

Administration: Individual.

Price Data, 2006: $95 per complete kit including examiner's manual (59 pages) and 25 summary/response forms; $55 per manual; $45 per 25 summary/response forms.

Time: (5–10) minutes.

Comments: Appropriate raters include teachers, parents, teacher assistants, or other qualified person who work closely with the child and are well acquainted with the child's language characteristics.

Authors: James E. Gilliam and Lynda Miller.

Publisher: PRO-ED.

Review of the Pragmatic Language Skills Inventory by THOMAS W. GUYETTE, Professor and Chair, and DONNA J. KELLY, Associate Professor, Department of Audiology and Speech Pathology, University of Arkansas at Little Rock and University of Arkansas for Medical Sciences, Little Rock, AR:

DESCRIPTION. The authors state that the Pragmatic Language Skills Inventory (PLSI) "helps [to] identify" (examiner's manual, p. 2) children with pragmatic language disorders between 5 and 12 years of age. It has four uses: (a) to identify students with disorders, (b) to document progress on pragmatic abilities, (c) to select intervention targets, and (d) to collect data, which may be used for research purposes. The PLSI is described as a standardized, norm-referenced instrument that is completed through teacher/caregiver ratings of a child's skills. The authors report that the 45-item inventory, which utilizes a 9-point scale, can be completed in 5–10 minutes. This measure is composed of three subscales, each of which contains 15 items. The Classroom Interaction Skills subscale probes a wide assortment of skills such as figurative language, topic maintenance, explanations, story writing, and slang. The Social Interaction Skills subscale taps a students' understanding of classroom rules, consequences of rule breaking, and conversational turn taking; and the Personal Interaction Skills subscale documents information on a child's ability to initiate communication, request help, play verbal games, and use nonverbal communication.

The PLSI is designed to be scored and interpreted by a qualified professional (e.g., speech-language pathologist, school psychologist); however, the individual completing the ratings is relatively free to vary. The manual states that the inventory may be completed by "a classroom teacher, parent, teacher assistant or other qualified person who works closely with the child and who is well acquainted with the child's language characteristics" (p. 5). However, in the opinion of these reviewers, the knowledge and skills expected of the rater are inconsistent with that statement. For example, the manual states that individuals who are rating a child's pragmatic skills "should have been trained in its use" (p. 6) and should have had "sufficient" opportunities to observe a child's pragmatic abilities in a variety of settings. It also states the raters "must have experience working with and observing average children's interactions and must be able to assess what 'average' behavior is for the age and gender of the child being rated" (p. 6). According to the manual, raters do not require any special training in order to make the PLSI ratings, but raters should have basic knowledge of behavioral rating scales and should become thoroughly familiar with the test manual prior to completing the survey.

The directions advise the raters to "read the items on the Summary/Response Form at least twice, think about the behavior described, and rate how frequently the child behaves in the manner described by each item" (examiner's manual, p. 6).

Raters are asked to rank their "impressions" of the child being evaluated on a 9-point scale with 1–3 designated as below average, 4–6 designated as average, and 7–9 designated as above average. The manual states that raters will generally feel "certain and confident" (p. 6) about how to respond on each of the 45 items. However, raters may also obtain information about a child's skills though observation and/or interviewing parents and teachers. Completing the PLSI would clearly take substantially more than 5–10 minutes if observation of the child and/or teacher interviews are necessary. Given that the PLSI taps a wide range of skill areas (e.g., writing a good story; maintaining a topic; understanding of simple similes, metaphors and idioms; comprehension of figurative language; obtaining the meaning of texts that explain how something works) it is difficult to imagine a single individual who feels confident about rating a child across all 45 items. Instructions for deriving percentile ranks and standard scores from the raw scores are provided in the examiner's manual. There is some confusion in the examiner's manual in regard to the scored response form. It appears that the scores for the Social Interaction Skills subscale and the Personal Interaction Skills subscale were mixed up (see pages 12–13 of the manual).

DEVELOPMENT. Limited information concerning the development of this instrument is provided, and the information that is provided often lacks sufficient detail for evaluation. The authors reported starting with 80 specific pragmatic behaviors, which they derived from a literature review. These 80 items were first reviewed by a "group" of speech-language pathologists, and then they were subsequently reviewed by experts in test construction at Pro-ED. It is not clear how the 80-item test pool was reduced to the current 45-item test. The authors did not report collecting any pilot data on the 80-item test pool nor did they provide any information suggesting that the final 45 items were derived from an item analysis. Finally, several of the 45 items in the inventory are not "traditionally" regarded as pragmatic skills (e.g., understanding slang expressions; comprehending simple similes, metaphors, and idioms; and understanding figurative language).

TECHNICAL. The manual states that the pragmatic skills of 1,175 children, between the ages of 5 and 12 years, were rated in 35 different states. The 38 raters included teachers, educational diagnosticians, speech-language pathologists, psychologists, and "other school personnel" (p. 19). According to these raters, 1,019 students were considered to be average, 61 were identified as gifted and talented, and 95 had been previously diagnosed with a variety of disabilities (e.g., mental retardation, blindness, hearing impairment, attention-deficit/hyperactivity disorder, emotional disturbance, learning disability, health impairment, autism, and multiple handicaps). The demographic characteristics (e.g., age, geographic location, race/ethnicity, gender) of the 1,175 children who were rated are provided for inspection.

The PLSI examiner's manual reports three reliability studies. The first of these is the use of the coefficient alpha, which evaluates the level at which test items correlate with one another. Second, reliability was examined using the test–retest method. In this study, the raters of 76 children filled out the PLSI evaluation form twice, one week apart. In the third reliability study, the authors examined interrater reliability. In this study, the same student was evaluated by two teachers who each knew the child "well enough to make a rating" (examiner's manual, p. 27). In all three studies, the reliability coefficients were adequate. However, in both the test-retest and interrater reliability studies, the populations tested were not well described and there was a critical lack of methodological detail that made it difficult to evaluate the significance of these findings.

Several different types of validity information were also presented (e.g., item discrimination, criterion-related, construct identification, and factor analysis). Again, correlations were generally in the adequate range. In the two concurrent criterion-related validity studies, the authors chose the Test of Pragmatic Language (TOPL) by Phelps-Terasaki and Phelps-Gunn (1992) as the criterion test. In the first study, 21 students (all average) were examined using both tests. In the second concurrent validity study, 30 children with diverse backgrounds (some with disabilities) were again given both the PLSI and the TOPL. Again, more detail regarding the methods used in these studies is needed before they can be appropriately evaluated. Also, the authors need to present information that justifies their use of the TOPL as the criterion test.

COMMENTARY AND SUMMARY. The PLSI taps a wide range of pragmatic behaviors for children between 5 and 12 years of age through report. Although the authors state that the survey can be completed in 5–10 minutes, it seems unlikely that a rater would be able to accurately complete each of the 45 items from memory. It seems as though valid administration of the instrument would entail both classroom observation and teacher interview. The rater's knowledge of the language abilities of a child participant appears to be overly demanding. Few, if any, formal child-participant tests are able to provide valid and reliable information about constructs such as a child's ability to write a good story, understand slang expressions, or comprehend simple similes, metaphors, and idioms. Given the vast knowledge required by the PLSI rater (e.g., of typical and atypical language development for children between the ages of 5 and 12 years of age, of how to complete formal behavioral rating scales, of how to observe the pragmatic targets of interest in context), it is strongly suggested that PSLI raters have a thorough grounding in normal and disordered school-age language skills.

Although the manual provides information in support of the instrument's reliability and validity, it is unclear how a survey instrument can validly measure such a wide range of language behaviors across the 5- to 12-year age range. The rater is expected to know what the test authors meant on items such as "Getting the meaning from teacher's lectures," "Giving oral book reports," "Following verbal directions," "Make-believe or pretending" and "teasing others appropriately." The rater is also expected to "have a good grasp of what is typical or average behavior for the child's age and gender" (examiner's manual, p. 6). It would have been helpful if the authors, in the development of this test, had collected normative data on each of the specific pragmatic behaviors across the 7-year age range. It seems problematic to assume that a parent, teacher's assistant, or classroom teacher would know when a child was advanced, average, or behind on the sorts of pragmatic abilities probed on the PLSI.

REVIEWERS' REFERENCE

Phelps-Terasaki, D., & Phelps-Gunn, T. (1992). *Test of Pragmatic Language.* Austin, TX: PRO-Ed.

Review of the Pragmatic Language Skills Inventory by AIMÉE LANGLOIS, Professor, Department of Child Development, Humboldt State University, Arcata, CA:

DESCRIPTION. The Pragmatic Language Skills Inventory (PLSI) is designed to identify children between 5 and 12 years of age who have pragmatic language disorders. It can also be used to specify therapy goals for these children, conduct follow-up evaluations, and document progress. In addition, it is deemed a "promising instrument" (examiner's manual, p. 4) for research. The test includes three subscales that determine a child's pragmatic language skills in Classroom, Social, and Personal Interactions, respectively.

The test takes less than 10 minutes to administer by an individual who rates on a 9-point scale the child's pragmatic skills on 45 items (15 in each subscale) and assigns each a score from 1 to 9. This individual, known as a "rater," bases his or her score on his or her knowledge of the child and that of children of the same age and gender regarding a particular skill (e.g., writing a good story, taking turns in conversation, asking for help or favors). After the rater has assigned scores for all 45 items, an "examiner" adds the scores for each subscale to compute a total raw score for that subscale; the examiner then derives percentile ranks and standard scores by using tables provided in an appendix. Finally, the standard scores for the three subscales are summed to determine a child's Pragmatic Language Index (PLI) and an overall percentile rank. To help parents and others understand the meaning of the standard and percentile scores, a table on the summary/response form describes a range of pragmatic language skills from "Very Poor" to "Very Superior" based on these scores.

The authors specify that the rater must be an individual who knows the tested child very well and is thus familiar with that child's language skills; as such, raters can be parents, teachers, teacher assistants, etc. However, the authors caution that scoring the individual scales, deriving standard and percentile scores, and interpreting results must be left to licensed professionals familiar with "quantitative and qualitative information" (examiner's manual, p. 5). It is emphasized that these professionals, identified as examiners, must carefully choose raters on the basis of their knowledge about specific children, their observation skills, and their accuracy in rating test items.

The test is easy to learn with clear instructions and examples for rating children and scoring results. The summary/response form is also easy to use. In addition to the three subscales completed by the rater, it includes an interpretation and recommendation page on which examiners can write their interpretations, as well as "recommendations for further assessment, and suggestions for appropriate intervention" (examiner's manual, pp. 13-14).

DEVELOPMENT. The authors offer a sound rationale for the development of the PLSI and its use. The test is founded on long-standing theories of pragmatic language, which are delineated in the test manual. These theories guided the selection of test items specific to school-age children. Following a thorough review of the literature, the authors designed their first version of the test, which they submitted for a critical analysis to practicing clinicians. On the basis of the feedback obtained, they modified the test and submitted it to two academicians for further review. After making additional changes, the authors submitted the test to "experts in test construction" (examiner's manual, p. 30) for further analysis. The PLSI with its 45 test items results from this rigorous review process.

TECHNICAL.

Standardization. The PLSI was standardized on 1,175 students (610 boys, 565 girls) between 5 and 12 years of age. The sample represents the U.S. population of school-age children with respect to geographic region, gender, race, ethnicity, and disability status. The authors provide a table showing that the percentage of individuals in each group is consistent with that reported by the U.S. Census Bureau in 2001 for the same group.

Reliability. The authors evaluated the coefficient alpha, test-retest, and interrater reliability of the PLSI. Coefficient alpha, a measure of the internal consistency of a test (Brown, 2002), was computed for the three subscales' standard scores and the PLI. Results revealed coefficients that range from .96 to .99, which indicates that the test has high internal consistency and that the standard errors of measurement are relatively small. Test users can thus make recommendations based on test results in confidence.

Test-retest reliability was determined by administering the test on two different occasions a week apart to 76 students. Results yielded "very large," significant (p <.01) correlations for each subscale's standard score and the PLI. Test users, therefore, know that a child's scores remain stable from one administration to the next (r = .78–.91)

and, conversely, that changes in a child's scores reflect either growth or regression in pragmatic skills.

Interrater reliability was determined by correlating the scores assigned by two examiners who knew well the 76 children involved in the test-retest reliability study. As qualified professionals they also computed the raw scores and PLSIs. Significant (p < .01) correlations from .85 and .90 were obtained and are deemed "very large." Clinicians are, therefore, sure that results obtained by different raters reflect a child's pragmatic abilities.

Validity. The authors attended to several types of validity in the development of the test: content, criterion, and construct. As described above, they provide evidence of content validity by indicating that they reviewed the literature on pragmatic language skills following which they conducted a three-step review process of an experimental version of the test.

The authors established that the PLSI has concurrent validity by correlating the scores of 51 children with their performance on the Test of Pragmatic Language (TOPL). Results were significant and indicate that the PLSI measures constructs similar to those assessed by the TOPL.

Construct validity was assessed in a variety of ways. An exploratory factor analysis examined "the relationships of the items to their respective subscales" (examiner's manual, p. 33); this analysis revealed that three factors defined 73% of the test variance and that each factor indicated a pragmatic domain that was used to identify a PLSI subscale. Other analyses include the intercorrelation of PLSI subscale standard scores (high), the relationship of subscale items to subscale scores (high), and the correlation of the test's subscale standard scores with the PLI (high). The authors discuss this aspect of validity at some length and provide tables to illustrate their findings. The evidence provided along with the discussion that pertains to it show that the PLSI has high construct validity.

The validity of the test was additionally assessed by comparing test scores for a group of 40 students with disabilities, a group of 45 gifted and talented students, and the normative sample. The results showed that gifted and talented students obtained "above average" scores, students with disabilities obtained scores ranging from "very poor" to "below average," and that the normative sample's scores were "average." These results not only show the well-known relationship between pragmatic language skills and other abilities but also further support the test's validity, which thus ensures that the PLSI can accurately identify children who have pragmatic language disabilities and those who do not. As is hoped by the authors, early identification of children with such disorders should allow them "to receive the treatment they need to prevent their problems from developing into full blown disabilities" (examiner's manual, p. 37).

COMMENTARY AND SUMMARY. The PLSI as a means to identify pragmatic language disorders in 5- to 12-year-old students has many strengths. First and foremost, its standardization with a representative sample of the U.S. population indicates that the test can be used with children from multiple backgrounds. Second, the test reflects a well-established construct. Third, the manual provides step-by-step administration, scoring, and interpretation instructions as well as comprehensive information about the PLSI standardization, reliability, and validity. Finally, the record forms are clear and easy to follow for the many individuals who are likely to administer, score, and interpret the test. The only issue about this tool is that raised by the authors regarding the selection of an individual who knows a child well enough to rate accurately his or her pragmatic skills *and* the exclusive role of the examiner in interpreting results. Given the high correlations among the subscales, one might question their discriminant validity. The authors are to be commended for designing such a powerful, useful, and yet simple test.

REVIEWER'S REFERENCE

Brown, J. D. (2002). Statistics corner: Questions and answers about language testing statistics: The Cronbach alpha reliability estimate. *Shiken: JALT Testing & Evaluation SIG Newsletter, 3*(1), 16-18. Retrieved May 18, 2006, from http://www.jalt.org/test/bro_13.htm

[152]

Pre-Reading Inventory of Phonological Awareness.

Purpose: "Designed to assess phonological awareness in young students."
Population: Ages 4.0–6.11.
Publication Dates: 2000–2003.
Acronym: PIPA.
Scores, 6: Rhyme Awareness, Syllable Segmentation, Alliteration Awareness, Sound Isolation, Sound Segmentation, Letter–Sound Knowledge.
Administration: Individual.

Price Data, 2007: $160 per complete kit including manual (2003, 82 pages), stimulus book, and 25 record forms; $49 per 25 record forms; $120 per stimulus book; $89 per manual.
Time: (25–30) minutes.
Authors: Barbara Dodd, Sharon Crosbie, Beth McIntosh, Tania Teitzel, and Anne Ozanne.
Publisher: The Psychological Corporation, A Harcourt Assessment Company.

Review of the Pre-Reading Inventory of Phonological Awareness by DAVID P. HURFORD, Director of the Center for the Assessment and Remediation of Reading Difficulties and Professor Psychology and Counseling, Pittsburg State University, Pittsburg, KS:

DESCRIPTION. The Pre-Reading Inventory of Phonological Awareness (PIPA) is a diagnostic instrument to assess the phonological awareness of young children ages 4 years to 6 years, 11 months. The PIPA comprises six subtests: Rhyme Awareness, Syllable Segmentation, Alliteration Awareness, Sound Isolation, Sound Segmentation, and Letter-Sound Knowledge. Preschool children's performances on these subtests and subtests like them have been linked to reading acquisition ability during the early elementary grades.

The PIPA is intended to: (a) assess phonological awareness of young children, (b) identify children who have difficulty with phonological awareness skills, and (c) assist in the planning of instructional interventions designed to improve the phonological awareness of the child with deficiencies in phonological awareness.

No special skills are required to administer the PIPA other than experience in scoring, interpretation, and assessment of early literacy skills in young students, and an understanding of the importance of standardization principles.

Each of the six subtests of the PIPA requires approximately 4 or 5 minutes to administer, thus the PIPA can be completed in approximately 25 to 30 minutes.

The PIPA provides raw scores, ranges, percentile ranges, and category descriptions (i.e., Emerging/Below Basic, Basic, and Proficient) for each subtest. The PIPA record form provides sections for identifying information (e.g., student's name, sex, school, grade, teacher, and test administrator; age [date tested, date of birth, chronological age]); optional information (race/ethnicity, special education status, migrant status, Title 1 status, LEP status, and a place for "other district criteria"), and the student profile (subtest raw scores, percentile ranges, and a graph to mark the percentiles to indicate the category classifications: Emerging/Below Basic, Basic, or Proficient).

DEVELOPMENT. The PIPA was standardized with a norming group of 450 children that was very similar to the demographic characteristics of the population of the United States. Seven percent of the sample was composed of children who were receiving early childhood special education, English as a Second Language education, special education, occupational therapy, physical therapy, and/or speech-language therapy. Four percent of the sample was composed of children who had ADHD, developmental delays, learning disabilities, limited English abilities, receptive and/or expressive language difficulties, and/or articulation disorders.

TECHNICAL. Reliability was assessed with internal consistency, test-retest, and interscorer reliability. Internal consistency was assessed by computing split-half correlation coefficients for each subtest by age (4-0 to 4-5, 4-6 to 4-11, 5-0 to 5-5, 5-6 to 5-11, 6-0 to 6-5, 6-6 to 6-11, and all ages combined). The average correlation coefficients across all age groups ranged from .82 (Rhyme Awareness and Alliteration Awareness) to .96 (Letter-Sound Knowledge).

Test-retest reliability was assessed with a group of 75 children randomly selected from the standardization sample ranging in age from 4-0 to 6-11 with an average of 5 years, 6 months. The test-retest interval averaged 13 days and ranged between 7 to 28 days. In most cases, the same examiner administered both administrations of the test and retest. The demographic characteristics of this group were quite similar to the standardization sample and the United States population. The average stability coefficients, correlation coefficients between the first and second administrations of the subtests, ranged from .67 (Syllable Segmentation) to .97 (Letter-Sound Knowledge). Although the stability coefficients were of moderate strength, Cohen's D estimates of effect size were quite small, ranging between -.03 and .10. These values indicate very small mean differences between the first and second administrations of the subtests.

Interrater reliability was assessed by examining the results of two individuals who independently scored 40 PIPA assessments that were randomly selected from the standardization sample prior to assessment. The 40 PIPA assessments had been audiotaped so that the raters could complete the PIPA subtests from the audiotaped information. The interrater correlations ranged from .82 (Syllable Segmentation) to .98 (Rhyme Awareness). Although a single interrater reliability value was not presented, the various coefficients from the subtests indicate appropriate levels of interrater reliability.

Validity was assessed by providing evidence for content validity, internal structure, and criterion-related validity. With regard to content validity, the subtests included on the PIPA have either been used for, or are very similar to, tasks that have been used to tap phonological awareness in the research literature. There is ample evidence that these tasks assess phonological awareness and can accurately identify children who have deficiencies in phonological awareness.

The internal structure of the PIPA was assessed by examining the intercorrelations between the subtests. Because all of the subtests were developed to assess some aspect of phonological awareness, there were, as expected, at least moderate relationships between all of the subtests. The weakest correlation was between Syllable Segmentation and Sound Segmentation (.42), which theoretically and practically have less in common than the other subtests. The strongest correlations were between Letter-Sound Knowledge and Alliteration Awareness (.78), and Letter-Sound Knowledge and Sound Isolation (.78). Each of the three subtests measures the ability to name letters that represent sounds or individual sounds.

Criterion-related validity was assessed by examining a group of children's PIPA subtest scores and their subtest scores from the Early Reading Diagnostic Assessment, Second Edition (ERDA-2). Because phonological awareness measures are known to be good predictors of success in reading acquisition, there should be a relationship between the PIPA and ERDA-2 subtest scores. To assess criterion-related validity, 48 kindergarten and 48 first-grade children were assessed with both the PIPA and ERDA-2. Order of testing was counterbalanced so that approximately half of the children were assessed with the PIPA and then the ERDA-2, and the other half were first assessed with the ERDA-2 and then the PIPA. The correlations between the various subtests of the PIPA and ERDA-2 were consistent with criterion-related validity. The subtests that were tapping similar constructs yielded correlation coefficients that were moderately strong (e.g., Letter Recognition [ERDA-2] and Letter-Sound Knowledge [PIPA], .81; Rhyming [ERDA-2] and Rhyme Awareness [PIPA], .71). The subtests that were tapping dissimilar constructs yielded correlation coefficients that were quite weak (e.g., Letter Recognition [ERDA-2] and Syllable Segmentation [PIPA], -.01; Target Words [ERDA-2] and Syllable Segmentation [PIPA], .07; Word Opposites [ERDA-2] and Sound Isolation [PIPA], .03). Although the correlation coefficients were moderately related between the subtests of the ERDA-2 and PIPA for the kindergarten children, the various subsets for the first graders were much weaker ranging between .01 (Pseudoword Decoding [ERDA-2] and Sound Isolation [PIPA]) to .53 (Pseudoword Decoding [ERDA-2] and Sound Segmentation [PIPA]). However, the relationships were expected by the authors to be weaker for the first graders because the PIPA assesses phonological awareness and the ERDA-2 for first graders emphasizes reading rather than phonological awareness. In fact, the subtests that were more likely to be tapping similar constructs did have higher correlation coefficients (e.g., Letter Recognition [ERDA-2] and Letter-Sound Knowledge [PIPA], .45).

Validity was also assessed by examining classification consistency between the PIPA and the ERDA-2, which both classify the student's performance based on their percentile rankings (i.e., PIPA: percentile ranks of 70 to 99 = Proficient, 30 to 69 = Basic, and 0 to 29 = Emerging for 4- and 5-year-olds, or Below Basic for 6-year-olds; ERDA-2: percentile ranks of 70 to 99 = Proficient, 30 to 69 = Basic, and 0 to 29 = Emerging for kindergarten children, and Below Basic for first, second, and third graders). Classification consistency was evaluated by examining the degree of consistency of the classification each student was given by test (PIPA vs. ERDA-2) and by subtest. Agreement between the tests and subtests ranged between 23.0% (PIPA Letter-Sound Knowledge and ERDA-2 First-Grade Letter Recognition) and 62.5% (PIPA Rhyme Awareness and ERDA-2 Kindergarten Rhyming) for an average agreement of 44.4% for the three-category classification scheme. Although the classification consistency

was rather poor, the authors also examined the classification data by assigning "Needs Intervention" based on percentile scores between 0 and 39 and "Does Not Need Intervention" based on percentile scores above 39. The consistency of classification for this two-by-two classification scheme ranged from 43.8% (PIPA Syllable Segmentation and ERDA-2 Kindergarten Syllables) to 81.3% (PIPA Rhyme Awareness and ERDA-2 Kindergarten Rhyming) for an average agreement of 65.8%. These values are still rather unimpressive. Even widening the range of scores, the PIPA is not extraordinarily predictive. In fact, if one makes the arguments that (a) phonological awareness is closely aligned with reading acquisition, (b) performance on the PIPA adequately taps phonological awareness, and (c) the performance on the ERDA-2 represents behaviors that are closely related to skills necessary for reading, given that it is a test of early reading diagnosis, then there should be a very close correspondence between the individuals that the ERDA-2 indicates "Needs Intervention" and the individuals the PIPA indicates "Needs Intervention." It could further be argued that because the First-Grade ERDA-2 assesses behaviors more closely related to reading, one of the behaviors that the PIPA is hoped to predict, and because phonological awareness deficiencies should be indicative of difficulties of later reading problems, the PIPA should identify more children in need of intervention than does the ERDA-2. In fact, the ERDA-2 identifies two (e.g., ERDA-2 First-Grade Syllables and PIPA Syllable Segmentation) to five (e.g., ERDA-2 First-Grade Phonemes and PIPA Sound Isolation) times more children in need of intervention than does the PIPA. This seems problematic.

There is no assessment of item discrimination, or item bias with reference to gender or race. It would also add considerable evidence for validity if construct validity was assessed by utilizing age and group differentiation. Age differentiation is another means to demonstrate the validity of results from the test. Phonemic awareness abilities should improve with age. No evidence was presented for age differentiation. Group differentiation, like age differentiation, can be used to support validity as well. A test of phonemic awareness should be able to differentiate between groups of young children who are known to have reading difficulties and those who do not have reading difficulties. No evidence was presented to support construct validity in this regard either, although the classification consistency information presented above came close. Unfortunately, the classification consistency data did little to support validity. In conclusion, the case for validity was not strongly established.

COMMENTARY. The stimulus materials for the PIPA are appropriate for the age of the child to be assessed. However, the Sound Segmentation subtest requires manipulatives, five counters (e.g., small equal-sized blocks), that the test administrator must provide. For standardization purposes, it would seem that the manipulatives should be identical for each administration. Thus, the PIPA would best be served if the test developers provided the manipulatives and based their standardization protocol with these manipulatives. Then possible differences in the various ways that the manipulatives might affect each child would be neutralized.

The manual is appropriately written. It provides specific and useful information regarding the administration of the PIPA.

SUMMARY. The PIPA assesses the phonemic awareness abilities of children aged 4 years to 6 years, 11 months of age with adequate levels of reliability. The case for validity was not adequately supported. Although the authors appropriately argue that the subtests that are included in the PIPA represent tasks that have been found in the research literature to assess phonemic awareness, the evidence to support validity needs strengthening.

Review of the Pre-Reading Inventory of Phonological Awareness by MAURA JONES MOYLE, Assistant Professor of Speech Language Pathology & Audiology, Marquette University, Milwaukee, WI:

DESCRIPTION. The Pre-Reading Inventory of Phonological Awareness (PIPA) is a norm-referenced diagnostic test of phonological awareness for children ages 4 years, 0 months to 6 years, 11 months in prekindergarten through first grade. The primary purposes of the PIPA are to establish a baseline of phonological awareness for preliterate children prior to formal instruction in reading, and to identify older students with poor phonological awareness who are at risk for reading failure. The PIPA consists of six subtests—Rhyme Awareness, Syllable Segmentation, Alliteration Awareness, Sound Isolation, Sound Segmentation, and Letter-Sound Knowledge–designed to assess the principal components of phonological awareness (syllable, onset-rime, and phoneme awareness) and grapheme-phoneme (letter-sound) knowledge. The subtests can be administered separately and are reported to take 4 to 5 minutes each. Administration of the entire test requires 25 to 30 minutes.

The PIPA can be administered by teachers, speech-language pathologists, or other educational professionals familiar with standardized assessments. Items are scored as correct, incorrect, or no response. Each subtest includes an "Item Analysis" table to assist the examiner in identifying strategies the student may have used in responding, and to identify specific areas of strength and weakness. The raw score of each subtest can be converted into a percentile range, which corresponds to one of three categories of phonological awareness achievement: (a) *Emerging* (if the child is 4 or 5 years old) or *Below Basic* (if the child is 6 years old), (b) *Basic*, or (c) *Proficient*. Scores in the 0 to 29th percentile range represent Emerging or Below Basic skill level, and students who score within this range are considered to be at risk of not meeting developmental expectations. Scores in the 30th to 69th percentile range correspond to Basic skill development; however, the authors recommend that any student falling below the 40th percentile should receive phonological awareness intervention. Children who score in the 70th to 99th percentile range are considered to be Proficient in their phonological awareness skills.

DEVELOPMENT. The PIPA is an adaptation of the Preschool and Primary Inventory of Phonological Awareness, developed in the United Kingdom. The rationale for testing phonological awareness is based on the well-documented finding that early phonological awareness ability is highly predictive of later reading achievement in children. A satisfactory review of the literature is provided to support the selection of phonological awareness skills measured by the subtests of the PIPA, and the subtest order reflects the typical developmental sequence of phonological awareness abilities. Although the authors provide explanations of the rationale, design, and test format of each subtest, minimal information is provided regarding item development. For example, items in the Syllable Segmentation subtest are described as words that are unlikely to be in young children's vocabularies; however, the process for verifying this assumption is not explained. Test items were analyzed using percent-correct statistics, item-to-tal correlations (point biserials), and age-to-age progressions in mean item scores. All items are reported to perform satisfactorily, although specific results are not provided; therefore, no items were omitted after standardization. In addition, subtest raw score means generally increased with age among children in the standardization sample, suggesting that the test items are sensitive to developmental growth.

TECHNICAL. The standardization sample consists of 450 children, 75 children in each of six age groups. The distribution of the sample across gender, race/ethnicity, region, and parent's years of education reflects the demographic characteristics of school children in the United States (U.S. Bureau of the Census, 2000). Although the norming sample of the PIPA includes children from several racial and ethnic groups, the proportion of minority children included may not be large enough to consider the test appropriate for use with children from diverse linguistic and cultural backgrounds (Wyatt, 2002). For example, the PIPA norming sample includes 74 African American children, or only 16.44% of the total. In addition, the norms are not tabulated according to ethnicity or dialect, making it impossible to compare a dialect speaker to his or her linguistic and cultural peers. Recent research investigating the standardized assessment of phonological awareness skills demonstrated that children who spoke African American English scored significantly below expected norms on the Test of Phonological Awareness (TOPA), even though their basic reading skills were within normal limits (Thomas-Tate, Washington, & Edwards, 2004). Therefore, it is important to account for differences in the phonological systems of children who speak nonmainstream English when assessing phonological awareness skills.

Test-retest reliability analysis (time interval range of 7 to 28 days with mean of 13 days) of the PIPA subtests resulted in mean stability coefficients ranging from fair (.67) to excellent (.97). Mean internal consistency reliability (i.e., split-half) coefficients ranged from good (.82) to excellent (.96). Interscorer agreement percentage ranged from .82 to .98. To establish content validity, the authors reviewed literature supporting their choice of phonological awareness skills assessed by the

PIPA. In sum, the measures included are those that have been shown to identify children with phonological awareness deficits and to predict reading failure. Validity based on internal structure is demonstrated by examining intercorrelations among the PIPA subtests. Results indicate that similar subtests were more highly correlated than subtests that tap into more distinct skills. Overall, the six subtests were moderately to highly correlated (.42—.78) suggesting that they measure similar, but not completely overlapping skills. Criterion-related validity was measured by comparing performance on the PIPA to the Early Reading Diagnostic Assessment, Second Edition (ERDA-2), in a subset of 96 children. Overall, the PIPA subtests were more highly correlated with the ERDA-2 subtests for kindergarten children (-.01–.81) than for first grade students (-.03–.53). The authors predicted that this finding would be the case, given that reading (rather than phonological awareness) is the focus of instruction for first graders.

Classification consistency between the PIPA and the ERDA-2 was examined for selected subtests (i.e., subtests that measure a similar skill). Both tests provide three levels of achievement classification–Emerging/Below Basic, Basic, or Proficient. Exact classification consistency on paired subtests ranged from 23%—63%. When looking at children who differed by no more than one category, the accuracy increased to 90%—98%. The rate of agreement between "Needs Intervention" (i.e., children scoring below the 40th percentile) and "Does Not Need Intervention" (i.e., children scoring at the 40th percentile and above) was also examined for selected subtests of the PIPA and the ERDA-2. The agreement rates ranged from 44% to 81%.

COMMENTARY. A robust relationship between early phonological awareness skills and later reading achievement has been consistently demonstrated in the literature (e.g., Gillon, 2004). Therefore, assessments of phonological awareness are needed to identify children accurately who may be at risk of reading failure. The PIPA appears to be a carefully designed instrument that provides a comprehensive view of children's phonological awareness skills and letter-sound knowledge. Instructions for test administration, scoring, and interpretation are straightforward. Results from the PIPA can be used to gather baseline data, identify children with deficits, and assist in intervention planning. The PIPA is unique in that it includes norms for children as young as 4 years of age.

Despite its strengths, the PIPA could be improved along several dimensions. With respect to test development, no information is provided on the development of individual stimulus items. More importantly, no specific information is provided in terms of the appropriateness of the test for children from culturally and linguistically diverse backgrounds.

As far as scoring and interpretation, the raw score of each PIPA subtest is converted into a percentile range, rather than a specific percentile rank and/or corresponding standard score. A single score or rank would facilitate comparisons of the PIPA to other standardized tests for both clinical and research purposes. In addition, the PIPA provides norms only for individual subtests, and does not provide an overall composite score. In terms of clinical application, the authors recommend intervention for students whose percentile range scores are below the 40th percentile. This guideline should be interpreted with caution given that it is based on a single source (Good et al., 2001), and does not correspond to eligibility criteria required by most school districts for receiving special education services (e.g., 10th percentile or below).

In terms of concurrent validity (i.e., comparing the test to similar measures), the PIPA is compared only to the ERDA-2, and the correlations between the tests are generally modest in strength. Comparing the PIPA to other measures of phonological awareness would add support to its claim of validity. Classification consistency between the PIPA and the ERDA-2 is less than ideal (especially given that there are only three categories of achievement), and the consistency between "Needs/Does Not Need Intervention" is also lower than would be desired. Also, these comparisons were made concurrently, so the predictive value of the PIPA for later reading achievement has yet to be established.

SUMMARY. The PIPA is a well-designed, comprehensive test of phonological awareness skills that is normed on children as young as 4 years of age. Caution should be taken when using the test with children who speak nonmainstream English, and it is hoped that future editions of the test will address issues of linguistic and cultural diversity. Also, additional evidence regarding criterion-related validity and the predictive value of the PIPA for reading achievement would add to the value of the test.

REVIEWER'S REFERENCES

Gillon, G. (2004). *Phonological awareness: From research to practice.* New York: The Guilford Press.
Good, R. H., III, Kaméenui, E. J., Francis, D., Fuchs, L., O'Connor, R., Simmons, D. C., & Torgeson, J. (2001). *Analysis of reading assessment measures coding form: Item by item narrative description.* Retrieved July 22, 2006, from University of Oregon, Institute for the Development of Educational Achievement Web site: http://idea.uoregon.edu/assessment/assessment_forms.html
Thomas-Tate, S., Washington, J., & Edwards, J. (2004). Standardized assessment of phonological awareness skills in low-income African American first graders. *American Journal of Speech-Language Pathology, 13,* 182-190.
Wyatt, T. (2002). Assessing communicative abilities of clients from diverse cultural and language backgrounds. In D. Battle (Ed.), *Communication disorders in multicultural populations* (3rd ed.; pp. 415-459). Boston: Butterworth-Heinemann.

[153]

Pre-Referral Intervention Manual—Third Edition.

Purpose: To provide appropriate intervention strategies for learning and behavior problems.
Population: Grades K–12.
Publication Dates: 1988–2006.
Acronym: PRIM-3.
Scores: Not scored.
Administration: Individual.
Price Data, 2006: $101 per complete kit including manual (2006, 570 pages), 50 learning and behavior problem checklists, and 50 intervention strategies documentation forms; $36 per manual; $35 per 50 learning and behavior problem checklists; $30 per 50 intervention strategies documentation forms; $225 per Pre-Referral Intervention Manual CD-ROM.
Time: Administration time not reported.
Comments: Intervention strategies in 13 areas: Memory/Abstractions/Generalizations/Organizations, Listening, Speaking, Reading, Writing, Spelling, Mathematical Calculations, Academic Performance, Interpersonal Relationships, Depression and Motivation, Inappropriate Behavior Under Normal Circumstances, Rules and Regulations, Group Behavior.
Authors: Stephen B. McCarney and Kathy Cummins Wunderlich.
Publisher: Hawthorne Educational Services, Inc.
Cross References: For reviews by Anthony W. Paolitto and Gabriele van Lingen of an earlier form, see 13:236.

Review of the Pre-Referral Intervention Manual—Third Edition by ROSEMARY FLANAGAN, Assistant Professor/Director, Masters Program in School Psychology, Adelphi University, Garden City, NY:

[Editor's Note: The Pre-Referral Intervention Manual—Third Edition is a framework for conducting clinical interviews to plan interventions rather than a psychological measure per se.

Therefore, the instrument no longer meets the Buros Institute criteria for review. The review that follows is made available, however, in the interest of continuity. Given that the criteria employed in MMY reviews are intended for psychological and educational measures, some aspects of the review below may be less appropriate than is typical.]

DESCRIPTION. The Pre-Referral Intervention Manual—Third Edition (PRIM-3) contains 219 areas of potential school difficulty for which interventions are offered for school learning and behavior problems. The PRIM-3 is used to provide assistance to children who demonstrate concerns that are not of the severity to warrant referral to conduct an assessment for special education eligibility. An eight-step model for prereferral services (Graden, Casey, & Christenson, 1985) is presented that outlines the process from the initial concern expressed by the classroom teacher, to team meetings, use of the manual, intervention selection, and implementation and evaluation of an intervention. The model includes continuing a strategy that proves effective; a referral for evaluation for special education is made when the strategy is ineffective. No direction is offered to aid in deciding the duration of an intervention or the number of interventions that might be attempted prior to referral for possible special education placement. Accompanying the manual is a learning and behavior problem checklist to be completed by the child's teacher(s). The checklist contains 219 items that are identical to the 219 areas of learning and behavior for which interventions are proposed. The PRIM-3 is not scored and thus the technical properties cannot be commented upon.

The learning and behavior problems are categorized according to the following areas: Memory, Abstractions, Generalizations, and Organization; Listening; Speaking; Reading; Writing; Spelling; Mathematical Calculations; Interpersonal Relationships; Academic Performance; Depression/Motivation; Inappropriate Behavior Under Normal Circumstances; Rules and Expectations; and Group Behavior. A form to document intervention strategies is also available. Included in the manual are sample forms that could facilitate study skills development or support behavioral interventions. Information for teachers to guide instructional modifications and to plan and conduct behavioral interventions is also included.

The items appear to be reasonable interventions for the stated difficulties. For example: For a student who is not accepted by other students, one possible intervention is: "Do not criticize. When correcting the student, be honest, yet supportive. Never cause the student to feel negatively about himself/herself" (manual, p. 329). For a youngster who cannot tell time: "Make certain the student understands all concepts involved in telling time (e.g., counting by 15s, 10s, 5s; the big hand and the little hand, etc.)" (manual, p. 214).

The PRIM-3 provides lists of interventions for the same areas as were provided in the PRIM-2 (McCarney, Wunderlich, & Bauer, 1993). It can be readily used for its intended purpose as a source book for school-based teams and classroom teachers. The rationale for the revision is not stated in the manual, nor is it stated that the PRIM-3 is a revision. The revision primarily includes an increase in the number of items in the various areas; in some instances, the increase in items is substantial. The interventions offered are generally less complex at the beginning of the list as compared to those at the end of the list for any given area of concern. Use of the checklist and the form to document interventions permits a structured and organized approach to intervention selection, although no guidelines are offered for intervention selection based on characteristics of the child. Some school professionals may find the documentation of intervention attempts useful, although a similar result could be accomplished without using the test materials. Nevertheless, in addition to its stated purpose, the PRIM-3 may be useful as a source book for school psychologists and other school personnel who prepare reports and may offer instructional recommendations. In this regard, it may be particularly useful to the novice professional.

COMMENTARY. There are concerns about the PRIM-3. Many of the same criticisms made of the prior edition remain. The checklist is essentially a list of concerns not anchored or referenced normatively. The absence of scoring makes it considerably more difficult to evaluate the PRIM-3 overall or any of the suggested interventions, rendering it impossible to comment on its construct, concurrent, or predictive validity. The content does have face validity. The age levels for which the interventions might be used are not specified. The basis for selection of the items or the rationale for number of items per particular category was not specified. Moreover, there continues to be an absence of information as to whether any of the interventions are empirically supported. This shortcoming could have been addressed by providing references to the relevant literature. It appears that critiques of the second edition did not influence the development of the third edition. More important, however, is that given the mandates for schools to use evidence-based interventions, the PRIM-3 is likely to offer little utility to practitioners.

SUMMARY. The PRIM-3 is an updated and expanded version of the PRIM-2. Although it has utility for its stated purpose, its results do not reflect the current zeitgeist regarding the use of empirically supported interventions. Useful information for intervention development may be obtained. It should not be used as a screening device for possible referral to special education.

REVIEWER'S REFERENCES

Graden, J. K., Casey, A., & Christenson, S. L. (1985). Implementing a pre-referral intervention system: Part I: the model. *Exceptional Children, 51,* 377-384.
McCarney, S. B., Wunderlich, K. C., & Bauer, A. M. (1993). The Pre-Referral Intervention Manual (2nd ed.). Columbia, MO: Hawthorne.

[154]

Preschool Child Observation Record, Second Edition.

Purpose: Designed to create a "picture of children's development and abilities."

Population: Ages 2-6 to 6-0 years.

Publication Dates: 1992-2003.

Acronym: COR.

Scores: 7 areas: Initiative, Social Relations, Creative Representation, Movement/Music, Language and Literacy, Mathematics/Science, Total.

Administration: Indivdual or group.

Price Data, 2006: $174.95 per complete kit including 2 Observation Items manuals (2003, 45 pages), user's guide, What's Next? Planning Children's Activities Around Preschool Child Observations Guide, 25 Child Anecdotes booklets, 25 Parent Guide booklets (includes Spanish version), 1 Class Summary form, 25 Child Information and Developmental Summary forms, 50 Parent Report forms (includes Spanish version), Preschool COR poster, High/Scope Preschool Key Experiences poster, 2 complete desk posters, and 2 sets of COR category tabs; $14.95 per 2 Observation Items manuals; $15.95 per user's guide; $16.95 per What's Next? Planning Children's Activities Around Preschool Child Observations Guide; $39.95 per 25 Child Anecdotes booklets; $39.95 per 25 Parent Guide booklets (includes Spanish version); $11.95 per 1 Class Summary form and 25 Child Information and Developmen-

tal Summary forms; $16.95 per 50 Parent Report forms (includes Spanish version); $5.95 per Preschool COR poster; $5.95 per High/Scope Preschool Key Experiences poster; $8.95 per 2 complete desk posters.

Foreign Editions: Parent Guide booklets (2003) and Parent Report forms available in Spanish.

Time: Untimed.

Comments: This test is to be completed by teachers and parents/guardians; previous version was entitled High/Scope Child Observation Record for Ages 2 1/2–6.

Authors: High/Scope Educational Research Foundation.

Publisher: High/Scope Educational Research Foundation.

Cross References: For reviews by Glen P. Aylward and Mary Mathai Chittooran of an earlier version, see 14:167.

Review of the Preschool Child Observation Record, Second Edition by JEAN N. CLARK, Associate Professor of Educational Psychology, University of South Alabama, Mobile, AL:

DESCRIPTION. The Preschool Child Observation Record (COR), Second Edition is an observation instrument targeting children aged 2 1/2 to 6 years of age. The 32 categories for observation are arranged under six assessment variables, as follows: Initiative (making choices and planning, solving problems with materials, initiating play, and taking care of personal needs); Social Relations (relating to adults, relating to other children, resolving interpersonal conflict, and understanding and expressing feelings); Creative Representation (making and building models, drawing and painting pictures, and pretending); Movement and Music (moving in various ways, moving with objects, feeling and expressing steady beat, moving to music, and singing); Language and Literacy (listening to and understanding speech, using vocabulary, using complex patterns of speech, showing knowledge about books, using letter names and sounds, reading, and writing); and Mathematics and Science (sorting objects, identifying patterns, comparing properties, counting, identifying position and direction, identifying sequence, change and causality, identifying materials and properties, and identifying natural and living things).

Each category has five hierarchical levels, and the number corresponding to the level is the "score" for that particular observation. The "Child Anecdotes" is the data record. It contains the date and observer name, the observed category and level, and supporting anecdotal records, which the user manual says are critical. A class summary sheet contains columns for three dated sets of observations per year.

Both the user guide and the description booklet contain sample anecdotal comments, sample child behaviors, and descriptions of incidents to help the observer assess levels and categories to which anecdotes belong.

Parents and teachers are urged to complete the instrument and to attend a minimum 2-day training course. In addition, there is an activity planning book for preschool teachers, with suggested activities that help children learn the skills that are assessed by the instrument.

DEVELOPMENT. The original Preschool COR was published in 1992 (see reviews by Aylward & Chittooran, 2001). According to the user manual, the new edition contains "expanded sections assessing the foundations of language, literacy, mathematics, and science and a teacher guide" (p. 2).

The authors cite three main purposes for the development of the instrument: increasing number of those children attending preschool programs, the limitation of other assessment instruments to language or academic school readiness skills, and the premise that assessment should be directly tied to instruction. In answer to the above-cited needs, the Preschool COR contains instructions, samples, charts, checklists, and summary sheets so that parents, preschool workers, and teachers can use the instrument in any setting where children can be observed including the home, Headstart centers, nursery schools, Pre-K programs, day care centers, or preschools. The six assessment areas include traditional language and academic content such as Mathematics and Science, as well as assessment components in Movement and Music, Creativity, Initiative, and Social Relations. Finally, the instrument is accompanied by a planning guide, which contains specific lesson plans and activities to teach skills at all five levels of the 32 categories.

TECHNICAL. To assess the COR, 20 Headstart staff members used the instrument in observing 160 children in Spring 2002 and 233 children in Fall 2002. Surprisingly, in the reported analyses Initiative and Social Relations were combined, as were Creative Representation and Move-

ment; the category of Language and Literacy remained intact, as did the category of Mathematics and Science. No explanations were offered for this revision. After the spring data analysis ($n = 154$), 11 of the 32 items were revised in some way before the Fall data collection and analysis ($n = 230$).

Reliability. Interrater reliability was computed in the fall sample on 20 teachers and teacher assistants who assessed 41 children (17.8%), with Pearson product-moment reliability coefficients of .69 (Initiative and Social Relations), .70 (Creative Representation and Movement and Music), .79 (Language and Literacy), and .73 (Mathematics and Science). However, the observations differed both in what the adults were assessing, and the level assigned to target behaviors (user manual, p. 32). Therefore, it is questionable as to whether these results reflect psychometric descriptions of interrater scoring techniques.

Alpha coefficients (internal consistency reliability) yielded Spring scores of .82 (Initiative and Social Relations), .79 (Creative Representation and Movement and Music), .85 (Language and Literacy), and .88 (Mathematics and Science). On the revised Fall 2002 version, coefficients were .75, .80, .80, and .75, respectively.

Validity. Construct validity, which the authors call internal validity (user guide, p. 32) was reported from the Spring 2002 data only. Using principal components confirmatory factor analysis, four factors were found: Factor 1 contained six of the eight mathematics and science items ($n = 81$) with correlations of .58 (lowest: identifying patterns) to .74 (highest: identifying position and direction). Items related to Sorting Objects and Counting were below the .40 level of acceptance. Factor 2 contained five of eight items related to Language and Literacy ($n = 133$), with correlations of .41 (lowest: listening to and understanding speech) to .80 (highest: using letter names and sounds). Three items were not included because they did not correlate at the minimum .40 level: using vocabulary, using complex patterns of speech, and demonstrating knowledge about books. Factor 3 consisted of six of the eight items related to Initiative and Social Relations (.44–.74), and Factor 4 contained four of the eight items related to Creative Representation and Movement and Music (.45–.70).

Convergent validity, which the authors called external validity, was assessed using the Fall 2002 instrument with 28 Headstart children (12%), comparing COR scores with the Cognitive Skills Assessment Battery (CSAB; Boehm & Slater, 1981). The CSAB produces scores in three general areas: Basic Information (identify name, birthdate, address, and telephone number), Cognitive Skills (identify body parts, colors, shapes; recall words and sentences; muscle control; vocabulary; discriminating symbols, sounds, and words), and Response During Assessment (task persistence, attention span, and confidence). These three variables produced coefficients of .44, .49. and .47, respectively, in relation to Initiative and Social Relations on the COR, and .63, .52, and .67 , respectively with Language and Literacy on the COR.

Other assessments. To assess the developmental nature of the COR, the four variables used in the COR analysis were reported to be "weakly but significantly" (user's manual, p. 34) correlated with age: .25 for Initiative and Social Relations, .16 for Creativity and Movement and Music, .33 for Language and Literacy, and .28 for Mathematics and Science. The method for obtaining these scores was not described. Finally, the items were assessed for gender neutrality (that neither boys nor girls would tend to score more highly on any given item). No significant gender-related differences were reported.

COMMENTARY. The materials that accompany the instrument are thorough in explaining the procedure for assessing and documenting developmental observations. At least one anecdotal record is required as documentation for valid recording of each observational assessment; however, the task is time-consuming. In addition, there is reportedly marked differentiation in interpretation of behaviors and observations (user manual, p. 32), even among those who were trained to use the instrument. An analysis of correspondence between level of training and reliability of results is recommended because the assessments are based solely on observation and interpretation.

The parent guide is written in both English and Spanish, and is clear and straightforward. Parents are encouraged to document and share anecdotal records from home, and teachers are encouraged both to include parent reports in their records and to share their own findings with parents. However, teachers are cautioned against sharing level scores of children, but are advised to focus on developmental descriptions (p. 27). Such withholding may be questionable because many parents can comprehend the procedure, could add possible insight, and could use the information to focus their interactions with children in the home and other settings.

Psychometrically, the authors have attempted a thorough treatment of the data collected, using a variety of assessment means and data interpretation. However, several questions remain. First, collecting the sample data at one basic site means the results may not be generalizable to programs other than Headstart, to other regions, or to other programs that differ in any of several factors (size, clients, level of teacher training, program organization and administration).

An inherent problem with the data analysis is that the instrument presents six distinguishable variables, yet the analysis involves collapsing four variables into two dyad sets for purposes of analysis. A second general problem is that what the authors called "internal validity" is computed on the Spring 2002 data, before revision of 11 items; however, other analyses are presented for Fall 2002, or for both administrations.

In assessing convergent (external) validity, the COR was compared statistically to the CSAB. However, descriptions of the three categories do not parallel the COR semantically or conceptually. No discussion is offered about the method or choice of content that fed the data analysis. A suggestion would be to either conduct an expert interrater reliability test for content comparison, or to choose an instrument with a closer correspondence to the items on the COR.

SUMMARY. The Preschool COR, Second Edition, is a comprehensive and relatively novel instrument for assessing and recording developmental data on preschool children. Although the authors state that the instrument is to be used neither as a diagnostic nor screening tool, the recorded observations and anecdotal support provide a critical and useful profile of the developmental progress of children in a variety of areas. The 32 items represent four academic-related and four cognitive-social-related categories, assessed in five progressively complex levels. The companion website crosswalks COR-2 curriculum with standards from 17 states and reports further other studies involving the instrument.

The revised COR is flexible in use and application. However, the data are limited and the statistical analysis does not always follow sound psychometric practice. However, with attention to several areas as cited, the instrument could prove to be an asset in recording and documenting important developmental milestones in the life of preschoolers.

REVIEWER'S REFERENCES

Aylward, G. P. (2001). [Review of the High Scope Child Observation Record for Ages 2 1/2-6.] In B. S. Plake & J. C. Impara (Eds.), *The fourteenth mental measurements yearbook* (pp. 542–544). Lincoln, NE: Buros Institute of Mental Measurements.

Boehm, A. E., & Slater, B. R. (1981). Cognitive Skills Assessment Battery (Second Edition). New York: Teachers College, Columbia University.

Chittooran, M. M. (2001). [Review of the High Scope Child Observation Record for Ages 2 1/2-6.] In B. S. Plake & J. C. Impara (Eds.), *The fourteenth mental measurements yearbook* (pp. 544–546). Lincoln, NE: Buros Institute of Mental Measurements.

Review of the Preschool Child Observation Record, Second Edition by LEAH M. NELLIS, Director, Blumberg Center for Interdisciplinary Studies in Special Education, Indiana State University, Terre Haute, IN:

DESCRIPTION. The Preschool Child Observation Record (COR) is an observational instrument designed for use by staff in early childhood and preschool programs serving children aged 2 1/2 to 6 years. The instrument is aligned with the key experiences articulated in the High/Scope Curriculum framework and consists of 32 items in six categories—Initiative, Social Relations, Creative Representation, Movement and Music, Language and Literacy, and Mathematics and Science. According to the user guide, the COR can be utilized to monitor children's development over time, guide curriculum and class activities, and evaluate curriculum, classrooms, and programs.

As a tool for observational assessment, the COR requires users to take brief notes, referred to as anecdotes, and collect portfolio items that reflect a child's "significant daily behaviors" (user guide, p. 17). The collected anecdotes and portfolio items are then cross-referenced with categories and items to determine the best fit(s). A developmental rating is then assigned for each anecdote/ portfolio item using a 5-point scale ranging from simple (1) to complex (5). The COR Observation Items contains descriptive statements for each of the five levels to assist the user. Users are encouraged to collect anecdotes/portfolio items during the daily routine and throughout the year. Summary forms are available for completion and involve the user assigning a developmental level for each COR item. Although the user guide encourages the user to use as much evidence as possible,

it is permissible to use just one anecdote/portfolio item to determine a developmental level if the user is sure that the anecdote reflects typical behavior. If multiple anecdotes are available for a particular COR item, users are directed to choose the anecdote that reflects the highest level of behavior demonstrated. Item ratings within categories are then averaged to generate a category average.

DEVELOPMENT. The current version of the COR (2003) is a revision of the 1992 version, which was designed in response to a call by the early childhood community for authentic assessment tools reflecting all key areas of development. The revision began with a 2001 survey of 25 national early childhood leaders regarding critical characteristics of assessment instruments for young children. The High/Scope project staff responded to the survey results, the needs of users, and the Head Start Outcomes Framework in revising the COR. Limited information is provided regarding the development of the COR although two studies are described in general terms. The reader is referred to a website for further details regarding the studies. There is reference to item revisions but specific information is not provided. In addition, the user guide states that factor analysis supported four categories, instead of the six categories retained in the COR. The four categories (each containing eight items) were utilized for data aggregation and statistical purposes.

TECHNICAL. The user guide summarizes two studies conducted through what appears to be one county agency in Michigan in the spring and fall of 2002. The COR was completed by Head Start staff at the agency for 160 children in the spring and 233 children in the fall. Revisions to the COR were made between the spring and fall data collections. The spring 2002 sample was primarily older preschool children (73.6% were aged 4 years, 6 months to 5 years, 5 months) with approximately 1% being aged 3 years to 3 years, 5 months. The fall 2002 sample included more younger children (14.2% aged 3 years to 3 years, 5 months, 17.7% aged 3 years, 6 months to 3 years, 11 months, 35.3% aged 4 years to 4 years, 5 months, and 29.3% aged 4 years, 6 months to 4 years, 11 months) although the 5 years to 5 years, 5 months group was underrepresented (2.6%) and the over 5 years, 5 months group was not present. In addition, the user guide reported that 12% of the anecdotes used in the fall study had been incorrectly scored and needed to be rescored by project staff. It is unclear how these inaccuracies were discovered and how the accuracy of other ratings can be ensured. The studies are also impacted by incomplete ratings during both studies. For example, all COR items were rated for 41% of the spring sample and 26% of the fall sample.

Results from the two studies are presented as evidence of reliability and validity. The user guide presented internal consistency and interobserver agreement data as evidence of reliability. Moderate internal consistency reliability coefficients ranging from a low of .75 (Math and Science; Initiative and Social Relations) to a high of .80 (Creative Representation, Movement, and Music; Language and Literacy) were reported. Interrater agreement was addressed by examining correlation coefficients between teacher and assistant teacher ratings for 41 children. Correlations between the two ranged from .69 to .79 for the different scales.

Validity evidence included a confirmatory factor analysis and concurrent validity study. As mentioned previously, the factor analysis was interpreted as supporting a four-factor model accounting for 50% of the variance. The correlation between the COR and the Cognitive Skills Assessment Battery was investigated using a sample of 28 Head Start students. However, the presented data suggest that fewer completed cases were actually analyzed for the total COR ($n = 10$) and some COR categories ($n = 12$). Low to moderate correlations were reported ranging from a low of .22 to a high of .67.

COMMENTARY. The COR represents a tool designed to support the authentic assessment of young children, which is essential for conducting meaningful and functional information for families and educators. The COR is based upon a well-regarded early childhood curriculum and includes materials to assist users in linking COR ratings with instructional planning and sharing information with families. Two areas of concern are noted for further consideration. First, the rating system may increase the likelihood for error and spurious results. Although descriptive statements for each developmental level and item are provided, there is considerable latitude in terms of the number of observations required and the determination of a summary developmental level. This potential for fluctuation in ratings will be especially problematic if using the instrument to assess growth and development. Second, the psychometric evidence was limited and based upon studies involving nonrepresentative samples and various technical weaknesses (i.e., number of completed ratings). Further research regarding the validity and reliability of the COR should be conducted.

SUMMARY. The COR offers structure for the observation of young children and is integrated into an early childhood curriculum. Thus, the COR would clearly support teaching staff in reviewing curriculum and planning activities. The development of more specific scoring procedures and continued research appear to be needed to support the use of the COR for the purpose of assessing a child's developmental level and growth over time.

[155]
Preschool Program Quality Assessment, Second Edition.

Purpose: "Designed to evaluate the quality of early childhood programs and identify staff training needs."
Population: Center-based early childhood education settings.
Publication Dates: 1998–2003.
Acronym: PQA.
Administration: Individual or group.
Forms, 2: A, B.
Price Data, 2006: $25.95 per complete kit including administration manual (2003, 32 pages), Form A—Classroom Items, Form B—Agency Items, and set of Index Tabs; $12.95 per administration manual; $6.95 per Form B—Agency items; $6.95 per Form A—Classroom Items; $1.95 per index tab set.
Time: Administration time not reported.
Comments: "Based on classroom observations and interviews with teaching and administrative staff."
Authors: High/Scope Educational Research Foundation.
Publisher: High/Scope Educational Research Foundation.
  a) FORM A—CLASSROOM ITEMS.
  Scores, 5: Learning Environment, Daily Routine, Adult-Child Interaction, Curriculum Planning/Assessment, Classroom Score.
  b) FORM B—AGENCY ITEMS.
  Scores, 4: Parent Involvement/Family Services, Staff Qualifications/Development, Program Management, Agency Score.
Cross References: For reviews by Michael B. Bunch and William J. Sauser, Jr. of an earlier version, see 15:198.

Review of the Preschool Program Quality Assessment, Second Edition by ABIGAIL BAXTER, Associate Professor Department of Leadership and Teacher Education, University of South Alabama, Mobile, AL:

DESCRIPTION. The Preschool Program Quality Assessment, Second Edition (PQA) is a rating scale for assessing the "quality of early childhood programs and [to] identify staff training needs" (administration manual, p. 1). It is a revision of the Program Implementation Profile (PIP; High/Scope, 1989) and the Preschool Program Quality Assessment (PQA) involving rewording confusing items and combining redundant ones. There are two forms and scoresheets: Form A—Classroom Items and Form B—Agency Items. The PQA can be used by trained independent evaluators, program staff as a self-assessment, or students (in training programs). Form A has 39 items in four areas (Learning Environment, Daily Routine, Adult-Child Interaction, Curriculum Planning and Assessment), and Form B has 24 items in three areas (Parent Involvement and Family Services, Staff Qualifications and Staff Development, Program Management). For each item there are multiple indicators (2–9 per item). Form A includes pages for classroom diagrams and noting discrepancies between posted classroom schedules and actual routines.

Rater training is not specified in the manual, and careful reading of the test manual and several practice observations and interviews should adequately prepare raters. Training is offered by the publishers, and an Internet link is included in the manual.

Raters should schedule an entire day to complete the PQA. They should spend half a day on classroom observation and collecting supporting evidence for rating the first three areas of Form A. The other half day entails interviewing classroom teachers for the fourth section of Form A and directors for Form B. The interviews use standard questions. Form B is completed once for multiple classrooms within programs.

For Form A, raters collect information for each of the rows of indicators for each item and record them on the scoresheet or form. After the observation is complete, each indicator is rated on a 5-point scale that is anchored at three points. Next, each item is scored on a 5-point scale based upon a rubric (found in the manual and scoring forms) related to the indicator ratings. Item

scores are then copied into the scorebook's summary sheet. A similar procedure is used for Form B. A "Total Classroom Score" is the sum of all Form A rated items. The "Average Classroom Score" is the Total Classroom Score divided by the number of items rated.

DEVELOPMENT. The PQA is the result of work, begun in the 1980s, to quantify the quality of early childhood settings. The manual says little about its development, except that it has been used in "over 800 preschool and child care centers" (administration manual, p. 9), and the content was chosen to reflect best practices in working with young children. The items are both research-based and field-tested (High/Scope) and assess multiple dimensions of caring for young children. Items measure program structure and implementation, which are important for licensing requirements, and capture the child's experiences in the setting.

The PQA assesses some Head Start Program Performance Standards (U.S. Department of Health & Human Services, 1996, 2002). Thus, Head Start programs can use it to meet regulatory requirements for self-assessment, program reviews, training and program development plans, and monitoring and improving program quality. The concordance between the standards for the PQA and Head Start is documented.

TECHNICAL. Information about the development of the PQA is sparse without a description of how items were chosen. All reliability and validity estimates are from two Michigan field tests. There is sparse description of the types of children and/or centers included in the field tests except that 272 Michigan School Readiness Program (MSRP), Head Start, and private child care classrooms were involved. The second field test included two cohorts, and it is unclear if there were repeated measurements of classrooms within these two cohorts. One field test had 2,000 children but the size of the other is not reported. The inclusion only of children from Michigan is limiting. Finally, there is no information about how "typical" these classrooms were, another important factor.

Two reliability analyses are presented for the PQA. Interrater reliability was reported for 10 classrooms. Raters had a 3-day training session to establish reliability for the original PQA. Percent agreements (exact, and within a point) for the two older versions were all 79% and above. For the second edition, Pearson correlations between two raters in 10 classrooms are reported instead. Because of the small sample only three of the seven areas were included and all correlations were significant. The reliance on these correlational data does not sufficiently demonstrate interrater reliability. Two raters could rank consistently yet have consistent differences in the level of performance. Percent agreement should have been included for the PQA also. Internal consistency was assessed for Form A and Parent Involvement and Family Services from Form B, and the total PQA scores. All coefficient alphas were acceptable except for two areas for the smallest field-test site ($N = 19$ classrooms). There are no test-retest reliability coefficients so it may be difficult to use the PQA longitudinally. Theoretically, the stability of the quality of the early childhood settings is important to document because an important influence on the development of children is consistency of the caregiving environment. Classroom teachers are aware of being observed during the PQA, but test-retest reliability would ensure that there was some stability in the caregiving environment. This need is an even greater concern if the PQA is used to document classrooms' improved quality. Without evidence of stability of the areas across time, it is difficult to attribute observed changes in quality to anything but chance.

Confirmatory factor analysis with 150 classrooms using all items except those relating to Staff Qualifications and Staff Development and Program Management, which were excluded because they reflected agencies not classrooms, yielded a five-factor solution, accounting for 58% of the variance. The manual claims that the factors replicated the five areas assessed. However, data presented in the manual do not support this finding. Daily Routine did not make up one factor, but loaded on four of the five factors. Moreover, the text and a table in the manual are not entirely consistent regarding the loadings of two items relative to "small-group time" and "large-group time."

The concurrent validity of the five classroom areas was established through correlations with the Teacher Beliefs Scale (Burts, Hart, Charlesworth, & Kirk, 1990). Correlations were in the expected directions and all but one (Learning Environment/Appropriate Practices) were significant. Predictive validity of the PQA was established by the correlation between PQA classroom items and children's development as assessed in kindergarten with the Child Observation Record (High/Scope, 1992).

The psychometric properties of two areas (Staff Qualifications and Staff Development, Program Management) were never analyzed because insufficient data were available. These areas are important components of the overall quality of early childhood settings. Not having evidence of the PQA's reliability and validity for these areas limits its utility.

COMMENTARY. The PQA areas, items, and indicators adequately sample the characteristics of quality child care settings. Completing the PQA involves a large time commitment for observations and interviews but results in a higher quality assessment than tools completed in less time. Rating and scoring the PQA is also time-consuming but relatively straightforward. The information provided to programs through the PQA should justify its use.

There are psychometric and practical concerns, however. Raters need to be trained, but it is unclear if raters must be trained by High/Scope or if they can self-train. Reliability studies report 3 days of training for raters. This training requirement if meant for all, although not unreasonable, may likely either result in choosing another tool for self-assessment or inappropriate use of the PQA. Familiarizing oneself with the instrument should not be difficult for well-trained external evaluators, who may be the best suited for this tool.

The reliability data presented are weak. There is no test-retest reliability, an important measure for such a tool. The interrater reliability estimates answer part of the question, but information on raters' actual scoring agreements is missing. The correlations alone are not acceptable evidence of interrater reliability. The factor analysis also appears problematic. The text in the manual does not match some data presented in the manual. Questionable items in the Daily Routine and Adult-Child Interaction areas have been modified, but no evidence is presented that these modifications changed the factor structure and "fixed" the problems. The lack of psychometric information on the Staff Qualifications and Staff Development and the Program Management areas also is of concern. These areas are important components of quality early childhood programs and no reliability and validity evidence in these areas limits the utility of the PQA.

SUMMARY. The PQA is the third revision of a tool measuring the quality of early childhood education settings. Although it has a strong theoretical and practical grounding, it has psychometric problems. Completing the PQA is a relatively labor-involved process that requires attention to several dimensions of these settings. This requirement, combined with the complex nature of the observer training, may not make it a practical tool for community-based programs. Problems with the reliability and validity should also limit its use.

REVIEWER'S REFERENCES

Burts, D. C., Hart, C. H., Charlesworth, R., & Kirk, L. (1990). A comparison of frequencies of stress behaviors observed in kindergarten children in classrooms with developmentally appropriate versus developmentally inappropriate instructional practices. *Early Childhood Research Quarterly, 5,* 407-423.

High/Scope Educational Research Foundation. (1989). High/Scope Program Implementation Profile (PIP). Ypsilanti, MI: High/Scope.

High/Scope Educational Research Foundation. (1992). High/Scope Child Observation Record (COR) for Ages 2 1/2–6. Ypsilanti, MI: High/Scope.

U.S. Department of Health and Human Services. (1996). Administration got Children and Families, Head Start Bureau, Program Performance Standards for the Operation of Head Start Programs by Grantee and Delegate Agencies. *Federal Register,* November 05, 57210-57227. Washington, DC: U.S. Government Printing Office.

U.S. Department of Health and Human Services. (2002). Administration got Children and Families, Head Start Bureau, Program Performance Standards and Other Regulations. *Federal Register,* October. Available online from http://www2.acf.dhhs.gov/programs/hsb.performance/index.htm

Review of the Preschool Program Quality Assessment, Second Edition by STEPHEN B. JOHNSON, Psychometrician, CASTLE Worldwide, Morrisville, NC:

DESCRIPTION. The Preschool Program Quality Assessment, Second Edition (PQA) is intended for review and assessment of preschool classrooms and programs, whether engaged in High/Scope, HeadStart, or other initiatives. The PQA is designed for use by a trained outside evaluator or can be used by those interested in assessing their own classrooms or agencies. It is an assessment tool that focuses on best practices in early childhood education and consists of two forms: Form A (Classroom Items) and Form B (Agency Items), which in total rate 63 areas of best practice. Administration time is approximately 1 day per classroom and at least 1 day for the agency and requires raters trained in interview and observation techniques.

Form A focuses on four areas of classroom practice—Learning Environment (9 items), Daily Routine (12 items), Adult-Child Interactions (13 items), and Curriculum Planning and Assessment (5 items). Form B focuses on three agency areas— Parent Involvement and Family Services (10 items), Staff Qualifications and Staff Development (7 items), and Program Management (7 items).

Scoring is by hand and is conducted for each classroom and agency. Each item of the PQA consists of a statement followed by a series of indicator "rows." An item typically consists of two to four rows. For each indicator the rater is presented with descriptions that define Level 1, 3, and 5 (lower, middle, and upper). The rater collects and records supporting evidence for each indicator and assigns one of the three levels. Using scoring rules based on the number indicators and their levels, the rater assigns a quality level from 1 (low) to 5 (high) for each item.

Each form also provides a summary sheet for raters to record the total items rated and total score. Using the summary sheet a rater determines an average classroom and agency score based on the number of items that could be rated.

Training in the use of the PQA is highly recommended. High/Scope provides a 3-day training program.

As of 2006, the PQA (2nd Ed.) costs $25.95 per kit, which includes the administration manual, Form A, and Form B. Forms and manuals can be purchased separately.

DEVELOPMENT. The PQA (2nd Ed.) is a modification of the PQA, itself a successor of the Program Implementation Profile (PIP). The intent of the instrument is to provide a tool to capture program quality for assessment of compliance with licensing regulations, and to "capture children's experiences in the physical and interpersonal learning environment" (administration manual, p. 1).

The PQA's theoretical foundations are based on the work of David Weikart and his colleagues in the 1960s (e.g., Weikart, Deloria, Lawser, & Wiegerink, 1970), itself a reflection of Jean Piaget's work. This framework views the role of early childhood education as providing an environment in which children "initiate and engage in learning activities that contribute to their cognitive, affective, and physical development" and where adults are actively involved in gauging "the child's developmental status and present[ing] intellectual challenges intended to stretch the child's understanding" (Schweinhart, 2003).

The PQA (2nd Ed.) was also designed to reflect standards of both the National Association for the Education of Young Children (NAEYC) and Head Start Performance Standards (HSPS), standards that focus on a balance of child-initiated and adult-directed activities.

TECHNICAL. The administration manual provides an overview of the different studies used to support the development of both the original PQA and PQA, Second Edition. Evidence for reliability and validity are separately presented. The second edition was field tested in two research projects. The first was based upon a cohort of 2,000 children in 19 classrooms in 2000 (MSRP-2) and designed to assess the relationship between program quality and child development effects. The second (MFDPCS) comprised a total of 253 classrooms and was designed to assess the effectiveness of full-day and part-day programs across a variety of public and private situations.

Reliability is presented both as interrater agreement and an assessment of internal consistency using coefficient alpha. Interrater reliability was assessed by paired observations of 10 of the 19 MSRP-2 study classrooms, though only three sections could be assessed due to sample size. The coefficients that resulted were: Learning Environment (.57), Daily Routine (.75), and Adult-Child Interaction (.74). Coefficient alphas for five constructs (Learning Environment, Daily Routine, Adult-Child Interactions, Curriculum Planning and Assessment, and Parent Involvement and Family Services) are provided based on ratings of 185 classrooms drawn from both field studies. They ranged from .65 to .95 and averaged .93.

Validity evidence is provided through four mechanisms, a confirmatory factor analysis (CFA), relationship with other measures of program quality, relationships between ratings of program quality and child development outcomes, and mapping items of the PQA with Head Start Performance Standards (HSPS). The CFA used a sample size ranging from 134–152 classrooms to assess the first five constructs, although sample size restrictions did not support analysis of the Staff Qualifications and Staff Development and Program Management dimensions. Five factors emerged that accounted for 58% of the variance with factor loadings ranging from .43 to .82. The CFA resulted in the modification of an unspecified number of Daily Routine items, and an Adult-Child Interaction item was added to the form.

Relationships between the "PQA" and the Early Childhood Environment Rating Scale (ECERS; Harms & Clifford, 1980), the Caregiver Interaction Scale (CIS; Arnett, 1989), the Teacher Beliefs Scale (Burts, Hart, Charlesworth, & Kirk, 1990), the Developmental Indicators for the Assessment of Learning, Revised (DIAL-R; Mardell-Czudnowski & Goldenberg, 1990), and the High/Scope Child Observation Record (COR; High/Scope Educational Foundation, 1992) are provided. The majority of correlations are described as between .28 to .65, with most in the .40 to .50 range.

Finally the manual provides a detail map linking the items of the PQA with 12 HSPS. All PQA items aligned with at least one HSPS.

COMMENTARY. The authors of the PQA (2nd Ed.) have both a long pedigree and a strong commitment to providing an assessment tool grounded in theory and backed by evidence. It is a clearly valuable tool for assessing preschool programs that are based on Head Start or NAEYC standards. The PQA also offers individual teachers or agency staff a tool to help monitor their programs on a continuous basis, and the structured approach to evidence collection and analysis would be excellent skills for any teacher or administrator to learn.

The PQA is not, however, for the weak of heart. It requires a level of training and/or practice to administer that demands strong commitment from agencies and individuals. However, there is evidence to show that observation of another's practice will significantly improve one's own practice (e.g., Sasson, & Austin, 2005).

There are four pieces of evidence missing from the manual. First, to enhance the leap of faith that prior studies, such as those linking the original PQA with the ECERS provide appropriate validity evidence for the PQA (2nd Ed.), a small scale study on the correlation of ratings between the different forms would be warranted. Furthermore, because both the ECERS and DIAL have seen modifications since the initial PQA studies it may be appropriate to conduct new studies. Second, more details about the item development phase would be useful (for example, who developed and reviewed the PQA items, who reviewed the entire instrument, and was a panel of outside experts involved or was it all "in-house"?). Third, the authors have left a large piece of validity evidence off the table in their mapping of the items to the HSPS: information that describes how the mapping was conducted. For example, were external reviewers involved, it would greatly enhance the validity evidence of the instrument. Finally, it is also customary to provide interfactor correlations among the factors that resulted from the confirmatory factor analysis. The evidence for a five-factor solution was underwhelming; four factors seemed more appropriate, but a factor correlation table may have helped clarify this.

SUMMARY. The second edition of the PQA offers a solid, grounded tool in the assessment of preschool programs. Evidence for the validity and reliability of the instrument is developing well, though requires a little more clarity. The PQA requires an investment in time and staff resources that agencies and teachers may be reluctant to undertake. However, the potential of the instrument to develop a teacher and agency mindset about evidence should more than offset this investment.

REVIEWER'S REFERENCES

Arnett, J. (1989). Caregivers in day care centers: Does training matter? *Journal of Applied Developmental Psychology, 10*, 541-552.

Burts, D. C., Hart, C. H., Charlesworth, R., & Kirk, L. (1990). A comparison of the frequencies of stress behaviors observed in kindergarten children in classrooms with developmentally appropriate versus developmentally inappropriate instructional practices. *Early Childhood Research Quarterly, 53*, 407-423.

Harms, T., & Clifford, R. M. (1980). The Early Childhood Rating Scale. New York: Teachers College Press.

High/Scope Educational Research Foundation. (1992). High/Scope Child Observation Record (COR) for Ages 2 1/2–6. Ypsilanti, MI: High/Scope Press.

Mardell-Czudnowski, C., & Goldenberg, D. S. (1990). Developmental Indicators for the Assessment of Learning–Revised. Circle Pines, MN: American Guidance Services, Inc.

Sasson, J. R., & Austin, J. (2005). The effects of training, feedback, and participant involvement in behavioral safety observations on office ergonomic behavior. *Journal of Organizational Behavior Management, 24*(4), 1-30.

Schweinhart, L. J. (2003) *Validity of the High/Scope Preschool Education Model.* High/Scope Educational Research Foundation, Ypsilanti, MI. Retrieved August 21, 2006, from http://www.highscope.org/Research/high_scope_curriculum/curriculum_research06.htm

Weikart, D. P., Deloria, D., Lawser, S., & Wiegerink, R. (1970). *Longitudinal results of the Ypsilanti Perry Preschool Project.* Ypsilanti, MI: High/Scope Press.

[156]

Psychoeducational Profile: TEACCH Individualized Psychoeducational Assessment for Children with Autism Spectrum Disorders—Third Edition.

Purpose: Designed as a measure of autism and related developmental disabilities.
Population: Ages 6 months to 7 years 5 months.
Publication Dates: 1979–2005.
Acronym: PEP-3.
Administration: Individual.
Price Data, 2006: $450 per complete kit including examiner's manual, guide to item administration, picture book, 10 examiner scoring/sumary booklets, 10 response booklets, 10 caregiver report forms, and object kit; $61 per examiner's manual; $41 per guide to item administration; $41 per picture book; $28 per 10 examiner scoring/summary booklets; $19 per 10 response booklets; $19 per 10 caregiver report forms; $266 per object kit.
Time: (45–90) minutes.

Comments: Includes a norm-referenced scale and parent/caregiver scale; caregiver "must be an adult who is familiar with the behavior of the child being evaluated."
Authors: Eric Schopler, Margaret D. Lansing, Robert J. Reichler, and Lee M. Marcus.
Publisher: PRO-ED.

a) PERFORMANCE PART.
1) *Developmental Abilities.*
Scores: 6 subscales: Cognitive Verbal/Preverbal, Expressive Language, Receptive Language, Fine Motor, Gross Motor, Visual-Motor Imitation.
2) *Maladaptive Behaviors.*
Scores: 4 subscales: Affective Expression, Social Reciprocity, Characteristic Motor Behaviors, Characteristic Verbal Behaviors.
3) *Composites.*
Scores: 3 subscales: Communication, Motor, Maladaptive Behaviors.
b) CAREGIVER REPORT.
1) *Clinical Sections.*
Scores: 3 subtests: Problem Behaviors, Personal Self-Care, Adaptive Behavior.
Comments: Includes two sections estimating child's current developmental level in several areas and the degree of problems in different diagnostic categories.

Cross References: See T5:2111 (2 references); for reviews by Pat Mirenda and Gerald Tindal of an earlier edition, see 12:316 (2 references); for reviews by Gerald S. Hanna and Martin J. Wiese of the original edition, see 11:317.

Review of the Psychoeducational Profile: TEACCH Individualized Psychoeducational Assessment for Children with Autism Spectrum Disorder—Third Edition by PAT MIRENDA, Professor, Department of Educational and Counseling Psychology and Special Education, University of British Columbia, Vancouver, British Columbia, Canada:

DESCRIPTION. The Psychoeducational Profile—Third Edition (PEP-3) is designed to evaluate the learning strengths and weaknesses of children who are on the autism spectrum. It intended to be used primarily as a tool for planning individualized education programs (IEPs); secondary uses include information to confirm the diagnosis and assessing the results of educational interventions over time. The test is normed for children ages 2 years through 7 1/2 years.

The PEP-3 kit consists of a detailed and well-organized manual, a guide to item administration, the related forms, and set of toys and learning materials. Only a few additional items are needed prior to administration (i.e., small edibles, tissues, food and drink snack items, and light switch). For the Performance subtests, the examiner observes, evaluates, and records the child's responses in the context of structured play activities, assigning scores of 2 (passing), 1 (emerging), or 0 (failing) for each task. In the end, this assessment results in subtest scores, developmental age scores, percentile ranks, and developmental/adaptive levels (mild, moderate, severe) for six areas of development and four areas of maladaptive behavior. In addition, this edition of the PEP includes a Caregiver Report that can be used to collect information about (a) the caregiver's perceptions of the child's current developmental levels and diagnosis, (b) Problem Behaviors, (c) Personal Self-Care skills, and (d) Adaptive Behavior skills. Scores from the latter three sections can be transformed into percentile ranks and developmental/adaptive levels (appropriate, mild, severe). Finally, standard scores, percentile ranks, developmental ages, and developmental/adaptive levels (mild, moderate, severe) can be determined in three Composite areas (Communication, Motor, and Maladaptive Behaviors).

Like its predecessors, the PEP-3 is designed to address some of the challenges typically faced by examiners of children with autism spectrum disorders. Tasks in each of the developmental areas are designed at different levels of difficulty, to increase the likelihood that the child will experience success with at least some of them. The tasks are not timed and many do not require oral language ability. The items in the PEP-3 can be presented out of order if necessary, allowing the examiner to be flexible to meet the individual child's needs. Basals and ceilings are not used, and the examiner may credit easier items without administering them. For some tasks, the examiner may use verbal directions, gestures, demonstrations, and/or physical guidance to communicate to the child what he or she is supposed to do.

DEVELOPMENT. The PEP-3 manual states that the test "combines the latest research data on autism with the established information required for making diagnostic and prescriptive recommendations" (p. viii). No specific information about the theoretical model that underlies the developmental subtests is provided. The authors state that the Maladaptive Behaviors Composite and the items on the Problem Behaviors and Adaptive Behavior

subtests parallel the criterion domains for autism on the DSM-IV-TR, but no specific information is available about how these subscales were constructed.

TECHNICAL.

Standardization. The most significant improvement in the PEP-3 is in the psychometric area, with the addition of normative samples of 407 individuals with autism or other pervasive developmental disorders from 21 states and 148 normally developing children (ages 2–6) from 15 states. The characteristics of both samples compared favorably to data available in the 2001 U. S. Census with regard to race, ethnicity, family income, and educational level of parents. Although the percentages of the samples were not representative in terms of geographic region, no statistical differences among the four regions were found in tests of raw scores comparisons. The ratio of males to females in the autism sample was 4:1, which is congruent with current prevalence data.

Reliability. Three types of reliability data are reported in the manual: internal consistency, test-retest, and interrater. Internal consistency reliability was calculated for all of the subtests and composites using the autism sample at 11 age intervals (ages 2–12). The average coefficient alphas equaled or exceeded .90 for the Performance subtests, .84 for the Caregiver Report subtests, and .97 for the Composites, all of which are indicative of high reliability. In addition, coefficient alphas were calculated separately for the normally developing sample and for six unique gender, racial, and ethnic subgroups from the autism sample (males, females, Hispanics, Whites, Blacks, and other races), with high (i.e., >.76) coefficients reported for all subtests across subgroups. Test-retest reliability was measured using 33 children with autism (ages 4–14) from three states who were tested with a time lapse of 2 weeks between each administration. The test-retest coefficients for raw scores were all ≥.94, indicating a high degree of reliability. Interrater reliability for the Caregiver Report was examined with 29 children with autism, 2 children with Asperger syndrome, and 9 normally developing children, ages 2–10, from seven states. Two parents of each child completed the Caregiver Report independently, and polychoric correlations for each item on the problem behavior, personal self-care, and adaptive behavior subtests were then calculated. The mean coefficients were .85 for Problem Behavior, .90 for Personal Self-Care, and

.78 for Adaptive Behavior (one item from this subtest was excluded from the calculation). These results indicate that different caregivers appear to interpret the items on the Caregiver Report similarly and provide similar responses.

Validity. The manual also provides a number of indications of test validity. With regard to content-description validity, information is provided about a rationale for the selection of subtest items. In addition, item-total score Pearson correlations for each subtest were calculated for a subgroup of the autism sample at age intervals between 2–12 years. All (100%) of the PEP-3 subtests achieved item discrimination scores of ≥.35 (93% had scores of .50 or higher), which can be considered acceptable. Item difficulty was also examined and was found to be adequate, overall. Finally, to examine item bias, a logistic regression procedure using the entire autism sample was applied to each of the items in all of the PEP-3 subtests. Comparisons were made between males and females; Black versus non-Black subjects, and Hispanic versus non-Hispanic subjects. In the end, only four of the item comparisons were significant at the .001 level and had large effect sizes; however, none of the four items appeared to be gender-related, ethnocentric, or related to racial or ethnic stereotypes.

Concurrent validity was examined by comparing scores on the PEP-3 to those obtained on the 1984 version of the Vineland Adaptive Behavior Scales, the Childhood Autism Rating Scale (CARS), the Autism Behavior Checklist (2nd edition), and the Brief Ability Rating Scale (BARS). Correlations between PEP-3 scores and scores on all four criterion tests were high, in the expected direction, and (for the most part) significant at the .05 level. Thus, it appears that scores from the PEP can be used with a similar degree of confidence as those from these four measures.

Construct validity—the extent to which underlying traits of a test can be identified and the extent to which these traits reflect the theoretical model upon which the test is based—is supported with information from several sources. First, tables for the autism sample and the normally developing sample are provided to summarize the correlations between chronological age and raw scores on each of the seven developmental subtests, all of which are both significant at the .05 level and in the moderate to very high range. Evidence is also

provided that the normally developing sample performed better on the subtests than the autism sample (as would be expected). Intersubtest correlations for the raw scores (with age partialed out) range from .39 to .90 with a mean of .68 across 68 coefficients, indicating that the subtests are intercorrelated but probably measure different aspects of developmental skills or maladaptive behaviors. In addition, a maximum-likelihood confirmatory factor analysis was conducted using the raw scores of the autism sample, to validate empirically the PEP-3 composites (Communication, Motor, and Maladaptive Behavior). All indexes supported the fit of the model to the data, and all of the subtest factor loadings were large and significantly different from zero.

COMMENTARY. The strengths of this edition of the PEP-3 far outweigh its weaknesses. The vastly improved psychometric data and the detail with which they are presented in the manual are especially important. The manual provides clear and useful information about scoring and summary procedures. The PEP-3 materials are interesting, engaging, and (for the most part) durable, and are likely to be appealing even to children with significant developmental delays.

There are also some weaknesses that require attention. Although the authors state that the PEP-3 can be used to collect information to confirm a diagnosis of autism, few psychometric data are provided to back up this claim. Two of the three "autism measures" that were used to examine construct validity (the CARS and the BARS) were written by the same authors, and the latter is an experimental scale without psychometric data itself. To claim usefulness with regard to diagnosis, it would have been preferable to compare the relevant PEP-3 subscales to "gold standard" instruments such as the Autism Diagnostic Observation Schedule (Lord, Rutter, DiLavore, & Risi, 2002) and the Autism Diagnostic Interview—Revised (LeCouteur, Lord, & Rutter, 2003). In addition, some of the information needed by evaluators is not readily available in the manual (e.g., there are implications that the measure can be used with children under age 2 or over age 7.5, but this is not clear). Finally, although one case study is provided to illustrate how to use PEP-3 information for educational planning, the child used for this illustration is a preschooler. It would have been more helpful to see an example of a school-age child for whom educational planning is likely to be more challenging, given the wider discrepancy between developmental and chronological age.

SUMMARY. By providing the test materials as part of the standard package, adding the Caregiver Report, establishing standard scores for the Composites, updating the manual and test items, and, most importantly, providing comprehensive reliability and validity data, the PEP-3 authors have substantially improved this unique assessment tool. The PEP-3 has now moved beyond its former status as a potentially useful educational planning tool to become a reliable and valid instrument that has the potential for widespread use with children with autism spectrum disorder and can serve multiple functions.

REVIEWER'S REFERENCES

LeCouteur, A., Lord, C., & Rutter, M. (2003). Autism Diagnostic Interview—Revised. Los Angeles, CA: Western Psychological Services.
Lord, C., Rutter, M., DiLavore, P. C., & Risi, S. (2002). Autism Diagnostic Observation Schedule. Los Angeles, CA: Western Psychological Services.

Review of the Psychoeducational Profile: TEACCH Individualized Psychoeducational Assessment for Children with Autism Spectrum Disorders—Third Edition by LEAH M. NELLIS, Director, Blumberg Center for Interdisciplinary Studies in Special Education, Indiana State University, Terre Haute, IN:

DESCRIPTION. The Psychoeducational Profile—Third Edition (PEP-3) is an individualized assessment based upon the Treatment and Education of Autistic and related Communication-handicapped CHildren (TEACCH) program at the University of North Carolina at Chapel Hill. The PEP-3 is designed to assist in the diagnosis of autism and other pervasive development disorders (PDDs) and in the development of individualized educational programming for children between the ages of 2 and 7 1/2 years. The PEP-3 consists of both direct assessment, referred to as a Performance component, and a rating scale to be completed by the child's caregiver. The Performance part is organized into three composites—Communication, Motor, and Maladaptive Behaviors. Composites are derived from 10 subtests (six measuring the developmental abilities of Cognitive Verbal/Preverbal, Expressive Language, Receptive Language, Fine Motor, Gross Motor, and Visual-Motor Imitation and four measuring maladaptive behaviors of Affective Expression, Social Reciprocity, Characteristic Motor Behaviors, and Characteristic Verbal Behaviors). Com-

posed of two sections, the Caregiver Report requires the respondent to estimate the child's developmental level and degree of difficulty in various diagnostic categories and to respond to items in three subtests—Problem Behaviors, Personal Self-Care, and Adaptive Behavior.

The examiner's manual outlines administration and scoring procedures for the Performance component of the PEP-3; however, the need for flexibility in administration is noted and examiners are encouraged to utilize judgment regarding starting levels and credit for items below entry. Standardized administration directions for direct assessment items are included and should be followed as outlined in the manual. Items are scored as 0, 1, 2 and can be interpreted both normatively and clinically. Developmental subtest scoring is based upon the following three levels: passing (score of 2), emerging (score of 1), and failing (score of 0). The three levels for the Maladaptive Behavior subtests are appropriate (score of 2), mild (score of 1), and severe (score of 0). Developmental ages for all subtests on the Performance Part and the Caregiver Report are available based upon norms from a "normally developing sample" (examiner's manual, p. 11). Further, percentile ranks based upon an "autism comparison sample" are also available (p. 11). Subtest standard scores are utilized to derive composite scores, but users are cautioned not to interpret subtest standard scores because they were derived on highly skewed distributions (p. 21). Instead, users are directed to interpret percentile ranks, developmental ages, composites, and the profile of individual item passing and emerging scores.

DEVELOPMENT. The PEP-3 is based upon the original PEP (1979) and the PEP-R (1990). The PEP-3 revisions were made to improve the psychometric properties, increase family input and collaboration, assess what is referred to as special learning strengths and teachable skills (such as restricted interests), and include normative data for both a typically developing and autism spectrum disorder sample. The PEP-3 kit includes most of the toys and materials needed to administer the assessment, which is an improvement from earlier versions that required users to gather multiple materials. The examiner's manual notes that items and subtests were both added and deleted, although specific information regarding item development and analysis is not provided, and it is unclear whether the same sample is used for various analyses.

TECHNICAL. Two normative samples were utilized during development of the PEP-3. A sample of 407 individuals with autism or other PDDs forms the basis for determining percentile ranks and was used for both validity and reliability studies. The sample was primarily white (71%), male (80%), and identified as autistic (95%). Although the PEP-3 is designed for ages 2 to 7 1/2 years, this sample included individuals ranging in age from 2 to 21 years. The sample of normally developing children provides the basis for determining developmental ages and composite scores and reportedly included 148 children. The demographics for these 148 children were 84% white, 53% male, and 88% without a disability. The remaining 12% were identified with a learning disability, speech-language impairment, or "other disability." The age range of the normally developing sample was 2 through 6 years. There is no explanation regarding the source of the diagnostic status for children in either sample.

The manual reports high internal consistency (coefficient alpha) reliability for the autism sample with average coefficients ranging from a low of .84 (Problem Behaviors on the Caregiver Report) to a high of .99 (Communication Composite). Internal consistency reliability was investigated across racial groups although the sample was primarily white (71%). Internal consistency coefficients for individual subtests were generally lower for the normally developing sample, ranging from a low of .75 (Affective Expression) to a high of .94 (Cognitive Verbal/Preverbal). Test-retest data are presented for 33 children with autism with high correlation coefficients (ranging from .94 to .99). Interrater agreement was investigated for the Caregiver Report for 40 children (31 of which were identified with autism or PDD). Polychoric correlations were interpreted by the authors but were not reported in the manual. The authors conclude that the results indicate high interrater reliability.

Various studies were conducted to provide evidence of content, criterion-predictive, and construct validity. Different samples were utilized for the various studies and in some cases the sample is not well described in terms of age, sample size, and disability status. The sample for many of the studies appears to have consisted solely of individuals with autism disorder. One exception is a study conducted to investigate the PEP-3's ability to differentiate between normally developing children and those with autism spectrum disorder. Percentile rank medians were reported as evidence of group differentiation. A confirmatory factor analysis was conducted using the autistic sample and interpreted as support for the three-composite structure of the performance part of the PEP-3.

COMMENTARY. The PEP-3 has a strong theoretical basis in the TEACHH model and offers the administration flexibility often needed in clinical and educational practice. Many of the revisions made to this third edition will be highly beneficial to PEP-3 users. The attempts to strengthen the scoring and psychometric properties of the instrument are to be commended although the utility of the various scores is currently unknown. Users will need to be cognizant of the purpose for which the PEP-3 is being administered and to select the most appropriate score(s) accordingly. The descriptions of the standardization samples were inconsistent in some places (for example, sample size of the normally developing children) and vague (validity studies) in others. Further, the composition of the samples (age range, disability category) is problematic. The inclusion of an autism spectrum sample is beneficial although the sample appears to be skewed, given that 25% percent of the sample was described as falling in the "severe" range (examiner's manual, p. 22).

SUMMARY. The PEP-3 offers a viable assessment option for children with autism spectrum disorders, especially when the focus is on programming and identifying specific strengths and needs. The utility of the normative comparisons made possible by the revisions to the PEP-3 is less certain based on the existing research. Further research regarding the validity and reliability of the PEP-3 should be conducted.

[157]

Psychopathic Personality Inventory—Revised.

Purpose: Designed to help "assess psychopathic personality traits."

Population: Ages 18—86.

Publication Date: 2005.

Acronym: PPI-R.

Scores, 15: 8 Content scores (Machiavellian Egocentricity, Rebellious Nonconformity, Blame Externalization,

Carefree Nonplanfulness, Social Influence, Fearlessness, Stress Immunity, Coldheartedness), Total, 4 Validity scores (Virtuous Responding, Deviant Responding, Inconsistent Responding 15, Inconsistent Responding 40), 3 Factor scores (Self-Centered Impulsivity, Fearless Dominance, Coldheartedness).

Administration: Individual or group.

Price Data, 2007: $210 per introductory kit including professional manual (166 pages), 25 item booklets, 25 response forms, and 25 scoring summary forms; $72 per professional manual; $46 per 25 response forms; $55 per 25 reusable item booklets; $46 per 25 scoring summary forms.

Time: (20—30) minutes.

Comments: "PPI-R scores and profiles should not be used as the sole basis for diagnostic and treatment decisions that require the integration of information from varying sources."

Authors: Scott O. Lilienfeld and Michelle R. Widows.

Publisher: Psychological Assessment Resources, Inc.

Review of the Psychopathic Personality Inventory-Revised by GERALD E. DeMAURO, Managing Educational Assessment Scientist, American Institutes for Research, Voorheesville, NY:

DESCRIPTION. The self-report Psychopathic Personality Inventory–Revised (PPI-R) is a revision of the PPI designed to reduce reading load, eliminate cultural idioms, reword or eliminate items with poor psychometric properties, and develop new items borrowed (with permission) from the Multidimensional Personality Questionnaire (Tellegen, 1978/1982) for the Stress Immunity and Unlikely Virtues validity scales. The Total PPI-R score is a combination of eight constituent content scales: Machiavellian Egocentricity, Social Influence (called Social Potency on the PPI), Coldheartedness, Carefree Nonplanfulness, Fearlessness, Blame Externalization (called Alienation on the PPI), Rebellious Nonconformity (called Impulsive Nonconformity on the PPI), and Stress Immunity. Three factor scores are also available: Self-Centered Impulsivity, Fearless Dominance, and Coldheartedness (the same as the content score).

DEVELOPMENT. The PPI development was based on a series of considerations designed to sample the domain: (a) Dimensions of psychopathy were delineated avoiding criminal antisocial behaviors; (b) the test was structured to minimize socially desirable or undesirable responding; and

(c) a 4-point Likert-type format was used to eliminate central tendency in option selection.

Each stage of PPI test development was guided by principal components factor analyses with orthogonal (Varimax) and oblique rotations. Items were decomposed to the eight scales of the PPI-R. The Recaptured Item Technique (Meehl, Lykken, Schofield, & Tellegen, 1971) provided an independent validation of the factor labels. Exploratory factor analyses of PPI-R data generated by the norming sample, using both Promax and Varimax rotations, decomposed the scores to three superordinate factors accounting for 47% of the variance: Self-Centered Impulsivity, Fearless Dominance, and Coldheartedness.

The three rounds of PPI test development used samples of 241 male students (mean age = 20.4 years), 253 male students (mean age = 20.8 years), and 610 students consisting of 249 men (mean age = 21.7 years) and 361 women (mean age = 22.1 years). The raw scores were standardized within gender in the final round to avoid spurious effects in factor analysis.

Each round of development retained items that loaded .3 or higher on any factor or on the Total score, using principal components analyses. Items with slightly lower correlations were rewritten. Test development proceeded through four stages: (a) Of the original 136 items, 28 were deleted and 7 were rewritten; (b) additional items were written bringing the total to 188, 35 of which were deleted and 6 rewritten; (c) in the third round, 210 items were administered, 45 were deleted, and 5 new items were added to improve coverage of the domain; and (d) factor analyses identified eight content scales and three validity scales for 187 items.

An embedded 10-item Deviant Response (DR) scale was used to identify aberrant response patterns and eliminated between 3.4% and 5.4% of the respondents. A Variable Response Inconsistency scale was developed in the third round of test development and used to eliminate respondents from validity studies. An embedded 14-item Unlikely Virtues scale (see Tellegen, 1978/1982) was used as a variable in later analyses.

After eliminating respondents for validity scale anomalies, the tryout sample was 683 undergraduates, 256 men and 427 women. Principal axis factor analysis with Promax rotation identified eight factors. Items were retained if they loaded .15 or higher on the Total score and .3 or higher on a content scale. Some items with slightly lower correlations were retained to improve domain coverage. A 40-item Inconsistent Responding scale was developed to augment the 15-item scale and increase internal consistency.

TECHNICAL.

Reliability. Composite reliability coefficients, for the norming sample of 985 community and college examinees and for 154 inmate offenders, are reported for Total score (.93 and .86, respectively), the Self-Centered Impulsivity factor score (.92 and .91, respectively), and the Fearless Dominance factor score (.91 and .76, respectively). Test-retest and alpha coefficients are also reported for Total score and the eight content scales. Test-retest coefficients for 51 members of the norming sample over an interval ranging from 12 to 45 days ranged from .82 for Coldheartedness to .95 for Social Influence. The coefficients for the Self-Centered Impulsivity and Fearless Dominance factor scores and for the Total score were .92, .95, and .93, respectively.

Alpha coefficients for written (.95) and computerized (.92) forms of the PPI-R are reported (Sandler, 2004). Content scale coefficients for these two forms ranged from .75 to .90. Over a 3-week interval, the test-retest coefficients were .94 (written then computerized) and .90 (computerized then written), and the 16 content scale coefficients ranged from .66 to .91, with 13 values at or above .80.

Validity. Abundant validity evidence is reported to address discriminant and convergent properties of the PPI-R test scores. Studies of the PPI also support the construct evidence of validity, but these are not summarized here for the sake of brevity. The greatest obstacle to interpreting these findings is the multidimensionality of the psychopathy construct. Among the eight content scales, only Machiavellian Egocentricity and Rebellious Nonconformity yielded as many as four correlations of .3 or higher with the other seven scales. Blame Externalization, Carefree Nonplanfulness, and Fearlessness yielded two of seven correlations greater than .3. Social Influence, Stress Immunity, and Coldheartedness were not correlated .3 or higher with any of the scales. Stress Immunity had negative correlations with four of the other seven scales. This raises serious questions about the interpretation of a Total score.

Sources of validity evidence include correlations of the PPI-R Total, content, and factor scores with two global measures of psychopathy, Levenson's Self-Report Psychopathy Scale (Levenson, Kiehl, & Fitzpatrick, 1995) and the Self-Report Psychopathy Scale-II (SRP-II; Hare, 1991) and with two personality measures, the NEO Five Factor Inventory (NEO-FFI; Costa & McCrae, 1992) and the Personality Assessment Inventory (PAI; Morey, 1991). Correlations also are reported with measures of other constructs.

Based on the community/college and inmate samples, all eight content scales were significantly related to the SRP-II Total score. Seven of the scales were related to Levenson's Primary Psychopathy, SRP-II Factor 2, the Anti-Social Personality Disorder scale of the OMNI-IV Personality Disorder Inventory (Loranger, 2001), a measure of pathology. Six of the eight scales were related to Levenson's Secondary Psychopathy score, and four of the scales were related to the SRP-II Factor 1.

The PPI-R Total score was related to PAI Mania, Antisocial Features, and Aggression. Each of the eight content scores, as well, was positively or negatively related ($r \geq .35$) to those component scores of these personality measures consistent with theory.

The Self-Centered Impulsivity factor score was negatively related ($r \leq -.35$) to NEO-FFI Agreeableness and Conscientiousness and to PAI Treatment Rejection. It was positively related ($r \geq .35$) to 11 of the 18 PAI scales. The Fearless Dominance factor score was positively related to NEO-FFI Extraversion and negatively related to PAI Somatic Complaints, Anxiety, Anxiety-Related Disorders, and Depression. It was also negatively related to NEO-FFI Neuroticism. Convergence of PPI-R scores with scores on other instruments and with measures of behavior provides evidence in support of the construct validity of the PPI-R. The interpretation of the correlational studies could be facilitated by providing reliability estimates for the scores correlated and also providing the intercorrelations of external measures to enable an evaluation of their dimensionality.

Evidence supporting the use of the validity scales includes scoring differences in relation to response instructions, and correlations with corresponding scales of the PAI. Randomly completed protocols exceeded recommended cutoff scores on the 15-item (72.5%) and 40-item (78.5%) Inconsistent Responding scales.

Standardization. The 683 undergraduate item tryout protocols were supplemented with 329 adults who were representative of the 2002 U.S. population in race/ethnicity and education. Of these, 27 were eliminated for missing demographic information or extreme validity scale values, bringing the final sample to 985. An offender sample of 154 men also was tested to provide clinicians with comparative data.

Final item selection employed the same factor analytic criteria described above. The final PPI-R version consisted of 154 items in eight content scales and four validity scales.

Separate norms were developed by gender for the community sample in response to higher scores obtained by males. Within-gender norms also were developed for ages 18–24, 25–29, 30–39, 40–49, 50–59, and 60 years or older. Because there were no demographic differences in the offender sample, only one set of norms was developed for this group.

COMMENTARY. The validity argument rests most heavily on the convergent and discriminant properties of an instrument designed to assess a multidimensional construct. The dimensions of the construct, in turn, represent characteristics held important in the literature. Greater precision might be realized through profile analyses relating ranges of scores across Content areas to a theoretical framework. Similarly, although the test authors discourage the use of a single cutoff score, it is clear that reference to an informal normative cutoff score is common. Another approach is to set standards to describe the ranges of performance based on theory. This technique is common in educational achievement testing and could increase the interpretability of scores. It offers the advantage, as well, of defining the degree of psychopathy in criterion, rather than normative terms.

SUMMARY. The PPI-R has been developed through careful review of the theoretical bases for a multidimensional aspect of personality. The psychometric consequences are large and difficult. Nevertheless, the instrument provides enough support for interpreting scores to make it a valuable tool for counseling and research. Some suggestions are offered to enable the instrument to provide more criterion-related information.

REVIEWER'S REFERENCES

Costa, P. T., Jr., & McCrae, R. R. (1992). *Revised NEO Personality Inventory (NEO PI-R) and NEO Five-Factor Inventory (NEO FFI): Professional manual.* Odessa, FL: Psychological Assessment Resources.
Hare, R. D. (1991). The Self-Report Psychopathy Scale-II. Unpublished test, University Of British Columbia, Vancouver, Canada.
Levenson, M. R., Kiehl, K. A., & Fitzpatrick, C. M. (1995). Assessing psychopathic attributes in a noninstitutionalized population. *Journal of Personality and Social Psychology, 68,* 151-158.
Loranger, A. W. (2001). *OMNI Personality Inventories professional manual.* Lutz, FL: Psychological Assessment Resources, Inc.
Meehl, P. E., Lykken, D. T., Schofield, W., & Tellegen, A. (1971). Recaptured-Item Technique (RIT): A method for reducing somewhat the subjective element in factor naming. *Journal of Experimental Research in Personality, 5,* 171-190.
Morey, L. C. (1991). *The Personality Assessment Inventory professional manual.* Odessa, FL: Psychological Assessment Resources.
Sandler, J. C. (2004). *Computer equivalency of the psychopathic Personality Inventory—Revised in a nonincarcerated population.* Unpublished master's thesis, Castleton State College, Castleton, VT.
Tellegen, A. (1978/1982). *Brief manual for the Multidimensional Personality Questionnaire.* Unpublished manuscript, University of Minnesota.

Review of the Psychopathic Personality Inventory—Revised by S. ALVIN LEUNG, Professor, Department of Educational Psychology, The Chinese University of Hong Kong, Hong Kong, China:

DESCRIPTION. The Psychopathic Personality Inventory—Revised (PPI-R) is an improved version of the Psychopathic Personality Inventory (PPI). The PPI-R aimed to achieve the same objectives as its predecessor, which are to delineate and operationalize the global structure and specific components of psychopathic personalit, and to offer a "time efficient and easily administered measure of psychopathy that could be used in clinical and nonclinical settings" (professional manual, p. 5). The PPI-R is shorter than the PPI in length, and item wording has been simplified to accommodate individuals with lower reading skills.

The items and instructions of the PPI-R are written at a fourth-grade reading level, and the instrument could be administered to adults in forensic, clinical, and nonclinical settings. The PPI-R has 154 items, consisting of eight Content scales, which are Machiavellian Egocentricity (ME, 20 items), Rebellious Nonconformity (RN, 16 items), Blame Externalization (BE, 15 items), Carefree Nonplanfulness (CN, 19 items), Social Influence (SOI, 18 items), Fearlessness (F, 14 items), Stress Immunity (STI, 13 items), and Coldheartedness (C, 16 items). The sum of the Content scale scores becomes the PPI-R Total raw score. Three factor scores, named Self-Centered Impulsivity (sum of ME, RN, BE, CN), Fearless Dominance (sum of SOI, F, and STI), and Coldheartedness (C score), could also be computed by aggregating the specified Content scale raw scores. These three higher order factors were identified via exploratory factor analysis of the eight Content scales scores from the normative data. There are four validity scales, which are Virtuous Responding (VR, 13 items), Deviating Responding (DR, 10 items), and two Inconsistent Responding scales (choice of a 15-item or a 40-item scale). A 4-point Likert scale is used (false, mostly false, mostly true, and true). The professional manual states that if there were more than 30 invalid items, the PPI-R protocol would be considered invalid.

The interpretation of the PPI-R should be done by qualified professionals with training in clinical psychology or psychiatry. The administration of the PPI-R requires a reusable item booklet, a carbonless response form, and a scoring summary form. There is no time limit in completing the instrument, but most individuals can finish in 20 to 30 minutes. Raw scores for each of the scales and factor scores are computed by following steps outlined in the response form. Based on the raw scores, T scores, percentile scores, and 90% confidence intervals of each score (with the exception of the Inconsistent Responding scores in which only raw scores are used) are obtained from the norm tables provided in the professional manual. All scores are recorded in the scoring summary form, where a profile can be plotted.

For score interpretation, a T score of 50 is the mean, and T scores of 60 and 70 would be one and two standard deviations above the mean, respectively, based on the community/college norm. In general, higher scores indicate a more "pronounced" level of exhibiting the measured traits. There is no interpretive specification of different levels of T elevation, and the authors recommend that "clinical and research users of the PPI-R examine the full range of Total, Content scale, and factor scores" (professional manual, p. 20) instead of relying on specified cutoffs. The PPI-R Total score should be viewed as a global indicator of psychopathy, and elevations in the Content scales should be used to understand the basis of the elevation, especially when the PPI-R Total score is moderately elevated. In the case of an extremely elevated Total score, all or most of the Content scales are likely to be elevated as well. There is a caution that users should not interpret an extremely low PPI-R Total score as an indication of pathology.

T scores are not used to report the two Inconsistent Responding scores (IR15 and IR40). The absolute raw score difference between each

the 15 or 40 paired-items are aggregated, and interpretive comments of Acceptable, Atypical (aggregated score higher than 95% of the normative sample), or Highly Atypical (aggregated score higher than 99% of the normative sample) are given based on the value of the aggregated score. Highly Atypical protocols are considered invalid, and Atypical protocols are considered questionable as far as validity is concerned.

DEVELOPMENT. The original version of the PPI used a personality-based approach to measure psychopathy, incorporating an "antisocial-desirability manipulation" (professional manual, p. 29) in which items were phrased to give an impression that they were measuring desirable or normative attributes. Consistent with the literature on psychopathy, items addressing antisocial and criminal behavior were excluded. Initially, items were reviewed by independent groups who matched the items with the named scales. College students were used as normative samples, and exploratory factor-analytic techniques were conducted to determine item affiliation to scales. The resultant PPI consisted of 187 items, with eight subscales and three validity scales.

The PPI-R followed the same structure of the PPI. A majority of the items remained unchanged or were only slightly modified to increase clarity and ease in understanding. Twenty-six experimental items were added for the purpose of expanding and increasing the internal consistency of the Stress Immunity scale, Virtuous Responding scale (called Unlikely Virtuous scale in the PPI), and Inconsistent Responding scale. This process resulted in a 213-item tryout version.

The tryout version was administered to undergraduate students ($N = 683$, 256 men and 427 women), and principal axis exploratory factor analysis and item-score correlations were conducted. The same eight factors as the PPI emerged from the analysis, and factor loadings and item-score correlations were used as criteria to assign items to scales. This process resulted in a 167-item instrument that was then administered to a group of community adults ($N = 329$, gender of participants not specified) who received a payment for participation. The data collected from the community adults were combined with the college student data ($N = 683$) from the earlier tryout version to form the standardization sample. Another round of exploratory factor analysis and item-scale correlation was conducted with this sample, and 13 items were deleted to form a 154-item instrument with eight Content scales, three Factor scores, and four Validity scales.

TECHNICAL. The normative sample of the PPI-R was a combination of the college sample and the community sample used in developing the PPI-R items and scales (N = 985, 408 men and 577 women, see description above), and one can estimate from the size of the college sample that college students (N = 683, about 70% of normative sample) are overrepresented in the norm group. The test authors report that the normative sample matched the 2002 U.S. Census proportions for race/ethnicity and educational level, yet no figures were presented to substantiate this claim. Gender and age differences were found in the PPI-R Total score and several Content scales, and separate gender and age norms were recommended. It was reported that the PPI-R test scores were not related to race/ethnicity.

The PPI-R was administered to men (N = 154) who were offenders (aged 18 to 57) in a prerelease treatment facility. Data from this sample could be used to provide another normative perspective for individuals in the correctional system. However, because the size of the offender sample is small, and norms for women are not available, its usefulness is rather limited.

Internal consistency estimates (alpha coefficients) of PPI-R Total scores were .92 and .84 for the community/college and offender samples, respectively. The mean alpha coefficient of the eight Content scales was .84 (range from .78 to .87) for the community/college sample and .77 (range from .71 to .83) for the offender samples. The mean alpha coefficients for the three Factor scores were .87 and .82 for the two samples, respectively. The alpha coefficients for the VR, DR, IR15, and IR40 validity scores for the community/college sample were .72, .52, .33, and .53, respectively; for the offender sample, coefficients were .24, .29, .40, and .57, respectively. The low internal consistency reliability of the four validity scales is an important limitation of the instrument, suggesting that items in these scales might not be measuring themes that are cohesive in nature.

The test-retest correlation (N = 51, average of 19.9 days, range of 12 to 45 days) of the PPI-R Total score was .93, and for the eight Content scales, the mean correlation was .89 (range between .82 and .95). The mean test-retest correlation of the three Factor scores was .90.

The PPI-R manual reviews evidence concerning validity of the PPI as well as the PPI-R, as changes to items were considered minor and the relevance of earlier findings would still apply to the revised instrument. Evidence presented on the validity of the PPI-R focused mainly on convergent and discriminant validity, based on data collected from the normative samples. The PPI-R Total score and the Content scale scores of participants in the community/college and offender normative samples correlated significantly with a number of psychopathy-related measures, including the Primary and Secondary Psychopathy scales of Levenson's Self-Report Psychopathy Scale, Self-Report Psychopathy Scale-II, and the Antisocial Personality Disorder scale of the OMNI-IV Personality Disorder Inventory. The relationship between PPI-R scores and selected personality measures was also examined. For example, the PPI-R Total and Content scores correlated negatively with the Agreeableness scale of the NEO Five-Factor Inventory, and the Stress Immunity scale of the PPI-R associated most strongly with the Neuroticism scale of the latter instrument. The PPI-R Total score was found to correlate highly with the Antisocial Features, Mania, and Aggression scales of the Personality Assessment Inventory (PAI). Meanwhile, the PPI-R scores were found to correlate with measures of interpersonal problems, sensation seeking, trait anxiety, and alcohol and substance dependence.

In order to establish the relevance of the PPI-R validity scales, undergraduate students (N = 40) were asked to respond to the PPI-R items using one of the following approaches: honest responding, positive impression management, negative impression management, and speeded responding. In general, the findings supported the validity of the scales, and response style manipulations resulted in differences in validity scores that were consistent with research predictions. In a different study (N = 154), the Virtuous Responding scale correlated positively with the Positive Impression Management scale of the PAI, and the Deviant Responding scale correlated positively with the Inconsistency and Infrequency scales of the PAI.

COMMENTARY. The PPI-R is designed to be a measure of psychopathy for use in clinical and nonclinical settings. It is, however, unclear under what circumstances the instrument should be used clinically and nonclinically. Two of the three case illustrations presented in the PPI-R manual involve the use of the PPI-R to assess individuals in correctional settings. If the most central application of the PPI-R were in correctional settings, then there should be more research devoted to examining its validity for individuals being served in forensic and correctional systems. At this point, the PPI-R does not appear to be an instrument most suited for that population, especially when the adult and college normative sample of PPI-R consisted of a high proportion of college students, and the offender normative sample was limited in size ($N = 154$) and in gender representation (all males).

It is equally unclear what purposes the PPI-R could serve in nonclinical settings, and under what specific circumstances the assessment of psychopathy would be needed and relevant (e.g., employee selection, screening). It seems that in many settings, a more comprehensive assessment of personality is more preferable and practical than assessing a specific domain within personality (i.e., psychopathy) that is clearly based on a "deficit" and "disease" perspective.

The practical implications of the PPI-R scores have yet to be spelled out. The test authors acknowledge that a self-report measure of psychopathy could be used as a supplement to, but not as a substitute for, other assessment approaches such as semistructured interviews in which a full spectrum of data could be incorporated into the process. However, it is not clear *how* the PPI-R scores could be used to supplement other forms of assessment, and what implications could be derived from the scores in relation to treatment and intervention.

A fundamental conceptual query is "what is psychopathy?" The authors of the PPI-R used "an exploratory approach" to test construction in which exploratory factor analysis is employed "not merely as a means of selecting items but also a means of clarifying and modifying the constructs themselves" (professional manual, p. 5). The test authors should not stop at exploratory factor analysis, and there should be further efforts to validate the emerging framework using strategies such as confirmatory factor analytic techniques, and to connect the components of PPI-R with key concepts established in the literature on psychopathy.

In order to enrich the meaning and application of the instrument, the conceptual foundation of the instrument should be expanded and strengthened.

SUMMARY. The PPI-R is a self-report measure designed to assess different facets of psychopathic personality in clinical and nonclinical settings. There is some preliminary evidence that supports the reliability and convergent and discriminant validity of the instrument based on data collected from the normative samples. Additional evidence on the construct validity of the instrument is needed, especially from samples involved in the correctional system in which the PPI-R might have the greatest application. There is also a need to further delineate the conceptual foundation of the instrument so as to enrich its application. The PPI-R should not be used as the sole instrument to identify and diagnose psychopathic personality. Other assessment strategies should be used to develop a comprehensive picture of a person for diagnostic purposes.

[158]

Psychosocial Evaluation & Threat Risk Assessment.

Purpose: Designed to "assist school personnel in … determining the nature and degree of violence risk among students."
Population: Ages 11—18.
Publication Date: 2005.
Acronym: PETRA.
Scores, 15: 4 Domain scores (Psychological Domain, Ecological Domain, Resiliency Problems Domain, Total Domain), 8 Cluster scores (Depressed Mood, Alienation, Egocentrism, Aggression, Family/Home, School, Stress, Coping Problems), 2 Response Style Indicator scores (Social Desirability, Inconsistency), PETRA Threat Assessment Matrix score.
Administration: Individual or group.
Price Data, 2007: $115 per introductory kit including professional manual (2005, 85 pages), 25 rating forms, and 25 score summary/profile forms; $50 per professional manual; $50 per 25 rating forms; $25 per 25 score summary/profile forms.
Time: (10—15) minutes.
Author: Jay Schneller.
Publisher: Psychological Assessment Resources, Inc.

Review of the Psychosocial Evaluation and Threat Risk Assessment by MICHAEL FURLONG, Professor and Chair, Department of Counseling, Clinical, and School Psychology, and DIANE TANIGAWA,

Doctoral Candidate, University of California, Santa Barbara, Santa Barbara, CA:

DESCRIPTION. The Psychosocial Evaluation and Threat Risk Assessment (PETRA) is a 60-item (4 items are scored on two subscales and 4 items are used only for response consistency checks) self-report measure "designed to aid in the determination of threat risk through assessment of threat content and contextual risk factors associated with school violence among middle and high school students ages 11 to 18 years" (professional manual, p. 5). The instrument provides three "domain" scores (Psychological, Ecological, and Resiliency Problems) and a Total score. Domain scores are interpreted as falling in the Normal Range, Mild Clinical Risk (T-scores 60–69), Significant Clinical Risk (T-scores 70–79), and Very Significant Clinical Risk (T-scores of 80 and above), for each gender by four age groups (ages 11–12, 13–14, 15–16, and 17–18). The Psychological domain consists of four "clusters": Depressed Mood, Alienation, Egocentrism, and Aggression. The Ecological domain consists of two clusters: Family/Home and School. The Resiliency Problems domain consists of two clusters: Stress and Coping Problems. Standardized scores for clusters are not provided but raw scores can be expressed as Low ($\leq 33^{rd}$ percentile), Average (34th–74th percentile), High (75th–89th percentile), or Very High ($\geq 90^{th}$ percentile). Critical items and a Threat Assessment Matrix (TAM) are used to express global clinical judgments about threat severity. Inconsistency and social desirability "Response Style Indicators" are provided. Only one missing or invalid response for each cluster and Response Style Indicator is permissible. The scoring sheet under the answer sheet and carbon paper correct reverse scores, but raw scores (using a 4-point Likert scale) must be tallied and transferred to the score summary sheet. Missing or invalid responses may be replaced with the mean cluster raw score. Conversion and qualitative classification tables by gender and age are provided. Interpretation of the PETRA is described as a five-step process, and case illustrations are provided.

DEVELOPMENT. The first step identified psychosocial characteristics of school shooters from two studies by the FBI and the U.S. Secret Service before examining other literature on school violence and the validity of self-report measures. DSM-IV-TR content was used to generate items for the Aggression and Depressed Mood clusters. The initial pilot instrument, with 110 items, was administered to 25 undergraduate students for feedback. Reviews from the undergraduates and a separate expert panel reduced the number of items from 110 to 78. No explanation is provided for how the number of items was reduced from 78 to 60.

TECHNICAL.

Norming. A total of 8,483 responses were obtained from 10 schools, representing a diverse student population from southern Florida. The normative sample included 1,770 students (56% female) and was drawn from the larger sample; however, the only explanation for using this subsample was "convenience." A confusing point is that some of the selected subsample cases had missing responses. Given the size of the original sample pool, it was possible to use cases with complete responses and even to form random subsamples for cross-validation analyses. The normative sample consisted of students from various ethnicities: 33% identified as Caucasian, 27% identified as African American, 21% indicated as "Other," and 19% identified as Hispanic. No explanation is provided as to why there was no purposeful sampling to equate the numbers of males and females and provide balance across grade and ethnicity. Normative conversion tables are provided by age and gender (not ethnicity) because preliminary analyses showed significant but small differences for these variables.

Internal consistency. Coefficient alphas by age group ranged from .79–.82 for the Psychological domain, .66–.72 for the Ecological domain, .72–.78 for the Resiliency Problems domain, and .86–.90 for the Total domain. For males and females the alphas are .79 and .81 for the Psychological domain, .70 and .72 for the Ecological domain, .73 and .76 for the Resiliency Problems domain, and .87 and .89 for the Total domain. Coefficient alphas by ethnicity ranged from .75–.84 for the Psychological domain, .65–.74 for the Ecological domain, .68–.78 for the Resiliency Problems domain, and .84–.90 for the Total domain. The alpha coefficients are highest for Caucasians and lowest for the African Americans.

Test-retest stability. Corrected stability coefficients (between 7 and 10 days from a nonclinical sample of 59 students) are .82 for the Psychological domain, .79 for the Ecological domain, .84 for the Resiliency Problems domain, and .85 for the

Total domain. Corrected stability coefficients for the clusters range from .63 to .88.

Construct validity. Correlations between the clusters and the domains are provided in the examiner's manual by gender. Correlations between the clusters and Psychological domain did not vary greatly. Correlations between Depressed Mood, Alienation, Egocentricism, and Aggression and the Psychological domain ranged from .48–.81; however, correlations between the other clusters and the Psychological domain ranged from .45–.71. Correlations between clusters Family/Home and School and the Ecological domain ranged from .81–.88 and were much higher than the correlations between the other clusters and the Ecological domain ($r = .21–.53$). Correlations between clusters Stress and Coping Problems and the Resiliency Problems domain ranged from .70–.94. Unlike the other clusters, for males and females, correlations between Depressed Mood and the Resiliency Problems domain were greater than .70. The lack of any formal statistical analyses of the PETRA's construct validity is a major limitation. The scale includes four items that have double loadings, and one can only presume that this represents the results of some unreported exploratory factor analysis or a similar analysis. As such, the manual is incomplete without presenting the analytic results and, given the available sample, the inclusion of further analyses such as confirmatory factor analyses.

Discriminant validity. Significant differences were found between a clinical sample (from an outpatient mental health treatment facility) and a matched control sample on all the domains and five of the eight clusters (Depressed Mood, Alienation, Aggression, Family/Home, and Coping Problems). Significant differences were not found between the two groups in clusters Egocentricism, School, and Stress. A limitation is that the comparison/control group used in this analysis was not a school-referred sample and had just 29 clinical cases, only some of whom expressed a threat towards others.

Concurrent validity. Statistically significant correlations between the PETRA and two other measures of psychosocial functioning (Achenbach Youth Self Report [Child Behavior Checklist]; Behavior Assessment Scale for Children–2) were obtained from a nonclinical sample. Statistically significant correlations between the PETRA and

measures on depression and suicidal ideation were obtained from a clinical sample.

COMMENTARY.

Strengths. The PETRA provides scores and qualitative classifications in different areas of psychosocial functioning, highlights critical items for follow-up, assesses the validity of the responses (items measuring social desirability and inconsistency), and describes a clinical judgment process for assessing the severity of the level of a threat made by an adolescent. Professionals in schools will appreciate the information gained from the self-report measure and the structure of the five-step process in interpreting the PETRA. The score summary sheet organizes the information in easily readable tables and charts, and the Threat Assessment Matrix checklist assists school personnel in identifying the severity of the threat. Professionals will appreciate the relative ease in administering and scoring the PETRA.

Weaknesses. "The primary purpose of the PETRA is to help keep threats of violence from becoming acts of violence by providing the clinician with a tool to assist in assessing the magnitude of both the threat content and the context in which it was made" (professional manual, p. 7). However, the PETRA also suggests its use in assessing self-harm and/or psychosocial functioning and in research in school violence, including a way to monitor progress from intervention. Evidence for its utility in these areas is not provided in the professional manual, and there are no research studies suggesting that the PETRA is superior to other measures that are designed specifically to assess self-harm, psychosocial functioning, or progress from intervention. A "test and measures" and "keyword" search of the PETRA in PSYCHINFO produced zero results.

The manual presents several case studies showing how schools used the PETRA. However, no information is provided to guide the user in how to integrate its use into an overall response by a school threat assessment team. In fact, one case study mentioned how a youth who was referred to the principal for writing a provocative essay for an English class was reluctant to complete the PETRA but was informed by a school psychologist that, "his honest participation would be taken into consideration when deciding what type of administrative action was to be taken" (professional manual, p. 26). Such central issues in threat assessment as to how to address student rights and to obtain informed consent for such clinical assessments are not discussed in the manual.

There are some technical weaknesses of the PETRA. Although there are statistically significant correlations between the clusters and their respective domains in the PETRA and between the PETRA and other measures of psychosocial functioning, there are also relatively low correlations as well that appear to compromise the construct and concurrent validity of the PETRA. Also, three of the eight clusters (Egocentricism, School, Stress) did not differentiate those from the clinical sample from those in the nonclinical sample. Future studies should continue to investigate the validity of the domains, clusters, and items of the PETRA. In particular, the validity of the cluster Egocentricism needs to be further examined.

SUMMARY. The PETRA assesses psychosocial functioning, highlights critical items for follow-up, contains items to measure social desirability and inconsistency, and describes a method to evaluate clinically the severity of a threat made in a school context. As a measure of psychosocial functioning, other scales (such as the Behavior Assessment System for Children—Second Edition [BASC-2]; 17:21) have much greater research support. As a procedure to judge the severity of threat presented by a youth in a particular context, supporting evidence is limited. Until empirical research further substantiates the PETRA's construct validity and there is evidence supporting its sensitivity and specificity with respect to evaluating the severity of threat made by students at school, other procedures should be considered, such as those offered by panelists who were on the FBI (Cornell et al., 2004; Cornell & Sheras, 2006) and Secret Service school shooter study groups (Borum, Bartel, & Forth, 2005; Fein et al., 2002).

REVIEWERS' REFERENCES

Borum, R., Bartel, P., & Forth, A. (2005). Structured Assessment of Violence Risk in Youth. Odessa, FL: Psychological Assessment Resources.

Cornell, D., & Sheras, P. (2006). *Guidelines for responding to student threats of violence.* Longmont, CO: Sopris West.

Cornell, D., Sheras, P., Kaplan, S., McConville, D., Douglass, J., Elkon, A., McKnight, L., Branson, C., & Cole, J. (2004). Guidelines for student threat assessment: Field-test findings. *School Psychology Review, 33,* 527-546.

Fein, R., Vossekuil, B., Pollack, W., Borum, R., Modzeleski, W., & Reddy, M. (2002). *Threat assessment in schools: A guide to managing threatening situations and to creating safe school climates.* Washington, DC: U.S. Department of Education, Office of Elementary and Secondary Education, Safe and Drug-Free Schools Program and U.S. Secret Service, National Threat Assessment Center.

*Review of the Psychosocial Evaluation & Threat Risk Assessment by GEORGETTE YETTER, As-*sistant Professor, School of Applied Health and Educational Psychology, Oklahoma State University, Stillwater, OK:

DESCRIPTION. The Psychosocial Evaluation & Threat Risk Assessment (PETRA) is a new screening instrument designed for secondary school students ages 11 to 18 who threaten violence against themselves or others in school. The goals of the PETRA are "determining the nature and degree of violence risk among students" (professional manual, p. 1) and "providing the clinician with a tool to assist in assessing the magnitude of both the threat content and the context in which it was made" (professional manual, p. 7).

The PETRA consists of 60 self-report items rated on 4-point Likert scales. Fifty of the items are grouped into three domains: Psychological (25 items), Resiliency Problems (18 items), and Ecological (11 items). These domain scores are summed to produce an overall Total Domain score. Domain scores are reported both as T-scores and as qualitative classifications (normal, mild clinical risk, significant clinical risk, very significant clinical risk). The manual identifies 8 items from the domain scales as "Critical Items." It recommends that school staff attend particularly carefully to Critical Item responses, as they are felt to be indicative of a need for further assessment.

Each domain consists of several item clusters. The Psychological domain includes Depressed Mood (4 items), Alienation (6 items), Egocentrism (5 items), and Aggression (10 items). The Resiliency Problems domain contains Coping Problems (6 items) and Stress (12 items). The Ecological domain is made up of Family/Home (5 items) and School (6 items). The Family/Home cluster asks about parental supervision and involvement in their lives and discipline practices in the home; the School cluster asks about access to weapons and drugs at school, how well students like school, teacher fairness, and security. Some PETRA items represent multiple clusters and domains. Two items from Stress are also included in Alienation, and two others appear in Depressed Mood. Cluster scores are reported both as percentile ranks and as categorical descriptors (low, average, high, or very high).

Ten PETRA items are not included in domain or cluster scores. These Response Style Indicators include 7-item Social Desirability and 12-item Inconsistency scales (6 item pairs). Nine other Response Style items are scored on domain scales. The PETRA classifies Response Style Indicator scores as "typical," "atypical," or "very atypical."

The PETRA also provides guidelines to classify informally the nature of a student's threat using the "Threat Assessment Matrix." Following a rubric developed by the Federal Bureau of Investigation (O'Toole, 1998), threats are classified as "low," "medium," or "high" risk, according to their specificity, directness, and plausibility.

Students complete the PETRA by circling numbers from 0 to 3 to indicate whether they "disagree a lot," "disagree a little," "agree a little," or "agree a lot" with each PETRA item. Responses are reproduced using carbonless paper to a scoring sheet attached to the back of the response sheet. Manual scoring involves totaling items, transferring totals to a separate score summary sheet, and looking up T-scores and qualitative classifications. The response sheet took this reviewer's teenage son about 10 minutes to complete. Scoring also can be completed in about 10 minutes.

DEVELOPMENT. The PETRA is based on a school violence model proposing that youth who experience psychological and environmental stressors and who lack personal resilience are more vulnerable to problems coping with stress. For these adolescents, stressful experiences, particularly victimization, may trigger academic problems, depression, hostility, or other difficulties, which have the potential to result in school violence.

Items initially were developed based on a review of the school violence literature and on the DSM-IV-TR (American Psychiatric Association, 2000) diagnostic criteria for aggression and depression. Some of the initial items subsequently were revised or eliminated based on judgments of their validity by eight experts in education and psychology and by 25 students enrolled in an undergraduate psychology course. The structural coherence of the resulting instrument was investigated by analyzing the correlations of the items with the cluster scores and the relationships of the clusters with the domain scores.

TECHNICAL.

Standardization. The PETRA was administered to over 18,000 youth ages 11 to 18. These students were enrolled in five middle schools and five high schools in a single public school district. Nearly half (47%) of the test protocols that were administered were completed and returned. The

psychometric analyses of the PETRA were carried out on a subset of 1,770 students randomly selected from among these completed protocols.

Reliability. The manual reports data regarding the internal consistency of the PETRA's domains. For youth in all age groups, the reported coefficient alpha reliability coefficients are adequate for the Psychological domain (alpha = .79 to .82) and fair for Resiliency Problems (alpha = .72 to .78). By contrast, the alpha coefficients reported for the Ecological domain (alpha = .66 to .72) are far lower than the minimum of alpha = .80 that is desired for screening measures (Anastasi & Urbina, 1997), throwing into question its coherence. Also, although the internal consistency appears adequate for Caucasian, Hispanic, and "Other" ethnicity youth, for African American youth the alpha reliabilities are consistently and substantially lower for all three domains. In fact, for African Americans the alpha coefficients reported for both Ecological and Resiliency Problems are below alpha = .70, suggesting that the PETRA is less reliable for African Americans than for members of other racial and ethnic groups. No reliabilities or item-total correlations for cluster scores are provided, making it impossible to determine objectively how well the items fit the clusters to which they were assigned.

The manual also describes correlations between cluster scores and domain scores. With the exception of Egocentrism, which correlates strongly with only the Psychological domain score, moderate to high correlations ($r = .37$ to .92, median $r = .59$) were found between all clusters and domains. The manual attributes these intercorrelations to relationships among the underlying constructs. Of greater concern is an arbitrariness in the assignment of the Depressed Mood and Alienation clusters to the Psychological domain: their Pearson correlations with Resiliency Problems are equally high or higher—perhaps not surprising, because these clusters, although assigned to the Psychological domain, share several items with the Stress cluster of the Resilience domain. An alternative explanation for intercorrelations among so many scales is that the constructs measured are not well defined. This possibility seems particularly salient because the items were assigned to clusters and domains solely on the basis of clinical judgment and face validity. These concerns about the structural integrity of the PETRA are unlikely to be resolved until the PETRA is readministered to a broad sample of youth and its items subjected to a factor analysis.

Test-retest reliability of the PETRA was investigated. The correlations for all domain scores were adequate ($r = .79$ to $.85$) over a period of 7 to 10 days. The stability of the cluster scores consistently showed fairly high test-retest stability over this relatively brief period.

Validity. The PETRA's discriminant validity was explored by comparing responses of 29 high-risk youth receiving treatment at an outpatient facility (all of whom had previously threatened or attempted violence against themselves or another person) with those of a demographically matched sample of typical youth. Although all domain scores discriminated between the two samples, three clusters failed to do so—Egocentrism, School, and Stress.

Concurrent validity was evaluated by comparison with the Child Behavior Checklist and Behavior Assessment System for Children-2 on a sample of typical students, and with the Clinical Assessment of Depression, Children's Depression Inventory, and Suicidal Ideation Questionnaire for a sample of high-risk youth. Overall, the concurrent validity of the PETRA appears adequate.

COMMENTARY. Recent publications of the Federal Bureau of Investigation (O'Toole, 2000) and the U.S. Secret Service and U.S. Department of Education (Dwyer, Osher, & Warger, 1998) identify a variety of "early warning signs" to assist school staff and other adults in identifying youth at risk for committing violent acts. Although the PETRA addresses many of these early warning signs, it omits others, including belonging to a closed social group, prejudiced attitudes toward other ethnic and racial groups, a tendency to dehumanize others, and lack of trust (Dwyer, Osher, & Warger, 1998; O'Toole, 2000). The manual fails to provide a rationale for selecting and omitting variables in the development of the instrument. To this reviewer's knowledge, there is no objective basis for believing that the factors omitted are, in fact, less predictive of acts of violence than those included.

In light of the extensive literature on the impact of home, school, peers, and community factors in adolescents' engagement in violence (Gottfredson, 1987; Hyman & Perone, 1998), the inclusion of an Ecological domain on the PETRA

is to be commended. However, the Ecological domain, in its present form, is inadequate.

First, as mentioned above, there are weaknesses with its psychometric properties. Ecological items showed rather low internal consistency, particularly for African American students. Also, the School cluster score failed to discriminate between typical students and high-risk youth.

Secondly, the fact that the norm group was drawn from a single school district has a significant potential impact on the validity of the normed scores, particularly for the School cluster. Because many aspects of school practices and environments are impacted by district-level policies and local values, the norm group's School cluster responses surely reflected their district's values and practices. To the extent that this culture diverges from others across the U.S., normative comparisons on a national level are problematic.

Third, both the depth and breadth of the Ecological domain need to be strengthened. Research has identified prominent school-level risk and protective factors that the PETRA does not address. These include overcrowding; inadequate adult supervision; the tolerance for students with special needs at a school; an orderly, disciplined school environment; communication of high achievement expectations for students; and committed and caring teachers (Dwyer, Osher, & Warger, 1998; Gottfredson, 1987; Hyman & Perone, 1998; O'Toole, 1998). The PETRA also would do well to assess the communities where adolescents reside. For instance, the widespread availability of lethal weapons, prevalence of gangs, and "cultural values that encourage violence as a legitimate means of responding to conflict" all impact on the likelihood that youth will engage in violent acts (Furlong, Bates, & Smith, 2001, p. 128; O'Toole, 1998). To assess students' risk for violence adequately, the PETRA should address environmental influences as comprehensively as it assesses within-student factors (for which existing, well-validated instruments such as the Child Behavior Checklist [Achenbach & Rescorla, 2001] may be more appropriate).

A final concern pertains to the possibility of inadvertent misuse of the PETRA to profile students inappropriately as potentially violent. Although the manual states that the PETRA should be used only after a threat is made, to assess the seriousness of the threat and to make appropriate mental health referrals for students, it may seem tempting for schools to administer the PETRA in an attempt to identify students likely to commit violent acts when no threat has been made. Many students who never engage in violence exhibit risk factors, and identifying students as potentially violent in the absence of a threat would overlabel and stigmatize them (Bailey, 2001; Vossekuil, Fein, Reddy, Borum, & Modzeleski, 2002). Not only would such use of the PETRA be unethical and harmful to students, it might, in fact, increase feelings of alienation and resentment toward their school (Bailey, 2001).

SUMMARY. The PETRA is a new instrument for students ages 11 to 18. It applies a "threat risk assessment" approach, originally developed by law enforcement professionals, to help guide school officials in evaluating and managing students who express the intent to harm themselves or others at school. Although the PETRA addresses a broad set of factors known to predict acts of school violence, it lacks both the depth and the breadth to perform this task adequately. This reviewer has substantial concerns about the validity of this instrument for its intended use and its documentation, and secondary concerns regarding the potential for the PETRA to be inadvertently misused to inappropriately profile students as at-risk of committing violent acts.

REVIEWER'S REFERENCES

Achenbach, T., & Rescorla, L. (2001). *Manual for the ASEBA school-age forms & profiles.* Burlington: University of Vermont, Research Center for Children, Youth, and Families.
American Psychiatric Association. (2000). *Diagnostic and statistical manual of mental disorders* (4th ed., text revision). Washington, DC: Author.
Anastasi, A., & Urbina, S. (1997). *Psychological testing* (7th ed.). Upper Saddle River, NJ: Prentice Hall.
Bailey, K. A. (2001). Legal implications of profiling students for violence. *Psychology in the Schools, 38,* 141-155.
Dwyer, K., Osher, D., & Warger, C. (1998). *Early warning, timely response: A guide to safe schools.* Washington, DC: U.S. Department of Education.
Furlong, M. J., Bates, M. P., & Smith, M. C. (2001). Predicting school weapon possession: A secondary analysis of the Youth Risk Behavior Surveillance Survey. *Psychology in the Schools, 38,* 127-139.
Gottfredson, D. C. (1987). An evaluation of an organization development approach to reducing school disorder. *Evaluation Review, 11,* 739-763.
Hyman, I. A., & Perone, D. C. (1998). The other side of school violence: Educator policies and practices that may contribute to student misbehavior. *Journal of School Psychology, 36,* 7-27.
O'Toole, M. E. (2000). *The school shooter: A threat assessment perspective by the Critical Incident Response Group, National Center for the Analysis of Violent Crime, FBI.* Quantico, VA: Federal Bureau of Investigation.
Vossekuil, B., Fein, R. A., Reddy, M., Borum, R., & Modzeleski, W. (2002). *The final report and findings of the Safe School Initiative: Implications for the prevention of school attacks in the United States.* Washington, DC: U.S. Secret Service and U.S. Department of Education.

[159]

Putney Auditory Comprehension Screening Test.

Purpose: Designed to "assess auditory comprehension in severely physically disabled patients."

Population: Adults.
Publication Date: 2002.
Acronym: PACST.
Score: Total score only.
Administration: Individual.
Price Data, 2006: £62 per complete kit including manual (23 pages) and 25 questionnaire/scoring sheets; £33 per 50 questionnaire/scoring sheets.
Time: Untimed.
Comments: Requires only the ability to provide verbal or nonverbal "yes" or "no" responses.
Authors: J. G. Beaumont, Julia Marjoribanks, Sarah Flury, and Tracey Lintern.
Publisher: Harcourt Assessment [England].

Review of the Putney Auditory Comprehension Screening Test by JEFFERY P. BRADEN, Professor of Psychology, North Carolina State University, Raleigh, NC, and HAILEY E. KROUSE, Graduate Student in Psychology, North Carolina State University, Raleigh, NC:

DESCRIPTION. The Putney Auditory Comprehension Screening Test (PACST) is a 60-question screening measure designed to assess the auditory comprehension of individuals with severe visual and/or physical impairments. Unlike other tests of auditory comprehension, the PACST claims not to require the examinee to have adequate vision, discernable speech, reliable episodic memory, accurate time/space orientation, or sufficient fine motor ability to manipulate test materials. Instead, the PACST only requires an individual to indicate, in some manner, a "yes" or "no" response. The PACST claims to be appropriate for individuals with severe brain injury, stroke, Huntington's disease, or advanced multiple sclerosis.

Prior to test administration, the examiner must gather some preliminary information about the examinee. This information is needed to form questions that target biographical information and can be assessed for accuracy. In addition, the examiner should be familiar with the examinee's method of communication and, if applicable, assistive technology devices.

The first six questions of the PACST target the examinee's biographical data. The following 54 questions inquire about a variety of topics, and systematically vary correct response (yes vs. no), syntactic complexity, and congruity of semantic link (close vs. distant). The PACST manual provides directions to be given prior to administration, and examiners are advised to simplify directions if needed. However, guidelines for simplifying the directions are not provided. Test questions should be presented in order, starting with four practice items. The practice items help verify that the examinee understands the test directions, and the examiner understands examinee responses. However, directions for what to do if the examinee responds incorrectly to practice questions (e.g., provide answer, rephrase question) are not offered. Test questions may be repeated as necessary, and examiners should encourage examinees to guess at answers. Correct responses are provided on the scoring sheet. The response is to be circled if correct, or marked with an "X" if incorrect. The one-page scoring sheet is simple and easy to read. However, preliminary directions for the test are not provided on the scoring sheet.

The number of correct responses is added to yield a total score. Scores fall into one of the following three categories: the normal range (i.e., 57–60), impaired but above chance (i.e., 40–56), and performance at chance (i.e., 39 or below). Scores of less than 21 imply performance at levels worse than chance, perhaps indicating confusion between what constitutes a "yes" versus "no" answer. The manual also provides guidelines for assessing change over time.

DEVELOPMENT. The manual describes the test construction process, a nonclinical "standardization" sample, and a clinical validation sample. Native English ($N = 200$) speakers with no history of neurological impairment provided data for subsequent PACST item selection, and for establishing the "normal range" classification. Demographic data collected on the pilot participants included sex, age, socioeconomic status (SES), and level of education, but the manual does not report participant ethnicity nor explain recruitment procedures completely.

A total of 258 questions were developed according to linguistic criteria (see manual, p. 6). Participants completed a brief questionnaire assessing demographic and biographical information. Next, they were instructed to answer questions using only "yes/no" responses; to focus on accuracy, not speed; and to report if they felt questions were ambiguous. Information on the number of questions reported as ambiguous by the participants is not included. The 10 biographical questions were presented by an examiner, and the remaining 248 questions were presented in random order via computer. The computer recorded response latencies, and an examiner coded whether responses were correct. All participant responses were oral.

The developers excluded data for 6 participants from subsequent analyses, either because 10% or more of their responses were incorrect, or because their response latencies exceeded 1500 milliseconds, producing a final sample of 194 participants. The 258 questions were divided into six categories according to mean response latency. Test developers selected 9 questions from each category, excluding questions for which more than 8 people (i.e., 4%) responded incorrectly. They also selected 6 of 10 biographical questions for inclusion; the manual does not specify how questions were selected when more than the required number met these criteria. The 54 items assessing knowledge of common information are arranged from fastest to slowest response times, under the assumption that response latencies provide an independent estimate of item difficulty (which the data provided and logic supports). Confidence limits for chance ($p < .05$) performance on the 60 questions were calculated to identify random responding (i.e., a raw score range of 21 to 39).

TECHNICAL.

Standardization. The PACST is not a norm-referenced test, in that it does not purport to discriminate between individual performance differences observed in the general population. Rather, it seeks to discriminate normal from abnormal responders. Therefore, test development began with a nonclinical ($N = 194$) sample. An independent clinical validation sample of 112 residents at a neuro-disability hospital in England was also obtained to assess reliability and validity. Demographic data were collected for residents' age, years since diagnosis, years since admission, sex, educational attainment, and socioeconomic status. However, information regarding participants' race, ethnicity, and communication modalities is not included in the manual, nor was there a systematic effort to describe the degree to which either the normal or the clinical sample compares to or represents the general population or the population for which the test is intended.

Reliability. Two types of reliability are provided. First, internal consistency estimates drawn from the normal sample ($N = 194$) for the full 60 questions, and the subset of 54 questions not linked to examinees' unique biographic data, are excellent (alpha = .92). Second, test-retest stability for the clinical validity sample (N = 112) was sampled on three, 1-month intervals. Stability for the entire group is excellent (r_{xy} = .91 to .93). The mean total scores for the second (M = 53.45) and third (M = 53.06) test administrations were higher than the mean total score for the first administration (M = 52.57). Oddly, internal consistency is not reported for the clinical (N = 112) sample. Data for a subsample of residents (n = 52) scoring in the "impaired" range are presented separately. These results mirror those of the entire group, but produce lower values (i.e., stability coefficients range from .78 to .80, and gains from first to subsequent testing were about 2 points rather than 1). The manual (p. 11) offers a 6-point score difference between tests as the criterion for significant change at the p < .05 level, but does not explain how this was calculated (e.g., using confidence intervals vs. empirical data).

Validity. Two types of validity evidence are provided: content and relationships to other variables. With respect to content validity evidence, the developers argue (with some justification) that few adults would lack the knowledge needed to score in the normal range (i.e., obtain at least 57 correct responses), although independent analysis using judges to review for potential bias are not reported. With respect to relationships to other variables, two types of information are provided. First, the clinical sample has a high (57%) proportion of individuals below the normal range (vs. 0% in the nonclinical sample). Second, correlations with external judgments by ward managers (r_{xy} = .47–.52) and speech therapists (r_{xy} = .57–.83) are statistically significant and in expected directions, with lower correlations likely to be due to narrower sampling approaches and expertise of judges. Oddly, no specificity or sensitivity data are provided. Assuming that none of the nonclinical sample had auditory comprehension deficits, the specificity of the PACST appears to be excellent (i.e., 0% scored in the clinical range); however, sensitivity cannot be estimated without independent estimation of auditory comprehension deficits in the clinical sample. Assuming that all clinical sample members should exhibit deficits (an extreme assumption), the sensitivity can be no less than 57% and is most likely higher.

COMMENTARY AND SUMMARY. The PACST provides a quick, inexpensive, and reliable estimate of auditory comprehension. One particularly appealing feature of the test is the wide range of client differences in perception and response modalities incorporated into test design. In contrast, most auditory comprehension tests require retelling, other linguistic responses, or elaborate motor sequences to demonstrate comprehension; the PACST, therefore, provides an attractive alternative to those other tests. The data provided largely support the reliability and validity of the instrument, although the theoretical justification for item and test design is implicit rather than explicit. Evidence is not available to describe clinical sensitivity, possible interactions between ethnic dialects or exposure to knowledge and test scores, nor whether different response modalities influence the reliability and validity of results. Given the available data, the PACST is a promising instrument, but more evidence is required to provide strong endorsement of the PACST.

Review of the Putney Auditory Comprehension Screening Test by DANIEL C. MILLER, Professor, Texas Woman's University, Denton, TX:

DESCRIPTION. The Putney Auditory Comprehension Screening Test (PACST) was designed as a screening tool to assess for auditory comprehension in adult patients with severe physically disabling conditions (e.g., severe brain injury, brainstem stroke, Huntington's disease, or advanced multiple sclerosis). The main purpose of the PACST was to provide an objective measure of auditory comprehension that did not rely on a patient's orientation, episodic memory, visual skills, or the physical manipulation of the test material.

The PACST was designed for adults ages 18 to 90 years. The test is composed of 60 questions that require the patient to respond with an answer of "yes" or "no." The first 6 questions relate to biographical information, such as the patient's name, where he or she lives, and so on. The remaining 54 questions are questions such as "Do dogs fly?" or "Is a table an example of a piece of furniture?" The total score is the sum of the correct responses across the 60 items. Scores that fall within the 57–60 range are classified as "performance within normal range." Scores that fall within the 40–56 range are classified as "performance impaired but above chance." Scores that are 39 or below are classified as "performance at chance." The PACST may be used to assess for improvement or deterioration of a medical condition. Based on a 2-week test-retest reliability, the threshold of +/-6 raw score points is the threshold for determined improvement or deterioration.

DEVELOPMENT.

Initial piloting of items. Two hundred participants identified as normal, ranging in age from 16 to 65, took part in the initial piloting of the test items. The mean age of the sample was 41.6 with an equal number of men and women represented in the sample. English was the primary language spoken by these participants and they had no known neurological deficits. The test authors did not indicate the geographical representativeness of the initial pilot sample.

Two hundred and fifty-eight questions were administered to the pilot group. The questions were designed to meet the following criteria: (a) they require only a yes/no response, (b) the target response would be unambiguous, (c) episodic memory ability would be minimized, (d) orientation to time or space would be minimized, and (e) the items would be representative of a range of semantic functions (e.g., biographical, categories, descriptions, comparatives, time/sequence, abstract, general knowledge). Participant responses to all questions were digitally recorded via a computer in order to capture the response latency for each item. The computer also recorded the errors made by the participants and the order of the items administered.

Five independent variables were identified that related to the sentence stimuli: (a) target response (yes/no); (b) length of the sentence (3–5 words, 6–8 words, or 9–12 words); (c) semantic link between the target response and the semantics of the sentence; (d) the type of question asked (biographical, category, description, comparative, time/sequence, abstract, or general knowledge); and (e) syntactic complexity. After examining the statistical analysis of the data, nine questions from each of the four categories (sentence length, semantic link, question type, or syntactic complexity) that had a maximum of 4% incorrect responses were included in the final version of the test. The internal consistent measure, Coefficient alpha, for these 54 final test items was equal to .92. When the 6 biographical items were added to the final measure the alpha still remained as .92.

TECHNICAL.

Standardization. Participants in the clinical standardization of the PACST were all patients from the Royal Hospital for Neuro-disability in Putney, England. The PACST was administered to 112 patients on three separate occasions, 1 month apart. The mean age of the clinical sample was 52.31 with a standard deviation of 15.30 and a range of 18 to 90 years of age. The mean number of years since diagnosis was 20.50 with a standard deviation of 16.49 and a range of 1 to 79 years. The average number of years since admission was 9.13 with a standard deviation of 7.81 and a range of .5 to 48 years. There were 62 males and 50 females in the clinical sample. Analyses of the data revealed that there was not a significant difference between the sexes on overall test performance. There was a significant effect for age of the patient, with the older patients performing better than the younger ones. There was also a significant effect for education level and socioeconomic status, with the more educated and those with higher socioeconomic status performing better on the test.

Reliability. The test-retest reliability correlation coefficients for the entire normative data set: normal controls and the clinical sample were .93 for the 4-week retest and .91 for the 8-week retest. The test-retest reliability correlation coefficients for the clinical sample only were .79 for the 4-week retest and .78 for the 8-week retest.

Validity. To evaluate the validity of the PACST within a subset of the clinical sample, the ward managers and the speech and language therapists who worked with the patients on a regular basis were asked to rate each patient's auditory comprehension and the consistency of their yes/no responses. The correlation between the ward manager's rating of the patient's auditory comprehension and the patient's PACST score was statistically significant ($p < .001$) and produced a moderate correlation coefficient ($r = .48$). The speech and language therapist's view of the patient's auditory comprehension skills and the actual PACST scores was also statistically significant ($p < .001$) and also produced a moderate correlation coefficient ($r = .57$). The rating of the patient's consistency in giving yes/no responses by the ward managers compared to the actual PACST performance was not significant; however, the speech and language therapist's ratings of the patient's yes/no response consistency compared to the actual PACST performance was significant ($r = -.38, p < .04$).

The difficulty of the items was also examined by splitting the questions into quarters. Analyses revealed that the last quarter of the items were the most difficult for the entire normative sample as well as the clinical sample. The test authors discussed whether fatigue effects on the test might or might not account for this finding.

COMMENTARY. The purpose of the PACST was to provide a test of auditory comprehension that minimized any extraneous factors such as the patient's orientation, episodic memory, visual skills, or the physical manipulation of the test material. The PACST was piloted on an initial sample of normal control test takers (*n* = 200) as a means of testing out a pool of test items and reducing the number of items included on the final version of the test based on the psychometric properties of the test. The PACST was then administered to a clinical group of inpatient adults (*n* = 112), all of whom were residents at the Royal Hospital for Neuro-disability in Putney. Further validity studies will need to be conducted to test for the generalizability and utility of the PACST beyond the limits of the standardization sample. The test authors did report significant age differences and socioeconomic (SES) effects on the PACST scores, yet there are no separate norms for age groups or considerations made for differences in SES. The test-retest reliability coefficients and measures of internal stability appear to be adequate. The validity of the PACST could be better demonstrated by correlating the test with other measures of auditory comprehension.

SUMMARY. The Putney Auditory Comprehension Screening Test (PACST) was designed to measure auditory comprehension within an inpatient adult population at the Royal Hospital for Neuro-disability in Putney, England. The test appears to have adequate reliability, but there has been no published research demonstrating the effectiveness of the test with other clinical samples. Also, the authors report significant age differences in the standardization sample, yet do not provide separate norms for different age groups. The PACST should be reviewed as a research instrument until further clinical validation studies have been conducted and published.

[160]

The Pyramids and Palm Trees Test.

Purpose: Designed "to assess a person's ability to access detailed semantic representations from words and from pictures."
Population: Ages 18–80.

Publication Date: 1992.
Scores: Total score only.
Administration: Individual.
Price Data, 2007: £105.44 per complete kit including manual, 25 scoring sheets, word card, and stimulus book; £15.28 per 25 scoring sheets.
Time: Administration time not reported.
Authors: David Howard and Karalyn Patterson.
Publisher: Harcourt Assessment [England].

Review of The Pyramids and Palm Trees Test by ARTURO OLIVAREZ, JR., Associate Professor of Educational Psychology, and ALLISON BORODA, Graduate Assistant, Texas Tech University, Lubbock, TX:

DESCRIPTION. The Pyramids and Palm Trees Test was developed by David Howard and Karalyn Patterson. The primary purpose of the test is to ascertain a person's ability to access detailed semantic representations directly found in a series of words and pictures. The actual test consists of stimuli in the form of triads. The examinee is supposed to match correctly the bottom two stimuli (picture or words) with the top stimulus. For example a *writing ink container* has to be matched to a *pencil* or a *fountain pen*. The test consists of 52 triads or items. The two choices within an item are always semantic coordinates, whereas the object on top of each test item is typically from a different semantic category. The object on top is denoted the *given item* and the two choices are referred to as the *target* and the *distractor*. Examinees must select one of the bottom pictures (words) on the basis of some underlying property or association that is shared with the given item. The test allows examinees to tackle each triad on the basis of partial information; however, the participant is only able to perform with consistent accuracy if they are able to retrieve complete and correct semantic information from the three items in each triad (manual, p. 5).

The test booklet's pages are divided in half. The top half contains the given item, which can be presented as either a word or a picture. The bottom half presents the target and the distractor choices. These item choices may also be given as pictures or words. By combining the different presentation modalities, six distinct versions of the test may be administered. The first version includes pictures only. The second version of the test includes words only. The third version may include written words as the given item and pictures as alternatives. In the fourth, the administrator may choose to use the picture as a given item and written words as choices. If the administrator were to choose spoken words as the given item and either pictures or written words as choices, then two additional versions of test administration are possible. If the administrator uses a spoken word as the given item and two pictures as choices, then this would be considered a fifth version of the test. Finally, a sixth version of the test may be given if the administrator uses a spoken word as the given item and two written words as choices. These administration versions or options permit the examiner to determine a participant's processing of language and where any breakdown with negative to semantic organization may occur, thus enabling an occupational therapist or psychologist to establish an appropriate treatment program.

The administration and scoring sections of the manual provide a detailed description of how the exam administrator should conduct each of the testing sessions. The manual emphasizes the importance of ensuring that the examinees clearly understand the task so as to avoid poor performances due to their failure in comprehension of the task instructions. The test is not timed; the task is finished when the participant completes all 52 items, including the three practice triads. The administrator is encouraged to provide feedback during practice items only. When unsure of the association for a given test item, the participant is encouraged to guess. One-half of a point is allocated to participants who completely refuse to answer an item. All 52 test triads must be attempted by the examinee in order to consider the test administration valid. For purposes of cross-referencing test performance from a single individual, a different version of the test may be given at an interval of at least 1 week to reduce the impact of practice effects. The total score is computed by tallying the number of correct responses adding scores of .5 for refusals (essentially omits). Application of the Binomial Test provides the following cutoff values for performance on The Pyramids and Palm Trees Test. An "expected by chance" score is ascribed to an individual examinee who obtains at least half of the items correct; a score of 33 is "better than chance" at the $p < .05$ level; a score of 35 at the $p < .01$ level; and a score of 38 or better at $p < .001$. In the event of change in performances, especially in cases in which an examinee performs better in a latter version of the test, the earlier version should be re-administered a week later. However, the manual discourages repeated testing of a person over a short period of time.

DEVELOPMENT. The test was developed by two respected researchers in the field of cognitive neuropsychology with backgrounds in aphasia and semantic dementia. A cursory review of their work appears to indicate that the developers have an extensive background in their respective fields and that the present instrument is the result of many years of research in the area of language impairment in brain injury populations. The authors' work also relies on contributions within the "organization of semantic knowledge postulates [of] partially independent representational systems for words and objects" (manual, p. 11) from Warrington (1975), Beauvois (1982), Morton and Patterson (1980), Patterson and Shewell (1987), and Shallice (1987). Their framework is partially illustrated in the manual with a general description of the separate systems for lexical and object semantics. The test developers acknowledge that this system is not "universally" accepted by researchers such as Cohen, Kelter, and Woll (1980) and Humphreys and Riddoch (1984).

The manual provides brief information about the administration of 60 original test triads in two versions only (three pictures and three words). These original triads were administered to control groups of normal adults. Of the 60 triads only 52 were selected for assessment and interpretation with the mean scores of 98-99% correct responses whereas the performance of the "not normal" participants yielded less than 94% correct responses. A much earlier group of patients ($n = 13$) undergoing rehabilitation for traumatic brain injury reported performances with not one of the patients making more than three errors on the three-picture version of the test. The authors emphasize that it is the "pattern of performance" (manual, p. 9) that is of significance when using the test results with brain injury patients. The authors of the test provide a detailed set of instructions as to the meaning of the test's total score. A given patient performs consistently well if he or she is able to (a) recognize all three test items, (b) retrieve conceptual/semantic information from the items, and (c) perform the appropriate association with the given item while ignoring other semantic information such as similarities between target and distractor items. Unfortunately, the test's total score is less informative and useful when participants fail to make the appropriate semantic associations between the triad items. The authors offer a variety of reasons for this failure in performance and add that "determining the kind of problem that underlies the subject's difficulty depends on the overall pattern of performance" (manual, p. 10) for any of the six or more versions in which the test is able to be administered. According to the manual, the number of possible patterns that may result from a combination of deficits is large. However, the authors provide up to nine different profiles including brief descriptions and interpretations. The authors conclude that The Pyramids and Palm Trees Test "cannot be unequivocally related to a specific underlying level of impairment" (manual, p. 15).

TECHNICAL. The test can be administered by test administrators with a minimum set of qualifications that may include credentialed psychologists, occupational therapists, and speech and language therapists. This information is gathered from the publishing company's 2004 catalogue rather than the test manual. The authors provide a very brief description of the intended audience within the manual. They claim that the test "has been used extensively with clinical populations which include subjects with aphasia, agnosia and progressive dementias" (manual, pp. 9-10). However, the authors do not provide specific empirical normative data as to how the test has functioned. Additionally, the manual provides no description of the theoretical, empirical, or practical justification or basis for the test's triads. A simple search in PsychInfo and Google's Scholar engine attest to the wide use of The Pyramids and Palm Trees Test in the area of cognitive neuropsychology. However, in the journal articles that these reviewers were able to access, there was no mention of the test's construct validity, internal consistency, test-retest, and/or split-half reliability indices. The manual itself does not include a technical section where the psychometric properties of a test are typically addressed. No other source was found attesting to the overall utility and efficacy of the test in the 14 years since its introduction.

COMMENTARY. There are aspects that make The Pyramids and Palm Trees Test an important assessment tool for use with individuals with head injury and other conditions such as Alzheimer's disease. The user of the test can easily

determine the degree to which a participant can access meaning from pictures and words. The extracted information may enable the tester to establish whether a participant's performance or failure in naming or pointing to a named picture is due to difficulty in retrieving semantic information from the pictures and words. However, there are some troubling issues that need to be addressed. First, although this is clearly a widely used test in this area of research, it lacks a clear description of any theoretical background. There is also no precise explanation of what construct the test is measuring due to a lack of operational definitions. This omission seems important in light of the possibility of separate systems for lexical and object semantics. Although it is recognized that the population typically needing this type of assessment tends to be small, there is no excuse for the lack of research into its psychometric properties after 14 years and a substantial number of test users. Second, its wide use in research attests to how many respected researchers view it; yet, this popularity is not sufficient and scientifically expedient to make use of the test as a whole and of the test scores as reliable and valid measures. Third, the manual is wanting in scope for presenting detailed technical psychometric information regarding the test's many versions. Finally, just because the test is easy and simple does not make it informative for test users or patients who may benefit from the results as discrete evidence of progress or impairment.

This area of research is neither simple nor clear cut. There are many complex factors affecting the performance of any given patient. For instance, the standardization sample does not account for or even address the potential confounding influence of multiple impairments due to brain injury or degenerative disease. Impairments due to brain injury rarely occur in pure form. The Pyramids and Palm Trees Test does not acknowledge the potential influence of motor or production systems that could influence a participant's ability to respond correctly to items on the test. The challenge continues to be ever present for practitioners as well as researchers to develop measures that afford them the luxury of less complex and ambiguous measurement of these debilitating human conditions.

A final note is warranted regarding the quality of pictures used in the test. Many of the pictures are sketchy. In one test item, the quality of the pictures may differ for the target and the alternatives, resulting in the respondent choosing the item that is easiest to distinguish. In addition, some of the pictures represent items that are out-of-date. In one case, a picture representing a source of heat depicts an old-fashioned, stand-alone radiator. Unless the respondent has come in contact with such a device, they may be unfamiliar with its function.

SUMMARY. Even with its current weakness, The Pyramids and Palm Trees Test serves an important role in assisting occupational, speech, and language therapists to help diagnose a patient's degree of difficulty accessing meaning from pictures and words. From the brief review of the literature citing use of the test, one notices that this test is seldom the only measure used. Rather, it is one of several similar assessments gauged at tapping the particular condition of the individuals in question. This fact is important because the participants' conditions are no small challenge for the researcher and practitioner. Further studies should make efforts to address more specifically some of the issues addressed previously.

REVIEWERS' REFERENCES

Beauvois, M-F. (1982). Optic aphasia: A process of interaction between vision and language. *Philosophical Transactions of the Royal Society of London, B298,* 35-47.

Cohen, R., Kelter, S., & Woll, G. (1980). Analytical competence and language impairment in aphasia. *Brain and Language, 10,* 331-347.

Humphreys, G. W., & Riddoch, M. J. (1984). Routes to object constancy: Implications from neurological impairments of object constancy. *Quarterly Journal of Experimental Psychology, 36,* 385-415.

Morton, J., & Patterson, K. E. (1980). A new attempt at an interpretation, or an attempt at a new interpretation. In M. Coltheart, K. E. Patterson, & J. C. Marshall (Eds.), *Deep dyslexia.* London: Routledge and Kegan Paul.

Patterson, K. E., & Shewell, C. (1987). Speak and spell: Dissociations and word class effects. In M. Coltheart, G. Sartori, & R. Job (Eds.), *The cognitive neuropsychology of language.* London: Lawrence Erlbaum Associates.

Shallice, T. (1987). Impairments of semantic processing: Multiple dissociations. In M. Coltheart, G. Sartori, & R. Job (Eds.), *Deep dyslexia.* London: Routledge and Kegan Paul.

Warrington, E. K. (1975). The selective impairment of semantic memory. *The Quarterly Journal of Experimental Psychology, 27,* 635-657.

[161]
Rapid Automatized Naming and Rapid Alternating Stimulus Tests.

Purpose: "Designed to estimate an individual's ability to see a visual symbol … and name it accurately and rapidly."
Population: Ages 5-0 to 18-11.
Publication Date: 2005.
Acronym: RAN/RAS.
Scores, 6: Rapid Automatized Naming (Objects, Colors, Numbers, Letters), Rapid Alternating Stimulus (2-Set Letters and Numbers, 3-Set Letters/Numbers and Colors).
Administration: Individual.

Price Data, 2006: $130 per complete kit including examiner's manual (112 pages), 50 record forms, and set of 6 cards; $60 per examiner's manual; $50 per 50 record forms; $25 per set of 6 cards.
Time: (5–10) minutes.
Authors: Maryanne Wolf and Martha Bridge Denckla.
Publisher: PRO-ED.

Review of the Rapid Automatized Naming and Rapid Alternating Stimulus Tests by RUSSELL N. CARNEY, Professor of Psychology, Missouri State University, Springfield, MO:

DESCRIPTION. The Rapid Automatized Naming and Rapid Alternating Stimulus Tests (RAN/RAS Tests) consist of six brief, individually administered tests of naming speed. Naming speed, in turn, is viewed as representing how rapidly one can integrate visual and language processes. The RAN portion comprises four tests, each prompted by a set of familiar stimuli (i.e., either Objects, Colors, Numbers, or Letters). Each set consists of five high-frequency items (e.g., randomly repeated to yield 50 items per set). The RAS portion comprises two tests, each prompted by a set of familiar stimuli. One of these, "2-Set Letters and Numbers," consists of 50 alternating letters and numbers. The second, "3-Set Letters, Numbers, and Colors," consists of 50 alternating letters, numbers, and colors. Each of the six tests is presented by way of a glossy, folded cardboard sheet that the authors refer to as a stimulus card. The cover (8.5 X 11 inches) has 10 practice items presented in two rows of 5. Unfolded, the sheet (17 X 11 inches) displays the actual test: 5 rows, with each containing 10 of the stimulus items.

Administration requires the six stimulus cards, an examiner record form, and a stopwatch. Simple directions for administration are conveniently printed on the examiner's record form, and personnel with only minimal training in assessment (e.g., classroom teachers) can administer the test. The 10 items on each cover serve as a "practice run" in order to check that the child can identify the items and so that he or she understands to work as quickly and accurately as possible (the examiner is advised not to give the test if the child cannot read the set of 10 items on a test's cover). Once the practice items are completed, the examiner unfolds the stimulus card to display the 50 stimuli. The examinee is directed to read the items as quickly as possible without making mistakes. The examiner says "go" and then records the time it takes the student to read through the 50 items. A friendly administrative element is that, if the student gets confused on a test, they can start over—the goal is to time the student's best performance through the 50 items of each test. The examiner records the time, the number of errors, and the number of self-corrections in the boxes on the examiner record form. The latter two do not figure into the score but are used for clinical interpretation. Some guidelines for interpretation are included in the manual. All five tests are said to take only 5 to 10 minutes to administer.

According to the examiner's manual, there are three main uses for this test:

> "(a) early identification of children at risk for reading and learning difficulties; (b) ongoing assessment of processes underlying naming speed and reading fluency; and (c) measurement of the development, intactness, and efficiency of the basic word-retrieval system." (p. 5)

The raw score on each test consists of the total time in seconds required by the examinee to name the 50 items. The six raw scores can then be converted to normalized standard scores (mean = 100, SD = 15), age and grade equivalents, and percentile ranks. A conversion table is also provided that converts the standard scores to NCE scores, T-scores, z-scores, and stanines.

DEVELOPMENT. Naming-speed research has a long history and can trace its roots back to the late 1800s. Over the years, it has been studied in a variety of fields (e.g., education, psychology, neurology, reading research, and speech pathology). The current RAN/RAS Tests are based on rapid naming tasks initially developed by the authors in the 1970s and 1980s (Denckla & Rudel, 1976; Wolf, 1986). The RAN/RAS Tests were normed on 1,461 individuals, across 26 states, and with ages 5-0 to 18-11.

TECHNICAL. As defined by the *Standards for Educational and Psychological Testing* (AERA, APA, & NCME, 1999), test reliability "refers to the consistency of such measurements when the testing procedure is repeated on a population of individuals or groups" (p. 25). Hence, the authors calculated test-retest (time-sampling) reliability using a sample of 216 students in four states, ages 7-0 to 17-11. The sample consisted primarily of white children (non-Hispanic) who did not have an exceptionality. The RAN/RAS Tests were administered twice, with approximately 2 weeks between administrations. Corrected reliability coefficients ranged from .81 to .98 for different levels (i.e., elementary, middle, high school, and all ages). The uncorrected values were not much lower, ranging from .76 to .98. Standard errors of measurement (*SEM*s) are provided based on the corrected test-retest reliability coefficients. A succinct explanation as to how the *SEM*s may be used to produce various confidence intervals (68%, 90%, and 95%) is provided in the examiner's manual. A second type of reliability, interscorer reliability, was also examined. It ranged from .98 to 99. Clearly, this simple instrument can be reliably scored.

According to the *Standards for Educational and Psychological Testing* (AERA, APA, & NCME, 1999), validity "refers to the degree to which evidence and theory support the interpretations of test scores entailed by proposed uses of tests" (p. 9). The test authors examined three types of validity: content, criterion-related, and construct. Content validity gets at whether a test covers the right material and is built into the test during its development. In this instance, the objects, colors, numbers, and letters that comprise the tests were all high frequency items that had been used in prior research. Criterion-related validity evidence is provided by way of an earlier correlation study between the RAN Letters and Numbers Tests and the Rapid Digit Naming and Rapid Letter Naming subtests of the Comprehensive Test of Phonological Processing. The latter subtests represent another device getting at rapid naming. That study (2001) found a correlation of .72 between the digit naming tests, and of .71 between the letter naming tests. (This study could also be viewed as consistency evidence in terms of construct validity.) Further predictive studies are mentioned in the examiner's manual under construct validity.

Construct validity has to do with how well the test gets at the construct in question. It is usually demonstrated by providing various lines of logical evidence. In this regard, the authors of the RAN/RAS Tests provide four arguments. First, one would expect that as children grow older, their measured times on the RAN/RAS Tests would decrease, and they do. An examination of this yielded correlations ranging from -.48 to -.64 across the five tests.

Second, scores on the RAN/RAS Tests should distinguish between good and poor readers. Here, the manual provides a table (pp. 34–35) listing 14 studies (1972–1995) that found group differences on naming speeds supporting this proposition. It appears that 11 of these studies used the RAN, or RAN and RAS Tests per se. The remainder used similar tasks.

Third, because each of the five tests of the RAN/RAS Tests get at visual-verbal processing speed, they should correlate with each other. Again, evidence regarding this is provided via an intercorrelation matrix in the examiner's manual (p. 37). Correlations here ranged from .54 to .83.

Finally, and of importance, the RAN/RAS Tests should correlate with tests of reading ability. Numerous studies are provided in the examiner's manual that show significant correlations between the RAN/RAS Tests and various tests of reading ability. For example, the RAN/RAS Tests and the Woodcock-Johnson Psycho-Educational Battery—Revised Letter-Word Identification had corrected correlations ranging from .40 to .68 (with uncorrected values ranging from .34 to .56).

COMMENTARY. I like the simplicity of these tests. The naming task is straightforward, and the format is similar across all six. The administration is easy and direct by way of the examiner record form. As the manual notes, school personnel ranging from classroom teachers to reading specialists and school psychologists can administer this instrument. I would certainly concur that minimal training is required.

Despite the short administration time (5–10 minutes), the instrument has quite good test-retest reliability. In the elementary school sample, the corrected reliability coefficients were in the .80s to .90s. The middle school sample yielded corrected coefficients almost entirely in the .90s. The high school sample was even better, with the corrected reliability coefficients in the mid- to high .90s. I appreciated the fact that both corrected and uncorrected coefficients were provided. My only complaint here is that the sample used for this reliability study did not include children with exceptionalities. It would be worthwhile to get an estimate of test-retest reliability using a sample of children with exceptionalities because this test is intended for use with at-risk children.

I believe the test to be a valid measure of naming speed, which in turn can be used for such things as identifying children at risk for reading problems, ongoing assessment, and the measurement of children's word-retrieval systems. The authors of this test, Wolf and Denckla, have done much of the seminal work in this area, and they bring extensive expertise to the test's development. Given its history, it is not surprising that the examiner's manual states that these tests are sometimes referred to as the "gold standard of naming tests" (p. 1).

A minor concern might be the discrepancy between the format of the cover practice items and the format of the 50 items inside each test. That is, on the cover, each row consists of 5 items. Inside, however, the student is confronted with rows of 10 items. This could be confusing — especially to young children. However, the instructions attempt to eliminate any confusion by directing the examiner to "Move your finger across the whole top row to be sure the examinee does not stop at the crease in the middle of the [unfolded] stimulus card" (examiner's manual, p. 11). A second criticism might be the provision of age and grade equivalent scores, which have often been criticized as being easily misinterpreted. However, the examiner's manual rightly advises users to interpret them with caution, and provides several references in that regard.

SUMMARY. The Rapid Automatized Naming and Rapid Alternating Stimulus Tests (RAN/RAS Tests) are based on 30 years of research and clinical evidence. They constitute quick, easily administered, reliable measures of naming speed. And of more importance, the tests appear to be valid for their stated purposes: identifying children at risk for reading/learning problems, ongoing assessment, and the measurement of children's word-retrieval systems. The examiner's manual suggests that the tests are an "important addition to any prediction battery or diagnostic assessment of oral and written language for ages over 5 years" (p. 1). After reviewing these tests, I am inclined to agree.

REVIEWER'S REFERENCES

American Educational Research Association, American Psychological Association, & National Council on Measurement in Education. (1999). *Standards for educational and psychological testing.* Washington, DC: American Educational Research Association.

Denckla, M. B., & Rudel, R. G. (1976). Naming of objects by dyslexic and other learning-disabled children. *Brain and Language, 3,* 1–15.

Wolf, M. (1986). Rapid alternating stimulus naming in the development of dyslexias. *Brain and Language, 27,* 360–379.

Review of the Rapid Automatized Naming and Rapid Alternating Stimulus Tests by RAYNE A.

SPERLING, *Associate Professor of Educational Psychology, and NICHOLAS D. WARCHOLAK, PhD Candidate, Pennsylvania State University, University Park, PA:*

DESCRIPTION. The Rapid Automatized Naming and Rapid Alternating Stimulus Tests (RAN/RAS) are used to measure naming speed or one's ability to attend to a visual stimulus and rapidly and accurately retrieve its name. Slower naming speed has been correlated with some reading deficits (e.g., Manis, Doi, & Bhadha, 2000; Wolf, Bowers, & Biddle, 2000). The complete RAN/RAS kit contains an examiner's manual, response sheets, and six test cards. A researcher or practitioner can easily administer the RAN/RAS individually in just a few minutes. Students' time of completion is the outcome as measured by a stopwatch. The manual proposes three main uses of the RAN/RAS tests.

The primary purpose supported by the literature and practice is the first purpose, the early identification of children with reading disabilities. The second and third uses proposed in the manual are for assessment of ongoing processes and for measurement of basic naming. There is less support for these uses of the tests. The well-developed and easily followed manual provides a sound description of what the tasks are and how they have been used in the past. The RAN/RAS manual also provides norms for children with average abilities ages 5 through 18.

DEVELOPMENT. Variations on the tasks in the RAN/RAS kit have been used for more than 25 years. Information from the assessment is used to assist in screening individuals who may be at risk for a reading disability and both practitioners and researchers have employed the use of rapid naming tasks for this purpose. The use of such tasks is also very common in the research literature (e.g., Cirino, Israelian, Morris, & Morris, 2005; Schatschneider, Carlson, Francis, Foorman, & Fletcher, 2002). The tasks used here mirror those found in the literature, and the addition of the two- and three-stimuli tasks is of particular benefit to those conducting research on the double deficit hypothesis (e.g., Cirino et al., 2005; Spector, 2005; Vukovic, Wilson, & Nash, 2004). Care was taken in the development of the RAN/RAS tasks in that the objects for the naming task were selected based upon previous research. These objects were selected as stimuli based upon frequency of use, membership in family semantic categories, and ease in articulation as they are single syllable words (examiner's manual, p. 4). Other than the selection of the objects used in this task, the colors, numbers, and letters are commonly found in other rapid naming tasks and are grounded in previous research (e.g., Manis et al., 2000; McBride-Chang & Manis, 1996; Wiig, Zureich, & Chan, 2000).

TECHNICAL. The developers took great care in assuring that the norming sample represented children in schools in the United States. The 6-month norms provided in the manual are particularly helpful and relevant given the primary purpose of the assessment is to screen reading disabilities and the majority of administrations are likely with children in the 5- to 8-year age range. Regarding reliability estimates, the manual provides strong test-retest reliability estimates at 2 weeks, which is an appropriate time frame given the nature of the assessment. These reliability coefficients ranged from $r = .81$ through $r = .98$. The manual also provides interscorer reliability based upon completed assessments. To obtain this reliability a correlation was calculated between an administrator's previously recorded response sheets and a second scorer. Given the ease of scoring the assessment and the fact that recorded information is easily translated, these reliability coefficients provide very little information. A more appropriate reliability assessment would be to have two administrators assess the same learner simultaneously. Although one would suspect reasonable reliability across administrators, the lack of such a reliability analysis is a weakness in the development and reporting of the assessment and should be addressed in future work with these tests. Additional research and development with this assessment could also consider alternate forms of the tests.

Regarding validity, the content validity evidence is solid and the RAN/RAS tasks are consistent with many similar tasks found in the literature. Regarding the criterion-prediction validity, the manual provides correlations with similar tasks as found in the CTOPP ($r = .71$ and $r = .72$). The magnitude of these correlations does indicate validity support for the RAN/RAS. The manual further addresses correlations among the RAN tasks in the normative study as well as in data from independent research samples (see examiner's manual, Table 4.9, p. 37). These correlations are as would be expected and are consistent within the normative sample and across other administrations. Taken independently and together these correlations lend some support for the validity of the tasks as found in the RAN/RAS. The manual confirms an expected negative correlation between age and performance. The correlations between reading tasks and the RAN/RAS tests are, as expected, more moderate, but still lend support for the RAN/RAS tests.

COMMENTARY. Rapid naming tasks share a strong research base that has emerged from both research and practice. The double deficit hypothesis, as examined in recent research (e.g., Cirino et al., 2005; Spector, 2005; Sunseth & Greig Bowers, 2002; Vukovic et al., 2004; Wimmer, Mayringer, & Landerl, 2000; Wolf & Bowers, 2000), can also be examined through the RAN/RAS tests. The provision of 6-month norms for those learners ages 5 through 8 is especially critical given this is the age when most learners will be screened. The manual also provides norms for older learners through age 18. The least stable task in the assessment is likely the Objects task due to prior knowledge assumptions required. The Objects task and the multiple stimuli tasks are critical for those interested in stimuli that have not reached a level of automaticity that the Numbers, Letters, and Colors have for many learners. There is not much to suggest what it means to be "good" or superior on these tasks and how such performance should be interpreted. Some may misinterpret that being very superior should predict being a great reader and as such other reading problems may be discounted. Care should be taken in interpreting those that are above average and the manual should reflect this.

There are some minor concerns with the administration of the materials. For example, the materials as designed present a heavy glare and lighting should be assessed prior to administration. Although easily administered, one should practice prior to giving the exam. There is some question about what an administrator is supposed to do when the examinee skips a stimulus in the test. In our practice administrations this did occur with relative frequency. Although not stated, the manual suggests that a re-administration is warranted. There is no mention in the manual regarding the effects of repeated practice on the task and how retesting may actually hinder the validity of the score.

Another critique of the test is the descriptive ratings that are given to learners on the form. As noted, there is little evidence that being above average on this task is predictive of better achievement, aptitude, or any other outcome. Therefore, to rate someone as superior seems irrelevant. One additional concern is that those with speech disfluencies, that is, those with production difficulties such as stuttering, may be artificially flagged for reading disabilities and those administering the assessment may not be aware of other speech or language concerns. As with any measure, the data from this assessment should be used as only one piece in the diagnosis of and instructional proscription for children.

SUMMARY. The RAN/RAS is a well-designed, easy-to-administer assessment. Generally, practitioners and researchers have used self-generated rapid naming tasks or those found in assessment batteries to measure rapid naming ability. Therefore, some of the main benefits of the RAN/RAS over existing measures are that it is self-contained, rather economical, and easy to administer and score versus the alternatives. The manual is easy to follow and succinctly presents pertinent information to those who may want to administer the assessments. Practitioners and researchers can administer the tests with little practice or formal training. The psychometric properties of the instrument as packaged here are sound. One additional overall benefit of the rapid naming tasks such as those presented here are that they are quickly administered and therefore can provide relevant information in a short time frame. As such, these tests are ideal for practitioners concerned about effective use of instructional time. Overall, the RAN/RAS tests can contribute to both practice and current research.

REVIEWERS' REFERENCES

Cirino, P. T., Israelian, M. K., Morris, M. K., & Morris, R. D. (2005). Evaluation of the double-deficit hypothesis in college students referred for learning difficulties. *Journal of Learning Disabilities, 38,* 29–43.

Manis, F. R., Doi, L. M., & Bhadha, B. (2000). Naming speed, phonological awareness, and orthographic knowledge in second graders. *Journal of Learning Disabilities, 33,* 325–333,374.

McBride-Chang, C., & Manis, F. R. (1996). Structural invariance in the associations of naming speed, phonological awareness, and verbal reasoning in good and poor readers: A test of the double deficit hypothesis. *Reading and Writing, 8,* 323–339.

Schatschneider, C., Carlson, C. D., Francis, D. J., Foorman, B. R., & Fletcher, J. M. (2002). The relationship of rapid automatized naming and phonological awareness in early reading development: Implications for the double-deficit hypothesis. *Journal of Learning Disabilities, 35,* 245–256.

Spector, J. (2005). Instability of double-deficit subtypes among at-risk first grade readers. *Reading Psychology, 26,* 285–312.

Sunseth, K., & Greig Bowers, P. (2002). Rapid naming and phonemic awareness: Contributions to reading, spelling, and orthographic knowledge. *Scientific Studies of Reading, 6,* 401–429.

Vukovic, R. K., Wilson, A. M., & Nash, K. K. (2004). Naming speed deficits in adults with reading disabilities: A test of the double-deficit hypothesis. *Journal of Learning Disabilities, 37,* 440–450.

Wiig, E. H., Zureich, P., & Chan, H. H. (2000). A clinical rationale for assessing rapid automatized naming in children with language disorders. *Journal of Learning Disabilities, 33,* 359–374.

Wimmer, H., Mayringer, H., & Landerl, K. (2000). The double-deficit hypothesis and difficulties in learning to read a regular orthography. *Journal of Educational Psychology, 92,* 668–680.

Wolf, M., & Bowers, P. G. (2000). Naming-speed processes and developmental reading disabilities: An introduction to the special issue on the double-deficit hypothesis. *Journal of Learning Disabilities, 33,* 322–324.

Wolf, M., Bowers, P. G., & Biddle, K. (2000). Naming-speed processes, timing, and reading: A conceptual review. *Journal of Learning Disabilities, 33,* 387–407.

[162]
Reading Fluency Indicator.

Purpose: A brief, individually administered test of oral reading fluency that measures rate, accuracy, comprehension, and prosody.
Population: Grades 1–12.
Publication Date: 2004.
Acronym: RFI.
Scores: Total Reading Time, Total Miscues, Total Comprehension Passage Level, Words Read per Minute, Miscue Descriptive Analysis (Addition, Omission, Provided Word, Repetition, Reversal, Substitution), Prosody Rating System, Comprehension Descriptive Analysis (Literal Comprehension Questions, Inferential Comprehension Questions).
Administration: Individual
Levels, 10: P, K, 1–6, M, H.
Price Data, 2006: $154.99 per starter set including manual (42 pages), passage book, and 30 progress record forms; $82.99 per passage book; $30.99 per 20 progress record forms; $82.99 per manual.
Time: (5–10) minutes.
Comments: May be used as supplement to the Group Reading Assessment and Diagnostic Evaluation (15:113); "criterion-referenced."
Author: Kathleen T. Williams.
Publisher: Pearson.

Review of the Reading Fluency Indicator by ALICE CORKILL, Associate Professor, Department of Educational Psychology, University Nevada–Las Vegas, Las Vegas, NV:

The Reading Fluency Indicator (RFI) is described as an oral reading fluency assessment. Reading Fluency is defined in accordance with current conceptualizations and is measured via reading speed, miscues (error rates), comprehension, and prosody (expression). The test is an individually administered instrument that should assist teachers and other educational specialists to screen for fluency levels and monitor fluency development. It is, therefore, designed to be admin-istered to the same examinee on multiple occasions so that fluency progress may be tracked.

The test consists of four reading passages for each level that may be tested. The 10 levels include: Prekindergarten; Kindergarten; Grades 1 through 6 (6 levels); Grades 7 and 8 (1 level referred to as Level M); and Grades 9 through 12 (1 level referred to as Level H). The result is a set of 40 passages. Each passage is followed by four comprehension questions. Two types of questions follow each passage: literal and inferential. At the Prekindergarten, Kindergarten, and Grade 1 levels the comprehension questions include three literal questions and one inferential question. At Grade Levels 2, 3, and 4 the comprehension questions include two of each type. At Grade Levels 5, 6, Level M, and Level H the examinee is asked one literal question and three inferential questions. Although the two types of questions have been incorporated on the exam, which type of question an examinee answers correctly plays only a minor role in the scoring system because a total comprehension score is what is recorded. The test manual instructs that examinees who score 3 or 4 correct are performing at a level equal to 75% of fluent readers on the same passage. Examinees who correctly answer 1 or 2 of the comprehension items correctly are considered to be performing similarly to 25% of fluent readers on the same passage. The test manual does not describe how these values were acquired.

The exam is administered in two portions. First the passage level for the examinee must be determined. This assessment is performed using a word list test that is included in the RFI. The examiner must determine which word list to use with the examinee using one of two methods. If the examinee has recently taken the Group Reading Assessment and Diagnostic Evaluation (GRADE), his or her score may be used to determine which word list is most appropriate. To assist with this transformation, a needlessly confusing table with an almost incomprehensible example is provided in the test manual. The second option is to begin with the first and simplest word list and work forward. Each of 10 word lists consists of 10 words that correspond to the 10 reading passage levels described above. The examinee is instructed to read each word aloud while the examiner records correct and incorrect responses. The appropriate passage level for an examinee is determined by identifying the word list beyond which an examinee would make two or more mistakes in reading. For example, if the examinee misreads or does not know 2 of the 10 words in the Level 4 word list, the examinee would read a passage designated Level 3.

After the appropriate passage level has been determined, the examinee reads one passage out loud and then reads the comprehension questions out loud and selects a response that is recorded by the examiner. The passage is not available to the examinee when she or he is reading or answering the comprehension questions.

While the examinee is reading the passage, the examiner is required to determine the examinee's reading speed. This calculation is accomplished by establishing how many words the examinee can read in 60 seconds. Examinees are instructed to read the passage out loud at a comfortable speed. They are specifically instructed to not try to read as fast as they can. If the examinee reads the passage in less than 60 seconds, the examiner records how long it took the examinee to read the passage. If the examinee requires more than 60 seconds to read the passage, the examiner is required to indicate where the examinee was in the passage at the 60-second interval. An unnecessarily complicated formula is provided for calculation of reading speed (Word Count Per Minute). Indeed the example provided in the test manual calculates WCPM for an examinee who took 110 seconds to read a passage although the worksheet provided to examiners to assist in the calculation in Appendix C indicates that the formula is to be used for examinees who read the passage in less than 60 seconds. In either case, the formula works but it is somewhat confusing. The WCPM may be converted to a stanine for comparison with examinees from the norm sample through use of a table provided in the test manual.

The reading passages may or may not be accompanied by an illustration. The illustrations were designed so that they would not provide extraneous cues to the passage content. The font size of the passages is larger for the lower level passages, shifts to a smaller font for Level 2, and makes a final shift to a smaller font for Level 4. The passages are relatively interesting and the questions that follow each passage are directly related to the passage and fairly easy to answer. The reading passages for Level P (Prekindergarten)

average 29 words in length. Reading passages become progressively longer as the level increases finishing with an average of 177 words per passage for Level H (Grades 9 through 12). Although there are four passages for each level, no data or analyses related to passage level equivalence are provided. In addition, no readability information is available.

The examiner may elect to collect optional reading fluency information—miscues and prosody—during testing. Miscues may be recorded as a global score—a simple tally of the total number of errors—or based on the type of error made by the examinee. Six types of miscues are identified and examples are given: (a) addition—the examinee inserts a word in a passage sentence; (b) omission—the examinee omits a word or part of a word; (c) provided word—the examiner is instructed to provide words to the examinee if she or he cannot read the word within 3 seconds; (d) repetition—the examinee repeats a word or phrase; (e) reversal—the examinee transposes two words while reading; and (f) substitution—the examinee substitutes one word for another. A simple marking scheme is suggested to help examiners denote the miscue. The total number of miscues may be transformed into a quartile score through use of a table provided in the test manual.

A prosody (expressiveness) rating is achieved by comparing examinee performance to four descriptions available in the test manual. The examinee's reading rate, phrasing, pitch, word stress, and duration are incorporated into the prosody rating. The examiner assigns a rating on a 4-point scale. Descriptions of what each rating indicates are available in the test manual.

Each test booklet comes with a student summary form. The summary form provides space for entering test data for four separate testing occasions. The summary form includes tables for recording a student's test results as well as test date, birth date, and age. The test manual describes a needlessly complicated method for determining the student's exact age (years, months, days). Nowhere in the test manual is a rationale provided for this calculation. Furthermore, due to the way in which the stanines and quartile scores were acquired, an examinee's age is irrelevant in calculating these standard scores or in interpreting test results.

No reliability or validity information is provided. The test was normed on a sample of 386 students from the states of Iowa, Massachusetts, New Mexico, New York, and Texas that the test manual suggests represent four geographic regions of the United States: northeast, north central, south, and west. Regional numbers are not included in the test manual. Only students who had achieved a stanine score of 6 or higher on the GRADE were included in the norm sample to ensure that all readers who participated in the norm sample would be fluent readers so that comparison of examinees to the norm sample would be a comparison to individuals considered fluent. The norm sample includes roughly 43 students per grade level with the exception of Grades 2 ($n = 77$) and 6 ($n = 28$). Roughly equal numbers of male and female students participated. Ages 7 and 8 are likely overrepresented in the sample ($n = 61$; $n = 60$, respectively) with ages 16 and 18 being underrepresented ($n = 11$; $n = 6$, respectively; average number of participants per age = 30).

Students in the norm sample were assigned a passage level through use of the word list test. The test manual reports that students read all four passages at the assigned level and answered all of the questions. According to the information provided in the test manual, however, each set of passages was read by no fewer than 54 students with Passages 37 through 40 (Level H, Grades 9 through 12) having been read by 131 individuals. However, a total of only 60 students from Grades 9 through 12 are reported as being included in the norm group. Considering age groups instead results in a total of 55 students age 15 through 18. In neither approach—age group nor grade level— is a total of 131 examinees who would have read the Level H passages achieved. Even if all Grade 7 and 8 students read the Level H passages, it would yield a total of 110. Therefore, it is unclear how this sample of 386 students falling into the grade and age groups reported in the test manual resulted in more than 700 readings of the RFI passages. Nevertheless, the test manual reports that the stanines created for total reading time were developed based on this sample as were the quartile scores for miscues.

The Reading Fluency Indicator has the potential to provide teachers and other educational specialists with a quick, easy, and systematic process for monitoring student progress with respect to reading rate, types of errors made, and comprehension. Until or unless reliability and validity evidence is acquired, however, it cannot be recommended for use. In addition, issues related to how the instrument was normed and the equivalence of passages must be addressed.

Review of the Reading Fluency Indicator by GEORGE ENGELHARD, JR., Professor of Educational Measurement and Policy, Emory University, Atlanta, GA:

DESCRIPTION. The Reading Fluency Indicator (RFI) is a brief, individually administered test developed to measure oral reading fluency in the areas of rate, accuracy, comprehension, and prosody (proper expression) for students in Grades 1 to 12 (ages 5–18). The RFI includes 160 items classified into 10 RFI reading levels (P, K, 1–6, M, H). Each of the 10 RFI levels consists of four passages of similar difficulty level, and four comprehension questions per passage. Scores are available for the following: Oral Reading Time, Total Miscues, Words Correctly Read per Minute (WCPM score), Total Comprehension Score, and Prosody Rating. Stanine scores are available for Total Reading Time by passage, and quartile scores are available for Total Miscues by passage. The author estimates that administering the RFI takes about 5–10 minutes. Directions are provided for the examiner with clear and easy-to-understand scoring guidelines The author provides helpful advice on how to obtain scores for each student. The RFI can be used by itself, or as a supplement to the Group Reading Assessment and Diagnostic Evaluation (GRADE) Test (Williams, 2001). Users are provided with a manual that describes how to administer and score the RFI, and the manual also discusses potential uses of the RFI.

According to the author, "the RFI is a criterion-referenced assessment tool designed for screening and monitoring students' reading rates, accuracy, and comprehension while reading orally to a trained examiner" (manual, p. 19). Specifically, the author recommends using the RFI for placement into instructional groups for reading instruction, for development of oral reading fluency goals by special education teachers creating Individual Education Plans, for identification of oral reading errors in order to provide teachers with help planning interventions to remediate oral reading difficulties, and also for screening and monitoring growth in oral reading fluency. Essentially, "the RFI is designed to be a fluency screening and monitoring tool" (manual, p. 3).

DEVELOPMENT. The development of the RFI was guided by current conceptualizations of oral reading fluency. These views of oral reading fluency include the idea that fluency is defined as the ability to read orally with speed, accuracy, and proper expression (National Reading Panel, 2000), as well as the idea that fluency includes comprehension (Thurlow & van den Broek, 1977). The content of the RFI is aligned with this view of oral reading fluency, and the RFI provides information on reading speed, accuracy (miscue analysis of number and types of errors), comprehension, and expression (prosody rating). The test blueprint called for the use of graded passages specifically written for the RFI rather than authentic passages from the published literature. The 40 passages are graded in order to correspond to the 10 levels of the GRADE test (Williams, 2001). Each passage is followed by four comprehension questions in multiple-choice format (four answer choices). A panel of four senior consultants reviewed the passages and items. Scant details are provided regarding the activities of these senior consultants.

TECHNICAL. Minimal normative information is provided for the RFI. This is somewhat surprising because norm-referenced scores (stanines for oral reading time and quartiles for miscues) are featured in the RFI. The sample for developing norms is based on two separate phases. First, the GRADE test (Williams, 2001) was administered to 993 students in Grades 1–12 during the fall of 2003. Second, students with Comprehension Composite Scores on the GRADE test of 6 and above were given the RFI (N = 386). According to the author, students with scores of 6 and above are defined as "fluent readers" (manual, p. 30), and therefore the norm-referenced scores used in the RFI indicate the location of students in this group of 386 fluent readers. This is a very small and specialized norm group, and users should be very cautious about interpreting the stanine and quartile scores.

Empirical evidence regarding passage difficulty and RFI levels is not provided. The author recommends using a graded word list to determine where the examiner should start administering the RFI; however, no information is provided regarding the source of this word list or evidence regarding whether or not this list provides useful starting points for testing students.

No information is provided regarding score reliability, and the potential sources of error variance in the RFI scores related to content sampling and scorer differences. Minimally, the author should provide evidence regarding within scorer agreement (same scorer rating the same students on two separate occasions) and between scorer agreement (two scorers rating the same students on one occasion). Overall, the reliability and generalizability of the RFI scores are unknown. Given the amount of testing time (5–10 minutes), the small number of items administered to each student, and the high inference nature of some of the scores (e.g., the prosody rating), the RFI scores are likely to have very low reliability estimates.

Because there are no reliability estimates reported in the manual, it is not possible to calculate the standard errors of measurement for the scores. This omission is very problematic because one of the major recommended uses of the RFI is to measure changes in oral reading fluency over time. It is not possible to separate random fluctuations in student scores from meaningful changes in student scores without some sense of the stability of the RFI scores over time.

Evidence regarding the validity of the RFI scores is also not provided. Insufficient information makes it difficult for potential users to determine whether or not the RFI will be useful in making decisions and recommendations about their students. Minimally, the author should provide content-related evidence by providing more information regarding the table of specifications used to guide the development of the RFI. This elaboration should include more information regarding the activities and results from the four senior consultants who evaluated the content of the RFI. No information regarding bias or sensitivity reviews is reported in the manual. Future research with the RFI should examine differential item functioning (DIF) for the items and passages across relevant subgroups, such as African American students, English Language Learners, and students with various learning disabilities. These DIF studies are very important because many students with reading difficulties may be included within these subgroups.

COMMENTARY. There is essentially no technical information provided regarding the psychometric characteristics of the RFI. Without evidence regarding the reliability and the validity of the RFI scores for its recommended uses, the psychometric quality of the RFI is unknown. Combining the RFI with results from other assessments, such as the GRADE test (Williams, 2001) that was developed by the same author, may provide useful results for teachers. No supporting evidence is provided for the use of the RFI as a stand-alone measure of oral reading fluency, or as a supplement to other reading assessments. The use of the RFI as a stand-alone screen cannot be recommended until additional information is provided regarding the psychometric quality of this assessment.

Although the author can defend the use of a specialized norm group defined as fluent readers on the GRADE Test (Williams, 2001), this assembly is not the typical group of students that would be given the RFI. The target group that is most likely to respond to the RFI will be weak and nonfluent readers. A normative sample based on the full range of oral reading fluency would be preferable and should be added in the future. This normative sample should represent the full range of achievement in oral reading fluency, and this sample should also be used to provide standard item analyses for the 160 items on the RFI. The lack of empirical information (e.g., p-values and item discriminations) is a significant flaw that makes it virtually impossible to judge the psychometric adequacy of the RFI scores for accomplishing its intended purposes.

The author claims that the RFI is a criterion-referenced assessment; however, it is not clear how the author is using this term. Criterion-referenced scores obtain their meaning based on a comparison between student performance and a judged cut score or performance standard. In evaluating criterion-referenced performance standards, it is essential to describe the judges or panelists who set the performance standard (Stone, 2006). The manual recommends using scores of 3 or 4 correct on each passage with the inference that scoring at this level is "equivalent to that of at least 75% of the fluent readers on the same passage" (manual, p. 22). This definition appears to be norm-referenced, and the inference questionable given the small number of students in the specialized norm-group described in the manual.

Scoring is based on judgments of a 5–10 minute oral performance by a student. This assessment is a high inference activity for examiners. For example, it is possible that sources of error due to regional and cultural variations in student accents and language usage may negatively influence the scores. The administration of the RFI to fluent readers, as was done for the specialized norms, may mask many of the potential problems when administering the RFI to nonfluent readers. Information regarding psychometric quality and the utility of the RFI scores might be very different if data were obtained from nonfluent readers rather than fluent readers.

Even a brief look at the history of reading assessment (Engelhard, 2001) indicates that both reading theory and measurement theory have played roles in the creation of reading tests. The RFI appears to be theoretically grounded, but the lack of psychometric and measurement data is a significant omission regarding the development and refinement of the RFI.

SUMMARY. In summary, the RFI manual does not currently provide sufficient information to evaluate the psychometric quality of the test. Future versions of the RFI should provide evidence regarding psychometric quality as indicated by the *Standards for Educational and Psychological Testing* (AERA, APA, & NCME, 1999). Users should be extremely cautious in selecting the RFI because the manual provides no evidence regarding the reliability and validity of the RFI scores to inform decisions regarding student placement into reading groups for reading instruction, the development of oral reading fluency goals for Individual Education Plans, the identification of oral reading errors, and the screening and monitoring of student growth in oral reading fluency.

REVIEWER'S REFERENCES

American Educational Research Association, American Psychological Association, & National Council on Measurement in Education. (1999). *Standards for educational and psychological testing*. Washington, DC: American Educational Research Association.

Engelhard, G. (2001). Historical view of the influences of measurement and reading theories on the assessment of reading. *Journal of Applied Measurement, 2*, 1-26.

National Reading Panel. (2000). *Teaching children to read: An evidence-based assessment of the scientific research literature on reading and its implications for reading instruction* (National Institute of Health Pub. No. 00-4769). Washington, DC: National Institute of Child Health and Human Development.

Stone, G. E. (2006). Whose criterion standard is it anyway? *Journal of Applied Measurement, 7*(2), 160-169.

Thurlow, R., & van den Broek, P. (1977). Automaticity and inference generation. *Reading and Writing Quarterly, 13*, 165-184.

Williams, K. T. (2001). Group Reading Assessment and Diagnostic Evaluation. Circle Pines, MN: American Guidance Service, Inc.

[163]
Reading Progress Tests.

Purpose: Designed to "provide a continuous measure of individual and group progress in reading comprehension."

Population: Ages 5-0 to 12-2.

Publication Dates: 1996–1997.

Acronym: RPT.

Scores: Total score only.

Administration: Group.

Price Data, 2002: £12.99 per Stage One manual (1996, 48 pages); £13.50 per Stage Two manual (1997, 47 pages); £14.99 per Stage One specimen set; £16.99 per Stage Two specimen set.

Time: (20) minutes per test.

Authors: Denis Vincent, Mary Crumpler, and Mike de la Mare.

Publisher: Hodder & Stoughton Educational [England].

   a) STAGE ONE.

   1) *Literacy Baseline.*

   Purpose: "To provide a 'baseline' from which to measure subsequent progress."

   Population: Children in first term of their first year of compulsory schooling (ages 5-0 to 6-4).

   Price Data: £6.99 per 10 copies.

   2) *RPT Test 1.*

   Purpose: Constructed to "assess developing reading skills."

   Population: Year 1 (ages 5-8 to 7-2).

   Price Data: £6.99 per 10 copies.

   Time: (45–50) minutes.

   3) *RPT Test 2.*

   Population: Year 2 (ages 6-8 to 8-1).

   Price Data: £6.99 per 10 copies.

   b) STAGE TWO.

   1) *RPT Test 3.*

   Population: Year 3 (ages 7-8 to 9-2).

   Price Data: £6.99 per 10 copies; £11.50 per 10 Test 3 broadsheets.

   2) *RPT Test 4.*

   Population: Year 4 (ages 8-8 to 10-2).

   Price Data: £6.99 per 10 copies; £11.50 per 10 Test 4 broadsheets.

   3) *RPT Test 5.*

   Population: Year 5 (ages 9-8 to 11-2).

   Price Data: £6.99 per 10 copies; £11.50 per 10 Test 5 broadsheets.

   4) *RPT Test 6.*

   Population: Year 6 (ages 10-8 to 12-2).

   Price Data: £6.99 per 10 copies; £11.50 per 10 Test 6 broadsheets.

Review of the Reading Progress Tests by SHARON deFUR, Associate Professor of Curriculum and Instruction/Special Education, The College of William and Mary, Williamsburg, VA:

DESCRIPTION. The Reading Progress Tests (RPT), normed on school-aged children in England and Wales, include seven sequential but parallel developmental reading comprehension tests. The Stage One manual provides administration, scoring, and interpretation guidelines for the Literacy Baseline Test and RPT 1 and 2; the Stage Two manual provides the same for the RPT 3 through 6. The Literacy Baseline Test designed for children in their first year of school (ages 5 years, 0 months to 6 years, 4 months) establishes a literacy baseline for each student as well as for each teacher's class. The RPT 1 through RPT 6 provide subsequent annual reading comprehension progress testing up to Grade 6 (RPT age range 5 years, 8 months to 12 years, 2 months).

All seven tests use objective test booklet paper-and-pencil responses and can be group or individually administered and scored by a classroom teacher. The teacher manages the time allotted, but there is no penalty for extended time. According to the test authors, the Literacy Baseline Test can typically be completed in about 20 minutes whereas the Reading Progress Tests may take 45–50 minutes. No specialized credentials are required to use these tests.

The Literacy Baseline Test includes 40 response opportunities; the skills tested include phonological awareness, rhyming, literacy concepts, letter names, letter sounds, picture/word matching, and simple spelling. The number of items on the RPT ranges from 32 response options on the RPT 1 to 54 on the RPT 6; the increasing difficulty for all years is congruent with the range of age-appropriate expectations. All tests of the RPT assess vocabulary understanding, sequencing, inference, factual judgment, text reasoning, cloze comprehension measures, text comparison (not on RPT 1), and word meanings (not on RPT 2).

The manual is reasonably teacher friendly, but scoring and interpretation would be best done by an educator at least minimally schooled in basic research methods. Using the raw scores and tables provided in the manuals and with careful review, conscientious teachers could calculate a standardized score yielding a percentile equivalent, a reading-age equivalent, and a reading-ability level.

Confidence levels are stated for each test to promote confidence in the interpretation of the standardized scores and to caution test users regarding overinterpretation of the findings. Furthermore, the manuals provide a process for determining progress between test administrations. Progress scores yield progress quotients scaled with a mean of 100 or scores that can be interpreted in terms of percentiles. The Stage One manual offers two case studies to illustrate teacher use of the test results. The authors suggest that the RPT can confirm average progress, act as a screening tool for individuals who score very low or very high, and can measure progress of those whose reading comprehension is significantly below expectations. However, according to the authors, neither the Literacy Baseline Test nor the RPT are intended to be diagnostic for individual reading skills, but only an overall measure of reading comprehension.

DEVELOPMENT. Development of the RPT began in 1994 and the materials were then copyrighted in 1996 after field-testing with subgroups of children from England and Wales using teacher test administrators. Rather than traditional progress-monitoring tests that use the same probes in repeated tests, these tests were developed to assess progress in reading comprehension using probes that were similar in format and concept assessment from one test to another while attempting to meet the interest and developmental levels of most children at each grade level.

The results from field-testing from more than 1,000 student respondents enabled the authors to construct standardized scores and reading-age equivalents for the Literacy Baseline Test. First-year progress tests (1 year later) identified the questions that were most predictive of reading comprehension progress as well as selected the most appropriate items to measure the reading comprehension constructs. According to the authors, the tests represent repeated measures of the same skills.

TECHNICAL. Future users of these tests should assume that the items are culturally representative of England and Wales in the mid-1990s. No demographic data are provided other than that the norm group was representative of school-aged children in England and Wales.

Because these tests were designed to measure similar reading comprehension constructs consistently, the authors estimated the internal consistency of the measures. Using KR-20, they documented a high degree of internal consistency between the RPT tests (reliability measures ranged from .90 to .95). These values indicate that the items are measuring the domain effectively.

The authors claim the predictive validity of the tests is proven by the correlation between the Literacy Test Baseline and succeeding RPT 1 and RPT 2. Unfortunately, although they cite correlation coefficient(s) that imply respectful correlations (ranging from .61 to .80 from the Literacy Baseline to the RPT or between the RPT level tests), such values would appear to be indicative of alternative-forms reliability rather than predictive validity, although they provide some indication of construct validation, too.

Regarding content validity, scholars of reading literacy would undoubtedly agree that the test items across the RPT match the skill expectations found in most evidence-based reading practices. To the authors' credit, they devised comparable content across the RPT. This content includes: (a) vocabulary/matching; (b) auditory sequencing to who, what, why; (c) inference/reflection; (d) true-false-doesn't say; (e) reasoning questions; (f) cloze test of reading comprehension; (g) read across/ compare multiple texts; and (h) higher level vocabulary questions. Additionally, the authors report correlations of the RPT with national measures of reading in England and Wales. The correlations (ranging from .50–.60) suggest that performance on the RPT could generally predict student outcomes on potentially high stakes assessments for England and Wales.

Of importance to international readers of this review is the fact that although the spoken language of England and Wales may parallel North American English, the vocabulary used in the RPT reflects the language and culture of England, Wales, and perhaps other Commonwealth Nation countries. Respondents (a) for whom English is not their native language, (b) who have not been raised in the normed or Commonwealth settings, or (c) whose culture has not included English/ Welsh vocabulary may inappropriately receive lower scores due to some surprising cultural linguistic distinctions. For example, students are asked to match the following to pictures: (a) tin [in the U.S.A., this would be can]; (b) sweet [in the U.S.A., this would be candy]; and (c) tart [in the U.S.A., this might be pie]. Also, Mum is used for "mom";

Gram for "Grandmother"; and "pudding" to mean sausage-like preparations made with minced meat or various other ingredients stuffed into a bag or skin and boiled, rather than a sweet dessert. The Stage Two tests, although entertaining, require a developed sense of humor and parody as well as imagination to respond to the higher level questioning. All of the content used was consistent with the stated purpose, yet it is important for users of these instruments to remember that the test items are not culture free.

COMMENTARY. The Literacy Baseline Test and RPT minimally offer teachers in England and Wales, and perhaps other Commonwealth countries, a relatively simple reading comprehension progress-monitoring strategy whereby individual and class comprehension progress can be evaluated from school entry until exit from primary school. Only nominal written responses are required for age-appropriate progress to be determined. The authors neither examine nor promote item-level-analysis diagnostic interpretation of student responses, although the potential to do so could be present given the large number of students participating in the primary studies for these instruments.

The option for group administration offers both an individual progress-monitoring choice as well as a group score while providing teachers and administrators with valuable clues from which to plan individual and classroom-based strategies. The developmental theme-based format offers an intriguing alternative test condition for teachers and students that differs from typical repeated curriculum-based measures. Additionally, given the current age of accountability where progress monitoring is receiving increased attention internationally, the Literacy Baseline and RPT present schools and teachers a framework from which to assess and plan reading comprehension interventions and programs. Although these tests reflect English and Welsh vocabulary usage and cultural understandings, their model for progress monitoring can inform future test developers whose interest is annual progress monitoring. This approach is of particular interest and importance during the evolving international education emphasis on children's response to varying interventions (RPT) and to monitoring academic progress.

Nonetheless, at the time of this review, these tests are now 10 years old, and although reading literacy concepts have changed little in this time period, the critical theme approach of these tests that capture the age-appropriate interests of children may need revision to remain current with up-to-date interests of children and youth as well as require updated norms that reflect current demographics and reading literacy skills of elementary-aged children.

SUMMARY. These tests offer teachers and administrators a reliable and valid set of objective, primarily group-administered tests from which to assess baseline entry skills of reading comprehension for early attendees (age 5-0). Furthermore, these assessments provide an ongoing progress evaluation for individual students with each subsequent year. Although the test manuals do not promote item-level analysis, the tests do reflect a microcosm of reading comprehension skills that will be needed for later school success of elementary-aged students.

[164]
Ready to Learn: A Dyslexia Screener.

Purpose: Designed as a screening instrument for underlying early learning and prereading skills "so that children at risk for developing reading problems can be identified early."

Population: Ages 3-6 to 6-5.

Publication Dates: 1996–2004.

Scores: 16 subscale scores: (Rapid Naming, Bead Threading and Paper Cutting, Corsi Frog, Balance, Phonological Discrimination, Digit Span, Rhyming, Sound Order, Teddy & Form Matching, Vocabulary, Shape & Letter Copying [optional for ages 3-6 to 4-5], Repetition [optional for ages 3-6 to 4-5], Digit Naming [optional for ages 3-6 to 4-5], Letter Naming [optional for ages 3-6 to 4-5], First Letter Sound [ages 4-6 to 6-5], Postural Sound [ages 4-6 to 6-5]), Risk Index [one score for each of the above scale scores].

Administration: Individual.

Price Data, 2006: $250 per complete kit including manual (2004, 109 pages), 25 record forms, audio CD, stimulus book, set of manipulatives, and soft case; $110 per manual; $43 per 25 record forms; $12 per audio CD; $80 per stimulus book; $43 per set of manipulatives; $18 per Balance Test manipulative; $6.50 per CORSI Frog manipulative; $18 per 13 beads and a cord manipulative.

Time: (30–45) minutes.

Comments: This test can be completed in two sessions if necessary.

Authors: Angela J. Fawcett, Rod I. Nicolson, and Ray Lee.

Publisher: The Psychological Corporation, A Harcourt Assessment Company.

Review of Ready to Learn: A Dyslexia Screener
by R. ANTHONY DOGGETT, Assistant Professor
of Educational Psychology, and KRISTIN N.
JOHNSON-GROS, Assistant Professor of Educa-
tional Psychology, Mississippi State University,
Starkville, MS:

DESCRIPTION AND DEVELOPMENT. Ready to Learn: A Dyslexia Screener is a pre-school instrument designed to screen the underlying early learning and prereading skills of children ranging in age from 3 years, 6 months to 6 years, 5 months of age. The instrument is the U.S. adaptation of The Pre-School Screening Test (PREST; Fawcett, Nicolson, & Lee, 2001), The Dyslexia Early Screening Test (DEST; Nicolson & Fawcett, 1996), and The Dyslexia Early Screening Test—Second Edition (DEST-2; Nicolson & Fawcett, 2004), all of which were standardized in the United Kingdom. According to the authors, the primary goal in developing the subtests that are included on Ready to Learn: A Dyslexia Screener was to "construct a quick, enjoyable, and easy to administer test that would provide professionals with risk indices for school failure and, for children age 4:6 [4 years, 6 months] and older, risk indices for reading failure associated with dyslexia and other learning difficulties" (manual, p. 1). Other goals identified by the authors included providing the examiner with a profile of strengths and weaknesses based on the child's performance to use for instructional support planning within the school setting, establishing a measure of baseline performance prior to the receipt of intervention services, and serving as a basis for the request of formal assessment of the student for diagnostic purposes.

Ready to Learn: A Dyslexia Screener contains 16 brief subtests. Some of the subtests are designed to measure prerequisite subskills and knowledge for reading and writing readiness, and others are designed to assess neurocognitive constructs including working memory and automaticity. The Rapid Naming subtest assesses rapid auditory processing. The Phonological Discrimination, First Letter Sounds, Rhyming, and Sound Order subtests measure phonemic awareness and phonological skills. The Bead Threading and Shape & Letter Copying subtests assess fine motor skills along with the Corsi Frog subtest, which also evaluates visual working memory. The Balance and Postural Stability subtests assess balance and cerebellar functioning. The Digit Span subtest assesses a child's verbal working memory whereas the Repetition subtest evaluates the child's auditory working memory. The Teddy and Form Matching subtest evaluates the child's visual discrimination abilities. The Vocabulary subtest measures the child's receptive vocabulary. The Digit Naming subtest evaluates the child's knowledge of numbers whereas the Letter Naming subtest assesses the child's knowledge of letters both of which evaluate early numeracy and literacy skills. Ten of the subtests are designed for use with children ranging in age from 3 years, 6 months to six years, 5 months whereas four subtests (e.g., Shape & Letter Copying, Repetition, Digit Naming, and Letter Naming) are optional for ages 3 years, 6 months to 4 years, five months and two subtests (e.g., First Letter Sound and Postural Stability) are for use with children only in the 4 years, 6 months to 6 years, 5 months age range. Reading to Learn: A Dyslexia Screener takes approximately 30–45 minutes to administer depending on the age of the child, and the assessment can typically be conducted in one session. However, the authors noted that the screener may be administered in two sessions if the child appears to be restless or tired. The authors noted that no more than 2 days should pass between testing sessions. Parents or guardians may accompany the child into the testing session; however, they must remain out of view and refrain from interacting with the child during the assessment. School psychologists, qualified teachers, and other professionals who have obtained training in the administration of assessment instruments may administer Reading to Learn: A Dyslexia Screener and interpret the results.

Several scores are obtained from Reading to Learn: A Dyslexia Screener. First, raw scores are converted into age-appropriate Risk Index Scores. Each subtest score falls into one of three possible risk categories, which include Green, Yellow, and Red. Scores in the Green category indicate performance in the normal range (i.e., performance above 25% of age peers) and suggest that the child is at low risk for reading difficulty. Scores in the Yellow category indicate performance that is below average (i.e., performance between 11% and 25% of age peers) and suggest that the child is at moderate risk for reading difficulty. Scores in the Red category indicate performance that is well below average (i.e., performance that falls below 11% of age peers) and suggest that the child is at high risk for reading difficulty. The record form also provides a graph on the last page of the 8-page form that allows the examiner to plot the raw scores providing a profile of strengths and weaknesses for each student that can be reviewed when developing instructional strategies to address the child's needs. To aid in identifying instructional needs, the risk profile is grouped according to the unique content being evaluated, which includes knowledge and attainment (e.g., Vocabulary, Digit Naming, Letter Naming), Phonological awareness and Prereading skills (e.g., Rapid Naming, Phonological Discrimination, Digit Span, Rhyming, Repetition, First Letter Sound), motor skills (e.g., Bead Threading & Paper Cutting, Balance, Shape & Letter Copying, Postural Stability), and auditory and visual processing (e.g., Sound Order, Corsi Frog, Teddy & Form Matching). The manual also provides scaled growth scores with a mean of 10 and a standard deviation of 3 intended to assess growth in student performance on the subtests across time. However, the authors noted that growth in performance should not be assessed within an interval shorter than 6 months.

Reading to Learn: A Dyslexia Screener is accompanied by a 109-page, well-written manual, complete with seven chapters discussing the purpose, development, administration, scoring, interpretation, reliability, validity, and standardization of the instrument. Additionally, a chapter containing a case study is included in the manual, which aids in the interpretation of the scores and provides a list of resources for support. The authors of the manual provided thorough discussions about the theoretical and empirical basis for the inclusion of items, development of the subtests, and normative and validation procedures.

TECHNICAL.

Norming-standardization procedures. A total of 510 children ranging in age from 3 years, 6 months to 6 years, 5 months were included in the standardization sample. The sample was stratified along key demographic variables including sex, parent education level, race/ethnicity, and geographic region based on the data provided by the October 2000, school enrollment supplement of the U.S. Census current population survey. Approximately 4% of the children in the standardization sample were diagnosed with a language im-

pairment, developmental delay, or being at risk for developmental delay. Additionally, data were collected on clinical samples of 92 children considered at risk for delay or previously diagnosed with developmental or language delay.

Reliability. The manual reports internal consistency, test-retest reliability, and interscorer agreement scores. Internal consistency estimates were obtained using the split-half method corrected by the Spearman-Brown formula. Overall, reliability coefficients were moderate to strong correlations with a range from .56 to .93 and a majority of the lower scores being obtained for children in the oldest (e.g., 5 years, 6 months to 6 years, 5 months) age group. Test-retest reliability was evaluated in a study of 66 children who were administered the instrument on two occasions across an interval that ranged from 2 to 23 days with a median retest interval of 7 days. Children from all age ranges were tested, and the sample consisted of 42% female and 58% male with 51% being White, 21% African American, 17% Hispanic, 8% Asian, and 3% being of other ethnic or racial origin. Data obtained for test-retest reliability suggested that scores maintained adequate stability across administrations with small differences in scores and small effect sizes. One exception was noted for the Postural Stability subtest where the test-retest reliability score was .38. The authors noted that many of the examiners did not perform the recalibration of the balance tester properly, which greatly affected the reliability estimate for this subtest. The authors further reported that a study conducted with 26 children in the United Kingdom where the test examiners were trained to recalibrate the balance tester after each use had a stability coefficient of .83 (Nicolson & Fawcett, 2004). Interscorer agreement scores were not obtained for the Shape and Letter Copying subtest due to the subjective nature of scoring required for this subtest. Data obtained on 490 children revealed intraclass correlations that ranged from .83 to .92 across all ages.

Validity. The investigation of the internal structure of the instrument revealed that it had strong psychometric properties as subtests that were designed to measure similar constructs yielded strong correlations with each other whereas weak correlations were obtained between subtests designed to measure other dissimilar constructs. Using the normative sample, convergent and divergent validity was addressed through correlational studies with three other well known instruments including the Bracken School Readiness Assessment (BSRA; Bracken, 2002), Early Screening Inventory—Revised (ESIR; Meisels, Marsden, Wiske, & Henderson, 1997) and the Wechsler Preschool and Primary Scale of Intelligence—Third Edition (WPPSI-III; Wechsler, 2002). A review of the clinical studies revealed that children in the clinical groups performed differently from matched controls on subtests that measured motor and processing skills. For example, children diagnosed with language impairment, developmental delay, or at-risk for developmental delay all performed lower on the Balance and Repetition subtests. Finally, experts in gender studies and minority studies were consulted to ensure that items on the screener were not biased toward any group and results from the bias study with 422 children revealed no concerns with bias. Detailed information on the validity of the instrument is included in the manual for the interested reader.

COMMENTARY. Strengths of Ready to Learn: A Dyslexia Screener include (a) easy administration and scoring, (b) user-friendly manual that is well-organized and employs graphics to convey technical information and artwork to assist in administration of items, (c) summary and profile forms that aid in interpretation and explanation of results, (d) adequate standardization sample, (e) overall moderate to strong reliability and validity evidence, and (f) inclusion of resources in the manual to assist in potential remediation of identified concerns. Weaknesses include lower internal consistency scores for children in the 5 years, 6 months to 6 years, 5 months age range and a lower stability coefficient for the Postural Stability subtest.

SUMMARY. Ready to Learn: A Dyslexia Screener is designed to "provide insight into a child's strengths and weaknesses in relation to phonological awareness, working memory, motor skills, and visual and auditory processing" (manual, p. 39). The instrument contains 16 subtests that yield risk index scores, a risk profile, and growth index scores. Although efficient for use as a screener of potential academic problems, the instrument will be best utilized as a component of a thorough assessment battery for individuals suspected of experiencing delays or meeting criteria for a disorder. Most of the goals that were provided by the authors appear to be met by aiding in instructional

planning and as a screener for diagnostic questions. Although the authors suggested that the instrument can be used for a baseline measure of performance, the utility of the instrument for this purpose is somewhat limited due to the fact that at least 6 months must pass between administrations. As such, more sensitive measures would need to be utilized in between administrations to establish growth in a more formative manner. Finally, further investigation with populations and instruments other than those used by the authors will continue to provide valuable information about the psychometric properties and clinical utility of the instrument.

REVIEWERS' REFERENCES

Bracken, B. A. (2002). Bracken School Readiness Assessment. San Antonio, TX: The Psychological Corporation.
Fawcett, A. J., Nicolson, R. I., & Lee, R. (2001). The Pre-School Screening Test. London: The Psychological Corporation.
Meisels, S. J., Marsden, D. B., Wiske, M. S., & Henderson, L. W. (1997). Early Screening Inventory—Revised. Ann Arbor, MI: Rebus Inc.
Nicolson, R. I., & Fawcett, A. J. (1996). The Dyslexia Early Screening Test. London: The Psychological Corporation.
Nicolson, R. I., & Fawcett, A. J. (2004). The Dyslexia Early Screening Test—Second Edition. London: The Psychological Corporation.
Wechsler, D. (2002). Wechsler Preschool and Primary Scale of Intelligence—Third Edition. San Antonio, TX: The Psychological Corporation.

Review of Ready to Learn: A Dyslexia Screener by KATHLEEN M. JOHNSON, Psychologist, Lincoln Public Schools, Lincoln, NE:

DESCRIPTION. Ready to Learn: A Dyslexia Screener is an individually administered preschool screening test designed by the authors to provide a brief method for identifying risk indices for possible school failure (i.e., reading failure, dyslexia, and other learning difficulties). Additionally, Fawcett, Nicolson, and Lee (the test authors) report that this screening instrument provides examiners with a profile of strengths and weaknesses to guide early intervention and provides data on which to base a request for diagnostic assessment if needed. Ready to Learn is the U.S. adaptation of the authors' previous U.K. publications (The Pre-School Screening Test, 2001; The Dyslexia Early Screening Test, 1996; and The Dyslexia Early Screening Test—Second Edition, 2004) and has been standardized with a U.S. normative sample. It is intended to be used by school psychologists and other qualified professionals who are trained to administer and interpret individual educational and psychological assessments.

Ready to Learn is designed for children 3 years, 6 months to 6 years, 5 months of age. The screening instrument consists of 16 brief subtests, which can be administered in 30–45 minutes depending on the child's age. Materials that come with the test kit include: the test manual, record forms, stimulus book, balance testing device, wooden beads and a string, a CD recording used for one subtest, and a plastic frog. The examiner also needs the following items for each administration: a stopwatch, a small container to hold the beads, several blank sheets of unlined paper, a primary pencil or crayon, safety scissors, a CD player with speakers, a copy of the paper-cutting sheet from the manual, and a kitchen scale for calibrating the balance testing device.

The Ready to Learn subtests and their intended purposes are as follows: (a) Rapid Naming (RN—time needed to name a page of line drawings to assess rapid auditory processing), (b) Bead Threading and Paper Cutting (BTPC—beads threaded in one minute and cutting accuracy on two items to assess fine motor skills), (c) Corsi Frog (CF—imitate visual motor sequences to assess visual working memory and fine motor skills), (d) Balance (BAL—stand on one foot while responding to directions to assess balance and cerebellar functioning), (e) Phonological Discrimination (PD—discriminate between beginning and ending word sounds to assess phonemic awareness), (f) Digit Span (DS—repeat sequences of numbers to assess verbal working memory), (g) Rhyming (RHY—discriminate between rhyming and non-rhyming word sets to assess phonological skills), (h) Sound Order (SO—discriminate the auditory presentation of paired sounds to assess auditory discrimination), (i) Teddy and Form Matching (TFM—recognize target pictures among distracters to assess visual discrimination), (j) Vocabulary (VOC—identify a picture to match a spoken word to assess receptive vocabulary), (k) Shape and Letter Copying (SLC—copy simple shapes and letters to assess fine motor skills), (l) Repetition (REP—repeat simple sentences to assess auditory working memory), (m) Digit Naming (DN—name numerals printed on a page to assess academic knowledge), (n) Letter Naming (LN—name letters on a page to assess academic knowledge), (o) First Letter Sound (FLS—identify the beginning sound of words to assess phonemic awareness), and (p) Postural Stability (PS—maintain balance when slight pressure is applied to back to assess balance and cerebellar functioning). Subtests 11–14 are optional for children ages 3 years, 6 months to 4 years, 5 months and

Subtests 15 and 16 are intended only for children 4 years, 6 months to 6 years, 5 months old. All of the subtests are brief; the longest subtest has 16 items and most have 10 or fewer items. Ten of the 16 subtests have practice items with feedback, in addition to the verbal instructions and demonstrations. The authors categorize the subtests into four general groups for theoretical and interpretive purposes: knowledge and attainment (VOC, DN, LN), phonological and prereading skills (RN, PD, DS, RHY, REP, FLS), motor skills (BTPC, BAL, SLC, PS), and auditory and visual processing (SO, CF, TFM).

The manual contains detailed administration and scoring instructions, a sample case (with scoring, interpretation, and remediation information), and technical information. The examiner instructions are highlighted and easy to follow in both the manual and the stimulus book. The multipage record form is well organized for recording purposes and has summary pages for examining subtest scores in relation to each other both numerically and graphically. The raw score for each subtest is used to identify one of three age-appropriate risk levels for that subtest. The Red Risk Index corresponds to high risk for learning/reading difficulties and a score below the 11th percentile in the standardization sample. The Yellow Risk Index corresponds to moderate risk for learning/reading difficulties and a score that is between the 11th and 25th percentile. The Green Risk Index corresponds to low risk for learning/reading difficulties and a score that is above the 25th percentile. The risk index categories thus reflect the areas of relative strength and weakness displayed by a child. The authors recommend that overall risk of reading difficulty for a child be determined by the total number of subtests falling in the Red and Yellow risk categories (i.e., at least one-third of the subtests fall in the Red category or over one-half of subtests fall in the Red and Yellow categories combined). There is no composite score for the instrument. Using the data from the children 5 year, 0 months to 5 year, 5 months old in the sample, scaled growth scores for each subtest are also provided (Mean = 10, SD = 3). The authors state that these scores can be used to monitor a child's progress over time with repeated testing; Fawcett, Nicolson, and Lee suggest that an increase of 3 scaled score points (1 SD) or greater indicates significant skill growth.

However, the authors also state that the minimum time interval between testing sessions should be 6 months because of potential practice effects. As a result, it appears that the test could be used for pretest/posttest purposes with young students, but not for progress monitoring as typically defined in current literature (Good & Kaminski, 2002).

DEVELOPMENT. Ready to Learn is the combined result of various parts of previous screening tests published by the authors in the U.K. (The Pre-School Screening Test, The Dyslexia Early Screening Test, and The Dyslexia Early Screening Test—Second Edition) along with other subtests added or revised based upon feedback from examiners and teachers in the U.K. during the last decade. In the test manual, Fawcett, Nicolson, and Lee provide a description of each subtest along with what a strength or weakness on the subtest may indicate about learning. Some information about the origin of each task and previous research on the subtests is also provided. The standardization sample included 510 children selected to be a close approximation to the U.S. Census data from October 2000. The sample was stratified for relevant variables and included 4% of children diagnosed as having developmental delay, being at risk for delay, or having a language impairment. A description of the norm development process is provided in the manual as well.

TECHNICAL. Reliability and validity evidence is summarized by the authors in the test manual. Internal consistency reliability coefficients were calculated for all but two subtests using the split-half method on the normative sample data. The brevity of the Bead Threading and Paper Cutting subtest (only three items) and speeded aspect of Rapid Naming prevented the use of a measure of split-half internal consistency. The average coefficient values for the subtests range from .68 (Vocabulary) to .91 (Letter Naming) with a median coefficient value of .80. The authors describe the test as having strong internal consistency although the coefficient values for 8 of the 16 subtests are below .80. It is noted in the manual that some issues, such as item difficulty (e.g., Shape and Letter Copying for ages 3 years, 6 months—3 years, 11 months) and the restricted range of scores (e.g., mastery of the Balance items for ages 5 years, 6 months—6 years, 5 months) negatively impacted the coefficient values. Test-retest reliability was established by calculating sta-

bility coefficients for 66 children who were tested twice with a median retest interval of 7 days. The stability coefficient for Postural Stability was significantly lower (.38) than all the other values, and the authors reported it was likely due to the inconsistent recalibration of the balance testing device by the examiners prior to each testing session. The stability coefficients of the other 15 subtests ranged from .71 (Teddy & Form Matching) to .97 (Letter Naming) with a median coefficient of .86.

Validity evidence for Ready to Learn is documented by the authors on the basis of its internal structure (subtest intercorrelations), as well as correlations with other readiness, screening, and cognitive assessments. The subtest intercorrelations provide evidence of convergent validity among several academic readiness and other prereading skills (e.g., rhyming, phonological discrimination, sound order, repetition, and letter and number naming). Most of the subtests assessing motor skills have lower intercorrelations with the other subtests. Strong correlations between Ready to Learn subtest scores and other measures of academic readiness and concept knowledge were found in concurrent validity studies. Correlations were moderate to low between Ready to Learn subtests and IQ scores. Validity studies in clinical settings indicated that larger numbers of children with language impairments (than matched controls) performed in the Red risk category on subtests related to auditory and phonological processing skills. Children with developmental delays performed more poorly overall than matched controls, as would be predicted. The authors point out the possibility that lower scores on the Balance and Repetition subtests, earned by children with various learning difficulties, indicates processing problems (e.g., cerebellar impairment, working memory problems, weak/slow auditory processing) underlying dyslexia and other academic delays. Item-bias studies were used to identify and review problematic items.

COMMENTARY. Ready to Learn is a revised and updated screening instrument and a U.S. adaptation of the authors' previous U.K. measures (The Pre-School Screening Test, The Dyslexia Early Screening Test, and The Dyslexia Early Screening Test—Second Edition). The directions for administration and scoring procedures are effectively detailed in the materials. Most of the subtests appear to be fairly easy to administer and score, with the exception of the Postural Stability subtest because it requires special calibration of the balance testing device. The calibration is difficult to complete despite the detailed directions provided in the manual. Improvements in this edition of the instrument include technical data that support the reliability and validity of the instrument. The authors acknowledge that Ready to Learn should be used for screening rather than diagnostic purposes. Some of the Ready to Learn subtests (e.g., Phonological Discrimination, Letter Naming, Rapid Naming) more than others are closely aligned with the essential literacy skills as identified in current research and associated evidence-based assessment methods (National Reading Panel, 2000). The other subtests (e.g., Postural Stability, Digit Span, Balance) appear to be more theoretical in nature, processing-based, and somewhat more distant from the display of specific pre-academic skills. Teachers working with young students assess several of these areas within the literacy curriculum and may not need this type of screening instrument to help identify those students at risk for more general learning difficulties. The Ready to Learn results should be combined with effective curriculum-based assessment if the overall goal is to prevent academic failure due to possible learning difficulties. Despite the authors' suggestion that this instrument can be used to monitor a child's progress over time, additional assessment methods would likely be needed for planning specific instructional interventions and monitoring learning progress (Good & Kaminski, 2002).

SUMMARY. Ready to Learn is a relatively brief, individually administered screening instrument designed to assess a child's risk for developing reading and learning difficulties. It purports to provide data that, if needed, can support early referral for either proactive intervention or further assessment for the diagnosis of learning difficulties. Subtest scores are assigned to one of three risk categories, the most significant of which (Red Risk Index) indicates subtest skill levels at or below the 11th percentile for same-age peers. Ready to Learn may be useful for early childhood assessment teams to help identify areas of strength and weakness for intervention purposes, but it is not particularly useful for progress monitoring. The technical data presented in the manual support the reliability and validity of the instrument as a learning readiness screening instrument.

REVIEWER'S REFERENCES

Fawcett, A. J., Nicolson, R. I., & Lee, R. (2001). The Pre-School Screening Test. London: The Psychological Corporation.
Good, R. H., & Kaminski, R. A. (Eds.). (2002). *Dynamic indicators of basic early literacy skill* (6th ed.). Eugene, OR: Institute for the Development of Educational Achievement.
National Reading Panel. (2000). *Report of the National Reading Panel: Teaching students to read: An evidence-based assessment of the scientific research literature on reading and its implications for reading instruction.* Bethesda, MD: National Institute of Child Health and Human Development, National Institute of Health.
Nicolson, R. I., & Fawcett, A. J. (1996). The Dyslexia Early Screening Test. London: The Psychological Corporation.
Nicolson, R. I., & Fawcett, A. J. (2004). The Dyslexia Early Screening Test—Second Edition. London: The Psychological Corporation.

[165]
Risk-Sophistication-Treatment Inventory.

Purpose: Designed to assess juvenile offenders' risk for dangerousness, sophistication-maturity, and amenability to treatment.
Population: Juvenile offenders ages 9–18.
Publication Dates: 1998–2004.
Acronym: RSTI.
Scores, 12: Risk for Dangerousness (Violent and Aggressive Tendencies, Planned and Extensive Criminality, Psychopathic Features, Total), Sophistication-Maturity (Autonomy, Cognitive Capacities, Emotional Maturity, Total), Treatment Amenability (Psychopathology-Degree and Type, Responsibility and Motivation to Change, Consideration and Tolerance of Others, Total).
Administration: Individual.
Price Data, 2007: $174 per introductory kit including professional manual (2004, 109 pages), 25 interview booklets, and 25 rating forms.
Time: (50–65) minutes for semistructured interview; [15–20] minutes for rating form.
Comments: Semistructured interview and rating scale.
Author: Randall T. Salekin.
Publisher: Psychological Assessment Resources, Inc.

Review of the Risk-Sophistication-Treatment Inventory by JOHN S. GEISLER, Professor Emeritus, Department of Counselor Education and Counseling Psychology, Western Michigan University, Kalamazoo, MI:

DESCRIPTION. The Risk-Sophistication-Treatment Inventory (RSTI) is a 45-item instrument that can be used to assess the functioning of juvenile offenders (ages 9–18) in order to make informed and appropriate judgments as to their placement and disposition. The RSTI consists of five elements: (a) a semistructured interview (using an interview booklet protocol), (b) personal information (school, treatment, police, and assessment records), (c) information from parents/guardians, (d) other related data (e.g., psychological reports; aptitude, achievement, and intelligence test scores), and (e) a structured rating form. The rating form consists of three primary scales–Risk for Dangerousness, Sophistication-Maturity, and Treatment Amenability (15 items each) and one supplementary scale–Criminal Sophistication (derived from additional scoring of the SM items). Each item is scored on a 3-point Likert scale basis. In addition to the three primary scales, nine subscale scores (clusters) are also obtained. The clusters are grouped under the primary scales as follows (with related number of items): Risk for Dangerousness (Violent and Aggressive Tendencies—5, Planned and Extensive Criminality—6, and Psychopathic Features—4); Sophistication-Maturity (Autonomy—4, Cognitive Capacities—6, and Emotional Maturity—5); and Treatment Amenability (Psychopathology-Degree and Type—5, Responsibility and Motivation to Change—5, and Consideration and Tolerance of Others—5). Scoring on each item is done by a clinician and is based on material gained from the first four elements listed above. The material considered as part of this review consisted of a professional manual, interview booklet, and rating form.

Raw and converted scores (T scores and percentiles) are derived from scoring the rating form (RF). Raw scores (range = 0 to 30) are computed for the three primary and nine cluster subscales. The raw scores for the three primary scales are converted into linear T scores; the nine cluster scores are converted into percentiles. The primary scale T scores ($N = 591$) are further divided into range groupings: Risk for Dangerousness, Sophistication Maturity, and Treatment Amenability—below 41 (LOW), 41–59 (MIDDLE), 60 and above (HIGH); for the nine cluster subscales–below the 25th percentile (LOW), 25th–74th percentiles (MIDDLE), above the 75th percentile and higher (HIGH).

The scoring of the rating form is very much dependent on the quality and quantity of information gleaned from the semistructured interview and collateral sources, and the skill of the clinician. The interview is the primary source of information. The clinician is required to have a graduate-level education and training with special emphasis in interviewing, the use of psychological assessments, and diagnostic skills related to children and adolescents. The developer of the RSTI provides a thorough description of the scoring protocols, process, and criteria for each of the 45 items

(professional manual, pp. 14–29). Six case studies are presented in the manual.

DEVELOPMENT. Previous theories and empirical studies by the developer (and colleagues) led to the origination of the three major scales (Risk for Dangerousness, Sophistication-Maturity, and Treatment Amenability). Prior to the selection of the original RSTI items, advice and consultation was sought from 745 experts involved in working with juveniles: clinicians, judges, and forensic specialists. One hundred thirty-five items from psychological literature and case law related to juveniles were selected for analysis. "Psychologists from the Child and Adolescent Clinical Psychology section (Division 53 of the American Psychological Association) … and forensic diplomats" (professional manual, p. 62) were also used as consultants with respect to item selection. Items were reviewed for their importance and relevance vis-à-vis the three primary scales. In addition, exploratory and confirmatory factor analyses were conducted and the results compared to the opinions of clinicians and judges. "The model was tested separately for the judges and for the psychologists to further understand the similarities and differences in the ratings between these two groups. The revised three factor model showed an acceptable fit" (professional manual, p. 64). The results of these studies resulted in the identification of the nine subscale clusters.

TECHNICAL. Reliability, validity, and descriptive data were collected on samples of juvenile offenders in Dade County, FL ($N = 138$), Tuscaloosa, AL (detention center, $N = 125$ and $N = 114$; medical facility, $N = 145$), and Madison, WI (treatment center, $N = 126$). The original normative groups totaled 648, with 591 complete data sets (473 males, 118 females). The racial/ethnic composition was African American (52%), Caucasian, (34%), Hispanic (11%), and Others (2%).

Alpha coefficients ranged from .73 to .79 across all three primary scales ($N = 591$). Individual item-with-Total Score correlation coefficients were reported for all 45 items and ranged from .20 to .68. Interrater reliability coefficients for the primary scales, using a two-way random-effects model ranged from .73 to .94. Sample sizes for these data ranged from 114 to 145 in four separate studies. The Criminal Sophistication supplemental rating scale correlation coefficient range was from .60 to .70.

The results of construct validity studies were also reported. The Risk for Dangerousness scale scores were correlated with: (a) juveniles' past criminal activities, (b) antisocial behaviors, (c) rates of behavior chronicity, (d) demographic variables, (e) scores on the Adolescent Psychopathy Scale, (f) scores on the Revised Interpersonal Adjective Scales-Big Five (personality factors), (g) aggression assessments, and (h) scores on the Hare Psychopathy Checklist–Youth Version (PCL-YV). Sophistication-Maturity scale scores were correlated with: (a) the PCL-YV, (b) the Kaufman Brief Intelligence Test, (c) the BarOn Emotional Quotient Inventory: Youth Version, and (d) the Sternberg Triarchic Abilities Test. The developers also reported the results of studies correlating TA scale scores with: (a) the BarOn Inventory, (b) treatment compliance measures, and (c) psychopathy measure scores. Most of the correlations were in the expected direction and were of a low magnitude. Research study sample sizes ranged from 114 to 145. Approximately 40% of the correlation coefficients reached either the .01 or .05 levels of significance.

The developers reported on research that was designed to determine if there were statistically significant RSTI mean scale score differences between juveniles who were transferred from juvenile to adult courts ($N = 30$) and those who were not transferred ($N = 96$). A multivariate analysis of variance (MANOVA) revealed that transferred juveniles had higher mean scores on the Risk for Dangerousness and Sophistication-Maturity scales (and the Criminal Sophistication ratings) and lower mean scores on Treatment Amenability ($p < .05$). Two additional studies had similar results.

COMMENTARY. The developer of the RSTI is to be congratulated for the attempt to develop an instrument to assist professionals in the juvenile justice system with their deliberations regarding the management and disposition of cases. Of particular note is the quality of the professional manual, rating form, and semistructured interview booklet. The manual is comprehensive, well written, readable, and complete. The section in the manual on the scoring, the criteria for scoring, and the descriptions of each of the items on the rating form is especially noteworthy. The interview booklet deserves special commendation. The booklet contains questions, prompts, suggestions for probing, and provides guidance in order to gather as much information as possible from respondents. It is detailed and very comprehensive. The rating form is easily understood, readable, and clear. The only exception is the scoring of the supplemental material on the page where the Sophistication-Maturity scores are obtained. It is assumed that the scoring of this supplemental material will lead to a score on the Criminal Sophistication supplementary rating scale, but this formulation is not well defined. Very little information is provided on this scale, its development, reliability, validity, and utility. Its usefulness is problematic and questionable. The author needs either to provide detailed information on this scale or to eliminate it from the instrument. It is also suggested that Chapters 4 (Standardization and Normative Information) and 5 (Test Development) be relocated as Chapters 3 and 2, respectively. It makes logical sense to have test development as well as standardization and normative information at the beginning of the manual.

The qualifications of the clinicians who will be using this instrument are clearly and unambiguously prescribed. Clinicians must have advanced training and skills in assessment. Directions are clear and understandable as to how the instrument is to be used by clinicians, judges, and persons who are in positions of authority. Guidelines on how to conduct individual or group interpretations with juvenile clients are missing, however.

Although the primary purpose of the instrument is to assess the functioning of juvenile offenders for use in placement decisions, the instrument can also be used for assisting juveniles to gain insight into their beliefs, attitudes, and behaviors. The provision of material to assist clinicians with individual interpretations would be a welcome addition to the RSTI materials.

The developer claims that the normative sample groups are representative of juvenile offenders, yet no data are offered to support this claim. The normative samples from Dade County, FL; Tuscaloosa, AL; and Madison, WI may not be nationally representative. A broader base of sample groups is necessary in order to make a claim of a national distribution.

The reliability, validity, and factor analysis data are acceptable. The coefficient alpha and interrater reliability correlation coefficients are in the acceptable range. Many of the sources for the validity studies are from sources other than the developer. The material on reactive and proactive aggression in the manual, although interesting, does not advance the case for validity of the RSTI. Although some of the reported correlation coefficients between conduct disorders, psychopathology, and reactive and proactive aggression and personality variables with certain scales of the RSTI are statistically significant, they may not mean the coefficients are meaningful (e.g., .21 may be statistically significant [$p < .05$] but may have little or no "significance" in terms of utility). The developers should be cautioned against making claims that certain RSTI scales and cluster subscales assess personality dimensions and psychopathology (e.g., Psychopathic Features and Psychopathology-Degree and Type). The reported validity data do not support such a claim. The MANOVA data on the mean score differences between transferred and nontransferred males was most interesting; however, the sample size was small ($N = 126$) and only males were included, which makes generalizations tenuous at best. Additional predictive studies showing the relationship between the RSTI scales and outcome measures (treatment results, recidivism rates, school performance, attitudes, reduction in criminal behavior, etc.) would be extremely helpful. Because the primary purpose of the RSTI is to assess juvenile offender functioning, the results of longitudinal studies would help to determine the efficacy of the instrument. The author also provides "Five goodness-of-fit indexes for the conceptual structure of the three RSTI scales" (professional manual, p. 81). However, the table containing this information is confusing and appears incomplete.

The RSTI scoring systems need to be modified. The derivation of raw scores poses no problem (except the Criminal Sophistication scale). However, the same cannot be said about the normative scale conversions (male $N = 473$, female $N = 118$). The developer has chosen to use a percentile system for the nine cluster subscales and a T score system for the three primary scales (using different gender scores). Mixing two normative conversion systems can cause confusion and is probably not justified. In addition, using percentile scores with subscales containing as few as four items is problematic (e.g., raw scores of 0, 1, 2, 3, 4, 5, 6, and 7 all receive a percentile score of 1 or less on the Risk for Dangerousness male conver-

sion table). Also, the converted scores are grouped into ranges (Low, Middle, High) whose criteria are different. The score ranges for the cluster scales are different than the primary scales (the Middle score range for the cluster scores is the middle 50% [approximately] of scores, the Middle score range for the primary scales is 68% [approximately]). One solution is to increase the number of persons in the samples (the female norm group contains only 118 individuals). A second solution is to use only one normative system. A third solution is to drop the Low, Middle, High groupings entirely. The best solution is to have longitudinal data available so that predictive criterion scores could be established that would differentiate levels of dispositional success. The RSTI is a commendable instrument for which the efficacy would be greatly enhanced if follow-up research studies were generated and reported in the manual. A very complete item reference list of almost 200 references is included in the manual.

Review of the Risk-Sophistication-Treatment Inventory by STEVEN I. PFEIFFER, Professor and Director of Clinical Training, PhD Program in Combined Counseling and School Psychology, Florida State University, Tallahassee, FL:

DESCRIPTION. The Risk-Sophistication-Treatment Inventory (RSTI) is a 45-item test designed for use by clinicians to assess the functioning of juvenile offenders, ages 9 to 18, in three areas: level of risk the youth poses to the community (Risk for Dangerousness scale), level of maturity (Sophistication-Maturity scale), and amenability to treatment (Treatment Amenability scale). All items are rated on a 3-point scale. The purpose of the RSTI is twofold: to provide a clinically useful assessment for juvenile offenders; and to provide a standardized measure that addresses juvenile justice/legal questions, such as whether a juvenile should be considered for transfer to adult court.

Juvenile courts look to forensic psychologists and other mental health professionals for information on whether, and to what degree, a given youth poses a danger to the community. Juvenile court judges also are interested in the level of cognitive and emotional maturity of a juvenile offender, particularly in cases involving the question of transfer to adult court. And the juvenile justice system is interested in information on which youth are most amenable to treatment (i.e., have better prognoses and more likely to respond favorably to psychotherapeutic interventions). The RSTI is designed to provide this information.

Use of the inventory requires advanced graduate training with specific clinical expertise in forensic practice. The rating form consists of 45 items with 15 items for each of the three scales (Risk for Dangerousness, Sophistication-Maturity, Treatment Amenability). A 32-page interview booklet is provided to assist the clinician in conducting a semistructured clinical interview. In addition to conducting a semistructured interview, the clinician will need to review the youth's file (school records, police records, detention records, prior psychological testing, probation reports, etc.) and consult with parents and teachers to obtain the relevant information to rate all 45 items.

The RSTI yields a T score, percentile rank, and "offender range" (low, middle, high) for each of the three scales. In addition, the score summary sheet provides low, middle, and high offender ranges for each of the three clusters within each of the three scales. Risk of Dangerousness consists of Violent and Aggressive Tendencies, Planned and Extensive Criminality, and Psychopathic Features; Sophistication-Maturity consists of Autonomy, Cognitive Capacities, and Emotional Maturity; Treatment Amenability consists of Psychopathology–Degree and Type, Responsibility and Motivation to Change, and Consideration and Tolerance for Others.

DEVELOPMENT. The development of the RSTI was guided by careful consideration of the theoretical and empirical literature on serious juvenile delinquency and related topics (e.g., conduct disorder, aggression, violence, resilience, and competence), and by review of relevant statutes and appellate cases pertaining to transfer criteria. *Kent v. United States* (1966) originally raised the issues of risk for dangerousness, sophistication-maturity, and amenability to treatment, and is duly cited in the manual. Test development followed a carefully delineated set of procedures. First, an extensive review of the literature and input from experts operationalized the three constructs (scales) and set the stage for generating an initial pool of items. Two separate prototypical analyses were conducted that rated items considered central to each of the three constructs. This led to some item "pruning" (e.g., "hyperactivity," "promiscuous sexual behavior" and "glib/superfi-

cial charm" were eliminated because they were given low prototypical ratings).

The next step entailed conducting a series of preliminary exploratory factor analyses. This was followed by running a set of confirmatory factor analyses, which supported each of the three superordinate factors. This led to the three-factor, 45-item final version.

TECHNICAL. The manual is comprehensive and well-written. The manual provides quite detailed and extensive information on theory and research related to juvenile forensic issues. The rationale for and research underlying the RSTI is clear and compelling. The normative sample consists of 648 youth. Thoughtful norming procedures generated a sample representative of young offenders across a variety of juvenile facilities and settings, based on important demographic, psychological, and criminal offenses. However, the normative sample for females ages 9 to 13 is quite small (19), compromising interpretation of scores for young females.

The RSTI evidences acceptable but not very high internal consistency, with coefficient alpha values for the three scales ranging from .73 to .79. Standard error of measurement values are also acceptable, although not exceptionally small, ranging from 4.58 to 5.20. Interrater reliability was evaluated in four validity studies. Interclass correlation coefficients ranged from .84 to .94 for Risk for Dangerousness, .73 to .82 for Sophistication, and .83 to .92 for Treatment Amenability. A supplemental scale, Criminal Sophistication (derived from secondary ratings from the Sophistication-Maturity and Treatment Amenability scales), obtained relatively lower interrater values, ranging from .60 to .70 ($M = .64$). This supplemental scale appears to be more challenging for clinicians to rate.

The manual provides considerable construct and criterion-related validity in support of the three RSTI scales. A significant number of studies are cited that provide significant correlations between the three RSTI scales and related constructs (e.g., involvement in criminal behavior, age at onset of violent offenses, conduct disorder symptoms, reactive and proactive aggression, dominance, affiliation, extraversion, agreeableness, and psychopathy). Confirmatory factor analysis provides additional support for the structure of the three RSTI scales; goodness-of-fit indexes for all subclass structures were above .97, consistent with data that fit the hypothesized cluster structures of the inventory. The manual does not provide any direct evidence of the validity for the Treatment Amenability scale.

COMMENTARY. The RSTI is a well-conceived test. The development of the RSTI is marked by a notable marriage of theory, research, and clinical experience. There is no alternative test for the juvenile offender that measures risk for dangerousness, level of maturity, and amenability to treatment. The RSTI has taken a significant step forward in providing forensic psychologists and other clinicians with a standardized inventory to assist in the difficult decisions asked of practitioners who work with this uniquely challenging population. Juvenile court judges and personnel within the juvenile justice system will appreciate and value the information provided by the inventory.

Although the manual reports considerable evidence in support of the test's technical adequacy, further validation studies are imperative to determine just how well the test does what it is purported to do. Risk for dangerousness and amenability to treatment remain fuzzy psychological constructs. Whenever one intends to predict future behavior, particularly elusive behaviors such as the likelihood of committing a violent crime, or one's motivation to change and willingness to disclose personal concerns/issues in treatment, the accuracy of such predictions is influenced by many variables. A clinician can never expect that any one test can make accurate, fool-proof predictions without incorporating considerable collateral information and sound clinical judgment (and luck). The RSTI does appear to be a valuable tool to assist the forensic clinician in making these challenging opinions for the court.

SUMMARY. The RSTI is an ambitious and well-conceived test that provides valuable information on a juvenile offender's risk for dangerousness, sophistication-maturity, and treatment amenability. These are three areas where the juvenile court and juvenile justice system look to be informed by forensic psychologists and other mental health professionals. The manual is comprehensive and provides extensive information on the rationale and research underlying the RSTI. The rating form is clear, concise, and very well organized. A detailed interview booklet is provided that can be used during a semistructured interview to collect data to complete the rating form. Test

users will need to obtain supervised experience working with the juvenile offender population before they are comfortable and competent completing ratings on many of the items that can be difficult to rate.

REVIEWER'S REFERENCE

Kent v. United States, 383 U.S. 541 (1966).

[166]

Rivermead Assessment of Somatosensory Performance.

Purpose: "Designed to provide therapists and doctors with a brief, quantifiable and reliable assessment of somatosensory functioning after neurological disorders such as stroke, MS, peripheral neuropathies, head injury and spinal cord injury."

Population: Age 18 and over.
Publication Date: 2000.
Acronym: RASP.
Scores: Total score only.
Subtests, 7: Sharp/Dull Discrimination, Surface Pressure Touch, Surface Localization, Temperature Discrimination, Movement, Direction Proprioception Discrimination, Sensory Extinction, Two-Point Discrimination.
Administration: Individual.
Price Data, 2006: £184 per complete kit including manual, 25 scoring sheets, reference card, 2 aesthesiometers/neurometers, 2 neurotemps, two-point discriminator/neurodisk, and 30 neurotips; £35 per 50 scoring sheets.
Time: (25–35) minutes.
Authors: Charlotte E. Winward, Peter W. Halligan, and Derick T. Wade.
Publisher: Harcourt Assessment [England].

Review of the Rivermead Assessment of Somatosensory Performance by THOMAS M. DUNN, Associate Professor of Psychological Sciences, University of Northern Colorado, Greeley, CO:

DESCRIPTION. As its name implies, the Rivermead Assessment of Somatosensory Performance (RASP) is an instrument that assesses touch, pressure, temperature, and proprioception. These senses are notoriously difficult to measure adequately, but the RASP was designed to be a clinician friendly, standardized assessment of somatosenory performance using reliable measurement devices that produce scores that can be compared to norms. The RASP's quite innovative contribution to assessing the somatosenses is the development of three different devices to help quantify reliably stimulation arising from the skin.

From these three devices, seven subtests have been developed that "originate from established clinical practice and most have been used in a variety of unstandardized formats in medicine for well over a century" (manual, p. 4).

The three devices are the Neurometer, Neurotemp, and the Two-point Neurodisc. Two Neurometers are used for the Sharp/Dull Discrimination, Pressure, Surface Localization, and Sensory Extinction subtests. The Neurometers look like ball point pens, but are loaded with a "Neurotip" that has both a sharp and a dull end. The Neurometers are calibrated to produce the same reliable pressure from use to use. The sharp end of the Neurotip is single use only and disposal is required in a "sharps" container. The Neurotemps have plastic grips for nickel-plated copper disks. One disk is run under hot water or immersed in boiling water, the other is put into a refrigerator or placed into cold water. Embedded thermometers in each device read either a "hot" or "cold" range, with the "hot device" heated to about 120 degrees (F) and the "cold" device cooled to about 42 degrees (F). Obviously, these devices are used on the subtest of Temperature Discrimination. Finally, a single "Neurodisc" is a "four-pointed two-point discriminator" (manual, p. 6) that has 3, 4, and 5mm fixed distances between two points used on the Two-point Discrimination subtest (p. 6). No device is needed for the remaining subtest, Proprioception (both Movement and Direction Discrimination). The Neurometer, Neurotemp, and Two-Point Neurodisc are part of a test kit also containing a manual, scoring blanks, Neurotips, a laminated anatomical reference chart, and answer cards to use with patients who are unable to answer by voice.

Each of the above mentioned subtests contains multiple trials testing the surfaces of the face, hands, and feet, alternating from one side of the body to the other. Ultimately, 10 anatomically referenced test regions (measuring approximately $25mm^2$) are assessed for each subtest. All testing is done with the patient's eyes closed. Correctly identified stimuli from the affected and unaffected sides are counted. Patients may respond verbally, to pictures or words, or use hand signals. Scores from seven subtests are individually compared to norms derived from both a clinical sample and a nonclinical group. Two subtests also contain a variety of "sham" trials. These are instances when the clinician deliberately withholds a stimulus while giving a verbal cue to the patient that a stimulus is about to be applied. When a high number of "sham" touches are endorsed, this may mean that the patient is unreliable. The RASP can be given in its entirety, or only subtests of interest to the clinician can be administered.

DEVELOPMENT. The RASP is in its first edition (Copyright 2000). Minimal justification for test development and content is offered in the test manual. The manual states that senses selected are distinct and nonhierarchical. It should be noted that the RASP subtests closely follow widely accepted notions about the somatosenses. Developing norms for the RASP started with screening stroke patients from four hospitals in the United Kingdom. Initially, this group contained more than 400 patients, but the final clinical comparison group generated from the initial screening numbered 100. Only patients with the solitary diagnosis of a first-time stroke presenting with unilateral signs were included in the clinical group. The group was evenly divided between those with left- and right-sided lesions. An age-matched, nonclinical comparison group of 50 individuals with no pathology was also recruited.

TECHNICAL. As previously mentioned, the RASP used two relatively small comparison groups. The clinical group was divided into those with left- or right-sided deficits. Considerable effort was undertaken to assure that these clinical patients had no other impairment apart from history of cerebral vascular accident. Both the left- and right-sided groups were comparable in age, time elapsed since the stroke, and gender. The age-matched control group was slightly younger, but free from neurological deficit. The performance of the three groups (right-sided deficit, left-sided deficit, and intact control) is reported in means, medians, ranges, and standard deviations. Following testing, the patient's scores are compared to normative performance for each subtest. Patients who score two standard deviations below the mean performance are considered to be impaired. Clinical cutoff scores indicating impairment are listed.

Interrater reliability is reported to be quite high ($r = .92$). The RASP also has a measure for patient reliability. In addition, test authors consider the possibility that test results may not always be a true indicator of patient ability. For example, the patient may be fatigued from a long day of testing and may not put forth good effort. Whatever the reason, the authors include data to determine if the patient's presentation is atypical, suggesting that the patient is not reliable.

Validity data are absent from the manual. Although the authors suggest that RASP subtests were based on somatosensory tests that have been employed in medicine for more than 100 years, no data are reported to support concurrent (or any other) form of validity. Construct validity is not established. The rationale for building specific subtests appears sound. To be fair, there are few other standardized tests in this domain making validity evidence difficult to collect.

COMMENTARY. Formal assessment of somatosensory functioning is an overlooked domain in neuropsychology, probably because there are few standardized measures available to the clinician. The RASP would be a welcome addition to the test libraries of those who specialize in cognitive rehabilitation following brain insult. It takes about 30 minutes to administer, follows a standardized protocol, and has norms from both a clinical and control group.

There are only a few (slight) drawbacks to the RASP. Namely, the authors consider their Neurotips to be "sharps" that need to be disposed of in an approved container. Although the Neurotip is not intended to pierce the skin (making the risk of blood-borne transmission of a communicable disease very small), it could cause a puncture wound if handled improperly. Clinicians working in hospitals may have ready access to sharps containers, but those working in other settings may have difficulty finding appropriate ways to dispose of these single-use items. The Neurotemp devices also may cause some consternation. These instruments are optimally prepped with ice and boiling water. Although they are reported to stay in the appropriate temperature range for a reasonable amount of time, finding ice and boiling water adds to the 30-minute administration time.

I also have some concern about the normative sample. Because the test was normed on relatively small groups who were all in their early 60s, it is not known how patients who are either much younger or much older than this sample would perform. It would be desirable to have a range of scores across age groups of nonimpaired subjects. As well, it would be convenient if attained scores could be easily converted into standard scores. All in all, these drawbacks are minor in comparison to significant benefit of using the RASP.

Review of the Rivermead Assessment of Somatosensory Performance by TIMOTHY J. MAKATURA, Consulting Psychologist, Allegheny Children's Initiative, Pittsburgh, PA:

The Rivermead Assessment of Somatosensory Performance (RASP) is a "standardized test battery designed to provide a ... brief, quantifiable and reliable assessment of somatosensory functioning after neurological disorders" (manual, p. 4). The authors report that the assessment of somatosensory functioning is a typical and necessary part of the assessment process following neurological insult and note that procedures for doing so have traditionally lacked objective and reliable measures. Therefore, a single standardized assessment seems to be necessary.

The RASP consists of seven objective, quantifiable subtests that are easy to administer and simple to score. The seven tests are divided into five primary tests including: Sharp/Dull Discrimination, Surface Pressure Touch, Surface Localization, Temperature Discrimination, and Movement and Direction Proprioception Discrimination, and two secondary subtests: Sensory Extinction and Two-Point Discrimination. In order to facilitate the standardization process, the RASP includes standardized devices including three new, quantifiable and custom-designed instruments, called the Neurometer, the Neurotemp, and the two-point Neurodisc. These instruments give the examiner the opportunity to present the same stimulus to all subjects in terms of pressure, temperature, and location.

DESCRIPTION. Seven subtests comprise the RASP. Each subtest involves a specific stimulus that is presented to some of the 10 anatomically referenced regions of the body. These 10 regions are specified in an appendix of the user's manual. The examiner is advised to generally follow an alternate pattern in delivering the stimuli by moving from the unaffected side of the body (left or right) to the affected side, head to foot. For each subtest, regions of the body to be tested are specified.

The Sharp/Dull Discrimination subtest requires the Neurometers and involves the face, hand, and foot regions of the body. Sharp and dull stimuli and sham trials are presented via the Neurometers to different areas of the body. The

Surface Pressure Touch subtest requires one Neurometer and involves the face, hand, and foot regions. Varied pressure is delivered via the Neurometer to different areas of the body. The Surface Localization subtest requires the Neurometer and involves the face, hand, and foot regions. Light pressure is applied to different parts of the body. The Sensory Extinction subtest requires the Neurometers and involves the face and hand regions of the body. Stimuli are presented to homologous regions of the body simultaneously. Two-Point Discrimination requires the two-point Neurodisc and involves the index finger tip of both hands. Two-point stimuli of varying distances are presented to the index finger. The Temperature Discrimination subtest requires the Neurotemps and involves the face, hand, and foot region. Warm and cold stimuli are presented via the Neurotemps to different areas of the body. The Proprioception Movement and Direction Discrimination subtests involve the detection of the joint being moved and the direction of that movement. In each of these subtests, the patient's eyes are closed and they are asked to identify and/ or localize the particular sensation. The scoring sheet also provides the sequence of administration for each particular stimulus.

TECHNICAL. The normative population for the RASP included 100 patients with a diagnosis of first-ever unilateral stroke. Fifty of these patients had left-sided lesions and 50 had right-sided lesions. Patients with bilateral signs, noncompliance, severe visual or hearing impairments, cognitive impairments, secondary neurological condition, comprehension difficulties, or previous stroke were excluded from this sample. In addition, a control group of 50 non-brain-damaged individuals was recruited from the hospital (employees) and local community. The group members were generally matched by age, gender, and time post onset. Tables are presented for each subtest that provide average score, standard deviation, and range for the right- and left-sided lesion groups.

Interrater reliability was established by correlating the total scores on the five primary RASP subtests of two different raters with the original research therapist for 15 different participants. The correlation was .92. A Bland and Altman distribution graph is also presented to demonstrate agreement between raters.

SUMMARY. Generally, the RASP seems to accomplish the goal of presenting a brief, reliable, and quantifiable test of somatosensory functioning. The assessment improves on typical methods of testing by taking a number of commonly used tests and providing a standardized method of administration. The greatest strength of this test is the inclusion of equipment that delivers reliable stimuli that may be repeated over time.

There are also some cautions and concerns regarding the RASP. First, the description of the new equipment as "quantifiable and custom-designed pieces of equipment" (manual, p. 4) seems to be somewhat inconsistent with the red plastic devices that are found in the kit. There are also questions regarding the durability of this equipment over time. Second, the psychometric properties that support these procedures seem to be limited. It is hoped that future research will further investigate the validity and reliabilities of this test. A final concern involves the choice of subtests that are included in this assessment. Although the authors make a reasonable argument regarding the need for a brief, standardized assessment, they do not provide a rationale for their selection of the specific tasks that comprise the RASP. It seems that a number of other tasks could have been included, and the reason for their noninclusion is perplexing. Nonetheless, the RASP is certainly a welcome addition to the informal tests and assessments that are currently used to evaluate somatosensory functioning.

[167]
The Rivermead Behavioural Memory Test—Extended Version.

Purpose: Designed "to predict everyday memory problems in people with acquired, non-progressive brain injury and monitor change over time."
Population: Ages 16—65.
Publication Dates: 1985—1999.
Acronym: RBMT-E.
Scores, 12: First Names, Second Names, Belongings and Appointments, Picture Recognition, Story (Immediate), Story (Delayed), Face Recognition, Route (Immediate), Route (Delayed), Messages (Immediate), Messages (Delayed), Orientation and Date.
Administration: Individual.
Forms: 2 versions: A, B.
Price Data, 2006: £295.50 per complete kit including manual (1999, 20 pages), 25 scoring sheets, 2 stimulus books, picture cards, and timer.

Time: (25–30) minutes.
Authors: Barbara A. Wilson, Linda Clare, Janet M. Cockburn, Alan D. Baddeley, Robyn Tate, and Peter Watson.
Publisher: Harcourt Assessment [England].

Review of The Rivermead Behavioural Memory Test-Extended Version by ANDREW S. DAVIS, Assistant Professor, Department of Educational Psychology, Ball State University, and W. HOLMES FINCH, Assistant Professor, Ball State University, Muncie, IN:

DESCRIPTION. The Rivermead Behavioural Memory Test—Extended Version (RBMT-E) is a standardized, norm-referenced memory test that is designed to assess and predict common everyday memory. Designed for use with adolescents through geriatric adults, this instrument is constructed to assess individuals with static, acquired neurological injuries, although it also could be used for individuals without brain injuries. Information on this instrument is collected through an examiner-examinee interaction with 11 subtests that assess a variety of memory abilities and the patient's orientation. The RBMT-E consists of two parallel versions, each designed to assess a patient's memory status before and after an intervention or another time interval.

Each of the subtests yields a "profile score" that is calculated based upon the examinee's raw score, and in some cases adjusted for age or IQ. Indeed, it is necessary to have a measure of IQ in order to score the RBMT-E; in a pilot study the authors utilized brief measures to estimate IQ. Although there are 11 subtests, immediate and delayed measures create 13 raw scores and 12 profile scores. Once all of the profile scores are obtained for each subtest, they are summed to form an overall profile score, which can be grouped into 1 of 5 categories, Impaired, Poor Memory, Average Memory, Good Memory, and Exceptionally Good Memory. These classifications are based upon a normative sample of 191 normal subjects who completed both parallel measures of the RBMT-E. Aside from the overall profile score, there are no composite indices such as visual memory, verbal memory, working memory, or procedural memory. Some of the subtests will be very familiar to neuropsychologists or psychologists who commonly give memory tests. For example, there is a measure of face recognition (with distracters during the presentation), a picture rec-

ognition task, a pairing of faces with names task, and a narrative story recall task (both immediate and delayed). The RBMT-E also includes "Orientation and Date" subtests, which very closely resemble traditional mental status examinations (time, date, place, current and past president, and autobiographical memory).

DEVELOPMENT. The RBMT-E is an adaptation of the Rivermead Behavioural Memory Test (RBMT; Wilson, Cockburn, & Baddeley, 1985; T7:2181) which has four parallel forms. The RBMT-E was created by merging the four parallel forms of the RBMT into two parallel forms in order to increase the difficulty of the original measure to account for ceiling effects. The authors note "the RBMT comprises tasks analogous to everyday situations that appear to be troublesome for memory impaired patients" (manual, p. 4). The authors of the RBMT-E cite several studies that examined the validity and utility of the RBMT, including a validity study in which 80 patients with brain injury demonstrated significant correlations between observed everyday memory problems and their scores on the RBMT. The test authors note that the RBMT was designed to be a screening test, and therefore may not be able to detect mild brain impairment. However, the authors seem to indicate that increasing the memory load of the RBMT would increase the sensitivity of the RBMT, which they accomplished by combining Versions A and B of the RBMT into Version 1 of the RBMT-E and Versions C and D of the RBMT into Version 2 of the RBMT-E.

The test authors indicated that a pilot study (de Wall, Wilson, & Baddeley, 1994, as cited in the test manual) was conducted with two groups of individuals, one middle aged (ages 40–55 years) and the other elderly (65–79 years). The test authors noted that de Wall et al. (1994) discovered that the RBMT-E was able to differentiate between these two groups despite minimal statistically significant differences in memory between the groups. It seems as if de Wall et al. (1994) used the test materials of the RBMT and combined the forms as described above. Unfortunately, the number of subjects who participated in this study and the outcome statistics are not provided in the test manual. Based on these positive results, the test authors seem to have concluded that further development of the RBMT-E was appropriate. The test authors cite three modifications they made to this early version of the RBMT-E: modifications to diminish floor and ceiling effects, standardizing the test instructions and materials, and collecting a normative sample. The test authors also note, "We also included 18 subjects of African-Caribbean and Asian origin to ensure the test was appropriate for a multiracial society such as the United Kingdom or the United States of America" (manual, p. 4). Additional pilot testing revealed that some subtests needed to be increased in difficulty to avoid ceiling effects.

TECHNICAL. The normative data for the RBMT-E were created based upon a study the authors report in the test manual. Both versions of the RBMT-E were administered in a counterbalanced fashion to 191 participants between the ages of 16 and 76, with a mean age of 39.4 years and a standard deviation of 15.45 years. They also estimated IQ with the National Adult Reading Test (NART; Nelson, 1982) or the Spot-the-Word subtest from the Speed and Capacity of Language Processing Test (SCOLP; Baddeley, Emslie, & Nimmo-Smith, 1992). The test authors concluded that, although 4 of the 12 raw scores for the two versions were statistically significantly different at the .01 level, there were minor differences between the two versions of the RBMT-E for the entire group. They also concluded that IQ differences and age differences were present for several of the subtests, and these were accounted for in creating the scoring system (converting raw scores to profile scores). In neither analysis do they provide effect size estimates, so their claim as to the modesty of these differences is not empirically supported. In addition, the elimination of these differences in the standardization process is neither fully justified nor described. The authors indicate that they used box plot analysis, although they do not describe this method in any detail, nor do they provide the reader with a reference. Given that this approach is not similar to the more commonly used method of translating raw scores to Z values and then converting them to a scale with specific mean and standard deviation (e.g., Thorndike, 2005), the authors should provide a much more detailed description of their approach.

Aside from age and location, the authors report minimal demographic information regarding their sample. Although estimates of IQ data were collected, no mean IQ is reported, and there are no reported ethnicity data or educational levels

for the normative sample. In addition, the authors do not sufficiently describe some design issues relevant to their study. For example, they noted that 191 subjects completed both forms of the instrument, and that 6 subjects completed only one version. However, they do not indicate how many of this latter group completed only Version 1 or Version 2. In addition, it is not clear why they included the scores produced by these individuals in the broader study, given that the goal of the research was to compare relative difficulty on the two versions of the instrument, and most of the subjects had completed both. Furthermore, the authors state that "roughly half the subjects had Version 1 first followed at least a week later by Version 2." The technical report does not make clear the range of waiting times between taking the two versions for most of the subjects. Although the reader may know that the subjects had to wait at least 1 week, there is no indication regarding the maximum waiting time. Finally, the authors do not indicate why they elected to use two different measures for IQ.

The results of the box plot analysis were not reported, although the test authors indicated they used this technique to create the five levels of possible outcome profile scores for raw scores from each subtest. As mentioned above, given the nonstandard nature of this approach to standardization, at the least the authors should provide references for this approach, if not a full-length discussion. In addition, it would have been helpful for the test authors to report the number of participants in each age group of their standardization sample; indeed, only some of the subtests take age into account when calculating profile scores. This may cause some hesitancy in the use of some of these subtests because, for example, some clinicians may be wary of using the same conversion tables for 20-year-old patients and 70-year-old patients on a measure of delayed story recall (one of the subtests with no age cutoff criteria).

The test manual provides no evidence of reliability for the RBMT-E, and although some reliability studies may exist for the RBMT, these are not reported in the test manual of the RBMT-E. There is one discriminating groups validity study reported in the manual for the RBMT-E. The authors compared the test scores of 45 patients with neurological impairment on the RBMT and the RBMT-E. The authors were interested in determining if some patients who scored in the normal range would demonstrate deficits on the RBMT-E (because one of the goals of creating the RBMT-E was to increase the sensitivity of the measure). Indeed, some of the brain-injured patients' scores showed a decline when tested on the RBMT-E, compared to their RBMT score. As with the description of the parallel forms of the instrument, some key information is left out of this part of the technical manual. Specifically, although data were collected on 45 impaired individuals, the authors state that "More detailed information was available for 34 of these patients" (manual, p. 7). It is not clear to what information they were referring, or why it was not available for the other subjects. Furthermore, the distribution of scores reported in the accompanying tables do not match either the 45 or 34 reported in the text. Therefore, the reader is left not knowing which subsample of the data is being discussed in the technical manual.

Aside from the discriminating groups validity study, there are no other reported validity studies for the RBMT. This includes a lack of content validity, concurrent validity, predictive validity, and construct validity studies that some practitioners may expect from their measures of memory assessment. The test manual does report the results of some validity studies from the RBMT, but these are brief descriptions and generally do not include the statistics from these studies. Consumers of the RBMT-E will likely feel compelled to read these studies themselves to assess the validity of the previous RBMT.

COMMENTARY. The RBMT-E occupies an important place in the pantheon of memory tests, in that it attempts to assess everyday common memory ability, and does indeed seem to have good face validity. There are a variety of constructs that are seemingly measured by the RBMT-E, including visual memory, verbal memory, procedural memory, immediate memory, delayed memory, orientation, and autobiographical memory. The RBMT-E is very easy to administer and score, and experienced examiners should be able to very quickly incorporate this measure into their assessment practices. The overall profile score is useful, and many of the subtests would seem to have direct implications for intervention. For example, difficulty on the Belongings task would prompt neuropsychologists and psychologists to alter the home environment to help patients remember where they have placed things, a common complaint in patients suffering from memory problems. Difficulty on the Appointments task would prescribe additional help in remembering and recalling details regarding scheduling.

Many clinicians who routinely use memory tests as part of their practice will be disappointed with both the normative sample of the RBMT-E and the lack of supporting psychometric studies reported in the test manual. For example, a commonly used memory measure, the Wechsler Memory Scale—Third Edition (WMS-III; Wechsler, 1997; T7:2751) has a standardization sample of 1,250 adults. The WMS technical manual also reports extensive demographic information for the standardization sample as well as multiple studies attesting to the reliability and the validity of the measure. Additionally, several of the subtests on the RBMT-E and the WMS are virtually identical with regard to the construct that they seemingly measure, and they are very similar in technique as well. For additional comparison, a widely used memory test for children is the Children's Memory Scale (CMS; Cohen, 1997; T7:476). The CMS has a normative sample of 1,000 children, and like the WMS, reports multiple studies regarding the psychometric properties of the instrument and also measures some similar constructs using techniques comparable to those of the RBMT-E. In sum, some examiners may feel more comfortable with other memory measures that have more extensive validation. However, the RBMT-E does include some tasks that are not found on other commonly used memory tests, and it is these real-world tasks that have direct implications for interventions that are the primary strength of the RBMT-E. Practitioners may find, after reviewing the studies referenced (though not described) in the technical manual, that these scales of the RBMT-E may be appropriate for their particular circumstances.

SUMMARY. The test authors have produced a memory test that is an extension of a previous memory measure that has been shown to be successful in assessing real world memory tasks in patients with acquired neurological injury. This easy to score and administer test will provide clinicians with a valuable tool for creating interventions for individuals with memory complaints. However, as with many new tests, many clinicians will not feel comfortable with the use of the RBMT-E if they expect large normative samples and extensive validation of their instruments. In addition, the calculation of standard scores should be better explained so that users of the instrument have some sense for how they can be interpreted.

REVIEWERS' REFERENCES

Baddeley, A. D., Emslie, H., & Nimmo-Smith, I. (1992). The Speed and Capacity of Language Processing Test (SCOLP). Bury St. Edmunds, England: Thames Valley Test Company.

Cohen, M. J. (1997). Children's Memory Scale. San Antonio, TX: The Psychological Corporation.

de Wall, C., Wilson, B. A., & Baddeley, A. D. (1994). The Extended Rivermead Behavioural Memory Test: A measure of everyday performance in normal adults. *Memory, 2,* 149-166.

Nelson, H. E. (1982). The National Adult Reading Test (NART). Windsor, UK: NFER-Nelson.

Wechsler, D. (1997). Wechsler Memory Scale—Third Edition. San Antonio, TX: The Psychological Corporation.

Thorndike, R. B. (2005). *Measurement and evaluation in psychology and education,* (7th ed.). Upper Saddle River, NJ: Pearson.

Wilson, B. A., Cockburn, J., & Baddeley, A. D. (1985). The Rivermead Behavioural Memory Test. Bury St. Edmunds, England: Thames Valley Test Company.

Review of the Rivermead Behavioural Memory Test—Extended Version by HARRISON KANE, Assistant Professor of Educational and School Psychology, and DANIEL KRENZER, Doctoral Candidate, Mississippi State University, Mississippi State, MS:

DESCRIPTION. The Rivermead Behavioural Memory Test—Extended Version (RBMT-E) is an individually administered test that provides an assessment of memory impairment of day-to-day types of tasks for people with acquired, nonprogressive brain injury and can be used to monitor change over time. The subtest tasks of the RBMT-E comprise tasks analogous to everyday tasks and situations that often appear troublesome for individuals with poor or disrupted memory. In contrast to many standardized tests of memory, which resemble laboratory tasks, the RBMT-E activities emphasize reality-based functions of memory such as face and name recognition, scheduling and remembering appointments, recalling borrowed items, remembering sequential directions, story and message recall, and answering typical orientation questions (e.g., time, place, and date). Six subtests are structured to demand immediate and delayed recall components of memory. To the extent possible, activities are adapted to be personally relevant and realistic for the examinee (e.g., items borrowed belong to the examinee).

Use of the RBMT-E is restricted to professionals with appropriate advanced training and credentials. The test also may be used by individuals under the supervision of qualified personnel. Administration procedures are standardized and fairly straightforward. With very little practice, the examiner should be able to follow them accurately without reference to the manual. Several of the subtests are administered under timed conditions. Importantly, despite that the RBMT-E is intended for patients with suspected neurological impairment, the authors fail to specify recommended accommodations for clinical groups that may require adaptations to the standardized administration format, such as patients with expressive aphasia and specific perceptual impairment. Test materials are compact and easily manipulated, and the format of the test allows for an easy transition between the subtests. Scoring procedures are simple and direct. Subtest raw scores are converted to profile scores (ranging from 0 to 4) that are calculated by reference to estimated IQ (Below Average, Average, and Above Average) and age (16 to 76 years) of the examinee. These subtest profile scores are averaged to obtain an overall profile score (ranging from 0 to 4), which translates into a categorical description of the examinee's global memory (i.e., Impaired, Poor, Average, Good, and Exceptional). However, the instructions for scoring are brief and may create some ambiguity for those test givers who are not familiar with psychological testing. Administration time is estimated to be 25 to 30 minutes.

DEVELOPMENT. The original Rivermead Behavioural Memory Test was developed in 1985. Since its publication, the RBMT has emerged as a widely accepted test of everyday memory functions, particularly in Europe. However, as a screening instrument, the RBMT demonstrated considerable ceiling effects, rendering it insufficiently sensitive to mild deficits in memory, such as those commonly due to brain damage or the introduction of a drug/stressor. Thus, the rationale for the development of the RBMT-E stemmed from an effort to enhance diagnostic sensitivity by increasing the depth and difficulty of information to be remembered by the examinee. Essentially, the authors combined the four parallel versions of the RBMT to form two extended versions, under the assumption that doubling the amount of material to be memorized naturally increases the level of difficulty to a point whereby ceiling effects are effectively eliminated. The resulting two parallel forms of the RBMT-E are intended to minimize any meaningful practice effects resulting from repeated testing.

Compared to other tests of memory, the RBMT-E strives exclusively for ecological validity, to the expense of explicit theory based on structure, function, or localization. Insofar as each subtest is equally weighted in arriving at an estimate of global memory, the structure of the test implies that relatively specific abilities contribute to a general factor of everyday memory functioning.

TECHNICAL. Drawing upon the four parallel versions of the original RBMT, two pilot studies (one of which is unpublished) were conducted in the selection and refinement of test items for the extended version. These studies are described very briefly in the test manual, with no mention of sample size or demographics, beyond stating that participants were "highly motivated" individuals ranging in age from 40 to 79 years. Two subsequent studies provided the standardization sample, as well as evidence of reliability and validity. The first study consisted of 191 examinees aged 16 to 76 years without a history of brain injury who were administered the two parallel forms of the RBMT-E. Rough estimates of IQ were obtained using the National Adult Reading Test and the Spot-the-Word subtest of The Speed and Capacity of Language Processing Test (SCOLP). Results indicate the parallel forms are highly similar and sensitive to the effects of age, IQ, and gender. The second study, consisting of 45 neurologically impaired subjects, was conducted to determine whether the comprehensive format of the RBMT-E is more sensitive than its predecessor in identifying mild disruptions in behavioral memory. Approximately 66% of the individuals previously identified with the RBMT as demonstrating Normal memory were correspondingly classified with the RBMT-E. Similarly, approximately 72% of the subjects were classified as having Poor or Impaired memory across both instruments.

COMMENTARY. In contrast to many clinical memory tests that seem to be extensions of laboratory tests requiring the memorization of unrelated words, numbers, or paragraphs, the RBMT-E is designed to identify directly the memory problems encountered by patients in their daily lives. Intuitively, this characteristic of the RBMT-E would be advantageous in designing and monitoring meaningful interventions that are acceptable to patients and easily communicated to nonpsychologists. Compared to its predecessor,

the RBMT-E appears somewhat more sensitive to mild disturbances in memory. Therefore, the RBMT-E seems well suited as a practical complement to information gained from clinical observations and more traditional tests of memory. Alternate forms allow for the monitoring of progress with little influence of practice effects.

The RBMT-E possesses a number of limitations that warrant caution in its use. Evidence of reliability and validity is sparse. Inexplicably, although the information is available, the authors do not report reliability coefficients for the alternate forms of the RBMT-E. Simple calculations conducted for this review find most reliability coefficients to be on the order of .95 for all subgroups included in the standardization sample. Comparisons with the original RBMT reveal that the extended version demonstrates reasonable diagnostic sensitivity, with 72% of patients demonstrating poor and impaired memory being categorized similarly by both instruments. However, these results also indicated the RBMT-E was not particularly successful in distinguishing between different etiologies (e.g., stroke, closed head injury, and viral encephalitis). Aside from two studies conducted in 1994, no other studies supportive of the psychometric characteristics or clinical utility of the RBMT-E are reported. Several studies are noticeably absent. For example, there are no reported comparisons of the RBMT-E with other widely used standardized instruments, such as the Paired Association Learning Tests, the Wide Range Assessment of Memory and Learning, or the Wechsler Memory Scale. Thus, the authors fail to supply strong evidence of convergent or divergent validity. Similarly, the authors made no attempt to establish test-retest reliability or interrater reliability. The highly restricted range in the profile scores (0 to 4) prevent factor analyses that would confirm the construct validity and psychometric structure of the test. Apparently, the authors expect users to rely on clinical judgment and the established reliability and validity of the original RBMT to infer the technical adequacy of the RBMT-E. Detailed information of the standardization sample is absent. Importantly, the standardization sample is so small as to impede meaningful comparisons to any reference group. For example, of the participants in the standardization who completed both forms of the RBMT-E, the reference group for the lowest performers consists of only four individuals. Although the authors do not provide this information, when the established and cumulative effects of cognitive ability, gender, ethnicity, and age are considered, the standardization sample is spread so thin that norm-referenced interpretations are tenuous at best. Additionally, the absence of standard errors obviates detailed contrasts of strengths and weaknesses among the subtests. The restricted range of standard scores permits only broad classification, rather than a fine-grained assessment of strengths and weaknesses.

SUMMARY. The RBMT-E consists of 12 subtests, each composed of common daily tasks that are difficult for individuals with acquired, nonprogressive brain injury. As a comprehensive norm-referenced measure of everyday memory, the RBMT-E is not recommended. Norms are scant and dated. Convincing evidence of reliability and validity is limited. It seems, however, to be an adequate and fairly sensitive screening procedure for memory problems encountered in daily life. If fatigue and limited endurance of the patient are concerns, the original RBMT remains the preferred instrument.

[168]

Sales Potential Inventory.

Purpose: "Designed to help select top sales performers and determine the sales ability levels of current employees in any external or internal sales position."

Population: Job applicants and employees in sales positions.

Publication Dates: 2000–2001.

Acronym: S.P.I.

Scores, 2: S.P.I. score, Deception Scale score.

Administration: Group.

Price Data, 2005: $79.99 per starter kit including administrator's manual (2001, 28 pages), 5 tests, and 1 test log; $9.29 per 10 tests (volume discount available); $9.29 per 10 test logs for the online test version (volume discount available); $29.99 per administrator's manual.

Time: (15–20) minutes.

Comments: Online and pencil-and-paper versions of test are available; online version includes interpretive reports and follow-up interview questions.

Author: J. M. Llobet.

Publisher: G. Neil.

Review of the Sales Potential Inventory by KATHY E. GREEN, Professor of Education, University of Denver, Denver, CO:

DESCRIPTION. The purpose of the Sales Potential Inventory (SPI) is to identify and improve businesspersons' sales skills. Specifically, the two stated purposes are to assist in the selection of qualified applicants for sales positions and in identifying deficiencies in sales skills so that performance can be improved. The SPI is claimed to enhance equal employment opportunities by providing an objective and standardized process for employee selection. The SPI is intended for use with older adolescents or adults who would qualify for employment as salespersons. The SPI can be group administered in a paper version and can also be administered on-line. The scoring sheet is attached to the SPI as a carbonless copy, and examinee answers appear as checkmarks on the scoring sheet. Each response to the 30 selection-type items has a 1, 2, 3, or 4-point value. Responses are summed over each of four columns of items, with the grand total written in a box on the scoring sheet. In addition, five "deception items" are included. Keyed responses to those items are counted to create a 0- to 5-point Deception score, used to alert employers to the need to follow up with interview questions as the SPI score may be misleading. The SPI is presented as a fold-open booklet, with items on the inside facing pages. The booklet presentation makes responding and scoring straightforward. The 35 items could probably be answered in 10 minutes or less, though there is no time limit specified for completion.

Higher scores are interpreted as a greater likelihood of better sales ability. Although the administrator's manual provides a table of norms, it points out that norms and benchmarks are likely to differ by business type and geographical location. Therefore, companies are advised to develop their own norms. It is also mentioned that assessment information should be used in combination with other selection data to create a complete picture of the applicant or employee. No cutoff scores are suggested.

DEVELOPMENT. SPI items were written to assess sales-related attitudes, behavioral dispositions, and sales techniques, with five added items assessing the tendency to "fake good." Primary items were created based on review of the personnel selection literature, task analyses of in-person and telephone sales positions, interviews with successful salespersons, review of training materials for sales positions, and observation of specific jobs.

Items were written to assess the identified skills and personality characteristics. The administrator's manual provides minimal additional information regarding item development, piloting, revision, or functioning. It is stated that items were updated since the SPI's introduction in 1992, but no specific information is provided about individual items. The publisher's website, however, notes that test development items are selected that are the most highly predictive of job performance and that contribute to internal consistency, resulting in retention of 1/4 to 1/3 of the original item pool. No theoretical basis is provided for scale development, and no rationale or empirical evidence are provided for the decision to combine items assessing attitudes, dispositions, and sales techniques into a single score. Though data were apparently available to conduct a factor analysis, such data were not reported.

TECHNICAL. A norm table with scale scores and percentile conversion is based on responses of 706 employees. The norming sample included sales representatives from several organizations (customer service, telemarketing, office equipment sales, and telecommunications). Although the SPI is intended for use both with job applicants and employees, the norming sample comprised employees only. Using the norm table to interpret applicants' scores may be questionable, particularly if scores on the SPI are affected by sales training. Information concerning norms is vague and incomplete, and score distributions are not described, with no evidence that variables such as age, education, sales experience, industry, or job title were considered.

Items are phrased both negatively and positively. The relationship of most items to sales potential is predictable. Astute test-takers could easily inflate their scores if they chose to, and it is not clear that deception items, which query behavioral dispositions, would identify faking.

Internal consistency reliability was estimated as .61, with no information provided about the size or composition of the sample upon which that estimate was based. An internal consistency reliability estimate of .61 is inadequate for a measure used for individual placement or selection. No other forms of reliability were reported. Reliability may be low due to summing over items assessing multiple constructs (e.g., skills, attitudes).

Five small validity studies are reported in the administrator's manual. Concurrent criterion-related validity coefficients were .70 for customer service, .65 for telemarketing, .33 for office equipment sales, .33 for marketing, and .40 for credit union sales with the criterion being either sales performance as rated by a supervisor *or* sales conversion rate (percentage of sales attempts that yielded a sale). Sample sizes ranged from 17 to 44 sales employees. Three other studies, with, respectively, 97, 110 and 110, telecommunications, business, and consumer sales representatives, showed correlations of from .19 to .38 between SPI total score and individual items assessing sales knowledge, skills, and abilities. No explanation is offered for the broad range of validity coefficients, and it seems the SPI may be more predictive of sales potential in some businesses than in others. Correlations between SPI scores and individual item scores were low to moderate, which would be expected with the restricted variance likely with a single-item criterion. Validity evidence, though quite limited, is positive. The administrator's manual bases a claim that the SPI is "an accurate predictor of a wide variety of sales-oriented behaviors" (p. 18) on this evidence, which seems to be an overstatement. Finally, SPI mean scores were examined by race, with only minor differences found among African American, White, and Hispanic sales representatives.

COMMENTARY. Several concerns about the SPI limit its value. First, reliability is low. Nunnally (1994) recommends a minimum reliability of .90–.95 for tests used in selection. The SPI attempts to measure three potentially distinct concepts with no evidence (e.g., from a confirmatory factor analysis) that items assessing those concepts form a one-dimensional measure. Second, items are subject to socially desirable responding. Third, all data reported in support of validity and reported norms come from employees and not job applicants, thus no real information was available to judge SPI effectiveness as a selection tool for job applicants. No information is reported about gender, education, or work experience relative to SPI scores. Fourth, no theoretical basis for the measure was provided nor any reference to the literature.

SUMMARY. The SPI is easy to use and score. The developers have attempted to provide an objective measure free from adverse impact to aid in the employee selection and development process, and have discussed legal aspects of selection in the administrator's manual. The developers are careful to state that multiple measures need to be used in employee selection. SPI items are clearly written and related to sales, with some support for validity. However, reliability is inadequate for a selection tool, no theoretical basis is provided for the SPI, and information about measure development and structure is lacking. Although the SPI has potential and is one of a very few measures in this area, structure and reliability for samples of job applicants (not just employees) need to be supported before it is recommended for general use.

REVIEWER'S REFERENCE

Nunnally, J. C. (1994). *Psychometric theory* (3rd ed.) New York: McGraw-Hill.

[169]

Scales for Identifying Gifted Students.

Purpose: "Designed to assist school districts in the identification of students as gifted."
Population: Ages 5–18 years.
Publication Date: 2004.
Acronym: SIGS.
Scores: 7 areas: General Intellectual Ability, Language Arts, Mathematics, Science, Social Studies, Creativity, Leadership.
Administration: Individual.
Forms, 2: Home Rating Scale, School Rating Scale.
Price Data, 2006: $150 per complete kit including manual (57 pages), 25 Home Rating Scale forms, 25 School Rating forms, and 25 Summary forms; $65 per manual; $35 per 25 Home Rating Scale forms; $35 per 25 School Rating Scale forms; $20 per 25 Summary forms.
Foreign Language: Available in a Spanish-speaking version.
Time: (10–15) minutes.
Comments: This test "is designed to be completed by a teacher, counselor, or other professional who has an opportunity to observe the student for an extended period of time."
Authors: Gail R. Ryser and Kathleen McConnell.
Publisher: Prufrock Press Inc.

Review of the Scales for Identifying Gifted Students by MICHAEL S. MATTHEWS, Assistant Professor, Gifted Education Program, Department of Special Education, The University of South Florida, Tampa, FL:

DESCRIPTION. The Scales for Identifying Gifted Students (SIGS) is a rating scale designed to help identify academically gifted learners. Although procedures vary, states often mandate a behavior rating scale as part of the gifted identification process.

The SIGS has two forms, a Home and a School scale, both for use with students ages 5 through 18. A parent, teacher, or other adult who knows the student well may complete these forms. Each has seven subscales, which may be completed independently. Subscales include General Intellectual Ability, Language Arts, Mathematics, Science, Social Studies, Creativity, and Leadership.

Although instructions differ slightly, the content and presentation of the two forms are otherwise identical. Each subscale consists of 12 statements rated on a 5-point Likert scale from *None* (scored 0) to *Much More* (scored 4). Administration is untimed, but 10 to 15 minutes is suggested to complete a single subscale, implying approximately an hour to complete an entire form. On both forms, the respondent is asked to provide supporting examples for any subscale with six or more responses of *Much More*. Responses are summed within each subscale, yielding raw scores of 0 to 48.

Raw scores may be interpreted with reference to two sets of national norms, one based on general education students and the other based on students identified as gifted by their local schools. Conversion tables, divided by age (5–13 or 14–18 years), yield percentile ranks as well as standard scores on a typical IQ scale ($M = 100$, $SD = 15$). A summary sheet allows the user to examine scores from home and school simultaneously.

DEVELOPMENT. SIGS subscales follow the categories of giftedness in two recent federal definitions, with the exception that artistic giftedness is present in both federal definitions but is not assessed by the SIGS. The authors developed a list of characteristics for each subscale area based on a review of relevant literature, other rating scales, and content-area standards. These lists of characteristics then were revised based on content reviews conducted by professionals in gifted education; the number of experts who provided this feedback and how they were chosen is not stated. Based on the revised lists of characteristics, the authors developed 125 items for the initial version of the SIGS.

This initial version was administered to General and Gifted norm groups representative of the school-age U.S. population with regard to ethnicity, race, and geographic region. Each subscale was reduced to 12 items based on differential item functioning results and/or item discrimination coefficients below .40. It appears that results from the initial administration were reused to develop standard scores and percentile ranks for the revised 84-item form.

TECHNICAL.

Standardization. The authors present minimal demographic data for the norming sample; for example, race is presented simply as White, African American, or Other. On the School Rating Scale (SRS), only 20 of the 921 students in the General norm sample were categorized as "other," suggesting the SIGS standardization may have limited applicability to diverse populations. In the Gifted norm sample, only 50 of 1,055 students (4.7%) described their ethnicity as "other" on the school rating scale (SRS). Given the generally high rates of gifted program participation by some Asian student populations, and the much lower participation by students from other nonmainstream backgrounds, the omission of this information is perplexing.

Hispanic versus non-Hispanic participation is expressed in a separate table. Based on the data provided, it does not appear to be possible to determine whether these individuals were representative of the U.S. Hispanic population in terms of either current geographic locale or country of origin. The publisher has indicated that the Spanish-language translation provided in an appendix is suitable for use with Mexican-American students, although no supporting information is provided in the test manual.

Standard scores for the general norm sample were derived using polynomial regression. Due to the skew of gifted sample results, the authors calculated standard scores for this group using a linear transformation rather than one based on the normal distribution. These standardization methods appear to be appropriate choices. Gifted norms are useful primarily to minimize ceiling effects, as when contemplating accelerated educational placement for learners whose scores fall in the top few percentile ranks according to General norms.

Reliability. Reported internal consistency reliability for the SIGS is high. All scale coefficients are at or above .85 and they average above .90. Test-retest reliability studies used a 2-week interval and small samples of 37 to 61 individuals. Coefficients ranged from .58 (Social Studies) to .77 (General Intellectual Ability) for elementary and middle school students, and ranged from .68 (Science) to .93 (Social Studies) for high school students. For reasons that are unclear, the Social Studies subscale varied from least to most reliable across age groups.

No test-retest reliability was presented for the Mathematics subscale of the School Rating Scale (SRS), although a coefficient of .74 is reported for this area on the Home Rating Scale (HRS). The HRS test-retest reliability coefficients ranged from .66 (leadership) to .93 (Science and Social Studies). The two test-retest studies for the SRS and one study for the HRS were all based on a 2-week retest interval.

Interrater reliability between the Home and School scales was compared in two studies with large sample sizes of (respectively) 676 gifted students and 639 students not so identified. In the first study, correlations between parent and teacher ratings ranged from .43 to .53. Correlations in the second study ranged from .49 to .60. Because items on the two forms are identical, these relatively low correlations may reflect differences between teacher and parent perceptions. No comparisons were made within parents or within teachers, so it is difficult to judge whether the SRS/HRS differences are due to observing students in different contexts or to other causes. It would be interesting to know whether the gender of the parent filling out the form had any influence on these results.

Validity. The SIGS manual offers evidence of convergent, discriminant, item functioning, and predictive validity. Results from the SRS were correlated with measures of ability or aptitude including the Wechsler Intelligence Scale for Children, Third Edition (WISC-III), the Test of Cognitive Skills, Second Edition (TCS-2), the Cognitive Abilities Test (CogAT), the Otis-Lennon School Ability Test (OLSAT), and the Torrance Tests of Creative Thinking-Figural (TTCT-Figural). Sample sizes for these comparisons were quite small, ranging from 23 to 53, and no more than 5 African American and 8 Hispanic students were involved. Similar rates and results are reported for the HRS. These comparisons were based on students from the Gifted norm sample, using standard scores calculated from the General norms tables. This analysis appears unusual, but is probably an appropriate decision because there are no "gifted" norms for the comparison measures.

Correlations for General Intellectual Ability, a core attribute of most definitions of giftedness, ranged from .48 to .73 for the HRS and from .51 to .59 for the SRS. SIGS Creativity subscales correlated with the TTCT-Figural in the .60s for both SRS and HRS forms.

Some SIGS subscales differed in expected directions from other subscales; for example, the Science subscale has little relationship to Creativity as measured by the TTCT-Figural. Other differences were less clear; the SIGS SRS in Mathematics is less strongly correlated with the OLSAT School Ability Index (.38) than is the Creativity subscale of the SIGS SRS (.47). These relationships might arise from variations in the gifted identification criteria used in different states. For example, some states routinely assess creativity but others do not. Because the two SIGS norm groups are not disaggregated by state, it is not possible to determine the origin of these differences.

Differential item functioning analysis was carried out on the initial 125-item norming version of the SIGS. It is unclear whether this analysis was based on results from the Gifted group, the General group, or both groups combined. It is also unclear whether this process was carried out separately for Home and School scales, which one might expect to have led to the retention of different items for the two scales. Comparisons and items rejected through DIF analysis included African Americans versus non-African Americans (8 items), Hispanics versus non-Hispanics (6 items), and males versus females (21 items).

The authors of the manual present data that successfully support the predictive validity of the SIGS. A comparison of scores of gifted students (based on the General norms) with scores of students in the General group found differences larger than one standard deviation, in the expected direction, in all areas for both the Home and School scales of the SIGS.

COMMENTARY. The Scales for Identifying Gifted Students appears to be suitable for identifying gifted potential among white or African American students, and it may also be appropriate for use with students from other backgrounds. Specifically, how the measure performs with Asian, Native American, or gifted learners with specific learning disabilities remains unknown.

Due to the limited description provided, users also would be advised to proceed with caution in assessing Hispanic students with the SIGS.

Statistical evaluations supporting the SIGS have been selected thoughtfully, but are not always presented in sufficient detail to support fully the authors' conclusions. The suitability of the SIGS for monitoring student progress, or as a component of research studies with gifted learners, is also unclear based on the evidence its authors have presented. Using results obtained from the 125-item version to establish norms for the 84-item form seems questionable, as does the untested Spanish-language translation provided in an appendix. The uncritical application of direct translations is problematic for several reasons, not least of which is the likelihood of mischaracterizing students' abilities. Although the authors' intent in providing it is commendable, the Spanish translation merits its own independent development and evaluation process.

SUMMARY. Individuals in gifted education hold high hopes for this measure but will likely be disappointed by the lack of detail provided to support its use. There is little evidence that the SIGS would be in appropriate for identifying at least some gifted learners; however, there is not sufficient evidence to recommend unconditionally its use with school populations that are becoming increasingly diverse. Presenting exactly the same items for School and Home rating scales is problematic, because it suggests the possibility of inconsistencies in the standardization process. Because several alternatives are available, the user should carefully consider measures such as the Gifted Rating Scales (Pfeiffer & Jarosewich, 2003; 16:95), the Gifted Evaluation Scale—Second Edition (McCarney & Anderson, 1989; 14:156); and the widely used Scales for Rating the Behavioral Characteristics of Superior Students—Revised (Renzulli et al., 2002) before determining to use the SIGS.

REVIEWER'S REFERENCES

McCarney, S. B., & Anderson, P. D. (1989). *Gifted Evaluation Scale, Second Edition, technical manual.* Columbia, MO: Hawthorne Educational Services.

Pfeiffer, S. I., & Jarosewich, T. (2003). Gifted Rating Scales. San Antonio, TX: The Psychological Corporation.

Renzulli, J. S., Smith, L. H., White, A. J., Callahan, C. M., Hartman, R. K., Westberg, K. L., et al. (2002/1976). Scales for Rating the Behavioral Characteristics of Superior Students (rev. ed.). Mansfield Center, CT: Creative Learning Press.

Review of the Scales for Identifying Gifted Students by SANDRA WARD, Professor of Education, The College of William and Mary, Williamsburg, VA:

DESCRIPTION. The Scales for Identifying Gifted Students (SIGS) is a norm-referenced rating scale developed to help practitioners identify gifted students between the ages of 5—18 years. The authors assert that the SIGS also can be used to monitor the progress of gifted students and for research.

The SIGS includes a School Rating Scale (SRS) and a Home Rating Scale (HRS). Both rating scales assess talent in seven areas, including General Intellectual Ability, Language Arts, Mathematics, Science, Social Studies, Creativity, and Leadership. For each area there are 12 Likert-scale items that the respondents rate from 0 (*never exhibits behavior in comparison to his/her age peers*) to 4 (*exhibits the behavior much more in comparison to his/her age peers*). Thus, one might conclude that the respondent needs to know the typical occurrence of these behaviors in the population. The SRS should be completed by a teacher or other professional who has had daily contact with the student for at least 6 weeks. Teachers should complete the SRS for the academic subjects that they teach. The HRS is completed by parents, guardians, and/or caregivers. The technical manual includes a Spanish version of the HRS in the appendix.

The authors provide specific instructions for administration of the SIGS in the technical manual. These directions also can be found on the rating scales. The instructions are straightforward and easy to follow. The authors provide a definition for each numerical rating on the HRS and SRS to guide respondents. The scoring procedures for the SIGS are uncomplicated and well explained. The examiner sums the ratings in each domain for a specific scale. The sum of the columns is the raw score for that scale. The authors also provide directions for scoring scales when one or two items are not completed. The raw score for each scale is converted to a standard score (mean of 100, standard deviation of 15) and a percentile rank, using tables in the appendix of the manual. Standard scores and percentile ranks can be determined based on a General norm sample or a Gifted norm sample. For identification purposes, the authors recommend use of the General norm sample. The authors caution against using the SIGS as a sole criterion for identifying giftedness. The Summary Form of the SIGS provides space for the inclusion of additional data from other sources.

DEVELOPMENT. The authors of the SIGS cite the Improving America's Schools Act of 1994 (P.L. 103-382) and National Excellence: A Case for Developing America's Talent (USDOE, 1993) as sources for their definitions of gifted and talented. However, it remains unclear how they discerned these seven areas of talent included in the measure.

Initial lists of characteristics for each of the seven areas were derived from a literature review, standards of educational organizations, and other gifted rating scales. These lists were reviewed by experts in the field, and the lists were refined based on the feedback. The authors do not provide any information on the number or qualifications of the experts or the level of agreement necessary for an item to be maintained. The norming version of the SIGS included 18 items per scale, except for the Leadership area, which included 17 items.

A positive aspect of the scale's development was the use of differential item functioning. In the analyses, the authors examined item discrimination characteristics, and they deleted items with discriminant coefficients less than .40. However, only three categories of race were tested. More comprehensive analyses would have included other demographic factors such as socioeconomic status. The final version of the SIGS included 12 items per scale.

TECHNICAL. The SIGS was standardized based on data collected between spring of 2002 and spring of 2003. Data were collected on two samples of students: (a) a General norm sample, including students in general education classrooms; and (b) a Gifted norm sample, including students identified as gifted by their school districts. The General norm sample included 921 students for the SRS and 774 students for the HRS with a 75% overlap between the two samples. The Gifted norm sample included 1,055 students for the SRS and 811 students for the HRS with a 72% overlap between the two samples. Both the HRS and SRS samples were stratified within 3 age bands (5—9 years, 10—13 years, and 14—18 years). The samples were stratified to match the 2001 U.S. Census for geographic region, gender, ethnicity, and race. Although the authors contend that both the General and Gifted norm samples are representative of the U.S. population, they do not provide any Census or other data for comparison purposes.

The internal consistency reliability coefficients reported in the manual are sufficient for the intended purpose of the SIGS. The average coefficient alphas were equal to or greater than .90 for each scale across both norm samples. In the few cases where the internal consistency reliability coefficients dropped below .90 for individual scales or age groups, the values were still equal to or greater than .85.

Test-retest reliability for the HRS of the SIGS was computed on 37 gifted students ages 5 through 18 with a 2-week test-retest interval. The correlations ranged from .66 (Leadership scale) to .93 (Science and Social Studies scales). Test-retest reliability of the SRS of the SIGS was computed based on two samples of gifted students with a 2-week test-retest interval. The first sample included 61 elementary and middle school students, and the second sample included 46 high school students. The correlations for the elementary and middle school sample ranged from .61 (Science scale) to .77 (General Intellectual Ability scale). The correlations for the high school sample ranged from .68 (Science scale) to .92 (Leadership scale). The low test-retest coefficients raise some concerns about the consistency across teachers' and parents' ratings of the same student over time. Furthermore, test-retest reliability coefficients were computed on small samples of gifted students. The authors provide no evidence of the stability of the SIGS for the General norm group or over a longer time period.

Interrater reliability of the SIGS was computed on two samples. The first sample included 676 gifted students between the ages of 5 and 18. The second sample included 639 students who were not identified as gifted. The correlations between teacher and parent ratings for the gifted sample ranged from .43 (General Intellectual Ability scale) to .53 (Mathematics scale). The correlations between teacher and parent ratings for the nongifted sample ranged from .49 (Language Arts and Creativity scales) to .60 (Social Studies scale). These correlations fall in the moderate range, but they do indicate a large degree of variability in teacher and parent ratings of the same student. The authors should have compared mean ratings of parents and teachers as another indicator of agreement.

The authors provide evidence to support the convergent validity of the SIGS; however, all of their studies were completed with the Gifted norm sample. Consequently, the validity of the SIGS for the General norm sample remains unknown. The individual scales of the SIGS, SRS, and HRS were correlated with accepted standard measures of ability and creativity. The validity studies indicated that the scales of the SIGS SRS correlated significantly with the instruments in these domains. In most instances the appropriate scales of the SIGS correlated highest with the instrument being used as the criterion. The authors also report moderate to large correlations among the scales of the HRS and SRS. These results provide evidence of convergent validity, but they call into question the separateness of the individual scales of the SIGS.

The authors provide results of a group differentiation study to support the use of the SIGS to discriminate between gifted and nongifted students. A comparison of scores on each scale of the General norm group with the Gifted norm group indicated that the Gifted norm group scored more than one standard deviation higher than the General norm group. A difference of one standard deviation indicates that the SIGS is differentiating between the groups. The authors computed a series of t-tests with a suppressed alpha at .003 to control for error with many comparisons. A multivariate test could have been used to better control error. Additionally, Table 3.23 (p. 33 of the manual) that reports the results of this study is incorrect. The values listed under Mean, Gifted Norm Sample are actually the standard deviations of the General norm sample, and the values listed under Standard Deviations, General Norm Sample are actually the means of the Gifted norm sample.

COMMENTARY. The SIGS is a user-friendly rating scale that can be completed by teachers and parents to assist in the identification of students 5–18 years old who qualify for gifted services. The SIGS is easy to administer, score, and interpret. The examiner can use the Summary Form to synthesize data collected from the SIGS as well as other sources. Although the authors emphasize diverse areas of giftedness and include seven areas of talent in the scale, they do not provide a strong theoretical model or rationale for these seven areas of talent. The SIGS is standardized on both a General norm sample and a Gifted norm sample. For identification purposes, the General norm sample should be used to compute scores. Both norm samples are large and stratified on relevant dimensions. Although the authors claim representativeness to the 2001 U.S. Census data, these data are not provided in the manual. The internal consistency reliability of the instrument is robust. However, lower test-retest reliabilities and interrater reliabilities indicate variability in ratings across time and raters. The authors provide adequate evidence for convergent validity of the SIGS for the Gifted norm group only. The results of similar validity studies with the General norm sample should be reported. The authors provide evidence that the SIGS differentiated between gifted and nongifted samples; however, it remains unclear whether the seven scales of the SIGS are sensitive enough to monitor changes in a student's progress as the authors claim. A factor analysis confirming the existence of seven separate scales (areas of talent) would strengthen the instrument's validity. The high correlations among the seven areas do not support the separateness of the scales. Thus, caution is warranted in their individual interpretation.

SUMMARY. Based on the data provided on the technical adequacy of the SIGS, users should use the instrument cautiously for the identification of gifted students. At best, the SIGS should be used as a screening instrument as part of a comprehensive battery of assessment techniques. The reviewer was unable to ascertain the representativeness of the norm sample. Although internal consistency reliability is strong, test-retest and interrater reliabilities are weaker. Evidence for convergent validity is provided for only the Gifted norm sample. Additionally, more evidence is needed for the separate scale scores. Data presented in the manual suggest a considerable overlap among the seven scales. A confirmatory factor analysis to support the existence of separate scales is recommended.

[170]

Self-Appraisal Questionnaire.

Purpose: "Multi-dimensional self-administered questionnaire designed to predict violent and non-violent offender recidivism among correctional/forensic populations and to assist with the assignment of these populations to appropriate treatment/correctional programs and different institutional security levels."
Population: Male offenders, age 18 and older.
Publication Date: 2005.
Acronym: SAQ.
Scores, 8: Criminal Tendencies, Antisocial Personality Problems, Conduct Problems, Criminal History, Alcohol/Drug Abuse, Antisocial Associates, Anger, Total.
Administration: Individual or group.
Price Data, 2006: $75 per complete kit including technical manual (80 pages) and 25 QuikScore forms; $52 per technical manual; $38 per 25 QuikScore forms.
Time: (10–15) minutes.
Comments: Can be administered verbally.
Author: Wagdy Loza.
Publisher: Multi-Health Systems Inc.

Review of the Self-Appraisal Questionnaire by PHILLIP L. ACKERMAN, Professor of Psychology, Georgia Institute of Technology, Atlanta, GA:

DESCRIPTION. The Self-Appraisal Questionnaire (SAQ) is a 72-item self-report measure, administered with paper and pencil in either individual or group settings. The questionnaire is designed to assess risks and needs of incarcerated male adults aged 18 or older. The questionnaire is self-paced and can be completed in about 15 minutes. The individual selects "true" or "false" for each statement. The test is hand-scored, with a carbonless copy second sheet, which indicates the scale for each item. Seven subscale scores are obtained, including "Criminal Tendencies, Antisocial Personality Problems, Conduct Problems, Criminal History, Alcohol/Drug Abuse, Antisocial Associates, and Anger" (technical manual, p. x). A total score is also computed, based on all but the Anger subscale. Several items can be compared against existing case records to determine the validity of the individual's responses (i.e., questions relating to the offender's criminal history can be checked against the criminal record for that individual). The SAQ is intended to be used in support of a variety of case management applications (e.g., evaluation of risk for recidivism, security placement decisions, diagnoses of psychiatric conditions, decision making regarding mental health treatments). In addition, the manual indicates that the "SAQ can be used as a pre- and post-treatment" assessment measure" (technical manual, p. 2).

DEVELOPMENT. The SAQ was developed with consideration of both theoretical and empirical perspectives. The general theoretical principle behind the measure is to assess several key constructs that have been established as correlates of recidivism, with additional attention to those constructs that appear to be amenable to change. An initial pool of items were developed from the theoretical approach, which were then subjected to evaluation by subject-matter experts (SMEs). Item tryouts were used to further refine the measure based on additional SME evaluations. Items were retained if they showed high item-subscale correlations, reasonable base rates (i.e., between .15 and .85 probability of responding), and 75% agreement among the SME about subscale classification.

TECHNICAL.

Norms. Extensive norms are provided for American (N = 3,703) and Canadian (N = 938) samples. Details are presented on age, sentence length, and ethnic background for each sample, as are means, standard deviations, and frequency distributions for each subscale and total scores for the norming groups. Percentile rank conversion tables for each scale are also presented for both American and Canadian norming groups. Although references are provided for recent studies of female samples, the manual does not provide any norming information for this population.

Reliability/validity. Extensive reliability and validity data are presented in the manual. Coefficient alphas (which represent an amalgamation of item homogeneity and reliability information) indicate that the individual scales vary from highly heterogeneous scales (alpha = .31 for Antisocial Associates) to relatively homogeneous scales (alpha = .80 for Criminal Tendencies). The individual scales are not highly correlated with one another, indicating relatively good differentiation. No factor analysis of the scales is presented, but the apparent positive manifold among the scales (i.e., they are all positively correlated with one another) and alpha coefficient of around .90 for total score is consistent with the sense that a general factor is dominant in the overall questionnaire. Test-retest reliability after 1 week is reported for two small samples (N < 40), with generally high values.

Validity information is manifold and thorough. The manual reports on several efforts to assure "face validity" (p. 43), which is important for this particular instrument, because the SAQ is intended to be transparent to the individual completing the questionnaire. Construct validity is supported by subscale correlations with extant measures of antisocial attitudes related to criminal behavior, psychopathy, and risk/need factors. The manual provides indications of both convergent and discriminant validity across several extant

measures, and it provides breakdowns of high and low scorers for different criterion groups (e.g., those with low or high number of prior convictions, and those separated into nonviolent and violent groups). Case study illustrations are also provided. Predictive validity information is provided for 2-year and 5-year studies—both correlations and base rate information are presented in the manual. Moreover, very detailed information is presented about validity (in terms of recidivism predictions) in the context of receiver operating characteristics (ROC) functions, risk ratios, and relative improvement over chance—critical components for the assessment of the utility of the measure for the application of predicting risk for this population. Although the norming samples have adequate representation of majority and minority groups, there is no information about differential validity for the different groups, except for citations to two studies and a statement that the SAQ is "robust to ethnic diversity" (technical manual, p. 34).

COMMENTARY. The manual provides an exemplary degree of detail and supporting evidence regarding the development, norms, and technical quality of the SAQ, especially in light of the fact that this is a recently developed instrument. The documentation and supporting empirical evidence presented, along with a sensitivity to issues of application, such as base rates and relative improvement over chance, represent valuable components of the overall package. These are so often ignored in other test manuals. The evidence provided by the publisher indicates that this instrument may be a highly valuable tool to be used in conjunction with other information for several interrelated decisions (e.g., placement of convicted adult males and treatment decisions/plans). The manual does not overstate the utility of the measure, but places the critical information for easy access in the manual in a highly readable fashion. There is only one salient shortcoming in the manual, and that pertains to the suggested use of the instrument for pre-/posttreatment assessments. The manual indicates that roughly half of the items are "dynamic in nature, and thereby permit the assessment of change" (technical manual, p. x). However, there was no information presented that supported this particular claim, nor were there any empirical data associated with changes due to treatment effects. It was not even clear which scales are dynamic and which are likely to be stable over the course of treatment or long time intervals. It would be critical to have validation data (both construct and criterion) that distinguish between stable and dynamic components of the measure, before the use of the instrument for pre-/post-treatment evaluations could be supported.

SUMMARY. The SAQ represents an integration of several different indicators of risk/needs for a population of incarcerated adult males. By designing the assessment so that the incarcerated individuals complete it themselves, the instrument avoids problems inherent in subjective clinical judgments (e.g., see Meehl, 1954; Meehl & Rosen, 1955). The supporting reliability and validity information provided in the manual suggests that the measure has good psychometric properties for risk prediction purposes. The dynamic components of the SAQ are not yet well articulated or validated, nor are there normative data for female adult samples. Overall, the instrument appears to represent a valuable integrated assessment of several risk predictors in a convenient package for quick administration and interpretation.

REVIEWER'S REFERENCES

Meehl, P. E. (1954). *Clinical vs. statistical prediction: A theoretical analysis and a review of the evidence.* Minneapolis: University of Minnesota Press.
Meehl, P. E., & Rosen, A. (1955). Antecedent probability and the efficiency of psychometric signs, patterns, or cutting scores. *Psychological Bulletin, 52,* 194-216.

Review of the Self-Appraisal Questionnaire by RITA BUDRIONIS, *Licensed Clinical Psychologist, Licensed Sex Offender Treatment Provider, Director Dominion Sex Offenders Program, Associate Professor at Old Dominion University in Norfolk, VA:*

DESCRIPTION. The Self-Appraisal Questionnaire (SAQ) is a self-report actuarial instrument designed to assist in identifying offenders within correctional and forensic populations who are at risk for violent and nonviolent recidivism. The SAQ is also intended to serve as a treatment guide addressing dynamic factors along with stable factors, identifying and targeting treatment needs, projecting level of institutional security needed for the offender, and also in research as a pre- and posttreatment measure. This instrument is a 72-item self-report assessment procedure that requires a fifth grade reading level. It consists of 6 subscales that measure criminogenic/risk need areas along with an anger scale. It is intended for use by correctional personnel, mental health professionals, and case management personnel. The author recommends that interpretation be done by a

psychologist or another mental health specialist trained in forensic assessment. Age range is 18 years and older.

Directions for administering the test are clearly written and generally easy to follow. Estimated time for completion of this procedure is approximately 15 minutes. Clerical staff can score the SAQ with minimal training. Scoring takes less than 5 minutes. Scale scores are calculated by hand or calculator. Seven subscale scores result along with a total score. If literacy is an issue, the SAQ can be administered orally. The subscales are: Criminal Tendencies, Antisocial Personality Problems, Conduct Problems, Criminal History, Alcohol/Drug Abuse, Antisocial Associates, and Anger. The Anger scale is not included in the total score and there are several validity items (no formal scale).

DEVELOPMENT. The SAQ was developed to predict release outcome for offenders in the form of a self-report measure. Other measures are available for recidivism prediction; however, these tend to be more costly with clinician time such as the Psychopathy Checklist—Revised, Violence Risk Appraisal Guide, and Level of Service Inventory—Revised.

The underlying premise of the SAQ is that there are certain factors that are associated to recidivism of criminal behavior similar across cultures and populations and that some of these factors are amenable to change. The SAQ was initially developed by choosing constructs, such as conduct problems, which through research had been associated with recidivism. After consultation with correctional psychologists and staff, and development of an item pool, offenders were administered the experimental items. Items that showed strong correlation with their subscales were retained. After item selection was completed, correctional psychologists and a case manager assisted in selecting the final items that resulted in six scales used for prediction and an Anger scale to address anger management needs.

TECHNICAL. Overall studies done by the test author and his colleagues have found that the SAQ has shown generally good reliability and validity. In the original Canadian normative sample, there were high levels of test-retest reliability ranging from a reliability coefficient of .95 for Total SAQ score and .69 to .95 for the six recidivism subscales (time interval of 1 week). Internal consistency of the subscales as measured by the unweighted mean coefficient alphas ranged from .77 to .53 of the recidivism subscales. This later study involved over 4,000 offenders in five countries and was supportive of the original Canadian sample. The research has also generally been supportive of the unidimensionality of the subscales other than the Criminal Tendencies subscale, which appeared to be composed of three factors. There were no data addressing the effect of reading the SAQ aloud to respondents and how this modality may influence responses, nor how many of the respondents have had the test read to them.

In addition, the manual describes four levels of risk for each subscale developed "from follow-up studies over 2- and 5-year periods and clinical experience" (technical manual, p. 15). In the Interpretation section of the manual, recommendations of "no treatment necessary" for low individual subscale scores such as "Antisocial Associates" are based on this vaguely defined foundation. There are few or no research data to support these recommendations.

The drawbacks of these scale demarcations include a lack of empirically based cutoff scores. Low, Low-Moderate, High-Moderate, or High-Risk determination appears to be based on the author's discretion and clinical acumen.

COMMENTARY. The SAQ has several advantages over a number of other actuarial forensic recidivism instruments. It is easy and quick to administer, taking only 15 minutes. Clerical staff with little special training can quickly and easily administer it. It can be administered in a group or individual setting.

One of the most significant concerns regarding this instrument is the paucity of studies replicating these results with researchers who are independent of the test developer. The only published independent study (Mitchell & MacKenzie, 2006) found inadequate levels of internal consistency within the SAQ subscales as well as with scale multidimensionality. In addition, neither the subscales nor the total SAQ score predicted recidivism. The sample used in this study differed, however, from the prior populations used by evaluating minority, inner-city drug dealers. In the Canadian developmental sample, SAQ scores were strongly correlated with 2-year recidivism ($r = .59$) and moderately correlated with 1-year recidivism rates for Singapore females ($r = .24$). This discrepancy could be due to factors such as respondent deception, sample variability attenuation, or individual sample characteristics; however, these contrasting results question how well the SAQ will generalize in high-risk and other samples.

SUMMARY. In summary, the SAQ is a promising tool for assisting with assessment of recidivism risk with a research-based foundation, clear instructions, and applicability in a wide variety of forensic and clinical situations. This tool has the potential for encouraging research data in a number of venues; however, generalizability to other samples is a concern along with the lack of independent studies replicating the test developer's results.

REVIEWER'S REFERENCE

Mitchell, O., & MacKenzie, D. L. (2006). Disconfirmation of the predictive validity of the Self-Appraisal Questionnaire in a sample of high-risk drug offenders. *Criminal Justice and Behavior, 33*, 449–466.

[171]

Service Ability Inventory.

Purpose: Designed "to select job applicants who have a service orientation … to determine the service skill levels of current employees."

Population: Current and prospective employees.

Publication Dates: 1999–2004.

Acronym: S.A.I.

Scores, 7: Service Orientation, Interpersonal Skills, Tolerance for Stress, Team Skills, Patience, Coping Skills, Deception Scale.

Administration: Individual or group.

Price Data, 2005: $79.99 per starter kit including 5 tests, administrator's manual (2004, 32 pages), and 1 test log.

Time: (20–25) minutes.

Comments: Online and paper-and-pencil versions of test are available; online version includes interpretive reports and follow-up interview questions.

Author: J. M. Llobet.

Publisher: G. Neil.

Review of the Service Ability Inventory by MICHAEL B. BUNCH, Senior Vice President, Measurement Incorporated, Durham, NC:

DESCRIPTION AND DEVELOPMENT.

General. The Service Ability Inventory (S.A.I.), developed by J. M. Llobet, consists of a set of test forms and an administrator's manual. The test itself is composed of 35 statements on a specially printed, self-scoring form. Five of the 35 statements form a Deception Scale, whereas the other 30 constitute the main body of the Service Ability Inventory. Each statement, purported to have no right or wrong answers, is scored on a 1–4 scale to yield a score ranging from 30 to 120. The total test can be administered in about 20 minutes.

The S.A.I. scale. The 30 items making up the S.A.I. scale are generally face valid and straightforward. I administered the test to a senior manager of a national retail chain, and she found the statements both relevant and difficult to fake. The scenarios in the statements are realistic and easy to understand.

The Deception Scale. The five items making up the Deception Scale are a bit more difficult to connect to the underlying scale. The manual offers little explanation for the selection of these five particular items, and their content is general enough that they might well be taken from a generic deception scale from any personality test. In the end, it may be that scores on the Deception Scale are irrelevant, as suggested in the manual.

TECHNICAL. The 30-page manual tells how to administer and interpret results of the S.A.I. It provides background information and a rationale for the creation of the inventory. It also contains norms for S.A.I. scores and a general guideline for interpreting Deception Scale scores. Reliability coefficients are reported, as are seven validity studies. Both internal consistency (.67) and test-retest (.71) coefficients are reported. The validity studies include factor analyses, correlations with criterion variables (such as supervisor ratings), correlations with KSAs (knowledge, skills, and abilities), and comparisons of scores of incumbents at various levels of service. The manual also describes an adverse-impact study involving Caucasian, Black, and Hispanic examinees (negligible differences in scores).

COMMENTARY. The publisher (G. Neil) has assembled a reasonably effective and efficient screening tool to assess the service orientation of job applicants. The inventory itself is easy to use, short, and face valid. The manual is generally effective in providing useful information about the inventory, although in some instances, some information is missing or overstated. For example, I would consider an internal consistency coefficient of .67 or a test-retest coefficient of .71 insufficiently high for individual decisions. Such coefficients would be useful only if there were several times as many applicants as there were jobs.

The publisher also refers to "validity coefficients" in all the validity tables, when "correlation" or "correlation coefficient" would have been more

accurate. In each instance, the significance level of the coefficient is reported, and it is always less than .05, and generally less than .01, even when the correlation itself is only .2 or .3 (indeed, the highest correlation reported is .67, for S.A.I. scores vs. employer ratings of service orientation for a sample of 10 manufacturing/sales safety equipment employees). In reality, even the highest reported correlation explains less than half the variance in scores or ratings. The lowest correlation between S.A.I. scores and employer ratings was .35 (for real estate services), or a shared variance of only 12.25%. Sales performance showed even less overlap: a correlation of .31, to which the publisher adds "(p<.001)," even though inventory scores account for only 9.61% of the variation in sales. The p values seem impressive; other interpretations, though perhaps more appropriate, seem less so.

Perhaps the most important component of the manual is the norms table. Although scores hypothetically range from 30 to 120, scores of 76 or less are all assigned a percentile rank of 1, and scores above 105 are assigned a percentile rank of 100, making the effective score range of the inventory about 30 points wide. The norming sample ($N = 742$) yielded a mean of 92 with a standard deviation of 5.73, which would put 95% of the scores between 81 and 103 (which the norms table verifies). That would seem to leave a lot of the score points unused and discrimination even within the effective range somewhat awkward. An even shorter version of the inventory might be created from just those items that do discriminate, or the nondiscriminating items might be replaced by more discriminating items (which could easily have a positive impact on both the internal consistency and test-retest reliability of the test).

The one graphic representation of validity study data (p. 11 of the manual, no figure number) greatly magnifies small differences among criterion groups by eliminating most of the score range. Potential users who are aware of this misuse of statistics will ignore the graph and turn instead to the data, presented over the next few pages. Those who are not aware of the misuse may be misled.

SUMMARY. In spite of some of the technical deficiencies of the reliability and validity studies cited in the manual, I would recommend the S.A.I. under two conditions. First, the selection ratio should be highly favorable to the employer (at least twice as many applicants as available positions). The items have a high degree of face validity, and when the number of applicants is large, relative to the number of positions available, the test should help identify the top half or third of candidates. With a less favorable selection ratio, the effective score range is too narrow, and the inventory would likely be unable to make the fine distinctions in the region of the cut and would not be cost effective. Second, I would recommend that each employer who chooses to use this instrument conduct his or her own validity study, as the publisher suggests. The validity studies cited in the manual offer good suggestions regarding criterion variables that each employer might use.

The real value of the inventory may be its use as an icebreaker, providing the interviewer with something concrete with which to begin the interview (assuming the examinee has gotten this far). The manual recommends asking examinees why they responded as they did to certain statements in the inventory, which is indeed a good strategy, not only for the insights into the individual candidate but for the standardizing effect this practice may have on a set of interviews.

To improve the utility of the S.A.I. for future users, I would recommend that the publisher seek a different balance between sales pitch and technical rigor in the manual. This means a more open interpretation of correlation coefficients (i.e., percent shared variance rather than significance test results, which are largely a function of sample size and can easily make an essentially nonexistent relationship appear to be compelling, and abandoning the term "validity coefficient") as well as a bit more modesty with respect to bar graphs. The test has potential; it deserves a manual that illustrates its good qualities without overselling them.

Review of the Service Ability Inventory by DENICE WARD HOOD, Associate Professor of Educational Psychology, Northern Arizona University, Flagstaff, AZ:

DESCRIPTION. The Service Ability Inventory (S.A.I.) is an untimed, self-administered inventory consisting of 35 service-related situations or statements followed by multiple-choice response options. The inventory includes a 5-item "deception scale" to identify examinees attempting to "fake good" by providing socially desirable re-

sponses. The S.A.I. measures personality tendencies related to service-related employment and can be used to assess both employees and job applicants. The service-related situations were derived from job analyses of service-oriented jobs, as well as interviews with individuals who had experienced one or more (positive or negative) service situations. The examinee reads each situation or statement and selects the answer or action that would be *most typical* of her or him. The test developers estimate that the test will take approximately 20–25 minutes to complete. The section score is calculated by adding up all the point values. Unanswered items are scored as 1 point. The higher the scale score, the more service-oriented the individual is likely to be. Scores can range from 106+ to below 76. Norms are provided rather than cutoffs (pass/fail). Limitations in the areas of service skills or customer service orientation are indicated by a low scale score. The inverse is indicated by a high scale score. The S.A.I. is available in paper and online versions. The paper version (Version 2000) was utilized for this review. The S.A.I. (paper version) is a two-part form that makes a copy of the examinee's responses. The "carbon" form includes the scoring guide for the test administrator.

DEVELOPMENT. The S.A.I. was developed in 1992 to assist organizations in identifying individuals who have a strong service orientation. The administrator's manual provides minimal information related to the development of the S.A.I. The development process described indicated that the 35 situations were "derived from job analyses of service-oriented jobs, as well as interviews with individuals who had experienced one or more memorable (positive or negative) service situations" (administrator's manual, p. 6). The inventory was developed to identify applicants who demonstrate the skills needed for exceptional customer service, including a willingness to help others, an ability to work well within a team, and the ability to perform consistently under pressure. Service Orientation is defined as "the individual has good interpersonal skills, is a team player, has a helping disposition, is patient and can handle stressful situations" (administrator's manual, p. 11). The test publisher's website states that the S.A.I. measures the following: Service Orientation, Interpersonal Skills, Tolerance for Stress, Team Skills, Patience, Coping Skills, and includes the Deception Scale. It is unclear how these factors converge to form this construct.

The S.A.I. was revised "to increase internal consistency" (administrator's manual, p. 25) although the manual does not contain information on which items were changed. The reported correlation for the original and revised S.A.I. was .63.

TECHNICAL. The S.A.I. consists of 11 items that describe situations for which the examinee is asked to select, from among four responses, behaviors that would be most typical for them. The other 24 items are statements for which the examinee indicates his or her level of agreement (*strongly agree* to *strongly disagree*). There were 742 employees who participated in the validity and norm studies but the norm sample was not described in the administrator's manual. No further discussion of the individuals who comprised this sample was provided; therefore, it is unknown the extent to which this sample matched the intended examinee population. There is no evidence to suggest that ethnicity, gender, or age were considered in the norm-setting process. The percentile score and its corresponding S.A.I. score (based on the norm sample) were included in the manual. The developer "strongly recommends" (administrator's manual, p. 15) that users "validate their own data" by creating company-specific norms, because an organization's applicant pool may differ from the norming sample. However, information on this norming sample was not provided. The manual presented the results of seven validity studies that utilized Concurrent Validation Methodology, which the author indicates is in compliance with the Uniform Guidelines of Employee Selection Procedures. This procedure entails administering the test to current employees while performance data are collected at the same time. The researchers then examine the relationship between the performance ratings and the test scores to determine the extent to which the inventory can predict performance. Validity is determined by the extent to which performance is positively correlated with the inventory. That is, individuals with high scores on the inventory would have high performance ratings and those with low scores would have low ratings.

The initial validity study involved 134 customer service representatives from four different types of companies in the business sector. Validity in this context would be inferences made on the extent to which the test predicts job performance related to service ability. A factor analysis of 17 job dimension ratings was conducted "to determine which dimensions would best define service orientation" (administrator's manual, p. 18) but the corresponding job dimensions are not provided in the manual. Based on the factor analysis, the 17 dimensions were distilled down to 4 dimensions that comprise the "service-orientation factor." Service Orientation is defined as the sum of these four job performance ratings.

The results of six additional validity studies were presented in the manual. These included (#2) correlations between the S.A.I. scores and service orientation for five companies (sample sizes ranged from 10 to 134); (#3) a telecommunications company ($n = 97$); (#4) 110 different sales representatives from the same company as #3; (#5) Knowledge, Skills, and Abilities (KSA) ratings of 110 business sales representatives. Three of the validity studies involved different sets of employees at a telecommunication company. Two validation studies were conducted with the revised S.A.I. Validity Study #6 repeated the same process as #1 but included the updated items administered to 90 customer service representatives. Study #7 involved 198 Customer Service Associates (CSAs) being administered the S.A.I. and performance data being collected.

The validity coefficients ranged from .35, $p < .002$ (real estate services) to .67, $p < .02$ (manufacturing/sales safety equipment) for the four companies in the initial study. The combined validity coefficient for the companies was .41, $p < .00$. For evidence of reliability, the developers offer the results of a test-retest analysis ($r = .71$, $p < .001$). No time interval was provided in the manual. An unspecified internal consistency analysis provided a reliability of .67.

To address the possibility of adverse impact on race, the average S.A.I. scores for Black, Hispanic, and White examinees were presented. "Independent t-tests demonstrated that there were no significant differences between the average scores" (administrator's manual, p. 30). Because these samples are only identified by race, it is not clear if these individuals represent the total number of all participants in the validation studies.

COMMENTARY. According to the Society for Industrial and Organizational Psychology (SIOP) "the essential principle in the evaluation of any selection procedure is that evidence be accumulated to support an inference of job relatedness." The S.A.I. administrator's manual indicates that test developers met these criteria providing multiple sources of evidence by demonstrating the relationship between S.A.I. scores and job performance. Information on the demographic representativeness of the sample was not provided. Validity Study #6 referred to the revision of the S.A.I. that was undertaken to increase internal consistency. Some items were updated but the manual does not identify which items.

The administrator's manual contains information instructing users to adhere to federal, state, and local laws regarding recordkeeping. Users are cautioned to conduct their own validation study if it is determined that adverse impact in the selection process has occurred.

SUMMARY. The Service Ability Inventory is a 35-item test that was developed to "identity individuals who have a strong service orientation" (administrator's manual, p. 5), which can be used with both job applicants and current employees. The S.A.I. can be utilized as part of the interview process as well as a method to follow up examinees' responses. Test users are encouraged to conduct their own validation studies creating their own norms and benchmarks. Employment and promotion decisions should not be based on a single test and should comply with all EEOC procedures to ensure that the inventory is being used and interpreted appropriately.

REVIEWER'S REFERENCE

Society for Industrial and Organizational Psychology, Inc. (No date). *Principles for the validation and use of personnel selection procedures* (4th Ed.). Retrieved March 25, 2006 from http://www.siop.org/bookspubs.htm

[172]
The Severe Impairment Battery.

Purpose: Designed "to assess severe dementia in the elderly."
Population: Ages 51–91.
Publication Date: 1993.
Acronym: SIB.
Scores, 7: Attention, Orientation, Language, Memory, Visual-Spatial Ability, Construction, Total.
Administration: Individual.
Price Data, 2007: £238.48 per complete kit including manual (16 pages), 25 scoring sheets, stimulus cards, plastic shapes, spoon, cup, and full distractor pack in bag; £60.51 per 25 score sheets.
Time: 20 minutes.
Comments: Test takes into account specific behavioral and cognitive deficits associated with severe dementia; provides an assessment of social interaction skills abstracted from the Communication Activities in Daily Living Scale (T7:635).
Authors: J. Saxton, K. L. McGonigle, A. A. Swihart, and F. Boller.
Publisher: Harcourt Assessment [England].

Review of the Severe Impairment Battery by BRAD M. MERKER, Neuropsychology Post-Doctoral Fellow, University of Oklahoma Health Sciences Center, Oklahoma City, OK, and JOHN LINCK, Neuropsychology Post-Doctoral Fellow, University of Oklahoma Health Sciences Center, Oklahoma City, OK:

DESCRIPTION. The Severe Impairment Battery (SIB) is a 40-item test, administered by paper and pencil, using an interview format. The test is designed to assess "a range of cognitive functioning in patients who are unable to complete standard neuropsychological tests" (manual, p. 4). The SIB samples a wide variety of low-level tasks that take into account the specific behavioral and cognitive deficits associated with severe dementia. The test items consist of simple single-step commands presented in association with gestural cues. For example, examinees are asked to "tell me all the things you like to eat" (Item 13) and "is that a hat or cup?" (Item 19). The test yields a total score and six major subscale scores. Examiners are provided with a total score ranging from 0–100 and subscale scores assessing the following functional domains: Attention, Orientation, Language, Memory, Visuospatial Ability, and Construction. In addition, scores are derived for brief evaluations of praxis, orienting to name, and social interaction skills. To facilitate interpretation, the authors recommend using a cutscore of less than 63 to classify examinees as "very severely impaired," which corresponds to an MMSE (Folstein, Folstein & McHugh, 1975) score in the range of 0–4. Total administration time is estimated to be 20 minutes.

DEVELOPMENT. The Severe Impairment Battery was initially developed as an experimental measure (Saxton et al., 1990) and is now in its third version. The second version's total score ranged from 0–133, whereas the most recent version's total score ranges from 0–100. The SIB was designed to have a lower floor than preexisting measures and to be used as a more in-depth measure of low-level functioning across commonly assessed cognitive domains in patients with severe dementia. Materials furnished by the developer (including a manual, test protocols, and test stimuli) provide little information on the development of any of the three versions of the SIB. The developers provide no rationale behind the selection of the cognitive domains included in the measure, no definitions of the scales, and no empirical or theoretical information regarding how items were created and selected for inclusion in each of the scales. Additionally, several items appear to belong on more than one scale. For instance, one item on the Memory subscale asks examiners to provide their name to the examinee, repeat their name again, and then immediately ask the examinee for their name. No rationale is offered in the manual about how these items fit together to measure the individual scale constructs or how the scales fit together to measure the overarching construct of dementia.

TECHNICAL. No normative information is presented in the manual. The developers recommend using a cutscore of less than 63 as a means of classifying individuals as "very severely impaired." Unfortunately, the developers fail to discuss their rationale or the methodology for determining this cutscore. Based on the research cited in the manual, it appears that this cutscore is the mean score of 28 patients administered the second version of the test and who have MMSE scores in the range of 0–4. As a result, test users are cautioned when interpreting scores from the third version of the test as it remains unclear whether or not a cutscore of 63 (on the second version) or a corresponding score of 47 (on the third version) is valid for classifying patients as "very severely impaired."

Reliability and validity studies reported in the manual are based on the second version of the SIB, rather than the most recent version of the test. The developers propose that the changes made from the second to third versions of the test included items being dropped or rescored. The test authors assert that the changes "are minor and the validity and reliability data are assumed to apply to the new version" (manual, p. 6). No information on internal consistency is provided in the manual for any of the three versions of the test. Instead, developers provide information on interrater and test-retest reliability. Interrater reliability using two naïve raters was generally high, ranging from .89 (praxis) to 1.0 (orienting to name) with the total score having an interrater

reliability of .99. The second version of the test also appears to have adequate test-retest reliability over a period of 1 month, although a few of the scales had unacceptably low reliability coefficients (orientation, orienting to name). In general, reliability coefficients ranged from .06 (orientation) to .90 (total score), with most scales having moderate to high stability over time.

Evidence to support the validity of the SIB is limited. Support for the underlying constructs of the SIB was provided in the form of convergent validity. The SIB, MMSE, and the Mattis Dementia Rating Scale (Mattis, 1988) were administered to a sample of patients meeting the criteria for probable or possible dementia. The SIB and MMSE were moderately correlated ($r = .76$, $n = 70$), whereas the SIB and MDRS were more highly correlated ($r = .88$, $n = 55$). Additional validity reported in the manual highlighted a French version of the SIB administered to a sample of demented patients in Paris, France. As expected, the French version had high interrater reliability, test-retest reliability, and was highly correlated with the MMSE. Information pertaining to the underlying factor structure of the SIB was not furnished in the manual.

COMMENTARY. On the whole, the SIB fills a long-standing gap in neuropsychological assessment by allowing clinicians to assess severely demented individuals. This being said, it is rare that a patient presents to an outpatient setting for evaluation with an MMSE below 4. Given the measure is designed for use with severely demented patients, the SIB appears most appropriate for use in long-term nursing home facilities, acute rehabilitation hospitals, and in research settings. The SIB has the potential to become a valuable tool in the clinician's armamentarium if the developers can delineate reliable change and provide further clarification on the classification levels of severe dementia. Some of the measure's strengths include: ease of administration, the ability to assess multiple low levels skills, the manual's suggestions on establishing and maintaining rapport, the scoring format, which allows for cues and partial points, and the test's capacity to sample a vast array of cognitive domains.

Despite these strengths, the SIB has numerous limitations of which clinicians should be cognizant before using this measure in clinical practice. First, the manual provides reliability and validity data for only the 133-point version instead of the most recent 100-point version. This raises the question as to whether the recommended cutscore of 63 is appropriate for use with the most recent version of the SIB. Second, information on how the items were created, the rationale for the inclusion of items within domains, the decision process surrounding the determination of domains, the definition of domains, and the test's underlying factor structure are absent and should be present. Finally, the manual (copyrighted in 1993) makes it difficult to determine the measure's true merits. Developers noted that "additional reliability and validity studies are being carried out" (manual, p. 8), yet to date an updated manual has not been published. Based on a review of the literature that identified several studies utilizing the SIB including a short version, Italian version, German version, and a factorial validation of the SIB, an update of the current manual is suggested.

SUMMARY. The SIB is a 40-item, easy-to-administer measure of cognitive functioning for use with severely demented individuals. The test purportedly assesses six major cognitive subscales (i.e., Attention, Memory, Language, Visual-Spatial Abilities, Construction, and Orientation) plus three brief evaluations of praxis, social interaction, and orienting to name, yielding a Total Score and subscale scores. In its present form, limited reliability and validity data provided in the manual restrict the utility of the SIB outside of long-term nursing home facilities and research settings. Before clinicians can be confident in using the SIB in more diverse settings and with more diverse patient populations an updated manual that includes additional reliability and validity evidence using the third version of the test is needed.

REVIEWERS' REFERENCES

Folstein, M. F., Folstein, S. E., & McHugh, P. R. (1975). Mini-Mental State: A practical method for grading the cognitive state of patients for the clinician. *Journal of Psychiatric Research, 12,* 189–198.

Mattis, S. (1988). *DRS: Dementia Rating Scale professional manual.* New York: Psychological Assessment.

Saxton, J., McGonigle-Gibson, K. L., Swihart, A. A., Miller, V. J., & Boller, F. (1990). Assessment of the severely-impaired patient: Description and validation of a new neuropsychological test battery. *Psychological Assessment: A Journal of Consulting and Clinical Psychology, 2,* 298–303.

[173]
Social Responsiveness Scale.

Purpose: Designed to help "establish the diagnosis of autism spectrum conditions."
Population: Ages 4–18 years.
Publication Date: 2005.
Acronym: SRS.

Scores, 6: Social Awareness, Social Cognition, Social Communication, Social Motivation, Autistic Mannerisms, Total.
Administration: Group or individual.
Price Data, 2007: $91 per complete kit including 15 Parent AutoScore forms, 15 Teacher AutoScore forms, and manual (69 pages); $50 per manual; $38.50 per 25 Parent AutoScore forms; $38.50 per 25 Teacher AutoScore forms, bulk discounts available; Computerized components: $115.50 per 25-use Windows SRS scoring CD, bulk discounts available; $16.50 per 100 PC answer sheets; $22 per Continuing Education Questionnaire and Evaluation Form.
Time: (15–20) minutes.
Comments: This test is to be completed by a parent, teacher, or other custodial caretaker.
Authors: John N. Constantino and Christian P. Gruber.
Publisher: Western Psychological Services.

Review of the Social Responsiveness Scale by FRANCINE CONWAY, *Assistant Professor of Psychology, Adelphi University, Garden City, NY:*

DESCRIPTION. The Social Responsiveness Scale (SRS) is a 65-item questionnaire designed to be used in the identification of childhood disorders within the autism spectrum and to screen for and support clinical diagnoses in this area. The test authors suggest the SRS may be used to clarify diagnostic ambiguities in children between the ages of 4 and 18 years who have developmental disorders. The SRS is completed by either a parent or teacher knowledgeable of the child's behavior. The child's behavior is rated on a Likert scale of 1 to 4 for each item on the questionnaire. Items are characteristic of autism spectrum disorders and include domains of interpersonal behavior, communication, and repetitive/stereotypic behaviors associated with the disorders. The test includes an SRS profile sheet that contains the 65 test items, scoring sheet, and tables for converting raw scores to standard scores. Forms are available for parents and teachers, each specifying T-score conversion norms for males and females. The test is also accompanied by a manual detailing administration, scoring, and interpretation guidelines, as well as information on the test's development and psychometric properties.

A wealth of examples regarding completion of the scoring forms are provided in written and figural formats. The authors also include several case examples of how the test may be applied to a range of diagnostic categories occurring within the spectrum, including (a) the identification of Pervasive Developmental Disorders—Not Otherwise Specified, (b) undiagnosed Asperger's Disorder, (c) severity of autistic symptoms below the diagnostic threshold, (d) conflicting scores on the SRS and Autism Diagnostic Observation Schedule, and (e) Autism Spectrum Condition identified by parent and teacher SRS report. Simply put, the SRS offer a continuum on which a range of autism spectrum behaviors can be identified.

DEVELOPMENT. The SRS test manual describes the test's development in a clear manner. The development includes the authors' generation of a list of SRS items consistent with their clinical experience, a review by potential users of the test and clinical experts including "special education teachers, school psychologists, clinical child psychologists, neuropsychologists, pediatricians, child neurologists, child psychiatrists and parents of children with autism, Asperger's and PDD-NOS" (manual, p. 26). Although the authors report the experts' review was systematic, no further information is provided. There was no mention of the SRS items having been piloted prior to final test construction.

TECHNICAL.

Standardization. The standardization procedure included an *N* of 1,636 participants in several studies conducted in mostly large diverse metropolitan cities. The technical report provided adequate details of the five epidemiological studies. Group differences for the type of rater (i.e., teachers or parents), gender, and age were analyzed. Furthermore, the authors wisely completed analyses that checked for significant differences among participants of the five studies, which allowed them to combine and compare the studies.

Reliability. Reliability evidence was drawn from three comparisons that assessed internal consistency, construct temporal stability, and interrater reliability. Internal consistency reliability of SRS items for normative parent and teacher ratings, as well as its use for clinical diagnosis, was obtained. Alpha coefficients ranged from .93 to .97. *T*-scores analyses showed that mean ratings by different groups were not significantly different. Construct temporal stability was assessed using a 17-month delay. Baseline measures were highly correlated with maternal reports (.85 for males, .77 for females) in the months following the initial measure. Interrater reliability was obtained on three different raters (mother, father, and teacher) during test development. Three tables in the test manual's technical guide provide SRS reliability coefficients.

Validity. Evidence of validation is generally based on the repeated use of the measure in research studies where the SRS was compared with clinical interviews. The authors argue that the SRS demonstrated discriminant validity, as the SRS has been found to distinguish children with autism spectrum disorders from children with other psychiatric diagnoses. In addition, the SRS has been concurrently validated with the Autism Diagnostic Interview—Revised (ADI-R) where differences in mean scores among those with developmental disorders differed significantly from those with the diagnosis ($F = 72.95$, $df = 2,58$; $p < .0001$). Structural components of the SRS were also validated in epidemiological twin studies. Deficits in social behavior, verbal communication, and stereotypic repetitive behaviors were found to be consistently present in twins. Treatment subscales were added to the SRS after it had been validated. Specific symptom domains were established and shown to be reliable through internal consistency measures, which ranged from .77 to .92.

COMMENTARY. The SRS is a well-designed test for identifying characteristics of autism spectrum disorders. Given its Likert-type scale format, it is easy to use and provides an appropriate screening measure for autistic disorders. The authors' selection of test items is the most questionable aspect of test development. Admittedly, there was some effort to receive input from potential users. A more detailed explanation of the item selection processes and possibly piloting of items would strengthen scale development. Nonetheless, psychometric properties, such as rigorous reliability and validation efforts, compensate for any questions that may have arisen during its development.

General administration procedures allow individuals familiar with the child's behavior (teachers and parents) to serve as respondents. Appropriately, a note of caution appears on the SRS profile sheet encouraging users of the test to be familiar with the materials in the test manual.

SUMMARY. The test developers did a thoughtful job in conducting reliability and validity studies that support the psychometric integrity of the SRS. The inclusion of subscales that inform treatment is a useful feature of the test. Should there be another edition of this test, more details should be presented on item selection processes. The SRS promises to be a sound and useful measure in distinguishing a range of autism spectrum disorders.

Review of the Social Responsiveness Scale by JOHN J. VENN, Professor of Special Education, University of North Florida, Jacksonville, FL:

DESCRIPTION. The Social Responsiveness Scale (SRS) is a 65-item rating scale for measuring the severity of autism spectrum symptoms in children from 4 to 18 years of age. The SRS was designed for completion by a parent, teacher, or other primary caregiver who knows the child well. It can be completed in about 15 to 20 minutes. The instrument provides an overall picture of a child's social behavior as it occurs in natural social settings. The SRS subscales evaluate social awareness, social information processing, capacity for reciprocal social communication, social anxiety/avoidance, and autistic preoccupations and traits.

The SRS is best used as a screening instrument in clinical and educational settings. It was designed for screening children who may be at risk for autism spectrum conditions and for use with other diagnostic tools as part of a battery of assessments in the process of conducting clinical diagnosis of children with autism and related disorders. It is also useful as a research instrument and as an intervention tool for measuring the progress of children in response to intervention. Because it was developed to measure autism spectrum behaviors, it is also helpful in evaluating Asperger's disorder, Pervasive Developmental Disorder Not Otherwise Specified (PDD-NOS), and Schizoid Personality Disorder of Childhood. In addition, the scale can help professionals identify subthreshold autistic symptoms in children with a wide variety of psychological problems. Although the SRS is completed by a parent or teacher, responsibility for scoring and interpreting SRS results rests with professionals who have education, training, and experience in autism spectrum conditions and in the use of psychological tests.

The SRS yields an overall score and five treatment subscale scores. The SRS subscales measure Social Awareness, Social Cognition, Social Communication, Social Motivation, and Autistic Mannerisms. Raw scores for the total test and the subscales are converted into *T*-scores. Total *T*-scores of 76 and higher fall into the severe range and suggest the presence of an autism spectrum condition. *T*-scores of between 60 and 75 are in the moderate range and may suggest presence of mild autism spectrum disorders such as PDD-NOS or Asperger's Disorder. Scores of 59 or less are in the normal range and suggest the absence of an autism spectrum condition. Because the SRS is a screening test, care should be taken to avoid using it in isolation to identify children with disorders. Instead it should be used together with other appropriate diagnostic tools and procedures in the process of classifying children and determining if they qualify for special services. The SRS provides separate norms for parents and teachers and for males and females. Interpretation of SRS results is best when using scores from more than one rater. Interpretation of subscales scores should be done cautiously because of the low reliabilities associated with subtest scoring. This characteristic is typical of most instruments of this type.

The SRS administration and scoring procedures are well documented and straightforward. The manual provides clear directions for having parents, teachers, and primary caregivers complete the scale. The SRS uses a four-point system from *not true* to *almost always true* for rating each of the 65 behaviors. The scoring procedure is efficient and takes about 5 minutes to complete using a scoring worksheet. Raw scores are converted to *T*-scores and are plotted on a profile sheet that shows strengths and weaknesses in specific social behaviors; these may help in developing priorities for intervention.

DEVELOPMENT. The developers created the SRS based on their clinical experience with children who had pervasive developmental disorders. It was first used as a research tool in several clinical investigations of autism spectrum conditions. The norms for the instrument were developed in part with data from these studies. Originally called the Social Reciprocity Scale and later renamed as the Social Responsiveness Scale, the instrument was designed to help identify a wide range of deficits in reciprocal social behavior as it occurs naturally in social interaction. After developing the initial items, a panel of experts reviewed them. The reviewers included special education teachers, school psychologists, child psychologists, neuropsychologists, pediatricians, child neurologists, child psychiatrists, and parents of children with autism, Asperger's, and PDD-NOS.

TECHNICAL. Information about some aspects of the SRS norming process is vague. The manual indicates that the SRS norms were developed from five different large-scale research studies over a period of several years. The total sample used to develop the norms included more than 1,600 children. Three of the studies involved random samples of more than 800 twins from Missouri. However, these studies were conducted to examine intergenerational transmission of autistic traits rather than for normative research. It appears the decision to use these data to develop the norms was made later. A fourth study, which was conducted for normative purposes, involved 272 children from a suburban Midwestern school district. These four studies all generated parent report data. A fifth study was conducted to compile teacher report data although an unspecified amount of teacher report data was collected previously during earlier clinical investigations. The fifth study involved 552 students from a large suburban school district in the Midwest and a large urban district in the West. Because data analysis conducted by the developers indicated the presence of significant differences in scores by rater (parent or teacher) and by the gender of the rater, separate norms were developed for parents and for teachers, and the norms were further separated by the rater's gender. Other variables such as ethnicity, age, and education were taken into consideration in the norm setting process. According to the information in the manual the norms did not require age stratification because there was no evidence of systematic age differences within the sample. Unfortunately, information about the ethnic background of the children who participated in the first three twin studies was not available. As a result, the ethnic representation of that part of the sample had to be estimated. Most of the scores used to develop the norms were from children in Missouri, especially children who lived in and around St. Louis. Additional normative data were obtained subsequently from school children in Missouri and California.

The manual describes investigations of three types of reliability. These included study of internal consistency of SRS scores, a construct temporal stability investigation, and an examination of interrater agreement. The internal consistency study estimated split-half reliability using ratings completed by more than 1,000 parents and 500 teachers. The alpha coefficients from this study were .93 and .94 from the parent ratings and .97 and .96 from the teacher ratings. A third data set from a clinical sample of 281 child psychiatric patients with and without autism spectrum conditions yielded a coefficient of .97. These data provide strong evidence to support the split-half reliability of SRS total scores. In contrast, alpha coefficients for the SRS subscales ranged from .77 to .92 with a median coefficient of .87. These lower subscale values suggest the need for caution when interpreting subscale scores. The construct temporal stability was estimated using a sample of 379 children. Construct temporal stability is similar to test-retest reliability except that the delay between the two administrations of the test is generally several months to a year rather than a shorter intervening delay. To estimate the construct temporal stability of SRS scores, the children were given the SRS twice with an average delay of 17 months between the first and second administrations. The retest temporal stability for the parent report SRS scores in twins yielded correlations of .85 for the 102 boys in the study and .77 for the 277 girls in the study. The interrater agreement of SRS scores also was considered during SRS development. This study included 62 children and involved having both parents of the children and the child's teacher complete the SRS. The results of the analysis yielded correlation coefficients of .91 between mothers and fathers, .82 between mothers and teachers, and .75 between fathers and teachers. Although the results of these studies provide some initial evidence of reliability, more research is needed to clearly establish the test-retest and interrater reliability of the instrument.

Several studies provide the basis for evaluating the validity of SRS scores. These include an investigation of reciprocal social behavior, a concurrent validity study, studies of the effectiveness of the SRS as a measure of autistic traits, and an examination of the validity of SRS subscale scores. The reciprocal social behavior study was the initial research that launched the SRS as a rating scale and provided preliminary evidence of the discriminant validity of the instrument. This study (Constantino, Przybeck, Friesen, & Todd, 2000) involved 158 children who were psychiatric patients with and without autism spectrum conditions and 287 randomly selected children from a metropolitan school district. The children were placed into six groups for the analysis. The groups were 4–7-year-old school children, 8–14-year-old school children, children with PDD-NOS, autistic children who were verbal, autistic children who were nonverbal, and clinical controls. The distributions of SRS scores among the six groups were essentially smooth and continuous suggesting a continuous distribution of deficits among the groups. Further evidence of the validity of the SRS was provided in a concurrent validity study (Constantino, Davis, et al., 2003). This clinical research investigation compared the SRS with the Autism Diagnostic Interview—Revised (ADI-R) in 61 child psychiatric patients. The correlations between SRS scores and ADI-R algorithm scores for DSM-IV criterion sets were mostly in the .70 range. This study provided initial evidence of the concurrent validity of the SRS as a tool for measuring autistic traits. The developers also used data from a number of other studies to establish the effectiveness of the SRS as a measure of the construct of autistic traits (Constantino, et al., 2004; Constantino, Hudziak, & Todd, 2003; Constantino & Todd, 2000; Constantino & Todd, 2003). According to the SRS developers, results from these investigations support the existence of a single continuously distributed underlying factor that explains most of the variance in SRS scores. The developers used this finding to conclude that the SRS is an effective measure of overall autistic traits in children. In contrast to the conclusion about the construct validity of the SRS total scores, the treatment subscale scores may not clearly measure separate dimensions of autistic behavior. In fact, the SRS treatment subscales, which were added to the instrument after the total score was developed and validated, are highly correlated with each other. For this reason many questions exist about the utility of the subtest scores, and evaluators should exercise much caution when conducting subscale score analysis. Overall, the developers conducted a substantial number of analyses to establish the validity of the SRS as a new instrument for assessing autism and related disorders.

COMMENTARY. The successful use of the SRS in large scale research studies demonstrates that the rating scale has a clear focus and provides consistent, effective scores that discriminate among children with and without autism spectrum disorders. The instrument features straightforward administration, scoring, and interpretation guidelines that make it easy to compare scores across settings and raters. For example, mental health professionals responsible for making screening and diagnostic decisions may use different raters to achieve consensus about where a child's behavior falls within a range of autism spectrum behaviors. There are previously noted concerns about the subscales, such as a lack of differentiation between subscale scores and questions about the utility of subscale scoring. The value of the norm sample seems compromised in several ways. First, details about the norm development process are lacking. Second, the norms were developed over a period of several years using different studies rather than through a specifically designed norm development procedure. Most of the children who participated in the norm sample were from one Midwest area of the country. Finally, much of the data used to develop the norms was taken from studies that were not designed to yield normative information. Because of the process used to develop the norms, the norm sample may not be representative of the general population. Evaluators should use SRS scores cautiously, keeping in mind these limitations.

SUMMARY. The SRS developers have produced a rating scale that can be administered, scored, and interpreted in an efficient, cost effective manner. Although the SRS is a new instrument, it has already been used in an impressive variety of research studies examining autism spectrum disorders. The main benefit of the SRS in comparison with other instruments used to assess autism spectrum conditions is the 1 to 4 rating protocol. In contrast to scales with simple yes/no scoring systems, the SRS approach estimates where a child falls within a range of behavior. Thus the instrument may suggest the severity of autistic social impairment. The SRS does suffer from technical deficiencies, most notably weaknesses in the norm development process. Overall, however, the SRS is a much needed new rating scale for screening children who may have autism or related disorders. The SRS is helpful as one tool in a battery of instruments used in the process of identifying children with autism spectrum disorders, and it has demonstrated validity as a research tool. Because the SRS is a screening instrument, it has limited utility as a tool for identifying areas in need of intervention and for measuring child progress.

REVIEWER'S REFERENCES

Constantino, J. N., Davis, S. A., Todd, R. D., Schindler, M. K., Gross, M. M., Brophy, S. L., Metzger, L. M., Shoushtari, C. S., Splinter R., & Reich, W. (2003). Validation of a brief quantitative genetic measure of autistic traits: Comparison of the Social Responsiveness Scale with the Autism Diagnostic Interview—Revised. *Journal of Autism and Developmental Disorders, 33*, 427-433.

Constantino, J. N., Gruber, C. P., Davis, S., Hayes, S., Passanante, N., & Przybeck, T. (2004). The factor structure of autistic traits. *Journal of Child Psychology and Psychiatry, 45*, 719-726.

Constantino, J. N., Hudziak, J. J., & Todd, R. D. (2003). Deficits in reciprocal social behavior in male twins: Evidence for a genetically independent domain of psychopathology. *Journal of the American Academy of Child and Adolescent Psychiatry, 42*, 458-467.

Constantino, J. N., Przybeck, T., Friesen, D., & Todd, R. D. (2000). Reciprocal social behavior in children with and without pervasive developmental disorder. *Journal of Developmental and Behavior Pediatrics, 21*, 2-11.

Constantino, J. N., & Todd, R. D. (2000). The genetic structure of reciprocal social behavior. *American Journal of Psychiatry, 157*, 2043-2045.

Constantino, J. N., & Todd, R. D. (2003). Autistic traits in the general population: A twin study. *Archives of General Psychiatry, 60*, 524-530.

[174]

Sources of Stress Scale [2006 Revision].

Purpose: Designed as "an instrument to identify origins of perceived and current anxiety, to quantify the intensity of such stresses, and to determine the pattern of such perceptions for predictions and subsequent interventions."

Population: High school and adults.

Publication Dates: 1986–2006.

Acronym: S.O.S.S.

Administration: Group.

Price Data, 2006: $30 per 25 scales; $.40 per answer sheet; $30 per test manual (2006, 37 pages); $.30 per scoring scale; $.50 per answer sheet; $.25 for profile charts.

Time: [5–15] minutes per scale.

Comments: Self-rating scale.

Authors: Louise M. Soares and Anthony T. Soares.

Publisher: Castle Consultants.

a) CORPORATE EXECUTIVE FORM.

Scores: 12 categories: Daily Issues, Professional Issues, Internal Personnel, Outside Influence, Changes, Finances/Money, The Future, Health, My Personal Life, Myself, Personal Relationships, Time Management.

b) GRADUATE STUDENT FORM.

Scores: 12 categories: Campus Life, Academic Activities, Field Experiences, College Personnel, plus last 8 categories from *a* above.

c) CORPORATE EXECUTIVE FORM.

Scores: 12 categories: Daily Issues, Professional Issues, Internal Personnel, Outside Influence, Changes, Finances/Money, The Future, Health, My Personal Life, Myself, Personal Relationships, Time Management.

d) HIGH SCHOOL FORM.

Scores: 12 categories: Extracurricular Activities, Academic Activities, Life at School, High School, plus last 8 categories from *a* above.

e) NURSING FORM.

Scores: 12 categories: Same as *a* above.

f) PARENT FORM.

Scores: 12 categories: Children, Family Issues, Spouse/Partner, Work/Job/Occupation, plus last 8 categories from *a* above.

g) POLITICIAN FORM.

Scores: 12 categories: Same as *a* above.

h) SCHOOL ADMINISTRATOR FORM.

Scores: 12 categories: Instructional Leadership, Organizational Issues, Legal & Political Issues, Resource Allocation, plus last 8 categories from *a* above.

i) SENIOR CITIZEN FORM.

Scores: 12 categories: Same as *f* above but including Quality of Life Issues and excluding Work/Job/Occupation.

j) TEACHER FORM.

Scores: 12 categories: Classroom Issues, Professional Issues, School Issues, plus last 9 categories from *a* above.

k) YOUNG ADULTS FORM.

Scores: 12 categories: Same as *f* above.

Cross References: For reviews by JoAnn Murphey and Wesley E. Sime of an earlier edition, see 15:235.

Review of the Sources of Stress Scale [2006 Revision] by DEBORAH BANDALOS, Professor of Educational Psychology, University of Georgia, Athens, GA:

DESCRIPTION. The Sources of Stress Scale (S.O.S.S) is a self-report scale designed to measure perceptions of stressors and their relative strengths within specific groups. The scale was not designed to be a measure of stress or anxiety per se, but rather a measure of "areas in the environmental field perceived as causing stress" (S.O.S.S. test manual, p. 6). At the time of this review, there were separate versions of the scale for five role-related (graduate student, high school student, young adult, parent, and senior citizen) and six occupational (corporate executive, factory worker, nurse, politician, school administrator, and teacher) groups. The various scales contain a common core of items addressing the areas of Personal Relationships, Changes, Finances, Time Management, The Future, The Self, Health, and Personal Life, along with four additional scales focusing on activities or experiences that are specific to that role or occupation. Using this format, sources of stress emanating from different areas can be compared in terms of their relative saliencies for an individual. In addition, common stressors can be compared across role-related and/or occupational groups.

Although the test author briefly alludes to use of the scale in prediction and intervention, there is no information presented on how the scale might be used in interventions or what it might be used to predict. There is also no information on its validity for these purposes. In fact, the proposed uses of the scale are not provided in the manual, although the author does state that the scale would allow one to "look at common, external, identified sources [of stress] across groups in certain environments and across time" (manual, p. 6). Lacking any other information regarding proposed uses of the scale, I would suggest that those choosing to use the S.O.S.S. confine such usage to research purposes.

The self-report format of this scale consists of a system of checks, in which one check indicates the item represents a major source of stress and two checks indicates a very strong source of stress. Lack of any checks presumably indicates that the item is not a source of stress at all, although this is not stated explicitly. This response format lacks any categories for low or moderate levels of stress and is therefore strongly skewed toward the high end of the stress continuum. It is not clear why such a response format was chosen. The S.O.S.S. is scored by simply counting up the number of check marks in each of the 12 areas, or "clusters," as they are termed, on the scale. With 8 items for each of the 12 clusters, there are 96 items on the total scale. Directions for plotting the cluster scores on a graph for comparison of levels of stress relating to different areas are provided, and the user is encouraged to obtain such profiles. Although much is made of the score profiles, information on their development and psychometric properties is completely lacking. Tables for converting scores to stanines and T-scores are also provided, "for ease of comparison to other psychological assessments" (manual, p. 34). However, it should be noted that the conversions provided are not similar to those of most psychological assessments due to the lack of an important component: a description of the reference group. In fact, it is not at all clear how the conversion tables were derived. T-scores of 20–80 are provided only in multiples of 10 (i.e., 20, 30, 40, etc.) along with their raw score equivalents, given in ranges. No information on how these scores were obtained is provided. The same is true of the stanines. Moreover, it appears that the same set of T-scores and stanine conversions is to be used for all 11 versions of the S.O.S.S. This is surprising because the manual presents evidence to show that the score profiles for the different role- and occupation-related groups are quite different. In any case, because the meaning of transformed scores depends on the characteristics of the reference group, I see no utility in the use of the transformations provided. Those choosing to use the S.O.S.S. would do better to conduct their own transformations, assuming their sample is large enough to support this action.

DEVELOPMENT. The current version of the S.O.S.S. represents the third revision of this scale, in which the 6 occupation-related versions of the scales were developed. As noted previously, the addition of these 6 scales resulted in a total of 11 versions of the S.O.S.S. Information provided in the manual regarding the revisions is quite sketchy, as is information regarding the development of the scale overall. The manual simply states that items were developed based on "previous instrumentation, student responses, expert testimony, and interrater agreement" (manual, p. 6). However, as no further information is provided on any of these sources, no evaluation is possible. The section of the manual on "theoretical background," although more detailed than most other sections of the manual, relies on outdated references to make the point that an instrument such as the S.O.S.S. is needed. Further, there is no factor analytic or other evidence offered in the manual to indicate that the 12 clusters are either differentiable or internally consistent. From my reading of the content, some of the items might arguably fit in more than one of the clusters.

TECHNICAL. Although review by "experts" is mentioned several times in the manual, the qualifications of these experts and the results of their reviews are not described. The potential user of the scale apparently must be satisfied with the assertion that experts were consulted. Values of both internal consistency and test-retest reliability are provided, based on several samples. Values for the 12 scale clusters are not provided, so I assume that the reported values are for the total scale. Values for internal consistency range from .81 to .93 across various samples. These values are generally quite good, although with 96 items one would expect high values for this type of reliability. Test-retest reliability for an 8-week period ranged from .83 to .95, and over a 6-month period the values ranged from .80–.94. These values indicate strong stability of the total scale scores. It should be noted, however, that many of the values reported were based on samples that were quite small, ranging from 15 to 98, with a median sample size of 40.

I found the validity information to be quite puzzling. Coefficients are provided for "content" and "construct" validity, with no explanation. The values appear to represent correlation coefficients, although this is conjecture on my part. The manual provides absolutely no information regarding the validity studies that yielded the values provided, so it is not possible to make use of or to evaluate this information. For all practical purposes, there really is no validity information available.

COMMENTARY. The author of the S.O.S.S. is either unsophisticated in her knowledge of psychometric principles or has chosen to ignore them. Descriptions of the proposed uses of the scale and of the scale development are woefully inadequate. Score conversions are provided with no information on the reference group used to obtain them, or, for that matter, any information at all on how they were obtained. Twelve score "clusters" are described but there is no factor analytic or other information pertaining to their distinctness. The reliability of the scale appears to be its one strong point and appropriate coefficients were reported, but many of these are based on very small samples. Reliability was apparently assessed only for the total scale; no information on the reliability of "cluster" scores is provided. Validity information is presented with such a lack of detail that it is impossible to evaluate.

SUMMARY. The concept of focusing on the sources, rather than the manifestations, of stress is potentially a useful one for those working in clinical environments. However, those interested in using such an instrument should look elsewhere. The current version of the S.O.S.S. lacks adequate information in nearly all the areas in which a potential user might be interested. This is particularly distressing in light of the fact that similar problems were detailed in an earlier review of this instrument, and little appears to have been done in the interim to address them.

Review of the Sources of Stress Scale [2006 Revision], by JERRELL C. CASSADY, Associate Professor of Psychology, and MOLLY M. JAMESON, Doctoral Candidate, Department of Educational Psychology, Ball State University, Muncie, IN:

DESCRIPTION. According to the authors, the Sources of Stress Scale (S.O.S.S.) is intended to serve three purposes: identify the origins of perceived and current anxiety, quantify the intensity of the stressors, and determine patterns of these perceptions. The S.O.S.S. is actually a set of 11 similar versions, or "forms," designed to specifically target individuals in a variety of professions (e.g., teacher, nurse, political figures) or life stages (e.g., young adult, high school, senior citizen). For each chosen form, the S.O.S.S. provides both a self-assessment version and a significant other rating version. The significant other rating form, referred to as the observational version, is identical to the self-assessment in response guidelines. The only difference between the self- and other-ratings provided on the S.O.S.S. is driven by the introductory script at the top of the administration protocol.

For each form, the individual is rated on 12 dimensions of stress that are somewhat specific to their position in life. For all users, 8 of the 12 dimensions are the same: Personal Relationships, Changes, Finance, My Personal Life, Myself, Time Management, The Future, and Health. The remaining 4 dimensions, or clusters, vary across the users. For each of the 12 dimensions of stress, there are 8 identified potential stressors and one open-ended "other" option. The user is directed to mark each potential source of stress with one checkmark if it is a source of stress. If the potential source of stress is a "very strong" source, the user is to mark with two checkmarks. Hence, each dimension of stress sources has nine possible sources with each producing a "score" of 0, 1, or 2 in the strength of stress rating (possible range 0–18).

Suggestions for using the data generated from the scale include plotting the raw scores on a graph and developing a stress profile. The goal of this plotting is to identify the high points of stress for the individual. In addition, the authors claim a simple combinatory score (adding all 12 dimensions) can provide a composite profile to determine overall level of stress for the individual. The manual provides suggested stanine and *T*-score transformation values that are intended to align the values on this scale with standardized tests.

DEVELOPMENT. The manual accompanying the S.O.S.S. outlines a 20-year process of development for the scale. Although a variety of revisions have been offered in that time period, the bulk of the revisions focus on the development of new forms or general areas of stress to be considered for the target populations.

There is little empirical support or theoretical justification for the changes offered to the scale through the development phase. There is an intuitive sensibility to the items that were added to the S.O.S.S. over the years, and the increase in the number of professions has been reasonable. However, there is no evidence that the items added to the scale over time have been the product of a detailed analysis of the populations in question.

The manual outlines some of the procedures used to develop the scale, including university-based research for graduate and undergraduate students. The results of those analyses did not appear to affect the structure or format of the scale over time, but were used to identify gender and group differences.

Overall, the development process cannot be characterized as empirical or theoretical, based on the available information. Furthermore, standard procedures for scale validation have not been followed sufficiently to provide confidence that the sources of stress identified in this scale are the most relevant for each population in question. For instance, one source of validation for the 2001 version's differing age-focused forms was the family profile of a family of five (listed as daughter, son, father, wife, mother-in-law). Threats to validity with the use of a single family are significant; moreover, the case study provides a perilous issue in the overall S.O.S.S. That is, which form or version should individuals take when they fit multiple criteria? The wife in this example took the "Young Adult" version, whereas her son took the Graduate Student version and her husband took the "Family" version (now called Parent).

TECHNICAL. The technical manual provides insufficient evidence to conclude that the scale is reliable and valid for its intended use. The authors provide several estimates of test-retest reliability throughout the technical information manual. However, these estimates are offered based on small sample sizes. For instance, in the 2005 analysis of test-retest reliability over 8 weeks and 6 months, the reliability estimates were high, but were based on an average number of 28 participants in each professional category. In that same report, concurrent validity evidence was offered for the corporate executives, factory workers, nurses, politicians, school administrators, and teachers by comparing S.O.S.S. scores with job performance for a given month. There is insufficient information to identify the variable of "job performance," but more concerning is that this measure does not provide an indication of concurrent validity for a stress scale. The correlation generated in those estimates provides an indication of how tightly stress and job performance follow one another. A comprehensive search of the literature generated no evidence of an alternative published account validating the S.O.S.S. against another established stress measure.

The scoring suggestions provide guidelines for stanine and T-score transformations based on the raw score values received when completing the test. However, there is no evidence to support the determination of the values. Given the small number of individuals referenced in the validation studies, it is questionable that the offered values are a durable population estimate.

COMMENTARY. We found little value in the S.O.S.S. as a clinical tool. There is insufficient evidence provided to demonstrate that the scale has been developed with either a theoretical or empirical basis. It appears to be an intuitive instrument that can provide a casual user (perhaps in a human resources capacity) general and basic information about areas of stress in an individual's life. There may be value in this scale in research or evaluation studies, given the availability of alternate forms and significant other ratings.

Further validation work on the scales would improve the technical information dramatically. In particular, subjecting the instrument to a series of factor analyses, larger scale validation studies, and aligning it with a relevant theoretical basis would be useful.

SUMMARY. The information generated by the S.O.S.S. is generally interesting and illustrative. There are serious questions regarding the validity of the scale, and there are unresolved issues in scaling and appropriate administration to individuals who fit the criteria for different versions of the scale.

[175]

The Speed and Capacity of Language Processing Test.

Purpose: "Designed to provide a wholistic measure of the efficacy of language comprehension."

Population: Ages 16–65.

Publication Date: 1992.

Acronym: SCOLP.

Scores, 2: The Speed of Comprehension Test, The Spot-the-Word Test.

Administration: Individual.

Price Data, 2006: £92 per complete kit including manual (16 pages), 3 acetates, and 6 packs of 25 scoring sheets; £18 per 25 scoring sheets (specify Speed of Comprehension Test A, Speed of Comprehension Test B, Speed of Comprehension Test C, Speed of Comprehension Test D, Spot-the-Word Vocabulary Test A, or Spot-the-Word Vocabulary Test B).

Time: Untimed.

Comments: Each subtest comes with different versions for the purpose of retesting: The Speed of Comprehension Test has 4 versions (A, B, C, D) and The Spot-the-Word Test has 2 versions (A, B).

Authors: Alan Baddeley, Hazel Emslie, and Ian Nimmo-Smith.

Publisher: Harcourt Assessment [England].

Review of The Speed and Capacity of Language-Processing Test by KAY B. STEVENS, Associate Professor of Education, Texas Christian University, Fort Worth, TX, and J. RANDALL PRICE, Professor of Psychology, Richland College, Dallas, TX:

DESCRIPTION. The Speed and Capacity of Language-Processing Test (SCOLP) was published in 1992 and is described as a "wholistic" screening measure of acquired brain damage in adults ages 16 to 80. The test claims to measure the slowing of cognitive processes by differentiating between examinees who have "always been slow" (manual, p. 4) and those who have lost cognitive processing speed due to insult to the brain such as injury, drug/alcohol use, and disease. Two subtests are included: The Speed of Comprehension Test and The Spot-the-Word Test. Both subtests are given to examinees. No specific information is provided regarding examiner qualifications. The test is quick and easy to administer and score.

The Speed of Comprehension subtest requires the examinee to read silently, as quickly as possible, a series of 100 true/false sentences while marking the "true" sentences. The content in the sentences consists of "knowledge that is likely to be available to all subjects" (manual, p. 4). The raw score is the number of sentences read in 2 minutes. Errors are not counted unless the error rate is more than 10%. The number of sentences read is converted to a scaled score and/or percentile score adjusted according to age ranges. If the error rate exceeds 10% (which is rare), the authors suggest further clinical investigation into such conditions as illiteracy or dyslexia. Alternative methods for administering this subtest and cautions related to test alterations are addressed.

The Spot-the-Word subtest is not timed and requires the examinee to read silently 60 pairs of words—one word being a real word and the other a nonsense word (e.g., "brul"—a string of letters that are "pronounceable" and look like a word). The examinee is instructed to "spot" and mark the real word in the pair. The number of correct responses is converted to a scaled score and/or percentile score adjusted according to age ranges.

The subtest results are combined into a discrepancy score by subtracting The Speed of Comprehension subtest scaled score from The Spot-the-Word subtest scaled score. If the result is a positive number, the resulting discrepancy scaled score is converted to a percentile-range score with lower percentile ranges showing "evidence of impaired speed of processing" (manual, p. 9).

The test kit consists of a 16-page manual including limited descriptions of test background, administration, scoring, and validity and reliability studies, as well as a scoring key. Score-conversion tables yield scaled and percentile scores adjusted for age ranges for both subtests. Percentile range scores are provided for the discrepancy score. Four forms of The Speed of Comprehension subtest and two forms of The Spot-the-Word subtest are provided for repeated testing. A protocol page is located on the back of each Speed of Comprehension test.

DEVELOPMENT. The format of The Speed of Comprehension subtest was originally developed by Collins and Quillian in 1969 to assess semantic memory; however, the current authors conclude that the test is a rapid but sensitive neuropsychological measure of verbal processing speed related to fluid intellectual functioning. A low score on The Speed of Comprehension subtest may be due to "an intrinsically low level of verbal competence or a decrement from a previously high level of ability" (manual, p. 7). In contrast, the authors state that The Spot-the-Word subtest "gives a relatively robust estimate of crystallized verbal intelligence" (manual, p. 9). According to the manual, the SCOLP can detect acquired brain damage by comparing the results of The Speed of Comprehension subtest to results of The Spot-the-Word subtest. The underlying rationale centers on the general hypothesis that a fluid measure of information processing will be affected by damage to the brain, but that a measure of crystallized verbal intelligence will not. Therefore, if the examinee's score on The Speed of Comprehension subtest is substantially lower than the examinee's score on The Spot-the-Word subtest, insult to the brain is likely the cause of the slowed information processing.

The manual describes five nonpublished, non-peer-reviewed studies conducted by the test developers. Although these studies are presented as evidence of the reliability and validity of the SCOLP, they are more accurately viewed as pilot testing projects. The poorly described samples are small, and the evidence provided in four of the studies is limited to concurrent validity correlations of The Speed of Comprehension subtest with existing measures of verbal fluency and semantic memory and concurrent validity correlations of The Spot-the-Word subtest with existing measures of crystallized intelligence. The fifth study describes the collection of normative data on the SCOLP.

TECHNICAL. Information related to the norm group is *extremely* limited and outdated, and does not meet the educational and psychological testing standards (AERA, APA, & NCME, 1999). The norm sample included 224 individuals representing the "Registrar General's six social class bands" (manual, p. 12) ages 16 to 80. Explanation for the social class scale was not provided and is likely not an entity generally understood in countries outside the United Kingdom. Participants were divided into male and female and each gender group was then divided into six socioeconomic classes. The test developers do not describe how or when the normative sample was obtained but acknowledge that it came from the MRC Applied Psychology Unit volunteer subject panel. Based upon our own research, the authors of this review believe that the normative sample likely came from paid volunteers who registered with the

Medical Research Council (MRC), a publicly funded research organization located in Cambridge, United Kingdom.

Reliability data obtained from limited pilot studies with The Speed of Comprehension subtest revealed adequate split-half (.84 to .87) and strong parallel form (.93) reliability. Pilot studies with The Spot-the-Word subtest yielded marginal to adequate internal consistency (.78 to .83) and parallel form (.78) reliability coefficients.

Validity data obtained from the pilot studies revealed adequate concurrent validity between The Speed of Comprehension subtest and unnamed measures of category fluency and color naming ranging from .52 to .56, respectively. Also, The Speed of Comprehension subtest was found to correlate with the Mill Hill Vocabulary Scale (.51) and an unnamed measure of category speed (.55). Finally, the correlation between The Speed of Comprehension subtest and Raven's Matrices was nonsignificant, suggesting support for the notion that the subtest is not simply a measure of general intelligence. Validity data obtained from the pilot studies on The Spot-the-Word subtest supported the hypothesis that the subtest is more strongly related to crystallized intelligence, as its age-corrected correlation with the crystallized Mill Hill Vocabulary Scale equaled .86, than with the more fluid AH4 intelligence test (.60). Validity data were also reported in the normative data study. The Speed of Comprehension subtest was significantly correlated with The Spot-the-Word subtest (.57), a modified grammatical reasoning assessment (.60), and a revised form of the NART (.60). The importance of these correlations for validity remains unclear. It seems that the strength of the correlations of "fluid" and "crystallized" tests weakens the differences in the constructs, but no discussion regarding these correlations is offered. The Speed of Comprehension correlated negatively with age (-.19), which is consistent with typical age-related decline on measures of fluid abilities. Two forms (A & B) of The Spot-the-Word subtest were correlated with a modified version of the NART yielding coefficients ranging from .83 to .86.

COMMENTARY. Although the SCOLP is based on an interesting premise with potential usefulness, the problems with the current version are so serious and numerous that they preclude a complete description here. Problem examples include but are not limited to: (a) the age of information in the test manual (14 years old); (b) the absence of background information and affiliations related to the authors; (c) a manual fraught with omissions, inconsistencies, errors, vagueness, and poorly written descriptions; (d) inconsistencies among terms describing important constructs; (e) a limited and inadequately described normative sample; (f) concurrent validity studies involving unnamed and modified measures; and (g) the relative absence of peer-reviewed research attempting to validate the test with brain-damaged individuals (documenting its purpose). The manual fails to meet the *Standards for Psychological and Educational Testing* (AERA, APA, & NCME, 1999). Due to the problems, these reviewers opine the test has limited usefulness for screening or diagnostic purposes in the U.S. or other countries outside the United Kingdom, and due to other problems we doubt its clinical usefulness anywhere.

The authors of this review strongly recommend that the authors of this instrument respond to the problems listed above. Perhaps other interested researchers will find the SCOLP fertile ground for research projects aimed at developing a test that has the potential for screening individuals with brain damage due to acquired injury or disease. In a brief review of the literature these reviewers found one study examining the SCOLP (Saxton et al., 2001) and five examining The Spot-the-Word subtest (Baddeley, Emslie, & Nimmo-Smith, 1998; Law & O'Carroll, 1998; Lucas, Carstairs, & Shores, 2003; Watt & O'Carroll, 1999; Yuspeh & Vanderploeg, 2000). The studies revealed mixed reviews related to test/subtest technical quality; however, they are important in establishing the appropriate use of the test and future research; a review of the extant literature should be included in a revised test manual.

SUMMARY. The subtests of the SCOLP are somewhat unique in what they purport to measure and in their proposed ability to discriminate between acquired brain damage versus low premorbid intellectual functioning. We see potential in the use of this instrument for screening brain damage as well as in the assessment of effort using its forced-choice responding format. However, a complete test revision addressing the *extreme* technical problems must occur before its use as a norm-referenced test is recommended.

REVIEWERS' REFERENCES

American Educational Research Association, American Psychological Association, & National Council on Measurement in Education. (1999). *Standards for educational and psychological testing.* Washington, DC: American Educational Research Association.

Baddeley, A., Emslie, H., & Nimmo-Smith, I. (1993). The Spot-the-Word Test: A robust estimate of verbal intelligence based on lexical decision. *British Journal of Clinical Psychology, 32,* 55–65.

Law, R., & O'Carroll, R. E. (1998). A comparison of three measures of estimating premorbid intellectual level in dementia of the Alzheimer type. *International Journal of Geriatric Psychiatry, 13,* 727–730.

Lucas, S., Carstairs, J., & Shores, E. A. (2003). A comparison of methods to estimate premorbid intelligence in an Australian sample: Data from the Macquarie University Neuropsychological Normative Study (MUNNS). *Australian Psychologist, 38,* 227–237.

Watt, K. J., & O'Carroll, R. E. (1999). Evaluating methods for estimating premorbid intellectual ability in closed head injury. *Journal of Neurology, Neurosurgery, and Psychiatry, 66,* 474–479.

Saxton, J. A., Ratcliff, G., Dodge, H., Pandav, R., Baddeley, A., & Ganguli, M. (2001). Speed and Capacity of Language Processing Test: Normative data from an older, American community-dwelling sample. *Applied Neuropsychology, 8,* 193–203.

Yuspeh, R. L., & Vanderploeg, R. D. (2000). Spot-the-Word: A measure for estimating premorbid intellectual functioning. *Archives of Clinical Neuropsychology, 15,* 319–326.

[176]
Stanford-Binet Intelligence Scales for Early Childhood, Fifth Edition.

Purpose: Designed to assess intelligence and cognitive abilities.

Population: Ages 2 years to 7 years, 3 months.

Publication Date: 2005.

Acronym: Early SB5.

Scores, 14: Full Scale IQ (Nonverbal IQ, Verbal IQ), Nonverbal IQ (Nonverbal Fluid Reasoning, Nonverbal Knowledge, Nonverbal Quantitative Reasoning, Nonverbal Visual-Spatial Processing, Nonverbal Working Memory); Verbal IQ (Verbal Fluid Reasoning, Verbal Knowledge, Verbal Quantitative Reasoning, Verbal Visual-Spatial Processing, Verbal Working Memory); Abbreviated Battery IQ (Nonverbal Fluid Reasoning, Verbal Knowledge).

Administration: Individual.

Price Data, 2006: $355 per complete package including manual (282 pages), Item Book 1, Item Book 2, 25 record forms, manipulatives kit, child card, layout card, and carrying case; $49.50 per 25 record forms; $54.50 per manual.

Time: (15–50) minutes.

Comments: Adaptation of Stanford-Binet Intelligence Scales, Fifth Edition (16:233).

Author: Gale H. Roid.

Publisher: Riverside Publishing.

Review of the Stanford-Binet Intelligence Scales for Early Childhood, Fifth Edition by CHRISTOPHER A. SINK, Professor and Chair, School Counseling and Psychology, Seattle Pacific University, Seattle, WA, and CHRISTIE EPPLER, Assistant Professor, School Counseling and Psychology, Seattle Pacific University, Seattle, WA:

DESCRIPTION. The Stanford-Binet Intelligence Scales for Early Childhood, Fifth Edition (Early SB5) is a norm-referenced test battery measuring intelligence and cognitive abilities of young children, ages 2 years, 0 months through 7 years, 3 months. According to the test manual, the battery is intended to be a shorter version of the Stanford-Binet Intelligence Scales, Fifth Edition (SB5; Roid, 2003; see also Bain & Allin, 2005 and Pomplun & Custer, 2005), yet preserving "the full usefulness of the SB5's features and functionality … [and] providing cost and test administration benefits for this specialized subgroup" (Early SB5 manual, p. viii). Moreover, assuming a proper level of discretion, the Early SB5 is designed to identify in young children developmental disabilities and exceptionalities, and provide useful information for intervention planning (e.g., individual educational plans) and for contexts involving research and forensic work. In short, the battery was developed to appraise a child's cognitive assets and limitations in the most efficient and reliable way in the briefest amount of time.

The test manual summarizes the enhancements made to the Early SB5 and the SB5 from the Stanford-Binet Intelligence Scales, Fourth Edition (SB IV). For example, the Early SB5 and the SB5 have (a) five factors—Fluid Reasoning (FR), Knowledge (KN), Quantitative Reasoning (QR), Visual-Spatial Processing (VS), and Working Memory (WM) instead of the SB IV's four indexes; (b) more child-friendly materials and protocols; (c) five subtests that require only minimal nonverbal responses; (d) items that measure a wider range of ability level (i.e., very low functioning to very high giftedness); and (e) upgraded the test's usefulness.

Unlike the SB5, the Early SB5 includes these helpful modifications: (a) a Test Observation Checklist, (b) items that assess a range of ability levels in young children, (c) a software program that individualizes test results for caregivers, and (d) a condensed format and a single-volume test manual.

The Early SB5 battery must be individually administered to young children by highly experienced examiners who ask the children to respond to each item either verbally, nonverbally, or by performing a task. Because examiners can administer all or some of the battery's subscales, the mean testing time may range from 15 minutes for the battery's abbreviated version (Abbreviated Battery IQ or ABIQ) to upwards of 50 minutes to obtain a child's Full Scale IQ (FSIQ). Test items are categorized into either a Nonverbal (NV) or Verbal (V) domain, with each composed of the five factors/subtests mentioned above.

The manual clearly explains the instructions for item administration and scoring. Raw scores for each subtest are totaled on the record form and converted to age-group normative scaled scores (M = 10, SD = 3). Examinees receive a NVIQ, VIQ, FSIQ, and five factor scores (FR, KN, QR, VS, and WM), which are then summarized as (a) standardized scores (M = 100, SD = 15) and placed within examiner-determined confidence intervals (e.g., 90% or 95% CIs) and (b) percentile ranks. Subtest scaled and standard scores are readily profiled in coherent graphs. Trained examiners can also conduct qualitative analyses on domain and subtest score differences. In addition to manual scoring, a computer software program is available. It should be noted, however, there is no space on the record form for examiners to record their qualitative impressions and metacognitions; they simply indicate "fully correct," "partially correct," or "incorrect." There are supplementary scoring options outlined in the test manual as well (e.g., ABIQ, change-sensitive scores based on item response scaling theory). The items and their administration should be comprehensible to well-educated clinicians, psychometricians, and psychologists. Finally, the manual clearly articulates how the derived scores should be carefully interpreted and contextualized for disparate subgroups of young children.

DEVELOPMENT. The Early SB5's development is systematically overviewed in the manual covering such key topics as the battery's assumptions, purpose, and foci as well as the subtests' strong theoretical and research underpinnings and their nature and function. Specifically, the test development process involved five stages conducted over a 7-year period. The planning phase included an extensive review of intelligence theory and research, followed by a series of three pilot studies. Subsequently, a "tryout" edition was tested. Once problematic issues were resolved, the measure went through a comprehensive standardization process, leading to the public release of the Early SB5. Throughout the process, careful attention was given to (a) examiner recommendations and user ratings during item selection, (b) limiting potential item bias (e.g., gender, ethnic, cultural, religious, regional, and socioeconomic disparities), (c) maintaining high within-factor/subtest internal consistency and interscorer reliability coefficients, as well as high item discrimination indexes, (d) ensuring appropriate item difficulty for the 2- to 7-year age range, and (e) increasing the validity of the test for its intended uses.

TECHNICAL. General information presented in the test manual about the norming process was well documented. In particular, the Early SB5 subtests were selected from the SB5, which were standardized on a nationally representative sample of 4,800 examinees ages 2 to 85 and older, with 1,400 of the sample under age 6 and approximately 1,660 age 7 years, 3 months or younger. The sample largely corresponds to the percentages of age, gender, ethnicity (i.e., 65.5% White/Anglo-American, 12.5% Black/African American, 13.0% Hispanic, 4.8% Asian, and 4.3% Other), geographic locale, and socioeconomic levels enumerated by the 2001 U.S. Census Bureau. Additionally, a relatively small number of validity cases were collected on a wide range of learners with special needs (e.g., n = 373, students with learning disabilities; n = 202, students with intellectually giftedness; n = 154, students with mental retardation).

As expected with a "high stakes" measure, the information presented in the Early SB5 manual concerning reliability and validity of the SB5 battery is compendious and well supported. Internal consistency coefficients were computed across age levels. For children ages 2 to 7 years, the reliability coefficients ranged from mid-.70s to mid-.90s for the five Nonverbal and five Verbal subtests. These coefficients for the broader IQ indexes (FIQ, NIQ, and VIQ) using the norms for children ages 2 to 7 years consistently ranged from the mid- to high-.90s. Slightly lower magnitudes were realized for the Abbreviated Battery IQ, ranging from .89 (3-year-olds) to .92 (5- and 6-year-old examinees). Reliability coefficients for the factor index scores were also acceptable for the young examinees, ranging from the mid-.80s to the mid-.90s. The standard errors of measurement (*SEM*) for the subtest scaled scores, IQ scores, and factor index scores (norm group of 2- to 7-year-olds) were relatively small, approximately 1.0 *SEM*

for the 10 subtests, 2.1 to 3.6 *SEM* for the different IQ indexes, and 3.0 to 5.6 *SEM* for the factor index scores.

As reported in the manual, the test-retest reliability across subtests, IQ indexes, and factor score indexes were assessed to establish the Early SB's temporal stability over a 1- to 39-day period (*Mdn* = 5 days) using 96 respondents, ages 2 to 5, from the original standardization sample. The corrected stability coefficients were adequate for the 10 subtests, ranging from .76 (FI) to .91 (WM and KN). Similar stability coefficients were reported for an older sample group (*N* = 87, ages 6 to 20, *Mdn* = 8 days between testing). The examinees' gender and ethnicities were also tabled within the stability data.

Interscorer agreement (interrater reliability) coefficients were summarized for SB5 (Tryout Edition and Standardization Edition), varying from .74 to .97 (*Mdn* = .90). Regrettably, these indexes were not disaggregated for the Early SB5 data or for the sample of younger children, ages 2 to 7.

Although the manual fails to detail the evidence specifically collected to document the Early SB5's validity, the empirical support for the validity of the SB5, its "parent," is more than sufficient and well documented (Pomplun & Custer, 2005; Early SB5 manual). For example, the Early SB5 manual provides more than adequate evidence of the SB5's content validity and criterion-related (predictive and concurrent) validity. Specifically, criterion-related validity was demonstrated by the moderate to high correlations (e.g., approximately *rs* ranging from .40 to .90) found between examinees' scores on the SB5 and their scores on the SB IV and other measures of cognitive ability (e.g., Wechsler Preschool and Primary Scale of Intelligence—Revised, Wechsler Intelligence Scale for Children—Third Edition, Woodcock-Johnson III Tests of Cognitive Ability). Predictive validity was demonstrated by correlating SB5 scores with measures of academic achievement (e.g., Woodcock-Johnson III Tests of Achievement, Wechsler Individual Achievement Test—II), yielding coefficients in the acceptable moderate to high range (approximate *rs* ranging from .33 to .84). Furthermore, the SB5's criterion-related validity was demonstrated with special groups of examinees (e.g., students with autism, developmental delays, English language learners, intellectual giftedness, learning disabilities, mental retardation).

Using Cronbach and Meehl's (1955) expansive and generally accepted definition, Roid (in the Early SB5 manual) explicated the salient evidence demonstrating the SB5's—and by inference the Early SB5's—construct validity. First, the sophisticated analyses of age trends or growth curves reflecting changes in examinee responses showed clear differences in SB5 scores across age groups. Second, tables documenting the positive moderate to strong intercorrelations among SB5 subtest scaled scores, IQ scales, and factor index scores (ages 2 years, 0 months to 5 years, 11 months and 6 years, 0 months to 10 years, 11 months) suggest that the battery (a) taps various factors of the same general construct (i.e., general ability or *g*) and (b) is multidimensional in nature. Finally, the Early SB5's construct validity was further examined through the use of confirmatory maximum likelihood factor analyses on the examinees' subtest data. Key goodness-of-fit indexes suggested that for the 2-to-5 and 6-to-10 age groups, the appropriateness of the SB5's five-dimension model was supported. Cross-battery confirmatory factor analyses among subtest data germane to the SB5 and the Woodcock Johnson III and the Woodcock Johnson III Tests of Cognitive Ability also offered further evidence for the SB5's construct validity.

COMMENTARY. The value of the Early SB5's scores to accurately estimate general intelligence and its various cognitive subcomponents of young children is substantial. The battery has numerous strengths overviewed above, including its strong theoretical underpinnings and psychometric properties, as well as the Early SB5's practical utility with the 2-to-7 year age group. Moreover, assuming the reader is highly educated in child development, assessment methods, and psychometrics, the test manual is relatively easy to follow and use. Test administration and scoring appear to be straightforward. For clinicians and school personnel who lack sufficient time to hand score the battery, we suggest using the publisher's computer software.

There are several caveats to using the Early SB5 with young children. First, examiners must be diligent in maintaining the ethical standards of psychological assessment. Second, close attention and scrutiny must be paid to the children's responses and affectations, as well as to their level of interest, energy, and motivation from moment to moment. Third, test scores must be carefully interpreted in light of the various contextual factors influencing cognitive performance (e.g., developmental history, living conditions, familial background) and to the potential limitations and negative short- and long-term consequences of assigning IQ scores to young children.

SUMMARY. The developers of the Early SB5 continue the long-standing Stanford-Binet tradition of producing technically superior and highly serviceable measures of cognitive ability. The battery can be administered and scored in a relatively efficient manner. The test manual provides strong and convincing empirical evidence for the Early SB5's reliability and validity across a variety of sample groups. Although more research is needed to confirm the Early SB5's utility with preschool and early elementary-age children, in time the battery may become a valuable component in clinical and neuropsychological assessments, where there is a need for an early diagnosis of cognitive delay. If administered with the appropriate level of caution and professional expertise, the Early SB5 can be, therefore, given to young children in clinical and school settings.

REVIEWERS' REFERENCES

Bain, S. K., & Allin, J. D. (2005). Stanford-Binet Intelligence Scales, Fifth Edition [test review]. *Journal of Psychoeducational Assessment, 23,* 87–95.
Cronbach, L. J., & Meehl, P. E. (1955). Construct validity in psychological tests. *Psychological Bulletin, 52,* 281–302.
Pomplun, M., & Custer, M. (2005). The construct validity of the Stanford-Binet 5 measures of working memory. *Assessment, 12,* 338–346.
Roid, G. H. (2003). Stanford-Binet Intelligence Scales, Fifth Edition. Itasca, IL: Riverside Publishing.

Review of the Stanford-Binet Intelligence Scales for Early Childhood, Fifth Edition by JOHN J. VACCA, Assistant Professor of Individual and Family Studies, University of Delaware, Newark, DE:

DESCRIPTION. The Stanford-Binet Intelligence Scales for Early Childhood, Fifth Edition (Early SB5) is an individually administered test of intelligence for young children (2 years to 7 years, 3 months). There are a total of 10 subtests that when combined yield a Full Scale IQ, Nonverbal IQ, and a Verbal IQ. The intended usage of the Early SB5 is for developmental and neuropsychological evaluations and research. Results can provide useful data in the determination of formal diagnoses such as mental retardation or learning disabilities. The developers state that professionals using the Early SB5 or instruments like it should be extremely cautious in accurately portraying the assessment results, the potential influence of measurement error, and the limits of interpretation when working with young children.

Average testing time can vary depending on the scales that are administered. The total time ranges from 15 to 50 minutes or longer. Included in the Early SB5 is a materials kit. Items in the kit include manipulatives (e.g., cubes, formboard, small toys, cups), two easel-style stimulus books, and an examiner's manual.

The information contained in the examiner's manual clearly addresses the following: order of administration (including completion of appropriate routing subtests), basal and ceiling rules, criteria for timed items, and use of testing materials (e.g., toys, cubes). General scoring for subtest scores and the three IQs (Nonverbal, Verbal, and Full Scale) can be completed either by hand or through a computer program. There are clearly marked tables at the end of the manual to assist the examiner in identifying corresponding standard scores for each raw score that has been tallied. The computer-scoring program follows a similar rubric as seen with the conventional hand-scoring procedures. However, in addition, five descriptive reports can be generated to illustrate a child's performance. These include an Interpretive Worksheet, a Score Summary Report, an IQ and Factor Index Descriptive Report, a Narrative Report, and a Parent Report. Finally, the author recommends that the Parent Report never be sent out by itself without an accompanying parent meeting at which time impressions of the examiner and interests of the family can be shared.

DEVELOPMENT. The pedagogical development of the Early SB5 is based on the combined works of Cattell, Horn, and Carroll, now regarded as the CHC model of intelligence. This model highlights the integration of fluid-reasoning skills, crystallized abilities, as well as g (general intelligence = Quantitative Reasoning, Short-Term Memory, Visual Processing).

The publication of the Stanford-Binet Intelligence Scales, Fifth Edition (SB5) and Early SB5 represents the completion of a 7-year process involving extensive planning (literature reviews, expert advice, and user surveys), pilot studies, tryout edition, standardization edition, and final copy. Along with the direct involvement of Horn and Carroll, renowned scholar and developer in assessment Richard W. Woodcock worked very closely with the developers, especially early on in the 7-year project. An impressive table outlining all of the steps that were carried out in each year

is provided in the manual. Clearly, the author gathered data from all different perspectives (pedagogical to clinical) in their work in publishing the SB5 and Early SB5.

Close to 400 children were involved at various stages in each of the three pilot studies that were conducted in developing the test. Rasch analyses were then completed using the pilot data and items from the SB IV in order to link items in the new SB. The author indicates that an "Excellent model-data fit" was found and items were produced to fill in any gaps. In combination, the Rasch analysis helped lead the development of the Tryout Edition of the Early SB5. Eight original experimental subtests were eliminated given their incompatibility with identified factors.

Finally, scoring studies, including those addressing fairness and item development were also carried out. In sum, the final version not only represents the completion of many rigorous psychometric studies, but it also represents close scrutiny taken by the developers to account for major issues of bias including freedom from gender, race/ethnicity, culture, and religion contamination. In comparison to the 1,000 items from the pilot and tryout phases, reportedly 375 items were used in the Standardization Edition, and following the deletion of additional items from this item sample, 293 items were selected for the final published version.

TECHNICAL.

Standardization. The norming sample consisted of 4,800 participants, who ranged in age from 2 to 99. Stratification (based on U.S. Census data) was carried out to include appropriate representation across gender, race/ethnicity, geographic region, and socioeconomic level. Data were collected from the participants over a one-year period (2001–2002). The four U.S. Census regions were utilized for both the selection of examiners and participants. The author made sure to obtain individuals who represented both rural and urban areas across the country. Approximately 400 examiners (100 per Census region) were selected to be involved in the norming studies. They assisted in the recruitment of participants from schools, childcare centers, and senior centers. Five percent of the participants were enrolled in special education and were mainstreamed for at least 50% of their day. The author specified that no special accommodations or adaptations were provided, no matter the severity level of a disability. The following groups of children were excluded, however: those children considered to have severe medical conditions, limited English proficiency, severe sensory and/or communicative deficits, hearing or visual deficits, orthopedic or traumatic brain injury, and severe behavior disturbance (including autism). Interestingly, the children in the aforementioned group were included in validity studies but not in the normative sample for the test itself. A total of 1,365 children were involved in the validity study. Twenty-seven percent of the participants had learning disabilities, 15% were identified as gifted, and roughly 10% were identified as having speech-language impairments, mental retardation, developmental delay, autism, or ADHD.

Reliability. Reliability coefficients were calculated for each score and for each major age group. Split-half coefficients were determined across subtests (these values were subsequently corrected using Spearman-Brown formula). Average coefficient values were also calculated by averaging the Fisher's z transformed values for each age group. Excellent reliability was determined for the Full Scale IQ with coefficients ranging from .97 to .98. Similar values were reported for the Nonverbal and Verbal IQs as well as the factor scores with values ranging from .90 to .96. Analysis of test-retest reliability (with median administration interval of 5 days) yielded moderate to strong coefficient values (.66 to .93). Interscorer agreement was remarkably high as well with values mainly above .74.

Validity. Information is reported for content-, criterion-, and construct-validity. For content validity, the author reports that evidence was gathered and confirmed model-data fit and content relevance especially with respect to the results received from the Rasch procedures. Convincing data are reported for criterion-referenced validity when compared with the Stanford Binet IV and L-M, Wechsler Preschool and Primary Scales of Intelligence, Wechsler Intelligence Scale for Children-III, and the Woodcock-Johnson III Tests of Cognitive Abilities. Analysis of the Full Scale IQ derived from the SB5 across differing ages correlates highly with that derived from the Stanford Binet IV and L-M as well as the Full Scale IQs from both of the Wechsler series. Similar values

were documented when compared with the General Intellectual Ability derived from full administration of the Woodcock-Johnson III Tests of Cognitive Abilities. The author is commended for his aggressive efforts in designing and implementing representative validity studies to demonstrate degrees of relatedness between the SB5 and similar measures. Such data enable practitioners to feel more confident in analyzing assessment data gathered with very young children and making appropriate recommendations for interventions that support the ongoing development of the child. Studies on construct related validity produced data that support the heavy loading of g throughout the SB5. Theoretically, loadings of g are expected to increase across the age span and thus values at higher ages do not tend to drop below .50. With children under 5, it can be common for validity values to fluctuate and fall below the .50 level given the variance in rates of development for this age span. However, values determined in validity analyses for the SB5 were consistently higher than .5 and ranged from .60 to .69.

COMMENTS AND SUMMARY. The developers are to be commended for the lengths they went to not just in the development of the tool itself but also in the documentation of its validity with research on child development. They clearly adhered to recommended principles for test development as specified in the *Standards for Educational and Psychological Testing* (AERA, APA, & NCME, 1999). Further, the author was cognizant of current practices in early childhood assessment such as the need to include multiple measures when collecting data on children and the need to collaborate across individuals including the family to reflect the whole child. Only with the inclusion of how children function in their natural environments, the expectations and priorities of their families, and the data collected from curriculum-based and criterion-based measures can results from the Early SB5 be appropriately analyzed. The development of the Early SB5 is a welcome contribution to the field.

REVIEWER'S REFERENCE

American Educational Research Association, American Psychological Association, & National Council on Measurement in Education. (1999). *Standards for educational and psychological testing.* Washington, DC: American Educational Research Association.

[177]

Stanford English Language Proficiency Test.

Purpose: Designed to evaluate "the listening, reading, writing, speaking, and comprehension skills" of English language learners.

Population: Grades preK–12.

Publication Dates: 2005-2006.

Acronym: Stanford ELP.

Administration: Individual or group.

Forms, 3: A, B, C.

Levels, 6: Readiness, Preliteracy, Primary, Elementary, Middle Grades, High School.

Restricted Distribution: Distribution is restricted to accredited schools and school districts.

Price Data, 2007: $45 per Exam kit including Test Booklet, Directions for Administering, Screening Test, Screening Test Directions, Response Booklet (Readiness—High School), Practice Test, and Practice Test Directions for Administering; $7 per Practice Test Directions for Administering; $12.30 per 10 Practice Test packs; $14.40 per 5 Screening tests; $7 per Screening Test Directions for Administering; $42.80 per cassettes (standardized recording of all directions and stimuli for Listening, Speaking, and Writing [Forms A, B, C–Primary, Elementary, Middle Grades, High School]); $12.80 per Directions for Administering; $39 per 10 machine-scorable test packs (Form A—Preliteracy, Primary); $39 per 10 machine-scorable test packs (Form B—Primary); $39 per 10 machine-scorable test packs (Form C—Primary); $27.80 per 10 machine-scorable response booklet packs (Form A—Readiness, Elementary, Middle Grades, High School); $27.80 per 10 machine-scorable response booklet packs (Form B or C—Elementary, Middle Grades, High School); $11.20 per Speaking booklet (Form A, B, or C—Primary); $46.90 per 10 reusable test packs (Form A, B, or C—Elementary, Middle Grades, High School); $7.50 per class record; $23.50 per response keys (Form A, B, or C); $33.50 per Speaking/Writing Training Manual with DVD for Readiness–Preliteracy and Primary–High School; $50 per teacher Pre-and Post-Test Online Training; $45 per technical report/manual (2005, 191 pages); new technical manuals available Fall 2007 for SELP/SSLP Readiness–Preliteracy and SELP/SSLP Primary–High School.

Foreign Language Edition: Stanford Spanish Language Proficiency Test edition available.

Comments: Test requires the use of a cassette player. [Editor's Note: The Readiness level test and an expanded Preliteracy level test were published in 2006. These materials were not available to the 17th MMY reviewers.]

Authors: Harcourt Assessment, Inc.

Publisher: Harcourt Assessment, Inc.

a) READINESS.

Population: PreK.

Subtests, 4: Listening, Basic Academic Concepts, Writing, Speaking.

Scores, 6: Listening, Speaking, Comprehension (Listening and Basic Academic Concepts), Social (Listening and Speaking), Early Academic (Basic Academic Concepts and Writing), Productive (Speaking and Writing).

Time: (40) minutes.

b) PRELITERACY.

Population: Grade K–beginning 1.

Subtests, 5: Listening, Speaking, Early Reading, Early Writing, Writing.

Scores, 6: Listening, Speaking, Comprehension (Listening and Basic Academic Concepts), Early Academic (Basic Academic Concepts and Writing), Productive (Speaking and Writing).

Time: (90) minutes.

c) PRIMARY.

Population: Grades K—2.

Subtests, 5: Listening, Speaking, Reading, Writing Conventions, Writing.

Scores: 8 scales: 5 Content scales (Listening, Speaking, Reading, Total Writing [Writing conventions, Writing], Comprehension [Listening and Reading]), 3 Communication scales (Social [Listening, Speaking], Academic [Reading, Writing Conventions, Writing], Productive [Speaking, Writing]).

Time: (85–95) minutes.

d) ELEMENTARY.

Population: Grades 3–5.

Subtests: Same as Primary.

Scores: Same as Primary.

Time: Same as Primary.

e) MIDDLE GRADES.

Population: Grades 6–8.

Subtests: Same as Primary.

Scores: Same as Primary.

Time: (95–105) minutes.

f) HIGH SCHOOL.

Population: Grades 9–12.

Subtests: Same as Primary.

Scores: Same as Primary.

Time: Same as Middle Grades.

Review of the Stanford English Language Proficiency Test by DIXIE McGINTY, Associate Professor of Educational Research, Western Carolina University, Cullowhee, NC:

DESCRIPTION. The Stanford English Language Proficiency Test (Stanford ELP) is a criterion-referenced assessment of English language proficiency designed for English language learners in Grades K–12. The test is based on the 1997 version of the standards of the Teachers of English to Speakers of Other Languages (TESOL) and on individual state standards for English as a Second Language (ESL). Its primary purpose is to determine whether the student possesses the English language skills necessary to function in instructional settings in English. The publisher's suggested uses include screening for placement at the beginning of a school year, determining annual yearly progress of English language learners, and measuring program effectiveness. Three forms are available; according to the publisher, these are "parallel in content and structure" (technical manual, p. 13).

The full test is available at four levels: Primary (Grades K–2), Elementary (3–5), Middle Grades (6–8), and High School (9–12). Each of these includes subtests in Listening, Speaking, Reading, Writing Conventions, and Writing. For each subtest, an examinee receives a developmental scale score and a performance level (Pre-Emergent, Emergent, Basic, Intermediate, or Proficient). Detailed descriptions of the performance levels are provided in the technical manual. In addition to the levels described above, a brief, individually administered Pre-Literacy Level is available for kindergarten students.

Except for the Speaking subtest, the Primary through High School levels are group-administered. The Listening, Reading, and Writing Conventions subtests consist of a total of 60 or 68 multiple-choice items, depending on the test level. Writing is assessed through two extended-response items, which may be scored locally or by the publisher. The Speaking subtest, which must be individually administered, consists of 19 performance-based oral items, to be scored by the teacher/examiner according to criteria outlined in the administration guide. Oral stimuli for the Listening, Writing, and Speaking subtests may be either read aloud by the examiner from a script or presented through audio recordings provided by the publisher. The test is untimed; the publisher's estimated times are 90 minutes for the Primary and Elementary Levels and 100 minutes for the Middle Grades and High School Levels.

DEVELOPMENT. According to the technical manual, development of the test began with reviews of state English language development objectives, recent research in second language acquisition, and publications of national professional organizations. Test blueprints were developed by the publisher and reviewed by an external advisory board of national ESL experts. Items were written by ESL content specialists and practicing teachers trained by Harcourt as item writers, guided by detailed item specifications. All items were reviewed by content experts, measurement specialists, and editorial specialists. After items were assembled into field test forms, they were reviewed by the advisory board for appropriateness of content as well as for possible bias/sensitivity issues related to language group, gender, culture, or religion. It appears that this review took place without empirical data on the items.

The manual reports that an initial field test was conducted in May 2002, but no details are given. Items were selected for the final forms based on match to the instructional standard being tested, psychometric properties, and other criteria set forth in the test specifications. Forms A and B were released in 2003, followed by Form C in 2004.

Performance levels were set by an expanded advisory board using a modified Angoff (1971) procedure conducted via the Internet during a 10-day period in January 2003. To their credit, the publishers have included in the manual considerable detail about the standard-setting procedure.

TECHNICAL. A national study of the Stanford ELP was conducted in the spring through fall of 2003 for the purposes of equating the forms and the levels, establishing statistical reliability and validity, and providing descriptive statistics on items and subtests. Participants included students from 26 states, representing a wide variety (15) of the most prevalent world languages. The levels of the test were vertically equated to yield one continuous score scale. Horizontal equating of the three forms was accomplished through a Rasch-based analysis utilizing a counterbalanced design in which each student completed two forms of the test.

Because this test is intended to determine whether a student is capable of functioning in an English instructional setting, the most compelling validity evidence would be data showing the relationship between scores on the test and actual performance in school. This type of evidence is not available for this test; it is admittedly difficult to collect. Overall, however, validity evidence for the test is strong, centering on test content, internal structure, and relationships to other variables.

The test was developed with the involvement of content experts using standards-based test blueprints, and all items were reviewed for their match to the instructional standard being addressed. In a few aspects, evidence is described only vaguely. The manual states that "individual state English as a Second Language (ESL) standards provide the foundation for the test" (p. 5), but does not specify which states' standards were considered. With regard to internal structure, the manual emphasizes the importance of item discrimination indexes such as point-biserial correlation coefficients, yet no actual discrimination values for the test's items are provided.

Patterns in correlations between different pairs of subtest scores strongly support the test's construct validity. Solid validity evidence is also provided by correlations (ranging from .76 to .80) between scores on the Stanford ELP and the Stanford Diagnostic Reading Test and by statistically significant performance differences between nonnative and native English-speaking students who took the Stanford ELP.

Reliability evidence is limited to internal consistency indices and standard error of measurement values. Whole-test alpha reliability coefficients ranged from .92 to .96 for all forms and levels, indicating strong internal consistency. The manual provides neither test-retest nor alternate-forms reliability estimates. The latter, in particular, is a very serious omission because the publisher is marketing three forms of the test.

COMMENTARY. Among the test's strengths are its face validity, attractively formatted materials, and clear, thorough administration instructions. Potential users should be aware of several limitations, however.

First, although one might assume from the test development process that the three forms of the test are parallel, the publisher has provided no evidence to support this claim. Testing using more than one form of this test is thus not recommended until the publisher can supply alternate-forms reliability estimates and equating information, because we cannot be confident that an examinee's score will not depend on which form of the test is taken. Similarly, caution is urged in interpreting gains or growth measured by the test, because test-retest reliability coefficients are also lacking.

Second, the vertically equated scaled scores and the performance levels established through the standard-setting procedure do not always correspond in a logical way, leading to difficulties in interpretation, particularly when adjacent test levels are compared. For example, teachers will likely wonder why a *ninth*-grade student who receives a scaled score of 670 on the Speaking subtest is classified as "proficient," but an *eighth*-grade student with the same scaled score is classified as only "intermediate" (see Table G.2 in the technical manual).

Third, users who desire a test reflecting the TESOL standards should be aware that the Stanford ELP is based on the original 1997 version of the standards, which have since been revised. The current edition of the standards includes a new focus on academic language needed for the core content areas of language arts, mathematics, science, and social studies (TESOL, 2006). Though the test does measure academic language proficiency in a more general sense, it does not include items that specifically address all four content areas named above.

SUMMARY. An appealing test with strong face validity, the Stanford ELP is a promising addition to the array of currently available tests of English-language proficiency. It is hoped that the publisher will continue collecting empirical data to support its validity and reliability, and that the technical documentation for the test will be refined. Potential users are urged to consider carefully the caveats in the preceding section before making a final decision to purchase this test.

REVIEWER'S REFERENCES

Angoff, W. H. (1971). Scales, norms, and equivalent scores. In R. L. Thorndike (Ed.), *Educational measurement* (2nd ed., pp. 508–600). Washington, DC: American Council on Education.
Teachers of English to Speakers of Other Languages (TESOL). (2006). *PreK-12 English language proficiency standards: An augmentation of the WIDA English language proficiency standards.* Alexandria, VA: Author.

Review of the Stanford English Language Proficiency Test by GERALD TINDAL, Professor, University of Oregon, Eugene, OR:

MATERIALS. The Stanford English Language Proficiency Test is composed of five subtests: (a) Listening, (b) Writing Conventions, (c) Reading, (d) Writing, and (e) Speaking. Only the last subtest (Speaking) is individually administered and only one subtest (Writing) uses a constructed-response format; all others are group administered selected-response, multiple-choice tests. The entire test is estimated to take 90 minutes (with subtests varying from 15 to 20 minutes).

The Listening subtest aurally presents students with words, short speeches, or scenarios with the student being directed to select an answer from various pictures or graphics that depict a situation. Responses are scored as correct or incorrect according to the match of the option with the question or picture.

The Writing Conventions subtest addresses spelling, usage, capitalization, punctuation, conventions, and word usage at the word and sentence level. A range of tasks are presented in which students look at words, pictures, and sentences to select a correct response. Conventions are scored as correct or incorrect according to the match of the option with the question or picture.

Reading is divided into three areas: (a) decoding, (b) vocabulary, and (c) comprehension. Reading tasks vary from matching a word with a picture to answering a question given a statement or a brief passage. The comprehension reading passages sample narrative, information, and functional stories. Reading items are scored as correct or incorrect according to the match of the option with the question or picture.

Writing is a constructed response in which students compose a response to a picture or graphic prompt reflecting word choice, sentence structure, organization, and fluency. The student's composition is scored on a 4-point scale of mastery that focuses on conventions, length-complexity, and vocabulary.

Speaking is designed to assess repetition of words and phrases (accuracy, fluency, naturalness of rhythm and rate, and overall intelligibility), sentence completion, story telling, and social interaction. Some items on the test are scored on a 2-point rating scale of fluency; other items are scored on a 2-point rating scale of structure and vocabulary in sentence completion; one item is scored using a 4-point scale of story telling; and finally a 2-point scale is used for social interaction.

Three levels of the test are available: (a) Primary (Grades K–2), (b) Elementary (Grades 3–5), and (c) Middle-High (Grades 6–8 and 9–12). Three forms are available and each form contains 60 multiple-choice items (Listening, Writing Conventions, Reading), 2 extended response items (Writing), and 19 performance items (in the Speaking subtest).

Extensive materials are presented to support a clear and standardized administration: (a) screening tests, (b) practice booklets, (c) directions for administration, and (d) response booklets. Within the administration booklet, materials are organized into general directions to help plan the administration by preparing the materials and familiarizing the student, coding the booklets, and administering the test (including verbatim wording).

TEST DEVELOPMENT. The technical manual is organized around test development, test structure and content framework, technical information on test scores, performance levels, and standard setting. This information is presented for both the English and Spanish Language Proficiency Tests.

The test development information presents a brief section on research conducted on second language acquisition. Only three references are used in this section and they are all quite dated. Some of the statements made are stronger than the support presented. For example, "The idea that what students learn in one language is available in a second language has solid support" (p. 6). This statement is marginally supported with three references, two of them quite dated (1982 and 1991). Indeed, the test is based on this premise of a strong relation between literacy in a native language and proficiency in learning English.

As stated by the publisher, the test was developed through a comprehensive review and careful analysis of early language development curricula and educational objectives. Blueprints were based on Harcourt's analyses (though no documentation is provided); then these blueprints were reviewed by national experts (though no names were provided nor were any credentials presented). An advisory board was listed with seven individuals. The blueprints specified grade levels and standards addressed, as well as number of items at each standard to ensure appropriate breadth of content and reliability. The following information was specified in the blueprints: (a) standards tested, (b) number of items per test form, (c) acceptable range of p-values, (d) number and/or percentage of items within acceptable p-values, (e) number and/or percentage of items within specified levels of knowledge, and (f) other psychometric criteria. Test specifications were then considered in developing the final test, including item format, content restrictions, option requirements, and sample items.

Content match (between instructional standards and curricula with test items) was conducted using Webb's (1997) dimensions: (a) Categorical

Concurrence, (b) Range-of-Knowledge, (c) Depth-of-Knowledge Consistency, (d) Balance of Representation, and (e) Source of Challenge. No information was presented about specific standards.

The publisher described the process for developing items using content specialists and item writers. No information on their qualifications or the process of training was presented. The advisory board conducted a content review and sensitivity/bias review. Finally, the technical manual included Harcourt's policy on the use of accommodations for limited English Proficient students. The range of accommodations allowed was relatively narrow (breaks, extended time, repeating directions, and individual testing).

The publishers noted that the layout of the test was designed to be clean, colorful, and flexibly administered. The publisher provides the following data on technical adequacy.

The National Research Program described in the technical manual presents data collected from Spring 2003 through Fall 2003. The publisher notes that test administration occurred in 70 school districts from 26 states. In an appendix, the following statistics are displayed in tables: count, mean raw score, standard deviation, KR20 reliability coefficient, item difficulty levels, item discrimination indices, coefficient alpha, and the standard error of measurement (*SEM*). A brief section on vertical scaling also is presented (for students in Grades 3, 6, and 9). Scaled scores and cut score ranges are described and the appendix includes extensive tables on converting raw scores to scaled scores. Finally, a number of score-reporting options are presented. Little information is provided on the standardization sample about geographic region, ages-grades, ethnicities, or language proficiency.

For every subtest and level (Primary, Elementary, Middle, and High), p values are presented along with averages, standard deviations, standard error of measure, alpha coefficients of internal consistency (which tend to range in the high .80s to the mid .90s), and KR20 coefficients (ranging from the mid .70s to mid .80s). (KR20 is a special case of coefficient alpha for use with dichotomously scored items.)

A comparison of native and nonnative speakers was performed. Significant differences were reported at every grade level for Listening, Writing Conventions, and Reading. No data were reported for Speaking or Writing. The correlation coefficients between the Stanford English Language Proficiency Test and the Stanford Diagnostic Reading Test ranged from .76 to .80.

The correlation coefficients between the English Language Proficiency Test and the Abbreviated Reading subtest of the Stanford Achievement Test series (9th edition) ranged from .33 to .53. Correlations between subscores of the English Language Proficiency Test within each of the levels ranged from .52 to .992 (Primary), .61 to .93 (Elementary), .66 to .95 (Middle), and .63 to .95 (High School).

A comparison of proficiencies was performed to link ELL student and native speaker performance in Grades 2–4. Nonproficient students scored lower than proficient students on the English Language Proficiency Test. Reliability coefficients were presented for Forms A and B and every level for the whole test. Coefficients ranged from .92 to .95.

Finally, a standard-setting process was used to determine appropriate cut scores for proficiency at five levels (Pre-Emergent, Emergent, Basic, Intermediate, and Proficient). Using a modified Angoff procedure, judges estimated how threshold students would perform in each of the five levels. For each item, the judges estimated the percentage of threshold students who would answer it correctly (or perform on the rubric). These data were averaged and a second round of discussions was used to review the distributions and adjust their estimates. Final judgments were then made on the cut scores. No information is provided about the standard-setting panels, their training, experience in teaching second language, or their geographic location.

COMMENTS AND SUMMARY STATEMENT. The Stanford English Language Test is a well-organized test that may provide useful information for school personnel in determining a student's level of proficiency. The test is well organized with support materials and is very professionally designed with a variety of tasks for students to respond and display skills in Listening, Writing Conventions, Reading, Writing, and Speaking. The test comes with very detailed tables for interpreting performance on scaled scores and making judgments about proficiency according to five levels: Pre-Emergent, Emergent, Basic, Intermediate, and Proficient. The technical data on the test are fairly minimal, which is surprising given the considerable experience in the industry by the publisher.

The test was developed on the premise that proficiency in a native language is critically relevant for gaining (and predicting) proficiency in a second language. Yet, the research presented on this topic was quite dated and minimally covered.

The content-related evidence is very weak, with no specific standards displayed in the technical manual; although an alignment approach was discussed in the technical manual, no data are presented on any of the constructs (categorical concurrence, range of knowledge, depth of knowledge consistency, balance of representation, or source of challenge). The normative sample is inadequately described. No reliability data are presented on decision consistency, which is far more important than any other type, given the purpose of the test.

Criterion-related evidence is inadequate as the measures were in-house (e.g., other Stanford tests) and focused on reading and achievement rather than a robust and demanding analysis using an outside measure of language proficiency.

The standard-setting process is not sufficiently described with little technical information presented on the outcomes, other than the final performance descriptors for each of the proficiency levels. The qualifications of the judges are not presented nor are descriptions of their training presented.

In summary, educational professionals should use this test at their own risk until the publishers present more convincing and specific data on critical issues such as the demographics of the standardization sample, content-related evidence, decision consistency reliability, more robust criterion-related evidence, and more precise information on the standard-setting processes and outcomes.

REVIEWER'S REFERENCE

Webb, N. L. (1997). *Criteria for alignment of expectations and assessments in mathematics and science education* (Research Monograph No. 8). Council of Chief State School Officers.

[178]

The Strong Narrative Assessment Procedure.

Purpose: Designed to "evaluate language and narrative skills of students with diverse impairments such as language, learning, and cognitive challenges."

Population: Grades K–8.
Publication Date: 1998.
Acronym: SNAP.
Scores, 56: Awareness of Story Structure (Setting Includes Place and Time, Identification of Central Characters), Major Plot Episodes (Statement of Problem, Statement of Plan to Solve Problem, Statement of Problem Resolution), Use of Stylistic Devices (Formal Beginning of Story, Formal Conclusion), Coherence (Logical Story Consequence, Correct Sequence of Events, Use of Transition Terms), Total Story Retelling, Responses to Comprehension Questions (Factual, Inferential), Length (Number of C-units, Number of Words), Syntax (Average Words per C-unit, Total Number of Clauses, Number of Subordinate Clauses, Number of Clauses per C-unit, Number of Adverbial Clauses, Number of Nominal Clauses, Number of Relative Clauses, Complex Subordination, Cohesion (Number of Incomplete/Erroneous Reference Cohesion Ties, Number of Complete Reference Cohesion Ties, Total Reference Cohesion Ties, Percentage of Incomplete/Erroneous Reference Ties, Successful Revisions of Reference Ties, Total Number of Conjunction Cohesion Ties, Number of Additive Ties, Number of Temporal Ties, Number of Causal Ties, Number of Adversative Ties, Percentage of Additive Ties, Percentage of Temporal Ties, Percentage of Causal Ties, Percentage of Adversative Ties, Examples of Types of Conjunction Cohesion Ties, Examples of Conjunction Cohesion Ties Used Erroneously, Story Grammar (Total Number of Story Grammar Components, Number of Settings, Percentage of Settings, Number of Initiating Events, Percentage of Initiating Events, Number of Internal Responses, Percentage of Internal Responses, Number of Plans, Percentage of Plans, Number of Attempts, Percentage of Attempts, Number of Consequences, Percentage of Consequences, Number of Reactions, Percentage of Reactions, Number of Complete Episodes, Results of Story Retelling Questionnaire).
Administration: Individual or group.
Price Data, 2006: $99 per complete kit including manual (221 pages), 4 Mercer Mayer books, and 2 audiocassettes (1 story per side).
Time: 45(40–60) minutes per battery.
Comments: This test requires the use of a cassette tape player; 4 picture books/stimulus stories include: A Boy, A Dog and A Frog; Where Are You?; One Frog Too Many; Frog Goes to Dinner.
Author: Carol J. Strong.
Publisher: Thinking Publications.

Review of the Strong Narrative Assessment Procedure by NATALIE RATHVON, Assistant Clinical Professor, The George Washington University, Washington, DC, and Private Practice Psychologist and School Consultant, Bethesda, MD:

DESCRIPTION. The Strong Narrative Assessment Procedure (SNAP) is an individually administered instrument designed to assess narrative discourse skills and plan interventions for students with language disorders, learning disabilities, severe cognitive impairments, and other special needs in elementary and middle school. According to the manual, the stimulus materials have been successfully used with students from kindergarten through Grade 8, but data for interpreting performance are available only for samples of examinees ages 7 through 10. Narrative discourse samples are obtained by having examinees listen to a tape-recorded story while looking at a wordless picture book and then retell the story to the examiner. According to the author, the materials and procedures provide a consistent assessment context so that students' progress in story retelling can be monitored over time. Materials include an examiner's manual in a three-ring binder, four small paperback picture books, and two audiocassettes. Examiners must provide an audiocassette recorder and a blank audiocassette.

Administration. Administration procedures are designed to elicit language samples under naive listener conditions. The examiner introduces the task with a practice story, which is not scored. After asking the examinee to look at the picture book and listen to the tape-recorded story accompanying it, the examiner explains that he or she has to leave the room for a few minutes. After the examinee has listened to the 4-minute story, the examiner returns and asks the examinee to retell the story and answer 10 comprehension questions (5 factual, 5 inferential). The responses are tape-recorded, and the examinee is not permitted to look back at the book. The examiner then repeats the procedure with one of the three test books, which are numbered but can be used in any order. The examinee is prompted to turn the page by a frog's croak on the tape (all of the stories involve frogs), but the nature of the prompt is explained only by the narrator, not by the examiner. This omission may be in the interest of maintaining the fiction that the examiner has not heard the story, but it could have a negative impact on the performance of children with attentional or language comprehension problems. The author notes that some students will need an aide to turn the pages, but not all practitioners have access to paraprofessionals during testing sessions, and this modification must be considered in the light of considerations about confidentiality and test validity.

Although the author cites several studies from the 1980s reporting that naive listener conditions produce the most comprehensive story retellings, the absence of a supervising adult may introduce sources of construct-irrelevant variance, and children's levels of attention and engagement cannot be evaluated if the examiner is out of the room. Moreover, leaving a child unattended in a testing room raises ethical and legal concerns. The sample report in the manual states that the student was "observed discreetly" (p. 89), but the author does not indicate how this observation was achieved, and few test users are likely to have access to a testing room with an observational window. The author describes two other procedures for establishing a naïve listener condition that permit an adult to remain in the room—one in which the student retells the story into the tape recorder for a specific listener, such as a teacher, parent, or sibling, and one in which a second aide (not the page-turning aide) serves as the listener and provides neutral prompts. Although the first procedure has been used in research (e.g., Naremore, 1997), the second is likely to increase interexaminer variance, given the probability of differences in prompting between a paraprofessional and a trained clinician. Moreover, no data are presented to demonstrate the equivalence of the various assessment conditions on retelling quality.

Scoring. Although the SNAP yields only raw scores, scoring is anything but a SNAP! The examiner audiotapes and transcribes the retelling and responses to the comprehension questions, and after initial transcription, replays the audiotape to check the transcription for accuracy. The examiner then segments the transcript into C-units (meaningful communication units) and scores the retelling in terms of syntax, utterance length, fluency, cohesion, and story grammar, as well as scoring the response to the comprehension questions. The manual provides detailed instructions for transcribing, segmenting, and analyzing the retellings; practice exercises for each set of analyses; and several reproducible forms, including a Transcription and Analysis Worksheet, a Story Retelling Questionnaire, and a Narrative Assessment Worksheet for summarizing and recording the scores. Despite these supports, opportunities for interscorer inconsistency abound because of the length and complexity of the scoring process, even with the "basic" analysis, which omits cohesion and story grammar analyses. For example, 12 separate steps are required to calculate the percentage of incomplete/erroneous reference ties, which is only 1 of 56 scores that can be calculated.

The author claims that examiners can elicit and tape-record one story retelling in 10 to 15 minutes and that skilled users can transcribe, segment, and analyze the data in another 45 minutes. Both estimates appear highly optimistic, especially if examiners administer the practice story and listen to the retelling a second time to check for accuracy, as the manual advises. The learning curve is very steep, and practitioners will need to make a major investment of time and effort before they can achieve this level of efficiency.

The manual discusses translating assessment results into intervention, with guidelines for writing reports, setting long-term goals and objectives, and linking treatment goals to instruction. Although the sample report is based on the same 10-year-old student whose performance is analyzed in the earlier scoring examples, the manual does not reproduce his Narrative Assessment Worksheet, so that users must refer back to the previous chapters to understand how the obtained scores were translated into report form.

Interpretation. Two sets of field test data are provided for interpretive purposes. For examinees ages 8 through 10, 21 scores for story retelling comprehension, fluency, length, syntax, and cohesion measures may be compared to story-specific raw score means and standard deviations for the normal language students in a sample of 78 examinees ages 8 through 10. For 7-year-old examinees, 26 comparisons for story-telling measures are available for a sample of 26 students. Analyzing retellings for 7-year-old examinees is complicated by the fact that the score categories on the Narrative Assessment Worksheet correspond to the data tables for the sample of 8- to 10-year-olds and do not include some of the scores reported for the 7-year-old group. Scores on each measure are classified as "adequate" or "inadequate," the latter defined as scores falling more than one standard deviation below the mean for the students with normal language in the samples. The normal-language groups in both samples include only 13 students per age level, which falls far below acceptable levels for subgroup size.

The manual also includes a Story Retelling Questionnaire to permit a brief analysis of story grammar scores. Story grammar scores on the questionnaire are compared to pretest story retelling scores for a group of 50 students ages 9 through 11 who participated in a study of cross-age reading (Fox & Wright, 1997), with scores falling within one standard deviation of pretest means classified as inadequate. Although the manual describes the students as reading disabled, they are identified only as poor readers in the original article, and no evidence is presented to support the use of these scores to identify children with language impairments. In fact, interpreting examinee performance using any of the data sets is likely to result in misidentification and/or overidentification, for reasons discussed in the technical section below.

No field test data are provided for interpreting responses to the comprehension questions for examinees ages 8 through 10. According to the author, students with normally developing language generally achieve 100% accuracy on the factual questions and 80% to 100% on the inferential questions, but no empirical evidence is provided in support of these guidelines. Raw score means and standard deviations for the number of factual and inferential questions answered correctly are provided for the 26 students in the 7-year-old sample, but as with the other samples, the group is far too small to permit reliable or valid comparisons. Moreover, although the author notes that 4 of the 39 language-impaired students in the 1988 field testing were reluctant to speak during all four sessions, no cautions regarding the interpretation of SNAP results for children with very low verbal productivity are provided.

DEVELOPMENT. The SNAP is based on the author's doctoral research (Strong, 1989). Stimulus stories were written and recorded for four wordless picture books (Mayer, 1967, 1969, 1974; Mayer & Mayer, 1975) that have been used extensively in studies of narrative discourse. Stories were designed to be equivalent in terms of length, syntactic complexity, cohesive density, and story grammar complexity. Field test data were collected in 1988 from 78 students aged 8 through 10 (39 with normally developing language and 39 with mild to severe language impairments) enrolled in a school district in northern Utah. The 312 narrative samples were analyzed in terms of stability of length and cohesion (Strong, 1989; Strong & Shaver, 1991) and later reanalyzed using measures of fluency, syntax, and story grammar (Strong, 1990). Additional data were collected in 1998 for another Utah sample of 26 seven-year-olds (13 with normally developing language and 13 with language impairments). All of the field-test language samples were obtained using a slide-tape presentation of the four storybooks rather than the procedures in the SNAP. The author does not discuss how this difference in administration may have contributed to differences in performance compared with the procedures in this version of the SNAP.

TECHNICAL ADEQUACY.

Field test data. For the 1988 field test sample, parental permission was first obtained for 39 "accessible" (manual, p. 100) students with language impairments, after which 39 normal-language students matched for gender and age were randomly selected from each classroom in which a language-impaired student was enrolled or from the school in the case of retained students with language impairments. Mean IQ scores are presented by age for the language-impaired group, and Peabody Picture Vocabulary Test–Revised (PPVT–R) means are presented by age for both groups, but no other demographic information is included. Sample characteristics for the 7-year-old group are presented only for gender and PPVT–R scores. Data for interpreting responses to comprehension questions were taken from the 1997 study cited above (Fox & Wright, 1997). Although not mentioned in the SNAP manual, study participants were enrolled in a school in a rural, southeastern U.S. community with a high poverty rate and low levels of parent education, which may have resulted in deflated means and reduced score variance. In addition, the manual describes the students as reading disabled, whereas in the article, they are described only as poor readers. Using data from any of these samples to interpret examinee performance is likely to result in misidentification and/or overidentification for several reasons. First, for the 1988 and 1998 samples, means and standard deviations are presented separately for students with normal language and students with language impairments at each age level. Thus, examinee scores for most measures (scores are combined across age levels for two measures) are compared to only 13 children per age interval,

which falls far below the minimum size of 100 per age subgroup necessary to ensure score stability and an adequate representation of infrequent characteristics. The 1-year group intervals for the 1998 sample are too broad for use with children around 7 years old, and the 1988 sample data are now well beyond the 12-year criterion for norm recency (Rathvon, 2004). Moreover, examinee scores are compared to scores for students with normal language, which is likely to result in overidentification of language impairment because of inflated means.

The author does acknowledge that the data "do not meet the essential requirements for standardized test construction" (manual, p. 108) in terms of size and representativeness and advises users to develop their own norms if their examinee populations differ markedly from students in the field test sample or are of different ages. Nevertheless, interpretive guidelines direct users to compare examinee performance to that of normal-language field-test age peers. Similarly, the Narrative Assessment Worksheet provides space for recording means and standard deviations for normal-language age peers, and the sample report discusses the student's performance in reference to these scores. The guidelines for constructing local norms should be clarified. The manual recommends assessing 10 or more students per grade level, which is adequate for classroom-level norms but well below the recommended minimum of 20 for grade-level local norms (Stewart & Kaminski, 2002).

Reliability. Reliability evidence is very limited. Internal consistency is not evaluated. The four stories are highly similar in terms of number of C-units, number of major episodes, and other relevant variables, but correlations between the four sets of scores are not presented. Transcription agreement between the author and an unidentified coder was 100% for 64% of the 312 retellings for the 1988 sample, whereas there was no more than a three-word disagreement for the other 36% of the retellings. Intercoder agreement for segmentation of randomly selected transcripts and resegmentation of 11 additional randomly selected transcripts averaged 99% for both sets of comparisons after disagreements were resolved. Average intercoder agreement between the author and a set of trained coders (number unspecified) for 30% of the 1998 retellings was above 90% for transcription, segmentation, and all coding types. Although not discussed in the manual, agreement among three teacher scorers for pretest retellings in the 1997 study was .96.

Validity. Validity evidence based on test content includes a chapter discussing the rationale for assessing narrative language, studies on the elicitation of narrative discourse samples, and research on the SNAP elicitation task. The wordless picture books with black-and-white illustrations have been used extensively as a generative story-telling measure in narrative language research (e.g., Berman & Slobin, 1994; Botting, 2002). The illustrations are delightful, and the stories written for them are just as charming. Unfortunately, the male narrator reads the stories in a somber, almost lugubrious tone and with little expression, which may fail to engage some children. In addition, the main character in all of the books is male, and he and all of the other characters are Caucasian. The manual includes a brief discussion of cultural differences in narration but provides no data to support the assertion that the SNAP has utility for assessing English learners. Evidence that representatives from various demographic groups reviewed the materials and procedures for possible linguistic, cultural, gender, or racial/ethnic bias during the development and field-testing process is also absent.

No evidence is presented to document the SNAP's relationship to other validated language tests or contextually relevant measures such as teacher ratings and school grades or its utility in predicting future language outcomes. Construct-related validity is also limited. Differences among mean scores for the three age groups in the 1988 sample were in the expected direction and statistically significant for only 6 of the 21 measures, calling into question the developmental nature of the skills being measured, although subgroup sizes are so small that firm conclusions cannot be drawn. Group differentiation analyses also yielded mixed results. When scores were combined for the four stories, only 13 of the 21 scores (62%) significantly discriminated between normal-language and language-impaired groups. For the 7-year-old sample, nearly half of the measures (12 of 26) did not discriminate significantly between the two groups. No evidence that the SNAP can differentiate between individual children with and without language impairments is presented.

COMMENTARY. In recent years, there has been increasing interest in standardizing story re-telling tasks for diagnostic screening purposes and developing normative data that can be used to evaluate narrative language performance and monitor the progress of children receiving language services compared with normal developmental patterns (Botting, 2002; Gazella & Stockman, 2003; Scott & Windsor, 2000), especially in view of evidence that narrative language measures are among the strongest predictors of prognosis for children with language impairment (Botting, Faragher, Simkin, Knox, & Conti-Ramsden, 2001). Unfortunately, the SNAP's ability to contribute to this effort is limited by serious psychometric problems. Although the SNAP is described as a procedure rather than a test and the samples as yielding field-test rather than normative data, interpretive guidelines, forms, and report examples focus on comparing examinee performance to scores from small groups of normal-language-age peers in those samples, which is likely to result in overidentification. Although there is some limited evidence for interscorer reliability and stability, no evidence of internal consistency is presented. Although students with language impairments scored lower than students with normal language on the majority of measures in both field-test samples, the diagnostic utility of the SNAP remains uncertain because the samples fall short of minimum standards for recency, size, representativeness, and other critical factors. The SNAP also rates low in usability. Using the SNAP for screening, diagnostic, or intervention planning purposes is not supported by the evidence provided, although the information obtained may be of interest to clinicians seeking narrative discourse samples to supplement information obtained using standardized language tests.

SUMMARY. The Strong Language Narrative Assessment Procedure (SNAP) is one of several recent efforts to develop instruments that yield more standardized samples of text-level discourse skills. Although the author has created a structured procedure for eliciting and analyzing language samples using an attractive set of wordless picture books, there is insufficient evidence that the procedure yields consistent or clinically useful results. Evidence of reliability across items, occasions, and assessors is limited or absent. The field test samples provided for interpreting examinee performance are psychometrically unsound and are likely to contribute to overidentification and misidentification. Practitioners who are interested in assessing narrative language skills in school-age populations may wish to consider the Test of Narrative Language (Gilliam & Pearson, 2004; 16:247), which has good specificity and sensitivity and is rapidly becoming the standard measure in studies of text-level discourse.

REVIEWER'S REFERENCES

Berman, R., & Slobin, D. (Eds.). (1994). *Relating events in narrative.* Hillsdale, NJ: Erlbaum.

Botting, N. (2002). Narrative as a tool for the assessment of linguistic and pragmatic impairments. *Child Language Teaching and Therapy, 18,* 1–22.

Botting, N., Faragher, B., Simkin, Z., Knox, E., & Conti-Ramsden, G. (2001). Predicting pathways of specific language impairment: What differentiates good and poor outcome? *Journal of Child Psychology and Psychiatry, 42,* 1013–1020.

Fox, B. J., & Wright, M. (1997). Connecting school and home literacy experiences through cross-age reading. *The Reading Teacher, 50,* 396–403.

Gazella, J., & Stockman, I. J. (2003). Children's story retelling under different modality and task conditions: Implications for standardizing language sampling procedures. *American Journal of Speech-Language Pathology, 12,* 61–72.

Gilliam, R. B., & Pearson, N. A. (2004). Test of Narrative Language. Austin, TX: PRO-ED.

Mayer, M. (1967). *A boy, a dog and a frog.* New York: Dial Books for Young Readers.

Mayer, M. (1969). *Frog, where are you?* New York: Dial Books for Young Readers.

Mayer, M. (1974). *Frog goes to dinner.* New York: Dial Books for Young Readers.

Mayer, M., & Mayer, M. (1975). *One frog too many.* New York: Dial Books for Young Readers.

Naremore, R. C. (1997). Making it hang together: Children's use of mental frameworks to structure narratives. *Topics in Language Disorders, 18*(1), 16–31.

Rathvon, N. (2004). *Early reading assessment: A handbook for practitioners.* New York: Guilford Press.

Scott, C. M., & Windsor, J. (2000). General language performance measures in spoken and written narrative and expository discourse of school-age children with language learning disabilities. *Journal of Speech, Language, and Hearing Research, 43,* 324–339.

Stewart, L. H., & Kaminski, R. (2002). Best practices in developing local norms for academic problem solving. In A. Thomas & J. Grimes (Eds.), *Best practices in school psychology IV* (pp. 737–752). Bethesda, MD: National Association of School Psychologists.

Strong, C. J. (1989). *Stability of oral cohesion skills of language-impaired and normally developing school-aged children.* Unpublished doctoral dissertation, Utah State University, Logan.

Strong, C. J. (1990). *Stability of story-grammar, syntax, and fluency skills of language-impaired and normally developing school-aged children.* Unpublished report submitted to the American Speech-Language Hearing Foundation for 1989 New Investigator Award. Rockville, MD: ASHA Foundation.

Strong, C. J., & Shaver, J. P. (1991). Stability of cohesion in the spoken narratives of language-impaired and normally developing school-aged children. *Journal of Speech and Hearing Research, 34,* 95–111.

Review of the Strong Narrative Assessment Procedure by ANNITA MARIE WARD, Associate Professor, Salem International University, Bridgeport, WV:

DESCRIPTION. The Strong Narrative Assessment Procedure (SNAP) is an assessment tool designed for use by speech/language professionals who work at the elementary or middle school level. The assessment is administered individually and it involves students listening to a story while looking at a storybook. After listening to the story, a student retells it without reference to the book. The retelling is taperecorded and then analyzed for certain linguistic features. Each analysis is compared to mean scores and standard deviations of the same analysis of retellings by children who have normal linguistic development. Judgments are then made about the examinee's linguistic development, the need for intervention, and the type of intervention that should be offered if intervention is needed.

Four storybooks are provided as part of the materials needed to administer the assessment. The books have no words but a tape of each book's story is also provided. Needed and provided as part of the assessment materials are practice exercises for segmenting and analyzing students' narratives, a reproducible narrative assessment worksheet for summarizing and recording a student's syntax, sentence length, fluency, complexity, cohesion, and story grammar. Instructions are provided for eliciting, transcribing, and analyzing story retellings.

A testing/reference manual has been provided by the publisher, Thinking Publications. The manual is 206 pages long with 6 of those pages being reference pages.

The manual offers 10 steps for the narrative assessment. The examiner is told to give the examinee a storybook and then turn on a tape that tells the story of that particular storybook. The examiner then leaves the room and returns once the tape has finished. The examiner next takes the book away from the child and asks the child to tell the story he or she has heard. The child's retelling is tape-recorded as are responses to the 10 comprehension questions the examiner asks once the retelling is completed. Ten comprehension questions for each of the four storybooks, 5 factual and 5 inferential, are provided in the testing manual.

The examiner transcribes the retelling and segments it into communication units (C-units). C-units are defined as "one main clause … with all of its subordinate clauses attached to it" (manual, p. 15). Rules for segmenting C-units are offered in the testing manual. The examiner must count and record the number of words in each C-unit and then analyze those units for fluency, complexity, cohesion, length, syntax, and story grammar. Responses to comprehension questions are also recorded and judged for accuracy. The test manual also explains how to analyze for comprehension, fluency, and length; how to analyze for cohesion; and how to analyze for story grammar.

Fluency is defined as "the flow of language used to retell the story" (manual, p. 25) and story grammar as "the structural and content relationships that exist within stories, giving them shape" (manual, p. 63). Cohesion is defined as "the linguistic devices (grammar and vocabulary) that create connections (or 'ties') between and among sentences" (manual, p. 49).

All information gained from the analyses is recorded on the narrative assessment worksheet. In analyzing accuracy of responses to comprehension questions the examiner is told to make a judgment about whether or not the response is accurate based on information found in an appendix of the manual. From this analysis the examiner is told to "form an initial opinion about the adequacy of overall language comprehension skills" (manual, p. 27). The examiner analyzes fluency by counting the number of pauses per C-unit and has to judge whether self-corrections, abandoned utterances (starts/revisions, repetitions, fillers, and asides), and mazes detract from the retelling. The manual tells the examiner to make such judgments based on experience. Examples in the manual help guide the examiner in judging whether or not retellings can be considered fluent. In order to determine whether or not the examinee's total number of C-units and fluency fall within the normal range, the examiner uses means and standard deviations from appendices in the manual to compare an examinee's number of C-units and fluency to those of students of normal language development who participated in a pilot study of the SNAP. The manual provides guidance on how to write a report on the results of the assessment analyses as well as recommendations for interventions based on the analyses.

TEST DEVELOPMENT. "In the winter of 1988 SNAP stimulus stories and procedures were field tested" (manual, p. 99) using retellings from 78 students, aged 8–10 years. A later field test was conducted in the winter of 1998 to elicit and analyze retellings from 26 seven-year-old children. The results of this study are described in the testing manual.

During the 1988 field study, students participated in four sessions, a session for each of the storybooks. The four sessions occurred at 2-week intervals. The 312 narrative samples that were gathered were analyzed to establish the stability of length and cohesive adequacy measures over time. A later procedure reanalyzed the samples using measures of fluency, syntax, and story grammar. Thirty-nine of the students in the 1988 study had been identified by a northern Utah school system as having mild to severe language impairments. These students all had IQs higher than 85 and were not identified as emotionally, socially, or intellectually handicapped and were not identified as behaviorally disordered.

Thirty-nine students, randomly chosen from classrooms enrolling linguistically impaired participants but who were not themselves identified as linguistically impaired, also participated in the study. These students all had IQs higher than 85 and were not identified as emotionally, socially, or intellectually handicapped and were not identified as behaviorally disordered.

All participants in the field study were administered the Peabody Picture Vocabulary Test—Revised (PPVT-R). The mean scores for the PPVT-R for the students with normal language development was higher at every age level than the mean scores for students who had been identified as linguistically impaired. Analysis found the difference between the means for the two groups to be statistically significant.

During the field study the stories were presented from a rear-projection slide projector and students listened to the stories using headsets. Examiners taped students' retelling of stories and transcribed them. A second person listened to tapes to establish accuracy of transcriptions. For 64% of transcriptions there was complete agreement on accuracy; on 36% of transcriptions agreement was reached after transcribers relistened to tapes; 3% of tapes had to be discarded as agreement could not be reached due mostly to unintelligible words or sequences.

Tapes from the 1988 field test were coded for number of C-units; number of words; number of subordinate clauses; number of adverbial clauses; number of nominal clauses; number of relative clauses; number of incomplete, complete, and erroneous reference cohesion ties; number of complete episodes; number of conjunction cohesion ties; and number of story grammar components. No significant differences were found between the two groups of students on percentage of additive conjunctions, percentage of temporal conjunctions, percentage of causal conjunctions, percentage of settings, percentage of plans, percentage of consequences, or percentage of reactions.

As the data from the field studies were collected in only one geographical area with relatively small samples, the testing manual admits they may not be generalizable to groups that have characteristics different from members of the samples; therefore, the testing manual explains to examiners how to conduct their own field studies on the SNAP.

TECHNICAL. No technical report was offered with the testing/reference manual. Results of the field studies were presented. These studies compared analyses of retellings of stories by language-impaired students to analyses of retellings of the same stories by students who exhibited normal language development (i.e., the later group of students had not been identified by their school system as language-impaired). Children from these two groups were paired for gender and age. Both groups of students were enrolled in public schools in northern Utah, and the language-impaired students had been identified as language-impaired based on a 1981 United States Department of Education definition that a student is to be considered language impaired if that student "performed at least one standard deviation below the mean on two or more measures of oral expression or listening comprehension in one or more of three areas—morphology, syntax, and semantics" (manual, p. 100).

Reliability and validity. The manual offers no information on the validity of the SNAP as a language assessment tool. And no information is provided on the reliability of testing results obtained from various administrations.

COMMENTARY. The goals for the SNAP, according to the manual, relate to eliciting story retellings from elementary and middle school children and analyzing those retellings for certain linguistic features. After these analyses have been performed, users of the assessment are advised to take appropriate information from the field test data contained in the appendices of the manual to compare results from an individual analysis to means and standard deviations found within the appendices. However, there is no clear explanation in the testing manual as to how the comparison between the results of an individual analysis and this statistical information is to be made.

Moreover, for some analyses that test administrators are directed to perform, such as analyzing comprehension scores, there is no direction to use comparative statistical data. In the case of the results of comprehension questioning, test

users are told that they should form their own judgment about the adequacy of responses. The author of the test suggests that her own professional opinion after giving language tests for a decade is that children with normal language development score 100% on factual questions and 80% to 100% on inferential questions! From this information the conclusion is drawn that students' comprehension should be scored as "adequate" if they score 80% or higher on the factual and inferential comprehension questions.

But aside from the issue of scoring the comprehension responses, we have to wonder if it is possible to assess listening comprehension in the manner in which the SNAP attempts to assess it. On this assessment students listen to a story, retell it, and then are asked questions about it. Thus, listening comprehension may not be assessed so much as memory or interest. If students cannot respond to comprehension questions, they may not have a linguistic deficit so much as a memory deficit. In fact, this entire assessment is based on students' ability to remember. That is, the retellings that are scored for certain linguistic features are all based on memory with no reference to the storybook the students viewed while they listened to the story that they are later asked to retell.

No field study data are available for scoring the analyses of story structure. The testing manual recommends that the examiner should compare an analysis of an individual's story structure to the results of a study done by Fox and Wright in 1997. A table in the testing manual shows the means and standards deviations for the story structure analysis on children, ages 9 to 11, who participated in the referenced 1997 study. However, according to the table these participants had been identified as *reading disabled, not linguistically impaired.* The ability to recall a story's structure may be the same among linguistically impaired children as it is among reading disabled children or it may not be the same. However, if the SNAP is being used to identify linguistically impaired children, surely measures and scores should relate directly to that goal.

These issues related to scoring the comprehension and story structure analyses are indicative of an overall problem of the SNAP. It is not really clear from information provided by the publisher what the SNAP is designed to measure and, therefore, even the test developer has shown difficulty in assigning meaning to the multitude of measurements and analyses this assessment involves. Language is complex and has many aspects that can be loosely identified as phonological, syntactical, semantic, communicative, and pragmatic. Language impairments or disorders then are likely not of one type. We can identify some of these impairments or disorders as auditory discrimination problems, language processing problems, social/communicative problems, etc. As language itself is complex, then the sources of linguistic problems are complex and are likely varied. For example, auditory discrimination problems may have a physical basis; language processing problems may have both physical and cognitive sources; communicative/social problems may come about as a result of cognitive and social problems. These examples suggest that a linguistic assessment must not only reflect and be complex as the SNAP looks and is, but such an assessment must also reflect the complexity of language problems and the complexity of their sources as the SNAP does not. The task the SNAP is based upon is as much a memory task and a literacy task as it is a language task. Students must be able to remember a story in order to retell the story, and they must have had significant literacy experiences in order to tell a story and identify the structure of that story. Students' failures to provide accurate retellings will affect the analyses of their retellings. These analyses will be interpreted in terms of students' linguistic development but, in fact, students who are identified as linguistically impaired as a result of the analyses may not really have impaired language development as much as they have memory problems or a low level of literacy development. The developer of the SNAP does not acknowledge this complexity and has made no effort to establish the validity of the SNAP as a language assessment tool. Indeed, the overemphasis in the analyses on syntactical structures makes it likely that, even if the SNAP were valid as a linguistic assessment tool, it would identify linguistic problems of only a certain nature—those that relate to volume of production and elaboration—and would miss problems that relate to language processing, auditory discrimination, social communication, and pragmatics.

SUMMARY. The testing/reference manual for the SNAP presents some interesting research and ideas related to the syntactical structures used by both language-impaired children and children

of normal linguistic development. However, the test developer offers no evidence that this assessment tool is valid as a measurement of children's linguistic development. The analyses that the assessment requires are time-consuming and require not only a general knowledge of linguistic development but specific technical knowledge of English grammar and of specific conventions of discourse such as cohesive ties, all of which are explained throughout the testing/reference manual. The field tests that are detailed in the manual are applicable only to a certain population as the samples for the tests are small and consist only of children from one geographical area. The manual advises test users to conduct their own field tests if their populations differ from those of the samples that were used in the SNAP field tests. Why users should go to such an extent when other valid tests exist to identify linguistic impairments and developmental delays is less than entirely clear.

[179]

Stroop Color and Word Test [Adult and Children's Versions, Revised].

Purpose: Designed to test "the ability of the individual to separate the word and color naming stimuli."
Publication Dates: 1978–2003.
Scores, 4: Word, Color, Color-Word, Interference.
Administration: Individual or group.
Forms, 2: Children's Version, Adult Version.
Price Data, 2006: $85 per complete kit including manual and 25 test booklets (specify Children's or Adult Version); $35 per manual (specify Children's [2003, 35 pages] or Adult Version [2002, 72 pages]); $55 per 25 test bookets (specify Children's or Adult Version); $25 per computerized scoring; $80 per Spanish test booklet; $40 per Spanish manual.
Foreign Language Edition: Spanish version available.
Time: (5—15) minutes.
Publisher: Stoelting Co.
   a) CHILDREN'S VERSION.
      Population: Ages 5—14 years.
      Authors: Charles J. Golden, Shawna M. Freshwater, and Zarabeth Golden.
   b) ADULT VERSION.
      Population: Ages 15 years and older.
      Authors: Charles J. Golden and Shawna M. Freshwater.
Cross References: See T5:2516 (122 references) and T4:2582 (40 references); for reviews by James R. Evans and George W. Hynd of an earlier edition of the Adult version, see 9:1196 (15 references); see also T3:2319 (1 reference).

Review of the Stroop Color and Word Test by MARK ROYBAL, Adjunct Professor of School Psychology, National University, San Diego, CA:

DESCRIPTION. The current Stroop Color and Word Test is reportedly an updated norm-referenced standardized version of the initial Stroop test, which was published in 1978. The present manual is an effort to "update both scoring and interpretive strategies … as well as to improve clinical awareness of the meaning of Stroop scores" (manual, p. i). Initially, the Stroop Color and Word Test was used as a research tool for experimental purposes; however, its use has now expanded into the clinical arena. The authors ambitiously claim that the Stroop Color and Word Test would "be useful in the identification of several significant disorders" (children's manual, p. ii), such as ADD/ADHD, Oppositional Defiant Disorder, frontal lobe injuries, stress, and personality disorders.

The renewed version comes with two separate manuals for clinical and experimental uses: an Adult version for ages 15 and up, and a Children's version for ages 5–14. The new test version uses a three-color format with a modified scoring system for adults. The Stroop Color and Word Test consists of a front-page record form and three subtests. Each subtest is composed of a 5 x 20 matrix of items and is offered on a separate page: The Word test contains the names of colors printed in black ink; the Color test is presented with semantically meaningless symbols (XXXX) printed in colored ink; and the Color-Word test is composed of words from the first page, printed in the colors from the second page, with the restriction that the words and colors do not match (the word "RED" is presented in green or blue). Comparison scores across the three subtests render a Color-Word Interference Effect score that reportedly identifies individual differences within and among specifically defined populations.

Administration and scoring are straightforward; however, calculating T-scores using the Predicted score and Residual score was confusing and convoluted. An example would help the scoring and conversion process. The test, which can be administered in less than 5 minutes in group or individual settings, has two scoring methods: (a) the time to complete 100 items, or (b) the number of items completed in 45 seconds. New norms are included in both manuals. The children's version uses T-scores, drawn from means and standard deviation, by age, whereas the adult T-scores are tabled, based on multiple regression equations, utilizing education and age. The chapter on Common Patterns of Stroop Scores in Clinical Interpretation is prefaced with a clear caveat—scores should be interpreted "as part of a larger test battery rather than by itself" (manual, p. 9). The following chapter presents Case Examples that appear to be testimonials that lack any supportive data.

DEVELOPMENT. Conceptual development, standardization, and evaluation are critical stages of test development. The updated standardized form of the Stroop test appears to have succeeded with concept development, but failed with standardization (data collection, research questions, sample description and representativeness) and evaluation (consistency of test items and administration order).

TECHNICAL. Reliability is reported in terms of internal consistency and test-retest. Test-retest reliabilities were based on intervals ranging from 1 minute to 10 days. The author (1975) reported reliabilities of .88, .79, and .71 (N = 450) for the group version and reliabilities of .86, .82, and .73 (N = 30) for the individual version. The Color-Word Interference reliability scores in these samples were all in the .70 range. The data are difficult to interpret because of the limited information presented. Small sample sizes, brief time intervals, and limited analyses make the individual version findings suspect.

It is unclear what the authors of the Stroop test intend to measure. Is it intended to measure the difference between an innate color-naming organic ability versus a learning skill or is it intended to differentiate a variety of behavior responses from one behavioral response? The Stroop phenomenon continues to remain a mystery. Consequently, validity in the technical sense is lacking; however, there does appear to be face validity in what the Stroop appears to measure, but what it actually measures is unknown. The extensive literature cited appears to be a mixed bag of research findings that include modified test forms, administrative changes, and altered test items.

Norm-referenced tests are standardized using a clearly defined population that allows the user to compare individual scores to the stratified norm group. Unfortunately, both the Adult and

Children's versions lack essential data about the number of subjects, their racial or ethnic status, their gender, and the geographic regions they represent. It is difficult to determine the appropriateness (relevance) of a given subject's score to an unspecified population.

COMMENTARY. The Stroop Color-Word test, which is based on the competing-response hypothesis, has an extensive history of research-supported reviews that has produced a wide range of scientific literature. The Stroop Effect phenomenon, which occurs when speed and accuracy are slower (interference) with color-word stimuli than with reading color names, has been used to differentiate normal, non-brain-damaged subjects from brain-damaged subjects, identifies good flexibility, evaluates stress, cognition, and psychopathology. The brevity of the test and its scoring format have attracted researchers and clinicians to use this test.

SUMMARY. The Stroop Color Word test appears to be similar to the first edition with the exception of the updated norm tables, scoring, and interpretive strategies. Unfortunately, the manual appears to have maintained its monograph format, which puts it at odds with industry standards and test users' expectations. In addition, the norms are not clearly defined or described, and it appears that some support studies did not use the standard protocol for administration, and failed to provide appropriate interpretation strategies for the clinician. The use of the Stroop Color-Word test as a research tool has generated voluminous studies and should continue in that mode; however, its use as a clinical tool is questionable and is not recommended.

Review of the Stroop Color and Word Test [Adult and Children's Versions, Revised] by LOUISE M. SOARES, Professor of Educational Psychology, University of New Haven, West Haven, CT:

DESCRIPTION. The Stroop Color and Word Test assesses an individual's ability to sort information on three levels or scales: (a) identification of the words of colors printed in black ink; (b) naming of the colors (red, blue, green) of the nonwords written as XXXX; and (c) producing the names of the color words that are printed in another color. This last scale is interesting but it is not unexpected that slower times are recorded and an interference effect noted (e.g., saying the ink is blue when the color name printed is red). Each of these levels appears on one page with 100 items in five columns of 20, for a total of 300 items. Two versions are available—one for individuals over age 15 and a child's version for individuals aged 5 to 14. The items are the same for both versions; only the scoring is different. Administration time varies from 10 to 15 minutes for impaired participants on one scale to 45 seconds for groups of presumably normal participants. The participants are handed the test booklet and told to read aloud down the columns until they are told to stop (after 45 seconds). The individuals are then told to circle the item they last read. In group arrangements, the participants are told to read the words to themselves and then circle the last word read to themselves after being told to "stop." Scoring instructions are sufficiently clear for both versions. The Stroop Test yields three basic scores that are converted to T-scores for comparative purposes. Translating the raw scores to T-scores is especially helpful for comparisons of ages and for interpretations of results.

DEVELOPMENT. The literature base is extensive, though most of it predates the first standardized version of the test (1975), which resulted from the collection of basic normative data between 1974 and 1977. The earliest versions generally consisted of 10 rows and 10 columns on each page, using five colors. It was said to be useful in countless studies for identifying individual differences "in cognitive and personality research, in experimental psychopathology, and in the diagnosis and understanding of organic brain dysfunction" (manual, p. 1). In most cases, the identification process is horizontal rather than vertical. In other words, the results of the Stroop scores may reinforce the findings of other more sophisticated instruments rather than the other way around. No construct is provided or defined. In the Preface the author writes that the Stroop phenomenon "continues to remain somewhat of a mystery" and that it has become a "pop-icon of sorts" (manual, p. i).

TECHNICAL. Evidence supporting validity and reliability of the Stroop Color and Word Test is absent and insufficient, respectively. No validity data are offered. Limited data are offered related to test-retest reliability and alternate forms reliability. The test-retest coefficients were reported in 1965 and 1975, covering periods from 1 minute to 10 days. The coefficients ranged from .69 to .89

with different forms of the test. The same information appears in both manuals.

COMMENTARY. The lack of validity data has many implications in terms of confirmation to all other research that the scores presumably provide or are "useful in investigating a wide range of basic psychological processes in normal and dysfunctional people (manual, p. 2). However, because the test was designed to measure—simply put—"the ability of the individual to separate the word and color naming stimuli" (manual, p. 2), how can it possibly be useful to detect "residual functional deficits" (manual, p. 27)? And "medial-frontal infarctions" (manual, p. 30)? And as "an indicator of dementia severity" (manual, p. 32)? And the effects of Parkinson's disease (manual, p. 34), Turner Syndrome (manual, p. 35), schizophrenia (manual, p. 37), hemispheric asymmetry (manual, p. 40), depression (manual, p. 39), and so forth? It is difficult to fathom that 45 seconds of administration time can accomplish all that is claimed. If it is possible, far more evidence needs to be presented. The manual for the Children's Version adds claims for autism, learning disorders, attention deficit disorder, social impulsivity, and other conditions.

Reliability claims are also in doubt (manual, p. 8). The time interval used in test-retest reliability studies is too brief to be meaningful, and the coefficients from different forms should not be considered equivalent. No means and standard deviations were provided, nor estimates of the standard error of measurement.

The administration instructions are clear and apply to both adults' and children's versions. However, for young children they are overly long, wordy, and could be viewed by some participants as intimidating. Individuals are expected to read the words in the column "out loud." The one who administers the test can verify what word they were doing when saying "Stop. Circle the item you are on." For the group administration, the individuals are to read the words "to yourself," and follow the instructions of circling the word when hearing "Stop." There is no verification of how far any child went; so each child could circle any word.

The Children's version may be too long for young children—the same 300 items as in the Adult version. Not only do many children in the early grades continue to struggle with reading anything that long, they also tire more easily.

SUMMARY. I find no incontrovertible evidence that this test performs better than any other test to identify problems in semantic processing or to diagnose alleviation of the problems. Too much claim is made by the author(s) for the probative value of the Stroop test as part of a battery of tests in clinical diagnoses. Insufficient evidence is provided for such claims. Construct clarification and validity data are missing; reliability data are inadequate.

The Stroop test is a creative rendition of the observation that the individual tends to separate the word and color stimuli. Especially interesting is the interference effect that results from reading a color name, say "red," when it is printed in "blue" ink. There is no denying that the test has become popular and is used in many research and clinical collaborations. However, much more work needs to be done to legitimize its usefulness other than to maintain its "pop-icon" status.

[180]
Structured Inventory of Malingered Symptomatology.

Purpose: Designed as a screening measure of malingering to assess symptoms of both feigned psychopathology and cognitive function.
Population: Ages 18 and over.
Publication Date: 2005.
Acronym: SIMS.
Scores, 6: Neurologic Impairment, Affective Disorders, Psychosis, Low Intelligence, Amnestic Disorders, Total.
Administration: Individual.
Price Data, 2007: $120 per complete kit including professional manual (46 pages) and 25 response forms; $68 per professional manual; $60 per 25 response forms.
Time: (10–15) minutes.
Comments: This test can be self-administered.
Authors: Glenn P. Smith and Michelle R. Widows.
Publisher: Psychological Assessment Resources, Inc.

Review of the Structured Inventory of Malingered Symptomatology by THOMAS M. DUNN, Associate Professor of Psychological Sciences, University of Northern Colorado, Greeley, CO:

DESCRIPTION. The Structured Inventory of Malingered Symptomatology (SIMS) is a 75-item test described as a screening instrument used to detect malingering. The SIMS is self-administered, with the patient answering true/false questions directly on the test. Most patients finish the

SIMS in less than 15 minutes. The test's five scales, each with 15 items, cut across a number of clinical presentations and the measure is purported to be useful both in assessments of cognitive functioning and when considering the presence of psychopathology. The five scales of the SIMS are Psychosis, Neurologic Impairment, Amnestic Disorders, Low Intelligence, and Affective Disorders. A summary score is then computed with all five scales added together for a "Total" scale. The critical items of each scale are generally symptoms that are highly unusual, atypical, or inconsistent with the particular condition being malingered. For example, the Affective Disorder scale includes the item, "When my depression becomes too severe, I go out for long walks or do some form of exercise to relieve the tension." The Amnestic Disorder scale contains the item, "I cannot remember whether or not I have been married." Those who are blatantly malingering are thought to endorse items like these, even though such examples rarely occur with depression or memory impairment.

Although no special training is required to administer the SIMS, the traditional caution is given in the manual that results should only be interpreted by a qualified clinician. Scoring the instrument is completed by simply tearing open the test booklet and adding critical items that have been endorsed on the five scales and getting a grand sum to compute the "Total" score. There is no conversion from raw scores to standard scores. The booklet indicates clinical cutoff scores and if the number of critical items endorsed is higher than the cutoff score, the patient is thought to have completed the test in a suspicious manner. The authors are very clear that the SIMS should be used only as a screening instrument and that "Diagnosis of malingering should not be based on SIMS findings in isolation" (professional manual, p. 5). Clinicians are encouraged to perform a more in-depth evaluation of their patient when SIMS scores are high.

DEVELOPMENT. The SIMS is in its first edition (copyright 2005). It has been in development since 1991 when it was conceived. Item development started in earnest in 1993 with the generation of a pool of 200 potential test items. These items were developed after identifying qualitative characteristics of malingering that were found both in the literature and as part of other instruments. To be included in the item pool, the characteristic had to load onto one of the five SIMS scales and have been included in at least two studies. Nine clinical psychologists were then asked to sort the items into one of the five categories that would become the SIMS scales. The 15 items with highest agreement among the nine raters for placement into a category or domain made the final cut to be included in the test.

TECHNICAL. Once the test items were written and categorized, the SIMS was validated with a relatively small, nonclinical sample of 476 undergraduate students at four universities and community colleges. It is not clear where these schools are located. The validation sample was predominantly female (71%) and Caucasian (89.7%). Almost 9% were described as African American, and the remainder were Asian American, Native American, or Latino. Individuals in the normative sample were then sorted into one of six experimental conditions or a seventh "honest responders" control group. Those in the experimental groups were then asked to simulate having a particular impairment: psychosis, amnesia, depression, low intelligence, or neurological impairment. Finally, a "fake bad" group was instructed to malinger "abnormality." After being administered the SIMS, the normative group was then divided into developmental and cross-validation groups. The use of college student analogs (asked to simulate impairment) is common in the malingering literature, but it is unclear if such a small sample size is adequate when norming a test for malingering.

The selection of a developmental group allowed for the empirical derivation of clinical cutoff scores for each scale that effectively separates the simulated malingerers from the control group. The malingering groups were also collapsed together and compared against the control group, giving a cutoff score on a "Total" scale as well. The clinical cutoff scores are quite low, as more than two items endorsed on four of the five scales meet criteria for malingering. More than five items on the Affective Disorders scale meet criteria. These data were then used to compute sensitivity, specificity, and efficiency percentages for the five scales and for the Total score. Not surprisingly, the Total scale had the highest efficiency with a 94.96 percentage. The analysis was repeated on the cross-validation study with almost identical results.

Reliability for the SIMS is reported for both internal consistency and stability over time. An alpha coefficient was computed with the developmental sample data to establish internal consistency. Alphas ranged from .88 on the Total scale to .82 for the Psychosis scale. Test-retest reliability is less certain. The authors report a coefficient of .72 for a 3-week interval between testing sessions. However, this coefficient was derived from a Dutch translation for the test, using the original norms, with only 24 female participants. Worse, these participants were all control subjects and responding honestly to the items in both testing sessions. Because this instrument is designed to assess people who are not responding truthfully, it is difficult to predict how stable the measurement of a malingered performance would be over time.

Construct validity for the SIMS was established by computing group scale mean scores and finding statistical significance between each instructional condition (e.g., Psychosis, Neurologic Impairment) including the honestly reporting control condition. The authors conclude that this analysis provides evidence for the scales to differentiate between honest responding and simulated malingering as well as to differentiate between different domains of feigned symptoms. The SIMS also proved to be able to differentiate among college students who were simulating a malingered condition, others who were taking the test honestly, and a third subsample of Dutch psychiatric inpatients ($n = 10$). Further studies are cited regarding the SIMS' ability to discriminate between simulated malingerers, prison inmates identified by clinical staff as malingering, defendants undergoing competency to stand trial suspected of malingering, and an adolescent offender sample.

Studies of convergent and discriminant validity found that the SIMS is highly correlated with outdated or uncommon measures used to assess a malingered profile. The SIMS Total scale score is reported to have a correlation coefficient of .84 with the MMPI F scale. A more moderate correlation was found with the 16PF faking bad scale ($r = .45$).

COMMENTARY. The SIMS purports to fill a gap in test instruments by providing a screening measure for malingering that has test items to assess both feigned symptoms of cognitive impairment and psychopathology. Other attractive features of this measure are its reasonable price, self-administration in less than 15 minutes, scoring that requires only a few minutes, and straightforward interpretation.

The SIMS also has some weaknesses. First, it is likely that patients who would endorse the highly atypical symptoms comprising the SIMS scales will also demonstrate a variety of other inconsistencies and signals to the clinician that their presentation is not genuine. Because this instrument provides only cutoff scores (from a normative sample of only a few hundred college students simulating malingering), it cannot quantify degree of faking. This failure is unfortunate, as its only purpose is to verify to a suspicious psychologist that further assessment is necessary.

It is also concerning that the clinical cutoff scores derived for the SIMS were generated from nonclinical participants who were mostly female college students. Although the SIMS manual does include promising empirical studies using clinical samples, no clinical subjects were included in the normative group. None of the studies, however, include data about how patients from a neuropsychological sample perform on the SIMS.

The assessment of possible malingering is a daunting task. There are a variety of reasons why a patient presents as not being honest about their symptoms. As the authors point out, it takes a thinking clinician and multiple pieces of evidence to complete the picture of true malingering. Although the SIMS is one more tool for the clinician to use when performing assessments, it is best used in conjunction with a thorough test battery, more than one clinical interview, a complete medical and educational record review, and the incorporation of information from a variety of sources.

Review of the Structured Inventory of Malingered Symptomatology by RONALD J. GANELLEN, Associate Professor, Northwestern University Medical School, Chicago, IL:

DESCRIPTION. One issue to be considered during any psychological evaluation, and sometimes the primary issue in a forensic evaluation, is assessment of response validity. As pointed out by Widows and Smith in the Manual for the Structured Inventory of Malingered Symptomatology (SIMS), assessment of response validity is not a trivial issue as estimates of the incidence of malingering in forensic samples on average fall in a range between 15% and 30% (Mittenberg, Patton,

Canyock, & Condit, 2002). Given what is at stake for the individuals being examined, for social institutions such as prisons and insurance carriers, and for society, these findings highlight the need for clinicians to have available objective, well-validated tools to use to detect deliberate fabrication or exaggeration of symptoms of psychopathology and cognitive and memory impairment.

The SIMS is a brief, self-report inventory written at a fifth-grade reading level and developed to be used in clinical and forensic settings as a self-administered screening measure of malingered psychological, intellectual, and neuropsychological problems. Widows and Smith intend the SIMS to cover multiple dimensions of psychological functioning, including psychosis, affective disorders, amnesia, low intellectual functioning, and neuropsychological impairment. They appropriately caution users that a determination of malingering should not be based on scores from the SIMS alone, but should be based on information obtained from multiple sources, including other validated assessment instruments.

DEVELOPMENT. The SIMS targets five domains of psychological functioning that may be exaggerated or faked during an evaluation. A pool of 200 items was initially developed by the authors to be representative of bizarre, unusual, illogical, or highly atypical symptoms of a psychotic disorder, affective disorder, neurologic disorder, amnestic disorder, and low intelligence. Nine judges sorted each of these items in terms of which one of these five domains of pathology it reflected. Items were then assigned to one of the five domains of pathology on the basis of percentage agreement among judges. A minimum agreement of 66.7% was required for items to be retained; items were discarded if the agreement rate among judges was lower. If an item was rated as belonging to more than one domain, rank ordering was used.

The authors selected 15 items to form a scale for each of the five domains of pathology the SIMS targets. Thus, the SIMS has a total number of 75 items, which are scored on five nonoverlapping scales. A total SIMS score is also calculated by summing the raw scores from all five scales. It should be noted that the SIMS does not contain any scales that allow one to determine whether an individual was attentive when completing this measure, was able to read and understand test items, and/or responded in a consistent manner.

TECHNICAL. The interrater reliability for each of the five scales was described as being excellent. Similarly, the internal consistency for each SIMS scale was found to be quite high.

Once the 75 items making up the five SIMS scales were selected, the SIMS was administered to a sample of 238 predominantly female undergraduates. Participants were assigned to one of seven conditions: honest responding, simulated psychosis, simulated depression, simulated amnesia, simulated neurologic impairment, simulated low intelligence, or simulated faking bad. Before completing the SIMS, simulators read a vignette that provided a hypothetical incentive for malingering and information about the condition they were instructed to feign. The number of participants in each group was not specified.

Scores produced by the honest responders were contrasted with scores produced by each malingering group to identify cutoff scores for the SIMS scale corresponding to the instructional set (e.g., the Psychosis scale for the group instructed to feign a psychotic disorder). Cutoff scores were established to maximize accurate identification of the honest and malingering group. An investigation of cutoff scores showed that endorsement of few items would result in classification of malingering. For instance, an individual is identified as malingering if more than one item on the Psychosis scale or more than two items on the Neurologic Impairment, Amnestic Disorders, or Low Intelligence scales are endorsed.

The utility of the SIMS cutoff scores was investigated in additional analyses combining all malingering conditions (e.g., simulated psychosis, simulated neurologic impairment) into one group. The combined malingering group was compared to honest responders on each of the five SIMS scales and the SIMS Total score and diagnostic efficiency statistics were computed. The SIMS Total score was found to be the best indicator distinguishing honest from malingering participants. Individual SIMS scales also identified malingering, although they were less sensitive and less specific than the Total score. Similar results were obtained in a cross-validation sample of 238 undergraduates.

The SIMS manual reviews a number of studies comparing simulators instructed to feign psychopathology or neuropsychological impairment to honest responders. These studies, which primarily involved undergraduate students, provided findings consistent with those described above.

COMMENTARY. Although these findings provide preliminary evidence supporting the use of the SIMS Total score to distinguish malingered from honest responding, there are several issues that require further study before one can have confidence that the SIMS accurately differentiates between genuine and feigned psychological and neuropsychological problems. For instance, the authors do not provide information about the scores bona fide patients with no incentive to exaggerate or fabricate symptoms earn on SIMS scales. Thus, we do not know how patients with schizophrenia score on the SIMS Psychosis scale, how depressed patients score on the SIMS Affective Disorder scale, nor how patients with documented neuropsychological deficits scores on the SIMS Neurologic Impairment scale. These data would answer a relevant question that needs to be addressed given what appears to be the low thresholds for identification of malingering mentioned above (e.g., malingering is suspected if more than one item is endorsed on the Psychosis scale or if more than two items are endorsed on the Neurologic Impairment scale).

Findings from a study conducted by Edens, Otto, and Dwyer (1999) suggest that although the SIMS effectively identified simulated malingering, it was less effective in distinguishing between truly symptomatic individuals and those fabricating symptoms. Given these findings, Edens et al. (1999) cautioned that currently established cutoffs for SIMS scale scores carry a risk of false positive identification of malingering when used in clinical populations.

These findings should give one pause; although the reason to administer the SIMS is to provide objective information to differentiate between feigned and genuine psychological difficulties, the Edens et al. (1999) findings suggest that positive SIMS scores may be produced both by individuals who are malingering *and* by individuals who are accurately reporting symptoms of psychopathology. Widows and Smith conceded that these findings indicate that "the SIMS may be less than optimal for differentiating malingering from emotional distress or psychopathology" (professional manual, p. 29), but suggested such false positive errors may be "rectified through the use of more extensive follow-up malingering instruments" (professional manual, p. 29).

Lewis, Simcox, and Berry (2002) present related findings. They administered the SIMS, the Minnesota Multiphasic Personality Inventory-2 (MMPI-2), and the Structured Interview of Reported Symptoms (SIRS) to a sample of 55 men seen during a pretrial psychological evaluation. Study participants were classified as responding honestly or feigning psychopathology based on their scores on the SIRS. Although malingerers produced significantly higher mean scores on all SIMS scales than honest responders, in some cases elevated scores on the SIMS Total scale did not accurately identify participants as responding honestly or malingering.

Interestingly, Lewis et al. (2002) found that SIMS Total scores *below* the established cutoff accurately identified 100% of the individuals who were not faking. These findings suggest that although one can be very confident that low scores on the SIMS Total score provide strong evidence to rule out malingering, the significance of high scores is ambiguous. The practical application of this finding is the following: When the SIMS is administered as a screening instrument individuals who obtain a low SIMS Total score are unlikely to be feigning symptoms and do not require further evaluation, whereas those scoring above the cutoff require more extensive evaluation to reach an accurate determination of response validity.

Although the studies summarized in the SIMS manual provide evidence supporting the construct validity of the SIMS, one must also consider its incremental validity. In other words, one has to weigh whether the SIMS adds information above and beyond what can be learned from other, widely used measures of response validity, such as the MMPI-2 validity scales. To date, no studies have examined whether the SIMS provides information to identify malingered neuropsychological deficits that add to information derived from established tests of feigned impairment, such as the Test of Memory Malingering (TOMM; Tombaugh, 1996).

Lewis et al. (2002) administered both the SIMS and the MMPI-2 in the forensic sample described above. They investigated the incremental validity of the SIMS by entering the SIMS Total score after MMPI-2 validity scales into a regression analysis predicting honest or malingering group status. Adding the SIMS Total score did not produce a significant increase in the variance accounted for. This finding suggests one may not learn much from the SIMS that cannot be learned from the MMPI-2. Although further study of this issue is needed, these findings should be considered when deciding whether it is cost-effective to administer both the MMPI-2 and the SIMS during an evaluation.

SUMMARY. The SIMS was developed to be used as a screening measure of exaggerated or fabricated psychopathology and neuropsychological impairment. The available evidence suggests it has considerable promise to meet this goal when concerns about the veracity of problems in psychological adjustment are at issue. Data supporting the use of the SIMS to identify feigned cognitive and memory impairment are relatively sparse. Before clinicians can embrace the SIMS, additional research is needed to investigate the response patterns of individuals honestly reporting symptoms of both psychological and neuropsychological difficulties to determine whether published cutoff scores are appropriate or should be modified. Interpretation of SIMS scores should be approached with some caution. In a screening situation, SIMS scores below established cutoff levels may be viewed as providing strong evidence that an individual is *not* faking, whereas clinicians should be aware that the significance of scores above the cutoff may reflect either valid or exaggerated responding and signals a need to obtain additional information from multiple sources to rule in or rule out malingering. As the SIMS does not appear to add additional information to what can be learned from other, well-validated measures of response validity such as the MMPI-2, it may not be cost-effective to plan to administer both instruments during a comprehensive evaluation.

REVIEWER'S REFERENCES
Edens, J. F., Otto, R. K., & Dwyer, T. (1999). Utility of the Structured Inventory of Malingered Symptomatology in identifying persons motivated to malinger psychopathology. *Journal of the American Academy of Psychiatry and the Law, 27,* 387-396.
Lewis, J. L., Simcox, A. M., & Berry, D. T. R. (2002). Screening for feigned psychiatric symptoms in a forensic sample by using the MMPI-2 and the Structured Inventory of Malingered Symptomatology. *Psychological Assessment, 14,* 170-176.
Mittenberg, W., Patton, C., Canyock, E. M., & Condit, D. O. (2002). Base rates of malingering and symptom exaggeration. *Journal of Clinical and Experimental Neuropsychology, 24,* 1094-1102.
Tombaugh, T. N. (1996). Test of Memory Malingering: TOMM. North Tonawanda, NY: Multi-Health.

[181]
Team Skills (Form A-C).
Purpose: To evaluate a candidate's ability to work as a member or leader of a team.

Population: Applicants and incumbents for jobs requiring knowledge of team principles.
Publication Dates: 1998–2001.
Scores: Total score only covering 7 areas: Conflict Resolution, Group Dynamics, Team Decision Making, Productivity and Motivation, Communication Skills, Leader & Member Skills, Interpersonal Skills.
Administration: Group.
Price Data, 2006: $13 per consumable self-scoring test booklet (minimum order of 20); $24.95 per manual (2001, 13 pages).
Time: (60) minutes.
Comments: Self-scoring instrument.
Author: Roland T. Ramsay.
Publisher: Ramsay Corporation.

Review of the Team Skills (Form A-C) by GERALD TINDAL, Professor, University of Oregon, Eugene, OR:

The Ramsay Corporation published the Team Skills (Form A-C) in October 1998. This review is based on an analysis of a manual for administration and scoring as well as a self-scoring booklet.

On the first page of the introduction of the administration and scoring manual, which is 13 pages in length, the author notes that the test "was developed for use with Supervisor (any industry) as defined in the Dictionary of Occupational Titles (U.S. Department of Labor, 1992, p. 2) and empowered employees" (p. 1). The test is designed to "measure the knowledge and skills required to work successfully in teams" (manual for administration & scoring, p. 3). Later, in the specific directions to the examinee, the author notes that the test consists of "a series of exercises to be used in employee selection" (manual for administration & scoring, p. 5).

DEVELOPMENT. The development section appears on the second page of the manual, in which seven areas of team skills and knowledge are listed as subtests: (a) Conflict Resolution, (b) Group Dynamics, (c) Team Decision Making, (d) Productivity and Motivation, (e) Communication Skills, (f) Leader & Member Skills, and (g) Interpersonal Skills. Each subtest has 5 items. (The test consists of 35 items in total.) No test blueprint is provided.

The administration directions appear on pages 3 and 5 and comprise an introduction, testing conditions, preparation, and general directions to the test examiner. A stopwatch is required, although the verbatim directions state that "there is no time limit on this test, but it should take you no longer than 1 hour" (manual for administration & scoring, p. 6). The examiner also is directed to mark the time taken on each test booklet, although this information is never related to the construct being measured. Otherwise, the general directions consist of a series of inane paragraphs guiding the examiner to be clear (but casual), objective, follow directions exactly, observe the examinee, note any significant behavior, avoid distractions, collect the booklets, and remain with the examinee ("The examiner is to stay in the testing room with the examinees at all times. This is imperative" [p. 4]).

The self-scoring booklet is designed to be torn into a cover page (with the "bubbles" marked) and inside page (with the "bubbles" marked and aligned to the subtest totals). Each subtest is totaled as the sum of all five items. A table is provided for recording the sum of all five items for each subtest. A troublesome aspect of the test is that the answers cannot be changed once they are marked (the examinee is admonished to "NOT ERASE ANY ANSWERS," manual for administration & scoring, p. 5). Presumably, this restriction is because the response booklet is a form using "no carbon required" (NCR) paper. The "items" include a statement or situation and then four options (one of which is presumably correct), a common multiple-choice format.

TECHNICAL ADEQUACY. Technical information is reported in the manual and includes the following:

Reliability data (for Form A) are reported from scores collected in May 1997. A total of 1,168 individuals took the test; Kuder-Richardson 20 (KR-20) reliability coefficients are reported (with an average of .71), and a standard error of measurement of 2.4. Item analysis data are reported for each of the 35 items, including both difficulty (ranging from .04 to .92) and point-biserial coefficients (ranging from .02 to .50). In this table, a note appears that "items 8, 9, & 11 have been changed since this analysis" (manual for administration & scoring, p. 8); this is presumably because of the low values though many other items also are quite low.

Validity data include content-related information that is quite informal. "The content of the test is assured when the behaviors required on the test are also required on the job. It is a paper-pencil form of a work sample" (manual for administration & scoring, p. 9). This is the entirety of

what is addressed in content-related evidence. Criterion-related evidence includes two studies from other researchers. The authors note that the test has not been part of a criterion-related validation study. Construct validity is addressed with an assertion that "the construct measured is knowledge of team practices and principles. No formal studies of construct validity have been conducted" (manual for administration & scoring, p. 9).

Normative data are reported on 1,168 individuals (readers are only told that this group was composed of males and females). Otherwise, the only data reported are cumulative percentages for raw scores attained.

COMMENTARY. The reliability data are completely inadequate. KR-20 is not the type of reliability needed for a screening decision (e.g., employee selection). Consistency of decisions is far more important. Furthermore, the internal consistency of items within each subtest should be reported. Also, test-retest is very important in determining whether the measured construct is stable. Finally, no information is reported about the participants of the reliability study: how the study was conducted, in what settings participants were tested, how the examiners were trained, or anything about the demographics of the participants.

The validity data are completely inadequate. The constructs are not defined as a basis for defining the items. At the very least, validity data should include test specifications (content-related evidence including alignment with jobs requiring supervision), internal structures (particularly given the subtests that are used), response processes, and criterion-related evidence (other measures, both paper-and-pencil and performance examinations). Basically, the authors have failed to investigate the instrument.

The normative data are completely inadequate. No demographic information is reported (race-ethnicity, geographic distribution, ages, occupations, socioeconomic levels, or education levels, etc.).

SUMMARY. Probably the most embarrassing statement of failure on the part of the author to consider anything remotely related to technical adequacy is the last page under the title Future Research: "Ramsay Corporation would be very happy to receive any normative data, test results, or validation information. This will enable updating of manuals and more extensive information for test users" (manual for administration & scoring, p. 13).

This test really should not be used in any circumstance. It is poorly designed and formatted with no redeeming qualities. It is unfortunate that tests like this appear in the test markets without the possibility of charges being placed on the author/publisher of false advertising and failure to substantiate the claims being made.

[182]

The Test of Everyday Attention for Children.

Purpose: To measure "selective attention, sustained attention and attentional switching."
Population: Ages 6–16.
Publication Date: 1998.
Acronym: TEA-Ch.
Scores: 9 subtests: Sky Search, Score!, Creature Counting, Sky Search DT, Map Mission, Score DT, Walk/Don't Walk, Opposite Worlds, Code Transmission.
Administration: Individual.
Forms, 2: A, B.
Price Data, 2006: £355.50 per complete kit including manual, 25 scoring sheets, cue book, stimulus cards and maps, and 2 audiotapes; £81 per 50 scoring sheets.
Time: (55–60) minutes.
Authors: Tom Manly, Ian H. Robertson, Vicky Anderson, and Ian Nimmo-Smith.
Publisher: Harcourt Assessment [England].

Review of The Test of Everyday Attention for Children by MERILEE McCURDY, Assistant Professor of Educational Psychology, and AMANDA ALBERTSON, Graduate Student in Educational Psychology, University of Nebraska-Lincoln, Lincoln, NE:

The Test of Everyday Attention for Children (TEA-Ch) is an individually administered assessment instrument for measuring the levels of attention in children between 6 and 16 years of age. The TEA-Ch was adapted from the original Test of Everyday Attention (TEA; Robertson, Ward, Ridgeway, & Nimmo-Smith, 1994; 17:183), which was developed to measure adult attention. The nine subtests included in the TEA-Ch were developed to measure a child's ability to maintain their attention to achieve assessment goals. These subtests provide separate measures of three types of attention, including focused (selective) attention, sustained attention, and attentional control/switching. Selective attention is described as the ability to resist distraction, whereas sustained attention is the ability to keep one's mind focused on a task, and attentional switching is the ability to switch the focus of attention from one task to another. The authors created the TEA-Ch to assist in the identification of specific types of attention problems; therefore, aiding in more specific treatment development.

The TEA-Ch assessment was designed to be "game-like" and to minimize the need for skills such as memory, language, and comprehension, so as to objectively measure a child's level of attention. The manual indicates that administration of the entire assessment requires approximately 1 hour. However, the instrument offers the administrator the option to screen each of the attention factors using only four of the nine subtests, which allows for a shorter assessment period.

Scoring of the TEA-Ch is an objective task generally requiring the scorer to determine the total number of items correct within a subtest. However, scoring difficulty increases on four of the subtests that require completion time to be accounted for in addition to the number of correct items. The Procedural Guide and Scoring Sheet aids in the administration and scoring of the assessment. This form prompts the use of standardized instructions and allows space for scoring of individual items. Additionally, the Score Summary on the front page of the Procedural Guide and Scoring Sheet provides an area for raw scores, scaled scores, and percentile bands to be displayed for all subtests.

DEVELOPMENT OF THE TEA-CH. The TEA-Ch was developed to assess three different types of attention in children, including selective attention, sustained attention, and attentional switching. The TEA-Ch manual refers to current research suggesting that different types of attention rely on different brain systems. Specifically, the manual referred to lesion and functional imaging studies conducted by Posner and Peterson (1990) that have provided evidence for at least three attentional systems within the brain. This finding suggests that damage or inefficiency in one system will not automatically lead to poor functioning in another. Thus, the TEA-Ch is used to identify children experiencing attention concerns in one or all of the three areas.

Additionally, the manual refers to difficulties with attention being a common characteristic of several childhood disorders, including Attention Deficit/Hyperactivity Disorder, Autism, and Traumatic Brain Injury, among others. The manual also claims that the patterns of attention deficits vary across different disorders, which may provide another rationale for assessing different types of attention in children.

TECHNICAL.

Standardization. The normative sample for the TEA-Ch consisted of 293 Australian children and adolescents between the ages of 6 years, 7 months and 16 years of age. Of these 293 children, 147 were female and 146 were male. Six age bands were identified with 29 to 58 children in each age band, with fewer children in the oldest and youngest age groups. Children were excluded from the normative sample if they had a head injury or neurological illness, developmental delay or sensory loss, referral for attention or learning problems, or special education needs. A sample (*n* = 160) was administered an intelligence screener with the median standard score of 107.5. The manual did not include information on race or geographic region, nor did the manual indicate how well the sample represented the Australian population. However, the small sample size and numerous exclusions would not appear to represent the continent's population adequately.

Reliability. The assessment was re-administered to 19% of the sample between 5 and 20 days after the initial assessment to obtain test-retest/alternate forms correlation coefficients. The coefficients ranged between .57 on the Creature Counting subtest and .87 on the Same World subtest. These coefficients are considered to be moderately high, but should be interpreted cautiously given the short time interval between administrations. The authors acknowledge that attention skills of children can change quickly over time. Therefore, they recommend that retests be administered 20 days following the first administration or that more than one retest be given. No other tests of reliability conducted on the TEA-Ch were included in the manual.

Validity. Structural equation modeling was used to assess the validity of the TEA-Ch instrument. The authors indicate that this method provided a measure of "the extent to which the separate factors of selective attention, sustained attention and attentional control attract distinct patterns of performance" (manual, p. 34). The

relationship between the observed scores in the TEA-Ch and these three variables were examined, providing measures of the fit of the hypothetical model to the observed data. Results of structural equation modeling indicated that selective attention, sustained attention, and attentional control alone "form a good fit of the patterns of performance observed in a large group of children" (manual, p. 35).

To test the validity of the TEA-Ch, 96 children from the normative sample were administered additional measures of attention. The other measures included The Stroop Task (Trenerry, Crosson, DeBoe, & Leber, 1989), Trails Test (Spreen & Strauss, 1991), and Matching Familiar Figures Test (MFFT; Arizmendi, Paulsen, & Domino, 1981). The correlations between the scores on the additional measures of attention and the scores on the TEA-Ch were then analyzed. Results indicated strong correlations between tests and certain relevant TEA-Ch subtests, as well as several moderate correlations and several nonsignificant correlations. These results were said to be expected due to the differences in types of attention that the tests assess. In most cases, the analyses indicated significant correlations between the subtests and the tests that measured similar factors of attention.

A second evaluation of validity examined the relationship of the TEA-Ch subtests to intelligence and academic achievement. The claim was made that evidence of a strong correlation between the assessment of attention intelligence would indicate that additional assessments of attention, such as the TEA-Ch, were unnecessary. To examine the relationship between the TEA-Ch and four subtests from the Wechsler Intelligence Scale for Children—Third Edition (WISC-III), evaluations of 160 children were examined. Results indicated very few statistically significant correlations between TEA-Ch subtests and scores obtained from the WISC-III subtests. However, the Creature Counting and Map Mission subtests displayed significant correlations with WISC–III Full Scale Intelligence Quotient and the WISC-III subtests administered. In addition, TEA-Ch subtest scores were compared to measures of academic attainment in the same manner that they were compared to WISC-III scores. One-hundred-sixty children were administered the Wide Range Achievement Test—Revised (WRAT-R)

Reading, Spelling, and Arithmetic subtests. There were few significant correlations between TEA-Ch subtests and the WRAT-R scales. However, the Score!, Sky Search DT, Walk/Don't Walk, and Code Transmission subtests were correlated in a statistically significant manner with all of the WRAT-R scales.

Special populations. Two final examinations were performed, which compared children diagnosed with ADHD and Traumatic Brain Injury to control children from the original normative sample. These control children were matched to the special populations using WISC-III subtests. In each evaluation using the TEA-Ch (except one subtest), the control children outperformed the children with ADHD or TBI (although some differences were not statistically significant). This information provides initial data indicating that the TEA-Ch may be useful in identifying areas of attention problems. However, these samples were exceptionally small (ADHD = 24; TBI = 18), and should be reviewed with caution.

COMMENTARY. The TEA-Ch is a tool that was developed with the intention of "more clearly identifying the patterns of attentional problems" (manual, p. 6) a child or youth might be experiencing. The authors state that this cognitive assessment instrument should not be used for diagnostic purposes but rather to identify strengths and weaknesses of the attention skills in children and adolescents. The goal of this instrument is to provide useful information for treatment planning and development. These statements by the authors represent valid and responsible recommendations that should be followed by users of the TEA-Ch. However, treatment directions based on assessment data were not provided by the authors, which would have been useful and would have further increased the treatment utility of the measure. Unfortunately, most users will have difficulty using the assessment data for treatment planning and clinical decision making. In addition, the TEA-Ch has not undergone a complete psychometric evaluation, and the materials and instructions could benefit from modification.

Although current research is reflected in development of the tool, the normative sample does not appear to represent the population of interest adequately. For example, the sample includes 293 Australian children and excludes several groups of children, including those who were referred for attention or learning problems. In fact, it seems that by excluding children with attention or learning concerns from the normative sample, the test does not provide an adequate basis for evaluating attention concerns with children for whom the assessment was designed. In addition, the small normative sample impacts the quality of all reliability and validity examinations.

With regard to reliability and validity, a very large age range exists in the children who are given this assessment. It would have been useful if reliability and validity were examined separately among different age-bands instead of for the entire sample of children, which would have provided information about the ages for which the test is most appropriate. Unfortunately, the small normative sample size probably hindered these evaluations. In addition, other forms of reliability should be examined in addition to the test-retest/alternate forms information provided.

Finally, the measures of attention to which it was compared for validity purposes were not recent. The most recent assessment, the Trails Test, was 8 years old by the time the TEA-Ch was published. It can be concluded that the tests of attention to which the TEA-Ch was compared were not based on current research. To validate an assessment, it should be correlated with assessments that are based on current research and are widely used (e.g., Conners' Continuous Performance Test; Conners & MHS Staff, 2000).

The TEA-Ch is contained in a bulky kit and requires additional materials including a tape recorder. Of concern is the use of the tape recorder, a device that is becoming increasingly less common as technological advances reduce their need. In the near future, tape recorders may not be easily purchased. Although the included audiotape emits interesting sounds that may be fun for children, it seems that a more readily available system could gather the same information. The Procedural Guide and Scoring Sheet provides for a convenient document on which the administrator is provided with directions to be read to the child, and an area for scoring student responses. However, several of the subtests require very detailed and complicated instructions. These instructions are often lengthy, and it seems that children with attention deficits may have difficulty concentrating on and understanding the directions. Even with the provided practice items, confusion with the directions may not be captured by the administrator, leading to poor subtest performance. Furthermore, the language used in subtest instructions is not language that is familiar to all children. For example, the words "tread" and "trodden" are used in the directions for the Walk/Don't Walk subtest. These words would not appear to be universally understood and may be confusing for children who are not familiar with such terminology. In addition, the phrase "next go" is used to refer to continuing on to the next item, which again may be confusing for children. Universal language should be used as frequently as possible, so as not to confuse children from other parts of the world or from less affluent environments.

Although one of the objectives of this assessment was to minimize the need for skills such as memory, language, and comprehension, it seems that these skills are necessary. Many subtests require the child or adolescent to count sounds occurring at various time intervals. This task appears to require short-term memory skills to retain information on the current number of sounds until a new sound is emitted. In addition, for children to complete the tasks, they must understand the directions, which requires both language and oral comprehension skills. Eliminating the need for skills such as memory, language, and comprehension is a large feat for any assessment tool, and it cannot be assumed that the TEA-Ch has accomplished this task.

SUMMARY. Overall, the purpose of this assessment is to identify attention strengths and weakness to inform treatment planning. Although the TEA-Ch may have strong face validity with some users, caution should be applied. The normative sample of the TEA-Ch is inadequate and the reliability data are not comprehensive. Future versions or normative updates are recommended to provide a more comprehensive evaluation of the TEA-Ch. Because the TEA-Ch is based on the TEA, any concerns regarding the reliability and validity of the TEA would also be relevant to the TEA-Ch. For that reason, potential users of the TEA-Ch need to familiarize themselves thoroughly with the strengths and weaknesses of the TEA.

REVIEWERS' REFERENCES

Arizmendi, T., Paulsen, K., & Domino, G. (1981). The Matching Familiar Figures Test—A primary, secondary, and tertiary evaluation. *Journal of Clinical Psychology, 37*, 812–818.

Conners, C. K., & MHS Staff. (2000). Conners' Continuous Performance Test II. Toronto: Multi-Health Systems.

Posner, M. I., & Peterson, S. E. (1990). The attention system of the human brain. *Annual Review of Neuroscience, 13*, 25–42.

Robertson, I. H., Ward, A., Ridgeway, V., & Nimmo-Smith, I. (1994). Test of Everyday Attention. Bury St Edmunds, UK: Thames Valley Test Company.

Spreen, O., & Strauss, E. (1991). *A compendium of neuropsychological tests.* Oxford: Oxford University Press.

Trenerry, M. R., Crosson, B., DeBoe, J., & Leber, W. R. (1989). Stroop Neurological Screening Test. Odessa, FL: Psychological Assessment Resources.

Review of the Test of Everyday Attention for Children by MARTIN J. WIESE, Licensed Psychologist/Certified School Psychologist, Lincoln Public Schools, Lincoln, NE:

DESCRIPTION. The TEA-Ch is a downward extension of the Test of Everyday Attention (TEA; 17:183) for adults and it provides a standardized, norm-referenced assessment of attention for children and adolescents between the ages of 6 and 16. The TEA-Ch attempts to make available an objective measure of attention and bridge the gap between computerized tests of attention (Continuous Performance Test, Test Of Variables of Attention, IVA) and subjective behavior rating scales (Conners Rating Scale, Attention Deficit Disorder Evaluation Scale, Child Behavior Checklist, Behavior Assessment System for Children). The TEA-Ch has two parallel forms (A & B) that are administered in a familiar easel format. It does not require use of a computer but a cassette tape player is required. The authors also attempted to reduce the influence of memory, language, and comprehension on the child's attention. Administration of nine subtests takes about 1 hour and yields 13 age-scaled scores that measure focused (selective) attention, sustained attention, and attentional control/switching.

Focused (selective) attention is defined as the ability to resist distraction and to discriminate essential from nonessential information. It is measured with two subtests entitled Sky Search and Map Mission. Sky Search requires the child to find and circle "target" spaceships on a sheet filled with "targets" and very similar "distractor" spaceships as quickly as possible. This performance is compared to the child's performance on a sheet with no "distractor" spaceships. Map Mission is a timed (1 minute) cancellation task that requires the child to circle small "target" symbols on a map and ignore all other symbols.

Sustained attention is the ability to maintain attention and complete relatively routine and uninteresting tasks. There are five subtests of sustained attention: Score!, Walk/Don't Walk, and Code Transmission, and two dual tasks, Sky Search DT and Score! DT. Score! requires the child to count the number of scoring sounds they hear on a recorded tape. Long gaps between sounds make the task fairly boring and tedious. Walk/Don't Walk also requires sustained attention to tones on a recorded tape and requires the child to advance one step along a paper path, using a pen, after each "target" tone but inhibit responses to "distractor" tones. Code Transmission is the most monotonous and demanding of the sustained attention subtests. A very long (12 minutes) series of numbers is presented on cassette tape, and the child must listen for the target number pair (i.e., two 7s in a row) and then tell the examiner the number that preceded the number pair.

Sky Search DT and Score! DT are dual tasks that require the child to perform two things at once. Sky Search DT combines the Sky Search task with the Score! task, and the child must find "target" spaceships while keeping count of "target" scoring sounds. Score! DT combines the task of counting scoring sounds while listening for animal names.

Attentional switching is defined by the authors as "the ability to switch the focus of attention smoothly between one thing and another" (manual, p. 5). Two subtests measure attentional switching: Creature Counting and Opposite Worlds. Creature Counting is a counting test, and the child must switch counting, forward and backward, figures on a printed page (the child reverses direction when an arrow is encountered on the page). Opposite Worlds measures the speed with which children can make a cognitive reversal (say "one" when they see the number 2 and "two" when they see a 1). This speed is compared to the child's performance when simply naming the numbers (say "one" when they see the number 1).

The child's raw scores on each subtest are converted to age scaled scores (mean of 10 and standard deviation of 3) and percentile ranks. Normative tables are provided for six age bands and are divided by sex. There are no tables providing index or domain scores (Selective Attention, Sustained Attention, or Attentional Switching) nor is there a method to obtain a composite or total test score.

DEVELOPMENT. The TEA-Ch is based on the author's provisional theory that an individual's attentional processes can be broken down into three areas: selective attention, sustained attention, and attentional switching. Items and subtests from the adult TEA were modified for administration to children and adolescents.

TECHNICAL. The normative sample of the TEA-Ch is composed of 293 Australian children and adolescents stratified into six age-bands: 6 years, 0 months to 15 years, 11 months. Children with head injury, developmental delay, attention or learning problems, or those receiving special education services were excluded from the normative sample. No other demographic information is provided (sex, ethnicity, and parent education level), nor do the authors describe how members of the sample were obtained or who completed the standardization testing.

Reliability. It appears that alternate form reliabilities for individual subtests were calculated. Both Form A and Form B were administered to 55 children (with the second administration between 5 and 20 days after the first administration). Correlation coefficients range from .57 to .87. The highest reliabilities were obtained on the scores that measure completion time of several tasks.

Validity. A structural equation model (factor analysis) demonstrates a close fit to the author's a priori three-factor model (selective attention, sustained attention, and attentional control/switching). Ninety-six children from the standardization sample were also administered additional tests of attention including a Stroop task, Trails test, and Matching Familiar Figures Test (MFFT) as a test of concurrent validity. Comparisons and regression analysis revealed that both the Stroop Test and Trails Test (which measure selective attention skills) correlate highly with the Sky Search and Map Mission subtests. In addition, the MFFT (which requires inhibiting responses and measures impulsivity) correlated well with the Creature Counting and Opposite Worlds subtests as predicted by the authors.

The authors note that the TEA-Ch is an objective, cognitive measure of attention, designed to identify strengths and patterns of attentional weaknesses in children with suspected attention difficulties and consequently guide treatment and management plans. It is not intended for the initial identification of children with ADHD or ADD, which are psychiatric diagnoses. One study is reported that demonstrates that the TEA-Ch subtests were able to discriminate 24 ADHD boys from a matched control sample. A separate study also demonstrated that the TEA-Ch subtests were able to discriminate 18 children with Traumatic Brain Injury from a matched control group.

SUMMARY. The TEA-Ch provides a standardized, objective measure of attentional processes in children. In its favor, it does not rely on subjective observations of teachers or parents, and it does not require use of a computer to administer. It may be useful in discerning strengths and weaknesses in a child's attention, but treatment planning based on the results seems questionable given the theoretical and, as yet, unproven hypothesis of three distinct attentional processes (selective attention, sustained attention, and attentional switching). In its present form the TEA-Ch may be most useful as a research tool. With its limited normative sample (specific to Australian children), relatively weak-alternate form reliabilities (none exceed .87) for some subtests, and theoretical assumptions about the nature of attention problems, the TEA-Ch cannot be recommended for use in developing appropriate treatment programs for children with attention problems.

[183]

The Test of Everyday Attention.

Purpose: To measure "selective attention, sustained attention and attentional switching."
Population: Ages 18–80.
Publication Date: 1994.
Acronym: TEA.
Scores, 9: Map Search, Elevator Counting, Elevator Counting with Distraction, Visual Elevator, Elevator Counting with Reversal, Telephone Search, Telephone Search While Counting, Lottery, Total.
Administration: Individual.
Forms, 3: A, B, C.
Price Data, 2006: £269.50 per complete kit including manual (32 pages), 25 scoring sheets, cue book, stimulus cards and maps, 3 CDs, and 1 videotape; £41.50 per 50 scoring sheets.
Time: (45–60) minutes.
Authors: Ian H. Robertson, Tony Ward, Valerie Ridgeway, and Ian Nimmo-Smith.
Publisher: Harcourt Assessment [England].

Review of the Test of Everyday Attention by WILLIAM D. SCHAFER, Affiliated Professor (Emeritus) of Measurement, Statistics, and Evaluation, University of Maryland, College Park, MD:
DESCRIPTION.
Purpose and nature. According to the manual, the Test of Everyday Attention (TEA) is the first norm-referenced test that assesses several independent attention systems. These are selective attention, sustained attention, attentional switching, and divided attention. The authors acknowledge that little is known about the correlates of these different systems but anticipate that the availability of the measures may lead to research that can support both new understandings and clinical uses. The authors believe that the use of common, day-to-day activities as contexts make the assessments seem relevant to examinees, who may range from young normal through early Alzheimer's populations. There are three individually administered versions if needed for repeated testing; because of practice effects, they are to be administered in a prescribed order. The battery requires about 45 minutes to complete and yields scores from eight subtests.

Map Search requires the examinee to search for and circle on a 29 cm. by 41 cm. road map as many instances of a standard symbol (e.g., knife and fork for a restaurant; pump for a filling station; 80 are present in all) as possible in 2 minutes. The score is the number circled. This is intended as a selective attention measure.

In Elevator Counting, the examinee imagines himself or herself in an elevator with an inoperable floor indicator, but which emits a tone when a new floor is reached. They always begin on the first floor and the tones are tape-presented. When prompted, the examinee indicates which floor the elevator is at. This subtest is scored according to the number of correct strings and is intended as a measure of sustained attention.

The Elevator Counting with Distraction adds high tones that must be ignored to the earlier Elevator Counting subtest. This is intended as a measure of auditory selective attention and is scored by the number of correct strings.

In the Visual Elevator subtest, examinees are presented with drawings of elevator doors on a template with arrows indicating how they are to move through the drawings. Every now and then there is a drawing of an arrow, either up or down, in place of an elevator door. Beginning with "one" (first floor), the examinee vocally counts up as he or she moves through the diagrams, but says "up" or "down" as appropriate when a drawing of an arrow is encountered, and is to reverse direction if the arrow is opposite to the current direction of counting. This subtest is intended as a measure of attentional switching. It yields two scores: number of strings correct and time per switch.

Elevator Counting with Reversal is the same as the Visual Elevator subtest except that the prompts are presented from an audiotape. The score is the number of strings correct. This subtest is intended as a measure of auditory-verbal working memory.

In the Telephone Search subtest the examinee searches through the listings like those in a telephone directory, but each name is followed by a pair of symbols, sometimes the same and sometimes different. The examinee is shown a pair of identical symbols to search for and is to circle all instances, starting at the upper left and moving to the lower right without going back, and indicating when finished. The score is the time-per-target, the time taken to complete the task divided by the number of correctly circled symbol pairs. It is intended to assess selective attention.

The Telephone Search While Counting subtest is the same as the Telephone Search subtest except that strings of tape-presented tones are added. The examinee is asked also to count the number of tones in each string verbally. The time-per-target score (found as in the previous subtest) is divided by the ratio of number of strings correct divided by number of strings answered (correct or incorrect) and subtracted from the Telephone Search time-per-target score to yield a dual task decrement score that is intended as a measure of divided attention.

In the Lottery subtest, the examinee listens to a tape-presented series of lottery codes that are all of the form, two letters followed by three numbers. The examinee is to listen for codes that end with a target pair of identical digits and to write down the two letters of all codes that end with the target digits. The score is the number correct out of 10 and is intended as a measure of sustained attention.

DEVELOPMENT.

Equating. The three forms present virtually identical tasks with only trivial differences. Scale scores were developed based on the prescribed order of administration of the three forms, A followed by B, followed by C, as needed.

Norms. The norming sample consisted of 154 normal volunteers divided into four age bands; there is no information on how they were selected and recruited. All 154 took Form A, 118 of them took Form B 1 week later, and 39 of those who took Form B also took Form C 1 week later. Form C is interpreted only through comparison with Form B. The age group sizes of the original 154 range from 35 participants (ages 35–49) to 43 participants (ages 65–80). These sizes are clearly too small for clinical interpretation. Moreover, it is unclear which population(s) the sample represents.

Scales. Appendices in the manual have tables that are used to obtain the scale scores corresponding to the raw scores on each subtest separately by age group and form. Subtest scale scores ranging from 1 to 19 were developed to correspond to equivalent percentile ranges in the norming sample.

TECHNICAL COMMENTARY.

Reliability evidence. Test-retest reliability estimates were developed for the norm group as well as for a sample of 74 unilateral stroke patients. The coefficients generally support use of the test, at least for research purposes. However, there is no information about the potential sizes of conditional standard errors of measurement, which may or may not be largest in score ranges where practitioners most need accuracy.

Validity evidence. The manual presents evidence that the TEA subtests are reasonably independent of hearing and visual difficulties (within reason) and that the relationship between TEA subtests and general aptitude is mediated by age, justifying age-group norms. The scores of stroke victims and controls separately by two age groups generally show clear differences, and some subtests show differences between age and aptitude-matched controls and closed-head-injured groups.

A factor analysis of the TEA subtests along with external measures of attention generally supports a four-factor structure: (a) visual selective attention/speed (Map Search, Telephone Search Time per Target), (b) attentional switching (Visual Elevator Number Correct), (c) sustained attention (Lottery, Elevator Counting, Telephone Search Dual Task Decrement), and (d) auditory-verbal working memory (Elevator Counting with Reversal, Elevator Counting with Distraction). External tests load on all but the third factors.

These studies are all based on rather small samples and use statistical significance as the criterion for group differences. Although they can be calculated from the data given, presentation of effect sizes would help readers evaluate the magnitudes of these differences. Further, validity evidence of other types, particularly consequential, would be valuable in order to justify clinical use of the TEA.

Utility. The test seems easy to administer and score and reasonably engaging for the examinee. The manual has clear directions and there is a helpful videotape accompanying the materials that demonstrates administration.

COMMENTARY AND SUMMARY. The TEA combines assessments of constructs measured by other assessments as well as sustained attention. The availability of these measures within a single instrument should prove attractive to potential users.

Although the materials for testing are well designed and appear easy to use, the scoring and norms as well as the reliability and validity evidence are based on data from very limited samples. Moreover, because the scoring system reflects characteristics of the distributions of data from samples that are both small and unrepresentative of well-defined populations, data from larger and more interesting samples may lead to fundamental changes in how the raw data from examinees should be processed.

The publication date for the manual is 1994. Between then and now it should have been possible to administer the battery to a wider population. If the authors' original anticipation of both primary and clinical research using their test has been realized, there should by now be new information available that could be incorporated into a revision of the manual; such effort seems overdue. Until that evidence is presented, the TEA seems best described as a promising research instrument but as yet unproven as a clinical tool.

Review of the Test of Everyday Attention by TERRY A. STINNETT, Professor, School Psychology, Oklahoma State University, Stillwater, OK:

The Test of Everyday Attention (TEA), published in 1994, is claimed to be the first noncomputerized norm-referenced comprehensive test of attention available to clinicians and researchers. The TEA introductory kit examined for this review included a package of 25 record forms, an administration and technical manual, a spiral-bound booklet of stimulus cards, two map templates, three simulated telephone book pages, three parallel forms of cassette tapes of aural test stimuli, and one VHS training video tape. The audiotape cassettes have since been changed to CD format. The publisher suggests a user qualification of Level B is needed to use this test and, in general,

professionals working in the area of neurological impairment may have interest in the TEA. The TEA is relatively expensive; the start-up package advertised on the Harcourt Assessment website is US $496 with a package of 50 record forms at $78. The instrument was developed to measure three independent aspects of attention including selective attention, sustained attention, and attentional switching in persons 18 through 80 years of age. There is also a divided attention test in the TEA. The authors indicate the test may be useful for examination of attention problems in general and for gauging prognostic outlook for recovery of function and daily life function in patients following brain injury. At the time the TEA was released there was an absence of such measures and limited information available about the correlates of attention problems. Clinicians working with patients in these areas needed tests of attention for diagnostic purposes and treatment monitoring, whereas researchers needed such a test to develop further and more complete theoretical understanding of the constructs of attention.

DESCRIPTION. The TEA, which can be administered in 45 minutes to 1 hour, is an individually administered test of attention containing eight subtests. The TEA subtests are based on activities that are common for many adults such as reading telephone directories, scanning maps, and listening to lottery numbers as if in a broadcast. The test is designed to allow for three parallel forms (labeled A, B, and C) so that it could be used in a serial fashion with the same client. The three forms must be given in A-B-C order because there are some practice effects on repeating different forms of the subtests and separate norms are used for Version A and Version B. For test interpretation the raw scores on the subtests are converted to scaled scores (mean = 10, standard deviation = 3), which can range from 1–19, and they can also be converted to approximate percentile ranks. The norm tables for each subtest contain shaded areas, which represent problematic performance on each of the tests.

Map Search (MS), designed as a measure of selective attention, is a timed subtest requiring that the participant quickly and accurately scans a color map of the Philadelphia, Pennsylvania area for simple symbols (Form A—knife and fork, Form B—screwdriver and wrench, or Form C—gasoline pump). The map templates are sized

16.25 inches by 11.75 inches and are in a plastic sleeve for protection. There are two different maps to allow for the three versions of the subtest. The examinee circles the correct stimuli with a marker on the plastic sleeve. The examiner should be sure to remember to keep the map in the sleeve because the marker is not easily erased from the maps themselves and will leave a stain on the material. Examinees are given 2 minutes total for the task, and there are 80 correct stimuli on the map for each version of the subtest. Initially the examinee is asked to circle the stimuli with a red marker, and after 1 minute has elapsed the examiner gives him or her a blue marker for the remainder of the task. This switching allows for calculation of a 1-minute and a 2-minute (total) score. The number of correct stimuli circled in red is the 1-minute raw score, and the number of correct stimuli circled in blue is added to the number of correct red circles to yield the 2-minute score.

Elevator Counting (EC), a measure of auditory sustained attention, requires the participant to listen for and count a series of tape-recorded tones as if the tones designated different floors in an elevator. No tape recorder is furnished with the test, so examiners must provide their own. There are two practice items at the beginning of the tape to orient the examinee to the task demands, and there are seven actual items or strings of tones for the participant to count. After each item the examiner simply asks how many tones or "floors" the participant counted. One raw score point is awarded for each correct string. The practice strings are not included in the total score. This subtest has a low ceiling effect so no scaled scores or percentile rank conversions are provided in the manual. A raw score of 7 is interpreted as "normal," a score of 6 is "doubtful," and a score of 5 or less is interpreted as "definitely abnormal" (manual, p. 15). The EC task was developed as a variation of a task initially reported by Wilkins, Shallice, and McCarthy (1987) as a measure of right-frontal-lobe-based sustained attention.

Elevator Counting with Distraction (ECD), designed as a task of selective attention, requires the examinee to count low tones while ignoring high tones as if the low tones designated different floors passed in an elevator. As in the EC subtest there are two practice trials administered before the subtest begins. The raw score is simply the number of correct items out of 10. The authors note that the examinee needs to be able to discriminate high from low tones. Obviously, this test is particularly sensitive to influence from hearing impairment so examiners need to ascertain that the examinee has adequate auditory acuity. Raw scores for this subtest can be converted to scaled scores and approximate percentile ranks.

Visual Elevator (VE) is purported to be a test of attentional switching or cognitive flexibility. Each VE item is on a separate page in the stimulus card booklet. These items contain a number of squares that have a picture of elevator doors or large vertical arrows that point either up or down. The participant is required to count up and down as he or she follows the series of visually presented elevator doors. The doors represent different "floors." Interspersed among the elevator door stimuli are the large arrows, which signify that the examinee is to switch directions to the opposite way he or she was counting. The examiner points to each stimulus square on the page in the series and only moves to the next stimulus after the examinee has made a response. Note that each item is timed from the onset of the examinee's first verbal response until the last verbal response is made. The subtest yields an accuracy score (VE1), which is the number of final "floor" numbers correct out of 10 not including the two practice items. There is also a timing score (VE2) for this subtest, which is the total number of seconds for the correct items divided by the number of switches in each item. The number of switches is the number of large arrows in each item.

Elevator Counting with Reversal (ECR) is the auditory equivalent to the VE task, provides a measure of attentional switching/cognitive flexibility, and requires auditory-verbal working memory. However, in the ECR task the examinee is signaled to count upwards by the presentation of a high-pitched tone instead of a large upward-pointing arrow. Likewise, the examinee is signaled to count downward by the presentation of a low-pitched tone, while the floors are represented by the same tone as in the EC and ECD subtests described earlier. The tones are presented at a fixed speed from the audiotape. There are 3 practice items and 10 actual items. The authors do indicate that this test may be too difficult for patients who have severe brain damage. Raw scores for this subtest can be converted to scaled scores and approximate percentile ranks.

Telephone Search (TS), a test of selective attention, requires the examinee to look for key symbols that represent various services while searching through a large page from a simulated phone directory. There are three different phone pages to allow for the three versions of the test. The versions of the task use different symbols (Version A—plumbers pages, Version B—restaurants, or Version C—hotels pages). Two symbols (star, circle, square, or cross) are on the phone page next to each instance of the service for which the examinee has been instructed to search. The subtest is timed (up to 4 minutes), and the examinee is instructed to work as quickly as possible. The examinee is simply required to circle with a marker directly on the page only those services that are indicated by two identical symbols appearing together (i.e., two stars, two circles, etc.). The templates are the same dimensions as the MS templates and are sized 16.25 inches by 11.75 inches. These are laminated for protection and easy cleaning after use. The raw score is the number of correct responses divided by the amount of time used, which gives a time per target score. Raw scores for this subtest can be converted to scaled scores and approximate percentile ranks.

Telephone Search While Counting (TSC) reflects sustained attention but also yields an estimate of dual task decrement performance or divided attention. The subtest requires the examinee to again search for pairs of identical symbols on a simulated telephone page, but he or she must perform another simple task at the same time. The examinee simultaneously counts strings of tones presented from audiotape. The original time per target TS score is subtracted from a TSC weighted time per target score to provide the estimate of dual task decrement performance. This TSC time per target score is weighted based on the accuracy of the examinee's tone counting. Scores for this subtest can be converted to scaled scores and approximate percentile ranks.

The Lottery subtest is a measure of sustained attention for auditory information. The task simulates listening to lottery numbers by radio. The examinee listens to a 10-minute series of letters and numbers presented by audiotape. The stimuli always begin with two letters and end with three numbers (Version A, 5-5; Version B, 8-8; Version C, 3-3). For example, the examinee listens for strings that end in the numbers 5-5 and

writes down the two letters that preceded the 5s. There are 10 target stimuli in the 10-minute period. The responses are considered correct if at least one of the letters is given and it is given in the correct position. As with most of the TEA subtests the raw scores are converted to scaled scores and approximate percentile ranks.

TECHNICAL. The standardization sample is inadequate on a number of dimensions and is a significant weakness of the TEA. This aspect is a critical deficit, which significantly limits the generalizability of TEA results. The sample is geographically restricted to the United Kingdom, and it is unclear from exactly where the sample participants were solicited. There is not much descriptive information presented about the standardization sample members. The test also needs renorming because the standardization sample is at least 13 years old. Furthermore, it is based on only 154 "normal" volunteers aged 18 to 80 years of age, which is too small to be representative of the range of examinees likely to be assessed with the TEA. Additionally, users of the TEA need to exercise extreme caution because the age-group norms are based on miniscule numbers. The standardization sample was subdivided into four age groupings, and separate age norms are reported for each subtest. The ages are 18 to 34, 35 to 49, 50 to 64, and 65 to 80 years. There are approximately equal numbers of people in each age group ($n = 39$, $n = 35$, $n = 37$, $n = 43$ for each age group, respectively). Only "normal" individuals are included in the standardization sample, and this is also a concern because many of the subtests suffer from low ceiling effects and are more appropriate for use with individuals who have brain injury and/or cognitive impairments. The ceiling effects highlight the need for clinical norms for the test in addition to the general norms. The manual reports that the sample included 69 males and 85 females, but sex-based norms are not provided. The manual does report the number of people at each age group who scored above a standard score of 100 ($n = 100$) and below 100 ($n = 54$) on the National Adult Reading Test, which is suggested in the manual to be an estimate of intellectual functioning for members of the standardization sample. However, users of the TEA should be skeptical of this score as a measure of cognitive ability as it likely reflects primarily crystallized ability. There are no other demographic data or descriptions of the standardization sample, and this is a striking weakness for the test.

Test-retest reliability estimates based on the performances of 118 members of the standardization sample with a 1-week interval are presented for Versions A with B of TEA. These coefficients ranged from .59 (TSC) to .86 (MS and TS) in this sample. The coefficients were not calculated for EC or Lottery subtests because there was little variance in performance in the "normal" sample due to a ceiling effect. There are also Version A–B alternate-forms reliability estimates for 74 unilateral stroke patients. These coefficients ranged from .41 (TSC) to .90 (VE1) in this sample. The VE2 coefficient was not calculated and the ECR subtest was not administered. The TSC dual decrement task had inadequate test-retest reliability—.59 for normal participants and .41 for stroke patients. The authors indicated that this might be accounted for due to a learning effect from one administration to the next in the normal participants, which would have reduced variance. They also explain that the stroke patients had extreme difficulty with this task (floor effect), which could have reduced the variance in this sample. The alternate-forms reliability of Version C with B was also estimated following a week based on a subsample of participants (n = 39) in the normal standardization group. These coefficients ranged from .61 (TSC) to .90 (TS). Ceiling effects were again evidenced on the EC and Lottery subtests so no coefficients were calculated. In general, the reliabilities of the TEA subtests are suspect both in terms of the magnitude of the coefficients and in terms of length of interval between test-retest. Also these reliability coefficients are not simple test-retest estimates in the purest sense because they were based on alternate forms of certain subtests. Salvia and Ysseldyke (1998) recommend that reliability coefficients should be at least .90 for individual diagnostic purposes. One procedural safeguard to address the poor reliabilities would be to use the standard errors of measurement when describing an examinee's obtained score. The standard errors of measurement are omitted in the TEA manual. Given that the reliabilities (test-retest and alternate-forms) are marginal and that more error than is desirable is likely in the obtained scores, this relative low reliability is an important oversight. Crawford, Sommerville, and Robinson (1997) examined the

TEA psychometric properties to develop procedures for the quantitative analysis of subtest profiles for the TEA. They provided tables based on the standard error of the difference and standard deviation of the difference for TEA subtests to determine the critical values needed to detect reliable and abnormal differences between a subtest and the examinee's mean subtest score. They also elaborated a method to analyze TEA profiles by providing individual comparison standards for an individual client's performance.

The TEA fares better in terms of construct validity. The test authors conducted a principal-components analysis based on the standardization sample data to examine the test's underlying structure and a varimax (orthogonal) rotation was specified (Robertson, Ward, Ridgeway, & Nimmo-Smith, 1994, 1996). The 154 "normal" participants were administered the TEA, the Stroop Test, the d2 visual search task, Trails B, the Wisconsin Card Sorting Test, Backward Digit Span, and the Paced Auditory Serial Addition Test. A four-factor solution was derived, which accounted for 62.4% of the variance in performance. The first factor is described as visual selective attention/speed and included MS, Stroop Test, TS, Trails B, and d2 total. The second factor, described as attentional switching, included VE and Wisconsin Categories. The Lottery, EC, and TS dual task decrement subtests all loaded on the third factor, which is described as sustained attention. ECD Backward Digit Span and PASAT 2 second tasks loaded on the fourth factor, which is labeled as auditory-verbal working memory. Examination of the factor loading coefficients in the manual indicates this solution appears quite interpretable. MS and TS loaded strongly on visual selective attention speed (.84 and -.80) and did not cross load on the other three factors. Likewise, VE loaded only on the attentional switching factor (.78) and Lottery, EC, and TS dual task decrement only on the sustained attention factor (.70, .56, and -.72, respectively). The fourth factor, auditory-verbal working memory, was composed of the EC, with both the reversal and distraction scores loading (.62 and .52) on it; however, ECR cross loaded on the visual selective attention/speed factor (.49). Others have also examined the underlying structure of the TEA with fairly comparable results (Bate, Mathias, & Crawford, 2001; Chan, Lee, & Hoosain, 1999). Chan et al. (1999) and Bate et al.

(2001) also reported four factor solutions and named the factors visual selective attention, attentional switching, sustained attention, and divided attention. Neither of these research groups reported an auditory-verbal working memory factor as did the test authors. Bate et al. (2001) provided a good comparison of the subtest factor loadings across the three studies for interested readers. In general, the test does appear to measure different aspects of the construct of attention. However, because there is a limited number of subtests available on the TEA to represent these factors and some were represented by a single subtest, users should be cautious in identifying attentional deficits on the basis of a single subtest score to represent the broader constructs hypothesized from the factor analyses.

The TEA has also been shown to have clinical utility for discriminating clinical groups from normal control groups. Bate et al. (2001) reported that performance on the TEA MS and TS subtests was significantly different for patients with traumatic brain injury and education-matched controls suggesting a deficit in visual selective attention. Bate et al. also found that when the traumatic brain injury group was divided into early injury (less than 1 year post injury) versus late injury (more than 1 year post injury) subgroups, the early injury subgroup had significantly poorer performance on the Lottery subtest, indicating possible recovery of function for sustained attention beyond 1 year post injury. Allain, Forgeau, Zied Kefi, Etcharry-Bouyx, and Le Gall (2002) found that the performance of closed-head injury patients was significantly worse than matched controls on all subtests of the French version of the TEA indicating attentional problems are a salient characteristic of severe closed-head injury. Likewise, Chan (2000) found that most of the TEA subtests were effective in differentiating closed-head injury patients in Hong Kong from "normal" matched control participants. He also concluded that the TEA could discriminate closed-head injury patients in terms of sustained attention, selective attention, divided attention, and attentional switching. Cantagallo and Zoccolotti (1998) studied the Italian version of the TEA and concluded that the TEA was a valid assessment for use with middle-aged and older individuals. They found a significant age effect in a sample of people aged 20 to 69 years. They reported significantly decreasing

scores for those over 50 years of age. Females were also noted to score worse than males on three TEA subtests.

SUMMARY. The TEA test materials are well made and packaged. The test is relatively expensive. The administration and scoring of the test appear to be relatively straightforward. There is not much information presented in the manual to guide naïve users to a sophisticated level of interpretation, and the test would be better utilized by practitioners and researchers with expertise in dealing with patients with brain injury and the theoretical underpinnings of the construct of attention. Some of the TEA subtests suffer from ceiling problems and therefore will not be too helpful with relatively "normal" clients. The TEA standardization data are badly in need of revision, and the current norms are a significant weakness for the test. On the other hand, there is an accumulation of evidence to support the construct validity of the TEA, and the TEA has also been shown to be able to differentiate "normal" control subjects from various clinical groups. However, until the test is updated it is probably best that it remain as a research tool for examining attentional deficits in adult patients with brain injury.

REVIEWER'S REFERENCES

Allain, P., Forgeau, M., Zied Kefi, M., Etcharry-Bouyx, F., & Le Gall, D. (2002). Evaluation des troubles attentionnels chez des traumatisés crâniens sévères: intérêt d'une adaptation francophone du 'Test of Everyday Attention.' *Revue de Neuropsychologie, 12*(3), 401-435. Retrieved January 29, 2007 from the PsycINFO database.

Bate, A. J., Mathias, J. L., & Crawford, J. R. (2001). Performance on the Test of Everyday Attention and standard tests of attention following severe traumatic brain injury. *The Clinical Neuropsychologist, 15*, 405-422.

Cantagallo, A., & Zoccolotti, P. (1998). Il Test dell'Attenzione nella vita Quotidiana (T.A.Q.): Il contributo alla standardizzazione italiana. *Rassegna di Psicologia, 15*(3), 137-147. Retrieved January 29, 2007 from the PsycINFO database.

Chan, R. C. K. (2000). Attentional deficits in patients with closed head injury: A further study to the discriminative validity of the Test of Everyday Attention. *Brain Injury, 14*, 227-236.

Chan, R. C. K., Lee, T. M. C., & Hoosain, R. (1999). Application of the Test of Everyday Attention in Hong Kong Chinese: A factor structure study. *Archives of Clinical Neuropsychology, 14*, 715-716.

Crawford, J., Sommerville, J., & Robertson, I. (1997). Assessing the reliability and abnormality of subtest differences on the Test of Everyday Attention. *British Journal of Clinical Psychology, 36*(4), 609-617.

Robertson, I. H., Ward, T., Ridgeway, V., & Nimmo-Smith, I. (1996). The structure of normal human attention: The Test of Everyday Attention. *Journal of International Neuropsychological Society, 2*, 525-534.

Salvia, J., & Ysseldyke, J. E. (1998). *Assessment* (7th ed.). Boston, MA: Houghton Mifflin Company.

Wilkins, A. J., Shallice, T., & McCarthy, R. (1987). Frontal lesions and sustained attention. *Neuropsychologia, 25*, 359-365.

[184]

Test of Problem Solving 3: Elementary.

Purpose: Designed to assess children's critical thinking and problem solving skills.
Population: Ages 6.0—12.11.
Publication Dates: 1984–2005.
Acronym: TOPS 3.

Scores, 7: Making Inferences, Sequencing, Negative Questions, Problem Solving, Predicting, Determining Causes, Total.
Administration: Individual.
Price Data: Available from publisher.
Time: (35–40) minutes.
Authors: Linda Bowers, Rosemary Huisingh, and Carolyn LoGiudice.
Publisher: LinguiSystems, Inc.
Cross References: See T5:2710 (8 references).

Review of the Test of Problem Solving 3: Elementary by PATTI L. HARRISON, Professor of School Psychology, The University of Alabama, Tuscaloosa, AL:

DESCRIPTION. The Test of Problem Solving 3: Elementary (TOPS 3) is described as a diagnostic instrument to measure language-based problem solving and critical thinking of children ages 6 years through 12 years, 11 months. During administration, 18 photographs (e.g., a sick child with his father, a girls' basketball practice, a lightning storm) in an attractive stimulus book are shown to examinees. Examiners present several questions about each photograph, for a total of 96 test questions that require thinking skills in six task areas: Making Inferences, Sequencing, Negative Questions, Problem Solving, Predicting, and Determining Causes. Items reportedly were selected to represent common situations and to allow for a variety of experiences and cultural backgrounds. However, some items appear be more relevant for some children's experiences than those of other children (e.g., questions that address recycling, shin guards in soccer, the starting signal in a track event).

Examiners score responses to each question as 2, 1, or 0. The scoring guide in the test form contains a very brief list of criteria and sample responses; a scoring guide also appears in the test manual, but instead of providing expanded scoring information, simply repeats criteria and samples in the test form. Although the sample responses are described as not inclusive and examiners are instructed to use clinical judgment in scoring items, the lack of expanded scoring information and samples could impact reliable scoring of the instrument. Similarly, the test manual notes that examiners are allowed to prompt unclear responses of children, but provides little guidance regarding responses that should be prompted and how to prompt.

Following administration, examiners total item scores to obtain raw scores in each of the six task areas. The procedure has potential for errors because examiners must calculate totals across 14 pages in the test record. Raw scores are converted to age equivalents, percentile ranks, and standard scores ($M = 100$, $SD = 15$) for the six task areas and total test. General information about interpretation of these types of scores is offered in the test manual, but the information is not linked to TOPS 3: Elementary test performance. Uses of test scores for diagnosis are not addressed in interpretation guidelines. Several pages in the test manual are devoted to a rationale for teaching problem solving and thinking, but there are no specific instructions for linking TOPS 3: Elementary results to teaching.

DEVELOPMENT. The TOPS 3: Elementary is the third edition of a test that was first published in 1984 and revised in 1994. The authors describe their use of a 2, 1, 0 item scoring system in the 1984 version, a 1, 0 item scoring system for the 1994 version, and a return to a 2, 1, 0 item scoring system for the current edition. The test authors note that the assessment taps four major types of thinking (creative, decision making, problem solving, and critical thinking), but conclude that little agreement exists about specific skills in these areas. The six TOPS 3: Elementary task areas were based on skills identified in literature and results of an item pool study, but the content foundation is discussed only briefly in the test manual.

TECHNICAL. The test manual includes information about an item pool study and standardization study. The item pool study, conducted with 690 children, was used to identify criteria for item responses of 2, 1, and 0 and to evaluate items for difficulty, discrimination, age progression, bias, and fairness, although little information is provided about the procedures and results. The standardization study included 1,406 children from 46 states. Numbers of standardization participants by age, gender, race/ethnicity, and family income are reported. The sample is described as reflecting current census numbers, but census data are not reported for comparison to the standardization sample. Numbers of participants in high, middle, and low income groups are listed, but definitions for these groups are not provided. Also, additional demographics (e.g., community size, region of the country) used in typical test standardizations are not reported. Children from general education and special education were included in the standardization sample, but there is no information about the numbers of children from each population; this is an important oversight, because test performance can differ greatly for children in general and special education, and the inclusion of large numbers of children in special education can impact normative scores.

Normative data reported for the standardization sample raise concerns. A table of means, medians, and standard deviations by 1-year age groups on the six task areas and total test indicates small mean differences between some age groups for some task areas (e.g., means for 10-, 11-, and 12-year-olds on several task areas are very similar) and suggest that some tasks areas do not show an adequate developmental progression. The inadequate developmental progression is reflected in the age equivalent norms tables. The authors provide many appropriate cautions about using age equivalents. However, the age equivalent norms tables indicate that raw score differences of 1–2 points are associated with large age equivalents; for example, raw scores of 20, 21, and 22 for the predicting task area are equal to age equivalents of 8-9, 10-2, and 12-7, respectively. Age equivalent norms should not have been provided for this test, perhaps, given the lack of developmental progression for some tasks.

Percentile rank and standard score tables are provided for 1-year age intervals across the range of 6 years to 12 years, 11 months; 3- to 6-month intervals are more commonly used for tests that measure developmental constructs for children. Norms tables for standard scores and percentile ranks suggest a lack of test floor or ceiling for some task areas (e.g., although standard scores across age groups range from "<54" to 138, 70 is the lowest possible standard score for the Problem-Solving task area for 6-year-olds and 116 is the highest possible standard score for the Predicting task area for 12-year-olds).

Internal consistency, test-retest, and interrater reliability studies are reported. Little information is provided about the test-retest study, and the amount of time between test administrations is not reported. Test-retest reliability coefficients are based on small samples of 13–23 participants in each age group and range from .28 to .95

for the six task areas and .64 to .95 for total test, suggesting low test-retest reliability for some age groups. Standard errors of measurement for raw scores are reported with test-retest reliability data, but instructions for using these in interpretation of test scores are not provided. Internal consistency coefficients range from .36 to .80 for the six task areas across age groups. Interrater reliability was evaluated by a study in which seven examiners scored 26 randomly selected test forms. Although the test authors note that comparisons of scoring every item resulted in 50,688 comparisons, the table reporting agreement from 88–90% between pairs of examiners is not clear; it is not apparent if the percentages are average item agreements for each pair of examiners or reflect some other type of comparison.

Several types of validity are described. The authors support content validity based on extensive review of tests and the literature; however, as noted earlier in this review, little information is provided to support the content foundation for the test. Contrasted groups validity was investigated by comparing test scores of children from the standardization sample and children with language disorders; results from these small samples of children indicate significant mean differences for most task areas and total scores. The manual reports item-task correlations, as well as intercorrelations between task areas and between each task area and total test. The quite high intercorrelations between task areas, generally in the .70s to .80s for youngest and oldest age groups and .50s to .60s for middle age groups, and high task-total test correlations, generally in the .80s, suggest that the tasks areas are not as heterogeneous as is desirable and may not be measuring distinct constructs. There are no validity studies, such as factor analyses, to support structure of the test and validate separate scores for the test's six task areas. A number of analyses were conducted to investigate race and socioeconomic differences. The authors concluded that, in general, socioeconomic differences were found to be significant more often than race.

COMMENTARY AND SUMMARY. The TOPS 3: Elementary provides attractive materials that potentially result in an enjoyable test administration for children. However, there are a number of concerns that result in cautions about its use. Little information is provided about the foundation for the six task areas assessed by the test. Some test items may not be relevant for the background and experiences of all children. Scoring criteria and sample responses are limited. Little information for interpretation of test scores is provided. Important characteristics about the standardization sample, especially the numbers of children in general and special education, are not described. Norms indicate that some task scores do not demonstrate adequate developmental progression, which results in wide age equivalent differences associated with small raw score differences for some tasks. Standard scores, reported in 1-year intervals only, demonstrate limited test floors and ceilings for some ages. Reliability studies are not described adequately, and a number of coefficients are low. Task intercorrelations and correlations with total test suggest that the six task areas are not measuring distinct constructs. Overall, the stated purpose of the test as a diagnostic instrument is not supported by technical information provided in the test manual.

[185]

Test of Silent Contextual Reading Fluency.

Purpose: Designed as a quick and accurate method of assessing silent reading ability.
Population: Ages 7 to 18 years.
Publication Date: 2006.
Acronym: TOSCRF.
Scores: Total score only.
Administration: Group or individual.
Forms: 4 equivalent forms: A, B, C, D.
Price Data, 2006: $200 per complete kit including examiner's manual (98 pages), 25 Student record Forms A, 25 Student record Forms B, 25 Student record Forms C, and 25 Student record Forms D; $55 per examiner's manual; $45 per 25 Student record forms.
Time: (10) minutes.
Authors: Donald D. Hammill, J. Lee Wiederholt, and Elizabeth A. Allen.
Publisher: PRO-ED.

Review of the Test of Silent Contextual Reading Fluency by LISA F. SMITH, Senior Research Fellow, University of Otago, Dunedin, New Zealand:

DESCRIPTION. The Test of Silent Contextual Reading Fluency (TOSCRF) is designed to measure silent reading ability of school-age children. Four equivalent forms of the TOSCRF are composed of passages of increasing difficulty and length, ranging from preprimer to adult levels.

All passages were adapted from the Gray Oral Reading Tests—Fourth Edition (GORT-4; Wiederholt & Bryant, 2001) and the Gray Silent Reading Tests (Wiederholt & Blalock, 2000). The passages are presented in uppercase letters with neither punctuation nor spacing between words and examinees are asked to draw lines between the words.

The TOSCRF can be administered individually or in groups. Total administration time, including practice items, is approximately 10 minutes; actual testing time is 3 minutes. It yields a single raw score that is the sum of the correctly identified words. Standard scores, percentile ranks, age, and grade equivalents are provided on easy-to-interpret tables. The total score for the TOSCRF has a mean of 100 and a standard deviation of 15, with descriptive ratings given for the standard scores based on standard deviation units for IQ. Using a metric that is identical to IQ may promote misinterpretation of what is being measured by the TOSCRF. The suggestion that reading ability is analogous to intelligence poses both philosophical and empirical problems.

The examiner's manual provides detailed instructions for scoring, methods for ensuring interrater reliability in scoring, and 10 fully completed tests for practice scoring. This thoroughness is commendable, but brings into question whether the TOSCRF is truly quick and easy to score. Some of the scoring problems could be avoided by monitoring the practice items with examinees, especially emphasizing the need to make straight lines between letters and not over them. Other guidance is not clearly explained, for example, why tests with skipped rows should not be scored. And, although cautions about practice effects are given (see examiner's manual, p. 3), examiners are advised that students who may have been adversely affected during testing should be, "retested using an alternate form of the TOSCRF sometime later that day or another day" (examiner's manual, p. 11). With regard to score interpretation, no rationale is provided for assertions such as, students who do well have been read to often at home, or students who do not do well will be likely to show deficiencies across all reading skills. Examiners are also encouraged to try to identify factors that could lead to a low score on the TOSCRF, ranging from dyslexia to cerebral insults. Some of the factors listed are quite likely outside many examiners' expertise.

DEVELOPMENT. The TOSCRF is a new instrument. The authors request that clinicians and researchers using the test submit copies of their research and suggestions for improvements to the test.

TECHNICAL.

Standardization. The norming sample included $n = 1,898$ students from 23 states. The majority of the midwestern, southeastern, mountain, and southwestern states are not represented. Nevertheless, for the most part, the sample appears to be representative of nationwide statistics as reported in U.S. Census information (2002) with regard to geographic region, gender, family income, educational level of parents, and exceptionality status. The sample was also stratified by age with selected demographics and family income.

Reliability. Evidence of reliability is provided using alternate forms (immediate and delayed), test-retest, and interrater scoring. For alternate forms (immediate administration), data from the examinees in the norming sample were used. Examinees took all four forms of the test in one session without complete counterbalancing of forms. The test orderings were ABCD, BCDA, CDAB, and DABC, thus bringing into question potential problems with practice effects. The reliability coefficients ranged from .82 to .88 by age level and from .76 to 96 for selected subgroups. For test-retest reliability, $n = 85$ examinees in Austin, Texas took all forms of the TOSCRF with approximately 2 weeks between testing times. No description of counterbalancing is offered. Reliabilities range from .82 to .95. Any generalization about stability over time should be tentative, given the sample characteristics and the acknowledgement by the authors that the increase of scores from Time 1 to Time 2 might reflect a practice effect. The evidence for alternate forms (delayed administration) is questionable. The same $n = 85$ examinees in Austin, Texas that took part in the test-retest study then took all forms of the TOSCRF "after the passage of 2 weeks" (examiner's manual, pp. 30–31). Evidence of interrater reliability for $n = 4$ scorers was high.

Validity. In terms of content validity, the format of the TOSCRF is more analogous to games like hidden puzzles than reading actual text. As such, it is not a strong reflection of what the authors intend. However, some evidence of content validity might be inferred in that the test uses sentences adapted from the GORT-4 (Wiederholt & Bryant, 2001) and the Gray Silent Reading Tests (Wiederholt & Blalock, 2000).

For evidence of criterion-related validity, the TOSCRF was compared to archival scores on the Woodcock-Johnson III (WJ-III; Woodcock, McGrew, & Mather, 2001), the GORT-4 (Wiederholt & Bryant, 2001), and the Stanford Achievement Test Series—Ninth Edition (Stanford 9; Harcourt Brace Educational Measurement, 1996) for $n = 262$ examinees in Texas and New York representing various subgroups (e.g., regular education, learning disabled). The majority of this sample (83.5%) was male. In addition, the TOSCRF was administered with either the Test of Silent Word Reading Fluency (TOSWRF; Mather, Hammill, Allen, & Roberts, 2004) or the Test of Word Reading Efficiency (TOWRE; Torgesen, Wagner, & Rashotte, 1999) to samples from Texas, Florida, Arizona, and Massachusetts ($n = 181$, 63.5% male). Average uncorrected correlations across all forms of the TOSCRF ranged from .48 with the GORT-4 to .76 with the TOSWRF. The authors provide corrected correlations but these would be inappropriate in this instance because the underlying validity question is how closely the measures are related, not the constructs they represent. The findings also indicate that despite the items from the TOSCRF coming from the GORT-4, there may be fundamental differences between these measures. The authors also compare standardized scores from the TOSCRF to a global measure generated from a combination of the other measures, via an independent samples t-test. The findings show that the means of the standard scores are similar. The authors interpret this as evidence of validity, but this support seems weak at best.

For evidence of construct validity, the authors examine performance on the TOSCRF in terms of age, subgroups, other reading tests, school achievement, and intelligence. Mean raw scores by age increase for the most part; however, standard deviations are large and the mean scores drop at age 18. The authors explain this decrease by saying, "Many students this age who are still in school have been retained over the course of their school experience due to poor grades" (examiner's manual, p. 43). Substantiation for this argument is not offered. Scores for the subgroups are acceptable, but the authors rank order the subgroups without a rationale for doing so. For measures of school achievement, subtests of the Stanford 9 and the WJ-III were used. For intelligence, the Wechsler Intelligence Scale for Children—Third Edition (Wechsler, 1991) was used. Uncorrected correlations with the TOSCRF were mostly small to moderate; corrected correlations were understandably better. The authors also provide evidence of the specificity and sensitivity (looking at true and false positives, true and false negatives) of the TOSCRF in detecting students with reading problems when compared to a global measure using the other tests. As the authors point out, the results are reasonably good for a measure that only takes 10 minutes to administer.

COMMENTARY/SUMMARY. The stated uses for the TOSCRF are rather sweeping. The authors claim that the test "can be used confidently to identify both poor and good readers...to measure contextual fluency in a comprehensive reading assessment, to monitor reading development, and to serve as a research tool" (examiner's manual, p. 2). They state that for poor readers, the TOSCRF can estimate the degree of reading deficits. It is clear that the TOSCRF has the potential to live up to its claim as a time-efficient and cost-effective screening tool.

The TOSCRF is acceptable as a quick screening measure for students, as one part of a testing program. Overall, it does not reflect reading skills as encountered in daily life, and its evidence of reliability and validity need more substantiation. Furthermore, large areas of the United States and many subgroups were not represented in the norming sample of the TOSCRF; interpretation of scores for these areas and groups should be made with caution. It should be noted that the TOSWRF (Mather, Hammill, Allen, & Roberts, 2004) is a nearly identical measure that takes a similar amount of time to administer and is less expensive than the TOSCRF. In addition, another measure, such as the TOWRE (Torgesen, Wagner, & Rashotte, 1999) or the GORT-4 (Wiederholt & Bryant, 2001), may be more representative of reading skills.

REVIEWER'S REFERENCES

Harcourt Brace Educational Measurement. (1996). Stanford Achievement Test Series—Ninth Edition. San Antonio, TX: Author.
Mather, N., Hammill, D. D., Allen, E. A., & Roberts, R. (2004). Test of Silent Word Reading Fluency. Austin, TX: PRO-ED.
Torgesen, J. K., Wagner, R., & Rashotte, C. A. (1999). Test of Word Reading Efficiency. Austin, TX: PRO-ED.
U.S. Bureau of the Census. (2002). The statistical abstract of the United States: 2002 (122nd ed.). Washington, DC: Author.

Wechsler, D. (1991). Wechsler Intelligence Scale for Children—Third Edition. San Antonio, TX: Psychological Corp.
Wiederholt, J. L., & Blalock, G. (2000). Gray Silent Reading Tests. Austin, TX: PRO-ED.
Wiederholt, J. L., & Bryant, B. R. (2001). Gray Oral Reading Tests—Fourth Edition. Austin, TX: PRO-ED.
Woodcock, R. W., McGrew, K. S., & Mather, N. (2001). Woodcock-Johnson III. Itasca, IL: Riverside.

Review of the Test of Silent Contextual Reading Fluency by LOUISE M. SOARES, Professor of Educational Psychology, University of New Haven, West Haven, CT:

DESCRIPTION. The Test of Silent Contextual Reading Fluency (TOSCRF) is a new test (2006) that measures silent reading ability and, in particular, the speed of students to recognize individual words in passages that have no word or sentence breaks and no punctuation. The manual states that it is useful in "identifying poor readers, measuring contextual fluency in a comprehensive reading assessment, and to monitor reading development" (p. 2). It contains four equivalent forms, each of which can be completed in approximately 10 minutes.

DEVELOPMENT. Little about the development of the TOSCRF is described in its own test manual. Some of the history of this measure may be gleaned from the authors' acknowledgement that the passages students read in the current test are adaptations from passages in the Gray Oral Reading Tests—Fourth Edition (2001) and the Gray Silent Reading Tests (2000). The senior author of these two instruments is Wiederholt, who is one of the authors of the TOSCRF. The other two authors of the TOSCRF—Hammill and Allen—are credited with two other tests that were used to develop this new scale—Illinois Test of Psycholinguistic Abilities—Third Edition (2001) and Test of Silent Word Reading Fluency (2004). This last measure named was also used as part of its construct validity studies. Therefore, in terms of this test, the development of the scale is not directly known.

TECHNICAL. The construct of the TOSCRF is clear, as noted in its description. The testing of the construct is suitable and efficiently accomplished. The administrative instructions are easily followed. The scoring procedures are troublesome, however. The instructions are indeed "quick and easy" (manual, p. 8), but the rules for skipped rows, misplaced lines, and self-corrections are not reassuring. The interpretive factor alone could be risky. Some older children could do well because of experience with Web pages and e-mail messages where everything runs together. The authors do attempt to account for situational and examinee error, but younger children may not have the necessary finger dexterity to write in the lines that separate the words. Children who have been taught to read by the whole language reading method could very well have problems in identifying words. Some may still have trouble in focusing on the printed page. The authors might try to apply a bit more spacing between all the letters.

The authors supply ample evidence for reliability and validity of the instrument and provide multiple conversions that help examiners. Their samples are large ($N = 1,898$), taken from various sections of the country. Reliability analysis was conducted over all four tests using the methods of alternate forms, both immediate and delayed administrations (2 weeks) and test-retest (2 weeks). The corrected median coefficients over the four forms ranged from .81 to .87. The authors acknowledge that the 2-week interval could be responsible for "the presence of practice effects" (examiner's manual, p. 30), and recommend that the interval should be 2 months; but they did not follow their own advice.

Validity coefficients were obtained with content, criterion-predictive, and construct analyses. The statistical support is impressive until the authors discuss the relationships between the TOSCRF with types of reading and intelligence. Table 6.3 in the manual demonstrates the highest coefficients (.85 and .70, judged to be "very large") between the new test with the TOSWRF and TOWRE, both of which were antecedents of the current test. Global Reading also resulted in a coefficient of .70, which only accounts for 49% of the variance. The comparison of the GORT-4 test and Stanford 9 Total Reading were lower—.67 and .68, respectively. The correlations between TOSCRF and the WISC were significant but lower with a corrected coefficient for the total score of .50, accounting for 25% of the variance.

COMMENTARY. In terms of scoring, the authors seem to dismiss the potential for major variations in examiners' judgments in scoring practices. In an attempt to offset the charge of subjectivity, the authors used four staff members from the test's publisher to score independently a subset of the protocols from students in the normative sample. The authors believe that the resulting coefficients of .99 for the four test forms in a test-

retest arrangement "provide strong evidence supporting the test's scorer reliability" (manual, p. 83). This statement would have more credibility if experienced scorers had come from outside the publisher's realm. In terms of both validity and reliability analyses, the authors were thorough and comprehensive, although it is not entirely convincing to substantiate construct validity of a silent reading fluency test by correlating it with an established intelligence test (Wechsler Intelligence Scale for Children; WISC).

SUMMARY. The TOSCRF seems to be a quick (10 minutes), accurate, and cost-efficient test for assessing the silent reading ability of students. It has a broad and comprehensive foundation of research. The test manual is both informative and thorough. Problems that require more attention include scoring, although the authors seem to dismiss this as a procedure that requires attention. Another problem is validity analysis, particularly when trying to match reading fluency to intelligence, as noted above. The authors acknowledge that their work is at "only the initial stage in studying the test's validity" (examiner's manual, p. 49).

[186]

Test of Supervisory Skills.

Purpose: Designed to measure an individual's understanding of "the roles and responsibilities of a first-line supervisor."

Population: Business supervisors and potential business supervisors.

Publication Date: 2004.

Acronym: TOSS.

Scores, 8: Management of Performance Quality, Staffing/Personnel Actions, Communications, Interpersonal Relations, Problem Analysis/Resolution, Project Planning, Direct Supervision, Total.

Administration: Individual or group.

Price Data, 2005: $29.95 per technical and administrative manual; $50 per 10 question booklets; $75 per 25 answer sheets.

Time: (30–45) minutes.

Comments: Available in paper-and-pencil and Web-based versions.

Authors: Erich P. Prien and Leonard D. Goodstein.

Publisher: HRD Press, Inc.

Review of the Test of Supervisory Skills by AYRES G. D'COSTA, Associate Professor, Quantitative Research, Measurement, and Evaluation in Education, The Ohio State University, Columbus, OH:

DESCRIPTION. The Test of Supervisory Skills (TOSS) is a test of knowledge of supervisory skills. It consists of a question booklet with 70 statements such as: "*Allow more* experienced subordinates to divide work assignments with a new employee." Each statement is rated on a separate answer sheet (with an attached pressure-sensitive scoring key) using a 3-point Likert scale: *Ineffective, Neutral,* or *Effective*.

Question booklets and answer sheets (with the attached pressure-sensitive scoring key) are marketed in bundles of 10. The copyright holder is indicated as Performance Management Press.

The test can be scored by a local administrator using the scoring instructions presented. It appears (from page 5 where a negative score possibility is mentioned) that the "guessing" correction made for wrong answers (by multiplying by 2) is unusual. Incidentally, this correction is mentioned but not technically justified in the manual.

DEVELOPMENT. According to the 10-page technical manual, the Test of Supervisory Skills (TOSS) was originally titled the "Elements of Supervisory Skills Test" (EOS) and marketed under this title "for some time" (p. 1). No indication is provided as to when this original test was first produced, but it is stated that in 2004 the title was changed to a more appropriate title, and the test itself was revised to conform to the 1999 AERA-APA-NCME *Standards*. It is not clear whether the original 70 test statements were also changed in 2004.

The technical and administrative manual indicates that the rationale for TOSS is based upon the belief that a good supervisor can discriminate between effective and ineffective practices. Data were gathered on job tasks, including skills and areas of knowledge, from more than 20 job analyses conducted "in a variety of job settings, including manufacturing, service and educational institutions" (p. 1). These 20 job analyses are not referenced in the manual, nor are they presented and summarized. Factor analyses (again not referenced nor presented) are said to reveal the following seven factors: (a) Management of Performance Quality, (b) Staffing/Personnel Actions, (c) Communications, (d) Interpersonal Relations, (e) Problem Analysis/Resolution, (f) Project Planning, and (g) Direct Supervision.

There are 10 items per factor scale, thus a total of 70 items for the entire test. The items are arranged in order; thus Items 1 to 10 relate to the first scale, Management of Performance Quality; Items 11 to 20 to the second scale, Staffing/Personnel Actions, etc. The items are stated to be designed to reflect the job behaviors, skills, and knowledge comprised in each scale. It is indicated that this test is suitable for entry-level applicants to supervisory positions to determine their readiness, as well as for more experienced individuals to determine their strengths and training needs.

TECHNICAL. The manual presents test-retest reliability of .80 (n = 75) with a 2-week retest interval, and an internal consistency (KR-20) measure based on n = 191 as .94, both of which are respectable. The content validity of the 10 scales is based on the representativeness and coverage of the items that were selected on the basis of being related to each of the 10 factor scales. This is obviously judgmental, and the authors do not present any empirical assessment of the homogeneity of the scales based on item-scale correlations.

Further evidence of the validity of the test is presented in terms of correlations with six existing tests, four of which were developed by the first author Prien. Although the manual describes these analyses as evidence of construct validity, they might be more appropriately described as a concurrent criterion validity process. The correlations reported range from a meager .02 to a modest .33. Five of these six correlations are reported as statistically significant at the .01 level, which is not surprising given the large numbers of subjects (640, 630, 465, 234, 660, 661). The discussion does not recognize this fact, nor does it mention the low overlap (based on the squared correlation coefficients) that these low correlations indicate.

The validity discussion does include correlations with two cognitive measures, which are relatively high (.41, .35). This finding led to the justified conclusion that TOSS has a Spearman 'g' component, and therefore "intelligence is highly important in successful supervision, at least in understanding the nature of the tasks at hand" (manual, p. 5). The manual further reports predictive criterion validity of .49 and .21 with job performance ratings.

Finally, the manual compares percentile equivalents for hourly employees (n = 529) versus supervisors/managers (n = 1,606) and points out the significant mean score difference between them (p < .01).

COMMENTARY. TOSS appears to be a reasonable test of supervisory skills, especially given the claims of its basis in job analyses. However, there is need for more extensive technical analyses, especially in terms of justifying the seven scale constructs. The factor analyses need to be presented and discussed, not just mentioned. Each of the seven subscales needs evidence of validity and reliability, especially if they are to be utilized for diagnostic purposes.

SUMMARY. TOSS claims to be a measure of supervisory knowledge with seven subscales, with limited utility in selection and personnel development.

REVIEWER'S REFERENCE

American Educational Research Association, American Psychological Association, & National Council on Measurement in Education. (1999). *Standards for educational and psychological testing*. Washington, DC: AERA.

Review of the Test of Supervisory Skills by JOHN W. FLEENOR, Director of Knowledge Management, Center for Creative Leadership, Greensboro, NC:

DESCRIPTION. According to its publisher, the Test of Supervisory Skills (TOSS) is a reliable and valid measure of the skills and behaviors that characterize effective supervision. The instrument is designed to be administered both to applicants for entry-level supervisory positions and to more experienced supervisors. It may be potentially useful for identifying strengths and weaknesses in current supervisors for training and development purposes. The TOSS provides scores on seven factors that are thought to be related to the essential components of supervisory behavior: (a) Management of Performance Quality, (b) Staffing/Personnel Actions, (c) Communications, (d) Interpersonal Relations, (e) Problem Analysis/Resolution, (f) Project Planning, and (g) Direct Supervision.

DEVELOPMENT. The theoretical foundation of the instrument is based on the premise that individuals who understand what constitutes good supervisory practices will be able to discriminate between effective and ineffective supervisory behaviors. Individuals who are able to make this distinction are thought to be more likely to be effective supervisors. Conversely, individuals who are deficient in this area are less likely to be effective supervisors.

The development of the TOSS began with a series of job analyses of first-line supervisory positions. The analyses identified the competencies and tasks that represent the essential functions of supervisory jobs. Factor analyses of these skills and tasks resulted in the seven factors that comprise the scales of the instrument.

Each scale of the TOSS consists of 10 items, for a total of 70 items. The items on each scale are balanced between effective and ineffective behaviors. Each item is scored in a positive or negative direction based on the correlation of that item with ratings of supervisory effectiveness.

TECHNICAL. A 10-page manual (2004), written by the test authors, presents information on the theory, development, reliability and validity, administration, scoring, and interpretation of the TOSS.

The instrument can be administered individually or in groups. There is no time limit for the test, which usually takes about 1 hour to complete. Respondents indicate whether each of the 70 behavioral items represents effective or ineffective supervisory behavior, using a 3-point scale with a neutral option. They respond to each item directly on the provided answer sheet.

Administrators can easily score the TOSS by removing the top page of the answer sheet, revealing a scoring sheet. The manual presents two sets of norms based on samples of 529 hourly employees and 1,606 supervisors. When interpreting scores, administrators use the appropriate norm table in the manual to convert the respondents' raw scores to percentile scores.

The authors report the usual estimates of reliability, including internal consistency and test-retest reliabilities. Internal consistency reliability (KR-20) was calculated using the scores of the sample of 191 employed adults. Test-retest reliability (2-week interval) was calculated using a subsample ($n = 75$) of the group described above. These reliabilities were in the acceptable range (.94 for internal consistency and .80 for test-retest reliability).

As is necessary for any instrument used for employee selection, the authors conducted multiple criterion-related validity studies of the TOSS. Its scores were found to correlate .49 with supervisory ratings ($n = 84$), .21 with ratings of employee relationships ($n = 129$), and .21 with employees receiving an annual performance bonus ($n = 71$).

Additionally, the authors conducted a number of construct validation studies for the instrument. With sample sizes greater than 500, an average correlation of .38 was found between the TOSS and two measures of cognitive ability. With similar sample sizes, however, somewhat lower corrections were found between the TOSS and six other measures of supervisory skills (mean r = .21).

COMMENTARY. The TOSS appears to be a useful measure of supervisory skills. Its authors are well known in the field of industrial and organizational psychology, and their extensive experience is reflected in the development of the instrument.

The TOSS appears to have utility as a selection instrument for first-line supervisors and as a developmental tool for experienced supervisors. The test is a short, easily scored instrument with a straightforward interpretation. A strength of the instrument is its scales, which are based on extensive job analyses of supervisory positions. The scales were derived through a series of factor analyses of the job analysis data. Extensive validation studies were conducted, which indicate that the TOSS is fairly highly correlated with cognitive ability, and more modestly correlated with other measures of supervisory skills. This is an indication that the test is heavily loaded on the factor of general mental ability. It could be that respondents with higher levels of mental ability are better able to distinguish between the effective and ineffective supervisory behaviors presented on the test. The reported reliability values are acceptable; however, it is recommended that more extensive reliability studies be conducted.

SUMMARY. The TOSS is recommended as a measure of supervisory skills for use in employee selection and development. Users may want to conduct local validation studies to ensure that the instrument is valid for the jobs in their organizations.

[187]

Tests of Adult Basic Education, Forms 9 & 10.

Purpose: "Designed and developed to provide achievement scores that are valid for most types of adult education decision-making."
Population: Adults.
Acronym: TABE.
Subtests, 4–11: Pre-Reading (Level L), Reading, Mathematics Computation, Applied Mathematics, Language, Language Mechanics (optional), Vocabulary (optional), Spelling (optional), Science/Social Studies (Level A), Algebra/Geometry (Level A), Writing (Level A).
Administration: Individual or group.

Editions, 2: Complete Battery, Survey.
Forms, 2: 9, 10.
Price Data, 2006: $36 per 25 hand-scored SCOREZE answer sheets; $31 per 50 CompuScan answer sheets; $16 per 25 Individual Diagnostic Profiles; $32 per review materials; $19 per test directions book; $27 per 25 examinee books; $4 per group record sheet; $19 per norms book; $21 per Technical Report CD (116 pages printed); $24.50 per 25 Getting to Know TABE Workbooks; $60 per Guide to Administering TABE 9 & 10 book; $40 per TABE Teacher's Guide for Reading and Language: Linking Assessments to Learning book; $40 per TABE Teacher's Guide for Mathematics: linking Assessments to Learning book; $46 per 10 consumable test books; $46 per 10 reusable test books; $35 per audio tape; $19 per large print test directions; $58 per large print test book; $57 per 25 large print SCOREZE answer sheets; $8 per online test administration (bulk discounts available).
Special Editions: Form 9 is available in Large Print, Braille, and Audio.
Comments: Both forms available online.
Author: CTB/McGraw-Hill.
Publisher: CTB/McGraw-Hill.

a) COMPLETE BATTERY.
Purpose: Designed to "assess skill levels and help determine appropriate career or training programs."
Publication Dates: 1957–2004.
Levels, 4–5: L (Limited Literacy), E (Easy), M (Medium), D (Difficult), A (Advanced).
Scores, 4: Total Mathematics (Mathematics Computation, Applied Mathematics), Total Battery (Pre-Reading/Reading, Total Mathematics, Language).
Price Data: $101 per 25 Complete Battery test books; $42 per Complete Battery scoring stencils; $236 per Braille Complete Battery Test book; $48 per Writing test book; $16 per Writing Assessment and scoring manual; $72 per Science/Social Studies test book; $13 per Science/Social Studies test directions; $32 per 25 Science/Social Studies SCOREZE answer sheets; $23.50 per 50 Science/Social Studies CompuScan answer sheets; $21.25 per Science/Social Studies scoring stencils; $72 per Algebra/Geometry test book; $13 per Algebra/Geometry test directions; $32 per 25 Algebra/Geometry SCOREZE answer sheets; $23.50 per 50 Algebra/Geometry CompuScan answer sheets; $21.25 per Algebra/Geometry scoring stencils; $16 per Science/Social Studies and Algebra/Geometry tables book.
1) Pre-Reading.
Scores, 4: Match Letters, Recognize Letters, Recognize Beginning/Ending Sounds, Middle Sounds.

Levels: Level L only.
Time: 13(23) minutes.
2) Reading.
Scores, 4–5: Interpret Graphic Information, Words in Context, Recall Information, Construct Meaning, Evaluate/Extend Meaning [Levels E-A only].
Time: 32(42) minutes for Level L; 50(60) minutes for Levels E-A.
3) Mathematics Computation.
Scores, 2–6: Add Whole Numbers [Levels L-M], Subtract Whole Numbers [Levels L-M], Multiply Whole Numbers [Levels E-D], Divide Whole Numbers [Levels E-D], Decimals [Levels E-A], Fractions [Levels M-A], Integers [Levels D, A], Percents [Levels D, A], Order of Operations [Level A], Algebraic Operations [Level A].
Time: 15(25) minutes for Level L; 24(34) minutes for Levels E-A.
4) Applied Mathematics.
Scores, 6–9: Number & Number Operations, Computation in Context, Estimation [Levels E-A], Measurement, Geometry & Spatial Sense, Data Analysis, Statistics & Probability [Levels E-A], Patterns/Functions/Algebra, Problem Solving & Reasoning [Levels E-A].
Levels: Level L only.
Time: 45(55) minutes for Level L; 50(60) minutes for Levels E-A.
5) Language.
Scores, 6: Usage, Sentence Formation, Paragraph Development, Capitalization, Punctuation, Writing Conventions.
Levels: Levels E-A only.
Time: 55(65) minutes.
6) Vocabulary.
Scores, 3: Word Meaning, Multi-Meaning Words, Words in Context.
Levels: Levels E-A only.
Time: 14(24) minutes.
Comments: This subtest is optional.
7) Language Mechanics.
Scores, 2: Sentences/Phrases/Clauses, Writing Conventions.
Levels: Levels E-A only.
Time: 14(24) minutes.
Comments: This subtest is optional.
8) Spelling.
Scores, 3: Vowel, Consonant, Structural Unit.
Levels: Levels E-A only.
Time: 10(20) minutes.
Comments: This subtest is optional.
9) Science/Social Studies.
Scores: Scores not presented.
Level: Level A only.

Time: Administration time not reported.
Comments: This subtest is optional.
10) Algebra/Geometry.
Scores: Scores not presented.
Level: Level A only.
Time: Administration time not reported.
Comments: This subtest is optional.
11) Writing.
Scores: Scores not presented.
Level: Level A only.
Time: 45(55) minutes.
Comments: This subtest is optional.
b) SURVEY.
Purpose: Provides a skill snapshot for placement information.
Publication Dates: 1987–2004.
Levels, 4: Same as Complete Battery except for omission of Level L.
Scores, 2: Same as Complete Battery.
Price Data: $101 per Survey test book; $42 per Survey scoring stencils; $212 per Braille Survey test book.
1) Reading.
Scores, 5: Same as Complete Battery.
Time: 25(35) minutes.
2) Mathematics Computation.
Scores, 5–6: Same as Complete Battery.
Time: 15(25) minutes.
3) Applied Mathematics.
Scores, 9: Same as Complete Battery.
Time: 25(35) minutes.
4) Language.
Scores, 6: Same as Complete Battery.
Time: 25(35) minutes.
5) Language Mechanics.
Scores, 3: Same as Complete Battery.
Time: 14(24) minutes.
Comments: This subtest is optional.
6) Vocabulary.
Scores, 3: Same as Complete Battery.
Time: 14(24) minutes.
Comments: This subtest is optional.
7) Spelling.
Scores, 3: Same as Complete Battery.
Time: 10(20) minutes.
Comments: This subtest is optional.
c) LOCATOR TEST.
Purpose: Designed to "help teachers in assigning the level of the TABE test to administer."
Subtests, 4: Reading, Mathematics Computation, Applied Mathematics, Language.
Scores: Total score only.
Price Data: $58 per 2 Practice Exercise and Locator Test books; $21 per Practice and Locator Test scoring stencils; $130 per Braille Practice Exercise and Locator Test books.

Time: 37(47) minutes for Complete Battery; 35(45) minutes for Survey.

d) WORD LIST.

Scores: Total score only.

Price Data: $26 per Word List Test book; $58 per large print word list.

Time: 15(25) minutes.

e) PRACTICE EXERCISE.

Scores: Not scored.

Price Data: Same as *c* above.

Time: 20(30) minutes.

Cross References: For reviews by Michael D. Beck and Bruce G. Rogers of an earlier edition, see 13:343; for reviews by Robert W. Lissitz and Steven J. Osterlind of an earlier edition, see 11:446 (2 references); for reviews by Thomas F. Donlon and Norman E. Gronlund of an earlier edition, see 8:33 (1 reference); for a review by A. N. Hieronymus and an excerpted review by S. Alan Cohen of an earlier edition, see 7:32.

Review of the Tests of Adult Basic Education, Forms 9 & 10 by JUDITH A. MONSAAS, Executive Director for P-16 Assessment and Evaluation, University System of Georgia, Atlanta, GA:

DESCRIPTION. The Tests of Adult Basic Education (TABE) are "designed and developed to provide achievement scores that are valid for most types of adult education decision-making" (TABE technical report, p. 2). TABE has core content measures covering Reading, Mathematics Computation, Applied Mathematics, and Language. Optional supporting measures include Vocabulary, Language Mechanics, and Spelling. Additional Advanced-Level tests include Science, Social Studies, Algebra/Geometry, and Writing. TABE 9 & 10 consists of selected-response items "organized by content categories that reflect current trends in adult education, national standards, and adult curricula" (manual, p. 2). The content of these tests is written to be interesting and relevant to adults. Both paper-and-pencil and computer-based versions of the tests are available as are large print, audio, and Braille editions of TABE Form 9.

There are five levels for TABE 9 & 10: L (Limited Literacy–Pre-Reading), E (Easy), M (Medium), D (Difficult), and A (Advanced). These tests measure Prose Literacy, Document Literacy, and Quantitative Literacy. The TABE also has a Locator Test with the four core test areas consisting of items from TABE Levels E, M, D, and A. The Locator Test is to help assign the level of the TABE test to examinees. In addition to the complete battery just described, there are shorter TABE 9 & 10 Survey Tests that provide less diagnostic information.

According to the TABE Technical Report, the TABE is both criterion-referenced and norm-referenced and can be used to place examinees in adult education classes or other adult instructional programs, to predict GED scores, and for pre- and posttesting to measure growth and evaluate programs. Both norms and curricular objectives mastery information are provided.

DEVELOPMENT. The test development of TABE 9 & 10 Core and Optional tests is described as having seven stages: assessment design, item writing, item review, item tryout, item analysis, test selection, and national norming. The content validity section describes the procedures used to design the TABE 9 & 10; this process included reviewing current curricula and standards, knowledge and skills emphasized in instructional materials, trends in adult education, goals of adult basic education programs, and features in the GED 2002. Anchor items from the TABE 7 were also included for linking with earlier TABE editions. Although the process for developing the test design is clearly described, it would have been helpful if the authors had provided an actual copy of the test blueprint. In developing the item pool, items were written that focused on content of interest and relevance to adults; careful procedures were in place to reduce any inaccurate or stereotypical portrayal of any individual or group. Items were reviewed by diverse groups representing business and industry as well as various gender and racial/ethnic groups.

The TABE 9 & 10 tryout items were administered to more than 27,000 adult examinees from 43 states and 288 institutions including adult basic education institutions, adult and juvenile correction institutions, and vocational/technical colleges. Item analyses were conducted including item difficulty, distracter analysis, discrimination analyses, and omit rates. The tryout items were scaled and calibrated using the three-parameter IRT model. The test characteristic curve method was used to place estimated parameters on a scale from which the anchor items were drawn. Differential item function (DIF) analysis studies were conducted for African Americans, Hispanics, Whites, males, and females. This information along with the other bias reviews and item statistics was used to select those items to construct the final tests. The steps in the test development, item selection, and test form development are clearly described and incorporate test specifications and psychometric procedures that are consistent with current standards of test development. The last step in the test development, norming, is also described in the manual.

The test items and materials are well written with clear manuals for administering and scoring all forms and levels of the tests. The tests can be sent to CTB/McGraw-Hill for computer scoring or there are several local scoring options including scan sheets, hand scoring stencils, and a SCOREZE answer sheet that allows for quick scoring. The Individual Diagnostic Profile provides norm-referenced and criterion-referenced interpretation of the tests. The norm-referenced scores include percentiles and stanines. The "Objectives Mastery Summary" provides a criterion-referenced interpretation that is tied to subtopics on each test. Note that these are not really "objectives" but topics within the general content area (e.g., Interpreting Graphic Information on the Reading Test). These "objectives" are rated N for Nonmastery, P for Partial Mastery, or M for Mastery. The content is clear and detailed enough to have useful diagnostic value for a teacher. The items appear to have face validity in that they reflect the types of problems that adults solve and the types of materials that adults read and interpret. A qualified teacher or administrator could easily administer and score these tests after having carefully read the appropriate administration and scoring manual. The Diagnostic Profiles make interpretation of the test results clear as well.

TECHNICAL.

Norms. The TABE 9 & 10 national norming sample was selected from more than 400 institutions and included more than 34,000 examinees from 46 states. The sample was selected from varied programs such as adult basic education, adult secondary education, ESL programs, alternative high schools, juvenile and adult correction facilities, and vocational/technical programs. Tables show the sample by type of program, gender and racial/ethnic group, age group, disability and type/level of testing accommodation, ESL, and level of the TABE 9 & 10. Two sets of reference group norms are provided: TABE-All and TABE-Juvenile (ages 14–20). The sample is quite large and diverse, and although not random, appears to be representative of the population for which the TABE is intended.

The three parameter logistic IRT model was used to calibrate the standardization data. Both TABE 9 & 10 were equated, and items were scaled together and equated to TABE 7. The TABE 9 & 10 scores were transformed to the TABE 7 score scale.

Several types of scores are available including scale scores, grade equivalents (GEs), percentile ranks and stanines, and normal curve equivalents (NCEs). The latter three score reporting methods are available separately for the TABE-All and the TABE-Juvenile groups. The grade equivalent scores are equated to the TABE 7, and no information is provided on how these were originally determined. According to Rogers (1998), a reviewer of TABE 7 & 8, the GEs were determined by a study equating the TABE with the California Achievement Test using sound equating procedures. The manual provides an additional table comparing the TABE to GED 2002 scores; this table may be useful for certain adult education programs. No normative data are included on the three advanced-level tests in Science/Social Studies, Algebra/Geometry, and Writing—a notable omission.

There is no information provided on how the gradations for the criterion-referenced interpretation of the TABE were determined. Description of how the Non-Mastery, Partial Mastery, and Mastery levels were set would have provided important support for this test score interpretation.

Reliability. Reliability was determined primarily using internal consistency (KR-20) analyses and the standard error of measurement (*SEM*). The KR-20s and *SEM*s were provided for the complete battery and the survey tests at each level. The KR-20s were acceptable and were, predictably, higher for the complete battery than for the survey tests and optional tests, which are somewhat shorter. IRT Standard Error Curves demonstrated that the subtests by level are performing as expected with smaller *SEM*s in the center of the distribution and larger at the extreme scores. No reliability data were provided for the three advanced-level tests. In addition to the reliability estimates reported above, rater reliability should have been provided for the advanced-level Writing test.

Validity. The test development process clearly provides the content-related validity evidence to support the use of the TABE 9 & 10 Core and Optional Tests. The procedures for developing the Locator Test cut points are also clearly described and appropriate. Three methods were used for this analysis: using smoothed density functions, canonical discriminant analysis, and Item Characteristic Curves (ICC). According to the technical manual, the cut scores from these three methods were analyzed and "found to be highly comparable" (p. 14).

Patterns of correlations among the TABE 9 & 10 subtests provide construct validity support. Correlations between the GED 2002 and the TABE support the criterion-related validity of the tests though it must be noted that TABE 9 & 10 are linked to the GED 2002 through the TABE 7. Again, no validity information is provided on the three advanced tests.

COMMENTARY AND SUMMARY. The core and optional tests of the TABE 9 & 10 appear to be well developed with strong psychometric characteristics. The tests appear to be easy to administer, score, and interpret. The norm groups are large and diverse and reflect the type of examinee for whom the test is targeted. There does not appear to be a strong foundation associated with the mastery scores, and these should be used and interpreted with caution. Several types of information are needed (e.g., validity, reliability) before the three Advanced Level supplementary tests can be recommended for use.

REVIEWER'S REFERENCE

Rogers, B. (1998). [Review of the Tests of Adult Basic Education, Forms 7 & 8.] In B. S. Plake & J. C. Impara (Eds.), *The thirteenth mental measurements yearbook* (pp. 1083–1085). Lincoln, NE: Buros Institute of Mental Measurements.

[188]

Tower of London—Drexel University: 2nd Edition.

Purpose: A neuropsychological instrument "designed to assess higher-order problem solving—specifically, executive planning abilities—in children and adults."

Population: Ages 7–80.

Publication Dates: 1999–2005.

Acronym: TOL^{DX} 2nd Ed.

Scores, 8: Total Move Score, Total Correct Score, Total Time Violation, Total Rules Violation, Total Initiation Time, Total Execution Time, Total Problem-Solving Time, Total Stimulus-Bound.

Administration: Individual.

Forms, 2: Adult, Child.

Price Data, 2007: $278 per complete kit including technical manual (2005, 104 pages), 2 peg boards with beads, 25 child record forms, and 25 adult record forms; $242 per complete adult kit including technical manual, 2 peg boards with beads, and 25 adult record forms; $242 per complete child kit including technical manual, 2 peg boards with beads, and 25 child record forms; $87 per technical manual; $42 per 25 child or adult record forms.

Time: (10–15) minutes.

Comments: Administered individually by clinicians; special instructions for mentally challenged populations.

Authors: William C. Culbertson and Eric A. Zilmer.

Publisher: Multi-Health Systems, Inc.

a) CHILD.

Population: Ages 7–15.

b) ADULT.

Population: Ages 16 and older.

Cross References: For reviews by Carolyn M. Callahan and James P. Van Haneghan of the previous edition, see 15:267.

Review of the Tower of London-Drexel University: 2nd Edition by BRAD M. MERKER, Neuropsychology Post-Doctoral Fellow, University of Oklahoma Health Sciences Center, Oklahoma City, OK, and JOHN LINCK, Neuropsychology Post-Doctoral Fellow, University of Oklahoma Health Sciences Center, Oklahoma City, OK:

DESCRIPTION. The Tower of London-Drexel University (TOL^{DX} 2nd Edition) is a modification of a long-standing measure of executive functioning (Shallice, 1982). The current version (TOL^{DX}) was designed as an individually administered test of executive functioning with emphasis placed on measuring executive problem solving, planning, impulse control, attentional allocation, cognitive flexibility, abstraction, rule governed behavior, and self-monitoring. The test is suitable for use with both children and adults ranging in age from 7–80. Each version of the test begins with a demonstration item followed by 2 practice items and proceeds to 10 items of increasing difficulty.

To administer the test, two tower boards, two sets of different colored beads, a manual, stopwatch, and the appropriate child or adult record form are required. Using a three-peg tower structure board, the examiner places three beads on one tower board in the desired configuration. The examinee then uses the second tower board to move their three colored beads from the designated start position to the desired end position denoted by the examiner's tower board in as few moves as possible. The examinee is required to follow two basic rules while completing the task: He or she cannot move more than one bead at a time and cannot place more beads on the peg than it will hold. On each trial the examinee is allowed 2 minutes; however, if after 1 minute they have not completed the problem, a Time Violation is scored. All 10 items are administered to the examinee, and testing can be completed in approximately 10–15 minutes.

The TOL^DX scoring system includes eight indices: Total Moves, Total Correct, Initiation Time, Execution Time, Total Problem-Solving Time, Time Violations, Total Rule Violations, and Stimulus-Bound Responses. Raw scores are converted to standard scores and percentiles based on the examinee's age. Additionally, qualitative observations can be made of the examinee's problem-solving approach, attention and activity, and personal-emotional-social behaviors using a 5-point Likert scale. TOL^DX interpretation requires a thorough understanding of neuropsychology and the developers caution clinicians from solely using one test for diagnostic and treatment decisions. Alternatively, they suggest when making diagnostic decisions examiners include information from various sources such as additional testing, clinical interviews, and medical findings. Four case studies exemplifying the use of the TOL^DX as part of a comprehensive neuropsychological battery are provided within the manual. Cases illustrate the use of the TOL^DX when examining patients diagnosed with Oppositional Defiant Disorder/ADHD, overanxious disorder, closed head injury, and frontal lobe tumor.

DEVELOPMENT. The second edition of the TOL^DX is not unlike its predecessor and earlier versions of the Tower test (e.g., Tower of Hanoi, Tower of Toronto). Throughout the manual, the developers emphasize the development of executive function skills from childhood through early adulthood and the need for a measure of executive functioning that assesses both normal development and neurological dysfunction. The current version of the test contains several modifications from the original including the addition of a Stimulus-Bound score for older adults, extended normative data extending up to 80-year-olds, as well as additional empirical data further supporting the validity of the test. Initially, 26 problem configurations were created and administered to 256 college students. Based on the individual test items and their correlation with the total move score, 10 items with a .50 level of difficulty were selected to comprise the adult version of the TOL^DX. For the child version, 15 items from the pool of 26 items were selected for administration to children. Using the aforementioned criteria, 10 of the 15 items were selected to comprise the child version. In developing the test, the authors introduced problems requiring six and seven moves in an effort to increase the ceiling and sensitivity of the TOL^DX for older children.

TECHNICAL. The normative sample for the TOL^DX consisted of 990 individuals ages 7–80 drawn from the Northeastern parts of the United States and Canada. Age ranges are broken down into nine groups with ns ranging from 39 (60–80-year-olds) to 192 (30–39-year-olds). The sample was equally represented with regard to gender. The ethnic/racial breakdown of the normative sample is adequate, although individuals of Hispanic origin accounted for only 1% of the total sample. Despite having a large sample size, the standardization sample does not adequately represent some populations. Additional normative data drawn from the elderly, rural, and Hispanic populations would further increase the utility of the test with these underrepresented populations.

In addition to the normative sample, data were collected on two groups of children with ADHD for the purposes of gathering ADHD youth normative data. However, little descriptive information on the two samples is provided in the test manual, thus reducing the utility of the data when evaluating individuals with suspected ADHD. The developers also make mention of a study (Kennedy, 2000, 2003) using a modified TOL^DX with 64 adults with mental retardation of varying severity. The administrative protocol, test items, and normative data for use with individuals with cognitive limitations are provided in the test manual.

Reliability. Limited reliability information is provided in the manual. Test-retest reliability with an interval ranging from 5–92 days using a sample of 31 individuals diagnosed with ADHD demonstrated moderate (Total Move, $r = .80$) to poor (Total Rule Violation, $r = .24$) stability over time. Additional test-retest reliability evidence using a sample of individuals diagnosed with Parkinson's disease ranged from moderate (Execution Time, r

= .81) to poor (Rule Violations, *r* = .28) with a mean interval of 136.9 days. No test-retest reliability or other forms of reliability are reported for the normative group.

Validity. Evidence supporting criterion and construct validity of the TOL^{DX} is provided in the manual. Criterion validity is demonstrated in two ways. First, TOL^{DX} scores of normal and ADHD children were compared. As expected, the ADHD children in four age groups performed significantly worse than their age-matched peers, requiring a significantly greater number of moves, additional time, and committing substantially more rule violations. Using a subsample of normal and ADHD children, the derived discriminant analysis produced an overall classification rate of .78. Sensitivity and specificity were found to be .76 and .81, respectively, suggesting that the TOL^{DX} has an acceptable classification rate for making individual diagnostic decisions. Convergent validity evidence was established by comparing performance of the TOL^{DX} with the d^2 Test of Attention (a measure of select and sustained attention). Significant, albeit low, correlations suggest the TOL^{DX} measures attentional allocation as well as other cognitive abilities. Discriminant evidence was established by showing that insignificant intercorrelations existed with the Wechsler Adult Intelligence Scale—Revised (WAIS-R) Information and Picture Completion subtests. Finally, the developers highlighted a study undertaken to determine the relationship of the TOL^{DX} to mental status, cognitive ability, and adaptive status of patients with Parkinson's disease. Again, as predicted, the TOL^{DX} was found to be unrelated to a measure of intelligence, a measure of verbal learning and memory, and the Stroop Color Word Test, but significantly related to measures of general mental status (MMSE), adaptive status, executive functioning (i.e., Trail Making Test Part B), and activities of daily living.

Factor support for the TOL^{DX} was established by examining the relationship of the TOL^{DX} with other neuropsychological measures for the original sample of ADHD children. The neuropsychological battery primarily consisted of measures of executive functioning, attention, memory, and intelligence. Significant correlations ranging from .57 to -.54 existed between the TOL^{DX} scores and other measures of executive functioning. Alternatively, correlations with the

Wechsler Intelligence Scale for Children—Third Edition (WISC-III) were low and generally insignificant, whereas correlations with memory measures were unexpectedly significant. The developers explained the unforeseen relationship of the TOL^{DX} with memory measures as resulting from examinees generating and deploying organized search strategies. Factor analysis with oblique rotation was conducted using ADHD subjects' performance on the TOL^{DX}. The analysis revealed a four-factor solution that accounted for 66% of the variance. The four factors were: executive concept formation/flexibility, memory, executive planning/control, and psychometric intelligence. No evidence supporting construct validity is provided in the test manual for normal samples or for samples with documented frontal lobe damage.

COMMENTARY. The second version of TOL^{DX} appears to be a well-constructed and theoretically sound measure of executive functioning useful when assessing both children and adults with suspected neurological dysfunction. The test is easy to administer, score, and interpret and can be completed in under 15 minutes. Test users are provided with eight quantitative scores and are able to qualitatively rate examinees on their problem-solving approach; attention/activity; and personal, emotional, and social behavior. The extension of the upper age range to 80, the inclusion of a Stimulus-Bound score, and the additional validity evidence provided in the test manual represent commendable improvements over its predecessor. Its other strengths include: validity data for ADHD and Parkinson's patients, normative data for a sample of mentally handicapped individuals with mental retardation, and the inclusion of four interpretative cases.

Unfortunately, the TOL^{DX} continues to have several limitations that reduce the test's utility in clinical practice. First, Hispanics and elderly individuals are not adequately represented in the normative sample. The low number of individuals included in these groups raises concerns over whether the normative data accurately represent the general population. Second, minimal reliability and validity evidence is provided for individuals with suspected frontal lobe dysfunction (i.e., Parkinson's disease). Additional reliability, validity, and normative data for individuals with documented frontal lobe injuries (e.g., brain tumors, traumatic brain injuries) would provide further support for the psychometric soundness of the test. Finally, although the developers provide evidence of the test's psychometric properties using ADHD and Parkinson's samples, additional studies are needed using normal examinees with diverse backgrounds.

SUMMARY. The developers of the TOL^DX modified a long-standing measure of executive functioning (Shallice, 1982) and made several improvements in the second edition that have increased the measure's utility in clinical settings. The test has numerous strengths that make it especially useful when assessing neurological dysfunction in both adults and children. Reliability and validity evidence is generally adequate, although Hispanics, elderly, and individuals from rural areas are considerably underrepresented in the normative sample. At the present time, if examiners are cognizant of the test's limitations and the test is used alongside other measures of neuropsychological functioning, the TOL^DX can provide helpful information when faced with making diagnostic and treatment decisions.

REVIEWERS' REFERENCES

Kennedy, C. H. (2000). *The neuropsychology of sexual consents.* Unpublished doctoral dissertation, Drexel University, Philadelphia, PA.
Kennedy, C. H. (2003). Legal and psychological implications in the assessment of sexual consent in the cognitively impaired population. *Assessment, 10,* 352–358.
Shallice, T. (1982). Specific impairments of planning. *Philosophical Transactions of the Royal Society of London, B298,* 199–209.

Review of the Tower of London—Drexel University: 2nd Edition by GREGORY SCHRAW, Department of Educational Psychology, University of Nevada—Las Vegas, Las Vegas, NV:

DESCRIPTION. The Tower of London—Drexel University: 2nd Edition (TOL^DX) provides a test of higher order problem-solving skills, especially executive planning abilities, which include the delineation, organization, and integration of behaviors that are necessary to achieve a goal. The TOL^DX is believed to assess frontal lobe functioning in normal and clinical populations; thus, the TOL^DX provides a measure of the development of frontal-executive planning in children and adults, ranging from age 7 to age 80.

The TOL^DX consists of 10 timed problems using a three-peg board in which the test-taker is asked to arrange three colored beads to match a specific pattern. Some configurations require more moves than others; thus, they are more complex and require more time and executive planning. Each participant is administered a demonstration problem and two practice problems prior to the 10-item test. Administration time ranges from 10 to 15 minutes; scoring and interpretation for a skilled test administrator requires an additional 10 minutes.

DEVELOPMENT. The TOL^DX evolved from the classic Tower of Hanoi problem and was modified initially by Shallice (1982) to standardize problem difficulty and to make the test quick and efficient to administer. The current version was modified further to make the test suitable for a wide range of test takers.

The TOL^DX yields eight separate scores based on three critical dimensions, including movement performance, rule adherence, and temporal efficiency. Movement performance refers to how accurately a test taker executes the desired move. Rule adherence refers to whether time (e.g., a 120-second limit per problem) and rule (e.g., placing too many beads on a peg) violations occur. Temporal efficiency refers to how long it takes to solve a problem correctly without violations. The eight scores that are reported in the TOL^DX consist of Total Move, Total Correct, Total Rule Violation, Total Time Violation, Total Initiation Time, Total Execution Time, Total Problem-Solving, and Total Stimulus-Bound scores. The manual explains each of these scores in detail.

TECHNICAL. The TOL^DX is accompanied by a 94-page test manual, complete with information about administration, scoring, reliability and validity, interpretation, development, and standardization of the test. The test manual is clearly written and concise. Four case studies are considered in detail, which include special clinical cases of children and adults with closed head injuries, frontal lobe tumors, and psychological disorders.

The manual provides limited reliability and validity data. One study examined the test-retest reliability of 31 children with ADHD over intervals ranging from 5 to 92 days. Total Correct ($r = .42$), Total Time Violation ($r = .67$), and Total Rule Violation ($r = .24$) test-retest correlations were below the standard benchmark of $r = .70$. However, the Total Move score yielded a test-retest correlation of .80. The test authors describe the Total Move score as the primary measure of executive planning. No information is provided regarding the internal consistency of each of the eight subscores across the 10 target problems. In contrast, a study of 35 patients with Parkinson's disease showed test-retest correlations above .70

for all of the standard scores except the total correct score, which yielded a correlation of $r = .59$.

Both construct and criterion-related validity are discussed. One study using 129 ADHD children examined the intercorrelations among TOL^{DX} subscores, the Wisconsin Card Sorting Task, the Wechsler Intelligence Scale for Children-III, Stroop Color and Word test, and the Selective Reminding Test. An exploratory factor analysis yielded four factors, with the three selected TOL^{DX} subscales all loading above .60 on the same factor. The factor was labeled the executive planning/control factor, which correlated .42 with an executive concept formation/flexibility factor, which included a high loading from the Wisconsin Card Sorting Task. This result suggests that the TOL^{DX} assesses executive skills similar to the Wisconsin Test.

Regarding criterion-related validity, one study compared 446 normal children to 115 ADHD children using the TOL^{DX} subscales. Normal children had lower Total Move scores, higher Total Correct scores, and lower Total Execution Time scores than ADHD children. This finding suggests that the TOL^{DX} subscales discriminate between normal and ADHD children in the expected direction. A separate study compared 37 healthy men to 65 male patients with Parkinson's disease. The healthy controls performed more accurately and faster than the patients with Parkinson's disease. This study supported the claim that the TOL^{DX} discriminates between healthy and ill children.

COMMENTARY. The strengths of the TOL^{DX} include easy administration and scoring, a well-written manual, and the intuitive simplicity of the TOL^{DX} problems.

Weaknesses include lack of a clear theoretical framework and insufficient reliability and validity evidence. Test interpretation would be enhanced if the authors explained the executive planning process in more detail and provided a theoretical model of the process. Currently, it is difficult to tell whether the TOL^{DX} measures executive planning as claimed, or simply measures problem-solving accuracy that does not necessarily include executive planning components. In addition, linking executive planning to the vast research literature on problem solving would clarify what the TOL^{DX} purports to measure. Incomplete reliability and validity evidence poses a serious problem for the TOL^{DX}. Only two reliability stud-

ies are presented in the test manual. About half of the resultant reliability coefficients were below the .70 criterion used by researchers and clinicians. There also is a lack of predictive validity evidence. Comparing performance on the TOL^{DX} to traditional problem-solving measures would greatly enhance diagnostic utility of the instrument.

SUMMARY. Overall, the TOL^{DX} provides a quick measure of planning accuracy and efficiency. It provides specific information about total number of problems solved correctly, total time, and total problem-solving errors. These measures provide a benchmark for comparing different groups of learners.

REVIEWER'S REFERENCE

Shallice, T. (1982). Specific impairments of planning. *Philosophical Transactions of the Royal Society of London, B298*, 199–209.

[189]

Transition Planning Inventory (Updated Version).

Purpose: Designed to help identify "preferences and interests and areas of transition strength and needs."

Population: Students with disabilities who desire to plan for the future.

Publication Dates: 1997–2006.

Acronym: TPI-UV.

Scores: Ratings in 9 areas: Employment, Further Education, Daily Living, Leisure Activities, Community Participation, Health, Self-Determination, Communication, Interpersonal Relationships.

Administration: Group or individual.

Forms, 5: Student, Home, School, Profile and Further Recommendations, Modified Form for Students with Significant Disabilities.

Versions, 2: Paper and pencil, Computer.

Price Data, 2007: $175 per complete kit including Administration and Resource Guide (2006, 184 pages), 25 Profile and Further Assessment Recommendation forms, 25 School forms, 25 Home forms, 25 Student forms, Informal Assessments for Transition Planning resource, and Case Studies in Transition Planning book; $24 per Administration and Resource Guide; $25 per 25 Profile and Further Assessment Recommendation forms; $25 per 25 School forms; $25 per 25 Home forms; $25 per 25 Student forms.

Foreign Language Editions: Home forms available in Spanish, Chinese, Japanese, and Korean.

Time: (15–30) minutes per form.

Comments: The Home and Student forms can be administered independently, individually (assisted), in small groups, or orally; Student, Home, School, and Profile and Further Recommendations forms should all be used when working with students without significant disabilities.

Authors: Gary M. Clark and James R. Patton.
Publisher: PRO-ED.
Cross References: For reviews by Robert K. Gable and by Rosemary E. Sutton and Theresa A. Quigney of an earlier form, see 14:400.

Review of the Transition Planning Inventory (Updated Version) by PAM LINDSEY, Associate Professor, Curriculum and Instruction, Tarleton State University, Stephenville, TX:

DESCRIPTION. The Transition Planning Inventory: Updated Version (TPI-UV) is described as a formal assessment and planning tool for use with students with disabilities in individualized educational planning. It focuses on the major areas of transition from school to adult life as defined by federal law and research literature. The updated version of the original reflects the standards of the current revision of the Individuals with Disabilities Education Act (IDEA, 2004).

The TPI-UV consists of 46 transition planning statements organized according to the domains of transition identified by IDEA and reported in the literature, namely, Employment, Postsecondary Education/Training, Daily Living, Leisure Activities, Community Participation, Health, Self-Determination, Communication, and Interpersonal Relationships. Each area has three or more items related to knowledge, skills, or behaviors associated with successful transition or adjustment to adult status. The instrument is to be completed by a team of people including the student; his or her parents, guardians, or caregivers; and one or more professionals from his or her school. The test authors report that the rating forms were unchanged from the original TPI; however, new features were added to this version in response to reported themes from users over the past 7 years. New features include a computerized version, modified student form for those with significant disabilities, revisions to the Planning Notes and Further Assessment Recommendations forms, revisions to the descriptions about the intent and meaning of each transition statement, and translations of the Home form into four languages.

The TPI-UV uses a 6-point Likert-scale format to determine the rater's levels of agreement with the transition statements. The raters may choose a rating of 0 (*strongly disagree*) to 5 (*strongly agree*) for each statement in each domain. The ratings indicate the student's present levels of performance in each of the domains. The TPI-UV has three forms for completion and comparison: School form, Home form, and Student form. All may be completed independently by the respondent or administered orally by a designated interviewer. There is also space on the protocol for planning notes and recommendations for the need for further assessment.

A full description of each domain is provided along with a separate manual of case studies that guide respondents in interpreting the ratings for transition planning. The manual also describes the target groups for whom the TPI-UV is most appropriate.

Because the TPI-UV is a respondent instrument, user qualifications are listed by respondent. A minimum of three persons should be involved in the completion of the inventory, namely, the student, his or her primary care providers, and at least one teacher or other school personnel directly involved with the student. The test authors suggest that student preparation for completing the instrument is advised, and the manual describes a suggested preparation process.

DEVELOPMENT. The TPI-UV is the most current version (copyright, 2005) of an instrument that has been under development since 1997. The descriptions of each domain of transition are comprehensive and easily understood by the reader. The domains of transition are based on legislative mandates and current best practice in transition planning for students with disabilities. Transition planning is defined as a team approach for assessing a student's current levels of performance in each domain and his or her likelihood for successful transition to adult/community life.

Items for each domain were chosen by "surveying" other transition assessment instruments and through comments of practitioners and nonpractitioners from the field. The respondents evaluated the items in relation to their responsiveness to meet the needs of the schools for transition planning.

The TPI-UV used a total of 310 cases for the field-test group. These individuals represented a mixed group in terms of ethnicity; however, information was not provided concerning the types of disabilities represented in the sample.

TECHNICAL. As previously stated, the 46 items on the original TPI were not changed. Features were added based on field input. The inventory consists of 46 statements organized by the nine domains of transition.

The reliability data appear to be adequate with content and time sampling data revealing coefficient alphas ranging from a low of .71 to a high of .95. Two forms of reliability data are presented, namely, content and time sampling. Time sampling data measure the consistency of student performance over time. Thirty-six students were used to investigate the time sampling reliability. The reliability reported was adequate with a low of .70 and high of .98.

Content validity was established by looking at similar instruments and through practitioners' and nonpractitioners' comments. In addition, criterion-related and concurrent validity were discussed; however, the discussion did not indicate that either was established.

Overall, the technical data reported in the manual appear to support with some degree of confidence the reliability and validity of the instrument to help parents, students, and school personnel in planning for students' transition to adult life. Because the TPI-UV is an inventory/interview-constructed instrument, its reliability and validity are highly dependent on the truthfulness and accurate observations of the respondents.

COMMENTARY. As with all self-reports, the inherent problem is response bias related to all interview/inventory instruments. The test authors suggest that more than one school professional may add reliability to the rating and further that respondents' ratings of an individual should not be in comparison with his or her nondisabled peers. The test authors also clearly suggest that the TPI-UV should be used as one data source for effective transition planning.

The instrument is easy to give and score and the case study examples are very helpful in interpreting specific profiles. The instructions for comparing respondents' ratings and creating a student profile are clear.

The transition statements for each domain are very broad and open to a great deal of interpretation and respondent bias. For example, in the Communication domain, "has needed speaking skills" (administration and resource manual, p. 16) is a rated item. This item begs the question "needed for what?" Many of the items are similarly structured.

SUMMARY. The TPI-UV has some merit as a broad screening instrument. It may help participants more closely define the domains of transition skills and perhaps identify areas of concern. The case studies are very helpful in analyzing the results.

Review of Transition Planning Inventory (Updated Version) by JULIA Y. PORTER, Associate Professor of Counselor Education, Mississippi State University, Meridian, MS:

DESCRIPTION. The Transition Planning Inventory (Updated Version) (TPI-UV) assesses the transition strengths and needs of students with disabilities who are preparing to move from high school to postschool settings. This inventory assesses a student's current competency on nine transition domains using 46 items. Three rating forms are completed for each student: (a) Student form completed by the student; (b) Home form completed by the parent/guardian; and (c) School form completed by school personnel. Data collected using this multiple-perspective rating approach are recorded on the Profile and Further Assessment Recommendations form, which is then used to develop a transition action plan for the student.

Data collected by the TPI-UV include student input about interests and needs related to transition planning, which is a specified requirement in the Individuals with Disabilities Education Act of 2004 (IDEA 2004). Each respondent, including the student, is asked to rate the current competency level of the student from 0–5. A response of 0–2 indicates levels of need in an area, and responses of 3–5 indicate levels of competency in an area.

For the TPI-UV to be useful in transition planning, the respondents for each of the three forms need to understand the item terminology and respond honestly to each item. After responses are recorded and reviewed, collaboration is required to reach consensus on a transition action plan for the student.

Administration methods for the forms include pencil-and-paper administration, oral administration, or computer administration. Administration options include independent self-administration, guided self-administration, and oral administration. The test administrator needs to be familiar with the items on the TPI-UV to be able to answer questions about the items. The TPI-UV is available in four languages (Spanish, Chinese [Mandarin], Korean, and Japanese), and copies of the different language forms are available in the administration guide and may be copied.

Additional resources included in the TPI-UV kit include the books "Informal Assessments for Transition Planning" and "Case Studies in Assessment for Transition Planning." There is also a TPI Modified form for Students with Significant Disabilities and a Planning Notes form.

A computerized version of the TPI-UV is available separately from the TPI-UV kit. The computerized version reports average ratings on competency items in addition to student, home, and school scores.

DEVELOPMENT. The test developers designed the TPI-UV as an assessment and planning tool for school personnel to use with students with disabilities to plan transition services. The TPI-UV is designed to rate individuals on their current level of competency and not to compare individuals. Guidelines and scripts are available in the administration manual to facilitate administration of the TPI-UV. Test developers recommend administering the TPI-UV annually because student competencies and interests change. Triangulation of data from the Student form, Home form, and School form provides the best information for transition planning. However, the TPI-UV may be used with data from only the Student form and School form.

The nine transition domains assessed in the TPI-UV are: Employment, Further Education/Training, Leisure Activities, Daily Living, Community Participation, Health, Self-Determination, Communication, and Interpersonal Relationships. The TPI-UV presents eight choices per test item (Competency rating 0–5, DK [Don't Know], and NA [Not Applicable]). Approximate testing time for self-administration is 15–20 minutes for the Student form and Home form and 10–15 minutes for the School form. More information about the theoretical base used to develop the assessment forms would be useful to test administrators when comparing the TPI-UV with other instruments for test selection (Whiston, 2005).

Factors cited by the test developers that could affect assessment results include: (a) communication skills of respondents, (b) values of the parent/guardian, (c) instrument items that may not apply to a particular student, (d) differences in rater responses, and (e) getting parent/guardian to return the Home form.

TECHNICAL. Because the TPI-UV is an individualized screening inventory designed for planning purposes, the test developers did not establish norms. They did conduct field testing to address the validity and reliability of the forms before the first TPI was published in 1997. In 1995–1996, 844 respondents (288 students, 227 parent/guardians, and 329 school personnel) participated in the primary field testing. Content sample reliability was established using alpha coefficients which ranged from .70 to .95. The School form had the highest reliability coefficients and the Student form had the lowest alpha coefficients. Test developers noted that although some students overestimate their competency on items, any discrepancies in form responses may be addressed in an Individualized Education Plan (IEP) meeting and/or Transition Planning meeting.

Test-retest reliability coefficients ranged from .70 to .98 with the School form receiving the highest test-retest reliability coefficients and the Student form receiving the lowest coefficients (the test-retest interval was 7–10 days).

Content validity was addressed through item selection. Items were selected from a pool of 250 items that describe behaviors associated with adult adjustment and desired adult outcomes. The 250 items were drawn from a review of literature about adult adjustment of persons with disabilities and transition needs. Test developers selected a smaller number of items (49) to make the TPI more efficient to administer. The 49 items were reviewed by experts (22 practitioners who provide direct services in school settings and 20 nonpractitioners in higher education or special education administration). Based on the expert reviews, items were revised or deleted, which resulted in the 46 items selected for the TPI. The experts also were asked to rate the purpose and utility of the TPI and how well it would meet the needs of schools in transition planning. A majority of respondents said the TPI would be effective.

Test developers reported conducting criterion-related validity tests and reported that there were some significant correlations between the TPI-UV and the Wechsler Intelligence Scale for Children-III and the Vineland Adaptive Behavior Scales. Test developers did not provide results because of the small number of participants in the study who had usable data ($N = 48$ out of 310). Further, test developers reported that they are conducting additional validity studies. Additional reliability and validity data would help test administrators evaluate the appropriateness of the TPI-UV for their needs (American Educational Research Association, American Psychological Association, & National Council on Measurement in Education, 1999).

COMMENTARY. The TPI-UV is a useful screening and data collection tool for systematically addressing transition needs of students with disabilities, for identifying a student's need for further assessment on a particular transition domain, for helping develop transitional goals for a student, and for helping develop linkage goals for students. Resource materials included in the test kit and administration guide provide detailed examples of appropriate uses for assessment results from this instrument as well as recommendations of additional assessment instruments that may be used for additional assessment of competency needs identified by the TPI-UV. The TPI-UV may be used for an IEP or TP meeting to facilitate development of student transition plans and to provide documentation for compliance with IDEA 2004 as part of a student's file.

SUMMARY. The TPI-UV was designed to measure current competency of adolescents with disabilities (physical and mental) who are preparing to transition from a high school setting to other settings in the community such as postsecondary education or work. The TPI-UV is appropriate for use with individuals who have language deficiencies. The administration guide included with the test materials offers practical guidelines and examples for effectively using the TPI-UV for transition planning. Especially useful are the over 600 transition goals included in Appendix E of the administrator's guide that correlate with the nine domains assessed by the TPI-UV. These goals may be used to help set appropriate transition goals for students based on the composite results reported on the Profile and Further Assessment Recommendations form.

REVIEWER'S REFERENCES

American Educational Research Association, American Psychological Association, & National Council on Measurement in Education. (1999). *Standards for educational and psychological testing.* Washington, DC: American Educational Research Association.

Whiston, S. C. (2005). *Principles and applications of assessment in counseling* (2nd ed.). Belmont, CA: Wadsworth/Thomson Learning.

[190]

Trauma Assessment Inventories.

Purpose: "Designed to screen for Posttraumatic Stress Disorder" and designed to assess "Cognitive and emotional aspects of guilt associated with a specific traumatic event."

Population: Ages 18 years and older.

Publication Date: 2004.

Administration: Individual.

Price Data, 2007: $192.50 per complete kit including Screening Kit and Treatment Kit; Computerized Components: $96 per 20-use CD for Computer Scoring Only; $40 per 25 AutoScore forms (specify screening or treatment); $16.50 per 100 computerized answer sheets (specify screening or treatment).

Author: Edward S. Kubany.

Publisher: Western Psychological Services.

a) SCREENING KIT.

Purpose: "Designed to screen for Posttraumatic Stress Disorder."

Price Data: $109 per complete screening kit including 25 AutoScore forms, 25 test forms, and screening manual (47 pages); $44 per screening manual.

Time: (10-20) minutes.

Comments: This test can be abbreviated if time constraints are an issue.

1) *Traumatic Life Events Questionnaire.*

Acronym: TLEQ.

Scores, 3: Count of Events, Count of Events Associated with Fear or Hopelessness, Occurrences.

Price Data: $29 per 25 test forms.

2) *PTSD Screening and Diagnostic Scale.*

Acronym: PSDS.

Scores, 7: Criterion A, Criterion B, Criterion C, Criterion D, PSDS Symptom Score, Criterion E, Criterion F.

b) TREATMENT KIT.

Purpose: Designed to assess "Cognitive and emotional aspects of guilt associated with a specific traumatic event."

Price Data: $88 per complete treatment kit including 25 AutoScore forms, 25 test forms, and treatment manual (59 pages); $52 per treatment manual.

Time: Administration time not reported.

1) *The Trauma-Related Guilt Inventory.*

Acronym: TRGI.

Scores, 6: Global Guilt, Distress, Guilt Cognitions (Wrongdoing, Insufficient Justification, Hindsight-Bias/Responsibility).

Comments: This test is written at a 5th-grade reading level.

Review of the Trauma Assessment Inventories by JAMES P. DONNELLY, Assistant Professor, Department of Counseling, School & Educational Psychology, University at Buffalo, Amherst, NY, and KERRY DONNELLY, Clinical Neuropsychologist, VA Western New York Healthcare System, Buffalo, NY:

DESCRIPTION. The Trauma Assessment Inventories include three instruments to facilitate assessment of different aspects of trauma experience depending on the clinical need: Screening via The Traumatic Life Events Questionnaire (TLEQ), DSM diagnosis with the PTSD Screening and Diagnostic Scale (PSDS), and cognitively oriented treatment using The Trauma-Related Guilt Inventory (TRGI). The screening and diagnostic instruments (TLEQ and PSDS) are packaged and sold together (the "screening kit"); the TRGI treatment inventory (the "treatment kit") can be ordered separately. The author of all three inventories is Edward Kubany, Ph.D., who has focused his clinical activity and research on assessment and treatment of traumatic stress, especially with veterans, for more than a decade.

The TLEQ manual makes the case that traumatic events are far more frequent than is generally known and that a brief structured self-report in the clinical setting may be a very efficient way to obtain trauma history. The instrument includes 22 items with specific events such as motor vehicle accidents, war, sudden death of a close relative or friend, domestic violence, and similar events. Each item includes a set of contingent follow-up questions to assess frequency of occurrence and severity of emotional consequences. The 23rd item allows the respondent to identify any other event not previously listed and concludes with a summary item in which the respondent indicates which of the prior events was the most distressing. The event cited in the last item then becomes the focus of the DSM-oriented PSDS, as well as the TRGI assessment if cognitive-behavioral treatment is under consideration. The PSDS includes 38 items covering the six criteria for a diagnosis of PTSD in the DSM-IV. The PSDS is the most recent version of a measure previously called the Distressing Event Questionnaire (Kubany, Leisen, Kaplan, & Kelly, 2000). The TRGI includes 32 statements that describe guilt-related thoughts and feelings and produces six subscale scores.

These measures were developed on adult populations, but only one of the instruments, the PSDS, specifically refers to age considerations in administration in advising usage for individuals age 18 or over. The TRGI is written at a fifth grade reading level. Reading criteria for the TLEQ and PSDS are sixth and eighth grade levels, respectively. English language fluency is assumed. All three instruments are available in paper and computer versions. A brief version of the TLEQ is accomplished by instructing respondents to complete only unshaded items on the response form, reducing completion time to about 7 minutes. Administration by a trained technician and interpretation by a clinical professional is recommended.

DEVELOPMENT. The description of the development of the TLEQ in the manual is brief, but it appears that the identification and refinement of items was deliberate and thorough. The primary effort involved examination of the literature and related instruments along with extensive pilot testing (over 1,000 protocols). The final item set was completed after a review by a panel of seven PTSD experts to obtain feedback on the quality of item wording and adequacy of sampling of traumatic events. The 38 items of the PSDS were directly based on PTSD criteria in the DSM-IV. Once again, items were reviewed by PTSD experts. The TRGI was built more from the "ground up" than the two diagnostic instruments, presumably because the construct is more recent and so that interval level scales reflecting aspects of trauma-related guilt could be employed in contrast to the categorical judgments (primary traumatic event, diagnosis) facilitated by the screening kit.

The TRGI item development process included integration of relevant thoughts and feelings identified in prior studies, related instruments, clinician expertise, and semistructured interviews with trauma survivors. Ultimately, an initial pool of 120 items was reduced to a test set of 40 and a final set of 32 covering six constructs (subscales are Global Guilt, Distress, and four on specific guilt-cognitions including Hindsight Bias/Responsibility, Insufficient Justification, Wrongdoing, and a General subscale). The establishment of the six scales was based on factor analysis of three samples (two college groups with Ns of 200 and 125 and one battered women support group sample of 100). Item analysis with these samples was aimed at retention of items that met six criteria: variability in response evident in no more than 50% of respondents selecting any particular response anchor, item correlations below .9 with all other items, factor loading of .5 on primary factor with .3 or greater difference between primary and all other factors, and review of expected clinical utility of each item. The final 32-item set was said to produce a "robust and very stable" (TRGI manual, p. 26) four-factor solution that included 22 of the items. Unfortunately, the otherwise complete report in the manual does not include tables of the factor analysis results, and the text is limited in describing these analyses.

TECHNICAL.

The TLEQ. Because the TLEQ does not produce scale scores, the psychometric analysis focused on temporal consistency of reports of trauma in several samples, as well as content validity. Temporal consistency was examined in four samples over varying intervals from 5 days to 2 months. The samples included 51 Vietnam combat veterans, 49 residential substance abuse patients, 62 college students, and 42 members of a support group for battered women. Each item (traumatic event + emotional consequences) was assessed in terms of percent agreement and Cohen's kappa. The lowest temporal consistency levels were observed in the "other accident" category, with percent agreement ranging from 63 to 88 and kappa coefficients from .27 to .59. The interpretation of these numbers suggests that recall of particulars from a large and varied set is more complex than from a singular traumatic event, such as a life-threatening illness. The simple percentage agreement numbers may be more informative than coefficient kappa because: (a) kappa assumes that raters are independent (here they are the same people) and (b) kappa coefficients can be quite low even when agreement is actually high, depending on such parameters as cell size and base rate. The primary validity issue addressed in the manual is content validity. The case in favor of content validity is primarily made through the argument that the set of events in the TLEQ is more comprehensive than other similar measures, and that sample estimates of exposure to traumatic events tend to be higher with the TLEQ than other methods, including interviews. In addition, the instrument significantly discriminated between women with and without PTSD in a support group for battered women ($N = 61$).

The PSDS. Reliability studies on the PSDS included internal consistency of symptom reports, test-retest correlations, and temporal stability in terms of diagnosis based on PSDS score. All of these reliability analyses suggest good to excellent consistency of this instrument. Coefficient alpha estimates were above .80 for all clusters of PTSD symptoms in a sample of Vietnam veterans ($N = 120$), and four samples of women who had experienced domestic violence and other forms of abuse (Ns = 82, 75, 74, and 24). The lowest alpha estimates were .69 for clusters C and D in the veterans group. Test-retest correlations were examined in samples of battered women support group participants and veterans with varying time intervals (no indication is given as to why the intervals vary) averaging about 10 and 17 days, respectively. Another study examined the consistency of response over a 1-week period when paper and computer versions were utilized. In this study, 76 individuals from a variety of outpatient settings were given the alternate test formats 1 week apart. The correlation of total symptoms between the two versions was .81, and there was also good consistency in terms of classification in terms of PTSD diagnosis.

Validity of the PSDS was examined in homogeneous and heterogeneous populations with similar validity questions addressed in both kinds of samples. Diagnostic accuracy was studied by comparing PSDS responses to those obtained from a structured clinical interview (the Clinician-Administered PTSD scale). Analyses included sensitivity, specificity, and positive and negative predictive power. In addition to examining the ability of two scoring methods to discriminate between PTSD presence versus absence, the author broke down the accuracy data by sample and gender. Interestingly, for all samples except battered women, the optimal cutoff score for the symptom total was 26; for the women who had suffered sexual trauma, the optimal cutoff was 18. The extensive tables provided on these analyses are informative and provide good evidence of discriminant validity. In addition, convergent validity was shown to be good via correlations with previously developed clinical scales in both the homogeneous and heterogeneous samples, and again the reporting in the manual is complete.

The TRGI. Reliability of the TRGI is reported in terms of internal consistency and temporal stability. Internal consistency (coefficient alpha) is given for five samples including two groups of combat veterans and three groups of individuals who had experienced physical abuse trauma (Ns range from 68 to 269). Of the 30 coefficients (five samples by six subscales), only two were below .70, and 21 were at least .80. Smaller samples of college students (N = 32) and veterans (N = 69) were given the TRGI twice, with approximately 1 week between administrations. Test-retest correlations ranged from .73 to .86 across the six subscales and two samples. Validity studies have included discriminant validity demonstrating significant discrimination of PTSD diagnosis (in terms of mean differences between groups and Receiver Operating Characteristics [ROC] curve studies) as well as sensitivity to change in a randomized treatment study of cognitive therapy with PTSD patients.

COMMENTARY. In reviewing these instruments as a set we come away impressed with the likely clinical utility of these measures. They appear to have adequate psychometric support and the test manuals are generally well written and complete (some exceptions were noted above). The TRGI manual includes additional treatment material that may be quite useful in practice. There is the potential concern of investigator bias when so much of the supporting data have come from a single source, but the procedures followed in development of these measures meet generally accepted standards, and in some instances exceed them. One minor criticism is that we have seen other WPS manuals use the same overly general and outdated comments regarding effect size.

SUMMARY. As the test manual warns, no self-report instrument should be used by itself to make a diagnosis of PTSD. Nonetheless, the Trauma Assessment Inventories constitute a psychometrically sound set of tools for initial identification of traumatic experiences and for evaluation of posttraumatic symptoms. In addition, the TRGI appears to be a well-developed tool for assessment and treatment of guilt-related thoughts and feelings of trauma survivors in the context of cognitively oriented therapy.

REVIEWERS' REFERENCE

Kubany, E. S., Leisen, M. B., Kaplan, A. S., & Kelly, M. P. (2000). Validation of a brief measure of posttraumatic stress disorder: The Distressing Event Questionnaire (DEQ). *Psychological Assessment, 12*, 197-209.

Review of the Trauma Assessment Inventories by CARL J. SHEPERIS, Assistant Professor of Counselor Education, and APRIL K. HEISELT, Assistant Professor of Counselor Education, Mississippi State University, Starkville, MS:

DESCRIPTION. The Trauma Assessment Inventories set contains three instruments including the screening kit, composed of the Traumatic Life Events Questionnaire (TLEQ) and PTSD Screening and Diagnostic Scale (PSDS), and the treatment kit containing the Trauma-Related Guilt Inventory (TRGI; TLEQ, PSDS, and TRGI) designed to work in conjunction with one another to assist clinicians in making determinations about Posttraumatic Stress Disorder (PTSD) and the guilt associated with trauma survivors. The complete set or individual components are available for purchase. Additional manuals, testing forms, answer sheets, and computerized components for the Trauma Assessment Inventories are also available from the publisher.

The TLEQ is a 24-item self-report questionnaire used as a brief screener for PTSD symptomology. Respondents answer questions that address their exposure to 21 traumatic life events, indicating if and how often (i.e., once, twice, three times, four times, five times, or more than five times) particular life events occurred. Respondents are also asked about the presence of feelings of intense fear, helplessness, or horror in relation to those events. The TLEQ concludes with an open-ended question that asks respondents to indicate the one event that caused them the most distress. The TLEQ takes approximately 10 to 15 minutes to complete and can be administered to individuals with a sixth grade reading level.

The PSDS, a 38-item self-report questionnaire, is employed to assess the severity of the experienced event reported in the open-ended section of the TLEQ. Clinicians also may use the PSDS in reference to a given trauma. The PSDS contains 17 key components that match the six criteria for PTSD as defined by the fourth edition of the *Diagnostic and Statistic Manual of Mental Disorders* (American Psychiatric Association, 1994). Respondents use a 5-point Likert scale (i.e., *"absent or did not occur"* to *"present to an extreme or severe degree"*) to indicate the severity of symptoms they have experienced over a 30-day period. Respondents also indicate when their symptoms began and the length of time they have continued. The PSDS is designed for respondents who are 18 years of age or older with an eighth-grade reading ability. Both the TLEQ and the PSDS have abbreviated and long versions.

The TRGI is designed for clinicians who treat PTSD, and can be used to identify guilt-related feelings associated with traumatic events. The TRGI is a 32-item self-report questionnaire that employs a 5-point Likert scale (i.e., "*extremely true*" to "*not true at all*") to make determinations about respondent guilt feelings. TRGI items are scored on three separate dimensions: Global Guilt, Distress, and Guilt Cognitions.

The TLEQ and PSDS can be administered either via computer or in pencil-and-paper format. Because of the nature of the questions regarding traumatic experiences, the author suggests that trained clinicians debrief with respondents following the completion of the TLEQ. Clinicians clarify the specific event they want respondents to refer to when completing the PSDS. Although technicians can administer self-report inventories, interpretation of the results should be carried out by professionals with psychometric training.

The TLEQ and PSDS are self-report questionnaires that do not result in standardized scores. Users of the TLEQ can generate a rough index of the magnitude and severity of the trauma reported by respondents. These include the number of TLEQ events that have occurred in the life of a respondent; the number of TLEQ events that both occurred and evoked intense fear, helplessness, or horror; and the total number of events reported by the respondents and tallied by clinicians. Much like the TLEQ, there are no standardized scores for the PSDS. Clinicians also may consider symptom ratings in order to obtain informal measures of respondent distress.

The TRGI employs an Auto Score form whereby users transfer responses to the appropriate scale column. Scores are summed to determine raw scores in each of the six response value areas, although no separate general guilt cognition scores are interpreted on the TRGI. Raw scores are then plotted to normalized *T*-scores with a mean of 50 and standard deviation of 10. Average scores range between 45T and 55T. Users of the TRGI should review the content of the information provided by respondents contributing to high TRGI scores. The trauma assessment inventories also may be scored via computer.

DEVELOPMENT. Instrument development for the TLEQ was approached from a theoretical stance. Items were created following a review of relevant literature, examination of instruments that assess exposure to traumatic events, collecting open-ended responses from more than 1,000 completed preliminary TLEQ versions, and evaluating pilot item content. Content validity for the TLEQ and PSDS were established through the use of expert-review panels consisting of published PTSD experts and clinical psychologists specializing in PTSD.

The TRGI was developed using four sources including a review and analysis of guilt literature, examination of guilt scales, and structured interviews and clinical work with trauma survivors. An initial pool of 120 items was created to reflect the six dimensions of guilt. From this pool, a 40-item preliminary TRGI was prepared and distributed to two samples of college students who reported experienced traumas and 100 battered women attending support groups.

TECHNICAL. Four studies were conducted in order to determine the test-retest reliability of the TLEQ. Populations in the studies included: 51 Vietnam combat veterans (5- to 45-day test-retest intervals), 49 men and women in a residential substance abuse program (2-month interval), 62 college students (1-week interval), and 42 women attending support groups for battered women (2-week interval). Across the samples most items indicated adequate temporal stability, especially as it related to items asking about childhood physical abuse (kappas = .63 to .91), witnessing family violence (kappas = .60 to .79), childhood sexual abuse by someone more than 5 years older (kappas = .70 to .90), and stalking (kappas = .59 to .84). Poorest temporal consistency was related to nonmotor vehicle accidents. High test-retest reliability was found as it related to the reports of intense fear, horror, and helplessness as related by the women attending support groups for battered women. It should be noted that the samples used in these studies were relatively small.

Content validity procedures for the TLEQ were not clearly delineated in the manual. The author of the manual claimed that content validity was established because a large portion (93% in one study and over 99% in another) reported having experienced traumatic events. This reasoning is circular and does not clearly provide evidence of content validity.

Internal consistency for the PSDS was tested on 120 male Vietnam combat veterans and four groups of women including: 82 women sexually abused by a household member before the age of 18 who had received services in the previous year from an agency or provider that serves incest survivors; 75 women sexually assaulted after the age of 12 who received services in the previous year from an agency that serves rape victims; 74 women abused by an intimate partner who received services in the previous year from an agency that serves battered women; and 24 women with histories of prostitution, substance abuse, and sexual abuse. Alpha coefficients for each criterion ranged from .80 to .98. Test-retest reliability was assessed with 52 Vietnam combat veterans. Test-retest interval was from 5 to 45 days. The test-retest correlation coefficient for total PSDS symptoms was .95. The test-retest also was assessed with 54 women receiving support group counseling services from a nonprofit community agency that serves battered women. The test-retest interval ranged from 7 to 21 days and initial test-retest coefficient for total PSDS symptom scores was .83.

Two studies were conducted to determine the validity of the PSDS. One study, consisting of a homogeneous patient group of 120 Vietnam combat veterans, was conducted to compare structured interview assessments with protocol results. The PSDS correctly classified the PTSD status of 86% of the sample. An additional study found that when using a score of 18 or higher for making a PTSD diagnosis, the PSDS correctly classified PTSD status of between 83% and 93% of the four samples of women and 90% of the combined sample of 255 women.

To determine test-retest reliability the TLEQ and TRGI were distributed to 60 college students enrolled in an undergraduate psychology class. One week later the test was given to 32 students (23 students did not report trauma exposure and did not complete the TRGI and 5 others were dismissed due to missing data). Test-retest correlation coefficients for the Global Guilt, Distress, and Guilt Cognition scales were .73 or above. Test-retest correlations also were given to a sample of 69 military veterans. The interval for this group was 8 days and the coefficients for the Global Guilt, Distress, and Guilt Cognition scales were .84 or above, indicating strong test-retest reliability. In samples of 74 Vietnam combat veterans and 68 women in battered women's support groups the Guilt Cognitions scale significantly correlated with measures of depression and PTSD.

COMMENTARY. The TLEQ produces no formal scores. Instead it relies on respondents' reports of their experiences. Thus, users are cautioned that the PSDS should not be the sole instrument used to determine PTSD. Future research needs to be conducted in order to determine the extent of content-validity. Of particular importance with regard to the TRGI is that item development was based on a limited number of clinical interviews (Beckham, Feldman, & Kirby, 1998, p. 779). There is a paucity of research on the TLEQ, PSDS, and TRGI. Thus, further research is needed to determine the reliability and functionality of the instruments.

SUMMARY. The Trauma Assessment Inventories set including the TLEQ, PSDS, and TRGI comprise a low cost inventory set that is relatively easy to score and can provide seemingly accurate estimates of PTSD symptomology. It should be noted that none of these instruments alone should be used to diagnose PTSD as additional factors can mitigate diagnosis. Because the sample sizes employed during instrument development were small, more peer-reviewed research is needed in order to eliminate questions of validity for these instruments. Some aspects of the test manuals are confusing with regard to scoring procedures. However, illustrations in the test manuals prove useful.

REVIEWERS' REFERENCES

American Psychiatric Association. (1994). *Diagnostic and statistical manual of mental disorders* (4th ed.). Washington, DC: Author.
Beckham, J., Feldman, M., & Kirby, A. (1998). Atrocities exposure in Vietnam combat veterans with chronic posttraumatic stress disorder: Relationship to combat exposure, symptom severity, guilt, and interpersonal violence. *Journal of Traumatic Stress, 11*, 777-785.

[191]

Trauma Symptom Checklist for Young Children.

Purpose: Designed "to assess trauma symptoms in children."

Population: Ages 3–12 years.

Publication Dates: 1999–2005.

Acronym: TSCYC.

Scores, 11: Validity scales (Response Level, Atypical Response), Clinical scales (Anxiety, Depression, Anger/Aggression, Posttraumatic Stress-Intrusion, Posttraumatic Stress-Avoidance, Posttraumatic Stress-Arousal, Posttraumatic Stress-Total, Dissociation, Sexual Concerns).

Administration: Group.

Price Data, 2007: $185 per introductory kit including professional manual (2005, 61 pages), 25 item booklets, 25 hand-scorable answer sheets, 25 profile forms (Male & Female Ages 3–4 Years), 25 profile forms (Male & Female Ages 5–9 Years), and 25 profile forms (Male & Female Ages 10–12 Years); $285 per scoring program (CD-ROM) including unlimited scoring, reports, and profiles.

Time: (15–20) minutes.

Comments: Instrument is answered by the child's parents and/or care takers.

Author: John Briere.

Publisher: Psychological Assessment Resources, Inc.

Review of the Trauma Symptom Checklist for Young Children by KAREN MACKLER, School Psychologist, Lawrence Public Schools, Lawrence, NY:

DESCRIPTION. The Trauma Symptom Checklist for Young Children (TSCYC) is a 90-item, paper-and-pencil test, administered to parents or caretakers individually or in groups. The purpose of the test is to assess behaviors, feelings, or experiences associated with being the victim of or exposed to trauma in children ages 3–12 years of age. All items are rated from 1 to 4 relative to how often the caretaker believes the child has experienced each item within the past month. Questions are presented in English, at a 6.8-grade-equivalent reading level. The measure generates scores for two validity scales: Response Level and Atypical Response, and eight clinical scales: Anxiety (ANX), Depression (DEP), Anger/Aggression (ANG), Posttraumatic Stress-Intrusion (PTS-I), Posttraumatic Stress-Avoidance (PTS-AV), Posttraumatic Stress-Arousal (PTS-AR), Posttraumatic Stress-Total (PTS-TOT), Dissociation (DIS), and Sexual Concerns (SC). In addition to a total scale, the Response Level validity scale assesses the tendency to portray a child as psychologically healthy at all times, whereas the Atypical Response scale assesses the tendency to rate the child as being especially disturbed.

Nonclinical staff may administer and score the measure, but only trained clinicians should interpret results. There is no time limit for this test. The respondent is required to circle each response on a separate answer sheet. The evaluator then transfers the numerical responses onto a grid, broken down by scale. Most scales result in a raw score generated by summing the numerical responses endorsed by the respondent. If three or more items on a particular scale were left blank, the overall score for that scale is not computed. If less than three were left out, the scorer assigns a value of 1 for that item. The Response Level scale raw score is computed by counting how many items were rated 1 or left blank, whereas the Posttraumatic Stress-Total scale raw score is computed by totaling the raw scores from the Posttraumatic Stress-Intrusion, Posttraumatic Stress-Avoidance, and the Posttraumatic Stress-Arousal. After obtaining the raw scores for each scale, the evaluator plots the scores on a profile sheet corresponding to the gender and age (3–4, 5–9, 10–12 years) of the child. These scores can then be compared using T-scores, where a T-score of 50 is average, 65 or over is a possible concern, and 70 or over is clinically significant.

There is also a Diagnosis Worksheet on the initial scoring sheet for assessing the likelihood of Posttraumatic Stress Disorder. The worksheet follows the criteria set forth in the *Diagnostic and Statistical Manual of Mental Disorders, Fourth Edition, Text Revision (*DSM-IV-TR; American Psychiatric Association, 2000). Results of this worksheet indicate whether a diagnosis of PTSD is warranted.

DEVELOPMENT. The initial version of the TSCYC was a 120-item downward expansion and adaptation of the Trauma Symptom Checklist for Children (TSCC; Briere, 1996), a multiscale self-report measure of sexually related symptoms related to trauma. The measure was adjusted to be a caretaker response measure, especially helpful for younger children or those with poor reading skills. The content of the TSCYC was expanded to cover all relevant DSM-IV-TR posttraumatic intrusion, avoidance, and hyperarousal criteria. Although the items need to be answered relative to a month's time frame as the DSM stipulates, the measure does not conform to the DSM in that it does not require the rater to respond to all items based on a single trauma. Experts in the field of trauma were asked which questions could be deleted, and a validation sample of caregivers were given the measure as well. Thirty items demonstrating "the least psychometric quality or construct relevance were removed" (professional manual, p. 27).

A validation sample consisting of 219 caretakers, affiliated with six centers dealing with this population rated children having a mean age of 7.1. Racial composition was highly mixed with 62% nonwhite respondents. The majority of the children rated were female (62%), as was the gender of the caretakers (91%). Seventy percent of the caretakers were biological parents, 99% lived with the child being rated, and the modal number of hours spent per week with the child was 41–60 hours. Due to the predominantly female respondent group, care should be taken when using the measure with males. It may be that boys were less likely to receive assistance after experiencing sexually related trauma, for a variety of reasons.

TECHNICAL. Three samples are generally cited for the reliability and validity data. Internal consistency reliability for the Response Level scale is relatively and consistently high for the three samples cited, ranging from .73 to .86. The range was much greater for the Atypical Response scale, ranging from .36 to .93, which might be a reflection of the lower endorsement rates of the items. The author states that children at the upper range of the scale (10–12 years) had more variable scores on this scale, which increased the overall variability in the standardization sample statistics. The clinical scales had strong alpha coefficients, ranging from .78 to .93 across the three studies.

A random sample of 33 people from the standardization sample was used to determine test-retest reliability. The checklist was readministered from 1 to 13 days after the initial administration. Correlation coefficients were corrected for variability of the standardization sample, resulting in coefficients that ranged from .68 to .96.

Intercorrelations between scales ranged from .45 for the Sexual Concerns with the Dissociation scales to .90 between PTS-Avoidance to PTS-Total. The Response Level scale was negatively correlated with all scales, ranging from -.09 to -.46.

Caretakers filling out the measure in the standardization sample were asked if their child had experienced a highly upsetting or traumatic event; 42.3% of the caretakers responded yes. Regardless of the amount of time after the event, all scales received higher scores, which only shows that caretakers believing that their child experienced trauma found them to be responsive to that trauma.

Patterns emerged between scale scores and type of trauma. Childhood sexual abuse was found to be associated with PTS-I, PTS-AV, PTS-TOT, and SC scales; physical abuse with PTS-I, PTS-AR, PTS-TOT, and DIS, and witnessing violence with PTS-I, PTS-AR, PTS-AV, and PTS-TOT and negatively associated with the SC scale. Other studies showed predictive ability of the scales to discriminate between abused children and nonabused children.

Discriminant validity was also assessed in several studies, to assess concurrent validity and divergent validity. Concurrent validity was found with three other measures used to assess children's behaviors: The CBCL, the CSBI, and the CDC. The Posttraumatic Stress scales are unique to this measure and so could not be directly evaluated. Divergent validity was found between this measure and the TSCC, which was used as a foundation. The author contends that this may be due to the difference between a self-report measure and a checklist completed by a parent.

Two studies were conducted to determine diagnostic utility of the PTSD worksheet. Results are encouraging, but further research needs to be conducted in this area specifically.

COMMENTARY. The TSCYC is a unique measure that could play an important role in assessing mental health function in children too young or too traumatized to respond to more traditional self-report measures or a structured interview. The instrument demonstrates adequate reliability and validity to be used as an empirical tool as part of a comprehensive assessment of a child's level of functioning following a traumatic event experienced firsthand or witnessed. As noted by the author, there is the possibility that the caretaker might want to over- or underestimate the functioning levels of the child(ren) in question, but the validity scales give some assurance that the scores are valid.

The PTSD worksheet is a nice addition that gives a more data-driven approach to a DSM diagnosis, versus relying solely on parent interviews and clinical judgment. Readministration of the measure after a period of treatment might prove to be informative as well. As stated earlier, more studies need to be conducted in this area.

The design of the measure itself is somewhat problematic. First, the respondent has to answer the questions on a separate answer sheet, which may lead to incorrect answers being given to a question. This would be difficult to monitor, especially if the measure is being administered in a group setting. Second, despite the carbonless format, the answers have to be transcribed yet again by the scorer. Each answer has to be written into the correct line for each scale. The procedure is time-consuming and leaves another opportunity for error. Finally, the resulting scores are only raw scores, and must be transposed yet again to a separate profile sheet, where *T*-scores are finally available. Perhaps the whole scoring system could be put onto a computer program, in order to limit the amount of data processing an administrator must do.

SUMMARY. The Trauma Symptom Checklist for Young Children (TSCYC) provides a standardized format for obtaining information about a child's functioning after a recent traumatic event. Filled out by a caretaker, the evaluator is able to get information from children as young as 3 years of age, and from children who may not be able to fill out a self-report measure or who might be too traumatized to give very much information at all. The inclusion of a worksheet aimed at assessing the possibility of a PTSD diagnosis is a helpful part of a comprehensive evaluation of a child involved in or exposed to a traumatic event. Given the nature of this measure, the more information received about the child's levels of functioning, the better the treatment plan will be.

REVIEWER'S REFERENCES
American Psychiatric Association. (2000). *Diagnostic and statistical manual of mental disorders* (4th ed., text revision). Washington, DC: Author.
Briere, J. (1996). Trauma Symptom Checklist for Children. Odessa, FL: Psychological Assessment Resources.

Review of the Trauma Symptom Checklist for Young Children by TERRY A. STINNETT, Professor, School Psychology, Oklahoma State University, Stillwater, OK:

DESCRIPTION. The Trauma Symptom Checklist for Young Children (TSCYC) is a 90-item parent/caretaker rating scale designed to quickly assess trauma and posttraumatic stress symptomology in children aged 3 through 12. The TSCYC materials in the introductory kit include a user's manual, item booklets, answer sheets, and age- and gender-specific profile forms. The introductory kit is reasonably priced. The professional manual contains the test description, administration and scoring, interpretation, normative information and tables, and development and validation information. The reusable item booklets contain the items to which the informant responds on separate single-use carbonless answer/scoring sheets. The appropriate profile form can be used to graph the TSCYC data. There are three separate age-by-gender profile forms from which to select to summarize the respondent's ratings, dependent upon the age and gender of the child. The TSCYC is scored by hand; there is a CD-ROM scoring program that includes unlimited scoring,

reports, and profiles, but it was not included in the introductory kit and therefore was not reviewed with the start-up kit.

The TSCYC was developed to serve as a trauma-specific psychological test. General broadband behavior and emotional screening instruments typically do not include trauma items; therefore, the development of child self-report trauma scales are needed to supplement and to also capture the child's subjective understanding and reaction to a traumatic event (Evans & Oehler-Stinnett, 2006). Particular attention was given to include trauma-specific symptoms, appropriate normative data, and multiple checks to determine the validity of the rater's report. The test author reports that a significant percentage of children have been exposed to maltreatment or traumatic events and there are few commercially available standardized parent or self-report instruments to assess the impact of trauma on children. The use of parent/caretaker raters for the TSCYC circumvents some of the problems of using self-report with children less than 8 years of age related to cognitive and developmental limitations and/or reading comprehension. The rater indicates on a 4-point Likert-scale (1 = *not at all*; 2 = *sometimes*; 3 = *often*; 4 = *very often*) for each item how often the symptom was estimated to occur during the previous month. The materials are straightforward, well designed, and easy to use.

The TSCYC contains two validity and eight clinical scales. There is also a Posttraumatic Stress-Total (PTS-TOT) score, which evaluates the overall level of post-traumatic stress disorder (PTSD) symptomology in the child. The validity scales assess intentional or inadvertent misreporting by the rater of the child's functioning. Response Level (RL, nine items) estimates the rater's tendency to underreport typical problems that can result in an excessively positive view of the child. RL items include behaviors that most caregivers would commonly endorse for their child. Therefore, a high RL score may indicate the caregiver could lack insight or be defensive or avoidant about reporting problems for the child. Atypical Response (ATR, nine items) reflects the rater's tendency to endorse unusual or relatively high levels of trauma symptoms in the child. The result may be an excessively negative view of the child. This can sometimes be accounted for by a generalized negative overreporting style or a desire to present the child as particularly distressed. The ATR scale also contains a very informative item that indicates how familiar the rater is with the child based on report of hours spent in the same place with the child. The TSCYC Anxiety scale (ANX, nine items) was designed to indicate the degree of worry and fear displayed by the child. High scores on ANX may be generally accounted for by the presence of anxiety disorder, trauma-specific fears, or anxious hyper-arousal, which is often present with PTSD. The test author indicates that, because the ANX items refer to danger and fears of potential trauma, high scores may also indicate prior victimization or that the child has witnessed violence against others. The Depression scale (DEP, nine items) item content reflects feelings, cognitions, behavior, and verbalizations that are associated with sadness, unhappiness, or other depressive symptomology the child may display. The test author indicates that high scores on this scale may signify a depressive episode or dysthymic disorder, or grief associated with a loss or trauma. There is an Anger/Aggression scale (ANG, nine items) designed to indicate the degree of anger and aggressive behavior observed in the child. The scale reflects externalizing behaviors such as hitting, throwing, yelling, destroying things, and temper tantrums. The test author suggests that children who have been exposed to chronic abuse and neighborhood violence may show elevated scores on this scale. There are posttraumatic stress clinical scales that make the TSCYC unique from other widely used assessments for child behavior problems such as the Behavior Assessment System for Children—II (17:21) rating scales and the Achenbach System of Empirically Based Assessment rating scales (16:3). The TSCYC includes a Posttraumatic Stress-Intrusion scale (PTS-I, nine items), a Posttraumatic Stress-Avoidance scale (PTS-AV, nine items), and a Posttraumatic Stress-Arousal scale (PTS-AR, nine items). Those PTS scales are summed to yield the Posttraumatic Stress-Total (PTS-TOT), which reflects the total amount of posttraumatic re-experiencing, avoidance, and hyperarousal behaviors observed in the child. PTS-I items can signify that the child is having intrusive posttraumatic memories, flashbacks, recurrent nightmares, and fearful reactions to environmental stimuli that may remind him or her of a previously experienced traumatic event. PTS-I item content reflects

undercontrolled irrational behaviors, crying, aggression, and panic attacks. Elevations on the scale indicate that posttraumatic thoughts and behaviors are likely observed in the child. The PTS-AV scale can indicate the extent to which the child employs cognitive, behavioral, and emotional avoidance strategies to avoid distress and anxiety associated with the posttraumatic event. Item content for the PTS-AV scale includes social withdrawal and avoidance, oppositional behavior, denial of a traumatic event, nonresponsiveness in treatment when the past traumatic event is discussed or reduced or absent emotional response to the traumatic event. PTS-AR items can be a sign of the hyperarousal the child displays. A high score on the PTS-AR scale can indicate the child is easily startled, hyperactive, and tense. There are items that indicate attention and concentration problems, sleep problems, hypervigilance, and preoccupation with danger. The test author cautions that these symptoms also can be present with generalized anxiety rather than indicative of posttraumatic stress and that they can overlap with symptoms of Attention Deficit Hyperactivity Disorder. Therefore, additional information needs to be gathered before attributing an elevated score to posttraumatic stress. The TSCYC also includes a Dissociation (DIS, nine items) scale with items that indicate preoccupation and detachment, inattentive nonresponsiveness, and withdrawal and disengagement from the external environment. The test author indicates that the scale is not intended to evaluate significant dissociative disorders; rather it is designed to detect disruptions in the experience and response to the external environment consistent with children who have experienced traumatic events. Examining the scale item content reveals that items reflect inattentiveness, being in a daze, spacing out, being absent-minded, and other symptoms that are commonly observed in children with ADHD–Inattentive type. The final clinical scale, Sexual Concerns (SC, nine items), evaluates the amount of sexual distress and preoccupation observed in the child. Item content for the SC scale taps thoughts and feelings that would be inappropriate when present in children and may indicate prior or ongoing sexual victimization.

Raw scores are converted to *T*-scores and percentile ranks using the professional manual appendices. Raw scores also may be converted to *T*-scores directly on the profile forms but percentile ranks are not available on these forms. The test author reports that for all of the clinical scales except the PTS-TOT, T-scores of ≤ 64 are within normal limits, from 65 to 69 are potential problem areas, and T-scores ≥ 70 are clinically significant. For the PTS-TOT score, a T-score ≥ 70 suggests a severe posttraumatic presentation, whereas scores from 65 through 69 indicate a mild to moderate degree of PTSD stress with a likelihood that at least one PTSD cluster of the TSCYC will be elevated.

DEVELOPMENT. The initial version of the TSCYC was adapted from the Trauma Symptom Checklist for Children (TSCC; Briere, 1996) and expanded to allow for reports from caregivers of children who are as young as 3 years of age. The TSCYC has the same scales as the TSCC with the addition of the PTS-I, PTS-AR, and PTS-AV scales to reflect the *Diagnostic and Statistical Manual of Mental Disorders, Fourth Edition—Text Revision* (DSM-IV-TR; APA, 2000) criteria for PTSD, which is an improvement over the TSCC. The author attempted to have the TSCYC reflect the six symptom groups of the TSCC at the scale level; no attempt was made to match TSCC items. Thirty of the preliminary 120 items of the TSCYC were eliminated on the basis of a two-step process. First, 11 expert clinicians in the area of trauma and child abuse suggested certain items could be eliminated from the scale, and second, internal consistency analyses of the items were used to assess construct relevance and to maximize the psychometric qualities of the items included in the TSCYC. The readability level of the final item set is reported to be at the 6.8-grade level.

TECHNICAL.

Standardization. A stratified normative sample designed to match the 2002 U.S. Census data was gathered following e-mail solicitation from a national marketing research company. Potential participants indicated their ethnicity, the parental education level in the household, geographic region of residence, and the age and gender of children living in the home. Participants were included on a first-response basis in the sample until all demographic cells were full. About 95% of those who responded and who met the criteria for inclusion completed the TSCYC. Informed consent was furnished for those participants who met the demographic requirements for inclusion, and they completed a TSCYC scale online for a given randomly selected child in their

family. The standardization sample is based on 750 children who were rated with the TSCYC. The majority of the raters were women (61.1%). The sample matches the Census data well on the selected demographic variables specified by the test author for the sampling design. There were an equal number of boys and girls ($n = 375$) and approximately even numbers of children at each separate age level in the sample. There were significant gender and age differences on the TSCYC ratings and separate norms were developed by gender and age. Breakpoints for the ages 3–4 years ($n = 150$), 5–9 years ($n = 370$), and 10–12 years ($n = 230$) were used for the norms. The normative data for each scale are reported for the six combinations of age and gender. The test author also reported a significant multivariate effect for race on the TSCYC but it accounted for less than 3% of the variance in ratings by the standardization sample. These effects occurred on the RL, ATR, PTS-I, ANX, and DEP scales. Because of the minuscule amount of variance for which race accounted in TSCYC ratings, the test author did not calculate separate norms by race. A table in the professional manual (Table 4.4) specifies the racial/ethnic composition of each age grouping in the standardization sample by gender to allow comparison to the U.S. Census data target proportions used in the test development. Two additional studies are reported in the manual that examined the psychometric properties of the TSCYC. These were completed independent from the standardization sample. Briere et al. (2001) in a validation study had clinicians from six child advocacy centers, child abuse programs, or child trauma centers solicit participants ($N = 219$) at their sites based on the regular intake procedures in use. Fifty-six percent of these children had sexual abuse histories, 35% had been physically abused, and 46% had witnessed parental domestic violence. Gilbert (2004) studied 339 abused children between 3 and 12 years of age who were in an ongoing treatment program.

Reliability. Internal consistency (coefficient alpha) estimates for the clinical scales across all three studies were good and were consistent across the studies. The standardization sample alphas ranged from .78 (ANX) to .92 (PTS-TOT); the validation sample alphas ranged from .81 (SC) to .93 (PTS-TOT); the Gilbert (2004) alphas ranged from .82 (PTS-I, PTS-AV, SC) to .92 (PTS-

TOT, DIS). The validity scale alphas for the RL scale were adequate across the three studies (.80, .73, and .86, respectively) but the ATR scale alphas were inconsistent across the three studies. The standardization sample alpha for the ATR scale was excellent (.93) but inadequate in the validation and Gilbert studies (.36 and .46, respectively). The internal consistency estimates do provide some evidence of construct validity for the test. However, until the test is factor analyzed there is no way to determine whether the test overdefines the constructs of interest.

Use of the TSCYC in a repeated fashion over time might be helpful in treatment, but caution is warranted because the test-retest reliability estimates are variable across the subscales. Temporal stability for the instrument is important because posttraumatic symptoms may emerge directly after the traumatic event and then dissipate over time or reoccur if there is exposure to reminders of the traumatic event. TSCYC test-retest reliability was calculated from a randomly selected subset of the standardization sample (n = 33) with a 1- to 13-day interval reported between the first and second administration of the scale. Users might have more confidence in the temporal stability of the test if the time interval was constant for all of the participants, if the interval was at a minimum of 2 weeks between each test administration, and if a larger sample had been used. The corrected reliability coefficients for the clinical scales ranged from .68 (PTS-I) to .96 (ANG, DIS, SC) and the PTS-TOT was reported to be .87. Reliability coefficients of at least .90 have been recommended as necessary for individual diagnostic purposes (Salvia & Ysseldyke, 1998) and only DEP, ANG, PTS-AR, DIS, and SC meet that criterion. However, test users are not likely to make a diagnosis of PTSD or judge the degree of PTSD symptomology presented by a child on the basis of scores from the TSCYC alone. Nevertheless, one assessment procedural safeguard would be to use the standard errors of measurement to provide confidence intervals when describing the child's obtained score. The standard errors of measurement and confidence intervals are omitted in the TSCYC. Given that the test could be used in repeated fashion with the same child, this information would be a helpful addition to the technical information presented in the manual.

Validity. The TSCYC clinical scales were highly correlated in the normative sample and ranged from .45 to .90. Table 5.3 presents these correlations in the professional manual. The high degree of intercorrelation among the subscales also suggests that factor analyses are needed to further examine the test's structure. This type of analysis could also allow for the estimation of unique variance for each of the TSCYC scales. The convergent and divergent validity of the TSCYC is better established than its construct validity. The TSCYC has been shown to discriminate children who have experienced trauma from those who have not. Forty-two percent of the children in the standardization sample were reported by their caretakers to have undergone a highly upsetting or traumatic event (n = 317), and the remainder of the sample had not (n = 433). Discriminant function analysis was conducted and yielded structure coefficients for the clinical scales ranging from .36 (SC) to .83 (DEP). Follow-up univariate ANOVAs indicated there were significant differences in the expected direction between those children who had and those who had not had traumatic or upsetting experiences on every TSCYC scale except for the ATR subscale. The test manual did not report the classification results. The number of functions yielded in the analyses was not reported either, which could have informed users of the TSCYC in more detail about the underlying empirical and theoretical structure of the test.

Gilbert (2004) also examined the power of the TSCYC for predicting 45 children who had experienced sexual abuse from 45 children who had not. The children were matched on gender, age, and ethnicity. Logistic regression analyses were conducted and combinations of TSCYC scales successfully predicted 76% of the abused children and 87% of the nonabused children. Gilbert also found differences between the matched abused and nonabused children on the PTS-I, PTS-AV, PTS-AR, PTS-TOT, ANX, DEP, ANG, and SC scales. Effect sizes for these differences were respectable (Cohen's *d* ranged from .69 to 1.03 for the analyses). Certain TSCYC scales have been found to be significantly correlated with measures that tap similar constructs (Gilbert, 2004). ANX and DEP were most related to the Child Behavior Checklist (CBCL; Achenbach, 1991) Anxiety/Depression scale, and ANG was most related to the CBCL Aggression scale. Gilbert also reports the TSCYC DIS scale was most related to—and all of the TSCYC PTS scales were related to—the Child Dissociative Checklist (CDC; Putnam, Helmers, & Trickett, 1993). The SC scale was most related to the Child Sexual Behavior Inventory (CSBI; Friedrich, 1998), and Becker, Pears, and Freyd (2001) also reported the DIS scale to be related to two post hoc dissociation scales in the parent report form of the CBCL. These studies provide evidence for the concurrent validity of the TSCYC. However, the TSCYC was not as related to its parent scale (TSCC) as might have been expected. TSCYC scales and TSCC scale correlations ranged from .12 to .40. The TSCYC is a parent/caregiver rating scale whereas the TSCC is a child self-report. Agreement among parent, teacher, other adults, and child self-reports is often very poor for instruments that measure child and adolescent behavior and emotional problems in general (Achenbach, McConaughy, & Howell, 1987). Clinicians can use these different ratings to determine the pervasiveness of the symptomology by comparing measures based on different informant sources, but the poor relationship of the clinical scales among the TSCYC and the TSCC is somewhat disappointing.

The capacity of the TSCYC to diagnose PTSD has also been examined. Pollio, Glover-Orr, and Wherry (2002) found in 33 children aged 4 to 12 years that the weighted combination of PTS-I, PTS-AV, and PTS-AR correctly predicted 95% of the children without PTSD and 73% of those with PTSD as measured by the Diagnostic Interview for Children and Adolescents. When the remaining TSCYC scales were added to the equation, 100% of the children without PTSD were correctly identified, but the percentage of correct classification for those with PTSD remained at 73%. Finally, the diagnostic accuracy of the scale was examined by Gilbert, Briere, Taylor, and Viglione (2004). In a subsample (n = 90) from the Gilbert (2004) study a PTS-TOT raw score of 40 yielded a sensitivity of .72 and a specificity of .75 when identifying children who had been identified with PTSD on the UCLA PTSD Index.

Study of the incremental validity of the TSCYC scales in conjunction with other widely used systems such as the BASC II and the Achenbach rating scales would provide additional support for adding the TSCYC to an assessment.

COMMENTARY AND SUMMARY. The TSCYC may be a helpful addition to the repertoire of clinicians who need to assess PTSD symptomology in young children or to researchers in the area of child trauma and PTSD. The standardization sample is current and mirrors the 2002 U.S. Census data well on the selected demographic variables. The test-retest reliability estimates are somewhat lower than needed for diagnostic purposes but not so low that the test could not be used in the context of a multifactored assessment to aid in diagnosis and decision making. However, the short time interval reported to be used for calculating the test-retest reliability of the scale is of some concern. Those who give the instrument in serial fashion to the same children should be cautious. The test has sufficient internal consistency, but more construct validity evidence needs to be accumulated. The TSCYC scales are highly intercorrelated. Exploratory factor analyses could help better demonstrate the TSCYC's underlying empirical structure as well as provide evidence of the subtest specificity of its subscales. There is evidence of discriminant and convergent validity for the TSCYC. The subscales are related to other independent measures of similar constructs as expected, but surprisingly not too related to the TSCC. The TSCC measures a number of the same constructs as the TSCYC although the TSCC is a self-report measure and the TSCYC is a parent/caretaker report form. The TSCYC also has been shown to discriminate children who had experienced an upsetting or traumatic event from those who had not, abused from nonabused children, and children who were identified with PTSD on the UCLA PTSD Index from those who were not indicated. More evidence of the ability of the TSCYC to add incremental information above that which can be acquired with the widely used broad-band behavior and emotional problem assessment measures would also add to the merits of this test.

Assessment of PTSD in children typically includes the three DSM domains of re-experiencing, avoidance, and arousal, which are represented on the TSCYC. A thorough evaluation needs to include information about the child's play behavior (Smith-Stover & Berkowitz, 2005), interpersonal alienation, interference with daily functioning, physical/psychosomatic symptoms, and sense of foreshortened future (Garner-Evans & Oehler-Stinnett, 2006). However, those domains are not represented or minimally represented on the TSCYC. Nonetheless, there continues to be a dearth of instruments available to assess trauma and PTSD symptomology in young children. Overall, the test shows good promise for research and clinical application. The TSCYC is recommended for clinicians and researchers alike who may have an interest in trauma and PTSD in children. For those who are interested, Smith-Stover and Berkowitz (2005) and Evans and Oehler-Stinnett (2006) offer excellent and more detailed reviews of issues related to assessment of traumatic and PTSD symptomology in young children including the most widely used instrumentation in the area.

REVIEWER'S REFERENCES

Achenbach, T. M. (1991). *Manual for the Child Behavior Checklist/4-18 and 1991 Profile.* Burlington: University of Vermont, Department of Psychiatry.

Achenbach, T. M., McConaughy, S. H., & Howell, C. T. (1987). Child/adolescent behavioral and emotional problems: Implications of cross-informant correlations for situational specificity. *Psychological Bulletin, 101,* 213-232.

American Psychiatric Association. (2000). *Diagnostic and statistical manual of mental disorders* (4th ed., text revision). Washington, DC: Author.

Becker, K. A., Pears, K. C., & Freyd, J. J. (2001, April). *Analyses of post-traumatic stress and dissociation scales for children.* Poster presented at the meeting of the Society for Research in Child Development, Minneapolis, MN.

Briere, J. (1996). *Trauma Symptom Checklist for Children professional manual.* Odessa, FL: Psychological Assessment Resources.

Briere, J., Johnson, K., Bissada, A., Damon, L., Crouch, J., Gil, E., Hanson, R., & Ernst, V. (2001). The Trauma Symptom Checklist for Young Children (TSCYC): Reliability and association with abuse exposure in a multi-site study. *Child Abuse and Neglect, 25,* 1001-1014.

Evans, L., & Oehler-Stinnett, J. J. (2006). Children and natural disasters: A primer for school psychologists. *School Psychology International, 27,* 33-55.

Friedrich, W. N. (1998). *The Child Sexual Behavior Inventory professional manual.* Odessa, FL: Psychological Assessment Resources.

Garner-Evans, L., & Oehler-Stinnett, J. (2006). Structure and prevalence of PTSD symptomology in children who have experienced a severe tornado. *Psychology in the Schools, 43,* 283-295.

Gilbert, A. M. (2004). *Psychometric properties of the Trauma Symptom Checklist for Young Children (TSCYC).* Ph.D. dissertation, Alliant International University, San Diego, United States—California. Retrieved January 03, 2007, from ProQuest Digital Dissertations database. (Publication No. AAT 3118171).

Gilbert, A, M, Briere, J., Taylor, N., & Viglione, D. J. (2004). *Characteristics of PTSD and trauma-related symptoms in children as measured by the Trauma Symptom Checklist for Young Children and the UCLA PTSD Index.* Unpublished manuscript.

Pollio, E. S., Glover-Orr, L. E., & Wherry, J. N. (2002). *Assessing posttraumatic stress disorder using the Trauma Symptom Checklist for Young Children.* Paper presented at the San Diego Conference on Child Maltreatment, San Diego, CA.

Putnam, F. W., Helmers, K., & Trickett, P. K. (1993). Development, reliability, and validity of a child dissociation scale. *Child Abuse and Neglect, 17,* 731-741.

Salvia, J., & Ysseldyke, J. E. (1998). *Assessment* (7th ed.). Boston, MA: Houghton Mifflin Company.

Smith-Stover, C., & Berkowitz, S. (2005). Assessing violence exposure and trauma symptoms in young children: A critical review of measures. *Journal of Traumatic Stress, 18,* 707-717.

[192]

Verb and Sentence Test.

Purpose: "Developed to investigate disorders affecting the production and comprehension of verbs and sentences."

Population: People with aphasia, aged 18–80 years.

Publication Date: 2002.

Acronym: VAST.

Scores: 10 subtests: Verb Comprehension, Sentence Comprehension, Grammaticality Judgement, Action Naming, Verb Finite, Verb Infinitive, Sentence Construction, Anagrams Without Picture, Anagrams With Picture, *Wh*-Anagrams.

Administration: Individual.

Price Data: Available from publisher.

Time: (180) minutes for complete battery.

Comments: Subtests may be administered individually.

Authors: Roelien Bastiaanse, Susan Edwards, and Judith Rispens.

Publisher: Harcourt Assessment [England].

Review of the Verb and Sentence Test by SHAWN K. ACHESON, Associate Professor of Neuropsychology, Department of Psychology, Western Carolina University, Cullowhee, NC:

DESCRIPTION. The Verb and Sentence Test (VAST) is a traditional individually administered paper-and-pencil measure of language functioning in aphasic adults aged 18 to 80 years. The 10 subtests are designed to assess various aspects of verb production and comprehension in those with all types of aphasia. The central purpose of the VAST is to provide linguistically grounded information to clinicians that will help direct the process of therapy and rehabilitation rather than the simple diagnosis of aphasia. The test may be administered in its entirety in a little more than 3 hours. However, there are no composite scores to be calculated so the test may be used more effectively in a piecemeal fashion. In addition, there are no standard score conversions to be made for individual subtests. The administration manual provides a table of cutoff scores for each of the subtests. No explanation is provided regarding the development of these cutoff scores. Similarly, discussion related to the process of standardized administration is limited. The VAST authors recommend a very flexible approach to administration and scoring with the proviso that notes are made regarding those procedures and that they are followed again on retest.

DEVELOPMENT. The VAST is based on an earlier Dutch version. Both versions are explicitly based on a linguistic model of verb production and comprehension both individually and when embedded within a sentence. The authors describe three aims in development of the VAST. Using the VAST, the examiner should be able to: (a) obtain basic linguistic information concerning the client's aphasia, (b) use results from the VAST to guide the therapy process, and (c) use the VAST with clients with many different aphasic syndromes, except those with severe or global aphasias. Of these aims, the second appears to have been the central and guiding force. In fact, all VAST subtests can be related to known therapies.

Items on the original Dutch version were selected based on the performance of 50 non-brain-damaged participants. Items that were correctly completed by at least 90% of these individuals were retained in the final Dutch version of the test. The implicit assumption was that healthy speakers should be able to complete all items correctly. This final version was reported to have been administered to a group of non-brain-damaged speakers, a group of aphasics, and a group of nonaphasic participants with right hemisphere damage. However, no information is provided about how the results of those participants were used or evaluated. The English version of the VAST is based on a translation of the Dutch items. Items that could not be translated or linguistically irrelevant items were dropped from the VAST.

TECHNICAL. The standardization sample is inadequate by any standard. In developing the English-language version, only 79 nonaphasic and 25 aphasic individuals were used. Moreover, not all subtests were administered to every participant. Each subtest was administered to only 20–34 nonaphasic controls and 16–25 aphasics. Sixty-four percent of the aphasic sample were male and only 39% of the nonaphasic sample were male. The mean age for the aphasic sample was slightly older than the nonaphasic sample (68.4 yrs. [16.08 s.d.] vs. 55.57 yrs. (8.32 s.d.]). The mean number of years of education was slightly lower for the aphasic sample (11.6 [1.87 s.d.] vs. 13.55 [2.93 s.d.]). There was also considerable variability among the members of the aphasic group in terms of how long they were post aphasia onset. Individuals were between 2 and 257 months post onset ($M = 40$, s.d. = 55.1).

Alpha coefficients (reliability) are reported to be acceptable (.78–.95) on 8 of the 10 subtests. The VAST authors did not report values for the remaining 2 subtests because they were constructed of only 10 items each. Validity on the VAST is limited to a series of correlations between the VAST and the Token Test. Eight of the 10 correlations (-.47 to -.71) are statistically significant ($p \leq .05$). One correlation approached significance (Verb Comprehension, -.41; $p \leq .10$). The

correlation between the Sentence Construction subtest and the Token Test (-.36) was not significant. These correlations were based on the performance of 16 aphasic participants.

COMMENTARY. The validity of this instrument needs further investigation. Unlike reliability, validity is largely a hallmark of how a test is used, not a measure of some internal characteristics of the test or its items. The demonstration of validity reported by the authors is one of construct validity. This type of validity attempts to establish the similarity of constructs assessed by different tests. Unfortunately, by the authors' own admission, there is no other test that currently measures the same construct as that measured by the VAST. This is one of their selling points and therefore makes any measure of construct validity inconsequential. Fortunately, there are a host of other forms of validity, now collectively referred to as incremental validity, that would have been more relevant. For example, the authors might have tried to demonstrate that the specific information provided by the VAST actually improves therapy outcome relative to similar therapy performed in the absence of that information.

Overall, the Verb and Sentence Test is built around an interesting and important theoretical model. However, it is a relatively new model of psycholinguistics that does not yet appear to be firmly established. In addition, there is inadequate standardization, both in the normative group and in the test administration. Although reliability should be considered generally adequate, there is insufficient demonstration of the test's validity. The method used to establish validity was inappropriate in light of the novelty of the underlying constructs measured by the VAST. All of that said, I believe there is great promise for future iterations of this instrument. Much work remains to be done in terms of establishing its validity, and clarifying and operationalizing the administration of each of the subtests.

SUMMARY. The VAST is a 10-subtest measure of language production and comprehension specifically designed to provide information to speech language pathologists and clinical linguists that might benefit the therapy process. It is well grounded in a novel model of psycholinguistics but lacks sufficient demonstration of validity to make it a useful instrument in clinical practice today.

Review of the Verb and Sentence Test by
MILDRED MURRAY-WARD, *Dean, College of
Education, California State University Stanislaus,
Turlock, CA:*

DESCRIPTION. The Verb and Sentence
Test (VAST) is a clinical and research assessment
of persons with disorders affecting production and
comprehension of verbs and sentences. According
to the authors, the VAST is an adaptation of the
Werkwooden-en Zinnentest (WEZT) by
Bastiaanse, Maas, and Rispens (2000). The target
group is primarily composed of those persons with
all types of aphasia, including those with very mild
aphasia. The authors state that the VAST can be
used to investigate the nature of language disorders for a wide range of aphasic persons, establish
baselines against which language change or the
effectiveness of therapy can be calibrated, or to
motivate therapy (manual, 2002, p. 4).

Interestingly, the authors caution that the
VAST is less appropriate for persons with severe
or global aphasia. They also indicate that although
there are assessments for diagnosing type of aphasia and underlying causes of aphasia, little attention is given to sentence processing and verbs.

The test content focuses on linguistic production and comprehension. In the test manual,
the authors state that nouns and verbs are central
to sentence meaning and carry semantic and syntactic meaning, called "lemma," with verb lemma
being more complex. The VAST reveals the ability to recognize or retrieve a verb and its meaning,
form grammatical structure, and map grammatical
roles onto semantic roles.

The VAST focuses on production and comprehension at the single word and sentence level.
The items are organized into 10 tests to be selected by the examiner as most appropriate for
each examinee. These tests are organized under
Comprehension or Production areas. The 3 Production tests include: Verb Comprehension (selecting action represented in verb spoken by examiner), Sentence Comprehension (pointing to a
picture matching a sentence read by the examiner), and Grammaticality Judgment (identifying
which of sentences read by examiners are gram-
matically "good" or "bad"). For Comprehension,
the 7 tests include: Action Naming (naming an
action presented in a picture), Verbs Finite (supplying verbs in sentences read aloud and presented
in a picture), Verb Infinite (supplying verbs in

sentences read aloud and presented in a picture),
Sentence Construction (oral picture description),
Sentence Anagram With Pictures (using word
cards to make a sentence describing the picture),
Sentence Anagrams Without Pictures (making
sentences from word cards), and *Wh*-Anagrams
(using a picture and word cards to create a question that matches the pictures).

Most persons complete all 10 tests, although
the authors suggest that some tests are more suited
to persons with specific types of difficulties. The
entire battery requires approximately 3 hours to
complete. The test manual provides detailed directions for scoring the response of examinees in
each test area. Sample case studies, including
each person's profile of scores, are provided to
guide the examiner. Suggestions for therapy
follow each case.

DEVELOPMENT. The content of the VAST
was designed to parallel the structure of the WEZT.
The authors carefully described the rationale and
theoretical basis for inclusion of various types of
items based on research conducted on the nature
of types of aphasia. In addition, the authors clearly
indicated content that was not included in the
VAST and the rationale for exclusions.

The original Dutch version was administered to 50 non-brain-damaged persons who varied in age, gender, and educational level. All
individual items answered correctly by at least 90%
of this non-brain-injured group were retained, and
the remaining items were removed. The final
version was then used with 40 non-brain-injured
individuals, 35 aphasic speakers, and 6 nonaphasic
speakers with a lesion on the right hemisphere.
The introduction of the last group was made to
assure that errors made by aphasics were not due
to brain damage.

The English version was normed on 80 non-
brain-damaged and 25 aphasic persons. With the
non-brain-damaged speakers a type of matrix sampling method was used in which at least 20 participants completed each subtest. The 25 aphasic
persons were chosen because they possessed one
single lesion in the left hemisphere, were at least 2
months beyond initial onset, and had no other
cognitive disorders. No attempt was made to choose
persons based on type or severity of aphasia. These
persons were also tested using a type of matrix
sample method in which between 16 and 20 persons took each subtest. Although age, gender,

years of education, and time of post-onset were collected, the two groups were not matched on these variables because the Dutch study showed no relationship between performance and these variables. Data from the aphasic group revealed significantly lower performances on all tests compared to the non-brain-damaged group.

TECHNICAL.

Standardization. As described under the development section, the VAST has been standardized with aphasic and nonaphasic populations. Data on validity and reliability are presented in the manual.

Reliability. Reliability for the VAST was estimated using alpha coefficients for 8 of the 10 subtests that contained at least 20 items. The remaining tests of finite verbs and infinitives in sentences each contained only 10 items. Internal consistency indices so obtained ranged from .78 for Verb Comprehension to .95 for *Wh*-Anagrams. No test-retest or other reliability procedures were conducted.

Validity. The authors explored the VAST's validity using a concurrent validity procedure. A total of 16 aphasic persons completed the Token Test from the Aachen Aphasia Test (English version; Miller, DeBleser, & Willmes, in press). The Token Test is generally used to establish the severity of aphasia, with higher scores indicating more severe aphasia. Therefore, high scores on the VAST should be negatively correlated with scores on the Token Test. In fact, all tests of the VAST were negatively correlated with the Token Test, with correlations ranging from -.36 for Sentence Construction to -.71 for Sentence Comprehension. All but the Sentence Construction correlations were statistically significant, at $p < .05$ levels or better.

COMMENTARY. The VAST is an important tool in assessing aphasics. The test appears relatively easy to administer and the authors have described the function of each test section to assist the examiner in determining which tests are suitable for an examinee. The manual clearly described the theoretical and research base for the test. Validity evidence suggests that the test discriminates between non-brain-damaged and aphasic speakers. The internal consistency reliability coefficients for the individual tests are at generally acceptable levels.

However, some limitations in the test's development require that it be used with caution.

First, because the VAST is derived from a Dutch instrument, examiners should review the pictures for any possible cultural factors that could impact interpretation of the actions described in the pictures. Second, although the authors present clinical examples of results and suggestions for how to address the examinee's condition, there is no validity evidence for the profiles presented. Third, because no test-retest reliability study has been completed on the VAST's stability and sensitivity to treatment, a major purpose of the instrument has no technical data to support this use. The test authors themselves caution the user in measuring client improvement. They recommend applying McNemar-tests if one is interested in pre/post or change uses.

SUMMARY. The VAST is an interesting instrument that fills a need in tests for aphasics in the areas of production and comprehension of verbs and sentences. The instrument is an adaptation of the Werkwooden-en Zinnentest (WEZT) by Bastiaanse, Maas, and Rispens (2000). The VAST presents good validity evidence, but only partial reliability evidence to support its use in measuring change in aphasics. Therefore, examiners should use the instrument with caution for that purpose, following the guidelines recommended by the authors.

REVIEWER'S REFERENCES

Bastiaanse, R., Maas, E., & Rispens, J. (2000). De Werkwoorden-en Zinnentest (WEZT). Lisse: Swets & Zeitlinger.
Miller, N., DeBleser, R., & Willmes, K. (in press). The English language version of the Aachen Aphasia Test.

[193]

VIEW: An Assessment of Problem Solving Style.

Purpose: Designed to assess "problem-solving styles."
Population: Ages 12 years and older.
Publication Dates: 2002–2004.
Scores, 3: Orientation to Change, Manner of Processing, Ways of Decoding.
Administration: Individual or group.
Price Data, 2006: $25 per manual (70 pages); $165 per complete kit including facilitator's guide (219 pages) and 10 paper copies of VIEW (required for all first-time orders); $90 per 10 paper copies; $50 per set-up fee for on-line access; $90 per 10 on-line uses; discounts available for nonprofit schools, religious organizations, college and university faculty, and researchers.
Foreign Editions: Information regarding translated tests available from publisher.
Time: (10–15) minutes.
Authors: Edwin C. Selby, Donald J. Treffinger, Scott G. Isaksen, and Kenneth J. Lauer (technical manual only).
Publisher: Center for Creative Learning, Inc.

Review of the VIEW: An Assessment of Problem Solving Style by GREGORY SCHRAW, Professor, Department of Educational Psychology, University of Nevada, Las Vegas, Las Vegas, NV:

DESCRIPTION. The VIEW: An Assessment of Problem Solving Style provides a measure of preferences for solving problems based on a 34-item self-report scale. The VIEW provides scores on three factors that collectively purport to comprise problem-solving style, including Orientation to Change (OC), Manner of Processing (MP), and Ways of Deciding (WD).

The Orientation to Change scale includes 18 items and indicates which of two general styles for problem solving characterize the individual. One is the "Explorer" style, which is characterized by someone who likes to think in a divergent manner, explores multiple options, and considers a variety of possibilities in the problem-solving process. The second is the "Developer" style, which is characterized by someone who is systematic, incremental, and focuses on practical aspects of problem solving.

The Manner of Processing scale is based on eight items and indicates whether a person prefers to work externally (i.e., collaborating with others during the problem-solving process) or internally (i.e., thinking and working alone during all or most of the problem-solving process).

The Ways of Deciding scale is based on eight items. It provides information about whether an individual prefers to focus on people (i.e., maintaining harmonious relationships) or tasks (i.e., focusing on the logic of decisions and how things will be carried out) when making decisions during problem solving.

DEVELOPMENT. The VIEW is based on the Creative Problem Solving (CPS) framework developed by Isaksen, Dorval, and Treffinger (2000). Unfortunately, the CPS framework is neither described in detail in the facilitator's guide nor in the technical manual although descriptions may be found elsewhere. Thus, the underlying rationale for what aspects of problem solving the VIEW measures is not entirely clear and understanding it would involve reading beyond these two documents. The Facilitator's Guide does not relate the VIEW or the CPS framework to existing theories of problem solving, although in the technical manual, the authors suggest that the VIEW provides information about the psychology of the person generally, including the individual's learning style, cognitive style, and psychological type.

The main goal of the VIEW is to situate a person within a 2 (Orientation to Change) X 2 (Manner of Processing) X 2 (Ways of Deciding) problem-solving style matrix. It is purported that each person fits best into one of the eight mutually exclusive cells in the matrix. The manual provides the approximate proportion of individuals who have completed the VIEW who fall into each of the eight cells. Understanding one's problem-solving style presumably helps the individual solve problems more effectively, and helps organizations utilize human resources with greater efficiency.

The VIEW consists of 34 items, each with differential statements that represent opposite ends of a continuum. For example, Item 21 allows an examinee to indicate whether he or she has a preference for being cautious or being spontaneous. Each item allows the examinee to select from seven bubbles that best describe one's preference. The three bubbles to the left indicate strong, usual, or slight preference for the "cautious" end of the continuum. The center bubble indicates neutrality. The three bubbles to the right indicate strong, usual, or slight preference for the "spontaneous" end of the continuum.

TECHNICAL. The VIEW takes approximately 10–15 minutes to complete and is appropriate for ages 12 and above. The VIEW includes score sheets, a 150-page facilitator's guide, and a 67-page technical manual. The guide and manual are clearly written and suitable for nontechnical test administrators. One problem is that the guide and manual do not provide conceptual or technical detail.

The facilitator's guide includes sections on the VIEW's three dimensions, feedback and interpretation, responding to questions, training and instruction, and applications. The guide is very easy to understand and provides practical and useful information.

The technical manual includes sections on the VIEW's purpose, conceptual foundations, reliability, and validity. The manual is easy to read but only minimally informative to a testing expert.

The manual provides limited reliability and validity data. One study examined the test-retest reliability of 48 middle school children. Correlations for the OC, MP, and WD scales were .90, .65, and .60, respectively. A different study using 49 undergraduates reported correlations of .83,

.84, and .75 for the OC, MP, and WD scales. It is not clear whether the higher reliability coefficients for the college students are due to the age of the students or the homogeneity of the sample. Internal consistency using coefficient alpha for a sample of 3,676 unspecified examinees yielded scores of .88, .85, and .84 for the OC, MP, and WD scales.

Both construct and criterion-related validity are discussed. Regarding criterion-related validity, one study using 191 unspecified examinees indicated that individuals high on the Explorer dimension preferred the Informal Design dimension on the Productivity Environmental Preference Survey (PEPS; Dunn, Dunn, & Price, 1991). However, no data are provided for this study other than a brief verbal description. A study with 118 North Carolina high school students reported significant correlations between the VIEW and the Dunn and Dunn Learning Style Inventory, but did not provide a correlation table. Another study with 20 students at an urban New York University reported correlations between the VIEW and the Myers-Briggs Type Indicator. The OC scale correlated .67 with Sensing/Intuition; the MP scale correlated .59 with Extraversion/Introversion; and the WD scale correlated .49 with the Thinking/Feeling scale.

The construct validity of the VIEW was assessed in an exploratory factor analysis of the 34-item instruments completed by 3,676 unspecified examinees. Principal components analysis was used with a varimax rotation. This analysis yields a three-factor solution explaining about 42% of the sample variation. Most items had item-to-factor loadings of .50 or higher, and virtually all items had item-to-factor loading higher than .30. There were three items that loaded on two components, although each item had a much larger loading on one of the components.

COMMENTARY. The strengths of the VIEW include (a) easy administration and scoring, and (b) a well-written manual. Weaknesses include (a) lack of a clear theoretical framework and (b) insufficient validity evidence. Test interpretation would be enhanced if the authors related the three factors measured by the VIEW to a model of problem-solving, and to research on problem-solving effectiveness. The validity evidence presented in the technical manual is not adequate by contemporary standards. Specifically, the criterion-related validity studies are few, have

small sample sizes, and describe results without actually presenting data.

SUMMARY. Overall, the VIEW provides a quick measure of problem-solving preferences. It is not clear whether the 2 X 2 X 2 matrix possesses eight mutually exclusive cells. It is also not clear whether individuals with one profile perform differently than other individuals. Understanding problem-solving preferences may be helpful to an individual or to an employer, but more information is needed about the accuracy of this classification scheme.

REVIEWER'S REFERENCES

Dunn, R., Dunn, K., & Price, G. (1991). Productivity Environmental Preference Survey. Lawrence, KS: Price Systems, Inc.
Isaksen, S. G., Dorval, K. B., & Treffinger, D. J. (2000). *Creative approaches to problem solving: A framework for change* (2nd ed.). Dubuque, IA: Kendall/Hunt.

Review of the VIEW: An Assessment of Problem Solving Style by MARK A. STAAL, Chief, Special Operations & Aerospace Psychology, Air Force Special Operations Command, Hurlburt Field, FL:

DESCRIPTION. The VIEW: An Assessment of Problem Solving Style is a 34-item questionnaire, administered either by paper-and-pencil or as an on-line, web-based assessment. All of the VIEW's questions are based on the following "stem" statement, "When I am solving problems, I am a person who prefers...." Responses to each item fall along a continuum (a 7-point Likert scale) suggesting which statement most accurately describes each person's own approach to problem solving.

The VIEW yields three score dimensions. The first is "Orientation to Change (OC)"–the person's perceived preferences for managing change and solving problems. This index is broken down further into categories of "Explorer" and "Developer." These terms are used to describe one's change management and problem-solving style. The second dimension is "Manner of Processing (MP)"–the person's self-reported work preference. Manner of Processing is split between perceived external orientation (e.g., prefers to problem solve with others) and internal processing (e.g., prefers problem solving alone). The third and final index is "Ways of Deciding (WD)"–which describes the individual's emphasis given to people or tasks when making decisions and problem solving. Each dimension is discussed in detail in the VIEW's technical manual.

At the core of the VIEW's theoretical structure is the Creative Problem Solving (CPS) framework reportedly used throughout educational and organizational systems. In brief, this framework supports the notion that individuals differ in the way they approach problem solving: They require varying levels of structure and information, they frame and understand obstacles in different ways, and they process these elements in ways that are stylistically unique. In addition to CPS, the VIEW's authors also claim conceptual influence in the measurement's development from contemporary personality and learning theories (e.g., problem-solving styles, cognitive styles, personality types).

The manual describes the minimum qualifications for the VIEW user to include an undergraduate degree; coursework in testing, measurement, and statistics; and a statement regarding the proper uses of the inventory as well as a commitment to its responsible and ethical use. The manual does not provide a rationale for these qualifications. Although no time limit is noted, the manual estimates a 10–15-minute length to completion. The VIEW's creators claim that anyone with at least a sixth-grade proficiency in English (ages 12–adult) can take the questionnaire. This range is somewhat confusing in that the age range provided for the total normative sample is 12 to 82. The VIEW also comes with a facilitator's guide that expands upon aspects of the technical manual and provides guidance to test users for its administration and interpretation.

DEVELOPMENT. The VIEW's technical manual was published in 2004, although the Center for Creative Learning (the VIEW's publisher) has produced a "2005 Technical Update" (2006). The original technical manual provides a discussion of the inventory's conceptual and theoretical underpinnings, its development (reliability and validity), and an extensive reference list for the user. The manual details a four-stage process of development dating from 1997 when the earliest version of the instrument was first created (then known as the Indicator of Problem Solving Style). The current form of the VIEW was completed in 2001, and validation studies were conducted in 2002. Since that time it appears that research on the instrument has continued along with data gathering, expanding its normative database to over 10,000 respondents. Although the VIEW's developers state the inventory is unbiased and appropriate for use with individuals from a variety of ethnic/cultural backgrounds, the manual also states that continued research into this area is

desired and that its normative sample is one of "convenience and opportunity" (2005 technical update, p. 5) and neither random nor representative.

Normative data for the VIEW are based on the response of 10,151 participants (ranging in age from 12 to 82, mean of 39.8, SD of 11.6). Although the manual indicates that it is NOT appropriate for use with children under the age of 12, given the mean and SD of the database one can only assume that there are very few children or adolescents with whom to compare prospective underage test users. The VIEW's manual states that it has been field-tested with students, educators, church leaders, and a variety of managers. The unusual step of specifying "church leaders" as one of the inventory's normative groups was not explained further. Moreover, there was no attempt in the manual to describe further "managers" or "educators." A further description of the normative sample would be of value to the user. Of those in the sample, approximately 43% were male and 57% were female.

The VIEW was recently produced in Dutch, French, and Chinese (Korean and Japanese are in process). However, validation data for these alternative editions were not available for critical review.

TECHNICAL. The VIEW's manual provides a brief overview of several reliability studies. Unfortunately, these tend to be somewhat limited in size ranging from 23 to 49 participants. Test-retest correlations among these studies range from .60 (with 1 month between testings) to .93 (with 2 months between testings) across dimensions and samples, most often ranging in the .80s. In general, it appears that the MP and WD dimensions have slightly lower test-retest reliability than measures of OC. Although one test-retest study was also carried out over a 12-month period, the others were conducted with either 1- or 2-month intervals. Measures of internal consistency using coefficient alpha estimates are also provided. The results suggest the VIEW is internally consistent (coefficients range from .82 to .87 for each dimension).

The VIEW's developers describe the multi-iterative process the inventory has gone through to get to this point. It has been refined over time from its earliest version as an 18-item, single-dimension questionnaire, to a 30-item, then 40-item, and finally 34-item, three-dimensional measure. Through this process the item pool has been refined using rational analysis in the context of its theoretical underpinnings. Moreover, items have been worded for maximum dimensional discrimination.

Under the subheading of "Evidence based on test content," the authors describe a number of studies seeking to establish the VIEW's construct validity. Construct validation helps determine the extent to which a test may be said to measure a theoretical construct or trait. This process is often accomplished through the use of convergent or divergent validation. In other words, construct validity can be established by either determining whether test items correlate highly with other measures (convergence) that have been demonstrated to measure a similar construct/trait or by determining whether test items correlate poorly with instruments (divergence) that have been demonstrated to measure a different construct/trait. However, the studies mentioned in this section of the VIEW's manual provide little empirical support for the instrument's construct validity. For example, in one study, VIEW dimensions were compared to reported problem-solving choices. The results suggested that the way participants perceived their problem solving was similar to the way they actually solved problems. Recall that the VIEW is a self-report measure of perceived problem-solving style. Therefore, confirming that there is a strong similarity between how people perceive themselves and how they actually behave is interesting, but inadequate to confirm the VIEW's validity.

In a second study, researchers examined the relationship between the VIEW's three dimensions of style and participants' self-ratings on various personality-type indicators. Researchers found significant correlations between how people rated their problem-solving style on the VIEW and how they rated themselves on personality-type descriptors. It is somewhat unclear as to how these findings validate the VIEW because the various personality-type indicators examined were not designed to be used in this manner. Comparing lists of personality-type or style descriptors and finding coherence among them is not the same as correlating two different tests that purport to measure the same or similar constructs. A third study was mentioned in the manual; however, adequate details of that study were not provided and therefore it is difficult to evaluate its contribution in supporting the VIEW's validation.

Finally, under the subheading "Evidence based on relations to other variables," the manual provides a series of cross-validation studies further aimed at establishing the construct validity of the measure. Although the previous section failed to provide adequate empirical support, this section is quite good. Performance on the VIEW is compared to performance across a variety of other "style" measures and personality-type indicators.

In terms of internal structure, the VIEW's developers provide convincing support for their three-dimensional factors. A principal-components analysis with a Varimax rotation was conducted on the total sample verifying this structural model. Test items across each factor loaded between < .30 and .75 on their proposed dimension while loading typically below .10 on other dimensions.

COMMENTARY. The VIEW appears to be what it purports to be, a measure of problem-solving style preference. As such, it may be beneficial for individuals interested in exploring their own approach to problem solving across the three dimensions incorporated by the instrument, namely their Orientation to Change, their Manner of Processing, and their Ways of Deciding. However, the VIEW is a self-report instrument with straightforward face validity, and therefore, it simply groups users' self-perceptions into three style categories. These three categories appear to be largely independent from one another and the technical manual does a good job in establishing this fact. However, their coherence as complementary elements associated with problem-solving style, although rationally sound, remains somewhat lacking of empirical support.

SUMMARY. The developers of the VIEW have taken a complex and dynamic construct (creative problem solving, problem-solving style) and attempted to dismantle it into three component dimensions (OC, MP, and WD). They have done an admirable job in refining the instrument over time, validating their structural model, and providing adequate validation support. Their conceptual and theoretical case has rational appeal, but limited empirical support. Moreover, although the developers cogently argue for the value of the instrument and its uses, they provide little evidence for its practical employment. For example, it would be helpful to potential users to include research in its validation that demonstrates its usefulness as a measure and not just its correlation to other measures. Such additions to the research base and the manual would be very desirable and are recommended.

REVIEWER'S REFERENCE

Treffinger, D. J. (2006). VIEW: An Assessment of Problem Solving Style (2005 technical update). Sarasota, FL: Center for Creative Learning, Inc.

[194]

Visual Motor Assessment.

Purpose: "Designed to identify visual-motor problems in children and adults."

Population: Ages 6 and older.

Publication Dates: 1962–2006.

Acronym: ViMo.

Scores, 5: Total Rotation Score, *T*-Score, Total SPCD (Separation of the Circle-Diamond Figure), Total DCD (Distortion of the Circle-Diamond Figure), Total DD (Distortion of the Dot Figure).

Administration: Individual.

Price Data, 2007: $100 per complete kit including technical manual (104 pages), 25 record forms, and 2 sets of test cards; $60 per technical manual; $37 per 25 record forms.

Time: (5–15) minutes.

Comments: Formerly known as the Minnesota Percepto-Diagnostic (MPD) Test.

Author: Gerald B. Fuller.

Publisher: Multi-Health Systems, Inc.

Cross References: For information on the Minnesota Percepto-Diagnostic Test, see T5:1699 (2 references), T4:1647 (6 references), 9:719 (3 references), 8:872 (22 references), T2:1485 (17 references), and P:475 (19 references); for reviews by Richard W. Coan and Eugene E. Levitt of the original edition of the Minnesota Percepto-Diagnostic Test, see 6:231 (2 references).

Review of the Visual Motor Assessment by MARK ROYBAL, Adjunct Professor of School Psychology, National University, San Diego, CA:

DESCRIPTION. The Visual Motor Assessment (ViMo) was designed to identify and evaluate the degree of visual-motor impairment in children and adults. The new version now includes over 12,000 respondents. This clinical and educational instrument was formerly known as the Minnesota Percepto-Diagnostic (MPD) Test, which was published in 1969. The test manual describes the elements necessary for sound test development. The addition of several new diagnostic groups, scoring refinements, interpretive improvements, normative data for both children and adults, and historical information framing the development of the ViMo appear fundamentally adequate. The addition of case examples and research studies enhances its appeal.

The basic premise of this intersensory phenomenon (Fuller, 1969), which has been established for over 35 years, suggests that the interchange between two different sense modalities when copying geometric forms (Wertheimer Gestalt figures) can result in error patterns (rotation and configuration) that indicate normal development, neurological impairment, and emotional overlays or learning disabilities. Error patterns are scored according to the degree a copied figure is rotated from original placement, whereas configuration is based on separation and distortion. A refined interpretive feature allows for "testing the limits" (manual, p. 13) by the clinician.

Conflated stratified normative data (1969, 1982, and 2004) are provided for children ages 6 thru 14 (nine age groups for rotation and three age groups for low IQ) and for adults over 16 years of age. The children's data are adjusted for age and IQ, which tends to ensure the suitability of test results. In order to insure that the five cohort populations were drawn from a population with the same distribution "a Kolmogorov-Smirnov two sample test was used" (manual, p. 36).

ADMINISTRATION AND SCORING. The Visual Motor Assessment is administered in paper-and-pencil format. In addition, its nonverbal format can be used with individuals from different environmental and educational backgrounds. The ViMo can be administered in less than 10 minutes; however, there are no time limits. The author unequivocally states that the ViMo can be used as a "screening tool" (manual, p. xii) or part of a comprehensive neuropsychological evaluation. As a cautionary note, the manual states that interpreters "must have MHS b-level qualifications" (manual, p. 1). Second drawings may be requested if the clinician is testing the limits and attempting to distinguish between schizophrenic patients and brain-damaged patients. In addition, the second drawings can help identify problems of visual perception (input), execution (motor), or integration (memory). These second efforts are not scored, but are used only for refined interpretations.

Participants are asked to copy a geometric pattern from six different cards with a strict adherence to paper position, card placement, and correctness of the drawings. Each card has one-of-two geometric figures: (CD) a connected circle and diamond, and (D) a conical formation of dots. The raw rotation scores are converted into *T*-scores with adjustments made to age and IQ for the child cohorts. In addition, a Four-Step Assessment Process is provided to help "in differentiating between different diagnostic categories" (manual, p. xii).

DEVELOPMENT. The Visual Motor Assessment has gone through a number of moderate revisions that have enhanced its ability to identify and differentiate between and among specific populations. First, the provincial title of Minnesota Percepto-Diagnostic Test (1969) was replaced with a more appropriate title: the Visual Motor Assessment (2004). Second, the rationale was applied to carefully chosen Gestalt figures. For example, the rationale for the ViMo is based on Gestalt psychology and focuses on the perceptual reactions (rotation and configuration) of the human organism. The concept, which is presented in a laudable manner, suggests that subjects (children and adults) when copying certain geometric forms would perform consistently within their maturational development level or bio-emotional state.

After much experimentation with several Wertheimer figures the most cohesive and stable figures were selected for the test. This selection process should assure the examiner that test results are an accurate reading of the subject's visual-motor perceptual processing abilities; however, the majority of the research studies supporting the author's theoretical position are dated (1962).

Third, the conflated normative data were expanded in 2004 by the addition of a mixed Special Education group (1,766), and a group of adults (289) with schizophrenia. Refined configuration scores are reported to include African Americans, Hispanics, and Native Americans. No further descriptions are provided as far as proportional representation of these groups. Although the author drew subjects from 22 states, it is unclear whether these subjects are representative of the national population. Their age, gender, SES, geographic regions, and racial and ethnic status were not reported. Relevance is impossible to ascertain.

TECHNICAL. Reliability is reported in terms of split-half for children and test-retest for both children and adults. The typical even-odd procedure for split-half reliabilities was abandoned for two modified procedures: (a) two CD figures and one D figure, and (b) two D figures and one CD figure. The split-half reliability coefficients for the first procedure ranged from .52 to .75; whereas the second procedure, which split the test into CD figures versus D figures, resulted in coefficients of .40 to .73. The test-retest procedure for children was administered on two occasions, 1-year apart; a second procedure for adults and children was set apart for a 3-month period. The 1-year period reliabilities (coefficients of stability) ranged from a low of .49 to .65; the adult coefficients of stability for the 3-month period ranged from .72 to .86, and the children's coefficients were .53 to .72. Clearly, the ViMO's stability (3-month period) for adult populations over time is more reliable than its stability for children. Clinicians, however, prefer reliabilities above .80 for psychoeducational tasks and .90 for decision-making tasks.

There were a number of dated validity studies reported, most of which support the author's claim that the ViMo can identify and differentiate between and among various specifically defined populations. In a 1962 study, using the degrees of rotation (MPD) with several hundred adults, the assessment was able to identify 90% of the normals, 80% of the personality disordered, and 82% of the organics. Concurrent studies comparing the ViMo with the Luria-Nebraska Neuropsychological Battery—Children's Revision (LNNB-CR) resulted in very low correlations (.10–.27). When comparing the ViMo with other visual-motor tests and achievement tests, the correlations were below acceptable levels for perceptual abilities (average: -.34–.37) and academic skills (-.18–.56).

COMMENTARY. The Visual-Motor Assessment, which is based on the perceptual principle of Gestalt psychology (Wertheimer), has an extensive history of research that supports its ability to identify and differentiate between individuals who have normal visual perception, emotional disturbance, schizophrenia, or brain damage. The Visual Motor Assessment, which uses degrees of rotation and errors of configuration as indicators of perceptual performance, appears to be a worthy screening assessment for assessing high-risk children and adults. Its norms lack some relevance, which poses a substantial concern for prospective users. The quick administration and the score interpretations (testing the limits) with Case Examples may augment the clinicians' efforts. The use of the terms "culturally-deprived children" or "cultural deprivation" (manual, p. 54) is dated and offensive. These children are not deprived of culture, but rather lack opportunity and face impoverishment. The ViMo manual contains omissions. The administration and scoring sections were clearly presented, whereas the conflated norms were not well defined or described. Complicating things further are the inherent weaknesses of using cohort populations (brain-damaged, personality disorder) that are extremely heterogeneous and with possible diagnostic inaccuracies. Technical data are archaic. Reliability coefficients were uneven and validity coefficients were poor.

SUMMARY. The ViMo provides a rapid assessment of visual motor impairment in children and adults. It is relatively easy to administer and score, and fairly inexpensive. It may have clinical and educational utility if assessors use it as a screening device and use it with considerable caution.

REVIEWER'S REFERENCE

Fuller, G. B., Sharp, H., & Hawkins, W. F. (1969). The Minnesota Percepto-Diagnostic Test (MPD): Age norms and IQ adjustments. *Journal of Clinical Psychology, 23,* 456–461.

Review of the Visual Motor Assessment by KAY B. STEVENS, Associate Professor of Education, Texas Christian University, Fort Worth, TX, and J. RANDALL PRICE, Professor of Psychology, Richland College, Dallas, TX:

DESCRIPTION. The Visual Motor Assessment (ViMo) is a screening instrument designed for individuals 6 years of age and older. Examinees copy three versions of two of Wertheimer's designs (three circle-and-diamond figures and three dot-pattern figures) presented individually on cards. No test booklet is required; examinees draw designs on white letter-size paper using a pencil. The test has no time limits but generally takes approximately 10 minutes. Drawings are examined for two types of errors: rotation errors and configuration errors. Rotation errors are assessed on all six designs by using a protractor to determine the degrees of rotation within the examinee's drawings. Children's raw rotation scores are converted to *t*-scores adjusted for age and IQ; adult's actual rotation raw scores are used without conversion because "no differences in adult scores based on age or IQ in the developmental sample were found" (manual, p. 12). Configuration errors include separations and distortions. Separation errors apply to the circle-diamond designs and concern the space between the circle and the diamond. Distortion errors apply to all designs and are measured using clinical judgment based on dichotomous scoring; a score of one indicates error(s) and zero indicates no error(s). Configuration scores are addressed in the description of normative data including children and adults, but no derived scores are available

leaving test users only norm-referenced rotation scores to interpret. All scores are ultimately compared to score ranges with specified cutoff points. Rotation score ranges include diagnostic categories. For example, adult scores of 0 to 20 indicate normal perception, 21–59 personality disturbance, and 60 to 150 schizophrenia or brain damage; *t*-score ranges for normal and clinical populations of children also are provided.

DEVELOPMENT. The 2006 ViMo is a revision of the Minnesota Percepto-Diagnostic Test first standardized in 1969 (MPD) and revised in 1982 (MPD-R). The test is based on four principles of Gestalt perception: inhomogeneity, interaction of figure-ground, laws of grouping, and pragnanz, all of which are briefly described in the manual. Readers with no or minimal background knowledge in this area may find this reading esoteric. The manual states that the primary reasons for the 2004 revision were to (a) update norms, (b) compare results across versions, (c) improve and refine test properties, and (d) report research conducted since the previous revision. The most recent normative data were collected in 2004 with no significant differences in those data and the data collected in 1969 and 1982; therefore, all data were combined to make up the normative group for the 2006 revision. The 2006 revision added 3,169 children and 888 adults to the norm group. Two new clinical groups were added including a group of children receiving special education services and a group of adults with schizophrenia. In addition, 14 research-study summaries were added to the test manual since the 1989 revision: 10 peer-reviewed studies of which the test author is the author or co-author, 2 peer-reviewed studies conducted by other authors, 1 unpublished dissertation, and 1 unpublished manuscript.

TECHNICAL. Normative data for children and adults are separated in the manual.

Children. A brief and incomplete description of the groups of children in the standardization sample and how they were selected is available in the manual. Groups include children between the ages of 6 and 14 who were categorized as (a) normal (*n* = 6,600), (b) emotionally disturbed (*n* = 1,150), (c) schizophrenic (*n* = 298), (d) brain damaged (*n* = 367), and (e) in special education (*n* = 1,766). The manual states that children with emotional disturbance were randomly selected from "child guidance clinics, mental health centers, residential treatment centers and private practice facilities" (p. 35). Children with schizophrenia were selected who had been "officially diagnosed as schizophrenic by psychiatric and psychological staff" (manual, p. 35). The children with brain damage were selected who had a formal diagnosis of organic brain syndrome with documented neurological findings. Children served by special education were in their first year of special education and diagnosed with learning disabilities and/or behavioral problems according to state criteria. No information regarding gender, racial or ethnic background, socioeconomic status, geographic location, or types of communities from which the groups were selected is available.

Split-half and test-retest reliability measures were conducted with children, but other than the number of children in each age group, no further information on the participants was provided. Split–half reliability coefficients ranged from .52 to .75. Test-retest reliability coefficients with an interval of 1-year ranged from .49 to .65. Test-retest reliability coefficients with an interval of 3 months ranged from .53 to .72. No chapter or section of the manual is labeled validity data. However, research studies using the previous versions of the test (MPD, MPD-R) were summarized. The majority of the studies were published prior to the last manual of the test; only 14 recent studies were reported. For example, two studies concerning children with brain damage authored or co-authored by the test developer were reviewed. One showed that the MPD-R correctly differentiated 74% of brain-damaged from emotionally impaired children. The second study presented data suggesting that the MPD-R more accurately differentiated brain-damaged and psychiatric children than did the Bender-Gestalt. One study concerned the MPD-R scores of adolescents previously identified as schizophrenic versus those of adolescents with depression or personality disorders. Other studies with children concerned differences in MPD-R scores in Black, Hispanic, and White children as well as with Papago, Hopi, and Navajo children. Also, one study indicated that children with articulation disorders had poorer rotation scores than a control group. No other new studies of concurrent, construct, or predictive validity were reported.

Adults. Two thousand eighty-five individuals made up the adult normative sample including 835 adults considered to be normal, 510 with personality disturbance, 451 with brain damage, and 289 with schizophrenia. The mean age range was 29.11 to 52.32 and years of education ranged from 8.71 to 13.5. The manual states that adult samples were taken from 22 states representing the Midwest, East, South, and West. No information regarding gender, racial or ethnic background, socioeconomic status, geographic location, or types of communities from which the groups were selected is available.

Test-retest reliability was determined 3 months apart on 950 normal adults (.86), 270 adults with personality disorders (.81), 95 adults with brain damage (.72), and 87 adults with schizophrenia (.79).

Two studies with adults, published since the last manual, addressed the differentiation, by the MPD-R, of known groups of patients with organic brain damage and personality disturbances. No new studies of concurrent, construct, or predictive validity were reported.

COMMENTARY. The manual's explanations of procedures and descriptions of samples are inadequate in numerous instances. The following represent only a few examples: (a) Six thousand-six hundred normal children came from the combined 1969, 1982, and 2004 samples; however, only 4,000 normal children were used to establish the *t*-score conversions. No explanation is given for the underlying rationale for this decision, and no description was provided for how these 4,000 children were chosen. (b) On the split-half and test-retest reliability data for children, no description of the sampling procedure is provided nor is it clear if these groups included children with disabilities or not. (c) This test is recommended for discriminating children with emotional disorders, brain damage, and schizophrenia; however, no reliability data were reported designating these subpopulations. Test-retest reliability data are reported, however, for the aforementioned subpopulation. (d) The manual fails to provide *t*-scores for adults; instead, raw scores are used. The test developer's rationale for this omission appears unsupported in psychometric theory.

More important, in the opinion of these reviewers, the nature of the test construct measured by and the recommended uses of the ViMo are of dubious value. Current psychometric consensus is that drawing tests have serious limits to the amount of information they can provide. The use of a simple drawing test to discriminate brain dysfunction is based on an antiquated notion that drawing tests could discriminate individuals with brain damage. Lezak (2004) points out that drawing tests leave many cognitive functions unexamined and ignore the fact that every type of drawing task has been successfully performed by many cognitively impaired individuals. Furthermore, Anastasi and Urbina (1997) reviewed the use of drawing tasks to identify emotional disturbance and concluded that "most experts agree that drawings should be used only to generate hypotheses and that they must be interpreted in the context of other information about the individual" (p. 430). Reviewers (Coan, 1965; Levitt, 1965) of the MPD, an earlier version of the ViMo, concluded that the MPD manual did not include adequate data on the use of the MPD as a screening instrument with clinical as opposed to previously identified experimental groups. Some data have now been provided on error rates in actually discriminating normal individuals from those with brain damage or schizophrenia. These reviewers conclude that the MPD had interesting possibilities for research but no important clinical use at that time in its development. Little has changed since that time.

REVIEWERS' REFERENCES

Anastasi, A., & Urbina, S. (1997). *Psychological testing* (7th ed.). Upper Saddle River, NJ: Prentice-Hall, Inc.

Coan, R. (1965). [Review of the Minnesota Percepto-Diagnostic Test.] In O. K. Buros (Ed.), *The sixth mental measurements yearbook* (pp. 470-471). Highland Park, NJ: The Gryphon Press.

Levitt, E. (1965). [Review the of Minnesota Percepto-Diagnostic Test.] In O. K. Buros (Ed.), *The sixth mental measurements yearbook* (pp. 471-472). Highland Park, NJ: The Gryphon Press.

Lezak, M., Howieson, D., & Loring, D. (2004). *Neuropsychological assessment* (4th ed.). New York: Oxford University Press.

[195]

The Visual Object and Space Perception Battery.

Purpose: Designed to assess visual object and space perception.

Population: Adult.

Publication Date: 1991.

Acronym: VOSP.

Scores: 9 tests: Shape Detection Screening Test, Incomplete Letters, Silhouettes, Object Decision, Progressive Silhouettes, Dot Counting, Position Discrimination, Number Location, Cube Analysis.

Administration: Individual or group.

Price Data, 2007: £174.32 per complete kit including manual, 25 scoring sheets, and 3 stimulus books; £19.39 per 25 scoring sheets.

Time: Untimed.

Comments: Tests may be administered separately, in groups, or as a complete battery.

Authors: Elizabeth K. Warrington and Merle James.

Publisher: Harcourt Assessment [England].

Review of The Visual Object and Space Perception Battery by AYRES G. D'COSTA, Associate Professor, Quantitative Research, Measurement, and Evaluation in Education, The Ohio State University, Columbus, OH:

DESCRIPTION. The Visual Object and Space Perception (VOSP) Battery, intended as part of a neurological assessment of brained-damaged patients, consists of four tests of object perception and four tests of space perception, as follows: Test 1: Incomplete Letters; Test 2: Silhouettes; Test 3: Object Decision; Test 4: Progressive Silhouettes; Test 5: Dot Counting; Test 6: Position Discrimination; Test 7: Number Location; and Test 8: Cube Analysis.

The VOSP test battery attempts to identify highly specific impairments of cognitive function in patients following brain damage. However, the test manual warns that "visual object and space perception can only be meaningfully assessed in patients with adequate visual sensory capabilities" (manual, p. 9). Therefore, the Shape Detection Screening Test must first be administered as a screening device before the VOSP can be meaningfully utilized. This screening test is an adaptation of Warrington and Taylor's (1973) test of figure/ground perception.

The VOSP comes with a technical manual, a packet of manually scorable answer sheets, and three spiral-bound test binders. It is untimed, individually administered by qualified personnel, and is intended for adults ages 20 to 69.

DEVELOPMENT. The technical manual indicates that the VOSP was developed, validated, and standardized using patients from the Psychology Department of the National Hospital for Neurology and Neurosurgery, London, U.K. It further states that "although a theoretical issue was the original motivation for each of these tests, it was their pragmatic strength in terms of their selectivity and sensitivity that determined their selection and inclusion in this battery" (p. 7). Each of the eight tests was devised to focus on one component of visual perception, while minimizing the involvement of other cognitive skills. In other words, the manual does not present a theoretical rationale for the selection of the set of eight tests other than a pragmatic one, namely that such diagnostic information is useful for clinical purposes.

The eight tests were standardized and validated as individual tests using two samples of patients with diagnosed extra-cerebral neurological conditions. However, patients with medical conditions that might compromise cognitive function were excluded. All individuals in the samples were educated in British schools, and were tested for their adult reading achievement level. The VOSP tests have not been revised since 1991.

TECHNICAL.

Generalizability/sampling information. The technical manual provides statistical data for the two standardization samples that offer limited generalizability bases for external validity or wider utility of this test battery. Demographic summaries are available by sex, age, and social class for a total sample size of 200 for Sample 1 and 150 for Sample 2. The two samples are evenly distributed by gender and age. Social class is, as expected, normally distributed.

In addition, clinical details are provided in terms of lesions in the right and left hemispheres for two series of tested groups. Again, almost equal *n*s are noted for the right and left hemispheric lesion groups.

Technical information is provided for each of the eight tests of the VOSP. Each section presents the technical background justifying the inclusion of the specific test. It also presents the procedure used for developing the test. A subsequent paragraph summarizes how the test is administered, followed by a section on results which indicates that age-based norms (means, standard deviations) are presented in the Appendix. A *z*-test and a chi-square test were conducted to demonstrate validity based on the statistical significance of the results. Most of the tests of significance reported in the test manual for the eight tests appear to be statistically significant. However, some statistical tests were reported without discussion as nonsignificant (e.g., for Tests 3, 6, 7, and 8). Alpha levels range from .05 to .001. No reliability data are presented for any of the eight tests.

COMMENTARY. The VOSP appears to have reasonable utility in medical settings as a diagnostic instrument for patients with history of brain damage. It may be useful for clinicians who need specificity regarding cognitive impairments following brain damage. The psychometric data available at this time are somewhat limited. The tests were constructed in 1991 and there appear to be no follow-up analyses done since. The analyses reported are based on two samples totaling fewer than 400 subjects. It would be helpful to know if the tests have been in use since 1991 and what experience of clinical and psychometric successes they have had.

No reliability information is provided for any of the tests. Another major limitation is the lack of an overall theoretical framework that might help provide a context for this assessment. Given the many advances in this field over recent years, the VOSP tests and their clinical bases could be seriously dated. The references presented in the test manual generally belong in the 1970s and earlier.

SUMMARY. The VOSP is a test battery with eight subtests, developed and published in the U.K., designed to assess specific perceptual impairments following brain damage. Each test assesses one component of visual perception, while minimizing the involvement of other cognitive skills. It is based on the premise, for instance, that patients with right-hemisphere lesions are impaired (as compared with patients with left-hemisphere lesions) on tasks of object and space perception.

This test battery is simple to use, can be manually scored, and claims to have practical clinical utility. Age-based norms for use are provided in the test manual. The technical support of these claims is somewhat limited and dated. This test may have limited application to medical situations.

REVIEWER'S REFERENCE

Warrington, E. K., & Taylor, A. M. (1973). Contribution of the right parietal lobe to object recognition. *Cortex, 9,* 152–164.

[196]

Visual Patterns Test.

Purpose: Designed to measure "short term visual memory."

Population: Ages 13–92.

Publication Date: 1997.

Acronym: VPT.

Score: Total score only.

Administration: Individual.

Forms: 2 parallel forms: A, B.

Price Data, 2006: £70 per complete kit including manual (12 pages), stimulus cards, and response sheet; £35 per 50 scoring sheets.

Time: [10] minutes.
Authors: Sergio Della Sala, Colin Gray, Alan Baddeley, and Lindsay Wilson.
Publisher: Harcourt Assessment [England].

Review of the Visual Patterns Test by VALENTINA McINERNEY, Professor of Educational Psychology, School of Psychology, University of Western Sydney, Sydney, Australia:

DESCRIPTION. The Visual Patterns Test (VPT) is a measure of short-term, nonverbal memory. It has been designed specifically to target examinees' recall of visual images per se, separate from any need to recall any spatial elements such as their position. The rationale given for making this distinction is based on evidence of separate locations in the brain for neural activity associated with the functions of visual and spatial memory. In this context, the target populations for use of the VPT are those with brain damage due to degenerative disease or injury, and for whom differentiation between specific memory functions that may be impaired has particular clinical and research value.

The VPT is a short (up to 10 minutes) paper-and-pencil test comprising: (a) a 12-page manual, (b) two parallel-form (A and B) sets of 21 stimulus cards displaying increasingly complex black-and-white checkerboard patterns; and (c) four double-sided, laminated, response sheets showing blank grids, which are to be photocopied by the examiner for use in the testing situation.

No information is given as to the appropriate level of training required to administer the VPT, but given its simplicity, clinical training would not seem to be required. The interpretation of scores should be made by a clinician, however, especially in relation to adjusting raw scores for age and years of formal education. In addition, it would be for a clinician to decide how low a score should be to warrant further investigation. In this context, the developers recommend that a score at the 10th percentile might fall into this category, whereas at the 5th percentile, a score would be considered unusually low and suggestive of *short-term visual memory* impairment.

When administering the VPT, each stimulus card is shown to the examinee for 3 seconds and then covered up. There are three patterns at each level of difficulty. The examinee is requested to demonstrate recall of each pattern in turn by filling in squares on a blank grid of the same size

and shape on the response sheet. The developers point out that there is no set time limit for responding. Once the response is made, the target card is uncovered by the examiner. If the pattern was incorrectly recalled, the manual states that the examinee "should be encouraged to add or delete filled squares until the numbers agree" (manual, p. 8). The reason for this is not explained, nor is it made clear for how long to "encourage" the examinee to try to recall missing squares or how to avoid the danger of telling the examinee when the "numbers agree." The testing procedure finishes when the examinee cannot correctly recall any of the three patterns at a given level.

The raw VPT score is obtained by recording the number of correctly filled squares in the largest, most complex grid recalled by the examinee, with the maximum possible being 15. It is noted that only one grid needs to be reproduced correctly out of the three possible at each level of difficulty. The developers acknowledge that for "research purposes a more sensitive measure of recall would be provided by the mean of the complexities of, say, the last three patterns recalled" (manual, p. 8). No reasons are given for accepting a far less stringent measure of visual memory span for an examinee in a clinical setting. As the norms provided for the VPT were derived from this scoring method, it could be argued that the test capitalizes on one-off, chance recall by examinees.

The developers recommend that for examinees over 50 years of age, the raw VPT score should be adjusted to take into account age and years of formal education. This is because a significant positive correlation ($r = +.42$) was found between education and VPT score, and a significant negative correlation ($r = -.55$) was found between age and VPT score. In this context, a correction increment, or K-value, is to be added to the raw score, the detailed rationale for which is provided in the appendix. A table in the manual provides K-values for persons aged 50 to 95 who have had from 8 to 13 years of formal education.

DEVELOPMENT. The VPT was derived from previous matrices tests in which varied arrangements of similar elements are presented (Phillips, 1983; Phillips & Baddeley, 1971; Warrington & James, 1967). Due to the lack of complexity of such matrices, examinees need to store only a picture of a pattern in their memory. In this way, spatial processing is eliminated and the need for language skills to aid memory is minimized. The VPT is described as "essentially a paper-and-pencil version of an automised test" (manual, p. 5) developed by Wilson, Weidmann, Hadley, and Brooks in 1989. Unfortunately, details of the extent to which the VPT has been modified from this original test are not given.

Other tests of nonverbal short-term memory used in clinical practice are the Corsi Blocks Test (Corsi, 1972) and the Visual Scan subtest of the Wechsler Memory Scale (Wechsler, 1987), both of which require the examinee to reproduce a spatially presented sequence of events. An alternative to these tests is the Motor-Free Visual Perception Test (3rd ed.; Colarusso & Hammill, 2003; 16:152), which assesses visual perception through multiple-choice response formats. This test does not require any physical manipulation such as the filling in of grids by examinees in the VPT, or the tapping of blocks in the Corsi Blocks Test. The developers of the VPT do not provide any theoretical justification for examinees needing to use only motor skills to demonstrate their recall of patterns.

TECHNICAL. Standardization of Version A of the VPT was derived from a sample of 345 healthy British examinees. Version B was also tested with 204 examinees and was shown to be equivalent in difficulty to Version A. Given the latter comparatively smaller sample, the authors of the VPT have chosen to provide the statistical data for only Version A, the larger sample. In this context, the age range of participants was 13 to 92 years, with 54% of the sample aged less than 35 years—a positive skew. There were 159 males and 186 females in the sample, with a statistically significant lower mean score reported for females. This difference is described as having little practical significance as it equates to less than one point on the VPT.

Overall, the validity of the norming process of the VPT is poor for a number of reasons: There are no dates given for the testing of either version; no information is provided as to whether the examinees tested on each of Versions A and B were from different populations or on what bases they were determined to be healthy; no rationale is given for the selection of participants, specifically, the extent to which it was random. Other important details that are omitted include geographical locations, socioeconomic backgrounds, ethnicities, and reasons for participation.

Such lack of data to verify the representative nature of the sample severely compromises one's faith in the standardization of the VPT. Another concern is the lack of norm groupings by age, admittedly difficult given the relatively small sample used. Given recent research using fMRI scans to examine structural brain maturation during adolescence (see Blakemore & Choudhury, 2006) such norms would be of considerable value to clinicians and researchers in interpreting the scores of young people during puberty and adolescence.

Test-retest reliability of the VPT was assessed with a sample of 50 healthy British examinees aged 20–81 years. Reliability coefficients of .75 for Version A and .73 for Version B were obtained. Parallel-forms reliability was assessed using 194 healthy British examinees aged from 13–92 years. The coefficient was found to be .81. For 76 healthy Italian examinees aged from 15–86 years, the parallel-forms reliability coefficient was .88, whereas for 45 Italian brain-lesioned patients aged from 19–86 years, it was .75. Such reliabilities must be seriously questioned as no details are given about the samples or about the interval between administrations of the test, a factor that would create bias from practice effects. As Dikmen, Heaton, Grant, and Temkin (1999) point out in this context, when only correlation coefficients are presented as estimates of test-retest reliability, interpretations made by clinicians about memory improvement or deterioration for individuals will be very limited because test-retest intervals and samples used in instrument development will differ markedly from their patients. In this context, Dikmen et al. (1999) advise that "For a clinician interested in determining whether an observed change is likely by chance, the information needed is also the average practice effects and standard deviation of the change … to calculate the Reliable Change Index adjusted for practice effects" (p. 9).

Evidence of construct validity is presented from research conducted by the authors of the VPT themselves (reported in the manual as Della Salla, Gray, Baddeley, Wilson, Boyd, & Allamano, in preparation; published as Della Salla, Gray, Baddeley, Allamano, & Wilson, 1999). It appears that this research formed the technical basis from which the manual was derived.

One other empirical study is cited to support the construct validity of the VPT as a measure of visual memory span, distinct from spatial memory.

This is the work of Logie and Pearson (1997), in which children in age groups of 5–6, 8–9, and 11–12 years were compared using their performance on a "task which involved apparatus similar to that used for Corsi block span" (Logie & Pearson, 1997, p. 6) and "a 'visual span' procedure that was a modified version of that used by Logie et al. (1990) with adults and by Wilson, Scott and Power (1987) with young children" (Logie & Pearson, 1997, p. 6).

The VPT developers claim that "converging evidence for the distinctness of the abilities measured by the VPT and the *Corsi Blocks* tests comes from a developmental study by Logie and Pearson (in press), who found that the score differential in favor of the VPT increases markedly with age, suggesting that the two sets of skills have different developmental trajectories" (manual, p. 7). Given that neither the VPT nor the Corsi Blocks Test were used in this study, the case for validity of the VPT is undermined. The developers of the VPT report that for a clinical sample of 45 Italian brain-lesioned patients, the correlation between the VPT and the Corsi Blocks Test was moderately strong (.60), offering limited support for discriminative validity.

COMMENTARY. Overall, the normative information provided for the VPT is lacking and quite dated, especially given the current and pervasive use of digital, visual media across cultures, genders, ages, and education levels. This test should be restandardized using a much broader cross-section of such groups, especially children and adolescents, who are underrepresented in the current norms. In addition, it is recommended that the VPT be redeveloped to provide more alternatives for examinees who might be motor-impaired to demonstrate their nonverbal short-term memory recall. In light of the *Standards for Educational and Psychological Testing* (AERA, APA, & NCME, 1999; Parts 1, 2), methodological limitations of the VPT raise serious doubts about its validity and reliability. As Dikmen et al. (1999) warn, problems caused by these limitations would include failing to detect real memory changes in research situations, incorrectly diagnosing improvement or deterioration in a patient on repeated tests, or classifying patients as impaired or not impaired based on single administrations of measures. For these reasons, the VPT should not be the sole measure used for diagnostic purposes.

SUMMARY. The VPT is easily administered, scored, and language/culture free. The alternative versions may be used cautiously for retest purposes, with the interval being longer than 1 day to reduce practice effects. There is not strong evidence for construct validity of the VPT as a measure of distinctly visual (rather than spatial) memory for brain-injured patients. The test may be of some value, however, as part of a battery of nonverbal short-term memory tests used in a clinical situation.

REVIEWER'S REFERENCES

American Educational Research Association, American Psychological Association, & National Council on Measurement in Education. (1999). *Standards for educational and psychological testing.* Washington, DC: American Educational Research Association.

Blakemore, S., & Choudhury, S. (2006). Development of the adolescent brain: Implications for executive function and social cognition. *Journal of Child Psychology and Psychiatry, 47,* 296–312.

Colarusso, R. P., & Hammill, D. D. (2003). Motor-Free Visual Perception Test (3rd ed.). Novato, CA: Academic Therapy Publications.

Corsi, P. M. (1972). *Human memory and the medial temporal region of the brain.* Ph.D. Dissertation, McGill University, Montreal.

Della Salla, S., Gray, C., Baddeley, A., Allamano, N., & Wilson, L. (1999). Pattern span: A tool for unwelding visuo-spatial memory. *Neuropsychologia, 37,* 1189–1199.

Dikmen, S. S., Heaton, R. K., Grant, I., & Temkin, N. R. (1999), Test–retest reliability and practice effects of Expanded Halstead–Reitan Neuropsychological Test Battery. *Journal of the International Neuropsychological Society, 5,* 346–356.

Logie, R. H., & Pearson, D. G. (1997). The inner eye and the inner scribe of visuo-spatial working memory: Evidence from developmental fractionation. *European Journal of Cognitive Psychology, 9,* 241–257.

Logie, R. H., Zucco, G., & Baddeley, A. D. (1990). Interference with visual short-term memory. *Acta Psychologica, 75,* 55–74.

Phillips, W. A. (1983). Short-term visual memory. *Philosophical Transactions of the Royal Society of London, 302,* 259–309.

Phillips, W. A., & Baddeley, A. D. (1971). Reaction time and short-term visual memory. *Psychonomic Science, 22,* 73–74.

Warrington, E. K., & James, M. (1967) Disorders of visual perception in patients with localized cerebral lesion. *Neuropsychologia, 5,* 253–266.

Wechsler, D. (1987). The Wechsler Memory Scale—Revised. San Antonio, TX: The Psychological Corporation.

Wilson, J. T. L., Scott, J. H., & Power, K. G. (1987). Developmental differences in the span of visual memory for pattern. *British Journal of Developmental Psychology, 5,* 249–255.

Wilson, J. T. L., Weidmann, K. D., Hadley, D. M., & Brooks, D. N. (1989). The relationship between visual memory function and lesion detected by magnetic resonance imaging after closed head injury. *Neuropsychology, 3,* 255–265.

Review of the Visual Patterns Test by STEVEN R. SHAW, Assistant Professor of Educational and Counseling Psychology, McGill University, Montréal, Québec, Canada:

DESCRIPTION. The Visual Patterns Test (VPT) is a measure of short-term visual memory designed for persons aged 13 to 92 years. Short-term memory impairment is one of the most common manifestations of brain damage from either accident or degenerative disease. Short-term memory has distinct verbal or nonverbal components. Measures of nonverbal short-term memory are typically loaded on spatial processing abilities in addition to simple visual short-term memory. The purpose of the VPT is to measure visual short-term memory parsed from spatial short-term memory.

The task consists of a stimulus grid presented to the examinee for 3 seconds and then removed from view. The grids range in size from a 2 x 2 matrix to a 5 x 6 matrix. Patterns of squares within the grids are darkened, similar to a checkerboard. Patterns are designed so that one half of the total possible squares are darkened. The examinee's task is to darken squares on a blank white grid equal in size to that of the stimulus grid to match the design of the stimulus grid. For each level of complexity (i.e., size of the matrix) there are three patterns (i.e., items).

The VPT is a brief test. The manual reports that administration time is approximately 10 minutes. However, there are 42 possible items comprising 14 levels of complexity for each version. There is no time limit for responding, and examinees may correct responses, if they so desire. After the examinee finishes marking squares on the grid, the target pattern is uncovered. Therefore, the examinee is given feedback after each item. In three practice administrations with healthy adults conducted by the reviewer, administration times ranged from 18 to 32 minutes. Administration time may be longer for persons with a reflective response style, apraxia, or other motor impairment. Testing continues until the examinee fails to recall correctly any of the three patterns at any given level of complexity.

Scores are reported as "raw visual span" (i.e., the level of complexity of the largest grid to which examinee responded correctly for at least one of the three items). Scores are reported as raw scores and percentile ranks. Raw scores are adjusted for effects of age and number of years of formal education. A significant positive correlation ($r = .42$) between the VPT and number of years of formal education is reported. There is also a significant negative correlation ($r = -.55$) between the VPT and age. A table is included in the manual indicating by how many points the raw VPT score is to be adjusted.

DEVELOPMENT. Clinical psychologists frequently use tests such as the Corsi Blocks Test (Corsi, 1972) and the Visual Span subtest from the Wechsler Memory Scale (Wechsler, 1987) to assess nonverbal components of short-term memory. Based on several studies cited in the manual there is an important theoretical and clinical difference between spatial nonverbal short-term memory and visual nonverbal short-term memory. The VPT was designed so that the examinee is required to view and reproduce the appropriate design in the frontoparallel plane, which effectively removes the spatial component from the test. The result is a test of nonverbal short-term memory that exclusively assesses visual memory.

TECHNICAL.

Standardization. The two parallel forms of the VPT were normed independently. Version A was normed on 345 healthy British examinees. Version B was normed on 204 British examinees. Examinees' mean age was 41.95 years. The age distribution of the sample is skewed with 54% of the examinees being 35 years of age or younger. For Version A, the norm sample consists of 159 males and 186 females. Gender breakdown for Version B is not provided. No additional data on socioeconomic status, urban versus rural status, or ethnic group status are reported.

Reliability. The reliability of the VPT is reported as test-retest reliability and parallel forms reliability. Test-retest reliability was based on a sample of 50 healthy British examinees aged 20 to 81 years tested over two occasions. The test-retest reliability coefficient of Version A was found to be .75 and the test retest reliability coefficient of Version B was .73. Mean time between first and second testing was not reported. Parallel forms reliability estimates based on healthy examinees came from two studies. In Study 1, a sample of 194 healthy British examinees aged 13 to 92 years yielded a parallel forms reliability coefficient of .81. In Study 2, a sample of 76 healthy Italian examinees aged from 15 to 86 years yielded a parallel forms reliability .88. Also reported was a study using a clinical sample of 45 Italian brain-damaged patients aged 19 to 86 years, which resulted in parallel forms reliability estimates of .75. Detailed description of the examinees used for the reliability studies was not included. It is not clear whether the examinees in the reliability studies also were part of the norm sample.

Validity. The primary validity data presented consist of correlations with the Corsi Blocks Test (Corsi, 1972). Version A and B correlate with the Corsi Blocks Test .37 and .42, respectively. The authors' interpretation of the moderate correlation between the Corsi Blocks Tests and the VPT are that results support the conclusion that the VPT measures visual as opposed to spatial nonverbal short-term memory, because the Corsi Blocks

Test is purported to assess both visual and spatial short-term memory. Perhaps there is additional evidence supporting this conclusion. However, based on the research reported in the test manual evidence supporting the validity of the proposed interpretation of the VPT is not compelling. Two case studies and descriptions of manuscripts that are either in press or in preparation were also described, but not in sufficient detail to add support to the validity of the VPT.

There is a positive correlation of the VPT with years of education and negative correlation of the VPT with age. This supports the validity of the VPT as a sensitive measure of some aspect of memory functioning. In addition, statistically significant gender differences were found on the VPT. However, the authors dismissed this finding as too small for clinical relevance.

COMMENTARY. The VPT is a neuropsychological instrument with the barest description of psychometric properties presented in the manual. There are simply not enough data presented on reliability, validity, or norming procedures upon which to evaluate the technical quality. Although there is sufficient need for a measure of short-term visual memory in neuropsychological assessment, there is not enough background or supportive research reported to indicate that the VPT contributes to theoretical understanding or clinical decision making. The VPT appears to be a neuropsychological instrument, for which development is still in progress. At this point, the VPT should be used primarily on an experimental basis and in neuropsychological research.

SUMMARY. The VPT is a measure of short-term visual memory. Making the distinction between short-term spatial memory and short-term visual memory is an important theoretical and clinical neuropsychological contribution. However, the manual for the VPT does not contain sufficient information to assess the psychometric characteristics of this measure. Moreover, there is also inadequate information presented to determine if the VPT distinguishes between short-term spatial memory and short-term visual memory. This is an interesting and important research question. However, that question is not answered in the text of the VPT manual.

REVIEWER'S REFERENCES

Corsi, P. M. (1972). *Human memory and the medial temporal region of the brain.* Unpublished dissertation. McGill University, Montreal.
Wechsler, D. (1987). The Wechsler Memory Scale—Revised. San Antonio, TX: The Psychological Corporation.

[197]

Wechsler Intelligence Scale for Children—Fourth Edition Integrated.

Purpose: "Designed to assess the cognitive ability and problem-solving process of children."

Population: Ages 6-0 to 16-11.

Publication Dates: 1971–2004.

Acronym: WISC-IV Integrated.

Scores, 47: Verbal Comprehension Index (Similarities, Vocabulary, Comprehension, Information [supplemental], Word Reasoning [supplemental], Index), Perceptual Reasoning Index (Block Design, Picture Concepts, Matrix Reasoning, Picture Completion [supplemental], Index), Working Memory Index (Digit Span, Letter-Number Sequencing, Arithmetic [supplemental], Index), Processing Speed Index (Coding, Symbol Search, Cancellation [supplemental], Index), Full Scale IQ, Process Subtests (Similarities Multiple Choice, Vocabulary Multiple Choice, Picture Vocabulary Multiple Choice, Comprehension Multiple Choice, Information Multiple Choice, Block Design No Time Bonus, Block Design Multiple Choice, Block Design Multiple Choice No Time Bonus, Block Design Process Approach, Elithorn Mazes, Elithorn Mazes No Time Bonus, Digit Span Forward, Digit Span Backward, Visual Digit Span, Spatial Span Forward, Spatial Span Backward, Letter Span Nonrhyming, Letter Span Rhyming, Letter-Number Sequencing Process Approach, Arithmetic With Time Bonus, Arithmetic Process Approach-Part A, Arithmetic Process Approach-Part A With Time Bonus, Arithmetic Process Approach-Part B, Written Arithmetic, Cancellation Random, Cancellation Structured, Coding Copy).

Administration: Individual.

Price Data, 2007: $999 per complete basic kit including administration manual (2004, 487 pages), technical and interpretive manual (2004, 343 pages), WISC-IV stimulus book 1, WISC-IV Integrated stimulus books 2 and 3, block design set, 25 WISC-IV record forms, 10 WISC-IV Integrated record forms, 10 WISC-IV response book 1, 10 WISC-IV response book 2, 10 WISC-IV Integrated response book 3, Block Design Process Approach Grid Overlays, Visual Digit Span Item Card and Sleeve, Spatial Span Board, and scoring templates; $120 per integrated administration manual; $120 per technical and interpretive manual; $55 per 10 record forms; $37 per 10 response books; $475 per integrated writer; $79 per rolling case; $275 per integrated scoring assistant software.

Time: (65–80) minutes for the 10 core subtests; Additional time required for supplemental subtests; (3–23) minutes for Process subtests.

Comments: Combination of the Wechsler Intelligence Scale for Children—Fourth Edition (16:262) and the revised and renormed Wechsler Intelligence

Scale for Children—Third Edition as a Process Instrument; guidelines are provided for administering test to children who are deaf or hard of hearing.

Authors: David Wechsler, Edith Kaplan, Deborah Fein, Joel Kramer, Robin Morris, Dean Delis, and Arthur Maelender.

Publisher: The Psychological Corporation, A Harcourt Assessment Company.

Cross References: For reviews by Susan J. Maller and Bruce Thompson of the WISC-IV, see 16:262; see also T5:2862 (740 references); for reviews by Jeffrey P. Braden and Jonathan Sandoval of an earlier edition, see 12:412 (409 references); see also T4:2939 (911 references); for reviews by Morton Bortner, Douglas K. Detterman, and by Joseph C. Witt and Frank Gresham of an earlier edition, see 9:1351 (299 references); see also T3:2602 (645 references); for reviews by David Freides and Randolph H. Whitworth, and excerpted reviews by Carol Kehr Tittle and Joseph Petrosko, see 8:232 (548 references); see also T2:533 (230 references); for reviews by David Freides and R. T. Osborne of the original edition, see 7:431 (518 references); for a review by Alvin G. Burnstein, see 6:540 (155 references); for reviews by Elizabeth D. Fraser, Gerald R. Patterson, and Albert I. Rabin, see 5:416 (111 references); for reviews by James M. Anderson, Harold A. Delp, and Boyd R. McCandless, and an excerpted review by Laurance F. Shaffer, see 4:363 (22 references).

Review of the Wechsler Intelligence Scale for Children—Fourth Edition Integrated by RONALD A. MADLE, Licensed Psychologist, Mifflinburg, PA, and Adjunct Associate Professor of School Psychology, The Pennsylvania State University, University Park, PA:

DESCRIPTION. The Wechsler Intelligence Scale for Children—Fourth Edition Integrated (WISC-IV Integrated) is a measure of cognitive ability for children from 6 years and 0 months to 16 years and 11 months. As suggested by the name, it enhances the Wechsler Intelligence Scale for Children—Fourth Edition (WISC-IV; 16:262) by including standardized measures of test behavior, problem-solving style, and cognitive processes—many updated from the WISC-III as a Process Instrument (WISC-III PI).

WISC-IV users will find the instrument to be quite familiar. The heart of the WISC-IV Integrated uses the same 10 core and 5 supplemental subtests and it yields the same higher level scores: Full Scale IQ, Verbal Comprehension Index (VCI), Perceptual Reasoning Index (PRI), Working Memory Index (WMI), and Processing Speed Index (PSI). All composites use the traditional mean of 100, standard deviation of 15 metric. The WISC-IV Integrated, however, adds 16 process subtests, as well as qualitative and quantitative observations and error scores, to provide more measures of cognitive processes. (In this review, process subtests are distinguished from the core and supplemental [WISC-IV] subtests by an asterisk [*] preceding the name.)

The complete WISC-IV Integrated kit includes an Administration and Scoring Manual, a Technical and Interpretive Manual, three stimulus books, WISC-III and WISC-IV Integrated record forms, three response booklets, several scoring keys, 12 red and white blocks, a Spatial Span Board, Block Design Process Grid Overlays, and pencils. Owners of the WISC-IV can purchase an add-on kit to make it into a WISC-IV Integrated testing unit.

As a Level C test, substantial graduate training and supervision in assessment, as well as familiarity with the *Standards for Educational and Psychological Testing* (AERA, APA, & NCME, 1999), is required to administer, score, and interpret it. As with the WISC-IV, the easel-based Administration and Scoring Manual contains understandable instructions for administration and scoring.

Initial administration involves completing the 10 WISC-IV core subtests, an administration that takes about 65 to 80 minutes, to obtain the FSIQ and the four Index scores. Some or all of the supplemental subtests may then be administered in another 10 to 15 minutes. The crux of the WISC-IV Integrated is then giving some or all of the process subtests, often in a second session, to clarify responding and to test hypotheses. The process subtests take from 3 to 23 minutes each to administer; nearly 3 hours would be needed if all were administered. Detailed information about selecting process subtests for hypothesis testing is presented in the Technical and Interpretive Manual. As in the WISC-IV, supplemental subtests can be substituted for core subtests according to strict rules; process subtests, on the other hand, can never be substituted.

In addition to Similarities, Vocabulary, Comprehension, Information, and Word Reasoning subtests, the WISC-IV Integrated includes five Verbal domain process subtests: *Similarities Multiple Choice, *Vocabulary Multiple Choice, *Picture Vocabulary Multiple Choice, *Comprehension Multiple Choice, and *Information Multiple Choice. The Perceptual domain includes three more process subtests: *Block Design Multiple Choice, *Block Design Process Approach, and *Elithorn Mazes, in addition to the Block Design, Picture Concepts, Matrix Reasoning, and Picture Completion subtests. The Working Memory subtests (Digit Span, Letter-Number Sequencing, Arithmetic) are supported by *Visual Digit Span, *Spatial Span, *Letter Span, *Letter-Number Sequencing Process Approach, *Arithmetic Process Approach, and *Written Arithmetic. Finally, the Processing Speed subtests include *Coding Recall and *Coding Copy in addition to Coding, Symbol Search, and Cancellation.

Description of the process subtests would be too lengthy for this review. Their character can be seen in two adaptations of Block Design. *Block Design Multiple Choice is a multiple-choice version. The child looks at a picture of a constructed block design and selects the matching composition from four response options within a specified time limit. This format, of course, reduces demands on certain abilities, such as motor skills. Another variation can be seen in *Block Design Process Approach. As with Block Design, the child first constructs designs from red and white blocks. In a second part, however, incorrect items are readministered using grid overlays to assist the child in assembling the design. Similar adaptations are used in other subtests where additional aids, such as multiple-choice options, are used (e.g., *Multiple Choice Information) or modalities are changed or supplemented (e.g., *Visual Digit Span and *Spatial Span).

If all process subtests are administered there are a total of 26 process scores, as well as longest span and sequence scores on most Working Memory subtests, available for analysis and interpretation. Some analysis is normative and based on the process subtest scaled scores. For other parts, differences between two subtests are used to describe the child's intraindividual strengths and weaknesses. Some process scores are interpreted based on frequency of occurrence or base rate tables alone. At the most detailed level of analysis the process observation and error scores are interpreted.

DEVELOPMENT. The WISC-IV and WISC-IV Integrated shared a number of goals such as updating theoretical foundations, enhancing clinical utility, improving psychometric prop-

erties, increasing developmental appropriateness, and increasing user friendliness. Development of the WISC-IV Integrated, however, was offset to allow the WISC-IV process to guide the development of the WISC-IV Integrated. The WISC-IV Integrated development goals and process were grounded in prior efforts in developing the WISC-III PI, as well as the WAIS-R as a Neuropsychological Instrument. It is based on the process approach to assessing intelligence as recently promoted by Edith Kaplan (1988).

Early in the process a number of experts in clinical neuropsychology, psychological assessment, clinical psychology, and school psychology were consulted to develop a conceptual plan for the test. This process resulted in the retention and updating of 12 subtests from the WISC-III PI and the development of 4 more subtests to correspond to new WISC-IV core subtests. Of these subtests, 7 are adaptations of core and supplemental subtests and 6 are variations. Adaptations use original item content while variations consist of novel item content; both modify the mode of presentation or response mode. Three more subtests were developed to expand the construct coverage or provide other information relevant to the child's performance. Following this development effort the process included the traditional steps of piloting and standardization.

TECHNICAL. The Technical and Interpretive Manual consists of a number of parallel chapters. Chapters 1 through 5 cover the WISC-IV; chapters 6 to 10 are the WISC-IV Integrated versions of the same topics. Only Chapter 11—Interpretive Considerations—integrates the various subtests in a single combined chapter.

Standardization. The WISC-IV uses two overlapping standardization samples. The composition of both samples was based on the March 2000 U.S. Census distribution for race/ethnicity, parent education level, and geographic region. Both samples closely approximated the national sample on stratification variables. The WISC-IV section was standardized using the full 2,200 individuals with 200 per age group, equally split by gender. The WISC-IV Integrated portions, on the other hand, were based on a smaller sample of 730 individuals. Many of these individuals, but not all, were also included in the WISC-IV sample. The WISC-IV Integrated sample used 50 participants in the two youngest groups with 70 at each age thereafter, with an equal number of males and females in each group.

Reliability. WISC-IV reliability was based on the entire sample of 2,200 people, whereas the WISC-IV Integrated reliabilities used the 730 examinees. Internal consistency estimates using the split-half method with Spearman-Brown correction (test-retest reliability for speeded subtests [mean interval of 32 days]) was excellent for the FSIQ, with coefficients of .96 or .97 at every age. At the composite level the average coefficients across ages were quite good as well, ranging from .94 for the VCI to .88 for the PSI. Average reliability coefficients for the core and supplemental subtests across age groups ranged from .79 to .90. Coefficients for the 26 WISC-IV Integrated scaled process scores were similar (.67 to .91) to the core and supplemental subtests across age groups, although 9 of the scores had coefficients below .80. WISC-IV Integrated reliabilities were also computed using data from the several validity group studies. These coefficients averaged .66 to .96 across all groups, suggesting that the subtests are equally reliable in clinical and normative subjects.

Test-retest reliability information was estimated using a sample of 243 children across several age groups with a retesting interval of 32 days (range = 13 to 63 days). At the composite level, the index reliabilities ranged from .84 to .95, whereas the FSIQ coefficient was .91 or higher for each age group. Although the coefficients ranged from .63 (Arithmetic, ages 8–9) to .95 (Vocabulary, ages 14–16), most were in the .70s to .80s. Test-retest reliabilities were reported in the manual, however, for the majority of the process scores by age group.

Validity. The Technical and Interpretive Manual presents validity evidence for the WISC-IV and the WISC-IV Integrated in separate chapters. Validity evidence specific to the process subtests is more limited and, unfortunately, the reader is directed to the WISC-III PI Manual for additional validity evidence.

Both chapters cover evidence of validity based on research, theoretical literature, author and expert reviews, and response processes. A series of intercorrelation studies are then presented that show generally expected relationships (e.g., low to moderate correlations among subtests and higher correlations of subtests with the scales to which they are assigned) for all parts of the test. The process subtests showed lower systematic relation-ships, ostensibly because some share variance with other domains so they can shed additional light on component cognitive processes. For example, although Coding Recall was designed to provide supplemental information about the Processing Speed domain, it has a strong incidental memory component as well, resulting in additional correlation with the WMI.

Exploratory and confirmatory factor analyses are presented for the core and supplemental subtests (WISC-IV). The exploratory factor analyses showed expected loadings on the four WISC-IV domains, with confirmatory factor analyses demonstrating the four-factor model resulted in a better fit than other models using one through five factors. Process subtests were not included in the factor analyses.

The WISC-IV validity chapter also presents a number of studies investigating correlations with several Wechsler intelligence scales (WISC-III, WPPSI-III, WAIS-III, WASI). The WISC-IV Full Scale correlated .89 with the WISC-III Full Scale with an average decrease of 2.5 points, whereas the four-factor correlations ranged from .72 to .87. Very similar correlations were also found for the WPPSI-III, WAIS-III, and WASI. The remaining studies demonstrated lower but still substantial correlations with the WIAT-II, Children's Memory Scale, Gifted Rating Scale, and Adaptive Behavior Assessment System, Second Edition, and low correlations with the BarOn EQ, as would be expected. Finally, a number of studies covering various clinical groups (e.g., intellectual gifted, mentally retarded, learning disordered, and so forth) produced expected results.

Fifteen special group studies demonstrated expected normative levels across the WISC-IV Full Scale and Indices. For example, previously identified gifted children had high IQs (FSIQ = 123.5) whereas mentally retarded children showed lower than average scores (Mild FSIQ = 60.5 and Moderate FSIQ = 46.4). Other groups also showed results that are generally consistent with expected functioning. Thirteen of the 15 studies also included process subtests. For all subtests, specific patterns were detected by locating the process subtests that had the largest effect size differences for group means. As an example, children with Mixed Receptive-Expressive Language Disorders showed large effect sizes for process subtests in the Verbal and Working Memory domains. The majority of findings again were consistent with theoretical expectations and prior research.

Several of the special groups were also administered concurrent measures, notably the WIAT-II for children with reading or mathematics disorders and the Clinical Evaluation of Language Fundamentals, Fourth Edition (CELF-4) for language-disordered children. Reading-disordered children showed high correlations with Word Reading, Reading Comprehension, Pseudoword Decoding, and the Reading Composite, as well as depressed WMI scores that correlated moderately with Reading Comprehension. Similar patterns were observed with process subtests in the same domains. Children with mathematics disorders, contrary to predictions based on prior research, showed the strongest performance on the WMI. VCI and PSI showed the strongest correlations with the WIAT-II Mathematics Composite. In terms of process subtests, not surprisingly the highest correlations with the measures of math on the WIAT-II were with *Written Arithmetic. For language-disordered children it was found that the VCI score was the lowest and there were high correlations between the CELF-4 scores and the VCI and WMI Indices. Again, process scores in the same domains showed moderate to high correlations with the CELF-4 Core Language score.

The results of the validity studies, although providing initial evidence of validity, will need additional research to strengthen the empirical validity base of the WISC-IV Integrated at the process subtest level.

COMMENTARY AND SUMMARY. Due to the high degree of overlap, the WISC-IV Integrated shares many of the same strengths and weaknesses as the WISC-IV, such as updated theoretical foundations, updated norms, and so forth. The recent reviews by Maller (2005) and Thompson (2005) provide detailed information about the WISC-IV that is germane to the WISC-IV Integrated. Generally, however, this piece of the WISC-IV Integrated provides a well-designed measure of intellectual ability that will continue to be widely accepted in various fields of applied psychology.

How the unique aspects of the WISC-IV Integrated (i.e., the process subtests) will be viewed is likely to be highly dependent upon the potential user's beliefs about cognitive assessment. Those who favor a g-loaded, psychometric approach and eschew profile analysis will want to "just say no"

(McDermott, Fantuzzo, Glutting, Watkins, & Baggaley, 1992) to the WISC-IV Integrated, but this group clearly is not the target audience. For a more process-oriented examiner, however, the WISC-IV Integrated should provide a rich base of information for the generation and testing of various hypotheses about an individual child's cognitive functioning. For these practitioners the WISC-IV Integrated should provide a way of increasing the statistical precision of information often obtained by more informal "testing the limits." Though not based on an identical norm group, the WISC-IV Integrated should limit sources of error due to factors such as difference in the age of norms, different norm sampling plans, and so forth. There is every reason to expect that the WISC-IV Integrated will be well-accepted by many examiners who strive to tease out the cognitive factors that affect performance in academic and other settings. Even those who adhere to Cattell-Horn-Carroll theory should be able to apply the findings to that framework.

Even though the WISC-IV Integrated can improve the psychometric precision of a clinical approach, several problems still suggest the need for a cautious approach. For example, although some interpretation relies on normative scores, some also relies heavily on difference scores (e.g., Information versus Multiple-Choice Information) or comparisons that have lower reliabilities. The reliability and validity data for these scores in the manual are limited. In addition, there is minimal empirical information in the manual supporting the validity of the interpretations that may emerge from the various comparisons that can be made. Many interpretations still may be based more on clinical lore than on empirical findings (Kamphaus, 1998).

REVIEWER'S REFERENCES

American Educational Research Association, American Psychological Association, & National Council on Measurement in Education. (1999). *Standards for educational and psychological testing.* Washington, DC: Educational Research Association.
Kamphaus, R. W. (1998). Intelligence test interpretation: Acting in the absence of evidence. In A. Prifitera & D. H. Saklofske (Eds.), *WISC-III Clinical use and interpretation: Scientist-practitioner perspectives* (pp. 39–57). Academic Press.
Kaplan, E. (1988). A process approach to neuropsychological assessment. In T. Boll and B. K. Bryant (Eds.) Clinical neuropsychology and brain function: Research, measurement, and practice. The Master lecture series, Vol. 7 (pp. 127–167). Washington, DC: American Psychological Association.
Maller, S. J. (2005). [Review of the Wechsler Intelligence Scale for Children–Fourth Edition.] In R. A. Spies & B. S. Plake (Eds.), *The sixteenth mental measurements yearbook* (pp. 1093–1096). Lincoln, NE: Buros Institute of Mental Measurements.
McDermott, P. A., Fantuzzo, J. W., Glutting, J. J., Watkins, M. W., & Baggaley, A. R. (1992). Illusions of meaning in the ipsative assessment of children's ability. *Journal of Special Education, 25,* 504–526.
Thompson, B. (2005). [Review of the Wechsler Intelligence Scale for Children—Fourth Edition.] In R. A. Spies & B. S. Plake (Eds.), *The sixteenth mental measurements yearbook* (pp. 1096–1097). Lincoln, NE: Buros Institute of Mental Measurements.

Review of the Wechsler Intelligence Scale for Children—Fourth Edition Integrated by JOYCE MEIKAMP, Professor of Special Education, and CAROLYN H. SUPPA, Professor of Counseling, Marshall University Graduate College, South Charleston, WV:

DESCRIPTION. The Wechsler Intelligence Scale for Children—Fourth Edition Integrated (WISC-IV Integrated) is a merger of the Wechsler Intelligence Scale for Children–Fourth Edition (WISC–IV) and the revised and renormed Wechsler Intelligence Scale for Children-Third Edition Process Instrument (WISC–III PI). It is an individual assessment of both the intellectual and cognitive processes of children aged 6 years, 0 months to 16 years, 11 months. Thorough examinations of the WISC–IV are included in the previous edition of this publication; therefore, this review is focused on the additive components and applications of the WISC–IV Integrated.

In addition to the composite score and four index scores of the WISC-IV, the WISC-IV Integrated includes optional process scores from subtests theoretically based in the process-oriented approach to cognitive assessment. This approach considers a broader definition of intelligence, is contextualized to daily life and culture, and is less atomistic. Thus the process approach to intelligence testing evaluates substandard performances in relation to individual cognitive processes like test-taking behaviors and problem-solving strategies that may contribute to task performance. All or selected process subtests may be employed when a low scaled score is obtained on a corresponding subtest or when a child displays inconsistent or atypical performance. Results may be used to investigate low scores, detect cognitive strengths and weaknesses, set baselines for performance, monitor changes in cognitive functioning over time and determine recommendations for accommodation.

The WISC-IV Integrated is organized by four cognitive domains: Verbal, Perceptual, Working Memory, and Processing Speed. There is a corresponding Index score for each domain as well as a Full Scale IQ Score. Each domain comprises three types of subtests: core, supplemental, and optional—which are referred to as the process subtests. The core and supplemental subtests are taken from the WISC-IV. Core subtests are to be administered when deriving composite scores.

Should a core subtest be invalidated, a supplemental subtest may be substituted per instructions in the manual. The process subtests include revised WISC-III PI subtests, as well as new subtests designed to correspond to WISC-IV subtests, with the exception of one scale—Block Design Process Approach (BDPA)—which remains intact from the WISC-III PI. The process subtests may not be used as substitutes for core subtests as they are designed only for the provision of additional measures of cognitive abilities and hypotheses testing and are not included in the Index scores. The process subtests are not necessarily designed to measure the same construct as the core and supplemental subtests but are designed to give further explanation to a child's performance on certain subtests.

Seven process subtests are adaptations to the core and supplemental subtests (Similarities Multiple Choice, Vocabulary Multiple Choice, Picture Vocabulary Multiple Choice, Comprehension Multiple Choice, Information Multiple Choice, Arithmetic Process Approach, and Written Arithmetic). Each contains the same item content as its corresponding core or supplemental subtest but is modified in mode of presentation or response format. Six process subtests are variations of the core and supplemental subtests (Block Design Multiple Choice, Block Design Process Approach, Visual Digit Span, Spatial Span, Letter Span, and Letter-Numbering Sequencing Process Approach). These include novel item content and modifications to the mode of presentation or response format. Three process subtests are designed to expand the scope of construct coverage (Elithorn Mazes) or to provide information that may be related to the child's performance on other subtests (Coding Recall and Coding Copy).

The Verbal Domain includes three core subtests (Similarities, Vocabulary, and Comprehension) and two supplemental subtests (Information and Word Reasoning). There are five process subtests in the Verbal Domain (Similarities Multiple Choice, Vocabulary Multiple Choice, Picture Vocabulary Multiple Choice, Comprehension Multiple Choice, and Information Multiple Choice).

The Perceptual Domain is composed of three subtests (Block Design, Picture Concepts, and Matrix Reasoning) and one supplemental subtest (Picture Completion). The three Process subtests in this domain are Block Design Multiple Choice, Block Design Process Approach, and Elithorn Mazes.

Included in the Working Memory domain are two core subtests (Digit Span and Letter-Number Sequencing) and one supplemental subtest (Arithmetic). The six process subtests are Visual Digit Span, Spatial Span, Letter Span, Letter-Numbering Sequencing Process Approach, Arithmetic Process Approach, and Written Arithmetic.

In the Processing Speed domain are two core subtests (Coding and Symbol Search) and one supplemental subtest (Cancellation). The two process subtests include Coding Recall and Coding Copy.

Because typically only some of the process subtests are selected for an individual evaluation, no standard order has been established for the process subtests. The manual suggests that the process subtests from different domains be interspersed to emulate the order of the standardization sample, to maintain variety and interest and to decrease susceptibility to practice and interference effects. The Block Design Process Approach subtest should be administered last in the testing order to avoid order or practice effects.

Administration time for the core WISC-IV subtests is stated to be 65–80 minutes with 10–15 minutes expected for the completion of the supplemental subtests. Administration time for process subtests varies with the number of subtests administered and ranges from 3–23 minutes each. Tables displaying the required times for various percentages of the standardization samples are presented in the Administration and Scoring Manual. Also provided is a Technical and Interpretive Manual that presents detailed information. Both manuals are well-organized and user-friendly.

Special group studies to enhance clinical utility were included in the standardization of the WISC-IV Integrated. The 13 special group samples were limited in size but included children with: (a) Mental Retardation–Moderate Severity; (b) Reading Disorder; (c) Reading and Written Expression Disorder; (d) Mathematics Disorder; (e) Reading, Written Expression, and Mathematics Disorder; (f) Learning Disorder coexisting with Attention Deficit/Hyperactivity Disorder; (g) Attention Deficit/Hyperactivity Disorder; (h) Expressive Language Disorder; (i) Mixed Receptive-Expressive Language Disorder; (j) Open Head Injury; (k) Closed Head Injury; (l) Autistic Disorder; and (m) Asperger's Disorder.

Also to enhance clinical utility and to provide information on the links between cognitive processing and other relevant constructs between these special groups, children from some of the special groups studies were administered both the WISC-IV Integrated and another relevant instrument such as the Wechsler Individual Achievement Test—Second Edition (WIAT-II).

To increase developmental appropriateness, some instructions were simplified; teaching sample and/or practice items were added; and outdated items and artwork were revised or removed. Similar wording for instructions is used across all subtests and other administration procedures were simplified such as changing the layout of the stimulus book to reduce examiner reach and thus potentially reduce visual interference. Also, to increase user friendliness, verbal domain process subtest administration and scoring instructions appear in Stimulus Books 2 and 3.

The redesigned record form includes all elements of the WISC-IV as well as the WISC-IV Integrated process subtests and analysis. The last four pages of the form are detachable and are helpful when analyzing results without including test items or examinee's responses.

Age-corrected standard scores for the scaled and composite scores of the WISC-IV Integrated are provided. Tables reflecting the relations of scaled scores to standard deviations from the mean, percentile rank equivalents, confidence intervals of the composite scores, and test-age equivalents are provided in the manual to assist with interpretation. Detailed steps and suggested procedures for basic profile analysis also are provided and describe process-level discrepancy comparisons useful for refuting or confirming hypotheses based on the referral question and other information.

Administration and scoring requirements are the same as those for the WISC-IV with the exception of the need for additional instruction in the recording of process information. Due to the clinical judgment used in profile analysis, interpretation should be limited to practitioners who are experienced in the process approach and skilled in the integration of collateral information when answering the referral question. Suitability and fairness issues including guidelines for administration to children who are deaf or hard of hearing are provided in the manuals.

TECHNICAL. Because the WISC-IV Integrated process subtests are adaptations or variations of the WISC-IV subtests, the research for the WISC-IV Integrated was conducted in conjunction with the WISC-IV. Detailed information on the research programs for both scales is provided in the manuals and it was evident that appropriate standards were followed for the research stages.

Although all of the core and supplemental subtests are based on the WISC-IV standardization sample, all of the process scores (with the exception of the BDPA retained from the WISC-III PI) were derived from new data. The BDPA remains based in normative data from the WISC-III PI, which is reprinted in the WISC-IV Integrated manual. The sample was based in older census data. The differences in the data for this subtest should be considered because older norms may inflate scores.

A WISC-IV Integrated standardization edition was created and administered to a stratified sample of 730 children aged 6 years through 16 years and 11 months as well as to samples of children from the special groups. The standardization samples were representative of the March 2000 U.S. Bureau of Census data stratified according to age, sex, race/ethnicity, parent education level, and geographic region. Regardless of population demographics, some states still appear underrepresented with just one or two sampling sites. Asians and other races/ethnicity groups are not represented in the samples for many age groups, particularly in relation to geographic region and parent education level. The standardization sample for the special groups was 371. However, when this sample is assigned to the 13 groups, the group samples were small (Ns range from 14 to 45 per group) although they are reasonably representative of U.S. Census data. Detailed demographic and inclusion criteria are presented in the manual.

Evidence of reliability for the scaled process scores of the WISC-IV Integrated is similar to that provided for the WISC-IV. Most evidence of internal consistency was obtained using the split-half method with no description given for group division. Because Cancellation and Coding Copy are processing speed subtests, test-retest stability coefficients were used as the reliability estimate for the related process scores. For the overall standardization sample, average reliability coefficients range from .67 to .91.

Validity evidence for the WISC-IV Integrated builds on the extensive research supporting the WISC-IV and the WISC-III PI with additional literature reviews and expert input. Evidence of convergent and discriminate validity was based on two correlational studies performed on the WISC-IV Integrated normative sample—one to evaluate the relationships between the core and supplemental subtest scaled scores and the scaled process scores and one to evaluate the intercorrelations of the scaled process scores. These data support initial evidence of both convergent and discriminate validity.

Evidence of the relationships to WISC-IV Integrated test scores and related external variables was evaluated by administering other measures such as the WIAT-II to some of the special groups. However, additional research with more and varied samples is needed to increase clinical utility of the results.

COMMENTARY. The increased employment of the process-oriented approach to assessment is evidenced by the expanding range of process instruments and methods developed for the purpose of assessing cognitive processes according to a broader concept of intelligence and an expanded vision of learning. Although the theoretical basis for this approach supports enhanced clinical utility and applicability of cognitive assessment to case conceptualization, it is not without its critics who particularly desire increased reliability and validity evidence.

Because the process approach to standardized testing is a more recent development, further research is needed to provide information on the cognitive processes and test-taking behaviors that may contribute to test performance. However, the WISC-IV Integrated benefits from the psychometric and measurement methods of the WISC-IV as well as the research and resources of other Wechsler scales. It expands on the positives of the newer edition of the WISC by minimizing the emphasis on timed tasks and by decreasing potential speed confounding effects. However, it should be noted that many of these efforts are attempted through the use of multiple-choice questions that actually may complicate the cognitive performance of some children who might be conflicted by additional alternate responses. The manuals provide helpful guidelines for interpreting results and are straightforward regarding possible limitations of the approach. Good suggestions for further study also are provided.

When using a process approach for cognitive assessment, it is important to determine whether scores actually reflect a deficiency on a particular task or measurement error. Also, caution should be exercised when generalizing results from the special groups to other samples due to their limited standardization samples.

SUMMARY. If the WISC-IV Integrated is used in conjunction with other assessments and information, it provides a systematic observation of a child's unique problem-solving strategies and can assist the experienced clinician in determining an individual child's strengths and weaknesses, setting baselines for performance, monitoring changes over time and determining recommendations for accommodations. However, because assessment is not considered a single event, ongoing case consultation, outcome evaluation and assessment of developmental changes are crucial to effective long-term implementation of recommendations resulting from profile analysis.

[198]
The Wessex Head Injury Matrix.

Purpose: "Designed to assess and monitor recovery in patients after severe head injury."
Population: Ages 16 and over.
Publication Date: 2000.
Acronym: WHIM.
Scores: Not scored.
Administration: Individual.
Price Data, 2006: £69 per complete kit including manual and 25 scoring sheets; £71 per 50 scoring sheets.
Time: Untimed.
Authors: Agnes Shiel, Barbara A. Wilson, Lindsay McLellan, Sandra Horn, and Martin Watson.
Publisher: Harcourt Assessment [England].

Review of The Wessex Head Injury Matrix, by SANDRA D. HAYNES, Dean, School of Professional Studies, Metropolitan State College of Denver, Denver, CO:

DESCRIPTION. The Wessex Head Injury Matrix (WHIM) is a 62-item behavioral scale "designed to assess and monitor recovery in patients after severe head injury" (manual, p. 4) to help make meaningful predictions of recovery and to aid in treatment planning. Assessments can take place from the earliest stage of recovery on.

Any member of the medical treatment team dealing with patients with severe head injury can complete the scale by observing the patient's behavior although when learning to conduct observations, paired observations are suggested. Results of these observations are recorded as either observed, indicated by a check mark in the box next to the behavior description, or not observed, indicated with a cross mark in the box. Once 10 cross marks in a row are recorded, testing is discontinued for that observation session. Behaviors that are impossible to obtain for a specific patient should not be recorded (e.g., visual behaviors for a patient who is blind). There are enough boxes to record up to 15 observations of each behavior allowing for multiple observations over a period of time and by different observers. Each behavior is operationally defined on the test protocol to help with decision making and to ensure interrater reliability.

Although not formally delineated, the scale is divided into four sections. The first section comprises basic responses, some of which are reflexes. The other three comprise responses that are more purposeful in nature. The second section focuses on social interaction, the third on recovery of attention and cognitive organization, and the fourth, orientation and continuous memory and emergence from posttraumatic amnesia. The behaviors on the last three sections, for the most part, must be elicited. Some may be elicited by the presence of someone in the room or from internal cues such as hunger. Others require the test administrator to ask the patient questions or give commands. Some of the behavior indicators require props that are not or cannot be included in the testing materials. For example, props that are not included are a large bright object, bell or whistle or buzzer, playing cards, coins, a plastic toy, and pen and paper. In addition, patient-specific material must be obtained including objects that are meaningful to the patient, list of questions compiled by the patient's family, and a magazine that the patient would find interesting.

There is no scoring per se for the WHIM. Rather, a series of observations are analyzed to determine what the patient can do and how quickly the patient is recovering. Results are then summarized. Observed patterns of recovery are included in the manual's appendix for comparison.

DEVELOPMENT. The WHIM was constructed based on data from 88 patients with severe brain injury. The patients ranged in age from 14–67 and had experienced severe traumatic brain injury from a variety of causes. Data were collected via daily observation and recording of behaviors during recovery. Recovery behaviors were identified, ordered, and operationally defined. The 62 items were selected from an initial pool of 147 items after review and discussion by researchers and some retesting with the patients, although this part of test construction was not adequately covered in the manual.

TECHNICAL.

Standardization. No standardization group was identified outside of the 88 patients used for item construction.

Reliability. Estimates of reliability were obtained using a sample of 18 patients comparable in age to the original sample of 88. Interrater reliability and test-retest reliability were assessed. Percentage agreement and Kappa statistics were used for both analyses. Kappa statistics measure the proportion of rater's agreement to disagreement. Reported Kappa scores were .86 for interrater reliability and .74 for test-retest reliability. No scores were reported for percentage agreement but the values were judged to be acceptable by the authors.

Validity. Other than selecting behaviors for face validity, no measures of validity were addressed in the manual or other test materials.

COMMENTARY. The major strength of the WHIM is its focus on behaviors that can help clinicians develop individualized rehabilitation plans over an array of functions (e.g., social, cognitive) for persons with severe head injury. However, the efficacy of this claim needs further research. Administration and scoring are straightforward. Assessing recovery over time with a variety of observers is also a plus.

The manual is brief. Information on psychometric properties is limited. Additional supporting interpretive comments would make the test more useful in clinical situations, especially with regard to using the results to develop treatment plans.

SUMMARY. On the surface, the WHIM appears to be a good tool for measuring recovery in patients with severe head trauma. As stated in the manual (p. 4), "(a) it covers a wide range of real life skills, (b) it can be administered by observation, and its focus is on what the subject does or does not do... (c) it examines behaviours in the areas of motor ability, cognitive skills, and social interaction." More research into the efficacy of the instrument is needed.

Review of the Wessex Head Injury Matrix by H. DENNIS KADE, *Director, Developmental & Behavioral Health, Norfolk Department of Public Health, and Adjunct Assistant Professor, Old Dominion University, Norfolk, VA:*

DESCRIPTION. The Wessex Head Injury Matrix (WHIM) is a hierarchical 62-item behavioral measure of recovery after severe head injury. Motor, cognitive, and social functioning are included, but there are no formal subscales. Any multidisciplinary staff qualified to provide care for a patient in coma can administer and interpret the WHIM. The assessment is based on observations lasting from 5 minutes to several hours because it is acceptable to give credit for a behavior observed at any time during the day rather than just during a formal observation period.

The examiner completes the WHIM by simply checking which behaviors the patient can and cannot do. The highest behavior achieved is the preferred summary of the patient's performance and no cumulative scoring system is used. However, the total number of behaviors observed during one evaluation is noted because trends may reflect level of responsiveness after considering changes in context and duration of the assessment.

The purpose of the WHIM is to monitor progress and set treatment goals from the earliest stages of recovery from severe head injury. The developers emphasize its value for documenting small gains and evaluating behavior regardless of whether impairment has cognitive or physical origins. It is intended to fill the gap between the Glasgow Coma Scale (GCS) used initially and the point in time when a patient might be able to complete standardized ability tests. The rating form includes operational definitions of each behavioral item. Some readily available stimulus materials are not supplied with the test kit. Patient-specific materials such as a photograph and a magazine of interest and questions provided by the family need to be collected for each case. A minimum of 30 seconds is allowed for a response to a stimulus. Items are arranged hierarchically; administration is discontinued after failures on 10 consecutive items.

DEVELOPMENT. The WHIM was developed using patient observation and testing with everyday life tasks similar to the Portage Scale (Wilson, 1988). Daily observations were made from the end of sedation until hospital discharge concerning spontaneous behaviors, responses to naturally occurring stimuli, and responses to stimuli provided by the examiner. Stimuli were chosen that were easy to use and had face validity. The recovery process of 88 patients (73 males) aged 14 to 67 years (median of 26) with severe traumatic brain injury (TBI) causing 6 or more hours of coma was used to generate a hierarchy of operationally defined behaviors in the order in which they occurred. Beginning with reflexive behaviors these include basic purposeful behaviors, obeying commands, social communication, attention and cognitive organization, orientation, and continuous memory function. The initial behavioral observation was reduced to 147 items that were temporarily divided into 10 subscales. These were collapsed into a single main scale of 62 items. Further details on item development are not provided.

TECHNICAL. Motor vehicle accidents were the most common cause of injury in the patient sample on which the WHIM was standardized and 85 had some form of acceleration-deceleration trauma. The remaining 3 patients had "other" causes of brain injury. This sample matches the traditional population with severe traumatic brain injuries, but does not include blast-related cases prevalent in some populations such as recent war casualties who could produce a different behavioral hierarchy of recovery (Taber, Warden, & Hurley, 2006). Other demographic information such as ethnic or cultural background is not provided.

The only evidence of reliability provided by the developer was a 9-month study of 18 patients aged 16 to 65 years with the same inclusion criteria as the group on which the scale was developed. Percentage agreement is mentioned, but only Kappa statistics (where 1 represents perfect agreement and 0 indicates agreement at a chance level) are reported between two raters based on 2 to 46 assessments on each patient. An excellent mean interrater Kappa level of .86 is reported. A lower mean test-retest statistic of .74 is attributed to the desired sensitivity of the scale to changes between assessments. The time interval between these test-retest observations is not reported.

The developers recommend new users observe the patient in pairs and discuss their rating choices. No information is provided on the adequacy of this approach for producing reliable results among new test users.

Interpretation of results focuses on patient capabilities at a behavioral item level and on trends occuring across observations. The WHIM manual gives four examples of use with individual patients and trend data of five different recovery patterns. No formal validity studies subsequent to the development of the WHIM are reported.

COMMENTARY. The value of the WHIM as a measure of recovery from severe head injury lies in its hierarchical arrangement of many items that might allow a more detailed documentation of progress. However, its ability to predict progress is not yet documented by the developers. Equally important, conceptual clarification of differences between vegetative and minimally conscious states has been made subsequent to the publication of the WHIM (Giacino et al., 2002; Giacino & Kalmar, 2005). Other authors (Wilson, Graham, & Watson, 2005) have discussed the WHIM in this context, but formal validity studies need to address the ability of such coma recovery measures to make this distinction.

The reliability of the measure in use will depend on the examiner's ratings of patient behavior and this would be facilitated by the inclusion of training materials. Despite operational definitions, an element of examiner judgment is often present. For example, an examiner may need to determine whether the patient's vocalization represented an attempt to attract attention or was unrelated to the presence of others. The patients presented in the manual exemplify interpretation; no materials are provided that a new examiner could use to practice rating. Developers of observational measures such as the WHIM should consider including a DVD depicting behaviors that the new user could rate to determine personal interrater reliability with the developers.

SUMMARY. The WHIM certainly goes a step beyond the commonly used Glasgow Coma Scale (GCS) designed by Teasdale and Jennett (1974) for emergency room use and the Ranchos Los Amigos or Levels of Cognitive Functioning Assessment Scale (known as the LCFS/LOCF/ LOCFAS/Ranchos/ or RL/RLA) developed by Hagen, Malkmus, and Durham (1972) and used in many postacute settings. The WHIM shows potential with its detail and hierarchical organization, but needs further validation.

There are numerous other scales readers may wish to consider in measuring the changes associated with emergence from coma, but there are few published studies supporting their technical merits (Duff, 2001). The Disability Rating Scale (DRS) and its expansion, the Coma/Near Coma Scale (CNCS), allow tracking patients up to higher levels of functioning than the WHIM (Rappaport, 2005; Rappaport, Dougherty, & Kelting, 1992; Rappaport, Hall, Hopkins, Belleza, & Cope, 1982). The JFK Coma Recovery Scale has been revised to discriminate vegetative and minimally conscious states (Giacino, Kalmar, & Whyte, 2004).

REVIEWER'S REFERENCES

Duff, D. (2001). Review article: Altered states of consciousness, theories of recovery, and assessment following a severe traumatic brain injury. *Axone, 23,* 18-23.

Giacino, J. T., Ashwal, S., Childs, N., Cranford, R., Jennett, B., Katz, D. I., Kelly, J. P., Rosenberg, J. H., Whyte, J., Zafonte, R. D., & Zasler, N. D. (2002). The minimally conscious state: Definition and diagnostic criteria. *Neurology, 58,* 349-353.

Giacino, J. T., & Kalmar, K. (2005) Diagnostic and prognostic guidelines for the vegetative and minimally conscious states. *Neuropsychological Rehabilitation, 15*(3-4), 166-174.

Giacino, J. T., Kalmar, K., and Whyte, J. (2004). The JFK Coma Recovery Scale—Revised: Measurement characteristics and diagnostic utility. *Archives of Physical Medicine and Rehabilitation, 85,* 2020-2029.

Hagen, C., Malkmus, D., & Durham, P. (1972). Ranchos Los Amigos Levels of Cognitive Functioning Scale. Downey, CA: Communications Disorders Service, Ranchos Los Amigos Hospital.

Rappaport, M. (2005). The Disability Rating and Coma/Near-Coma scales in evaluating severe head injury. *Neuropsychological Rehabilitation, 15,* 442-453.

Rappaport, M., Dougherty, A. M., & Kelting, D. L. (1992). Evaluation of coma and vegetative states. *Archives of Physical Medicine and Rehabilitation, 73,* 628-634.

Rappaport, M., Hall, K. M., Hopkins, K., Belleza, T., & Cope, D. N. (1982). Disability rating scale for severe head injury: Coma to community. *Archives of Physical Medicine and Rehabilitation, 63,* 118-123.

Taber, K. H., Warden, D. L., & Hurley, R. A. (2006). Blast-related traumatic brain injury: what is known? *The Journal of Neuropsychiatry & Clinical Neurosciences, 18*(2), 141-145.

Teasdale, G., & Jennett, B. (1974). Assessment of coma and impaired consciousness: A practical scale. *Lancet, 2,* 81-84.

Wilson, B. A. (1988). Adapting 'Portage' for neurological patients. *International Rehabilitation Medicine, 7,* 6-8.

Wilson, C. F., Graham, L. E., & Watson, T. (2005). Vegetative and minimally conscious states: Serial assessment approaches in diagnosis and management. *Neuropsychological Rehabilitation, 15*(3-4), 431-441.

[199]

The WH Question Comprehension Test: Exploring the World of WH Question Comprehension for Students With an Autism Spectrum Disorder.

Purpose: Designed to indicate a student's competence in WH question form comprehension through appropriate match of question form and response.

Population: Ages 3 and up with cognitive impairments.

Publication Dates: 2002-2004.

Scores: 6 areas: Who, What, Where, When, Why, How.

Administration: Individual.

Price Data, 2006: $25 per combination test booklet/manual (2004, 175 pages).

Time: (20-30) minutes.

Comments: Test can be administered in multiple sessions if necessary.

Author: Beverly Vicker.

Publisher: Indiana Resource Center for Autism.

Review of The WH Question Comprehension Test: Exploring the World of WH Question Comprehension for Students with an Autism Spectrum Disorder by FRANCINE CONWAY, Assistant Professor of Psychology, Adelphi University, Garden City, NY:

DESCRIPTION. The WH Question Comprehension Test (WH) is a structured interview format test consisting of six WH categories with 10 items each. Test items are designed to provide screening information for interested parties regarding the range of a participant's comprehension of WH Question forms including Who, What, When, Where, Why, and How. All of the items are open ended and require participants to provide a response without any prompts. The test items are administered by the interviewer who then notes the interviewee's response. For each of the six categories, scores are generated on the degree to which the responses match the question form.

The WH is meant to be an informal screening assessment of the respondent's comprehension of WH form questions. Nonetheless, the author recommends that the examiner should be a licensed speech and language pathologist. However, if it is necessary to encourage cooperation of the examinee, an appropriate adult can participate in the test administration while being coached by the licensed professional.

Two forms of recording occur during and after the test administration. During the test, verbatim recording of the examinee's response to each of the WH categories can be noted on the test's response form. Each response is scored using a match system (+, +/-, -) or a score point system (0, -3) to indicate the extent to which the response matches the question form or is an indication of completeness of the responses, respectively. Once all the data have been collected, summary reports of the response to WH are generated. Summaries are organized to provide either a range of correct responses for each of the WH categories, error responses, or mismatches. Interpretation of the test's findings and observed behavior of the participant can be included in an optional section.

This section allows the examiner to offer commentaries on semantic information, pragmatic knowledge, expressive ability, syntax/morphology, and phonological use/perception. The final summary in the test is an optional report on "next steps," which includes intervention strategies (formal and informal) and plans to report the results of the test.

DEVELOPMENT. The WH item bank was developed by the generation of a list of questions presumably by the author, about common events and activities of the child. According to the author's report, "each question that was generated was controlled for complexity of grammar" (p. 9). The 120 items were piloted on three groups of participants representing: (a) typical development (ages 3–6), (b) specific language impairments 9 ages 4–7) and (c) mild to moderate cognitive impairments (ages 8–20). The final items were presented to a fourth group of individuals with Autism Spectrum Disorder (ages 4–12). Of the initial list of 120 questions, 60 items were selected. The item set resulting from the pilot contains six categories with 10 questions each that focus on a WH question form. The authors allude to the level of difficulty, relevance to the child's personal experience, and universality of the experience (p. 145) being the guiding factors in item selection. However, information about the selection and elimination process is noticeably absent. According to the author's own admission, the universality of children's experience is not a valid assumption and there is a lack of generalizability to other cultures.

TECHNICAL. The study was piloted on a small sample size of 93 individuals between 3–20 years of age; this small sample limits its generalizability. Furthermore, the study's pilot sample consisted of three main groups that were unevenly represented. For example, the number of participants in the Typical Development ($n = 54$), Specific Language Impairment ($n = 11$), and Cognitive Impairment ($n = 28$) groups is unbalanced and seldom overlap in terms of their ages. The Autistic group was not included in the pilot. Although these decisions, on the surface, seem unusual, the author's failure to provide a reasoned thoughtful explanation for these decisions in piloting the test items raises concerns. Furthermore, other than age, no demographic information, such as gender or ethnic composition, is available for the norming sample.

Item selection was not subjected to any statistical scrutiny. Descriptive statistics comparing the norming groups' performance of WH Questions were offered. However, these comparisons would be more meaningful if the analysis to determine significance of group differences was conducted. Furthermore, analyses that compared differences between the norming sample and impaired samples to the group of interest (i.e., Autistic group) would greatly improve our understanding of the between-group comparisons that the author presents.

Reliability and validity tests of the items were not done. Information on interrater reliability is critical to the design of the test where an examinee's open-ended responses are being determined as matches or mismatches with WH Question forms. Although the author does not provide information on whether data were collected by multiple raters, including this information in the developmental phase of the test would greatly enhance reliability of the test items.

COMMENTARY. The WH Question Comprehension Test compares favorably as a screening instrument in terms of ease of use. The test seems to have good face validity in that it clearly addresses WH question categories. The authors present this instrument as an informal screening of WH Questions, but its presentation contrasts with its administrative requirements and potential uses. That the author insists that the test should be administered by a licensed speech and language pathologist conveys the importance of the screening activity and the need for skilled abilities. Furthermore, the test allowance for intervention strategies (both formal and informal) speaks to the potential significance of this test.

In view of these professional parameters and significant test implications, the test lacks basic psychometric properties that would support its application. Unclear explanation of the procedures used in the test's development, as well as the absence of reliability and validity analyses are some of the major weaknesses of the WH. Moreover, the comparison groups used seemed convenient but of little relevance to the test construction goals.

An initial review of the items suggests it is appropriate to the test's goals. However, its applicability is complicated by the lack of clear guidelines pertaining to interpretation. For example, once the summaries of matches and error responses have been recorded, the user is left to guess how this information should be interpreted. Presumably, the summary responses are organized to provide the examiner with a sense of areas of strengths and weaknesses. However, this explanation is not explicitly stated and is left to the discretion of the examiner. In fact, very few conclusions can be drawn beyond the examinee's performance on individual test items. It is unclear how this information can be interpreted to obtain a gestalt of the examinee's comprehension of each WH category.

SUMMARY. The test developer can be credited with the insight and efforts that were made to promote the assessment of WH Questions to the verbal realm compared to previous tests that included visual stimuli. The strength of this study's development is the author's inclusion of some relevant research in the area of WH Questions. However, the test requires extensive standardization, reliability, and validity measures to establish its psychometric properties.

Review of The WH Question Comprehension Test: Exploring the World of WH Question Comprehension for Students with an Autism Spectrum Disorder by DOREEN W. FAIRBANK, Professor of Psychology, Meredith College, Raleigh, NC:

DESCRIPTION. Beverly Vicker, M.S., a Speech Language Consultant as part of the Indiana Resource Center for Autism, developed The WH Question Comprehension Test: Exploring the World of WH Question Comprehension for Students with an Autism Spectrum Disorder. The WH Question Comprehension Test is an interviewer-administered test for individuals with developmental delay, specific language impairment, and autism spectrum disorders that assesses an individual's ability to answer WH questions. WH questions include who, what, where, when, why, and how. The test is appropriate for individuals whose typical nonecholalic utterances average at least 2.0 morphemes or units of meaning. The age range is from 3 years old through adulthood. The test consists of 60 open-ended questions, divided into the six WH formats, and can be administered in 20 to 30 minutes by a licensed speech language pathologist. The WH Question Comprehension Test booklet includes the examiner's instructions, a reproducible set of the 60 open-ended questions divided into each of the six WH categories, the

corresponding response form, and intervention suggestions with reproducible materials. There are 10 questions for each of the WH formats (who, what, where, when, why, and how). The sections may be used in any order. The manual gives several suggestions for presentation order depending on the level and cooperativeness of the individual being tested. The examiner presents the questions orally to the individual. After the individual's response, another question from that section is given until all 10 questions are completed. The test can be given in one or several administrations and the manual discusses several types of adaptations and modifications that can be made in the test administration protocol. Scoring is based on a 3–0 scale: A correct answer is given a plus (+) or 3 points; a partially correct answer is given a plus-minus (+/-) or 2 points; a vague, emerging developmental answer is given a plus-minus (+/-) or 1 point (a value that is only available in the "How" subtest); and an incorrect value is given a minus (-) or 0 points. The examiner records the exact response on the record form and scores the response based on the correctness of the question/answer match. The accuracy of the answer can also be recorded but is optional to the examiner. The examiner rates incorrect answers on the type of error that occurred; for example, the answer could be an associative or repetitive response or the individual just answers with extraneous comments or with "I don't know." After the completion of the 60 questions, the examiner transfers the information to a five-part Summary of Responses form. The first section, Range of Correctness, separates the individual's answers into each of the WH sections and gives the total number of responses in each of the 3–0 scoring categories. The next section, Summary of Error Responses, gives the number of mismatch responses, of no responses, of associative comments, gestured responses, extraneous comment, or don't know responses for each of the six WH question types. The third section, Categorical Mismatch Summary, gives the number for each WH question that was substituted for a different type of WH question, for example, "When do you sleep?" and the response is "in a bed" (i.e., a when question that was mismatched for a where question). The fourth section, which is optional, is the Summary of Miscellaneous Observations, which includes the following sections: comprehension of semantic information, pragmatic knowledge such as repair strategies, ability to express thought/ideas, syntax/morphology use, phonological use/perception, and other information. The last section is Next Steps and is an optional section. The sections are information to be shared with, informal intervention strategies to consider, formal intervention strategies to consider, and the schedule reassessment date.

DEVELOPMENT. The WH Question Comprehension Test was published in 2002 and 2004 as part of the WH Question Comprehension Project of the Indiana Resource Center for Autism. It was developed as a result of observations through parent and teacher reports that many students on the autism spectrum, although verbal, had difficulty with WH questions. The test also could be used to examine the incorrect response to determine patterns, or so on. The pilot test contained a list of 120 questions and was administered during three stages. Stage I included 54 typically developing 3- to 6-year-olds. Stage II assessed 11 children aged 4–7 with specific language impairment. Stage III included 28 children with either mild cognitive impairment (8–11 years of age) or moderate cognitive impairment (8–20 years of age). The original 120 questions were reduced to the final edition of 60 questions before Stage IV was completed. This stage assessed 28 children within the autism spectrum disorder (aged 4–12 years). The manual gives generalizations and observations from the four developmental stages of the test. The results indicated that this test is a viable tool to use with a variety of individuals to screen for the first step in acquisition of WH question comprehension competency and also demonstrates the error response pattern for the autism spectrum disorder group.

TECHNICAL. The standardization of this test was based on the data (121 participants) obtained during the four stages of test development. The manual suggests that local norms should be developed to see how the individual being tested compares to the typical representatives of their community or school. Validity and reliability data are not given in the manual.

COMMENTARY. The WH Question Comprehension Test: Exploring the World of WH Question Comprehension for Students with an Autism Spectrum Disorder appears to be an adequate instrument for examining an individual's ability to answer WH questions. The manual also provides information and suggestions for developing lesson plans focusing on each type of WH question. Additional studies should be conducted to strengthen the standardization of this test.

SUMMARY. The WH Question Comprehension Test: Exploring the World of WH Question Comprehension for Students with an Autism Spectrum Disorder is an individually administered screening instrument intended for use with individuals with developmental delay, specific language impairment, and autism spectrum disorders, ages 3 years to adulthood. The instrument is administered by a licensed speech/language pathologist and consists of 60 open-ended WH questions. The test is self-contained and the examiner does not need to gather materials before administering the test. The manual describes the data collected during the test development but does not contain information regarding standardization, reliability, and validity. The instrument's results along with the suggested interventions provided in the manual may provide important information to a speech/language pathologist regarding the individual's ability to understand the linguistic skills of the WH questions and to enhance program development in this area.

[200]
Wiig Assessment of Basic Concepts.

Purpose: "Designed to evaluate a child's understanding and use of basic word opposites and related concepts."

Publication Date: 2004.

Acronym: WABC.

Scores, 10: Scores in 7 areas (Color/Shape, Size/Weight/Volume, Distance/Speed/Time, Quantity/Completeness, Location/Direction, Condition/Quality, Sensation/Emotion/Evaluation), Receptive raw score, Expressive raw score, Total raw score.

Administration: Individual.

Price Data, 2006: $179 per complete kit including Level 1 and Level 2 Storybooks, 50 Level 1 record forms, 50 Level 2 record forms, clipboard with calculator, Puppy Bank reinforcer with 30 Doggy Dog tokens, 75 WABC stickers, and tote bag; $29.96 per 50 Level 1—A Day at the Zoo record forms; $29.96 per 50 Level 2—A Day at the Park record forms; $4.95 per 75 WABC stickers; $14.95 per clipboard.

Time: (10–15) minutes.

Author: Elisabeth H. Wiig.

Publisher: Super Duper Publications.

a) LEVEL 1: A DAY AT THE ZOO.
Population: Ages 2-6 to 5-11 years.
b) LEVEL 2: A DAY AT THE PARK.
Population: Ages 5-0 to 7-11 years.

Review of the Wiig Assessment of Basic Concepts by CAROL M. McGREGOR, Content Development Specialist, The Learning House, Louisville, KY:

DESCRIPTION. The Wiig Assessment of Basic Concepts (WABC) is a norm-referenced assessment tool designed to determine the use and understanding of word opposites and related concepts required in communication and instruction of young children. The test provides standard scores, percentile ranks, and age equivalents. It is attractively packaged in a colorful carrying case and the materials within are large, bright, age-appropriate pictures that invite child responses in an interactive format. There are two levels of the test presented in story book format: Level 1, A Day at the Zoo (2 years, 6 months to 5 years, 11 months) and Level 2, A Day at the Park (5 years, 0 months to 7 years, 11 months). Level 1 contains 30 items and Level 2 contains 32 items. The last page of the record form provides an analysis of items by category. The test is untimed but should take 10–15 minutes to administer. The test was designed for use by speech-language pathologists, childhood educators, and teachers who are trained in assessment and treatment of language disorders, understand basic concept development, and are familiar with test administration and scoring. Although it is stated that under supervision, other childhood educators can administer this test, scoring and interpretation should be provided by those well trained in the use of tests.

The kit contains the two story texts, different colored forms for Levels 1 and 2, a colorful clipboard with calculator on which to keep the record form, a metal bank of tokens and some stickers for motivating reluctant youngsters, and the examiner's manual.

The items in both levels are grouped into seven semantic categories: Color/Shape, Weight/Volume, Distance/Speed/Time, Quantity/Completeness, Location/Direction, Condition/Quality, and Sensation/Emotion/Evaluation.

DEVELOPMENT. The design process for the WABC is to use pairs of words chosen from the first 3,000 words acquired by children based on frequency of use found in literature and clinical experiences. Word pairs share opposite meanings but represent common concepts (location, time).

Responses are given first by pointing (considered a receptive response) and then by naming (considered an expressive response). Wiig believes that having both of these types of responses is important to determining level of understanding. She assumes that being able to perform both of these responses demonstrates understanding. Over 200 licensed and practicing preschool teachers from quadrants of the U.S. responded to a survey indicating the importance of the word pairs in early childhood education for children ages 3 to 5. Word pairs for the final version of the WABC were influenced by these teachers' input. The WABC's purpose is to be a developmental and educational assessment tool rather than a diagnostic tool for determining eligibility for special education services. Wiig states that quantitative and qualitative results from this assessment tool are seen as providing educators and speech-language pathologists with a means to compare a child's understanding of basic word concepts to normal peers in order to determine need for further support, assessment, or intervention.

TECHNICAL. The WABC was pilot tested using 60 children with normal language development and 12 children considered to have language disorders. Items for the standardization test were added or deleted based on item analysis and examiner input from the pilot study.

The standardization version of the WABC contained 36 items for Level 1 and 37 items for Level 2. Twelve hundred children were selected for the standardization sample by age, gender, race, socioeconomic status, and language spoken at home to approximate the U.S. Census 2000 data. The author states that English was purposely oversampled as the test was not intended to be a bilingual test.

Validity. Face validity was determined by engaging the 200+ preschool teachers to judge the importance and relevance of the items to be used. Final item selection was affected by their judgments.

Concurrent validity was established by comparing results of the WABC with the Boehm Test of Basic Concepts—3 Preschool (Boehm, 2001) and Boehm Test of Basic Concepts (Boehm, 2000). The Pearson's *r* and Spearman's *rho* were used for all pairwise raw scores, Spearman's *rho* for pairwise percentile rank scores. Results for Level 1 and Level 2 indicated significant correlation ($p = < .01$) between the Boehm-3 Preschool and Boehm Test raw scores and the WABC Level 1 raw scores.

The lowest correlation (.56) was between Boehm raw scores and WABC Expressive scores, which was not unexpected because the Boehm is designed as a receptive measure.

Predictive validity was proven by calculating percentage measures of Levels 1 and 2 of the WABC based on Specificity, Sensitivity, and Total Correctly Identified. On both Levels 1 and 2, clinical and normal groups were age and sex matched. Levels of Specificity, Sensitivity, and Total Correctly Identified were calculated at Standard Score (SS) 85 (-1 *SD* below the mean) and at SS 77 (-1.5 *SD* below the mean). For both levels, the measures of Specificity, Sensitivity, and Total Accuracy were higher (between 96% and 100%) when a SS of 85 was used, a more liberal cutoff criterion. At the SS of 77 cutoff, Specificity and Total Accuracy remained high (between 93%–100%) whereas Sensitivity decreased to 86% and 88%, respectively, although that remains in the high range.

Internal consistency. Internal consistency was determined using coefficient alpha. For Level 1, Receptive alphas ranged from .72 to .85 and Expressive alphas ranged from .82 to .87. Total Items alphas ranged from .87 to .91. For Level 2, Receptive alphas ranged from .59 to .82; Expressive alphas ranged from .82 to .87; and Total Item alphas ranged from .83 to .91. The test author suggests that level of acquisition of basic concepts should be based on total test score.

Reliability. Using test-retest, reliability was established at .89 (Receptive), .90 (Expressive), and .93 for Total test on Level 1 indicating a high level of reliability. For Level 2, reliability was established at .78 (Receptive), .89 (Expressive), and .92 for Total test indicating a moderate to high level of reliability. The intervals for these correlational studies ranged from 14 to 30 days.

Interrater reliability was established using speech-language pathologists. Correlation coefficients of .99 and 1.00 between pairs of examiners indicated high consistency of results when using trained examiners.

COMMENTARY. Dr. Wiig's considerable knowledge and experience in the area of language development and language disorders gives credence to her facility for understanding how to provide an appropriate measure of young children's understanding of basic concepts. Along with having an assessment tool that has been properly sampled and proven appropriate, the WABC is also designed to be interesting and enticing to children. From the colorful carrying case, all materials are bright and designed to motivate children to want to get involved. Regarding usability, record forms and directions are simple and easy to understand, and norm tables are clear and easy to use. The test is practical and provides useful information to both teachers and speech-language pathologists for appropriate educational program planning.

There is a question as to the inclusion of children from homes where Spanish is spoken. Because the test was not meant to be given to individuals who are English-language learners, this information seems superfluous. The other concern is the low number of children included in the sample population for ages 2 years, 6 months to 2 years, 11 months. Confidence in results at this age group would be higher if the sample was larger and similar to the numbers included in the other age groups.

SUMMARY. The Wiig Assessment of Basic Concepts is a two-level, 62-item, norm-referenced developmental tool designed to assess young children's ability to understand basic language concepts from ages 2 years, 6 months to 7 years, 11 months. It is designed for speech-language pathologists and early childhood educators for the purpose of determining any language concerns that would indicate the need for special instructional design. Early childhood educators may administer the test but only those trained in testing and who have skills in language development should interpret results. Validity and reliability are adequate. Materials are attractive to young children and easy for examiners to use. An advantage that this test has over some others is that it is designed to assess both the receptive and expressive skills of young children.

REVIEWER'S REFERENCES

Boehm, A. (2000). Boehm-3: Boehm Test of Basic Concepts (3rd ed.). San Antonio, TX: The Psychological Corporation.
Boehm, A. (2001). Boehm-3 Preschool: Boehm Test of Basic Concepts (3rd ed.). San Antonio, TX: The Psychological Corporation.

Review of the Wiig Assessment of Basic Concepts by THOMAS McKNIGHT, Psychologist, Private Practice, Spokane, WA:

DESCRIPTION. According to the test author, this instrument is "an innovative norm-referenced assessment designed to evaluate a child's understanding and use of basic word opposites and related concepts" (examiner's manual, p. 1). The instrument allows children to demonstrate their knowledge of concepts by pointing to objects, animals, or persons (receptive) and naming the locations, basic attributes, and features of the items (expressive). The material is presented in storybook form and the drawings are well done and colorful. The instrument consists of two levels. Level 1 is appropriate for children 2 years, 6 months through 5 years, 11 months; Level 2 is appropriate for children 5 years, 0 months to 7 years, 11 months, and the overlap serves good purpose. Raw scores are converted to standard scores and percentile rank. Raw scores are also converted to age-equivalent scores for those institutions that still require such values but the manual contains no cautions regarding use of age-equivalent scores.

The Wiig Assessment of Basic Concepts (WABC) is clearly designed for individual assessment. Although the author noted the format might "tempt examiners to use the storybooks and test stimuli for teaching" (examiner's manual, p. 7), there is specific notation that such use might invalidate future use of the instrument and "should not be done" (examiner's manual, p. 7). Time to use the instrument is unclear and likely impacted by the child's age, attention span, motivation, and the skill of the examiner.

DEVELOPMENT. Initial design of the instrument included identifying a list of related word pairs or groups of words, from a list of the "first three thousand words acquired by children based on frequency of occurrence" (examiner's manual, p. 35) but there is no citation in the manual documenting these "first three thousand words." A large group of preschool teachers were then asked to rate word concepts in order of importance. However, a number of concepts, never reviewed by these teachers, were included in the final version of the instrument. Pilot study of the WABC used 60 children. The manual reports that the standardization sample included 1,200 children representing geographical areas, mother's educational level, race, gender, SES status, and language spoken in home.

TECHNICAL ASPECTS. Although, as noted above, the reported standardization sample was 1,200 children, there is indication that the total number of children was 1,144, based on the mother's educational level. The manual indicates that the standardization sample "on which norms are based" (p. 43) included more than 1,400 children, 729 for Level 1 and 763 for Level 2. Although the author noted the sample "closely approximates the U.S. Census 2000 Data, in a number of ways" (manual, p. 37), close inspection of various tables found a number of areas where the approximation was somewhat marginal. Except for the age range of 2 years, 0 months to 2 years, 11 months, the sample size for each age is adequate.

Face validity of the instrument is good, likely reflecting the input from preschool teachers in the pilot study. Concurrent validity, using the Boehm-3 with Level 1 ($n = 31$), might be considered modest with Pearson's r ranging from .56 to .75 for raw scores. There is some improvement, using 25 children, between Level 2 and the Boehm-3, with Pearson's r ranging from .70 to .74 for raw scores. Spearman's rho is equally unimpressive. Predictive validity, using 32 controls and 32 children in a language disorder group, was excellent when -1.0 SD was used as the cutoff point and, as expected, less impressive when -1.5 SD was used.

Test-retest reliability was established, using 58 children with Level 1 and 62 children with Level 2; the retest interval ranged from 14–30 days. For Level 1, correlations were .89 and .90 for Receptive and Expressive raw scores, respectively. For Level 2, correlations were .78 and .89 for Receptive and Expressive raw scores, respectively. Correlations for total scores were somewhat higher, for both groups. Interrater reliability was calculated using three speech-language pathologists (SLPs), all of whom listed the responses of 66 children. Correlations between pairs of the SLPs indicated correlations near 1.00 (.99 or 1.00). The authors rightly concluded that this represented high agreement among well-trained examiners.

COMMENTARY. Concurrent validity, between the WABC and the Boehm-3, is rather modest and additional study is needed. Initial studies indicate predictive validity is high and interrater reliability is excellent. Test-retest reliability is adequate. The overlap of Levels 1 and 2 is an excellent idea, allowing for collection of better information about children who are close to the cutoff ages for each level.

SUMMARY. The WABC appears to be a useful instrument, when assessing the knowledge of basic concepts of preschool children and somewhat older children with possible developmental delay. The skillful drawings and bright colors will appeal to the children for whom the instrument was designed. Preschool teachers, school psychologists, and speech pathologists will find it useful. Additional validity and reliability studies, using larger numbers of children, are needed.

[201]
Woodcock-Johnson III® Diagnostic Reading Battery.

Purpose: "Measures important dimensions of phonological awareness, phonics knowledge, reading achievement, and related oral language abilities."
Population: Ages 2–80+.
Publication Date: 2004.
Acronym: WJ III DRB.
Scores, 8: Basic Reading Skills, Reading Comprehension, Phonics Knowledge, Phonemic Awareness, Oral Language Comprehension, Brief Reading, Broad Reading, Total Reading.
Subtests, 10: Letter-Word Identification, Passage Comprehension, Word Attack, Reading Vocabulary, Reading Fluency, Spelling of Sounds, Sound Awareness, Sound Blending, Oral Vocabulary, Oral Comprehension.
Administration: Individual.
Price Data, 2007: $397.25 per complete kit with carrying case including test book, audio CD package, comprehensive manual (197 pages), software package, and 25 test records and subject response booklets; $61.25 per 25 test records and subject response booklets; $67 per comprehensive manual; $146 per scoring and reporting program (Windows/Mac).
Time: (60) minutes.
Comments: Composed of 8 tests from the WJ III Tests of Achievement and 2 tests from the WJ III Tests of Cognitive Abilities (see Woodcock-Johnson III; 15:281); includes software for scoring and printing reports.
Authors: Fredrick A. Schrank, Nancy Mather, and Richard W. Woodcock.
Publisher: Riverside Publishing.

Review of the Woodcock-Johnson III® Diagnostic Reading Battery by CONNIE ENGLAND, Associate Professor/Department Chair, Grad Counseling & Guidance, Lincoln Memorial University, Knoxville, TN:

DESCRIPTION. The Woodcock-Johnson III Diagnostic Reading Battery (WJ III DRB) is composed of selected tests from the Woodcock-Johnson III (WJ III; Woodcock, McGrew, & Mather, 2001a). With the exception of Test 8 (Sound Blending) and Test 9 (Oral Vocabulary derived from the WJ III Test of Cognitive Abilities; WJ III COG; Woodcock, McGrew, & Mather, 2001c), most of the tests for the current WJ III DRB come from the standard and extended batteries of Form B of the WJ III Tests of Achievement (WJ III ACH; Woodcock, McGrew, & Mather, 2001b).

The WJ III DRB is a set of 10 individually administered tests designed to measure specific aspects of the reading process: phonological awareness, phonics knowledge, reading achievement, and related oral language abilities. The WJ III DRB also includes two tests of oral language ability: Oral Vocabulary and Oral Comprehension.

Unique to the WJ III DRB are the intra-reading and intra-battery discrepancy procedures. These procedures are used to examine a participant's relative strengths and weaknesses among four areas of reading: Basic Reading Skills, Reading Comprehension, Phonics Knowledge, and Reading Fluency (treated as a cluster in the intra-reading discrepancy procedure.) In this procedure each standard score (SS) is compared with a predicted score that is based on the average of the other four tests (or five tests, in the case of Reading Fluency). In the intra-battery discrepancy procedure the examiner gains insight into the examinee's strengths and weaknesses related to six broad areas of reading-related abilities. To employ this analysis all 10 tests must be administered. Analysis of cluster discrepancy is similar to the intra-reading discrepancy procedure.

The components of the WJ III DRB are: test book, comprehensive manual, test record, subject response booklet, audio recording, and scoring and reporting program. The scoring and reporting program generates a score report, summary and table of scores report, parent report, age/grade profile, standard score/percentile rank profile, and classroom report. (A more in-depth discussion of the comprehensive nature of the scoring and interpretation aspect of this is provided in the Technical section of this review.) The manual states that with appropriate training and supervision, classroom teachers or aides under the supervision of a qualified and experienced examiner could administer some or all of the tests. The manual warns, however, that diagnostic decision making is recommended only for trained educational examiners.

DEVELOPMENT. The battery contains 10 tests. Eight are from Form B of the standard and extended versions of the WJ III Tests of Achievement: Letter-Word Identification, Passage Comprehension, Word Attack, Reading Vocabulary, Reading Fluency, Spelling of Sounds, and Sound Awareness. Two are from the WJ III Tests of Cognitive Abilities: Sound Blending and Oral Vocabulary. Extensive information relevant to the content of the WJ III DRB is available in the detailed descriptions of each area test, which lends support to their inclusion in this measure. The manual's underlying rationale for the design of the various tests and clusters was to select tests that measure different aspects of reading achievement or reading–related ability.

The WJ III DRB manual provides a table illustrating (a) the tests that are included in the various interpretive clusters and (b) discrepancy procedures for each test. Information included in the intra-reading discrepancy procedure provides a pattern of skill development that can be used to "substantiate the 'unexpectedness' of a [reading] difficulty by comparing and contrasting a subject's performance in one area with the average of his or her performance in the other areas included in the procedure" (comprehensive manual, p. 14). Intra-battery procedures present a comparison of the predicted score that is based on the average of the other eight tests (or nine in the case of Reading Fluency).

TECHNICAL. "Normative data for the WJ III DRB are the same date gathered from 8,818 subjects in more than 100 geographically diverse U.S. communities during the standardization of the Woodcock-Johnson III (Woodcock, McGrew, & Mather, 2001a)" (comprehensive manual, p. 89). A three-stage sampling procedure was selected to approximate the distribution of the U.S. population. According to the authors it would be impractical to reach this goal through random sampling. Details of the three-stage sampling procedure are available in the WJ III technical manual (McGrew & Woodcock, 2001).

A unique characteristic of the WJ III DRB is the use of a continuous-year procedure of testing that provides norms based on data gathered throughout the school year. Grade and age equivalents, percentile ranks, and standard scores are thus based on the distribution of scores at each examinee's exact chronological age and grade placements. For example, "WJ III DRB percentile ranks and standard scores are based on the distance a subject's score is from the median value for the reference group at any tenth of a year for grades K.0 to 18.0, at any month for ages 4-0 to 90" (comprehensive manual, p. 95).

According to the manual, reliability characteristics (i.e., standard error of measurement, internal consistency, and test-retest) meet or exceed the basic standards for both individual placement and programming decisions. Because tests included in the WJ III DRB's reliability estimates are a reflection of previously reported data submitted by the larger tests from which it was extrapolated, the WJ III Tests of Achievement and WJ III Tests of Cognitive Abilities, adequate reliability for the WJ III DRB is assumed with little further discussion. For example, standard errors of measurement are listed for each test and cluster score at each age range. Internal consistency reliability coefficients and test-retest reliability range from $r = .58$ to $.99$ for all tests at all age levels. Median cluster reliabilities are between $r = .83$ to $.90$ or higher. For a more comprehensive look at reliability estimates the reader is referred to the *Fifteenth Mental Measurements Yearbook* reviews of the WJ III (Cizek, 2003; Sandoval, 2003).

Support for the content, concurrent, and construct validity of the WJ III DRB is presented in a variety of correlational studies. All 10 tests selected for inclusion in the WJ III DRB demonstrate moderate to high intercorrelations between the broad construct of language proficiency and reading abilities. The lowest correlations occurred at the younger ages and become progressively higher through the older ages. "This suggests that levels of oral language and reading become more similar in individuals as they progress through school and mature into adulthood" (comprehensive manual, p. 98). Research comparing the WJ III DRB with the reading clusters from the Wechsler Individual Achievement Test (WIAT) and the Kaufman Test of Educational Achievement (KTEA) revealed moderate to strong correlations and suggests that its clusters measure the same conceptual domains as do similar batteries of reading and related abilities. Furthermore, studies with the WJ III Tests of Cognitive Abilities (WJ III COG), Wechsler Intelligence Scale for Children—Third Edition (WISC-III), Differential Ability Scales (DAS), and Wechsler Preschool and Primary Scale of Intelligence—Revised (WPPSI-R) suggest strong correlations with measures of cognitive-academic-language proficiency (CALP). Additionally, the Brief Reading, Broad

Reading, Basic Reading, and Phonics Knowledge clusters of the WJ III DRB discriminated between students with and without learning disabilities.

A significant aspect of the WJ III DRB is the fact that one of the longest chapters in the manual, 23 pages, is devoted to Scores and Interpretation. The manual's wide range of interpretive information covers each test and cluster by providing a four-tiered hierarchy used in evaluating test performance data. Level 1 consists of behavioral observations during testing and error analysis of individual responses; both are intended to provide a description of the examinee's reaction to the test and to evaluate performance on finely defined skills at the item content level. This level presents qualitative information that can be used to support hypotheses regarding an examinee's reading ability and language proficiency. Level 2 describes the examinee's level of development with respect to the norm group and provides information regarding developmental strengths and weaknesses. Scores at this level include raw scores, test or cluster W scores, age equivalents, and grade equivalents. Level 3 gives criterion-referenced information on the examinee's proficiency on tasks of average difficulty to peers. Such scores as Test or Cluster W DIFF scores (the difference between an individual's ability and the ability of the average person at his or her age or grade), Relative Proficiency Index (RPI) scores (allows statements to be generated about a subject's predicted quality of performance on tasks similar to the ones tested), CALP (i.e., cognitive-academic language proficiency) level scores, and Instructional Zone provide developmental information on typical tasks that would be perceived by the examinee as "easy," or "very difficult." At this level "placement decisions based on a criterion of significantly good or poor proficiency" can be made as well as "prediction of performance with similar tasks" (comprehensive manual, p. 67). Level 4 presents information concerning the examinee's relative standing within the group. Rank order data to include Standard Scores (*T* and *z* scores) NCE, Discrepancy SD DIFF, and Percentile Ranks provide information on the examinee's relative positioning in the group as well as assists in placement decisions based on a criterion of significantly high or low standing.

COMMENTARY AND SUMMARY. The WJ III's examiner's manual states that, "the tests, clusters, factors, and scales of the WJ III provide more precise measures and a wider breadth of coverage of human cognitive abilities than are found in any other system of psychological and educational assessment" (McGrew & Woodcock, 2001, p. 2). To that end it is no surprise that the WJ III Tests of Achievement (R) have long acted as the benchmark for educators and clinicians in the assessment of overall achievement. With the development of this pared-down version of the WJ III, however, an additional expectation is that the WJ III DRB provides the next step toward designing interpretive assessment reports able to discern discrete changes in performance and assist in the development of appropriate interventions. Additional research demonstrating the utility of the WJ III DRB's extensive scoring methods in the planning and development of reading interventions would greatly enhance our knowledge of how best to evaluate response to treatment data and further clarify classification assessment based on RTI.

REVIEWER'S REFERENCES

Cizek, G. J. (2003). [Review of the Woodcock-Johnson III.] In B. S. Plake, J. C. Impara, & R. A. Spies (Eds.), *The fifteenth mental measurements yearbook* (pp. 1020–1024). Lincoln, NE: Buros Institute of Mental Measurements.
McGrew, K. S., & Woodcock, R. W. (2001). *Technical Manual: Woodcock-Johnson III.* Itasca, IL: Riverside Publishing.
Sandoval, J. (2003). [Review of the Woodcock-Johnson III.] In B. S. Plake, J. C. Impara, & R. A. Spies (Eds.), *The fifteenth mental measurements yearbook* (pp. 1024–1028). Lincoln, NE: Buros Institute of Mental Measurements.
Woodcock, R. W., McGrew, K. S., & Mather, N. (2001a). Woodcock-Johnson III. Itasca, IL: Riverside Publishing.
Woodcock, R. W., McGrew, K. S., & Mather, N. (2001b). Woodcock-Johnson III Tests of Achievement. Itasca, IL: Riverside Publishing.
Woodcock, R. W, McGrew, K. S., & Mather, N. (2001c). Woodcock-Johnson III Tests of Cognitive Abilities. Itasca, IL: Riverside Publishing.

Review of the Woodcock-Johnson III® Diagnostic Reading Battery by HOWARD MARGOLIS, Professor Emeritus of Literacy and Special Education, Queens College of the City University of New York, New York, NY, and Reading and Special Education Consultant, Voorhees, NJ, and ANTONIA D'ONOFRIO, Professor, Center for Education, School of Human Service Professions, Widener University, Chester, PA:

DESCRIPTION. The Woodcock-Johnson III Diagnostic Reading Battery (WJ III DRB) "is a comprehensive set of individually administered tests ... selected from the Woodcock-Johnson III" (comprehensive manual, p. 1). Its 10 norm-referenced tests measure both reading and reading-related abilities, such as oral vocabulary. Its norms are applicable to examinees age 2 to 90 years of age, though not all tests are applicable for preschool children. In addition to offering two discrepancy procedures (intra-reading and an intra-battery) that the WJ III does not, it also offers four new clusters: Brief Reading, Total Reading, Phonics Knowledge, and Oral Language Comprehension.

The WJ III DRB's 10 tests are, in recommended order of administration: Letter-Word Identification, Passage Comprehension, Word Attack, Reading Vocabulary, Reading Fluency, Spelling of Sounds, Sound Awareness, Sound Blending, Oral Vocabulary, and Oral Comprehension. However, it is not the tests themselves, but the eight clusters derived from the tests that "provide the primary basis for interpretation" (comprehensive manual, p. 12). The eight clusters are Basic Reading Skills, Brief Reading, Broad Reading, Oral Language Comprehension, Phonemic Awareness, Phonics Knowledge, Reading Comprehension, and Total Reading. The advantage of these clusters is that they "minimize the danger of generalizing from the score for a single, narrow ability to a broad, multifaceted ability. Cluster interpretation results in greater validity because more than one component of a broad ability comprises the score that serves as a basis for interpretation" (comprehensive manual, p. 12). Moreover, cluster scores are more reliable and more consistent than individual tests, allowing for greater confidence in decision making.

Clusters allow examiners simultaneously to gain both a broader and finer view of an examinee's reading and related abilities; this can help examiners better understand the examinee's reading abilities and avoid unnecessary testing. For example, the Reading Comprehension cluster is composed of the Passage Comprehension and Reading Vocabulary tests; the Oral Language Comprehension cluster is composed of the Oral Vocabulary and Oral Comprehension tests. The relationship between the two clusters is moderately high for school-age children (all coefficients in the mid .70s). If fifth graders score well-below average on the Reading Comprehension cluster, but well-above average on the Oral Language Comprehension cluster, their poor Reading Comprehension performance is probably not caused by oral language difficulties; their knowledge of vocabulary and syntax should allow them to understand reading materials as well as average-achieving fifth graders. Theoretically, their reading comprehension difficulties may be caused by word identification difficulties, which in turn may be caused by difficulties with phonics and phonemic awareness.

A quick review of their performance on the clusters related to word identification—Basic Reading Skills and Phonics Knowledge—should provide initial answers; a poor performance on either suggests examining their component test scores and, in some cases, further assessment.

Examiners need not administer all the WJ III DRB's tests. Instead, examiners are encouraged to be "selective" (comprehensive manual, p. 20). For example, if a fourth grader has historically recognized words accurately and quickly, and does well on the Phonics Knowledge cluster, administering the Sound Awareness and Sound Blending tests (the Phonemic Awareness cluster) makes little sense as a high Phonics Knowledge score suggests mastery of Phonemic Awareness, its prerequisite cluster. Theoretically, if this fourth grader scored well-above average on the Letter-Word Identification test, it may be unnecessary to administer the Word Attack and Spelling of Sounds tests, which constitute the Phonics Knowledge cluster. Again, by history and test performance, this fourth grader has demonstrated the prerequisite knowledge and skills. Similarly, to use time effectively, examiners are encouraged not to administer all of a test's items, but to use suggested starting points based on the estimated ability of examinees.

The WJ III DRB has many purposes. The comprehensive manual describes several: research, psychometric training, guidance, screening, diagnosis, program planning, and progress monitoring. To achieve these, the WJ III DRB provides a variety of derived scores and profiles that the WJ III DRB's software (WJ III DRB Scoring and Reporting Program, included with each kit) can readily calculate and include in the software's interpretative reports. Compared to scores derived from other norm-referenced tests, these scores may be particularly helpful in monitoring progress as they are derived from "data gathered throughout the school year, as opposed to norms based on data gathered at, perhaps, two points in the school year and then presented as fall and spring norms" (comprehensive manual, p. 5). Although the WJ III DRB aims to serve many purposes, one appears primary—to identify specific reading difficulties and their causes. Thus the battery's name: Diagnostic Reading Battery.

Administering the WJ III DRB does not require graduate training in reading. Aides and teachers can administer it as long as they are properly trained and supervised by "appropriately certified or licensed" examiners (comprehensive manual, p. 107). To this end, the comprehensive manual provides a chapter dedicated to training examiners. Interpretation, however, requires far more expertise, expertise that is typically characterized by "an applicable graduate-level program of study that includes, at a minimum, a practicum-type course covering administration and interpretation of norm-referenced tests of reading achievement" (comprehensive manual, p. 107).

TECHNICAL. Standardization of the WJ III DRB was based on the stratified random selection of 8,818 participants from 100 "geographically diverse U.S. communities" (comprehensive manual, p. 89). This wide sampling allowed (a) indexing scores to representative comparison groups and (b) generalizing to a broader population of potential examinees. Participants were further selected within age/grade classifications: preschool (ages 2–5 years), kindergarten through 12th grade; college/university students; and adult subjects (20–80+ years). Stratification variables were also differentiated for census region, community size, sex, race, Hispanic origin, and parents' level of education. A subject weighting procedure was employed to better ensure that the statistical norms were representative of the national population. Subject weights were computed for all levels of each of the stratification variables (e.g., census region), making the percentage of participants in each strata proportional to population percentages for equivalent groups. Subject weights were then used to compute test norms, thereby correcting for the overrepresentation of any group.

Norms. Means, standard deviations, and numerous derived scores (e.g., grade equivalents, age equivalents, percentile ranks, standard scores) are reported for each test and test cluster. Test clusters were created by combining tests of similar underlying competencies (comprehensive manual, p. 98); this grouping, the authors postulate, allows for generalization to a more representative pool of reading competencies. For example, Letter-Word Identification and Word-Attack were combined to create the Basic Reading Skills cluster; Oral Vocabulary and Oral Comprehension were combined to create the Oral Language Comprehension cluster.

The WJ III DRB also uses continuous-year norms obtained by testing throughout a year instead of one or two times during the year. According-ing to the comprehensive manual, continuous-year norms effectively eliminate errors of measurement introduced by contextual variables arising from discrete test administration.

Reliability. As the value of a coefficient assessing test-retest reliability drops, the percentage of error variance in test scores conversely rises, indicating that a test is less stable. Lower internal consistency reliability coefficients similarly indicate reduced consistency among the items and scales on a test. Salvia, Ysseldyke, and Bolt (2007) posit that when making important decisions about individual children, "the minimum standard should be .90" (p. 141).

The comprehensive manual reports that for age groups 4 to 7 years, 8 to 10, 11 to 13, and 14 to 17, only 1 of 24 test-retest reliability coefficients for test administered a year apart equaled or exceeded .90; 13 of 24 fell between .59 and .79. Thus, most of the WJ III DRB tests showed only moderate reliability. For clusters, the 1-year test-retest picture was far better: For different age groups, 6 of 12 test-retest reliability coefficients equaled or exceeded .90; 6 of the 12 fell in the .80s. Most likely, this pattern of greater reliability for clusters is influenced by the greater number of items in clusters.

In addition to reporting test-retest reliability coefficients for individual age groups, the manual reports test-retest reliability coefficients for a group composed of all the examinees from the individual age groups. When interpreting the reliability coefficients for this group, called "All Ages" (p. 97), examiners should consider the possibility that these coefficients were inflated; this may have been caused by the larger range of responses due to the wide age range. Reliability coefficients for All Ages may mask test instability for specific age groups, such as adolescents.

The internal consistency of 8 of the 10 WJ III DRB tests was assessed by calculating the split-half reliability for each test, and then applying the Spearman-Brown prophecy formula to correct for test length. For the Reading Fluency and Spelling of Sounds tests, Rasch procedures were used to estimate the unique values of the standard error of measurement (*sem*) for examinees' raw scores. The coefficients for tests were quite varied for preschool and school-age groups (ages 2 through 19 years), ranging from the mid .60s to the high .90s. For these groups, 73% of the coefficients assessing the internal consistency of clusters were .90 or higher; the remaining coefficients fell in the .80s. Consequently, examiners should be able to generalize information gained from clusters to similar tasks. Overall, these coefficients support the manual's position that "for most important decisions," examiners should emphasize the interpretation of clusters (p. 97).

Validity. The content validity of the WJ III DRB is arguably demonstrated both by strategies for item development and by the content validation procedures described in its comprehensive manual. Specifically, the manual claims that items are comprehensive in terms of content and item difficulty; their selection was based on expert opinion and item validation studies. For most items "an open-ended design" was used to "closely parallel the requirements of language performance in real-life" (p. 98).

The comprehensive manual describes four studies that investigated the WJ III DRB's criterion-related validity: its correlation with independent tests of similar or related content. When investigating statistical validity, some would posit that intertest correlations should be moderate, to establish that a statistical connection exists among tests of related content and skills, and to show that the tests are not redundant measures. To a large degree, the validity studies yielded moderate correlations.

One study found that for 52 children in Grades 1 through 8, five of the WJ III DRB clusters were moderately correlated with reading-related tests and clusters from the Kaufman Test of Educational Achievement (KTEA) and the Wechsler Individual Achievement Test (WIAT). A second study reported correlations between six of the WJ III DRB's clusters and clusters from the WJ III Tests of Cognitive Abilities and the Wechsler Intelligence Scale for Children—Third Edition (WISC-III), for children in Grades 3 through 5. Of the 162 coefficients, 82 (50.6%) ranged between .50 and .75. A third study tested subgroups of young children from a larger group (n = 202; mean age = 52.7 months; SD = 12.6) to assess the relationship between three WJ III DRB tests and measures of intelligence. The coefficients for WJ III General Intellectual Ability, one of the measures of intelligence, and Letter-Word Identification ranged from .59 to .62; for Word Attack, from .49 to .52; for Passage Comprehension, from

.25 to .27. For two of these three WJ III DRB tests, all coefficients were moderate.

Obviously, a great deal of astute, meticulous work went into developing the WJ III DRB's items and standardizing the battery. Its standardization is excellent. And its reliability is moderately stable for individual tests and more so for clusters. Unfortunately, the information supporting its validity is sparse and far less impressive—many more validity studies are needed. These studies should go beyond simply correlating the WJ III DRB with similar norm-referenced measures. Correlating two similar norm-referenced reading measures, or two norm-referenced measures that purportedly measure unrelated constructs, will likely yield expected results. More important would be (a) to compare the WJ III DRB's instructional levels to the ability of examinees to read different materials; (b) to see how WJ III DRB test or cluster scores relate to examinees' abilities to master different skills (e.g., sound blending); (c) to see if improved WJ III DRB scores generalize to improved reading of lengthier, more complex materials; and (d) to assess, in a controlled experiment with high internal validity, the effectiveness of using the WJ III DRB to design remedial interventions. Such information is critical for establishing the WJ III DRB's validity as a diagnostic battery.

COMMENTARY. The comprehensive manual, or examiner's manual, is well organized and clearly written. It provides a wealth of information about the WJ III DRB, including explicit instructions on how to administer it and interpret results. It also provides examiners with excellent, straightforward guidance on testing that can be particularly helpful to new examiners. For example, new examiners might well benefit from recommendations such as: "After the initial practice sessions, strive for a brisk testing pace. Inefficient testing procedures can be boring for a subject and can invite distraction and increase testing time" (comprehensive manual, p. 18). Importantly, the comprehensive manual provides considerable guidance on how to make accommodations for examinees with a wide range of difficulties that might influence test results, such as English Language Learners and children with physical impairments. Such guidance is critically important when testing children for special education eligibility and for diagnosing reading difficulties.

The WJ III DRB's materials—the comprehensive manual, the standard test book that examinees read from and respond to, and the standard test record—are very informative and well laid out, which makes administration relatively easy. Moreover, the standard test record provides both a Test Session Observation checklist for characterizing the examinee's general behavior and, for five tests, a Qualitative Observation checklist for best characterizing the examinee's behavior as it relates to each test's particular tasks. These checklists can make test observations more precise and relevant, which is often critical to validly interpreting quantitative data.

Eight of the WJ III DRB's 10 tests appear to measure what they are purported to measure in a straightforward manner. Two, however, Reading Fluency and Passage Comprehension, may cause examiners to make invalid conclusions.

According to the comprehensive manual, "Reading Fluency measures the person's ability to read simple sentences … quickly, decide whether the statement is true, and then circle Yes or No" (p. 11). This test differs from many other measures of reading fluency in that it is not limited to the number of words read correctly per minute. Nor does it assess expression (e.g., phrasing and intonation). Instead, it simultaneously measures the speed with which an examinee silently identifies words in context, reasons, and decides. Thus, an examinee who can identify words quickly, but who ponders and slowly decides on answers might resemble a slow reader, leading to recommendations for instructional strategies to increase the examinee's speed of word identification; here, the recommendation would be erroneous as the low fluency score was caused by slower-than-average speed in reasoning or in decision making (slow decision making is characteristic of extremely reflective youngsters or some youngsters who greatly fear making mistakes), not slow speed of word identification. This, however, should not be viewed as a flaw of the test, but of interpretation. Perhaps this problem could be prevented if the test was renamed.

The second half of the Passage Comprehension test, designed for examinees whose ability level is second grade or above, uses a modified cloze procedure to assess examinees' understanding of short passages. The procedure has examinees silently read a short passage and orally provide the missing word. The mean number of words in the passages on the first page of this test section is 3.67 words ($SD = 1.15$); the mean on the last page, presumably the most difficult, is 28.75 words ($SD = 5.74$). The modified cloze task differs greatly from common reading tasks, for example, answering questions about or summarizing much longer, much more complicated reading selections. Hence, using examinees' performances on this short, narrow, and relatively simple cloze task to predict how well they comprehend lengthier, more complicated reading materials may often be faulty, even when examinees' scores for Passage Comprehension and Reading Vocabulary are combined into scores for the Reading Comprehension cluster.

The WJ III DRB's authors argue that reading passages and answering questions is confounded by many variables (e.g., cognition, background knowledge, language processing); thus it is not a pure measure of comprehension. Although their point is well taken, their argument that their cloze procedure is a less contaminated, better measure of reading comprehension is not convincing. Like reading lengthy passages, cloze also involves variables related to cognition, background knowledge, and language processing. A counter argument can be made that if the authors are right, it is unlikely that performance on a narrow cloze task will reliably generalize to broader, longer, more complex reading tasks that purportedly represent the same construct plus additional challenges. In line with this hypothesis, Carlisle and Rice (2004) noted that cloze has two distinct limitations: (a) it correlates only moderately with multiple-choice comprehension questions; (b) it is "not ideal if one wants to assess understanding and recall of ideas and information in natural passages" (p. 535). Spear-Swerling (2004) concluded that "emphasizing a single format [like cloze] could be misleading …. Basing evaluations of reading comprehension on more than one format … seems preferable to reliance on a single format " (p. 142). Likewise, Rathvon (2004) noted that no one testing procedure is sufficient to provide a full understanding of comprehension: "Given the diversity of formats and psychometric characteristics, it is not surprising that research comparing norm-referenced reading comprehension tests has consistently found that different tests yield significantly different scores for the same set of examinees" (p. 164).

Given the limitations of cloze, if school personnel use WJ III DRB scores to identify students' instructional levels for reading comprehension, as the comprehensive manual suggests, they may be quite disappointed unless they limit instructional activities to modified cloze tasks of less than 30 words—an indefensible practice. In this sense, the Passage Comprehension test falls short of meeting the WJ III DRB's definition of content validity: "the extent to which the content of a test represents the domain it is designed to measure" (comprehensive manual, p. 97). Nevertheless, if viewed as a narrow, limited measure of reading comprehension, it can help examiners understand—if only partially—an examinee's current comprehension abilities.

As previously noted, the comprehensive manual is well organized and clearly written. Nevertheless, it has one weakness that those who interpret the battery need to consider: It fails to indicate prominently and definitively that generalizing from its tests and clusters to other tasks can be problematic. A careful, heedful reading of Chapter 5 of the manual indicates that interpretations of test results should not go far beyond the tasks themselves and that diagnosing reading problems should not depend entirely on the WJ III DRB: "With the WJ III DRB … grade and age scores reflect the actual level of task difficulty a student can perform and thus are useful for instructional planning" (p. 73). "The [Relative Proficiency Index or RPI predicts the] … quality of performance on tasks similar to the ones tested" (p. 74). "Finally, testing is just one part of the total assessment process. [Examiners need to] compare and integrate test results with information from many sources" (comprehensive manual, p. 87). It is unfortunate this guidance is not prominently and definitively displayed, as a single, integrated statement, in one or several places in the comprehensive manual and in the WJ III DRB's software-generated reports. Looking at the first statement above about grade and age scores, one is given only a minimal, opaque, easily overlooked hint that generalization is limited. It is not until one reads the sentence about RPIs on page 74—"The RPI allows statements to be generated about a subject's predicted quality of performance on tasks *similar* to the ones tested" [italics added]—and inferentially combines the two statements, that a picture of limited generalizability begins to emerge.

Notwithstanding the criticism that the WJ III DRB's report-generating software fails to warn examiners that the battery's tests and clusters have limited generalizability, all who use the battery should consider using its software—it can reduce calculation errors, save a great deal of time, and produce reports that help to identify the examinee's strengths and weaknesses. Its reports are well organized, well focused, concise, and meaningful. But like all automated reports, they can easily be used in a robotic, unreflective manner (which the first reviewer has often observed). Clearly, such usage is not the WJ III DRB's fault, but that of examiners who forget that any psychological or educational test is only a sample of descriptive behavior representing one moment in time and that no automated report can sufficiently convey a full understanding of an examinee's history, strengths, and needs, especially those of an examinee with complex reading problems. Viewing any test battery as a definitive measure of the constructs it attempts to measure gives the battery far more credit than it deserves. Thus, one solution is to add an addendum to the WJ III DRB's reports, an addendum that briefly, but prominently, discusses the limitations of the test results and, when reasonable, supplements them with both information from additional sources and validated conclusions.

SUMMARY. Despite the need for more validity studies, the WJ III DRB appears to be a fine test that can help qualified examiners (e.g., learning consultants, reading specialists) gain an overall understanding of examinees' reading abilities and identify their weaknesses, especially if examiners focus on clusters rather than individual tests. Like all tests, however, the WJ III DRB should not be used alone. It needs to be supplemented by other quality measures of reading ability, especially measures that more accurately reflect the reading demands placed on students (e.g., the need to comprehend and respond to lengthier, more complex reading materials). Such tests include the Qualitative Reading Inventory-4 (Leslie & Caldwell, 2006) and the Stieglitz Informal Reading Inventory (Stieglitz, 2002).

Together with tests that more closely approximate typical reading activities, a knowledgeable, informed examiner—who engages in diagnostic teaching, who observes the examinees in different instructional situations, who is familiar with the local reading curricula and the skills and orientations of the instructors, and who arranges to have the examinee's reading progress carefully monitored—should be able to use the WJ III DRB to gather the information needed to help many examinees improve their reading abilities. To accomplish this, the WJ III DRB can be an excellent tool for examiners, but it should not be used alone.

REVIEWERS' REFERENCES

Carlisle, J. F., & Rice, S. M. (2004). Assessment of Reading Comprehension. In C. A. Stone, E. R Silliman, B. J. Ehren, & K. Apel (Eds.), *Handbook of language and literacy: Development and disorders* (pp. 521-540). New York: Guilford.

Leslie, L., & Caldwell, J. (2006). Qualitative Reading Inventory–4. Boston: Allyn & Bacon.

Rathvon, N. (2004). *Early reading assessment: A practitioner's handbook.* New York: The Guilford Press.

Salvia, J., Ysseldyke, J. E., & Bolt, S. (2007). *Assessment in special education* (10th ed.). Boston: Houghton-Mifflin Company.

Spear-Swerling, L. (2004). Fourth graders' performance on a state-mandated assessment involving two different measures of reading comprehension. *Reading Psychology, 25,* 121-148.

Stieglitz, E. L. (2002). The Stieglitz Informal Reading Inventory: Assessing reading behaviors from emergent to advanced levels (3rd ed.). Boston: Allyn & Bacon.

[202]
Woodcock-Muñoz Language Survey—Revised.

Purpose: Designed "to provide a broad sampling of proficiency in oral language, language comprehension, reading and writing."

Population: Ages 2–90+.

Publication Dates: 1993–2005.

Acronym: WMLS-R.

Scores, 7: Picture Vocabulary, Verbal Analogies, Letter Word Identification, Dictation, Understanding Directions, Story Recall, Passage Comprehension.

Administration: Individual.

Forms, 3: English A, English B, Spanish.

Price Data, 2007: $323.50 per English complete kit including test book, 25 test records, dictation worksheet, manual (2005, 174 pages), audio compact disc, and a software and reporting program; $323.50 per Spanish complete kit including test book, 25 test records, dictation worksheet, manual (2005, 174 pages), audio compact disc, and a software and reporting program; $40.75 per 25 test records.

Foreign Language Editions: Also available in Spanish.

Time: (45–50) minutes.

Comments: There is a computer program for scoring and generating narrative reports for any combination of tests from the test.

Authors: R. W. Woodcock, A. F. Muñoz-Sandoval, M. L. Ruef, and C. G. Alvarado.

Publisher: Riverside Publishing.

Cross References: For reviews by Linda Crocker and Chi-Wen Kao of an earlier edition, see 13:364.

Review of the Woodcock–Muñoz Language Survey—Revised by JAMES DEAN BROWN, Professor of Second Language Studies, University of Hawai'i at Manoa, Honolulu, HI:

DESCRIPTION. The Woodcock-Muñoz Language Survey–Revised (WMLS-R) is an individually administered collection of tests that provide "a broad sampling of proficiency in oral language, language comprehension, reading, and writing" (comprehensive manual, p. 1) in two forms (A & B) for English and one form for Spanish (which was adapted from the English forms). The seven WMLS-R tests are Picture Vocabulary, Verbal Analogies, Letter-Word Identification, Dictation, Understanding Directions, Story Recall, and Passage Comprehension. Scores can also be generated for the following 11 "academic language clusters" (derived by combining items from various tests): Oral Language, Reading-Writing, Broad English/Spanish Ability, Listening, Oral Expression, Reading, Writing, Language Comprehension, Applied Language Proficiency, Oral Language–Total, and Broad English/Spanish Ability–Total.

The three test books (one for each form, packaged in sturdy four-ring binders) contain picture and word cards that serve as stimuli in testing the examinees. The test stimuli are on one side of each card and teacher's directions are on the other, so the teacher and examinee can sit across from each other. The test records for each form contain a cover page (with spaces for identifying, language exposure, language use, and test session information) and spaces for the teacher to record the examinee's responses on the seven WMLS-R tests. The dictation worksheets provide areas for recording identifying information as well as spaces for students to draw and write their answers for the Test 4 dictation. The comprehensive manual provides an overview of the WMLS-R; descriptions of the tests and academic language clusters; general administration and scoring procedures; specific administration and scoring directions; information about scoring and interpretations; development, standardization, equating, and technical characteristics; as well as examiner training guidelines and practice exercises. The audio compact disc provides CD-formatted audio for the Test 5 Understanding Directions and Test 6 Story Recall for all three forms. The Scoring and Reporting Program is a CD-ROM computer program that is only available for the Windows operating system. Easy to install, it allows teachers to create records for each student's biodata information, and the seven scores each for an English form and a Spanish form, the students' language exposure and use responses, and the teacher's test session observations. Individual reports can then easily be generated in "standard reports," age/grade profiles, standard score/percentile rank profiles, or parent reports. Reports can also be produced for various groups, test dates, teachers, or schools. All of these reports can be previewed or sent to a printer, file, or word processor.

All in all, the Scoring and Reporting Program is a useful database and score-reporting program. Although data entry is somewhat tedious and time-consuming, many benefits can be derived from having all this test information in a single database.

DEVELOPMENT. According to the manual, special attention was paid to creating items and test directions that "would be deemed appropriate in the skill areas tested and age range covered" (comprehensive manual, p. 73). A group of unspecified "professionals" from various parts of the U.S. reviewed and gave recommendations on the English items and test directions, and similar "professionals" from several parts of the Spanish-speaking world served the same purposes for the Spanish items and test directions.

The standardization samples for the two English forms (n = 8,818) and the Spanish form (n = 1,157) are described in terms of age, geographical location, community size, sex, race, Hispanic background, types of school, parents' level of education, and other variables.

TECHNICAL. The items for the WMLS-R "were Rasch calibrated" (comprehensive manual, p. 80). Very little information is given about exactly how the items were Rasch calibrated (i.e., what computer program/algorithm was used, which fit statistics were used, how misfitting persons and items were dealt with). However, considerably more information is provided about how Rasch analysis was used to equate the three forms.

Adequate descriptive and reliability statistics are given for each of the seven tests and separately for the 11 academic language clusters. These are given for all scores taken together and also broken down by age groups ranging from 2 to 80+. All possible intercorrelations of the tests and academic clusters are also given either in the text of the manual or in its appendices.

The median (across age groups) split-half reliabilities (adjusted) for the seven tests ranged from .76 to .97. The median (across age groups) reliabilities (using Mosier's procedures for weighted composites) for the 11 academic language clusters ranged from .88 to .98.

The validity of the WMLS-R is defended in a very clearly described test content coverage chart. Criterion-related validity is explored separately through four different studies: one for preschool students, another for school-age students, a third for university students, and a final one for bilingual students. A wide variety of descriptive statistics are presented in each of these studies along with correlation coefficients between WMLS-R test scores and academic cluster scores with various criterion measures including verbal, nonverbal, mathematics, total achievement, and IQ tests. This shotgun approach generally shows that the scores generated by the WMLS-R are moderately correlated with other verbal measures and less so with nonverbal measures.

The authors claim confidently that the WMLS-R can be used to measure language proficiency in English and/or Spanish, English/Spanish language dominance, change in English/Spanish language abilities, need for bilingual education or ESL services, readiness for English-only instruction, eligibility for gifted programs, results to assist in educational planning, proficiency and gain for program evaluation purposes, and English/Spanish language proficiency for research studies.

COMMENTARY. A number of potential concerns exist in the design of the WMLS-R. First, the test is administered on an individual basis. Administering all seven tests individually would take a great deal of time.

Second, the examiner training guidelines and practice exercises in the last chapter of the manual are very important. Indeed, given the complexity of administering and scoring the tests, these guidelines and the attendant training would most probably prove mandatory.

Third, entering the data into the Scoring and Reporting Program is somewhat tedious and time-consuming.

Fourth, in the Scoring and Reporting Program, it is not possible to import scores from or export to other spreadsheet, database, or statistical programs. Scores can be exported, but only to text (.txt) files. It would be helpful if they could be exported, at least to very common formats like Excel.

Fifth, in several places, although the authors say the items "were Rasch calibrated," no information is provided for exactly how that was done, and nothing is said about how misfitting items and persons were identified and dealt with.

Sixth, although the content validity arguments for the validity of the WMLS-R are reasonably convincing, the shotgun approach to examining the criterion-related validity of the WMLS-R does not ultimately prove very convincing, especially given the wide variety of purposes for which the authors claim the WMLS-R can be used.

SUMMARY. In deciding about adopting this test, teachers and administrators should keep in mind that the WMLS-R must be administered on an individual basis; the examiner training will probably be essential; there are many components to keep track of; entering data into the Scoring and Reporting Program is time-consuming even though a variety of useful reports can eventually be generated; importing or exporting from that program is only possible as text files; teachers will probably have to explain why all examinees are not taking all items; the authors do not explain how the tests "were Rasch calibrated" or how misfitting items and persons were dealt with; and, although the content validity arguments are fairly convincing, the shotgun criterion-related validity arguments are less so, especially given the wide variety of purposes for which the authors say the test can be used.

On a more positive note, the WMLS-R does provide "a broad sampling of proficiency in oral language, language comprehension, reading, and writing" (comprehensive manual, p. 1). Indeed, these tests measure many aspects of language use including a number of aspects of communicative and productive language use. Thus, teachers who have ESL or bilingual Spanish/English students of any age and have ample time to devote to the testing process may find these tests quite useful. In addition, because the WMLS-R is packaged in a very appealing way with sturdy binders, good artwork, and appealing CD packaging, it should prove interesting to the students and turn out to be quite durable.

Review of the Woodcock-Muñoz Language Survey—Revised by SALVADOR HECTOR OCHOA, Professor, University of Texas-Pan American, Edinburg, TX:

DESCRIPTION. The Woodcock-Muñoz Language Survey–Revised (WMLS-R) is substantially different from its predecessor, the Woodcock-Muñoz Language Survey (1993, 2001 renormed only), given that it has been expanded to seven subtests and includes new items and norms. The seven subtests of the WMLS-R English and Spanish forms include: Picture Vocabulary/Vocabulario Sobre Dibujos, Verbal Analogies/Analogias Verbales, Letter Word Identification/Identificacion de Letras y Palabras, Dictation/Dictado, Understanding Directions/Comprension de Indicaciones, Story Recall/Rememoracion de Cuentos, and Passage Comprehension/Comprension de Textos. These seven subtests are combined in different ways to yield the following 11 cluster scores: Oral Language, Reading-Writing, Broad English Ability, Listening, Oral Expression, Reading, Writing, Language Comprehension, Applied Language Proficiency, Oral Language–Total, and Broad English Ability–Total.

The WMLS-R can be used in several different ways. The test manual outlines the following nine purposes in which the test can be used: (a) "determining English and/or Spanish language proficiency"; (b) "determining oral language dominance of bilingual (English and Spanish) subjects"; (c) "monitoring growth or change in English and/or Spanish language ability"; (d) "determining eligibility for bilingual education/ ESL services"; (e) "assessing readiness of English language learners for English-only instruction"; (f) "determining eligibility for accelerated or gifted and talented programs"; (g) "assisting in educational planning"; (h) "evaluating program effectiveness"; and (i) "describing subjects' language characteristics in research studies" (comprehensive manual, pp. 5-7).

The manual provides sufficient and easy-to-understand information on how to administer this test. The examiner is not required to administer all seven subtests. If all seven subtests are given, the manual states that it will take between 35 and 45 minutes to give a particular version of the WMLS-R. One particularly notable feature included is that the test manual provides additional helpful test administration guidelines for children with the following special needs: attentional and behavioral difficulties, hearing impairments, visual impairments, and physical impairments.

A strength of the WMLS-R is that it provides various types of scores. The WMLS-R yields the following norm-referenced scores: age and grade equivalent scores, standard scores (mean of 100 and standard deviation of 15), and percentiles. The WMLS-R also provides a relative proficiency index (RPI) score. The RPI score "predicts a person's percentage of success on a [given] . . . task that the reference group (subjects of the same age or grade) would perform with 90% success" (comprehensive manual, p. 60). Thus, if a child were to earn an RPI of 40, this score would indicate that he or she would be predicted to achieve only 40% mastery on the tasks where his or her peers would achieve 90% mastery. Moreover, each language version of the WMLS-R yields a cognitive academic language proficiency (CALP) score. A student's CALP score ranges from 1 to 6 to indicate the following six levels of language proficiency: negligible, very limited, limited, fluent, advanced, and very advanced. The examiner can also obtain qualitative information about the child's language by completing the language use questionnaire on the front cover of the protocol. This questionnaire seeks information about the extent that the child's utilizes English and Spanish. A parent form is also available in English and Spanish.

DEVELOPMENT. The WMLS-R is based on the Cummins (1984) theoretical work of language proficiency, which states that there are two types of language proficiency: basic interpersonal communication skills (BICS) and cognitive academic language proficiency (CALP). CALP is the type of language proficiency that children need to be successful in academic settings.

The manual fails to provide specific information regarding how test items were developed and selected for the English version of the WMLS-R. The manual states that professionals throughout the United States reviewed items and provided their recommendations for inclusion. The manual, however, fails to specify how many "professionals" and to describe their specific qualifications. Additionally, no information regarding the criteria used by professionals for item selection was provided.

With respect to the Spanish version of the WMLS-R, the manual states that professionals from "several regions of the Spanish-speaking world as well as Spanish fluent professionals in the United States" (p. 73) were consulted to examine test items. The manual, however, does not indicate the number of professionals who provided consultation on item selection and their specific qualifications. The WMLS-R test manual does specify that the tests of the Spanish version of the WMLS-R "are adaptations of the parallel tests in English" (p. 77). In particular, each item included on the Spanish version was "scaled to their empirical difficulty in English" (p. 77). This scaling was performed utilizing the Rasch model. The manual does not provide specific data to demonstrate that the Spanish version was equally calibrated to the English version.

TECHNICAL.

English version. The same sample used to norm the Woodcock-Johnson–III Tests of Cognitive Ability (Woodcock, McGrew, & Mather, 2001b) and Woodcock Johnson–III Tests of Achievement (Woodcock, McGrew, & Mather, 2001a) was used for the English version. Thus, although this test was published in 2005, the norming procedures were conducted from 1996 to 1999. The standardization sample for the English version comprised 8,818 individuals with a sufficient number of individuals at each age level/ group. The sample was selected on the basis of 10 stratifying factors that included: geographical region, "community size," gender, race, Hispanic status, "type of elementary school," "type of college/university," "education of adults," "occupational status of adults," and "occupation of adults in the labor force" (comprehensive manual, pp. 74-75). The sample appears to be reflective of the United States population.

The manual provides substantial information about the internal consistency reliability of the English version. The manual reported reliability coefficients at each age from 2 to 19 years (when appropriate), for seven 10-year intervals (20–29 to 70–79), and for 80 and above. The median internal consistency reliability coefficients across all age groups for the seven subtests varied from .76 for the Story Recall subtest to .97 for the Letter Word Identification subtest. The median internal consistency reliability coefficients across age groups for the 11 cluster scores ranged from .88 for the Oral Language and Language Comprehension clusters to .98 for the Broad English Ability total cluster. All internal consistency reliability coefficients for the 11 cluster scores are reasonable. No test-retest reliability data were provided.

The test manual provides information regarding the content, concurrent, and construct validity of the English version. With respect to content validity, the manual provides a blueprint of the topic area to be covered by each subtest as well as the stimuli (auditory or visual) and the response mode that is required of the examinee. Three concurrent validity studies were conducted on the following three age groups: preschool, school age, and college level. With respect to the preschool study, the WMLS-R Oral Language-Total cluster score correlated .67 with the Differential Ability Scales (DAS) Verbal Ability score and .69 with the Wechsler Preschool and Primary Scale of Intelligence—Revised (WPPSI-R) Verbal IQ. With a school-age cohort, the WMLS-R Broad English Ability Cluster score correlated .80 with the Wechsler Intelligence Scale for Children–III Verbal IQ. With respect to the college sample, the WMLS-R Broad English Ability Cluster score correlated .81 with the Wechsler Adult Intelligence Scale– III (WAIS-III) Verbal IQ and .60 with the Oral and Written Language Scales (OWLS). Moreover, the WMLS-R Reading-Writing Cluster score correlated .90 with the Wide Range Achievement Test–Third Edition (WRAT-III) Reading score and .81 with the WRAT-III Spelling score. This reviewer considers all of these validity coefficients to be in the acceptable range. Construct validity was demonstrated by growth curves for each subtest that clearly revealed age progression. The test authors state that the CALP should correlate with school academic success because it "is an important prerequisite for school success" (comprehensive manual, p. 92). Correlations between the WMLS-R Broad English Ability–Total cluster and the WJ-III Total Achievement score were .83, .91, .89, .89, and .88 for Grades 1, 2, 3–4, 5–7 and 8–12, respectively. Again, this reviewer believes that the validity coefficients are all in the acceptable range. No factor-analytic studies were reported to support the 11 cluster scores on the English version.

Spanish version. The sample used to equate the Spanish version with the English version of the WMLS-R consisted of 1,157 individuals. Only 85 members (7%) of the sample were from three states in the United States. The remainder of the sample was obtained from the following countries: Mexico, Argentina, Panama, Costa Rica, Colombia, and Puerto Rico.

The manual failed to provide information regarding the socioeconomic status, gender, educational attainment, age, type of schooling attended, and geographical location (urban/rural) of this sample. The manual provides no information regarding the reliability and validity of the revised Spanish version of the WMLS-R. Instead, the manual provides data from the earlier WMLS comprehensive manual. The authors state: "Because the results and implications are still informative, the study is described here" (comprehensive manual, p. 85). Reporting psychometric data from an earlier version and stating that it is still informative for this revised Spanish version is not acceptable because the revised version is composed of new items and new subtests have been added.

COMMENTARY.

English version. This test has strengths that merit discussion. The major strength of this test is its solid psychometric properties. The norming sample is reflective of the United States population. There is sufficient evidence provided to demonstrate the internal consistency reliability, content validity, concurrent validity, and construct validity of this measure. Moreover, the WMLS-R was developed with an appropriate theoretical framework regarding second language acquisition. This measure yields qualitative, norm-referenced, and CALP scores, which can be very helpful to educators. Additional research regarding the factor structure and the test-retest reliability of this version are needed.

Spanish version. This version of the test has serious limitations because the manual does not provide sufficient information regarding psychometric properties, calibration data, or demographic information regarding the calibration sample. Additional research is needed to establish the reliability and validity of the Spanish version.

SUMMARY. The test authors should be commended for developing a test that is based on a theoretical framework of second language acquisition that is considered to be appropriate and relevant by experts in this discipline. The English version of this test is appropriate to use. Given that the Spanish version has been calibrated to the English version of this test, this version is very promising. However, additional research regarding the psychometric properties of this version is needed before it can be recommended.

REVIEWER'S REFERENCES

Cummins, J. (1984). *Bilingualism and special education: Issues in assessment and pedagogy*. Austin, TX: PRO-Ed.

Woodcock, R. W., McGrew, K. S., & Mather, N. (2001a). Woodcock-Johnson III Tests of Achievement. Itasca, IL: Riverside Publishing.

Woodcock, R. W., McGrew, K. S., & Mather, N. (2001b). Woodcock-Johnson III Tests of Cognitive Abilities. Itasca, IL: Riverside Publishing.

[203]
The Word Test 2: Elementary.

Purpose: Designed to assess expressive vocabulary and semantics.

Population: Ages 6.0–11.11.

Publication Dates: 1981–2004.

Scores, 7: Associations, Synonyms, Semantic Absurdities, Antonyms, Definitions, Multiple Definitions, Total.

Administration: Individual.

Price Data: Available from publisher.

Time: (30) minutes.

Authors: Linda Bowers, Rosemary Huisingh, Carolyn LoGiudice, and Jane Orman.

Publisher: LinguiSystems, Inc.

Cross References: See T5:2911 (6 references) and T4:2983 (2 references); for reviews by Mavis Donahue and Nambury S. Raju of the original edition, see 9:1393.

Review of The Word Test 2: Elementary by DARRELL L. SABERS, Professor of Educational Psychology, and HUAPING SUN, Doctoral Student, University of Arizona, Tucson, AZ:

DESCRIPTION. The WORD Test 2: Elementary, A Test of Expressive Vocabulary and Semantics is a complete revision of The WORD Test and The WORD Test-Revised. This new test has six tasks—Associations, Synonyms, Semantic Absurdities, Antonyms, Definitions, and Flexible Word Use—each with 15 items. All items are scored zero or one, with Associations and Flexible Word Use requiring two correct responses to get an item score of one. There are no basal or ceiling rules, and thus it is expected that each student be given all 90 items. The test is designed for children of ages 6 through 11, and for some older children whose functional language abilities are within the performance range of the test.

The WORD Test 2: Elementary is packaged attractively with an easy-to-read manual and an easy-to-use record form for administration and scoring. The directions for administering are clear, with some varied optional prompts to help keep the children engaged. The test is administered to an individual child who responds verbally to spoken questions. Limited clinical judgment is needed for determining the scoring of some responses,

and thus the authors appropriately suggest that only professionals should administer the test. However, the fairness of the scoring criteria may be questioned. As a synonym for "repair," "fix" or "rebuild" or "mend" is correct; however, "fixes" or "rebuilds" or "mends" is incorrect (examiner's manual, p. 24). Nothing in the directions suggests to a 6-year-old child why the other responses would be scored zero. The administration and scoring of the test takes approximately 30 minutes, and it is allowable to give the examinee a break after completion of a task if required.

Scores available for students are percentile ranks and standard scores for 6-month age intervals, and also age equivalents. These three scores are provided for each task and for the total score when all six tasks have been administered. No interpretation of a total score based on a subset of the six tasks is provided. Because there is no description of the norming or standardization populations from which the samples of students were selected, these derived scores are not meaningful. The description of the standardization samples suggests that regions of the nation and range of socioeconomic status were ignored. No explanation is given for these omissions, and regular and special education participants were not differentiated in the sampling process.

In addition to the lack of information supporting the normative data, there is a serious problem with the ceiling effect of the test. There are not enough hard items to measure children aged 8 and older with good language skills. According to the manual, a perfect raw score of 15 on the Associations subtest corresponds to the 90th percentile for the 7 years, 6 months to 7 years, 11 months age group whereas the same raw score is equal to the 93rd percentile for the 8 years to 8 years, 5 months age group. It is absurd that the same raw score results in a higher percentile rank for an older age group, a result of the percentile ranks not being "smoothed" as Raju (1985) noted in a prior *Mental Measurements Yearbook* review of the original version of The WORD Test. Due to the truncated range of scores for older age groups, the standard errors of measurement (*SEMs*) for many subtests appear suspect. For instance, the *SEM* of the Associations subtest for the 11 years, 6 months to 11 years, 11 months age group is .90. A raw score of 14 on Associations for that age group is equivalent to the 47th percentile. However, one who earns 1 more point in the raw score is at the 71st percentile (highest percentile rank for the age group) whereas one who scores 1 point less in the raw score is at the 24th percentile. The ceiling effect plus the decision not to report standard scores for raw scores of zero for subtests creates a restriction of variability in reported scores; thus the standard deviations of the subtest scores at some ages are unknown. The description of the standard scores as having means of 100 and standard deviations of 15 for all ages and all tasks is not correct. We suggest calculating midinterval percentile ranks (Nitko, 2001, p. 400) and reporting standard scores for raw scores of zero on subtests to partially address the problem of restricted scoring range.

DEVELOPMENT. The six tasks are identical to those in the original version of The WORD Test, though the name of the sixth task, Multiple Definitions, has been changed to Flexible Word Use. All the items in the new test are dichotomously scored, whereas scores of 0, 1, and 2 were possible for each item of Associations in the original test. No rationale is provided for this change.

Overall, information about test development is insufficient in the manual. Evidence of content validity is missing. Other than the claim that the tasks and words come from school curricula for Grades 1 through 6, there is no evidence regarding how the collection of items was derived from the curricula. The item selection study might have helped test developers to collect possible responses and make scoring guidelines comprehensive. The same problems of the standardization and normative study also exist in the item selection study. Namely, there is no mention of how parts of the country and participants of different socioeconomic status were included in the sample. The percentage of special education students in the sample is also unknown. Thus, test users have little confidence that the item selection study is really based on a "national" sample.

TECHNICAL. To the authors' credit, test-retest reliability coefficients and *SEM*s for each task and the total test at 6-month age intervals are reported. But the time interval between the two testings is not mentioned. The lowest test-retest reliability coefficient is .37 in the Flexible Word Use task for the 11 years to 11 years, 5 months age group. The manual explains that several reliability indexes may be spuriously low because of the restricted scoring range of the group. On the other hand, test users should keep in mind that reliability indexes might be spuriously high for the young age groups. The KR20 estimates of internal consistency reliability for each task are also presented, ranging from .63 to .84.

Interscorer reliability is of big concern for a test to assess expressive language ability, even though the manual suggests only professionals be eligible to administer and score the test. Unfortunately, the 97.8% of agreement in scoring six protocols among nine speech-language pathologists provides no convincing evidence of high interscorer reliability. It is unclear how 2,520 total comparisons for the first protocol and 4,050 total comparisons for the other five protocols were determined. Besides, the protocol scoring comparison ignores examiner variability during the test administration.

A major problem with this test is the lack of validity evidence. We do not agree that a point-biserial correlation between item score and task score is an index of validity. With 15 items for each task, item-rest correlations are more desirable to examine item discrimination, which would be lower than item-total correlations shown in the manual. The test description suggests that the specific tasks are constructed to identify strengths and weaknesses in a child's language; so low intertask correlations are desired. However, given that the intertask correlations are of about the same magnitude as the interitem reliabilities of the tasks, the corrected-for-attenuation correlations among the tasks average greater than .90, thus making the authors' interpretation that "the tasks do assess separate language functions" (examiner's manual, p. 59) suspect. The title "Average Task Intercorrelations and Average Correlations Between Tasks and Total Test" in the examiner's manual is misleading. Because each table presents task intercorrelations and correlations between tasks and total test for one age interval, "average" here makes no sense at all. Contrasted-groups validity information was obtained by comparing a sample of students from the normative population with a "matched sample" of language-disordered students receiving special services, but there is no mention of how the samples were matched. No convergent validity or discriminant validity data are available to support that this test measures students' expressive vocabulary and semantic abilities but not other cognitive abilities.

The statistical analysis of ethnic differences in test performance is not justified. Examinations of differential item functioning of ethnic groups, when done correctly, are based on matching groups based on performance on some measure before comparing success rates on individual items. It is not important to compare overall test scores of different groups because the reasons for those differences cannot be isolated from poverty and lack of comparable schooling. What is of interest is whether a certain item discriminates against a target group when another measure shows the groups are comparable. No data reported suggest that such an analysis was run. In addition, although group comparisons are presented, there is no description of the groups compared. The statistical power of tests conducted is ignored in this manual, and many nonsignificant differences may be due to lack of power. The size of the minority groups is too small to conduct these studies properly, and that fact does not seem to justify the extensive presentation of irrelevant data to support a false claim.

COMMENTARY. The discontinue rule in the original test that three consecutive items missed ends the administration of a subtest was not criticized in the previous review, so it is curious to see it no longer used in the current version. It is difficult to support a decision to administer all 90 items to a student who completes the test with only 1 or a few items correct. Given the difficulty of the subtest Flexible Word Use, where 26% of the 6 years to 6 years, 5 months age group scored zero, why should one administer that entire task to a child who has scored only a single point on the previous 75 items? As one educator put it, that would be like saying to a child "OK, you cannot swim across the pool; so try to swim across the lake." Bracey (2006) has a chapter on "Testing: A major source of data—and maybe child abuse" that could use this test as an example if anyone would follow directions and administer all 90 items in this case.

The section of the manual, Discussion of Performance, provides suggestions for remediation for the six tasks. This discussion includes excellent strategies for teaching the skills necessary for performing the tasks, but there is no caution about how implementing these teaching strategies would affect the validity of the scores from future administrations of the test to those children. A particular need for this caution is evident in strategies for teaching Absurdities, where the content of the test is used in the discussion (examiner's manual, p. 47). As described by Mehrens and Kaminski (1989), test validity is not independent of the exposure to instruction on the content in achievement tests.

SUMMARY. The examiner's manual states: "Be skeptical of a published test documentation that is vague, confusing, or incomplete" (p. 45). We are skeptical of the WORD Test 2: Elementary for those and other reasons. Perhaps the potential users of this test should just examine the words and tasks to see if the test measures meaningful word knowledge and use. It would pass such an inspection for many educators, and those approving the content could use the test for measuring the progress of their students in the same way as they might use a classroom test. In such a use, the standard scores, percentile ranks, and age equivalents should be ignored, and instruction on the tasks of the test would not cause inferences to be invalid. Educators using the test in this manner rather than as a standardized test with national norms might not be disappointed, and their students might gain considerably from the suggestions for instruction found in the examiner's manual (pp. 47–49).

REVIEWERS' REFERENCES
Bracey, G. W. (2006). *Reading educational research: How to avoid getting statistically snookered.* Portsmouth, NH: Heinemann.
Mehrens, W. A., & Kaminski, J. (1989). Methods for improving standardized test scores: Fruitful, fruitless, or fraudulent? *Educational Measurement: Issues and Practice, 8,* 14–22.
Nitko, A. J. (2001). *Educational assessment of students* (3rd ed.). Upper Saddle River, NJ: Merrill Prentice Hall.
Raju, N. S. (1985). [Review of The WORD Test.] In J. V. Mitchell, Jr. (Ed.), *The ninth mental measurements yearbook* (pp. 1772–1773). Lincoln, NE: Buros Institute of Mental Measurements.

[204]

Work Orientation and Values Survey.

Purpose: Identifies and categorizes 32 work values, reflecting survey taker's approach to world of work.

Population: Adult and teenage job seekers and career planners.

Publication Date: 2002.

Acronym: WOVS.

Scores, 8: Earnings and Benefits, Working Conditions, Time Orientation, Task Orientation, Mission Orientation, Coworker Relations, Supervisor Relations, Managing Others.

Administration: Group or individual.

Price Data, 2006: $24.95 per 25 inventories including copy of administrator's guide (8 pages).

Time: (15–20) minutes.

Comments: Self-administered and self-scored.
Author: Robert P. Brady.
Publisher: JIST Publishing, Inc.

Review of the Work Orientation and Values Survey by ALAN C. BUGBEE, JR., Director of Psychometrics, American Society for Clinical Pathology, Chicago, IL:

DESCRIPTION. The Work Orientation and Values Survey (WOVS) is an attitude scale designed to assess a person's values and how they relate to that person's choice of an occupation and/or how that person can improve their working situation relative to their values. This instrument is an extension of the work of Ginzberg, Ginsburg, Axelrad, and Herma (1951) and Super (1957), which found that people's beliefs have direct and substantial effects on what type of work they enjoy and how well they do at their choice of work. The survey is based on the well-demonstrated theory that personal values are stable and enduring and that by knowing these values, relative to employment and the type of work a person wants to do, that person can find "good" or "best" fit with an occupation. This will yield satisfied workers who will enjoy their jobs and do well at them.

The WOVS is a self-administered and self-scored survey. Its intended audiences are adults and high school students. Its focus is on career planning and vocational counseling (administrator's guide, p. 1). According to the administrator's guide (p. 3) and the survey (pp. 4, 5-6), the WOVS measures eight Work Values, which the guide refers to as constructs. These are: Earnings and Benefits, Working Conditions, Time Orientation, Task Orientation, Mission Orientation, Managing Others, CoWorker Relations, and Supervisor Relations. Each of these is measured by four items, laid out systematically in the survey.

The scale consists of 32 phrases (i.e., "Job security," "Seeing that others do their job," "Getting a good evaluation"). The test taker is asked to rate how important each of the statements is to them in their work. The ratings use a 5-point Likert-type scale, with the options Very Important, Important, Somewhat Important, Of Little Importance, and Not Important. The test taker is asked to circle the numeric value that corresponds to their choice—5 for *Very Important* to 1 for *Not Important*—for each item. The survey is untimed, although the takers are asked to "quickly answer each item honestly and go on to the next one until you have rated all 32" (survey, p. 2).

The WOVS involves five steps. In the first step, the examinee completes the survey. The second step has the examinee complete the scoring form. This involves entering the value (1 to 5) from the survey on to the corresponding place on the scoring form. For example, the Work Value "Working Conditions" consists of Questions 2, 15, 23, and 26 on the survey. The test taker enters the values they gave for these questions into the corresponding boxes.

Step 3 is the summation of the values in Step 2. These become the total score for each of the eight Work Values. Step 4 is the creation of the examinee's WOVS profile. This profile uses the total scores for each Work Value to show the relative importance of them to the test taker. The examinee puts an "X" over the number that corresponds to their Work Value. This shows them where their Work Values fit in the eight different measures.

Step 5 consists of a number of parts. The first part, "Understand and Use the WOVS Results," gives a brief explanation of how to interpret the outcomes of the survey relative to the normative values for each of the eight measures. It also provides an exercise for the test takers to put their results for the eight measures in the order that these measures apply to the examinee.

Step 5 continues with the next part, "You Can Change or Adjust Work Values to Meet Long Term Goals." Here, a chart of the eight Work Values is presented. The examinees are asked to lay out how they can fit their particular Work Values to long-term career objectives. The test taker is asked to list his or her minimum for each Work Value (i.e., "In the At Least column below, write the minimum that you would accept for that Work value if a situation met your other values reasonably well," p. 6). In addition, examinees are asked to write the conditions that they would prefer. In Earnings and Benefits, for example, this would include the lowest acceptable salary and minimum benefits, followed by the preferred and expected salary and benefits. Performing this exercise in all eight areas is expected to help the test taker find a medium for their personal work values and employment.

The last part of Step 5 asks examinees to write their responses to three questions. The first asks which values are most important to them in career planning and why they are most important. The second question asks them whether their answers to the WOVS questions suggest that they need more training, education, or experience, and, if so, in what kind. The third question asks what they can do in their current employment to meet their work values or improve their situation.

The administrator's guide (pp. 5–7) presents "interpretation tips" and suggests that these can be shared with the examinees, in conjunction with the information provided by the survey. This section presents some information about how the WOVS was developed and what the results can mean.

DEVELOPMENT. As previously mentioned, the WOVS was developed following the path established by Ginzberg, Ginsburg, Axelrad, and Herma (1951) and Super (1957) that a person's values are important in the kind of work they do and their employment situation. The guidebook presents a brief summary (one page) of the research that supports this view. Other than this, no technical information is presented. Information about how the scales were developed is absent. From the brief report on prior research, it appears that this survey grew out of the author's previous work in this area.

TECHNICAL.

Standardization. Two normative tables are available for the WOVS. The table presented in the administrator's guide (p. 4) applies to adults. This norm is for comparison of the test takers to the sample (n = 74) population, ages 18 to 65, from Michigan, Ohio, and Indiana. The guide states that this sample is from urban, suburban, small town, and rural areas. No information is presented on how the sample was selected, why it is from such a small geographic area, or whether it is intended to be representative of a larger population, such as the Midwest or the United States.

The other normative information is only available on the publisher's website (www.jist.com/WOVS_HSNorms.pdf). This is not mentioned in the guide. This norm uses a larger sample (n = 310) than the adult sample. It covers urban, suburban, rural, and small town schools. There is no mention from where the sample is taken.

Tables for both normative sets show raw scores and T-scores for each of the eight Work Values. Both tables provide the average raw score and T-score (50) and raw score and T-score (10) standard deviation for the normative sample in each of the categories. No mention is made about why T-score conversion was used. All of the discussions in the guide and the survey refer only to the raw scores.

Reliability. The WOVS administrator's guide presents test-retest reliability for each of the eight Work Value categories. The sample used for the reliability analysis may be the same one used for the adult normative sample. It is the same size (n = 74) and comes from the same area—central and southern Michigan, northeastern Indiana, and northwestern Ohio. Whether this sample is "sufficiently large" enough for this summated rating scale is uncertain (Likert, 1974).

The test-retest (no interval noted) reliabilities range from a low of .81 (Working Conditions) to a high of .86 (Task Orientation). No overall reliability for the total survey is reported. No reliability information at all is presented for the high school sample.

Validity. The briefly (four sentences) reported validity evidence for the WOVS is based on content validity. This content validity was examined by having three expert judges ("who represented more than 50 years' experience in career counseling, vocational assessment, career development, and/or vocational rehabilitation," administrator's guide, p. 3) sort the 32 survey statements into the Work Values category where they best fit. This type of sorting is usually done with a large number of different statements to judge which ones are the best in order to build an attitude scale (Thurstone, 1974).

COMMENTARY. The Work Orientation and Values Survey is an interesting use of people's attitudes about work and how this fits with the type of work they do. It attempts to assess eight different areas of Work Values in a brief (32 items) form. It presents an interesting (and brightly multicolored) survey form that allows the user to complete the survey and scale their responses as they fit into the eight Work Values. It also leads them towards thinking about how their values fit with their current work situation and how to adjust their values to accomplish their long-term goals.

Unfortunately, due to the paucity of information about how the scale was developed and its technical properties (e.g., reliability and validity evidence), it is uncertain whether it accomplishes what it is intended to do. For example, its validity evidence, as reported, is strictly content-based. At the very least, this fails to fulfill the standards for technical quality (American Educational Research Association, American Psychological Association, & National Council on Measurement in Education, 1999, Standards 1.7, 1.10, 1.11).

The apparent application of the test results to adults and high school students is not adequately explained. Indeed, the normative information for high school students is only available via the internet. It is presented without explanation of how the sample was selected.

SUMMARY. The Work Orientation and Values Survey is a brief 32-item Likert-type scale designed to measure eight Work Values. The instrument is intended to help adults and high school students find a "fit" between their particular work values and their personal career goals. Unfortunately, the WOVS lacks a lot of important information. This lack makes it difficult to know whether or not it is doing what it is intended to do. With stronger and more complete information on its validity, reliability, development, and application, the WOVS could prove to be a very useful measure.

REVIEWER'S REFERENCES

American Educational Research Association, American Psychological Association, & National Council on Measurement in Education. (1999). *Standards for educational and psychological testing.* Washington, DC: American Educational Research Association.

Ginzberg, E., Ginsburg, S. W., Axelrad, S., & Herma, J. L. (1951). *Occupational choice: An approach to a general theory.* New York: Columbia University Press.

Likert, R. (1974). The method of constructing an attitude scale. In G. M. Maranell (Ed.), *Scaling: A sourcebook for behavioral scientists* (pp. 233–243). Chicago: Aldine Publishing Co.

Super, D. E. (1957). *The psychology of careers.* New York: Harper.

Thurstone, L. L. (1974). A law of comparative judgment. In G. M. Maranell (Ed.), *Scaling: A sourcebook for behavioral scientists* (pp. 81–92). Chicago: Aldine Publishing Co.

Review of the Work Orientation and Values Survey by BERT A. GOLDMAN, Professor, University of North Carolina at Greensboro, Greensboro, NC:

DESCRIPTION. The Work Orientation and Values Survey (WOVS) developed by Robert P. Brady is a 32-item, self-report instrument that identifies the importance a person places on eight work-related values, which are recorded on a profile by following an easy-to-use, four-step procedure. Step 5 instructs respondents to prioritize the eight work values based upon the importance the respondents assign to each. Respondents are next instructed to adjust their work values to meet long-term goals by assigning, on a 4–20 scale, their least value, and their preferred value for each of the eight work values. Following this step, the respondents are requested to consider other things

such as: what work values they think are most important in their long-term career planning and why; do their responses on the WOVS suggest that they need more training, education, or work experience, and if so what kind; and finally they are asked what they can do in their current job or situation to better meet their most important work values or to improve their present situation.

This self-report instrument was designed to be used in career development, pre-employment, human resources, vocational counseling, job development, work adjustment, job satisfaction, job retention, and disability management.

DEVELOPMENT. Seminal interest by Brady in the general area of valuing elements appears to have occurred in 1971 when he examined selected variables affecting the vocational development of elementary school children. He cites several of his own studies and those of other researchers, all of whom focused on values as holding a critical place in career planning. Thus in 2001, Brady and Reinink introduced the WOVS as a quantitative approach for self-directed planning and career counseling that is usually administered by a vocational professional, but which can also be self-administered for self-directed exploration and planning purposes.

TECHNICAL. Norms for the WOVS were developed using an 18- to 65-years-of-age sample population from Michigan, Ohio, and Indiana. The number of people comprising this sample population is given as 74, but no reason is given for selecting the sample from these three states. Further, this information suggests that, on the average, only 24 or 25 persons were selected from each state, which when divided by the four locales, suggests that only about 8 persons were drawn from each locale in each of the three states. When these are spread over the broad age range of 18 to 65, the sample could hardly be a representative one. In addition, there is no description of the selection process.

Raw scores and their corresponding T-scores based upon a mean of 50 and a standard deviation of 10 comprise the norms. This reviewer questions the value of these norms given the preceding discussion of sample size. Further, it appears that because the respondents generate a profile in Step 4, which can be interpreted using an ipsative approach, this, then, is what should be of value to the respondents rather than the norms.

Content validity was examined by providing three experienced career counselors with operational definitions of the eight work-related values and having them independently assign each of the 32 survey items to one of the eight work-related values. Brady reports complete agreement was reached among the three counselors. However, this approach may not reveal the validity of the eight work-related values because they were created from only 32 survey items, which may not be the complete domain of work-related values. For example, are there gender differences with regard to work-related values? If so, this may call for expansion of the number of items and/or values. Further, a factor analysis should be conducted to statistically determine the underlying structure of the work-related values.

Test-retest reliability coefficients of .81 to .86 provided an acceptable range obtained from what appears to be the same 74 people who comprised the norm group. However, no specific confirmation of this N is given nor is information provided on the time interval between administrations.

COMMENTARY. Robert P. Brady created a self-report instrument enabling adults 18 to 65 years of age to identify and determine the importance of eight values in their present job as well as in their future career plans. Five steps for completing the self-report instrument are numbered and are clearly laid out, making them easy to follow within a relatively brief amount of time. There are two additional steps that should be numbered as Steps 6 and 7 to convey a more accurate picture of the extent of work required for completion of the survey.

The administrator's guide states that respondents indicate the importance of each of the 32 statements on a 5-point Likert-type scale ranging from 1 (*of no importance*) to 5 (*very important*). This is an ordinal scale, not a Likert scale because a Likert scale always ranges from some degree of Disagreement to some degree of Agreement.

No information is given to indicate how the 32 items comprising the WOVS were actually selected and whether there was any field-testing of the items. There is no specific statement indicating the age range of those for whom the WOVS is designed, although an age range was used in the development of norms.

SUMMARY. Although the Work Orientation and Values Survey is a self-report instrument with good reliability, some demonstrated validity, and relatively easy administration, it provides only one element for present job analysis and for use in career planning. Elements of greater importance for these major considerations, in this reviewer's opinion, would be such attributes as overall intellectual ability, specific aptitudes, achievements, personality traits, and interest/disinterests. Further, because the WOVS could provide supplementary information useful to a respondent, the respondent, who obtains the assistance of a career counselor, would be the one best served.

[205]

Workplace Skills Survey.

Purpose: Designed to provide "information regarding basic work ethics and employment skills."
Population: Job applicants and employees.
Publication Date: 1998.
Acronym: WSS.
Scores, 7: Communication, Adapting to Change, Problem Solving, Work Ethics, Technological Literacy, Teamwork, Composite.
Administration: Individual or group.
Price Data, 2007: $43 per introductory kit including 5 reusable test booklets, 20 answer/score sheets, and technical manual (9 pages); $32 per 20 answer/score sheets; $18 per 10 reusable test booklets.
Time: 20 minutes.
Author: Industrial Psychology International Ltd.
Publisher: Industrial Psychology International Ltd.

Review of the Workplace Skills Survey by JEAN P. KIRNAN, Professor of Psychology, The College of New Jersey, Ewing, NJ:

[Note: The reviewer gratefully acknowledges the contributions of Brian Kirby to this critique. His hard work and insights are greatly appreciated.]

DESCRIPTION. The purpose of the Workplace Skills Survey (WSS) is to assess nontechnical skills related to success in the workplace. This measure is designed for individuals 16 years of age or older who are planning on entering the workforce. The instrument produces a total score along with separate subscores for the six employability skills of Communication, Adapting to Change, Problem Solving, Work Ethics, Technological Literacy, and Teamwork. Although its stated use is for job applicants, the publisher's website suggests that scores can also be used for adult education and training programs (Industrial

Psychology International, 2000). In stark contrast to traditional employment tests, the WSS moves beyond the job knowledge, academic skill, and general mental ability measures long used in employee selection, and instead, attempts to measure more specific skills required of most workers in virtually all work settings.

The WSS allows 20 minutes for the completion of 48 multiple-choice items. The items present an interesting mix tapping into general workplace knowledge, work etiquette, conflict resolution, supervisor-employee interactions, scheduling, flow chart reading, professional correspondence, customer service, communication, and appropriate workplace behavior. The items have a high degree of face validity and fairly represent women and ethnic minorities in various work scenarios. Some of the items are transparent and thus are susceptible to social desirability or impression management. No attempt is made to detect or correct for such response errors.

Answers are recorded on a separate two-page answer sheet. The test taker circles their answers on the top sheet and a carbon sheet transfers responses to a detachable second page that contains scoring guidelines. Scoring of the answer sheet is very easy and can be accomplished quickly by the test administrator. The scorer merely needs to separate the two sheets and tally the correct responses. Determining subscores is made simple through the use of a color-coded system. Raw scores are calculated and then converted to stanines using a chart that appears on the second page of the answer sheet. The reusable booklet helps to reduce costs.

DEVELOPMENT. There is little information as to the construction of the WSS items, except that they are designed to tap into competencies identified in an earlier report by the Department of Labor (Department of Labor, 2000). The SCANS report identified 20 competencies and 17 fundamental skills. It would be useful for the publisher to indicate how the WSS items and subscores map onto these competencies. In the validity section of the manual reference is made to a pool of 120 items that were administered to a sample of 764 community college students. Item response theory was used to analyze the items and establish norms, ultimately identifying the final 48 items. However,

the origin of those 120 items and demographic information on the 764 respondents is lacking.

Raw scores can be transformed to stanines using a chart at the bottom of the second page of the answer sheet or to T-scores using a conversion table in the manual. It is reported that stanine scores are based on a reference population of high school graduates. This reviewer assumes that the T-scores are based on the same sample. This is insufficient information for the normative sample. Demographics such as gender, ethnicity, age, years in employment, type of jobs held, date tested, and geographical location as well as sample size are needed to properly interpret the WSS scores. Without such information, the scores are hard to interpret. It would be far better to have norms based on workers in jobs that utilize these skills. The manual states that a typical high school graduate would achieve a stanine of 5 or a T-score of 50, whereas a graduate of a 2- or 4-year program (one assumes this means college) will score 6–7 on the stanine and 55–60 on the T-score. It is unclear how the typical scores were determined because the normative sample is never fully described.

TECHNICAL. A study of internal consistency was conducted to demonstrate reliability of the WSS. This produced a correlation of .90 for total score in a sample of 472 community college students. The publisher should report separate reliability estimates for the six subscores in addition to total score reliability. This is especially critical given the small number of items (eight per subscale).

There are no validation studies reported for the WSS. The WSS is purported to measure six competencies that are needed in today's workplace. There is no evidence to support the construct validity of the WSS; how does one know that it actually measures communication, adapting to change, problem solving, work ethics, technological literacy, or teamwork? Nor is there any research to support the predictive validity of the instrument (that someone who scores high on these measures will, in fact, be a better worker than someone who scores low).

Tests used in employee selection are subject to federal guidelines and thus should report on potential impact to protected groups. Data on mean scores, as well as prediction should be provided separately for gender and racial groups.

COMMENTARY. The WSS is a simple-to-use, quick measure of six workplace competencies that would seem to be relevant in a variety of jobs. However, good face validity and low cost are insufficient reasons to recommend a test's use. The instrument lacks evidence of appropriate reliability at the subscale level, provides insufficient information about norm groups, and reports no validity research.

SUMMARY. The WSS attempts to measure an interesting array of knowledge and skills that would be useful in a wide variety of work settings. The measurement of such nontechnical workplace skills would greatly complement the traditional selection tools of general mental ability and job knowledge and is an avenue worth pursuing. However, the insufficient psychometric research and limited normative data leave this reviewer no choice but to not recommend the instrument.

REVIEWER'S REFERENCES

Industrial Psychology International. (2000). Workplace Skills Survey. Retrieved March 4, 2006, from http://www.metritech.com/IPI/ipi_home.htm
U. S. Department of Labor Employment and Training Administration. (2000). Skills and tasks for jobs: A SCANS report for America 2000 (1999). Retrieved March 4, 2006, from http://wdr.doleta.gov/opr/fulltext/document.cfm?docn=6140

Review of the Workplace Skills Survey by WILLIAM I. SAUSER, JR., Associate Dean and Professor, Business and Engineering Outreach, Auburn University, Auburn, AL:

DESCRIPTION. An individual has earned her high school diploma or GED, developed her academic and technical skills in community college (or another skill-building program), and is now interested in entering the world of work. But does she have the general workplace skills needed to function effectively in the workplace? If not, what areas of expertise must she strengthen before being prepared for success as an employee?

It is questions like these that the Workplace Skills Survey (WSS) is intended to help answer. The Survey itself comes in two forms, a 48-item, 20-minute timed test that can be self-scored, and a 56-item, 50-minute timed test that can be scored electronically by the test publisher. Both versions are laid out attractively in easy-to-read booklets, and both versions provide clear instructions for administration in either a group or individual setting. According to the manual, "People whose reading ability is at or above the 6th-grade level should have little trouble with the test" (p. 3). This reviewer believes, however, that individuals with less well-developed literacy skills will have considerable difficulty completing all of the items in the time allowed. Naturally, noncompletion will affect the examinee's scores on the various dimensions and the composite total.

The WSS is not intended to measure academic ability; instead it seeks to assess workplace readiness of adults and adolescents in terms of abilities to "work effectively with others, understand time management techniques, interact with technology, show up for work, follow instructions, and demonstrate a host of non-technical skills that make the difference between success or failure on the job" (manual, pp. 2–3). The items consist of issues and scenarios that frequently occur in the typical workplace; the examinee is asked to evaluate the problem and select the best of the four choices provided for each item. As noted in the manual, the items often require the examinee to refer to "authentic workplace materials, such as memos, forms, and charts" (p.3) displayed in the test booklet. The self-scored version of the WSS yields normative stanine and *T*-scores for six dimensions (Communication, Adapting to Change, Problem Solving, Work Ethics, Technological Literacy, and Teamwork) plus an overall composite stanine score presumably measuring workplace readiness. The electronically scored version provides these plus scores on career planning and job attainment.

DEVELOPMENT. Information provided by the publisher about the development of the WSS is sketchy at best. The manual (p. 2) refers to a 1991 report from the U.S. Department of Labor, *What Work Requires of Schools: A SCANS Report for America 2000*, as the inspiration for the selection of dimensions to be measured by the WSS, but does not discuss how the actual items were created. The manual (p. 4) does indicate that "a total of 120 items were field-tested on a sample of 764 community college students," and that these items were analyzed using item response theory (specifically the Rasch model). The *T*-score and stanine norms provided apparently resulted from "several years' experience with a statewide program that annually assessed in excess of 10,000 high school and community college students" (manual, p. 4). Clearly this level of detail is not sufficient to make a careful assessment of the Survey's usefulness. Although the items possess a level of face validity, and the dimensions seem reasonable, there is no real evidence upon which to base a conclusion that the WSS samples content that may be required for functioning successfully in a typical workplace. The publisher is encouraged to provide more details about the development of the WSS in the manual, or at least to refer the interested reader to supplemental material that provides such a description.

TECHNICAL. Technical information about the psychometric properties of the WSS is woefully inadequate. As noted above, details about the development of the instrument are quite minimal and—other than the face validity—there is no basis provided in the manual to support a judgment that the WSS measures with any scientific accuracy the dimensions of workplace readiness it claims to address. The administrator's manual for the longer (electronically scored) version does indicate that items range in difficulty from 20 to 60 and that seven items (eight in the self-scored version) relate to each dimension scored. There is no evidence provided for test-retest reliability, nor is there even one or more correlation coefficients supplied to support the belief that the two forms of the Survey are parallel. Evidence supporting any form of validity claims (content, construct, criterion-related) is absent from the manual. There is no evidence presented to support the conclusion that the various dimensions scored are truly independent from one another. In fact, the instructions to sum the stanine scores for each dimension to produce an overall composite score suggest to this reviewer that the publisher believes the instrument may actually be unidimensional, or at least the scales are highly intercorrelated.

The manual is silent about the interpretation of the dimension and composite scores, other than to indicate on a supplemental sheet of paper that stanine scores of 1-2-3 are Below Average, whereas those of 4-5-6 are Average and those of 7-8-9 are Above Average. There is no information provided in the manual to help the examinee or his or her vocational counselor to develop a plan to strengthen workplace skills that are "below average," or to capitalize on skills that are "above average." This omission is a glaring deficiency for an instrument that purports to be helpful in preparing individuals to succeed in the world of work.

COMMENTARY. Workplace readiness is an extremely important concept. High schools, community colleges, and other educational institutions devoted to preparing students to become productive contributors in the workplace are hungry for instruments to help them assess the effectiveness of their work. Potential employees desire to know how well prepared they are to enter the workplace, and what additional skills they need to develop if they are to succeed. Employers are always interested in instruments that can help them identify recruits with the potential to succeed on the job. Clearly then, there is a market for a well-developed, psychometrically sound instrument that can be used to measure with meaningful results the dimensions of workplace readiness. Such an instrument would be useful for vocational guidance, self-development, program evaluation, and perhaps even employee selection. The WSS may have some promise as a useful instrument for one or more of these purposes, but it needs to be much more carefully researched and documented before it is ready to be marketed for any of these uses.

The test publisher is commended for seeking to meet an important need, and for devising an instrument that—on its face—shows some promise of meeting this need. On the other hand, the publisher should devote much more effort and energy to examining the psychometric properties of the WSS and documenting them in the manual if this instrument is to gain any credibility for use by vocational counselors, job seekers, or employers. Instructions about how to interpret and use the instrument must also be developed and provided. At present the WSS appears to be in an early stage of development. Future research with this instrument may be warranted, but this reviewer cannot recommend the WSS for professional use in its present form.

SUMMARY. The Workplace Skills Survey is an attractively presented instrument designed to assess workplace readiness along six important dimensions—Communication, Adapting to Change, Problem Solving, Work Ethics, Technological Literacy, and Teamwork. It is a multiple-choice instrument that comes in two forms, a 48-item version that can be self-scored and a 56-item version that can be scored electronically. Both forms make use of charts, forms, memos, and other means of conveying information commonly found in the workplace. Both versions yield T-scores and stanine scores. Unfortunately, details about the development of the WSS and evidence of its psychometric quality are not adequately presented in the manual, and there is no clear reason to believe that the instrument is useful for any of the purposes for which it is presumably intended—vocational counseling, program evaluation, employee screening, and individual assessment of ability. Given this inadequacy, the WSS is not suitable for professional use for any of these purposes. The instrument does appear to have promise, however, and the publisher is encouraged to structure a careful program of research and documentation to justify possible use of the instrument for professional purposes.

[206]
Y-OQ-30.1 [Youth Outcome Questionnaire—Omni Version].

Purpose: Designed to measure "the treatment process for children and adolescents receiving any form of behavioral health treatment including psychoactive medications."
Population: Ages 12–18 years.
Publication Dates: 1998–2002.
Acronym: Y-OQ-30.1.
Scores: Total score only.
Administration: Individual or group.
Restricted Distribution: Requires licensure from American Professional Credentialing Services LLC.
Price Data, 2006: Licensing cost available from publisher; $25 per administration and scoring manual (2003, 21 pages); $25 per test.
Foreign Language Editions: English, Spanish, and French editions available.
Time: (2–15) minutes.
Comments: Test can be parent-reported and self-reported.
Authors: Gary M. Burlingame, Bruce W. Jasper (manual only), Gary Peterson (manual only), M. Gawain Wells, Curtis W. Reisinger, G. S. (Jeb) Brown (manual only).
Publisher: OQ Measures LLC.

Review of the Y-OQ-30.1 [Youth Outcome Questionnaire—Omni Version] by SANDRA LOEW, Associate Professor, University of North Alabama, Florence, AL:

DESCRIPTION. The Y-OQ-30.1 [Youth Outcome Questionnaire—Omni Version] is a single-page, 30-question form that can be filled out by parents, adolescents, or other persons such as teachers or therapists, that measures the treatment progress of children or adolescents. This instrument is a shortened version of the 64-item Youth Outcome Questionnaire (16:283). It is designed to be used at intake, during the course of treatment, and at the end of treatment for behavioral and psychiatric problems. It is a behavioral analysis record that tracks progress being made in treatment and helps determine when treatment is complete. Scoring is simple addition of the items with a higher score indicating higher levels of distress.

A licensing fee is required in order to purchase and use this test. Each administration of the test is an additional cost.

DEVELOPMENT. The Y-OQ-30.1 was developed to address the need that mental health care providers have to show the effectiveness of treatments they offer. This shortened version of the Youth Outcome Questionnaire (Y-OQ) takes less time to fill out, yet provides the information from all affected parties such as adolescents, parents, and treatment providers. The Y-OQ-30.1 is based on extensive research and statistical analysis of the Y-OQ that allowed the test developers to shorten that version yet maintain the psychometric properties of the longer version. Adolescents, parents, and teachers are more likely to answer the shortened version, thereby allowing for multiple testing opportunities to provide increased information about behavioral changes.

TECHNICAL. The Parent-report community standardization sample was taken largely from the Western U.S. in the Rocky Mountain region. The Parent-report clinical sample came from the Western region, the Eastern seaboard, and other areas of the U.S. The Self-report community sample was also taken from the Rocky Mountain region and the Self-report clinical sample was from that Western region with the addition of clients in treatment along the Eastern seaboard. It is stated in the manual that the cutoff scores "are based on large and diverse samples" (p. 5), yet the manual does not provide demographic information, other than age and gender, for those samples. There is a significant difference between the community and clinical samples with the clinical sample showing more symptoms than the community sample.

There seem to be significant gender differences in the Parent-report clinical sample. However, the manual does not provide practitioners with the information necessary to compensate for gender differences when scoring and interpreting this instrument.

Using coefficient alpha, the internal consistency of the Y-OQ-30.1 was .96 for the Parent-report and .93 for the Self-report. These indices are appropriate reliability estimates and are quite good. Criterion-related validity compares the Y-OQ-30.1 to the Child Behavior Checklist with a correlation coefficient of .76, which is adequate.

Research was also performed to assess the sensitivity of the instrument to change, which is an important aspect of this assessment. The results showed statistically significant improvement between pretest and posttest scores. The comparison of the community and the clinical samples showed statistical significance that also indicates some evidence of construct validity.

COMMENTARY. The strengths of the Y-OQ-30.1 are that it is a short questionnaire that is easy to read, score, and interpret. It seems to be a sensitive tool that allows treatment providers to evaluate how the treatment is progressing. It also can be used to document to those paying for mental health services for adolescents that the treatment is moving toward a positive outcome.

Probably the weakness of the Y-OQ-30.1 is that it lacks the psychometric evidence necessary to support the premise that it provides valid information. The manual does not provide enough information for a practitioner to make an informed choice concerning this assessment tool.

Although the Y-OQ-30.1 is a shortened version of the very respectable Y-OQ, there is limited information that allows the practitioner to assume that this version is just as good, but shorter.

The normative sample is mostly from the Western U.S. and there is no information concerning the demographics of that sample. If the manual explained to practitioners how to adjust for those gender and age differences, it would be a significant improvement.

SUMMARY. The Y-OQ-30.1 is a one-page questionnaire that holds great promise. It is short and easily filled out by adolescents, parents, and teachers, thereby allowing its use at intake, during treatment, after treatment, and for follow-up. However, the psychometric properties of this instrument are not yet adequately documented for widespread use.

Ongoing research is occurring. Practitioners who would like to contribute to that research should do so but should be extremely careful about decisions that they make using a not quite fully validated assessment instrument.

Review of the Y-OQ-30.1 [Youth Outcome Questionnaire-Omni Version] by W. JOEL

SCHNEIDER, Assistant Professor of Psychology, and MARK E. SWERDLIK, Professor of Psychology, Illinois State University, Normal, IL:

DESCRIPTION. The Y-OQ-30.1 [Youth Outcome Questionnaire-Omni Version] is a brief rating scale designed to provide clinicians and/or administrators (perhaps especially those in managed-care settings) with information about changes in general psychological distress and conduct problems in children and adolescents. Parent-report (for ages 4–17) and Self-report (for ages 12–18) versions are available. The instrument consists of 30 items originally taken from the 64-item Youth Outcome Questionnaire (16:283). These 30 items capture a wide range of symptoms such as somatic concerns, relationship turmoil, violent behavior, substance use, hyperactivity, depression, anxiety, hopelessness, and more. The Y-OQ-30.1 does not have any subscales. The total score is a simple sum of the raw scores from the 30 Likert-scale items. Empirically determined cut scores indicate likely clinical status and a reliable change index indicates how many points a score can fluctuate from one administration to the next before a change is to be considered clinically significant.

DEVELOPMENT. The Y-OQ-30.1 is a subset of the 64 items that comprise the Youth Outcome Questionnaire. Thirty items were selected based on the following considerations: (a) Items had to be both relevant and sensitive to therapeutic interventions; (b) the final item pool had to measure a wide variety of symptoms, particularly general symptoms observed across many diagnostic categories; (c) symptoms measured had to be directly relevant to the quality of life of the individual being rated; and (d) items needed to be written at a fourth grade reading level or lower.

Several different community and clinical samples were used to derive the norms for the Y-OQ-30.1. Most of the samples were taken from the U.S. Rocky Mountain region, primarily from midsized cities in Utah and Idaho. The community samples for the Parent version come from about 650 parents who participated in a random-selection telephone survey and 462 parents from a single elementary school. About 530 adolescents who had never received mental health treatment were recruited from their schools to provide community norms for the Self-report version of the Y-OQ-30.1. Given the data collection methods used, it is reasonable to assume that these participants are broadly representative of people living in the Rocky Mountain region (and possibly the U.S. as a whole). However, no demographic data are provided in the test manual to support that assumption.

Data from clinical samples were collected from a wide variety of settings in the U.S. Rocky Mountain region and Eastern seaboard. Over 3,800 Parent-report protocols were collected from parents with children receiving services from community, outpatient, or inpatient mental health care settings. Over 1,300 adolescents receiving services in inpatient, outpatient, or community mental health care settings also completed the Self-report protocols. Data collection from other regions in the U.S. is ongoing.

TECHNICAL. The internal consistency (coefficient alpha) of the Y-OQ-30.1 was high (.92–.94) for both the Self- and Parent-report measures and for both community and clinical samples. A subset ($N = 106$) of the community sample completed the measure twice over an average period of about 3 weeks. Test-retest reliability was .80 for the Parent-report version and .91 for the Self-report version. As is common with behavior rating scales, interrater reliability differed depending on the nature of the dyad. Parents generally agreed with each other ($r = .71, N = 70$) on the severity of their children's symptom levels. Adolescents tended to agree more with their mothers ($r = .58, N = 61$) than with their fathers ($r = .45, N = 43$) as to the severity of their distress (Dunn, Burlingame, Walbridge, Smith, & Crum, 2005).

The optimum cut scores discriminated between the community and clinical samples (Parent-report cut score of 29: sensitivity = .80, specificity = .75; Self-report cut score of 30: sensitivity = .70, specificity = .63). The mean total scores were significantly higher for groups expected to have higher rates of psychopathology (i.e., community < outpatient < inpatient samples).

The Y-OQ-30.1 total score is a measure of general distress and behavioral disturbance. It was never intended to be a psychometrically pure (i.e., unidimensional) index. Indeed, it may measure as many as five broad factors (Dunn et al., 2005) but the subscales that might otherwise be formed to measure these factors would not be reliable enough for use in clinical decisions for individuals.

The Parent version of the Y-OQ-30.1 correlated strongly ($r = .76, N = 423$) with the Child Behavior Checklist (Achenbach, 1991) total score.

Thus, it appears that the Y-OQ-30.1 is reasonably reliable, sensitive to differing levels of psychopathology, and strongly correlated with at least one well-validated measure of mental and behavior problems in children and adolescents.

COMMENTARY. It appears that the Y-OQ-30.1 is an efficient and inexpensive tool that appears to be a reasonable choice for clinicians needing to track overall improvements in children and adolescents receiving psychological and behavioral treatment. Although it was designed specifically to help clinicians needing to provide managed-care providers with regular updates on patient progress, explicit and formal tracking of overall distress can focus both the clinician and client in ways otherwise unlikely to occur. Indeed, sharing with clients a graph of their improvements over the course of therapy can be a powerful intervention in and of itself.

Even though a measure may have many excellent features, it is the responsibility of the clinician to be aware of the limitations of the instrument. Although it can reliably measure overall distress and disturbance, the Y-OQ-30.1 is not, nor was it designed to be, a diagnostic instrument that can assist in fine-grained differential diagnoses.

The norms are probably representative of urban residents in the U.S. Rocky Mountain region but the details in the manual needed to support even that assumption are scant. Unfortunately, most U.S. clinicians from other regions are probably not sure how similar that population (typically white, middle class, and Mormon) is to the population in their own communities. Given that the Y-OQ-30.1 is a very general measure, it is unlikely that the norms are radically different from those of other regions, although data are needed to support this supposition. Furthermore, the absolute level of the total score is of less concern than the relative changes in the score over the course of treatment. Even so, national and local norms would give clinicians greater confidence in their interpretations of the data as they use the measure.

Thus far, there are no data available to suggest that the use of the Y-OQ-30.1 results in better treatment outcomes. It is not clear that managed-care decision makers stand on solid ground when decisions are made based on Y-OQ-30.1 data.

SUMMARY. The Y-OQ-30.1 [Youth Outcome Questionnaire] is a brief (30-item) measure of general distress and behavior disturbance in children and adolescents (ages 4 to 18). The Parent-report version is available for the full age range and the Self-report version is available for adolescents. Its primary purpose is to track overall changes over the course of treatment rather than to be used as a diagnostic instrument. Despite some concerns about the representativeness of the standardization sample, it appears that the Y-OQ-30.1 may be reasonably well suited for the purposes for which it was designed.

REVIEWERS' REFERENCES

Achenbach, T. M. (1991). *Manual for the Child Behavior Checklist and 1991 Profile.* Burlington: University of Vermont, Department of Psychiatry.
Dunn, T. W., Burlingame, G. M., Walbridge, M., Smith, J., & Crum, M. J. (2005). Outcome assessment for children and adolescents: Psychometric validation of the Youth Outcome Questionnaire 30.1 (Y-OQ-30.1). *Clinical Psychology and Psychotherapy, 12,* 388-401.

[207]

Y-OQ-SR 2.0 [Youth Outcome Questionnaire—Self Report].

Purpose: Designed to "assess behavior change as the adolescent clients themselves perceive it."
Population: Ages 12–18 years.
Publication Dates: 1999–2005.
Acronym: Y-OQ-SR 2.0.
Scores, 7: Intrapersonal Distress, Somatic, Interpersonal Relations, Social Problems, Behavioral Dysfunction, Critical Items, Total.
Administration: Individual or group.
Restricted Distribution: Requires licensure from American Professional Credentialing Services LLC.
Price Data, 2006: Licensing cost available from publisher; $25 per administration and scoring manual (1999, 15 pages); $25 per test.
Foreign Language Editions: English, Spanish, and French editions available.
Time: (7–15) minutes.
Authors: M. Gawain Wells, Gary M. Burlingame, Paul M. Rose (manual only), and Michael J. Lambert (test only).
Publisher: OQ Measures LLC.

Review of Y-OQ-SR 2.0 [Youth Outcome Questionnaire—Self-Report] by JOHN S. GEISLER, Professor Emeritus, Department of Counselor Education and Counseling Psychology, Western Michigan University, Kalamazoo, MI:

DESCRIPTION. The self-report version of the Youth Outcome Questionnaire (Y-OQ-SR 2.0) is a 64-item, paper-and-pencil measure of mental health treatment progress for adolescents ages 12–18. The manual copyright date is 1999 and the copyright date for the instrument is 2005.

This measure is used to assess the self-reported beliefs, attitudes, feelings, moods, and behaviors of adolescents during the previous 7 days using a 5-point (0–4) Likert scale. It may be administered and scored (individually or in groups) by nonclinical personnel. No criteria are presented with respect to the qualifications of persons who interpret the scores. A Total Score and six subscale scores (Intrapersonal Distress, Somatic, Interpersonal Relations, Critical Items, Social Problems, and Behavioral Dysfunction are generated (raw scores only). There is a description of the purposes and features for each subscale. Only one form is available. The publishers indicate that the information in the manual is preliminary in nature and that additional studies are underway.

The Y-OQ-SR 2.0 was not designed to measure psychopathology, rather it was designed to assess the changes in attitudes, beliefs, and behaviors of the target population over the period of time adolescents are in treatment programs. The statements are in the first person, singular format and are straightforward in nature. Responses are scored as follows: *Never or Almost Never* (0), *Rarely* (1), *Sometimes* (2), *Frequently* (3), and *Almost Always or Always* (4). The instructions indicate that those completing the measure should respond to every statement. The answer sheet must be hand scored by summing the scores for each subscale. Eight items are reverse scored because they assess healthy behaviors and beliefs. The raw scores for these items are not scored as 0, 1, 2, 3, or 4. These scores are transformed as follows: 0 = 2, 1 = 1, 2 = 0, 3 = -1, and 4 = -2. No explanation is provided as to why the reversed scored items are on a different numerical scale (-2 to +2). If the adolescent completing the inventory fails to respond to four or fewer items, then substitute values can be inserted for those omissions by determining the mean scores of the answered items and using this "created" score (nearest whole number) for the missing response(s). If five or more items do not have responses, the scores are considered invalid. The number of items/scale was not reported. The items are randomly placed on the answer sheet so that respondents cannot identify those items as belonging to a given scale.

DEVELOPMENT. The instrument was designed to be a companion and parallel instrument to the parent/guardian version (Y-OQ). The priorities in development were: brief administration time (approximately 7 minutes), sensitivity to change over short time periods, nominal cost, and high psychometric standards.

Materials provided by the developers (a manual and an answer sheet) provide less than minimal information regarding the development of the items, the rationale for scale development, the underlying psychological constructs, and reports of field testing. No empirical time sequence (repeated measures) studies were reported. The developers indicate that three adolescent groups who were in a partial hospitalization program (no Ns provided) were asked to describe what they believed was the intent of the "questions" (statements). Questionable statements were then reworded.

Four sample groups were used for research purposes and not to develop normative scores (e.g., percentiles, stanines). These groups were from the intermountain section of some western states. The four groups were composed of adolescents from: (a) a residential mental health program, (b) an outpatient substance abuse treatment agency, (c) a partial hospitalization program, and (d) junior and senior high schools. The school sample students were described as "community normal (untreated)" (manual, p. 6). It is assumed that this sample was to be seen as a control, referent group. The developers reported the total number of participants in the samples were $N = 1,334$ although some discrepancies exist. One table listed a total of 1,255 participants; two tables in the manual combined reported 1,332 participants; and one table listed 1,334 as the total number of participants (with sample sizes of 512, 291, 224, and 228, which totals 1,255).

TECHNICAL. The developers indicated that reliability was assessed using "Chronbach's [sic] alpha with the entire sample of adolescents (N = 1,334)" (manual, p. 11) across all four sample groups. Yet they also indicated that the Total Score reliability estimate was .96 across only three groups. Reliability coefficient estimates were reported to be: Total Score, .96; Intrapersonal Distress, .91; Somatic, .73; Interpersonal Relations, .77; Social Problems, .84; Behavior Dysfunction, .78; and Critical Items, .81. It is possible that these high estimates could be the result of the similarity of item content. The authors also indicated that such high reliability coefficients are indicative of a "strong single factor underlying the

several subscales of the questionnaire" (manual, p. 11). No validity evidence was presented.

Information on the means and standard error of the means for the four sample groups for total and scale scores was presented. No standard deviations of group scores were listed. Standard deviations are much more important than the standard error of the mean for purposes of analysis. ANOVA information on gender differences within the community group and patient group was presented. (The Interpersonal Relations total mean score was reported to be 7.436E-02 [sic], which makes no sense.) An ANOVA with respect to age group differences (three categories) was conducted across all four groups. An F ratio was reported; however, it was unclear to which scale score (or Total Score) it is related. No F ratios were listed in the ANOVA age group differences table. However, the standard deviations were listed.

A cutoff score system was described. The three treatment groups' combined mean scores were compared to the "community" group mean scores to determine what the cutoff scores (significant differential between groups) would be for the total scores and the six scale scores. All of these cutoff scores were reported in the text. The authors also reported that these same cutoff scores were also listed in tabular form. However, the cutoff scores in the text did not match the cutoff scores in the table (e.g., Total Score 47 vs. 34.1526). (Also, the male [N = 192] Somatic mean score was 4.5781, the female [N = 319] Somatic score was 6.0188, and the reported combined mean score was 1.1996, which is a mathematical impossibility.)

The developers also provided information on the calculation of a change score index (Reliable Change Index), which could be utilized to determine the level of treatment improvement (if any) across time. Index change scores were developed for all seven scores. However, the developers did not take the next step and report the results of longitudinal research studies (i.e., the validity and utility of the instrument with treatment groups were not established).

COMMENTARY AND SUMMARY. First, a comment needs to be made about the quality of the manual. The errors (syntax, spelling, word usage, format, style, tabular presentations, and mathematical) are quite numerous and must be corrected before the manual can be said to be a professional publication. A strong editorial hand needs to be employed.

A psychological foundation for scale and item development needs to be in place. There is little justification or rationale for the Y-OQ-SR 2.0 scales. Perhaps the rationale for the Y-OQ (parent/guardian) instrument could be utilized, but it was not included in the materials provided. In any event, because the Y-OQ-SR 2.0 can be used as a standalone instrument, construct validity must be established. Empirical data and studies need to be provided to support scale development. Factor analysis would be one tool that could be utilized. Information about the development of the items is missing.

Validity data are sadly lacking. There is no supportable evidence reported that indicates that the scales are measuring what they are purported to be measuring (e.g., the developers state that the nine-item Critical Items scale assesses "change [*sic*] in paranoia, obsessive-compulsive behaviors, hallucination [*sic*], delusions, suicide, mania, and eating disorders," manual, p. 3). It is extremely difficult to imagine that a nine-item scale can measure changes in the factors cited. Can suicide potential be accurately assessed with one item?

The developers also provide a unique, but unsupportable, solution to missing responses. They indicate that the administrator can calculate substitute responses by determining the mean of the actual responses to scale items and inserting this mean score for the missing information. An eight-item scale could have two missing responses. The developer's solution to this problem would be to determine the mean score for the remaining six responses and substitute this created mean response for the two missing responses. This procedure is highly problematic.

The authors of the manual indicate that the instrument is to be utilized to track the progress of adolescents who are receiving mental health services. Two of the normative treatment groups cited were composed of youths who were receiving mental health services in either a residential or partial hospitalization program. Members of the third normative treatment group were receiving substance abuse treatment services. It is suggested that members of this treatment group may or may not be receiving mental health treatment services to the same degree as are members of the first two groups. The equivalency of the three groups is questionable.

It is recommended that electronic scoring be employed for the Y-OQ-SR 2.0. Hand scoring can lead to scoring errors. On the scoring sheet one of the item responses (#45) could be scored on one of two scales because the scoring boxes are adjacent to each other. It is also recommended that normative scores be available to those who wish to use them. Guidelines should also be developed for those professionals who wish to interpret the score results on an individual or group basis.

The developers should be commended for cautioning against using the Y-OQ-SR 2.0 for diagnostic and mental health screening because the percent of true and false positives (relative to the Total Score cutoff) does not justify its use for these purposes. Even though the developers indicate that the instrument does not assess psychopathology, some of the terminology used to describe the scale items suggests otherwise—"anxiety, depression, emotional distress, paranoia, obsessive-compulsive disorders, hallucination, delusions, mania, eating disorders, and sexual problems" (manual, p. 3). They also suggest that high scores may be indicative of the need for inpatient, partial hospitalization, or residential care.

The use of this instrument is not warranted or justified at this time. Its use should be restricted solely for research and development purposes. Until such time as (a) more rigorous and thorough reliability, validity (content, construct, and predictive) and longitudinal studies are reported; and (b) the manual is revised and significantly improved, its usefulness is questionable and highly problematic.

Review of the Y-OQ-SR 2.0 [Youth Outcome Questionnaire—Self-Report] by JOSEPH C. KUSH, Associate Professor, Duquesne University, Pittsburgh, PA:

DESCRIPTION. The Y-OQ-SR 2.0 [Youth Outcome Questionnaire-Self Report] version 2.0 is a self-report, paper-and-pencil measure, designed to assess the therapeutic progress of adolescents receiving mental health treatment. The questionnaire is designed for adolescents ages 12–18 and requires approximately 7 to 10 minutes to be completed. The instrument consists of 64 questions that are presented in a 5-point Likert scale format and is designed to assess behavioral change to assist with progress tracking and outcome measurement.

The Y-OQ-SR 2.0 is intended to be a companion to the Youth Outcome Questionnaire

(Burlingame, Wells, Lambert, & Cox, 1996; 16:283) a parallel scale completed by the parent/guardian of the adolescent. Both scales produce a total score as well as six subscale scores: Intrapersonal Distress, Somatic, Interpersonal Relations, Critical Items, Social Problems, and Behavioral Dysfunction. Although not included in the administration and scoring manual for the Y-OQ-SR 2.0, the *Sixteenth Mental Measurements Yearbook* reviews (Green, 2005; Hattie, 2005) of the Youth Outcome Questionnaire indicate that the development of the subscales was based upon: (a) a meta-analysis comparing treated and untreated children; (b) a series of focus groups of an unspecified number of clients and parents, and 10 outpatient provider groups; and (c) an examination of the behavior change goals derived from an unspecified number of hospital records. In this regard, it would be fair to say that the development of the Y-OQ-SR 2.0 subscales was primarily pragmatic; the scale remains primarily atheoretical in nature.

Directions for administration are not standardized, the administration directions simply state, "The Y-OQ-SR 2.0 requires no instruction beyond those printed on the answer sheet." These instructions direct the respondent to "Read each statement carefully and decide how true this statement is during the past 7 days." The Y-OQ-SR 2.0 manual provides no indication of the readability level of the scale, a significant limitation given the high comorbidity of academic achievement difficulties often experienced by adolescents with emotional and behavioral impairments. Although the administration directions do alert clinicians to be cautious in their explanation of the purpose for completing the instrument and to encourage clients to complete the scale honestly, there are no provisions for what to do if the adolescent is unfamiliar with a word or phrase or is unable to read the questions. It is not stated explicitly whether or not it would be appropriate for the examiner to read the questions aloud to the adolescent.

Although the administration and scoring manual indicates that, "Scoring the Y-OQ-SR is a fairly simple, straightforward procedure" (manual, pp. 4–5), the actual calculations are in fact a bit tedious. Total and subscale scores are calculated by adding the corresponding item values; however, the subscales contain different numbers of questions, and some items are weighted and some are negatively scored. As a result the subscales are represented by an inconsistent number of questions and range of possible scores: Intrapersonal Distress (17 questions, range -4 to 68); Somatic (8 questions, range 0 to 32); Interpersonal Relations (10 questions, range -6 to 34); Critical Items (9 questions, range 0 to 36); Social Problems (8 questions, range -2 to 30); Behavioral Dysfunction (11 questions, range -4 to 40); and Total Score (64 questions, range -16 to 240). Resulting scores are not able to be put into any type of common metric such as z-scores, T-scores, or percentiles. This omission will greatly limit the ability of the Y-OQ-SR 2.0 results to be compared to other behavior rating scales.

The standardization sample(s) described in the Y-OQ-SR 2.0 manual is presented in a somewhat confusing/contradicting manner. The manual indicates that four independent samples were collected, all from the Intermountain Western United States. One of the samples termed the "Community" sample was drawn from junior and senior high school students who had never received mental health treatment. A table in the manual indicates that the size of the Community sample was 512 although within the text it appears to be 1,334 minus 821 or 513. Within this population 49% of the students were male and 51% were female. The "Clinical" sample (55% male and 45% female) was drawn from a community health center ($N = 224$), a partial hospital setting ($N = 291$), and an outpatient substance abuse treatment agency ($N = 228$). Although balanced, these proportions do not reflect the fact that males typically far outnumber females in adolescent treatment facilities. As would be expected, the untreated control group received a statistically significant lower Total Score than the three clinical populations. It is noteworthy to point out that reliable differences did not emerge among the three clinical groups. Again, although these samples total 743, another place in the text indicates that the clinical sample consisted of 821 adolescents. The apparent miscalculations of something as simple as the size of the normative population serve to create an unfortunate question about the accuracy of the more technical aspects of the instrument.

Three major factors significantly limit the generalizability of the Y-OQ-SR 2.0 given its deficient standardization procedure. First, all subjects were drawn from the Western region of the

United States. Second, the ethnic makeup of the standardization sample is not reported. Third, although the authors indicate that "schools were chosen whose children came from a broad spectrum of SES levels" (manual, p. 6), no attempt was made to stratify the standardization sample for socioeconomic status, a factor highly correlated with psychopathology.

RELIABILITY. A single paragraph is contained in the user's manual to describe the reliability of the Y-OQ-SR 2.0. Internal consistency estimates of the instrument were assessed using Cronbach's (misspelled in the manual as Chronbach) coefficient alpha. Alpha coefficients were generally high with a reported reliability of .96 for the entire sample. Subscale coefficient alphas were reported as: Intrapersonal Distress, .91; Somatic, .73; Interpersonal Relations, .77; Critical Items, .81; Social Problems, .84; and Behavioral Dysfunction, .78. No subscale intercorrelations are reported.

Unfortunately, the Y-OQ-SR 2.0 fails to provide any evidence of test-retest reliability. This omission is especially alarming because the authors state, "While the Y-OQ-SR 2.0 was not designed to be a diagnostic device, but specifically to track therapeutic change" (manual, p. 12). Clinicians are provided no guidance for determining what constitutes normal variability across time for the total scale score or for any subscales. In the absence of published test-retest reliability data, potential users of the Y-OQ-SR 2.0 will be unable to ascertain whether changes in scores over time reflect normal developmental fluctuations, measurement errors associated with the instrument, abnormal etiology, or true therapeutic change.

VALIDITY. Data to support the validity of the Y-OQ-SR 2.0 are equally lacking. The user's manual reports no evidence of any type of convergent, discriminant, predictive, or construct validity. Although an exploratory factor analysis of the original Y-OQ (Burlingame, Wells, Lambert, & Cox, 2004) revealed two underlying factors for the total scale, the Y-OQ-SR 2.0 purports to identify the original, atheoretically derived, six subscales. This result is puzzling on two accounts. First, the authors actually acknowledge this limitation, "like the Y-OQ, the overall very high reliability estimate of the Y-OQ-SR suggests a strong single factor underlying the several subscales of the questionnaire" (manual, p. 11), but make no attempt to

correct for this limitation. Second, this statement occurs in the reliability section of the manual; the authors apparently do not understand the relationship between internal consistency reliability estimates and factorial or construct validity for an instrument.

The Y-OQ-SR 2.0 manual also fails to provide evidence of predictive validity for the instrument. Clinicians will therefore be unable to derive even basic diagnostic decisions when utilizing the Y-OQ-SR 2.0. Additionally, the test manual provides no evidence of incremental validity, or the extent to which information obtained from the scale increases the accuracy of predictions derived from other sources of information. Additionally, the authors make no mention of the limitations associated with self-report instruments (e.g., responses may be distorted by social desirability and so on) and how these data might be combined, and possibly improved, with information from other behavior rating scales completed by parents or teachers.

The single attempt at addressing issues of validity occurs in a section describing sensitivity (proportion of members of clinical groups correctly identified) and specificity (proportion of members of the normal group correctly identified). The administration and scoring manual indicates that the Y-OQ-SR 2.0 correctly identified clinical group members 66% of the time and normal group members 74% of the time when utilizing a cutoff score of 46. These values are quite low and the authors are correct when they point out, "Thus the current information suggests that the Y-OQ-SR presently *should not* be utilized for screening purposes, in that one-third of the clinical cases would be missed and one-fourth of the non-clinical cases would be identified as clinical" (manual, p. 12).

Finally, the Y-OQ-SR manual indicates there were no Total Score differences between male and female adolescent respondents. However, females did produce a higher score on the Intrapersonal Distress and Somatic subscales whereas males produced higher scores on both the Interpersonal Relations and Social Problems subscales. With regard to age-related differences, the authors found that younger adolescents exhibited higher subscale and Total Scale scores than did mid- and late-adolescents. No firm explanation is provided, rather the authors conclude the obvious that "younger adolescents were either experiencing overall greater difficulties or... were more willing to report greater difficulties" (manual, p. 10).

SUMMARY. The Y-OQ-SR 2.0 is an atheoretical, self-report instrument designed to assess the treatment progress of adolescents receiving mental health treatment. The scale possesses numerous psychometric shortcomings that significantly limit the usability of the instrument. With the exception of internal consistency reliability data, there are currently no other empirical data to support the utility of the instrument, most notably test-retest reliability. Similarly, evidence of the validity of the instrument is also not provided. The utility of information derived from the subscales (several of which contain inappropriately small numbers of items and low internal consistency reliabilities), over and above what is provided from the Total Scale score, is also lacking. Gender differences and age-related differences of several of the subscales serve to magnify the questionable utility of the subscales. Perhaps the single most important characteristic of the scale is the evidence that total scores differ significantly between normal, outpatient, and inpatient populations. However, this factor is outweighed by the fact that the scale tends to underidentify true pathology and to overidentify normal adolescents as needing clinical services. Until significant psychometric improvements can be incorporated into the Y-OQ-SR 2.0 it does not appear appropriate as a diagnostic or screening tool.

REVIEWER'S REFERENCES

Burlingame, G. M., Wells, M. G., & Lambert, M. J. (1996). *Administration and scoring manual for the Y-OQ.* Wilmington, DE: American Professional Credentialing Services.
Burlingame, G. M., Wells, M. G., Lambert, M. J., & Cox, J. C. (2004). Youth Outcome Questionnaire (Y-OQ). In M. E. Maruish (Ed.), *The use of psychological testing for treatment planning and outcome assessment* (3rd ed.). Mahwah, NJ: Lawrence Erlbaum Associates.
Green, S. K. (2005). [Review of the Youth Outcome Questionnaire (Y-OQ-2.01)]. In R. A. Spies & B. S. Plake (Eds.), *The sixteenth mental measurements yearbook* (pp. 1180–1182). Lincoln, NE: Buros Institute of Mental Measurements.
Hattie, J. (2005). [Review of the Youth Outcome Questionnaire (Y-OQ-2.01)]. In R. A. Spies & B. S. Plake (Eds.), *The sixteenth mental measurements yearbook* (pp. 1182–1183). Lincoln, NE: Buros Institute of Mental Measurements.

[208]

Youth Program Quality Assessment.

Purpose: "Designed to evaluate the quality of youth programs and identify staff training needs."
Population: Youth-serving programs.
Publication Date: 2005.
Acronyms: Youth PQA.
Administration: Individual or group.
Forms, 2: A, B.

Price Data, 2006: $39.95 per complete kit including administration manual (35 pages), Form A—Program Offering Items, and Form B—Organization Items; $19.95 per administration manual; $10.95 per Form A—Program Offering Items; $10.95 per Form B—Organization Items.
Comments: This test is based on observations and interviews by either "independent raters or as a self-assessment."
Authors: High/Scope Educational Research Foundation.
Publishers: High/Scope Educational Research Foundation.

a) FORM A—PROGRAM OFFERING ITEMS.
Purpose: "Focuses on youth experiences during a program offering."
Scores, 5: Safe Environment, Supportive Environment, Interaction, Engagement, Total.
Time: (120) minutes.
b) FORM B—ORGANIZATION ITEMS.
Purpose: "Assesses the organization's infrastructure."
Scores, 4: Youth Centered Policies/Practices, High Expectations for All Students/Staff, Access, Total.
Time: (60) minutes.

Review of the Youth Program Quality Assessment by GEORGETTE YETTER, Assistant Professor, School of Applied Health and Educational Psychology, Oklahoma State University, Stillwater, OK:

DESCRIPTION. The Youth Program Quality Assessment (Youth PQA) for Grades 4–12 is "an assessment of best practices in after-school programs, community organizations, schools, summer programs and other places where youth have fun, work, and learn with adults" (High/Scope, 2005a). The Youth PQA was developed to structure and guide program evaluation efforts. The test manual indicates that the Youth PQA can be used in several ways: (a) to guide independent assessment of a youth program by a rater from outside the organization, (b) to assist staff in self-evaluating their own program, or (c) to enable older youths to evaluate their programs under supervision from program staff.

General structure. Comprehensive evaluation of a youth program requires completion of both Form A (Program Offering, 60 items) and Form B (Organization, 43 items). Form A measures youth experiences in the program, and it is rated through direct observation of program delivery. Form B evaluates organizational supports for the program. It is rated based on a program administrator's responses to a series of 74 structured interview questions.

Scales and subscales. Form A contains four subscales: Safe Environment, Supportive Environment, Interaction, and Engagement. Each subscale assesses several program components. The Safe Environment subscale assesses five components: "Psychological and emotional safety is promoted" (2 items); "Physical environment is safe and free of health hazards" (4 items); "Appropriate emergency procedures and supplies are present" (6 items); "Program space and furniture accommodate the activities offered" (4 items); and "Healthy food and drinks are provided" (3 items). The six components measured by the Supportive Environment scale include "Staff provide a welcoming atmosphere" (3 items); "Session flow is planned, presented, and paced for youth" (5 items); "Activities support active engagement" (4 items); "Staff support youth in building new skills" (2 items); "Staff support youth with encouragement" (3 items); and "Staff use youth-centered approaches to reframe conflict" (4 items). The Interaction subscale measures four components: "Youth have opportunities to develop a sense of belonging" (4 items); "Youth have opportunities to participate in small groups" (3 items); "Youth have opportunities to act as group facilitators and mentors" (3 items); and "Youth have opportunities to partner with adults" (2 items). The Engagement subscale measures "Youth have opportunities to set goals and make plans" (2 items); "Youth have opportunities to make choices based on their interests" (2 items); and "Youth have opportunities to reflect" (4 items).

Form B is made up of three subscales, each assessing four program components. Youth-Centered Policies and Practices measures "Staff qualifications support a positive youth development focus" (5 items); "Program offerings tap youth interests and build multiple skills" (3 items); "Youth have an influence on the setting and activities in the organization" (3 items); and "Youth have an influence on the structure and policy of the organization" (5 items). High Expectations for Youth and Staff evaluates the components of "Organization promotes staff development" (5 items); "Organization promotes supportive social norms" (3 items); "Organization promotes high expectations for young people" (2 items); and "Organization is

committed to ongoing program improvement" (4 items). The Access subscale assesses "Staff availability and longevity with the organization support youth-staff relationships" (3 items for Grades 4–12); "Schedules are in effect" (3 items); "Barriers to participation are addressed" (3 items); and "Organization communicates with families, other organizations, and schools" (3 items).

Scoring procedure. The test manual recommends that programs use multiple raters to complete Form A and one rater for Form B. Evaluators rate items after observing youth in their program settings and conducting a structured interview with an administrator. All items are assigned a rating of 1, 3, or 5. Specific descriptors are provided to anchor these ratings. Item scores are averaged to obtain subscale scores. Scores above 3 are considered above average; those below 3 are below average. Subscale scores are compared to identify program strengths and weaknesses.

Time to complete. According to the test manual, an experienced rater can complete Form A in "a minimum of" 3 hours (2 hours to observe and collect written evidence and 1 hour to score), and 2 hours for Form B (1 hour to complete the interview and 1 hour to score). It recommends that program evaluators learn to complete the Youth PQA most reliably and quickly by attending formal training sessions offered by High/Scope.

Evidence of the time required to complete the Youth PQA was provided in a report describing its use for self-assessment by 24 after-school programs run by 21st Century Community Learning Centers. Several programs indicated that despite having received one day of training from High/Scope on observation and scoring, the observation and scoring procedures seemed too time-consuming (High/Scope, 2005b). The time investment for observation and scoring varied widely among the programs, ranging from 5.5 hours (by a rater "very familiar" with the Youth PQA) to 28–30 hours. It is apparent that the time demands for administering and scoring the Youth PQA can be high for staff not very familiar with the instrument.

DEVELOPMENT.

Theoretical foundations. The empirical literature shows that high-quality out-of-school programs for children and youth ages 6 to 18 share certain practices: a clear mission; high expectations; positive social norms; a safe and healthy environment; small enrollment; well-trained personnel; low staff turnover; appropriate content and pedagogy; opportunities for youth to engage; appropriate structure; supportive relationships; empowerment practices that support autonomy; opportunities for skill building; and coordination with family, school, and community (Bodilly & Beckett, 2005). High/Scope organized these quality indicators into a hierarchical model, the "Pyramid of Program Quality" (Akiva, 2005). The Youth PQA reflects this model, and it comprehensively addresses these best practice components.

The Youth PQA items initially were developed by adapting the Preschool PQA, an assessment tool developed for young children (High/Scope, 2003; 17:155). These items were later modified following feedback from a committee of youth development experts (Akiva, 2005).

TECHNICAL.

Reliability and validity. The Youth PQA was validated on 140 youth programs offered by 51 organizations in Michigan. "Most... were after-school programs that met weekly or daily over several months" (High/Scope, 2005a, p. 1). The programs addressed diverse content areas and included a range of approaches (e.g., mentoring, residential care, school-based). Half the programs were located in urban areas and one-third in suburban neighborhoods. The 1,635 participating youth were between 10 and 18 years old and they represented varied ethnic and racial groups.

Two factor analyses investigated the coherence of the component scores that make up the Supportive Environment, Interaction, and Engagement scales. Although these analyses were performed on small samples, the structural coherence of the Supportive Environment and Engagement scales was reasonable. However, the Interaction scale was of questionable integrity, in that several of its clusters appeared to more appropriately represent Supportive Environment. Safe Environment and Access were not included in the factor-analytic results. These "catchall" subscales (High/Scope, 2005b) were retained despite "less than optimal" psychometric performance (administration manual, p. 16), due to their empirical and theoretical importance.

A factor analysis also analyzed the structural integrity of the component scores that make up the Youth-Centered Policies and Practices, High Expectations, and the Access subscales. The sample size was quite small, but these subscales showed plausible structure. Additional analyses certainly are needed to investigate further the structural integrity of all the subscales. The manual provides no validity evidence supporting the adequacy of the items for representing their respective components.

Three validity studies were conducted, as completed by independent raters. The first study explored its concurrent validity through correlations with the Youth Survey (Youth Development Strategies, Inc.). Statistically significant correlations were obtained with Safe Environment, Interaction, Engagement, and Youth-Centered Policies and Practices. Interpretation of these relationships is clouded, however, by an almost complete lack of information about the Youth Survey on the website to which the manual refers. A second validity study explored correlations with informal ratings of program quality by experts. Ratings of 13 organizations by seven experts were strongly linked with Safe Environment, Supportive Environment, Interaction, and Engagement. A final investigation examined the ability of Form A to differentiate between programs in which personnel had completed training in participatory programming from those in which staff had not received this training. Programs in which workers had completed 4 days of High/Scope training received higher PQA ratings, compared with programs where the employees had not attended training.

The manual provides no validity evidence for the Youth PQA when used by program staff or youth for program self-assessment. However, a separate study describes the use of the PQA for self-assessment purposes by 24 Michigan 21st Century after-school programs. Although the self-assessment ratings evidenced positive bias, the internal consistency of the Supportive Environment, Interaction, and Engagement subscales were, in the opinion of this reviewer, acceptable (High/Scope, 2005b). These findings suggest that the Youth PQA may be a useful tool for self-evaluation by youth programs.

COMMENTARY. The youth out-of-school program literature has clearly articulated the need for an instrument for evaluating program effectiveness. Overall, the Youth PQA is promising, particularly given its solid convergence with the empirical findings on effective youth programs. The Youth PQA is a newly developed instrument. Some of its subscales, notably Safe Environment and Access, show structural weaknesses. Other scales, particularly High Expectations for Youth and Staff, lack strong validity evidence. Nevertheless, the Supportive Environment, Interaction, and Engagement subscales have real potential for helping youth programs to make valuable improvements in the services they provide to children and youth. More research is needed to validate and refine the Youth PQA, particularly the items that make up the component scores. Pending further analyses, interpretation of individual component scores is not advised.

SUMMARY. The Youth PQA for Grades 4–12 is a promising instrument developed to evaluate youth out-of-school programs. This instrument has the potential to be useful for serving as the framework for program evaluation both by outside evaluators and by youth programs for the purpose of self-evaluation. Nevertheless, further refinement of this instrument is needed. Programs considering the adoption of the Youth PQA are cautioned that this instrument has the potential to be time-consuming, especially when used by raters inexperienced in its use.

REVIEWER'S REFERENCES

Akiva, T. (2005, Fall/Winter). Turning training into results: The new Youth Program Quality Assessment. *High/Scope ReSource*. Retrieved September 2, 2006, from www.highscope.org

Bodilly, S., & Beckett, M. K. (2005). *Making out-of-school time matter: Evidence for an action agenda*. The RAND Corporation. Retrieved September 3, 2006, from http://www.wallacefoundation.org/WF/KnowledgeCenter/KnowledgeTopics/Out-Of-SchoolLearning/Costs_Of_OST_Programs.htm

High/Scope Educational Research Foundation. (2003). *High/Scope Program Quality Assessment—Preschool Version* (2nd ed.). Ypsilanti, MI: High/Scope Press.

High/Scope Educational Research Foundation. (2005a). *Youth Program Quality Assessment validation study: Findings for instrument validation*. Retrieved September 2, 2006, from www.highscope.org

High/Scope Educational Research Foundation. (2005b). *Measuring quality in Michigan's 21st Century after-school programs: The Youth PQA self-assessment pilot study*. Retrieved September 2, 2006, from www.highscope.org

[209]
Youth Risk and Resilience Inventory.

Purpose: Designed "to identify individual assets or resilience factors" and "screen for the presence of risk factors such as teasing, intimidation, bullying, physical abuse, violence, and victimization; to identify signs of emotional stress; and to assess their impact on the individual."
Population: Ages 10 to 17.
Publication Date: 2006.
Acronyms: YRRI.
Scores, 2: Risk Factor, Resilience Factor.
Administration: Individual or group.
Price Data, 2006: $23.95 per complete kit including 25 test booklets and administrator's guide (8 pages); bulk discounts are available.
Time: Administration time not reported.

Comments: There is an optional "My Journal" section at the end of the test; this option does not affect the numeric scores.
Authors: Robert P. Brady.
Publishers: JIST Publishing, Inc.

Review of the Youth Risk and Resilience Inventory by MERITH COSDEN, Professor of Counseling, Clinical and School Psychology, University of California—Santa Barbara, Santa Barbara, CA:

DESCRIPTION. The Youth Risk and Resilience Inventory (YRRI) is a 54-item, self-report inventory designed to assess the number and types of stressors and protective factors experienced by children and adolescents. Thirty-six of the items assess risk factors and the remaining 18 assess resilience. The risk items cover external risks present in the home, school, or community; interpersonal risks associated with the quality and quantity of relationships; and intrapersonal risk factors, including distress and dysphoria. All items are presented as short, declarative statements, with respondents asked to rate how well the statement describes them using a 1 to 5 scale corresponding to *never, seldom, sometimes, often,* and *very often.* The risk and protective items are interspersed and presented in five blocks. The administrator's guide states that the blocks were designed for easy self-scoring, and the items in these blocks are not grouped to represent specific types of risk and protective factors.

The YRRI response form is designed for self-response. Respondents can read the instructions on the form and then circle the numbers that represent their responses. The form also provides respondents with the opportunity to total their scores. Items that assess risk factors are colored yellow, and items that assess protective factors are green, so that respondents can easily obtain subtotals for each. There is also a scale provided on the form that indicates the category in which the scores place the youth in terms of very low to very high risk, and very low to very high strength. There has been no study of the validity of these designations. Finally, there is a section at the end of the answer sheet for youth to write a brief description of any problems they have at home, at school, or in the community.

DEVELOPMENT. According to the administrator's guide, the items in the scale were created after review of numerous studies on factors that place youth at risk, and factors that have a protective impact on youth facing adversity. A large, and appropriate, set of studies are cited. No additional information is provided, however, with regard to how particular items were selected or created, or whether there were other items that were tested and deleted. There is also little information provided on the manner in which the normative sample was obtained. The norms are based on a sample of 76 youth ages 10 to 19. This is a small normative sample given the age span covered and the need to represent youth with a range of risk and protective factors. Further, although the youth are described as representing urban, suburban, and rural areas, the extent to which they do so is unclear. Youth were described as having been referred for assessment by a teacher, caseworker, counselor, or mental health worker. It would appear from the analyses provided in the administrator's guide that students with and without risk were compared, but the method of sampling students not at-risk is not described.

TECHNICAL. The reliability of the YRRI was assessed by looking at its internal consistency. The coefficients were adequate for both the Risk Factor scale and the Resilience Factor scale. Alternate form and test-retest reliability coefficients were not reported.

Evidence supporting content and concurrent-criterion validity is provided in the administrator's guide. The author indicates that content validity is evident because the items were based on a review of the literature on risk and protective factors related to social, behavioral, and medical outcomes. Although the face validity of the items indicates that they emerged from this literature, the possible exclusion of other items, or oversampling some areas, is not addressed.

Evidence of criterion validity of the YRRI is based on a series of analyses in which at-risk youth identified by teachers, counselors, shelters, or abuse treatment programs were compared to students who were not at-risk. The t-test analyses presented in the administrator's guide reveal significant differences between students identified as at-risk and students who are not at-risk on both the Risk and Resilience subscales. The degrees of freedom provided in the tables indicate that there were no more than 80 students in each analysis, inclusive of both at-risk and not at-risk subgroups.

The administrator's guide also provides a list of critical items that address concerns such as sexual abuse that need immediate action. Items that cluster in specific areas of concern, such as depression and anxiety, and situational problems at home, in school, or in the community, are also identified. This allows the assessor to visually assess specific areas of need. There are also caveats provided in the administrator's guide on the possibilities of youth responding in ways that provide false positive (exaggerated need statements) or false negative (minimizing or denial) outcomes.

COMMENTARY. Assessing risk and protective factors is important for developing intervention plans for youth experiencing behavioral problems at home, at school, or in the community. Understanding specific risk factors can help concerned adults identify the genesis of problems, while understanding protective factors may provide areas of strength on which to build. One asset of the YRRI is that it assesses both risk and resilience, and it does so with separate items, not just opposing responses to the same items. Although the YRRI is easy to administer and can provide some interesting information on at-risk youth, its psychometric properties, beyond its internal consistency, are not well established. In particular, the self-scoring opportunity provided for youth, and the categories provided to them on which to rate their needs and strengths, is a serious concern because these categories may provide invalid information, causing concern or confusion. Validity evidence derives from a series of analyses that employ insufficient sample sizes. From these, it is not possible to conclude that the assessment is a valid indicator of risk and protective factors in youth. There are other problems with the validity analyses as well. First, the number of youth in each group (at-risk and not at-risk) is not provided, making it difficult to evaluate the quality of the comparison group. Second, the degrees of freedom change with each analysis, suggesting that the number of youth in each analysis is different. It is unclear whether the individuals in each analysis are from nonoverlapping samples, or from the same sample. The lack of information about referral sources for both at-risk and comparison groups leaves the composition of the groups ambiguous. Simply, the sample size is too small and unspecified to support use of *t* scores and risk categories for comparative purposes.

The YRRI is probably best used as an adjunct to a psychosocial interview. To develop norms that can differentiate youth with and without serious risk, it would be necessary to have a normative sample that included youth who were not at-risk. Future development of the norms of the YRRI and subsequent study of the validity of its categories may yield additional uses for this scale.

SUMMARY. The YRRI is an easily administered, self-report inventory in which youth respond to items describing potential risk and protective factors in their lives. Although the items have strong face validity, the small size of the normative sample, poor descriptions of how students were sampled, and limited study of the validity of the scales and their classifications, suggest that the instrument is better used for descriptive than comparative purposes. It is recommended that use be limited to descriptive item analysis in conjunction with a clinical interview until more research on the validity and utility of the scale is conducted and reported.

Review of the Youth Risk and Resilience Inventory by TIMOTHY R. KONOLD, Associate Professor of Research, Statistics, and Evaluation, University of Virginia, Charlottesville, VA:

DESCRIPTION. The Youth Risk and Resilience Inventory (YRRI) is a 54-item, self-report screening measure designed for use with school-aged children 10 to 17 years of age. The YRRI is intended to help identify the presence of a variety of risk (e.g., bullying, violence, and victimization) and emotional stress factors across different situations including home, school, and community. In addition, resilience or protective factors are assessed by the YRRI, including such things as goal setting and supportive relationships.

The response protocol is brightly colored with large text, and readability should not be a problem for most users who fall within the intended age group. Respondents rate the frequency with which each of 54 statements applies to them on a 5-point scale ranging from *never* to *very often*. The scoring protocol is accompanied by a 5-page (excluding references) administrator's guide that includes an introduction to the YRRI, evidence of psychometric

properties in the form of validity and reliability studies, administration directions, scoring directions, suggested interpretive frameworks.

Thirty-six of the 54 items can be combined to form a global measure of risk, and the remaining 18 items serve as measures of resilience. Beyond these global measures, users are encouraged to examine responses to individual items pertaining to Depression, Anxiety, Victimization, False Negatives, False Positives, Situation, and Critical items. Raw score to *T*-score conversions are available, at the mean and one standard deviation increments, for the two global measures.

DEVELOPMENT. According to the YRRI administrator's guide, items on the Risk scale are said to have been constructed from research reported in the social, behavioral, and medical literature. Items on the Resilience scale were more heavily influenced by research in the fields of behavioral and social sciences. Numerous references are provided to users that suggest the sources consulted during the item construction phase. The test author does not specify how this literature was used to inform the actual items (or scales) that appear on the YRRI. Little or no theoretical or empirical support is provided in the administrator's guide for understanding the composition of the various scales (e.g., depression, anxiety, victimization) beyond an examination of the items that comprise them.

The author indicates that Flesch's (1949) approach for evaluating readability revealed that language of the items was accessible to this age group. However, no information is provided to suggest the statements were subjected to empirical item analyses or expert review.

TECHNICAL. Information pertaining to the norming process and score interpretations is limited. Norms are provided in the form of average raw and *T*-scores for both the global Risk and Resilience scales. In addition, raw and *T*-scores are provided at one standard deviation increments. *T*-scores for values falling between these points are not provided. Descriptors are provided as interpretive guidelines at each of these score points. For example, on the Risk scale, youth scoring at the mean are said to be at "average risk" (administrator's guide, p. 4). Those scoring one standard deviation above the mean (+1*SD*) are said to be "at risk," +2*SD* at "high-risk," and +3*SD* at "extreme risk." The lack of description provided for the categories in general make it difficult for users to know the meaning or implications of high or extreme risk. No empirical studies are reported in the administrator's guide to indicate that youth at these score points are more vulnerable than youth at other score points on the scale.

It is also important to note that these score points are based on a very small normative sample of $N = 76$ youth ranging in age from 10–19 years. A sample size this small renders the normative score points and assigned descriptors unstable. Separate tables are not provided by age/grade, and no explanation is provided as to why scores would not be expected to differ as a function of age and grade. T-scores were obtained through a normalization of the raw score distributions, making it difficult to determine the actual percentage of youth falling at or above certain reported score points (percentiles are not provided).

The biggest problem with the description of the normative sample is that users are not told whether the normative sample and resulting cut score points are based on $N = 76$ youth that are not at-risk, youth that have been previously identified as being at risk, or a combination of the two groups. This is has direct implications for judging the relative severity of individual scores.

Reliability. Evidence of reliability is presented in the form of internal consistency estimates and standard errors of measurement. Reported internal consistency estimates are generally in the acceptable range (i.e., > .80) for the Risk and Resilience scales. No estimates are provided for the other scales purportedly measured on the YRRI. In addition, no estimates of score consistency over time (i.e., test-retest reliability) are provided for any of the scales.

Validity. The section on validity is a bit shorter than what might typically be expected for a published instrument. It is widely recognized that validity refers to the accumulation of evidence to support the interpretation of test scores in the context of their purpose. For organizational purposes, this evidence is often grouped under well known categories (e.g., content, criterion, construct). The YYRI administrator's guide describes validity evidence in terms of content and concurrent-criterion. There is some evidence in the administrator's guide that item construction was informed from a review of

the literature on risk and resilience as investigated across a variety of disciplines. Although encouraging in many ways, the connection between this body of literature and how risk is operationally defined through the use of the items appearing on the YRRI is not made.

Evidence of concurrent validity is presented in the form of group difference comparisons of YRRI scores between externally identified at-risk versus nonrisk groups. These analyses address whether scores on the YRRI are able to reliably discriminate between groups that should possess different levels of Risk indicators. Two studies are reported along these lines, the results of which generally support higher levels of risk factors as measured by the YRRI among youth identified as being at risk by teachers, case workers, counselors, and substance abuse treatment centers in comparison to those youth who were not identified by these external sources as being at risk. The ability of the YRRI to discriminate between at-risk youth and non-at-risk youth as identified by a domestic violence program was less convincing.

Resilience scores from the YRRI were also compared between these two groups that were identified from a variety of sources. Here, resilience scores were generally lower among students identified as being at-risk by teachers and substance abuse treatment centers. Differences between groups identified by school counselors and domestic violence programs were less pronounced.

COMMENTARY/SUMMARY. The measurement of risk and resilience is important to understanding youth and providing the necessary treatment mechanisms to help them succeed. At present, however, the current version of this instrument falls short on several levels. First, there is a lack of theoretical justification that establishes these items as the best items to assess risk and resilience among youth. There is little information pertaining to item try outs and why certain items are grouped together to form different scales. Second, the size of the normative sample ($N = 76$) is inadequate to cover a 7-year age span and reveal stable descriptions of score points suggestive of qualitatively distinct categories of risk and resilience. Information pertaining to the degree of skewness and/or kurtosis in the normative sample would help users better understand the extent of nonnormality that may have been realized in the standardization sample. It is unclear what the reported descriptive labels ("at-risk," "high risk," "extreme risk") indicate in terms of being at risk, at risk for what, in what contexts, and how they are distinct from one another in terms of their concurrent and/or predictive usefulness. Equally important, the degree to which the normative sample was composed of at-risk youth is not addressed. This makes it difficult to determine whether the normative frameworks for interpreta-tion are adequate. Third, the reported psychomet-ric information pertaining to the instrument's reliability and validity is generally favorable. However, many important aspects related to errors of measurement (reliability) and the appropriateness of test score use (validity) are not included. No evidence of stability over time is reported, and no empirical evidence is provided to support that the instrument is measuring what is intended (construct validity).

REVIEWER'S REFERENCE

Flesch, R. (1949). *The art of readable writing*. New York: MacMillan.

APPENDIX

TESTS LACKING SUFFICIENT TECHNICAL DOCUMENTATION FOR REVIEW

Effective with The Fourteenth Mental Measurements Yearbook *(2001), an additional criterion was added for tests reviewed in* The Mental Measurements Yearbook. *Only those tests for which at least minimal technical or test development information is provided are now reviewed. This list includes the names of new and revised tests received since publication of* The Sixteenth Mental Measurements Yearbook *that are lacking this documentation. The publishers have been advised that these tests do not meet our review criteria.*

[210]

Alleman Leadership Development Questionnaire.
Publisher: Silverwood Enterprises, LLC.

[211]

Alleman Mentoring Activities Questionnaire.
Publisher: Silverwood Enterprises, LLC.

[212]

Alleman Relationship Value Questionnaire.
Publisher: Silverwood Enterprises, LLC.

[213]

Applicant Productivity Profile.
Publisher: Pearson Performance Solutions [No reply from publisher; status unknown].

[214]

The Assessment of Personal Goals.
Publisher: Mind Garden, Inc.

[215]

Basic Banking Skills Battery.
Publisher: Pearson Performance Solutions [No reply from publisher; status unknown].

[216]

Bilingual Two-Language Assessment Battery of Tests.
Publisher: Branden Publishing Co.

[217]

Bloomer Learning Test—Neurologically Enhanced.
Publisher: Brador Publications, Inc. [No reply from publisher; status unknown].

[218]

Career & Life Explorer.
Publisher: JIST Publishing, Inc.

[219]

Cortical Vision Screening Test.
Publisher: Harcourt Assessment [England].

[220]

Criterion Validated Written Test for Emergency Medical Practitioner.
Publisher: Vantage McCann Associates.

[221]

Criterion Validated Written Test for Fire Medic.
Publisher: Vantage McCann Associates.

[222]
Criterion Validated Written Tests for Firefighter [Revised].
Publisher: Vantage McCann Associates.

[223]
Criterion Validated Written Tests for Police Officer [Revised].
Publisher: Vantage McCann Associates.

[224]
Customer Service Profile.
Publisher: Pearson Performance Solutions [No reply from publisher; status unknown].

[225]
Domestic Situation Inventory.
Publisher: JIST Publishing, Inc.

[226]
Drafter (CAD Operator).
Publisher: Ramsay Corporation.

[227]
Employee Productivity Index.
Publisher: Pearson Performance Solutions [No reply from publisher; status unknown].

[228]
Fire Promotion Tests—Complete Service [Revised].
Publisher: Vantage McCann Associates.

[229]
Fox Adds Up.
Publisher: CTB/McGraw-Hill.

[230]
Fox in a Box—Second Edition.
Publisher: CTB/McGraw-Hill.

[231]
Fox Letters and Numbers.
Publisher: CTB/McGraw-Hill.

[232]
Instructional Style Indicator [Revised].
Publisher: Consulting Resource Group International, Inc.

[233]
Insurance Selection Inventory.
Publisher: Pearson Performance Solutions [No reply from publisher; status unknown].

[234]
Language Assessment Skills Links Benchmark Assessment.
Publisher: CTB/McGraw-Hill.

[235]
Language Assessment Skills Links K-12 Assessments.
Publisher: CTB/McGraw-Hill.

[236]
Law Enforcement Applicant Inventory.
Publisher: Pearson Performance Solutions [No reply from publisher; status unknown].

[237]
Leadership Skills Inventory [Revised] [Consulting Resource Group International, Inc.].
Publisher: Consulting Resource Group International, Inc.

[238]
Learning Style Indicator [Revised].
Publisher: Consulting Resource Group International, Inc.

[239]
Management Aptitude Test.
Publisher: Pearson Performance Solutions [No reply from publisher; status unknown].

[240]
Management Readiness Profile.
Publisher: Pearson Performance Solutions [No reply from publisher; status unknown].

[241]

MultiCraft Trainee Test.
Publisher: Ramsay Corporation.

[242]

Observation Ability Test for the Police Service.
Publisher: Vantage McCann Associates.

[243]

Office Skills Assessment Battery.
Publisher: Pearson Performance Solutions [No reply from publisher; status unknown].

[244]

Partners in Play: Assessing Infants and Toddlers in Natural Contexts.
Publisher: Thomson Delmar Learning.

[245]

Personal History Checklist for Adolescents.
Publisher: Psychological Assessment Resources, Inc.

[246]

Planning, Organizing, & Scheduling Test, Revised Edition.
Publisher: HRD Press, Inc.

[247]

Police Promotion Tests—Complete Service [Revised].
Publisher: Vantage McCann Associates.

[248]

Power Reading Assessment Kit.
Publisher: National Reading Styles Institute, Inc.

[249]

Quick Style Indicator.
Publisher: Consulting Resource Group International, Inc.

[250]

Retail Management Applicant Inventory.
Publisher: Pearson Performance Solutions [No reply from publisher; status unknown].

[251]

Sales Style Indicator [Revised].
Publisher: Consulting Resource Group International, Inc.

[252]

Standardized Bible Content Tests, Forms I and J.
Publisher: Association for Biblical Higher Education.

[253]

Station Employee Applicant Inventory.
Publisher: Pearson Performance Solutions [No reply from publisher; status unknown].

[254]

Stress Indicator & Health Planner [Revised].
Publisher: Consulting Resource Group International, Inc.

[255]

SuperSelect.
Publisher: Pearson Performance Solutions [No reply from publisher; status unknown].

[256]

Telemarketing Applicant Inventory.
Publisher: Pearson Performance Solutions [No reply from publisher; status unknown].

[257]

Transition-to-Work Inventory.
Publisher: JIST Publishing, Inc.

[258]

Values Preference Indicator [Revised].
Publisher: Consulting Resource Group International, Inc.

[259]

Work Preference Match: A Career Exploration Tool.
Publisher: JIST Publishing, Inc.

TESTS TO BE REVIEWED FOR THE EIGHTEENTH MENTAL MEASUREMENTS YEARBOOK

By the time each new Mental Measurements Yearbook *reaches publication, the staff at the Buros Institute have already collected many new and revised tests destined to be reviewed in the next* Mental Measurements Yearbook. *Following is a list of tests that meet the review criteria and that will be reviewed, along with additional tests published and received in the next year, in* The Eighteenth Mental Measurements Yearbook.

A-4 Police Officer Video Test
Administrative Series Modules
The Awareness of Social Inference Test

B-3R, B-4R, B-5, B-5a Firefighter Tests
BRIGANCE Diagnostic Assessment of Basic Skills–Revised Spanish Edition
Bruininks-Oseretsky Test of Motor Proficiency, Second Edition
Burks Behavior Rating Scales, Second Edition

C-BDQ Correctional Officer Background Data Questionnaire
C-1 and C-2 Correctional Officer Tests
Cigarette Use Questionnaire
Clinical Evaluation of Language Fundamentals–4 Screening Test
Customer Service Skills Inventory

D-1, D-2, and D-3 Police Officer Tests
Diagnostic Assessments of Reading, Second Edition

ElecTest (Form A, Form A-C, & Form B)
Expressive Vocabulary Test, Second Edition

Koppitz Developmental Scoring System for the Bender Gestalt Test, Second Edition

Millon College Counseling Inventory

P-BDQ Police Officer Background Data Questionnaire

P-Det 1.0 and 2.0 Police Detective Tests
P-1SV and P-2SV Police Officer Tests
Parenting Relationship Questionnaire
Peabody Picture Vocabulary Test, Fourth Edition
PL-1 and PL-2 Police Administrator Tests (Lieutenant)
The ProfileXT Assessment
PST-100SV and PST-80SV Public Safety Telecommunicator Tests
PSUP 1.1, 2.1, and 3.1 Police Supervisor Tests (Corporal/Sergeant)
PsychEval Personality Questionnaire

Report Completion Exercise for Firefighter, Police Officer, and Correctional Officer
Roberts-2

School Motivation and Learning Strategies Inventory
701 and 702 Fire Supervisor Tests (Lieutenant)
The Social Problem-Solving Inventory for Adolescents
SPELL-2: Spelling Performance Evaluation for Language and Literacy—Second Edition

Test of Adolescent and Adult Language, Fourth Edition
Test of Memory and Learning, Second Edition
Test of Preschool Early Literacy
The Token Test for Children, Second Edition

Vineland Adaptive Behavior Scales, Second Edition

NEW TESTS REQUESTED BUT NOT RECEIVED

The staff of the Buros Institute endeavor to acquire copies of every new or revised commercially available test. Descriptions of all tests are included in Tests in Print *and reviews for all tests that meet our review criteria are included in* The Mental Measurements Yearbook. *A comprehensive search of multiple sources of test information is ongoing, and test materials are regularly requested from publishers. Many publishers routinely provide review copies of all new test publications. However, some publishers refuse to provide materials and others advertise tests long before the tests are actually published. Following is a list of test titles that have been requested but not yet provided.*

The ABC Inventory-Extended
The Abel Assessment for Interest in Paraphilias
The Abel Assessment for Sexual Interest
Abilities Forecaster
Ability Profiler
Ability Test
Accuracy Level Test
AccuRater
AccuVision
Achiever
ACS California Chemistry Diagnostic Test
ACS Chemistry in the Community (Chem Com) Curriculum, High School Chemistry
ACS Examination in Instrumental Methods
ACT Assessment
Actions, Styles, Symbols in Kinetic Family Drawings
Acumen Leadership WorkStyles
Acumen Team Skills
Acumen Team WorkStyles
Adaptability Test [Revised]
Adaptiv Resilience Factor Inventory
Adjective Rating Scale
Admitted Student Questionnaire and Admitted Student Questionnaire Plus
Adolescent & Child Urgent Threat Evaluation
Adolescent Chemical Dependency Inventory
The Adolescent Multiphasic Personality Inventory
Adolescent SASSI-A2
Adolescent Self-Report and Projective Inventory
Adult Child Distortion Scale
Adult Health Nursing
Adult Measure of Essential Skills
Adult Memory and Information Processing Battery
Adult Presentence Evaluation
Adult Pretrial Test
Adult Self-Perception Profile
Advanced Management Tests
Advanced Placement Examination in Comparative Government and Politics
Advanced Placement Examination in Computer Science
Advanced Placement Examination in Economics
Advanced Placement Examination in Environmental Science
Advanced Placement Examination in Government and Politics
Advanced Placement Examination in Macroeconomics
Advanced Placement Examination in Microeconomics
Advanced Placement Examination in Psychology
Advanced Placement Examination in Statistics
Advanced Placement Examination in United States Government and Politics
Advanced Placement Program: Psychology
The Advanced Problem Solving Tests
Algebra
Allied Health Aptitude Test
American Health and Life Styles
The American Tobacco Survey
Anatomy and Physiology
Aphasia Screening Test
Apperceptive Personality Test
Applied Natural Sciences
Applied Technology Series
APTICOM
Aptitude Assessment
Aptitude Test Battery for Pupils in Standards 6 and 7
Aptitude Test for International Secondary Students
The Arabic Speaking Test
The Area Coordinator Achievement Test
Areas of Change Questionnaire
Arithmetic Index [Revised]
Arithmetic Test, Form A
Arizona Basic Assessment and Curriculum Utilization System for Young Handicapped Children
Armed Services Vocational Aptitude Battery
Armstrong Naming Test
Assertiveness Profile
Assessing Semantic Skills Through Everyday Themes
Assessment of Collaborative Tendencies
Assessment of Competencies and Traits
Assessment of Grandparenting Style
Assessment of Information and Communication Literacy

Assessment of Organizational Readiness for Mentoring
Assessment of Sound Awareness and Production
Assessment of Stuttering Behaviors
The Assessment, Evaluation, and Programming System for Infants and Children
Associational Fluency
Attention Battery for Children
Attention Index Survey
Attitude Survey
Auditory Perception Test for the Hearing Impaired
Auditory-Visual Single-Word Picture Vocabulary Test–Adolescent
Authentic Assessment for the Intermediate Level in French
Authentic Assessment for the Intermediate Level in Spanish
Authentic Writing Screener
Autism Diagnostic Interview—Revised
Auto Technician

The b Test
Baccalaureate Achievement
Basic Academic Evaluation
Basic Inventory of Natural Language
Basic Nursing Care I and II
The BASICS Behavioral Adjustment Scale
Basics in Nursing I, II, III
Battelle Developmental Inventory—Spanish
Behavior Forecaster
Behavior Style Analysis
Behavioral Characteristics Progression (BCP) Assessment Record
Behavioral Intervention Plan
Bell Relationship Inventory for Adolescents
Bilingual Classroom Communication Profile
Bilingual Health and Developmental History Questionnaire
Bilingual Language Proficiency Questionnaire
Bilingual Vocabulary Assessment Measure
BldgTest
Building Maintenance Test
Business English Assessment
Business Personality Indicator

C.I.T.E. Academic Learning Styles
The California Critical Thinking Dispositions Inventory [Revised]
California Critical Thinking Skills Test [Revised]
The California Measure of Mental Motivation
The California Reasoning Appraisal
California Self Evaluation Scale
Caliper Profile
Call Center Survey
The Call Centre Battery
Callier-Azusa Scale: H Edition
CAMDEX: The Cambridge Mental Disorders of the Elderly Examination

Campbell Leadership Index—Revised
Campbell-Hallam Team Leader Profile
Candidate and Officer Personnel Survey
Care of the Adult Client
Care of the Client During Childbearing and Care of the Child
Care of the Client with a Mental Disorder
Career Automotive Retailing Scale
Career Competency Scale for College Students
Career Competency Scale—Sales and Marketing
Career Concerns Checklist: College Edition
The Career Exploration Inventory: A Guide for Exploring Work, Leisure, and Learning, Third Edition
Career Finder
Career Guidance Inventory II
Career Interest Profiler
Career Mapper
Career Personality Questionnaire
Career Portfolio Builder
Career Preference Scale
Career Selection Questionnaire
Career Values Scale
Caregiver-Administered Communication Inventory
Cellular Technician
Change Agent Questionnaire
Change Management Effectiveness Profile
Change Style Indicator
Chemical Abuse Scale
Chemical Reading
Chemistry
Chemistry Test
Child and Adolescent Diagnostic Scales
Child and Adolescent Functional Assessment Scale
Child Health Nursing
Child Health Questionnaire
Child Observation Record (COR) for Infants and Toddlers
Child-focused Toddler and Infant Experiences: Revised Form
Children's Interaction Matrix
Children's Self-Report and Projective Inventory
CLEP Education Assessment Series
CLEP Subject Examination in Freshman College Composition
Clerical Aptitudes [Revised]
Clerical Series Test Modules
Clerical Series Test: Oral Instructions Forms Completion
Clerical Test Battery
Clinician-Administered PTSD Scale
Clinician-Administered PTSD Scale for Children and Adolescents
Clock Drawing
Cloze Reading Tests 1-3, Second Edition
CNC Math (Trig. Test)
CNC Operator

Computer Programmer Aptitude Battery
The Concise Learning Styles Assessment
Concussion Resolution Index
Conflict Style Instrument
Copeland Symptom Checklist for Attention Deficit Disorders
COPS Interest Inventory (1995 Revision)
Corporate Communication Assessment
Corporate Ethics Audit
Counterproductive Behavior Index
CPI 260
Creativity Questionnaire
Creativity/Innovation Effectiveness Profile
The Creatrix Inventory [Revised]
Cree Questionnaire [Revised]
Crichton Vocabulary Scale, 1988 Revision
Criterion Validated Written Tests for Firefighter [Revised]
Criterion-Referenced Articulation Profile
Critical Thinking in Clinical Nursing Practice–PN
Critical Thinking in Clinical Nursing Practice–RN
Critical Thinking Test
CRT Skills Test
Cultural Diversity and Awareness Profile
Culture for Diversity Inventory
Culture for Diversity Inventory
Customer Satisfaction Practices Tool
Customer Service Aptitude Profile
Customer Service Commitment Profile
Customer Service Listening Skills Exercise
Customer Service Simulator
Customer Service Skills Assessment
Customer Service Styles Survey
Customer Service Survey

Data Entry and Data Checking Tests
Data Entry Test
Dealing With Conflict Instrument
DecideX
Defendant Questionnaire
Denison Leadership Development Survey
Denison Organizational Culture Survey
DEST: Dental Ethical Sensitivity Test
Detention Promotions Test–Complete Service [Revised]
Developmental Eye Movement Test
Developmental Inventory of Learned Skills
Developmental Reading Assessment
Diagnostic Assessments of Reading, Second Edition
The Diagnostic Inventory of Personality and Symptoms
Diagnostic Prescriptive Assessment
Diagnostic Readiness Test–PN
Diagnostic Readiness Test–RN
Diagnostic Test for High School Math
Diagnostic Test for Pre-Algebra Math
Differential Aptitude Tests for Schools

Differential Assessment of Autism & Other Developmental Disorders
Dimensional Assessment for Patient Placement Engagement & Recovery
Dimensional Assessment of Personality Pathology—Basic Questionnaire
The Dimensions of Depression Profile for Children and Adolescents
The Discovering Diversity Profile and Facilitator's Kit
Disruptive Behavior Rating Scale
Diversity & Cultural Awareness Profile
Diversity Survey
Do What You Are Self Discovery Assessment
The Dot Counting Test
Draw A Person Questionnaire
Drug Store Applicant Inventory
Drug/Alcohol Attitude Survey
Dynamic Assessment and Intervention: Improving Children's Narrative Abilities
Dynamic Factors Survey
Dynamic Occupational Therapy Cognitive Assessment for Children
Dyslexia Screener

Early Literacy Diagnostic Test
Edinburgh Reading Tests [2002 Update]
Edinburgh Reasoning Series
Educational Development Series [1997-1998 Norms]
Educational Interest Inventory II
Educators Survey
Efron Visual Acuity Test
Elect. & Inst. Technician
Electrical Technician I
Electrical Technician II
Elementary Student Opinion Inventory
Emo Questionnaire [Revised]
Emotional Competence Inventory—University Edition
Emotional Intelligence Profile
Emotional Intelligence Questionnaire: General and General 360°
Emotional Intelligence Questionnaire: Managerial and Managerial 360°
Emotional Intelligence Style Profile
Emotional Quotient Scale for Children
Emotional Quotient Scale for Employee
Emotional Smarts!
Employee Adjustment Survey
Employee Empowerment Survey
Employee Evaluation of Management Survey
Employee Opinion Survey
Employee Productivity Profile
Employee Wellness Evaluation
Empowerment Management Inventory
Endler Multidimensional Anxiety Scales [including EMAS Social Anxiety Scales]
English and Citizenship Test
Entry Level Police Officer Examination

Infant/Preschool Play Assessment Scale
Influencing Skills Index
The Influencing Skills Inventory
Influencing Skills Profile
Influencing Strategies and Styles Profile
The Influencing Style Clock
Information and Communications Technology Literacy Assessment
Initial Assessment: An Assessment for Reading, Writing and Maths [New Version]
In-Law Relationship Scale
Instruments for Assessing Understanding & Appreciation of Miranda Rights
Integrity Survey
Intercultural Communication Inventory
Interest Check List
Interest Inventory
Interest/Skills Checklist
Internal Customer Service Survey
InterSurvS
Intuitive Mechanics (Weights & Pulleys) [Revised]
Inventory of Gambling Situations
Inventory of Leadership Styles
Inventory of Marital Conflict (IMC)
Inventory of Parent-Adolescent Conflict
Inventory of Parent-Child Conflict
Inventory of Premarital Conflict (IPMC)
Inventory of Program Stages of Development
Inventory of Religious Activities and Interests
Inventory of School Effectiveness
Invest in Your Values
Inwald Personality Inventory–Clinical
Inwald Personality Inventory–Short Version
Inwald Survey 2
Inwald Survey 2-Adolescent Version
Inwald Survey 3
Inwald Survey 4
Inwald Survey 6
Inwald Survey 8
The Iowa Developing Autonomy Inventory
Iowa Writing Assessment
IPI Performance Appraisal Questionnaires
Ironworker

The Janus Competency Identification & Assessment System
The Japanese Speaking Test
Job and Vocational Attitudes Assessment
Job Effectiveness Prediction System
Job Requirements Questionnaire
Job Skills Training Needs Assessment
Job Values Inventory
Job-O Enhanced
Jonico Questionnaire
Judgment of Line Orientation
The Julia Farr Services Post-Traumatic Amnesia Scale
Jung Type Indicator

Junior Scholastic Aptitude Test Battery (Standard 5)
Juvenile Presentence Evaluation
Juvenile Pretrial Test
Juvenile Substance Abuse Profile
Juvenile Treatment Outcome

Kaleidoscope Profile for Educators
The Kaufman Speech Praxis Test for Children
Kendrick Assessment of Cognitive Ageing
The Kendrick Assessment Scales of Cognitive Ageing
Kindergarten Readiness Checklists for Parents
Kuder Career Search
Kuder Skills Assessment
Kuhlmann-Anderson Tests [1997 norms/standards]

Laboratory Technician (Mfg.)
Langdon Adult Intelligence Test
Language Assessment for Grades 3 & 4
Language Processing Test-Revised
[Law Enforcement] Personal History Questionnaire
LEAD (Leader Effectiveness and Adaptability Description) Instrument: Self/Other
Leadership Competency Inventory [Revised]
Leadership Development Profile
Leadership Development Series
Leadership Effectiveness Analysis
Leadership Effectiveness Profile
Leadership in Nursing
Leadership Opinion Questionnaire [Revised]
Leadership Qualities Scale
Leadership Scale: Staff Member/Manager
Leadership Skills Test
Leadership Versatility Index
The Learning Disability Diagnostic Inventory
Leatherman Leadership Questionnaire II
Legendary Service Leader Assessment
Life Events Scale for Children
Life Style Inventory
Lifespace Access Profile
Lifestyle Questionnaire [Selby MillSmith]
Linking Skills Index
Linking Skills Profile
Listening & Literacy Index
Listening Effectiveness Profile
The Listening Test
Literacy Probe 7–9
Logramos
Lore Leadership Assessment II
Lowenstein Occupational Therapy Cognitive Assessment Battery [Revised]

MacArthur Competence Assessment Tool for Treatment
The MacArthur Competence Assessment Tool—Criminal Adjudication
Machinist Test—Form AC
Macmillan Group Reading Test 9-14

Maculaitis Assessment of Competencies II
Major Field Tests
Management & Supervisory Skills
Management Behavior Assessment Test
Management Candidate Profile
Management Development Questionnaire
Management Effectiveness Profile
Management Practices Inventory
Management Style Indicator
Management Training Needs Analysis
Managerial and Professional Job Functions Inventory [Revised]
The Managerial and Professional Profiles
Managing Performance
Marriage Assessment Inventory
Marysville Test of Language Dominance
Maternity and Child Health Nursing
Maternity Infant Nursing
Math Grade-Placement Tests
Mathematical Achievement Test
Matson Evaluation of Social Skills With Youngsters
Matson Evaluation of Social Skills with Youngsters, Hard of Hearing Version
The McQuaig System
The Meade Movement Assessment
Measure of Individual Differences in Dominance-Submissiveness
Measures of Guidance Impact
Measures of Individual Differences in Temperament
Mechanical Aptitudes [Revised]
Mechanical Repair Apprentice Battery
MecTest (A Test for Maintenance Mechanics)–Form AU-C
Medical College Admission Test
Meeker Structure of Intellect Screening for Learning & Thinking Abilities
Meeting Effectiveness Inventory Self/Other
Meeting Effectiveness Questionnaire
Member Satisfaction Survey
Memory and Concentration Test
Memory Complaints Inventory for Windows
Mental Health Concepts
Metric Assessment of Personality
Michigan Screening Profile of Parenting
Michigan State Suggestibility Profiles
Microbiology
Millwright Test
Mini-Hilson Life Adjustment Profile
Minnesota Cognitive Acuity Screen
Minnesota Developmental Programming System Behavioral Scales
Missouri Aptitude and Career Information Inventory
Missouri Comprehensive Student Needs Survey
Mobile Equipment Mechanic
Mobile Equipment Operator
Moray House Tests
Mortimer-Filkins Test for Problem Drinkers

Motivation Questionnaire
Motive-A Motivational Analysis
Movement ABC
MR/DD Profile
The MSFI College of Law Admission Test
Multi-Digit Memory Test
Multidimensional Personality Questionnaire
Multifactor Leadership Questionnaire for Teams for Research
Multi-Level Management Surveys
Multiphasic Environmental Assessment Procedure [Revised]
Music Teacher Self-Assessment

National Assessment of Educational Progress–Released Exercises
The National Corrections Officer Selection Test
The National Firefighter Selection Test & National Firefighter Selection Test—Emergency Medical Services
The National First- and Second-Line Supervisor Tests
The National Police Officer Test [Revised]
Natural Sciences in Nursing
NCTE Cooperative Test of Critical Reading and Appreciation
Negotiating Style Instrument
Negotiation Style Instrument
Networking & Relationship Building Profile
Neuropsychological Aging Inventory
The New Jersey Test of Children's Reasoning
The New Jersey Test of Reasoning [Adult Version]
New Reading Analysis
New Workers Inventory
NOCTI Experienced Worker Assessments
NOCTI Job Ready Assessments
NOCTI/The Whitener Group Industrial Assessments
The Nonspeech Test
Nonverbal Form [Revised]
Nonverbal Reasoning [Revised]
Normal Nutrition
Normative Adaptive Behavior Checklist—Revised
Norris-Ryan Argument Analysis Test
NTE Specialty Area Tests: School Social Worker
Numeracy Progress Tests
Numerical Computation Test
Nurse Aide (Assistant) Program
Nursing Care During Childbearing and Nursing Care of the Child
Nursing Care in Mental Health and Mental Illness
Nursing Care of Adults with Pathophysiological Disturbances–Part I and II
Nursing Care of Adults, Parts I, II, and III
Nursing Care of Children
Nursing the Childbearing Family

O'Neill Talent Inventory
Objective Risk Taking Test

Occupational Interest Profile
Occupational Motivation Questionnaire
Occupational Personality Profile
Occupational Preference Inventory
Office Skills Profile
Office Skills Tests [Revised]
Ohio Vocational Competency Assessment
Online Sales Effectiveness Profile
The Opportunities-Obstacles Profile
Oral Communication Battery
Organisational Transitions
Organizational Assessment Survey
Organizational Character Index
Organizational Climate Survey
Organizational Focus Questionnaire
Organizational Justice Inventory
Organizational Survey System
OSHA Violations Safety Test
Outcome Assessment and Reporting System

P.A.S.S. III Survey
Pacesetter
Pair Behavioral Style Instrument
Parent Opinion Inventory, Revised Edition [1995 Edition]
Parental Involvement in Education Scale
Parenting Needs Inventory for Parents
Parenting Stress Inventory
Parker Team Development Survey
Parolee Inventory
Partner Power Profile
Partnering Development Assessment
Passport
Paternal Role Survey
Pathognomonic Scale
Pathways to Independence, Second Edition
PCA Checklist for Computer Access
Pediatric Symptoms Checklist
Perceived Competence Scale for Children
Perceptual Archetypal Orientation Inventory
Performance Coaching
Performance Management Assessment System
Performance On-Line
Performance Skills Quality Teams Assessment
Performer
Personal Audit [Revised]
Personal Competency Framework
Personal Directions
Personal Dynamics Profile
Personal Effectiveness Profile
Personal Interest and Values Survey
Personal Learning Profile
Personal Productivity Assessment
Personal Profile Analysis
Personal Stress & Well-being Assessment
Personal Success Profile
The Personality Preference Profile

Personality Questionnaire
Personnel Security Standards Psychological Questionnaire
Personnel Selection Inventory
Personnel Selection Inventory [Revised]
The PETAL Speech Assessment
Pharmacology in Clinical Nursing
The Phonological and Reading Profile—Intermediate
Phonological Awareness & Reading Profile
The Phonological Awareness Profile
The Phonological Awareness Test
Phonological Screening Assessment
Physical Assessment
Pictorial Inventory of Careers
Pictorial Reasoning Test [Revised]
Picture Interest Exploration Survey
Pikunas Adult Stress Inventory
PIP Developmental Charts, Second Edition
PipeTest
PLAN [Revised]
The Play Observation Scale [Revised]
Plice Officer Morale Survey
Plotkin Index
Plumber-Pipefitter Test
PM Benchmark Kit
PN Fundamentals
PN Pharmacology
Police Administrator (Assistant Chief) 566
Police Administrator (Captain) 565
Police Administrator (Chief) 568
Police Administrator (Lieutenant) 564
Police Corporal/Sergeant Examination 562 and 563
Police Officer Examinations 175.1 and 175.2
Police Officer: A-2
Police Radio Dispatcher
Polymath Intellectual Ability Scale
Portland Digit Recognition Test [Revised]
Positive and Negative Syndrome Scale [Revised]
Post-Heroic Leadership
Power and Performance Measures
Power Perception Profile
The Praxis Series: Professional Assessments for Beginning Teachers
Pre-Admission Examination–PN
Pre-Admission Examination–RN
Precision Handling Performance Assessment Unit
Precision Measurement
Predictive Index
The Predictive Reading Profile
Predictive Sales Survey
The Preliminary Hindi Proficiency Test
The Preliminary Japanese Speaking Test
Pre-Post Inventory
The Press Test [Revised]
The Prevue Assessment
Pro Care
Probity/Honesty Inventory

The Self-Perception Profile for Adults
Self-Perception Profile for Children
Self-Perception Profile for Learning Disabled Students
Seligman Attributional Style Questionnaire
Senior South African Individual Scale–Revised
Sensorimotor Performance Analysis
SEPO (Serial Position) Test for the Detection of Guilty/
  Special Knowledge
Serial Digit Learning
Servant Leadership Inventory Forms A&B
Service Skills Indicator
The Sexual Abuse Interview for the Developmentally
  Disabled
SF-12: Physical and Mental Health Summary Scales
SF-36: Physical and Mental Health Summary Scales
The Shapes Analysis Test
The Shorr Couples Imagery Test
The Shorr Parent/Child Imagery Test
Short Tests of Clerical Ability [Revised]
SigmaRadius 360° Feedback
Situational Leadership II Leadership Skills Assessment
Situational Leadership® [Revised]
Six Factor Automated Vocational Assessment System
16+ PersonalStyle Profile
Skil Scale Inventory
SkillCheck Professional Plus
Skillscape
Slosson Auditory Perceptual Skill Screener
Slosson—Diagnostic Math Screener
Slosson Intelligence Test—Primary
Slosson Intelligence Test—Revised (SIT-R3)
Slosson Oral Reading Test—Revised 3
Slosson Phonics and Structural Analysis Test
Slosson Visual Perceptual Skill Screener
Slosson Visual-Motor Performance Test
Slosson Written Expression Test
Slosson-Diagnostic Math Screener
Social Communication Questionnaire
Social Competency Rating Form
The Social Support Scale for Children
Socially Appropriate and Inappropriate Development
SON–R2 1/2–7 and SON-R 5 1/2–17
Space Thinking (Flags) [Revised]
Spanish Articulation Measures
Spanish Language Assessment Procedures [Revised 1995
  Edition]
The Spanish Speaking Test
The Spanish Structured Photographic Expressive Lan-
  guage Test 3
The Spanish Structured Photographic Expressive Lan-
  guage Test–II
The Spanish Structured Photographic Expressive Lan-
  guage Test–Preschool
Spanish Test for Assessing Morphologic Production
Special Abilities Scales
Specialty Practice Tests: End-of-Course Exams
Spectrum CPI 260 Instrument

Sr. Maint. Tech. Pipefitter
Staff Burnout Scale for Police and Security Personnel
The Staffordshire Mathematics Test
Stages of Concern Questionnaire
Stanford Spanish Language Proficiency Test
Stanford Writing Online Version 1.0
Station Manager Applicant Inventory
Step One Survey
Stephen's Oral Language Screening Test
Stones: Concepts About Print Test
Story Recall Test
Strategic Leadership Type Indicator [including 360-
  Degree Feedback Profile]
Strong Interest and Skills Confidence Inventory
Strong Interest Explorer—Self-scorable
Structured Photographic Expressive Language Test—
  Preschool 2
Structured Photographic Expressive Language Test 3
Student Aspiration Inventory
Student Instructional Report II
Student Opinion Inventory, Revised Edition [1995
  Edition]
Subordinate Behavior Rating
Substance Abuse Questionnaire
Super's Work Values Inventory—Revised
Supervise Ability Scale
Supervisor's Role Rating
Supervisory Aptitude Test
Supervisory Proficiency Tests
Supervisory Simulator
Supervisory Skills Test
The Supplementary Shorr Imagery Test
Support Staff Opinion Inventory
SureHire
Survey of Beliefs
Survey of Goals for Student Learning
Survey of Implementation
Survey of Instructional and Organizational Effective-
  ness
Survey of Interpersonal Values [Revised]
Survey of Personal Values [Revised]
The Survey of Quality Values in Practice
System for Testing and Evaluation of Potential
System of Interactive Guidance Information, Plus
Systematic Assessment of Voice

Tajma Personality Profile
Tangent Screen
TapDance
Teacher and Student Technology Surveys
Teacher Opinion Inventory, Revised Edition [1995
  Edition]
Teacher Performance Assessment [2006 Revision]
Team Assessment System
Team-Building Effectiveness Profile
Team Climate Inventory
Team Culture Analysis

Team Effectiveness Inventory
Team Empowerment Practices Test
Team Leader Competencies
Team Leader Skills Assessment
Team Management Index
Team Management Profile
Team Member Behavior Analysis
Team Performance Index
Team Performance Profile
Team Performance Questionnaire
Team-Review Survey
Team Skills Indicator
Team Success Profile
Teambuilding Effectiveness
Technology and Internet Assessment
Temperament Comparator [Revised]
Temporal Orientation
TerraNova Online
Tertiary Education Mathematics Test
Tertiary Writing Assessment
Test Alert (Test Preparation)
Test of Academic Achievement Skills—Revised
Test of Adult Literacy Skills
Test of Auditory Processes
Test of Auditory Reasoning and Processing Skills
Test of Auditory-Perceptual Skills, Revised
Test of Auditory-Perceptual Skills, 3rd Edition
Test of Auditory-Perceptual Skills, Upper Level
The Test of Everyday Reasoning
Test of General Intellectual Skills
Test of Grammatical and Syntactical Skills
Test of Handwriting Skills
Test of Inductive Reasoning Principles
Test of Mechanical Concepts [Revised]
Test of Oral Reading and Comprehension Skills
Test of Pictures/Forms/Letters/Numbers Spatial Orientation and Sequencing Skills
Test of Problem Solving—Adolescent
Test of Problem Solving-Revised-Elementary (TOPS-R)
Test of Relational Concepts [Norms for Deaf Children]
Test of Semantic Skills—Intermediate
Test of Semantic Skills—Primary
Test of Silent Reading Skills
Test of Visual-Motor Skills, Revised
Test of Visual-Motor Skills—Upper Level
Test of Visual-Motor Skills (Upper Level) Adolescents and Adults
Test of Visual-Perceptual Skills (Non-Motor): Revised
Test of Visual-Perceptual Skills (Non-Motor), 3rd Edition
Test of Visual-Perceptual Skills (Non-Motor) Upper Level: Revised
Test of Visual-Perceptual Skills, Upper Level
Tests in Aspects of Literacy and Numeracy
Tests of General Educational Development [The GED Tests] [Revision]

The Texas Oral Proficiency Test
The ACT Evaluation/Survey Service [Revised]
Theological School Inventory
Thinking Creatively with Sounds and Words
360 By Design
360 Degree Assessment and Development
360° Feedback Assessment
Thurstone Temperament Schedule [Revised]
Thurstone Test of Mental Alertness [Revised]
Time Management Effectiveness Profile
Time Management Inventory
Titmus Stereo Fly Test
Tobacco Use Survey
Took Knowledge & Use
Torrance Tests of Creative Thinking [with 1998 norms]
Total Quality Management Survey
TotalView
TotalView Assessment System
Training Needs Assessment for Modern Leadership Skills
Training Needs Assessment Test
Training Proficiency Scale
Triage Assessment for Psychiatric Disorders
Truck Driver Inventory
Trustworthiness Attitude Survey
The Two Cultures Test
Types of Work Index
Types of Work Profile

Undergraduate Assessment Program: Business Test
Understanding Communication [Revised]
Urban District Assessment Consortium's Alternative Accountability Assessments

Value Assessment Scale
Value Development Index Form A and Form B
Value Development Index Form C
Values and Motives Questionnaire
Verbal Form [Revised]
Victim Index
Visual Form Discrimination
The Vocabulary Gradient Test
Vocational Interest, Experience and Skill Assessment (VIESA), 2nd Canadian Edition

Warehouse & Shipping Reading
Welder, Repair & Maint.
What About You?
Window on Work Values Profile
Winterhaven Visual Copy Forms and Visual Retention Test
Wonderlic Interactive Skills Evaluations, Keyboard and Office Skills
Wonderlic Interactive Skills Evaluations, Software Skills
Word Processing Aptitude Battery
The WORD Test-Adolescent

The WORD Test-R (Elementary)
The Word Test—R and The Word Test—Adolescent
Words List
Work Habits, Attitudes and Productivity Scale [Employee and Student Editions]
Work Keys Assessment
Work/Life Values Checklist
Work Preference Questionnaire

Work-Readiness Cognitive Screen
Work Skills Series Manual Dexterity
Work Team Simulator
Working Together: An Assessment of Collaboration
Workplace Ergonomics Profile
Workplace Skills Survey
Workplace Skills Survey—Form E
Wright & Ayre Stuttering Self-Rating Profile

DISTINGUISHED REVIEWERS

Based on the recommendation of our National Advisory Council, the Buros Institute of Mental Measurements is now making special recognition of the long-term contributions made by individual reviewers to the success of the Mental Measurements Yearbook series. To receive the "Distinguished Reviewer" designation, an individual must have contributed to six or more editions of this series beginning with The Ninth Mental Measurements Yearbook. *The first list below includes those who have contributed to six or more editions as of the current* Seventeenth Mental Measurements Yearbook. *On the following page is a list of those who qualified with their contribution to* The Sixteenth Mental Measurements Yearbook *(note that some reviewers are on both lists). By virtue of their long-term service, all these individuals exemplify an outstanding dedication in their professional lives to the principles of improving the science and practice of testing.*

Phillip A. Ackerman
Caroline M. Adkins
Mark A. Albanese
Jeffrey A. Atlas
James T. Austin
Laura L. B. Barnes
Albert M. Bugaj
Michael B. Bunch
Carolyn M. Callahan
Karen T. Carey
Janet F. Carlson
Joseph C. Ciechalski
Gregory J. Cizek
Alice J. Corkill
Kevin D. Crehan
Rik Carl D'Amato
Ayres G. D'Costa
Gerald E. DeMauro
Beth Doll
George Engelhard, Jr.
Doreen Ward Fairbank
John W. Fleenor
Michael J. Furlong
Ronald J. Ganellen
Bert A. Goldman
Richard E. Harding
Patti L. Harrison
Robert W. Hiltonsmith
Jeffrey A. Jenkins
Michael G. Kavan
Jean Powell Kirnan
Frederick T. L. Leong
S. Alvin Leung
Matthew E. Lambert

Steven H. Long
Cleborne D. Maddux
Koressa Kutsick Malcolm
Rebecca J. McCauley
M. David Miller
Patricia L. Mirenda
Judith A. Monsaas
Paul M. Muchinsky
Salvador Hector Ochoa
Steven I. Pfeiffer
James W. Pinkney
Bruce G. Rogers
Darrell L. Sabers
Vincent J. Samar
Jonathon Sandoval
Eleanor E. Sanford-Moore
William I. Sauser, Jr.
Diane J. Sawyer
William D. Schafer
Gene Schwarting
Steven R. Shaw
Eugene P. Sheehan
Jeffrey K. Smith
Stephanie Stein
Terry A. Stinnett
Gabrielle Stutman
Mark E. Swerdlik
Gerald Tindal
Roger L. Towne
Michael S. Trevisan
T. Steuart Watson
William K. Wilkinson
Claudia R. Wright

DISTINGUISHED REVIEWERS FROM THE SIXTEENTH MENTAL MEASUREMENTS YEARBOOK

Phillip A. Ackerman
Mark A. Albanese
Jeffrey A. Atlas
James T. Austin
Stephen N. Axford
Patricia A. Bachelor
Laura L. B. Barnes
Ronald A. Berk
Brian F. Bolton
Gregory J. Boyle
Michael B. Bunch
Linda K. Bunker
Janet F. Carlson
JoEllen V. Carlson
C. Dale Carpenter
Joseph C. Ciechalski
Gregory J. Cizek
Mary M. Clare
Kevin D. Crehan
Gerald E. DeMauro
Beth Doll
George Engelhard, Jr.
Deborah B. Erickson
Robert Fitzpatrick
John W. Fleenor
J. Jeffrey Grill
Richard E. Harding
Patti L. Harrison
Michael R. Harwell
Allen K. Hess
Jeffrey A. Jenkins
Samuel Juni
Randy W. Kamphaus
Michael G. Kavan
Timothy Z. Keith
Mary Lou Kelley
Jean Powell Kirnan
Howard M. Knoff
Joseph G. Law, Jr.

Frederick T. L. Leong
S. Alvin Leung
Rick Lindskog
Cleborne D. Maddux
Koressa Kutsick Malcolm
Rebecca J. McCauley
William B. Michael
Kevin L. Moreland
Anthony J. Nitko
Janet A. Norris
Judy Oehler-Stinnett
D. Joe Olmi
Steven I. Pfeiffer
G. Michael Poteat
Nambury S. Raju
Paul Retzlaff
Cecil R. Reynolds
Bruce G. Rogers
Michael J. Roszkowski
Darrell L. Sabers
Jonathon Sandoval
Eleanor E. Sanford
William I. Sauser, Jr.
Diane J. Sawyer
Gene Schwarting
Jeffrey K. Smith
Jayne E. Stake
Stephanie Stein
Terry A. Stinnett
Richard B. Stuart
Hoi K. Suen
Mark E. Swerdlik
Michael S. Trevisan
Wilfred G. Van Gorp
T. Steuart Watson
William K. Wilkinson
Claudia R. Wright
James E. Ysseldyke
Sheldon Zedeck

CONTRIBUTING TEST REVIEWERS

SHAWN K. ACHESON, Associate Professor of Neuropsychology, Department of Psychology, Western Carolina University, Cullowhee, NC

PHILLIP L. ACKERMAN, Professor of Psychology, Georgia Institute of Technology, Atlanta, GA

CAROLINE M. ADKINS, Professor Emeritus, School of Education, Hunter College, City University of New York, New York, NY

EUGENE V. AIDMAN, Senior Research Scientist, Defense Science and Technology Organisation & Senior Lecturer, University of Adelaide, Adelaide, Australia

MARK A. ALBANESE, Professor of Population Health Sciences, University of Wisconsin School of Medicine and Public Health, Madison, WI

AMANDA ALBERTSON, Graduate Student in Educational Psychology, University of Nebraska-Lincoln, Lincoln, NE

KATHLEEN D. ALLEN, Assistant Professor of Education, St. Martin's University, Lacey, WA

MARTIN W. ANDERSON, Director of Administration, Connecticut Department of Administrative Services, Hartford, CT, and Adjunct Professor, University of New Haven, West Haven, CT

DOLORES J. APPL, Associate Professor, College of Education, Health, and Rehabilitation, University of Maine at Farmington, Farmington, ME

MICHELLE ATHANASIOU, Professor of School Psychology, University of Northern Colorado, Greeley, CO

JAMES A. ATHANASOU, Faculty of Education, University of Technology, Sydney, Australia

JEFFREY A. ATLAS, Clinical Psychologist, SCO Family of Services, Queens, NY

JAMES T. AUSTIN, Senior Research Specialist, Center on Education and Training for Employment, College of Education and Human Ecology, The Ohio State University, Columbus, OH

DEBORAH BANDALOS, Professor of Educational Psychology, University of Georgia, Athens, GA

LAURA L. B. BARNES, Associate Professor of Research, Evaluation, Measurement, and Statistics, Oklahoma State University, Tulsa, OK

LAUREN R. BARTON, Early Childhood Researcher, Early Childhood Program, Center for Education and Human Services, SRI International, Menlo Park, CA

SHERI BAUMAN, Associate Professor, Department of Educational Psychology, University of Arizona, Tucson, AZ

ABIGAIL BAXTER, Associate Professor, Department of Leadership and Teacher Education, University of South Alabama, Mobile, AL

SCOTT F. BEERS, Assistant Professor, Curriculum and Instruction, Seattle Pacific University, Seattle, WA

MICHAEL D. BIDERMAN, Professor of Psychology, University of Tennessee at Chattanooga, Chattanooga, TN

BRUCE BISKIN, Director of Learning Assessment, Thomas Edison State College, Trenton, NJ

ALLISON BORODA, Graduate Assistant, Texas Tech University, Lubbock, TX

JEFFERY P. BRADEN, Professor of Psychology, North Carolina State University, Raleigh, NC

LINDA E. BRODY, Johns Hopkins University, Center for Talented Youth, Baltimore, MD

JAMES DEAN BROWN, Professor of Second Language Studies, University of Hawai'i at Manoa, Honolulu, HI

BETHANY A. BRUNSMAN, Assessment/Evaluation Specialist, Lincoln Public Schools, Lincoln, NE

RITA BUDRIONIS, Licensed Clinical Psychologist, Licensed Sex Offender Treatment Provider, Director Dominion Sex Offenders Program, Associate Professor at Old Dominion University in Norfolk, VA

ALBERT M. BUGAJ, Professor of Psychology, University of Wisconsin–Marinette, Marinette, WI

ALAN C. BUGBEE, JR., Director of Psychometrics, American Society for Clinical Pathology, Chicago, IL

MICHAEL B. BUNCH, Senior Vice President, Measurement Incorporated, Durham, NC

MATTHEW K. BURNS, Associate Professor of Educational Psychology, University of Minnesota, Minneapolis, MN

CAROLYN M. CALLAHAN, Commonwealth Professor of Education, University of Virginia, Charlottesville, VA

KAREN CAREY, Professor of Psychology, California State University, Fresno, CA

JANET F. CARLSON, Professor, Department of General Academics, Texas A&M University at Galveston, Galveston, TX

RUSSELL N. CARNEY, Professor of Psychology, Missouri State University, Springfield, MO

HEIDI M. CARTY, Associate Director, Student Research & Information, University of California, San Diego, San Diego, CA

JERRELL C. CASSADY, Associate Professor of Psychology, Department of Educational Psychology, Ball State University, Muncie, IN

TIFFANY D. CHANDLER, Doctoral Candidate, School Psychology Program, Mississippi State University, Starkville, MS

MARY (RINA) M. CHITTOORAN, Associate Professor and Chair, Department of Educational Studies, Saint Louis University, St. Louis, MO

ROBERT CHRISTOPHER, Professional, Clinical and Forensic Assessments, LLC, Sparks, NV

DAVID F. CIAMPI, Adjunct Professor, International Homeland Security Defense Coalition and Homeland Security Project, Region 6, MA

JOSEPH C. CIECHALSKI, Professor, East Carolina University, Greenville, NC

GREGORY J. CIZEK, Professor of Educational Measurement and Evaluation, University of North Carolina–Chapel Hill, Chapel Hill, NC

JEAN N. CLARK, Associate Professor of Educational Psychology, University of South Alabama, Mobile, AL

LORRAINE CLEETON, Faculty Mentor in the Ph.D. Program in Education, Walden University, Minneapolis, MN

D. ASHLEY COHEN, Clinical Neuropsychologist, Forensic Psychologist, CogniMetrix (private practice), San Jose, CA

THEODORE COLADARCI, Professor of Educational Psychology, University of Maine, Orono, ME

COLLIE CONOLEY, Professor of Counseling Clinical and School Psychology, University of California, Santa Barbara, Santa Barbara, CA

FRANCINE CONWAY, Assistant Professor of Psychology, Adelphi University, Garden City, NY

ALICE CORKILL, Associate Professor, Department of Educational Psychology, University of Nevada-Las Vegas, Las Vegas, NV

MERITH COSDEN, Professor of Counseling, Clinical and School Psychology, University of California, Santa Barbara, Santa Barbara, CA

ANDREW A. COX, Professor, Counseling and Psychology, Troy University, Phenix City, AL

KEVIN D. CREHAN, Professor of Educational Psychology, University of Nevada, Las Vegas, Las Vegas, NV

RIK CARL D'AMATO, M. Lucile Harrison Professor of Excellence, School of Applied Psychology and Counselor Education, College of Education and Behavioral Sciences, University of Northern Colorado, Greeley, CO

AYRES G. D'COSTA, Associate Professor, Quantitative Research, Measurement, and Evaluation in Education, The Ohio State University, Columbus, OH

MOIRA DALY, Lecturer of Communication Sciences, University of Vermont, Burlington, VT

ANDREW S. DAVIS, Assistant Professor, Department of Educational Psychology, Ball State University, Muncie, IN

GARY J. DEAN, Professor and Chairperson, Department of Adult and Community Education, Indiana University of Pennsylvania, Indiana, PA

SANDRA F. DEAN, Instructor, Pennsylvania Highlands Community College, Indiana, PA

SHARON deFUR, Associate Professor of Curriculum and Instruction/Special Education, The College of William and Mary, Williamsburg, VA

GEORGE J. DEMAKIS, Associate Professor of Psychology, University of North Carolina at Charlotte, Charlotte, NC

GERALD E. DeMAURO, Managing Educational Assessment Scientist, American Institutes for Research, Voorheesville, NY

GYPSY M. DENZINE, Associate Dean and Professor of Educational Psychology, Northern Arizona University, Flagstaff, AZ

R. ANTHONY DOGGETT, Assistant Professor of Educational Psychology, Mississippi State University, Starkville, MS

BETH DOLL, Professor of Educational Psychology, University of Nebraska-Lincoln, Lincoln, NE

JAMES P. DONNELLY, Assistant Professor, Department of Counseling, School & Educational Psychology, University at Buffalo, Amherst, NY

KERRY DONNELLY, Clinical Neuropsychologist, VA Western New York Healthcare System, Buffalo, NY

ANTONIA D'ONOFRIO, Professor of Education, Center for Education, School of Human Service Professions, Widener University, Chester, PA

ANTHONY T. DUGBARTEY, Visiting Assistant Professor, Department of Psychology, University of Victoria, Victoria, British Columbia, and Forensic Psychologist, Forensic Psychiatric Services Commission, Victoria, British Columbia, Canada

THOMAS M. DUNN, Associate Professor of Psychological Sciences, University of Northern Colorado, Greeley, CO

IBRAHIM DUYAR, Assistant Professor of Educational Administration, University of Arkansas at Little Rock, Little Rock, AR

CHER N. EDWARDS, Assistant Professor, School Counseling and Psychology, Seattle Pacific University, Seattle, WA

RICK EIGENBROOD, Assistant Dean for Graduate Studies and Assessment, Seattle Pacific University, Seattle, WA

ARTHUR S. ELLEN, School Psychologist, New York City Department of Education, New York, NY

GEORGE ENGELHARD, JR., Professor of Educational Measurement and Policy, Emory University, Atlanta, GA

CONNIE ENGLAND, Associate Professor/Department Chair, Grad Counseling and Guidance, Lincoln Memorial University, Knoxville, TN

CHRISTIE EPPLER, Assistant Professor, School Counseling and Psychology, Seattle Pacific University, Seattle, WA

DOREEN W. FAIRBANK, Professor of Psychology, Meredith College, Raleigh, NC

W. HOLMES FINCH, Assistant Professor, Department of Educational Psychology, Ball State University, Muncie, IN

ROSEMARY FLANAGAN, Associate Professor/Director, Masters Program in School Psychology, Adelphi University, Garden City, NY

JOHN W. FLEENOR, Director of Knowledge Management, Center for Creative Leadership, Greensboro, NC

STEPHEN J. FREEMAN, Professor and Chair, Department of Counseling, Texas A&M University–Commerce, Commerce, TX

BRUCE FRUMKIN, Director, Forensic and Clinical Psychology Associates, South Miami, FL

MICHAEL FURLONG, Professor and Chair, Department of Counseling, Clinical, and School Psychology, University of California, Santa Barbara, Santa Barbara, CA

RONALD J. GANELLEN, Associate Professor, Northwestern University Medical School, Chicago, IL

MARY L. GARNER, Associate Professor of Mathematics, Kennesaw State University, Kennesaw, GA

ADRIENNE GARRO, Assistant Professor of Psychology, Kean University, Union, NJ

JOHN S. GEISLER, Professor Emeritus, Department of Counselor Education and Counseling Psychology, Western Michigan University, Kalamazoo, MI

BERT A. GOLDMAN, Professor, University of North Carolina at Greensboro, Greensboro, NC

JORGE E. GONZALEZ, Assistant Professor, Department of Educational Psychology, Texas A&M University, College Station, TX

THERESA GRAHAM, Adjunct Faculty, University of Nebraska-Lincoln, Lincoln, NE

KATHY E. GREEN, Professor of Education, University of Denver, Denver, CO

MALINDA HENDRICKS GREEN, Professor, College of Education, University of Central Oklahoma, Edmond, OK

THOMAS GUYETTE, Professor and Chair, Department of Audiology and Speech Pathology, University of Arkansas at Little Rock and University of Arkansas for Medical Sciences, Little Rock, AR

THOMAS EMERSON HANCOCK, Everett School District, Everett, WA

RICHARD E. HARDING, Director of Research, Kenexa Technology, Inc., Lincoln, NE

PATTI L. HARRISON, Professor of School Psychology, The University of Alabama, Tuscaloosa, AL

KEITH HATTRUP, Associate Professor of Psychology, San Diego State University, San Diego, CA

THEODORE L. HAYES, Principal Selection Research Scientist, The Gallup Organization, Washington, DC

REBEKAH HAYNES, Research Graduate Assistant, Texas A&M University, College Station, TX

SANDRA D. HAYNES, Dean, School of Professional Studies, Metropolitan State College of Denver, Denver, CO

APRIL K. HEISELT, Assistant Professor of Counselor Education, Mississippi State University, Starkville, MS

CARLEN HENINGTON, Associate Professor of School Psychology, Mississippi State University, Mississippi State, MS

ROBERT W. HILTONSMITH, Professor of Psychology, Radford University, Radford, VA

KATHRYN E. HOFF, Associate Professor, Psychology Department, Illinois State University, Normal, IL

THOMAS P. HOGAN, Professor of Psychology, University of Scranton, Scranton, PA

DENICE WARD HOOD, Associate Professor of Educational Psychology, Northern Arizona University, Flagstaff, AZ

WILLIAM R. HORSTMAN, Forensic Neuropsychologist, Private Practice, San Francisco, CA

ANITA M. HUBLEY, Associate Professor of Measurement, Evaluation, and Research Methodology, University of British Columbia, Vancouver, British Columbia, Canada

DAVID P. HURFORD, Director of the Center for the Assessment and Remediation of Reading Difficulties and Professor Psychology and Counseling, Pittsburg State University, Pittsburg, KS

MOLLY M. JAMESON, Doctoral Candidate, Department of Educational Psychology, Ball State University, Muncie, IN

MARC JANOSON, President, Forensic Psychology PC, New York, NY

JEFFREY A. JENKINS, Associate Professor, Roger Williams University, Bristol, RI

STEPHEN B. JOHNSON, Psychometrician, CASTLE Worldwide, Morrisville, NC

KATHLEEN M. JOHNSON, Psychologist, Lincoln Public Schools, Lincoln, NE

KRISTIN N. JOHNSON-GROS, Assistant Professor of Educational Psychology, Mississippi State University, Starkville, MS

H. DENNIS KADE, Director, Developmental & Behavioral Health, Norfolk Department of Public Health, and Adjunct Assistant Professor, Old Dominion University, Norfolk, VA

ASHRAF KAGEE, Professor of Psychology, Stellenbosch University, Matiland, South Africa

HARRISON KANE, Assistant Professor of Educational and School Psychology, Mississippi State, MS

MICHAEL G. KAVAN, Associate Dean for Student Affairs and Associate Professor of Family Medicine, Creighton University School of Medicine, Omaha, NE

DONNA J. KELLY, Associate Professor, Department of Audiology and Speech Pathology, University of Arkansas at Little Rock and University of Arkansas for Medical Sciences, Little Rock, AR

KEVIN R. KELLY, Head, Department of Educational Studies, Purdue University, West Lafayette, IN

JEAN P. KIRNAN, Professor of Psychology, The College of New Jersey, Ewing, NJ

TIMOTHY R. KONOLD, Associate Professor of Research, Statistics, and Evaluation, University of Virginia, Charlottesville, VA

S. KATHLEEN KRACH, Assistant Professor, University of Nevada, Las Vegas, Las Vegas, NV

DANIEL KRENZER, Doctoral Candidate, Mississippi State University, Mississippi State, MS

HAILEY E. KROUSE, Graduate Student in Psychology, North Carolina State University, Raleigh, NC

JODY L. KULSTAD, Adjunct Professor, Seton Hall University, South Orange, NJ

JOSEPH C. KUSH, Associate Professor, Duquesne University, Pittsburgh, PA

MATTHEW E. LAMBERT, Assistant Clinical Professor of Neuropsychiatry, Texas Tech University, Health Sciences Center, Lubbock, TX

SUZANNE LANE, Professor of Research Methodology, University of Pittsburgh, Pittsburgh, PA

AIMÉE LANGLOIS, Professor, Department of Child Development, Humboldt State University, Arcata, CA

COURTNEY LeCLAIR, Doctoral Student in Educational Psychology, University of Nebraska-Lincoln, Lincoln, NE

FREDERICK T. L. LEONG, Professor of Psychology, Michigan State University, East Lansing, MI

S. ALVIN LEUNG, Professor, Department of Educational Psychology, The Chinese University of Hong Kong, Hong Kong, China

JOHN LINCK, Neuropsychology Post-Doctoral Fellow, University of Oklahoma Health Sciences Center, Oklahoma City, OK

PAM LINDSEY, Associate Professor, Curriculum and Instruction, Tarleton State University, Stephenville, TX

SANDRA LOEW, Associate Professor, University of North Alabama, Florence, AL

SUSAN LONBORG, Professor of Psychology, Central Washington University, Ellensburg, WA

STEVEN LONG, Speech Pathology and Audiology, Marquette University, Milwaukee, WI

KAREN MACKLER, School Psychologist, Lawrence Public Schools, Lawrence, NY

CLEBORNE D. MADDUX, Foundation Professor of Counseling and Educational Psychology, University of Nevada, Reno, Reno, NV

RONALD A. MADLE, Licensed Psychologist, Mifflinburg, PA, and Adjunct Associate Professor of School Psychology, The Pennsylvania State University, University Park, PA

JENNIFER N. MAHDAVI, Assistant Professor of Special Education, Sonoma State University, Rohnert Park, CA

TIMOTHY J. MAKATURA, Consulting Psychologist, Allegheny Children's Initiative, Pittsburgh, PA

KORESSA KUTSICK MALCOLM, School Psychologist, Augusta County Public Schools, and Adjunct Faculty Member, Mary Baldwin College, Staunton, VA

HOWARD MARGOLIS, Reading and Special Education Consultant, Voorhees, NJ, and Professor Emeritus of Literacy and Special Education, Queens College of the City University of New York, New York, NY

MICHAEL S. MATTHEWS, Assistant Professor, Gifted Education Program, Department of Special Education, The University of South Florida, Tampa, FL

KEVIN J. McCARTHY, Staff Psychologist, State of Louisiana, Department of Health and Hospitals, ELMHS Facility, Jackson, LA

REBECCA J. McCAULEY, Professor of Communication Sciences, University of Vermont, Burlington, VT

MERILEE McCURDY, Assistant Professor of Educational Psychology, University of Nebraska-Lincoln, Lincoln, NE

DIXIE McGINTY, Associate Professor of Educational Research, Western Carolina University, Cullowhee, NC

CAROL M. McGREGOR, Content Development Specialist, The Learning House, Louisville, KY

VALENTINA McINERNEY, Professor of Educational Psychology, School of Psychology, University of Western Sydney, Sydney, Australia

THOMAS McKNIGHT, Psychologist, Private Practice, Spokane, WA

TAWNYA MEADOWS, Assistant Professor of Psychology, University of Nebraska Medical Center, Omaha, NE

FREDERIC MEDWAY, Professor of Psychology, University of South Carolina, Columbia, SC

JOYCE MEIKAMP, Professor of Special Education, Marshall University Graduate College, South Charleston, WV

BRAD M. MERKER, Neuropsychology Post-Doctoral Fellow, University of Oklahoma Health Sciences Center, Oklahoma City, OK

DANIEL C. MILLER, Professor, Texas Woman's University, Denton, TX

M. DAVID MILLER, Professor of Educational Psychology, College of Education, University of Florida, Gainesville, FL

PAT MIRENDA, Professor, Department of Educational and Counseling Psychology and Special Education, University of British Columbia, Vancouver, British Columbia, Canada

RAMA K. MISHRA, Department of Psychiatry, Medicine Hat Regional Hospital, Alberta, Canada

JUDITH A. MONSAAS, Executive Director for P-16 Assessment and Evaluation, University System of Georgia, Atlanta, GA

DAVID MORSE, Professor, Counseling, Educational Psychology and Special Education, Mississippi State University, Mississippi State, MS

MAURA MOYLE, Assistant Professor of Speech Language Pathology & Audiology, Marquette University, Milwaukee, WI

PAUL M. MUCHINSKY, Joseph M. Bryan Distinguished Professor of Business, The University of North Carolina at Greensboro, Greensboro, NC

MILDRED MURRAY-WARD, Dean, College of Education, California State University Stanislaus, Turlock, CA

LEAH M. NELLIS, Director, Blumberg Center for Interdisciplinary Studies in Special Education, Indiana State University, Terre Haute, IN

SALVADOR HECTOR OCHOA, Professor, University of Texas-Pan American, Edinburg, TX

ARTURO OLIVAREZ, JR., Associate Professor of Educational Psychology, Texas Tech University, Lubbock, TX

AMY M. OLSON, Doctoral Student, University of Arizona, Tucson, AZ

ALLISON OSBORN, Doctoral Student, University of Nebraska-Lincoln, Lincoln, NE

SANDYE M. OUZTS, Graduate Student in Psychology, North Carolina State University, Raleigh, NC

GRETCHEN OWENS, Professor of Child Study, St. Joseph's College, Patchogue, NY

VICKI S. PACKMAN, Senior Assessment Analyst, Salt River Project, Phoenix, AZ

L. CAROLYN PEARSON, Professor of Educational Foundations, University of Arkansas at Little Rock, Little Rock, AR

JAMES A. PENNY, Senior Psychometrician, CASTLE Worldwide, Morrisville, NC

STEVEN I. PFEIFFER, Professor and Director of Clinical Training, PhD Program in Combined Counseling and School Psychology, Florida State University, Tallahassee, FL

JAMES W. PINKNEY, Professor of Counselor and Adult Education, East Carolina University, Greenville, NC

DAVID J. PITTENGER, Associate Provost for Academic Administration, The University of Tennessee at Chattanooga, Chattanooga, TN

JULIA Y. PORTER, Associate Professor of Counselor Education, Mississippi State University, Meridian, MS

SHAWN POWELL, Director, Wyoming National Guard Youth ChalleNGe Program, Guernsey, WY, and Graduate Lecturer, University of Northern Colorado, Greeley, CO

J. RANDALL PRICE, Professor of Psychology, Richland College, Dallas, TX

PAM RAMSDEN, Senior Lecturer, University of Bolton, Bolton, Lancashire, England

CRYSTAL M. RAMSAY, Doctoral Student, Pennsylvania State University, University Park, PA

NATALIE RATHVON, Assistant Clinical Professor, The George Washington University, Washington, DC, and Private Practice Psychologist and School Consultant, Bethesda, MD

SEAN REILLEY, Assistant Professor of Psychology, Morehead State University, Morehead, KY

ELIZABETH KELLEY RHOADES, Associate Professor of Psychology at West Texas A&M University, Canyon, TX

SHARON ANN RICHARDSON, Assistant Professor of Educational Leadership, University of Arkansas at Little Rock, Little Rock, AR

BRUCE G. ROGERS, Professor Emeritus of Educational Psychology, University of Northern Iowa, Cedar Falls, IA

MARK ROYBAL, Adjunct Professor of School Psychology, National University, San Diego, CA

DARRELL L. SABERS, Professor of Educational Psychology, University of Arizona, Tucson, AZ

VINCENT J. SAMAR, Associate Professor, Department of Research, National Technical Institute for the Deaf, Rochester, NY

JONATHAN SANDOVAL, Professor of Education, University of the Pacific, Stockton, CA

ELEANOR E. SANFORD-MOORE, Vice-President of Research and Development, MetaMetrics, Inc., Durham, NC

WILLIAM I. SAUSER, JR., Associate Dean and Professor, Business and Engineering Outreach, Auburn University, Auburn, AL

DIANE J. SAWYER, Murfree Professor of Dyslexic Studies, Middle Tennessee State University, Murfreesboro, TN

WILLIAM D. SCHAFER, Affiliated Professor (Emeritus) of Measurement, Statistics, and Evaluation, University of Maryland, College Park, MD

MICHAEL J. SCHEEL, Associate Professor, Department of Educational Psychology, University of Nebraska-Lincoln, Lincoln, NE

W. JOEL SCHNEIDER, Assistant Professor of Psychology, Illinois State University, Normal, IL

GREGORY SCHRAW, Professor, Department of Educational Psychology, University of Nevada, Las Vegas, Las Vegas, NV

GENE SCHWARTING, Associate Professor, Education/Special Education, Fontbonne University, St. Louis, MO

STEVEN R. SHAW, Assistant Professor of Educational and Counseling Psychology, McGill University, Montreal, Quebec, Canada

EUGENE P. SHEEHAN, Dean, College of Education and Behavioral Sciences, University of Northern Colorado, Greeley, CO

CARL J. SHEPERIS, Assistant Professor of Counselor Education, Mississippi State University, Starkville, MS

WES SIME, Professor, Emeritus, University of Nebraska-Lincoln, Lincoln, NE

CHRISTOPHER A. SINK, Professor and Chair, School Counseling and Psychology, Seattle Pacific University, Seattle, WA

JANET SMITH, Associate Professor, Department of Psychology and Counseling, Pittsburg State University, Pittsburg, KS

JEFFREY SMITH, Professor, The University of Otago, Dunedin, New ZealandLISA F. SMITH, Senior Research Fellow, University of Otago, Dunedin, New Zealand

RUSSELL W. SMITH, Senior Psychometrician, Alpine Testing Solutions, Henderson, NV

KATHARINE SNYDER, Associate Professor of Psychology, Methodist College, Fayetteville, NC

LOUISE M. SOARES, Professor of Educational Psychology, University of New Haven, West Haven, CT

LORAINE J. SPENCINER, Professor of Special Education, University of Maine at Farmington, Farmington, ME

RAYNE A. SPERLING, Associate Professor of Educational Psychology, Pennsylvania State University, University Park, PA

DONNA SPIKER, Program Manager, Early Childhood Program, Center for Education and Human Services, SRI International, Menlo Park, CA

MARK A. STAAL, Chief, Special Operations & Aerospace Psychology, Air Force Special Operations Command, Hurlburt Field, FL

STEPHANIE STEIN, Professor and Chair of Psychology, Central Washington University, Ellensburg, WA

KAY B. STEVENS, Associate Professor of Education, Texas Christian University, Fort Worth, TX

JAY R. STEWART, Director and Associate Professor Rehabilitation Counseling Program, Division of Intervention Services, Bowling Green State University, Bowling Green, OH

TERRY A. STINNETT, Professor, School Psychology, Oklahoma State University, Stillwater, OK

GABRIELLE STUTMAN, Private Practice, Westchester and Manhattan, NY

HUAPING SUN, Doctoral Student, University of Arizona, Tucson, AZ

CAROLYN H. SUPPA, Professor of Counseling, Marshall University Graduate College, South Charleston, WV

MARK E. SWERDLIK, Professor of Psychology, Illinois State University, Normal, IL

DIANE TANIGAWA, Doctoral Candidate, Department of Counseling, Clinical, and School Psychology, University of California, Santa Barbara, CA

ROBERT M. THORNDIKE, Professor of Psychology, Western Washington University, Bellingham, WA

GEOFFREY L. THORPE, Professor of Psychology, University of Maine, Orono, ME

GERALD TINDAL, Professor, University of Oregon, Eugene, OR

STEPHANIE D. TISCHENDORF, Senior Program Associate, Center on Education and Training for Employment, College of Education and Human Ecology, The Ohio State University, Columbus, OH

JOHN TIVENDELL, Professor of Psychology, Université de Moncton, Moncton, New Brunswick, Canada

RENEE M. TOBIN, Assistant Professor of Psychology, Illinois State University, Normal, IL

ROGER L. TOWNE, Associate Professor, Department of Communication Sciences and Disorders, Worcester State College, Worcester, MA

MICHAEL S. TREVISAN, Professor, Educational Psychology, Washington State University, Pullman, WA

JOHN J. VACCA, Assistant Professor of Individual and Family Studies, University of Delaware, Newark, DE

JAMIE E. VANNICE, Doctoral student in School Psychology, School of Applied Psychology and Counselor Education, University of Northern Colorado, Greeley, CO

JOHN J. VENN, Professor of Special Education, University of North Florida, Jacksonville, FL

DOLORES KLUPPEL VETTER, Professor Emerita, University of Wisconsin-Madison, Madison, WI

ROMEO VITELLI, Private Practice, Hamilton, Ontario, Canada

THERESA VOLPE-JOHNSTONE, Clinical and School Psychologist, Pleasanton Unified School District, Pleasanton, CA

JUSTIN M. WALKER, Doctoral Student in School Psychology, School of Applied Psychology and Counselor Education, University of Northern Colorado, Greeley, CO

NICHOLAS D. WARCHOLAK, PhD Candidate, Pennsylvania State University, University Park, PA

SANDRA WARD, Professor of Education, The College of William and Mary, Williamsburg, VA

ANNITA MARIE WARD, Associate Professor, Salem International University, Bridgeport, WV

T. STEUART WATSON, Professor and Chair, Department of Educational Psychology, Miami University, Oxford, OH

TONYA S. WATSON, Assistant Professor, Department of Family Studies and Social Work, Miami University, Oxford, OH

BART L. WEATHINGTON, Assistant Professor of Psychology, University of Tennessee at Chattanooga, Chattanooga, TN

KATHERINE WICKSTROM, Assistant Professor, Department of Educational Psychology, Miami University, Oxford, OH

MARTIN J. WIESE, Licensed Psychologist/Certified School Psychologist, Lincoln Public Schools, Lincoln, NE

WILLIAM K. WILKINSON, Consulting Educational Psychologist, Boleybeg, Barna, County Galway, Republic of Ireland

BEVERLY J. WILSON, Associate Professor, Graduate Psychology, Seattle Pacific University, Seattle, WA

MYRA N. WOMBLE, Associate Professor of Workforce Education, University of Georgia, Athens, GA

JAMIE G. WOOD, Associate Professor of Psychology, Pittsburg State University, Pittsburg, KS

CLAUDIA R. WRIGHT, Professor Emerita, California State University, Long Beach, Long Beach, CA

GEORGETTE YETTER, Assistant Professor, School of Applied Health and Educational Psychology, Oklahoma State University, Stillwater, OK

SUZANNE YOUNG, Associate Professor of Educational Research, University of Wyoming, Laramie, WY

MICHAEL J. ZICKAR, Associate Professor of Psychology, Bowling Green State University, Bowling Green, OH

INDEX OF TITLES

This title index lists all the tests included in The Seventeenth Mental Measurements Yearbook. *Citations are to test entry numbers, not to pages (e.g., 54 refers to test 54 and not page 54). Test numbers along with test titles are indicated in the running heads at the top of each page, whereas page numbers, used only in the Table of Contents but not in the indexes, appear at the bottom of each page. Superseded titles are listed with cross references to current titles, and alternative titles are also cross referenced.*

Some tests in this volume were previously listed in Tests in Print VII *(2006). An* (N) *appearing immediately after a test number indicates that the test is a new, recently published test, and/or that it has not appeared before in any Buros Institute publication other than* Tests in Print VII. *An* (R) *indicates that the test has been revised or supplemented since last included in a Buros publication.*

Abbreviated Torrance Test for Adults, 1 (N)
Abuse Disability Questionnaire, 2 (N)
Academic Intervention Monitoring System, 3 (N)
Achievement Motivation Inventory, 4 (N)
Air Conditioning Specialist (Form SWA-C), 5 (N)
Alleman Leadership Development Questionnaire, 210
Alleman Mentoring Activities Questionnaire, 211
Alleman Mentoring Scales Questionnaire, see Alleman Mentoring Activities Questionnaire, 211
Alleman Relationship Value Questionnaire, 212
Amsterdam Short-Term Memory Test, 6 (N)
Anger Disorders Scale, 7 (N)
Applicant Productivity Profile, 213
Applicant Risk Profiler, 8 (N)
The Assessment of Aphasia and Related Disorders, Second Edition, see Boston Diagnostic Aphasia Examination—Third Edition, 29
Assessment of Classroom Communication and Study Skills, 9 (N)
The Assessment of Personal Goals, 214
The Assessment of Phonological Processes—Revised, see Hodson Assessment of Phonological Patterns—Third Edition, 87
Attention Deficit Disorders Evaluation Scale—Third Edition, 10 (R)
The Autobiographical Memory Interview, 11 (N)

The Balloons Test, 12 (N)
Basic Achievement Skills Inventory, 13 (N)
Basic Banking Skills Battery, 215
Batería III Woodcock-Muñoz™, 14 (R)
Bateria Woodcock Psico-Educativa en Español [Woodcock Spanish Psycho-Educational Battery], see Batería III Woodcock-Muñoz™, 14
Batería Woodcock-Muñoz—Revisada, see Batería III Woodcock-Muñoz™, 14
Battelle Developmental Inventory Screening Test, see Battelle Developmental Inventory™, 2nd Edition, 15
Battelle Developmental Inventory™, 2nd Edition, 15 (R)
Battery for Health Improvement 2, 16 (R)
Bayley Scales of Infant and Toddler Development—Third Edition, 17 (R)
Bayley Scales of Infant and Toddler Development—Third Edition, Screening Test, 18 (R)
Bayley Scales of Infant Development, Second Edition, see Bayley Scales of Infant and Toddler Development—Third Edition, 17
Bayley Scales of Infant Development, see Bayley Scales of Infant and Toddler Development—Third Edition, 17
Becker Work Adjustment Profile: 2, 19 (R)

INDEX OF ACRONYMS

This Index of Acronyms refers the reader to the appropriate test in The Seventeenth Mental Measurements Yearbook. *In some cases tests are better known by their acronyms than by their full titles, and this index can be of substantial help to the person who knows the former but not the latter. Acronyms are only listed if the author or publisher has made substantial use of the acronym in referring to the test, or if the test is widely known by the acronym. A few acronyms are registered trademarks (e.g., SAT); where this is known to us, only the test with the registered trademarks is referenced. There is some danger in the overuse of acronyms. However, this index, like all other indexes in this work, is provided to make the task of identifying a test as easy as possible. All numbers refer to test numbers, not page numbers.*

CLASSIFIED SUBJECT INDEX

The Classified Subject Index classifies all tests included in The Mental Measurements Yearbook *into 18 major categories: Achievement, Behavior Assessment, Developmental, Education, English and Language, Fine Arts, Foreign Languages, Intelligence and General Aptitude, Mathematics, Miscellaneous, Neuropsychological, Personality, Reading, Science, Sensory-Motor, Social Studies, Speech and Hearing, and Vocations. This Classified Subject Index for the tests reviewed in* The Seventeenth Mental Measurements Yearbook *includes tests in 14 of the 18 available categories. (The categories of Fine Arts, Foreign Languages, Science, and Social Studies had no representative tests in this volume.) Each category appears in alphabetical order and tests are ordered alphabetically within each category. Each test entry includes test title, population for which the test is intended, and the test entry number in* The Seventeenth Mental Measurements Yearbook. *All numbers refer to test numbers, not to page numbers. Brief suggestions for the use of this index are presented in the introduction and definitions of the categories are provided at the beginning of this index.*

Achievement

Tests that measure acquired knowledge across school subject content areas. Included here are test batteries that measure multiple content areas and individual subject areas not having separate classification categories. (Note: Some batteries include both achievement and aptitude subtests. Such batteries may be classified under the categories of either Achievement or Intelligence and Aptitude depending upon the principal content area.)

See also Fine Arts, Intelligence and General Aptitude, Mathematics, Reading, Science, and Social Studies.

Behavior Assessment

Tests that measure general or specific behavior within educational, vocational, community, or home settings. Included here are checklists, rating scales, and surveys that measure observer's interpretations of behavior in relation to adaptive or social skills, functional skills, and appropriateness or dysfunction within settings/situations.

Developmental

Tests that are designed to assess skills or emerging skills (such as number concepts, conservation, memory, fine motor, gross motor, communication, letter recognition, social competence) of young children (0-7 years) or tests which are designed to assess such skills in severely or profoundly disabled school-aged individuals. Included here are early screeners, developmental surveys/profiles, kindergarten or school readiness tests, early learning profiles, infant development scales, tests of play behavior, social acceptance/social skills; and preschool psychoeducational batteries. Content specific screeners, such as those assessing readiness, are classified by content area (e.g., Reading).

See also Neuropsychological and Sensory-Motor.

Education

General education-related tests, including measures of instructional/school environment, effective schools/teaching, study skills and strategies, learning styles and strategies, school attitudes, educational programs/curriculae, interest inventories, and educational leadership.

Specific content area tests (i.e., science, mathematics, social studies, etc.) are listed by their content area.

English and Language

Tests that measure skills in using or understanding the English language in spoken or written form. Included here are tests of language proficiency, applied literacy, language comprehension/development/proficiency, English skills/proficiency, communication skills, listening comprehension, linguistics, and receptive/expressive vocabulary. (Tests designed to measure the mechanics of speaking or communicating are classified under the category Speech and Hearing.)

Fine Arts

Tests that measure knowledge, skills, abilities, attitudes, and interests within the various areas of fine and performing arts. Included here are tests of aptitude, achievement, creativity/talent/giftedness specific to the Fine Arts area, and tests of aesthetic judgment.

Foreign Languages

Tests that measure competencies and readiness in reading, comprehending, and speaking a language other than English.

Intelligence and General Aptitude

Tests that measure general acquired knowledge, aptitudes, or cognitive ability and those that assess specific aspects of these general categories. Included here are tests of critical thinking skills, nonverbal/verbal reasoning, cognitive abilities/processing, learning potential/aptitude/efficiency, logical reasoning, abstract thinking, creative thinking/creativity; entrance exams and academic admissions tests.

Mathematics

Tests that measure competencies and attitudes in any of the various areas of mathematics (e.g., algebra, geometry, calculus) and those related to general mathematics achievement/proficiency. (Note: Included here are tests that assess personality or affective variables related to mathematics.)

Miscellaneous

Tests that cannot be sorted into any of the current MMY categories as listed and defined above. Included here are tests of handwriting, ethics and morality, religion, driving and safety, health and physical education, environment (e.g., classroom environment, family environment), custody decisions, substance abuse, and addictions. (See also Personality.)

Neuropsychological

Tests that measure neurological functioning or brain-behavior relationships either generally or in relation to specific areas of functioning. Included here are neuropsychological test batteries, questionnaires, and screening tests. Also included are tests that measure memory impairment, various disorders or decline associated with dementia, brain/head injury, visual attention, digit recognition, finger tapping, laterality, aphasia, and behavior (associated with organic brain dysfunction or brain injury).

See also Developmental, Intelligence and General Aptitude, Sensory-Motor, and Speech and Hearing.

Personality

Tests that measure individuals' ways of thinking, behaving, and functioning within family and society. Included here are projective and apperception tests, needs inventories, anxiety/depression scales; tests assessing substance use/abuse (or propensity for abuse), risk taking behavior, general mental health, emotional intelligence, self-image/-concept/-esteem, empathy, suicidal ideation, schizophrenia, depression/hopelessness, abuse, coping skills/stress, eating disorders, grief, decision-making, racial attitudes; general motivation, attributions, perceptions; adjustment, parenting styles, and marital issues/satisfaction.

For content-specific tests, see subject area categories (e.g., math efficacy instruments are located in Mathematics). Some areas, such as substance abuse, are cross-referenced with the Personality category.

Reading

Tests that measure competencies and attitudes within the broadly defined area of reading. Included here are reading inventories, tests of reading achievement and aptitude, reading readiness/early reading ability, reading comprehension, reading decoding, and oral reading. (Note: Included here are tests that assess personality or affective variables related to reading.)

Science

Tests that measure competencies and attitudes within any of the various areas of science (e.g., biology, chemistry, physics), and those related to general science achievement/proficiency. (Note: Included here are tests that assess personality or affective variables related to science.)

Sensory-Motor

Tests that are general or specific measures of any or all of the five senses and those that assess fine or gross motor skills. Included here are tests of manual dexterity, perceptual skills, visual-motor skills, perceptual-motor skills, movement and posture, laterality preference, sensory integration, motor development, color blindness/discrimination, visual perception/organization, and visual acuity. (Note: See also the categories Neuropsychological and Speech and Hearing.)

Social Studies

Tests that measure competencies and attitudes within the broadly defined area of social studies. In cluded here are tests related to economics, sociology, history, geography, and political science, and those related to general social studies achievement/proficiency. (Note: Also included here are tests that assess personality or affective variables related to social studies.)

Speech and Hearing

Tests that measure the mechanics of speaking or hearing the spoken word. Included here are tests of articulation, voice fluency, stuttering, speech sound perception/discrimination, auditory discrimination/comprehension, audiometry, deafness, and hearing loss/impairment. (Note: See Developmental, English and Language, Neuropsychological, and Sensory-Motor.)

Vocations

Tests that measure employee skills, behaviors, attitudes, values, and perceptions relative to jobs, employment, and the work place or organizational environment. Included here are tests of management skill/style/competence, leader behavior, careers (development, exploration, attitudes); job- or work-related selection/admission/entrance tests; tests of work adjustment, team or group processes/communication/effectiveness, employability, vocational/occupational interests, employee aptitudes/competencies, and organizational climate.

See also Intelligence and General Aptitude, and Personality and also specific content area categories (e.g., Mathematics, Reading).

ACHIEVEMENT

Basic Achievement Skills Inventory; Grades 3 & 4, 5 & 6, 7 & 8, 9–12, and ages 8 to 80; 13

Comprehensive Testing Program 4; Grades 1–2, 2–3, 3–4, 4–5, 5–6, 6–7, 7–8, 8–9, 9–10, 10–11; 52

Fast Track; Adults; 71

Iowa Tests of Basic Skills®, Forms A and B; Grades K–9; 93

Performance Series; Grades 2-10; 143

Tests of Adult Basic Education, Forms 9 & 10; Adults; 187

Wechsler Intelligence Scale for Children—Fourth Edition Integrated; Ages 6-0 to 16-11; 197

BEHAVIOR ASSESSMENT

Attention Deficit Disorders Evaluation Scale—Third Edition; Ages 4-18; 10

Behavior Assessment System for Children [Second Edition]; Ages 2-25; 21

Behavior Evaluation Scale—Third Edition; Ages 4-19; 22

Behavior Rating Inventory of Executive Function—Adult Version; Ages 18-90; 23

Clinical Assessment of Attention Deficit–Adult; Ages 19-79; 46

Clinical Assessment of Attention Deficit–Child; 8-18 years; 47

Dutch Eating Behaviour Questionnaire; Ages 9–adult; 60

Gilliam Autism Rating Scale—Second Edition; Ages 3-22; 78

IVA+Plus [Integrated Visual and Auditory Continuous Performance Test]; Ages 6 to adult; 96

PDD Behavior Inventory; Ages 1-6 to 12-5; 142

Pre-Referral Intervention Manual—Third Edition; Grades K-12; 153

Social Responsiveness Scale; Ages 4-18 years; 173

Transition Planning Inventory (Updated Version); Students with disabilities who desire to plan for the future; 189

The Wessex Head Injury Matrix; Ages 16 and over; 198

DEVELOPMENTAL

EDUCATION

ENGLISH AND LANGUAGE

Stanford English Language Proficiency Test; Grades preK-12; 177

The Strong Narrative Assessment Procedure ; Grades K-8; 178

Woodcock-Muñoz™ Language Survey–Revised; Ages 2–90+; 202

The WORD Test 2: Elementary; Ages 6.0-11.11; 203

INTELLIGENCE AND GENERAL APTITUDE

Abbreviated Torrance Test for Adults; Adults; 1

Batería III Woodcock-Muñoz™; Ages 2–90+; 14

Cambridge Prospective Memory Test; Ages 16 and over; 36

Detroit Tests of Learning Aptitude—Primary, Third Edition; Ages 3–9; 55

Draw-A-Person Intellectual Ability Test for Children, Adolescents, and Adults; Ages 4-0 to 89-11; 59

Gifted and Talented Evaluation Scales; Ages 5-18; 77

James Madison Test of Critical Thinking; Grades 7-12+; 97

Kaufman Brief Intelligence Test, Second Edition; Ages 4-90; 102

The MIDAS: Multiple Intelligences Developmental Assessment Scales [Revised]; Ages 6–9, ages 9–14, ages 15–19, ages 20 and up; 123

The Middlesex Elderly Assessment of Mental State; Adults; 124

The Pyramids and Palm Trees Test; Ages 18-80; 160

Scales for Identifying Gifted Students; Ages 5-18 years; 169

Stanford-Binet Intelligence Scales for Early Childhood, Fifth Edition; Ages 2 years to 7 years, 3 months; 176

Test of Problem Solving 3: Elementary; Ages 6.0-12.11; 184

VIEW: An Assessment of Problem Solving Style; Ages 12 years and older; 193

Wiig Assessment of Basic Concepts; Ages 2-6 to 7-11 years; 200

MATHEMATICS

Group Mathematics Assessment and Diagnostic Evaluation; Grades K–12; 83

Iowa Algebra Aptitude Test™, Fifth Edition; Grades 7–8; 92

Orleans-Hanna Algebra Prognosis Test, Third Edition; Grades 7–11; 138

MISCELLANEOUS

Abuse Disability Questionnaire; Women ages 18 years and older; 2

Child and Adolescent Risk Evaluation: A Measure of the Risk for Violent Behavior; Ages 2–19; 40

Five Factor Wellness Inventory; Elementary, high school, and adults; 74

Group Environment Scale, Third Edition; Group members and leaders; clinicians, consultants, and program evaluators; 82

Gudjonsson Suggestibility Scales; Ages 6 and over; 84

Infant/Toddler Environment Rating Scale—Revised Edition; Infant/toddler day care centers; 89

The Level of Service Inventory—Revised [2003 Norms Update]; Ages 16 and older; 107

Level of Service/Case Management Inventory: An Offender Assessment System; Offenders ages 16 and over; 108

NEUROPSYCHOLOGICAL

PERSONALITY

READING

SENSORY MOTOR

SPEECH AND HEARING

VOCATIONS

PUBLISHERS DIRECTORY
AND INDEX

This directory and index gives the names and test entry numbers of all publishers represented in The Seventeenth Mental Measurements Yearbook. *Current addresses are listed for all publishers for which this is known. This directory and index also provides telephone and FAX numbers and e-mail and Web addresses for those publishers who responded to our request for this information. Please note that all test numbers refer to test entry numbers, not page numbers. Publishers are an important source of information about catalogs, specimen sets, price changes, test revisions, and many other matters.*

Association for Biblical Higher Education
5575 S. Semoran Blvd., Suite 26
Orlando, FL 32822-1781
Telephone: 407-207-0808
FAX: 407-207-0840
E-mail: exdir@abhe.org
Web: www.abhe.org
Test: 252

Ballard & Tighe Publishers
P.O. Box 219
Brea, CA 92822-0219
Telephone: 800-321-4332
FAX: 714-255-9828
E-mail: info@ballard-tighe.com
Web: www.ballard-tighe.com
Test: 94

The Basic Skills Agency
Commonwealth House
1-19 New Oxford Street
London WC1A 1NU
England
Test: 71

Birkman International, Inc.
3040 Post Oak Blvd., Suite 1425
Houston, TX 77056
Telephone: 800-215-2760
FAX: 713-963-9142
E-mail: sales@birkman.com
Web: www.birkman.com
Test: 28

Brador Publications, Inc.
P.O. Box 149
Scotland, CT 06264
Test: 217

BrainTrain
727 Twin Ridge Lane
Richmond, VA 23235
Telephone: 804-320-0105
FAX: 804-320-0242
E-mail: info@braintrain.com
Web: www.braintrain.com
Test: 96

Branden Publishing Co.
P.O. Box 812094
Wellesley, MA 02482
Telephone: 781 235-3634
FAX: 781 790-1056
E-mail: branden@brandenbooks.com
Web: www.brandenbooks.com
Test: 216

Castle Consultants
111 Teeter Rock Road
Trumbull, CT 06611
Telephone: 203-375-5353
FAX: 203-375-2999
E-mail: cassie@castleconsultants.us
Web: www.castleconsultants.us
Test: 174

Center for Applied Linguistics
4646 40th Street, NW
Washington, DC 20016-1859
Telephone: 202-362-0700
FAX: 202-363-7204
E-mail: info@cal.org
Web: www.cal.org
Test: 27

Center for Creative Learning
4921 Ringwood Meadow
Sarasota, FL 34235
Telephone: 941-342-9928
FAX: 941-342-0064
E-mail: info@creativelearning.com
Web: www.creativelearning.com
Test: 193

Consulting Resource Group International, Inc.
P.O. Box 8000, PMB 386
Sumas, WA 98295-8000
Telephone: 604-852-0566
FAX: 604-850-3003
E-mail: info@crgleader.com
Web: www.crgleader.com
Tests: 68, 99, 144, 232, 237, 238, 249, 251, 254, 258

Creative Learning Press, Inc.
P.O. Box 320
Mansfield Center, CT 06250
Test: 106

The Critical Thinking Co.
P.O. Box 1610
Seaside, CA 93955-1610
Telephone: 800-458-4849
FAX: 831-393-3277
E-mail: info@criticalthinking.com
Web: www.criticalthinking.com
Test: 97

CTB/McGraw-Hill
20 Ryan Ranch Road
Monterey, CA 93940-5703
Telephone: 831-393-0700
Web: www.ctb.com
Tests: 187, 229, 230, 231, 234, 235

Curriculum Associates, Inc.
153 Rangeway Road
P.O. Box 2001
North Billerica, MA 01862-0901
Telephone: 800-225-0248
FAX: 800-366-1158
E-mail: info@cainc.com
Web: www.curriculumassociates.com
Tests: 31, 32, 33, 34

The Devine Group, Inc.
10200 Alliance Road, Suite 310
Cincinnati, OH 45242
Test: 56

Educational & Psychological Consultants, Inc.
1715 West Worley Street, Suite #A
Columbia, MO 65203-2603
Telephone: 573-446-6232
E-mail: kuncej@missouri.edu
Test: 145

Educational Records Bureau
220 East 42nd Street, Suite 100
New York, NY 10017-5006
Telephone: 212-672-9800
FAX: 212-370-4096
E-mail: info@erbtest.org
Web: www.erbtest.org
Tests: 52, 69

Elbern Publications
P.O. Box 9497
Columbus, OH 43209
Telephone: 614-231-1950
FAX: 614-237-2637
E-mail: ebecker@insight.rr.com
Test: 19

English Language Institute
University of Michigan
TCF Building, Suite 350
401 East Liberty Street
Ann Arbor, MI 48104-2298
Telephone: 734-764-2416
FAX: 734-763-0369
E-mail: melabelium@umich.edu
Web: www.lsa.umich.edu/eli/
Test: 67

Enterprise Management Ltd.
4531 Roanoak Way
Palm Harbor, FL 34685
Telephone: 727-934-9810
E-mail: mlippitt@enterprisemgt.com
Web: www.enterprisemgt.com
Test: 104

G. Neil
720 International Parkway
P.O. Box 450939
Sunrise, FL 33345-0939
Telephone: 800-999-9111
FAX: 954-846-0777
E-mail: hrassessments@gneil.com
Web: www.gneil.com
Tests: 8, 44, 168, 171

H&H Publishing Company, Inc.
1231 Kapp Drive
Clearwater, FL 33765-2116
Test: 105

Harcourt Assessment
1 Procter Street
London WC1V 6EU
United Kingdom
Telephone: +44 (0)20 7911 1960
FAX: +44 (0)20 7911 1961
E-mail: info@harcourt-uk.com
Web: www.harcourt-uk.com
Tests: 11, 12, 24, 25, 36, 58, 60, 61, 70, 79, 85, 111,
    124, 131, 159, 160, 166, 167, 172, 175, 182, 183,
    192, 195, 196, 198, 219

Harcourt Assessment, Inc.
19500 Bulverde Road
San Antonio, TX 78259-3701
Telephone: 800-211-8378
FAX: 877-576-1816
Tests: 138, 147, 149, 177

Hawthorne Educational Services, Inc.
ATTN: Adina Laird, Dir. of External Relations
800 Gray Oak Drive
Columbia, MO 65201
Telephone: 800-542-1673
FAX: 800-442-9509
E-mail: adina_laird@hes-inc.com
Web: www.hes-inc.com
Tests: 10, 22, 153

Hay Group
Hay Resources Direct
116 Huntington Avenue
Boston, MA 02116-5712
Telephone: 800-729-8074
FAX: 617-927-5008
E-mail: Haytrg@haygroup.com
Web: www.hayresourcesdirect.haygroup.com
Test: 66

High/Scope Educational Research Foundation
600 North River Street
Ypsilanti, MI 48198-2898
Telephone: 734-485-2000
FAX: 734-485-0704
E-mail: info@highscope.org
Web: www.highscope.org
Tests: 62, 154, 155, 208

Hodder & Stoughton Educational
Hodder Headline PLC
338 Euston Road
London NW1 3BH
England
Telephone: 0207 873 6000
FAX: 0207 873 6299
E-mail: chas.knight@hodder.co.uk
Web: www.hoddertests.co.uk
Test: 163

Hogrefe & Huber Publishers
875 Massachusetts Avenue
7th Floor
Cambridge, MA 02139
Telephone: 800-228-3749
FAX: 425-823-8324
E-mail: HH@HHPUB.COM
Web: WWW.HHPUB.COM
Test: 4

Houghton Mifflin Company
College Division, Education
222 Berkeley Street
Boston, MA 02116-3764
Telephone: 617-351-5000
FAX: 617-351-1134
E-mail: college_educ@hmco.com
Web: http://education.college.hmco.com
Test: 35

HRD Press, Inc.
22 Amherst Road
Amherst, MA 01002–9709
Telephone: 800-822-2801
FAX: 413-253-3490
E-mail: info@hrdpress.com
Web: www.hrdpress.com
Tests: 115, 121, 186, 246

Indiana Resource Center for Autism
Indiana Institute on Disability and Community
2853 East Tenth Street
Bloomington, IN 47408-2696
Test: 199

Industrial Psychology International, Ltd.
4106 Fieldstone Road
P.O. Box 6479
Champaign, IL 61826-6479
Telephone: 800-747-1119
FAX: 217-398-5798
E-mail: IPI@METRITECH.COM
Web: WWW.METRITECH.COM
Test: 205

JIST Publishing, Inc.
8902 Otis Avenue
Indianapolis, IN 46216-1033
Telephone: 800-648-5478
FAX: 800-547-8329
E-mail: info@jist.com
Web: www.jist.com
Tests: 50, 98, 100, 204, 209, 218, 225, 257, 259

LinguiSystems, Inc.
3100 4th Avenue
East Moline, IL 61244-9700
Telephone: 800-776-4332
E-mail: testing@linguisystems.com
Tests: 103, 184, 203

Master Publishing, Inc.
6125 West Howard Street
Niles, IL 60714-3401
Telephone: 847-763-0916
FAX: 847-763-0918
E-mail: TROTTER@FIRSTPOINTKIDS.COM
Web: www.firstpointkids.com
Test: 141

Mind Garden, Inc.
855 Oak Grove Ave., Suite 215
Menlo Park, CA 94025
Telephone: 650-322-6300
FAX: 650-322-6398
E-mail: info@mindgarden.com
Web: www.mindgarden.com
Tests: 74, 82, 130, 214

Multi-Health Systems, Inc.
P.O. Box 950
North Tonawanda, NY 14120-0950
Telephone: 800-456-3003
FAX: 888-540-4484
E-mail: CUSTOMERSERVICE@MHS.COM
Web: www.mhs.com
Tests: 7, 26, 41, 107, 108, 109, 129, 170, 188, 194

Multiple Intelligences Research and Consulting, Inc.
1316 South Lincoln Street
Kent, OH 44240
Telephone: 330-677-8534
E-mail: sbranton@kent.edu
Web: www.miresearch.org
Test: 123

National Reading Styles Institute, Inc.
P.O. Box 737
Syosset, NY 11791-0737
E-mail: nick@nrsi.com
Test: 248

NFER-Nelson Publishing Co., Ltd.
The Chiswick Centre/9th Floor
414 Chiswick High Road
London W4 5TF
England
Tests: 38

OQ Measures LLC
P.O. Box 521047
Salt Lake City, UT 84152-1047
Telephone: 1-888-647-2673
Tests: 136, 137, 206, 207

Organization Analysis and Design LLC
168 High Street
Norwell, MA 02061
Test: 135

Pearson
5601 Green Valley Drive
Minneapolis, MN 55437
Telephone: 800-627-7271 or 952-681-3232
FAX: 800-632-9011 or 952-681-3299
Web: www.pearsonassessments.com
Tests: 13, 16, 20, 21, 30, 83, 102, 125, 126, 162

Pearson Performance Solutions
One North Dearborn, Suite 1600
Chicago, IL 60602
Tests: 213, 215, 224, 227, 233, 236, 239, 240, 243, 250, 253, 255, 256

Personal Strengths Publishing
P.O. Box 2605
Carlsbad, CA 92018-2605
Telephone: 800-624-7347
FAX: 760-602-0087
E-mail: mail@PersonalStrengths.com
Web: www.PersonalStrengths.com
Tests: 72, 73

PITS: Psychologische Instrumenten Tests en Services
Postbus 1084
2302 BB Leiden
The Netherlands
Telephone: ++ (0)71-5318786
FAX: ++ (0)71-5728165
E-mail: info@pits-online.nl
Web: www.pits-online.nl
Tests: 6, 148

PRO-ED
8700 Shoal Creek Blvd.
Austin, TX 78757-6897
Telephone: 800-897-3202
FAX: 800-397-7633
E-mail: info@proedinc
Web: WWW.PROEDINC.COM
Tests: 29, 55, 59, 75, 77, 78, 80, 86, 87, 110, 151, 156, 161, 185, 189

Prufrock Press Inc.
P.O. Box 8813
Waco, TX 76714-8813
Telephone: 800-998-2208
FAX: 800-240-0333
E-mail: info@prufrock.com
Web: www.prufrock.com
Test: 169

Psychological Assessment Resources, Inc.
16204 N. Florida Avenue
Lutz, FL 33549-8119
Telephone: 800-331-8378
FAX: 800-727-9329
E-mail: custsupp@parinc.com
Web: www.parinc.com
Tests: 23, 46, 47, 48, 64, 88, 142, 150, 157, 158, 165, 180, 191, 245

The Psychological Corporation, A Harcourt Assessment Company
19500 Bulverde Road
San Antonio, TX 78259-3701
Telephone: 800-211-8378
FAX: 800-232-1223
E-mail: customer_care@harcourt.com
Web: www.PsychCorp.com
Tests: 3, 17, 18, 42, 43, 49, 57, 63, 81, 95, 140, 152, 164, 197

Ramsay Corporation
Boyce Station Offices
1050 Boyce Road
Pittsburgh, PA 15241-3907
Tests: 5, 39, 51, 65, 90, 112, 113, 114, 116, 117, 118, 119, 120, 127, 128, 181, 226, 141

Research Press
P.O. Box 9177
Champaign, IL 61826
Telephone: 800-519-2707
FAX: 217-352-1221
E-mail: rp@researchpress.com
Web: www.researchpress.com
Test: 40

Riverside Publishing
Attn: Rob Elsey
3800 Golf Road, Suite 100
Rolling Meadows, IL 60008
Telephone: 800-323-9540
FAX: 630-467-7192
Web: www.riversidepublishing.com
Tests: 14, 15, 54, 92, 93, 132, 176, 201, 202

Scantron Corporation
110 West A Street, Suite 800
San Diego, CA 92101
Telephone: 800-722-6876
FAX: 619-615-0522
E-mail: marjorie–reynolds@scantron.com
Web: www.scantron.com
Test: 143

Scholastic Testing Service, Inc.
480 Meyer Road
Bensenville, IL 60106-1617
Telephone: 1-800-642-6787
FAX: 630-766-8054
E-mail: stesting@email.com
Web: www.ststesting.com
Tests: 1, 91

SIGMA Assessment Systems, Inc.
P.O. Box 610984
Port Huron, MI 48061-0984
Telephone: 800-265-1285
FAX: 800-361-9411
E-mail: SIGMA@SigmaAssessmentSystems.com
Web: www.SigmaAssessmentSystems.com
Tests: 37, 133, 146

Silverwood Enterprises, LLC
P.O. Box 363
Sharon Center, OH 44273
Telephone: 330-239-1646
FAX: 330-239-0250
E-mail: silverasoc@aol.com
Tests: 210, 211, 212

Sopris West
4093 Specialty Place
Longmont, CO 80504-5400
Telephone: 800-547-6747
FAX: 303-776-5934
E-mail: WWW.SOPRISWEST.COM
Web: WWW.SOPRISWEST.COM
Test: 76

Stoelting Co.
620 Wheat Lane
Wood Dale, IL 60191-1164
Telephone: 630-860-9700
FAX: 630-860-9775
E-mail: psychtests@stoeltingco.com
Web: www.stoeltingco.com/tests
Tests: 2, 122, 179

Super Duper Publications
P.O. Box 24997
Greenville, SC 29616-2497
Telephone: 800-277-8737
FAX: 800-978-7379
E-mail: custserv@superduperinc.com
Web: www.superduperinc.com
Tests: 45, 200

Taylor & Francis
Rankine Road
Basingstoke
Hampshire RG24 8PR
England
Test: 84

Teachers College Press
1234 Amsterdam Avenue
New York, NY 10027
Telephone: 212-678-3929
FAX: 212-678-4149
E-mail: tcpress@tc.columbia.edu
Web: www.teacherscollegepress.com
Test: 89

Thinking Publications
424 Galloway Street
P.O. Box 163
Eau Claire, WI 54702-0163
Tests: 9, 53, 178

Thomson Delmar Learning
Executive Woods
5 Maxwell Drive
P.O. Box 8007
Clifton Park, NY 12065-2919
Test: 244

Vantage McCann Associates, Inc.
110 Terry Drive
Newtown, PA 18940-1850
Telephone: 267-759-1197
FAX: 215-579-8391
Web: www.vantagemccann.com
Tests: 220, 221, 222, 223, 228, 242, 247

Western Psychological Services
12031 Wilshire Blvd.
Los Angeles, CA 90025-1251
Telephone: 310-478-2061
FAX: 310-478-7838
Web: www.wpspublish.com
Tests: 101, 134, 139, 173, 190

INDEX OF NAMES

This index indicates whether a citation refers to authorship of a test, a test review, or a reviewer's reference for a specific test. Numbers refer to test entries, not to pages. The abbreviations and numbers following the names may be interpreted as follows: "test, 73" indicates authorship of test 73; "rev, 86" indicates authorship of a review of test 86; "ref, 45" indicates a reference in one of the "Reviewer's References" sections for test 45. Reviewer names mentioned in cross references are also indexed.

SCORE INDEX

This Score Index lists all the scores, in alphabetical order, for all the tests included in The Seventeenth Mental Measurements Yearbook. Because test scores can be regarded as operational definitions of the variable measured, sometimes the scores provide better leads to what a test actually measures than the test title or other available information. The Score Index is very detailed, and the reader should keep in mind that a given variable (or concept) of interest may be defined in several different ways. Thus the reader should look up these several possible alternative definitions before drawing final conclusions about whether tests measuring a particular variable of interest can be located in this volume. If the kind of score sought is located in a particular test or tests, the reader should then read the test descriptive information carefully to determine whether the test(s) in which the score is found is (are) consistent with reader purpose. Used wisely, the Score Index can be another useful resource in locating the right score in the right test. As usual, all numbers in the index are test numbers, not page numbers.

RIGHTS AND RESPONSIBILITIES OF TEST TAKERS: GUIDELINES AND EXPECTATIONS

PREAMBLE

The intent of this statement is to enumerate and clarify the expectations that test takers may reasonably have about the testing process, and the expectations that those who develop, administer, and use tests may have of test takers.

Tests are defined broadly here as psychological and educational instruments developed and used by testing professionals in organizations such as schools, industries, clinical practice, counseling settings and human service and other agencies, including those assessment procedures and devices that are used for making inferences about people in the above-named settings.

The purpose of the statement is to inform and to help educate not only test takers, but also others involved in the testing enterprise so that measurements may be most validly and appropriately used. This document is intended as an effort to inspire improvements in the testing process and does not have the force of law. Its orientation is to encourage positive and high quality interactions between testing professionals and test takers.

The rights and responsibilities listed in this document are neither legally based nor inalienable rights and responsibilities such as those listed in the United States of America's Bill of Rights. Rather, they represent the best judgments of testing professionals about the reasonable expectations that those involved in the testing enterprise (test producers, test users, and test takers) should have of each other.

Testing professionals include developers of assessment products and services, those who market and sell them, persons who select them, test administrators and scorers, those who interpret test results, and trained users of the infor-

mation. Persons who engage in each of these activities have significant responsibilities that are described elsewhere, in documents such as those that follow (American Association for Counseling and Development, 1988; American Speech-Language-Hearing Association, 1994; Joint Committee on Testing Practices, 1988; National Association of School Psychologists, 1992; National Council on Measurement in Education, 1995).

In some circumstances, the test developer and the test user may not be the same person, group of persons, or organization. In such situations, the professionals involved in the testing should clarify, for the test taker as well as for themselves, who is responsible for each aspect of the testing process. For example, when an individual chooses to take a college admissions test, at least three parties are involved in addition to the test taker: the test developer and publisher, the individuals who administer the test to the test taker, and the institutions of higher education who will eventually use the information. In such cases a test taker may need to request clarifications about their rights and responsibilities. When test takers are young children (e.g., those taking standardized tests in the schools) or are persons who spend some or all their time in institutions or are incapacitated, parents or guardians may be granted some of the rights and responsibilities, rather than, or in addition to, the individual.

Perhaps the most fundamental right test takers have is to be able to take tests that meet high professional standards, such as those described in Standards for Educational and Psychological Testing (American Educational Research Association, American Psychological Association, & National Council on Measurement in Education, 1999) as well as those of other appropriate professional associations. This statement should be used as an adjunct, or supplement, to those standards. State and federal laws, of course, supersede any rights and responsibilities that are stated here.

REFERENCES

American Association for Counseling and Development (now American Counseling Association) & Association for Measurement and Evaluation in Counseling and Development (now Association for Assessment in Counseling). (1989). *Responsibilities of users of standardized tests: RUST statement revised.* Alexandria, VA: Author.

American Educational Research Association, American Psychological Association, & National Council on Measurement in Education. (1999). *Standards for educational and psychological testing.* Washington, DC: American Educational Research Association.

American Speech-Language-Hearing Association. (1994). *Protection of rights of people receiving audiology or speech-language pathology services.* ASHA (36), 60-63.

Joint Committee on Testing Practices. (1988). *Code of fair testing practices in education.* Washington, DC: American Psychological Association.

National Association of School Psychologists. (1992). *Standards for the provision of school psychological services.* Author: Silver Springs, MD.

National Council on Measurement in Education. (1995). *Code of professional responsibilities in educational measurement.* Washington, DC: Author.

The Rights and Responsibilities of Test Takers: Guidelines and Expectations

Test Taker Rights and Responsibilities Working Group of the Joint Committee on Testing Practices August, 1998

As a test taker, you have the right to:

1. Be informed of your rights and responsibilities as a test taker.
2. Be treated with courtesy, respect, and impartiality, regardless of your age, disability, ethnicity, gender, national origin, religion, sexual orientation or other personal characteristics.
3. Be tested with measures that meet professional standards and that are appropriate, given the manner in which the test results will be used.
4. Receive a brief oral or written explanation prior to testing about the purpose(s) for testing, the kind(s) of tests to be used, if the results will be reported to you or to others, and the planned use(s) of the results. If you have a disability, you have the right to inquire and receive information about testing accommodations. If you have difficulty in comprehending the language of the test, you have a right to know in advance of testing whether any accommodations may be available to you.
5. Know in advance of testing when the test will be administered, if and when test results will be available to you, and if there is a fee for testing services that you are expected to pay.
6. Have your test administered and your test results interpreted by appropriately trained individuals who follow professional codes of ethics.
7. Know if a test is optional and learn of the consequences of taking or not taking the test, fully completing the test, or canceling the scores. You may need to ask questions to learn these consequences.
8. Receive a written or oral explanation of your test results within a reasonable amount of time after testing and in commonly understood terms.
9. Have your test results kept confidential to the extent allowed by law.
10. Present concerns about the testing process or your results and receive information about procedures that will be used to address such concerns.

As a test taker, you have the responsibility to:

1. Read and/or listen to your rights and responsibilities as a test taker.
2. Treat others with courtesy and respect during the testing process.
3. Ask questions prior to testing if you are uncertain about why the test is being given, how it will be given, what you will be asked to do, and what will be done with the results.

4. Read or listen to descriptive information in advance of testing and listen carefully to all test instructions. You should inform an examiner in advance of testing if you wish to receive a testing accommodation or if you have a physical condition or illness that may interfere with your performance on the test. If you have difficulty comprehending the language of the test, it is your responsibility to inform an examiner.

5. Know when and where the test will be given, pay for the test if required, appear on time with any required materials, and be ready to be tested.

6. Follow the test instructions you are given and represent yourself honestly during the testing.

7. Be familiar with and accept the consequences of not taking the test, should you choose not to take the test.

8. Inform appropriate person(s), as specified to you by the organization responsible for testing, if you believe that testing conditions affected your results.

9. Ask about the confidentiality of your test results, if this aspect concerns you.

10. Present concerns about the testing process or results in a timely, respectful way, if you have any.

The Rights of Test Takers: Guidelines for Testing Professionals

Test takers have the rights described below. It is the responsibility of the professionals involved in the testing process to ensure that test takers receive these rights.

1. Because test takers have the right to be informed of their rights and responsibilities as test takers, it is normally the responsibility of the individual who administers a test (or the organization that prepared the test) to inform test takers of these rights and responsibilities.

2. Because test takers have the right to be treated with courtesy, respect, and impartiality, regardless of their age, disability, ethnicity, gender, national origin, race, religion, sexual orientation, or other personal characteristics, testing professionals should:

a. Make test takers aware of any materials that are available to assist them in test preparation. These materials should be clearly described in test registration and/or test familiarization materials.

b. See that test takers are provided with reasonable access to testing services.

3. Because test takers have the right to be tested with measures that meet professional standards that are appropriate for the test use and the test taker, given the manner in which the results will be used, testing professionals should:

a. Take steps to utilize measures that meet professional standards and are reliable, relevant, useful given the intended purpose and are fair for test takers from varying societal groups.

b. Advise test takers that they are entitled to request reasonable accommodations in test administration that are likely to increase the validity of their test scores if they have a disability recognized under the Americans with Disabilities Act or other relevant legislation.

4. Because test takers have the right to be informed, prior to testing, about the test's purposes, the nature of the test, whether test results will be reported to the test takers, and the planned use of the results (when not in conflict with the testing purposes), testing professionals should:

a. Give or provide test takers with access to a brief description about the test purpose (e.g., diagnosis, placement, selection, etc.) and the kind(s) of tests and formats that will be used (e.g., individual/group, multiple-choice/free response/performance, timed/untimed, etc.), unless such information might be detrimental to the objectives of the test.

b. Tell test takers, prior to testing, about the planned use(s) of the test results. Upon request, the test taker should be given information about how long such test scores are typically kept on file and remain available.

c. Provide test takers, if requested, with information about any preventative measures that have been instituted to safeguard the accuracy of test scores. Such information would include any quality control procedures that are employed and some of the steps taken to prevent dishonesty in test performance.

d. Inform test takers, in advance of the testing, about required materials that must be brought to the test site (e.g., pencil, paper) and about any rules that allow or prohibit use of other materials (e.g., calculators).

e. Provide test takers, upon request, with general information about the appropriateness of the test for its intended purpose, to the extent that such information does not involve the release of proprietary information. (For example, the test taker might be told, "Scores on this test are useful in predicting how successful people will be in this kind of work" or "Scores on this test, along with other information, help us to determine if students are likely to benefit from this program.")

f. Provide test takers, upon request, with information about re-testing, including if it is possible to re-take the test or another version of it, and if so, how often, how soon, and under what conditions.

g. Provide test takers, upon request, with information about how the test will be scored and in what detail. On multiple-choice tests, this information might include suggestions for test taking and about the use of a correction for guessing. On tests scored using professional judgment (e.g., essay tests or projective techniques), a general description of the scoring procedures might be provided except when such information is proprietary or would tend to influence test performance inappropriately.

h. Inform test takers about the type of feedback and interpretation that is routinely provided, as well as what is available for a fee. Test takers have the right to request and receive information regarding whether or not they can obtain copies of their test answer sheets or their test materials, if they can have their scores verified, and if they may cancel their test results.

i. Provide test takers, prior to testing, either in the written instructions, in other written documents or orally, with answers to questions that test takers may have about basic test administration procedures.

j. Inform test takers, prior to testing, if questions from test takers will not be permitted during the testing process.

k. Provide test takers with information about the use of computers, calculators, or other equipment, if any, used in the testing and give them an opportunity to practice using such equipment, unless its unpracticed use is part of the test purpose, or practice would compromise the validity of the results, and to provide a testing accommodation for the use of such equipment, if needed.

l. Inform test takers that, if they have a disability, they have the right to request and receive accommodations or modifications in accordance with the provisions of the Americans with Disabilities Act and other relevant legislation.

m. Provide test takers with information that will be of use in making decisions if test takers have options regarding which tests, test forms or test formats to take.

5. Because test takers have a right to be informed in advance when the test will be administered, if and when test results will be available, and if there is a fee for testing services that the test takers are expected to pay, test professionals should:

a. Notify test takers of the alteration in a timely manner if a previously announced testing schedule changes, provide a reasonable explanation for the change, and inform test takers of the new schedule. If there is a change, reasonable alternatives to the original schedule should be provided.

b. Inform test takers prior to testing about any anticipated fee for the testing process, as well as the fees associated with each component of the process, if the components can be separated.

6. Because test takers have the right to have their tests administered and interpreted by appropriately trained individuals, testing professionals should:

a. Know how to select the appropriate test for the intended purposes.

b. When testing persons with documented disabilities and other special characteristics that require special testing conditions and/or interpretation of results, have the skills and knowledge for such testing and interpretation.

c. Provide reasonable information regarding their qualifications, upon request.

d. Insure that test conditions, especially if unusual, do not unduly interfere with test performance. Test conditions will normally be similar to those used to standardize the test.

e. Provide candidates with a reasonable amount of time to complete the test, unless a test has a time limit.

f. Take reasonable actions to safeguard against fraudulent actions (e.g., cheating) that could place honest test takers at a disadvantage.

7. Because test takers have the right to be informed about why they are being asked to take particular tests, if a test is optional, and what the consequences are should they choose not to complete the test, testing professionals should:

a. Normally only engage in testing activities with test takers after the test takers have provided their informed consent to take a test, except when testing without consent has been mandated by law or governmental regulation, or when consent is implied by an action the test takers have already taken (e.g., such as when applying for employment and a personnel examination is mandated).

b. Explain to test takers why they should consider taking voluntary tests.

c. Explain, if a test taker refuses to take or complete a voluntary test, either orally or in writing, what the negative consequences may be to them for their decision to do so.

d. Promptly inform the test taker if a testing professional decides that there is a need to deviate from the testing services to which the test taker initially agreed (e.g., should the testing professional believe it would be wise to administer an additional test or an alternative test), and provide an explanation for the change.

8. Because test takers have a right to receive a written or oral explanation of their test results within a reasonable amount of time after testing and in commonly understood terms, testing professionals should:

a. Interpret test results in light of one or more additional considerations (e.g., disability, language proficiency), if those considerations are relevant to the purposes of the test and performance on the test, and are in accordance with current laws.

b. Provide, upon request, information to test takers about the sources used in interpreting their test results, including technical manuals, technical reports, norms, and a description of the comparison group, or additional information about the test taker(s).

c. Provide, upon request, recommendations to test takers about how they could improve their performance on the test, should they choose or be required to take the test again.

d. Provide, upon request, information to test takers about their options for obtaining a second interpretation of their results. Test takers may select an appropriately trained professional to provide this second opinion.

e. Provide test takers with the criteria used to determine a passing score, when individual test scores are reported and related to a pass-fail standard.

f. Inform test takers, upon request, how much their scores might change, should they elect to take the test again. Such information would include variation in test performance due to measurement error (e.g., the appropriate standard errors of measurement) and changes in performance over time with or without intervention (e.g., additional training or treatment).

g. Communicate test results to test takers in an appropriate and sensitive manner, without use of negative labels or comments likely to inflame or stigmatize the test taker.

h. Provide corrected test scores to test takers as rapidly as possible, should an error occur in the processing or reporting of scores. The length of time is often dictated by individuals responsible for processing or reporting the scores, rather than the individuals responsible for testing, should the two parties indeed differ.

i. Correct any errors as rapidly as possible if there are errors in the process of developing scores.

9. Because test takers have the right to have the results of tests kept confidential to the extent allowed by law, testing professionals should:

a. Insure that records of test results (in paper or electronic form) are safeguarded and maintained so that only individuals who have a legitimate right to access them will be able to do so.

b. Provide test takers, upon request, with information regarding who has a legitimate right to access their test results (when individually identified) and in what form. Testing professionals should respond appropriately to questions regarding the reasons why such individuals may have access to test results and how they may use the results.

c. Advise test takers that they are entitled to limit access to their results (when individually identified) to those persons or institutions, and for those purposes, revealed to them prior to testing. Exceptions may occur when test takers, or their guardians, consent to release the test results to others or when testing professionals are authorized by law to release test results.

d. Keep confidential any requests for testing accommodations and the documentation supporting the request.

10. Because test takers have the right to present concerns about the testing process and to receive information about procedures that will be used to address such concerns, testing professionals should:

a. Inform test takers how they can question the results of the testing if they do not believe that the test was administered properly or scored correctly, or other such concerns.

b. Inform test takers of the procedures for appealing decisions that they believe are based in whole or in part on erroneous test results. Inform test takers, if their test results are under investigation and may be canceled, invalidated, or not released for normal use. In such an event, that investigation should be performed in a timely manner. The investigation should use all available information that addresses the reason(s) for the investigation, and the test taker should also be informed of the information that he/she may need to provide to assist with the investigation.

c. Inform the test taker, if that test taker's test results are canceled or not released for normal use, why that action was taken. The test taker is entitled to request and receive information on the types of evidence and procedures that have been used to make that determination.

The Responsibilities of Test Takers: Guidelines for Testing Professionals

Testing Professionals should take steps to ensure that test takers know that they have specific responsibilities in addition to their rights described above.

1. Testing professionals need to inform test takers that they should listen to and/or read their rights and responsibilities as a test taker and ask questions about issues they do not understand.

2. Testing professionals should take steps, as appropriate, to ensure that test takers know that they:

a. Are responsible for their behavior throughout the entire testing process.

b. Should not interfere with the rights of others involved in the testing process.

c. Should not compromise the integrity of the test and its interpretation in any manner.

3. Testing professionals should remind test takers that it is their responsibility to ask questions prior to testing if they are uncertain about why the test is being given, how it will be given, what they will be asked to do, and

what will be done with the results. Testing professionals should:

a. Advise test takers that it is their responsibility to review materials supplied by test publishers and others as part of the testing process and to ask questions about areas that they feel they should understand better prior to the start of testing.

b. Inform test takers that it is their responsibility to request more information if they are not satisfied with what they know about how their test results will be used and what will be done with them.

4. Testing professionals should inform test takers that it is their responsibility to read descriptive material they receive in advance of a test and to listen carefully to test instructions. Testing professionals should inform test takers that it is their responsibility to inform an examiner in advance of testing if they wish to receive a testing accommodation or if they have a physical condition or illness that may interfere with their performance. Testing professionals should inform test takers that it is their responsibility to inform an examiner if they have difficulty comprehending the language in which the test is given. Testing professionals should:

a. Inform test takers that, if they need special testing arrangements, it is their responsibility to request appropriate accommodations and to provide any requested documentation as far in advance of the testing date as possible. Testing professionals should inform test takers about the documentation needed to receive a requested testing accommodation.

b. Inform test takers that, if they request but do not receive a testing accommodation, they could request information about why their request was denied.

5. Testing professionals should inform test takers when and where the test will be given, and whether payment for the testing is required. Having been so informed, it is the responsibility of the test taker to appear on time with any required materials, pay for testing services and be ready to be tested. Testing professionals should:

a. Inform test takers that they are responsible for familiarizing themselves with the appropriate materials needed for testing and for requesting information about these materials, if needed.

b. Inform the test taker, if the testing situation requires that test takers bring materials (e.g., personal identification, pencils, calculators, etc.) to the testing site, of this responsibility to do so.

6. Testing professionals should advise test takers, prior to testing, that it is their responsibility to:

a. Listen to and/or read the directions given to them.

b. Follow instructions given by testing professionals. Complete the test as directed.

c. Perform to the best of their ability if they want their score to be a reflection of their best effort.

d. Behave honestly (e.g., not cheating or assisting others who cheat).

7. Testing professionals should inform test takers about the consequences of not taking a test, should they choose not to take the test. Once so informed, it is the responsibility of the test taker to accept such consequences, and the testing professional should so inform the test takers. If test takers have questions regarding these consequences, it is their responsibility to ask questions of the testing professional, and the testing professional should so inform the test takers.

8. Testing professionals should inform test takers that it is their responsibility to notify appropriate persons, as specified by the testing organization, if they do not understand their results, or if they believe that testing conditions affected the results. Testing professionals should:

a. Provide information to test takers, upon request, about appropriate procedures for questioning or canceling their test scores or results, if relevant to the purposes of testing.

b. Provide to test takers, upon request, the procedures for reviewing, re-testing, or canceling their scores or test results, if they believe that testing conditions affected their results and if relevant to the purposes of testing.

   c. Provide documentation to the test taker about known testing conditions that might have affected the results of the testing, if relevant to the purposes of testing.

9. Testing professionals should advise test takers that it is their responsibility to ask questions about the confidentiality of their test results, if this aspect concerns them.

10. Testing professionals should advise test takers that it is their responsibility to present concerns about the testing process in a timely, respectful manner.

Members of the JCTP Working Group on Test Taker Rights and Responsibilities:

Kurt F. Geisinger, PhD (Co-Chair); William Schafer, EdD (Co-Chair); Gwyneth Boodoo, PhD; Ruth Ekstrom, EdD; Tom Fitzgibbon, PhD; John Fremer, PhD; Joanne Lenke, PhD; Sharon Goldsmith, PhD; Kevin Moreland, PhD; Julie Noble, PhD; James Sampson Jr., PhD; Douglas Smith, PhD; Nicholas Vacc, EdD; Janet Wall, EdD.

Staff liaisons: Heather Fox, PhD, and Lara Frumkin, PhD